EHRS Electronic health record system
EI Emotional intelligence
EIS Executive information system
EMAR Electronic medication administration record
EMDS Essential Medical Data Set
EMIC Emergency Maternal and Infant Care Program
EMPI Enterprise-wide master patient index
EMR Electronic medical record
EOC Episode-of-care
EPA Equal Pay Act of 1963
EPA SRS Environmental Protection Agency Substance Registry System
EPO Exclusive provider organization
ERA Electronic remittance advice
ERD Entity relationship diagram
ES Expert system
FASB Financial Accounting Standards Board
FDA Food and Drug Administration
FECA Federal Employees' Compensation Act
FEP Blue Cross and Blue Shield Federal Employee Program
FI Fiscal intermediary
FLSA Fair Labor Standards Act of 1938
FMLA Family and Medical Leave Act of 1993
FOIA Freedom of Information Act
FTE Full-time equivalent
GAAP Generally accepted accounting principles
GAAS Generally accepted auditing standards
GASB Government Accounting Standards Board
GIS Geographic information system
GMDN Global Medical Device Nomenclature
GPCI Geographic practice cost index
GPWW Group practice without walls
GUI Graphical user interface
HAVEN Home Assessment Validation and Entry
HCPCS Healthcare Common Procedure Coding System
HCPD Health care provider dimension
HCUP Healthcare Cost and Utilization Project
HEDIS Health Plan Employer Data and Information Set
HH PPS Home health prospective payment system
HHA Home health agency
HHRG Home health resource group
HHS Department of Health and Human Services
HI Hospitalization insurance (Medicare Part A)
HIE Health information exchange
HIM Health information management
HIMSS Health Information Management and Systems Society
HIPAA Health Insurance Portability and Accountability Act of 1996
HIPDB Healthcare Integrity and Protection Data Bank
IHS Indian Health Service
HIS Hospital information system
HIT Health or healthcare information technology
HITSP Health Information Technology Standards Panel
HL7 Health Level Seven
HMIS Health management information system
HMO Health maintenance organization
HOLAP Hybrid online analytical processing
HTML HyperText Markup Language
HUGN Human Genome Nomenclature
ICD-10-CM International Classification of Diseases, Tenth Revision, Clinical Modification
ICD-10-PCS International Classification of Diseases, Tenth Revision, Procedure Classification System
ICD-9-CM International Classification of Diseases, Ninth Revision, Clinical Modification
ICD-O International Classification of Diseases for Oncology
ICF International Classification on Functioning, Disability and Health
ICNP International Classification for Nursing Practice
ICPC-2 International Classification of Primary Care
ICR Intelligent character recognition
ICSI Institute for Clinical Systems Improvement
IDN Integrated delivery network
IDR Intelligent document recognition
IDS Integrated delivery system
IEEE Institute of Electrical and Electronics Engineers
IFHRO International Federation of Health Record Organizations
IMIA International Medical Informatics Association
IOM Institute of Medicine
IPA Independent practice association
IPF Inpatient psychiatric facility
IPO Integrated provider organization
IPSD Inpatient service day
IRB Institutional review board
IRF Inpatient rehabilitation facility
IRR Internal rate of return
IRVEN Inpatient Rehabilitation Validation and Entry
IS Information system
ISO United Nations International Standards Organization
ISS Injury Severity Score
IT Information technology
K-NN K-nearest neighbor
LOINC Logical Observation Identifier Names and Codes
LOS Length of stay
LTCH Long-term care hospital
LUPA Low-utilization payment adjustment
MBO Management by objectives

Health Information Management

Concepts, Principles, and Practice

Third Edition

Kathleen M. LaTour, MA, RHIA, FAHIMA
Shirley Eichenwald Maki, MBA, RHIA, FAHIMA
Editors

The Web sites listed in this book were current and valid as of the date of publication. However, Web page addresses and the information on them may change or disappear at any time and for any number of reasons. The user is encouraged to perform his or her own general Web searches to locate any site addresses listed here that are no longer valid.

ISBN: 978-1-58426-217-6
AHIMA Product Number AB103309

AHIMA Staff:

Claire Blondeau, MBA, Senior Editor
Katie Greenock, Editorial and Production Coordinator
Ashley Sullivan, Assistant Editor
Pamela Woolf, Developmental Editor
Ken Zielske, Director of Publications

American Health Information Management Association
233 North Michigan Avenue, Suite 2150
Chicago, Illinois 60601-5800

ahima.org

Contents

Detailed Table of Contents

PART II
Healthcare Information Development

PART III
Aggregate Healthcare Data

PART IV
Comparative Healthcare Data

PART VI
Management of Health Information Services

Appendices, Glossary, and Index

About the Editors and Authors

Kathleen M. LaTour, MA, RHIA, FAHIMA, is an assistant professor and chair of the department of healthcare informatics and information management (HIIM) at the College of St. Scholastica in Duluth, Minnesota. She is an active member of the Minnesota Health Information Management Association, where she was selected as the Distinguished Member in 1992. She has served as chair and member of many AHIMA councils and as a member of AHIMA's Board of Directors from 1993 to 1997. She participated in the development of the AHIMA Model Curricula for both bachelor's- and master's-level programs. She is currently a member of AHIMA's Health Information Exchange Practice Council and is a CAHIIM accreditation reviewer. She has authored several articles and contributed a chapter to Health Information Management Technology: An Applied Approach, second edition, a textbook published by AHIMA in 2006. She was awarded fellowship in AHIMA in recognition of sustained contributions to the field of HIM and, in 2004, was co-recipient of AHIMA's Legacy Award. She currently serves on the board of the Community Health Information Collaborative (CHIC) in Duluth and on the Standards Workgroup of the Minnesota Department of Health eHealth Initiative.

Shirley Eichenwald Maki, MBA, RHIA, FAHIMA, is an assistant professor in the department of healthcare informatics and information management at the College of St. Scholastica in Duluth. From 2002–2008, she served as project director for The ATHENS Project, a health sciences EHR curriculum project funded by a grant from the U.S. Department of Education, Title III program. She is the 2001 recipient of the College of St. Scholastica's Max H. Lavine Award for Teaching Excellence. She has served as chair and member of many AHIMA councils and committees, most recently as chair of the Research Committee, a member of the Nominating Committee, and project manager for AHIMA's HIM Researcher Training Institute in 2007 and 2008. A former AHIMA Board member and former president of AHIMA, she was awarded the association's Distinguished Member Award in 1998. She has held the position of director of education and accreditation at AHIMA. She serves on the Ambulatory EHR Working Group of the Certification Commission on Health Information Technology (CCHIT). She recently co-authored the text, *Using the Electronic Health Record in the Health Care Provider Practice* published in 2008 by Delmar Cengage Publishing. She was awarded fellowship in AHIMA in recognition of sustained contributions to the field of HIM and, in 2004, was co-recipient of AHIMA's Legacy Award.

Margret K. Amatayakul, MBA, RHIA, CHPS, FHIMSS, is president of Margret\A Consulting, LLC, in Schaumburg, Illinois, a consulting firm specializing in computer-based patient records and associated HIM standards and regulations, such as HIPAA. She has more than thirty years of experience in national and international HIM. A leading authority on electronic health record (EHR) strategies for healthcare organizations, she has extensive experience in EHR selection and project management, and she formed and served as executive director of the Computer-based Patient Record Institute (CPRI). Other positions held include associate executive director of AHIMA, associate professor at the University of Illinois, and director of medical record services at the Illinois Eye and Ear Infirmary. She is a much-sought-after speaker, has published extensively, and has earned several professional service awards. Amatayakul also serves as an adjunct faculty member of the College of St. Scholastica and the University of Illinois at Chicago.

Rita K. Bowen, MA, RHIA, CHPS, has nearly 30 years of experience in healthcare information management. She is currently the privacy officer for the Erlanger Health System in Chattanooga, Tennessee, and has previously held positions as director of health information services, director of medical records, marketing director, and medical records consultant at various hospitals and medical services companies throughout the United States. Bowen has an MA in health information management technology from the College of Saint Scholastica and earned her bachelor's degree in medical science from Emory University in Atlanta. She has a continuous history of activities with AHIMA and the Tennessee HIMA. She has served on AHIMA's Board of Directors since 2006, as president-elect in 2009, and as president in 2010.

Elizabeth D. Bowman, MPA, RHIA, has served as a professor in the HIIM program at the University of Tennessee Health Science Center in Memphis for more than 30 years and was appointed the interim chair of the department in 2006. She received a bachelor's degree from Millsaps College and a master's degree in public administration with a concentration in healthcare administration from the University of Memphis. Bowman is a co-editor of the last six editions of the *Tennessee Health Information Management Association Legal Handbook.* She has served as chair of the AHIMA Assembly on Education and received the AHIMA Educator Award in 1999. She is a recipient of the Tennessee Health Information Management Association's Distinguished Member Award. In addition, she has served as a commissioner on the Commission on Accreditation for Health Informatics and Information Management Education and as chair of the commission in 2007. She frequently presents seminars and legal updates for HIIM professionals.

Bonnie S. Cassidy, MPA, RHIA, FAHIMA, FHIMSS, CPHQ, received a BS degree in medical record administration from Daemen College in Amherst, New York, and a master's degree from Cleveland State University. A member of the AHIMA Board of Directors, she recently chaired the AHIMA Fellowship Review Committee and was a member of the EHR Transformation Workgroup, the Panel of Accreditation Surveyors for The Commission on Accreditation for Health Informatics and Information Management Education (CAHIIM), and the Clinical Terminology and Classification Practice Council. In addition, she has served as chair of the AHIMA Nominating and Professional Development committees; HIM Steering; QMS Roles and Functions committees; and the Data Quality, E-Health and Corporate Communications and Marketing Task Forces of AHIMA. Her achievements include the AHIMA 2000 Legacy Award, AHIMA's 1995 Professional Achievement Award, and the Distinguished Member Award from the Ohio Health Information Management Association (OHIMA), where she is a past president. In 2005, she was appointed to the Certification Commission for Health Information Technology Work Group on the Certification Process. She has represented the HIM profession on many levels, including as a frequent contributor to the *Journal of AHIMA* and as a presenter at AHIMA educational sessions and annual conventions. Her career has included working as a practitioner for two major teaching hospitals, a consultant for three professional service companies, adjunct faculty for two HIT programs, and vice-president of business development for an HIM-focused consulting company. Currently, she is president of Cassidy & Associates Consulting.

Nadinia Davis, MBA, CIA, CPA, RHIA, FAHIMA, is the Director of Health Records Services for Merit Mountainside Hospital in Montclair, New Jersey, and an adjunct instructor of Healthcare Finance Systems in the Health Informatics Department at the University of Medicine and Dentistry of New Jersey. She previously was an assistant professor of HIM at the College of Natural, Applied, and Health Sciences at Kean University in Union, New Jersey. She has worked as a coding consultant and auditor in acute settings and as director of medical records at a rehabilitation institute. Prior to her HIM career, Davis worked in the financial services industry, most recently as an internal auditor. She is a former president and a Distinguished Member of NJHIMA, as well as a former member of the AHIMA Board of Directors. She was a coauthor of *Introduction to Health Information Technology,* a contributor to *Effective Management of Coding Services,* and editor and contributor to *Workbook to Accompany Essentials of Health Care Finance.* Davis has been an active member of the New Jersey Society of Certified Public Accountants, and is currently serving on the Executive Committee of the Board of Trustees.

Margaret M. (Maggie) Foley, PhD, RHIA, CCS, is a clinical associate professor in the department of health information management at Temple University in Philadelphia. She has more than 20 years experience in various aspects of health information management. She has held the position of Director of Medical Records for a large acute care teaching hospital and a psychiatric facility. She is a member of the inaugural class of AHIMA's HIM Researcher Training Institute, 2007 and 2008. She has also held various volunteer positions in national, state, and local health information management professional associations. Recently, she has served on the AHIMA ICD-10-CM Implementation Task Force, the AHIMA Clinical Terminology and Classification Practice Council, and as a member of the PHIMA Executive Board.

Matthew J. Greene, RHIA, CCS, is functional analyst/HIM specialist and data content team leader for the Department of Veterans Affairs Health Data Repository project. Prior to this position, he was a coder and HIM manager at the Buffalo, New York, and Salt Lake City VA healthcare systems. He received a BS in medical record administration from Daemen College in Amherst, New York. He was awarded the 2004 Distinguished Member Award from the Utah Health Information Management Association (UHIMA). Currently, Greene is serving his second year as director of acute care for UHIMA. In addition, he has volunteered for several AHIMA initiatives, including the eHIM Workgroup and the ICD-10-CM Field Test, and he is an active member of the Health Level Seven (HL7) Medical Record/Information Management, Structured Documents, and EHR Technical committees. He also has been a workgroup volunteer for the eGov Consolidated Health Informatics (CHI) initiative.

J. Michael Hardin, PhD, is professor of statistics in the Department of Information Systems, Statistics, and Management Science at the University of Alabama in Tuscaloosa. In addition, he is adjunct professor of health informatics in the Department of Health Services Administration at the University of Alabama at Birmingham (UAB). Prior to these positions, Hardin served for 13 years as professor of health informatics, biostatistics, computer science, and preventive medicine at UAB and was selected as scholar in residence at Loyola University of Chicago. Moreover, he has been a visiting scholar at Trinity College, University of Dublin. A frequent speaker at AHIMA national meetings in the areas of database design, data modeling, and data mining, he has given more than 30 presentations on various topics related to data mining and data warehousing and has taught decision support in health informatics for the past seven years. He has authored or coauthored more than 90 publications and has served as a consultant to several major companies in the area of Medicare program integrity and utilization review.

Laurinda B. Harman, PhD, RHIA, is an associate professor and chair of the Department of Health Information Management at the College of Health Professions at Temple University in Philadelphia. She has been an HIM professional and educator for 40 years and has directed HIM baccalaureate programs at George Washington University in Washington, DC, and The Ohio State University in Columbus. Dr. Harman was a faculty member in the health information technology program at Northern Virginia Community College and served as director of education and human resource development for the Department of Health Care Sciences at George Washington University. She edited *Ethical Challenges in the Management of Health Information* and received the AHIMA 2001 Triumph Legacy Award for this important health information resource. The second edition was published in 2006. She contributed chapters to *Health Informatics Research: Practices and Innovative Approaches*; *Health Information Management: Concepts, Principles, and Practice;* and *Health Information Technology: An Applied Approach;* AHIMA publications. Dr. Harman is on the editorial board of *Perspectives in Health Information Management*, has contributed articles to *Journal of American Health Information Management Association* and has delivered presentations at several AHIMA National Conventions. She received a bachelor of science degree in biology with a concentration in medical record administration from Daemen College in Buffalo, New York, a master of science degree in education at Virginia Polytechnic and State University in Blacksburg, Virginia, and a PhD in human and organizational systems at Fielding Graduate University in Santa Barbara, California.

Anita C. Hazelwood, MLS, RHIA, FAHIMA, is a Professor in the Health Information Management Department at the University of Louisiana at Lafayette and has been a credentialed Registered Health Information Administrator (RHIA) for more than 30 years. Anita has actively consulted in hospitals, nursing homes, physician's offices, clinics, facilities for the mentally retarded, and in other educational institutions. She has conducted numerous ICD-9-CM and CPT coding workshop throughout the state for hospitals and physicians' offices and has written numerous articles and co-authored chapters in several HIM textbooks. Anita has co-authored two books titled *ICD-9-CM Coding and Reimbursement for Physicians' Services* and *ICD-10-CM Preview* for which she won AHIMA's Legacy Award in 2003. Anita has been a member of the American Health Information Management Association (AHIMA) for 32 years and has served on various committees and boards. Anita is a member of the Louisiana Health Information Management Association (LHIMA) and was selected as its 1997 Distinguished Member. She has served throughout the years as president, president-elect, treasurer, strategy manager and board member and has directed numerous committees and projects.

Loretta A. Horton, MEd, RHIA, received a medical record technician certificate from Research Hospital and Medical Center and a bachelor's degree in psychology from Rockhurst College, both in Kansas City, Missouri; a health information administration certificate from Stephens College in Columbia, Missouri; and a master's degree in education, with an emphasis in curriculum and instruction, from Wichita State University in Wichita, Kansas. She also has completed graduate work in sociology at the University of Nebraska in Omaha. Currently, Loretta is coordinator of the health information technology program at Hutchinson Community College in Hutchinson, Kansas. Previously, she worked in a variety of health information settings, including acute care and mental health, and has consulted with long-term care, mental retardation, home health, hospice, and prison systems. Additionally, she has worked as an instructor in the health information administration program at the College of St. Mary in Omaha, Nebraska, and for 3M (Code 3) as a marketing and training coordinator in Salt Lake City. Loretta has been active in component state organizations as well as the American Health Information Management Association. She has served on the Item Writing Task Force for the Council on Certification and currently serves on the Council on Accreditation.

Diana Lynn Johnson, PhD, is an assistant professor in the Computer Science/Information Systems Department at the College of St. Scholastica where she teaches systems analysis, technology ethics, and computer programming to both health informatics and information management students and computer science students. She has previously held positions as academic technology coordinator, senior systems development analyst, systems analyst, and programmer/analyst. She has been a technology educator for 16 years and has received the Business Professionals of America Faculty Award, the College of St. Scholastica Tassie McNamara Faculty Award, and is a multiple year honoree in Who's Who Among America's Teachers. She earned a master's degree in educational media and technology from the College of St. Scholastica and a doctorate in education with a specialization in instructional design from Capella University. She is a member of the Association for Computing Machinery and Delta Kappa Gamma International.

Elizabeth Layman, PhD, RHIA, CCS, FAHIMA, is professor and chair in the Department of Health Services and Information Management at East Carolina University, Greenville, North Carolina. She previously worked at Hennepin County Medical Center and the University of Minnesota

Hospitals, both in Minneapolis, from 1974 through 1990. Dr. Layman worked in several departments, such as third-party reimbursement, credit and collections, account auditing, outpatient registration, inpatient admissions, research studies, and quality management. In 1990, Dr. Layman joined the faculty of the Medical College of Georgia in Augusta. While on the faculty, she also consulted for the Physicians' Practice Group. Dr. Layman successfully sat for the first CCS examination in 1992. In 2001, she was awarded the designation of Fellow of the American Health Information Management Association, one of the first two individuals in the country to receive this award. She is the co-author of *Principles of Healthcare Reimbursement*, published by AHIMA in 2006, and for which she and her co-author were recipients of AHIMA's Legacy Award in 2007. She contributed chapters to the 2nd edition of *Health Information Management: Concepts, Principles, and Practice*, and *Health Informatics Research Methods: Principles and Practice*, both AHIMA publications. She was the first editor of *Perspectives in Health Information Management* and has delivered presentations at numerous AHIMA events. She earned her baccalaureate degree from the University of Minnesota. While working, she returned to school to earn her associate's degree in medical record technology. She completed St. Scholastica's progression program to earn her postbaccalaureate certificate in health information administration. She earned her master's degree in organizational leadership from the College of St. Catherine's and her doctorate in higher education from Georgia State University.

Madonna M. LeBlanc, MA, RHIA, is an assistant professor in the health informatics and information management program at the College of St. Scholastica in Duluth, Minnesota. From 2003-2008 she served as the HIIM department's designated faculty lead for the ATHENS Project—a health sciences effort to integrate an electronic health record system into professional curricula as a teaching/learning tool. Prior to her teaching role, she managed health information services at St.Mary's/Duluth Clinic Health System in Superior, Wisconsin. Her responsibilities included a broad spectrum of acute care HIM functions, from physician education to Joint Commission survey coordination. Her field experience also includes cancer registry and physician peer administration. She is a graduate of the College of St. Scholastica's Master's program in health information management. Madonna has served the Minnesota Health Information Management Association (MHIMA) as a member of the Board of Directors, president-elect in 2004-2005, president in 2005-2006 and serving since 2005 as MHIMA's community education coordinator for AHIMA's myPHR campaign.

Susan E. McClernon, MHA, FACHE, currently serves as the CEO/President of Innovative Healthcare Leadership, a healthcare consulting firm based in Duluth, MN. Sue previously served as a chief operating officer/administrator for large tertiary hospitals, including St. Mary's Medical Center in Duluth, Minnesota, and Brackenridge Hospital in Austin, Texas. Brackenridge Hospital was named a Top 100 Hospital in 2001, 2002, and 2003 by Modern Healthcare's Solucient Benchmarking process during Sue's tenure as administrator. She is an active Fellow in the American College of Healthcare Executives and was named Hospital Administrator of the Year in 2007 by HCAAM/MHA. She received her bachelor's degree in healthcare management from the College of St. Scholastica and her master's degree in healthcare administration from the University of Minnesota. She is currently pursuing her doctoral degree in health research, policy, and administration through the University of Minnesota School of Public Health. Sue has also been active in the American Hospital Association and Catholic Healthcare Association.

Pamela K. Oachs, MA, RHIA, is an assistant professor in the College of St. Scholastica's healthcare informatics and information management department. She teaches courses related to health information technology, system development and implementation, workflow redesign, healthcare management, and applied research. She has most recently participated in a collaborative student/faculty grant promoting the use of a personal health record in vulnerable populations. She has more than 15 years of healthcare experience. Her career has included a variety of positions, both managerial and professional, in the areas of utilization management, quality improvement, medical staff credentialing, Joint Commission coordination, information technology, project management, and patient access. She has been involved in system implementations, both small and large, in a variety of healthcare settings. She has served on the Board of Directors of the Minnesota Health Information Management Association and the Northeastern Minnesota Health Information Management Association.

Susan L. Parker, MEd, RHIA, currently serves as the AHIMA Career Counselor. She has been actively involved in the HIM industry for more than 25 years. She is currently owner of Seagate Consultants, a recruiting firm focused on health information management. Susan assists in establishing career action plans reflective of individual goals. Susan served on AHIMA's Board of Directors from 2000–2003.

Karen R. Patena, MBA, RHIA, is a clinical assistant professor and undergraduate program coordinator in the HIM program, Department of Biomedical and Health Information Sciences, College of Applied Health Sciences, at the University of Illinois at Chicago (UIC). She earned an MBA from DePaul University and is currently pursuing a doctorate degree at UIC. She is an alumnus of the University of Illinois health information management program. Previously, Patena was director of the independent study division of AHIMA and a faculty member at Indiana University and Prairie State College. She also has extensive experience in hospital medical record department management, including computer systems planning and implementation. Her areas of expertise include management, quality improvement and TQM, and the use of computers in healthcare and systems analysis. She has presented numerous tutorials at local, state, and national levels on the use of the Internet in HIM. She currently serves on the panel of accreditation surveyors for the Commission on Accreditation for Health Informatics and Information Management Education (CAHIIM)

Rebecca B. Reynolds, EdD, RHIA, is an associate professor and program director of the graduate program in health informatics and information management. She is past-president of the Tennessee Health Information Management Association and has served on the AHIMA Nominating Committee. She is a recipient of the Tennessee Health Information Management Association's Distinguished Member Award and the Outstanding New Professional Award. Reynolds was a 2006 recipient of AHIMA's Faculty Development Stipend Award and is a member of the inaugural class of AHIMA's HIM Research Training Institute. She received a master's degree in healthcare administration and her EdD in higher education leadership from the University of Memphis. She is currently on the Editorial Review Board for *Perspectives in Health Information Management* and most recently co-edited and co-authored the *Fundamentals of Law for Health Informatics and Information Management* textbook published by AHIMA.

Lynda A. Russell, EdD, JD, RHIA, CHP, is privacy manager at Cedars-Sinai Medical Center in Los Angeles. She holds a baccalaureate degree in medical record science from the Medical College of Georgia, a master's and doctorate in educational administration and supervision from the University of Central Florida, and a JD from the University of Florida. A member of the California Bar, she is licensed to practice before the Superior Court of California and the Federal Court of the Central District of California. She is certified in healthcare privacy. Russell has been an HIM professional for more than 30 years and has been active professionally on the national, state, and local levels. She served as president of the Florida Health Information Management Association and of the California Health Information Association (CHIA). She has held numerous local, state, and national committee appointments, including chair of AHIMA's Educational Strategy Committee and AHIMA's Component State Association Advisory Committee as well as chair of CHIA's Editorial Board. Russell is an adjunct instructor with the Santa Barbara City College HIT Program. She also serves as a frequent speaker and has published widely on a variety of health information and related topics, including HIPAA.

Patricia B. Seidl, RHIA, CCDM, has more than nine years of project management experience and is currently working in clinical research data management for Astellas Pharma, Inc. She has 18 years of experience in information technology as a systems analyst and project manager. Seidl previously served as an adjunct professor for the project management certificate program at the College of St. Scholastica and was a contributing author to *Special Edition: Using Microsoft Project 2000.* She received a bachelor's degree from the College of St. Scholastica and an associate of applied science degree in computer science from the University of Southern Colorado.

Carol Marie Spielman, MA, RHIA, has served in numerous HIM leadership roles for more than 30 years, including director of HIM at a northern Minnesota healthcare system comprising four hospitals and more than 20 clinics, director of HIM at a long-term respiratory care hospital in St. Paul, director of HIM at mental health facilities in West Virginia and North Dakota, and director of HIM at a critical access hospital in northern Michigan. She has directed the computer application selection process, application implementation, the report design and distribution process, and updates and ongoing maintenance for numerous clinical registries in the areas of cancer, cardiology/cardiac surgery, and trauma, in addition to the Medicare quality measures. She has co-led healthcare system information management teams in preparation for numerous Joint Commission surveys. She recently served on healthcare system leadership teams to plan for the implementation of the Epic electronic health record at three of the system's hospitals, and to evaluate requests for new clinical registries based on an internally designed criteria set. She has worked in healthcare sales, has served on numerous college advisory boards for HIM and related programs. She has served as board member and newsletter editor for the Minnesota Health Information Management Association, and recently served as the Minnesota Epic User's Group chairperson for HIM. She is currently the radiology and lab/pathology reimbursement analyst for St. Mary's Duluth Clinic Health System in Duluth, Minnesota, and adjunct faculty in the health information and informatics masters program at the College of St. Scholastica.

David X. Swenson, PhD, is an associate professor in the management department at the College of St. Scholastica, where he teaches strategic management, organizational development, leadership, and principles of management. He is also clinical associate professor of behavioral sciences at the University of Minnesota Medical School and a forensic psychologist in private practice. He has worked in the field of psychology for more than 35 years. In addition, he has served as director of student development at the College of St. Scholastica, director of clinical services at the Human Resource Center of Douglas County, Wisconsin, and co-director of a training and consulting partnership. He has authored more than 80 publications, including *Stress Management for Law Enforcement.* A doctoral graduate of the University of Missouri at Columbia in counseling and personnel services, Swenson also has master's degrees in management and educational media and technology and is a diplomate in forensic psychology.

Carol A. Venable, MPH, RHIA, FAHIMA, is a professor and department head of HIM at the University of Louisiana at Lafayette and has been an HIM professional for nearly 30 years. She is actively involved with AHIMA's Assembly on Education (AOE), Panel of Accreditation Surveyors, and several other committees, as well as the Louisiana Health Information Management Association, where she has held many leadership positions and was selected as Distinguished Member in 1991. In addition, she is a member of the Society for Clinical Coding (SCC). Previously, she was director of medical records at Lafayette General Medical Center, has consulted in a variety of healthcare facilities and educational institutions, and conducts coding workshops for hospitals and physician offices. Venable has written, coauthored, and edited numerous publications, including AHIMA's *ICD-9-CM Diagnostic Coding and Reimbursement for Physician Services* and *ICD-10-CM Preview*, for which she was awarded AHIMA's Legacy Award in 2003. She frequently serves as a reviewer for publishers of HIM-related textbooks, certification exams, and electronic materials.

Karen A. Wager, DBA is an associate professor in the department of health administration and policy at the Medical University of South Carolina in Charleston, where she received a master's degree in health information administration and finance. In 1998, she received a doctorate of business administration from the University of Sarasota. She is a member of AHIMA and has served on various association committees. She was president of the South Carolina Health Information Management Association (SCHIMA) from 1991 to 1992.

Amy L. Watters, MA, RHIA, is an assistant professor and director of the HIM graduate program at the College of St. Scholastica. She has more than 10 years of HIM experience. Her career has included a variety of positions, including release of information experience, HIM and admitting management experience in acute care settings, product management experience at a software and consulting firm, and HIPAA security experience at a multi-specialty physician group. She has served on the board of the Minnesota Health Information Management Association and is currently serving as president of the Northeastern Minnesota Health Information Management Association.

Vicki L. Zeman, MA, RHIA, is academic coordinator of professional practice experience for the Department of Healthcare Informatics and Information Management at the College of St. Scholastica in Duluth, Minnesota. An HIM professional for 30 years, she practiced in a variety of settings for 13 years before becoming an educator. Her last six years in practice were focused on the area of hospitalwide quality improvement. She is co-coordinator of the Personal Health Key Project, funded by the Minnesota Community Foundation Vision Grant, which promotes the use of a personal health records in the St. Scholastica campus community. While serving as an instructor in the HIM program for 17 years, she also served as the coordinator of the RHIT to RHIA progression program.

Preface

Health information management (HIM) professionals play a critical role in the delivery of healthcare in the United States through their focus on the collection, maintenance and use of quality data to support the information-intensive and information-reliant healthcare system. HIM professionals practice in an increasingly diverse set of roles in a wide variety of healthcare settings: provider and payer organizations, public and private agencies—research, licensing, accreditation, etc., and vendor organizations which provide health IT products, as well as consulting and outsourcing services. As managers of healthcare data and information systems, HIM professionals collaborate with other members of the healthcare team to ensure that an individual's health data and information is accurate, complete, accessible, confidential, and secure. The dynamic nature of the HIM profession reflects the continuous change that characterizes the healthcare delivery system as a whole.

Although expansion of the HIM profession is a positive and rewarding trend, it poses unique challenges for preparing students in educational programs to assume a variety of positions within the healthcare industry. The need to respond to change has driven the efforts of the American Health Information Management Association (AHIMA) to develop model curricula for associate-, baccalaureate-, and master's-level education. The model curricula create clear boundaries between the various levels of HIM education in terms of content, program outcomes, and professional competencies. The accreditation process for HIM programs and the certification examinations for RHIAs and RHITs support these deliberately defined differences in content and competencies at the different levels of professional education.

This textbook is designed to reflect HIM practice at the baccalaureate level with emphasis on the core set of skills and knowledge set forth in the AHIMA model curriculum. Its topics reflect the recommended content as defined in the Model Curriculum for Baccalaureate Degree Programs in Health Information Management. The content and organization of the text allow for the effective integration of dynamic concepts into an existing HIM curriculum. It also serves as a resource for current practitioners in the field who seek to update or expand their knowledge base in one or more content areas reflected in the evolving professional body of knowledge.

All the content areas of the AHIMA Model Curriculum for Baccalaureate Programs are covered in this text with the exception of those related to the biomedical sciences (anatomy, physiology, pathophysiology/disease processes, medical terminology, pharmacology, and so on), basic human resources management principles, and the skill-development aspects of classification systems. The editors recognize that in some content areas, specialized content-specific textbooks may be required as additional resources, especially for developing competence in coding, the use of basic computer systems, and human resources management.

Central to the organization of this text is the information management model created by the Joint Commission. This model presents HIM as an incremental process that begins with the collection of patient-specific data, followed by the aggregation of data to generate information, the development of comparative data, and, finally, the utilization of such data and derived information to increase knowledge and support decision making.

In combination, use of the AHIMA model curriculum and the Joint Commission information management model as the foundations of this textbook ensures that the content is covered in a logical and systematic way. The structure of each chapter is designed to help students apply concepts and principles in practice in an organized and systematic way. The features used to accomplish this goal include the following:

- Examples and case studies used throughout the text reflect the contemporary spectrum of HIM practice environments.
- Some chapters begin with a Theory into Practice section, which includes a case study. The case study gives the learner an appreciation of how the major concepts and principles in the chapter are applied in a practice-based situation.
- Each chapter contains Check Your Understanding sections that allow learners to verify their command of the information presented in the chapter. Answers appear in appendix C.
- Many chapters contain a Real-World Case developed from today's top stories in healthcare delivery.

The text is presented in six parts. Part I introduces the concepts of informatics and information management as they apply to the healthcare industry. It also introduces the profession of health information management.

Chapter 1 introduces the concept of HIM, discusses the overall characteristics and challenges of today's modern healthcare environment, and provides a short history of AHIMA.

Chapter 2 provides an overview of the organizations that deliver, finance, and regulate healthcare services in the United States. It focuses on the impact of accreditation, licensure, regulation, reimbursement systems, and legal and ethical issues in creating the environment for managing and delivering healthcare services. This chapter provides a context for the concepts and applications presented in the remainder of the text.

Chapter 3 introduces the field of informatics as it is applied in healthcare. The chapter surveys the emerging technologies in the clinical environment (for example, imaging, natural language processing, artificial intelligence, and Web technologies). It explores the major issues associated with computerizing clinical data and presents an overview of the types of computer applications used to support clinical decision making. It also identifies the barriers and limitations associated with computerized clinical decision support.

Chapter 4 introduces the body of knowledge, competencies, and ethical principles that constitute the core of the HIM profession's contributions to the healthcare industry. The education, certifications, and associations that are identified with the HIM profession are discussed, as are the functions and roles of HIM professionals.

Chapter 5 introduces the concept of information as an organizational asset that must be managed effectively to provide and sustain its value. The chapter discusses the components of the Joint Commission information management model. It presents the principles, tools, and techniques used to develop data, to create a database infrastructure and establish reporting capabilities that meet the needs of the various types and levels of information systems users within an organization. The essential characteristics of quality data as well as the principles, regulations, and techniques associated with ensuring data security are presented as the primary concerns of information managers. Knowledge management applications, data warehousing, and data mining are also discussed.

Chapter 6, introduces the process of information systems development. It begins with a discussion of information systems planning as a component of an organization's strategic planning effort. This chapter focuses on the information systems life cycle: its phases, the activities within each phase, and the unique and complementary roles of information technology staff, information management professionals, and information users in the information systems development effort.

Part II focuses on the development of health information systems from the perspective of individual patients. It addresses the development of personally identifiable health information and the basic concepts of managing health records in both a manual and a computerized environment in today's healthcare facilities.

Chapter 7 addresses healthcare information standards, including the concept of converting data into information in the healthcare environment. It also explores the development of uniform standards that guide data collection in healthcare. It discusses healthcare data sets, including the history, purpose, and use of each. It also introduces emerging healthcare informatics standards that support the transition from paper-based to computer-based health records.

Chapter 8 focuses on the content and structure of patient-specific data and personally identifiable data and information, as collected in individual health records. It addresses data sources, capture of data in a health record, and documentation requirements. This chapter also addresses management issues related to paper-based record systems, including clinical documentation issues, medical word processing as a tool for documentation, forms design, storage and retrieval systems, and chart tracking.

Chapter 9 focuses on the development of electronic health records (EHRs), including issues related to the transition from paper-based records to electronic or computer-based records. Data capture, imaging, security, and user needs are among the topics addressed. Issues related to the creation and maintenance of computer-based patient records also are discussed.

Chapters 10 and 11 focus on the legal and ethical concepts and issues related to healthcare information systems and HIM practice. Current legal and regulatory issues are explored, including issues related to privacy, confidentiality, security, and access to healthcare data. Work processes related to release of information policies and procedures are addressed. Ethical issues such as those related to computerization of clinical information, the coding–reimbursement connection, and vendor–organization relationships are among those discussed in chapter 11.

Part III focuses on the conversion of patient-specific data and information into aggregate data used for analysis, statistics, and research, as well as clinical and administrative decision making.

Chapter 12 focuses on secondary or impersonal uses of healthcare data, that is, data that have been abstracted from individual health records and captured in healthcare databases. Included in this chapter are secondary records such as indexes, registers, and registries, as well as exploration of data sources, data capture, and the healthcare information infrastructure. Information management concepts are applied to healthcare database development.

Chapter 13 provides an introduction to classification systems for healthcare data including ICD-9-CM, CPT, and SNOMED. Emerging clinical vocabularies are introduced, and the concept of data representation in computer-based systems is explored, as is medical linguistics as a basis for clinical classifications and vocabularies.

Chapter 14 provides an overview of the uses of coded data and health information in reimbursement systems. Included in this chapter are issues related to coding management, case-mix management, billing procedures, and severity-of-illness classifications. Methods for managing the quality of coded data are addressed.

Part IV introduces the development and use of comparative data in healthcare and focuses on the development of statistical and research methodologies. It addresses professional competencies put forth in the AHIMA Model Curriculum for HIA programs.

Chapter 15 emphasizes the collection, use, presentation, and verification of statistical healthcare data. Fundamentals of descriptive and inferential statistics are covered, as are standard formulae for facility-based statistics. This chapter focuses on the practical application of descriptive and inferential statistics in a healthcare environment and the application of information management concepts in developing comparative data.

Chapter 16 addresses basic research methods as they are applied to healthcare information. The chapter focuses on the steps in developing a research project, including defining a research problem, performing a literature review, determining research design and methodology, selecting measurement instruments, analyzing data, and presenting study results. Library research techniques and data search and access also are addressed.

Chapter 17 addresses the collection and use of aggregate data in the analysis and evaluation of healthcare services. Topics such as clinical quality assessment, clinical outcomes management, critical pathways and case management, utilization review, and risk management systems are explored. The chapter focuses on healthcare data as a resource in clinical decision making.

Part V explores knowledge-based healthcare data and information and applies the concepts of knowledge management to the use of healthcare information for biomedical and research support as well as for expert systems and decision support. The process of converting knowledge assets into wisdom to create a learning organization is explored.

Chapter 18 presents concepts associated with acquiring clinical knowledge-based data. This chapter addresses national research policy development, medical/health research and investigation, and research protocol data management. The role of HIM professionals in a research environment is explored.

Chapter 19 addresses the application of artificial intelligence concepts to support administrative, executive, and clinical decision making. Specifically, the chapter focuses on the various types and classes of decision support systems being used in healthcare and how they are being used. The concepts of data warehousing and data mining, as they apply to decision support systems, are discussed. Emerging career opportunities for HIM professionals in decision support areas are explored.

Part VI addresses the tools, techniques, and strategies utilized in managing health information services. It provides an overview of human resources management and focuses on applications of both operational and human resources management principles in the healthcare setting.

Chapter 20 introduces the management discipline, the evolution of management thought, and the functions of management. It presents the principles and basic tools associated with each management function. The relationship between management functions and skills within the various levels of management in an organization is discussed. Communications and problem-solving models and techniques are explored.

Chapter 21 addresses leadership theory and functions, traits related to leadership effectiveness, and key differences between the concepts of managing and leading. The role of a leader in positively facilitating the transition of people through organizational change is explored.

Chapter 22 focuses on the systems nature of work processes in organizations. It introduces the concepts, tools, and techniques associated with designing (and redesigning) effective and efficient work processes, as well as those associated with implementing new or revised work processes. Performance measurement and performance improvement in terms of productivity, quality measurement, benchmarking, and work process redesign are presented as major topics.

Chapter 23 discusses the implementation of appropriate policies, procedures, and practices in each of the seven human resources (HR) activity areas: HR planning and analysis; equal employment opportunity; staffing; HR development; compensation and benefits; health, safety, and security; and employee and labor/management relations. Effective recruitment, selection, and hiring practices also are discussed, as well as job orientation and performance review.

Chapter 24 focuses on training and retaining employees in a highly competitive labor environment and with a rapidly diversifying workforce pool. Topics include orientation programs, staff development programs, continuing education needs identification, and employee retention strategies. A departmental training and development model is presented. Trends in staffing are explored, including flexible scheduling, job sharing, home-based work, and outsourcing.

Chapter 25 focuses on the concepts and tools associated with planning and controlling the financial resources required to operate a department or work unit within a healthcare organization. Basic financial and managerial accounting principles, concepts, and reporting are explained. Operations, labor, and capital budgeting processes and techniques are presented. Organizational and departmental financial performance measures are reviewed, with a special emphasis on accounts receivable management. The role(s) that HIM professionals play in the financial management of the organization is explored.

Chapter 26 addresses project management. The focus is on the various aspects of a project that must be integrated to effectively move it from an idea to a functioning reality. The organization and processes that must be put in place to effectively manage a project are defined. The requisite skill set of project managers as well as the tools and techniques used by effective project managers are explored. The impact that the project context, stakeholder needs and expectations, and competing demands have on the project manager's work is highlighted.

Chapter 27 focuses on the role of the health information professional and manager as a visionary leader and strategist for a department and an organization. The principles of strategic management are presented. Models for strategic planning and techniques for implementing a strategic management philosophy into a department or organization are explored.

Four appendixes follow Part VI. Appendix A features sample health record documentation forms. Appendix B features the 2004 AHIMA Code of Ethics and the 2008 Standards for Ethical Coding. Appendix C provides an answer key to the student self-study Check Your Understanding exercises within each chapter. In this edition, Appendix D is on the enclosed CD-ROM only. It contains a list of HIM-related Web resources with live URL links for easy access.

A complete glossary of HIM terms is included at the end of this book. Throughout the text chapters, boldface type is used to indicate the first substantial reference to key terms included in the glossary. A detailed content index is also included. Frequently used abbreviations, acronyms, and initials are spelled out on the inside covers of the book for easy reference.

Acknowledgments

The editors and publications staff would like to express appreciation to the many authors who contributed chapters to this textbook. They willingly shared their expertise, met tight deadlines, accepted feedback, and contributed to building the body of knowledge related to health information management. Writing a chapter is a time-consuming and demanding task, and we are grateful for the authors' contributions.

We would also like to thank authors who contributed to previous editions of this textbook:

Mehnaz Farishta, MS
Susan H. Fenton, MBA, RHIA
Sandra R. Fuller, MA, RHIA
Michelle A. Green, MPS, RHIA, CMA
Linda L. Kloss, MA, RHIA, CAE
Mary Cole McCain, MPA, RHIA
Carol E. Osborn, PhD, RHIA
Kam Shams, MA
Andrea Weatherby White, PhD, RHIA
Frances Wickham Lee, DBA, RHIA

We also would like to thank the following reviewers who lent a critical eye to this endeavor.

Current edition reviewers:

June E. Bronnert, RHIA, CCS, CCS-P
Jill Burrington-Brown, MS, RHIA
Michelle L. Dougherty, RHIA, CHP
Jill S. Clark, MBA, RHIA
Kathy DeVault, RHIA, CCS
Angela K. Dinh, MHA, RHIA
Claire Dixon-Lee, PhD, RHIA, FAHIMA
Melanie A. Endicott, MBA/HCM, RHIA, CCS
Susan H. Fenton, MBA, RHIA
Beth Hjort, RHIA, CHPS
Karen Kostick, RHIT, CCS, CCS-P
Donald T. Mon, PhD, FHIMSS
Dan Rode, MBA, FHFMA
Stephen A. Sivo, PhD
Mary H. Stanfill, RHIA, CCS, CCS-P
Lou Ann Wiedemann, MS, RHIA, CPEHR
Maggie Williams, MA

Previous edition reviewers also include:

Donna Bowers, JD, RHIA, CHP
Christopher G. Chute, MD, DrPH
Leslie A. Fox, MA, RHIA, FAHIMA
Jennifer Garvin, PhD, RHIA, CPHQ, CCS, FAHIMA
Kathy Giannangelo, RHIA, CCS
Barry S. Herrin, CHE, Esq.
Susan Hull, MPH, RHIA, CCS, CCS-P
Lolita M. Jones, RHIA, CCS
Carol Ann Quinsey, RHIA, CHPS
Harry Rhodes, MBA, RHIA, CHPS
Rita A. Scichilone, MHSA, RHIA, CCS, CCS-P, CHC
Valerie Watzlaf, PhD, RHIA, FAHIMA
Ann Zeisset, RHIT, CCS-P, CCS

Finally the editors wish to acknowledge the guidance, patience, and expertise of Pamela Woolf, Developmental Editor. She is the glue that held the entire project together. The editors also wish to thank Senior Editor Claire Blondeau, MBA, who filled this role for the second edition.

Foreword

To Tomorrow's Health Information Leaders:

Publication of the third edition of *Health Information Management Concepts, Principles, and Practice* comes at a time of unprecedented focus on healthcare information. The United States and many nations are investing in health information and communications technology as a strategy to improve the quality and safety of patient care and manage system costs. Health information management (HIM) has become a top line issue in health systems across the world and in the United States. Significant financial investment is finally ramping up—and not a moment too soon.

The Institute of Medicine published the landmark study "To Err is Human" in 1999. In 2000, the U.S. National Committee of Vital and Health Statistics called for development of a national health information infrastructure. In 2004, former President George W. Bush called for widespread adoption of interoperable electronic health records (EHRs) within 10 years and appointed a national coordinator for health information technology. Federal leadership, combined with substantial private-sector leadership, produced progress in accelerating standards development, certification of EHRs, implementation of first generation regulations for privacy and security, and testing of interoperable solutions. However, physician adoption did not ramp up at the level required to achieve the goal of EHRs for all citizens by 2014. Despite disappointing adoption rates to date, support for digital health information continues to grow as a bipartisan issue in Washington, D.C. and in nearly all state capitals.

In February 2009, President Barack Obama signed the American Recovery and Reinvestment Act into law (Public Law 111-5) providing the first significant funding in the United States for health information and communication technology and related programs. Holding to the goal of EHRs for all citizens by 2014, PL 111-5 includes nearly $20 billion for provider loans and grants to defray some of the physician and hospital costs to acquire and implement certified EHRs. It also sets up a national plan to govern and coordinate national policy and standards to provide technical assistance and shared learning through research. Importantly, it acknowledges the significance of developing a workforce capable of implementing and optimizing the use of systems and using information to improve care. *You* are part of that critical workforce as your professional preparation comes at a time when demand for health information management professionals has never been stronger. You will implement and optimize the use of systems, safeguard personal information, and learn to use vital health data to improve patient care and the health of the population.

In the 82 years since the HIM field was created, the role of the health information management professional has never been more expansive or more relevant. Research shows that HIM professionals practice in 40 work settings and more than 100 job titles. The importance of these roles will continue to expand as HIM shifts from process management to highly valued knowledge work. *Health Information Management: Concepts, Principles, and Practice* is a compendium of the knowledge, skills, and competencies that you need to succeed as an HIM professional. In this Third Edition, Editors Shirley Eichenwald Maki, MBA, RHIA, FAHIMA, and Kathleen M. LaTour, MA, RHIA, FAHIMA have revised and rethought each chapter so it reflects the latest developments of this fast-paced field. They have designed this text to provide comprehensive coverage of the "science" of health information management and then added the "art" through a rich variety of case studies and exercises. They assembled content experts representing the breadth of information management in healthcare today and the foundational concepts and principles that will enable today's students to solve tomorrow's problems.

The context within which information is managed—the healthcare system; concepts of informatics, information, and information systems management; and the profession of health information management—is expertly covered by contributors Bonnie S. Cassidy, MPA, RHIA, FAHIMA, FHIMSS; Amy L. Watters, MA, RHIA; Susan Parker, MEd, RHIA; Diana Lynn Johnson, PhD; Carol Marie Spielman, MA, RHIA; and Karen A. Wager, DBA.

The sources, types, and standards for health information and the legal and ethical requirements for electronic health information are covered by experts from the field and from academia including Rita A. Scichilone, MHSA, RHIA, CCS, CCS-P, CHC-F; Rebecca B. Reynolds, EdD, RHIA; Elizabeth D. Bowman, MPA, RHIA; Margret K. Amatayakul, MBA, RHIA, CHPS, CPEHR, FHIMSS; Lynda A. Russell, EdD, JD, RHIA, CHP; Rita K. Bowen, MA, RHIA, CHPS; and Laurinda B. Harman, PhD, RHIA.

Managing and deriving value from aggregate and comparative data, including the use of data for quality improvement and research is addressed by Elizabeth D. Bowman, MPA, RHIA; Matthew J. Greene, RHIA, CCS; Margaret M. Foley, PhD,

RHIA, CCS; Anita C. Hazelwood, MLS, RHIA, FAHIMA; Carol A. Venable, MPH, RHIA, FAHIMA; Loretta A. Horton, MEd, RHIA; Elizabeth Layman, PhD, RHIA, CCS, FAHIMA; Vicki L. Zeman, MA, RHIA; Valerie Watzlaf, PhD, RHIA, FAHIMA; J. Michael Hardin, PhD; and Uzma Raja, PhD.

Management, leadership, and strategy is ably discussed by practice and academic leaders including David X. Swenson, PhD; Pamela K. Oachs, MA, RHIA; Madonna M. LeBlanc, MA, RHIA; Karen R. Patena, MBA, RHIA; Nadinia Davis, MBA, CIA, CPA, RHIA, FAHIMA; Patricia B. Seidl, RHIA, CCDM; and Susan E. McClernon, MHA, CHE.

Opportunities for health information professionals continue to expand to include areas of information management subspecialties such as executive leadership, health data analytics, quality improvement, revenue cycle management and compliance, privacy and security management, information systems and policy management, and education. This text is dedicated to you, the health information management student. You are tomorrow's professional leaders, and your efforts will ensure that health information and communications technology investments deliver on their promise to improve health and the quality of healthcare. This text also is dedicated to those who built and nurtured this profession and its legacy of service. As we complete the transition from a paper-based to computer-based healthcare information system, we will be fulfilling the dream of our profession's leaders: high-quality healthcare through high-quality information.

Linda L. Kloss, MA, RHIA, FAHIMA
Chief Executive Officer
American Health Information
Management Association

Part I

Informatics and Health Information Management

Chapter 1
Introduction

Shirley Eichenwald Maki, MBA, RHIA, FAHIMA, and Kathleen M. LaTour, MA, RHIA, FAHIMA

The field of health information management (HIM) has been a recognized field of professional study for 75 years. It was originally called medical record science and members of the profession were originally called medical record librarians. From its inception, the mission of the profession was to elevate the standards of clinical recordkeeping in hospitals, dispensaries, and other healthcare facilities. Since its founding, the professional association, now known as the American Health Information Management Association (AHIMA), and the professionals affiliated with it have been advocates for the effective management of clinical data and health records to ensure their confidentiality, integrity, and availability in every type of healthcare setting. HIM professionals serve the healthcare industry and the public by managing, analyzing, and utilizing the information vital for patient care, and making it accessible to healthcare providers when and where it is needed (Johns 2006). AHIMA and its members strive to support the delivery of "quality healthcare through quality information" (AHIMA 2008).

Beginning with the managed care movement in the 1980s, effective information management began to emerge as a top priority for healthcare institutions. Subsequently, events affecting healthcare delivery and the management of healthcare delivery services have placed even greater pressure on healthcare organizations to improve their information-handling capacity and functionality. Johns (2006) emphasizes that the healthcare industry now fully recognizes the importance of information flow across departmental boundaries and the necessity of broad dissemination throughout the organization. Currently, there are significant government and industry initiatives focused on the goal of improving the delivery of healthcare by "bringing timely health information to, and aiding communication among, those making health decisions for themselves, their families, their patients, and their communities" (NCVHS 2001). These initiatives have been supported through a series of public and private endeavors to address critical elements in accomplishing the goal. The efforts include a series of Institute of Medicine reports, the Department of Health and Human Services (HHS) recommendations for creating a National Health Information Infrastructure, the Markle Foundation's Connecting for Health, and efforts toward standards development. This chapter provides a brief introduction to the HIM profession and focuses on the changing nature of its core domain of practice. It sets the stage for the remaining chapters by providing a context for the broad range of topics that must be addressed in a textbook whose purpose is to describe the concepts, principles, and practices associated with the HIM profession in its current state of transformation. (A full discussion of the HIM profession and related professional associations is presented in chapter 4.)

The Modern Healthcare Environment

In the 1990s, several forces at work in the U.S. healthcare industry had a transformational effect on the HIM profession. During that decade, competition among healthcare providers was stimulated by major changes in the reimbursement system used by Medicare and Medicaid (two federally mandated healthcare programs). Integrated healthcare delivery systems also began to emerge as significant organizational models, and managed care delivery systems continued to expand. As a result of these developments, the availability of timely and accurate clinical information has become critical to the viability of healthcare organizations. Medical and administrative staffs recognize that the information gathered from clinical records is an invaluable organizational asset. They also understand that this information represents an important quality indicator and a vital tool for efficiently managing the business of healthcare in a tight financial environment.

The wise application of increasingly sophisticated computer technology also has received increased attention among healthcare professionals and organizations. Technology is the obvious solution to the industry's need for greater efficiency in managing the ever-increasing volume of healthcare data. In addition, as diverse healthcare decision makers look for flexibility in how to access and analyze vast electronic repositories of clinical data, advanced decision support technology is critical to meeting that demand.

Today, these trends continue to affect the practice of health information management and healthcare in general as:

- The federal government strategic vision includes every American having an interoperable electronic health record (EHR) by the year 2014. In his first message to Congress in January 2009, President Obama pledged economic stimulus support to the development of HIT initiatives.
- State governments and regional public/private partnerships work to establish health information exchange (HIE) systems that facilitate the transfer of health information among authorized parties to enhance the quality of care and reduce the cost of healthcare services.
- Payers pilot healthcare reimbursement systems that provide incentives for healthcare organizations to implement health information technologies (HIT) to support quality-of-care programs.
- Regulators and accreditation agencies focus on the use of computer-based information technologies to improve patient safety and reduce the number of medical errors.
- Healthcare consumers are creating and maintaining personal health records (PHRs) with the support of many employers, healthcare providers, third-party payers, and independent HIT vendors to facilitate access to more complete and accurate information for continuing care.
- Workforce shortages place greater emphasis on technological systems for improving productivity of the healthcare workforce.
- Integrated information system (IS) solutions as well as clinician-friendly hardware and applications are continuing to evolve.
- The Internet and its derived technologies make connectivity across otherwise disparate information systems accessible and affordable for healthcare organizations.

Contemporary Health Information Management

The HIM profession is the only profession that has as its core professional mission the quality of the data collected and maintained in the course of delivering healthcare services. Although clinical and allied healthcare professionals depend on the availability of high-quality data to perform clinical decision making, their primary concern is providing diagnostic and therapeutic services, not managing clinical information. The administrators and managers of healthcare organizations also use collected clinical information to plan and manage healthcare services, but managing the quality of the data they use is not their major concern. Similarly, computer scientists and technicians are concerned primarily with the performance of software and hardware configurations; researchers are concerned primarily with the development of scientific solutions to important questions; third-party payers are concerned primarily with the control of financial resources; and policy makers are concerned primarily with incentives for cost-effectiveness, social justice, and ethical practice. Although they all rely on high-quality data, only the HIM profession is charged with ensuring the availability of high-quality data for a variety of uses and users.

In an information-intensive environment embedded within a technology supported framework, HIM professionals must continuously build and market their unique knowledge base and competencies in the following areas:

- Practice standards, laws, and regulations related to ensuring the accuracy, completeness, integrity, privacy, and security of healthcare information
- The legal health record, as the business record for each healthcare organization
- Healthcare data standards
- Healthcare data analytics and reporting methods
- Clinical coding, classification, and reimbursement systems
- Health record and information systems design, functions, and maintenance
- Organizational and cross-disciplinary modes of functioning to achieve quality and productivity goals

Once applied in a world of paper-based records and manual systems, the HIM knowledge base and competencies are now needed to effectively transition vital clinical data resources into electronic clinical repositories and EHR systems. These modern technological systems support both the operational and strategic needs of the organization's workforce and decision makers. In addition, "The shift to electronic practice has enlivened the profession and opened doors to new work settings . . . such as biotechnology, public health, pharmaceuticals, and government" (Wilhelm and Dixon-Lee 2007, 25). (Chapter 4 discusses emerging roles for HIM professionals.)

Today the HIM profession remains committed to its original mission to elevate health record standards and practices. It does so, however, in a healthcare environment that is becoming more and more technology driven in both its work processes and information flow, as well as more and more dependent on the quality and accessibility of the information contained within clinical records. HIM professionals work to ensure that their communities and customers are provided high-quality and cost-effective healthcare information services.

HIM skills and competencies are needed by all organizations that use person-specific or aggregate patient data. The national push to adopt health information technology will accelerate the demand for a qualified HIM workforce (Kloss 2005).

Working in strong collaborative partnerships with specialists in information technologies and with specialized healthcare data and information users (physicians, nurses, pharmacists, therapists, administrators, researchers, policy makers, and others), health information managers have become key players within the emerging discipline of healthcare informatics. Healthcare informatics focuses on designing and implementing technology-based information systems to support the specialized activities associated with each type of healthcare worker. For example, nursing informatics focuses on systems that support the work of nurses, and medical informatics focuses on systems that support the work of physicians. Similarly, consumer informatics systems support the activities of patients, long-term care residents, and healthcare clients (Shortliffe, et al. 2000).

Thus, to carry on the important legacy of their predecessors, today's HIM professionals support an adapted vision of their unique contribution. They build and maintain an accompanying set of strengthened competencies for the healthcare industry they serve. They envision how the concepts, principles, and practices at the core of the HIM knowledge base and competencies continue to apply in their changing work environment and settings. In addition, they assess their adaptive strengths and weaknesses relative to that vision and, most important, they take action to position themselves appropriately to contribute their unique expertise to the organizations they serve.

Summary

The HIM profession began with the founding of the Association of Record Librarians of North America in 1928. The association's original goal was to improve clinical recordkeeping in healthcare facilities. The association, now known as the American Health Information Management Association, and a new generation of HIM professionals have inherited a powerful legacy from those original medical records pioneers. Today, HIM professionals have an extraordinary opportunity and obligation to build on their professional legacy by elevating the standards for clinical data and information systems in a healthcare environment that demands integrated, computer-based, user-focused data repositories and warehouses. The viability and vitality of the HIM profession in the future depends on the commitment of current and future professionals to think and act strategically in order to address the data and information needs of an evolving healthcare industry. To meet that challenge, HIM professionals must continually update their knowledge base and competencies through self-assessment and commitment to lifelong learning, and they must actively take part in their professional organizations' activities at the local, regional, state, and national levels.

References

AHIMA. Vision. 2008. http://www.ahima.org/about/mission.asp.

Blum, B.I. 1986. *Clinical Information Systems.* New York: Springer-Verlag.

Johns, M.L. 2006. Introduction. Chapter 1 in *Health Information Management Technology: An Applied Approach,* 2nd ed. Chicago: AHIMA.

Kloss, L. 2005. Supply and demand: A challenge for healthcare and HIM. *Journal of AHIMA.* 76(5):23.

NCVHS. November 1, 2001. *A Strategy for Building the National Health Information Infrastructure.* Washington, DC.

Protti, D.J. 1984. Knowledge and skills expected of health information scientists: A sample survey of prospective employers. *Methods of Information in Medicine* 23(4):204–208.

Shortliffe, E.H., L.E. Perreault, G. Wiederhold, and L.M. Fagan, eds. 2000. *Medical Informatics: Computer Applications in Health Care and Biomedicine.* New York: Springer-Verlag.

Wilhelm, C. and C. Dixon-Lee. 2007. A new blueprint for HIM education. *Journal of AHIMA.* 78(8):25.

Chapter 2
The U.S. Healthcare Delivery System

Bonnie S. Cassidy, MPA, RHIA, FAHIMA, FHIMSS

Learning Objectives

- Understand the history of the healthcare delivery system from ancient times to the present
- Know the basic organization of the various types of hospitals and healthcare organizations
- Recognize the impact of managed care on healthcare providers
- Recognize the impact of external forces on the healthcare industry
- Identify the various functional components of an integrated delivery system
- Describe the systems used for reimbursement of healthcare services
- Recognize the role of government in healthcare services

Key Terms

Accreditation
Acute care
Ambulatory care
American Association of Medical Colleges (AAMC)
American College of Healthcare Executives (ACHE)
American College of Surgeons
American Health Information Management Association (AHIMA)
American Hospital Association (AHA)
American Medical Association (AMA)
American Nurses Association (ANA)
Average length of stay (ALOS)
Behavioral healthcare
Biotechnology
Blue Cross and Blue Shield Association
Case management
Centers for Medicare and Medicaid Services (CMS)
Chief executive officer (CEO)
Chief financial officer (CFO)
Chief information officer (CIO)
Chief nursing officer (CNO)
Chief operating officer (COO)
Clinical privileges
Commission on Accreditation of Health Informatics and Information Management Education (CAHIIM)
Conditions of Participation
Continuous quality improvement (CQI)
Continuum of care
Deemed status
Evidence-based medicine
Extended care facility
Health savings accounts
Health systems agency
Home healthcare
Hospice care
Hospital Survey and Construction Act (Hill-Burton Act)
Integrated delivery network (IDN)
Integrated delivery system (IDS)
Investor-owned hospital chain
Joint Commission
Long-term care
Malpractice
Managed care
Managed care organization (MCO)
Medicaid
Medical device
Medical staff bylaws
Medical staff classifications
Medicare
National Committee for Quality Assurance (NCQA)
National Institutes of Health (NIH)
National Practitioner Data Bank (NPDB)
Peer review
Peer review organization (PRO)
Physician assistant (PA)
Postacute care
Prospective payment system (PPS)
Public Health Service (PHS)
Quality improvement organization (QIO)
Reengineering
Rehabilitation services
Skilled nursing facility (SNF)
Subacute care
Tax Equity and Fiscal Responsibility Act (TEFRA)
Telehealth
TRICARE
Utilization Review Act
Workers' compensation

A broad array of healthcare services is available in the United States today, ranging from simple preventive measures such as vaccinations to complex lifesaving procedures such as heart transplants. An individual's contact with the healthcare delivery system often begins with family planning and prenatal care before he or she is born and continues through end-of-life planning and hospice care.

Healthcare services are provided by physicians, nurses, and other clinical providers who work in ambulatory care, acute care, rehabilitative and psychiatric care, and long-term care facilities. Healthcare services also are provided in the homes of hospice and home care patients. Assisted living centers, industrial medical clinics, and public health department clinics also provide services to many Americans.

Integrated delivery systems (IDSs) provide a full range of healthcare services along a continuum of care to ensure that patients get the right care at the right time from the right provider. The continuum extends from primary care providers to specialist and ancillary providers. The goal of IDSs is to deliver high-quality and cost-effective care in the most appropriate setting (Sloane et al. 1999, 9). Most hospitals are integrated into their communities through ties with area physicians and other healthcare providers, clinics and outpatient facilities, and other practitioners. Almost half of the nation's hospitals are tied to larger organizational entities, such as multihospital and integrated healthcare systems (IHCSs), integrated delivery networks (IDNs), and alliances. A network or IDN is a group of hospitals, physicians, other providers, insurers, or community agencies that work together to deliver health services (AHA 2004).

In 2002, there were more than 1,300 **acute care** hospitals (27 percent of the total) in networks (AHA 2004). Multihospital systems include two or more hospitals owned, leased, sponsored, or contract managed by a central organization. In 1985, 27.5 percent of hospitals were system members; by 2002, this figure had risen to 46 percent (AHA 2004). Within the context of healthcare, an alliance is a formal organization usually owned by shareholders or members that works on behalf of its individual members to provide services and products and to promote activities and ventures (AHA 1999). In 2000, there were more than 3,300 hospitals in group-purchasing organizations (the dominant kind of alliance). The same hospitals can be registered in more than one category (AHA 2000).

In 2002, there were 321 multihospital or integrated healthcare systems in the United States. The majority were not-for-profit, including religious (56) and secular (209) systems. Fifty-one systems were investor owned, and five were operated by the federal government (Jonas and Kovner 2005, 232). From 1997 to 2005, the total number of hospitals that provided acute care services remained relatively constant, with a negligible drop from 5,350 in 1997 to 5,213 in 2005 (HFMA 2008). This chapter discusses the origin of the healthcare industry in the United States and examines the history from the 1800s to the 21st century. Included in this history is the impact of external forces that have shaped the healthcare system of today.

History of Western Medicine

Modern Western medicine is rooted in antiquity. The ancient Greeks developed surgical procedures, documented clinical cases, and created medical books. Before modern times, European, African, and Native American cultures all had traditions of folk medicine based on spiritual healing and herbal cures. The first hospitals were created by religious orders in medieval Europe to provide care and respite to religious pilgrims traveling back and forth from the Holy Land. However, it was not until the late 1800s that medicine became a scientific discipline. More progress and change occurred during the twentieth century than over the preceding 2,000 years. The past few decades have seen dramatic developments in the way diseases are diagnosed and treated as well as the way in which healthcare is delivered.

Before the advent of modern Western medicine, epidemics and plagues were common. Epidemics of smallpox, measles, yellow fever, influenza, scarlet fever, and diphtheria killed millions of people. Bubonic plague spread periodically through Europe and killed millions more. Disease was carried by rodents and insects as well as by the travelers who moved along intercontinental trade routes.

The medical knowledge that had been gained by ancient Greek scholars such as Hippocrates was lost during the Middle Ages. The European Renaissance, a historical period beginning in the 14th century, revived interest in the classical arts, literature, and philosophy as well as in the scientific study of nature. This period also was characterized by economic growth and concern for the welfare of workers at all levels of society. With this concept came a growing awareness that a healthy population promoted economic growth.

North America's First Hospitals

Early settlers in the British colonies of North America appointed commissions to care for the sick, to provide for orphans, and to bury the dead. During the mid-1700s, the citizens of Philadelphia recognized the need for a place to provide relief to the sick and injured. They also recognized the need to isolate newly arrived immigrants who had caught communicable diseases on the long voyage from Europe.

In Philadelphia, Benjamin Franklin and other colonists persuaded the legislature to develop a hospital for the community. It was the first hospital in the British colonies of North America. The Pennsylvania Hospital was established in Philadelphia in 1752. (Almost 200 years earlier, Hernando Cortez established the first hospital in Mexico, and it still serves patients today.)

Over its first 150 years, the Pennsylvania Hospital served as a model for the organization of hospitals in other communities. The New York Hospital opened in 1771 and started its first register of patients in 1791. Boston's Massachusetts General Hospital opened in 1821.

Standardization of Medical Practice

Human anatomy and physiology and the causes of disease were not well understood before the twentieth century. At one time, it was believed that four basic fluids, called humors, determined a person's temperament and health and that the imbalances in the proportion of humors in the body caused disease. The therapeutic bleeding of patients was practiced until the early twentieth century. Early physicians also treated patients by administering a variety of substances with no scientific basis for their effectiveness.

An individual's early medical education consisted of serving as an apprentice to an established practitioner. Just about anyone could hand out a shingle and call himself a physician. The medical profession recognized that some of its members achieved better results than others, and leaders in the profession attempted to regulate the practice of medicine in the late 1700s. The first attempts at regulation took the form of licensure. The first licenses to practice medicine were issued in New York in 1760. By the mid-1800s, however, efforts to license physicians were denounced as being undemocratic, and most states removed penalties for practicing medicine without a license.

As the population of the United States grew and settlers moved westward, the demand for medical practitioners far exceeded the supply. To staff new hospitals and serve a growing population, many private medical schools appeared almost overnight. By 1869, there were 72 medical schools in the United States. However, these schools did not follow an established course of study and some graduated students with as little as six months of training. The result was an oversupply of poorly trained physicians.

The American Medical Association (AMA) was established in 1847 to represent the interests of physicians across the United States. However, the AMA was dominated by members who had strong ties to the medical schools and the status quo. Its ability to lead a reform of the profession was limited until it broke its ties with the medical schools in 1874. At that time, the association encouraged the creation of independent state licensing boards.

In 1876, the **American Association of Medical Colleges** (AAMC) was established. The AAMC was dedicated to standardizing the curriculum for U.S. medical schools and to developing the public's understanding of the need to license physicians.

Together, the AMA and the AAMC campaigned for medical licensing. By the 1890s, 35 states had established or reestablished a system of licensure for physicians. At that time, 14 states decided to grant licenses only to graduates of reputable medical schools. The state licensing boards discouraged the worst medical schools, but the criteria for licensing continued to vary from state to state and were not fully enforced.

By the early twentieth century, it had become apparent that improving the quality of American medicine required regulation through curriculum reform as well as licensure. However, the members of the AMA were divided on this issue. Conservative members continued to believe that the association should stay out of the area of regulation. Progressive members supported the continued development of state licensure systems and the creation of a standardized model for medical education.

The situation attracted the attention of the Carnegie Foundation for the Advancement of Teaching. The president of the foundation offered to sponsor and fund an independent review of the medical colleges then operating in the United States. Abraham Flexner, an educator from Louisville, Kentucky, undertook the review in 1906.

Over the following four years, Flexner visited every medical college in the country and carefully documented his findings. In his 1910 report to the Carnegie Foundation, the AMA, and the AAMC, he described the poor quality of the training provided in the colleges. He noted that medical school applicants often lacked knowledge of the basic sciences. Flexner also reported how the absence of hospital-based training limited the clinical skills of medical school graduates. Perhaps most important, he reported that huge numbers of graduates were being produced every year and that most of them had unacceptable levels of medical skill. He recommended closing most of the existing medical schools to address the problem of oversupply.

Several reform initiatives grew out of Flexner's report and from recommendations made by the AMA's Committee on Medical Education. One of the reforms required medical school applicants to hold a college degree. Another required that medical training be founded in the basic sciences. Reforms also required that medical students receive practical, hospital-based training in addition to classroom work. These reforms were carried out in the decade following Flexner's report, but only about half of the medical schools actually closed. By 1920, most of the medical colleges in the United States had met rigorous academic standards and were approved by the AAMC.

Today, medical school graduates must pass a test before they can obtain a license to practice medicine. The licensure tests are administered by state medical boards. Many states now use a standardized licensure test developed in 1968 by the Federation of State Medical Boards of the United States. However, passing scores for the test vary by state. Most physicians also complete several years of residency training in addition to medical school.

Specialty physicians also complete extensive postgraduate medical education. Board certification for the various specialties requires the completion of postgraduate training as well as a passing score on a standardized examination. The most common medical specialties include the following:

- Internal medicine
- Pediatrics
- Family practice
- Cardiology
- Psychiatry
- Neurology
- Oncology
- Radiology

The most common surgical specialties include:

- Anesthesiology
- Cardiovascular surgery
- Obstetrics and gynecology
- Orthopedics
- Urology
- Ophthalmology
- Otorhinolaryngology
- Plastic and reconstructive surgery
- Neurosurgery

Some medical and surgical specialists undergo further graduate training to qualify to practice subspecialties. For example, the subspecialties of internal medicine include endocrinology, pulmonary medicine, rheumatology, geriatrics, and hematology. Physicians also may limit their practices to the treatment of specific illnesses. For example, an endocrinologist may limit his or her practice to the treatment of diabetes. Surgeons can work as general surgeons or as specialists or subspecialists. For example, an orthopedic surgeon may limit his practice to surgery of the hand, surgery of the knee, surgery of the ankle, or surgery of the spine.

Some physicians and healthcare organizations employ **physician assistants** (PAs) and surgeon assistants (SAs) to help them carry out their clinical responsibilities. Such assistants may perform routine clinical assessments, provide patient education and counseling, and perform simple therapeutic procedures. Most PAs work in primary care settings, and most SAs work in hospitals and ambulatory surgery clinics. PAs and SAs always work under the supervision of licensed physicians and surgeons.

Standardization of Nursing Practice

In the nineteenth century and the first part of the twentieth century, religious organizations sponsored more than half of the hospitals in the United States. Members of religious orders often provided nursing care in these organizations. As the U.S. population grew and more towns and cities were established, new hospitals were built. Older cities also grew, and city hospitals became more and more crowded.

In the late 1800s, nurses received no formal education and little training. Nursing staff for the hospitals was often recruited from the surrounding community and many poor women who had no other skills became nurses. The nature of nursing care at that time was unsophisticated. Indeed, the lack of basic hygiene often promoted disease. Many patients died from infections contracted while hospitalized for surgery, maternity care, and other illnesses.

In 1868, the AMA called the medical profession's attention to the need for trained nurses. During the years that followed, the public also began to call for better nursing care in hospitals.

The first general training school for nurses was opened at the New England Hospital for Women and Children in 1872. It became a model for other institutions throughout the country. As hospital after hospital struggled to find competent nursing staff, many institutions and their medical staffs developed their own nurse training programs.

The responsibilities of nurses in the late nineteenth and early twentieth centuries included housekeeping duties. Nurses also cooked meals for patients in kitchens attached to each ward. Direct patient care duties included giving baths, changing dressings, monitoring vital signs, administering medications, and assisting physicians. During this time, nurses were not required to hold a license to practice.

In 1897, a group of nurses attending the annual meeting of the American Society of Superintendents of Training Schools for Nursing founded the Nurses Associated Alumnae of the United States and Canada. In 1911, the organization was renamed the **American Nurses Association** (ANA). During the early meetings of the association, members established a nursing code of ethics and discussed the need for nursing licensure and for publications devoted to the practice of nursing.

At the turn of the twentieth century, nurses also began to organize state nursing associations to advocate for the registration of nurses. Their goal was to increase the level of competence among nurses nationwide. Despite opposition from many physicians who believed that nurses did not need formal education or licensure, North Carolina passed legislation requiring the registration of nurses in 1903. Today, all 50 states have laws that spell out the requirements for the registration and licensure of nursing professionals.

Modern registered nurses (RNs) must have either a two-year associate's degree or a four-year bachelor's degree from a state-approved nursing school. Nurse practitioners, researchers, educators, and administrators generally have a four-year degree in nursing and additional postgraduate education in nursing. The postgraduate degree may be a master's of science or a doctorate in nursing. Nurses who graduate from nonacademic training programs are called licensed practical nurses (LPNs) or licensed vocational nurses (LVNs). Non-degreed nursing personnel work under the direct supervision of registered nurses. Nurses in all 50 states must pass an exam to obtain a license to practice.

Today's RNs are highly trained clinical professionals. Many specialize in specific areas of practice such as surgery, psychiatry, and intensive care. Nurse-midwives complete advanced training and are certified by the American College of Nurse-Midwives. Similarly, nurse-anesthetists are certified by the Council on Certification and Council on Recertification of Nurse Anesthetists. Nurse practitioners also receive advanced training at the master's level that qualifies them to provide primary care services to patients. They are certified by several organizations (for example, the National Board of Pediatric Nurse Practitioners) to practice in the area of their specialty. According to the American Hospital Association (2008), hospitals today have an estimated 116,000 RN vacancies with projections of a U.S. shortage of 1 million RNs by 2020.

Standardization of Hospital Care

In 1910, Dr. Franklin H. Martin suggested that the surgical area of medical practice needed to become more concerned with patient outcomes. He had been introduced to this concept in discussions with Dr. Ernest Codman. Codman was a British physician who believed that hospital practitioners should track their patients for a significant amount of time after treatment so that they could determine whether the end result had been positive or negative. Codman also supported the use of outcome information to identify the practices that led to the best results for patients.

At that time, Martin and other American physicians were concerned about the conditions in U.S. hospitals. Many observers felt that part of the problem was related to the lack of organization in medical staffs and lax professional standards. In the early twentieth century, before the development of antibiotics and other pharmaceuticals, hospitals were used mainly by physicians who needed facilities in which to perform surgery. Most nonsurgical medical care was still provided in the home. It was natural, then, for the force behind improved hospital care to come from surgeons.

The push for hospital reforms eventually led to the formation of the **American College of Surgeons** in 1913. The organization faced a difficult task. In 1917, the leaders of the college asked the Carnegie Foundation for funding to plan and develop a hospital standardization program. The college then formed a committee to develop a set of minimum standards for hospital care. It published the formal standards under the title of the Minimum Standards.

During 1918 and part of 1919, the college examined the hospitals in the United States and Canada just as Flexner had reviewed the medical colleges a decade earlier. The performance of 692 hospitals was compared to the college's Minimum Standards. Only 89 of the hospitals fully met the college's standards; some of the best-known hospitals in the country failed to meet them.

Adoption of the Minimum Standards was the basis of the Hospital Standardization Program and marked the beginning of the modern **accreditation** process for healthcare organizations. Basically, accreditation standards are developed to reflect reasonable quality standards. The performance of each participating organization is evaluated annually against the standards. The accreditation process is voluntary. Healthcare organizations choose to participate in order to improve the care they provide to their patients.

The American College of Surgeons continued to sponsor the hospital accreditation program until the early 1950s. At that time, four professional associations from the United States and Canada decided to join forces with the college to create a new accreditation organization. This organization was called the Joint Commission on Accreditation of Hospitals. The associations were the American College of Physicians, the AMA, the American Hospital Association (AHA), and the Canadian Medical Association. The new organization was formally incorporated in 1952 and began to perform accreditation surveys in 1953.

The Joint Commission continues to survey several different types of healthcare organizations today, including:

- Acute care hospitals
- Long-term care facilities
- Ambulatory care facilities
- Psychiatric facilities
- Home health agencies

Several other organizations also perform accreditation of healthcare organizations. These include the American Osteopathic Association (AOA), the Commission on Accreditation of Rehabilitation Facilities (CARF), and the Accreditation Association for Ambulatory Healthcare (AAAHC).

Professionalism of the Allied Health Professions

After the First World War, many of the roles previously played by nurses and nonclinical personnel began to change. With the advent of modern diagnostic and therapeutic technology in the middle of the twentieth century, the complex skills needed by ancillary medical personnel fostered the growth of specialized training programs and professional accreditation and licensure.

According to the AMA's definition, *allied health* incorporates the healthcare-related professions that function to assist, facilitate, and complement the work of physicians and other clinical specialists. The Health Professions Education Amendment of 1991 describes allied health professionals as health professionals (other than RNs, physicians, and PAs) who have received a certificate, an associate's degree, a bachelor's degree, a master's degree, a doctorate, or postdoctoral training in a healthcare-related science. Such individuals share responsibility for the delivery of healthcare services with clinicians (physicians, nurses, and PAs).

Allied health occupations are among the fastest growing in healthcare. The number of allied health professionals is difficult to estimate and depends on the definition of allied health. Unlike medicine, women dominate most of the allied health professions, representing between 75 and 95 percent in most of the occupations. All 50 states require licensure for some allied health professions (physical therapy, for example). Practitioners in other allied health professions (occupational therapy, for example) may be licensed in some states, but not in others.

The following list briefly describes some of the major occupations usually considered to be allied health professions (Jonas and Kovner 2005, 446–448):

- *Clinical laboratory science*: Originally referred to as medical laboratory technology, this field is now referred to more appropriately as clinical laboratory science. Clinical laboratory technicians perform a wide array of tests on body fluids, tissues, and cells to assist in the detection, diagnosis, and treatment of diseases and illnesses.
- *Diagnostic imaging technology:* Originally referred to as x-ray technology and then radiologic technology, this field is now more appropriately referred to as diagnostic imaging. The field continues to expand to include nuclear medicine technologists, radiation therapists, sonographers (ultrasound technologists), and magnetic resonance technologists.
- *Dietetics*: Registered dietitians (RDs) (sometimes called clinical nutritionists) are trained in nutrition. They are responsible for providing nutritional care to individuals and for overseeing nutrition and food services in a variety of settings, ranging from hospitals to schools.
- *Emergency medical technology*: Emergency medical technicians (EMTs) are responsible for providing a wide range of services on an emergency basis for cases of traumatic injury and other emergency situations and in the transport of emergency patients.
- *Health information management:* Health information management (HIM) professionals (formerly called medical record managers) oversee health record systems and manage health-related information to ensure that it meets relevant medical, administrative, and legal requirements. Health records are the responsibility of registered health information administrators (RHIAs) and registered health information technicians (RHITs).
- *Occupational therapy*: Occupational therapists (OTs) evaluate and treat patients whose illnesses or injuries have resulted in significant psychological, physical, or work-related impairment.
- *Physical therapy*: Physical therapists (PTs) evaluate and treat patients to improve functional mobility, reduce pain, maintain cardiopulmonary function, and limit disability. PTs treat movement dysfunction resulting from accidents, trauma, stroke, fractures, multiple sclerosis, cerebral palsy, arthritis, and heart and respiratory illness. Physical therapy assistants work under the direction of PTs and help carry out the treatment plans developed by PTs.
- *Respiratory therapy*: Respiratory therapists evaluate, treat, and care for patients with breathing disorders. They work under the direction of qualified physicians and provide services such as emergency care for stroke, heart failure, and shock, as well as treat patients with emphysema and asthma.
- *Speech-language pathology and audiology*: Speech-language pathologists and audiologists identify, assess, and provide treatment for individuals with speech, language, or hearing problems.

Check Your Understanding 2.1

Instructions: On a separate piece of paper, write down the word or term that correctly completes each of the sentences.

1. The ancient ___ developed surgical procedures, documented clinical cases, and created medical books.
   a. Egyptians
   b. Greeks
   c. Phoenicians
   d. Chinese
2. The ___ was established in 1847 to represent the interests of physicians across the United States.
   a. American Association of Medical Colleges
   b. American College of Surgeons
   c. Committee on Medical Education
   d. American Medical Association
3. Today, medical school students must pass a test before they can obtain a ___ to practice medicine.
   a. degree
   b. residency
   c. specialty
   d. license
4. The first general training school for ___ was opened at the New England Hospital for Women and Children in 1872.
   a. nurses
   b. physician assistants
   c. surgical specialists
   d. surgeons
5. Modern ___ must have either a two-year associate's degree or a four-year bachelor's degree from a state-approved nursing school.
   a. nurse practitioners
   b. licensed vocational nurses
   c. registered nurses
   d. licensed practical nurses
6. In 1910, Dr. Franklin H. Martin suggested that the surgical area of medical practice needed to become more concerned with ___.
   a. patient care
   b. professional standards
   c. patient outcomes
   d. nonsurgical medical care
7. Adoption of the Minimum Standards marked the beginning of the modern ___ process for healthcare organizations.
   a. accreditation
   b. licensing
   c. reform
   d. educational
8. According to the AMA's definition, ___ incorporates the healthcare-related professions that function to assist, facilitate, and complement the work of physicians and other clinical specialists.
   a. home health
   b. nursing care
   c. ambulatory care
   d. allied health

Modern Healthcare Delivery in the United States

Until the Second World War, most healthcare was provided in the home. Quality in healthcare services was considered a product of appropriate medical practice and oversight by physicians and surgeons. Even the Minimum Standards used to evaluate the performance of hospitals were based on factors directly related to the composition and skills of the hospital medical staff.

The twentieth century was a period of tremendous change in American society. Advances in medical science promised better outcomes and increased the demand for healthcare services. But medical care has never been free. Even in the best economic times, many Americans have been unable to take full advantage of what medicine has to offer because they cannot afford it.

Concern over access to healthcare was especially evident during the Great Depression of the 1930s. During the Depression, America's leaders were forced to consider how the poor and disadvantaged could receive the care they needed. Before the Depression, medical care for the poor and elderly had been handled as a function of social welfare agencies. During the 1930s, however, few people were able to pay for medical care. The problem of how to pay for the healthcare needs of millions of Americans became a public and governmental concern. Working Americans turned to prepaid health plans to help them pay for healthcare, but the unemployed and the unemployable needed help from a different source.

Effects of the Great Depression

The concept of prepaid healthcare, or health insurance, began with the financial problems of one hospital, Baylor University Hospital in Dallas, Texas (AHA 1999, 14). In 1929, the administrator of the hospital arranged to provide hospital services to Dallas's schoolteachers for 50 cents per person per month. Before that time, a few large employers had set up company clinics and hired company physicians to care for their workers, but the idea of a prepaid health plan that could be purchased by individuals had never been tried before.

The idea caught on quickly, and new prepaid plans appeared across the country. Eventually, these plans became known as Blue Cross plans when the blue cross symbol used by some of the new plans was adopted officially as the trademark for all the plans in 1939.

Another type of prepaid plan, called the Blue Shield plan, was subsequently developed to cover the cost of physicians' services. The idea for the Blue Shield plans grew out of the medical service bureaus created by large lumber and mining companies in the Northwest. In 1939, the first formal Blue Shield plan was founded in California.

Growth in the number of Blue Cross/Blue Shield plans continued through the Depression and boomed during the World War II. During the war-related labor shortages, employers began to pay for their employees' memberships in the "Blues" as a way to attract and keep scarce workers.

The idea of public funding for healthcare services also goes back to the Great Depression. The decline in family income during the 1930s curtailed the use of medical services by the poor. In 10 working-class communities studied between 1929 and 1933, the proportion of families with incomes under $150 per capita had increased from 10 to 43 percent. A 1938 Gallup poll asked people whether they had put off seeing a physician because of the cost. The results showed that 68 percent of lower-income respondents had put off medical care, compared with 24 percent of respondents in upper-income brackets (Starr 1982, 271).

The decreased use of medical services and the inability of many patients to pay meant lower incomes for physicians. Hospitals were in similar trouble. Beds were empty, bills went unpaid, and contributions to hospital fund-raising efforts tumbled. As a result, private physicians and charities could no longer meet the demand for free services. For the first time, physicians and hospitals asked state welfare departments to pay for the treatment of people on relief.

The Depression posed a severe test for the AMA. It was no easy matter to maintain a common front against government intervention when physicians themselves were facing economic difficulties. Because of the economic hardships, many physicians were willing to accept government-sponsored health insurance. In 1935, the California Medical Association endorsed the concept of compulsory health insurance because health insurance promised to stimulate the use of physicians' services and help patients pay their bills.

The AMA's response to the economic crisis emphasized restricting the supply of physicians, rather than increasing the demand for their services by instituting mandatory health insurance. The AMA reacted by pushing for the closure of medical schools and reductions in the number of new medical students.

By the mid-1930s, however, the AMA began to adjust its position on health insurance. Instead of opposing all insurance, voluntary or compulsory, it began to define the terms by which voluntary programs might be acceptable. Although accepting health insurance plans in principle, the AMA did nothing to support or encourage their development.

The push for government-sponsored health insurance continued in the late 1930s during the administration of President Franklin D. Roosevelt. However, compulsory health insurance stood on the margins of national politics throughout the New Deal era. It was not made part of the new Social Security program, and it was never fully supported by President Roosevelt.

Postwar Efforts toward Improving Healthcare Access

After World War II, the issue of healthcare access finally moved to the center of national politics. In the late 1940s, President Harry Truman expressed unreserved support for a national health insurance program. However, the issue of compulsory health insurance became entangled with America's fear of communism. Opponents of Truman's healthcare program labeled it "socialized medicine," and the program failed to win legislative support.

The idea of national health insurance did not resurface until the administration of Lyndon Johnson and the Great Society legislation of the 1960s. The Medicare and Medicaid programs were legislated in 1965 to pay the cost of providing healthcare services to the elderly and the poor. The issues of healthcare reform and national health insurance were again given priority during the first four years of President Bill Clinton's administration in the 1990s. However, the complexity of American healthcare issues at the end of the twentieth century doomed reform efforts.

Influence of Federal Legislation

During the twentieth century, Congress passed many pieces of legislation that had a significant impact on the delivery of healthcare services in the United States. Many of these legislative efforts are described in the following subsections.

Biologics Control Act of 1902

Direct federal sponsorship of medical research began with early research on methods for controlling epidemics of infectious disease. The Marine Hospital Service performed the first research. In 1887, a young physician named Joseph Kinyoun set up a bacteriological laboratory in the Marine Hospital at Staten Island, New York. Four years later, the Hygienic Laboratory was moved to Washington, D.C. It was given authority to test and improve biological products in 1902 when Congress passed the Biologics Control Act. This act regulated the vaccines and sera sold via interstate commerce. That same year, the Hygienic Laboratory added divisions in chemistry, pharmacology, and zoology.

In 1912, the service, by then called the U.S. Public Health Service, was authorized to study chronic as well as infectious diseases. In 1930, reorganized under the Randsdell Act, the Hygienic Laboratory became the **National Institutes of Health** (NIH). In 1938, the NIH moved to a large, privately donated estate in Bethesda, Maryland (Starr 1982, 340).

Today, the mission of the NIH is to uncover new medical knowledge that can lead to health improvements for everyone. The NIH accomplishes its mission by conducting and supporting medical research, fostering communication of up-to-date medical information, and training research investigators. The organization has played a vital role in recent clinical research on treatment of the following diseases:

- Heart disease and stroke
- Cancer
- Depression and schizophrenia
- Spinal cord injuries

Social Security Act of 1935

The Great Depression revived the dormant social reform movement in the United States as well as more radical currents in American politics. Unionization increased and the American Federation of Labor abandoned its long-standing opposition to social insurance programs. The Depression also brought to power a Democratic administration. The administration of Franklin D. Roosevelt was more willing than any previous administration to involve the federal government in the management of economic and social welfare.

Even before Roosevelt took office in 1933, a steady movement toward some sort of social insurance program had been growing. By 1931, nine states had passed legislation creating old-age pension programs. As governor of New York, Roosevelt endorsed unemployment insurance in 1930. Wisconsin became the first state to adopt such a measure early in 1932.

Although old-age pension and unemployment insurance bills were introduced into Congress soon after his election, Roosevelt refused to give them his strong support. Instead, he created a program of his own. In June 1934, he announced that he would appoint a Committee on Economic Security to study the issue comprehensively and report to Congress in January 1935. The committee consisted of four members of the cabinet and the federal relief administrator and was headed by the secretary of labor, Frances Perkins.

Although Roosevelt indicated in his June message that he was especially interested in old-age and unemployment programs, the committee included medical care and health insurance in its research. From the start, the prevailing sentiment on the committee was that health insurance would have to wait. Abraham Epstein was the founder of the American Association for Social Security and a leading figure in the social insurance movement. In an article published in October 1934, he warned the administration that opposition to health insurance was strong. He advised the administration to be politically realistic and cautious on health insurance.

Sentiment in favor of health insurance was strong among members of the Committee on Economic Security. However, many members of the committee were convinced that adding a health insurance amendment would spell defeat for the entire Social Security legislation. Ultimately, the Social Security bill included only one reference to health insurance as a subject that the new Social Security Board might study. The Social Security Act was passed in 1935.

The omission of health insurance from the legislation was by no means the act's only conservative feature. It relied on a regressive tax and gave no coverage to some of the nation's poorest people, such as farmers and domestic workers. However, the act did extend the federal government's role in public health through several provisions unrelated to social insurance. It gave the states funds on a matching basis for maternal and infant care, rehabilitation of crippled children, general public health work, and aid for dependent children under the age of 16.

Hospital Survey and Construction Act of 1946

Passage of the **Hill-Burton Act** was another important development in American healthcare delivery. Enacted in 1946 as the **Hospital Survey and Construction Act**, this legislation authorized grants for states to construct new hospitals and, later, to modernize old ones. The fund expansion of the hospital system was to achieve a goal of 4.5 beds per 1,000 persons. The availability of federal financing created a boom in hospital construction during the 1950s. The hospital system grew from 6,000 hospitals in 1946 to a high of approximately 7,200 acute care hospitals.

Growth in Number of Hospitals

The number of hospitals in the United States increased from 178 in 1873 to 4,300 in 1909. In 1946, at the close of World War II, there were 6,000 American hospitals, with 3.2 beds available for every 1,000 persons.

In 2002, there were 4,927 hospitals in the United States, with a total of 821,000 beds. Of the $1.4 trillion spent on healthcare in 2001, hospital costs totaled $415 billion or 32 percent. The majority of the hospitals in the U.S. are nonprofit or owned by local, state, or federal governments (Jonas and Kovner 2005, 224).

Decline in Number of Hospitals

During the 1980s, medical advances and cost-containment measures caused many procedures that once required inpatient hospitalization to be performed on an outpatient basis. Outpatient hospital visits increased by 40 percent with a resultant decrease in hospital admissions. Fewer patient admissions and shortened lengths of stay (LOS) resulted in a significant reduction in the number of hospitals and hospital beds. Healthcare reform efforts and the acceptance of managed care as the major medical practice style of U.S. healthcare resulted in enough hospital closings and mergers to reduce the number of government and community-based hospitals in the United States to approximately 5,000 (Sultz and Young 2004, 68).

Public Law 89-97 of 1965

In 1965, passage of a number of amendments to the Social Security Act brought Medicare and Medicaid into existence. These two programs have greatly changed how healthcare organizations are reimbursed. Recent attempts to curtail Medicare and Medicaid spending continue to affect healthcare organizations.

Medicare (Title XVIII of the Social Security Act) is a federal program that provides healthcare benefits for people 65 years old and older who are covered by Social Security. The program was inaugurated in 1966. Over the years, amendments have extended coverage to individuals who are not covered by Social Security but who are willing to pay a premium for coverage, to the disabled, and to those suffering from chronic kidney disease.

The companion program, **Medicaid** (Title XIX of the Social Security Act), was established at the same time to support medical and hospital care for persons classified as medically indigent. Originally targeted to recipients of public assistance (primarily single parent families and the aged, blind, and disabled), Medicaid has expanded to additional groups so that it now targets poor children, disabled, pregnant women, and very poor adults (including those 65 years of age and over). The only exception to these expansions was passage of the Personal Responsibility and Work Opportunity Reconciliation Act of 1996 (PRWORA, P.L. 104-193, 1996), which changed eligibility for legal and illegal immigrants (Jonas and Kovner 2005, 56). Medicaid today is a federally mandated program that provides healthcare benefits to low-income people and their children. Medicaid programs are administered and partially paid for by individual states. Medicaid is an umbrella for 50 different state programs designed specifically to serve the poor. Beginning in January 1967, Medicaid provided federal funds to states on a cost-sharing basis to ensure that welfare recipients would be guaranteed medical services. Coverage of four types of care was required: inpatient and outpatient services, other laboratory and x-ray services, physician services, and nursing facility care for persons over 21 years of age.

Many enhancements have been made in the years since Medicaid was enacted. Services now include family planning and 31 other optional services such as prescription drugs and dental services. With few exceptions, recipients of cash assistance are automatically eligible for Medicaid. Medicaid also pays the Medicare premium, deductible, and coinsurance costs for some low-income Medicare beneficiaries.

Four million individuals were enrolled in Medicaid during 1966, its first year of implementation. By December 2002, 39.7 million people were enrolled in Medicaid programs. In 2002, the states and the federal government expended $250.4 billion on Medicaid, most of which was directed toward the elderly, the blind, or the disabled. Elderly and disabled participants comprised about one-quarter of the Medicaid rolls, yet the program expends almost three-quarters of all funds on this group (Jonas and Kovner 2005, 56–57).

The following excerpt is from *National Scorecard on U.S. Health System Performance, 2008*:

> Overall, the *National Scorecard on U.S. Health System Performance, 2008,* finds that the U.S. is losing ground in providing access to care and has uneven health care quality. The Scorecard also finds broad evidence of inefficient and inequitable care. Average U.S. performance would have to improve by more than 50 percent across multiple indicators to reach benchmark levels of performance.
>
> Closing performance gaps would bring real benefits in terms of health, patient experiences, and savings. For example:
>
> - Up to 101,000 fewer people would die prematurely each year from causes amenable to healthcare if the U.S. achieved the lower mortality rates of leading countries.
> - Thirty-seven million more adults would have an accessible primary care provider, and 70 million more adults would receive all recommended preventive care.
> - The Medicare program could potentially save at least $12 billion a year by reducing readmissions or by reducing hospitalizations for preventable conditions.
> - Reducing health insurance administrative costs to the average level of countries with mixed private and public insurance systems (Germany, the Netherlands, and Switzerland) would free up $51 billion, or more than half the cost of providing comprehensive coverage to all the uninsured in the U.S. Reaching

benchmarks of the best countries would save an estimated $102 billion per year.

Studies further document the cost in lives and lost productivity from the nation's failure to provide secure health insurance to all. Based on areas within the U.S. that achieve superior outcomes at lower costs, it should be possible to close gaps in healthcare quality and access, and to reduce costs significantly.

Several implications for policy emerge from the Scorecard findings:

Notably, all of the quality indicators showing significant improvement have been targets of national and collaborative efforts to improve, informed by data with measurable benchmarks and indicators reached by consensus. Conversely, there was failure to improve in areas such as mental healthcare, primary care, hospital readmission rates, or adverse drug events for which focused efforts to assess and improve at the community or facility level are lacking. Further, the continued failure to adopt interoperable health information technology (HIT) makes it difficult to generate the information necessary to document performance and monitor improvement efforts.

Hospital readmission rates and rates of potentially preventable hospitalizations for ambulatory care-sensitive conditions remain high and variable across the country, as do total costs for the chronically ill. Studies indicate that it is possible to prevent hospitalization or rehospitalization with better primary care, discharge planning, and follow-up care—an integrated, systems approach to care.

Multiple indicators highlight the fact that the U.S. has a weak primary care foundation. Investing in primary care with enhanced capacity to provide patients with round-the-clock access, manage chronic conditions, and coordinate care will be key steps in moving to more organized care systems.

However, current payment incentives for hospitals, physicians, and nursing homes do not support coordination of care or efficient use of expensive, specialized care. Information also fails to flow with patients across sites of care due to lack of health information technology and information exchange systems. These inefficiencies require innovative payment policies as well as care delivery approaches to improve outcomes for patients and to use resources more efficiently.

The 2008 National Scorecard documents the human and economic costs of failing to address the problems in our health system. Recent analysis suggests it could be possible to insure everyone and achieve significant savings with improved value over the next decade. Healthcare expenditures are projected to double to $4 trillion, or 20 percent of national income, over the next decade, and millions more U.S. residents are on a path to becoming uninsured or underinsured, absent new policies. We need to change directions, starting with the recognition that access to care, healthcare quality, and efficiency are interrelated.

Aiming higher and moving on a more positive path will require strategies targeting the multiple sources of poor health system performance. These strategies include:

- Universal and well-designed coverage that ensures affordable access and continuity of care, with low administrative costs
- Incentives aligned to promote higher quality and more efficient care
- Care that is designed and organized around the patient, not providers or insurers
- Widespread implementation of health information technology with information exchange
- Explicit national goals to meet and exceed benchmarks and monitor performance
- National policies that promote private-public collaboration and high performance

Rising costs put families, businesses, and public budgets under stress, pulling down living standards for middle- as well as low-income families. New national policies that take a coherent, whole-system, population view are essential for the nation's future health and economic security. (Commonwealth Fund 2008)

Public Law 92-603 of 1972

Utilization review (UR) was a mandatory component of the original Medicare legislation. Medicare required hospitals and **extended care facilities** to establish a plan for UR as well as a permanent UR committee. The goal of the UR process was to ensure that the services provided to Medicare beneficiaries were medically necessary.

In an effort to curtail Medicare and Medicaid spending, additional amendments to the Social Security Act were instituted in 1972. Public Law 92-603 required concurrent review for Medicare and Medicaid patients. It also established the professional standards review organization (PSRO) program to implement concurrent review. PSROs performed professional review and evaluated patient care services for necessity, quality, and cost-effectiveness.

Three major eras occurred in healthcare policy from 1975 to 2000. Like an archeological site, these eras have mostly accumulated on top of one another, rather than fully replacing that which precedes them. The health policy eras can be identified as the following (Etheredge 2001; Siegel and Channin 2001):

- *Age of Traditional Insurance* (1965–1982), which began with the enactment of Medicare and Medicaid and which was based on open-ended, fee-for-service health insurance
- *Age of Regulated Prices for Government Programs* (1983–1992), which was launched with the enactment of the Medicare DRG (diagnosis-related group) system
- *Age of Markets, Purchasing, and Managed Care* (1993–2000), the era that has seen the population move to managed care plans in both the private and public coverage programs
- *Information Age* (2000–present), the arrival of the new millennium has thrust the healthcare delivery system into the "information age." Improving the delivery of healthcare both in a quantitative and qualitative sense will depend on improving management of digital information within and among healthcare institutions (Siegel and Channin 2001)

Health Systems Agency (HSA)

The Health Planning and Resources Development Act of 1974 called for a new local organization, the **health systems agency** (HSA), to have broad representation of healthcare providers and consumers on governing boards and committees. Although the governance structure required participation by consumers, interested parties from the provider groups dominated the discussions. HSAs were fundamentally unsuccessful in materially influencing decisions about service or technology expansion. Their decisions became undeniably political, and attempts to achieve consensus based on real service needs were counterbalanced by community interests in economic and employment expansions. Concurrent with attempts to slow cost increases through a planning approach, a number of other legislative initiatives took shape that were directly related to concerns over Medicare costs and service quality (Sultz and Young 2004, 39, 242). The legislation that created the HSAs, or nationwide system of local health planning agencies, was repealed in 1986.

Utilization Review Act of 1977

In 1977, the **Utilization Review Act** of 1977 made it a requirement that hospitals conduct continued-stay reviews for Medicare and Medicaid patients. Continued-stay reviews determine whether it is medically necessary for a patient to remain hospitalized. This legislation also included fraud and abuse regulations.

Peer Review Improvement Act of 1982

The Peer Review Improvement Act of 1982 redesigned the PSRO program and renamed the agencies **peer review organizations** (PROs). At this time, hospitals began to review the medical necessity and appropriateness of certain admissions even before patients were admitted. PROs were given a new name in 2002 and are now called **quality improvement organizations** (QIOs). They currently emphasize quality improvement processes. Every state and territory, as well as the District of Columbia, now has its own QIO. The mission of the QIO is to ensure the quality, efficiency, and cost-effectiveness of the healthcare services provided to Medicare beneficiaries in its locale.

Tax Equity and Fiscal Responsibility Act of 1982

In 1982, Congress passed the **Tax Equity and Fiscal Responsibility Act** (TEFRA). TEFRA required extensive changes in the Medicare program. Its purpose was to control the rising cost of providing healthcare services to Medicare beneficiaries. Before this legislation was passed, healthcare services provided to Medicare beneficiaries were reimbursed on a retrospective, or fee-based, payment system. TEFRA required the gradual implementation of a **prospective payment system** (PPS) for Medicare reimbursement.

In a retrospective payment system, a service is provided, a claim for payment for the service is made, and the healthcare provider is reimbursed for the cost of delivering the service. In a PPS, a predetermined level of reimbursement is established before the service is provided.

Prospective Payment Act (1982)/ Public Law 98-21 of 1983

The PPS for acute hospital care (inpatient) services was implemented in 1983, according to Public Law 98-21. Under the inpatient PPS, reimbursement for hospital care provided to Medicare patients is based on diagnosis-related groups (DRGs). Each case is assigned to a DRG on the basis of the patient's diagnosis at the time of discharge. For example, under inpatient PPS, all the cases of viral pneumonia would be reimbursed at the same predetermined level of reimbursement no matter how long the patients stayed in the hospital or how many services they received.

Prospective payment systems for other healthcare services provided to Medicare beneficiaries have been gradually implemented in the years since 1983. Implementation of the ambulatory payment classification system for hospital outpatient services, for example, began in 2000.

Consolidated Omnibus Budget Reconciliation Act of 1985

The Consolidated Omnibus Budget Reconciliation Act of 1985 made it possible for the Healthcare Financing Administration (HCFA) to deny reimbursement for substandard healthcare services provided to Medicare and Medicaid beneficiaries. (HCFA's name was changed to the **Centers for Medicare and Medicaid Services** [CMS] in 2001.)

Omnibus Budget Reconciliation Act of 1986

The Omnibus Budget Reconciliation Act of 1986 requires PROs to report instances of substandard care to relevant licensing and certification agencies.

Healthcare Quality Improvement Act of 1986

The Healthcare Quality Improvement Act established the **National Practitioner Data Bank** (NPDB). The purpose of the NPDB is to provide a clearinghouse for information about medical practitioners who have a history of malpractice suits and other quality problems. Hospitals are required to consult the NPDB before granting medical staff privileges to healthcare practitioners. The legislation also established immunity from legal actions for practitioners involved in some peer review activities.

Omnibus Budget Reconciliation Act of 1989

The Omnibus Budget Reconciliation Act of 1989 instituted the Agency for Healthcare Policy and Research. The mission of this agency is to develop outcome measures to evaluate the quality of healthcare services.

Omnibus Budget Reconciliation Act of 1990

The Omnibus Budget Reconciliation Act of 1990 requires PROs to report actions taken against physicians to state medical boards and licensing agencies.

Health Insurance Portability and Accountability Act of 1996

The Health Insurance Portability and Accountability Act (HIPAA) of 1996 addresses issues related to the portability of health insurance after leaving employment, as well as administrative simplification. One of HIPAA's provisions was the creation of the Healthcare Integrity and Protection Data Bank (HIPDB). Its mission is to inform federal and state agencies about potential quality problems with clinicians and with suppliers and providers of healthcare services.

Mental Health Parity Act of 1996

The Mental Health Parity Act of 1996 (MHPA) is a federal law that may apply to two different types of coverage (CMS 2008a):

- Large group self-funded group health plans (CMS has jurisdiction over self-funded public sector [non-federal governmental] plans while the Department of Labor 866-444-3272 has jurisdiction over private sector self-funded group health plans.)
- Large group fully insured group health plans.

A decade after enactment of the Mental Health Parity Act of 1996, Congress is again considering the issue. Today's discussion is occurring in a new environment. Effective new treatment strategies have transformed the practice of behavioral healthcare, and health insurance plans are using a new generation of tools to promote optimal care. Health plans offer customized programs to encourage members to use effective care on an ongoing basis. They provide a variety of flexible benefit options for members, and they use advanced information systems to communicate with behavioral health practitioners about best practices.

A summary of some of the current key objectives of HHS include the following:

- *Accelerate personalized healthcare*: Focus on an effective healthcare delivery system provided at a lower cost, and is technology enabled.
- *Recruit, develop, retain, and strategically manage a world-class HHS workforce*: Focus on meeting and exceeding the human resource expectations of HHS.
- *Modernize Medicaid*: Focus on a fair and equitable Medicaid program that exists without fraud in all states.
- *Turn adversity to advantage for the New Orleans health system*: Provide support and assistance to the citizens of New Orleans and encourage and support the rebuilding of its healthcare system.
- *Improve financial performance*: Focus on continuous quality improvement in meeting the expected HHS standards and guidelines.
- *Promote health information technology* (HIT): Work on electronic health record (EHR) adoption throughout the U.S., with a focus on an interoperable nationwide health information network. This goal can only be achieved if the system is created that supports consumer privacy and risk protections.
- *Expand electronic government*: Secure all aspects of systems to protect information entrusted to HHS and prepare IT systems and processes for disaster recovery and response.
- *Harness the power of transparent healthcare*: Make additional information available to the public regarding the price and quality of services that Medicare pays for and facilitate the development of successful health information exchange (HIE) programs.
- *Emphasize prevention and healthy living*: Establish scientifically-based physical activity guidelines for healthy Americans.
- *Broaden health insurance and long-term care coverage*: Increase the percentage of adults and children who have access to quality healthcare services through private health insurance, and increase the awareness of the need for long-term care planning.
- *Emphasize faith-based and community solutions*: Support community-based approaches to reduce health disparities that affect racial, ethnic, and underserved populations.

Biomedical and Technological Advances in Medicine

Rapid progress in medical science and technology during the late nineteenth and twentieth centuries revolutionized the way healthcare was provided. The most important scientific advancement was the discovery of bacteria as the cause of infectious disease. The most important technological development was the use of anesthesia for surgical procedures. These nineteenth century advances formed the basis for the development of antibiotics and other pharmaceuticals and the application of sophisticated surgical procedures in the twentieth century.

To further medical advances in the twenty-first century, the NIH sought the input of more than 300 recognized leaders in academia, industry, government, and the public to create a "Roadmap" program to accelerate biomedical advances, create effective prevention strategies and new treatments, and bridge knowledge gaps. The program, which involves a plethora of NIH Institutes and Centers, has three main strategic initiatives (NIH 2005):

- New Pathways to Discovery, which includes a comprehensive understanding of building blocks of the body's cells and tissues and how complex biological systems operate; structural biology; molecular libraries and imaging; nanotechnology; bioinformatics and computational biology
- Research Teams of the Future, including interdisciplinary research, high-risk research, and public-private partnerships
- Re-engineer the Clinical Research Enterprise

Through these efforts, NIH will boost the resources and technologies needed for twenty-first century biomedical science.

Figure 2.1 offers a timeline of key biological and technological advances at a glance.

Although surgical procedures were performed before the development of anesthesia, surgeons had to work quickly on conscious patients to minimize risk and pain. The availability of anesthesia made it possible for surgeons to develop more advanced surgical techniques. The use of ether as an anesthetic was first recorded in 1842. At about the same

Figure 2.1. Key biological and technological advances in medicine

Time	Event
1842	First recorded use of ether as an anesthetic
1860s	Louis Pasteur laid the foundation for modern bacteriology
1865	Joseph Lister was the first to apply Pasteur's research to the treatment of infected wounds
1880s–1890s	Steam first used in physical sterilization
1895	Wilhelm Roentgen made observations that led to the development of x-ray technology
1898	Introduction of rubber surgical gloves, sterilization, and antisepsis
1940	Studies of prothrombin time first made available
1941–1946	Studies of electrolytes; development of major pharmaceuticals
1957	Studies of blood gas
1961	Studies of creatine phosphokinase
1970s	Surgical advances in cardiac bypass surgery, surgery for joint replacements, and organ transplantation
1971	Computed tomography first used in England
1974	Introduction of whole-body scanners
1980s	Introduction of magnetic resonance imaging
1990s	Further technological advances in pharmaceuticals and genetics; Human Genome Project
2000s	NIH creates roadmap to accelerate biomedical advances, create effective prevention strategies and new treatments, and bridge knowledge gaps in the 21st century

time, nitrous oxide was introduced for use during dental procedures and chloroform was used to reduce the pain of labor. By the 1860s, the physicians who treated the casualties of the American Civil War on both sides had access to anesthetic and pain-killing drugs.

In the 1860s, Louis Pasteur began studying a condition in wine that made it sour and unpalatable. He discovered that the wine was being spoiled by parasitic growths. His research proved that tiny, living organisms (called bacteria) increase through reproduction and cause infectious disease. Pasteur also demonstrated that bacteria could be destroyed by the application of heat and certain chemicals (for example, alcohol). In doing so, he laid the foundation for modern bacteriology. After 20 years of research into the biology of microorganisms, Pasteur began studying human diseases. In 1885, he developed a vaccine that prevented rabies.

Although the importance of cleanliness had been known since early times, the role that microorganisms played in disease was not understood until Pasteur conducted his research. In 1865, Joseph Lister was the first to apply Pasteur's research to the treatment of infected wounds. Lister began by protecting open fractures from infection by treating the wounds with carbolic acid (a disinfectant). His discovery was called the antiseptic principle. Antisepsis reduced the mortality rate in Lister's hospital after 1865 from 45 to 12 percent. He published his results in 1868, and soon carbolic acid was being used to prevent bacterial contamination during surgery.

During the 1880s and 1890s, physical sterilization using steam was developed. This technological advance had a major impact on surgery and in other areas throughout the hospital. The sterile operative technique was further advanced through the introduction of rubber surgical gloves in 1898. Other advances included the use of sterile gowns, masks, and antibiotics and other drugs.

In 1895, the well-known physicist Wilhelm Roentgen made observations that led to the development of x-ray technology. He found that he could create images of the bones in his hand by passing x-rays through his hand and onto a photographic plate. Radiographic technology is used extensively today to diagnose illnesses and injuries.

Many advances in laboratory testing occurred during the twentieth century. Equipment that allows the rapid laboratory processing of diagnostic and prognostic examinations was developed, and the number of diagnostic laboratory procedures increased dramatically. For example, studies of prothrombin time were first made available in 1940, electrolytes in 1941 through 1946, blood gas in 1957, creatine phosphokinase in 1961, serum hepatitis in 1970, and carcinoembryonic antigen (the first cancer-screening test) in 1974.

Diagnostic radiology and radiation therapy have undergone huge advances in the past 50 years. An enormous advance first used in 1971 in England was an imaging modality called computed tomography (CT). The first CT scanners were used to create images of the skull. Whole-body scanners were introduced in 1974. In the 1980s, another powerful diagnostic tool was added, magnetic resonance imaging (MRI). MRI is a noninvasive technique that uses magnetic and radio-frequency fields to record images of soft tissues.

Surgical advances have been remarkable as well. Cardiac bypass surgery was developed in the 1970s, as were the techniques for joint replacement. Organs are now successfully transplanted and artificial organs are being tested. New surgical techniques have included the use of lasers in ophthalmology, gynecology, and urology. Microsurgery is now a common tool in the reconstruction of damaged nerves and blood vessels. The use of robotics in surgery holds great promise for the future (Sloane et al.1999, 6–7).

Biotechnology is "the field devoted to applying the techniques of biochemistry, cellular biology, biophysics, and molecular biology to addressing practical issues related to human beings, agriculture, and the environment" (*Stedman's Medical Dictionary* 2000).

A pharmaceutical or drug company is a commercial business and is referred to as *Pharma*. Two examples of companies in the field of biotechnology are Pharma and medical device companies. These companies conduct research, develop, market and/or distribute drugs, for the healthcare industry.

A medical device company produces **medical devices** which can be defined as an instrument or apparatus intended for use in the diagnosis of disease or for a treatment of a condition. A medical device is used by a physician for a patient that has a condition where a body part does not achieve any of its primary intended purposes such as a heart valve. Medical devices can be used for life support, such as anesthesia ventilators, as well as for monitoring of patients, such as fetal monitors, and other uses such as incubators.

Check Your Understanding 2.2

Instructions: On a separate piece of paper, match the descriptions with the appropriate legislation.

1. ___ Hospital Survey and Construction (Hill Burton) Act
2. ___ Tax Equity and Fiscal Responsibility Act
3. ___ Public Law 89-79 of 1965
4. ___ Utilization Review Act
5. ___ Omnibus Budget Reconciliation Act of 1989
6. ___ Public Law 92-603 of 1972
7. ___ Healthcare Quality Improvement Act of 1986
8. ___ Omnibus Budget Reconciliation Act of 1990

a. Amendments to the Social Security Act that brought Medicare and Medicaid into existence
b. Authorized grants for states to construct new hospitals
c. Required concurrent review for Medicare and Medicaid patients
d. Required hospitals to conduct continued-stay reviews for Medicare and Medicaid patients
e. Established the National Practitioner Data Bank
f. Required peer review organizations to report actions taken against physicians to state medical boards and licensing agencies
g. Required extensive changes in the Medicare program to control the rising cost of providing healthcare services to Medicare beneficiaries (PPS general implementation)
h. Instituted the Agency for Healthcare Policy

Professional and Trade Associations Related to Healthcare

A number of trade and professional associations currently influence the practice of medicine and the delivery of healthcare services in the United States. Descriptions of a few of the numerous healthcare-related professional and trade associations that currently influence healthcare issues are provided here.

American Medical Association (AMA)

The **American Medical Association** (AMA) was founded in 1847 as a national voluntary service organization. Today, the AMA has more than 815,000 physician members from every area of medicine. The organization is headquartered in Chicago. For more than 161 years, the AMA has pursued its mission to promote the art and science of medicine and the betterment of public health. Today, that longstanding commitment continues to inspire the AMA's efforts to uphold the highest standards in patient care, practice management, and professionalism. In 2007, as the largest organization of physicians in the country, the AMA marked its eighth consecutive year of financial growth, with net operating results of $24.4 million. Its key objectives are:

- Become the world leader in obtaining, synthesizing, integrating, and disseminating information on health and medical practice
- Remain the acknowledged leader in promoting professionalism in medicine and setting standards for medical ethics, practice, and education
- Continue to be an authoritative voice and influential advocate for patients and physicians
- Continue to be a sound organization that provides value to members, related organizations, and employees

In addition, the AMA acts as an accreditation body for medical schools and residency programs. It also maintains and publishes the Current Procedural Terminology (CPT) coding system. CPT codes are used as the basis of reimbursement systems for physician services and other types of healthcare services provided on an ambulatory basis.

American Hospital Association (AHA)

The **American Hospital Association** (AHA) was founded in 1899. At its first meeting, eight hospital superintendents gathered in Cleveland, Ohio, to exchange ideas, compare methods of hospital management, discuss economics, and explore common interests and new trends. The original group was called the Association of Hospital Superintendents. Its mission was "to facilitate the interchange of ideas, comparing and contrasting methods of management, the discussion of hospital economics, the inspection of hospitals, suggestions of better plans for operating them, and such other matters as may affect the general interest of the membership" (AHA 1999, 110).

The Association of Hospital Superintendents adopted a new constitution in 1906 and a new name, the American Hospital Association. At that time, it had 234 members. Its major concerns were developing hospital standards and building the management skills of it members.

Today, the mission of the AHA is to advance the health of individuals and communities. The association has a current membership of approximately 5,000 hospitals and healthcare institutions, 600 associate member organizations, and 40,000 individual executives active in the healthcare field. Its headquarters are located in Chicago.

The AHA publishes *Coding Clinic,* which provides official ICD-9-CM coding advice.

Joint Commission

Since its beginning in 1952, the **Joint Commission** has continually evolved to meet the changing needs of healthcare organizations. The organization changed its name from the Joint Commission on Accreditation of Hospitals (JCAH) to the Joint Commission on Accreditation of Healthcare

Organizations (JCAHO) in the late 1980s to the Joint Commission in 2006 in recognition of changes in the U.S. health delivery system. Today, the Joint Commission is the largest healthcare standards-setting body in the world. It conducts accreditation surveys in more than 19,500 facilities, including ambulatory care facilities, long-term care facilities, behavioral health facilities, healthcare networks, and managed care organizations as well as acute care hospitals (Joint Commission 2007).

In the late 1990s, the Joint Commission moved away from traditional quality assessment processes and began emphasizing performance and quality improvement. Its ORYX initiative reflected the new approach. The goal of the ORYX initiative was to incorporate the ongoing collection of quality and performance data into the accreditation process.

Today, the Joint Commission's standards give organizations substantial leeway in selecting performance measures and improvement projects. Outcome measures document the results of care for individual patients as well as for specific types of patients grouped by diagnostic category. For example, an acute care hospital's overall rate of postsurgical infection would be considered an outcome measure. The outcome measures must be reported to the Joint Commission via software from vendors that the Joint Commission has approved for this purpose.

Blue Cross and Blue Shield Association

The forerunner of the **Blue Cross and Blue Shield Association** was a commission instituted by the AHA in 1929. In 1960, the commission was replaced by the Blue Cross Association and ties to the AHA were broken. In 1982, the Blue Cross Association merged with the National Association of Blue Shield Plans to become the Blue Cross and Blue Shield Association. Blue Cross and Blue Shield brands are the nation's oldest and largest family of health benefits companies and one of the most recognized brands in the health insurance industry, serving more than 99 million people in the United States, Washington DC, and Puerto Rico.

American College of Healthcare Executives (ACHE)

The **American College of Healthcare Executives** (ACHE) is an organization for healthcare administrators. Like most of the organizations previously discussed, it is headquartered in Chicago. Its mission is to serve as "the professional membership society for healthcare executives; to meet members' professional, educational, and leadership needs; to promote high ethical standards and conduct; and to enhance healthcare leadership and management excellence."

ACHE has nearly 30,000 members internationally. It also publishes books and textbooks on healthcare services management.

American Nurses Association (ANA)

The ANA was founded in 1897. Headquartered in Washington, D.C., the ANA is a professional association as well as the strongest labor union active in the nursing profession. It represents the interests of the nation's 2.9 million RNs (ANA 2008). The ANA's mission is to work for the improvement of health standards and the availability of healthcare services, to foster high professional standards for nurses, to stimulate and promote the professional development of nurses, and to advance the economic and general welfare of its members. Their mission is to "advance the nursing profession by fostering high standards of nursing practice, promote the rights of nurses in the workplace, project a positive and realistic view of nursing" (ANA 2008).

American Health Information Management Association (AHIMA)

The **American Health Information Management Association** (AHIMA) is the professional membership organization for managers of health record services and healthcare information. It was founded in 1928 under the name of the Association of Record Librarians of North America. In 1929, the association adopted a constitution and bylaws. Its name was changed to the American Medical Record Association in 1970 and then to AHIMA in 1991.

Today, with headquarters in Chicago, the association has more than 52,000 members. Its mission is to be the "professional community that improves healthcare by advancing best practices and standards for health information management and the trusted source for education, research, and professional credentialing" (AHIMA 2008). The association's vision is "quality healthcare through quality information." (AHIMA 2008)

The association is the sponsoring organization for the **Commission on Accreditation of Health Informatics and Information Management Education** (CAHIIM), which accredits two- and four-year programs in health information management. AHIMA also offers an approval program for master's programs in HIM and coding specialist programs. Additionally, it certifies health information professionals as registered health information technologists (RHITs) for graduates of two-year programs and registered health information administrators (RHIAs) for graduates of baccalaureate programs. Finally, AHIMA offers credentialing examinations for coding professionals as certified coding specialists (CCSs), certified coding specialists for physicians' services (CCS-Ps), certified health care privacy and security specialists (CHPS), certified coding associates (CCAs), and Health Data Analysis (HDA).

Other Healthcare-Related Associations

Many other healthcare-related associations in the United States serve their professional members by providing educational, certification, and accreditation services. The best known include the following:

- American Osteopathic Association
- American Dental Association

- American College of Surgeons
- American League for Nursing
- American Society of Clinical Pathologists
- American Dietetic Association
- Commission on Accreditation of Rehabilitation Facilities
- American Association of Nurse Anesthetists

Check Your Understanding 2.3

Instructions: On a separate piece of paper, match each organization with the appropriate description.

1. ___ American College of Healthcare Executives
2. ___ American Hospital Association
3. ___ American Medical Association
4. ___ American Nurses Association
5. ___ American Health Information Management Association
6. ___ Blue Cross and Blue Shield Association

a. Part of this organization's mission is to "enhance healthcare leadership and management excellence."

b. This organization was originally called the Association of Hospital Superintendents.

c. This organization was originally a commission instituted by the AHA in 1929.

d. This association was founded in 1928 under the name of the Association of Record Librarians of North America.

e. Part of this organization's mission is to work for the improvement of health standards and the availability of healthcare services.

f. This organization's mission is to promote the art and science of medicine and to improve public health.

Healthcare Providers and Settings

According to the U.S. Department of Labor, a healthcare provider or health professional is an organization or person who delivers proper healthcare in a systematic way professionally to any individual in need of healthcare services (29 CFR 825.118).

Healthcare Institutions and Services

Healthcare delivery is more than hospital-related care. It can be viewed as a continuum of services that cuts across services delivered in ambulatory, acute, sub-acute, long-term, residential, and other care environments. This section describes several of the alternatives for healthcare delivery along this continuum.

Organization and Operation of Modern Hospitals

The term *hospital* can be applied to any healthcare facility that has the following four characteristics:

- An organized medical staff
- Permanent inpatient beds
- Around-the-clock nursing services
- Diagnostic and therapeutic services

Most hospitals provide acute care services to inpatients. **Acute care** is the short-term care provided to diagnose and treat an illness or injury. The individuals who receive acute care services in hospitals are considered inpatients. Inpatients receive room-and-board services in addition to continuous nursing services. Generally, patients who spend more than 24 hours in a hospital are considered inpatients.

The **average length of stay** (ALOS) in an acute care hospital is 30 days or less. (Hospitals that have ALOSs longer than 30 days are considered long-term care facilities. Long-term care is discussed in detail later in this chapter.) With recent advances in surgical technology, anesthesia, and pharmacology, the ALOS in an acute care hospital is much shorter today than it was only a few years ago. In addition, many diagnostic and therapeutic procedures that once required inpatient care can now be performed on an outpatient basis.

For example, before the development of laparoscopic surgical techniques, a patient might be hospitalized for 10 days after a routine appendectomy (surgical removal of the appendix). Today, a patient undergoing a laparoscopic appendectomy might spend only a few hours in the hospital's outpatient surgery department and go home the same day. The influence of managed care and the emphasis on cost control in the Medicare and Medicaid programs also have resulted in shorter hospital stays.

In large acute care hospitals, hundreds of clinicians, administrators, managers, and support staff must work closely together to provide effective and efficient diagnostic and therapeutic services. Most hospitals provide services to both inpatients and outpatients. A hospital outpatient is a patient who receives hospital services without being admitted for inpatient (overnight) clinical care. Outpatient care is considered a kind of ambulatory care. (Ambulatory care is discussed later in this chapter.)

Modern hospitals are extremely complex organizations. Much of the clinical training for physicians, nurses, and allied health professionals is conducted in hospitals. Medical research is another activity carried out in hospitals.

Types of Hospitals

Hospitals can be classified in many different ways according to the

- Number of beds
- Type of services provided
- Type of patients served
- For-profit or not-for-profit status
- Type of ownership

Number of Beds

A hospital's number of beds is based on the number of beds that it has equipped and staffed for patient care. The term *bed capacity* is sometimes used to reflect the maximum number of inpatients for which the hospital can care. Hospitals with fewer than a hundred beds are usually considered small. Most of the hospitals in the United States fall into this category. Some large, urban hospitals have more than 500 beds. The number of beds is usually broken down by adult beds and pediatric beds. The number of maternity beds and other special categories may be listed separately. Hospitals also can be categorized on the basis of the number of outpatient visits per year. Table 2.1 compares the type of ownership and size of hospitals from 1975 to 2005.

Type of Services Provided

Some hospitals specialize in certain types of service and treat specific illnesses. For example:

- *Rehabilitation hospitals* generally provide long-term care services to patients recuperating from debilitating or chronic illnesses and injuries such as strokes, head and spine injuries, and gunshot wounds. Patients often stay in rehabilitation hospitals for several months.
- *Psychiatric hospitals* provide inpatient care for patients with mental and developmental disorders. In the past, the ALOS for psychiatric inpatients was longer than it is today. Rather than months or years, most patients now spend only a few days or weeks per stay. However, many patients require repeated hospitalization for chronic psychiatric illnesses. (Behavioral healthcare is discussed in detail later in this chapter.)
- *General acute care hospitals* provide a wide range of medical and surgical services to diagnose and treat most illnesses and injuries.
- *Specialty hospitals* provide diagnostic and therapeutic services for a limited range of conditions (for example, burns, cancer, tuberculosis, or obstetrics and gynecology).

Type of Patients Served

Some hospitals specialize in serving specific types of patients. For example, children's hospitals provide specialized pediatric services in a number of medical specialties.

For-Profit or Not-for-Profit Status

Hospitals also can be classified on the basis of their ownership and profitability status. Not-for profit healthcare organizations use excess funds to improve their services and to finance educational programs and community services. For-profit healthcare organizations are privately owned. Excess funds are paid back to the managers, owners, and investors in the form of bonuses and dividends.

Type of Ownership

The most common ownership types for hospitals and other kinds of healthcare organizations in the United States include the following:

- *Government-owned hospitals* are operated by a specific branch of federal, state, or local government as not-for-profit organizations. (Government-owned hospitals are

Table 2.1. Type of ownership and size of hospital 1975 vs 2005

Type of Ownership and Size of Hospital	1975	2005
Hospitals	**Number**	**Number**
All hospitals	7,156	5,756
Federal	382	226
Nonfederal	6,774	5,530
Community	5,875	4,936
Nonprofit	3,339	2,958
For profit	775	868
State-local government	1,761	1,110
6–24 beds	299	370
25–49 beds	1,155	1,032
50–99 beds	1,481	1,001
100–199 beds	1,363	1,129
200–299 beds	678	619
300–399 beds	378	368
400–499 beds	230	173
500 beds or more	291	244
Beds	**Number**	**Number**
All hospitals	1,465,828	946,997
Federal	131,946	45,837
Nonfederal	1,333,882	901,160
Community	941,844	802,311
Nonprofit	658,195	561,106
For profit	73,495	113,510
State-local government	210,154	127,695
6–24 beds	5,615	6,316
25–49 beds	41,783	33,726
50–99 beds	106,776	71,737
100–199 beds	192,438	161,593
200–299 beds	164,405	151,290
300–399 beds	127,728	126,899
400–499 beds	101,278	76,894
500 beds or more	201,821	173,856
Occupancy Rate	**Percent**	**Percent**
All hospitals	76.7	69.3
Federal	80.7	66.0
Nonfederal	76.3	69.5
Community	75.0	67.3
Nonprofit	77.5	69.1
For profit	65.9	59.6
State-local government	70.4	66.7
6–24 beds	48.0	33.5
25–49 beds	56.7	47.1
50–99 beds	64.7	59.0
100–199 beds	71.2	63.2
200–299 beds	77.1	67.7
300–399 beds	79.7	70.1
400–499 beds	81.1	71.2
500 beds or more	80.9	75.9

Sources: AHA Annual Survey of Hospitals. Hospital Statistics, 1976, 1981, 1991–2007 editions. © 1976, 1981, 1991–2007: Used with the permission of Health Forum LLC, an affiliate of the AHA; CDC http://www.cdc.gov/nchs/data/hus/hus07.pdf#092; National Center for Health Statistics Health, United States, With Chartbook on Trends in the Health of Americans 2007.

sometimes called public hospitals.) They are supported, at least in part, by tax dollars. Examples of federally owned and operated hospitals include those operated by the Department of Veterans Affairs to serve retired military personnel. The Department of Defense operates facilities for active military personnel and their dependents. Many states own and operate psychiatric hospitals. County and city governments often operate public hospitals to serve the healthcare needs of their communities, especially those residents who are unable to pay for their care.
- *Proprietary hospitals* may be owned by private foundations, partnerships, or investor-owned corporations. Large corporations may own a number of for-profit hospitals, and the stock of several large U.S. hospital chains is publicly traded.
- *Voluntary hospitals* are not-for-profit hospitals owned by universities, churches, charities, religious orders, unions, and other not-for-profit entities. They often provide free care to patients who otherwise would not have access to healthcare services.

Organization of Hospital Services

The organizational structure of every hospital is designed to meet its specific needs. For example, most acute care hospitals are made up of a board of directors, a professional medical staff, an executive administrative staff, medical and surgical services, patient care (nursing) services, diagnostic and laboratory services, and support services (for example, nutritional services, environmental safety, and HIM services).

Board of Directors

The board of directors has primary responsibility for setting the overall direction of the hospital. (In some hospitals, the board of directors is called the governing board or board of trustees.) The board works with the chief executive officer (CEO) and the leaders of the organization's medical staff to develop the hospital's strategic direction as well as its mission, vision, and values:

- *Mission:* A statement of the organization's purpose and the customers it serves
- *Vision*: A description of the organization's ideal future
- *Values*: A descriptive list of the organization's fundamental principles or beliefs

Other specific responsibilities of the board of directors include the following:

- Establishing bylaws in accordance with the organization's legal and licensing requirements
- Selecting qualified administrators
- Approving the organization and makeup of the clinical staff
- Monitoring the quality of care

The board's members are elected for specific terms of service (for example, five years). Most boards also elect officers, commonly a chairman, vice-chairman, president, secretary, and treasurer. The size of the board varies considerably. Individual board members are called directors, board members, or trustees. Individuals serve on one or more standing committees such as the executive committee, joint conference committee, finance committee, strategic planning committee, and building committee.

The makeup of the board depends on the type of hospital and the form of ownership. For example, the board of a community hospital is likely to include local business leaders, representatives of community organizations, and other people interested in the welfare of the community. The board of a teaching hospital, on the other hand, is likely to include medical school alumni and university administrators, among others.

Increased competition among healthcare providers and limits on managed care and Medicare and Medicaid reimbursement have made the governing of hospitals especially difficult during the past two decades. In the future, boards of directors will continue to face strict accountability in terms of cost containment, performance management, and integration of services to maintain fiscal stability and to ensure the delivery of high-quality patient care.

Medical Staff

The medical staff consists of physicians who have received extensive training in various medical disciplines (for example, internal medicine, pediatrics, cardiology, gynecology and obstetrics, orthopedics, and surgery). The medical staff's primary objective is to provide high-quality care to the patients who come to the hospital. The physicians on the hospital's medical staff diagnose illnesses and develop patient-centered treatment regimens. Moreover, physicians on the medical staff may serve on the hospital's governing board, where they provide critical insight relevant to strategic and operational planning and policy making.

The medical staff is the aggregate of physicians who have been granted permission to provide clinical services in the hospital. This permission is called **clinical privileges**. An individual physician's privileges are limited to a specific scope of practice. For example, an internal medicine physician would be permitted to diagnose and treat a patient with pneumonia, but not to perform a surgical procedure. Most members of the medical staff are not actually employees of the hospital. However, many hospitals do directly employ radiologists, anesthesiologists, and critical care specialists.

Medical staff classification refers to the organization of physicians according to clinical assignment. Depending on the size of the hospital and on the credentials and clinical privileges of its physicians, the medical staff may be separated into departments such as medicine, surgery, obstetrics, pediatrics, and other specialty services. Typical medical staff classifications include active, provisional, honorary, consulting, courtesy, and medical resident assignments.

Officers of the medical staff usually include a president or chief of staff, a vice-president or chief of staff-elect, and a secretary. These offices are authorized by vote of the entire active medical staff. The president presides at all regular meetings of the medical staff and is an ex officio member of all medical staff committees. The secretary ensures that accurate and complete minutes of medical staff meetings are maintained and that correspondence is handled appropriately.

The medical staff operates according to a predetermined set of policies. These policies are called the **medical staff bylaws**. The bylaws spell out the specific qualifications that physicians must demonstrate before they can practice medicine in the hospital. The bylaws are considered legally binding. Any changes to the bylaws must be approved by a vote of the medical staff and the hospital's governing body.

Administrative Staff

The leader of the administrative staff is the CEO or **chief executive officer**. The CEO is responsible for implementing the policies and strategic direction set by the hospital's board of directors. He or she also is responsible for building an effective executive management team and coordinating the hospital's services. Today's healthcare organizations commonly designate a **chief financial officer** (CFO), a **chief operating officer** (COO), and a **chief information officer** (CIO) as members of the executive management team.

The executive management team is responsible for managing the hospital's finances and ensuring that the hospital complies with the federal, state, and local regulations, standards, and laws that govern the delivery of healthcare services. Depending on the size of the hospital, the CEO's staff may include healthcare administrators with job titles such as vice-president, associate administrator, department director or manager, or administrative assistant. Department-level administrators manage and coordinate the activities of the highly specialized and multidisciplinary units that perform clinical, administrative, and support services in the hospital.

Healthcare administrators may hold advanced degrees in healthcare administration, nursing, public health, or business management. A growing number of hospitals are hiring physician executives to lead their executive management teams. Many healthcare administrators are fellows of the American College of Healthcare Executives.

Patient Care Services

Most of the direct patient care delivered in hospitals is provided by professional nurses. Modern nursing requires a diverse skill set, advanced clinical competencies, and post-graduate education. In almost every hospital, patient care services constitute the largest clinical department in terms of staffing, budget, specialized services offered, and clinical expertise required.

Nurses are responsible for providing continuous, around-the-clock treatment and support for hospital inpatients. The quantity and quality of nursing care available to patients are influenced by a number of factors, including the nursing staff's educational preparation and specialization, experience, and skill level. The level of patient care staffing is also a critical component of quality.

Traditionally, physicians alone determined the type of treatment each patient received. However, today's nurses are playing a wider role in treatment planning and **case management**. They identify timely and effective interventions in response to a wide range of problems related to the patients' treatment, comfort, and safety. Their responsibilities include performing patient assessments, creating care plans, evaluating the appropriateness of treatment, and evaluating the effectiveness of care. At the same time that they provide technical care, effective nursing professionals also offer personal caring that recognizes the patients' concerns and the emotional needs of patients and their families.

A registered nurse qualified by advanced education and clinical and management experience usually administers patient care services. Although the title may vary, this role is usually referred to as the **chief nursing officer** (CNO) or vice-president of nursing or patient care. The CNO is a member of the hospital's executive management team and usually reports directly to the CEO.

In any nursing organizational structure, several types of relationships can be identified, including the following:

- *Line relationships* identify the positions of superiors and subordinates and indicate the levels of authority and responsibility vested with each position. For example, a supervisor in a post-operative surgical unit would have authority to direct the work of several nurses.
- *Lateral relationships* define the connections among various positions in which a hierarchy of authority is not involved. For example, the supervisors of pre-operative and post-operative surgical units would have parallel positions in the structure and would need to coordinate the work they perform.
- *Functional relationships* refer to duties that are divided according to function. In such arrangements, individuals exercise authority in one particular area by virtue of their special knowledge and expertise.

Diagnostic and Therapeutic Services

The services provided to patients in hospitals go beyond the clinical services provided directly by the medical and nursing staff. Many diagnostic and therapeutic services involve the work of allied health professionals. Allied health professionals receive specialized education and training, and their qualifications are registered or certified by a number of specialty organizations.

Diagnostic and therapeutic services are critical to the success of every patient care delivery system. Diagnostic services include clinical laboratory, radiology, and nuclear medicine. Therapeutic services include radiation therapy, occupational therapy, and physical therapy.

Clinical Laboratory Services

The clinical laboratory is divided into two sections: anatomic pathology and clinical pathology. Anatomic pathology deals with human tissues and provides surgical pathology, autopsy, and cytology services. Clinical pathology deals mainly with the analysis of body fluids, principally blood, but also urine, gastric contents, and cerebrospinal fluid.

Physicians who specialize in performing and interpreting the results of pathology tests are called pathologists. Laboratory technicians are allied health professionals trained to operate laboratory equipment and perform laboratory tests under the supervision of a pathologist.

Radiology

Radiology involves the use of radioactive isotopes, fluoroscopic and radiographic equipment, and CT and MRI equipment to diagnose disease. Physicians who specialize in radiology are called radiologists. They are experts in the medical use of radiant energy, radioactive isotopes, radium, cesium, and cobalt as well as x-rays, and radioactive materials. They also are expert in interpreting x-ray, MRI, and CT diagnostic images.

Radiology technicians are allied health professionals trained to operate radiological equipment and perform radiological tests under the supervision of a radiologist.

Nuclear Medicine and Radiation Therapy

Radiologists also may specialize in nuclear medicine and radiation therapy. Nuclear medicine involves the use of ionizing radiation and small amounts of short-lived radioactive tracers to treat disease, specifically neoplastic disease (that is, nonmalignant tumors and malignant cancers). Based on the mathematics and physics of tracer methodology, nuclear medicine is widely applied in clinical medicine. However, most authorities agree that medical science has only scratched the surface in terms of nuclear medicine's potential capabilities.

Radiation therapy uses high-energy x-rays, cobalt, electrons, and other sources of radiation to treat human disease. In current practice, radiation therapy is used alone or in combination with surgery or chemotherapy (drugs) to treat many types of cancer. In addition to external beam therapy, radioactive implants, as well as therapy performed with heat (hyperthermia), are available.

Occupational Therapy

Occupational therapy is the medically directed use of work and play activities to improve patients' independent functioning, enhance their development, and prevent or decrease their level of disability. The individuals who perform occupational therapy are credentialed allied health professionals called occupational therapists. They work under the direction of physicians. Occupational therapy is made available in acute care hospitals, clinics, and rehabilitation centers.

Providing occupational therapy services begins with an evaluation of the patient and the selection of therapeutic goals. Occupational therapy activities may involve the adaptation of tasks or the environment to achieve maximum independence and to enhance the patient's quality of life. An occupational therapist may treat developmental deficits, birth defects, learning disabilities, traumatic injuries, burns, neurological conditions, orthopedic conditions, mental deficiencies, and psychiatric disorders. Within the healthcare system, occupational therapy plays various roles. These roles include promoting health, preventing disability, developing or restoring functional capacity, guiding adaptation within physical and mental parameters, and teaching creative problem solving to increase independent function.

Physical Therapy and Rehabilitation

Physical therapy and rehabilitation have expanded into many medical specialties. Physical therapy can be applied in most disciplines of medicine, especially in neurology, neurosurgery, orthopedics, geriatrics, rheumatology, internal medicine, cardiovascular medicine, cardiopulmonary medicine, psychiatry, sports medicine, burn and wound care, and chronic pain management. It also plays a role in community health education. Credentialed allied health professionals administer physical therapy under the direction of physicians.

Medical **rehabilitation services** involve the entire healthcare team: physicians, nurses, social workers, occupational therapists, physical therapists, and other healthcare personnel. The objective is to either eliminate the patients' disability or alleviate it as fully as possible. Physical therapy can be used to improve the cognitive, social, and physical abilities of patients impaired by chronic disease or injury.

The primary purpose of physical therapy in rehabilitation is to promote optimal health and function by applying scientific principles. Treatment modalities include therapeutic exercise, therapeutic massage, biofeedback, and applications of heat, low-energy lasers, cold, water, electricity, and ultrasound.

Respiratory Therapy

Respiratory therapy involves the diagnosis and treatment of patients who have acute or chronic lung disorders. Respiratory therapists work under the direction of qualified physicians and surgeons. The therapists provide such services as emergency care for stroke, heart failure, and shock patients. They also treat patients with chronic respiratory diseases such as emphysema and asthma.

Respiratory treatments include the administration of oxygen and inhalants such as bronchodilators. They set up and monitor ventilatory equipment and provide physiotherapy to improve breathing.

Ancillary Support Services

The ancillary units of the hospital provide vital clinical and administrative support services to patients, medical staff, visitors, and employees.

Clinical Support Services

The clinical support units provide the following services:

- Pharmaceutical services
- Food and nutrition services
- HIM (health record) services
- Social work and social services
- Patient advocacy services
- Environmental (housekeeping) services
- Purchasing, central supply, and materials management services
- Engineering and plant operations

HIM services are managed by credentialed health information management professionals—RHIAs and RHITs. The pharmacy is staffed by registered pharmacists and pharmacy technologists. Food and nutrition services are managed by registered dietitians (RDs), who develop general menus, special-diet menus, and nutritional plans for individual patients. Social work services are provided by licensed social workers and licensed clinical social workers. Patient advocacy services may be provided by several types of healthcare professionals, most commonly, registered nurses and licensed social workers.

Administrative Support Services

In addition to clinical support services, hospitals need administrative support services to operate effectively. Administrative support services provide business management and clerical services in several key areas, including:

- Admissions and central registration
- Claims and billing (business office)
- Accounting
- Information services
- Human resources
- Public relations
- Fund development
- Marketing

Organization of Ambulatory Care

Ambulatory care is the preventative or corrective healthcare services provided on a nonresident basis in a provider's office, clinic setting, or hospital outpatient setting (AHIMA 2010).Ambulatory care encompasses all the health services provided to individual patients who are not residents in a healthcare facility. Such services include the educational services provided by community health clinics and public health departments. Primary care, emergency care, and ambulatory specialty care (including ambulatory surgery) can all be considered ambulatory care. Ambulatory care services are provided in a variety of settings, including urgent care centers, school-based clinics, public health clinics, and neighborhood and community health centers.

Current medical practice emphasizes performing healthcare services in the least costly setting possible. This change in thinking has led to decreased utilization of emergency services, increased utilization of nonemergency ambulatory facilities, decreased hospital admissions, and shorter hospital stays. The need to reduce the cost of healthcare also has led primary care physicians to treat conditions they once would have referred to specialists.

Physicians who provide ambulatory care services fall into two major categories: physicians working in private practice and physicians working for ambulatory care organizations. Physicians in private practice are self-employed. They work in solo, partnership, and group practices set up as for-profit organizations. Today, the majority of healthcare provided in the United States is by physicians in small physician practices.

Alternatively, physicians who work for ambulatory care organizations are employees of those organizations. Ambulatory care organizations include health maintenance organizations, hospital-based ambulatory clinics, walk-in and emergency clinics, hospital-owned group practices and health promotion centers, freestanding surgery centers, freestanding urgent care centers, freestanding emergency care centers, health department clinics, neighborhood clinics, home care agencies, community mental health centers, school and workplace health services, and prison health services.

Ambulatory care organizations also employ other healthcare providers, including nurses, laboratory technicians, podiatrists, chiropractors, physical therapists, radiology technicians, psychologists, and social workers.

Private Medical Practice

Private medical practices are physician-owned entities that provide primary care or medical and surgical specialty care services in a freestanding office setting. The physicians have medical privileges at local hospitals and surgical centers but are not employees of those healthcare entities.

Hospital-based Ambulatory Care Services

In addition to providing inpatient services, many acute care hospitals also provide various ambulatory care services.

Emergency Services and Trauma Care

There was an annual average of 4,500 emergency departments (EDs) operating in the United States during 2003 and 2004. Over one-half of EDs saw less than 20,000 patients annually, but 1 out of 10 had an annual visit volume of more than 50,000 patients (Burt and McCaig 2006). Hospital-based emergency departments provide specialized care for victims of traumatic accidents and life-threatening illnesses. In urban areas, many also provide walk-in services for patients with minor illnesses and injuries who do not have access to regular primary care physicians.

Many physicians on the hospital staff also use the emergency care department as a setting to assess patients with problems that may either lead to an inpatient admission or require equipment or diagnostic imaging facilities not available in a private office or nursing home. Emergency services function as a major source of unscheduled admissions to the hospital.

Outpatient Surgical Services

Generally, ambulatory surgery refers to any surgical procedure that does not require an overnight stay in a hospital. It can be performed in the outpatient surgery department of a hospital or in a freestanding ambulatory surgery center. The increased number of procedures performed in an ambulatory setting can be attributed to improvements in surgical technology and anesthesia and the utilization management demands of third-party payers. The American Hospital Association reported that more than 22 million operations were performed in community hospitals in 1990. And for the first time, it said, a majority of these operations—51 percent—were done on an outpatient basis that did not require a hospital stay (Leary 1992). The shift from inpatient to outpatient surgery accelerated in the 1980's, growing at a rate of more than 10 percent a year. In 1980, for instance, 3 million same-day surgical procedures were performed, as compared with nearly 16 million operations involving hospital stays. Although the growth rate of outpatient surgery has slowed to about 7 percent a year, health experts project that by the end of the decade, 65 percent to 70 percent of surgery will be done on a same-day basis.

Outpatient Diagnostic and Therapeutic Services

Outpatient diagnostic and therapeutic services are provided in a hospital or one of its satellite facilities. Diagnostic services are those services performed by a physician to identify the disease or condition from which the patient is suffering. Therapeutic services are those services performed by a physician to treat the disease or condition that has been identified.

Hospital outpatients fall into different classifications according to the type of service they receive and the location of the service. For example, emergency outpatients are treated in the hospital's emergency or trauma care department for conditions that require immediate care. Clinic outpatients are treated in one of the hospital's clinical departments on an ambulatory basis. And referral outpatients receive special diagnostic or therapeutic services in the hospital on an ambulatory basis, but responsibility for their care remains with the referring physician.

Community-based Ambulatory Care Services

Community-based ambulatory care services refer to those services provided in freestanding facilities that are not owned by or affiliated with a hospital. Such facilities can range in size from a small medical practice with a single physician to a large clinic with an organized medical staff (Masters and Nester 2001).

Among the organizations that provide ambulatory care services are specialized treatment facilities. Examples of these facilities include birthing centers, cancer treatment centers, renal dialysis centers, rehabilitation centers, and so on.

Freestanding Ambulatory Care Centers

Freestanding ambulatory care facilities provide emergency services and urgent care for walk-in patients. Urgent care centers (sometimes called emergicenters) provide diagnostic and therapeutic care for patients with minor illnesses and injuries. They do not serve seriously ill patients, and most do not accept ambulance cases.

Two groups of patients find these centers attractive. The first group consists of patients seeking the convenience and access of emergency services without the delays and other forms of negative feedback associated with using hospital services for nonurgent problems. The second group consists of patients whose insurance treats urgent care centers preferentially compared with physicians' offices.

As they have increased in number and become familiar to more patients, many of these centers now offer a combination of walk-in and appointment services.

Freestanding Ambulatory Surgery Centers

Generally, freestanding ambulatory surgery centers provide surgical procedures that take anywhere from 5 to 90 minutes to perform and that require less than a four-hour recovery period. Patients must schedule their surgeries in advance and be prepared to return home on the same day. Patients who experience surgical complications are sent to an inpatient facility for care.

Most ambulatory surgery centers are for-profit entities. They may be owned by individual physicians, managed care organizations, or entrepreneurs. Generally, ambulatory care centers can provide surgical services at lower cost than hospitals can because their overhead expenses are lower.

Public Health Services

Although the states have constitutional authority to implement public health, a wide variety of federal programs and laws assist them. The Department of Health and Human Services (HHS) is the principal federal agency for ensuring health and providing essential human services. All its agencies have some responsibility for prevention. Through its 10 regional offices, HHS coordinates closely with state and local government agencies, and many HHS-funded services are provided by these agencies as well as by private-sector and nonprofit organizations.

The Office of the Secretary of HHS has two units important to public health: the Office of the Surgeon General of the United States and the Office of Disease Prevention and Health Promotion (ODPHP). ODPHP has an analysis and leadership role for health promotion and disease prevention.

The surgeon general is appointed by the president of the United States and provides leadership and authoritative, science-based recommendations about the public's health. The surgeon general has responsibility for the **public health service** (PHS) workforce (Jonas and Kovner 2005, 108–109).

Home Care Services

Home healthcare is the fastest-growing sector to offer services for Medicare recipients. The primary reason for this is increased economic pressure from third-party payers. In other words, third-party payers want patients released from the hospital more quickly than they were in the past. Moreover, patients generally prefer to be cared for in their own homes. In fact, most patients prefer home care, no matter how complex their medical problems. Research indicates that the medical outcomes of home care patients are similar to those of patients treated in **skilled nursing facilities** (SNFs) for similar conditions.

In 1989, Medicare rules for home care services were clarified to make it easier for Medicare beneficiaries to receive such services. Patients are eligible to receive home health services from a qualified Medicare provider when they are homebound, when they are under the care of a specified physician who will establish a home health plan, and when they need physical or occupational therapy, speech therapy, or intermittent skilled nursing care.

Skilled nursing care is defined as both technical procedures, such as tube feedings and catheter care, and skilled nursing observations. Intermittent is defined as up to 28 hours per week for nursing care and 35 hours per week for home health aide care. Many hospitals have formed their own home healthcare agencies to increase revenues and at the same time allow them to discharge patients from the hospital earlier.

Voluntary Agencies

Voluntary agencies provide healthcare and healthcare planning services, usually at the local level and to low-income patients. Their services range from giving free immunizations to offering family planning counseling. Funds to operate such agencies come from a variety of sources, including local or state health departments, private grants, and different federal bureaus.

One common example of a voluntary agency is the community health center. Sometimes called neighborhood health centers, community health centers offer comprehensive, primary healthcare services to patients who otherwise would not have access to them. Often patients pay for these services on a sliding scale based on income or according to a flat rate, discounted fee schedule supplemented by public funding.

Some voluntary agencies offer specialized services such as counseling for battered and abused women. Typically, these are set up within local communities. An example of a voluntary agency that offers services on a much larger scale is the Red Cross.

Long-term Care

Generally speaking, **long-term care** is the healthcare rendered in a nonacute care facility to patients who require inpatient nursing and related services for more than 30 consecutive days. Skilled nursing facilities, nursing homes, long-term care facilities and rehabilitation hospitals are the principal facilities that provide long-term care. Rehabilitation hospitals provide recuperative services for patients who have suffered strokes and traumatic injuries as well as other serious illnesses. Specialized long-term care facilities serve patients with chronic respiratory disease, permanent cognitive impairment, and other incapacitating conditions.

Long-term care encompasses a range of health, personal care, social, and housing services provided to people of all ages with health conditions that limit their ability to carry out normal daily activities without assistance. People who need long-term care have many different types of physical and mental disabilities. Moreover, their need for the mix and intensity of long-term care services can change over time.

Long-term care is mainly rehabilitative and supportive rather than curative. Moreover, healthcare workers other than physicians can provide long-term care in the home or in residential or institutional settings. For the most part, long-term care requires little or no technology.

Long-term Care and the Continuum of Care

The availability of long-term care is one of the most important health issues in the United States today. There are two principal reasons for this. First, thanks to advances in medicine and healthcare practices, people are living longer today than they did in the past. The number of people who survive previously fatal conditions has been growing, and more and more people with chronic medical problems are able to live reasonably normal lives. Second, there was an explosion in birth rate following World War II. Children born during that period, the so-called "baby-boomer generation," are in or entering their 50s today. These factors combined indicate that the need for long-term care can only increase in the years to come.

As discussed earlier, healthcare is now viewed as a **continuum of care**. That is, patients are provided care by different caregivers at several different levels of the healthcare system. In the case of long-term care, the patient's continuum of care may have begun with a primary provider in a hospital and then continued with home care and eventually care in a SNF. That patient's care is coordinated from one care setting to the next.

Moreover, the roles of the different care providers along the patient's continuum of care are continuing to evolve. Health information managers play a key part in providing consultation services to long-term care facilities with regard to developing systems to manage information from a diverse number of healthcare providers.

Delivery of Long-term Care Services

Long-term care services are delivered in a variety of settings. Among these settings are SNFs or nursing homes, residential care facilities, hospice programs, and adult day-care programs.

Skilled Nursing Facilities or Nursing Homes

The most important providers of formal, long-term care services are nursing homes. SNFs, or nursing homes, provide medical, nursing, and, in some cases, rehabilitative care around the clock. The majority of SNF residents are over age 65 and quite often are classified as the frail elderly.

Many nursing homes are owned by for-profit organizations. However, SNFs also may be owned by not-for-profit groups as well as local, state, and federal governments. In recent years, there has been a decline in the total number of nursing homes in the United States, but an increase in the number of nursing home beds.

Nursing homes are no longer the only option for patients needing long-term care. Various factors play a role in determining which type of long-term care facility is best for a particular patient, including cost, access to services, and individual needs.

Residential Care Facilities

New living environments that are more homelike and less institutional are the focus of much attention in the current long-term care market. Residential care facilities now play a growing role in the continuum of long-term care services. Having affordable and appropriate housing available for elderly and disabled people can reduce the level of need for institutional long-term care services in the community. Institutionalization can be postponed or prevented when the elderly and disabled live in safe and accessible settings where assistance with daily activities is available.

Hospice Programs

Hospice care is provided mainly in the home to the terminally ill and their families. Hospice is based on a philosophy of care imported from England and Canada that holds that during the course of terminal illness, the patient should be able to live life as fully and as comfortably as possible but without artificial or mechanical efforts to prolong life.

In the hospice approach, the family is the unit of treatment. An interdisciplinary team provides medical, nursing, psychological, therapeutic, pharmacological, and spiritual support during the final stages of illness, at the time of death, and during bereavement. The main goals are to control pain, maintain independence, and minimize the stress and trauma of death.

Hospice services have gained acceptance as an alternative to hospital care for the terminally ill. The number of hospices is likely to continue to grow because this philosophy of care for people at the end of life has become a model for the nation.

Adult Day-Care Programs

Adult day-care programs offer a wide range of health and social services to elderly persons during the daytime hours. Adult day-care services are usually targeted to elderly members of families in which the regular caregivers work during the day. Many elderly people who live alone also benefit from leaving their homes every day to participate in programs designed to keep them active. The goals of adult day-care programs are to delay the need for institutionalization and to provide respite for the caregivers. They are also known as day health centers.

Data on adult day-care programs are still limited, but there were approximately 3,400 programs in 2002 (Partners in Caregiving 2002). Most adult day-care programs offer social services, crafts, current events discussions, family counseling, reminiscence therapy, nursing assessment, physical exercise, activities of daily living, rehabilitation, psychiatric assessment, and medical care. Major study findings include the following:

- The average overall enrollment in adult day centers was 42 participants; average daily attendance was 25. The average length of stay was 2 years.
- Among adult day centers, 78 percent reported that they were nonprofit organizations; 22 percent reported that they were for-profit organizations.
- Among adult day centers, 37 percent provide a social model of care (with no nursing services provided), 21 percent provide a medical model (providing nursing services and in some instances rehabilitation therapy), and 42 percent provide a combined social and medical model. Centers exclusively serving individuals with dementia constituted 20 percent.
- The three major problems cited by adult day center providers are inadequate funding, difficulty recruiting and retaining staff, and difficulty maintaining census and attendance levels needed to cover operating costs.

Despite providers' stated concerns about under-utilization, the study concluded that the number of adult day centers (3,407) falls short of the number needed to serve the population of adults with chronic, debilitating illnesses and their family caregivers (Partners in Caregiving 2002).

Behavioral Health Services

From the mid-nineteenth century to the mid-twentieth century, psychiatric services in the United States were based primarily in long-stay institutions supported by state governments, and patterns of practice were relatively stable. Over the past 45 years, however, remarkable changes have occurred. These changes include a reversal of the balance between institutional and community care, inpatient and outpatient services, and individual and group practice.

The shift to community-based settings began in the public sector, and community settings remain dominant. The private sector's bed capacity increased in the 1970s and 1980s, including psychiatric units in nonfederal general hospitals, private psychiatric hospitals, and residential treatment centers for children. Substance abuse centers and child and adolescent inpatient psychiatric units grew particularly quickly in the 1980s, as investors recognized their profitability. In the 1990s, the growth of inpatient private mental health facilities leveled off, and the number of outpatient and partial treatment settings increased sharply. Although the number of mental health organizations providing 24-hour services (hospital inpatient and residential treatment) increased significantly over the 32-year period from 1970 to 2002, the number of psychiatric beds provided by these organizations decreased by more than half, from 524,878 in 1970 to 211,199 in 2002 (Foley et al. 2004)

Residential treatment centers for emotionally or behaviorally disturbed children provide inpatient services to children under 18 years of age. The programs and physical facilities of residential treatment centers are designed to meet patients' daily living, schooling, recreational, socialization, and routine medical care needs.

Day-hospital or day-treatment programs occupy one niche in the spectrum of **behavioral healthcare** settings. Although some provide services seven days per week, many programs provide services only during business hours, Monday through Friday. Day-treatment patients spend most of the day at the treatment facility in a program of structured therapeutic activities and then return to their homes until the next day. Day-treatment services include psychotherapy, pharmacology, occupational therapy, and other types of rehabilitation services. These programs provide alternatives to inpatient care or serve as transitions from inpatient to outpatient care or discharge. They also may provide respite for family caregivers and a place for rehabilitating or maintaining chronically ill patients. The number of day-treatment programs has increased in response to pressures to decrease the length of hospital stays.

Insurance coverage for behavioral healthcare has always lagged behind coverage for other medical care. Although treatments and treatment settings have changed, rising healthcare costs, the absence of strong consumer demand for behavioral health coverage, and insurers' continuing fear of the potential cost of this coverage have maintained the differences between medical and behavioral healthcare benefits.

Although the majority of individuals who are covered by health insurance have some outpatient psychiatric coverage, the coverage is often quite restricted. Typical restrictions include limits on the number of outpatient visits, higher copayment charges, and higher deductibles.

Behavioral healthcare has grown and diversified, particularly over the past 40 years, as psychopharmacologic treatment has made possible the shift away from long-term custodial treatment. Psychosocial treatments continue the process of care and rehabilitation in community settings. Large state hospitals have been supplemented, and in many cases replaced, by psychiatric units in general hospitals, new outpatient clinics, community mental health centers, day-treatment centers, and halfway houses. Treatment has become more effective and specific, based on our growing understanding of the brain and behavior. Advances in the biological and behavioral sciences continue to improve opportunities for diagnosing, treating, and preventing psychiatric disorders (Jonas and Kovner 1999, 243–273).

Check Your Understanding 2.4

Instructions: On a separate piece of paper, match the descriptions provided with the terms to which they apply.

1. ___ Behavioral health service
2. ___ Public health service
3. ___ Home care service
4. ___ Hospice program
5. ___ Skilled nursing facility
6. ___ Voluntary agency
7. ___ Residential care facility
8. ___ Day-treatment program
9. ___ Continuum of care
10. ___ Freestanding ambulatory care center

a. Fastest-growing sector of Medicare
b. Provides emergency services and urgent care for walk-in patients
c. Represents a reversal in the balance between institutional and community care
d. Designed to meet patients' daily living, schooling, recreational, socialization, and routine medical care needs
e. Has an analysis and leadership role for health promotion and disease prevention.
f. Provides healthcare and healthcare planning services usually at the local level and to low-income patients
g. Provides alternatives to inpatient care or serves as transition from inpatient to outpatient care or discharge
h. Care provided mainly in the home to the terminally ill and their families
i. Care provided by different caregivers at several different levels of the healthcare system
j. Healthcare rendered in a nonacute care facility to patients who require inpatient nursing and related services for more than 30 consecutive days

---

Integrated Delivery Systems

Many hospitals have responded to local pressures by rapidly merging, acquiring, and entering into affiliations and other risk-sharing reimbursement agreements with other acute and nonacute providers, hospital-based healthcare systems, physicians and physician group practices, and managed care organizations. Transactions have included mergers of nonprofit organizations into either investor-owned or other nonprofit entities.

The goal of **integrated delivery systems** (IDSs) or **integrated delivery networks** (IDNs) is to organize the entire continuum of care, from health promotion and disease prevention to primary and secondary acute, tertiary care, long-term care, and hospice care, to maximize its effectiveness across episodes of illness and pathways of wellness. A premium is placed on integration and holistic care.

Managed care and healthcare organization integration have placed enormous pressure on information systems. The need for cost data, as well as the integration of data from the various components of integrated systems, has placed many demands on systems technology and personnel. A healthcare provider that cannot completely analyze the cost of delivery when dealing with an insurer is at a distinct disadvantage. Similarly, an inability to integrate patient data across a system can produce increased costs, inefficiencies, and even medical errors.

An IDS combines the financial and clinical aspects of healthcare and uses a group of healthcare providers, selected on the basis of quality and cost management criteria, to furnish comprehensive health services across the continuum of care (AHIMA 2010). In an integrated health delivery network, various types of organizations are connected along a continuum of care through horizontal and vertical integration. Depending on where you are in the United States, an IDN may also be called integrated health system, integrated delivery system (network), integrated care system (network), organized delivery system, community care network, integrated healthcare organization, integrated service network, or population-based integrated delivery system. These are all essentially referring to the same thing.

Information Needs of IDNs

The role of computers has changed rapidly in healthcare organizations, just as it has in many service organizations. The more advanced systems, once called data-processing centers, became management information systems. As computer operations became more powerful and complex, it became possible to think about creating new services or greatly improving existing ones. Innovations were considered strategic uses of information systems because they helped an organization to compete or achieve its goals. Hospitals and integrated health systems have begun to use computers to serve in new functions. For example, a hospital can offer physicians the opportunity to connect to its computer system. Thanks to virtual private networks, a physician can connect to an integrated health system's intranet and work within the system in a private and secure environment without worrying about the downtime often experienced on the Internet.

The emergence of IDNs has placed enormous pressure on the need for integrated information systems. The need for financial information, as well as the integration of data from the various components of integrated systems, has placed many demands on systems technology and personnel. An IDN must be able to integrate patient data across a system in an effort to analyze ways to reduce costs and inefficiencies. Healthcare providers must have access to their own data and be able to understand their own cost data to be competitive with insurance companies.

The role of IT and information management changed dramatically from the 1990s to 2008 for healthcare organizations. Business process improvement and transformation were considered strategic uses of IT because they were converting data to information and analyzing it to their own customized needs. "Interoperable systems provide clinicians with secure and efficient access to the comprehensive patient information they need to make fully informed clinical decisions," said Joyce Sensmeier, vice president, informatics, at Health Information Management Systems Society (HIMSS). "These systems are the foundation of the comprehensive electronic health record and nationwide and regional health information networks." (e-MDs 2008).

Health Information Exchange (HIE) is an initiative by healthcare professionals and industry to improve the way computer systems in healthcare share information. HIE promotes the coordinated use of established standards such as Digital Imaging and Communication in Medicine (DICOM) and Health Level 7 (HL7) to address specific clinical needs in support of optimal patient care. Systems developed in accordance with HIE communicate with one another better, are easier to implement, and enable care providers to use information more effectively. Physicians, medical specialists, nurses, administrators and other care providers envision a day when vital information can be passed seamlessly from system to system within and across departments and made readily available at the point of care. HIE is designed to make their vision a reality by improving the state of systems integration and removing barriers to optimal patient care.

Why HIE Is Necessary

Optimal patient care requires efficient access to all relevant information. Despite the advanced state of technology, however, healthcare enterprises have not yet begun to realize the full potential of computer systems to reduce medical errors, improve the efficiency of care providers, and enhance the overall quality of clinical care. To do so requires a framework for information sharing that meets the needs of care providers as well as patients—and gains acceptance among the companies that build the systems they rely on.

Standards provide the basis for such a framework, but alone do not solve the problem. In any standard there are gaps, options, room for conflicting interpretations. No standard maps perfectly to the complex and ever-changing information domain of a healthcare enterprise. Filling the gap between standards and systems integration has, until now, required expensive, site-specific interface development. To close that gap, a process for building a detailed framework for the implementation of standards is needed. HIE provides that process and promotes integration within and across all units of the healthcare enterprise, although it began in 1998 with a focus on radiology.

Barriers to IDN Integration

It takes many years to truly integrate these new, often hospital-sponsored aggregations of facilities and services into integrated systems for the delivery of healthcare. Barriers to doing so include:

- Failure to understand the new core business
- Inability to overcome the hospital paradigm, as it may not be consistent with system priorities
- Ambiguous roles and responsibilities throughout the system
- Inability to "manage" managed care
- Inability to execute the strategy
- Lack of alignment or match between various components, such as orientation toward the market versus managerial control of strategy

The success of a strength is highly dependent on system investments in IT, managerial leadership, and empowerment and shared-system ownership with physicians (Jonas and Kovner 1999, 173–175).

The Future of Integrated Delivery Networks

Hospitals in the United States will most likely continue to affiliate with others in large local systems; and there may be enhanced identification of hospitals as part of regional and national chains, depending on financial incentives and other messages in the environment, including antitrust regulation (that is, on how far hospitals are allowed to combine, by law, into monopolies or oligopolies). There probably will be a variety of models in the future, together with a reaffirmation by hospitals of their functions in local communities, regardless of ownership or membership in larger systems. The history of hospitals suggests that they will continue to expand wherever possible rather than contract and that they will continue to be controlled by shifting coalitions of community interests, business interests, physicians, third-party payers, trustees, administrators, politicians, and lobbyists. One of the key issues is the availability and channeling of hospital income.

In 2009, President Barack Obama announced administration plans to convene a health summit to initiate extensive reforms to the U.S. healthcare system that would broaden coverage, cut costs, and support EHR adoption (Obama 2009).

Check Your Understanding 2.5

Instructions: On a separate piece of paper, indicate whether the statements below are true or false (T or F).

1. ___ Ambulatory care is the short-term care provided to diagnose and treat an illness or injury.
2. ___ The influence of managed care and the emphasis on cost -control in the Medicare and Medicaid programs have resulted in shorter hospital stays.
3. ___ Hospitals can be classified on the basis of their type of ownership.
4. ___ Government hospitals are operated by a specific branch of federal, state, or local government as for-profit organizations.
5. ___ The board of directors has primary responsibility for setting the overall direction of the hospital.
6. ___ Medical staff classification refers to the organization of physicians according to clinical assignment.
7. ___ A registered nurse qualified by advanced education and clinical and management experience usually administers patient care services.
8. ___ Physicians who specialize in radiology are called radiology technicians.
9. ___ Occupational therapy is made available in acute care hospitals, clinics, and rehab centers.
10. ___ The ancillary units of the hospital provide vital clinical and administrative support services to patients, medical staff, visitors, and employees.

Forces Affecting Hospitals

A number of recent developments in healthcare delivery have had far-reaching effects on the operation of hospitals in the United States.

Subacute Care

Subacute care represents a new movement in healthcare. In the past, the term was used in reference to the services provided to hospitalized patients who did not meet the medical criteria for needing acute care. Today, it refers to the level of skilled care needed by patients with complex medical conditions, typically Medicare patients who have multiple medical problems.

Traditionally, nursing homes, home care providers, and rehabilitation facilities have provided subacute care. Now some hospitals are developing subacute units in response to changing demographics that make it a cost-effective alternative to inpatient acute care.

Development of Peer Review and Quality Improvement Programs

The goal of high-quality patient care is to promote, preserve, and restore health. High-quality care is delivered in an appropriate setting in a manner that is satisfying to patients. It is achieved when the patient's health status is improved as much as possible. Quality has several components, including the following:

- Appropriateness (the right care is provided at the right time)

- Technical excellence (the right care is provided in the right manner)
- Accessibility (the right care can be obtained when it is needed)
- Acceptability (the patients are satisfied)

Peer Review

In **peer review,** a member of a profession assesses the work of colleagues within that same profession. Peer review has traditionally been at the center of quality assessment and assurance efforts. The medical profession's peer review efforts have emphasized the scientific aspects of quality. Appropriate use of pharmaceuticals, postoperative infection rates, and accuracy of diagnosis are among the measures of quality that have been used. Peer review is a requirement of both CMS and the Joint Commission.

Quality Improvement

Quality improvement (QI) programs have been in place in hospitals for years and have been required by the Medicare and Medicaid programs and accreditation standards. QI programs have covered medical staff as well as nursing and other departments or processes.

Efforts to encourage the delivery of high-quality care take place at the local and national levels. Such efforts are geared toward assessing the efforts of both individuals and institutions. Currently, professional associations, healthcare organizations, government agencies, private external quality review associations, consumer groups, managed care organizations, and group purchasers of care all play a role in trying to promote high-quality care.

Growth of Managed Care

Managed care is a generic term for a healthcare reimbursement system that manages cost, quality, and access to services. Most managed care plans do not provide healthcare directly. Instead, they enter into service contracts with the physicians, hospitals, and other healthcare providers who provide medical services to enrollees in the plans.

Managed care systems control costs primarily by presetting payment amounts and restricting patient access to healthcare services through precertification and UR processes. (Managed care is discussed in more detail in chapter 14.) Managed care delivery systems also attempt to manage cost and quality by:

- Implementing various forms of financial incentives for providers
- Promoting healthy lifestyles
- Identifying risk factors and illnesses early in the disease process
- Providing patient education

Restructuring initiatives and increased use of technology have streamlined operations and improved operational efficiencies over recent years for the managed care industry. Humana is one of the nation's largest healthcare plan providers in the United States, with approval from The Centers for Medicare and Medicaid Services (CMS) to offer the Medicare Part D prescription drug plan (PDP) to the more than 42 million Medicare eligible beneficiaries. Humana's new product design has, in recent years, focused on meeting the demand for greater self determination by employers and members for varying levels of co-payments, deductibles, coinsurance, benefits levels, and price (Kallos 2008).

Efforts at Healthcare Reengineering

During the 1980s and 1990s, healthcare organizations attempted to adopt **continuous quality improvement** (CQI) processes. Lessons learned from other areas of business were applied to healthcare settings. **Reengineering** came in many varieties, such as focused process improvement, major business process improvement, and business process innovation, total quality management (TQM), and CQI. Regardless of its approach, every healthcare organization attempted to look inside and think "process" as opposed to traditional "department" thinking. Healthcare organizations formed cross-functional teams that collaborated to solve organizational problems. At the same time, the Joint Commission reengineered the accreditation process to increase its focus on process and systems analysis. Gone were the days of thinking in a "silo." All of those silos were turned over, and healthcare teams learned from each other. The drivers of reengineering included cost reduction, staff shortages, and implementation of technology. Healthcare quality improvement is divided into three related activities: quality improvement (including process improvement, CQI, TQM, Six Sigma); quality control (audits, ISO 9001, statistical process control); and quality planning (new products and services) (Carlson 2002).

Emphasis on Patient-focused Care

Patient-focused care is a concept developed to contain hospital inpatient costs and improve quality by restructuring services so that more of them take place in the nursing units (patient floors) and not in specialized units in dispersed hospital locations. The emphasis is on cross-training staff in the nursing units to perform a variety of functions for a small group of patients rather than one set of functions for a large number of patients. Some organizations have achieved patient-focused care by assigning multiskilled workers to serve food, clean patients' rooms, and assist in nursing care. However, some organizations have experienced low patient satisfaction with this type of worker because the patients are confused and do not know who to ask to do what.

Hospital staff spend most of their time performing activities in the following nine categories:

- Medical, technical, and clinical procedures
- Hotel and patient services
- Medical documentation

- Institutional documentation
- Scheduling and coordination
- Patient transportation
- Staff transportation
- Management and supervision
- Ready-for-action activities

A study at Lakeland Regional Medical Center, a 750-bed hospital in central Florida, found that medical, technical, and clinical activity consumed one-sixth of the center's personnel-related costs. The study also showed that almost twice that amount of time was spent writing things down. Scheduling and coordination took as much time as medical activity, and ready-for-action activities consumed even more (Jonas and Kovner 1999, 2005).

The study suggested that restructuring services at Lakeland would reduce the number of staff required for patient care activities from 2,200 to 1,200 and improve care. The amount of physical space allotted to each unit would be sufficient to contain a minilab, diagnostic radiology rooms, linen and general supply, stockrooms, and so on. If such changes were carried out, medical documentation could be reduced by almost two-thirds, scheduling and coordination service by more than two-thirds, and ready-for-action time by two-thirds (Jonas and Kovner 1999, 2005).

Hospitals have had difficulty in fully and rapidly implementing patient-focused care for the following reasons: the high cost of conversion; the extensive physical renovations required; resistance from functional departments; and other priorities for management, such as mergers and considering potential mergers.

Check Your Understanding 2.6

Instructions: On a separate piece of paper, write the best terms to complete the following sentences.

1. Today, ___ refers to the level of skilled care needed by patients with complex medical conditions, typically Medicare patients who have multiple medical problems.
   a. acute care
   b. ambulatory care
   c. subacute care
   d. high-quality care
2. Quality has several components, including appropriateness, technical excellence, ___, and acceptability.
   a. accuracy of diagnosis
   b. continuous improvement
   c. connectivity
   d. accessibility
3. ___ programs have been in place in hospitals for years and have been required by the Medicare and Medicaid programs and accreditation standards.
   a. Quality assurance
   b. Peer review
   c. Managed care
   d. Quality improvement
4. ___ is a generic term for a healthcare reimbursement system that manages cost, quality, and access to services.
   a. Quality improvement
   b. Subacute care
   c. Managed care
   d. Patient-focused care
5. Recent evidence indicates that the quality of care provided under managed care systems may differ across ___.
   a. population groups
   b. healthcare settings
   c. medical facilities
   d. integrated delivery systems
6. ___ attempts to contain hospital inpatient costs and improve quality by restructuring services.
   a. Continuous quality improvement
   b. Patient-focused care
   c. Managed care
   d. Acute care
7. Managed care and healthcare organization integration have placed enormous pressure on ___.
   a. integrated delivery systems
   b. acute care facilities
   c. rehabilitation facilities
   d. information systems

Licensure, Certification, and Accreditation of Healthcare Facilities

Under the 10th Amendment of the U.S. Constitution, states have the primary responsibility for public health, which includes disease and injury prevention, sanitation, water and air pollution, vaccination, isolation and quarantine, inspection of commercial and residential premises, food and drinking water standards, extermination of vermin, fluoridation of municipal water supplies, and licensure of physicians and other healthcare professionals. Each state has a division or agency that is dedicated to promoting high-quality patient care and safety in healthcare facilities and outpatient services by conducting regular on-site surveys. State and federal licensing and certification programs require that high-performance standards be met in the provision of medical care and in the construction and maintenance of the healthcare facility.

State Licensure

Licensure gives legal approval for a facility to operate or for a person to practice within his or her profession. Virtually every state requires that hospitals, sanatoria, nursing homes, and pharmacies be licensed to operate, although the requirements and standards for licensure may differ from state to state. State licensure is mandatory. Federal facilities such as those of the Department of Veterans Affairs (VA) do not require licensure.

Although licensure requirements vary, healthcare facilities must meet certain basic criteria that are determined by state regulatory agencies. These standards address such concerns as adequacy of staffing, personnel employed to provide services, physical aspects of the facility (equipment, buildings), and services provided, including health records. Licensure typically is performed annually, and facilities must usually meet the minimum acceptable standards for operation.

Certification for Medicare Participation

In 1965, the Social Security Act established both Medicare and Medicaid. Medicare was the responsibility of the Social Security Administration (SSA), but federal assistance to the state Medicaid programs was administered by the Social and Rehabilitation Service (SRS). SSA and SRS were agencies in the Department of Health, Education, and Welfare (HEW). In 1977, the Health Care Financing Administration (HCFA) was created under HEW to effectively coordinate Medicare and Medicaid. In 1980, HEW was divided into the Department of Education and the Department of Health and Human Services (HHS). In 2001, HCFA was renamed the Centers for Medicare and Medicaid Services (CMS), an agency of HHS.

CMS maintains oversight of the survey and certification of nursing homes and continuing care providers (including hospitals, nursing homes, home health agencies, end-stage renal disease facilities, hospices, and other facilities serving Medicare and Medicaid beneficiaries) and makes available to beneficiaries, providers and suppliers, researchers, and state surveyors information about these activities. In November 2002, CMS began a national Nursing Home Quality Initiative (NHQI). The goals of the initiative are essentially twofold: to provide consumers with an additional source of information about the quality of nursing home care by providing a set of MDS-based quality measures on Medicare's Nursing Home Compare Web site, and to help providers improve the quality of care for their residents by providing them with complementary clinical resources, quality improvement materials, and assistance from the QIOs in every state (CMS 2005). The quality initiative, an important component of CMS's comprehensive strategy to improve the quality of care provided by America's nursing homes, is a four-prong effort that consists of (CMS 2005):

- Regulation and enforcement efforts conducted by state survey agencies and CMS
- Improved consumer information on the quality of care in nursing homes
- Continual, community-based quality improvement programs designed for nursing homes to improve their quality of care
- Collaboration and partnership to leverage knowledge and resources

Many nursing homes have already made significant improvements in the care being provided to residents by taking advantage of these materials and the support of QIO staff (CMS 2005). From the beginning of this Nursing Home Quality Initiative, CMS has insisted that the quality measures are dynamic and will continue to be refined as part of CMS's ongoing commitment to quality

To be eligible for Medicare and Medicaid reimbursement, providers must demonstrate compliance with the **Conditions of Participation**, which is the process of certification. Certification is the process by which government and nongovernment organizations evaluate educational programs, healthcare facilities, and individuals as having met predetermined standards. The certification of healthcare facilities is the responsibility of the states. However, Title XVIII of the Medicare Act specifies that facilities accredited by the Joint Commission and the American Osteopathic Association must be deemed in compliance with the Medicare Conditions of Participation for Hospitals; those accredited are said to have deemed status.

Voluntary Accreditation

Accreditation is a voluntary system of institutional or organizational review performed by an independent body created for the purpose of evaluating the work quality of the subject agencies, using written criteria (Jonas and Kovner 1999, 527).

The Joint Commission operates voluntary accreditation programs for hospitals and other healthcare services. It certifies hospitals as having met the Conditions of Participation required for reimbursement under the federal Medicare program. The definition of federal **Deemed Status** is as follows:

> In order for healthcare organizations to participate in and receive payment from the Medicare and Medicaid programs, [they] must be certified as complying with the Conditions of Participation, or standards, set forth in federal regulations (Joint Commission 2007).

A majority of state governments recognize the Joint Commission accreditation as a condition of licensure and receiving Medicaid reimbursement. Inspections are typically triannual with accreditation and survey findings made publicly available. The standards are based on the premise that healthcare organizations exist to maximize the health of the people they serve while using resources efficiently. When an organization is found to be in substantial compliance with the Joint Commission standards, accreditation may be awarded for up to three years. Hospitals must undergo a full survey at least every three years.

The Joint Commission publishes accreditation manuals with standards for hospitals, non-hospital-based psychiatric and substance abuse organizations, long-term care organizations, home care organizations, ambulatory care organizations, and organization-based pathology and clinical laboratory services.

Much like the Joint Commission, the American Osteopathic Association (AOA) Hospital Accreditation Program accreditation is a voluntary program that accredits osteopathic hospitals. Those hospitals that are accredited are recognized by the HHS as having deemed status and thus are eligible to receive Medicare funds (AOA 2005). AOA has been accrediting healthcare facilities for more than 30 years under Medicare. It is one of only two voluntary accreditation programs in the United States authorized by CMS to survey hospitals under Medicare. In addition, the program is a cost-effective, user-friendly means to validate the quality of care provided by a facility.

The AOA accreditation program was developed in 1943 and 1944 and implemented in 1945. Under this program hospitals were surveyed each year. In this manner, the AOA was able to ensure that osteopathic students received their training through rotating internships and residencies in facilities that provided high-quality patient care. In 1995, the AOA applied for and received deeming authority to accredit laboratories within AOA-accredited hospitals under the Clinical Laboratory Improvement Amendments of 1988. AOA also has developed accreditation requirements for ambulatory care and surgery, mental health, substance abuse, and physical rehabilitation medicine facilities (AOA 2005).

Reimbursement of Healthcare Expenditures

Together, the Medicare and Medicaid programs and the managed care insurance industry have virtually eliminated fee-for-service reimbursement arrangements.

Evolution of Third-party Reimbursement

The evolution of third-party reimbursement systems for healthcare services began more than 60 years ago. The evolution created a need for systematic and accurate communications between healthcare providers and third-party payers. Commercial health insurance companies (for example, Aetna) offer medical plans similar to Blue Cross/Blue Shield plans. Traditionally, Blue Cross organizations covered hospital services and Blue Shield covered inpatient physician services and a limited amount of office-based care. Today, Blue Cross plans and commercial insurance providers cover a full range of healthcare services, including ambulatory care services and drug benefits. (Healthcare reimbursement systems are discussed in more detail in chapter 14.)

Most commercial health insurance is provided in the form of group policies offered by employers as part of their fringe benefit packages for employees. Unions also negotiate health insurance coverage during contract negotiations. In most cases, employees pay a share of the cost and employers pay a share.

Individual health insurance plans can be purchased but usually are expensive or have limited coverage and high deductibles. Individuals with preexisting medical conditions often find it almost impossible to get individual coverage.

Commercial insurers also sell major medical and cash payment policies. Major medical plans are directed primarily at catastrophic illness and cover all or part of treatment costs beyond those covered by basic plans. Major medical plans are sold as both group and individual policies. Cash payment plans provide monetary benefits and are not based on actual charges from healthcare providers. For example, a cash payment plan might pay the beneficiary $150 for every day he or she is hospitalized or $500 for every ambulatory surgical procedure. Cash payment plans are often offered as a benefit of membership in large associations such as the American Association of Retired Persons (AARP).

Government-sponsored Reimbursement Systems

Until 1965, most of the poor and many of the elderly in the United States could not afford private healthcare services. As a result of public pressure calling for attention to this growing problem, Congress passed Public Law 89-97 as an Amendment to the Social Security Act. The amendment created Medicare (Title XVIII) and Medicaid (Title XIX). Medicare and Medicaid are not issuers of health insurance. They are public health plans through which individuals obtain health coverage.

Medicare

Medicare was first offered to retired Americans in July 1966. Today, retired and disabled Americans who are eligible for Social Security benefits automatically qualify for Medicare coverage without regard to income. Coverage is offered under two coordinated programs: hospital insurance (Medicare Part A) and medical insurance (Medicare Part B).

Medicare Part A is financed through payroll taxes. Initially, coverage applied only to hospitalization and home healthcare. Subsequently, coverage for extended care in nursing homes was added. Coverage for individuals eligible for Social Security disability payments for over two years and those who need kidney transplantation or dialysis for end-stage renal disease also was added.

Medical insurance under Medicare Part B is optional. It is financed through monthly premiums paid by eligible beneficiaries to supplement federal funding. Part B helps pay for physician's services, outpatient hospital care, medical services and supplies, and certain other medical costs not covered by Part A. At the present time, Medicare Part B does not provide coverage of prescription drugs. (Medicare Parts A and B are discussed in greater detail in chapter 14.) In January 2006, Medicare Part D was implemented to provide prescription drug coverage for Medicare beneficiaries who select this option.

Medicaid

Medicaid is a medical assistance program for low-income Americans. The program is funded partially by the federal government and partially by state and local governments. The federal government requires that certain services be provided and sets specific eligibility requirements.

Medicaid covers the following benefits:

- Inpatient hospital care
- Outpatient hospital care
- Laboratory and x-ray services
- SNF and home health services for persons over 21 years old

- Physician's services
- Family planning services
- Rural health clinic services
- Early and periodic screening, diagnosis, and treatment services

Individual states sometimes cover services in addition to those required by the federal government.

Services Provided by Government Agencies

Federal health insurance programs cover health services for several additional specified populations.

TRICARE, which was originally referred to as the Civilian Health and Medical Program for the Uniformed Services (CHAMPUS), pays for care delivered by civilian health providers to retired members of the military and the dependents of active and retired members of the seven uniformed services. The Department of Defense administers the TRICARE program. The program also provides medical services to active members of the military.

The Veteran's Administration (VA) provides healthcare services to eligible veterans of military service. The VA hospital system was established in 1930 to provide hospital, nursing home, residential, and outpatient medical and dental care to veterans of the First World War. Today, the VA operates more than 950 medical centers throughout the United States. The medical centers are currently being organized into 22 Veterans Integrated Service Networks (VISNs) to increase the efficiency of their services.

Through the Indian Health Service, HHS also finances the healthcare services provided to Native Americans living on reservations across the country.

State governments often operate healthcare facilities to serve citizens with special needs, such as the developmentally disabled and mentally ill. Some states also offer health insurance programs to those who cannot qualify for private healthcare insurance. Many county and local governments also operate public hospitals to fulfill the medical needs of their communities. Public hospitals provide services without regard to the patient's ability to pay.

Workers' Compensation

Workers' compensation is an insurance system operated by the individual states. Each state has its own law and program to provide covered workers with some protection against the costs of medical care and the loss of income resulting from work-related injuries and, in some cases, illnesses. The first workers' compensation law was enacted in New York in 1910. By 1948, every state had enacted such laws. The theory underlying workers' compensation is that all accidents that occur at work, regardless of fault, must be regarded as risks of industry and that employer and employee should share the burden of loss (Jonas and Kovner 1999, 41).

Insurance

Healthcare insurance was created to spread risk over a large pool of people, and to protect assets in the event of a catastrophic illness or injury. Health insurance guards against financial devastation in the face of serious health problems. In the United States, there are more than 200 million people covered by private health insurance (Edelson 2006). Of those, 53 percent are self-insured and 47 percent are fully insured. As for employers providing health insurance benefits for their employees, the 2007 data reflects that 96 percent of the large employers offer health insurance for their employees, with only 43 percent of small employers (Edelson 2006).

Managed Care

The growth of managed care in the United States has had a tremendous impact on healthcare organizations and healthcare professionals. Managed care is a broad term used to describe several types of prepaid healthcare plans. Common types of managed care plans include health maintenance organizations (HMOs), preferred provider organizations (PPOs), and point-of-service (POS) plans.

Members of HMOs pay a set premium and are entitled to receive a specific range of healthcare services. In most cases, employers and employees share the cost of the plan. Coverage can be provided for an individual employee or his or her whole family. HMOs control costs by requiring members of the plan to seek services only from a preapproved list of providers, who are reimbursed at discounted rates. The plans also control access to medical specialists, expensive diagnostic and treatment procedures, and high-cost pharmaceuticals. They generally require preapproval for specialty consultations, inpatient care, and surgical procedures.

The development of managed care was an indirect result of the federal government's enactment of the Medicare and Medicaid laws in 1965. Medicare and Medicaid legislation prompted the development of **investor-owned hospital chains** and stimulated the growth of university medical centers. Both of these furthered the corporate practice of medicine by increasing the number of management personnel and physicians employed by hospitals and medical schools (Kongstevdt 1993, 3–5).

The new healthcare programs for the elderly and poor laid the groundwork for increased corporate control of medical care delivery by third-party payers. This was done through the government-mandated regulation of fee-for-service and indemnity payments for healthcare services. After years of unchecked healthcare inflation, the government authorized corporate cost controls on hospitals, physicians, patients, prospective payment systems, and the resource-based relative value scale.

Further federal support for the corporate practice of medicine resulted from passage of the HMO Act of 1973. Amendments to the act enabled managed care plans to increase in numbers and expand enrollments through healthcare programs financed by grants, contracts, and loans. After passage of the HMO Act, strong support for the HMO concept came from business; the executive, legislative, and judicial branches of government; and several states where managed care proliferated, such as California, some northeastern states, and particularly Minneapolis and St. Paul, Minnesota.

Bipartisan support for managed care was based on the concept that HMOs can decrease costs and encourage free-market competition in the medical care arena with only limited government intervention. One measure of success of this policy can be found in the virtual disappearance of some 17 national health insurance bills introduced into Congress in the early 1970s (Kongstevdt 1993, 3–5).

Impact of Managed Care Organizations

With more and more Americans receiving their health insurance through **managed care organizations** (MCOs), the responsibilities of primary care providers have changed. In the fee-for-service model, the primary care provider is responsible only for the patients actually seen in his or her office, and a practice is viewed as being made up of individual patients. In a fully capitated managed care setting, however, particularly when the provider is paid through a capitation system rather than by a modified fee-for-service system, he or she is responsible for providing care to a defined population of patients assigned by the MCO. The MCO may audit the provider's practice to determine whether standards of care are being met. In the capitated MCO setting, providers are often held responsible for each patient on their panels, whether or not the patient ever comes to the office to be seen. Thus, if the standard of care set by the MCO for a pediatric practice requires that 90 percent of children receive all their immunizations by two years of age, the denominator used in assessing compliance with this goal is the total number of children two years of age and older in the provider's panel, not just the children actually seen in the provider's office. Standards of care, benchmarks against which the adequacy of care provided by the primary care practitioner is judged, exist for preventive services. Although quality assurance measures have been required in hospital settings for a long time, it has only been since 1991, with the advent of standards of accreditation for MCOs set by the **National Committee on Quality Assurance** (NCQA), the accrediting body for MCOs, that widespread monitoring of standards of care in ambulatory settings has begun to gain acceptance (Jonas and Kovner 2005, 240).

The advent of managed care appeared to tame healthcare cost inflation during the early and mid-1990s, but costs are once again rising rapidly. In particular, the total cost of pharmaceuticals is skyrocketing. The managed care industry faces continued financial challenges. At the same time, it remains under intense public scrutiny and is facing continued attempts at increased government legislation and regulation. In addition, for many years costs increased faster than premiums could rise to cover them. Thus, escalating costs have forced employers to ask workers to pay for a larger share of healthcare. Political and market forces and the weakness of any stabilizing influences are eroding the ability of managed care firms to control underlying healthcare costs.

From 1960 to 2002, national healthcare spending rose from $27 billion to $1.6 trillion. Within that time period, the population of the United States rose from 186 million to 285 million and the gross domestic product (GDP) rose from $527 billion to $10.4 trillion. One thing that stands out from these numbers is the fact that healthcare spending outgrew the population. According to the statistics, per capita spending on healthcare during that same time period increased from $143 per person to $5,440 per person (Jonas and Kovner 2005, 630).

By several measures, healthcare spending continues to rise at the fastest rate in our history. In 2007, total national health expenditures were expected to rise 6.9 percent—two times the rate of inflation (NCHC n.d.). Total spending was $2.3 trillion in 2007, or $7600 per person. Total healthcare spending represented 16 percent of the gross domestic product (GDP). U.S. healthcare spending is expected to increase at similar levels for the next decade reaching $4.2 trillion in 2016, or 20 percent of GDP. The annual premium for an employer health plan covering a family of four averaged nearly $12,100. The annual premium for single coverage averaged over $4,400 (NCHC n.d.).

Although nearly 47 million Americans are uninsured, the United States spends more on healthcare than other industrialized nations, and those countries provide health insurance to all their citizens (California Health Care Foundation 2005). Moreover, despite the incredible investment America continues to make in healthcare, an astounding 15 percent of Americans lack healthcare coverage altogether. See figure 2.2 for an overview and breakdown of the 2008 annual health insurance premiums for U.S. covered workers.

Although managed care deserves much of the credit for taming the rampant, double-digit healthcare inflation of the 1980s and early 1990s, the relief from rising medical bills that Americans enjoyed for several years is over, and increases in premiums have both HMOs and employers, especially smaller ones, scrambling for countermeasures. The following excerpt is taken from the National Conference of State Legislature's Health Insurance and the States (2008):

> For most Americans, market-based health insurance remains the predominant form of health coverage. According to the most recent detailed census report (2007, published August 2008), of 299,106,000 total Americans:
>
> The number of people with health insurance increased to 253.4 million in 2007 up from 249.8 million in 2006.
>
> - 201,897,000 people (67.5 percent) were covered by private market health insurance.
> - 177,367,000 people (59.3 percent) were enrolled in employer based insurance.
> - 26,620,000 people (8.9 percent) were enrolled in "individual market" or direct purchase health insurance.
> - By comparison, 83,151,000 people (27.8 percent) were covered by some form of government insurance.
>   —39,481,000 were counted in Medicaid in 2007. In 2003, *6,419,000* of Medicaid recipients also had some type of private insurance according the Census Bureau. (Note: Medicaid

agencies provided services to over 50 million individuals in 2006; see NCSL's Medicaid Overview for resources and updates)

—41,276,000 were enrolled in Medicare in 2007. According the Census Bureau, in 2003, *21,777,000* of Medicare enrollees also had some type of private insurance, such as "Medi-Gap" supplemental policies or retiree benefits from a former employer.

—10,767,000 were enrolled in military healthcare.

—45,657,000 were counted as "not covered at any time during the year."

Consumer-Driven Healthcare

An emerging issue in the private insurance market is that of consumer-driven healthcare. This strategy seems to be gaining momentum in an effort to both allow employees more choice in their healthcare decisions and to stabilize healthcare costs. The design of consumer-driven plans varies, but, essentially, employers provide employees with a "personal care account," which is a fixed amount and offered in the form of a voucher, refundable tax credit, higher wages, or some other transfer of funds. Employees may choose their own services and providers as well as manage their annual spending. If an employee uses up all the funds in his or her personal care account, he or she is responsible for expenses up to a deductible, at which point wraparound or catastrophic coverage starts. A deductible places a minimum amount at which major medical expenses will be covered (Jonas and Kovner 2005, 69).

Health Savings Accounts (HSAs)

Health savings accounts (HSAs), also called medical savings accounts, offer participants the opportunity to control how their healthcare dollars are spent. HSAs were created by the Medicare bill signed by President Bush in December 2003, and are designed to help individuals save for future qualified medical and retiree health expenses on a tax-free basis.

The benefit of an HSA is that the member pays for the deductible with pretax dollars, which allows a member to save the money that ordinarily would have gone to pay taxes. When members pay off the deductible, the insurance company begins to pay. The money in the HSA earns interest and is owned by the member who holds the account (Health Insurance Carriers 2005). Industry estimates indicate that the number of individuals covered by HSA-eligible health plans increased significantly between 2004 and 2007. HSA participation also increased between 2004 and 2005, with estimates

Figure 2.2. Annual health insurance premiums for U.S. covered workers 2008

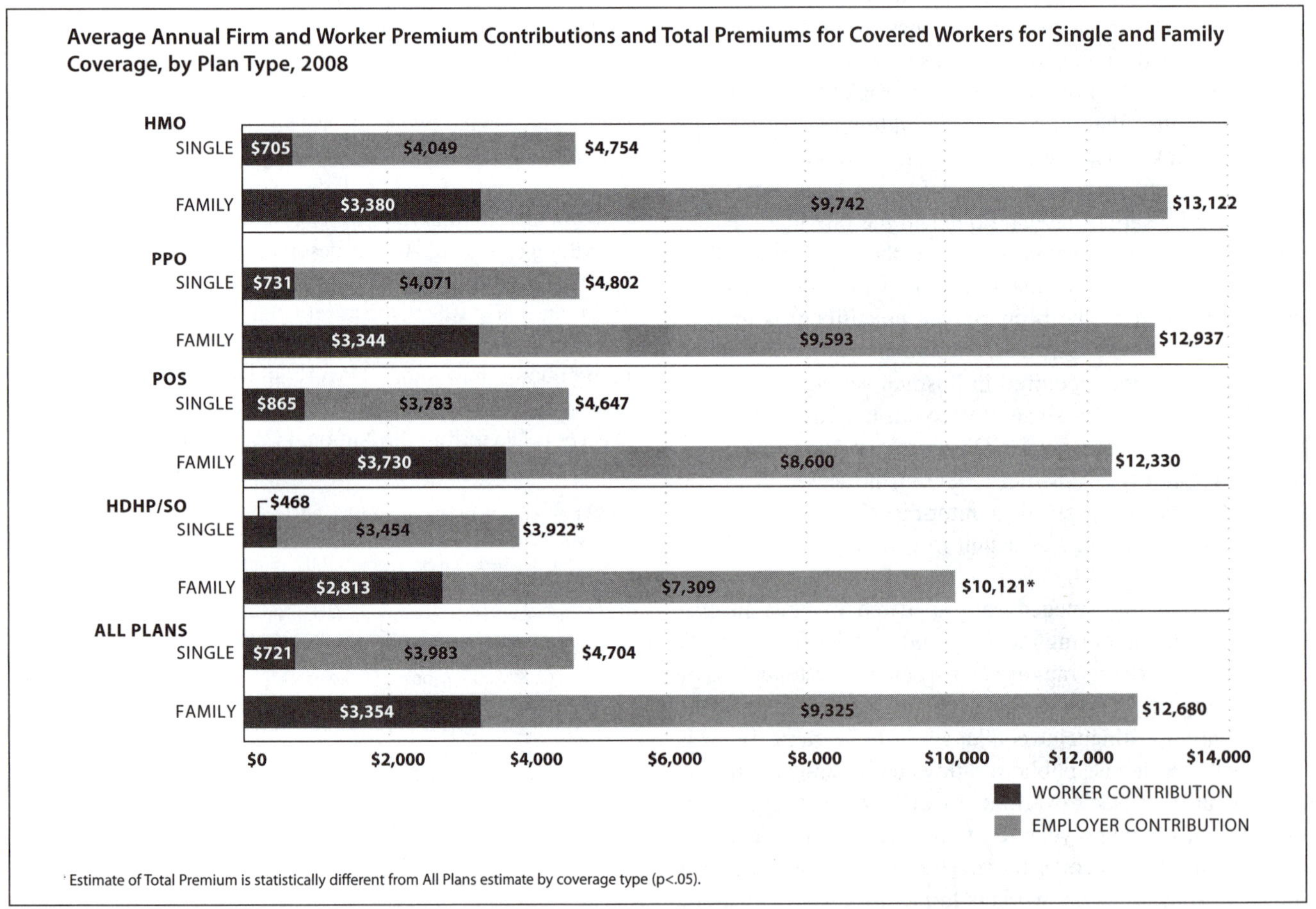

Source: Kaiser/HRET Survey of Employer-Sponsored Health Benefits, 2008.

of continued growth through 2007. Nevertheless, many HSA-eligible health plan enrollees have not opened HSAs (GAO 2008). See figure 2.3 for an overview of the estimated lives covered by HSA-eligible plans from September 2004 to January 2007. Between January 2007 and January 2008, the fastest growing market for HSA/HDHP products was small-group coverage (AHIP 2008).

Continued Rise in Healthcare Costs

The main reason for continued rise in healthcare costs is that spiraling healthcare costs have, in effect, lessened workers' wages. Even though workers are producing more, inflation-adjusted median family income has dipped 2.6 percent—or nearly $1,000 annually since 2000. Employees and employers are getting squeezed by the price of healthcare. The struggle to control health costs is viewed as crucial to improving wages and living standards for working Americans. Employers are paying more for healthcare and other benefits, leaving less money for pay increases. Benefits now devour 30.2 percent of employers' compensation costs, with the remaining money going to wages, the Labor Department reported (GAO 2008). That is up from 27.4 percent in 2000. Since 2001, premiums for family health coverage have increased 78 percent, according to a 2007 report by the Kaiser Family Foundation. Premiums averaged $12,106, of which workers paid $3,281, according to the report (Fletcher 2008).

The catalysts for employers' annual cost for healthcare coverage increases include the cost of prescription drugs, medical innovation, and a growing acceptance of higher-premium health plans that offer greater flexibility in choice of providers. One way that employers attempted to control costs was to implement monitoring and preventive care plans for conditions such as diabetes and heart disease.

As mentioned, the United States continues to spend more on healthcare than any other developed nation. The average per capita healthcare spending among 30 member nations of the Organization for Economic Cooperation and Development is less than half as much.

Moreover, the United States is seeing greater growth in spending from one year to the next than other developed nations. Despite the higher costs, however, Americans have a much higher incidence of obesity and their average life expectancy is slightly lower than that of people in Japan, Iceland, Sweden, and Canada.

Healthcare prices in the United States are influenced by many factors. Supply and demand is greatly influenced by insurance companies and health plans. Patients' bargaining power is greatly decreased because providers can negotiate different charges depending on the payer. Many cash-strapped Americans abandon their expensive private healthcare plans and choose not to be insured at all. Unfortunately, patients who are not covered by MCOs are typically charged much higher rates for care. For example, a hospital might charge a set price of $1,900 for a CT scan procedure when billing an individual not covered by a managed care contract but discount the cost to $1,200 for someone who is covered. This is because managed care companies insist on negotiated rates for care (Plunkett Research 2003).

Figure 2.3. Estimated lives covered by HSA-eligible plans, September 2004 to January 2007

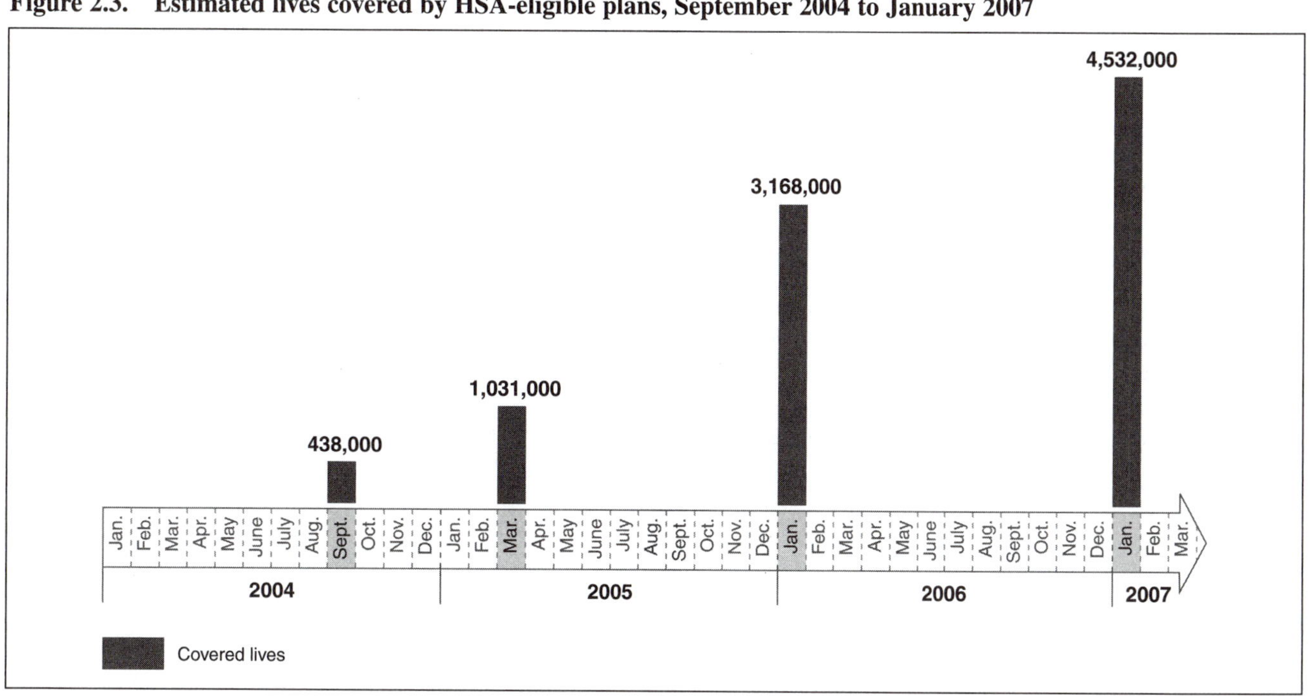

Source: America's Health Insurance Plans.

Payer Changes

Employers are fighting back, partly by establishing new benefits methods that can accomplish much more than simply raising workers' copayments. For example, many major firms are showing their employees how to use the Internet to obtain better information about diseases and prevention. Insurance providers are using the Internet as a resource as well. For example, Humana's Web-based Emphesys benefits system puts everything from monthly payments to participating physicians to claims on the Internet at a substantial decrease in cost. Some employers are even hiring in-house physicians and nurses to provide primary care in the workplace.

Cost and Quality Controls

The federal government became involved in the quality of care and malpractice issues through the establishment of the National Practitioner Data Bank (NPDB) under the Healthcare Quality Improvement Act of 1986. Congress enacted this legislation to

- Moderate the incidence of malpractice
- Allow the medical community to demonstrate new willingness to weed out incompetents
- Improve the base of timely and accurate information on medical malpractice

The act required hospitals to request information from the data bank whenever they hire, grant privileges, or conduct periodic reviews of a practitioner. (See chapter 10 for additional discussion of malpractice and other legal issues affecting HIM)

Check Your Understanding 2.7

Instructions: Indicate on a separate piece of paper whether the statements below are true or false (T or F).

1. ___ Blue Cross plans and commercial insurance providers cover a full range of healthcare services.
2. ___ Most commercial health insurance is provided in the form of group policies offered by employers as part of their fringe benefit packages for employees.
3. ___ Today, retired and disabled Americans who are eligible for Social Security benefits automatically qualify for Medicare coverage.
4. ___ Medicaid is a medical assistance program for upper-income Americans.
5. ___ The Department of Defense administers the TRICARE program.
6. ___ Employers provide employees with a personal care account in consumer-driven healthcare.
7. ___ The development of managed care was an indirect result of the federal government's enactment of the Medicare and Medicaid laws in 1965.
8. ___ The federal government became involved in the quality of care and malpractice issues through the establishment of the National Practitioner Data Bank under the Healthcare Quality Improvement Act of 1986.

Future of American Healthcare

The American healthcare industry is at a crossroads today as a result of several significant factors, including:

- The commercial health insurance and managed care industries face continued challenges, both financially and in terms of public perception.
- Medicare and Medicaid programs are in need of reform to deal with a rapidly aging population.
- Subacute and postacute care services segments continue to grow and present new challenges to the industry.
- Healthcare industry is entering what will long be remembered as the beginning of the Biotech Era.
- Development of evidence-based medicine calls for greater integration of all professions associated with healthcare, including purchasing and management.
- Malpractice insurance costs for physicians are spiraling out of control.

Commercial Health Insurance Industry

One major challenge facing the healthcare industry is the questionable image of managed care companies in general. Supporters of managed care contend that its structure offers higher-quality care at a lower cost. On the other hand, critics of managed care argue that the system risks lives by allowing plan managers to question—and sometimes reverse—the decisions made by medical professionals while emphasizing cost control at the expense of quality; thus sabotaging the bond of trust that should exist between doctor and patient. Additionally, many detractors of managed care are concerned about the trend of mergers creating huge managed care companies. Some metropolitan markets are dominated by as few as two major health plans. Critics are equally concerned about the lack of autonomy of physicians who are forced to deal with the growing power of managed care giants.

While both supporters and critics make valid arguments, sweeping generalizations about the state of managed care are inherently flawed because no two managed care plans are exactly alike. Neither society nor consumers can afford to turn back the clock to the considerably more expensive, traditional fee-for-service system in which high-quality preventive care was largely nonexistent and patient care was generally provided without regard to cost.

Medicare and Medicaid Programs and an Aging Population

The future obligations of Medicare and Medicaid are significant enough to cause vast problems for the federal budget. Reforms are vital. Meanwhile, the number of seniors covered by Medicare will continue to grow at an exceedingly high rate and new prescription coverage costs will add to the government's financial problems.

Millions of dollars in potential profits are lost as hospitals and health systems write off record amounts of revenues to bad debt. Costs also are being forced upward by legislation passed in response to the overall public mistrust of managed care firms. Moreover, total healthcare expenditures are driven up by the aging baby-boomer generation and the scope and total amount of available healthcare.

In the wake of the tremendous growth of all aspects of the healthcare industry from 1945 onward, efficiency, competition, and productivity were, regretfully, largely overlooked. Much of this occurred because such a large portion of the healthcare bill is paid by federal and state governments. According to CMS, total Medicare and Medicaid program outlays in 2007 reached $600 billion. Of this, total outlays in FY 2007 for Medicaid was $332.2 billion with one out of every 5 persons enrolled in Medicaid in the United States (CMS 2008).

Growth of Subacute and Postacute Care Services

Spending for home healthcare, hospital-based and freestanding nursing facilities has been growing rapidly. Subacute care providers have been growing in number and capacity (President's Advisory Commission 1998). **Postacute care**, also called subacute care or transitional care, is a type of short-term care provided by many long-term care and rehabilitation facilities and hospitals. Subacute care is often referred to as care that falls between acute care and traditional skilled nursing home care. It is needed immediately after, or instead of, hospitalization and includes medical services such as short-term rehabilitation, ventilator care/respirator care, intravenous therapy, wound management, and cardiac rehabilitation. This may include rehabilitation services, specialized care for certain conditions (such as stroke and diabetes), and postsurgical care and other services associated with the transition between the hospital and the home. Residents of these units often have been hospitalized recently and typically have more complicated medical needs.

The goal of subacute care is to discharge residents to their homes or to a lower level of care. Subacute care usually lasts between 15 and 100 days, and is covered by Medicare. Some nursing homes have been providing short-term rehabilitation services and ventilator/respirator care for years. However, there recently has been a significant increase in the number of facilities offering these and other subacute services (CDC 2004).

Biotech Era

Biotechnology is shifting the U.S. healthcare paradigm from a society "struggling to meet the escalating health problems of an aging population to one that focuses on wellness by preventing or delaying the onset of disease" (Burrill 2005). Almost 80 percent of the nation's healthcare spending is for chronic care. With advances in systems biology, this is shifting toward more personalized medicine focused on prevention, and eventually could lead to "a future in which an individual's genetic makeup can be determined to help tailor safer, more effective, cost-efficient treatments" (Burrill 2005).

New tools and a better understanding of how biological systems work is expected to create new treatments for everything from obesity, memory loss, and aging to cancer and cardiovascular illnesses. However, "safety issues in the pharmaceutical industry will continue to dominate the headlines" (Burrill 2005).

Overall, an outcome of the improvements made to the U.S. healthcare system in the twentieth century is a much longer, healthier life. Increased healthcare costs are typically incurred at the end of life. (See figure 2.4.) Much of the focus of biotechnology is directed at improving the care for chronic diseases of the elderly (Lynn and Adamson 2003).

Development of Evidenced-based Best Practices and Outcomes

Physicians are caught between the desire for high-quality care and the desire for cost control on the part of payers, including HMOs, Medicare, and Medicaid. The cost-versus-care debate has spawned an energetic movement to improve the quality of healthcare in the United States, much of it centered on patients' rights.

Evidence-based medicine is the conscientious, explicit, and judicious use of current best evidence in making decisions about the care of individual patients. The practice of evidence-based medicine means integrating individual clinical expertise with the best available external clinical evidence from systematic research. Evidence-based healthcare extends the application of the principles of evidence-based medicine to all professions associated with healthcare, including purchasing and management (Centre for Evidence-based Medicine 2005).

The importance of measuring and monitoring healthcare quality is essential, yet quantifying healthcare quality is complex. The entire process of quality assessment requires judgment and choices that should be influenced by physicians' clinical realities of medical care. It is assumed as well as essential that healthcare providers possess the knowledge to participate actively in the assessment of healthcare quality. Assessing quality requires the development and application of performance measures that are explicit standards of care against which actual clinical care is judged. Given the availability of evidenced-based guidelines for the management of

Figure 2.4. Americans' healthcare expenditures are concentrated in the final part of the life span

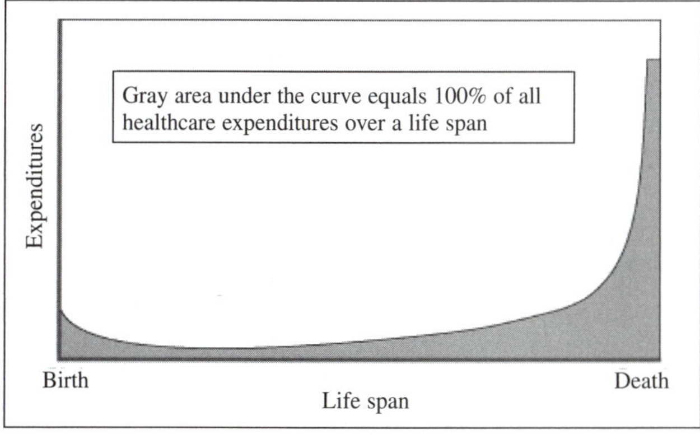

Source: Lynn and Adamson 2003.

patients, there is a natural inclination to use these consensus statements as a basis for developing performance measures for the evaluation of healthcare quality. Guidelines are not performance measures. Rather, they are written to suggest diagnostic or therapeutic interventions for most patients in most circumstances. The use of guideline recommendations in diagnosing and treating individual patients is left to the discretion of the physician. In contrast, performance measures are standards of care that imply that physicians are in error if they do not care for patients according to these standards. Therefore, in addition to stating an explicit diagnostic or therapeutic action to be performed, performance measures must define how to practically identify those patients for whom a specific action should be taken (American Heart Association 2000).

The Agency for Healthcare Research and Quality (AHRQ) promotes evidence-based practice in everyday care through establishment of 12 evidence-based practice centers (EPCs), which develop evidence reports and assess healthcare technology. Because of the EPC program, AHRQ became a "science partner" with private and public organizations (AHRQ 2004).

Malpractice Insurance Costs for Physicians

Malpractice is the improper or negligent treatment of a patient, as by a physician, resulting in injury, damage, or loss. Garner (2004) defines malpractice as:

> The failure of rendering professional services to exercise that degree of skill and learning commonly applied under all the circumstances in the community by the average prudent reputable member of the profession with the result of injury, loss or damage to the recipient of those services or to those entitled to rely upon them.

Medical malpractice liability insurance premiums have increased in recent years, with a trend toward increasingly large plaintiffs' awards and higher losses for insurers. Premiums have risen both because insurance companies face increased costs to pay claims (from growth in malpractice awards) and because of reduced income from the insurance companies' investments and other short-term factors. Rapidly rising malpractice premiums may influence physicians, especially those in high-risk fields, to stop practicing medicine, thus reducing the availability of healthcare in some parts of the country (Beider and Hagen 2004).

New Models of Healthcare Delivery

Telehealth is a new platform on which healthcare provision can be reshaped to meet the challenges of an aging population and more demanding and discerning patients and citizens. It involves automating all routine healthcare processes, from monitoring blood sugar levels to administering drugs, and extending the distribution of more complex and expert medical expertise by using videoconferencing to deliver consultations or surgical support. Following both these paths delivers benefits to healthcare provisioning, enabling medical staff to work more effectively, whatever their level of expertise or responsibility. Telehealth provides medical staff with a tool to eradicate mundane and low-value healthcare processes and maximize their core skills and expertise. The same level of automation that is routine among financial and retail verticals, for example, is not as prevalent within the healthcare community. Changes underway have the potential to fundamentally change the delivery of healthcare in the near and long term (HBS Consulting 2003).

Telehealth is now extending beyond the collection of vital signs. The most important factor in any telehealth-based disease management system is its clinical content. Ideally, the clinical content will provide two-way communication of not just physiological information (namely vital signs) but education and compliance information as well. Rich clinical content provides diagnosis-specific information, including programs for co-morbidity diagnoses, that takes patient responses into account when determining the next question. For instance, if a CHF patient does not demonstrate an understanding of the significance of shortness of breath or the importance of taking medications each day, the system uses branching logic to transmit appropriate educational information. This individualizes each encounter the patient has with the telehealth system.

Daily documentation of patient information using telehealth technology allows the care provider to track health patterns over time and detect deviations in patient data that may indicate a decline in health before it becomes acute. A telehealth system can provide alerts that are activated when patient-specific baselines exceed a given parameter–weight, for instance. This is practically impossible in the traditional care delivery model. Having baselines is not enough, though. The homecare agency must be able to modify baselines easily to ensure alerts are kept to a minimum and only signify a truly serious situation. Taken together, detailed health tracking and alerts allow agencies to fully understand the overall health of the patient (Utterback 2005).

The evolution of telehealth is not only expected to reshape the delivery of consultations, monitoring, and treatments, but it also is expected to reshape access to healthcare services by healthcare providers, patients, and citizens. Healthcare delivery is no longer controlled—and will be less and less controlled—by secondary and primary healthcare providers.

Summary

Throughout history, humans have attempted to diagnose and treat illness and disease. As populations settled into towns and cities, early folk medicine traditions eventually led to the establishment of formalized entities specifically designed to care for the sick. In the American colonies, enlightened thinkers such as Benjamin Franklin soon saw the need to establish hospitals and to regulate the practice of medicine. The nineteenth century saw the growth of organizations dedicated to standardizing medical practice and ensuring consistency in the quality of healthcare delivery. Organizations such as the AMA and the ANA were created to represent the interests of their members and to further ensure the quality of their services.

The twentieth century ushered in a completely new concept in the provision of healthcare: prepaid health plans. For the first time, Americans could buy health insurance. However, during the Great Depression of the 1930s and World War II, it became obvious that millions of Americans could not afford to pay for healthcare. After the war, the federal government began to study the problem of healthcare access for all Americans. Finally, during the Johnson administration in the 1960s, Congress passed amendments to the Social Security Act of 1935 that created the Medicare and Medicaid programs. These programs were designed to pay for the cost of healthcare services to the elderly and the poor.

As the healthcare industry has grown, so have efforts to regulate it. Some regulation has come from professional and trade associations that are associated with the industry. However, much regulation has come from the federal government, particularly with regard to the Medicaid and Medicare programs. Moreover, the types and variety of healthcare services that are available today have increased dramatically. Every new type of service, and every new way to provide it, brings complex issues that must be addressed in order to ensure that Americans receive the highest-quality healthcare possible at the most affordable price.

Passage of the Medicare and Medicaid programs and establishment of the managed care industry have had a tremendous impact on the way that healthcare in the United States is delivered and paid for. The ramifications of these changes on the American healthcare industry have yet to be fully appreciated. The only thing that is certain is that the American healthcare system continues to be a work in progress.

References

29 CFR 825.118: "What is a "health care provider?" 1995.

3DQuote.com. 2000. Blue Cross national. http://www.3dquote.com/blue-cross-national-info.htm.

Agency for Healthcare Research and Quality. 2004 (Sept.). *Evidence-based practice centers overview.* Rockville, MD: AHRQ. http://www.ahrq.gov/clinic/epc.

America's Health Insurance Plans Center for Policy and Research. 2008 (April 1). http://www.ahipresearch.org/pdfs/2008_HSA_Census.pdf.

American Health Information Management Association. 2008. Mission, Values, and Vision. http://www.ahima.org/about/mission.asp.

American Health Information Management Association. 2010. *Pocket Glossary of Health Information Management and Technology.* 2nd ed. Chicago:AHIMA.

American Heart Association. 2000. Measuring and improving quality of care: A report from the American Heart Association/American College of Cardiology first scientific forum on assessment of healthcare quality in cardiovascular disease and stroke. *Stroke* 31(4):1002–1012. http://www.circ.ahajournals.org/cgi/content/full/101/12/1483.

American Hospital Association. 2004 (Oct. 25). Fast Facts on U.S. Hospitals from *AHA Hospital Statistics.* http://www.aha.org/aha/resource_center/fast-facts/fast_facts_US_hospitals.html.

American Hospital Association. 1999. *100 Faces of Healthcare.* Chicago: Health Forum.

American Hospital Association. 2008. Report on Workforce Challenges. http://www.aha.org/aha/content/2008/pdf/08-issue-workforce.pdf.

American Medical Association. 2001. American Medical Association Physician Masterfile, December 2000. http://www.ama-assn.org/ama1/pub/upload/images/373/internettable.gif.

American Nurses Association. 2008. About ANA. http://nursingworld.org/FunctionalMenuCategories/AboutANA.aspx.

American Osteopathic Association. 2005. http://www.do-online.osteotech.org/index.cfm.

Beider, P. and S. Hagen. 2004 (Jan. 8). Limiting tort liability for medical malpractice. Washington, D.C.: Congressional Budget Office. http://www.cbo.gov.

Burrill, G.S. 2005 (June 20). Healthcare in transition: Biotech drives major changes. Paper presented at BIO 2005, Philadelphia. http://www.sev.prnewswire.com/biotechnology/20050619/NYSU00419062005-1.html.

Burt, C.W. and L.F.McCaig. 2006. Staffing, capacity, and ambulance diversion in emergency departments: United States, 2003–04. Advance data from vital and health statistics; no 376. Hyattsville, MD: National Center for Health Statistics.

California Health Care Foundation. 2005 (March 2). Health Care Costs 10—2005. http://www.chcf.org.

Carlson, Bob. 2002 (Oct.) It's Not the Road You Take – It's Getting There That Counts. *Managed Care.* http://www.managedcaremag.com/archives/0210/0210.quality.html.

Centers for Disease Control. 2004. Health care in America: Trends in utilization. http://cdc.gov/nchs/datawh/nchsdefs/postacutecare.htm.

Centers for Medicare and Medicaid Services. 2005 (March 4). U.S. Department of Health and Human Services. http://www.cms.hhs.gov/NursingHomeQualityInits.

Centers for Medicare and Medicaid Services. 2008 (Oct. 17). Actuarial Report: Financial Outlook on Medicaid, Dept of HHS, CMS. http://www.cms.hhs.gov/ActuarialStudies/downloads/MedicaidReport2008.pdf.

Centers for Medicare and Medicaid Services. 2008a. The Mental Health Parity Act. http://www.cms.hhs.gov/HealthInsReformforConsume/04_TheMentalHealthParityAct.asp.

Centre for Evidence-Based Medicine. 2005. Glossary of terms in evidence-based medicine. Oxford: Institute of Health Sciences. http://www.cebm.net/glossary.asp.

Commonwealth Fund. 2008 (July). Why Not the Best? Results from the National Scorecard on U.S. Health System Performance, 2008. The Commonwealth Fund Commission on a High Performance Health System.

Davis, K. and A. Shih. 2008 (April). Get Organized: How to Streamline Health Care Delivery. The Commonwealth Fund. http://www.commonwealthfund.org/aboutus/aboutus_show.htm?doc_id=680551.

Dicken, J.E. 2008 (April 1.) Letter to the Honorable Henry A. Waxman, Chairman, Committee on Oversight and Government Reform, House of Representatives and the Honorable Pete Stark, Chairman, Subcommittee of Health, Committee on Ways and Means, House of Representatives. *Health savings accounts: Participation increased and was more common among individuals with higher incomes*, United States Government and Accountability Office, Washington , DC. 5.

e-MDs. 2008 (April 28). e-MDs Participates in 2008 Integrating the Healthcare Enterprise Connectathon. http://www.e-mds.com/news.

Edelson, E. 2006 (May 30). More Young People Going Without Health Insurance. *Washington Post.* http://www.washingtonpost.com/wp-dyn/content/article/2008/05/30/AR2008053001645.html.

Etheredge, L. 2001. *On the Archeology of Health Care Policy: Periods and Paradigms, 1975–2000.* Washington, D.C.: The National Academies Press. http://www.nap.edu/books/NI000569/html/1.html.

Fletcher, M. 2008 (Mar. 24).The Rising Health Costs Cut Into Wages. *Washington Post*, A01. http://www.washingtonpost.com/wp-dyn/content/article/2008/03/23/AR2008032301770.html.

Foley, D.J., R.W. Manderscheid, J.E. Atay, J. Maedke, J. Sussman, and S. Cribbs. 2004. Chapter 19: Highlights of Organized Mental Health Services in 2002 and Major National and State Trends. In *Mental Health, United States, 2004.* DHHS Publication No. (SMA) 06-4195. http://mentalhealth.samhsa.gov/publications/allpubs/sma06-4195/chapter19.asp.

Garner, B.A., ed. 2004, *Black's Law Dictionary.* 8th ed. St. Paul, MN: West Group.

HBS Consulting. 2003. http://www.hbs-consulting.com.

Healthcare Financial Management Association. 2008 (Oct. 7). Declining capacity in acute care hospitals may indicate problems. FindArticles.com. http://findarticles.com/p/articles/mi_m3257/is_6_61/ai_n19311763.

Health Insurance Carriers. 2005. Health Savings Accounts. http://www.health-insurance-carriers.com/hsa.html.

Joint Commission. 2007 *Comprehensive Accreditation Manual for Hospitals.* Oakbrook Terrace, IL: Joint Commission.

Jonas, S. and A.R. Kovner. 2005. *Healthcare Delivery in the United States.* 8th ed. New York: Springer.

Jonas, S. and A.R. Kovner. 1999. *Healthcare Delivery in the United States.* 6th ed. New York: Springer.

Kallos, C. 2008 (June 10). Zacks Equity Research, Managed Care Industry: Positioned for Growth. http://seekingalpha.com/article/80722-managed-care-industry-positioned-for-growth.

Kongstevdt, P. 1993. *The Managed Care Handbook.* Gaithersburg, MD: Aspen.

Leary, W.E. 1992 (July 1). Outpatient Surgery on the Rise; Regulation Doesn't Keep Pace. *New York Times.*

Lynn, J. and D.M. Adamson. 2003. White paper: Living well at the end of life: Adapting health care to serious chronic illness in old age. Santa Monica, CA: RAND. http://www.rand.org/pubs/white_papers/2005/WP137.pdf.

Masters, P.A. and C. Nester. 2001 (Jan.). A Study of Primary Care Teaching Comparing Academic and Community-based Settings. *Journal of General Internal Medicine* 16(1): 9–13.

The National Coalition on Health Care (NCHC). Health Insurance Costs. http://www.nchc.org/facts.

National Conference of State Legislatures. 2008 (Oct. 20). Health Insurance and the States. http://www.ncsl.org/programs/health/healthmc.htm.

National Institutes of Health. 2005. NIH Roadmap: Accelerating medical discovery to improve health. Frequently asked questions. http://www.nihroadmap.nih.gov/faq.asp.

Obama, B. 2009. Speech to Joint Session of Congress Feb. 24, 2009.

Partners in Caregiving: The Adult Day Services Program. 2002. National Study of Adult Day Services, 2001–2002. Winston-Salem, NC: Wake Forest University School of Medicine. Funded by Robert Wood Johnson Foundation. http://www.rwjf.org/newsroom/featureDetail.jsp?featureID=183&type=2.

Pitts, S.R. and R.W. Niska. 2008 (Aug.). National Hospital Ambulatory Medical Care Survey, Emergency Department Summary 2006. National Health Statistics Report, Number 7. http://www.cdc.gov/nchs/data/nhsr/nhsr007.pdf.

Plunkett Research. 2003 (Dec.). *Plunkett's Health Care Industry Almanac.* 2004 ed. Houston, TX: Plunkett Research, Ltd.

Poisal, J.A., et al. 2007 (Feb. 21). Health Spending Projections Through 2016: Modest Changes Obscure Part D's Impact. *Health Affairs.* W242–253.

President's Advisory Commission on Protection and Quality in the Health Care Industry. 1998 (March 12). Improving health care quality in an industry in transition. In *Quality First: Better Health Care for All Americans.* http://www.hcqualitycommission.gov/final.

Siegel, E.L. and D.S. Channin. 2001. Integrating the Healthcare Enterprise: A Primer; Part 1: Introduction. *Radiographics* 21:1339–1341. http://radiographics.rsnajnls.org/cgi/content/full/21/5/1339.

Sloane, R.M., B.L. Sloane, and R. Harder. 1999. *Introduction to Healthcare Delivery Organization: Functions and Management.* 4th ed. Chicago: Health Administration Press.

Starr, P. 1982. *The Social Transformation of American Medicine.* New York: Basic Books.

Stedman's Medical Dictionary. 2000. http://www.stedmans.com.

Sultz, H.A. and K.M. Young. 2004. *Healthcare USA—Understanding its Organization and Delivery.* 4th ed. Sudbury, MA: Jones and Bartlett.

United States Government Accountability Office (GAO). 2008 (Apr. 1). Health Savings Accounts: Participation Increased and Was More Common among Individuals. GAO Report, GAO - 08-744R. http://www.gao.gov/new.items/d08474r.pdf.

Utterback, K. 2005 (Jan./Feb.). Supporting a New Model of Care with Telehealth Technology. *Home Telehealth.* http://tie.telemed.org/articles/article.asp?path=homehealth&article=telehealthTechnology_ku_tpr05.xml.

Chapter 3
Informatics in Healthcare

Amy L. Watters, MA, RHIA, Pamela K. Oachs, MA, RHIA, and Deborah Kohn, MPH, RHIA, CHE, CPHIMS, FHIMSS

Learning Objectives

- Understand the field of informatics as it is being applied in healthcare
- Identify the major issues associated with computerizing health data and information
- Learn the types of computer applications and technologies being used to support the delivery of healthcare and the management of health data and information
- Identify the barriers and limitations associated with computerized health data and information
- Develop a working knowledge of the emerging technologies that support the creation and maintenance of electronic health record (EHR) systems
- Prepare for assuming a leadership role in the development of improved healthcare information systems, integrated patient information systems, and decision support tools

Key Terms

Analog
Application programming interface (API)
Application service provider (ASP)
Applied healthcare informatics
Artificial intelligence (AI)
Audit trails
Autocoding
Automated forms-processing (e-forms) technology
Bar-coding technology
Bit-mapped data
CareMaps
Clinical care plans
Clinical informatics
Clinical information system (CIS)
Clinical messaging system
Clinical pathways
Clinical practice guidelines
Clinical workstation
Clinical/medical decision support system
Clinician/physician Web portals
Computer output laser disk/enterprise report management (COLD/ERM) technology
Computer-assisted coding
Consumer health
Consumer informatics
Content
Continuous speech input
Data
Data marts
Data mining
Data repositories
Data types
Data warehouses
Data warehousing
Decision support systems
Dental informatics
Diagnostic image data
Digital
Digital signature management technology
Discrete data
Document
Document image data
Document-imaging technology
Document management technology
e-commerce
e-health
Electronic data interchange (EDI)
Electronic document/content management system
Electronic medical record (EMR)
Electronic records management technology
Encryption
Enterprise master patient index (EMPI)
Evidence-based medicine
Executive information system (EIS)
Expert decision support system
Extensible Markup Language (XML)
Extranets
Firewalls
Free-text data
Geographic information system (GIS)
Gesture recognition technology
Health information exchange (HIE)
Health information management (HIM)
Health information technology (HIT)
Health 2.0
Healthcare informatics
HyperText Markup Language (HTML)
Identity management
Informatics
Information
Information management
Information science
Information systems (ISs)
Intelligent character recognition (ICR) technology
Intelligent document recognition (IDR) technology
Interoperability
Interoperable
Interoperate
Intranets
Logical (or conceptual) repository
Management information system (MIS)
Mark sense technology
Master patient index (MPI)
Medical informatics
Metadata
Motion or streaming video/frame data
Multimedia
Natural language processing technology
Neural networks
Nursing informatics
Object-oriented database
Online/real-time analytical processing (OLAP)
Online/real-time transaction processing (OLTP)
Open source technology
Optical character recognition (OCR) technology
Outcomes management
Par level
Patient/consumer Web portals
Personal digital assistant PDA)
Personal health record (PHR)
Physical data repository
Physiological signal processing systems
Pixel
Point-of-care information systems
Protocol
Public Key Infrastructure (PKI)
Radio frequency identification (RFID)
Raster image
Real audio data
Record locator service (RLS)
Regional health information organization (RHIO)
Relational database
Secure messaging systems
Software as a Service (SaaS)
Speech recognition technology
Structured data
Taxonomy
Text mining
Unstructured data
Vector graphic (or signal tracing) data
Web content management systems
Web portal
Web services
Web 2.0
Web-based systems and applications
Wireless technology
Workflow technology

The rapid deployment of computer technology to manage **data** and **information** continues to impact healthcare delivery systems and services. This means that well-trained and skilled individuals with knowledge about both healthcare and computerized information technologies are needed to design, develop, select, and maintain health information management (HIM) systems.

This chapter introduces the field of **informatics** as it is currently being applied in the healthcare industry. Also, it describes the current and emerging technologies used to support the delivery of healthcare and the management and communication of patient information. Finally, this chapter discusses health information management as a component of the health informatics infrastructure and the partnerships that HIM professionals will forge with information technology (IT) and health informatics professionals in the future.

The Field of Informatics

Informatics is the science of **information management**. It uses computers to manage data and information and support decision-making activities. The management of data and information includes the generation, collection, organization, validation, analysis, storage, and integration of data, as well as the dissemination, communication, presentation, utilization, transmission, and safeguarding of information.

Healthcare informatics is the field of **information science** concerned with the management of all aspects of health data and information through the application of computers and computer technologies. The healthcare industry is information intensive. One needs to spend only a day with a healthcare provider or clinician to realize that the largest percentage of healthcare professional activities relates to managing massive amounts of data and information. This includes obtaining and documenting information about patients, consulting with colleagues, staying abreast of the current literature, determining strategies for patient care, interpreting laboratory data and test results, and conducting research.

The influence of healthcare informatics is broad. **Health information technology** (HIT) is having a huge impact not only on the complex financial and administrative aspects of healthcare, but also on its unique clinical practices. For example, computer information systems, which provide communication and information management for such functions as order entry, results retrieval, care planning, and charting, are installed in every kind of healthcare organization—from major academic teaching hospitals and integrated delivery networks and systems to post–acute care facilities, physician practices, and managed care organizations. Historically, the healthcare industry has not valued healthcare informatics to the same degree that other industries have. The healthcare industry has been perceived as slow to both understand computerized information management and to incorporate it effectively into the work environment. Perhaps this is because the data and information requirements of the healthcare industry are more demanding than those of other industries in a number of areas. These areas include implications of violations of privacy, support for personal values, responsibility for public health, complexity of the knowledge base and terminology, perception of high risk and pressure to make critical decisions rapidly, poorly defined outcomes, and support for the diffusion of power (Stead and Lorenzi 1999, 343).

Recently, the concept of **applied healthcare informatics** has emerged, which emphasizes the use of the computer-based applications in delivering and documenting healthcare services (AMIA 2005). Therefore, for HIM, applied healthcare informatics is the application of healthcare information technology to HIM. As this concept evolves, the healthcare industry will continue to take note of HIM's contribution to this growing field. In addition, HIM's position within the broad healthcare informatics domain will continue to be reinforced.

Check Your Understanding 3.1

Instructions: Answer the following questions on a separate piece of paper.

1. How are the disciplines of information management and informatics related? How are they different?
2. Why are data and information so crucial to a healthcare professional's daily work?
3. Why is the healthcare industry perceived as being less proactive than other industries in the area of computerized information systems? How can this perception be changed?

The Informatics Revolution in Healthcare

Revolution is an overused word, but when applied to the effect of all that is or is becoming **digital,** automated, or electronic in the healthcare industry, it is entirely accurate. Over the past several decades, established relationships, value chains, and strategies have been radically altered or swept away within the healthcare industry by computer technology.

Evolution of Healthcare Informatics

The term *informatics* was adopted in the early 1970s when European universities and research institutions offered programs to focus on the introduction and application of computers and computer **information systems** (ISs) in society. Likewise, the term *healthcare informatics*—the intersection of computer information systems and healthcare—was based on an idea born in Europe. However, since the mid-1980s, some of the most original and creative minds in the healthcare professions in the United States have engaged in healthcare informatics research and development, giving rise to it as a discipline in its own right. Today, the goal of this discipline is to understand the structure, dynamics, design, implementation, and ongoing maintenance of information systems that are composed of people, technology, and organizational factors. This allows the appropriate flow and use of information to be individually optimized for every task in every context for every user in any organization (Turley et al. 2001, 48). Thus, the discipline's focus today is on the development, implementation, and use of computer-based applications that support ever-changing business and workflow processes that, in turn, support specific types of users in performing their work or meeting their needs.

For example, some users of healthcare informatics (for example, physicians) work in clinical medicine or medical research, where the term **medical informatics** is commonly used. Other users work in nursing, where **nursing informatics** is the commonly recognized term. Some users work in dentistry (**dental informatics**). **Clinical informatics** is a more general term that has gained acceptance. It applies to a variety of clinician users, including physicians, nurses, pharmacists, clinical laboratory scientists, and therapists. Even **consumer informatics** is beginning to be used as computer information systems begin to connect individuals and their healthcare providers. Consequently, the generic term *healthcare informatics* is seen as the broader domain, which stresses the interdisciplinary nature of the discipline and underscores the need to involve all healthcare professionals and consumers (patients) in developing, using, and maintaining effective computer information systems.

The value proposition of healthcare informatics can be defined as the study, creation, and implementation of healthcare business and workflow processes designed to improve the communication and use of healthcare data and information, as well as to improve the management of the data and information. Thus, the value proposition serves the clinical, technical, administrative, commercial, and public aspects of healthcare. As such, applied healthcare informatics can make it possible to achieve better outcomes for the healthcare delivery industry. Structures and communication methods allow information to be linked to healthcare work processes and managed as an organizational asset. Data-mining techniques and filters locate information and limit reports to the immediate context. Presentation and data display functionality can enhance healthcare users' analysis techniques and adapt to individual learning styles. Education and training programs are beginning to produce people who know how to develop effective information-enabled work processes.

Health information managers are well positioned to play key roles in ensuring acceptance of healthcare informatics within the healthcare industry. They have the knowledge base and skills needed to exploit the computerized information systems and technologies for their unique practical and strategic functional capabilities. Therefore, HIM professionals can leverage chief information officers, the health information technology industry, and the field of healthcare informatics as partners to enable administrators, clinicians, and consumers to use data and information to improve health, healthcare, and healthcare delivery systems.

Examples of Calls to Action and Informatics Successes

Calls to action for the use of information technologies to improve the healthcare delivery system are not new. The 1990s began with the Institute of Medicine's (IOM) report, which was based on the findings of its Committee on Improving the Patient Record, which championed the computer-based patient record (CPR) (Dick and Steen 1991). (CPRs, with its more current term, electronic health records [EHRs], are discussed in detail in chapter 9.) The second portion (Title II) of Public Law 104-191, the Health Insurance Portability and Accountability Act of 1996 (HIPAA), addressed the requirements to support electronic information exchange with goals of administrative efficiency and process improvement. It also mandated the protection of health information maintained and communicated in electronic information systems.

In early 2000, two additional IOM reports based on the findings of its Committee on Quality of Health Care in America were published. The first report, "To Err is Human: Building a Safer Healthcare System," shocked the nation with its estimated number of deaths each year resulting from preventable medical errors (Kohn et al. 1999). The second, follow-up report, "Crossing the Quality Chasm: A New Health System for the 21st Century," called for transforming America's "failing" healthcare industry (IOM 2001). Each of these calls to action identified IT needs and the potential for IT benefits.

The IOM's third report, "Leadership by Example: Coordinating Government Roles in Improving Health Care Quality," argued that the federal government should lead the development of clinical standards for measuring care and proposed financial incentives for organizations that improve quality (IOM 2002). This report called for five "demonstration" projects, including IT development, to help coordinate the exchange of healthcare information across the industry. The fourth report, "Patient Safety: Achieving a New Standard for Care" (IOM 2003) called for the Consolidated Health Informatics (CHI) initiative of the Department of Health and Human Services (HHS), the Department of Defense (DoD), and the Department of Veterans Affairs (VA) to work with the National Committee on Vital and Health Statistics (NCVHS) to identify appropriate clinical data standards that will make health information uniform and understandable to all. In addition, this report mandated that EHRs "operate seamlessly as part of a national network of health information that is accessible by all healthcare organizations" (NCVHS 2001).

Examples of healthcare informatics successes are steadily growing. Charge collection and billing, automated laboratory testing and reporting, clinical documentation, computerized provider order entry (CPOE), patient and provider scheduling, diagnostic imaging, and secondary data use make up a distinguished healthcare informatics "success" list, proving what is doable and supporting further investment. Still, many of the healthcare informatics calls to action and successes have not produced compelling outcomes, especially those outcomes related to improving the quality of healthcare for more individuals at an affordable cost. Therefore, today's task for informatics is to design, develop, and implement computer information systems that enable healthcare organizations to accomplish visions for providing the highest-quality care in the most effective way.

Nationwide Health Information Network

The Nationwide Health Information Network (NHIN; formerly known as the National Health Information Infrastructure [NHII]) is a government-sponsored initiative designed to improve the effectiveness, efficiency, and overall quality of health and healthcare in the United States by developing a comprehensive, interconnected, knowledge-based network of **interoperable** information systems among all sectors of the healthcare industry. It is also referred to as the Medical Internet, which allows providers of care to electronically exchange data among all electronic health records so that a complete, electronic health record can be assembled whenever and wherever a patient presents for care.

The NHIN was mentioned first by the IOM in its seminal report, "The Computer-based Patient Record: An Essential Technology for Health Care" (Dick and Steen 1991). A decade later, the NHIN was defined further by the NCVHS in its report, "Information for Health: A Strategy for Building the NHII" (NCVHS 2001). Following September 11, 2001, and the much publicized anthrax attacks, the NHIN gained national attention in both public and private sectors when the need for enhanced public health surveillance and response became more visible and immediate. Consequently, the IOM's fourth quality report, "Patient Safety: Achieving a New Standard for Care," additionally asserted that a NHIN "should be the highest priority for all healthcare stakeholders" (IOM 2003).

HHS provided initial guiding principles and requirements for this national network. Based on these and other requirements, in 2004, the Center of Information Technology Leadership determined that over the 10 years required to build a national system of healthcare information exchange a hefty $276 billion would be spent, with another $16.5 billion per year in operating costs (2004). However, a fully implemented and standardized NHIN, consisting of machine-interpretable data (that is, structured messages, standardized content or data) would deliver national savings of $77.8 billion per year. This savings takes into account interface and system costs, including acquisition and maintenance, as well as savings primarily due to decreased redundancy and administrative time. Savings from improved patient safety and quality of care are not considered in this number (Walker et al. 2005, 16). (See table 3.1.)

Table 3.1. Annual savings with a NHIN

Provider Type	Net Value, Starting at Year 11
Hospitals/Clinician Offices	$33.5 billion
Payers	$21.6 billion
Laboratories	$13.1 billion
Imaging Centers	$ 8.2 billion
Pharmacies	$ 1.3 billion
Public Health	$ 0.1 billion
TOTAL	**$77.8 billion**

© Deborah Kohn 2005.

Significant barriers to achieving the NHIN by 2014 exist. Such barriers include a lack of standards allowing for **interoperability** and data sharing, insufficient funding, a lack of ongoing economic incentives needed to sustain infrastructure operations, and public concern over privacy. In late 2004, the HHS Office of the National Coordinator for Health Information Technology (ONC) published a request for information (RFI) to seek public comment about how to develop the NHIN—more than 500 responses were received. A summary report was released in 2005.

The interoperability and data-sharing strategies available to support the NHIN are fundamentally no different from those available to individual healthcare provider organizations. However, to develop the NHIN, healthcare organizations must carefully weigh public concerns over privacy as well as cross, multi-organizational concerns over the continued ownership, control, and competitive business advantage their existing data provide them.

Consequently, in late 2004, HHS stipulated that the NHIN must be built incrementally from collaborative, local, and regional efforts in the public and private sectors. As a result, today's NHIN focus is to begin with a network of connected, public and private regional health information organizations (RHIOs; formerly known as local health information infrastructures [LHIIs]) or health information exchanges (HIEs), each facilitating exchange of health information in a "region." NHIN activities on the national level focus on the development and adoption of standards and economic incentives that will promote the growth of these regional, health information exchange infrastructures.

Health Information Exchange

Health information exchange (HIE) is the ability to move healthcare information electronically between disparate healthcare information systems while maintaining the accuracy of the information being exchanged (AHIMA 2007). It is the electronic movement of health information among organizations according to agreed upon standards and protocols (NAHIT 2008). HIM professionals' skills and knowledge beyond the technical focus are important for achieving success in any HIE initiative. HIM professionals play an important role in asking pertinent HIE questions to ensure data quality, privacy, security, and patient safety. For example:

- What data or information will be exchanged?
- How will access to the data or information be authorized and authenticated?
- Who will control data authorization and authentication?
- How is data ownership defined?
- What data quality indicators have been established and how will they be measured?
- What is the plan for data or information communication and interaction with patients/consumers?

Regional Health Information Organizations and Health Information Exchanges

Regional health information organizations (RHIOs) are healthcare provider, payer, and patient collaboratives that regionally exchange healthcare information. They serve anywhere from approximately 500,000 to more than 1 million lives. Typically, a RHIO is made up of diverse healthcare stakeholders providing and receiving services in a medical referral area (for example, sometimes this area is identified as one served by a regional emergency medical services organization). As such, RHIOs are bigger and fewer than the earlier local health information organizations (LHIOs). However, RHIOs typically are no larger than a state.

Many developing RHIOs and larger health information exchanges (HIEs) favor a decentralized or "federated" approach to their technical architectures for exchanging healthcare information. This model is not the fully integrated, monolithic, centralized database model of most healthcare provider organizations. Instead, it consists of distinct, distributed, disparate, and decentralized databases "linked together" by a centralized **record locator service** (RLS) and, perhaps, with **application programming interfaces** (APIs). An API is a set of definitions or protocols used by programmers to write applications which allow one piece of computer software to communicate with another (AHIMA 2006).

The Markle Foundation's 2006 Connecting for Health Common Framework, which proposes to facilitate the exchange of healthcare information in RHIOs and HIEs, is a set of standards, policies, and methods intended to ensure secure and reliable connectivity between healthcare systems and to enable RHIOs and HIEs to connect and grow into the NHIN. An RLS is a key infrastructure component of the Common Framework to support this connectivity and interoperability (Connecting for Health 2006).

Distinct, distributed, disparate, and decentralized databases and systems linked by RLSs allow RHIO and HIE participants to search for health records on each of the other systems using patient indexing and identification software. In turn, the records remain intact in source systems where the information is initially created. RLSs only contain information (such as pointers or locators) about where patient-authorized information can be found and not the actual information the records contain.

Authorized users of an established RHIO or HIE can search the RLS, find and select the patient, and then cue the communication application to generate a real-time message to all participating databases that contain data for the patient. The databases receive the request message and send back all appropriate data to the requestor in real time (AHIMA 2007). Release of information (ROI) from one entity to another is subject to authorization requirements between those parties; in certain sensitive treatment situations patients or providers might choose not to share information. Patients may also choose to opt out of participating in a RLS at all.

As such, the federated model allows information sharing to occur without requiring a unique, national patient identifier and allows contributing organizations to retain ownership and control of their data. The federated model has other advantages. For example, data ownership is managed by defining business policies and access rules. In addition, new computer systems typically are not required, allowing for an easier transition to regional EHRs.

Unfortunately, the federated model consists of several drawbacks. Because there is no centralized database, no unified data model, and no standardized codification, decision support and many reporting capabilities are limited. In addition, the federated approach typically requires more coordination to implement. For example, RHIO and HIE stakeholders often have to accept diverse regional infrastructures and workflows. Consequently, today, a hybrid "centralized—federated" technical architecture model is commonly deployed.

The ultimate goal of RHIOs and HIEs is to enhance the quality and safety of patient care. Therefore, HIM professionals play a key role by getting involved in RHIOs and HIEs by creating policies, establishing processes, developing communication plans, and ensuring that solid HIM principles are addressed.

Check Your Understanding 3.2

Instructions: Answer the following questions on a separate piece of paper.

1. What is the goal of healthcare informatics? How does healthcare informatics benefit a healthcare organization?
2. Describe at least two major reports published by the IOM that have each served as a call to action in healthcare informatics.
3. What initiative is referred to as the *Medical Internet* and what is its purpose?
4. What barriers exist to achieving the NHIN within the next 10 years?
5. What can the HIM professional offer to the development of RHIO and HIE initiatives?
6. Describe the federated approach that many RHIOs and HIEs are taking to develop their technical architectures for regional healthcare information exchange. What are the advantages and disadvantages of this approach?

Current and Emerging Information Technologies in Healthcare

To examine the information resources and systems that enable healthcare organizations to accomplish their visions in the most effective way, HIM professionals must possess fundamental knowledge of computer-based information systems' components. This includes possessing knowledge of system hardware, software, and service components; communication and networking components; the Internet and its derived technologies; and system architectures. For the purposes of this chapter, it is assumed that students have acquired this basic knowledge through other, generic computer system courses and related textbooks.

Next, it is appropriate that HIM professionals review some of the current and emerging information technologies used to support the delivery of healthcare as well as the management and communication of health data and information within the healthcare setting. To do this, five categories of current and emerging technologies in healthcare are discussed in this chapter:

- Different types of data and formats
- Efficient access to, and flow of, data and information
- Managerial and clinical decision making
- Diagnosis, treatment, and care of patients
- Security of data and information

Supporting Different Types of Data and Formats

The information technologies currently in use for healthcare applications, as well as the new technologies being developed, consist of different data types and formats that are all used to support the creation, storage, dissemination, and analysis of information in every healthcare setting.

Different Data Types and Formats

Healthcare informatics professionals have agreed that an EHR system is not one or even two or more "products." Rather, it is a concept that consists of a plethora of integrated, component information systems and technologies. The automated files that make up the EHR system's component information systems and technologies consist of different **data types**, and the data in the files consist of different data formats. (See chapter 5 for a complete discussion of data types and data formats.)

Some data formats are structured and some are unstructured. For example, the data elements in a patient's automated laboratory order, result, or demographic or financial information system are coded and alphanumeric. Their fields are predefined and limited. In other words, the type of data is discrete, and the format of these data is structured. Consequently, when a healthcare professional searches a database for one or more coded, **discrete data** elements based on the search parameters, the engine can easily find, retrieve, and manipulate the element.

However, the format of the data contained in a patient's transcribed radiology or pathology result, history and physical (H&P), or clinical note system using word-processing technology is unstructured. **Free-text data**, as opposed to discrete, **structured data**, are generated by word processors, and their fields are not predefined and limited. Consequently, when a healthcare professional searches unstructured text, the search engine cannot easily find, retrieve, and manipulate one or more data elements embedded in the text.

Likewise, the format of the data contained in a patient's dictated radiology or pathology result, H&P, or clinical note system using speech recognition technology (real-time speech in, text out) is unstructured. However, the speech recognition technology's engine takes the unstructured, free-text-based speech data and codifies them, often with the help of templates. Hence, the format of the outputted text data becomes structured, with predefined and limited fields. Search engines then easily can find, retrieve, and manipulate one or more data elements embedded in the text.

Diagnostic image data, such as a digital chest x-ray or a computed tomography (CT) scan stored in a diagnostic image management system, represent a different type of data called **bit-mapped data**. However, the format of bit-mapped data also is unstructured. Saving each bit of the original image creates the image file. In other words, the image is a **raster image**, the smallest unit of which is a picture element or **pixel**. Together, hundreds of pixels simulate the image.

Some diagnostic image data are based on **analog**, photographic films, such as an analog chest x-ray. These analog films must be digitally scanned, using film digitizers, to digitize the data. Other diagnostic image data are based on **digital** modalities, such as computed radiography (CR), CT, magnetic resonance (MR), or nuclear medicine.

Document image data are yet another type of data that are also bit mapped, and the format of which is unstructured. These data are based on analog paper **documents** or on analog photographic film documents. Most often, analog paper-based documents contain handwritten notes, marks, or signatures. However, such documents can include preprinted documents (such as forms), photocopies of original documents, or computer-generated documents available only in hard copy. Analog photographic film-based documents (that is, photographs) are processed using an analog camera and film, similar to analog chest x-rays. Therefore, both the analog paper-based and the photographic film-based documents must be digitally scanned, using scanning devices that are similar to facsimile machines.

In addition, the EHR system's component information systems and technologies consist of other data types, the formats of which are also unstructured. **Real audio data** consist of sound bytes, such as digital heart sounds. **Motion or streaming video/frame data**, such as cardiac catheterizations, consist of digital film attributes, such as fast forwarding. The files that consist of **vector graphic (or signal-tracing) data**, are created by saving lines plotted between a series of points, accounting for the familiar ECGs, EEGs, and fetal traces.

When more than one **unstructured data** type is present in an information system, the data and system they represent are referred to as **multimedia**. Clearly, the EHR system is multimedia.

Figure 3.1 shows the different types of data and their sources found in EHR system component information systems.

Speech Recognition Technology

For more than 20 years, the concept of generating an immediately available, legible, final, signed note or report based on computer speech input has been the catalyst for the development and application of different forms of speech recognition technology in healthcare. The technology remains approximately 98 percent accurate (Nuance Communications 2008). Typically, systems offering approximately 98 percent accuracy still may not be acceptable for efficient and often lengthy clinical dictation purposes. Consequently, many still consider speech recognition an emerging technology.

Today, speech recognition technology is speaker independent with continuous speech input. Speaker independence does not require extensive training. The software is already trained to recognize generic speech and speech patterns. **Continuous speech input** does not require the user to pause between words to let the computer distinguish between the beginning and ending of words. However, the user is required to be careful in the enunciation of words.

Although speech recognition vocabularies are expanding due to faster and more powerful computer hardware, only limited clinical vocabularies have been developed. Limited vocabulary-based speech recognition systems require the user to say words that are known or taught to the system. In healthcare, limited clinical vocabulary-based specialties such as radiology, emergency medicine, and psychiatry have realized significant benefits for dictation from the technology.

In general, there are two types of speech recognition technology systems:

- *Orders-based* speech recognition technology system primarily is used by the Radiology, Pathology, and other related service departments where ordered test results are dictated.
- *Encounters-based* speech recognition technology system primarily is used by HIM, Emergency, and other related service departments where encounter information is dictated.

Speech recognition technology systems can be deployed in several ways. One is *front-end clinician editing*. The key advantage of this type of deployment is that immediate speech authentication eliminates transcription turn-around-times (TATs). One disadvantage of this type of deployment is that many clinicians cannot tolerate the (typically) time-consuming learning curve. Another is *full or partial back-end transcriptionist editing* (also known as speech with correctionists or editors). The key advantage of this type of deployment is that, typically, dictators are not aware that their dictation is being routed through the speech recognition technology system and subsequently "back-end edited" by transcriptionists or correctionists. One disadvantage of this type of deployment

Figure 3.1. CPR data types and their sources

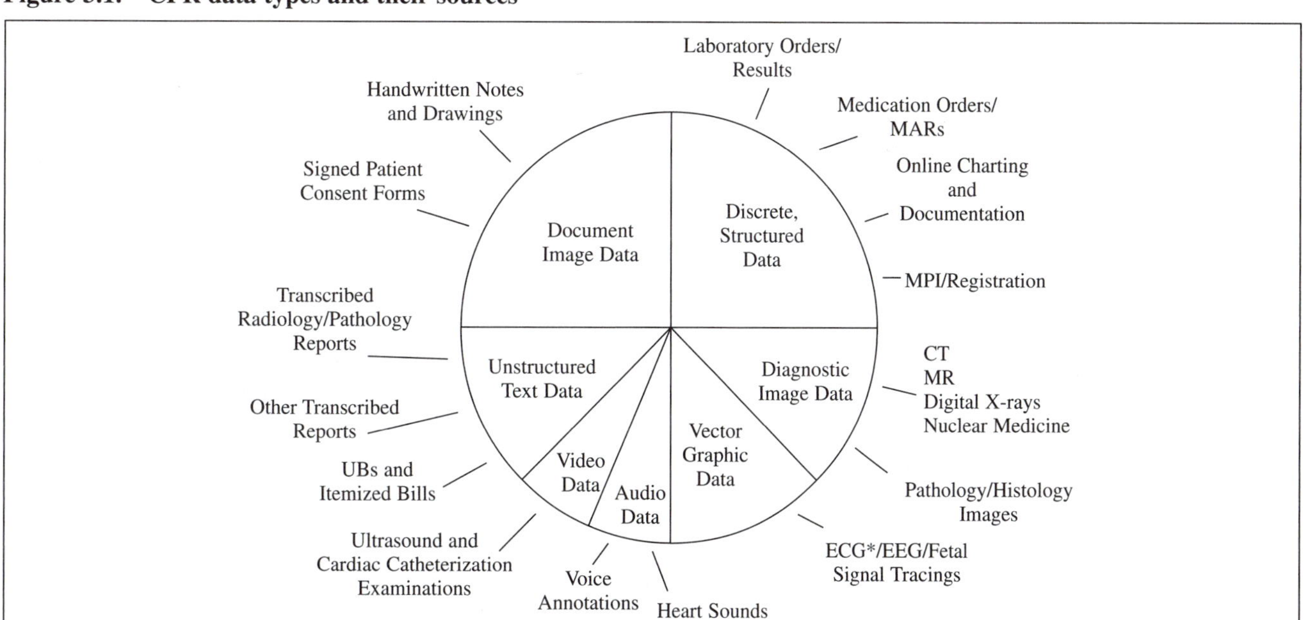

*ECG is the more correct term, but EKG is more widely used.

is that even the best speech recognition technology systems using this type of deployment include TATs.

Other areas in healthcare have realized significant benefits from speech recognition input technology for specific programs. These programs include data-entry systems, navigating through pathways, pulling down menus, editing text, autodialing phone numbers, and completing multiple-choice-based forms. This usually requires exchanging data with the other applications through seamless, but complex, interfaces.

The ultimate goal in speech recognition technology is to be able to talk to a computer's central processor and rapidly create vocabularies for applications without collecting any speech samples (in other words, without training). It includes being able to talk at natural speed and intonation and in no specific manner. It also includes having the computer understand what the user wants to say (the context of the word or words) and then apply the correct commands or words as coded data in a structured format. Finally, it includes identifying a user's voice and encrypting the voiceprint. Over the next years and decades, clinical vocabularies and algorithms will continue to improve, true speaker independence will be achieved, and natural language understanding will ultimately make structured dictation a reality.

Natural Language Processing Technology

One could argue that **natural language processing technology** is another name for **speech recognition technology.** When one talks at natural speed without pausing between words, the *natural language* voice bytes are, indeed, processed by this technology. However, natural language processing technology is more than speech recognition technology.

Natural language processing technology considers sentence structure (syntax), meaning (semantics), and context to accurately process and extract free-text data, including speech data for application purposes. As such, it differs from simple Boolean word search programs that often complement speech recognition technology-based systems. For example, the narratives "no shortness of breath, chest pain aggravated by exercise" and "no chest pain, shortness of breath aggravated by exercise" look the same to a Boolean word search engine when looking for occurrences of "chest" and "pain" in the same sentence. This Boolean word search approach retrieves approximately 20 percent of the answer 20 percent of the time. It is rife with false positives and false negatives.

On the other hand, natural language processing technology knows the difference in the narratives' meanings. For example, for health record coding applications, it teaches computers to understand English well enough to "read" transcribed reports and notes and then find certain key concepts (not merely words) by identifying the many different phrasings of the concept. By "normalizing" these concepts, different phrases of the same content can all be compared with one another for statistical purposes. For example, "the patient thinks he has angina" and "the doctor thinks the patient has angina" have different meanings from a coding perspective (Schnitzer 2000, 96). By employing statistical or rules-based algorithms, natural language processing technology can then compare and code these similar expressions accurately and quickly.

Autocoding and **computer-assisted coding** are the terms commonly used to describe natural language processing technology's method of extracting and subsequently translating dictated and then transcribed free-text data, or dictated and then computer-generated discrete data, into ICD or CPT codes for clinical and financial applications such as patient billing and health record coding. **Text mining** and data mining are the terms commonly used to describe the process of extracting and then quantifying and filtering free-text data and discrete data, respectively.

Early results of several formative studies suggest that natural language processing technology improves health record coding productivity and consistency without sacrificing quality (Warner 2000, 78). More recent studies suggest that quality remains in question when natural language processing is used (AHIMA 2004). Despite the studies' outcomes, vendors continue to integrate natural language processing technology within health record coding reference tools, coding guidelines, drug databases, and legacy information systems to provide complete patient billing, health record coding, and other applications with little or no human intervention.

Check Your Understanding 3.3

Instructions: Answer the following questions on a separate piece of paper.

1. Provide an example of structured and unstructured data formats and an example of discrete and free-text data types.
2. What is a key advantage to structured data when searching a database?
3. What are the similarities and differences between a diagnostic image and a document image?
4. Provide a healthcare example for each of the following data types: real audio data, motion or streaming data, signal or vector graphic data.
5. What is the difference between (a) speech recognition technology and natural language processing technology and (b) natural language processing searching and Boolean searching?

Supporting Efficient Access to, and Flow of, Data and Information

A plethora of current and emerging information technologies are used to support efficient access to, and flow of, healthcare data and information. For purposes of this chapter, the following technologies are highlighted:

- Automatic recognition technologies
- Electronic data interchange (EDI) and e-commerce
- Enterprise master patient indexes and identity management
- Data repositories
- Electronic document/content management systems
- Secure messaging systems
- Web-derived technologies and applications

- Application service providers (ASPs) and Software as a Service (SaaS)

Automatic Recognition Technologies

Several technologies are used in healthcare to recognize analog items automatically, such as tangible materials or documents, or to recognize characters/symbols from analog items. Character/symbol recognition technologies recognize electronically scanned characters or symbols from analog items, enabling the identified data to be quickly, accurately, and automatically entered into digital systems. Other recognition technologies identify the actual items.

Character/Symbol Recognition Technologies

Character/symbol recognition technologies include bar-coding, optical character recognition (OCR), and gesture recognition technologies.

Bar-Coding Technology

Almost three decades ago, the bar code symbol was standardized for the healthcare industry, making it easier to adopt **bar-coding technology** and to realize its potential. Since then, bar-coding applications have been adopted for labels, patient wristbands, specimen containers, business/employee/patient records, library reference materials, medication packages, dietary items, paper documents, and more. Benefits have been realized by the uniform consistency in the development of commercially available software systems, fewer procedural variations in healthcare organizations using the technology, and the flexibility to adopt standard specifications for functions while retaining current systems. Because virtually every tangible item in the clinical setting, including the patient, can be assigned a bar code with an associated meaning, it is not surprising to find bar coding as the primary tracking, identification, inventory data-capture, and even patient safety medium in healthcare organizations.

With bar-coding technology, an individual's computer data-entry rate can be increased by eight- to twelve-fold in applications such as patient medication tracking, supply requisitioning, or chart/film tracking. For example, a function such as hand-keying paper chart/film locations into a computer that once took a healthcare professional eight hours to perform now can be done in 30 to 45 minutes with bar-coding technology.

In addition to eliminating time, bar-coding technology eliminates most of the mounds of paperwork (worksheets, count sheets, identification sheets, and the like) that are still associated with traditional computer keyboard entry. When bar-coding systems are interfaced to these types of healthcare information systems, the bar code can be used to enter the data, especially repetitive data, saving additional processing time and paper generation.

More importantly, the data input error rates with bar coding are as close to zero as most IT professionals think is possible. For all intents and purposes, bar-coded data, with an error rate of approximately three transactions in 1 million, can be considered error free. Thus, it is a most effective remedy for medication errors when used to ensure that the right medication dose is administered to the right patient.

Optical Character Recognition Technology

Like bar coding, **optical character recognition (OCR) technology** was invented to reduce manual data input, or hand-keying. OCR technology recognizes machine-generated characters (for example, preprinted numbers and letters) by interpreting the scanned, bit-mapped shapes of the characters' images and then converting the characters into computer-processable codes. OCR technology was initially used to automatically identify financial accounts consisting of preprinted Arabic numbers and Roman letters using the E13B font on thousands of paper-based documents, such as bank checks.

OCR has since been perfected to recognize the full set of preprinted typeset fonts as well as point sizes. Moreover, it performs well with different Germanic and Romance languages. The best OCR systems compensate for imperfectly formed characters and scanned pages by employing characteristics such as de-skewing, broken character repair, and redaction. De-skewing "straightens" oblique characters, broken character repair "fixes" incomplete characters, and redaction "hides" superfluous characters. OCR is used to perform everything from indexing scanned documents to digitizing full text. Its ability to dramatically reduce manual data input, or hand-keying, while increasing input speed represents the best aspect of this technology.

Unfortunately, like other technologies, OCR has been perfected but is not perfect. The approximately 98 percent recognition rate realized by most OCR systems (Prime Recognition 2008) may not be sufficient for the kind of text recognition applications OCR software is designed to perform. In addition, after an analog document is scanned by OCR technology, the data become unstructured, free-text data. As with all unstructured text data, when a healthcare professional needs to search the text, the search engine cannot easily find, retrieve, and manipulate one or more data elements embedded in text.

Gesture Recognition Technology

The recognition of constrained or unconstrained, handwritten, English language free text (print or cursive, upper- or lower-case, characters or symbols) typically stored on paper-based, analog documents is known as **intelligent character recognition (ICR) technology**. The recognition of hand-marked characters in defined areas of, typically, paper-based analog documents is known as **mark sense technology**. Collectively, these technologies are referred to as **gesture recognition technologies**.

Mark sense technology detects the presence or absence of hand-marked characters on analog documents. Consequently, it is used for processing analog questionnaires, surveys, and tests, such as filled-in circles by Number 2 pencils on SAT exam forms.

ICR technology is quite an elaborate information-processing technique. An operation such as the detection of lines or the beginnings of words in sections of handwritten text can be accomplished with relative ease in the normal case. However, subsequent tasks turn out to be extraordinarily complicated. These include segmentation of the words into individual characters and assignment of the individual characters to a definite class of characters, such as words. Consequently, ICR error rates remain high. As such, ICR technology is being adopted slowly, primarily into the data-entry activities of certain types of pen-based computer devices, such as handheld devices.

Neural networks remain the leading ICR technology. These networks are modeled on the way synapses work in the brain: processing information by recognizing patterns of signals. As such, they adapt themselves into shifting configurations based on what they encounter. In other words, they change as they grow and learn.

Consequently, for each handwritten character or symbol recognized by ICR technology, a confidence level is expressed internally as a percentage and a user picks the threshold below which he or she wants to flag uncertain characters or symbols. Like speech recognition technology, a training or setup period is required for this emerging technology.

Other Recognition Technologies

Automatic recognition technologies that identify actual items include radio frequency identification (RFID) and intelligent document recognition (IDR) technologies.

Radio Frequency Identification Technology

Radio frequency identification (RFID) technology allows cars to zip through toll plazas without stopping to tender cash and is the alert buzzer that sounds if someone tries to leave a department store before a salesperson removes the plastic tags. The technology is rapidly evolving, primarily in the consumer products industry.

RFID technology works in the following manner: Chips that emit radio signals are embedded in analog items and products. The signals are read and captured by receivers installed in ceilings or toll booths. The receivers act as data collectors and send the signals to PCs on a network, allowing the items and products to be tracked.

RFID's applicability in the healthcare industry is limited only by the imagination. Like bar codes, it is being used to track moveable patients, clinicians, medications, and equipment. As such, in a wireless environment, conceivably, RFID could replace bar codes for these applications.

However, today, the question surrounding RFID is its business value. First, healthcare organizations must install wireless networks with the required access points. However, this is occurring at a rapid rate, despite RFID. Second, today, passive RFID tags—those that become activated when they are in close proximity to a "reader," similar to a bar code reader—cost around 10 to 20 cents each (RSA Laboratories 2007a). In comparison, bar code stickers cost around 1 cent (Barcode Factory 2008). For example, today if every medication dose in a healthcare organization were to be RFID tagged, the costs remain substantial when compared to bar code tags. On the other hand, RFID users only have to go to the nearest computer and click on an icon to locate patients, clinicians, or equipment.

Privacy and security of RFID technology is also a consideration. A RFID system presents important security challenges. RFID tags are so small and easily embedded that consumers may not even be aware if they are carrying them or that a RFID system is in place. Also because the RFID tag reading is not a visible process, it is difficult to know when security and privacy policies are adhered to or breached (RSA Laboratories 2007b).

Intelligent Document Recognition Technology

Recently, an automatic recognition technology has been developed to recognize types of analog documents or forms, eliminating the need for bar codes or other characters/symbols that identify the documents or forms. **Intelligent document recognition (IDR) technology** trains itself to identify document or form types and to sort the information accordingly for subsequent data entry. This training process requires a period of continuously scanning each type of document or form. As such, the pattern of document and form layouts and information locations educates the system to recognize the document or form for future recognition situations.

Electronic Data Interchange and E-Commerce

Electronic data interchange (EDI) allows the transfer (incoming and outgoing) of information directly from one computer to another by using flexible, standard formats. These formats function as a common language among many different healthcare "trading" or "business" partners (payers, government agencies, financial institutions, employer groups, healthcare providers, suppliers, and claims processors) who have agreed to exchange the information electronically but use a wide variety of application software with incompatible native formats. In the healthcare industry, with its traditionally strong reliance on paper-intensive processes, the goal of EDI is to eliminate the administrative nightmares of transferring paper documents back and forth between these partners and then hand-keying the information into the partners' disparate computer systems.

No EDI story has been told more often than that of the former American Hospital Supply Corporation (AHSC) in the late 1970s. AHSC pioneered an electronic connection with its customer hospitals that reinforced its position as the country's largest distributor of hospital supplies. Beginning as a "dumb terminal"-based utility for transmitting electronic purchase orders, over time this proprietary system evolved into a PC-based information system that served as the gateway for what became Baxter Healthcare's purchase orders and confirmations.

By the late 1980s, the healthcare industry's business partners expanded their EDI linkages beyond purchase orders to electronic invoices and payments. At the same time, the American National Standards Institute (ANSI) chartered the Accredited Standards Committee (ASC) X12 to create standard, electronic formats for all business transactions. ASC X12's Insurance Subcommittee (X12 N) Healthcare Task Group developed many standard healthcare transactions, including healthcare claims (837), healthcare payments and remittance advices (835), and healthcare claim status requests (276).

However, acceptance by the healthcare industry to use these standards as the tools for conducting business electronically was atrociously slow. The unfortunate outcome of the industry's self-imposed obstacles to the adoption of standards-based EDI increased the need for paper-based and telephone callback business processes, resulting in even higher costs and less efficiencies than the older, manual systems. So, in 1991, the Workgroup for Electronic Data Interchange (WEDI), a public and private task force, was established by HHS to develop an action plan for healthcare standards-based EDI: standardizing and implementing electronic data exchange to reduce the healthcare industry's inefficient administrative processes and increasing costs. WEDI's 1993 report underscored the need to establish uniform content and coding so that healthcare data could be exchanged quickly, easily, and inexpensively via interconnecting networks. Also, the report recommended industry-wide, standards-based EDI implementation guidelines. Such guidelines included establishing unique identification numbers for patients, providers, and payers; ensuring security to protect confidential medical and financial information; and enabling eligibility checking, verification of claim status and copayments, and referral information. The then HHS Secretary Louis Sullivan proposed that standards-based EDI would decrease paperwork and result in savings of $4 to $10 billion annually (HHS 1993). These WEDI/HHS recommendations and proposals became the drivers that forced the enactment of Title II, Administrative Simplification, of HIPAA.

HIPAA's proposed rule on the EDI and coding standard transaction set was published in August 2000. Its original compliance date was extended to October 2003, when the regulation was officially implemented. The rule mandates that healthcare "covered entities" and"business partners" implement a common standard (ASC X12 N) for the transfer of information and accept the standard-based electronic transaction. This regulation does not apply to the transfer of data and information within a healthcare organization, but it does apply to the transfer of data and information external to and between healthcare organizations.

By 2000, the term *EDI* (but not the concept) had become somewhat dated. With the mid- to late 1990s introduction and widespread acceptance of the Internet and its derived technologies, such as the Web, the term **e-commerce** began to replace the term *EDI*. Today, e-commerce is used to describe the integration of all aspects of business-to-business (B2B) and business-to-consumer (B2C) activities, processes, and communications, including EDI.

In addition, the term **e-health** is now used to describe the application of e-commerce in the healthcare industry. Several principles and concepts of e-health directly relate to EDI principles and concepts. These include the links among the healthcare trading and business partners; the links to healthcare equipment and supply vendors, providers, and health plans; and the transactions for exchanging data on healthcare eligibility, referrals, claims, and so forth. As recently as August 2008, the Healthcare Information and Management Systems Society (HIMSS) proposed using the EDI principles and e-commerce concepts of HIPAA's transaction exchange network to improve and promote the exchange of clinical data and information. A HIMSS (2008) white paper titled, *The NHIN Highway is Already Paved: The Existing HIPAA Transaction Exchange Network is an Able Solution for the Conveyance of Clinical Information* calls for the existing claims clearinghouse network for HIPAA financial and administrative transactions to be expanded to become the national network for clinical transactions. The white paper argues that the EDI and clearinghouse industry has been developing its network for 25 years and that its vendors are covered under the existing HIPAA transactions, privacy, and security rules. Consequently, RHIOs and HIEs could benefit from a strong coordination with this existing network.

Enterprise Master Patient Indexes and Identity Management

Too often, breakdowns in patient identification cause patient record errors that threaten data integrity. The most common error occurs when healthcare provider organization registration personnel fail to locate existing patient information in the organization's **master patient index** (MPI), including the patient's unique identification number. The patient is then assigned another record (in other words, a duplicate record) and a new file is created in the database. When this error occurs, it is unclear into which database file the patient's data should be entered. This often results in unnecessary duplicate tests, billing problems, and increased legal exposure in the case of adverse treatment outcomes.

Another common error occurs when registration personnel incorrectly register a patient under another person's existing, unique identification number. This error of overlay results in the merging of two different patients' data into one file. The clinical risks are obvious.

As healthcare organizations continue to come together into integrated delivery networks (IDNs), the probability increases that information about a patient is spread across multiple databases and in multiple formats. In addition, the information is updated and accessed by multiple transaction processing systems and personnel. This causes problems when the IDN begins to assemble information about a patient in order to deliver care across diverse systems and encounters. Longitudinal applications, such as the EHR system, cannot be successful.

Consequently, healthcare provider organizations are developing strategic initiatives for **enterprise master patient**

indexes (EMPIs). In the broad sense, this involves the increasingly important service referred to as **identity management**.

EMPIs provide access to multiple repositories of information from overlapping patient populations that are maintained in separate systems and databases. This occurs through an indexing scheme to all unique patient identification numbers and information in all the organizations' databases. As such, EMPIs become the cornerstones of healthcare system integration projects.

EMPIs work in two ways. At the back end, EMPIs coordinate recordkeeping. The indexes receive information from multiple systems that need no modification. The receiving is often performed through an integration gateway or engine. The enterprise index tests to see whether the patient is identified in all of the systems; if not, it may assign a unique identification number or other, related identifier as well as correlate records throughout the enterprise.

At the front end, EMPIs receive requests from existing registration systems to send data to these systems. Usually, these existing registration systems need some reprogramming to enable them to request and receive data from the EMPI. Currently, there is no consistent, accepted trigger event and standard data format to do this.

EMPI building is complex. Variations in information systems, data capture, and organizational goals and objectives present multiple challenges to integrating patient data. For example, EMPI building involves a multitude of decision points. These include deciding whether to employ centralized or distributed data storage; whether to maintain limited, additional information such as allergies and encounter histories or robust information such as problem lists; and whether to establish batch processing or real-time communication between the registration system and the EMPI.

In addition, EMPIs include complex capabilities. These capabilities include merging records pertaining to the same person using probabilistic matching and algorithms, maintaining source systems' pointers, removing duplicate records, and providing a common user interface. Finally, after technical and organizational issues are overcome, the purely operational tasks of linking patients across multiple entities and episodes of care and maintaining these linkages are difficult and can be costly.

Data Repositories

Data repositories are powerful databases that exist in every industry and are designed to store large amounts of data. Typically, these databases are organized into data fields, data records, and data files.

Typically, the model of these databases is relational. In other words, the data are stored physically in the database using two-dimensional tables that create a relation. The format of the data is usually structured, and the type of data is discrete. Therefore, this model forces the database architect to predict how many data fields, records, and files will be stored about a particular event.

Some **relational databases** contain binary large objects (BLOBs) in their tables that consist of unstructured data, such as free-text data, bit-mapped data, real audio data, streaming video data, or vector graphic data. More commonly, relational databases contain pointers in their tables that indicate other, physical data repositories containing the unstructured data.

Another model of these databases is the **object-oriented database**. An object can contain several types of unstructured data. Typically, these data types are stored in the database tables with specific behavior rules or procedures. For example, streaming video data are stored in the database tables with "fast-forward" or "rewind" behavior rules. This model cannot force the database architect to predict how many data fields, records, and files will be stored about a particular event.

Typically, in healthcare provider organizations, the term *data repository* is used to refer to databases that are relational and store structured, discrete, clinical, administrative, and financial data. As such, the repositories storing clinical data are often called clinical data repositories (CDRs), the repositories storing patient financial data are often called financial data repositories (FDRs), and so on. Sometimes one data repository physically stores all the organization's structured and discrete clinical, administrative, and financial data related to patients.

To provide continuous, high-quality care for patients, all the physical data repositories in healthcare provider organizations must be linked logically. These repositories include the relational databases that store structured, discrete, patient clinical, administrative, and financial data as well as the object-oriented databases that store unstructured, patient free-text, bit-mapped, real audio, streaming video, or vector graphic data. The EMPI primary index keys, the patients' unique identification numbers, are the links.

In addition, the organizations' logically linked, physical data repositories must be designed to allow **online/real-time transaction processing** (OLTP) of the data stored in the repositories. In other words, the data are entered into the repositories by the organizations' various "feeder" applications, and the users must be able to manipulate, update, retrieve, and otherwise act on the data in real time while the data are stored in the repositories. This requires data repositories to include tools designed to perform intricate data searches and retrievals.

For example, a healthcare provider organization's CDR typically incorporates powerful, centralized, relational database management technology. In an online/real-time mode, the CDR allows providers of care to access and manipulate patient-structured and discrete, administrative, and clinical data, such as patient demographic data, physician orders, nursing care plans, and laboratory, radiology, or pathology results. It also allows providers to access and manipulate unstructured, free-text patient data, such as transcribed clinical report data.

Electronic Document/Content Management Systems (ED/CM)

A **document** is any analog or digital, formatted, and preserved "container" of data or information, collectively referred to as **content**. The document is a well-worn and very useful human construct. It really has not changed much in 5,000 years. People like doing some very basic things using documents, things that do not change just because document data and information were once contained on stone tablets and, today, are electronic and contained in spreadsheets, e-mail messages, and laboratory test result reports.

For example, people like to exchange documents, read documents, and know what the documents mean. One reason why many healthcare professionals still resist using data and information systems to accomplish their daily work functions and processes is that viewing or reading an information system's data (informational representations of the system's transactions) is, plainly, unaccommodating to the human eye. Unless the data are formatted, accompanied by print-like qualities, such as headings or bolding, and contained in documents, data are difficult to interpret.

It is for this reason that documents, and not data, are required for evidentiary disclosure and discovery purposes. To settle legal disputes, the transaction *presentation, not representation,* is required for all business record documents. In healthcare organizations, this involves the retrieval of the bill document, the consultation report document, the photograph document, the image document, and so on.

An **electronic document/content management system** (ED/CM) is any electronic system that manages an organization's analog and digital documents and content (that is, not just the "data") to realize significant improvements in business work processes. Like most information systems, the ED/CM system consists of a number of component technologies that support both digital and analog document and content management. These component technologies are discussed in the following sections.

Document-Imaging Technology

Document-imaging technology is one, and only one, of the many ED/CM system component technologies. This technology electronically captures, stores, identifies, retrieves, and distributes documents that are not generated digitally or are generated digitally but are stored on paper for distribution purposes. Currently, in healthcare provider organizations, documents that typically are not generated in a digital format, are stored on paper, and are candidates for this technology include handwritten physician problem lists and notes; "fill-in-the-blank" typeset nursing forms; preprinted Conditions of Treatment forms; and external documents (documents from the outside).

By digitally scanning (faxing) the documents, the technology converts the analog data on the document into digital, bit-mapped, document images, discussed in a previous section of this chapter. As more and more documents are created, distributed, and stored digitally, the dependence on, and use of, this technology decreases.

Document Management Technology

For every type of document as well as for every section or part of a document, **document management technology** automatically organizes, assembles, secures, and shares documents. Some of the more common document management technology functions include document version control, check in-check out control, document access control, and text and word searches.

Electronic Records Management Technology

Business records are bound by legal and regulatory requirements. Consequently, formats for long-term preservation, storage media for long-term viability, and strategies for record migration and accessibility are required. **Electronic records management technology** include components that must ensure the authenticity, security, and reliability of an organization's electronic records. For example, mass storage is required for the massive amounts of structured and unstructured data as well as the large number and kind of documents stored in ED/CM systems. The major, mass storage medium used in ED/CM systems is magnetic, including disk (for example, Redundant Array of Independent Disks [RAID], Network Attached Storage [NAS], Content Addressable Storage [CAS]) or tape options. For extraordinarily large amounts of data and lengthy document archive requirements, the optical medium might be used, including Compact Disk-Read Only Memory (CD-ROM), CD-Recordable, Digital Versatile Disk (DVD; read only or recordable), or magneto-optical-based Write Once Read Many (WORM) options.

In addition, ED/CM system records must be properly classified under appropriate categories so that appropriate legal and regulatory retention rules can be applied. Users must determine how to identify and declare these records so that the records and record documents can be deleted, purged, or destroyed at a defined point in their life cycle.

Workflow and Business Process Management (BPM) Technology

Business Process Management (BPM) technology allows computers to add and extract value from document content as the documents move throughout an organization. The documents can be assigned, routed, activated, and managed through system-controlled rules that mirror business operations and decision processes. For example, in healthcare organizations, **workflow technology** automatically routes electronic documents into electronic in-baskets of its department clerks or supervisors for disposition decisions.

Computer Output Laser Disk/Enterprise Report Management (COLD/ERM) Technology

Computer output laser disk/enterprise report management (COLD/ERM) technology electronically stores, manages, and distributes documents that are generated in a digital format and whose output data are report-formatted and print-stream originated. Unfortunately, documents that are candidates for this technology too often are printed to paper or microform for distribution and storage purposes. COLD/ERM technology not only electronically stores the report-formatted documents but also distributes them with fax, e-mail, Web, and traditional hard-copy print processes. One of the more recent trends for ERM is to store the coded, report-formatted output data natively and convert the data to **Extensible Markup Language** (XML) or **HyperText Markup Language** (HTML) when needed. In healthcare provider organizations, such documents generated by COLD/ERM technology typically include "green bar" financial system reports, Uniform Bills (UBs)/CMS (formerly known as HCFA) 1500s, laboratory cumulative result summary reports, and transcribed, word-processed medical reports.

Automated Forms-Processing (e-forms) Technology

Automated forms-processing (e-forms) technology allows users to electronically enter data into online forms and electronically extract the data from the online forms for various data-manipulation purposes. Powerful contextual verification processes have made such operations highly accurate. In addition, the form document is stored in a form format, as the user sees it on the screen, for ease of interpretation.

Digital Signature Management Technology

Digital signature management technology offers both signer and document authentication for analog or digital documents. Signer authentication is the ability to identify the person who digitally signed the document. Implementation of the technology is such that any unauthorized person will not be able to use the digital signature. Document authentication ensures that the document and the signature cannot be altered (unless both the original document and the change document are shown). As such, document authentication prevents the document signer from repudiating that fact.

Secure Messaging Systems

Messaging systems electronically deliver data and information to users. As such, e-mail systems are messaging systems. However, **secure messaging systems** eliminate the security concerns that surround e-mail but retain the benefits of proactive, traceable, and personalized messaging. These systems are not transaction (data) processing systems. Also known as secure notification delivery systems, these systems store and forward content to users in an asynchronous, "anytime" mode.

In healthcare, secure messaging systems are often referred to as **clinical messaging systems** because these systems are important, pervasive tools that are included in a broad set of contextual collaboration tools for clinicians. Other clinical collaboration tools include synchronous, real-time tools, such as instant messaging, chat servers, and Web/media conferencing. However, secure clinical messaging is the most heavily used because it crosses time zones, can be done in each clinical user's own time frame, and gives clinical recipients time to think over and then respond to issues, such as notifications of abnormal laboratory test results. In addition, clinical messaging does not require all participants to be available at the same time and eliminates the scheduling problems associated with the real-time tools.

Secure clinical messaging systems work in the following manner: When a **clinical information system** (CIS) generates a patient alert regarding a possible drug interaction or an anomalous test result, the secure clinical messaging system immediately routes the alert, along with patient data, to a caregiver's designated pager number, fax machine number, telephone number, or e-mail address. In turn, clinicians can securely send these alerts to other, related clinicians. Also, messages can be automatically escalated to the next available caregiver if the original caregiver does not respond within a predefined time frame. In addition, messages can be tracked throughout the care delivery network.

Most of today's secure clinical messaging systems fall into one of four architectures: peer-to-peer networking, a message staging server installed inside the network's firewall, a staging server installed outside the firewall (usually hosted), and a wholly outsourced service. A message staging server installed on an organization's virtual private network (VPN) works best for larger organizations that collaborate regularly with the same business partners. A hosted staging server works best for smaller organizations that benefit from a pre-message payment plan. When a secure clinical messaging system's staging server is installed inside the network's firewall, the server can act as a "will call" window for authenticated viewing (Tabar 2003).

Web-derived Technologies and Applications

It is an understatement that the Internet has transformed the healthcare industry and its stakeholders. Likewise, it is an understatement that the Internet will continue to grow, change, and influence everything in the 21st century. Because of this relatively new phenomenon, having only made its impact beginning in the late 1990s, the full range of social, economic, political, cultural, and historical perspectives regarding what we today know as healthcare and information management will continue to be drastically transformed in less than a tenth of the time it took to change over the last half century and in ways that, today, are unimaginable.

Consequently, for HIM professionals to take advantage of the opportunities afforded by the Internet phenomenon, it is important to review some of the many, current technologies and applications that have been developed only because of the Internet and its two dominant applications/**protocols**: e-mail (Simple Mail Transfer Protocol [SMTP]) and the World Wide Web (HyperText Transfer Protocol [HTTP]). For the purposes of this chapter, the following Web-derived technologies and applications are highlighted: Web-based information systems, Web portals, Web-based intranets and extranets, Web content management systems, and Web services.

Web-based Information Systems and Applications

In past decades, healthcare information system (HIS) vendors were forced to migrate their existing systems and products from proprietary, centralized processing-based architectures running on mainframe computers, minicomputers, and microcomputers to open, client/server-based architectures. This required a lot of time and money in terms of company research and development (R&D). In many cases, it involved a total rewrite of the systems' code. For those HIS companies that designed their systems based on client/server architectures, they, too, were required to expend a lot of R&D time and money. This was because such firms typically had to transition from 16- to 32-bit hardware and software components, which also involved a total rewrite of the systems' code.

Ironically, at the same time that thousands of computer components were being "thickened" to 32 bits, maintaining thick client workstations and their multitude of corresponding servers became an IT department's worst nightmare. Also, during this time, the Internet and its derived technologies began to be introduced, offering a simpler and more cost-effective alternative to computer system development and maintenance.

However, the mass introduction and acceptance of the Internet and its derived technologies once again forced HIS companies to make another transition: to Web browser-based or Web native architectures. This, again, required a lot of R&D. In all cases, it involved a total rewrite of the systems' code.

Unfortunately, many HIS companies with legacy or client/server-based systems no longer could afford to make the next transition to Web browser-based or Web native architectures. Consequently, many of these companies began to transition their existing systems and products to Web browser-based or Web native architectures by Web-enabling the systems.

With Web enabling, the HIS companies did not rewrite their systems' code in the newer, Web native programming languages, such as HTML, SGML, XML, or Java and its derivatives. Instead, when an authorized user logs on to the system, he or she is presented with a Web page. From the Web page, the companies' systems applications (for example, applications written in Microsoft's 32-bit Visual Basic) are launched.

Web browser-based or **Web native systems** are more complex. These are systems where companies have either written or rewritten their systems' code using one or more of the above-mentioned, Web native programming languages. In Web browser-based or Web native systems, the Web browser acts as the primary desktop interface for access to a healthcare organization's repositories. The Web browser is used to display and query (for example, to drill down via hypertext) information stored in databases as quickly as client/server-based systems. (For comparison purposes, in Web browser-based or Web native systems, the retrieval application typically resides on the server. In client/server-based systems, the retrieval application typically is loaded on standard, thick client workstations.)

Web browser-based or Web native systems accept data inputs from other systems and send them to other databases over the network using plug-ins or display controls, such as Active X or CORBA. These systems are OLTP systems and have been proven to reduce network administration and workstation maintenance costs.

Web Portals

No one information system (IS) can provide all the applications, data types, and data formats needed by all of the healthcare industry's diverse healthcare organizations and users. Consequently, healthcare provider organizations maintain multiple, disparate "feeder" applications for their data repositories. Depending on their size and systems acquisition philosophies, some healthcare provider organizations maintain and often integrate large numbers of disparate feeder applications, and others maintain and integrate at least two or three.

Each disparate feeder application for the repository has a unique user interface, uses different data nomenclature, and takes limited advantage of data standards. Therefore, it is not only difficult to integrate the information from the disparate systems into the repositories, but it is also difficult for the organizations' users to learn and interact with the different systems.

Consequently, the concept of the **clinical workstation** evolved during the early 1990s so that one single point of access to the data in the repositories and to the applications "feeding" the data into the repositories would be deployed at the clinician's workstation or desktop. This single point of access would include a common user interface to view the information from the disparate applications as well as to launch the applications.

During this time, Microsoft's Windows operating system products became ubiquitous for PC client workstations. Consequently, the Windows-based graphical user interface (GUI) was originally deployed at the clinical workstation. However, with the mid- to late-1990s introduction and widespread acceptance of the Internet and its derived technologies, the Web browser began to be deployed as the user interface of choice.

Today, the term *clinical workstation* is still used to describe the presentation of healthcare data and the launching of applications in the most effective way for healthcare providers. However, for all intents and purposes, the concept of Web-based, clinician/physician portals has replaced the concept of the clinical workstation.

A **Web portal** is a single point of personalized access (an entryway) through which to find and deliver information (content), applications, and services. Web portals began in the consumer market as an integration strategy rather than a solution. Portals offered users of the large, public, online Internet service provider Web sites, such as AOL, fast, centralized access (via a Web browser) to an array of Internet services and information found on those Web sites.

Consequently, like clinical workstations, **clinician/physician Web portals** first were seen as a way for clinicians to easily access (via a Web browser) the healthcare provider organizations' multiple sources of structured and unstructured data from any network-connected device. Like clinical workstations, clinician/physician Web portals evolved into an effective medium for providing access to multiple applications as well as the data. And because clinician/physician portals are based on Internet technologies, they became the access points to sources of data and applications both internal and external to the organization.

In short, clinician/physician Web portals have become, and can be considered analogous to, internal, private Webs. As such, the portals provide centralized security both internal and external to the organization. This is accomplished by restricting access to data and applications contained within the portal to authorized users. Examples of authorized users for healthcare provider organizations include a role (for example, physician), an individual (for example, Chris Jones, MD), a group of individuals (for example, all the physicians in the organization), a department (for example, internal medicine), or a group of departments (for example, surgical subspecialties).

In addition, clinician/physician Web portals provide simplified, automated methods of creating **taxonomy**, or classifying data. Consumer portals, such as Yahoo.com, provide good examples of this, whereby files and data corresponding to food, fashion, and travel are organized for easy access. Finally, true clinician/physician Web portals have at least one search engine and allow customization at the role and individual level. As such, search engines must be able to search e-mails, file servers, Web servers, and databases; and customization must allow users to create individual, relevant views. The clinical benefits of these portal features and functions are obvious.

With the success of clinician/physician Web portals, a growing number of healthcare provider and payer organizations have established Web portals for their patients/members. Each participant receives an account on the Web portal with a unique log-in and password. Typical payer-based portal uses include accessing membership information and choosing a primary care physician. Typical provider-based portal uses include requesting prescription renewals, scheduling appointments, and asking questions of providers via secure messaging. Increasingly, **patient/consumer Web portals** are allowing patients to pay their bills online and to securely view all or portions of their provider-based, electronic medical record, such as current medical conditions, medications, allergies, and test results.

Although patients/members access the portals over the Internet, all the information, including the secure messaging applications, resides on the provider's or payer's secured servers. As such, these portals dovetail well with HIPAA, which empowers patients/consumers with the authority to determine who can have access to their healthcare information. Also, patients can use the portal to notify providers if their EHR is incorrect. As consumers seek to take a larger role in their healthcare, such patient/member "entryways" to information (content), applications, and services are expected to become more common.

Intranets and Extranets

Web-based information systems and applications cannot continue to proliferate without creating Web-based **intranets** designed to enhance communication among an organization's internal employees and facilities and Web-based **extranets** designed to enhance communication among an organization's external business partners. This is true because intranets link every employee within an organization via an easy-to-navigate, comprehensive network devoted to internal business operations and extranets link an organization's external business partners with the same, comprehensive network, but one that is devoted to external business operations.

Just as Web portals are analogous to internal, private Webs, Web-based intranets are analogous to internal, private Internets. Access to data and applications contained within the intranet is restricted to authorized users. Restricted access to intranets by authorized users provides assurances that the general Internet public cannot access this private, secure network. However, through its intranet, a healthcare organization can access the Internet's servers for general Internet mail and messaging.

Like Web portals, Web-based intranets are growing at an astounding rate. They offer better security than use of the "public" Internet. Moreover, they are less expensive to implement and easier to use than most private networks of proprietary mail and messaging software products. In fact, today, intranets have become so important that almost every healthcare provider organization uses them as some form of development platform.

For example, private, secure networks provide every healthcare organization employee with basic information, such as message boards, employee handbooks, manuals, mail, cafeteria menus, newsletters, directories, and contact lists. Also, they are used for the development of the organization's EHR. Here, the challenge is to evolve from the intranet's "static," informational, and brochureware-based Web pages to "dynamic" Web pages where authorized intranet users can access the private network's Web-based applications from anywhere and at anytime. This requires a powerful, stable infrastructure that can handle the transmission of larger amounts of data and support dynamic applications during times of peak use. It also requires continuous management of all the information and content on the intranet so that its users can find what they need to do their jobs better and so that the intranet information is kept current.

Extranets connect intranets that exist outside an organization's firewall. For example, typically, an IDN's autonomous care facilities (for example, acute care, long-term care, home healthcare), each with its own intranet, need to communicate between and among themselves via secure e-mail or other collaboration tools. As such, the facilities connect the various intranets and form an extranet.

Another example is when organizations connect to their external suppliers of equipment or trading partners so that they can exchange information. In a hospital, the companies that supply medical equipment for the hospital can, with an extranet, "peer into" the **par levels** (the accepted, standard inventory levels for all supplies and equipment in an organization) of the hospital's supply inventory to determine when the various supply par levels are getting lower and it is time to reorder. Thus, forming an extranet prevents a hospital employee from having to check inventory and write a reorder. In this example, the hospital's supplier or trade partner can peer into only this portion of the hospital's intranet and automatically send the supplies when needed.

Web Content Management Systems

Publishing a few static or dynamic pages on an organization's intranet- or extranet-based Web site is relatively easy. However, getting a group of people to do this effectively is challenging. Getting many groups of people to create the pages, track the revisions, set up the workflow, and scale and secure the intranet and extranet's framework is quite difficult from an organizational perspective.

Web content management systems label and track the exponential increase in and variety of information that is placed on a Web site so that the information can be easily located, modified, and reused. These systems are a critical component in personalizing an organization's Web-based intranet and extranet, Web portal, and page content for site users and visitors. They also provide crucial versioning and globalization capabilities. *Versioning* enables each of the Web site's content components to be tracked individually. Then, as the content changes, each iteration of the content can be identified and the overall Web site can be recreated as it existed at any specific point in time. *Globalization* enables the look and feel of an organization's Web site to be managed centrally, while specific content is managed for local requirements, such as regional healthcare language or procedure differences.

Web Services

Web services technology is a platform for software applications (or services) whose basic communication mechanism is XML, the universal language of the Web and the accepted format for data exchange over the Internet. In addition, Web services technology utilizes Web-based infrastructure protocols, such as HTTP and transmission control protocol/Internet protocol (TCP/IP). As such, Web services technology allows programs written in different languages and on different operating systems to communicate with each other in a standards-based way. In other words, Web services technology is an open, standardized way of integrating disparate, Web browser-based and other applications.

By using XML messages to format and tag data, Web services technology allows for data interchange without the need for translation. In addition, the messages use system-independent vocabularies and protocols, such as Simple Object Access Protocols (SOAP), to transfer the data; Universal Description, Discovery, and Integration (UDDI) to list what services are available; and Web Services Description Language (WSDL) to describe the services available.

Unlike traditional Web-based client/server architecture, such as a Web server/Web page system, Web services technology does not provide the user with a GUI, such as the browser. Instead, it shares business logic, data, and processes through a programmatic interface across a network.

Healthcare organizations have been gradually installing Web services to ease integration of disparate Web-based and legacy applications, often written in incompatible languages. This ensures that the organizations' applications **interoperate** and that healthcare organizations can more easily choose tools for important interorganizational and regional data sharing. (See figure 3.2.)

Like other, traditional technologies and systems, Web-derived technologies and applications have inherent benefits. Similarly, the issues surrounding the successful deployment of the technologies and applications in healthcare provider organizations are complex. For example, technical hurdles that must be overcome in using intranets, portals, and Web content management systems are found at every point of the compass; some are obvious and some are hidden. More important, implementation of the business processes that breathe new life into healthcare organizations via these technologies and systems is difficult. Developing and using Web-derived technologies and applications takes time and commitment, usually without obvious, upfront, hard-dollar benefits.

Open Source Technology

Open source software products are applications whose source (human-readable) code is freely available to anyone who is interested in downloading the code. Advantages of **open source technology** include its availability, it extensibility to be customized, and the collaborative nature of the product in which a community of developers and users can interact, review and improve upon each other's ideas. Disadvantages of open source include the need for skilled developers within an organization to take advantage of the benefits noted earlier as well as a lack of dependable technical support.

Figure 3.2. Web services

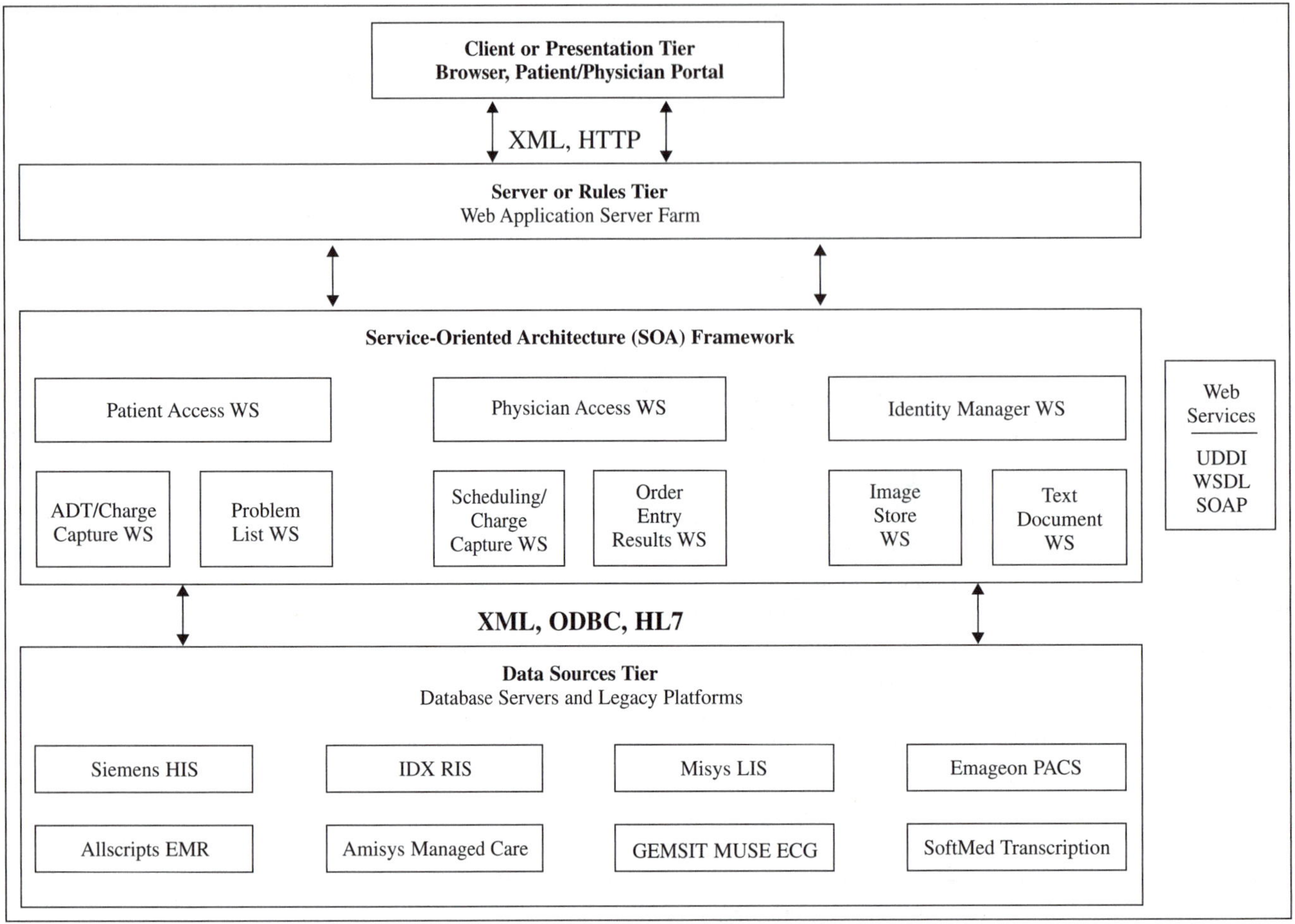

According to the open source definition maintained by Open Source Initiative (2006), 10 criteria must be met to qualify a software program as *open source*.

- Free redistribution: Free redistribution is allowed and royalty payments are prohibited.
- Source code: The program must include source code.
- Derived works: Modifications and derived works are allowed.
- Integrity of author's source code: The integrity of the original source code must be preserved.
- No discrimination against any person or groups: The license must not discriminate against any person or group.
- No discrimination against fields of endeavor: The license must not restrict anyone from making use of the program in a specific field of endeavor.
- Distribution of license: The license remains with the program even if it is redistributed.
- License must not be specific to a product: The rights attached to the program must not depend on the program's being part of a particular software distribution.
- License must not restrict other software: The license must not insist that all other programs distributed on the same medium must be open source software.
- License must be technology-neutral: No provision of the license may be predicated on any individual technology or style of interface.

Application Service Providers/Software as a Service

Application service providers (ASPs) are service firms that deliver, manage, and remotely host ("remote hosting" being a common term associated with ASPs) standardized (prepackaged) applications software through centralized servers via a network, not exclusively, but more commonly, the Internet. Also known as **Software as a Service** (SaaS), software is provided through an outsourcing contract. As such, the ASP/SaaS is viewed as a type of outsourcing. The contract is based on fixed, monthly usage, "rental-like" fees (for example, flat rate and per registered user fees) or transaction-based fees (for example, per transaction or percentage of revenue). The emphasis of this arrangement is on the functional use, rather than on the ownership, of a system (Nussbaum 2001, 3).

ASPs/SaaSs share many characteristics with the other types of outsourcing. The former service bureaus of the 1980s and 1990s, which provided remote time-sharing services, existed during a time when hardware costs and knowledge to operate the hardware were expensive and not widely available. Service bureaus were a type of outsourcing that allowed healthcare provider organizations to concentrate management attention on its core business of patient care and not become distracted or diverted into IT challenges.

Times changed, and the high connectivity costs plus substantial monthly fees associated with service bureaus became less attractive than smaller, more robust and flexible systems that could be operated locally. But the concept of outsourcing did not dissipate. The remote computing option became an extension of the service bureau concept. Currently, this type of outsourcing is offered by many of the major HIS vendors. The difference is that remote computing outsourcing requires a substantial cadre of healthcare organization–employed and local IT professionals to operate the organization's software while the system's hardware and software reside in the vendor's data center.

The appeal of the ASP/SaaS to both IT buyers and sellers is based on its position as a type of outsourcing somewhere between remote computing and full-asset outsourcing, which involves the transfer of all staff, long-term relationships, and accountability from internal IT management to a contracted third party. For example, major capital IT expenditures are the responsibility of the ASP/SaaS. Consequently, healthcare organizations no longer need to fund large, upfront IT expenditures. Traditionally, chief financial officers crafted leases or similar arrangements to help mitigate some of the cash flow impact of IT purchases. However, the ASP/SaaS is also responsible for all the systems' maintenance and upgrades, which, under a leasing arrangement, are the responsibility of the healthcare organization. In addition, the ASP/SaaS offers various payment methods, such as fixed monthly fees or transaction-based fees. Consequently, the ASP/SaaS outsourcing model permits a more predictable monthly cost, potentially over a shorter duration.

Since ASPs and SaaSs are both remotely hosted, today many people use the terms synonymously. However, if one were to technically differentiate the two, one could say that the ASP hosts one, individual instance of an application on one server. By contrast, the SaaS hosts several, different instances of an application on one server.

Although the ASP/SaaS model offers many benefits, a number of issues must be understood as detracting from its appeal. Perhaps the least favorable aspect of the ASP/SaaS outsourcing model is the likelihood that the healthcare organization must accept a standard, off-the-shelf product. For the ASP/SaaS to maintain its system efficiently and effectively for all its customers, often users are not allowed the level of customization or tailoring to which they are accustomed. Often healthcare organizations lose control on the time of system upgrades as well as the response time for changes to the software. The ASP/SaaS may be faced with conflicting priorities among its customers in terms of demand for specific features and functions.

Given the need for integration and interfacing between and among a healthcare organization's disparate ISs, it is not a trivial exercise to consider how to integrate and interface ASP/SaaS offerings into healthcare organizations' existing or future IT environments. Virtually all ASPs/SaaSs in healthcare limit their deliveries to their owned applications. Where multiple source applications are delivered and customer owned, virtually none is provided with a common user interface.

It is also not trivial to change an ASP/SaaS in the event it files for bankruptcy or no longer participates with its customers in a partner-based relationship. Last but not least, security is a major concern, with the healthcare organization still maintaining full responsibility for firewalls and HIPAA compliance.

Many ASP/SaaS delivery models reflect the application breadth, source, level of integration, interfaces, customer risks, and associated services. Thus, the delivery of the ASP/SaaS model varies based on the organization's current environment and value. Currently, the most significant targets for ASP/SaaS consideration appear to be healthcare provider organizations with smaller investments in IT or those that have difficulty retaining technical expertise and resources. This includes physician practices, small acute or specialty care facilities, and stand-alone clinics.

Check Your Understanding 3.4

Instructions: Answer the following questions on a separate piece of paper.

1. Provide a healthcare example for each of the following automatic recognition technologies: bar coding, OCR, ICR, RFID, and IDR.
2. How are the concepts of EDI, e-commerce, and e-health interrelated?
3. What is driving the heightened interest in EMPI technology within the healthcare industry?
4. What types of data are commonly maintained in an object-oriented database associated with a clinical data repository?
5. What is an ED/CM system? Explain the value of the following technologies: document-imaging technology, workflow and BPM technology, COLD/ERM technology, automated forms technology, and digital signature management technology.
6. Explain why secure clinical messaging is often preferred over real-time tools such as instant messaging or chats?
7. How are Web browser-based systems different from Web-enabled systems?
8. What is the primary purpose of the clinical workstation and the clinician/physician portal?
9. How do Web portals established by providers or payers assist consumers in taking a larger role in their healthcare?
10. What is the difference between an intranet and an extranet? Provide an example of how each can be used in healthcare.
11. Describe the benefits and drawbacks of open source technology.
12. What are the benefits and drawbacks of choosing to use the ASP/SaaS model for providing IT applications to a healthcare organization?

Supporting Managerial and Clinical Decision Making

Many current and emerging information technologies are used to support managerial and clinical decision making. For the purposes of this chapter, the following technologies and systems are highlighted:

- Data warehouses and data marts
- Decision support systems
- Artificial intelligence

Data Warehouses and Data Marts

Data warehouses are large, centralized, enterprise-wide collections of all the historical, demographic, and transactional data and information about businesses that are used to support managerial or, in the case of healthcare provider organizations, clinical decision-making processes. **Data warehousing** is the acquisition of all the business data and information from potentially multiple, cross-platform sources, such as legacy databases, departmental databases, and online transaction-based databases, and then the warehouse storage of all the data in one consistent format. **Data mining** is the probing and extracting of all the business data and information from the warehouse and then the quantifying and filtering of the data for analysis purposes.

Like data repositories, data warehouses are powerful databases. And, like data repositories, typically the format of the data in the warehouse is structured and the type of data is discrete.

However, the model of the data warehouse database is typically subject oriented. In other words, the data within the data warehouse are organized along subject lines (customer, product, patient, clinician) rather than along operational lines (accounting, management, medicine, surgery) in order to be accessible and useful across the enterprise. For example, healthcare provider organizations use data warehouses to centrally organize patient information, to establish wellness plans supporting community medicine, and to reduce costs.

In addition, the data are stored in the warehouse database using multidimensional tables rather than two-dimensional tables that create a relation as in relational databases. For example, if a surgeon performs a certain procedure several times during a period of time, the data query also may need to include the average length of stay (ALOS) for the procedure. Therefore, the warehouse data must be structured so that the identifying data (such as a procedure, time period, or ALOS) reside in the database dimension headers (which are comparable to the row and column headers of a spreadsheet) rather than being repeated for each record as in relational databases. This multidimensional model, sometimes referred to as a physical cube, lends itself to trend analysis and forecasting.

Generally, for day-to-day operations, a healthcare organization needs relatively current data and each operational unit needs only its own data. That is why relational and object-oriented database models for data repositories are well-suited for OLTP. But for large-scale, retrospective data analysis, for which **online/real-time analytical processing** (OLAP) is designed, a healthcare organization generally needs not just its current status, but also a historical record over time or time variance, encompassing all the organizational operating units by subject for comparison purposes.

In addition, for large-scale data analysis, a healthcare organization generally requires summary data, not detail data. Using the above surgeon and procedure example, the data query may need to know only the summary figure for the ALOS.

Finally, warehouse data, when correctly recorded, cannot be updated like repository data. Generally, only two kinds of operations occur in a data warehouse: data warehousing and data mining. This is referred to as the nonvolatility of warehouse data.

In healthcare, data warehouses have been used primarily for the following applications (Henchey 1998, 68):

- *Clinical management*: For example, every day, patient clinical data are fed into the warehouse from multiple sources to contribute to enterprise-wide best practices and to identify areas of excessive variation from best practices.
- *Operations management*: For example, sophisticated analytical tools, such as cost accounting, case-based budgeting, and variance analysis tools, are included with the warehouse to determine new healthcare market opportunities.
- *Outcomes management*: For example, data mining is conducted to study patient health status or other factors, such as satisfaction, that contribute to clinical outcomes.
- *Population management*: For example, to proactively manage the health of plan members, data mining helps the organization to predict utilization or identify at-risk members requiring case management.
- *Revenue management*: For example, the data warehouse assists healthcare financial analysts in addressing all the different contractual and regulatory reimbursement formulas. With revenue based on a mix of several dimensions, such as fee-for-service, capitation, and risk pooling, only the data warehouse can provide a complete picture of the enterprise's revenue stream and the factors controlling it.

A data warehouse cannot simply be bought and installed. Its implementation requires the integration of many products within its architecture. For example, often data warehouses require advanced data warehousing and mining techniques and tools. The software must be able to locate data that often are stored on multiple servers that may include any type of machine or operating system. The software must be able to maintain **metadata** (indexed data about the data), such as what indexes the acquired data uses. Further, the software must be able to recognize data duplication and exceptions as well as issue alerts when data are not present or have been corrupted.

Data marts can be thought of as miniaturized data warehouses. Data marts are usually geared to the needs of a specific department, group, or business operational unit. Because data marts are considerably smaller in both size and complexity than data warehouses, some healthcare organizations build data marts as a way of testing data warehouses on smaller, more focused scales. What many are finding, though, is that data marts can easily proliferate into a collection of incompatible data stores with accessibility or utility limited to the department or operational unit that designed the mart.

Decision Support Systems

Decision support systems (DSSs) are interactive computer systems that intend to help decision makers use data and models to identify and solve problems and make decisions. A great deal of innovation is occurring related to DSSs, and the technologies of which they are comprised are changing rapidly.

Generally, DSSs are based on either a data repository model or a data warehouse model. Both transfer data from an operational environment (either in real time or retrospectively, in batches at fixed intervals) to a decision-making environment, and both organize the data in a form suitable to decision support applications.

Power (1997) suggests that DSSs can be classified based on one or more of the following five categories:

- *Communications-driven DSSs* emphasize communications, collaboration, and shared decision-making support. A simple Internet bulletin board or threaded e-mail is the most elementary level of functionality in this type of DSS.
- *Data-driven DSSs* emphasize access to and manipulation of internal, and sometimes external, structured business data. Simple file systems accessed by query and retrieval tools provide the most elementary level of functionality in this type of DSS.
- *Document- or graphics-driven DSSs* focus on the retrieval and management of unstructured business data. Basic document- or graphics-driven DSSs exist in the form of Web-based search engines.
- *Knowledge-driven DSSs* can suggest or recommend actions to decision makers. These DSSs are person-to-computer systems with specialized problem-solving expertise. The expertise consists of knowledge about a particular domain, understanding of problems within that domain, and skill at solving some of those problems.
- *Model-driven DSSs* emphasize access to and manipulation of a model, for example, statistical, financial, optimization, and simulation models. Simple statistical and analytical tools provide the most elementary level of functionality in this type of DSS.

A wide variety of DSSs and related tools and technologies exist in healthcare, most of which can be classified as hybrids of the preceding categories. These systems include, but are not limited to, clinical/medical decision support systems, management information systems (MISs), executive information systems (EISs), geographic information systems (GISs), and expert decision support systems.

Clinical/Medical Decision Support Systems

Typically, **clinical/medical decision support systems** are data driven. They assist clinicians in applying new information to patient care through the analysis of patient-specific clinical/medical variables. Clinical/medical decision support systems can be characterized simply by providing reminders and alerts, clinical guideline advice, therapy critiquing, or benchmarking tools. However, many of these systems are used to enhance diagnostic efforts and, thus, quality of care, by including computer programs that provide extensive differential diagnoses based on the clinical/medical data and information entered by the clinician (Barnett et al. 1987). Many systems streamline workflow processes and enhance efficiencies. Other forms of clinical/medical decision support systems seek to prevent medical errors and improve patient safety. These DSSs include tools such as antibiotic management programs and anticoagulation dosing calculators (Hunt et al. 1998).

For years, clinical/medical decision support systems have been the subject of industry criticism. Clinicians complain that the system tools often are populated with general, textbook-type information that is not actionable or that the tools contain too much information that distracts the clinicians. Also, some systems simply do not blend well into care processes and are perceived as a source of additional work by already busy clinicians. In some instances, the tools are so complicated that clinicians cannot use them effectively. In addition, often the systems have been architected and executed only partially, resulting in limited functionality and unmet expectations (Krohn 2004).

Management Information Systems

Typically, **management information systems** (MISs) refer to the broad range of data-, document-, or knowledge-driven DSSs that provide information concerned with an organization's administrative functions (in other words, those functions that are associated with the provision and utilization of services). In addition, DSS-based MISs enable management to interrogate the computer on an ad hoc basis for various kinds of information within the organization so as to predict the effect of potential decisions. As such, DSS-based MISs provide information to people who must query these systems to make disposition decisions about valuable resources in a timely, accurate, and complete manner. Such systems are crucial for the effective administration of any organization and include, but are not limited to, general accounting and financial systems, customer relationship management (CRM) systems, enterprise resource planning (ERP) systems, and operations and plant management systems.

Executive Information Systems

Executive information systems (EISs) are DSSs that support the decision making of senior managers. As such, they provide direct online access to timely, accurate, and actionable information about aspects of a business that are of particular interest to a senior healthcare manager. Typically, this information is provided in a useful and navigable format so that managers can identify broad strategic issues and then explore the information to find the root causes of those issues. According to Kelly (2001), the following EIS features and functions are essential:

- Specifically tailored to executives' information needs
- Capable of accessing data about specific issues and problems
- Capable of aggregating data into meaningful reports
- Provide extensive online analysis tools, including trend analysis, exception reporting, and drill-down or data-mining capabilities
- Capable of accessing a broad range of internal and external data
- Easy to use (typically mouse or touch screen driven)
- Capable of being used directly by executives without assistance
- Capable of presenting information in a graphical form

Geographic Information Systems

In the strictest sense, **geographic information systems** (GISs) are DSSs capable of assembling, storing, manipulating, and displaying geographically referenced data and information. In other words, GISs identify data according to their locations. The applications of GIS in healthcare extend from practical community-based services to sophisticated studies on a global scale. For example, pediatricians consult community-based GISs to observe neighborhoods with high concentrations of lead and decide whether lead screenings would be appropriate for certain patients.

Expert Decision Support Systems

Expert decision support systems (also referred to as systems that use principles of artificial intelligence) use a set of rules or encoded concepts to construct a reasoning process. Such rules or concepts are based on knowledge developed from consultation with experts on a problem and the processing or formalizing of this knowledge in such a manner that the problem can be solved. In other words, expert DSSs provide the kind of problem analysis and advice that an expert might provide if he or she were present as a consultant.

Some of the various rules-based processing techniques used by expert DSSs are neural networks and data mining, defined earlier in this chapter. Other techniques include (Siwicki 1996, 47):

- *Fuzzy logic:* A rules-based system that mimics human thought and enables a computer to "think" in inexact terms rather than in a definitive, either-or manner
- *Genetic algorithms:* Tools that examine data and determine by programmed stipulations which data best match a stated goal and which data do not
- *Symbolic reasoning:* A method of deduction that follows an explicit line of inferences

Expert systems "learn" based on the continual addition of data to the system. Therefore, in its simplest model, the technologies of speech recognition or ICR can be considered expert. These technologies adapt themselves into shifting configurations based on what they encounter, and they change as they grow and learn.

Artificial Intelligence

In other disciplines and industries, the term *artificial intelligence* is often used synonymously with the term *expert decision support systems*. Because expert decision support systems, especially those using neural network techniques, "learn" as humans do by processing information through recognizing patterns of signals, there are only a few differentiators.

The field of **artificial intelligence** (AI) is the branch of computer science concerned with endowing computers with the ability to simulate human intelligence and behavior. As such, AI attempts to understand intelligence and intelligent entities and then design computer systems to perform functions normally associated with language, learning, reasoning, and problem solving.

This involves developing systems that think and act like humans. This human-centered approach to AI involves empirical science, which, in turn, involves hypothesis creation and experimental confirmation. This also involves developing systems that think and act rationally. A rationalist approach to AI involves a combination of mathematics and engineering.

Exploring and furthering the application of AI to clinical situations is lofty because of the vital and crucial nature of medical science as well as the need for accurate and timely data and information to support clinical decisions. Consequently, AI to support clinical decision making focuses on the gathering, availability, security, and use of medical information throughout the human life cycle and beyond.

Check Your Understanding 3.5

Instructions: Answer the following questions on a separate piece of paper.

1. What features differentiate a data warehouse from a data repository?
2. What is the primary difference between expert decision support systems and, more common in healthcare, clinical decision support systems?
3. What functional capabilities are associated with applications that use artificial intelligence technology?

Supporting the Diagnosis, Treatment, and Care of Patients

Many current and emerging information technologies are used to support the diagnosis, treatment, and care of patients.

For the purposes of this chapter, the following technologies are highlighted:

- Physiological signal processing systems
- Point-of-care information systems
- Mobile and wireless technology and devices
- Automated care plans, clinical practice guidelines, clinical pathways, and protocols
- Telemedicine/telehealth
- Electronic health record (EHR) systems
- Computer-based patient information and education

Physiological Signal Processing Systems

The human body is a rich source of signals that carry vital information about underlying physiological processes. Traditionally, such signals have been used in clinical diagnosis as well as in the study of the functional behavior of internal organs.

Earlier in this chapter, **physiological signal processing systems**, such as ECG, EEG, EMG, and fetal trace systems, were mentioned because these systems store data based on the body's signals and create output based on the lines plotted between the signals' points. The data type used by these systems is referred to as signal tracing or vector graphic data.

Physiological signal processing systems measure biological signals. Also, they help to integrate the medical science of analyzing the signals with such disciplines as biomedical engineering, computer graphics, mathematics, diagnostic image processing, computer vision, and pattern recognition. The integration of these disciplines allows these systems to electronically compile measurement equations, estimate the signals' parameters, and characterize the feedback elements. For example, the computer-based analysis of the neuromuscular system, the definition of cardiovascular system models, the control of cardiac pacemakers, the regulation of blood sugar levels, and the development of artificial organs not only serve patient diagnostic and care purposes, but they also support the development and simulation of instrumentation for physiological research and clinical investigation.

Point-of-Care Information Systems

Computer systems that allow healthcare providers to capture and retrieve data and information at the location where the healthcare service is performed have come a long way since hard-wired computer terminals with green screens were first placed at the patient's bedside more than 25 years ago. Functionally, almost every type of patient clinical and administrative application has been introduced to provide care services at the bedside, in the exam room, at the home, or even on the patient, as in medical monitoring. Technologically, massive changes have occurred in these systems' platforms, footprints, and networking capabilities.

For example, many acute care facilities have installed clinical **point-of-care information systems** that, among other services, provide online medication order entry, profiles, administration schedules, and records. The records include information about medications not given (with reasons) as well as related information such as fluid balances, physical assessments, laboratory test results, and vital signs. All medications, including unit doses, are bar coded and scanned at or near the patient's bedside along with the patient's wristband and the caregiver's identification badge. This prompts a safety edit, documents administration of the medication, and generates the charge. Other acute care facilities have installed administrative point-of-care (or service) systems that have eliminated admitting areas. Inpatients are greeted at the door with their room assignments, and roving admissions representatives visit patients in the assigned rooms to complete all the admission procedures.

Typically, point-of-care information systems use portable, handheld, wireless devices to enable entry of the data by a bar code scanner, keypad, or touch screen. Also, the devices are used to upload and download information to and from hard-wired workstations. Retrieval of the data occurs at the wireless device or on wall-mounted or portable, cart-based computers. The data also can be entered and retrieved on hard-wired workstations located in areas outside the point of care, such as central areas at patient care units, back offices, central or satellite pharmacies, and physician lounges, homes, and offices.

Mobile and Wireless Technology and Devices

Perhaps the biggest influence on, as well as challenge for, point-of-care information systems and their use comes from recent, significant advances in **wireless technology** and smaller, mobile devices. For the healthcare industry, the successful integration of wireless technology and smaller, mobile devices with point-of-care software supports and enhances the clinician's decision-making processes.

True wireless systems use wireless networks and wireless devices to access and transmit data in real time. At the basic level, wireless technology is based on the use of radio waves. For the purposes of this chapter, the technology is divided into two categories: (1) regulated and unregulated, and (2) wide area and in-building.

For the general benefit of the country, Congress has charged the Federal Communications Commission (FCC) with regulation of the radio spectrum. This regulation encompasses licenses for the use of the radio frequencies for commercial radio, television, walkie-talkies, and mobile telephones. Specific portions of the radio spectrum may be assigned to specific users, such as individual radio stations, or set aside for general and usually low power use, such as citizens' band (CB) radio.

For years, healthcare organizations have used in-building wireless point-of-care information systems, such as telemetry systems. These systems were based on existing technologies and use a portion of the radio spectrum reserved for industrial, scientific, and medical purposes (ISM band). Individual licenses are not required for these types of systems.

Also, provider organizations have long used wide-area wireless technology to support ISs, such as point-of-care systems. This technology involves microwave systems that are based on fixed, point-to-point wireless technology used to connect buildings in a campus network. Microwave systems are regulated and require licenses and compliance with FCC procedures.

Until recently, most in-building wireless systems were proprietary. However, adoption of the IEEE 802.11 wireless technology standard has begun to provide a reasonable level of standardization. The IEEE 802.11 standard allows data transmission speeds up to 11 megabits per second, is relatively low power, and does not require licenses for installation and use. The IEEE 802.11b is an international standard that provides a method for wireless connectivity to fixed and portable devices within a local area. As such, this standard allows interoperability among multiple vendor products.

But it is the widespread adoption of cellular telephone technology that has significantly advanced the development of wireless technology and, consequently, its support for point-of-care systems. A brief look at most healthcare organizations today turns up mobile phones, two-way pagers, Internet-enabled telephones (also known as smart phones), and **personal digital assistants** (PDAs).

Currently, the majority of these mobile devices are used to meet personal, individual needs. For wireless technology and the smaller mobile devices to be integrated into larger corporate projects such as point-of-care information systems, they must significantly enhance the function and use of existing ISs. Ironically, existing ISs in use by healthcare provider organizations, including point-of-care information systems, were not designed to support clinician workflow but, instead, were developed to automate specific functions, as previously described. As a result, often clinicians must access multiple systems to retrieve the information they need and spend 10 minutes each day simply logging on.

On the other hand, mobile devices improve this paradigm by allowing clinicians to use a device personalized to their individual workflows, such as clinical (for example, e-prescribing), dictation, and billing workflows, not functions. In addition, mobile devices provide clinicians the information they need anytime, anywhere, and on any network-addressable device.

Therefore, increasingly, healthcare organizations are taking advantage of wireless technology and mobile devices. Impediments that have prevented a more widespread use of the technology and devices for point-of-care systems and other workflows include:

- Impediments preventing widespread use of wireless technology
  - Vendor difficulty in packaging wireless technology with specific clinical software applications that demonstrate a significant return on investment and add value to the clinician
  - The use of proprietary wireless technology
  - Inconsistent technology deployment
  - The need to make a large investment for the deployment of wireless technology on a wide scale
  - The need to make a large investment for the underlying network infrastructure to support wireless technology
- Impediments preventing widespread use of smaller, portable, point-of-care devices
  - Battery life, including how and when batteries will be recharged
  - Device weight and where the devices will be stored when not in use
  - Securing the device(s) (for example, requiring that all such devices are encrypted with secure passwords; this simple step might eliminate what is today one of the largest sources of data breaches when these devices are lost or misplaced.)
  - Screen real estate
  - Application functionality (for example, how the data are delivered in bits and are not presented in a page-oriented fashion, how the processing of the data must be transactional, and how an abundance of frivolous graphics or poor-quality content cannot be tolerated)

Automated Clinical Care Plans, Practice Guidelines, Pathways, and Protocols

The terms used to describe practice mandates, care process guides and documents, disease management (also known as chronic care improvement), decision algorithms, and quality improvement tools are not well standardized. They tend to be used informally and interchangeably, resulting in miscommunication among healthcare professionals.

Consequently, when **clinical care plans**, practice guidelines, pathways, and protocols are automated and used by multidisciplinary teams, patient care can be affected unless the definitions are uniformly applied. For example:

- Healthcare providers create clinical care plans for individual patients for a specific time period. Typically, clinical care plans are based on provider training.
- Clinical practice guidelines are recommendations based on systematic statements or clinical algorithms of proven care options. Often professional organizations and associations, health plans, and government agencies such as the Agency for Health Care Policy and Research develop these guidelines.
- For a specific time period, clinical (or critical) pathways or **CareMaps** delineate standardized, day-to-day courses of care for a group of patients with the same diagnosis or procedure to achieve consistent outcomes. Typically, pathways or CareMaps are developed by the local healthcare organization or health plan.
- Clinicians often use the term *protocol* to refer to the written documents that guide or specify a practice, including **clinical practice guidelines** and **clinical pathways**. Strictly speaking, however, protocols are more detailed

care plans for individual patients based on investigations performed by professional societies, drug companies, or individual researchers (Bufton 1999, 258).

Providers now recognize the enormous variation in how they diagnose, treat, and care for patients. Consequently, there is a trend to adopt **evidence-based medicine** and **outcomes management** based on more use of guidelines, formalized pathways, and protocols. Automating these guidelines, pathways, and protocols for easier access and use is the first step. Also, there is a trend to incorporate care plans into providers' notes. This is being recognized as automated clinical documentation systems are being introduced into and used by more healthcare organizations.

In short, care plans, guidelines, pathways, and protocols, as well as formularies and other knowledge bases, are becoming automated for easier access and use and for easier maintenance. In particular, practice guidelines and knowledge bases that are available through subscriptions from agencies, societies, and research companies can be kept more current because users can incorporate periodic downloads into their transaction-based or analytic systems.

The challenge for automated care plans, practice guidelines, pathways, and protocols is that, like clinical workstations and Web portals, no one form of clinical documentation or one view of the information suits everyone or all situations. For example, the wide variability of clinical documentation is obvious in H&Ps versus consultations. Such documentation suits some providers, but not others, or some situations, but not all. Similarly, views of data are requested in page, narrative, table, flowchart, or graphic formats. Therefore, automated plans, guidelines, pathways, and protocols require customization capabilities to help individuals and groups better share knowledge to reach similar decisions about patient care. Automated drawing tools and anatomical diagrams are other documentation options.

Another challenge is that it is difficult to convert intricate clinical care processes and guideline, pathway, and protocol content into computer architecture. An even higher level of complexity occurs when the content is merged with reengineered processes, instead of just automating the existing or status quo processes. This is because these actions represent a translation of specific and conceptual clinical information and interpretations into data fields. Therefore, it is recommended that clinicians work with IS analysts, such as health information managers, to ensure that the integrity of the clinical content is preserved during the conversion.

In addition, the task of seamlessly embedding reminders, alerts, or defaulted, guideline-based clinical orders into ISs as well as the care processes is challenging. According to Bufton (1999, 266), this requires in-depth knowledge of the following:

- Computer system's capabilities and limitations, such as data dictionaries, field lengths, screen builders, and data retrieval, analysis, and reporting capabilities
- Processes of care, local caseloads, and local practice environments
- Many diverse guidelines, pathways, and protocols

Telemedicine/Telehealth

Interactive, patient–provider consultations across gulfs of time and space represent what is often referred to as classic telemedicine or telehealth. However, the field has always encompassed a plethora of strategies for moving clinical knowledge and expertise instead of moving people. As such, telemedicine/telehealth systems, like EHR systems, are concepts made up of several cost-effective technologies used to bridge geographic gaps between patients and providers.

In other words, telemedicine/telehealth is not videoconferencing technology. Rather, it is clinically adequate, interactive, media conferencing (for example, video conferencing) integrated with other technologies. It can be dynamic and include interactive (or real-time processing) technology, or it can be static and include store-and-forward (or batch processing) technology. It includes telecommunications and remote control-based biomedical technologies. It utilizes in-room systems, roll-abouts, desktop systems, and handheld units. Often it is integrated with component technologies of the EHR system and derived technologies of the Internet. The access and ability to transmit patient records and the integration with reference databases on the Internet all play into the telemedicine/telehealth model.

Telemedicine/telehealth is not a new way to deliver healthcare. It takes existing ways of delivering healthcare and enhances them, such as enhancing patient–provider consultations via "electronic house calls." It extends care to underserved populations, whether they are located in rural or urban areas, and redefines the healthcare organization's community. It transfers clinical information between places of lesser and greater medical capability and expertise.

Like medicine in general, telemedicine/telehealth technology is made up of a number of specialties and subspecialties. Some examples include:

- Telecardiology
- Teledermatology
- Telehome healthcare
- Teleneurology
- Telenursing healthcare
- Teleophthalmology
- Telepathology
- Telepsychiatry
- Teleradiology
- Telesurgery

The telemedicine/telehealth specialty that has been around for the longest time and, perhaps, is the most notable is teleradiology. Even today, spurred by a rising demand for sophisticated imaging tests as well as a smaller pool of radiologists from which to recruit, teleradiology is taking advantage of the speedy Internet transfer of medical data to outsourced, foreign radiologists who provide preliminary interpretations of scans during their normal business hours. In addition, since the early 1990s, the University of Pittsburgh Medical Center, the Mayo Clinic, and other prestigious provider organizations have employed dynamic telepathology interactions. Teleradiology and telepathology specialties are considered first-generation telemedicine/telehealth systems and services because they do not rely on patient interaction.

The second-generation telemedicine/telehealth systems and services involve those specialties relying on patient interaction and consultations. These include teleophthalmology, telepsychiatry, telehome healthcare, and so on.

The latest generation of telemedicine/telehealth systems and services involves patient interaction beyond the consultation. For example, in October 2001, telesurgeons in New York City performed the world's first complete (that is, from start to finish) telesurgery by successfully operating on the gallbladder of a patient in France. This was accomplished by sending high-speed signals through fiber-optic cables across the Atlantic Ocean to robots in a Strasbourg clinic.

As both a clinical and technological endeavor, telemedicine/telehealth plays a key role in the integration of managing patient care and in the more efficient management of the information systems that support it. However, overcoming multiple technical challenges remains a concern. These challenges include the lack of systems interoperability and network integration as well as metropolitan broad bandwidth limitations. Other challenges that require overcoming complex behavioral, economic, and ethical constraints are physician resistance; lack of consistent, proven cost-effectiveness; lack of consistent, proven medical effectiveness; and concerns for safety.

Electronic Health Record (EHR) Systems

In 1991, the Institute of Medicine (IOM) defined the computer-based patient record (CPR) as "an electronic patient record that resides in a system specifically designed to support users by providing accessibility to complete and accurate data, alerts, reminders, clinical decision support systems, links to medical knowledge, and other aids" (Dick and Steen 1991, 11). Fortunately, by the end of the millennium, a common definition of the CPR was under way by various groups: a system consisting of "electronically stored information about an individual's lifetime health status and healthcare. It replaces the paper medical record as the primary record of care, meeting all clinical, legal and administrative requirements. . . . [It] provides reminders and alerts, linkages with knowledge sources for decision support, and data for outcomes research and improved management of healthcare delivery" (Dick et al.1997, 11).

Fortunately, there also was agreement that the CPR system was not one or even two or more products. According to Dick and Steen, the CPR system is a "set of components that form the mechanism by which patient records are created, used, stored and retrieved. . . . It includes people, data, rules and procedures, processing and storage devices, and communication and support facilities" (1991, 12). The CPR system is "an evolving concept that responds to the dynamic nature of the healthcare environment and takes advantages of technological advances" (Dick et al. 1997, 11). In other words, the CPR system is a concept consisting of an array of integrated, component information systems and technologies.

However, only within the last few years did a universal understanding of the CPR system's components emerge, and, along with that, a new, universal term for the CPR system: the electronic health record (EHR) system. In a recent report, the National Alliance for Health Information Technology (NAHIT) defines both the **electronic medical record** (EMR) and the EHR. An EMR is defined as, "an electronic record of health-related information on an individual that can be created, gathered, managed, and consulted by authorized clinicians and staff within one healthcare organization." (NAHIT 2008, 6) An EHR is defined as, "an electronic record of health-related information on an individual that conforms to nationally recognized interoperability standards and that can be created, managed, and consulted by authorized clinicians and staff across more than one healthcare organization." (NAHIT 2008, 6). Over time, it is expected that the term *EMR* will become obsolete due to the ultimate requirement for interoperability.

During summer 2003, the IOM was commissioned to provide an EHR System (EHR-S) Functional Needs and Priority by Care Settings model for a standardized EHR. In addition, HHS enlisted the Health Level 7 (HL7) standards development organization to create an EHR-S Functional Model and Standard based on the findings of the IOM and to ballot the Functional Model and Standard by 2004. (HL7 is the organization that develops, by a voluntary consensus process, standards for patient *clinical* electronic data interchange. Founded in 1987, HL7 consists of a large, broad healthcare IT membership. In addition, HL7 was accredited in 1994 by the International Standards Organization's [ISO] American National Standards Institute [ANSI].) During spring 2004, HL7's second Draft Standard for Trial Use on the EHR-S Functional Model and Standard was passed by its members. After a period of two years wherein the draft standard was tested, it was balloted and adopted as a fully accredited standard. Today this accredited standard serves as one of the resources to the Certification Commission for Healthcare Information Technology's (CCHIT's) development of EHR functional criteria.

The significance of this achievement cannot be understated. The EHR-S Functional Model and Standard laid the foundation for the first-generation, standards-based EHR and defined the system's components as elements of an IT infrastructure by which the patient's EHR is created and managed. This infrastructure represents an aggregation of information from multiple, often disparate, databases and systems within and across the healthcare enterprise. It incorporates a messaging standard for common representation of all pertinent patient data. Stored data are indexed with sufficient detail to support retrieval for patient care delivery, management, and analysis. It includes hardware, application software, system software, user interfaces, networks, communications protocols, and so on.

EHR System Infrastructure

Technically, the EHR system infrastructure consists of multiple **physical data repositories**. Typically, these repositories are organized into data fields, data records, and data files. They store structured, discrete, clinical, administrative, and financial data as well as unstructured, patient free-text, bitmapped, real audio, streaming video, or vector graphic data. They must be linked to form one **logical (or conceptual) repository**. Typically, the EMPI primary index keys constitute these links. (See figure 3.3.)

Technically, the EHR system infrastructure also consists of multiple data types, information systems, software applications, and technologies. Examples of multiple data types were given earlier in this chapter. Examples of multiple information systems include most of those discussed in this chapter, such as clinical information systems, HISs, ambulatory care information systems, electronic document and content management systems, picture archive and communication systems, telemedicine systems, patient appointment and resource scheduling systems, physiological signal processing systems, registration and eligibility and enrollment systems, and DSSs. Examples of multiple software applications and technologies also include most of those discussed in this chapter, such as workflow and secure messaging software, security and access to ITs, single log-on software, Web-derived technologies, and digital or electronic signature software.

Today, most healthcare organizations have installed at least one or more EHR system infrastructure component technologies or systems. However, unfortunately, the existing components may not be integrated or interfaced.

Typically, several EHR system infrastructure components are implemented in healthcare organizations in parallel. Solely technical attributes of EHR system infrastructure component systems and technologies must not be considered when determining whether and when to implement the various components. Instead, the value of the component to improve the quality of patient care, the fiscal priorities of the organization, the available technical and organizational resources, and the unique business motives and strategies of the organization must be considered.

EHR System Attributes and EHR System Functionality Standards

The 1991 IOM report identified 12 attributes for the CPR system. These attributes represented the elements essential to provide the required functionality that would support healthcare providers with a robust CPR system.

Since then, the attributes have been revised and expanded, most notably those included in the EHR-S Functional Model and Standard. (The EHR-S Functional Model and Standard is discussed in detail in chapter 9.) However, for historical context, it is important to review the original CPR system attributes so that HIM professionals can ensure their completeness as tools with enhanced utility for providing high-quality patient care in light of the ever-changing healthcare environment and technological advances.

Following are the 1991 IOM report's 12 attributes for the CPR system (Dick and Steen 1991):

- Offers a problem list
- Measures health status and functional levels (in other words, it measures clinical outcomes)
- Documents clinical reasoning and the rationale for patient care decisions
- Provides longitudinal and timely linkages with other patient records
- Protects the privacy of the individual by guaranteeing that the information is confidential (in other words, indicating that the information is sensitive) and the confidential information is secure (for example, by providing audit trail capabilities)

Figure 3.3. Physical and logical data repositories for CPR systems

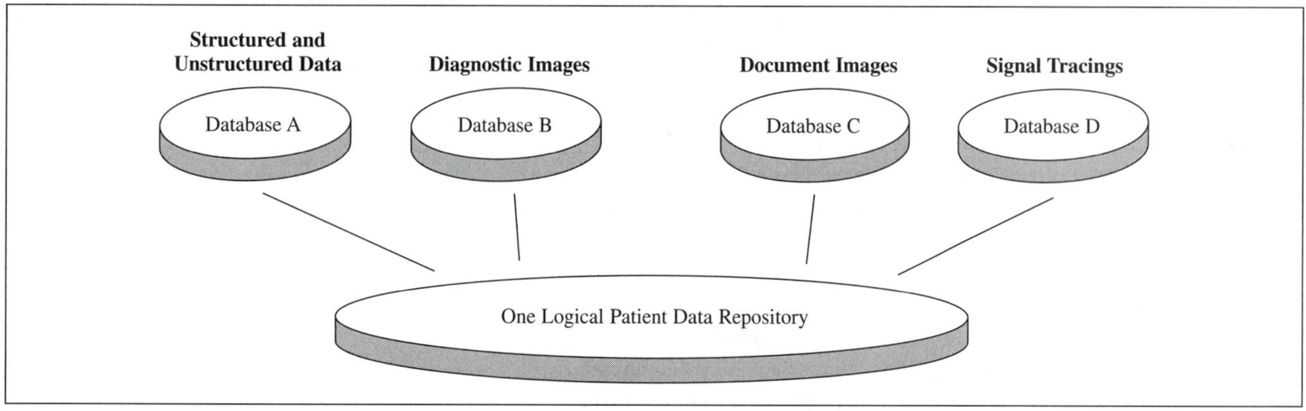

- Provides continuous, authorized user access
- Supports simultaneous, multiple user views into the CPR
- Supports timely access to local and remote information resources
- Facilitates clinical problem solving, using specific rule sets or decision support systems
- Supports direct data entry by providers of care, especially physicians
- Supports practitioners in measuring or managing costs and improving quality
- Is flexible to support existing and evolving clinical specialty needs

According to Dick and Andrews (1995, 66, 78), revised and expanded CPR system attributes were considered crucial to the establishment of robust CPR (and now, EHR) systems. If any one of the attributes were ignored or inadequately addressed in the design and development of the CPR system, the CPR might be jeopardized. Some of these subattributes include:

- A substantial, flexible, and extensible clinical data dictionary.
- A well-designed CDR so that the CDR is capable of supporting the extensive and diverse needs of all healthcare practitioners.
- An array of powerful input capabilities to allow for the direct data entry of caregivers at the point of care.
- A user-friendly, ergonomically designed presentation of the information for all intended users, including a presentation tailored to the type of individual and to personal preferences.
- Automated, intelligent support that anticipates and facilitates all clinical processes and thinking.

Current Status of Electronic Health Record Systems

No one disputes the fact that EHR systems have the potential to improve care quality and patient safety at lower costs. Furthermore, technologically, the chances of realizing the EHR vision are better today than ever before, primarily thanks to the advent of the Internet and its derived technologies model. As such, much can be done today to prepare and continue to implement the EHR system's component systems and technologies.

However, today, several years after the original IOM report, EHR systems remain far from the various standards for patient medical records. In addition, it is anticipated that still more years will pass before most healthcare organizations fully install EHR systems and, therefore, fully realize the systems' potential. "Recent surveys suggest that EHR implementation was between 17 to 24 percent in physicians' offices in an ambulatory setting. EHR use in any format in hospital settings was estimated to be 20 to 25 percent, and the use of computerized physician order entry (CPOE) was about 15 percent." (Houser and Johnson 2008).

Some HIT professionals argue that, as originally defined and agreed to, a CPR/EHR system is not what is needed and that the system's objective should not be a theoretical ideal or concept but, rather, a focus on specific patient care processes and related systems and technologies that produce immediate, clear benefits and value (Drazen 2001). For example, implementing clinical DSSs, CPOE systems, medication administration systems, and patient registry systems can provide huge advantages in patient care and safety.

On the other hand, most HIT professionals agree that the biggest challenge in implementing all the processes and related systems and technologies is the inability to seamlessly share information between the various systems and technologies, even with well-established messaging and other standards. This lack of systems interoperability has been caused by the standards' lack of information models for the management of the data, leading to enormous standards flexibility. As such, this flexibility has led most healthcare IS developers to interpret and implement the standards in a conflicting, nonuniform, and proprietary manner. Therefore, despite significant standards development and compliance efforts, healthcare organizations have been left with thwarted attempts for reliable, quick, and cost-effective EHR systems.

Some HIT professionals argue that interoperability must precede any EHR use. They view the risk of implementing processes and systems as an opportunity that might lead irreversibly to treatment of health information as a proprietary asset of delivery systems. They believe that if standards are not solidified and built into EHR systems now, a generation of investment will be wasted (Brailer 2005).

To address this issue, the Healthcare Information Technology Standards Panel (HITSP) was founded in 2005, to serve as a cooperative partnership between the public and private sectors for the purpose of achieving a widely accepted and useful set of standards to enable and support widespread interoperability among healthcare software applications. The Panel's work is driven by a series of priorities issued by the American Health Information Community (AHIC). HITSP produces recommendations and reports which are intended to be applicable to the developing Nationwide Health Information Network for the United States (NHIN), as well as to community and regional HIE networks (Healthcare Information Technology Standards 2008).

Another challenge is that EHR system quantitative returns on investment have not been consistently demonstrated. Consequently, there remains a bewildering array of EHR initiatives, activities, and debates, with only a few proving to be good assessment vehicles. For example, provider organizations continue to buy huge, difficult-to-implement systems from one large vendor for millions of dollars, which does little to restore the confidence that there will be a future market for other, more focused products, especially those products that must focus on smaller provider organizations, such as physician offices.

As long as the healthcare industry continues to do this and as long as interoperability remains elusive, EHR systems will advance, but not quickly or cost-effectively.

Computer-based Patient Information and Education

During the past decade, the use of e-commerce (in other words, the use of the Internet and its derived technologies to integrate all aspects of business-to-business and business-to-consumer activities, processes, and communications) has transformed every vertical market industry. In the healthcare industry, the following examples illustrate this transformation:

- Increasing numbers of patients access the Internet for information about healthcare providers, treatment options, and personal health information (PHI).
- Health Web sites provide patients with tools to develop and maintain personal, online health records independent of providers.
- Healthcare providers and patients correspond via e-mail, with each viewing and contributing information to the health record.
- Health plans, disease-specific groups, and professional associations use Web sites to provide education and interact with patients.

E-Health

Simply stated, e-health is the application of e-commerce to the healthcare industry. E-health offers businesses and consumers the opportunity to provide or engage in a number of services, including:

- PHRs
- Patient appointment scheduling
- Patient registration
- Previsit health screening, evaluations, and assessments
- Postvisit patient education
- Information on health conditions, diseases, wellness, or new healthcare developments
- Support for handheld, point-of-care devices

E-health offers businesses and consumers clear, potential benefits, including:

- Enabling patients and staff to do more with less support
- Streamlining managed care contract administration, EDI, and claims processing
- Building relationships and brand equity with patients, physicians, and affiliated providers
- Improving access to vital patient information
- Reducing care costs
- Improving care delivery
- Building market image and position
- Improving employee productivity and morale
- Facilitating pharmaceutical research, clinical trials, and regulatory submission
- Promoting direct contact with patients

Healthcare organizations must be able to provide high-quality services through e-health to realize the preceding benefits. Although most organizations have the necessary technology to provide these services, e-health initiatives are often hindered by an organization's culture to accept the profound changes that e-health can bring about.

Following are key qualities required of an e-health culture:

- *Quick*: The growth of e-health requires that organizations respond more quickly to communications from patients and customers. Because of e-health technologies' speed and ease of use, the people served by healthcare organizations have come to expect equally fast replies. To promote this level of speed within the organization's culture, healthcare professionals must support and encourage quick decision making, helping the organization to become accustomed to a faster pace of operation.
- *Patient focused and service oriented*: Although all healthcare organizations are in the business of serving people, many information systems still are not truly patient focused and thus not e-compatible. As e-health technologies continue to allow patients to seek help through a wider variety of sources, organizations that, in the past, did not provide high-quality service through patient-centered systems are going to fall behind. To promote greater patient focus and service orientation in the organization's culture, healthcare professionals must determine where the service shortcomings lie and then make the necessary improvements. For example, a new e-health-based patient appointment and resource scheduling system will not enhance patient service if patients still have to wait an hour to be seen by a provider after they arrive at the point of service.
- *Partnership-friendly*: To implement many of the e-health technologies and systems to support the delivery of healthcare and the management and communication of health data within the healthcare organization, many partnerships and outsourcing relationships with vendors have developed. To promote better relationships with these partners, healthcare organizations must develop other partnerships for purposes other than technology. As such, an organization that is comfortable working with all kinds of partners has a much broader range of tools available because it employs high-tech means to improve service to patients.

As the wave of e-health continues, the challenge to HIM professionals is clear. They can understand the potential of e-health in the industry and can control and direct its power to the benefit of their customers, health plan members, and patients. Or they can allow the technologies to roll uncontrolled through and around their organizations (for example, not establishing strict policies and procedures for PHI included in e-mail messages). If they choose the latter, they will effectively hand over their rich knowledge base and expert skills to faster-moving, better-focused professionals, some of whom may not even exist yet.

Consumer Health

E-commerce and e-health are the key contributors to a more consumer-driven healthcare delivery system. To address this development, many organizations are gearing their healthcare delivery approaches toward **consumer health**; that is, providing services that accommodate a more knowledgeable patient while helping them to become more informed and to participate as a partner in their own healthcare. Not only do patients have access to medical information and content online, but they also have access to tools that allow them to better manage their own health information. For example, AHIMA has turned its focus to consumer education through its production of a public education presentation kit titled "Your Personal Health Information: How to Access, Manage, and Protect It" (MyPHR 2008). The kit provides HIM leaders with complete materials for an hour-long presentation to the general public (AHIMA e-HIM Personal Health Record Work Group 2005). In addition, companies like Microsoft and Google have developed free, Web-based programs to help consumers store and manage their health information. Consumer health is driving the healthcare and technology industries to use their creative efforts to offer electronic solutions that further engage patients and permit them to be successful managers of their own health.

Personal Health Records

Personal health records (PHRs) electronically populate elements or subsets of PHI from provider organization databases into the electronic records of authorized patients, their families, other providers, and sometimes health payers and employers. A range of people and groups maintain the records, including the patients, their families, and other providers. The development of PHRs parallels the consumer-centrism described earlier and long evident in other vertical market industries, such as banking, where consumers maintain and examine their activities 24 hours a day in a secure electronic environment.

PHRs come in a variety of forms and formats, with no standard design or model yet to emerge. In recent years, AHIMA has vigorously promoted the use of PHRs and has provided definitions and attributes for standardization.

For example, AHIMA defines the PHR as "an electronic, lifelong resource of health information needed by individuals to make health decisions. Individuals own and manage the information in the PHR, which comes from healthcare providers and the individual. The PHR is maintained in a secure and private environment, with the individual determining rights of access. The PHR does not replace the legal record of any provider" (AHIMA 2005).

In addition, AHIMA (2005) suggests that the following attributes describe more completely the ideal PHR:

Functionality

- Aids the transition from paper to electronic recordkeeping
- Allows the individual to refill prescriptions electronically
- Addresses the major issues of health literacy skills (reading and writing) in the context of culture and language
- Allows selective retrieval and formatting of information by individuals or agents
- Is portable (remains with the individual)
- Helps the individual organize PHI
- Educates the individual about PHI
- Assists the individual with decision making and health management and wellness (for example, reminders of health activities, health risk assessments, and public health and patient safety alerts)
- Is flexible and expandable to support evolving health needs of the individual and family

Format and Content

- Dynamic record that is continuously updated
- Standard format is electronic
- Incorporates paper documents and other media formats
- Linked with, or contains copies of, provider's legal or electronic records
- Original and immediate source of information is identifiable
- Includes dates of entry and occurrence of all information
- Contains lifelong health information
- Not considered a complete record
- Not restricted by any one format
- Not the legal record or EHR of a provider
- Not restricted by culture or language
- Providers use their professional judgment, as they do with any patient-supplied history, for clinical decision support or health management of the individual

Privacy Access and Control

- Private and secure
- Controlled by the individual
- Accessible any place and time by individual
- Accessible in an emergency
- Individual has primary responsibility for the information

Maintenance and Security

- Audit trail shows what information was viewed, by whom, and when
- Amendable by original source as a means of maintaining record integrity
- Individual decides what is incorporated into his or her record

Interoperability

- Achieves easy, accurate, and consistent exchange with others by using communication and health vocabulary standards
- Standard-driven to support evolving HIT

11/9

- Supports structured data collection from individual and stores information using a defined vocabulary
- Links to supportive educational, management, productivity, and quality knowledge bases

Currently, the most common PHR variations and models include:

- *Shared data record*: The shared data record model consumes the largest number of PHRs and is the most effective. Here, both provider (or employer or health plan) and patient maintain the record. In addition, the provider (or employer or health plan) supports the record. As such, the patient receives and adds information over time. The focus of this model is to keep track of health events, medications, or specific physiological indicators, such as exercise and nutrition.
- *EHR extensions*: The EHR extensions model extends the EHR into cyberspace so that an authorized patient can access the provider's record and check on the record's content. Often this model also allows an authorized patient to extract data from the healthcare provider's record. The record is still maintained by the provider but is available to the patient in an online format.
- *Provider-sponsored information management*: The provider-sponsored information management model represents provider-sponsored information management by creating communication vehicles between patient and provider. Such vehicles can include reminders for immunizations or flu shots, appointment scheduling or prescription refill capabilities, and monitoring tools for disease management in which regular collection of data from the patient is required.

Recently, the preceding models have been enhanced by the introduction of software platforms that propose to store a patient's PHR in a health "vault" or "bank." Under these models, data can be added and viewed electronically by the patient and any other individuals or healthcare providers to whom the patient allows permission. Software giants Google and Microsoft have created health vaults or banks for patients to store health data from various healthcare organizations, such as physicians and pharmacies, in one location. They have partnered with prestigious providers of the aforementioned PHR models, such as the Cleveland Clinic and the Mayo Clinic, respectively, to import medical information into the patients' own, secure account.

Several issues are at stake. The first is whether a provider organization will be willing to work with a PHR. For example, increasing consumer demand for useful PHRs will make it mandatory that an EHR system be capable of sending and receiving data from a PHR. Another issue is whether a patient can trust the network that is transmitting his or her information. Currently, large-scale deployment and adoption of Internet-based PHRs remains slow because of ongoing privacy and security challenges, especially with PHR or PHR-related software vendors that are not considered HIPAA "covered entities." Such vendors cannot be held accountable to comply with HIPAA's existing patient privacy and information security regulations.

In 2002, the American Society for Testing and Materials (ASTM) Committee E31 (Healthcare Informatics), Subcommittee 26 established a standard for PHRs on the Internet. Content for the standard was based on the e-health tenets developed by AHIMA in 2000. In 2007, HL7 announced the approval of the Personal Health Record System Functional Model (PHR-S FM) as a Draft Standard for Trial Use. The PHR-S FM defines the functions that may be present in PHR systems and provides guidelines that facilitate HIE among different PHR systems and between PHR and EHR systems.

PHRs have tremendous implications for the future of HIM professionals. HIM professionals will become the custodians of the online dimension of PHRs and their information on top of the organization's EHR system and paper records. Consequently, HIM professionals must answer a number of questions as they begin to create PHRs for patients/consumers, link PHRs to education and the healthcare community, and integrate the PHRs with other patient or health plan member information. For example (Hagland 2001):

- Who will be the stakeholders who will be developing and implementing PHRs?
- How will the PHRs fit into the organization's existing culture and processes for patient information access?
- If the organization has installed component technologies of the EHR system, how will PHRs integrate with those existing components?
- How will PHRs fit into the organization's strategic IT plan?
- What will be the privacy, security, and confidentiality dimensions of the PHRs?
- What will be the budgetary implications?
- What will be the organization's marketing and public relations implications?
- What will be the medicolegal implications?
- If an outsourcing partner maintains the PHRs at least partly or fully, what will be the practical and strategic implications of that decision?

Web 2.0

Web 2.0 is considered the second generation of Internet-based services that emphasizes online collaboration and sharing among users. Some of these applications and technologies include blogs, social networks, content communities, wikis, and podcasts. Web 2.0 tools are characterized by being highly collaborative and participative, using multiple data sources and multimedia, and connecting communities through conversation and an open environment that is virtually available at any time. Although the first generation of Internet services was passive in nature, the Web 2.0 users are actively engaged through the creation of their own content, participating in discussions and communities, and sharing their own videos, photos, and information.

In the healthcare industry, Web 2.0 technologies and tools commonly are referred to as **Health 2.0**. Many consumers and providers are using Health 2.0 tools to better manage their health and that of their patients. Blogs are used to share clinical education information, wikis are used as healthcare reference tools, podcasting is used to provide continuing education for healthcare providers, and social networking is used by patients to develop condition-related communities.

On the other hand, legal and ethical issues must be considered with the use of such technologies and tools. For example, the privacy of the patient and the confidentiality and transparency of the information must be addressed. Additionally, liability issues and the value of intellectual property come into play. Because the nature of Web 2.0/Health 2.0 is inherently open and collaborative, Web 2.0/Health 2.0 restrictions are few, and there is little control over data and information that is available for open distribution. Consequently, while the power of the Web 2.0/Health 2.0 technologies and tools is clear, also is the importance of harnessing its power for the greater good of the healthcare industry.

Check Your Understanding 3.6

Instructions: Answer the following questions on a separate piece of paper.

1. Provide at least five distinct examples of diagnostic tests that involve physiological signal processing.
2. What patient data are typically collected and viewed (accessed) by care providers using point-of-care systems?
3. What is driving the increased use of computerized care protocols in healthcare?
4. Describe how second- and third-generation telehealth applications differ in functionality from first-generation applications such as teleradiology.
5. Why is it that an electronic medical record created by scanning or faxing analog paper documents into digitized, bitmapped images does not fit the description of a CPR as defined in the 1991 and 1997 IOM reports?
6. Why is HL7's EHR-S Functional Model and Standard significant?
7. Provide at least five examples of services healthcare organizations are offering their customers utilizing e-health technology?
8. What are the characteristics of an e-health culture in a healthcare organization?
9. Describe the differences among the following three common models for the PHR: shared data record, EHR extensions, and provider-sponsored information management.
10. Describe the ways consumers use Web 2.0/Health 2.0 tools to manage their health and the subsequent issues that must be managed by healthcare providers.

Supporting the Security of Data and Information

Many current and emerging information technologies are used to support the security of healthcare data and information. They are the same technologies used to support the security of data and information in most vertical market industries. What sets the healthcare vertical market industry apart is the application of the technologies according to the second portion (Title II) of HIPAA, which mandates the protection of health information.

For the purposes of this chapter, the following technologies are highlighted:

- Encryption and cryptography
- Biometrics technology
- Firewall systems
- Audit trails

Encryption and Cryptography

Computer technology's greatest strengths also are its greatest weaknesses. For example, computer technology, especially the Internet and its derived technologies, easily allows anyone to send and receive information. However, it also easily allows anyone to intercept a transmission.

Cryptography is an applied science in which mathematics transforms intelligible data and information into unintelligible strings of characters and back again. **Encryption** technology uses cryptography to code digital data and information. This is so that the information can be transmitted over communications media and the sender of the information can be sure that only a recipient who has an authorized decoding "key" can make sense of the information.

There are two broad categories of encryption. The first category is symmetric or single-key encryption. Here, each computer uses software that assigns a secret key or code. One computer uses the key to code the message, and the other computer uses the same key to decode the message before the recipient can read it. This form of encryption requires both computers to have the same key.

The second category is asymmetric or **public key infrastructure** (PKI) encryption. PKI does not require that both computers have the same key to decode messages. A private key is known to one computer, which gives a public key to the other computer with which it wants to exchange encrypted data. The public key can be stored anywhere it is convenient, such as on a Web site or within an e-mail. The second computer decodes the encrypted message by using the public key and its own private key.

To prevent abuse, some type of authority is needed to serve as a trusted third party. A certification authority (CA) is an independent licensing agency that vouches for the individual's identity and relationship to the individual's public key. Acting as a type of electronic notary public, a CA verifies and stores a sender's public and private encryption keys and issues a digital certificate or "seal of authenticity" to the recipient.

These keys come in various strengths or levels of security. The strengths vary not only according to the algorithm that codes the data, but also on how well the encoding and decoding keys are maintained. The more bits a key has, the harder it is to break the code without massive computer assistance.

For Internet sites, the use of private and public keys is handled behind the scenes by users' computer browsers and the Web servers for the sites. For example, when a healthcare Internet user performs an online, interactive business transaction, a secure socket layer (SSL) PKI is used to exchange sensitive healthcare data and information.

PKI is becoming the de facto encryption technology for secure data transfers and online authentication. As such, its use will enable healthcare organizations to meet HIPAA's regulations concerning the security of data and electronic signatures.

Biometrics Technology

Biometrics technology verifies a person's identity by measuring (comparing different mathematical representations of) biological and physical features or traits unique to the individual. For example, in signature verification technology, the biometrics of a handwritten signature are measured to confirm the identity of an individual. In data access technology, the biometrics of a hand (hand geometry), fingerprint (fingerprint matching), eye (iris or retinal scanning), voice (voice verification), or facial feature (facial image recognition) are measured to confirm the individual's identity.

Unique, positive identification or verification without the fear of replication or duplication for access to confidential health information is critical. As such, HIPAA requires a mechanism to ensure the authentication of the user and to restrict the user only to those systems that he or she is authorized to access. But because positive identification is so reliable as a personal identifier, individuals might feel that their privacy is threatened or compromised.

Fingerprint matching is the oldest and most popular type of biometrics technology. Everyone has unique, immutable fingerprints made of a series of ridges, furrows, and minute points or contours on the surface of the finger that form a pattern. Retinal scanning is quite accurate because it involves analyzing the layer of blood vessels at the back of the eye. But it is not as popular an identification technology because of the close contact users must make with a scanning device and thus is unfriendly for users wearing eyeglasses or contact lenses. Iris scanning is less intrusive than retinal scanning but is considered clumsy to use.

Facial image recognition requires an unobtrusive, digital camera to develop a dynamic, facial image of the user. Unfortunately, matching dynamic images is not as easy as matching static images, such as two or more fingerprints or iris scans. Therefore, positive identification based on multiple biometrics technologies currently has the most promising potential for authentication purposes.

Firewall Systems

Firewalls are hardware and software security devices situated between the routers of a private and public network. They are designed to protect computer networks from unauthorized outsiders. However, they also can be used to protect entities within a single network, for example, to block laboratory technicians from getting into payroll records. Without firewalls, IT departments would have to deploy multiple-enterprise security programs that would soon become difficult to manage and maintain.

Firewalls originated during the 1980s and were used to screen a network's incoming data from unwanted, outside addresses. At that time, networks were not large and complicated. Consequently, firewalls were not foolproof and were easy to circumvent.

By contrast, today's massive and complex networks demand firewall systems fortified with software applications that, for example, authenticate users, encrypt messages, scan for viruses and spyware, and produce audit trails. Technically, most firewalls are made up of proxy and filtering services. Proxy services are special-purpose programs allowing network administrators to permit or deny specific applications or features of applications. They screen user names and all information that attempts to enter or leave the private network. Filtering allows the routers to permit or deny decisions for each piece of information that attempts to enter or leave the private network.

Firewalls are based on pre-established rules that allow or deny access to the network or exchange of information between the networks. As such, firewalls enforce security policies so that everything not explicitly permitted is denied. For example, firewall systems determine which inside services may be accessed from the outside, which outsiders are permitted access to the permitted inside services, and which outside services may be accessed by insiders. For a firewall to be effective, all traffic to and from the networks must pass through the firewall, where it can be inspected.

The firewall itself must be immune to penetration. Unfortunately, a firewall cannot offer protection after an attacker has gotten through or around it.

Audit Trails

Audit trails are chronological sets of records that provide evidence of computer system utilization. Data are collected about every system event, such as log-ins, log-outs, file accesses, and data extractions. As such, audit trails are used to facilitate the determination of security violations and to identify areas for improvement. Their usefulness is enhanced when they include trigger flags for automatic, intensified review.

Today, audit trails serve as strong impediments to computer data abuse. For example, the presence of these tools promotes awareness that people who access confidential information can be tracked and held accountable.

Care must be taken to determine which audited data elements are required by law or which ones are exceptions. Following are some suggested data elements to track activity in healthcare information system audit trails:

- Date and time of event
- Patient identification
- User identification
- Access device used
- Type of action (view or read, print, update or add)
- Identification of patient data access by a category of content

- Source of access and software application used
- Reason for access by category (patient care, research, billing)

Practical issues concerning the use of audit trails involve trust. For example, healthcare organizations must be able to distinguish between users who access patient records for patient care and those who access them for unauthorized purposes. Frequent sampling by organizational managers or "tiger teams" is one way to determine system usage within an environment of trust. Delegating to users the responsibility to examine their own audit histories is another way to determine this. It is recommended that the results of audit trails be published and included in employee performance reviews.

Check Your Understanding 3.7

Instructions: Answer the following questions on a separate piece of paper.

1. What is public key infrastructure and why is it receiving so much attention within the healthcare industry?
2. What are the benefits and drawbacks of using each of the following human features for authentication purposes: fingerprints, iris images, and facial images?
3. Firewalls protect network access by employing proxy and filtering services. What are proxy services and filtering services?
4. What are two practical ways to instill user trust in healthcare organizations when deploying IS audit trails?

Healthcare Informatics and Health Information Management

Health information management (HIM) is the healthcare industry's professional field that ensures that high-quality data and information are available to every type of authorized user who depends on the data and information to deliver high-quality healthcare services and to make high-quality healthcare-related decisions. HIM professionals serve not only the healthcare industry, but also the public. By managing, compiling, analyzing, and utilizing data from many sources, HIM professionals identify ways to better utilize healthcare resources, more accurately provide patient billing and reimbursement services, reveal public health patterns, and establish new medical treatments vital for improved patient care and administrative purposes.

Trained HIM professionals manage the quality of the data and information content, including its timeliness, appropriateness, accuracy, relevance, and integrity. In addition, HIM professionals develop policies to meet information management standards as mandated by the government and other regulatory and accrediting organizations. Most important, HIM professionals work diligently to protect the privacy of the individual and the confidentiality of the data and information they make available to legitimate users.

Historically, healthcare and healthcare-related data and information have been collected, stored, and transmitted using paper-based systems. Currently, paper-based systems are still commonly used for data and information management purposes in healthcare organizations. Consequently, in this time of transition between paper-based and computer-based systems, managing part manual, part electronic systems (often referred to as "hybrid" systems) is providing HIM professionals with significant challenges. Because healthcare informatics is concerned with the management of all aspects of health data and information in computer-based systems, it clearly includes HIM as one of its components. And, as more and more healthcare and healthcare-related data and information are being collected, stored, and transmitted using computer technologies, the HIM discipline is increasingly being integrated into the domain of healthcare informatics.

HIM professionals must be intimate partners with HIT professionals, who, together, form strong alliances with each type of authorized user (physicians, nurses, clinicians, dentists, consumers, and administrators) to develop and implement the required hardware and software and the required data and information infrastructure (content and format) to support their unique needs as well as the overall needs of the healthcare organization. In this context HIM professionals will continue to assume a leadership role in the development, implementation, and use of improved healthcare information systems, integrated patient information systems, accurate decision support tools, or any of the current and emerging information technologies highlighted in this chapter.

Check Your Understanding 3.8

Instructions: Answer the following question on a separate piece of paper.

1. The HIM discipline is becoming a professional field within the domain of healthcare informatics. What is driving this transition?

Real-World Case

Six months after the merger of two of Chicago's large acute care organizations, Diane Samuels was appointed Chief Information Officer (CIO) of the merged entity. The CIO from one of the merged acute care organizations had accepted an offer from an employer in the area of the country from which he had moved two years ago. The CIO from the other merged acute care organization resigned after 10 years of service when he was not chosen CIO of the merged entity.

In interviewing for the position, Diane learned that:

- One of her predecessors had recommended that the clinical information systems of the two acute care organizations be merged by 2010.
  - One of the CISs in one of the acute care organizations, City General (CG), was installed about 15 years ago. This system was not HIPAA security compliant and it lacked important CIS features, such as alerts and reminders.
  - It was estimated that $10 million would be saved following the merger of the two CIS systems.

- Her boss, the CEO of the merged entity, had committed to its board that expenses would be reduced during fiscal year 2008 by the $10 million that was expected to be saved following the merger.

When Diane began her new position, she knew she needed to make a number of critical decisions regarding the CISs. At first, she thought that in order to merge the two CISs, she could either implement into CG the existing CIS at the other acute care organization, University Medical Center (UMC), or implement an entirely new CIS in both facilities.

However, Diane quickly learned the following information:

- If the choice were made to implement the UMC CIS into CG, the existing UMC CIS would need to be significantly rewritten to "fit" into CG and its environment of existing systems. This appeared risky because there had been inadequate documentation of the many changes that had been made to CG's environment of existing systems that were interfaced to the old, current system. Further, UMC's existing CIS could create technical problems in CG's existing environment of "other" systems' operating systems.
- CISs are closely integrated with registration systems. Therefore, at UMC, extensive work had already been completed on a new registration system using GE's (formerly IDX's) Flowcast software, which had been specifically designed to integrate acute care facility inpatient and outpatient registration. UMC's objective was to eventually integrate this hospital registration system with the UMC physician offices' registration system. Therefore, implementing UMC's CIS into CG would require that CG's existing registration system also be converted to GE's Flowcast. The usual time to undertake such a project is two years.
- Both UMC's and CG's CIS hardware leases and software licenses were due to terminate in about six months. Both lease contracts forced the hospitals to both purchase the existing (and out of date) hardware and software (which may not allow system integration) at a cost of approximately $10 million.
- If the choice were made to implement an entirely new CIS in both facilities, a new system would cost approximately $50 million. However, it would serve both hospitals and, according to vendors, have a better chance of achieving full integration.
- Aside from the dollars, the IT staff at CG had a poor track record of implementing new systems. In addition, the IT department had a vacancy rate of 50 percent.

Diane met with her staff and, after researching several companies that offered both products and services, she solicited request for proposals (RFPs) from the following three companies:

- Dak Systems Consulting, the leading company in healthcare systems integration services, refused to bid on the systems integration required for a new CIS at both facilities. This was because of the risks and time constraints involved in designing, implementing, and testing the system before the leases and year terminated.
- GE proposed that its new, recently redeveloped CIS be implemented in both facilities. After all, this system was developed to integrate into GE's registration system, which was already installed at UMC and most likely would need to be installed at CG anyway. In addition, the merged entity would get a much better price than $50 million for purchasing this new system. Unfortunately, GE was unable to provide evidence of successful installation of its recently redeveloped CIS not only at a similar, large delivery network, but anywhere.
- Cerner Corporation was the leading provider of CISs for large acute care facilities and integrated delivery networks. Cerner proposed that its CIS be installed in both acute care organizations and strongly recommended that its registration system replace CG's existing and old registration system as well as UMC's existing and new registration system. Unfortunately, aside from the UMC CIS's high price tag, Cerner's registration system had not been chosen the year before when UMC was evaluating new registration systems. This was because UMC believed that Cerner did not have as extensive experience as GE in integrating both hospital and physician office registration systems.

Finally, Diane could outsource management of any new CIS, but it was unlikely that an outsourcing firm would guarantee that a new CIS would be in place before the leases expired and the year ended.

The stakes surrounding Diane's recommendation to her CEO could not be higher in terms of dollars or her career.

Summary

The informatics revolution has changed the healthcare delivery system. Technology has advanced exponentially, allowing healthcare providers to use new methods to care for their patients. Patients, in turn, have become well armed with information about their health and healthcare options, and are utilizing new tools, such as the PHR and Web 2.0, to manage their care. These advances lead to opportunities and challenges as the industry focuses on strengthening the infrastructure and improving interoperability. Consequently, the data and information demands on the healthcare industry require that informatics address all aspects of healthcare, including financial, administrative, and clinical. Health information managers are knowledgeable about both healthcare and computerized information technologies. This positions them to lead the way as technology continues to advance and governmental, and other organizations, call for more effective and efficient healthcare delivery.

References

AHIMA e-HIM Personal Health Record Work Group. 2005. Practice brief: Defining the personal health record. *Journal of AHIMA* 76(6):24–25.

AHIMA e-HIM Personal Health Record Work Group. 2005. Practice brief: The role of the personal health record in the EHR. *Journal of AHIMA* 76(7):64A–D.

American Health Information Management Association. 2000. AHIMA's basic operational tenets for protecting the privacy of personal health information on the Internet. http://www.ahima.org/infocenter/guidelines/tenets.asp.

American Health Information Management Association. 2004. Practice brief: Delving into computer-assisted coding. *Journal of AHIMA* 75(10).

American Health Information Management Association. 2006. *Pocket Glossary of Health Information Management and Technology*. Chicago:AHIMA.

American Health Information Management Association. 2007. Practice brief: HIM principles in health information exchange. *Journal of AHIMA* 78(8).

American Medical Informatics Association. 2005. http://www.amia.com.

Barcode Factory. 2008. http://www.barcodefactory.com/website/pc/home.asp.

Barnett, G.O., J. Cimino, J. Hupp, and E. Hoffer. 1987. DXplain: An evolving diagnostic decision-support system. *Journal of the American Medical Association* 258(1):67–74.

Brailer, D.J. 2005 (Jan. 19). Interoperability: The key to the future health care system. *Health Affairs*–Web Exclusive. http://www.content.healthaffairs.org/cgi/content/full/hlthaff.w5.19/DC1.

Bufton, M. 1999. Electronic health records and implementation of clinical practice guidelines. In *Electronic Health Records: Changing the Vision.* Edited by G.F. Murphy, M.A. Hanken, and K.A. Waters. Philadelphia: W.B. Saunders Company.

California HealthCare Foundation. 1999. National survey: Confidentiality of medical records. http://www.ehealth.chcf.org.

Center of Information Technology Leadership. 2004. *The Value of Healthcare Information Exchange and Interoperability*. Boston: Partners HealthCare.

Connecting for Health. 2006. Record locator service: Technical background from the Massachusetts Prototype Community. http://www.connectingforhealth.org/commonframework/docs/T6_RecordLocator.pdf.

Department of Health and Human Services. 1993 (Nov. 23). Press release: A push toward paperless processing in healthcare. *HHS News*.

Dick, R., and W. Andrews. 1995. Point of care: An essential technology for the CPR. *Healthcare Informatics* 12(5):64–66, 78.

Dick, R.S., and E.B. Steen, eds. 1991. *The Computer-based Patient Record: An Essential Technology for Health Care*. Washington, D.C.: National Academy Press.

Dick, R.S., E.B. Steen, and D.E. Detmer, eds. 1997. *The Computer-based Patient Record: An Essential Technology for Health Care*. Rev ed. Washington, D.C.: National Academy Press.

Drazen, E. 2001. Is this the year of the computer-based patient record? *Healthcare Informatics* 18(2):94–98.

Goldman, J., and Z. Hudson. 2000. Virtually exposed: Privacy and e-health. *Health Affairs* 19(6):140–148.

Hagland, M. 2001. Getting more personal. *Journal of AHIMA* 72(8):35.

Health Insurance Portability and Accountability Act of 1996. Public Law 104-191. http://www.access.gpo.gov/nara/cfr/index.html.

Healthcare Information and Management Systems Society. 2008. The NHIN Highway Is Already Paved: The Existing HIPAA Transaction Exchange Network Is an Able Solution for the Conveyance of Clinical Information. A White Paper by the HIMSS Financial Systems Steering Committee. http://www.himss.org.

Healthcare Information Technology Standards Panel. 2008. http://www.histp.org.

Henchey, P. 1998. Maximizing ROI in data warehouses. *Advance for Health Information Executives* 2(1):60–70.

Houser, S.H., and L.A. Johnson. 2008 (May 16). Perceptions regarding electronic health record implementation among health information management professionals in Alabama: A statewide survey and analysis (Electronic version). *Perspectives in Health Information Management* (5). http://www.pubmedcentral.nih.gov/articlerender.fcgi?artid=2394577.

Hunt, D., R. Haynes, S. Hanna, and K. Smith. 1998. Effects of computer based clinical decision support systems on physician performance and patient outcomes: A systematic review. *Journal of the American Medical Association* 280(15):1339–1346.

Institute of Medicine, Committee on Quality of Health Care in America. 2001. *Crossing the Quality Chasm: A New Health System for the 21st Century.* Washington, D.C.: National Academy Press.

Institute of Medicine, Committee on Quality of Health Care in America. 2002. *Leadership by Example: Coordinating Government Roles in Improving Health Care Quality.* Washington, D.C.: National Academy Press.

Institute of Medicine, Committee on Quality of Health Care in America. 2003. *Patient Safety: Achieving a New Standard of Care.* Washington, D.C.: National Academy Press.

Kelly, F. 2001. Implementing an executive information system (EIS). http://www.dssresources.com.

Kohn, L.T., J.M. Corrigan, and M.S. Donaldson, eds. 1999. *To Err Is Human: Building a Safer Health System.* Washington, D.C.: National Academy Press.

Krohn, R. 2004. Clinical decision support systems. *Journal of Healthcare Information Management* 18(4):10–11.

MyPHR. 2008. http://www.myphr.com.

National Alliance on Health Information Technology. 2008 (April 28). *Defining Key Health Information Technology Terms*. Report to the Office of the National Coordinator for Health Information Technology.

National Committee on Vital and Health Statistics. 2001. Information for health: A strategy for building the NHII. http://www.aspe.hhs.gov/sp/nhii/Documents/NHIIReport2001/default.htm.

Nuance Communications. 2008. Dragon Medical: Speech-enable the practice's EMR for faster, more efficient and profitable clinical documentation. [Product sheet]. http://www.nuance.com/naturallyspeaking/pdf/ds_DNS10_Medical.pdf.

Nussbaum, G. 2001. Bitten by the ASP: Application service providers. *Proceedings of the Healthcare Information and Management Systems Society*. Vol. 1 (Session 7), 1–9. Chicago: HIMSS.

Open Source Initiative. 2006. The open source definition. http://www.opensource.org/docs/osd.

Power, D.J. 1997. What is a DSS? *The Online Executive Journal for Data-Intensive Decision Support* 1(3). http://www.taborcommunications.com/dsstar/971021/100015.html.

Prime Recognition. 2008. OCR Software Accuracy Comparison. http://www.primerecognition.com/augprime/ocr_accuracy_compare.htm.

RSA Laboratories. 2007a. A Primer on RFID. http://www.rsa.com/rsalabs/node.asp?id=2116.

RSA Laboratories. 2007b. Protecting consumer privacy. http://www.rsa.com/rsalabs/node.asp?id=2119.

Schnitzer, G. 2000. Natural language processing: A coding professional's perspective. *Journal of AHIMA* 71(9):95–98.

Siwicki, B. 1996. Artificial intelligence: A new generation of health care applications. *Health Data Management* 4(4):47–52.

Stead, W. and M. Lorenzi. 1999. Health informatics: Linking investment to value. *Journal of the American Medical Informatics Association* 6(5):341–348.

Tabar, P. 2003. Get the message? *Healthcare Informatics* 20(5):50.

Turley, J., C. Johnson, T. Johnson, and J. Zhang. 2001. A clean slate: Initiating a graduate program in health informatics. *MD Computing* 18(1): 47–48.

Walker, J., E. Pan, D. Johnston, J. Adler-Milstein, D. W. Bates, and B. Middleton. 2005 (Jan. 19). The value of health care information exchange and interoperability. *Health Affairs*–Web Exclusive. http://www.content.healthaffairs.org/cgi/content/full/hlthaff.w5.10/DC1.

Warner, H. 2000. Can natural language processing aid outpatient coders? *Journal of AHIMA* 71(8):78–81.

Chapter 4
The Health Information Management Profession

Susan Parker, MEd, RHIA

Learning Objectives

- Understand the professional definition of health information management (HIM)
- Recognize the components of HIM
- Differentiate HIM from information technology and health library science
- Identify the types of data relevant to the HIM profession
- Identify the functions within the HIM professional domain
- Understand the media and forms in which health information is found and must be managed
- Recognize the components of the HIM body of knowledge
- Identify the characteristics of a profession that apply to HIM
- Identify the key HIM professional associations
- Understand the importance of a professional code of ethics and what the HIM Code of Ethics means
- Recognize the importance of lifelong learning in the HIM profession
- Know the process and benefits of certification and the requirements for maintaining certification
- Recognize the importance of continuing education and the options available to HIM professionals

Key Terms

Access control
American Health Information Management Association (AHIMA)
American Medical Informatics Association (AMIA)
Association for Healthcare Documentation Integrity (AHDI)
Association of Clinical Documentation Improvement Specialists (ACDIS)
Body of Knowledge (BoK)
Certification
Certified coding associate (CCA)
Certified coding specialist (CCS)
Certified coding specialist–physician-based (CCS–P)
Certified Health Data Analyst (CHDA)
Certified in healthcare privacy and security (CHPS)
Certified professional in health information management systems (CPHIMS)
Clinical data
Clinical data specialist
Clinical project manager
Coded data
College of Healthcare Information Management Executives (CHIME)
Commission on Accreditation for Health Informatics and Information Management Education (CAHIIM)
Consultant
Continuing education
Data capture
Data dictionary
Data display
Data integrity specialist
Data modeling
Data quality management
Data quality manager/data quality analyst
Data resource administrator
Demographic data
Electronic health information management (e-HIM)
Epidemiological data
Financial data
Health information management (HIM)
Health information manager/director
Health science librarians/medical librarians
Healthcare Information Management and Systems Society (HIMSS)
Informatics
Information privacy coordinator/privacy officer
Information technology professionals
International Federation of Health Record Organizations (IFHRO)
International Medical Informatics Association (IMIA)
Medical informatics professionals
National Cancer Registrars Association (NCRA)
Nosology
Patient information coordinator
Personal health record (PHR)
Process and workflow modeling
Profession
Reference data
Registered health information administrator (RHIA)
Registered health information technician (RHIT)
Research and decision support analyst
Research data

In 1928, the Association of Record Librarians of North America was organized under the sponsorship of the American College of Surgeons. The objective of the new organization was "to elevate the standards of clinical records in hospitals, dispensaries, and other distinctly medical institutions" (Huffman 1941, 18). This precursor to the **American Health Information Management Association** (AHIMA) began to define the qualifications, duties, and training for individuals working in medical records. In 1941, Huffman categorized the responsibilities of the medical record librarian as (185–187):

- Organization and management
- Numbering, filing, and cross-indexing
- Ethics and medicolegal
- Statistics, comparative studies, and research
- Secretarial duties
- Correlation of the medical records library and the medical reference library

Many of these elements are still included in today's professional definition of health information management (HIM). Other elements of the 1941 definition are irrelevant or of limited importance. The longevity of this professional definition documents the unique role of the health information manager and the resilience of the profession through time.

This chapter focuses on the professional definition and scope of HIM practice. It also discusses the characteristics of a profession, such as belonging to professional organizations, and provides specific examples that apply to HIM.

Professional Definition

In the past 50 years, numerous changes have affected the responsibilities of the health information manager. The advent of computers, government sponsorship and regulation of healthcare, advances in medical practice, and socioeconomic changes and progress in higher education have all affected the **health information management** (HIM) profession. In 2000, AHIMA's Committee on Professional Development completed the most recent update of the professional definition for HIM. (See figure 4.1.) Changes in the healthcare environment, information technology (IT), and information management continue to have an impact on the practice of health information management.

> Health information management improves the quality of healthcare by ensuring that the best information is available to make any healthcare decision. Health information management professionals manage healthcare data and information resources. The profession encompasses services in planning, collecting, aggregating, analyzing, and disseminating individual patient and aggregate clinical data. It serves the healthcare industry including: patient care organizations, payers, research and policy agencies, and other healthcare-related industries (Russell 2001, 48B).

HIM professionals are not limited to healthcare data found in industries and organizations. In 2008, the National Alliance for Health Information Technology's (NAHIT) research resulted in the **personal health record** (PHR) definition development by the Office of the National coordinator for Health Information Technology. This definition describes an electronic record wholly managed by the consumer, conforming to nationally recognized standards and capable of exchanging information with multiple sources. PHRs offer HIM professionals boundless opportunities as the industry transitions to a national health information network (AHIMA 2008a).

HIM deals primarily with data and information that is created during the diagnosis and treatment of individual patients. Closely related, but different, fields include information technology, medical library science, and health informatics.

The IT field provides computing hardware, software, and data transmission technology for all industries, including healthcare. Although HIM professionals routinely work with **information technology (IT) professionals** and study some computer science topics, HIM does not require the same depth of computer knowledge and skill that IT does.

Health library science is a specialized area of library science that evolved from the enormous volume of reference materials published in medical and health literature. Health science librarians provide access to library resources and teach people how to use them. (Chronicle Guidance Publications 1999, 8). **Health science librarians and medical librarians** provide health information about new medical treatments, clinical trials and standard trials procedures to physicians, allied health professionals, patients, consumers and corporations (Medical Library Association 2008). The provision of reference material to aid in health decision making is an increasingly important function of computer-based patient records (IOM 1997, 88). As clinicians' demand for point-of-care access to health literature increases, HIM professionals work closely with health science librarians to integrate these types of health information resources for specific patients or patient populations into electronic health record (EHR) systems.

Biomedical and health informatics seeks to understand and promote the effective organization, analysis, management, and use of information in healthcare (American Medical Informatics Association 2008). **Medical informatics professionals** are physicians who specialize in the application of electronic information processing to medical practice. It is the "field that concerns itself with the cognitive, information processing and communication tools of medical practice, education and research including the information science and technology to support these tasks" (Greenes and Shortliffe 1990).Other disciplines also are developing postgraduate informatics specialties such as nursing informatics, dental informatics, and pharmacy informatics. Health informatics at the graduate level is concerned with the design and application of computer-based technologies and information systems, problem-solving techniques, analytic methods, and systems thinking to meet the information needs of the

Figure 4.1. Professional definition of HIM

Health Information Management: Professional Definition
Developed by the 1999 and 2000 Committees on Professional Development

Effective January 2001

Health information management improves the quality of healthcare by ensuring that the best information is available to make any healthcare decision. Health information management professionals manage healthcare data and information resources. The profession encompasses services in planning, collecting, aggregating, analyzing, and disseminating individual patient and aggregate clinical data. It serves the following healthcare stakeholders: patient care organizations, payers, research and policy agencies, and other healthcare-related industries.

HEALTH	Domain Description	Unique Impact
The field of health is broad, including everything from birth to death and wellness to illness. Health information management deals largely with patient data.	Health information includes: • **Clinical data** captured during the process of diagnosis and treatment. • **Epidemiological databases** that aggregate data about a population. • **Demographic data** used to identify and communicate with and about an individual. • **Financial data** derived from the care process or aggregated for an organization or population. • **Research data** gathered as a part of care and used for research or gathered for specific research purposes in clinical trials. • **Reference data** that interacts with the care of the individual or with the healthcare delivery systems, like a formulary, protocol, care plan, clinical alert or reminder, etc. • **Coded data** that is translated into a standard nomenclature or classification so that it may be aggregated, analyzed, and compared.	Health information professionals manage a variety of types of information across the healthcare industry. Their expertise uniquely impacts the value of this data as evidenced in the examples below: • **Clinical Data**—Organization of information supports direct patient care and serves a variety of industry needs like reimbursement, planning, and research. • **Epidemiological Databases**—Aggregate statistics reveal disease trends. • **Demographic Data**—Attention to data quality provides unique identification of patients in a healthcare enterprise and accurate information available to run the business of healthcare. • **Financial Data**—Understanding the clinical context of costs and the rules for reimbursement improves organizational decision making. • **Research Data**—Planning for future use of data improves the quality and reduces the cost of data capture and analysis. • **Reference Data**—Providing current literature and research outcomes enhances clinical knowledge at the point of care and in operational decision making. • **Coded Data**—Aggregate statistics enhance analysis for epidemiological patterning. Combining knowledge of the clinical content, documentation principles, coding systems, and data use provides accurate information for the industry.
INFORMATION	**Domain Description**	**Unique Impact**
Health information is captured and stored in a variety of media and forms.	The management of information relates to all of these forms: • **Data**—Individual and aggregate • **Reports** • **Medical records**—An aggregation of reports and data that describe an individual patient usually within one delivery site or system • **Data dictionaries** • **Vocabularies** Information may be stored using a variety of media: • **Paper** • **Databases** • **Microfilm/microfiche** • **Computer stored**	**FORMS** **Data** • Healthcare generates enormous amounts of data that are only useful if well managed. **Reports** • Summarization of data into relevant reports quickly communicates vital information. **Medical Records** • Developing uniform definitions of the most critical information gathered about a patient to create a legal document. **Data Dictionary** • Creating standards to define critical content. **Vocabularies** • Defining the language of healthcare. **MEDIA** **Paper** • Managing the historic and pervasive method of healthcare communication. **Databases** • Constructing relevant collections of data. **Microfilm/Microfiche** • Reduction of storage space required for maintaining legal documents. **Computer Stored** • Assuring preservation of a legal standard when applying new technologies.

(Continued on next page)

Figure 4.1. (Continued)

MANAGEMENT	Domain Description	Unique Impact
Management of health information uniquely stems from a knowledge of clinical, management, and informatics principles and is performed by individuals focused at the strategic, management, and technical levels.	**PLANNING** **Administration** • Managing data collection and storage • Managing information retrieval and release **Policy Development** • Establishing security, confidentiality, retention, integrity, and access standards • Developing training programs that empower others to carry out the information policies • Advocating for privacy, confidentiality, and access **Strategic Planning** • Identifying the organization or projects that need information support for current and future strategic operations and initiatives • Planning capture, storage, and display of data to ensure operational effectiveness, including use of technology **INFORMATICS** **Data Modeling** • Determining data needs and identifying the relationships among these data **Process and Work-Flow Modeling** • Identifying the flow of work and information required to perform a function including: decomposition diagrams, dependency diagrams, and data flow **Data Capture and Display Design** • Focusing on system design, screen design, report design, and forms design **Data Dictionary Maintenance** • Maintaining dictionary design, standardization, update, and dissemination **Access Control** • Designing, implementing, and monitoring the map between information and user access **Data Quality Management** • Effecting the collection, application, warehousing, and analysis of data to improve information quality **Nosology** • Analyzing and interpreting disease and procedure classifications and terminologies for accuracy of translation of healthcare data **TECHNICAL** **Classification and Coding** • Assigning the appropriate code or nomenclature term for categorization **Abstracting** • Compiling the pertinent information from the medical record based on predetermined data sets **Registry Development** • Assembling a chronological set of data for an express purpose **Storage** • Implementing and providing oversight of electronic and paper-based filing systems **Retrieval** • Making accessible information that is stored in various media and sites **Release** • Appropriately responding to requests for information based on laws and policy **Analysis** • Performing qualitative and quantitative analysis of documentation against standards and policy	**PLANNING** **Administration** • Reducing the cost of health information • Successfully implementing an enterprisewide master person index **Policy Development** • Participating in national policy discussions on health information privacy • Drafting organizational policies that conform with state and federal regulations **Strategic Planning** • Initiating market position strategies influenced by sound outcomes data • Ensuring easy access to health information by care providers across an enterprise **INFORMATICS** **Data Modeling** • Improving access to healthcare data • Improving the quality of information **Process and Work-Flow Modeling** • Ensuring faster access to cash through improved revenue cycles • Providing for less time spent by clinicians in charting; more time for patient care **Data Capture and Display Design** • Improving patient safety through reduced documentation error • Reducing training time for clinicians in how to chart **Data Dictionary Maintenance** • Making accurate and timely data available for clinical and business decisions • Increasing access to data **Access Control** • Protecting patients' right to privacy • Complying with state and federal laws and regulations • Improving access when appropriate **Data Quality Management** • Consistently and methodically improving the quality of data • Improving decision making influenced by reliable information **Nosology** • Providing access to clinically relevant aggregate data **TECHNICAL** **Classification and Coding** • Reducing the threat of fraud and abuse litigation • Improving data accuracy • Establishing processes for accurate reimbursement **Abstracting** • Providing access to key data at the patient and aggregate levels **Registry Development** • Providing information to support long-term care of chronic disease • Providing research information for the value of treatment of chronic disease **Storage** • Reducing costs of storing records • Complying with state and federal laws **Retrieval** • Making information available for healthcare emergencies • Providing the most cost-effective access to information **Release** • Protecting patients' rights to privacy of health information • Reducing risk of litigation from inappropriate release **Analysis** • Allowing for meaningful interpretation of statistical data • Presenting both business and clinical information with appropriate content and context review
		EXTENDED ROLES *As with any robust profession, individuals evolve into divergent roles to develop, support, and nurture aspects of the profession. Although related to the profession, additional skills are developed to contribute to health information management without directly managing health information. For example, they support the core definition by:* • *Teaching others to manage health information* • *Developing and marketing products and services that help to manage health information* • *Developing software that manages health information* • *Consulting with others in the management of health information*

Source: AHIMA 2005a.

healthcare industry. Health informatics is a broad, transdisciplinary field, of which HIM is a related specialty at the graduate level.

Scope of Health Information

Health information begins at birth and ends at death. It is a collection of information from multiple sources with a wide variety of uses. Health information includes data from the individual patient record as well as aggregate data on a patient population that can span the globe. Within the professional definition of HIM, health information includes the following types of data:

- **Clinical data**, the most common type of health information, document the signs, symptoms, diagnoses, impressions, treatments, and outcomes of the care process. They are captured during diagnosis and treatment and are stored in the medical record. Clinical data serve a variety of industry needs beyond direct patient care, including reimbursement, planning, and research. They may be collected and stored in paper or electronic formats. Although the health information manager rarely collects or uses clinical data directly in the delivery of care, one of the principal roles is that of developing systems that collect accurate and timely information and make it available to decision makers.
- **Epidemiological data** are used to describe health-related issues or events, such as disease trends found in specific populations or general analytics of population health. The information then may be used to inform the public or to generate actions that could affect a trend. For example, data on the incidence of sexually transmitted diseases might be used to measure the impact of a teen education program. HIM professionals could establish systems to transmit such information accurately and appropriately while maintaining patient confidentiality. They also could be involved in data analysis and display.
- **Demographic data** provide statistical information about a population, such as age, place of residence, gender, and so on. Accurate and complete demographic data perform two important information functions in healthcare. First, data such as age and gender have their own value when combined with clinical information. For instance, a gender designation can make a diagnosis commonplace, rare, or impossible. Breast cancer, a common diagnosis in a certain age of female, is rare, albeit possible, in males. However, pregnancy is only possible in females. Second, demographic data may be used to uniquely identify individuals so that all the other health information attributed to them can be collected and accessed accurately.
- **Financial data** are either derived from the care process or aggregated for an organization or population. Healthcare is a business. Health care spending has increased at a faster rate of growth than the gross domestic product, inflation, and population. The latest data available shows that total national spending on healthcare rose to $1.67 trillion (HHS 2004). Although accounting and financial management are not within the HIM domain, understanding the relationship among clinical services, costs, and the rules for reimbursement is vital to the health information manager role.
- **Research data** may be collected as a part of care and then used in research or collected for specific research purposes in clinical trials. HIM professionals play a role in the collection and use of research data from existing records. In addition, they consider research needs when planning for future types and uses of data as a research tool. In this way, HIM professionals improve access to data and reduce the costs of research at the same time.
- **Reference data** are commonly created and maintained by someone outside health information management. They interact with the care of the individual or with the healthcare delivery system in the form of a formulary, protocol, care plan, clinical alert, or reminder. The nursing staff or the medical staff generally create care plans; the pharmacy normally administers the formulary, although ensuring that reference data are available for the care provider is a critical HIM role. Health information managers also are responsible for incorporating elements of this static information into the patient's medical record to support clinical documentation and may be part of the clinical documentation improvement team.
- **Coded data** are data that have been translated into a standard nomenclature or classification so they can be aggregated, analyzed, and compared. To facilitate the analysis of large amounts of information, coded data frequently are grouped into meaningful categories. The categories may be as simple as M for male and F for female or as extensive as those used to code diagnoses and procedures. The grouping may be simplistic, as in age range, or as complex as the methodology used in prospective payment systems.

HIM professionals may have responsibilities that require specialization in one of these data types or require engaging with multiple data types and services. In all cases, HIM professionals perform a variety of tasks associated with ensuring the availability of high-quality data and information to support the healthcare industry.

Check Your Understanding 4.1

Instructions: Answer the following questions on a separate piece of paper.

1. What factors have influenced the change in the professional definition of health information management (HIM)?
2. What are the differences between HIM professionals and IT professionals?
3. What role does the HIM professional play in working with clinical data?
4. How does the HIM professional's role differ from roles assumed by other healthcare professionals and what makes HIM unique?
5. How are reference data different from other types of healthcare data?

Domains of Health Information Management Practice

The management of health information is based on knowledge of clinical practice, information management principles, and informatics concepts. Health information management can be practiced at the planning level, addressing the administrative aspects of health information systems, including policy development. When focused on informatics, HIM includes several functions that are required to develop and administer computer-based information systems. When practiced at a technical level, HIM manipulates data to be used by others for a variety of decision-making purposes. (Refer to figure 4.1.)

Planning

The practice of HIM at the planning level involves the administration of information systems and the development of policies to ensure that those systems are administered effectively and confidentially today as well as in the future.

Administration

HIM involves the administration of systems that collect and store data and the management of information retrieval and release. Effective administration of these systems makes information available and ensures appropriate access, security, and confidentiality. Effective administration of health information systems also increases healthcare delivery efficiency because it reduces clinical time and streamlines business processes. Administrative responsibilities may involve staff, space, equipment, and procedures for a large integrated delivery system or may be focused on ensuring the effective utilization of a single information resource, such as managing a cancer registry.

Policy Development

Along with the administration of systems and people, the development of policies specific to health information is among the HIM professional's job functions. **Policy development** includes:

- Establishing data security, confidentiality, retention, integrity, and access standards
- Developing training programs that empower others to carry out the information policies
- Advocating for data privacy, confidentiality, and appropriate access

Strategic Planning

Finally, strategic planning for future information needs is a role for the HIM professional. This role involves identifying information needs for an organization or a project to support current and future strategic operations, initiatives, or compliance with regulations or laws. It also involves planning the capture, storage, and display of data to ensure operational effectiveness, including the use of technology.

Informatics

Informatics is the science of information management in a computer-based environment. It involves the use of computers to automate the collection, storage, utilization, and transmission of information.

Those information management tasks that involve handling data and information fall into the arena of informatics. These tasks include:

- **Data modeling**: Determining data needs and identifying the relationships among the data
- **Process and workflow modeling**: Identifying the flow of work and information required to perform a function, including decomposition diagrams, dependency diagrams, and data flow
- **Data capture and data display**: The function of system design, screen design, report design, and form design
- **Data dictionary**: Dictionary design, standardization, update, and dissemination
- **Access control**: Designing, implementing, and monitoring the map between information and user access
- **Data quality management:** The collection, application, warehousing, and analysis of data to improve information quality
- **Nosology**: Interpreting disease and procedure classifications and terminologies for accurate translation of healthcare data

These HIM (informatics) functions can be illustrated using a simple information systems example. A patient presents to the emergency department and needs to be registered. Data modeling would indicate what information is needed to identify the patient, to collect insurance information for payment, to provide demographic information needed for patient care, and to identify the person the patient would want contacted in the event his or her condition worsened. An example of the relationship among the data might be that the patient's address is the same for identification, billing, and contact purposes. Thus, this information would need to be collected only once.

Continuing with the example, process and workflow modeling would involve identifying how this information is collected. In the emergency department, a critical patient may have a different process model than a patient with a less serious condition. Certain information, such as name and date of birth, might need to be collected before any clinical treatment could begin, whereas insurance information could be collected after initial emergency treatment, prior to discharge.

Data capture and data display for collecting the registration information might involve a form the patient fills in and returns to the registration clerk. It is easy to see how such a form should be designed to easily transform written patient information to the data fields on a computer screen. Also, information should be collected in the most convenient manner for the patient. As consumers utilize PHRs, HIM informatics functions for data capture and display will become an increasingly significant tool.

A data dictionary defines all the unique data elements in the data set. For instance, the data field for a Social Security number would indicate that it is nine characters long, numeric, and the unique identifier assigned by the Social Security Administration. Having a complete and specific data dictionary allows for data field design and editing. An edit for the Social Security number would be to ensure that all the characters are numbers. A data dictionary also may record other types of data attributes (for example, weight recorded in pounds rather than grams) or stipulate that an entry must be authenticated or signed by the person collecting the information.

Access control is a critical function within HIM relative to information security. This function maps the relationship between information and the individuals authorized to use it. It may be established at a variety of levels. For instance, an attending physician may have access to a patient's entire medical record, but a lab technician may have access to lab data only. Understanding the information contained in the medical record and the roles of the different individuals authorized to use it allows the health information manager to design mechanisms that enable users to access the information they need and also safeguard patient confidentiality.

In the emergency department example, it is clear how data quality management plays a key role in high-quality care and the effective delivery of medicine. Data quality management considers each of the steps of the data cycle: collection, application, warehousing, and analysis. HIM professionals first look at how the data are used and then design the required data set, through data modeling, to ensure that they are collected at the most logical point. Application (use) of the data is considered to ensure that the information is available when and where it is needed. Warehousing (storage) of the data ensures that the information from this emergency visit is available for a follow-up visit to either the patient's primary care provider or the hospital inpatient unit should the patient require hospitalization. Making the data available for analysis may be required to determine staffing levels in the emergency department, to address quality of care concerns, or to improve patient satisfaction questionnaires.

Nosology, the final informatics function in the HIM professional definition, does not deal directly with the information collected in the emergency department encounter. As a nosologist, the HIM professional puts in place a standard terminology or description of the diagnoses and procedures used so that information can be stored and analyzed. Suppose the HIM professional wanted to find all the patients who came to the emergency department for a myocardial infarction. Care providers use a number of different terms to refer to a myocardial infarction, including an MI, a heart attack, a coronary, and so on. By developing and using a standard terminology to describe this condition, the nosologist can ensure that every case of myocardial infarction will be found.

Technical Functions

There are many technical functions that fall into the HIM scope of practice. Much of this technical work is the focus of the associate-level education in the HIM field. For example, health information technicians are commonly engaged in the following activities:

- *Classification and coding*: The process of assigning the appropriate code or nomenclature term for categorization
- *Abstracting*: The function of compiling the pertinent information from the medical record based on predetermined data sets
- *Registry development*: The process of assembling a chronological set of data for an express purpose
- *Storage*: Implementation and oversight of computer-based and paper-based filing systems
- *Retrieval*: The process of making information stored in various media and sites accessible
- *Release*: The function of appropriately responding to requests for information based on laws and policy
- *Analysis*: The process of conducting qualitative and quantitative analysis of documentation against standards and policy

Health Information Media and Forms

The final domain of HIM professional practice concerns the forms in which health data are captured and stored. The management of information relates to all the following forms:

- Data (individual and aggregate)
- Reports
- Health records
- Data dictionaries
- Clinical vocabularies

Information may be stored using a variety of media, including electronic (computer systems), database, microfilm or microfiche, and paper.

Check Your Understanding 4.2

Instructions: Answer the following questions on a separate piece of paper.

1. What benefits are gained from HIM planning?
2. How are data modeling and process or workflow modeling related?
3. What are some of the elements of a data dictionary?
4. What are some examples of how understanding the content of health information relates to the informatics functions?

Health Information Management Body of Knowledge

Merriam-Webster's Collegiate Online Dictionary (2008) defines knowledge as "the fact or condition of knowing something with familiarity gained through experience or association." Therefore a **body of knowledge** (BoK) would be the collected resources, knowledge, and expertise within and related to a profession. A BoK is usually made up of knowledge areas that represent a taxonomy of relevant concepts. Most BoKs also reference a significant amount of supporting literature. The HIM profession has a strong body of knowledge starting at entry-level degree programs and building through the Foundation of Record Education (FORE) BoK reference library.

There are distinct curriculum models for each educational level within the field: associate, baccalaureate, and master's degrees. The health information administration (HIA) model (baccalaureate level) is presented in figure 4.2 and can be categorized into 15 topics:

- Health data structure, content, and standards
- Healthcare information requirements and standards
- Clinical classification systems
- Biomedical sciences
- Reimbursement methodologies
- Healthcare statistics, biomedical research and quality management—healthcare statistics and research
- Quality management and performance improvement
- Health services organization and delivery

Figure 4.2. AHIMA knowledge clusters for health information management baccalaureate degree program

AHIMA KNOWLEDGE CLUSTERS for HEALTH INFORMATION MANAGEMENT

Baccalaureate Degree Program

The knowledge clusters serve as the basis of curriculum development and learning objectives for academic programs in health information management. Bloom's Taxonomy is a classification system that provides a standard system of classifying the learning outcome level expected of a content area (knowledge cluster) within an educational experience and provides constructive help on building a curriculum. Bloom's Taxonomy helps to specify learning objectives so that it becomes easier to plan learning experiences and prepare evaluation devices.

Bloom's Taxonomy	Explanation
1 = Knowledge: The remembering (or recalling) of appropriate, and previously learned information	• Observation & recalling information • Classifications & categories (of major ideas) • Knowledge of major principles and theories of subject matter • Learning objectives phrasing: list, define, describe, identify, match, select, label, reproduce, state
2 = Comprehension: Grasping the meaning of information	• Translate knowledge into a new context • Interpret facts, infer causes • Predict consequences • Learning objectives phrasing: convert, discuss, estimate, explain, generalize, give examples, restate in own words, summarize, distinguish, differentiate, interpret
3 = Application: Applying previously learned information to new situations to solve problems	• Identify the best answer • Solve problems using required skills or knowledge • Determine, discover, assess, articulate • Learning objectives phrasing: apply, demonstrate, calculate, solve, modify, change, classify, discover, solve, teach, utilize
4 = Analysis: Breaking down information and inferring (or finding evidence) to support divergent conclusions	• Break down, differentiate, discriminate • Recognize, infer, point out • Illustrate, outline, prioritize • Learning objectives phrasing: diagram, distinguish, organize parts, recognize hidden meanings, identify components, arrange, select, explain, infer, prioritize
5 = Synthesis: Applying prior knowledge and skills to create a new or original whole	• Use old ideas to create new ones • Predict and draw conclusions • Adapting divergent knowledge toward a new synthesis • Learning objectives phrasing: adapt, anticipate, collaborate, combine, compare, compose, design, devise, facilitate, negotiate, reconstruct, reorganize, substitute, revise, design, invent
6 = Evaluation: Judging the value of material based on personal values and opinions resulting in an end product	• Assess value of theories and presentations • Make choices based on reasoned argument • Verify the value of evidence presented • Learning objectives phrasing: Appraise, decide, recommend, convince, judge, support, conclude, critique, defend, reframe

Figure 4.2. (Continued)

Knowledge Cluster Content
Biomedical Sciences
■ Anatomy (3)
■ Physiology (3)
■ Medical Terminology (5)
■ Pathophysiology (4)
■ Pharmacotherapy (4)
I.A. Health Data Structure, Content, and Standards
1. Structure and use of health information (individual, comparative, aggregate) (5)
2. Health information media (paper, electronic/computer-based; e-health-personal, web-based) (5)
3. Type and content of health record (paper, electronic, computer-based, e-healthpersonal, web-based) (5)
4. Data quality assessment and integrity (5)
5. Secondary data sources (registries and indexes; databases – such as MEDPAR, NPDB, HCUP) (4)
6. Healthcare data sets (such as OASIS, HEDIS, DEEDS, UHDDS, UACDS, NEDSS, NMMFS) (4)
7. Health information archival systems (5)
8. National Healthcare Information Infrastructure (NHII) (5)
9. Data collection tools (such as forms; computer input screens; other health record documentation tools) (5)
I.B. Healthcare Information Requirements and Standards
1. Standards and regulations for documentation (such as JCAHO, CARF, COP, AAAHC, AOA) (5)
2. Health information standards (such as HIPAA, ANSI, ASTM, LOINC, UMLS, MESH, Arden Syntax, HL-7) (5)
I.C. Clinical Classification Systems
1. Healthcare taxonomies, clinical vocabularies, terminologies/nomenclatures (such as ICD-9-CM, ICD-10, CPT, SNOMED-CT, DSM-IV) (4)
2. Medicare Severity Diagnosis Related Groups (MS-DRGs) (4)
I.D. Reimbursement Methodologies
1. Clinical data and reimbursement management (5)
2. Compliance strategies and reporting (e.g. National Correct Coding Initiative) (4)
3. Chargemaster management (4)
4. Casemix management (4)
5. Audit process (such as compliance and reimbursement) (5)
6. Payment systems (such as PPS, DRGs, APCs, RBRVS, RUGs) (4)
7. Commercial, managed care and federal insurance plans (4)
II.A. Healthcare Statistics, Biomedical Research and Quality Management—Healthcare Statistics and Research
1. Statistical analysis on healthcare data (5)
2. Descriptive statistics (such as means, standard deviations, frequencies, ranges, percentiles) (5)
3. Inferential statistics (such as t-tests, ANOVAs, regression analysis, statistical process control, reliability, validity) (5)
4. Vital statistics (5)

(Continued on next page)

Figure 4.2. (Continued)

Knowledge Cluster Content
5. Epidemiology (4)
6. Data reporting and presentation techniques (5)
7. Computerized statistical packages (5)
8. Research design/methods (such as quantitative, qualitative, evaluative, outcomes) (5)
9. Knowledge-based research techniques (such as Medline, CMS, libraries, web sites) (5)
10. National guidelines regarding human subjects' research (4)
11. Institutional review board process (IRB) (5)
12. Research protocol data management (4)
II.B. Quality Management and Performance Improvement
1. Quality assessment and management tools (such as benchmarking, ORYX, SQC) (5)
2. Utilization and resource management (4)
3. Risk Management (4)
4. Disease management process (such as case management, critical paths) (4)
5. Outcomes measurement (such as patient, customer satisfaction, disease-specific) (5)
III.A. Health Services Organization and Delivery
1. Organization of healthcare systems (5)
2. Components and operation of healthcare organizations including e-health delivery (5)
3. Accreditation standards (such as JCAHO, AOA, NCQA, CARF, CHAP, URAC) (5)
4. Regulatory and licensure requirements (such as COP, state health departments) (5)
III.B. Healthcare Privacy, Confidentiality, Legal and Ethical Issues
1. Legislative and legal system (4)
2. Privacy, confidentiality, security principles, policies and procedures (5)
3. Health information laws, regulations, and standards (such as HIPAA, e-health, JCAHO, state laws) (5)
4. Elements of compliance programs (5)
5. Professional and practice related ethical issues (5)
IV.A. Information Technology and Systems
1. Computer concepts (hardware components, systems architectures, operating systems and languages, and software packages and tools) (4)
2. Communications technologies (networks—LANS, WANS, VPNs; data interchange standards—NIST, HL-7) (4)
3. Internet technologies (Intranet, web-based systems, standards – SGML, XML) (4)
4. Data, information and file structures (data administration, data definitions, data dictionary, data modeling, data structures, data warehousing, database management systems) (5)
5. Data storage and retrieval (storage media, query tools/applications, data mining, report design, search engines) (5)
6. Data security (protection methods—physical, technical, managerial, risk assessment, audit and control program, contingency planning, data recovery, Internet, web-based, and e-Health security) (5)

Figure 4.2. (Continued)

IV.B. Applied Health Informatics
1. Leading development of health information resources and systems (4)
2. Brokering of information services (5)
3. Clinical, business and specialty systems applications (administrative, clinical decision support systems, electronic health record and computer-based health record systems, nursing, ancillary service systems, patient numbering systems at master and enterprise levels) (5)
4. Systems development (planning, analysis and design, customization, selection/procurement, implementation, integration, support, testing and evaluation, auditing and monitoring) (5)
5. Human factors and user interface design (4)
6. Systems Life Cycle (systems analysis, design, implementation, evaluation, and maintenance) (5)
V.A. Organization and Management
1. Principles of management (5)
2. Negotiation techniques (4)
3. Communication and interpersonal skills (5)
4. Team/consensus building (5)
5. Professional development for self and staff (4)
6. Problem solving and decision making processes (5)
VI.A. Human Resources Management
1. Employment laws (4)
2. Principles of human resources management (recruitment, supervision, retention, counseling, disciplinary action) (5)
3. Workforce education and training (4)
4. Performance standards (5)
VI.B. Financial and Resource Management
1. Healthcare finance (payer mix, bond rating, investment, capitalization) (3)
2. Accounting principles (4)
3. Budget process (capital and operating) (5)
4. Cost/benefit analysis (5)
VI.C. Strategic Planning and Organizational Development
1. Strategic leadership, management and planning (4)
2. Organizational behavior (4)
3. Business building (entrepreneurialism—building your own business; entrepreneurialism—championing best practices, processes, services within your organization) (3)
4. Change management (4)
5. Organizational assessment and benchmarking (4)
VI.D. Project and Operations Management
1. Process reengineering and work redesign (4)
2. Project management (5)

- Healthcare privacy, confidentiality, security, legal, and ethical issues
- Health information technology and systems
- Organization and management
- Human resources management
- Financial and resource management
- Strategic planning and organizational development
- Project and operations management

These 15 topics are the foundational body of knowledge for a baccalaureate prepared health information management professional. The curriculum at all degree levels is routinely examined and updated to ensure its relevance to the field. The **Commission on Accreditation of Health Informatics and Information Management Education** (CAHIIM) accredits educational institutions that offer associate and baccalaureate degrees in health information administration and health information technology. CAHIIM also accredits advanced education in HIM at the master's degree level. This accreditation process ensures that the appropriate curriculum is being taught, along with other essential elements of a high-quality educational experience.

Two elements make this curriculum unique: (1) the specialization to healthcare throughout the curriculum, and (2) the combination of studies in the biomedical sciences, management, and information fields. In addition to this specific HIM curriculum, HIM students are required to have an understanding of additional general education topics to prepare them for the workplace, including:

- Oral and written communications
- Social sciences
- Arts and humanities
- Microcomputer literacy, including word processing, spreadsheets, database management, and graphics and presentation
- Natural sciences
- Mathematics

These content areas do not represent individual courses but, rather, define the scope of instruction required of all accredited HIA programs.

The American Health Information Management Association (AHIMA) offers resources to support the BoK for the profession through the FORE Library. The AHIMA online HIM BoK resource contains:

- *Journal* articles from the past 20 years
- Periodicals published by AHIMA
- Practice briefs, position statements, guidelines, and white papers
- Job descriptions and other relevant association information
- Government publications
- Links to other HIM documents
- Practice guidance reports on current electronic health information topics

Check Your Understanding 4.3

Instructions: Answer the following questions on a separate piece of paper.

1. In which knowledge cluster would a health information administration student learn about HIPAA regulations?
2. What is the purpose of health services organization and delivery in the HIA curriculum?
3. What are the elements within health data structure, content, and standards?
4. List all the curriculum topics that are important to performing research.

Characteristics of a Profession

The term **profession** may be defined in a number of ways. *Merriam-Webster's* Collegiate Online Dictionary defines it as "a calling requiring specialized knowledge and often long and intensive academic preparation" (2008). The world is changing, as are the traditional boundaries associated with professions. In Thomas Friedman's book *The World is Flat* (2005) the indicators point toward a much more global empowerment than has ever been experienced before. The health information management profession is continually addressing this future within its dynamic core professional characteristics. In *The Qualifying Association*, Millerson describes a profession as "a type of higher grade, non-manual occupation, with both subjectively and objectively recognized occupational status, possessing a well-defined area of study or concern and providing a definite service, after advanced training and education" (1964, 10). Whether using Friedman or Millerson's definition, there are certainly characteristics of a profession that apply to HIM:

- Professional associations
- Code of ethics
- Unique body of knowledge that must be learned through formal education
- System of training with entry by examination or other formal prerequisites (certification)
- Professional cohesion
- Professional literature

Professional Associations

Accepting the rewards of a profession means accepting its responsibilities. One of the ways to ensure professional success is through membership in a professional association. Professional associations provide a rich environment for learning, contributing, and networking. The following professional associations are particularly important to individuals working in the field of HIM.

American Health Information Management Association

AHIMA represents more than 53,000 members. Association membership includes HIM professionals credentialed in the field as well as those with an interest in health information management and a willingness to abide by the AHIMA Code of Professional Ethics (appendix B). HIM professionals serve the healthcare industry and the public by managing, analyzing, and utilizing data vital for patient care and making them accessible to healthcare providers when they are needed most.

AHIMA members play many diverse roles, yet share a common purpose: to provide reliable and valid information that drives the healthcare industry. They are specialists in administering information systems, managing medical records, and coding information for reimbursement and research. As leaders in the field of HIM, AHIMA members work to ensure that healthcare is based on accurate and timely information. AHIMA is the oldest and largest of the membership associations in health information. Since its creation in 1928, AHIMA has undergone numerous changes and significant development. (See figure 4.3.) Building on the profession's strong tradition, AHIMA members also are prepared to be a driving force in a changing healthcare industry. Health information is not a paper document maintained in one location and accessible only through one mechanism. HIM professionals permeate the fabric of healthcare to provide a vital link for practitioners, consumers, and payers. Although much has evolved in the field of HIM, the central vision of AHIMA remains constant: "to provide quality healthcare through quality information." (AHIMA 2008b). AHIMA seeks to attain that vision by:

- Supporting members with practice guidance and lifelong learning opportunities
- Providing a professional network through Communities of Practice (CoP) for members to reach out to their colleagues

Figure 4.3. AHIMA timeline (name changes, credentials awarded)

1928 (Oct. 11)	Association of Record Librarians of North America (**ARLNA**) founded.
1929	*Bulletin of the Association of Record Librarians of North America* published.
1933	Registered Record Librarian (**RRL**) credential established.
1934	First professional baccalaureate program approved at the College of St. Scholastica, Duluth, MN.
1938 (Dec)	*Bulletin, American Association of Medical Record Librarians*, replaces the *Bulletin of the Association of Record Librarians of North America.*
1944	Name of association changed to American Association of Medical Record Librarians (**AAMRL**) when Canadian members formed their own organization.
1944 (Dec.)	*Journal of the American Association of Medical Record Librarians* replaces *Bulletin, American Association of Medical Record Librarians.*
1953	Accredited Record Technician (**ART**), credential established.
1953	First schools for medical record technicians approved: St. Francis Hospital, Breckenridge, MN, Marymount Hospital, Garfield Heights, Ohio, St. Benedict's Hospital, Ogden, UT.
1954	Certified Record Librarian (**CRL**) designation established to recognize RRLs who had been in the field for at least 15 years and had made significant contributions to the profession. It was discontinued in 1964 because the general membership thought its use detracted from that of the RRL.
1964 (Jan)	*Medical Record News, the Journal of the American Association of Medical Record Librarians* replaces *Journal of the American Association of Medical Record Librarians.*
1970	Name of association changed to American Medical Record Association (**AMRA**).
1970 (Feb)	*Medical Record News, the Journal of the American Medical Record Association* replaces *Medical Record News, the Journal of the American Association of Medical Record Librarians.*
1978	Registered Record Administrator (**RRA**) credential replaces the Registered Record Librarian (RRL) credential.
1980 (Aug)	*Journal of the American Medical Record Association* replaces *Medical Record News.*
1991	Name of association changed to American Health Information Management Association (**AHIMA**).
1991 (Nov)	*Journal of the American Health Information Management Association* (*Journal of AHIMA*) replaces *Journal of the American Medical Record Association.*
1992	Certified Coding Specialist (**CCS**) credential established.
1997	Certified Coding Specialist–Physician-based (**CCS-P**) credential established.
1999	Fellow of the American Health Information Management Association (**FAHIMA**) designation established to recognize members who have made significant and lasting contributions to the HIM profession.
1999	First master's degree program approved by CAHIIM at the College of St. Scholastica, Duluth, MN.
2000	Registered Health Information Technician (**RHIT**) credential replaces the Accredited Record Technician (ART) credential; Registered Health Information Administrator (**RHIA**) credential replaces the Registered Record Administrator (RRA) credential.
2001	Certified Coding Associate (**CCA**) entry-level coding credential established.
2002	Certified in Healthcare Privacy (**CHP**) credential created.
2002	Certified in Healthcare Security (**CHS**) credential, sponsored by HIMSS and administered by AHIMA created.
2002	Certified in Healthcare Privacy and Security (**CHPS**) credential, sponsored jointly by AHIMA and HIMSS, created.
2004	*Perspectives in Health Information Management* (PHIM) research journal published.
2005	CAHIIM took responsibility for specialized programmatic accreditation of HIM programs.
2008	PHIM name changed to Health Informatics and Information Management Research.
2008	Certified Health Data Analyst (CHDA) credential approved by the House of Delegates.

Source: AHIMA 2008.

- Guaranteeing excellence to the healthcare industry through certification and relevant resources
- Disseminating best practices and innovations
- Promoting education and research in the field
- Providing public policy leadership
- Advocating for the profession and for HIM issues

AHIMA supports a system of component organizations in every state plus Washington, D.C. and Puerto Rico. Component state associations (CSAs) provide their members with local access to professional education, networking, and representation. They also serve as an important forum for communicating national issues and keeping members informed of regional affairs that affect HIM.

American Medical Informatics Association

The **American Medical Informatics Association** (AMIA) is a membership organization composed of individuals, institutions, and corporations that develop and use biomedical and health informatics to improve healthcare. Founded in 1990, AMIA was created when the American College of Medical Information and the Symposium on Computer Applications in Medical Care merged. Its members include physicians, nurses, computer and information scientists, biomedical engineers, medical librarians and academic researchers, educators, and students. AMIA represents the United States at the **International Medical Informatics Association** (IMIA). Further, AMIA sponsors educational sessions and publishes the *Journal of the American Medical Informatics Association.*

Association of Clinical Documentation Improvement Specialists

The **Association of Clinical Documentation Improvement Specialists** (ACDIS) was formed in 2007 as a community in which clinical documentation improvement professionals could communicate resources and strategies to implement successful programs and achieve professional growth. The mission is to bring CDI specialists together for improvement. Members receive electronic resources, have access to online discussions, and have access to e-learning courses for continuing education credit. ACDIS also offers annual educational conferences.

Association for Healthcare Documentation Integrity

The **Association for Healthcare Documentation Integrity** (AHDI), formerly American Association for Medical Transcription (AAMT), was established in 1978 and refocused in 1999 as the profession of medical transcription evolved. AHDI's mission is to set standards for education and practice in clinical documentation, ensuring the highest level of accuracy, privacy, and security while improving patient safety and quality of care for consumers. Membership is open to any person employed in or involved in the field of healthcare documentation and data capture. AHDI also certifies medical transcriptionists.

College of Healthcare Information Management Executives

The **College of Healthcare Information Management Executives** (CHIME) was formed in 1992, through a collaborative effort by the Healthcare Information Management and Systems Society (HIMSS) and the Center for Health Information Management (CHIM). CHIME serves two purposes: (1) to serve the professional development needs of healthcare chief information officers (CIOs), and (2) to advocate more effective use of information management within healthcare.

CHIME offers its members professional development opportunities through its biannual CIO Forums, research, and through courses in IT strategies, architecture, and best practices. Other resources include member-to-member surveys, online reference documents, and various presentations made available online.

Healthcare Information and Management Systems Society

The **Healthcare Information Management and Systems Society** (HIMSS) provides leadership in healthcare for the management of technology and management systems. Members include healthcare professionals in a variety of healthcare settings, including hospitals, corporate healthcare systems, clinical practice groups, vendor organizations, and consulting firms. HIMSS offers membership to individuals, organizations and healthcare providers, corporations and affiliates for non-profit associations, and professional organizations. Although HIMSS offers a variety of benefits, it is best-known for its annual conference and exhibition, which is the largest in the industry. HIMSS supports 46 chapters across the U.S. and Canada. HIMSS also offers **certified professional in health information management systems** (CPHIMS) certification.

International Federation of Health Record Organizations

The **International Federation of Health Record Organizations** (IFHRO) supports national associations and health records professionals to improve health records. Established in 1968 as a forum to bring together national organizations, IFHRO continues to focus on global issues affecting health information. IFHRO has a partnership with IMIA and is affiliated with the World Health Organization (WHO). IFHRO is organized into six regions, consistent with the World Health Organization: Europe, Americas, South East Asia, Western Pacific, Eastern Mediterranean, and Africa. Although national membership is reserved for one association per country, individuals may be associate members of IFHRO. A world congress is sponsored every three years and attracts HIM professionals from all over the globe.

International Medical Informatics Association

The mission of IMIA is to promote informatics in healthcare and biomedical research; advance and nurture international cooperation. To accomplish this, their objectives are to stimulate research, development, and application, to move informatics from theory into practice, disseminate knowledge and technology, promote education, and represent the field of health informatics with the WHO and other international professional and governmental organizations. Generally, membership to IMIA is limited to organizations, societies, and corporations. IMIA sponsors a conference, MEDINFO, every three years and engages multiple working groups to advance its mission.

National Cancer Registrars Association

The **National Cancer Registrars Association** (NCRA) was chartered in 1974, and its more than 4,500 members represent the various types of institutions that have an interest in cancer management. NCRA sponsors an annual conference designed to improve registrars' professional expertise. NCRA also sponsors a certification, the certified tumor registrar (CTR), for individuals working in this field. AHIMA developed the Cancer Registry Management formal education program in a collaborative partnership with NCRA.

Code of Ethics

An important element of any profession is its commitment to a code of ethics. Today's HIM professionals can face a variety of ethical dilemmas regarding payment and reimbursement systems, confidentiality and privacy, facility accreditation and licensure, and fair practices. A formal code of ethics ensures that professionals understand and agree to uphold an ethical standard that puts the best interests of the profession before their personal best interests.

AHIMA has developed a code of ethics for certified HIM professionals. (See chapter 11 and Appendix E). A violation of the code of ethics is grounds for disciplinary action, including revocation of credentials. Alleged violations of the code are subject to a formal peer review process. These processes are separate from legal or administrative procedure. AHIMA's Code of Ethics was revised in 2008.

Education

An educational requirement is part of the definition of a profession. Indeed, completing a profession's educational requirements is fundamental to gaining entry into the field. Additionally, ongoing education is a responsibility of any professional. This is especially true of HIM professionals challenged by new regulations, revolutionary technologies, and an industry in transition. In 2004, the AHIMA House of Delegates passed a resolution calling for its members to embrace lifelong learning (2004a):

> That AHIMA members make the commitment to lifelong learning and professional development so that HIM professionals continue to be vital players in ensuring quality healthcare through quality information.

This learning may be formal education through the pursuit of a master's or doctoral degree. Ongoing professional development also can be demonstrated through **continuing education** (CE) gained from conferences, workshops, reading, or distance learning activities. Seeking challenging work assignments and making professional development a goal when making career choices all contribute to an individual's professional development.

Certification

Certification is a process by which a nongovernment agency or association recognizes the competence of individuals who have met certain qualifications as determined by the agency or association. In HIM, AHIMA certification provides both personal validation and validation to employers and consumers of professional competence. Specifically, certification:

- Demonstrates to colleagues and superiors a dedication to high-quality healthcare and to the highest standards of HIM.
- Presents solid evidence to employers that an employee has trained and been tested to implement best practices and apply current technology solutions, advancing the organization.
- Sets a person apart from non-credentialed job candidates. In recent AHIMA-sponsored research groups, healthcare executives and recruiters cited these reasons for preferring credentialed personnel: (1) assurance of current knowledge through continued education, (2) possession of field-tested experience, and (3) verification of base-level competency.
- Has value for employers because it supports a worker's ability to uphold industry standards and regulations, thereby potentially saving organizations from fines and penalties due to errors or noncompliance.
- Catalyzes career development by augmenting resumes and adding recognition to candidates' capability. Because credentials appear after a person's name, they announce expertise with every signature.

To achieve AHIMA certification, individuals must meet certain eligibility requirements and successfully complete an examination. AHIMA credentials currently are divided into three practice areas: HIM, Coding, and Healthcare Privacy and Security, offering six credential opportunities, as described in the following subsections.

Registered Health Information Administrator

Registered health information administrators (RHIAs) are skilled in the collection, interpretation, and analysis of patient data. Additionally, they receive the training necessary to assume managerial positions related to these functions. RHIAs interact with all levels of an organization—clinical, financial, administrative—that use patient data in decision making and everyday operations.

A recent AHIMA member survey revealed that more than half of all HIM professionals work in acute care hospitals (53.3 percent), which, while not surprising, indicates the growing diversity of opportunities available for RHIAs. (See figure 4.4.) RHIAs enjoy job placement in a broad range of settings that span the continuum of healthcare, including clinics, integrated healthcare delivery systems, long-term care facilities, behavioral or mental health facilities, hospice, home health centers, and ambulatory surgical centers. RHIA's and HIM professionals also are employed in non-provider settings such as vendors, corporate compliance, government health agencies, insurers and managed care, billing companies, and pharmaceutical firms. Prospects are especially strong in these settings for RHIAs who possess advanced degrees in business or health administration.

To become eligible to take the RHIA examination, applicants must meet one of the following educational requirements:

- Hold a baccalaureate degree or post baccalaureate certificate from a health information administration (HIA) program accredited by CAHIIM
- Hold a degree from a foreign HIA baccalaureate program with which AHIMA has a reciprocity agreement

The RHIA exam is offered continually at computer testing sites located throughout the country and arrangements can be made for international testing sites. An application must

Figure 4.4. HIM professional work settings

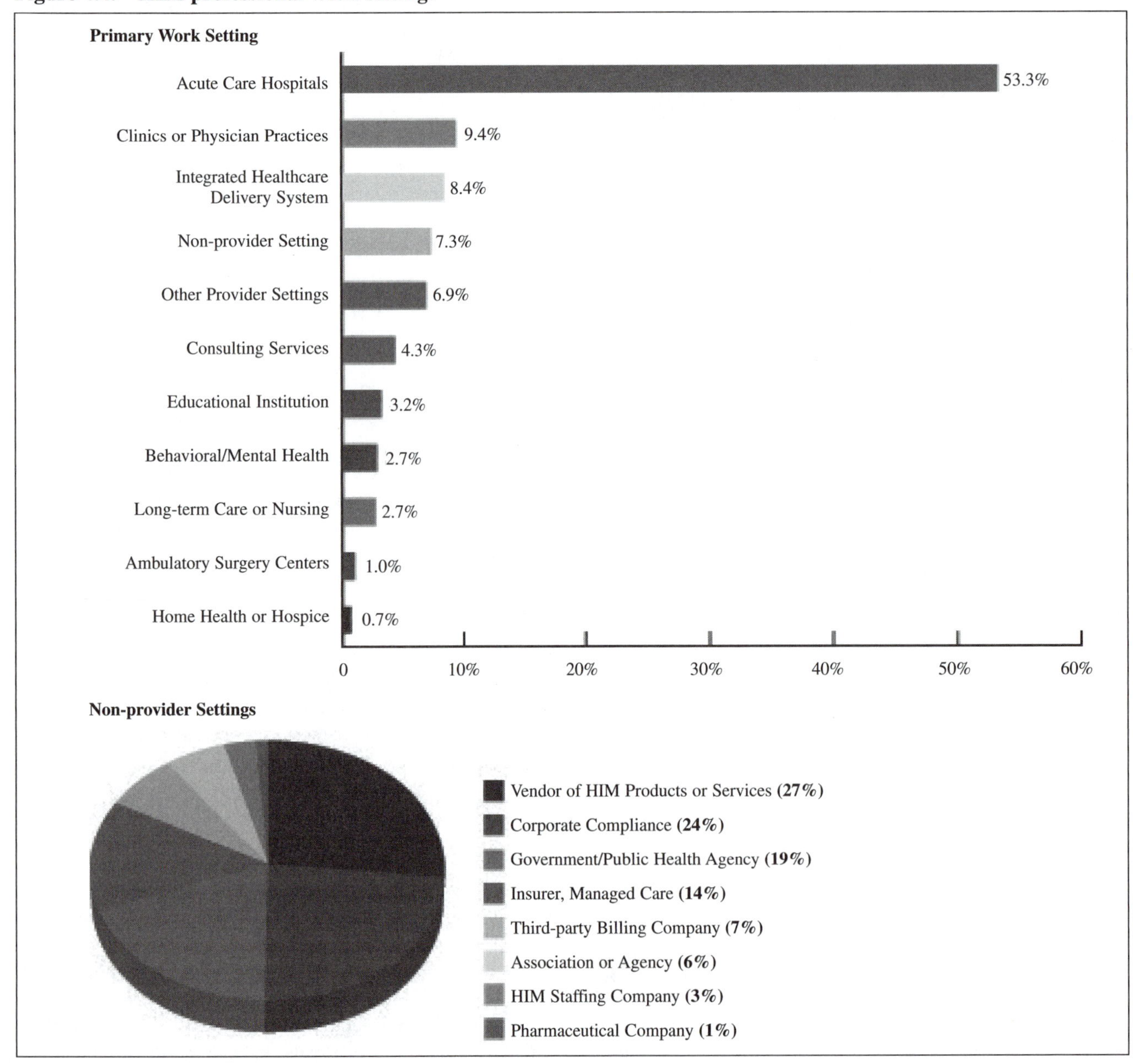

Source: AHIMA Salary Survey 2008e.

be filed with AHIMA, and then an identification number and password are assigned.

Registered Health Information Technician

Registered health information technicians (RHITs) are health information technicians who ensure the quality of medical records by verifying their completeness, accuracy, and proper entry into computer systems. RHITs also may use computer applications to assemble and analyze patient data for the purpose of improving patient care or controlling costs. These technicians often specialize in coding diagnoses and procedures in patient records for reimbursement and research. Moreover, they may serve as cancer registrars, compiling and maintaining data on cancer patients. In a recent AHIMA membership survey, the majority of RHIT respondents held job titles in one of the following categories: coding/technician or manager/supervisor. With experience, the RHIT credential holds solid potential for advancement to management positions, especially when combined with a bachelor's degree.

Employment opportunities exist for RHITs in any organization that uses patient data or health information, including pharmaceutical companies, law and insurance firms, and health product vendors.

RHITs can look forward to expanding career opportunities in health information technology. According to the Bureau of Labor Statistics, HITs can expect an almost 30 percent growth rate by 2014 (Martiniano and Moore 2006).

RHIT eligibility requires an associate degree in HIM from a CAHIIM-accredited program or graduate from an HIM program approved by a foreign association with which AHIMA has a reciprocity agreement.

Certified Coding Associate

Certified coding associates (CCAs) are entry-level coders certified in the knowledge required to code. They are tested in their understanding of anatomy and physiology, pathophysiology, medical terminology, medical documentation, and the principles of classification systems. This credential creates the first step of a coding career ladder that could lead to a CCS or a CCS–P with more training and experience. Moreover, CCAs may choose to expand their interests in HIM beyond coding and continue their education by attaining a degree in HIM and applying for the RHIT or RHIA credential.

Certified Coding Specialist

Certified coding specialists (CCSs) are professionals skilled in classifying medical data from patient records, generally in the hospital setting. CCSs review patient records and assign numeric codes for each diagnosis and procedure. They must possess expertise in the ICD-9-CM coding system and the surgery section within the CPT coding system. In addition, the CCS must be knowledgeable in medical terminology, disease processes, and pharmacology.

Hospitals or medical providers report coded data to insurance companies or the government (Medicare and Medicaid recipients) for reimbursement of their expenses. Coding accuracy is highly important to healthcare organizations because of its impact on revenues and in the description of health outcomes. Accordingly, the CCS credential demonstrates tested data quality and integrity skills in a coding practitioner. The CCS certification exam assesses mastery or proficiency in coding rather than entry-level skills.

Certified Coding Specialist–Physician-based

The **certified coding specialist–physician-based** (CCS–P) has expertise in physician-based settings such as physician offices, group practices, multispecialty clinics, or specialty centers. The CCS–P reviews patient records and assigns numeric codes for each diagnosis and procedure. To perform this task, he or she must possess in-depth knowledge of the CPT coding system and familiarity with the ICD-9-CM and HCPCS Level II coding systems. The CCS–P is also expert in health information documentation, data integrity, and quality. Because patients' coded data are submitted to insurance companies or the government for expense reimbursement, the CCS–P plays a critical role in the health provider's business operation. Moreover, the employment outlook for this coding specialty looks highly favorable with the growth of managed care and the increase in non-hospital health services delivery options.

Certified in Healthcare Privacy and Security

The **certified in healthcare privacy and security** (CHPS) credential denotes advanced competency in designing, implementing, and administering comprehensive privacy and security protection programs in all types of healthcare organizations. The CHPS certification offers expanded career opportunities as well as credibility and recognition regarding privacy and security of health information. In a recent survey, 70 percent of healthcare executives agree that credentialed employees help reduce exposure to fraud and abuse charges. Those wanting to earn this credential will need to meet one of the following eligibility requirements:

- Baccalaureate degree and minimum of four years experience in healthcare management
- Masters or related degree (JD, MD, PhD) and two years experience in healthcare management
- Health information management credential (RHIA or RHIT) with a baccalaureate or higher degree and a minimum of two years experience in healthcare management

Certified Health Data Analyst

The Certified Health Data Analyst (CHDA) designation denotes advanced competencies in acquiring, managing, analyzing, interpreting, and transforming data into accurate, consistent, and timely information while balancing the "big picture" strategic vision with day-to-day details. CHDA-certified professionals exhibit broad organizational knowledge and the ability to communicate with individuals and groups at multiple levels, both internal and external. Eligibility to write this examination requires that the applicant meet one of the following requirements:

- Baccalaureate degree or higher and a minimum of five years of healthcare data experience
- RHIA and a minimum of one year of healthcare data experience

Certification Maintenance

In addition to original educational requirements for certifications, credentialed health information management professionals are required to participate in continuing education. The purpose of a CE program is to offer the public a form of assurance that individuals practicing a profession maintain competence following certification. In the health professions, maintaining competence is especially critical because of the rapid growth in technology, changes in social policies, and the expanding roles of health professionals in all areas of healthcare.

Participants are responsible for self-assessment of their personal strengths and weaknesses and can individualize CE programs to ensure their own professional competence. The number of CE hours that can be obtained in any particular activity is unlimited but there is a minimum required number of total hours. It is recommended that participants attempt to increase their knowledge and skills through a balanced variety of educational methods.

Continuing Education Requirements

All degree-based AHIMA credentialed professionals, RHIAs and RHITs regardless of AHIMA membership, maintain their credentials through:

1. *Completion of acceptable CE credits during a two-year period (cycle)*: RHIAs must earn 30 CE clock hours/credits, and RHITs must complete 20 CE clock hours. Eighty percent of all CE units must be earned within the HIM domain. The AHIMA Web site offers a link for domain explanation. (Refer to figure 4.2.)

   To receive credit, activities must be completed within the assigned cycle period. All cycles begin on January 1 and end on December 31 the following year. Individuals holding multiple credentials must earn 10 CE credits for each additional certification above the number required for their initial certification, not to exceed 60. Coding credential maintenance requires annual self-assessment.
2. *Payment of CE assessment fees:* AHIMA members are charged a CE assessment with annual membership dues. Nonmembers pay a CE fee set by the AHIMA Board of Directors.
3. *Validation of CE report*: Participants must submit their CE report forms (figure 4.5) to AHIMA by January 31, following the end of the CE cycle. The report may be completed online or by using the paper form and returning it to AHIMA. (Participants should keep a photocopy or a printout of the form.) Participants who are not audited will receive a CE validation certificate to retain as evidence of meeting CE requirements. Participants selected for audit do not meet requirements until they comply with the audit procedures. A CE validation certificate will be forwarded to audited participants after documentation has been received and approved.

Reporting Requirements and Cost

Approximately two months before the two-year cycle report is due, a Continuing Education Report form is mailed to the credential holder. Participants must record the number of CE credits received in each of the core content areas, the number of hours received in other HIM areas, and the total hours earned during the reporting period.

Although only the number of hours earned needs to be reported, it is important that participants maintain complete personal files of CE activities in case they are audited. AHIMA provides a CE tracking form for members.

Currently, AHIMA members holding degree-based credentials (RHIA, RHIT, or coding credentials) currently pay an annual $10 assessment with their membership dues and up to $72.50 for CHPS credential maintenance. Non-AHIMA members are assessed a CE maintenance fee as set by the Board of Directors.

Revocation and Restoration of Certification

If a credentialed HIM professional does not maintain their credential for two consecutive CE cycles (four years), the candidate will be required to apply and retake the applicable examination. If four years or less, candidates can complete the Intent to Restore Credential application, pay all appropriate restoration fees, and obtain the required number of CEs to reinstate a credential.

During restoration, an individual is listed as a restoration candidate for a maximum period of one year. No one may use the RHIT or RHIA credential after it has been revoked. The Council on Certification (COC) can revoke credentials of any individual failing to comply with AHIMA's Code of Ethics. COC-revoked credentials may not be restored.

Continuing Education Audits

As CE hours are entered into the membership files, approximately 2 percent of the candidates are randomly selected for audit. An individual selected for audit is required to submit verifiable documentation for each activity listed on the CE report form. Auditors will seek verification of attendance or participation, content description, and CE credits earned. Thus, CE participants are advised to retain all records in their files for at least one year following the cycle end date.

Prior Approval of Activities

Unless otherwise indicated, programs or activities do not need prior approval from AHIMA. If the program or activity has not received AHIMA prior approval, candidates can judge for themselves whether it meets AHIMA requirements. The AHIMA Web site offers CE Qualifying Activities guidance.

Figure 4.5. Partial excerpt of AHIMA's CE reporting form

CONTINUING EDUCATION TRACKING FORM

This tracking form is provided for your records only. Approximately two months before your two-year cycle report is due, a Continuing Education Report Form will be mailed to you. Although you will only need to report the number of continuing education units earned, it is important that you maintain a complete personal file. Individuals whose report forms are audited (approximately 2% of the reporting population) will be required to produce program descriptions and verification of participation.

Instructions:

Each program/activity must be calculated separately. Record whole hours only.
When calculating the total hours for each program, add the program hours only (lunch and breaks cannot be included). Add whole numbers (hours) first. Then add all fractional hours (minutes) and convert to whole hours. If any fractional time remains equal to 45 minutes or more, that time may be rounded up to one hour. Fractional time less than 45 minutes may not be counted for CE credit.

Number	Program Title and Sponsor	Location	Dates	Hours Earned	HIM Domain

(Continued on next page)

Figure 4.5. (Continued)

CONTINUING EDUCATION UNITS (CEUS)

Instructions: *List the number of continuing education units (CEUs) you earned in each category during the reporting period. Indicate the number of hours in the space provided.*

Technology: __________

Application of existing and emerging technologies for the collection of clinical data, the transformation of clinical data to useful health information, and the communication and protection of information.

Management Development: __________

Application of organizational management theory and practices as well as human resource management techniques, to improve departmental adaptability, innovation, service quality, and operational efficiency.

Clinical Data Management: __________

Application of data analysis techniques to clinical databases in order to evaluate practice patterns, assess clinical outcomes and assure cost-effectiveness of healthcare services.

Performance Improvement: __________

Study of fundamental organizational changes and how they are functionally organized or how they deliver patient care, with special focus on the requisite changes made in health information systems and services.

External Forces: __________

Knowledge of strategies that organizations and health information management professionals have employed to effectively address emerging legislative, regulatory, or other external party actions that potentially impact the collection and use of health data.

Clinical Foundations: __________

Understanding of human anatomy and physiology, the nature of disease processes in humans, and the current methods of diagnosis and treatment of acute and chronic medical conditions and diseases.

Privacy and Security __________

Understanding and application of current healthcare regulations which promote protection of medical information and the electronic transmission of health information; to act as the patient's advocate for their understanding of his or her rights in regard to protected health information.

TOTAL: __________

Professional Cohesion

Another aspect of a profession is professional cohesion, which is characterized by the members of a profession acting in a unified way. The existence of a professional association is one expression of professional cohesion as it embodies the members of the profession who act as a profession rather than as individuals. Professional cohesion can be witnessed in AHIMA's position statements or in advocacy positions that are taken with regulators or legislators. The recognition and adoption of best practices is another example of professional cohesion.

Professional Literature

The final element of a profession is the existence of professional literature. This textbook is one example of professional literature. The *Journal of the American Health Information Management Association* is the best-known source of HIM knowledge. Published since the 1930s, it is distributed to all AHIMA members and is available by subscription to nonmembers. Despite the fact that several other companies publish books and periodicals dealing with HIM, research and publication of HIM topics is in short supply when compared to other professions. This is an area of opportunity for HIM professionals to contribute to the professional BoK.

The *Journal of Health Informatics and Information Management Research* is an online research journal published by AHIMA and indexed in PubMed and AHIMA's Web site.

Check Your Understanding 4.4

Instructions: Answer the following questions on a separate piece of paper.

1. In what way is AHIMA addressing a more global future?
2. Why might someone belong to more than one professional association?
3. What are some of the key services provided by AHIMA?
4. What are examples of international health information associations?
5. What is a CSA and one benefit of membership?
6. How is the importance of continuing education addressed in the AHIMA's Code of Ethics?
7. How does AHDI differ from ACDIS?
8. What are the benefits of certification, and how does one maintain it?
9. Which professional associations offer certification?
10. Who is eligible for RHIA certification?
11. How frequently are certification records audited?
12. How does someone report CE activities?

Current and Evolving Professional Roles

Workforce research has confirmed that HIM professionals hold 200 different job titles in 40 types of organizations ranging from hospitals to veterinary clinics (Wing and Langelier 2004). This underscores how fundamentally HIM is changing. The U.S. Department of Labor, Bureau of Labor Statistics continues to project HIM as one of the high growth health occupations. Just 20 years ago, almost all HIM professionals worked in acute care hospitals. Today that number is just over 50 percent. For decades, we differentiated "traditional" from "nontraditional" practice; today, this distinction is irrelevant. HIM skills and competencies are needed by all organizations that use person-specific or aggregate patient data. The adoption of health IT will further accelerate the demand for a well qualified HIM workforce. (See figure 4.6.)

Vision 2006 was an extensive project envisioning HIM practice and roles as projected in 1996. This strategic document provided the foundation for HIM practice role definition. In 2003, AHIMA convened a task force to articulate a vision for an e-HIM future. **Electronic health information management** (e-HIM) addresses the nature of HIM practices and professional roles emerging within the health care industry as it transitions from paper-based to computer-based health information systems. In 2007, AHIMA published *Vision 2016: A Blueprint for Quality Education in Health Information Management* to outline an educational strategy required to bring new professionals into the field with the degree and level of training required to meet the knowledge and competency requirements of HIM in a healthcare system that is supported by a fully functional and interoperable electronic health information infrastructure.

Traditional HIM practice has been based on physical records, files filled with paper forms and documents. The future state of health information is electronic, patient-centered, comprehensive, longitudinal, accessible, and credible. Traditional medical records have become electronic health records (EHRs). HIM professionals play a variety of critical roles in the transition from paper to electronic records. In 2007, HIM professionals approved a resolution to apply their skills and knowledge in data capture methods, compliance, performance measurement, revenue cycle management, and data quality management. HIM professionals are partnering with clinical, legal, and information technology to address the legal business issues for the health record.

Figure 4.6. e-HIM professional roles

Business process engineer Clinical data analyst/clinical documentation coordinator Clinical research/trials associate Compliance officer Data quality manager Data sets, nomenclature and classification standards manager Data translator Instructor/trainer Educator Healthcare consumer advocate Health data/information resource manager	Health information services manager (director, assistant director, supervisor) Health information system applications designer/trainer, marketing and sales manager/implementation and support manager Privacy/security officer Project manager Quality Improvement manager Reimbursement manager Revenue cycle manager

Source: AHIMA Framework for HIM Education 2004.

Exciting career opportunities will emerge. HIM workgroups continually convene to provide best practice and help more clearly define the HIM professionals expanded opportunities. The e-HIM Work Group developed an extensive report projecting new roles in 2005. *Vision 2016* further identifies projected as well as current job titles by credential and degree level. These roles provide additional, expanded career opportunities. (Figure 4.7 shows a member profile for baccalaureate and advanced degree statistics.) The following is a selection of job titles and brief descriptions as identified through *Vision 2006*, *Vision 2016*, 2005 e-HIM Work Group, and member-driven research. This is by no means a complete list of job titles, but it does provide a sample of HIM opportunities.

- A **health information manager/director** in an integrated delivery system is responsible for the enterprise-wide direction of HIM functions. The role may be a line or staff management position. It includes working with the CIO and IS users to advance systems, methods, and applications support and to improve data quality, access, confidentiality, security, and usability.
- A **clinical data specialist** concentrates on assuring accurate and complete coding, validating the information contained in databases for internal and external uses, and providing information for clinical research across the entire integrated healthcare delivery system.
- A **patient information coordinator** helps consumers manage their personal health information, including personal health histories and release of information. This individual also helps customers understand managed care services and access to health information resources. With the growth of PHRs, consumers may learn to rely on the competency of the PI coordinator.
- A **clinical project manager** is responsible for managing and frequently participating in defining the scope of work, developing project plans, and maintaining schedules. This person will finalize the budget, develop plans for minimizing risks, and will be responsible for implementing improvement processes.
- A **data quality manager/data quality analyst** is responsible for data management functions that involve formalized continuous quality improvement activities for data integrity throughout the organization, beginning with the data dictionary and policy development, as well as data quality monitoring and audits. This role in particular may grow exponentially in light of the area of developing health information exchange (HIE).
- **Information privacy coordinator/privacy officer** will work in collaboration with managers to assess risks to health information security and privacy, monitor organizational privacy compliance issues, and establish policy and procedures to address security risks. The information privacy coordinator will develop training and monitor programs to ensure employee awareness.
- **Data integrity specialist** is responsible for assuring quality and accuracy of medical information in any form, electronic or hybrid. Frequently electronic health record systems make duplicate systems easier, the data integrity specialist identifies and resolves potential concerns such as fraud duplication, misfiles and other integrity issues associated with data management (AHIMA e-HIM Task Force 2003).
- A **consultant** broadly encompasses many aspects of HIM. Typically a consultant will be employed outside of the healthcare provider arena, working for an external firm or independently. Consultants may be responsible for operational assistance with e-HIM conversions, revenue cycle and coding auditing, compliance, privacy and security, or any of the HIM-related functions.
- A **data resource administrator** represents the next generation of records and data management and uses technological tools such as the computer-based patient record, data repositories, and data warehouses to meet current and future care needs across the continuum, provide access to the needed information, and ensure long-term data integrity and access.
- *A* **research and decision support analyst** ensures the quality of data and information generated through clinical investigations and other research projects. The decision support specialist provides clinicians and senior managers with information for decision making and strategy development. Both specialists use a variety of analytical tools.

In an information-driven healthcare world, roles for HIM professionals shift and expand continuously. The one constant of the HIM profession is its responsibility for advancing the quality of health information and assuring its availability in response to the needs of the healthcare industry.

Real-World Case

Jane Rogers, age 31, is supervisor for clinical coding in the health information service at Memorial Medical Center in Chicago. She left her job as a clinical coder at Community General Hospital six months ago to take this newly created position. Jane graduated from the Health Information Administration program at Chicago University 10 years ago and is credentialed as a RHIA and CCS by AHIMA. Jane is excited about the field and plans to sit for the Certified Health Data Analyst (CHDA) credential. Jane knows the HIM field with which she is so familiar plays a significant role in the data-driven healthcare arena. She wants to be able to share her expertise and help her employer with more than simply coding the data. She is an active member in good standing of the association and serves on the Coding Roundtable for the Chicago Area Health Information Management Association. The position at Memorial was a significant promotion, increasing her salary by $11,000 a year and offering her a

Figure 4.7. Member profile, Baccalaureate degree and advanced degree statistics

AHIMA Members with Baccalaureate Degrees		
Job Titles	**#**	**%**
Coding Professional	1,854	18.5%
Director	1,816	18.1%
Other	1,390	13.9%
Manager	1,246	12.4%
Consultant	810	8.1%
Supervisor	405	4.0%
Coordinator	341	3.4%
Administrator/CEO/COO	219	2.2%
Systems Analyst	217	2.2%
Data Quality Analyst	196	2.0%
HIM Faculty	174	1.7%
Assistant Director	169	1.7%
Project Manager	156	1.6%
Compliance Officer	149	1.5%
Assistant Administrator/VP/AVP	110	1.1%
Medical Record Analyst	109	1.1%
Registrar	105	1.0%
Privacy Officer	81	0.8%
Transcriptionist	73	0.7%
Team Leader	68	0.7%
Nurse	65	0.6%
Sales Representative	47	0.5%
DRG Coordinator	42	0.4%
Customer/Client Representative	34	0.3%
IS/MIS Director	34	0.3%
Assistant Manager	33	0.3%
Client Support Specialist	26	0.3%
Chief Information Officer	16	0.2%
Information Security Officer	13	0.1%
Chief Financial Officer	6	0.1%
Case Mix Analyst	3	0.0%
Safety Officer	3	0.0%
Doctor	1	0.0%
TOTAL RESPONSES	**10,011**	

AHIMA Members with Master's or Doctoral Degrees		
Job Titles	**#**	**%**
Director	598	26.6%
HIM Faculty	259	11.5%
Manager	242	10.8%
Consultant	218	9.7%
Coding Professional	144	6.4%
Administrator/CEO/COO	103	4.6%
Assistant Administrator/VP/AVP	87	3.9%
Other	86	3.8%
Compliance Officer	58	2.6%
Coordinator	57	2.5%
Project Manager	53	2.4%
Assistant or Assoc Director	43	1.9%
Supervisor	41	1.8%
Systems Analyst	35	1.6%
Privacy Officer	33	1.5%
Chief Information Officer	26	1.2%
Analyst- various	24	1.1%
Specialist-various	19	0.8%
Chief Executive Officer	17	0.8%
IS/MIS Director	12	0.5%
Coding Consultant	11	0.5%
Data Quality Analyst	11	0.5%
Clinical Data Specialist	10	0.4%
Registrar	9	0.4%
Nurse	7	0.3%
Attorney	6	0.3%
Chief Financial Officer	6	0.3%
Customer/Client Representative	6	0.3%
Doctor	6	0.3%
Auditor-various	5	0.2%
Client Support Specialist	5	0.2%
Information Security Officer	5	0.2%
Clinical Research Assistant	2	0.1%
TOTAL RESPONSES	**2,244**	

Source: AHIMA 2007a.

chance to be a supervisor; and it has the added the potential to grow if she attains the CHDA credential. The new level of earnings allowed Jane to live on her own and to purchase her own car, a four-year-old bright-red Saturn.

Jane reports to Steve Murray, manager of patient accounts and the health information service. Steve is the nephew of Memorial's chief financial officer, John Murray III. John was hired as the CFO 10 years ago when the medical center was in significant financial trouble. Steve has an MBA from the University of Chicago but, unlike most managers at Memorial including his uncle, no formal training in health informatics, health information, or financial management. However, he is young and ambitious and has shown himself to be an effective manager. He has streamlined operations in patient accounts and health information services, increasing revenues by 20 percent, increasing collections and cash flow, automating many functions, and reducing clerical staff.

Jane is responsible for the staff that review medical records of patients treated at Memorial to identify the diagnoses and procedures involved in inpatient, outpatient, and emergency treatment. Staff assign codes that are the basis for the bills submitted for reimbursement to the federal and state government and to private insurance companies.

Steve told Jane that her first priority was to make coding functions more current. Further, he wanted to cut in half the 20 or more days that it currently took to complete coding and billing functions. To that end, Jane reorganized processing procedures, helped the staff utilize the computerized coding system more effectively, taught staff new techniques for speeding up record review, and had achieved her goal within one financial quarter. In a meeting with Steve at the end of her three-month probationary period, Jane was awarded a $1,000 spot bonus for her achievement. Even John Murray, the CFO stopped by to congratulate her. Jane was so proud of her achievement that she presented her approaches at the monthly meeting of the Coding Roundtable and posted a short article to the Chicago area Community of Practice. Jane was thrilled to receive words of encouragement from many of her colleagues.

With processing now running smoothly, Jane turned to coding accuracy. She undertook a study in which she randomly sampled the coded records of all six of her coding staff and recoded them herself without looking at the original codes. She found that accuracy rates ranged from 78 to 92 percent. Although benchmark standards are difficult to come by, Jane knew that the coders at Community General met a standard of 90+ percent and that their evaluations and merit increases depended on maintaining it. Despite standard guidelines for correct code assignment, payer requirements do not always conform to them. Payers are constantly issuing instructions about what codes they will and will not accept, and coders sometimes do not have the latest instructions. Further, medical record documentation is not always clear or complete and although they do use a computerized system, accurate code assignment requires some individual judgment. Because the codes assigned to a case determine reimbursement, it is possible to increase the organization's revenue by using codes representing more complex diagnoses or procedures. These must be supported by documentation in the medical record. However, code assignment is seldom a black-and-white decision, and thus it is possible to assign unsupported codes, thereby increasing reimbursement, and also to fail to assign an appropriate code, thereby decreasing reimbursement.

In her weekly meeting with Steve, Jane reviewed the findings and proposed a plan for retraining and ongoing data quality control, including an adjusted compensation plan that would reward accurate work by her staff members. Her plan also called for developing a set of written guidelines that would reinforce Memorial's official guidelines and be presented to administration and the medical staff for approval. In this way, the coders would be reminded of how important their role is in assuring quality data, they would be reminded of the ground rules, and they would have a solid basis on which their performance was to be measured. Steve indicated that he would support the plan provided it did not result in slower processing time or reduced levels of reimbursement. Jane agreed to make certain that training did not slow down processing. She also suggested that improving accuracy would likely have a neutral effect on reimbursement because coders were undoubtedly missing reimbursable diagnoses and procedures.

With her plan in hand, Jane thought it would be wise to focus on the clinical areas most vulnerable to inaccurate coding. She began by conducting another interrater reliability study of cardiac surgery cases because these cases always present a challenge to coders. Again, she found wide variability in coder performance, this time ranging from 68 to 89 percent. She developed guidelines and obtained approval for them from the cardiac surgery clinical staff and administration. Then, she conducted a training program for her staff, who were paid overtime to attend so they did not fall behind in their work.

With another success under her belt, Jane next tackled the area of respiratory disease, another area of coding complexity and a major clinical service at Memorial, representing nearly 10 percent of its discharges. Further, Jane knew from reading her *Journal of the American Health Information Management Association* that bacterial pneumonia was the focus of investigations of Medicare fraud and abuse being conducted by the Department of Justice (DoJ). In fact, a number of healthcare organizations had paid substantial fines for having coded pneumonia cases with codes not supported by documentation in the medical records. Jane pulled a sample of records coded as "bacterial pneumonia," "other bacterial pneumonia," and "viral pneumonia." She worked late into the night for a week coding, recoding, checking, and double-checking her findings, which showed that cases were being consistently coded with the "bacterial" and "other bacterial" codes even though very few of the records had culture reports verifying bacterial infection. She calculated that with 150 cases a year and $5,000 in additional billings per case, this pattern of inaccurate coding was resulting in $750,000 in unsubstantiated revenue. The sheer volume of such cases made it unlikely that Memorial could claim random error if the DOJ chose to investigate.

Jane spent the weekend rechecking her findings and preparing a report with guidelines for accurate coding. She decided she had better talk to the coding staff before her regular weekly meeting with Steve on Monday afternoon. So first thing Monday morning, she met with her staff and reviewed her findings. Jane was shocked when Sally, the most tenured coder nodded and said, "We're just doing what we're told." When pressed, Sally acknowledged that the chief of respiratory medicine, Dr. Barrows, and Steve Murray had met with the coding staff the year before to discuss the coding of pneumonia cases. Jane asked, "Do you have anything in writing from the meeting?" "No," Sally replied, "they just told us that there were other ways to determine bacterial pneumonia than by culture and that Memorial was the major referral center for treating bacterial pneumonia." Needing time to digest what she had learned, Jane rescheduled her meeting with Steve, claiming a headache and upset stomach. She went home early to consider what to do next.

Concluding that the best approach would be to let the facts speak for themselves and hoping perhaps Steve did not understand what he had asked of the coding staff, Jane presented her report to Steve the next day along with her pneumonia coding guidelines. Steve was quiet and did not interrupt her, taking notes as she went through her findings. She concluded by saying, "Steve, we must implement the new guidelines at once, and we must also submit corrected bills for the cases we inaccurately submitted over the past year. This is the only way we can be sure that a fraud and abuse investigation will not be brought against Memorial." Steve replied, "Thank you, Jane. I'd like a copy of the report, and I'll discuss it with Dr. Barrows and our CFO, John Murray. We'll get back to you. In the meantime, don't say anything about this to anyone."

Three weeks have passed, and Steve has canceled three weekly meetings in a row and barely spoken to Jane when they meet informally in the hallway or cafeteria. He has asked no further questions and has given no indication of his intention to act on Jane's findings or proposals for action.

Summary

Health information managers work with clinical, epidemiologic, demographic, financial, research, reference, and coded healthcare data. Health information administrators plan information systems, develop policy, and identify current and future information needs. In addition, they apply the science of informatics to the collection, storage, use, and transmission of information.

HIM professionals prepare for their careers by mastering a well-defined body of knowledge expressed in a formal curriculum offered through CAHIIM-accredited academic programs. This curriculum covers, though is not limited to, content that addresses biomedical sciences, informatics, management, and research principles. When they are finished with their formal education, most HIM professionals achieve certification by passing a certification examination offered by AHIMA. Maintenance of certification demonstrates a lifelong commitment to continuing education and adherence to the HIM Code of Ethics.

As the professional association that represents most health information managers, AHIMA provides numerous services to its members and to the healthcare industry. Through certification of individual members, AHIMA ensures a qualified workforce. AHIMA works to improve healthcare by disseminating best practices, promoting research, and providing public policy leadership.

The HIM profession continues to evolve and change in response to healthcare trends, information technology, and government regulation. In the 1980s, most HIM professionals worked in hospitals; today, almost half of AHIMA's members work outside hospitals in a growing variety of health information practice sites. Health information management is a dynamic profession facing many current and future challenges, transitions, and opportunities. The conversion from paper files to electronic records has brought with it a shift in roles (from managers and supervisors to more high-level technical specialists) and broadened opportunities for HIM leaders.

References

AHIMA e-HIM Task Force. 2003. Vision of the e-HIM future: A report from the AHIMA e-HIM Task Force. Supplement to *Journal of AHIMA*.

American Health Information Management Association. 2004a. http://library.ahima.org/xpedio/groups/secure/documents/ahima/bok1_025460.hcsp?dDocName=bok1_025460.

American Health Information Management Association. 2004b. AHIMA timeline. http://library.ahima.org.

American Health Information Management Association. 2005a. Health information management: Professional definition. http://www.ahima.org/infocenter.

American Health Information Management Association. 2005b. HIM baccalaureate degree knowledge cluster content and competency levels. http://www.ahima.org/academics.

American Health Information Management Association. 2005c. Model curriculum, framework for HIM education. http://www.cahiim.org/resources/documents/HITBaccModelCurriculum.pdf#page%3D1.

American Health Information Management Association/FORE. 2005d. *Embracing the Future, New Times, New Opportunities for Health Information Managers*. http://www.ahima.org/fore/professional documents.

American Health Information Management Association. 2007a (Sept.). *Vision 2016: A Blueprint for Quality Education in Health Information Management*. http://www.ahima.org emerging issues.

American Health Information Management Association. 2007b (Oct.). AHIMA Resolution on Quality Data and Documentation in the EHR. House of Delegates. submitted by AHIMAs Physician Practice Council, approved by House of Delegates.

American Health Information Management Association. 2008a (June). Defining the Personal Health Information Management Role. Personal Health Record Practice Council. www.ahima.org.

American Health Information Management Association. 2008b. Mission. http://www.ahima.org.

American Health Information Management Association. 2008c. Code of Ethics. http://www.ahima.org/code of ethics.

American Health Information Management Association.2008d. FORE Library: HIM Body of Knowledge. http://www.ahima.org /fore/about.

American Health Information Management Association. 2008e. Salary Survey. http://www.ahima.org/salarystudy.

American Medical Informatics Association. 2008. http://www.amia.org.

Association for Clinical Documentation Improvement Specialists. 2007. http://www.cdiassocation.com.

Association for Healthcare Documentation Integrity. 2008. http://www.ahdionline.org.

Chronicle Guidance Publications. 1999. Health Sciences Librarians Brief 516, 8–11. Moravia, NY: Chronicle Guidance Publications.

College of Healthcare Information Management Executives. 2008. http://www.cio-chime.org.

Commission on Accreditation for Health Informatics and Information Management Education (CAHIIM). http://www.cahiim.org.

Friedman, T. L. 2005. *The World Is Flat, A Brief History of the Twenty-First Century*. New York: Farrar, Straus and Giroux.

Greenes, R.A. and E.H. Shortliffe. 1990. Medical informatics: An emerging academic discipline and institutional priority. *Journal of the American Medical Association* 263(8):1114–1120.

Health and Human Services. Effects of Health Care Spending on the U.S. Economy, 2004, Trends in Health Care Spending. http://aspe.hhs.gov/health/costgrowth.

Health Information Careers. 2008. http://www.healthinformationcareers.com.

Health Information Management and Systems Society. 2008. http://www.himss.org.

Huffman, E.K. 1941. *Manual for Medical Records Librarians.* Chicago: Physicians' Record Company.

Institute of Medicine, Committee on Improving the Patient Record in Response to Increasing Functional Requirements and Technological Advances. 1997. *The Computer-Based Patient Record: An Essential Technology for Health Care.* Washington, D.C.: U.S. National Academy of Sciences.

International Federation of Health Records Organizations. 2007. www.ifhro.org.

International Medical Informatics Association. 2008. www.imia.org.

Martiniano, R. and J. Moore. 2006 (June). Health Care Employment Projections: An Analysis of Bureau of Labor Statistics Occupational Projections, 2004–2014. The Rensselaer, NY: Center for Health Workforce Studies, School of Public Health, University at Albany. http://chws.albany.edu.

Medical Library Association. 2008 (Oct.). http://www.mlanet.org.

Merriam-Webster's Online Collegiate Dictionary. 2008. http:// www.merriam-webster.com.

Millerson, G. 1964. *The Qualifying Association: A Study in Professionalization.* London: Routledge & Paul.

National Cancer Registrar's Association. 2008. http://www.ncra-usa.org.

Russell, L.A. 2001. Not what we were in 1928: A new professional definition. *Journal of AHIMA* 72(4):48A–48D.

Russell, L. and Patena, K.. 2004. "Preparing tomorrow's professionals: A new framework for HIM education." *Journal of AHIMA* 75(6) 23–26.

Sager, A. and D. Socolar. 2005. Health care costs absorb one-quarter of economic growth, 2000–2005. Boston University School of Public Health, Health Reform Program. http://www.healthreformprogram.org.

Wing, P. and M.H. Langelier. 2004. The future of HIM: Employer insights into the coming decade of rapid change. *Journal of AHIMA* 75(6):28–32.

Wing, P. and E. Salsberg. 2002. How trends shape the work force today and tomorrow. *Journal of AHIMA* 73(4):38.

Chapter 5
Data and Information Management

Diana Lynn Johnson, PhD,
and Carol Marie Spielman, MA, RHIA

Learning Objectives

- Understand the difference between data, information, and knowledge
- Discuss the basic principles of information management
- Discuss the Joint Commission-based information management model
- List and give examples of ten characteristics of quality data as outlined by AHIMA
- List and give examples of the Essential Principles of Healthcare Documentation as developed by the Medical Record Institute Consensus Workgroup on Health Information Capture and Report Generation
- Discuss how the design of a database can affect data quality
- Compare a relational database and its characteristics with other database models
- Discuss how data modeling, particularly using an entity relationship diagram (ERD), can help ensure high-quality data
- Discuss the role of a data dictionary in ensuring both the quality of enterprise-wide data and data within a specific database application
- Describe and compare the roles of database administrator, data administrator, data resource manager, and data analyst
- Discuss how to ensure the integrity and security of data within a database
- Apply principles of effective data display
- Apply principles for making effective presentations

Key Terms

Aggregate data
Attributes
Authorization management
Comparative data
Conceptual data model
Crosswalk
Data
Data administrator
Data analyst
Data definition language (DDL)
Data dictionary
Data integrity
Data manipulation language (DML)
Data map
Data modeling
Data models
Data quality model
Data resource manager
Database
Database administrator
Database life cycle (DBLC)
Database management system (DBMS)
Derived attribute
Documentation
Enterprise Content and Records Management (ECRM)
Entity
Entity relationship diagram (ERD)
Explicit knowledge
Foreign key
Information
Information capture
Information management
Integrity constraints
Key attribute
Knowledge
Knowledge management
Knowledge-based information
Logical data model
Many-to-many relationship
Normalization
Object
Object-oriented database (OODB)
Object-oriented database management system (OODBMS)
One-to-many relationship
One-to-one relationship
Patient-specific data
Physical data model
Primary key
Referential integrity
Relational database
Relational database management system (RDBMS)
Report generation
Structured query language (SQL)
System catalog
Tacit knowledge
Ten characteristics of data quality
Unified modeling language (UML)
User-centered design

Health information managers have numerous roles within the healthcare industry. Most, if not all, of these roles involve managing data and information shared by a diverse and sometimes widely dispersed group of users. These data are the heart of the healthcare environment and vital to decision making processes surrounding both patient care and the business of healthcare. Meeting the challenge of managing the data and information for these purposes is not a simple task. Users have different information needs and may even have different data definitions. These different needs and definitions must be addressed in developing effective healthcare information systems.

This chapter introduces data and information as organizational assets that must be managed effectively to provide and sustain their value. It looks at the relationship between data and information, a Joint Commission-based model for managing healthcare information, other principles of healthcare information management, issues related to measuring data quality in a healthcare setting, basic database design, a few key concepts related to database management (data dictionaries, data management roles, ensuring the security and integrity of databases), and some basic principles of effective data and information display and presentation.

From Data to Information to Knowledge

Where does **information** come from? The simple answer is that information is processed data. **Data** are the raw facts, generally stored as characters, words, symbols, measurements, or statistics. Unprocessed data are not very useful for decision making. Take, for example, the numerals 6, 5, and 0. What do they mean? If seen together as 650, the data might be processed into the number six hundred fifty. When processing this number further by looking it up in the International Classification of Diseases Ninth Revision, Clinical Modification (ICD-9-CM) codebook or entering it into an encoder software program, it takes on even more meaning. It is now known that 650 is the code that represents a completely normal delivery of a single infant.

Is this information? That depends. When looking for a particular patient's diagnosis to process a claim, 650 may, in fact, be providing the information an insurance clerk needs. However, for the medical researcher looking for patient characteristics that contribute to completely normal deliveries, 650 on one patient's chart is not yet "processed" enough to provide useful information.

Where does data end and information begin? How are the two concepts related? Do the data collected and stored affect the information available within the organization? To answer these questions, one must first know who needs the data or information to perform what job function or functions. What people and what decisions are involved?

Information is a valuable asset at all levels of the healthcare organization. Personnel, both clinical and support staff, who perform the day-to-day operations related to patient care or administrative functions rely on information to do their jobs. This is truly the information age, and nowhere is this more apparent than in healthcare. Healthcare managers at both the middle management level and the executive level make extensive use of information, both to carry out day-to-day operations and in strategic planning for the organization. An interesting point to think about is that the same data may actually provide different information to different users. In other words, one person's data may be another person's information.

To illustrate this point, consider a small data set that represents some patient demographic data. It might be a subset of data from a hospital master patient index (MPI) system. (See table 5.1.)

This single set of data could be used at all levels of the hospital, beginning with the admissions process, a day-to-day operation of the facility. Admission personnel would use the data set to verify previous admissions or the spelling of a name. They also would be responsible for data entry and updating the MPI to ensure that it contains accurate, timely data. The MPI data set, as is, would provide useful information to the admissions personnel.

At the middle management level, the director of outpatient services might want information about where recent patients live and how far they travel to use this hospital. He or she might further process or query the data set to classify patients by zip code. After the query is completed, the director of outpatient services has useful information to help identify where patients live.

Table 5.1. Subset of a master patient index table

MRN	Last Name	First Name	Middle Name	DOB	Payment Type	Zip Code
096543	Jones	Georgia	Louise	11/21/1957	Self	29425
065432	Lexington	Milton	Robert	08/12/2000	Private	29425
467345	Lovingood	Jill	Karen	10/14/1992	Medicaid	29401
678543	Martin	Chloe	Mary	05/30/1978	Private	29465
234719	Martin	John	Adams	06/22/1961	Private	29401
786543	Nance	Natalie	JoAnn	11/27/1922	Medicare	29464

The CEO is interested in patient mix as well, but wants to see trend data over time showing the percentage of Medicare patients versus the percentage of private-pay and nonpaying patients. Again, the same data set is used, but the query process is more complex and the data set must be linked to another data set that contains payment information. The data in the MPI data set must be processed more extensively before any truly useful information is available to meet the CEO's needs. Moreover, the data from the MPI might be used in strategic planning for the hospital. Any number of complex queries about the patient population could contribute to strategic marketing or development decisions. The organization might even combine the MPI data set with external data sets using sophisticated decision support systems (DSSs) that compare its performance with the performance of other facilities in the region or state.

As information systems have evolved and become more complex, organizations are more aware of the importance of managing electronic data among numerous information systems. **Enterprise Content and Records Management** (ECRM) is:

> The strategy, technology, and processes for managing information assets facilitated by information technology. . . . Today's ECRM tools address all electronic content, including e-mail, with full life-cycle controls and integrate retention management approaches to ensure organizational compliance. These solutions support the ability to imbed content classification, retention rules, and integrate with collaboration tools (Strong 2008, 39).

Some texts include a third, higher level in the data-to-information hierarchy: **knowledge** (See figure 5.1). Lau defines knowledge as "information combined with experience, context, interpretation, and reflection" (2004, 2). AHIMA e-HIM Workgroup on Computer-Assisted Coding defines **knowledge management** as "capturing, organizing, and storing knowledge and experiences of individual workers and groups within an organization and making this information available to others in the organization" (2004, 2). This definition illustrates that there are two types of knowledge: explicit and tacit. **Explicit knowledge** is knowledge that is easily communicated and stored, for example documents and procedures. **Tacit knowledge** is personal knowledge that is not easily communicated or stored. Employees' experiences, habits, and skills are examples of tacit knowledge. Unless employee tacit knowledge is captured and stored, it is lost when an employee leaves the organization—hence the need for knowledge management.

People use knowledge to make decisions. In the preceding 650 example, the medical researcher might use his or her experience (tacit knowledge), diagnostic rules (written or not), and statistical rules (explicit knowledge) to determine the relationships between patient characteristics and the 650 diagnosis. Computer systems that combine an expert knowledge base and some type of rule-based decision analysis component are sometimes referred to as knowledge management systems to differentiate them from more traditional transaction-based or analytical information systems. Although computerized DSSs in healthcare are not always knowledge management systems, knowledge management systems are almost always used for decision support. (See chapter 19 for more information on decision support systems.)

The value of knowledge management in the healthcare setting is obvious when healthcare explicit and tacit knowledge are identified. To illustrate this, consider the explicit knowledge that may be available in the healthcare setting: procedure manuals, research results, clinical guidelines, policies, computer programs, and training materials. This explicit knowledge is easily recorded, stored, and shared in electronic databases or libraries. Now consider the tacit knowledge, most of which is in the minds of individuals: employee experience, skills, judgment, and guiding principles. The predicted large number of healthcare worker retirements and the shortage of healthcare workers (Bureau of Labor Statistics 2008) illustrate the need to capture, store, and distribute the tacit knowledge of employees.

Dr. Francis Lau (2004) has developed a knowledge management framework for the healthcare environment which addresses both explicit and tacit knowledge. It includes the core concepts of knowledge production, use, and refinement within a social context influenced by individual and organizational values and preferences. Figure 5.2 illustrates how the concepts are interrelated and iterative:

- *Knowledge production* includes the creation, organization, and storage of knowledge.

Figure 5.1. From data to knowledge

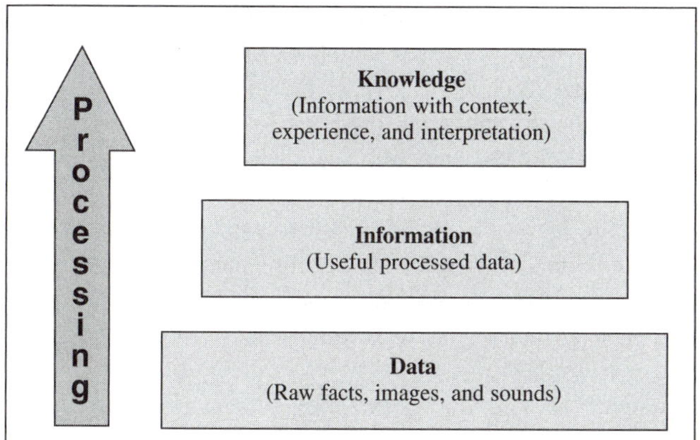

Figure 5.2. A conceptual knowledge management framework in healthcare

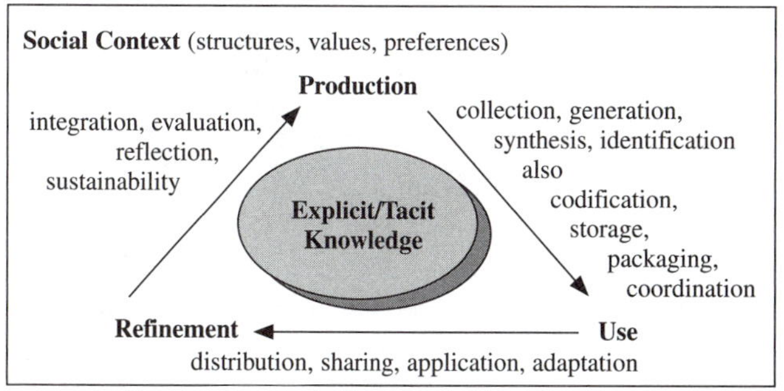

Source: Lau 2004, 3.

- *Knowledge use* includes the distribution and sharing of knowledge.
- *Knowledge refinement* includes the evaluation, adaptation, and sustainability of knowledge.

Healthcare faces many changes. Consumers are more informed; there is a need to increase efficiency, reduce costs, and improve quality; the industry is changing its focus from curing to preventing illnesses; there is a healthcare worker shortage; and there has been an increase in the generation of medical data, information, and knowledge. Managing this data, information, and knowledge is essential to addressing these changes.

Check Your Understanding 5.1

Instructions: Answer the following questions on a separate piece of paper.

1. Give an example of data that are found in a patient medical record. How could these data become information?
2. Explain the statement that "one person's information can be another person's data."
3. What is the value of Enterprise Content and Records Management (ECRM) to a large organization?
4. Give specific examples of explicit and tacit knowledge in healthcare. Why would it be important to manage these?

Joint Commission Model for Managing Information

The Joint Commission's mission is to improve patient safety and the quality of healthcare by accrediting hospitals and other healthcare organizations in the United States. The Joint Commission recognizes that **information management** is important to safe, quality care. According to the Joint Commission (2008), "the goal of the information management function is to support decision making to improve patient outcomes, improve healthcare documentation, improve patient safety, and improve performance in patient care, treatment, and services, governance, management, and support processes" (IM-1). The Joint Commission evaluates and accredits healthcare organizations using a set of standards and has an entire chapter in its 2009 *Comprehensive Accreditation Manual for Hospitals* dedicated to information management. The Joint Commission introduces the Information Management (IM) standards by emphasizing the importance of accurately capturing, categorizing, filing, maintaining, and securing healthcare information. The Joint Commission's first IM standard is "the hospital plans for managing information" (2009, IM-3). "Planning is the most critical part of the organization's information management process" (Joint Commission 2009, IM-3) and it is important that all areas of the hospital collaborate and are involved. The Joint Commission describes four elements of performance to address the importance of planning for managing information (2009, IM-3).

- Identifying internal and external information needs to provide safe, quality care
- Identifying data and information flow
- Using information to guide development of processes to manage information
- Including the appropriate people to participate in assessing, selecting, integrating and using information management systems for the delivery of care, treatment and services

The Joint Commission (2009) has IM standards regarding the information continuity process which address the hospital's preparation for information system interruptions. Other IM standards include: ensuring the accuracy, currency, availability, integrity, security, and privacy of health information, and effectively managing the collection and dissemination of information.

The Joint Commission (2008) model for managing information displayed in figure 5.3 includes four types of healthcare data shown as inputs: patient-specific, aggregate, comparative, and knowledge-based.

Patient-specific data and information can be linked to a specific patient through a unique identifier, such as a medical record number or hospital account number. Patient-specific data and information are used to "facilitate patient care, treatment, and services; serve as a financial and legal record; aid in research; support decision analysis; and guide professional and hospital performance improvement. This information is maintained as a paper record or as electronic health information" (Joint Commission 2008, IM-12).

Aggregate data and information come from patient-specific information, but generally there are no patient identifiers and the data or information is presented in summary form. Results of a quality improvement study using summarized patient data is an example of aggregate information.

Comparative data and information are used for benchmarking or other comparisons within or across healthcare organizations. They do not include patient identifiers and are generally presented as summary data or statistics. The data and information falling into this category (unlike simply aggregate) are generally used to measure performance against an internal or external standard.

Knowledge-based information is a "collection of stored facts, models, and information that can be used for designing and redesigning processes and for problem solving" (Joint Commission 2008, IM-12). When the term is used by the Joint Commission IM standards, it refers to the information found in the relevant clinical, scientific, and management literature.

All four types of healthcare data must be considered in the healthcare facility's overall plan for managing information.

The Joint Commission model for managing information begins with a needs assessment and ends with information use. The ultimate goal of any healthcare information system is to produce high-quality information that can be used effectively to meet the organization's needs. There are many

Figure 5.3. Joint Commission Management of Information Model

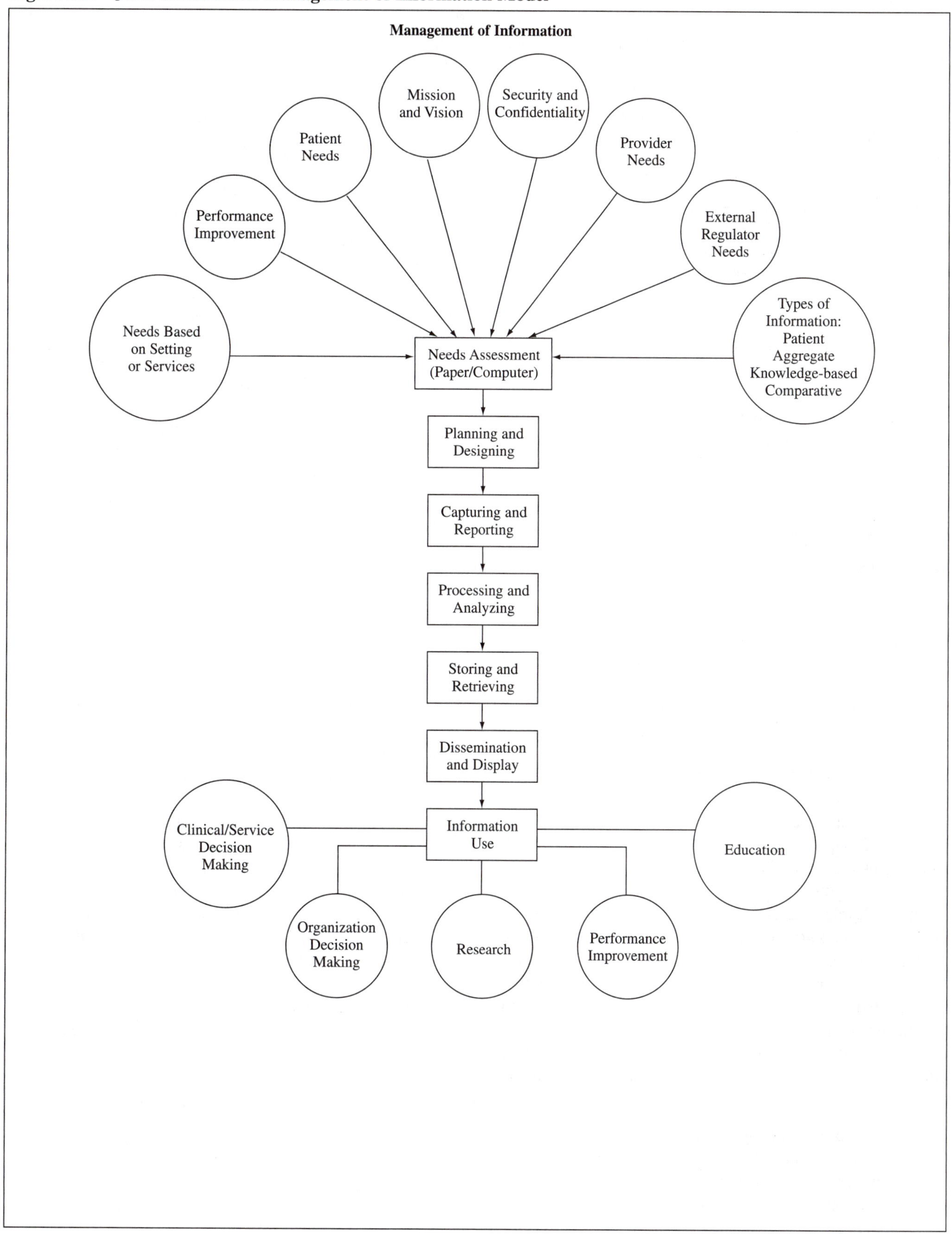

Source: Joint Commission 2008.

different, specific uses of healthcare information. The Joint Commission IM model (refer to figure 5.3) identifies five categories of uses: clinical decision making, organizational decision making, research, performance improvement, and education (of patients, families, and healthcare providers).

The needs assessment is organization specific. Clearly, although they likely have some data and information needs in common, a 50-bed critical access hospital has different needs than a multi-facility academic healthcare center. There is no "one size fits all" in planning how to manage a healthcare organization's information. After determining its information needs (based on the inputs identified in the model), the healthcare organization must plan and design its information systems (ISs). The Joint Commission does not dictate that the ISs must be computer-based, but it does expect them to meet certain standards, whether they are paper-based or fully electronic. In planning and designing ISs that will meet its identified needs, the healthcare organization must consider not only how to capture and report its information, but also how to ensure its privacy, integrity, security, availability, currency, accuracy, and how to disseminate it (Joint Commission 2009).

Basic Principles of Information Management

Healthcare functions revolve around collecting, analyzing, making decisions using data and information, and auditing for data integrity. Internal uses of this data and information include: creating a medical history; ensuring the patient receives proper care; communicating between providers; recommending procedures; generating billing information; creating legal documentation; giving accrediting, licensing, and governmental agencies information; and identifying trends and assisting with research. In addition, healthcare marketing or advocacy groups, such as Healthgrades or the Leapfrog Group respectively, may access aggregate healthcare claims data, add their own analysis and interpretation, and post it to public Web sites to assist consumers with personal health-related decisions. With so many different uses of healthcare data and information, it is critical that healthcare organizations manage their information resources wisely. Before the design and development of any IS, it is important to understand and embrace some basic principles of information management beyond the Joint Commission model.

In one well-known source, Austin and Boxerman (2003) cite three "overarching" principles for managing information resources:

- Treat information as an essential organizational resource, on a par with human resources, financial resources, and capital facilities and equipment.
- Obtain top executive support for IS planning and management.
- Develop an IS strategic vision and plan.

These three principles may be considered steps in setting the stage for effective information management within the healthcare organization. However, planning for information systems involves other important considerations, including:

- The value of information lies in its application to decision making within the organization.
- High-quality data is the foundation of high-quality information.
- Integration of systems enhances IS quality and efficiency.
- Information users must be involved in defining needs and designing information systems.

All of these principles are highly intertwined. Strategic IS planning is key to managing information resources wisely and ensuring that systems are compatible with one another and can be integrated. Moreover, planning ensures that the ISs the organization is developing are in line with its overall mission, goals, and strategic plan. The entire strategic IS planning process is only effective if the organization's top-level executives are supportive and actively involved.

It is the enterprise-wide nature of information that dictates the importance of systems integration and user involvement in defining and designing ISs. Too often, ISs are built for one particular unit within the organization, which can lead to inefficient management of information or even inaccurate information. If the users are not involved in every aspect of systems design and development, the resulting IS may function very well technically but be of no use to anyone. Increasingly, organizations are realizing the value of user involvement in the design of IS systems. **User-centered design** is a concept that involves the user throughout the entire design and development process. Involving the user throughout the entire process enables the developers to make sure the users' needs are met. In healthcare, user-centered design translates to patient-centered, caregiver-centered, support staff-centered, employee-centered, and the like.

Which is worse, a technically weak and cumbersome computer system that provides the information needed or a technically savvy system that does not? Invariably, end users choose the cumbersome system that provides the right information. (See chapter 6 for a more complete discussion of strategic IS planning.)

Check Your Understanding 5.2

Instructions: Answer the following questions on a separate piece of paper.

1. Why does the Joint Commission IM model begin with a needs assessment?
2. According to the Joint Commission IM model, what items are considered in a hospital's information management needs assessment? What are the basic categories of information used in the model?
3. What are the basic principles of information management?
4. Why is it particularly important for healthcare organizations to understand the basic principles of information management?
5. Why is user-centered design important?

Data Quality

The concept of data quality is closely tied to the ability of a healthcare IS to support decision making at all levels of the organization. The adage "garbage in, garbage out" is true. This section discusses the importance of establishing data quality standards and introduces two sets of guidelines that can be used for this purpose.

How can one know when data quality has been achieved? The quality of data is tied to the use, or application, of the data. Again, high-quality data is the foundation of high-quality information and the value of information lies in its application to decision making within the organization.

> Consider for a moment an organization with sophisticated healthcare information systems that affect every type of healthcare information, from patient-specific to knowledge-based. What if the quality of the documentation going into the systems is poor? What if there is no assurance that the reports generated from the systems are accurate or timely? How would the users of the systems react? Are those information systems beneficial or detrimental to the organization in achieving its goals? (Wager et al. 2005, 43).

A healthcare organization cannot have high-quality healthcare information without first establishing that it has high-quality healthcare data. We know that clinical providers and administrative staff gather healthcare information. Much of this clinical information is recorded in patient records and subsequently coded for purposes of reimbursement and research. As noted in the discussion of the Joint Commission model for managing information (refer to figure 5.3), information is used by many areas: clinical/service decision-making, organizational decision-making, research, performance improvement, and education. Poor-quality data collection and reporting can affect patient care, communication among providers and patients, documentation, revenue generation (due to problems with reimbursement), outcomes evaluation, research activities, or public reporting.

The problems with poor-quality patient care data are not strictly limited to the patient health record. In a recent, well-circulated report, the Medical Records Institute (MRI) identified five major functions that are affected by poor-quality documentation (MRI 2002). These functions are found not only at the healthcare organizational level, but also throughout the healthcare environment.

> Patient safety is affected by inadequate information, illegible entries, misinterpretations, and insufficient interoperability.
>
> Public safety, a major component of public health, is diminished by the inability to collect information in a coordinated, timely manner at the provider level in response to epidemics and the threat of terrorism.
>
> Continuity of patient care is adversely affected by the lack of shareable information among patient care providers.
>
> Healthcare economics are adversely affected, with information capture and report generation costs currently estimated to be well over $50 billion annually.
>
> Clinical research and outcomes analysis are adversely affected by a lack of uniform information capture that is needed to facilitate the derivation of data from routine patient care documentation (MRI 2002, 2).

The MRI report identifies healthcare documentation as having two basic parts**: information capture** and **report generation. Information capture** is "the process of recording representations of human thought, perceptions, or actions in documenting patient care, as well as device-generated information that is gathered and/or computed about a patient as part of health care" (MRI 2002, 2). Some means of information capture in healthcare organizations are handwriting, speaking, word processing, touching a screen, pointing and clicking on words or phrases, videotaping, audio recording, and generating digital images through x-rays and scans.

Report generation "consists of the formatting and/or structuring of captured information. It is the process of analyzing, organizing, and presenting recorded patient information for authentication and inclusion in the patient's healthcare record" (MRI 2002, 2). In order to have high-quality documentation that results in high-quality data, both information capture and report generation must be considered.

Data Quality Standards

Before an organization can measure the quality of the information it produces and uses, it must establish data standards. That is, data can be identified as high-quality only when they conform to a recognized standard. Ensuring this conformance is not as easy as it might seem because no universally recognized set of healthcare data quality standards exists today. One reason for this is that the quality of the data needed in any situation is driven by how the data or the information that comes from the data will be used. For example, in a patient care setting the margin of error for critical lab tests must be zero or patient safety is in jeopardy. However, a larger margin of error may be acceptable in census counts or discharge statistics. Healthcare organizations must establish data quality standards specific to the intended use of the data or resulting information.

Although no universally adopted healthcare data quality standards exist, two organizations have published guidance that can assist healthcare organizations in establishing their own data quality standards. In *Healthcare Documentation: A Report on Information Capture and Report Generation,* the MRI has published a set of "essential principles of healthcare documentation," (2002, 9) and the American Health Information Management Association (AHIMA) has published the data quality management model (Wager et al. 2005).

MRI Principles of Healthcare Documentation

AHIMA defines **documentation** as "the methods and activities of collecting, coding, ordering, storing, and retrieving information to fulfill future tasks." (AHIMA 2007, 66). The MRI report states that many steps must be taken to ensure the quality of healthcare documentation (and, thus, the quality of healthcare data). It lists the essential principles to which healthcare organizations should adhere as they establish healthcare documentation and information systems (and their accompanying policies). (See figure 5.4.) The MRI

Figure 5.4. MRI Consensus Workgroup Essential Principles of Healthcare Documentation

For optimal information capture and report generation, it is important to establish a set of documentation principles to be implemented on a national/international basis. This report recommends that all healthcare documentation must meet the following "Essential Principles of Healthcare Documentation."

Unique identification of patient

Systems, policies, and practices should:

- Provide unique identification of the patient at the time of recording or accessing the information.
- Provide within and across organizations:
  –Simple and easy methods to identify individuals and correct duplicate identities of the same individual.
  –Methods to distinguish among individuals, including those with similar names, birth dates, and other demographic information.
  –Linkages between different identifications of the same individual.

Accuracy

Systems, policies, and practices should:

- Promote accuracy of information throughout the information capture and report generation processes as well as during its transfer among systems.
- Require review to assure accuracy prior to integration in the patient's record.
- Include a means to append a correction to an authenticated document, without altering the original.
- Require the use of standard terminology so as to diminish misinterpretations.

Completeness

Systems, policies, and practices should:

- Identify the minimum set of information required to completely describe an incident, observation, or intent.
- Provide means to ensure that the information recorded meets the legal, regulatory, institutional policy, or other requirements required for specific types of reports (for example, history and physical, operative note).
- Link amendments to the original document (that is, one should not be able to retrieve an original document without related amendments [or vice versa] or notification that such amendments exist and how to access them).
- Discourage duplication of information.
- Discourage nonrelevant and excessive documentation.

Timeliness

Systems, policies, and practices should:

- Require and facilitate that healthcare documentation be done during or immediately following the event so that:
  –Memory is not diminished or distorted.
  –The information is immediately available for subsequent care and decision making.
- Promote rapid system response time for entry as well as retrievability through:
  –Availability and accessibility of workstations.
  –User-friendly systems and policies that allow for rapid user access.
- Provide for automatic, unalterable time, date, and place stamp of each:
  –Documentation entry, such as dictation, uploading, scanning (original, edits, amendments).
  –Access to the documentation.
  –Transmittal of the documentation.

Interoperability

Systems, policies, and practices should:

- Provide the highest level of interoperability that is realistically achievable.
- Enable authorized practitioners to capture, share, and report healthcare information from any system, whether paper- or electronic-based.
- Support ways to document healthcare information so that it can be correctly read, integrated, and supplemented within any other system in the same or another organization.

Retrievability (the capability of allowing information to be found efficiently)

Systems, policies, and practices should:

- Support achievement of a worldwide consensus on the structure of information so that the practitioner can efficiently locate relevant information. This requires the use of standardized titles, formats, templates, and macros, as well as standardized terminology, abbreviations, and coding.
- Enable authorized data searches, indexing, and mining.
- Enable searches with incomplete information (for example, wild card searches, fuzzy logic searches).

Authentication and accountability

Systems, policies, and practices should:

- Uniquely identify persons, devices, or systems that create or generate the information and that take responsibility for its accuracy, timeliness, etc.
- Require that all information be attributable to its source (that is, a person or device).
- Require that unsigned documents be readily recognizable as such.
- Require review of documents prior to authentication. "Signed without review" and similar statements should be discouraged.

Auditability

Systems, policies, and practices should:

- Allow users to examine basic information elements, such as data fields.
- Audit access and disclosure of protected health information.
- Alert users of errors, inappropriate changes, and potential security breaches.
- Promote use of performance metrics as part of the audit capacity.

Confidentiality and Security

Systems, policies, and practices should:

- Demonstrate adherence to related legislation, regulations, guidelines, and policies throughout the healthcare documentation process.
- Alert the user to potential confidentially and security breaches.

RECOMMENDATION #1: Fund, create, and promote a practical implementation guide for the dissemination, teaching, and adoption of the "Essential Principles of Healthcare Documentation" by practitioners, providers, vendors, and healthcare organizations, as well as regulatory bodies and medical schools.

Source: MRI 2002.

recommends that these principles be uniformly adopted by healthcare organizations.

It is noteworthy that the MRI takes the position that when practitioners interact with electronic resources, their ability to adhere to these principles is increased. All documentation records data and information, which needs to be retrieved in order to be used. The MRI argues that all healthcare information should be indexed "to facilitate both clinical and administrative retrieval" (MRI 2002, 16). This is difficult to do with unstructured, free text, such as handwriting, e-mails, and transcription. As electronic medical records are implemented and information capture methods become more interactive, the ability to retrieve information will improve. Table 5.2 shows documentation styles and major information capture methods.

AHIMA Data Quality Model

AHIMA (1998) has published a **data quality model** and an accompanying set of general data characteristics. The model is used as a framework for the design of management processes and data quality measures. There are some similarities between the AHIMA characteristics and the MRI essential principles (refer to figure 5.4). However, one difference is that AHIMA strives to include all healthcare data and limits characteristics to clinical documentation. (See figures 5.5 and 5.6.)

The AHIMA model (1998) includes the following **ten characteristics of data quality**:

- *Accuracy:* Data that are free of errors are accurate. Typographical errors in discharge summaries or misspellings of names are examples of inaccurate data.
- *Accessibility*: Data items should be easily obtainable and legal to access with strong protections and controls built into the process.
- *Comprehensiveness*: All required data items are included. Ensure that the entire scope of the data is collected and document intentional limitations.
- *Consistency:* Data quality needs to be consistent. A difference in the use of abbreviations provides a good example of how the lack of consistency can lead to problems. For example, a nurse may use CPR to mean cardiopulmonary resuscitation one time and computer-based patient record another time, leading to confusion if the chart were audited.
- *Currency:* Many types of healthcare data become obsolete after a period of time. A patient's admitting diagnosis is often changed by the time he or she is discharged. If a clinician needed a current diagnosis, which one would he or she choose?
- *Definition*: Clear definitions should be provided so that current and future data users will know what the data mean. Each data element should have clear meaning and acceptable values.
- *Granularity:* Data granularity is sometimes referred to as data "atomicity," which means that the individual data elements cannot be further subdivided; they are "atomic." For example, a typical patient's name should generally be stored as three data elements—last name, first name, middle name ("Smith," "John," and "Allen")—and not as a single data element ("John Allen Smith"). Again, granularity can be related to the purpose for which the data are collected. Although it is possible to subdivide a person's birth date into separate fields for the month, date, and year, this is usually not desirable. Birth date is at the lowest level of granularity when used as a patient identifier.
- *Precision:* Precision often relates to numerical data. It denotes how close to an actual size, weight, or other standard a particular measurement is. Some healthcare data must be very precise. For example, in figuring drug dosage, it would be unacceptable to round up to the nearest gram if the drug were to be dosed in milligrams.

Table 5.2. Documentation styles and major information capture methods

	Free Text	Structured Text	Interactive Text
Handwriting	Mostly free text	Paper forms	N/A
Transcription	Mostly free text	Macros and normals	N/A
Speech Recognition	Free text	Templates	Interactive templates
Direct Input	Free text	Mostly structured text	More interactive

Source: MRI 2002.

Figure 5.5. AHIMA data quality management model

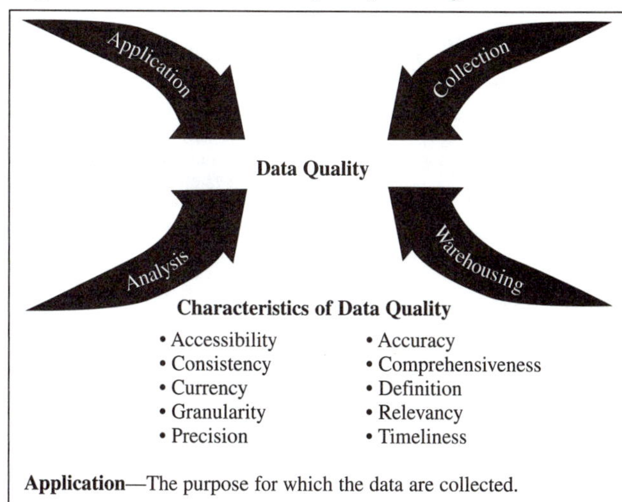

Application—The purpose for which the data are collected.

Collection—The processes by which data elements are accumulated.

Warehousing—Processes and systems used to archive data and data journals.

Analysis—The process of translating data into information utilized for an application.

Source: AHIMA 1998.

Figure 5.6. AHIMA characteristics of data quality

Characteristic	Application	Collection	Warehousing	Analysis
Data Accuracy Data are the correct values and are valid.	To facilitate accuracy, determine the application's purpose, the question to be answered, or the aim for collecting the data element.	Ensuring accuracy involves appropriate education and training and timely and appropriate communication of data definitions to those who collect data. For example, data accuracy will help ensure that if a patient's sex is female, it is accurately recorded as female and not male.	To warehouse data, appropriate edits should be in place to ensure accuracy. For example, error reports should be generated for inconsistent values such as a diagnosis inappropriate for age or gender. Exception or error reports should be generated and corrections should be made.	To accurately analyze data, ensure that the algorithms, formulas, and translation systems are correct. For example, ensure that the encoder assigns correct codes and that the appropriate DRG is assigned for the codes entered. Also, ensure that each record or entry within the database is correct.
Data Accessibility Data items should be easily obtainable and legal to collect.	The application and legal, financial, process, and other boundaries determine which data to collect. Ensure that collected data are legal to collect for the application. For example, recording the age and race in medical records may be appropriate. However, it may be illegal to collect this information in human resources departments.	When developing the data collection instrument, explore methods to access needed data and ensure that the best, least costly method is selected. The amount of accessible data may be increased through system interfaces and integration of systems. For example, the best and easiest method to obtain demographic information may be to obtain it from an existing system. Another method may be to assign data collection by the expertise of each team member. For example, the admission staff collects demographic data, the nursing staff collects symptoms, and the HIM staff assigns codes. Team members should be assigned accordingly.	Technology and hardware impact accessibility. Establish data ownership and guidelines for who may access data and systems. Inventory data to facilitate access.	Access to complete, current data will better ensure accurate analysis. Otherwise results and conclusions may be inaccurate or inappropriate. For example, use of the Medicare case mix index (CMI) alone does not accurately reflect total hospital CMI. Consequently, strategic planning based solely on Medicare CMI may not be appropriate.
Data Comprehensiveness All required data items are included. Ensure that the entire scope of the data is collected and document intentional limitations.	Clarify how the data will be used and identify end-users to ensure complete data are collected for the application. Include a problem statement and cost-benefit or impact study when collected data are increased. For example, in addition to outcome it may be important to gather data that impact outcomes.	Cost-effective comprehensive data collection may be achieved via interface to or download from other automated systems. Data definition and data precision impact comprehensive data collection (see these characteristics below).	Warehousing includes managing relationships of data owners, data collectors, and data end-users to ensure that all are aware of the available data in the inventory and accessible systems. This also helps to reduce redundant data collection.	Ensure that all pertinent data impacting the application are analyzed in concert.
Data Consistency The value of the data should be reliable and the same across applications.	Data are consistent when the value of the data is the same across applications and systems such as the patient's medical record number. In addition, related data items should agree. For example, data are inconsistent when it is documented that a male patient has had a hysterectomy.	The use of data definitions, extensive training, standardized data collection (procedures, rules, edits, and process) and integrated/interfaced systems facilitate consistency.	Warehousing employs edits or conversion tables to ensure consistency. Coordinate edits and tables with data definition changes or data definition differences across systems. Document edits and tables.	Analyze data under reproducible circumstances by using standard formulas, scientific equations, variance calculations, and other methods. Compare "apples to apples."

Figure 5.6. (Continued)

Characteristic	Application	Collection	Warehousing	Analysis
Data Currency The data should be up-to-date. A datum value is up-to-date if it is current for a specific point in time. It is outdated if it was current at some preceding time yet incorrect at a later time.	The appropriateness or value of an application changes over time. For example, traditional quality assurance applications are gradually being replaced by those with the more current application of performance improvement.	Data definitions change or are modified over time. These should be documented so that current and future users know what the data mean. These changes should be communicated in a timely manner to those collecting data and to the end-users.	To ensure current data are available, warehousing involves continually updating systems, tables, and databases. The dates of warehousing events should be documented.	The availability of current data impacts the analysis of data. For example, to study the incidence of diseases or procedures, ICD-9-CM codes may be used. Coding practices or the actual code for a disease or procedures may change over time. This should be taken into consideration when analyzing trends.
Data Definition Clear definitions should be provided so that current and future data users will know what the data mean. Each data element should have clear meaning and acceptable values.	The application's purpose, the question to be answered, or the aim for collecting the data element must be clarified to ensure appropriate and complete data definitions.	Clear, concise data definitions facilitate accurate data collection. For example, the definition of patient disposition may be "the patient's anticipated location or status following release or discharge." Acceptable values for this data element should also be defined. The instrument of collection should include data definitions and ensure that data integrity characteristics are managed.	Warehousing includes archiving documentation and data. Consequently, data ownership documentation and definitions should be maintained over time. Inventory maintenance activities (purging, updates, and others), purpose for collecting data, collection policies, information management policies, and data sources should be maintained over time also.	For appropriate analysis, display data needs to reflect the purpose for which the data were collected. This is defined by the application. Appropriate comparisons, relationships, and linkages need to be shown.
Data Granularity The attributes and values of data should be defined at the correct level of detail.	A single application may require varying levels of detail or granularity. For example, census statistics may be utilized daily, weekly, or monthly depending upon the application. Census is needed daily to ensure adequate staffing and food service. However, the monthly trend is needed for long-range planning.	Collect data at the appropriate level of detail or granularity. For example, the temperature of 100° may be recorded. The granularity for recording outdoor temperatures is different from recording patient temperatures. If patient Jane Doe's temperature is 100°, does that mean 99.6° or 100.4°? Appropriate granularity for this application dictates that the data need to be recorded to the first decimal point while appropriate granularity for recording outdoor temperatures may not require it.	Warehouse data at the appropriate level of detail or granularity. For example, exception or error reports reflect granularity based on the application. A spike (exception) in the daily census may show little or no impact on the month-to-date or monthly reports.	Appropriate analysis reflects the level of detail or granularity of the data collected. For example, a spike (exception) in the daily census resulting in immediate action to ensure adequate food service and staffing may have had no impact on analysis of the census for long-range planning.
Data Precision Data values should be just large enough to support the application or process.	The application's purpose, the question to be answered, or the aim for collecting the data element must be clarified to ensure data precision.	To collect data precise enough for the application, define acceptable values or value ranges for each data item. For example, limit values for gender to male, female, and unknown; or collect information by age ranges.		

(Continued on next page)

Figure 5.6. (Continued)

Characteristic	Application	Collection	Warehousing	Analysis
Data Relevancy The data are meaningful to the performance of the process or application for which they are collected.	The application's purpose, the question to be answered, or the aim for collecting the data element must be clarified to ensure relevant data.	To better ensure relevancy, complete a pilot of the data collection instrument to validate its use. A "parallel" test may also be appropriate, completing the new or revised instrument and the current process simultaneously. Communicate results to those collecting data and to the end-users. Facilitate or negotiate changes as needed across disciplines or users.	Establish appropriate retention schedules to ensure availability of relevant data. Relevancy is defined by the application.	For appropriate analysis, display data to reflect the purpose for which the data were collected. This is defined by the application. Show appropriate comparisons, relationships, and linkages.
Data Timeliness Timeliness is determined by how the data are being used and their context.	Timeliness is defined by the application. For example, patient census is needed daily to provide sufficient day-to-day operations staffing, such as nursing and food service. However, annual or monthly patient census data are needed for the facility's strategic planning.	Timely data collection is a function of the process and collection instrument.	Warehousing ensures that data are available per information management policy and retention schedules.	Timely data analysis allows for the initiation of action to avoid adverse impacts. For some applications, timely may be seconds. For others it may be years.

Source: AHIMA 1998.

- *Relevancy:* Data must be relevant to the purpose for which they are collected. Accurate, timely data may be collected about a patient's color preferences or choice of hairdresser, but are they relevant to the patient's care?
- *Timeliness:* Timeliness is a critical dimension in the quality of many types of healthcare data. Take, for example, a patient's discharge diagnoses recorded as ICD-9-CM codes. These codes must be recorded in a timely manner in order to facilitate reimbursement for the healthcare facility.

Data Quality Requirements for Information Systems

In addition to the ten characteristics of data quality, AHIMA has also published data quality best practices (AHIMA e-HIM Workgroup on Assessing and Improving Healthcare Data Quality in the EHR 2007):

- Access permissions: Define and enforce access to the data.
- Data dictionary: A data dictionary exists and each data element is defined. The definitions are communicated to all staff.
- Standardized format**:** Use a standardized format to ensure consistency.
- State and federal laws: All laws, regulations, accreditation standards, and policies are followed.
- Data integrity: Implement policies and procedures throughout the patient encounter to ensure data integrity.

It already has been noted that users must be involved in defining their information needs and designing information systems. One of the first steps in systems analysis is to identify the users' specific data needs. As a part of this process, it is important to identify the level of quality the user requires for each data element. Another way to view this is to evaluate the use of the data along the AHIMA model's ten characteristics of data quality. This evaluation eventually will be translated into technical performance requirements for the IS.

Consider a patient encounter in an electronic health record (EHR) system. Figure 5.7 applies AHIMA model's ten characteristics of quality data to the activities of a patient encounter: registration, assessment, treatment, follow-up, information management, and information exchange. Each phase has a data quality checkpoint because ensuring data quality is an ongoing process.

Check Your Understanding 5.3

Instructions: Answer the following questions on a separate piece of paper.

1. Compare and summarize the similarities and differences between the AHIMA Data Quality Model (refer to figure 5.6) and the MRI Essential Principles of Documentation (refer to figure 5.4).
   a. What data quality characteristics do they both list?
   b. What is the major difference between these two sets of guidelines? Are they compatible with one another?
2. List the ten characteristics of data quality.
3. Give one example of the importance of each of the 10 characteristics of data quality in ensuring the quality of patient information.

Figure 5.7. Applying AHIMA's ten data characteristics to a patient encounter

Data Characteristics	Registration **Data Quality Checkpoint:** Identification (ID) Validation (identity proofing)	Assessment **Data Quality Checkpoint:** History and physical (H&P)	Treatment **Data Quality Checkpoint:** Medication reconciliation	Follow-up **Data Quality Checkpoint:** Discharge/ Transfer/ Referral (DTR) record with patient instructions	Information Management **Data Quality Checkpoint:** Audit log of unauthorized access to the patient record	Information Exchange (external) **Data Quality Checkpoint:** Information from external sources
Accuracy—Ensures data have the correct value, are valid, and attached to the correct patient record.	Photo ID or two other forms of identification used.	Authentication by author licensed by the state. Patient demographics (five core-data elements (i.e., name [first, middle initial, last], date of birth, gender, Social Security number, medical record number) against that of the record.	List is current and the source of information is noted.	Policies exist defining the components of the DTR record (e.g., correct patient ID, location for follow-up/ongoing care, patient instructions for self-care, diet, activity, and current medication regimen and allergies).	Periodic system security audits conducted to prevent unauthorized alteration or loss of data.	Incoming records matched against requests for information and validated.
Accessibility—Data items should be easily obtainable and legal to access with strong protections and controls built into the process.	Record of ID validation for each patient encounter exists (i.e., mandatory flag indicating the ID was validated and checked against the master person index).	Available to the right person, in the right place, at right time, for the right purpose as allowed by state and federal law.	Clinical history that pulls the data from previous encounters is available for verification and usage in patient care (e.g., check and verify patient meds with prior record).	Information is made available to patient and patient-authorized organization/ individual responsible for ongoing care at conclusion of visit/ stay.	End user authentication achieved by system signature, date/time stamp.	Data available in PDF format only and linked to appropriate patient record by note in system.
Comprehensiveness—All required data items are included. Ensure that the entire scope of the data is collected and document intentional limitations.	Source and date of ID validation noted. Flag addressed. Multiple discriminations that would further ID the patient such as mother's maiden name included.	Includes all components required by regulatory/ accrediting agencies, medical staff rules, and bylaws.	Data needed for treatment as defined by regulatory/ accrediting agencies, medical staff rules, and bylaws is available at the point of service (e.g., for each medication the name, dosage, route, timing, duration are documented).	Record includes all components required by regulatory agencies/ accrediting bodies, medical staff rules, and bylaws. Verification of patient/SO understanding of instructions is documented by licensed author	Includes user's login ID and date and time of access and the content accessed.	Policies note external data cannot be certified as comprehensive.
Consistency—The value of the data should be reliable and the same across applications.	Standards exist for ID search criteria (e.g., full name search, partial name search).	Required content is the same and available across the encounter and between applications (e.g., the allergy stated in the H&P should the same throughout the patient stay).	Data values are coordinated across the continuum of care (e.g., the translation of a patient's medication list to a required formulary is verified each time a translation occurs).	Process exists ensuring DTR data is consistent with data in other parts of the medical record.	A plan and schedule exists for audits and follow-up.	Policies address the use of external data because it may not meet internal definitions.

(Continued on next page)

Figure 5.7. (Continued)

Data Characteristics	Registration Data Quality Checkpoint: Identification (ID) Validation (identity proofing)	Assessment Data Quality Checkpoint: History and physical (H&P)	Treatment Data Quality Checkpoint: Medication reconciliation	Follow-up Data Quality Checkpoint: Discharge/Transfer/Referral (DTR) record with patient instructions	Information Management Data Quality Checkpoint: Audit log of unauthorized access to the patient record	Information Exchange (external) Data Quality Checkpoint: Information from external sources
Currency—The data should be up-to-date.	Policies exist ensuring the latest ID data is entered and validated.	Information is updated in real-time or within a certain timeframe (i.e., information is synchronized every 30 minutes). When auto-population of data occurs, author validates and updates as necessary and a notation is captured by the system of this occurrence.	Medications taken by the patient are verified against the previous record and updated as necessary.	Policies exist to ensure the most current data are entered and verified for each component.	Verify data classes are clearly and appropriately defined and consistent with current business needs and requirements (e.g., public, sensitive, private, confidential).	Policies note data from external source will not be current. Relying on dates within documentation is suspect in electronic form.
Definition—Clear definitions should be provided so that current and future data users will know what the data mean. Each data element should have clear meaning and acceptable values.	A policy and procedure for updating, communicating, disseminating, and implementing the data dictionary exists (e.g., standards exist to ensure the same patient name and ID flows across all modules of the system including use of hyphens, apostrophes, etc.).	Guidelines defining H&P content (e.g., those by an accrediting agency) are available to authors and noted in the application user guide.	Standardized formulary exists.	Standardized data definitions for each required component of the DTR are clearly defined.	A storage security assessment and audit procedure integrated with other security practices once the major elements of storage security have been defined appropriately for your organizations.	Policies note any agreements with other providers as to definitions of the data.
Granularity—The attributes and values of data should be defined at the correct level of detail.	A policy and procedure for updating, communicating, disseminating, and implementing the data dictionary exists (e.g., truncation does not occur and values are clearly understood).	Components of the H&P as defined by the chosen standard (e.g., CMS E/M guidelines) are documented.	Attributes for each medication (e.g., dosage, form, route, etc.) are defined.	Content of the DTR is defined so all required information for each component is captured (e.g., for medications: brand/generic name, dosage, route, frequency; for activities allowed description of examples).	A storage security assessment and audit procedure is integrated with other security practices once the major elements of storage security have been defined appropriately for your organizations.	Policies note beyond what would be expected from the current standards there is no assurance of the values assigned to data (e.g., laboratory values from another source may not be expressed in the same manner as receiving facility).
Precision—Data values should be just large enough to support the application or process.	Standard policies exist ensuring the same set of rules apply to the ID data values for capture, storage, display, and reporting.	Data obtained by the provider support the degree of patient complexity.	Checks are done to ensure what is ordered is what is given to the patient.	Policies exist to allow prepopulated fields (e.g., discharge medication list, instructions) as well as free text to facilitate data capture (e.g., name/location of organization to provide ongoing care).	Changes are identified and potential security impact assessed.	As directed by HIPAA, the sending organization sends only the minimum necessary information requested.

Figure 5.7. (Continued)

Data Characteristics	Registration **Data Quality Checkpoint:** Identification (ID) Validation (identity proofing)	Assessment **Data Quality Checkpoint:** History and physical (H&P)	Treatment **Data Quality Checkpoint:** Medication reconciliation	Follow-up **Data Quality Checkpoint:** Discharge/ Transfer/ Referral (DTR) record with patient instructions	Information Management **Data Quality Checkpoint:** Audit log of unauthorized access to the patient record	Information Exchange (external) **Data Quality Checkpoint:** Information from external sources
Relevancy—The data are meaningful to the performance of the process or application for which they are collected	Standard policies exist requiring the capture of all demographic data that reflects the information needed for ID validation. Standard algorithm for pulling up the patient exists.	Data obtained by the provider support the plan of care (e.g., significant positive/ negative findings).	Express relationships to established standards meet the patient/client needs, achieve the organizations goals and produce benefits exist.	Policies exist requiring the DTR to contain data relevant and necessary for coordination of ongoing care of the patient.	Compliance with specified controls and procedures verified.	Policies note beyond what would be expected from the current standards there is no assurance of the receipt of meaningful data.
Timeliness—Timeliness is determined by how the data are being used and their context.	Real-time updates of ID are performed.	Documented at the time of encounter by the authorized provider and available for patient care.	Patient's medications are available for patient care.	Record is documented at the conclusion of the patient encounter and made available to the patient and patient-authorized organization/ individual responsible for ongoing care.	Conduct audits on a regularly scheduled routine and as needed.	Policies note data from external source will never be timely in the sense of context because the receiver would not be defining the context.

Source: AHIMA e-HIM Workgroup on Assessing and Improving Healthcare Data Quality in the EHR 2007.

Database Design and Management

Knowledge of database design and management is important in the healthcare field. Health information management (HIM) professionals who understand database design and management will be able to actively participate with the IS department in the design, development, and maintenance of the facility databases. This database knowledge will enhance the communication and interaction between the HIM and IS professionals.

Today's healthcare information systems are generally built on an underlying **database** structure. A database structure stores information about entities (tables), attributes (columns), and relationships between entities (Pratt and Adamski 2008). This type of IS structure can be found in computer applications ranging from an enterprise-wide clinical data repository to a small desktop application designed to track delinquent signatures on patient records. A **database management system** (DBMS) is a collection of computer software that manages and controls access to the data in the database. Regardless of the scope or size of the database used in an application, the theoretical constructs are the same and a good database design is equally important.

"A database that meets all user requirements does not just happen" (Rob and Coronel 2009, 10). The structure of the database must be designed carefully. In a well-designed database, data is entered once and stored in one place. Anyone who accesses the data gets the most updated version. A poorly designed database can lead to redundant data and information errors, which in turn can lead to poor management or patient care decisions. Data redundancy occurs when the same data is stored in multiple locations resulting in unnecessary duplicate data.

Revisit the master patient index (MPI) subset (refer to table 5.1) that was described earlier. Think of it as representing a portion of a table within a database that provides the data for an integrated hospital-wide IS. Assume that this table stores all patient demographic information. This should be the only place where the patient's name, date of birth, and address are stored. If this information is needed in other applications, such as billing, the unique identifier (in this case, the medical record number [MRN]) should be used to link the table to other tables with the accounting and billing information. Storing a data element in one location within the database enables accurate data updates and deletions.

Suppose there was a separate storage table for patient demographic information for each department-level application. The patient's demographic information would be stored in a billing database and in the MPI database. If a patient's name was misspelled or a birth date was incorrect, someone would have to go to each table separately and update the information. Updating the MPI without also updating the billing database would lead to reports yielding inconsistent, if not inaccurate, results. How would anyone know which table had the correct information?

It is no exaggeration to say that a poorly designed database can lead to poor decision making. The database is the source from which information is created. To repeat, one of the basic principles of information management is that the value of information lies in its application to decision making within the organization.

Database Life Cycle

Chapter 6 introduces the concept of a systems development life cycle (SDLC), which is used in systems analysis to illustrate the stages of development for an IS. The general SDLC provides a framework for developing any type of IS project. When dealing with a database project, the SDLC is often referred to as the **database life cycle** (DBLC) (Rob and Coronel 2009). The phases of the DBLC correspond to those of the general SDLC but include the specific tasks needed to develop an effective database.

Figure 5.8 illustrates a six-phase DBLC. The phases of this life cycle are as follows (Rob and Coronel 2009):

1. *Database initial study:* The database developer meets with key users and develops a list of user requirements. Technical requirements are discussed, and an analysis of how this database fits with existing systems is conducted.
2. *Database design:* The type of database is determined (relational or object oriented, for example). Conceptual-level and logical-level data models are developed during this phase. User interface also is designed. User–developer interaction is critical during this phase. Depending on the scope of the project, a prototype database may be developed and tested.
3. *Database implementation:* The database is actually loaded onto the network or workstation where it will reside. Test users are assigned user and access rights at the time of implementation.
4. *Testing and evaluation:* The importance of testing the database and evaluating the results of the testing cannot be overemphasized. Many times, even after careful design, problems are not discovered until the database is being used in a live environment.
5. *Database operation:* After the database is implemented, tested, and evaluated, it can be put into full operation.
6. *Database maintenance and evolution:* In this last phase of the cycle, the database must be continually maintained, evaluated for its usefulness and efficiency, and updated as enhancements or changes are required.

Figure 5.8. Six-phase database life cycle

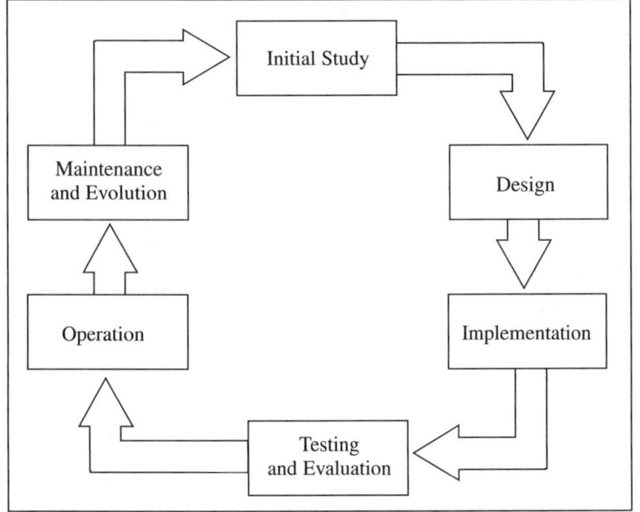

It is important to recognize that this life cycle is an iterative, rather than a sequential, process. Each phase can lead to modifications in other phases. This chapter focuses on activities related primarily to the design phase, although the design phase is closely related to the other phases of the SDLC. For example, the importance of user involvement in defining the objectives and constraints of the database cannot be overemphasized. Moreover, users are critical to development of a complete and accurate data dictionary. (Data dictionaries are defined and discussed later in this chapter.) Compare the database life cycle (refer to figure 5.8) to the Joint Commission IM model (refer to figure 5.3). The database life cycle or many life cycles would be contained within the iterative IM model. Each application selected by the organization that utilized a database would have included one or more database life cycles.

Data models, which are pictures or abstractions of real conditions, are used extensively during database design. A good analogy for a data model is a blueprint of a new building. No reputable builder would construct a building without a detailed blueprint. Of course, some changes may occur along the way, but the basic foundation and ways in which the building units will be put together are worked out in the blueprint. The use of data models facilitates communication between the technically oriented database designer and the end users. A data model allows the designers and users to visualize the database design. The concept that "a picture is worth a thousand words" applies. Data models also enable the individuals involved in database design to explore the features and characteristics of the database before actual implementation occurs.

Types of Databases

Before beginning a more detailed discussion of using and developing data models, the common types of databases and their associated DBMSs should be defined. This section defines and describes two database structures: relational and object oriented. Two other structures, hierarchical and network, are older types that no longer have a significant presence in the database market. They may be found as legacy systems within healthcare organizations but not in newer systems.

Relational Database Structure

The **relational database** model was developed in 1970 (Rob and Coronel 2009). It was not considered a practical design at the time because it required significant processing power. As computers became more powerful in the late 1980s and

1990s, the relational database became the predominant type used in healthcare and in other industries. A relational database is implemented through a **relational database management system** (RDBMS). The major advantage of the RDBMS is that it allows a database designer to operate at a logical, rather than a physical, level. (See section on levels of data models.) Microsoft Access is an example of an RDBMS for developing desktop applications. Oracle, DB2, and Sybase are examples of more robust systems for developing larger applications.

The RDBMS consists of three distinct components: the interface, the data manipulation "engine," and the tables. (See figure 5.9.) The interface component allows the users to utilize the data and is developed using a wide variety of software. In Microsoft Access, for example, Visual Basic for Applications (VBA) is built into the RDBMS and is used to create the forms and reports that comprise the majority of the user interface. The tables within a relational database are created using a special type of software, a **data definition language** (DDL). In between the user interface and the data tables is the database engine, the component that retrieves, edits, and updates the data from its underlying tables. The type of software used for these functions is called a **data manipulation language** (DML).

The most common language used for both DDL and DML for relational databases today is **structured query language** (SQL). All RDBMSs support SQL, and many RDBMS vendors have created extensions to the language that are specific to their product. SQL can be used to create, modify, delete, and query data in the database. The SQL used in Access looks slightly different from the SQL used in Oracle. SQL is a nonprocedural, or fourth-generation, language. The user specifies what must be done, but not how it is to be done. In other words, the SQL user does not have to know about the complex actions that actually are occurring when an SQL command is executed by the computer (Rob and Coronel 2009). SQL uses verb commands such as "create," "delete," "select," or "update." Using the master patient index table from table 5.1, the following illustrates an example SQL query that lists the patients' names and payment type for all patients with payment type of Private:

Figure 5.9. RDBMS components

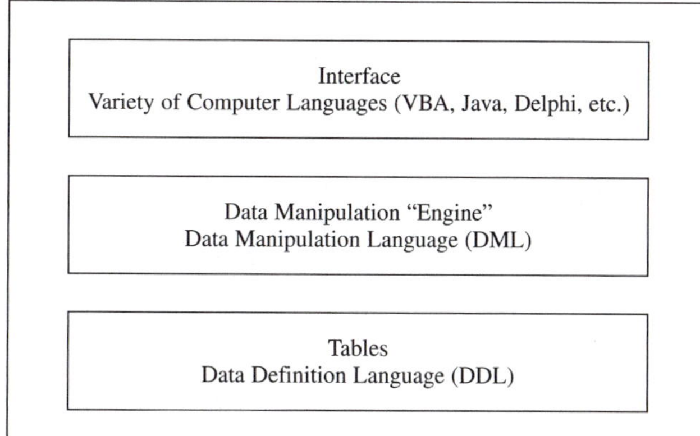


```
SELECT First_Name, Last_Name, Payment_Type
FROM MasterPatientIndex
WHERE Payment_Type = 'Private';
```

The results of the SQL query are:

First_Name	Last_Name	Payment_Type
Milton	Lexington	Private
Chloe	Martin	Private
John	Martin	Private

Tables (sometimes called relations) provide the foundation of a relational database. Each table consists of rows and columns similar to a spreadsheet. Rows represent each record within the table, for example information about one patient; columns represent the data fields or **attributes** of each table, for example the last names of patients. Figure 5.10 illustrates the concepts of table, column, and rows. A relational database consists of multiple tables, which is illustrated in figure 5.11.

Tables in a relational database are related to one another by sharing a common field, or **key attribute**. In the earlier example involving the MPI and the billing system, these two tables could be linked by the key attribute, MRN.

The relational database has several advantages over its predecessors, the network and hierarchical databases. The most important advantages include (Rob and Coronel 2009):

- *Structural independence:* It is possible to make changes to the database structure without affecting how the RDBMS accesses the data. In other words, data elements

Figure 5.10. Illustration of table, row, and column in a subset of the Patient Master Index

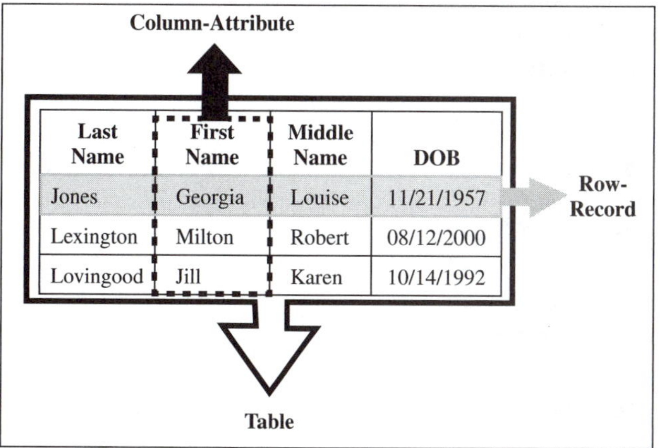

Figure 5.11. Relational database

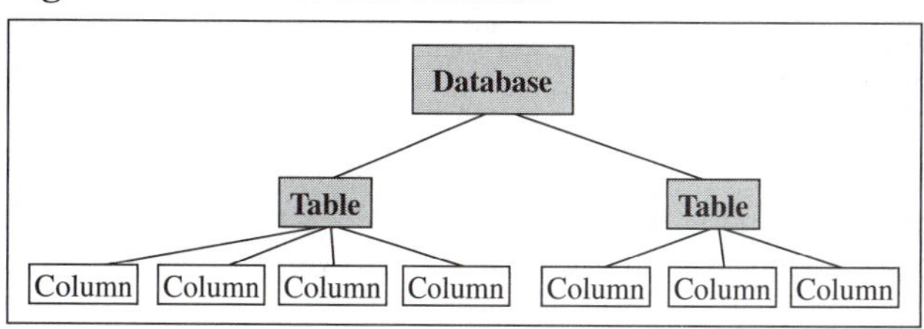

can be changed in the tables without affecting the data manipulation features or interface with the user.

- *Improved conceptual simplicity:* Through its use of logical tables, the relational database makes it easier for the developer and the user to understand the data.
- *Easier database design, implementation, management, and use:* Relational databases are much easier to design and manage than their predecessors were.
- *Ad hoc query capability:* The common data manipulation language, SQL, is simple to use and understand because it so closely resembles the English language.
- *A powerful database management system:* A good RDBMS makes it possible to hide a system's physical complexity from the developer and the user.

Object-Oriented Database Structure

The newest type of database structure is the **object-oriented database** (OODB). The basic component in the OODB is an object, not a table. An **object** includes both data and their relationships within a single structure; it is conceptually more difficult to understand than a table. **Object-oriented database management systems** (OODBMSs) utilize classes and subclasses that "inherit" characteristics from the parent class. The goal of using objects in programs and database management systems is to promote reuse of program code and to store the data with the methods (procedures) that use the data. "Pure" object-oriented databases are not yet common in the healthcare market, but there are applications with object-oriented components built upon relational databases. This hybrid database type is referred to as an *object-relational database*.

Data Models

Data modeling serves as a link between "real" things about which the organization wants to collect and maintain data and the actual database structure. One of the problems with database design is that designers, programmers, and users do not necessarily see data the same way. Different users have different views of the organization's data, depending on their particular needs. Different views of data can lead to poorly constructed information systems that fail to meet the needs of many users. Ensuring that communication among designers, programmers, and users is as unambiguous as possible can prevent this. Data modeling is an excellent communication tool for reducing complex data structures to easy-to-understand pictures or abstractions.

Levels of Data Models

There are three levels of data models: conceptual, logical, and physical. These levels are based on the degree of abstraction represented by the data model. The **conceptual data model** is the one with the highest level of abstraction. In other words, it is neither hardware nor software dependent. In theory, the same conceptual model can be developed whether the organization develops its database as a relational database or as an object-oriented database. The conceptual model also implies that it defines requirements for the entire enterprise or organizational unit under consideration. End users should be intimately involved in the development of conceptual data models. The level of abstraction should be high enough that end users with little or no computer programming experience can visualize the data requirements.

The next level of data model is the **logical data model**. The logical data model is still hardware independent but will be drawn to match the type of database management system (DBMS) that will be used. There are differences in the way logical models are depicted, depending on whether the DBMS is relational or object oriented. For example, the **entity relationship diagram** (ERD), described in detail later in this chapter, was developed to depict relational database structures. It can be used to depict conceptual-level models for any type of database but would only be used to model a relational database at the logical level. A common notation used for modeling object-oriented databases is **unified modeling language** (UML). UML can be used to depict a conceptual data model and a logical OODB model.

Another characteristic of the logical data model is that it is drawn to represent a view of the data by a specific group within the enterprise, for example, a department or a unit within a department. Of course, the logical data model should be based on the conceptual model for the enterprise. Another way to think about logical data models is that they are components of the conceptual model with more DBMS-related detail.

The **physical data model** is concerned with the lowest level of abstraction, including how data are physically stored on storage devices (Rob and Coronel 2009). As relational and object-oriented databases have become more widely used, the physical data model has decreased in importance. One of the strengths of the relational and object-oriented databases is that they do not require the physical modeling details required by the older hierarchical and network database structures.

Data Modeling Process

The importance of data modeling cannot be overstated. Not only does the data model serve as a communication tool among IS developers and users, but it also provides the developer an opportunity to work out conceptual and design issues and problems prior to beginning the actual design process. This is an important step in ensuring the quality of the data and, subsequently, the quality of the information that can be gathered from the IS. The data themselves constitute the most basic units within an IS.

As stated earlier, one of most common data models, the ERD, is associated with relational database design. The ERD modeling technique is used to develop both conceptual and logical data models for relational databases. Several different sets of notations are used for drawing an ERD. Two of the most common methods are the Chen model and the Crow's foot model. Peter Chen developed his notation for ERDs in the 1970s (Rob and Coronel 2009). The Crow's foot mode is based on the same modeling concepts as the original Chen model. However, the Crow's foot model depicts the data relationships at a slightly higher level of abstraction than the Chen model does. The models used for illustration throughout this chapter are drawn using the Crow's foot symbols.

Figure 5.12 illustrates a simple ERD drawn using the conventions associated with the Chen model and the Crow's foot symbols. These models show that the relationship between the data table (or entity) HOSPITAL and the data table (or entity) DIVISION is one to many. A one-to-many relationship means that for every instance of HOSPITAL stored in the database, many related instances of DIVISION may be stored. Reading the diagram in the other direction, each instance of DIVISION stored in the database is related to only one instance of HOSPITAL. Think about a multi-hospital system that has three hospitals—A, B, and C. Each hospital has multiple divisions within it, and each specific division (for example, the finance division in A) is related to only one hospital.

Although a detailed discussion of the conventions and steps associated with developing an ERD are beyond the scope of this chapter, the basic steps for developing an ERD for a simple end-user database is outlined. An ERD is a graphical representation of the entities, attributes, and relationships that a database comprises. It is used as a planning and communication tool throughout the database development process. As stated earlier, an ERD can be used as a conceptual-level data model for any type of database and as a logical-level data model for a relational database. This discussion examines a simple ERD being developed for a patient-tracking system in a rural healthcare system that operates three clinics. The proposed tracking system will be developed as a relational database. Its purpose is to track patient visits within the three clinics.

Entities

Entities in the ERD are represented by a rectangle. An **entity** is a person, place, or thing about which data are to be collected in the database being designed. What would the entities for the patient-tracking database be?

Another way to think about entities is that they eventually will be transformed into the tables within the database. The entities for the visit-tracking database would be PATIENT, CLINIC, and VISIT. There could be more entities, depending on the data to be stored. For example, if one wanted to collect information about the provider of care for the visit, one would likely have an entity, PROVIDER, or even two entities, PHYSICIAN and NURSE. Selecting the entities for an ERD depends on the purpose of the proposed database. This example limits data collection to VISIT, PATIENT, and CLINIC.

Attributes

Attributes are the characteristics or data elements to be collected about each entity. They can be depicted in an ERD as oval shapes coming off an entity. This method is not practical when there are many attributes per table; therefore, many designers use a separate list to document attributes. In the Crow's foot notation, attributes are sometimes listed within the entity rectangle.

What would be some likely attributes in this example? For the PATIENT table, one would want to store a unique identifier for the patient, such as a medical record number. This unique identifier is called a **primary key**. A primary key cannot be duplicated within the table and cannot contain a null value. Each table row or record within the database must have a unique primary key.

Continuing with the example, one also would want to store at least basic demographic information such as address, phone number, and date of birth. Figure 5.13 shows simplified, partial lists of attributes for the three tables. Attributes become the fields or column headings within the data tables of a relational database. Notice that the names of the attributes in figure 5.13 adhere to a common naming convention for database fields. The name of the table makes up the first part of the name followed by an underscore. This way, it is easy to identify where a particular data element is stored by looking at its names. Also note that these attributes are all atomic, meaning they cannot be further subdivided.

Another type of attribute is a **derived attribute**. Derived attributes are not stored in the database table but, instead, are calculated when the database is accessed. An example of a derived attribute is age. A patient's age at the time of a visit could be calculated using the date of birth attribute, the admission date, and the visit date. A patient's current age could be calculated using date of birth and today's date.

Figure 5.12. ERD notations demonstrating Crow's Foot and Chen Models

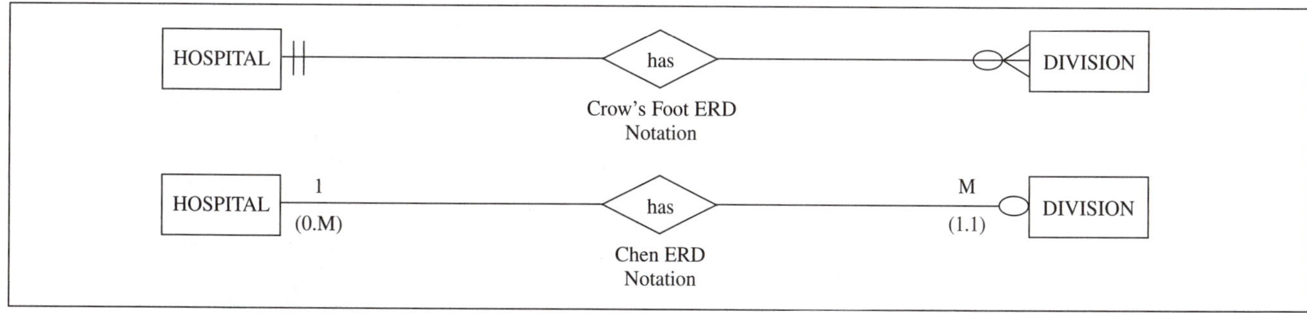

In this example, the primary key (PK) for PATIENT, PATIENT_MRN, is repeated in VISIT, as is the PK for CLINIC, CLINIC_ID. These keys are called **foreign keys** (FK) in the VISIT table. Foreign keys allow relationships between tables. By having the foreign keys in VISIT, the information in PATIENT and CLINIC is linked through the VISIT table. Figure 5.14 illustrates the ERD for this example.

Relationships

Relationships are represented in an ERD by a diamond shape or as text across the relationship line. The name of the relationship is usually a verb that describes the relationship between two or more of the entities in the diagram. A conceptual ERD contains three types of relationships:

- One-to-one relationship
- One-to-many relationship
- Many-to-many relationship

Figure 5.13. Partial attribute lists for PATIENT, VISIT, and CLINIC

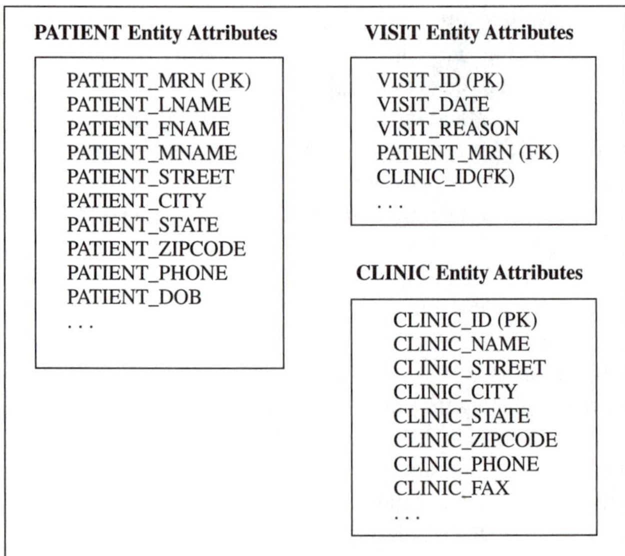

PATIENT Entity Attributes

PATIENT_MRN (PK)
PATIENT_LNAME
PATIENT_FNAME
PATIENT_MNAME
PATIENT_STREET
PATIENT_CITY
PATIENT_STATE
PATIENT_ZIPCODE
PATIENT_PHONE
PATIENT_DOB
. . .

VISIT Entity Attributes

VISIT_ID (PK)
VISIT_DATE
VISIT_REASON
PATIENT_MRN (FK)
CLINIC_ID(FK)
. . .

CLINIC Entity Attributes

CLINIC_ID (PK)
CLINIC_NAME
CLINIC_STREET
CLINIC_CITY
CLINIC_STATE
CLINIC_ZIPCODE
CLINIC_PHONE
CLINIC_FAX
. . .

Figure 5.14. Sample ERD

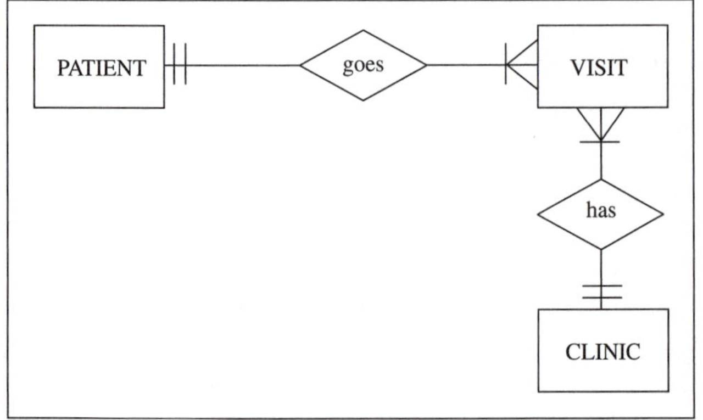

A **one-to-one relationship** exists when an instance of an entity (a row or record) is associated with one instance of another entity, and vice versa. This type of relationship is illustrated in figure 5.15; these relationships are taken from a current bed assignment database. There is only one bed per patient and one patient per bed. One-to-one relationships are rare in logical-level data models because they often indicate that a separate entity is unnecessary. Often a one-to-one relationship can be implemented as an attribute or field within a single table. In other words, a field, PATIENT_BED, could be added in the PATIENT table in this example to collect this information.

The **one-to-many relationship** exists when one instance of an entity is associated with many instances of another entity. In the example shown in figure 5.14, the relationship between PATIENT and VISIT is one-to-many. For each instance of PATIENT in the database, there could be many instances of VISIT. In other words, each patient may have many visits, but each visit is associated with only one patient. The relationship between CLINIC and VISIT is also one-to-many. For each instance of CLINIC, there can be many VISITS, but each visit occurs in only one clinic. One-to-many relationships also can be optional. In this example, however, they are not because each patient must have a visit before he or she is entered into the database and each clinic must have visits before it is entered into the database.

Whether a relationship is optional is determined by the business rules of an organization. If one said that patients were entered into the database before they had any visits, this relationship would change to optional. This might occur in a family-oriented clinic where children or spouses of patients were registered but never seen.

A **many-to-many relationship** occurs only in a data model developed at the conceptual level. In the example shown in figure 5.14, suppose the need for a separate VISIT entity was not recognized. The relationship between PATIENT and CLINIC is many-to-many. For each instance of PATIENT, there could be many instances of CLINIC because patients can be seen in more than one clinic. For each instance of CLINIC, there could be many PATIENTS because the clinic sees many patients. Figure 5.16 shows the many-to-many relationship between PATIENT and CLINIC.

Figure 5.15. One-to-one relationship

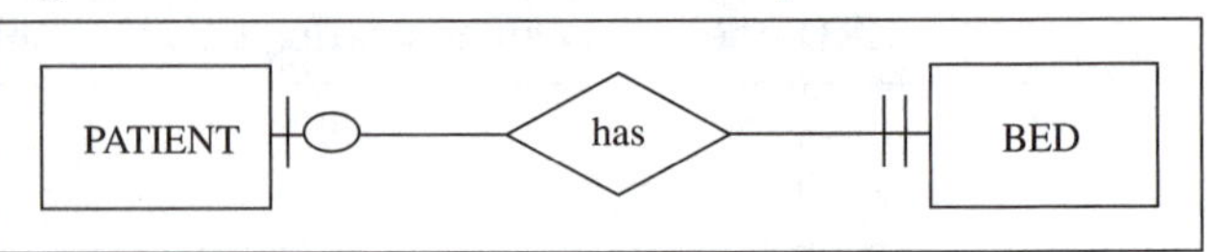

Figure 5.16. Many-to-many relationship

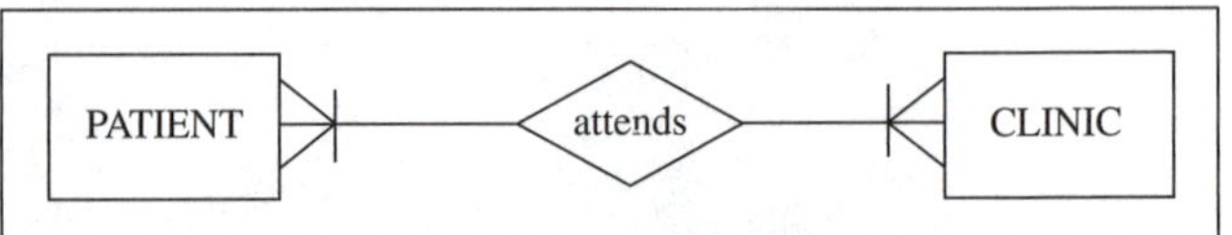

Well-structured databases consist primarily of one-to-many relationships. Many-to-many relationships cannot be implemented in a relational database and, as discussed, one-to-one relationships are rare. The process of ensuring that the data model can be implemented as relational tables in a database is called **normalization**. By normalizing the data tables to ensure that data are stored in only one location, except for the planned redundancy inherent in key attributes, database developers decrease the possibility of data anomalies resulting from additions and deletions.

Check Your Understanding 5.4

Instructions: Answer the following questions on a separate piece of paper.

1. Why is database design and management knowledge important to the HIM professional?
2. Which type of database is the most common today?
3. How does database design affect the quality of the data stored in the database?
4. What is a data model?
5. Discuss the differences among a conceptual-level, logical-level, and physical-level data model.
6. What are some common uses of an ERD? What is UML?
7. Define the basic components of an ERD.
8. How are the entities and relationships depicted in an ERD?
9. Using the Crow's foot notation, draw an ERD to depict the following relationship: Each patient has one physician, but each physician has many patients.

Data Dictionary Used as a Tool in Controlling Data Quality

Important tools for use in controlling the quality of data in healthcare are the data dictionary and the data map or crosswalk. AHIMA (e-HIM Workgroup on EHR Data Content 2006) defines a **data dictionary** as "a descriptive list of names (also called representations or displays), definitions, and attributes of data elements to be collected in an information system or database" (64A). A data dictionary is like a map of the database. Whenever a set of data is created, it should have an accompanying data dictionary. A data dictionary can ensure consistency by standardizing definitions.

Data map or **crosswalk** "are terms used to describe the connections, or paths, between classifications and vocabularies" (Bryant 2006, 9) For example, when a healthcare researcher is studying the effectiveness of an imaging technology, such as Magnetic Resonance Imaging for diagnosing cancer from 1998 to 2008, the researcher uses the Magnetic Resonance Imaging codes from the International Classification of Diseases, 9th Revision, Clinical Modification (ICD-9-CM), to conduct this study. ICD-9-CM is updated each year as science and technologies advance, and as new diseases and treatments are discovered. The ICD-9-CM coding classification in 1998 was notably less detailed than ICD-9-CM in 2008. To help the researcher ensure study validity and integrity, the researcher will rely on the data map, or crosswalk that "connects" the ICD-9-CM codes across the span of the study to ensure that an ICD-9-CM code in 1998 has, in essence, the same meaning as the ICD-9-CM code it is mapped or crosswalked to in 2008. (Chapter 13 provides additional information on classifications and vocabularies.)

Types of Data Dictionaries

There are two general types of data dictionaries: the DBMS data dictionary and the organization-wide data dictionary.

DBMS Data Dictionary

The DBMS data dictionary is developed in conjunction with development of the database. Modern DBMSs have built-in data dictionaries that go beyond data definitions and store information about tables and data relationships. These integrated data dictionaries are sometimes referred to as **system catalogs**, reflecting their technical nature.

Figure 5.17 shows a portion of a designer-defined data dictionary developed in Microsoft Access for the simplified PATIENT table discussed earlier. The database developer would use this portion of the software to define the data to be stored in the database's system catalog.

A typical data dictionary associated with a DBMS allows for at least documentation of the following:

- Table names
- All attribute or field names
- A description of each attribute
- The data type of the attribute (text, number, date, and so on)
- The format of each attribute, such as DD_MM_YYYY for the date
- The size of each attribute, such as 12 characters in a phone number with dashes
- An appropriate range of values, such as integers 100000–999999 for the health record number
- Whether the attribute is required
- Relationships among attributes

Other descriptions that might be stored in the data dictionary associated with a database include:

- Who created the database?
- When the database was created?
- Where the database is located?
- What programs can access the database?
- Who the end users and administrators of the database are?
- How access authorization is provided to all users?

Organization-wide Data Dictionary

The second type of data dictionary is developed outside the framework of a specific database design process. This data dictionary serves to promote data quality through data consistency across the organization. Individual data element definitions are agreed upon and defined. This leads to better-quality data and facilitates the detailed, technical data dictionaries that are integrated with the databases themselves. Ideally, every healthcare organization will develop a data dictionary to define common data and their formats. This organization-wide document becomes a valuable resource for IS development.

Looking at the MPI example discussed earlier (refer to table 5.1), what would need to be defined for each field? Although everyone may think they know the definition of a Last Name, can they all agree that it will be stored as no more than 25 characters? How should the Middle Name be handled? Will it be the maiden name for married women? Is the medical record number to be stored with leading zeros? All these issues can be settled with the development of an organization-wide data dictionary.

Another challenge for healthcare managers results from interorganizational projects or the merger of healthcare organizations. Suppose a multi-facility organization wanted to merge its MPI systems. Imagine the challenges involved in not only defining data elements, but also in uncovering existing definitions. If the organizations in question built other systems based on internal MPI definitions all of these systems would need to be analyzed and changed.

Development of Data Dictionaries

The health information manager should be a key member of any data dictionary project team. Developing a data dictionary can be an overwhelming task in light of the diversity of data users and the size and scope of some healthcare organizations.

To assist with the development of data dictionaries, AHIMA has published recommended guidelines (AHIMA e-HIM Workgroup on EHR Data Content 2006).

- *Design a plan*: Preplan the development, implementation, and maintenance of the data dictionary.
- *Develop an enterprise data dictionary*: Integrate common data elements across the entire institution to ensure consistency.
- *Ensure collaborative involvement*: Make sure there is support from all key stakeholders.
- *Develop an approvals process:* Ensure a documentation trail for all decisions, updates, and maintenance.

Figure 5.17. Partial data dictionary for PATIENT table

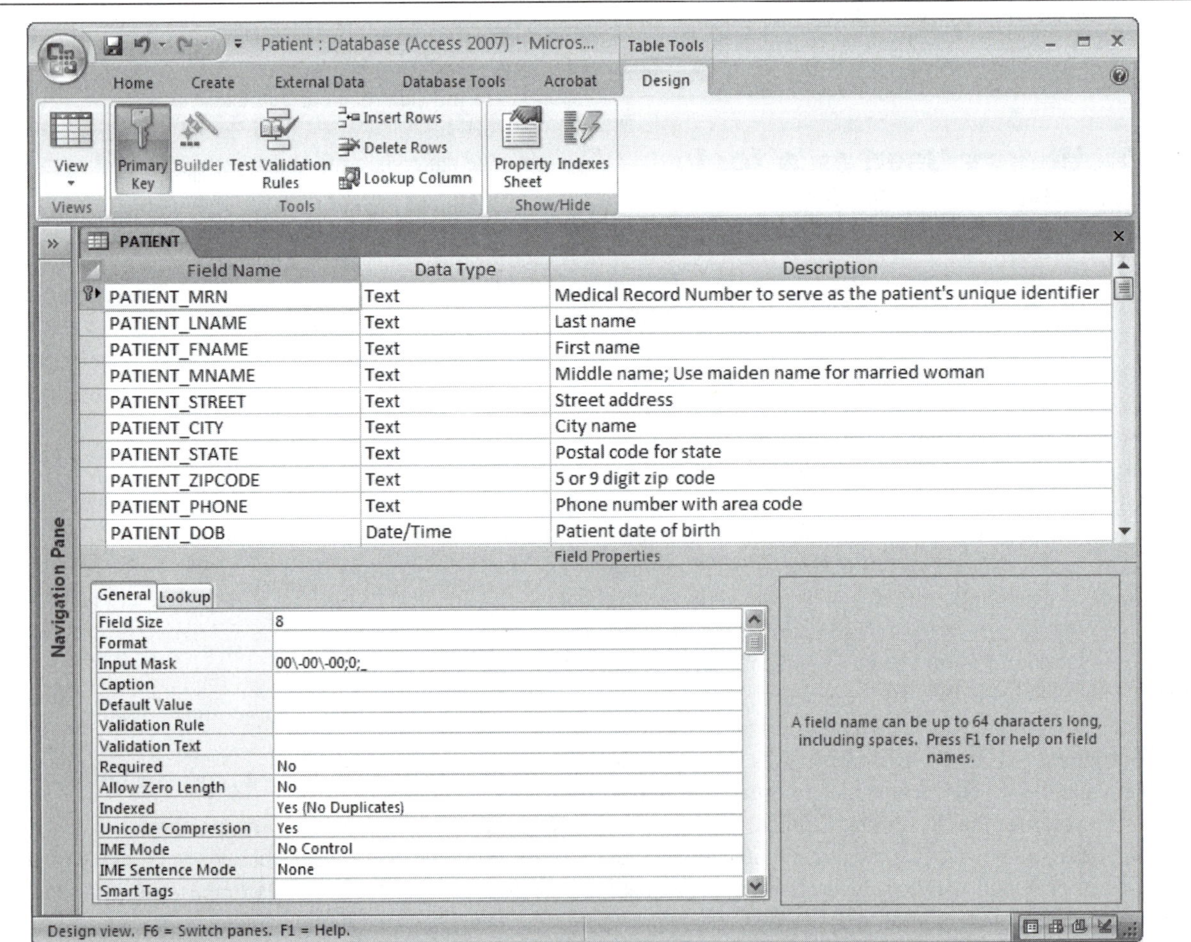

- *Identify and retain details of data versions*: Version control is important.
- *Design for flexibility and growth.*
- *Design room for expansion of field values.*
- *Follow established ISO/International Electrotechnical Commission (IEC) 11179 guidelines for metadata registry*: To promote interoperability follow standards.
- *Adopt nationally recognized standards.*
- *Beware of differing standards for the same concepts.*
- *Use geographic codes and conform to the National Spatial Data Infrastructure and the Federal Geographic Data Committee.*
- *Test the information system*: Develop a test plan to ensure the system supports the data dictionary.
- *Provide ongoing education and training.*
- *Assess the extent to which the data elements maintain consistency and avoid duplication.*

Check Your Understanding 5.5

Instructions: Answer the following questions on a separate piece of paper.

1. What is a data dictionary? What is its importance in ensuring data quality?
2. What type of information would be listed in an organization-wide or enterprise-wide data dictionary? What other types of information would be stored in a system catalog?
3. What is a data map or crosswalk?
4. What are AHIMA's recommended guidelines for development of data dictionaries?

Roles in Data Management

This chapter focuses on the importance of maintaining high-quality data that will lead to high-quality information and decisions. High-quality data do not just happen. Healthcare organizations must establish mechanisms and policies for managing their data resources. Such mechanisms and policies must encompass not only the technical aspects of implementing and maintaining the databases within the organization, but also ensure that the data conform to established standards of quality. Several roles within the healthcare IS team can be used to manage the quality of healthcare data. These include database administrator, data administrator, data resource manager (AHIMA 1999) and data analyst (AHIMA 2005).

Database Administrator

The technical aspects of managing a database are usually assigned to a **database administrator** (DBA). Typical DBA functions include defining and developing the database, implementing the technical aspects of the DBMS, monitoring the performance of the database, creating and enforcing the security measures associated with the DBMS, and managing the system catalogs or data dictionaries that are internal to the DBMS (Johns 2003).

DBAs typically have information technology (IT) backgrounds and may not be equipped to deal with managing the less technical side of data quality, particularly healthcare data. This has led some healthcare organizations to create a new position—the data administrator (DA).

Data Administrator

According to Johns (2003), the functions of the **data administrator** include:

- Planning for the database, including identifying the major entities, attributes, and relationships among entities and developing the conceptual data models for the organization
- Evaluating and selecting an appropriate DBMS
- Managing an enterprise-wide data dictionary
- Training database users
- Developing and implementing database security policies and procedures

The DA must work closely with the DBA, but the focus of the DA role is on managing the data and the database rather than on the technical implementation and maintenance issues that are the DBA's responsibility.

Data Resource Manager

In 1998, AHIMA described an emerging data management role for HIM managers in its Vision 2006 document—the **data resource manager** (DRM). AHIMA (1999, 111) defines a DRM as the person who "uses technical tools, such as computer-based health record systems, data repositories, and data warehouses . . . (to) ensure that the organization's information systems meet the needs of those who provide and manage patient services along the continuum of care and that the organization's data resources are secure, accessible, accurate, and reliable."

The role of the DRM is specifically defined as having two primary goals: (1) to provide leadership for the data resource management functions and (2) to ensure that the data are secure, accessible, accurate, and reliable.

The DRM role is similar to the DA role described by Johns (2003), with a few differences in focus. As defined by AHIMA, the DRM is not only concerned with managing the quality and security of the healthcare data in an organization, but is also very involved in retrieving data from the systems within the organization. The skill set required to perform the data resource management function in a healthcare organization includes a thorough understanding of health information administration and a working knowledge of the technical aspects of health information systems, particularly databases and DBMSs. The DRM should be comfortable as a participant in healthcare database management and design. Further, he or she should have a thorough understanding of HIM issues such as confidentiality, access, release of information, and security.

Data Analyst

In the findings of their Health Information Management Workforce Study (AHIMA 2005), AHIMA recognizes that healthcare providers are increasingly utilizing health information for a variety of decisions and benchmarking measurements. Public reporting of health care information by government, marketing, and patient advocacy organizations has emphasized the need for accurate data, and health care organizations are increasing their reliance on health information management professionals to provide data analysis.

AHIMA defines a **data analyst** as a professional who investigates and compiles data for different purposes, "including clinical research, data auditing, quality assessment, cost estimation, risk assessment, physician practice monitoring, management of resources, and reimbursement mechanisms" (AHIMA 2005, 5).

Check Your Understanding 5.6

Instructions: Answer the following questions on a separate piece of paper.

1. Discuss the differences and similarities in the roles of the database administrator, the data administrator, the data resource manager, and the data analyst.
2. Which of the discussed roles would be most appropriate for a health information manager? Explain your answer.

Safeguards for Ensuring Data Integrity and Security

Nowhere is ensuring the integrity and security of data more important than in healthcare. Healthcare organizations have an obligation to protect patient privacy and to maintain the confidential nature of the physician–patient relationship. Healthcare privacy and confidentiality are regulated by state and national laws and standards, as well as by standards of care. Other chapters in this text discuss confidentiality and privacy from a legislative and regulatory perspective. This section focuses on the safeguards that should be implemented in a healthcare database system.

Data Integrity

Databases contain rules known as **integrity constraints** that must be satisfied by the stored data. **Data integrity** happens when all of the data in the database conform to all integrity constraint rules. Database integrity constraints include:

- *Data type*: The data entered into a field should be consistent with the data type for that field. For example, if a field is a numeric field, it should only accept numbers. If it is a date field, it should only accept a legitimate date.
- *Legal values*: Many fields have a limited number of "legal" values. For example, a health record number may only be entered as 000001 through 999999.
- *Format*: Certain fields, such as dates, must be entered in a certain format, such as MM/DD/YYYY.
- *Key constraints*: Constraints placed on the primary and foreign keys within the database. A foreign key, for example, cannot be entered into the database unless a corresponding primary key already exists. This concept is called **referential integrity** (Pratt and Adamski 2008).

These constraints help ensure that the originally entered data and changes to these data follow certain rules. DBMSs today include the functionality to enforce integrity constraints (Pratt and Adamski 2008). After the parameters for the types of integrity have been set within the database, users cannot violate them. For example, they cannot enter nonnumeric data into a number field. An error message will result. Likewise, a user cannot add a VISIT entry to the database described earlier unless a corresponding PATIENT has already been entered.

Data Security

Data security ensures the confidentiality, integrity, and availability of the data (Rob and Coronel 2009). Modern DBMSs have built-in mechanisms to enforce security rules. Within healthcare organizations, most of the database systems are shared with multiple users. This makes implementing the security features of the DBMS critical.

Protecting the security and privacy of data in the database is called **authorization management**. Two of the important aspects of authorization management are user access control and usage monitoring (Rob and Coronel 2009).

User access control features within the database are designed to limit access to the database or some portion of it. According to Rob and Coronel (2009), they generally provide the DBA or DA responsible for security with the tools to:

- Define each user of the database. The DBA can create log-in information for each user.
- Assign passwords to users.
- Define user groups. By defining user groups, the DBA can limit access to certain groups. For example, some users may have read-only privileges. These users can see the data in the database but cannot enter or change them. Other users may be granted read-write privileges, so they can enter and change data.
- Assign access privileges. This can be done according to user groups as described above or on an individual basis. The highest level of privilege is the administrative level, which should be reserved for the DBA. Persons with administrative permissions can change the underlying structure of the database.

This list represents the security features that are part of the DBMS. The database also can be secured at the network operating system level. In many cases, a database user will first log in to the network system with one log-in and password and then log in to the database with a second log-in and password. The database also can be secured through physical security protections, such as locked rooms, password-protected workstations, surveillance video, and voice recognition. The level of sensitivity of the data within the database should determine the level of security.

Usage monitoring is another aspect of authorization management. One of the most common ways that database administrators monitor database use is to use audit trails to determine whether there have been any actual or attempted access violations. The audit trails should be able to tell the DBA when and where the attempted breech occurred.

Check Your Understanding 5.7

Instructions: Answer the following questions on a separate piece of paper.

1. What is data integrity?
2. How is data integrity different from data security?
3. What do the authorization management features in a DBMS do?

Effective Data Display and Presentation

The MRI (2002) report on healthcare documentation reminds us that there are two major components to the documentation process: information capture and report generation. However, many methods are used for clinical and administrative report generation and transmission in healthcare. For example, many reports are disseminated in a standard document format, such as Microsoft Word, rich text, or pdf. The reports also might be generated directly from the database system, such as Microsoft Access or Oracle, a report-writing application such as Crystal Reports, or a spreadsheet such as Microsoft Excel. Moreover, different types of reports are suited for the different types of healthcare information. Patient-specific information to be filed in a paper-based medical record would commonly be printed in a document format with an individual focus; aggregate and comparative reports are more likely to include statistical and graphical information.

Health information managers also may be required to make presentations or provide information for others to make presentations based on aggregate and comparative data. These types of presentations often are supported by the use of presentation software such as Microsoft PowerPoint. To fully explore the various technologies and best practices for preparing high-quality reports and presentations is beyond the scope of this chapter. However, the following section introduces some basic principles for displaying data, particularly graphical data, and for creating slides for presenting data.

Principles of Data Display

In his seminal work, *The Visual Display of Quantitative Information*, Edward Tufte (2001, 13) outlined the features of an "ideal" graph. Graphical displays should

- Show the data
- Induce the viewer to think about the substance rather than the methodology, graphic design, the technology, or other things
- Avoid distorting what the data have to say
- Present many numbers in a small space
- Make large data sets coherent
- Encourage the eye to compare different pieces of data
- Reveal the data at several levels of detail
- Serve a reasonably clear purpose
- Be closely integrated with the statistical and verbal descriptions of the data set

With the advent of easy-to-use software packages, such as Excel, any user can create a professional-looking graph with ease. However, this ease does not negate the need for the user to understand the data being displayed and to select the appropriate format. Examine the data set presented in table 5.3, which shows the average number of admissions per month to a healthcare facility for one year.

The graphs in figures 5.18, 5.19, and 5.20 were created using Microsoft Excel to represent these data. Which one is the most effective for showing a comparison of the average admissions for the year?

The bar graph is a clear, accurate representation of the data. No unnecessary information or misleading three-dimensional aspects are given. The scale begins at zero and is not distorted. What about the pie chart? This is a totally inappropriate use of a pie chart. A pie chart is only used to show part or percentages of a whole. What does this chart tell you? What is the "whole" to which you are comparing? If you wanted to have a chart to show the breakdown for a

Table 5.3. Average facility admissions by month

Month	Admissions
January	999
February	780
March	923
April	834
May	800
June	959
July	845
August	902
September	1,005
October	782
November	966
December	1,027

Figure 5.18. Bar chart created to show the average number of patient admissions in one year by month

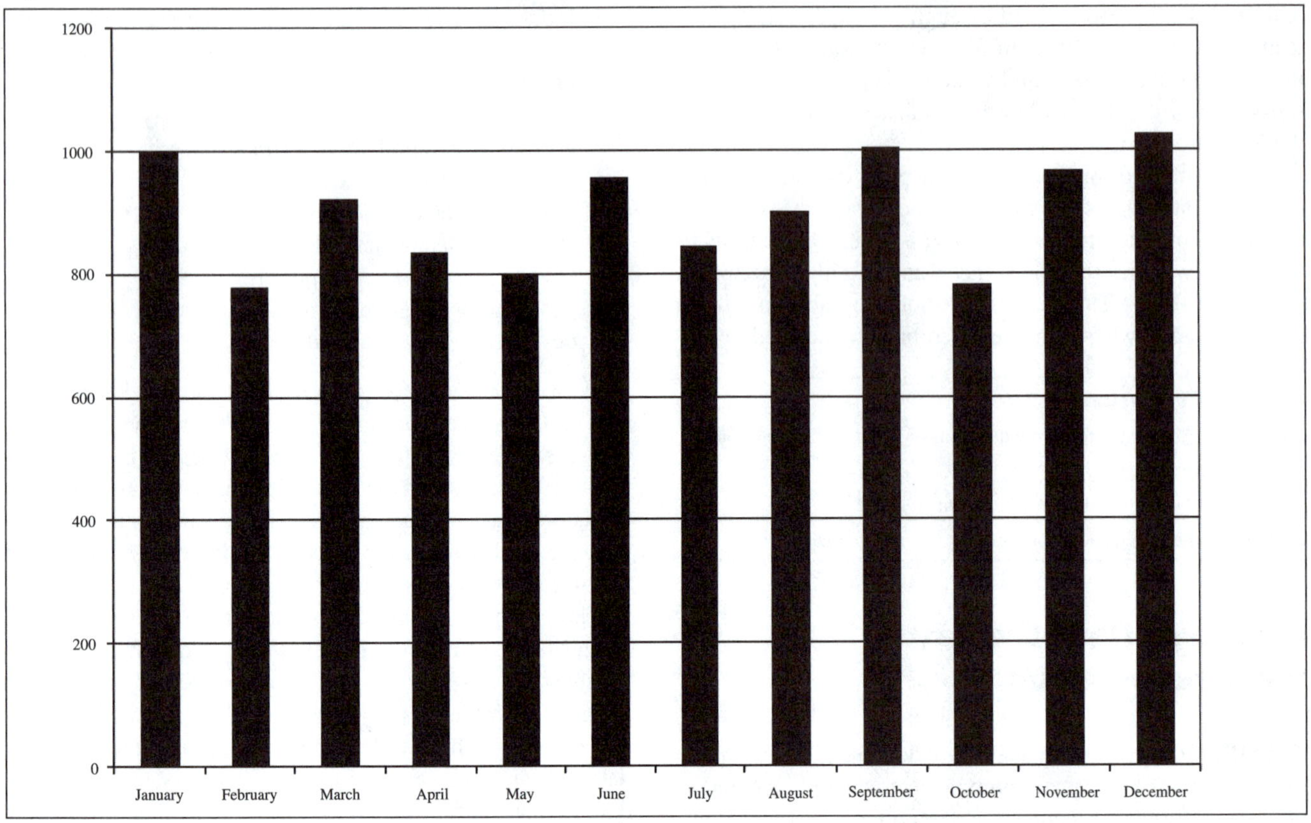

month's admissions by race, a pie chart might be appropriate. (See figure 5.21.)

What about the line chart? At first glance, you might have chosen this as the best graph. However, on closer look, the scale for the chart is distorted, exaggerating the differences in average admissions. Consider the line graph in figure 5.22, which displays the same data. Which one (figure 5.20 or figure 5.22) adheres to Tufte's admonishment to avoid distorting what the data have to say?

Tufte (2001, 51) also provided a list of principles for graphical excellence. He stated that graphical excellence:

- Is the well-designed presentation of interesting data—a matter of *substance*, of *statistics*, and of *design*
- Consists of complex ideas communicated with clarity, precision, and efficiency
- Gives the viewer the greatest number of ideas in the shortest time with the least ink in the smallest space

Principles of Creating Effective PowerPoint Presentations

Any number of sources provide guidance in developing effective PowerPoint presentations. A search of the Internet or a trip to the library will yield a variety of resources. Mills (2007) covers both designing and giving a presentation and creating a PowerPoint presentation. According to Mills (2007, 5), there are seven steps that should be followed for designing and giving presentations:

1. Define your purpose: Why are you presenting?
2. Profile your audience: Know your audience's needs and motivations.
3. Map your structure: Structure your story.
4. Add drama and impact: Liven up the presentation with anecdotes, stories or visuals.

Figure 5.19. Pie chart created to show the average number of patient admissions in one year by month

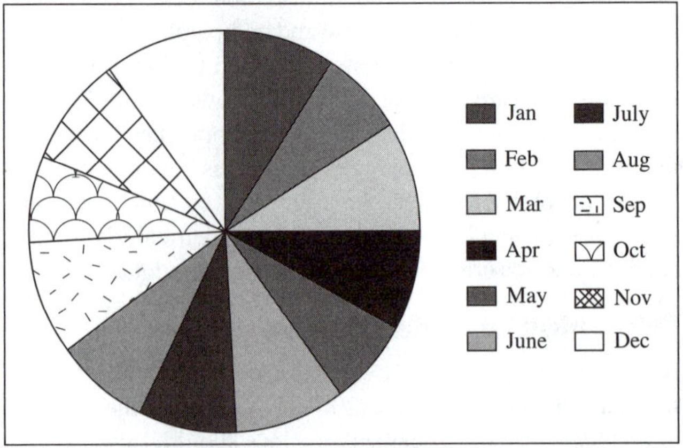

Figure 5.20. Line chart created to show the average number of patient admissions in one year by month

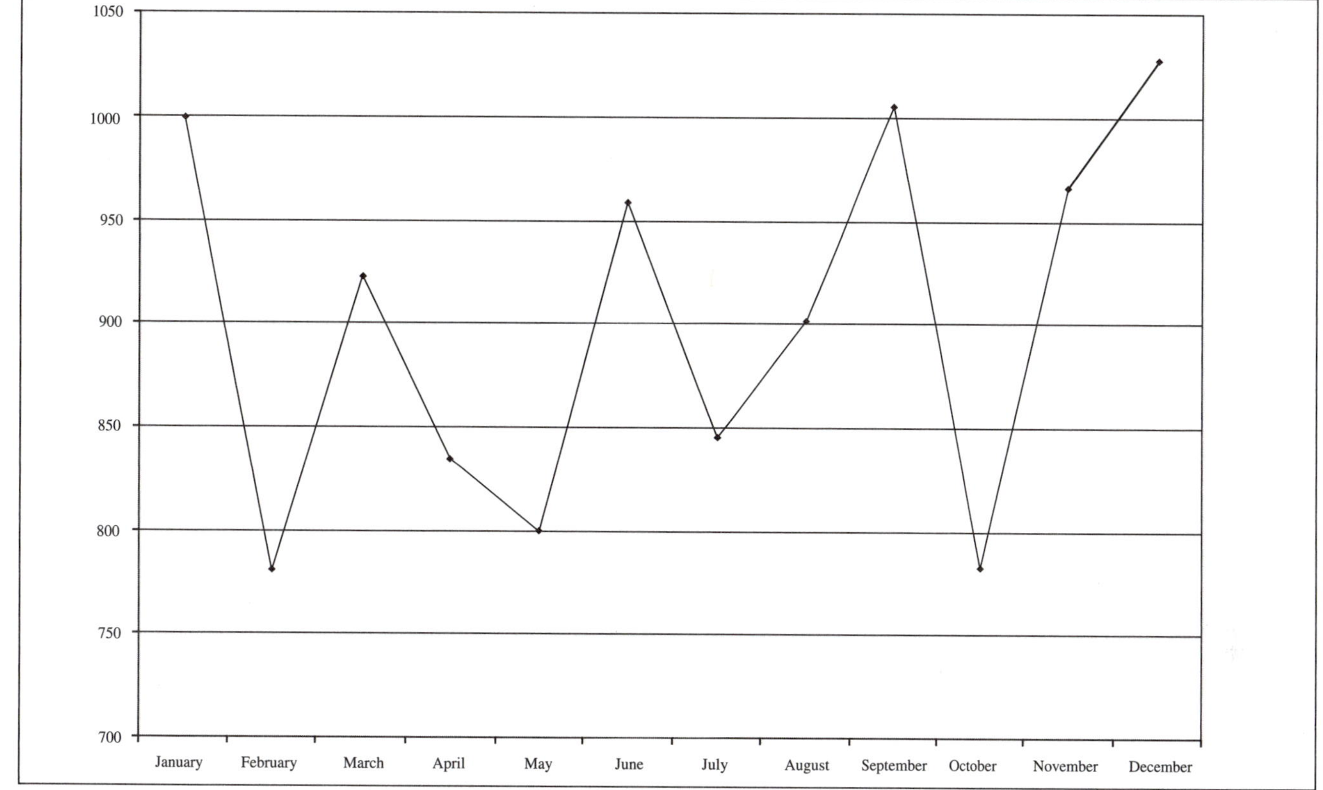

5. Rehearse until perfect: The more you rehearse, the better you get.
6. Deliver with style: The way you deliver is as important as the content.
7. Review and revise: Learn from your mistakes.

When the word *presentation* is heard, the program Microsoft PowerPoint comes to mind. It is important to remember that PowerPoint is just one tool that can be used for presentations. The phrase *death by PowerPoint* seems common in the business environment. One way to avoid being part of a *death by PowerPoint* presentation is to remember that PowerPoint is not a good medium for reading. It is important to avoid putting too much information on a slide. Only the main ideas should be included. The PowerPoint presentation is intended to *support* a presentation, not *be* the presentation. Mills (2007) gives six strategies to optimize the impact of a PowerPoint presentation:

- Align PowerPoint with the way the brain works: Use both the visual and verbal channels of the brain and avoid information overload.
- Segment your story into bites: Presenting a few slides, slowly and calmly, works the best.
- Make clear to your viewer the location and direction of the presentation: Use graphics to inform viewers where they have been and where they are going.
- Use visuals to persuade: Keep your text to the bare essentials and convert words into visuals wherever possible.
- Purge all but essential text and audiovisual effects: Less is more. (See figure 5.23 for an example of a slide that is too busy.)
- Dice and sequence complex visuals: Present one point per slide. (See figures 5.24 and 5.25 for an improved display of information from figure 5.23.)

There are many resources on creating PowerPoint presentations. Some books center on the PowerPoint software and the formatted presentations that are created. Some authors

Figure 5.21. Admissions by race

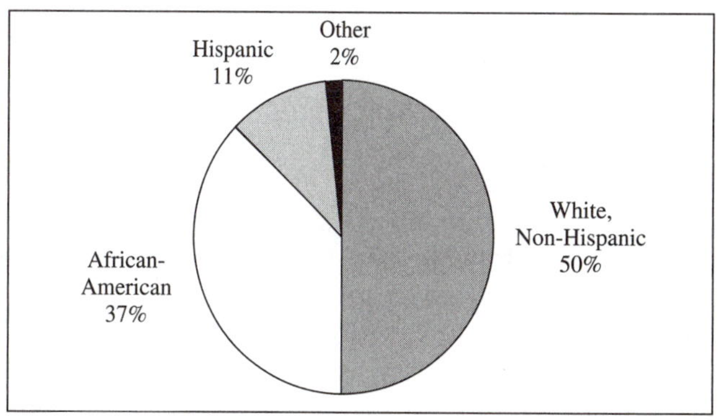

Figure 5.22. Line chart without distortion

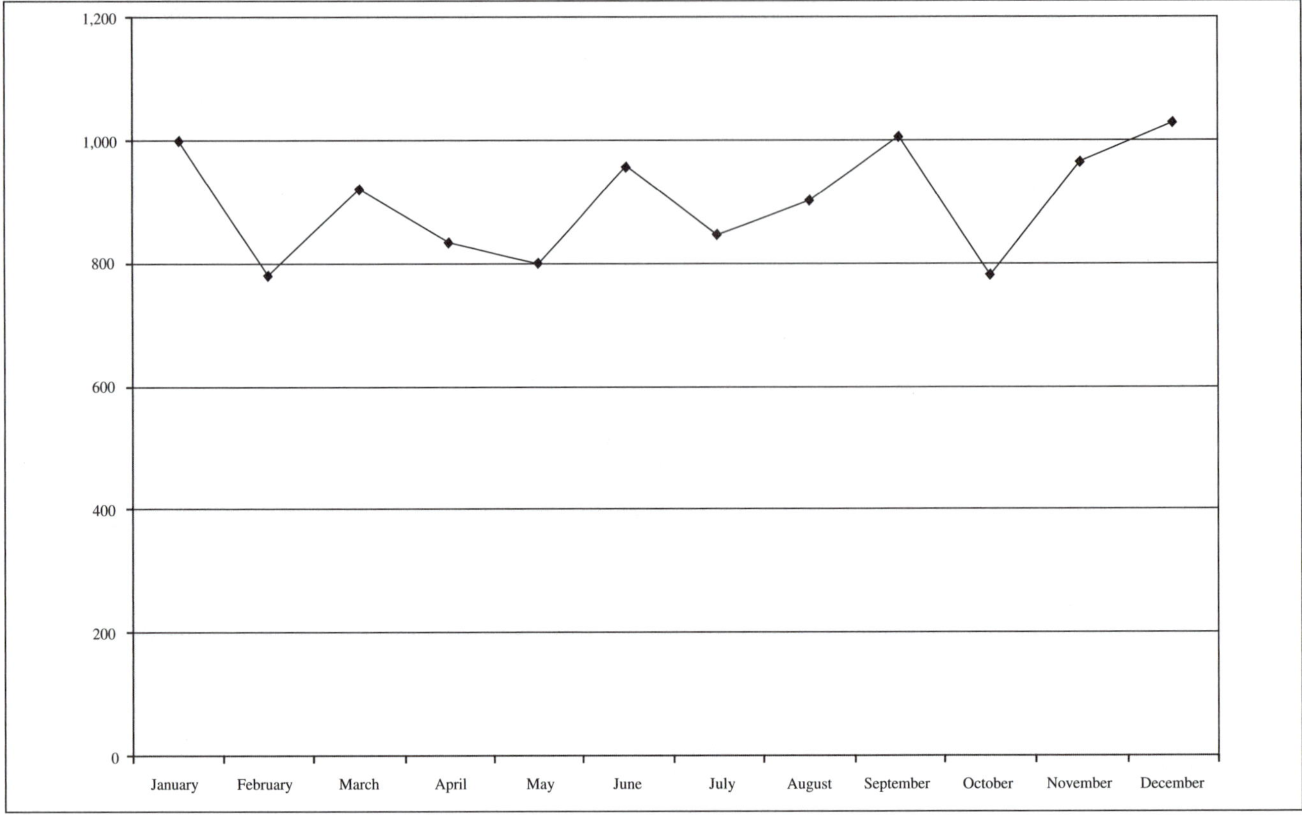

write about the act of the presentation itself and view PowerPoint as just one tool that could be used. Reynolds (2008) has written *Presentation Zen: Simple Ideas on Presentation Design and Delivery*. He writes about an approach to designing and delivering presentations that advocates giving up the past PowerPoint template deck of slides method for a creative, story-based method. The key to an effective presentation, no matter what the presentation mode, is to focus on presenting the right information to the right audience in a way that is clear, useful, and interesting.

Check Your Understanding 5.8

Instructions: Answer the following questions on a separate piece of paper.

1. What are the features of an "ideal" graph?
2. What are the basic guidelines for graphical excellence?
3. List and give examples of the steps for designing and giving presentations.
4. List and give examples of strategies to optimize the impact of PowerPoint presentations.

Real-World Case

Medical Associates (MA) is a physician group for a large academic medical center located in the southeastern United States. It provides services ranging from prevention and wellness to highly specialized care at outpatient clinics and facilities both on the medical center campus and in the surrounding community. Several years ago, after a major lawsuit involving the possibility of coding and billing inconsistencies, the MA executive committee voted to adopt a formal organizational compliance plan, with the goal of ensuring that the group's physicians, providers, and billing staff understood their legal responsibilities with regard to professional billing. One of the key features of the plan was to provide "coordinated training of clinical staff and billing personnel concerning applicable billing requirements and MA policies."

As outlined in the MA compliance plan, approximately 3,000 clinical and nonclinical employees need compliance education and training. Each of approximately 20 departments has a compliance coordinator responsible for tracking its employees' compliance education to ensure that all pre-established yearly requirements are met. Employees with patient care responsibilities must accrue four hours of training per year—one hour of general training and three hours of training related specifically to billing compliance. However, different categories of employees may have different training requirements. For example, some nonclinical employees need only one hour of general training. Any of this training can be obtained in a number of different settings: sessions offered by the employee's own department, departmental meetings with a compliance topic discussed, sessions offered by another department, sessions offered by the Compliance Office, videotape sessions, Internet sessions, or reading articles and other documents. Every employee must have documented evidence, including a signed attendance sheet, that he or she actually attended approved educational sessions to accrue the hours. Another complicating factor in maintaining quality-tracking records is that each training session may count for more than one type of training. Some sessions may last for only 15 minutes, others for three hours.

Figure 5.23. Busy PowerPoint slide

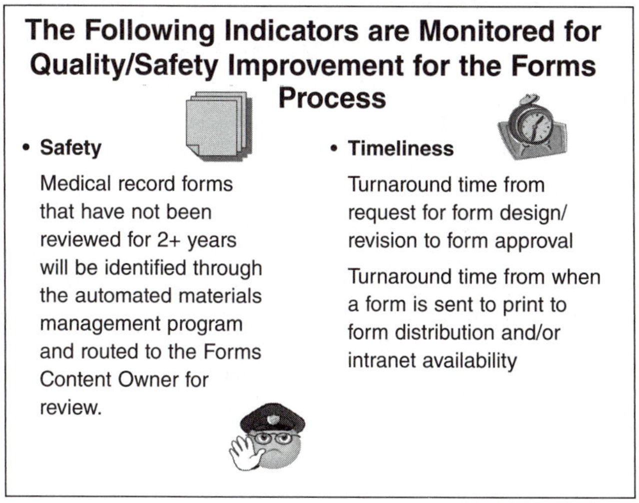

The Following Indicators are Monitored for Quality/Safety Improvement for the Forms Process

- **Safety**

  Medical record forms that have not been reviewed for 2+ years will be identified through the automated materials management program and routed to the Forms Content Owner for review.

- **Timeliness**

  Turnaround time from request for form design/ revision to form approval

  Turnaround time from when a form is sent to print to form distribution and/or intranet availability

Figure 5.24. Improved PowerPoint slide set (first)

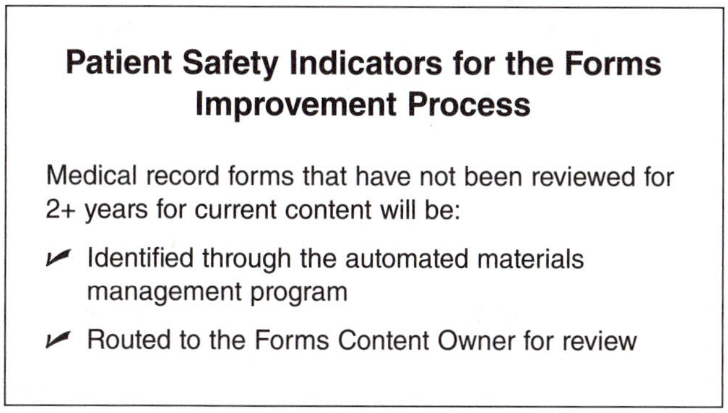

Patient Safety Indicators for the Forms Improvement Process

Medical record forms that have not been reviewed for 2+ years for current content will be:

- Identified through the automated materials management program
- Routed to the Forms Content Owner for review

Figure 5.25. Improved PowerPoint slide set (second)

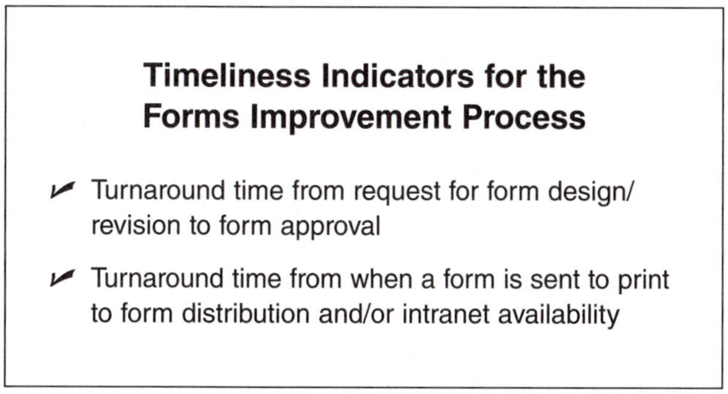

Timeliness Indicators for the Forms Improvement Process

- Turnaround time from request for form design/ revision to form approval
- Turnaround time from when a form is sent to print to form distribution and/or intranet availability

Originally, each department developed its own system for tracking employees. Recognizing that the education tracking and documentation would be an arduous task, several MA departments developed Excel applications for tracking and reporting; others developed small Access databases for this purpose.

Several significant issues emerged as compliance coordinators gained experience in tracking and reporting compliance education for their departments. They began to recognize a need to share their data across departments. As they began to share their spreadsheets and small databases, they soon realized that there were no standard definitions for the fields within the disparate tracking systems and no means for easily uploading one department's data into another's system. Multiple problems related to redundant data were identified. Any one employee might have education documented in more than one department's education-tracking system. The MA Compliance Office had to spend a great deal of time trying to clean and merge the data that came in from the various departments. The central Compliance Office could not easily identify who actually needed what type of education. These issues and others led the MA Compliance Office to consider the development of a central, shared database for all coordinators to use.

After several months of planning, a centralized, shared compliance education database was developed. Figure 5.26 shows the underlying table structure of its final version. In addition, a user-friendly interface was developed for data entry and information retrieval. The database was designed as a relational database, and the relationships are included in the schema. The infinity symbol shows the "many" sides of each one-to-many relationship. Because of the relational nature of the database, redundancy was reduced and the chance for data-entry update and deletion errors was all but eliminated.

The centralized education database has worked well for the MA compliance coordinators since its implementation a year ago. Multiple standard reports have been developed. These can be customized to show data by department, by cost center, or by divisions within departments. The MA compliance coordinators meet periodically to discuss multiple issues, including database issues. The database developer has continued to work under contract for MA compliance and has made various enhancements to the interface and standard reports. However, the underlying data structure has remained the same. The MA Compliance Office has expressed its confidence in the quality of the data and, consequently, in their reports since the database was implemented. The departmental coordinators also are happy in knowing that each employee for whom they are responsible is only in the database one time and that regardless of which department provided the education, they can track the total required hours accrued.

Figure 5.26. Relational schema for compliance education database

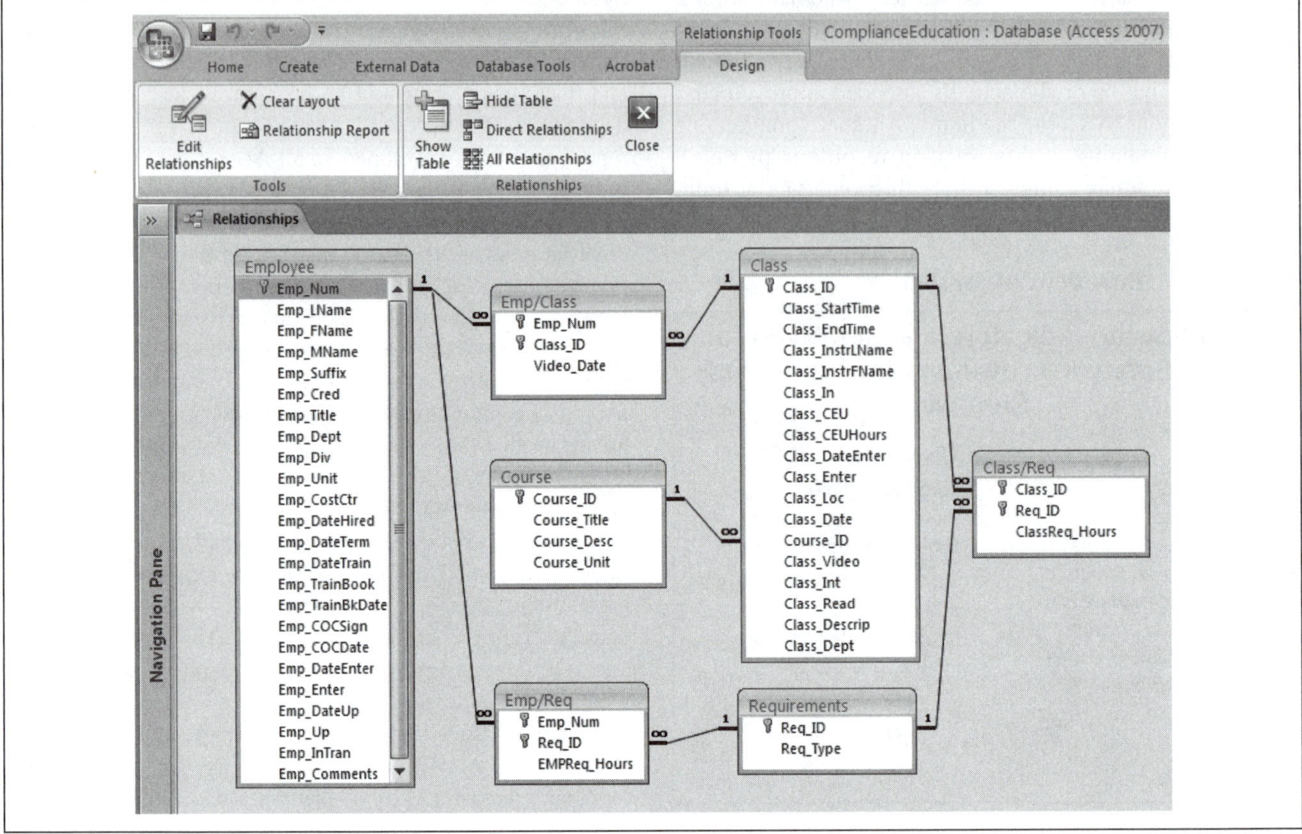

Summary

Health information managers must manage information that is shared by diverse and widely dispersed groups of end users. Information is derived from data, or raw facts. Knowledge is derived from information by combining it with experience and interpretation. Information and knowledge are then used by any number of individuals within a healthcare organization in making decisions about patient care. Thus, data, information, and knowledge are valuable resources that must be managed carefully following certain basic principles. Essential to the management of information is the organization's ability to ensure the quality of the data it maintains. Data quality is evaluated by comparing its characteristics to recognized standards. Although no single set of nationally recognized standards for healthcare data quality exists, two organizations, AHIMA and the Medical Records Institute, have published guidelines. Eventually, the evaluation of the data is translated into technical performance requirements for the information system.

Data quality can be controlled through multiple mechanisms. It can be controlled through effective database design found in computer applications. The design organizes the data in a way that facilitates their use. Two common types of database structures are the relational database and the object-oriented database. Each database structure is implemented through a specific management system. Key to database design is the process of data modeling, which links the "real" things about which the organization wants to collect and maintain data and the database structure.

An important tool in controlling data quality is the data dictionary. There are two general types: the DBMS (database management system) data dictionary, which is developed at the same time the database is developed, and the organization-wide data dictionary, which promotes data consistency throughout the organization.

To manage their data resources, healthcare organizations must set up mechanisms and policies that address not only database implementation and maintenance, but also standards of data quality. The roles of HIM professionals continue to evolve. AHIMA periodically surveys HIM professionals about their roles and publishes articles to disseminate the results.

References

American Health Information Management Association. 1998. Practice brief: Data quality management model. *Journal of AHIMA* 69(6).

American Health Information Management Association. 1999. *Evolving HIM Careers.* Chicago: AHIMA.

American Health Information Management Association. 2005. Embracing the future: New times, new opportunities for health information managers. Summary findings from the HIM workforce study. http://www.ahima.org/fore/professional/documents/Embracing-all.pdf#page%3D1.

American Health Information Management Association. 2007. Practice brief: Data standards, data quality, and interoperability. *Journal of AHIMA* 78(2): 65–68.

AHIMA e-HIM Workgroup on Computer-Assisted Coding. 2004. Delving into computer-assisted coding. Appendix G: Glossary of Terms. *Journal of AHIMA* 75(10): Web extra.

AHIMA e-HIM Work Group on EHR Data Content. 2006. Practice brief: Guidelines for developing a data dictionary. *Journal of AHIMA* 77(2): 64A–D.

AHIMA e-HIM Work Group on Assessing and Improving Healthcare Data Quality in the EHR. 2007. Practice brief: Assessing and improving EHR data quality. *Journal of AHIMA* 78(3): 69–72.

Austin, C.J. and S.B. Boxerman. 2003. *Information Systems for Health Services Administration*. 6th ed. Chicago: Health Administration Press.

Bureau of Labor Statistics, U.S. Department of Labor. 2008. *Career Guide to Industries, 2008-09 ed.* http://www.bls.gov/oco/cg/cgs035.htm.

Bryant, G. 2006. Testimony of Gloryanne Bryant, RHIA, CCS, Corporate Director for Coding and Health Information Management Compliance Catholic Healthcare West, to the Health Subcommittee of the Committee on Ways and Means US House of Representatives. http://www.ahima.org/icd10/documents/MicrosoftWord-TestimonyofGloryanneBryant_4_.pdf.

Johns, M.L. 2003. *Information Management for Health Professions*. 2nd ed. Albany, NY: Delmar.

Joint Commission. 2008. *Comprehensive Accreditation Manual for Hospitals: The Official Handbook*. Oakbrook Terrace, IL: Joint Commission Resources.

Joint Commission. 2009. *Comprehensive Accreditation Manual for Hospitals: The Official Handbook*. Oakbrook Terrace, IL: Joint Commission Resources.

Lau, F. 2004. Toward a conceptual knowledge management framework in health. *Perspectives in Health Information Management* 1(8).

Medical Records Institute. 2002. *Healthcare Documentation: A Report on Information Capture and Report Generation*. Boston: Medical Records Institute.

Mills, H. 2007. *Power Points! How to Design and Deliver Presentations that Sizzle and Sell*. New York, NY: AMACOM.

Pratt, P.J. and J. Adamski. 2008. *Concepts of Database Management*. 6th ed. Cambridge, MA: Course Technology, Thomson Learning.

Reynolds, G. 2008. *Presentation Zen: Simple Ideas on Presentation Design and Delivery*. Berkeley, CA: New Riders.

Rob, P. and C. Coronel. 2009. *Database Systems: Design, Implementation, and Management*. 8th ed. Boston, MA: Course Technology, Thomson Learning.

Strong, K.V. 2008. Enterprise Content and Records Management. *Journal of AHIMA* 79(2):39.

Tufte, E.R. 2001. *The Visual Display of Quantitative Information*. 2nd ed. Cheshire, CT: Graphics Press.

Wager, K.A., F.W. Lee, and J.P. Glaser. 2005. *Managing Health Care Information Systems: A Practical Approach for Health Care Executives*. San Francisco: Jossey-Bass.

Chapter 6
Information Systems Development

Karen A. Wager, DBA

Learning Objectives

- Understand the importance of strategic information systems planning to healthcare organizations
- Describe the purpose and major activities within each phase of the systems development life cycle: analysis, design, implementation, and maintenance and evaluation
- Identify the resources needed to effectively manage information systems within healthcare organizations
- Know the roles and responsibilities of information system professionals
- Identify the health information manager's role in planning, selecting, and implementing healthcare information systems

Key Terms

Administrative information systems
Analysis phase
Application service provider (ASP)
Application systems analyst
Chief information officer (CIO)
Chief information security officer (CISO)
Chief information technology officer (CITO)
Chief medical informatics officer (CMIO)
Clinical information systems
Clinical systems analyst
Database administrators
Design phase
Electronic health record (EHR)
Electronic medical record (EMR)
Implementation phase
Information system (IS)
Information technology (IT)
Maintenance and evaluation phase
Master Planning or Steering Committee
Network administrators
Programmers
Request for information (RFI)
Request for proposal (RFP)
Strategic IS planning
Systems analyst
Systems development life cycle (SDLC)
Webmasters

Healthcare organizations are under increased pressure to control costs and improve efficiency. At the same time, they are experiencing increased demands to ensure patient safety, reduce medical errors, improve the quality of care, promote access, and ensure compliance with privacy and security regulations. Many healthcare organizations are looking to **information system** (IS) technology to help them respond to these pressures and provide high-quality services in a more cost-effective manner.

Oftentimes, however, healthcare organizations have far more IS priorities than they have resources to allocate to them. How should decisions be made regarding which IS initiatives to support? How can healthcare administrators be reasonably assured that the information systems selected will meet their organization's current and future needs and be accepted by end users? What process will the organization use to select and implement a new system? After the decision is made to implement an IS, what resources are needed to adequately maintain and support it?

This chapter introduces a framework for addressing these important questions, including a description of the process that should be used to select a new IS, large or small. It also describes the people, policies, and organizational structure needed to maintain information systems and to manage information resources effectively. Finally, it discusses strategic information systems planning, the systems development life cycle, information resource management, and the role of the health information managers in planning, selecting, and implementing healthcare information systems.

Definition of Terms

Two broad categories of healthcare information systems described in this chapter are administrative and clinical systems. **Administrative information systems** contain primarily administrative or financial data and are commonly used to support the management functions or general operations of a healthcare facility (Wager et al. 2005). Examples include human resource management systems, materials management, patient billing, and staff scheduling. Administrative information systems were the first computerized systems implemented in most healthcare organizations. A recent survey by the American Hospital Association (2007) shows that 97 percent of hospitals have administrative applications in place that support the patient revenue cycle (registration, billing, electronic claims, and credit collections) and nearly three-quarters have patient scheduling and supply chain management applications.

In contrast to these administrative systems, **clinical information systems** (or applications) contain primarily clinical or health-related data that are used to diagnose, treat, monitor, and manage patient care. Examples of clinical applications include ancillary departmental systems (such as pharmacy, radiology, and laboratory medicine) as well as **electronic medical record** (EMR) systems, computerized provider order entry, medication administration, and nursing documentation. Most U.S. hospitals have pharmacy, radiology, and laboratory information systems in place (AHA 2007). Approximately 11 percent of hospitals are estimated to have fully functional EMR systems, yet nearly two-thirds of hospitals report having only partially implemented them. In the ambulatory care setting, only 4 percent of physician practices have extensive, fully functional EMRs and 13 percent have a basic system (Donald 1989; DesRoches et al. 2008). A *basic system* is defined as a computerized system for capturing health information and data, order entry for prescriptions, and results management for viewing laboratory and radiology results. A fully functional EMR system has all the functions of the basic system but also includes order entry for laboratory and radiology tests, electronic prescribing, and decision support capabilities (DesRoches et al. 2008).

Both administrative and clinical information systems may provide decision support capabilities to the end user. For example, one of the key attributes of an EMR system is its ability to alert the provider when two drugs should not be taken in combination or when a patient is due for a health maintenance examination such as a mammogram or bone density scan. Decision support features such as these can serve as tools in enabling the provider to manage the patient's care more effectively. Furthermore, most healthcare organizations are grappling with how to effectively select and implement clinical decision support systems (such as EMR and computerized provider order entry [CPOE] systems) into the care process. When the term EMR is used in this chapter, it is used in reference to a unique organization's system. The term **electronic health record** (EHR) is used when referencing a system that shares information across organizations (NAHIT 2008). See chapter 9 for a full discussion of EMRs and EHRs.

Today's Environment and the Growing Demand for Healthcare Information Systems

In 2007, healthcare spending reached $2.7 trillion, or $7,600 per person, representing 16 percent of the gross domestic product (GDP) (Poisal et al. 2007). In addition to rising healthcare costs, between 44,000 and 98,000 people die in hospitals each year as the result of medical errors (IOM 2000). Early estimates indicated that nearly 7,000 people die each year from medication errors alone, about 16 percent more deaths than the number attributable to work-related injuries. Even more staggering is the fact that more than 57,000 Americans die needlessly each year because they do not receive appropriate healthcare and, of this number, 90 percent die because of known conditions such as high blood pressure or elevated cholesterol that are not adequately monitored and controlled (NCQA 2003).

Containing healthcare costs and addressing patient safety issues have become national priorities. In response to a call issued by President Bush in 2004, the nation is seeking transparency of cost and quality information, as well as the widespread adoption of EHRs to become the standard within the next decade. The Centers for Medicare and Medicaid Services (CMS), the Joint Commission, and the National Committee for Quality Assurance are but a few examples of the agencies that now require healthcare providers to report performance in key quality indicators. For example, hospitals routinely report the degree to which they adhere to a range of clinical performance indicators, such as what percent of patients with acute myocardial infarction receive an aspirin at admission. Hospitals' performance in adhering to performance indicators is information that is now publicly available, which promotes transparency of quality and cost information to consumers, payers, and purchasers of care so individuals and communities are empowered to make more informed decisions.

To further the president's goal of widespread adoption of EHRs, in 2004 the Office of the National Health Information Technology Coordinator (ONC) was established. Numerous public and private agencies and organizations are currently working together to overcome the barriers that have impeded the widespread use and adoption of EHRs (and related systems) in healthcare in the past. In addition to the ONC, some of the key federal agencies involved with furthering the adoption and interoperability of EHR systems include the American Health Information Community, Healthcare Information Technology Standards Panel (HITSP), and the Certification Commission on Healthcare Information Technology (CCHIT).

How achievable is the president's call? Although estimates vary, most studies show that only 4 to 20 percent of healthcare facilities have implemented an EMR or other clinical decision support systems such as CPOE (Brailer and Terasawa 2003; 2007; DesRoches et al. 2008). It is not for their lack of benefit to patient care. Numerous studies have shown that the use of EMR-related systems can improve quality, decrease costs, and improve service and satisfaction (Bates and Gawande 2003; Bates et al., 1999; Barlow et al. 2004; Brailer and Terasawa 2003; Teich et al. 2000).

Despite the many benefits, major barriers to widespread adoption of EMR-type systems exist. The three primary barriers are (1) the high cost of acquiring and supporting systems, (2) a lack of sufficient standards and interoperability concerns, and (3) organizational and behavioral resistance (Wager et al. 2005). Acquiring an EMR system (or other IS) is a significant investment of time, resources, and people. Besides the up-front capital needed to acquire the system, significant costs are associated with implementing and maintaining the system, as well as the time, effort, and personnel resources devoted to redesigning processes and incorporating the system into the care process.

For the small physician practice (fewer than five physicians), it is difficult to make a business case for independent EMR adoption. Coupled with the cost issue is the fact that IS technology failures are common in healthcare. One-third to one-half of all healthcare IS projects fail (Brailer and Terasawa 2003). Likewise, many healthcare organizations have diverse and competing IS priorities and many initiatives never get off the ground due to lack of sufficient buy-in from clinical staff.

Such barriers can—and will—be overcome. However, they require that healthcare managers and leaders assume an active role in ensuring that their organizations are well equipped and prepared for change. Healthcare managers need to ask themselves the following questions:

- What are the strategic goals of the organization? What type(s) of information systems are needed to enable the organization to achieve its goals? To what degree are the IS goals aligned with the organization's overall strategic goals?
- How should decisions be made regarding which IS initiatives to support? What criteria or methods will be used? How will the organization make capital budget decisions?
- How can the organization be reasonably assured that the IS selected will meet its current and future needs and be accepted by end users?
- After the decision is made to implement an IS, what resources are needed to adequately maintain and support it?

Strategic Information Systems Planning

No board of directors would ever recommend building a new healthcare facility without an architect's blueprint and a comprehensive assessment of community/market needs and resources. The architect's blueprint helps ensure that the new facility has a strong foundation, a well-planned organizational basis, and the potential for growth and expansion. The assessment helps ensure that there is a need for the new facility and that adequate resources are available to support it.

Similarly, it is critical that the organization's IS plans be well aligned and integrated with its overall organizational strategic plans. To develop a blueprint for IS technology, the healthcare organization should engage in strategic IS planning. **Strategic IS planning** is the process of identifying and prioritizing IS needs based on the healthcare organization's mission and strategic goals.

Until recent years, few healthcare organizations have engaged in strategic planning for information systems. If an IS plan existed at all, it probably had been developed by the IS department staff, people who had not participated in the organization's overall strategic planning process. Having two separate plans often led to redundant systems, duplication of effort, and the acquisition of information systems that could not interact with each other.

Today, healthcare leaders recognize the importance of aligning business strategy with IT strategy (Wager et al. 2005). A recent survey of healthcare information technology (HIT) professionals found that 87 percent reported that a strong level of integration exists between IS strategies and overall organizational strategy. Yet only 37 percent of respondents indicated that their IS strategic plan is a component of the organization's strategic plan (HIMSS 2008). Ross and Weill (2002) published an article in *Harvard Business Review* entitled "Six IT Decisions Your IT People Shouldn't Make." They studied IT management practices at hundreds of companies around the world and found that although a number of factors distinguish top-performing companies, the most important factor is that senior managers take a leadership role in a handful of IT decisions. Two of these key decisions include defining the strategic role that IT will play in the company and making clear decisions about which IT initiatives will and will not be funded. These same principles apply to healthcare senior managers and organizations as well.

Different approaches or methods for developing a strategic IS planning process can be used. The following sections present a generic approach. Factors such as the type, size, and complexity of the organization as well as the decision-making philosophy of its leadership team are certainly important components in determining how to establish IS priorities.

Strategic Planning Process

As the senior leadership team engages in strategic planning discussions, they should ensure that IS leadership is also engaged in these discussions. In particular, they should examine the organization's view of the role that IS technology will play in the organization's future. To what extent, if any, will HIT enable the organization to achieve its strategic goals? Historically, this has not been the approach to systems development within healthcare. Many information systems were developed or acquired by healthcare organizations in a rather piecemeal fashion. Early systems were primarily administrative or financial in nature and often developed in-house by what was then the data processing department. With the advent of microcomputers in the mid-1980s, healthcare organizations began to invest more extensively in **clinical information systems.** However, these systems were often purchased from outside vendors based on individual department needs and not on the needs of the organization as a whole or on its strategic plans. For example, the radiology department might have purchased the best radiology IS on the market and the laboratory department purchased the best laboratory IS, with little, if any, consideration of whether the organization had an appropriate **information technology** (IT) infrastructure to adequately support the two systems. The systems were thought of quite independently.

Today, it is vital that the leadership team adopt a systemwide perspective on information management and view each major IS acquisition within the context of the larger picture; that is, how the system supports the organization's overall mission and strategic goals. A direct alignment should exist between the strategic goals of the organization and major IS initiatives. The goal is to build systems that support the goals of the organization, not disparate applications that do not "talk to each other." In fact, the lack of connectivity or interoperability among applications is one of the most frequently cited complaints among clinicians and administrators.

To help ensure that information systems support the organization's strategic plan and are not acquired in isolation, healthcare leaders examine both the external and internal environment and business plans before establishing IS priorities or making IS investments.

Generic Approach

The following steps represent a generic approach to developing a strategic IS plan. (See figure 6.1.) This approach can be modified or adapted to meet the healthcare organization's individual needs. The steps include the following:

1. Review the organization's strategic plan and assess the organization's current external and internal environment.
2. Identify the organization's mission, strategic goals, and objectives and assess its IS needs.
3. Establish IS priorities.
4. Gain approval from the organization's leaders (executive management and board of directors) of the prioritized plan for completing IS projects.

Reviewing the Strategic Plan and Assessing the External and Internal Environment

To begin the planning process, the IS Steering Committee should review the organization's current strategic plans, goals, and objectives and evaluate its current external environment. The overall strategic plan should include an environmental assessment that analyzes the external forces that may affect the organization. External forces include changes in reimbursement methodologies, new government regulations, and changes in the demographics or healthcare needs of the community.

An environmental assessment should also be performed to explore emerging technologies and their potential impact on the ways the healthcare organization delivers its services. In conducting this assessment, a subgroup of the committee may want to review the literature, visit trade shows, network with colleagues in the field, or meet with leading vendors in the marketplace. A number of consultant groups also can provide vendor/product information to the organization.

In addition to the external environmental assessment, it is equally important that the IS steering committee conduct an internal environmental assessment of the organization's current IS environment. The committee should consider questions such as:

- Which information systems are currently used within the organization?
- To what extent do these systems meet the needs of end users?

- Which systems are likely to need replacement or upgrades? Which ones are likely to become obsolete within the next few years?
- To what extent is the organization able to support and maintain its current systems? Does it have the people, equipment, and network infrastructure needed to support its current systems?
- To what degree are the current systems cost-effective and efficient?
- How well do the existing information systems support the organization's strategic goals?

As part of the analysis of the current internal environment, the committee may also compare the organization's IT functionality and performance against external benchmarks. For example, the committee might compare the organization's ratio of end users to technical support personnel with industry averages. It also might compare the organization's performance in key areas with the performance of other, similar organizations. The committee might want to consider the following questions:

- How secure are patient information systems?
- How much downtime does the facility experience?
- How much IT staff time is spent troubleshooting system problems?
- In what ways, if any, have the major systems adversely affected patient care?
- To what degree are existing systems in compliance with the Health Insurance Portability and Accountability Act (HIPAA) privacy and security regulations?

It is essential that the organization evaluate existing systems to accurately identify its needs, problems, and opportunities for improvement. Otherwise, it runs the risk of installing a new IS to fix a perceived problem only to discover that the new system never addressed the actual problem and, instead, created a host of new problems.

Figure 6.1. Strategic information systems planning process

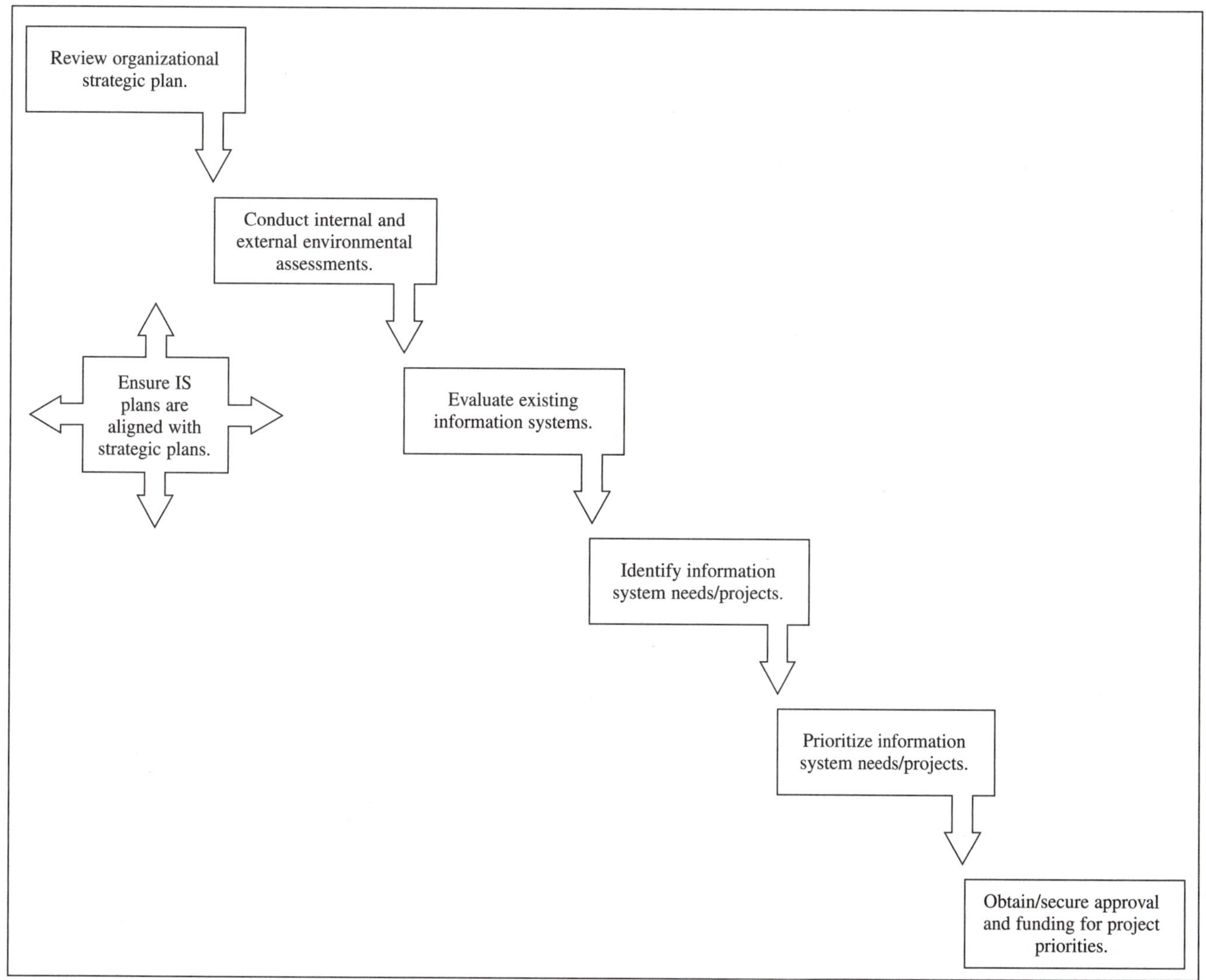

Identifying IS Needs and Prioritizing IS Projects

After the committee has developed a thorough understanding of the organization's strategic goals, environment, emerging information technologies, and existing information systems, it should identify IS needs throughout the organization. This internal needs assessment can be formal or informal. For example, if the committee wants to conduct a formal assessment, it might conduct structured interviews with key users or administer surveys in key areas throughout the organization. A less formal approach would be to ask all IS steering committee members to list the information needs within their respective areas. The outcome of this assessment is a fairly comprehensive list of the organization's information management needs. Eventually, the list can be used to identify projects and establish IT priorities.

The next step in the planning process is to establish priorities. Again, the committee might take different approaches to accomplish this important task. One approach is to identify all proposed IS projects and hold an intensive retreat where all interested stakeholders (IS steering committee members and other interested clinicians and staff) score and rank each project. Sufficient information concerning each project should be given to the stakeholders ahead of time to help them make informed choices. (See chapter 9 for a discussion specific to EHR planning considerations and migration strategies.)

Gaining Approval for the Plan

When using either the generic approach or another approach to setting priorities, the strategic IS planning process should result in a list of identified project priorities. These priorities should then be developed further and forwarded to the senior administration and the board of directors for approval and funding. It is important to note that the priority list is not static. It should be reviewed periodically and modified accordingly based on changes in the environment and the growing needs of the organization.

Role of a Master Planning or Steering Committee

Generally the leadership team will establish an interdisciplinary oversight committee to guide and manage the strategic planning process. This **Master Planning or Steering Committee** would likely have representation from the key clinical and administrative areas of the organization such as the medical staff, nursing, pharmacy, radiology, and other ancillary areas as well as finance, administration, IT, and health information management. The composition of the master planning committee may vary, but its primary goal is to make high level decisions regarding the implementation of the strategic plan, and ensure all efforts are coordinated and communicated at all levels within the facility. Who should lead the Master Planning Committee? That too can vary considerably—it is important to select a chairperson that possesses strong leadership skills, is well respected within the organization, and maintains a "big picture" view of the organization's strategic plans.

Check Your Understanding 6.1

Instructions: Answer the following questions on a separate piece of paper.

1. Why is strategic planning for information systems important to organizations in today's healthcare environment? What risks are associated with not having an IS plan?
2. Who should be involved in the strategic planning process? Who should lead the effort?
3. Why is it important for the IS plan to be integrated with the healthcare organization's overall strategic plan?
4. Why is it important for healthcare organizations to examine their existing information systems? What aspects of the existing system(s) should be examined during the planning process?
5. How might a healthcare organization approach prioritizing its IS projects or needs?

Information Systems Development

After establishing IS priorities as part of the strategic plan, the healthcare organization should follow a structured project management process for selecting and implementing new systems. The structured approach enables the organization to identify viable alternatives, gain user buy-in, select a system that meets the needs of the users, and implement the system in a well-organized, systematic way.

Because several new system projects may be going on simultaneously and people may be involved in more than one project, it is important that the projects be organized and managed consistently. Ideally, the IT staff or the project leader should maintain a project repository for every IS initiative. Included in the project repository would be all minutes, notes, survey results, and other relevant information used in managing the project. The project repository is particularly important in healthcare organizations that experience high turnover among IT staff. (See chapter 26 for a full discussion of project management principles, processes, and tools.)

Systems Development Life Cycle

One process for IS development is the **systems development life cycle** (SDLC). Although there are many different models of the SDLC, all generally include a variation of the following four phases: analysis, design, implementation, and maintenance and evaluation. As the activities that occur in each phase are discussed, it should become apparent that the process does not end when the new IS is implemented. Rather, the SDLC is an ongoing process that requires continuing assessment and planning. Figure 6.2 illustrates the cyclical nature of the SDLC.

Like the strategic IS planning process, the SDLC involves the participation of numerous people with diverse backgrounds and areas of expertise. Depending on the nature and scope of the project, representatives from the key clinical and administrative areas should be involved. For example, if the organization plans to replace its pharmacy IS, the process

Figure 6.2. Systems development life cycle

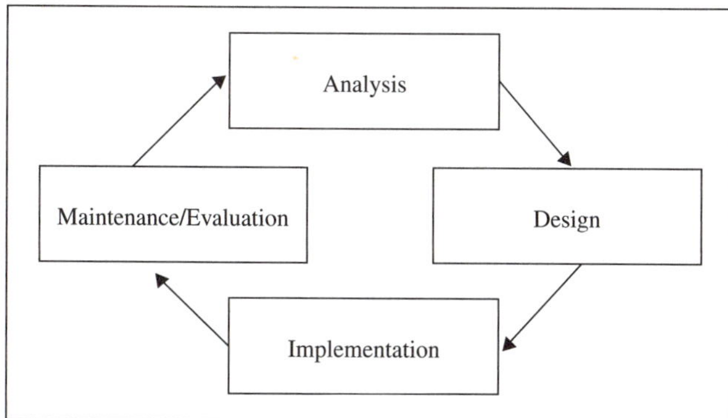

might include individuals from the medical staff, nursing, and other ancillary areas that depend on or use pharmacy information, in addition to key people from the pharmacy department. Representatives from IT and HIM services also should be involved.

Analysis Phase

After senior administration or the board gives the go-ahead for the project, the **analysis phase** begins. During the analysis phase, the need for a new IS is explored further, problems with the existing system are solidified, and user needs are identified. The primary focus in this beginning phase of the SDLC is on the business problem, independent of any technology that can or will be used to implement a solution to that problem.

In this phase, it is important to examine the current system and to identify opportunities for improvement or enhancement. Even though an initial assessment was completed as part of the strategic information planning process, the analysis phase of the SDLC involves a more extensive evaluation. Typically, the existing system is evaluated by asking routine users to identify its strengths and limitations. Completion of this task can help ensure that the organization does not make a significant investment in a new system only to later discover that what was needed was better communication, additional training, and more extensive technical support, and not a new information system.

When it is clear that a new IS is needed, the next step is to assess the information needs of users and to define functional requirements. It is best to have a structured method for accomplishing this task. For example, the project team might administer a questionnaire, conduct focus groups, or hold joint-requirements planning sessions. A joint-requirements planning session is a highly structured group meeting that is conducted to analyze problems and define functional requirements. Whatever method or combination of methods is used to solicit user input, the process should result in a detailed list of user specifications.

Design Phase

After the users' needs have been identified, the process generally moves into the **design phase.** During this phase, consideration is given to how the new system will be designed or selected. Questions to ask include:

- Will the new system be built in-house?
- Will the organization hire an outside developer to build the system?
- Will the facility purchase an IS from a vendor, or lease it from a vendor or **application service provider** (ASP)—a company or firm that deploys, manages, and remotely hosts prepackaged software through centrally located servers, often on a fixed, per user basis or on a per transaction fee basis?

Due to time, cost, and personnel restraints, most healthcare organizations first look at what IS products are available in the vendor community. For this reason, this discussion focuses on selecting an IS from a vendor rather than building one in-house. In the rare situation that a facility decides to build a system in-house, it is generally because the facility's needs are unique and it has the technical expertise to design and support the system.

A facility that wishes to explore the systems available in the vendor community might begin by obtaining information from exhibits at professional conferences, directories or publications, the Internet, vendor user groups, consulting firms, and contacts with colleagues in the health information systems (HIS) industry. A **request for information** (RFI) is generally sent to a fairly extensive list of vendors that are known to offer products or systems that meet the organization's needs. The RFI is used to obtain general product information and to prescreen vendors. Responses to the RFI are used to narrow the list to a smaller number of vendors who will be invited to respond to the **request for proposal** (RFP).

The RFP generally includes much more detail on the system's requirements and provides guidelines for vendors to follow in bidding. According to Wager, et al. (2005), for a major system acquisition, the RFP generally includes:

- Instructions for vendors, including the proposal deadline and contract information, specific instructions for completing the RFP, and any stipulations with which the vendor must comply
- Organizational objectives, including the type of system or application being sought, and how it will fit into the organization's strategic plans and goals
- Background of the organization, including a description of the facility (size, type of patient services, patient volume, and so forth) and an inventory of applications and the network infrastructure
- System goals and requirements, including a description of the system characteristics and the features that are desired or required
- Vendor qualifications, including background information, experience, number of installations, annual financial reports, and standard contract

- Proposed solution, including a description of how the vendor believes its product meets the organization's goals and needs
- Criteria to be used in evaluating the RFP
- General contractual requirements, including warranty information, payment, schedule, and penalties for failure to meet schedules specified in the contract
- Pricing and support

Moreover, it is a good idea to ask about the number of planned installations during the same time period and how staffing and other support issues will be managed if multiple implementations are under way at the same time.

Concurrent with development of the RFP, the project team should establish the criteria with which to evaluate the vendors' responses to the RFP. For example, the team may want to evaluate the extent to which each vendor's product meets the functional requirements of the new system, the vendor's track record of performance, and the extent to which the vendor's philosophy of systems development is congruent with the organization's IT strategy. In addition, the team may want to evaluate system reliability, costs, and projected benefits.

Evaluation of the vendor and its products should not depend solely on its response to the RFP. Other formal and informal mechanisms should be used to evaluate each vendor and its products. For example, the project team may hold vendor presentations, check references, attend user group meetings, and make site visits to other facilities that use the product. The purpose of these activities is to gather as much relevant information as possible to make an informed decision. Interested clinicians, administrators, and other end users, as well as members of the project team, should have the opportunity to participate in as many of these activities as possible.

As part of the system selection process, the project team should conduct a cost-benefit analysis for each viable alternative. Costs should include acquisition costs (for example, hardware, software, network, and training) in addition to operating or maintenance costs (for example system upgrades, technical support, supplies, and equipment). Most costs can be identified and measured reasonably accurately. However, the benefits to implementing an IS can be much more difficult to identify. Some benefits, such as increased productivity or improved access to information are tangible and can be measured (albeit not easily); others are intangible and very difficult to quantify. For example, a new EMR system might lead to improved employee morale or increased patient satisfaction, but these potential benefits might be more difficult to isolate and quantify. Consequently, when comparing different vendor systems or alternatives, it is important to evaluate and measure costs and benefits to the fullest extent possible. A variety of standard cost-benefit analysis methods may be used to evaluate different IT options that are beyond the scope of this book. *Systems Analysis and Design* (Whitten and Bentley 2007) provides a fairly complete explanation of different cost-benefit analysis methods.

When the top two or three vendors have been identified, leadership within the healthcare organization generally initiates the contract negotiation process. It is generally a good idea to begin contract negotiations with more than one vendor. This provides leverage during the negotiation process and affords the organization an alternative should it and the vendor not agree on the terms of the contract. A host of very detailed and technical issues are generally addressed in the contract: everything from when the system is to be delivered and installed, to training and support, to warranties and guarantees, to who is responsible for ensuring that the product interfaces with other institutional systems. Internal legal counsel generally reviews the contract carefully before it is signed and commitments are made.

Implementation Phase

After contract negotiations have been finalized, the **implementation phase** begins. In this phase, a comprehensive plan for implementing the new system is developed. An interdisciplinary implementation team is generally established and led by a project manager. The implementation team will likely include some of the same individuals involved in selecting the new system, but other key people should be involved in the process as well.

Ideally, the project manager should be someone who is well respected and knowledgeable, has experience with implementing new systems, and has the political influence and power to make things happen. He or she also should have strong organizational and communication skills and be able to work effectively with everyone involved in the implementation including the vendor, clinicians, and senior management. The importance of selecting the right person to lead the effort cannot be overemphasized. Even though a good implementation does not guarantee user acceptance of the new system, a poor implementation can lead to frustration, dissatisfaction, and disillusionment. Some organizations never recover fully from a disastrous system implementation.

One of the implementation team's priorities is to identify all the tasks that must be completed before the go-live date. Depending on the type of system, the number of users, and the complexity of the conversion process, the tasks may vary in scope and complexity. However, many system implementation projects require at least the following tasks:

- Preparing the site (for example, work-flow patterns, noise, space, telephone lines, and electrical power)
- Installing the necessary hardware and software
- Preparing data tables
- Building interfaces
- Establishing an IT infrastructure (for example, stable network, secure database) to support the system
- Ensuring that adequate security and confidentiality practices are in place
- Training managers, technical staff, and other end users
- Testing the new system
- Identifying and correcting errors

- Preparing documentation to support system use (for example, procedure manuals)
- Implementing conversion plans
- Developing and testing backup and disaster recovery procedures

Although each of these major tasks is very important, a few should be highlighted to stress their relevance to the implementation phase. First, it is critical to thoroughly test any new system before the go-live date. This means testing, testing, and retesting the new system with real patient data, not sample data the vendor may have provided or your institution may have created. Even though it is nearly impossible to identify and correct all the errors before a system goes live, it is essential to identify and correct as many of them as possible. It is often much easier to correct a problem in the test mode than after the system is fully operational.

Second, adequate training is essential. A healthcare organization may be implementing a solid, highly reputable new system, but if the staff who will be using it are not thoroughly trained, the system's implementation can result in dissatisfaction and low morale. For any new system to be successful, it must be accepted and used by the staff. Different organizations and vendors might use different approaches to training, but one common approach is to train the trainer. This approach involves identifying key people in the various functional areas (for example, nursing units, laboratory, and billing), training them on the system, and then having them train others in their area (with guidance from the vendor or a "super user").

The train the trainer method can be effective because after the vendor is gone, staff must be available who are comfortable with the system and can assist others. It is equally important to allow adequate time for training. Staff should not have to squeeze in training on their lunch break, with little or no time to practice using the new system. Just as it is important to use real data in testing the system, it is critical to give staff practice using the new system with real patients or real data.

In addition to providing training, the organization must have the IT infrastructure and processes in place to support the system. The infrastructure should include a stable network, a sufficient number of workstations appropriately located throughout the organization, adequate security measures, up-to-date procedural manuals, and a process for reporting problems with the system.

Finally, it is important to develop plans for converting the old system to the new one. Conversion to a new system often requires major changes in the workflow and organizational structure and places increased demands on staff during this period. Therefore, it is essential to plan appropriately for the conversion and to ensure that adequate technical and support staff members are available to assist managers and end users, as needed.

Throughout the implementation process, many tasks or activities may occur simultaneously; others will need to be completed before other activities can begin. Because of the number of different tasks occurring, it is generally a good idea for the project manager to use a Gantt chart or project management tool that identifies the major tasks, their estimated start and completion dates, the individuals responsible for performing them, and the resources needed to complete them. Again, activities or tasks that depend on the completion of other tasks should be readily identified. Project management software such as Microsoft Project is useful in creating Gantt charts, is easy to use, and enables the manager to track project resources (for example, staff, equipment) and expenditures. Figure 6.3 is an example of a Gantt chart for an IS implementation project.

Maintenance and Evaluation Phase

The final phase of the SDLC is the **maintenance and evaluation phase.** Regardless of how well designed and tested a new system may be, errors or bugs inevitably occur after it goes into operation. IT support staff must be available to find potential problems and take steps to correct them. Whether the technical staff are in-house or employed through a contract service, well-trained staff must be available to maintain or support the new system. For critical systems such as patient care or clinical information systems, technical support should be available 24 hours a day, seven days a week. Sufficient technical staff also should be available to oversee system backups and upgrades, replace outdated equipment, respond to new regulatory requirements, and provide ongoing training and assistance. Nearly 25 percent of the total technical staff time may be devoted to maintenance activities when several information systems are in place.

As the organization hires new people, its technical or support staff must be available to train them on the system. Likewise, all staff will need additional training on a regular basis to ensure that they are current with system upgrades, enhancements, and new features or procedures. Ideally, the organization should have a plan in place outlining how staff will receive initial and ongoing training on any new or existing IS. Many healthcare organizations now appoint an individual within key clinical and administrative departments whose primary role is to ensure that the department staff has adequate training and technical support available to them. For example, the radiology department might have a radiological technician with strong computer skills who serves as the information technician and assists and trains other staff in the department. Such an approach can be effective in increasing response time to user requests and alleviating user frustration.

In addition to providing adequate training and support, the healthcare organization should monitor data quality and integrity and ensure that the system is secure and safe. Specifically, emergency backup procedures should be in place in the event the system fails or goes down for any reason. All staff should know what to do in such circumstances. The backup procedures should be well documented and readily available to staff. If forms are utilized during downtimes, clear instructions on what to do with them should be available when the system is restored.

Figure 6.3. Sample Gantt chart of an IS implementation project

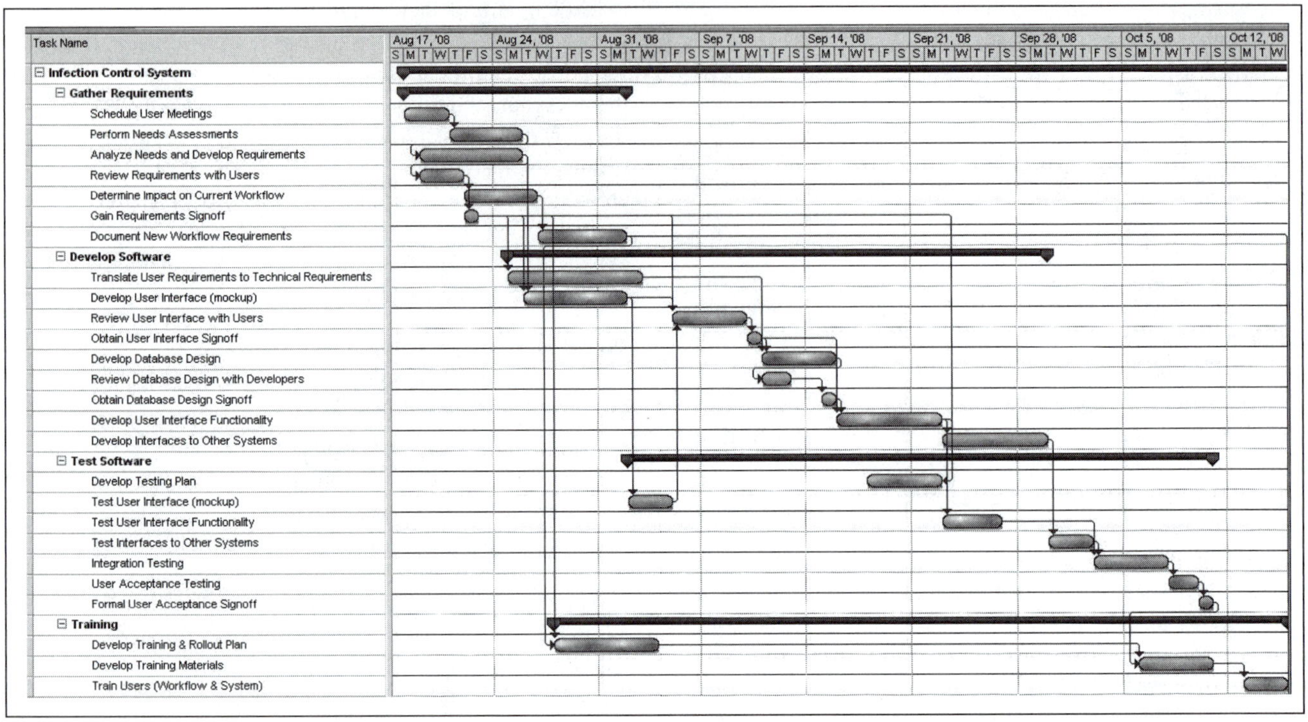

Task Name
⊟ **Infection Control System**
⊟ **Gather Requirements**
Schedule User Meetings
Perform Needs Assessments
Analyze Needs and Develop Requirements
Review Requirements with Users
Determine Impact on Current Workflow
Gain Requirements Signoff
Document New Workflow Requirements
⊟ **Develop Software**
Translate User Requirements to Technical Requirements
Develop User Interface (mockup)
Review User Interface with Users
Obtain User Interface Signoff
Develop Database Design
Review Database Design with Developers
Obtain Database Design Signoff
Develop User Interface Functionality
Develop Interfaces to Other Systems
⊟ **Test Software**
Develop Testing Plan
Test User Interface (mockup)
Test User Interface Functionality
Test Interfaces to Other Systems
Integration Testing
User Acceptance Testing
Formal User Acceptance Signoff
⊟ **Training**
Develop Training & Rollout Plan
Develop Training Materials
Train Users (Workflow & System)

Source: Medical University of South Carolina

However, maintaining and supporting the new systems is not enough. Information systems should be evaluated on an ongoing basis to determine if they are contributing to the institution's overall goals and meeting user needs. Healthcare administrators today are demanding to know whether the return on investment (ROI) to the organization has been realized since system implementation. Being able to measure ROI is becoming increasingly important as healthcare institutions struggle to manage limited resources more effectively. Consequently, as a part of the system evaluation process, institutions are looking at the organizational, technological, and economic impact of information systems on the enterprise as a whole. The Agency for Healthcare Quality and Research (AHRQ) recently published a Health Information Technology toolkit that can serve as a useful resource in guiding the organization through the evaluation process (Cusack and Poon 2007).

HIM Contributions to IS Development

Health information managers can make unique contributions to the SDLC process. Because HIM professionals understand the origins and content of patient data contained in health records as well as the financial impact of coding, they are in an ideal position to speak to the need to integrate clinical and financial information. HIM professionals also have a broad understanding of healthcare organizations and their major components and frequently interact with clinicians and administrators who need access to relevant information for decision-making purposes.

Perhaps the best way to describe the different contributions HIM professionals could make to the SDLC is to walk through a simple example. Let's say that the healthcare organization has decided to select and implement an enterprise-wide EMR system within the next two years. During the analysis phase, the HIM professional could assist in identifying problems with the current health record system and in assessing the needs of various user groups. Because this individual understands the major components of an EMR system and many of the problems associated with paper-based health record systems, he or she could assist the project team in identifying user specifications for the RFP.

During the design phase, the HIM professional could share knowledge and insight into the EMR selection process. Most likely, he or she would attend several professional conferences each year to visit vendor exhibits, network with colleagues throughout the nation, and attend educational sessions on various aspects of EMR development and implementation. The HIM professional could return to the institution with the insight and lessons learned from others in the field. Throughout the EMR selection process, the HIM professional could attend vendor demonstrations, conduct site visits, and evaluate vendor responses to the RFP. In addition, he or she could provide valuable input when addressing security and confidentiality issues.

During the implementation phase of the EMR project, the HIM professional should become part of the implementation team or could participate in system-building activities such as:

- Developing a data dictionary
- Performing data mapping

- Designing electronic forms and reports
- Testing the system
- Training staff
- Identifying technical errors
- Developing backup and disaster recovery plans
- Ensuring that all staff members are aware of patient confidentiality and system security

Finally, in the maintenance and support phase, the HIM professional could evaluate the system's impact on the department's operations and on the quality of the data residing in the EMR, identify and communicate problems to the appropriate individuals, and develop an ongoing training program for staff. HIM professionals could also serve as application system analysts, as the liaisons between the IS staff and the end-users in training, support, and ongoing enhancement to the system. These are just a few of the many ways in which a HIM professional could make significant contributions to the SDLC of a new system.

Check Your Understanding 6.2

Instructions: Answer the following questions on a separate piece of paper.

1. What is the relationship between strategic information systems planning and the systems development life cycle?
2. Identify the four main phases of the SDLC and describe the purpose or intent of each.
3. What is the difference between an RFI and an RFP?
4. Briefly describe the HIM professional's contributions to the SDLC.

Management of Healthcare Information System Resources

Managing information resources is a vital function of any healthcare organization. Within hospitals or health systems, an in-house information services or information systems department often coordinates this function, although a growing number of healthcare organizations outsource IT functions to outside vendors such as an application service provider (ASP) (Fortin and MacDonald 2006). Outsourcing IT might be particularly attractive to small rural hospitals or small physician practices that may not have the in-house technical expertise to implement and support information systems.

Most larger healthcare organizations have an IS department that provides a wide range of technical support functions to users throughout the organization. These functions include systems development and implementation, systems support and maintenance, user support, database administration, communications and network administration, and Web support. Figure 6.4 shows a typical organizational structure for an IS department and the following sections describe some of the key positions within that structure.

IS Management Team Chief Information Officer

Generally, the IS department is managed by the **chief information officer** (CIO) or director of IS, who in turn reports to the chief executive officer (CEO) or some other senior-level individual. The CIO is responsible for helping to lead the strategic IS planning process, managing the major functional units within the IS department, and overseeing the management of information resources throughout the enterprise.

Chief Medical Informatics Officer

An emerging position is the **chief medical informatics officer** (CMIO). Individuals assuming CMIO positions are typically physicians who have medical informatics training. Generally, the role of the CMIO is to provide physician leadership and direction in the deployment of clinical applications in healthcare organizations.

Figure 6.4. Typical organizational structure for IS department

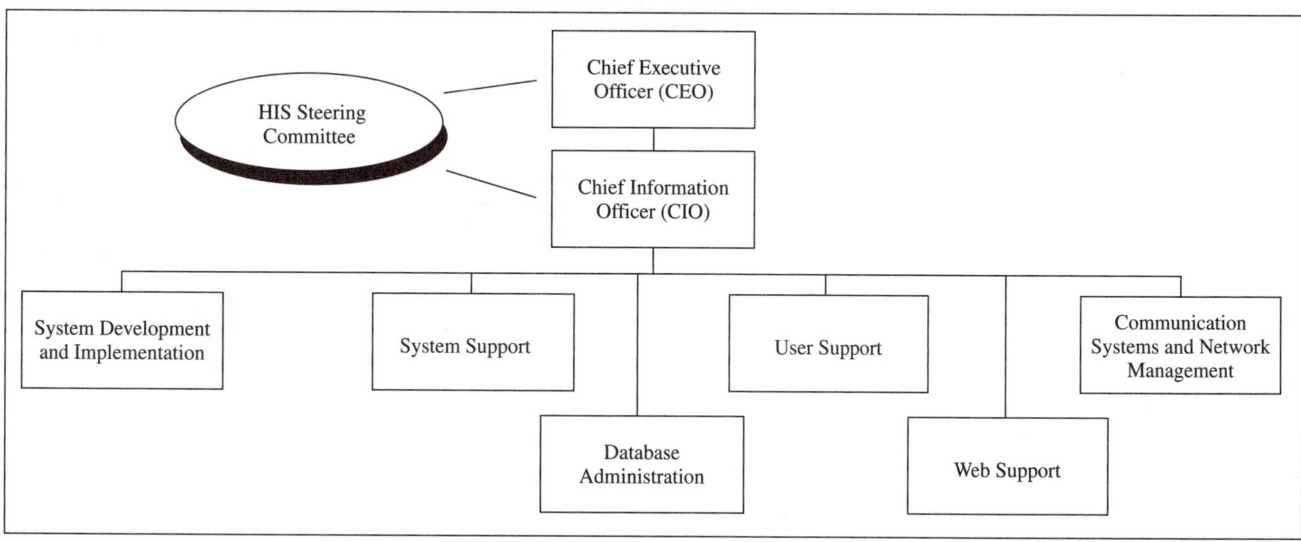

Chief Information Technology Officer

Another relatively new position is the **chief information technology officer** (CITO). The purpose of this role is to guide the organization's decisions related to technical architecture. For example, the CITO might be involved in determining which operating systems or network technologies the organization will support. This individual also typically keeps current on the latest technology developments and their applicability or potential use in the organization.

Chief Information Security Officer

Chief information security officer (CISO) is yet another emerging IT leadership role. The need for a CISO has grown as a direct result of the organization's need to be compliant with HIPAA security regulations. The CISO's primary responsibility is to ensure that the healthcare organization has an effective information security plan and that appropriate measures are in place to ensure that the organization's information systems are secure and safe from tampering or misuse (Wager et al. 2005).

IS Technical Staff

In years past, most of the staff working in the IS department typically had backgrounds in programming and computer science. Today, the department is likely to include individuals with unique sets of skills and specialized areas of interest. These positions include:

- **Systems analysts***:* Systems analysts investigate, analyze, design, develop, install, evaluate, and maintain the healthcare organization's information systems. These individuals typically are involved in all aspects of the SDLC and serve as a liaison among end users and programmers, **database administrators,** and other technical personnel. Systems analysts with a clinical background in nursing, medicine, or other health professions, including HIM, are often called **clinical systems analysts or application systems analysts.** They understand the language of clinicians and generally have an in-depth understanding of the patient care process.
- **Programmers**: Programmers are responsible primarily for writing program codes and developing applications. In general, they perform the function of systems development and work closely with system analysts.
- **Network administrators:** Network administrators are involved in installing, configuring, managing, monitoring, and maintaining network applications. They are responsible for supporting the network infrastructure and controlling user access.
- **Database administrators:** Database administrators are involved in database design, management, security, backup, and user access. They are responsible for the technical aspects of managing a database.
- **Webmasters:** Webmasters are the most recent additions to the IS department. They provide support to Web applications and to the healthcare organization's intranet and Internet operations. Some of their responsibilities include designing and constructing Web pages, managing hardware and software, and linking Web-based applications to the organization's existing information systems.

All IS staff must have an opportunity to stay up to date in the IS field by attending conferences, gaining certification in specialized areas, and enrolling in formal academic or continuing education courses. IT applications serving the healthcare industry are emerging at a phenomenal rate, so the professional development of IS staff is critical.

HIM Professional Roles in Information Technology

As healthcare organizations move toward EMR system implementation, HIM professionals are finding career opportunities within the IT department. In June 2005, the American Health Information Management Association's (AHIMA) HIM Practice Transformation e-HIM Work Group published an article titled "EHR Career Opportunities: Sample HIM Job Descriptions." This article identifies some of the types of positions closely aligned with the IT organizational structures that are held by experienced HIM professionals and by new graduates (for example, clinical applications coordinator, enterprise application specialists, and integration architect). (See figure 6.5.) Each of these positions reflects the valuable contribution the HIM body of knowledge brings to the healthcare organization's IT department as it implements EMR systems and is required to manage an increasing variety and volume of clinical data for numerous internal and external users.

That unique HIM body of knowledge includes knowledge of:

- Existing and emerging requirements related to privacy and confidentiality of health information
- Applicable federal and state EHR-related laws, accreditation standards, and data and vocabulary standards
- Critical activities related to the integrity of the master patient index file
- Clinical data requirements of both internal and external data users
- Interdepartmental and interdisciplinary clinical data and the information workflow

Figure 6.6 shows how HIM professionals' skills overlap to make them uniquely qualified for e-HIM roles.

Figure 6.5. EHR career opportunities: Sample HIM job descriptions

Clinical Analyst
- Format, design, and build relevant clinical content into appropriate workflows
- Lead discussions on clinical and functional design with multidisciplinary teams
- Provide key knowledge on implementation of standardized, streamlined clinical content
- Design clinical content for software applications across all care processes (including documentation, ordering, alerting and notification actions, reporting needs)
- Develop future state process and knowledge structures
- Test and troubleshoot problems within the applications
- Develop detailed content design documents
- Facilitate validation sessions with clinical researchers
- Develop and publish supporting documentation
- Exhibit excellent written and verbal communication skills

Clinical Applications Coordinator
- Implement and support multiservice software packages
- Manage the customization of site parameters
- Address integration issues with other software packages
- Review site parameters and local tables with each service for accuracy and completeness
- Coordinate implementation of new software products that cover these functions
- Analyze and evaluate processes related to information flow
- Provide training to all services on current software applications and new features
- Ensure training is scheduled for new users
- Coordinate efforts to correct deficiencies and errors that occur in the electronic record

Clinical Project Manager, Senior Project Manager
- Manage the scope of work, objectives, and other project management activities of assigned projects
- Finalize project budget and scope of work
- Act as primary project contact with sponsor to ensure appropriate communication channels are maintained and reporting schedules adhered to
- Manage project budget to meet financial and company goals (realization targets); identify and develop change orders
- Develop project plans, schedules, and other scope definition documents for assigned projects as outlined in the project operations database
- Maintain project management information and tracking systems
- Coordinate and evaluate the probability and impact of risks
- Develop plans for minimizing risk impact on project objectives
- Implement improvement processes for assigned projects

Clinical Research Associate
- Monitor activities at clinical study sites to ensure adherence to good clinical practices, standard operating procedures, and study protocols
- Review regulatory documents as required and prepare site visit reports
- Manage multiple projects
- Work both independently and in team environments
- Participate in the study development and start-up process, including reviewing protocols and designing or reviewing study follow-up
- Prepare informed consent forms
- Develop study documents
- Organize and present at investigator meetings
- Work with management on monitoring strategy
- Develop project-specific clinical research associate training
- Participate in clinical training programs and maintain awareness of developments in the field of clinical research

Clinical Vocabulary Manager
- Create, maintain, and implement terminologies, validation files, and maps for a variety of use cases in the EHR
- Perform ongoing review of the auto and manual encoder systems for terminology and classification systems, including methods and processes, and implement recommendations for improving and optimizing the encoding process
- Assist in the analysis of the enterprise's classification and grouping system assignment trends and use data from classification and grouping systems to assist in decision making
- Proactively monitor developments in the field of clinical terminologies and medical vocabularies
- Recommend the most appropriate classification or terminology systems to meet all required information reporting needs
- Possess expertise in clinical terminology, medical vocabulary, and classification systems and skill in mining, deriving, or engineering clinical ontologies

Enterprise Applications Specialist
- Possess knowledge of existing and emerging requirements related to privacy and confidentiality of health information
- Possess knowledge of existing EHR policies and procedures associated with the collection and distribution of clinical data via the repository
- Facilitate the identification, creation, implementation, and maintenance of organization policies and procedures related to the EHR
- Serve as a clinical information liaison to facilitate communication between clinical caregivers and technical implementation teams
- Maintain current knowledge of applicable federal and state EHR-related laws and accreditation standards; monitor and communicate changes to ensure organizational adaptation and compliance
- Serve as EHR consultant to the organization
- Manage multiple projects simultaneously
- Coordinate and assemble appropriate personnel for task force assignments related to EHR projects and issues
- Coordinate activities related to the integrity of the master patient index file
- Provide development guidance and coordination to ensure clinical data generated and stored in disparate clinical systems is made available in the EHR when appropriate
- Work cooperatively with the administrative director of HIM and other applicable organizational entities to ensure policies and procedures meet or exceed existing legal and regulatory requirements as related to the EHR and accepted medical record standards of practice
- Work cooperatively with privacy and security officer to ensure compliance with all existing and emerging requirements related to privacy and confidentiality of health information

Health Systems Specialist
- Possess knowledge of automated data processing
- Process file structures
- Implement applications
- Possess knowledge of data communication principles and techniques
- Develop and analyze data
- Prepare recommendations resulting from special studies

Health Information Services Department Technician
- Possess knowledge of hospital and departmental policies and procedures
- Exercise excellent communication skills
- Perform regulatory and accreditation review for the health information services department
- Summarize findings and report results
- Provide technical and administrative assistance for other health information services functions

(Continued on next page)

Figure 6.5. (Continued)

Information Privacy Coordinator
- Monitor organizational information privacy compliance issues
- Work in collaboration with managers of technical information security to assess risks to health information security and privacy
- Establish policies and procedures to address privacy and security risks
- Draft information privacy policies and procedures and champion their approval and adoption by operational departments
- Develop training and monitoring programs to ensure employee awareness of and compliance with health information privacy policies and procedures

Integration Architect (Implementation)
- Manage the integration of all vendor applications at a single client site
- Work closely with client and installation teams to ensure the smooth and seamless flow of information and data across all client domains
- Manage the oversight and design of test scenarios, the installation process, and timely conversion of systems, which requires:
  –Clinical system integration experience
  –Installation experience with numerous clinical applications
  –Consulting experience
  –Clinical experience

Optical Imaging Coordinator
- Assist in the implementation of new systems
- Train users and provide follow-up training when required
- Monitor workflow
- Function as a liaison between health informatics and information services departments

Process Improvement Engineer
- Educate customers and transfer knowledge
- Diagnose and resolve problems
- Anticipate and address customer needs
- Function as an effective team leader
- Function as an effective team facilitator and methodology advisor
- Act as an effective team member
- Acquire and apply superior skills to achieve quality outcomes
- Respond to changing circumstances
- Manage highly complex projects

Records and Information Coordinator
- Provide reference services to all departments and levels of personnel and process incoming information
- Sort, classify, and verify coded material for integration into systems
- Create and maintain logs, computerized indexes, and databases to provide accurate status and retrieval information

Risk Management Specialist
- Assess and prevent risks that threaten the ongoing viability of the organization
- Analyze and improve patient safety and thorough managing functions
- Collect and disseminate patient safety lessons
- Lead the intervention of patient safety issues

Senior Document Coordinator
- Provide support for the processing of adverse event reports through tracking and data entry
- Generate reports
- Manage records
- Participate in continuous improvement of departmental processes and procedures
- Track timelines for completion of adverse event processing and enter data into safety database

Solution Analyst
- Provide support for clients and vendor associates working directly on client projects
- Possess expertise in field investigation and the successful resolution of service requests
- Develop education and knowledge transfer materials
- Provide documentation for requirements modeling and functional design, test products, which requires:
  –Background in healthcare, sciences, or information systems
  –Ability to work on multiple projects simultaneously
  –Effective written and verbal communication skills

Solution Consultant
- Provide in-depth solution and functionality knowledge support for the sales process
- Initiate contact with clients and make sales demonstrations of solution functionality, which are customized and specific to benefits sought by the client
- Provide input on the development of marketing materials
- Take part in knowledge transfer from the sales team to the project implementation team, requiring:
  –Strong understanding of a hospital organization
  –Background in clinical information systems
  –Formal presentation experience at the executive level as well as with physicians and nurses
  –Experience presenting IT solution demonstrations

Systems Analyst
- Determine client's business and technical requirements
- Identify appropriate stakeholders
- Consult with client on alternatives to target business needs and opportunities
- Evaluate, recommend, and redesign processes
- Collect and define requirements
- Translate functional design documents
- Participate in the technical design, test planning, and user documentation processes
- Participate in analysis of client-identified issues or problems, which may require changes to procedures, standards, or systems
- Analyze business and user needs, document requirements, and revise existing systems logic difficulties as necessary
- Work with users and peers in planning, developing, implementing, and supporting new or existing applications
- Analyze and re-engineer business processes

Source: AHIMA 2005.

Figure 6.6. HIM skills overlap e-HIM roles

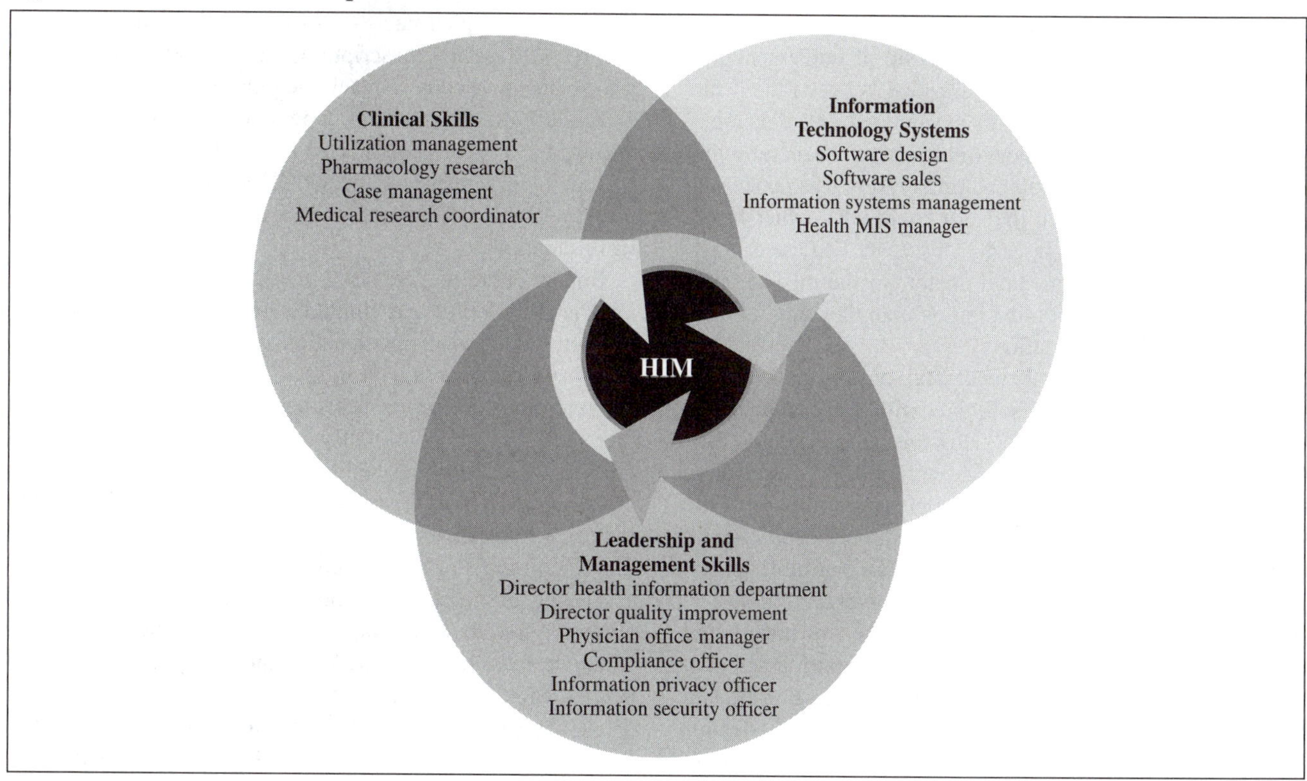

Source: AHIMA 2005.

Real-World Case

Brian Hutchinson, MHA an alumnus of the Master in Health Administration (MHA) program at the Medical University of South Carolina, wrote the following original case study. It has been adapted for educational use and is used with permission.

Sunnybrook Medical Center (SMC) is an 850-bed acute and long-term care facility located in Inner City, California, that is composed of many departments, including surgery, rehabilitation, geriatric psychiatry, and long-term care. Its patient volume is approximately 100,000 visits per year, and the emergency department sees 20,000 visits a year. The medical staff is composed of 125 active attending physicians, 50 salaried (18 full-time, 32 part-time), and 100 residents. Most physicians admit solely to SMC and are single practitioners, located on-site or within 10 miles of SMC.

The hospital identified as one of its goals the desire to implement a computerized provider order-entry (CPOE) system. This goal emerged from that fact that the hospital had been experiencing high turnover of pharmacists who were unhappy with the paper order system, long delays in medications reaching patients, patient safety concerns, and the fact that the clinic staff spent too much time dealing with the paper orders. Therefore, it was felt that implementation of a CPOE system would facilitate patient safety and enable providers to deliver higher-quality care. By defining a broad set of goals, SMC was able to define specific objectives of what it wanted the CPOE system to accomplish. Specifically, SMC wanted to reduce the turnaround time for patient medication, to eliminate transcription errors, to reduce the time clinical staff spent on paper orders, to improve the workflow among the different departments of the hospital, to provide decision support tools for physicians, and to increase pharmacists' job satisfaction and retention.

In 2004, SMC began implementation of a 100 percent CPOE system with an interface to the pharmacy computer system. SMC completed implementation in two phases. The first took 18 months and was piloted in the Traumatic Brain Injury unit of rehabilitation medicine. This site was selected because it had a longer average length of stay, a small number of attending physicians and residents, and a dedicated core of nurses. All these factors allowed for a comprehensive evaluation of the CPOE system in this unit within a controlled environment. After successfully implementing the system in the pilot area, SMC implemented the CPOE in each area of the hospital. Then, in 2008, the final phase involved installation of an interface from the CPOE to the computerized pharmacy system.

Before implementation, SMC recognized the barriers that inhibit successful CPOE implementation. The barriers to quality transformation are: no ownership of the system, personnel shortages, fear of system failures, low expectations, poor senior leadership, little physician engagement, and lack of standardized work processes. SMC's solutions to these barriers started with a shared vision and support from upper management that the entire hospital could buy into; thus, the entire hospital could take ownership in implementation of the CPOE. Next, SMC built a bridge between the "suits and coats" (administrators and physicians) and developed a physician-led performance improvement structure that showed the medical staff that administration was concerned about their issues and that the staff could take ownership in improving the hospital. In SMC's case, its CEO and president happened to be a medical doctor, so the medical staff felt more connected to administration than they might otherwise feel in other organizations.

After the senior management and physicians were on board, SMC used model software with tools capable of adapting to the needs of SMC. However, in order to do this, SMC needed to select a vendor whose flexibility would allow the CPOE system to adapt to the people and processes of the organization. When this was established, the hospital could focus on creating an IT team that would be careful to understand the importance of the clinical processes.

The IT team included a system champion, who understood the CPOE system and had the capacity to support the clinical staff, representatives from management and line staff, and vendor operations. Moreover, SMC involved the IT department in committees that helped manage change throughout their organization so that the IT staff would understand the needs of the hospital.

Lastly, SMC realized that for a CPOE system to meet its objectives, the work processes related to medication order entry had to be error free. Physicians at SMC had historically relied on nurses to administer orders in some cases. For example, an order written QAM for insulin should be administered before breakfast, not at 10 a.m. This might not seem like a hindrance, but computers are essentially dumb and correct information must be entered precisely. Moreover, the hospital wanted to have a more accurate audit trail to ensure that its practices were consistent with Leapfrog recommendations and The Joint Commission standards.

In 2008, the interface connecting the pharmacy system to the CPOE system was installed. Before this time, pharmacists had to reenter physician orders from a printout they received from the CPOE system into the existent pharmacy system. This was very labor and time intensive. The time it took to administer a medication to the patient could be as long as 48 hours, with it taking 8 to 24 hours for the pharmacist to review the medication. Needless to say, this was highly inefficient and costly, both financially and in terms of patient satisfaction and quality of care. Yet, when the interface was implemented in 2008, the time it took for medication to be administered to patients decreased to approximately one hour for pharmacist review and another hour to reach the patient. This dramatic decrease in time was due to the reduction in the medical management work flow. Before the interface was implemented, the workflow consisted of 10 steps, of which ordering comprised 39 to 49 percent. After implementation, the ordering processes were simplified to include only the physicians and pharmacists, not the medication administration record (MAR) transcription, nurse review, and the time it took the chart copy to reach the pharmacy.

In addition, the hospital experienced a $50 million loss during a two-year period. However, SMC remained committed to implementing the CPOE system. Eventually, its investment paid off with higher revenues and its objectives were satisfied.

Implementation decreased medical errors due to both improved legibility and clinicians being alerted to potential problems, such as allergic reactions and adverse drug interaction, from safeguards built in the CPOE system. In addition, the retention of pharmacists improved and job satisfaction increased. So SMC was left with a dedicated team of pharmacists, which eliminated its need for agency personnel. In addition, the pharmacists could now focus on patient care instead of dispensing activities, resulting in a 50 percent increase in the number of medication-related interventions.

During the implementation process, SMC learned many lessons. First, the entire organization, including senior management, must be committed. Second, a phased-in approach offered SMC a chance to minimize the impact of glitches and technical problems. Third, having a strong partnership between the IS staff and the clinical staff was critical. SMC also found that it was important for the IS staff to understand the clinical and technical components of the clinicians' work. Fourth, it is important for an organization to plan for a high level of physical on-site support. Fifth, an organization should reengineer and streamline its workflow in order for a CPOE system to be successful. Sixth, having a system champion who is a clinician to aid in the transition process is critical. Last, the vendor must provide support and flexibility.

SMC's experiences provide valuable information for organizations seeking to implement a CPOE system. SMC shows how successful implementation must start with senior-level management arriving at a consensus on a vision and fully supporting it. Moreover, a relationship must exist between administration and the clinical staff that fosters understanding. In addition, SMC shows the importance of strategic planning when implementing any information system. If the CEO at SMC had not taken the bold step of acquiring the CPOE system, which put the hospital in financial crisis for two years, SMC would never have realized the gains in revenue and healthcare quality. In conclusion, it is necessary to have an IT vendor who is both flexible and knowledgeable throughout the entire implementation process.

Summary

In today's environment, healthcare organizations look to IS technology as a way to help them provide high-quality care in a cost-effective manner. However, healthcare managers at all levels often find that they are competing with their colleagues for limited IS resources. Senior administrators are encouraging healthcare managers to work together to build integrated ISs that will support patient care and enable them to control costs across the enterprise. Clearly, in today's environment, information systems should not be developed or selected in isolation. Healthcare organizations should engage in strategic IS planning to ensure that systems are available to support their goals and plans and to prioritize IS needs. The IS plans should be well aligned and integrated with the organization's overall strategic plans. This process should involve key stakeholders throughout the organization, including clinicians and administrators and HIM and information technology leaders.

After the decision has been made to develop or select a new information system, a project manager should be appointed to oversee and manage the SDLC process. Again, key stakeholders throughout the organization should be involved in the analysis, design, implementation, and maintenance and support phases of the SDLC. Adequate technical and organizational resources should be in place to ensure that the new systems are sufficiently maintained and supported. Moreover, systems should be reviewed and evaluated on a continuing basis to determine their technological, organizational, and economic impact on the enterprise.

References

American Hospital Association . 2007. Continued Progress: Hospital use of information technology. American Hospital Association, Chicago.

Barlow, S., J. Johnson, and J. Steck. 2004. The economic effect of implementing an EMR in an outpatient clinical setting. *Journal of Healthcare Information Management* 18(1):46–51.

Bates, D., and A. Gawande. 2003. Improving safety with information technology. *New England Journal of Medicine* 348(25):2526–2534.

Bates, D., G. Kuperman, J. Rittenberg, J. Teich, J. Fiskio, N. Ma'luf, et al. 1999. A randomized trial of computer-based intervention to reduce utilization of redundant laboratory tests. *American Journal of Medicine* 106(2):144–150.

Brailer, D. and E. Terasawa. 2003. *Use and Adoption of Computer-based Patient Records*. Oakland, CA: California HealthCare Foundation.

Cusack, C. M. and E. G. Poon. 2007. *Evaluation Toolkit: Health Information Technology.* Boston: AHRQ National Resource Center for Health Information Technology. 1–37.

DesRoches, C., E. Campbell, et al. 2008. Electronic health records in ambulatory care—A national survey of physicians. *New England Journal of Medicine* 359(1):50–60.

Donald, J. 1989. Prescribing costs when computers are used to issue all prescriptions. *British Medical Journal* 299: 28–30.

Fortin, J. and K. MacDonald. 2006. *Physician Practices: Are Application Service Providers Right for You?* Oakland, CA: California HealthCare Foundation.

HIMSS. 2008. 19th Annual 2008 HIMSS Leadership Survey: CIO Results Final Report (sponsored by Cisco).

Institute of Medicine, Committee on Quality of Health Care in America. 2000. *To Err is Human: Building a Safer Health System.* Washington, DC: National Academy Press.

National Alliance for Health Information Technology. 2008. Defining Key Health Information Technology Terms: Report to the Office of the National Coordinator for Health Information Technology. The National Alliance for Health Information Technology. 1–40. Chicago.

National Committee for Quality Assurance. 2003. *The State of Healthcare Quality: Industry Trends and Analysis.* Washington, DC: NCQA.

Poisal, J. A., C. Truffer, et al. 2007. Health spending projections through 2016: Modest changes obscure part D's impact. *Health Affairs* 26(2): 2242–2253.

Ross, J. W. and P. Weill. 2002. Six IT decisions your IT people shouldn't make. *Harvard Business Review* 80(11): 84–91.

Teich, J.P., P. Merchia, J. Schimiz, G. Kuperman, C. Spurr, and D. Bates. 2000. Effects of computerized physician order entry on prescribing practices. *Archives of Internal Medicine* 160: 2741–2747.

Wager, K., F. Lee, et al. 2005. *Managing Health Care Information Systems: A Practical Approach for Health Care Executives.* SanFrancisco: Jossey-Bass.

Whitten, J. and L. Bentley. 2007. *Systems Analysis and Design Methods.* Chicago: McGraw-Hill/Irwin.

Part II

Healthcare Information Development

Chapter 7
Healthcare Information Standards

*Kathleen M. LaTour, MA, RHIA, FAHIMA,
and Rita A. Scichilone, MHSA, RHIA, CCS, CCS-P, CHC-F*

Learning Objectives

- Explain healthcare data sets and describe their purpose
- Recognize the basic data sets used in acute care, ambulatory care, long-term care, emergency care, and home care settings
- Describe the unique use of the Minimum Data Set for Long-Term Care and Resident Assessment Protocols in defining and addressing the care of residents in long-term care facilities
- Identify the purpose and use of the Health Plan Employer Data and Information Set (HEDIS)
- Explain the intent of the ORYX initiative and give examples of the core measures identified through ORYX
- Recognize the key players in current efforts to develop standards for electronic health records (EHRs)
- Define the term *healthcare information standards* and explain vocabulary standards, content and structure standards, technical standards (message format, electronic data interchange, transaction, communication), medication standards, and privacy and security standards
- Recognize the impact of the Health Insurance Portability and Accountability Act of 1996 (HIPAA) on the development of health informatics standards
- Explain the relationship of core data elements to healthcare informatics standards in electronic environments
- Describe current federal initiatives to support EHR development and to create a national health information network (NHIN)
- Explain the concepts of interoperability and connectivity as they relate to the federal initiatives to create a national health information data structure
- List important strategic objectives from the Federal Health Technology Strategic Plan
- Recognize the continuity of care record core data set
- Describe the structure of the Nationwide Health Information Network

Key Terms

Accreditation
Accreditation Standards Committee X12
Aggregate data
American College of Radiology and the National Electrical Manufacturers Association (ACR-NEMA)
American Health Information Community (AHIC)
American National Standards Institute (ANSI)
American Society for Testing and Materials (ASTM)
ASTM Standard E1384-02a
Bills of Mortality
Center for Drug Evaluation and Research Data Standards (CDER) Manual
Centers for Medicare and Medicaid Services (CMS)
Certification Commission for Health Information Technology (CCHIT)
Clinical Document Architecture (CDA)
Common Framework
Consolidated Health Informatics initiative (CHI)
Continuity of Care Record/Document (CCR/CCD)
Core data elements
Core measure
Data
Data content standards
Data dictionary
Data elements
Data Elements for Emergency Department Systems (DEEDS)
Data set
Department of Health and Human Services (HHS)
Digital Imaging and Communication in Medicine (DICOM)
Electronic data interchange (EDI)
Essential Medical Data Set (EMDS)
Extensible markup language (XML)
Health care provider dimension (HCPD)
Health information exchange (HIE)
Health Information Security and Privacy Collaboration (HISPC)
Health information standards
Health Information Technology Standards Panel (HITSP)
Health Insurance Portability and Accountability Act of 1996 (HIPAA)

Health Level Seven (HL7)
Health Plan Employer Data and Information Set (HEDIS)
Healthcare information standards
Hospital discharge abstract system
Identifier standards
Information
Inpatient
Institute of Electrical and Electronics Engineers (IEEE)
International Organization for Standardization (ISO)
Joint Commission
Long-term care
Medicare prospective payment system
Message format standards
Metadata registry
Minimum Data Set for Long Term Care–Version 2.0 (MDS 2.0)
National Alliance for Health Information Technology
National Center for Health Statistics (NCHS)
National Committee for Quality Assurance (NCQA)
National Committee on Vital and Health Statistics (NCVHS)
National Council on Prescription Drug Programs (NCPDP)
National Drug Code (NDC) directory
National Information Infrastructure-Health Information Network Program (NII-HIN)
National provider identifier (NPI)
Nationwide Health Information Network (NHIN)
Nomenclature
Office of the National Coordinator of Health Information Technology (ONC)
ORYX initiative
Outcomes and Assessment Information Set (OASIS)
Outpatient
Personal health dimension (PHD)
Picture archiving and communication systems (PACS)
Population health dimension (PHD)
Privacy standards
Regional health information network (RHIN)
Regional health information organization (RHIO)
Resident assessment protocols (RAPs)
RxNorm
Security standards
Semantic clinical drug (SCD)
Social Security number (SSN)
Standards development organizations (SDOs)
Structure and content standards
Transaction standards
Uniform ambulatory care data set (UACDS)
Uniform hospital discharge data set (UHDDS)
Unique identification number
Vocabulary standards
X12N

Data and information pertaining to individuals who use healthcare services are collected in virtually every setting where healthcare is delivered. **Data** represent basic facts and measurements. In healthcare, these facts usually describe specific characteristics of individual patients. The term *data* is plural. Although the singular form is datum, *data element* is frequently used to describe a single fact or measurement. For example, age, gender, insurance company, and blood pressure are all **data elements** concerning a patient. **Information** refers to data that have been collected, combined, analyzed, interpreted, or converted into a form that can be used for specific purposes. In other words, data represent facts; information represents meaning.

In healthcare settings, data are stored in the individual's health record whether that record is in paper or electronic format or a hybrid combination of paper and electronic documents. The numerous data elements in the health record are then combined, analyzed, and interpreted by the patient's physician and other clinicians. For example, test results are combined with the physician's observations and the patient's description of his or her symptoms to form information about the disease or condition that is affecting the patient. Physicians use both data and information to diagnose diseases, develop treatment plans, assess the effectiveness of care, and determine the patient's prognosis.

Data about patients can be extracted from individual health records and combined as **aggregate data.** Aggregate data are used to develop information about groups of patients. For example, data about all of the patients who suffered an acute myocardial infarction during a specific time period could be collected in a database. From the aggregate data, it would be possible to identify common characteristics that might predict the course of the disease or provide information about the most effective way to treat it. Ultimately, research using the aggregate data might be used for disease prevention. For example, researchers identified the link between smoking and lung cancer by analyzing aggregate data about patients with a diagnosis of lung cancer; smoking cessation programs grew from the identification of the causal effect of smoking on lung cancer and a variety of other conditions.

The first known efforts to collect and use healthcare data to produce meaningful statistical profiles date back to the 17th century. In the early 1600s, Captain John Graunt gathered data on the common causes of death in London. He called his study the **London Bills of Mortality** (WHO n.d.). However, few systematic efforts were undertaken to collect statistical data about the incidence and prevalence of disease until the mid-20th century, when technological developments made it possible to collect and analyze large amounts of healthcare data.

Modern efforts at standardizing healthcare data began in the 1960s. At that time, healthcare facilities began to use computers to process larger amounts of data than could be handled manually. The goal was to make comparisons among data from multiple providers. It soon became evident that healthcare organizations needed to use standardized, uniform data definitions in order to arrive at meaningful data comparisons.

The first data standardization efforts focused generally on hospitals and specifically on hospital discharge data. The intent of the efforts was to standardize definitions of key data elements commonly collected in hospitals. Discharge data were collected in **hospital discharge abstract systems.** These systems used databases compiled from aggregate data about all of the patients discharged from a particular facility. The need to compare uniform discharge data from one hospital to the next led to the development of **data sets**, or lists of recommended data elements with uniform definitions.

There is an old saying, "You can't compare apples and oranges." When we attempt to compare terms that do not have the same definition it is like comparing apples and oranges. Standardizing data elements and definitions makes it possible to compare the data collected at different facilities. For example, when data are standardized, the term "admission" means the same thing at City Hospital and at University Hospital. Because both hospitals define admission in the same way, then the hospitals can be compared with each other on such things as the number of admissions or the percentage of occupancy each has had.

Today, hospitals and other healthcare organizations collect more data and develop more information than ever before. Moreover, data and information from the health records of individual patients are used for more purposes than ever before. The demand for information is coming from users within the organizations as well as from external users such as third-party payers, government agencies, **accreditation** organizations, and others. The extensive use of information within and across organizational boundaries demands standards that promote interoperable electronic interchange of data and information. Information standards are critical in the migration to electronic health records (EHRs), as described in chapter 9.

The data sets originally developed to support uniform data collection are inadequate for an electronic environment and many public and private organizations have been actively engaged in the process of developing **healthcare information standards** to support EHR development and information interchange. Healthcare information standards development is a dynamic process that evolves on a continuous basis as key players in the standards development community negotiate, refine, and revise standards. The critical importance of healthcare information standards has been recognized in recent federal initiatives including the **Consolidated Health Informatics initiatives** (CHI) as well as efforts of the **Office of the National Coordinator of Health Information Technology** (ONC).

According to a report entitled "Toward a National Health Information Infrastructure" by the **National Committee on Vital and Health Statistics** (NCVHS 2000),"if information in multiple locations is to be searched, shared, and synthesized when needed, we will need agreed-upon information guardians that can exchange data with each other . . . we will need equitable rules of data exchange so that competitors (within or between healthcare provider systems, health information management companies, or health Web services) will be willing to connect and share data" (NCVHS 2000).

This chapter describes the initial efforts at developing standardized data sets for use in different types of healthcare settings, including acute care, ambulatory care, long-term care, and home care. It explores the recent national initiatives related to interoperability and connectivity of healthcare information systems that will support widespread implementation of EHR and the ultimate establishment of the Nationwide Health Information Network (NHIN) that will improve patient care, increase safety, and optimize both clinical and administrative decision making. This chapter addresses the evolution of health information standards that are the foundation of this vision.

Standardized Healthcare Data Sets

The concept of data standardization became widely accepted during the 1960s and, under the leadership of the **National Center for Health Statistics** (NCHS) and the NCVHS in collaboration with other organizations, data sets were developed for a variety of healthcare settings. Data sets for acute care, long-term care, and ambulatory care were the first to be created. In healthcare, data sets have two purposes: (1) to identify the data elements that should be collected for each patient and (2) to provide uniform definitions for common terms. The use of uniform definitions ensures that data collected from a variety of healthcare settings will share a standard definition.

The standardization of data elements and definitions makes it possible to compare the data collected at different facilities. Comparison data are used for a variety of purposes, including external accreditation, internal performance improvement, and statistical and research studies. However, data sets are not meant to limit the number of data elements that can be collected. Most healthcare organizations collect additional data elements that have meaning for their specific administrative and clinical operations.

Uniform Hospital Discharge Data Set

In 1969, a conference on hospital discharge abstract systems was sponsored jointly by the NCHS, the National Center for Health Services Research and Development, and Johns Hopkins University. Conference participants recommended that all short-term general hospitals in the United States collect a minimum set of patient-specific data elements. They also recommended that these data elements be reflected in all databases formulated from hospital discharge abstract systems. They called the list of patient-specific data items the **Uniform Hospital Discharge Data Set** (UHDDS).

In 1974, the federal government adopted the UHDDS as the standard for collecting data for the Medicare and Medicaid programs. When the Prospective Payment Act was enacted in 1983, UHDDS definitions were incorporated into the rules and regulations for implementing diagnosis-related groups (DRGs). A key component was the incorporation of the definitions of principal diagnosis, principal procedure, and other significant procedures, into the DRG algorithms. As a result, accurate assignment of a DRG is dependent on accurate selection and coding of the principal diagnosis and principal procedure and the appropriate sequencing of other significant diagnoses and procedures. The NCVHS revised the UHDDS in 1984. The new UHDDS was adopted for all federal health programs in 1986.

The intent of the UHDDS is to list and define a set of common, uniform data elements. The data elements are to be collected in the health records of every hospital inpatient. They are subsequently abstracted from the health record and included in databases that describe aggregate patient characteristics. Because UHDDS data definitions are a component of DRGs and required to accurately calculate DRG payment, short-term, general hospitals in the United States generally collect patient-specific data in the format recommended by the UHDDS.

The UHDDS has been revised several times since 1986. The current version includes the recommended data elements shown in figure 7.1.

Uniform Ambulatory Care Data Set

Ambulatory care includes medical and surgical care provided to patients who return to their homes on the same day they receive the care. It is provided in physicians' offices, medical clinics, same-day surgery centers, outpatient hospital clinics and diagnostic departments, emergency treatment centers, and hospital emergency departments (EDs). Patients who receive ambulatory care services in hospital-based clinics and departments are referred to as **outpatients**. Patients admitted to hospitals for overnight stays are referred to as **inpatients.**

Since the 1980s, the number and the length of inpatient hospitalizations have declined dramatically. At the same time, the number of healthcare procedures performed in ambulatory settings has increased. There are several reasons for this trend:

- Technological improvements in diagnostic and therapeutic procedures and the development of short-acting anesthetics have made it possible to perform many medical and surgical procedures in ambulatory facilities. Surgical procedures that once required inpatient hospitalization and long recovery periods are now being performed in same-day surgery centers.
- Third-party payers have extended coverage to include most procedures performed on an outpatient basis.
- The **Medicare prospective payment system** limits reimbursement for inpatient care and, in effect, encourages the use of ambulatory or outpatient care as an alternative to more costly inpatient services.

Like hospitals, ambulatory care organizations depend on the availability of accurate data and information. A standardized data set to guide the content and structure of ambulatory health records and data collection systems in ambulatory care was needed.

In 1989, the NCVHS approved the **Uniform Ambulatory Care Data Set** (UACDS). The committee recommended its use in every facility where ambulatory care is delivered. Several of the data elements that make up the UACDS are similar to those used in the UHDDS. For example, the UACDS data elements that describe the personal identifier, residence, date of birth, gender, and race and ethnicity of the patient are the same as the definitions in the UHDDS. The purpose of keeping the same demographic data elements is to make it easier to compare data for inpatients and ambulatory patients in the same facility.

However, the UACDS also includes data elements specific to ambulatory care, such as the reason for the encounter with the healthcare provider. The UACDS also includes optional data elements to describe the patient's living arrangements and marital status. These data elements (shown in figure 7.2) are unique to the UACDS. Ambulatory care practitioners need information about the living conditions of their patients because patients and their families often need to manage at-home nursing care, for example, activity restrictions after a surgical procedure. Hospital staff provides such nursing services in acute care settings.

The goal of the UACDS is to improve data comparison in ambulatory and outpatient care settings. It provides uniform definitions that help providers to analyze patterns of care. The data elements in the UACDS are those most likely to be needed by a variety of users. Unlike the UHDDS, the UACDS has not been incorporated into federal regulations. Therefore, it is a recommended, rather than a required, data set and, in practical terms, it has been subsumed by other data definition efforts, most notably the core data elements recommended as part of the NHIN, which is described later in this chapter.

Minimum Data Set for Long-term Care and Resident Assessment Protocols

Uniform data collection is also important in the long-term care setting. **Long-term care** incorporates the healthcare services provided in residential facilities for individuals who are unable to live independently owing to chronic illness or disability. Long-term care facilities also provide dietary and social services as well as housing and nursing care.

For a long-term care facility to participate in the Medicare and Medicaid programs, the **Centers for Medicare and Medicaid Services** (CMS) requires the development of a comprehensive functional assessment for every resident. From this assessment, a nursing home resident's plan of care is developed.

The **Minimum Data Set for Long-term Care–Version 2.0** (MDS 2.0) is a federally mandated standard assessment

Figure 7.1. UHDDS data elements

Data Element	Definition/Descriptor
01. Personal identifier	The unique number assigned to each patient within a hospital that distinguishes the patient and his or her hospital record from all others in that institution.
02. Date of birth	Month, day, and year of birth. Capture of the full four-digit year of birth is recommended.
03. Sex	Male or female
04. Race and ethnicity	04a. Race American Indian/Eskimo/Aleut Asian or Pacific Islander Black White Other race Unknown 04b. Ethnicity Spanish origin/Hispanic Non-Spanish origin/Non-Hispanic Unknown
05. Residence	Full address of usual residence Zip code (nine digits, if available) Code for foreign residence
06. Hospital identification	A unique institutional number used across data collection systems. The Medicare provider number is the preferred hospital identifier.
07. Admission date	Month, day, and year of admission
08. Type of admission	Scheduled: Arranged with admissions office at least 24 hours prior to admission Unscheduled: All other admissions
09. Discharge date	Month, day, and year of discharge
10 & 11. Physician identification • Attending physician • Operating physician	The Medicare unique physician identification number (UPIN) is the preferred method of identifying the attending physician and operating physician(s) because it is uniform across all data systems.
12. Principal diagnosis	The condition established, after study, to be chiefly responsible for occasioning the admission of the patient to the hospital for care.
13. Other diagnoses	All conditions that coexist at the time of admission or that develop subsequently or that affect the treatment received and/or the length of stay. Diagnoses that relate to an earlier episode and have no bearing on the current hospital stay are to be excluded.
14. Qualifier for other diagnoses	A qualifier is given for each diagnosis coded under "other diagnoses" to indicate whether the onset of the diagnosis preceded or followed admission to the hospital. The option "uncertain" is permitted.
15. External cause-of-injury code	The ICD-9-CM code for the external cause of an injury, poisoning, or adverse effect (commonly referred to as an E code). Hospitals should complete this item whenever there is a diagnosis of an injury, poisoning, or adverse effect.
16. Birth weight of neonate	The specific birth weight of a newborn, preferably recorded in grams.
17. Procedures and dates	All significant procedures are to be reported. A significant procedure is one that is: • Surgical in nature, or • Carries a procedural risk, or • Carries an anesthetic risk, or • Requires specialized training. The date of each significant procedure must be reported. When more than one procedure is reported, the principal procedure must be designated. The principal procedure is one that is performed for definitive treatment rather than one performed for diagnostic or exploratory purposes or is necessary to take care of a complication. If two procedures appear to be principal, the one most closely related to the principal diagnosis should be selected as the principal procedure. The UPIN must be reported for the person performing the principal procedure.
18. Disposition of the patient	• Discharged to home (excludes those patients referred to home health service) • Discharged to acute care hospital • Discharged to nursing facility • Discharged home to be under the care of a home health service (including a hospice) • Discharged to other healthcare facility • Left against medical advice • Alive, other; or alive, not stated • Died All categories for primary and other sources are: • Blue Cross/Blue Shield • Other health insurance companies • Other liability insurance • Medicare • Medicaid • Worker's Compensation • Self-insured employer plan • Health maintenance organization (HMO) • CHAMPUS • CHAMPVA • Other government payers • Self-pay • No charge (free, charity, special research, teaching) • Other
19. Patient's expected source of payment	Primary source Other sources
20. Total charges	All charges billed by the hospital for this hospitalization. Professional charges for individual patient care by physicians are excluded.

Source: Adapted from Hanken and Water 1994.

Figure 7.2. UACDS data elements

Data Element	Definition/Descriptor
Provider identification, address, type of practice	Provider identification: Include the full name of the provider as well as the unique physician identification number (UPIN). Address: The complete address of the provider's office. In cases where the provider has multiple offices, the location of the usual or principal place of practice should be given. Profession: • Physician, including specialty or field of practice • Other (specify)
Place of encounter	Specify the location of the encounter: • Private office • Clinic or health center • Hospital outpatient department • Hospital emergency department • Other (specify)
Reason for encounter	Includes, but is not limited to, the patient's complaints and symptoms reflecting his or her own perception of needs, provided verbally or in writing by the patient at the point of entry into the healthcare system or in the patient's own words recorded by an intermediary or provider at that time.
Diagnostic services	All diagnostic services of any type.
Problem, diagnosis, or assessment	Describes the provider's level of understanding and the interpretation of the patient's reasons for the encounter and all conditions requiring treatment or management at the time of the encounter.
Therapeutic services	List, by name, all services done or ordered: • Medical (including drug therapy) • Surgical • Patient education
Preventive services	List, by name, all preventive services and procedures performed at the time of encounter.
Disposition	The provider's statement of the next step(s) in the care of the patient. At a minimum, the following classification is suggested: 1. No follow-up planned 2. Follow-up planned • Return when necessary • Return to the current provider at a specified time • Telephone follow-up • Return to referring provider • Refer to other provider • Admit to hospital • Other

Source: Adapted from Hanken and Water 1994.

form used to collect demographic and clinical data on nursing home residents. It consists of a core set of screening and assessment elements based on common definitions. To meet federal requirements, long-term care facilities must complete an MDS for every resident at the time of admission and at designated reassessment points throughout the resident's stay.

The MDS uses some of the same data elements and definitions used in other data sets. However, it is far more extensive and includes more clinical data than either the UHDDS or the UACDS. The data collected via the MDS are used to develop care plans for residents and to document placement at the appropriate level of care.

The MDS organizes data according to 20 main categories. Each category includes a structured list of choices and responses. The use of structured lists automatically standardizes the data that are collected. The major categories of data collected in the MDS include:

- Demographic information
- Identification and background information
- Cognitive patterns
- Communication and hearing patterns
- Vision patterns
- Mood and behavior patterns
- Psychosocial well-being
- Physical functioning and structural problems
- Continence in past 14 days
- Disease diagnoses
- Health conditions
- Oral and nutritional status
- Oral and dental status
- Skin condition
- Activity pursuit patterns
- Medications
- Special treatments and procedures
- Discharge potential and overall status
- Assessment information
- Therapy supplement for Medicare Prospective Payment System (PPS)

The data collected via the MDS are used to develop a **Resident Assessment Protocol** (RAP) summary for each resident. The MDS provides a structured way to organize resident information and develop a resident care plan. Problems identified through the assessment process are documented and a RAP is triggered. For each triggered RAP, the facility must describe the following factors:

- Nature of the condition (may include presence or lack of objective data and subjective complaints)
- Complications and risk factors that affect the decision to proceed to care planning
- Factors that must be considered in developing individualized care plan interventions
- Need for referrals or further evaluation by appropriate healthcare professionals

Nursing home personnel use the data from the MDS and RAP to plan, carry out, and assess the care given to individual residents. The **Department of Health and Human Services** (HHS) is currently in the process of developing MDS version 3.0. MDS 3.0, scheduled for implementation in 2009, represents a significant revision and is focused on "implementing standardized assessment . . . for facilitating care management in nursing homes" (HHS 2008).

Outcomes Assessment Information Set (OASIS)

In 1999, the Health Care Financing Administration (HCFA) (renamed the Centers for Medicare and Medicaid Services [CMS]) implemented a standardized data set for use in the home health industry. The **Outcomes and Assessment Information Set** (OASIS) is designed to gather data about Medicare beneficiaries who are receiving services from a home health agency. OASIS includes a set of core data items that are collected on all adult home health patients. The data are used in measuring patient outcomes in order to assess the quality of home healthcare services. Under the prospective payment program for home health, implemented in 2000, data from OASIS also form the basis of reimbursement for provided services.

OASIS data are grouped into the following categories:

- Demographics and patient history
- Living arrangements
- Supportive assistance
- Respiratory
- Neurological
- Psychological
- Integument
- Pain
- Activities of Daily Living (ADLs) and Instrumental Activities of Daily Living (IADLs)
- Medications
- Elimination status
- General information
- Emergent care

Data collected through OASIS are used to assess the patient's ability to be discharged or transferred from home care services and to evaluate the quality and outcome of services given to the patient.

Data Elements for Emergency Department Systems

Emergency and trauma care in the United States have become sophisticated over the past few decades. Emergency services represent a significant part of the healthcare delivery system. As emergency and trauma care services have been developed, it has become increasingly important to collect relevant aggregate data. Many states require the reporting of trauma cases to state agencies.

In 1997, the Centers for Disease Control and Prevention (CDC), through its National Center for Injury Prevention and Control (NCIPC), published a data set called **Data Elements for Emergency Department Systems** (DEEDS). This data set was developed with input from the American College of Emergency Physicians, the Emergency Nurses Association, and the American Health Information Management Association (AHIMA). Its stated purpose is to support the uniform collection of data in hospital-based emergency departments and to substantially reduce incompatibilities in emergency department records.

DEEDS recommends the collection of 156 data elements in hospitals that offer emergency care services. As with the UHDDS and UACDS, this data set contains recommendations on both the content and the structure of the data elements to be collected. The data are organized into the following eight sections:

- Patient identification data
- Facility and practitioner identification data
- Emergency department payment data
- Emergency department arrival and first-assessment data
- Emergency department history and physical examination data
- Emergency department procedure and result data
- Emergency department medication data
- Emergency department disposition and diagnosis data

DEEDS incorporates national standards for electronic data interchange so its implementation in an EHR system can facilitate communication and integration with other information systems (NCIPC2008).

Essential Medical Data Set

The **Essential Medical Data Set** (EMDS) was created as a complement to DEEDS. It was developed as part of the **National Information Infrastructure-Health Information Network Program** (NII-HIN) in 1997. The EMDS gives healthcare providers a concise medical history data set for each individual patient. The goal is to enhance the effectiveness of emergency care. The EMDS is different from DEEDS in that DEEDS is designed to collect data about a specific emergency encounter while EMDS is designed to create a health history for an individual patient.

The EMDS is intended for use in EHR systems. During the course of an emergency, the emergency department's information system queries a data repository for the patient's past medical history. The documentation for the visit is recorded according to the DEEDS format, and the data are sent to a regional data repository when the emergency care episode is complete.

Emergency care often has a critical impact on patient survival. Therefore, it is important to collect standardized, comparable data. These data then can be used to assess the effectiveness of treatment modalities, response time, and patient survival rates.

Trauma registries and statewide trauma database systems have grown incrementally over the past several years. State departments of public health as well as the federal agencies involved in oversight of emergency care are interested in statistical data about the efficacy of emergency treatment. Collecting standardized data in the emergency care system is fundamental to meaningful analysis of information about emergency care.

Standardized Data Collection Efforts

The following three initiatives do not represent the development and promulgation of information standards; however, each is an initiative in which standardized data are collected and used in assessing utilization, quality, and cost of healthcare for selected populations. As such, they are worth addressing in this chapter. HEDIS and ORYX are addressed in detail in Chapter 17.

Health Plan Employer Data and Information Set

The **Health Plan Employer Data and Information Set** (HEDIS) is sponsored by the **National Committee for Quality Assurance** (NCQA). HEDIS is a set of standard performance measures designed to provide purchasers and consumers of healthcare with the information they need for comparing the performance of managed healthcare plans.

HEDIS is designed to collect administrative and claims data as well as health record review data. The data are used to analyze and assess the outcomes of treatment. HEDIS collects standardized data about specific health-related conditions or issues so that the success of various treatment plans can be assessed and compared. HEDIS data form the basis of performance improvement efforts for health plans. HEDIS data also are used to develop physician profiles. The goal of physician profiling is to positively influence physician practice patterns.

HEDIS contains more than 50 measures related to conditions such as heart disease, cancer, diabetes, asthma, chlamydia infection, smoking cessation, and menopause counseling. It includes data related to patient outcomes in addition to data about the treatment process used by the clinician in treating the patient.

Standardized HEDIS data elements are abstracted from health records in clinics and hospitals. The health record data are combined with enrollment and claims data and analyzed according to HEDIS specifications.

The purpose of HEDIS is to collect standardized data about specific health-related conditions or issues so that the success of various treatment plans can be assessed and compared. HEDIS data form the basis of performance improvement efforts for health plans. HEDIS data also are used to develop physician profiles. The goal of physician profiling is to positively influence physician practice patterns.

An example of a focused HEDIS review is diabetes care and treatment. Other examples of HEDIS clinical measures include:

- Adolescent immunizations
- Smoking cessation programs
- Antidepressant medication management
- Breast cancer screening
- Cholesterol screening after a heart attack
- Prenatal care during the first trimester

Data from HEDIS studies are often released publicly by health plans to document substantial positive effects on the health of their clients. Results are compared over time and with data from other sources. From the data, health plans determine opportunities for performance improvement and develop potential interventions.

HEDIS is an example of a population-based data collection tool. It illustrates the need for developing standardized data definitions and uniform collection methods. It also emphasizes the importance of data quality management.

Core Measures for ORYX

The **Joint Commission** is one of the largest users of healthcare data and information. Its primary function is the accreditation of hospitals and other healthcare organizations. In 1997, the Joint Commission introduced the **ORYX initiative** to integrate outcomes data and other performance measurement data into its accreditation processes. (The initiative was named ORYX after an African animal that can be thought of as a different kind of zebra.) The goal of the initiative is to foster a comprehensive, continuous, data-driven accreditation process for healthcare facilities.

The ORYX initiative uses nationally standardized performance measures to improve the safety and quality of healthcare.

The goal of the ORYX initiative is to integrate outcomes and other performance measures into the accreditation process through data collection about specific core measures (Joint Commission 2009). The **core measures** are based on selected diagnoses and conditions such as diabetes mellitus, the outcomes of which can be improved by standardizing care. They include the minimum number of data elements needed to provide an accurate and reliable measure of performance. Core measures rely on data elements that are readily available or already collected. Chapter 17 explores current ORYX core measure studies.

Health Information Exchange (HIE) Initiatives

As the world becomes more connected and its people move around more than at any other time in history, there is an increasing need to exchange information among organizations. Communication and data content standards make it possible to exchange health information using electronic networks that reach across the country and around the world. Technology standards lay the foundation for these networks and data standards enhance the utility and value of the process. As the second decade of the Millennium approaches, advances in consensus-based standards are making connectivity possible and improving continuity of care and patient safety.

A variety of models and initiatives have been developed and launched with varying degrees of success. Regional health information organizations (RHIOs) developed and maintained HIE standards in an attempt to share information and make it available where needed. These organizations bring together healthcare stakeholders within a defined region and govern the HIE process for the purpose of improving care in that community (HHS n.d.). As sophistication and utility of the Internet (based on standards) increases, there will be a number of new standards development activities emerging that affect health information management in all settings. The concept of a national health information infrastructure (NHII) is designed to bring information to and aid communication among all stakeholders in the process. The infrastructure requires technology investment for success but also requires fundamental change in business process, information sharing, and adoption of standards. Interoperability is a common thread in all discussion concerning health information technology (HIT). Without the proper standards and infrastructure to facilitate systems that are able to reliably exchange information an interoperable environment fostering safer and less costly systems cannot occur.

Federal Support Activities for Standards Development: Nationwide Health Information Network (NHIN)

The implementation of standards across the healthcare industry in the United States and creation and continued development of the **Nationwide Health Information Network** (NHIN) establish exchange standards to support electronic health record availability for the person wherever needed. All healthcare is delivered at the local level so a "network of networks" is envisioned to link the location of care with information held on the individual receiving the care wherever it is stored.

The standardized collection of common data elements can provide valuable information about the effectiveness of interventions and treatments for specific diseases. Healthcare providers are able to compare their success rates with those of other providers to determine areas for performance improvement. Measures of quality and effectiveness can be analyzed and compared concerning medications, procedures, or other types of health interventions. This type of analysis can provide critical information that will eventually have a positive impact on clinical outcomes and cost control.

In 1998, the NCVHS produced the concept paper "Assuring a Health Dimension for the National Information Infrastructure" that discussed a conceptual model of a nationwide network of health information. In 2001, NCVHS began to explore the feasibility of a national health information infrastructure (NHII) that would allow the electronic exchange of health information. The goal of this initiative was to offer a technology solution that would increase patient safety, reduce medical errors, increase efficiency and effectiveness of healthcare, and contain costs (Mon 2005). The NHII initiative launched an industry-wide discussion on how to exchange information electronically in a secure and standard fashion (Mon 2005). This discussion focused attention on the necessity of developing standards to facilitate the definition, collection, exchange, and use of data and information. The NCVHS serves as the statutory public advisory body to the Secretary of the HHS in the area of health data and statistics, and work continues to transform the current healthcare delivery system to support enhanced HIE.

According to the NCVHS report "Information for Health: A Strategy for Building the National Health Information Infrastructure" (NCVHS 2001), the NHII includes not just technologies but, more importantly, values, practices, relationships, laws, standards, systems, and applications that support all facets of individual health, healthcare, and public health. It emphasizes the criticality of implementing national **health information standards** as a foundation of a system that supports connectivity and interoperability. The terminology for describing the local or regional networks has evolved over the last decade from subnetworks to the more general use of HIEs to describe the process. Past efforts at standards development have been disparate with varying degrees of industry leadership and limited federal influence or funding. Under the NHIN, initiative efforts are focused on creating standards and defining a universal language of health information to flow through networks. As the process spreads and matures, maintaining universality is critical as development and electronic health record (EHR) implementation accelerates. A key tenet for healthcare delivery in the 21st century is to collect information once at the point of care and repurpose it many times for a variety of health related needs.

There have been diverging opinions on how to accomplish the objective. Consensus building for universal health information interoperability architecture occurs at the federal, state and local levels. Key public and private organizations are actively working to make the concept of a national health information network a reality while selected regional organizations are successfully sharing data between organizations and care settings. In 2007, through ONC, six additional contracts were awarded to advance Cooperative Agreements for additional participants in the trial implementations. These activities advance the standards and create suitable infrastructure to support interoperable EHRs.

In 2004, President George W. Bush issued Executive Order 13335. This order called for widespread interoperable EHRs within 10 years (2014) and it established the ONC. The presidential directive to the National Coordinator was to develop and implement a strategic plan to guide the nationwide implementation of interoperable HIT in both the public and private sectors (Thompson and Brailer 2004). The **American Health Information Community** (AHIC), also referred to as "the Community," was formed in 2005 for leadership toward a connected system and standards development. AHIC initially formed workgroups in the following areas: biosurveillance, consumer empowerment, chronic care, and EHRs. A year later, two additional groups were added: the Biosurveillance Data Steering Group as a sub-workgroup within the biosurveillance workgroup (since renamed Population Health and Clinical Care Connections workgroup), and the Confidentiality, Privacy and Security workgroup. The confidentiality work group was created as a resource responsible for addressing issues relevant to all the workgroups. Also in 2006, the AHIC launched the Quality workgroup to address the need for the development of quality measures; and a Personalized Healthcare workgroup was created to develop and make recommendations on standards for interoperable integration of genomic test information into personal EHRs. During 2008, this organization was incorporated into a public–private entity to continue its efforts. The new organization was initially called the AHIC Successor, Inc, then was renamed the National eHealth Collaborative (NeHC) in January 2009 to bring the views of consumers, government, and industry into a shared focus on what is needed to enable the development of a secure and reliable exchange of electronic health information nationwide. It is important for HIM professionals to become involved in standards use and when possible development; following the activities of this organization is one way to be involved in the process.

The Community workgroup meetings are open to the public. Notices for each meeting appear in the *Federal Register*. Members of the public can listen to the meetings via the Internet, and the public has the opportunity to submit comments at the end of each meeting. ONC provides a conference room at the HHS in Washington, D.C. so that all who are interested can listen to the meetings. Registration is not required for Internet access to meetings. In order to attend in person a meeting held at an HHS building, a sign-in process at the security desk at the building entrance and proper identification (photograph) is required.

Soon after the office was established, ONC gathered broad input from key stakeholders about how the NHIN should be designed. AHIMA responded as a member of a thirteen organization collaborative of major healthcare and information technology organizations. This collaborative recommended general adoption of a set of tools critical to achieving an interoperable environment that supports modern healthcare practice, including precisely defined and uniform technical standards as well as common policies and methods. This set of tools is called the **Common Framework** (Kloss 2005b). The nationwide heath information network is being constructed incrementally using internet technology with particular emphasis on confidentiality and security of data. A key element is that the network is private, secure, and built on patient control and authorization. Personal information would remain with the healthcare provider and accessed and exchanged only as needed and with proper authorization and security (Kloss 2005b).

Federal initiatives and programs support development of local or **regional health information organizations** (RHIOs). RHIOs may also be referred to as **regional health information networks** (RHINs), community health information networks, and (most commonly) HIE. A RHIO is a networked community (with the community defined at the local or regional level) that includes physician offices, hospitals, nursing homes, pharmacies, and, in some cases, payers, vendors, or other healthcare-related agencies. The purpose of a RHIO is to give regional healthcare providers access to clinical information for all patients in the defined region across a decentralized technology environment. Such organizations are formed in response to local and regional needs and each operates independently, both in the choice of network design and in its access model. The goal of RHIOs is consistent with the goal of NHIN: improved quality of care, increased patient safety, reduction of medical errors, and cost savings. The Electronic Healthcare Network Accreditation Commission (EHNAC) is expected to accredit HIE and RHIO community health data network partnerships and other groups promoting data sharing across multiple stakeholders.

Advancing a Foundation for Health Information Sharing

Soon after the office was created, the ONC issued a series of three-year government contracts focused on the four key areas identified by the healthcare industry as key to HIE development: EHR certification, data standards, NHIN architecture, and privacy and security (Carol 2005). Contracts were awarded to public-private groups to address three of the key areas, which are graphically represented in figure 7.3.

- **Certification Commission for Health Information Technology** (CCHIT) was funded to develop criteria and evaluation processes to certify EHRs and the infrastructure or network components through which they interoperate. CCHIT serves as the recognized U.S. certification authority for EHRs and the networks used to exchange EHR data. CCHIT was founded in 2004, with support from three leading industry associations in healthcare information management and technology: AHIMA, the Healthcare Information and Management Systems Society (HIMSS), and the **National Alliance for Health Information Technology** (NAHIT). In October 2006, HHS officially designated CCHIT as a Recognized Certification Body (RCB). The **American National Standards Institute** (ANSI) was awarded a contract to convene the National **Health Information**

Technology Standards Panel (HITSP). This organization serves as a cooperative partnership between the public and private sectors for achieving a wide acceptance and usable standards. HITSP's specific mission is to enable and support widespread interoperability among healthcare software applications as they interact in a local, regional, and NHIN for the United States. Progress toward serving the clinical information and business requirements for health information sharing may be followed by reviewing the most current library of interoperability. HITSP panel activities are sponsored by ANSI in cooperation with HIMSS, Advanced Technology Institute (ATI), and Booz Allen Hamilton. Funding is provided via a contract from HHS.

- The **Health Information Security and Privacy Collaboration** (HISPC) project received federal funding about the same time as HITSP. This project originally included 3 phases and 34 states and territories in the United States. In the first phase, the 34 teams followed a defined process to assess variances in organization-level business policies and state laws that affect health information exchange. The second phase focused on identification and proposal of practical solutions while preserving privacy and security requirements in the applicable federal and state laws. In 2008, the third phase, developing detailed plans and implementing solutions, was underway.
- **Core data elements** and **data content standards** support the development of networked health information systems. There are three interactive and interdependent dimensions that the NHII vision continues to address. These dimensions provide a means for conceptualizing the capture, storage, communication, processing, and presentation of information for each group of information users:
  - Personal health dimension
  - Healthcare provider dimension
  - Population health dimension

Details are found in the report from NCVHS entitled, "Toward a National Health Information Infrastructure" (NCVHS 2000b). The three dimensions described are a useful division for considering health data management requirements in HIM roles and the future environment and practices for health record management.

- **Personal Health Dimension** (PHD): Core content of the PHD will be controlled by the individual both in the initial input of data and in the ability to edit personal data. Individuals will select data elements that are relevant to their specific age, gender, health history, health and wellness concerns, and other factors. The core content in table 7.1 represents a minimum data set; the plan is to develop standards for a PHR and **data dictionary** that supports a consistent format that will allow healthcare providers to access the data as needed and as authorized by the individual. In July 2008, CCHIT released recommendations for certification of PHRs.
- **Health Care Provider Dimension** (HCPD): The HCPD includes information that is captured during the patient care process and concurrently integrates this information with clinical guidelines, protocols, and selected information that the provider is authorized to access from the PHR, as well as information from the population health dimension that is relevant to the patient's care (NCVHS 2000). The HCPD would be useful to providers in any and all care settings. Core content of the HCPD is delineated in table 7.2. There is overlap between the dimensions as healthcare providers share data with the other stakeholder groups.

Figure 7.3. Core health data elements proposed for standardization

1. Personal/Unique Identifier[2]
2. Date of Birth
3. Gender
4. Race and Ethnicity
5. Residence
6. Marital Status
7. Living/Residential Arrangement[1]
8. Self-Reported Health Status[2]
9. Functional Status[2]
10. Years of Schooling
11. Patient's Relationship to Subscriber/Person Eligible for Entitlement
12. Current or Most Recent Occupation and Industry[2]
13. Type of Encounter[2]
14. Admission Date (inpatient)
15. Discharge Date (inpatient)
16. Date of Encounter (outpatient and physician services)
17. Facility Identification[1]
18. Type of Facility/Place of Encounter[1]
19. Health Care Practitioner Identification (outpatient)[1]
20. Provider Location or Address of Encounter (outpatient)
21. Attending Physician Identification (inpatient)[1]
22. Operating Clinician identification[1]
23. Health Care Practitioner Specialty[1]
24. Principal Diagnosis (inpatient)
25. Primary Diagnosis (inpatient)
26. Other Diagnoses (inpatient)
27. Qualifier for Other Diagnoses (inpatient)
28. Patient's Stated Reason for Visit or Chief Complaint (outpatient)[2]
29. Diagnosis Chiefly Responsible for Services Provided (outpatient)
30. Other Diagnoses (outpatient)
31. External Cause of Injury
32. Birth Weight of Newborn
33. Principal Procedure (inpatient)
34. Other Procedures (inpatient)
35. Dates of Procedures (inpatient)
36. Procedures and Services (outpatient)
37. Medications Prescribed
38. Disposition of Patient (inpatient)[1]
39. Disposition (outpatient)
40. Patient's Expected Sources of Payment[1]
41. Injury Related to Employment
42. Total Billed Charges[1]

[1]Element for which substantial agreement has been reached but for which some amount of additional work is needed.

[2]Element which has been recognized as significant but for which considerable work remains to be undertaken.

A lack of footnote indicates that these elements are ready for implementation.

Source: http://ncvhs.hhs.gove/ncvhsr1.htm.

- **Population Health Dimension** (PHD): The PHD acknowledges the importance of population-based health data and resources that are necessary to improve public health. This data will help public health professionals identify public health threats, assess population health, focus programs and policies on well-defined health problems, inform and educate individuals about health issues, evaluate programs and services, conduct research to address health issues, and perform other public health services (NCVHS 2000). In 2008, the CDC awarded three contacts for HIEs to build data-sharing operations designed to deliver data to public health authorities. This funding was made in conjunction with the program led by ONC to attain trial implementations of the NHIN. Core content of the population health dimension is identified in the community health dimension in table 7.3.

Table 7.1. Core content of the personal health dimension

Personal Health Record	• Personal identification information • Emergency contact information • Lifetime health history; summary of caregiver records from all sources of care, including immunizations, allergies, family history, occupational history, environmental exposures, social history, medical history, treatments procedures, medication history, outcomes • Lab results (e.g., EKGs) or links to results (MRI results at a radiology department data warehouse, digital images of biopsy slides, or digital video of coronary angiography) • Emergency care information (e.g., allergies, current medications, medical/surgical history summary) • Provider identification and contact information • Treatment plans and instructions • Health risk factor profile, recommended clinical preventative services, and results of those services • Health insurance coverage information
Other Elements	• Correspondence: records of patient–provider communication, edits made to PHR, or concerns about accuracy of information in health care provider medical records • Instructions about access by other persons and institutions • Audit log of individuals/institutions who access electronic records • Self-care trackers: nutrition, physical activity, medications, dosage schedules • Personal library of quality health information resources • Healthcare proxies, living wills, and durable power of attorney for health care
Elements from the Community Health Dimension	• Local public health contact information • Local healthcare services (e.g., walk-in clinics) • Environmental measures and alerts pertinent to an individual's home, neighborhood, school, and workplace

Source: NCVHS 2000.

Table 7.2. Core content of the health care provider dimension

Patient Record Elements	• Personal identification information • Sociodemographic identifiers (gender, birthday, age, race/ethnicity, marital status, living arrangements, education level, occupation) • Health insurance information (including covered benefits) • Legal consents or permissions • Referral information • Correspondence • Patient history information (may include longitudinal history from PHD, immunizations, allergies, current medications) • Stated reason for visit • External causes of injury/illness • Symptoms • Physical exams • Assessment of patient signs and symptoms • Diagnoses • Laboratory, radiology, and pharmacy orders • Laboratory results • Radiological images and interpretations • Record of alerts, warnings, and reminders • Operative reports • Vital signs from ICU • Vital signs from PHD • Treatment plans and instructions • Progress notes • Functional status • Discharge summaries • Instructions about access • Audit log of individuals who accessed patient record • Patient amendments to patient record • Provider notes, such as knowledge of patient, patient-provider interactions, patient's access to services
Other Elements That Support Clinical Practice	• Protocols, practice guidelines • Clinical decision-support programs • Referral history
Elements from the Community Health Dimension	Depending on the patient, the HCPD would include additional contextual information necessary for understanding, treating, and planning the care of the patient: • Aggregate data on the healthcare of community members • Community attributes affecting health (e.g., economic status and population age) • Community health resources (e.g., home health services) • Community health (e.g., possible environmental hazards at home, work, school, or in the community at large)

Source: NCVHS 2000.

Table 7.3. Core content of the community health dimension

Public Health Data	• Infant mortality, immunization levels, and communicable disease rates • Environmental, social, and economic conditions • Measures related to public health infrastructure, individual healthcare providers, and healthcare institutions • Other summary measures of community health • Registries • Disease surveillance systems • Survey data • Data on Healthy People objectives and Leading Health indicators
Information from the HCPD (with personally identifiable information removed except under legally established public health protocols and strict security)	• Health status and outcomes, health events, health risks, health behaviors, and other individual characteristics • Healthcare utilization and access, health insurance status • Health care of community members
Other Elements	• Directories of community organizations and services • Planning, evaluation, and policy documents • Compendia of laws and regulations • Material to support public education campaigns • Practice guidelines and training materials for public health officials

Source: NCVHS 2000.

Shortly after the release of this report, an additional report entitled "Uniform Data Standards for Patient Medical Record Information" was published (NCVHS 2000a). At the present time, there are no "at large" health vocabularies designated as a national standard challenging the creation of uniform health records. The lack of adoption of a national standard vocabulary for healthcare use makes it difficult to develop universal clinical decision support. Additional collaboration between stakeholder groups is needed in standards development to coordinate healthcare terminology standards and **message format standards** to obtain greater semantic precision for HIE.

The transition from paper to EHRs necessitates the transition from legacy data sets toward a comprehensive core data set for continuity of care (figure 7.4) that maps back to EHR functions (AHIMA 2004). Efforts and workgroups continue in a variety of standard organizations and professional societies toward data content standards that support legal requirements, continuing care, quality of care measurement, and patient safety. Table 7.4 describes two goals outlined in the ONC-Coordinated Federal Health Information Technology Strategic Plan: 2008–2012.

Figure 7.4. Continuity of care record core data set

- Patient administrative and clinical data
- Basic information about the patient's payer
- Advance directives
- Patient's sources of support
- Patient's current functional status
- Problems
- Family history
- Social history
- Alerts
- Medications
- Medical devices or equipment need by patient
- Immunization history
- Vital signs, as appropriate
- Results of laboratory, diagnostic, and therapeutic results
- Diagnostic and therapeutic procedures
- Encounters
- Plan of care
- Healthcare providers

Source: Adapted from HIMSS 2003.

Table 7.4. Summary of health IT strategic goals and objectives: 2008–2012

Goal 1: Patient-focused Healthcare	**Objective 1.1:** Facilitate electronic exchange, access, and use of electronic health information, while protecting the privacy and security of patients' health information.	**Objective 1.2:** Enable the movement of electronic health information to support patients' health and care needs.	**Objective 1.3:** Promote nationwide deployment of electronic health records (EHRs) and personal health records (PHRs) and other consumer health IT tools.	**Objective 1.4:** Establish mechanisms for multi-stakeholder priority-setting and decision-making.
Goal 2: Population Health	**Objective 2.1:** Advance privacy and security policies, principles, procedures, and protections for information access in population health.	**Objective 2.2:** Enable exchange of health information to support population-oriented uses.	**Objective 2.3:** Promote nationwide adoption of technologies to improve population and individual health.	**Objective 2.4:** Establish coordinated organizational processes supporting information use for population health

Source: The ONC-Coordinated Federal Health Information Technology Strategic Plan: 2008–2012: http://www.hhs.gov/healthit/resources/HITStrategicPlanSummary.pdf.

In 2007, HHS awarded contracts to nine regional and state HIEs to begin trial implementations of the NHIN. Figure 7.5 illustrates the NHIN structure and relationships between regional and national efforts. When available, HHS plans to place specifications and testing materials in the public domain so all organizations can guide efforts to adopt interoperable health information sharing.

Check Your Understanding 7.1

Instructions: Answer the following questions on a separate piece of paper.

1. What is the difference between patient-specific data and aggregate data?
2. Why is it important for data from various sources to be defined in a standardized or uniform way?
3. How do a data set and core data elements make it possible to standardize data in healthcare organizations?
4. What organization initially took the lead in developing a minimum data set for hospitals and continues to play an active role in this area?
5. What role has the growth of technology played in the development of data sets and core content definitions?
6. How does the MDS indicate potential problems that must be addressed by the nursing home patient's caregivers?
7. What is the primary difference between DEEDS and the EMDS?
8. What is the common purpose for the use of data generated through HEDIS and ORYX?
9. Why does each of these outcomes measurement systems focus on the collection of clinical data elements in their databases?
10. What is the purpose of the NHIN and how do the three core content areas support that role?

Standards to Support Interoperability and Connectivity

The original NCVHS uniform data sets (for example, UHDDS, UACDS) have been the industry standard for data collection, but they were created for use in paper-based (manual) health record systems. These data sets alone can no longer accommodate the data requirements of the current healthcare delivery system. The demands of electronic health records and clinical information systems require a number of minimum data sets and data content standards. The Federal Health Architecture (FHA) and health information exchange activities have clearly identified the need to develop standards that support connectivity and interoperability. Because federal agencies are responsible for the costs of a significant amount of healthcare services, FHA from the ONC is active in championing standards development through HITSP. Thompson and Brailer (2004) stated that "without an interoperable infrastructure to allow for the secure movement of health information, the adoption and use of EHRs will not realize their full benefits." An interoperable infrastructure requires coordinated and secure HIE, including the business, governance, and technical delivery methods to support it; a set of intercommunication tools and services for common architecture development; the diffusion of product standards into deployed products; privacy and security assurances; and connectivity infrastructure.

Figure 7.5. Graphic representation of the Nationwide Health Information Network (NHIN)

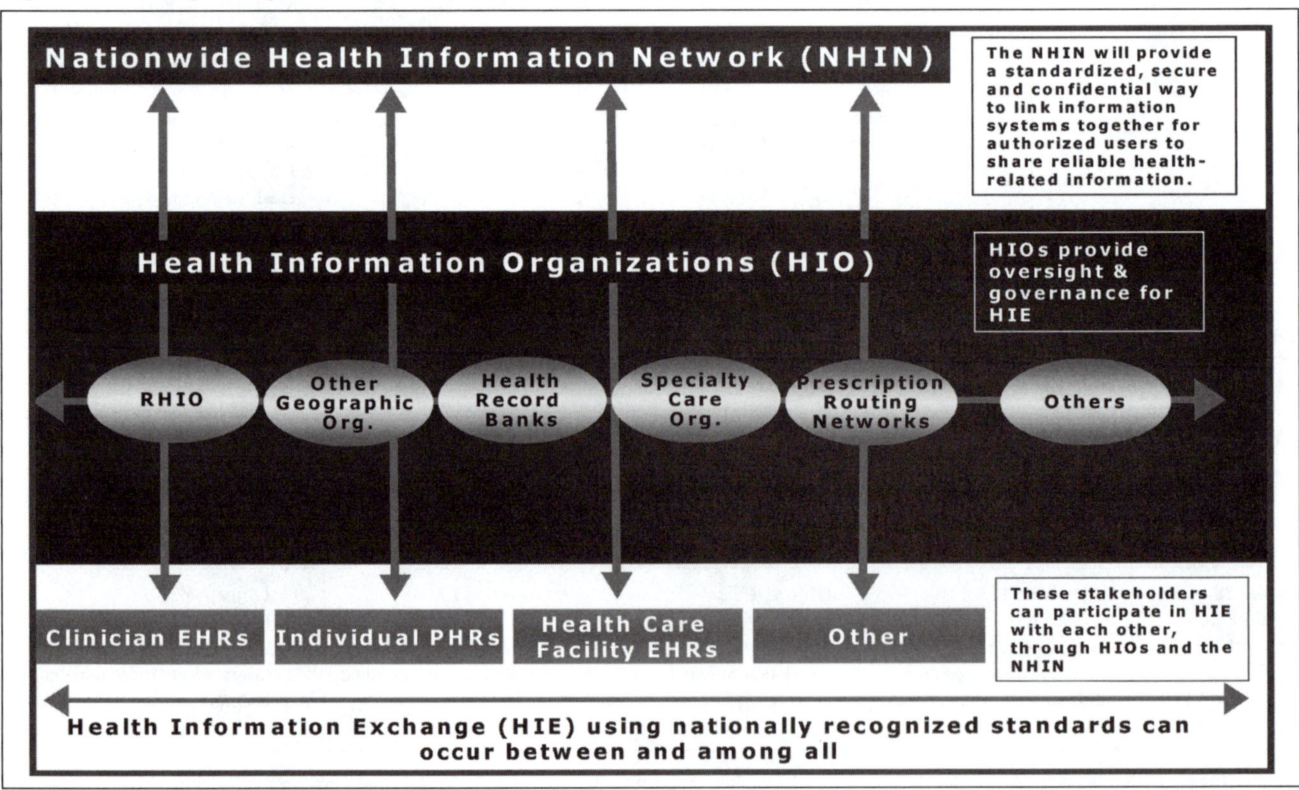

Source: National Alliance for Health Information Technology -Report to the Office of the National Coordinator for Health Information Technology. 2008. Defining Key Health Information Technology Terms. http://www.hhs.gov/healthit/documents/m20080603/10_2_hit_terms.pdf.

To fulfill current demands for information and to implement a workable nationwide system, information standards are critical, including the following list of standards important to HIM:

- Message format standards from HL7 and authoritative standards organizations
- Clinical data representation standards (including the vocabularies, clinical classification systems, and terminologies discussed in chapter 13)
- Technical standards such as electronic data interchange and e-commerce
- Medication terminology standards and medicine reconciliation procedures
- Overarching data privacy and security standards, including those that were promulgated as part of the **Health Insurance Portability and Accountability Act of 1996** (HIPAA).

In the United States, when HITSP selection of interoperability specification standards occurs, it is followed by submission to the Secretary of the HHS for review. Following confirmation by the Secretary there is a designated planning and testing period for the standard (usually one year) for industry use and refinement. Following this period the standards are officially recognized by the Secretary for adoption in all federal agencies. In this fashion the federal government is helping public and private stakeholders build a strong foundation for interoperable HIT investment to support EHRs and HIE.

Data Needs in an Electronic Environment

Healthcare organizations often have evolved into environments where several different computer systems are used at the same time performing different operational requirements. For example, a hospital's laboratory system might be entirely separate from its billing system. In fact, the various departments of large healthcare organizations often use different operating systems and are serviced by different vendors as they purchase the "best of breed systems" for a specific use case, then link them together with interfaces to share data. In addition to operating multiple systems, it is an ongoing challenge to integrate information from legacy systems operating on old platforms with state-of-the art information systems because of the rapid advancement of information management and communication technologies.

Healthcare organizations must integrate data that originate in various storage locations within facilities as well as in repositories outside the facility affecting operations and decision support. They also must be able to respond to requests to transfer information to other facilities, payers, accrediting and regulating agencies, quality improvement organizations, and other information users. In 2007, the American Medical Informatics Association (AMIA) developed the Secondary Uses and Re-Uses of Healthcare Data: Taxonomy for Policy Formulation and Planning document. This document illustrates the broad use of healthcare data for purposes other than direct patient care.

Goals for an interconnected healthcare delivery system can be accomplished only when every system is using common data standards first described in the NCVHS (2000) report "Uniform Data Standards for Patient Medical Records Information." Thompson and Brailer (2004) expressed the federal commitment to standards in their statement that "A key component of progress in interoperable health information is the development of technically sound and robustly specified interoperability standards and policies." They cite the development of the Consolidated Health Informatics (CHI): a joint initiative of the HHS, the Department of Defense (DoD), and the Veterans Administration (VA). The CHI initiative created 25 standards to be used in conjunction with the federal health architecture programs within the ONC. Additional interoperability specifications are now being released regularly in the United States as part of the HITSP process.

Healthcare Information Standards

Healthcare information standards describe accepted methods for collecting, maintaining, and transferring healthcare data elements between computer systems. These standards provide a common language that facilitates and supports:

- Exchanging information
- Sharing information
- Communicating within and across disciplines and settings
- Integrating disparate data systems
- Comparing information at a regional, national, and international level
- Linking data in a secure environment

Standards are the building blocks of effective health information systems and effective public health and healthcare delivery systems. They lay the foundation for disease surveillance, monitoring the health and healthcare of populations, performing outcomes research, providing for decision making, and policy development. The long-term vision for optimal healthcare exchange in place for almost a decade is to enhance the comparability, quality, integrity, and utility of health information from a wide variety of public sources through uniform data policies and standards (NCVHS 2001). Imagine trying to follow a recipe with no standard measurements, instructions that were not organized in any particular order or using any specific structure—standard information models, data structures, and transactions are important to avoid confusion, streamline clinical workflow, and promote better care procedures.

Health information standards fall into five categories: information standards, including content and structure of the electronic health record and message format standards; clinical data representation standards, including vocabularies, clinical classification systems, and terminologies as discussed in chapter 13; technical standards such as electronic data interchange or e-commerce; medication standards; and data privacy and security standards, including those that were promulgated as part of HIPAA. International, national, state and regional or local standards ensure communication and efficiency and minimization of duplication of effort along the continuum of healthcare. It is especially important to note that healthcare is provided locally and standards must be adopted at the local level to achieve the full benefit. The first step for HIM professionals is to be aware of and promote the use of recognized standards when beneficial, even in the absence of a federal mandate.

Content and Structure of Electronic Health Records

Structure and content standards establish and provide clear and uniform definitions of the data elements to be included in electronic health record systems. Moreover, they specify the type of data to be collected in each data field, the width of each data field, and the content of each data field. Standards are a consistent way to record and share health information. The e-Health Initiative (eHI) defines a standard as a well-defined approach that supports a business process, has been agreed upon by experts, and has been publicly vetted. The e-Health Blueprint: Building Consensus for Common Action involved more than 200 organizations in its development and is a solid approach towards building a better system.

EHR data standards include various types of e-Health standards including terminology, information interchange and messaging, data content, security, privacy, transactions and claims standards, identifiers for organizations and individuals, functionality, process, workflow, and information models.

Health Level Seven

Health Level Seven, Inc. (HL7) is an international not-for-profit, ANSI-accredited, standards-developing organization. HL7 provides a comprehensive framework and related standards for the exchange, integration, sharing, and retrieval of electronic health information that supports clinical practice and the management, delivery, and evaluation of health services. As a result of their broadened mission, HL7 developed the HL7 Electronic Health Record System (EHR-S) Functional Model and Standards that address the content and structure of an EHR. "Level Seven" refers to the highest level of the **International Organization for Standardization** (ISO) communications model for Open_Systems Interconnection (OSI)—the application level. The application level addresses the definition of the data to be exchanged, the timing of the interchange, and the communication of certain errors to the application. The seventh level supports such functions as security checks, participant identification, availability checks, exchange mechanism negotiations and, most importantly, data exchange structuring.

Workgroups comprised of volunteers are responsible for defining the HL7 standard protocol. Both the organization and the standard itself are referred to as HL7. The HL7 standard consists of rules for transmitting demographic data, orders, patient observations, laboratory results, history and physical observations and findings. It also includes message rules for appointment scheduling, referrals, problem list maintenance, and care plans. Membership in HL7 is available to anyone interested in the development of a cost-effective approach to system connectivity.

In 2004, the EHR-S Functional Model and Standards passed an ANSI Draft Standards for Trial Use. Since that time, additional standards have been established and are listed on the HL7 Web site. There is an EHR-S Registry web site that lists all of the current profiles. The purpose of the functional model is to provide a foundation for common understanding of possible and useful functions of EHR systems. Ongoing additional work is adding to this model and adapting to new technology and medical developments as they emerge.

The HL7 **Clinical Document Architecture** (CDA) provides an exchange model for clinical documents (such as history and physicals, operative reports, discharge summaries and progress notes) and brings the healthcare industry closer to the realization of an electronic health record. The CDA utilizes XML (Extensible Markup Language), the HL7 Reference Information Model (RIM), and coded vocabularies to make documents machine readable, so they can be easily parsed and processed electronically. It also makes documents human readable so they can be easily retrieved and used by the people who need them. CDA documents can be displayed using XML-aware Web browsers or wireless applications such as cell phones. The CDA was adopted in May 2004, as a federal health information interoperability standard to identify standards and terminologies used to define the messaging architecture and syntax of clinical text documents (NAHIT 2005). The Clinical Document Architecture for Clinical Document Types (sometimes referred to as CDA 4 CDT) initiative supports standardization for medical information exchange, and establishes standard ways of identifying and organizing discrete clinical data. This standard enables location and retrieval of clinical information inside electronic health records. Implementation guides developed, balloted, and published by HL7 provide specifications for specific use cases.

American Society for Testing and Materials (ASTM) E31 Committee

The **American Society for Testing and Materials** (ASTM) develops standards for a variety of industries in the United States. The ASTM Technical Committee on Healthcare Informatics E31 is charged with the responsibility for developing standards related to the EHR. E31 works through subcommittees assigned to various aspects of this endeavor. Of interest to the HIM Community is the work of the subcommittee on Healthcare Data Management, Security, Confidentiality, and Privacy (E31.25) who developed Standard Practice for Content and Structure of the Electronic Health Record (EHR). Other examples include the Health Information Transcription and Documentation Committee (E31.22) who developed the standards: E2344 Standard Guide for Data Capture through the Dictation Process and E2364 Standard Guide for Speech Recognition Products in Health Care. Also, the Committee on Healthcare Information Capture and Documentation (E31.15) developed standard E2117 Standard Guide for Identification and Establishment of a Quality Assurance Program for Medical Transcription and E2369 Standard Specification for **Continuity of Care Record** (CCR).

ASTM Standard E1384-02a identifies the content and structure for EHRs. The scope of this standard covers all types of healthcare services, including acute care hospitals, ambulatory care, skilled nursing facilities, home healthcare, and specialty environments. It applies to short-term contacts such as EDs and emergency medical care services as well as long-term care such as primary care physicians with long-term contact.

The following purposes are outlined for the ASTM Practice for Content and Structure of the EHR:

- Identify the content and logical data structure and organization of an EHR consistent with currently acknowledged patient record content. The record carries all health-related information about a person over time. It may include history and physical, laboratory tests, diagnostic reports, orders and treatments documentation, patient identifying information, legal permissions, and so on. The content is presented and described as data elements or as clinical documents. This standard is consistent with Extensible Markup Language (XML). See Document Type Definition (DTD) 2.1 and W3CXML Schema 1.0.
- Explain the relationship of data coming from diverse sources (for example, clinical laboratory information management systems, order entry systems, pharmacy information management systems, dictation systems), and other data in the EHR as the primary repository for information from various sources.
- Provide a common vocabulary for those developing, purchasing, and implementing EHR systems.
- Provide sufficient content from which data extracts can be compiled to create unique setting views.
- Map the content to selected relevant biomedical and health informatics standards (ASTM 2008).

The ASTM Committee 31 also developed the CCR specification, which is categorized as Electronic Health Records standard E2369. The CCR standard is a core data set of relevant current and past information about a patient's health status and healthcare treatment. The CCR was created to help communicate that information from one provider to another for referral, transfer, or discharge of the patient or when the patient wishes to create a personal health record. Data from a CCR may also be incorporated into a personal health record. Because it utilizes XML codes, it enhances interoperability and allows its preparation, transmission, and viewing in multiple ways. The CCR is designed to be organized and transportable. It is sponsored by a consortium of healthcare organizations, practitioners, and other stakeholders. ASTM and HL7 collaboratively developed the **Continuity of Care Record/Document** (CCR/CCD) to leverage clinical document architecture (CDA) with the CCR specifications. HITSP has created the HITSP Summary Documents Using HL7 **Continuity of Care Document** (CCD) Component (HITSP 2008). As the use of the CCR/CCD combination increases, this data set is likely to become the common HIE methodology between the EHR and PHR systems.

Identifier Standards

Identifier standards recommend methods for assigning **unique identification numbers** to individuals, including patients, healthcare providers (for example, physicians and dentists), corporate providers (healthcare organizations), and healthcare vendors and suppliers. Identifiers usually use a combination of numeric or alphanumeric characters such as a hospital number or a billing number. The **National Provider Identifier** (NPI) is a HIPAA Administrative Simplification Standard. This number is a unique identification number for covered healthcare providers. Covered healthcare providers and all health plans and healthcare clearinghouses will use these identifier numbers in the administrative and financial transactions adopted under HIPAA. The NPI is a 10-position, intelligence-free numeric identifier (10-digit number). Intelligence free means that the numbers do not carry other information about healthcare providers, such as the state where they live or practice, or in which specialty they may be qualified. As of May 2007 (May 2008, for small health plans), the NPI was required in lieu of legacy provider identifiers in the HIPAA standards transactions.

It is generally agreed that unique identification numbers are needed for patients, but there is no consensus on the method of identification. HIPAA regulations require unique identification numbers that can be used across information systems although individual patient identifiers have not been adopted due to a number of factors. Much of the controversy relates to the use of the **social security number** (SSN) as the identifier for patients. This identifier was not designed as a universal identifier and the Social Security Administration is adamant in its opposition to using the SSN for purposes other than those identified by law. Due to the evolution of the use of this number as an identifier or source for identity confirmation it is a target for identity thieves. Other sources for identity confirmation in healthcare being explored include biometrics (fingerprint, iris, retinal scans) with some installations operational using this technology. Smart cards and implantable systems are other technologies to watch to increase security and patient identification and security in the future. Universal identifiers are culture specific and may be influenced by the allowed use of such a number and the protection afforded against misuse.

Clinical Representation Standards

Clinical representation standards include clinical terminology, classification and vocabulary systems, lab and clinical observation codes such as LOINC, drug codes, as well as health informatics standards for information modeling, and metadata. Standard terminology systems establish common definitions for medical terms to encourage consistent descriptions of an individual's condition in the health record.

Medical terminology is extremely complex, and establishing universal medical **vocabulary standards** is a challenging task. Various synonymous medical terms are often used in different areas of the country. In fact, medical terminology often varies between physicians working in the same organization, depending on where and when each physician was trained and in which medical specialty he or she practices. For example, one physician might describe a patient's diagnosis as Parkinson's disease, another might describe it as Parkinsonism, and a third might use the term paralysis agitans. All three terms describe the same disease but using the terms interchangeably would adversely affect data quality and make retrieval more challenging. In addition, data comparison among the physicians' patients would be difficult, if not impossible.

The use of clinical classification coding systems, for example International Classification of Diseases (ICD) or Current Procedural Terminology (CPT) codes to represent health-related conditions and procedures is common in healthcare for indexing and administrative use. The use of standardized, uniform terminology for data capture and reporting is critical to accurate information storage and retrieval. Terminology and vocabulary standards adoption enhanced by technology advancement sets the stage for future automated coding systems that facilitate a higher degree of data integrity than is possible with traditional code assignment and reporting workflow. The development of vocabularies, terminologies, and classification systems as well as drug codes, laboratory and clinical observation codes, information modeling, and metadata are thoroughly explored in chapter 13. Entire code sets are often featured as HL7 standard value sets allowing an electronic system to restrict data selections to a defined set of valid choices and minimize system changes for code set updates.

Currently there is no "master set" of data elements that would facilitate HIE at the highest level of interoperability. More work toward the adoption of a standard integrated set of data elements and terminologies will advance HIE and enhance clinical representation in electronic environments. For more information about the use of clinical terminologies and classification systems see chapter 13.

Technical Standards

The ANSI is a private, non-profit organization that coordinates voluntary standards in the United States. Many standards developers and participants support ANSI as the central body responsible for the identification of a single consistent set of voluntary standards called American National Standards. ANSI provides an open forum for all concerned interests to identify specific business needs, plan to meet those needs, and agree on standards. Although ANSI itself does not develop standards, its approval of standards does indicate that the principles of openness and due process have been followed in the approval process and that a consensus of those participating in the approval process has been achieved. Most **standard development organizations** (SDOs) use the formal balloting process defined by ANSI.

ANSI also sponsors the HITSP work towards interoperability specifications and is the official U.S. representative to the International Organization for Standardization (ISO). ISO standards are voted on by country rather than individual members. In 1998, ISO created the Technical Committee 215–Health Informatics Organization, f ISO TC 215 as part of a United States delegation to the larger organization. AHIMA members are represented in this technical committee charged with advancement of internationally recognized standards.

Electronic data interchange (EDI) is the electronic transfer of information, such as health claims transmitted electronically, in a standard format between trading partners. EDI originated when a number of industries identified cost savings through the electronic transmission of business information. They were convinced that the standardization of formatted information was the most effective means of communicating with multiple trading partners. EDI allows entities within the healthcare system to exchange medical, billing, and other information and to process transactions in a manner that is fast and cost-effective. With EDI there is a substantial reduction in handling and processing time compared to paper, and the risk of lost paper documents is eliminated. EDI also can eliminate the inefficiencies of handling paper documents, which would significantly reduce administrative burden, lower operating costs, and improve overall data quality. In recent years the term EDI has often been replaced by the term *e-commerce*.

In 1979, ANSI chartered a new committee, known as the **Accredited Standards Committee** (ASC) X12, Electronic Data Interchange (referred to as ASC X12N or **X12N**). The charge of the committee was to develop uniform standards for the electronic interchange of business transactions. In 2008, the HHS issued a proposed rule to adopt the X12 standard version 5010 and the National Council for Prescription Drug Programs standard version D.0 for electronic transactions including healthcare claims. The updated X12 transaction standards were needed to support the migration to ICD-10-CM and ICD-10-PCS coding systems in the U.S. X12N and the drug programs to advance electronic processing involving prescriptions.

One of the purposes of the HIPAA Administrative Simplification rules was to standardize information exchange, and in August 2000, the HHS published regulations for electronic transactions. These regulations apply to transactions that occur between healthcare providers and healthcare plans and payers (Rode 2001). The long-term goal of the **transaction standards** is to allow providers and plans or payers to seamlessly transfer data back and forth with little intervention. To do this, HHS has adopted the electronic transactions standards of ASC X12 Insurance Subcommittee (Accredited Standards Committee Health Care Task group [X12N]).

The work of ASC X12 is conducted primarily by a series of subcommittees and task groups whose major function is the development of new, and the maintenance of existing, EDI standards. The standards adopted for EDI are called ANSI ASC X12N and include:

- Professional/institutional X12N 837 Healthcare Claim Transactions, version 4010/5010
- X12N 835 Health Care Claim (HCC) Payment/Advice (or remittance advice, RA) transactions
- X12N 837 Coordination of Benefits (COB) transactions

To implement the HIPAA administrative simplification provisions, the above transaction standards are included under part 162 of title 45 of the Code of Federal Regulations (CFR) as the standard for processing electronic healthcare claims, coordination of benefits, and remittance advice (RA) transmissions.

Logical Observation Identifiers Names and Codes (LOINC)

LOINC is a well-accepted set of terminology standards that provide a standard set of universal names and codes for identifying individual laboratory and clinical results. It is managed by the Regenstrief Institute in Indianapolis and was developed using a semantic data model. LOINC codes are widely acceptable and are included in the consolidated health informatics standards. The LOINC vocabulary is maintained as a single table structure and the database and supporting materials are available for download. The Regenstrief LOINC Mapping Assistant (REMLA) is also available as a program for searching and viewing the LOINC database. Like other contemporary clinical terminologies, LOINC codes are designed to work efficiently in electronic environments. (More information about LOINC is available in chapter 13.)

Institute of Electrical and Electronics Engineers (IEEE) 1073

The **Institute of Electrical and Electronics Engineers** (IEEE) 1073 provides for open systems communications in healthcare applications, primarily between bedside medical devices and patient care information systems, optimized for the acute care setting. The IEEE 1073 Series was adopted as a federal health information interoperability standard for electronic data exchange. Increasingly there are personal health monitoring devices that interface with other devices including electronic health records for data capture and remote monitoring. As the health record includes more direct interaction with machines and their output, the collaboration and cooperation between device standards and health informatics standards organizations is expected.

Digital Imaging and Communications in Medicine

Through a cooperative effort between the **American College of Radiology and the National Electrical Manufacturers Association** (ACR-NEMA), **Digital Imaging and Communications in Medicine** (DICOM) was originally created to permit the interchange of biomedical image waveforms and related information. These organizations define the health record to include not only textual, coded, and numeric information (linguistic), but also a detailed, structured record of image-related information. DICOM is part of the Medical Imaging Technology Alliance (a division of NEMA).

The information associated with each image is the standard administrative and billing information used today—patient name, procedure code, and so on. Combined with the open protocol, this protocol provides for data interchange, not data understanding. The companies who developed the exchange standard now have taken another step and suggested a mapping and terminology resource to index the content of biomedical images in a clinically relevant manner.

DICOM is used by most medical professions that utilize imaging within the healthcare industry including cardiology, dentistry, endoscopy, mammography, ophthalmology, and orthopedics. DICOM was adopted as the federal health information interoperability messaging standard for imaging in March 2003 (Alliance Standards Directory 2005). Important to the field of medical imaging are **picture archiving and communication systems** (PACS). PACS are computers or networks dedicated to the storage, retrieval, distribution, and presentation of medical images. The most common format today for storage of images is the DICOM standard. In 2006, the Alliance Standards Directory was donated by NAHIT to the National Institute of Standards and Technology (NIST). NIST included this body of work in its Healthcare Standards Landscape Web-application and database.

Medication Standards

Medications are used extensively to prevent and treat medical conditions in the United States and around the world. Physicians, payers, and pharmacies communicate with one another to assure that ordered medications are prescribed, administered, and reimbursed as the clinician intended. Research studies are frequently conducted to determine the efficacy of various drugs; removal of certain categories of drugs from the market due to unforeseen adverse effects has focused attention on medication issues and has underscored the need for accurate and accessible information about all pharmaceutical treatments. Terminology standards are discussed in chapter 13.

Food and Drug Administration (FDA)

The FDA administers the **National Drug Codes (NDC) Directory**. HIM professionals should be familiar with this resource. The current edition of the NDC Directory is limited to prescription drugs and insulin products that have been manufactured, prepared, propagated, compounded, or processed by registered establishments for commercial distribution.

Structured Product Labeling (SPL) is a document markup standard approved by HL7 and adopted by FDA as a mechanism for exchanging medication information. In 2006, the selection of SNOMED CT as one of the terminologies of choice for the highlights section of the Structured Product Labeling (SPL) was announced by the FDA. The choice of SNOMED CT was made to facilitate a one-to-one mapping between concepts and codes commonly used in electronic health records and the same concepts and codes used in the electronic prescribing information found in the SPL's highlights section.

FDA Center for Drug Evaluation and Research Data Standards (CDER) Manual

The FDA **Center for Drug Evaluation and Research Data Standards (CDER) Manual** is a compilation of standardized nomenclature monographs that have been reviewed and approved by the CDER Nomenclature Standards Committee (NSC). **Nomenclature** is a recognized system of terms used in a science or art that follows pre-established naming conventions.

These CDER nomenclature standards are considered binding upon all new automated databases, and upon all existing automated databases when undergoing a major redesign. Use of the nomenclature standards is strictly voluntary for static existing databases. Some of the current CDER automated databases that use these nomenclature standards include the Center-wide Oracle Management Information System (COMIS), the Division Files System (DFS), the Drug Product Reference File (DPRF), the Drug Registration and Listing System (DRLS), the Developers and Distributors System (DADS), the Special Products Online Tracking System (SPOTS), and the Phase 4 Tracking System. More information about the CDER manual and process is available from the FDA Web site. Table 7.5 includes examples of FDA CEDR drug nomenclature monographs.

Table 7.5. Examples of FDA CDER drug nomenclature monographs

Drug Nomenclature Monographs	Monograph Number
Drug Classification	C-DRG-00101
Dosage Form	C-DRG-00201
Route of Administration	C-DRG-00301
Ingredient Name	C-DRG-00401
Proprietary Name	C-DRG-00402
Animal Common Names	C-DRG-00403
Animal Cell Tissue Fluid Biomolecule	C-DRG-00404
Biotechnology Origin	C-DRG-00405
Potency	C-DRG-00501
Indications	C-DRG-00601

Source: FDA 2005.

National Council for Prescription Drug Programs

The **National Council for Prescription Drug Programs** (NCPDP) is a not-for-profit ANSI-accredited Standards Development Organization consisting of more than 1,500 members representing chain and independent pharmacies, consulting companies and pharmacists, database management organizations, federal and state agencies, health insurers, health maintenance organizations (HMOs), mail service pharmacy companies, pharmaceutical manufacturers, pharmaceutical services administration organizations, prescription service organizations, pharmacy benefit management companies, professional and trade associations, telecommunication and systems vendors, wholesale drug distributors, and other parties interested in electronic standardization within the pharmacy services sector of the healthcare industry. The NCPDP SCRIPT standard is used for transmitting prescription information electronically between prescribers, providers, and other organizations or agents. The standard addresses the electronic transmission of new prescriptions, changes of prescriptions, prescription refills, prescription fill status notifications, cancellation notifications, relaying of medication history, and transactions used in long-term care.

Semantic Clinical Drug (SCD) of RxNorm

RxNorm provides standardized names for clinical drugs (active ingredient plus strength plus dose form) and for dose forms as administered. It provides links from clinical drugs to their active ingredients, drug components (active ingredient plus strength) and some related brand names. RxNorm is produced in consultation with the FDA, the VA, and the HL7 standards development organizations. RxNorm is only released in the UMLS Metathesaurus.

The **Semantic Clinical Drug (SCD)** is a subset of RxNorm for the ingredient plus strength and dose form. An example is: Fluoxetine 4mg/mL Oral Solution. The SCD of RxNorm was adopted as a federal healthcare information interoperability standard for clinical drug nomenclature.

LOINC Clinical Special Product Labeling (SPL)

The Structured Product Labeling (SPL) specification purpose is to facilitate the submission, review, storage, dissemination, and access to product labeling information. The CHI

Structured Product Labeling (SPL) sections standard is the LOINC Clinical SPL section terminology. The terminology for product labeling sections referenced in the SPL is maintained within LOINC Clinical system.

Privacy and Security Standards

HIPAA mandated the adoption of privacy and security protection for identifiable health information. HIPAA **privacy standards** have been implemented throughout the healthcare industry. They are addressed thoroughly in chapter 10.

Security standards ensure that patient-identifiable health information remains confidential and protected from unauthorized disclosure, alteration, or destruction. Effective security standards are especially important in computer-based environments because patient information is accessible to many users in many locations.

Security standards are addressed in detail in chapter 9 as they relate to the EHR Many standards organizations—most notably, the ASTM and HL7—have developed security standards, but no single standard currently addresses all of the HIPAA provisions.

Standards Development

Many organizations are directly involved in the development of healthcare information standards and invest in resources required to develop, distribute, and maintain the standards for use by others. These organizations are referred to as **standards development organizations** (SDOs). Both private organizations and government agencies are involved in the process of developing standards. Most standards are created through a voluntary consensus process that involves identifying the need for a standard, negotiating the content of the standard, and drafting a proposed standard. The final standard is published after undergoing a comment and revision period. This process facilitates wide adoption and improved utility.

A number of organizations play key roles in coordinating standards development. They do not develop standards but, rather, coordinate the efforts of other SDOs. ANSI coordinates the development of voluntary standards in a variety of industries, including healthcare. Most SDOs in the United States are members of ANSI. The ISO coordinates international standards development. ANSI represents the United States at the ISO with technical advisory group (TAG) committee 215 (Health Informatics) generating interest for HIM professionals. There are currently nine work groups within ISO 215 working on healthcare-related standards.

Many organizations are involved in the process of setting standards within specific industries and areas of expertise. The U.S. healthcare industry is no exception. Table 7.6 provides a list of several of the organizations that are actively involved in developing standards for health-related information management. Both private and government organizations influence the development of standards by taking positions on proposed standards and setting policies that lend credibility to standards. The government agencies that influence standards development include the CMS, the Food and Drug Administration (FDA), the Agency for Health Care Policy and Research (AHCPR), the Office of the Assistant Secretary for Planning and Evaluation (ASPE), and the CDC/NCHS.

There are published directories of healthcare standards including HCS Online published by the ECRI Institute. The NAHIT has provided definitions important to standards development through a consensus process. There is also a listing of standards in the United States Health Information Knowledgebase (USHIK). This is a health metadata registry funded and directed by the Agency for Healthcare Research and Quality with management support in partnership with the CMS. USHIK provides and maintains a metadata registry of health information data element definitions, values, and information models that enable browsing, comparison, synchronization, and harmonization within a uniform query and interface environment. The USHIK is populated with the data elements and information models of SDO and other healthcare organizations in such a way that public and private organizations can harmonize information formats with healthcare standards.

This organization also contains data element information for government initiatives supporting the use and implementation of data standards (for example, HIPAA) and the CHI initiative. The USHIK established a metadata registry methodology based on International Organization for Standardizations (ISO)/International Electrotechnical Commission (IEC) 11179 Information Technology-Specification and Standardization of Data Elements.

A **metadata registry** is used to store characteristics of data that are necessary to clearly describe, inventory, analyze, and classify data. A health metadata registry supports data sharing with cross-system and cross-organization descriptions of common units of health data. This process assists users to form common understanding of a data unit's meaning, representation, and identification.

At present, one of the most challenging aspects of the standards movement is the area of standards harmonization. There are many initiatives occurring in the United States as well as in the international community, resulting in duplication and competition among organizations. Harmonization of these efforts will be critical if the movement toward PHRs for individuals, EHRs at all points of care, and networked health information systems at both the regional and national level are to move forward. The ONC has been charged with the responsibility of leading efforts toward standards harmonization. It will take the cooperation and collaboration of many, especially the HIM profession that is built on the foundation of standards development, to accomplish the reform needed to achieve the goals outlined.

Table 7.6. Standards development organizations

Organization	Types of Standards	Description
Accredited Standards Committee X12 Data Interchange Standards Association (DISA) 333 John Carlyle Street, Suite 600 Alexandria, VA 22314 Telephone: (703) 548-7005 www.disa.org	Electronic data interchange for billing transactions The committee's particular area of focus has been computer-to-computer communications between healthcare providers and third-party payers	Chartered in 1979 by ANSI, the X12N subcommittee develops and maintains X12 standards, interpretations, and guidelines. X12N is one of the standards for EDI that is specified in the regulations of the Health Insurance Portability and Accountability Act of 1996. Subgroups of X12N include: *WEDI: Workgroup on Electronic Data Exchange* WEDI has been the prime mover in the development of insurance industry standards. In 1995, WEDI became a private standards advocacy group. *HIBCC: Health Industry Business Communications Council*
American College of Radiology–National Electrical Manufacturers Association (ACR-NEMA) American College of Radiology 1891 Preston White Drive Reston, VA 20191 Telephone: (703) 648-8900 www.acr.org National Electrical Manufacturers Association 1300 N. Seventeenth Street, Suite 1847 Rosslyn, VA 22209 Telephone: (703) 841-3200 www.nema.org	Exchange of digitized images	ACR is a professional association, and NEMA is a trade association. They have worked collaboratively to develop the Digital Imaging and Communications in Medicine (DICOM) standard, which promotes a digital image communications format and facilitates development by the American College of Radiology of picture archive and communications systems. DICOM may be used for electronic exchange of x-rays, computed tomography (CT), magnetic resonance imaging (MRI), ultrasound, nuclear medicine, and other radiology images. Work is under way to support other diagnostic images.
American Society for Testing and Materials (ASTM) 100 Barr Harbor Drive West Conshohocken, PA 19428 Telephone: (610) 832-9585 www.astm.org	Multiple health informatics standards, including clinical content of patient records, exchange of messages about clinical observations, data security and integrity, healthcare identifiers, data modeling, clinical laboratory systems, Arden syntax (a coding system), and system functionality	Organized in 1898, the ASTM is one of the largest SDOs in the world. It provides a forum for vendors, users, consumers, and others to develop standards for a wide range of materials, products, systems, and services. It is composed of more than 140 subcommittees or working groups identified as E31 and E32. Since 1990, Committee E31 on Healthcare Informatics has developed standards for health information and health information systems. Standard E1384, discussed earlier, is a product of the E31 subcommittee of ASTM.
Health Level Seven (HL7) 3300 Washtenaw Avenue, Suite 227 Ann Arbor, MI 48104 Telephone: (734) 677-7777 www.hl7.org	Electronic interchange of clinical, financial, and administrative information among disparate health information systems	HL7 is an ANSI-accredited SDO. Level 7 refers to the highest level of the Open System Interconnection (OSI) model of the International Standards Organization. The HL7 standard addresses issues that occur within the seventh, or application, layer.
Institute of Electrical and Electronics Engineers (IEEE) 445 Hoes Lane P.O. Box 1331 Piscataway, NJ 08855-1331 Telephone: (732) 981-0060 www.ieee.org	Medical device information and general informatics format	The IEEE's Medical Data Interchange Standard (MEDIX) is a standard set of hospital system interface transactions based on the ISO standards for all seven layers of the OSI model. Another IEEE standard for a medical information bus (MIB) links bedside instruments in critical care with health information systems.
National Council on Prescription Drug Programs (NCPDP) 4201 N. Twenty-fourth Street, Suite 365 Phoenix, AZ 85016 Telephone: (602) 957-9105 www.ncpdp.org	Data interchange and processing standards for pharmacy transactions	The NCPDP has defined standards for transmitting prescription information from pharmacies to payers for prescription management services and for receiving approval and payment information back in near-real time. Other standards address adverse drug reactions and utilization review.

Adapted from Brandt 2000, 39.

Check Your Understanding 7.2

Instructions: Answer the following questions on a separate piece of paper.

1. What is the difference between a data set and a healthcare information standard?
2. What changes in the healthcare industry have prompted the focus on developing healthcare information standards?
3. How would ASTM Standard E1384-02a and the HL7 EHR-S Functional Standard be helpful during the development of an EHR system?
4. What SDOs have been most active in developing structure and content standards for EHRs?
5. Describe the difference between an EHR and EMR according to the project contracted to NAHIT from ONC.

Evolving and Emerging Health Information Standards

The development of healthcare information standards is far from complete. The task is critically important to the widespread development of electronic health record systems and, ultimately, to implementation and use of a national health information infrastructure. Leading standards groups are continuously working to reach consensus on a variety of standards, but many issues are still to be resolved. As breakthroughs occur in communication technology, information management innovation will take advantage of time saving and cost saving workflow shortcuts. This will affect certain jobs within the profession, but it is expected that for every position lost to automation or improved, at least two more will emerge to manage the changes. HIM professionals just have to be sure to keep on learning since the pace of innovation and change is rapid.

Extensible Markup Language

A key technology tool for enabling data sharing is called **extensible markup language** (XML). XML was developed as a universal language to facilitate the storage and transmission of data published on the Internet. Markup languages communicate electronic representations of paper documents to computers by inserting additional information into text (Sokolowski 1999). The best-known markup language is hypertext markup language (HTML), which is used to convert text documents into Internet-compatible format.

Pothen and Parmanto (2000) describe XML as "an easy-to-learn, standardized mark-up language with customizable tags that describe data within documents." In other words, XML provides a context for data through the use of a tag. In the context of health data, XML tags each item of data with a descriptor that differentiates, for example, between a number that is a SSN from a number that represents the medical record number. XML allows data to be communicated from one computerized system to another without losing the integrity of the data. In addition, XML provides structure and rules that are "important for healthcare informatics because they will provide context for narrative text, a document information model, agreement on high-level structures, and a facility for standardizing formats" (Sokolowski 1999, 22). In other words, XML enables suitably coded documents to be read and understood without difficulty by both humans and machines. It is an open standard for meta languages controlled by the World Wide Web Consortium (W3C) (Schroeter 2008).

As EHRs continue to evolve in somewhat disjointed manner (as described in chapter 9), XML has the potential to solve some of the difficulties posed by the lack of standardized vocabulary and the need to transmit data among disparate computer systems. Some of the characteristics that make XML relevant to the development of an EHR were described by Pothen and Parmanto (2000):

- XML combined with existing classification systems such as ICD-9-CM can improve the completeness of health records by providing a clear description of the content of data in the record
- XML allows data in the health record to be organized in a meaningful and searchable form

XML also can serve as a standard for exchange of health information over the Web because it is not impeded by disparate computer systems. A test project conducted in Canada utilized XML for data exchange among three remote health-related organizations that each used a different set of applications, databases, and technology. The organizations mapped each system to standard templates in XML and were able to seamlessly transfer data from one location to the other (Smith 2001). The implementation of XML within the healthcare industry has the potential to address many of the issues of both vocabulary and transmission.

The National Institute for Science and Technology (NIST) has a number of projects that inform the future of information management science. One of the projects is the Health Care Standards Landscape that provides a useful resource for emerging technology and standards activities including XML conformance testing.

Check Your Understanding 7.3

Instructions: Answer the following questions on a separate piece of paper.

1. What is the relationship between healthcare information standards and the coding of healthcare data?
2. What is the reason for creating a unique identification number for every healthcare consumer?
3. Why is use of the SSN as a unique identification number not appropriate?
4. What characteristics of XML make it a potential solution for many of the problems of storing and transmitting health information?

Real-World Case

HIM expertise plays a critical role in standards development. Many standards development organizations rely on participation by organizational representatives bringing unique perspectives to the process so that standards created by collaboration meet the common good for all stakeholders.

AHIMA promotes and coordinates participation in standards work important to the HIM profession and its members. Some members are employed by standards development organizations or for companies that directly support them. Other HIM professionals serve on committees or work groups that enable them to represent the views of the profession as well as the interests of their employer. It is important that the HIM voice be heard as standards are developed that impact representation of health data, protect the confidentiality and privacy of the patient, and assure reliability of the health record to meet both clinical and business requirements.

The Minimum Data Set for long-term care reporting is being revised to incorporate changes in practice and technology that were not available when it was developed. Standard terminologies including SNOMED CT and LOINC are expected to make the MDS more interoperable and easier to interface with electronic health record systems so that data can be collected more efficiently and re-used for more than one purpose.

In 2006, the HHS invested in research to determine how this data set could work more efficiently by linking the data elements in the MDS 2.0 to CHI standard terminologies.

A report entitled "Standardizing the MDS with LOINC and Vocabulary Matches" is available from http://aspe.hhs.gov/daltcp/reports/2007/MDS-LOINC.htm. An additional report entitled "Making the 'Minimum Data Set' Compliant with HIT Standards" is found at http://aspe.hhs.gov/daltcp/reports/2006/MDS-HIT.htm.

Work continues with future versions of the MDS to incorporate emerging standards and technology assistance to improve quality and efficiency for data capture and sharing. The CMS continues to explore new data elements and structures for the minimum data set and expects to finalize the MDS. A demonstration program for post-acute care reform began in 2007 and continues in 2008 with the Continuity Assessment Record Evaluation (CARE), so this could be an emerging standard for the future.

Case Study Assignment

You are the Director of HIM for an Integrated Healthcare Delivery System. Your chief medical informatics officer, Mary Watson, is creating a strategic plan for the skilled care services available in the system including the skilled care unit affiliated with the Flagship hospital, swingbed services offered by the three rural hospitals, and the five nursing homes with skilled care beds that are part of your system.

1. What health information standards will you want to become familiar with in order to understand information management needs for the future for these facilities?
2. What skills might the HIM professionals in your organizations require to assist the clinical staff in these facilities with health record management and completion of the data set?
3. Mary has heard something about a new assessment called CARE. What can you find out for her that will help her with strategic planning?

Develop an executive summary presentation for Mary that outlines the key standards to monitor for long-term care.

Summary

According to Brandt (2000), "The vision is clear: a longitudinal, or lifetime, health record for each person that is computer-based, secure, readily accessible when needed, and linked across the continuum of care [is needed]. In reality, we are a long way from that model." At the end of the first decade of the 21st century, a comprehensive electronic health record for every citizen is not yet a reality. It is impossible to develop a longitudinal EHR that meets Brandt's specifications without standards that guide the development. The complexity of technology, the variations in computer platforms from one system to the next, and the differing (and sometimes conflicting) data needs of users demand flexible health data/information systems. The systems must be able to store volumes of data in a standardized format, communicate across vendor-specific systems, and keep data in a secure manner that protects individual privacy and information confidentiality.

The need for standardized data definitions was recognized in the 1960s, and the NCVHS took the lead in developing uniform minimum data sets for various sites of care. As technology has driven the development of the data/information systems, the early data sets have been supplemented with healthcare information standards that focus on electronic health record systems. A number of standards-setting organizations are involved in developing uniform definitions, data fields, and views for health record content and structure. Identifier, clinical representation, technical, medication, privacy and security standards have been created and implemented. These standards are dynamic and in constant development by various groups. Standards development generally takes place as a consensus-driven process among various interested parties. In most cases, implementation is voluntary. However, there are many groups involved in standards development and competition exists among those groups. One of the major efforts of the ONC is standards harmonization that consolidates a useful and accepted set of national IT standards.

Some data sets and standards have been incorporated into federal law and are thus required for use by affected healthcare organizations. For example, in 1983, the standardized definitions of the UHDDS were incorporated into the Prospective Payment Act (PL98-603) and are still required for reporting inpatient data for reimbursement under the Medicare program.

HIPAA mandated the incorporation of healthcare information standards into all electronic or computer-based health information systems. Of particular importance under HIPAA are transaction/messaging standards for communication of data across systems, privacy standards that protect individual privacy and confidentiality, security standards that ensure that data is accessed only by those who have a specific right to access, and identifier standards that offer methods of identifying both individual patients as well as healthcare providers. The rules and regulations for HIPAA are still in development, and, to date, the transaction, privacy, and security standards have been implemented. Other standards are still under development.

The development of health information standards to support the development of electronic health records gained national support through federal initiatives aimed at developing a strategic plan to guide the nation's implementation of interoperable health information technology in both the public and private sectors. The ONC has been given a mandate to advance the development, adoption, and implementation of healthcare information technology nationally through collaboration among public and private interests and to ensure that these standards are consistent with current efforts to set HIT standards for use by the federal government (Thompson and Brailer 2004).

Work will continue on the development of healthcare informatics standards to support continued development of electronic health records and health information exchange. It is a complex task and a dynamic one with constant activity in the development, modification, negotiation, and implementation process. The rapid growth of technology and the increasing need for healthcare data/information makes the task a daunting one. According to Kloss (2005) "The EHR is seen as essential for safe, effective care and a building block to wire the healthcare system. Now we need to better understand the prerequisites for interoperability so technology investments deliver on their promises. It is not sufficient to automate health records within organizations; there must be interconnectivity among providers and between providers and patients."

References

American Health Information Management Association. 2006a. *Pocket Glossary of Health Information Management and Technology*. Chicago: AHIMA,142.

AHIMA e-HIM Work Group on Regional Health Information Organizations (RHIOS). 2006b. Practice Brief: Using the SSN as a patient identifier. *Journal of AHIMA* 77(3):56A–D. http://library.ahima.org/xpedio/groups/public/documents/ahima/bok1_030976.hcsp?dDocName=bok1_030976.

AHIMA e-HIM Workgroup on Core Data Sets as Standards for the EHR. 2004. Practice brief: E-HIM strategic initiative: Core data sets. *Journal of AHIMA* 5(8):68A–D. http://library.ahima.org/xpedio/groups/public/documents/ahima/bok1_023159.hcsp?dDocName=bok1_023159.

American Medical Informatics Association (AMIA). 2007. Secondary Uses and Re-Uses of Healthcare Data: Taxonomy for Policy Formulation and Planning Document. http://www.amia.org/inside/initiatives/healthdata/2007/amiataxonomyncvhs.pdf.

American Society for Testing and Matierials (ASTM) Committee E31 on Healthcare Informatics. 2008. http://www.astm.org/COMMIT/COMMITTEE/E31.htm.

Brandt, M.D. 2000. Health informatics standards: A user's guide. *Journal of AHIMA* 71(4):39–43.

Carol, R. 2005. Short term forecast: Experts speak up on ONC's RFI, RFPs and the year ahead. *Journal of AHIMA*. 76(9):42–44, 46, 48, 50.

Centers for Medicare and Medicaid. Nursing Home Quality Initiatives. 2008. http://www.cms.hhs.gov/nursinghomequalityinits/25_nhqimds30.asp.

Centers for Medicare and Medicaid. Overview of the Medicare Post Acute Care Payment Reform Initiative.2008. http://www.cms.hhs.gov/DemoProjectsEvalRpts/downloads/PACPR_RTI_CMS_PAC_PRD_Overview.pdf.

Connecting for Health. Common Framework.2008 http://www.connectingforhealth.org/commonframework.

Consolidated Health Informatics Standards. 2008. http://www.hhs.gov/healthit/chiinitiative.html.

eHealth Initiative Blueprint: Building Consensus for Common Action. 2008. http://www.ehealthinitiative.org/blueprint.

Electronic Healthcare Network Accreditation Commission. 2008. http://www.ehnac.org/pr_2008-0818.html.

Food and Drug Administration Center for Drug Evaluation and Research (FDA CDER). 2008. National Drug Code Frequently Asked Questions. http://www.fda.gov/cder/ndc.

Food and Drug Administration Center for Drug Evaluation and Research. 2008. *CDER Data Standards Manual*. http://www.fda.gov/cder/dsm.

Health Information Technology Standards Panel. http://www.hitsp.org/about_hitsp.aspx.

Health Level Seven (HL7) ANSI Approved Standards. http://www.hl7.org.

Joint Commission. 2009. *Comprehensive Accreditation Manual*. Oakbrook Terrace, IL.

Kloss, L. 2005a. Standardized data: The difference for EHR solutions. *Journal of AHIMA* 76(2):23.

Kloss, L. 2005b. The NHIN comes into focus. http://www.hitsp.org/about_hitsp.aspx.

Mon, D.T. 2005. An update on the NHIN and RHIOs. *Journal of AHIMA* 76(6):56–57, 59.

National Council on Prescription Drug Programs. Basic Guide to Standards NCPDP. http://www.ncpdp.org/pdf/Basic_guide_to_standards.pdf.

National Alliance for Health Information Technology. Defining Key Health Information Technology Terms. Report to the Office of the National Coordinator for Health Information Technology.2008. http://www.nahit.org/images/pdfs/HITTermsFinalReport_051508.pdf.

National Center for Injury Prevention and Control. 2008. Data elements for emergency department systems, Release 1.0. Atlanta, GA: CDC and HHS. http://www.cdc.gov/ncipc/pub-res/deedspage.htm.

National Committee on Vital and Health Statistics. 2000a. Uniform Data Standards for Patient Medical Record Information. http://ncvhs.hhs.gov/hipaa000706.pdf.

National Committee on Vital and Health Statistics. 2000b. Toward a national health information infrastructure: Interim report. Washington, D.C.: HHS. http://www.ncvhs.hhs.gov/NHII2kReport.htm.

National Committee on Vital and Health Statistics. 2001. Information for health: A strategy for building the national health information infrastructure. Washington, D.C.: HHS. http://www.aspe.hhs.gov/sp/nhii.

National Library of Medicine. Unified Medical Language System: Rx Norm. 2008. http://www.nlm.nih.gov/research/umls/rxnorm.

Pothen, D.J. and B. Parmanto. 2000. XML furthers CPR goals. *Journal of AHIMA* 71(9):24–29.

Research Triangle Institute. Health Information Security and Privacy Collaboration: Executive Summary. 2008. http://privacysecurity.rti.org/Portals/0/HISPC_Exec_Summary_2008.pdf.

Rode, D. 2001. Understanding HIPAA transactions and code sets. *Journal of AHIMA* 72(1):26–32.

Schroeter, G. 2008. How XML is Improving Data Exchange in Healthcare. XML—the Site. http://www.softwareag.com/xml/library/schroeter_healthcare.htm.

Smith, D.A. 2001. Data transmission: a world of possibilities. *Journal of AHIMA* 72(5):26–27.

Sokolowski, R. 1999. XML makes its mark. *Journal of AHIMA* 70(10): 21–24.

Thompson, T.G. and D.J. Brailer. 2004. The decade of health information technology: Delivering consumer-centric and information-rich healthcare—Framework for strategic action. Washington, DC: HHS.

United States Department of Health and Human Services. Assuring a Health Dimension for the National Information Infrastructure. http://www.hhs.gov/healthit/documents/m20080603/10_2_hit_terms.pdf.

United States Department of Health and Human Services. HHS Officially Recognizes Certification Body to Evaluate Electronic Health Records. http://www.dhhs.gov/news/press/2006pres/20061026a.html.

United States Department of Health and Human Services.(HHS) MDS 3.0 for Nursing Homes. 2008. http://www.cms.hhs.gov/NursingHomeQualityInits/25_NHQIMDS30.asp.

Watzlaf, V.J.M., X. Zeng, C. Jarymowycz, and P.A. Firouzan. 2004 (January). Standards for the content of the electronic health record. *Perspectives in Health Information Management*. http://library.ahima.org/xpedio/groups/public/documents/ahima/bok1_022297.html.

World Health Organization. (n.d.) History of the Development of ICD. http://www.who.int/classifications/icd/en/HistoryOfICD.pdf.

Chapter 8
Paper-based and Hybrid Health Records

Rebecca B. Reynolds, EdD, RHIA
and Elizabeth D. Bowman, MPA, RHIA

Learning Objectives

- Describe the traditional (paper-based) health record and the hybrid health record and identify its primary uses and users
- Describe the transition from the paper record to the hybrid record to the electronic health record and the impact of the transition on the flow of health record information
- Identify the organizations and standards for the content of the health record
- Describe the major content areas of the health record, including administrative and demographic data, clinical data, and specialized content
- Outline the flow of health record information from initial encounter to final format
- Contrast methods that providers use to contribute information to the health record
- Give examples of general requirements for the primary documentation required in most health records, including the history and physical examination, progress notes, orders, and discharge summary
- Define quantitative and qualitative record analysis
- Define the purposes of the following processes: concurrent analysis and discharge analysis, open-record review, record review, point-of-care review, and continuous record review
- Compare an incomplete health record and a delinquent health record
- Identify forms and documentation requirements specific to facilities other than acute care hospitals, including ambulatory care, home care, hospice care, rehabilitation care, and long-term care facilities
- Explain the role of the health information management (HIM) professional in the forms control program
- Compare internal and external (contract) medical transcription services
- Summarize how new developments such as telecommuting and voice recognition technology will change the role of the medical transcriptionist
- Define the unit, serial, and serial-unit systems of record numbering and filing and the appropriate use of each, including methods of number assignment
- Explain the basic rules of terminal digit (TD) filing and the advantages of using TD filing concepts for productivity
- Describe policies and procedures on health record storage, retention, and destruction
- Define the functions of the master patient index

Key Terms

Accreditation Association for Ambulatory Health Care (AAAHC)
Administrative information
Advance directive
American College of Surgeons (ACS)
Association of Healthcare Documentation Integrity (AHDI)
Authentication
Authorization
Autoauthentication
Bar coding
Bylaws
Care path
Case manager
Certified medical transcriptionist (CMT)
Chart tracking
Charting by exception
Closed records
Closed-record review
Compliance
Computerized provider order entry (CPOE) system
Concurrent analysis
Conditions of Participation
Consent
Consultation
Continuous record review
Contract service
Delinquent health record
Demographic information
Digital dictation
Discharge analysis
Discharge summary
Disposition
Do not resuscitate (DNR) order
Electronic signature
Emergency Medical Treatment and Active Labor Act (EMTALA)
Enterprise-wide master patient index (EMPI)
Family numbering
History
Hybrid record
Incentive pay
Informed consent

Integrated health record
Licensure
Longitudinal health record
Master patient index (MPI)
Medical transcription
Medicare
Microfilming
National Association for Home Care (NAHC)
National Hospice and Palliative Care Organization (NHPCO)
Notice of Privacy Practices
Ongoing records review
Open-record review
Optical imaging technology
Outsourcing
Overlap
Overlay
Personal digital assistants (PDAs)
Point-of-care review
Principal diagnosis
Problem-oriented medical record (POMR)
Progress notes
Qualitative analysis
Quantitative analysis
Queuing
Retention
Retention schedules
Scanning
Serial numbering system
Serial-unit numbering system
Source-oriented health record
Straight numeric filing system
Telestaffing
Terminal-digit filing system
Transcription
Unique identifier
Unit numbering system
Universal chart order
Voice recognition technology

The patient health record is in the process of transitioning from a paper-based to an electronic format. Indeed, most healthcare facilities currently maintain their health records using a combination of the two formats (sometimes referred to as a hybrid health record system) in order to accommodate the many different ways in which patient information is provided. Today's health records include computer printouts as well as handwritten notes. A recent survey of the American Hospital Association's most wired hospitals and health systems in the United States revealed that the majority of these facilities have a hybrid health records. Data now arrive via electronic transfer from computerized laboratory or radiological testing or examination, through direct voice entry into a word-processing system, and from provider wireless devices and handheld personal computers. But as this chapter describes, the paper-based health record is a long way from being obsolete. The momentum to move away from paper is increasing dramatically, but a fully operational electronic health record (EHR) for all types of healthcare providers and facilities remains a future goal for the healthcare system.

This chapter traces the evolution of the health record and describes the different kinds of information it contains and the different formats in which it is kept. The chapter also focuses on the health information management professional's role in managing patient information, from the creation and storage of information to its long-term retention and eventual destruction, and in ensuring its accuracy, completeness, and security. Finally, this chapter describes the functions of the master or enterprise patient index, which is critical for proper patient identification and record location.

Evolution of the Health Record

The paper-based patient health record has evolved as medicine and medical technology have evolved. Once simply the notation of the patient's name and a brief description of his or her illness or injury, today the health record is a detailed collection of handwritten entries, transcribed reports, electronic data, and computer printouts reflecting the contributions of numerous healthcare providers.

Historical Overview

Health records have existed as long as there has been a need to communicate information about patient treatment. Archeological evidence indicates that maintaining information on patient care and treatment techniques is an ancient art.

Health records are maintained by all organizations that deliver healthcare services, including physician and provider offices, long-term care facilities, emergency clinics, rehabilitation facilities, home health agencies, behavioral health facilities, correctional institutions, and numerous types of delivery systems and organizations. Records vary depending on the type of facility. Healthcare records in acute care hospitals, for example, require rapid documentation by many providers. Patients are often in the hospital for life-threatening injuries or conditions, and many different providers access and record information in the patients' health records, on average, within a five-day time span. Records in nonacute care hospital settings have many of the same forms found in the acute care settings. The records also will contain many specialized forms to meet requirements related to those settings. Although format and content of the health record may differ among healthcare settings, all providers of care must maintain information to meet patient care needs and to comply with relevant laws, standards, and regulations.

Today's HIM professional is responsible for records that contain more paper than ever before and are maintained in a variety of formats other than paper. There is an increasing demand to share information among providers on a regional basis to improve continuity of care. The multiple formats of today's records are a challenge to the goal of uniform sharing of information. The skills of the HIM professionals are in great demand to ensure the quality of shared information.

Documentation and Maintenance Standards for the Health Record

Health records provide proof of what has been done for the patient. As the complexity of care has evolved, so has the need for improved documentation. Standards for record documentation and maintenance have been established and are refined and revised constantly. These standards and regulations have a major impact on what is documented in the health record.

The American College of Surgeons and the Joint Commission

The **American College of Surgeons** (ACS) provided the impetus for standardizing health records when it developed minimum standards for hospitals early in the twentieth century. It was evident to the ACS that standards were needed because candidates for membership were unable to produce proof of their experience with various types of surgical cases. Records were either nonexistent or of poor quality. The ACS Minimum Standard of 1917 included specific requirements for maintaining patient health records. The Joint Commission (formerly known as the Joint Commission on Accreditation of Healthcare Organizations) standards for documentation evolved from this original standard.

The Joint Commission is the successor organization to the ACS in the area of standardization. It assumed responsibility for the accreditation process in 1952 as a joint effort of the ACS, the American College of Physicians, the American Medical Association, and the American Hospital Association. Initially responsible for the accreditation of hospitals, the Joint Commission has since expanded its accreditation process to home health, long-term care, and other types of healthcare facilities.

The major source of information on the hospital or any healthcare facility is the health record. Joint Commission surveyors routinely review the health records of current patients to obtain knowledge about the facility's performance and process of care.

Medicare (CMS) Conditions of Participation

In 1965, the federal government passed legislation creating the **Medicare** program that provides healthcare insurance coverage to Americans over 65 years of age. Since then, the legislation has been expanded to cover persons disabled for two years as well as persons with chronic kidney disease. The Centers for Medicare and Medicaid Services (CMS), known as the Health Care Financing Administration (HCFA) until 2001, is the division of the federal Department of Health and Human Services responsible for developing and enforcing regulations regarding the participation of healthcare providers in the Medicare program.

The regulations for health record content and documentation were originally established in the **Conditions of Participation**. As health record documentation became increasingly important, CMS began to focus on reviewing it for medical necessity and compliance with the decision-making rules established by the federal government. In addition, CMS published guidelines for documenting **histories** and physical examinations and medical decision making that affect physician reimbursement.

State Licensure

Every state has certain **licensure** regulations that healthcare facilities must meet in order to remain in operation. Licensure regulations may include very specific requirements for the content, format, retention, and use of patient records. These regulations are established by state governments, usually under the direction of state departments of health.

Internal Standards

Bylaws, rules, and regulations are developed by the medical staff and approved by the board of trustees or governing body in every type of healthcare facility. In addition to describing the organization's manner of operation, bylaws outline the content of patient health records, identify the exact personnel who can enter information in health records, and restate applicable Joint Commission and CMS requirements. In addition, bylaws describe the time limits for completing patient health records. Surveyors review the bylaws to ensure that healthcare facilities abide by their own established rules and regulations and that the bylaws are in agreement with current Joint Commission standards. All medical staff personnel are required to abide by the approved bylaws.

The Modern Health Record

The modern health record includes the contributions of numerous healthcare providers. In addition, it includes information provided by the patient or a person acting on his or her behalf describing the reasons for the patient's visit to the healthcare provider and other pertinent background facts. The modern health record is patient centered, meaning that the patient is the focus of all documentation on the activities that revolve around him or her while under the provider's care.

Definition of the Health Record

The information in the health record must outline and justify the patient's treatment, support diagnosis of the patient's condition, describe the patient's progress and response to medications and services, and explain the outcomes of the care provided. As documentation of all the activities that revolve around the patient, the health record promotes continuity of care among all the providers who treat the patient.

The health record itself is the property of the healthcare facility. However, the patient has the right to be informed about the use of his or her protected health information (PHI). Federal Health Insurance Portability and Accountability Act (HIPAA) regulations require that the patient be notified of the uses of PHI through the notice of privacy practices.

Functions of Health Records and Health Information

To providers, the health record is valuable as the principal source of information in determining care for the patient. To the healthcare facility, it is valuable as a primary source of information in determining the reimbursement for care.

The primary functions of the health record are as follows:

- Facilitate the ongoing care and treatment of individual patients
- Support clinical decision making and communication among clinicians
- Document the services provided to patients in support of reimbursement
- Provide information for the evaluation of the quality and efficacy of the care provided
- Provide information in support of medical research and education
- Help facilitate the operational management of the facility
- Provide information as required by local and national laws and regulations

Ongoing Care and Treatment of Individual Patients

The most important use of the health record is patient care, and the person to whom the record is of most value is the patient. When physicians were the only caregivers, they knew the patient and family and decided how detailed the patient's records needed to be. Often a small card or a ledger listing the patient's problem at a particular time was all the record keeping physicians needed. As healthcare has come to depend on technology and the skilled personnel to use it, health records have become more complex. Patients often have multiple caregivers. Providers cannot remember all the information provided by the available technology to a large number of patients, and fast access to past information about the patient's care is vital to the continuity of care.

Clinical Decision Making and Communication

Health information serves the vital function of allowing all the patient's providers to enter and analyze information and to make decisions. Each member of the healthcare team has equal access to the information and can review what others are doing and communicate with them through the record. Thus, the health record is the healthcare team's primary reference and communication tool.

Reimbursement

Information in the health record is used to document the services provided to the patient so that coding and payment for the care provided can be made by those responsible for the bill. Insurance companies, managed care organizations, and CMS require that specific information be submitted to support the bill and to prove that the care provided was medically necessary.

Evaluation of the Quality and Efficacy of Care

The health record is used as a legal document to assess the quality of care rendered by the healthcare provider. The documentation in the record provides information for accrediting and licensing activities. The content of the health record also provides evidence of compliance with evidence-based medicine guidelines.

Medical Research and Education

Data from many health records can be aggregated (combined) and analyzed for research studies and provide statistical information on medical conditions and treatment modalities. As an example, public health agencies that need health information need data on certain diseases and conditions to develop prevention and control procedures as well as to monitor disease trends. Moreover, the information in health records serves to provide continuing education for students in a variety of health professions.

Operational Management

Information gathered from health records helps facilities plan for the future based on the types of patients and diagnoses treated. Aggregate statistical information provides data on the use of services, provider patterns, and other important issues. Management often uses the information to make comparisons with other facilities. Finally, the quality of information in the health record aids managerial decision making in terms of improving the quality of patient care.

Legal Purposes

The health record serves the legal interests of the patient, the provider, and the facility. It serves as evidence in legal cases addressing the treatment received by the patient or the extent of injuries. It serves to prove the patient's allegations in a malpractice case and also is used by the clinical provider and the facility to defend the care they provided the patient. The record is admissible as evidence under the business records provision because the documentation occurs routinely as part of the healthcare facility's daily operation.

The Longitudinal Health Record

The **longitudinal health record** is a record compiled about an individual from birth to death. It is valuable because all the information about a patient is maintained and accessible.

It serves as a reference of past history and avoids repetition of details and duplication of testing for the same conditions. Moreover, the longitudinal health record helps to prevent medical errors because information on allergies, drug interactions, surgeries, and past medical problems can be made available before treatment decisions are made. The physician can review the details of a patient's care and retrieve information needed at a later date.

A longitudinal health record is difficult to achieve in a paper-based record system because the patient typically has records at a variety of provider locations, such as physician offices, clinics, and hospitals, each of which often has a totally separate record system. The different records are not linked, making it difficult to access all needed patient information. Hybrid records do not improve this access issue as they are generally flat, text files and cannot be integrated into other healthcare provider systems. A longitudinal electronic health record would be especially valuable because it would allow information to be accessed from different locations. Many efforts are presently underway to develop the capability to share patient information electronically in order to improve quality, safety, and continuity of care.

Responsibility for Quality Documentation

The provider of care is responsible for ensuring that entries made in the record are of high quality. Although the facility's medical staff bylaws establish the rules and regulations for record content, the individual care providers are ultimately responsible for the quality of entries they make and authenticate. Figure 8.1 presents general documentation guidelines that every provider who writes or enters information in the patient health record should follow.

The quality of provider entries includes legibility. If an entry cannot be read, it must be assumed that it cannot or was not used in the patient care process.

The HIM professional is responsible for ensuring that providers understand the regulations and standards for proper documentation and for educating providers as changes occur. He or she should be involved in training residents and others who enter information so that standards are maintained and the record remains in its proper format.

The facility's administration is responsible for providing the equipment and support personnel to assist physicians in proper documentation. For HIM services, this includes computers, dictation and **transcription** equipment and services, as well as HIM staff members who assist in creating a high-quality record for accurate coding and billing for the facility's reimbursement.

Except in facilities owned by individuals or the government, a board of trustees or governing board has ultimate legal responsibility for the quality of care rendered in the facility. However, responsibility for patient care decisions and documentation of these decisions is delegated to the physician responsible for the patient.

Figure 8.1. Guidelines for documenting and maintaining the patient health record

These guidelines are considered standard or typical health information practices. Individual facilities develop their own policies based on institutional needs and laws and regulations.

1. All entries in the health record must be authenticated to identify the author (name and professional status) and dated.
2. No erasures or deletions should be made in the health record.
3. All entries in the paper health record should be in ink. Photocopying or scanning should be considered when colored ink or colored forms are used because some colors do not reproduce well.
4. Blank spaces should not be left in progress/nursing notes. If blanks are left, they should be marked out with an X so that additional information cannot be inserted on the paper out of proper date sequence.
5. If a correction must be made in a paper health record, one line should be neatly drawn through the error, leaving the incorrect material legible. The error then should be initialed and dated so that it is obvious that it is a corrected mistake.
6. The original report should always be maintained in the health record. Cumulative laboratory reports or computerized nursing notes may be replaced with the latest cumulative report. Faxed copies of admission orders and histories and physicals may be used as originals in the record. The usual signature requirements should be followed.
7. All blanks on forms should be completed, especially on consent forms.
8. When health records are filed incomplete (as directed by medical staff/health record committee policy), a statement should be attached to indicate that this is the case. The statement should be signed by the chief of staff/chair of the health record committee as specified in the policy.
9. Chart folder labeling, dotting, or other methods of identifying at a glance a particular type of patient, such as one with a drug or alcohol diagnosis or HIV-positive status, should be discouraged to prevent inadvertent breaches of patient confidentiality.

Check Your Understanding 8.1

Instructions: Answer the following questions on a separate sheet of paper.

1. What is the primary purpose of patient health information?
2. What are six other purposes or uses of patient health information?
3. What is the role of each of the following in the development of standards for health information: Joint Commission, Centers for Medicare and Medicaid Services, state licensure, and medical staff bylaws?
4. Why is a longitudinal health record valuable, and why is a longitudinal health record in a hybrid system difficult to achieve?
5. Who is responsible for ensuring the quality of health record documentation?

Content of the Health Record

All health records contain information that can be classified into two broad categories: administrative/demographic data and clinical data. All health record entries must be legible, complete, dated, and authenticated according to the healthcare organization's policies. Health records may be paper-based, electronic, or hybrid (a combination of formats). As health records evolve from paper to electronic and imaging formats, the term **hybrid record** is used to describe the record information format. Because the hospital record is the most complex in content, it will be used in describing the content of the record.

Administrative and Demographic Information

Administrative and demographic information is generally found on the front page of the paper health record and on the log-in screen in an electronic health record (EHR). The information entered provides facts that identify the patient and data related to payment and reimbursement and other operational needs of the healthcare facility. This information is entered into the system by administrative staff when the patient presents for care or may be entered electronically by the patient or staff from a physician's office.

Demographic Data

Demographic data represent one type of **administrative information**. Demographic data are collected prior to, or at the time of, admission or treatment at a healthcare facility. This is the first information the facility collects. Payment information also is part of the administrative information. Administrative information also includes the various **consents** for treatment and the use of patient information, notification of patient rights, and other nonclinical information.

Demographic information is a type of administrative information. Demographic information includes facts such as:

- Patient's name
- Patient's address
- Patient's telephone number
- Patient's date of birth
- Patient's next of kin
- Other identifying information specific to the patient

A **unique identifier** number is assigned to each health record. Facilities use the unique identifier to ensure that all information about the patient is inserted in the correct record or that the correct record is accessed when a query is entered into the computer system. Demographic information helps to specifically identify the patient and can be aggregated from many patients to provide statistical information that is vital for planning, research, statistics, and other needs.

Demographic information may be entered directly into the computer by admission or registration personnel. In cases where the patient is coming to the facility for elective, or voluntary, treatment or an operative procedure, he or she can provide this information prior to arrival at the facility. The patient usually provides the information directly, but in cases where the patient is a minor or is incapacitated or in an emergency situation, another individual may provide the information. In such cases, the record must state the name and relationship of the person providing the information in case the information has to be verified or amended.

The demographic information in a totally paper-based health record environment is usually on the first page, which is called the face sheet or front sheet. This information is often found on the initial computer screen in facilities that have EHRs.

Consent to Treatment

Through the consent process, the patient agrees to undergo the treatments and procedures to be performed by clinical caregivers. A general consent is often part of the admission or entry process into the healthcare facility. However, this general consent does not replace the individual consent forms the patient must complete and sign for each operation or special procedure to indicate that he or she is fully informed about the care to be provided. Written consents signed by the patient for experimental drugs and treatment and for participation in research also must be included in the health record. Refusal of treatment or procedures likewise must be written to ensure that the consequences of the decision to refuse treatment have been explained and the patient is aware of them.

Consent to Use or Disclose Protected Health Record Information

With regulatory changes put into place under HIPAA, upon admission to the facility or prior to treatment by the provider, patients must be informed about the use of individually identifiable health information. This **Notice of Privacy Practices** must explain and give examples of the uses of the patient's health information for treatment, payment, and healthcare operations, as well as other disclosures for purposes established in the regulations. (See appendix C.) If a particular use of information is not covered in the Notice of Privacy Practices, the patient must sign an **authorization** form specific to the additional disclosure before his or her information can be released. (See figure A.21 in appendix A.) HIPAA and the Privacy Rule are discussed in Chapter 10.

Consent to Special Procedures

In cases where the patient is coming to the facility for a specific procedure, an **informed consent** spelling out the exact details of the treatment must be signed by the patient or his or her legally authorized representative. This consent must show that the patient, or the person authorized to act for the patient, understands exactly what the procedure, test, or operation is going to be, including any possible risks, alternative methods, and outcomes.

Advance Directives

An **advance directive** is a written document, such as a living will, that states the patient's preferences for care in the event that the patient's condition prevents him or her from making care decisions. It also can be in the form of a durable power of attorney for healthcare in which the patient names another person to make medical decisions on his or her behalf in the event he or she is incapacitated. When the patient has a written advance directive, its existence must be noted in the health record. Patients or family members may bring the document to the facility to show the patient's wishes in case of terminal disease, traumatic injury, or cardiac arrest.

The advance directive can be included as a part of the health record, although its inclusion may not be required. There may be documentation by the physician of a discussion with the patient or the family about the patient's wishes, rather than a formal written document.

Patients must be informed that they have the right to have an advance directive. Further, they must be notified of the provider's policies regarding its refusal to comply with advance directives.

Acknowledgment of Receipt of Patient's Rights Statement

CMS requires that Medicare patients be informed of their rights, including the right to know who is treating them, the right to confidentiality, and the right to be informed about treatment. The patient's rights statement also must explain the patient's right to refuse treatment, to participate in care planning, and to be safe from abuse. The patient must sign a statement that these rights have been explained, and the signed statement must be made part of the health record. States often have laws and regulations regarding the rights that must be explained to patients, such as the right to privacy in treatment, to refuse treatment, and to refuse experimental treatments and drugs.

Property and Valuables List

Although facilities encourage patients to leave jewelry and other valuables at home, patients often will have with them property such as clothing, dentures, eyeglasses, hearing aids, and other personal articles. Patients may be asked to list these items and sign a release of responsibility form to absolve the facility of responsibility for loss or damage to their personal property. This form then becomes part of the patient health record.

Clinical Data

Clinical data include information related to the patient's condition, course of treatment, and progress. The patient health record includes mainly clinical data.

Medical History

The **history** is a summary of the patient's illness from his or her point of view. Its purpose is to allow the patient or his or her authorized representative to give the physician as much background information about the patient's illness as possible. The physician usually tailors the physical examination to symptoms described in the patient's history and begins an assessment. Thus, the history provides a base on which the physician can develop a plan of care.

Documentation guidelines for histories and physical examinations and medical decision making published by CMS affect physician reimbursement and are discussed further in chapter 14.

Components of the Medical History

The medical history has several components, including the following:

- *Chief complaint*: Told in the patient's own words (or those of the patient's representative), the chief complaint is the principal reason the patient is seeking care.
- *Present illness*: This component addresses what the patient feels the problem is and includes a brief description of the duration, location, and circumstances of the complaint.
- *Past medical history*: This consists of questions designed to gather information about past surgeries and other illnesses that might have a bearing on the patient's current illness. The physician asks about childhood and adult illnesses, operations, injuries, drug sensitivities, allergies, and other health problems.
- *Social and personal history*: The social history uncovers information about habits and living conditions that might have a bearing on the patient's illness, such as marital status, occupation, environment, and so on. Consumption of alcohol or tobacco products also may affect a patient's health. This section also should address the patient's psychosocial needs.
- *Family medical history*: The questions in this component allow the physician to learn whether other family members have conditions that might be considered genetic. Common questions concern cardiovascular diseases or conditions, renal diseases, history of cancer or diabetes, allergies, health of immediate relatives, and ages of relatives at death and causes of their deaths.
- *Review of systems*: This component consists of questions designed to cue the patient to reveal symptoms he or she may have forgotten, did not think were important, or neglected to mention when providing the historical information.

It is important that the person recording the history document whether the information was given by the patient or by another person in cases where the patient is unable to communicate.

Physical Examination

The physical examination is the actual comprehensive assessment of the patient's physical condition through examination and inspection of the patient's body by the physician. Its purpose is to obtain initial signs and symptoms so that appropriate treatment can begin. The end of the physical examination should include the impression, a list of the patient's problems based on the information obtained and the initial plan for the patient's care while in the hospital.

Components of the Physical Examination

The physical examination is conducted by observing the patient, palpating or touching the patient, tapping the thoracic and abdominal cavities, listening to breath and heart sounds, and taking the blood pressure. In a comprehensive physical examination, each body system of the patient is examined thoroughly. If the patient is admitted for a particular procedure, a more focused physical examination may take place.

Time Frame of the History and Physical Examination

The facility must have a policy that establishes a time frame for completing the history and physical. Most facilities set the time frame as the first 24 hours following admission and require that the history and physical be completed by the provider who is admitting the patient. Joint Commission and CMS require that the history and physical examination must be completed no more than 30 days before or 24 hours after admission and the report must be placed in the record within 24 hours after admission. If the history and physical have been completed within the 30 days prior to admission, there must be an updated entry in the medical record that documents an examination for any changes in the patient's condition, and this entry must be included in the record within the first 24 hours of admission. This is called an *interval history*. CMS rules specify that the history and physical examination be completed by the physician or other qualified individual who has medical staff privileges in accordance with state law and hospital policy. State licensure laws vary on the acceptable time frame for completion of the history and physical.

Joint Commission requires the history and physical examination to be recorded and made part of the patient health record prior to any operative procedure. When the physician chooses to dictate the history and physical, the dictated report must be transcribed and attached to the chart before the procedure. When the report is dictated but not transcribed, a written preoperative note covering the history and physical is acceptable only in an emergency. The physician must write an explanation of the emergency circumstances.

The HIM professional is responsible for ensuring that the most stringent time requirements are followed so that the facility is in **compliance** with state and federal laws and regulations, licensure standards, CMS Conditions of Participation, and accreditation requirements for the specific type of facility. Table 8.1 lists the information usually included in a complete medical history, and table 8.2 shows the information usually documented in the report of a physical examination.

Diagnostic and Therapeutic Orders

Physicians' orders direct the healthcare team. Orders may be for treatments, ancillary medical services, laboratory tests, radiological procedures, medications, devices, related materials, restraint, or seclusion. Orders change according to the patient's needs and responses to previous treatment. In the case of medications, the physician orders a specific drug in a particular dosage stating how often the drug is to be given, by what means (orally, intravenously, or by other method), and for how long. Certain categories of medications, such as narcotics and sedatives, have an automatic time limit or stop order. This means that these medications will be discontinued unless the physician gives a specific order to continue the medication. This method prevents patients from receiving drugs for a longer period of time than is necessary.

Orders for tests and services must demonstrate the medical necessity and explain the reason for the order. This expla-

Table 8.1. Information usually included in a complete medical history

Components of the History	Complaints and Symptoms
Chief complaint	Nature and duration of the symptoms that caused the patient to seek medical attention as stated in his or her own words
Present illness	Detailed chronological description of the development of the patient's illness, from the appearance of the first symptom to the present situation
Past medical history	Summary of childhood and adult illnesses and conditions, such as infectious diseases, pregnancies, allergies and drug sensitivities, accidents, operations, hospitalizations, and current medications
Social and personal history	Marital status; dietary, sleep, and exercise patterns; use of coffee, tobacco, alcohol, and other drugs; occupation; home environment; daily routine; and so on
Family medical history	Diseases among relatives in which heredity or contact might play a role, such as allergies, cancer, and infectious, psychiatric, metabolic, endocrine, cardiovascular, and renal diseases; health status or cause and age at death for immediate relatives
Review of systems	Systemic inventory designed to uncover current or past subjective symptoms that includes the following types of data: • *General:* Usual weight, recent weight changes, fever, weakness, fatigue • *Skin:* Rashes, eruptions, dryness, cyanosis, jaundice; changes in skin, hair, or nails • *Head:* Headache (duration, severity, character, location) • *Eyes:* Glasses or contact lenses, last eye examination, glaucoma, cataracts, eyestrain, pain, diplopia, redness, lacrimation, inflammation, blurring • *Ears:* Hearing, discharge, tinnitus, dizziness, pain • *Nose:* Head colds, epistaxis, discharges, obstruction, postnasal drip, sinus pain • *Mouth and throat:* Condition of teeth and gums, last dental examination, soreness, redness, hoarseness, difficulty in swallowing • *Respiratory system:* Chest pain, wheezing, cough, dyspnea, sputum (color and quantity), hemoptysis, asthma, bronchitis, emphysema, pneumonia, tuberculosis, pleurisy, last chest x-ray • *Neurological system:* Fainting, blackouts, seizures, paralysis, tingling, tremors, memory loss • *Musculoskeletal system:* Joint pain or stiffness, arthritis, gout, backache, muscle pain, cramps, swelling, redness, limitation in motor activity • *Cardiovascular system:* Chest pain, rheumatic fever, tachycardia, palpitation, high blood pressure, edema, vertigo, faintness, varicose veins, thrombophlebitis • *Gastrointestinal system:* Appetite, thirst, nausea, vomiting, hematemesis, rectal bleeding, change in bowel habits, diarrhea, constipation, indigestion, food intolerance, flatus, hemorrhoids, jaundice • *Urinary system:* Frequent or painful urination, nocturia, pyuria, hematuria, incontinence, urinary infections • *Genitoreproductive system:* Male—venereal disease, sores, discharge from penis, hernias, testicular pain, or masses; female—age at menarche, frequency and duration of menstruation, dysmenorrhea, menorrhagia, symptoms of menopause, contraception, pregnancies, deliveries, abortions, last Pap smear • *Endocrine system:* Thyroid disease; heat or cold intolerance; excessive sweating, thirst, hunger, or urination • *Hematologic system:* Anemia, easy bruising or bleeding, past transfusions • *Psychiatric disorders:* Insomnia, headache, nightmares, personality disorders, anxiety disorders, mood disorders

Table 8.2. Information usually documented in the report of a physical examination

Report Components	Content
General condition	Apparent state of health, signs of distress, posture, weight, height, skin color, dress and personal hygiene, facial expression, manner, mood, state of awareness, speech
Vital signs	Pulse, respiration, blood pressure, temperature
Skin	Color, vascularity, lesions, edema, moisture, temperature, texture, thickness, mobility and turgor, nails
Head	Hair, scalp, skull, face
Eyes	Visual acuity and fields; position and alignment of the eyes, eyebrows, eyelids; lacrimal apparatus; conjunctivae; sclerae; corneas; irises; size, shape, equality, reaction to light, and accommodation of pupils; extraocular movements; ophthalmoscopic exam
Ears	Auricles, canals, tympanic membranes, hearing, discharge
Nose and sinuses	Airways, mucosa, septum, sinus tenderness, discharge, bleeding, smell
Mouth	Breath, lips, teeth, gums, tongue, salivary ducts
Throat	Tonsils, pharynx, palate, uvula, postnasal drip
Neck	Stiffness, thyroid, trachea, vessels, lymph nodes, salivary glands
Thorax, anterior and posterior	Shape, symmetry, respiration
Breasts	Masses, tenderness, discharge from nipples
Lungs	Fremitus, breath sounds, adventitious sounds, friction, spoken voice, whispered voice
Heart	Location and quality of apical impulse, trill, pulsation, rhythm, sounds, murmurs, friction rub, jugular venous pressure and pulse, carotid artery pulse
Abdomen	Contour, peristalsis, scars, rigidity, tenderness, spasm, masses, fluid, hernia, bowel sounds and bruits, palpable organs
Male genitourinary organs	Scars, lesions, discharge, penis, scrotum, epididymis, varicocele, hydrocele
Female reproductive organs	External genitalia, Skene's glands and Bartholin's glands, vagina, cervix, uterus, adnexa
Rectum	Fissure, fistula, hemorrhoids, sphincter tone, masses, prostate, seminal vesicles, feces
Musculoskeletal system	Spine and extremities, deformities, swelling, redness, tenderness, range of motion
Lymphatics	Palpable cervical, axillary, inguinal nodes; location; size; consistency; mobility and tenderness
Blood vessels	Pulses, color, temperature, vessel walls, veins
Neurological system	Cranial nerves, coordination, reflexes, biceps, triceps, patellar, Achilles, abdominal, cremasteric, Babinski, Romberg, gait, sensory, vibratory
Diagnosis(es)	

nation is required because payers may not reimburse the facility if the reason for the test or treatment is not properly documented.

The legibility of orders is important to ensure that they are clearly understood by the personnel who must carry them out. Some facilities use a **computerized provider order entry (CPOE) system.** Verbal orders that are entered into the paper record or computer system by nonphysician personnel must be signed or authenticated by the provider authorized to give orders.

Clinicians Authorized to Give and Receive Orders

Orders must be written by the physician or verbally communicated to persons authorized to receive and record verbal orders either in person or by telephone. The person accepting the order should record the order, sign it and give his or her title, such as RN, PT, LPN, as appropriate. In some states, certified registered nurse practitioners and physician assistants are allowed to write or give verbal orders.

Medical staff policies and procedures must specifically state the categories of personnel authorized to accept orders. Verbal orders for medication are usually required to be given to, and to be accepted only by, nursing or pharmacy personnel. Some categories of personnel that may accept verbal or oral orders for services within the specific area of practice include physical therapists, registered nurse anesthetists, dietitians, and medical technologists.

The time the order was given should be in writing. Some facilities do not allow verbal orders for treatments or procedures that might put the patient at risk. The Joint Commission requires verbal orders to be repeated by the person accepting them to verify that they are clearly understood.

Signatures on Orders

Generally, orders must be dated and authenticated manually or electronically by the treating provider or providers responsible for the patient's care and who either wrote or gave the orders. In the case of verbal or telephone orders, the provider should sign them as soon as possible after giving them. Many facilities require the ordering provider to indicate that the telephone orders are accurate, complete, and final by authenticating them in writing or electronically within 24 hours. The timing requirements for signatures on orders are governed by state law, facility policy, accreditation standards, and government regulations and may vary from facility to facility. CMS regulations state that in the absence of state law, the time limit for authentication will be within 48 hours.

For years, HIM department personnel carefully reviewed each order and marked those with missing signatures so that each could be individually signed by the responsible provider after discharge. However, signing orders after discharge does not affect the patient's care process, so many facilities no longer routinely review orders for signature following patient discharge. A review of orders is part of the concurrent or **open-record review** process; thus, orders can be signed in a timely manner and providers with patterns of unsigned orders can be detected. A comparison of orders to laboratory and other ancillary reports and to nursing documentation is another way to ensure that all orders are carried out.

Some facilities are developing standing, or standard, orders for certain procedures that all physicians can use when performing the particular procedure. Other facilities require an additional order to implement the standing orders, and still others allow a registered nurse to initiate the standing orders because the medical staff has previously approved them.

CMS regulations provide a five-year exception to the rules regarding signatures on verbal orders. This exception allows verbal (telephone or oral) orders to be signed by another provider responsible for the patient's care even if the order did not originate with that provider. The CMS rules retain the current requirements that the use of verbal orders should be infrequent and used only when the orders cannot be written or given electronically. The CMS regulations further state that verbal orders must only be accepted by persons authorized by hospital polices and procedures and state and federal law.

Special Types of Orders

Do not resuscitate (DNR) orders must contain documentation that the decision to withhold cardiopulmonary resuscitation (CPR) was discussed, when the decision was made, and who participated in the decision. This discussion is often documented in the **progress notes**. Generally, patients are presumed to have consented to CPR unless a DNR order is present in the record. Do not resuscitate orders may be part of the advance directives in the record.

Orders for seclusion and restraint, including drugs used for restraint, must comply with facility policies and CMS regulations, state laws, and Joint Commission requirements. These should never be standing or as-needed orders but, instead, such drugs must be ordered only when necessary to protect the patient or others from injury or harm. Specific time limits for these orders must be followed, and there must be continuous oversight of the patient under restraint or seclusion.

Discharge Orders

Discharge orders for hospital patients must be in writing and can only be issued by a physician. When a patient leaves against medical advice, this fact should be noted in lieu of a discharge order because the patient was not actually discharged. In the case of death, some facilities require that a discharge to the morgue order be written.

Clinical Observations

Clinical observations of the patient are documented in the health record in several areas, including progress notes, consultation reports, and ancillary notes, as described here.

Medical Services

Progress notes are chronological statements about the patient's response to treatment during his or her stay in the facility. Facility procedures and policies must state exactly what categories of personnel are allowed to write or enter information into progress notes. Generally, these personnel include physicians, nurses, physical therapists, occupational therapists, respiratory therapists, social workers, case managers, registered dietitians (RDs), nurse anesthetists, pharmacists, radiologic technologists, speech therapists, and others providing direct treatment or consultation to the patient. Each person authorized to enter documentation into the progress notes must write or enter his or her own note, authenticate and date it, and indicate authorship by signing his or her full name and title. In some cases all types of practitioners record progress notes on a common form (integrated progress notes) while in other record formats there may be separate sections for physician, nursing, and therapy progress notes.

Each progress note should review changes in the patient's condition, findings based on the facts of the case, test results, and response to treatment, as well as an analysis of the findings. The final part of the note contains the decisions or actions planned for future care. When writing in a paper patient record, providers must avoid leaving blank spaces between progress notes to prevent information from being added out of sequence.

Flowcharts are an effective way to illustrate the patient's progress and can be computerized to demonstrate progress or to keep track of certain data. Many physicians and other providers use handheld personal computers to maintain ongoing flowchart information about patients, such as blood glucose levels over time.

How often progress notes are written depends on the patient's condition, and the frequency is generally established by the healthcare facility or payers of care. In a hospital, the physician primarily responsible for the patient's care is often required to write a progress note daily. Doing so shows the physician's involvement and that he or she is aware of changes in the patient's condition.

Consultations are additional opinions of specialists. The attending physician may request that the specialist see the patient and prepare a consultation report. Each consultant is responsible for writing, dictating, or entering his or her own report. The report should show evidence of the consultant's review of the record examination of the patient and any pertinent findings, opinions, and recommendations. Moreover, the documentation should show that the physician requesting the consultation reviewed the report.

Nursing Services

Nursing personnel have the most frequent contact with patients, and their notes provide the complete record of the patients' progress and condition and demonstrate the continuity of care. Licensed registered nurses, licensed practical nurses (sometimes called licensed vocational nurses), and nursing assistants record the patient's vital signs and facts of the physician's orders being carried out, observe the patient's response to treatment interventions, and describe the patient's condition and complaints as well as the outcome of care as reflected in the patient's status at discharge or termination of treatment. The method most commonly used by nurses to enter notes is narrative detailed documentation.

Nursing personnel begin recording information in the health record when the patient is admitted to the facility. They coordinate the patient's care to ensure that orders are carried out. The initial nursing assessment must summarize the date, time, and method of admission; the patient's condition, symptoms, and vital signs; and other information. Nurses may use a variation of the SOAP (subjective, objective, assessment, and plan) notes from the problem-oriented medical record format (discussed later in this chapter) when recording notes. All nursing notes must be signed by the individuals who provided the service or observed the patient's condition. Full names and titles are required with each entry.

Charting by exception, or focus charting, is a method of charting only abnormal or unusual findings or deviations from the prescribed plan of care. A complete assessment is performed every shift or every eight hours. When events differ from the assessment or the expected norm for a particular patient, the notes should focus on that particular event and include the data, assessment, intervention, and response. Flow sheets and care plans may be used to illustrate changes in the patient's condition. The purpose of charting by exception is to reduce repetitive record keeping and documentation of normal events. Bedside terminals and direct input of monitoring information and other computerization of nursing observations and medication distribution save nurses a great deal of time because information does not have to be rewritten numerous times.

Medication records are maintained by nursing staff for all patients and include medications given, time, form of administration, and dosage and strength. The records are updated each time the patient is given his or her medication. The health record must reflect when a medication is given in error, indicating what was done about it and the patient's response. Adverse drug reactions must be fully documented and reported to the provider and to the performance improvement or risk management program according to guidelines established by the facility.

Flow sheets are often used in addition to narrative notes for intake and output records showing how much fluid the patient consumed and how much was eliminated. In addition, blood glucose records are often flowcharted for ease of comparison. Degree of pain is another aspect of the patient's condition that is commonly flowcharted.

Nurses are responsible for maintaining records of patient transfers (to surgery, to another room, or level of care) as well as visits to physician or treatment offices and other locations outside the facility.

Case managers are nurses, social workers, or other personnel who are responsible for assisting the patient through the care process. The case management process improves quality of care because care is scheduled in an orderly way and fragmentation is reduced. Hospitals, managed care organizations, and other facilities use case managers to improve coordination of care, scheduling, and discharge planning. Many facilities use predetermined **care paths** that are specific to diagnoses or conditions; case managers ensure that patients receive care according to the care path. Care paths are also called clinical pathways, critical paths, and clinical algorithms.

Ancillary Services

Laboratory and radiology reports and reports from other ancillary services, such as EKGs (electrocardiographs) and EEGs (electroencephalographs), must be signed by the physician responsible for the interpretations. A pathologist is responsible for the work of the pathology laboratory; a radiologist is responsible for the work of the radiology department. Many states have separate **retention schedules** for the actual x-rays that differ from the retention time frames for other health records. The typed interpretations of the radiology or other reports become part of the health record and are kept as long as the health records are kept. Images may be part of a computerized picture archiving communication system (PACS) which have a separate retention schedule than the health record.

The laboratory conducts tests on blood, urine, sputum, and other body fluids. Many specialized tests are performed in the laboratory to provide information the physician can use to make a diagnosis, including analyses of specimens removed during surgery. Laboratory results in a computerized environment are available to the provider as soon as they are entered into the computer. In most facilities, a laboratory summary of computerized results is generated consistently throughout the patient's stay, with a final summary completed after discharge. These multipage summaries are printed and made part of the patient health record. Some facilities use manually completed laboratory forms divided into an original and several copies. The original report is the one that should be included in the record. Most facilities require the original laboratory report to be placed in the health record within 24 hours. In many hybrid systems, this information is computer output to laser disk (COLD) fed into the hospital information system rather than being kept as a print-out in the final record. HIM personnel must ensure all COLD fed reports come from the source of primary system into the system which maintains the legal health record. This transfer of data may require interfaces and requires oversight to ensure the information is part of the permanent record.

Healthcare facility policies and procedures must state that the practitioner approved by the medical staff to interpret diagnostic procedures, such as nuclear medicine procedures, MRIs, EEGs, and EKGs, should sign and date his or her interpretations. The interpretations then become part of the health record. Scans and videotapes, tracings, or other actual recordings are often COLD fed directly into the hospital information system. Providers may view such recordings, but the recordings do not become part of the permanent record. It is important that all tests or procedures ordered have corresponding reports in the health record.

Orders and records of services rendered to patients from rehabilitation, physical therapy, occupational therapy, audiology, or speech pathology should be included in the record as appropriate to the patient. These reports must contain evaluations, recommendations, goals, course of treatment, and response to treatment. Nutritional care plans need to be developed in compliance with a physician order and information on nutrition and diet should be included in the discharge plan and transfer orders.

Surgical Services

The operative section of the health record includes the anesthesia record, the intraoperative record, and the recovery record. The history and physical examination, informed consents signed by the patient or his or her authorized representative, and the postoperative progress note also are part of the documentation about the operative procedure. Every patient's record must include a complete history and physical examination prior to any surgery or invasive procedure unless there is an emergency. When the history and physical report is dictated, it must be included in the record.

Moreover, the anesthesiologist or the certified registered nurse anesthetist must write a pre-anesthesia evaluation or an updated evaluation prior to surgery. This evaluation must cover information on the anesthesia to be used, risk factors, allergy and drug history, potential problems, and a general assessment of the patient's condition. An intraoperative anesthesia record must be maintained of all events during surgery, including complete information on the anesthesia administration, blood pressure, pulse, respiration, and other monitors of the patient's condition. Finally, after surgery, the appropriate anesthesia personnel must write a postoperative anesthesia follow-up report. Outpatient surgical cases also must include post-anesthesia evaluations. Records of post-anesthesia visits should indicate any unusual events or complications of anesthesia. CMS regulations state that any individual qualified to administer anesthesia can complete the post-anesthesia evaluation rather than limiting the post-anesthesia documentation completion to the individual who actually administered the patient's anesthesia.

The operative report itself must be written or dictated by the surgeon immediately after surgery and must include the names of the surgeon and assistants, technical procedures performed, findings, specimens removed, estimated blood loss, and postoperative diagnosis. The surgeon must enter a brief postoperative progress note in the record immediately after surgery before the patient leaves the operating suite to enable follow-up care. Most facilities have dictation areas near the operative suite or cardiac catheterization laboratories to allow surgeons to dictate the operative reports immediately. However, the written postoperative progress note must be completed to provide information for patient care until the transcribed report is placed in the patient record, usually 12 to 24 hours after surgery. The postoperative progress notes and the dictation and transcription of operative reports must be carefully monitored to ensure that this documentation is placed in the health record in a timely manner.

Pathology reports are required for cases in which a surgical specimen is removed or expelled during a procedure. The medical staff and a pathologist must decide which specimens require both a microscopic and macroscopic (gross or with the naked eye) evaluation of the tissue and which require a gross examination only. These reports are part of the operative section of the health record and must be signed by the pathologist. The preoperative diagnosis and pathological diagnosis can then be compared for quality of care purposes.

Information on the patient's discharge from the postoperative or post-anesthesia care unit must be documented and signed by the licensed independent practitioner responsible for the discharge or by the provider verifying that the patient is ready for discharge according to specific discharge criteria. The operative section also will contain data on implants, including product numbers, and additional information for follow-up.

Organ Transplantation

CMS requires hospitals to inform families of the opportunity to donate organs, tissues, or eyes. All patients meeting the United Network of Organ Sharing (UNOS) criteria must be evaluated and the documentation must be part of the health record. Facilities participating in the transplant program are required to share patient information and provide access to health records to representatives of approved Organ Procurement Organizations (OPO). Documentation showing that the organ procurement organization has been notified regarding a patient near death must be included in the health record so that anatomical gifts can be preserved and used. Samples forms and other information are available on the UNOS Web site.

Conclusions at Termination of Care

At the time of discharge, the physician must summarize the patient's condition at the beginning of treatment and basic information about tests, examinations, procedures, and results occurring following treatment. This conclusion at termination of care is called the discharge summary.

Discharge Summary

The **discharge summary**, also called the clinical resume, provides details about the patient's stay while in the facility and is the foundation for future treatment. It is prepared when the patient is discharged or transferred to another facility or when the patient expires. The summary states the patient's reason for admission and gives a brief history explaining why he or she needed to be hospitalized. Pertinent laboratory, x-ray, consultation, and other significant findings, as well as the patient's response to treatment or procedures, are included. In addition to a description of the patient's condition at discharge, the discharge summary delineates specific instructions given to the family for future care, including information on medications, referrals to other providers, diet, activities, follow-up visits to the physician, and the patient's final diagnoses. The discharge summary must be authenticated and dated by the physician.

Some facilities require the final diagnoses to be recorded and the discharge summary to be dictated or written at the time of discharge. The information in the discharge summary is extremely important to meet the facility's coding, billing, and reimbursement needs. In some facilities, a paper discharge summary form with an outline of contents is used to ensure that all items are included. A copy of the discharge form including follow-up instructions should be provided to the patient or caregivers at discharge.

When a patient expires in the hospital, the facility often requires the physician who pronounced death to write a note that gives the time and date of death. The death note is in addition to the discharge summary required in all death cases no matter how long the patient was in the facility.

A discharge summary is not typically required for patients who are in the hospital for 48 hours or less. Such patients usually have a short-stay or short-service record or a final discharge progress note. This one-page form can be used to record the history and physical examination, the operative report, the discharge summary, and discharge instructions. When the patient is admitted to the facility, the reason for admission must be recorded. When the patient dies 48 hours or less after admission, the short-stay record is insufficient and a complete discharge summary must be prepared. Most facilities do not require a discharge summary for normal newborns and obstetrical cases without complications, as long as there is a final progress note.

Typically, the discharge summary must be completed within 30 days after discharge; however, facility policy may require a quicker completion date. When a patient is transferred, the physician should complete the discharge summary within 24 hours.

At the time of discharge, the principal diagnosis and other diagnoses should be recorded completely without symbols or abbreviations on the health record summary sheet (the face sheet) or discharge summary or on another form prescribed by the facility. The **principal diagnosis** is defined as the condition determined, after study, to be chiefly responsible for occasioning the patient's admission to the hospital.

Healthcare facilities must determine what information goes with the patient when he or she is transferred to another level of care such as a rehabilitation or skilled nursing facility. When the transfer is to an affiliated institution that is part of the same healthcare system, the original patient record is transferred with the patient and new orders are written at the receiving institution to initiate care. A discharge summary is generally required.

Discharge Plan

Discharge planning information regarding further treatment of the patient should be part of the acute care health record. The discharge planning process begins at admission and must include information on the patient's ability to perform self-care as well as other services needed by the patient. The case manager, the social worker, utilization review personnel, or nursing personnel may write this plan.

Records Filed with the Health Record

In the past, there was much debate about whether patient records received from other facilities should be made part of the receiving facility's health record. Some facilities released the information from all facilities because all of it was used in treatment decisions. Other facilities maintained that they were responsible only for the information originating in their own facilities and had requestors obtain original records from the originating facility. HIPAA regulations now require that all information, including information from other facilities, is part of the health record. It is important for healthcare facilities to develop polices to determine exactly what health information mailed, faxed, or personally brought to the facility by the patient or patient's family becomes part of the receiving facility's designated health record. A good practice is to have the attending physician review copies and note which documents should be made permanent parts of the record. Any extraneous copies, x-rays, or other information should be returned to the patient. Personal health records (PHRs) will create new challenges for HIM professionals. As consumers use technology to create PHRs, HIM professionals must determine when and how to incorporate electronic PHRs into the facility's health record.

Facilities maintain information on the release of information from the patient record explaining what was released, to whom the information was released, and the date. This required information is often filed with the health record but should not be released when the patient record is released. Federal regulations now require that facilities provide an "accounting of disclosure" under the HIPAA regulations, but most facilities have traditionally maintained this type of information. (See figure A.22 in appendix A.)

Specialized Health Record Content

The content of the patient health record varies according to the type of care provided. Many facilities offer specialized services requiring special documentation that is not found in every patient's record. Joint Commission standards and regulations often specify particular content to include in the record. The following sections describe various specialized services and their records.

Obstetrical Care

The prenatal record, which is kept in the physician's office to document prenatal care as it occurs, serves as the history and physical for an obstetrical patient. When the patient requires a Cesarean section, however, the record must include a full history and physical or a detailed admission progress note explaining the need for a Cesarean section.

A labor and delivery record indicates the name of the patient, maiden name, date of delivery, sex of infant, name of physician, name of persons assisting, any complications, type of anesthesia used, name of person administering anesthesia, and names of others present at delivery. In the case of a stillborn infant, a separate patient record is not created; rather, information is recorded in the mother's delivery record.

Neonatal Care

Newborns are considered separate patients with separate health records. The newborn patient record must include an admission examination and a discharge examination. Usually, special chart forms for progress notes, orders, and nursing notes are included. When the patient has been in the newborn intensive care unit, a complete discharge summary is required.

Emergency Care

Emergency health records may be filed separately or incorporated into the health record when the patient is admitted to the same facility. When the records are filed separately, the emergency record must be available when the patient is readmitted or seeks care in the future. Most of the emergency information is recorded on one sheet in a paper health record format. Additional sheets may include laboratory, radiology, and other tests; consent forms; and follow-up instructions.

The content of the emergency health record should generally include the following items:

- Identification data
- Time of arrival
- Means of arrival (by ambulance, private automobile, or police vehicle)
- Name of person or organization transporting patient to the emergency department
- Pertinent history, including chief complaint and onset of injury or illness
- Significant physical findings
- Laboratory, x-ray, and EKG findings
- Treatment rendered
- Conclusions at termination of treatment
- Disposition of patient, including whether sent home, transferred, or admitted
- Condition of the patient upon discharge or transfer
- Diagnosis upon discharge
- Instructions given to the patient or the family regarding further care and follow-up
- Signatures and titles of the patient's caregivers

When the patient leaves before being seen or against medical advice (AMA), this fact should be noted on the emergency department form. Consent forms for treatment also must be included in the record. In cases where the patient is in critical condition or otherwise unable to sign the consent, an explanation should be documented. A copy of the emergency record should be made available to the provider of follow-up care.

Most states require facilities to maintain an additional chronological record or to register all patients visiting the emergency department with name, date, time of arrival, and record number. This registration also includes the names of patients who were dead on arrival.

Emergency patients must be made aware of their rights. Transfer and acceptance policies and procedures must be delineated to ensure that facilities comply with the **Emergency Medical Treatment and Active Labor Act** (EMTALA) and state regulations regarding transfers. Patients cannot be transferred or refused treatment for reasons related to ability to pay or source of payment nor can hospitals determine that space is unavailable based on ability to pay or source of payment. Anyone who requests or requires an examination must be provided an appropriate medical screening examination by hospital staff to determine whether a medical emergency exists. Further, the hospital must stabilize the medical emergency by ensuring an airway and ventilation, by controlling hemorrhage, and by stabilizing or splinting fractures before a patient can be transferred. The hospital must maintain screening examinations for a period of five years. Non-emergency patients are typically examined by the triage nurse or other emergency department staff, and referred to a minor medical clinic, physician office, or other non-emergency patient care facility.

Appropriate transfer means that the receiving hospital agrees to receive the patient and provide appropriate medical treatment. Records must be provided to the receiving hospital, and the patient or responsible person must understand the medical necessity of the transfer.

Ambulatory or Outpatient Care

Ambulatory or outpatient care means that patients move from location to location and do not stay overnight. Ambulatory or outpatient care may be given in a freestanding clinic, a clinic that is part of a larger hospital system, or a physician or other provider office. When patients are in a clinic affiliated with a hospital, the entire health record should be available. Joint Commission requires ambulatory patients to have a summary list by the third visit that includes known diagnoses, conditions, procedures, drug allergies, and medications. It also requires each ambulatory care record to contain a history and physical examination, operative reports, diagnostic and therapeutic procedures, consultations, follow-up notes, observations of patients, and discharge notes at the conclusion or termination of treatment. Contents vary depending on the treatment received.

Ambulatory facilities that only perform surgery are called ambulatory surgery centers (ASCs). Patients having surgery at any type of ambulatory facility must have a history and physical examination prior to surgery, consents, an operative note, a postoperative progress note, and the same anesthesia information as an operative patient in the hospital. In addition, the record must document instructions for postoperative care and postoperative follow-up. Clinics often call patients after surgery to check on their condition, and these calls should be documented in the record. The **Accreditation Association for Ambulatory Health Care** (AAAHC) requires that the history and physical examination, laboratory reports, radiology reports, operative reports, and consultations be signed in a timely manner. Laboratory and other reports must be included in the patient record as soon as possible.

Traditionally, physician office records have been less comprehensive than hospital medical records. Physicians must develop standardized formats and comprehensive documentation practices.

Behavioral Health Care

Behavioral health records, also known as mental health records or psychiatric records, must include diagnostic and assessment information related to both the patient's mental condition and his or her physical health.

Home Health Services

According to the **National Association for Home Care** (NAHC), the term *home care* covers many types of services "delivered at home to recovering, disabled, chronically or terminally ill persons in need of medical, nursing, social, or therapeutic treatment and/or assistance with the essential activities of daily living" (NAHC 2005). Physicians order home care services that may include visits from many types of healthcare providers, including physical and occupational therapists and nurses. Patient health records must contain a legible record of each visit describing what was done to or for the patient during the visit. The providers working with patients must develop and document periodic plans of care. Specific forms developed by CMS are used in home care to document and update the plan of care.

Hospice Care Services

The **National Hospice and Palliative Care Organization** (NHPCO) defines hospice care as a "team-oriented approach to expert medical care, pain management, and emotional and spiritual support expressly tailored to the patient's needs and wishes" (NHPCO 2005). Because hospice care is delivered to patients with all types of terminal illnesses, the family is involved in the care and support is given by the hospice organization. Hospice services are provided in numerous types of settings, including homes, hospitals, and long-term care facilities (NHPCO 2005). Special documentation for the election of hospice care is required for CMS to reimburse for services.

Rehabilitation Services

Rehabilitation covers a wide range of services provided to build or rebuild the patient's abilities to perform the usual activities of daily life. Among these services are physical therapy, occupational therapy, and speech therapy.

Physical therapists work in numerous types of facilities, ranging from acute care to long-term care and patient homes, setting goals for patients and helping them reach their goals by building muscle strength and respiratory and circulatory efficiency. Their patients include those who have been disabled for a number of reasons, including birth defect, trauma, and illness. Treatments include exercise, manipulation, heat therapy, light therapy, the use of electricity, and therapeutic massage. In addition to setting treatment goals, physical therapists have to document patient progress.

Occupational therapists are part of the rehabilitation team and work with patients to restore their ability to perform the usual functions of daily life, such as eating, dressing, preparing food, working, and handling other activities specific to the patient. Speech therapists and other specialized therapists are important members of the rehabilitation team and work together to achieve a variety of patient goals. Rehabilitation professionals must assess patients and provide services based on a plan of care for each patient.

Rehabilitation Services may be accredited by either the Joint Commission or the Commission on Accreditation of Rehabilitation Facilities (CARF). CARF standards are specific to rehabilitation facilities. The organization provides accreditation surveys and awards accreditation based on compliance with the standards.

Long-term Care

Long-term care describes the care provided for extended periods of time to patients recovering from illness or injury. Long-term care facilities offer a combination of services, ranging from independent living to assisted living to skilled nursing care. Rehabilitation services are often part of the long-term care plan. The long-term care record must document a comprehensive assessment that includes items in the Minimum Data Set (MDS) to meet CMS requirements stated in 42 CFR 483.20. (Chapter 7 addresses MDS standards for data collection.)

In addition, long-term facilities must meet state requirements. Individualized patient care plans must be developed and included in the health record. These plans must cover the potential for rehabilitation, the ability to perform activities of daily living, medications prescribed, and other aspects of care.

As with acute care facilities, the frequency of progress notes depends on the patient's condition. The focus in long-term care is on the achievement of goals. The HIM functions are similar to those in other types of facilities, but a great deal of concurrent review is required. Paper records of patients who have been in the facility for an extended period of time must be divided with the most current information maintained on the nursing unit, with the rest filed elsewhere to save space at the nursing station.

Check Your Understanding 8.2

Instructions: On a separate piece of paper, match the contents with the appropriate part of the record by placing the letter for the form in the blank preceding the description of the form's content.

1. ___ Directions given for drugs, devices, and healthcare treatments
2. ___ Comprehensive assessment of patient to determine signs and symptoms
3. ___ Records maintained by physical therapists, speech therapists, respiratory therapists, and other providers of special services
4. ___ Protocol for the process of care
5. ___ Summary of background information about the patient's illness
6. ___ Statement of patient's wishes or instructions for care
7. ___ Conclusions at the termination of care
8. ___ Observations of the patient's response to treatment
9. ___ Record that must contain the time and means of arrival and the name of the person transporting the patient to the facility
10. ___ Opinions of specialists

a. Care path
b. History
c. Physical examination
d. Orders
e. Consultations
f. Nursing notes
g. Advance directives
h. Emergency record
i. Discharge summary
j. Ancillary notes

Format of the Paper-based and Hybrid Health Record

The term *format* refers to the organization of information in the health record. There are many possible formats, and most facilities use a combination of arrangements. During the patient care process, the paper-based health record is often in a different format than after the patient is discharged. This is especially true in facilities with a hybrid health record that in some cases scan the paper portions of the record after the discharge of the patient. Regardless of the media of the health record, a systematic format for the health record ensures all users of the health record can easily locate the patient information required for their needs.

Source-oriented Health Records

The **source-oriented health record** is the conventional or traditional method of maintaining paper-based health records. In this method, health records are organized according to the source, or originating, department that rendered the service (for example, all lab reports are filed together; all radiological reports are filed together, and so on).

When the patient is in active treatment in the hospital, for example, the record is often maintained in reverse chronological order, with the most recent information in the front of each record section. Tabs allow easy reference to the grouped reports, enabling staff to quickly find the patient's response to treatment.

After the patient is discharged, many facilities rearrange the record in chronological order. However, the arrangement is still source oriented with all labs together, all progress notes together, and all other related reports filed together in date order. Figure 8.2 shows the arrangement of forms for records maintained in a large acute care hospital. Sometimes facilities leave the record in the same format as it was maintained while the patient was in the facility rather than spend the time rearranging the forms. This is called **universal chart order**. Many hybrid health record systems are source oriented and maintain the organization and format of the health record by scanning and indexing the forms based on the "tabs" from the paper-based health record.

Problem-oriented Health Records

Lawrence Weed developed the **problem-oriented medical record** (POMR) in the 1970s. The POMR is comprised of the problem list, the database (the history and physical examination and initial lab findings), the initial plan (tests, procedures, and other treatments), and progress notes organized so that every member of the healthcare team can easily follow the course of patient treatment (Weed 1970).

A distinctive feature of the POMR is the problem list, which serves as the record's table of contents. All relevant problems—medical, social, or other—that may have an impact on the patient are listed with a number. As problems are resolved, the resolution is noted; new problems are added as they occur. The problem list serves as a permanent index that providers can quickly check to review the status of past and current problems. Entries in the record include the number of the problem addressed.

The most recognizable component of the POMR is the SOAP format, which is a method for recording progress notes. SOAP is an easy acronym that helps providers remember the specific and systematic decision-making process. *S* stands for subjective findings and includes statements from the patient's viewpoint such as symptoms. The subjective findings are followed by objective findings (the *O* in the acronym) such as laboratory and test results as well as observations and findings from the physical examination. *A* stands for assessment, which consists of appraisals and judgments based on the findings and observations. The *P* stands for plan, which states the methods to be followed in addressing the problems. Although the full POMR as championed by Weed has not been adopted universally, many physicians and providers routinely use the SOAP method or an adaptation of it to document progress notes and also include a problem list in the record.

Integrated Health Records

The content of the **integrated health record** is arranged in strict chronological order. Different types of information and sources of information are mixed together according to the dates on the entries. The order of the record is determined by the date the information was entered, the date of the service,

Figure 8.2. Patient record content

This is not a complete list but does show the types of forms found in most acute care hospitals.

- Admission record (face sheet)
- Discharge diagnosis information
- Identification data
- General conditions of admission form
- Medicare statements
- History
  - Chief complaint
  - Present illness
  - Review of systems
  - Past history
  - Family history
  - Social history
- Physical examination
- Impression or working diagnosis (part of history and physical or admission note)
- Plan of care (part of history and physical or admission notes)
- Prenatal and labor record
  - Labor and delivery summary
  - Admission assessment
  - Labor progress record
  - Infant identification sheet
- Physician office record
- Copies of records from other facilities
- Reports of tests and results
  - Laboratory
    - Transfusions
    - Bone marrow
    - Toxicology
    - Other special reports
  - Radiology includes scans, ultrasounds, arteriograms, MRI, and so on
    - EEG
    - EKG
    - Echocardiograms
    - Treadmills
    - Holter monitor
    - Doppler
- Therapy reports
  - Physical therapy
  - Occupational therapy
  - Cardiac rehabilitation
  - Respiratory therapy
  - GI lab
  - Cardiac catheterization
  - Other specialty areas
- Progress notes, clinical observations, and patient's response to care
- Consultation reports
- Informed consent
- Anesthesia record
- Operative room clinical record
- Intraoperative report
- Postoperative or recovery record
- Pathology report
- Discharge summary
- Final diagnosis
- Death
  - Consent for autopsy
  - Autopsy report, if done
  - Release of body
- Discharge instructions
- Discharge medication orders
- Nursing notes and observations
  - Medication administration records
  - Graphic charts
  - Intake-output, temperature, pulse, respirations (vital signs)
- Nursing assessments
  - Admission assessments
  - Care plans
  - Critical pathways
- Records of donation or receipt of transplants or implants
- Advance directives (if brought to the facility by the patient)
- Living will (if brought to the facility by the patient)
- Power of attorney
- Special consents
  - Anatomical gifts
  - AMA release
  - Leave of absence
  - Consent to photograph
- Emergency record
  - Demographic information
  - Treatment record
    - Triage assessments
    - Nurses' notes
    - EKG
- Newborn records
  - Admission record
  - Discharge summary
  - Consultation
  - Consents
  - Physician orders/progress notes
  - Lab
  - Radiology
  - Newborn record
  - Estimated gestational age
  - Medication record
  - Initial assessment
  - Labor and delivery record
  - Infant identification—footprints and photographs
  - Newborn ICU delivery room
  - Flow sheet
- Observation, neonatal, ICU
- Nursery progress record
- Pediatrician selection form

Source: Methodist Health Systems, Memphis, TN.

or the date the report was received, not by the source department; and the record gives the sequence of the patient's care as delivered. Although this system makes it difficult to find a particular document unless one knows the date, it does provide a better picture of the story of the patient's care. Physician offices often use this format.

Strengths and Weaknesses of Paper-based Health Records

The main benefit of paper-based health records is that they are the usual way that records are maintained and, therefore, familiar to all users. Providers do not need technological training to begin documenting in the record. Written documentation is not affected by system outages.

However, paper-based records have numerous disadvantages. The main disadvantage is that only one person at a time can access information. In addition, there are problems with tracking and monitoring locations of the paper record on the patient floors, within the HIM department, and when it is checked out of the HIM department. The filing of loose and late-arriving reports also presents a problem. Attaching loose reports is not always a priority in a busy patient care area, and this can result in numerous loose pieces of paper arriving in the HIM department. HIM personnel must route or deliver the forms to the patient care treatment area if the patient is still present in the facility or personnel must sort and file stacks of loose paper forms. Organizing loose reports and attaching them to many individual records can be a formidable job. An entire record or a volume of a paper record can be lost or misfiled, making important patient information unavailable to providers when they need it.

The creation of shadow or duplicate systems is also a problem with paper-based health record systems. Some providers are so concerned about the possibility that records can be lost or not located in a timely manner that they create additional records by copying the original records or keeping a separate set of notes. Providers may want to maintain duplicate information for billing purposes. These notes may never become part of the original record or the provider may rely on only the duplicate shadow record without referencing the entire original record, which may have additional information.

Strengths and Weaknesses of Hybrid Health Records

The main benefit of hybrid health record systems is that they maintain the format of the paper-based record after the discharge of the patient. Some facilities with hybrid records keep the paper format for the portion of the record that was created on paper while other facilities scan the paper portions of the record after discharge. However, unlike facilities that maintain part of the hybrid record in a paper-based format permanently, those facilities that scan the paper portions of the hybrid record provide hybrid records with many of the advantages of electronic health records. These advantages include more rapid and simultaneous access by providers; less manpower required to file loose paperwork, purge the records and look for missing paper records, and less space required to archive than paper-based records. Also physicians may remotely access the hybrid record for record completion. Hybrid record systems thus typically reduce the number of incomplete and delinquent health records since physicians do not have to wait until the record is available to come to the HIM department to complete records.

Scanned hybrid records are not as advanced as electronically created records and often cannot be searched for content. They are typically comprised of imaged reports and not separate fields that can be searched. Figure 8.3 lists the steps in the usual flow of the paper-based health record in a traditional acute care facility.

Figure 8.3. Steps in the flow of the paper-based patient health record following discharge

1. Records of discharged patients arrive or are delivered to HIM department.
2. Receipt of records is verified by comparing discharge lists to actual charts received.
3. Folder corresponding to records is pulled.
4. Record is assembled according to prescribed format ensuring that all pages belong to the correct patient and that forms are in correct date order.
5. Deficiencies such as signatures, reports needing completion, and so on are assigned to the responsible provider.
6. Diagnoses and procedures are coded.
7. Record is held for final completion by providers either in incomplete chart area or some other filing area.
8. Charts are rechecked after the providers have done their work to ensure that all have been completed.
9. The complete record is filed in the permanent filing area.

Check Your Understanding 8.3

Instructions: On a separate piece of paper, fill in the blanks with the appropriate terms.

1. ___ This is the conventional or traditional method of maintaining paper-based health records.
2. ___ This record is maintained in the same format while the patient is hospitalized and after discharge.
3. ___ This record is maintained in strict chronological order.
4. ___ This record begins with a problem list that serves as the table of contents for the record.
5. ___ This organization provides care to patients who are terminally ill.
6. ___ These services include physical therapy, occupational therapy, and speech therapy.
7. ___ These services range from independent living to assisted living and skilled nursing care.
8. ___ These duplicate notes or copies often do not become a part of the original record.

Staffing of the Health Information Department

The HIM department's organization varies according to the type of facility. Long-term care facilities may have a very small HIM department with one person in charge or with responsibility for records that are assigned as part of an administrative position. Some long-term care facilities use outside consultants to handle the functions of record keeping.

In contrast, large acute care facilities often employ many HIM professionals, including a department director. Other HIM professionals manage specific areas or functions such as coding, analysis, assembly, transcription, release of information (ROI), imaging, storage, filing, and retrieval. In addition, large facilities sometimes use contract personnel to perform transcription, coding, ROI, and other activities.

In facilities with large ambulatory patient populations and paper-based record systems, health records frequently move in and out of the HIM department. Records must be pulled from the file for clinic appointments and for walk-in patients without appointments; the records need to be delivered and picked up, and then re-filed. Any reports of tests or treatments that arrive separately from the record must be attached to the record quickly. Patients may have several appointments in several different clinics, resulting in many transfers of patient records to various providers. Tracking chart location is critical because so many providers, including resident physicians, use the record.

Management of Health Record Content

The HIM professional manages health record content through oversight responsibilities of **medical transcription** services to produce clinical reports that become part of the health record. The responsibilities for incomplete records include analyzing and monitoring incomplete records to ensure that they are properly completed to meet facility standards and patient healthcare needs, as well as controlling the design and production of forms to ensure that all health records are in a standardized format.

Transcription

Completion of the health record is greatly enhanced by the sophisticated dictation and transcription equipment in use today. Physicians and other providers first dictate the necessary reports, including, but not limited to, history and physical examinations, operative reports, discharge summaries, consultations, progress notes, clinic notes, pathology reports, and radiology reports. The dictated report then is transcribed to produce final printed output or COLD fed data into the electronic system to become a part of the legal health record. Personnel who type, that is, transcribe, the dictation are called medical transcriptionists. Facilities should encourage providers to dictate so that reports can be created and later accessed electronically.

Components of a Transcription System

The system encompasses both the dictation and transcription process. The physician or provider dictates into a variety of devices, including a telephone by calling a special number connected to the facility's dictation system or by using a special phone dedicated only to dictation. The dictation also may be recorded using a separate handheld recorder onto a cassette tape that is delivered to the department. Input from personal computers (PCs) or handheld personal computer devices called **personal digital assistants** (PDAs) is becoming more prevalent. Whatever the means of input by the dictator, a transcriptionist retrieves the dictated voice input and transcribes the content. The transcription may be performed on-site at the facility or off-site from a remote location. The final product, the transcribed report, is sent for review to the physician or provider, who authenticates it as the final approved original for inclusion in the legal health record. **Authentication** may be done on the printed report or electronically in the computer system. The facility's policies must specify that the signature or authentication indicates that the physician or provider who dictated the report has reviewed and corrected it (if necessary) and approves the content of the report.

Digital dictation is the process by which voice sounds are recorded and converted into a digital format. The physician or provider begins the dictation process using a telephone, a microphone attached to a PC, or a hands-free microphone. The dictator enters digits to indicate certain basic information, such as identification of the dictator, identification of the patient, and the type of report to be dictated (a history and physical examination, a discharge summary, an operative report, and so on).

The dictator then speaks and the dictation is transmitted to a computer that digitizes the voice. After the voice sounds have been digitized, the dictation is accessed by the transcriptionist who transcribes the report by listening to the voice and converting it to typed output. Special software features allow the transcriptionist to produce reports with as few keystrokes as possible, using techniques such as word expanders. Word expanders are shortened versions of phrases. For example, the keystrokes WDWN are changed to produce typed output as "well-developed, well-nourished." Some facilities use normal reports or macros so that the dictator can direct the transcriptionist to edit and tailor to the individual patient.

Digital systems allow the dictated information to be prioritized so that reports that have to be completed quickly are produced first. The dictation can be easily located by utilizing identifying information that is provided by the dictator. Digital systems automatically time-stamp the date and time the work was dictated and the date and time the transcription was started and completed. Random access by the transcriptionist allows the workload to be shared and distributed among several transcriptionists. Providers and other appropriate staff can dial-in and listen to the recorded information rather than wait until the final report is transcribed. Coders can listen to the dictated information and code from the discharge summary and other dictated reports rather than wait for the actual transcribed reports. The transcribed report can be faxed automatically to the physician's office, printed out in the transcription area, printed out to clinics or patient floors, COLD fed into the electronic health record (EHR), and integrated to the chart completion system.

Providers can review transcribed documents online and may have editing capabilities. In some systems, both the original and the final edited versions become part of the legal patient health record.

Turnaround times for transcribing dictated reports for different types of work are developed by the HIM department, administration, and physicians in order to meet patient care needs. For example, history and physical examination reports have a strict turnaround time due to Joint Commission requirements that require them to be attached to the record prior to surgery. Typical turnaround times include 12 hours or less for operative reports and 24 to 48 hours for discharge summaries and other reports. Consultation reports also often have a very short turnaround time. Operative reports, on the other hand, may be assigned a turnaround time of two to three days. And discharge summaries may have a lower priority for transcription if the digital system allows coders and other personnel to access and listen to them. Turnaround times are utilized as key indicators in assessing the quality and productivity of the transcription area.

Planning for and Selecting Transcription Equipment

When purchasing or upgrading a dictation and transcription system, the HIM professional must be aware of the long-range consequences of this important decision. Equipment vendors can provide a wealth of information based on their experience working in various facilities. They can help the HIM department determine the number of ports, or entry points, that need to be available based on the number of dictators and transcriptionists requiring simultaneous access. The system needs to have sufficient accessibility to avoid collision, which would prevent a dictator or transcriptionist from gaining access to the system. Immediate access for all users, whether dictating or transcribing, is critical to the system's success. When dictators call in, a digital channel selector automatically selects an available line without input from the dictator.

In addition, it is important to anticipate the amount of recording time necessary to meet current needs and to have sufficient space available to meet future needs. Recording time is often stored on two drives so that backup, or redundancy, is available in case one drive fails. Dictation and transcription systems need to interface with existing hospital information systems (HISs) to ensure that a method exists to automatically download identification information from the **master patient index** (MPI). Physicians or providers and transcriptionists do not have to enter a great deal of information to bring up the correct patient, which promotes accuracy and consistency in patient identification. Security also needs to be in place to ensure that only authorized persons can access the system. Security methods may include a single-authentication system (user name and password) or two-factor authentication (user name and password with a secure token).

The facility must have vendor support to ensure that the system is operational at all times. Transcription systems should be designed so that the transcriptionists can work independently if the general facility information system is not working. Although entering patient information without the connection to the general information system will require greater effort, the work can continue to be generated.

Transcription systems may be designed to archive, or save, dictated information for any length of time. Some facilities archive for 90 days and others for six or more months. Long periods of storage may cause the system to work more slowly, but the advantage is continued access. Even if dictated reports are not attached to the paper or hybrid health records, the people who need the information for coding and billing purposes, quality studies, indexes, registries, and other operational needs can still access and utilize the information.

Transcription services may be centralized or decentralized. In a decentralized system, pathology, radiology, and other departments in addition to health information management may have their own transcriptionists. Some HIM departments have centralized transcription areas that transcribe reports for the entire facility or for all facilities in an integrated system. Moreover, some transcription departments perform work for physician offices in order to generate revenue. The transcription department must consider every possible customer and analyze every possible location for dedicated dictation stations, including nurses' stations, clinics, operative areas, and workrooms in the HIM department. Further, every acceptable format (for example, separate tapes of different sizes or downloads from PCs or PDAs) must be determined and policies established for the types of recordings that are allowed. Using a variety of input devices will cause productivity problems and prevent full utilization of the dictation and transcription system's capabilities. In physician offices and clinics, cassette tapes are used more often for dictation than in larger facilities.

The HIM professional must fully understand the dictation and transcription system application. A **certified medical transcriptionist** (CMT) may supervise the transcription area, but the manager of the HIM department is ultimately responsible for the work produced. Before purchasing any large system, the HIM professional should interview references and visit similar facilities to see the system in operation. Often the vendor will arrange these site visits. The HIM professional also might visit facilities that are using the equipment under consideration but have not been specifically recommended by the vendor. Further, he or she might attend trade shows and seminars and narrow the field of products to avoid confusion. In addition, he or she should include the people who will actually use the system in the decision-making process.

Issues in the Management of Transcription Services

Although transcription is just one function of the HIM department, it often requires a great deal of the department's attention and resources. A backlog of dictated minutes waiting to be transcribed is an issue that needs constant monitoring to be sure turnaround times are met. History and physical examination reports and operative reports have accreditation and regulatory time limitations. Quick turnaround time from dictation to transcribed report is important because providers must be able to retrieve information when it is needed for patient care.

Recruitment and retention of qualified medical transcriptionists are major problems for HIM professionals. Transcription equipment is expensive to acquire and maintain, and the equipment and technology are changing rapidly. Skilled medical transcriptionists who can accurately transcribe dictation are in short supply, and the role of the medical transcriptionist is evolving. This evolution is discussed in the following sections.

Internal versus Outsourcing Transcription

The facility must decide whether to handle transcription services in-house, to contract with (or outsource to) transcription companies outside the facility, or to use a combination of internal and contract services.

Outsourcing to transcription service companies, or **contract services**, is on the rise. Some healthcare facilities routinely contract all or a portion of their workload; others use the contract service on an as-needed basis for peak times and to accommodate overflow work. The major advantage to a contract service is that it can save the facility money in terms of salaries, fringe benefits, equipment, depreciation, floor space, maintenance, workstations, supplies, and reference materials. Furthermore, use of an outside service can eliminate problems associated with overloading the system with increased dictation prior to a Joint Commission survey or at times when medical residents change clinical service rotations in a teaching facility. Although outsourcing transcription services is an attractive option, it must be analyzed carefully. The major disadvantages to outsourcing are the loss of control over the transcription service, the potential security risks, and the high cost of contract transcription services.

When selecting a contract service, the HIM professional should become as familiar with the company as possible. A growing number of offshore companies or U.S.-based companies send work via the Internet to transcription personnel in other countries. Such companies must provide assurance that their transcriptionists are bonded, trained in confidentiality, and well supervised.

The manner in which the company handles a sudden influx of work is important because this is one of the major reasons why healthcare facilities use outside transcription companies. The exact method and rationale for billing and counting the final product also is extremely important. The HIM professional should question the exact definitions of a line, word, page, keystroke, minutes, or bytes or whether style requirements such as capitalizing, boldface, or underlining are an additional charge.

The counting method should be fully explained in the contract. Most companies charge by the line, but the definition of a line may be 65 characters rather than a physical line. For example, if physical lines are counted and the facility is paying $0.13 to $0.18 per line, the costs can add up in situations where one word on a line is considered a line. Using a smaller font to increase the amount of typing per line may be more costly because a smaller type may scan into an imaging system or microfilm poorly. Some companies base their charge on turnaround time, with an increased cost per line when transcription is completed within a shorter time frame. For example, the charge for transcription within 48 hours would be $0.10 a line; within 24 hours, $0.12 a line; and within 8 hours, $0.18 a line. In addition, the company may include electronic storage costs for dictation.

Billing can be complicated and the HIM professional must determine the true cost of the outside contract company's service so that he or she can compare alternatives accurately. The distribution and delivery method and the number of copies provided by the company must be evaluated because reprints might cost as much as the original transcribed document. Some companies transmit information back to the facility to be printed by the facility or send information via the Internet, fax, overnight delivery service, or courier. The contract needs to state whether the facility or the company will pay for the transmission service. Also, there may be an additional charge for corrections. If the facility allows physicians or providers to dictate on other devices instead of directly into the dictation system, this also may affect the cost.

In addition, the facility must assess how the outside company's equipment will integrate with the facility's current hospital information system, for example, with regard to phone lines, software, and interface with the electronic record system, if one exists. If the printing is to be done in the facility, responsibility for printer maintenance and supply costs must be determined. The quality of the work performed by the contract company must be evaluated in terms of content, proper abbreviation use, typing and spelling errors, general appearance, correction of grammatical errors, and correct spelling of physician and patient names. Some companies provide several levels of proofreading, including by a physician. However, proofreading also must be performed by the healthcare facility on at least a sample of the reports, and the facility must maintain the voice files so that quality checks can be performed on the outside service's work to ensure that what was dictated was what was actually typed. The HIM professional must make sure the work is closely monitored.

Even with a contract service, the health information manager still has oversight responsibility for the outside contract service and quality control. Facility personnel must file the printed reports in the health record and distribute them to residents, referring physicians, and consultants, as appropriate. Further, contracts must be carefully reviewed to ensure that contract services provide for the security of patient information.

The HIM professional also must ensure fast and easy access to the system. If physicians and coders have the ability to listen to dictation prior to transcribing, this capability should not change when transcription is outsourced.

Staffing of the Transcription Area

When the healthcare facility chooses to do transcription internally, the staff must be carefully selected to ensure that transcription is of high quality. Each applicant for a transcription position should be tested using the kind of work to be performed to confirm that he or she can type from the voice files. In addition, the applicant must have excellent concentration skills, excellent hearing skills, and excellent proofreading and editing skills. CMS has developed guidance for remote workers and this information is a good resource for developing policies and procedures to provide access for remote workers.

Applicants who are CMTs are in great demand. The Medical Transcription Certification Commission grants certification upon the successful completion of an examination. The requirements for this voluntary examination are experience or formal education or both. The CMT must maintain currency and certification by earning continuing education (CE) hours. Proprietary business schools and community colleges offer formal educational programs and are excellent sources for transcriptionists. A healthcare facility's offer to allow students to obtain clinical experience at the facility is an excellent way to attract applicants. Some healthcare facilities offer on-the-job training to persons with excellent typing skills.

The **Association of Healthcare Documentation Integrity** (AHDI), formerly the American Association for Medical Transcription (AAMT), has a model curriculum for formal educational programs. The curriculum includes the study of medical terminology, anatomy and physiology, medical science, operative procedures, instruments, supplies, laboratory values, reference use and research techniques, and English grammar. All applicants should have knowledge of the areas of the model curriculum.

In addition, the AHDI produces a bimonthly journal and has excellent reference materials. CE opportunities are available for transcription professionals. Transcriptionists must be given the opportunity to participate in CE activities and to be updated in new medical procedures, tests, and terminology.

The AHDI has a model job description with three defined levels for the professional transcriptionist. Some facilities may use these levels as a guide for levels of classification of personnel and promotions.

Telestaffing, or telecommuting, is a growing alternative for medical transcriptionists and many other healthcare workers. In telestaffing, personnel are allowed to work from home or some other remote location. This has been very successful for healthcare facilities, although remote transcriptionists require special supervisory attention. They need to feel that they are part of the HIM department. The supervisor must ensure ongoing communication with telestaffing employees via e-mail or by bringing them to the facility for CE meetings and interaction with other departmental personnel. Some healthcare facilities offer telecommuting only to employees who have been with them for a period of time, fully understand the system, and are known to be responsible and dependable. Transcriptionists working outside the healthcare facility use a telephone line or cable connection to access the system. The facility may supply the transcriptionist with the telephone line, the computer workstation, and reference materials. Transcriptionists working from home must be held to the same production and quality standards as in-house transcriptionists and must be fully trained in the security and confidentiality of healthcare information.

Determining the number of transcriptionists needed in relation to the number of providers dictating is challenging and depends on the types and amount of information typed, the specialties of the facility, whether the facility is a teaching hospital or a clinic, and the types of non-transcription duties assigned to the transcriptionists, among other factors. In a clinic or physician office, transcription may be done as part of a larger job. The HIM professional must determine the acceptable turnaround time (TAT) for different types of dictated reports; often referred to as work types. There is a range of definitions of TAT and often variation occurs at various healthcare facilities and various settings. According to the July 2008 AHIMA white paper, "Transcription Turnaround Time for Common Document Types," common TAT varies from 8 to 24 hours based on the work type of the dictated report. Most healthcare facilities codify the acceptable TAT for various work types in the medical staff bylaws. The failure of the responsible provider to dictate the report in the required timeframe often results in a deficiency in the health record. Once a report is dictated, there are factors that may contribute to noncompliance with approved TATs including staffing, work volume changes, transcription anomalies, implementation of new technology or equipment, and TAT expectation changes.

Productivity Management

Payment methods for transcriptionists vary depending on whether the transcriptionist works for a healthcare facility or a contract service. Entry-level transcriptionists may be paid by the hour. Some contract services pay transcriptionists more per hour for straight production typing, but the transcriptionists may not have the benefits that are available to the employees of a healthcare facility. The ADHI has excellent current information about productivity. This should be referenced to ensure the current standards are utilized.

Quality is a vital part of productivity management in transcription. The supervisor must review the quality of work produced on a regular basis. Among the items to review are punctuation errors, omitted dictation, misspelled words or medical terms, and formatting errors. An analysis of each transcriptionist's errors will target those areas that need improvement. The *Book of Style for Medical Transcription* is often used as the standard for defining and measuring medical transcription errors.

Speech and Voice Recognition

Speech or **voice recognition technology** is used increasingly as the accuracy of output improves. In voice recognition technology, the spoken word is transmitted immediately to a database and converted to typed output, which eliminates the need for the transcriptionist to listen to and type the information. The quality of the output is very dependent on the quality of the dictation. The speaker must speak clearly and distinctly. The role of the transcriptionist will change as this new technology increases in accuracy. In time, the transcriptionist will become primarily an editor and proofreader. Speech recognition technology may be utilized on the front-end where the person dictates through a microphone or headset apparatus connected to a PC. As the person dictates, the words appear on the screen and are corrected if they are not displayed correctly. The document is correct when completed and the dictator controls the entire process. The facility may still require the document to be sent to a transcriptionist or other person who controls its distribution.

This method also requires training of the individual who is dictating and the dictator may feel that this process is too slow and takes too much physician time. In back-end speech recognition, after the physician dictates in the usual manner, the audio is sent as a draft text along with the voice file to the transcriptionist who serves as an editor to listen to the audio in comparison with the displayed text and to make changes to the text document. This document then goes back to the dictating provider for approval. The advantage is that the person dictating does not have to change dictation behavior. Back-end speech recognition (also called *server-based speech recognition*) does not improve productivity because editing is as time-consuming as transcribing. Radiology departments and other departments that have many repetitive reports have utilized speech recognition technology more effectively than the general facility.

Incentive Programs

Because of the competition for Certified Medical Transcriptionists, many healthcare facilities offer **incentive pay** plans to reward transcriptionists for high productivity. For example, a hospital may require a transcriptionist to type eight hours a day and produce 1,200 lines of typed output for a base monthly salary. Beyond 1,200 lines, the transcriptionist may earn a bonus of $0.06 per line, with the bonus cents per line increasing to the point where a transcriptionist typing 2,001 lines would receive a bonus of $0.12 per line. However, the quality of the work must remain at 98 percent accuracy based on regular quality review.

For fairness in the incentive system, work must be rotated so that each transcriptionist has the opportunity to perform different kinds of work from different providers. Providers for whom English is a second language may produce dictation that is more difficult to transcribe. Moreover, some providers are not careful in their dictation, which requires more listening and replaying. Operative reports may be more difficult to transcribe than discharge summaries.

The proponents of incentive pay plans believe that monetary incentives increase productivity, reduce turnover, provide fair and equitable pay, and motivate employees. In this payment method, highly productive transcriptionists are paid for what they produce.

Evaluation of the Effectiveness and Efficiency of Transcription Services

The effectiveness and efficiency of transcription services are judged primarily by turnaround time and accuracy in typing the dictation. History and physical examinations and operative reports have time limitations set forth in Joint Commission regulations. Discharge summaries are valuable sources of information for coding, billing, and reimbursement. With EMR systems, the dictated information and transcribed documents are accessible to all providers and healthcare personnel who need to refer to them. The success of the transcription service depends on both the cooperation of the providers who dictate and the skills of the medical transcriptionists.

Check Your Understanding 8.4

Instructions: Answer the following questions on a separate sheet of paper.

1. What are the advantages of using a contract transcription system? What are the advantages of having transcription performed in-house?
2. What are the formal educational requirements for a certified medical transcriptionist?
3. How will speech recognition technology change the job of the medical transcriptionist?
4. What are the four benefits of an incentive pay plan?
5. What factors must be considered when determining the number of transcriptionists a healthcare facility needs?

Abstracting

Abstracting is the compilation, usually in an electronic database, of pertinent information extracted from the patient record. The purpose of abstracting is to make information from the patient record readily available for internal and external reporting needs. Abstracting supports the secondary use of patient data for registries, public reporting, research and other purposes. It is important for the HIM professional to understand the mission of the facility when determining both the amount of information to abstract from the health record and the appropriate staff required for the abstracting.

Abstracting Process for Paper-based and Hybrid Health Records

In a facility with paper-based and hybrid health records there are typically administrative systems for registration, coding, and billing and some clinical systems with electronic processes that require data input through an abstracting process. In these cases, the HIM professional may be required to abstract more information than in facilities with more advanced electronic health record systems which provide electronic query functions. The process of abstracting begins with defining the needs and the purposes for the abstracted information. For the creation of indices information about the treating physician and procedures performed this information may be a combination of information from other systems that integrates into the abstracting system. For example, a paper-based facility may have an ADT (admission, discharge, and transfer) system which captures basic demographic information about the patient and the treating physician. After discharge, this information is available in the abstracting system, and the coder then assigns codes to the encounter. This information is stored with the demographic information; however, the coder may have to enter the names of the physicians who performed the surgeries or procedures during the hospital stay. Also, the coder may verify the discharge status entered in the system with that documented in the health record. If the facility is a teaching facility, the names of the residents and fellows involved in the care of the patient may also be included in the abstracting system.

Incomplete Record Control

Health records must be complete in order to provide all the information that is necessary for patient care, billing, and reimbursement. The HIM department must verify that all records are received from the nursing floor, including records of any previous admissions that were sent to the nursing unit. After the records arrive in the HIM department, their location must be carefully tracked until they reach final storage in the filing area or are scanned.

The business office notifies the HIM department of bills that are waiting for information from the physician so that the record can be coded and the bill prepared. The administration places a great deal of pressure on the HIM department to process bills in a timely manner so that revenue can be generated for the facility. In turn, the HIM professional must motivate physicians to provide the information the department needs to do its work. Incomplete records are less of a problem in most healthcare facilities with hybrid or electronic health records. However, monitoring incomplete health records is a constant challenge for the HIM professional.

Quantitative Analysis

Quantitative analysis, often called **discharge analysis,** is a review of the health record for completeness and accuracy. It is generally conducted retrospectively, that is, after the patient's discharge from the facility or at the conclusion of treatment. Quantitative analysis also may be done while the patient is in the facility, in which case it is referred to as concurrent review or **concurrent analysis.** Concurrent analysis means that the record is analyzed during the patient's stay in the healthcare facility. It has the advantage of HIM or other personnel being present on the floors where the physicians see patients. HIM personnel can remind providers to complete items in the record and to sign orders and progress notes. Some facilities have HIM personnel physically located on the nursing floors to monitor record completion closely. Other facilities have HIM personnel visit patient care areas to obtain signatures and ensure that loose reports are placed in the health record. Discharge analysis serves as an additional check to ensure that the record is complete and that all information belongs to the patient. The concurrent review and discharge analysis review typically analyze the health records for the same documentation.

One component of the discharge analysis process is to assemble the record which is the arrangement of the forms in the paper-based health record in a standard permanent sequence for filing. The order of the forms in the record is unique to each hospital. This order also may differ from the sequencing of forms while patients are under active treatment when convenient reference to certain information is needed. While in active use, the health record is arranged with the most current information on top as follows: orders, progress or clinic notes, operative notes, medications, graphic sheets, nursing notes, consultations, ancillary forms, consents, history and physical, demographic information, and face sheet. The order differs according to the facility, but the record forms the provider prepares and writes on most frequently are on top to allow for quick entry of orders and progress notes. Labeled tabs divide the chart into sections to assist in finding needed documents.

When the patient is discharged or treatment is terminated, the record arrives in the HIM department, where it is immediately assembled for filing for a paper-based record, or assembled and prepared for scanning in the case of the hybrid health record. The face sheet and demographic information are on top, followed by the history and physical examination, the discharge summary, ancillary reports, consents, operative reports, progress notes in date order with the earliest orders first, orders in date order, nursing notes in date order, and so forth.

Many facilities leave the record in the order in which it arrives in the HIM department rather than spend the time to rearrange it. This system is called universal chart order or uniform chart order. The benefits of the universal chart order system are that time is saved in the HIM department and providers can find the parts of the record they need more easily because the arrangement remains the same.

A facility moving to universal chart order must involve nursing and physicians in the decisions about chart arrangement because they use the record as a reference for patient care every day. Labeled dividers and a standard table of contents help ensure that everyone who works with the chart knows the proper arrangement. In the hybrid health record system, the pages of the record are checked for bar codes for indexing according to the labeled dividers and tabs in the paper-based health record.

Quantitative analysis involves several additional steps. The record forms must be reviewed individually to make sure they belong to that particular patient. Organizing the paper forms is an important step. Forms are often intermingled and usually separated into a source-oriented format. Preliminary laboratory reports may be discarded when there is a final cumulative summary report.

Each facility must develop its own procedures for quantitative analysis. Responsibility for completion of the record must be assigned to each responsible provider. This is called *deficiency assignment*. The deficiencies, or parts of the record needing completion or signature, are entered into the HIS or on paper worksheets attached to the incomplete, or deficient, health record.

Moreover, the record must be reviewed to ensure that certain basic reports that are common to all patient records are present, including the history and physical, progress notes, orders, nursing notes, and discharge summary. Other reports (for example, operative reports, diagnostic tests, consultations, and so on) may be included depending on the patient's course of treatment. Quantitative analysis also includes a review for authentication that may be done by written signature, rubber stamp facsimile (unacceptable to CMS), computer password, or initials, and must include the professional title of the individual responsible for the entry.

Any corrections to the record must be entered properly. In paper records, the provider should draw a single line through the error, add a note explaining the error, initial and date the error with the date it was discovered, and enter the correct information in chronological order. For electronic entries, a procedure should be followed that explains how to correct errors and enter addenda to the health record. In cases of medical identify theft, when someone presents using another's identity, the record must be identified so the appropriate health information is entered into the correct health record. This is a growing area of concern for the HIM professional, and procedures and guidance will continue to evolve until a standard of practice is established.

Criteria for Adequacy of Documentation

Documentation must reflect the care rendered to the patient and the patient's response to care. It must be timely and legible and authenticated by the person who wrote it. The health record is considered a legal document and a business record because it records events at or about the time they happen. Timeliness and legibility are two of the main areas of focus for accreditation and licensure bodies. Personnel in the HIM department analyze the health record for timeliness, accuracy, and completeness of entries in the health record. There are many patient safety concerns as discussed in Chapter 17 of this text. However, one patient safety issue that relies on proper documentation is the use of abbreviations in the health record. The health record must be analyzed to ensure that symbols and abbreviations used in documentation have been approved by the medical staff and have only one clear meaning. The HIM department staff often analyze the health record for adequacy of documentation during (concurrent analysis) and after (discharge analysis) the patient's stay in the hospital.

Authentication of Health Record Entries

Authentication means to prove authorship and can be done in several ways. Signatures handwritten in ink are the most common method for signing paper-based health records. The Joint Commission allows rubber-stamp facsimile signatures when there is a statement verifying that the physician is the only one who will use the stamp and will maintain control of it. CMS specifically forbids the use of rubber stamps as an authentication method.

An **electronic signature** or e-signature is defined by AHIMA as, "the system for assigning electronic documents by entering a unique code or password that verifies the identity of the healthcare practitioner and creates an individual signature on the record" (AHIMA e-HIM Work Group on Implementing Electronic Signatures 2003). A statement ensuring that the password is controlled and used only by the responsible provider should be required to protect patient confidentiality and to ensure that others do not use it. Password security is critical. Electronic signatures will be used more frequently as more documents in the record are produced by, and remain in, the system but do not become part of the paper record. Facilities that scan paper records of discharged patients into imaging systems must make it clear to physicians that these are images of papers that can be viewed but not edited.

Autoauthentication is a policy that allows the physician or provider to state in advance that dictated and transcribed reports should automatically be considered approved and signed when the physician does not make corrections within a certain period of time. Another variation of autoauthentication is that physicians authorize the HIM department to send a weekly list of documents needing signatures. The list is then signed and returned to the HIM department. Some facilities use autoauthentication even though the Joint Commission does not approve it. The objection is that evidence cannot be provided that the physician actually reviewed and approved each report. Facilities that use these methods of autoauthentication state that the physician offices automatically receive copies of transcribed reports and thus providers have the ability to review the reports before the deadline or before signing the list of reports.

Signatures in teaching hospitals are especially important to show that the attending physician responsible for the patient is actively involved in the patient's care. Signatures are generally required on all reports completed by residents and medical students. In electronic signature programs, the attending physician's co-signature should be entered after the resident has reviewed and signed the report to confirm the attending physician's participation.

Record Completion Policies and Procedures

The health record is not complete until all its parts are assembled, organized, and authenticated. The HIM professional, the administration, and the medical staff must develop record completion policies and procedures and include them in the medical staff bylaws. Although the facility's governing body has overall responsibility for patient care, responsibility for the delivery and documentation of patient care is delegated to the medical staff. The medical staff and the individual physician have primary responsibility for completing the health record to document the process of care that was rendered.

Most facilities have a committee in place composed of members of the medical staff, the administration, nursing, and other provider disciplines with responsibility for ensuring that medical staff members follow the established rules and regulations for health records. This committee may be the health record committee, the quality committee, or some other committee responsible for ensuring compliance with rules and regulations. The HIM professional should serve on the committee and generally assist the physician or provider committee chair by preparing the agenda and minutes for meetings.

The HIM professional also assists the committee by preparing reports on the status of record completion and problems with the flow of the record through the facility. Reports regarding the percentage of incomplete and delinquent health records are important to ensure that accreditation standards are met on an ongoing basis. The findings from various types of record review, including concurrent reviews and retrospective reviews, are presented to the committee and discussed. The committee often plays a key role in the approval of forms and electronic templates so that the standard form and format of the health record can be maintained.

The committee chair may communicate directly with physicians or other medical staff members to solve problems related to record completion. The committee can be a valuable resource to the HIM professional because it has representation from every area that enters documents into the patient record. Committee members can often assist the HIM department in acquiring equipment and personnel needed to properly perform its responsibilities. The committee generally reports to the executive committee of the medical staff and makes recommendations for executive staff action to improve patient record services.

Qualitative Analysis

In **qualitative analysis**, HIM personnel carefully review the quality and adequacy of record documentation and ensure that it is in accordance with the policies, rules, and regulations established by the facility, the standards of licensing and accrediting bodies, and government requirements. Like quantitative analysis, qualitative analysis may be done concurrently or retrospectively.

Qualitative analysis is a more in-depth review of health records than quantitative analysis, although the processes may overlap somewhat, depending on the facility. When qualitative analysis is done while the patient is in the facility or under active treatment, it is called **open-record review, ongoing records review**, **point-of-care review**, or **continuous record review**. Joint Commission requires an open-record review to ensure that its documentation standards are met at the point of care delivery. HIM personnel as well as case management personnel, nurses, physicians, and other providers should participate in the open-record review process. This review process looks at requirements such as presence of the history and physical examination prior to surgery, completion of the postoperative note, and many other aspects of the care process as documented in the health record. Open-record review should be done on an ongoing basis.

Qualitative review also is performed on **closed records**. **Closed-record review** means that the qualitative review is done retrospectively following discharge or termination of treatment. The benefit of open-record review is that problems in the care process that are revealed through the review can be corrected immediately. Closed-record review is an important way to obtain information about trends and patterns of documentation.

Role of Health Information Management Professionals

CMS and state licensure standards require healthcare facilities to have an HIM department with a designated person having administrative responsibility for health records. This requirement includes having the staff, equipment, and policies and procedures to ensure that records are current and accurate and that information is accessible.

The HIM department works closely with the business department regarding chart completion. The business department and the entire organization depend on the HIM staff to work with physicians and other healthcare professionals to provide the necessary information so that bills can be finalized in a timely manner. Bills are usually sent within two to three days after discharge. The health information manager receives daily notification of accounts that need information, and procedures must be established to expedite the flow of information for payment purposes.

Role of the Medical Staff

Medical staff members are responsible for developing bylaws governing their operation. The requirements for documentation and completion of health records as well as penalties for not adhering to these rules are included in the medical staff bylaws. Each member of the medical staff signs a statement that he or she will abide by the bylaws, and each is responsible for documentation.

Management of Incomplete Records

The HIM professional is responsible for ensuring that health records, whether manual or electronic, are readily accessible and that adequate equipment and personnel are available to facilitate record completion. No matter how well staffed and well organized the HIM department is, it can only facilitate the process. The providers are responsible for the documentation and must dictate, authenticate, and otherwise complete the patient health record.

Storage, Retrieval, and Tracking of Incomplete Records

Facilities provide access to incomplete records in various ways. Paper-based records needing completion must be maintained in an area that is easily accessible to physicians. They may be arranged alphabetically by the last name of the responsible physician or filed in numerical order. Filing by physician name enables physicians to go directly to their own boxes to access and complete their own records.

One disadvantage of alphabetic filing by physician name is that completion is often delayed because the record may remain in one physician's box until it is completed and moved to the next box. In a facility with many specialists or many residents, maintaining incomplete records in numerical order by the patient's record number works well because the records are accessible to all providers who need to complete them. Other facilities file incomplete records alphabetically by the patient's last name. Still other facilities immediately file the records into the general file area, using a combination of filing methods. In a combination method, when only one provider needs to work on a record, it is filed under that provider's name. When several physicians need to work on the records, a numerical system is used. The advantage is that records are all filed in one area for ease of location by the clerical staff.

In systems with incomplete records filed, clerical staff must be available to assist providers and to ensure that the portions of the record that need to be completed are actually done. When incomplete records are filed numerically, the facility might require physicians to call before arriving at the department so that the needed records can be pulled. Some HIM personnel speed up record completion by taking records to physicians' offices located on the hospital campus.

With the hybrid health record system, the paper-based portion of the record may be scanned at discharge of the patient into the HIS and providers are allowed to electronically authenticate incomplete records. This method is convenient for the providers as deficient health records may be simultaneously routed to multiple providers via workflow software. It is more efficient than the paper-based routing of health records as it requires fewer HIM personnel to locate, transport, and re-file the paper-based health record. It is also more efficient for the providers who may access, authenticate, and complete the hybrid health record remotely. Hybrid health record systems have decreased the health record delinquency rates in many facilities.

The completion time clock begins running when the patient is discharged, expires, or when treatment is terminated. Records are considered deficient or incomplete immediately at discharge. Some facilities choose to begin the time clock after the records are reviewed quantitatively by the HIM staff and made available to the providers; however, regulations and standards do not provide for "extra" time for analysis or transcription delays, computer system downtime, or physician unavailability. Healthcare facility policies and medical staff bylaws must define when incomplete or deficient records become delinquent.

Delinquent health records are those records that are not completed within the specified time frame, for example, within 14 days of discharge. A delinquent record is similar to an overdue library book. The definition of a delinquent chart varies according to the facility, but most facilities require that records be completed within 30 days of discharge as mandated by CMS regulations and Joint Commission standards. Some facilities require a shorter time frame for completing records because of concerns about timely billing. **Chart tracking** of the location of incomplete and delinquent records as they move through the completion process is vital because many people need access to the records of recently treated patients.

Policies and Procedures on Record Completion

Numerous methods may be used to encourage the timely completion of records. Joint Commission specifies that the number of delinquent records cannot exceed 50 percent of the average number of discharges, so keeping the number of delinquent charts as low as possible is a constant challenge for HIM staff. Concurrent analysis by HIM or other facility personnel can help speed up completion time. Using case managers to work with physicians on chart completion issues while the patient is in the facility, for example, helps reduce the burden on the HIM department. HIM professionals rely on medical staff committees, such as the health record committee, chiefs of medical services, and medical staff leaders to motivate providers to complete records. As previously discussed, hybrid health records alleviate some of the past issues with completion of the health record.

Many facilities limit the retrospective checking and flagging of incomplete items in the HIM department to the discharge summary, history and physical examination, operative reports, consultations, and clinical reports. Nursing information is not reviewed nor are signatures on progress notes and orders checked. Less detailed analysis is done after discharge due to the increased emphasis on open-record review when patients are in the facility under active treatment. Requiring physicians to sign notes and orders retrospectively does not affect the process of patient care and treatment or ensure that adequate documentation is available at the time patient care is provided. The HIM department should continue to monitor a sample of notes and orders to ensure that signatures are present to comply with established facility policies, accreditation standards, and regulations. Corrective measures should be developed when there is a pattern of missing signatures.

As mentioned earlier, penalties for noncompletion of health records must be included in medical staff bylaws. Penalties such as suspension of admission privileges or surgical privileges for the individual physician or a physician group and the levying of fines per incomplete chart or per day must be explained in the bylaws. Some hospitals make health record completion a condition of continued membership on the medical staff and suspend physicians who do not comply with the rules regarding completion. Suspended physicians must reapply for staff membership. Some states require that physicians suspended three times in a year be reported to the state medical board. However, in some small facilities or in facilities where a physician is responsible for many admissions, it is difficult to enforce the rules regarding suspension of admitting privileges.

Each facility must have a policy in place for dealing with situations where records remain incomplete for an extended period. The HIM director can be given authority to declare that a record is complete for purposes of filing when a provider relocates, dies, or has an extended illness that would prevent the record from ever being completed. Every effort should be made to have a partner or physician in the same specialty area complete the chart so that coding, billing, and statistical information is available. In teaching hospitals, residents sometimes leave before charts are completed and they become difficult to locate. Thus, many facilities require departing residents to obtain clearance from the HIM department before the end of the residency period. The medical staff committee responsible for health record functions also may review long-standing incomplete charts and direct that they be filed even though incomplete.

Physician Notification Processes

Most healthcare facilities notify physicians of records that need completion on an escalating basis. For example, the first notice reminds the physician that records need completion; the second describes the penalties for noncompliance; the third limits the admission or operative privileges of the physician and might include suspension of even emergency admission privileges, and the fourth gives a warning regarding suspension or removal from the medical staff. Finally, the physician may be considered to have forfeited staff membership and will have to reapply for membership. Some teaching facilities withhold paychecks for residents or refuse to approve vacations until all of the physician's charts are complete.

The HIM department is responsible for counting incomplete charts and preparing lists of those providers who have delinquent records and those whose privileges have been suspended. Extensions are often granted when physicians are out of town, sick, have a death in the family, and so on. The handling of physician suspensions requires a great deal of tact and cooperation among the HIM professional, the medical staff leadership, and the administration.

Forms Design and Management

The management and design of forms used in the healthcare environment is a concern of all providers. Forms must be developed and approved in a careful, systematic process to ensure that they meet facility standards, are compatible with imaging and **microfilming** systems, and do not duplicate information on existing forms. (Examples of commonly used health record forms are provided in appendix A of this book.) HIM department personnel must be constantly vigilant to ensure that only approved forms become part of the permanent health record. Unapproved forms do not have the necessary form numbers or bar codes needed for imaging and indexing systems. Small forms and folded flowcharts create problems when records are handled and utilized. Oversize forms create problems in microfilming or optical imaging because special preparation is required to ensure that all information is filmed or scanned. As health records move toward an electronic format, the forms design process becomes the process of designing computer views for entry of data, but the principles of control still apply. Facilities with hybrid health records have to transition existing forms into templates for the EHR. This transition requires a lot of input and expertise from HIM personnel.

Principles of Forms Design

A well-designed form improves the reliability of the data entered on it. A form should be designed to collect information in a consistent way and to remind providers of information that needs to be included. Many paper record forms consist of a single sheet. Other specialty forms, such as a unit-set form or a multipart form, have multiple-sheet forms preassembled in either carbon or carbonless sets. With spot carbons in unit-set forms, only part of the information on the original is visible on the copy. For example, when the face sheet is the first page of a unit set and is printed on the computer, the carbon can be positioned so that the copy for a clinical department would have only the patient identification information and not the financial information.

Continuous-feed forms use a series of forms separated with perforations that can be printed by a printer without having to load the paper for each form printed. The forms then can be separated and distributed. Continuous-feed forms can be used for both single sheets and multiset forms.

Most forms include similar basic components and all should contain at least a heading to describe the contents and purpose of the form, instructions on how to complete it, and spaces to enter required and optional information. General guidelines to follow when designing forms include:

- The form should be easy to complete.
- Instructions on completion and use of the form should be included.
- The form should have a heading with a title that clearly identifies its purpose.
- The facility's name and address should appear on each page of the form.
- The name, patient identification number, and other identifying information should be present on each form. Most facilities now use **bar coding** as identifying information.
- Bar coding also should be included in indexing the form for random access in an optical scanner or microfilming system. Bar codes are generally printed directly on the document or on a label affixed to the document.
- The form number and date of revision should be included to ensure that the form being used is the correct and most current version.
- Outdated forms should be recalled and eliminated.
- The physical layout of the form should be logical. When a clerk is entering information as the patient gives it, the form should be organized to match the way the information is requested.
- Personal and address data and other items of information that relate to one another should be placed together (for example, the patient's city, state, and zip code).
- Font selection should be standardized. Some experts recommend all capital letters.
- Margins should be left for hole punches to allow the documents to be placed in folders or chart holders. The holes may be on the left-hand side of the form, at the top, or both, depending on the types of folders or binders used.
- Ruled lines may be used to outline sections of forms to allow for easy entry of data or to separate areas of the form.
- Shading can be used to separate and emphasize areas of the form.
- Check boxes and fields can be used to provide space for the collection of data.

Careful consideration also should be given to including information on the backs of forms. Facilities that are **scanning** and imaging paper records must have the bar-coded patient identification information on the back of the form to ensure proper indexing into the imaging system. Even though scanners can scan both sides of a document, the ability to index and thus access the information must be ensured.

Forms Control Systems

Facilities must develop strict guidelines and processes for forms control. Word-processing programs and programs specifically designed for forms design have made the process easier than in the past. Providers often design their own non-approved forms, which may appear in the paper record when it arrives in the HIM department. These unauthorized forms affect the patient care process as well as procedures in the department. The person who designed the form may be unaware of the interrelated processes that are affected by changing it. A bar code identifying the type of form may not be available.

Forms control systems must:

- Provide for the development of forms according to established guidelines
- Control the printing and use of forms
- Guide providers in designing forms according to established guidelines
- Prevent staff from changing or designing forms that duplicate existing forms or could be combined into other forms

Forms control is critical to the transition toward hybrid and EHR systems. The transition to electronic records usually begins with creating a hybrid health record by using an imaging system to gather information about existing forms and to ensure that all forms can be properly scanned and indexed. Without indexing, the information cannot be easily retrieved. The forms control process also should establish processes for forms inventory, forms identification, forms analysis, and forms purchasing.

Forms Inventory

The first step in the forms control process is the forms inventory. This process involves gathering each form and all of its editions to ensure that the most current version is used. A subject file is a good idea for bringing together all the forms used by each of the areas, such as all admissions or registration forms, all operative forms, and all nursing forms. Organizing in this manner can prevent new forms from being developed when current forms have the needed information, assist in finding ways to combine forms with related information, and serve as a reminder that information changed on one form must be changed on related forms.

Forms Identification

The second part of the forms control process is forms identification. This process involves assigning each form a distinct title that reflects its use. In paper systems, a forms number is also assigned to indicate that the form has been approved. The date and the source department are usually included with the number. Bar coding and labels with complete bar-coded information about the form are becoming more prevalent as facilities prepare for the computerization of forms. A numerical listing of forms should be maintained.

Forms Analysis

Forms analysis involves the continuous review and revision of forms. The forms analysis process is often initiated because of procedural problems, such as when providers are not receiving the information they need to do their work. Forms assist in guiding processes and ensuring that complete information is obtained and recorded. Flowcharting the development and distribution of the forms is helpful in determining whether a form is still useful, whether the information it contains is current, and whether it meets the current requirements of the facility.

Forms Purchasing

Purchasing and printing comprise the fourth part of the forms control process. A policy should be in place stating that forms cannot be ordered or reordered without approval of the forms committee or some other group or individual responsible for purchasing and printing approval. Some facilities now use just-in-time production of forms where copies of forms can be printed at the patient-care area rather than having to maintain a large inventory of paper forms. This inventory of forms becomes obsolete when any change is made to the form.

Check Your Understanding 8.5

Instructions: Answer the following questions on a separate sheet of paper.

1. What are quantitative analysis and qualitative analysis? What purpose do they serve?
2. How does concurrent review facilitate record completion?
3. What is universal chart order, and why is it being adopted by healthcare facilities?
4. What is the difference between open- and closed-record reviews?
5. Why is the finance department concerned about the timely completion of records?
6. In what two ways do HIM departments store incomplete health records? How do the two storage systems work?
7. What is the difference between an incomplete record and a delinquent record?
8. How does the HIM professional help providers to complete health records?
9. What three methods do facilities use to authenticate health records? How does each method work?
10. Why have some facilities stopped notifying providers about orders and progress notes needing signatures?
11. Why is forms control a critical responsibility of the HIM professional?
12. What are the four parts of the forms control process?
13. Why is it important for those providers wanting a new form to go through the approval process?
14. How are bar codes and labels used in forms?

Creation, Storage, and Retention of Paper-based and Hybrid Health Records

Healthcare organizations need policies covering the distribution and storage of health records to ensure that the records can be located quickly when they are needed for patient care and other uses. Controlling the storage of paper-based and hybrid health records is critical to patient care. The quality of patient care as well as the image and reputation of the HIM department may depend on the speed with which patient health information can be retrieved.

Management of paper-based and hybrid health records includes three processes: creation and identification, storage and retrieval, and retention and disposition.

Health Record Creation and Identification

As discussed earlier, the health record is created when the patient is first admitted to or treated in a healthcare facility. Every patient is assigned a specific identification number, and the health record is initiated with the collection of admission or registration information. As data and information about the patient's care and condition are documented, the record grows. The record remains in active use for the purposes of patient care, clinical coding, billing, statistical analysis, and other operational processes until the episode of care ends.

Health Record Identification Systems

For the correct health record to be quickly retrieved when it is needed, each record must be assigned a unique identifier. The choice of record identification system is tied to the organization's filing system and other core information systems.

Alphabetic versus Numeric Patient Identifiers

Small healthcare facilities, such as physician offices, often use a simple alphabetical identifier: the patient's last and first names. This identifier is also used for filing of medical records in strict alphabetical order by the patient's last name. Alphabetical systems are more appropriate for facilities with a smaller number of records. Most healthcare organizations use a record identification system that assigns a numerical identifier to each patient.

Serial Numbering System

In a **serial numbering system**, each patient receives a new number at each visit, and numbers are assigned in straight numerical sequence to consecutive patients in the order in which they arrive for treatment. Each time a patient is treated by the facility, a new number is issued to link the patient to that particular visit or admission. This system is often used by clinics and physician offices.

Unit Numbering System

In a **unit numbering system,** the patient is assigned a number during the first encounter for care and keeps it for all subsequent encounters. The number may be assigned automatically by the computer program. Some facilities, such as Veterans Affairs facilities, use the patient's Social Security number as the unit number because it is a unique permanent number already assigned to the patient. However, due to patient privacy concerns and increases in identify theft, the use of the Social Security number is not recommended for other hospitals. Most large facilities use a unit numbering system. If facilities change from a serial to a unit numbering system, it is important to pick a start date and move forward from that point. As patients are readmitted, they are assigned a new number that then becomes the permanent unit number and all records are brought forward and linked under the new number.

Serial-Unit Numbering System

In a **serial-unit numbering system**, the patient is issued a different number for each admission or encounter for care and the records of past episodes of care are brought forward to be filed under the last number issued. This creates a unit record that contains information from all the patient's encounters. Because this system requires a great deal of shifting of records and changing of numbers, it is not as commonly used as the unit numbering system.

Family Numbering System

Family numbering is a type of unit numbering system. In this system, the entire family is assigned one number and all information on visits by any family member is filed in one location. This system may be appropriate for use in family practice settings, but care must be taken to preserve patient privacy.

Health Record Filing Systems

Most healthcare facilities use numerical filing systems for permanent storage of paper-based health records. Small facilities, such as physician offices and clinics, often use alphabetic filing; larger facilities generally use numerical filing systems.

Straight Numeric Filing System

In a **straight numeric filing system**, records are filed in numerical order according to the number assigned. The major shortcoming of straight numeric filing is that most of the file activity is where the most recent numbers have been assigned since records of recent hospitalizations or visits are the ones most in use.

Terminal-Digit Filing System

In a **terminal-digit filing system**, records are filed according to a three-part number made up of two-digit pairs. The basic terminal-digit filing system contains 10,000 divisions, made up of 100 sections ranging from 00–99 with 100 divisions within each section ranging from 00–99. In a terminal-digit filing system, the shelving units (filing space) is equally divided into 100 sections.

In terminal-digit filing, the record number is placed into terminal-digit order when the health record is ready for filing. The number is broken down into two-digit pairs and is read from right to left. For example, the number 670187 would be written as 67-01-87. The first pair of digits on the right (87) is called the primary number or the terminal-digit number, the second pair of digits (01) is called the secondary number, and the third pair of digits (67) is called the tertiary or final number.

The primary number is considered first for filing. The primary numbers range from 00 to 99 and represent the 100 sections of the filing area. Because many records will be filed in each section, each section needs to be further subdivided, first according to the secondary number and then according to the tertiary number. As shown in figure 8.4, a record numbered 67-01-87 would be filed in section 87, in subsection 01, and then in numerical sequence for 67 (after 66-01-87 and before 68-01-87). All records with the tertiary and secondary numbers of 01-87 would be filed within this part of the file.

Consider three patients who were admitted to a facility and were issued the following numbers in sequence: 67-01-87, 67-01-88, and 67-01-89. In a terminal digit system, these records would be added to three different filing sections of the 100 sections of the file rather than all being filed at the end as in a straight numerical system. (See figure 8.5). In a standard terminal-digit filing area, there will be 10,000 guides to index the primary number sections and secondary number subdivisions so that behind each guide, all records will have the same final four digits. The guides are set up vertically with the digits above the line on the guide representing the division (secondary number) and the digits below the line representing the section (primary number). An index guide tab marked with 67 above the line and 80 below would indicate the 67 division of the 80 section.

The advantage of terminal-digit filing is that filing shelves fill equally rather than at the end of the shelving units, as is the case with conventional straight numerical filing. There will be one record with the primary number 00, one with 01, and so on through 99 for every 100 consecutive numbers issued to patients. For every 100 records added to the file, each section of the file will be increased by only one record. The task of shifting (moving records) to alleviate overcrowding at the end of the shelving unit is reduced because the sections are filed evenly across the sections. One hundred consecutively numbered folders would be removed from 100 separate locations. Thus, the even distribution of records throughout the filing space can be maintained and misfiles can be reduced because clerks need to remember only two numbers at a time.

Another advantage of terminal-digit filing is that the department's workload can be evenly distributed among filing personnel. Certain sections can be designated for each employee. For example, if a department has five file clerks, each could be given responsibility for a specific section, with clerk one responsible for section 00–19, clerk two responsible for section 20–39, and so on. In addition to maintaining the assigned sections, each clerk would file loose reports and keep the records in order, handle requests for information from patient records, and perform other duties.

Terminal-digit filing can be adapted to various types of numbering systems. A six-digit number is most common, but some facilities, such as VA facilities, use a longer number. The VA uses the Social Security number as the basis for terminal-digit filing. For example, number 401-80-1530 could be adapted to serve as a terminal digit by dividing it so that 30 is the primary number, 15 is the secondary number, and 40180 is the tertiary number. The files do not expand as evenly because there is no facility control over the assignment of numbers to patients.

Another advantage of terminal-digit filing concepts is for random distribution of voice files for transcription and health records for coding. The primary digits of the system are randomly assigned to staff so that difficult to understand dictators and difficult to code records are randomly assigned. Terminal-digit filing concepts may also be utilized to distribute loose paperwork filing and the doctors' incomplete area.

Figure 8.4. Filing of patient record 67-01-87 in a terminal digit system

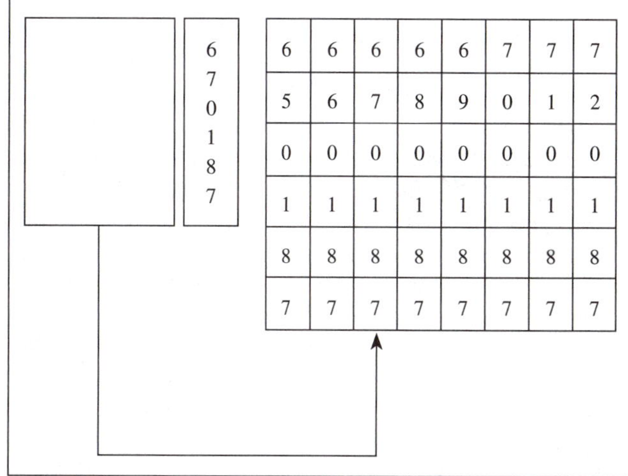

Figure 8.5. Filing of three consecutive patient records under the terminal digit system

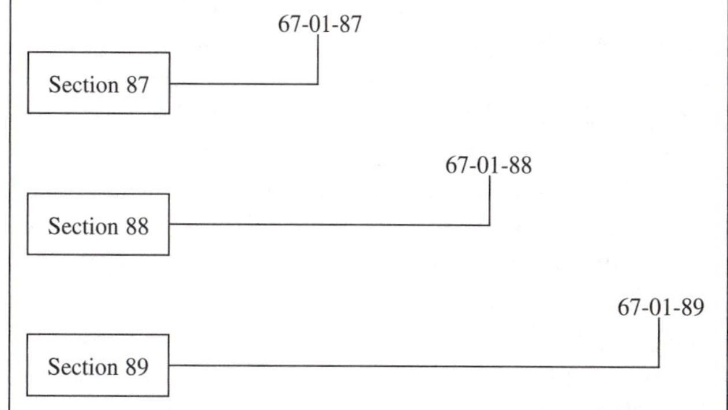

Health Record Storage and Retrieval

The HIM department is responsible for ensuring that the health record is available when needed by the provider for patient care. No matter how well organized and well managed the HIM department is, the timeliness of record delivery to providers is the measure of the quality of the department's services. The hybrid state of the health record makes reproduction of the health record more difficult since the health record may be stored in various formats within the same facility.

Health Record Storage

Storage is the application of efficient procedures for the use of filing equipment and storage media to keep records secure and available to those providers and other healthcare personnel authorized to access them. Record storage equipment can range from numerous types of file cabinets to open shelves of various heights and types.

Planning for health record storage is a major responsibility for the HIM professional. He or she must maintain a leadership role in ensuring that sufficient, conveniently accessible space is available for the storage of paper records. Ways must be provided to consistently maintain sufficient filing room by moving inactive records or by microfilming or imaging records. With hybrid records in which some parts of the record are electronic, the paper sections of the record may be smaller and take less filing space than records that are entirely paper-based.

Because space is expensive, administrators and facilities management personnel are always looking for ways to better use it. The HIM professional must make sure that health records are not located in poor environmental conditions where they can be either damaged or difficult to locate. For example, health records should not be stored in areas where pipes and flammable substances are located. Subbasements without proper flooring and temperature control, parking garages, and non-temperature-controlled commercial storage units are not appropriate storage locations for health records. Water, pests, and mold are all potential problems. Temperature and humidity control are important to prevent mold. The storage area must be clean and dust free and located away from food and trash in order to prevent bugs such as paper mites. Chemical treatments for mold and pests can cause problems for workers who must sort through and locate records for patient treatment. The HIM professional must be firm in the need to protect the original records for the duration of the legally required period. The potential need for the health records should be considered when deciding to send records to an off-site storage facility. Many companies specialize in the storage of vital records and provide the proper conditions for the protection of records as well as access to records.

HIM professionals have had to deal with the restoration of paper records damaged by water resulting from hurricanes, earthquakes, and tornadoes. There are companies that specialize in the restoration of records and can handle disaster recovery. Moreover, some companies negotiate contracts ensuring that the healthcare provider is first in line for recovery efforts should a disaster occur. Paper is extremely fragile when wet and indirect circulation of air is critical; dehumidification and perhaps vacuum freezing are considerations in the restoration process. With a hybrid record in which part of the record is in an electronic format, methods must be utilized to ensure the physical security of those parts of the record also.

Health Record Retrieval

Retrieval is concerned with locating requested records and information. It involves signing out or checking out records from the filing area and tracking those that are not returned within the specified time period. A number of excellent software systems are available for tracking patient records.

HIM personnel must be able to quickly determine the exact location of a specific health record at any time. Facilities should have strict policies and procedures in place that specify who is permitted to check out records from the filing area. Past records are generally requested when patients are readmitted or appear for appointments. Large clinics create a lot of activity in the filing area because records must be pulled in advance for patient appointments.

The filing area should be audited periodically to ensure that files are in correct order, regardless of the filing system used. Loose reports should be attached, and those awaiting attachment should be sorted and organized to facilitate retrieval. Audits of the record tracking system should be conducted to ensure that the health record is still under the responsibility of the person named in the system.

Statistics on the ratio of number of requests to number of health records in the file should be maintained to demonstrate the activity in the filing area. Statistics on the ratio of the number of health records located to the number of records requested provide evidence of the filing function's accuracy and quality.

Health Record Filing and Storage Equipment

Filing equipment vendors are the HIM professional's best resource in planning a filing area that makes the best use of the available space. Open-shelf filing is the least expensive option for health record storage. Shelves are usually arranged back to back just as shelving is in a library. Shelving uses space more efficiently because only 30 to 36 inches are needed for each aisle. When standard file cabinets with drawers are used, aisles should be at least five feet wide to allow two facing file cabinets to be opened at the same time and to allow personnel who need to work in the same area to pass. Lateral files with drawers and doors also require sufficient aisle space for opening the individual drawers and allowing personnel to pass.

Many facilities use open-shelf files mounted on tracks to conserve valuable space. These are referred to as movable files, and many different styles are available. The main consideration is whether the files open electronically or manually. With movable files mounted on tracks, more sections of files can be installed because the floor space for many fixed aisles is not needed. The files in a mobile unit can be opened one aisle at a time. With permanently installed open shelves, there are fixed aisles between each shelf. Whatever type of shelving is selected, the shelves must handle the heavy weight of paper-based health records, which may require reinforced flooring.

The estimated number of file shelves needed is based on several factors. One consideration is the average size of individual records. The volume of patients and the number of repeat visits or readmissions affect the potential expansion of each individual patient record. The type of facility also affects the size of individual records. Acute care facilities with extensive ancillary services and more acutely ill patients have larger individual patient records, as do facilities specializing in transplants, cancer, and other chronic diseases. When unit records are organized in a terminal-digit filing system, there must be adequate expansion space in each division of the filing area to allow for expansion of individual records. Hybrid records in which portions of the records are maintained solely in electronic format are smaller than totally paper-based records.

It is the responsibility of the HIM professional to ensure that the vendors' estimates for filing space are adequate. The number of linear filing inches is the key factor. When there are existing records, the average size of the individual records can be easily calculated by measuring the number of files on a random sampling of shelves. The usable space must be measured from the inside of the panels so that the true number of linear filing inches is reflected. For example, one standard three-foot-wide shelf would have approximately 33 linear inches available for filing, not 36 linear inches. Allowance also should be made for file guides, which also reduce the number of linear filing inches.

An example might be that of a department expanding into another filing area. The department has selected eight-shelf open shelves that are 36 inches wide with 33 inches of actual filing space on each shelf. The department's present health records have been measured in random areas of the existing files and average two inches in thickness. With 5,000 discharges anticipated each year and a projection of five years, 25,000 records will need to be stored (5,000 × 5 = 25,000). Because records average a two-inch thickness, 50,000 filing inches are needed (25,000 × 2 = 50,000). Because each eight-shelf unit will have 264 linear filing inches available, the number of inches needed, 50,000, must be divided by 264 to determine the number of filing units that must be purchased, which will be 190.

Storage space is at a premium, and many facilities have several locations for storage of health records. This can create retrieval problems when health records are at distant locations or off-site. Much personnel time can be spent walking or driving to off-site locations. Some facilities contract with commercial storage companies to store inactive records; commercial storage companies can provide transportation of health records to the facility.

Many facilities use color coded file folders in their filing system—different colors representing numbers or letters depending on the filing system—and the colors appear on the folders and guides. The records in a particular section are in blocks of color. This method allows misfiles to be identified quickly. Vendors of file folders have endless possibilities of color-coding different pairs of numbers and letters. The colors selected to represent particular digits must be permanent and continued when new folders are ordered or else the advantage of color-coding will be lost.

Health Record Retention and Disposition

Retention involves determining the schedule to be followed to protect and preserve active and inactive records. **Disposition** involves the process of destroying the records once the end of the retention period has been reached. Establishing policies that incorporate state and federal laws and maintaining a disaster plan are part of the disposition process. The transfer and destruction of records, optical scanning, and microfilming are all part of this stage. Facilities must be careful to monitor record maintenance so that health records are moved continuously out of active storage as they become inactive or reach maximum retention periods. Health records cannot be stored indefinitely because storage area is expensive. Older records also may not be as useful in the patient care treatment process.

In looking at retention requirements, it is important to look at the requirements for secondary as well as primary records. Primary records are the original health records in whatever form they are kept; secondary records are byproducts of the original information such as indexes, physician profiles, databases, billing information, and other reports or queries.

Accreditation and the Legal Health Record Retention Requirements

AHIMA recommends that retention of health information be based on the needs and requirements of the facility, such as legal requirements, continued patient care, research, education, and other legitimate uses. Joint Commission asserts that the length of health record retention depends on laws, regulations, and the use of health records for care and for other purposes such as research and education.

State laws, CMS regulations, and other federal regulations, accreditation standards, and facility policies and procedures must also be reviewed when establishing a retention schedule. The HIM professional must adhere to the strictest time limit if the recommended retention period varies among different laws and regulations. In addition to the length of time for maintaining health records, the HIM professional must consider the required length of retention for other documentation such as immunization records, mammography records, x-rays and radiographs, and the records of minors and incompetent patients.

CMS requires health records to be maintained for at least five years, according to 42 CFR 482.24(b). This requirement includes committee reports, physician certification and recertification reports, radiologist records (printouts, films, scans, and other images), home health agency records, long-term care records, laboratory records, and any other records that document information about claims. The Occupational Safety and Health Administration (OSHA) requires records of employees with occupational exposure to be maintained for the duration of employment plus 30 years. The statutes of limitation (deadline for filing a lawsuit) in various types of legal actions are important considerations in developing a retention schedule.

The facility or provider is responsible for maintaining the health record. When the facility or provider cannot produce a record, it must be able to prove that the loss was unintentional. Other departments rely on the expertise of the HIM professional to assist them in developing record retention procedures. A retention plan for the facility must be carefully written and included in the departmental policy and procedure manual to ensure that record destruction is part of the normal course of business and that no one particular health record or group of health records is singled out for destruction.

Retention Requirements for Ancillary Materials

E-mail messages and faxes are used for instructions, information about appointments, and the reporting of information. These must be printed or archived and included in the health record.

Images, such as complete readouts or "strips" from EEGs, EKGs, fetal monitors, Holter monitors, treadmill tests, EMGs, echocardiograms, videotapes, and other imaging records, do not have to be kept within the physical health record but must be retrievable for as long as legally required. The original interpretations of the results must actually be part of the physical patient health record. Facilities may have computerized systems that COLD feed the results into the imaging system so that the actual images are available to physicians and other providers. These images are not always of diagnostic quality in some scanning systems, so ancillary departments should maintain the information for the appropriate retention period. State law should be reviewed to determine the handling of other images. In many states, these are handled the same way that radiologist's records are handled.

Fetal monitoring strips create storage problems for many HIM departments. They are part of the mother's record, but because the strips relate to the newborn, they should be maintained according to the length of time stipulated for a minor's records. Because these strips are not compatible with imaging systems, some facilities have digital systems software to maintain and store fetal monitoring strips within the labor and delivery area.

Magnetic tapes containing the digital versions of MRI and CT studies are not considered permanent health records as long as a hard copy of the final images (radiographic film) is placed in the patient's health record. The signed interpretation of the studies must be maintained in the record for the full retention period required by law. According to 21 CFR 900.12 (c)(4), mammograms must be maintained for 5 to 10 years, depending on whether additional mammograms are performed. State laws may require a retention period for mammograms of 20 to 30 years. This is another example of the HIM professional having to ensure that the longer time period is followed when retention schedules are determined.

Microfilming or optical and electronic imaging technology is allowed by most state laws and is an acceptable method of maintaining patient health records. Because the images are of some documents, computerized results, and other test results, each type of work to be imaged must be carefully considered.

Destruction and Transfer of Health Records

After time limits for retention have been reached, the HIM professional must decide on the destruction process for health records, which must ensure that health records are burned, shredded, or destroyed in such a way that protected health information is not revealed. It is important to document the method of destruction, the date, and that fact that record destruction is part of the normal course of business with no one particular health record or group of health records singled out for destruction.

When the facility is closed or sold, its health records are transferred to the successor provider, meaning the entity or individual that purchases the facility. In ambulatory care settings or physician offices, patients are informed of their options to transfer their records to another provider of choice before their health records are transferred to the successor provider. When a physician leaves a group practice, patients should be given the choice to transfer their health records and move with the physician or to have the health records and the responsibility for care transferred to another provider in the group.

Development of a Record Retention Program

Figure 8.6 lists the objectives of a record retention program. The program must ensure that health records are retained; that inactive records are maintained; that retention is cost-effective in terms of storage space, equipment, and personnel; that a formal health record destruction process is in place; and that retention periods are established. A task force or committee might be established with representation from administration, medical staff, health information services, risk management, and legal counsel to give consideration to the needs of all groups who use patient health information. Figure 8.7 lists some of the elements to consider. These include looking carefully at all of the record's uses and the cost of space.

Figure 8.6. Objectives of a record retention program

- To ensure retention and preservation of all valued health records
- To maintain noncurrent records of continuing value for uniform time periods and in designated locations
- To ensure cost-effectiveness in record storage space, equipment, and personnel
- To dispose of unnecessary records by developing an orderly, controlled, and confidential system of record destruction
- To establish record retention periods consistent with patient care, regulatory requirements, and other legal considerations

Figure 8.7. Elements to consider in the preservation of records

- Patient value for continued care
- Record usage in the facility as guided by the patient population and activity of its medical staff
- Legal value as determined by the statute of limitations
- Research value
- Historical value
- Volume and cost to maintain hard-copy storage versus microfilm, optical disk, or remote storage
- Storage and safety standards
- Contractual arrangements with payers

The HIM director is generally responsible for implementing the retention program. However, other individuals may be charged with the shared responsibility of implementing the program in some facilities. Some facilities establish a task force to oversee the record retention program, sometimes chaired by an HIM professional.

The steps in developing a record retention program include:

1. Conduct an inventory of the facility's records
2. Determine the format and location of record storage
3. Assign each record a retention period
4. Destroy records that are no longer needed

Conducting an Inventory of Records

The first step in establishing a record retention program is to carefully and completely inventory the records or categories of records that are maintained. In this phase, it is important to determine all the locations and formats of patient information, including images, videotapes, e-mails, tracings, computerized records, and other formats. The inventory also must include the records and registries maintained by all departments. A comprehensive list of all software and versions used also should be maintained so that health records, documents, and images can be retrieved in the future. Specialized computer systems used by individual departments should be included.

Determining Storage Format and Location

Determining the format and location of storage is the second step in retention program development. Facilities may choose to retain records in paper format or on hard copy and store them either on-site or in off-site contract storage. Off-site contract storage should be located at a distance far enough away from the facility to ensure that a disaster affecting the facility will not also affect the storage location.

One storage mechanism for inactive records is microfilming. Microfilming is the process of recording miniaturized images of a patient health record on film. The images are usually filmed by a special camera onto rolls of 16-millimeter film. The microfilmed images may be stored permanently on the rolls, which may be stored either in boxes labeling the first and last patient numbers on a roll or inserted into special cartridges. Roll film contains information on many patients and cannot be changed. The images are often indexed according to type of form at the time of filming to allow for quicker retrieval of information.

An alternative to storing microfilm rolls in cartridges is to store images in microfilm jackets. The roll film would be cut into strips and inserted into the channels of the jackets. The microfilm jacket has the advantage of serving as an individual folder for storing the records of one patient. Additional filmed images can be added to the jacket or changed. The jackets are usually four by six inches and have a strip at the top on which to record the patient's name and number. Because the strips can be color-coded, the jackets can be filed in filing cabinets or electric files using the same filing and numbering system the facility uses for paper records.

Microfilm cameras also can film directly onto a microfiche film format. Like the microfilm jacket, the microfiche has the advantage of having only one patient's information available on the sheet of fiche. However, its disadvantage is that patient information cannot be updated because the images are filmed directly onto the microfiche itself. The most common size of fiche is a four-by-six-inch sheet, with space for the patient's name and number.

Many facilities use a combination of microfilm formats to accommodate technology and equipment changes. The microfilming of records has many advantages, including the following:

- Microfilming saves space, which is the primary reason why facilities use it.
- Health records can be retrieved and retained for a long period of time.
- It is simple to duplicate microfilm records in order to provide security or backup copies, and paper copies can be printed from reader printer equipment.
- Microfilm is legally admissible as the original document.

The facility also must consider disadvantages when deciding whether to microfilm records. These issues include the following:

- Although microfilming saves a great deal of storage space, it is expensive. For example, preparing the records for filming is a major cost that involves removing staples, checking identification, adjusting oversized or overlapping forms for filming, repairing sheets, and other tasks.

- Special equipment is needed to read and copy microfilm.
- Personnel must be available in patient care areas or in the HIM department to find the microfilm jackets, microfiche, or roll microfilm and to locate the exact information needed.

Microfilming can be done on-site by facility personnel or under contract with a microfilming company. When the facility decides to have the microfilming done in-house, it must take into account the costs of equipment, labor and training, supplies, and maintenance.

On the other hand, when the facility decides to use an outside contract microfilming company, the contract should specify who performs the preparation and packs the boxes of records. After records have been transported to the outside contract company, the facility must be able to retrieve the patient's information at any time in case he or she is readmitted or appears for treatment. When records are to be indexed, the contract should fully explain the indexing procedure to ensure that needed documents are accessible. The contract also should specify the turnaround time for filming. Moreover, film returned to the facility must be carefully analyzed to ensure its quality and legibility before the original record is destroyed. The company microfilming the records usually handles their destruction after the facility has audited the returned film. The cost of microfilming is generally based on the number of images filmed.

A second storage mechanism is optical scanning. Records can be scanned into optical scanning equipment or digitally transferred. The imaging process converts paper or microfilm documents into a computer-readable digital format. The facility must determine what information can be fed directly into the imaging system, for example, registration and face sheet, discharge summary, and all other dictated and transcribed reports. Digitized information, including that produced by laboratory and radiology can be "COLD-fed" into the imaging system. COLD now refers to a variety of technologies related to digitized input and output. Optical scanning produces an image of the record that can be indexed and quickly retrieved and simultaneously viewed by many providers. This is not a true electronic record because the image cannot be changed after it has been permanently archived.

Imaging involves preparing, or prepping, the documents, which must be done before the records are scanned. Staples must be removed, papers repaired, and each page checked to ensure the presence of a bar code on both the front and back of every form in the record. The scanning process involves inserting the paper into the optical scanner so that both the front and back pages are scanned at the same time. Two types of scanners are usually used for health records: flatbed scanners and automatic document-feed scanners. The type of scanner used depends on the volume to be scanned. Flatbed scanners are usually slower than automatic document-feed scanners but require less preparation of individual documents.

Indexing involves identifying each individual page. Indexing is critical. If the image is not indexed to the proper patient and the proper form for that admission, the information cannot be retrieved. Image and indexing inspection is important to make sure the image is legible.

The scanner is the device that actually scans a human-readable document and uses software to make a picture of the document. After being scanned, records must be verified and generally are not submitted to the final stored archive until the physician completes them. After records are archived in the imaging system, they cannot be changed. While waiting to be archived, images can be added or indexing changed.

Facilities assign personnel to handle the tasks of preparation and scanning. Emergency department reports, outpatient reports, and reports submitted from physicians often do not have the proper patient numbers or encounter numbers, and all of this identifying information must be entered so that each form in the record can be properly indexed and retrieved. A concern for HIM professionals is that scanning equipment from one vendor may not work with equipment from another vendor. The long-term storage capability of optical disk has not been evaluated for long-term quality because the technology is still evolving.

Beginning an imaging system requires detailed planning. Decisions must be made about converting existing records or whether only information from a certain date forward will be imaged. In addition, security backups of images should be available. Health records should be on the type of optical storage using WORM, "write once, read many," technology. This means that the data cannot be erased or altered. Rewritable or erasable **optical imaging technology** is not appropriate for health records.

Although imaging has the advantages of rapid retrieval and simultaneous access, it is not an easy process to implement. Loose materials and late-arriving information still must be scanned and indexed. Moreover, problems still exist with recovering charts from the nursing areas after discharge and with unapproved forms being developed and included in the record that cannot be indexed because they do not have bar coding. The HIM department still must perform open-record review and check forms for signatures. In other words, the traditional functions of the HIM department do not change. While the patient is in the facility or in active treatment, the record is paper. The imaging system does not convert the paper into images until after patient discharge or termination of treatment.

Using an imaging system does change the workflow in the facility. The record can be accessed remotely and by more than one provider, which means that physicians spend less time in the HIM department completing records. The record can be queued to HIM employees or others to complete specific tasks such as coding. **Queuing** involves a process of making the record available to a particular user. Because the record is available remotely, HIM employees, such as coders and transcriptionists, are able to work from home or at locations away from the main facility.

Imaging is a key part of the progression to an electronic document management system and ultimately to the electronic health record because it provides providers with quick access to pictures such as x-rays, MRIs, and other documents rather than having to wait for the paper copy. This type of quick access to images improves safety and quality of care.

Assigning a Retention Period

After all departments have been inventoried, the third step is to assign a retention period for each type of record. The retention period should be defined as time in active files, time in inactive storage, and total time before destruction.

As discussed previously, state and federal laws and regulations must be reviewed to ensure that records are maintained for the longest length of time required. Many states recommend that patient health records be retained for 10 years following patient discharge or death. There are usually special requirements for minor patients. For example, the state of Tennessee requires that the records of minors or mentally disabled patients be maintained until the age of majority plus one year, or a total of 10 years, whichever is longer. Therefore, the record of a newborn in Tennessee would be maintained until the patient reaches the age of majority, which is 18 years plus one year or a total of 19 years.

The retention period should reflect the scope and needs of the facility, along with the preliminary costs associated with microfilming, imaging, and other methods of maintaining and storing records. Storage mechanisms should be selected that protect records and provide ease of access and employee safety.

Protection of paper-based, microfilmed and hybrid health records during the legally required retention period is extremely important and needs to be considered before a disaster occurs or a situation occurs where a health record in storage cannot be found. In addition, as discussed earlier, health records can be destroyed or may be unusable due to water damage, extremes of heat and humidity, and damage caused by airborne chemicals and insects. Natural disasters such as floods, hurricanes, and earthquakes should also be considered when determining how and where to store paper medical records. Records should be stored in areas that have clear aisles and doorways, and boxes or shelves should be well marked and indexed so that needed records can be found. Fire extinguishers should be easily accessible. Transportation and availability of health records back to the facility must also be considered.

Commercial storage vendors should be selected carefully to ensure that records are protected from unauthorized access. Policies for security of all satellite record storage areas must be developed and business associate agreements (Discussed in Chapter 10) signed regarding timely access to, and retrieval of, health records.

In facilities utilizing an imaging system, the general rule is usually that paper records should be boxed up after all paper is scanned, indexed, and released in the electronic document management system (EDMS), stored for no longer than six months, and then destroyed. An organization may influence skeptics of destroying the paper by demonstrating quality processes on the front end—during scanning and indexing. The EDMS totally transitions a facility in terms of the legal medical record, and the legal definition is no longer based upon paper.

Destroying Unnecessary Records

Destroying records that are not needed is the fourth step in developing a record retention program. There must be a rule that no patient health information can be destroyed or thrown away without approval of the HIM director or other authorized committee or person, according to facility policy. The HIM professional must be alert to changes in departmental administration or departmental relocation or remodeling because departments often use these events to clean out files, which could result in the destruction of needed patient information.

The destruction of patient records must be done as part of the facility's usual business. When the required retention schedule has been satisfied, a complete list of records to be destroyed should be compiled and submitted to the individual designated to authorize the destruction. Outsourcing of destruction to shredding companies should be carefully monitored to protect patient confidentiality. The destruction of computerized records should follow security guidelines to ensure that the information is destroyed permanently. Facilities must maintain basic information about the patient in the master patient index (MPI), which is maintained permanently even though the corresponding health record is destroyed.

The American Health Information Management Association (AHIMA) recommends that records be destroyed in such a way that the information cannot possibly be reconstructed. The destruction should be documented, and the documentation should include the following:

- Date of destruction
- Method of destruction (shredding, burning, or other means)
- Description of the disposed record series of numbers or items
- Inclusive dates covered
- A statement that the records were destroyed in the normal course of business
- The signatures of the individuals supervising and witnessing the destruction

AHIMA further recommends that facilities maintain destruction certification documents permanently. Such certificates may be required as evidence that records were destroyed in the regular course of business. When facilities fail to apply destruction policies uniformly or when destruction is contrary to policy, courts may allow a jury to infer that the facility destroyed its records to hide evidence.

Check Your Understanding 8.6

Instructions: Answer the following questions on a separate piece of paper.

1. What is the difference between a serial numbering system and a unit numbering system?
2. What are two advantages of terminal-digit filing over straight numerical filing?
3. What are the main factors in determining how long to maintain a health record?
4. What is the major advantage of microfilming health records?
5. What is the major advantage of optical imaging in the chart completion process?
6. What are the four primary steps in a record retention program?

Master Patient Index

The master patient index (MPI) is a permanent database including every patient ever admitted to or treated by the facility. Even though patient health records may be destroyed after legal retention periods have been met, the information contained in the MPI must be kept permanently. The MPI is also referred to as the master person index, the master name file, the **enterprise-wide master person or patient index** (EMPI), regional master patient index (RMPI) and the master patient database. Whatever it is called, the MPI is an important key to the health record because it contains the patient's identifying information including patient name and health record number.

Each facility has an MPI, which is used as the key to locating patient information, for all patients who have been registered or treated at any location in the facility. The MPI can be a simple manual file containing cards with basic identification information about the patient or it can be a sophisticated computerized system. In a computer-based MPI, the database associates the patient with the particular number under which patient treatment information can be located. The index also helps to control number assignments to ensure that former patients with unit numbers are not inadvertently assigned a new number.

The challenges in maintaining the master patient index are many. For example, patients may not remember previous admissions or may have been admitted under a different name. A person other than the patient may have provided incorrect information, resulting in a new number being assigned when the patient returns for an appointment or is readmitted to the hospital. Sometimes patients use different middle initials or a nickname rather than a given name, or their names may have many possible spellings or may be hyphenated. Babies may have names changed, first and last names can be reversed, and outside laboratories may use different data. Basic demographic information such as addresses can be abbreviated incorrectly. In some cases, patients do not speak the same language as the clerk entering the information, resulting in miscommunication and incorrect data. Facilities that have either merged or separated must keep information on patients treated and often have problems combining information from two computer systems into one master patient index. Facilities may have manual card files that have been microfilmed in the past or may use a variety of formats over time, from index cards, to microfilmed cards on rolls or microfiche, to a computerized database.

The challenge for facilities is to maintain a correct and current MPI so that each patient has a unique identifier number. Duplication and overlays and overlaps are a major problem. An **overlap** occurs when a patient has more than one medical record number assigned across more than one database. An **overlay** occurs when one patient record is overwritten with data from another patient's record. The goal is to have a true longitudinal record from birth to death, and the MPI serves as the link to information and certainty of identification that are critical to the quality and safety of patient care. Healthcare facilities have hired HIM professionals as EMPI coordinators or have hired consultants to clean and maintain EMPI systems to ensure that the correct information on the correct patient is available to the provider and others who need it. The sharing of data is a worthy goal, but incorrect information can adversely affect the quality and safety of care; thus, accuracy of the MPI is a critical issue. There is a movement toward a uniform patient identifier that would be used nationwide, although this idea raises concerns about compromising patient confidentiality.

The MPI usually includes the following information:

- Patient's full name and any other names the patient uses
- Patient's date of birth
- Patient's complete address
- Patient's phone numbers including cellular phone number
- Patient's health record number
- Patient's billing or account number
- Name of the attending physician
- Dates of the patient's admission and discharge or the date of the visit or encounter
- Patient's disposition at discharge or the conclusion of treatment
- Patient's marital status
- Patient's gender
- Patient's race
- Name of the patient's emergency contact

Other information may be included to further identify the patient and ensure that his or her name is linked to the proper record number. Some facilities include the mother's maiden name as another way to link the patient health record number and information to the proper patient. Many facilities develop a standard of five common fields to search for each new entry in the MPI and to review the MPI database for potential duplicate entries.

Controls for accuracy of the MPI include limiting access to the index and limiting the ability to make changes to a few key personnel. The first key to maintaining an accurate index is to obtain the correct information in the beginning, but there are numerous problems, such as situations when the patient is unable to provide the correct information or when items are entered improperly. In the past, when only HIM personnel assigned numbers, there was more control; today, numbers are entered by many different personnel to patients entering the facility through many areas such as the emergency department, the inpatient admissions area or the outpatient clinic. The more people involved in entering data, the greater the potential for error.

When a patient's record or healthcare information cannot be located, his or her care may be compromised. Without prior information, the physician and other providers might duplicate tests or treatments. A second record for the same patient is then created under a new number, which adds to the problem of bringing the parts of the patient record together. Research to "clean up" duplicate numbers and other errors is among the HIM professional's responsibilities.

As electronic information exchange becomes more prevalent, it is critical that the master patient indexing system correctly identifies the patient. One possible way to exchange healthcare information among facilities would be to utilize an MPI as an additional technical layer infrastructure serving as an umbrella to connect and provide access to computerized patient information at different facilities. Although the MPI consists of demographic information, it is the first step in ensuring that correct clinical information about the correct patient is shared. The MPI becomes the link among multiple computer systems that must be able to share information with each other. This process is complicated within one facility with many computer systems, but when multiple facilities try to share information, the EMPI or RMPI is a prerequisite to linking together the data within their various computer systems.

Check Your Understanding 8.7

Instructions: Answer the following questions on a separate piece of paper.

1. Why is the MPI considered the key index in the HIM department?
2. Why is accurate information critical for the MPI?
3. What are some of the reasons why incorrect information is obtained?
4. What is the consequence of a patient having duplicate health record numbers?

Real-World Case

A recently hired director of health information management is facing a difficult challenge. The hospital is in the process of converting to an electronic health record and there is a lot of confusion about what to do with the paper health records. The HIM professional is being asked to give up the current file room space to make room for a new diagnostic imaging machine and needs to plan how to archive the paper health records. The hospital administrator just wants to "get rid" of all these old records.

Summary

Although healthcare facilities are working toward an electronic medical record, many facilities still have paper-based or hybrid records. Regardless of its format, the patient health record is the foundation for most of the decisions made in any healthcare facility. Decisions relative to patient care and financial reimbursement depend on the quality of documentation in the health record. The health record is the communication tool among the members of the patient's healthcare team. It is evidence of what was done for the patient, and the information it contains is used to evaluate the quality of care and to provide important information for research and public health needs. The information in the healthcare record protects the legal interests of both the patient and the facility. The traditional saying, "if it wasn't documented, it wasn't done," is a reminder of how important the record is for the patient, the facility, and the numerous other users of the record and the information it contains.

Ensuring that the health record meets current regulatory, legal, accrediting, and licensing standards as well as the facility's bylaws and polices is an ongoing challenge for the HIM professional. He or she must continuously educate and update providers on changes affecting documentation. Records must be reviewed both while the patient is in active treatment and after treatment to ensure that they meet the current requirements. It is important to analyze and process paper-based or hybrid health records efficiently to ensure that complete information is available for billing and reimbursement purposes. Facilitating the completion of health records by providers is a key factor in ensuring that needed information can be provided to all authorized users.

Facilities use a variety of formats for storing health records to ensure that they are available for future use. As technology has changed, so have the methods of maintaining and storing patient records. Records may be copied onto different types of microfilm stored in cabinets on rolls or on microfiche, scanned or maintained in the HIS. The facility may have a recently installed imaging system. Healthcare information includes videotapes, graphic results, videos, and images from specific computerized test results.

The master patient index may be maintained in many formats also including partially on cards that have been microfilmed and on different types of microfilm. The MPI is the key to finding the correct patient's information.

The HIM professional has been incrementally transitioning from managing paper health records to managing information in a variety of media and formats. The transition is ongoing, and HIM professionals must take a leadership role in ensuring that needed health information from the patient's past continues to be available for use in the future.

References

42 CFR 483.20: Code of Federal Regulations.

Abraham, P.R. 2001. *Documentation and Reimbursement for Home Care and Hospice Programs.* Chicago: AHIMA.

AHIMA Ambulatory Care Section. 2001. *Documentation for Ambulatory Care.* Rev. ed. Chicago: AHIMA.

AHIMA e-HIM Work Group on Implementing Electronic Signatures. 2003 (Oct. 20). Practice brief: Implementing electronic signatures. *Journal of AHIMA*–Web exclusive.

AHIMA e-HIM Work Group on Speech Recognition in the EHR. 2003 (Oct. 20). Practice brief: Speech recognition in the electronic health record. *Journal of AHIMA*–Web exclusive.

AHIMA MPI Task Force. 2004. Practice brief: Building an enterprise master person index. *Journal of AHIMA* 75(1):56A–56D.

AHIMA/MTIA Joint Task Force. 2008 (July). Transcription Turnaround Time for Common Document Types. http://library.ahima.org.

American Health Information Management Association. 2005. *Documentation and Reimbursement for Behavioral Healthcare Services.* Chicago: AHIMA.

Association of Healthcare Documentation Integrity (AHDI). http://www.ahdionline.org.

Burrington-Brown, J. and G. Hughes. 2003 (June). Practice brief: Disaster planning for health information. *Journal of AHIMA*–Web exclusive.

Clark, J.S., ed. 2004. *Documentation for Acute Care.* Rev. ed. Chicago: AHIMA.

Horton, L. 2007. *Calculating and Reporting Healthcare Statistics.* Chicago: AHIMA.

Hughes, G. 2002 (Nov.). Practice brief: Destruction of patient health information. *Journal of AHIMA*–Web exclusive.

James, E. 2004. *Documentation and Reimbursement for Long-Term Care.* Chicago: AHIMA.

Joint Commission. 2008. *Comprehensive Accreditation Manual for Hospitals.* Oak Brook Terrace, IL: Joint Commission.

Marrelli, T.M. 2000. *Nursing Documentation Handbook.* 3rd ed. St. Louis: Mosby/YearBook.

National Association for Home Care. 2005. http://www.nahc.org.

National Hospice and Palliative Care Organization. 2005. http://www.nhpco.org.

Peden, A. 2005. *Comparative Records for Health Information Management.* 2nd ed. Clifton Park, NY: Thompson Delmar Learning.

Rhodes, H. 2002 (June 24). Practice brief: Retention of health information. *Journal of AHIMA*–Web exclusive.

Rinehart-Thompson, L.A. 2008. Storage media profiles and health record retention practice patterns in acute care hospitals. *Perspectives in Health Information Management.* 5(9): 1–13.

Tegan, A., et al. 2005. Practice brief: The EHR's impact on HIM functions. *Journal of AHIMA* 76(5):56C–H.

United Network for Organ Sharing. http://www.unos.org/data/about/collection.asp.

Weed, Lawrence L. 1970. *Medical Records, Medical Education, and Patient Care.* Cleveland, OH: Case Western Reserve University.

Other Suggested Resources

AHIMA e-HIM Work Group on Maintaining the Legal EHR. 2005 (Nov.-Dec.). Update: Maintaining a legally sound health record—paper and electronic. *Journal of AHIMA* 76(10): 64A–L.

AHIMA e-HIM Work Group on Electronic Document Management as a Component of EHR, 2003. Electronic Document Management as a Component of the Electronic Health Record. http://library.ahima.org.

Brodnik, et al. 2009. *Fundamentals of Law for Health Informatics and Information Management.* Chicago: AHIMA.

Chapter 9
Electronic Health Records

Margret K. Amatayakul, MBA, RHIA, CHPS, FHIMSS

Learning Objectives

- Describe the evolution of the electronic health record (EHR) and its supporting technologies
- Identify terms and concepts associated with EHRs
- Describe technologies that support and supplement EHRs
- Discuss EHR system challenges and the supporting roles of health information management (HIM) professionals in addressing these challenges
- Develop an appreciation for the planning and implementation aspects of EHRs
- Provide examples of EHR systems as they may be implemented in various types of care settings

Key Terms

Access controls
Ancillary system applications
Application service provider (ASP)
Architecture
ASTM Continuity of Care Record (CCR)
Audit controls
Authentication
Availability
Bar-code medication administration record (BC-MAR) system
Bridge technology
Certification Commission for Healthcare Information Technology (CCHIT)
Change management
Client/server architecture
Clinical data repository (CDR)
Clinical data warehouse (CDW)
Clinical decision support (CDS)
Clinical document architecture (CDA)
Clinical messaging
Clinical transformation
Computer output to laser disk (COLD)
Computerized provider order entry (CPOE)
Confidentiality
Context-sensitive
Contingency planning
Continuity of care document (CCD)
Dashboard
Data exchange standards
Data quality management
Digital Imaging in Communications in Medicine (DICOM)
E-Discovery
E-forms
Electronic health record (EHR)
Electronic medical record (EMR)
Electronic medication administration record (EMAR) system
Enterprise (or electronic) content and records management (ECRM)
E-prescribing (e-Rx)
Financial and administrative applications
Foundational applications (for EHR)
Health information exchange (HIE)
Health Level Seven (HL7)
Healthcare Information Security and Privacy Collaboration (HISPC)
Healthcare Information Technology Standards Panel (HITSP)
Heuristic thought
Hospital information system (HIS)
Human–computer interface
Hybrid record
Information technology (IT) acquisition strategy
Institute of Medicine (IOM)
Integration
Integrity
Interface
Interoperability
Knowledge base
Laboratory information system (LIS)
Legacy system
Legal health record
Longitudinal
Medication reconciliation
Message format standards
Migration path
National Council for Prescription Drug Programs (NCPDP)
Nationwide health information network (NHIN)
Online analytical processing (OLAP)
Online transaction processing (OLTP)
Order communications
Personal health record (PHR)
Pharmacy information system (PIS)
Picture archiving and communication system (PACS)
Point-of-care (POC) patient charting system
Practice management system (PMS)
Protected health information (PHI)
Protocol
Radiology information system (RIS)
Redundancy
Redundant arrays of independent (or inexpensive) disks (RAID)
Registry
Remote connectivity
Results management systems
Results review systems
Risk analysis
Semantics
SMART goals
Smart peripherals
Source systems
Specialty clinical applications
Structured data
Syntax
Unstructured data
Vocabulary
Web portal
Web Services Architecture (WSA)
Workflow
eXtensible Markup Language (XML)

Although the concept of the electronic health record (EHR) has been around since the late 1960s, it has only been since the late 1990s that it has become a serious goal for many provider organizations. This goal was further solidified in President Bush's 2004 State of the Union address, which referenced the importance of EHRs and created the goal of an EHR for all Americans by 2014, with the help of significant federal government initiatives. The concept of capturing clinical data from multiple sources for use at the point of care in clinical decision-making has been difficult to achieve because there are many unique challenges in health information computing.

Health information computing is not just about quickly "crunching" numbers to produce a bank balance or to calculate an airplane weight for takeoff. Health information is largely textual. However, computers do not manipulate narrative text as easily as numbers. Moreover, health information is contextual. A given word may have different meanings when associated with other words (for example, red may indicate embarrassment when describing a face or it may indicate infection when describing a lesion). This makes it difficult for computers to "read" and interpret narrative information. Yet, narrative is the predominant form of documentation in paper-based records. Users must adapt to a significant change in how they enter data to take full advantage of an EHR.

Furthermore, healthcare professionals who need to use computers are very mobile. They move to examining rooms, to the surgery suite with a patient on a gurney, or even to patients in their homes. Other workers are mobile, but their data requirements are generally more limited (such as in the package delivery industry). Handheld, wireless devices have begun to be deployed successfully in healthcare computing only recently, but they still are not ideal. Finally, most computerization has been built on the assumption that there are standard ways of doing things. Computers can process an enormous amount of data very rapidly when standard terms and standard processes are being used. However, the human body is anything but standard. Healthcare is as much an art as it is a science. It has taken time for sophisticated computational processes to be developed that essentially allow the computer to "learn" processes through pattern analysis, thus supporting humans as they engage in **heuristic thought** processes when diagnosing and treating patients.

Perhaps the biggest challenge is not about the technology at all, but the people, policy, and process issues that arise as organizations grapple with the changes that automating information—not just the chart—has on daily **workflows** and processes. Unfortunately, many organizations approach the implementation of an EHR from the perspective of yet another technology, rather than as a part of a much broader clinical transformation. The Joint Commission (Pryor et al. 2006) defines **clinical transformation** as "a comprehensive, ongoing approach to care delivery excellence that offers value while measurably improving quality, enhancing service, and reducing costs through the effective alignment of people, process, and technology."

This chapter focuses on the importance of the EHR and its supporting technologies. It describes what forms EHRs take and how they integrate the roles of information technology (IT) and traditional health information management (HIM) into truly an information management (IM) program that supports clinical transformation. The chapter also emphasizes the importance of an integrated view of IM within a hospital, clinic, or other care delivery organization, as well as across care delivery organizations in integrated delivery networks (IDNs) and beyond to personal health records (PHRs) for consumer empowerment, health information exchange (HIE), and, ultimately, a nationwide health information network (NHIN) for value-driven healthcare.

Theory into Practice

Dr. Smith is at home having breakfast with her family. Before heading off to the hospital to check on patients and then to the office, she decides to clear as much from her inbox as possible this morning since she plans to attend a local medical society meeting this evening and wants to leave her office early. She logs onto her computer at home using a secure Web portal and first reviews all of the lab results that came in since yesterday. She approves most for posting to her patients' personal health records, but tasks her office receptionist to arrange a call with one of the patients for today if possible.

In Dr. Smith's inbox she sees a message from a colleague, Dr. Jones, who is requesting a consult for a patient with an especially severe condition. Dr. Jones has used his practice management system to check and receive prior authorization from the patient's health plan for the consult and used his EHR to forward the patient's health summary via the Continuity of Care Document standard to Dr. Smith for her review. In addition to this message, Dr. Smith's office is also requesting approval for renewal of a medication for a patient who is out of town. In responding to the renewal request, an alert informs Dr. Smith that the patient is also due for a checkup, so this information is sent back to the office scheduling system for contacting the patient to make an appointment within the next 10 days. Further checking her inbox, Dr. Smith notes that there is an e-mail from another colleague wanting to chat before the meeting this evening about a new treatment regime that appears promising. Not having seen the literature on this, Dr. Smith checks the National Library of Medicine archives on the Internet for any possible articles. Finding a few, she tags them for printing in the office. Finally, Dr. Smith plans on reviewing and signing the two discharge summaries she dictated yesterday so they may be electronically fed into those patients' records but before she has a chance to do this she receives an instant message concerning a patient in the hospital whose condition is deteriorating rapidly.

Not wanting to delay treatment for this patient until she arrives at the hospital, Dr. Smith engages the charge nurse in an exchange of information, including a streaming video of the patient's latest vital signs. Dr. Smith decides to move the patient to critical care and places a series of orders for the patient. She is aided in her medication reconciliation process by access to a comprehensive list of the patient's past medications that is supplied by the health plan that Dr. Smith, as a member of the health information exchange organization in the community, receives as well as current medications from the hospital bar-code medication administration record system. In addition, while placing an order for a specific medication via the hospital's portal to its computerized provider order entry system with its clinical decision support system, Dr. Smith is alerted that the medication she entered is contraindicated with another drug the patient is taking, so she makes an adjustment. As it is now time for her to leave, she quickly sets a reminder to review the two transcribed documents at lunch time and logs off the system.

This scenario reflects the growing trends of **remote connectivity**; clinical messaging; integration of voice, data, and video; use of knowledge sources; work flow tasking, clinical decision support, and integration of the components of the EHR with multiple external sources and uses of health information.

Evolution of the Electronic Health Record

The EHR is as much a concept as a product to buy or a system to build. In its landmark work, the **Institute of Medicine** (IOM) defined the **electronic health record** (EHR), then called the computer-based patient record (CPR), as a record "that resides in a system specifically designed to support users by providing accessibility to complete and accurate data, alerts, reminders, clinical decision support systems, links to medical knowledge, and other aids. This definition encompasses a broader view of the patient record than is current today, moving from the notion of a location or device for keeping track of patient care events to a resource with much enhanced utility in patient care (including the ability to provide an accurate longitudinal account of care), in management of the healthcare system, and in extension of knowledge" (IOM 1991). In addition, the IOM provided the caveat that "merely automating the form, content, and procedures of current patient records will perpetuate their deficiencies and will be insufficient to meet emerging user needs" (IOM 1991 reaffirmed by the IOM in a 1997 update to its original patient record study).

As with any revolutionary system, the EHR has suffered somewhat from multiple different interpretations and rapid development of products that did not fully meet the vision. When the IOM first released its report, vendors rushed to market such products. They were often more vaporware than reality or were limited in true EHR functionality. In fact, some of them were so disappointing or cumbersome to use that they may have discouraged potential users to such an extent that they may be unwilling to try again.

Today, there is a much better understanding of the complexity of what an EHR is and how it may help achieve the following goals:

- Improve the quality of healthcare through data availability and links to knowledge sources
- Enhance patient safety with context-sensitive reminders and alerts, clinical decision support, automated surveillance, chronic disease management, and drug and device recall capability
- Support health maintenance, preventive care, and wellness through patient reminders, health summaries, tailored instructions, educational materials, and home monitoring and tracking capability
- Increase productivity through data capture and reporting formats tailored to the user; streamlined workflow support; and patient-specific care plans, guidelines, and protocols
- Reduce hassle factors and improve satisfaction for clinicians, consumers, and caregivers by managing scheduling, registration, referrals, medication refills, and work queues and by automatically generating administrative data
- Support revenue enhancement through accurate and timely eligibility and benefit information, cost-efficacy analysis, clinical trial recruitment, rules-driven coding assistance, external accountability reporting and outcomes measures, and contract management
- Support predictive modeling and contribute to development of evidence-based healthcare guidance
- Maintain patient confidentiality and exchange data securely among all key stakeholders

EHR Terms

Still today, there remains the challenge of developing, implementing, and truly achieving the goals set forth for EHR, especially as it is recognized that these goals extend information technology beyond a single care delivery organization across the continuum of care as well as to consumers directly. The result continues to be the use of a variety of terms in an attempt to describe the stage at or purpose for which an organization or vendor is using or developing a product—perhaps so as not to overstate capabilities or set false expectations.

In 2008, the National Alliance for Health Information Technology (NAHIT) published a set of terms and definitions to help the industry achieve consensus on terminology, especially surrounding the use of electronic *health* record versus electronic *medical* record. While it is too early to determine whether the definitions will be widely adopted, it is interesting to note that some vendors who have used the term electronic medical record in their advertising have already started changing their product names to EHR.

Electronic health record (EHR) is the term used in this textbook to describe a comprehensive system of applications that afford access to **longitudinal** (from birth to death) health information about an individual across the continuum of care, assist in documentation, support clinical decision making, and provide for knowledge building. This is consistent with the definition of EHR proposed by NAHIT, which states "an electronic record of health-related information on an individual that conforms to nationally recognized interoperability standards and that can be created, managed, and consulted by authorized clinicians and staff across more than one healthcare organization" (NAHIT 2008).

Electronic medical record (EMR) has been a popular term, but with multiple meanings. In some contexts, EMR refers to physician office systems and in other contexts it refers to systems that rely heavily on document imaging and other electronic content management (especially in hospitals). The NAHIT defines this term as "an electronic record of health-related information on an individual that can be created, gathered, managed, and consulted by authorized clinicians and staff within one healthcare organization." (NAHIT 2008, 6). The key difference between the terms EHR and EMR as suggested by NAHIT is in EHR being interoperable and EMR not. **Interoperability** refers to the ability of two different systems to exchange data with each other. Unfortunately, many care delivery organizations are challenged with systems not being as interoperable as desired within their own organization, let alone with other organizations, hence the popularity of the more limited EMR term.

Neither of the NAHIT's definitions of EHR or EMR addresses the functionality that contributes to enhanced utility beyond that of paper-based records that the IOM originally envisioned. In 2004, however, the standards development organization, **Health Level Seven** (HL7), adopted the term *EHR* in its EHR-System Functional Model and has described a highly functional system. EHR is the only term used by the federal government in its efforts to promote adoption of health information technology, including requiring "interoperable EHRs" as certified by the **Certification Commission for Healthcare Information Technology** (CCHIT) in federal incentive programs. Although the term *record* is still used in all of these references to convey a rather confined set of information, the term *health* broadens the concept of the record containing only information about medical care to all information about maintaining health, wellness, and prevention of illness and injury important to an individual.

In addition to these definitions, there has been no resolution regarding whether an EMR and an EHR are really two different systems or if one is a precursor to the next. Some hospitals have adopted not only both terms, but two separate systems. They use components of an EHR during the period of patient care, and then electronically feed or print out and scan documents to achieve a totally paperless state, which they call their EMR. If this begins to feel very confusing, the sad state of affairs is that, indeed, there is a lot of confusion!

EHR Key Concepts

Perhaps the best approach to reduce confusion about what is an EHR is to recognize that the EHR is the end state desired by all, and that it may be built on and complemented by many different technologies and applications—some of which are fully interoperable and others that can be made accessible for viewing even if they are not fully capable of sharing data across the systems. This highlights two other important concepts to be distinguished: structured, or discrete, data and unstructured data. **Structured data** are the values of variables that the computer can process. For example, in the sentence, "This is a three-month-old female with a cough," the age, sex, and chief complaint are variables. If "three-month," "female," and "cough" are entered into fields for age, sex, and chief complaint, respectively, they may be encoded by the computer for easy processing. The numeric age (three) may be captured as is, with a code to represent month (as opposed to day or year). The sex may be designated as F or M, 1 or 2, or some other coding system as designated by the designer of the system. The chief complaint may be coded by ICD, SNOMED, or other **vocabulary**. When these three elements are entered, they may be processed in many ways in the EHR. For example, age may be used to calculate the appropriate dose of a medication (the computer may contain the ability to process a rule such as "for patients under the age of three months, reduce adult dose by half for this medication"). Another example of structured data occurs when a birth date is entered, and the computer always calculates the age of the patient according to the current date, thus eliminating the need for the age of the patient to be entered into the system. Structured data are essential for all forms of **clinical decision support** (CDS) and for producing both internal reports for patient recall (such as for visit reminders and drug or device recalls), quality improvement, and research, as well as to meet external accountability reporting.

Unstructured data include narrative notes, which may be typed into comment fields, or dictated, transcribed, or handwritten into an electronic system, as well as images (scanned documents or medical images). Although unstructured data may be indexed for later retrieval and viewing, they are not as easily processed as structured data. Today, **enterprise (or electronic) content and records management** (ECRM) systems are becoming increasingly sophisticated. These systems enable scanning and indexing of paper documents and other content in digital form. These systems may appear as if they are causing structured data processing to occur. For example, a form that contains allergy information in a given location on the form may have that allergy information individually indexed and then made available for the system to display as a reminder about allergies in designated locations. However, the system would not be able to run a report on how many food allergies were recorded for patients having an adverse reaction to a specific drug because that allergy information was only unstructured data in a specific location, not a structured variable with multiple values—including specific types of foods, medications, bee venom, and others. While this may not seem like an important report to run, it may be performed as part of post-marketing drug surveillance. For example, the advice to avoid grapefruit juice when taking Lipitor came about by identifying drug reactions caused by food.

The difference between structured data and unstructured data is very important. While not everything recorded about a patient needs to be in structured format, it is essential to carefully think through what data might ultimately be needed in CDS and for reporting purposes, especially as increasing quality measurement and reporting requirements are unfolding from the federal government, payers, and others.

A final concept to understand in approaching EHR is that the EHR is not a single piece of software or one application. Rather, it is the ability for many applications to exchange and process data. These applications may vary by type of care delivery organization.

In hospitals, the CCHIT is certifying "hospital EHRs" only if they have **foundational applications** coupled with **electronic medication administration record** (EMAR) and **computerized provider order entry** (CPOE) systems. Foundational applications include those that capture patient and provider demographic and administrative information (such as from a Registration-Admission Discharge Transfer [R-ADT]), maintain and create custom patient lists (including master person index [MPI] system), maintain problem lists, retain allergy information, manage medication lists, access and view test results during the ordering process (so the laboratory and radiology departments must also have information systems), and perform **medication reconciliation** (that is, checking medications each time a patient transfers to another level of care). Obviously, for CPOE and EMAR to be viable there must at least be a pharmacy information system capable of receiving orders and generating information for medication administration. The CPOE and EMAR systems themselves must include clinical decision support functionality, such as to display an allergy alert when ordering a medication or to indicate a medication is overdue for administration. CCHIT has not yet incorporated functionality for other forms of information capture, display, and use, such as for performing nursing assessments, capturing history and physical exam information, or recording progress notes, vital signs, or other information. CCHIT just began certifying inpatient EHR products in 2007, and the criteria for certification are expected to expand in subsequent years to include applications for these other functions, as well as specialty services such as intensive care, labor and delivery, and the like. In hospitals, many of the applications that support CPOE and EMAR and other applications have been relatively stand-alone applications. They each may have received patient demographic data and some may have had **order communications** directed to them. As more of the components are in place, hospitals typically look for tighter **integration** of data and adoption of CDS systems. CDS systems include context-specific templates that drive data collection; alerts about clinical conditions, such as indications and contraindications concerning medications or changes in patient vital signs; reminders, potentially about health maintenance and wellness protocols; and many other forms of clinical help. In general, CDS systems require two key things: structured data and a clinical data repository (CDR), or a special form of relational database that can integrate all the data from disparate applications (discussed later in this chapter).

In ambulatory settings, the EHR may be a more integrated set of applications for the full range of processes performed in outpatient departments, clinics, physician offices, and the like. Physician offices typically have a **practice management system** (PMS) that manages many of the foundational elements of registering a patient, scheduling an appointment, capturing charges, billing, and so on. This will feed into the EHR that enables maintaining a problem list, medication list, allergy information, and immunization information; capturing history and physical exam information, care plans, patient progress, and visit notes; ordering tests, procedures, therapies, nursing services, and consults (using an application that is essentially CPOE); and writing prescriptions. **E-prescribing** (e-Rx) is a special type of ordering application that generates a prescription to be filled by a retail pharmacy that is not exactly equivalent to a medication order that is directed to the clinical pharmacy in a hospital.

In addition to these two primary types of EHRs, there are those that require special functionality for emergency departments, long-term care, home care, and other types of care delivery organizations. The **personal health record** (PHR) is another application which may be a supplement to an EHR or a system separate from the care delivery organization. The PHR is a means for individuals to compile information about their health, the care they have received, and other factors important to them. PHRs can be an important adjunct to EHRs. Many providers are looking at ways to provide patients with more information about their care and to receive information from individuals that may be useful for their care. Some providers are concerned that PHRs are not standardized and often not structured in a manner amenable to electronic processing in EHRs; others have expressed liability concerns. PHRs may contain more information than a provider has the time (or is reimbursed for time) to review at any given care encounter or may be lacking information vital to the care of the patient. However, PHRs can be extremely valuable for patients with chronic illness, individuals who may be unable to relate health history except via a PHR carried by a caregiver, or individuals who are highly mobile. HL7 has created a PHR-System Functional Model and CCHIT has plans to start certifying PHRs in 2009. It is likely that PHRs will see greater adoption in the near future.

Check Your Understanding 9.1

Instructions: On a separate piece of paper, indicate whether each answer is true or false. If the statement is false, change the statement so it reads true or explain why it is false.

1. An EHR is the same as an EMR.
2. *EHR* is the term that describes interoperability required by federal government incentive programs.
3. Some providers are concerned about the liability that PHRs may introduce into their practice of medicine.
4. An example of structured data would be the value of the diastolic blood pressure.
5. CDS depends on the integration of structured data.
6. Hospital EHR systems tend to be built from many clinical computing components.
7. The federal government most commonly uses the term *electronic medical record* to distinguish physician office systems from hospital-based health information technology (HIT).
8. Structured data are generally encoded by the computer for processing.
9. Both hospitals and clinics use e-prescribing systems to order medications.
10. For a CPOE system to be included in an EHR certified by CCHIT, it must include clinical decision support functionality.

EHR Functionality

Three important work products have contributed significantly to today's better understanding of how an EHR should function. These are from the IOM, HL7, and CCHIT. In 2003, the IOM again contributed to the body of knowledge surrounding EHRs when it responded to a federal government request to describe EHR key capabilities. It identified eight core functionalities and developed a spreadsheet of how they could be rolled out across four types of healthcare organizations (hospitals, ambulatory care, nursing homes, and care in the community [PHR]) over an eight-year time frame. The core functionalities are (IOM 2003):

- Health information and data
- Results management
- Order entry and management
- Decision support
- Electronic communication and connectivity
- Patient support
- Administrative processes
- Reporting and population health management

The 2003 IOM work was then given to the HL7 standards development organization for them to enhance and ballot as a standard. This was done in 2004, as the EHR System Functional Model Draft Standard for Trial Use (DSTU), and was finalized as an ANSI-accredited standard in 2007. The model is depicted in figure 9.1.

The HL7 EHR-System Functional Model (EHR-S FM) includes approximately 60 pages of functions, their descriptions, rationale for inclusion, and citations, where applicable. The work incorporates not only the IOM key capabilities but enhances these with greater administrative functionality and explicit security requirements to ensure confidentiality as well as the integrity of and availability to the data. The preface to the HL7 EHR-S FM notes that the functions described are visionary and that not every vendor will, or would be expected to, incorporate all functions. This clearly recognizes that the EHR is still very much in development and that organizations must take a **migration path** through various applications, technologies, and operations to achieve the benefits cited for an EHR.

In order to assist organizations in acquiring products that meet a minimum set of functionality, the CCHIT has formed to establish criteria, test products against the criteria, and provide certification of EHRs. The organization was formed in 2005, with an investment from American Health Information Management Association (AHIMA) and the Healthcare Information Management and Systems Society (HIMSS). It also received federal government funding for some of its start-up operations and expects to be self-sustaining when the initial investment and grant funds have been depleted. The CCHIT began certifying products in 2006. The criteria they develop to use in the certification process are based on HL7 as well as other standards.

Migration Path

Because an EHR is essentially a set of functional components and the means to get them to work together, each organization should recognize that a migration path is necessary to ultimately reach its goals for clinical transformation through EHR. This migration path may be considered a strategic

Figure 9.1. HL7 EHR-System Functional Model

Direct Care	DC.1	Care Management
	DC.2	Clinical Decision Support
	DC.3	Operations Management and Communication
Supportive	S.1	Clinical Support
	S.2	Measurement, Analysis, Research and Reports
	S.3	Administrative and Financial
Information Infrastructure	IN.1	Security
	IN.2	Health Record Information and Management
	IN.3	Registry and Directory Services
	IN.4	Standard Terminologies & Terminology Services
	IN.5	Standards-based Interoperability
	IN.6	Business Rules Management
	IN.7	Workflow Management

Source: Health Level Seven 2007. Copyright 2007 by Health Level Seven,® Inc

plan, but is somewhat different than the traditional IT strategic plan that focuses only on applications and technology. Because the EHR is a tool to use for clinical transformation, the migration path should also reflect the operational elements of people, policy, and process changes to address improvements in clinical quality, patient safety, evidence-based practices, cost of care, productivity, and user satisfaction. The migration path should identify specific, measurable goals along a realistic time line given the organization's current culture, information technology infrastructure, financial capability, and other strategic imperatives. (See figure 9.2.)

Many hospitals are starting their EHR migration by to adopting **bridge technology** such as ECRM and **clinical messaging** that provides some, but not all, of the benefits of EHR, and many physician offices are rushing to market to buy an EHR that they really do not understand. Little study has been done on the impact that adoption of any of the technology has on the organization, whether it be the ability to move forward with other EHR components in a hospital or to actually use the EHR in the office. Indeed, many organizations are making investment decisions that will be difficult for them to change as time goes on and their requirements get more sophisticated.

This is not to imply that bridge technology is inappropriate or that physician offices are not at all prepared for an EHR. Bridge technology serves a very useful purpose and may be the most appropriate strategy for a given organization. However, a formal review should be made of the EHR goals, current and planned applications, current and planned technology, and organizational culture and readiness. It should be understood that ECRM, for example, perpetuates the paper record, but makes information more accessible. Some organizations actually believe that instituting ECRM (as its primary strategy) sets an organization back in its quest for an EHR because it does not encourage use of data capture and retrieval technology. (It should be noted that some ECRM support for EHR will always be necessary, as there will be external documents to scan, e-mail messages to save, some—though hopefully a decreasing amount—of transcription to store, and the like.)

In constructing a migration path, the first step should be explicitly documenting what the organization wants to accomplish by automating its clinical systems. For instance, a hospital may have some goals to improve its near-miss medication error rate by 80 percent using the **bar-code medication administration record** (BC-MAR) system, which adds positive patient identification and drug information to EMAR to carry out automated reminders for the five rights of medication management (right patient, right medication, right dose, right route, and right time); to reduce unnecessary diagnostic studies tests by 10 percent by providing results to providers at the same time an order is placed; and to have

Figure 9.2. An example migration path for an EHR

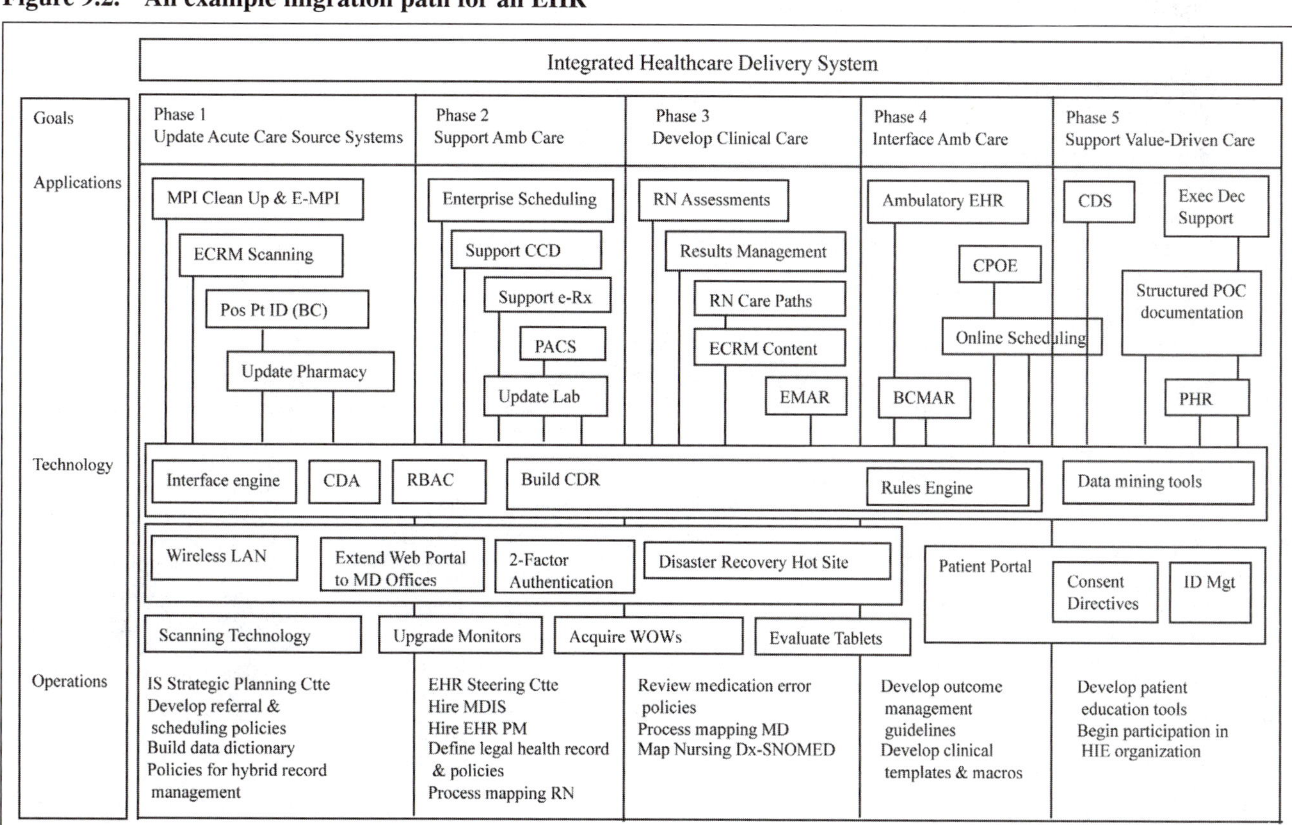

nurses spend 50 percent less time on paperwork by using a single nurse assessment template that distributes data to all other applicable users that could increase time spent on patient education by half an hour for each patient. Writing **SMART goals** ensure that goals are specific, measurable, attainable, realistic, and timely. These goals should help the hospital identify the needed functionality in the components of the EHR they acquire, identify the specific technology requirements to support those functions, and set expectations for people to adopt new policies and processes to ensure the goals' achievement and, therefore, provide value back to the organization for its investment.

The second step in constructing a migration path should be describing the current state of the organization's applications, technology, and operations. Then the organization should determine what applications, technology, and operational elements are needed to achieve each of its goals for clinical transformation.

Once the migration path is developed, it should be reviewed regularly and updated as needed. It becomes the roadmap for all decisions relative to going forward with clinical transformation. Achieving consensus on the migration path keeps organizations from making reactive decisions. Except for unanticipated changes in current applications, technology, or operations, the migration path should be relatively stable and enable the organization to be proactive in its path to achieving benefits from EHR. Every organization has its own migration path. There is no one right or wrong path, only one that is most appropriate for a particular organization given its current situation and future goals. Unfortunately, many organizations are not taking the approach of strategically planning for an EHR but, rather, are responding to external pressures, acquiring whatever their vendor offers, or implementing a system they consider temporary, never retiring any of their information systems. The investment not only in acquiring any technology, but also in taking the time and making the effort to implement and gain adoption of a system is immense and often considered too great to ever abandon. Even when a vendor retires a product, a healthcare organization is more likely to find a way to work with the system than to buy a replacement, fearing the effort it will take to get a new system working satisfactorily.

EHR Foundation: Financial and Administrative and Ancillary Support Systems

Clearly, if the definition of EHR includes the ability to capture data from multiple sources, all source data must be in electronic form. Collectively these are called **source systems**, and there are several types. (See figure 9.3.) Most hospitals and many physician offices have **financial and administrative applications** (such as [R-ADT], patient accounting, MPI, order communication, and the like), and many have **ancillary system applications** that are largely operational, or departmental, but also generate clinical information (such as **laboratory information systems** [LISs], **radiology infor-**

Figure 9.3. Source systems feeding data to the inpatient EHR

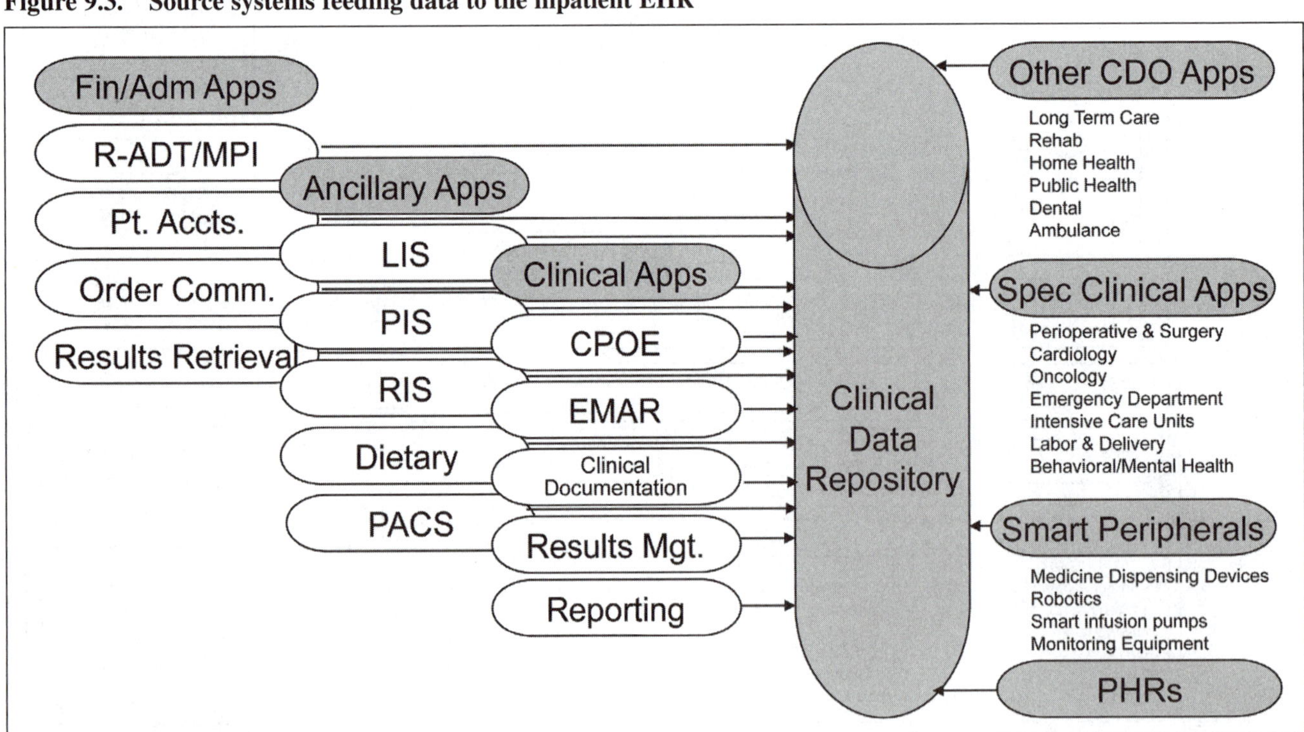

mation systems [RISs], **pharmacy information systems** [PISs], and so on). As the migration path toward EHR is considered, it is important to recognize the primary purpose of ancillary systems—to help manage the operations of the departments in which they are used. For example, while LISs obviously produce lab results, they do many other things in order to produce the results: They must receive the order for the test, assign an accession number to the order and specimen if the specimen accompanies the order, generate a specimen collection list and bar code labels for the specimen collection vials, schedule phlebotomists to collect the specimens from the patient, and interface with auto analyzers that run the tests to download the results. Once the results of the tests are available and quality checked, the system prints results or otherwise makes the results available for viewing by the ordering provider. In addition to these basic features, LISs manage workload balancing, supplies inventories, Medicare medical necessity checking, billing, public health reporting, and generate custom reports for clinical or quality management. PISs and RISs perform equivalent functions for the departments in which they are used. In addition, there are other departments that may have their own applications, such as a blood bank, nutrition and food services, housekeeping, and others.

In addition to such ancillary systems, there are also **specialty clinical applications**, such as for intensive care, perioperative or surgical services, cardiology, oncology, emergency medicine, labor and delivery, infection control, and others. Many of these specialty clinical applications have been less mainstream, in that they are less widely used and frequently not able to be integrated as well with financial and administrative data or other ancillary systems. Even more recently, care delivery organizations are acquiring **picture archiving and communication systems** (PACS) that digitize medical images. They are also acquiring **smart peripherals**, which are medical instruments that have information processing components including medication dispensing devices, robotics, smart infusion pumps, and vital signs monitoring equipment.

Many hospitals and physician offices do not have all source data automated or the ability for all source systems to communicate with one another or integrate all source data together. It may be prudent for an organization to address these issues prior to adopting additional applications or appropriate to consider strategic replacement of systems where current systems are old and there is little vendor support for a comprehensive EHR. Part of the benefit of an EHR migration path is that it is easy to see dependencies between applications and their technology, as well as the operational elements needed. For instance, a clinical messaging application requires not only a portal, but increased bandwidth for users of the portal. In addition, policies are needed for when clinical messaging should be used and when a phone call or actual visit to the patient is essential. A striking example of dependencies is illustrated by a critical access hospital that wanted to acquire a BC-MAR system as part of its quest to achieve an EHR. However, critical access hospitals are short stay (less than 96 hours), very small (25 beds or less), and often meet only CMS requirements (not Joint Commission accreditation). As a result, many critical access hospitals (1,292 as of December 2007) do not employ full-time pharmacists, do not stock large inventories of drugs, and often buy needed drugs from local retail pharmacies or mail order houses. They may not have a fully functioning PIS, they often do not buy drugs in unit dose packages (which are more expensive), and without a full time pharmacist do not have the necessary oversight to do their own packaging. The cost of buying drugs in unit dose form or acquiring a unit dose packaging system and increased pharmacist consulting time is often prohibitive—making acquisition of the BC-MAR form of EMAR not feasible for that critical access hospital.

Systems to Support Access to Clinical Information

Because many care delivery organizations do not have a full complement of source systems, or even those that are sufficient to support the major clinical components of an EHR, they often use bridge technology to enhance access to patient information. These interim applications may include ECRM systems, clinical messaging, access to knowledge bases, and registries, before acquiring all the necessary source systems. In some cases, providers interact fairly well with the systems and in other cases the systems primarily enhance financial and administrative processes.

ECRM systems greatly improve financial and administrative processes after discharge, where many departments need access to the patient's chart, where there are record completion responsibilities for several providers, and where access to clinical information may be needed in immediate outpatient or emergency department follow up. ECRM systems utilize content management technology and document imaging.

Where feasible, content that already exists in electronic form can be fed electronically (formerly referred to as **computer-output-to-laser-disk** [COLD]) into a repository for viewing via the ECRM system. This would include digital dictation, transcribed documents, voice files from speech dictation, e-mail, e-fax, and other non-document content. Coupling electronic feeds from such systems with scanning documents that only exist on paper enables the organization to virtually eliminate paper charts. Many hospitals do eliminate their paper charts, although they need to check their state evidentiary requirements, as some states require paper documents to be retained for a specified period of months after scanning—presumably the period of time that will see the most use of the scanned images and, therefore, the ability to identify any missing items or other scanning issues. This does not, however, preclude the organization from performing complete quality checks on its scanning process. Although data in image form are not readily processable in CDS systems, they do have the benefit of making information available to multiple users simultaneously. It is also possible to add workflow technology to these systems that can be used to queue work among staff or between departments.

Clinical messaging is another technology that bridges the gap between stand-alone, ancillary systems and a comprehensive EHR. With clinical messaging, secure Web-based technology is used to exchange remotely (such as from the hospital to a physician office) scanned or electronically fed documents or results from source systems, as well as e-mail messages among users.

Access to **knowledge bases** is another form of bridge technology. In this, clinicians are provided access to the medical literature, clinical practice guidelines, evidence-based healthcare information, drug knowledge bases, and other clinical information not associated with a given patient. In some cases, this support is simply a pre-defined set of Internet "favorites" or content that has been specifically gathered and provided through the organization's intranet. In other cases, the knowledge is provided through a subscription service that formats the content in useful ways and keeps it current. For example, access to drug knowledge is popular with both physicians and nurses—and may be updated daily. Once clinical EHR applications are acquired, knowledge bases can be integrated with patient-specific data for CDS. They can also provide instructions for patients that can be produced in a variety of languages, include special instructions where co-morbid conditions exists, and even incorporate the patient's picture if so desired by the organization.

Use of a **registry** is a final form of bridge technology. A registry is a collection of a limited set of information about a patient and often disease specific—such as for diabetes, heart disease, or other chronic illnesses. These are more popular in physician offices than hospitals as an interim step to a fully functional EHR. Typically, use of a registry requires a staff member to abstract data from the paper chart or the office to then use **e-forms** (using optical character recognition) to collect specific data for the registry. When the patient is next seen, staff will print out an update of the information in the registry that usually includes such items as chronic disease reminders. Registries can also be used for quality assessment, patient recall, and research. Because their data are not collected electronically at the point of care, they cannot serve all the same CDS services of an EHR. They also place an added burden on staff to enter and retrieve the data.

Systems to Provide Provider–Patient Connectivity

Some of the clinical messaging systems utilize **Web portals** (secure gateways to a local area network [Internet] based on Internet technology) to provide secure connectivity. This technology is a step up from clinical messaging because not only may messages be exchanged, but direct access to certain applications may be provided. For example, if the hospital has a CPOE system, providers may be granted access to the system through a provider portal. This enables them to enter orders as if they were in the hospital, based on organizational policy. (Some organizations may wish to limit the nature of the orders permitted through such a portal. Since the portal does not require the physical presence of the provider, some hospitals have concerns that physicians may not visit the patients as often as appropriate given the portal services.)

Both clinical messaging and Web portals may be set up by the organization for use by patients as well. For example, patients may be able to exchange secure e-mail messages with their providers, such as to request a drug refill, for access to a results retrieval system, scheduling system, patient health summary, or for tailored instructions for taking medications, wound care, and so on. PHRs are becoming popular with some patients and the federal government, health plans, and employers are promoting their use for value-driven healthcare. They come in many forms. The majority of individuals who retain a PHR do so today on paper form, keeping paper copies of discharge summaries or printouts of instructions. There are, however, an increasing number of PHR vendors selling directly to consumers. These may be fairly unsophisticated, where patients can direct providers to send an e-fax to a given Web site or they can upload documents or enter information themselves. Others are quite comprehensive, where the vendor provides for both direct feeds from a provider or health plan as well as structured templates for the individual to enter their own data. Health plans are particularly interested in populating these PHRs with problem lists and medication lists from claims data. While there are some concerns about how accurate this information may be, certainly the fact that the health plan can provide this information across all providers is attractive. Together with the patient, the health plan can then provide more direct disease management support. In these more comprehensive forms of PHRs, the source of the data is identifiable and the data entered by any given source is only able to be altered by that source—maintaining the integrity of all data. Finally, there are also PHRs that are "tethered" to, or directly coordinated with, the EHR in a provider setting. Although these may only contain the information from that one provider, the ability for the patient to enter their own data can be an aid to the provider. Certainly, the patient can log on in advance of a visit or at a kiosk in the waiting room and enter their own medical history, family history, history of present illness, and respond to structured questions that provide a review of systems. This saves considerable documentation time during the visit, where this information only needs to be reviewed and validated. The time savings can then be spent on more thorough examination, treatment planning, and education.

Although most care delivery organizations do not roll out Web portals or PHRs until after they have gone further down their migration path with more of the clinical applications, the nature of the application and technology is no different at whatever point these are implemented. In fact, many organizations are finding it desirable to move implementation of these systems further up in their migration to take advantage of patient data entry as well as the expectation that patients who are more aware of quality and cost of healthcare will be more informed consumers. Such systems are also of great interest to **health information exchange** (HIE) organizations forming to interconnect disparate care delivery organizations within a given locale, region, or state.

Point of Care and Clinical Decision Support Systems

In addition to capturing data from multiple sources, the final component of the EHR definition is that it be used as the primary source of information and decision support at the point of care. Certainly, some of the bridge technology strategies support this part of the EHR definition, although in many cases the applications' intent is not always carried out. For example, documents may be scanned and other data electronically fed into a repository for access at the nursing station, but clinicians may continue to use only printouts to review data and rely fully on paper for documentation. Perhaps the biggest hurdle for new users of EHRs is adapting to using them at the point of care. This requires recognition that documenting at the point of care is best for patients because it is there that reminders and alerts can be acted upon immediately. It is also necessary for users to recognize that while it may take a bit more time to document on a computer, the documentation is more complete, accurate, and timely, as well as yielding downstream time savings.

Because **point-of-care (POC) patient charting systems** guide the user in the necessary data to collect in the context of the specific patient (using **context-sensitive** templates that react to the nature of the data being entered and that tailor the template to the specific data entry needs), the documentation is complete. In fact, the result is that it sometimes takes a little longer to enter data on the computer. Physicians often believe that entering short orders takes longer in a CPOE system because they have to take more steps to log on, find the patient, comply with the requirements of the template (in this case, standing order requirements) for complete documentation, and then log off. Physicians who complain, however, should be reminded that the number of calls from nurses and pharmacists with questions is significantly reduced because the orders are now more complete and the risk of error is reduced. (Longer orders appear to take an equal or lesser amount of time to enter because of economies of scale.)

In addition to enhanced completeness, point-of-care documentation is more accurate because one does not have to rely upon memory or scribbled notes to document the information, potentially, several hours after the fact. At one hospital, nurses found that where their nursing admission assessment once took over an hour to complete, it now took about half the time, they were sure it was more accurate, and they did not have to reenter much of the same data throughout the rest of the admission.

The biggest incentive for documenting at the point of care is the CDS element of EHR applications. CDS is frequently embedded as an integral part of CPOE, e-prescribing, EMAR/BC-MAR, point-of-care patient charting, and other individual applications, such as in a pharmacy information system that provides the pharmacy staff with information on potential drug contraindications. In addition to the CDS that may exist in any one application, more robust CDS applications work with data supplied from multiple applications in an integrated manner. Whatever form CDS takes, it must be carefully planned because too many alerts and reminders can be annoying—in fact, that is called *alert fatigue*. However, no alerts can result in healthcare professionals believing they are being used as clerical data entry staff. CDS must be accurate, timely, and specific to the patient's needs.

Staging the implementation of CDS is a key component of the migration path and includes elements of software applications, technology (such as using wireless tablets or computers on wheels), and operational needs; including the need for teams of physicians and nurses to review the rules that fire the alerts and reminders and for staff to keep the CDS system up-to-date as clinicians become accustomed to their use and then want additions, deletions, or changes as new evidence-based medical knowledge and best practices emerge, or as national goals are revised. The diabetes HbA1c test results are a good example of this. For providers to participate in the Physician Quality Reporting Initiative (PQRI) and earn a 1.5 percent incentive on Medicare claims, they were required to track the percent of patients with HbA1c levels over 9.0 percent; yet in Minnesota, where they have a highly refined quality improvement program, they are expecting to see HbA1c measures below 7.0 percent to meet standard. The American Association of Clinical Endocrinologists recommends a target HbA1c of 6.5 percent for people with diabetes. However, there is some recent evidence that suggests attempting to lower HbA1c levels to as normal as possible may not be best for children, the elderly, and those with certain medical conditions. HIM professionals can help their organizations be aware of such differences and potential changes. Also, always using the actual value of the HbA1c, rather than a relative value (for example, more than 9.0 percent or "within normal limits") helps reporting in a changing environment.

Clearly, tracking the latest scientific information and making decisions for the organization is critical. However, the rewards of CDS use are great. CDS contributes not only to patient safety and quality of care, but productivity and reduced hassle factors as well. For instance, physician offices find they are able to reduce the time spent on managing prescription refills by half or more with an e-prescribing system including clinical drug reminders and alerts. Difficult differential diagnosis situations are aided by software that can scan reams of medical literature much more quickly than a human could, even if willing to take the time that often is not available. CDS can contribute to EHR user satisfaction because users know there are controls built in to help them apply their professional knowledge in effective and efficient ways.

Legacy Systems and Their Impact on EHRs

Virtually all hospitals and many clinics have some existing information system applications before they approach adoption of an EHR. These are often referred to as **legacy systems**, in part because of their age and in part because they often are focused on financial and administrative processes and lack the ability to integrate data with newer, clinical systems. It may be difficult to believe, but legacy systems based on mainframe computer technology with DOS-based or other proprietary operating system software still exist in use today. As the care delivery organization moves to more clinical systems, this frequently requires them to revamp their technology to newer, **client/server architecture** or to use other, third-party software to create a Windows environment.

In addition to older architecture, early efforts to develop products for hospitals were made by vendors developing **hospital information systems** (HISs) largely modeled from other industries' accounting systems. Products for the ambulatory settings were largely billing and practice management systems (PMSs). Once these vendors approached more robust departmental systems and clinical systems to support EHRs, they found that they were lacking in the new technologies to support more sophisticated processes and often did not have clinicians on staff to guide them in the needed functionality. The result was less than desirable products, in some cases producing unintended consequences that have subsequently been published as cautions for the industry. For example, some of the legacy system vendors pushed quickly to enter the CPOE market when the IOM reported on the huge number of medication errors in this country in its *To Err is Human* report (2000). However, these systems were built with the predominant hospital patient in mind—not addressing the need to calibrate drugs for infants. The result was several widely publicized reports on infant mortality resulting from such systems. While these were certainly unfortunate and the vendor clearly should have studied processes more closely in their target market, such incidents also point to the need for thorough planning by the organizations acquiring such projects and for professional judgment in their use. EHRs are tools and should support busy professionals; yet such professionals cannot abdicate their responsibility for ensuring proper patient care. On the ambulatory side and perhaps with not as tragic results (but still with potentially dire financial consequences), an example of a similar nature is being found in some of the quality reviews conducted after EHR implementation. In these cases, some physicians are performing more detailed histories, reviewing more systems in a review of systems, and documenting others that may not be medically necessary because the system has been built to prompt them for documentation to increase their reimbursement.

Another element of legacy system impact on EHRs is the development of acute care and ambulatory care systems independent of each other. Although there are distinct differences in workflow and computing needs for acute care versus ambulatory care, the fact that these products were being developed independently also meant that they were generally unable to exchange data seamlessly across the settings. Although Web-based technology can help exchange health information among hospitals and clinics or physician practices, systems have to be upgraded to accommodate this function. When such a focused development approach is coupled with the fact that the vendors largely started with financial and administrative expertise, often the result has been the acquisition of more clinically based products through merging with or acquiring other companies. So while various components offered by a single vendor may bear the same name, they may not come from the same development platform and do not work seamlessly together.

However, buying all applications from a vendor that has developed all of its own components can present other challenges. The components in these suites of products are likely to be well integrated among themselves, but highly proprietary. This means that if the vendor does not have a specific application a care delivery organization desires, it either needs to wait for the vendor to develop it or acquire it from another company and either use it as a stand-alone application or attempt to interface it with the primary suite of products—often a difficult and expensive task.

IT Acquisition Strategies

So, while the legacy of information system use in healthcare in the U.S. may be strong, it also puts the U.S. in a weak position with respect to making significant advancements with new technology, as other countries have no legacy environment. This situation has led to U.S. care delivery organizations approaching EHRs from one of four perspectives, or **information technology** (IT) **acquisition strategies**. The first strategy is often described as "best-of-fit." In a best-of-fit environment, one vendor's suite of products is used, and there is heavy reliance on the vendor to move forward along an EHR migration path. The second strategy, which is essentially the opposite, is "best-of-breed" strategy, where many, if not all, source systems are from different—presumably the "best"—vendors for the component being acquired. Where necessary, the organization has interfaced these systems so that some data are passed from one to another (typically demographic data from the financial system to [some of] the administrative systems and charges from administrative systems to the financial system). In some cases, the different systems do not exchange data electronically, so data in one system that are needed by another system may have to be rekeyed. A third strategy that many organizations are considering today is called "dual core," where the financial and administrative systems—which are usually the oldest but most stable—are retained in their legacy **architecture** and new technology is acquired for the clinical components of the EHR. The two cores are then interfaced. Finally, a more recent phenomenon is the "rip-and-replace" IT acquisition strategy, where, as much as possible, all older applications are replaced with new applications from a single vendor, with newer architecture and more clinically oriented approaches.

While this may seem like a very costly endeavor, it can be cost effective if systems are so old that they will soon be retired by the vendor anyway and where constant maintenance of interfaces is hugely expensive. (See figure 9.4.)

Health Information Systems for Other Types of Healthcare Institutions

Although hospitals and clinics have generally been the early adopters of EHRs, other types of healthcare providers, as well as payers, are adopting various forms of EHRs as well. Behavioral health facilities find the integration of data from multiple sources especially helpful in coordination of care. Home health agencies have for some time adopted handheld devices to capture data in compliance with regulatory requirements. Long-term care facilities have a more difficult time affording systems, but their highly structured data-reporting requirements also make them good candidates for simple EHR systems. Finally, health plans collect a tremendous amount of data about individuals from claims, direct feeds from commercial labs, as well as claims attachments. These health plans are creating databases that can be sorted by patients as their EHRs for disease management, or data in aggregate can be used for predictive modeling.

Still, it is important to note that the many forms of EHRs that exist in the different health environments are generally stand-alone with respect to the organization in which they reside, with little exchange among different organizations. Even among components of an integrated delivery network (IDN), not all systems communicate with one another. This is changing as HIE organizations, such as regional health information organizations (RHIOs), form. HIE organizations are a fairly new concept intended to support care across the continuum within a geographical community, region, or state. HIE within the organization is accomplished in a variety of ways, but frequently through portal technology. The federal government envisions a **nationwide health information network** (NHIN) whereby health information may be exchanged securely and seamlessly to authorized parties across the country. In the absence of a national patient identifier, this will require a sophisticated patient identification process and record locator service, in addition to stronger privacy and security controls. (See the Technologies section in this chapter and in chapter 7.)

Check Your Understanding 9.2

Instructions: On a separate piece of paper, match the EHR benefits with the functions that support them. Several of the functions will support more than one benefit.

Benefits:

A. Enhance patient safety
B. Improve quality of care
C. Increase productivity
D. Maintain patient confidentiality
E. Reduce hassle factors
F. Support health maintenance
G. Support predictive modeling
H. Support revenue enhancement

Functions:

1. ___ Context-specific reminders
2. ___ Data availability
3. ___ Evidence-based healthcare
4. ___ External accountability reporting
5. ___ Medication refills
6. ___ Security
7. ___ Tailored instructions to patients
8. ___ Workflow support

Figure 9.4. IT acquisition strategies

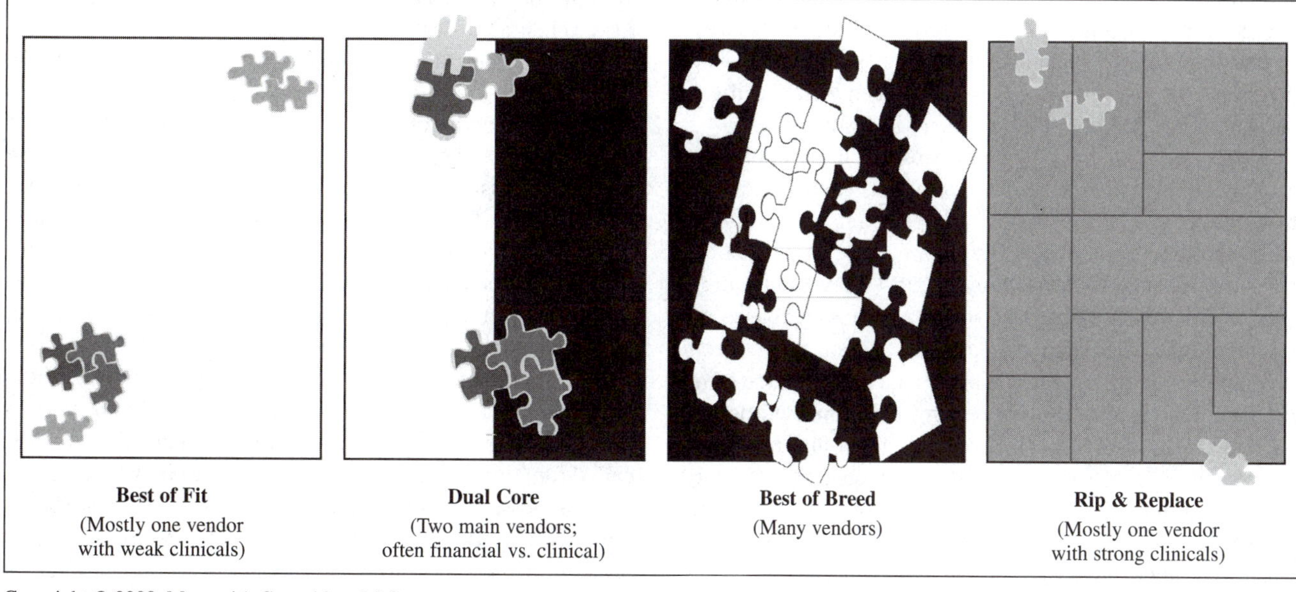

Technologies that Support the EHR

From the description of the evolution of EHR and its functionality, it should be clear that an EHR is not simply a computer software package or program. Unlike ancillary systems, such as LISs or admitting systems that basically perform one major function for one department, an EHR system may be viewed as the "engine" that integrates all other systems.

To serve its function of capturing data from multiple sources and converting them into timely, usable information, the EHR embodies many different technologies. These technologies include databases, data exchange standards, vocabulary standards, image processing, data retrieval technology, data capture technology, **data quality management**, CDS, communications and networking, storage, and security.

Databases

There are essentially two ways to integrate data for an EHR. One is to collect all the data needed in a central database, process them there, and disperse results from there; the second is to keep data in independent systems and use **data exchange standards** to access the data.

Integration of data from multiple independent systems into a central database is generally considered more appropriate for a comprehensive EHR. This not only provides access to data but integrates them in a manner that makes them more readily processable in real time and for CDS. In order to collect and process data in this integrated manner, a database is used that incorporates special indexing and management functions to capture, sort, process, and present information back to users—specific to a patient and in a split second of time! Such a database is called a data repository. To distinguish repositories that focus on clinical information (instead of financial or administrative data), the term **clinical data repository** (CDR) is used. CDRs are relational databases that have been optimized to perform **online transaction processing** (OLTP). Each and every time a user enters data, retrieves data, views data, and is supplied an alert specific to a given patient that action is considered a transaction.

A CDR is typically used for processing transactions and even though they may be very complex, each transaction does not require processing an immense amount of data at one time. When complex analyses are to be performed on data, a **clinical data warehouse** (CDW) may be the more appropriate database structure to use. Data warehouses are designed to receive data (often as an extraction of data from a repository) and perform complex, analytical processes on the data. This processing is referring to as **online analytical processing** (OLAP). Data can be mined and processed in many ways. For example, a data warehouse may be used for clinical quality improvement, best practice guideline development, or pay-for-performance (P4P) data reporting. It is not to suggest that reports cannot be generated from any individual application or from a CDR; however, complex, analytical processing requires numerous data and a great amount of time to process, which will degrade the processing power of the CDR and frustrate users. Hence, small organizations that do not acquire a CDW tend to generate fewer complex reports, process them at night or on weekends when the CDR is less active, or rely on external CDWs to which they send data for processing. For example, the Centers for Medicare and Medicaid Services (CMS) maintains a CDW of all Medicare claims. Many states have various registries (such as immunization, trauma, tumor, and the like) to which care delivery organizations contribute data and receive various reports.

Databases and their structures are more fully described in chapter 5. Data warehousing is addressed further in chapter 19.

Data Exchange Standards and Vocabulary Standards

The second way to achieve an EHR is by retaining all the data in the various independent, departmental system databases and using data exchange standards to view data from each system. This approach to EHR is generally considered an interim approach because it primarily facilitates viewing of information and limited sharing of data among applications—primarily patient demographics. As a result, processing the data is limited to the processing capability of only one application at a time. Consequently, different medications could be compared in a PIS, but lab results from an LIS could not be integrated into the PIS for processing for drug-lab checking.

While exchanging data across different applications is fairly limiting, it is important to recognize that data exchange standards are still required to smoothly move data from an application system to a repository and back. For example, a hospital may have an LIS and a PIS. As it acquires a CPOE system, the data from the LIS and PIS flow into the repository. When an order is written, it also enters the repository. There, the order may be compared with data from the LIS and PIS. CDS rules may process the data to determine that a medication being ordered is contraindicated for the patient because of abnormal liver function studies. An alert will fire from the repository to the provider entering the order about this situation. The provider then can make whatever adjustments in the order that may be necessary. The repository then directs the medication order to the PIS where pharmacy operations can be performed, including generating a charge, updating the inventory, and so on. (See figure 9.5.)

Data exchange standards have typically been called message format standards because their primary intent was to move a "message" from one system to another. This is also called functional interoperability. For example, when the PIS sends a message that a drug has been removed from stock for a particular patient, it sends a charge message to the patient accounting system. (Note: As medication administration is becoming automated as well, some hospitals are shifting medication charge capture from the pharmacy to the bedside. In this way, the charge is not created until the drug is actually administered. However, wherever the charge is captured, a message must be sent to the patient accounting system.)

Message format standards ensure that the structure and format of data are the same, as they are being transmitted from one system to another. This data structure and format is called **syntax**. Each proprietary system has its own syntax. For systems to exchange data or "talk" to one another, the syntax must be made the same. As an example, in figure 9.6 two different systems are attempting to convey the same information, but using different field names (patient name versus individual name) and different element names (middle initial versus middle name) and sequencing the elements differently.

System developers use message format standards to create **interfaces** between systems. The predominant message format standard used to create interfaces in health information systems is HL7. However, there are other standards development organizations that develop standards for specific, niche areas. For example, **Digital Imaging and Communications in Medicine** (DICOM) develops standards for the exchange of digital images (that is, in PACS). Standards for financial and administrative transactions (namely, claims, eligibility, remittance advice, and the like) are developed by ASC X12. Another increasingly important standards creator for care delivery organizations is the **National Council for Prescription Drug Programs** (NCPDP), which develops protocols for claims and eligibility transactions between retail pharmacies and payers, but more recently developed the SCRIPT standard for use in e-prescribing systems. Unfortunately, these standards development organizations are independent and often do not attempt to harmonize their standards with each other. A good example of the impact of this is in the area of medication ordering. When a provider enters orders into a CPOE system in a hospital, the system uses an HL7 interface from the CPOE to the information system in the hospital's clinical pharmacy. However, when a provider writes a prescription in an e-prescribing system to be sent to a retail pharmacy, the prescription must be written in the NCPDP SCRIPT protocol for the retail pharmacy to receive. HL7 and NCPDP standards are not compatible with one another so that the provider cannot use the CPOE to write a prescription or the e-prescribing system to write a medication order. Clearly this needs to change, especially as more and more information is expected to be shared across the continuum of care. The **Healthcare Information Technology Standards Panel** (HITSP) formed in 2005 as a private organization funded by the federal government to address standards harmonization and gaps, especially in light of using a nationwide health information network (NHIN). The result has been favorable thus far with, for example, HL7 and NCPDP working on a way to bring alignment between their messaging standards—although a final, harmonized standard does not yet exist.

Figure 9.5 Example of a clinical data repository

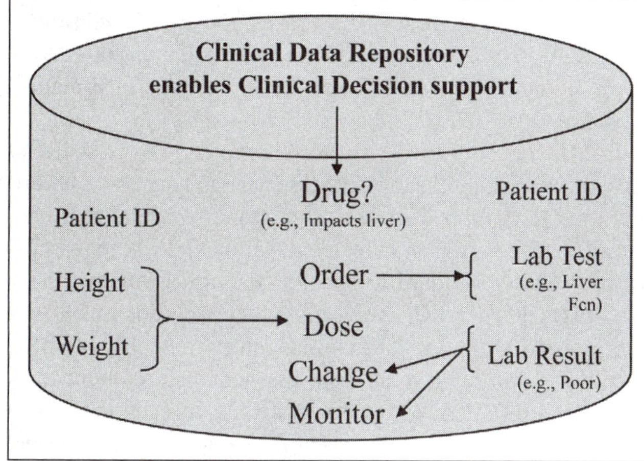

Figure 9.6. Different systems attempting to convey the same information

System A	System B
Patient's Name: Last, First, Middle Initial	Individual's Name: First, Middle, Last

An interface, then, is a software program that maps data from one system to another, in accordance with the message format standard **protocol** so that the data can be sent either from one system to another (unidirectional interface) or between two systems (bidirectional interface). However, some of these standards, HL7 in particular, have a lot of optionality. As a result, even two systems that are HL7 compliant may not be fully interoperable (that is, able to exchange data easily). Writing an interface between two systems can be very challenging because it requires not only someone who knows how to do the computer programming involved, but also someone to negotiate between the two different vendors whose systems are being interfaced. It is for these reasons that interfaces have been very expensive, sometimes costing tens of thousands of dollars (with some of that money going to each of the two vendors). Additionally, interfaces must be kept up to date. Each time one of the two systems that have been interfaced is upgraded by its vendor, the interface must be checked and potentially modified to ensure that the change in one system is reflected in the capability to communicate the message to the other system. Of course, the problem is further compounded—and sometimes impossible to solve—when the vendors do not use HL7 or use two different standards. Although the syntaxes illustrated in figure 9.6 may seem subtle, they are sufficiently different as to render the two systems unable to communicate with one another without an interface.

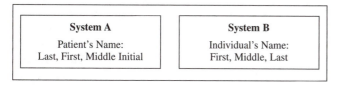

Because of the cost and complexity of building interfaces between systems, some hospitals are reluctant to buy systems that have not been created by their primary vendor. However, it should be noted that buying systems from a single vendor may not necessarily mean they are fully integrated (integration referring to the ability to exchange data without an interface). A company may have bought another company in order to add a particular product to its product line. Although it will write an interface from the purchased product to its own product line in advance of selling the system to the end user, these interfaces may be limited in scope or may not work with other vendor systems a given hospital may have.

To date, message format standards have been limited to exchanging whatever data were sent from one system to another. There was no reconciliation that the terminology used in one system was the same in the other system. The data were not standardized. A common vocabulary was not referenced. Most recently, the industry has come to realize that for one clinical system to use another clinical system's data, terms must have the same meaning. **Semantics** indicates that the content of a message has a common meaning. When a message format standard specifies the vocabulary with which the data are encoded, the functionality is called semantic interoperability. HL7 Version 3 has begun to embed vocabulary references into its message format standard.

Continuing the example illustrated in figure 9.5, the LIS may encode lab result data using the Logical Observations Identifiers Names and Codes (LOINC) vocabulary. The CPOE system may present clinical drug choices to the ordering provider via RxNorm vocabulary. The PIS may use National Drug Codes (NDCs) to maintain its drug inventory. However, knowing which vocabulary is used to express each data element in the process can ensure proper understanding by the respective user and system, and mapping can occur among the standard vocabularies. For example, a map from RxNorm codes to NDC codes ensures that both clinical treatment and pharmacy inventory needs are met.

While data exchange standards are challenging today, there is the expectation that applications will ultimately be moved to a **Web Services Architecture** (WSA) that can take advantage of **eXtensible Markup Language** (XML) constructs. XML is a specification for creating custom markup languages that uses a set of annotations to text that gives instructions regarding how text is to be displayed. HL7 v3 messages are based on an XML encoding syntax. However, the message standard is not backward compatible with its Version 2.x protocols, hence, until such time that care delivery organizations move from client/server architectures to WSA, the value of HL7 Version 3 messaging component is somewhat limited for use in structured data exchange. The HL7 Version 3 **Clinical Document Architecture** (CDA), however, enables documents to be transported using HL7 Version 2.x, HL7 Version 3, DICOM, MIME attachments to e-mail, http, or ftp. As a result, it has become much more widely used in ECRM systems and for creation of the **Continuity of Care Document** (CCD), which is the result of harmonizing the **ASTM International Continuity of Care Record** (CCR) standard content for referrals with the HL7 CDA standard for document construction. The CCD is now widely used in creating PHRs.

Data exchange standards are described more fully in chapter 7 and vocabulary standards in chapter 13.

Electronic Content and Records Management (ECRM)

In addition to being an application that supports digital content management and document imaging, ECRM can also be considered a set of technology. While in the past care delivery organizations may have focused on document-imaging systems to scan existing documents and store them for viewing through a computer workstation, the functionality of ECRM systems has evolved considerably. Document imaging systems frequently were department-based, often being used primarily for archiving records; or focused on a limited set of functions across a few departments, such as for revenue cycle management. Today, ECRM systems work with CDR and can store digital content and scanned documents into a CDR alongside structured data. The content and documents can be more finely indexed, so that, indeed, an allergy recorded on a document can be moved to other locations, for instance, always present when a CPOE application is accessed, included in ECRM technology to manage the flow of work throughout an organization, document version control—perhaps as different levels of signature are applied or a document has a correction applied to it or an amendment associated with it. Behind the scenes, the ECRM can manage retention of content and documents so that various levels of archiving can be achieved to better manage information storage.

ECRM systems are widely used in many industries. Those that have been adopted in healthcare need to have the software modified to support clinical information management needs. Because of this, HL7 has created the clinical document architecture (CDA) standard to specify how a document should be constructed. The CDA specifies that each document that conforms to its standard has a mandatory textual part which ensures human interpretation of the document contents and optional structured parts (for software processing). The structured parts are intended to utilize standard vocabularies. As recommended by the National Committee on Vital and Health Statistics (NCVHS) to the Department of Health and Human Services (HHS), these include SNOMED, LOINC, RxNorm, and the Universal Medical Device Nomenclature System (UMDNS). Additional discussion of electronic content and record management is presented in chapter 3.

Clinical images are pictures generated by medical devices such as x-rays, EKG monitors, and others. They are stored in PACS in digital images. Clinical images from PACS can be viewed through standard monitors if great detail is not required. Diagnostic-quality viewing of such images requires special monitors with high-resolution. However, even more can be accomplished with clinical images than just their viewing. With monitors that have full-motion video capability coupled with PACS software, images can be rotated, enlarged, sliced, colored, measured, and enhanced in other ways as well as viewed simultaneously with other images. Because of these capabilities, many radiologists, cardiologists, and others who use such images find PACS superior to standard radiology film.

Data Retrieval Technology

Because most applications used in clinical departments of hospitals today primarily provide for data retrieval, technology to support this functionality is maturing. Retrieval technology may be as basic as a lookup, where a query is made to access certain data from a specific system (for example, a lab result on a certain patient from the LIS). The desired patient may be selected from a list or by entering his or her name or medical record number.

More sophisticated retrieval technologies enable a user to use navigational tools that permit selection of a specific data element, to make a customized table, or even to graph results. They may also access several different types of data from different source systems through a single application screen. Hence, a medication list may be viewed from the same application screen as the lab results. There may be windows for different types of data from different sources, or there may be predesigned or customizable screens that permit viewing a specific user's preferred set of data. The most sophisticated retrieval technology, coupled with a CDR, permits not only viewing of data by type, but also manipulation of several different types of data, such as plotting lab results on a graph against medication administration, vital signs, and so on. The CCHIT distinguishes basic **results review systems** from the more sophisticated **results management systems**.

One disadvantage to using a computer to view information is the inability to flip quickly through multiple pages of data. Clinicians have learned to rapidly scan a patient's record to both get an overall picture of the patient and to find specific data. Although this capability is available via computer through specific search features, color, and other navigational tools, they are not yet everyday tools used by all clinicians. Many users find it easier to use a printout of the electronically stored data to look at results. Unfortunately, such printouts create a number of problems. Multiple copies of the same information may be printed and filed in the record, making it more voluminous. Worse is the situation where some of the printouts have been annotated so that two copies of the same printout may have different data on them. If one of the duplicates gets destroyed, vital information may be lost. Destruction of copies even with no documentation on them is an added burden. The situation where some data are on paper and some data are in electronic form is called a **hybrid record**.

However, as more clinicians become accustomed to the computer, the key to achieving true usability of an EHR is to pack as much information on a single screen as possible. Figure 9.7 provides an example of the Veterans Health Affairs (VHA) VistA Computerized Patient Record System (CPRS) cover sheet view. This is an excellent example of the ability of a computer to pull together information needed about a patient on one screen. These summary screens often serve as a **dashboard**, or launching pad, to be able to drill down to further detail about a given aspect of the patient's care, such as to view a structured progress note from a previous appointment, to get access to the complete lab report, to go directly to a data entry screen to start capturing history of present illness data or enter an order, to retrieve a stored document, or to set up a task for a nurse, scheduler, or other team member. (This dashboard functionality is common, although not illustrated directly in figure 9.7.) Although it may seem cleaner or more user-friendly to have fewer data on any given screen, the reverse has actually proved to be true; although the layout of such a dense screen must be carefully designed.

Thus, an important characteristic of retrieval technologies is that of screen layout and the ability to customize or tailor the layout to the preference of the user. Many EHR systems display a tailored screen based on the user's log-on. Thus, when Dr. Jones logs on, his personally preferred screen layout is displayed. The ability to drill down to greater detail is also important; but, again, caution must be applied to avoid having so many pathways through data that the user gets lost and cannot effectively go back to an original screen. Research has also shown that three levels of screen layers are about the most anyone can use effectively.

A word about color, animation, icons, and sound is also appropriate in a discussion of retrieval technologies. Color can be very helpful in navigating a screen to find desired data, but the number of people (especially men) who are color-blind must be considered. Color should never be relied on solely to convey any critical alerts; instead, color should be accompanied by a special icon, animation, or sound. Icons can be very effective in guiding users, but they must be large enough to be seen clearly and should be intuitive. Unfortunately, few standard symbols can be used in creating icons for health information systems. Of all the navigational elements available, sound may be the least used in healthcare because of the many medical devices that routinely emit sounds and have special sound alarms.

Data Capture Technology

If it is difficult to get clinicians to retrieve data from EHR systems, it has been even more difficult to get them to enter data. This is changing, although not as rapidly as one would like. Many clinicians have never learned to type and consider typing or any other form of keyboard use to be a clerical function. Even clinicians who are willing and able to type still often find data entry on a computer more challenging and time-consuming than handwriting or dictating.

Figure 9.7. Example of patient cover sheet view

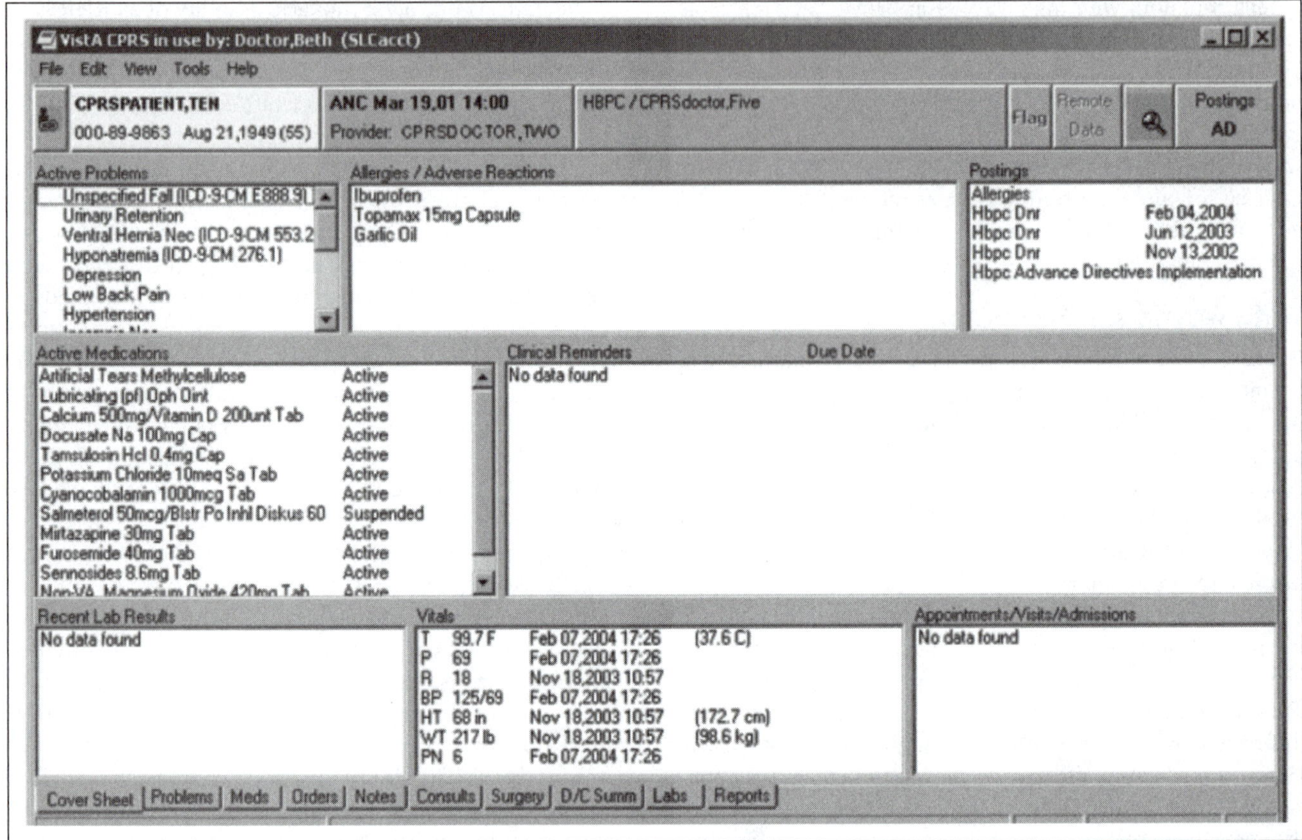

Unfortunately, no ideal solution has yet been found to support data capture effectively for all users in all environments. However, there are a few key considerations. Most important, data entry must return value to the user. If the user can obtain decision support at the time of data entry that is valuable to him or her, data entry will be more palatable. However, the decision support must facilitate and not interfere with the flow of information processing. Clinicians are more inclined to enter data when they can see that the direct result of their data entry is a benefit to their subsequent work (for example, it prompts for billing support data or automatically generates tailored instructions to the patient). However, if data entry is perceived to take longer than traditional recording, even if its purpose is laudable (such as to have more legible data to improve patient safety), it will be a hard sell.

Several technologies can help make data capture easier. Collectively, these are often called **human–computer interfaces** because of their importance in getting clinicians to perform data entry. They include:

- *Structured data entry through point-and-click fields, drop-down menus, structured templates, or macros:* In addition to making data entry easier, structured data entry makes data processing easier. Devices supporting such data entry include the mouse, touch screen, and a stylus (used on a tablet computer). If the data are further codified to a standard vocabulary, that makes them much more valuable in processing, although not always as easy to use from a user perspective. SNOMED, for instance, is a highly robust and comprehensive vocabulary—but is often too detailed for everyday clinical use. Some EHR vendors are starting to adopt other, non-standard vocabularies, yet able to be mapped to SNOMED, so that data entry is made user-friendly while the data are compatible with more sophisticated functionality. While structured data is essential for CDS and reporting, there are many times when a narrative form of the information is desirable. Some EHR vendors also map structured data to phrases, sentences, or even paragraphs, so that when the structured data are entered, the system can display the data embedded in a narrative note. This may scroll along the bottom of the screen as data entry occurs, or be generated as a separate note at the end of the data entry process. An alternative to the formation of the narrative in this manner is the use of a macro, where the user enters a code or key word which generates narrative that contains variables to be updated for the specific patient. For example, by entering "cc" a provider may be presented with a paragraph that states "This is a <age> year old, <race> <sex> presenting to the office with <chief complaint> of <number> <units> duration." The user then would enter the variable data, perhaps to produce a sentence that reads "This is a 12-year-old white male presenting to the office with left ear ache of two days duration."

- *Speech and handwriting recognition:* Speech and handwriting recognition is another alternative form of data entry that can be very effective for certain clinicians. It is not the panacea of which every clinician dreams, but where data entry is fairly repetitive and the vocabulary fairly limited, speech or handwriting recognition devices can be effectively trained. In some cases, speech recognition has improved to where it has become a replacement for dictation. In some of these cases, the user reviews the speech as it is being converted to type and makes any needed corrections; in other cases, the speech is sent to a special device where it generates type for a "correctionist" to review and edit. Such use of speech recognition produces digital content, not structured data. However, speech recognition can also be used as commands, where a command invokes structured data entry. Handwriting recognition is similar to speech recognition, where the system is taught to recognize a user's handwriting. Some tablet computers have been able to convert handwriting to type fairly successfully, but because of the need for somewhat greater precision than normal handwriting, most tablet computers are used today to capture and retain the handwriting or to aid structured data entry.
- *Handheld and wireless devices:* Handheld devices, such as tablet computers, personal digital assistants (PDAs), and smart phones may utilize any of the other forms of data entry, from keying and selecting from a list to speech and handwriting recognition. Their use is growing in popularity, but still not necessarily the total answer for everyone. Tablets are generally easy for mobile professionals to have readily available, though they are still fairly heavy, have hot spots, and, when used in a wireless environment—which is typical—may experience network drops. PDAs may be limited in terms of the volume of data they can store and their processing capabilities. The size of both the screen and the keypad also may be smaller than desirable. Unless tablets or PDAs are wireless, their ability to communicate or link to primary information systems is limited to when they are docked to a workstation. Handheld devices also can run out of battery power. Extra batteries and charging are required. However, handheld devices are ideal for certain limited functions, such as writing prescriptions or for use in capturing a home health data set, and as they are becoming more sophisticated and wireless, they are becoming popular. Still, many healthcare organizations find it just as effective to mount a notebook computer to a cart and move it with the user. These sometimes are affectionately called COWs (computers on wheels) or WOWs (wireless on wheels). For the less mobile healthcare professional, desktop computer workstations are still the mainstay.
- *Direct data capture from a medical device attached to a patient:* This is yet another important means of capturing certain kinds of data, such as vital signs. Special medical devices (such as a pacemaker) are even able to be connected to a standard telephone for capturing data or checking on the device's status from a remote location.
- *Patient data entry:* Incorporating patient-generated data into the EHR is just now starting to be used. In some systems, patients can log on to a Web site from home or at a kiosk in private waiting area, enter data in accordance with a context-specific template, and submit the data to their provider. At the care delivery site, the provider reviews and validates the information, and it becomes part of the EHR. In the past, providers have been somewhat reluctant to incorporate patient-generated information. There were misunderstandings that the patients could access and change the entire content of the provider's records. Moreover, there were misperceptions that the information may be too voluminous or erroneous. However, with more focus on patient-centric care and consumer empowerment, this is changing. Providers are also finding that patient entry of data reduces their own data entry version. Some studies have suggested that patients are more complete and honest when recording on a computer. They may feel less intimidated or rushed. Especially helpful have been EHR components that provide for automated informed consent, where the patient can go through a consent form thoroughly, be shown pictures, and even in some cases speak to a live person via a chat service. When completed by the patient, the information is reviewed one more time by the provider, and both patient and provider sign off—either with a digitized signature (image of a signature, such as used in the retail industry) or a pre-assigned UserID and password.
- *Natural language processing (NLP):* NLP may be considered a special form of data entry. It is the capability of a computer to apply very sophisticated mathematical and probabilistic formulas to narrative text and convert the text to structured data. Although text processing is becoming more feasible, the technology has a long way to go before it can be used routinely.

Data Quality Management

As more clinicians perform more data entry for mission critical applications, it is becoming increasingly important to assure the quality of the data entered. It is easy to click the wrong item, enter too many or too few digits in a number, copy narrative from one note to create another and not change all the required variables, under use structured data in favor of comments fields, or override CDS. HIM professionals should assist their care delivery organizations in updating policies and procedures that describe the required documentation practices for the EHR, which build on and refine documentation practices for paper-based records. The organization should also require checks and balances in the EHR to support data quality (such as valid values for a field, alerts to enter data for a required field, check internal consistency for right and left, and so on), and utilize regular data quality audits. For example, if it is found that a comment field is repeatedly used to enter a specific data value that is already on the drop-down menu, this may mean the EHR cannot process that data, defeating the purpose of enhanced utility in EHRs. This is a user training issue that must be addressed. Many clinicians really do not appreciate that the EHR is more than an automated chart. They often are so grateful that they can access data they previously could not that they forget there are many other benefits that rely on structured data. However, if the findings of the audit reveal that the value placed in the comment field is one that is not on the drop-down menu and occurs frequently, there should be consideration for adding the choice or identifying it as a synonym, as applicable. Again, many new users will not think about how the system can be improved. They assume that what they are given is something with which they must work. The result can be some growing unhappiness that the EHR is not doing more than the paper chart is for the level of effort they put forth in learning to use it. Documentation audits should also look for completeness, timeliness, internal consistency, and other factors that have typically been evaluated in paper documentation. For example, do all patients on a unit appear to have been given their morning meds only seconds apart? This is not feasible in walking from room to room, so it is possible that nurses have found a workaround where they are scanning all the meds at the nursing unit instead of at the point of care—defeating the medication five rights of ensuring right patient, right drug, right dose, right route, and right time. In addition to reviewing the EHR itself, it is important to walk around and see how users are using the EHR. This should be done periodically, and not just after go-live, but when upgrades or even slight modifications are applied. For example, a desired fix may necessitate a slight change in the placement of a data entry field, which can cause an unexpected workflow change. While such a change to the EHR should be communicated via pop-up at the time of log in, choosing that day to do a workaround provides the extra emphasis on the commitment and support the organization is making in its EHR and clinical transformation initiative. Walking around also can demonstrate that those responsible for the technology and compliance are approachable. Just as in the paper world, documentation audits and walkarounds should not be punitive, but serve to enhance the EHR's usefulness.

A special case of data quality centers on the common practice of data reuse in computers. Because it is easy to copy and paste, clinicians soon learn to use this capability where it exists. As mentioned earlier, such a practice often results in not fully addressing all the required variables. Even if the a data element copied from one record to another does not contribute to a medical error, the inconsistency or incomplete documentation can result in the questioning of the entire record if the record is brought to court. Many organizations are disabling this capability where they can, or monitoring for it with applicable sanctions. Yet others have found that the practice is sufficiently useful so they put users on notice that they are individually at risk for errors that may result. Clearly, each organization should do a risk analysis to address such issues for itself. Data quality and the components of a data quality model are addressed in chapter 5.

Clinical Decision Support

A great deal of importance has been placed on the role of CDS in EHRs. CDS systems directly address patient safety and healthcare quality improvement issues. They also aid in bringing value to the user. CDS systems depend on analytical tools that process structured data in many sophisticated ways. Special analytical tools include reminders and alerts, clinical guideline advice, benchmarking, expert system resources, and diagnostic or procedural investigative tools. CDS systems often depend on an elaborate set of rules, or logical pathways, to trigger reminders or to direct data through a pathway. These rules may be defined by the healthcare organization using them, or they may be acquired from the EHR vendor, via subscription to a knowledge base (such as a drug knowledge base [DKB]), or through associations, government agencies, or health plans that compile evidence-based health research into best practice guidance. A full discussion of decision support technology is provided in chapter 19.

A critical element of maintaining an EHR is to keep CDS up to date. There are many ways such systems can become obsolete or not function properly. Obviously, if a rule directs a clinician to perform certain diagnostic examinations or studies are based on best practices and the best practices change, the rule needs to change as well. The medical literature is replete with examples of where new evidence has suggested that an old treatment modality is not as effective as a newer one or where a correlation once believed to have existed between certain factors no longer appears to be true. In addition to keeping rules current, it is important to ensure that each rule has the correct information to process. For example, in an emergency situation where a patient presents with chest pain, there are several possible diagnoses, each based in a different bodily system, including cardiac, respiratory, digestive, and so forth. If a CDS system requires a specific set of data to be collected for every patient presenting with chest pain and all data requirements are met, the CDS will operate properly. However, if one data element is not entered, the rule either may not fire when it should or it may fire when unnecessary, causing an annoyance. If clinicians routinely override the rule and identify such inconsistencies in the rule firing, they will lose trust in all the CDS and the purpose of CDS is lost. Many organizations will not permit a required field to be overridden for this reason. Other organizations allow the override but have the EHR produce an alert that indicates that CDS has been negated due to lack of information, so that the users are advised that they are on their own for making the applicable decision. However, even in cases where all necessary data are entered and a rule fires appropriately, physicians may need to override the rule. For example, it may be that a patient is allergic to a medication, but having tried other medications and in consultation with the patient it is agreed to give a lower dose of the medication with heightened monitoring. This is a legitimate clinical reason for the override. Some organizations do not require explicit documentation of the rationale for overriding an alert, citing that such rationale was not previously required. However, with EHRs retaining metadata that the rule fired could be an issue in a lawsuit, where an attorney may question why attention was not paid to the alert. Even if this never happens, the fired alert is likely to cause a nurse or pharmacist to double-check with the provider, and that ensuing telephone call and potential delay in getting medication to the patient could be eliminated by a simple acknowledgment that the alert was purposely overridden. The EHR should enable a pop-up for the rationale to be recorded by one simple click. Just the same, there are times when rules themselves need to be modified or turned off. In some cases, certain clinicians find certain rules highly repetitive and annoying. In evaluating whether a rule should be changed, a designated clinical committee should review the rule to determine whether its impact on the ultimate result warrants the change. It is also possible, however, to fire rules in accordance with classes of users. For example, when a house staff member logs on, he or she could have more CDS than when an attending physician logs on; or certain specialties may want more rules than others.

HIM professionals should be actively engaged in documentation audit and walkarounds, can help evaluate the use of rules, and trace the impact of a change in any data element to the ultimate use of the data in CDS. This also should be a part of the organization's information systems change control, or configuration management, process where all changes to the system are fully documented. In the information technology department, change control is often used to prioritize requested changes and track that they have been performed, but they do not always retain the documentation describing who or why the change was made. This can be important in managing subsequent changes as well.

System Communication and Networks

Obviously, the backbone of an EHR is the hardware and software on which the system runs. The term *architecture* refers to the configuration, structure, and relationships of all components of a computer system. Three main types of architecture are used in creating an EHR:

- *Mainframe architecture* utilizes a single large computer to process data received from terminals into which data are entered. Mainframe systems tend to be considered legacy systems because they are the configuration of older applications. In general, mainframe architecture is limited in its ability to support the extensive transaction processing required of an EHR and is rarely found anymore in care delivery organizations.
- *Client/server architecture* uses a combination of computers to capture and process data. Servers are computers with powerful processors. They typically will house all the application software and store all active data captured by all the clients (typical desktops, tablets, PDAs, or other computers used to enter and retrieve data) throughout the network. Servers work for multiple clients, who have less powerful processors (and in some cases have minimal processing capability of their own, in which case they are called thin clients). (See chapter 3 for further discussion of architecture and networks.)
- *Web services architecture* (WSA) is the next generation of computing structures. It is a way of integrating Web-based applications using open standards over an Internet protocol backbone. WSA allows organizations to share data across different system platforms behind a firewall without being tied to one operating system or programming language. Chapter 3 provides a foundational discussion of Web-based applications in healthcare.

Storage Technology

The volume of data captured by information systems in general, and in particular by EHRs, is becoming immense. In addition, there is a growing expectation that data should be accessible in real time for very long periods of time. Finally, as clinicians become dependent on the computer for all their data needs, they will not tolerate downtime or delays for retrieving archived data.

As a result, managing data storage has become an increasingly important issue. Where in the past data were retained online for, at most, a matter of days after discharge or a visit, and a backup was made daily and stored on tape, an EHR virtually demands that data be retained online forever, be instantaneously retrievable, and be backed up continuously—both locally and in a remote environment for disaster recovery.

A storage device is a machine that contains storage media. Tape drives are the oldest form of storage device and are rapidly becoming obsolete because data are stored sequentially, making retrieval slow. Generally, tapes must be mounted by a person to a tape drive and connected to the central processor for use. Disk drives are the most common storage device today. Disk technology has moved rapidly from magnetic disks to optical disks of many different forms. Many servers contain optical disk drives that can store very large volumes of data. Still, the result of storing data on the same server that is used to process data in the various applications slows down the server. As a result, disks are being organized in **redundant arrays of independent (or inexpensive) disks**, called RAID, so that a great volume of data can be stored.

It is also being discovered that magnetic media is somewhat faster than optical media, even though the capacity of magnetic media is less. Also, storage devices are being organized into their own storage area networks (SANs) so that they can be accessible from any server on the network; these may be both local and remote. When such technology is deployed, however, there also must be software that manages the SAN, to keep track of where data are stored, and moves older data to less expensive but still accessible storage locations. The result of the huge demand for storage and all the available options has led to storage management becoming an entire domain within information technology services.

In addition to being accessible, data must have continuously **availability**. As noted, when paper backup no longer exists in a paperless EHR environment, there must be assurance that the computer system is available to users at all times. To achieve such availability, an EHR must have full **redundancy**, accomplished through "mirrored processing" and automated failover in servers, as well as backup and network redundancy. This means that as data are entered and processed by one server, they are simultaneously being entered and processed by a second server. Should the primary server crash, the system fails over to the second server and can continue processing as if (at least from the user's point of view) nothing had happened. Obviously, the servers still must be monitored and when the primary server goes down, someone must be ready to perform repairs or replace it as rapidly as possible. Some organizations invest in yet a third redundant server. Server redundancy, however, is not the only redundancy needed to keep everything up and running. Backup power support of various types is essential. Many hospitals have their own backup generator, but those acquiring an EHR find they need a second generator to back up just the information technology. Backup network technology and services is also critical. Even for a small physician office, having a broadband connection for every day, with a DSL backup may be prudent.

So, although storage media are cheap, healthcare has had a tendency to store all electronic data making storage management an increasingly expensive proposition. The introduction of an EHR should trigger a review of the organization's retention schedule, with an eye toward potentially enabling a realistic retention schedule for electronic data. Another element of the retention schedule should be to understand the impact of e-Discovery and address what will be retained for what period of time. **E-Discovery** refers to Amendments to Federal Rules of Civil Procedure and Uniform Rules Relating to Discovery of Electronically Stored Information, which many states are also adopting; wherein audit trails, the source code of the program, metadata ("data about data"), and any other electronic information that is not typically considered the legal health record (see next section in this chapter) is subject to a motion for compulsory discovery. Care delivery organizations should follow their retention policies to the letter, documenting the rationale for any given variation. E-Discovery and legal health records in an electronic environment are fully discussed in chapter 10.

Two examples serve to illustrate: Nurses have long used a card system for annotating their care plans for their patients —in pencil, so they may be updated as needed. On discharge, these are discarded. This has been the standard of practice, but in an EHR, the care plans are recorded permanently. It may be feasible to delete these from the EHR. But it is yet another new step, which some nurses may always remember to do and others may not; and some nurses may choose to delete or not based on certain circumstances they perceive to be important. The inconsistency of the practice is subject to question. Because the EHR will record this, it is probably better to retain the information. Another example relates to documentation of system crashes in the information technology department. There has been more than one incident of a lawsuit lost when an information system activity log could not be produced for the court as proof of the timing of a system crash in comparison to the timing of a specific data entry, dictation, transcription, or signature of a document.

Check Your Understanding 9.3

Instructions: On a separate piece of paper, spell out each of the following abbreviations for technology used in the EHR:

1. CDR
2. CDS
3. CDW
4. COW
5. ECRM
6. RAID
7. SAN

Define the following EHR technology concepts:

8. Client/server architecture
9. Full server redundancy
10. Integration
11. Interface
12. Semantic interoperability
13. Source systems
14. Storage management

Security Controls

Security controls need to be put in place to address confidentiality, data integrity, and availability—often referred to as the CIA of security. Every individual has private information he or she does not share with anyone, including innermost thoughts, dreams, and feelings. When some of this information is shared with someone else in confidence, a condition called **confidentiality** is established. Sometimes this confidential information is written down or placed into a computer system. To ensure that confidential information can be accessed only by those to whom the individual has given permission, security measures are put into place. In healthcare, in addition to affording confidentiality to private health information as well as other personal information such as protecting against identity theft, security measures protect the **integrity** of the information (so that it is not altered in any way) and ensure its availability (so that it is accessible when needed for subsequent care and other legitimate purposes).

An EHR system can afford better security for confidential information because access controls, authentication systems, audit trails, and other measures exist where they do not in a paper environment. However, because some of the controls have been viewed as an annoyance and attention to deploying them has not always been as careful and thorough as necessary, breaches of confidentiality and security incidents do occur. And because of an increasing rate of identity theft, state governments are cracking down by the only means they have—the adoption of data breach notification laws requiring security incidents relating to any private information be made public so that consumers can take appropriate action to protect themselves. Unfortunately, reporting of such incidents has also had the effect of making consumers increasingly more concerned about any of their private information—financial, social, and certainly medical—being compromised. As a result, many care delivery organizations are adopting more stringent security controls, sanctions, and other formal processes to aid in data protection. Attention to security and privacy is essential as the move is made to EHRs. The Hippocratic Oath has directed physician protection of private information for centuries. Moreover, every provider has instituted security measures as part of his or her standard business practices. The Health Insurance Portability and Accountability Act (HIPAA) of 1996 requires specific attention to security and privacy. HIPAA uses the term **protected health information** (PHI) to describe individually identifiable health information held by a covered entity or business associate on behalf of the covered entity and which is protected through confidentiality, integrity, and availability measures required under the HIPAA regulations. Unfortunately, HIPAA does not cover all personal health information that now may be held in locations apart from any covered entity, such as PHRs, life insurers, schools, and the like. A number of advocacy organizations are pushing for HIPAA to be broadened in scope or for Congress to enact broad-sweeping federal privacy legislation. The enactment of the Genetic Information Nondiscrimination Act (GINA) of 2008 takes a step in the right direction as it protects against discriminatory use of genetic information in health insurance and employment, while enabling individuals to take advantage of personalized medicine.

HIPAA Privacy Requirements

HIPAA privacy requirements include specific policies and procedures on uses and disclosures of PHI, individuals' rights with respect to their information (including the right to access, restriction requests, amendment requests, and others) and privacy management. Although most of HIPAA's privacy requirements are accomplished through administrative and operational activities, EHR technology can assist in carrying out a number of the privacy standards. For example, because patients have the right to request restrictions on who may use and disclose PHI, a means to institute special access provisions must be in place to follow such requests, allowing access perhaps only to the creator of the data or to a few given users with special authorization. In the paper environment, restrictions may have been accomplished by putting a special note on the chart cover, which may not be very effective when many individuals involved in treating a patient have access to all parts of the medical record. An EHR provides highly effective controls for its minimum necessary requirements, where specific categories of information and under specific conditions are identified for specific classes of persons who may access the information. Because the minimum necessary requirement does not pertain to disclosures for healthcare treatment, some care delivery organizations have interpreted this so broadly as to include that any healthcare professional may have access to any patient. It must observed, however, that not every clinician has a treatment relationship with every patient. In an emergency, the EHR should have emergency access procedures that can be invoked by a simple additional click on a pop-up window, for instance, indicating the nature of the emergency. This function is often called "break-the-glass," after the action one takes to break the glass to reach a fire alarm. This usually also generates a special audit trail that can be reviewed later to assure that the situation was truly an emergency. Having such a strong control has been a huge deterrent for the curious. In another example, when a patient requests confidential communication, there needs to be a way to notify providers that an alternate address or phone number must be used to contact the patient concerning certain information. Again, a note on the chart cover may be the only available solution in the paper environment, but a flag that pops up on a computer screen or that automatically routes calls or correspondence would provide much greater assurance that the patient's request is being carried out. Many technical measures are available to help protect patient privacy. HIPAA privacy measures are also discussed in chapter 10.

HIPAA's security requirements are generally more technical than the privacy requirements, but they also require establishing policies to direct how the technical tools will be applied. Again using the example of access controls, a policy will need to be established on how access is authorized, who establishes the access controls, and what each user is authorized to access. Access profiles are established as a matter of policy. For example, some hospitals decide to control nurse access to patient information by the floor on which the nurse is working. Within nursing, there may be controls on who may view information and who may view and enter information. Laboratory technicians may be given access only to those patients for whom a laboratory test order has been placed. Their access might be limited to viewing only certain information about the patient, such as diagnosis and current medications, and entering information only into the laboratory component of the information system.

Privacy and security measures are especially being scrutinized as care delivery organizations become involved with health information exchange (HIE) organizations. HIE organizations are generally not considered covered entities, but rather business associates. Because this is one step removed from covered entity status, many covered entities want to see stronger security controls. In addition, there is increasing emphasis on consumer empowerment and the need to enable consumers to be more directive in who may have access to particular information. Many states have enacted new consent requirements for disclosure, and some states are looking at their existing consent requirements as being too stringent and not permitting HIE. A recent federal government initiative was the **Healthcare Information Security and Privacy Collaboration** (HISPC), which is a partnership consisting of a multi-disciplinary team of experts and the National Governor's Association (NGA) working with approximately 40 states to assess and develop plans to address variations in organization-level business policies and state laws that affect privacy and security practices which may pose challenges to interoperable health information exchange. The United States has what has been described as a "crazy quilt" of state laws relating to authorizations and consents for use and disclosure of individually identifiable health information. The disparity in state laws has virtually resulted in every covered entity getting an authorization for every disclosure, including for treatment, payment, and healthcare operations which is not required under HIPAA.

Now that HIE organizations would serve to be the exchange agent for health information, there are increasing concerns about ensuring proper authorization for uses and disclosures. Some HIE organizations are constructing their processes around a PHR service, directly giving consumers total control over who may have access to specific information. Even when a HIE organization is not tightly aligned with a PHR, many are enabling individuals to provide their own consent directives as to whether they want their data to be included in the HIE organization exchange capabilities (called *opt in*), whether they do not want their data to be exchanged via the HIE organization (*opt out*), or if they do want to be included in the exchange service, to whom data may be disclosed and under what circumstances ("quilted" consent directive). (It should be noted that HIE organizations would not hold health information in one massive database but either would provide direction to where information is located among the participants or would use a bank vault type of structure to manage health information for many different organizations—much like the application service provider or remote connectivity option provided by many information systems vendors today.)

HIPAA Security Requirements

HIPAA requires that every provider conduct a security **risk analysis** to determine the appropriate level of security controls to put into place. A risk analysis is a systematic process of identifying security measures to afford protections given an organization's specific environment, including where the measures are located, what level of automation they have, how sensitive the information is that needs protection, what remediation will cost, and many other factors.

Risk is the potential for harm. It is composed of vulnerabilities and threats. Vulnerabilities are potential avenues of attack, or gaps in controls. For example, in the paper environment, an unlocked back door to the file room is an avenue of attack. In a computer system, a vulnerability may be as obvious as not having a firewall on the network or not backing up a computer system, but it may also be as subtle as overlooking when a password is shared or accepting the fact that the vendor does not provide break-the-glass functionality.

Threats include targets, agents, and events. The nature of potential threats is often more difficult to evaluate in the vulnerability-threat equation of risk. As a result, care delivery organizations either go overboard on their controls or believe it will not happen to them and do not institute appropriate controls. It is important to understand the nature of the organization, its surroundings, and other factors as threats are identified. For instance, being a care delivery organization in hurricane-plagued New Orleans is an obvious threat that care delivery organizations in other parts of the country may not face. However, being located near a major highway or a construction site can result in accidents that wreck havoc with power or sewer lines. Some care delivery organizations that are near universities identify student hackers as more of a threat than if they were located in the central business district of a major city.

A target is what might be attacked. HIPAA identifies three targets: confidentiality, integrity, and availability (CIA). Many security experts include a fourth target—accountability. Accountability refers to the fact that a person who has accessed a system, entered data, or otherwise used a system is associated with that action and held responsible for it. HIPAA includes this as part of the other three forms of targets.

An agent is a means of attack. Frequently, agents are individuals who have access to PHI, knowledge of security weaknesses, and motivation to cause harm. However, it should be noted that there are other forms of agents that do not necessarily intend to do harm, do not result in harm, or are physical agents. For example, a person who has access to an information system may inadvertently do something resulting in a breach of confidentiality, an integrity problem, or a lack of availability. Moreover, access, alteration, or unavailability could have resulted in harm but did not. Finally, there are acts of nature, such as fire or flood that cause harm. Despite that many consumers believe the greatest risk with their personal information being in electronic form is a hacker, this is not the case. The biggest risk is internal, and most often from the curious; although there is a growing concern surrounding medical identity and credit card theft and selling data, such as to unscrupulous attorneys or to pharmaceutical manufacturers—but again, primarily from those internal to the organization.

An event is the form of harm. Inappropriate access that causes a breach of confidentiality, modification of data that causes an integrity problem, denial of service that renders information unavailable, and repudiation that allows an individual to disavow responsibility for an action are forms of harm.

A risk analysis studies each vulnerability and determines its associated threats. Generally, when doing a risk analysis, the combination of threat and vulnerability is assigned a risk level to help determine what mitigation steps should be taken and in what priority order. The risk level may be a numeric score or a relative value statement, such as high, medium, and low. Obviously, those with the highest score or relative importance would receive the greatest resources and first attention (Amatayakul 2009). (See figure 9.8.) Many care delivery organizations conducted a risk analysis in the early 2000s when compliance with the HIPAA Privacy and Security Rules was first required and have not done another one since that time. This is not only dangerous because threats and vulnerabilities can change over time and especially with enhanced information system use, but it is a compliance issue as well. The HIPAA Security Rule requires "periodic technical and nontechnical evaluation, based initially on the standards and subsequently in response to environmental or operation changes affecting the security of ePHI." (45 CFR §164.308(8)).

HIPAA security requirements are categorized into standards and implementation specifications. Standards describe what must be addressed. The implementation specifications describe how the standards can be implemented. Some implementation specifications are marked *required*, meaning they must be implemented as described in the regulation. Other implementation specifications are marked *addressable*, meaning the organization may determine how it can best implement the standard. It is important to note that addressable implementation specifications are not optional; they must be addressed but can be addressed in accordance with organizational risk needs. The security requirements also fall into three sections: administrative safeguards, physical safeguards, and technical safeguards. Finally, the security requirements were written to be technology neutral, recognizing that new technology is always surfacing and knowing that repeatedly modifying regulations is impossible for the federal government. As a result, many of the requirements appear vague. It is important for HIM professionals to help keep their organizations on top of new requirements. For instance, in the summer of 2008, the Drug Enforcement Administration (DEA) issued proposed rules that would allow prescriptions for controlled substances (for example, narcotics) to be written electronically—where heretofore such prescriptions required a wet signature. The proposed regulations require two-factor **authentication**, including something the provider knows (for example, a password) and something the provider keeps (that is, a physical token, which may be a smart card, smart phone, and the like). In planning for adoption of e-prescribing, such added security measures must be factored into the budget as well as the convenience afforded by not having to switch to paper for controlled substances.

Administrative Safeguards

Administrative safeguards cover policies, procedures, contracts, and plans for security. In addition to the security risk analysis already mentioned, HIPAA requires ongoing risk management, application of appropriate sanctions against workforce members who fail to comply with the security policies and procedures of the covered entity (CE), and IS activity review, wherein audit logs, access reports, and security incident reports are regularly reviewed for problems. In

Figure 9.8. A security risk analysis

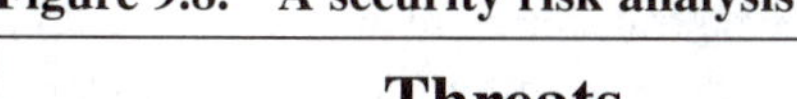
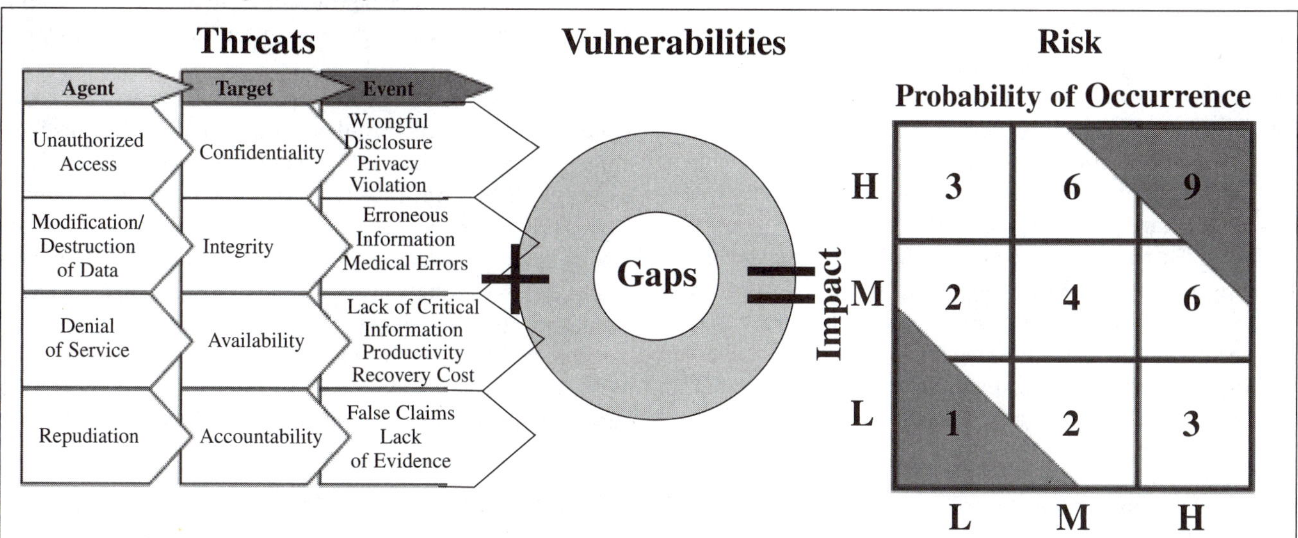

addition to this ongoing activity, HIPAA's evaluation standard requires a periodic technical and nontechnical evaluation of security measures in response to environmental or operational changes affecting the security of PHI in electronic form (ePHI). The CE must assign responsibility for the development and implementation of security policies and procedures to a security official and must have a security awareness and training program in place.

Policies associated with information access management include appropriate clearance procedures and supervision of, and termination procedures for, members of the workforce. Policies and procedures must be in place to authorize, establish, and modify access when there is a change in the workforce member's duties. These access management standards are very important and often troublesome for healthcare organizations because of the many different types of workforce members (including full- and part-time employees, staff working second shifts, temporary staff who may serve for short blocks of time and then return months later, volunteers, students, members of the medical staff, and staff with multiple roles—in some cases providing treatment and in other cases providing case review for short periods of time). In addition, there are often a number of people involved in processing members of the workforce, where this is not always a tight chain of command. Because access authorization is time consuming and complex, it is often not performed on a timely basis when people change jobs or terminate on their own. Every change in a workforce member's status should be considered urgent with respect to modifying or terminating access.

Contingency planning is another administrative security requirement. Applications should be categorized by criticality and backup plans, disaster recovery plans, and emergency mode operations plans developed in accordance with the criticality of the application and its information. These plans should be tested and revised routinely in accordance with the results of the tests. While HIPAA refers to contingency planning with respect to information system applications, other forms of contingency planning are important to institute in the event of a significant power outage or other disaster. These include returning to paper-based processes if necessary. HIM professionals need to address the issues of how such paper contingencies are carried out and how the information is loaded back into the EHR.

Just as in the Privacy Rule, the Security Rule requires business associate (BA) agreements with persons or entities that would have access to ePHI as part of their contractual responsibilities to the CE. The BA agreement relative to security requires the BA to appropriately safeguard the ePHI and to report to the CE any security incident of which it becomes aware.

Physical Safeguards

Physical safeguards obviously have to do with protecting the environment, including ensuring that applicable doors have locks that are changed when needed and that fire, flood, and other natural disaster preparedness is in place (for example, fire alarms, sprinklers, smoke detectors, raised cabinets). Other physical controls include badging and escorting visitors and other typical security functions such as patrolling the premises, logging equipment in and out, and camera-monitoring key areas. HIPAA does not provide many specifics on physical facility controls, but does require a facility security plan with the expectation that these matters will be addressed.

Workstation use and security are important physical safeguards. CEs are expected to implement policies and procedures that specify the proper functions to be performed, the manner in which they are to be performed, and the physical attributes of the surroundings of a specific workstation or class of workstation that can access ePHI. Although HIPAA does not define *workstation,* healthcare organizations should consider a workstation to contain not only desktop computers, but also any human–computer interface that provides the ability to access, enter, or process ePHI. Members of the workforce who use workstations should know how to safeguard them, including ensuring that virus protection software is upgraded; that log-in failure is noticed; and how to create, change, and safeguard passwords.

Media and device controls also are important parts of physical safety. Many providers are evaluating whether they really need all the printers they have, how to dispose of confidential trash (including nonrecyclable containers with labels, paper awaiting shredding, and so on), and whether all workstations need the capability of saving to disk drives or USB drives. USB (universal serial bus) ports are now widely prevalent on all computers and can connect not only tiny hard drives containing as much 8 GB of memory or more but other devices that everyone carries today, such as personal digital assistants (PDAs) and smart phones. Some organizations are disabling USB ports as a result. Certainly, whenever a device must be discarded, or even transferred to another user within the organization, it should have its disk drive thoroughly erased.

Because so many security incidents have occurred surrounding use of laptops, other portable and mobile devices, remote storage services, and remote access capabilities, CMS issued a HIPAA Security Guidance document in December 2006, providing specific cautions and recommendations for policy development, heightened training, and addressing incidents. It also strongly recommended possible risk management strategies including two-factor authentication, increased backup, password protection for all files, encryption for all portal devices, strong physical security protections for mobile devices, and prohibition against transmission of ePHI via open networks, such as the Internet.

Technical Safeguards

There are five technical security standards. These include access controls, audit controls, integrity, person or entity authentication, and transmission security. The first four typically refer to data "at rest," that is, when data are stored in a database or even in a temporary location in a computer, such as cache memory. Transmission security obviously addresses the special needs to protect ePHI as it is being transmitted over an electronic communications network.

Access controls require unique user identification, emergency access procedures, automatic log-off, and encryption and decryption of data.

Although most organizations assign unique user identification to every user, often these unique user IDs are not always used. This requirement has met with concern in some hospital departments where it was common practice to share a single log-on for convenience sake and in some physician office settings where there may not be a staff member who knows how to establish (then modify and terminate as applicable) a unique user ID, or where there is an interest in saving money by having few users identified for license purposes.

The user ID provides the access privileges for which a user has been authorized. HIPAA permits organizations to select the strength of the access controls they adopt. Some common examples include:

- *User-based access control* basically gives a person access by his or her name so that every user is assigned a specific set of privileges. This can be difficult to manage and frequently results in everyone being assigned the same access privileges.
- *Role-based access control* establishes parameters by what role an individual plays (nurse, physician, pharmacist).
- *Context-based access control* is the strongest form of access control. It not only establishes a profile based on who the person is and what role he or she is playing, but also on what specific information may or may not be accessed. In some cases, this can be linked to location and time of day as well. For example, "Nurse Jones may access patients on 3W during first shift, and in the emergency department on second shift if signed in for ED duty."

Emergency access procedures refer to steps taken for obtaining necessary ePHI during an emergency. Many organizations have difficulty understanding or carrying out this requirement. It must be understood that the security access controls reflect the Privacy Rule minimum necessary requirements such that a treatment, payment, or healthcare operations (TPO) relationship must exist for access to ePHI. The emergency access procedure provides for access when such a TPO relationship has not existed but then suddenly does exist. Sometimes emergency access procedures are carried out in a procedural manner, where the IT department or help desk must be called to provide access. This is clearly not very responsive if, in fact, there is a true medical emergency. More technical mechanisms to provide this access include break the glass, as earlier described. Unfortunately, many of today's ISs do not have break-the-glass capability, or if they do, the physicians are still resistant. Break the glass really only works effectively when access controls are very specific and when mechanisms are in place to clearly and always identify treatment relationships.

Person or entity authentication is closely related to access controls. Entity authentication refers to the password or other means to prove the identity of a person or other computer system (entity) needing access to ePHI. In most cases, a password has been used, although tokens, biometrics, callback procedures, and PINs also are permitted. Although not the strongest method of authentication, passwords can be strengthened through several means. First, they should never be shared and strong sanctions should be in place to enforce this. A strong password is one that is extremely difficult to guess. If the password is strong, it does not need to be changed frequently. In fact, that will only encourage people to write a password down, making it accessible to others. Ideally, there should be a system of single sign-on, where one password will get a user into every application to which he or she is authorized access. Because of the great mix of old and new applications in healthcare, this is rarely achievable. However, users may be encouraged to synchronize their passwords to the extent possible. Systems also should log off automatically after a period of inactivity to prevent anyone from seeing what is currently on a screen and to prevent others from using someone's log-on.

Audit controls are the mechanisms that record and examine activity in information systems. HIPAA does not specify what form of audit controls must be used, how or how often they must be examined, or how long they must be retained (although HIPAA does require that all documentation associated with the standards be retained for six years). Ideally for an EHR, there should be the ability to audit both viewing of data as well as any entry of data, although most systems today can only audit data entry. (Note: Entry includes not only the entry of new data, but also the entry of any correction. Erroneous data can be hidden from normal viewing with only an annotation that there was an error, but the data must never be deleted.)

Integrity refers to data not being altered or destroyed as they are captured, retained, processed, or transmitted in electronic form. Integrity is accomplished through technical measures, such as check-digits, hash totals, and other forms of edits on the underlying digital representation of the data to ensure that data are accurate and complete.

The transmission security standard requires the CE to guard against unauthorized access to ePHI being transmitted over an electronic communications network. It includes two addressable implementation specifications: integrity controls and encryption. As a matter of good business practices, most healthcare organizations have addressed security for their LAN through private cabling, their WAN through leasing private telephone lines, and for any network that utilizes the Internet through virtual private network (VPN) technology. A VPN is a security service that creates an encrypted tunnel in the Internet through which data can pass securely. The VPN requires special access controls and authentication procedures. When a healthcare organization permits access to the open Internet, it will utilize a firewall that examines each message and blocks those messages that do not meet specified security criteria.

HIPAA does not require use of a digital signature, although some healthcare organizations are beginning to experiment with this, especially for e-mail. It is important to note that three types of signatures may be used in computer systems:

- *Digitized signature* is generally considered the weakest type of signature. It is an image of a handwritten signature. Digitized signatures are commonly used in retail stores where they are captured on a signature pad and the clerk is supposed to compare the signature to the signature on the back of the credit card.
- *Electronic signature* is generally considered to be a userID and password or other form of authentication (such as token, biometric, callback procedure, and so on). In addition to the fact that HIPAA does not require more than this, the Electronic Signatures in Global and National Commerce Act (ESIGN) permits an electronic signature to be any "electronic sound, symbol, or process, attached to or logically associated with a contract or other record and executed or adopted by the person with the intent to sign the record." (CMS 2007). This definition encompasses digitized signature, even though it is considered very weak.
- *Digital signature* is a process that uses encryption to ensure that the elements that comprise the electronic signature are not altered. There are various forms of digital signature. The most common is an asymmetric key operation in which a pair of keys (passwords or other forms of authentication) is used, one on the sender side and one on the receiver side, to ensure that the signature is legitimate. When digital signature utilizes a digital certificate authorized by a certificate authority and other formal protocols to manage the keys, the process is called public key infrastructure (PKI). PKI is generally considered the strongest form of digital signature because the certificate authority acts as a notary to the keys and can revoke them at any time. PKI may encrypt not only the passwords, but also the content of the message itself, thus affording both strong authentication and data integrity. Digital signatures and PKI are not yet widely adopted, primarily because there is no single standard for everyone to use. As a result, a hospital might not be able to transmit messages to a physician's office if both used different digital signature technology.

Check Your Understanding 9.4

Instructions: On a separate piece of paper, provide an example of how each of the following privacy and security requirements can be carried out in the EHR:

1. Minimum necessary use requirement
2. Individual right to request restriction
3. Confidentiality of PHI when transmitted over the Internet
4. Emergency operation procedures
5. Authentication

Identify each statement below as characteristic of one or more of the following types of signature:

Z = Digitized signature
E = Electronic signature
D = Digital signature

6. ____ Minimum required by HIPAA authentication requirement
7. ____ Utilizes encryption to protect the signature
8. ____ Permitted by the ESIGN law
9. ____ PKI is an example
10. ____ Biometrics is an example

EHR System Challenges

The greatest advantage of an EHR is its contribution to the quality of care and patient safety. Greatly enhanced access to data is its current most important feature. Beyond the ability to retrieve data is the capability to use data. In the past, most clinicians did not truly value information as a tool to help them care for patients, except for limited, short-term results data. For the most part, recording information about patient care was viewed as a necessary evil. However, if such information could guide clinicians' work, communicate to others better, and help avoid errors, the EHR should truly become the much-enhanced utility that the IOM originally envisioned.

The greatest disadvantages of an EHR are directly related to its greatest advantages: Enhanced use and usability make the EHR a significant investment not only in direct cost, but also in gaining executive support, clinician adoption, system building, training, and maintenance. In addition, there are still some lingering concerns about legal and regulatory aspects and heightened privacy and security concerns.

Cost-Benefit, ROI, and Financing

EHR systems are undoubtedly expensive, even as costs are decreasing. The cost of an EHR system for a hospital is very difficult to generalize because a single system is not purchased. Rather, source systems are integrated into a repository and other applications are acquired that collectively comprise the EHR. Costs also vary over time. However, estimates range from \$3 to \$4 million for a small community hospital with generally a single vendor, \$10 to \$15 million or more for a small to medium-sized community hospital with a best-of-breed situation, to upwards of \$100 million for a large IDN to acquire the hardware, software, and human resources to fully implement an EHR. For physician offices, the cost is somewhat easier to estimate because the system being purchased is generally more self-contained. For very small practices (one to three physicians), an EHR may cost around $10,000 to $15,000 per physician. Costs go up as the practice increases in size because of the increase in complexity. There are generally more source systems to interface, and often the practices want greater customizability and more comprehensive functionality. Costs for such systems range from $25,000 to $50,000 or more per physician (also depending on whether a practice management system is acquired or replaced as part of the EHR acquisition).

As previously noted, the benefits of these systems are often difficult to quantify. Their primary benefits are quality and patient safety. However, there are other benefits that do accrue specific financial rewards. For hospitals, there can be an impact on the clerical workforce, admissions personnel, billers, transcriptionists, couriers, and other support staff, although many staff can be redeployed doing document scanning, data pre-load prior to go-live, documentation audits, and other activities, especially if staff are interested in acquiring new knowledge and skills. Costs of storing paper charts should be reduced. Although nurses are rarely, if ever, eliminated, overtime and temporary staff costs may be reduced or eliminated. The impact on nursing is much more that their time is freed up to perform more professional nursing functions. This has a downstream benefit to patient safety and quality of care. Hospitals also generally find improvements in charge capture, reduced repetitive tests, use of lower-cost drugs, shorter lengths of stay because actions can be more timely, and other savings from clinical decision support. Bed turnover time may be reduced, discharge planning may be improved, and the ability to handle surges in patient load may be easier. Still, the greatest impact is the reduction in errors of all types, which ultimately impacts the bottom line through better positioning for contracting, improved likelihood of better accreditation and licensure outcomes, and, more recently, incentives offered by Medicare and other payers, especially for physician offices but also for hospitals. For physician offices, many of these same benefits apply. In addition, some offices find that they can see more patients in a day because of productivity improvements. Other offices are able to add physician extenders (for example, nurse practitioners or physician assistants) using freed-up paper chart storage space, thus enhancing revenues to the group. Level of service (E/M) coding support generally improves revenues from 2 to 3 percent to as much as 10 to 20 percent, depending on the quality of coding performed prior to EHR adoption and sometimes the specialty of the practice.

However, the benefits must be weighed against not only the cost of the EHR, but also other factors that go into the total cost of ownership (TCO). For example, more staff trained in health informatics may be necessary. Other IT support staff needs may increase or be outsourced. Even the most rudimentary of EHR systems require some effort to implement. Data dictionaries must be created, rules must be reviewed, templates must be reviewed or developed, screen layouts potentially may have to be customized, reports have to be structured, and there is extensive testing. These activities are often referred to as system build, or system configuration. To not just implement the system but to gain full adoption by all intended users, there must be considerable process mapping and workflow analysis and redesign. Training is required for everyone, even for those who may have used another EHR system, because not only is each one different, but also every implementation is different due to the variations in source systems, customizations, and organizational preferences. (Today, almost every new physician has done a rotation through a Veterans Health Affairs facility that has a robust EHR, so as these physicians enter the work force, there will be an increasing surge of interest in EHRs. In fact, many find that having an EHR is now contributory to successful recruitment of physicians, nurses, and other healthcare professionals. Finally, because an EHR is a clinical system, it must be kept current with the latest evidence-based medicine, new and recalled drugs, new terms for new diseases, and new processes and workflows brought about by external factors, such as reimbursement or patient needs.

The result of a cost-benefit analysis should be the ability to perform return on investment (ROI) analysis. The easiest measure to calculate is the payback period. This is the cash flow (additional cash inflows less cash outflows due to the EHR) compared to the cost of the investment for the period of time it takes to achieve a positive difference. Generally, payback periods of from two to five years are tolerable. Longer payback periods are difficult to justify. Internal rate of return (IRR) and net present value (NPV) also may be calculated. These ROI measures require a financial calculator or a spreadsheet to factor into the cost-benefit equation the time value of money. If the IRR or NPV for an EHR investment is greater than the IRR or NPV on other investments, the EHR is considered a good investment. Alternatively, many care delivery organizations are recognizing that an EHR must now be considered a cost of doing business. Reduced costs to abstract data to participate in the increasing quality measurement and reporting requirements plus the emphasis on patient safety and quality are difficult to quantify, but are essential to address.

Most vendors will attempt to provide ROI analysis for their clients. However, caution should be applied in interpreting these results because they typically assign a monetary value to every benefit, whether actual savings will result or the benefit will only yield greater value. For example, many vendors will calculate nurse full-time equivalent (FTE) savings, even though no nurses will be eliminated. Although this can provide a good comparison between systems, the expected savings cannot be "taken to the bank." And, in some cases, these savings do need to factor into bank loans or lines of credit for financing the investment.

Other financing options in addition to using cash reserves from operations or loans include acquiring the EHR through an **application service provider** (ASP) model, funding part of it through grants or looking to philanthropy or donations. The ASP model, sometimes called remote hosting, is both a financing and an acquisition strategy. With an ASP, the vendor hosts the data center hardware and application software so that upfront and ongoing maintenance costs for the organization are minimized in return for a monthly fee. A good way to compare the ASP financing and acquisition model to the typical license agreement is to consider the ASP as renting an apartment and the license agreement the purchase of a house. In the ASP, rent accumulates over time to frequently be more than the actual cost of the house. The ASP generally offers less flexibility (you cannot paint the balcony on your apartment with pink and purple stripes when the rest of the building is green), but considerably less need for in-house IT expertise (you can call maintenance when there is a leaky faucet). However, the biggest concern providers have had about ASPs is that the data reside with the ASP. This may actually be a more secure environment than a given provider could hope to provide. Unfortunately, however, especially small ASPs have been known to go out of business, leaving providers without access to their data (worst case) or with their data and no application software to support them (best case). Doing thorough due diligence not only on the product being acquired but the vendor's viability is essential. Contractual agreements need to be carefully worked out so that the provider is assured of getting access to the data and the software needed to at least continue processing until the data can be migrated to another vendor's application. Unfortunately, when an ASP goes out of business, it is often due to bankruptcy, so there is little hope of compensation for disruption of service or conversion. Grants and donations are increasingly becoming available. Federal and state governments have been interested in promoting EHR adoption and so several initiatives are providing grants, no- or low-cost loans, and Stark Law and Anti-kickback statutes have had exceptions built into them for providers to be donated EHR software and support (but not hardware) or e-prescribing systems, such as from the hospitals with which they are affiliated or from health plans.

Executive Commitment

Executives, obviously, are acutely aware and concerned about ROI and financing issues. They sometimes feel powerless to ensure that the EHR is adopted in a manner that will, in fact, achieve the expected benefits. However, executives can be the crucial factor in adoption and benefits realization if they demonstrate their commitment and support, establish appropriate expectations, and generally foster a culture of quality and productivity improvement. Implementing an EHR system into an adversarial environment is risky. In fact, many believe that implementing only a mediocre EHR product in a good environment can have better results than implementing the best EHR in a poor environment. People, policy, and process are the key to success and are driven by executive leadership.

Therefore, many ask how executive support can be gained if it is not already present. (If it is present, it is highly likely that the organization is well on its way to achieving a successful EHR already.) Often, without executive leadership recognizing its own issues, little can be done from only a small segment of the organization desiring an EHR. There really needs to be a groundswell of support for the EHR before the executive posture is likely to change. This groundswell must include the medical staff and potentially even the community of patients, health plans, and businesses at large. One of the most successful implementations of an EHR engaged community leaders in helping to fund and motivate adoption.

Clinician Adoption

Although cost and executive commitment are essential ingredients in moving forward with an EHR, clinician adoption is the keystone to achieving results. Clinicians include physicians, nurses, pharmacists, technicians, therapists, and all others who use clinical information to treat patients. Although each may be challenged in special ways, it is probably the physician community that is most challenged, followed by the nursing community that needs the most training.

Physician Concerns with EHR Adoption

For physicians, the EHR represents a monumental change to old habits. Virtually everything physicians do today concerning documentation is changed by an EHR. Consider only the need to select the patient for whom to write a medication order. In the paper environment, the correct patient's chart may have been presented to the physician by a member of the nursing staff or a blank sheet of paper could be used to write orders when the chart could not be immediately located. The physician did not have to select Mary Gonzalez from a list of patients that might also include Marie Gomez. The mere fact that care must be taken to distinguish between two relatively similar names is not the norm for the physician and requires a thought process that could be considered distracting from the processing of medication selection and dosage calculation, which is more likely uppermost in the physician's mind. This may seem a minor inconvenience in light of the fact that the system could return contraindication information that normally would have resulted in a phone call from the pharmacist, which simply delays the distraction to another point in time. Yet old habits die hard! The system, then, must be carefully programmed to be intuitive and include as many failsafe measures as possible, but not so many that they are distracting or delay the intended action on the system.

In many cases, physicians must be convinced of the value of the EHR through either using an EHR in their own practice or peer pressure. Typically, physician champions are identified and expected to lead the charge. Sometimes, however, physician champions can be looked upon as mavericks by their peers, or they may be brought into the picture too late in the process, which can cause resentment to build in the medical staff. In either case, physician leadership may be required to build trust in the system. Many organizations are beginning to identify the need for a medical director of information systems (MDIS) or chief medical informatics officer (CMIO) who would spend a good portion of time on EHR system selection and implementation and then maintenance, including training peers, ensuring the CDS system is appropriate and kept current, and troubleshooting system issues. Many MDISs recognize the importance of process improvement and support process mapping and other strategies to support change. However, hospitals must recognize that engaging the medical staff early is critical to success. Many hospitals still dictate that a CPOE system will be acquired and used without seeking the advice and support of the medical staff. Unfortunately, this strategy is rarely successful with clinical information systems. (This strategy is not even successful when the system affects employed physicians and other clinicians, such as an electronic medication administration record system expected to be used by nurses.)

It is interesting to note that physicians tend to be more willing to adopt EHR systems in their own office practice than they are in the hospital or hospitals with which they are affiliated. There are several reasons for this. Perhaps foremost is the fact that the hospital system is just that, a system designed to support an institution, not necessarily an individual. There are significant differences between systems designed for physician offices and hospitals. These differences reflect the many differences in workflow between these two kinds of care. (See table 9.1.)

A physician views the office EHR from an ownership perspective and the hospital EHR from an indentured servant perspective. Couple that with the fact that the hospital system is different from the office system, representing a second system to learn, and one can appreciate the challenge a physician has in using a hospital system. The most successful situation is one in which the office and hospital systems look and function very similarly. This, of course, can be aided by using a standard user interface and providing remote connectivity to accustom the physician to the look and feel of the hospital system.

Table 9.1. Differences in hospital and physician's office workflow

	Hospital	Physician's Office
Workflow	Tightly coordinated	Loosely coordinated
Communication	Formal	Informal
Primary user	Nurse	Physician
Data content	Comprehensive	Fragmented
Data volume	High density	Low density
Data source	Multiple, disparate	Patient/provider generated
Information flow	Location centric	Geographically dispersed
Data input	Mobile	Stationary
IS decision making	Administration	Physicians

Physicians also are concerned about security and privacy issues, as well as patient perception issues. Today's information systems have typically been secured by virtue of the fact that they contain minimal patient data, few people know how to use them, and they are closed systems. They do not connect to the outside world. As use and users expand, security must be enhanced to better protect privacy. On the other hand, however, security measures must not be so onerous as to make EHRs even more formidable to learn and use. Many physicians find loss of productivity, and hence revenue, a major concern as they get ready to use an EHR in their offices. Frequently, it is necessary to schedule fewer patients to be seen in a day for the first few weeks after go-live. If thorough planning, early engagement of all members of the office team, careful attention to processes and workflows, advance pre-load of key data, and mandatory training are instituted, most offices find that physicians can return to normal workloads within a few weeks or a month or so.

Some physicians, and other clinicians, also have expressed concern about patient acceptance of computers. Will the patient perceive the computer to be a barrier between patient and clinician? Many clinicians are finding that patients actually expect them to use a computer, or at least are not surprised when they do. In fact, some patients are starting to make an EHR a criterion on which they select their doctor. This is as true for elderly patients as young ones, especially as many of the elderly patients have younger members of the family caring for them. They want the convenience of e-mail and even e-visits, being able to schedule appointments themselves, and appreciate the ability to enter blood sugar diaries or medication tracking. Many providers find that computers add value to the patient encounter. Clinicians who make the computer a barrier because they do not use it well will surely create a barrier for their patients. However, the computer can be used to engage and provide the patient with instantaneous information and instructions. Showing the patient a graph of personal data can be a powerful motivator. Instructions tailored specifically to the patient can improve his or her compliance with a treatment regime.

Nursing Staff Concerns with EHR Adoption

Physicians are not the only users of EHRs. Certainly, their concerns are critical, but attention must be paid to nurse issues, in both hospitals and physician offices.

In hospitals, nursing staff are the primary users of the EHR, yet very few nurses have the opportunity to learn about and evaluate various EHR systems from a nursing perspective. Although many physicians go to conferences and begin to see these systems and hear presentations from peers, nurses have less opportunity for such exposure. Moreover, physicians are starting to acquire EHRs for use in their own offices; hospital-based nurses have no such opportunity. Physician adoption is critical, but it should not be assumed that nurses will necessarily adopt the EHR without issues of their own. A good way to gain nurse support for the EHR is to engage them early in the process. Nurses that represent mainstream nursing need to be prominent members of the EHR selection committee. They need the opportunity to see and hear what issues may arise and how they can be overcome. Amazingly, many systems are not nurse-friendly. Care has not been taken to address special charting issues. For example, nurses depend on trended data to discern changes in their patients' statuses. If corrections made to data cannot be incorporated into the trend lines appropriately, their ability to monitor such trends is at risk. As an example, one system correctly identified where an error had occurred but placed the newly corrected information at the end of the trend line, not at the point of error. This was very difficult for nurses to use because they wanted to see the trend over time, not have to make mental adjustments for the fact that a certain data point should be somewhere else.

It is not uncommon to find nurses left out of the EHR decision-making process in physician offices (much as physicians are left out of the EHR decision-making process in the hospital). Again, this is a mistake because nurses are the ones who will likely use the EHR for a considerable portion of their work and will be expected to support the physician in learning to use the EHR.

Legal and Regulatory, Hybrid Record, and Legal Health Record Issues

Although many states have not adopted specific statutes relating to EHRs, many have updated their statutes to address electronic information in general. Other states are generally silent on whether health information is in paper or electronic form because the statutes are old and generally assumed a paper form. The Federal Rules of Civil Procedure and Uniform Rules Relating to Discovery of Electronically Stored Information that most states have also enacted set the foundation for use of electronic information systems. Every organization needs to review its own statutes, but EHRs are generally believed to be legally acceptable for use, so long as special safeguards on their accuracy and integrity are applied. HIM professionals are in the best position to advise their organizations on appropriate ways to carry out these safeguard procedures. As previously mentioned, they may include audits of how templates are completed and how CDS systems are used.

Safeguard procedures also may need to include how hybrid record situations are managed. If part of the official, legal record is deemed electronic and part paper, indications may need to be included in the paper record when content is in electronic form. Some hospitals use a table of contents at the beginning of the paper chart indicating the location of all content (paper or online). The location of information also will change over time, as initially only lab results may be available online, and later, nursing notes, and so on. HIM professionals must be vigilant about managing the use of printouts of electronic content as they significantly increase processing time and cost and do pose a patent safety risk if documentation is recorded on the paper. Some organizations have taken to filling printers in nursing stations and physician lounges with different colored paper to remind users that they should not be used for documentation and must be shredded after use. The opposite concern of using printouts during patient care is that they may be so discouraged that clinicians may avoid reviewing the information at all. This can add a burden to nursing staff that may be asked to read results to the clinicians and can pose a risk of misinterpreting information that is read. The worst case is where some results may not be reviewed at all.

Decisions also need to be made about whether the electronic part of the record will ultimately be printed and incorporated into the paper chart, or will remain online exclusively. Some hospitals have been printing and then scanning the printouts of the electronic parts of EHRs that cannot be electronically fed directly into an ECRM system. This obviously contributes to cost, but if the majority of information is not in electronic form, it may be the most prudent approach to ensuring that all content of the record is in one location.

So while many hospitals will live through a hybrid record situation for some period of time, certain portions of EHRs may have to be converted to paper or signed on paper in certain circumstances and in certain states. For example, state boards of pharmacy generally control the form and format of a prescription. Standards for electronic prescribing care now are regulated by the federal government through the introduction of payment for outpatient drugs for Medicare beneficiaries under Part D, created by the Medicare Modernization Act (2003). However, until regulations proposed by the DEA are adopted, prescriptions for controlled substances will still require a wet signature. In some states or by hospital policy, the clinical pharmacy may also only accept paper copies of orders.

In addition to the above exceptions, many courts still require the production of a paper record in response to a subpoena or court order. Taking a laptop into the courtroom to view an EHR is not commonplace at all. Furthermore, there are issues of connectivity, privacy through incidental disclosures, and the risk that more than the legal health record may be accessible without a motion for further discovery.

AHIMA has been active in helping organizations define their **legal health record** (LHR), which they define as the "subset of all patient-specific data created or accumulated by a healthcare provider that may be released to third parties in response to legally permissible requests." (AHIMA 2005). This definition has arisen from the fact that EHRs contain more information than has typically been considered the business record of the organization, representing what was done for the patient and by whom. The EHR contains metadata that is administrative or operational in nature and may also be used to house other forms of communications with patients, health plans, and the like. AHIMA has been instrumental in having HL7 develop a Legal EHR-System Functional Profile, which is an adjunct to its EHR-System Functional Model. Released in June 2007 as a draft standard for trial use, it is expected to receive user comments over the course of the next two years, and then become an ANSI-accredited standard. In addition to specifying what constitutes a LHR, the Functional Profile helps organizations determine how to construct a legal presentation of the EHR that is admissible in court (Servais 2008). Chapter 10 provides a full discussion of the legal issues relating to the EHR.

e-HIM and Roles in EHR

The EHR represents both exciting times and potentially scary times for HIM professionals. Certainly, HIM professionals recognize the burdens of paper records and the important benefits that accrue from EHRs with much enhanced utility. Still, HIM professionals may be concerned that they are not in the best position to advise their organizations on new ways that information management may need to be carried out in the new EHR world. They are sometimes left out of the planning process—at least until it is almost too late to correct an issue discovered after the fact! Finally, HIM professionals may find their departmental base of staff eroding, as many of the traditional functions can be automated; or faced with the challenge of a significant retraining effort. Those who traditionally pull and file charts now need to learn how to use ECRM systems. Release of information staff may become patient educators as more patients may be able to access information themselves. Automated coding (especially in physician offices) may give way to traditional coding. Transcription services will be decreased with point-of-care charting methods. Some transcriptionists are already doing speech dictation correction rather than transcription; and there will likely be different ways to monitor for incomplete charts as EHRs provide inboxes to physicians advising them of deficiencies.

However, HIM professionals who adopt the e-HIM role will find many new and interesting functions. The e-HIM professional is in the best position to urge the organization to adopt a migration path, rather than reactively acquire applications which have dependencies not yet addressed. The HIM professional is typically the only member of the organization that sees all aspects of the health record and so can advise when one application depends on another for certain information. HIM professionals are trained in workflow and process improvement, and can best anticipate where there may be changes that others do not recognize. HIM professionals are intimately familiar with data flows as well. Even where quality, risk management, and executive decision making may be in separate departments today, the HIM professional is frequently called on to determine the accuracy of reports, interpret findings, and offer suggestions for additional analysis. All of the data quality and documentation auditing described in this chapter are functions for e-HIMs. HIM professionals have also been the official custodian of the record in most organizations, and in addition to maneuvering through all of the hybrid record and LHR issues, described earlier, as they continue to fulfill this role they also need to take more of a data stewardship role—ensuring the data are accurate and complete, that the data are privacy- and security-protected, and that users value the data as information assets of the organization. Data stewardship is a function that every person who has access to PHI must take on, but e-HIM professionals should heavily promote this function. In fact, with HIPAA sometimes being a "dirty word," if not at least a tired mantra, data stewardship that encompasses HIPAA and other accountabilities and responsibilities for data can be one way to refresh the HIPAA principles for the organization. Finally, HIM professionals have traditionally been an interface with patients with respect to information rights, certainly when they are the designated information privacy official, but even when not—and long before HIPAA. As consumer empowerment takes hold and patients have ever greater access to their information and maintain their own PHRs, e-HIM professionals should be there to assist them. AHIMA's myPHR.org Web site is a good place to start to help patients navigate these new waters.

One important consideration in fulfilling new roles in the EHR environment is the need to be very collegial. Today, some HIM professionals have close working relationships with the IT department and patient financial services in the hospital. However, this is not true in all cases, and the HIM professional may have to work hard to foster better relationships with these departments and others. For some time, the Joint Commission has merged its IT and HIM standards into one IM standard, recognizing that each department has a role to play, but the end result must be a single approach to managing the information assets of the organization. In addition to working closely with the IT department, some HIM professionals find themselves becoming part of the IT department and even in a few cases the chief information officer (CIO). While the intent of becoming an e-HIM professional should not be to take over the IT department, it is essential to coordinate closely with the IT department. Both IT professionals and e-HIM professionals have their own unique knowledge and skill sets that are different and essential, while contributing to the overarching goals for IM in general and EHR in particular. In addition to a close working relationship between HIM and IT departments, e-HIM professionals will find themselves working much more closely with other departments, especially nursing and physicians—in positive rather than adversarial roles of demanding chart completion. Once again, however, HIM professionals may be surprised that these departments also have a stand-alone mentality—believing that only physicians or nurses best know physician and nursing information needs. So e-HIM professionals will need to prove value to these groups to ensure doctors and nurses get the value they need from the e-HIM professional. Really making an effort to regularly join in with different professionals and understanding their concerns and needs is very important. Not only should e-HIM professionals conduct walkarounds to help an EHR implementation, but they need to make an effort to regularly communicate with the different departments that will be impacted by the EHR. Sometimes this means delegating HIM departmental work to staff within the department, spending less time on non-essential tasks, or cultivating relationships outside of the work environment to network with the staff in these departments, and finding creative ways to ingratiate the HIM professional and department staff into these departments.

In addition to a collegial relationship within the hospital, it is also necessary to cultivate relationships with the physician offices. HIM professionals already know the physicians, and there is an opportunity for e-HIM professionals to help them with their EHR vendor selection, implementation, and adoption. Such relationships will strengthen the e-HIM professionals' knowledge of EHRs and their ability to coordinate hospital and physician office communications, garner trust for sharing data, and resolve issues where they occur.

A final consideration faced by some HIM professionals is how they can participate more fully in the planning, implementation, and benefits realization for EHRs. HIM professionals may have to assume a more assertive stance and truly market their services. Similar to marketers, the HIM professional needs to find the right product to provide and then target it to the right person in a highly positive manner. HIM professionals who distribute articles of interest, volunteer for a project, or even produce a report on some of the issues currently facing the organization find that they can demonstrate their value in a very positive manner. Unfortunately, some of the best skills HIM professionals have to offer are in the area of protection—legal, privacy, and data quality—and these are not always valued by everyone in the organization. These issues also have not necessarily been well-addressed by EHR vendors. As a result, users who are excited about using the EHR sometimes do not want to be bothered with details of what should constitute a legal health record, how corrections should be made in an EHR, and so on. HIM professionals who approach the EHR with such concerns can sometimes be viewed as negative, and this may come across as not supportive of the EHR. This is the last thing e-HIM professionals want, but in order to overcome some of these perceptions it may be necessary to do some soul searching and be flexible. Flexibility, thinking outside the box, and being aware that things can be different and yet produce the same results is important. However, different processes do not always translate into the same results, and e-HIM professionals have an obligation to point this out. Doing so in manner that is constructive may take some fine-tuning and rehearsal of what, where, when, and how to address these issues.

Check Your Understanding 9.5

Instructions: Answer the following questions on a separate piece of paper.

1. List five areas of physician resistance that need to be overcome when adopting an EHR.
2. Differentiate between the payback period and internal rate of return for calculating return on investment for an EHR.
3. Compare the ASP and acquisition models of financing an EHR.
4. Discuss the importance of executive commitment in the adoption of an EHR.
5. What are the two key regulatory issues for EHR?

EHR System Planning and Acquisition

Dwight D. Eisenhower is quoted as having said: "In preparing for battle, I have always found that plans are useless, but planning is indispensable." A recent study of chief technology officers indicated that 10 percent do not do strategic technology planning. They contend that strategic planning is a frustrating, time-consuming endeavor that distracts from, rather than contributes to, the real work of building and maintaining an adequate technology infrastructure. Still, the majority of those surveyed indicated that good planning helped achieve impressive outcomes with a minimum of frustration.

Many understand that an EHR is not a technology or an event but, rather, a journey toward goals aided by technology. Some call this a migration path; others view it as a strategic plan or an evolution along a set of generations (although some would prefer a revolution) (Gillespie 2003).

EHR Readiness

As an organization approaches the acquisition of an EHR, it is very important to assess its readiness, plot its migration path, and develop a plan of action. Organizations would be well advised to inventory their applications, technical capabilities, staffing resources, and reporting needs. However, there is potentially nothing more important than taking a soul-searching look at the organization's culture of **change management** and process improvement. It cannot be emphasized enough that the organization's culture of responsiveness is a critical factor in EHR adoption. In fact, there is as key distinction between implementation and adoption. Technology can be installed and applications configured, but getting users to actually use the EHR to its fullest extent is different and takes considerable people skills. Adoption may actually take more time and effort than all of the implementation elements combined.

Organizational Goals for EHR Systems

A large measure of an organization's readiness for the EHR is its understanding and articulation of goals for the EHR. Every member of the organization must understand what an EHR is. There should be a common understanding and clearly stated definition. The EHR is not an administrative or financial system; rather, it is a set of clinical components designed to support direct patient care. Clinicians who bypass the system for printouts or use clerical support for data entry are not achieving the benefit of the EHR and are undermining achievement of its goals. An organization that does not monitor achievement of goals to take corrective action is setting itself up for failure. EHRs can be powerful in helping an organization achieve its strategic initiatives, but they must be managed carefully.

After the organization establishes its EHR goals, it can better determine its overall approach to acquiring an EHR. An EHR migration path should be constructed, and all system selections should be made in relationship to the path. Organizations that develop a migration path are generally able to make support system selections that are more in line with their ultimate EHR requirements. An EHR migration path should address the following:

- What is the organization's current readiness? What applications does it currently have, what technology supports these applications, and what operational elements (EHR steering committee, physician champions, medical director of IS, nurse informaticists, e-HIM professionals, practice guidelines, evidence-based knowledge resource utilization, process mapping, and so on) are in place?
- What additional applications are needed, and in what sequence?
- What changes to existing applications must be made?
- Are interfaces required? Is there a repository? Is there a warehouse?
- Will the technical architecture support an EHR, or will a major investment in hardware need to be made first?
- Is the network sufficient to support all EHR users, or will this need to be enhanced?
- What operational changes need to be adopted? Will changes need to be made in policies and procedures in support of an EHR? Are staff resources available to support both implementation and ongoing maintenance requirements?

It is not uncommon to find organizations without a migration path floundering in their EHR acquisition. They typically are reactive rather than proactive. Information systems have typically been requested and used by individual departments, and often this is expected to continue in an EHR environment. This information silo mentality must be changed in an EHR environment that requires all systems to work together, not be duplicative, and be acquired in the sequence that most appropriately addresses the organization's EHR goals. For example, a hospital with a document-imaging system should not approve a radiology department's request for a separate document-imaging system just because its PACS vendor is attempting to make a sale. Likewise, the HIM department would not need a chart-tracking system if a document-imaging system was going to be implemented within the next year. Yet, an organization without an EHR migration path might not be able to see the overall picture and focus the organization on working together.

EHR Planning and Project Management

An EHR migration path can be developed by an EHR steering committee or can be a precursor to the appointment of an EHR steering committee. If a great deal of infrastructure needs to be put into place prior to EHR acquisition, it may be appropriate to do that prior to forming an EHR steering committee. However, an EHR steering committee can begin to address the operational issues simultaneously with the technical infrastructure issues. Process mapping, gaining acceptance of practice guidelines, and adopting other standards can take considerable time.

An EHR steering committee should be composed of representatives of all direct users as well as those who support such users. The committee is often chaired by a clinician. Other clinical representatives must be present and representatives of IT and HIM are essential for representing IM issues. Responsibility for IM does not shift from HIM to IT or individual departments just because the EHR is a clinical system—it is still the organization's business record, despite enhanced utility it should provide.

At some point, the organization will need an EHR project manager. When direct planning begins, someone needs to provide oversight that all elements are working together. Although an EHR project manager is critical during implementation, an organization is often best served when such an individual starts early in the planning stages and potentially remains in place at least through benefits realization. A project manager can be appointed from within the organization, hired from outside, or contracted with for a period of time. An internal candidate knows the organization but may also carry some "baggage." However, the position can be an excellent opportunity for someone interested in new challenges. An EHR is really a series of ongoing projects, so the project manager rarely needs to be concerned about finishing the project and not having a job. An external candidate has to get up to speed rapidly on the organization's culture but often is viewed as a more neutral party in negotiating among the different departmental silos that reflect current information system use today. The third option, contracting for a project manager, is often used in a small organization where the position of project manager is likely to be short-term. The risks in using a contract project manager include that the project manager may not be devoted exclusively to one organization's project and may not impart the learning to existing staff necessary for them to continue to maintain the system. This can be guarded against by requiring staff to be trained, but is often a secondary part of the project and frequently the outcome is not as successful as desired.

A project manager must have skills that may be different from those required of an operational manager. The project manager must have excellent communication, facilitation, negotiation, and leadership skills, while often not being the project leader (who is more likely the chair of the EHR steering committee). He or she must be skilled at delegating, diligent about following up, comfortable with escalating issues, able to see the big picture, and yet comfortable attending to highly detailed task monitoring. A project manager does not have to be highly skilled in information technology but should have a working knowledge of what can and cannot be accomplished. He or she will work with the IT department and the vendor's implementation team, which will provide the IT expertise needed for the specific product. The project manager does not have to be a clinician but should have a thorough understanding of healthcare and the nature of clinical information and associated processes. Finally, the project manager should be well grounded in project management and process-mapping tools. Becoming an EHR project manager is an excellent opportunity for e-HIM professionals, but it is not a simple promotion. HIM professionals need to demonstrate their ability to adapt to programmatic responsibility and their strong interest in persevering for the duration of the project.

Vendor Selection

Healthcare organizations acquire EHR systems in a variety of ways. Some organizations build their own systems. This is especially true of more academic, research-based environments. Many of these have multiple source systems, some of which are homegrown and others of which are licensed from one or more vendors. If the organization does not believe a product exists on the market that addresses its needs, it may consider acquiring a repository and then creating the applications that will integrate data into the repository, run queries, provide CDS, and so on. Developing a system from scratch is becoming much less common as more sophisticated commercial products are introduced into the marketplace. Because it is sometimes difficult to hire and retain highly qualified IT staff, building a system from scratch is also costly and time-consuming. Vendors can provide commercial-grade products and economies of scale that simply are not available to individual organizations.

Other organizations buy a fully integrated HIS and upgrade as the vendor supplies more functionality toward the ultimate goal of the EHR. Many smaller hospitals and physician office practices find this to be a suitable solution. The advantage is that the vendor provides a tried-and-true solution. The disadvantage is that these systems generally are fairly basic, meeting minimum requirements of everyone rather than trying to address any special needs, or developing very advanced, customizable applications that are beyond the typical small organizations' capabilities to implement and get adopted.

Still other organizations prefer a best-of-breed or dual core IT acquisition strategy. They go to market to find a vendor or vendors who will supply the clinical applications that comprise an EHR.

As previously noted, EHRs for physician offices are much more likely to integrate all components into a bundled package. There may be some individual, often optional, modules, but the vendor selection is more straightforward.

An organization approaching EHR vendor selection typically goes through a lengthy process of analyzing EHR functionality. Although EHRs are not yet commodity products, EHR vendors with CCHIT certification have a core set of functionality that does not vary considerably among vendors. What the organization should look for is the vendor's ability to be a good partner in EHR implementation. The vendor must have the core functionality desired and also should be ready to help the organization overcome adoption issues, address process changes, and support ongoing maintenance and upgrades well into the future. Organizations may review the IOM core functionality and HL7 EHR System Functional Model to help them determine their functional requirements. Beyond that, however, significant due diligence will be necessary to determine other key factors in deciding on a vendor.

Key selection criteria might include:

- Functionality
- Vendor viability
- Vendor support
- Training availability
- Implementation support
- Technology or architecture
- Vision (research and development momentum)
- Integration
- Vendor's clinical culture
- ROI potential

Except for the ROI potential, cost is not identified as a criterion for EHR selection. Cost is undoubtedly important, but it should not be used in the basic selection. Vendors have many ways to price products, and because the products are not commodities there is considerable room for price negotiation as well as many financing options. The lowest bidder is likely to have the lowest ranking in most of the functionality. When the functionality does not support the user community, ROI will not be achieved, resulting in a significant investment for very little return.

Most organizations use a formal request for proposal (RFP) process to solicit information from vendors on how they can meet the criteria. This may then be accompanied by product demonstrations. From there, most organizations are able to narrow their choice down to a finalist and backup. Due diligence in the form of site visits, corporate visits, reference checks, credit checks on owners of the vendor company, and other steps need to be performed before a final contract is negotiated to ensure that the organization is getting the product it wants.

EHR System Implementation

After a system has been selected, system implementation includes initial planning, hardware and software installation, system build, testing, and user training. Because the EHR directly affects clinical processes, process improvement, workflow redesign, and potentially even space layout are affected.

Initial Planning

After the contract is negotiated for an EHR system, initial planning will take place. This is the time that a comprehensive implementation plan is produced and a communication plan is developed to ensure that all stakeholders are kept up to date with the EHR implementation progress and engaged appropriately in various aspects of the project. A project governance structure may be implemented with various domain teams that support the EHR steering committee. This includes assigning responsibility and accountability for making the myriad of decisions that must be made during the course of the implementation. Domain teams must be populated with all applicable representatives of the end users impacted. This is often a process that is not performed well. For example, an EMAR may be viewed as a nursing system; yet without pharmacy working alongside the nurses, differences in how drugs are dispensed, vocabulary differences in drug names, and the like are not fully identified and prepared for. The relationship with the vendor is another planning task. A "war room" may need to be designated where everyone can work on the project. An issues management system needs to be developed so that resolution of the myriad of issues that occur can be made harmoniously with the vendor. Finally, most organizations also set up a formal training room, and often start end user training with basic computer skills.

Hardware and Software Installation

The next step in implementation is the acquisition and installation of the additional hardware required for the EHR. This often includes upgrades to the network, new servers, additional backup and disaster recovery services, bar code readers, printers, scanning devices, and, of course, human computer interfaces for various users. Next, the vendor will generally load the software onto the servers. The software is then ready for configuration to the care delivery organization's specific needs. During this time, super users within the organization are identified and trained on system build—usually in an intensive period of time at the vendor's location. Super users typically are clinicians who serve as a bridge between the ultimate end users of the EHR components and the IT staff.

System Build

System build is the term typically used to describe the configuration of the applications to fit the care delivery organization's environment. System build should begin with process mapping and workflow analysis. These will identify the data input and output requirements and what changes need to be made both in the EHR components and in the processes and workflows performed by the users. System build is the process whereby the organization's unique data and clinical standards are designed into the system. System build can take many months of detailed process mapping, data dictionary build, screen design or screen design refinements, template development, review of CDS rules, design of reports, and many other aspects of ultimately being able to use the system.

System Testing

It should be clear that a system as complex as an EHR must be tested thoroughly. There may be several levels of testing, from evaluating that a screen has been built correctly to the fact that data can be passed from one component to another. Testing should follow the flow of data through all systems and through all decision points. Stress testing also may be performed to ensure that the system works not only in the test environment where there are minimal data and few users, but also will work when the system is live and many users are using it simultaneously. Generally, there is an acceptance testing process that addresses all aspects of the system, including adoption rates. This acceptance testing procedure usually triggers a final payment or sign-off on acceptance and should occur from one to three months at a minimum after go-live.

End User Training

End user training is essential. Super users are often used in a train-the-trainer mode. It is important to recognize that users learn in different ways. For example, nurses may do well in a classroom session where the experience can be shared. On the other hand, physicians often require one-on-one, private instruction. In fact, physicians often learn best when a system is intuitive and they can learn on their own. Nevertheless, learning on one's own carries risk—either that they will not take the time to learn, or that they will learn bad habits or only what they think they need to know, which may not be sufficient. To support all end users, there must be some formal training, sufficient online help, and ultimately strong support during go-live. However implementation is managed, training is key to using the system and does not end at go-live. Ongoing training and reinforcement of regular users hones their skills and helps them to learn new things on an ongoing basis. It helps prevents workarounds where users may attempt to revert to old ways of doing things that often can lead to taking more time to use the EHR, and frequently does not afford them all the benefits of the EHR.

Data Conversion, Chart Conversion, Roll Out Planning, and Go-Live

The entire implementation process is not totally sequential. Data conversion, chart conversion, roll out planning, and go-live are frequently planned well in advance, but then implemented after all system build and end user training take place.

Data conversion is the movement of existing electronic data from an old system to a new system. If the EHR implementation entails new applications for admissions and registration or billing (or practice management in a physician office), there will very likely need to be considerable conversion of data from the old systems to the new ones. A MPI clean-up project is often performed at this time as well, especially if the implementation entails a move to an enterprise-wide MPI. Data housed in various source systems may also need to be converted. Data conversion is not an easy or perfect process. Because the old systems will not have all the functionality of the new system, there may be gaps in data or data fields that do not match from the old to the new. Data conversion is a tedious process that must be thoroughly tested. In some cases, it is so difficult to perform that organizations may start at least some of their new system usage from scratch. For example, while patient demographic data are often converted, the accounts receivable may not be converted—the hospital or office retaining a license to use the old system until the accounts are paid, or they may only do a balance forward.

Paper chart conversion is a key issue for EHR implementation; especially in physician offices where access to the last visit information is critical, especially for patients with chronic disease. There are several approaches. Some organizations use document imaging as both an interim solution to achieving improved access to information and a means to make old paper charts accessible in an EHR environment. This is the most common way to address the need to bring paper records into the EHR environment. The issue then becomes what parts of the paper record to scan and how far back to scan them. There are no right answers across the board; the organization needs to consider its readmission and revisit rate and use of records (for example, for patient care only or research and education as well). In some cases, the organization may decide to scan the entire records of active patients so that they have a solid archive. In other cases, the organization (typically a physician office) may decide to scan only parts of active patients' paper records and pull the paper records if other information is needed.

If an organization is adopting an EHR where there are considerable discrete data and a repository supporting CDS, it may want to abstract some or all of certain records so that the data are not only accessible for viewing, but also are available for processing. In this case, the organization may hire abstractors or expect clinicians to perform their own abstracting. Again, issues arise concerning what data need to be abstracted and how far back the abstracting must be performed. Abstracting is generally more expensive than scanning, so it should be performed judiciously. Of course, a combination of scanning and abstracting can be used. For example, it may be desirable in an ambulatory environment to abstract the problem list, medication list, allergies, and immunizations and then scan other key documents. Continuing to pull the paper charts is yet another possible way to address how old information is made available to clinicians. Some consider this the least expensive way to make information available, but it may not be if one considers the issues of the hybrid record. Continuing to pull paper charts not only does not reduce this cost, but creates patient safety risk if documentation continues to be performed in the paper chart. In addition, there is the potential that continuing to pull the chart continues a dependency on paper for those who are more resistant to using the computer.

There are numerous ways in which installations can be rolled out—by special users, by department, by nursing unit, by site, or by function. Often the vendor has the best recommendation and should be considered an important guide. This issue also should be evaluated during site visits and reference checks. A few organizations have started to consider adopting a "big bang" approach to their roll out. In this case, all of the EHR component applications are implemented at once, although still usually by department, nursing unit, and others. A big bang approach has significant advantages in that it reduces the use of the hybrid record and end users learn and experience the entire process at once. Alternatively, it can be a huge undertaking to train and support even phases of user rollout on all applications. There are concerns that some users cannot learn or at least adapt to this much change at once. Each organization needs to evaluate its organizational culture to help them assess the best approach.

Go-live is the final stage that culminates the implementation. This is the time that the applications are turned on and users are expected to start using the system. This needs to be staged very carefully. Testing must have been done thoroughly—although it is likely there will be bugs and process and workflow issues to be ironed out as all the end users start to actually use the system. There is usually a go-live rehearsal. The day of go-live, and for some period of time afterwards, usually requires extra support staff to be available near the end users. Go-live is usually performed in an ambulatory environment at time when it is quieter; although hospitals do not often have such a luxury. Celebrating a successful go-live is also an important element. In fact, celebration of the project's milestones throughout the implementation helps all staff performing the implementation through this tedious and stressful time. Celebrating can take many forms, but should be built into the organization's EHR project communication plan.

Benefits Realization, Course Correction and Ongoing Maintenance, Upgrades, and Enhancements

Benefits realization should be the culmination of the implementation. This is the point in time when the organization believes all end users are trained, the system has gone live, and there has been some period of time to get acclimated and adopt as much of the process changes and functionality as possible. The original goals are then reviewed to determine whether they have been met. Some goals may be in the form of financial rewards—where there is a specific return on investment to be achieved. Many goals for EHRs are related to patient safety and quality, yet still need to be specific and measurable, and should be evaluated that they are being met. Goals may be staged over time. For instance, in a physician office, the office may set a goal to reduce transcription by 50 percent within the first year of adoption, then to 85 percent within the second year. In a hospital, it may be that 75 percent of all medication orders and 30 percent of all other orders are entered on the CPOE system within three months of go-live, with full utilization by the end of the first year. If these milestones are not met, the organization then needs to determine why they were not met and take steps to correct course. Is it a system problem, user training issue, resistance to change, or technology issue? Sometimes an organization will not correctly anticipate the bandwidth necessary to support all the new users. Other times, the system configuration needs changing—even after careful system build tasks have been performed. Sometimes also, the goals may have been unrealistic, in which case they should be modified—but still specific and measurable. A solid management theory that "you cannot manage what you cannot measure" is true in an EHR project. If an organization cannot determine whether goals have been met, there is a management issue.

The importance of ongoing system maintenance dovetails directly with benefits realization. As previously mentioned, a clinical system demands constant updating. New drugs, new procedures, new codes, new processes, and many other factors mean continual upgrading of the software itself from the vendor and reconfiguration by the user organization. Even things that may seem minor can be major factors in maintenance. For example, if a particular CDS system alert is set to page a physician and a given physician gets a new pager, the system will need to be reset to send the page to the correct pager. This example may seem minor, but it is a major issue when the alert is a serious situation that is overlooked because the page was not received.

In addition to regular maintenance, the vendor will supply upgrades, and organizations look for enhancements. It seems the EHR project never ends! And, in fact, it must be remembered that the EHR really is not a project—but a clinical transformation program that is much broader and more encompassing of the changes needed to achieve value-driven healthcare.

Check Your Understanding 9.6

Instructions: On a separate piece of paper, list in order of sequence the steps in planning and acquiring an EHR.

___ a. Develop a request for proposal.

___ b. Describe the EHR migration path.

___ c. Appoint a project manager.

___ d. Define the vision of the EHR for the organization.

___ e. Establish goals to be achieved by the EHR.

___ f. Assess organizational readiness for an EHR.

___ g. Train users.

___ h. Conduct vendor demonstrations.

___ i. Perform system build.

___ j. Plan paper chart conversion.

___ k. Determine the EHR return on investment.

___ l. Perform due diligence.

Future Directions of Health Information Technologies

This chapter represents both currently available technology and future directions. This is because all the technology described here is in use somewhere, but not necessarily adopted all in one place or as widely as desired.

Today, it appears that information technology is beginning to be more broadly adopted for clinical information computing. Factors that are contributing to heightened interest and EHR use include a critical mass of support systems, more manageable human–computer interfaces, pervasive use of the Internet, the IOM patient safety reports, HIPAA standards, and, perhaps most important, federal government initiatives that have created new opportunities for EHR system use. The federal government is identifying numerous incentive and sanction programs to encourage adoption of e-prescribing in physician offices and EHR throughout healthcare. The government, health plans, and employers are promoting consumer empowerment where the consumer is becoming much more knowledgeable and involved. The government is also more concerned than ever about public health and the need for surveillance systems to monitor for potential bioterrorism. If nothing else, the cost of healthcare is still a significant driver of the government's interest in productivity improvement.

An EHR depends on having a critical mass of support systems. All patient care areas, ancillary departments, and support services must be automated and supply data to a CDR (or be fully integrated). More and more hospitals and physician offices are beginning to have all the necessary source systems in place to support a repository and eventually an EHR.

One of the most critical precursors to an EHR is the need for a user-friendly human-computer interface and other more manageable (and affordable) technologies. The healthcare industry has always been reactive rather than proactive when it comes to new technology. Even new medical technology undergoes years of testing before it is considered safe enough to use on patients. This reluctance to use new technology, coupled with the lack of graphical user interfaces, mobile devices, data capture tools, and online application processing capabilities, truly has held back EHR adoption. Thanks to the Internet and e-commerce, many new technologies are becoming more realistic for healthcare.

The explosion of Internet use and e-commerce has resulted in more widespread use of computers in general and in particular by providers (who are realizing the value of enhanced communications through the Internet) and patients (who are demanding connectivity with their providers).

The biggest spurt of interest in EHR, and perhaps the most compelling for providers, grew out of the IOM reports on patient safety. As a result of these reports describing the extent of medical errors and their cause and potential cure, external pressure has been brought to bear on providers by employers and payer contracting groups. Caution must be applied, however, to recognize that many levels of automation can help reduce medical errors. CPOE can achieve greater legibility without a full EHR. However, a robust decision support system that is a component of an EHR identifies contraindications, provides information on more efficacious medications, and offers best practice guidelines (FCG 2003).

Interestingly, HIPAA has had minimal impact on achieving the EHR. The goal of HIPAA was to actually "encourage the development of a health information system." The transaction and code sets regulation has required a change in claims but has done little else in the way of promoting information system use. Privacy and security regulations are written to be more supportive of health information exchange in a secure manner, yet many organizations are either confused or concerned about potential breeches and, in some cases, have used the regulations as an excuse not to proceed with more clinical computing.

Patient medical record information (PMRI) standards, which were a part of HIPAA, have been recommended by the National Committee on Vital and Health Statistics (NCVHS) but have not as yet been made into regulations (NCVHS 2002). HITSP has made specific recommendations for message format standards for achieving interoperability, standard vocabularies for data comparability, and data quality standards. Interoperability is critical to integrating data from disparate systems to support EHRs. Standard vocabularies ensure that content in disparate systems carries the same meaning. Data quality standards ensure internal consistency, accuracy, completeness, reliability, and timeliness.

There is every indication that the EHR's time has finally come. The future will include complete automation of support systems and use of Internet-based technology to make EHR adoption more affordable and easier to use. More than anything else, ROI is finally beginning to be recognized.

Real-World Case

A hospital already has a homegrown HIS that includes basic patient registration and billing functions. It also supports nursing personnel in order to facilitate communication with the laboratory, pharmacy, and radiology departments so they may receive and process orders. The LIS is interfaced with the HIS so that laboratory results can be viewed from it. A special program was developed recently to supply clinical guidelines for the treatment of diabetes and heart disease that are printed out by nursing personnel for each applicable patient and placed in his or her paper health record. The HIM department is scanning the contents of the medical record for coding and archival purposes. However, the scanned documents cannot be viewed through the HIS because the two systems do not communicate with one another. Access to archived documents is made available through dedicated workstations on the nursing units, selected other areas of the hospital, and to physician offices through a Web portal. The hospital also has several other, smaller and independent systems for its emergency department, nutrition services, surgery scheduling, and rehab, although these are also all stand-alone systems. Physicians who are members of the hospital's medical staff have access to the HIS from their offices to review lab results, electronically fed dictation and scanned documents, and to schedule patients for surgery. The physicians have also started using an e-prescribing system supplied to them by the health plan, which is contributing to significant savings through encouraged use of generic equivalents for brand name drugs, as well as a patient safety improvement with better drug knowledge that helps them avoid contraindications. Clinical components that comprise an EHR have been acquired, starting with the basic CCHIT requirements for foundational systems, CPOE and EMAR. It is important that the hospital plan be interoperable with existing systems and with future acquisition of EHRs by their medical staff members. The hospital also anticipates joining the newly formed HIE organization to extend its ability to care for patients across the continuum of care, even when that care is provided by a different care delivery organization.

Summary

An EHR is both a reality today and a goal for tomorrow. For some organizations, the reality of an EHR is an interim solution or bridge technology, intended to support valid benefits of automation, yet falling short of the goals many have espoused for patient safety, quality of care improvements, productivity enhancements, rising healthcare costs, and homeland security issues. For others, the EHR reality is a continual migration path sometimes dictated by internal organizational issues and sometimes limited by vendor offerings. These migration paths often begin with the challenge of interfacing source systems, building a repository, getting clinicians to perform data entry, and building and achieving adoption of clinical decision support systems. Still, the EHR as envisioned by its early pioneers and carried forward by the Institute of Medicine and now federal government initiatives is very much a goal of all healthcare organizations.

References

45 CFR §164.308(8) Standard: Evaluation.

AHIMA e-HIM Work Group on the Legal Health Record. 2005. Update: Guidelines for defining the legal health record for disclosure purposes. *Journal of AHIMA* 76(8):64A–G.

Amatayakul, M.K. 2009. *Electronic Health Records: A Practical Guide for Professionals and Organizations*. 4th ed. Chicago: AHIMA.

Amatayakul, M.K. 2009. *Guide to HIPAA Privacy and Security Auditing: Practical Tools and Tips to Ensure Compliance*. 2nd ed. Marblehead, MA: HCPro.

Amatayakul, M.K., S.S. Lazarus, T. Walsh, and C.P. Harley. 2004. *Handbook for HIPAA Security Implementation.* Chicago: AMA Press.

ASTM International. ASTM E2369-05 Standard Specification for Continuity of Care Record (CCR). http://www.astm.org/Standards/E2369.htm.

Certification Commission for Healthcare Information Technology, 2007. Functionality Criteria for 2007 Certification of Inpatient EHRs Final. http://www.cchit.org.

Certification Commission for Healthcare Information Technology, 2007. Ambulatory Functionality 2007 – Final Criteria for 2007 Certification of Ambulatory EHRs. http://www.cchit.org.

Cohen, M.R., and M. Amatayakul. 2004. EHR corner: Segmenting the EHR market. *ADVANCE for Health Information Executives* 8(6):22.

Conn, J. 2007 (July 30). What does a chief medical information officer do? *Modern Healthcare.*

Connecting for Health, Markle Foundation. 2006. Connecting Americans to Their Health Care: A Common Framework for Networked Personal Health Information.

Department of Health and Human Services. CMS. 2007. CR5971. www.cms.hhs.gov/Transmittals/downloads/R248PI.pdf.

Department of Health and Human Services. 2008 (June 3). The ONC-Coordinated Federal Health Information Technology Strategic Plan: 2008–2012.

First Consulting Group. 2003. Computerized physician order entry: Costs, benefits and challenges.

Gillespie, G. 2003 (July). Helpful tips for CIOs who take on the universe. *Health Data Management.* 29–38.

HarrisInteractive. 2007 (March 26). Many U.S. Adults are Satisfied with Use of Their Personal Health Information. *Harris Poll®* #27.

Health Level Seven. 2007. *EHR System Functional Model.* Ann Arbor, MI: Health Level Seven.

Health Level Seven. 2007 (June). *Legal Electronic Health Record-System Functional Profile.* Registration Release 1 (v1.0). Ann Arbor, MI: Health Level Seven.

Health Level Seven. 2007 (November). *PHR-System Functional Model, Release 1 DSTU.* Ann Arbor, MI: Health Level Seven.

Institute of Medicine. 1991. *The Computer-based Patient Record: An Essential Technology for Health Care.* Washington, DC: National Academy Press.

Institute of Medicine. 2000. *To Err is Human: Building a Safer Health System.* Washington, DC: National Academy Press.

Institute of Medicine. 2003. Key capabilities of an electronic health record system. Letter Report. Washington, DC: IOM. http://www.nap.edu/books/NI000427/html.

Medicare Prescription Drug, Improvement, and Modernization Act of 2003. Title I: Medicare Prescription Drug Benefit. Baltimore: CMS.

National Alliance on Health Information Technology. 2008 (April 28). Defining Key Health Information Technology Terms. Report to the Office of the National Coordinator for Health Information Technology. 6.

National Alliance on Health Information Technology. 2008 (April 28). Defining Key Health Information Technology Terms http://www.nahit.org/images/pdfs/HITTermsFinalReport_051508.pdf.

National Committee on Vital and Health Statistics. 2002 (Feb. 27). Letter report to the secretary of HHS reporting on issues related to the adoption of uniform data standards for patient medical record information (PMRI). http://www.ncvhs.hhs.gov/020227lt.htm.

P.L. No. 106-229, 114 Stat. 464. 2000. (Codified at 15 U.S.C. § 7001 et seq.) Electronic Signatures in Global and National Commerce Act.

Pryor, D.B., et al. 2006. The clinical transformation of Ascension Health: Eliminating all preventable injuries and deaths. *Joint Commission Journal on Quality and Patient Safety* 32(6):299–308(10).

Servais, C.E. 2008. *The Legal Health Record.* Chicago: AHIMA.

Strong, K. 2008. Enterprise content and records management. *Journal of AHIMA* 80(2):38–42.

Thompson, T.G., and D.J. Brailer. 2004 (July 21). The decade of health information technology: Delivering consumer-centric and information-rich health care. Framework for strategic action. http://www.hhs.gov/healthit/frameworkchapters.html.

Chapter 10
Legal Issues in Health Information Management

Lynda A. Russell, EdD, JD, RHIA, CHP,
and Rita Bowen, MA, RHIA, CHPS

Learning Objectives

- Define terms specific to civil litigation
- Diagram the state and federal court systems
- Describe the sources of law
- Explain the difference between civil law and criminal law
- Describe the process for a civil case and the process for a criminal case
- Discuss liability for a tort as it relates to healthcare
- Discuss liability for breach of contract as it relates to healthcare
- Discuss the legal aspects of a health record
- Discuss the purposes for retaining health records
- Outline the basic principles for releasing confidential health information with or without patient authorization
- Identify the required elements of an authorization for the disclosure of confidential health information
- Analyze various requests for confidential health information and determine whether patient authorization is required
- Elaborate on the role of the health record in medical staff appointments and privileges
- Discuss management of the use and disclosure of information process and function
- Explain the health information administrator's relationship with the risk manager in reducing facility liability
- Discuss difficulties and challenges in defining the legal health record (LHR)
- Elaborate on responding to e-discovery requests

Key Terms

Administrative law
Case law
Circuit
Civil law
Common law
Contract law
Controlled Substances Act
Court of Appeals
Covered entity (CE)
Credentialing process
Criminal law
Default judgment
Defendant
Designated record set
e-discovery
Electronic health record (EHR)
Evidence
Federal Register
Felony
Freedom of Information Act (FOIA)
Health Insurance Portability and Accountability Act of 1996 (HIPAA)
Incident
Individually identifiable health information
Interrogatories
Judge-made law
Jurisdiction
Legal health record
Licensure
Litigation
Metadata
Misdemeanor
Motion for summary judgment
National Practitioner Data Bank
Negligence
Plaintiff
Preemption
Privacy Act of 1974
Privacy Rule
Privilege
Privileging process
Prosecutor
Protected health information (PHI)
Request for production
Restitution
Spoliation
Standard of care
Statute of limitations
Statutory (legislative) law
Tort
Trier of fact
Veterans Health Administration (VHA)

The U.S. legal system consists of three related subsystems: a judicial system, a regulatory system, and an administrative system.

The *judicial system* affords a person or entity the opportunity to bring a civil action against another person or entity believed to have caused harm to the original party. An individual can bring a wide variety of actions against an alleged wrongdoer. The judicial system also affords a person or entity charged with criminal wrongdoing the opportunity to defend himself or herself against those charges. In this way, the judicial system provides an avenue for a wronged party to seek retribution or to clear his or her name.

The *regulatory system* controls many activities related to industry, in particular, the healthcare industry. These controls exist as statutes or as regulations derived from, or promulgated pursuant to, statutes. Often the statutes set forth what action is required, and the regulations set forth how that action is to be met.

The *administrative system* controls governmental administrative operations. Federal and state administrative agencies enact regulations that have the same force of law that statutory laws do.

Understanding the American judicial, regulatory, and administrative subsystems within the legal system gives a health information management (HIM) professional an appreciation for the health record as a legal document and its role in each of these subsystems.

This chapter explains the basic workings of the U.S. legal system. It then identifies the legal principles that apply to healthcare in general and to health information administration in particular. Furthermore, the chapter describes how health records are used in legal proceedings. Finally, it discusses medical staff appointments and privileging.

Because it is impossible to summarize the infinite variety of state laws, the text is based on applying the **Privacy Rule** under the **Health Insurance Portability and Accountability Act of 1996** (HIPAA) (HIPAA-a). HIM professionals must consult their individual state statutes, codes, and regulations for specific applications that may have been declared more stringent than HIPAA and thus not preempted by HIPAA.

Introduction to the Legal System

To understand the role of the HIM professional in protecting confidential health information, one must first understand the principles for disclosing such information. Because many disclosures are made as part of **litigation**, the HIM professional should be very comfortable with the legal process. The following sections present the basics about the sources of American law, the court system, the legal process, and the types of actions encountered in healthcare.

Sources of Law

The laws that rule all Americans' lives come from many sources, which results in a rather complex legal system. Overall, there is a federal legal system and 50 individual state legal systems. Regardless of the source, the legal system is a process through which members of society settle disputes. These disputes may be between private individuals and organizations or between either of these entities and the government, whether state, federal, or both.

Constitutional Law

Much of the law governing society is set out in the state and federal constitutions. The Constitution of the United States is the highest law in the land. It takes precedence over constitutions and laws in the individual states and local jurisdictions (Pozgar 2007). The Constitution defines the federal government's general organization and grants powers to it. It also places limits on what federal and state governments may do. State constitutions have the same effect within the borders of each state. Some state constitutions are very elaborate and govern everything from state lotteries to retirement plans for state workers.

Common Law

English common law is the primary source of many legal rules and principles and was based initially on tradition and custom. **Common law**, also known as **judge-made law** or **case law**, is regularly referred to as unwritten law originating from court decisions where no applicable statute exists. Before the Norman Conquest in 1066, English laws primarily addressed violent crimes. After the Norman Conquest, a legal system began to develop that included a jury hearing complaints from the king's subjects (Pozgar 2007).

After the American Revolution, Louisiana was the only state that did not adopt all or part of the existing English common-law principles (Pozgar 2007). States created after the Revolution vary in their treatment of English common law, but most have adopted the common law in effect as of a certain date. As a matter of technical legal practice, this date of adoption can make a difference in how a lawsuit is resolved if the only source of law on the subject in the state is the English common law. These cases of "first impression" are rare. Louisiana is the exception because it bases much of its common law on the French (Code of Napoleon) and Spanish civil law systems (Pozgar 2007). States continue to add to the body of common law through court decisions (also referred to as a court's holding) when existing statutes do not apply to the issue before the court. Because each state adds to the common law within its boundaries, there is no body of national common law. Thus, a common-law principle established in one state has no effect in another state unless the second state also adopts the principle. Even then, it may be applied differently. After a court establishes a new common-law principle, that principle becomes a precedent for future cases addressing the same issues. The body of common law in a given state is continually evolving through being modified, overturned, abrogated, or created by court decisions.

Statutory Law

By contrast, **statutory (legislative) law** is written law established by federal and state legislatures. It may be amended, repealed, or expanded by the legislature. Statutory law also may be upheld or found by a court to violate or conflict with the state or federal constitution. Further, it may be found to conflict with a different state law or a federal law.

Courts also interpret laws in terms of how they apply to a given situation. Thus, statutory law may be "revised" by a court ruling in terms of its constitutionality and applicability. However, if the legislature disagrees with the court's interpretation, it can revise the statute. The legislative revision then becomes the law versus the court's revision based on its interpretation.

Administrative Law

Federal and state legislatures often delegate their legislative authority to regulate in technical or complex areas to appropriate federal and state administrative agencies. These agencies are empowered to enact regulations that have the same force of law that statutory law has and can impose criminal penalties for noncompliance. Accordingly, **administrative law** is the branch of law that controls governmental administrative operations (Pozgar 2007). Such administrative agencies include licensing and accrediting bodies, Medicare, Medicaid, and other federal and state government programs.

Federal administrative agencies function under the Administrative Procedures Act, which sets forth the following (Pozgar 2007):

- The procedures under which administrative agencies must operate
- The procedural responsibilities and authority of administrative agencies
- The legal remedies for individuals or entities harmed by agency actions

The act also requires administrative agencies to make agency rules, opinions, orders, records, and proceedings available to the public (Administrative Procedures Act §552). The publication used to accomplish this is the ***Federal Register***, which is issued by the U.S. Government Printing Office every business day. The information that agencies must publish includes the following:

- Their organizational structure and the location where the public can obtain information
- Formal and informal procedures and forms and instructions for using them
- General statement of applicability
- Amendments, revisions, or repeals of any of this information

Furthermore, agencies must publish proposed administrative rules and revisions to existing rules for which they are delegated the responsibility and authority to enact. These rules or revisions are published in the *Federal Register* for a comment period during which the public is invited to make comments on the applicability and impact of the proposed rules on a given person, group of persons, or entity. After the comment period ends, the applicable administrative agency may or may not finalize the rules. If the rules are finalized, the notice and the final rule are published in the *Federal Register*. The final rule is also codified and published in the appropriate code section. The Medicare Conditions of Participation regulations and HIPAA's Administrative Simplification rules are examples of healthcare-related information regulations published in the *Federal Register*. Such regulations and administrative decisions can be subject to judicial review when questions arise regarding whether an agency has overstepped its bounds in interpreting the law (Pozgar 2007).

Most states have similar administrative procedure acts, but few have as elaborate a system for the adoption of new regulations as the federal government.

The Court System

The American court system is composed of the state court system and the federal court system. The nature of the issue determines which court has **jurisdiction** over the issue. Matters in the following three categories belong only to federal courts: federal crimes, such as racketeering and bank robbery; constitutional issues; and civil actions where the parties do not live in the same state. Other civil and criminal cases are heard in the state court system.

State Court System

Typically, the state court system has several levels. In most states, the lowest level consists of specialty courts or local courts that hear cases involving traffic, small claims, and justice of the peace issues. State civil and criminal cases are initiated in the lower-level trial courts. These are referred to differently in different states, for example, as district trial courts or superior courts. New York's trial courts are called the "Supreme Court." Some trial courts at this level have limited jurisdiction and include courts such as probate, family, juvenile, surrogate, and criminal. Other trial courts at this same level have general jurisdiction. Decisions made in a court at this level may be appealed to the intermediate courts, usually known as the state appeals courts. State appellate courts have general jurisdiction; however, some states (such as Texas) divide their appellate courts into civil and criminal appellate jurisdiction, and others divide appellate courts by legal and equitable jurisdiction.

State legal systems also include a court at the highest level. These courts of last resort also are known by different terms in different states. Many are simply the Supreme Court of the state; others are the Supreme Judicial Court as in Massachusetts, and New York has the **Court of Appeals** as its highest court. These higher courts also have general jurisdiction over all cases heard in the state's trial and appellate courts. Decisions coming from the highest state court hearing a case become the law of that state unless a state legislative process enacts a statute to override the court's decision, or unless it is overturned by another case.

Federal Court System

The trial-level federal courts are the 94 U.S. district courts (trial courts). Included in the district courts are the bankruptcy courts. Because federal courts have exclusive jurisdiction over bankruptcy matters, such cases cannot be filed in a state court. Special federal courts have jurisdiction over specific matters. These courts include the U.S. Tax Court (hears cases involving federal tax matters only), the U.S. Customs Court (reviews administrative decisions made by customs officials), the U.S. Court of Appeals for the Armed Forces (the jurisdiction of which is limited to hearing appeals from court martials under the Uniform Code of Military Justice), and the U.S. Court of Federal Claims (hears certain claims against the government including those for money damages) (Pozgar 2007). The federal appellate level is composed of the U.S. Courts of Appeals, each covering a geographic area known as a **circuit**. The U.S. Supreme Court is the highest court in the U.S. legal system and hears appeals from the federal appellate courts and the various state courts of last resort.

The Legal Process

The HIM professional can better serve patient privacy interests if he or she has an understanding of the legal process. This understanding should cover both civil and criminal processes, as healthcare facilities sometimes are affected by criminal cases.

Civil Cases

Civil law involves relations between individuals, corporations, government entities, and other organizations. Most actions encountered in the healthcare industry are based in civil law. Typically, the remedy for a civil wrong is monetary in nature but also may include carrying out some action.

The party bringing the action or complaint in a civil case is the plaintiff. The plaintiff has the burden of proving the wrong, that the defendant did the wrong act, that the wrong did the plaintiff harm, the harm from the wrong, and the expected **restitution.** The plaintiff presents **evidence** before a judge or a jury that must be more compelling than that of the opposing side, the defendant. The plaintiff or an attorney on the plaintiff's behalf begins the process by filing a complaint in the appropriate court. Hereafter in this discussion, the term **plaintiff** refers collectively to the individual or entity bringing the action and that individual or entity's attorney. The plaintiff has a summons, including a copy of the filed complaint, served on the defendant. The defendant or an attorney on the defendant's behalf prepares an answer and files it in the same court where the original complaint was filed. Hereafter in this discussion, the term **defendant** refers collectively to the person or entity against whom an action has been brought and that person or entity's attorney.

A case may be resolved in five ways:

- A judge can dismiss the plaintiff's case for procedural reasons. The plaintiff's complaint may not set forth a claim recognized by law, the summons and complaint may not have been properly served on the defendant, or the defendant may not be subject to the court's jurisdiction (meaning that the court has no power to compel the defendant to do what it commands). The judge may permit the plaintiff to correct the error and refile the case.
- If the defendant fails to file a timely answer, the court will find in favor of the plaintiff and enter a **default judgment** against the defendant.
- A case may be settled out of court before it goes to trial or at any time during trial before the **trier of fact** (judge or jury) announces the decision.
- Presuming the case does not settle or is not dismissed or no default judgment is entered, the case will proceed with pretrial activities by both plaintiff and defendant. Such activities, known as pretrial discovery, include, but are not limited to, the taking of witnesses' depositions, the serving of **interrogatories** and **requests for production** on the opposing party, and the issuing of subpoenas, as necessary. The court (the judge assigned to the case) will set dates according to the law by which pretrial discovery must be completed. At the conclusion of this stage, in most cases one or both parties present **motions for summary judgment**, in which they argue that there are (or are not) any facts remaining in dispute and that one or the other is (or is not) entitled to a judgment being entered without the intervention of the trier of fact. If the judge grants such a motion, the case is over and has the same effect as if the case had proceeded to trial.
- If a motion for summary judgment is not successful or is not made, the case will proceed to trial before the trier of fact. In most civil cases, the plaintiff must prove his or her case by what is known as a "preponderance of the evidence." In simple terms, this means that there is enough evidence to tip the scales, even slightly, in favor of the plaintiff's case. This is a substantially lower standard of proof than a criminal case, in which the government must prevail "beyond a reasonable doubt." Upon conclusion of the trial, a verdict is given and a judgment rendered against the party determined to be wholly or partially liable for the harm. In civil cases, a verdict is more commonly referred to as being "liable" or "not liable." Either party may appeal the judgment to an appellate court and possibly even to the highest court in that state.

Criminal Cases

Criminal law addresses crimes that are wrongful acts against public health, safety, and welfare. Criminal laws also include punishment for those persons violating the law. Criminal cases involve matters between individuals or groups of people and the government. Crimes are either a felony or a misdemeanor as defined by state or federal law. **Felonies** are the more serious crimes and include, among others, murder, thefts of items or cash in excess of a certain set value (ordinarily $1,000), assault, and rape. **Misdemeanors** are lesser offenses and include disorderly conduct, thefts of small amounts of property, and breaking into an automobile. Information theft crimes (such as hacking, computer destruction, spamming, and the like) can be either misdemeanors or felonies. The criminal provisions of the HIPAA Privacy Rule have only felony crimes.

When law enforcement learns that a crime has or may have been committed, an investigation is begun. The government initiates a criminal action against those individuals or groups of people it believes have committed the crime based on the law enforcement investigation. When the **prosecutor** (prosecuting attorney), also known as the district or state attorney (depending on the state) or the U.S. attorney (in the federal system), determines sufficient evidence is present, he or she files charges against the defendant on behalf of the government. In some states, a grand jury must return an indictment for a felony crime to be prosecuted. The grand jury has the authority to issue subpoenas for its investigative process, and all evidence considered by the grand jury remains confidential unless an indictment is returned. The court arraigns the charged person on the prosecutor's charge, and the prosecutor prosecutes those charges against the defendant. The prosecutor has the burden of proving the charges against the defendant. In virtually all criminal cases, the government must prove the defendant's guilt beyond a reasonable doubt.

The accused defendant may plead guilty and be sentenced to probation or imprisonment and/or pay a fine. He or she also may plead not guilty, which results in a trial. Upon conclusion of the trial, a verdict of either guilty or not guilty is rendered. When a defendant is found not guilty, the charges are dismissed. A defendant found to be guilty is sentenced to probation or imprisonment and/or to pay a fine. In most jurisdictions, only a defendant who is found guilty at trial can proceed through the appellate process.

Actions Encountered in Healthcare

The healthcare industry is involved most often in civil cases and less often in criminal cases. Because government is increasing its investigations into and prosecutions for healthcare fraud and refusal to treat patients based on financial status, the healthcare industry will be faced with more criminal cases. However, this chapter focuses on civil actions. The types of civil legal actions that most typically affect the healthcare industry are torts and contracts. The vast majority of claims founded in tort and **contract law** are resolved without appearing in court, many before a lawsuit is filed.

Torts

A **tort** is an action brought when one party believes that another party caused harm through wrongful conduct and the party bringing the action seeks compensation for that harm. In addition to compensation, a second reason for bringing a tort action is to discourage the wrongdoer from committing further wrongful acts. Three categories of tort liability exist: negligence, intentional torts, and strict and products liability (Pozgar 2007). Most healthcare **incidents** arise in the negligent tort category.

Negligent Torts

Negligence results when a person does not act the way a reasonably prudent person would act under the same circumstances. A negligent tort may result from a person committing an act or failing to act as a reasonably prudent person would or would not in the given circumstances (Pozgar 2007). Typically, negligence is careless conduct that is outside the generally accepted standard of care. **Standard of care** is defined as what an individual is expected to do or not do in a given situation. Standards of care are established in a variety of ways: by professional associations, by statute or regulation, or by practice. Such standards are considered to represent expected behavior unless a court finds differently. Therefore, standards also are established by case law. Standards not established by a governmental body do not by themselves have the force of law.

In healthcare, the standard of care is the exercise of reasonable care by healthcare professionals having similar training and experience in the same or similar communities. However, some courts may define standards of care on a national level versus a community level.

Negligence also may occur in cases where an individual has evaluated the alternatives and the consequences of those alternatives and has exercised his or her best possible judgment. Thus, a person can be found negligent when he or she has failed to guard against a risk that he or she knew could happen. Furthermore, negligence can occur in circumstances where it is known, or should have been known, that a particular behavior would place others in unreasonable danger. Negligence may occur in the form of (Pozgar 2007, 29):

- *Malpractice*: Negligence or carelessness of a professional person, such as a nurse, pharmacist, physician, or accountant
- *Criminal negligence*: Reckless disregard for the safety of another; the willful indifference to an injury that could follow an act (in this respect, it is possible that conduct could at once create civil and criminal liability)

Negligence can further be categorized in other ways. For example, negligent torts can be categorized as (Pozgar 2007, 29):

- *Malfeasance*: The execution of an unlawful or improper act
- *Misfeasance*: The improper performance of an act resulting in injury to another
- *Nonfeasance*: The failure to act when there is a duty to act as a reasonably prudent person would act in similar circumstances

Further, negligence can be categorized by the degree of wrongdoing. *Ordinary negligence* is failure to do what a reasonably prudent person would do, or doing something that a reasonably prudent person would not do, in the same circumstances (Pozgar 2007, 29). *Gross negligence* is intentionally omitting care that would be proper or providing care that would be substandard or improper (Pozgar 2007, 29).

To recover damages caused by negligence, the plaintiff must show that all four elements of negligence are present (Pozgar 2007, 29):

- There must be a *duty of care*. For this element to be present in a medical malpractice case, a physician–patient, nurse–patient, therapist–patient, or other caregiver–patient relationship must exist at the time of the alleged wrongful act.
- There must have been a *breach of the duty of care*. The plaintiff must present evidence that the defendant acted unreasonably under the circumstances.
- The plaintiff must have *suffered an injury* as a result of the defendant's negligent act or failure to act. Injury includes not only physical harm, but also mental suffering and the invasion of a patient's rights and privacy.
- The plaintiff must show that the defendant's conduct *caused* the plaintiff's harm. As an example, varying from a recognized procedure is insufficient to justify the plaintiff's recovery of damages. The plaintiff must show that the variance was unreasonable and that it caused the harm.

When no statute exists to define what is reasonable, the trier of fact determines what a reasonably prudent person would have done. According to Pozgar (2007), "the reasonably prudent person represents the conduct of the average person in the community under the circumstances facing the defendant at the time of the alleged negligence" (Pozgar 2007, 31). The trier of fact considers characteristics such as age, sex, training, education, mental capacity, physical condition, and knowledge in defining the reasonably prudent person. After the behavior of a reasonably prudent person is defined for the given circumstances, the trier of fact compares the defendant's behavior against that definition. If the defendant's behavior meets or exceeds the definition, no negligence has occurred. On the other hand, if the defendant's behavior does not meet the reasonably prudent person standard and damages result, negligence has occurred. In such a case, the trier of fact must determine whether:

- The harm that would result from the failure to meet the reasonably prudent person standard could have been foreseen.
- The negligent act caused harm to the plaintiff.

Intentional Torts

Although most torts experienced in healthcare are based on negligence, an occasional intentional tort is committed that includes actions such as assault, battery, libel, slander, invasion of privacy, and false imprisonment. The element of intent is the difference between the intentional tort and the negligent tort. *Intent* means the person committed an act knowing that harm would likely occur.

A quick review of several intentional torts gives the reader an idea of how they may occur in a healthcare setting. The intentional torts discussed below include assault and battery, false imprisonment, defamation of character, fraud, invasion of privacy, and reckless infliction of mental distress.

Assault is a deliberate threat that is combined with the apparent present ability to cause physical harm to another person (Pozgar 2007, 38). For example, a large male nurse in the emergency department tells a frail elderly woman that he will break her arm if she does not do what he tells her to do. His comment is a deliberate threat, and his size gives him the apparent ability to harm the woman.

Battery is intentionally touching another person's body in a socially impermissible manner without that person's consent (Pozgar 2007, 38). In healthcare, laws regarding battery are especially important because of the requirement for consent for medical and surgical procedures. The hospital and the treating healthcare professionals may be held liable for harm caused by the lack of a proper patient consent. Even if the outcome of the procedure benefits the patient, touching the patient without proper consent may make the healthcare professional liable for battery.

False imprisonment is another intentional tort. A healthcare provider's efforts to prevent a patient from leaving a hospital may result in false imprisonment. This is not the case when a patient with a contagious disease or a mentally ill patient who is likely to cause harm to others is compelled to remain in the hospital (Pozgar 2007). There are limits to the actions staff can take to compel a patient not to leave a hospital. For example, staff may confine a person to protect them from harming themselves or others (Pozgar 2007, 38). The patient's insistence on leaving the facility should be documented in his or her health record, and the patient should be asked to sign a discharge against medical advice form that releases the facility from responsibility. When excessive force is used to restrain a patient, the healthcare provider may be held liable for both false imprisonment and battery (Pozgar 2007, 38).

Defamation of character is a false communication about someone to a person other than the person defamed that tends to injure that person's reputation (Pozgar 2007, 40). The communication may be either oral or written. *Libel* is the written form of defamation, and *slander* is the spoken form. To recover in an action for defamation, the plaintiff must prove that:

- The defendant made a false and defamatory statement about the plaintiff.
- The statement was not a "privileged" publication and was made to a third person.
- At least negligence occurred.
- Actual or presumed damages occurred.

Proof of special damages, including economic losses, is not required to recover in a defamation case. Special damages include economic losses. Courts also may find that the defamation caused injury to a person's reputation. However, there are four exceptions regarding harm to reputation. In these exceptions, the plaintiff is not required to show proof of actual harm to his or her reputation when the defendant allegedly performs one of the following acts (Pozgar 2007, 40):

- Accuses the plaintiff of a crime
- Accuses the plaintiff of having a loathsome disease
- Uses words that affect the plaintiff's profession or business
- Calls a woman unchaste

When slander is alleged, the plaintiff usually must prove special damages. However, if the slander refers to the plaintiff in a professional capacity, the plaintiff is not required to show actual harm because slanderous references to a person's professional capacity are presumed to be damaging to that person's professional reputation (Pozgar 2007, 42). As to the second exception, healthcare professionals are protected against claims of libel when complying with laws requiring the reporting of communicable diseases that the patient may consider loathsome (Pozgar 2007).

The defendant (the one being accused of defaming another) has two defenses available to a defamation action. The person making an alleged defamatory statement that harms another's reputation will not be liable for that statement if he or she shows the statement was true (Pozgar 2007). Secondly, the person making the allegedly defamatory communication can claim privilege if he or she is making the communication:

- In good faith
- On the proper occasion
- In the proper manner
- To persons who have a legitimate reason to receive the information

The defense of privilege is based on the person making the communication being charged with a higher duty. For example, in one case, a director of nurses wrote a letter to a nurse's professional registry stating that the hospital wanted to discontinue a particular nurse's services because narcotics were disappearing whenever the nurse was on duty (*Judge v. Rockford Memorial Hospital* 1958). The court found the communication to be privileged because the director of nurses had a legal duty to make the communication in the interests of society. Thus, the court denied the nurse's claim for damages.

Fraud is a prevalent concern in today's healthcare environment. It is defined as "a willful and intentional misrepresentation that could cause harm or loss to a person or property" (Pozgar 2007, 44). For example, physicians can be held liable for fraud if they claim that a particular procedure will cure a patient's ailment when they know it will not, or if they charge a third-party payer for a medical procedure they did not actually perform.

Invasion of privacy is another major concern in healthcare. A person's right to privacy is "the right to be left alone—the right to be free from unwarranted publicity and exposure to public view, as well as the right to live one's life without having one's name, picture, or private affairs made public against one's will" (Pozgar 2007, 45). The right to privacy is also the right to control personal information (McWay 2003, 118). The courts hold healthcare providers liable for negligent disregard for a patient's right of privacy, especially when patients cannot adequately protect themselves because of unconsciousness or immobility (Pozgar 2007, 45). One major actionable offense of concern in healthcare involving invasion of privacy is the release or disclosure of health information without patient authorization in circumstances when it is required. (See figure A.21 in appendix A.)

The *intentional or reckless infliction of mental distress* for which a person can be held liable includes mental suffering resulting from such things as despair, shame, grief, and public humiliation (Pozgar 2007). If the plaintiff shows that the defendant (the one inflicting the distress) intended to cause mental distress and knew or should have known that his or her actions would do so, the plaintiff can recover damages (Pozgar 2007).

The distinction between negligence torts and intentional torts is far from academic. In most state legal systems, punitive damages (those damages awarded to punish or deter wrongful conduct over and above compensation for injury) are limited in negligence cases and may, in fact, be capped in medical malpractice cases. However, most states permit punitive damages as a matter of right in cases of intentional torts, and these damages usually fall outside the scope of state laws capping jury awards or damages. Consequently, it is possible for a battery case involving a failure to obtain surgical consent (an intentional tort) to have more economic value than a medical malpractice case (a negligence tort) due to the presence or absence of punitive damages.

Strict and Products Liability

Strict liability occurs when some person or entity is held "responsible for damages their actions or products cause, regardless of 'fault' on their part" (Pozgar 2007, 46). Products liability is the legal doctrine under which a manufacturer, seller, or supplier may be liable to a buyer or other third party for injuries caused by a defective product (Pozgar 2007). The injured person may bring an action based in negligence, breach of warranty, or strict liability. To prevail in *negligence*, the plaintiff must show that there was a duty that was breached causing the injury. The manufacturer will not be held liable for injuries if they resulted from the user's negligent use of the product. Manufacturers will be held liable for injuries resulting from a bad product design (Pozgar 2007). Manufacturers often provide instructions on the proper use of their product. Should a manufacturer not provide these instructions, the manufacturer may be liable for negligence (Pozgar 2007). Defective packaging can be the basis for a finding in negligence. A manufacturer also has a duty to warn of dangers associated with normal, proper use of the product.

To recover under the theory of *breach of warranty,* the plaintiff must show there was an express or implied warranty (Pozgar 2007). Through an *express warranty*, the seller makes specific promises to the buyer. Whereas an *implied warranty* exists when the law implies such a warranty exists "as a matter of public policy" to protect the public from harm (Pozgar 2007, 48).

The third basis on which a plaintiff may base a product's liability claim is *strict liability,* which is liability without fault. To prevail, the plaintiff only must show an injury resulted while using the product in the proper manner. The plaintiff does not need to show negligence by the manufacturer. The elements for a strict liability case are (Pozgar 2007, 48):

- Product must have been manufactured by the defendant
- Product must have been defective at the time it left the hands of the manufacturer or seller
- Plaintiff must have been injured by the specific product
- Defective product must have been the proximate cause of the injury

Under strict liability, the manufacturer also may be held liable pursuant to the concept of *res ipsa loquitur* (the thing speaks for itself). To recover, the plaintiff must show (Pozgar 2007, 49):

- The product did not perform in the way intended
- Neither the buyer nor a third person had tampered with the product
- The defect in the product existed when it left the manufacturer

Defenses

A healthcare provider may raise a number of defenses in response to a lawsuit (McWay 2003, 55–60). These include the following:

- ***Statute of limitations***: A statutorily set time frame within which a lawsuit must be brought or the court must dismiss the case.
- *Good Samaritan:* Statutes that protect physicians and other rescuers from liability for their acts or omissions in providing emergency care in a nontraditional setting such as at an automobile accident site when no charge for services is made.
- *Contributory negligence*: The plaintiff's conduct contributed in part to the injury the plaintiff suffered and, if found to be sufficient, can preclude the plaintiff's recovery for the injury.
- *Comparative negligence*: The plaintiff's conduct contributed in part to the injury the plaintiff suffered, but the plaintiff's recovery is reduced by some amount based on his or her percentage of negligence.

The charitable immunity and governmental immunity defenses have been either significantly limited or abolished as defenses by state and federal laws.

Defenses in products liability cases include (Pozgar 2007, 49):

- Assumption of risk
- Intervening cause
- Contributory negligence
- Comparative fault
- Disclaimers

Contract

Suits under contracts are the other type of civil claim arising in the healthcare industry. A contract is an agreement, written or oral, that, in most cases, is legally enforceable through the legal system. Contracts must not violate state or federal policy or state or federal statute, rule, or regulation. Contract law is based on common law. However, some states have replaced common law with statutory law or administrative agency regulations. In those states, the statutes or administrative regulations control. One example of how contractual issues affect healthcare is a contract for services between the hospital and a contracting physician or a physician group, such as pathologists, radiologists, anesthesiologists, and emergency medicine physicians.

The elements of a contract must be stated clearly and specifically. A contract cannot exist unless all the following elements exist. There must be an *agreement* between two or more persons or entities. The agreement must include a valid offer, acceptance, and an exchange of consideration. In an *offer*, one party promises to either do something or not do something if the other party agrees to either do something or not do something (Pozgar 2007). The party making the offer must communicate it to the other party so that it can be accepted or rejected. There also must be *acceptance.* Acceptance requires the following to be valid (Pozgar 2007, 73):

- Meeting of the minds (parties must understand and agree on the terms comprising the contract)
- Definite and Complete (terms must be sufficiently complete for parties to understand the terms)
- Duration (the party making the offer (offeror) may revoke offer prior to a valid acceptance; revocation not effective until the party to whom the offer was made (offeree) receives the revocation; once offeree accepts offer, it cannot be revoked)
- Complete and Conforming (acceptance must be mirror image of the offer—not add, change, or delete any of the terms in the offer)

Finally, a contract must be supported by legal and bargained-for consideration. Each party "must give up something of value in exchange for something of value" (Pozgar 2007, 73).

The parties to a contract must have the capacity to enter into the agreement, such as being a competent adult, being of age of majority, not being incapacitated by medication or alcohol, and not being mentally incapacitated. The contract must be for a legal purpose. Finally, the contract must not violate public policy (Pozgar 2004, 90). A hospital contract with patients that attempts to limit their right to sue could be a contract to which a court would apply the unconscionable concept and hold the hospital liable.

A contract action arises when one party claims that the other party has failed to meet an obligation set forth in a valid contract. Another way to state this is that the other party has breached the contract. The resolution available is either compensation (money damages) or performance of the obligation. To succeed in a breach of contract action, the plaintiff must show (Pozgar 2007, 73):

- Parties entered into a valid contract
- Plaintiff performed as specified
- Defendant did not perform as specified
- Plaintiff suffered an economic loss as a result of the defendant's failure to perform

The defendant can raise a variety of defenses to a breach of contract action including waiver and default, conduct of the parties, and waiving rights under the agreement.

Check Your Understanding 10.1

Instructions: Answer the following questions on a separate piece of paper.

1. What are the four sources of laws governing Americans?
2. What types of cases are typically heard in the federal court system?
3. Which court is the court of last resort in the U.S. legal system?
4. What are the two most common types of civil cases experienced in healthcare?
5. In a court, who is the trier of fact?
6. What is the result of a trial called?
7. What types of cases are covered by criminal laws?
8. What are the roles of prosecutor and defendant in a criminal case? Who has the burden of proof?
9. What are the possible outcomes of a criminal case?
10. What are the three categories of tort liability? From which category do most healthcare cases arise?
11. What is the definition of a negligent tort?
12. What are the four elements of negligence?
13. How might false imprisonment occur in a hospital?
14. What defenses are available to a defendant accused of defamation of character?
15. Privacy is difficult to achieve in a healthcare setting. However, courts will hold healthcare providers liable for what type of invasion of privacy?
16. What is a contract?
17. What action must occur for a contract case to arise?

Legal Aspects of Healt Information Manageme

The field of health information manage and treat the patient's health record as a legal document. Thus, the HIM professional must have an understanding of all the regulations and statutes that affect the creation and maintenance of the health record.

Form and Content of the Health Record

The health record is a complete, accurate, and current report of the medical history, condition, and treatment that a particular patient receives during an encounter with a healthcare provider. (See chapter 9 and later in this chapter for a discussion of a legal health record.) In a hospital, the encounter may be on either an inpatient or outpatient basis. Moreover, it may be defined as one episode of treatment or an accumulation of all episodes of treatment in any setting that is part of the organization.

The health record is composed of two sections: the demographic section and the clinical section. Most of the information in the *demographic section* is collected at the time of admission or registration for treatment. It includes, among other items, the patient's name, sex, age, insurance information, and the person to contact in case of emergency. This information may be added to and changed throughout the patient's medical encounters. The *clinical section* comprises the patient's complaint, history of present illness, medical history, family history, social history, continuing documentation of ongoing medical care, report of diagnostic tests, x-ray reports, surgery and other procedure reports, consultant reports, nursing documentation, various graphs, and the final diagnoses. In some states, licensure regulations may specify the contents. In other states, the health record content is defined in broader terms.

Accrediting agency regulations or standards are one source for identifying health record content. (See appendix C.) The Joint Commission, the American Osteopathic Association (AOA), and other accrediting organizations include some level of requirements for health record content. The Medicare program's Conditions of Participation also include minimum requirements for health record content. However, some sources of regulations for health record content are more prescriptive than others are. For example, some regulations give details on the information to be retained, others specify the broad categories of information required, and still others state simply that the health record must be accurate, adequate, or complete. Most states have statutory or regulatory definitions of what a proper health record must contain, and many third-party payers also dictate how health records for their insured must be maintained and kept. The HIM professional must be aware of the most stringent definition of the health record content to which his or her particular organization is subject.

…also is important to heed requirements of agencies …d laws that regulate hospitals and have an impact on the process of creating and maintaining health records. The healthcare industry in general and hospitals in particular are extensively regulated by all levels of the government and by numerous agencies within each level of government. Additionally, they are regulated for accreditation purposes by nongovernment agencies. Quite often, hospitals are faced with conflicting requirements because of this multiple-regulation environment.

Regulatory (Licensure) Agencies

Typically, state legislatures have granted authority to a state administrative agency to

- Develop standards hospitals must meet
- Issue licenses to those hospitals that meet the standards
- Monitor continuing compliance with the standards
- Penalize hospitals that violate the standards

Licensure is issued for the organization as a whole. It addresses policies and procedures, staffing, and hospital building integrity among many other facets of the organization. Some states require additional licenses for specific services in the hospital. For example, laboratory, radiology, renal dialysis, and substance abuse services may require separate licenses in addition to the facility license. Additional state and federal laws apply to the use of drugs and medical devices.

Some states require separate licensure for hospital pharmacies whereas other states regulate hospital pharmacies through the general state hospital licensing system. Typically, the laws address dispensing and administering drugs to patients in the hospital and dispensing take-home drugs through an inpatient or outpatient hospital visit. Additionally, some regulations require sufficient staff members for the hospital pharmacy based on the hospital's size and scope of services.

Finally, some states require certain types of medical equipment to be separately licensed, such as x-ray equipment or medical waste disposal systems.

Hospitals cannot operate without a license. Those that violate the standards may lose their licenses or be penalized in other ways, such as with fines. Thus, licensure is government regulation that is mandatory for hospitals.

Accreditation Agencies

Accreditation is offered through nongovernment agencies. One of the most important accrediting agencies for hospitals is the Joint Commission. The Joint Commission develops standards that hospitals must meet to be accredited. The healthcare organization applies to the Joint Commission to be accredited, pays an accreditation fee, and submits to an extensive survey to ensure compliance with the Joint Commission's published standards. The Joint Commission addresses privacy, information security, confidentiality, ethical behavior, patient rights training and whether the hospital complies with applicable laws and regulations, and in a number of standards. The student should review the most current manual published by the Joint Commission for standards on these topics.

Effective January 2004, The Joint Commission introduced a self-assessment approach to showing compliance with privacy and confidentiality standards and elements of performance. The organization uses 12 months of concrete data to score itself on the elements of performance. The Joint Commission verifies those scores during a regular accreditation visit.

Similarly, the AOA accredits osteopathic hospitals and functions in much the same way that the Joint Commission does.

Accreditation is considered voluntary and is not legally mandated, but it is very important to healthcare organizations. Some states accept the Joint Commission or AOA accreditation as a basis for partial or full licensure with limited or no additional survey by the state agency. This "deeming" authority gives the Joint Commission a significant amount of power it would not otherwise have.

Whereas the Joint Commission and the AOA focus on the entire hospital, other accrediting agencies focus on specific services of the hospital. For example, there is a separate accreditation process for laboratory and radiology services in addition to that of the Joint Commission and the AOA.

The federal Medicare program also sets standards for hospitals in its Conditions of Participation. Although these are government regulations, participation in the Medicare program is considered voluntary. However, few, if any, hospitals elect not to participate in this program. Thus, a hospital must comply with these standards to receive payment from the Medicare program for covered services provided to Medicare beneficiaries. The Medicare program also recognizes organizations that have the Joint Commission or AOA accreditation as meeting most of the Conditions of Participation, and it grants them deemed status. A hospital would typically undergo an additional survey only if a special Medicare inspection finds noncompliance.

Statutory and Regulatory Law

There are many sources of law mandating the privacy of confidential health information. Some of these sources are discussed here.

Privacy

There is no right to privacy specifically stated in the U.S. Constitution. However, in 1965, the Supreme Court recognized an implicit constitutional right of privacy in *Griswold v. Connecticut* (1965). In this case, the court ruled that "the right to privacy limits governmental authority to regulate contraception, abortion, and other decisions affecting reproduction" (Miller 1986, 6–7). Some states also have recognized the right to privacy in their state constitutions (California Constitution, Article 1, Declaration of Rights, Section 1) (Arizona Constitution, Section 8 Right to privacy) (Florida Constitution, Article I, Section 23, Right of privacy).

On August 21, 1996, Congress enacted HIPAA. This legislation initially focused on making it easier for employees to retain health coverage when they changed jobs or their family status changed. The HIPAA legislation addressed waste, fraud, and abuse in the healthcare system. It also focused on simplifying the administration of health insurance (HIPAA-b) (Carter 2003, 1).

To address simplification, Congress added the Administrative Simplification provisions, which created a single federal standard electronic claims format for electronic data interchange (HIPAA-c). With these provisions, the legislature intended to improve the efficiency and effectiveness of the healthcare system (HIPAA-d). However, Congress continued to express concerns about privacy and security of patient information in an electronic environment (HIPAA-c). Consequently, HIPAA required HHS to develop and implement electronic transaction standards and to develop regulations to protect the privacy and security of **individually identifiable health information** (HIPAA-e) (Carter 2003, 1). As a result, HHS issued three sets of standards: Transactions and Code Sets (45 CFR §§160, 162), and Privacy, and Security (45 CFR §§160, 164). All rules for these three sets of standards have been promulgated and issued. Covered entities as defined in HIPAA were required to be in compliance with the Privacy Rule by April 14, 2003, with the Transactions and Code Sets Rule by October 16, 2003, and with the Security Rule by April 20, 2005. The compliance dates for small health plans were extended by one year for each set of rules. (HIPAA is covered in more detail later in this chapter.)

Another piece of federal legislation addressing a patient's right to privacy is the **Privacy Act of 1974**. This act gives individuals some control over the information collected about them by the federal government (Hughes 2002). It does not apply to records maintained by institutions in the private sector (McWay 2003). Under the Privacy Act of 1974, people have the right to (Hughes 2002):

- Learn what information has been collected about them
- View and have a copy of that information
- Maintain limited control over the disclosure of that information to other persons or entities

This act also applies to federal government healthcare organizations such as the **Veterans Health Administration** (VHA) and Indian Health Services and to record systems operated pursuant to a contract with a federal government agency (Hughes 2002).

Further, the **Freedom of Information Act** (FOIA) is a federal law through which individuals can seek access to information without authorization of the person to whom the information applies. This act applies only to federal agencies and not the private sector. The Veterans Administration and Defense Department hospital systems are subject to this act, but few other hospitals are. The only protection of health information held by federal agencies exists when disclosure would "constitute a clearly unwarranted invasion of personal privacy" (Miller 1986).

Despite the need for patient privacy, healthcare providers disclose health information to subsequent healthcare providers to the extent necessary to ensure continuity of patient care (Hughes 2003). Federal legislation that specifically provides for such disclosures includes, but is not limited to:

- Medicare Conditions of Participation for Hospitals
- Conditions of Participation for Clinics, Rehabilitation Agencies, and Public Health Agencies as Providers of Outpatient Physical Therapy and Speech-Language Pathology
- Conditions of Participation for Home Health Agencies
- Confidentiality of Alcohol and Drug Abuse Patient Records

As to privacy rights, the Conditions of Participation for Hospitals rule states that hospitals must have procedures to protect the confidentiality of patient records (Hughes 2002). Under this rule, hospitals must protect records against unauthorized access and alteration. Further, original records may be removed from the facility only in accordance with federal and state laws (Hughes 2002).

The Conditions of Participation for Clinics, Rehabilitation Agencies, and Public Health Agencies as Providers of Outpatient Physical Therapy and Speech-Language Pathology regulations permit the physician to provide medical information to the receiving facility (Hughes 2003).

The Conditions of Participation for Home Health Agencies also requires facilities to have written policies and procedures to safeguard health information against loss or unauthorized use (Hughes 2002). Furthermore, the Requirements for States and Long-Term Care Facilities give the resident or his or her legal representative the right to access information about the resident. Additionally, these regulations give the resident the right to personal privacy and confidentiality of personal and clinical records (Hughes 2002).

The Confidentiality of Alcohol and Drug Abuse Patient Records rule is a federal rule that applies to information created for patients treated in a federally assisted drug or alcohol abuse program (Hughes 2002). This rule specifically protects the identity, diagnosis, prognosis, or treatment of these patients (Hughes 2002). These rules generally prohibit redisclosure of health information related to this treatment except as needed in a medical emergency or when authorized by an appropriate court order or the patient's authorization (Rhodes and Hughes 2003). (See figure A.22 in appendix A.). The rule also specifies the circumstances under which information can be released without patient authorization and requires that language prohibiting redisclosure be attached to all released information concerning drug or alcohol treatment (Hughes 2002).

Other Federal Legislation

The Comprehensive Drug Abuse Prevention and Control Act of 1970, the **Controlled Substances Act**, controls the use of narcotics, depressants, stimulants, and hallucinogens (Pozgar

2007). Because this act affects the dispensing and administering of these specific drug categories, pharmacy staff must be well versed in this law and how it interacts with state licensing and regulatory laws and accrediting standards. The controlled substances are classified into schedules according to the extent to which they are controlled. Schedule I drugs are subject to the tightest controls; Schedule I–IV drugs may be dispensed only upon a practitioner's lawful order.

In the outpatient environment, a prescription that meets the requirements of the law is required. In the inpatient setting, an order in the health record satisfies this requirement for a lawful order. The practitioner signing the prescription or the order in the health record must be registered with the Drug Enforcement Administration (DEA) of the Department of Justice. State law determines which professionals may be classified as practitioners for this purpose.

The Food, Drug, and Cosmetic Act, which includes the Medical Device Amendments of 1976, covers products that are distributed in federal territory or transported in interstate commerce (Pozgar 2007, 242). Most equipment and supplies used in a hospital for patient care are regulated as devices under these regulations.

Retention of the Health Record

The health record serves several purposes and must be retained to meet those purposes. These purposes include:

- Most important, the health record is a tool used in the patient's continuing medical care because it provides complete and accurate information about the patient's previous care and treatment.
- It serves as a means of communication among the patient's healthcare providers—physicians, nurses, therapists, pharmacists, and technologists.
- It is used by the patient's healthcare providers as a basis for developing the plan of care. In addition, the health record may be reviewed after care is rendered to evaluate the quality of the care.
- It is a source of information for statistical, research, and educational purposes.
- It serves as a source of billing and financial reports and information because billing records must be supported by the documentation in the health record.
- It is valuable in legal proceedings because it reflects the care given (the treatments, procedures, and medications the patient received), includes statements made by the patient about the cause of his or her illness or injury, and shows any errors in judgment or treatment made by healthcare facilities or professionals.

These varied purposes influence how long health records must be kept, or their retention period. Federal and state laws and regulations often determine retention periods. In the absence of such laws, professional organizations offer guidance (Davis et al. 2004) (McWay 2003). Further, the advent of technology, in particular the move toward an electronic health record, will influence retention periods (McWay 2003). For those periods determined by state law, the state defines what the minimum retention period will be. Some states are more specific than others. For example, some states base the retention period, at least partially, on the statute of limitations for bringing a legal action. Some state and federal statutes and regulations set specific retention requirements for particular parts of the health record (for example, x-rays or mammography studies) or for particular patient types (for example, minors, mentally ill, deceased) (Davis, et al. 2004).

The HIM professional must be aware of the retention statutes and retention periods in his or her state of employment. In some cases, the organization may define a retention period that is longer than the period required by the state. The organization should base its retention policy on hospital and medical needs and any applicable statutes and regulations.

Retention also includes the safeguarding of confidential information maintained in health records. All hospital staff members with the right to access a patient's health record have an obligation to protect the confidentiality of patient information.

Check Your Understanding 10.2

Instructions: Answer the following questions on a separate piece of paper.

1. What are the two sections of a health record? What type of information is contained in each section?
2. What is the primary difference between licensure and accreditation of healthcare organizations?
3. What national patient information confidentiality standards were promulgated in December 2000?
4. On what basis can a plaintiff claim unauthorized disclosure of health information against a hospital?
5. What was the holding regarding privacy issued by the court in *Griswold vs Connecticut?*
6. What information can the HIM professional use to determine how long to retain health records?
7. What are the three sets of standards included in the HIPAA Administrative Simplification provisions that are addressed in the text?
8. In addition to HIPAA, what other pieces of legislation are discussed that address privacy?

Ownership and Control of the Health Record

Patients often believe they own their health record. The HIM professional must be able to advise the patient regarding the actual ownership and control of the physical health record and the patient's rights to the information contained in it.

Ownership of the Physical Record

The physical health record is considered the property of the healthcare provider, the physician, or the hospital that maintains it because it is the healthcare provider's business record. Yet, the patient and others have an interest in the information contained within the health record. The patient and others, as authorized under state and federal laws, rules, and regulations, have the right to access the information as discussed below and to control the use and disclosure of that information.

Redisclosure of health information is of significant concern to the healthcare industry. As such, the HIM professional must be alerted to state and federal statutes addressing this issue (Rhodes and Hughes 2003). A consent obtained by a hospital pursuant to the Privacy Rule in 45 CFR §164.506(a)(5) does not permit another hospital, healthcare provider, or clearinghouse to use or disclose information. However, the authorization content required in the Privacy Rule in 45 CFR §164.508(c)(1) must include a statement that the information disclosed pursuant to the authorization may be disclosed by the recipient and thus is no longer protected (45 CFR §164.508(c)(2)(iii).

Use and Disclosure of Patient Information

The HIPAA Privacy Rule addresses how and for what purposes **protected health information** (PHI) can be used. PHI is individually identifiable health information that covered entities or their business associates transmit or maintain in any form or format. The Privacy Rule covers information in oral, electronic, and paper formats (45 CFR §§164.500; 501 and 514). The covered entities include:

- Health plans that pay for medical care
- Healthcare clearinghouses that receive health information in a nonstandard format and convert the information into a standard format; or healthcare clearinghouses that receive health information in a standard format and convert the information into a nonstandard format
- Healthcare providers that electronically transmit any health information (45 CFR §§160.102–103)

The Privacy Rule is the first attempt at a national set of privacy protections. Although the HIPAA rules provide for preempting state law, it is not a true national standard for patient information privacy. In other words, it is not a ceiling. It is considered a floor because it permits exceptions to the state law **preemption** provisions (45 CFR §§160.201–205).

Prior to HIPAA, many states recognized patients' rights to access their own health records. Many states also recognized that various third parties have a legitimate need to access the confidential health information contained in a health record. These third parties include insurance companies for payment purposes, insurance companies when coverage has been applied for, government agencies to determine eligibility for healthcare programs, and so on. Furthermore, prior to HIPAA, many states also permitted patients to control access by all third parties except those to which the hospital is required to report information of a medical nature or as otherwise required by law.

The standard HIPAA rule is that it preempts state law if it is contrary to that state law except if one or more of the following conditions is met (45 CFR §§160.201–205):

- The secretary of HHS determines that the provision of state law is necessary to prevent fraud and abuse related to providing or paying for healthcare; to ensure appropriate state regulation of insurance and health plans; for state reporting on healthcare delivery or costs; or for public health, safety, or welfare if the intrusion into privacy is warranted when balanced against this need.
- The secretary of HHS determines that the provision of state law is for the purpose of regulating the manufacture, registration, distribution, dispensing, or other control of controlled substances.
- The provision of state law relates to the privacy of individually identifiable health information and is more stringent than a provision in the HIPAA Privacy Rule.
- The provision of state law provides for reporting disease or injury, child abuse, birth, or death, or for the conduct of public health surveillance, investigation, or intervention.
- The provision of state law requires a health plan to report, or to provide access to, information for management audits, financial audits, program monitoring and evaluation, or licensure or certification of facilities or individuals.

For purposes of the HIPAA preemption analysis, a state law is more stringent when, in general terms, it affords a patient more access to his or her medical information or more control over the disclosure of his or her medical information to third parties (45 CFR §160.203(b)). As an example, a state statute that requires a patient to consent to any disclosure of his or her medical information to an insurance company for purposes of payment would take precedence over the HIPAA rules, but a statute that prohibited a patient from receiving a copy of his or her health record (other than psychotherapy notes) would not.

Even though HIPAA is the first attempt at national privacy legislation, the HIM professional also must be aware of state laws affecting the use and disclosure of PHI. The Privacy Rule is discussed below in terms of patient rights, the types of disclosures that require the patient be given an opportunity to agree or object, uses and disclosures that require patient authorization, and uses and disclosures that do not require patient authorization.

Patient Rights

HIPAA provides patients with certain rights related to protecting their privacy and their PHI. It requires that every patient be provided a Notice of Privacy Practices (Notice) setting forth the following (45 CFR §164.520):

- How covered entities may use and disclose PHI
- The patient's rights regarding the covered entities' uses and disclosures
- The covered entities' obligations for protecting the patient's PHI

The Privacy Rule is very specific about the required contents of the Notice. The Notice must be provided upon request. Covered entities having a direct patient relationship with the patient must provide the patient a copy of the Notice at the time of the first service delivery, including service delivered electronically. In emergency situations, covered entities providing care must provide the Notice as soon as practicable after the emergency treatment situation is resolved. The **covered entity** (CE) is to make a good faith effort to obtain the patient's written acknowledgment of receipt of the Notice. This requirement also is delayed until practicable in emergency treatment situations. If receipt is not obtained for any reason, including patient refusal to provide the acknowledgment, the CE is required to document its good faith efforts and the reason why the acknowledgment was not obtained.

With reference to the previous discussion of more stringent state privacy laws, the Notice must be tailored specifically to disclose the effect of these more stringent standards. A generic disclosure that "state laws may affect your rights" is not sufficient.

A second right that the Privacy Rule provides patients is the right to access their own patient information (45 CFR §164.524). Although, as stated earlier, some states had given patients this right, under HIPAA all patients now have it. The information that patients have the right to access is termed the **designated record set**. The types of information that HIPAA does not provide access to are:

- Oral information
- Psychotherapy notes
- Information compiled in anticipation of, or for use in, a civil, criminal, or administrative action or proceeding
- PHI the CE maintains that is subject to or exempted from the Clinical Laboratory Improvements Amendment (CLIA) of 1988

This right of access applies to all three categories of CEs that actually create or receive PHI other than as a business associate of another CE.

The patient's request can be denied without giving the patient an opportunity to request review of the denial. In addition to the PHI types noted earlier to which the patient is not given access, access can be denied in the following circumstances:

- When the CE is a correctional institution or a CE acting under the direction of the correctional institution and such access would jeopardize the health, safety, security, custody, or rehabilitation of the individual or others
- When PHI was created or obtained during research that includes treatment (access is suspended while the research is in progress as long as the patient agreed to the access denial when consenting to participate in the research and the patient had been advised that the right would be reinstated upon completion of the research)
- When the PHI is contained in records subject to the Privacy Act of 1974 and is also not available for access under the Privacy Act

The Privacy Rule gives patients a third right, which is to request that the CE amend the designated record set (45 CFR §164.526). It provides that this request also can be granted or denied. Grounds for denying an amendment request include the following:

- The PHI was not created by the CE, unless the patient indicates that the originator is no longer available.
- The PHI is not part of the designated record set.
- The PHI would not be available for the patient to inspect.
- The PHI is accurate and complete.

One of the most striking features of this legislation is found in 45 CFR§164.528 wherein it gives a patient the right to obtain an *accounting of disclosures* of PHI made by a CE in the six years or less prior to the request date (45 CFR §164.528). An accounting does not need to include such disclosures as the following:

- To carry out treatment, payment, and healthcare operations
- To the patient who is the subject of the PHI
- Those that are incidental to treatment, payment, or healthcare operations
- Those pursuant to patient authorization
- For a facility directory or to family or caregivers
- For national security or intelligence purposes
- To correctional institutions or law enforcement under specific circumstances
- PHI included in a limited data set
- Those made prior to the compliance date for the CE

If disclosures have been made to an oversight agency or law enforcement official and the agency or official notifies the CE that including these disclosures in an accounting would likely impede the agency's activities, the CE must temporarily suspend the patient's right to receive the requested accounting. For each disclosure included in an accounting, the accounting report must include the disclosure date, the recipient's name and address, and a brief description of the PHI disclosed as well as the purpose of the disclosure. The Privacy Rule provides a specific procedure for multiple disclosures to the same person or entity for a single purpose or for research purposes.

Another right is that of requesting the CE to restrict the use of PHI to carry out treatment, payment, or healthcare operations; to those involved in the patient care; and for notification purposes (45 CFR §164.522(a)). Again, the CE is not required to agree to the requested restriction. If the CE agrees to the requested restriction, it must document the restriction and must maintain that documentation for six years. A patient also may request health plans and healthcare clearinghouses, which create or receive PHI other than as a business associate, to restrict uses and disclosures.

Moreover, patients are given the right to request that CEs communicate with them in a confidential manner or method (45 CFR §164.522(b)). Confidential communications may be either by an alternative means or at alternative locations. For example, a patient may request that any telephone contact be made only at work or that all written communication be sent to a post office box rather than to his or her home address. A CE that is a healthcare provider:

- Must accommodate reasonable requests
- May not require the patient to provide an explanation of the basis for the request
- May require the patient to place the request in writing

A CE that is a health plan also must accommodate reasonable requests. However, the health plan is permitted to require the patient to provide a statement that the disclosure of all or part of the information to which the request pertains could endanger the patient.

Check Your Understanding 10.3

Instructions: Answer the following questions on a separate piece of paper.

1. Who owns the physical health record?
2. Who owns the information contained in the health record, whether paper or computer-based?
3. What is the primary focus of the HIPAA Privacy Rule?
4. Who are the covered entities covered by the HIPAA Privacy Rule?
5. Does HIPAA preempt all state laws addressing privacy? Discuss your answer.
6. What information must be described in the Notice of Privacy Practices?
7. When are healthcare providers who have a direct relationship with the patient required to provide the patient with a copy of the Notice of Privacy Practices?
8. What formats of information are protected under HIPAA?
9. To what types of information is the patient not provided access?
10. What is the most striking feature of the Privacy Rule?
11. List five types of disclosures that do not need to be included in an accounting.
12. Can the patient's request to access his or her own health information be denied? Explain your answer.
13. Under the Privacy Rule, who may sign an authorization for the disclosure of information?
14. Discuss the circumstances listed in the Privacy Rule under which a facility may deny a patient's request for access to his or her own health information without providing the patient the opportunity to have the denial reviewed.
15. Explain the access to health information available to the news media.
16. Under what circumstances does the Privacy Rule permit disclosure of health information to a patient's employer?
17. What, if any, circumstances might make a healthcare provider liable for breach of confidentiality when reporting public health information?

Types of Disclosures Requiring Opportunity to Agree or Object

The Privacy Rule provides patients an opportunity to agree or object to specific types of disclosures (45 CFR §164.510). These do not require a written authorization; verbal authorization is acceptable. However, communication with the patient regarding these types of disclosures and the patient's decision should be documented in the health record or other appropriate manner of documentation.

Absent the patient's objection, a covered healthcare provider may use specific PHI to maintain a directory of patients in its facility. This information includes the patient's:

- Name
- Location in the provider's facility, including the emergency room
- Condition in very general terms that do not include specific medial information about the patient
- Religious affiliation

The general terms that can be used to indicate the condition include undetermined, good, fair, serious, critical, stable, died, and treated and released. The patient is not required to provide information regarding religious affiliation. The covered provider may disclose the name, location, and condition to anyone asking for the patient by name, including the news media. The covered provider may disclose these elements plus the religious affiliation to members of the clergy even if they do not ask for the patient by name. If the patient does not specifically express an objection to being included in the facility's directory, the PHI may be released as noted without the patient's consent or authorization.

When a patient is incapacitated or in an emergency situation and cannot object to being included in the facility's directory, the covered provider may disclose the information as noted if the disclosure is:

- Consistent with any previously expressed preference that is known to the provider
- In the patient's best interest as determined by the provider using professional judgment

If, during the patient's stay in the facility, he or she regains the capacity to make his or her own decisions, the provider must advise the patient about the facility's directory policies and provide the patient the opportunity to object to being included in it.

The covered provider also may obtain the patient's verbal agreement or objection to disclose PHI for the following purposes (45 §164.510):

- Disclosure to family, friends, or other caregivers identified by the patient relevant to their involvement with the patient's care. The requirement for patient authorization typically extends to a request by a patient's family members, including the spouse. However, healthcare providers may discuss general information about the patient's condition with family members without authorization unless the patient has instructed otherwise. If the patient is incapacitated, the physician and other caregivers may discuss health information and treatment plans with the next of kin or the patient's representative (however that is defined by a given state) to the extent necessary to make medical decisions on the incapacitated patient's behalf. The Privacy Rule permits the hospital to disclose to a family member, other relative, close personal friend, or any person identified by the patient health information directly relevant to that person's involvement in the patient's care or payment for healthcare (45 CFR §164.510(b)(1)(i)). (See further discussion under the section on use and disclosure with patient authorization.)

- The hospital may use or disclose health information to notify or assist in notifying (identifying or locating) a family member, a personal representative, or some other person responsible for the patient's care of the patient's location, general condition, or death (45 CFR §164.510(b)(1)(ii)). In such disclosures in situations of incapacity or emergency, the CE may exercise professional judgment to determine whether the disclosure is in the patient's best interest). State law defines who may serve as a personal representative.
- Disclosure to a public or private entity assisting in disaster relief efforts.

Check Your Understanding 10.4

Instructions: Answer the following questions on a separate piece of paper.

1. Does releasing information from the directory require the patient's written authorization? Explain your answer.
2. To whom can religious affiliation information be released?
3. Under what circumstances might the hospital disclose information from the directory if the patient is incapacitated or in an emergency situation?
4. Discuss whether the hospital can disclose information to family, friends, or other caregivers.

Use and Disclosure with Patient Authorization

Except as permitted or required under the HIPAA Privacy rule, a valid patient authorization is required for the use or disclosure of PHI (45 CFR §164.508(a)(1)). This requirement typically extends to a request by a patient's family members, including the spouse. The hospital must have clear policies and procedures for releasing confidential health information with patient authorization. These policies must provide for careful review of each request. They must provide for a careful review of the authorization to ensure that it meets all requirements stated in applicable state and federal statutes and regulations, depending on which requirements are more stringent. As provided in the Privacy Rule, the procedure must permit the opportunity for the patient to revoke an authorization at any time in writing, except to the extent that the hospital has relied on the authorization and taken action as a result of it (45 CFR §164.508(b)(5)(i)). It is good practice to require a patient to sign an authorization for releasing confidential health information to the patient on whom the information is maintained. Finally, all policies and procedures for releasing confidential health information with patient authorization must follow the guidelines established in the Privacy Rule discussed next unless state law supersedes HIPAA.

The Privacy Rule gives very detailed specifications for patient authorization to disclose confidential health information (45 CFR §§164.508(c)(1)–(4)). The authorization must include a specific description of the information to be used or disclosed. In addition, the name or other specific identification of the person(s) authorized to request and receive the requested information must be included. In addition, the authorization must include the expiration date or event that relates to the individual or the purpose of the use or disclosure. The patient must be given the right to revoke the authorization in writing, the exceptions to this right, and a description of how he or she may revoke it. The authorization also must advise the patient that information released pursuant to the authorization may be subject to redisclosure by the recipient and no longer protected. Finally, the patient must sign and date the authorization.

If a personal representative signs the authorization, a description of his or her authority to act for the patient must be included in the authorization form. Also, the form must be written in plain language. The patient must be advised that the hospital will not condition treatment, payment, enrollment in a health plan, or eligibility for benefits on his or her providing authorization for the requested information. The authorization must include a description of each purpose for the requested information. Furthermore, the authorization must contain a statement to the effect that the patient may inspect or copy the information and may refuse to sign it. The hospital must disclose to the patient whether disclosure of the information will result in direct or indirect remuneration to the facility from a third party. If there is remuneration, the authorization must state that such remuneration will result. Also, the patient is entitled to a copy of the signed authorization.

Authorizations for uses and disclosures of health information created for research that includes treatment of the patient must contain additional elements. For example, there must be a description of the extent to which the information will be used or disclosed to carry out treatment, payment, or healthcare operations. The authorization must further include a description of any health information that could be disclosed but will not be disclosed for facility directories or public health purposes. However, the facility may not include a limitation affecting its right to disclose information required by law.

If the facility has or intends to obtain a general consent or has provided or intends to provide the individual with a Notice of Privacy Practices, the authorization must refer to that consent or notice and state that the statements made are binding.

Pursuant to 45 CFR §164.508(b)(2), if any of the following circumstances pertain to the authorization, it is considered "defective":

- The expiration date has passed or the expiration event has occurred.

- The authorization is not completely filled out.
- The authorization has been revoked.
- Any required elements are missing.
- The authorization is combined with any other document to create a "compound authorization" except where permitted.
- The facility knows that material information included in the authorization is false.

For an unemancipated minor, the legal representative is the parent, guardian, or other person acting in *loco parentis.* For the incompetent adult, the conservator of the person (probate or psychiatric) or the attorney in-fact may serve as the legal representative. The patient's spouse or the person financially responsible for the patient may sign only for the limited purpose of enrolling the patient in a third-party payer plan. For a deceased patient, the executor, administrator, or other person with authority to act on behalf of the patient or of the patient's estate may sign an authorization for the disclosure of health information. In addition, there are many medical treatments for which a minor (whether or not emancipated) can self-refer under state and federal statutes and regulations. In most states, these treatments include outpatient mental health treatment, drug and alcohol testing and treatment, pregnancy counseling, and treatment for sexually transmitted diseases. In these circumstances, the minor, and not the minor's parent or guardian, controls the disclosure of health information.

To be valid, the written authorization must state the limitations, if any, on the types of health information to be disclosed. Further, it must state the specific uses and limitations, if any, on the use of the health information by the recipients.

The two categories of uses and disclosures that the Privacy Rule specifically refers to as requiring patient authorization are psychotherapy notes and marketing. Psychotherapy notes are those notes recorded in any medium by a mental health professional documenting or analyzing conversations from a private counseling session or a group, joint or family counseling session (45 CFR §164.508(a)(2)). These notes are maintained separately from the rest of the patient's health record. Psychotherapy notes exclude medication prescription and monitoring, counseling session start and stop times, the modalities and frequencies of treatment furnished, results of clinical tests, and any summary of the diagnosis, functional status, treatment plan, symptoms, prognosis, and progress to date (45 CFR §164.501). However, HIPAA does provide an exception to the authorization requirements for psychotherapy notes; in these circumstances no patient authorization is required:

- In treatment, payment, or healthcare operations:
  —Use by the originator of the treatment notes
  —Use or disclosure by the CE in its own training programs in which students, trainees, or practitioners in mental health learn under supervision
  —Use or disclosure by the CE to defend itself in a legal action or other proceeding brought by the patient
- As required or permitted as part of oversight of the originator of the psychotherapy notes

As defined in the Privacy Rule, marketing requires an authorization that contains the elements described earlier and an additional statement regarding direct or indirect payment by a third party. HIPAA defines marketing as a communication about a product or service that encourages recipients of the communication to purchase or use the product or service or as an arrangement between a covered entity and any other entity where the covered entity discloses PHI to the other entity, in exchange for direct or indirect remuneration, to permit the other entity to encourage recipients to purchase or use its product or service.

Even in these circumstances classified as marketing, HIPAA provides exceptions that are discussed in the next section.

Check Your Understanding 10.5

Instructions: Answer the following questions on a separate piece of paper.

1. Does the requirement for a written authorization for use and disclosure apply to obtaining information about family members, including the spouse?
2. List five elements that must be included in a HIPAA-compliant authorization for use and disclosure.
3. Discuss the elements required in an authorization for use and disclosure when health information is created for research that includes treatment.
4. Who can sign an authorization for use and disclosure when the patient is a minor?
5. For what two categories of uses and disclosures does HIPAA specifically require an authorization for uses and disclosures?

Use and Disclosure without Patient Authorization

The basic rule under HIPAA is that the healthcare facility may use or disclose PHI without an authorization for treatment, payment, or healthcare operations purposes (45 CFR §164.506(a)). Although health information can be released without patient authorization in these circumstances, such requests must be scrutinized carefully. Thus, healthcare facilities also must have clear policies and procedures for releasing confidential health information without patient authorization. For example, reporting required by statutes, whether federal or state, should be addressed. Information that can be released to the public without patient authorization should be specified. Typical mandatory disclosures that should be addressed in policies and procedures include those under court order and subpoena, whether served by a party to a suit or administrative proceeding, or by a government agency in the course of an investigation. Mandatory disclosure pursuant to orders by a board, commission, or administrative agency engaged in formal adjudication of a dispute should be included in policies and procedures. Additionally, policies should address releasing health information pursuant to an order by an arbitrator or arbitration panel carrying out arbitration under the law. Also, disclosure without patient authorization can occur pursuant to a search warrant. This type of disclosure should be detailed very carefully in policies and procedures. Disclosure of health information in response to requests in workers' compensation cases is controlled by state law and should be included in hospital policies. Finally, policies also must identify the categories of internal staff needing confidential health information to carry out their job duties. Policies also should specify the types of information needed and the reasons for permitting access. Policies and procedures should permit the opportunity for the patient to restrict how health information is used and disclosed to carry out treatment, payment, or healthcare operations (45 CFR §164.506(c)(4)(i)). All policies and procedures for releasing confidential health information without patient authorization must also follow the guidelines set in the Privacy Rule, again unless state law supersedes HIPAA.

As discussed in the patient's rights section of this chapter, patients and their representatives have access to PHI without signing an authorization form (45 CFR §164.524). In reality, many facilities may have the patient or patient's representative complete the authorization form as a means of documenting the request. Although care should be taken in releasing all health information to a patient, particular care should be taken in releasing specialized information such as information related to mental health, drug and alcohol abuse, and sexually transmitted diseases. Federal and some state statutes address some or all of these types of specialized information. The Privacy Rule in 45 CFR §164.524(a)(1) provides the patient's right of access to inspect and obtain a copy of health information, except for psychotherapy notes and information compiled in reasonable anticipation of, or for use in, a civil, criminal, or administrative action or proceeding.

Further, under the Privacy Rule, the hospital may deny access for other reasons, provided the patient is given a right to have such denials reviewed by a licensed healthcare professional designated by the hospital to act as a reviewing official and who did not participate in the original decision to deny. This reviewer must provide or deny access (45 CFR §164.524(a)(3)).

Numerous other types of disclosures of confidential health information may be made without patient authorization. These include disclosure for direct patient care purposes, for payment purposes, for healthcare operations activities, as required by law, and several others.

Disclosure for *direct patient care (treatment) purposes* is among the most common and most important disclosures without patient authorization. Those involved with patient care must have timely access to health information. In 45 CFR §164.501 and 45 CFR §§164.506(c)(1) and (2), the Privacy Rule permits the facility and healthcare providers to use or disclose confidential information for:

- Providing, coordinating, or managing healthcare and related services by one or more healthcare providers, including with a third party
- Consulting among healthcare providers relating to a patient
- Referring a patient for healthcare from one healthcare provider to another

Payment purposes is another important type of disclosure that may be made without patient authorization. The Privacy Rule permits the healthcare provider to use or disclose health information for payment purposes such as health plans obtaining premiums, determining coverage, and providing benefits. It also includes healthcare providers or health plans obtaining or providing reimbursement for services (45 CFR §164.501; 45 CFR §§164.506(c)(1) and (3)).

Healthcare operations consists of a number of activities carried out in a typical provider setting (45 CFR §164.501; 45 CFR §§164.506(c)(1), (4) and (5)). One activity that is important to a hospital is quality improvement (QI). Under HIPAA, QI is a standard healthcare operation and does not require the CE to obtain patient authorization to use confidential health information. Other healthcare operations functions include peer review; underwriting; medical review, legal services, and auditing; business planning, development, management, and administration; educational programs; and licensing and accreditation. Specifically, many organizations participate in educational activities for their medical staff members and their clinical and nonclinical staff members. Some also participate in formalized training programs for physicians, nurses, and allied health professionals. All these trainees require some level of access to confidential health information as part of their training (45 CFR 164.501). However, such access should be on a need-to-know basis. Typically, such use of confidential information does not require patient authorization.

In addition, because health records are considered hospital business records, the information in them has many administrative uses that are considered healthcare operations. Hospital professional, technical, and administrative staff should have access to these records on a need-to-know basis. Administrative uses include, but are not limited to, auditing, billing, filing, replying to inquiries, and defending litigation.

PHI may be disclosed without an authorization as required by law. The use or disclosure is limited to the requirements of the particular law under which is it is used or disclosed (45 CFR §164.512(a)(1)). In some cases, there is a common-law duty to disclose health information, for example, to warn persons of the presence of contagious disease. In many states, there also is a duty to warn an individual against whom a patient has made a credible threat to harm (*Tarasoff v. Board of Regents* 1976). In another case, a physician failed to warn his patient that she had contracted HIV through a blood transfusion. As a result, the hospital and the physician were sued three years later when the patient's sexual partner was exposed to the virus. The court held that the hospital was liable for the physician's failure to warn (Kadzielski 2004) (*Reisner v. Regents of the University of California* 1995).

These cases should not be confused. *Reisner* involved failure to warn a patient of a serious condition; *Tarasoff* involved failure to warn a third party about potential harm from his patient.

No authorization is needed to use or disclose PHI for public health activities (45 CFR §164.512(b)). Some health records contain information that is important to the public welfare. Such information must be reported to the state's public health service to ensure public safety. The Privacy Rule provides that the hospital or healthcare provider may disclose confidential health information to:

- A public health authority authorized to collect or receive information for preventing or controlling disease, injury, or disability
- A public health authority or other government authority authorized to receive reports of child abuse or neglect
- A person subject to the FDA
- A person who may have been exposed to a communicable disease or may be at risk of contracting or spreading a disease or condition (if the entity is authorized to notify such person (45 CFR §§164.512(b)(1)(i)–(iii)). Activities that are reported include:
  - Disease and injury reporting
  - Vital statistics reporting (births and deaths)
  - Public health investigation, surveillance, or intervention
  - Child abuse and neglect reporting (HIPAA specifically stated to follow state law (OCR 2000)
  - Product safety, quality, or effectiveness reporting to the FDA
  - Communicable disease reporting
  - Reporting to an employer in very limited circumstances regarding medical surveillance of the workplace or work-related illness or injury

The Privacy Rule addresses disclosure of health information in the last activity above in 45 CFR §164.512(b)(1)(v). The hospital may disclose information to an employer when one of the following conditions is met:

- The care provider is a member of the employer's workforce or provides healthcare to the patient at the employer's request.
- The care relates to a medical surveillance of the workplace or to a work-related illness or injury.
- The information that is disclosed consists of findings concerning a work-related illness or injury or a workplace-related medical surveillance.
- The employer needs the findings to comply with its obligations under federal and state laws.

The Privacy Rule also requires the hospital to provide written notice to the individual that health information relating to the workplace medical surveillance and work-related illnesses and injuries will be disclosed to the employer.

Reporting of other types of abuse, neglect, or domestic violence also is permitted under HIPAA (45 CFR §164.512(c); (OCR 2000) when required by law; when the patient agrees to the reporting; and when the CE, in its professional judgment, believes disclosure is necessary to prevent serious harm to the patient or other potential victims. Further, the CE may disclose in situations where the patient is incapacitated and law enforcement or some other public official authorized to receive such information indicates that the disclosure is not to be used against the patient and that immediate enforcement activity depends on the disclosure and would be adversely affected by waiting. Persons complying with reporting statutes are not considered to be making an unauthorized disclosure (HIPAA-f).

Health oversight agencies may receive PHI without authorization for their activities but must be authorized to oversee the healthcare system (public or private) or government programs in which health information is necessary to determine eligibility or compliance or to enforce civil rights laws for which health information is relevant. Health oversight agency activities include audits; civil, criminal, or administrative investigations or proceedings; licensure; disciplinary actions; inspections; or other activities necessary for appropriate oversight of any of the following entities (45 CFR §164.512(d)):

- Healthcare system
- Government benefit programs for which health information is relevant to beneficiary eligibility
- Entities subject to government regulatory programs for which information is necessary for determining compliance with program standards
- Entities subject to civil rights laws for which health information is necessary for determining compliance

A CE also may disclose PHI in judicial and administrative proceedings. Disclosing confidential health information in compliance with the legal process is typically provided for statutorily. Under the Privacy Rule in 45 CFR §§164.512(e)(i)–(iv), a hospital may disclose health information in the course of any judicial or administrative proceeding in response to any of the following:

- Court or administrative tribunal order if the hospital discloses only the health information expressly authorized by such order
- Subpoena, discovery request, or other lawful process not accompanied by a court or administrative tribunal order if the hospital receives satisfactory assurance that reasonable efforts have been taken to give notice of the request to the person who is the subject of the requested information or to secure a qualified protective order that meets specific requirements

A hospital can disclose health information in response to a lawful process without receiving the satisfactory assurance, discussed earlier, when it makes reasonable efforts to provide notice to the individual or to seek a qualified protective order (45 CFR §164.512(e)(v)).

Pursuant to the Privacy Rule in 45 CFR §164.512(f), the hospital may disclose health information to law enforcement officials without authorization for law enforcement purposes when one of the following conditions is met:

- Disclosure is required by law, including laws that require the reporting of certain types of wounds or other physical injuries.
- Disclosure is made in compliance with a court order, court-ordered warrant, subpoena, summons, or grand jury subpoena.
- Disclosure is made in response to an administrative request, that is, a subpoena or summons, a civil demand or an authorized investigative demand, or a similar process authorized under law.
- Purpose of the request is to identify or locate a suspect, fugitive, material witness, or missing person (information related to the individual's DNA or DNA analysis, dental records, typing, samples or body fluids, or tissue analysis may not be released).
- Disclosure is made in response to a law enforcement official's request for such information about an individual who is, or is suspected to be, a victim of a crime.
- Purpose of the disclosure is to alert law enforcement of the suspicion that a patient's death may have resulted from criminal conduct.
- Hospital believes the health information is evidence of criminal conduct that occurred on its premises.

When providing healthcare in an emergency situation, other than such emergency on the premises of the healthcare provider, the provider may disclose health information to law enforcement officials when it appears necessary to alert law enforcement to any of the following (45 CFR §164.512(f)(6)):

- Commission and nature of a crime
- Location of the crime or of the victim(s)
- Identity, description, and location of the perpetrator of the crime

Coroners, medical examiners, and funeral directors may receive PHI as necessary to carry out their duties with respect to decedents (45 CFR §164.512(g)). Such duties for a coroner or medical examiner include identifying a deceased person, determining a cause of death, or other duties as authorized by law. If it is necessary for a funeral director to have PHI prior to, and in reasonable anticipation of, the individual's death, the CE may disclose that information necessary to carry out the funeral director's function.

Organ Procurement Organizations

An *organ procurement organization* or a tissue bank processing the tissue of a decedent for transplantation into the body of another person also may be given health information. In 45 CFR §164.512(h) the Privacy Rule provides that a hospital may disclose health information to organ procurement organizations.

Research is another activity for which confidential health information is important. Hospital policy often requires that researchers' access to health information be documented as bona fide research. Such documentation may be provided through a recognized institutional review board's approval of the research. Many states and the federal government have established regulations for the protection of human subjects, including protecting confidential information [45 CFR §46.111(a)(7), protection of human subjects]. Any use of confidential health information for research purposes must comply with all such regulations, including those set forth in the Privacy Rule. Under the Privacy Rule in 45 CFR §164.512(i), researchers may use or disclose health information, as necessary, to prepare a research protocol or for research purposes. This section also provides that researchers may use or disclose health information for the purpose of research on such information for decedents. The facility that creates confidential health information for research that includes treatment of the patient must obtain an authorization for the use or disclosure of that information.

PHI may be disclosed to avert a serious threat to health and safety (45 CFR §164.512(j)). To do so, the CE must, in good faith, believe the use or disclosure is necessary to prevent or lessen a serious and imminent threat to the health and safety of a person or the public and is reasonably able to prevent or lessen the threat. Moreover, the CE may disclose PHI if it believes in good faith that the disclosure is necessary for law enforcement to identify or apprehend an individual because of a statement by a person admitting participation in a violent crime that the CE believes may have caused serious physical harm to the victim. Further, the CE may disclose PHI in cases where the individual has escaped from a correctional institution or from lawful custody.

PHI can be disclosed for specialized governmental functions (45 CFR §164.512(k)). These functions include:

- Military and veterans activities
- National security and intelligence activities
- Protective services to the president and heads of state
- Medical suitability determination (for example, security clearance purposes)
- Correctional and law enforcement custodial facilities for the health and safety of the patient, other inmates, or officers or employees at the correctional facility
- Government programs providing public benefits
- Workers' compensation programs to comply with state laws for the provision of benefits for work-related injuries or illness (45 CFR §164.512(l))

With regard to workers' compensation cases, statutes in some states permit the disclosure of health information without patient authorization, but some states require patient authorization or a subpoena from an administrative agency or court for release. It is important to be familiar with a particular state's laws before disclosing any health information in workers' compensation cases.

Without the patient's authorization, an organization may use only demographic data (name, address, and other contact information, date of birth, gender, insurance status, and so on) and dates of service to carry out fundraising activities (45 CFR §164.514(f)(1)). Demographic data do not include information about diagnoses, procedures, or the nature of the patient's illness or services. The organization may disclose this demographic data to a philanthropic foundation that raises funds for the organization (HIPAA-g). The organization also may provide such data to a business associate that conducts fundraising on behalf of the organization. Any fundraising materials sent to a patient must include instructions on how to opt out of receiving future fundraising materials.

As stated in the Use and Disclosure with Patient Authorization section, there are marketing exceptions to the requirement for an authorization. When the communication is a face-to-face encounter with a patient or when it involves a promotional gift of nominal value, no authorization is required (45 CFR §164.508(a)(3)). Furthermore, the Privacy Rule describes specific circumstances that are not considered marketing, such as (45 CFT §164.501):

- The covered entity describing its own health-related products and services
- Communications about entities participating in a healthcare provider network or health plan network, replacement of or enhancements to a health plan, and health-related products or services available only to a health plan enrollee that adds value to the benefits
- Communications about products and services related to a patient's treatment
- Communications for case management or care coordination
- Recommendations to the patient about alternative treatments, therapies, healthcare providers, or care settings

The Privacy Rule establishes the requirement for verifying the identity of the person receiving the PHI and his or her authority to have access to the requested information.

Penalties

Any person who believes that a CE is violating or has violated the HIPAA Privacy Rule may file a complaint by mail, fax, or e-mail with the Department of Health and Human Services (HHS) Office of Civil Rights (OCR) which enforces the Privacy Rules. Complaints to the OCR must:

- Be filed in writing (either on paper or electronically)
- Name the CE that is the subject of the complaint and describe the acts or omissions believed to be in violation of the applicable requirements of the Privacy Rule
- Be filed within 180 days of when the complainant knew that the act or omission complained of occurred (OCR may extend the 180-day period if "good cause" is shown.)

The OCR will investigate the complaint on behalf of the Secretary of the Department of Health and Human Services (HHS) (45 CFR §160.306(a)). The investigation may include the OCR reviewing pertinent policies, procedures, and other documents and the circumstances of the alleged violation (45 CFR §160.306(c)). If the investigation reveals the CE did not violate the HIPAA Privacy Rule, the Secretary will notify the CE. However, should the investigation reveal the CE did not comply with the Privacy Rule, the Secretary will first attempt to enter into an informal resolution (45 CFR §160.312(a)(1)):

- Voluntary compliance
- Corrective action
- Resolution agreement

Most Privacy Rule investigations have been concluded through these types of resolutions. Once the resolution is accepted, the OCR notifies the complainant and the CE in writing of the resolution result (OCR 2006).

If the CE and the Secretary are unable to resolve the issue informally, the Secretary will give the CE an opportunity to provide written evidence of mitigating factors or affirmative defenses (45 CFR §160.312(a)(3)(i)). In the event the CE does not resolve the issue to the OCR's satisfaction, the OCR may impose civil money penalties (CMPs) on the CE. Should CMPs be imposed, the CE may request a hearing before an HHS administrative law judge who decides if the penalties are supported by the evidence. The monetary penalties collected are deposited in the U.S. Treasury. The complainant does not receive any portion of CMPs collected from covered entity (OCR 2006).

The penalties for violating the HIPAA provisions are found at Title 42 of the United States Code. These provisions provide both civil fines and criminal fines and punishments. The general CMP for anyone violating the HIPAA rules is not more than $100 for each violation, with civil fines capped at $25,000 per calendar year for each provision violated (42 USC §1320d-5). Civil penalties may not be imposed when:

- The entity being held subject to the penalty can satisfy the secretary of HHS that the person violating the rule(s) did not know, and would not have known, that he or she violated them.
- The violation was not because of willful neglect and can be corrected within a 30-day period.
- The act is a violation of the criminal provisions (42 USC §1320d-6(a)) discussed here. This means both civil and criminal penalties may not be applied to a wrongdoer for the same violation.

Should the violation be classified as a criminal violation, penalties are assessed pursuant to 42 USC §1320d–6(a). The key to criminal violation is the concept of "knowingly" committing an act. This means purposefully committing an act or acting in willful disregard of the existence of the statutory scheme (Malone 2004). Any of the following actions are classified as criminal:

- Knowingly using or causing to be used a unique health identifier in violation of the rules

- Knowingly obtaining patient PHI in violation of the rules
- Knowingly disclosing patient PHI to another person in violation of the rules

Maximum penalties for criminal violations are set forth in 42 USC §1320d–6(b). The actual penalty imposed against someone convicted of a criminal violation is determined pursuant to the Federal Sentencing Guidelines (Malone 2004). The Sentencing Guidelines were established by the United States Sentencing Commission to establish "uniform punishment that is applied to similarly situated defendants upon conviction" (Malone 2004). The guidelines provide for the judge to consider the offense level and the defendant's criminal history in setting the sentence. They specify the following penalties:

- A fine of not more than $50,000, imprisonment for not more than one year, or both.
- If the violation is committed under false pretenses, the fine is not more than $100,000, imprisonment for not more than five years, or both.
- If the violation is committed with the intent to sell, transfer, or use PHI for commercial advantage, personal gain, or malicious harm, the fine is not more than $250,000, imprisonment for not more than ten years, or both.

There may be circumstances under which the OCR collaborates in an investigation or refers a matter for investigation to another agency. For example, the OCR will investigate in conjunction with the Centers for Medicare and Medicaid Services (CMS) any allegations in a complaint that could also be a violation of the HIPAA Security Rule (45 CFR Parts 160 and 164, Subparts A and C). CMS is the HHS agency responsible for enforcing the Security Rule. The OCR may actually refer a complaint to the Department of Justice (DOJ) for criminal investigation. This might result if the complaint contains information about a CE's action that could be a violation of the criminal provision of HIPAA (42 USC 1320d-6). Such actions involve the knowing disclosure or obtaining of protected health information in violation of the Rule (OCR 2006).

Check Your Understanding 10.6

Instructions: Answer the following questions on a separate piece of paper.

1. What three categories of uses and disclosures does HIPAA specifically *not* require an authorization for use and disclosure?
2. Under HIPAA, must a patient sign an authorization for use and disclosure before being permitted access to his or her own record? Explain your answer.
3. May PHI be used and disclosed without patient authorization for a hospital case manager to coordinate care with another healthcare provider such as a long-term care facility? Explain your answer.
4. List at least five uses and disclosures of PHI for which HIPAA does not require an authorization.
5. What common types of information must be reported for public health purposes?
6. What penalties can be enforced against a person or entity that willfully and knowingly violates the HIPAA Privacy Rule?

Use of Health Records in Litigation

This section discusses how the health record is used in litigation. The health record serves as documentation of care provided when the patient alleges wrongdoing against the hospital and healthcare providers in a lawsuit or seeks damages from another party who caused an injury or illness.

Admissibility of the Health Record

The health record may be valuable evidence in a legal proceeding. To be admissible, the court must be confident that the record

- Is complete, accurate, and timely (recorded at the time the event occurred)
- Was documented in the normal course of business
- Was made by healthcare providers who have knowledge of the "acts, events, conditions, opinions, or diagnoses appearing in it." (Adair et al. 2005, 64A)

The court must accept that the information was recorded as the result of treatment, not in anticipation of a legal proceeding. Furthermore, to be admissible, the health record must be pertinent and proper. The health record is considered hearsay because the healthcare providers made the entries in the record and not in court under oath (McWay 2003, 135–136). However, the judge or jury uses the exception to the hearsay rule of evidence codified in the Federal Rules of Evidence and the Uniform Rules of Evidence to determine what is pertinent and proper (McWay 2003, 135; AHIMA e-HIM Work Group on the Legal Health Record. 2005b)).

To have an electronic health record admissible, the court must be confident that the system from which the record was produced is accurate and trustworthy. Characteristics used to support a system's accuracy and trustworthiness are (Adair et al. 2005, 64A):

- The type of computer used and that computer's acceptance as standard and efficient equipment
- The record's method of operation
- The method and circumstances of preparation of the record

Medical witnesses may refer to the health record to refresh their recollection. The custodian of records, typically the health information manager, may be called as a witness to identify the record as the one subpoenaed. He or she also may be called to testify as to policies and procedures relevant to the following:

- Creation of the record including the system or process used
- Maintenance of the record to prevent it from being altered
- Maintenance of the record to prevent it from being accessed without proper authorization

The actual admissibility as evidence depends on the facts and circumstances of the case and the applicable state and federal rules of evidence.

The EHR and Court: e-Discovery

Health information management (HIM) professionals are beginning to experience a completely different approach to responding to requests for health records in litigation whether for depositions or as evidence in court. This new approach applies when the facility has a total electronic record or a hybrid record. What HIM professionals are experiencing is known as **e-discovery**, which is a pretrial process through which parties obtain and review electronically stored data. The e-discovery changes to the Federal Rules of Civil Procedure (FRCP) became effective December 1, 2006 (AHIMA e-HIM Work Group on e-Discovery 2006). Although the FRCP applies only to cases in federal district courts, states are beginning to implement similar e-discovery rules that apply to state civil and criminal cases. For example California enacted a Civil Discovery Act effective in January 2007.

The AHIMA Practice Brief, *The New Electronic Discovery Civil Rule*, is an excellent resource for how e-discovery, whether at the state or federal level, impacts the HIM professional (AHIMA e-HIM Work Group on e-Discovery 2006). Specifically, the AHIMA e-HIM Work Group identifies the key issues to be "the impact on disclosure processes, retention and destruction, spoliation, and business continuity planning." (AHIMA 2006, 68E).

In the past, HIM professionals could be involved in the pretrial discovery phase through a subpoena for records or for testifying at a deposition. With the advent of e-discovery, the HIM professional's involvement begins much earlier in the litigation stages with pretrial conferences. During pretrial conferences, attorneys for the parties meet to reach agreement on matters related to discovery, such as document discovery. Thus HIM and information technology (IT) professionals must work with the organization's attorney prior to a pretrial conference to identify relevant information and its availability (AHIMA 2006, 68B). Although the entity producing the electronically stored information (ESI) can object, it must produce the information in "the form in which it is ordinarily maintained or a reasonably usable form." (DeLoss 2008).

The healthcare organization must define what constitutes the legal health record for disclosure purposes (McClendon 2007). This is particularly important in the EHR environment. Through technology, vast volumes of information can be created and stored. Therefore, much more extensive information is subject to discovery than in the paper record environment. Any data stored electronically can serve as evidence, for example, text, information on PDAs, calendar files, Web sites, and the like (AHIMA 2008). The concept of "any and all records" has certainly taken on a whole new connotation with e-discovery.

HIM professionals must now be familiar with documents stored in what is termed "native file format," including **metadata** (AHIMA e-HIM Work Group on e-Discovery 2006, 68D) (DeLoss 2008). Metadata is data about the data—about the "content, context, location and other characteristics of data stored in a system (AHIMA e-HIM Work Group on e-Discovery 2006, 68E) (Servais 2008, 15). It includes information not previously available with paper documents such as the time stamp for accessing, creating entries in or changing electronic records. Metadata can be obtained as part of the discovery process in civil litigation (Servais 2008, 15).

The e-discovery rule will certainly impact retention and destruction of health information. Therefore, HIM professionals must work more closely with IT and other departments to establish and implement information management plans. These plans must address information contained in e-mail, voicemail, instant messages, document drafts, and shadow records (AHIMA e-HIM Work Group on e-Discovery 2006, 68E). Information management plans must also address disaster recovery and business continuity (AHIMA e-HIM Work Group on e-Discovery 2006).

The concepts of a legal hold and **spoliation** continue under the e-discovery rule. A legal hold is typically issued by a court when there is concern that information relevant to a legal proceeding or audit could be destroyed. This hold would suspend any normal disposition activities, including destruction. The following events can prompt the HIM professional to place a health record under a legal hold (DeLoss 2008):

- Complaints
- Civil investigative demands
- Subpoenas
- Demand letters
- Pre-litigation discussions with opposing counsel
- Preservation letter
- Written notice from opposing counsel
- Government investigation or inquiry

Spoliation is the "intentional destruction, mutilation, alteration, or concealment of evidence" (AHIMA e-HIM Work Group on e-Discovery 2006, 68E). The organization would have the burden of disputing spoliation allegations by showing that "information lost was a result of a good faith operation of the electronic system" (AHIMA e-HIM Work Group on e-Discovery 2006, 68E).

What does the HIM professional do to prepare for the eventuality of having to respond to an e-discovery request or subpoena? The AHIMA e-HIM Work Group on e-Discovery states that not only must HIM professionals be familiar with what the organization defines as its records (such as legal health record, business record, designated record set), but also with the location and types of information stored within various source systems and databases (AHIMA e-HIM Work Group on e-Discovery 2006, 68E) (Dimick 2007). Dimick (2007) recommends that HIM professionals start by reviewing the organization's information management plan. The HIM professional knows which departments feed clinical information into the legal health record whether in the paper or electronic format; they must now also become familiar with what systems are used by these different departments (Dimick 2007). According to DeLoss (2008), the locations in which information can be electronically stored both at home and at work include:

- Laptops and desktops
- Servers and shared drives
- Handheld devices such as PDAs and cell phones
- Removable storage devices such as flash drives, thumbnails, CDs
- Web sites
- Databases

DeLoss (2008) also addressed the location of ESI from the perspective of ancillary services, clinical services, remote access, personal equipment, and e-mail. With regard to ancillary services DeLoss (2008) noted the HIM professional must know or determine whether the information is integrated into the EHR or maintained separately. He also stated one should ask if external providers are networked and if data resides on equipment such as an MRI, digital x-ray, and the like (DeLoss 2008). When the HIM professional thinks of the clinical environment, DeLoss (2008) mentions equipment used to access the organization's EHR through remote access. He also mentions equipment such as IV medication pumps, dictation systems, robotics, emergency or "crash" situations, or personal health records (PHRs).

Complying with an e-discovery request or subpoena most likely involves many systems. This is no easy task because as Dimick (2007) points out, the standards for what will be discoverable and what electronic information needs to be part of the health record are still being developed. Dimick (2007) further states that HIM professionals should store only what's vital—if it's stored, it is likely subject to e-discovery. Having good policies, procedures, standards, information management plans, and such that are enforced is the place to start.

The AHIMA e-Discovery Task Force (2008) stated the organization must also develop a litigation response plan and it identified five key steps healthcare organizations should take to develop and implement such a plan:

- Evaluate applicable rules—federal, state, and local level e-discovery rules
- Form a litigation response team—an interdisciplinary group to implement and conduct ongoing review of the e-discovery process
- Analyze issues, risks, and challenges that may arise from e-discovery—this analysis is the basis for policy and procedure development
- Develop or revise organizational policies and procedures to incorporate e-discovery
- Develop and implement an ongoing monitoring and evaluation process to ensure continued compliance with policies and procedures

So just what is the role of the HIM professional in e-discovery? "While discoverable information will evolve with the creation of complex electronic record systems, the most advanced system means nothing to the e-discovery process if there aren't people who know how to store, manage, and access the information. That is where HIM professionals come in." (Dimick 2007, 3).

Privileges

Professional relationships between the patient and specific groups of caregivers further affect use of the record and its contents as evidence. These relationships are referred to as **privileges**. The information exchanged between patient and caregiver pursuant to a privilege is a confidential communication that the patient anticipates will be held confidential. One such widely recognized privilege is the physician–patient privilege. This privilege provides that the physician is not permitted to testify as a witness about certain information gained as a result of this relationship without the patient's consent.

The information included in the physician–patient privilege is insulated from the discovery process when there is no patient authorization, waiver, or an overriding law or public policy (Davis et al. 2004). The physician–patient relationship usually does not apply to court-ordered examinations or other examinations completed on behalf of other third parties, such as insurance companies (Miller 1986). Depending on the state, similar privileges exist between psychotherapist and patient, sexual assault victim and counselor, and domestic violence victim and counselor.

In states where these professional relationships are recognized, they apply when the caregiver is being compelled to testify as a witness concerning information obtained as a result of the relationship. However, these privileges do not preclude the caregiver from making reports as required by law.

Patient's Waiver of Privilege

The patient may release the caregiver from the privileges discussed through words or actions. This release is known as a waiver of the privilege. For example, a patient who placed his or her treatment at issue in a trial could not continue to claim a privilege to protect the information. The caregiver then could be compelled to testify regarding the information previously considered confidential.

Government's Right of Access to Health Records

The government, whether federal or state, has the right to access health information with or without patient authorization in certain circumstances. Healthcare providers must sign an agreement with HHS to receive payments for care provided to patients covered under the Medicare program (Miller 1986). Medicaid is a joint federal and state program to provide medical care to individuals unable to pay for care. Healthcare providers apply to the responsible state agency for a contract with the state to provide services to Medicaid recipients in return for payment for services provided (Miller 1986). Both HHS and the state Medicaid agency may request information from the health record to support the healthcare provider's bill submitted for payment. By signing up with Medicare or Medicaid, the patient gives permission for the healthcare provider to disclose confidential health information to the appropriate agency without further authorization.

The government also may require access to health information for other investigative purposes such as pursuant to the federal fraud and abuse statutes that require information-sharing arrangements to be undertaken in an arm's-length transaction and pursuant to a written agreement (Kadzielski 2004). An arm's-length transaction is a transaction in which "parties are dealing from equal bargaining positions, neither party is subject to the other's control or dominant influence, and the transaction is treated with fairness, integrity, and legality" (Trautmann 2003).

Another important federal statute for which the government may need access to health information as part of an investigation is the Emergency Medical Treatment and Active Labor Act. This act involves the transfer of uninsured individuals from one hospital emergency department to another for financial reasons (Kadzielski and Kogan 1997).

Individuals are personally liable for their own acts of unauthorized disclosure of confidential health information. The individual's liability is based on fault because he or she did something wrong or failed to do something he or she should have done. Employers also may be held liable for any job-related acts of their employees or agents. It must be distinguished that the hospital is not liable for a breach of confidentiality by the members of its medical staff because they are not employees or agents of the hospital. However, the hospital may be liable for the consequences of any unauthorized disclosure, whether by employees, agents, or medical staff members, because of the breach of its duty to maintain information confidential. The injured person benefits from these concepts of fault because he or she can sue the employer, the employee, or both.

Unauthorized disclosure by various healthcare professionals also may be addressed in professional licensing and certifying laws or regulations. These provisions subject the professional to potential discipline by the licensing or certifying agency for breach of confidentiality because it is considered unprofessional conduct.

Check Your Understanding 10.7

Instructions: Answer the following questions on a separate piece of paper.

1. What are the three methods by which a physician–patient privilege may be created?
2. What actions or requirements can release the care provider from the applicable privilege?
3. Give two examples of government access to health information with or without patient authorization.
4. What is metadata and why is it important in responding to a subpoena?
5. Discuss why the HIM professional will experience a significant change in responding to legal requests under e-discovery statutes (state or federal)?
6. If the custodian of records is called to testify pursuant to a subpoena, what can she or he testify to?

Case Law since HIPAA

There are a number of areas of uncertainty in the HIPAA regulations. Interpretation of these areas requires one to make a judgment call, a good faith effort to follow the regulations, and then take a wait-and-see approach to see if these areas are tested in the courts. Because at the time of this writing the final regulations have been effective for only a few years, case law since implementation of the Privacy Rule is still in flux.

Sample Cases

In *Law v. Zuckerman* (2004), a federal court in Maryland ruled that HIPAA preempted a state law that would have required a plaintiff's current doctor to discuss the patient's condition with the defendants' lawyer without notice to, or consent of, the patient. The court held that Maryland's law was not more stringent than the HIPAA regulations. In *In re PPA Litigation* (2003), a New Jersey state court ruled that HIPAA did not preempt the state-authorized practice of permitting defendants in personal injury cases to conduct information interviews with the plaintiff's treating physician where patient authorization requirements are not met. In this case, HIPAA-compliant authorization forms were not required by the court.

The first HIPAA privacy criminal prosecution occurred in *U.S. v. Gibson* (2004). In this case, an employee of the Seattle Cancer Care Alliance was charged with illegal disclosure of a patient's PHI in order to fraudulently obtain and make purchases with credit cards in the patient's name. Pursuant to the penalties discussed earlier, this disclosure was for personal gain and potentially subjected the defendant to a fine of up to $250,000 and up to 10 years in prison. The defendant pleaded guilty and entered into a plea bargain with the federal government that recommends 10 to 16 months in prison and requires full restitution to the patient and the credit card companies. In November 2004, under the HIPAA Privacy Rule, U.S. District Judge Ricardo Martinez sentenced the defendant to 16 months in prison, three years of supervised release, and more than $9,000 in restitution.

Of interest in this case is that the defendant is not a covered entity under HIPAA, but rather an employee of a CE that is subject to HIPAA. This case demonstrates that at least one U.S. attorney interprets the HIPAA criminal provisions as applying personally to members of the CE's workforce. There is still considerable debate as to whether the HIPAA criminal provisions apply to persons and organizations that are not CEs.

In the past few years more legal activity has occurred with HIPAA as the basis. While working as a nurse for the Northeast Arkansas Clinic, the defendant, Smith, accessed a patient's health information and gave the information to her husband. Her husband called the patient and threatened to use the information in an impending legal action. In December 2007, both Smith and her husband were indicted for conspiracy to wrongfully disclose individually identifiable information for personal gain and witness tampering (Park 2008). Smith pleaded guilty to the charges of wrongfully disclosing a patient's health information for personal gain.

The most significant recent legal action was the Federal Grand Jury indictment of a former University of California Los Angeles Medical Center employee on April 9, 2008 (*U.S. v. Jackson* 2008). Jackson was an Administrative Specialist with access to individually identifiable health information (protected health information or PHI). In 2006 and into 2007, Jackson illegally obtained PHI on celebrity patients and provided it to a national media outlet. She received at least $4,600 for the information. As discussed earlier, if found guilty in this federal criminal action, Jackson could be imprisoned for up to 10 years or fined not more than $250,000, or both.

Of even further significance is the fact that on July 16, 2008, HHS entered into its first corrective action plan with a covered entity for potential HIPAA privacy and security regulation violations (Lazzarotti 2008). This action followed the OCR and CMS investigation of more than 30 complaints from persons that the Seattle-based healthcare provider, Providence Health and Services, had notified of data breaches (Lazzarotti 2008). Providence Health and Services agreed to pay $100,000 and entered into a three-year corrective action plan (Lazzarotti 2008). Lazzarotti (2008) stated the notifications resulted when backup tapes, optical disks, and laptops that contained unencrypted electronic protected health information of more than 386,000 patients were lost or stolen after being taken from the covered entity's premises and left unattended. Through the Resolution Agreement, Providence Health and Services agreed to ensure it will safeguard patient identifiable electronically stored protected health information (Lazzarotti 2008). Further, because Providence Health and Services entered into the Resolution Agreement, HHS did not impose the potentially significant civil monetary penalties under HIPAA (Lazzarotti 2008).

The Release of Information Process and Function

Managing the release (use and disclosure) of information (ROI) process and function requires an attention to detail and constant vigilance. The ROI manager must constantly stay current with changes in local, state, and federal laws and regulations affecting the use and disclosure of PHI. Further, the ROI manager must be cognizant of the Joint Commission and other regulatory agency requirements regarding protecting a patient's confidentiality and privacy by protecting health information. The manager must constantly ensure that policies and procedures reflect all current local, state, and federal statutes and regulations, as well as regulatory agency requirements.

The ROI manager must provide education that reinforces the organization's policies and the importance of following them. Additionally, ROI staff must be provided with, and express an understanding of, the expectations for them to follow ROI policies and procedures.

The ROI manager must participate in the QI process. This can be used as one means of evaluating staff compliance with policies and procedures. Furthermore, the manager must gather statistics regarding performance (request turnaround time, number of requests processed per employee per month, number of subpoenas processed per employee per month, and so on). These statistics, among others, can be used as the basis for requesting additional staff or as part of the annual evaluation process. Completing requests according to departmental standards, which are based on regulations such as HIPAA or state law, demonstrates the individual employee's competence, or lack thereof, in his or her job.

In some organizations, the ROI functions are decentralized; that is, carried out in other areas in addition to the HIM department. Although having use and disclosure requests processed where the applicable record is maintained may seem the most efficient approach, such an organizational structure presents many management challenges. The ROI manager must ensure that all entities within the organization carrying out the ROI function are following standardized policies and procedures. This requires strong organizational and supervision skills.

The manager is responsible for participating with the organization's privacy officer to investigate any alleged violations of the HIPAA rules by ROI staff. The investigation should be conducted pursuant to the organization's investigation policy and may include involving the human resources (HR) department to impose disciplinary action pursuant to HR policies.

Finally, it is the manager's responsibility to establish an environment in which employees can be successful. Therefore, the ROI manager must develop and implement systems that support the employees' needs.

Check Your Understanding 10.8

Instructions: Answer the following questions on a separate piece of paper.

1. What uses can the ROI manager make of data collected?
2. In addition to the statistics mentioned above, list three other categories of statistics that would be useful to the ROI manager in managing this function.
3. What education should the ROI manager provide the ROI staff?
4. Does the ROI manager participate in investigating alleged HIPAA violations by ROI staff? Discuss your answer.

Medical Staff Appointments, Privileges, and Peer Review

Patients expect the physicians who treat them in hospitals to have been evaluated for competency in their selected area of medical practice. Patients expect to receive treatment at or above the acceptable standard of care. Hospitals use the medical staff appointment process to accomplish this evaluation.

Duty to Use Reasonable Care in Granting Staff Appointments

The hospital governing board typically is composed of members from the community and sometimes includes medical staff members. This body has final responsibility for the operation of the hospital. Because of its responsibility for managing the hospital and upholding a satisfactory standard of care, it has the legal duty to select medical staff members. The governing board must use reasonable care in approving a physician's application to be a staff member and grant clinical privileges before the physician can treat patients in the hospital. Typically, after the physician is granted initial medical staff membership, he or she must reapply for membership and privileging every year or every two years. It must be noted that medical staff members are not employees or agents of the hospital. However, even though they are independent of the hospital, they are accountable individually and collectively to the board for the quality of care they provide.

In *Darling v. Charleston Community Memorial Hospital* (1965), the court stated the "corporate negligence doctrine" under which the hospital had a duty to provide an adequately trained medical and nursing staff. The *Darling* case indicated the need for hospitals to have effective credentialing and continuing medical evaluation and review programs for all members of a professional staff" (Pozgar 2007, 134). This case specifically held that the governing board has the "duty to establish mechanisms for the medical staff to evaluate, counsel, and when necessary, take action against an unreasonable risk of harm to a patient arising from the patient's treatment by a physician" (Pozgar 2007, 162). Further, the *Darling* court held that based on the hospital's obligation to select high-quality physicians to be medical staff members, the hospital may be held liable for a patient's injury caused by a physician who does not meet those standards but was given medical staff membership and privileges.

Darling involved an 18-year-old college football player studying to be a teacher and coach who suffered a broken leg during a game. He was taken to a small, accredited community hospital where the only physician on duty in the emergency department was a general practitioner who had not treated a severe leg fracture for three years. The physician ordered x-rays that revealed fractures of both bones in the lower leg. The physician reduced the fractures and applied a full-leg plaster cast. The patient complained of pain, and the physician split the cast and visited the patient while in the hospital. However, the physician never called in a specialist because he thought it unnecessary. Two weeks later, the plaintiff was transferred to a larger hospital where he was treated by an orthopedic surgeon. The specialist found dead tissue in the fractured leg and removed dead tissue several times over the next two months. Ultimately, he was unable to save the leg and amputated it eight inches below the knee.

The plaintiff's father rejected any settlement and filed suit against the hospital and the physician. The physician was eventually able to settle, but the case against the hospital continued to trial. A judgment was returned against the hospital and upheld in the Illinois Supreme Court.

The hospital's governing board relies on the medical staff structure to conduct the actual evaluation of physicians applying for medical staff membership and to make recommendations regarding their suitability for membership. The mechanisms for selecting medical staff members pursuant to *Darling* and applicable state statutes indicate that peer review is the best system for monitoring physicians. Many states provide that peer review must be conducted in a reasonable and fair manner.

The Credentialing Process

The **credentialing process** is the screening process through which the medical staff evaluates a physician's application for medical staff membership. In this process, the medical staff validates the physician's credentials: medical education, including medical school, residencies, postdoctoral studies, and fellowships; license to practice; and medical practice experience. This process also includes reviewing and evaluating professional references and professional society membership. This process also applies to other licensed independent practitioners (for example, nurse practitioners and allied health practitioners).

One major step taken in this process is searching the **National Practitioner Data Bank** regarding judgments and settlements of claims of professional negligence regardless of the amount (Cohen 2004). Further, this process includes validating the physician's liability insurance. Having a license to practice medicine in a particular state does not give the physician the right to be a medical staff member in any hospital; rather, it is merely one required criterion. Credentialing criteria should be related directly to patient care and based on objective factors such as education, experience, and current competence (Kadzielski 2004, 198). To avoid the appearance of discrimination based on profession, credentialing criteria for different types of practitioners (radiologists, psychiatrists, orthopedists, and so on) should be objective and based on community standard of care (Kadzielski 2004, 198).

Federal laws in the form of the Medicare Conditions of Participation for Hospitals, home health agencies, and long-term care facilities, among others, set forth requirements for medical staff credentialing (Kadzielski 2004). Most states typically address medical staff appointments in licensing statutes or statutes specific for the selection of medical staff members or both. Further accreditation standards, such as those published by the Joint Commission, require physician credentialing prior to granting privileges to practice in a healthcare facility (Kadzielski 2004).

The Privileging Process

After a physician is determined to meet the criteria to be a medical staff member in a particular hospital, the medical staff must evaluate his or her quality of medical practice and determine the services and procedures he or she is qualified to provide. This is known as the **privileging process**. A physician's clinical privileges determine the services he or she may provide, such as what operations he or she may perform. The medical staff must have established a written definition of what it means to be granted the privilege to provide a particular service. Some hospitals grant privileges for specific procedures; others grant privileges for categories of procedures. Still other hospitals grant privileges based on levels of care, such as privileges to care for critical care patients. Another approach is to grant privileges by medical specialty based on the services a particular specialty is permitted to perform.

To evaluate a physician for privileging, a hospital may require the physician to obtain a consultation before performing specific procedures. Physicians also may be required to have operative procedures proctored by an observing or assisting physician. A hospital may require certification beyond a license, such as board certification in a particular medical specialty, before granting privileges for a physician to practice in that specialty.

As stated above, physicians must periodically reapply for medical staff membership. As part of the reapplication process, their privileges are reevaluated using established criteria. For example, the hospital may review, among other factors, the physician's blood usage patterns, lengths of stay, infection rates, complications and complication rates, health record documentation, and closed malpractice claims (Kurdwanowski and Schaedler 1997). The hospital also may review the outcome of focused studies, such as those discussed below. Moreover, physicians who have gained additional training since the last appointment may seek privileges not previously held. For any new privileges requested, the physician may be required to have consultation or proctoring performed. Most state statutes and the federal Health Care Quality Improvement Act require this collection and review of information in the privileging process (Davis et al. 2004).

The goal of privileging is to ensure that all physicians have the requisite training and experience to perform the requested services. This process also applies to other licensed independent practitioners (for example, nurse practitioners and allied health practitioners).

Accessibility and Confidentiality of Credentialing Files

In this discussion, *credentialing* is used as a collective term for the credentialing and privileging processes. In looking at accessibility to credentialing files, third parties, such as the Joint Commission, and state and federal regulatory organizations, may review credentialing files as part of their accrediting and licensing functions. Some states statutorily protect credentialing files from discovery in legal proceedings. However, when a plaintiff alleges negligent credentialing against a hospital, whether the protection will hold up comes into question (Davis et al. 2004). In such a circumstance, the hospital finds itself in the situation of attempting to protect the information in the credentialing files while at the same time needing those very same documents to defend it (Davis et al. 2004). Although statutory protections may be in place for credentialing information, facilities should be reluctant to share such information "because any subsequent disclosure of peer review committee records could result in a loss of this protection" (Kadzielski 2004, 205).

Confidentiality of QI and Concurrent Review Activities

As noted above, outcomes of focused studies may be used to evaluate a physician's application for continued medical staff membership and privileges to practice. These studies are usually conducted as part of the hospital's QI activities. QI is the process of improving medical care and potentially decreasing healthcare costs. (This process is discussed more fully in chapter 22.)

QI activities can be carried out on a concurrent review basis or on a retrospective basis. *Concurrent review* consists of evaluating medical care as it is being given. Concurrent review activities can be carried out in a variety of ways. One method is through case management (utilization review) that focuses on the appropriateness of the admission, the level of care, and length of stay (Miller 1986).

Retrospective review occurs after patient discharge. This review may take the form of a focused study based on a pattern of questionable care identified during concurrent review or other retrospective review activities. The questionable care leading to a focused study may be care provided by any caregiver, including physicians. The hospital has a responsibility to address any problems discovered through either review process. If a physician was the caregiver providing the questionable care and it is determined that he or she is not practicing at the expected level of care, an educational session may be conducted with the particular physician. If warranted, more stringent steps, such as suspension of the physician's medical staff privileges or medical staff membership termination, may be taken.

These review activities involve collecting outcomes and performance data on how a physician performed as a physician and may affect continued medical staff membership. Accordingly, the review files are considered confidential. Many states have statutes that specifically provide confidentiality to these types of files (Davis et al. 2004). California Evidence Code Section 1157 is an example of such a law. This statute protects from discovery the proceedings and records of organized peer review committees responsible for the evaluation and improvement of the quality of care.

Check Your Understanding 10.9

Instructions: Answer the following questions on a separate piece of paper.

1. After he or she completes an application, what is the process for granting a physician membership on the hospital medical staff?
2. What documentation is typically reviewed for the initial membership appointment?
3. What activities may a medical staff require of a physician in order to grant the physician privileges to provide a specific service?
4. As part of the reapplication process, what additional factors may the medical staff review in the privileges component?
5. Discuss circumstances in which confidential information in a credentialing file may be accessed.
6. Distinguish between concurrent and retrospective review activities.
7. What is the basis for maintaining QI and concurrent review files confidential?

Other Liability Issues

Hospitals and other healthcare providers face other liability issues. Hospital staff members have a duty to advise an appropriate member of administration when they become aware of any action or failure to act that is below the standard of care. The standard of care does not just apply to direct patient care. By definition, it applies to the safeguarding of patients' personal belongings whether or not they are placed in the direct care of the facility. For patient and staff personal belongings not placed in the direct care of the facility, the facility must have policies and procedures for addressing questions of theft by staff.

The standard of care also applies to the physical safety of the premises for patients, staff, visitors, vendors, and members of the general public who come onto the premises. Physical safety means being free from physical defects in buildings and grounds and from being harmed by patients, non-staff members, or staff members. Moreover, the hospital must address staff safety as it relates to treatment of violent or uncontrolled patients (for example, a patient under the influence of drugs or alcohol while being treated in the emergency department).

Electronic Health Records

The move toward a fully **electronic health record** (EHR) brings special liability issues with it. In particular, liability issues can be classified in two categories (McWay 2003, 215–216):

- Those in which the information in the EHR serves as proof in a lawsuit of the quality of patient care provided
- Those that arise from unauthorized access to, or the careless handling or maintenance of, patient information in a computerized environment

The first issue focuses on whether the EHR can be admitted as evidence. This raises the hearsay rule and how it can be overcome for electronically stored medical records. Although admissibility of such records has been tested on a limited basis, federal courts have allowed a computer printout into evidence where the foundation, trustworthiness, and accuracy requirements were shown to have been met (McWay 2003, 218).

The second issue focuses on the legal requirements to keep EHRs safe and secure. The EHR must be subject to all three components of the HIPAA Security Rule: administrative safeguards (policies, procedures, risk assessment (45 CFR §164.308)); physical safeguards (facility access control (45 CFR §164.310)); and technical safeguards (access control (45 CFR §164.312)).

The Legal Health Record

The 2006, AHIMA House of Delegates passed a resolution stating, among other supporting statements, that "AHIMA advocates that organizations define one set of health information that meets the legal and business needs of the organization and complies with state and federal laws and regulations" (AHIMA 2007b). However, what constitutes the **legal health record** (LHR)? The resolution does not define the specifics of an LHR. Therefore, the HIM professional reading the resolution is probably still uncertain of what constitutes the LHR. Is it the same for all like-facilities? Does the format i n which it is created and stored (paper, electronic, hybrid) determine what constitutes the LHR? Moving toward an EHR environment adds another dimension to defining the LHR.

Factors the HIM professional should consider in defining or assessing whether the current record is a LHR, regardless of format, include:

- Purpose of the health record
- State and federal laws, regulations, and standards defining health record content
- Internal documents
- Risks the organization faces if its health record does not meet business record or legal health record requirements or the rules of evidence especially if it is an EHR

Pursuant to the Federal Rules of Evidence (FRE) for business records, the health record qualifies as a business record. It is created and kept in the normal course of business; made at or near the time of the matter recorded; and made by a person within the business with knowledge of the events recorded (FRE 803(6)). The business is providing healthcare. As a business record the health record contains documentation of patient care, which can be used for continuity of care and for billing. Further, it serves as a communication tool for caregivers. The organization uses the health record for operational activities such as evaluating quality of care provided. The organization also uses the health record as a resource for medical research and education.

The health record as a business record can also serve as "testimony" in legal proceedings (AHIMA 2007c). The legal standards that control whether a record is admissible in court apply regardless of whether the health record is paper or electronic (AHIMA 2007a). Such standards include the presumption that information recorded in conjunction with business practices is trustworthy and has potential evidentiary value (Rinehart-Thompson et al. 2008). In other words, the rules of evidence requirements and health record content requirements are the standards. Thus the health record is the organization's "legal health record" (Rinehart-Thompson et al. 2008, 125).

State and federal laws, regulations, licensure requirements, and accrediting body standards defining health record content, maintenance, and documentation requirements are covered earlier in this chapter. A review of that section reveals these standards vary widely according to practice setting (Rinehart-Thompson et al. 2008) (Servais 2008). Rinehart-Thompson, Reynolds, and McCain (2008) also point out that internal documents such as the medical staff bylaws, rules, and regulations may contain documentation and retention requirements. These internal documents must also be considered when defining the LHR. Thus there is no boilerplate definition of the LHR—it is what it is as each organization defines it.

The LHR definition was much simpler to arrive at when only paper-based records were used. That definition focused on the content including other materials such as radiology films and other imaging documents (AHIMA 2005a). Those "simple" days are gone for most healthcare organizations; that definition applies today only in organizations that continue to function in a truly paper-based environment.

Servais (2008) states the LHR is a subset of "patient-specific data created and accumulated by a healthcare provider that may be released to third parties in response to legally permissible requests" (Servais 2008, 1). McClendon (2007) also states that the healthcare organization may define its LHR in terms of the data set to be released in response to a legal request such as a subpoena by cataloging and using policies and procedures to state what will be divulged pursuant to a legal request. Because most healthcare organizations have moved to some level of electronic health record, the LHR definition may include information in both paper and electronic format, typically referred to as a hybrid health record. In this situation, the organization must broaden its assessment of what makes up the LHR—consider which "data elements, electronic-structured documents, images, audio files, video files and paper documents" should be included (Rinehart-Thompson et al. 2008, 126). To define the legal EHR, McClendon (2007) suggests that HIM professionals can build on existing policies and procedures and listing of documents defining the paper-based LHR. AHIMA has developed a legal EHR policy template located in the AHIMA Body of Knowledge. The HIM professional must remember to also include the details of source EHR systems feeding what the organization has defined as it legal EHR (McClendon 2007). Servais (2008) points out that the organization must determine which data source will be considered the "source of truth" (Servais 2008, 2). Therefore, defining the LHR, regardless of format, is a multidisciplinary responsibility.

According to Amatayakul (2008), HIM professionals are involved in many EHR implementation activities including, but not limited to

- Auditing compliance with clinical guidelines
- Auditing changes in electronic documentation
- Managing data dictionary
- Designing and modifying templates, screens, and reports
- Managing access controls to EHR systems
- Testing legal admissibility of records
- Managing amendments to records
- Serving on the EHR development and implementation committees
- Serving as the EHR project manager

Amatayakul (2008) stated that HIM professionals must remember that data quality, which is the HIM professional's responsibility, is the key to ensuring a legal EHR.

Further, in 2003, organizations classified as covered entities under HIPAA were required to determine what constituted their **designated record set** (DRS). HIPAA defines the DRS as those medical records and billing records about an individual the covered entity maintains or that the covered entity uses to make decisions about individuals (45 CFR §164.501). Because the DRS may include documents from other providers and e-mail communications between providers and between provider and patient, the DRS potentially includes more information than what has historically been included in an organization's paper-based LHR. The organization must evaluate this information to determine whether it should be included in the definition of the organization's LHR.

The integrity of the health record is critical to it meeting the standards of evidence in a court of law and thus being classified as the organization's LHR. The integrity of the information stored in the health record means it is correct, accurate, and complete (Rinehart-Thompson et al. 2008, 132). Under the FRE, authenticity of the record means "it is what it purports to be" (Rinehart-Thompson et al. 2008, 133) (FRE 901(a)). Rinehart-Thompson, Reynolds, and McCain (2008) explain that those using the information stored in the health record rely on it being accurate; that it has not been changed either intentionally or accidentally. Thus the point of record completion (lock down) must be defined (Olenik 2008). Reliability is one of the standards the information must meet to be acceptable as evidence in court.

Rinehart-Thompson, Reynolds, and McCain (2008) further state that authenticity relates both to the information being created and the system being used to create and store that information. As to the system, reliability includes such features as user access controls, system security, access tracking and auditing capabilities, and operational stability (dependability and availability). These features are particularly important because the general concern is that electronically stored information can be easily changed. According to Olenik (2008), the organization must determine what the "original" record is:

- Paper documents
- Electronic information
- Imaged documents

Authenticity also means that in both the paper and EHR environments, there must be methods in place to verify the author of entries made in the health record. This process is typically referred to as authentication. In paper records authentication is most often accomplished by a handwritten signature and initials, both in ink. Authentication in an EHR is another matter. Electronic or digital signatures and computer keys are examples of authentication methods used in EHRs (Rinehart-Thompson et al. 2008; Servais 2008). An organization can also write in its policy that the auto-authentication process can be used. This process states that an entry is considered authenticated if the author fails to review and affirmatively approve or disapprove the entry within a specified time period (Rinehart-Thompson et al. 2008; Servais 2008). Whatever approach is decided upon, it must comply with applicable laws and regulations (Olenik 2008). Olenik (2008) provided one such example: "CMS Interpretive Guidelines for Hospitals 482.24(c)(1) *all entries must be legible and complete, and must be authenticated and dated promptly by the person (identified by name and discipline) who is responsible for ordering, providing, or evaluating the service furnished.*"

According to Rinehart-Thompson, Reynolds, and McCain (2008), when defining the LHR, a number of authentication issues must be considered. For example, countersignatures are required when one professional practices under the direct supervision of another. This second provider countersigns documentation authenticating the actions, documentation, and authentication of the first provider. Documents such as assessments require authentication by all staff members involved in the assessment. These multiple authentications may actually occur at different times.

Other issues that need to be considered when defining the LHR include (Rinehart-Thompson et al. 2008; Servais 2008):

- Accuracy of information–does the information reflect the "true, correct and exact description of the care provided?" (Rinehart-Thompson et al. 2008, 137)
- Abbreviations
- Legibility
- Changes (revisions, additions, deletions, and version management)
- Timeliness and completeness
- Printing

One major concern is the "cut and paste" function included in some systems. According to Olenik (2008), the risks include:

- Copying information to the wrong patient
- Copying information to the wrong encounter for the correct patient
- Inadequate identification of the original author and date of the entry
- Could be unethical or illegal in circumstances such as clinical trials

An EHR can be particularly effective in addressing some of these issues, such as abbreviations and legibility. Additionally, there are operational topics to be addressed (McClendon 2007; Servais 2008):

- Alterations to role-based access
- Authorship (attributing information creation to a specific person or entity) and authentication
- Policy and procedure development
- Designating the custodian(s) of records
- Non-repudiation
- Output formats
- Permanent archiving, retention, and destruction procedures
- System and network security
- Disaster recovery and business continuity

Servais (2008) further indicates that the organization's legal counsel should participate in determining the impact of including or excluding certain documents from the LHR.

In summary, the definition of a LHR for a specific organization boils down to what documents, data, and the like the organization determines it will disclose pursuant to a legal request and whether that information meets the rules of evidence requirements and health record content, maintenance, and retention requirements. As the LHR transforms from a paper-based record to an EHR, laws and regulations continually change as does technology. Prudent HIM professionals must monitor these changes to stay current so they can meet their obligations related to maintaining the integrity and security of the organization's LHR and EHR.

Incident Reports

A happening that is inconsistent with the standard of care is generally defined as an incident. As discussed above, standards of care are not related only to direct patient care. Therefore, incidents do not relate only to patient care. Anyone witnessing or involved in an incident should complete an incident report as soon as possible after the incident as a way to capture the details of what happened. The incident report is one tool staff can use to report unusual incidents to administration. Data should be collected from the incident reports and analyzed to determine whether trends are developing.

Because incident reports contain facts, hospitals strive to protect their confidentiality. In some states, incident reports are protected under statutes protecting QI studies and activities (Davis et al. 2004). They also may be protected under attorney–client privilege (Davis et al. 2004; McWay 2003). Protection under this doctrine may be based on whether the primary purpose of the incident report is to provide information to the hospital's attorney or liability insurer (Davis et al. 2004; McDonough 2004; McWay 2003).

To further ensure incident report confidentiality, no copies should be made and the original must not be filed in the health record nor removed from the files in the department responsible for maintaining them, typically risk management or QI (McDonough 2004) (McWay 2003). Also no reference to the completion of an incident report should be made in the health record. Such a reference would likely render the incident report discoverable because it is mentioned in a document that is discoverable in legal proceedings.

Relationship to Risk Manager

The health information manager and the risk manager should work as a team. The risk manager depends on the health information manager to alert him or her to potentially compensable events. These are events that could result in a settlement or judgment against the facility, further resulting in a payout of funds whether through insurance or from facility internal funds. Such events can be identified through coding and abstracting, and various health record review activities conducted by HIM department staff. The health information manager also can advise the risk manager when an attorney requests a copy of a health record. The risk manager then can review records identified by any of these methods to determine whether further action is necessary from a risk management standpoint.

Check Your Understanding 10.10

Instructions: Answer the following questions on a separate piece of paper.

1. Define incident as it relates to the healthcare environment.
2. Name two doctrines under which incident reports may be protected.
3. What characteristics of a medical record qualify these records to be "business records"?
4. Differentiate between "authenticity" and "authentication."
5. Discuss the various issues that should be considered when defining the legal health record.
6. Why should incident reports be protected?
7. Discuss the relationship between the health information manager and the risk manager.

Real-World Case

Adapted from a publication on the Internet discussing the subject of employers' practice of maintaining health information in the employees' personnel records (Small Business, Medical Investigations 2004).

Mary Beth Jones, RHIA professional, is the new director of the HIM department at a midsized hospital in an eastern state. She has recently learned that the HR department maintains detailed medical information in its personnel files. Additionally, she has learned that her employer routinely uses this information when collecting health information for its group insurance plan, when employees request time off for a medical leave, and as part of its substance abuse assistance program.

State law recognizes a duty of confidentiality to protect this information and to avoid dissemination to nonessential third parties. Moreover, it requires that employers maintain health records separately from personnel files and recognize a claim for negligent maintenance of personnel files if they are not maintained separately. Furthermore, employers in Mary Beth's state are prohibited from using or disclosing employee medical information unless (1) such disclosure is compelled by law, (2) the information is relevant to a lawsuit between employer and employee, or (3) disclosure is necessary to administer an employee benefit plan.

Summary

The basic court system is the same from one state to another. However, the health information management professional should become familiar with the differences that do exist for the state in which he or she works. This knowledge gives the HIM professional the ability to communicate effectively with legal counsel regarding health records and policies and procedures affecting health records when the inevitable lawsuit arises.

Knowledge that is more important and valuable to the HIM professional is of the statutes that control the use and disclosure of confidential health information. These statutes are both federal and state in nature. This area of law is constantly in flux and requires the HIM professional to constantly review the many available resources pertaining to such statutes, including publications and seminars. These resources also should address case law that may affect the ongoing applicability of federal and state statutes and regulations.

E-discovery statutes at the federal and at state level as available are having a significant impact on responding to subpoenas and other requests for information. E-discovery goes beyond the data that is visible in systems by including metadata. The concepts of legal hold and spoliation are very important to the HIM professional in responding under e-discovery statutes to a subpoena or other request.

In conjunction with e-discovery, the HIM professional must have an understanding of what constitutes the organization's electronic health record (EHR), including what systems are contained in the EHR. Included in all of this is knowing what makes up the organization's legal health record (LHR). According to the AHIMA House of Delegates in 2006, the LHR is one set of health information meeting the legal and business needs of the organization (AHIMA 2007b).

Another body of knowledge the HIM professional should develop is a clear understanding of licensure and accreditation standards that affect the creation, completion, maintenance, and protection of health records.

The HIM professional must ensure that health records policies and procedures are in place and enforced and that they reflect all statutes, regulations, and standards pertaining to health records, particularly those pertaining to the use and disclosure of confidential information.

Among the many members of the hospital staff with whom the HIM professional works, he or she must have a close relationship with the facility risk manager. The HIM professional can provide the risk manager tremendous assistance in identifying and addressing incidents that may place the facility at risk.

References

Adair, D., et al. 2005. Practice brief: Update: Maintaining a legally sound health record: Paper and electronic. *Journal of AHIMA* 76(10): 64A–L. http://www.ahima.org/e-him.

Administrative Procedures Act, 5 U.S.C.S. §500-576 (Law. Co-op. 1989).

AHIMA e-Discovery Task Force. 2008. Practice brief: Litigation response planning and policies for E-discovery. *Journal of AHIMA* 79(2): 69–75. http://www.ahima.org/e-him.

AHIMA e-HIM Work Group on Defining the Legal Health Record. 2005a. Practice brief: Guidelines for defining the legal health record for disclosure purposes. *Journal of AHIMA* 76(8): 64A–G. http://www.ahima.org/Privacy.

AHIMA e-HIM Work Group on e-Discovery. 2006. The electronic discovery civil rule. *Journal of AHIMA* 77(8): 68A–H.

AHIMA e-HIM Work Group on the Legal Health Record. 2005b. Practice brief: The legal process and electronic health records. *Journal of AHIMA* 76(9): 96A–D.

American Health Information Management Association. 2007a. Is your electronic record a legal record? Highlights from the 78th National Convention: Reaching New Heights. *Journal of AHIMA* 78(1): 54.

American Health Information Management Association. 2007b. Resolution on the legal health record. *Journal of AHIMA* 78(1): 53.

American Health Information Management Association. 2007c. The legal EHR: Trials and errors. *AHIMA Advantage* 11:4. http://www.ahima.org.

Amatayakul, M. 2008. EHRs in a changing environment. California Health Information Management Association 2008 State Convention and Exhibit. San Jose, CA: CHIA.

Arizona Constitution, Section 8, Right to privacy. http://azleg.state.az.us/const/2/8.htm.

California Civil Discovery Act. http://CaliforniaDiscovery.findlaw.com.

California Constitution, Article 1, Declaration of rights, Section 1. http://leginfo.ca.gov/.const/.article_1.

Carter, Patricia I. 2003. *HIPAA Compliance Handbook 2003*. Frederick, MD: Aspen Publishers.

Cohen, M. 2004. Statutes, standards, and regulations. In *Risk Management Handbook for Health Care Organizations*. 4th ed. Edited by Carroll, R. San Francisco: Jossey-Bass.

Darling v. Charleston Community Memorial Hospital, 33 Ill.2d 326, 211 N.E. 2d, 253 (1965).

Davis, K.S., J.C. McConnell, and E.D. Shaw. 2004. Data management. In *Risk Management Handbook for Health Care Organizations*. 4th ed. Edited by Carroll, R. San Francisco: Jossey-Bass.

DeLoss, G. E. 2008. Electronic health records: An overview of legal liability, discovery and donation issues. California Health Information Management Association 2008 State Convention and Exhibit. San Jose, CA: CHIA.

Dimick, C. 2007. E-Discovery: Preparing for the coming rise in electronic discovery requests. *Journal of AHIMA* 78(5): 24–29.

Florida Constitution, Article I, Section 23, Right of privacy. http://www.leg.state.fl.us.

FRE 803: Hearsay Exceptions: Availability of Declarant Immaterial (1975).

FRE 901: Requirement of Authentication or Identification (1975).

Griswold v. Connecticut, 381 U.S. 479 (1965).

Health Insurance Portability and Accountability Act of 1996. Public Law 104-191.

HIPAA-a. Public Law 104-191, 110 Stat. 1936 (codified in scattered sections of 18, 26, 29, and 42 U.S.C.).

HIPAA-b. Public Law 104-191, preface 110 Stat. at 1936.

HIPAA-c. 65 Fed. Reg. 82463 (Dec. 28, 2000).

HIPAA-d. Public Law 104-191, §261; 65 Fed. Reg. 82463 (Dec. 28, 2000).

HIPAA-e. Public Law 104-191, §§263, 264 (codified at 42 USC 1320d-2 to 1320d-8).

HIPAA-f. 65 Fed. Reg. 82484 (Dec. 28, 2000).

HIPAA-g. 65 Fed. Reg. 82718 (Dec. 28, 2000).

Hughes, G. 2002. Practice brief: Laws and regulations governing the disclosure of health information (updated). http://library.ahima.org.

Hughes, G. 2003. Practice brief: Transfer of patient health information across the continuum (updated). http://library.ahima.org.

In re PPA Litigation, 2003 WL 22203834 (NJ Super L 2003).

Judge v. Rockford Memorial Hospital, 17 Ill. App. 2d 365, 150 N.E. 2d 202 (1958).

Kadzielski, M.A. 2004. Physician and allied health professional credentialing. In *Risk Management Handbook for Health Care Organizations*. 4th ed. Edited by Carroll, R. San Francisco: Jossey-Bass.

Kadzielski, M.A. and E.I. Kogan. 1997. Physician and allied health professional credentialing. In *Risk Management Handbook for Health Care Organizations*. 2nd ed. Edited by Carroll, R. Chicago: American Hospital Publishing.

Kurdwanowski, F. and P.A. Schaedler. 1997. Internal and external relationships. In *Risk Management Handbook for Health Care Organizations*. 2nd ed. Edited by Carroll, R. Chicago: American Hospital Publishing.

Law v. Zuckerman, 307 F. Supp. 2d 705 (D. MD 2004).

Lazzarotti, J.J. 2008 (July). Hospital to Pay $100,000, Comply with 3-Year Corrective Action Plan for HIPAA Data Breach. http://www.jacksonlewis.com/legalupdates/article.cfm?aid=1448.

Malone, E.F. 2004. *Who Goes to Jail? A Guide for HIPAA Privacy Officers*. Chicago: AHIMA.

McClendon. K. 2007 (Feb.). Record Disclosure and the EHR: Defining and managing the subset of data disclosed upon request. *Journal of AHIMA* 78(2): 58–59.

McDonough, W.J. 2004. Systems for risk identification. In *Risk Management Handbook for Health Care Organizations*. 4th ed. Edited by Carroll, R. San Francisco: Jossey-Bass.

McWay, D.C. 2003. *Legal Aspects of Health Information Management.* Clifton, NY: Delmar.

Miller, R.D. 1986. *Problems in Hospital Law.* Rockville, MD: Aspen.

Office of Civil Rights. 2006. Compliance and Enforcement, How OCR Enforces the HIPAA Privacy Rule. http://www.hhs.gov/ocr/privacy/enforcement/hipaarule.html.

Office of Civil Rights. 2000. 65 *Federal Register* 82527.

Olenik, K. 2008. How to create your legal EHR policy. California Health Information Management Association 2008 State Convention and Exhibit. San Jose, CA: CHIA.

Park, Carolyne. 2008 (April 17). Nurse pleads guilty to privacy violation. *Arkansas Democrat Gazette.* http://library.ardemgaz.com/ArchiveSearch.asp?SearchWords=nurse-guilty&eventStartDate=04%2F17%2F2008&eventStopDate=04%2F17%2F2008.

Pozgar, G.D. 2004. *Legal Aspects of Health Care Administration.* Sudbury, MA: Jones and Bartlett.

Pozgar, G.D. 2007. *Legal Aspects of Health Care Administration.* Sudbury, MA: Jones and Bartlett.

Reisner v. Regents of the University of California, 37 Cal. Rptr2d 518 (1995).

Rhodes, H. and G. Hughes. 2003. Practice brief: Redisclosure of patient health information. Health Information Management Operations. *Journal of AHIMA* 74(4): 56A–C. http://www.ahima.org.

Rinehart-Thompson, L.A., R.B. Reynolds, K. Olenik, and M.C. McCain. 2008. The Legal Health Record: Maintenance, Content, Documentation, and Disposition. Chapter 7 in *Fundamentals of L aw for Health Informatics and Information Management.* Edited by Brodnik, M.S., L.A. Rinehart-Thompson, M..C. McCain, and R.B. Reynolds. Chicago: AHIMA.

Servais, C. 2008. *The Legal Health Record.* Edited by Olderman, N. and K. Trahan. Chicago: AHIMA.

Small Business, Medical Investigations. 2004 (July). http://www.findlaw.com/employmentbook/HFCHP5_e.html.

Tarasoff v. Board of Regents, 17 Cal.3d 425, 551 P.2d 334 (Cal. 1976).

Trautmann, Carl O. 2003. Small Business Dictionary. http://www.small-business-dictionary.org/default.asp?.

U.S. v. Gibson, CR 04-0374RFM (W.D. WA 2004).

U.S. v. Jackson, CR08-0-0430, U.S. District Court for the Central District of California, 2008.

45 CFR 46.111(a)(7): Research - Protection of Human Subjects, including Protecting Confidential Information. 2006 (Oct. 1).

45 CFR 160: General Administrative Requirements. 2000 (Dec. 28).

45 CFR 160.102-103. 2002 (Aug.14).

45 CFR 160.201–205: Preemption Provisions. 2002 (Aug. 14).

45 CFR §160.203(b): General Rules and Exceptions. 2002 (Aug. 14).

45 CFR 160.306(a): OCR Investigations–Right to File a Complaint. 2006 (Feb. 16).

45 CFR 160.306(c): OCR Investigations. 2006 (Feb. 16).

45 CFR 160.312(a)(1): Resolution where Non-Compliance is Indicated. 2006 (Feb. 16).

45 CFR 160.312(a)(3)(i): Mitigating Factors and Affirmative Defenses. 2006 (Feb. 16).

45 CFR 162: Transaction and Code Sets. 2000 (Aug. 17).

45 CFR 164 Subparts A and C: Security Rule. 2003 (Feb. 20).

45 CFR 164 Subpart E: Privacy of Individually Identifiable Health Information. 2003 (Feb. 20).

45 CFR 164.300: Security. 2003 (Feb. 20).

45 CFR 164.308: Security–Administrative Safeguards. 2005 (Oct. 1).

45 CFR 164.310: Security–Physical Safeguards. 2005 (Oct. 1).

45 CFR 164.312: Security–Technical Safeguards. 2005 (Oct. 1).

45 CFR 164.500: Privacy. 2002 (Aug. 14).

45 CFR 164.501: Definitions. 2003 (Feb. 20).

45 CFR 164.506(a): Permitted Uses and Disclosures. 2002 (Aug. 14).

45 CFR 164.506(a)(5): Consent. 2002 (Aug. 14).

45 CFR 164.506(c)(1): Treatment, Payment, and Health Care Operations. 2002 (Aug. 14).

45 CFR 164.506(c)(2): Treatment Activities of Health Care Provider. 2002 (Aug. 14).

45 CFR 164.506(c)(3): Payment Activities of Health Care Provider. 2002 (Aug. 14).

45 CFR 164.506(c)(4): Health Care Operations of Health Care Provider. 2002 (Aug. 14).

45 CFR 164.506(c)(4)(i): Health Care Operations of Health Care Provider. 2002 (Aug. 14).

45 CFR 164.506(c)(5): Treatment, Payment, and Health Care Operations in Organized Health Care Arrangement. 2002 (Aug. 14).

45 CFR 164.508(a)(1): Authorization—General Rule. 2002 (Aug. 14).

45 CFR 164.508(a)(2): Psychotherapy Notes. 2002 (Aug. 14).

45 CFR 164.508(a)(3): Marketing. 2002 (Aug. 14).

45 CFR 164.508(b)(2): Defective Authorizations. 2002 (Aug. 14).

45 CFR 164.508(b)(5)(i): Authorization Revocation. 2002 (Aug. 14).

45 CFR 164.508(c)(1) – (4): Authorization Content. 2002 (Aug. 14).

45 CFR 164.508(c)(2)(iii): Authorization Content—Core Elements and Requirements. 2002 (Aug. 14).

45 CFR 164.510: Opportunity to Agree or Object to Disclosures. 2002 (Aug. 14).

45 CFR 164.510(b)(1)(i): Uses and Disclosures for Involvement in the Individual's Care. 2002 (Aug. 14).

45 CFR 164.510(b)(1)(ii): Uses and Disclosures for Notification Purposes. 2002 (Aug. 14).

45 CFR 164.512(a)(1): Required by Law. 2002 (Aug. 14).

45 CFR 164.512(b): Public Health Activities. 2002 (Aug. 14).

45 CFR 164.512(b)(1)(i) – (iii): Communicable Disease Notification. 2002 (Aug. 14).

45 CFR 164.512(b)(1)(v): Disclosure to Employer. 2002 (Aug. 14).

45 CFR 164.512(c): Reporting Abuse, Neglect, Domestic Violence. 2002 (Aug. 14).

45 CFR 164.512(d): Health Oversight Activities. 2002 (Aug. 14).

45 CFR 164.512(e)(i) – (iv): Judicial or Administrative Proceeding. 2002 (Aug. 14).

45 CFR 164.512(e)(v): Judicial or Administrative Proceeding–Qualified Protective Order. 2002 (Aug. 14).

45 CFR 164.512(f): Law Enforcement. 2002 (Aug. 14).

45 CFR 164.512(f)(6): Law Enforcement—Perpetrator of Crime. 2002 (Aug. 14).

45 CFR 164.512(g): Decedents. 2002 (Aug. 14).

45 CFR 164.512(h): Procurement Organizations. 2002 (Aug. 14).

45 CFR 164.512(i): Research. 2002 (Aug. 14).

45 CFR 164.512(j): Avert Serious Threat. 2002 (Aug. 14).

45 CFR 164.512(k): Specialized Government Functions. 2002 (Aug. 14).

45 CFR 164.512(l): Workers Compensation. 2002 (Aug. 14).

45 CFR 164.514: De-identified Information. 2002 (Aug. 14).

45 CFR 164.514(f)(1): Fundraising. 2002 (Aug. 14).

45 CFR 164.520: Notice of Privacy Practices. 2002 (Aug. 14).

45 CFR 164.522(a): Restrict Use of Protected Health Information. 2002 (Aug. 14).

45 CFR 164.522(b): Confidential Communications. 2002 (Aug. 14).

45 CFR 164.524: Access to Own Protected Health Information. 2002 (Aug. 14).

45 CFR 164.524(a)(1): Patient Right of Access to Own Protected Health Information. 2002 (Aug. 14).

45 CFR 164.524(a)(3): Reviewable Grounds for Denial of Access to Own Protected Health Information. 2002 (Aug. 14).

45 CFR 164.526: Amend Designated Record Set. 2002 (Aug. 14).

45 CFR 164.528: Accounting of Disclosures. 2002 (Aug. 14).

42 USC 1320d-5: General Civil Money Penalties. 1996.

42 USC 1320d-6(a): Criminal Provisions. 2000.

42 USC 1320d-6(b): Maximum Penalties. 2000.

Chapter 11
Ethical Issues in Health Information Management

Laurinda B. Harman, PhD, RHIA

Learning Objectives

- Recognize core health information ethical problems, including those related to privacy and confidentiality; compliance, fraud, and abuse; clinical code selection and use; quality review; research and decision support; public health; managed care; clinical care; electronic health information systems; the management of sensitive information; the roles of manager, entrepreneur, and advocate; and business relationships with vendors
- Recognize the historical problems of research and ethics and the importance of diligence for future research endeavors
- Recognize the problems associated with the emerging ethical problem of medical identity theft
- Identify ethical principles and professional values that can guide health information management (HIM) professionals who must confront and respond to ethical problems
- Apply the AHIMA Code of Ethics to guide behaviors such as protecting privacy, advancing HIM knowledge and practice, advocating for others, and refusing to participate in or conceal unethical behaviors
- Follow the steps in an ethical decision-making process that can be used to resolve complex ethical problems

Key Terms

Autonomy
Beneficence
Bioethics
Blanket authorization
Confidentiality
Ethical agent
Ethical decision making
Ethicist
Ethics
Justice
Medical identity theft
Moral values
Need-to-know principle
Nonmaleficence
Privacy
Secondary release of information
Security

The responsibilities of the health information management (HIM) professional include a wide range of functions and activities. Regardless of the employer, such as healthcare facility, vendor, pharmaceutical company, or research firm, the HIM professional's core ethical obligation is to protect patient privacy and confidential communication. The documentation in the paper and electronic health information systems include many sacred stories that must be protected on behalf of the patient and the aggregate community of patients and consumers served by the healthcare system. The obligation to protect this information is at the center of the decisions made on behalf of patients, the healthcare team, peers, colleagues, the public, or the many other stakeholders who seek access to patient and consumer information (AHIMA 2004).

The terms in this chapter describe ethical principles that most people already know, although the terms themselves may not be familiar. For example, recognizing the importance of individuals being able to decide what happens to them is autonomy, doing good is included in the ethical principle of beneficence, not harming others is nonmaleficence, and treating people fairly is justice (Beauchamp and Childress 2001). This chapter provides the language and framework for understanding more about ethics within the context of dealing with complex health information issues. It also offers a step-by-step process that HIM professionals can use to make appropriate ethical choices and to analyze what is and is not justified from an ethical perspective.

Theory into Practice

With regard to one of the HIM professional's primary functions, how might ethical principles apply in the case of deciding whether to release patient information?

- **Autonomy** would require the HIM professional to ensure that the patient, and not a spouse or third party, makes the decisions regarding access to his or her health information.
- **Beneficence** would require the HIM professional to ensure that the information is released only to individuals who need it to do something that will benefit the patient (for example, to an insurance company for payment of a claim).
- **Nonmaleficence** would require the HIM professional to ensure that the information is not released to someone who does not have authorization to access it and who might harm the patient if access were permitted (for example, a newspaper seeking information about a famous person).
- **Justice** would require the HIM professional to apply the rules fairly and consistently for all and not to make special exceptions based on personal or organizational perspectives.

Moral Values and Ethical Competencies

Although most people probably have never undertaken a formal study of ethics, everyone is exposed to ethical principles, moral perspectives, and values throughout a lifetime. Individuals learn about basic **moral values** from families, religious leaders, teachers, the government, community organizations, and other groups that influence experiences and perspectives. Moral values are taught as "this is right and that is wrong." For example, some might consider it right to be nice to a neighbor and wrong to destroy the neighbor's property. However, these are not universal values. Others might consider it acceptable to be rude or mean to a neighbor they do not like and to destroy the neighbor's property. Applying this language to health information management, it is right—and a moral obligation—to protect the neighbor's privacy when you learn about diseases and conditions while working and it is wrong to share the neighbor's medical information with other neighbors, family, and friends.

HIM professionals should not make ethical decisions on behalf of others based solely on personal moral values or perspectives because not everyone shares the same moral perspectives or values. Professional responsibilities often require an individual to move beyond personal values. For example, an individual might demonstrate behaviors that are based on the values of honesty, providing service to others, or demonstrating loyalty. In addition to these, professional values might require promoting confidentiality, facilitating interdisciplinary collaboration, and refusing to participate or conceal unethical practices. Professional values could require a more comprehensive set of values than what an individual needs to be an **ethical agent** in his or her personal life. For example, an HIM professional who hears information about a friend at a party has a range of options. He or she can share the information, share only part of it, change it, or not confirm or share it with anyone. However, that same individual in his or her role as an HIM professional cannot share overheard information under any circumstances.

Ethics provides a language and a framework for formally discussing ethical issues, taking into account the values and obligations of others. Ethical discussion offers an opportunity to resolve conflicts when competing values are at stake. **Ethical decision making** requires people to explore choices beyond the perspective of simple right or wrong (moral) options. According to Glover, "ethics refers to the formal process of intentionally and critically analyzing the basis for one's moral judgments for clarity and consistency" (Glover 2006). When making health information decisions, HIM professionals must go beyond the personal right or wrong moral perspective and evaluate the many values and perspectives of others who are engaged in the decision to be made.

Ethical discussions outside the healthcare environment can be theoretical in nature, and the analysis of a problem does not necessarily result in an action. For example, **ethicists** could discuss whether to require all citizens living in a certain community to donate 10 hours a week to people in need as part of their civic duty. One ethicist might argue for a decision based on the ethical principle of beneficence, which would guide action to do good things for others. Another ethicist might argue for the same decision based on the principle of justice in which every citizen should contribute his or her fair share for the good of the whole. These discussions and decisions would not necessarily require an action but would help frame the ethical justification for a certain action.

In contrast, **bioethics** involves problems or issues regarding clinical care or the health information system that are never strictly theoretical in nature and must always result in a decision. HIM professionals cannot merely deliberate whether to release patient information, assign the correct code, or purchase a new software system. Rather, they must apply ethical principles and then do something. In short, ethics applied in the work environment cannot remain theoretical and must result in an action.

Ethical Foundations in Health Information Management

Ethical principles and values have been important to the HIM profession since its beginning in 1928. The first ethical pledge was presented in 1934, by Grace Whiting Myers, a visionary leader who recognized the importance of protecting information in medical records. The HIM profession was launched with recognition of the importance of privacy and the requirement of authorization for the release of health information:

> I pledge myself to give out no information from any clinical record placed in my charge, or from any other source to any person whatsoever, except upon order from the chief executive officer of the institution which I may be serving. (Huffman 1972, 135)

Today, it is the patient who authorizes the release of information and not the chief executive officer (CEO) of the healthcare organization, as was stated in the original pledge. The most important values embedded in this pledge are to protect patient privacy and confidential information and to recognize the importance of the HIM professional as a moral agent in protecting patient information (Rinehart-Thompson and Harman 2006). The HIM professional has a clear ethical and professional obligation not to give any information to anyone unless the release has been authorized.

Protection of Privacy, Maintenance of Confidentiality, and Assurance of Data Security

The terms privacy, confidentiality, and security are often used interchangeably. However, there are some important distinctions, including:

- **Privacy** is "the right of an individual to be let alone. It includes freedom from observation or intrusion into one's private affairs and the right to maintain control over certain personal and health information" (Harman 2006, 634).
- **Confidentiality** carries "the responsibility for limiting disclosure of private matters. It includes the responsibility to use, disclose, or release such information only with the knowledge and consent of the individual" (Harman 2006, 627–628). Confidential information may be written or verbal.
- **Security** includes "physical and electronic protection of the integrity, availability, and confidentiality of computer-based information and the resources used to enter, store, process, and communicate it. The means to control access and protect information from accidental or intentional disclosure" (Harman 2006, 635).

The HIM professional's responsibilities include ensuring that patient privacy and confidential information are protected and that data security measures are used to prevent unauthorized access to information. This responsibility includes ensuring that the release policies and procedures are accurate and up-to-date, that they are followed, and that all violations are reported to the proper authorities.

The Health Insurance Portability and Accountability Act (HIPAA) of 1996 establishes national standards for the privacy and security of health information. This law deals with privacy, information standards, data integrity, confidentiality, and data security (Rinehart-Thompson and Harman 2006). Although HIPAA was passed in 1996, it took five years before the Privacy Rule became effective in April 2001, with an April 2003 compliance date. Congress passed the statute and the U.S. Department of Health and Human Services (HHS) developed the regulations contained within the Privacy Rule (HHS 2003). The final HIPAA Security Rule regulations were published in the *Federal Register* in February 2003, and became effective in April 2005.

This legislation, which includes administrative simplification standards and security and privacy standards, has had—and will continue to have—a major impact on the collection and dissemination of information for years to come. This legislation has an enforcement program, and HIM professionals serve an important role to assure compliance. Although privacy is a right protected by the U.S. Constitution, each state can affect its own legislation regarding access to patient information. Preemptive federal legislation was needed so that all patient information would be protected regardless of where a patient lived or received healthcare. Moreover, this legislation protects individuals from losing their health insurance when leaving or changing jobs by providing insurance continuity (portability) and increases the federal government's authority over fraud and abuse in the healthcare arena (accountability) (Harman 2005).

Part of the impetus for HIPAA was the development of the electronic health record (EHR) (Amatayakul 2007; Dick et al.1997; Hanken and Murphy 2006; Johns 2002; Murphy et al. 1999). As patient information was moved to the electronic medium, integrated systems across the continuum of care were developed and information was released and redisclosed to many people and agencies needing access to it. Thus, standardized federal legislation became an imperative. HIPAA was designed to guarantee that information transferred from one facility to the next would be protected. The National Committee on Vital and Health Statistics (NCVHS) supports a National Health Information Infrastructure (NHII) so that patient care information can be transferred and protected in our integrated healthcare systems. As a result, patients benefit from the continuity of care and can control their personal health information (NCVHS 2001; Gellman 2004). See additional information about ethics, research and HIPAA later in this chapter and Chapter 10 for more information about HIPAA.

In an electronic environment, protecting privacy has become extremely difficult and patients are becoming increasingly concerned about the loss of privacy and their inability to control the dissemination of information about them. As patients become more aware of the misuses of information, they may become reluctant to share information with their healthcare team. This may, in turn, result in problems with the healthcare that is provided and the information given to researchers, insurers, the government, and the many other stakeholders who legitimately need to access to the information. Increasingly, patients are seeking anonymity and responding to issues related to the use and disclosure of health information for directory purposes; to family and close personal friends; for notification purposes such as disasters; and for other disclosures required by law such as public health, employer medical surveillance, and funeral directors (Hughes 2002a; Hughes 2002b; Rhodes 2001; AHIMA 2002).

Professional Code of Ethics

HIM professionals used the pledge as the basis for guiding ethical decision making until 1957, at which time the American Association of Medical Record Librarians' (AAMRL) House of Delegates passed the first Code of Ethics for the Practice of Medical Record Science. (See figure 11.1.) The first code of ethics combined ethical principles with a set of professional values to help support the decisions that HIM professionals had to make at work. The original Code of Ethics has been revised several times since 1957—in 1978, 1988, 1998, and 2004. (See figures 11.2, 11.3, and 11.4, respectively, and appendix B for the Code of Ethics).

Upon being awarded the credential of registered health information administrator (RHIA) by the American Health Information Management Association (AHIMA), the HIM professional agrees to follow the principles and values discussed in this chapter and to base all professional actions and decisions on those principles and values. Even if federal or state laws did not require the protection of patient privacy, the HIM professional would be responsible for protecting it according to the AHIMA's Code of Ethics.

Professional Values and Obligations

The ethical obligations of the HIM professional include the protection of patient privacy and confidential information. Core health information issues include what information should be collected; how the information should be handled, who should have access to the information, and under what conditions the information should be disclosed.

Figure 11.1. 1957 Code of Ethics for the Practice of Medical Record Science

[Note: Gender-neutral language was not used in the 1950s, so the male pronoun should be read as "he or she."]

As a member of one of the paramedical professions he shall:

1. Place service before material gain, the honor of the profession before personal advantage, the health and welfare of patients above all personal and financial interests, and conduct himself in the practice of this profession so as to bring honor to himself, his associates, and to the medical record profession.
2. Preserve and protect the medical records in his custody and hold inviolate the privileged contents of the records and any other information of a confidential nature obtained in his official capacity, taking due account of the applicable statutes and of regulations and policies of his employer.
3. Serve his employer loyally, honorably discharging the duties and responsibilities entrusted to him, and give due consideration to the nature of these responsibilities in giving his employer notice of intent to resign his position.
4. Refuse to participate in or conceal unethical practices or procedures.
5. Report to the proper authorities, but disclose to no one else, any evidence of conduct or practice revealed in the medical records in his custody that indicates possible violation of established rules and regulations of the employer or of professional practice.
6. Preserve the confidential nature of professional determinations made by the staff committee which he serves.
7. Accept only those fees that are customary and lawful in the area for services rendered in his official capacity.
8. Avoid encroachment on the professional responsibilities of the medical and other paramedical professions, and under no circumstances assume or give the appearance of assuming the right to make determinations in professional areas outside the scope of his assigned responsibilities.
9. Strive to advance the knowledge and practice of medical record science, including continued self-improvement, in order to contribute to the best possible medical care.
10. Participate appropriately in developing and strengthening professional manpower and in representing the profession to the public.
11. Discharge honorably the responsibilities of any Association post to which appointed or elected, and preserve the confidentiality of any privileged information made known to him in his official capacity.
12. State truthfully and accurately his credentials, professional education, and experiences in any official transaction with the American Association of Medical Record Librarians and with any employer or prospective employer.

American Association of Medical Librarians 1957.

Figure 11.2. 1977 AMRA bylaws and Code of Ethics

The medical record practitioner is concerned with the development, use, and maintenance of medical and health records for medical care, preventive medicine, quality assurance, professional education, administrative practices and study purposes with due consideration of patients' right to privacy. The American Medical Record Association believes that it is in the best interests of the medical record profession and the public which it serves that the principles of personal and professional accountability be reexamined and redefined to provide members of the Association, as well as medical record practitioners who are credentialed by the Association, with definitive and binding guidelines of conduct. To achieve this goal, the American Medical Record Association has adopted the following restated Code of Ethics:

1. Conduct yourself in the practice of this profession so as to bring honor and dignity to yourself, the medical record profession and the Association.
2. Place service before material gain and strive at all times to provide services consistent with the need for quality health care and treatment of all who are ill and injured.
3. Preserve and secure the medical and health records, the information contained therein, and the appropriate secondary records in your custody in accordance with professional management practices, employer's policies and existing legal provisions.
4. Uphold the doctrine of confidentiality and the individual's right to privacy in the disclosure of personally identifiable medical and social information.
5. Recognize the source of the authority and powers delegated to you and conscientiously discharge the duties and responsibilities thus entrusted.
6. Refuse to participate in or conceal unethical practices or procedures in your relationship with other individuals or organizations.
7. Disclose to no one but proper authorities any evidence of conduct or practice revealed in medical reports or observed that indicates possible violation of established rules and regulations of the employer or professional practice.
8. Safeguard the public and the profession by reporting to the Ethics Committee any breach of this Code of Ethics by fellow members of the profession.
9. Preserve the confidential nature of professional determinations made by official committees of health and health-service organizations.
10. Accept compensation only in accordance with services actually performed or negotiated with the health institution.
11. Cooperate with other health professions and organizations to promote the quality of health programs and advancement of medical care, ensuring respect and consideration for the responsibility and the dignity of medical and other health professions.
12. Strive to increase the profession's body of systematic knowledge and individual competency through continued self-improvement and application of current advancements in the conduct of medical record practices.
13. Participate in developing and strengthening professional manpower and appropriately represent the profession in public.
14. Discharge honorably the responsibilities of any Association position to which appointed or elected.
15. Represent truthfully and accurately professional credentials, education, and experience in any official transaction or notice, including other positions and duality of interests.

American Medical Record Association 1977.

Ethical obligations are central to the professional's responsibility, regardless of the employment site or the method of collection, storage, and security of health information. Health information ethical and professional values are based on obligations to the patient, the healthcare team, the employer, the interests of the public, and oneself, one's peers, and one's professional associations (Harman 1999).

Based on an analysis of the AHIMA Code of Ethics for 1957, 1977, 1988, 1998, and 2004, the following themes and values were identified (Harman and Mullen 2006).

Obligations to the Patient and the Healthcare Team

With regard to the patient and the healthcare team, the HIM professional is obligated to:

- *Protect health, medical, genetic, social, personal, financial, and adoption information*: Clinical information (for example, diagnoses, procedures, pharmaceutical dosages, or genetic risk factors) must be protected as well as behavioral information (for example, use of drugs or alcohol, high-risk hobbies, sexual habits). It is increasingly important to protect genetic and social information so that patients will not be vulnerable to the risks of discrimination.

Figure 11.3. 1988 AMRA bylaws and Code of Ethics

The medical record professional abides by a set of ethical principles developed to safeguard the public and to contribute within the scope of the profession to quality and efficiency in health care. This code of ethics, adopted by the members of the American Medical Record Association, defines the standards of behavior which promote ethical conduct.

1. The Medical Record Professional demonstrates behavior that reflects integrity, supports objectivity, and fosters trust in professional activities.
2. The Medical Record Professional respects the dignity of each human being.
3. The Medical Record Professional strives to improve personal competence and quality of services.
4. The Medical Record Professional represents truthfully and accurately professional credentials, education, and experience.
5. The Medical Record Professional refuses to participate in illegal or unethical acts and also refuses to conceal the illegal, incompetent, or unethical acts of others.
6. The Medical Record Professional protects the confidentiality of primary and secondary health records as mandated by law, professional standards, and the employer's policies.
7. The Medical Record Professional promotes to others the tenets of confidentiality.
8. The Medical Record Professional adheres to pertinent laws and regulations while advocating changes which serve the best interest of the public.
9. The Medical Record Professional encourages appropriate use of health record information and advocates policies and systems that advance the management of health records and health information.
10. The Medical Record Professional recognizes and supports the association's mission.

American Medical Record Association 1988.

Figure 11.4. 1998 AHIMA bylaws and Code of Ethics

AHIMA's Mission

The American Health Information Management Association is committed to the quality of health information for the benefit of patients, providers, and other users of clinical data. Our professional organization:

- Provides leadership in HIM education and professional development
- Sets and promotes professional practice standards
- Advocates patient privacy rights and confidentiality of health information
- Influences public and private policies including educating the public regarding health information
- Advances health information technologies

Guiding Principles

We are committed to the:

- Creation and utilization of systems and standards to ensure quality health information
- Achievement of member excellence
- Development of a supportive environment and provision of the resources to advance the profession
- Provision of the highest-quality service to members and health care information users
- Investigation and application of new technology to advance the management of health information

We value:

- The balance of patients' privacy rights and confidentiality of health information with legitimate uses of data
- The quality of health information as evidenced by its integrity, accuracy, consistency, reliability, and validity
- The quality of health information as evidenced by its impact on the quality of health care delivery

This Code of Ethics sets forth ethical principles for the HIM profession. Members of this profession are responsible for maintaining and promoting ethical practices. This Code of Ethics, adopted by the American Health Information Management Association, shall be binding on health information management professionals who are members of the Association and all individuals who hold an AHIMA credential.

I. Health information management professionals respect the rights and dignity of all individuals.

II. Health information management professionals comply with all laws, regulations, and standards governing the practice of health information management.

III. Health information management professionals strive for professional excellence through self-assessment and continuing education.

IV. Health information management professionals truthfully and accurately represent their professional credentials, education, and experience.

V. Health information management professionals adhere to the vision, mission, and values of the Association.

VI. Health information management professionals promote and protect the confidentiality and security of health records and health information.

VII. Health information management professionals strive to provide accurate and timely information.

VIII. Health information management professionals promote high standards for health information management practice, education, and research.

IX. Health information management professionals act with integrity and avoid conflicts of interest in the performance of their professional and AHIMA responsibilities.

American Health Information Management Association 1998.

- *Protect confidential information*: This involves ensuring that the information collected and documented in the patient information system is protected by all members of the healthcare team and by anyone with access to the information. This responsibility also includes protection of verbal communications on behalf of a patient and can involve communication with those in the legal profession, the media, or others who seek patient information.
- *Provide service to those who seek access to patient information*: Individuals who may request access to patient information include healthcare providers; insurance, research, or pharmaceutical companies; government agencies; and employers. Disclosure and redisclosure policies and procedures must be developed and followed. The HIM professional must ensure the honor of the profession before personal advantage and the health and welfare of patients before all other interests. He or she also must balance the many competing interests of all the stakeholders who want patient information, avoiding conflicts of interest.
- *Preserve and secure health information*: This includes obligations to maintain and protect the medium that stores the information, such as paper documentation, computer, microfilm, CD-ROM, and the EHR, including the protection of all databases and detailed secondary records and registries.
- *Promote the quality and advancement of healthcare*: As an important member of the healthcare team, the HIM professional provides valuable expertise in the collection of health information that will help providers improve the quality of care they deliver. The HIM professional should develop expertise in clinical medicine, pharmacology, biostatistics, and quality improvement methodologies so as to interpret clinical information and support research.
- *Function within the scope of responsibility and restrain from passing clinical judgment*: Sometimes healthcare data may indicate a problem with a provider of care, the treatment of a diagnosis, or some other problem. The HIM professional's obligation is to provide the data; however, the obligation of evaluating the significance of the data rests with those held accountable for the review of the data. The HIM professional should repeatedly, consistently, and accurately report the results of studies, regardless of the volatility of the research outcomes.

Obligations to the Employer

With regard to the employer, the HIM professional is obligated to:

- *Demonstrate loyalty to the employer*: The HIM professional can do this by respecting and following the policies, rules, and regulations of employment unless they are illegal or unethical.
- *Protect committee deliberations*: The HIM professional should be as committed to protecting committee con-

versations and decisions as he or she is to protecting patient information. Examples of such committees include medical staff and employer committees.

- *Comply with all laws, regulations, and policies that govern the health information system*: The HIM professional should keep up-to-date with state and federal laws, accrediting and licensing standards, employer policies and procedures, and any other standards that affect the health information system.
- *Recognize both the authority and the power associated with the job responsibility*. The HIM professional is the expert on privacy and confidentiality and must be present at strategic meetings with clinical providers, administrative staff, and financial and operations management personnel to be sure that HIM expertise is presented and understood. Unethical behaviors would be to hide and not be at the top-level strategic meetings, wait for the outcomes, and then complain about the decisions that were made, such as inappropriately releasing information to an employer. For example, the HIM professional cannot remain quiet and let others have the power to decide what information is released, what software is installed, or other important HIM decisions. HIM professionals do have both the power and the authority to say, "No, that is not acceptable" or "This is appropriate action."
- *Accept compensation only in relationship to work responsibilities*. Increasingly, there are groups or individuals who could benefit by having access to patient information and are willing to pay for such information. Access to databases with patient information on certain diagnoses such as AIDS or cancer could be sought by employers, commercial vendors, or others. The HIM professional must avoid the temptation to accept money for disclosing patient information or proprietary vendor secrets.

Obligations to the Public

With regard to the public interest, the HIM professional is obligated to:

- *Advocate change when patterns or system problems are not in the best interests of the patients*. The HIM professional should be a change agent and lead initiatives to change laws, rules, and regulations that do not ensure the integrity of patient information, including the protection of privacy and confidentiality. Moreover, the HIM professional should be proactive about protecting patients, the healthcare team, the organization, the professional association, peers, and himself or herself. State and national policy and legislative advocacy activities support this ethical obligation.
- *Report violations of practice standards to the proper authorities*. The HIM professional should not share information learned at work with family or friends or discuss such information in public places. The HIM professional should report the results of audits to the proper authorities only and bring potential or actual problems to the attention of those individuals responsible for the delivery and assessment of care and services.
- *Promote interdisciplinary cooperation and collaboration*. As an important member of the healthcare team, the HIM professional should work with others to analyze and address health information issues, facilitate conflict resolution, and recognize the expertise and dignity of his or her fellow team members.

Obligations to Self, Peers, and Professional Associations

With regard to self, peers, and professional associations, the HIM professional is obligated to:

- *Be honest about degrees, credentials, and work experiences*. The HIM professional should only report an acquired degree (such as a BS or MS) or successfully earned credentials (such as an RHIA or a CCS). Work experiences must be reported accurately and honestly.
- *Bring honor to oneself, one's peers, and one's profession*. This obligation refers to personal competency and professional behavior (for example, at professional meetings). The HIM professional should try to ensure that peers and colleagues are proud to have him or her on the health information team.
- *Commit to continuing education and lifelong learning*. The HIM professional's education should not stop when he or she has earned a degree or a credential. Rather, the HIM professional should continue to attend educational sessions to keep abreast of changing laws, rules, and regulations that affect the health information system. The HIM professional should be a lifelong learner and contribute to improving the quality of healthcare service delivery. HIM professionals can keep their credentials by meeting the ongoing certification requirements of AHIMA. Maintaining competency through self-improvement is an important directive that ensures the continuance of the profession.
- *Strengthen health information professional membership*. This obligation includes belonging to professional associations, actively participating on committees, making presentations, writing for publications, and encouraging others to seek health information management as a career.
- *Represent the health information profession to the public*. The HIM professional has a responsibility to advocate for the public interest in areas related to the principles and values of HIM practice. For example, HIM professionals serve an important role when advocating for needed legislation to protect privacy and confidentiality, educational manpower funding, or appropriate EHR applications.
- *Promote and participate in health information research*. For example, when problems are discovered with the

health information system, the HIM professional should conduct studies to clarify their sources and potential solutions.

Ethical Responsibilities of the HIM Professional

In general, the HIM professional's primary responsibilities include those related to designing and implementing a system to ensure the completeness, accuracy, and timeliness of health information. In support of these responsibilities, the HIM professional is accountable for complying with laws, rules, regulations, standards, and policies from many sources, including the government, accreditation and licensure organizations, and the healthcare facility. Some of the HIM professional's core ethical responsibilities include the following (Harman 2006):

- Protecting patient privacy and confidential information (Rinehart-Thompson and Harman 2006)
- Making appropriate decisions regarding the selection and use of clinical diagnostic and procedural codes (Schraffenberger and Scichilone 2006)
- Developing policies and procedures that ensure coding accuracy that supports clinical care and research and meets the requirements for reimbursement, while avoiding fraud and abuse violations (Rinehart-Thompson 2006)
- Reporting quality review outcomes honestly and accurately, even when the results might create conflict for an individual or an institution (Spath 2006)
- Ensuring that research and decision support systems are reliable (Johns and Hardin 2006)
- Releasing accurate information for public health purposes for patients with communicable diseases, such as AIDS or venereal disease, and assisting with the complexities of information management in the context of bioterrorism and the threat or reality of global diseases, such as smallpox or avian flu (Neuberger 2006)
- Supporting managed care systems by providing accurate, reliable information about patients and consumers, clinicians, healthcare organizations, and patterns of care, with special care devoted to issues related to access to information (Schick 2006)
- Facilitating the exchange of information for patients, families, and providers of care, especially for those affected by chronic and terminal illness, that ensure patient autonomy and beneficence (Tischler 2006)
- Ensuring that the EHR meets the standards of privacy and security according to HIPAA and other federal and state laws (Hanken and Murphy 2006), the standards of information security (Czirr et al. 2006), and software development (Fenton 2006)
- Ensuring that clinical data repositories, data marts, data warehouses, and EHRs meet the standards of the best practices of health information and database management (Lee et al. 2006)
- Participating in the development of integrated delivery systems so that patients can move across the continuum of care and the right information can be provided to the right people at the right time (Olson and Grant 2006)
- Working in the context of e-health technologies that allow consumers, patients, and caregivers to search for health information and advice, create and maintain personal health records, and conduct virtual consultations with their care providers (Baur and Deering 2006)
- Ensuring that health information technology systems, including EHRs, electronic prescribing, bedside bar coding, computerized provider order entry (CPOE), and clinical decision support systems reduce errors and improve quality (Bloomrosen 2006)
- Managing the protection of sensitive information, including genetic information (Fuller and Hudson 2006); drug, alcohol, sexual, and behavioral information (Randolph and Rinehart-Thompson 2006); and adoption information (Jones 2006)
- Developing moral awareness and nurturing an ethical environment in the context of managing a health information system (Flite and Laquer 2006)
- Serving as entrepreneur and advocate for patients, the healthcare team, and others who have interests in the health information system (Gardenier 2006; Helbig 2006)
- Working with vendors in the development of business relationships that ensure ethical processes when selecting and communicating with vendors, managing vendor relationships, and dealing with the contract negotiation process (Olenik 2006)

Ethical Issues Related to Medical identity Theft

Medical identity theft is an emerging ethical issue and has become the latest information crime. It is relatively easy to do, the stakes are high, the financial temptations are huge, it is difficult to detect and there are virtually no protections for the patient or providers that are victimized, at the present time. What is it, who commits the crime, what protections can be put into place, and what HIM advocacy roles are needed? (AHIMA e-HIM Work Group on Medical Identity Theft 2008; Nicholas et al 2008).

> Medical identity theft occurs when someone uses a person's name and sometimes other parts of their identity–such as insurance information or Social Security Number—without the victim's knowledge or consent to obtain medical services or goods, or when someone uses the person's identity to obtain money by falsifying claims for medical services and falsifying Medicare records to support those claims. (World Privacy Forum 2006b, 16)

Medical identity theft is committed by family, friends and acquaintances, and strangers who steal someone's identity in order to obtain medical care, services, or equipment, either because they do not have medical care or their insurance does not cover the needed services. Medical identity theft creates an ethical dilemma for the healthcare system because those involved can be working within the healthcare delivery system, including doctors, nurses, administrative staff, and health information and billing employees. The World Privacy Forum (2006b, 14) notes that:

> All levels of the medical system may be involved in medical identity theft. Doctors, clinics, billing specialists, nurses and other members of the medical profession have taken part in this crime, as have criminals who work in administrative positions inside the healthcare system to collect information and to carry out their crimes.

There was one case in California in which it was determined that medical record and billing employees had copied the identity information for cash for as little as $100 (FTC 2000). Those who commit the crime can earn money by using the patient information fraudulently. Medical information systems have multiple access points across the continuum of the healthcare system, making it almost impossible to detect and correct fraud. Medical identify theft deserves the attention of the HIM professional because the central problem is falsification of medical documentation that could adversely affect patient safety. Inaccurate information, such as an incorrect blood type or inaccurate documentation of prescriptions can kill patients (World Privacy Forum 2006b; Weaver, 2000); Office of Inspector General 2005; *United States v. Sample* 2000). Also, the "real" patients can be denied needed equipment (wheelchairs or walkers, and the like) because their records show that they have already received the equipment, when, in fact, the fraudulent user of their health information received the equipment.

The National Health Information Network (NHIN) could exacerbate the ease of committing this crime. Electronic systems with multiple centralized and decentralized databases could facilitate both the commission and hiding of this crime. Increasingly, physicians are becoming victims of this crime, with their name and license numbers stolen; and their signatures forged for writing prescriptions and documentation that will help criminals bill for services never rendered to patients.

HIPAA provides some modicum of protection but cannot begin to truly protect patient information or patients from being harmed. The problem becomes almost unsolvable in the context of secondary releases of false information for insurance, the increasing number of integrated systems and the development of medical clearinghouses. HIM professionals are in a strong position to be advocates on behalf of patients who are victimized by this crime. In addition, it places an obligation on the profession to be diligent in hiring practices, especially with the employees that report directly to HIM professionals. Once hired, the employees must have ongoing educational sessions on the importance of ethical behavior.

The Patient's Perspective

Many patients have been victimized by medical identity theft and the overwhelming reality is that there are few who can assist them in resolving the problem, as opposed to those who are victimized by financial identity theft. There are inadequate resources and knowledge in the private sector (police departments, insurance companies, bankers, and the like) as well as the lack of laws specific to medical identity theft. There have been preliminary protective and corrective recommendations for patients that have been initiated by the Federal Trade Commission (2005) and the Government Accountability Office (2005). Where are the HIM professionals in the context of this ethical problem?

The HIM Professional's Perspective

Because of the unique aspects of this crime, HIM professionals must be vigilant in the case of medical identity theft and work with the "real" patient to confirm and correct inaccurate information. If there is no previous medical record, there must be a way to identify the record as being fraudulent and refuse further release of the information, something easier said than done. HIM professionals can exacerbate the problem by refusing to work with the "real" patient. Does the HIM professional have the time, resources, and expertise to substantiate valid identification? The HIM professional must seek assistance in this process, if necessary, rather than just sending the patient away. Legal counsel should be sought.

Once information is in a patient's medical record, it is difficult to amend or remove that information. HIM professionals cannot ignore the false documentation in the medical records and information systems or the problems of duplicating these false entries in multiple databases as a result of secondary data uses. The Code of Ethics requires attestation as to the accuracy and validity of the data.

Patients need to be able to access and amend their medical records, if fraud has occurred. As patients maintain their own personal health record (PHR), they will become more aware of the fraud. They are in the best position to know that the documentation belongs to someone else, based on a review of medical or financial reports (AHIMA PHR n.d.; World Privacy Forum 2006a).

Even HIPAA, which was designed prior to this latest information crime, does not give the patient the right to request and assure the necessary amendment in all records. Covered entities are not required to account for disclosures related to treatment, payment, or healthcare. AHIMA (2006), as part of the 2006 State of HIPAA Compliance Survey noted:

> As in previous years, the accounting for disclosures requirement is reported to be a difficult one and is most often mentioned as needed modification. AHIMA and other groups have sought a recommendation for such an amendment from the National Committee on Vital and Health Statistics and the Office for Civil Rights, but at this time no amendment is expected in the near future.

Given this, HIM professionals should work toward the solution that all HIM systems should track all disclosures, even if not required by HIPAA and there should be guaranteed protection of all information and an accounting of all disclosures. Information security systems must account for protection of the information and audit trails that identify both internal and external disclosures to prevent fraud, rather than allow the EHR to exacerbate the problem (Sparrow 2000).

The health information system is extremely complex. Data can be entered manually, electronically, through PDAs, through wireless systems, or from laptops. Information systems cross geographical boundaries and utilize many different software and hardware applications for patient care and research. The AHIMA Code of Ethics requires that we protect the information across this continuum. The adage a few years ago was "follow the money." Today, the mantra must be "follow the information."

What can HIM professionals do as part of advocacy roles?

- Facilitate the patient's ability to review and correct errors in their medical records (not just the entries with which they disagree but those that are due to fraud and do not belong to their medical or treatment history). This information might also be in the pharmaceutical information system or within the insurance agency database.
- Prevent discrimination. Not only can medical errors affecting patient safety occur with medical identity theft, but there can also be discrimination in the life and health insurance systems. Do not obstruct patients' ability to review their records; we need to pay attention to their pleas, if they think that they are victims of medical identity theft. Make sure that patients have the right to amend their documentation and to assure systems that will facilitate this process.
- Reconsider the importance of analysis. The entire medical record was previously analyzed for accuracy and the medical record analyst could learn to identify falsification of information. Now, analysis often is limited to discharge summaries, operative reports, and other critical documents. Does the organization have systems in place, within the context of the EHR, that will prevent medical identity theft?
- Consider improving the HIPAA rules and regulations related to the accounting of disclosures to include problems related to internal participants.
- Participate in HIM research studies that will help identify occurrences and sources of medical identity theft.
- Conduct needed risk assessments as the NHIN becomes more of a reality—the electronic health record (EHR), can make this crime easier. Document and quantify this problem. Improper access to information and disclosures of false information could increase in the future as a result of the EHR.
- Build interdisciplinary collaborative teams to conduct this research, including healthcare providers, HIM professionals, privacy and security experts, legal representatives (both prosecution and defense), ethicists, HIPAA, identify theft and fraud experts, and patients who have been victimized.
- Design systems that can assess employees' integrity and accountability. Make sure the healthcare team and employees that work on behalf of patients respect the importance and sacredness of the information in a patient's medical records. Give them an understanding of the importance of ethics so that they will avoid the temptation of taking money for the information in the system. Ensure that there are no pressures on employees that will tempt them to participate in the fraud.
- Assure that colleagues understand and value the HIM Code of Ethics, which sets forth values and ethical principles and offers ethical guidelines to which professionals aspire and by which their actions can be judged. A code is important in helping guide the decision-making process and can be referenced by individuals, agencies, organizations, and bodies (such as licensing and regulatory boards, insurance providers, courts of law, agency boards of directors, government agencies, and other professional groups) (AHIMA Code of Ethics 2004).
- Consider establishing policies so that patients who are victim of medical identity fraud do not have to pay for the costs of duplicating their files. A 2006 AHIMA survey found that 63 percent of providers charge patients for copies and these costs can be up to $5 per page (although $1 is more common) (AHIMA 2006). Increasingly, healthcare facilities have abandoned the practice of charging patients for copies of their medical information, based on a rationale that it belongs to them and providing copies is an important customer service.

When HIM professionals think about identity, they typically think about the person and the story in an individual medical record. Emerging technologies are changing perceptions of a person's identity—the sum of our genetic and health information. HIM professionals are being challenged to understand and deal with issues that they have never faced before; and they must stay abreast of new and evolving issues that deal with identity. HIM professionals have ethical obligations to prevent problems with medical identity theft and to report those who participate in this crime. HIM professionalism and the Code of Ethics will help with emerging issues, now and in the future.

Ethical Issues Related to Documentation and Privacy

Just a few decades ago, only a few people created documentation in patient health records and still fewer wanted access to patient information after the episode of care was completed. In today's healthcare system, many providers document their decision-making process and patient outcomes in the health information system and many more people want access to that information. The HIM professional plays a critical role in developing policies and procedures to ensure the integrity of patient information, including appropriate and authorized access.

In addition to writing policies and procedures to ensure compliance with federal and state laws, accrediting and licensing agencies, and the bylaws of the healthcare facility, the HIM professional can serve many functions that support the integrity of data and the protection of privacy. As a member of the HIM team, the HIM professional can design and deliver educational sessions to the healthcare team to make them aware of the documentation and access rules and regulations. Sometimes educational sessions address the issue of avoiding participation in fraudulent or retrospective documentation practices. Retrospective documentation practices are those where healthcare providers add documentation after care has been given for the purpose of increasing reimbursement or avoiding a medical legal action.

Unacceptable documentation practices include backdating progress notes or other documentation in the patient's record and changing the documentation to reflect the known outcomes of care (versus what was done at the time of the actual care). It is the HIM professional's responsibility to work with others to ensure that patient documentation is accurate, timely, and created by authorized parties. The professional Code of Ethics requires the HIM professional to assure accurate and timely documentation.

Ethical Issues Related to Release of Information

Three primary ethical problems are pertinent to the release of information (ROI):

- Violations of the need-to-know principle
- Misuse of blanket authorizations
- Violations of privacy that occur as a result of secondary release of information procedures

In the past, the standard for ROI was the need to know. If an insurance company had a patient request to pay for surgery, the request was sent to the healthcare facility and the HIM professional carefully examined it for legitimacy. He or she would:

- Compare the patient's signature to the one collected upon admission to the facility
- Check the date to ensure that the request was dated after the occurrence so that the patient was aware of what was being authorized and released
- Verify the insurance company as the one belonging to the patient
- Review the request for what was wanted and whether the requestor was entitled to the information

The HIM professional then reviewed the documentation and provided the information requested. For example, the admission and discharge dates, the diagnoses of cholecystitis and cholelithiasis, and the surgical procedure of cholecystectomy were provided to the insurance company so that the bill could be paid.

Today, the process of abstracting needed information is virtually nonexistent, except for disability cases, and documentation is copied above and beyond the criterion of the **need-to-know principle**. For example, in response to the request to verify an admission for a cholecystectomy, the history and physical, the operative report, the discharge summary, and the laboratory report could be copied. That documentation could reveal social habits, genetic risks, and family history of disease that have nothing to do with the surgery. Patient privacy could be violated as a result of the release of the information through subsequent discrimination by insurers.

Another common ethical problem is misuse of **blanket authorizations**. Patients often sign a blanket authorization, which authorizes the release of information from that point forward, without understanding the implications. The requestor of the information then could use the authorization to receive health information for many years. The problem with the use of blanket authorizations is that there is no way for the patient to know that the information is being accessed. Patients cannot authorize the release of information in 2003 for diagnoses or care that has not yet been provided. For example, by 2009, the patient might have AIDS or cancer and might not want this information released.

A third problem is **secondary release of information** to others by the authorized recipient to an unauthorized party. This problem has increased in frequency since the computerization of health information. A legitimate request might be processed to pay for an insurance claim, but adequate safety and protections may not be in place for the information after it has been released. The initial requestor then could forward the information to others without patient authorization. The HIM professional cannot merely think about ROI within the context of the single request. The responsibility to "follow the information" is much more serious today than it was a few years ago. Does the HIM professional know who gains access to the information after it is released to an authorized requestor? If not, he or she may be contributing to the violations of patient privacy and a subsequent instance of discrimination by employers or insurance companies based on the information that was released.

Patients have increasingly expressed concerns about the use of blanket authorizations and secondary ROI by the initial requestor or receiving party. They fear that more information is being given out than is necessary and that they do not know about the many people and agencies that are gaining access to this information.

HIPAA has been designed to address several issues related to patient privacy, including a return to the need-to-know principle. The HIM professional needs to participate in the development of computerized systems that can replicate the original human decisions regarding ROI to release what is needed but not more. Although it is easier to just photocopy the information, the HIM professional needs to carefully consider the implications of doing this within the context of patient privacy. This situation has created an opportunity for HIM professionals to participate with other HIM professionals in efforts to correct these problems.

Because the HIM professional works in many employment sites throughout the healthcare delivery system, the ethical obligations extend into a variety of areas, as noted above. In fulfilling the responsibilities of the position, the HIM professional must apply ethical values when making decisions wherever he or she is positioned within the organization.

Check Your Understanding 11.1

Instructions: On a separate piece of paper, match the HIM professional's obligations to the following groups with the professional values expressed in AHIMA's Code of Ethics (appendix B).

a. Patients and the healthcare team
b. Employer
c. Public interest
d. Oneself and one's peers and professional associations

1. ___ Accept compensation only in relationship to responsibilities
2. ___ Advocate change
3. ___ Preserve and secure health information
4. ___ Be honest
5. ___ Commit to continuing education and lifelong learning
6. ___ Promote interdisciplinary cooperation and collaboration
7. ___ Promote and participate in research
8. ___ Demonstrate loyalty to employer
9. ___ Discharge association duties honorably
10. ___ Protect committee deliberations
11. ___ Stay within the scope of responsibility and restrain from passing clinical judgment
12. ___ Bring honor to self, peers, and profession
13. ___ Protect medical and social information
14. ___ Promote the quality and advancement of healthcare
15. ___ Represent the profession to the public
16. ___ Comply with laws, regulations, and policies
17. ___ Report violations of practice standards to the proper authorities
18. ___ Refuse to participate in or conceal unethical practices
19. ___ Provide service
20. ___ Strengthen professional membership
21. ___ Recognize authority and power
22. ___ Promote confidentiality

Ethical Decision-Making Matrix

HIM professionals must factor several criteria into their decision making, as illustrated in figure 11.5. These include, but are not limited to:

- *Cost*: Can the facility and the health information system afford the improvement in the system?
- *Technological feasibility*: Will the technological application provide accurate and reliable information for the decision-making process?

Figure 11.5. Ethical decision-making matrix

ETHICAL PROBLEM		
Steps	**Information**	
1. What is the question?		
2. What are the facts?	**KNOWN**	**TO BE GATHERED**
3. What are the values? Examine the shared and competing values, obligations, and interests in order to fully understand the complexity of the ethical problem(s).	**Patient:** **HIM Professional:** **Healthcare professionals:** **Administrators:** **Society:** **Other, as appropriate:**	
4. What are my options?		
5. What should I do?		
6. What justifies my choice?	***JUSTIFIED***	***NOT JUSTIFIED***
7. What can I do to prevent this ethical problem?		

Source: Harman 2006.

- *Federal and state laws*: Are there federal or state laws that must be considered before a change is made in the system?
- *Medical staff bylaws*: Are there rules or regulations unique to the facility that require or prohibit a decision?
- *Accreditation and licensing standards*: Which agencies have standards that are important to the decision being made? Do the standards allow or prohibit a certain action?
- *Employer policies, rules, or regulations*: Does the facility have policies, rules, or regulations that require or prohibit a decision?

Although these criteria must be assessed in the decision-making process, they cannot be used alone. Virtually every decision the HIM professional makes also must be based on ethical principles and professional values.

Ethicists provide assistance in this process. Glover (2006, 35, 38, 50) has proposed a seven-step process to guide ethical decision making. When faced with an ethical issue, the HIM professional should ask and answer all of the following questions. The questions represent the steps in the decision-making process.

1. What is the ethical question?
2. What facts do you know and what do you need to find out?
3. Who are the different stakeholders, what values are at stake, and what are the different obligations and interests of each of the stakeholders?

4. What options for action do you have?
5. What decision should you make and what core HIM values are at stake?
6. What justifies the choice and what are the value-based reasons to support the decision? What choice or choices cannot be justified?
7. What prevention options can be put into place so that this issue will not come up again?

When a decision must be made about an issue and only one choice is identified, the decision most likely will be based on an individual's narrow moral perspective of right or wrong. If it is an ethical problem, the decision makers must take into account the perspectives of competing stakeholders and their values. Decisions made without this model will not benefit from an ethical decision-making process that considers multiple options.

Check Your Understanding 11.2

Instructions: Using a, b, c, and so on, rearrange the steps of the ethical decision-making process in the correct order on a separate piece of paper.

1. ___ What decision should you make and what core HIM values are at stake?
2. ___ What facts do you know and what do you need to find out?
3. ___ What options for action do you have?
4. ___ What is the ethical question?
5. ___ What justifies the choice and what are the reasons to support the decision, based on values? What choice or choices cannot be justified?
6. ___ What prevention options can be put into place so that this issue will not happen again?
7. ___ Who are the different stakeholders, what values are at stake, and what are the different obligations and interests of each of the stakeholders?

Core Health Information Ethical Problems

Several problems face HIM professionals in today's complex world, including issues related to the use of information; computerized health information systems; the management of sensitive health information; process and strategies for decision making; and the HIM roles as manager, entrepreneur, and advocate. The business relationships with vendors can also create ethical tensions. There are issues raised because of the uses of information, including clinical code selection and use, quality review, research and decision support, public health, managed care, and clinical care (Harman 2006).

Ethical Issues Related to Coding

In the past, coding was done almost exclusively for clinical studies and quality assurance review processes. Although codes were provided for reimbursement purposes, the healthcare facility was reimbursed on the basis of usual, customary, and reasonable costs. The codes that were assigned became the basis of retrieval for clinical studies, the reimbursement system, and quality outcome reporting systems. Over time, healthcare facilities have continued to use the coding systems to retrieve information in health records for clinical and administrative studies, but they also have begun to use the codes for reimbursement purposes. After the codes became the basis for reimbursement, there were inherent incentives to code so that the greatest amount of reimbursement could be given. This placed the importance of accurate coding at the forefront of the ethical issues facing HIM professionals.

Ethical problems have risen in the past few years as a result of the direct linkage between coding and payments for care. Increased pressure has been put on HIM professionals who are coding to transmit inaccurate information, creating problems that are legal and ethical in nature. Problems include pressure to code inappropriate levels of service, discovering misrepresentation in physician documentation, miscoding to avoid conflicts, discovering miscoding by other staff, lacking the tools and educational background to code accurately, and being required by employers to engage in negligent coding practices (Schraffenberger and Scichilone 2006). In response to these issues, AHIMA passed standards that specifically address coding issues (refer to figure 11.4).

Failure to heed the complex rules of coding for reimbursement can lead to problems with compliance and with fraud and abuse for the HIM professional. If the HIM professional fails to establish adequate monitoring systems for accurate code assignment or submits a false claim, the consequences could include penalties such as fees and prison. The HIM professional must know the laws and the penalties for failure to follow the laws and, most importantly, have the expertise to develop preventive programs to ensure that the false claim is a nonoccurrence. Fraud and abuse problems include documentation that does not justify the billed procedure, acceptance of money for information, fraudulent retrospective documentation on the part of the provider to avoid suspension, and code assignment without physician documentation. An important role for the HIM professional is that of compliance officer (Rinehart-Thompson 2006).

Ethical Issues Related to Quality Management, Decision Support, Public Health, Managed Care, and Clinical Care

Many factors contribute to the ethical problems faced by quality management professionals, including the rising cost of healthcare, limited resources, and concerns with patient safety. Some of the common quality outcome problems include (Spath 2006):

- Inaccurate performance data that are inappropriately shared with the public
- Negative care outcomes, such as infections, that occur in the course of providing home healthcare
- Failure to check a physician's licensure status

- Incomplete health records hidden in preparation for accreditation or licensure surveys
- Patterns of inappropriate healthcare

The pressures to conceal information, discovered as an outcome of quality reporting systems and that could be potentially harmful to an employer and problems with patient safety require constant diligence and the courage to repeatedly report the truth. Research and decision support responsibilities include ensuring data integrity and confidentiality, assuring compliance with human subject research protocols, and maintaining and enhancing professional competence (Johns and Hardin 2006).

Career opportunities for the HIM professional are growing in public health systems. Careers in this area require an understanding of the government's role in the collection and use of health information. The government's responsibility to protect the health of the public sometimes competes with the need to protect patient privacy, such as in the case of reporting HIV status. State and local mandatory reporting requirements exist for certain conditions, including infectious and communicable diseases. The government needs this information to monitor, investigate, and implement interventions, when necessary. Sometimes problems arise when the public's right to know or duty to one's employer conflicts with patient privacy (Neuberger 2006). The HIM professional can provide invaluable assistance with public health initiatives that will contribute to environmental and personal health. This role requires constant advocacy so that the interests of both the public and the individual patient can be served. New threats of bioterrorism and global infections, such as SARS or avian flu, pose new ethical dilemmas in the management of health information. There will need to be a balance between protecting privacy of those injured and providing information to the government and healthcare professionals so that the medical crisis can be resolved.

There are many important ethical issues faced by the HIM professional working on behalf of managed care organizations. Problems arise if high-quality information is not provided so that commitments to patients, clinicians, and communities cannot be met. As with other situations, access to information is key to the problems faced by the HIM professional as he or she helps with the organization's strategies regarding pricing, access to providers, and quality of care. Job responsibilities in this work context include providing information about provider practices, providing patient clinical and demographic information, and establishing policies and procedures that provide for patient privacy (Schick 2006).

As the baby boomers age, there is an increasing number of patients who will require information in order to make difficult end-of-life decisions. Problems dealing with aging, frailty, autonomy of those near death, physician bias and equity, treatment choices, treatment goals and beneficence, advance care planning, palliative care, and managing pain are a few of the difficult decisions that must be made, and ethical decision-making is imperative (Tischler 2006).

Ethical Issues Related to Sensitive Health Information

All health information must be protected, but additional ethical issues have emerged around the release of sensitive information such as genetic, drug, and alcohol treatment; communicable disease; and psychiatric and adoption information. At least two levels of genetic information can be reported in an information system: presence of a disease, such as cystic fibrosis, and presence of a risk of disease, such as a genetic risk for breast cancer. Various state laws govern the use and release of genetic information and the HIM professional must be aware of them. In recent years, there have been growing concerns about discrimination in employment and insurance based on the misuse of genetic information (Fuller and Hudson 2006). The Genetic Information Nondiscrimination Act of 2008 was passed in Fall 2008 (HHS 2008). This took many years to pass and Government Relations for AHIMA worked extensively to facilitate passage of this important legislation. Other federal and state laws will need to be passed in order for patients to be fully protected in the context of genetic information and this is an important first step.

According to Fuller and Hudson (2006), the HIM professional must be aware of the following issues related to genetic information:

> (1) Genetic research and testing can give researchers, clinicians, and patients a means to prevent, treat, or screen for a disease. Often, however, individuals are reluctant to participate in genetic research and testing because they believe they cannot be sure of the privacy of the genetic information that will be obtained from them and placed in their medical records or in research records.
>
> (2) Insurers and employers may seek genetic information to identify at-risk individuals and deny them employment or insurance coverage, fire them, or raise their insurance premiums. Genetic information may also be sought in custody battles or in cases of third-party liability. Even when this information is not used to discriminate, individuals may be concerned about its disclosure because of its possibility of causing psychosocial harm, such as harm to family relationships.
>
> (3) It is difficult to provide special protections for genetic information as a category because it cannot be clearly separated from other medical information. Therefore, the best way to protect genetic information is to strengthen privacy and confidentiality protections for medical information in general and to enact antidiscrimination legislation.
>
> (4) The HIPAA Privacy Rule provides a basic level of privacy and confidentiality protection for protected health information. The Privacy Rule does not preempt state laws (including genetic antidiscrimination laws) that offer a higher level of privacy protection.
>
> (5) The generation of experimental data by a research protocol is not specifically addressed by most state laws.
>
> (6) HIM professionals have the responsibility to ensure that their practices are guided by state and federal laws and regulations to protect genetic information and by the ethical imperative to protect the privacy and confidentiality of patients.

One of the most important opportunities for an HIM professional is to become involved in resolving the above-stated issues on behalf of patients and the healthcare system.

Federal and state laws also govern the use of behavioral health information and special concerns with its use. The HIM professional must respond to the government, the police, and other agencies that seek drug, alcohol, sexual, or other behavioral information (Randolph and Rinehart-Thompson 2006). The inappropriate release of information can have serious discriminatory consequences, such as:

- The police officer presents an arrest warrant to a behavioral health facility. Do you confirm that the patient has been treated? What are the implications for patient privacy if you do?
- A patient with schizophrenia and assaultive behavior is about to be released from a healthcare facility. Do you have a responsibility to inform the girlfriend who has been assaulted in the past? What are your obligations to protect the privacy of the patient being released?

The ROI dealing with substance abuse, sexually transmitted diseases, and mental health require extra caution on the part of the HIM professional when developing release policies and procedures. There are often competing interests between public safety and patient privacy. How does one deal with law enforcement officials within this context? Federal and state legislation can provide some guidance, but often additional legal counsel must be sought.

The release of adoption information is another example of an issue in which laws are necessary, but insufficient, for solving the problems. Decisions cannot be made merely by following the legal rules. More and more often, access to adoption information is being requested by adopted children seeking their biological parents, and vice versa. Biological parents often look for children who could be organ donors or for other assistance. This issue reflects the complexities of releasing genetic and behavioral information because, increasingly, "self" is defined within genetic parameters and biological heritage is becoming more important in defining self. Access to adoption information raises the larger issue of familial access to information, regardless of adoptive status. If biological children can gain access to health information for their biological parent(s), why can't all children gain access to familial information? (Jones 2006). HIM professionals must be alert to these special needs and refrain from processing requests for adoption information without carefully considering the risks for violations of patient privacy, discrimination, or inappropriate access.

Ethical Issues Related to Research

There are many past and present problems with research and ethics. Human subjects have been mistreated, misinformed, and harmed in recent years, even though there are ethical codes, national and international agreements and agencies that review research proposals, with a focus of protecting research participants. These include the Nuremberg Code, the Helsinki Agreement (also known as the Declaration of Helsinki), the National Research Act of 1974 (Public Law 93–348), the Belmont Report, bioethics commissions, HIPAA, and IRB processes (Harman and Nielsen 2008, 341). See chapter 18 for a full discussion of the Nuremberg Code, the Declaration of Helsinki, the Belmont Report, and the IRB process.

The primary ethical principles that are engaged in research include respect for autonomy (self determination); beneficence (promoting good); nonmaleficence (do no harm); and justice (fairness) (Beauchamp and Childress 2001). The respect for autonomy requires an ability of the participant to understand and authorize the research through informed consent; beneficence means that benefit is possible; nonmaleficence means that patients will not be intentionally harmed; and justice requires fairness in the enrollment of participants (Harman and Nielsen 2008, 337).

Table 11.1 highlights some of the research projects and the ethical issues (Harman and Nielsen 2008, chapter 13).

As noted in table 11.1, mistreatment of vulnerable populations has happened too often. These populations include children; persons who are cognitively impaired, comatose, drug addicts, economically disadvantaged, elderly, institutionalized, non-English speaking employees, low literacy persons, minorities, or persons involved in illegal activities. Other groups include pregnant women, fetuses, neonates and in-vitro; prisoners and students (over the age of 18) (Harman and Nielsen 2008).

HIM professionals must be cautious when reviewing research protocols and take patient safety and protection seriously.

Ethical Issues Related to Electronic Health Record Systems

With a paper-based health record, access issues were relatively simple. Only one person at a time could access the information, and it was extremely difficult to collect and use data of an aggregate nature. With computerization, many requestors are allowed multiple, simultaneous access and it is relatively easy to share information across a continuum of care and with computerized systems well outside the boundaries of any individual care site. The advent of the electronic information system has presented complex challenges with regard to record integrity and information security, integrated linkage of information systems across a continuum of care, software development and implementation, and the protection of information in e-health systems (Harman 2006, 279–305, 403–419).

E-HIM affords information exchange that necessitate active participation on the part of HIM professionals, in both the public and private sectors. There are many ethical challenges, including developing and maintaining information and systems security, exchanging information within and across jurisdictions, executing technical and clinical services contracts, handling release of information, implementing and managing telehealth applications, maintaining and documenting compliance with HIPAA and state privacy rules, and maintaining the legal electronic medical record (Bloomrosen 2006).

As information systems became computerized and healthcare facilities began to link various health information systems, the temptation increased to sacrifice privacy and data integrity for the sake of business efficiency and timely access to information. There is an exponential increase in the risk to privacy and the protection of confidential information (Hanken and Murphy 2006). The HIM professional must do a thorough systems analysis of the independent systems and ensure that the merged systems meet the criteria of data integrity, information security, and ethical use of the information.

Information security carries additional burdens of ethical decision making. Many requestors such as insurance companies, government agencies, managed care organizations, and employers need health information to do their jobs. Unauthorized access to patient information becomes a constant challenge, given the need to balance the responsibility to protect information while giving others access to information

Table 11.1. Examples of research projects and ethical issues

Research Project	Event(s)	Ethical Issues
Jewish Chronic Disease Hospital Study	Live cancer cells were injected into patients with chronic diseases	Patients were not told about the cancer cells Consent was oral and not documented
Tuskegee Syphilis Study	African-American sharecroppers who had syphilis treatable with penicillin were not given the antibiotic, so that the natural progression of the disease could be monitored	Mistreatment of a vulnerable population Lack of informed consent Failure to treat
Willowbrook State School	Healthy children were intentionally inoculated with the hepatitis virus. Children were exposed to overcrowding, poor sanitary conditions, and physical and sexual abuse by the school's staff	Mistreatment of a vulnerable population
Holmesburg Prison Study	Pharmaceutical companies tested their products (drugs, soap, dioxin, tobacco, eye drops, psychotropic drugs, radioactive isotopes and other products) on prisoners who were paid more money than other prisoners and given special privileges	Mistreatment of a vulnerable population Lack of informed consent Long-range healthcare problems, with no compensation to the prisoners
Tearoom Trade Study	Homosexual men were misled regarding "protection" in a public restroom, license plates recorded, interviewed in homes, results published with participants able to be identified	Violation of autonomy, informed consent and the right to privacy Unacceptable deception The researcher acting as an "insider" misleading participants
Deceptive Marketing of Vioxx	Salesmen lied to physicians about cardiovascular risk Widespread advertisements in public domain to convince people to use Physicians who noted problems were offered positions of "consultant" which silenced them	Dishonesty to physicians and patients Motivation of profit more important than patient safety Company suppressed research results which indicated risks
Jesse Gelsinger Case	18-year-old with inherited metabolic disorder (managed with medication), enrolled in a gene therapy trial and died in 5 days	Risks not full explained (two patients already had serious side effects) Consent did not indicate that monkeys had died Jesse substituted for another participant who had dropped out Lab result, which would have excluded patient, did not Researchers had financial conflict of interest

Sources: Information for Jewish Chronic Disease Hospital Study, Willowbrook State School, Tuskegee Syphillis Study, and Tearoom Trade Study retrieved from http://www.humanresearch.msu.edu/participants/history.htm; Jesse Gelsinger Case was retrieved from http://www.circare.org/index.htm; Deceptive Marketing of Vioxx retrieved from http://www.ahrp.org/ethical/EthicalViolations.php; Holmsburg Prison Study retrieved from Homblum 2007, 1999.

within the context of job responsibilities. Internal requestors include, but are not limited to, patients, providers of care, financial agencies, and administrative and clinical personnel such as quality or risk management professionals. External stakeholders include other healthcare facilities, research institutes, accrediting and licensing agencies, and fiscal intermediaries (Czirr et al. 2006). The HIM professional must develop a comprehensive information security policy, including detailed audit trails of access and actions. Moreover, the policy must be monitored with consequences for violations. Increasingly, HIM professionals are being designated as the information security officers within a healthcare facility or healthcare system.

Development and implementation of software systems are inherently interdisciplinary in nature, and the process requires collaboration and conflict resolution. The physicians, the HIM professional, the information technology experts, and administrative personnel often have competing interests. The HIM professional is often in the position of carefully delineating the details of competing interests so that appropriate decisions can be made. This role of being able to see the systems' implications within the context of protecting privacy is invaluable (Fenton 2006). The HIM professional's role as interdisciplinary facilitator is crucial, which is why educational sessions on organizational development, team building, and conflict resolution are often key components of the HIM professional's continuing education program.

The expertise of the HIM professional includes data resource management because computerized information systems generate data repositories and huge amounts of health information of interest to many people. A primary focus of the HIPAA legislation is to ensure that systems are developed that protect privacy, threats of violations of information integrity, and unauthorized access. Data resource managers must have both HIM technical expertise and information technology expertise so that they can design and monitor systems that ensure data security and patient privacy. These functions are accomplished through the use of many decision-making tools, including databases, clinical data repositories, and data-mining tools, among others. The primary ethical dilemma involves balancing the competing interests of access and appropriate use of information (Lee et al. 2006).

As HIM systems became computerized, the capacity for developing integrated delivery systems across a continuum of care became technologically possible. HIM systems relied on paper-based systems in which each facility had its own health record and the only way to transmit information from one site of care to another was through copying procedures. Now, information can follow the patient and be instantly and simultaneously shared and made available as needed. This is both good news and bad. The segregated, independent systems had some inherent protections of privacy. The integrated computerized systems require HIM professional diligence to ensure protection of information and access to only those who have a need to know. Information management policies, rules, and procedures for individual healthcare entities must be compatible with those of other facilities, and often the issues of competing interests can create major ethical conflicts as to the appropriate action.

The master patient index presents a major problem because there is often no consistency among facilities in terms of how and what information is collected. If the information is to follow the patient, the individual systems must be accurate and compatible. Data quality issues include accuracy, comprehensiveness, consistency, currency, granularity, precision, relevancy, and timeliness (AHIMA 1998). Negotiation and problem-solving skills are an inherent requirement for the HIM professional working in an integrated delivery system (Olson and Grant 2006). The HIM professional must lead the organization in addressing data quality issues associated with implementing integrated information systems.

Last, but not least, the HIM professional's ethical expertise is needed in the burgeoning e-health systems. Some of the ethical issues the HIM professional faces in the work environment include the quality of online information, privacy protections, and equity and privacy. The issue of equity is important to e-health systems because not everyone has access to the information on the electronic systems. There cannot be equity when one patient instead of another can easily gain access to invaluable and voluminous information about symptoms, diseases, pharmaceutical interventions, and treatment options. Privacy can be an issue when patients reveal sensitive information to a Web site and have no idea what will happen to the information or who will have access to it. The opportunities for the HIM professional are unlimited given the problems of consumer access to information, quality of information provided, and access to information. This nontraditional advocacy role for HIM professionals is important in this emerging technological advancement (Baur and Deering 2006).

Roles of Manager, Entrepreneur, and Advocate

The HIM professional deals with daily complexities that require the need for understanding ethics. Problems such as late and absent employees, temptations at conventions and meetings, employees who should be terminated, and poor work performance are a few of the many dilemmas facing the busy HIM manager (Flite and Laquer 2006). As an entrepreneur, the HIM professional must understand the complexities of business practices intersecting with professional values and ethical principles. Common ethical dilemmas occur when establishing contracts, clarifying the roles of intrapreneur and entrepreneur, or acting as an independent contractor. Difficulties may arise when consulting for competitors (having access to sensitive information that might be of value to the competition), dealing with advertising, confronting unrealistic client expectations, or confusing profit versus not-for-profit motivations for decisions (Gardenier 2006).

HIM professionals have always been advocates for patients and providers, and the advocate role is important in today's healthcare delivery system. For the HIM professional, advocacy "is ethics in action: choosing to take a stand for and speak out for the rights or needs of a person, group, organization, or community" (Helbig 2006). For example, HIM problems that require advocacy include:

- Protecting the privacy of prominent citizens because it is more tempting to want access to the information of prominent citizens, such as elected officials and famous actors
- Demonstrating compassion for drug-dependent peers
- Protecting the work environment for HIM employees
- Ensuring that consent forms are properly designed so that patients understand what they are signing and so that patient information is protected from unauthorized secondary disclosure

The advocacy role requires HIM expertise, ethical expertise, and an understanding of the patient's bill of rights (Helbig 2006).

Business relationships with vendors also pose ethical dilemmas. What issues are raised when vendors are also friends? What is the appropriate use of gifts? Should some vendors be "preferred" when dealing with requests for proposals? How can you assure ethical dealings when negotiating contracts? (Olenik 2006).

Check Your Understanding 11.3

Instructions: On a separate piece of paper, match the ethical principle with its definition.

1. ___ Autonomy
2. ___ Beneficence
3. ___ Nonmaleficence
4. ___ Justice
5. ___ Moral values
6. ___ Ethical decisions
7. ___ Privacy
8. ___ Confidentiality
9. ___ Data security
10. ___ HIPAA

a. Right or wrong
b. Reasoned discourse
c. Right to be let alone
d. Promote good
e. Self-determination
f. Healthcare communication
g. Do no harm
h. Fairness in applying rules
i. Establishes privacy and security standards
j. Electronic protection of information

Real-World Case

Carol Wright is an outstanding manager. She has worked for C&S Pharmaceuticals for 15 years. She has received five promotions and is currently responsible for abstracting and quality operations. Carol has been quick to identify personnel problems and provides educational and instructional support to her staff.

Carol supervises Joan, who is often absent or late for work. When she does come to work she makes many mistakes, but she always seems to meet work standards prior to her performance reviews. Various forms of motivation, education, and administrative support have been offered to Joan in the past. This week, Joan failed to show up for three days without notifying the office. The company policy states that if an employee does not show up for work for three consecutive days without notifying the office by the end of the third business day (5 p.m.), the employee's employment shall be terminated.

On the third day, some managers may be anxiously waiting for the employee to call and explain the absence, but this was not the case with Carol. Carol had recognized that this employee was nonproductive, noncompliant, and met the criteria for job abandonment. Carol was prepared to terminate Joan, because she repeatedly demonstrated a clear disregard for the policy related to reporting to work. Carol no longer had any patience for Joan's behaviors. Carol was confident that the employee was not going to comply with the policy and that this would be an easy termination. She completed the termination paperwork based on job abandonment at 3 p.m. and left it on her desk for the 5 p.m. submission to the human resources department. At 4:30 p.m., Carol's secretary told her that Joan was on the telephone, but Carol did not accept the call. The paperwork was sent to the human resources department at 5 p.m. and Joan's employment was terminated the next day (Harman 2006, 510).

Summary

Ethical decision making is one of the health information professional's most challenging and rewarding job responsibilities. It requires courage because there will always be people who choose not tell the truth or do the right thing. HIM professionals must discuss these issues with their peer professionals and seek the advice of the professional association when necessary.

The HIM professional's job responsibilities inherently require an understanding of ethical principles, professional values and obligations, and the importance of using an ethical decision-making matrix when confronting difficult challenges at work. With this knowledge, the informed HIM professional can move from understanding problems based on a moral perspective only to understanding the importance of applying an ethical decision-making process. Ethical decision making takes practice and discussions with peers will help the HIM professional to build competency in this important area.

When making ethical decisions, the HIM professional should use the complete ethical decision-making matrix to consider all the stakeholders and their obligations and the important HIM professional values. More than one response can be given for any ethical issue as long as the complete matrix is applied. Just as there can be more than one "right" answer to a problem, there can be "wrong" answers, especially when an answer is based only on a moral value or the perspective of one individual or when the action violates ethical principles.

There will always be ongoing ethical problems, such as the protection of human subjects in research, and emerging or new ethical problems, such as medical identity theft, which require the constant diligence of the HIM professional.

Bioethical decisions involving the use of health information require action and such actions always require courage. The healthcare team, the patients, and the others who are served need to know that the HIM professional has the expertise and the courage to make appropriate ethical decisions.

References

AHIMA e-HIM Work Group on Medical Identity Theft. 2008. Practice Brief: Mitigating medical identity theft. *Journal of AHIMA* 79(7): 63–69.

Amatayakul, M.K. 2007. *Electronic Health Records: A Practical Guide for Professionals and Organizations*. 3rd ed. Chicago: AHIMA.

American Health Information Management Association. 2002. Practice brief: Consent for uses and disclosures of information. Updated from *Journal of AHIMA* 72 (5):64E–64G. http://www.ahima.org.

American Health Information Management. 2004. Code of Ethics. www.ahima.org/about/ethics.asp.

American Health Information Management Association. 2006. State of HIPAA Compliance. p.14. http://www.ahima.org/index.asp.

American Health Information Management Association. 2008 (Sept.). http://www.ahima.org/about/ethics.asp.

American Health Information Management Association. The state of HIPAA privacy and security compliance. http://www.ahima.org/emerging_issues/2006StateofHIPAACompliance.pdf.

American Health Information Management Association (n.d.). Personal Health Record (PHR). http://www.myphr.com.

Baur, C. and M.J. Deering. 2006. e-Health for consumers, patients and caregivers. Chapter 16 in *Ethical Challenges in the Management of Health Information*. 2nd ed. Edited by Harman, L.B. Sudbury, MA: Jones and Bartlett.

Beauchamp, T. and J. Childress. 2001. *Principles of Biomedical Ethics*. New York: Oxford University Press.

Bloomrosen, M. 2006. E-HIM: Information technology and information exchange. Chapter 17 in *Ethical Challenges in the Management of Health Information*. 2nd ed. Edited by Harman, L.B. Sudbury, MA: Jones and Bartlett.

Czirr, K., K. Rosendale, and E. West. 2006. Information security. Chapter 12 in *Ethical Challenges in the Management of Health Information*. 2nd ed. Edited by Harman, L.B. Sudbury, MA: Jones and Bartlett.

Department of Health and Human Services. 2003. Summary of the HIPAA Privacy Rule. *OCR Privacy Brief*. http://www.hhs.gov/ocr/privacysummary.pdf.

Department of Health and Human Services . 2008 (Oct.). Proposed Rules Genetic Information Nondiscrimination Act of 2008. *Federal Register* 73(198).

Dick, R.S., E.B. Steen, and D.E. Detmer, eds. 1997. *The Computer-Based Patient Record: An Essential Technology for Health Care*. Rev. ed. Washington, DC: National Academy Press.

Dixon, P. 2006 (May 3). Medical identity theft: The information crime that can kill you. The World Privacy Forum.

Federal Trade Commission. 2000 (Aug.18). http://www.ftc.gov/bcp/workshops/idtheft/comments/weaverlind.htm.

Federal Trade Commission. 2003 (Sept.). Identity theft survey report. http://www.consumer.gov/idetheft/pdf/synovaterreport.pdf.

Federal Trade Commission. 2005. Take charge: Fighting back against identity theft. http://www.ftc.gov/bcp/conloine/pubs/credit/idtheft.htm.

Fenton, S.H. 2006. Software development and implementation. Chapter 13 in *Ethical Challenges in the Management of Health Information*. 2nd ed. Edited by Harman, L.B. Sudbury, MA: Jones and Bartlett.

Flite, C. and S. Laquer. 2006. Management. Chapter 21 in *Ethical Challenges in the Management of Health Information*. 2nd ed. Edited by Harman, L.B. Sudbury, MA: Jones and Bartlett.

Fuller, B.P. and K.L. Hudson. 2006. Genetic information. Chapter 18 in *Ethical Challenges in the Management of Health Information*. 2nd ed. Edited by Harman, L.B. Sudbury, MA: Jones and Bartlett.

Gardenier, M. 2006. Entrepreneurship. Chapter 22 in *Ethical Challenges in the Management of Health Information*. Edited by Harman, L.B. Sudbury, MA: Jones and Bartlett.

Gellman, R. 2004 (June 23). When HIPAA meets NHII: A new dimension for privacy. Presentation to U.S. Department of Health and Human Services Data Council Privacy Committee, Washington, D.C.

Glover, J.J. 2006. Ethical decision-making guidelines and tools. Chapter 2 in *Ethical Challenges in the Management of Health Information*. 2nd ed. Edited by Harman, L.B. Sudbury, MA: Jones and Bartlett.

Government Accountability Office. 2005 (June). Identity theft rights: Some outreach efforts to promote awareness of new consumer rights are underway. GAO-05-710.

Hanken, M.A. and G. Murphy. 2006. Electronic patient record. Chapter 11 in *Ethical Challenges in the Management of Health Information*. Edited by Harman, L.B. Sudbury, MA: Jones and Bartlett.

Harman, L.B. 1999. HIM and ethics: Confronting ethical dilemmas on the job, an HIM professional's guide. *Journal of AHIMA* 71(5):45–49.

Harman, L.B. 2005. HIPAA: A few years later. *Online Journal of Issues in Nursing* 10(2). http://www.nursingworld.org/ojin/topic27/tpc27_2.htm.

Harman, L.B., ed. 2006. *Ethical Challenges in the Management of Health Information*. 2nd ed. Sudbury, MA: Jones and Bartlett.

Harman, L.B. and V.L. Mullen. 2007 (Oct.). Emerging HIM ethical issues. Presentation at AHIMA convention.

Harman, L.B. and V.L. Mullen. 2006. Professional values and the code of ethics. Chapter 1 in *Ethical Challenges in the Management of Health Information*. 2nd ed. Edited by Harman, L.B. Sudbury, MA: Jones and Bartlett.

Harman, L.B. and C.S. Nielsen. 2008. Research and ethics. In *Health Informatics Research methods: Principles and Practice*. Chicago: AHIMA.

Helbig, S. 2006. Advocate. Chapter 24 in *Ethical Challenges in the Management of Health Information*. 2nd ed. Edited by Harman, L.B. Sudbury, MA: Jones and Bartlett.

Hornblum, A.M. 1999. *Acres of skin: Human experiments at Holmesburg Prison*. New York: Routledge.

Hornblum, A.M. 2007. *Sentenced to science: One black man's story of imprisonment in America.* University Park, PA: Pennsylvania State University.

Huffman, E.K. 1972. *Manual for Medical Record Librarians.* 6th ed. Chicago: Physician's Record Company.

Hughes, G. 2002a (Nov.). Practice brief: Laws and regulations governing the disclosure of health information. Updated from *Journal of AHIMA* 72(5):64A–64C. Proprietary content from http://www.ahima.org.

Hughes, G. 2002b (Oct.). Practice brief: Required content for authorizations to disclose. Updated from *Journal of AHIMA* 72(10):72A–72D. Proprietary content from http://www.ahima.org.

Johns, M.L. 2006. Adoption information. Chapter 19 in *Ethical Challenges in the Management of Health Information.* 2nd ed. Edited by Harman, L.B. Sudbury, MA: Jones and Bartlett.

Johns, M.L. and J.M. Hardin. 2006. Research and decision support. Chapter 7 in *Ethical Challenges in the Management of Health Information.* 2nd ed. Edited by Harman, L.B. Sudbury, MA: Jones and Bartlett.

Jones, M.L. 2002. *Information Management for Health Professions.* 2nd ed. Albany, NY: Delmar.

Layman, E.J. and V.J.Watzlaf, eds. 2008. *Health informatics research methods: Principles and practice.* Chicago: AHIMA.

Lee, F.W., A.W. White, and K.A. Wager. 2006. Data resource management. Chapter 14 in *Ethical Challenges in the Management of Health Information.* 2nd ed. Edited by Harman, L.B. Sudbury, MA: Jones and Bartlett.

Long, K. 2006 (Dec. 4). The grave costs of medical identity theft. *ADVANCE*:22–23.

Maloney, A. 2008 (Feb. 11). Stop medical identity theft. *ADVANCE.* http://health-information.advanceweb.com/editorial/content.

Murphy, G., M.A. Hanken, and K.A. Waters. 1999. *Electronic Health Records: Changing the Vision.* Philadelphia: W.B. Saunders.

National Committee on Vital and Health Statistics. 2001. Information for health: A strategy for building the national health information infrastructure. http://www.aspe.hhs.gov/sp/nhii/Documents/NHIIReport2001/report11.htm.

Neuberger, B.J. 2006. Public health. Chapter 8 in *Ethical Challenges in the Management of Health Information.* 2nd ed. Edited by Harman, L.B. Sudbury, MA: Jones and Bartlett.

Nichols, C. et al. 2008. *Medical Identity Theft.* Chicago: AHIMA.

Office of Inspector General, Department of Health and Human Service, Criminal Actions. 2005 (Sept.). http://oig.hhs.gov/fraud/enforcement/criminal/05/0905.html.

Olenik, K. 2006. Vendor Relationships. Chapter 23 in *Ethical Challenges in the Management of Health Information.* 2nd ed. Edited by Harman, L.B. Sudbury, MA: Jones and Bartlett.

Olson, B. and K.G. Grant. 2006. Integrated delivery systems. Chapter 15 in *Ethical Challenges in the Management of Health Information.* 2nd ed. Edited by Harman, L.B. Sudbury, MA: Jones and Bartlett.

Randolph, S. J. and L.A. Rinehart-Thompson. 2006. Drug, alcohol, sexual, and behavioral health information. Chapter 20 in *Ethical Challenges in the Management of Health Information.* 2nd ed. Edited by Harman, L.B. Sudbury, MA: Jones and Bartlett.

Rhodes, H. 2001 (Updated). Practice Brief: Patient anonymity. *Journal of AHIMA* 72(5):64O–64R.

Rinehart-Thompson, L.A. 2006. Compliance, fraud, and abuse. Chapter 4 in *Ethical Challenges in the Management of Health Information.* 2nd ed. Edited by Harman, L.B. Sudbury, MA: Jones and Bartlett.

Rinehart-Thompson, L.A. and L.B. Harman. 2006. Privacy and confidentiality. Chapter 3 in *Ethical Challenges in the Management of Health Information.* 2nd ed. Edited by Harman, L.B. Sudbury, MA: Jones and Bartlett.

Schick, I.C. 2006. Managed care: Lessons in integration. Chapter 9 in *Ethical Challenges in the Management of Health Information.* 2nd ed. Edited by Harman, L.B. Sudbury, MA: Jones and Bartlett.

Schraffenberger, L.A. and R.A. Scichilone. 2006. Clinical code selection and use. Chapter 5 in *Ethical Challenges in the Management of Health Information.* 2nd ed. Edited by Harman, L.B. Sudbury, MA: Jones and Bartlett.

Sparrow, M. K. (2000). License to steal: How fraud bleeds America's health care system. Westview Press. chapters 5–8.

Spath, P.L. 2006. Quality review. Chapter 6 in *Ethical Challenges in the Management of Health Information.* 2nd ed. Edited by Harman, L.B. Sudbury, MA: Jones and Bartlett.

Tischler, J.F. 2006. Clinical care: End of life. Chapter 10 in *Ethical Challenges in the Management of Health Information.* 2nd ed. Edited by Harman, L.B. Sudbury, MA: Jones and Bartlett.

United States v. Sample, 213 F. 3d 1029, 2000 U.S. App.Lexis 11945. (8th Cir. 2000).

Weaver, L. 2000 (Aug. 18). Federal Trade Commission. Identity theft victim assistance workshop. http://www.ftc.gove/bcp/workshops/idtheft/comments/weaverlind.htm.

World Privacy Forum. 2006a (June 30). Access, amendment, and accounting of disclosures: FAQs for medical ID theft victims. http://www.worldprivacyforum.org/FAQ_medicalrecordprivacy.html.

World Privacy Forum. 2006b (June 5). Medical identity theft: What to do if you are a victim (or are concerned about it). http://www.worldprivacyforum.org/medidtheft_consumertips.html.

Part III

Aggregate Healthcare Data

Chapter 12
Secondary Records and Healthcare Databases

Elizabeth D. Bowman, MPA, RHIA

Learning Objectives

- Distinguish between primary and secondary data and between patient-identifiable and aggregate data
- Identify the internal and external users of secondary data
- Compare the facility-specific indexes commonly found in hospitals
- Describe the registries used in hospitals according to purpose, methods of case definition and case finding, data collection methods, reporting and follow up, and pertinent laws and regulations affecting registry operations
- Define the terms pertinent to each type of secondary record or database
- Discuss agencies for approval and education and certification for cancer, immunization, trauma, birth defects, diabetes, implant, transplant, and immunization registries
- Distinguish among healthcare databases in terms of purpose and content
- Compare manual and automated methods of data collection and vendor systems with facility-specific systems
- Assess data quality issues in secondary records
- Recognize appropriate methods for ensuring data security and the confidentiality of secondary records
- Discuss some of the other issues related to the collection and maintenance of secondary data such as transparency, ownership, and deidentification
- Identify the role of the health information management professional in creating and maintaining secondary records

Key Terms

Abbreviated Injury Scale (AIS)
Abstracting
Accession number
Accession registry
Activities of daily living
Agency for Healthcare Research and Quality (AHRQ)
Aggregate data
Autodialing system
Case definition
Case finding
Claim
Clinical trial
Collaborative Stage Data Set
Computer virus
Credentialing
Data confidentiality
Data security
Database
Deidentification
Demographic information
Disease index
Disease registry
Edit
Encryption
Facility-based registry
Food and Drug Administration (FDA)
Health services research
Healthcare Cost and Utilization Project (HCUP)
Healthcare Integrity and Protection Data Bank (HIPDB)
Histocompatibility
Incidence
Index
Injury Severity Score (ISS)
Interrater reliability
Master population/patient index (MPI)
Medical Literature, Analysis, and Retrieval System Online (MEDLINE)
Medicare Provider Analysis and Review (MEDPAR)
National Health Care Survey
National Practitioner Data Bank (NPDB)
National Vaccine Advisory Committee (NVAC)
Operation index
Patient-identifiable data
Physician index
Population-based registry
Primary data source
Protocol
Public health
Secondary data source
Staging system
Transparency
Traumatic injury
Unified Medical Language System (UMLS)
Vital statistics

As a rich source of data about an individual patient, the health record fulfills the uses of patient care and reimbursement for individual encounters. However, it is not easy to see trends in a population of patients by looking at individual records. For this purpose, data must be extracted from individual records and entered into specialized **databases** that support analysis across individual records. These data may be used in a facility-specific or **population-based registry** for research and improvement in patient care. In addition, they may be reported to the state and become part of state- and federal-level databases that are used to set health policy and improve healthcare.

The health information management (HIM) professional can play a variety of roles in managing secondary records and databases. He or she plays a key role in helping to set up databases. This task includes determining the content of the database or registry and ensuring compliance with the laws, regulations, and accrediting standards that affect the content and use of the registry or database. All data elements included in the database or registry must be defined in a data dictionary. In this role, the HIM professional may oversee the completeness and accuracy of the data abstracted for inclusion in the database or registry.

This chapter explains the difference between primary and secondary data sources and their uses. It also offers an in-depth look at various types of secondary databases, including **indexes** and registries, and their functions. Finally, the chapter discusses how secondary databases are processed and maintained.

Primary versus Secondary Data Sources and Databases

The health record is considered a **primary data source** because it contains information about a patient that has been documented by the professionals who provided care or services to that patient. Data taken from the primary health record and entered into registries and databases are considered a **secondary data source**.

Data also are categorized as either **patient-identifiable data** or **aggregate data**. The health record consists entirely of patient-identifiable data. In other words, every fact recorded in the record relates to a particular patient identified by name. Secondary data also may be patient identifiable. In some instances, data are entered into a database, along with information such as the patient's name, maintained in an identifiable form. Registries are an example of patient-identifiable data on groups of patients.

More often, however, secondary data are considered aggregate data. Aggregate data include data on groups of people or patients without identifying any particular patient individually. Examples of aggregate data are statistics on the average length of stay (ALOS) for patients discharged within a particular diagnosis-related group (DRG).

Purposes and Users of Secondary Data Sources

Secondary data sources consist of facility-specific indexes; registries, either facility or population based; and other healthcare databases. Healthcare organizations maintain those indexes, registries, and databases that are relevant to their specific operations. States as well as the federal government also maintain databases to assess the health and wellness of their populations.

Secondary data sources provide information that is not easily available by looking at individual health records. For example, if the HIM director doing a research study wanted to find the health records of 25 patients who had the principal diagnosis of myocardial infarction, he or she would have to look at numerous individual records to locate the number needed. This would be a time-consuming and laborious project. With a diagnosis index, the task would involve simply looking at the list of diagnoses in numerical order and selecting those with the appropriate diagnosis code for myocardial infarction for inclusion in the study.

Data extracted from health records and entered into disease-oriented databases can, for example, help researchers determine the effectiveness of alternate treatment methods. They also can quickly demonstrate survival rates at different stages of disease.

Internal users of secondary data are individuals located within the healthcare facility. For example, internal users include medical staff and administrative and management staff. Secondary data enable these users to identify patterns and trends that are helpful in patient care, long-range planning, budgeting, and benchmarking with other facilities.

External users of patient data are individuals and institutions outside the facility. Examples of external users are state data banks and federal agencies. States have laws that mandate cases of patients with diseases such as tuberculosis and AIDS be reported to the state department of health. Moreover, the federal government collects data from the states on vital events such as births and deaths.

The secondary data provided to external users is generally aggregate data and not patient-identifiable data. Thus, these data can be used as needed without risking breaches of confidentiality.

Check Your Understanding 12.1

Instructions: Answer the following questions on a separate piece of paper.

1. What is the difference between a primary data source and a secondary data source?
2. What is the difference between patient-identifiable data and aggregate data?
3. Why are secondary data sources developed?
4. What are the differences between internal users and external users of secondary data sources?

Facility-Specific Indexes

The secondary data sources that have been in existence the longest are the indexes that have been developed within facilities to meet their individual needs. These indexes enable health records to be located by diagnosis, procedure, or physician. Prior to extensive computerization in healthcare, these indexes were kept on cards. They now are usually computerized reports available from data included in databases routinely maintained in the healthcare facility. Most acute care facilities maintain indexes described in the following subsections.

Master Population/Patient Index

The **master population/patient index** (MPI), which is sometimes called the master person index, contains patient-identifiable data such as name, address, date of birth, dates of hospitalizations or encounters, name of attending physician, and health record number. Because health records are filed numerically in most facilities, the MPI is an important source of patient health record numbers. These numbers enable the facility to quickly retrieve health information for specific patients.

Hospitals with a unit numbering system also depend on the MPI to determine whether a patient has been seen in the facility before and therefore has an existing medical record number. Having this information in the MPI avoids issuance of duplicate record numbers. Most of the information in the MPI is entered into the facility database at the time of the admission/preadmission or registration process.

Disease and Operation Indexes

In an acute care setting, the **disease index** is a listing in diagnosis code number order for patients discharged from the facility during a particular time period. Each patient's diagnoses are converted from a verbal description to a numerical code, usually using a coding system such as the International Classification of Diseases, Ninth Revision, Clinical Modification (ICD-9-CM). In most cases, patient diagnosis codes are entered into the facility health information system as part of the discharge processing of the patient health record. The index always includes the patient's health record number as well as the diagnosis codes so that records can be retrieved by diagnosis. Because each patient is listed with the health record number, the disease index is considered patient-identifiable data. The disease index also may include other information such as the attending physician's name or the date of discharge. In nonacute settings, the disease index might be generated to reflect patients currently receiving services in the facility.

The **operation index** is similar to the disease index except that it is arranged in numerical order by the patient's procedure code(s) using ICD-9-CM or Current Procedural Terminology (CPT) codes. The other information listed in the operation index is generally the same as that listed in the disease index except that the surgeon may be listed in addition to, or instead of, the attending physician.

In many cases, facilities no longer have an actual listing for the diagnosis and operation indexes. Instead, they query the HIS system utilizing the ICD-9-CM code for the condition or operation needed.

Physician Index

The **physician index** is a listing of cases in order by physician name or physician identification number. It also includes the patient's health record number and may include other information, such as date of discharge. The physician index enables users to retrieve information about a particular physician, including the number of cases seen during a particular time period. As with the disease and operation indexes, facilities generally query the HIS system to obtain physician data.

Check Your Understanding 12.2

Instructions: Answer the following questions on a separate piece of paper.

1. How do HIM departments use facility-specific indexes?
2. What is the purpose of the master population/patient index? What types of information does it include?
3. What is the purpose of disease and operations indexes? What types of information do they include?
4. What is the purpose of the physician index? What types of information does it include?

Registries

Disease registries are collections of secondary data related to patients with a specific diagnosis, condition, or procedure. Registries are different from indexes in that they contain more extensive data. Index reports can usually be produced using data from the facility's existing databases. Registries often require more extensive data from the patient record. Each registry must define the cases that are to be included in it. This process is called **case definition**. In a trauma registry, for example, the case definition might be all patients admitted with a diagnosis falling into ICD-9-CM code numbers 800 through 959, the trauma diagnosis codes.

After the cases to be included have been determined through the case definition process described earlier, the next step in data acquisition is usually **case finding**. Case finding includes the methods used to identify the patients who have been seen and treated in the facility for the particular disease or condition of interest to the registry. After cases have been identified, extensive information is abstracted from the paper-based patient record into the registry database or fed from other databases and entered into the registry database.

The sole purpose of some registries is to collect data from the patient health record and to make them available to users. Other registries take further steps to enter additional information in the registry database, such as routine follow-up of patients at specified intervals. Follow-up might include rate and duration of survival and quality of life issues over time.

Cancer Registries

Cancer registries have a long history in healthcare. According to the National Cancer Registrars Association (NCRA), the first hospital registry was founded in 1926, at Yale-New Haven Hospital. It has long been recognized that aggregate clinical information is needed to improve the diagnosis and treatment of cancer. Cancer registries were developed as an organized method to collect these data. The registry may be *facility based* (located within a facility such as a hospital or clinic) or *population based* (gathering information from more than one facility within a geographic area such as a state or region).

The data from **facility-based registries** are used to provide information for the improved understanding of cancer, including its causes and methods of diagnosis and treatment. The data collected also may provide comparisons in survival rates and quality of life for patients with different treatments and at different stages of cancer at the time of diagnosis. In population-based registries, emphasis is on identifying trends and changes in the **incidence** (new cases) of cancer within the area covered by the registry.

The Cancer Registries Amendment Act of 1992 provided funding for a national program of cancer registries with population-based registries in each state. According to the law, these registries were mandated to collect data such as:

- Demographic information about each case of cancer
- Information on the industrial or occupational history of the individuals with the cancers (to the extent such information is available from the same record)
- Administrative information, including date of diagnosis and source of information
- Pathological data characterizing the cancer, including site, stage of neoplasm, incidence, and type of treatment

Case Definition and Case Finding in the Cancer Registry

As defined previously, case definition is the process of deciding what cases should be entered in the registry. In a cancer registry, for example, all cancer cases except certain skin cancers might meet the definition for the cases to be included. Skin cancers such as basal cell carcinomas might be excluded because they do not metastasize and do not require the follow-up necessary for other cancers included in the registry. Data on benign and borderline brain/central nervous system tumors also must be collected by the National Program of Cancer Registries (CDC 2008).

In the facility-based cancer registry, the first step is case finding. One way to find cases is through the discharge process in the HIM department. During the discharge procedure, coders or discharge analysts can easily earmark cases of patients with cancer for inclusion in the registry. Another case-finding method is to use the facility-specific disease indexes or the HIS system to identify patients with diagnoses of cancer. Additional methods may include reviews of pathology reports and lists of patients receiving radiation therapy or other cancer treatments to determine cases that have not been found by other methods.

Population-based registries usually depend on hospitals, physician offices, radiation facilities, ambulatory surgery centers (ASCs), and pathology laboratories to identify and report cases to the central registry. The population-based registry has a responsibility to ensure that all cases of cancer in the target area have been identified and reported to the central registry.

Data Collection for the Cancer Registry

Data collection methods vary between facility-based registries and population-based registries. When a case is first entered in the registry, an **accession number** is assigned. This number consists of the first digits of the year the patient was first seen at the facility, with the remaining digits assigned sequentially throughout the year. The first case in 2009, for example, might be 09-0001. The accession number may be assigned manually or by the automated cancer database used by the organization. An **accession registry** of all cases can be kept manually or provided as a report by the database software. This listing of patients in accession number order provides a way to monitor that all cases have been entered into the registry.

In a facility-based registry, data are initially obtained by reviewing and collecting them from the patient's health record. In addition to **demographic information** (such as name, health record number, address), patient data in a registry include:

- Type and site of the cancer
- Diagnostic methodologies
- Treatment methodologies
- Stage at the time of diagnosis

The stage provides information on the size and extent of spread of the tumor throughout the body. Historically, several different **staging systems** have been used. The American Joint Committee on Cancer (AJCC) has worked, through its Collaborative Stage Task Force, with other organizations with staging systems to develop a standardized data set, the **Collaborative Stage Data Set**, which uses computer algorithms to describe how far a cancer has spread (AJCC 2008).

After the initial information is collected at the patient's first encounter, information in the registry is updated periodically through the follow-up process discussed in the following section.

Frequently, the population-based registry only collects information when the patient is diagnosed. Sometimes, however, it receives follow-up information from its reporting entities. These entities usually submit the information to the central registry electronically.

Reporting and Follow-up for Cancer Registry Data

Formal reporting of cancer registry data is done through an annual report. The annual report includes aggregate data on the number of cases in the past year by site and type of cancer. It also may include information on patients by gender, age, and ethnic group. Often a particular site or type of cancer is featured with more in-depth data provided.

Other reports are provided as needed. Data from the cancer registry are frequently used in the quality assessment process for a facility as well as in research. Data on survival rates by site of cancer and methods of treatment, for example, would be helpful in researching the most effective treatment for a type of cancer.

Another activity of the cancer registry is patient follow-up. On an annual basis, the registry attempts to obtain information about each patient in the registry, including whether he or she is still alive, status of the cancer, and treatment received during the period. Various methods are used to obtain this information. For a facility-based registry, the facility's patient health records may be checked for return hospitalizations or visits for treatment. The patient's physician also may be contacted to determine whether the patient is still living and to obtain information about the cancer.

When patient status cannot be determined through these methods, an attempt may be made to contact the patient directly, using information in the registry such as address and telephone number of the patient and other contacts. In addition, contact information from the patient's health record may be used to request information from the patient's relatives. Other methods used include reading newspaper obituaries for deaths and using the Internet to locate patients through sites such as the Social Security Death Index and online telephone books. The information obtained through follow-up is important to allow the registry to develop statistics on survival rates for particular cancers and different treatment methodologies.

Population-based registries do not always include follow-up information on the patients in their databases. They may, however, receive the information from the reporting entities such as hospitals, physician offices, and other organizations providing follow-up care.

Standards and Agencies in the Approval Processes

Several organizations have developed standards or approval processes for cancer programs. (See table 12.1.) The American College of Surgeons (ACS) Commission on Cancer has an approval process for cancer programs. One of the requirements of this process is the existence of a cancer registry as part of the program. The ACS standards are published in the Cancer Program Standards (ACS 2008a). When the ACS surveys the cancer program, part of the survey process is a review of cancer registry activities.

The North American Association of Central Cancer Registries (NAACCR) has a certification program for state population-based registries. Certification is based on the quality of data collected and reported by the state registry. The NAACCR has developed standards for data quality and format and works with other cancer organizations to align their various standards sets.

The Centers for Disease Control and Prevention (CDC) also has national standards regarding completeness, timeliness, and quality of cancer registry data from state registries through the National Program of Cancer Registries (NPCR). The NPCR was developed as a result of the Cancer Registries Amendment Act of 1992. The CDC collects data from the NPCR state registries.

Table 12.1. Standard-setting or approval agencies for cancer registries

Agency	Type of Registry
American College of Surgeons (ACS)	Facility based
North American Association of Central Cancer Registries (NAACCR)	Population based
Centers for Disease Control and Prevention	Population based

Education and Certification for Cancer Registrars

Traditionally, cancer registrars have been trained through on-the-job training and professional workshops and seminars. The National Cancer Registrars Association (NCRA) has worked with colleges to develop formal educational programs for cancer registrars either through a certificate or associate degree program. A cancer registrar may become certified as a certified cancer registrar (CTR) by passing an examination provided by the National Board for Certification of Registrars (NBCR). Eligibility requirements for the certification examination include a combination of experience and education (NCRA 2008).

Trauma Registries

Trauma registries maintain databases on patients with severe traumatic injuries. A **traumatic injury** is a wound or other injury caused by an external physical force such as an automobile accident, a shooting, a stabbing, or a fall. Examples of such injuries would include fractures, burns, and lacerations. Information collected by the trauma registry may be used for performance improvement and research in the area of trauma care. Trauma registries are usually facility based but may, in some cases, include data for a region or state.

Case Definition and Case Finding for Trauma Registries

The case definition for the trauma registry varies from registry to registry but frequently involves the inclusion of cases with diagnoses from ICD-9-CM sections 800 through 959, the trauma diagnosis codes. To find cases with trauma diagnoses, the trauma registrar may query the HIS system looking for cases with codes in this section of ICD-9-CM. In addition, the registrar may look at deaths in services with frequent trauma diagnoses such as trauma, neurosurgery, orthopedics, and plastic surgery to find additional cases.

Data Collection for Trauma Registries

After the cases have been identified, information is abstracted from the health records of the injured patients and entered into the trauma registry database. The data elements collected in the abstracting process vary from registry to registry but usually include:

- Demographic information on the patient
- Information on the injury

- Care the patient received before hospitalization (such as care at another transferring hospital or care from an emergency medical technician who provided care at the scene of the accident or in transport from the accident site to the hospital)
- Status of the patient at the time of admission
- Patient's course in the hospital
- ICD-9-CM diagnosis and procedure codes
- Abbreviated injury scale (AIS)
- Injury severity score (ISS)

The **abbreviated injury scale** (AIS) reflects the nature of the injury and the severity (threat to life) by body system. It may be assigned manually by the registrar or generated as part of the database from data entered by the registrar. The **injury severity score** (ISS) is an overall severity measurement calculated from the AIS scores for the three most severe injuries of the patient (Trauma.org 2008).

Reporting and Follow-up for Trauma Registries

Reporting varies among trauma registries. An annual report is often developed to show the activity of the trauma registry. Other reports may be generated as part of the performance improvement process, such as self-extubation (patients removing their own tubes) and delays in abdominal surgery or patient complications. Some hospitals report data to the National Trauma Data Bank, a large database of aggregate data on trauma cases (ACS 2008b). An example of the use of such population data is the number of head injuries from motorcycle accidents in a state to encourage passage of a helmet law.

Trauma registries may or may not do follow-up of the patients entered in the registry. When follow-up is done, emphasis is frequently on the patient's quality of life after a period of time. Unlike cancer, where physician follow-up is crucial to detect recurrence, many traumatic injuries do not require continued patient care over time. Thus, follow-up is often not given the emphasis it receives in cancer registries.

Standards and Agencies for Approval of Trauma Registries

The American College of Surgeons certifies levels I, II, III, and IV trauma centers. As part of its certification requirements, the ACS states that the level I trauma center, the type of center receiving the most serious cases and providing the highest level of trauma service, must have a trauma registry (ACS 2008b).

Education and Certification of Trauma Registrars

Trauma registrars may be registered health information technicians (RHITs), registered health information administrators (RHIAs), registered nurses (RNs), licensed practical nurses (LPNs), emergency medical technicians (EMTs), or other health professionals. Training for trauma registrars is accomplished through workshops and on-the-job training. The American Trauma Society (ATS), for example, provides core and advanced workshops for trauma registrars. It also provides a certification examination for trauma registrars through its Registrar Certification Board. Certified trauma registrars have earned the certified specialist in trauma registry (CSTR) credential.

Birth Defects Registries

Birth defects registries collect information on newborns with birth defects. Often population based, these registries serve a variety of purposes. For example, they provide information on the incidence of birth defects to study causes and prevention of birth defects, to monitor trends in birth defects to improve medical care for children with birth defects, and to target interventions for preventable birth defects such as folic acid to prevent neural tube defects.

In some cases, registries have been developed after specific events have put a spotlight on birth defects. After the initial Persian Gulf War, for example, some feared an increased incidence of birth defects among the children of Gulf War veterans. The Department of Defense subsequently started a birth defects registry to collect data on the children of these veterans to determine whether any pattern could be detected.

Case Definition and Case Finding for Birth Defects Registries

Birth defects registries use a variety of criteria to determine which cases to include in the registry. Some registries limit cases to those birth defects found within the first year of life. Others include those children with a major defect that occurred in the first year of life and was discovered within the first five years of life. Still other registries include only children who were liveborn or stillborn babies with discernible birth defects.

Cases may be detected in a variety of ways, including review of disease indexes, labor and delivery logs, pathology and autopsy reports, ultrasound reports, and cytogenetic reports. In addition to information from hospitals and physicians, cases may be identified from rehabilitation centers and children's hospitals and from vital records such as birth, death, and fetal death certificates.

Data Collection for Birth Defects Registries

A variety of information is abstracted for the birth defects registry, including:

- Demographics
- Codes for diagnoses
- Birth weight
- Status at birth, including liveborn, stillborn, aborted
- Autopsy
- Cytogenetics results
- Whether the infant was a single or multiple birth
- Mother's use of alcohol, tobacco, or illicit drugs
- Father's use of drugs and alcohol
- Family history of birth defects

Diabetes Registries

Diabetes registries collect data about patients with diabetes for the purpose of assistance in managing care as well as for research. Patients whose diabetes is not kept under good control frequently have numerous complications. The diabetes registry can keep up with whether the patient has been seen by a physician in an effort to prevent complications.

Case Definition and Case Finding for Diabetes Registries

There are two types of diabetes mellitus: insulin-dependent diabetes (type I) and non-insulin-dependent diabetes (type II). Registries sometimes limit their cases by type of diabetes. In some instances, there may be further definition by age. Some diabetes registries, for example, only include children with diabetes.

Case finding includes the review of health records of patients with diabetes. Other case-finding methods include the reviews of the following types of information:

- ICD-9-CM diagnostic codes
- Billing data
- Medication lists
- Physician identification
- Health plans

Although facility-based registries for cancer and trauma are usually hospital based, facility-based diabetes registries are often maintained by physician offices and clinics because they are the main location for diabetes care. Thus, the data about the patient to be entered into the registry are available at these sites rather than at the hospital. Patient health records of diabetes patients in the physician practice may be identified through ICD-9-CM code numbers for diabetes (code numbers in category 250), billing data for diabetes-related services, medication lists for patients on diabetic medications, or identification of patients as the physician sees them.

Health plans also are interested in optimal care for their enrollees because diabetes can have serious complications when not managed correctly. They may provide information to the office or clinic on diabetic enrollees in the health plan.

Data Collection for Diabetes Registries

In addition to demographic information about the cases, other data collected may include laboratory values such as HbA1c. This test is used to determine the patient's blood glucose level for a period of approximately 60 days prior to the time of the test. Moreover, facility registries may track patient visits to follow up with patients who have not been seen in the past year.

Reporting and Follow-up for Diabetes Registries

A variety of reports may be developed from the diabetes registry. For facility-based registries, one report may keep up with laboratory monitoring of the patient's diabetes to allow intensive intervention with patients whose diabetes is not well controlled. Another report might be of patients who have not been tested within a year or who have not had a primary care provider visit within a year.

Population-based diabetes registries might provide reporting on the incidence of diabetes for the geographic area covered by the registry. Registry data also may be used to investigate risk factors for diabetes.

Follow-up is aimed primarily at ensuring that the diabetic is seen by the physician at appropriate intervals to prevent complications.

Implant Registries

An implant is a material or substance inserted in the body, such as breast implants, heart valves, and pacemakers. Implant registries have been developed for the purpose of tracking the performance of implants, including complications, deaths, and defects resulting from implants, as well as longevity.

In the recent past, the safety of implants has been questioned in a number of highly publicized cases. In some cases, implant registries have been developed in response to such events. For example, there have been questions about the safety of silicone breast implants and temporomandibular joint implants. When such cases arise, it has often been difficult to ensure that all patients with the implant have been notified of safety questions.

A number of federal laws have been enacted to regulate medical devices, including implants. These devices were first covered under Section 15 of the Food, Drug, and Cosmetic Act. The Safe Medical Devices Act of 1990 was passed and then amended through the Medical Device Amendments of 1992. These acts required facilities to report deaths and severe complications thought to be due to a device to the manufacturer and the **Food and Drug Administration** (FDA) through its MedWatch reporting system. Implant registries can help in complying with the legal requirement for reporting for the sample of facilities required to report.

Case Definition and Case Finding for Implant Registries

Implant registries sometimes include all types of implants but often are restricted to a specific type of implant such as cochlear, saline breast, or temporomandibular joint.

Data Collection for Implant Registries

Demographic data on patients receiving implants are included in the registry. The FDA requires that all reportable events involving medical devices include information on the following (FDA 2008):

- User facility report number
- Name and address of the device manufacturer
- Device brand name and common name
- Product model, catalog, and serial and lot number
- Brief description of the event reported to the manufacturer or the FDA

Thus, these data items also should be included in the implant registry to facilitate reporting.

Reporting and Follow-up for Implant Registries

Data from the implant registry may be used to report to the FDA and the manufacturer when devices cause death or serious illness or injury. Follow-up is important to track the performance of the implant. When patients are tracked through the registry, they can be easily notified of product failures, recalls, or upgrades

Transplant Registries

Transplant registries may have varied purposes. Some organ transplant registries maintain databases of patients who need organs. When an organ becomes available, an equitable way then may be used to allocate the organ to the patient with the highest priority. In other cases, the purpose of the registry is to provide a database of potential donors for transplants using live donors, such as bone marrow transplants. Posttransplant information also is kept on organ recipients and donors.

Because transplant registries are used to try to match donor organs with recipients, they are often national or even international in scope. Examples of national registries include the UNet of the United Network for Organ Sharing (UNOS) and the registry of the National Marrow Donor Program (NMDP).

Data collected in the transplant registry also may be used for research, policy analysis, and quality control projects.

Case Definition and Case Finding for Transplant Registries

Physicians identify patients needing transplants. Information about the patient is provided to the registry. When an organ becomes available, information about it is matched with potential donors. For donor registries, donors are solicited through community information efforts similar to those carried out by blood banks to encourage blood donations.

Data Collection for Transplant Registries

The type of information collected varies according to the type of registry. Pretransplant data about the recipient include:

- Demographics
- Patient's diagnosis
- Patient's status codes regarding medical urgency
- Patient's functional status
- Whether the patient is on life support
- Previous transplantations
- **Histocompatibility**—"a state of immunologic similarity (or identity) that permits successful homograft transplantation." (*Stedman's Online Dictionary*)

Information on donors varies according to whether the donor is living. For organs harvested from patients who have died, information is collected on:

- Cause and circumstances of the death
- Organ procurement and consent process
- Medications the donor was taking
- Other donor history

For a living donor, information includes:

- Relationship of the donor to the recipient (if any)
- Clinical information
- Information on organ recovery
- Histocompatibility

Reporting and Follow-up for Transplant Registries

Reporting includes information on donors and recipients as well as survival rates, length of time on the waiting list for an organ, and death rates. Follow-up information is collected for recipients as well as living donors. For living donors, the information collected might include complications of the procedure and length of stay (LOS) in the hospital. Follow-up information about recipients includes information on status at the time of follow-up (for example, living, dead, lost to follow-up), functional status, graft status, and treatment, such as immunosuppressive drugs. Follow-up is carried out at intervals throughout the first year after the transplant and then annually after that.

Immunization Registries

Children are supposed to receive a large number of immunizations during the first six years of life. These immunizations are so important that the federal government has set several objectives related to immunizations in Healthy People 2010, a set of health goals for the nation. These include increasing the proportion of children and adolescents who are fully immunized (Objective 14–24) and increasing the proportion of children in population-based immunization registries (Objective 14–26).

Immunization registries usually have the purpose of increasing the number of infants and children who receive proper immunizations at the proper intervals. To accomplish this goal, they collect information within a particular geographic area about children and their immunization status. They also help by maintaining a central source of information for a particular child's immunization history, even when the child has received immunizations from a variety of providers. This central location for immunization data also relieves parents of the responsibility of maintaining immunization records for their own children.

Case Definition and Case Finding for Immunization Registries

All children in the population area served by the registry should be included in the registry. Some registries limit their inclusion of patients to those seen at public clinics, excluding those seen exclusively by private practitioners. Although children are usually targeted in immunization registries, some registries do include information on adults for influenza and pneumonia vaccines.

Children are often entered in the registry at birth. Registry personnel may review birth and death certificates and adoption records to determine what children to include and what children to exclude because they died after birth. In some cases, children are entered electronically through a connection with an electronic birth record system. Accuracy and completeness of the data in the registry are dependent on the thoroughness of the submitters in reporting immunizations.

Data Collection for Immunization Registries

The National Immunization Program at the CDC has worked with the **National Vaccine Advisory Committee** (NVAC) to develop a set of core immunization data elements to be included in all immunization registries. The data elements are divided into required and optional. The required data elements include (CDC 2008a):

- Patient's name (first, middle, and last)
- Patient's birth date
- Patient's sex
- Patient's birth state and country
- Mother's name (first, middle, last, and maiden)
- Vaccine type
- Vaccine manufacturer
- Vaccination date
- Vaccine lot number

Other items may be included, as needed, by the individual registry.

Reporting and Follow-up for Immunization Registries

Because the purpose of the immunization registry is to improve the number of children who receive immunizations in a timely manner, reporting should emphasize immunization rates, especially changes in rates in target areas. Immunization registries also can provide automatic reporting of children's immunization to schools to check the immunization status of their students.

Follow-up is directed toward reminding parents that it is time for immunizations as well as seeing whether the parents do not bring the child in for the immunization after a reminder. Reminders may include a letter or postcard or telephone calls. **Autodialing systems** may be used to call parents and deliver a prerecorded reminder. Moreover, registries must decide how frequently to follow up with parents who do not bring their children for immunization. Maintaining up-to-date addresses and telephone numbers is an important factor in providing follow-up. Registries may allow parents to opt out of the registry if they prefer not to be reminded.

Standards and Agencies for Approval of Immunization Registries

The CDC, through its National Immunization Program, provides funding for some population-based immunization registries. The CDC has identified 12 minimum functional standards for population-based immunization registries (CDC 2008a), including:

- Electronically store data on all NVAC-approved core data elements
- Establish a registry record within six weeks of birth for each newborn child born in the catchment area
- Enable access to and retrieval of immunization information in the registry at the time of the encounter
- Receive and process immunization information within one month of vaccine administration
- Protect the confidentiality of healthcare information
- Ensure the security of healthcare information
- Exchange immunization records using Health Level Seven (HL7) standards
- Automatically determine the routine childhood immunization(s) needed, in compliance with current Advisory Committee on Immunization Practices (ACIP) recommendations, when an individual presents for a scheduled immunization
- Automatically identify individuals due or late for immunization(s) to enable the production of reminder or recall notifications
- Automatically produce immunization coverage reports by providers, age groups, and geographic areas
- Produce official immunization records
- Promote the accuracy and completeness of registry data

The CDC provides funding for population-based immunization registries.

Other Registries

Registries may be developed for any type of disease or condition. Examples of other types of registries that are commonly kept include HIV/AIDS and cardiac registries.

In addition, registries may be developed for administrative purposes. The National Provider Registry is an example of an administrative registry. Data collected for healthcare administrative purposes are discussed in the next subsection.

Check Your Understanding 12.3

Instructions: Answer the following questions on a separate piece of paper.

1. Why are registries created and maintained?
2. How is case definition different from case finding?
3. What is the difference between a facility-based registry and a population-based registry?

Answer questions 4 through 10 for each of the following registries: cancer, trauma, birth defects, diabetes, implant, transplant, and immunization.

4. What methods are used for case definition and case finding?
5. What methods of data collection are used?
6. What methods of reporting are used?
7. What methods of follow-up are used?
8. What standards are applicable, and what agencies approve or accredit the registry?
9. What education is required for registrars?
10. What certification is available for registrars? What agency/organization provides certification? What are the certification requirements?

Healthcare Databases

Databases may be developed for a variety of purposes. The federal government, for example, has developed a wide variety of databases to enable it to carry out surveillance, improvement, and prevention duties. Health information managers may provide information for these databases through data abstraction or from data reported by a facility to state and local entities. They also may use these data to do research or work with other researchers on issues related to reimbursement and health status.

There are concerns about collecting healthcare data in an environment without clear guidance about ownership of secondary data, unauthorized reuse of data, and spotty confidentiality and security regulations. Patients have concerns that secondary data collected about them may adversely affect their employment or ability to obtain health insurance. It is much more difficult for patients to determine what information about them is maintained in secondary databases than it is to view their primary health records. Although facilities utilize secondary data under the "healthcare operations" section of HIPAA, patients must be made aware of this practice through the Notification of Privacy Practices. Also, not all secondary data is protected under HIPAA.

National and State Administrative Databases

Some databases are established for administrative rather than disease-oriented reasons. Data banks are developed, for example, for **claims** data submitted on Medicare claims. Other administrative databases assist in the **credentialing** and privileging of health practitioners.

Medicare Provider Analysis and Review File

The **Medicare Provider Analysis and Review** (MEDPAR) file is made up of acute care hospital and skilled nursing facility (SNF) claims data for all Medicare claims. It consists of the following types of data:

- Demographic data on the patient
- Data on the provider
- Information on Medicare coverage for the claim
- Total charges
- Charges broken down by specific types of services, such as operating room, physical therapy, and pharmacy charges
- ICD-9-CM diagnosis and procedure codes
- DRGs

The MEDPAR file is frequently used for research on topics such as charges for particular types of care and analysis by DRG. The limitation of the MEDPAR data for research purposes is that it only contains data about Medicare patients.

National Practitioner Data Bank

The **National Practitioner Data Bank** (NPDB) was mandated under the Health Care Quality Improvement Act of 1986, to provide a database of medical malpractice payments; adverse licensure actions including revocations, suspensions, reprimands, censures, probations and surrenders of licenses for quality of care purposes only, and certain professional review actions (such as denial of medical staff privileges) taken by healthcare entities such as hospitals against physicians, dentists, and other healthcare providers (NPDB 2006). The NPDB was developed to alleviate the lack of information on malpractice decisions, denial of medical staff privileges, or loss of medical license. Because these data were not widely available, physicians could move to another state or another facility and begin practicing again with the current state or facility unaware of the previous actions against the physician.

Information in the NPDB is provided through a required reporting mechanism. Entities making malpractice payments, including insurance companies, boards of medical examiners, and entities such as hospitals and professional societies must report to the NPDB. The information to be reported includes information on the practitioner, the reporting entity, and the judgment or settlement. Information on physicians must be reported, but information on other healthcare providers, though not mandatory, also will be accepted. Monetary penalties may be assessed for failure to report.

The law requires healthcare facilities to query the NPDB as part of the credentialing process when a physician initially applies for medical staff privileges and every two years thereafter.

Healthcare Integrity and Protection Data Bank

Part of the Health Insurance Portability and Accountability Act (HIPAA) of 1996 mandated the collection of information on healthcare fraud and abuse because there was no central place to obtain this information. As a result, the national **Healthcare Integrity and Protection Data Bank** (HIPDB) was developed. The types of items that must be reported to the data bank include reportable final adverse actions such as (HHS 2008):

- Federal or state licensing and certification actions, including revocations, reprimands, censures, probations, suspensions, and any other loss of license, or the right to apply for or renew a license, whether by voluntary surrender, non-renewability, or otherwise
- Exclusions from participation in federal or state healthcare programs
- Any other adjudicated actions or decisions defined in the HIPDB regulations

There may be some overlap with the National Practitioner Data Bank, so a single report is made and then sorted to the appropriate data bank. Information to be reported includes information on the healthcare provider, supplier, or practitioner that is the subject of the final adverse action, the nature of the act, and a description of the actions on which the decision was based. Only federal and state government agencies and health plans are required to report, and access to the data bank is limited to these organizations and to practitioners, providers, and suppliers who may only query about themselves.

State Administrative Data Banks

States also frequently have health-related administrative databases. Many states, for example, collect either UHDDS or UB-04 data on patients discharged from hospitals located within their area. The Statewide Planning and Research Cooperative System (SPARCS) in New York is an example of this type of administrative database. It combines UB-04 data with data required by the state of New York.

National, State, and County Public Health Databases

Public health is the area of healthcare dealing with the health of populations in geographic areas such as states or counties. One of the duties of public health agencies is the surveillance of health status within their jurisdiction.

Databases developed by public health departments provide information on the incidence and prevalence of diseases, possible high-risk populations, survival statistics, and trends over time. Data for these databases may be collected using a variety of methods including interviews, physical examination of individuals, and review of health records. At the national level, the National Center for Health Statistics (NCHS) has responsibility for these databases.

National Health Care Survey

One of the major national public health surveys is the **National Health Care Survey**. To a large extent, it relies on data from patient health records. It consists of a number of databases, including:

- National Hospital Discharge Survey
- National Ambulatory Medical Care Survey
- National Survey of Ambulatory Surgery
- National Nursing Home Survey
- National Home and Hospice Care Survey

Table 12.2 lists the component databases of the National Health Care Survey, along with their corresponding data sources.

Data in the National Hospital Discharge Survey are abstracted manually from a sample of acute care hospitals or from discharged inpatient records or are obtained from state or other discharge databases. Items collected follow the Uniform Hospital Discharge Data Set (UHDDS), including demographic data, admission and discharge dates, and final diagnoses and procedures.

The National Ambulatory Medical Care Survey includes data collected by a sample of office-based physicians and their staffs from the records of patients seen in a one-week reporting period. Data included are demographic data, the patient's reason for visit, the diagnoses, diagnostic and screening services, therapeutic and preventive services, ambulatory surgical procedures, and medications and injections, in addition to information on the visit disposition and time spent with the physician.

Data for the National Survey of Ambulatory Surgery are collected on a representative sample of hospital-based and freestanding ambulatory surgery centers. Data include patient demographic characteristics; source of payment; information on anesthesia given; the diagnoses; and the surgical and non-surgical procedures on patient visits to hospital-based and freestanding ambulatory surgery centers. The survey consists of a mailed survey about the facility and abstracts of patient data.

The National Nursing Home Survey provides data on the facility, current residents, and discharged residents. Information is gathered through an interview process. The administrator or designee provides information about the facility. For information on the residents, the nursing staff member most familiar with the resident's care is interviewed. The staff member uses the resident's health record for reference in the interview. Data collected on the facility includes information on ownership, size, certification status, admissions, services, full-time equivalent employees, and basic charges.

Table 12.2. National healthcare databases

Database	Type of Setting	Content	Data Source	Method of Data Collection
National Hospital Discharge Survey	Hospital inpatient	Uniform Hospital Discharge Data Set	Discharged patient records	Abstract
National Ambulatory Medical Care Survey	Office-based physician practice	Data on the patient and the visit	State discharge databases Office-based physician records	Abstract
National Survey of Ambulatory Surgery	Hospital-based and freestanding ambulatory surgery centers	Data on the facility and patients	Facility response to survey and patient records	Survey and abstract
National Nursing Home Survey	Nursing Home	Data on the facility and current and discharged residents	Administrator Nurse caregiver	Interview
National Home and Hospice Care Survey	Home Health and Hospice	Facility data and patient data	Administrator Caregiver	Interview
National Electronic Disease Surveillance System (NEDSS)	Public Health Departments	Possible bioterrorism incidents	Local and state public health departments	Electronic surveillance

Both the current and discharged resident interviews provide demographic information on the resident as well as LOS, diagnoses, level of care received, **activities of daily living** (ADL), and charges.

For the National Home and Hospice Care Survey, data are collected on the home health or hospice agency as well as on its current and discharged patients. Data include referral and length of service, diagnoses, number of visits, patient charges, health status, reason for discharge, and types of services provided. Facility data are obtained through an interview with the administrator or designee. Patient information is obtained from the caregiver most familiar with the patient's care. The caregiver may use the patient's health record in answering the interview questions.

Because of the bioterrorism scares in recent years, the CDC is developing the National Electronic Disease Surveillance System (NEDSS), which serves as a major part of the Public Health Information Network (PHIN). It will provide a national surveillance system by connecting the CDC with local and state public health partners. This integrated system will allow the CDC to monitor trends from disease reporting at the local and state level to look for possible bioterrorism incidents.

Other national public health databases include the National Health Interview Survey, which is used to monitor the health status of the population of the United States and the National Immunization Survey, which collects data on the immunization status of children between the ages of 19 and 35 months living in the United States.

State and local public health departments also develop databases as needed to perform their duties of health surveillance, disease prevention, and research. An example of a state database is the infectious/notifiable disease database. Each state has a list of diseases that must be reported to the state, such as AIDS, measles, and syphilis, so that containment and prevention measures may be taken to avoid large outbreaks. As mentioned above, these state and local reporting systems will be connected with the CDC through NEDSS to evaluate trends in disease outbreaks. Statewide databases and registries also may collect extensive information on particular diseases and conditions such as birth defects, immunization, and cancer.

Vital Statistics

Vital statistics include data on births, deaths, fetal deaths, marriages, and divorces. Responsibility for the collection of vital statistics rests with the states. The states share information with National Center for Health Statistics (NCHS). The actual collection of the information is carried out at the local level. For example, birth certificates are completed at the facility where the birth occurred. They are then sent to the state. The state serves as the official repository for the certificates and provides vital statistics information to NCHS. From the vital statistics collected, states and the national government develop a variety of databases and statistics about vital events in the state or country.

One vital statistics database at the national level is the Linked Birth and Infant Death Data Set. In this database, the information from birth certificates is compared to death certificates for infants who die under one year of age. This database provides data to conduct analyses for patterns of infant death. Other national programs that use vital statistics data include the National Mortality Followback Survey, the National Survey of Family Growth, and the National Death Index (CDC 2008b). In some of these databases, such as the National Mortality Followback Survey, additional information is collected on deaths originally identified through the vital statistics system.

Similar databases using vital statistics data as a basis are found at the state level. Birth defects registries, for example, frequently use vital records data with information on the birth defect as part of their data collection process.

Clinical Trials Databases

A **clinical trial** is a research project in which new treatments and tests are investigated to determine whether they are safe and effective. The trial proceeds according to a **protocol**, which is the list of rules and procedures to be followed. Clinical trials databases have been developed to allow physicians and patients to find clinical trials. A patient with cancer or AIDS, for example, might be interested in participating in a clinical trial but not know how to locate one applicable to his or her type of disease. Clinical trials databases provide the data to enable patients and practitioners to determine what clinical trials are available and applicable to the patient.

The Food and Drug Administration Modernization Act of 1997 mandated that a clinical trials database be developed. The National Library of Medicine has developed the database, called ClinicalTrials.gov, which is available on the Internet for use by both patients and practitioners (NLM 2008). Information in the database includes the following:

- Abstracts of Clinical Study Protocols
  - Summary of the purpose of the study
  - Recruiting status
  - Criteria for patient participation
  - Location of the trial and specific contact information
- Additional Information (may help a patient decide whether to consider a particular trial)
  - Research study design
  - Phase of the trial
  - Disease or condition and drug or therapy under study

Each data element has been defined. For example, the brief summary gives an overview of the treatments being studied and types of patients to be included. The location of the trial tells where the trial is being carried out so that patients can select trials in convenient locations. Recruitment status indicates whether subjects are currently being entered in the trial or will be in the future or whether the trial is closed to new subjects. Eligibility criteria include information on the type of condition to be studied, in some cases the stage of the disease, and what other treatments are allowed during the trial or must have been completed before entering the trial. Age is also a frequent eligibility criterion. Study types include diagnostic, genetic, monitoring, natural history, prevention, screening, supportive care, training, and treatment (McCray and Ide 2000, 316). Study design includes the research design being followed.

A clinical trial consists of four study phases. Phase I studies research the safety of the treatment in a small group of people. In phase II studies, emphasis is on determining the treatment's effectiveness and further investigating safety. Phase III studies look at effectiveness and side effects and make comparisons to other available treatments in larger populations. Phase IV studies look at the treatment after it has entered the market.

Some clinical trials databases concentrate on a particular disease. The Department of Health and Human Services, for example, has developed the AIDS Clinical Trials Information Service (ACTIS). The National Cancer Institute sponsors the Physician Data Query (PDQ), a database for cancer clinical trials. These databases contain information similar to ClinicalTrials.gov. Although ClinicalTrials.gov has been set up for use by both patients and health practitioners, some databases are more oriented to practitioners. Clinical trials are discussed in chapter 18.

Health Services Research Databases

Health services research is research concerning healthcare delivery systems, including organization and delivery and care effectiveness and efficiency. Within the federal government, the organization most involved in health services research is the **Agency for Healthcare Research and Quality** (AHRQ). AHRQ looks at issues related to the efficiency and effectiveness of the healthcare delivery system, disease protocols, and guidelines for improved disease outcomes.

A major initiative for AHRQ has been the **Healthcare Cost and Utilization Project** (HCUP). HCUP uses data collected at the state level from either claims data from the UB-04 or discharge-abstracted data, including UHDDS items reported by individual hospitals and, in some cases, by freestanding ambulatory care centers. Which data are reported depends on the individual state. Data may be reported by the facilities to a state agency or to the state hospital association, depending on state regulations. The data are then reported from the state to AHRQ where they become part of the HCUP databases.

HCUP consists of a set of databases:

- Nationwide Inpatient Sample (NIS) consists of inpatient discharge data from a sample of hospitals in 35 states throughout the United States
- State Inpatient Database (SID) includes data collected by states on hospital discharges
- State Ambulatory Surgery Databases (SASD) includes information from a sample of states on hospital-affiliated ASCs and, from some states, data from freestanding surgery centers
- State Emergency Department Databases includes data from hospital-affiliated emergency departments (EDs)
- Abstracts for visits that do not result in a hospitalization
- Kids Inpatient Database (KID) is made up of inpatient discharge data on children younger than 19 years old

These databases are unique because they include data on inpatients whose care is paid for by all types of payers including Medicare, Medicaid, and private insurance as well as by self-paying and uninsured patients. Data elements include demographic information, information on diagnoses and procedures, admission and discharge status, payment sources, total charges, LOS, and information on the hospital or freestanding ambulatory surgery center. Researchers may use these databases to look at issues such as those related to the costs of treating particular diseases, the extent to which treatments are used, and differences in outcomes and cost for alternative treatments.

National Library of Medicine

The National Library of Medicine produces two databases of special interest to the HIM professional: MEDLINE and UMLS.

Medical Literature, Analysis, and Retrieval System Online

Medical Literature, Analysis, and Retrieval System Online (MEDLINE) is the best-known database from the National Library of Medicine. It includes bibliographic listings for publications in the areas of medicine, dentistry, nursing, pharmacy, allied health, and veterinary medicine. HIM professionals use MEDLINE to locate articles on HIM issues as well as articles on medical topics necessary to carry out quality improvement and medical research activities.

Unified Medical Language System

The **Unified Medical Language System** (UMLS) provides a way to integrate biomedical concepts from a variety of sources to show their relationships. This process allows links to be made between different information systems for purposes such as the electronic health record. UMLS is of particular interest to the HIM professional because medical classifications such as ICD-9-CM, CPT, and the Healthcare Common Procedure Coding System (HCPCS) are among the items included. UMLS is covered extensively in chapter 13.

Health Information Exchange

Health information exchange (HIE) initiatives have been developed in an effort to move toward a longitudinal patient record with complete information about the patient available at any point of care. This is patient-specific rather than aggregate data and is used primarily for patient care. Some researchers have looked at the amount of data available through the health information exchanges as a possible source of data to aggregate for research. Since HIE is a fairly new concept, it is important that HIEs take the time to develop policies and procedures covering the use of data collected for patient care for other purposes. Special attention needs to be paid to whether patients included in the HIE need to provide individual consent to be included when the data is aggregated for research or other purposes. Aggregated data can be deidentified to add another layer of protection for the patient's identity. A full discussion of HIE is included in Chapter 7.

Data for Performance Measurement

The Joint Commission, CMS, and some health plans are requiring healthcare facilities to collect data on core performance measures. These measures are "quantitative tools used to assess the clinical, financial, and utilization aspects of a healthcare provider's outcomes of processes" (AHIMA 2010). As such, they are secondary data. Facilities must determine how to collect these measures and how to aggregate the data for reporting purposes. Such measures may be used in the future as a basis for pay for performance. It is, therefore, extremely important that the data accurately reflect the quality of care provided in the facility.

Check Your Understanding 12.4

Instructions: Answer the following questions on a separate piece of paper.

1. What information is included in the Medicare Provider Analysis and Review File?
2. What limitations are encountered when using MEDPAR data in research?
3. Why was the National Practitioner Data Bank developed? What law requires its use? Why was the Healthcare Integrity and Protection Data Bank developed? What law requires its use?
4. What types of information must be reported to the National Practitioner Data Bank and the Healthcare Integrity and Protection Data Bank? Do the two data banks overlap in any way?
5. How do healthcare organizations use the NPDB? Who may use the Healthcare Integrity and Protection Data Bank?
6. How can the health information manager contribute to public health databases?
7. Which of the five National Health Care Survey databases use data from health records?
8. What is a clinical trial? Why are clinical trials databases developed? Which law mandated development of a national clinical trials database?
9. What is the source of data for the Healthcare Cost and Utilization Project?
10. Why is UMLS of interest to HIM professionals?
11. Why have health information exchange efforts been developed?
12. What type of data is included in HIEs?

Processing and Maintenance of Secondary Databases

Several issues surround the processing and maintenance of secondary databases. HIM professionals are often involved in decisions concerning these issues.

Manual versus Automated Methods of Data Collection

Although registries and databases are almost universally computerized, data collection is commonly done manually. The most frequent method is **abstracting**. Abstracting is the process of reviewing the patient health record and entering the required data elements into the database. In some cases, the abstracting may initially be done on an abstract form. The data then would be entered into the database from the form. In many cases, it is done directly from the primary patient health record into a data collection screen in the computerized database system.

Not all data collection is done manually. In some cases, data can be downloaded directly from other electronic systems. Birth defects registries, for example, often download information on births and birth defects from the vital records system. In some cases, providers such as hospitals and physicians send information in electronic format to the registry or database. The National Discharge Survey from the National Center for Health Statistics uses information in electronic format from state databases. As the electronic health record (EHR) develops further, less and less data will need to be manually abstracted since it will be available electronically through the EHR.

Vendor Systems versus Facility-Specific Systems

Each registry must determine what information technology solution best meets its needs. In some cases that will be a vendor-created product specifically for registries. In other cases, the registry system may be part of an overall facility health information system. It is important that either type of product is able to incorporate demographic and other pertinent information from the facility HIS system. In this way, time is saved and data integrity between the registry information and the HIS system is maintained. If registries utilize registry applications as part of a facility-wide HIS, it is important that the registry manager be included in the decision of which HIS system to purchase for the facility as well as in pertinent training and implementation decisions.

Data Quality Issues

Indexes, registries, and databases are only helpful when the data they contain are accurate. Decisions concerning new treatment methods, healthcare policy, and physician credentialing and privileging are made based on these databases. Incorrect data will likely result in serious errors in decision making. Several factors must be addressed when assessing data quality, including data validity, reliability, completeness, and timeliness.

Validity of the Data

Validity refers to the accuracy of the data. For example, in a cancer registry, the stage of the neoplasm must be recorded accurately because statistical information on survival rates by stage is commonly reported.

Several methods may be used to ensure validity. One method is to incorporate **edits** in the database. An edit is a check on the accuracy of the data, such as setting data types. When a particular data element, such as admission date, is set up with a data type of date, the computer will not allow other types of data, such as name, to be entered in that field. Other edits may use comparisons between fields to ensure accuracy. For example, an edit might check to see that all patients with the diagnosis of prostate cancer are listed as males in the database.

Reliability of the Data

Another factor to be considered in looking at data quality is reliability. Reliability refers to the consistency of the data. For example, all patients in a trauma registry with the same level, severity, and site of injury should have the same Abbreviated Injury Scale. Reliability is frequently checked by having more than one person abstract data for the same case. The results are then compared to identify any discrepancies. This is called an **interrater reliability** method of checking. Several different people may be used to do the checking. In the cancer registry, physician members of the cancer committee are called on to check the reliability of the data.

The use of uniform terminology is an important way to improve data reliability. This has been evident in case definition for registries. The criteria for including a patient in a registry must have a clear definition. Definitions for terms such as race, for example, must include the categories to be used in determining race. When uniform terms are not used, the data will not be consistent. Also, it will be impossible to make comparisons between systems when uniform terms have not been used for all data. A data dictionary in which all data elements are defined helps ensure that uniform data definitions are being followed. An example would be the term *discharge time*. Discharge time could be the time the physician writes the discharge order, the time the information about the discharge is entered into the ADT system, or the time the patient leaves the floor. The data dictionary could define it as the time the information is entered in the ADT system, and then everyone recording discharge time would be using the same time for that data element.

Completeness of the Data

Completeness is another factor to be considered in data quality. Missing data may prevent the database from being useful for research or clinical decision making. To avoid missing data, some databases will not allow the user to move to the next field without making an entry in the current one, especially for fields considered crucial. Looking at a variety of sources in case finding is a way to avoid omitting patients who should be included in a registry.

Timeliness of the Data

Another concept important in data quality is timeliness. Data must be available within a time frame helpful to the user. Factors that influence decisions may change over time, so it is important that the data reflect up-to-date information.

Data Security and Confidentiality Issues

Data security usually refers to the tools, including technological safeguards, used to ensure confidentiality of personal health information. **Data confidentiality** usually refers to an individual's right to information privacy and is accomplished through well-managed administrative privacy policies and practices and technology tools.

HIPAA-Covered Entities

When looking at data security and confidentiality issues, it is important to consider the HIPAA regulations for privacy and security. For HIPAA-covered entities, the data collection done by registries is considered part of "healthcare operations." The patient does not, therefore, have to sign an authorization for release of protected health information (PHI) to be included in the registry. Reporting of notifiable diseases to the state comes under "required reporting" and does not require patient authorization for release (Handling Cancer Registry Requests 2003, 7). Release of information to requestors other than the state will depend on the requestor. Data may be released to internal users, such as physicians for research, without the patient's consent as well because research also comes under healthcare operations. External users, such as the American College of Surgeons, collect aggregate data from facilities, so individual patient authorization is not required. Information about patients that may be included in registries or other secondary data sources and reported to outside entities must be included in the facility's Notice of Privacy Practices given to each patient on their initial encounter. Through this mechanism, patients are made aware that data about them may be reported to outside entities.

HIPAA security regulations also apply to data in registries and indexes. These regulations require policies in the areas of administrative, technical, and physical security, which are discussed here. (See chapter 10 for further discussion of privacy, security, and confidentiality.)

Entities Not Covered by HIPAA

Not all registries and databases are covered under HIPAA if they do not bill for patient care services. Central registries would be an example of a registry that is not covered under HIPAA. In such cases, the general norms for data security and confidentiality should be followed.

Data Security

Registries and secondary databases must ensure the security of the information that they maintain. A number of methods such as passwords and role-based access may be used to ensure that only authorized people have access to patient data in the facility's computer system. Loss of data is another important consideration in data security which could severely affect registries and secondary data sources. Although data sometimes are lost as a result of unauthorized access, more often they are lost in more routine ways such as computer malfunction or **computer viruses** which can cause data to be erased or lost.

Physical security of the system is a consideration that is required under the HIPAA security regulations. Computer terminals must be kept in areas that are not physically accessible to unauthorized people. Reports and printouts from the system should not be left where they can be seen. When they are no longer needed, they should be destroyed.

Technical security under HIPAA involves issues such as whether sensitive data need to be encrypted. **Encryption** is a method of scrambling data so that they cannot be read without first being decoded. An AIDS registry, for example, might want to use an encryption method to protect patient-identifiable information since AIDS data is considered sensitive.

Data Privacy and Confidentiality

Maintaining the privacy and confidentiality of health data is a traditional role of HIM professionals. When looking at methods to protect secondary records, patient-specific information requires more control than secondary databases that include only aggregate data because individual patients cannot be identified in aggregate data. Policies on who may access the data provide the basic protection for confidentiality.

The type of data maintained also may affect policies on confidentiality. For many of the government databases discussed earlier, the information is aggregate and the data are readily available to any interested users. For example, public health data are frequently published in many formats, including printed reports, Internet access, and direct computer access.

As is true of all employees working with patient data, employees working with data in indexes, registries, and databases should receive training on confidentiality. Further, they should be required to sign a yearly statement indicating that they have received the training and understand the implications of failure to maintain confidentiality of the data.

Deidentification

In some cases, users of secondary data will need to remove identifying data so that data can be used without violating the patient's privacy. This process is called **deidentification**. The HIPAA Privacy regulations indicate two ways to accomplish the deidentification.

- The covered entity can strip off certain elements to ensure that the patient's information is truly deidentified (HIPAA 2007).
- The covered entity can have an expert apply generally accepted statistical and scientific principles and methods to minimize the risk that the information might be used to identify an individual (Brodnik et. al. 2009).

Whichever method is utilized, it is important that a data set released as deidentified contain no information which would enable patients to be individually identified.

Transparency

Transparency refers to the degree to which patients included in secondary data sets are aware of their inclusion. In its report, *Toward a National Framework for the Secondary Use of Health Data*, the American Medical Informatics Association (2006) has recommended that full disclosure be the policy for all secondary uses of data.

Trends in the Collection of Secondary Data

The most significant trend in collecting secondary data is the increased use of automated data entry. Registries and databases are more commonly using data already available in electronic form rather than manually abstracting all data. As the computerized health record becomes more common, separate databases for various diseases and conditions such as cancer, diabetes, and trauma will become unnecessary. The patient health record itself will be a database that can be queried for information currently obtained from specialized registries.

Since not all data can currently be entered through automated means, other facilities are using existing technologies such as point of care data collection at the patient's bedside using wireless technology (Eisenhower 2005). Finally, secondary data collection is becoming more common and more secondary data is being collected about patients. Because of this fact, national stakeholders such as the American Medical Informatics Association and the National Center for Vital and Health Statistics are becoming more involved in setting national policy related to secondary data. One of the issues of concern is the ownership of secondary data. As stated in an AHIMA practice brief, "'Who can do what to which data and under which circumstances' is really the central question that must be asked in determining the rights and responsibilities of each stakeholder" (Burrington-Brown and Hjort 2007). Stakeholders include patients, health facilities, HIE organizations, vendors, governmental agencies, employers, and researchers. There is currently no clear-cut guidance on the sometimes conflicting rights and responsibilities of each stakeholder of the data. Additional issues include transparency, deidentification, and data privacy and confidentiality that were previously discussed.

As more secondary data is collected, the role of the HIM professional remains that of stewardship. According to the American Medical Informatics Association, data stewardship "encompasses the responsibilities and accountabilities associated with managing, collecting, viewing, storing, sharing, disclosing, or otherwise making use of personal health information" (NCVHS 2007). These are traditional roles for the HIM professional in relationship to primary data. It will be necessary for these roles to be expanded to encompass secondary data.

Check Your Understanding 12.5

Instructions: Answer the following questions on a separate piece of paper.

1. What factors must be considered when determining the quality of data?
2. Which errors in registries and other secondary databases can cause serious problems?
3. What methods and systems can be used to ensure the quality of secondary healthcare data?
4. What is the difference between security and confidentiality?
5. What methods might be used to control access to a health information system?
6. What types of data should be encrypted?
7. What methods can be used to ensure data confidentiality?
8. What trends are evident in the collection of secondary data?
9. Which types of registries and secondary data sources would be covered by HIPAA privacy and security regulations?
10. How are patients notified that data about them may be included in registries and databases and released to outside entities?
11. What is deidentification and what are two ways under HIPAA that deidentification may be accomplished?

Real-World Case

A hospital with a level I trauma center serving a tri-state area had an ongoing problem. It was required to provide care to all major trauma cases from the three states within its service area regardless of the patients' ability to pay. However, one of the states was unwilling to pay for the care provided to its indigent patients. Because trauma care can be extremely intensive and costly, the hospital was losing a lot of money.

To demonstrate the extent of the problem, the hospital administrator asked the trauma registrar to gather data on patients from the state unwilling to pay. The trauma registrar easily identified these patients and provided information by zip code on their location and the type and severity of their injuries. After the patients had been identified, the business office was able to calculate the cost to the hospital of providing their care. The administrator then presented this information to the state legislature to clearly outline the case for the state's obligation to pay for the care the trauma center provided to its indigent patients.

Summary

Health records contain extensive information about individual patients but are difficult to use when attempting to perceive trends in care or quality. For that reason, secondary records were developed. One type of secondary record is the index. An index is a report from a database that provides information on patients and supports retrieval by diagnosis, procedure, or physician. Health information management departments routinely produce indexes.

Disease registries are developed when extensive information is needed about specific diagnoses, procedures, or conditions. They are commonly used for research and to improve patient care and health status. From the database created through the data collection process, reports can be developed to answer questions regarding patient care or issues such as rates of immunization and birth defects. In some cases, patient follow-up is done to assess survival rates and quality of life after a disease or accident.

HIM professionals perform a variety of roles in relation to registries. In some cases, they work on setting up the registry. Moreover, they may work in data collection and management of registry functions. HIM professionals are well suited to such positions because of their background and education in management, health record content, regulatory and legal compliance, and medical science and terminology.

Today, organizations and institutions of all types commonly maintain databases pertaining to healthcare. At the federal level, some administrative databases provide data and information for decisions regarding claims and practitioner credentialing. Other databases focus on the public health area, using data collected at the local level and shared with states and the federal government. These databases assist in government surveillance of health status in the United States. Some databases, such as the clinical trials database, are mandated by law and help patients and providers locate clinical trials regardless of source or location.

Registries and databases raise a number of managerial issues. Data collection is often time-consuming, so some databases now use automated entry methods. In addition, decisions must be made between vendor and facility-specific products. Finally, the quality of the data is an important issue because the decisions made based on data in registries and databases depend on the data's validity, reliability, accuracy, and timeliness.

Another important issue related to registries and databases is data security. Facilities must adopt methods that will ensure controlled access to data as well as prevent the loss of data. Confidentiality is always of concern to the HIM professional, and steps must be taken to protect it.

In the future, separate registries and databases may become less common with the advent of the computer-based patient record. Essentially a large database, the electronic health record can be queried directly rather than having to first abstract data from the primary record into a secondary record.

References

American College of Surgeons. 2008a. Commission on cancer. http://www.facs.org/cancer.

American College of Surgeons. 2008b. Trauma programs. http://www.facs.org/trauma/index.html.

American Health Information Management Association. 2010. *Pocket Glossary of Health Information Management and Technology*, 2nd ed. Chicago, AHIMA.

American Joint Committee on Cancer. 2008. http://www.cancerstaging.org.

American Medical Informatics Association. 2003.

American Medical Informatics Association. 2006. *Toward a National Framework for the Secondary Use of Health Data*. Bethesda, MD: American Medical Informatics Association.

Brodnik, M., et al. 2009. *Fundamentals of Law for Health Informatics and Information Management.* Chicago: AHIMA.

Burrington-Brown, J. and B. Hjort. 2007. Health data access, use and control. *Journal of AHIMA* 78(5): 63–66.

Center for Devices and Radiological Health. 1996. Medical device reporting for user facilities. http://www.fda.gov/cdrh/mdruf.pdf.

Centers for Disease Control. 2008. National Program of Cancer Registries. http://www.cdc.gov/cancer/NPCR/publications.

Centers for Disease Control. 2008a. National immunization program. http://www.cdc.gov/vaccines/programs/iis/stds/coredata.htm1.

Centers for Disease Control. 2008b. National Center for Health Statistics. http://www.cdc.gov/nchs/nvss.htm.

Department of Health and Human Services. 2008. Fact sheet on the Healthcare Protection and Integrity Data Bank.

Eisenhower, C., et al. 2005. Data abstraction unplugged: Taking trauma registry to the point of care with wireless technology. *Journal of AHIMA* 76 (7): 42–45.

Food and Drug Administration. 2008. http://www.fda.gov/cdrh/medical devicesafety/index.html.

Garthe, E. 1997. Overview of trauma registries in the United States. *Journal of AHIMA* 68(7):26, 28, 30–31.

Handling cancer registry requests for information. *In Confidence* 11(8):7.

Health Insurance Portability and Accountability Security Regulations, 45 CFR.§164 (2007).

McCray, A. and N.C. Ide. 2000. Design and implementation of a national clinical trials registry. *Journal of the American Medical Informatics Association* 7(3):313–323.

National Cancer Registrars Association. 2005. http://www.ncra-usa.org.

National Committee on Vital and Health Statistics. 2007. Report to the Secretary of the U.S. Department of Health and Human Services on Enhanced Protection for Uses of Health Data: A stewardship framework for "Secondary Uses" of Electronically Collected and Transmitted Health Data.

National Library of Medicine. 2008. http://www.clinicaltrials.gov.

National Practitioner Data Bank for Adverse Information on Physicians and Other Health Care Practitioners: Reporting on Adverse and Negative Actions 2006 (Mar. 21) *Federal Register* 71 14135.

Osborn, C.E. 1999. Benchmarking with national ICD-9-CM coded data. *Journal of AHIMA* 70(4):59–69.

Ringer, D. and W. Cain. 2004. COC revises cancer standards, creates FORDS. *Advance for Health Information Professionals.*

http://www.health-information.advanceweb.com/common/EditorialSearch/AViewer.aspx?CC=28947.

Stedman's Medical Dictionary Online. 2008. http://www.stedmans.com/section.cfm/45.

Trauma.org. 2008. http://www.trauma.org.

U.S. Department of Health and Human Services. 2000. Healthy people 2010: Tracking healthy people 2010.

Chapter 13
Clinical Classifications and Terminologies

Matthew J. Greene, RHIA, CCS
and Margaret M. Foley, PhD, RHIA, CCS

Learning Objectives

- Differentiate among and identify the correct uses of classifications, nomenclatures, and terminologies
- Discuss the strengths and weaknesses of the classification systems currently required in the United States
- Identify clinical data representation and data retrieval needs and select a terminology most likely to meet these needs
- Understand the need for a terminology in an electronic health record (EHR) system
- Discuss the role of mapping among clinical terminologies
- Describe the characteristics of a sound clinical terminology

Key Terms

American Medical Association (AMA)
American Society for Testing and Materials (ASTM)
Breast Imaging Reporting and Data System Atlas (BI-RADS)
Centers for Medicare and Medicaid Services (CMS)
Clinical Care Classification (CCC)
Clinical terminology
College of American Pathologists (CAP)
Community of Practice (CoP)
Concept
Consolidated Health Informatics (CHI)
Context
Current Dental Terminology (CDT)
Current Procedural Terminology (CPT)
Digital Imaging and Communications in Medicine (DICOM)
Emergency Care Research Institute (ECRI)
Environmental Protection Agency (EPA) Substance Registry System (SRS)
European Committee for Standardization (CEN)
Extensibility
Food and Drug Administration (FDA)
Framework
General Equivalence Mapping (GEM)
Global Medical Device Nomenclature (GMDN)
Granularity
Health Insurance Portability and Accountability Act (HIPAA)
Health Level Seven (HL7)
Healthcare Common Procedure Coding System (HCPCS)
Human Genome Nomenclature (HUGN)
Human Genome Organisation (HUGO)
Inferencing
Interface Terminology
International Classification of Diseases (ICD)
International Classification of Diseases, 9th Revision, Clinical Modification (ICD-9-CM)
International Classification of Diseases, 10th Revision, Clinical Modification (ICD-10-CM)
International Classification of Diseases, 10th Revision, Procedural Coding System (ICD-10-PCS)
International Classification of Diseases, 11th Revision (ICD-11)
International Classification of Diseases for Oncology, 3rd Revision (ICD-O-3)
International Classification on Functioning, Disability, and Health (ICF)
International Classification of Primary Care (ICPC-2)
International Health Terminology Standards Development Organisation (IHTSDO)
Interoperability
Lexicon
Logical Observation Identifiers, Names and Codes (LOINC)
Medical Dictionary for Regulatory Activities (MedDRA)
Medical Subject Headings (MeSH)
Morbidity
Morphological
Morphology
Mortality
Multiaxial
National Cancer Institute (NCI) Thesaurus
National Center for Health Statistics (NCHS)
National Drug Code (NDC)
National Library of Medicine (NLM)
Nomenclature
Not Elsewhere Classified (NEC)
Not Otherwise Specified (NOS)
Orthographic
Patient medical record information (PMRI)
Permanence
Persistence
Polyhierarchy
Reference terminology
Relationship
RxNorm
Structured Product Labeling (SPL)
Syntactic
Systemized Nomenclature of Dentistry (SNODENT)
Systemized Nomenclature of Medicine-Clinical Terms (SNOMED CT)
Systematized Nomenclature of Medicine Reference Terminology (SNOMED RT)
Terminology
Topography
Transformation
UMLS Metathesaurus
UMLS Semantic Network
UMLS SPECIALIST Lexicon
Unified Medical Language System (UMLS)
Universal Medical Device Nomenclature System (UMDNS)
Vendor neutral
Vocabulary
World Health Organization (WHO)
World Organization of National Colleges, Academies, and Academic Associations of General Practitioners/Family Physicians (WONCA)

Healthcare is faced with many challenges, including an aging population, the need to conserve resources, medical knowledge that is increasing exponentially, and a consumer population with Internet access. To meet these challenges, healthcare organizations must have the ability to operate effectively and efficiently using the latest medical data and knowledge. Unfortunately, the healthcare industry in the United States has yet to fully agree on common terminologies that would allow healthcare facilities and practitioners throughout the country to exchange and use information reliably.

It is difficult to believe that the quest to classify **morbidity** and **mortality** is quite old. London parishes first began to keep death records in 1532. In 1662, John Graunt, a merchant, wrote *Natural and Political Observations . . . Made upon the Bills of Mortality.* His friend, Sir William Petty, was able to extrapolate from mortality rates an estimate of community economic loss caused by deaths. Two hundred years later, in *Notes on a Hospital,* Florence Nightingale wrote, "In attempting to arrive at the truth, I have applied everywhere for information, but in scarcely an instance have I been able to obtain hospital records fit for any purposes of comparison. If they could be obtained . . . they would show subscribers how their money was being spent, what amount of good was really being done with it, or whether the money was not doing mischief rather than good" (Barnett et al. 1993, 1046).

Many of the same issues remain in healthcare today. It is vitally important to be able to compare data for outcomes measurement, quality improvement, resource utilization, best practices, and medical research. These tasks can be accomplished only when healthcare has a common terminology that is easily integrated into the electronic health record (EHR).

This chapter examines the history and current practices of classification in the healthcare industry. It also addresses various clinical terminologies and the desired characteristics of a terminology.

Development of Classification Systems and Terminologies for Healthcare Data

As the discussion of classification systems and terminologies for healthcare data begins, it is important to have an understanding of several terms related to clinical content representation. Unfortunately, it is difficult to get complete agreement on definitions for even these basic concepts. However, there are some commonly accepted definitions. A classification is a "system that arranges similar diseases and procedures and organizes related entities for easy retrieval" (AMIA and AHIMA Terminology and Classification Policy Task Force 2007, 38). A **nomenclature** is a system of names or terms used for a particular discipline created to facilitate communication by eliminating ambiguity (*Merriam-Webster Online Dictionary* 2008; NCVHS 2005). The terms *classification* and *nomenclature* are often used interchangeably. However, Chute (2000) distinguishes the two: "classifications and nomenclatures can be more helpfully regarded as lying along a continuum, where the first categorizes and aggregates while the second supports detailed descriptions" (298). The Diagnostic Statistical Manual (DSM) is an example of a nomenclature which provides a listing of the terms and definitions (criteria) used to describe mental health disorders. The International Classification of Disease, 10th Revision is a classification system which organizes (categorizes) many of its disease entries by body system or etiology. For example, disorders related to the circulatory system are organized and classified within a single chapter.

In the generic sense a **terminology** is a "set of terms representing the system of concepts of a particular subject or field" (AHIMA 2010, 291). Obviously when working in healthcare, medical or clinical terminologies are of interest. Another generic term often used when discussing terminologies is **lexicon** which refers to the listings of words or expressions in a language (terminology) and information about the language such as definitions, related principles and description of (grammatical) structure (NLM 2008a). The pyramid in figure 13.1 illustrates how these terms are all related. A nomenclature can be less specific than a terminology, which is less specific than a language. So, while a classification or nomenclature categorizes and aggregates, a terminology represents the whole of a subject field.

It is important to recognize that the problem of multiple definitions and names is endemic in the field of healthcare terminology. A **clinical terminology** is defined as a set of standardized terms and their synonyms that record patient findings, circumstances, events, and interventions with sufficient detail to support clinical care, decision support, outcomes research, and quality improvement (AMIA and

Figure 13.1. Comparative level of detail in nomenclatures, terminologies, and languages

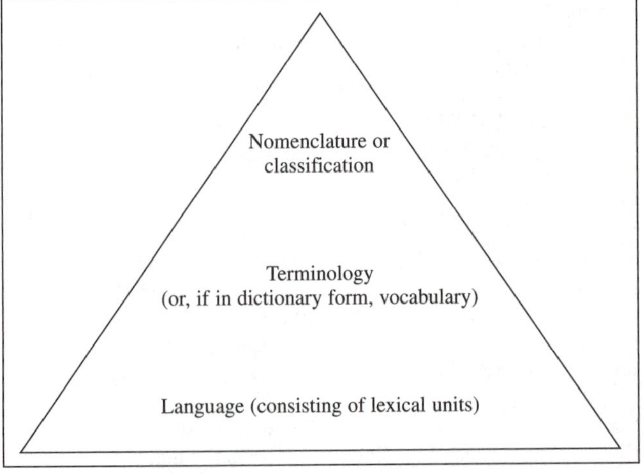

AHIMA Terminology and Classification Policy Task Force 2007, 41). Whereas a *clinical vocabulary* is "a formally recognized list of preferred medical terms"(AHIMA 2010, 55). The definition for the **vocabulary** is similar to that terminology except that it includes the meanings or definitions of words. Because of their very similar meanings, the terms clinical terminology and clinical vocabulary are often used interchangeably in practice. To further complicate the issue, many working within the field also often use "terminology" to refer to the entire spectrum of issues related to clinical data representation from classifications and nomenclatures to clinical terminologies (Chute 2000, 299).

Clinical classifications and terminologies serve different functions. For example, the classification systems ICD-9-CM and CPT represent similar procedures and diagnoses with single codes. This broad categorization of information is useful for functions such as billing and monitoring resource utilization. In contrast, terminologies support the capture and representation of information collected within an EHR at the time of documentation (Bowman 2005). Terminologies exist to represent topics ranging from nursing documentation and laboratory data to medical devices. This detailed level of data capture is useful to support functions such as clinical decision support and clinical alerts.

Depending on the purpose of a given classification or terminology, differences are also seen at the level of **granularity** (detail) used to represent content. For example, the CPT classification system has a single code (86003 Allergen specific IgE: quantitative or semiquantitative, each allergen) to report a laboratory test to detect a specific allergen. The same code is used regardless of the allergen (for example, food, weeds, dust). Whereas, LOINC (Logical Observation Identifier Names and Codes), a clinical terminology, provides many different codes (for example, 11195-5, 11196-3, 11197-1) to represent the test for each unique allergen (NLM 2008b). In this case, the LOINC representation of the allergen tests is more granular, that is, more specific.

Check Your Understanding 13.1

Instructions: Answer the following questions on a separate piece of paper.

1. What are the general functions of classifications and nomenclatures? Give examples of each.
2. How does a clinical terminology differ from a classification or nomenclature?

Current Systems of Classification and Nomenclature

Systems for classifying diseases have progressed through various stages since the first classification system was developed in the late 19th century. The following sections describe past, current, and near-future developments for a variety of classification systems.

International Classification of Diseases

The **International Classification of Diseases** (ICD) began as the Bertillon Classification of Diseases in 1893. In 1900, the French government convened an international meeting to update the Bertillon classification to the International List of Causes of Death. The goal was to develop a common system for describing the causes of mortality. The **World Health Organization** (WHO) became responsible for maintaining the ICD in 1948. Currently, ICD is used by more than 100 countries worldwide to classify diseases and other health issues. The classification system facilitates the storage and retrieval of diagnostic information and serves as the basis for compiling mortality and morbidity statistics reported by WHO members. The latest version of the International Classification of Diseases, the 10th edition (ICD-10), has been in use since 1994. In 1999, the United States began using ICD-10 to report mortality statistics under its agreement with WHO. ICD-10 is routinely updated by the WHO. The development of an 11th edition of ICD is underway. A significant difference in **International Classification of Diseases, 11th Revision** (ICD-11) is that it will be designed to include linkages to standardized healthcare terminologies to facilitate processing and use of the data for a variety of purposes such as research (WHO 2007).

International Classification of Diseases, 9th Revision, Clinical Modification

Developed by the **National Center for Health Statistics** (NCHS), the **International Classification of Diseases, 9th Revision, Clinical Modification** (ICD-9-CM) is a derivative work of the International Classification of Diseases, 9th Revision, as developed by WHO. ICD-9-CM is used in the United States only to code and classify diagnoses from inpatient and outpatient records, as well as inpatient procedures. Although diagnostic and procedural coding were the original functions of the system, ICD-9-CM also has been used to communicate provider reimbursement information on healthcare services since 1983. Today, coding for reimbursement is a vital part of healthcare operations. The official ICD-9-CM coding guidelines are published quarterly in Coding Clinic for ICD-9-CM by the Central Office on ICD-9-CM Coding of the American Hospital Association (AHA).

Changes and updates to ICD-9-CM are managed by the ICD-9-CM Coordination and Maintenance Committee, a federal committee co-chaired by representatives from the NCHS and the **Centers for Medicare and Medicaid Services** (CMS). The NCHS is responsible for Volumes 1 and 2 (diagnoses), and the CMS is responsible for Volume 3 (procedures). Figure 13.2 shows an example of a section of an entry in the Tabular Listing of Diseases (ICD-9-CM, Volume 1).

Both the public and private sectors are invited to make suggestions for modifications to ICD-9-CM, and meetings are open to the public. Modifications may be implemented on April 1 and October 1 of each year. However, to date, code updates have only been released in October.

International Classification of Diseases, 10th Revision, Clinical Modification

As with ICD-9-CM, the U.S. government modified the **International Classification of Diseases, 10th revision, Clinical Modification** (ICD-10-CM) for the reporting of morbidity data. ICD-10-CM contains a substantial increase in content over ICD-9-CM. Improvements in the content and format of the ICD-10-CM draft include:

- Additional information relevant to ambulatory care
- Expanded cause of injury codes
- New combination diagnosis/symptom codes to reduce the number of codes needed to fully describe a condition
- Greater specificity in code assignment
- Laterality information (right and left)
- Use of seven-digit alphanumeric format which facilitates expansion and revision of classification

Figure 13.2. Example of Volume 1 ICD-9-CM entry

TUBERCULOSIS (010–018)

Includes: infection by Mycobacterium tuberculosis (human) (bovine)

Excludes: *congenital tuberculosis (771.2)*
late effects of tuberculosis (137.0–137.4)

The following fifth-digit subclassification is for use with categories 010–018:

0 unspecified
1 bacteriological or histological examination not done
2 bacteriological or histological examination unknown (at present)
3 tubercle bacilli found (in sputum) by microscopy
4 tubercle bacilli not found (in sputum) by microscopy, but found by bacterial culture
5 tubercle bacilli not found by bacteriological examination, but tuberculosis confirmed histologically
6 tubercle bacilli not found by bacteriological or histological examination but tuberculosis confirmed by other methods [inoculation of animals]

§ 010 Primary tuberculous infection
010.0 Primary tuberculous infection
Excludes: *nonspecific reaction to tuberculin skin test without active tuberculosis (795.5)*
positive:
PPD (795.5)
tuberculin skin test without active tuberculosis (795.5)
010.1 Tuberculous pleurisy in primary progressive tuberculosis
010.8 Other primary progressive tuberculosis
Excludes: *tuberculous erythema nodosum (017.1)*
010.9 Primary tuberculous infection, unspecified

§ 011 Pulmonary tuberculosis
Use additional code to identify any associated silicosis (502)
011.0 Tuberculosis of lung, infiltrative
011.1 Tuberculosis of lung, nodular
011.2 Tub erculosis of lung with cavitation
011.3 Tuberculosis of bronchus
Excludes: *isolated bronchial tuberculosis (012.2)*
011.4 Tuberculous fibrosis of lung
011.5 Tuberculous bronchiectasis
011.6 Tuberculous pneumonia [any form]
011.7 Tuberculous pneumothorax
011.8 Other specified pulmonary tuberculosis
011.9 Pulmonary tuberculosis, unspecified
Respiratory tuberculosis NOS
Tuberculosis of lung NOS

§ Requires fifth-digit. See codes and definitions.

Figure 13.3 is an example of an entry in the Tabular Listing of Diseases, ICD-10-CM.

As of this writing, the Department of Health and Human Services (HHS) published a notice of proposed rulemaking which identified the replacement of ICD-9-CM with ICD-10-CM for diagnosis coding and ICD-10-PCS (International Classification of Diseases, 10th Revision, Procedural Coding System) for procedural coding. The proposed effective date for use of the ICD-10 code sets is October 1, 2013 (HHS 2008).

To facilitate the transition from ICD-9-CM, crosswalks have been developed, which link similar concepts in ICD-9-CM with those in ICD-10-CM or ICD-10-PCS. The crosswalks, called **General Equivalence Mappings** (GEMs), were developed by a coordinated effort of the NCHS, CMS, AHIMA, AHA, and 3M Health Information Systems. Four GEMs were created to handle translation of data between the 9th and 10th versions of the code sets. Two of GEMs crosswalk information from ICD-9-CM to the ICD-10 code sets for diagnoses and procedures. In the remaining two GEMs, ICD-10-CM and ICD-10-PCS serve as the source classifications. A clear one-to-one correspondence between an ICD-9-CM and ICD-10-CM code does not occur very often. Therefore, the GEMs provide information regarding the type of match such as a direct match, no match, an approximate match, or a one-to-many code linkage (Butler 2007).

Figure 13.3. Example of an ICD-10-CM entry

T40 Poisoning by, adverse effect of and underdosing of narcotics and psychodysleptics [hallucinogens]
Excludes2: drug dependence and related mental and behavioral disorders due to psychoactive substance use (F10.–F19.–)

The appropriate 7th character is to be added to each code from category T40
A initial encounter
D subsequent encounter
S sequela

T40.0 Poisoning by, adverse effect of and underdosing of opium
T40.0x Poisoning by, adverse effect of and underdosing of opium
T40.0x1 Poisoning by opium, accidental (unintentional)
Poisoning by opium NOS
T40.0x2 Poisoning by opium, intentional self-harm
T40.0x3 Poisoning by opium, assault
T40.0x4 Poisoning by opium, undetermined
T40.0x5 Adverse effect of opium
T40.0x6 Underdosing of opium

Source: NCHS 2007, 1929.

ICD-10-CM Field Test Study

AHIMA and the AHA collaborated on an ICD-10-CM Field Testing Project in 2003. The goal of this project was to assess the functionality of ICD-10-CM and its ability to describe conditions better than ICD-9-CM. Volunteers with adequate coding knowledge and experience with ICD-9-CM were recruited to code 50 records using both ICD-9-CM and ICD-10-CM. Procedural coding was not included in this study. Volunteers selected for the study were required to undergo several hours of training in regards to ICD-10-CM coding guidelines and how to use the reporting tool. After training, the volunteers were advised to select 50 medical records from various care settings to code. They were then required to submit the codes from both systems, the amount of time required to code each case in both systems, and any difficulties that they experienced with the ICD-10-CM system. The findings included the following key observations (AHIMA and AHA 2003):

- Clinical descriptors were found to be 71.7 percent better in ICD-10-CM than ICD-9-CM
- 76.3 percent of the respondents reported that ICD-10-CM was an improvement over ICD-9-CM
- 78.6 percent of the respondents suggested that ICD-10-CM should be implemented for coding conditions in 3 years or less
- 60 percent of the respondents recommended that coders would require 16 hours or less of training before using ICD-10-CM
- Over 50 percent of the respondents reported that there was no time difference required to code in both systems
- The respondents also reported that coding in ICD-10-CM may require less time if adequate coding tools and training are provided and when the coders become familiar with ICD-10-CM
- No significant change in documentation practices by clinicians will be required

International Classification of Diseases, 10th Revision, Procedural Coding System

In the mid-1990s, CMS awarded a contract to the 3M Health Information Systems group to develop a new procedural coding system to replace the Tabular List of Procedures, Volume 3 of ICD-9-CM. The classification developed, the **International Classification of Diseases, 10th Revision, Procedural Coding System** (ICD-10-PCS), is considered an improvement over ICD-9-CM, Volume 3 for many reasons including the use of standardized definitions, ease of expandability, ease of use and comprehensiveness. ICD-10-PCS uses very precise definitions. For example, a percutaneous approach is defined as "entry, by puncture or minor incision, of instrumentation through the skin or mucous membrane and any other body layers necessary to reach the site of the procedure" (CMS 2008a). This is a substantial improvement over ICD-9-CM in which a term could have a different meaning in different sections of the classification. For example, when referring to a percutaneous liver biopsy in ICD-9-CM, *percutaneous* means through the skin. However, percutaneous in the term *percutaneous coronary angioplasty* refers to an endoscopic percutaneous approach. The greater coverage of ICD-10-PCS is illustrated by the significantly larger number of codes. ICD-9-CM contains approximately 4,000 procedure codes and ICD-10-PCS contains over 86,000 (Averill et al. 2005) (CMS 2008a).

ICD-10-PCS is composed of seven-character alphanumeric codes. Each character can be one of 34 values (numbers 0 through 9 and the letters of the alphabet excluding I and O). The classification is divided into 16 sections, each of which covers a specific diagnostic area (for example, medical and surgical, radiation oncology, and mental health). Depending on the requirements of each section, the seven characters are assigned different meanings. For example, in the medical and surgical section, the fourth character represents the body part or region involved in the procedure; in the placement section, it represents the body region or orifice; and in the chiropractic section, it represents the body region (CMS 2008).

Figure 13.4 illustrates the meanings of each character of ICD-10-PCS codes in the medical surgical section of the classification.

Table 13.1 is an excerpt from a table used for code assignment in the medical and surgical section of ICD-10-PCS. All codes represented in the table begin with the three characters identified in the header 0FB and are completed with characters selected from each of the four columns depending upon the nature of the procedure being coded.

International Classification of Diseases for Oncology, 3rd Revision

The **International Classification of Diseases for Oncology** (ICD-O-3) is currently in its third revision. This classification is used for coding diagnoses of neoplasms in tumor and cancer registries and in pathology laboratories. The **topography** code describes the site of origin of the neoplasm and uses the same three- and four-character categories as in the neoplasm section of the second chapter of ICD-10. The **morphology** code describes the characteristics of the tumor itself, including cell type and biologic activity. The topography codes remain the same as in the previous edition, but the morphology codes have been thoroughly revised where necessary in the third edition.

Figure 13.4. Code structure of ICD-10-PCS medical and surgical codes

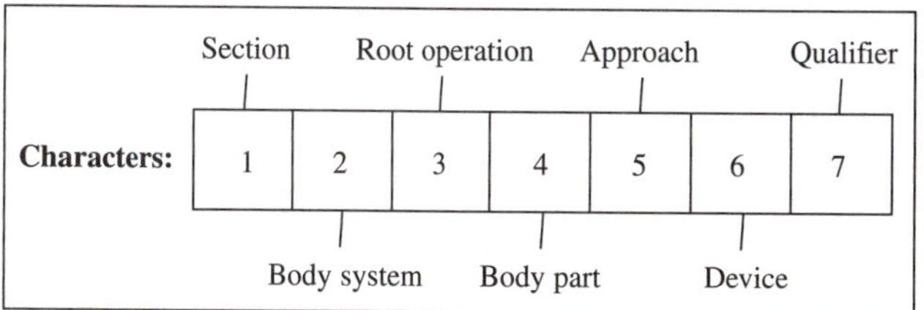

Source: CMS 2008, 1.6.

Table 13.1. ICD-10-PCS

0: MEDICAL AND SURGICAL F: HEPATOBILIARY SYSTEM AND PANCREAS B: EXCISION: Cutting out or off, without replacement, a portion of a body part			
Body Part Character 4	**Approach Character 5**	**Device Character 6**	**Qualifier Character 7**
0 Liver 1 Liver, Right Lobe 2 Liver, Left Lobe 3 Liver, Caudate Lobe 4 Gallbladder G Pancreas	0 Open 3 Percutaneous 4 Percutaneous Endoscopic	Z No Device	X Diagnostic Z No Qualifier
5 Hepatic Duct, Right 6 Hepatic Duct, Left 7 Hepatic Duct, Caudate 8 Cystic Duct 9 Common Bile Duct C Ampulla of Vater D Pancreatic Duct F Pancreatic Duct, Accessory	0 Open 2 Open Endoscopic 3 Percutaneous 4 Percutaneous Endoscopic 7 Via Natural or Artificial Opening 8 Via Natural or Artificial Opening Endoscopic	Z No Device	X Diagnostic Z No Qualifier

Source: CMS 2008.

To the greatest extent possible, ICD-O uses the nomenclature published in the WHO series, International Histological Classification of Tumors. ICD-O is under the purview of the heads of the WHO Collaborating Centres for Classification of Disease (WHO 2008a).

International Classification on Functioning, Disability, and Health

The **International Classification on Functioning, Disability, and Health** (ICF) is a classification of health and health related domains that describe body functions and structures, activities and participation. Three lists exist within ICF:

- Body functions and structure
- Domains of activity and participation
- Environmental factors that interact with all these components

ICD-10 and ICF are complementary, and users are encouraged to use them together to create a broader and more meaningful picture of the experience of health of individuals and populations (WHO 2008b). Table 13.2 provides examples of ICF self-care codes.

Current Procedural Terminology (CPT)

The **American Medical Association** (AMA) publishes the **Current Procedural Terminology** (CPT). According to the AMA, the purpose of CPT is "to provide a uniform language that accurately describes medical, surgical, and diagnostic services, and thereby serves as an effective means for reliable nationwide communication among physicians, patients, and third parties" (2008). CPT was first developed and published by the AMA in 1966. In 1983, the system was adopted by CMS as Level I of the Healthcare Common Procedure Coding System (HCPCS). Since that time, CPT has become widely used as a standard for outpatient and ambulatory care procedural coding in contexts related to reimbursement.

CPT is updated every year on January 1. The codebook is organized into chapters by specialty, body system, or service provided. The codes themselves consist of five digits, and the descriptions of the codes are often accompanied by inclusion and exclusion notes. Modifiers to the five-digit codes also are used extensively. CPT also contains two supplemental sections. The first, Category II codes, are optional codes used for performance measurement reporting purposes. The CPT Category III codes are temporary codes assigned to facilitate data collection for emerging technologies.

CPT is maintained by the CPT Editorial Panel, which is authorized to revise, update, and modify CPT. The majority of the panel are physicians, with the rest coming from industry and government. Supporting the work of the CPT Editorial Panel is the CPT Health Care Professionals Advisory Committee (HCPAC). The HCPAC includes participation in the CPT process from organizations representing limited-license medical practitioners and allied health professionals.

The AMA is responsible for developing and publishing the official guidelines for CPT. The association provides support in several ways. It publishes CPT Assistant, a monthly newsletter, and offers CPT Information Services, a telephone service that provides users with expert advice on code use. The association also conducts an annual CPT coding symposium (AMA 2008).

Healthcare Common Procedure Coding System

The **Healthcare Common Procedure Coding System** (HCPCS) is used to report services and supplies primarily for reimbursement purposes. The system is divided into two

Table 13.2. Examples of ICF self-care codes

Chapter	Description	Categories	Category Description	Subcategories
Self-Care	This chapter is about caring for oneself; washing and drying oneself; caring for one's body and body parts; dressing, eating, and drinking; and looking after one's health	d530 Toileting	Planning and carrying out the elimination of human waste (menstruation, urination, and defecation) and cleaning oneself afterwards.	**d5300** Regulating urination **d5301** Regulating defecation **d5302** Menstrual care **d5308** Toileting, other specified **d5309** Toileting, unspecified
		d540 Dressing	Carrying out the coordinated actions of putting on and taking off clothes and footwear in sequence and in keeping with climatic and social conditions, such as by putting on, adjusting, and removing shirts, skirts, blouses, pants, undergarments, saris, kimono, tights, hats, gloves, coats, shoes, boots, sandals, and slippers.	**d5400** Putting on clothes **d5401** Taking off clothes **d5402** Putting on footwear **d5403** Taking off footwear **d5404** Choosing appropriate clothing **d5408** Dressing, other specified **d5409** Dressing, unspecified

Source: WHO 2005.

sections referred to as levels. Level I of HCPCS is composed of the CPT codes as published by the AMA and represents medical services and procedures performed by physicians and other healthcare providers. Level II of the HCPCS contains codes which represent products, supplies and services not included in the CPT codes. The Level I (CPT) codes (other than the Category II and III codes) are five-digit numeric codes, whereas Level II codes are five-character alphanumeric codes. HCPCS codes may be reported with two-character modifiers.

Except for temporary codes (those beginning with G, K, or Q), HCPCS codes are updated every year on January 1. The HCPCS Level II codes can be downloaded from the HCPCS Web site. Table 13.3 contains examples of various types of HCPCS Level II codes (CMS 2008b).

Diagnostic and Statistical Manual of Mental Diseases

The Diagnostic and Statistical Manual of Mental Diseases (DSM) was first published by the American Psychiatric Association (APA) in 1952. The fourth and most recent complete revision was introduced in 1994. In 2000, the APA introduced DSM-IV-TR (Fourth Edition, Text Revision), which is the most current version available. The next edition of the DSM, DSM-V, is scheduled for publication in 2012 (APA 2008a).

DSM is a **multiaxial** coding system with five axes. Axis I includes the mental disorders or illnesses comparable to general medical illnesses. Axis II includes personality disorders. Axis III includes general medical illnesses. Axis IV covers life events or social problems that affect the patient. Axis V is the overall level of the patient's functioning, usually as determined by the Global Assessment of Functioning (GAF). Figure 13.5 provides an example of DSM-IV-TR codes and instructions.

Table 13.3. Examples of HCPCS Level II codes

HCPCS Level II Code	Code Title
A0130	Non-Emergency Transportation: Wheel-Chair Van
A4918	Venous Pressure Clamp, For Hemodialysis, Each
B4036	Enteral Feeding Supply Kit; Gravity Fed, per Day
C9228	Injection, Tigecycline, per 1 mg
D0272	Bitewings-Two Films
E0619	Apnea Monitor, with Recording Feature
G8293	Copd Patient without Spirometry Results Documented
J3370	Injection, Vancomycin Hcl, 500 mg
K0652	Skin Protection Wheelchair Seat Cushion, Width Less Than 22 Inches, Any Depth
L1825	Knee Orthosis, Elastic Knee Cap, Prefabricated, Includes Fitting And Adjustment
Q0480	Driver For Use with Pneumatic Ventricular Assist Device, Replacement Only
S0274	Nurse Practitioner Visit at Member's Home, Outside of a Capitation Arrangement

Source: CMS 2008.

Figure 13.5. Example of DSM-IV-TR codes

Diagnostic Criteria for Mental Retardation

A. Significantly subaverage intellectual functioning: an IQ of approximately 70 or below on an individually administered IQ test (for infants, a clinical judgment of significantly subaverage intellectual functioning).
B. Concurrent deficits or impairments in present adaptive functioning (i.e., the person's effectiveness in meeting the standards expected for his or her age by his or her cultural group) in at least two of the following areas: communication, self-care, home living, social/interpersonal skills, use of community resources, self-direction, functional academic skills, work, leisure, health, and safety.
C. The onset is before age 18 years.

Code based on degree of severity reflecting level of intellectual impairment:

317 Mild Mental Retardation: IQ level 50–55 to approximately 70

318.0 Moderate Mental Retardation: IQ level 35–40 to 50–55

318.1 Severe Mental Retardation: IQ level 20–25 to 35–40

318.2 Profound Mental Retardation: IQ level below 20 or 25

319 Mental Retardation, Severity Unspecified: when there is strong presumption of Mental Retardation but the person's intelligence is untestable by standard tests

The APA states two general uses for DSM: as a source of diagnostic information that enhances clinical practice, research, and education and as a tool for collecting and communicating accurate public health statistics. The APA updates DSM information to correspond to ICD-9-CM. According to the APA, the DSM will be updated to ICD-10-CM when it is implemented in the United States (APA 2008b).

The International Classification of Primary Care

The **International Classification of Primary Care** (ICPC-2) is a coding terminology for the classification of primary care developed by the **World Organization of National Colleges, Academies, and Academic Associations of General Practitioners/Family Physicians** (WONCA) International Classification Committee (WHO 2008c). According to WONCA, ICPC-2 has been developed as a tool for general practitioners and family doctors throughout the world. It has been mapped to ICD-10 so that conversion systems can be used. Extensive use has confirmed that it and ICD-10 are complementary rather than in competition. ICPC-2 includes a severity of illness checklist and functional status assessment charts (Jamoulle 1998). Table 13.4 depicts the four categories of diagnosis in primary care in ICPC.

Table 13.4. ICPC-2's four categories of diagnosis in primary care

Category	Description	Examples
1. Aetiological and pathological	The diagnosis has proven pathology or aetiology	Appendicitis, acute myocardial infarction
2. Pathophysiological	The diagnosis has a proven pathophysiological substrate	Presbycusis, hypertension
3. Nosological	The diagnosis depends on a symptom complex based on consensus between physicians	Depression, irritable bowel syndrome
4. Symptom	A symptom or complaint is the best medical label for the episode	Fatigue, eye pain

Current Dental Terminology

The **Current Dental Terminology** (CDT) is a reference manual maintained and updated annually by the American Dental Association. Included in the manual is the Code on Dental Procedures and Nomenclature (the Code) which is a classification system for dental treatment procedures and services. The Code has been designated as the national standard for reporting dental services by the Federal Government under the **Health Insurance Portability and Accountability Act** (HIPAA), and is recognized by third-party payers nationwide. The codeset is organized into 12 categories of service, each with its own series of five-digit alphanumeric codes (see table 13.5). Each category of service is divided into subcategories of generally recognized related procedures (ADA 2008).

National Drug Codes

The **Food and Drug Administration** (FDA) developed the **National Drug Codes** (NDCs) to serve as a universal product identifier for human drugs. It identifies the labeler/vendor, product, and trade package size. It is an approved HIPAA billing/financial transaction code set for reporting drugs and biologicals. In 2004, the NDCs were adopted as a federal healthcare information interoperability standard to enable the federal healthcare sector to share information regarding drug products (USHIK 2008).

Each drug product is assigned a unique 10-digit, 3-segment number. The three segments of an NDC represent:

- First segment—labeler code, assigned by the FDA. A labeler is a firm that manufactures, repacks, or distributes a drug product
- Second segment—product code, identifies a specific strength, dose form, and formulation for a particular firm.
- Third segment—package code, identifies package sizes. Both the product and package codes are assigned by the firm.

Table 13.5. Examples of CDT 2005 codes

Category of Service	Code Series	Example Code	Nomenclature	Descriptor (if applicable)
I. Diagnostic	D0100–D0999	D0277	Vertical bitewings–7 to 8 films	This does not constitute a full mouth intraoral radiographic series.
II. Preventive	D1000–D1999	D1320	Tobacco counseling for the control and prevention of oral disease	Tobacco prevention and cessation services reduce patient risks of developing tobacco-related oral diseases and conditions and improves prognosis for certain dental therapies.
III. Restorative	D2000–D2999	D2390	Resin-based composite crown, anterior	Full resin-based composite coverage of tooth.
IV. Endodontics	D3000–D3999	D3410	Apicoectomy/periradicular surgery–anterior	For surgery on root of anterior tooth. Does not include placement of retrograde filling material.
V. Periodontics	D4000–D4999	D4355	Full mouth debridement to enable comprehensive evaluation and diagnosis	The gross removal of plaque and calculus that interfere with the ability of the dentist to perform a comprehensive oral evaluation. This preliminary procedure does not preclude the need for additional procedures.
VI. Prosthodontics, removable	D5000–D5899	D5110	Complete denture–maxillary	
VII. Maxillofacial Prosthetics	D5900–D5999	D5984	Radiation shield	Synonymous terminology: radiation stent, tongue protector, lead shield. An intraoral prosthesis designed to shield adjacent tissues from radiation during orthovoltage treatment of malignant lesions of the head and neck region.
VIII. Implant Services	D6000–D6199	D6010	Surgical placement of implant body: endosteal implant	Includes second-stage surgery and placement of healing cap.
IX. Prosthodontics, fixed	D6200–D6999	D6794	Crown–titanium	
X. Oral Surgery	D7000–D7999	D7220	Removal of impacted tooth–soft tissue	Occlusal surface of tooth covered by soft tissue; requires mucoperiosteal flap elevation.
XI. Orthodontics	D8000–D8999	D8691	Repair of orthodontic appliance	Does not include bracket and standard fixed ortho appliances. It does include functional appliances and palatal expanders.
XII. Adjunctive General Services	D9000–D9999	D9230	Analgesia, anxiolysis, inhalation of nitrous oxide	

Source: ADA 2008.

The NDC will be in one of the following configurations: 4-4-2, 5-3-2, or 5-4-1 (see table 13.6). Each manufacturer defines the specific codes for their own products. Therefore, there is no uniform class hierarchy for the codes, and codes may be reused at the manufacturer's discretion (Hammond and Cimino 2001).

Table 13.6. Examples of NDC codes

Drug	NDC Code
Fluoxetine 100 mg Caps	00172-4363-70
Prenatal Plus Tab	0093-9111-01
Hydrocodone/APAP 7.5/500 mg Tab	00591-0385-05
Glycolax 3350 NF POW	62175-442-31
Flonase 0.05% Nasal Spray	00173-0453-01
Progesterone 600 mg Supp	51927-1046-00
Seraquel 100 mg Tab	00310-0271-10
Axert 12.5 mg Tab	00062-2085-06
Amitriptyline 25 mg Tab	00603-2213-32
Amoxicillin 400 mg/5 Susp	63304-0970-04

Check Your Understanding 13.2

Instructions: Answer the following questions on a separate piece of paper.

1. What was the original purpose of ICD-9-CM?
2. Name and describe the four characteristics of ICD-10-PCS that makes it an improvement over ICD-9-CM for a procedural coding system.
3. What is the primary function of CPT?
4. What does the topography code in ICD-O describe?

Healthcare Terminologies

Along with the many data standards discussed in chapter 7, healthcare terminologies facilitate health information exchange by standardizing the data collected. Through this standard representation of data, terminologies provide shared meaning and a sense of context for the information being used. In simple terms, this ability to exchange information between computer systems is referred to as **interoperability**.

A 2006 Presidential Executive Order calling for the promotion of quality and efficient healthcare provides a more detailed definition for interoperability as "the ability to communicate and exchange data accurately, effectively, securely, and consistently with different information technology systems, software applications, and networks in various settings, and exchange data such that clinical or operational purpose and meaning of the data are preserved and unaltered" (Bush 2006). Many experts have identified a lack of interoperability as a major obstacle to realizing the full potential of EHR systems and the exchange of health information (Ash and Bates 2005) (NCVHS 2005) (AMIA and AHIMA Terminology and Classification Policy Task Force 2007).

Interoperability is often described in levels. The NCVHS has identified three levels: basic, functional, and semantic. Basic interoperability relates to the ability to successfully transmit and receive data from one computer to another. The ability to understand or interpret the information being transmitted is not essential to basic interoperability. Functional interoperability refers to sending messages between computers with a shared understanding of the structure and format of the message. With functional interoperability, the receiving computer can store information in a similar data field because the nature (context) of the data being sent is understood. For example, the receiving computer could recognize that the information being sent is a lab result and store it accordingly. The NCVHS definition of semantic interoperability is similar to that of the Health Level Seven's (HL7) EHR Interoperability Work Group in which the information being transmitted is understood (NCVHS 2000) (EHR Interoperability Work Group 2007). So, building on the previous example, the receiving system would not only recognize that what was being sent is a lab value but would also understand the method used to calculate the value and the reference ranges for a normal result. The use of clinical terminologies in EHRs to provide standardized data is essential to achieving semantic interoperability. Progress is being made in the incorporation of clinical terminologies into EHR systems.

There are different types of clinical terminologies each of which serve unique purposes. Spackman, Campbell, and Cote (1997) defined a **reference terminology** for clinical data as "a set of concepts and relationships that provides a common reference point for comparison and aggregation of data about the entire healthcare process, recorded by multiple different individuals, systems, or institutions." A reference terminology provides a common source to which data captured through other terminologies and classifications can be mapped. This linkage back to a common source facilitates aggregation and comparison of data. SNOMED CT, a widely used reference terminology, is discussed later in this chapter. An **interface terminology** is concerned with facilitating clinician documentation within the standardized structure (for example, menus, drop-down boxes) needed for an EHR. An interface terminology provides a limited set of words and phrases in a manner that is consistent with a clinician's thought process used while documenting. Information represented by an interface terminology is often mapped to similar concepts in a comprehensive reference terminology. In this sense the interface terminology serves as a conduit between the natural language expression of the healthcare provider and the data as it is represented by the reference terminology (Rosenbloom et al. 2006).

The following section describes some of the terminologies being used more commonly in EHRs and their uses.

Systematized Nomenclature of Medicine-Clinical Terms (SNOMED CT)

The **Systematized Nomenclature of Medicine-Clinical Terms** (SNOMED CT) is a comprehensive multi-hierarchical concept-oriented clinical terminology owned, maintained, and distributed by the **International Health Terminology Standards Development Organisation** (IHTSDO), an international non-profit organization based in Denmark. Table 13.7 lists the top-level hierarchies into which SNOMED CT is organized.

The size of the terminology conveys how extensive it is. The 2008 release of SNOMED CT includes more than 315,000 active concepts, 806,000 active descriptions, and 945,000 defining relationships (IHTSDO 2008a; 2008b). A

Table 13.7. Example of SNOMED hierarchies

Clinical finding
• Finding *(Swelling of arm)*
• Disease *(Pneumonia)*
Procedure *(Biopsy of lung)*
Observable entity *(Tumor stage)*
Body structure *(Structure of thyroid)*
• Morphologically abnormal structure *(Granuloma)*
Substance *(Gastric acid)*
Pharmaceutical/biologic product *(Tamoxifen)*
Specimen *(Urine specimen)*
Qualifier value *(Right)*
Record artifact *(Death certificate)*
Physical object *(Suture needle)*
Physical force *(Friction)*
Environments/geographical locations *(Intensive care unit)*
Social context *(Organ donor)*
Situation with explicit content *(No nausea)*
Staging and scales *(Barthel index)*
Linkage concept
• Link assertion *(Has etiology)*
• Attributes *(Finding site)*
Special concept *(Inactive concept)*

Source: IHTSDO 2008.

concept is the most granular unit within a terminology. In SNOMED CT, it is specifically defined as "a single clinical meaning identified by a unique numeric identifier" (College of American Pathologists 2008). Multiple descriptions are oftentimes assigned to a single concept. For example, the descriptions heart attack, myocardial infarction, and cardiac infarction would all be linked to a single concept. **Relationships** describe how the concepts within SNOMED CT are linked to one another. An example of a relationship is that the concept *diabetes mellitus* is an *endocrine disorder*, another concept with a broader meaning (IHTSDO 2008c).

The current terminology—SNOMED CT—is the result of the evolution and combination of various classifications and terminologies over the past several decades. SNOMED was originally built on the Systematized Nomenclature of Pathology (SNOP), which was introduced in 1965. Like SNOP, SNOMED uses an alphanumeric, multiaxial coding scheme (Kudla and Blakemore 2001). In 1997, the College of American Pathologists (CAP) worked with a team of physicians and nurses from Kaiser Permanente to begin development of the **Systematized Nomenclature of Medicine-Reference Terminology** (SNOMED RT). One of the ways that SNOMED RT came to be recognized as a reference terminology was by the inclusion of an elementary mapping to ICD-9-CM (Kudla and Blakemore 2001). SNOMED also worked with the **Digital Imaging and Communications in Medicine** (DICOM) community, the Logical Observation Identifier Names and Codes (LOINC) system, and the various nursing vocabularies to further expand its content. In 2002, SNOMED RT and Clinical Terms, Version 3 (CTV3), also known as the Read Codes, merged to create the SNOMED–Clinical Terminology (CT) system. In 2007, the SNOMED CT intellectual property rights were transferred from the College of American Pathologist to IHTSDO.

HHS recommended SNOMED CT as part of a core set of **patient medical record information** (PMRI) terminology in 2003. Then in 2004, SNOMED CT was adopted as a federal information technology interoperability standard (IHTSDO 2008b):

- Describe specific nonlaboratory interventions and procedures performed or delivered
- Exchange results of laboratory tests between facilities
- Describe anatomical locations for clinical, surgical, pathological, and research purposes
- Diagnosis and problem lists
- Define terminology of the delivery of nursing care

Tables 13.8 and 13.9 illustrate level of detail comparisons between SNOMED CT concepts and codes to ICD-9-CM and CPT.

Examples of Implementations of SNOMED CT

A recent survey found that SNOMED CT is currently being used in EHR systems as a clinical reference terminology to capture data for problem lists, quality reporting alerts, warnings, or reminders generated by decision support, data retrieval, supporting data collection at the point of care, and for patient care assessments. The survey findings also indicated that current users of SNOMED CT plan to increase their usage of the terminology in the EHR over the next several years (Giannangelo and Fenton 2008). The Department of Veteran Affairs (VA) is using SMOMED CT for standardization of problem list entries, allergic reactions, and anatomy coding in autopsy reports. A subset of SNOMED CT terms that can be used to represent problem list entries documented within an EHR is available for download at the Unified Medical Language System's Web site. The list is being provided without any licensing or intellectual property restrictions in an effort to facilitate use of the SNOMED CT terms for problem list data representation (NLM 2008c). The incorporation of SNOMED CT into EHR applications is increasing (IHTSDO 2008d).

Table 13.8. SNOMED ICD clinical detail comparison: Specimen adequacy

SNOMED	Description	ICD
112631006	Specimen unsatisfactory for diagnosis	799.9
77289001	Insufficient tissue for diagnosis	
67736002	Specimen poorly fixed	
54192004	Specimen obscured by foreign material	
63038006	Specimen obscured by inflammation	
84567002	Specimen obscured by blood	
7667005	Specimen shows excessive cytolysis	

Source: CAP n.d.

Table 13.9. SNOMED CPT clinical detail comparison: Procedures

SNOMED-CT	Description	CPT
	Total abdominal hysterectomy with or without removal of tubes, with or without removal of ovaries	58150
86477000	–with removal of tube and ovary	
27950001	–with unilateral removal of ovary	
31545000	–with unilateral removal of tube	

Source: CAP n.d.

Logical Observation Identifiers, Names and Codes

Development of the **Logical Observation Identifiers, Names and Codes** (LOINC) began in February 1994. Today, LOINC is generally accepted as the exchange standard for laboratory results. The Regenstrief Institute maintains the LOINC database and its supporting documentation. Most healthcare facilities and reference laboratories use their own protocols for storing lab test and result information. The goal for LOINC is not to replace the laboratory fields in facility databases but, rather, to provide a mapping mechanism. The LOINC committee hoped that laboratories would create fields in their master files for storing LOINC codes and names as attributes of their own data elements. (Regenstrief Institute 2008). Each LOINC name identifies a distinct laboratory observation and is structured to contain up to six parts, including:

- Analyte/component (for example, potassium, hemoglobin)
- Kind of property measured or observed (for example, mass, mass concentration, enzyme concentration)
- Time aspect of the measurement or observation (a point in time versus an observation integrated over time)
- System and sample type (for example, urine, blood, serum)
- Type of measurement or observation scale (quantitative [a number] versus qualitative [a trait such as cloudy])
- Type of measurement or observation method used (for example, clean catch or catheter)

Table 13.10 provides an example of a LOINC code and the characteristics with its corresponding attributes.

The primary disadvantage to LOINC is that it may require significant modifications to work with a current laboratory information system that has been previously using its own protocols for lab data representation. A distinct advantage to using LOINC is that it enables the standardized communication of laboratory results. Large integrated delivery systems that have very diverse laboratory processing systems (the machines that perform the tests) will find it easier to maintain and use an EHR with LOINC-identified laboratory results.

LOINC is divided into two major sections: Lab LOINC and Clinical LOINC. Clinical LOINC includes entries for vital signs, hemodynamics, intake/output, EKG, obstetric ultrasound, cardiac echo, urologic imaging, gastroendoscopic procedures, pulmonary ventilator management, selected survey instruments, and other clinical observations.

In 2003, LOINC was adopted as a federal health information interoperability standard for the electronic exchange of laboratory test orders and drug label section headers using **Structured Product Labeling** (SPL) (Regenstrief Institute 2008).

Table 13.10. Example of a LOINC code and its attributes

LOINC number	10968-6
Component/Analyte	Smudge cells/100 leukocytes
Property	NFr (number fraction)
Time aspect	Pt (point in time)
System (sample type)	Bld (whole blood)
Scale type	Qn (quantitative—continuous numeric scale
Method type	Manual count

Source: Regenstrief Institute 2008.

Examples of LOINC Implementations

LOINC has been implemented in a number of different healthcare settings. Many large commercial laboratories such as Quest and LabCorp have adopted LOINC as an alternate format for reporting lab data. The Department of Veterans Affairs (VA) has implemented Lab LOINC as their primary coding system for laboratory tests and HL7 messages. The **Consolidated Health Informatics** (CHI) initiative has recommended the use of Clinical LOINC to fully specify document titles in text-based documentation (Regenstrief Institute 2008). Several healthcare facilities have reported successful use of LOINC to standardize the reporting of laboratory data (Baorto et al. 1998; Khan et al. 2006).

Clinical Care Classification

The **Clinical Care Classification** (CCC) system is a standardized, coded nursing terminology that identifies the discrete elements of nursing practice. CCC provides a unique **framework** and coding structure for capturing the essence of patient care in all healthcare settings.

The system consists of two interrelated terminologies: one to capture nursing diagnoses and outcomes and another to capture nursing interventions and actions. It is classified by 21 Care Components. The care components provide a standardized framework that links the CCC terminologies to each other and enables them to be mapped to other health-related classification systems. This increases the opportunities for health information and interoperability in the important area of nursing.

The CCC system can be used for a number of purposes. Primarily, it facilitates capturing standardized data with the electronic documentation of patient care at the point of care. It can be used to track nursing activities in patient care, clinical pathways, decision support, and the effect of nursing care on patient outcomes. Furthermore, it can be used to predict workload, resource needs, and determine costs of nursing care. This is difficult to capture without a standardized method for codifying nursing data.

The CCC also has applications in nursing education. It can be used to teach students how to document patient care electronically and the characteristics of a nursing terminology for documentation purposes. For the most part, nursing documentation is still primarily done on paper. Future nurses need to transition to the electronic health record and education is key.

Another important functionality the CCC provides is in the area of nursing research (table 13.11). It supports analy-

Table 13.11. Examples of CCC system nursing diagnoses

Code	Category	Diagnosis
A01	Activity Alteration	Change in or modification of energy used by the body
A01.1	Activity Intolerance	Incapacity to carry out physiological or psychological daily activities
A01.2	Activity Intolerance Risk	Increased chance of an incapacity to carry out physiological or psychological daily activities
O38.1	Activities of Daily Living (ADLs) Alteration	Change in modification of ability to maintain oneself
Q45.1	Acute Pain	Physical suffering or distress; to hurt
E12.1	Adjustment Impairment	Inadequate adaptation to condition or change in health status
U61.4	Adolescent Behavior Alteration	Change in or modification or normal standards of performing developmental skills and behavior of a typical adolescent from 12 years through 20 years of age
U61.5	Adult Behavior Alteration	Change in or modification or normal standards of performing developmental skills and behavior of a typical adult from 21 years through 64 years of age
L26.1	Airway Clearance Impairment	Inability to clear secretions/obstructions in airway
N58.2	Alcohol Abuse	Excessive use of distilled liquors

Source: Saba 2005.

sis and evaluation of patient outcomes, facilitates the design of expert systems, and the advancement of nursing practice knowledge. The CCC's standardized terminology allows much higher quality data for the research. It also allows the data to be captured and reviewed more quickly than paper documentation. Thus, the knowledge gained can be utilized to improve the nursing care provided to patients at the point of care (Saba 2008).

RxNorm

RxNorm is a standardized nomenclature for clinical drugs that provides information on a drug's ingredients, strengths, and form in which it is to be administered or used. It is produced by the National Library of Medicine and allows various systems using different drug nomenclatures to share data efficiently at the appropriate level of detail. RxNorm's standard names for clinical drugs are connected to the names of drugs present in many other controlled vocabularies, including those available in drug information sources today. These connections facilitate interoperability among the electronic health record systems that record or process data dealing with clinical drugs. (NLM 2008d). Examples of the linkages provided through RxNorm include from brand named and generic named clinical drugs to their active ingredients, drug components, and related brand names. They can also be connected to the FDAs NDCs (refer to table 13.6) for specific drug products and many of the drug vocabularies commonly used in pharmacy management and drug interaction (NIST 2008). This nomenclature provides a detailed level of codified data that facilitates interoperability between pharmacy systems. It allows these systems to check for drug–drug or drug–allergy interactions so that providers can avoid prescribing certain drugs and to give them other prescription choices with no adverse effects. This functionality is available today on a limited basis for patients that are treated in both the VA and Department of Defense (DoD) medical treatment facilities. It has already been shown to significantly decrease medication errors, duplicate prescriptions, and most importantly, improved patient safety.

MEDCIN

MEDCIN is a proprietary clinical terminology owned and maintained by Medicomp Systems. The system was initially developed by Peter Goltra in 1978 and has been updated regularly. Table 13.12 contains examples of a few of the MEDCIN approximately 270,000 clinical elements created with a strong focus on facilitating documentation by providing clinically relevant choices in a format that is consistent with the provider's clinical thought processes. Because of this feature, the system is considered to be an interface terminology (Bowman 2005; Fraser 2005). MEDCIN is licensed by EHR developers that incorporate the terminology into

Table 13.12. Examples of MEDCIN clinical elements

Code Number	Clinical Element
1931	Joint swelling, fingers, right hand
34183	Chronic interstitial cystitis
49339	Mechanical vitrectomy by pars plana approach
48618	Acetaminophen + Diphenhydramine
35034	Accident involving a motor vehicle, collision with another motor vehicle on the road

Source: Goltra 1997.

their EHR systems. For example, MEDCIN is the clinical terminology used by the DoD in its Armed Forces Health Longitudinal Technology Application (AHLTA) system. MEDCIN also identifies relationships through multiple hierarchies for each of its clinical elements. These linkages support other functionalities of the system such as clinical alerts, automated note generation, and computer-assisted coding for CPT evaluation and management codes (Goltra 1997; Medicomp Systems 2008).

Check Your Understanding 13.3

1. What is semantic interoperability?
2. Identify a clinical terminology that would be a good candidate to represent: a) laboratory data, b) nursing documentation, and c) problem list documentation.
3. What do the terms *concept* and *relationship* mean in the context of SNOMED CT?

Other Emerging Healthcare Terminologies, Classifications, and Nomenclatures

National Cancer Institute Thesaurus

The **National Cancer Institute (NCI) Thesaurus** (figure 13.6) contains the working vocabulary used in NCI data systems. It covers clinical, translational, and basic research as well as administrative terminology. In May 2004, the NCI Thesaurus was adopted as a federal healthcare information interoperability standard to describe anatomical locations for clinical, surgical, pathological, and research purposes (NAHIT 2005).

The NCI Terminology Browser displays the NCI Thesaurus. The Thesaurus is an open content vocabulary that is free to use with virtually no restrictions. It is built so that both humans and computers can interpret it (NCI 2004).

Figure 13.6. NCI thesaurus taxonomy concept details

Identifiers:	
Name	Pancreas
Code	C12393
Relationships to other concepts:	
Anatomic_Structure_Has_Location	Epigastric Region
Anatomic_Structure_is_Physical_Part-of	Gastrointestinal System
Information about this concept:	
Display_Name	Pancreas
Mitelman_Code	218
Preferred_Name	Pancreas
Semantic_Type	Body Part, Organ, or Organ Component
Subsource	ICD
Subsource	LASH
Subsource	Mitelman
Unified Medical Language System	C0030274

Source: NCI 2005.

Human Genome Nomenclature

The **Human Genome Nomenclature** (HUGN) provides data for all human genes which have approved symbols (see table 13.13). It is managed by the **Human Genome Organisation** (HUGO) Gene Nomenclature Committee (HGNC) as a confidential database containing over 16,000 records. Gene records can be searched on the Web by symbol or name to directly retrieve information on gene symbol, gene name, cytogenic location, OMIM (Online Mendelian Inheritance in Man) number and PubMed ID. Data are integrated with other human gene databases and approved gene symbols are carefully coordinated with the Mouse Genome Database (MGD). The online version of the database is updated weekly. HUGN was adopted as a federal health information interoperability standard for exchanging information regarding the role of genes in biomedical research and healthcare (NAHIT 2005).

Global Medical Device Nomenclature

Medical devices consist of such things as home blood pressure monitors, blood glucose devices, and ventilators. A standard is needed to inventory devices, document their use by healthcare providers, and regulate their availability and use in the community by public health agencies. Regulation involves approval and classifications of devices as well ensuring the safety and effectiveness of these products.

Table 13.13. Human genes with approved symbols: Single-letter amino acid codes

Amino Acid	Three-Letter Symbol	One-Letter Symbol
Alanine	Ala	A
Arginine	Arg	R
Asparagine	Asn	N
Aspartic Acid	Asp	D
Asn + Asp	Asx	B
Cysteine	Cys	C
Glutamine	Gln	Q
Glutamic Acid	Glu	E
Gln + Glu	Glx	Z
Glycine	Gly	G

Source: Wain et al. 2002.

The **Global Medical Device Nomenclature** (GMDN) is a collection of internationally recognized terms used to describe and catalogue medical devices and supplies. It provides the names, definitions, and unique codes for medical devices and supplies. The GMDN contains nearly 7,000 terms plus more than 10,000 synonyms. GMDN is currently divided into 12 categories that encompass all of these products (figure 13.7). As new product areas need to be included into this classification system, a new category will be allotted and that category then developed.

GMDN was developed through the harmonization of six established medical device terminologies including a previous version of the **Universal Medical Device Nomenclature System** (UMDNS). It is primarily used by regulatory agencies such as the Federal Drug Agency (FDA) in the United States. It is strongly supported by the FDA for communicating this data. They also recommend that the GMDN eventually replace the FDA terminology for devices. The nomenclature is used extensively outside the U.S. and is recognized by the European Committee for Standardization (CEN) and other international bodies.

Figure 13.7. GMDN device categories

The Standard allocates codes for a possible 20 categories. For this version of the GMDN 13 device categories are now established. These are:	
01	Active implantable devices
02	Anaesthetic and respiratory devices
03	Dental devices
04	Electro mechanical medical devices
05	Hospital hardware
06	In vitro diagnostic devices (IVD)
07	Nonactive implantable devices
08	Ophthalmic and optical devices
09	Reusable instruments
10	Single use devices
11	Technical aids for disabled persons
12	Diagnostic and therapeutic radiation devices
13	Obsolete terms
14	Vacant
15	Vacant
16	Vacant
17	Vacant
18	Vacant
19	Vacant
20	Vacant

Source: BSI Group 2004.

The Consolidated Health Informatics (CHI) group was an initiative to approve interoperability standards in the United States. CHI recommended that the GMDN and UMDNS be merged and the resulting terminology be adopted as the standard. The GMDN and UMDNS are similar in scope. The FDA and **Emergency Care Research Institute** (ECRI) are currently producing a map of UMDNS to GMDN to coordinate their practices that may lead to a merger in the near future. This should result in a terminology that enables the U.S. federal system to utilize one set of medical device names, definitions, and codes. These identifiers may also be used to communicate with foreign entities.

Universal Medical Device Nomenclature System

The Universal Medical Device Nomenclature System (UMDNS) is a standard international nomenclature and computer coding system for medical devices. It facilitates identifying, processing, filing, storing, retrieving, transferring, and communicating data about medical devices. It is primarily used by healthcare institutions. It has been adopted by many nations, including the entire European Union (EU). It is used in applications ranging from hospital inventory and work-order controls to national agency medical device regulatory systems. It is incorporated into the UMLS. See the section on the Global Medical device Nomenclature for the planned merger of these two nomenclatures (NAHIT 2005).

Environmental Protection Agency Substance Registry System

The **Environmental Protection Agency** (EPA) **Substance Registry System** (SRS) provides information on substances and how they are represented in the EPA's regulations and information systems. It provides a common basis for identification of chemicals, biological organisms, and other substances listed in EPA regulations and data systems, as well as substances of interest from other sources, such as publications. The EPA SRS was adopted as the federal health information interoperability standard for chemicals in May 2004 (see table 13.14) (NAHIT 2005).

Breast Imaging Reporting and Data System Atlas

Breast Imaging Reporting and Data System Atlas (BI-RADS) was designed to serve as a comprehensive guide providing standardized breast imaging terminology, a report organization, assessment structure, and a classification system for mammography, ultrasound, and MRI of the breast (NAHIT 2005). BI-RADS assessment categories are listed in table 13.15.

BI-RADS is the product of a collaboration effort among members of various committees of the American College of Radiology with cooperation from the National Cancer Institute, the Centers for Disease Control and Prevention, the FDA, and the **College of American Pathologists.** Results are compiled in a standardized manner that permits the maintenance and collection analysis of demographic, mammographic, and outcome data (ACR 2003).

Table 13.14. Example of an EPA SRS substance list

Name	Liquid Nitrogen (Containing)
Molecular Formula	[No Criteria Specified]
Type	All
Classification	All
Display Option	Substance Name
Sort Option	Name
Systematic Name	Nitrogen
EPA Registry Name	Nitrogen
Classification	Chemical
CAS number	7727-37-9
TSN	
ICTV	
EPA ID	
Compare?	

Source: EPA 2005.

Table 13.15. BI-RADS mammography assessment categories

Assessment	Category
a. Mammographic Assessment is Incomplete	0: Need Additional Imaging Evaluation and/or Prior Mammograms for Comparisons
b. Mammographic Assessment is Complete–Final Categories	1: Negative
	2: Benign Finding(s)
	3: Probably Benign Finding–Initial Short-Interval Follow-Up Suggested
	4: Suspicious Abnormality–Biopsy Should Be Considered
	5: Highly Suggestive of Malignancy–Appropriate Action Should Be Taken (Almost certainly malignant)
	6: Known Biopsy–Proven Malignancy–Appropriate Action Should Be Taken

Source: ACR 2003.

Medical Dictionary for Regulatory Activities

MedDRA, the **Medical Dictionary for Regulatory Activities**, is a pragmatic, medically valid terminology with an emphasis on ease of use for data entry, retrieval, analysis, and display, as well as a suitable balance between sensitivity and specificity within the regulatory environment. It was developed by the International Conference on Harmonisation (ICH) and is owned by the International Federation of Pharmaceutical Manufacturers and Associations (IFPMA) acting as trustee for the ICH steering committee.

MedDRA terminology applies to all phases of drug development, excluding animal toxicology. It also applies to the health effects and malfunction of devices.

Who should subscribe to MedDRA?

- Pharmaceutical companies
- Biotechnology companies
- Device manufacturers
- Regulatory authorities
- Contract research organizations
- Systems developers
- Other support service organizations

The Maintenance and Support Services Organization (MSSO) serves as the repository, maintainer, and distributor of MedDRA as well as the source for the most up-to-date information regarding MedDRA and its application within the biopharmaceutical industry and regulators. MedDRA subscribers submit proposed changes to the terminology. The MSSO includes a group of internationally based physicians who review all proposed subscriber changes and provide a timely response directly to the requesting subscriber (MSSO 2008).

SNODENT

The **Systematized Nomenclature of Dentistry** (SNODENT) is a clinical vocabulary developed by the American Dental Association (ADA) for data representation of clinical dentistry content. The need for interoperable dental information is increasing as the field of dentistry is moving more into the medical management of oral diseases. For example, dentists now sometimes perform saliva testing which is performed for the purpose of substance abuse and disease monitoring. This type of information may need to be shared with other healthcare providers. The ADA SNODENT editorial panel is responsible for maintaining the terminology (Furlong 2008).

Evaluation of Clinical Terminologies and Classification Systems

As HIM professionals search for ways to formalize the myriad types of data contained in EHRs, it helps to be able to evaluate the different classifications and terminologies. Certain characteristics are desirable. The first 12 characteristics listed here are taken from Cimino (1998). The final six are taken from Campbell, who presented additional requirements after his experience with implementing a terminology for Kaiser Permanente (Campbell et al. 1999). The characteristics are listed here:

- Content: The content of clinical classifications and terminologies should be determined by their intended use. It is wise to assume that the first identified need will never be the last or only need. It is far better to have too much content initially than to have too little to meet subsequent needs.
- Concept orientation: The content of terminologies and classifications should be oriented toward concepts rather than terms or code numbers. For example, "cold" can either be a disease (Chronic Obstructive Lung Disease or the common cold), or a feeling of temperature—these are three separate concepts.
- Concept **permanence**: Terminologies and classifications must be permanent if they are to be useful for longitudinal reporting. Concepts may be inactivated but must never be deleted.
- Nonsemantic concept identifier: No implicit or explicit meaning can be associated with the code numbers used in a classification system. Because primary healthcare systems are now computerized, the human ability to use a classification system without a computer is no longer necessary. For example, in ICD-9-CM code 250.xx is related to diabetes regardless of when the condition was put into ICD-9-CM. Thus, 250 has meaning.
- **Polyhierarchy**: Multiple relationships should exist for every concept. For example, bacterial pneumonia is both a pulmonary disease and an infectious disease.
- Formal definitions: Standardized definitions are necessary to ensure comparability among terminologies and classifications. They also reduce confusion.
- Reject Not Elsewhere Classified (NEC): **Not Elsewhere Classified** is not the same as **Not Otherwise Specified** (NOS). NOS means that there is no additional information. NEC means you have more information but no place to put it. It also means that any additional information will be lost forever if it is assigned the NEC label (for example, assigning "Pneumonia, NEC" when you know the bacterial agent causing the pneumonia, but ICD-9-CM doesn't accommodate it).
- Multiple granularities: Because classifications and terminologies must fulfill multiple purposes, the information in them may be specific or general so that all needs can be met.
- Multiple consistent views: Classifications and terminologies must accommodate more than one viewpoint to allow them to be multipurpose as well as to ensure continuity of care. When caring for the same patient, nurses want to use nurse speak and physicians want to use physician speak.
- Context representation: Words have different meanings when used in different contexts or as different grammatical parts of language. **Context** is determined by how the concepts relate to each other. For example, consider the term "cold." In the phrase "the patient is cold," cold is how the patient feels. In the phrase, "the patient has a cold," cold is a disease. The difference between the two phrases reflects the two different contexts of the word "cold."
- Graceful evolution: The days of yearly updates need to end soon. Future updates will have to be made monthly or, more likely, weekly. The growth of medical knowledge is exponential; classification systems and terminologies must to be able to keep up.
- Recognized redundancy: Classifications and terminologies need to accommodate redundancy.
- Licensed and copyrighted: Terminologies and classifications need to be copyrighted and licensed to control local modifications, which result in semantic drift and produce incomparable data.
- **Vendor neutral**: Classifications and terminologies must be vendor neutral so that they can be readily used as national standards by all vendors without conferring a competitive advantage to any one of them.
- Scientifically valid: Terminologies and classifications should be understandable, reproducible, and useful and should reflect the current understanding of the science.
- Adequate maintenance: A central authority that provides a rapid response to requests for new terms is essential to minimize the need for local enhancements and to keep terminologies and classifications current.
- Self-sustaining: Classifications and terminologies should be supported by public or endowment funding. Alternatively, licensing fees should be proportional to the value the system provides to users.
- Scalable infrastructure and process control: The tools and processes for maintaining a terminology or classification should be scalable, especially for a nationally standardized terminology.

ASTM Standard E 2087-00

HIM professionals should use all of their system analysis and data management skills when evaluating the appropriateness of a clinical terminology for a particular function or need. A helpful reference for evaluating the quality of a clinical terminology is the **American Society for Testing and Materials** (ASTM) Standard E 2087-00: Standard Specification for Quality Indicators for Controlled Health Vocabularies (ASTM International 2000). This standard covers the principal notions needed to assign value to a controlled vocabulary. It provides guidelines needed to build useful, maintainable vocabularies and improve terminology development. It specifies the minimum requirements and a starting point for developers. It is applicable in all areas of healthcare where clinical data is kept or utilized (ASTM 2000). The specific evaluation criteria from this standard are:

6. Evaluation

6.1 As we seek to understand quality in the controlled vocabularies that we create or use, we need standard criteria for the evaluation of these systems. All evaluations should reflect and specifically identify the purpose and scope of the vocabulary being evaluated.

6.2 Purpose and Scope: Important dimensions along which scope should be defined include:

6.2.1 Clinical Area of Use, Disease Area of Patients, and Expected Profession of Users—In what parts of healthcare is it intended to be used and by whom?

6.2.2 Primary Use—Includes: reporting for remuneration, management planning, epidemiological research, indexing for bibliographic, Web-based retrieval, recording of clinical details for direct patient care, use for decision support, linking of record to decision support, and the like.

6.2.3 **Persistence** and Extent of Use—Some vocabularies are intended, at least initially, primarily for a specific study or a specific site. If a vocabulary is intended to be persistent, there should be a means of updating or some kind of change management.

6.2.4 Degree of Automatic **Inferencing** Intended—Is it intended that classification be automatic? Is it intended that validation on input be possible and, if so, within what limits? If post-coordinated expressions are to be accepted, what can be inferred about them and what restrictions must be placed on them?

6.2.5 **Transformations** (Mappings) to Other Vocabularies—What transformations/mappings are supported for what intended purpose? For example, transformation for purposes of bibliographic retrieval may require less precision than transformation for clinical usage. What is the sensitivity and specificity of the mappings?

6.2.6 User/Developer **Extensibility**—Is it intended that the vocabulary be extended by users or applications developers? If so, within what limits? If not, what mechanisms are available for meeting new needs as they arise?

6.2.7 Natural Language Input or Output—Are they supported for analysis or input? To what level of competence are they supported, for example, stilted telegraphic presentation, idiomatic presentation, and such?

6.2.8 Other Functions—What other functions are intended? Examples include linkage to specific decision support systems, linkage to post-marketing surveillance, and the like.

6.2.9 Current Status—To what extent is the system intended to be finished or a work in progress? If different components of the terminology are at different stages of completion, how is this indicated?

National Library of Medicine's Role in Healthcare Terminologies

The **National Library of Medicine** (NLM) is the world's largest medical library. It collects materials in all aspects of biomedicine and healthcare, as well as works on biomedical aspects of technology, the humanities, and the physical, life, and social sciences. It is a standards-supporting/promoting organization that explores the uses of computer and communication technologies to improve organizations and the use of biomedical information. It is responsible for publishing Medical Subject Headings (MeSH), RxNorm, Semantic Clinical Drug (SDC) of RxNorm, and the Unified Medical Language Systems (UMLS) (NAHIT 2005).

Unified Medical Language System

The **Unified Medical Language System** (UMLS) is a government-funded project from the NLM. The UMLS has been in development since 1986. The purpose of the UMLS is "to facilitate the development of computer systems that behave as if they 'understand' the meaning of the language of biomedicine and health. The UMLS provides data for system developers as well as search and report functions for less technical users (NLM 2008e)." This goal is achieved through the three knowledge sources found in the UMLS: (1) the UMLS Metathesaurus, (2) the SPECIALIST Lexicon, and (3) the UMLS Semantic Network. More information on the UMLS can be obtained from the NLM Web site. When looking in-depth at the UMLS, it is important to keep in mind that it has been designed for computer use; its layouts and other structures are meant to be read by machines. It is not structured to be readable by humans.

UMLS Metathesaurus

The **UMLS Metathesaurus** contains information on biomedical concepts and terms from more than 100 controlled vocabularies and classifications used in health records, administrative health data, bibliographic and full-text databases, and expert systems. It preserves the names, meanings, hierarchical contexts, attributes, and interterm relationships present in its source vocabularies; adds certain basic information to each concept; and establishes new relationships among terms from different source vocabularies. Its source vocabularies include terminologies designed for use in health record systems; large disease and procedure classifications used for statistical reporting and billing; more narrowly focused vocabularies used to record data related to psychiatry, nursing, medical devices, adverse drug reactions, and so on; disease and finding terminologies from expert diagnostic systems; and some thesauri used in information retrieval.

Computer programs can use information in the Metathesaurus to interpret user inquiries, interact with users to refine their questions, identify the databases that contain information relevant to particular inquiries, and convert the users' terms into the vocabulary used by relevant information sources. The scope of the Metathesaurus is determined by the combined scope of its source vocabularies.

The Metathesaurus is produced by the automated processing of machine-readable versions of its source vocabularies, followed by human review and editing by subject experts. It is intended primarily for use by system developers but also can be a useful reference tool for database builders, librarians, and other information professionals.

UMLS SPECIALIST Lexicon

The **UMLS SPECIALIST Lexicon** is an English-language lexicon containing many biomedical terms. It has been developed in the context of the SPECIALIST natural language processing project at the NLM. The current version includes over 200,000 terms.

The lexicon entry for each word or term records syntactic, morphological, and orthographic information. (**Syntactic** refers to the formal properties of language; **morphological** refers to the study and description of word formation in a language, including inflection, derivation, and compounding; and **orthographic** refers to the correctness of spelling or the representation of the sounds of a language by written or printed symbols.) Lexical entries may be single-word or multiword terms. Entries that share their base form and spelling variants, if any, are collected into a single lexical record. The base form is the uninflected form of the lexical item—the singular form in the case of a noun, the infinitive form in the case of a verb, and the positive form in the case of an adjective or adverb.

UMLS Semantic Network

The **UMLS Semantic Network,** through its 135 semantic types, provides a consistent categorization of all concepts represented in the UMLS Metathesaurus. The 54 links between semantic types provide the structure for the network and represent important relationships in the biomedical domain. All information on specific concepts is found in the Metathesaurus; the network provides information on the basic semantic types assigned to these concepts and defines their possible relationships.

Examples of UMLS Implementation

The VA has used the UMLS Metathesaurus as a lookup tool for finding concepts, synonyms, and linkages to other terminologies in the data standardization of allergies data. They are also using the UMLS RxNorm for standardizing pharmacy data and are sharing that data with the Department of Defense as part of the Consolidated Health Data Repository (CHDR) interagency project. It has also been proposed to use UMLS as the mediation terminology for VA drug classes in the CHDR project. Vanderbilt University has used UMLS in their WizOrder order entry and decision support system.

Medical Subject Headings

Medical Subject Headings (MeSH) is the NLM's controlled vocabulary thesaurus. It consists of terms naming descriptors in a hierarchical structure that permits searching at various levels of specificity (NAHIT 2005). The descriptors exist in both alphabetic and hierarchical structures. It contains very broad headings, such as "Mental Disorders," and more specific levels, such as "Conduct Disorder." There are 22,568 descriptors in MeSH and more than 139,000 headings, called Supplementary Concept Records, within a separate thesaurus. Thousands of cross-references also exist. MeSH is used by the NLM for indexing articles from 4,600 of the world's leading biomedical journals for the MEDLINE/PubMed database. Each bibliographic reference is associated with a set of MeSH terms that describe the content of the item. Staff subject specialists are responsible for revising and updating the vocabulary on a continuous basis. MeSH is available in electronic format at no charge at www.nlm.nih.gov/mesh and a hard copy version is published each January (UMLS 2005).

Mapping Initiatives

As illustrated with this chapter's descriptions of widely varying clinical classifications and terminologies, no single system meets all needs. Maps which link related content in classifications and terminologies allow data collected for one purpose to be used for another. For example, a laboratory system that manages data using the LOINC terminology, can map the LOINC terms to CPT codes to be used for billing purposes. The NLM, within the framework of the UMLS, contains many sets of mapping among terminologies including a LOINC to CPT mapping and a SNOMED CT to ICD-9-CM (NLM 2008e).

Mapping is the process by which concepts and terms in one system are associated with concepts and terms that are the same or substantially similar in another system. Many maps are created to support a specific use case. For example, the map created for a reimbursement use case might be very different from a public health use case. This is even true if the two use cases were mapping between the same two systems. Therefore, successful mapping requires a thorough understanding of the intended use of the map (use case), the structure and purpose of the source, and target terminologies (Foley et al. 2007).

Most often, the links created in a map are categorized according the how closely the terms in each system are related (Imel 2002). Examples of these categories are:

- *One-to-One*: An exact match is made between the systems
- *Narrow-to-Broad*: A more granular term in the starting system maps to a more general term in the receiving system
- *Broad-to-Narrow*: A more general term in the starting system maps to a more granular term in the receiving system
- *Unmappable*: There is no match in the receiving system

Developing and maintaining maps that have been created between classifications and terminologies is a relatively new field, and best practices for validation and routine maintenance are still being developed. Maintenance of maps is resource intensive requiring review and updating, as necessary, of established links whenever a source or target terminology is updated. As electronic health records continue to evolve, the need for cross-system maps and for persons who understand map creation, validation, and maintenance will increase.

Health Level Seven Vocabulary Workgroup

The objective of the **Health Level Seven** (HL7) Vocabulary Workgroup is to identify, organize, and maintain coded vocabulary terms used in HL7 messages. It's goal is to provide an organization and repository for maintaining a coded vocabulary that, when used in conjunction with HL7 and related standards, will enable the exchange of clinical data and information so that sending and receiving systems have a shared, well defined, and unambiguous knowledge of the meaning of the data transferred. The purpose of the exchange of clinical data includes, but is not limited to: provision of clinical care, support of clinical and administrative research, execution of automated transaction-oriented decision logic (medical logic modules), support of outcomes research, support of clinical trials, and support of data reporting to government and other authorized third parties. To achieve this goal, the workgroup works cooperatively with all other groups that have an interest in coded vocabularies used in clinical computing. These groups include standards development organizations, creators and maintainers of vocabularies, government agencies and regulatory bodies, clinical professional specialty groups, vocabulary content providers, and vocabulary tool vendors (HL7 2007).

AHIMA Clinical Terminology and Vocabulary Community of Practice

The AHIMA Clinical Terminology and Vocabulary **Community of Practice** (CoP) is the community for those interested in clinical terminologies and vocabularies. It contains information of interest to health information management professionals as well as others interested in this topic. Like other CoPs, it includes sections for announcements, FAQs, links, resources, document collaboration, HIM Body of Knowledge, and discussion. Contributions to content and questions are always welcome and improve the usefulness of the community.

Check Your Understanding 13.4

Instructions: Answer the following questions on a separate piece of paper.

1. Why is concept of permanence important in clinical terminologies and classifications?
2. What is another name for context representation? What does the term mean?
3. What is the role of mapping in relation to clinical terminologies?

Real-World Case

Diane Parisian, RHIA, CCS, works at the National Aeronautics and Space Administration (NASA) Johnson Space Center in Houston, Texas. Diane's official employer is Wyle Laboratories. She is working on a longitudinal study of astronaut health. The goal of this study is to investigate the incidence of morbidity and mortality of astronauts and to determine whether the occupational exposures are related to an increased risk of morbidity or mortality.

Diane's title is coder/analyst. This is a fairly generic job title and her duties go beyond what a coder/analyst performs in a hospital setting. Her official job description includes entering data from many different sources into a research database. The research project entails getting as much past and present health information as possible about the astronauts, from any and all sources. The data is then encoded and entered into the database.

Although they currently use both ICD-9-CM and SNOMED CT, the researchers plan to eventually discontinue the ICD-9-CM coding. The researchers originally tried to used ICD-9-CM but found that it did not have enough detail. When they would search the database, they would retrieve irrelevant records. The researchers needed the data representation to be more accurate so they could be more efficient. NASA is hoping that as the electronic health record (EHR) becomes more prevalent and providers start using SNOMED CT, more information will be able to be shared electronically.

Diane received her Bachelor's in Health Information Management from the University of Texas Medical Branch (UTMB) in Galveston, TX. After graduation she worked as an area manager for a release of information company and was a coder at a hospital before the job at NASA. Diane found out about the job at NASA from a friend who saw the posting on the Internet. When they talked about the job Diane realized she lived close to NASA and even knew other health information managers who worked at NASA. She called her contact at NASA and while she knows that didn't get her the job, she believes it helped get her in the door for the interview. Diane decided she was ready for a new challenge and accepted the position.

When asked to describe her training for the position, Diane says most of it was on-the-job training. There is another coder/analyst who had already received SNOMED training and she trained Diane. Diane said that her understanding of coding, communication skills, and flexibility have been most useful in this position. The coding and classification skills learned for ICD-9-CM can be transferred to SNOMED CT. The communication skills necessary include technical writing, presentation skills, and the ability to get along with others. Diane has often had to work in teams on different projects and says she cannot image doing a job without these skills. The flexibility has been needed as Diane has had to take the lead on certain aspects of this project. Diane thinks she would have been better prepared for the job if she had had more training in database design and some basic programming.

The most unexpectedly frustrating part of the job has been coding with SNOMED CT. There are no instructions for coding with SNOMED CT as there are for ICD-9-CM, so now the NASA team is working with other experts in the field on the best methods for coding in SNOMED CT. The team was interested in making the data comparable but couldn't find anyone with an answer so they have decided to develop their own internal guidelines. To support these guidelines, they are developing their own software. This will assist the coders in getting the data in, so that the researchers can get information out. Diane is on the team developing the software and has been involved in writing technical requirements and use case documents. The most surprising thing about Diane's job is that she finds herself involved in many projects outside her normal duties—both HIM and non-HIM related projects. She says that her HIM and organizational skills transfer to other projects.

Diane sees terminologies and vocabularies as a huge opportunity for the future of health information management. She says we should not be afraid to venture into new territory. To quote her, "If we don't step up and deal with it, someone else will." Diane encourages everyone to keep up with the developments in the field of classifications and vocabularies.

Summary

A variety of classifications and terminologies exist to support different healthcare functions. Classifications are used to aggregate data for functions such as data analysis and reimbursement. Clinical terminologies play an essential role in capturing and sharing data in a manner that meets the requirements of semantic interoperability, which is essential for reliable health information exchange. Mapping is a function which allows for the reuse of data captured for one purpose to be used for other purposes. In order to reach the full potential of health information exchange, HIM professionals must participate in the development, implementation, and maintenance of information systems that use standard terminologies, nomenclatures, and classification systems.

References

American College of Radiology. 2003. BI-RADS Atlas. http://www.acr.org.

American Dental Association. 2008. *Current Dental Terminology, CDT-2009–2010*. Chicago: ADA.

American Health Information Management Association. 2010. *Pocket Glossary of Health Information Management and Technology*. 2nd ed. Chicago, IL: AHIMA.

American Health Information Management Association and American Hospital Association. 2003 (Sept. 23). *ICD-10-CM Field Testing Project: Report on Findings*. Chicago: AHIMA and AHA.

American Medical Association. 2008. CPT (Current Procedural Terminology). http://www.ama-assn.org/ama/pub/category/3113.html.

American Medical Informatics Association and American Health Information Management Association Terminology and Classification Policy Task Force. 2007 (June 27). Healthcare terminologies and classifications: An action agenda for the United States. *Perspectives in Health Information Management*. http://library.ahima.org/xpedio/groups/public/documents/ahima/bok1_032401.html.

American Psychiatric Association. 2008a. DSM-V: The Future Manual.

American Psychiatric Association. 2008b. Diagnostic and Statistical Manual. http://www.psych.org/MainMenu/Research/DSMIV.aspx.

American Society for Testing and Materials. 2008. Standard E 2087-00: Standard Specification for Quality Indicators for Controlled Health Vocabularies, ASTM International, West Conshohocken, PA, www.astm.org.

Ash, J. S. and D.W. Bates. 2005. Factors and forces affecting EHR system adoption: Report of a 2004 ACMI discussion. *Journal of the American Medical Informatics Association* 12(1):8–12.

ASTM International. 2000. ASTM E2087-00: Standard specification for quality indicators for controlled health vocabularies. West Conshohocken, PA: ASTM.

Averill, R.F., R.L. Mullin, B.A. Steinbeck, N.I. Goldfield, T.M. Grant, and R.R. Butler. 2005. *Development of the ICD-10 Procedure Coding System (ICD-10-PCS)*. 3M HIS Research Report 1-05. St. Paul, MN: 3M.

Baorto, D M., J J. Cimino, C A. Parvin, and M G. Kahn. 1998. Combining laboratory data sets from multiple institutions using the logical observation identifier names and codes (LOINC). *International Journal of Medical Informatics* 51(1):29–37.

Barnett, O.G., et al. 1993. The computer-based clinical record: Where do we stand? *Annals of Internal Medicine* 119(10):1046–1048.

Bidgood, W.D., Jr. 1997. Documenting the information content of images. Proceedings of the AMIA Annual Fall Symposium: 424–428.

Bowman, S. 2005 (Spring). Coordination of SNOMED-CT and ICD-10: Getting the most out of electronic health record systems. *Perspectives in Health Information Management* Chicago, AHIMA.

BSI Group. 2004. Global Medical Device Nomenclature (GMDN). http://www.gmdn.org.

Bush, G. W. 2006. Executive Order: Promoting Quality and Efficient Health Care in Federal Government Administered or Sponsored Health Care Programs. Washington, D.C.

Butler, R. 2007. The ICD-10 general equivalence mappings: Bridging the translation gap from ICD-9. *Journal of AHIMA* 78 (9):84–86.

Campbell, K.E., B. Hochhalter, J. Slaughter, and J. Mattison. 1999. Enterprise issues pertaining to implementing controlled terminologies. IMIA Conference Proceedings. Edmonton, AB: IMIA.

Centers for Medicare and Medicaid Services. 2008a. ICD-10-PCS 2008 Version What's New in this Release. http://www.cms.hhs.gov/ICD10/Downloads/pcs_whats_new_2008.pdf.

Centers for Medicare and Medicaid Services. 2008b. HCPCS General Information. http://www.cms.hhs.gov/MedHCPCSGenInfo/.

Chute, C.G. 2000. Clinical classification and terminology: Some history and current observations. *Journal of the American Medical Informatics Association* 70 (3):298–303.

Cimino, J.J. 1998. Desiderata for controlled medical vocabularies in the twenty-first century. *Methods of Information in Medicine* 37:394–403.

College of American Pathologists. 2008. SNOMED Terminology Solutions. http://www.cap.org/apps/cap.portal?_nfpb=true&_pageLabel=snomed_page.

Department of Health and Human Services. 2005. Administrative simplification transaction and code sets, frequently asked questions. http://aspe.hhs.gov/admnsimp/final/txfin01.htm.

Department of Health and Human Services. 2008. HIPAA Administrative Simplification: Modifications to Medical Data Code Set Standards to Adopt ICD-10CM and ICD-10-PCS. *Federal Register* 73 (164):49796–49832.

Department of Health and Human Services, Centers for Disease Control, National Center for Health Statistics. 2005. *International Classification of Diseases*. 10th Revision. http://www.hhs.gov.

Department of Veterans Affairs. n.d. http://www.va.gov.

EHR Interoperability Work Group. 2007. Coming to Terms: Scoping Interoperability for Health Care: Health Level Seven.

Environmental Protection Agency Substance Registry System. 2005. Substance List. http://www.epa.gov/srs.

Evans, K. 2004 (July 14). Statement to the subcommittee on technology, information policy, intergovernmental relations and the census. Washington, D.C.: U.S. House of Representatives.

Foley, M.M., C.Hall, K. Perron, and R. D'Andrea. 2007. Translation please: Mapping translates clinical data between the many languages that document it. *Journal of AHIMA* 78 (2):34–38.

Food and Drug Administration. n.d. http://www.fda.gov.

Fraser, G. 2005. Problem list coding in e-HIM. *Journal of AHIMA* 76 (7):68–70.

Furlong, A. 2008 (June 18). 2015 EHR deadline "just around the corner.'" *ADA News*.

Giannangelo, K., and S. H. Fenton. 2008. SNOMED CT survey: An assessment of implementation in EMR/EHR applications. *Perspectives in Health Information Management* 5:7.

Goltra, P.S. 1997. *MEDCIN: A New Nomenclature for Clinical Medicine*. New York: Springer-Verlag.

Hammond, W.E. and J.J. Cimino. 2001. Standards in medical informatics. In *Health Informatics*. Edited by Hannah, K.J. and M.J. Ball. New York: Springer-Verlag.

Health Level Seven. 2005. HL7 NLM contract announcement. http://www.hl7.org.

Imel, M. 2002. A closer look: The SNOMED Clinical Terms to ICD-9-CM mapping. *Journal of AHIMA* 73 (6):66–69.

International Health Terminology Standards Development Organisation. 2008a. *Second 2008 International Release of SNOMED CT Now Available*. http://www.ihtsdo.org/fileadmin/user_upload/Docs_01/News/Second_2008_International_Release_Press_Release.pdf.

International Health Terminology Standards Development Organisation. 2008b. *SNOMED 2008* Fact Sheet. http://www.cap.org/apps/docs/snomed/documents/january_2008_release.pdf.

International Health Terminology Standards Development Organisation. 2008c. SNOMED CT User Guide – July 2008 International Release.

International Health Terminology Standards Development Organisation. 2008d. Who is using SNOMED-CT? http://www.ihtsdo.org/snomed-ct/who-is-using-snomed-ct.

Jamoulle, M. 1998. ICPC-2: The international classification of primary care: An introduction. http://www.ulb.ac.be/esp/wicc/icpc2.html.

Khan, A.N., S. P. Griffith, C. Moore, D. Russell, A. C. Rosario, Jr., and J. Bertolli. 2006. Standardizing laboratory data by mapping to LOINC. *Journal of the American Medical Informatics Association* 13 (3):353–355.

Kudla, K.M. and M. Blakemore. 2001. SNOMED takes the next step. *Journal of AHIMA* 72(7):62–68.

Levin, R. 2004 (June 14). FDA related activities: Structured product labeling project for the daily med initiative. Drug Information Association annual meeting. http://www.fda.gov/cder/present/DIA2004/Levin_DailyMed.PPT.

Medicomp Systems, Inc. 2008. *MEDCIN*. http://www.medicomp.com/index_html.htm.

Merriam-Webster Online Dictionary. 2008. http://www.merriam-webster.com.

National Alliance for Health Information Technology. 2005. Alliance Standards Directory. http://www.hitsdir.org.

National Cancer Institute. 2004. NCI DTS browser. http://www.nciterms.nci.nih.gov/NCI Browser.

National Committee on Vital and Health Statistics. 2003 (Nov. 5). Letter to Tommy G. Thompson, Secretary, Department of Health and Human Services. http://www.ncvhs.hhs.gov/031105/t.htm.

National Committee on Vital and Health Statistics. 2005. NCVHS Subcommittee on Standards and Security. http://www.ncvhs.hhs.gov/stdschrg.htm.

National Institute of Standards and Technology. 2008. Health Information Technology (HIT) Implementation Testing and Support Web site for the Nationwide Health Information Network (NHIN) Initiative. http://xreg2.nist.gov/hit-testing.

National Library of Medicine. 2005. Fact sheet: Medical subject headings. http://www.nlm.nih.gov/pubs/factsheets/mesh.html.

National Library of Medicine. 2008a. Unified Medical Language System Glossary. http://www.nlm.nih.gov/research/umls/online%20learning/glossary.htm#l.

National Library of Medicine. 2008b. UMLS Knowledge Source Server Mappings: Draft LNC215 to CPT2005 Mapping. http://umlsks.nlm.nih.gov/uPortal/tag.b19c0fb661fa2381.render.userLayoutRootNode.uP?uP_fname=mappings-download.

National Library of Medicine. 2008c. UMLS Enhanced VA/KP Problem List Subset of SNOMED CT. http://www.nlm.nih.gov/research/umls/Snomed/snomed_problem_list.html.

National Library of Medicine. 2008d. RxNorm Overview. http://www.nlm.nih.gov/research/umls/rxnorm/overview.html.

National Library of Medicine. 2008e. UMLS 2008AA Documentation, Section 2 Metathesuarus. http://www.nlm.nih.gov/research/umls/meta2.html.

Regenstrief Institute, Inc. 2008. Logical Observation Identifiers Names and Codes. http://loinc.org.

Rosenbloom, S.T., R.A. Miller, K.B. Johnson, P.L. Elkin, and S.H. Brown. 2006. Interface terminologies: facilitating direct entry of clinical data into electronic health record systems. *Journal of the American Informatics Association* 13 (3):277–288.

Saba, V.K. 2008. Clinical Care Classification (CCC) System. http://www.sabacare.com.

Spackman, K.A., K.E. Campbell, and R.A. Cote. 1997. SNOMED RT: A reference terminology for health care. *Proceedings/AMIA Annual Fall Symposium* 640:4.

Unified Medical Language System. 2005. RxNorm. http://www.nlm.nih.gov/research/umls/rxnorm_main.html.

United States Health Information Knowledgebase. 2008. Consolidated Health Informatics. http://www.dcg.dnsalias.net/chi.

Wain, H.M., E.A. Bruford, R.C. Lovering, M.J. Lush, M.W. Wright, and S. Povey. 2002. Guidelines for Human Gene Nomenclature. *Genomics* 79(4): 464–470. http://www.gene.ucl.ac.uk/nomenclature/guidelines.html.

World Health Organization. History of the development of ICD. http://www.who.int/classifications/icd/en/HistoryOfICD.pdf.

World Health Organization 2007. Production of ICD-11: The overall revision process.

World Health Organization. 2008a. *International Classification of Diseases for Oncology,* 3rd Edition. http://www.who.int/classifications/icd/adaptations/oncology/en/index.html.

World Health Organization. 2008b. *International Classification of Functioning, Disability and Health*. http://www.who.int/classifications/icf/en.

World Health Organization. 2008c. *International Classification of Primary Care, Second edition (ICPC-2)*. http://www.who.int/classifications/icd/adaptations/icpc2/en/index.html.

Chapter 14
Reimbursement Methodologies

Anita C. Hazelwood, MLS, RHIA, FAHIMA
and Carol A. Venable, MPH, RHIA, FAHIMA

Learning Objectives

- Understand the historical development of healthcare reimbursement in the United States
- Describe current reimbursement processes, forms, and support practices for healthcare reimbursement
- Describe the difference between commercial health insurance and employer self-insurance
- Describe the purpose and basic benefits of the following government-sponsored health programs: Medicare Part A, Medicare Part B, Medicare Advantage, Medicaid, CHAMPVA, TRICARE, IHS, TANF, PACE, SCHIP, workers' compensation, and FECA
- Understand the concept of managed care and provide examples of different types of managed care organizations
- Identify the different types of fee-for-service reimbursement methods
- Understand ambulatory surgery center rates
- Describe prospective payment systems for various types of healthcare facilities and services
- Explain the elements of coding quality
- Differentiate between encoders, automated code assignment, and computer-assisted coding
- Describe the purpose of the fee schedules, chargemasters, and auditing procedures that support the reimbursement process

Key Terms

Accept assignment
Accounts receivable
Acute care prospective payment system (PPS)
Administrative services only (ASO) contracts
Advance Beneficiary Notice (ABN)
All patient DRGs (AP-DRGs)
All patient refined DRGs (APR-DRGs)
Ambulatory payment classification (APC) system
Ambulatory surgery center (ASC)
Ambulatory Surgery Center Prospective Payment System (ASC PPS)
Auditing
Automated code assignment
Balance billing
Balanced Budget Refinement Act (BBRA)
Blue Cross and Blue Shield (BC/BS)
Blue Cross and Blue Shield Federal Employee Program (FEP)
Bundled payments
Capitation
Case-mix group
Case-mix group (CMG) relative weights
Case-mix index
Categorically needy eligibility groups (Medicaid)
Chargemaster
Civilian Health and Medical Program of the Uniformed Services (CHAMPUS)
Civilian Health and Medical Program–Veterans Administration (CHAMPVA)
Claim
CMS-1500
Coding
Coinsurance
Comorbidity
Compliance
Compliance program guidance
Complication
Computer-assisted coding (CAC)
Coordination of benefits (COB) transaction
Cost outlier
Cost outlier adjustment
Current Procedural Terminology (CPT)
Department of Health and Human Services (HHS)
Diagnosis-related groups (DRGs)
Discharge planning
Discounting
DRG grouper
Emergency Maternal and Infant Care (EMIC) Program
Employer-based self-insurance
Encoder
Episode-of-care (EOC) reimbursement
Exclusive provider organization (EPO)
Explanation of Benefits (EOB)
External reviews (audits)

Federal Employees' Compensation Act (FECA)
Fee schedule
Fee-for-service basis
Fiscal intermediary (FI)
Fraud and abuse
Geographic practice cost index (GPCI)
Global payment
Global surgery payment
Group health insurance
Group model health maintenance organization
Group practice without walls (GPWW)
Hard-coding
Health maintenance organization (HMO)
Health Plan Employer Data and Information Set (HEDIS)
Healthcare Common Procedure Coding System (HCPCS)
Healthcare provider
Home Assessment Validation and Entry (HAVEN)
Home health agency (HHA)
Home health prospective payment system (HH PPS)
Home health resource group (HHRG)
Hospice
Hospital-Acquired Conditions (HAC)
Hospitalization insurance (HI) (Medicare Part A)
ICD-9-CM (International Classification of Diseases, Ninth Revision, Clinical Modification)
Indemnity plans
Independent practice association (IPA)
Indian Health Service (IHS)
Inpatient psychiatric facility (IPF)
Inpatient rehabilitation facility (IRF)
Inpatient Rehabilitation Validation and Entry (IRVEN) system
Insured
Insurer
Integrated delivery system (IDS)
Integrated provider organization (IPO)
Long-term care hospital (LTCH)
Low-utilization payment adjustment (LUPA)
Major diagnostic category (MDC)
Major medical insurance (catastrophic coverage)
Managed care
Management service organization (MSO)
Medicaid
Medical foundation
Medically needy option (Medicaid)
Medicare
Medicare Administrative Contractor (MAC)
Medicare Advantage
Medicare carrier
Medicare fee schedule (MFS)
Medicare Severity Diagnosis Related Groups (MS-DRGs)
Medicare Summary Notice (MSN)
Medigap
Minimum Data Set 2.0 (MDS)
National Committee for Quality Assurance (NCQA)
National conversion factor (CF)
National Correct Coding Initiative (NCCI)
Network model health maintenance organization
Network provider
Nonparticipating providers
Omnibus Budget Reconciliation Act (OBRA)
Outcome and Assessment Information Set (OASIS)
Out-of-pocket expenses
Outpatient code editor (OCE)
Outpatient prospective payment system (OPPS)
Packaging
Partial hospitalization
Payer of last resort (Medicaid)
Payment status indicator (PSI)
Per member per month (PMPM)
Per patient per month (PPPM)
Physician–hospital organization (PHO)
Point-of-service (POS) plan
Policyholder
Preferred provider organization (PPO)
Premium
Present on admission (POA)
Primary care manager (PCM)
Primary care physician (PCP)
Principal diagnosis
Principal procedure
Professional component (PC)
Programs of All-Inclusive Care for the Elderly (PACE)
Prospective payment system (PPS)
Public assistance
Relative value unit (RVU)
Religious Non-Medical Health Care Institutions (RNHCI)
Remittance advice (RA)
Resident Assessment Validation and Entry (RAVEN)
Resource Utilization Groups, Version III (RUG-III)
Resource-based relative value scale (RBRVS)
Respite care
Retrospective payment system
Revenue codes
Skilled nursing facility prospective payment system (SNF PPS)
Social Security Act
Staff model health maintenance organization
State Children's Health Insurance Program (SCHIP)
State workers' compensation insurance funds
Supplemental medical insurance (SMI) (Medicare Part B)
Tax Equity and Fiscal Responsibility Act of 1982 (TEFRA)
Technical component (TC)
Temporary Assistance for Needy Families (TANF)
Traditional fee-for-service reimbursement
TRICARE
TRICARE Extra
TRICARE Prime
TRICARE Prime Remote
TRICARE Senior Prime
TRICARE Standard
UB-04
Unbundling
Upcoding
Usual, customary, and reasonable (UCR) charges
Voluntary Disclosure Program
Workers' compensation

In the United States, very complex systems are used to pay healthcare organizations and individual healthcare professionals for the services they provide. This complexity is due in part to the variety of reimbursement methods in use today as well as the strict requirements for detailed documentation to support medical **claims**. The government and other third-party payers also are concerned about potential **fraud and abuse** in claims processing. Therefore, ensuring that bills and claims are accurate and correctly presented is an important focus of healthcare **compliance**.

A reimbursement claim is a statement of services submitted by a **healthcare provider** (for example, a physician or a hospital) to a third-party payer (for example, an insurance company or Medicare). The claim documents the medical and surgical services provided to a specific patient during a specific period of care. Accurate reimbursement is critical to the operational and financial health of healthcare organizations. In most healthcare organizations, health insurance specialists process reimbursement claims. Health information management (HIM) professionals also play an important role in healthcare reimbursement by:

- Ensuring that health record documentation supports services billed
- Assigning diagnostic and procedural codes according to patient record documentation
- Applying coding guidelines and edits when assigning codes or **auditing** for coding quality and accuracy
- Appealing insurance claims denials

This chapter reviews the history of healthcare reimbursement in the United States and explains the different reimbursement systems commonly used since the advent of the various types of **prospective payment systems.** It then discusses a variety of healthcare reimbursement methodologies with a focus on Medicare prospective payment systems. Finally, it explains how reimbursement claims are processed and the support processes involved.

History of Healthcare Reimbursement in the United States

Healthcare reimbursement in the United States has a long and complex history. Until the late 1800s, Americans paid their own healthcare expenses. Many people without the means to pay for care received charity care or no care at all. Over the past 100 years, a number of groups attempted to develop systems that would ensure adequate healthcare for every American. But the development of prepaid insurance plans and third-party reimbursement systems did not follow a straight path. The result is the complicated reimbursement system in place today.

Campaigns for National Health Insurance

The American Association of Labor Legislation (AALL) began the campaign for health insurance in the United States with the creation of a committee on social welfare. The committee held its first national conference in 1913 and drafted model health insurance legislation in 1915. The proposed legislation limited coverage to the working class and others who earned less than $1,200 a year, including their dependents. Coverage included the services of physicians, nurses, and hospitals; sick pay; maternity benefits; and a death benefit of $50 to pay for funeral expenses. Although the plan was supported by the American Medical Association (AMA), it was never passed into law.

During the 1930s, expanding access to medical care services became the focus of healthcare reforms. Hospital costs increased as the middle class used more hospital services. Medical care, especially hospital care, became a larger item in family budgets. The Committee on the Cost of Medical Care (CCMC) was formed to address concerns about the cost and distribution of medical care. It was funded by eight philanthropic organizations, including the Rockefeller, Millbank, and Rosenwald foundations. It first met in 1926 and stopped meeting in 1932. The CCMC's published research findings demonstrated the need for additional healthcare services. The committee recommended that national resources be allocated for healthcare and that voluntary health insurance be provided as a means of covering medical costs. However, like the AALL's earlier efforts, nothing came of the CCMC initiative.

In 1937, the Tactical Committee on Medical Care was formed. It drafted the Wagner National Health Act of 1939. The act supported a federally-funded national health program to be administered by states and localities. The Wagner Act evolved from a proposal for federal grants-in-aid to a plan for national health insurance. The proposal called for compulsory national health insurance and a payroll tax. Although the proposed legislation generated extensive national debate, Congress did not pass it into law.

In 1945, the healthcare issue received the support of an American president for the first time when Harry Truman introduced a plan for universal comprehensive national health insurance. Proposed compromises included a system of private insurance for those who could afford it and public welfare services for the poor. Truman's plan died in a congressional committee in 1946.

After the Second World War, private insurance systems expanded and union-negotiated healthcare benefits served to protect workers from the impact of unforeseen healthcare expenses. The Hill-Burton Act (formally called the Hospital Survey and Construction Act) was passed in 1946. This health facility construction program was instituted under Title VI of the Public Health Service Act. The program was designed to provide federal grants for modernizing hospitals that had become obsolete due to a lack of capital investment from the onset of the Great Depression (1929) to the end of World War II (1945). The program later evolved to address other types of infrastructure needs. In return for federal funds, facilities agreed to provide medical services free or at reduced rates to patients who were unable to pay for their own care.

Congress first introduced a bill to fund coverage of hospital costs for Social Security beneficiaries in 1948. In response to criticism from the AMA, the proposed legislation was expanded to cover physician services. The concept of federal health insurance programs for the aged and the poor was highly controversial. It was not until 1965 that President Lyndon Johnson signed the law that created federal healthcare programs for the elderly and poor as part of his Great Society legislation (also called the War on Poverty).

Title XVIII of the **Social Security Act**, or Health Insurance for the Aged and Disabled, is commonly known as Medicare. Medicare legislation was enacted as one element of the 1965 amendments to the Social Security Act. Medicare is a health insurance program designed to complement the retirement, survivors, and disability insurance benefits enacted under Title II of the Social Security Act. When it was first implemented in 1966 it covered most Americans over the age of 65. In 1973, several additional groups became eligible for Medicare benefits, including those entitled to Social Security or Railroad Retirement disability cash benefits for at least 24 months, most persons with end-stage renal disease (ESRD), and certain individuals over 65 who were not eligible for paid coverage but elected to pay for Medicare benefits.

Medicaid was designed as a cost-sharing program between the federal and state governments. It pays for the healthcare services provided to many low-income Americans. The program became effective in 1966 under Title XIX of the Social Security Act. It allowed states to add health coverage to their **public assistance** programs for low-income groups, families with dependent children, the aged, and the disabled. Because Medicaid eligibility is based on meeting criteria other than income, today the program covers only about 40 percent of the population living in poverty.

The Medicare and Medicaid programs were originally the responsibility of the Department of Health, Education, and Welfare, the predecessor to the **Department of Health and Human Services** (HHS). The Social Security Administration (SSA) administered the Medicare program, and the Social and Rehabilitation Service (SRS) administered the Medicaid Program. In 1977, administration of Medicare and Medicaid was transferred to a newly created administrative agency within HHS, the Health Care Financing Administration (HCFA). HCFA's name changed in 2001, and the agency is now the Centers for Medicare and Medicaid Services (CMS).

The demand for medical services grew tremendously during the 1970s and early 1980s. As a result, health insurance premiums and the cost of funding Medicare and Medicaid programs skyrocketed. By the mid-1980s, both private and government-sponsored healthcare programs had instituted cost-cutting programs.

Since 1983, CMS has developed the prospective payment system (PPS) to manage the costs of the Medicare and Medicaid programs. The PPS for inpatient acute care was the first to be implemented, followed by several others ranging from home health services to outpatient facility services. The most recently implemented system is the inpatient psychiatric facilities. Medicare and Medicaid reimbursement is discussed in more detail later in the chapter.

Private and self-insured health insurance plans have also implemented a number of cost-containing measures, most notably, **managed care** delivery and reimbursement systems. Managed care has virtually eliminated **traditional fee-for-service reimbursement** systems in just two decades. The implementation of managed care systems has had far-reaching effects on healthcare organizations and providers in every setting. However, hospitals have experienced the greatest financial pressure. Managed care is discussed in detail later in this chapter.

Development of Prepaid Health Plans

In 1860, Franklin Health Assurance Company of Massachusetts became the first commercial insurance company in the United States to provide private healthcare coverage for injuries that did not result in death. Within 20 years, 60 other insurance companies offered health insurance policies and by 1900, both accident insurance companies and life insurance companies were offering policies. These early policies covered loss of income and provided benefits for a limited number of illnesses (such as typhus, typhoid, scarlet fever, and smallpox).

Modern health insurance was born in 1929, when Baylor University Hospital in Dallas, Texas, agreed to provide healthcare services to Dallas schoolteachers. The hospital agreed to provide room, board, and certain ancillary services to the teachers for a set monthly fee of 50 cents. This plan is generally considered to be the first Blue Cross plan. Such plans were attractive to consumers and hospitals alike because they provided a way to ensure that patients would be able to pay for hospital services when they needed them. Payment was made directly to the hospital, not to the patient. In addition, coverage usually included a hospital stay for a specified number of days or for specific hospital services.

The Blue Cross plans contrasted with standard **indemnity plans** (insurance benefits provided in the form of cash payments) offered by private insurance companies that reimbursed, or indemnified, the patient for covered services up to a specified dollar limit. It was then the responsibility of the hospital to collect the money from the patient. Blue Shield plans were eventually developed by physicians. The plans were similar to Blue Cross plans except that they offered coverage for physicians' services.

Starting in the 1930s, and continuing through World War II, traditional insurance companies added health insurance coverage for hospital, surgical, and medical expenses to their accident and life insurance plans. During World War II, **group health insurance** was offered as a way to attract scarce wartime labor. Group health insurance plans provide healthcare benefits to full-time employees of a company. This trend was strengthened by the favorable tax treatment for fringe benefits. Unlike monetary wages, fringe benefits were not subject to income or Social Security taxes. Therefore, a pretax dollar spent on health insurance coverage was worth more than an after-tax dollar spent directly on medical services. After the war, the Supreme Court ruled that employee benefits, including health insurance, were a legitimate part of the labor–management bargaining process. Health insurance quickly became a popular employee benefit.

Although early health insurance policies covered expenses associated with common accidents and illnesses, they were inadequate for coverage of extended illnesses and lengthy hospital stays. To correct this deficiency, insurance companies in the early 1950s began offering **major medical insurance** coverage for catastrophic illnesses and injuries. Major medical insurance provides benefits up to a high-dollar limit for most types of medical expenses. However, it usually requires patients to pay large deductibles. It also may place limits on charges (for example, room and board) and may require patients to pay a portion of the expenses. Blue Cross and Blue Shield soon followed suit by offering similar plans.

Typically, the major medical insurance **policyholder** (or **insured**) paid a specified deductible—the amount the insured pays before the **insurer** assumes liability for any remaining costs of covered services. After the deductible had been paid, insured and insurer (third-party payer) shared covered losses according to a specified ratio, and the insured paid a **coinsurance** amount. Coinsurance refers to the amount the insured pays as a requirement of the insurance policy. For example, an insurance company may require the insured to pay a percentage of the daily costs for inpatient care.

According to the Washington Insurance Council (a nonprofit association of insurance companies and insurance professionals), by 1955, health insurance coverage continued to expand, and eventually 77 million Americans were covered by either an indemnity plan or a major medical plan. In subsequent years, insurance companies introduced high-benefit-level major medical plans, which limited out-of-pocket expenses. **Out-of-pocket expenses** are the healthcare expenses the insured is responsible for paying. After the insured pays an amount specified in the insurance plan (that is, the deductible plus any copayments), the plan pays 100 percent of covered expenses. Such health insurance plans are common today and have been expanded to include coverage for advanced medical technology.

According to the U.S. Census Bureau, the percentage of people covered by health insurance in 2006 was 84.2 percent, lower than in previous years. (See table 14.1.)

The lack of health insurance for so many Americans continues to be a serious concern. Because of the financial constraints brought about by changes in Medicare and Medicaid as well as managed care reimbursement, many hospitals are no longer able to provide charitable services. As a result, underfunded and overcrowded public hospitals are struggling to provide services to uninsured patients who cannot pay for their own care. In addition, many uninsured patients delay seeking medical treatment until they are extremely ill, with long-term consequences for their own health and for the healthcare system. Thousands of patients with chronic diseases such as diabetes and asthma are brought to hospital emergency departments every day because they do not have access to basic healthcare services.

Table 14.1. Health insurance coverage status: 1987–2006

Year	Total U.S. Population (000)	Number Covered (000)	Percentage Covered
2006	298,754	251,551	84.2
2005	295,895	250,623	84.7
2004	293,191	249,212	85.0
2003	288,280	243,320	84.4
2002	285,933	242,360	84.8
2001	282,082	240,875	85.4
2000	279,517	239,714	85.8
1999	274,087	231,533	84.5
1998	271,743	227,462	83.7
1997	269,094	225,646	83.9
1996	266,792	225,077	84.4
1995	264,314	223,733	84.6
1994	262,105	222,387	84.8
1993	259,753	220,040	84.7
1992	256,830	218,189	85.0
1991	251,447	216,003	85.9
1990	248,886	214,167	86.1
1989	246,191	212,807	86.4
1988	243,685	211,005	86.6
1987	241,187	210,161	87.1

Source: Based on U.S. Census Bureau information: www.census.gov/hhes/hlthins/historic/hihistt4.html.

One solution to the problem may be to expand government-sponsored healthcare programs. Another may be to create tax incentives to help individuals and small employers purchase private health insurance. For example, tax deductions could be offered to low-income people who buy their own insurance, or tax credits could be offered to small employers that offer health insurance coverage to employees.

Check Your Understanding 14.1

Instructions: Answer the following questions on a separate piece of paper.

1. How did the uninsured pay for healthcare services prior to implementation of government programs (for example, Medicare)?
2. Why did the Centers for Medicare and Medicaid Services develop prospective payment systems?
3. Using table 14.1, calculate the percentage change in health insurance coverage status from 2005 to 2006.
4. Which government agency administers the Medicaid and Medicare programs?
5. During World War II, how did employers try to increase wartime labor?

Healthcare Reimbursement Systems

Before the widespread availability of health insurance coverage, individuals were assured access to healthcare only when they were able to pay for the services themselves. They paid cash for services on a retrospective **fee-for-service basis**, in which the patient was expected to pay the healthcare provider after a service was rendered. Until the advent of managed care, capitation, and other PPSs, private insurance plans and government-sponsored programs also reimbursed providers on a retrospective fee-for-service basis.

Fee-for-service reimbursement is now rare for most types of medical services. Today, most Americans are covered by some form of health insurance and most health insurance plans compensate providers according to predetermined discounted rates rather than fee-for-service charges. However, some types of care are not covered by most health insurance plans and are still paid for directly by patients on a fee-for-service basis. Cosmetic surgery is one example of a medical service that is not considered medically necessary and so is not covered by most insurance plans. Many insurance plans also limit coverage for psychiatric services, substance abuse treatment, and the testing and correction of vision and hearing.

Commercial Insurance

Most Americans are covered by private group insurance plans tied to their employment. Typically, employers and employees share the cost of such plans. Two types of commercial insurance are commonly available: private insurance and **employer-based self-insurance**.

Private Health Insurance Plans

Private commercial insurance plans are financed through the payment of **premiums**. Each covered individual or family pays a pre-established amount (usually monthly), and the insurance company sets aside the premiums from all the people covered by the plan in a special fund. When a claim for medical care is submitted to the insurance company, the claim is paid out of the fund's reserves.

Before payment is made, the insurance company reviews every claim to determine whether the services described on the claim are covered by the patient's policy. The company also reviews the diagnosis codes provided on the claim to ensure that the services provided were medically necessary. Payment then is made to either the provider or the policyholder.

When purchasing an insurance policy, the policyholder receives written confirmation from the insurance company when the insurance goes into effect. This confirmation document usually includes a policy number and a telephone number to be called in case of medical emergency. An insurance policy represents a legal contract for services between the insured and the insurance company.

Most insurance policies include the following information:

- What medical services the company will cover
- When the company will pay for medical services
- How much and for how long the company will pay for covered services
- What process is to be followed to ensure that covered medical expenses are paid

Employer-based Self-Insurance Plans

During the 1970s, a number of large companies discovered that they could save money by self-insuring their employee health plans rather than purchasing coverage from private insurers. Large companies have large workforces, and so aggregate (total) employee medical experiences and associated expenses vary only slightly from one year to the next. Periods of rapid inflation in healthcare charges is the exception to this. The companies understood that it was in their best interest to self-insure their health plans because yearly expenses could be predicted with relative accuracy.

The cost of self-insurance funding is lower than the cost of paying premiums to private insurers because the premiums reflect more than the actual cost of the services provided to beneficiaries. Private insurers build additional fees into premiums to compensate them for assuming the risk of providing insurance coverage. In self-insured plans, the employer assumes the risk. By budgeting a certain amount to pay its employees' medical claims, the employer retains control over the funds until the time when grouper medical claims need to be paid.

Employer-based self-insurance has become a common form of group health insurance coverage. Many employers enter into **administrative services only (ASO) contracts** with private insurers and fund the plans themselves. The private insurers administer self-insurance plans on behalf of the employers.

Blue Cross and Blue Shield Plans

Blue Cross and Blue Shield (BC/BS) plans, also known as the Blues, were the first prepaid health plans in the United States. Originally, Blue Cross plans covered hospital care and Blue Shield plans covered physicians' services.

The first Blue Cross plan was created in 1929. In 1939, a commission of the American Hospital Association (AHA) adopted the Blue Cross national emblem for plans that met specific guidelines. The Blue Cross Association was created in 1960, and the relationship with the AHA ended in 1972.

The first Blue Shield plan was created in 1939, and the Associated Medical Care Plans (later known as the National Association of Blue Shield Plans) adopted the Blue Shield symbol in 1948. In 1982, the Blue Cross Association and the National Association of Blue Shield Plans merged to create the Blue Cross and Blue Shield Association.

Today, the Blue Cross and Blue Shield Association includes over 60 independent, locally operated companies with plans in 50 states, the District of Columbia, and Puerto Rico. The Blues offer health insurance to individuals, small businesses, seniors, and large employer groups. In addition, federal employees are eligible to enroll in the **BC/BS Federal Employee Program** (FEP) (also called the BC/BS Service Benefit Plan). The plan offers these two products to federal employees:

- **Preferred provider organization (PPO) plan**: Healthcare providers provide healthcare services to members of the plan at a discounted rate
- **Point-of-service (POS) plan**: Subscribers are encouraged to select providers from a prescribed network but are allowed to seek healthcare services from providers outside the network at a higher level of copayment

Government-Sponsored Healthcare Programs

The federal government administers several healthcare programs. The best known are Medicare and Medicaid. The Medicare program pays for the healthcare services provided to Social Security beneficiaries 65 years old and older as well as permanently disabled people, people with end-stage renal disease, and certain other groups of individuals. State governments work with the federal Medicaid program to provide healthcare coverage to low-income individuals and families.

In addition, the federal government offers three health programs to address the needs of military personnel and their dependents as well as Native Americans. The Civilian Health and Medical Program–Veterans Administration (CHAMPVA) provides healthcare services for dependents and survivors of disabled veterans, survivors of veterans who died from service-related conditions, and survivors of military personnel who died in the line of duty. TRICARE (formerly CHAMPUS, the Civilian Health and Medical Program–Uniformed Services) provides coverage for the dependents of armed forces personnel and retirees receiving care outside a military treatment facility. The Indian Health Service (IHS) provides federal health services to American Indians and Alaska natives.

Medicare

The original **Medicare** program was implemented on July 1, 1966. In 1973, Medicare benefits were expanded to include individuals of any age who suffered from a permanent disability or end-stage renal disease.

For Americans receiving Social Security benefits, Medicare automatically provides **hospitalization insurance** (HI) (Medicare Part A). It also offers voluntary **supplemental medical insurance** (SMI) (Medicare Part B) to help pay for physicians' services, medical services, and medical–surgical supplies not covered by the hospitalization plan. Enrollees pay extra for Part B benefits. To fill gaps in Medicare coverage, most Medicare enrollees also supplement their benefits with private insurance policies. These private policies are referred to as **Medigap** insurance. **Medicare Advantage** (formerly Medicare+Choice) was established by the Balanced Budget Act (BBA) of 1997 to expand the options for participation in private healthcare plans. Established in 2003, Medicare Part D covers prescription drugs.

According to CMS, approximately 19 million Americans were enrolled in the Medicare program in 1966. In 2005, approximately 40 million people were enrolled in Parts A or B (or both) of the Medicare program, and 6.4 million of the enrollees participated in a Medicare Advantage plan.

Medicare Part A

Medicare Part A is generally provided free of charge to individuals age 65 and over who are eligible for Social Security or Railroad Retirement benefits. Individuals who do not claim their monthly cash benefits are still eligible for Medicare. In addition, workers (and their spouses) who have been employed in federal, state, or local government for a sufficient period of time qualify for Medicare coverage beginning at age 65.

Similarly, individuals who have been entitled to Social Security or Railroad Retirement disability benefits for at least 24 months and government employees with Medicare coverage who have been disabled for more than 29 months are entitled to Part A benefits. This coverage also is provided to insured workers (and their spouses) with end-stage renal disease as well as to children with end-stage renal disease. In addition, some otherwise-ineligible aged and disabled beneficiaries who voluntarily pay a monthly premium for their coverage are eligible for Medicare Part A.

The following healthcare services are covered under Medicare Part A: inpatient hospital care, long-term care, skilled nursing facility (SNF) care, home health care, and hospice care. (See table 14.2.) Medicare Part A pays for inpatient hospital care and long-term care when such care is medically necessary. An initial deductible payment is required for each hospital admission, plus copayments for all hospital days following day 60 within a benefit period.

Each benefit period begins the day the Medicare beneficiary is admitted to the hospital and ends when he or she has not been hospitalized for a period of 60 consecutive days. Inpatient hospital care is usually limited to 90 days during each benefit period. There is no limit to the number of benefit periods covered by Medicare hospital insurance during a beneficiary's lifetime. However, copayment requirements apply to days 61 through 90. When a beneficiary exhausts the

Table 14.2. Medicare Part A benefit period, beneficiary deductibles and copayments, and Medicare payment responsibilities according to healthcare setting

Healthcare Setting	Benefit Period	Patient's Responsibility	Medicare Payments
Hospital (Inpatient)	First 60 days Days 61–90 Days 91–150 (these reserve days can be used only once in the patient's lifetime) Beyond 150 days	$1,024 annual deductible $256 per day $512 per day All costs	All but $1,024 All but $256/day All but $512/day Nothing
Skilled Nursing Facility	First 20 days Days 21–100 Beyond 100 days	Nothing $128 per day All costs	100% approved amount All but $128 per day Nothing
Home Health Care	For as long as patient meets Medicare medical necessity criteria	Nothing for services, but 20% of approved amount for durable medical equipment (DME)	100% of the approved amount, and 80% of the approved amount for DME
Hospice Care	For as long as physician certifies need for care	Limited costs for outpatient drugs and inpatient respite care ($5 per prescription and 5% for respite care)	All but limited costs for outpatient drugs and inpatient respite care
Blood	Unlimited if medical necessity criteria are met	First 3 pints unless you or someone else donates blood to replace what you use	All but first 3 pints per calendar year

Source: Adapted from *Medicare and You* 2008.

90 days of inpatient hospital care available during a benefit period, a nonrenewable lifetime reserve of up to a total of 60 additional days of inpatient hospital care can be used. Copayments are required for such additional days.

SNF care is covered when it occurs within 30 days of a three-day-long or longer hospitalization and is certified as medically necessary. The number of SNF days provided under Medicare is limited to 100 days per benefit period, with a copayment required for days 21 through 100. Medicare Part A does not cover SNF care when the patient does not require skilled nursing care or skilled rehabilitation services.

Care provided by a **home health agency** (HHA) may be furnished part-time in the residence of a homebound beneficiary when intermittent or part-time skilled nursing and/or certain other therapy or rehabilitation care is needed. Certain medical supplies and durable medical equipment (DME) also may be paid for under the Medicare home health benefit.

The Medicare program requires the HHA to develop a treatment plan that is periodically reviewed by a physician. Home health care under Medicare Part A has no limitations on duration, no copayments, and no deductibles. For DME, beneficiaries must pay 20 percent coinsurance, as required under Medicare Part B.

Terminally ill persons whose life expectancies are six months or less may elect to receive **hospice** services. To qualify for Medicare reimbursement for hospice care, patients must elect to forgo standard Medicare benefits for treatment of their illnesses and agree to receive only hospice care. When a hospice patient requires treatment for a condition that is not related to his or her terminal illness, however, Medicare does pay for all covered services necessary for that condition. The Medicare beneficiary pays no deductible for hospice coverage but does pay coinsurance amounts for drugs and inpatient **respite care**. (Respite care is any inpatient care provided to the hospice patient for the purpose of providing primary care-givers a break from their care-giving responsibilities.)

Medicare Part B

Medicare Part B (supplemental medical insurance) covers the following services and supplies:

- Physicians' and surgeons' services, including some covered services furnished by chiropractors, podiatrists, dentists, and optometrists; and services provided by the following Medicare-approved practitioners who are not physicians: certified registered nurse anesthetists, clinical psychologists, clinical social workers (other than those employed by a hospital or an SNF), physician assistants, and nurse practitioners, and clinical nurse specialists working in collaboration with a physician
- Services in an emergency department or outpatient clinic, including same-day surgery and ambulance services
- Home healthcare not covered under Medicare Part A
- Laboratory tests, x-rays, and other diagnostic radiology services, as well as certain preventive care screening tests
- Ambulatory surgery center (ASC) services in Medicare-approved facilities
- Most physical and occupational therapy and speech pathology services

- Comprehensive outpatient rehabilitation facility services and mental healthcare provided as part of a partial hospitalization psychiatric program when a physician certifies that inpatient treatment would be required without the partial hospitalization services. (A **partial hospitalization** program offers intensive psychiatric treatment on an outpatient basis to psychiatric patients, with an expectation that the patient's psychiatric condition and level of functioning will improve and that relapse will be prevented so that rehospitalization can be avoided.)
- Radiation therapy, renal dialysis and kidney transplants, and heart and liver transplants under certain limited conditions
- DME approved for home use, such as oxygen equipment, wheelchairs, prosthetic devices, surgical dressings, splints, and casts, walkers, and hospital beds needed for use in the home
- Drugs and biologicals that cannot be self-administered, such as hepatitis B vaccines and immunosuppressive drugs (plus certain self-administered anticancer drugs)
- Preventive services such as bone mass measurements, cardiovascular screening blood tests, colorectal cancer screening, diabetes services, glaucoma testing, Pap test and pelvic exam, prostate cancer screening, screening mammograms, and vaccinations (flu, pneumococcal, hepatitis B)

To be covered, all Medicare Part B services must be either documented as medically necessary or covered as one of several prescribed preventive benefits. Also, Part B services are generally subject to deductibles and coinsurance payments. (See table 14.3.) Certain medical services and related care are subject to special payment rules, for example:

- Deductibles for administration of blood and blood products
- Maximum approved amounts for Medicare-approved physical or occupational therapy services performed in settings other than hospitals
- Higher cost-sharing requirements, such as those for outpatient psychiatric care

It should be noted that the following healthcare services are usually not covered by Medicare Part A or B and are only covered by private health plans under the Medicare Advantage program:

- Long-term nursing care
- Custodial care
- Dentures and dental care
- Eyeglasses
- Hearing aids

Medicare Advantage

Medicare Advantage provides expanded coverage of many healthcare services. Although any Medicare beneficiary may

Table 14.3. Medicare Part B benefit deductibles and copayments and Medicare payment responsibilities according to type of service

Type of Service	Benefit	Deductible and Copayment	Medicare Payment
Medical expense	Physician's services, inpatient and outpatient medical and surgical services and supplies, and durable medical equipment (DME) Mental healthcare	$110 annual deductible, plus 20% of approved amount after deductible has been met, except in outpatient setting 50% of most outpatient care	80% of approved amount (after patient has paid $110 deductible) 50% of most outpatient care
Clinical laboratory services	Blood tests, urinalysis, and more	Nothing	100% of approved amount
Home healthcare	Intermittent skilled care, home health aid services, DME and supplies, and other services	Nothing for home care service 20% of approved amount for DME	100% of approved amount 80% of approved amount for DME
Outpatient hospital services	Services for diagnosis and treatment of an illness or injury	$135 annual deductible, plus a coinsurance amount for *each service* received during an outpatient visit. For *each* outpatient service received, the coinsurance amount cannot be greater than the Medicare Part A inpatient hospital deductible. The coinsurance amount is based on 20% of the national median charge for ambulatory payment classification associated with the service. Charges for items or services that Medicare does not cover	Payment based on ambulatory patient classifications/outpatient prospective payment system
Blood	Unlimited if medical necessity criteria are met	First 3 pints (if met under Part B, does not have to be met again under Part A)	All but first 3 pints

Source: Adapted from *Medicare and You* 2008.

receive benefits through the original fee-for-service program, most beneficiaries enrolled in both Parts A and B can choose to participate in a Medicare Advantage plan instead. Organizations that offer Medicare Advantage plans must meet specific requirements as determined by CMS.

Primary Medicare Advantage products include the following types of plans:

- *Managed care plans:* In a managed care plan, patients can only go to doctors, specialists, or hospitals on the plan's list, which is referred to as a network, except in an emergency. Patients also may have to choose a primary care doctor and need a referral to see a specialist, but they pay lower copayments and receive extra benefits.
- *PPO plans:* In a PPO plan, patients use doctors, specialists, and hospitals in the plan's network and can go to doctors and hospitals not on the list, usually at an additional cost. Patients do not need referrals to see doctors or go to hospitals that are not part of the plan's network and may pay lower copayments and receive extra benefits.
- *Private fee-for-service plans:* These plans allow beneficiaries to go to any doctor or hospital that accepts the terms of the plan's payment. The private company, rather than the Medicare program, decides how much it will pay and how much patients pay for services rendered.
- *Medical specialty plans:* Medical specialty plans provide more focused healthcare for specific people.

Medicare Prescription Drug Improvement and Modernization Act

The Medicare Prescription Drug Improvement and Modernization Act, also known as the Medicare Reform Bill, was signed into law by President George W. Bush in December 2003. This legislation provides seniors and individuals with disabilities with a prescription drug benefit, more choices, and better benefits under Medicare. Medicare drug plans are run by insurance companies and other private companies approved by Medicare. Each plan can vary in cost and drugs covered, and beneficiaries select their preferred plan.

Out-of-Pocket Expenses and Medigap Insurance

Medicare beneficiaries who elect the fee-for-service option are responsible for charges not covered by the Medicare program and for various cost-sharing aspects of Parts A and B. These liabilities may be paid by the Medicare beneficiary; by a third party, such as an employer-sponsored health plan or private Medigap insurance; or by Medicaid, when the person is eligible.

Medigap is private health insurance that pays, within limits, most of the healthcare service charges not covered by Medicare Parts A or B. These policies must meet federal and state laws.

The payment share for beneficiaries enrolled in Medicare Advantage plans is based on the cost-sharing structure of the specific plan they select. Most plans have lower deductibles and coinsurance than are required of Medicare fee-for-service beneficiaries. Such beneficiaries pay the monthly Part B premium and may pay an additional plan premium, depending on the plan.

For hospital care covered under Medicare Part A, a fee-for-service beneficiary's payment share includes a one-time deductible amount payable at the beginning of each benefit period. For 2008, the deductible is $1,024. This deductible covers the beneficiary's part of the first 60 days of each inpatient hospital stay. When continued inpatient care is needed beyond the 60 days, additional coinsurance payments ($256 per day in 2008) are required through the 90th day of a benefit period. Each Part A beneficiary also has a lifetime reserve of 60 additional hospital days that may be used when the covered days within a benefit period have been exhausted. Lifetime reserve days may be used only once, and coinsurance payments ($512 per day in 2008) are required.

For SNF care covered under Part A, Medicare fully covers the first 20 days in a benefit period. For days 21 through 100, a copayment ($128 per day in 2008) is required. Medicare benefits expire after the first 100 days of SNF care during a benefit period.

Home health care services require no deductible or coinsurance payment by the beneficiary. For any Part A service, the beneficiary is responsible for paying fees to cover the first three pints or units of nonreplaced blood per calendar year. The beneficiary has the option of paying the fee or arranging for the blood to be replaced by family and friends then paying 20 percent of the Medicare approved amounts for additional pints of blood.

Most beneficiaries covered by Medicare Part A pay no premiums. Eligibility is generally earned through the work experience of the beneficiary or of his or her spouse. In addition, most individuals over 65 who are otherwise ineligible for Medicare Part A coverage can enroll voluntarily by paying a monthly premium when they also enroll in Part B.

For Part B (refer to table 14.3), the beneficiary's payment share includes:

- One annual deductible ($135 in 2008)
- Monthly premiums ($96.40 to $238.40 per month depending on income in 2008)
- Coinsurance payments for Part B services (usually 20 percent of medically allowable charges)
- Any deductibles for blood products
- Certain charges above approved charges (for claims not on assignment)
- Payment for any services that are not covered by Medicare

Medicaid

Title XIX of the Social Security Act enacted **Medicaid** in 1965. The Medicaid program pays for medical assistance provided to individuals and families with low incomes and limited financial resources. Individual states must meet broad national guidelines established by federal statutes, regulations, and policies to qualify for federal matching grants under the Medicaid program. Individual state medical assistance agencies, however, establish the Medicaid eligibility standards for residents of their states. The states also determine the type, amount, duration, and scope of covered services; calculate the rate of payment for covered services; and administer local programs.

Medicaid policies on eligibility, services, and payment are complex and vary considerably among states, even among states of similar size or geographic proximity. Therefore, an individual who is eligible for Medicaid in one state may not be eligible in another. In addition, the amount, duration, and scope of care provided vary considerably from state to state. Moreover, Medicaid eligibility and services within a state can change from year to year.

Medicaid Eligibility Criteria

Low income is only one measure for Medicaid eligibility. Other financial resources also are compared against eligibility standards. Each state determines these standards according to federal guidelines.

Generally, each state can determine which groups Medicaid will cover. Each state also establishes its own financial criteria for Medicaid eligibility. However, to be eligible for federal funds, states are required to provide Medicaid coverage to certain individuals. These individuals include recipients of federally assisted income maintenance payments, as well as related groups of individuals who do not receive cash payments. The federal **categorically needy eligibility groups** include:

- Individuals eligible for Medicaid when they meet requirements for **Temporary Assistance for Needy Families** (TANF)
- Children below age six whose family income is at or below 133 percent of the federal poverty level (FPL) (the income threshold established by the federal government)
- Pregnant women whose family income is below 133 percent of the FPL (services are limited to those related to pregnancy-related medical care)
- Supplemental Security Income (SSI) recipients in most states
- Recipients of adoption or foster care assistance under Title IV-E of the Social Security Act
- Specifically protected groups (typically individuals who lose their cash assistance due to earnings from work or from increased Social Security benefits, but who may keep Medicaid for a period of time)
- Infants born to Medicaid-eligible pregnant women
- Certain low-income Medicare beneficiaries

States also have the option of providing Medicaid coverage to other categorically related groups. Categorically related groups share the characteristics of the eligible groups (that is, they fall within defined categories), but the eligibility criteria are somewhat more liberally defined. A **medically needy option** also allows states to extend Medicaid eligibility to persons who would be eligible for Medicaid under one of the mandatory or optional groups except that their income and resources are above the eligibility level set by their state. Individuals may qualify immediately or may "spend down" by incurring medical expenses that reduce their income to or below their state's income level for the medically needy.

In 1996, Congress passed the Personal Responsibility and Work Opportunity Reconciliation Act (also known as welfare reform). The act made restrictive changes in the eligibility requirements for SSI coverage. These changes also affected eligibility for participation in the Medicaid program.

The welfare reform act also affected a number of disabled children. Many lost their SSI benefits as a result of the restrictive changes. However, their eligibility for Medicaid was reinstituted by the BBA.

In addition, the welfare reform act repealed the open-ended federal entitlement program known as Aid to Families with Dependent Children (AFDC). TANF, which replaced AFDC, provides states with grant money to be used for time-limited cash assistance. A family's lifetime cash welfare benefits are generally limited to a maximum of five years. Individual states also are allowed to impose other eligibility restrictions.

Medicaid Services

To be eligible for federal matching funds, each state's Medicaid program must offer medical assistance for the following basic services:

- Inpatient hospital services
- Outpatient hospital services
- Emergency services
- Prenatal care and delivery services
- Vaccines for children
- Physicians' services
- SNF services for persons aged 21 or older
- Family planning services and supplies
- Rural health clinic services
- Home healthcare for persons eligible for skilled nursing services
- Laboratory and x-ray services
- Medical and surgical services of a dentist
- Pediatric and family nurse practitioner services
- Nurse-midwife services
- Federally qualified health center (FQHC) services and ambulatory services performed at the FQHC that would be available in other settings
- Early and periodic screening and diagnostic and therapeutic services for children under age 21
- States also may receive federal matching funds to provide some of the optional services, the most common being:
  - Diagnostic services
  - Clinic services

- Prescription drugs and prosthetic devices
- Transportation services
- Rehabilitation and physical therapy services
- Prosthetic devices
- Home care and community-based care services for persons with chronic impairments

The BBA also called for implementation of a state option called **Programs of All-Inclusive Care for the Elderly** (PACE). PACE provides an alternative to institutional care for individuals 55 years old or older who require a level of care usually provided at nursing facilities. It offers and manages all of the health, medical, and social services needed by a beneficiary and mobilizes other services, as needed, to provide preventive, rehabilitative, curative, and supportive care.

PACE services can be provided in day healthcare centers, homes, hospitals, and nursing homes. The program helps its beneficiaries to maintain their independence, dignity, and quality of life. PACE also functions within the Medicare program. Individuals enrolled in PACE receive benefits solely through the PACE program.

Medicaid–Medicare Relationship

Medicare beneficiaries who have low incomes and limited financial resources also may receive help from the Medicaid program. For persons eligible for full Medicaid coverage, Medicare coverage is supplemented by services that are available under their state's Medicaid program according to their eligibility category. Additional services may include, for example, nursing facility care beyond the 100-day limit covered by Medicare, prescription drugs, eyeglasses, and hearing aids. For those enrolled in both programs, any services covered by Medicare are paid for by the Medicare program before any payments are made by the Medicaid program because Medicaid is always the **payer of last resort**. Table 14.4 provides a comparison of the Medicare and Medicaid programs.

State Children's Health Insurance Program

The **State Children's Health Insurance Program** (SCHIP) (Title XXI of the Social Security Act) is a program initiated by the BBA. SCHIP (sometimes referred to as the Children's Health Insurance Program, or CHIP) allows states to expand existing insurance programs to cover children up to age 19. It provides additional federal funds to states so that Medicaid eligibility can be expanded to include a greater number of children.

SCHIP became available in October 1997, and is jointly funded by the federal government and the states. Following broad federal guidelines, states establish eligibility and coverage guidelines and have flexibility in the way they provide services. Recipients in all states must meet three eligibility criteria:

- They must come from low-income families.
- They must be otherwise ineligible for Medicaid.
- They must be uninsured.

States are required to offer the following services:

- Inpatient hospital services
- Outpatient hospital services
- Physicians' surgical and medical services
- Laboratory and x-ray services
- Well-baby and child care services, including age-appropriate immunizations

TRICARE

TRICARE is a healthcare program for active-duty members of the military and other qualified family members. Eligible retirees and their family members, as well as eligible survivors of members of the uniformed services, also are eligible for TRICARE.

The idea of medical care for the families of active-duty members of the uniformed military services dates back to the late 1700s. It was not until 1884, however, that Congress directed Army medical officers and contract surgeons to care for the families of military personnel free of charge.

Table 14.4. Comparison of Medicare and Medicaid programs

Medicare	Medicaid
Health insurance for people age 65 and older, or people under 65 who are entitled to Medicare because of disability or are receiving dialysis for permanent kidney failure	Health assistance for people of any age
Administered through fiscal intermediaries, insurance companies under contract to the government to process Medicare claims	Administered by the federal government through state and local governments following federal and state guidelines
Medicare regulations are the same in all states	Medicaid regulations vary from state to state
Financed by monthly premiums paid by the beneficiary and by payroll tax deductions	Financed by federal, state, and county tax dollars
For people age 65 and over, eligibility is based on Social Security or Railroad Retirement participation. For people under age 65, eligibility is based on disability. For people who undergo kidney dialysis, eligibility is not dependent on age	Eligibility based on financial need
Beneficiary responsible for paying deductibles, coinsurance or copayments, and Part B premiums	Medicaid can help pay Medicare deductible, coinsurance or copayment, and premiums
Hospital and medical benefits; preventive care and long-term care benefits are limited	Comprehensive benefits include hospital, preventive care, long-term care, and other services not covered under Medicare such as dental work, prescriptions, transportation, eyeglasses, and hearing aids

There was very little change in the provision of medical care to members of the military and their families until the Second World War, when the military was made up mostly of young men who had wives of childbearing age. The military medical care system could not handle the large number of births or the care of young children. So, in 1943, Congress authorized the **Emergency Maternal and Infant Care Program** (EMIC). The program provided maternity and infant care to dependents of service members in the lowest four pay grades.

During the early 1950s, the Korean conflict also strained the capabilities of the military healthcare system. As a result, the Dependents Medical Care Act was signed into law in 1956. Amendments to the act created the **Civilian Health and Medical Program of the Uniformed Services** (CHAMPUS) in 1966.

During the 1980s, the search for ways to improve access to top-quality medical care and at the same time control costs led to implementation of CHAMPUS demonstration projects in various parts of the country. The most successful of these projects was the CHAMPUS Reform Initiative (CRI) in California and Hawaii. Initiated in 1988, the CRI offered military service families a choice in the way their military healthcare benefits could be used. Five years of successful operation and high levels of patient satisfaction persuaded Department of Defense officials that they should extend and improve the CRI concepts as a uniform program nationwide.

The new program, known as **TRICARE,** was phased in nationally by 1998. TRICARE offers three options: TRICARE Prime, TRICARE Extra, and TRICARE Standard.

TRICARE Prime

Of the three options, **TRICARE Prime** provides the most comprehensive healthcare benefits at the lowest cost. Military treatment facilities, such as military base hospitals, serve as the principal source of healthcare and a **primary care manager** (PCM) is assigned to each enrollee.

Two specialized programs supplement TRICARE Prime. **TRICARE Prime Remote** provides healthcare services to active-duty military personnel stationed in the United States in areas not served by the traditional military healthcare system. (Active-duty personnel include members of the Army, Navy, Marine Corps, Air Force, Coast Guard, and active National Guard.) **TRICARE Senior Prime** is a managed care demonstration program designed to serve the medical needs of military retirees who are 65 years old or over, as well as their dependents and survivors.

TRICARE Extra

TRICARE Extra is a cost-effective preferred provider network (PPN) option. Healthcare costs in TRICARE Extra are lower than for TRICARE Standard because beneficiaries must select physicians and medical specialists from a network of civilian healthcare professionals working under contract with TRICARE. The healthcare professionals who participate in TRICARE Extra agree to charge a preestablished discounted rate for the medical treatments and procedures provided to participants in the plan.

TRICARE Standard

TRICARE Standard incorporates the services previously provided by CHAMPUS. TRICARE Standard allows eligible beneficiaries to choose any physician or healthcare provider. It pays a set percentage of the providers' fees, and the enrollee pays the rest. This option permits the most flexibility but may be the most expensive for the enrollee, particularly when the provider's charges are higher than the amounts allowed by the program.

CHAMPVA

The **Civilian Health and Medical Program–Veterans Administration** (CHAMPVA) is a healthcare program for dependents and survivors of permanently and totally disabled veterans, survivors of veterans who died from service-related conditions, and survivors of military personnel who died in the line of duty. CHAMPVA is a voluntary program that allows beneficiaries to be treated for free at participating VA healthcare facilities, with the VA sharing the cost of covered healthcare services and supplies. Because of the similarity between CHAMPVA and TRICARE, people sometimes confuse the two programs. However, CHAMPVA is separate from TRICARE and there are distinct differences between them. TRICARE is for individuals currently serving in the armed forces, and CHAMPVA is for retired military personnel.

Indian Health Service

The provision of health services to Native Americans originally developed from the relationship between the federal government and federally-recognized Indian tribes established in 1787. It is based on Article I, Section 8, of the U.S. Constitution and has been given form and substance by numerous treaties, laws, Supreme Court decisions, and executive orders.

The **Indian Health Service** (IHS) is an agency within the HHS. It is responsible for providing healthcare services to American Indians and Alaska natives. The American Indians and Alaska natives served by the IHS receive preventive healthcare services, primary medical services (hospital and ambulatory care), community health services, substance abuse treatment services, and rehabilitative services. Secondary medical care, highly specialized medical services, and other rehabilitative care are provided by IHS staff or by private healthcare professionals working under contract with the IHS.

A system of acute and ambulatory care facilities operates on Indian reservations and in Indian and Alaska native communities. In locations where the IHS does not have its own facilities or is not equipped to provide a needed service, it contracts with local hospitals, state and local healthcare agencies, tribal health institutions, and individual healthcare providers.

Workers' Compensation

Most employees are eligible for some type of **workers' compensation** insurance. Workers' compensation programs cover healthcare costs and lost income associated with work-related injuries and illnesses. Federal government employees are covered by the **Federal Employees' Compensation Act** (FECA). Individual states pass legislation that addresses workers' compensation coverage for nonfederal government employees. Some states exclude certain workers, for example, business owners, independent contractors, farm workers, and so on. Texas employers are not required to provide workers' compensation coverage.

Federal Workers' Compensation Funds

In 1908, President Theodore Roosevelt signed legislation to provide workers' compensation for certain federal employees in unusually hazardous jobs. The scope of the law was narrow and its benefits were limited. This law represented the first workers' compensation program to pass the test of constitutionality applied by the U.S. Supreme Court.

FECA replaced the 1908 statute in 1916. Under FECA, civilian employees of the federal government are provided medical care, survivors' benefits, and compensation for lost wages. The Office of Workers' Compensation Programs (OWCP) administers FECA as well as the Longshore and Harbor Workers' Compensation Act of 1927 and the Black Lung Benefits Reform Act of 1977.

FECA also provides vocational rehabilitation services to partially disabled employees. Employees who fully or partially recover from their injuries are expected to return to work. FECA does not provide retirement benefits.

State Workers' Compensation Funds

According to the American Association of State Compensation Insurance Funds (AASCIF), state workers' compensation insurance was developed in response to the concerns of employers. Before state workers' compensation programs became widely available, employers faced the possibility of going out of business when insurance companies refused to provide coverage or charged excessive premiums. Legislators in most states have addressed these concerns by establishing **state workers' compensation insurance funds** that provide a stable source of insurance coverage and serve to protect employers from uncertainties about the continuing availability of coverage. Because state funds are provided on a nonprofit basis, the premiums can be kept low. In addition, the funds provide only one type of insurance: workers' compensation. This specialization allows the funds to concentrate resources, knowledge, and expertise in a single field of insurance.

State workers' compensation insurance funds do not operate at taxpayer expense because, by law, the funds support themselves through income derived from premiums and investments. As nonprofit departments of the state or as independent nonprofit companies, they return surplus assets to policyholders as dividends or safety refunds. This system reduces the overall cost of state-level workers' compensation insurance. Numerous court decisions have determined that the assets, reserves, and surplus of the funds are not public funds but, instead, the property of the employers insured by the funds.

In states where state funds have not been mandated, employers purchase workers' compensation coverage from private carriers or provide self-insurance coverage.

Managed Care

Healthcare costs in the United States rose dramatically during the 1970s and 1980s. As a result, the federal government, employers, and other third-party payers began investigating more cost-effective healthcare delivery systems. The federal government decided to move toward PPSs for the Medicare program in the mid-1980s. Prospective payment as a reimbursement methodology is discussed later in this chapter. Commercial insurance providers looked to managed care.

Managed care is the generic term for prepaid health plans that integrate the financial and delivery aspects of healthcare services. In other words, managed care organizations work to control the cost of, and access to, healthcare services at the same time that they strive to meet high-quality standards. They manage healthcare costs by negotiating discounted providers' fees and controlling patients' access to expensive healthcare services. In managed care plans, services are carefully coordinated to ensure that they are medically appropriate and needed. (Managed care is also discussed in chapter 2.)

The cost of providing appropriate services is also monitored continuously to determine whether the services are being delivered in the most efficient and cost-effective way possible.

Since 1973, several pieces of federal legislation have been passed with the goal of encouraging the development of managed healthcare systems. (See table 14.5.) The Health Maintenance Organization Assistance Act of 1973 authorized federal grants and loans to private organizations that wished to develop **health maintenance organizations** (HMOs). Another important advancement in managed care was development of the **Health Plan Employer Data and Information Set** (HEDIS) by the **National Committee for Quality Assurance** (NCQA).

The NCQA is a private, not-for-profit organization that accredits, assesses, and reports on the quality of managed care plans in the United States. It worked with public and private healthcare purchasers, health plans, researchers, and consumer advocates to develop HEDIS in 1989. HEDIS is a set of standardized measures used to compare managed care plans in terms of the quality of services they provide. The standards cover areas such as plan membership, utilization of and access to services, and financial indicators. The goals of the program include:

- Helping beneficiaries make informed choices among the numerous managed care plans available

- Improving the quality of care provided by managed care plans
- Helping the government and other third-party payers make informed purchasing decisions

CMS offers several managed care options to Medicare and Medicaid enrollees. It began collecting HEDIS data from Medicare managed care plans in 1996.

Several kinds of managed care plans are available in the United States, including:

- Health maintenance organizations (HMOs)
- Preferred provider organizations (PPOs)
- Point-of-service (POS) plans
- Exclusive provider organizations (EPOs)
- Integrated delivery systems (IDSs)

Health Maintenance Organizations (HMOs)

An HMO is a prepaid voluntary health plan that provides healthcare services in return for the payment of a monthly membership premium. HMO premiums are based on a projection of the costs that are likely to be involved in treating the plan's average enrollee over a specified period of time. If the actual cost per enrollee were to exceed the projected cost, the HMO would experience a financial loss. If the actual cost per enrollee turned out to be lower than the projection, the HMO would show a profit. Because most HMOs are for-profit organizations, they emphasize cost control and preventive medicine.

Today, most employers and insurance companies offer enrollees some type of HMO option. The benefit to third-party payers and enrollees alike is cost savings. Most HMO enrollees have significantly lower out-of-pocket expenses than enrollees of traditional fee-for-service and other types of managed care plans. The HMO premiums shared by employers and enrollees also are lower than the premiums for other types of healthcare plans.

HMOs can be organized in several different ways, including the **group model HMO**, the **independent practice association** (IPA), the **network model HMO**, and the **staff model HMO**, or there can also be a combination of the staff, group, and network models.

Group Model HMOs

In the group model HMO, the HMO enters into a contract with an independent multispecialty physician group to provide medical services to members of the plan. The

Table 14.5. Federal legislation relevant to managed care

Year	Legislative Title	Legislative Summary
1973	Federal Health Maintenance Organization Assistance Act of 1973 (HMO Act of 1973)	• Authorized grants and loans to develop HMOs under private sponsorship • Defined a federally qualified HMO (certified to provide healthcare services to Medicare and Medicaid enrollees) as one that has applied for and met federal standards established in the HMO Act of 1973 • Required most employers with more than 25 employees to offer HMO coverage when local plans were available
1974	Employee Retirement Income Security Act of 1974 (ERISA)	• Mandated reporting and disclosure requirements for group life and health plans (including managed care plans) • Permitted large employers to self-insure employee healthcare benefits • Exempted large employers from taxes on health insurance premium
1981	Omnibus Budget Reconciliation Act of 1981 (OBRA)	• Provided states with flexibility to establish HMOs for Medicare and Medicaid programs • Resulted in increased enrollment
1982	Tax Equity and Fiscal Responsibility Act of 1982 (TEFRA)	• Modified the HMO Act of 1973 • Created Medicare risk programs, which allowed federally qualified HMOs and competitive medical plans that met specified Medicare requirements to provide Medicare-covered services under a risk contract • Defined risk contract as an arrangement among providers to provide capitated (fixed, prepaid basis) healthcare services to Medicare beneficiaries • Defined competitive medical plan (CMP) as an HMO that meets federal eligibility requirements for a Medicare risk contract but is not licensed as a federally qualified plan
1985	Preferred Provider Health Care Act of 1985	• Eased restrictions on preferred provider organizations • Allowed subscribers to seek healthcare from providers outside the PPO
1985	Consolidated Omnibus Budget Reconciliation Act of 1985 (COBRA)	• Established an employee's right to continue healthcare coverage beyond scheduled benefit termination date (including HMO coverage)
1988	Amendment to the HMO Act of 1973	• Allowed federally qualified HMOs to permit members to occasionally use non-HMO physicians and be partially reimbursed
1989	Health Plan Employer Data and Information Set (HEDIS)—developed by National Committee for Quality Assurance (NCQA)	• Created standards to assess managed care systems in terms of membership, utilization of services, quality, access, health plan management and activities, and financial indicators
1994	HCFA's Office of Managed Care established	• Facilitated innovation and competition among Medicare HMOs

providers usually agree to devote a fixed percentage of their practice time to the HMO. Alternatively, the HMO may own or directly manage the physician group, in which case the physicians and their support staff would be considered its employees.

Group model HMOs are closed-panel arrangements. In other words, the physicians are not allowed to treat patients from other managed care plans. Enrollees of group model HMOs are required to seek services from the designated physician group.

Independent Practice Associations (IPAs)

IPAs are sometimes called individual practice associations. In the IPA model, the HMO enters into a contract with an organized group of physicians who join together for purposes of fulfilling the HMO contract but retain their individual practices. The IPA serves as an intermediary during contract negotiations. It also manages the premiums from the HMO and pays individual physicians as appropriate. The physicians are not considered employees of the HMO. They work from their own private offices and continue to see other patients. The HMO usually pays the IPA according to a prenegotiated list of discounted fees. Alternatively, physicians may agree to provide services to HMO members for a set prepaid capitated payment for a specified period of time. Capitation is discussed later in this chapter.

The IPA is an open-panel HMO, which means that the physicians are free to treat patients from other plans. Enrollees of such HMOs are required to seek services from the designated physician group.

Network Model HMOs

Network model HMOs are similar to group model HMOs except that the HMO contracts for services with two or more multispecialty group practices instead of just one practice. Members of network model HMOs receive a list of all the physicians on the approved panel and are required to select providers from the list.

Staff Model HMOs

Staff model HMOs directly employ physicians and other healthcare professionals to provide medical services to members. Members of the salaried medical staff are considered employees of the HMO rather than independent practitioners. Premiums are paid directly to the HMO, and ambulatory care services are usually provided within the HMO's corporate facilities. The staff model HMO is a closed-panel arrangement.

Preferred Provider Organizations (PPOs)

PPOs represent contractual agreements between healthcare providers and a self-insured employer or a health insurance carrier. Beneficiaries of PPOs select providers such as physicians or hospitals, from a list of participating providers who have agreed to furnish healthcare services to the covered population. Beneficiaries may elect to receive services from nonparticipating providers but must pay a greater portion of the cost (in other words, higher deductibles and copayments). Providers are usually reimbursed on a discounted fee-for-service basis.

Point-of-Service Plans

POS plans are similar to HMOs in that subscribers must select a **primary care physician** (PCP) from a network of participating physicians. The PCP is usually a family or general practice physician or an internal medicine specialist. The PCP acts as a service gatekeeper to control the patient's access to specialty, surgical, and hospital care as well as expensive diagnostic services.

POS plans are different from HMOs in that subscribers are allowed to seek care from providers outside the network. However, the subscribers must pay a greater share of the charges for out-of-network services. POS plans were created to increase the flexibility of managed care plans and to allow patients more choice in providers.

Exclusive Provider Organizations

Exclusive Provider Organizations (EPOs) are similar to PPOs except that EPOs provide benefits to enrollees only when the enrollees receive healthcare services from **network providers**. In other words, EPO beneficiaries do not receive reimbursement for services furnished by nonparticipating providers. In addition, healthcare services must be coordinated by a PCP. EPOs are regulated by state insurance departments. In contrast, HMOs are regulated by state departments of commerce or departments of incorporation.

Integrated Delivery Systems

An **Integrated Delivery System** (IDS) is a healthcare provider consisting of a number of associated medical facilities that furnish coordinated healthcare services. Most IDSs include a number of facilities that provide services along the continuum of care, for example, ambulatory surgery centers, physicians' office practices, outpatient clinics, acute care hospitals, SNFs, and so on.

Integrated delivery systems can be structured according to several different models, including:

- Group practices without walls (GPWWs)
- Integrated provider organizations (IPOs)
- Management service organizations (MSOs)
- Medical foundations
- Physician–hospital organizations (PHOs)

Group Practices without Walls

Group practices without walls (GPWW) is an arrangement that allows physicians to maintain their own offices but to share administrative, management, and marketing services (for example, medical transcription and billing) for the purpose of fulfilling contracts with managed care organizations.

Integrated Provider Organizations

Integrated provider organizations (IPOs) manage and coordinate the delivery of healthcare services performed by a number of healthcare professionals and facilities. IPOs typically provide acute care (hospital) services, physicians' services, ambulatory care services, and skilled nursing services. The physicians working in an IPO are salaried employees. IPOs are sometimes referred to as delivery systems, horizontally integrated systems, health delivery networks, accountable health plans, integrated service networks (ISNs), vertically integrated plans (VIPs), and vertically integrated systems.

Management Service Organizations

Management Service Organizations (MSOs) provide practice management (administrative and support) services to individual physicians' practices. They are usually owned by a group of physicians or a hospital.

Medical Foundations

Medical foundations are nonprofit organizations that enter into contracts with physicians to manage the physicians' practices. The typical medical foundation owns clinical and business resources and makes them available to the participating physicians. Clinical assets include medical equipment and supplies as well as treatment facilities. Business assets include billing and administrative support systems.

Physician-Hospital Organizations

Physician–Hospital Organizations (PHOs), previously known as medical staff–hospital organizations, provide healthcare services through a contractual arrangement between physicians and hospital(s). PHO arrangements make it possible for the managed care market to view the hospital(s) and physicians as a single entity for the purpose of establishing a contract for services.

Check Your Understanding 14.2

Instructions: Answer the following questions on a separate piece of paper.

1. What is fee-for-service reimbursement? Why is it rarely used today as a reimbursement method?
2. How are private commercial insurance plans financed?
3. What process do most insurance companies use to reimburse healthcare services?
4. What are administrative services only contracts?
5. What federal program pays for healthcare services provided to financially needy individuals?
6. For which populations of individuals do TRICARE and CHAMPVA reimburse healthcare services?
7. Why is Medicare Part B referred to as supplemental medical insurance?
8. What federal legislation expanded Medicare options by creating Medicare Advantage?
9. What private health insurance pays (within limits) for most healthcare services not covered by Medicare Part A?
10. How did the Medicare and Medicaid programs come into effect? How are the two programs different?
11. How are Medicaid eligibility standards established?
12. What is the difference between a preferred provider organization and a point-of-service plan?
13. What is the purpose of the State Children's Health Insurance Program?
14. What type of Medicare coverage applies to inpatient hospitalization? To prescription eyeglasses? To emergency department visits? To dental care? To ambulatory surgery center service? To hospice care?
15. What is the difference between TRICARE Extra and TRICARE Prime?
16. How does state workers' compensation coverage differ from federal workers' compensation coverage?
17. What type of HMO model employs physicians and other healthcare professionals to provide healthcare services to members?
18. What is the difference between an independent practice association and a staff model HMO?
19. Define managed care and describe the various types of managed care programs available in the United States.
20. What do management service organizations do?

Healthcare Reimbursement Methodologies

As mentioned earlier in this chapter, about 85 percent of Americans are covered by some type of private prepaid health plan or federal healthcare program. Therefore, most healthcare expenses in the United States are reimbursed through third-party payers rather than by the actual recipients of the services. The recipients can be considered the "first parties" and the providers the "second parties." Third-party payers include commercial for-profit insurance companies, nonprofit Blue Cross and Blue Shield organizations, self-insured employers, federal programs (Medicare, Medicaid, SCHIP, TRICARE, CHAMPVA, and IHS), and workers' compensation programs.

Providers charge their own determined amounts for services rendered. However, providers are rarely reimbursed this full amount because third-party payers may have a unique reimbursement methodology. For example, commercial insurance plans usually reimburse healthcare providers under some type of **retrospective payment system**. In retrospective payment systems, the exact amount of the payment is determined after the service has been delivered. In a PPS, the exact amount of the payment is determined before the service is delivered. The federal Medicare program uses PPSs.

Fee-for-Service Reimbursement Methodologies

Fee-for-service reimbursement methodologies issue payments to healthcare providers on the basis of the charges assigned to each of the separate services that were performed for the patient. The total bill for an episode of care represents the sum of all the itemized charges for every element of care provided. Independent clinical professionals such as physicians and psychologists who are not employees of the facility issue separate itemized bills to cover their services after the services are completed or on a monthly basis when the services are ongoing.

Before prepaid insurance plans became common in the 1950s and the Medicare and Medicaid programs were developed in the 1960s, healthcare providers sent itemized bills directly to their patients. Patients were held responsible for paying their own medical bills. When prepaid health plans and the Medicare and Medicaid programs were originally developed, they also based reimbursement on itemized fees.

Traditional Fee-for-Service Reimbursement

In traditional fee-for-service (FFS) reimbursement systems, third-party payers or patients issue payments to healthcare providers after healthcare services have been provided (for example, after the patient has been discharged from the hospital). Payments are based on the specific services delivered. The fees charged for services vary considerably by the type of services provided, the resources required, and the type and number of healthcare professionals involved.

Payments can be calculated on the basis of actual billed charges, discounted charges, pre-negotiated rate schedules, or the usual or customary charges in a specific community.

For example, some third-party payers pay only the maximum allowable charges as determined by the plan. Maximum allowable charges may be significantly lower than the provider's billed charges. Some payers issue payments on the basis of **usual, customary, and reasonable (UCR) charges**. Commercial insurance and Blue Cross/Blue Shield plans often issue payments based on pre-negotiated discount rates and contractual cost-sharing arrangements with the patient.

For many plans, the health plan and the patient share costs on an 80/20 percent arrangement. The portion of the claim covered by the patient's insurance plan would be 80 percent of allowable charges. After the third-party payer transmits its payment to the provider, the provider's billing department issues a final statement to the patient. The statement shows the amount for which the patient is responsible (in this example, 20 percent of allowable charges).

The traditional FFS reimbursement methodology is still used by many commercial insurance companies for visits to physicians' offices.

Managed Fee-for-Service Reimbursement

Managed FFS reimbursement is similar to traditional FFS reimbursement except that managed care plans control costs primarily by managing their members' use of healthcare services. Most managed care plans also negotiate with providers to develop discounted **fee schedules**. Managed FFS reimbursement is common for inpatient hospital care. In some areas of the country, however, it also is applied to outpatient and ambulatory services, surgical procedures, high-cost diagnostic procedures, and physicians' services.

Utilization controls include the prospective and retrospective review of the healthcare services planned for, or provided to, patients. For example, a prospective utilization review of a plan to hospitalize a patient for minor surgery might determine that the surgery could be safely performed less expensively in an outpatient setting. Prospective utilization review is sometimes called precertification.

In a retrospective utilization review, the plan might determine that part or all of the services provided to a patient were not medically necessary or were not covered by the plan. In such cases, the plan would disallow part or all of the provider's charges and the patient would be responsible for paying the provider's outstanding charges.

Discharge planning also can be considered a type of utilization control. The managed care plan may be able to move the patient to a less intensive, and therefore less expensive, care setting as soon as possible by coordinating his or her discharge from inpatient care.

Episode-of-Care Reimbursement Methodologies

Plans that use **episode-of-care (EOC) reimbursement** methods issue lump-sum payments to providers to compensate them for all the healthcare services delivered to a patient for a specific illness or over a specific period of time. EOC payments also are called **bundled payments**. Bundled payments cover multiple services and also may involve multiple providers of care. EOC reimbursement methods include capitated payments, global payments, global surgery payments, Medicare ambulatory surgery center rates, and Medicare PPSs.

Capitation

Capitation is based on per-person premiums or membership fees rather than on itemized per-procedure or per-service charges. The capitated managed care plan negotiates a contract with an employer or government agency representing a specific group of individuals. According to the contract, the managed care organization agrees to provide all the contracted healthcare services that the covered individuals need over a specified period of time (usually one year). In exchange, the individual enrollee or third-party payer agrees to pay a fixed premium for the covered group. Like other insurance plans, a capitated insurance contract stipulates as part of the contract exactly which healthcare services are covered and which ones are not.

Capitated premiums are calculated on the projected cost of providing covered services **per patient per month** (PPPM) or **per member per month** (PMPM). The capitated premium for an individual member of a plan includes all the services covered by the plan, regardless of the number of services actually provided during the period or their cost. If the average member of the plan actually used more services than originally assumed in the PPPM calculation, the plan would show a loss for the period. If the average member actually used fewer services, the plan would show a profit.

The purchasers of capitated coverage (usually the member's employer) pay monthly premiums to the managed care plan. The individual enrollees usually pay part of the premium as well. The plan then compensates the providers who actually furnished the services. In some arrangements, the managed care plan accepts all the risk involved in the contract. In others, some of the risk is passed on to the PCPs who agreed to act as gatekeepers for the plan.

The capitated managed care organization may own or operate some or all of the healthcare facilities that provide care to members and directly employ clinical professionals. Staff model HMOs operate in this way. Alternatively, the capitated managed care organization may purchase services from independent physicians and facilities, as do group model HMOs. For example:

> The ABC HMO awarded a capitated contract to the XYZ Medical Center for a total compensation of $3,600,000 in the year 2004. According to the terms of the contract, the medical center agreed to provide comprehensive healthcare services to all 500 enrollees covered under the contract for 12 months. The medical center received lump-sum payments of $300,000 per month over the 12-month period. A large, multispecialty PHO owned by the hospital acted as primary care gatekeepers and provided medical services to the enrollees. Inpatient and outpatient services were provided directly by the medical center.

Global Payment

Global payment methodology is sometimes applied to radiological and similar types of procedures that involve professional and technical components. Global payments are lump-sum payments distributed among the physicians who performed the procedure or interpreted its results and the healthcare facility that provided the equipment, supplies, and technical support required. The procedure's **professional component** is supplied by physicians (for example, radiologists), and its **technical component** (for example, radiological supplies, equipment, and support services) is supplied by a hospital or freestanding diagnostic or surgical center. For example:

> Larry Timber underwent a scheduled carotid angiogram as a hospital outpatient. He had complained of ringing in his ears and dizziness, and his physician scheduled the procedure to determine whether there was a blockage in one of Larry's carotid arteries. The procedure required a surgeon to inject radiopaque contrast material through a catheter into Larry's left carotid artery. A radiological technician then took an x-ray of Larry's neck. The technician was supervised by a radiologist and both were employees of the hospital.
>
> *Professional component:* Injection of radiopaque contrast material by the surgeon
>
> *Technical component:* X-ray of the neck region
>
> *Global payment:* The facility received a lump-sum payment for the procedure and paid for the services of the surgeon from that payment.

Global Surgery Payments

A single **global surgery payment** covers all the healthcare services entailed in planning and completing a specific surgical procedure. In other words, every element of the procedure from the treatment decision through normal postoperative patient care is covered by a single bundled payment. For example:

> Tammy Murdock received all the prenatal, perinatal, and postnatal care involved in the birth of her daughter from Dr. Thomas Michaels. She received one bill from the physician for a total of $2,200. The bill represented the total charges for the obstetrical services associated with her pregnancy. However, the two-day inpatient hospital stay for the normal delivery was not included in the global payment, nor were the laboratory services she received during her hospital stay. Tammy received a separate bill for these services. In addition, if she had suffered a postdelivery complication (for example, a wound infection) or an unrelated medical problem, the physician and hospital services required to treat the complications would not have been covered by the global surgical payment.

Check Your Understanding 14.3

Instructions: Answer the following questions on a separate piece of paper.

1. What type of payment system is in place when the amount of payment is determined before the service is delivered?
2. What are usual, customary, and reasonable (UCR) charges based on?
3. Many insurance plans require patients to share costs for healthcare services. What is the most typical cost share ratio?
4. Which utilization control is most closely associated with managed fee-for-service reimbursement?
5. What would a managed care plan likely show when a group of patients uses more services than the plan originally calculated in its contract with the group?
6. What are bundled payments? What is another name for bundled payments?
7. Describe the concept of capitation and explain how capitated payments are calculated.

Medicare's Prospective Payment Systems

Congress enacted the first Medicare Prospective Payment System in 1983, as a cost-cutting measure. Implementation of the acute care prospective payment system resulted in a shift of clinical services and expenditures away from the inpatient hospital setting to outpatient settings. As a result, spending on non-acute care exploded.

Congress responded by passing the **Omnibus Budget Reconciliation Act** (OBRA) of 1986, which mandated that CMS develop a prospective system for hospital-based outpatient services provided to Medicare beneficiaries. In subsequent years, Congress mandated the development of PPSs for other healthcare providers.

Medicare's Acute Care Prospective Payment System

As mentioned, prior to 1983, Medicare Part A payments to hospitals were determined on a traditional FFS reimbursement methodology. Payment was based on the cost of services provided, and reasonable cost or per-diem costs were used to determine payment.

During the late 1960s, just a few years after the Medicare and Medicaid health programs were implemented, Congress authorized a group at Yale University to develop a system for monitoring quality of care and utilization of services. This system was known as **diagnosis-related groups** (DRGs). DRGs were implemented on an experimental basis by the New Jersey Department of Health in the late 1970s as a way to predetermine reimbursement for hospital inpatient stays.

At the conclusion of the New Jersey DRG experiment, Congress passed the **Tax Equity and Fiscal Responsibility Act of 1982** (TEFRA). TEFRA modified Medicare's retrospective reimbursement system for inpatient hospital stays by requiring implementation of the DRG PPS in 1983. Under DRGs, Medicare paid most hospitals for inpatient hospital services according to a predetermined rate for each discharge. Very simply, the DRG system was a way of classifying patients on the basis of diagnosis. Patients within each DRG were said to be "medically meaningful"—that is, patients within a group were expected to evoke a set of clinical responses which statistically would result in an approximately equal use of hospital resources. Originally there were 470 DRGs with changes made to the system each year. On October 1, 2007, the DRG system became the **Medicare Severity-Diagnosis Related Groups** (MS-DRGs).

At this time, several types of hospitals are excluded from Medicare's acute care PPS. The following facilities are still paid on the basis of reasonable cost, subject to payment limits per discharge or under a separate PPS:

- Psychiatric and rehabilitation hospitals and psychiatric and rehabilitation units within larger medical facilities
- **Long-term care hospitals** (LTCH), which are defined as hospitals with an average length of stay of 25 days or more
- Children's hospitals
- Cancer hospitals
- Critical access hospitals
- **Religious Non-Medical Health Care Institutions** (RNHCI)

To determine the appropriate MS-DRG, a claim for a healthcare encounter is first classified into one of 25 **major diagnostic categories** (MDCs). Most MDCs are based on body systems and include diseases and disorders relating to a particular system. However, some MDCs include disorders and diseases involving multiple organ systems (for example, burns). The number of MS-DRGs within a particular MDC varies.

The **principal diagnosis** is defined as the condition which, after study, is determined to have caused the admission of the patient to the hospital for care and it determines the MDC assignment. Within each MDC, decision trees are used to determine the correct MS-DRG. (See figure 14.1.) Within most MDCs, cases are divided into surgical MS-DRGs (based on a surgical hierarchy that orders individual procedures or groups of procedures by resource intensity) and medical MS-DRGs. Medical MS-DRGs generally are differentiated on the basis of diagnosis and age. Some surgical and medical MS-DRGs are further differentiated on the basis of the presence or absence of **complications** or **comorbidities** (CCs).

A complication is a secondary condition that arises during hospitalization and is thought to increase the length of stay by at least one day for approximately 75 percent of patients. A co-morbid condition is a condition that existed at admission and is thought to increase the length of stay at least one day for approximately 75 percent of patients. During the initial years of DRGs there was a standard list of diagnoses that were considered CCs. Each year new CCs are added and others deleted from the CC list.

Prior to the implementation of MS-DRGs, a comprehensive review of the CC list was performed and an important change to the CC concept was made. Each base MS-DRG can be subdivided in 1 of 3 possible alternatives:

- MS-DRGs with three subgroups Major Complication/ Comorbidity (MCC, CC, and non-CC; referred to as "with MCC,' "with CC," and "w/o CC/MCC)
  - MS-DRG 682 Renal Failure w MCC
  - MS-DRG 683 Renal Failure w CC
  - MS-DRG 684 Renal Failure w/o CC/MCC
- MS-DRGs with two subgroups (MCC and CC/non-CC); referred to as "with MCC' and "without MCC"
  - MS-DRG 725 Benign Prostatic Hypertrophy w MCC
  - MS-DRG 726 Benign Prostatic Hypertrophy w/o MCC
- MS-DRGs with two subgroups (non CC and CC/MCC); referred to as "with CC/MCC" and "without CC/MCC"
  - MS-DRG 294 Deep Vein Thrombophlebitis w CC/ MCC
  - MS-DRG 295 Deep Vein Thrombophlebitis w/o CC/ MCC

The increased number of classifications is intended to differentiate between the levels of resource consumption within a base MS-DRG group.

Under the **acute care prospective payment system** (PPS), a predetermined rate based on the MS-DRG (only one is assigned per case) assigned to each case is used to reimburse hospitals for inpatient care provided to Medicare and TRICARE beneficiaries. Hospitals determine MS-DRGs by assigning **ICD-9-CM** codes to each patient's principal diagnosis, comorbidities, complications, major complications, **principal procedure,** and secondary procedures. These code numbers and other information on the patient (age, gender, and discharge status) are entered into a grouper. A MS-**DRG grouper** is a computer software program that assigns appropriate MS-DRGs according to the information provided for each episode of care.

Reimbursement for each episode of care is based on the MS-DRG assigned. Different diagnoses require different levels of care and expenditures of resources. Therefore, each MS-DRG is assigned a different level of payment that reflects the average amount of resources required to treat a patient assigned to that MS-DRG. Each MS-DRG is associated with

Figure 14.1. Excerpt of MS-DRG decision tree for surgical MDC 06

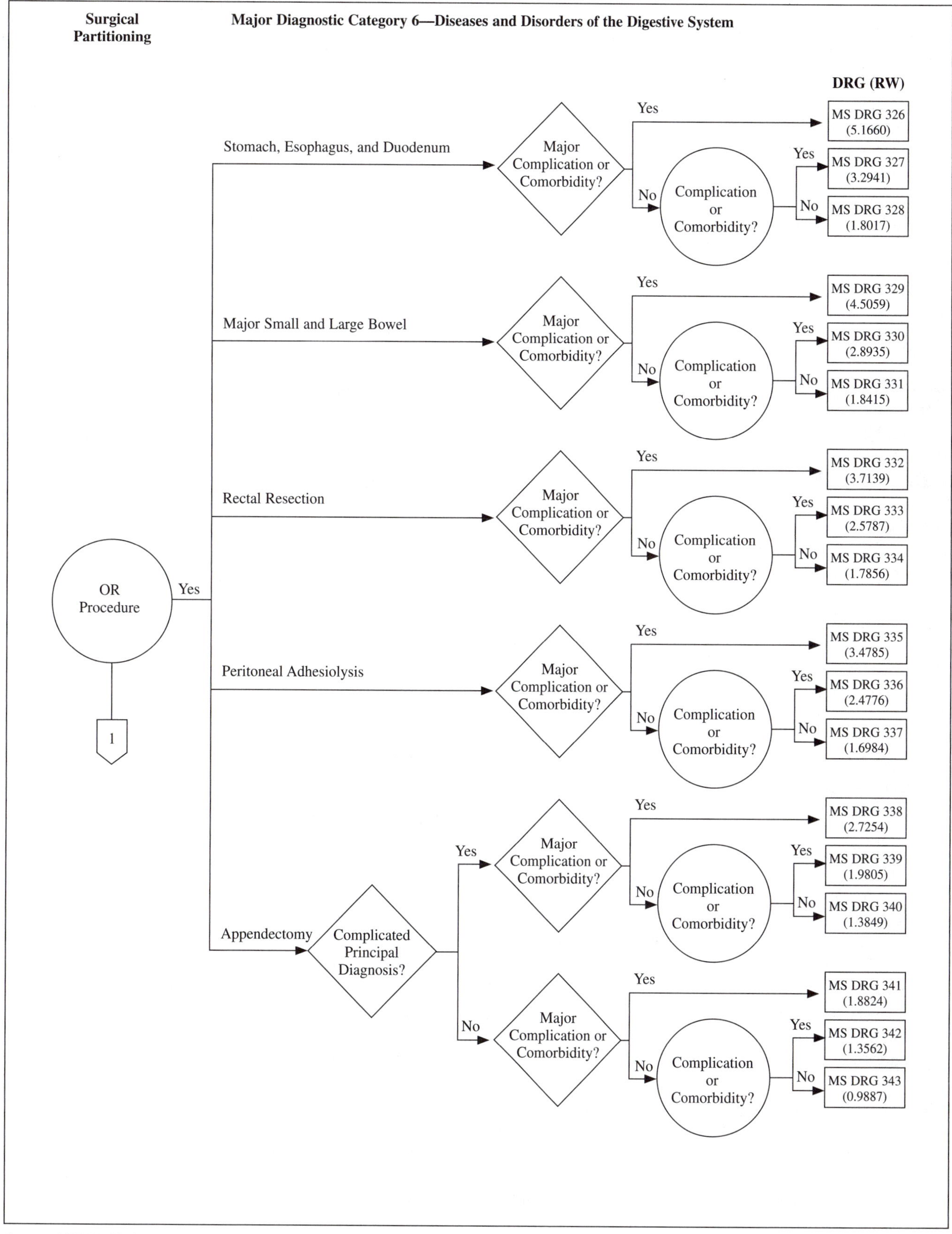

Source: AHIMA 2008.

a description, a relative weight, a geometric mean length of stay (LOS), and an arithmetic mean LOS. The relative weight represents the average resources required to care for cases in that particular MS-DRG relative to the national average of resources used to treat all Medicare patients. A MS-DRG with a relative weight of 2.000, on average, requires twice as many resources as a MS-DRG with a relative weight of 1.000. The geometric mean LOS is defined as the total days of service, excluding any outliers or transfers, divided by the total number of patients; the arithmetic mean LOS is defined as the total days of service divided by the total number of patients.

For example, MS-DRG 1, organized within MDC 01, is described as heart transplant or implant of heart assist system w MCC and has a relative weight of 23.4061, a geometric mean LOS of 29.1, and an arithmetic mean LOS of 40.2.

CMS adjusts the Medicare MS-DRG list and reimbursement rates every fiscal year (October 1 through September 30). There are currently 745 MS-DRGs.

In some cases, the MS-DRG payment received by the hospital may be lower than the actual cost of providing Medicare Part A inpatient services. In such cases, the hospital must absorb the loss. In other cases, the cost of providing care is lower than the MS-DRG payment and the hospital may receive a payment for more than its actual cost and, therefore, makes a profit. It is expected that, on average, hospitals will be reimbursed for their total costs in providing services to Medicare patients.

Special circumstances can also apply to inpatient cases and result in an outlier payment to the hospital. An outlier case results in exceptionally high costs when compared with other cases in the same DRG. For fiscal year (FY) 2008, to qualify for a **cost outlier**, a hospital's charges for a case (adjusted to cost) must exceed the payment rate for the MS-DRG by $22,650. The additional payment amount is equal to 80 percent of the difference between the hospital's entire cost for the stay and the threshold amount.

There can be further hospital specific adjustments resulting in add-on payments:

- Disproportionate Share Hospital (DSH): If the hospital treats a high percentage of low-income patients, it receives a percentage add-on payment applied to the MS-DRG-adjusted base payment rate.
- Indirect Medical Education (IME): If the hospital is an approved teaching hospital, it receives a percentage add-on payment for each case paid under MS-DRGs. This percentage varies depending on the ratio of residents to beds.
- New Technologies: If the hospital can demonstrate the use of a new technology that is a substantial clinical improvement over available existing technologies and the new technology is approved, additional payments are made. Hospitals must submit a formal request to CMS with a significant sample of data to demonstrate that the technology meets the high-cost threshold.

The MS-DRG system creates a hospital's **case-mix index** (types or categories of patients treated by the hospital) based on the relative weights of the MS-DRG. The case-mix index can be figured by multiplying the relative weight of each MS-DRG by the number of discharges within that MS-DRG. This provides the total weight for each MS-DRG. The sum of all total weights divided by the sum of total patient discharges equals the case-mix index. A hospital may relate its case-mix index to the costs incurred for inpatient care. This information allows the hospital to make administrative decisions about services to be offered to its patient population. For example:

> The hospital's case-mix report indicated that a small population of patients was receiving obstetrical services, but that the costs associated with providing such services was disproportionately high. This report along with other data might result in the hospital's administrative decision to discontinue its obstetrical services department.

An **all patient DRG** (AP-DRG) system was developed in 1988 by 3M Health Information Systems as the basis for New York's hospital reimbursement program for non-Medicare discharges. AP-DRGs are still used in a number of states as a basis for payment of non-Medicare claims. AP-DRGs use the patient's age, sex, discharge status, and ICD-9-CM diagnoses and procedure codes to determine a DRG that, in turn, determines reimbursement. 3M also has developed **all patient refined DRGs** (APR-DRGs) as an extension of the DRG concept. APR-DRGs adjust patient data for severity of illness and risk of mortality, help to develop clinical pathways, are used as a basis for quality assurance programs, and are used in comparative profiling and setting capitation rates (3M HIS 2002).

Hospital-Acquired Conditions and Present on Admission Indicator Reporting

The Deficit Reduction Act of 2005 (DRA) mandated a quality adjustment in the MS-DRG payments for certain hospital-acquired conditions. CMS titled the program "Hospital-Acquired Conditions and Present on Admission Indicator Reporting" (HAC and POA). Inpatient hospitals were required to submit POA information on diagnoses for inpatient discharges on or after October 1, 2007. The following hospitals are exempt from the POA indicator requirement: critical access hospitals, long-term care hospitals, Maryland waiver hospitals, cancer hospitals, children's inpatient facilities, inpatient rehabilitation facilities, and psychiatric hospitals.

Present on admission (POA) is defined as a condition present at the time the order for inpatient admission occurs—conditions that develop during an outpatient encounter, including the emergency department, observation or outpatient surgery, are considered as present on admission. A POA indicator is assigned to principal and secondary diagnoses and the external cause of injury codes. The reporting options that are available are

- Y = Yes, diagnosis was present at the time of inpatient admission
- N = No, diagnosis was not present at the time of inpatient admission
- U = Unknown, documentation is insufficient to determine if condition was present at the time of inpatient admission
- W = Clinically undetermined. The provider is unable to clinically determine whether the condition was present at the time of admission.
- Unreported/Not used = Exempt from POA reporting

Complete guidelines with examples are part of the *ICD-9-CM Official Guidelines for Coding and Reporting* and should be reviewed. The POA indicator guidelines do not provide guidance on when a condition should be coded but, rather, how to apply the POA indicator to the final set of diagnosis codes that have been assigned.

CMS identified eight **hospital-acquired conditions** (not present on admission) as "reasonably preventable," and hospitals will not receive additional payment for cases in which one of the eight selected conditions was not present on admission. This is termed the HAC payment provision. The eight originally selected conditions include:

- Foreign object retained after surgery
- Air embolism
- Blood incompatibility
- State III and IV pressure ulcers
- Falls and trauma
- Catheter-associated urinary tract infection
- Vascular catheter-associated infection
- Surgical site infection—mediastinitis after coronary artery bypass graft

Additional conditions were proposed for FY 2009 and these include:

- Surgical site infections following certain orthopedic procedures and bariatric surgery
- Certain manifestations of poor control of blood sugar levels
- Deep vein thrombosis (DVT)/Pulmonary embolism (PE) following total knee replacement and hip replacement procedures

Payment implications for the original eight conditions and the proposed additional conditions took place on October 1, 2008.

Resource-Based Relative Value Scale (RBRVS) System

In 1992, CMS implemented the **resource-based relative value scale** (RBRVS) system for physician's services such as office visits covered under Medicare Part B. The system reimburses physicians according to a fee schedule based on predetermined values assigned to specific services.

The **Medicare fee schedule** (MFS) is the listing of allowed charges that are reimbursable to physicians under Medicare. Each year's MFS is published by CMS in the *Federal Register.*

To calculate fee schedule amounts, Medicare uses a formula that incorporates the following **relative value units** for:

- Physician work (RVUw)
- Practice expenses (RVUpe)
- Malpractice costs (RVUm)

Sample 2008 RVUs for selected HCPCS codes are shown in table 14.6.

Payment localities are adjusted according to three **geographic practice cost indices** (GPCIs):

- Physician work (GPCIw)
- Practice expenses (GPCIpe)
- Malpractice costs (GPCIm)

Sample GPCIs for selected U.S. cities are shown in table 14.7.

Table 14.6. Sample 2008 RVUs for selected HCPCS codes

HCPCS Code	Description	Work RVU	Facility Practice Expense RVU	Malpractice Expense RVU
99203	Office visit	1.34	.43	.09
99204	Office visit	2.00	.71	.12
10080	I&D of pilonidal cyst, simple	1.19	1.10	.11
45380	Colonoscopy with biopsy	4.43	2.24	.35
52601	TURP, complete	15.13	8.43	.87

Table 14.7. Sample GPCIs for selected U.S. cities

City	Work GPCI	Practice Expense GPCI	Malpractice Expense GPCI
St. Louis	1.000	.943	1.001
Dallas	1.009	1.033	1.077
Seattle	1.014	1.109	.755
Philadelphia	1.016	1.102	1.492

A geographic cost index is a number used to multiply each RVU so that it better reflects a geographical area's relative costs. For example, costs of office rental prices, local taxes, average salaries, and malpractice costs are all affected by geography.

A **national conversion factor** (CF) converts the RVUs into payments. In 2008, the CF was $34.0682.

The RBRVS fee schedule uses the following formula:

[(RVUw × GPCIw) + (RVUpe × GPCIpe)
+ (RVUm × GPCIm)] × CF = Payment

As an example, payment for performing a repair of a nail bed (code 11760) in Birmingham, Alabama, in 2008, can be calculated. RVU values include:

- Work RVU (RVUw) = 1.60
- Practice expense RVU (RVUpe) = 1.43
- Malpractice RVU (RVUm) = 0.21

GPCI values include:

- Work GPCI (GPCIw) = 1.00
- Practice expense GPCI (GPCIpe) = 0.850
- Malpractice GPCI (GPCIm) = 0. 617
- National CF = $34.0682

The calculation is as follows:

(1.60 × 1.00) + (1.43 × 0.850) + (0.21 × 0.617) × $34.0682
1.60 + 1.2155 + 0.1295
2.945 × $34.0682
Fee schedule payment of $100.33

Medicare Skilled Nursing Facility Prospective Payment System

The BBA mandated implementation of a **skilled nursing facility prospective payment system** (SNF PPS). The system was to cover all costs (routine, ancillary, and capital) associated with covered SNF services furnished to Medicare Part A beneficiaries. Certain educational activities were exempt from the new system.

The SNF PPS was implemented on July 1, 1998. Under the PPS, SNFs are no longer paid under a system based on reasonable costs. Instead, they are paid according to a per-diem PPS based on case mix–adjusted payment rates. Per diem rates range from a high of about $630 to a low of about $160.

Medicare Part A covers posthospital SNF services and all items and services paid under Medicare Part B before July 1, 1998 (other than physician and certain other services specifically excluded under the BBA). Major elements of the SNF PPS include rates, coverage, transition, and consolidated billing. OBRA required CMS to develop an assessment instrument to standardize the collection of SNF patient data. That document is called the **Minimum Data Set** (MDS). MDS 2.0 is currently used but MDS 3.0 is scheduled for implementation on October 1, 2009.

The MDS is the minimum core of defined and categorized patient assessment questions that serves as the basis for documentation and reimbursement in an SNF. The MDS form contains a face sheet for documentation of resident identification information, demographic information, and the patient's customary routine.

Resource Utilization Groups

SNF reimbursement rates are paid according to **Resource Utilization Groups, Version III** (RUG-III) (a resident classification system) based on the MDS resident assessments.

The RUG-III classification system uses resident assessment data from the MDS collected by SNFs to assign residents to one of 53 groups. MDS data that classify patients into one of the upper 35 RUGs automatically justify the patients' admission to the SNF. Patients who are classified into the lower 18 RUGs are evaluated on a case-by-case basis.

Resident Assessment Validation and Entry

CMS developed a computerized data-entry system for long-term care facilities that offers users the ability to collect MDS assessments in a database and transmit them in CMS-standard format to their state database. The data-entry software is entitled **Resident Assessment Validation and Entry** (RAVEN). RAVEN imports and exports data in standard MDS record format; maintains facility, resident, and employee information; enforces data integrity via rigorous edit checks; and provides comprehensive online help. It includes a data dictionary and a RUG calculator.

Consolidated Billing Provision

The BBA includes a billing provision that requires an SNF to submit consolidated Medicare bills for its residents for services covered under either Part A or Part B except for a limited number of specifically excluded services. For example, when a physician provides a diagnostic radiology service to an SNF patient, the SNF must bill for the technical component of the radiology service because this is included in the SNF consolidated billing payment. The rendering physician must develop a business relationship with the SNF in order to receive payment from the SNF for the services he or she rendered. The professional component of the physician services is excluded from SNF consolidated billing and must be billed separately to the **Medicare carrier**. There are, of course, other exclusions to this provision, including physician assistant services, nurse practitioner services, and clinical nurse specialists when these individuals are working under the supervision of, or in collaboration with, a physician, certified midwife services, qualified psychologist services, and certified registered nurse anesthetist services. Other exclusions include hospice care, maintenance dialysis, selected services furnished on an outpatient basis such as cardiac catheterization services, CAT scans and MRIs, radiation therapy, and ambulance services. In addition, SNFs report **Healthcare Common Procedure Coding System** (HCPCS) codes on all Part B bills.

Medicare and Medicaid Outpatient Prospective Payment System

The **Outpatient Prospective Payment System** (OPPS) was first implemented for services furnished on or after August 1, 2000. Under the OPPS, the federal government pays for hospital outpatient services on a rate-per-service basis that varies according to the **ambulatory payment classification** (APC) group to which the service is assigned. The Healthcare Common Procedural Coding System (HCPCS) identifies and groups the services within each APC group. Services included under APCs follow:

- Surgical procedures
- Radiology including radiation therapy
- Clinic visits (E/M)
- ER visits
- Partial hospitalization services for the mentally ill
- Chemotherapy
- Preventive services and screening exams
- Dialysis for other than ESRD
- Vaccines, splints, casts, and antigens
- Certain implantable items

The OPPS does not apply to critical access hospitals (CAHs) or hospitals in Maryland that are excluded, IHS hospitals, hospitals outside the 50 states, the District of Columbia, and Puerto Rico.

The calculation of payment for services under the OPPS is based on the categorization of outpatient services into APC groups according to **Current Procedural Terminology** (CPT)/HCPCS codes. ICD-9-CM coding is not utilized in the selection of APCs. The more than 850 APCs are categorized into significant procedure APCs, radiology and other diagnostic APCs, medical visit APCs, and a partial hospitalization APC. Services within an APC are similar, both clinically and with regard to resource consumption, and each APC is assigned a fixed payment rate for the facility fee or technical component of the outpatient visit. Payment rates are also adjusted according to the hospital's wage index. Multiple APCs may be appropriate for a single episode of care as the patient may receive various types of services such as radiology or surgical procedures.

The OPPS **payment status indicators** (SIs) (see table 14.8) that are assigned to each HCPCS code and APCs play an important role in determining payment for services under the OPPS. They indicate whether a service represented by a HCPCS code is payable under the OPPS or another payment system and also whether particular OPPS policies apply to the code. Status indicator "N" refers to items and services that are "packaged" into APC rates. **Packaging** means that payment for that service is packaged into payment for other services and, therefore, there is no separate PAC payment. Packaged services might include minor ancillary services, inexpensive drugs, medical supplies, and implantable devices.

Discounting applies to multiple surgical procedures furnished during the same operative session. For discounted procedures, the full APC rate is paid for the surgical procedure with the highest rate and other surgical procedures performed at the same time are reimbursed at 50 percent of the APC rate. When a surgical procedure is terminated after a patient is prepared for surgery, but before induction of anesthesia, the facility is reimbursed at 50 percent of the APC rate. Modifier 73 should be appended to the procedure code

Table 14.8. OPPS payment status indicators and description of payment under OPPS

Status Indicator	Description of Payment under OPPS
SI A	Services paid under some other method (such as a fee schedule): • Ambulance services • Clinical diagnostic laboratory services • Nonimplantable prosthetic and orthotic devices • EPO for ESRD patients • Physical, occupation, and speech therapy • Routine dialysis services for ESRD patients provided in a certified dialysis unit of a hospital • Diagnostic mammography • Screening mammography
SI B	Codes that are not recognized by OPPS when submitted on an outpatient hospital Part B bill type
SI C	Inpatient procedures
SI D	Discontinued codes
SI E	Items, codes, and services not covered by Medicare
SI F	Corneal tissue acquisition; certain CRNA services and Hepatitis B vaccines
SI G	Pass-through drugs and biologicals
SI H	Pass-through device categories
SI K	Non-pass-through drugs, biologicals, and radiopharmaceutical agents; therapeutic radiopharmaceuticals, brachytherapy services, blood and blood products
SI L	Influenza vaccine; Pneumococcal pneumonia vaccine
SI M	Items and services not billable to the fiscal intermediary
SI N	Items and services packaged into APC rates
SI P	Partial hospitalization
SI Q	Packaged services subject to separate payment under OPPS payment criteria
SI S	Significant procedure, not discounted when multiple
SI T	Significant procedure, multiple reduction applies
SI V	Clinic or emergency department visit
SI Y	Nonimplantable durable medical equipment
SI X	Ancillary services

indicating that the procedure was discontinued. Modifier 74 is appended to the procedure code when a procedure is interrupted after its initiation or the administration of anesthesia. The facility receives the full APC payment.

The OPPS does pay outlier payments on a service-by-service basis when the cost of furnishing a service or procedure by a hospital exceeds 1.75 times the APC payment amount and exceeds the APC payment rate plus a fixed-dollar threshold. For CY 2008, the threshold was $1,575. If a provider meets both of these conditions, the outlier payment is calculated as 50 percent of the amount by which the cost of furnishing the service exceeds 1.75 times the APC payment rate.

Services that are identified with a status indicator "C" have been identified as inpatient only services and will not be reimbursed by Medicare when they are provided on an outpatient basis. This inpatient only list is updated each year.

Special payments are also made for new technology in one of two ways. Transitional pass-through payments are temporary additional payments that are made when certain drugs, biological agents, brachytherapy devices, and other expensive medical devices new to medicine are used. These new technology APCs were created to allow new procedures and services to enter HOPPS quickly even though their complete costs and payment information are not known. New technology APCs house modern procedures and services until enough data is collected to properly place the new procedure in an existing APC or to create a new APC for the service/procedure. Coding for E/M medical visits is difficult under the APC system. CMS states that each facility should develop a system for mapping the provided services furnished to the different levels of effort represented by E/M codes. As long as services furnished are documented and medically necessary and the facility is following its own system, which reasonably relates the intensity of hospital resources to the different levels of codes, CMS assumes that the hospital is in compliance with its reporting requirements.

Ambulatory Surgery Centers (ASCs)

For Medicare purposes, an **ambulatory surgery center** (ASC) is a distinct entity that operates exclusively for the purpose of furnishing outpatient surgical services to patients. An ASC is either independent or operated by a hospital. If it is operated by a hospital, it has the option of being covered under Medicare as an ASC or can continue to be covered as an outpatient surgery department. To be considered an ASC of a hospital it has to be a separately identifiable entity physically, administratively, and financially.

The Medicare Modernization Act (MMA) of 2003 extensively revised the ASC payment system with changes going into effect on January 1, 2008. The system is called the **Ambulatory Surgery Center Prospective Payment System** (ASC PPS).

ASCs must accept assignment as payment in full. Eighty percent of the payment comes from the government and 20 percent from the beneficiary.

Under the ASC payment system, Medicare will make payments to ASCs only for services on the ASC list of covered procedures. The surgical procedures included in the list are those that have been determined to pose no significant risk to beneficiaries when furnished in an ASC. The ASC payment includes services such as medical and surgical supplies, nursing services, surgical dressings, implanted prosthetic devices not on a pass-through list, and splints and casts. Examples of services not included in the ASC payment are brachytherapy, procurement of corneal tissue, and certain drugs and biologicals.

The payment rates for most covered ASC procedures and covered ancillary services are established prospectively based on a percentage of the OPPS payment rates while a small number of services are contractor-based, such as the pass-through items.

The HCPCS code is used as the basis for payment. Each HCPCS code falls into one of more than 1,500 ASC groups with each group having a unique payment. Medicare pays 80 percent of the wage-adjusted rate and the beneficiary is responsible for the other 20 percent. Similar to the OPPS, each HCPCS has a payment indicator that determines whether the surgical procedure is on the ASC list (A2); Brachytherapy source paid separately (H7); Device-intensive procedure paid at adjusted rate (J8); or Packaged service or item for which no separate payment is made (N1). These are just a few examples of some of the payment indicators; there are others.

Again, like the OPPS, there are guidelines for payment of terminated procedures. The following rules apply:

- 0 percent payment for procedures terminated for reasons before the ASC has expended substantial resources
- 50 percent payment for procedures that are terminated due to medical complications prior to anesthesia
- 100 percent payment for procedures that have started but are terminated after anesthesia is induced

Home Health Prospective Payment System

The BBA called for the development and implementation of a **home health prospective payment system** (HH PPS) for reimbursement of services provided to Medicare beneficiaries. The PPS for HHAs was implemented on October 1, 2000. Extensive changes were made in 2008.

OASIS and HAVEN

HHAs use the OASIS data set and HAVEN data-entry software to conduct all patient assessments, not just the assessments for Medicare beneficiaries. OASIS stands for **Outcome and Assessment Information Set**. It consists of data elements that (1) represent core items for the comprehensive assessment of an adult home care patient and (2) form the basis for measuring patient outcomes for the purpose of outcome-based quality improvement (OBQI). OASIS is a key component of Medicare's partnership with the home care industry to foster and monitor improved home health care outcomes. The Conditions of Participation for HHAs require that HHAs electronically report all OASIS data.

CMS also developed the OASIS data-entry system called HAVEN (**Home Assessment Validation and Entry**). HAVEN is available to HHAs at no charge through CMS's Web site or on CD-ROM. HAVEN offers users the ability to collect OASIS data in a database and transmit them in a standard format to state databases. The data-entry software imports and exports data in standard OASIS record format; maintains agency, patient, and employee information; maintains data integrity through rigorous edit checks; and provides comprehensive online help.

Home Health Resource Groups

Home health resource groups (HHRGs) represent the classification system established for the prospective reimbursement of covered home care services to Medicare beneficiaries during a 60-day episode of care. Covered services include skilled nursing visits, home health aide visits, therapy services (for example, physical, occupational, and speech therapy), medical social services, and nonroutine medical supplies. Durable medical equipment (DME) is excluded from the episode-of-care payment and is reimbursed under the DME fee schedule.

The classification of a patient into 1 of 153 HHRGs is based on OASIS data, which establish the severity of clinical and functional needs and services utilized. Grouper software is used to determine the appropriate HHRG (See table 14.9). For example:

> OASIS data collected on a 76-year-old male home care patient resulted in an HHRG of C2, F3, and S2. This HHRG is interpreted as a clinical domain of low severity, a functional domain of moderate severity, and a service utilization domain of low utilization.

The HHRG assigned as well as the type of supplies provided and the number of home health visits comprises the HIPPS code, which is the unit of payment for the episode of care.

Table 14.9. HHRG severity levels in three domains: clinical , functional, and service utilization

Domain	Score	Severity Level
Clinical	C1 C2 C3	Minimum severity Low severity Moderate severity
Functional	F1 F2 F3	Minimum severity Low severity Moderate severity
Service utilization	S1 S2 S3 S4 S5	Minimum utilization Low severity utilization Moderate utilization High utilization Maximum utilization

Episode of care reimbursements vary from $1,300 to almost $8,000 and are affected by treatment level and regional wage differentials. There is no limit to the number of 60-day episodes of care that a patient may receive as long as Medicare coverage criteria are met.

Low Utilization and Outlier Payments

When a patient receives fewer than four home care visits during a 60-day episode, an alternate (reduced) payment, or **low-utilization payment adjustment** (LUPA), is made instead of the full HHRG reimbursement rate. HHAs are eligible for a **cost outlier adjustment**, which is a payment for certain high-cost home care patients whose costs are in excess of a threshold amount for each HHRG. The threshold is the 60-day episode payment plus a fixed-dollar loss that is constant across the HHRGs.

Ambulance Fee Schedule

A new Medicare payment system for medically necessary transports effective for services provided on or after April 1, 2002, was included as part of the BBA. The payment system applies to all ambulance services including volunteer, municipal, private, independent, and institutional providers (hospitals, critical access hospitals, SNFs, and HHAs).

Ambulance services are reported on claims using HCPCS codes that reflect the seven categories of ground service and two categories of air service. Mandatory assignment is required for all ambulance service providers.

The seven categories of ground (land and water) ambulance services include:

- Basic life support
- Advanced life support, level 1
- Advanced life support, level 2
- Specialty care transport
- Paramedic intercept
- Fixed wing air ambulance
- Rotary wing air ambulance

Inpatient Rehabilitation Facility (IRF) Prospective Payment System

The BBA (as amended by the **Balanced Budget Refinement Act of 1999**) authorized implementation of a per-discharge PPS for care provided to Medicare beneficiaries by inpatient rehabilitation hospitals and rehabilitation units, referred to as **inpatient rehabilitation facilities** (IRFs). The PPS for IRFs became effective on January 1, 2002.

IRFs must meet the regulatory requirements to be classified as a rehabilitation hospital or rehabilitation unit that is excluded from the PPS for inpatient acute care services. To meet the criteria, an IRF must operate as a hospital. Requirements state that during the most recent, consecutive, and appropriate 12-month time period, the hospital will have treated an inpatient population of whom at least 75 percent required intensive rehabilitative services for treatment of one or more of the medical conditions specified in figure 14.2.

Figure 14.2. Medical conditions that are criteria for classification as inpatient rehabilitation facility

- Stroke
- Spinal cord injury
- Congenital deformity
- Amputation
- Major multiple trauma
- Fracture of femur (hip fracture)
- Brain Injury
- Neurological disorders including multiple sclerosis, motor neuron diseases, polyneuropathy, muscular dystrophy, and Parkinson's disease
- Burns
- Rheumatoid arthritis, osteoarthritis, polyarthritis
- Systemic vasculidities with joint inflammation
- Knee or hip replacement

Source: CMS 2007.

Patient Assessment Instrument

IRFs are required to complete a patient assessment instrument (PAI) upon each patient's admission and also discharge from the facility. CMS provides facilities with the **Inpatient Rehabilitation Validation and Entry** (IRVEN) system to collect the IRF-PAI in a database that can be transmitted electronically to the IRF-PAI national database. These data are used in assessing clinical characteristics of patients in rehabilitation settings. Ultimately, they can be used to provide survey agencies with a means to objectively measure and compare facility performance and quality and to allow researchers to develop improved standards of care.

The IRF PPS uses information from the IRF-PAI to classify patients into distinct groups on the basis of clinical characteristics and expected resource needs. Data used to construct these groups, called **case-mix groups** (CMGs), include rehabilitation impairment categories (RICs), functional status (both motor and cognitive), age, comorbidities, and other factors deemed appropriate to improve the explanatory power of the groups. There are currently 92 CMGs into which patients are classified.

CMG Relative Weight

An appropriate weight, called the **CMG relative weight**, is assigned to each case-mix group and measures the relative difference in facility resource intensity among the various groups. Separate payments are calculated for each group, including the application of case- and facility-level adjustments. Facility-level adjustments include wage-index adjustments, low-income patient adjustments, and rural facility adjustments. Case-level adjustments include transfer adjustments, interrupted-stay adjustments, and cost outlier adjustments.

Long-Term Care Hospital (LTCH) Prospective Payment System

The Balanced Budget Refinement Act of 1999 amended by the Benefits Improvement Act of 2000 mandated the establishment of a per discharge, DRG-based PPS for longer-term care hospitals beginning on October 1, 2002.

LTCHs are defined as having an average inpatient LOS greater than 25 days. Typically, patients with the following conditions are treated in LTCHs:

- Chronic cardiac disorders
- Neuromuscular and neurovascular diseases such as after-effects of strokes or Parkinson's disease
- Infectious conditions requiring long-term care such as methicillin-resistant Staphylococcus aureus
- Complex orthopedic conditions such as pelvic fractures or complicated hip fractures
- Wound care complications (traumatic, pressure, diabetic, and venous)
- Multisystem organ failure
- Immunosuppressed conditions
- Respiratory failure and ventilation management and weaning
- Dysphagia management
- Postoperative complications
- Multiple intravenous therapies
- Chemotherapy
- Pre-and postoperative organ transplant care
- Chronic nutritional problems and total parenteral nutrition issues
- Spinal cord injuries
- Burns
- Head injuries

MS-LTC-DRGs

Patients are classified into distinct diagnosis groups based on clinical characteristics and expected resource use. These groups are based on the current inpatient DRGs. There are approximately 650 LTC-DRGs. The payment system includes the following three primary elements:

- Patient classification into a MS-LTC-DRG weight.
- Relative weight of the MS-LTC-DRG. The weights reflect the variation in cost per discharge as they take into account the utilization for each diagnosis.
- Federal payment rate. Payment is made at a predetermined per discharge amount for each MS-LTC-DRG.

Adjustments

The PPS does provide for case-(patient) level adjustments such as short-stay outlier, interrupted stays, and high-cost outliers. Facility-wide adjustments include area wage index and cost of living adjustments.

A short-stay outlier is an adjustment to the payment rate for stays that are considerably shorter than the average length of stay (ALOS) for a particular MS-LTC-DRG. A case would qualify for short-stay outlier status when the LOS is between one day and up to and including five-sixths of the ALOS for the MS-LTC-DRG. Both the ALOS and the five-sixths of the ALOS periods are published in the *Federal Register.* Payment under the short-stay outlier is made using different payment methodologies. (See table 14.10 for examples of MS-LTC-DRGs and the ALOS for each.)

Table 14.10. Examples of MS-LTC-DRGs, relative weights, geometric ALOS, and short-stay outlier threshold

MS-LTC-DRG	Description	Relative Weight	Geometric ALOS	Short-Stay Outlier Threshold
9	Bone marrow transplant	1.2617	31.5	26.3
28	Spinal procedures w MCC	1.2617	31.5	26.3
114	Orbital procedures w/o CC/MCC	0.8596	25.2	21.0
132	Cranial/facial procedure w/o CC/MCC	1.7509	37.9	31.6
150	Epistaxis w MCC	0.8596	25.2	21.0
163	Major chest procedure w MCC	2.5063	33.5	27.9
181	Respiratory neoplasm w CC	0.6255	18.7	15.6
194	Simple pneumonia and pleurisy w MCC	0.7698	21.6	18.0

An interrupted stay occurs when a patient is discharged from the long-term care hospital and then is readmitted to the same facility for further treatment after a specific number of days away from the facility. There are different policies if the patient is readmitted to the facility within three days (called three-day or less interrupted-stay policy) or if the patient is away from the facility more than three days (called the greater than three-day interrupted-stay policy).

A high-cost outlier is an adjustment to the payment rate for a patient when the costs are unusually high and exceed the typical costs associated with a MS-LTC-DRG. High-cost outlier payments reduce the facility's potential financial losses that can result from treating patients who require more costly care than is normal. A case qualifies for a high-cost outlier payment when the estimated cost of care exceeds the high-cost outlier threshold which, for example, in 2009 was $22,960.

Inpatient Psychiatric Facilities (IPFs) Prospective Payment System

The Balanced Budget Refinement Act of 1999 mandated the development of a per diem PPS for inpatient psychiatric services furnished in hospitals and exempt units. The PPS became effective on January 1, 2005, establishing a standardized per diem rate to **inpatient psychiatric facilities** (IPFs) based on the national average of operating, ancillary, and capital costs for each patient day of care in the IPF. The system uses the same MS-DRGs as the acute care hospital inpatient system.

CMS is phasing in the PPS for existing facilities over a three-year period with full payments under the PPS beginning in the fourth year. The per diem payment is adjusted to reflect both patient and facility characteristics that cause significant cost increases.

Adjustments

Patient-level or case-level adjustments are provided for age, specified MS-DRGs, and certain comorbidity categories. Payment adjustments are made for eight age categories beginning with age 45 at which point, statistically, costs are increased as the patient ages.

The IPF receives an MS-DRG payment adjustment for a principal diagnosis that groups to one of 15 psychiatric MS-DRGs. (See table 14.11.) Seventeen comorbidity categories that require comparatively more costly treatment during an inpatient stay also generate a payment adjustment. The list of comorbidity categories and their associated ICD-9-CM diagnosis codes can be found in table 14.12.

In addition, there is a variable per diem adjustment to recognize higher costs in the early days of a psychiatric stay.

The IPF PPS also includes an outlier policy for those patients who require more expensive care than expected in an effort to minimize the financial risk to the IPF. Although the basis of the system is a per diem rate, outlier payments are made on a per case basis rather than on the per diem basis. Patients who are given electroconvulsive therapy (ECT) get an additional adjustment.

The PPS also includes regulations on payments when there is an interrupted stay, meaning the patient is discharged from an IPF and returns to the same or another facility before midnight on the third consecutive day. The intent of the policy is to prevent a facility from prematurely discharging a patient after the maximum payment is received and subsequently readmitting the patient.

Facility adjustments include a wage-index adjustment, a rural location adjustment, a teaching status adjustment, cost-of-living adjustment for Alaska and Hawaii, and a qualifying emergency department adjustment.

Check Your Understanding 14.4

Instructions: Answer the following questions on a separate piece of paper.

1. When did Congress enact the first Medicare prospective payment system?
2. What were Medicare Part A payments to hospitals based on prior to implementation of the diagnosis-related group PPS?
3. What type of diagnosis is the MS-DRG prospective payment rate based on?
4. What is the name of the computer software program that assigns appropriate MS-DRGs according to information provided for each episode of care?
5. What kinds of hospitals are excluded from the Medicare acute care PPS?
6. How are MS-DRGs organized?
7. What does case mix refer to? What is the relationship between MS-DRGs and case-mix groups?
8. What act mandated implementation of the skilled nursing facility PPS?
9. What are resident assessment data? From what are they collected?
10. What is the purpose of the resource-based relative value scale?
11. What types of hospitals are not reimbursed according to the outpatient prospective payment system?
12. What concept is applied when multiple surgical procedures are furnished during the same operative session?

Table 14.11. Psychiatric DRGs

MS-DRG	MS-DRG Description
056 057	Degenerative nervous system disorders w MCC Degenerative nervous system disorders w/o MCC
080 081	Nontraumatic stupor and coma w MCC Nontraumatic stupor and coma w/o MCC
876	OR procedure w principal diagnoses of mental illness
880	Acute adjustment reaction and psychosocial dysfunction
881	Depressive neuroses
882	Neuroses except depressive
883	Disorders of personality and impulse control
884	Organic disturbances and mental retardation
885	Psychoses
886	Behavioral and developmental disorders
887	Other mental disorder diagnoses
894	Alcohol/drug abuse or dependence, left AMA
895	Alcohol/drug abuse or dependence with rehabilitation therapy
896 897	Alcohol/drug abuse or dependence w/o rehabilitation therapy w MCC Alcohol/drug abuse or dependence w/o rehabilitation therapy w/o MCC

Table 14.12. Comorbidity categories affecting IPS payments

Category	ICD-9-CM Diagnosis Codes
Developmental disabilities	317, 318.0, 318.1, 318.2, and 319
Coagulation factor deficit	286.0 through 286.4
Tracheostomy	519.00 through 519.09; V44.0
Renal failure, acute	584.5 through 584.9, 636.30, 636.31, 636.32, 637.31, 637.32, 638.3, 639.3, 669.32, 669.34, 958.5
Renal failure, chronic	403.01, 403.11, 403.91, 404.02, 404.03, 404.12, 404.13, 404.92, 404.93, 585.3,585.4, 585.5, 585.6, 585.9, 586, V45.1, V56.0, V56.1, V56.2
Oncology treatment	140.0 through 239.9 with either 99.25 or a code from 92.21 through 92.29
Uncontrolled Type I diabetes mellitus w or w/o complications	250.02, 250.03, 250.12, 250.13, 250.22, 250.23, 250.32, 250.33, 250.42, 250.43, 250.52, 250.53, 250.62, 250.63, 250.72, 250.73, 250.82, 250.83, 250.92, 250.93
Severe protein calorie malnutrition	260 through 262
Eating and conduct disorders	307.1, 307.50, 312.03, 312.33, 312.34
Infectious diseases	010.01 through 041.10, 042, 045.00 through 053.19, 054.40 through 054.49, 055.0 through 077.0, 078.2 through 078.89, 079.50 through 079.59
Drug or alcohol-induced mental disorders	291.0, 292.0, 292.12, 292.2, 303.00, 304.00
Cardiac conditions	391.0, 391.1, 391.2, 402.01, 404.03, 416.0, 421.0, 421.1, 421.9
Gangrene	440.24, 785.4
Chronic obstructive pulmonary disease	491.21, 494.1, 510.0, 518.83, 518.84, V46.11, V46.12, V46.13, V46.14
Artificial openings—digestive and urinary	569.60 through 569.69, 997.5, V44.1 through V44.6
Severe musculo-skeletal and connective tissue disorders	696.0, 710.0, 730.00 through 730.09, 730.10 through 730.19, 730.20 through 730.29
Poisoning	965.00 through 965.09, 965.4, 967.0 through 969.9, 977.0, 980.0 through 980.9, 983.0 through 983.9, 986, 989.0 through 989.7

13. Which data set for patient assessments is used by the home health PPS?
14. What types of services are covered by the home health resource group classification system?
15. What PPS uses a Patient Assessment Instrument to gather data on patients?
16. What is the purpose of the IRVEN software?
17. To meet the definition of a long-term care hospital, what must the average length of stay be?
18. What is a short-stay outlier in relation to the LTCH PPS, and how is it calculated?
19. What other PPSs use the MS-DRGs currently used for inpatient hospitals?
20. The IPF prospective payment system identifies comorbidities that generate a payment adjustment. What are some of the other factors that generate adjustments with the IPF PPS?

Coding and the Reimbursement Process

Coding is the process of assigning numerical representations to clinical documentation (AHIMA 2010). As mentioned, many of the Prospective Payment Systems are based on the ICD-9-CM, CPT, or HCPCS codes. Therefore, complete and accurate coding has become central to the financial survival of the healthcare provider organizations.

The coding professional's first responsibility is to ensure the accuracy of coded data. To this end, AHIMA has established a code of professional ethics by which coders must abide.

Elements of Coding Quality

The quality of coded clinical data depends on a number of factors, including:

- Adequate training for everyone involved in the coding process, including coders, coding supervisors, clinicians, and financial personnel
- Adequate references and support resources, including up-to-date coding books, as well as subscription publications that communicate official guidelines (namely, *Coding Clinic for ICD-9-CM* and *CPT Assistant*) and, in some cases, encoders or other support software
- Accurate and complete clinical documentation that includes every pertinent condition and service provided to the patient
- The support of senior managers, who must understand how important the coding function is to the organization's continued existence
- A performance improvement plan for the coding function that ensures continuous quality improvement processes

When all of these components are present, the quality of coded clinical data can be evaluated according to the following elements:

- *Reliability*: The extent to which the data can be reproduced by subsequent measurements or tests (for example, coded clinical data are considered reliable when multiple coders assign the same codes to a record)
- *Validity*: The extent to which the coded data accurately reflect the patient's diagnoses and procedures (Bowman 2001)
- *Completeness*: The extent to which the coded data represent all of the patient's relevant diagnoses or procedures
- *Timeliness*: The extent to which the coded data are available within the timeframes required for billing purposes, decision support, and other uses

The quality of coded data relies on the quality of the clinical documentation. HIM professionals should work with the clinicians and other personnel to continue to improve its quality.

Coding Policies and Procedures

As with other organizational policies and procedures, coding policies and procedures are needed to promote consistency. Coding policies and procedures should include the following items:

- Directions for reviewing the record
- Instructions on how to address incomplete or conflicting documentation
- Instructions for communicating with physicians and developing physician queries and instructions for clarification and recording health record addenda
- Instructions on the actions to be taken when an appropriate code cannot be located
- Use of codes not required for reimbursement (optional codes)
- Standardized definitions or codes sets (for example, HIPAA requirements)
- Use of reference materials and books and instructions for updating
- Computerized data entry or other processes (Bowman 2001)

These items must be specified in policies and procedures so that coders know what is expected of them and so that the healthcare organization can ensure its compliance with government and payer requirements.

Quality Assessment for the Coding Process

Quality assessment for the coding process is also referred to as performance improvement for the coding process. It involves looking at more than just the assigned codes. As stated previously, accurate coding is essential to the economic survival of the healthcare organization; hence, ongoing efforts to improve the coding process should yield better economic benefits.

Baseline measurements of the current coding process need to be taken and benchmarks for improvement should be set up. For example, if the current process results in records being coded an average of 10 work-hours after arriving in the HIM department, a benchmark for improvement might be to code records in less than 8 hours. To establish valid internal coding data monitors, comparative data will be necessary. Comparative data can be obtained from a variety of sources, including state data organizations, hospital associations, peer review organizations, and the Medicare MedPar data, which can be obtained from the CMS. The National Health Information Resource Center and the National Association of Health Data Organizations are additional sources of information on health data.

Quality assessment of a process is generally ongoing. Even when the most ambitious goals for the most important measures have been accomplished, the measures should continue to be monitored. In addition, management should continually search for ways to improve the coding process through computerization or other methods.

Check Your Understanding 14.5

Instructions: Answer the following questions on a separate piece of paper.

1. What is the coder's primary responsibility?
2. What is the main factor in ensuring the quality of clinical coding?
3. Describe the quality assessment process for coding.

Application of Technology to the Coding Process

Recent technologies are having a considerable impact on the coding process, and new technologies hold promise for the future. Some of the most significant advances are discussed here.

Encoders

An **encoder** is a computer software program designed to assist coders in assigning appropriate clinical codes to words and phrases expressed in natural human language (Slee and Slee 1991). Initially developed during the era of paper-based health records, the principal purpose of encoders was to help ensure accurate reporting for reimbursement (Beinborn 1999).

Encoders come in two distinct categories: logic-based and automated codebook formats. A logic-based encoder prompts the user through a variety of questions and choices based on the clinical terminology entered. The coder selects the most accurate code for a service or condition (and any possible complications or comorbidities).

An automated codebook provides screen views that resemble the actual format of the coding system. This allows the coder to review code selections, notes, look-up tables, edits, and various other automated notations that help him or her choose the most accurate code for a condition or service. Although encoders can cite official coding guidelines and provide code optimization guidance, they require user interaction. Encoders promote accuracy as well as consistency in the coding of diagnoses and procedures.

A number of companies currently market encoder products. An up-to-date list of these products can be found in the annual coding issue of the *Journal of the American Health Information Management Association.*

Computer-Assisted Coding

AHIMA defines **computer-assisted coding** (CAC) as the use of computer software that automatically generates a set of medical codes for review, validation, and use based upon the documentation provided by the various providers of healthcare (AHIMA 2010, 62). With CAC, an electronic document is processed through a computer application to generate a list of procedure and diagnosis codes. There are two CAC applications designs: natural language processing (NLP) and structured data input. NLP uses a technology based on artificial intelligence that extracts pertinent data and terms from a text-based document and converts them into medical codes. The natural language processing technology used might be algorithmic (rules-based) or statistical. Schnitzer (2000) has stated that statistical approaches that can predict how an experienced coder might code a record and use machine learning techniques are superior to rigid rule sets. This opinion is congruent with the oft-heard argument that "coding is subjective". NLP is most commonly used in the medical specialties of radiology, pathology, and emergency medicine. According to the 2004 report of the AHIMA e-HIM Work Group on Computer-Assisted Coding, "CAC works best within medical domains that have a limited vocabulary. NLP-based tools in particular work best when there is a limited number of source documents that must be analyzed for code selection and less extensive coding guidelines."

Structured data input is used when menu selections and drop-down pick lists are used for documentation rather than handwritten or dictated notes. When a practitioner selects a certain term from a drop-down list, a code is automatically generated which is then reviewed by a coding professional.

According to Schnitzer, the advantages to using **automated code assignment** include:

- *Consistency*: Automated code assignment is consistently correct and consistently incorrect; thus, errors are easier to locate and fix once they are detected.
- *Accuracy*: As with medical knowledge, the amount of information that must be synthesized to correctly code patient records has increased substantially. Expert computer software programs can apply these rules and guidelines accurately.
- *Speed*: The computational power of computers can apply the many coding rules and guidelines efficiently.

Other benefits include a potential decrease in coding costs as overtime, vacation and other benefits might be decreased. In addition, when codes are available for billing more quickly, accounts receivables are improved and revenue increases.

It is important to note, however, that computer-assisted coding is not a magic bullet. For example, it cannot address the major obstacle facing today's human coder: the lack of accurate, complete clinical documentation. As Schnitzer (2000) put it, "If a service isn't appropriately documented, there no way for NLP to find it, assume it, or infer it." In addition, automated code assignment has not developed to the point where it can operate without substantial human interaction (Warner 2000).

There are advantages and disadvantages to implementing CAC. Each individual facility should determine if CAC would be beneficial to its operation. As CAC evolves so will the role of the HIM professional. However, the fear that coding professionals will become obsolete is unfounded. The expertise of coders will always be needed both for the review and the teaching of the software. Coders positions will be elevated rather than eliminated.

Emerging Technologies

As is apparent from the preceding subsection, the status quo will not continue for coding. A number of emerging technologies will likely be used to support the coding function.

Speech recognition is one candidate for improving the coding process as well as coding accuracy. As speech recognition improves and has the ability to accurately document what the clinician is saying, the ease of completely documenting healthcare services also improves. Schwager (2000) maintains that "speech recognition, combined with technology designed to extract and structure medical information (natural language processing) contained in narrative text, can automate the coding process used in reimbursement." He also discusses the possibility that the computerized patient record software could analyze the record in an interactive fashion, prompting the clinician for higher-quality documentation.

Handheld computers or personal digital assistants (PDAs) also are becoming commonplace. Many physicians and other healthcare professionals find them helpful. As computer systems continue to develop, it will only be a matter of time before these small units are used for data entry and other functions in healthcare organizations.

Check Your Understanding 14.6

Instructions: Answer the following questions on a separate piece of paper.

1. What is the difference between encoders and automated code assignment?
2. Name two emerging technologies and describe their impact on coding.

Processing of Reimbursement Claims

Understanding payment mechanisms is an important foundation for accurately processing claims forms. However, it is not enough just to understand payment mechanisms.

A facility's patient accounts department is responsible for billing third-party payers, processing **accounts receivable,** monitoring payments from third-party payers, and verifying insurance coverage. Medicare carriers and **fiscal intermediaries** (FIs) contract with CMS to serve as the financial agent between providers and the federal government to locally administer Medicare's Part A and Part B.

Coordination of Benefits

In many instances, patients have more than one insurance policy and the determination of which policy is primary and which is secondary is necessary so that there is no duplication of benefits paid. This process is called the coordination of benefits (COB) or the **coordination of benefits transaction**. The monies collected from third-party payers cannot be greater than the amount of the provider's charges.

Submission of Claims

According to the National Uniform Billing Committee (NUBC) more than 98 percent of hospital claims are submitted electronically to Medicare. The Administrative Simplification Compliance Act (ASCA), which was part of HIPAA, mandated the electronic submission of all healthcare claims with a few exceptions.

Healthcare facilities submit claims via the 837I electronic format which replaces the **UB-04** (CMS-1450) paper billing form. Physicians submit claims via the 837P electronic format, which takes the place of the **CMS-1500** billing form. For those healthcare facilities with a waiver of the ASCA requirements, UB-04 and CMS-1500 are used.

Explanation of Benefits and Medicare Summary Notice Remittance Advice

An **Explanation of Benefits** (EOB) is a statement sent by a third-party payer to the patient to explain services provided, amounts billed, and payments made by the health plan. Medicare sends a **Medicare Summary Notice** (MSN) to a beneficiary to show how much the provider billed, how much Medicare reimbursed the provider, and what the patient must pay the provider by way of deductible and co-payments. (See figure 14.3 for a sample Part B MSN.)

A **remittance advice** (RA) is sent to the provider to explain payments made by third-party payers (see figure 14.4). Payments are typically sent in batches with the RA sent to the facility and payments electronically transferred to the provider's bank.

Figure 14.3. Sample Medicare summary notice

CMS
CENTERS for MEDICARE & MEDICAID SERVICES
Medicare Summary Notice
Page 1 of 2
July 1, 2006

BENEFICIARY NAME
STREET ADDRESS
CITY, STATE ZIP CODE

CUSTOMER SERVICE INFORMATION

Your Medicare Number: 111-11-1111A

If you have questions, write or call:
Medicare (#12345)
555 Medicare Blvd., Suite 200
Medicare Building
Medicare, US XXXXX-XXXX

Call: 1-800-MEDICARE (1-800-633-4227)
Ask for Hospital Services
TTY for Hearing Impaired: 1-877-486-2048

BE INFORMED: Beware of "free" medical services or products. If it sounds too good to be true, it probably is.

This is a summary of claims processed from 05/15/2006 through 08/10/2006.

PART A HOSPITAL INSURANCE – INPATIENT CLAIMS

Dates of Service	Benefit Days Used	Non-Covered Charges	Deductible and Coinsurance	You May Be Billed	See Notes Section
Claim Number: 12435-84956-84556-45621 **Cure Hospital, 213 Sick Lane, Dallas, TX 75555** Referred by: Paul Jones, M.D.					a
04/25/06 – 05/09/06	14 days	$0.00	$876.00	$876.00	b, c
Claim Number: 12435-84956-845556-45622 **Continued Care Hospital, 124 Sick Lane, Dallas, TX 75555** Referred by: Paul Jones, M.D.					
05/09/06 – 06/20/06	11 days	$0.00	$0.00	$0.00	

PART B MEDICAL INSURANCE – OUTPATIENT FACILITY CLAIMS

Dates of Service	Services Provided	Amount Charged	Non-Covered Charges	Deductible and Coinsurance	You May Be Billed	See Notes Section
Claim Number: 12435-8956-8458 **Medicare Hospital, 123 Medicare Lane, Dallas, TX 75209** Referred by: Paul Jones, M.D.						d
04/02/06	L.V. Therapy (Q0081)	$33.00	$0.00	$6.60	$6.60	
	Lab (3810)	1,140.50	0.00	228.10	228.10	
	Operating Room (31628)	786.50	0.00	157.30	157.30	
	Observation Room (99201)	293.00	0.00	58.60	58.60	
	Claim Total	**$2,253.00**	**$0.00**	**$450.60**	**$450.60**	

(continued)

THIS IS NOT A BILL – Keep this notice for your records.

Figure 14.3. (Continued)

Your Medicare Number: 111-11-1111A

Notes Section:

a The amount Medicare paid the provider for this claim is $XXXX.XX.

b $776.00 was applied to your inpatient deductible.

c $30.00 was applied to your blood deductible.

d The amount Medicare paid the provider for this claim is $XXXX.XX.

Deductible Information:

You have met the Part A deductible for this benefit period.

You have met the Part B deductible for 2006.

You have met the blood deductible for 2006.

General Information:

You have the right to make a request in writing for an itemized statement which details each Medicare item or service which you have received from your physician, hospital, or any other health supplier or health professional. Please contact them directly, in writing, if you would like an itemized statement.

Compare the services you receive with those that appear on your Medicare Summary Notice. If you have questions, call your doctor or provider. If you feel further investigation is needed due to possible fraud and abuse, call the phone number in the Customer Service Information Box.

Appeals Information – Part A (Inpatient) and Part B (Outpatient)

If you disagree with any claims decisions on either Part A or Part B of this notice, your appeal must be received by **November 1, 2006**. Follow the instructions below:

1) Circle the item(s) you disagree with and explain why you disagree.

2) Send this notice, or a copy, to the address in the "Customer Service Information" box on Page 1. (You may also send any additional information you may have about your appeal.)

3) Sign here ____________________________ Phone number ____________________

Revised 08/06

Figure 14.4. Sample single-claim remittance advice

Medicare National Standard Intermediary Remittance Advice

FPE:	07/30/07
PAID:	01/25/08
CLM#	2
TOB:	111

PATIENT:	JOHN DOE					PCN:	235617
HIC:	123456			SVC FROM:	01/05/08	MRN:	124767
PAT STAT:	01	CLAIM STAT:	1	THRU:	01/06/08	ICN:	987654

CHARGES:		PAYMENT DATA: 140=DRG		0.000	=REIM RATE
1939.90	=REPORTED	2741.69	=DRG AMOUNT	0.00	=MSP PRIM PAYER
0.00	=NONCOVERED	2497.26	=DRG/OPER	0.00	=PROF COMPONENT
0.00	=DENIED	244.43	=DRG/CAPITAL	0.00	=ESRD AMOUNT
1939.90	=COVERED	0.00	=OUTLIER	0.00	=HCPCS AMOUNT
DAYS/VISITS:		0.00	=CAP OUTLIER	0.00	=ALLOWED AMOUNT
1	=COST REPT	768.00	=CASH DEDUCT	0.00	=G/R AMOUNT
1	=COVD/UTIL	0.00	=BLOOD DEDUCT	0.00	=INTEREST
0	=NONCOVERED	0.00	=COINSURANCE	-801.79	=CONTRACT ADJ
0	=COVD VISITS	0.00	=PAT REFUND	675.00	=PER DIEM AMT
0	=NCOV VISITS	0.00	=MSP LIAB MET	1973.69	=NET REIM AMT
ADJ REASON CODES:	CO A2 -801.79				
	PR 1 768				
REMARK CODES:	MA02				

Medicare Carriers

Medicare carriers process Part B claims for services by physicians and medical suppliers. Examples of carriers might include a state Blue Shield plan or commercial insurance companies or other organizations under contract with Medicare. Carriers are responsible for performing the following functions:

- Determining the charges allowed by Medicare
- Maintaining the quality of performance records
- Assisting in fraud and abuse investigations
- Providing education to providers, suppliers, and beneficiaries as necessary
- Making payments to physicians and suppliers for Part B–covered services

Medicare Fiscal Intermediaries

Medicare FIs process Part A claims and hospital-based Part B claims for institutional services, including inpatient hospital claims, SNFs, HHAs, and hospice services. They also process outpatient claims for supplemental medical insurance (Medicare Part B). Examples of FIs include Blue Cross and Blue Shield organizations and commercial insurance companies under contract with Medicare.

FIs are responsible for performing the following functions:

- Determining costs and reimbursement amounts
- Maintaining records
- Establishing controls
- Safeguarding against fraud and abuse or excess use
- Conducting reviews and audits
- Making payments to providers for covered services
- Providing education to facilities and beneficiaries as necessary

Medicare Administrative Contractors

Medicare administrative contractors (MACs) are newly established contracting entities that will administer Medicare Part A and Part B as of 2011. MACs will replace the carriers and fiscal intermediaries.

National Correct Coding Initiative (NCCI)

CMS implemented the **National Correct Coding Initiative** (NCCI) in 1996 to develop correct coding methodologies to improve the appropriate payment of Medicare Part B claims.

NCCI policies are based on:

- Coding conventions defined in the CPT codebooks
- National and local policies and coding edits
- Analysis of standard medical and surgical practice
- Review of current coding practices

The NCCI edits explain what procedures and services cannot be billed together on the same day of service for a patient. The mutually exclusive edit applies to improbable or impossible combinations of codes. For example, code 58940, Oophorectomy, partial or total, unilateral or bilateral, would never be used with code 58150, Total abdominal hysterectomy (corpus and cervix), with or without removal of tube(s), with or without removal of ovary(s). Modifiers may be used to indicate circumstances in which the NCCI edits should not be applied and payment should be made as requested. Modifier –59, for example, is used when circumstances require that certain procedures or services be reported together even though they usually are not.

Portions of the NCCI are incorporated into the **outpatient code editor** (OCE) against which all ambulatory claims are reviewed. The OCE also applies a set of logical rules to determine whether various combinations of codes are correct and appropriately represent services provided. Billing issues generated from these CCI and OCE edits often result in claim denials.

Check Your Understanding 14.7

Instructions: Answer the following questions on a separate piece of paper.

1. What is a COB transaction and what is its purpose?
2. What purpose does the remittance advice serve?
3. What is CMS-1500 used for? What is another name for this form?
4. What is the difference between a Medicare carrier and a fiscal intermediary? What functions is each responsible for performing?
5. What is a Medicare Administrative Contractor?
6. What is the purpose of the NCCI edits?
7. What are the NCCI policies implemented in 1996 to develop correct coding methodologies to improve appropriate payment of Medicare Part B claims based on?

Reimbursement Support Processes

Reimbursement support processes are routinely reviewed and revised by third-party payers to control payments to providers. Healthcare facilities also implement reimbursement support processes to make sure that they are receiving the level of reimbursement to which they are entitled. Third-party payers revise fee schedules and healthcare facilities revise chargemasters, evaluate the quality of documentation and coding, conduct internal audits, and implement compliance programs.

Management of the Fee Schedules

Third-party payers that reimburse providers on a fee-for-service basis generally update fee schedules on an annual basis. A fee schedule is a list of healthcare services and procedures (usually CPT/HCPCS codes) and charges associated with each. (See table 14.13.) The fee schedule (sometimes referred to as a table of allowances) represents the approved payment levels for a given insurance plan (for example, Medicare, Medicaid, and BC/BS).

Physicians, practitioners, and suppliers must notify Medicare by December 31 of each year whether they intend to participate in the Medicare program during the coming year. Medicare participation means that the provider or supplier agrees to accept assignment for all covered services provided to Medicare patients. To accept assignment means the provider or supplier accepts, as payment in full, the allowed charge (from the fee schedule). The provider or supplier is prohibited from **balance billing**, which means the patient cannot be held responsible for charges in excess of the Medicare fee schedule.

However, participating providers may bill patients for services that are not covered by Medicare. Physicians must notify a patient that the service will not be paid for by giving the patient a Notice of Exclusions from Medicare Benefits.

If a provider believes that a service may be denied by Medicare because it could be considered unnecessary, he must notify the patient before the treatment begins using an **Advance Beneficiary Notice** (ABN). (See figure 14.5.)

Nonparticipating providers (NonPARs) do not sign a participation agreement with Medicare but may or may not **accept assignment.** If the nonPAR physician elects to accept assignment, he or she is paid 95 percent (5 percent less than participating physicians) of the MFS. For example, if the

Table 14.13. Partial 2008 Medicare physician fee schedule payment amounts for Chicago, Illinois

Carrier Locality	CPT Code	Nonfacility Fee Schedule Amount	Facility Fee Schedule Amount
95216	10040	93.78	81.59
95216	10060	106.81	92.09
95216	10061	183.84	164.92
95216	10080	170.42	95.57
95216	10081	261.31	164.17
95216	10120	137.41	91.16
95216	10121	264.62	189.36

Source: CMS 2008.

Figure 14.5. Advance beneficiary notice (ABN)

Patient's Name: Medicare # (HICN):

ADVANCE BENEFICIARY NOTICE (ABN)

NOTE: You need to make a choice about receiving these health care items or services.

We expect that Medicare will not pay for the item(s) or service(s) that are described below. Medicare does not pay for all of your health care costs. Medicare only pays for covered items and services when Medicare rules are met. The fact that Medicare may not pay for a particular item or service does not mean that you should not receive it. There may be a good reason your doctor recommended it. Right now, in your case, **Medicare probably will not pay for –**

Items or Services:

Because:

The purpose of this form is to help you make an informed choice about whether or not you want to receive these items or services, knowing that you might have to pay for them yourself. Before you make a decision about your options, you should **read this entire notice carefully.**

Ask us to explain, if you don't understand why Medicare probably won't pay.

Ask us how much these items or services will cost you (**Estimated Cost: $**_______________), in case you have to pay for them yourself or through other insurance.

PLEASE CHOOSE **ONE** OPTION. CHECK **ONE** BOX. **SIGN & DATE** YOUR CHOICE.

Option 1. YES. I want to receive these items or services.

I understand that Medicare will not decide whether to pay unless I receive these items or services. Please submit my claim to Medicare. I understand that you may bill me for items or services and that I may have to pay the bill while Medicare is making its decision. If Medicare does pay, you will refund to me any payments I made to you that are due to me. If Medicare denies payment, I agree to be personally and fully responsible for payment. That is, I will pay personally, either out of pocket or through any other insurance that I have. I understand I can appeal Medicare's decision.

Option 2. NO. I have decided not to receive these items or services.

I will not receive these items or services. I understand that you will not be able to submit a claim to Medicare and that I will not be able to appeal your opinion that Medicare won't pay.

Date **Signature of patient or person acting on patient's behalf**

NOTE: Your health information will be kept confidential. Any information that we collect about you on this form will be kept confidential in our offices. If a claim is submitted to Medicare, your health information on this form may be shared with Medicare. Your health information which Medicare sees will be kept confidential by Medicare.

OMB Approval No. 0938-0566 Form No. CMS-R-131-G (June 2002)

MFS amount is $200, the PAR provider receives $160 (80 percent of $200), but the nonPAR provider receives only $152 (95 percent of $160).

NonPAR providers who choose not to accept assignment are subject to Medicare's limiting charge rule, which states that a physician may not charge a patient more than 115 percent of the nonparticipating fee schedule. The provider collects the full amount from the patient and Medicare reimburses the patient. Figure 14.6 illustrates the various fee schedules by type of provider.

Management of the Chargemaster

The **chargemaster** (table 14.14), also called the charge description master (CDM), contains information about healthcare services (and transactions) provided to a patient. Its primary purpose is to allow the provider to accurately charge routine services and supplies to the patient. Services, supplies, and procedures included on the chargemaster generate reimbursement for almost 75 percent of claims submitted for outpatient services alone.

The information that makes up a chargemaster line item may vary from one facility to another. There are, however, some common elements found in a typical chargemaster (Shraffenberger and Kuehn 2007). These include:

- *Item description*: Examples might be the evaluation and management visit, observation, or emergency room visit.
- *CPT/HCPCS code:* This code must correspond to the description of the service.
- *Revenue code*: The **revenue code** is a three-digit code that describes a classification of a product or service provided to the patient. These revenue codes are required by CMS for reporting services. (See table 14.15 for examples of revenue codes.)

Figure 14.6. Examples of physician reimbursement methodologies

Participating Provider	
Physician's fee	$180.00
MFS	$105.00
Medicare pays 80% of MFS or	$ 84.00
Patient pays 20% of MFS or	$ 21.00
Physician write-off ($180–$105)	$ 75.00
Nonparticipating provider who accepts assignment	
Physician's fee	$180.00
MFS	$105.00
Medicare nonPAR fee (95% of $105)	$ 99.75
Medicare pays 80% of nonPAR fee	$ 79.80
Patient pays 20% of nonPAR fee	$ 19.95
Physician write-off ($180–$99.75)	$ 80.25
Nonparticipating provider who does not accept assignment	
Physician's normal fee	$180.00
MFS	$105.00
Medicare nonPAR fee (95% of $105)	$ 99.75
Limiting charge (115% of $99.75)	$114.71
Patient billed	$114.71
Medicare pays patient (80% of nonPAR fee)	$ 79.80
Patient out of pocket ($114.71–$79.80)	$ 34.91

Table 14.14. Sample section from a chargemaster

		CPT/HCPCS Code					
Charge Code	Item Description	Insurance Code A	Insurance Code B	Insurance Code C	Revenue Code	G/L Key	Activity Date
2110410000	ECHO ENCEPHALOGRAM	76506	76506	Y7030	320	15	12/2/2006
2110410090	F/U ECHO ENCEPHALOGRAM	76506	76506	Y7040	320	15	12/2/2006
2110413000	PORT US ECHO ENCEPHALOGRAM	76506	76506	Y7050	320	15	12/2/2006
2120411000	ULTRASOUND SPINAL CONTENTS	76800	76800	Y7060	320	15	12/2/2006
2130401000	THYROID SONOGRAM	76536	76536	Y7070	320	15	1/1/2008
2151111000	TM JOINTS BILATERAL	70330	70330	Y7080	320	15	8/12/2007
2161111000	NECK LAT ONLY	70360	70360	Y7090	320	15	10/1/2006
2162111000	LARYNX AP & LATERAL	70360	70360	Y7100	320	15	10/1/2006
2201111000	LONG BONE CHLD AP	76061	76061	Y7110	320	15	8/12/2007
2201401000	NON-VASCULAR EXTREM SONO	76880	76880	Y7120	320	15	10/1/2006
2210111000	SKULL 1 VIEW	70250	70250	Y7130	320	15	1/1/2008
2210112000	SKULL 2 VIEWS	70250	70250	Y7140	320	15	8/12/2007
2210114000	SKULL 4 VIEWS	70260	70260	Y7150	320	15	8/12/2007
2211111000	MASTOIDS	70130	70130	Y7160	320	15	1/1/2008
2212111000	MANDIBLE	70110	70110	Y7170	320	15	12/2/2006
2213111000	FACIAL BONES	70140	70140	Y7180	320	15	12/2/2006
2213114000	FACIAL BONES MIN 4	70150	70150	Y7190	320	15	12/2/2006
2214111000	NASAL BONES	70160	70160	Y7200	320	15	1/1/2008
2215111000	ORBITS	70200	70200	Y7210	320	15	1/1/2008
2217111000	PARANASAL SINUSES	70220	70220	Y7220	320	15	1/1/2008

Table 14.15. Examples of UB-04 revenue codes

Revenue Code	Description
250	Pharmacy—General
251	Pharmacy—Generic Drugs
252	Pharmacy—Nongeneric Drugs
253	Pharmacy—Take-Home Drugs
260	IV Therapy—General
261	IV Therapy—Infusion Pump
262	IV Therapy—IV Therapy/Pharmacy Services
263	IV Therapy—IV Therapy/Drug/Supply Delivery
270	Medical/Surgical Supplies and Devices—General
271	Medical/Surgical Supplies and Devices—Nonsterile Supply
272	Medical/Surgical Supplies and Devices—Sterile Supply
273	Medical/Surgical Supplies and Devices—Take-Home Supplies
280	Oncology—General
289	Oncology—Other
290	DME—General
291	DME—Rental
292	DME—Purchase of New DME
293	DME—Purchase of Used DME
300	Laboratory—General
301	Laboratory—Chemistry
302	Laboratory—Immunology
303	Laboratory—Renal Patient (Home)
310	Laboratory Pathological—General
311	Laboratory Pathological—Cytology
312	Laboratory Pathological—Histology
320	Radiology—Diagnostic—General
321	Radiology—Diagnostic—Angiocardiography
322	Radiology—Diagnostic—Arthrography
360	Operating Room Services—General
361	Operating Room Services—Minor Surgery
362	Operating Room Services—Organ Transplant—Other Than Kidney
370	Anesthesia—General
371	Anesthesia—Incident to Radiology
372	Anesthesia—Incident to Other Diagnostic Services
410	Respiratory Services—General
411	Respiratory Services—Inhalation Services
412	Respiratory Services—Hyperbaric Oxygen Therapy

- *Charge amount*: This is the amount the facility charges for the procedure or service. It is not necessarily what the facility will be reimbursed by the third-party payer.
- *Charge or service code*: The charge or service code is an internally assigned number that is unique to the facility. It identifies each procedure listed on the chargemaster and identifies the department or revenue center that initiated the charge. The charge code can be very useful for revenue tracking and budget analysis.
- *General ledger key*: The general ledger key is a two- or three-digit number that assigns a line item to a section of the general ledger in the hospital's accounting system.
- *Activity/status date*: The activity/status date indicates the most recent activity of an item.

Chargemasters may allow more than one CPT/HCPCS code per item to differentiate between payment schedules for different payers.

The CDM can also be a tool for collecting workload statistics that can be used to monitor production and compile budgets. It is often used as a decision support tool to evaluate costs related to resources and to prepare for contract negotiations with managed care organizations.

The CDM relieves coders from coding repetitive services and supplies that require little, if any, formal documentation analysis. In these circumstances, the patient is billed automatically by linking the service to the appropriate CPT/HCPCS code (referred to as **hard-coding**). The advantage of hard-coding is that the code for the procedure will be reproduced accurately each time that a test, service, or procedure is ordered. The following services are typically hard-coded: radiology, laboratory, EEG and EKG, rehabilitative services, and respiratory therapy (Schraffenberger and Kuehn 2007).

Maintenance of the Chargemaster

The chargemaster must be updated routinely. Maintenance of the chargemaster is best accomplished by representatives from health information management, clinical services, finance, the business office or patient financial services, compliance, and information systems. The HIM professionals are generally consulted regarding the update of CPT codes. The CDM is updated when new CPT codes become available, when departments request a new item, and when the medical fee schedules or PPS rates are updated.

Some of the basic responsibilities of the CDM committee include (Rhodes 1999):

- Developing policies and procedures for the chargemaster review process
- Performing an annual chargemaster review when new CPT/HCPCS codes are available
- Reviewing key elements of the annual chargemaster review, including all CPT codes for accuracy, validity, and relationship to the CDM

- Reviewing all procedures and service descriptions for accuracy and clinical appropriateness
- Reviewing all revenue codes for accuracy and linkage to charge description numbers
- Ensuring that the usage of all HCPCS, CPT, and revenue codes is in compliance with Medicare guidelines or other existing payer contracts
- Reviewing all charge dollar amounts for appropriateness by payer
- Reviewing all charge description numbers for uniqueness and validity
- Reviewing all department code numbers for uniqueness and validity
- Performing ongoing chargemaster maintenance as the facility adds or deletes new procedures, updates technology, or changes services provided
- Establishing a procedure to allow clinical department directors to submit chargemaster change requests for new, deleted, or revised procedures or services
- Making sure there is no duplication of code assignment by coders and chargemaster-assigned codes in any department
- Reviewing all charge ticket and order-entry screens for accuracy against the chargemaster and appropriate mapping to CPT/HCPCS codes, when required
- Reviewing and complying with directives in Medicare bulletins, transmittals, Medicare manual updates, and official coding guidelines
- Complying with guidelines in the NCCI or other known coding or bundling edits
- Carefully considering any application that involves one charge description number "exploding" into more than one CPT/HCPCS code to prevent inadvertent unbundling and unearned reimbursement for services
- Reviewing and taking action on all RA denials involving HCPCS/CPT coding or HCFA (now CMS) coding guidelines

An inaccurate chargemaster adversely affects facility reimbursement, compliance, and data quality. According to an AHIMA practice brief (Rhodes 1999), negative effects that may result from an inaccurate chargemaster include overpayment, underpayment, undercharging for delivery of healthcare services, claims rejections, and fines or penalties. Chargemaster programs are automated and involve the billing of numerous services for high volumes of patients, often without human intervention. Therefore, it is highly likely that a single error on the chargemaster could result in multiple errors before it is identified and corrected, resulting in a serious financial impact.

Management of the Revenue Cycle

Revenue cycle management (RCM) involves many different processes and people, all working to ensure that the healthcare facility is properly reimbursed for the services provided. Effectively managing the revenue cycle is paramount to improving the revenues received by the facility. Delays in payment, denied claims, and other lost revenues tremendously impact the facility's financial health.

The revenue cycle involves many functions in addition to the process of billing. According to an AHIMA practice brief (Youmans 2004), the major functions typically include:

- Admitting, patient access management
- Case management
- Charge capture
- Health information management
- Patient financial services, business office
- Finance
- Compliance
- Information technology

Revenue Cycle Management (RCM) Committee

An effective method for managing the revenue cycle is through a RCM committee or team composed of individuals from all the departments involved in the revenue cycle. The HIM professional is an important player on this team. Various team members should analyze the revenue cycle indicators, which include:

- Value and volume of discharged, not final billed encounters
- Number of accounts receivable (AR) days
- Number of bill-hold days
- Percentage and amount of write-offs
- Percentage of clean claims
- Percentage of claims returned to provider
- Percentage of denials
- Percentage of accounts-missing documents
- Number of query forms
- Percentage of late charges
- Percentage of accurate registrations
- Percentage of increased point-of-service collections for elective procedures
- Percentage of increased DRG payments due to improved documentation and coding (Youmans 2004)

The HIM professional's area of expertise is varied and will be extremely useful in denials management, data analysis and presentation, write-off preparation, policy development, response to patient financial services requests, and review of OCEs and groupers.

Chapter 25 also addresses RCM in relation to the financial management of the facility.

Management of Documentation and Coding Quality

According to Deborah Elder (2000), manager of inpatient and outpatient coding services, Medical Management Plus, Inc., in Birmingham, Alabama:

> The importance of complete and accurate coding cannot be underestimated. ICD-9-CM and CPT-4 coding drives reimbursement and

also presents a mechanism by which external and internal agents evaluate utilization of services, quality of care, and the hospital's patient acuity level. This numerically abbreviated medical information is only as complete as the physician documentation and is only as accurate as the coder's translation. Coders have a monumental impact on the hospital and this impact will broaden as other healthcare services are converted to a prospective payment method of reimbursement, including Outpatient Services, Extended Care Facilities, and Home Health Agencies.

The cornerstone of accurate coding is physician documentation. According to an AHIMA practice brief (Prophet 2001), ensuring the accuracy of coded data is a shared responsibility between coding professionals and physicians. Accurate diagnostic and procedural coded data originate from collaboration between physicians, who have a clinical background, and coding professionals, who have an understanding of classification systems.

Complete, accurate, legible, and timely documentation should:

- Address the clinical significance of abnormal test results
- Support the intensity of patient evaluation and treatment and describe the thought processes and complexity of decision making
- Include all diagnostic and therapeutic procedures, treatments, and tests performed, in addition to their results
- Include any changes in the patient's condition, including psychosocial and physical symptoms
- Include all conditions that coexist at the time of admission, that subsequently develop, or that affect the treatment received and the length of stay. This encompasses all conditions that affect patient care in terms of requiring clinical evaluation, therapeutic treatment, diagnostic procedures, extended length of hospital stay, or increased nursing care and monitoring
- Be updated as necessary to reflect all diagnoses relevant to the care or services provided
- Be consistent and discuss and reconcile any discrepancies (this reconciliation should be documented in the medical record)
- Be legible and written in ink, typewritten, or electronically signed, stored and printed (Prophet 2001)

Physician Query Process

There are instances, however, when it is necessary to query the physician for clarification of data that may influence proper code assignment. This might include instances when there is conflicting or incomplete information in the record. Query forms have proved to be an effective means of communication with physicians. AHIMA cautions coders that these forms are used to improve documentation and understanding of the clinical situation, but not to increase reimbursement (Prophet 2001).

The facility should develop a standard form to be used in communicating with physicians. Characteristics of a good query form are noted in figure 14.7.

Figure 14.7. Characteristics of a good query form

The query form should:

- Be clearly and concisely written
- Contain precise language
- Present the facts from the medical record and identify why clarification is needed
- Present the scenario and state a question that asks the physician to make a clinical interpretation of a given diagnosis or condition based on treatment, evaluation, monitoring, and/or services provided. "Open-ended" questions that allow the physician to document the specific diagnosis are preferable to multiple-choice questions or questions requiring only a "yes" or "no" response. Queries that appear to lead the physician to provide a particular response could lead to allegations of inappropriate upcoding
- Be phrased such that the physician is allowed to specify the correct diagnosis. It should not indicate the financial impact of the response to the query. The form should not be designed so that all that is required is a physician signature
- Include patient name, admission date, medical record number, name and contact information (phone number and e-mail address) of the coding professional, specific questions and rationale, place for the physician to document his or her response, place for the physician to sign and date his or her response

Source: Prophet 2001, 88I–M.

Coding and Corporate Compliance

The federal government has initiated efforts to investigate healthcare fraud and to establish guidelines to ensure corporate compliance with the government guidelines. Part of the initiative involved providing healthcare organizations with guidelines for developing comprehensive compliance programs with specific policies and procedures.

History of Fraud and Abuse and Corporate Compliance in Healthcare

Probably the most pertinent fact in the history of corporate compliance related to healthcare organizations is that the federal government, specifically the HHS, is the largest purchaser of healthcare in the United States. Because one of the federal government's duties is to use the taxpayers' monies wisely, federal agencies must ensure that the healthcare provided to enrollees in federal healthcare programs is appropriate and is actually provided.

Several federal initiatives and pieces of legislation related to investigating, identifying, and preventing healthcare fraud and abuse have been passed. Interestingly, the basis of these initiatives and laws lies within the Civil False Claims Act, which was passed during the Civil War to prevent government contractors from overbilling for services provided. The original law was updated and reinforced in subsequent legislation and is still used to prosecute offenders.

Several government agencies are involved in detecting, prosecuting, and preventing fraud and abuse. Among them are the HHS, the Office of the Inspector General (OIG), the Department of Justice (the attorney general), the Federal

Bureau of Investigation (FBI), CMS, the Drug Enforcement Agency (DEA), the Internal Revenue Service (IRS), and state attorney generals.

Many initiatives are joint efforts among the agencies. For example, Operation Restore Trust, which began in 1995, is a joint effort of HHS, OIG, CMS, and the Administration on Aging. Operation Restore Trust spent only $7.9 million in the first two years to identify $188 million in overpayments to providers. It also led to implementation of special fraud alerts notifying providers of current investigative findings and to the **Voluntary Disclosure Program**.

The federal government began to actively investigate fraud in the Medicare program in 1977, with passage of the Anti-Fraud and Abuse Amendments of 1977 to Title XIX of the Social Security Act (SSA). However, detecting, preventing, and prosecuting fraud and abuse did not reach true prominence until the Health Insurance Portability and Accountability Act (HIPAA) of 1996, established Sections 1128C and 1128D of the SSA. Sections 1128C and 1128D authorized the OIG to conduct investigations, audits, and evaluations related to healthcare fraud. The BBA focused on fraud and abuse issues specifically relating to penalties.

The BBA also required that physicians and practitioners provide diagnostic information (to show medical necessity) prior to a facility performing lab or radiology services for a patient.

As previously mentioned, HIPAA expanded the OIG's duties to include:

- Coordination of federal, state, and local enforcement efforts targeting healthcare fraud
- Provision of industry guidance concerning fraudulent healthcare practices
- Establishment of a national data bank for reporting final adverse actions against healthcare providers

Significantly, HIPAA authorizes the OIG to investigate cases of healthcare fraud that involve private healthcare plans as well as federally funded programs; although, according to information on the OIG Web site, present policies restrict the OIG's investigative focus to cases of fraud that affect federally funded programs.

A major portion of HIPAA focused on identifying medically unnecessary services, upcoding, unbundling, and billing for services not provided. **Upcoding** is the practice of assigning a diagnosis or procedure code specifically for the purpose of obtaining a higher level of payment. It is most often found when reimbursement-grouping systems are used.

Unbundling is the practice of using multiple codes that describe individual components of a procedure rather than an appropriate single code that describes all steps of the procedure performed. Unbundling is a component of the NCCI.

HIPAA also expanded sanctions related to mandatory exclusion from Medicare, length of exclusion, failure to comply with statutory obligations, and anti-kickback penalties (Schraffenberger and Kuehn 2007).

Since February 1998 the OIG has continued to issue **compliance program guidance** for various types of healthcare organizations. The OIG Web site posts the documents that most healthcare organizations need to develop fraud and abuse compliance plans. The goal of compliance programs is to prevent accusations of fraud and abuse, make operations run more smoothly, improve services, and contain costs (Anderson 2000).

Elements of Corporate Compliance

In the February 23, 1998 *Federal Register*, the OIG outlined the following seven elements as the minimum necessary for a comprehensive compliance program:

- The development and distribution of written standards of conduct, as well as written policies and procedures that promote the hospital's commitment to compliance and address specific areas of potential fraud, such as claims development and submission processes, code gaming, and financial relationships with physicians and other healthcare professionals
- The designation of a chief compliance officer and other appropriate bodies, for example, a corporate compliance committee, charged with the responsibility for operating and monitoring the compliance program, and who report directly to the CEO and the governing body
- The development and implementation of regular, effective education and training programs for all affected employees
- The maintenance of a process, such as a hotline, to receive complaints and the adoption of procedures to protect the anonymity of complainants and to protect whistleblowers from retaliation
- The development of a system to respond to allegations of improper or illegal activities and the enforcement of appropriate disciplinary action against employees who have violated internal compliance policies, applicable statutes, regulations, or federal healthcare program requirements
- The use of audits or other evaluation techniques to monitor compliance and assist in the reduction of identified problem areas
- The investigation and remediation of identified systemic problems and the development of policies addressing the nonemployment or retention of sanctioned individuals

The OIG believes that a compliance program conforming to these elements above will not only "fulfill the organization's legal duty to ensure that it is not submitting false or inaccurate claims to government and private payers," but will also result in additional potential benefits, including, among others:

- Demonstration of the organization's commitment to responsible conduct toward employees and the community

- Provision of a more accurate view of behavior relating to fraud and abuse
- Identification and prevention of criminal and unethical conduct
- Improvements in the quality of patient care

The *Federal Register* published the supplemental compliance program guidance for hospitals in the January 31, 2005 issue. This document supplements rather than replaces the 1998 compliance program guidance (CPG) document. The supplemental CPG contains new compliance recommendations and an expanded discussion of risk areas, current enforcement priorities, and lessons learned in the area of corporate compliance.

For additional resources on compliance and fraud and abuse, see figure 14.8.

Relationship between Coding Practice and Corporate Compliance

Any corporate compliance program must contain references to complete and accurate coding. Many of the documented fraud and abuse convictions have centered on the coding function.

OIG Work Plan

At the beginning of each fiscal year, the OIG publishes guidance on its "special areas of concern" for the upcoming year. The OIG refers to this as its work plan. The table of contents for the 2008 Work Plan is shown in figure 14.9; the full plan can be found on the OIG Web site.

HIM Compliance Program

As mentioned above, one element of the corporate compliance program addresses the coding function. Because the accuracy and completeness of ICD-9-CM and CPT code assignment determine the provider payment, the reference to coding is not surprising. Thus, it is important that healthcare organizations have a strong coding compliance program. This coding compliance plan should be based on the same principles as that of the corporate-wide program. The basic elements of a coding plan should include:

- Code of conduct
- Policies and procedures
- Education and training
- Communication
- Auditing
- Corrective action
- Reporting

Code of Conduct

The HIM department should develop a code of conduct or perhaps adopt AHIMA's Standards of Ethical Coding.

Policies and Procedures

Policies and procedures that describe the facility's coding standards and functions should be documented in a coding compliance manual. Some of the items that should be included in this manual include policies on the following: ambiguous or incomplete documentation, rebilling of problem claims, use of official coding guidelines, issues where no official guidelines exist, and clarification of new or confusing coding issues.

Education and Training

Periodic and staff-appropriate education of staff is a key factor in a successful coding compliance program. Education for coders should be provided monthly (Schraffenberger and Kuehn 2007).

Areas that could be covered at training sessions include:

- The OIG work plan
- Clinical information related to problematic body systems, diagnoses, and procedures
- Changes to the PPSs
- Changes to ICD-9-CM, HCPCS Level II, and CPT codes
- Application of the Official Coding Guidelines
- Issues in *Coding Clinic for ICD-9-CM*
- Issues in *CPT Assistant*

All newly hired coding personnel should receive extensive training on the facility's and HIM department's compliance programs.

Education of the medical staff on documentation is likewise important to the success of any coding compliance program. Documentation education may be provided monthly, bimonthly, or quarterly depending on the importance of the issues covered (Schraffenberger and Kuehn 2007).

Examples of documentation problems that may need to be addressed with physicians include:

- Inconsistent documentation
- Incomplete progress notes
- Undocumented care
- Test results not addressed in physician documentation
- Historical diagnoses being documented as current diagnoses
- Long-standing, chronic conditions that are not documented
- Lack of documentation of postoperative complications
- Illegibility
- Documentation not completed on time (Bowman 2004)

Figure 14.8. Online compliance resources

Organization	Web site
Department of Health and Human Services, Office of the Inspector General	www.oig.hhs.gov
American Health Information Management Association	www.ahima.org
Health Care Compliance Association	www.hcca-info.org
National Health Care Anti-Fraud Association	www.nhcaa.org
Centers for Medicare and Medicaid Services	www.cms.hhs.gov
CMS Fraud Page	www.medicare.gov

Figure 14.9. HHS/OIG fiscal year 2005 work plan—Centers for Medicare and Medicaid Services

Medicare Hospitals
Hospital Capital Payments
Medicare-Dependent Hospital Program
Adjustments for Graduate Medical Education Payments
Nursing and Allied Health Education Payments
Inpatient Prospective Payment System Wage Indices
Payments to Organ Procurement Organizations
Inpatient Hospital Payments for New Technologies
Long-Term Care Hospital Payments for Interrupted Stays
Long-Term Care Hospital Short Stay Outliers
Special Payment Provisions for Patients Who Are Transferred to Onsite Providers and Readmitted to Long-Term Care Hospitals
Special Payment Provisions for Long-Term Care Hospitals Discharging Beneficiaries to Colocated or Satellite Providers
Critical Access Hospitals
Medicare Disproportionate Share Payments
Inpatient Psychiatric Facility Emergency Department Adjustments
Provider Bad Debts
Compliance with Medicare's Transfer Policy
Payments for Diagnostic X-Rays in Hospital Emergency Departments
Patient Care and Safety in Physician-Owned Specialty Hospitals
Oversight of the Joint Commission Hospital Accreditation Process
Medicare Secondary Payer

Medicare Home Health
Cyclical Noncompliance in Medicare Home Health Agencies
Accuracy of Data on the Home Health Compare Web Site
Accuracy of Coding and Claims for Medicare Home Health Resource Groups

Medicare Nursing Homes
Skilled Nursing Facility Consolidated Billing
Oversight of Medicare Skilled Nursing Facility Cost Reports
Medicare Hospice Care

Medicare Physicians and Other Health Professionals
Place of Service Errors
Evaluation and Management Services during Global Surgery Periods
Medicare Payments for Psychiatric Services
Services Performed by Clinical Social Workers
Medicare Payments for Selected Physician Services
Medicare "Incident to" Services
Appropriateness of Medicare Payments for Polysomnography
Long-Distance Physician Claims Associated with Home Health Agency and Skilled Nursing Facility Services
Assignment Rules by Medicare Providers
Business Relationships and the Use of Magnetic Resonance Imaging under the Medicare Physician Fee Schedule
Medicare Payments for Interventional Pain Management Procedures
Geographic Areas with High Utilization of Ultrasound Devices
Geographic Areas with a High Density of Independent Diagnostic Testing Facilities
Payments for High-Frequency Chiropractic Treatments
Physician Reassignment of Benefits

Medicare Medical Equipment and Supplies
Durable Medical Equipment Payments for Beneficiaries Receiving Home Health Services
Medicare Payments for Durable Medical Equipment Claims with Modifiers
Medicare Part B Payments for Home Blood Glucose Testing Supplies
Durable Medical Equipment Payments in South Florida
Comparison of Prices for the Negative Pressure Wound Therapy Pump
Payment Suspensions for Medical Equipment Suppliers
Durable Medical Equipment Claims Review in Comprehensive Error Rate Testing
Appropriateness of Medicare Reimbursement for Pressure-Reducing Support Surfaces
Medicare Payments for Power Wheelchairs
Supplier Purchase Prices for Power Wheelchairs in the Medicare Program
Part B Services in Nursing Homes: An Overview
Part B Services in Nursing Homes: Durable Medical Equipment
Part B Services in Nursing Homes: Enteral Nutrition Therapy
Part B Pricing of Enteral Nutrition Therapy

Medicare Part B Drug Reimbursement
Computation of Average Sales Price
Payments to Dialysis Facilities for Epogen
Monitoring Medicare Part B Drug Prices: Comparing Average Sales Prices to Widely Available Market Prices
Monitoring Medicare Part B Drug Prices: Comparing Average Sales Prices to Average Manufacturer Prices
Changes in Average Sales Price for Part B Drugs
Medicare Payment for Chemotherapy Drug Administration Services
Billing for Excessive Dosages of Prescription Drugs in Medicare Part B
Upselling of Inhalation Drugs by Suppliers

Medicare Part D Administration
Part D Dual-Eligible Demonstration Project
Duplicate Drug Claims for Hospice Beneficiaries
Medicare Part D Duplicate Claims
Duplicate Medicare Part A and Part B Claims Included with Part D Claims
Coordination and Oversight of Medicare Parts B and D to Avoid Duplicate Payments
Payments for Drugs under Medicare Part D during Part A Skilled Nursing Stays
Allocation of Employer Premiums under the Retirement Drug Subsidy Program
Allowable Costs under the Retirement Drug Subsidy Program
Actuarial Value of Retiree Prescription Drug Coverage
Rebates in the Retiree Drug Subsidy Program
State Contribution to Drug Benefit Costs Assumed by Medicare
Medicare Part D Reconciliations
Medication Therapy Management Program
Aberrant Part D Claims
Part D Catastrophic Coverage
Bid Submission by Part D Sponsors
Part D Negotiated Drug Prices and Price Concessions
Disenrollment of Deceased Beneficiaries
Implementation of Medicare Part D in Nursing Facilities
Prescription Drug Plan Marketing Materials
Comparing Drug Prices: Medicare Part D to Medicaid
Comparing Drug Prices: Medicare Part D to Medicare Part B Average Sales Prices
Medicare Part D Coordination of Benefits with Other Prescription Drug Coverage
Potential Fraudulent Drug Overutilization by Dual-Eligible Beneficiaries under Medicare Part D
Drug Prices on the Medicare Prescription Drug Plan Finder
Drug Utilization during the Medicare Part D Coverage Gap
Medicare Part D Explanation of Benefits Forms
Beneficiary Complaints about Medicare Prescription Drug Plans
Prescription Drug Plan Sponsors' Detection and Reporting of Fraud and Abuse

Other Medicare Services
Medicare Payments for Observation Services versus Inpatient Admission for Dialysis Services
Laboratory Services Rendered During an Inpatient Stay
Therapy Services Provided by Comprehensive Outpatient Rehabilitation Facilities
Emergency Health Services for Undocumented Aliens
Separately Billable Laboratory Services under the End Stage Renal Disease Program
Unallowable Payments to Terminated Medicare Providers/Suppliers

(Continued on next page)

Figure 14.9. (Continued)

Ambulance Services Used to Transport End-Stage Renal Disease Beneficiaries
Part B Therapy Payments for Home Health Beneficiaries
Pricing of Clinical Laboratory Tests
Part B Services in Nursing Homes: Mental Health Needs and Psychotherapy Services
Ambulatory Surgical Center Payment System

Medicare Advantage
Stabilization Fund
Managed Care Encounter Data
Follow-up on Adjusted Community Rate Proposals
Medicare Advantage Organization Bids
Frailty Payment Adjustments for Programs of All-Inclusive Care for the Elderly Organizations
Payments to Medicare Advantage Organizations for Deceased Enrollees
Medicare Advantage Lock-In Provisions
Medicare Advantage Special Needs Plans
Oversight of Medicare Advantage Plans' Marketing Practices

Medicare Contractor Operations
Preaward Reviews of Contract Proposals
Contractors' Administrative Costs
Fiscal Integrity of Quality Improvement Organizations
Contracting Operations
Contractors' Accounting System Audits
Contractors' Provisional Billing Rates
Pension Segmentation
Pension Costs Claimed
Unfunded Pension Costs
Pension Segment Closing
Postretirement Benefits and Supplemental Employee Retirement Plan Costs
Medicare Appeals Process: Administrative Law Judges
Medicare Appeals Process: Qualified Independent Contractor Reconsiderations
Contractors' Provider Education and Training Efforts
Medicare Summary Notice
Medicare and Medicaid Data Matching Project
Accuracy and Completeness of the National Provider Identifier
Recovery Audit Contractors: Reducing Medicare Improper Payments

Medicare Cross-Cutting Issues
Serious Medical Errors (Never Events)
Doctors' Office Quality Information Technology Initiatives

Medicaid Hospitals
Hospital Outlier Payments
Hospital Eligibility for Disproportionate Share Hospital Payments
States' Use of Disproportionate Share Hospital Payments
Provider Eligibility for Medicaid Reimbursement
Medicaid Disproportionate Share Hospital Payment Distribution

Medicaid Long-Term and Community Care
Billing for Medicaid Nursing Home Patients Transferred to Hospitals
Community Residence Rehabilitation Services
Assisted Living Facilities
Targeted Case Management
States' Use of Civil Monetary Penalty Funds
Medicaid Home Health Agency Claims
Inappropriate Medicaid Payments for Personal Care Services during Periods of Institutionalization
Medicaid Payments for Personal Care Services
Medicaid Payments for Medicare-Covered Home Health Services
State and Federal Oversight of Medicaid-Funded Assisted Living Facilities
Medicaid Adult Day Health Service Payments for Ineligible and Absent Beneficiaries

Medicaid Mental Health Services
Medicaid Supplemental Mental Health Payments to Prepaid Inpatient Health Plans
Early and Periodic Screening, Diagnosis, and Treatment of Mental Health in Medicaid Managed Care Plans

Medicaid/State Children's Health Insurance Program
Assessing Medicaid Eligibility for Children Enrolled in Separate State Children's Insurance Programs

Medicaid Prescription Drugs
Calculation of Average Manufacturer Prices
States' Medicaid Drug Claims
States' Use of the Average Manufacturer Price to Establish Medicaid Pharmacy Reimbursement
Pharmacies' Ability to Purchase Drugs at the Average Manufacturer Price
Postimplementation Review of the Federal Upper Limit Program
States' Accountability over Medicaid Drug Rebate Programs
Zero Dollar Unit Rebate Amounts
Additional Rebates of Brand-Name Drugs
Disputes within the Medicaid Prescription Drug Rebate Program
Assessing the Accuracy of Drug Type Classification in the Medicaid Drug Rebate Initiative File
States Collection of Medicaid Rebates for Physician-Administered Drugs

Other Medicaid Services
Family Planning Services
Medicaid Payments for Transportation Services
Medicaid Safeguards over Payments for Nonemergency Transportation Services
Medical Equipment
Medicaid Laboratory Tests
Adult Rehabilitative Services
Outpatient Alcoholism and Substance Abuse Services
Freestanding Inpatient Alcoholism and Substance Abuse Providers
Medical Services for Undocumented Aliens
Reimbursement Rates for Services Provided by Indian Health Service Facilities
Medicaid's Use of an All-Inclusive Rate for Reimbursing the Indian Health Service and Tribes for Prescription Drugs
Improper Medicaid Payments for Laboratory Services for Dual-Eligible Beneficiaries
Medicaid Physical and Occupational Therapy Services: Appropriateness of Payments
Use of Bundled Rates for Payment to Medicaid School-based Providers

Medicaid Administration
Contingency Fee Payment Arrangements
Upper Payment Limits—Flow of Funds
Medicaid Upper Payment Limits
Medicaid Payments for Services Provided Under Section 1115 Demonstration Projects
Medicaid Waiver Safety Net Care Pools
Medicaid Payments for Services Provided Under Section 1915(b) Managed Care/Freedom of Choice Waivers
Medicaid Payments Made for Ineligible Managed Care Members
Sections 1915(b) and (c) Concurrent Waivers
Medicaid Payments for Services Provided Under Section 1915(c) Home- and Community-based Service Waivers
Appropriateness of Level of Care Determinations for Home- and Community-based Services Waiver Recipients
Provider Enrollment Controls for Medicaid Home- and Community-Based Services Waiver Providers
State and Federal Oversight of Home- and Community-based Services
Additional Medicaid Payments to High-Volume Providers
Medicaid Provider Tax Issues
Physician Assistant Reimbursement

Figure 14.9. (Continued)

Medicaid Asset Transfers and Estate Recovery Provision for Nursing Home Care
Medicaid Eligibility in Multiple States
Medicaid Administrative Costs
Medicaid Claims at Enhanced Federal Financial Participation Rates
Medicare/Medicaid Credit Balances
Medicaid Management Information System Costs
Medicaid Statistical Information System Data Reporting
Medicaid and State Children's Health Insurance Program Payment Error Rate Measurement
Medicaid Managed Care Encounter Data: Reporting and Utilization
External Quality Review Organizations' Compliance with Federal Requirements
State Medicaid Third-Party Liability
Medicaid Enrollment of Working Disabled

Medicare and Medicaid Nursing Home Issues
Quality of Care and Corporate Compliance Programs in Nursing Homes with Corporate Integrity Agreements
Plan of Care: Addressing Minimum Data Set and Resident Assessment Protocols through Provided Services

Information Systems Controls
Annual OIG Reports to Congress on Medicare Contractor Information Systems Security Programs
Federal Information Security Management Act of 2002 and Critical Infrastructure Protection
Information Technology Planning to Support Medicare Fee-for-Service Contractor Reform
Smart Card Technology
Health Information Technology in Medicare and Medicaid—Security Issues
State-based Controls over Medicaid Payments and Program Eligibility
Medicare Contractor Information Technology Closeout Audits
Selected Medicare Part D General and Application Controls for Systems that Track True Out-of-Pocket Costs
Implementation of Medicare Part D at Small- and Medium-Size Plans and Plans New to Medicare
Point-of-Sale System for Handling Emergency Billing Under Medicare Part D
Oversight of System Conversions, Redesigns, and Transition of State Medicaid Management Information Systems
Medicaid Management Information Systems—Business Associate Agreements
Security Planning for Systems under Development
Claims-Processing Controls to Prevent Duplicate Payments for Medicaid Services

Medicare/Medicaid Gulf Coast Hurricane Response
Billing for Durable Medical Equipment in Hurricane-Affected Areas
Duplicate Medicaid Payments to Providers
Medicaid Payments for Evacuees
Uncompensated Care Costs
Financial Status of Hospitals in the New Orleans Area

Investigations
Health Care Fraud
Medicaid Program
Exclusions
Provider Self-Disclosure

Legal Counsel
Resolution of False Claims Act Cases and Negotiation of Corporate Integrity Agreements
Providers' Compliance with Corporate Integrity Agreements
Advisory Opinions, Fraud Alerts and Other Industry Guidance
Civil Monetary Penalties

Communication

Communication between the coding supervisor and the coding professionals is vital to ensure consistency in following coding policies and issues.

Internal Audits

Ongoing evaluation is critical to successful coding and billing for third-party payer reimbursement. In the past, the goal of internal audit programs was to increase revenues for the provider. Today, the goal is to protect providers from sanctions or fines. Healthcare organizations can implement monitoring programs by conducting regular, periodic audits of (1) ICD-9-CM and CPT/HCPCS coding and (2) claims development and submission. In addition, audits should be conducted to follow up on previous reviews that resulted in the identification of problems (for example, poor coding quality or errors in claims submission).

Auditing involves the performance of internal and **external reviews** to identify variations from established baselines (for example, review outpatient coding as compared with CMS outpatient coding guidelines). Internal reviews are conducted by facility-based staff (for example, HIM professionals), and external reviews are conducted by either consultants hired for this purpose (for example, corporations that specialize in such reviews and independent health information consultants) or third-party payers.

The scope and frequency of audits and the size of the sample depend on the size of the organization, available resources, the number of coding professionals, the history of noncompliance, risk factors, case complexity, and the results of initial assessments (Bowman 2004).

One of the elements of the auditing process is identification of risk areas. Some major risk areas include:

- MS-DRG coding accuracy
- Variations in case mix
- Discharge status (transfers versus discharges)
- Services provided under arrangement
- Three-day payment window, formerly called the 72-hour rule (Under this rule, diagnostic services provided within three days of admission should be included, bundled, in the DRG, whether or not they are related to the admission. Non-diagnostic services provided within three days of admission should be included in the DRG only if they are related to the admission.)
- All nondiagnostic services that are unrelated to the admission can be billed separately.
- Medical necessity
- Evaluation and management services
- Chargemaster description

Selecting types of cases to review also is important. Some examples of various case selection possibilities are found in figure 14.10.

Figure 14.10. Examples of various case selections for auditing

- Simple random sample
- Medical DRGs by high dollar and high volume
- Surgical DRGs by high dollar and high volume
- Medical DRGs without comorbid conditions or complications
- Surgical DRGs without comorbid conditions or complications
- Major diagnostic category by high dollar and high volume
- Most common diagnosis codes
- Most common procedure codes
- Significant procedure APCs by high dollar and high volume
- Unlisted CPT codes
- "Separate procedure" CPT codes reported in conjunction with related CPT codes
- Unusual modifier usage patterns
- Not elsewhere classified (NEC) and not otherwise specified (NOS) codes
- Highest-level evaluation and management (E/M) codes
- Consultation E/M codes
- Critical Care E/M codes
- Chargemaster review by service
- Superbill, encounter form, and charge sheet review by specialty

The frequency of audits depends on the individual facility; daily, weekly, monthly, or quarterly audits may be considered.

The results of the audits must be analyzed to determine the reason(s) for the coding errors. Focused reviews in one particular area may be necessary to review a higher volume of cases in which there were frequent errors. Certainly, focused reviews aimed at OIG target areas would be appropriate. Significant variations from baselines should prompt an investigation to determine cause(s).

Feedback on the results of audits should be presented to interested parties such as coding staff, supervisors, and physicians.

Corrective Action

Certainly, the goal of corrective action activities is the prevention of the same or a similar problem in the future. Typical corrective actions for resolving problems identified during coding audits include:

- Revisions to policies and procedures
- Development of additional policies and procedures
- Process improvements
- Education of coders, physicians, or other organizational staff depending on the nature of the identified problem
- Revision or addition of routine monitoring activities
- Revisions to the chargemaster
- Additions, deletions, or revisions to systems edits
- Documentation improvement strategies
- Disciplinary action (Bowman 2004)

Reporting

Documentation on coding compliance activities should be maintained and reported as stated in the policies and procedures. Certainly, adverse findings should be reviewed with the corporate compliance officer and steps taken as necessary to report these findings.

Check Your Understanding 14.8

Instructions: Answer the following questions on a separate piece of paper.

1. How often do third-party payers update fee schedules?
2. What does the term *accept assignment* mean?
3. Explain the difference between a participating provider, a nonparticipating provider who accepts assignment, and a nonparticipating provider who does not accept assignment.
4. What is the limiting charge rule?
5. What is a chargemaster, and why do healthcare facilities develop chargemasters?
6. How might an inaccurate chargemaster affect facility reimbursement?
7. What are the typical items on the charge description master?
8. Who is responsible for maintaining the charge description master?
9. Who and what are involved in revenue cycle management?
10. What are some characteristics of a good physician query form?
11. What do coding compliance programs concentrate on preventing? Which federal agency has established the precise steps that each healthcare facility must follow in establishing its compliance program?
12. What do the terms *upcoding* and *unbundling* mean in relation to coding?
13. What items might be covered during educational programs for the medical staff?
14. What major risk areas are related to coding and billing?
15. Describe some of the benefits of effective corporate compliance programs for healthcare organizations.

Real-World Case

Itemized charges on the UB-04 that are not supported by patient record documentation are unlikely to be reimbursed by a third-party payer. Examples of charges that would not be paid upon review of the patient record in comparison to the UB-04 include the following:

- Duplicate charges for services rendered one time only (for example, multiple charges for same service, such as surgery)
- Laboratory panel tests for which there should be a single charge
- Medications and diagnostic tests not prescribed by a physician
- Medications that a patient did not receive
- Tests repeated because of hospital error
- Services listed for dates after the patient was discharged from the facility
- Professional services performed by nurses or technicians (for example, equipment monitoring)

Summary

From its very beginnings, financial reimbursement for healthcare services has followed several paths. Among these are private pay, commercial insurance, employer self-insurance, and various government programs. The mixture of payment mechanisms has made healthcare reimbursement in the United States very complex.

As a consequence, the processing of medical claims can be complicated. How a claim is processed, what documentation is required, and how much reimbursement will be paid depend on the payer and the type of claim. Many attempts have been made to create a uniform healthcare claim that would accommodate all payment mechanisms. Claims processed for payment under Medicare have been consolidated into a uniform bill.

Healthcare organizations have developed several tools to help manage the billing and reimbursement process, including development of fee schedules and chargemasters. The HIM professional is frequently called on to provide expertise in the development, management, and auditing of these tools. In addition, organizations have recognized that ongoing evaluation of the entire billing process is essential to ensure accurate payment as well as to avoid fraud and abuse sanctions or fines. The HIM professional's work is likely to involve helping to develop such audit programs in addition to conducting the audits themselves.

Over the past two decades, the billing and reimbursement process has become an integral part of the job functions of many HIM professionals. The expertise given to the process to ensure accurate and timely claims submission is critical to the operations of any healthcare organization.

Payments for the delivery of healthcare services increased from $27 billion in 1960 to more than $2.3 trillion in 2007. In response, private insurers introduced managed care programs and the federal government implemented prospective payment systems to replace the costly per diem (or traditional fee-for-service) reimbursement methods. The federal government also incorporated managed care into its healthcare programs.

Health claims reimbursement processing has evolved from the submission of a handwritten CMS-1500 form to specially designed forms used for optical scanning purposes to electronic data interchange. Of recently enacted federal legislation affecting claims reimbursement processing, the NCCI and the OIG coding compliance programs have had the most effect on HIM professionals.

References

AHIMA e-HIM Workgroup on Computer-Assisted Coding. 2004. Delving Into Computer-Assisted Coding. *Journal of AHIMA* 75(10): 48A–H.

American Health Information Management Association. 2010. *Pocket Glossary of Health Information Management and Technology*. 2nd ed. Chicago: AHIMA.

American Medical Association. 2008. *Current Procedural Terminology,* 2008 ed. Chicago: AMA.

Anderson, S. 2000. Audit outpatient bills to get all the money you deserve. *Medical Records Briefing* 15(12):6.

Averill, R.F. 1999. Honest mistake or fraud? Meeting the coding compliance challenge. *Journal of AHIMA* 70(5):16–21.

Beinborn, J. 1999. Automated coding: The next step. *Journal of AHIMA* 70(7): 38–42.

Bowman, E. 2007. Coding, classification, and reimbursement systems. In *Health Information: Management of a Strategic Resource*. 3rd ed. Edited by Abdelhak, M. et al. Philadelphia: W.B. Saunders Company.

Bowman, S. 2004. *Health Information Management Compliance: A Model Program for Healthcare Organizations*. 3rd ed. Chicago: AHIMA.

Campbell, C., H. Schmitz, and L. Waller. 1998. *Financial Management in a Managed Care Environment.* Albany, NY: Delmar Thomson Learning.

Campbell, T. Opportunities for HIM in revenue cycle management. *Journal of AHIMA* 74(10):62–63.

Centers for Medicare and Medicaid Services.2008. http://www.cms.hhs.gov.

Coder's Desk Reference. 2008. Salt Lake City: Ingenix.

Davis, J.B. 2004. *Reimbursement Manual for the Medical Office: A Comprehensive Guide to Coding, Billing and Fee Management.* Los Angeles: Practice Management Information Corporation.

Dougherty, M. 2000. New home care PPS brings major changes. *Journal of AHIMA*, 71(10):78–82.

Elder, D. 2000. Coding: The key to compliance. Birmingham, AL: Medical Management Plus. http://www.mmplusinc.com.

Green, M.A., and J.C. Rowell. 2008. *Understanding Health Insurance: A Guide to Professional Billing.* Albany, NY: Delmar Cengage Learning.

Harkins, P.D. 2000 (Oct. 16). The alphabet soup of Medicare reimbursement. *Advance for Health Information Professionals*. 25.

Johnson, S.L. 2006. *Understanding Medical Coding: A Comprehensive Guide.* Albany, NY: Delmar Cengage Learning.

Kuehn, L. 2007. *CPT/HCPCS Coding and Reimbursement for Physician Services.* Chicago: AHIMA.

Lewis, M. 2008. *Working with Insurance and Managed Care Plans: A Guide for Getting Paid.* Los Angeles: Practice Management Information Corporation.

Medical Records Briefing. 2000. Make sure that your APC claim makes it through the OCE. *Medical Records Briefing* 15(9):1.

Medicare and You. 2008. Baltimore: CMS. http://www.cms.hhs.gov/partnerships/22my.asp.

Medicare Hospital Outpatient Payment System Quick Reference Guide. 2004. Baltimore: CMS. http://www.cms.hhs.gov.

National Committee for Quality Assurance. http://www.ncqa.org.

Newby, C. 2006. *From Patient to Payment.* New York: McGraw-Hill.

Palmer, K. 1999. A brief history: Universal health care efforts in the U.S.: Late 1800s to Medicare. http://www.pnhp.org.

Prophet, S. 2001. Practice brief: Developing a physician query process. *Journal of AHIMA* 72(9):88I–M.

Rhodes, H. 1999. Practice brief: The care and maintenance of charge masters. *Journal of AHIMA*, 70(7):supplement 2.

Rizzo, C.D. 2000. *Uniform Billing: A Guide to Claims Processing.* Albany, NY: Delmar Thomson Learning.

Role of the physician in the home health prospective payment system. 2000 (Nov. 7). Medicare Newsroom. http://www.hgsa.com.

Schnitzer, G.L. 2000. Natural language processing: A coding professional's perspective. *Journal of AHIMA* 71(9):95–98.

Schraffenberger, L. 2008. *Basic ICD-9-CM Coding.* Chicago: AHIMA.

Schraffenberger, L. and L. Kuehn. 2007. *Effective Management of Coding Services.* Chicago: AHIMA.

Schwager, R. 2000. Speech recognition propels transcription revolution. *Journal of AHIMA* 71(9): 64–68.

Slee, V.N., and D.A. Slee. 2008. *Health Care Terms.* 5th ed. St. Paul, MN: Tringa Press.

Smith, G. 2008. *Basic CPT/HCPCS Coding.* Chicago: AHIMA.

Spellman, H. 2008. Computer-Assisted Coding. *Code Write Community News.* July: 3–5.

3M Health Information Systems. http://www.3Mhis.com.

Valerius, J., N. Bayes, and C. Newby. 2004. *Medical Insurance: A Guide to Coding and Reimbursement.* New York: McGraw-Hill.

Warner, H.R. 2000. Can natural language processing aid outpatient coders? *Journal of AHIMA* 71(8):78–81.

Youmans, K. 2004. Practice brief: An HIM spin on the revenue cycle. *Journal of AHIMA* 75(3):32–36.

Part IV

Comparative Healthcare Data

Chapter 15
Healthcare Statistics

Loretta A. Horton, MEd, RHIA

Learning Objectives

- Define measurement
- Differentiate among nominal-level, ordinal-level, interval-level, and ratio-level data
- Identify various ways in which statistics are used in healthcare
- Differentiate between descriptive and inferential statistics
- Define hospital-related statistical terms
- Calculate hospital-related inpatient and outpatient statistics
- Define community-based morbidity and mortality rates
- Calculate community-based morbidity and mortality rates
- Define and calculate measures of central tendency and variability
- Describe the characteristics of the normal distribution
- Identify the relationships of measures of central tendency and variation to the normal distribution
- Display healthcare data using tables, charts, and graphs, as appropriate
- Calculate the case-mix index
- Locate healthcare-related state and federal databases on the Internet
- Use healthcare data collected from online databases in comparative statistical reports

Key Terms

Acute care
Ambulatory surgery center (ASC)
Average daily census
Average length of stay (ALOS)
Bar chart
Bed count
Bed count day
Bed turnover rate
Boxplot
Bubble charts
Case fatality rate
Case mix
Case-mix index (CMI)
Cause-specific death rate
Census
Consultation rate
Continuous variables
Crude birth rate
Crude death rate
Daily inpatient census
Descriptive statistics
Discrete variables
Encounter
Fetal autopsy rate
Fetal death (stillborn)
Fetal death rate
Frequency distribution
Frequency polygon
Gross autopsy rate
Gross death rate
Histogram
Hospital autopsy
Hospital autopsy rate
Hospital death rate
Hospital inpatient autopsy
Hospital-acquired (nosocomial) infection rate
Incidence rate
Infant mortality rate
Inferential statistics
Inpatient bed occupancy rate (percentage of occupancy)
Inpatient service day (IPSD)
Interval-level data
Length of stay (LOS)
Line graph
Maternal death rate (hospital based)
Maternal mortality rate (community-based)
Mean
Measures of central tendency
Median
Mode
National Vital Statistics System (NVSS)
Neonatal mortality rate
Net autopsy rate
Net death rate
Newborn (NB)
Newborn autopsy rate
Newborn death rate
Nominal-level data
Normal distribution
Nosocomial (hospital-acquired) infection
Notifiable disease
Occasion of service
Ordinal-level data
Outpatient visit
Pie chart
Population-based statistics
Postneonatal mortality rate
Postoperative infection rate
Prevalence rate
Proportion
Proportionate mortality ratio (PMR)
Range
Rate
Ratio
Ratio-level data
Referred outpatient
Scales of measurement
Scatter chart
Standard deviation
Stem and leaf plots
Total length of stay (discharge days)
Variability
Variance
Vital statistics

Complete and accurate information is at the heart of good decision-making. The health information management (HIM) professional has responsibility for ensuring that the data collected are accurate and organized into information that is useful to healthcare decision makers.

The primary source of clinical data in a healthcare facility is the health record. To be useful in decision-making, data taken from the health record must be as complete and accurate as possible. Data are compiled in various ways to help in making decisions about patient care, the facility's financial status, and facility planning, to name a few.

This chapter discusses common statistical measures and types of data used by organizations in different healthcare settings and data collection and reporting on a community, regional, and national basis. Methods and tools for graphically displaying data are then presented along with a discussion of normal distribution and descriptive statistics.

Theory into Practice

The Department of Quality Improvement at Community Hospital asked the HIM director to provide the hospital's Cesarean section (C-section) rate for the previous year. The hospital's goal is to keep their rate under 27 percent. The latest national statistics show the rate to be at 30.2 percent. During the previous year, the hospital recorded 210 deliveries. Of these, 48 were performed by Cesarean section. The C-section rate was 23 percent [(48/210) × 100]. The quality improvement coordinator is pleased that the hospital's complication rate is within the goal set by the hospital.

At this same hospital, the Cardiology physicians are asking to add a new Cardiac Catheterization Laboratory. The current laboratory currently accommodates 1,500 patients. They believe they could increase utilization by patients if they were able to add another laboratory. The associate administrator in charge of facility planning is using their state's recommendations that a cardiac catheterization lab is available 250 days a year for eight hours per day and that the average lab can service six procedures per day. He asks the HIM director to provide him with the number of patients that have been transferred to another facility for catheterizations over the past year. During the past year, 486 patients have been transferred for a cardiac catheterization at another facility. The associate administrator has met with the cardiologists and told them that he is planning to recommend a denial of their requests because the number of patients transferred does not justify the need for an additional laboratory. Figure 15.1 shows a line graph of the number of cardiac catheterization patients transferred to other hospitals and table 15.1 shows the transfers by medical specialty.

Introduction to Measurement

Before discussing statistical measures used in healthcare, it is important to understand what measurement is and how the data collected are classified. Measurement simply refers to

Figure 15.1 Community Hospital number of cardiac patients transferred to other hospitals

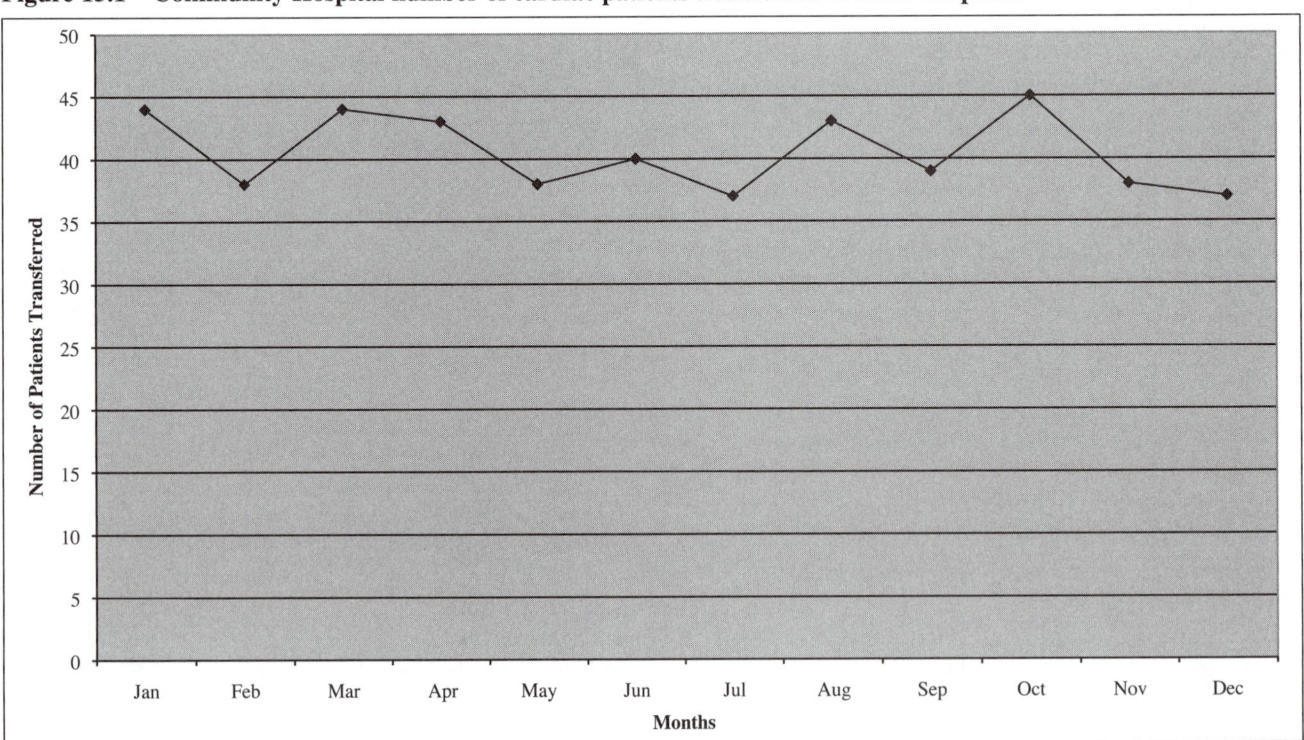

Table 15.1. Community Hospital, number of transfers for cardiac catheterizations by service, 20XX

	Family Practice	Internal Medicine	Cardiology	Total
January	5	17	22	44
February	6	15	17	38
March	8	14	22	44
April	9	14	20	43
May	7	15	16	38
June	5	14	21	40
July	6	10	21	37
August	8	10	25	43
September	10	6	23	39
October	9	9	27	45
November	4	8	26	38
December	3	15	19	37
Total	80	147	259	486

measuring an "attribute or property of a person, object, or event according to a particular set of rules" (Osborn 2005, 66). The result of the measurement will be numbers. And, the "particular set of rules" refers to what will be collected and how it will be collected so that the resulting numbers "will be meaningful, accurate, and informative" (Osborn 2005, 66). In other words, the process of collecting the data must be consistent in order to ensure the results are the same no matter who is collecting the data. If there is consistency in the data collection we will be able to make comparison in our own facilities and across facilities.

Data collected falls on one of four **scales of measurement:** nominal, ordinal, interval, or ratio. Furthermore, the data collected is described as either continuous or discrete. These characteristics influence the type of graphic technique that can be used to display the data and the types of statistical analyses that can be performed.

Nominal-level data fall into groups or categories. This is a scale that measures data by name only. The groups or categories are mutually exclusive, that is, a data element cannot be classified to more than one group. Some examples of nominal data collected in healthcare are related to patient demographics such as third-party payer, race, and sex. There is no order to the data collected within these categories.

Data that fall on the ordinal scale have some inherent order, and higher numbers are usually associated with higher values. In **ordinal-level data,** the order of the numbers is meaningful, not the number itself. Staging of a pressure ulcer is an example of a variable that has order. A pressure ulcer has four stages, with stage I being the least severe ulcer and stage IV being the most severe. In this example, the higher number is associated with the most severe type of pressure ulcer; however, we cannot measure the difference between the levels in exact numerical terms.

The most important characteristic of **interval-level data** is that the intervals between successive values are equal. On the Fahrenheit scale, for example, the interval between 20°F and 21°F is the same as between 21°F and 22°F. But because there is no true zero on this scale, we cannot say that 40°F is twice as warm as 20°F.

The **ratio-level data** is the highest level of measurement. On the ratio scale there is a defined unit of measure, a real zero point, and the intervals between successive values are equal. A real zero point means that there is an absolute zero. Only when a zero on a scale truly means the total absence of a property being assessed can that scale be described as ratio-level. For example, consider the variable "length of stay." **Length of stay** (LOS) has defined units of measurement, day, and a real zero point—0 days. Because there is a real zero point, we can state that an LOS of six days is twice as long as an LOS of three days. Multiplication on the ratio scale by a constant does not change its ratio character, but addition of a constant to a ratio measure does. For example, if we add two days to each LOS so that the stays are 8 and 5 days respectively, the ratio of their stays is no longer 2:1. However, if we multiply the respective lengths of stay by 2 (for example, 6 3 2 and 3 3 2), the ratio between the two lengths of stay remains 2:1.

The difference between the ratio and interval scales of measurement is that there is no true zero point on the interval scale.

This four-fold structure is a useful classification for data and the four levels are hierarchically arranged so that higher levels include the key properties of the levels so that ratio level data include the three key properties found in nominal, ordinal, and interval level data.

Discrete versus Continuous Data

Another way to classify data involves categorizing them as either being "discrete" or "continuous." Data that are nominal or ordinal are also considered discrete. **Discrete variables** are those that fall into categories. For example, the variable "gender" has two categories: male and female. The variable "third-party payer" has a number of categories, depending on the healthcare facility. Examples include Medicare, Medicaid, commercial insurance, and private insurance or self-pay.

Discrete variables can only take on a limited number of values and have gaps between successive values. In the pressure ulcer example, the ulcer can be a stage I, II, III, or IV (limited number of values). It cannot be staged as 2.5 or 3.2 as there are "gaps" between each stage. This is an example of a discrete variable that has order to its categories.

Continuous variables are either interval or ratio-level, but some ratio-level variables are discrete. For example, if you wanted to compare the number of patients on two different nursing units you could count 5 on one unit and 10 on another. This data are discrete. But you could also say that there are twice as many patients on one unit as there are on the other. And, there could be zero patients on one unit; this would be a true zero because it absolutely corresponds to the total absence of the variable you are assessing—the number of patients on each unit. With **continuous variables** there are no gaps in the measurement data. For example, an individual's weight may be 120 or 121 or any weight between 120 and 121. Continuous variables include fractions. Arithmetic operations—addition, subtraction, multiplication, and division—may be performed on continuous variables.

Check Your Understanding 15.1

Instructions: On a separate piece of paper, identify the scale of measurement for each of the following variables and indicate whether each variable is discrete or continuous.

1. ___ Zip code
2. ___ Blood pressure
3. ___ Heart Failure Classification I, II, III, IV
4. ___ Age
5. ___ Ethnicity
6. ___ Marital status
7. ___ Length of stay
8. ___ Discharge disposition (home, SNF, and so on)
9. ___ Weight
10. ___ Level of education
11. In the example given earlier in Theory into Practice, the associate administrator suggests expanding the hours of the Cardiac Catheterization Lab. How many additional hours must the Cardiac Catheterization Lab be open each day to accommodate the additional patients?
12. What percentage of Cardiac Catheterization Transfers is there for each of the services: Family Practice, Internal Medicine, and Cardiology?

Common Statistical Measures Used in Healthcare

Healthcare data are collected to describe the health status of groups or populations. The data reported about healthcare facilities and communities describe the occurrence of illnesses, births, and deaths for specific periods of time. Data that are collected may be either facility based or population based. The sources of facility-based statistics are **acute care** facilities, long-term care facilities, and other types of healthcare organizations. The population-based statistics are gathered from cities, counties, states, or specific groups within the population, such as individuals affected by arthritis.

Reporting statistics for a healthcare facility is similar to reporting statistics for a community. Rates for healthcare facilities are reported as per 100 cases or percent; a community rate is reported as per 1,000, 10,000, or 100,000 people. For example, if a hospital experienced 2 deaths in a given month and 100 patients were discharged in the same month, the death rate would be 2 percent ([2/100]/100). If there were 200 deaths in a community of 80,000 for a given period of time, the death rate would be reported as 25 deaths per 10,000 population ([200/10,000]/80,000) for the same period of time.

Ratios, Proportions, and Rates: Three Common Examples of Ratio-Level Data Worth Knowing

Many healthcare statistics are reported in the form of a ratio, proportion, or rate. These measures are used to report morbidity (illness), mortality (death), and natality (birthrate) at the local, state, and national levels. Basically, these measures indicate the number of times something happened relative to the number of times it could have happened. All three measures are based on formula 15.1. In this formula, x and y are the quantities being compared and x is divided by y. Further, 10^n is 10 to the nth power. The size of 10^n may equal 10, 100, 1,000, 10,000, and so on, depending on the value of n:

$$10^0 = 1$$
$$10^1 = 10$$
$$10^2 = 10 \times 10 = 100$$
$$10^3 = 10 \times 10 \times 10 = 1{,}000$$

Ratios

In a **ratio**, the quantities being compared, such as patient discharge status (x = alive, y = dead), may be expressed so that x and y are completely independent of each other, or x may be included in y. For example, the outcome of patients discharged from Community Hospital could be compared in one of two ways:

Alive/dead, or x/y
Alive/(alive + dead), or $x/(x + y)$

In the first example, x is completely independent of y. The ratio represents the number of patients discharged alive compared to the number of patients who died. In the second example, x is part of the whole $(x + y)$. The ratio represents the number of patients discharged alive compared to all patients discharged. Both expressions are considered ratios.

Proportions

A **proportion** is a particular type of ratio in which x is a portion of the whole $(x + y)$. In a proportion, the numerator is always included in the denominator. Figures 15.2 and 15.3 describe the procedures for calculating ratios and proportions.

Formula 15.1. General formula for calculating rates, proportions, and ratios

Ratio, proportion, rate = $x/y \times 10^n$

Figure 15.2. Calculation of a ratio; discharge status of patients discharged in a month

1. Define x and y:

   x = number of patients discharged alive
   y = number of patients who died

2. Identify x and y:

   $x = 235$
   $y = 22$

3. *Set up the ratio x/y:*

   235/22

4. Reduce the fraction so that either x or y equals 1:

   10.68/1

There were 10.68 live discharges for every patient who died.

Figure 15.3. Calculation of a proportion; discharge status of patients discharged in a month

1. Define x and y:

   x = number of patients discharged alive
   y = number of patients who died

2. Identify x and y:

   $x = 235$
   $y = 22$

3. Set up the proportion $x/x + y$:

   235/(235 + 22) = 235/257

4. Reduce the fraction so that either x or y equals 1:

   0.91/1

The proportion of patients discharged alive was 0.91.

Rates

Rates are often used to measure events over a period of time. Sometimes they also are used in performance improvement studies. Like ratios and proportions, rates may be reported daily, weekly, monthly, or yearly. This allows for trend analysis and comparisons over time. The basic formula for calculating a rate is shown in formula 15.2.

Healthcare facilities calculate many types of morbidity and mortality rates. For example, the C-section rate is a measure of the proportion, or percentage, of C-sections performed during a given period of time. C-section rates are closely monitored because they present more risk to the mother and baby and because they are more expensive than vaginal deliveries. In calculating the C-section rate, the number of C-sections performed during the specified period of time is counted and this value is placed in the numerator. The number of cases, or the population at risk, is the number of women who delivered during the same time period. This number is placed in the denominator. By convention, inpatient hospital rates are reported as the rate per 100 cases ($10^n = 10^2 = 10 \times 10 = 100$) and are expressed as percentages.

Figure 15.4 shows the procedure for calculating a rate. In the example, 33 of the 263 deliveries at Community

Formula 15.2. Calculating risk for contracting a disease

$$\text{Risk rate} = \frac{\text{Number of cases occurring during a given time period}}{\text{Total number of cases or population at risk during the same time period}}$$

Figure 15.4. Calculation of a rate; C-section rate for May 20XX

During May, 263 women delivered; of these, 33 deliveries were by C-section. What is the C-section rate for May?

1. Define the numerator (number of times an event occurred) and the denominator (number of times an event could have occurred):

   Numerator = total number of C-sections performed during the time period

   Denominator = total number of deliveries, including C-sections, in the same time period

2. Identify the numerator and the denominator:

   Numerator = 33
   Denominator = 263

3. Set up the rate:

   33/263

4. Multiply the numerator by 100 and then divide by the denominator:

   ([33 × 100]/263) = 12.5%

The C-section rate for May is 12.5 percent.

Hospital during the month of May were C-sections. In the formula, the numerator is the number of C-sections performed in May (given period of time) and the denominator is the total number of deliveries including C-sections (the population at risk) performed within the same time frame. In calculating the rate, the numerator is always included in the denominator. Also, when calculating a facility-based rate, the numerator is first multiplied by 100, and then divided by the denominator.

Because hospital rates rarely result in a whole number, they usually must be rounded. The hospital should set a policy on whether rates are to be reported to one or two decimal places. The division should be carried out to at least one more decimal place than desired.

When rounding, if the last number is five or greater, the preceding number should be increased one digit. In contrast, if the last number is less than five, the preceding number remains the same. For example, when rounding 25.56 percent to one decimal place, the rate becomes 25.6 percent because the last number is greater than five. When rounding 1.563 percent to two places, the rate becomes 1.56 percent because the last digit is less than five. Rates of less than 1 percent are usually carried out to three decimal places and rounded to two. For rates less than 1 percent, a zero should precede the decimal to emphasize that the rate is less than 1 percent, for example, 0.56 percent.

Check Your Understanding 15.2

Instructions: on a separate piece of paper, identify the following statements as a rate, a ratio, or a proportion.

1. Medicare admissions outnumber commercial insurance admissions 3 to 2.
2. At the annual state HIM meeting, 85 of the registrants were female and 35 were male. Therefore 0.71 percent of the registrants were female.
3. Of the 250 patients admitted in the last six months, 36 percent had Type II diabetes mellitus.

Statistical Data Used in Healthcare Facilities

Acute Care Statistical Data

In the daily operations of any organization, whether in business, manufacturing, or healthcare, data are collected for decision-making. To be effective, the decision makers must have confidence in the data collected. Confidence requires that the data collected be accurate, reliable, and timely. The types of data collected in the acute care setting are discussed in the following section.

Administrative Statistical Data

Hospitals collect data on both inpatients and outpatients on a daily basis. They use these statistics to monitor the volume of patients treated daily, weekly, monthly, or within some other specified time frame. The statistics give healthcare decision makers the information they need to plan facilities and to monitor inpatient and outpatient revenue streams. For these reasons, the HIM professional must be well versed in data collection and reporting methods.

Standard definitions have been developed to ensure that all healthcare providers collect and report data in a consistent manner. The *Pocket Glossary of Health Information Management,* developed by the American Health Information Management Association (AHIMA), is a resource commonly used to describe the types of healthcare events for which data are collected. It includes definitions of terms related to healthcare corporations, health maintenance organizations (HMOs), and other health-related programs and facilities. Some basic terms that HIM professionals should be familiar with include:

- *Hospital inpatient:* A patient who is provided with room, board, and continuous general nursing service in an area of the hospital where patients generally stay at least overnight.
- *Hospital newborn inpatient:* A patient who is born in the hospital at the beginning of the current inpatient hospitalization. Newborns are usually counted separately because their care is so different from that of other inpatients. Infants born on the way to the hospital or at home are considered hospital inpatients, not hospital newborn inpatients.
- *Inpatient hospitalization:* A period in a person's life during which he or she is an inpatient in a single hospital without interruption, except by possible intervening leaves of absence.
- *Inpatient admission:* The formal acceptance by a hospital of a patient who is to be provided with room, board, and continuous nursing service in an area of the hospital where patients generally stay overnight.
- *Inpatient discharge:* The termination of a period of inpatient hospitalization through the formal release of the inpatient by the hospital. The term includes patients who are discharged alive (by physician's order), who are discharged against medical advice (AMA), or who died while hospitalized. Unless otherwise indicated, inpatient discharges include deaths.
- *Hospital outpatient:* A hospital patient who receives services in one or more of the outpatient facilities when he or she is not currently an inpatient or home care patient. An outpatient may be classified as either an emergency outpatient or a clinic outpatient. An emergency outpatient is admitted to the emergency department of a hospital for diagnosis and treatment of a condition that requires immediate medical, dental, or other emergency services. A clinic outpatient is admitted to a clinical service of the clinic or hospital for diagnosis and treatment on an ambulatory basis.

Inpatient Census Data

Even though much of the data collection process has been automated, an ongoing responsibility of the HIM professional is to verify the **census** data that are collected daily. The census reports patient activity for a 24-hour reporting period. Included in the census report is the number of inpatients admitted and discharged for the previous 24-hour period as well as the number of intra-hospital transfers. An intra-hospital transfer is a patient who is moved from one patient care unit (for example, the intensive care unit) to another (for example, the surgical unit). The usual 24-hour reporting period begins at 12:01 a.m. and ends at 12:00 midnight. In the census count, adults and children (A&C) are reported separately from newborns.

Before compiling census data, however, it is important to understand their related terminology. The census is the number of hospital inpatients present at any one time. For example, the census in a 300-bed hospital may be 250 patients at 2:00 p.m. on May 1, but 245 an hour later. Because the census may change throughout the day as admissions and discharges occur, hospitals designate an official census-taking time. In most facilities, the official count takes place at midnight. The census-reporting time can be any other time, but it must be consistent throughout the healthcare facility.

The result of the official count taken at midnight is called the **daily inpatient census**. This is the number of inpatients present at the official census-taking time each day. Also included in the daily inpatient census are any patients who were admitted and discharged that same day. For example, if a patient was admitted to the cardiac care unit (CCU) at 1:00 p.m. on May 1 and died at 4.00 p.m. on May 1, he would be counted as a patient who was both admitted and discharged the same day.

Because patients admitted and discharged the same day are not present at the census-taking time, the hospital must account for them separately. If it did not, credit for the services provided these patients would be lost. The daily inpatient census reflects the total number of patients treated during the 24-hour period. Figure 15.5 displays a sample daily inpatient census report.

A unit of measure that reflects the services received by one inpatient during a 24-hour period is called an **inpatient service day** (IPSD). The number of IPSDs for a 24-hour period is equal to the daily inpatient census, that is, one service day for each patient treated. In figure 15.5, the total number of inpatient service days for May 2 is 230.

IPSDs are compiled daily, weekly, monthly, and annually. They reflect the volume of services provided by the healthcare facility: the greater the volume of services, the greater the revenues to the facility. Daily reporting of the number of IPSDs is an indicator of the hospital's financial condition.

As mentioned, the daily inpatient census is equal to the number of IPSDs provided for that day as shown here:

Day	Census	Same Day Admissions and Discharges	Inpatient Service Days
Day 1	240	0	240
Day 2	253	1	253
Day 3	235	2	237
Total			790

Figure 15.5. Daily inpatient census report—adults and children

May 2	
Number of patients in hospital at midnight, May 1	230
+ Number of patients admitted May 2	+ 35
− Number of patients discharged, including deaths, May 2	− 40
Number of patients in hospital at midnight, May 2	225
+ Number of patients both admitted and discharged, including deaths	+ 5
Daily inpatient census at midnight, May 2	230
Total inpatient service days, May 2	230

Thus, the total number of IPSDs for a week, a month, and so on can be divided by the total number of days in the period of interest to obtain the **average daily census.** In the preceding example, 730 IPSDs is divided by three days to obtain an average daily census of 243.3. The average daily census is the average number of inpatients treated during a given period of time. The general formula for calculating the average daily census is shown in formula 15.3.

In calculating the average daily census, adults and children (A&C) and **newborns** (NB) are reported separately. This is because the intensity of services provided to adults and children is greater than it is for newborns. To calculate the A&C average daily census, the general formula is modified as shown in formula 15.4. Many facilities use a whole number when calculating the census.

The formula for the average daily census for newborns is shown in formula 15.5. For example, the total number of IPSDs provided to adults and children for the week of May 1 is 1,729, and the total for newborns is 119. Using the formulas, the average daily census for adults and children is 247 (1,729/7) and for newborns it is 17 (119/7). The average daily census for all hospital inpatients for the week of May 1 is 264 ([1,729 + 119]/7). Table 15.2 compares the various formulas for calculating the average daily census.

Formula 15.3. Calculating the average daily census

$$\text{Average daily census} = \frac{\text{Total number of inpatient service days for a given period}}{\text{Total number of days in the same period}}$$

Formula 15.4. Calculating the average daily census for adults and children

$$\text{Average daily census for A\&C} = \frac{\text{Total number of inpatient service days for A\&C for a given period}}{\text{Total number of days for the same period}}$$

Formula 15.5. Calculating the average daily census for newborns

$$\text{Average daily census for NBs} = \frac{\text{Total number of inpatient service days for NBs for a given period}}{\text{Total number of days for the same period}}$$

Table 15.2. Calculation of census statistics

Indicator	Numerator	Denominator
Average daily inpatient census	Total number of inpatient service days for a given period	Total number of days for the same period
Average daily inpatient census for adults and children (A&C)	Total number of inpatient service days for A&C for a given period	Total number of days for the same period
Average daily inpatient census for newborns (NBs)	Total number of inpatient services days for NBs for a given period	Total number of days for the same period

Check Your Understanding 15.3

Instructions: Answer the following questions on a separate piece of paper.

1. Community Hospital reported the following statistics for adults and children at midnight April 1: Census 120; Admissions 22; Discharges 18; 1 patient admitted and died the same day. Calculate the following for April 2:
   a. Inpatient census
   b. Daily inpatient census
   c. Inpatient service days
2. Community Hospital reported the following statistics for their newborn unit at midnight April 1: Census 12: Births 6; Discharges 2; 1 Newborn born and transferred to the state University Hospital. Calculate the following for April 2:
   a. Inpatient census
   b. Daily inpatient census
3. Community Hospital reported the following statistics for their intensive care unit at midnight April 1: Census 10; Admitted directly from the ESD 2; 1 patient admitted and expired; 1 patient transferred from Surgery unit. Calculate the following for April 2:
   a. Inpatient census
   b. Daily inpatient census

Inpatient Bed Occupancy Rate

Another indicator of the hospital's financial position is the **inpatient bed occupancy rate,** also called the percentage of occupancy. The inpatient bed occupancy rate is the percentage of official beds occupied by hospital inpatients for a given period of time. In general, the greater the occupancy rate, the greater the revenues for the hospital. For a bed to be included in the official count, it must be set up, staffed, equipped, and available for patient care. The total number of inpatient service days is used in the numerator because it is equal to the daily inpatient census or the number of patients treated daily. The occupancy rate compares the number of patients treated over a given period of time to the total number of beds available for the same period of time.

For example, if 200 patients occupied 280 beds on May 2, the inpatient bed occupancy rate would be 71.4 percent ([200/{280 × 1}] × 100). If the rate were for more than one day, the number of beds would be multiplied by the number of days within that particular time frame. For example, if 1,729 IPSDs were provided during the week of May 1, the inpatient bed occupancy rate for that week would be 88.2 percent ([1,729/{280 × 7}] × 100).

The denominator in this formula is actually the total possible number of IPSDs. That is, if every available bed in the hospital were occupied every single day, this would be the maximum number of IPSDs that could be provided. This is an important concept, especially when the official **bed count** changes for a given reporting period. For example, if the bed count changed from 280 beds to 300, the bed occupancy rate would reflect the change. The total number of inpatient beds times the total number of days in the period is called the total number of **bed count days.** The general formula for the inpatient bed occupancy rate is shown in formula 15.6.

For example, in May the total number of inpatient service days provided was 7,582. The bed count for the month of May changed from 280 beds to 300 on May 20. To calculate the inpatient bed occupancy rate for May, the total number of bed count days must be determined. There are 31 days in May; therefore, the total number of bed count days is calculated as:

Number of beds, May 1–May 19 = 280 × 19 days = 5,320 bed count days
Number of beds, May 20–May 31 = 300 × 12 days = 3,600 bed count days
5,320 + 3,600 = 8,920 bed count days

The inpatient bed occupancy rate for the month of May is 85.0 percent ([7,582/8,920] × 100).

As with the average daily census, the inpatient bed occupancy rate for adults and children is reported separately from that of newborns. To calculate the total number of bed count days for newborns, the official count for newborn bassinets is used. Table 15.3 reviews the formulas for calculating inpatient bed occupancy rates.

It is possible for the inpatient bed occupancy rate to be greater than 100 percent. This occurs when the hospital faces an epidemic or disaster. In this type of situation, hospitals set up temporary beds that usually are not included in the official bed count. As an example, Community Hospital experienced

Formula 15.6. Calculating the inpatient bed occupancy rate

$$\text{Inpatient bed occupancy} = \frac{\text{Total number of inpatient service days for a given period}}{\text{Total number of inpatient bed count days for the same period}} \times 100$$

Table 15.3. Calculation of inpatient bed occupancy rates

Rate	Numerator	Denominator
Inpatient bed occupancy rate	Total number of inpatient service days for a given period × 100	Total number of inpatient bed count days for the same period
Inpatient bed occupancy rate for adults and children (A&C)	Total number of inpatient service days for A&C for a given period × 100	Total number of inpatient bed count days for A&C for the same period
Newborn (NB) bed occupancy rate	Total number of NB inpatient service days for a given period × 100	Total number of bassinet bed count days for the same period

an excessive number of admissions in January because of an outbreak of influenza. In January, the official bed count was 150 beds. On January 5, the daily inpatient census was 156. Therefore, the inpatient bed occupancy rate for January 5 was 104 percent ([156/150] × 100).

Bed Turnover Rate

The **bed turnover rate** is a measure of hospital utilization. It includes the number of times each hospital bed changed occupants. The formula for the bed turnover rate is shown in formula 15.7. For example, Community Hospital had 2,060 discharges and deaths for the month of April. Its bed count for April averaged 677. The bed turnover rate is 3.0 (2,060/677). This simply means that on average, each hospital bed had three occupants during April.

Check Your Understanding 15.4

Instructions: Answer the following questions on a separate piece of paper.

1. What is the inpatient bed occupancy rate for each of the following patient care units at Community Hospital for the month of June? (Calculate to one decimal point.)

Inpatient Unit	Service Days	Bed Count	Occupancy Rate
Medicine	580	36	________
Surgery	689	42	________
Pediatric	232	18	________
Psychiatry	889	35	________
Obstetrics	222	10	________
Newborn	212	15	________

2. Use the preceding information to determine the Occupancy Rate for Community Hospital—all Adults and Children (exclude newborns). Calculate to one decimal point.
3. On June 1, Community Hospital expanded the number of patient beds from 156 to 200. Use the following information to determine the Occupancy Rate for January to June; July to December; and the total for the year (non-leap year).

Months	Service Days	Bed Count
January–June	15672	156
July–December	25876	200

Length of Stay Data

Length of stay (LOS) data is calculated for each patient after he or she is discharged from the hospital. It is the number of calendar days from the day of patient admission to the day of patient discharge. When the patient is admitted and discharged in the same month, the LOS is determined by subtracting the date of admission from the date of discharge. For example, the LOS for a patient admitted on May 12 and discharged on May 17 is five days (17 – 12 = 5)

When the patient is admitted in one month and discharged in another, the calculations must be adjusted. One way to calculate the LOS in this case is to subtract the date of admission from the total number of days in the month the patient was admitted and then to add the total number of hospitalized days for the month in which the patient was discharged. For example, the LOS for a patient admitted on May 28 and discharged on June 6 is nine days ([May 31–May 28 = 3 days] + [June 1–June 6 = 6 days]; LOS = 9 days).

When a patient is admitted and discharged on the same day, the LOS is one day. A partial day's stay is never reported as a fraction of a day. The LOS for a patient discharged the day after admission also is one day. Thus, the LOS for a patient who was admitted to the ICU on May 10 at 9:00 a.m. and died at 3:00 p.m. on the same day is one day. Likewise, the LOS for a patient admitted on May 12 and discharged on May 13 is one day.

When the LOS for all patients discharged for a given period of time is summed, the result is the **total length of stay.** As an example, five patients were discharged from the pediatric unit on May 9. The LOS for each patient was as follows:

Patient	LOS
1	5
2	3
3	1
4	8
5	10
Total LOS	**27**

In the preceding example, the total LOS is 27 days (5 + 3 + 1 + 8 + 10). The total LOS is also referred to as the number of days of care provided to patients who were discharged or died (discharge days) during a given period of time.

The **average length of stay** (ALOS) is calculated from the total LOS. The total LOS divided by the number of patients discharged is the ALOS. Using the data in the preceding example, the ALOS for the five patients discharged from the pediatric unit is 5.4 days (27/5)

The general formula for calculating ALOS is shown in formula 15.8. As with the measures already discussed, the

Formula 15.7. Calculating the bed turnover rate

$$\text{Bed turnover rate} = \frac{\text{Total number of discharges, including deaths, for a given time period}}{\text{Average bed count for the same time period}}$$

Formula 15.8. Calculating the average length of stay

$$\text{Average length of stay} = \frac{\text{Total length of stay for a given period}}{\text{Total number of discharges, including deaths, for the same period}}$$

ALOS for adults and children is reported separately from the ALOS for newborns. Table 15.4 reviews the formulas for ALOS. Table 15.5 displays an example of a hospital statistical summary prepared by the HIM department using census and discharge data.

Check Your Understanding 15.5

Instructions: Complete the following exercise on a separate piece of paper.

Day	Number of Patients Discharged	Discharge Days
August 1	12	72
August 2	10	70
August 3	12	72
August 4	17	136
August 5	8	32
August 6	9	81
August 7	11	68
August 8	10	80
August 9	14	63
August 10	12	84

1. Calculate the total length of stay for the patient discharges and the average length of stay. Calculate to one decimal point.
   a. Total length of stay _______
   b. Number of patients discharged _______
   c. Average length of stay _______

Patient Care and Clinical Statistical Data

Thus far, this chapter has discussed statistical measures that are indicators of volume of services and utilization of services. The collection of data related to morbidity and mortality is also an important aspect of evaluating the quality of hospital services. Morbidity and mortality rates are reported for all patient discharges within a certain time frame. They also may be reported by service or by physician or other variable of interest in order to identify trends or problems that require corrective action. The most frequently collected morbidity and mortality rates are presented in this section.

Hospital Death (Mortality) Rates

The **hospital death rate** is based on the number of patients discharged, alive and dead, from the hospital. Deaths are considered discharges because they are the end point of a

Table 15.4. Calculation of LOS statistics

Indicator	Numerator	Denominator
Average LOS	Total LOS (discharge days) for a given period	Total number of discharges, including deaths, for the same period
Average LOS for adults and children (A&C)	Total LOS for A&C (discharge days) for a given period	Total number of discharges, including deaths, for A&C for the same period
Average LOS for newborns (NB)	Total LOS for all NB discharges and deaths (discharge days) for a given period	Total number of NB discharges, including deaths, for the same period

Table 15.5. Statistical summary, Community Hospital for the period ending July 20XX

Admissions	July 20XX		Year-to-Date 20XX	
	Actual	Budget	Actual	Budget
Medical	728	769	5,075	5,082
Surgical	578	583	3,964	3,964
OB/GYN	402	440	2,839	3,027
Psychiatry	113	99	818	711
Physical Medicine & Rehab	48	57	380	384
Other Adult	191	178	1,209	1,212
Total Adult	2,060	2,126	14,285	14,380
Newborn	294	312	2,143	2,195
Total Admissions	2,354	2,438	16,428	16,575
Average Length of Stay	**July 20XX**		**Year-to-Date 20XX**	
	Actual	Budget	Actual	Budget
Medical	6.1	6.4	6.0	6.1
Surgical	7.0	7.2	7.7	7.7
OB/GYN	2.9	3.2	3.5	3.1
Psychiatry	10.8	11.6	10.4	11.6
Physical Medicine & Rehab	27.5	23.0	28.1	24.3
Other Adult	3.6	3.9	4.0	4.1
Total Adult	6.3	6.4	6.7	6.5
Newborn	5.6	5.0	5.6	5.0
Total ALOS	6.2	6.3	6.5	6.3
Patient Days	**June 20XX**		**Year-to-Date 20XX**	
	Actual	Budget	Actual	Budget
Medical	4,436	4,915	30,654	30,762
Surgical	4,036	4,215	30,381	30,331
OB/GYN	1,170	1,417	10,051	9,442
Psychiatry	1,223	1,144	8,524	8,242
Physical Medicine & Rehab	1,318	1,310	10,672	9,338
Other Adult	688	699	4,858	4,921
Total Adult	12,871	13,700	95,140	93,036
Newborn	1,633	1,552	12,015	10,963
Total Patient Days	14,504	15,252	107,155	103,999
Other Key Statistics	**June 20XX**		**Year-to-Date 20XX**	
	Actual	Budget	Actual	Budget
Average Daily Census	485	492	498	486
Average Beds Available	677	660	677	660
Clinic Visits	21,621	18,975	144,271	136,513
Emergency Visits	3,822	3,688	26,262	25,604
Inpatient Surgery Patients	657	583	4,546	4,093
Outpatient Surgery Patients	603	554	4,457	3,987

period of hospitalization. In contrast to the rates discussed in the preceding section, newborns are not counted separately from adults and children.

Gross Death Rate

The **gross death rate** is the proportion of all hospital discharges that ended in death. It is the basic indicator of mortality in a healthcare facility. The gross death rate is calculated by dividing the total number of deaths occurring in a given time period by the total number of discharges, including deaths, for the same time period. The formula for calculating the gross death rate is shown in formula 15.9.

As an example, Community Hospital experienced 21 deaths (A&C and NBs) during the month of May. There were 633 total discharges, including deaths. The gross death rate is 3.3 percent ([21/633] × 100).

Net Death Rate

The **net death rate** is an adjusted death rate. It is calculated with the assumption that certain deaths should not "count against the hospital." The net death rate is an adjusted rate because it does not include patients who die within 48 hours of admission. The reason for excluding these deaths is that 48 hours is not enough time to positively affect patient outcome. In other words, the patient was not admitted to the hospital in a manner timely enough for treatment to have an effect on his or her outcome. The formula for calculating the net death rate is shown in formula 15.10.

Continuing with the preceding example of the 21 patients who died at Community Hospital, three died within 48 hours of admission. Therefore, the net death rate is 2.9 percent ([{21 – 3}/{633 – 3}] × 100 = 2.9%). The fact that the net death rate is less than the gross death rate is favorable to Community Hospital because lower death rates may be an indicator of better care.

Newborn Death Rate

Even though newborn deaths are included in the hospital's gross and net death rates, the **newborn death rate** can be calculated separately. Newborns include only infants born alive in the hospital. The newborn death rate is the number of newborns who died in comparison to the total number of newborns discharged, alive and dead. To qualify as a newborn death, the newborn must have been delivered alive. A stillborn infant is not included in either the newborn death rate or the gross or net death rate. The formula for calculating the newborn death rate is shown in formula 15.11.

Fetal Death Rate

In healthcare terminology, the death of a stillborn baby is called a **fetal death.** A fetal death is a death prior to the fetus's complete expulsion or extraction from the mother in a hospital facility, regardless of the length of the pregnancy. Thus, stillborns are neither admitted nor discharged from the hospital. A fetal death occurs when the fetus fails to breathe or show any other evidence of life, such as a heartbeat, a pulsation of the umbilical cord, or a movement of the voluntary muscles.

Fetal deaths also are classified into categories based on length of gestation or weight. (See table 15.6.) To calculate the **fetal death rate,** divide the total number of intermediate and late fetal deaths for the period by the total number of live births and intermediate and late fetal deaths for the same period. The formula for calculating the fetal death rate is shown in formula 15.12. For example, during the month of May, Community Hospital experienced 269 live births and 13 intermediate and late fetal deaths. The fetal death rate is 4.6 percent ([13/{269 + 13}] × 100).

Maternal Death Rate

Hospitals are also interested in calculating their **maternal death rate.** A maternal death is the death of any woman from any cause related to, or aggravated by, pregnancy or its management, regardless of the duration or site of the pregnancy. Maternal deaths that result from accidental or incidental causes are not included in the maternal death rate.

Maternal deaths are classified as either direct or indirect. A direct maternal death is the death of a woman resulting

Formula 15.9. Calculating the gross death rate

$$\text{Gross death rate} = \frac{\text{Total number of inpatient deaths (including NBs) for a given period}}{\text{Total number of discharges, including A\&C and NB deaths, for the same period}} \times 100$$

Formula 15.10. Calculating the net death rate

$$\text{Net death rate} = \frac{\text{Total number of inpatient deaths (including NBs) minus deaths} < 48 \text{ hours for a given period}}{\text{Total number of discharges (including A\&C and NB deaths) minus deaths} < 48 \text{ hours for the same period}} \times 100$$

Formula 15.11. Calculating the newborn death rate

$$\text{Newborn death rate} = \frac{\text{Total number of NB deaths for a given period}}{\text{Total number of NB discharges (including deaths) for the same period}} \times 100$$

Table 15.6. Classifications of fetal death

Classification	Length of Gestation	Weight
Early fetal death	Less than 20 weeks' gestation	500 g or less
Intermediate fetal death	20 weeks' completed gestation, but less than 28 weeks	501 to 1,000 g
Late fetal death	28 weeks' completed gestation	Over 1,000 g

from obstetrical (OB) complications of the pregnancy state, labor, or puerperium (the period including the six weeks after delivery). Direct maternal deaths are included in the maternal death rate. An indirect maternal death is the death of a woman from a previously existing disease or a disease that developed during pregnancy, labor, or the puerperium that was not due to obstetric causes, although the physiologic effects of pregnancy were partially responsible.

The maternal death rate may be an indicator of the availability of prenatal care in a community. The hospital also may use it to help identify conditions that could lead to a maternal death. The formula for calculating the maternal death rate is shown in formula 15.13. For example, during the month of May, Community Hospital experienced 275 maternal discharges. Two of these patients died. The maternal death rate for May is 0.73 percent ([2/275] × 100). Table 15.7 summarizes hospital-based mortality rates.

Check Your Understanding 15.6

Instructions: Using the data provided on deaths and discharges at Community Hospital for the past calendar year, answer the following questions on a separate sheet of paper. Calculate to two decimal points.

Total discharges, including deaths (A&C)	1,250
Total deaths (A&C)	22
Deaths less than 48 hours after admission (A&C)	5
Fetal deaths (intermediate and late)	4
Live births	150
Newborn deaths	2
Newborn discharges, including deaths	152
Maternal deaths (direct)	1
OB discharges, including deaths	155

1. ___ What is the gross death rate for adults and children?
2. ___ What is the net death rate for adults and children?
3. ___ What is the fetal death rate?
4. ___ What is the newborn death rate?
5. ___ What is the gross death rate for adults and children and newborns combined?
6. ___ What is the maternal death rate (direct)?

Autopsy Rates

An autopsy is an examination of a dead body to determine the cause of death. Another name that may be used is a post-mortem examination. Autopsies are very useful in the education of medical students and residents. In addition, they

Formula 15.12. Calculating the fetal death rate

$$\text{Fetal death rate} = \frac{\text{Total number of intermediate and late fetal deaths for a given period}}{\text{Total number of live births plus total number of intermediate and late fetal deaths for the same period}} \times 100$$

Formula 15.13. Calculating the maternal death rate

$$\text{Maternal death rate} = \frac{\text{Total number of direct maternal deaths for a given period}}{\text{Total number of maternal (OB) discharges, including deaths, for the same period}} \times 100$$

Table 15.7. Calculation of hospital-based mortality rates

Rate	Numerator (*x*)	Denominator (*y*)
Gross death rate	Total number of inpatient deaths, including NBs, for a given period × 100	Total number of discharges, including A&C and NB deaths, for the same period
Net death rate (institutional death rate)	Total number of inpatient deaths, including NBs, minus deaths < 48 hours for a given period × 100	Total number of discharges, including A&C and NB deaths, minus deaths < 48 hours for the same period
Newborn death rate	Total number of NB deaths for a given period × 100	Total number of NB discharges, including deaths, for the same period
Fetal death rate	Total number of intermediate and late fetal deaths for a given period × 100	Total number of live births plus total number of intermediate and fetal deaths for the same period
Maternal death rate	Total number of direct maternal deaths for a given period × 100	Total number of maternal (obstetric) discharges, including deaths, for the same period
Infant death rate	Number of deaths under one year of age during a given time period	Number of live births during the same time period

can alert family members to conditions or diseases for which they may be at risk.

Two categories of hospital autopsies are conducted in acute care facilities: hospital inpatient autopsies and hospital autopsies. A **hospital inpatient autopsy** is an examination of the body of a patient who died while being treated in the hospital. The patient's death marked the end of his or her stay in the hospital. A pathologist or some other physician on the medical staff performs this type of autopsy in the facility.

A **hospital autopsy** is an examination of the body of an individual who at some time in the past had been a hospital patient and was not a hospital inpatient at the time of death. A pathologist or some other physician on the medical staff performs this type of autopsy as well. The following sections describe the different types of autopsy rates calculated by acute care hospitals.

Gross Autopsy Rates

A **gross autopsy rate** is the proportion or percentage of deaths that are followed by the performance of autopsy. The formula for calculating the gross autopsy rate is shown in formula 15.14. For example, during the month of May, Community Hospital experienced 21 deaths. Autopsies were performed on four of these patients. The gross autopsy rate is 19.0 percent ([4/21] × 100).

Net Autopsy Rates

The bodies of patients who have died are not always available for autopsy. For example, a coroner or medical examiner may claim a body for an autopsy for legal reasons. In these situations, the hospital calculates a **net autopsy rate.** In calculating the net autopsy rate, bodies that have been removed by the coroner or medical examiner are excluded from the denominator. The formula for calculating the net autopsy rate is shown in formula 15.15. Continuing with the example in the preceding section, the medical examiner claimed three of the patients for autopsy. The numerator remains the same because four autopsies were performed by the hospital pathologist. However, because three of the deaths were identified as medical examiner's cases and removed from the hospital, 3 is subtracted from 21. The net autopsy rate is 22.2 percent ([4/{21 – 3}] × 100).

Hospital Autopsy Rates

A third type of autopsy rate is called the **hospital autopsy rate.** This is an adjusted rate that includes autopsies on anyone who may have at one time been a hospital patient. The formula for calculating the hospital autopsy rate is shown in formula 15.16. The hospital autopsy rate includes autopsies performed on any of the following:

- Bodies of inpatients, except those removed by the coroner or medical examiner. When the hospital pathologist or other designated physician acts as an agent in the performance of an autopsy on an inpatient, the death and the autopsy are included in the percentage.
- Bodies of other hospital patients, including ambulatory care patients, hospital home care patients, and former hospital patients who died elsewhere, but whose bodies have been made available for autopsy to be performed by the hospital pathologist or other designated physician. These autopsies and deaths are included in computations of the percentage.

Generally, it is impossible to determine the number of bodies of former hospital patients who may have died in a given time period. In the formula, the phrase available for hospital autopsy involves several conditions, including:

- The autopsy must be performed by the hospital pathologist or a designated physician on the body of a patient treated at some time at the hospital.
- The report of the autopsy must be filed in the patient's health record and in the hospital laboratory or pathology department.
- The tissue specimens must be maintained in the hospital laboratory.

Formula 15.14. Calculating the gross autopsy rate

$$\text{Gross autopsy rate} = \frac{\text{Total inpatient autopsies for a given period}}{\text{Total number of inpatient deaths for the same period}} \times 100$$

Formula 15.15. Calculating the net autopsy rate

$$\text{Net autopsy rate} = \frac{\text{Total number of autopsies on inpatient deaths for a period}}{\text{Total number of inpatient deaths minus unautopsied coroners' or medical examiners' cases for the same period}} \times 100$$

Formula 15.16. Calculating the hospital autopsy rate

$$\text{Hospital autopsy rate} = \frac{\text{Total number of hospital autopsies for a given period}}{\text{Total number of deaths of hospital patients whose bodies were available for autopsy for the same period}} \times 100$$

Figure 15.6 explains how to calculate the hospital autopsy rate.

Newborn Autopsy Rates

Autopsy rates usually include autopsies performed on newborn infants unless a separate rate is requested. The formula for calculating the **newborn autopsy rate** is shown in formula 15.17.

Fetal Autopsy Rates

Hospitals sometimes also calculate the **fetal autopsy rate.** Fetal autopsies are important for the clinician to determine the cause of the fetal loss and to the parents to determine if they need genetic counseling. Fetal autopsies are performed on stillborn infants who have been classified as either intermediate or late fetal deaths. This is the proportion or percentage of autopsies done on intermediate or late fetal deaths out of the total number of intermediate or late fetal deaths. The formula for calculating the fetal autopsy rate is shown in formula 15.18. Table 15.8 summarizes the different hospital autopsy rates.

Check Your Understanding 15.7

Instructions: Read the following scenario and answer the questions on a separate sheet of paper.

In April, Community Hospital experienced 25 inpatient deaths. Two of these were coroner's cases. One additional death was a former hospital patient who died in hospice and was autopsied by the hospital pathologist. Twelve autopsies were performed on the remaining deaths. Calculate to one decimal point.

1. ___ What is the gross autopsy rate for this month?
2. ___ What is the net autopsy rate for this month?
3. ___ What is the hospital autopsy rate?

Hospital Infection Rates

The most common morbidity rates calculated for hospitals are related to hospital-acquired infections, called **nosocomial infections.** The hospital must continuously monitor the number of infections that occur in its various patient care units because infection can adversely affect the course of a patient's treatment and possibly result in death. The Joint Commission requires hospitals to follow written guidelines for reporting all types of infections. Examples of the different types of infections are respiratory, gastrointestinal, surgical wound, skin, urinary tract, septicemias, and infections related to intravascular catheters.

Hospital-acquired Infection Rates

Hospital-acquired (nosocomial) infection rates may be calculated for the entire hospital or for a specific unit in the hospital. They also may be calculated for the specific types of infections. Ideally, the hospital should strive for an infection rate of 0.0 percent. The formula for calculating the hospital-acquired or nosocomial infection rate is shown in formula 15.19. For example, Community Hospital discharged 725 patients during the month of June. Thirty-two of these patients experienced hospital-acquired infections. The hospital-acquired infection rate is 4.4 percent ([32/725] × 100).

Postoperative Infection Rates

Hospitals often track their **postoperative infection rate.** The postoperative infection rate is the proportion or percentage of infections in clean surgical cases out of the total number of surgical operations performed. A clean surgical case is one in which no infection existed prior to surgery. The postoperative infection rate may be an indicator of a

Figure 15.6. Calculation of the hospital autopsy rate

In June, 33 inpatient deaths occurred. Three of these were medical examiner's cases. Two of the bodies were removed from the hospital and so were not available for hospital autopsy. One of the medical examiner's cases was autopsied by the hospital pathologist. Fourteen other autopsies were performed on hospital inpatients who died during the month of June. In addition, autopsies were performed in the hospital on:

- A child with congenital heart disease who died in the emergency department
- A former hospital inpatient who died in an extended care facility and whose body was brought to the hospital for autopsy
- A former hospital inpatient who died at home and whose body was brought to the hospital for autopsy
- A hospital outpatient who died while receiving chemotherapy for cancer
- A hospital home care patient whose body was brought to the hospital for autopsy
- A former hospital inpatient who died in an emergency vehicle on the way to the hospital

Calculation of total hospital autopsies:

1 autopsy on medical examiner's case
+14 autopsies on hospital inpatients
+ 6 autopsies on hospital patients whose bodies were available for autopsy

21 autopsies performed by the hospital pathologist

Calculation of number of deaths of hospital patients whose bodies were available for autopsy:

33 inpatient deaths
− 2 medical examiner's cases
+ 6 deaths of hospital patients

37 total bodies available for autopsy

Calculation of the hospital autopsy rate:

$$\frac{\text{Total number of hospital autopsies for the period}}{\text{Total number of deaths of hospital patients with bodies available for hospital autopsy for the period}} \times 100$$

$$(21 \times 100)/37 = 56.8\%$$

problem in the hospital environment or of some type of surgical contamination.

The individual calculating the postoperative infection rate must know the difference between a surgical procedure and a surgical operation. A surgical procedure is any separate, systematic process on or within the body that can be complete in itself. A physician, dentist, or some other licensed practitioner performs a surgical procedure, with or without instruments, to

- Restore disunited or deficient parts
- Remove diseased or injured tissues
- Extract foreign matter
- Assist in obstetrical delivery
- Aid in diagnosis

A surgical operation involves one or more surgical procedures that are performed on one patient at one time using one approach to achieve a common purpose. An example of a surgical operation is the resection of a portion of both the intestine and the liver in a cancer patient. This involves two procedures, removal of a portion of the liver and removal of a portion of the colon; but it is considered only one operation because there is only one operative approach or incision. In contrast, an esophagoduodenoscopy (EGD) and a colonoscopy performed at the same time are two procedures with two different approaches. In the former, the approach is the upper gastrointestinal tract; in the latter, the approach is the lower gastrointestinal tract. In this case, the two procedures do not have a common approach or purpose. The formula for calculating the postoperative infection rate is shown in formula 15.20.

Formula 15.17. Calculating the newborn autopsy rate

$$\text{Newborn autopsy rate} = \frac{\text{Total number of autopsies on NB deaths for a given time period}}{\text{Total number of NB deaths for the same period}} \times 100$$

Formula 15.18. Calculating the fetal autopsy rate

$$\text{Fetal autopsy rate} = \frac{\text{Total number of autopsies on intermediate and late fetal deaths for a given period}}{\text{Total number of intermediate and late fetal deaths for the same period}} \times 100$$

Table 15.8. Calculation of hospital autopsy rates

Rate	Numerator	Denominator
Gross autopsy rate	Total number of autopsies on inpatient deaths for a given period × 100	Total number of inpatient deaths for the same period
Net autopsy rate	Total number of autopsies on inpatient deaths for a given period × 100	Total number of inpatient deaths minus unautopsied coroner or medical examiner cases for the same period
Hospital autopsy rate	Total number of hospital autopsies for a given period × 100	Total number of deaths of hospital patients whose bodies are available for hospital autopsy for the same period
Newborn (NB) autopsy rate	Total number of autopsies on NB deaths for a given period × 100	Total number of NB deaths for the same period
Fetal autopsy rate	Total number of autopsies on intermediate and late fetal deaths for a given period × 100	Total number of intermediate and late fetal deaths for the same period

Formula 15.19. Calculating the nosocomial infection rate

$$\text{Hospital-acquired infection rate} = \frac{\text{Total number of hospital-acquired infections for a given period}}{\text{Total number of discharges, including deaths, for the same period}} \times 100$$

Formula 15.20. Calculating the postoperative infection rate

$$\text{Postoperative infection rate} = \frac{\text{Number of infections in clean surgical cases for a given period}}{\text{Total number of surgical operations for the same period}} \times 100$$

Consultation Rates

A consultation occurs when two or more physicians collaborate on a particular patient's diagnosis or treatment. The attending physician requests the consultation and explains his or her reason for doing so. The consultant then examines the patient and the patient's health record and makes recommendations in a written report. The formula for calculating the **consultation rate** is shown in formula 15.21.

Case-Mix Statistical Data

Case mix is a method of grouping patients according to a predefined set of characteristics. Medicare severity diagnosis-related groups (MS-DRGs) are often used to determine case mix in hospitals.

When calculating case mix using MS-DRGs, the **case-mix index** (CMI) is the average MS-DRG weight for patients discharged from the hospital. The CMI is a measure of the resources used in treating the patients in each hospital or group of hospitals. It may be calculated for all patients discharged, discharges by payer (table 15.9), or the discharges of particular physicians (table 15.10).

Table 15.11 provides an example of a case-mix calculation for 10 MS-DRGs at Community Hospital. The CMI is calculated by multiplying the number of cases for each MS-DRG by the relative weight of the MS-DRG, summing the result (751.7206) and dividing by the total number of cases (484). By convention, the CMI is calculated to five decimal points and rounded to four.

The CMI can be used to indicate the average reimbursement for the hospital. From table 15.9, the reimbursement is approximately 1.5670 times the hospital's base rate. It also is a measure of the severity of illness of Medicare patients. In table 15.9, you can see that Medicare patients, as expected, have the highest CMI at 2.0059.

Other data analyzed by MS-DRG include LOS and mortality rates. LOS and mortality data are benchmarked against the hospital's peer group and national data. The process of benchmarking involves comparing the hospital's performance against an external standard or benchmark. An excellent source of information for benchmarking purposes is the Healthcare Cost Utilization Project database (HCUPnet), which is available online. A comparison of hospital and national data for MS-DRG 293 appears in table 15.12.

Gross analysis of the data indicates that Community Hospital's mortality rate and average charges are better than the national average. But, at the same time, the ALOS is somewhat higher than the national average.

Check Your Understanding 15.8

Instructions: Using the following table, answer the following questions on a separate piece of paper. Calculate to one decimal point.

MS-DRG	MS-DRG Title	Rel. Wt.	No. of Pts.	Total Wt.
179	Respiratory infections and inflammations w/o CC/MCC	1.2754	5	
187	Pleural effusion w/ CC	1.1947	2	
189	Pulmonary edema and respiratory failure	1.3660	3	
194	Simple pneumonia and pleurisy w/ CC	1.0235	1	
208	Respiratory system diagnosis w/ ventilator support <96 hours	2.2463	1	
280	Acute myocardial infarction, discharged alive w/ MCC	1.7391	3	
299	Peripheral vascular disorders w/ MCC	1.2220	2	
313	Chest pain	0.5489	4	
377	G.I. hemorrhage w/ MCC	1.3367	1	
391	Esophagitis, gastroent and misc. digest disorders w/ MCC	0.9565	1	
547	Connective tissue disorders w/o CC/MCC	0.9054	1	
552	Medical back problems w/o MCC	0.7839	1	
684	Renal failure w/o CC/MCC	0.9835	1	
812	Red blood cell disorders w/o MCC	0.7780	2	
872	Septicemia w/o MV 96+ hours w/o MCC	1.3783	1	
918	Poisoning and toxic effects of drugs w/o MCC	0.6886	1	
Total			**30**	

1. ___ Last month, Community Hospital had 57 discharges from its Medicine unit. Four patients developed a urinary tract infection while in the hospital. Calculate the nosocomial infection rate for the last month.
2. ___ During June, Community Hospital had 149 discharged. Forty-seven patients had consultations from specialty physicians. What was the consultation rate for June?
3. ___ Dr. Green discharged 30 patients from Medicine Service during the month of August. The table below presents the number of patients discharged by MS-DRG. Calculate the total weight for each MS-DRG and the CMI for Dr. Green.

Formula 15.21. Calculating the consultation rate

$$\text{Consultation rate} = \frac{\text{Total number of patients receiving consultations for a given period}}{\text{Total number of discharges and deaths for the same period}}$$

Table 15.9. Case-mix index by payer, Community Hospital, 20XX

Payer	CMI	*N*
Commercial	1.8830	283
Government managed care	.9880	470
Managed care	1.4703	2326
Medicaid	1.3400	962
Medicare	2.0059	1776
Other	1.3251	148
Self-pay	1.3462	528
Total	1.5670	6503

Table 15.10. Case-mix of one physician, 20XX

Physician	CMI	*N*
A	1.0235	71
B	[illegible]	71
C	[illegible]	86
Total	1.2501	228

Table 15.11. Calculation of case-mix index for 10 MS-DRGs, Community Hospital, 20XX

MS-DRG	Number (*N*)	MS-DRG Weight	*N* × MS-DRG Weight
286	84	1.6667	140.0028
287	41	1.1412	46.7892
293	61	0.8765	53.4665
378	41	1.0195	41.7995
391	43	0.9565	41.1295
434	45	1.0125	45.5625
689	26	1.0587	27.5262
871	31	1.7484	54.2004
982	61	3.5417	216.0437
986	51	1.6706	85.2003
Total	484		751.7206
CMI			1.5531

Table 15.12. Benchmark data, Community Hospital vs. national average for MS-DRG 293, Heart failure and shock w/o CC/MCC

	ALOS	Mortality Rate	Average Charges
Community Hospital	4.8	0.3%	$20,042
National average	4.6	2.1%	$27,731

Ambulatory Care Statistical Data

Ambulatory care includes healthcare services provided to patients who are not hospitalized (that is, who are not considered inpatients or residents and do not stay in the healthcare facility overnight). Such patients are referred to as outpatients. Most ambulatory care services today are provided in freestanding physicians' offices, emergency care centers, and ambulatory surgery centers that are not owned or operated by acute care organizations. Hospitals do, however, provide many hospital-based healthcare services to outpatients. Hospital outpatients receive services in one or more areas within the hospital, including clinics, same-day surgery departments, diagnostic departments, and emergency departments.

Outpatient statistics include records of the number of patient visits and the types of services provided. Many different terms are used to describe outpatients and ambulatory care services, including:

- **Hospital ambulatory care:** Hospital-directed preventive, therapeutic, and rehabilitative services provided by physicians and their surrogates to patients who are not hospital inpatients or home care patients
- **Outpatient:** A patient who receives care without being admitted for inpatient or residential care
- **Hospital outpatient:** A patient who receives services in one or more of the facilities owned and operated by a hospital
- **Emergency outpatient:** A patient who is admitted to the emergency department or equivalent service of a hospital for diagnosis and treatment of a condition that requires immediate medical services, dental services, or related healthcare services
- **Clinic outpatient:** A patient who is admitted to a clinical service of a clinic or hospital for diagnosis or treatment on an ambulatory basis
- **Referred outpatient:** A patient who is provided special hospital-based diagnostic or therapeutic services on an ambulatory basis; the services are ordered by a referring physician and the responsibility for medical care remains with that physician rather than with the hospital
- **Outpatient visit:** A provision of services to an outpatient in one or more units or facilities located in or directed by the provider maintaining the outpatient healthcare services

- **Encounter:** A contact between a patient and a healthcare professional who has primary responsibility for assessing and treating the patient at a given contact and for exercising independent medical judgment
- **Occasion of service:** A specified, identifiable service involved in the care of a patient or consumer that is not an encounter; occasions of service may be the result of an encounter, for example, to fulfill physicians' orders for tests or procedures ordered as part of an encounter
- **Ambulatory surgery centers:** Hospital-based or freestanding surgical facilities that perform elective surgical procedures on patients who are classified as outpatients and who are typically released from the facility on the same day the surgery was performed; also referred to as short-stay surgery, one-day surgery, same-day surgery, or come-and-go surgery services

Public Health Statistics and Epidemiological Information

Just as statistics are collected in the healthcare organizational setting, they also are collected on a community, regional, and national basis. **Vital statistics** are an example of data collected and reported at these levels. The term *vital statistics* refers to the collection and analysis of data related to the crucial events in life: birth, death, marriage, divorce, fetal death, and induced terminations of pregnancy. These statistics are used to identify trends. For example, a higher-than-expected death rate among newborns may be an indication of the lack of prenatal services in a community. A number of deaths in a region due to the same cause may indicate an environmental problem.

These types of data are used as part of the effort to preserve and improve the health of a defined population—the public health. The study of factors that influence the health status of a population is called epidemiology.

National Vital Statistics System

The **National Vital Statistics System** (NVSS) is responsible for maintaining the official vital statistics of the United States. These statistics are provided to the federal government by state-operated registration systems. The NVSS is housed in the National Center for Health Statistics (NCHS) of the Centers for Disease Control and Prevention (CDC).

To facilitate data collection, standard forms and model procedures for the uniform registration of events are developed and recommended for state use through cooperative activities of the individual states and the NCHS. The standard certificates represent the minimum basic data set necessary for the collection and publication of comparable national, state, and local vital statistics data. The standard forms are revised about every 10 years, with the last revision completed in 2003. To effectively implement these new certificates, the NCHS is working with its state partners to improve the timeliness, quality, and sustainability of the vital statistics system, along with collection of the revised and new content of the 2003 certificates.

The certificate of live birth is used for registration purposes and is composed of two parts. The first part contains the information related to the child and the parents. The second part is used to collect data about the mother's pregnancy. This information is used for the collection of aggregate data only. No identification information appears on this portion of the certificate nor does it ever appear on the official certificate of birth. Pregnancy-related information includes complications of pregnancy, concurrent illnesses or conditions affecting pregnancy, and abnormal conditions and/or congenital anomalies of the newborn. Lifestyle factors such as use of alcohol and tobacco also are collected. Thus, the birth certificate is the major source of maternal and natality statistics. A listing of pregnancy-related information appears in figure 15.7.

Data collected from death certificates are used to compile causes of death in the United States. The certificate of death contains decedent information, place of death information, medical certification, and disposition information. Data on causes of death are classified and coded using the International Classification of Diseases (ICD). Beginning in 1999, the United States implemented ICD-10 for the coding of causes of death. Examples of the content of death certificates appear in figure 15.8.

A report of fetal death is completed when a pregnancy results in a stillbirth. This report contains information on the parents, the history of the pregnancy, and the cause of the fetal death. Information collected on the pregnancy is the same as that recorded on the birth certificate. To assess the effects of environmental exposures on the fetus, the parents' occupational data are collected. Data items related to the fetus include:

- Cause of fetal death, whether fetal or maternal
- Other significant conditions of the fetus or mother
- When fetus died (before labor, during labor or delivery, or unknown)
- Risk factors related to pregnancy

The report of induced termination of pregnancy records information on the place of the induced termination of pregnancy, the type of termination procedure, and the patient. (See figure 15.9.)

A tool for monitoring and exploring the interrelationships between infant death and risk factors at birth is the linked birth and infant death data set. This is a service provided by the NCHS. In this data set, the information from the death certificate (such as age and underlying or multiple causes of death) is linked to the information in the birth certificate (such as age, race, birth weight, prenatal care usage, maternal education, and so on) for each infant who dies in the United States, Puerto Rico, the Virgin Islands, and Guam. The purpose of the data set is to use the many additional variables available from the birth certificate to conduct a detailed analysis of infant mortality patterns.

Birth, death, fetal death, and termination of pregnancy certificates provide vital information for use in medical research,

Figure 15.7. Content of U.S. certificate of live birth, 2003

Child's Information
- Child's name
- Time of birth
- Sex
- Date of birth
- Facility (hospital) Name (if not an institution, give street address)
- City
- County

Mother's Information
- Current legal name
- Date of birth
- Mother's name prior to first marriage
- Birthplace
- Residence (state)
- County
- City
- Street number
- Zip code
- Inside city limits?
- Mother married?
- If no, has paternity acknowledgment been signed in the hospital?
- Social Security number (SSN) requested for child?
- Mother's SSN
- Father's SSN
- Education
- Hispanic origin?
- Race

Father
- Current legal name
- Date of birth
- Birthplace
- Education
- Hispanic origin?
- Race

Pregnancy History
- Date of first prenatal care visit
- Date of last prenatal care visit
- Total number of prenatal visits for this pregnancy
- Number of previous live births
- Mother's height
- Mother's pregnancy weight
- Mother's weight at delivery
- Did mother get WIC food for herself during this pregnancy?
- Number of previous live births
- Number of other pregnancy outcomes
- Cigarette smoking before and during pregnancy
- Principal source of payment for this delivery
- Date of last live birth
- Date of last other pregnancy outcome
- Date last normal menses began
- Risk factors in this pregnancy
- Infections present and/or treated during this pregnancy
- Obstetric procedures
- Onset of labor
- Characteristics of labor and delivery
- Method of delivery
- Maternal mortality

Newborn Information
- Birth weight
- Obstetric estimate of gestation
- Apgar score (1 and 5 minutes)
- Plurality
- If not born first (born first, second, third, etc.)
- Abnormal conditions of newborn
- Congenital anomalies of the newborn
- Was infant transferred within 24 hours of delivery?
- Is infant living at time of report?
- Is infant being breast fed at discharge?

Source: NVSS 2005.

Figure 15.8. Content of U.S. certificate of death, 2003

Decedent Information
- Name
- Sex
- Social Security number
- Age
- Date of birth
- Birthplace
- Residence (state)
- County
- City or town
- Street and number
- Zip code
- Inside city limit?
- Ever in U.S. armed forces?
- Marital status at time of death
- Surviving spouse's name (If wife, give name prior to first marriage)
- Father's name
- Mother's name (prior to first marriage)
- Decedent's education
- Hispanic origin?
- Race
- Informant's name
- Relationship to decedent
- Mailing address

Disposition Information
- Method of disposition
- Place of disposition (cemetery, crematory, other)
- Location
- Name and address of funeral facility

Place of Death Information
- Place of death
- If hospital, indicate inpatient, emergency room/outpatient, dead on arrival
- If somewhere other than hospital, indicate hospice, nursing home/long-term care facility, decedent's home, other
- Facility name
- City, state, zip code
- County

Medical Certification
- Date pronounced dead
- Time pronounced dead
- Signature of person pronouncing death
- Date signed
- Actual or presumed date of death
- Actual or presumed time of death
- Was medical examiner contacted?
- Immediate cause of death
- Due to ________
- Due to ________
- Due to ________
- Other significant conditions contributing to death
- Was an autopsy performed?
- Were autopsy findings available to complete the cause of death?
- Did tobacco use contribute to death?
- If female, indicate pregnancy status
- Manner of death
- For deaths due to injury:
- Date of injury
- Time of injury
- Place of injury
- Injury at work?
- Location of injury
- Describe how injury occurred
- If transportation injury, specify if driver/operator, passenger, pedestrian, other

Source: NVSS 2005.

Figure 15.9. Content of U.S. standard report of induced termination of pregnancy, 1997

Place of Induced Termination	Inside city limits?
Facility name	Zip code
Address (city, town, state, county)	Hispanic origin?
	Race
	Education
Patient Information	Date last normal menses began
Patient Identification	Clinical estimate of gestation
Age at last birthday	Previous pregnancies
Marital status	Live births
Date or pregnancy termination	Other terminations
Residence (city, town, state, county	Type of termination procedure

Source: NVSS 2005.

epidemiological studies, and other public health programs. In addition, they are the source of data for compiling morbidity, birth, and mortality rates that describe the health of a given population at the local, state, or national level. Because of their many uses, the data on these certificates must be complete and accurate.

Population-based Statistics

Population-based statistics are based on the mortality and morbidity rates from which the health of a population can be inferred. The entire defined population is used in the collection and reporting of these statistics. The size of the defined population serves as the denominator in the calculation of these rates.

Birth Rates and Measures of Infant Mortality

Two community-based rates that are commonly used to describe a community's health are the crude birth rate and measures of infant mortality. The official international definition of a live birth is the delivery of a product of conception that shows any sign of life after complete removal from the mother. A sign of life may consist of a breath or cry, any spontaneous movement, a pulse or heartbeat, or pulsation of the umbilical cord.

Rates that describe infant mortality are based on age. Therefore, the definitions for the various age groups must be strictly followed. Table 15.13 summarizes the calculations for community-based birth and infant mortality rates. These mortality or death rates are broken down as follows:

- **Crude birth rate:** As shown in formula 15.22, the crude birth rate is the number of live births divided by the population at risk. As the formula shows, community rates are calculated using the multiplier 1,000, 10,000, or 100,000. The purpose is to bring the rate to a whole number, as discussed earlier in the chapter. The result of the formula would be stated as the number of live births per 1,000 population. For example, if there were 7,532 live births in a community of 600,000 in 1999, the crude birth rate for that year would be 12.6 per 1,000 population ([7,532/600,000] × 1000).
- **Neonatal mortality rate:** The neonatal mortality rate can be used as an indirect measure of the quality of prenatal care and/or the mother's prenatal behavior (for example, alcohol, drug, or tobacco use). The neonatal period is the period from birth up to, but not including, 28 days of age. In the formula for calculating the neonatal mortality rate, the numerator is the number of deaths of infants under 28 days of age during a given time period and the denominator is the total number of live births during the same time period.
- **Postneonatal mortality rate:** The postneonatal mortality rate is often used as an indicator of the quality of the home or community environment of infants. The postneonatal period is the period from 28 days up to, but not including, one year of age. In the formula for calculating the postneonatal mortality rate, the numerator is the number of deaths among infants from age 28 days up to but not including one year during a given time period and the denominator is the total number of live births less the number of neonatal deaths during the same time period.
- **Infant mortality rate:** The infant mortality rate is the summary of the neonatal and postneonatal mortality rates. In the formula for calculating the infant mortality rate, the numerator is the number of deaths among infants under one year of age and the denominator is the number of live births during the same period. The infant mortality rate is the most commonly used measure for comparing health status among nations. All the rates are expressed in terms of the number of deaths per 1,000.

Death (Mortality) Rates

Other measures of mortality with which the HIM professional should be familiar include the following:

- **Crude death rate:** The crude death rate is a measure of the actual or observed mortality in a given population. Crude death rates apply to a population without regard to characteristics such as age, race, and sex. They measure the proportion of the population that has died during a given period of time (usually one year) or the number of deaths in a community per 1,000 for a given period of time. The formula for calculating the crude death rate is shown in formula 15.23.
- **Cause-specific death rate:** As its name indicates, the cause-specific death rate is the rate of death due to a specified cause. It may be calculated for an entire population or for any age, sex, or race. In the formula, the numerator is the number of deaths due to a specified cause for a given time period and the denominator is the estimated population for the same time period. Table 15.14 displays cause-specific death rates for men and women due to influenza and pneumonia for the year 2005. The cause-specific death rates for each age group are consistently higher for men than for women. This information could lead to an investigation of why men are more susceptible to death from pneumonia than women.

- **Case fatality rate:** The case fatality rate measures the probability of death among the diagnosed cases of a disease, most often acute illness. In the formula for calculating the case fatality rate, the numerator is the number of deaths due to a specific disease that occurred during a specific time period and the denominator is the number of diagnosed cases during the same time period. The higher the case fatality rate, the more virulent the infection.
- **Proportionate mortality ratio:** The proportionate mortality ratio (PMR) is a measure of mortality due to a specific cause for a specific time period. In the formula for calculating the PMR, the numerator is the number of deaths due to a specific disease for a specific time period and the denominator is the number of deaths from all causes for the same time period. Table 15.15 displays the PMRs for influenza pneumonia in the United States in 2005.
- **Maternal mortality rate:** The maternal mortality rate measures the deaths associated with pregnancy for a specific community for a specific period of time. It is calculated only for deaths that are directly related to pregnancy. In the formula for calculating the maternal mortality rate, the numerator is the number of deaths attributed to causes related to pregnancy during a specific time period for a given community and the denominator is the number of live births reported during the same time period for the same community. Because the maternal mortality rate is very small, it is usually expressed as the number of deaths per 100,000 live births.

Table 15.16 summarizes the calculations for these rates.

Table 15.13. Calculation of community-based birth and infant death (mortality) rates

Measure	Numerator (x)	Denominator (y)	10^n
Crude birth rate	Number of live births for a given community for a specified time period	Estimated population for the same community and the same time period	1,000
Neonatal death rate	Number of deaths under 28 days up to, but not including, one year of age during a given time period	Number of live births during the same time period	1,000
Postneonatal death rate	Number of deaths from 28 days up to, but not including, one year of age during a given time period	Number of live births during the same time period less neonatal deaths	1,000
Infant death rate	Number of deaths under one year of age during a given time period	Number of live births during the same time period	1,000

Formula 15.22. Calculating the crude birth rate

$$\text{Crude birth rate} = \frac{\text{Number of live births for a given community for a specified time period}}{\text{Estimated population for the same community and the same time period}} \times 10^n$$

Formula 15.23. Calculating the crude death rate

$$\text{Crude death rate} = \frac{\text{Total number of deaths for a population during a specified time period}}{\text{Estimated population for the same time period}} \times 10^n$$

Table 15.14. Cause-specific mortality rates by sex, due to influenza and pneumonia (ICD-10 codes J10–J18.9) age 45+ in the United States, 2005

	Women			Men		
Age Group	**Population**	**Deaths**	**Rate/100,000**	**Population**	**Deaths**	**Rate/100,000**
45–54	21,586,910	881	4.08	20,895,355	1,302	6.23
55–64	15,728,823	1,434	9.12	14,626,718	1,988	13.59
65–74	10,110,417	2,975	29.43	8,529,396	3,640	42.68
75–84	7,774,917	9,360	120.39	5,279,445	9,198	174.22
85+	3,492,142	19,465	557.39	1,603,796	10,797	673.22
Total	58,693,209	34,115	58.12	50,934,710	26,925	52.86

Source: CDC 2005.

Table 15.15. Proportionate mortality ratios for influenza and pneumonis (ICD-10 codes J10–J18.9) all ages, in the United States, 2005

Age Group	Influenza and Pneumonia Deaths	Total Deaths	PMR/100
0–4	375	33,196	1.13
5–14	106	6,602	1.61
15–24	172	34,234	0.50
25–34	354	41,925	0.84
35–44	934	84,785	1.10
45–54	2,183	183,530	1.19
55–64	3,422	275,301	1.24
65–74	6,623	398,355	1.66
75–84	18,563	686,665	2.70
85+	30,267	703,169	4.30

Source: CDC 2005.

Check Your Understanding 15.9

Instructions: Review the mortality data in the following and then answer the following questions on a separate piece of paper.

Sex Specific Death Rates, United States, 1999–2005				
	Female		Male	
Age Group	Population	Deaths	Population	Deaths
Less than 1 year	2,005,492	12,422	2,101,135	16,018
1–4 years	7,916,886	1,991	8,280,211	2,765
5–9	9,545,396	1,281	9,993,397	1,556
10–14	10,175,908	1,468	10,681,835	2,297
15–19	10,248,766	3,817	10,790,223	9,886
20–24	10,180,924	4,908	10,856,936	15,623
25–34	19,721,652	12,642	20,421,260	29,283
35–44	21,922,425	31,476	21,940,039	53,309
45–54	21,586,910	69,058	20,895,355	114,472
55–64	15,728,823	109,872	14,626,718	165,429
65–74	10,110,417	175,548	8,529,396	222,807
75–84	7,774,917	351,430	5,279,445	335,235
85 +	3,492,142	464,373	1,603,796	238,796
Total	150,410,658	1,240,286	145,999,746	1,207,476

Source: NVSR 2005.

1. ___ What is the crude death rate per 10,000 for men?
2. ___ What is the crude death rate per 10,000 for women?
3. ___ What is the crude death rate per 10,000 for the entire group?
4. ___ What is the crude death rate per 10,000 for men ages 35–44?
5. ___ What is the crude death rate per 10,000 for women ages 35–55?

Table 15.16. Calculation of community-based death (mortality) rates

Rate	Numerator (x)	Denominator (y)	10^n
Crude death rate	Total number of deaths for a population during a specified time period	Estimated population for the same time period	1,000 or 10,000 or 100,000
Cause-specific death rate	Total number of deaths due to a specific cause during a specified time period	Estimated population for the same time period	100,000
Case fatality rate	Total number of deaths due to a specific disease during a specified time period	Total number of cases due to a specific disease during the same time period	100
Proportionate mortality (ratio)	Total number of deaths due to a specific cause during a specified time period	Total number of deaths from all causes during the same time period	NA
Maternal mortality rate	Total number of deaths due to pregnancy-related conditions during a specified time period	Total number of live births during the same time period	100,000

Measures of Morbidity

Two measures are commonly used to describe the presence of disease in a community or specific location (for example, a nursing home): incidence and prevalence rates. Disease is defined as any illness, injury, or disability. Incidence and prevalence measures can be broken down by race, sex, age, or other characteristics of a population.

An **incidence rate** is used to compare the frequency of disease in populations. Populations are compared using rates instead of raw numbers because rates adjust for differences in population size. The incidence rate is the probability or risk of illness in a population over a period of time. The formula for calculating the incidence rate is shown in formula 15.24. The denominator represents the population from which the case in the numerator arose, such as a nursing home, school, or organization. For 10^n, a value is selected so that the smallest rate calculated results in a whole number. For example in a small population such as a nursing home you might select 100, in studying a larger population you might select 1,000. The **prevalence rate** is the proportion of persons in a population who have a particular disease at a specific point in time or over a specified period of time. The formula for calculating the prevalence rate is shown in formula 15.25. The prevalence rate describes the magnitude of an epidemic

Formula 15.24. Calculating the incidence rate

$$\text{Incidence rate} = \frac{\text{Total number of new cases of a specific disease during a given time period}}{\text{Total population at risk during the same time period}} \times 10^n$$

Formula 15.25. Calculating the prevalence rate

$$\text{Prevalence rate} = \frac{\text{All new and preexisting cases of a specific disease during a given time period}}{\text{Total population during the same time period}} \times 10^n$$

and can be an indicator of the medical resources needed in a community for the duration of the epidemic.

It is easy to confuse incidence and prevalence rates. The distinction is in the numerators of their formulas. The numerator in the formula for the incidence rate is the number of new cases occurring in a given time period. The numerator in the formula for the prevalence rate is all cases present during a given time period. In addition, the incidence rate includes only patients whose illness began during a specified time period whereas the prevalence rate includes all patients from a specified cause regardless of when the illness began. Moreover, the prevalence rate includes a patient until he or she recovers.

National Notifiable Diseases Surveillance System

In 1878, Congress authorized the U.S. Marine Hospital Service, the precursor to the Public Health Service, to collect morbidity reports on cholera, smallpox, plague, and yellow fever from U.S. consuls overseas. This information was used to implement quarantine measures to prevent the spread of these diseases to the United States. In 1879, Congress provided for the weekly collection and publication of reports of these diseases. In 1893, Congress expanded the scope to include weekly reporting from states and municipalities. To provide for more uniformity in data collection, Congress enacted a law in 1902 that directed the surgeon general to provide standard forms for the collection, compilation, and publication of reports at the national level. In 1912, the states and U.S. territories recommended that infectious disease be immediately reported by telegraph. By 1928, all states, the District of Columbia, Hawaii, and Puerto Rico were participating in the national reporting of 29 specified diseases. In 1961, the CDC assumed responsibility for the collection and publication of data concerning nationally notifiable diseases.

A **notifiable disease** is one for which regular, frequent, and timely information on individual cases is considered necessary to prevent and control disease. The list of notifiable diseases varies over time and by state. The Council of State and Territorial Epidemiologists (CSTE) collaborates with the CDC to determine which diseases should be reported. State reporting to the CDC is voluntary. However, all states generally report the internationally quarantinable diseases in accordance with the World Health Organization's International Health Regulations. Completeness of reporting varies by state and type of disease and may be influenced by any of the following factors:

- Type and severity of the illness
- Whether treatment in a healthcare facility was sought
- Diagnosis of an illness
- Availability of diagnostic services
- Disease-control measures in effect
- Public awareness of the disease
- Resources, priorities, and interests of state and local public health officials

Information that is reported includes date, county, age, sex, race and ethnicity, and disease-specific epidemiologic information; personal identifiers are not included. A strict CSTE Data Release Policy regulates dissemination of the data. A list of nationally notifiable infectious diseases appears in figure 15.10. The list is updated annually.

National morbidity data are reported weekly. Public health managers and providers use the reports to rapidly identify disease epidemics and to understand patterns of disease occurrence. Case-specific information is included in the reports. Changes in age, sex, race and ethnicity, and geographic distributions can be monitored and investigated as necessary.

Check Your Understanding 15.10

Instructions: Answer the following questions on a separate piece of paper.

1. Define incidence rate and prevalence rate.
2. What is a notifiable disease?
3. Calculate the incidence rate, per 100,000, for the following hypothetical data: In 20XX, 65,000 new cases of HIV were reported in the United States. The estimated population for 20XX was 296,410,404.

Presentation of Statistical Data

Collected data are often more meaningful when presented in graphic form (consider any of the acute or ambulatory care data previously described). How one presents such data will be governed by whether they are nominal, ordinal, interval or ratio.

Tables, charts, and graphs offer the opportunity to analyze data sets and to explore, understand, and present frequency

Figure 15.10. Nationally notifiable infectious diseases in the United States, 2009

- Acquired Immunodeficiency Syndrome (AIDS)
- Anthrax
- Arboviral neuroinvasive and non-neuroinvasive diseases
  - California serogroup virus disease
  - Eastern equine encephalitis virus disease
  - Powassan virus disease
  - St. Louis encephalitis virus disease
  - West Nile virus disease
  - Western equine encephalitis virus disease
- Botulism
  - Botulism, foodborne
  - Botulism, infant
  - Botulism, other (wound and unspecified)
- Brucellosis
- Chancroid
- *Chlamydia trachomatis*, genital infections
- Cholera
- Coccidioidomycosis
- Cryptosporidiosis
- Cyclosporiasis
- Diphtheria
- Ehrlichiosis/Anaplasmosis
  - Ehrlichia chaffeensis
  - Ehrlichia ewingii
  - Anaplasma phagocytophilum
  - Undetermined
- Giardiasis
- Gonorrhea
- *Haemophilus influenzae*, invasive disease
- Hansen disease (leprosy)
- Hantavirus pulmonary syndrome
- Hemolytic uremic syndrome, post-diarrheal
- Hepatitis, viral, acute
  - Hepatitis A, acute
  - Hepatitis B, acute
  - Hepatitis B, virus, perinatal infection
  - Hepatitis C, acute
- Hepatitis, viral, chronic
  - Chronic Hepatitis B
  - Hepatitis C Virus Infection (past or present)
- Human Immunodeficiency Virus (HIV) infection
  - HIV infection, adult (>=13 years)
  - HIV infection, pediatric (<13 years)
- Influenza-associated pediatric mortality
- Legionellosis
- Listeriosis
- Lyme disease
- Malaria
- Measles
- Meningococcal disease
- Mumps
- Novel influenza A virus infections
- Pertussis
- Plague
- Poliomyelitis, paralytic
- Poliovirus infection, nonparalytic
- Psittacosis
- Q fever
- Rabies
  - Rabies, animal
  - Rabies, human
- Rocky Mountain spotted fever
- Rubella
- Rubella, congenital syndrome
- Salmonellosis
- Severe Acute Respiratory Syndrome–associated Coronavirus (SARS–CoV) disease
- Shiga toxin-producing *Escherichia coli* (STEC)
- Shigellosis
- Smallpox
- Streptococcal disease, invasive, Group A
- Streptococcal toxic-shock syndrome
- *Streptococcus pneumoniae*, drug resistant, invasive disease
- *Streptococcus pneumoniae*, invasive disease non-drug resistant, in children less than 5 years of age
- Syphilis
  - Syphilis, primary
  - Syphilis, secondary
  - Syphilis, latent
  - Syphilis, early latent
  - Syphilis, late latent
  - Syphilis, latent, unknown duration
  - Neurosyphilis
  - Syphilis, late, non-neurological
  - Syphilitic Stillbirth
- Syphilis, congenital
- Tetanus
- Toxic-shock syndrome (other than Streptococcal)
- Trichinellosis (Trichinosis)
- Tuberculosis
- Tularemia
- Typhoid fever
- Vancomycin, intermediate *Staphylococcus aureus* (VISA)
- Vancomycin, resistant *Staphylococcus aureus* (VRSA)
- Varicella (morbidity)
- Varicella (deaths only)
- Vibriosis
- Yellow fever

Source: CDC, Nationally Notifiable Infectious Disease, United States 2009.

distributions, trends, and relationships in the data. The purpose of tables, charts, and graphs is to communicate information about the data to the user of the data.

Whatever type of graphic form is used, it should:

- Display the data
- Allow the user to think about the meaning of the data
- Avoid distortion of the data
- Encourage the user to make comparisons
- Reveal data at several levels, from a broad overview to the fine detail

Methods of displaying the data in graphic form are discussed in the following subsections.

Tables

A table is an orderly arrangement of values that groups data into rows and columns. Almost any type of quantitative information can be organized into a table. Tables are useful for demonstrating patterns and other kinds of relationships. In addition, they may serve as the basis for more visual displays of data, such as charts and graphs, where some of the detail may be lost. However, because tables are not very interesting, they should be used sparingly.

A useful first step is to prepare a table shell that shows how the data will be organized and displayed. A *table shell* is the outline of a table with everything in place except for the data. (See table 15.17) A table should contain all the information the reader needs to understand the data in it. It should have the following characteristics:

- It is a logical unit.
- It is self-explanatory and can stand on its own when photocopied or removed from its context.
- All sources are specified.
- Specific, understandable headings are provided for every column and row.
- Row and column totals are checked for accuracy.
- Blank cells are not left empty. When no information is available for a particular cell, the cell should contain a zero or a dash.
- Categories are mutually exclusive and exhaustive.

The data contained in tables should be aligned. Guidelines for aligning text and numbers include:

- Text in the table should be aligned at left.
- Text that serves as a column label may be centered.
- Numeric values should be aligned at right.
- When numeric values contain decimals, the decimals should be aligned.

The essential components of a table are summarized in figure 15.11.

Tables may contain information on one, two, or three variables. Tables 15.18 and 15.19 are examples of one- and two-variable tables, respectively.

Charts and Graphs

Charts and graphs of various types are the best means for presenting data for quick visualization of relationships. They emphasize the main points and analyze and clarify relationships among variables.

Several principles are involved in the construction of charts and graphs. When constructing charts and graphs, the following points should be considered:

- *Distortion:* To avoid distorting the data, the representation of the numbers should be proportional to the numerical quantities represented.
- *Proportion and scale:* Graphs should emphasize the horizontal. It is easier for the eye to read along the horizontal axis from left to right. Also, graphs should be greater in length than height. A useful guideline is to

Table 15.17. Table shell

TITLE							
		Sex				Total	
		Male		Female			
Box Head	**Age**	**Number**	**%**	**Number**	**%**	**Number**	**%**
Stub	*Row Variable*	→→→→→	→→→→→	→→→→→	→→→→→	→→→→→	→→→→→
	< 45			*Column Variable*			
↓	45–54			↓			
↓	55–64			↓			
↓	65–74			↓			
↓	75+			↓			

Source: HHS 1994.

Figure 15.11. Essential components of a table

Title	The title should be as complete as possible and should clearly relate to the content of the table. It should answer the following questions: • What are the data (e.g., counts, percentages)? • Who (e.g., white females with breast cancer; black males with lung cancer)? • Where are the data from (e.g., hospital, state, community)? • When (e.g., year, month)? A sample title might be: Site Distribution by Age and Sex of Cancer Patients upon First Admission to Community Hospital, 2000–2004
Box Head	The box head contains the captions or column headings. The heading of each column should contain as few words as possible but should explain exactly what the data in the column represent.
Stub	The row captions are knows as the stub. Items in the stub should be grouped to make it easy to interpret the data, for example, ages grouped into five-year intervals.
Cell	The cell is the box formed by the intersection of a column and a row.
Optional Items:	
Note	Notes are used to explain anything in the table that the reader cannot understand from the title, box head, or stub. They contain numbers, preliminary or revised numbers, or explanations of any unusual numbers. Definitions, abbreviations, and/or qualifications for captions or cell names should be footnoted. A note usually applies to a specific cell(s) within the table, and a symbol (e.g., ** or #) may be used to key the cell to the note. If several notes are used, it is better to use small letters than symbols or numbers. Note any numbers that may be confused with the numbers within the table.
Source	If data are used from a source outside the research, the exact reference to the source should be given. The source lends authenticity to the data and allows the reader to locate the original information if he or she needs it.

Source: HHS 1994.

Table 15.18. One-variable table, Community Hospital admissions by gender, 20XX

Gender	Number	Percentage
Male	3,141	46.0%
Female	3,683	54.0%
Total	6,824	100.0%

Table 15.19. Two-variable table, Community Hospital admissions by race and gender, 20XX

Race	Gender		Total
	Male	Female	
White	2,607	2,946	5,553
Non-white	534	737	1,271
Total	3,141	3,683	6,824

follow the three-quarter-high rule. This rule states that the height (y-axis) of the graph should be three-fourths the length (x-axis) of the graph.

- *Abbreviations:* Any abbreviations should be spelled out in notes.
- *Color:* Color may be used to highlight groupings that appear in the graph.
- *Print:* Both upper- and lowercase letters should be used in titles; the use of all capital letters can be difficult to read.

Bar Charts

Bar charts are used to display data from one or more variables. The bars may be drawn vertically or horizontally. The simplest bar chart is the one-variable bar chart. In this type of chart, a bar represents each category of the variable. For example, if the data in table 15.18 were displayed in a bar chart, "gender" would be the variable and "male and female" would be the variable categories. Bar charts are used for nominal or ordinal variables. Sometimes ratio data that is discrete tend to be represented with bar charts rather than histograms because they are not continuous. Figure 15.12 displays the data from table 15.18 as a bar chart. The length or height of each bar is proportional to the number of males and females admitted. Presentation of the data in a bar chart makes it easy to see that more females than males were admitted to Community Hospital.

Figure 15.13 displays the two-variable data from table 15.19 as a two-variable or grouped-variable bar chart in a three-dimensional format. Computer software makes it easy to present data in this way. However, presenting data in a three-dimensional format can be tricky. The reader may not always be able to estimate the true height of the bar. In a three-dimensional bar chart, the back edges of the bar appear higher than the front edge, as in figure 15.13. To make sure the reader correctly interprets the chart, the bars should include the actual values for each category.

Figure 15.14 presents guidelines for constructing bar charts.

Pie Charts

A **pie chart** is an easily understood chart in which the sizes of the slices of the pie show the proportional contribution of each part. Pie charts can be used to show the component parts of a single group or variable. Pie charts are intended for interval or ratio data.

To calculate the size of each slice of the pie, first determine the proportion that each slice is to represent. Multiplying the proportion by 360 (the total number of degrees in a circle) will give the size of each slice of the pie in degrees.

Figure 15.15 shows payer data collected on admissions to Community Hospital. The summary data for one year show that managed care was the payer for 39 percent of the patients, Medicare was the payer for 30 percent, Medicaid was the payer for 18 percent, government-managed care was the payer for 8 percent of the patients, and 5 percent of the patients had commercial insurance.

Figure 15.12. One-variable bar chart, Community Hospital admissions by gender, 20XX

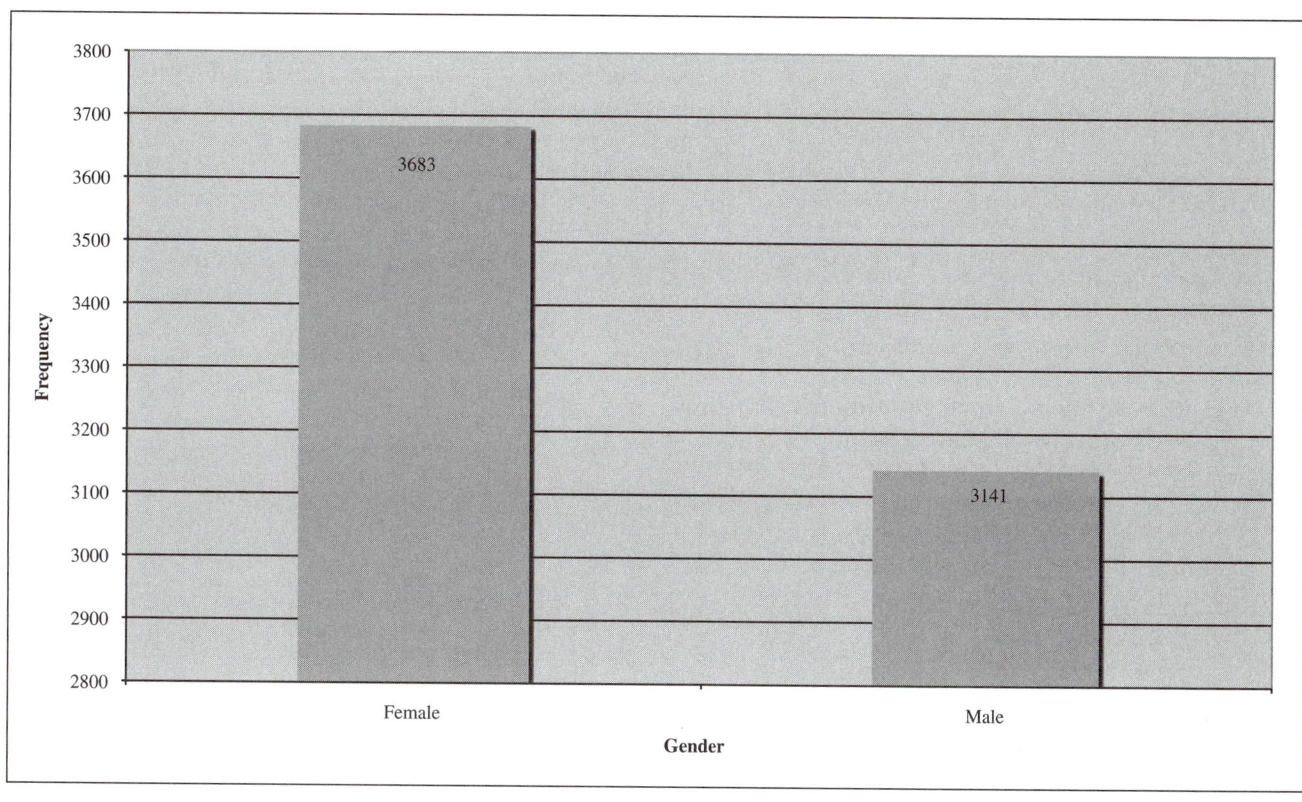

Figure 15.13. Two-variable bar chart, Community Hospital admissions by race and gender, 20XX

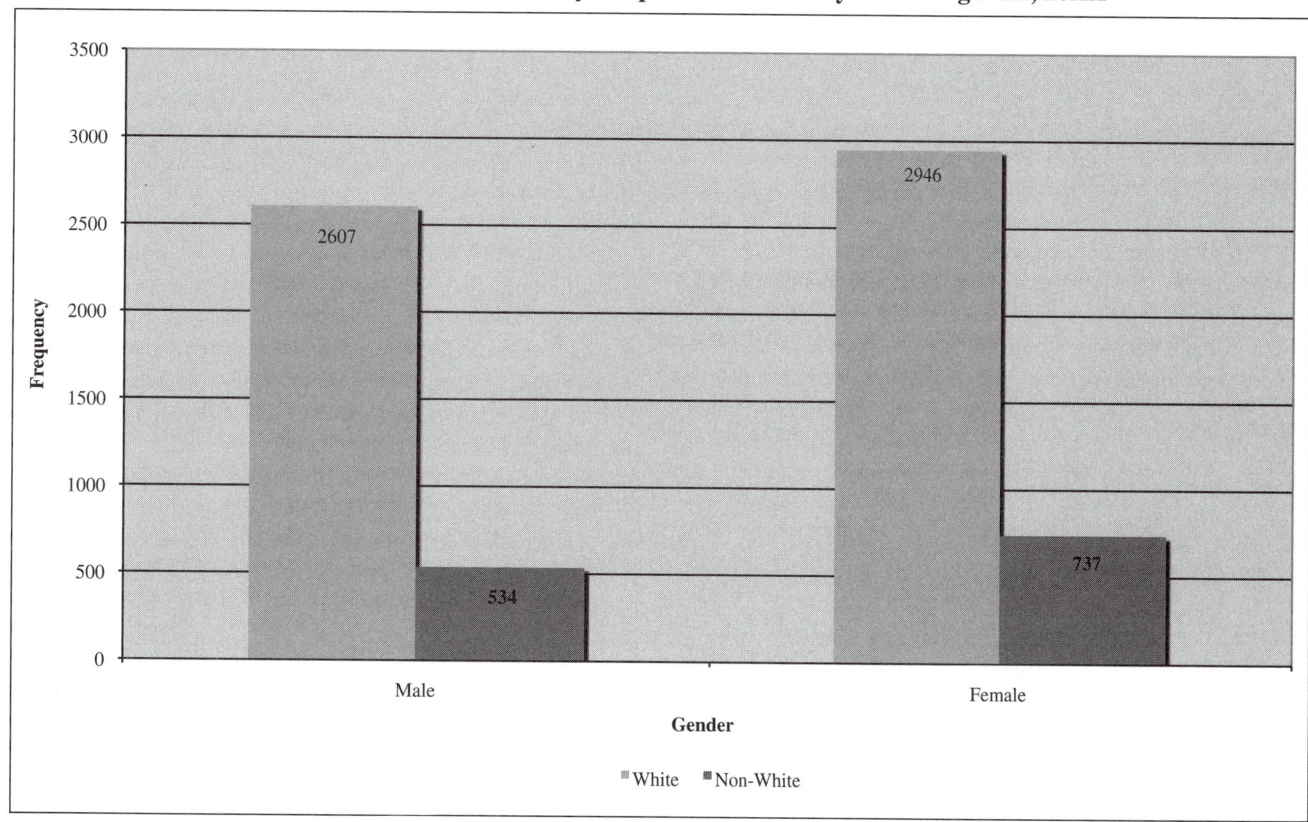

Figure 15.14. Guidelines for constructing a bar chart

When constructing a bar chart, keep the following points in mind:

- Arrange the bar categories in a natural order, such as alphabetical order, order by increasing age, or an order that will produce increasing or decreasing bar lengths.
- The bars may be positioned vertically or horizontally.
- The length of the bars should be proportional to the frequency of the event.
- Avoid using more than three bars (categories) within a group of bars.
- Leave a space between adjacent groups of bars, but not between bars within a group.
- Code different categories of variables by differences in bar color, shading, and/or cross-hatching. Include a legend that explains the coding system.

Figure 15.15. Pie chart, Community Hospital admissions by payer, 20XX

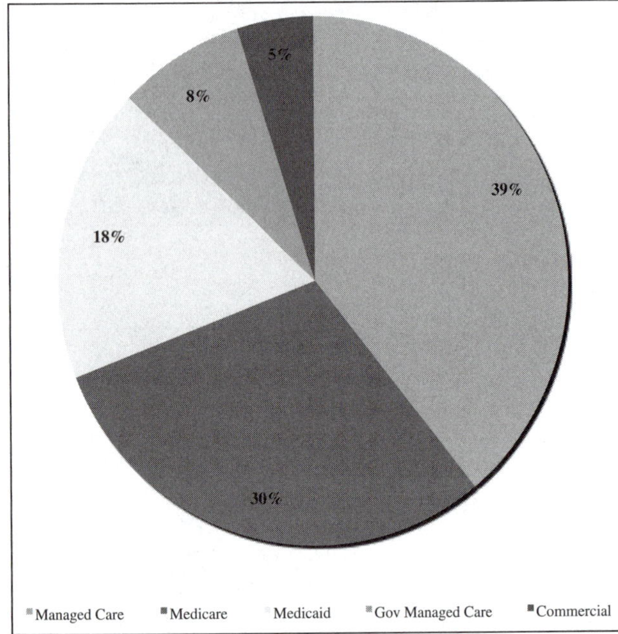

With 39 percent of the pie chart, the managed care category equals approximately 140° (360° × 0.39 = 140°). The Medicare category equals 108° (360° × 0.30 = 108°). The Medicaid category equals 65° (360° × 0.18 = 65°). The government-managed care category equals approximately 29° (360° × 0.08 = 29°). And commercial insurance equals 18° (360° × 0.05 = 18°). Taken together, the slices equal 360° (140° + 108° + 65° + 29° + 18° = 360°).

The slices of the pie should be arranged in some logical order. By convention, the largest slices begin at twelve o'clock. Computer software is available to make the construction of pie charts easy. The pie chart in figure 15.15 was prepared using Excel software.

Line Graphs

A **line graph** may be used to display time trends. The *x*-axis shows the unit of time from left to right, and the *y*-axis measures the values of the variable being plotted. A line graph does not represent a **frequency distribution**.

A line graph consists of a line connecting a series of points. Like all graphs, a line graph should be constructed so that it is easy to read. Selection of the proper scale, a complete and accurate title, and an informative legend is important. When a graph is too long and narrow, either vertically or horizontally, it has an awkward appearance and may exaggerate one aspect of the data.

A line graph is especially useful for plotting a large number of observations. It also allows several sets of data to be presented on one graph.

Either actual numbers or percentages may be used on the *y*-axis of the graph. Percentages should be used on the *y*-axis when more than one distribution is to be shown. A percentage distribution allows comparisons among groups where the actual totals are different.

When two or more sets of data are plotted on the same graph, the lines should be made different—solid or broken—for each set. However, the number of lines should be kept to a minimum to avoid confusion. Each line then should be identified in a legend located on the graph.

There are two kinds of time-trend data: point data and period data. Point data reflect an instant in time. Figure 15.16 displays point data—the total number of admissions for each year represented in the graph. Period data are averages or totals over a specified period of time, such as a five-year time frame. Table 15.20 summarizes period data for survival rates of patients diagnosed with kidney cancer. Figure 15.17 displays these period data in a line graph.

Histograms

A **histogram** is used to display a frequency distribution. It is different from a bar graph in that a bar graph is used to display data that fall into groups or categories (nominal or ordinal data). The categories are noncontinuous, or discrete. In a bar chart, the bars representing the different categories are separated. (Refer to figures 15.12 and 15.13.) On the other hand, histograms are used to illustrate frequency distributions of continuous variables, such as age or LOS. A continuous variable can take on a fractional value (for example, 75.345°F). With continuous variables, there are no gaps between values because the values progress fractionally. Histograms are used for interval or ratio variables.

In a histogram, the frequency distribution may be displayed as a number or a percentage. The histogram consists of a series of bars. Each bar has one class interval as its base and the number (frequency) or percentage of cases in that class interval as its height. A class interval is a type of category. It can represent one value in a frequency distribution (for example, three years of age) or a group of values (for example, ages three to five).

In histograms, there are no spaces between the bars. (See figure 15.18.) The lack of spaces between bars depicts the continuous nature of the distribution. The sum of the heights of the bars represents the total number, or 100 percent, of the cases. Histograms should be used when the distribution

Figure 15.16. Line graph with point data, Community Hospital admissions 2004–2008

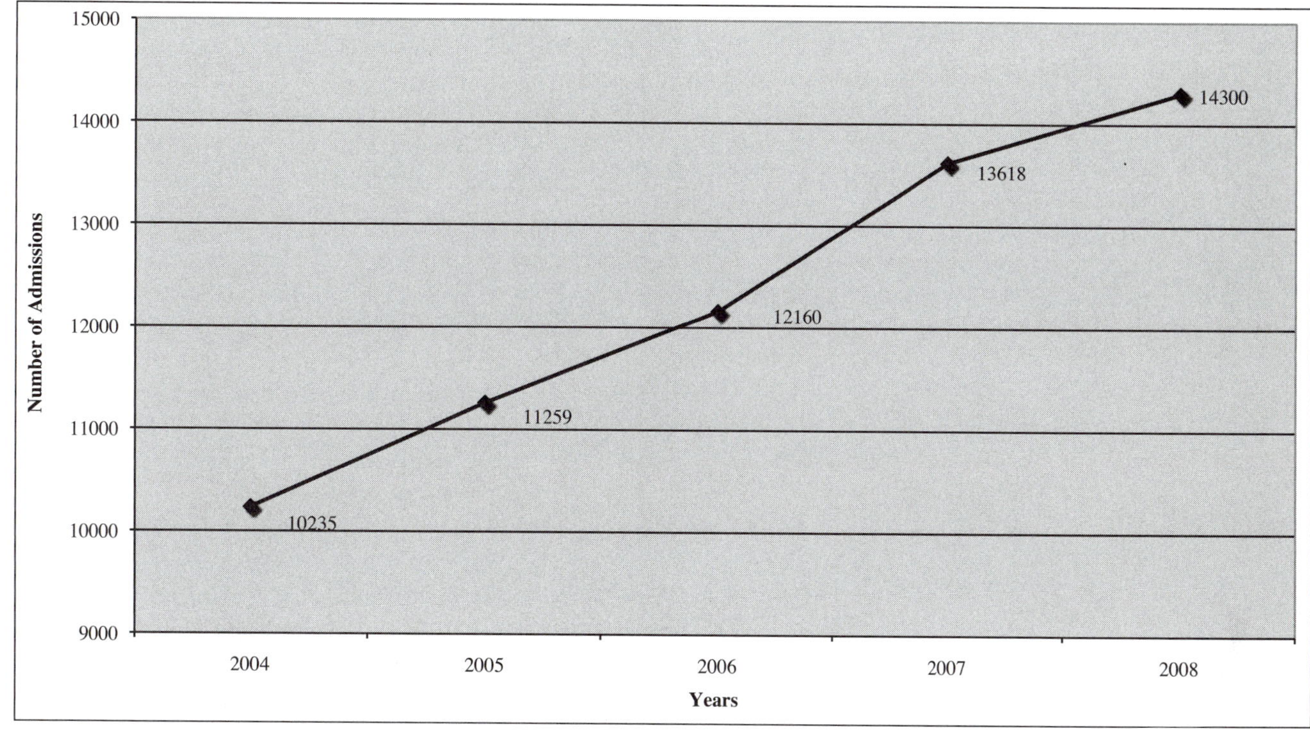

of the data needs to be emphasized more than the values of the distribution.

Frequency Polygons

A **frequency polygon** is an alternative to a histogram. Like a histogram, it is a graph of a frequency distribution, but in line form rather than bar form and is intended for interval or ratio data. The advantage of frequency polygons is that several of them can be placed on the same graph to make comparisons. Another advantage is that frequency polygons are easy to interpret.

When constructing a frequency polygon, the *x*-axis should be made longer than the *y*-axis to avoid distorting the data. The frequency of observations is always placed on the *y*-axis and the scale of the variable on the *x*-axis. The frequency polygon in figure 15.19 plots the same data that appear in the histogram in figure 15.18. Because the *x*-axis represents the entire frequency distribution, the line starts at zero cases and ends with zero cases.

Scatter Charts

Scatter charts, also called scatter plots or scatter diagrams, are used when one wants to determine if there is a relationship between two variables, such as charges and LOS. Data collected for scatter charts must be at the interval or ratio level of measurement. The data for the two variables are arranged in pairs; one of the two variables is plotted on the *x*-axis and the other variable is plotted on the *y*-axis. The closer the data points come to making a straight line, the stronger the relationship between the two variables. If the data points form a straight line from the lower left of the *x*-axis to the upper right on the *y*-axis, the relationship is positive. (See figure 15.20.) If the line begins at a high value on the *y*-axis and descends to a low value on the *x*-axis, the relationship is negative. (See figure 15.21.) If the data points are widely scattered, there is no relationship between the two variables. (See figure 15.22.)

Table 15.20. Sample five-year survival rates for kidney cancer by stage, for patients diagnosed between 2000 and 2008

Year of Diagnosis	Midpoint of Interval	Survival Rate (%)		
		Localized	Regional	Distant
2000–2002	2001	80	71	28
2003–2005	2004	84	74	29
2006–2008	2007	85	74	31

Bubble Charts

A **bubble chart** is a type of scatter plot with circular symbols used to compare three variables; the size of the symbol indicates the value of a third variable. In developing the chart, one variable is displayed on the vertical or *y*-axis, and two variables are displayed on the horizontal or *x*-axis. Data must be at the interval or ratio-level of measurement.

As an example, an administrator is interested in displaying the average charges for the five highest volume MS-DRGs in the organization. The number of discharges

Figure 15.17. Period data trend line: Survival rates for kidney cancer by stage for patients diagnosed from 2000–2008

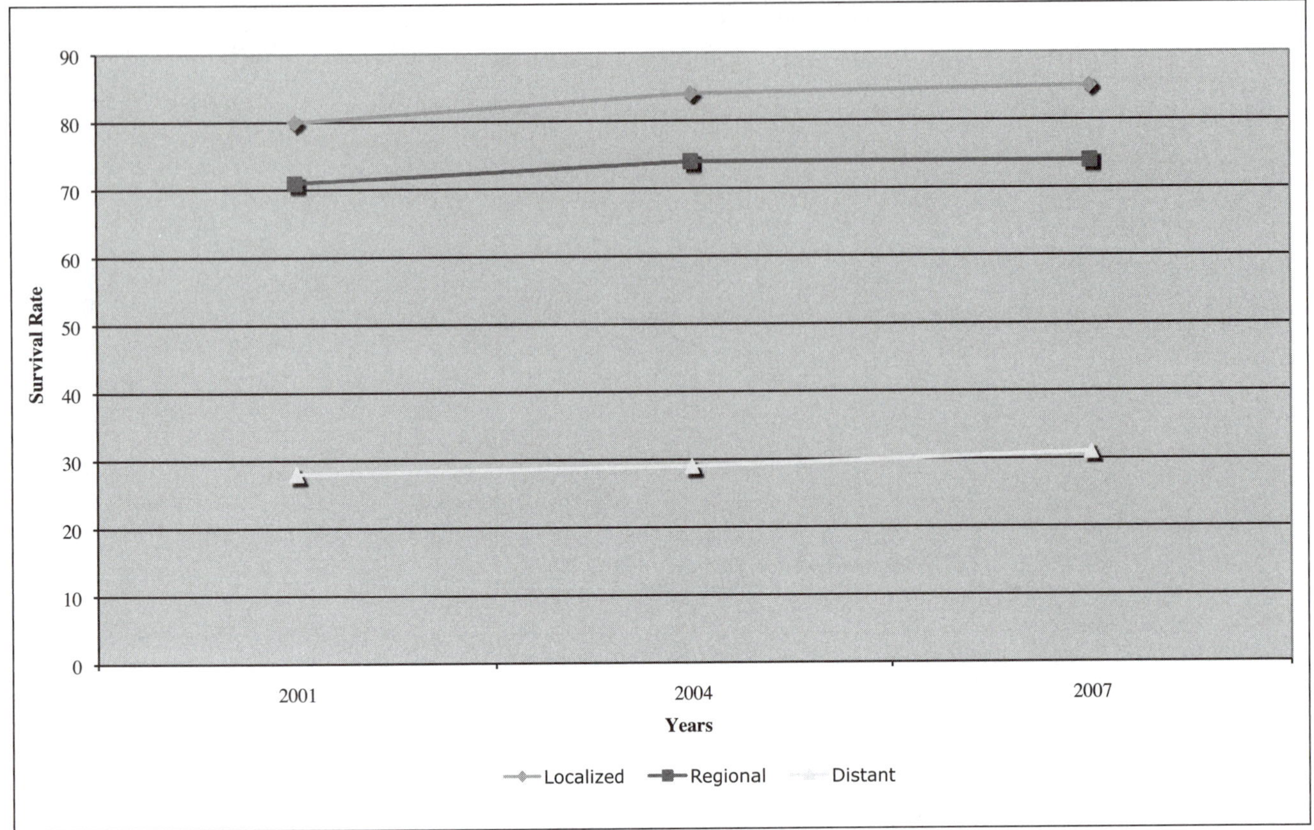

will be displayed on the *x*-axis, and average charges will be displayed on the *y*-axis. The size of the bubble indicates the percentage of total discharges for each MS-DRG. The data are displayed in table 15.21, and the corresponding bubble chart is displayed in figure 15.23. It can easily be seen that MS-DRG 795, Normal Newborn, has the highest proportion of overall discharges and the lowest average charges among the top-volume MS-DRGs.

Stem and Leaf Plots

In **stem and leaf plots,** data can be organized so that the shape of a frequency distribution is revealed. As an example, a stem and leaf plot will be constructed on the age of 12 patients discharged from MS-DRG 68, Nonspecific CVA and Precerebral Occlusion w/o Infarct w/o MCC. The ages are ranked in order from lowest to highest:

44 51 52 52 62 65 65 66 68 72 76 82

To develop the plot, break each number into two parts. The last number is called the leaf and the rest of the number is called the stem. Thus, for the number 51, 1 is the leaf and 5 is the stem, and for the number 125, 5 is the leaf and 12 is the stem. The data are then arranged in a table that looks somewhat like a T, with the stem portion in the first column and the leaf portion in the second column. For our data set, the stems are 4, 5, 6, 7 and 8. The leaf portion is then

Figure 15.18. Histogram, Community Hospital LOS of patients discharged from DRG 127, 20XX

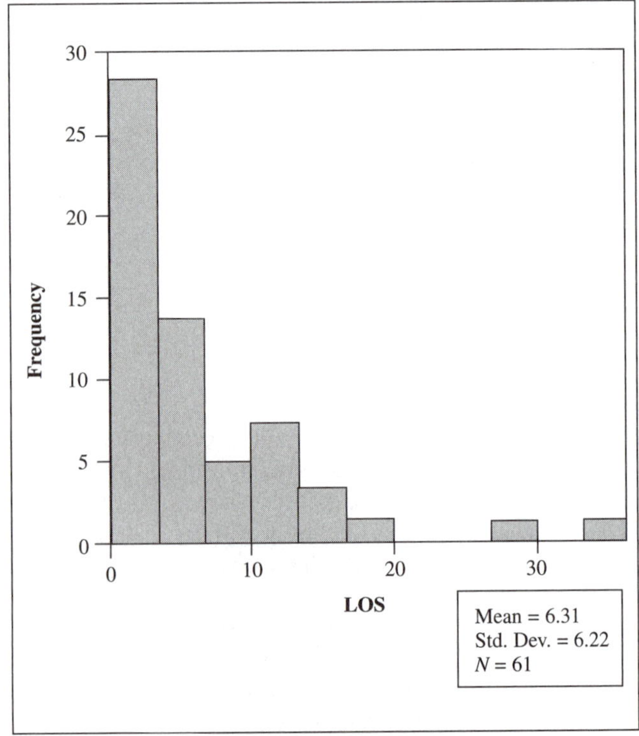

Figure 15.19. Frequency polygon, Community Hospital LOS of patients discharged from DRG 127, 20XX

filled in with the last digits that correspond to each stem as shown here:

Stem	Leaf
4	4
5	122
6	25568
7	26
8	2

The completed plot reveals the distribution of the data set. It can immediately be seen that the lowest value in the distribution is 44 and the highest is 82 and that there are five observations in the 60s age group. Turning the table on its side shows a fairly normal bell-shaped distribution.

			8		
L			8		
e			6		
a		2	5		
f		2	5	6	
	4	1	2	2	2
Stem	4	5	6	7	8

Boxplots

Boxplots are useful in summarizing a data set. In a boxplot, a single variable in two categories can be compared. The boxplot reveals the range, median, and the 25th and 75th percentiles for the distribution. To illustrate, patients discharged from MS-DRGs 66, Intracranial hemorrhage or cerebral infarction w/o CC/MCC, and 68, Nonspecific CVA & Precerebral Occlusion w/o Infarct w/o MCC, are compared with age as the variable.

The frequency distributions appear in figures 15.24 and 15.25. Twelve patients were discharged from MS-DRG 68 ranging in age from 44 to 82; 38 patients were discharged from MS-DRG 66 ranging in age from 22 to 86. The boxplot, shown in figure 15.26, displays these data side by side. Even though there are more discharges from MS-DRG 66 with a wider range in age, the median age for both MS-DRGs is similar, 62 and 65 respectively. The interquartile range (25th

Figure 15.20. Scatter chart, perfect positive relationship

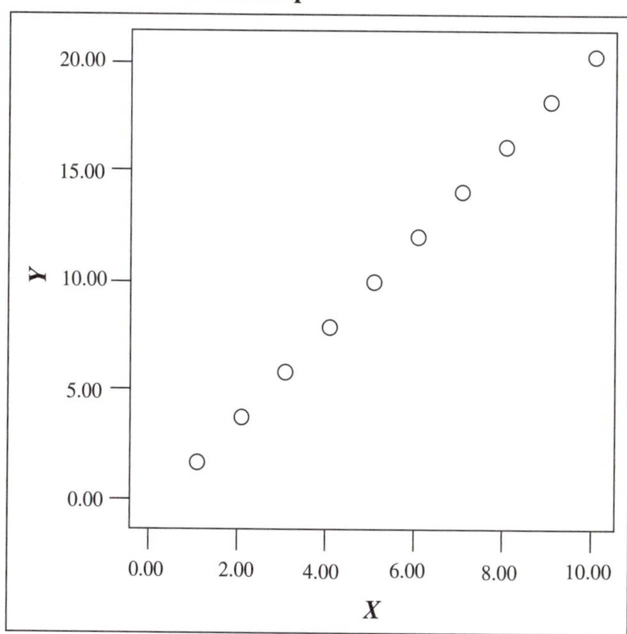

to 75th quartile) for both groups is age 52 to 72 for MS-DRG 66 and age 51 to 73 for MS-DRG 68.

Spreadsheets and Statistical Packages

Electronic spreadsheets, such as Microsoft Excel, and statistical packages, such as SPSS or SAS, can be used to facilitate the data collection and analysis processes. The advantage of using one of these tools is that charts and graphs can be formulated at the time the data are being analyzed. Instruction on the use of these tools is beyond the scope of this chapter; however, they are available on the market and readers are encouraged to learn how to use them.

Figure 15.21. Scatter chart, perfect negative relationship

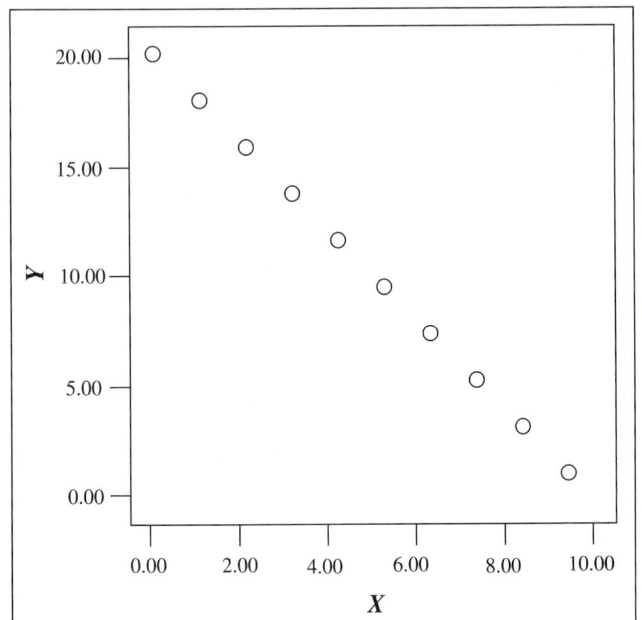

Figure 15.22. Scatter chart no relationship

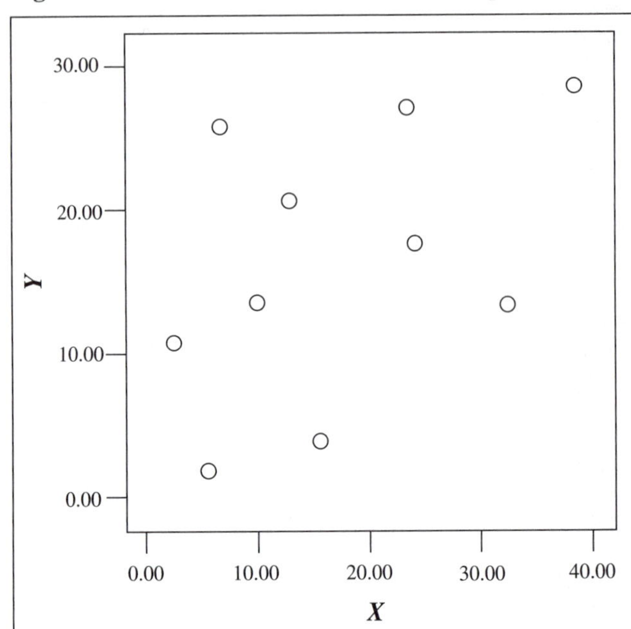

Table 15.21. Top five high-volume discharges, average charges, and percent of total discharges, Community Hospital, 20XX

MS-DRG	Number of Discharges	Average Charges	Percent of Total Discharges
795—Normal Newborn	637	$1,239	9.8%
946—Rehabilitation w/o CC/MCC	542	$21,517	8.4%
775—Vaginal Delivery w/o Complicating Diagnoses	505	$5,576	7.8%
293—Heart Failure and Shock w/o CC/MCC	287	$12,043	4.4%
766—Cesarean Section w/o CC/MCC	189	$7,626	2.9%

Figure 15.23. Bubble chart, top five high-volume discharges, average charges, and percent of total discharges, Community Hospital, 20XX

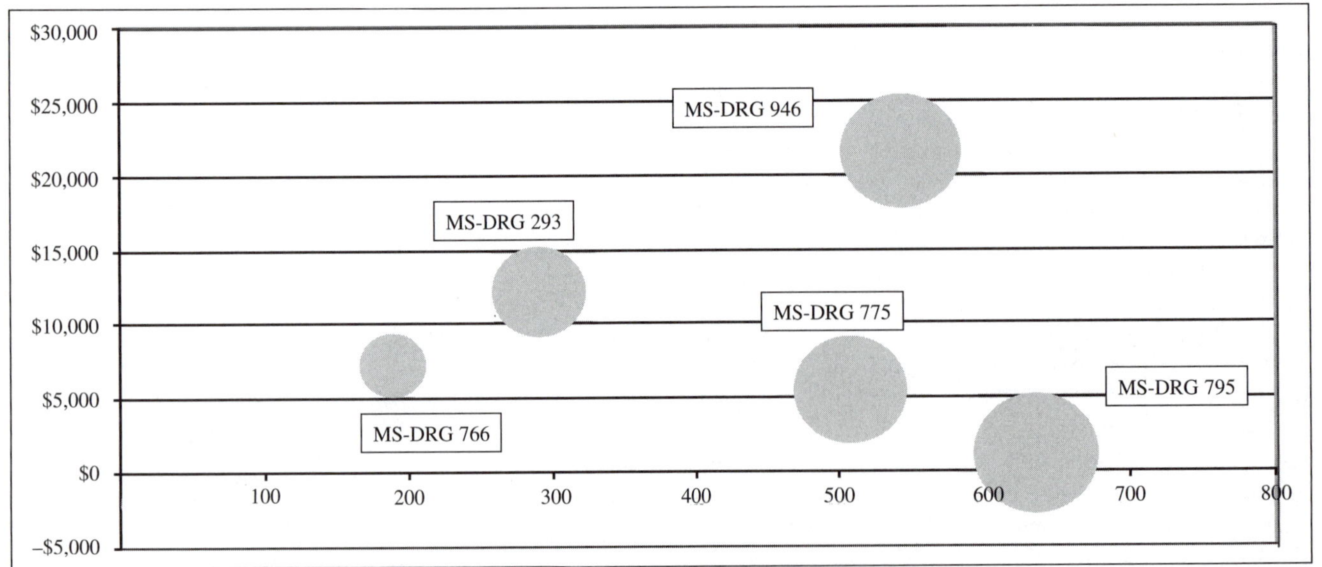

Check Your Understanding 15.11

Instructions: Complete the following sentences on a separate sheet of paper.

1. A presentation of data in rows and columns is a ___.
2. A graphic display technique used to display parts of a whole is a ___.
3. A graphic display technique used to show trends over time is a ___.
4. A graphic display technique used to display categories of a variable is a ___.
5. A graphic display technique that may be used to show the age distribution of a population is a ___.
6. A graphic technique that can visually compare the range of a variable between two categories is a ___.

Figure 15.24. Frequency distribution for age, MS-DRG 68 Nonspecific CVA and Precerebral Occlusion without Infarct without MCC

Age

N	Valid	12
	Missing	0
Median		65.00
Percentiles	25	52.00
	50	65.00
	75	71.00

Age

		Frequency	Percent	Valid Percent	Cumulative Percent
Valid	44	1	8.3	8.3	8.3
	51	1	8.3	8.3	16.7
	52	2	16.7	16.7	33.3
	62	1	8.3	8.3	41.7
	65	2	16.7	16.7	58.3
	66	1	8.3	8.3	66.7
	68	1	8.3	8.3	75.0
	72	1	8.3	8.3	83.3
	76	1	8.3	8.3	91.7
	82	1	8.3	8.3	100.0*
	Total	12	100.0*	100.0*	

*rounded

Figure 15.25. Frequency distribution for age, MS-DRG 66 Intracranial hemorrhage or cerebral infarction without CC/MCC

Statistics

Age

N	Valid	38
	Missing	0
Median		62.00
Percentiles	25	51.50
	50	62.00
	75	73.50

Age

		Frequency	Percent	Valid Percent	Cumulative Percent
Valid	22	1	2.6	2.6	2.6
	23	1	2.6	2.6	5.3
	26	1	2.6	2.6	7.9
	39	1	2.6	2.6	10.5
	44	1	2.6	2.6	13.2
	46	1	2.6	2.6	15.8
	47	1	2.6	2.6	18.4
	49	1	2.6	2.6	21.1
	50	1	2.6	2.6	23.7
	52	1	2.6	2.6	26.3
	55	1	2.6	2.6	28.9
	56	1	2.6	2.6	31.6
	57	3	7.9	7.9	39.5
	58	2	5.3	5.3	44.7
	60	2	5.3	5.3	50.0
	64	1	2.6	2.6	52.6
	68	2	5.3	5.3	57.9
	70	2	5.3	5.3	63.2
	71	2	5.3	5.3	68.4
	72	2	5.3	5.3	73.7
	73	1	2.6	2.6	76.3
	75	1	2.6	2.6	78.9
	76	1	2.6	2.6	81.6
	77	2	5.3	5.3	86.8
	78	1	2.6	2.6	89.5
	83	1	2.6	2.6	92.1
	84	1	2.6	2.6	94.7
	86	2	5.3	5.3	100.0*
	Total	38	100.0*	100.0*	

*rounded

Figure 15.26. Boxplot of age, DRGs 14 and 15

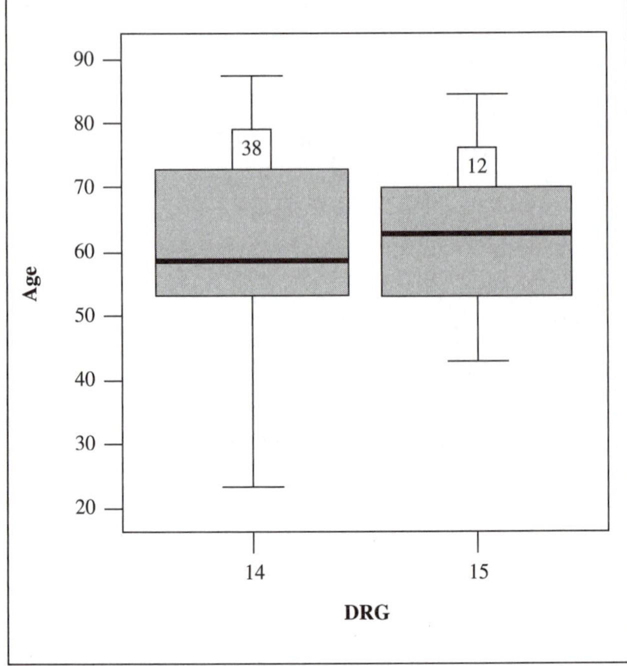

Descriptive Statistics

Measures of central tendency and measures of **variability** are used to describe frequency distributions. Measures of central tendency are measures of location; they indicate the typical value of a frequency distribution. Variation emphasizes differences and scattering around the typical value of a data set. Inferences about populations from samples are based on the variation of the observations in the data set.

Descriptive measures are computed from both populations and samples. A population is a group of persons or objects about which an investigator wants to draw a conclusion. A sample is a subset of a population. Measures that result from a compilation of data from populations are called parameters. Measures that result from samples are called statistics. For example, if an organization is interested in the average age of undergraduates enrolled at City University, all registered undergraduates would be the defined population. If the average age of the entire population of undergraduate students is calculated, the resultant average is a population parameter. However, if a sample is drawn from the registered undergraduate students and the average age is calculated, the resultant average is a sample statistic.

A variety of **descriptive statistics** are available to help a researcher summarize data for a variable in a frequency distribution. The choice of which descriptive statistics to use is determined, for the most part, by a variable's scale of measurement. Later, the shape of a variable's frequency distribution will be identified as another relevant factor.

Measures of Central Tendency—The Center of a Variable's Values

Measures of central tendency and variability also can be used to describe populations. Measures of central tendency discussed in this subsection are the mean, median, and mode. There are three measures of the center of a distribution of values. The most appropriate center to use can often be determined on the basis of the scale of measurement of the variable considered. Modes are used for nominal-level variables; medians for ordinal-level variables; and means are used for interval and ratio-level variables.

A frequency distribution shows the values that a variable can take and the number of observations associated with each value. For example, using LOS as the variable, five patients were discharged with the following lengths of stay:

Patient	LOS
1	2 days
2	3 days
3	4 days
4	2 days
5	3 days

The data displayed in the table above are referred to as a frequency distribution. A frequency distribution displays the number of times a particular observation occurs for the variable being measured. In this example, the number of times a certain LOS occurs is the variable of interest. The frequency distribution for LOS, in ascending order, is 2, 2, 3, 3, and 4 days.

Frequency distributions may be constructed for both discrete and continuous data. As an example, Community Hospital wants to construct a frequency distribution showing the LOS of patients who were discharged on May 10. LOS is a continuous variable falling on the ratio scale of measurement. The hospital wants to see how many of these patients were in the hospital for a particular LOS (for example, four days). The variable is the LOS, and the frequency is the number of times a particular LOS occurred among the patients discharged on May 10.

To construct the frequency distribution, list all the values that the particular LOS can take, from the lowest observed value to the highest. Then enter the number of times a discharged patient had that particular LOS. Table 15.22 shows a frequency distribution for LOS on May 10. Notice that the frequency distribution lists all the values for LOS between the lowest and the highest, even when there are no observations for some of the values. For example, there are no observations of patients spending three days in the hospital. Six patients have LOS of four days. The data in table 15.22 can be used to calculate measures of both central tendency and variability.

Mean

The **mean** is the arithmetic average of a frequency distribution. To calculate a mean, the data must fall on the interval or ratio scales of measurement. The mean is the sum of all scores in a frequency distribution divided by the number of scores. The symbol for the mean is X_i (pronounced x-bar).

Table 15.22. Calculation of the variance, LOS data

LOS	LOS − Mean (5.8) $(X - \bar{X})$	(LOS − Mean)² $(X - \bar{X})^2$
1	−4.8	23.04
1	−4.8	23.04
2	−3.8	14.44
2	−3.8	14.44
4	−1.8	3.24
4	−1.8	3.24
4	−1.8	3.24
4	−1.8	3.24
4	−1.8	3.24
4	−1.8	3.24
5	−0.8	0.64
5	−0.8	0.64
5	−0.8	0.64
5	−0.8	0.64
5	−0.8	0.64
5	−0.8	0.64
6	0.2	0.04
6	0.2	0.04
6	0.2	0.04
6	0.2	0.04
6	0.2	0.04
6	0.2	0.04
6	0.2	0.04
6	0.2	0.04
6	0.2	0.04
6	0.2	0.04
6	0.2	0.04
7	1.2	1.44
7	1.2	1.44
7	1.2	1.44
7	1.2	1.44
7	1.2	1.44
7	1.2	1.44
8	2.2	4.84
8	2.2	4.84
8	2.2	4.84
8	2.2	4.84
8	2.2	4.84
9	3.2	10.24
9	3.2	10.24
9	3.2	10.24
10	4.2	17.64
Total	0*	179.88

*rounded

$$s^2 = \sum_i^n (X_i - \bar{X})^2 / N - 1$$
$$= 179.88/41$$
$$= 4.39$$

The formula for calculating the mean in a frequency distribution is:

$$\bar{X} = \sum_i^n X_i / N$$

where Σ is summation, X_i is each successive observation from the first one in the frequency distribution, $i = 1$, to the last observation (n), and N is the total number of observations.

To calculate the ALOS for the data in table 15.22, substitute the appropriate figures into the following formula:

$$\bar{X} = \sum_i^n X_i / N$$

$$\bar{X} = \frac{1+1+2+2+4+4+4+4+4+4+5+5+5+5+5+5+6+6+6+6+6+6+6+6+6+6+6+7+7+7+7+7+7+8+8+8+8+8+9+9+9+10}{42}$$

$$\bar{X} = 245/42$$

$$\bar{X} = 5.8$$

The ALOS for patients discharged from Community Hospital on May 10 is 5.8 days (rounded).

Two disadvantages are associated with using the mean as the most typical value in a frequency distribution. First, in this example, the LOS for the 42 patients are integers (whole numbers). However, the ALOS is fractional (5.8), even though there is no fractional LOS. Fractional values are considered more a problem of interpretation than a result that is not meaningful. In this case, the ALOS is interpreted as, "On average, the ALOS for the patients discharged from the Community Hospital on May 10 is between 5 and 6 days."

Second, the mean is sensitive to extreme measures. That is, it is strongly influenced by outliers. For example, if the 10-day LOS were actually a 25-day LOS, the ALOS would increase to 6.2 days.

Thus, the average or arithmetic mean may not always be the most appropriate way to summarize the most typical value of a frequency distribution. The measure of central tendency selected to describe the typical value of a frequency distribution should be based on the characteristics of that particular frequency distribution.

Median

The **median** is the midpoint of a frequency distribution and falls in the ordinal scale of measurement. It is the point at which 50 percent of the observations fall above and 50 percent fall below. If an odd number of observations is in the frequency distribution, the median is the middle number. In the following frequency distribution, the median is 13. Three observations fall above the value of 13, and three fall below it:

10 11 12 **13** 14 15 16

If an even number of observations is in the frequency distribution, the median is the midpoint between the two middle observations. It is found by averaging the two middle scores ($[x + y]/2$). In the following example, the median is 13.5 ([13 + 14]/2):

10 11 12 **13** **14** 15 16 17

If the two middle observations take on the same value, the median is that value. When determining the median, it does not matter whether there are duplicate observations in the frequency distribution. Consider the following frequency distribution:

10 11 11 12 **13** **13** 14 15 16 17

In this frequency distribution, the median falls between the fifth and sixth observations. Therefore, the median is 13 ([13 + 13]/2).

Table 15.22 records LOS data for 42 patients. In this example, the median falls between the 21st and 22nd observations. Placed in order from lowest to highest, the distribution is as follows:

1 1 2 2 4 4 4 4 4 4 4 5 5 5 5 5 5 5 6 6 6 6 6 **6**
6 6 6 6 6 7 7 7 7 7 7 7 8 8 8 8 8 9 9 9 10

The median is 6 ([6 + 6]/2).

The median offers the following three advantages:

- Relatively easy to calculate
- Based on the whole distribution and not just a portion of it, as is the case with the mode
- Unlike the mean, it is not influenced by extreme values or unusual outliers in the frequency distribution

Mode

The **mode** is the simplest measure of central tendency. It is used to indicate the most frequent observation in a frequency distribution. The mode offers several advantages, including:

- Easy to obtain and interpret
- Not sensitive to extreme observations in the frequency distribution
- Is easy to communicate and explain to others
- Can be used with nominal-level data

However, there are also disadvantages, including:

- It may not be descriptive of the distribution when the most frequent observation does not occur very often, especially when the number of observations is large.
- It may not be unique. That is, more than one mode may be in a distribution. A frequency distribution may be unimodal, bimodal, or multimodal. When each observation occurs an equal number of times, the distribution does not have a mode.
- It does not provide information about the entire distribution, only the observation that occurs most frequently.

In table 15.22, the mode is 6 because 11 patients had lengths of stay of 6 days. To summarize, for the LOS data in table 15.22, the measures of central tendency are similar. The mean is 5.8 days, the median is 6 days, and the mode is 6 days. These statistics are summarized in table 15.23.

Table 15.23. Descriptive statistics for LOS data

N	Valid	42
	Missing	0
Mean		5.8333
Median		6.0000
Mode		6.00
Standard deviation		2.09432
Variance		4.386
Range		9.00
Minimum		1.00
Maximum		10.00

Measures of Variability—Spread of a Variable's Values

In addition to measures of central tendency, the hospital can use measures of variability to describe frequency distributions. These measures indicate how widely the observations are spread out around the measures of central tendency. The measures of spread increase with greater variation in the frequency distribution. The spread is equal to zero when there is no variation. The spread of a nominal-level's variable can only be depicted by frequency data. Ordinal-level data may also be displayed as frequencies, but sometimes it may help to calculate a range. Standard deviations and their squared values are used to represent interval and ratio-level data so long as such data are normally distributed; otherwise ranges are used for these kinds of data as well. This subsection discusses the following measures of spread: the range, the variance, and the standard deviation.

Range

The **range** is the simplest measure of spread. It is the difference between the smallest and largest values in a frequency distribution:

$$\text{Range} = X_{\max} - X_{\min}$$

The range for the LOS data in table 15.23 is 9 (10 – 1 = 9).

One disadvantage of the range is that it can be affected by extreme values, or outliers, in the distribution. Also, the range varies widely from sample to sample. Only the two most extreme observations affect its value, so it is not sensitive to other observations in the distribution.

Two frequency distributions may have the same range but differ greatly in variation. For example, the range for the following frequency distributions is 9 (10 – 1 = 9):

Distribution 1: 1 2 3 4 5 6 7 8 9 10

Distribution 2: 1 1.5 3 3.5 3.7 7 8 8.26 10 10

However, when the two distributions are compared, the second distribution has more variation than the first distribution. This is demonstrated when the variance is calculated. The variance for the first distribution is 9.1, and the variance for the second distribution is 11.8.

Variance

The **variance** of a frequency distribution is the average of the squared deviations from the mean. The variance of a sample is symbolized by s^2. The variance of a distribution is larger when the observations are widely spread. The formula for calculating the variance is:

$$s^2 = \frac{\sum (X - \overline{X})^2}{N - 1}$$

The squared deviations of the mean are calculated by subtracting the mean of the frequency distribution from each value in the distribution. The difference between the two values is squared, $(X - \overline{X})^2$. The squared differences are summed and divided by $N - 1$. The calculations for the variance for the LOS data are shown in table 15.23.

In the calculations for the variance, the sum of $(X - \overline{X})$ is equal to zero. This is because the mean is the balance point in the distribution. When a value is less than the mean, the difference is negative (1 – 5.8 = –4.8); when the value is greater than the mean, the difference is positive (6 – 5.8 = 0.2). Therefore, the sum of the differences from the mean is equal to zero. In this example, the sum approximates zero because the actual mean of 5.8333 was rounded to 5.8 for ease in calculation.

The concept of variance is meaningful in more advanced procedures, but in the case of describing the distribution of a single variable, the standard deviation is preferred.

Standard Deviation

The variance for the LOS data in table 15.23 is 4.39, but what does this mean? The interpretation of the variance is not meaningful at the descriptive level because the original units of measure—the lengths of stay—are squared to arrive at the variance. By calculating the square root of the variance, the data are returned to the original units of measurement. This is called the **standard deviation**, which is symbolized by s. The formula for the standard deviation is:

$$s = \sqrt{\frac{\sum (X - \overline{X})}{N - 1}}$$

The standard deviation for the LOS data is 2.1.

The standard deviation is the most widely used measure of variability in descriptive statistics. Because it is easy to interpret, it is the preferred measure of dispersion for frequency distributions. Most handheld calculators include features for calculating the variance and the standard deviation.

The measures of central tendency and variation may be calculated using a handheld calculator. Also, statistical packages such as SPSS are available for performing these and other descriptive and **inferential statistics.** The histograms were prepared using SPSS. The SPSS output for the LOS data appears in table 15.23. The slight differences between the handheld calculator results and the SPSS results in the mean, variance, and standard deviation are because of rounding.

Check Your Understanding 15.12

Instructions: Fifteen infants were born at Community Hospital during the week of December 1. Using a handheld calculator, determine the measures of central tendency and variability for the following infant birth weights (in grams):

2,450	2,750	2,600
2,540	2,815	2,540
2,300	1,735	1,720
2,715	1,800	2,780
2,400	2,485	2,640

1. ___ Mean
2. ___ Median
3. ___ Mode
4. ___ Range
5. ___ Variance
6. ___ Standard deviation

Normal Distribution

The **normal distribution** is actually a theoretical family of distributions that may have any mean or any standard deviation. It is bell-shaped and symmetrical about the mean. Because it is symmetrical, 50 percent of the observations fall above the mean and 50 percent fall below it. In a normal distribution, the mean, median, and mode are equal. The values of the normal distribution range from minus infinity ($-\infty$) to plus infinity ($+\infty$).

In the normal distribution, the standard deviation indicates how many observations fall within a certain range of the mean. The areas under the curve corresponding to one, two, and three standard deviations are 68.3 percent, 95.4 percent, and 99.7 percent.

Figure 15.27 shows an example of a normal distribution superimposed on a histogram. The center of the distribution, or mean, is 6. (The median and the mode also are 6.) The standard deviation is 2.45. This means that 68 percent of the observations in the frequency distribution fall within 2.45 standard deviations of 6 (6 ± 2.45). Thus, 68 percent fall between 3.55 and 8.45; 95 percent fall between 1.1 and 10.9; and 99.7 percent fall between 21.35 and 13.35.

As shown in figure 15.27, a characteristic of the normal distribution is that each tail of the curve approaches the x-axis but never touches it, no matter how far from center the line it is.

A histogram of the frequency distribution for the LOS data in table 15.23 is shown in figure 15.28. The distribution is more peaked than the normal distribution and so is considered kurtotic. *Kurtosis* is the vertical stretching of a distribution.

A skewed distribution is asymmetrical. Skewness is the horizontal stretching of a frequency distribution to one side or the other so that one tail is longer than the other. The longer tail has more observations. Because the mean is sensitive to extreme observations, it moves in the direction of the long

Figure 15.27. Histogram of normal distribution

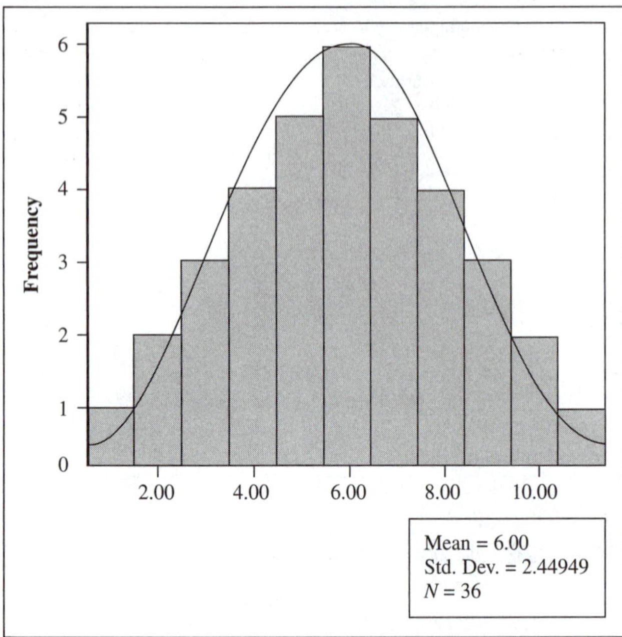

Figure 15.28. Histogram of LOS with superimposed normal curve

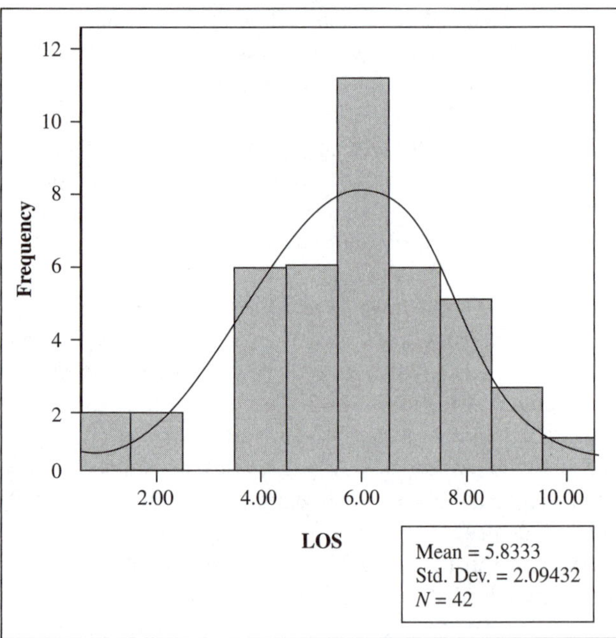

tail when a distribution is skewed. When the direction of the tail is off to the right, the distribution is positively skewed, or skewed to the right. When the direction of the tail is off to the left, the distribution is negatively skewed, or skewed to the left. When the mean and the median approximate one another (as with the LOS data), the distribution is not significantly skewed. A perfect normal distribution has a zero skew. If an interval or ratio-level distribution is skewed, the median may be more appropriate than the mean in representing the center of such a distribution.

Check Your Understanding 15.13

Instructions: Answer the following questions on a separate piece of paper.

1. What are the characteristics of a normal distribution?
2. What is the definition of the term *skewness*?

Real-World Case

The quality improvement committee of Community Hospital wanted to study MS-DRG 689 kidney and urinary tract infections w MCC, because of wide variations in LOS and total charges. The committee asked the HIM director to prepare a profile of patients discharged from MS-DRG 320. A summary of the patients discharged from MS-DRG 320 at Community Hospital was prepared using information found in the hospital's online database.

Summary

The nominal, ordinal, interval and ratio scales of measurement are discussed in this chapter. In nominal measure, names are given to objects or categories. Nominal data's measure of central tendency is the mode. Examples of nominal data include gender, marital status, health insurance type, race, and place of residence. In ordinal data the numbers given to categories represent rank order. The central tendency of ordinal data can be represented by its mode or its median. Examples of ordinal data include patient health status (that is, critical, stable, good) or opinion scales (strongly agree to strongly disagree). The most important characteristic of interval-level data is that the intervals between successive values are equal. Examples include temperature or years. The central tendency of a variable measured at the interval level can be represented by its modes, median, or mean. Ratio-level data is the highest level of measurement. On the ratio scale there is a defined unit of measure, a real zero point, and the intervals between successive values are equal.

Rates, ratios, proportions, and statistics are commonly used to describe community and hospital populations. They are considered to be descriptive statistics because they portray the characteristics of a group or population. Public health officials use community-based rates, ratios, and proportions to evaluate the general health status of a community. Morbidity and mortality rates are used as indicators of the accessibility and availability of healthcare services in a community.

Hospital-based rates are used for a variety of purposes. First, they describe the general characteristics of the patients treated at the facility. Hospital administrators use the data to monitor the volume of patients treated monthly, weekly, or within some other specified time frame. The statistics give healthcare decision makers the information they need to plan facilities and to monitor inpatient and outpatient revenue streams.

Graphic techniques are often used to summarize and clarify data. Data may be displayed in a variety of ways, for example, as charts, graphs, and tables. Graphic forms are effective ways to present large quantities of information.

The health information management professional is in a position to serve as a data broker for the healthcare organization. To do this, he or she must fully understand the clinical data that are collected and their application to the decision-making process. In addition, he or she must know what information is needed and how to provide it in a timely manner. With this knowledge, the HIM professional can become an invaluable member of the healthcare team.

References

Agency for Healthcare Research and Quality. 2010. AHRQ Profile: Quality research for quality healthcare. AHRQ publication no. 00-P005. Rockville, MD: AHRQ. http://ahrq.gov/about/profile.htm.

Agency for Health Care Policy and Research. 2000. HCUPnet: Healthcare cost and utilization project. Rockville, MD: AHRQ. http://hcup.ahrq.gov/HCUPnet.asp.

Centers for Disease Control and Prevention. 2005a. CDC Wonder Data Base. http://wonder.cdc.gov.

Centers for Disease Control and Prevention. 2005b. Division of Public Health Surveillance and Informatics. Nationally notifiable infectious diseases. United States, 20085. http://cdc.gov/ncphi/disss/nndss/phs/infdis2008.htmcdc.gov/epo/dphsi/phs/infdis2005.htm.

Department of Health and Human Services, Public Health Service. 1994. *Self-Instructional Manual for Cancer Registries, Book 7: Statistics and Epidemiology for Cancer Registries.* NIH Publication No. 94-3766. Washington, D.C.: HHS. http://seer.cancer.gov/training/manuals/Book7.pdf.

Ellerbruch, L. 2005. Department of Mathematics/Computer Science. Northern Michigan University, CS255 Computers in Elementary Education. Stem-and-Leaf Plot. http://ellerbruch.nmu.edu/cs255/jnord/stemplot.html.

Horton, L.A. 2007. *Calculating and Reporting Healthcare Statistics.* 2nd ed. Chicago: AHIMA.

Microsoft Corporation. 2005. Creating a Bubble Chart. http://office.microsoft.com/en-us/assistance/HA011170761033.aspx.

National Center for Health Statistics. 2008. Centers for Disease Control and Prevention. http://cdc.gov/nchs.

National Vital Statistics System. 2007. Centers for Disease Control and Prevention. http://cdc.gov/nchs/nvss.htm.

Osborn, C.E. 2005. *Statistical Applications for Health Information Management.* Sudbury, MA: Jones and Bartlett.

Chapter 16
Research Methods

Elizabeth Layman, PhD, RHIA, CCS, FAHIMA

Learning Objectives

- Describe basic research designs and methods used in the practice of health information management
- Formulate research problems in terms of research questions
- Search knowledge bases such as bibliographic databases
- Plan research projects appropriate to the research questions
- Conduct research projects using standard and suitable tools and techniques
- Present research findings in formats consistent with the purpose of the research
- Critically evaluate research studies in health-related fields

Key Terms

Abstract
Alternative hypothesis
Applied research
Basic research
Bivariate
Case study
Case-control (retrospective) study
Categorical data
Causal relationship
Causal-comparative research
Census survey
Cluster sampling
Common Rule
Confounding (extraneous, secondary) variable
Construct validity
Content analysis
Content validity
Continuous data
Control group
Convenience sampling
Correlational research
Cross-sectional
Data cleansing
Data mining
Deductive reasoning
Dependent variable
Descriptive research
Descriptive statistics
Discrete data
Double-blind study
Empiricism
Ethnography
Evaluation research
Experimental (study) group
Experimental research
External validity
Focus group
Focused studies
Generalizability
Grounded theory
Heterogeneity
Historical research
Hypothesis
Imputation
Independent variable
Inductive reasoning
Inferential statistics
Institutional review board (IRB)
Instrument
Internal validity
Interrater reliability
Interval data
Intervention
Interview guide
Interview survey
Intrarater reliability
Level of significance
Likert scale
Literature review
Longitudinal
Meta-analysis
Metric
Missing values
Mixed methods research
Model
Mortality (attrition)
Multivariate
Naturalism
Naturalistic observation
Negative (inverse) relationship
Nominal data
Nonparametric (distribution-free) technique
Nonparticipant observation
Nonrandom sampling
Null hypothesis
Observational research
One-tailed hypothesis
Operationalize
Ordinal data
Paradigm
Parametric technique
Parsimony
Participant observation
Peer review
Peer-reviewed (refereed) journal
Pilot study
Placebo
Positive (direct) relationship
Positivism
Power
Primary analysis
Primary source
Prospective
Protocol
Purposive sampling
Qualitative approach
Quantitative approach
Questionnaire survey
Random sampling
Randomization
Randomized clinical trial (RCT)
Ratio data
Reliability
Research
Research frame
Research method
Research methodology
Retrospective
Sample
Sample size
Sample size calculation
Sample survey
Scale
Scientific inquiry
Secondary analysis
Secondary source
Semantic differential scale
Semistructured question
Simple random sampling
Simulation observation
Stratified random sampling
Structured (close-ended) question
Survey
Systematic literature review
Systematic sampling
Target population
Test statistics
Theory
Treatment
Triangulation
Two-tailed hypothesis
Type I error
Type II error
Univariate
Unstructured (open-ended) question
Validity
Variable

Health information management (HIM) is an intersection of many different fields of study. Health information managers are business people in a health-related profession. Thus, health information managers draw on theories from the many fields associated with both business and healthcare, including management, organizational behavior, sociology, psychology, medical sciences, computer science, and decision support. In this chapter, **research** concepts are applied to healthcare settings and the role of the HIM professional as a researcher is explored.

The purpose of research is to create generalizable knowledge. Research answers questions and provides solutions to everyday problems. Research is not some vague, mysterious activity for geniuses, as some people believe; rather, it is a step-by-step method that ordinary people can use to collect reliable and accurate facts in order to generate valuable information.

Research into medicine and healthcare has greatly enhanced the quality and length of people's lives. For example, antibiotics, endoscopic surgery, and the Medicare inpatient prospective payment system, among many others, all are the result of research. Moreover, continued advances in effective treatments and efficient methods of healthcare delivery depend on future research.

HIM professionals are contributors to research studies. (See table 16.1.) They are experts on health data; the data's location, accuracy, and format; and other aspects of HIM practice. Their training and education provide specific research skills; and their professional values are supportive of research.

Knowledge of research also supports HIM practice. Understanding **research methods** aids HIM professionals whenever they use data or information to answer a question or to make a decision.

This chapter provides an overview of the role of research in HIM and healthcare and the development of theories and models. It also presents a step-by-step process for conducting research. Finally, the chapter addresses how HIM professionals can use the techniques of research to improve HIM practice and data quality.

Research in Medicine and Healthcare

The history of research in medicine and healthcare parallels the history of civilization. The use of the data in health records also follows the history of civilization.

History

The tradition of proposing rational explanations for the causes of disease dates back to 3500 B.C. The Egyptians recorded symptoms and cures for illnesses, and the Greeks continued the tradition. Indeed, Hippocrates, practicing medicine in about 400 B.C., wrote more than 50 books on health and disease. Similar advances occurred in India and China. Scientists and philosophers continued advances in medicine and health throughout the Middle Ages and the Renaissance.

In the United States, research in medicine and healthcare and interest in the research university evolved together. The present form of the research university emerged in the 1860s (Rudolph 1990, 332–334). Yale awarded the first doctoral degrees in the United States in 1861 (Rudolph 1990, 335). Cornell University was chartered in 1865; Johns Hopkins University was founded in 1867. In the 1890s, national learned societies and journals were established (Jencks and Riesman 1977, 14). The structuring of departments (such as biology, philosophy, and history) within the university was also established in the 1890s. By 1914, the two dozen leading U.S. universities had been established (Jencks and Riesman 1977, 13).

During the early 1900s, Flexner investigated the quality of medical education and recommended that many substandard medical schools be closed (1910, 16). He also described the ideal organization of medical education. Flexner recommended that medical schools be located in leading universities with associated hospitals and identified outstanding examples such as the Johns Hopkins University and the University of Michigan (1910, 47, 106–107). Today's academic health center was born from the union of medical schools, hospitals, and research universities.

Academic health centers became especially important after the federal government increased its funding for research in the 1950s. These federal research grants became important sources of revenue for universities. As conduits for federal funding, academic health centers became increasingly prominent in their universities. One major source of federal funding for medical research is the National Institutes of Health (NIH). Today, the NIH supports 50,000 grants totaling $28 billion related to medical research (NIH 2007). Thus, research, as means to raise funds, became an integral part of the academic enterprise. (See chapter 18 for a discussion of clinical (medical) research, including clinical trials.)

Health Record Data in Research

With the development of writing, ancient physicians and scribes could record diseases and their treatments. For example, as early as 3000 B.C., scribes recorded on papyrus the medical and surgical treatments of Egyptian physicians (Haas 1999, 578). (See figure 16.1.) In the Ebers papyrus, the treatment of urinary retention and excessive urination with myrrh and other herbs is recorded (Nickel 2005, 21). The Edwin Smith papyrus is a surgical textbook describing 48 surgical cases (Feldman and Goodrich 1999, 282).

More recently, health records became an integral part of the hospital standardization program of the American College of Surgeons (ACS). In 1918, the ACS began to evaluate the quality of care that a hospital provided by evaluating its health records. Since then, researchers have used health

Table 16.1. HIM contributions to research teams

HIM-Specific Skills	Research-Specific Skills	HIM Values
Knowledge of health record content Form and view design Expertise in classifications and nomenclatures Database query skills Professional collegiality	Ability to conduct literature reviews Knowledge of research protocols Capability to devise case-based algorithms Understanding of procedures of institutional review boards Knowledge of data collection protocols Written and oral communication of data, information, and knowledge	Accuracy Attention to detail Respect for patient rights and confidentiality Commitment to protecting health data privacy and security

Figure 16.1. Sample of Egyptian surgical treatment

Examination
If thou examinest a man having a gaping wound in his head, penetrating to the bone, smashing his skull, and rending open the brain of his skull, thou shouldst palpate his wound.

Diagnosis
Thou shouldst say concerning him: "An ailment not to be treated."

Treatment
Thou shouldst anoint that wound with grease. Thou shalt not bind it; thou shalt not apply two strips upon it: until thou knowest that he has reached a decisive point.

Source: Feldman and Goodrich 1999, 282.

records as a way to both log data during research and access existing data for their research.

Recently published studies demonstrate the use of health records in research. These studies used both paper-based and electronic health records (EHRs) and were conducted in athletic departments as well as hospital outpatient and emergency departments.

Bolin and Goforth described how team physicians and athletic trainers documented the sideline care of athletes (2005, 405). They surveyed the 11 member schools of the Atlantic Coast Conference on the evaluation of injuries, dispensation of medications, availability of health records, and means and timing of documentation. Of the 11 schools, 5 had EHRs, 6 briefly documented on the sideline during football games and then composed a full note after the game, and all 11 had access to the athletes' key medical data (allergies) on the sideline (406). The researchers recommended two ways to manage clinical information on the sideline: laminated cards and EHRs on hand-held computers (409).

Researchers investigated the feasibility of using a generic, structured data entry application in a hospital outpatient pediatric clinic (Roukema et al. 2006, 15). They had four pediatricians enter data for eight new patients into both the traditional paper record and the electronic health record. Only 44 percent of patient data was identical in the paper and electronic health records with the patient history lacking more data than the physical examination. The researchers speculated that, because of the narrative nature of patient histories, writing in the paper record was easier than navigating the electronic application (19). Another researcher also investigated the capture of clinical information in paper-based records and EHRs for emergency department care (Silfen 2006). However, in this study, the documentation systems were at two different community hospitals. The researcher evaluated the documentation systems' respective abilities to capture accurate data that could be subsequently coded to the American Medical Association's evaluation and management codes. There was no statistically significant difference in the accuracy rates of the two documentation systems (665). The researchers for both studies concluded that electronic capture of health data was feasible.

Although retrospective review of health records is a common method of research in healthcare, problems with this method have been identified. Researchers found that key data were not documented. For example, health information researchers found that data such as occupation, menopausal status, estrogen receptor and progesterone receptor values, and other items were not always documented in the health record or cancer registry abstract for African American women diagnosed with breast cancer (Watzlaf et al. 1996, 30–31). Other researchers also found that health records were incomplete (Berner et al. 2005, 43). The decision algorithms of clinical decision support systems (CDSSs) depend upon the data provided by health records. These researchers specifically examined the support system's recommendations for therapy in gastrointestinal bleeding. The absence of key data "resulted in inappropriate and unsafe recommendations" in almost 77 percent of encounters (Berner et al. 2005, 43). The researchers concluded that missing data can affect the accuracy of clinical decision support systems that were designed to reduce medication errors. Thus, there are obstacles in the use of health records as a primary data source in research.

Despite the problems identified, however, thousands of studies have followed methods similar to these studies. They demonstrate the importance of health record data in research and their potential for improving the quality of patient care.

Research Frame

A **research frame** is the overarching structure of the research project. Another term for the research frame is **paradigm**. A research frame comprises the theory or theories underpinning the study, the models illustrating the factors and relationships of the study, the assumptions of the field and the researcher, the methods, and the analytical tools. Research is conducted within frames.

Theories

A **theory** is the systematic organization of knowledge that predicts or explains behavior or events. Theories and research have a chicken-and-egg relationship. Theories are both the result and the foundation of research. Researchers begin with informed predictions or raw theories of what they believe will happen. As they collect observations and data, they refine their theories. Over time, the refined theories become more predictive of subsequent events than their previous embryonic versions.

Theories help people understand their world. Without theories, people are merely speculating. Although speculation may be informed by experiences and some facts, it is nevertheless speculation.

Apparent in all fields of study, theories explain what people have observed. In addition, they provide definitions, relationships, and boundaries. In other words, theories systematically organize everything people know about a concept. Formally defined, theories are:

- Concepts that are abstract ideas generalized from particular instances
- Interrelationships that are assumed to exist among these concepts
- Consequences that are assumed to follow logically from the relationships proposed in the theory (Amatayakul and Shah 1992, 8)

The best theories simplify the situation, explain the most facts in the broadest range of circumstances, and most accurately predict behavior (Singleton and Straits 2005, 20). Researchers in health information management use several different theories (see figure 16.2).

Overall, research theories are practical and efficient because they help researchers explain and predict many events in simple and precise terms. In other words, theories organize knowledge. When knowledge is organized, ordinary people can access and use it. Thus, everyone benefits.

Models

A **model** is a representation of a theory in visual format. Models can portray theories with objects, can be smaller-scaled versions, or can be graphic representations. A model includes all of a theory's known properties. AHIMA, for example, has a theory about what defines data quality. Experts at AHIMA have identified collection, analysis, application, and warehousing as the functions of data quality management and hypothesize that data quality will result if practitioners follow proper procedures within these activities. (See figure 16.3 for a model of the AHIMA theory.)

Research Methodology

Research methodology is the study and analysis of research methods and theories. Generally, there are two types of research: basic research and applied research. These two types are ends of a continuum, not separate entities. Therefore, the distinction between them is sometimes unclear. In essence, **basic research** focuses on the development of theories and their refinement whereas **applied research** focuses on the implementation of the theories in practice. For example, as applied researchers, some HIM professionals study questions they believe will improve health information practices in the continuum of care. Another way to differentiate basic and applied research is that basic research answers the question "why" and applied research answers the questions "what" and "how" (Gay et al. 2006, 6).

Figure 16.2. Theories used in health informatics and HIM research

- Adult learning theories
- Behavioral theories
- Change theories
- Diffusion of innovation
- Information processing or cognitive learning theories
- Information theories (Shannon and Weaver Information-Communication Model and Blum's model)
- Learning styles
- Learning theories
- Systems theory

Source: Englebardt, S.P., and R. Nelson. 2002. *Health Care Informatics: An Interdisciplinary Approach*. St. Louis, MO: Mosby, Inc. 5–25.

Figure 16.3. AHIMA's model of data quality

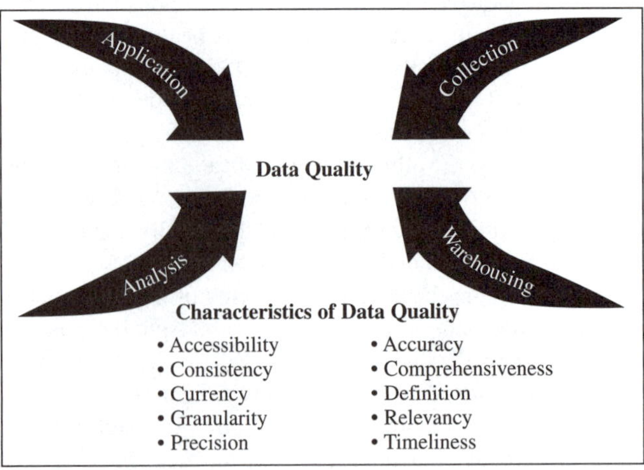

Source: AHIMA 1998.

Also, at a general level, researchers in research methodology have described two overarching approaches to research: the quantitative approach and the qualitative approach.

The **quantitative approach** is the explanation of phenomena through scientific inquiry and empiricism. **Scientific inquiry** involves making predictions, collecting and analyzing evidence, testing alternative theories, and choosing the best theory. **Empiricism** means "based on observed and validated evidence." For example, research based on experiments is empirical. Objective knowledge is the desired end result. As the word *quantitative* implies, the data often can be quantified and result in statistical or numerical results. Another name for the quantitative approach is **positivism**. A classic example of quantitative research is the human genome project.

Researchers in the **qualitative approach** interpret non-numerical observations. These non-numerical observations include words, gestures, activities, time, space, images, and perceptions. These observations are placed in context. Another term for the qualitative approach is **naturalism**. A classic example of qualitative research is Margaret Mead's anthropological study of the Polynesian culture of American Samoa in the early 1920s. Examples in medicine involve studies of near-death experiences, dying, and being a patient. Without qualitative research, healthcare personnel would not have learned that elderly, married patients cut their pills in half in order to share their prescriptions when they run out of money.

These two approaches to research are frames on a grand scale. Within both approaches, researchers make certain basic assumptions. (See table 16.2.) Some large topics require both approaches with many researchers conducting complementary studies.

An emerging third approach is called **mixed methods research** (Johnson and Onwuegbuzie 2004, 15). Mixed methods research combines quantitative and qualitative techniques within a single study and across related studies. Mixed methods research may be suited to investigations into complex phenomena in healthcare (McKibbon and Gadd 2004). An example is a study of the role of computerized physician order entry (CPOE) systems in introducing the risk of medication errors (Koppel et al. 2005, 1198). The researchers conducted a qualitative and quantitative study of the interaction between house staff and the CPOE system at a tertiary-care teaching hospital. They found that CPOE systems facilitated 22 types of medication error risks (Koppel et al. 2005, 1199).

Table 16.2. Comparison of assumptions in quantitative and qualitative research approaches

Quantitative	Qualitative
Single truth exists	Multiple truths exist simultaneously
Single truth applies across time and place	Truths are bound to place and time (contextual)
Researchers can adopt neutral, unbiased stances	Neutrality is impossible because researchers choose their topics of investigation
Chronological sequence of causes can be identified	Influences interact with one another to color researchers' views of the past, present, and future

The purpose of the research determines the approach. Research that investigates numerically measurable observations or tests a **hypothesis** is often quantitative; while research that is exploratory and preliminary often begins with a qualitative investigation.

Most advances in medicine have been the result of quantitative research. Quantitative research, with its scientific and evidence-based approach, is also the approach that HIM researchers often select.

Within both the quantitative and the qualitative approaches, researchers use inductive reasoning and deductive reasoning. **Inductive reasoning**, or induction, involves drawing conclusions based on a limited number of observations. For example, during his professional practice experience, a student might observe that all coders in the coding department at XYZ hospital had the RHIT credential. Thus, he might conclude that all coders have the RHIT credential. **Deductive reasoning**, or deduction, involves drawing conclusions based on generalizations. For example, all coders have the RHIT credential. Jane Doe is a coder. Therefore, Jane Doe must have the RHIT credential.

As the examples demonstrate, neither induction nor deduction alone is completely satisfactory. Used together, however, they are very effective and are the basis of the research.

Check Your Understanding 16.1

Instructions: Answer the following questions on a separate piece of paper.

1. What is research?
2. Why are health records important in research?
3. What are the three characteristics of a theory?
4. How does the phrase "keep it simple" apply to theories?
5. What are the advantages of models?
6. Why is the research conducted by HIM professionals considered applied research?
7. Why is it so important for researchers to know their purpose?
8. How do inductive reasoning and deductive reasoning differ?

Research Process

Conceptually, researchers participate in the following major activities:

- Defining the research question (problem)
- Summarizing prior pertinent knowledge
- Gathering data
- Analyzing the data
- Interpreting and presenting findings

However, because these major activities are so broad, most researchers divide them into more manageable components. Thus, the research process becomes orderly problem solving. In the verbal shorthand of researchers, these basic components are:

- Defining the research question (problem)
- Performing a literature review
- Determining a research design and method
- Selecting an instrument
- Gathering data
- Analyzing the data
- Presenting results

Defining the Research Question (Problem)

Research begins with defining the problem. Defining the problem is also known as specifying the research question. Whichever phrase is used, both mean that researchers must be crystal clear about what they are investigating. Vague notions lead to substandard research, which is a waste of time, effort, and energy for both researchers and participants.

The importance of investing time and effort in developing the research question cannot be overstated. Experts agree that "the key element, the starting point and the most important issue in developing research, is the research question" (Metz 2001, 13).

According to Metz, the criteria for a well-developed research question are:

- The question is clearly and exactly stated.
- The question has theoretical significance, practical worth, or both.
- The question has obvious and explicit links to a larger body of knowledge, such as a theory or a research model.
- The research's results advance knowledge in a definable way.
- The answer to the question or the solution to the problem is worthwhile.

The first step in developing the research question is to identify a general problem in an area of interest and expertise. Three excellent sources of meaningful problems exist:

- *Research models:* Research models show all the factors and relationships in a theory. Researchers can select one or two factors that other researchers have raised questions about or have found problematic. An added benefit is that the model suggests the relationships among all the factors. For example, researchers in health information management could use AHIMA's Model of Data Quality to develop a research problem. (Refer to figure 16.3.) These hypothetical researchers could investigate the relationship between collection and data quality. Finally, research models explicitly link to a larger body of knowledge, one of the criteria for a well-developed research question.
- *Recommendations of earlier researchers*: In journal articles, researchers specifically make recommendations for later research. Their research raises yet more questions that future researchers can answer.
- *Gaps in the body of knowledge:* A comprehensive review of the literature related to the problem or question will identify gaps or problematic areas. (See next section on performing a literature review.) For example, in journal articles, researchers often identify unintentional flaws in their own study that future researchers could correct in a replication study. Correcting the flaw in the subsequent study could produce more accurate and predictive results than were found in the original study. In health information management and other fields, entire articles have been dedicated to reviewing the literature. These literature review articles can be examined for research questions. Literature review articles related to health informatics and health information management have covered a wide range of topics. (See figure 16.4.)

In addition, researchers make recommendations for future research in master's theses and doctoral dissertations. Therefore, a careful and thoughtful reading of journal articles, literature review articles, master's theses, and doctoral dissertations can identify meaningful research problems.

The next step is to narrow the focus of the question to a manageable and researchable issue. Researchers clearly state the research problem or question in their article or paper in order to draw the reader into the topic. A helpful metaphor is the funnel. Researchers begin with a broad, general question and then gradually pinpoint the topic to their precise problem or question.

Moreover, an effective problem statement delimits or sets the boundaries of the problem. By clearly stating the study's area of investigation, researchers also specify the aspects of the problem that are beyond or outside the scope of their research. For example, the researcher might begin the problem statement with a general societal concern. Supporting citations would then come from the popular literature, opinion articles, and journal articles. Next, he or she would

Figure 16.4. Examples of topics of literature review in health informatics and HIM

- Trends in evaluation studies of health information systems and technology (Ammenwerth and de Keizer 2005)
- Information technology and improvement of clinical care (Sanders and Aronsky 2006; Young et al. 2007)
- Impact of electronic health records on productivity (Poissant et al. 2005)
- Use of clinical information-retrieval technology (Pluye et al. 2005)
- Access, use, quality, and types of consumer e-health initiatives (Strecher 2007)
- Representing time in medical natural language processing (Zhou and Hripcsak 2007)
- Management of multiple projects in healthcare research (Hopkins et al. 2007)

concentrate the discussion by explaining how this problem or question affects the field of health information management. Finally, he or she would state the research problem or question succinctly and accurately.

Clearly delineating the problem helps the researcher later in the research process when he or she is writing the hypothesis. The hypothesis is written after the researcher completes the literature review. In the hypothesis, the researcher operationalizes his or her research question. (See later section on statement of hypothesis.). **Operationalize** means formulating the question in terms that are capable of generating data and that satisfactorily capture the issues of the question or problem.

The last step in developing the research question or problem is to ensure that the issue has merit. Similar to substandard research, research on a trite issue about which no one cares is a waste of time, effort, and energy. Therefore, the key to defining the problem statement is to find a meaningful problem that needs a solution or a significant question that needs an answer.

Performing a Literature Review

A **literature review** is a systematic and critical investigation of the important information about a topic. After completing this orderly and organized approach to the literature, researchers know the following about a topic:

- Mainstream and lesser-known theories, theorists, and factors
- Key turning points in the development of ideas about the topic
- Typical research methods
- Major research instruments
- Appropriate analytical approaches

From the literature review, researchers are able to assess the competency of research studies and to identify gaps or holes in the field's body of knowledge. Because overviews identify gaps or discrepancies in a field's knowledge, they are both sources of problems or research questions that researchers can investigate and an excellent means to refine and focus a research question into a previously unexplored issue.

Literature review has three meanings. (See table 16.3.) In the first meaning, it is the process of identifying, reading, analyzing, summarizing, and synthesizing the writings of other researchers and thinkers. In the second and third meanings, the literature review is a product. It is the portion of a manuscript or an article in which researchers record their analysis and summary of the literature they have read. A literature

Table 16.3. Three meanings of "literature review"

Meaning	General Description	Example
One	Process	Identifying, reading, analyzing, summarizing, and synthesizing the works of researchers and experts
Two	Product—Portion of study's presentation	Excerpt from research article, Kesh, Someswar, and Wullianallur Raghupathi. 2004. Critical issues in bioinformatics and computing. *Perspectives in Health Information Management* 1(9):1–8. Bioinformatics is defined by the National Institutes of Health as the "research, development, or application of computational tools and approaches for expanding the use of biological, medical, behavioral or health data, including those to acquire, store, organize, archive, analyze, or visualize such data." The exponential growth in the amount of such data has necessitated the use of computers for information cataloging and retrieval; a more global perspective in the quest for new insights into health and disease and the resulting data mining also underscore the need for bioinformatics. Both sophisticated hardware and complex software play an increasingly critical role in the analysis of genomic data, and the accelerated maturation of the field of bioinformatics has implications for computing and life sciences professionals as well as the general public. Like computational biology, bioinformatics is anchored in the life sciences as well as computer and information sciences and technologies. Its interdisciplinary and integrative approach draws from fields such as mathematics, physics, computer science and engineering, biology, and behavioral science. The generally accepted subdisciplines include (1) development of new algorithms and statistics with which to assess relationships among members of large data sets; 2) analyses and interpretation of various types of sequences, domains, and structures; and (3) development and implementation of tools that enable efficient access and management of different types of information.
Three	Product—Entire research article or book	Citation in bibliographic databases includes publication type of "review" and number of references Edmonson, S.R., K.A. Smith-Akin, and E.V. Bernstam. 2007. Context, automated decision support, and clinical practice guidelines: Does the literature apply to the United States practice environment? [Review] [36 refs] *International Journal of Medical Informatics* 76(1):34–41. Dorr, D., L.M. Bonner, A.N. Cohen, R.S. Shoai, R. Perrin, E. Chaney, and A.S. Young. 2007, Informatics systems to promote improved care for chronic illness: A literature review. [Review] [40 refs] *Journal of the American Medical Informatics Association* 14(2):156–163. Systematic (integrative) review Meta-analysis

review article is a separate and independent peer-reviewed article. In a literature review article, the previously mentioned "portion" is expanded and refined into an entire article.

Both as a process and as a product, these overviews identify gaps or discrepancies in the body of knowledge for researchers.

Purpose of the Literature Review

The purpose of a literature review is to develop and present a strong knowledge base. The strong knowledge base can be used to:

- Conduct research
- Generate and analyze theories
- Develop evidence-based practice guidelines
- Develop curriculum
- Perform strategic planning
- Develop white (position) papers

The researcher comes to a complete understanding of the topic. This means that he or she can:

- Determine applicable theories, pertinent factors, and appropriate research designs and methods
- Outline a historical overview of a topic
- Explain the development and evolution of relevant theories
- Assess the thoroughness of literature reviews in published studies
- Relate theorists and researchers with their ideas and findings
- Differentiate between accepted theories and those outside the mainstream
- Discriminate between relevant and irrelevant factors
- Clarify concepts, recognize trends, explain debates, and identify confounding factors
- State advantages and disadvantages of various research methods
- Cite the strengths and weaknesses of various instruments
- Select appropriate techniques for analysis
- Identify competently conducted research and inadequately conducted research
- Detect the holes in the body of knowledge that his or her research can fill

Thus, the literature review results in the researcher "owning" this particular slice of the body of knowledge. He or she knows the theories; the names of the researchers, theorists, and collaborators; the sources of the data; common research designs; and gaps in the body of knowledge.

Process of the Literature Review

Researchers conducting a literature review identify, read, analyze, summarize, and synthesize knowledge and research of a topic and closely related topics. The process of a literature review is a systematic plan consisting of four steps:

1. Determine the literature to review.
2. Identify, categorize, organize, and obtain the literature.
3. Analyze the research questions, methods, and results presented in the literature.
4. Synthesize the information in the literature.

Sources of Information

In the first step, the researcher determines the literature to review. Sources of information include journals; periodicals; books, brochures, and book chapters; technical and research reports; proceedings of conferences; doctoral dissertations and master's theses; unpublished works; reviews; audiovisual media; and electronic media. (See figure 16.5.) These sources can be found in many bibliographic databases that

Figure 16.5. Sources of information

Periodicals
Abstract
Annual review
Cartoon
Journal
Magazine
Monograph
Newsletter
Newspaper
Press release

Books, Brochures, and Book Chapters
Book
Book chapter
Brochure
Dictionary
Encyclopedia
Legal citation
Manual
Map or chart
Pamphlet
Product insert
Published or archived letter

Technical and Research Reports
Government bulletin
Government report
Industry report
Issue brief
Monograph
Nongovernment agency report
Position paper
Reference report
University report
White paper
Working paper

Proceedings of Meetings
Conference
Meeting
Poster session
Symposium
Unpublished proceeding paper

Doctoral Dissertations and Master's Theses
Abstract of dissertation
Abstract of thesis
Dissertation
Thesis

Unpublished Works
Submitted manuscript
Unpublished letter
Unpublished manuscript
Unpublished raw data

Reviews
Book
Film
Video

Audiovisual Media
Address
Audiotape
Chart
Film
Lecture
Music recording
Performance
Published interview
Recorded interview
Slide
Speech
Television broadcast and transcript
Television series and transcript
Unpublished interview
Work of art

Electronic Media
Abstract on CD-ROM
CD-ROM
Computer program
Computer software
Electronic database
Internet Web site
Online abstract
Online book
Online journal
Software manual

index them. Because health information management combines theories from many academic fields, HIM researchers need to search a wide variety of databases that include sources related to management, organizational behavior, sociology, psychology, medical sciences, computer science, and decision support. Particularly helpful are databases that access the articles in journals related to medicine, health, health information management, health services administration, and bioinformatics. (See table 16.4)

The literature comprises primary and secondary sources. **Primary sources** are the original works of the researchers who conducted the investigation. The articles by Bolin and Goforth (2005) and by Silfen (2006) described earlier in this chapter are primary sources. Research-based articles in the *New England Journal of Medicine* or *Science* are other examples of primary sources. **Secondary sources** are summaries of the original works. Encyclopedias and textbooks are familiar secondary sources. Other examples of secondary sources are annual reviews (also sometimes called tertiary sources). Annual reviews summarize and synthesize current and recent knowledge on a topic. Examples from over 30 disciplines in the biomedical, life, physical, and social sciences are available online (Annual reviews). They may be special issues of print or electronic journals or entire books.

Table 16.4. Selected bibliographic databases with emphases in medicine, health, HIM, health services administration, and health informatics

Bibliographic Database	Description
ACM Digital Library (Association for Computing Machinery)	Journals, magazine, and conference proceedings from 1985, many full text
AltHealth Watch	International peer-reviewed and professional journals, many full text from 1990; also includes magazines, reports, proceedings, association and consumer newsletters, pamphlets, booklets, special reports, original research and book excerpts
Allied and Complementary Medicine (AMED)	Biomedical journals focused on alternative and complementary with relevant articles taken from other journals plus newspapers and books; includes English-language and European sources
Annual Reviews	Definitive academic resource for reviews in topics from biomedical, physical, and social sciences
BioMed Central	Peer-reviewed research of biology and medicine with immediate, barrier-free access from 1997
BioMedical Reference Collection, Comprehensive	Full-text journals including clinical medicine, psychiatry, psychology, nursing, allied health, public health, nutrition, and HIM
CINAHL (Cumulative Index of Nursing and Allied Health Literature)	Journals and publications in nursing, biomedicine, health sciences librarianship, consumer health, and allied health disciplines
Health Business FullTEXT Elite	Full-text journals on healthcare administration and other non-clinical aspects of healthcare management
Health Services Technology/Assessment Texts (HSTAT)	Free, Web-based full-text documents on health information for healthcare decision making
IEEE Xplore (Institute of Electrical and Electronics Engineers)	Full-text access to transactions, journals, magazines, and conference proceedings since 1952
Health Source: Nursing/Academic	Scholarly full-text journals, many focused on nursing and allied health; indexing, 1984–present; full text, 1990–present
LISTA (Library Information Science and Technical Abstracting)	Open access to periodicals, books, research reports, and conference proceedings from mid-1960s
MEDLINE	Authoritative source of information on medicine, nursing, allied health, dentistry, veterinary medicine, healthcare system, and preclinical sciences
OVID Healthstar (HSTR)	More than 3 million citations addressing health services, technology, administration, and research, published from 1975–present, from the National Library of Medicine. Includes both clinical and non-clinical topics in journal articles, government documents, newspaper articles, monographs, book chapters, technical reports, and meeting abstracts and papers
PubMed	Preeminent bibliographic biomedical database of the National Library of Medicine
SIAM Journals Online (Society for Industrial and Applied Mathematics)	Access to full-text journals from 1994

For literature reviews, primary sources are preferable to secondary sources.

The gold standard for a literature review is primary research in **peer-reviewed journals**. **Peer review** is the process that ensures that the information reported in the journal is of the highest quality (Colaianni 1994, 156). Journals may be peer-reviewed (also called research, refereed, academic, and professional) or nonpeer-reviewed (also called popular). In peer-reviewed journals, the articles are evaluated in manuscript form by experts in the field (peers) for quality prior to publication.

Both print and electronic journals are peer-reviewed. Examples of peer-reviewed journals are the *Journal of the American Medical Association,* the *New England Journal of Medicine, Science,* and the *Journal of the American Medical Informatics Association.* In the field of health information management, the major peer-reviewed journals are the *Journal of American Health Information Management Association* and *Perspectives in Health Information Management.* Thus, researchers must make a distinction between research (professional) literature and popular literature. Properly conducted and written literature reviews focus on primary sources in peer-reviewed journals.

Search Techniques

In the second step, researchers identify, categorize, organize, and obtain the literature. A systematic plan identifies the databases to search as well as all the terms used to query the databases. Categorizing includes listing all types of sources of information on the topic. Although traditional literature may constitute the major portion of the plan, other sources (such as videos, newscasts, and the Internet) can contribute and should be considered. Tables and lists are essential tools. The plan also includes organizing the documentation of the queries, the search terms, the results of the queries for each database, and the literature itself as it is received. This section focuses on the search techniques.

Procedure

The following steps describe the search procedure for refereed journal articles. Researchers can use similar tactics in other media and for popular literature.

1. Generate a list of key terms and synonyms (in the databases of medical literature these are medical subject headings or MeSH headings). Include synonyms and alternative formats and spellings (quality management, continuous quality improvement, performance improvement; manage, management; **meta-analysis**).
2. Generate a list of target databases (such as Ovid Healthstar, MEDLINE, CINAHL). An excellent database for health-related research is PubMed from the National Library of Medicine. HIM researchers provide detailed instructions on how to query this database (Fenton and Williams 2005, 60A).
3. Search each database with each term. Use an advanced "All Fields" search and document each search.
4. Use the "Limit" function to narrow the searches to refereed journals (also sometimes called academic journals). You can also "limit" to human subjects, English language, and time periods.
5. Scan the abstracts of the articles to determine whether the articles are applicable. Abstracts summarize research studies' major parts: context; objective; design, setting, and participants; **interventions**; main outcome measures; results; and conclusions.
6. Print articles from online journals and from print journals.
7. Copy articles from print journals (bring an adequate supply of change or purchase a copy card). Note that although it may be convenient or expedient to only use online articles, the resulting literature review will be incomplete and biased. In some cases, academic libraries offer document delivery in which the library staff scan the articles and send the articles electronically to the requester. Be sure to investigate the costs of this procedure as it may be expensive.
8. Read and analyze the literature obtained to date.
9. Identify key journal articles.
10. Obtain the references cited at the end of the key articles. Track their order and receipt.
11. Note the medical subject headings (MeSH headings) of the key articles. If the original list missed these terms, rerun the searches of the databases on the new terms.
12. Identify key researchers in the topic. Run advanced searches on "author." Obtain every researcher's articles and books on the topic.
13. Alphabetize all the copies of the articles by author. This strategy avoids duplication and allows prompt access.

To avoid rework during the manuscript's composition, researchers should capture all data about the source when they first obtain it. The various style manuals have different requirements. To meet all the requirements, researchers should be sure to note the following information about their sources:

- Full name of the author, including first name and middle initial or name (be aware that some entries in Web sites have authors)
- Full title of the journal, book, video, or Internet site
- Complete information about dates of publication, including the year, month, and season (be aware that some entries in Web sites are dated)
- Complete name and address of the publisher (for books and videos)
- Inclusive page numbers
- Volume number and issue number (sometimes these data are only on the front of the publication)
- Accurate URL and access date (for the Internet)

As a means to organize the literature review, researchers are strongly encouraged to invest in a bibliographic software package at the beginning of their research. Bibliographic software packages greatly assist researchers. Helpful features of these packages allow researchers to:

- Create their own personal bibliographic databases
- Utilize the packages' search engines that directly download citations into the researchers' personal bibliographic databases
- Import the contents of databases into word-processing software
- Transform bibliographic entries into the required style of the journal (styles editor)

Commonly used bibliographic packages include Reference Manager, EndNote, RefWorks, and ProCite. Reference manager "freeware" includes BiblioExpress and Scholar's Aid 2000 Lite. Zotero runs on Mozilla Foxfire and is easy to use.

Library Research

Students and instructors have access to sources of information and bibliographic databases through the holdings of their educational institutions' libraries. Libraries have extensive holdings that include books, reference manuals, maps, videotapes, audiotapes, and literary and other databases. Many libraries list their holdings on the Internet. Book holdings can typically be accessed through the library's catalog. The databases and online journals usually can be found under electronic resources. Libraries purchase licenses that allow their users access to the various databases. Just as different libraries have purchased different books, different libraries have purchased different licenses.

In addition, AHIMA members have access to the holdings of the Foundation for Research and Education (FORE) Library in the Body of Knowledge (BoK) of the Communities of Practice (CoP). These holdings include:

- Full-text articles from the *Journal of the American Health Information Management Association* since 1998
- One hundred twenty-five leading journals in healthcare and health information management
- A thousand books related to healthcare and health information management
- Limited access to some propriety bibliographic databases

There is also document delivery for a fee that varies by availability. Practice guidelines about e-HIM, the transition from paper health records to EHRs, also are available at the AHIMA Web site (AHIMA 2008).

Practitioners also may access sources of information and databases through their workplaces. Healthcare organizations have libraries or some arrangement to access to libraries. As employees, practitioners may access these resources.

Although Web sites may have information that has not been peer reviewed, they may have valuable government reports and other documents. Many libraries of colleges and universities, such as the University of South Carolina Beaufort Library (2007), have developed online tutorials on their Web sites that explain the features of various Internet search engines.

In the steps of the search procedure, this brief statement is made: "Read and analyze the literature obtained to date." The brevity of this statement in no way represents the task of reading and analyzing the literature. In this analytical task, researchers should be noting:

- Major theories and theorists
- Trends
- Concepts, factors, and variables
- Research designs and methods
- Populations and sampling techniques
- Accepted and commonly used instruments
- Appropriate statistical techniques
- Controversial issues within the topic

Researchers can record the key features of each article in a table. (See table 16.5.) From this tool, they can identify trends, common characteristics, and gaps.

Table 16.5. Summary of the literature

Author	Year	Design & Method	Time Frame	Sample & Response Rate	Statistical Techniques	Key Findings, Limitations, & Recommendations
X and Y	1980	Descriptive	One-shot	20 patients, convenience 100%	Means and percentages	• More smokers in dermatology clinic • Small convenience sample limits generalizability • Recommends larger random sample
A and B	1995	Correlational	One-shot	70 random subjects, 30%	Bivariate correlation	• Relationship between smoking and skin tone • Limitations of self-report and one-shot approach • Recommend longitudinal, experimental research
L, M, and N	2001	Quasi-experimental	1 year	40 subjects, 100%	ANOVA	• Skin tone of nonsmokers significantly more toned than skin tone of smokers • Generalizability limited because subjects from one socioeconomic class and one clinic • Recommend larger and more heterogeneous sample

Development of Literature Review

The development of the literature review is the synthesis of the data and information captured in the process of the literature review. The word *synthesize* cannot be emphasized enough. In today's world of data and information overload, mere narrative reviews, which are long summaries of previous studies, are not adequate. Readers require the knowledge that comes from the analysis and synthesis of the literature.

After completing the literature review, researchers develop its products. These products are written and may be either a portion of a journal article, paper, or presentation or an entire article or paper. However, in both forms, the well-developed literature review concisely and logically states what is known and unknown about a topic.

For both forms, the characteristics of a good literature review are:

- Comprehensiveness that is also relevant and focused
- Critique that includes strengths, weaknesses, limitations, and gaps
- Analysis
- Summary that is succinct and logical and comprises mainly primary sources
- Synthesis

Several common conventions guide the development of both forms of literature reviews. These conventions are detailed in the following paragraphs, with unique aspects of each form concluding this section.

In a complex or broad topic, researchers should briefly describe the strategy they used to identify literature. In addition, they should explain the scope of the literature review by explicitly stating both their inclusion and exclusion criteria. For example, a researcher could state, "The topic of health information systems is broad. This literature review focused on research articles related to mental health."

Researchers should make a conscious effort to identify, consider, and use an organizing function or factor for the literature review. Using the research model is one organizing function; chronology is another. Explicitly stating the order helps to guide and direct the reader. A coherent and logical order clarifies the topic.

In the literature review, the researcher identifies the key points or turning points in the development of knowledge about a topic. The literature included should be the research studies that either moved the topic forward or added new factors to the topic. However, important studies with contradictory findings also should be included. Otherwise, readers could interpret the absence of contradictory studies as bias. Evidence of bias detracts from the credibility of the literature review. Explanations of the contradictory findings, based on evaluation and analysis, might be suggested.

Moreover, the studies included in the research study should be pertinent. When tangential studies are included, their relevance should be explicitly stated. Generally, the least-related studies should be discussed first and the most-related studies discussed last.

Research studies that either were conducted inadequately or resulted in gaps or conflicting results should be included, especially if the researcher is rectifying the errors. Again, the researcher should specifically point out the inadequacies, gaps, or conflicting results.

Key research studies or turning-point studies should be described in greater detail than replication or duplicative studies. Enough information about the key studies (design, time frame, method, sample, response rate, statistical techniques, and findings) should be included so that the reader can evaluate their quality. Research that has the same findings with the same factors should be bundled. For example, the author could state, "Research (citation one, citation two, citation three, and so on) has shown that smoking is bad for skin tone."

Tradition and logic demand that researchers pay close attention to verb tense when they write the literature review. The tense of the verb situates the event or idea in time. Present tense expresses truths, accepted theories, and facts. Recent, valid studies also are explained in the present tense. For example:

- *Accepted theory*: Specific goals motivate employees more than vague goals.
- *Recent study*: Johnson's results illustrate the importance of specific goals.

Past studies with continued historical value can be described in the past tense. Including the date to situate the study is a common practice. For example:

- *Study of historical importance*: In 1972, the study of Smith et al. showed the importance of expectancy in motivation.

However, the easiest and safest rule is to use present tense for published studies and theories.

A table that briefly highlights the important features of the studies in the literature review is an effective tool. Readers can quickly see trends and gaps in the literature. The table lists each study in a row, with columns displaying its summary, advantages, and disadvantages. Another possible structure for the table is to use rows for the studies but substitute features of the studies in the columns. (Refer to table 16.5.)

As a portion of a journal article, paper, or presentation, the purpose of the literature review is to persuade the reader or audience of the necessity of the research study. The literature review should guide the reader and audience to reach the same conclusions that the researchers reached and the same question or problem. Moreover, the reader and audience should conclude that the logical and necessary next step is the research proposed by the researchers. A secondary purpose is to assure the reader or audience that the researcher has conducted a thorough and diligent review of all aspects of the topic. The thoroughness of the literature review lends credibility to both the researcher and the entire investigation. Finally, the literature review should conclude with a clear and exact statement of the hypothesis.

As an entire article, the literature review is a specialized type of research. Terms for this type of research are systematic literature review, integrative review, or meta-analysis. The **systematic literature review** is a methodical approach to literature review that reduces the possibility of bias. It is characterized by:

- Explicit search criteria to identify literature
- Inclusion and exclusion criteria to select articles and information sources
- Evaluation against consistent methodological standards

This analytical summary of the literature is an amplified and enhanced version of the paragraphs that form the literature review in other research articles.

The meta-analysis is a specialized kind of systematic review that introduces statistical techniques to combine the results of several studies. This type of review is discussed in greater detail in the subsection on research methods.

The literature review article is a distillation and synthesis of the current status of knowledge on a topic. "Systematic reviews establish whether scientific findings are consistent and can be generalized across populations, settings, and **treatment** variations" (Mulrow 1994, 597). Annual reviews are examples of analytical summaries of the literature. Examples of annual reviews can be found in journal articles or entire books.

More information on performing literature reviews is available in *Health Sciences Literature Review Made Easy* (Garrard 2007), which focuses on literature reviews in the health sciences.

Check Your Understanding 16.2

Instructions: Answer the following questions on a separate piece of paper.

1. What are the seven basic steps of research?
2. What are five characteristics of a well-developed research question?
3. What are three rich sources of meaningful research questions?
4. Why is conducting a literature review important for a researcher?
5. List five data sources, other than journal articles, that a researcher should consider when doing a comprehensive search.
6. Why would a researcher limit the search of journal articles to refereed journals?
7. Why would the director of health information services select the productivity standard recommended in a peer-reviewed journal rather than the productivity standard recommended in a popular magazine?
8. How do researchers use key terms (MeSH headings)?
9. Why would a researcher use bibliographic software?
10. Why should studies with contradictory results be included in the review of the literature?
11. In the review of the literature, what information about key studies should readers expect?

Determining a Research Design and Method

A research design is a plan for conducting research that appropriately manages variations and provides answers to the research question or problem. Researchers can investigate the same broad question or problem using several different research designs. The design chosen depends on the purpose of the research. An important point to remember is that how the problem or question is defined in the problem statement indicates the appropriate research design.

Researchers can choose from among many research designs. Moreover, different disciplines, such as history, medicine, and anthropology, tend to emphasize and use different designs. Certain designs are better suited to answer certain types of questions or to solve certain types of problems than other designs are. (See table 16.6.)

Similarly, certain research methods are more associated with one design than another. However, there is considerable overlap among the methods and their designs. Again, the purpose of the research determines the appropriate research method. Thus, the choice of both the research design and the research method depends on the research question or problem.

Research Designs

There are six common research designs: historical, descriptive, correlational, evaluation, experimental, and causal-comparative. These designs are particularly well suited to research in topics related to healthcare and, specifically, health information management. Which design is appropriate depends on the problem and the researcher's definition of the problem.

Historical Research

Historical research investigates the past. Researchers examine primary and secondary sources. Primary sources include wills, charters, reports, minutes, eyewitness accounts, letters, and e-mail records. Secondary sources are derived from primary sources; secondary sources summarize, critique, or analyze the primary sources. This chapter is a secondary source because it describes and summarizes the original reports of others. Primary sources are superior to secondary sources. An example of historical research in healthcare would be an investigation of the development of health insurance in the United States. Examining both primary and secondary sources, researchers in health information management could explore the founding of the professional association, the development of the code of ethics, or the establishment of the technical-level and the various specialty credentials.

Descriptive Research

Descriptive research determines and reports the current status of topics and subjects. Common tools used to collect descriptive data are **surveys**, interviews, and observations. The shortcomings of descriptive research include the lack of standardized questions, trained observers, and high-response rates. Examples of descriptive studies include polls of Americans' opinions concerning abortion, the patient's bill of rights, stem-cell research, and bioengineering.

In health information management, researchers also conduct descriptive studies. A very limited list of examples includes studies on the status of the composition of the HIM workforce, employee morale in HIS departments, coding accuracy, the extent of EHR implementation, and the types of tasks that HIM technicians and administrators perform.

Correlational Research

Correlational research determines the existence, the direction, and the degree of relationships among factors. For example, HIM professionals have conducted correlational studies on factors related to the adoption of health information technologies (Rosenthal and Layman 2008, 6) and to e-learning (Bell 2006, 4). Other correlational studies in health information management might investigate relationships between credential and coding accuracy, job satisfaction and educational level, and increased patient volumes and the level of organizational computerization.

The factors in correlational research and other research designs are called **variables**. The degree or strength of the relationship can range from 0.00 to 1.00 (or –1.00). A strength of 0.00 means absolutely no relationship. On the other hand, a strength of 1.00 (or –1.00) means a perfect relationship. For example a **positive (direct) relationship** 0.313 exists between the size of a physician practice and its utilization of the EHR (Rosenthal and Layman 2008, 19). A positive relationship means that the larger the physician practice the more likely the practice is to utilize an EHR. This direct relationship could also be expressed as the smaller the physician practice, the less likely its utilization of the EHR. Conversely, in a **negative (inverse) relationship**, the directions of the relationship are opposite (inverse). For example, researchers found increased adoption of health information technologies, particularly clinical information technologies, was associated with improved health outcomes (Menachemi et al. 2008, 56). The relationship between overall health information technology adoption and the post pancreatic resection mortality rate was –0.403. Thus, the higher the adoption of health information technologies, the lower the mortality rate after pancreatic resections.

Correlational research cannot establish causation. Correlational research can only detect the existence, the direction, and the degree of relationship. For example, in the research on utilization of EHRs in physician practices, the researchers could *not* state whether the practice size causes the use

Table 16.6 Designs of research and their applications

Design	Application	Method	Example in Healthcare
Historical	Understand past events	• Case study • Bibliography	• What factors led to the enactment of Medicare legislation? • How did events in the history of the American College of Surgeons affect the development of the field of health information management?
Descriptive	Describe current status	• Survey • Observation	• What barriers prevent healthcare personnel from using computers during the delivery of patient care? • How do coders use references and help screens when they code?
Correlational	Determine existence and degree of relationship	• Survey • Secondary analysis	• How are credential and performance related? • What is the relationship between provider satisfaction and EMR systems?
Evaluation	Evaluate effectiveness	• Case study	• How has implementation of an EMR system affected the enterprise's ability to deliver healthcare to underserved populations? • How has EDI reduced the costs of delivery of healthcare to Medicare patients?
Experimental	Establish cause and effect	• Randomized, double-blind, clinical trial • Pretest-posttest control group method • Solomon four-group method • Posttest-only control group	• Which group of molecules with innate immunity affects the risk and severity of invasive Blastomycosis dermatitidis infection? • Which dosage level of the medication is more efficacious and safer for immunocompromised patients with uncomplicated herpes zoster?
Causal-Comparative (Quasi-Experimental)	Detect causal relationship	• One-shot case study • One-group pretest-posttest • Static group comparison • Nonparticipant observation	• What is the effect of a coder training program on the case mix index? • What is the effect of having a working mother on childhood obesity?

of EHRs or whether the use of EHRs causes the practice size (Rosenthal and Layman 2008). Adding to the correlational researchers' difficulties, a third unlisted factor, such as geographic location, could affect both the practice size and the utilization of the EHR. This third unlisted factor is called a **confounding (extraneous, secondary) variable** because it confounds (confuses) interpretation of the data.

Researchers conducting correlational studies use surveys, standardized tests, observations, and secondary data. The important point to remember is that correlational research never establishes causal relationships.

Evaluation Research

Evaluation research examines the effectiveness of technologies, policies, products, programs, or organizations. Researchers examine several aspects of these objects (topics) of research, such as conceptualization, design, implementation, impact, and **generalizability** (Shi 2008, 212). For example, researchers might investigate the effectiveness of a new computer-assisted coding software. Educational programs also are often the focus of evaluation research. Often grants supporting public services require an evaluation of a service's effectiveness. Case studies are often associated with evaluation research.

In health information management, leaders of an integrated health delivery system could evaluate the effectiveness of aspects of different coding systems. HIM professionals examined the usefulness of the ICD-10-CM system in capturing public health diseases compared to ICD-9-CM (Watzlaf et al. 2007, 1). The researchers found that ICD-10-CM was more specific and captured public health diseases (reportable diseases and leading causes of morbidity and mortality) more fully than ICD-9-CM. However, coders were more likely to agree on the coding of some conditions in ICD-9-CM than in ICD-10-CM. Conditions more consistently coded in ICD-9-CM than ICD-10-CM were external causes of injury, diabetes, lower respiratory diseases, heart disease, and malignant neoplasms. The researchers noted, however, that this consistency may have been related to the coders' greater familiarity with ICD-9-CM than with ICD-10-CM. Finally, the researchers concluded that their findings had implications for improving the coding system and for educating coders on ICD-10-CM.

Experimental Research

Experimental research establishes causal relationships. A **causal relationship** shows cause and effect. For example, smoking (the cause) results in lung cancer (the effect). Characteristics of experimental research are:

- Control
- Manipulation of treatment
- Random assignment of subjects to groups

The key and defining characteristic of experimental research is control. Experimental researchers follow strict protocols to maintain control. Experimental research is the gold standard.

Researchers conducting experimental research select both independent variables and dependent variables. **Independent variables** are the factors that researchers manipulate directly; independent variables are antecedent or prior factors. **Dependent variables** are the measured variables; they depend on the independent variables. The dependent variables reflect the results that the researcher theorizes. They occur subsequently or after the independent variables. Therefore, the independent variable causes an effect in the dependent variable.

The independent variables that researchers manipulate are also called interventions or treatments. Researchers use the term *treatment* generically or broadly, beyond its usual meaning of therapy. Therefore, treatment could mean a physical conditioning program, a computer training program, a particular laboratory medium, or the timing of prophylactic medications.

In experimental research, researchers select subjects for comparison groups. The **experimental (study) group** comprises the research subjects. Another group, the **control group**, comprises the control subjects. The experimental subjects undergo the intervention of the research study. For comparison, the control subjects do not.

Important elements of experimental research are random sampling and randomization. Although the terms are similar, they represent two different procedures. **Random sampling** is the unbiased selection of subjects from the population of interest. (Random sampling is discussed in greater detail in the section on gathering data.) **Randomization** is the random allocation of subjects between experimental groups and control groups. Thus, step one is to select subjects from the population using random sampling and step two is to randomly assign these randomly selected subjects to experimental or control groups.

Random sampling and randomization characterize **double-blind studies**. A double-blind study is an extremely rigorous form of experimental research in which neither the researcher nor the subject knows to which group the subject belongs. Random selection and random allocation eliminate the effects of expectations and perceptions. For instance, a participant receiving a new heart medication may expect to have more energy and actually believe that he or she does have more energy. In addition, the researcher who knows the participant is receiving the new heart medication may perceive that the participant's color has improved. Thus, double-blind studies control bias because of false expectations and perceptions.

Double-blind studies are often used in the investigation of new drugs. When experimental and control groups are created, neither the participants nor the researchers know to which group the individual participants belong. In order to receive what appears to be the new drug, the participants in the control group are given a **placebo**. A placebo looks exactly like the new drug but, instead, contains harmless ingredients (sometimes called a sugar pill). Therefore, the expectations of the researchers and the participants do not bias the results.

Causal-Comparative Research

Causal-comparative research is a type of quasi-experimental design. *Quasi* means resembling or having some of the characteristics. Therefore, causal-comparative research resembles experimental research by having many, but not all, of its characteristics. However, causal-comparative research lacks two key characteristics of experimental research: manipulation of treatment and random assignment to a group.

Choosing causal-comparative research is correct when one of the three following situations exist:

- The variables cannot be manipulated (gender, age, race, birthplace).
- The variables should not be manipulated (accidental death or injury, child abuse).
- The variables represent different conditions that have already occurred (medication error, heart catheterization performed, smoking).

This research design is also called *ex post facto*, meaning **retrospective**. Examples of quasi-experimental research are case-control (retrospective) studies, field experiments, and natural experiments.

Epidemiologists investigating the development of disease often use **case-control (retrospective) studies**. In case-control studies, the epidemiologists look for characteristics and occurrences that are related to the subsequent development of a disease. In these studies, epidemiologists collect masses of data from health records and through interviews with both persons with the disease (cases) and persons without it (controls). HIM professionals are often involved with case-control studies because they are experts on the content of health records and at finding cases and controls using various clinical and administrative classification systems, such as ICD-9-CM, ICD-10, DSM, and SNOMED CT.

Researchers investigating the sociology of medicine often conduct field experiments by going into the site (field) and observing activities. The strength of this type of research is that participants tend to act more naturally in their real setting. An outstanding example of field research is the research on health practitioners' conversations overheard in elevators. Researchers rode hospital elevators all day, listening to and recording conversations. They found that patient confidentiality was severely breached.

Researchers conducting natural experiments wait for the event to occur naturally. For example, researchers interested in the effectiveness of triage in emergencies would wait for a disaster. Prior to the disaster, they would establish baseline data and tools for data collection. When the disaster occurs, they would record their observations of the actions and results.

In case-control studies, field experiments, and natural experiments, researchers relinquish control of the situations. For purists, however, the lack of randomization and control of treatment lessens the value of causal-comparative (quasi-experimental) research. The research only weakly determines causation. However, as the examples illustrate, in some situations, causal-comparative research is the only design that is logistically and ethically feasible. Causal-comparative research, then, determines the possibility of causal relationships.

Time Frame as an Element of Research Design

Another element of design cuts across all six types of design. This element is the time frame of the study. There are two pairs of time frames: retrospective versus prospective and cross-sectional versus longitudinal.

Studies within a retrospective time frame look back in time. For example, many early research studies of stress were retrospective. In these retrospective studies, the researchers measured the participant's level of stress and then asked the participant to reconstruct events that had occurred in a past period of time. Leadership studies in which the researcher asked the leader to list factors that led to his or her success are another example of a retrospective time frame. For some types of questions, such as those related to historic events, a retrospective design is the only possible design.

In **prospective** research studies, subjects are followed into the future to examine relationships between variables and later occurrences. For example, researchers identify individuals or subjects with certain variables and then follow these individuals or subjects into the future to see what occurs. Researchers conducted a study in which they prospectively assigned consecutively admitted patients to one of two groups (Oniki et al. 2003, 179). The nurses caring for one group of patients received periodic electronic reminders about the status of documentation on routine nursing tasks; the nurses caring for the other group did not receive the reminders (Oniki et al. 2003, 180). The researchers found fewer deficiencies in documentation for the electronic reminder group (Oniki et al. 2003, 181). Research studies with a cross-sectional design collect data at one point in time. **Cross-sectional** studies are snapshots and, as such, may collect data at an entirely unrepresentative point in time. The great advantage of cross-sectional studies is that they are efficient.

Longitudinal studies collect data from the same participants at multiple points in time. Cancer registries that collect data on cancer patients throughout their lifetimes are prime examples of longitudinal studies. Other longitudinal studies include studies of breast cancer and cardiovascular disease. For example, since 1976, the Nurses' Health Study has followed the health of more than 120,000 nurses (Field et al. 2007, 968).

The six types of research designs are not rigid boxes. Researchers often combine designs to address their particular research questions or problems. For instance, many studies include both descriptive and correlational findings. In describing their study, researchers also often state its time frame. Thus, a researcher would state that the study was descriptive, correlational, and cross-sectional. However, the key to classifying the design is to understand the purpose of the research.

Check Your Understanding 16.3

Instructions: Answer the following questions on a separate piece of paper.

1. What determines a researcher's choice of a research design?
2. Which research design would a researcher use to investigate the relationship between a supervisor's level of stress and the number of his or her subordinates?
3. What would be a direct relationship between the supervisor's level of stress and the number of his or her subordinates?
4. What is the key characteristic of experimental research?
5. How does quasi-experimental research differ from experimental research?
6. How do independent variables and dependent variables differ?
7. In a double-blind study, who knows which subjects are in the study group and which subjects are in the control group?
8. Why would a researcher choose a longitudinal study rather than a cross-sectional study?

Research Methods

A research method is the particular strategy that a researcher uses to collect, analyze, and present data. Particular methods are associated with certain designs, although considerable overlap exists. (Refer to table 16.6.) For example, researchers can use surveys in both descriptive and correlational designs.

Surveys

A survey is a common research method. Surveys are a form of self-report research in which the individuals themselves are the source of data. Surveys collect data about a population to determine its current status with regard to certain factors (Gay et al. 2006, 11). Surveys that collect data from all the members of the population are **census surveys**; surveys that collect data from representative members of the population are **sample surveys**.

HIM professionals conduct both types of surveys. For example, when surveying HIM program directors, researchers surveyed all the directors (Sasnett and Ross 2007, 4). On the other hand, when information about the members of the national association (a population of more than 40,000) is needed, researchers conduct only a sample survey. A census survey of a large population is generally beyond the resources of a solitary researcher or a small research team. For example, in an exploratory descriptive study, an HIM researcher surveyed a representative sample of 250 "most-wired" hospitals to investigate their record retention practices (Rinehart-Thompson 2008b, 2).

Survey research is further categorized as interview or questionnaire. Researchers conduct **interview surveys** by personally questioning the members of the **target population**. In **questionnaire surveys**, researchers create electronic or paper forms that include the questions.

Interviews

In interview surveys, researchers orally question the members of the population. Examples of interview surveys are telephone surveys, exit polls, and **focused studies**. Researchers can question members of the population as individuals or as a **focus group**. In focused studies, the researcher and the group members have a group discussion.

Researchers use a written list of questions called an **interview guide**. Using an interview guide ensures that all individuals or focus groups are asked the same questions. Researchers can strictly control the questions and responses or can allow a free-flowing conversation. They often record sessions and then transcribe the comments.

For example, researchers explored the effects of health information technologies on clinical tasks and workflows in ambulatory care settings (Leu et al. 2008, 372). The researchers interviewed executives and staff in eight ambulatory care settings (four community health centers, three health center networks, and one large primary care organization). The researchers selected sites that were national leaders and used a variety of health information technologies (Leu et al. 2008, 372). There were a total of 20 on-site, in-person interviews. The interviews were audiotaped and transcribed. The data were entered into specialized software for the analysis of textual, graphical, audio, and visual data. The analyses revealed that the participants described six clinical domains. In these clinical domains, the workflows must be fully operational for the health information technologies' deployment to be successful (Leu et al. 2008, 373). The researchers concluded that their study had implications for certification and evaluation of EHR systems, for identification of challenges to effective use and degree of adoption of EHR systems, and for educational curricula (Leu et al. 2008, 377).

Questionnaires

Questionnaire surveys also query members of the population. Rather than asking questions orally, researchers mail participants an electronic or print form to complete and return. Questionnaire studies are efficient because they require less time and money than interview studies do and because they allow the researchers to collect data from many more members of the target population. Moreover, Internet-based questionnaire studies further enhance efficiency because the subjects' answers are entered directly into the database, which eliminates a step for the researchers.

For example, HIM researchers conducted a Web-based survey of vendors of health information technologies (Giannangelo and Fenton 2008, 3). The purpose of the survey was to assess the vendors' integration or potential integration of SNOMED CT into their EHR and EMR products. Of the 408 vendors, 72 responded (18 percent). Of the respondents, 59 percent had obtained or planned to obtain a SNOMED CT license. However, only 20 percent of these respondents had made SNOMED CT operational in their computer applications. The most common reason provided by the 41 percent of respondents who did not plan to obtain a SNOMED CT license was the lack of market demand. The researchers concluded that additional emphasis is needed to promote the incorporation of SNOMED CT into EHR and EMR applications (Giannangelo and Fenton 2008, 7). In another example, researchers assessed the ways organizations that develop evidence-based clinical guidelines search the literature to capture relevant information (Deurenberg et al. 2008, 23). The researchers used a semi-structured questionnaire (see subsequent section on Features of Instruments) that asked the participants to provide information about their organization and its types of clinical guidelines, to indicate the databases and the search tools and evaluation methods they used, and to suggest ways to improve the search tools (Deurenberg et al. 2008, 24). One finding was that MEDLINE was a common database for all the guideline development organizations (Deurenberg et al. 2008, 28).

Observational Research

In **observational research**, researchers observe, record, and analyze behaviors and events. Highly detailed, observational research provides insights into what subjects do, how they do it, and why they do it. Usually classified as qualitative research, observational studies include a wide range of research techniques. Observational researchers may use **triangulation** to support their findings. Triangulation is the use of multiple sources or perspectives to investigate the same phenomenon. The multiple sources or perspectives include data (multiple times, sites, or respondents), investigators (researchers), theories, and methods (Bednarz 1985, 304). The results or conclusions are validated if the multiple sources or perspectives arrive at the same results or conclusions. This process lends credence to the research.

Observational research is used in many designs. For example, sociologists used a descriptive design to describe the culture of medical students (Becker et al. 1961). There are three common types of observational research: nonparticipant observation, participant observation, and ethnography.

Nonparticipant Observation

In **nonparticipant observation**, researchers act as neutral observers who neither intentionally interact with nor affect the actions of the population being observed. Of the three types of observational research, HIM professionals are more likely to encounter nonparticipant observation. Nonparticipant observation takes three common forms: **naturalistic observation**, simulation observation, and case study.

In nonparticipant observation, researchers also analyze the content of modes of communication, such as documentation, speech, body language, music, television shows, commercials, and movies. Research on the content of Web sites has become common. For example, researchers evaluated the Web accessibility of state vocational rehabilitation agencies (Sligar and Zeng 2008, 13). The purpose of the research was to assess whether the 80 Web sites (50 state sites, District of Columbia, and 29 sites for the blind) were accessible to people with disabilities. The researchers used software that incorporated Web Content Accessibility Guidelines (WCAG). Of the Web sites, seven (nine percent) did not comply with WCAG checkpoints (Sligar and Zeng 2008, 15). The researchers noted that because of the dynamic nature of the Internet, ongoing monitoring of the accessibility of Web sites is needed (Sligar and Zeng 2008, 17).

Also, using nonparticipant observation, researchers investigated how physicians used a hospital's multiple clinical information systems in their tasks (Sørby and Nytrøm 2005, 112–113). The hospital's clinical information systems were in both paper and electronic formats. In this study, physicians were observed as they processed 52 patients' discharges from the coronary care unit. The two nonparticipant observers (medical students) had researcher-designed check sheets upon which to record their observations. As the physicians performed the discharge process, the nonparticipant observers marked on the check sheets the clinical information sources and described the information retrieved. The researchers found low reliance on the EHR system. Of the 688 informational elements retrieved during the discharge process, 60 percent (412) were obtained from paper formats, 22 percent (151) from other humans (physicians, nurses, and patients), and 18 percent (125) from electronic formats (114–115). Moreover, observation revealed that the physicians actually used the EHR system less than they had reported on a subsequent survey (117). The researchers concluded that, to support physicians in their tasks, the EHR system could be improved, particularly the interfaces between applications (117).

In a naturalistic study, researchers reviewed the performance of collision avoidance systems from 73 real rear-end striking crashes (13) or rear-end striking near-crashes (60) (McLaughlin et al. 2008, 10). Collision avoidance systems rely on driving data from various sensors and indicators including radar, infrared laser, ultrasonic, machine vision, accelerator, speedometer, and brake and turn signals. Types of systems include parking assistance, forward collision warning (rear-end), and lane change and warning. Systems provide varying degrees of control from issuing warnings to taking control of the vehicle. The systems' driving data were entered into software that allowed the frame-by-frame review and analysis of the events. The researchers concluded that, based on the timing of the systems' alerts and human reaction times in the driving literature, just over 60 percent of the population would be able to avoid a collision (McLaughlin et al. 2008, 14).

Simulation observation is very similar to naturalistic observation except that the researchers stage the events rather than allowing them to occur naturally. Researchers can invent their own simulations or use standardized vignettes to stage the events. For example, researchers investigated how institutional policies and federal regulations for clinical research affect the configuration of an EHR (Kahn et al. 2007, 661–662). To identify potential problems in workflows, the researchers created a detailed clinical vignette (662). Included in the vignette were all the key steps of a prospective clinical trial. (See chapters 12 and 18.) Discussing policies, procedures, and workflows in terms of EHR configurations, resulted in definitions of the users' roles and access and the system's workflows and functional capabilities (Kahn et al. 2007, 663). Reviewing the vignette also revealed a lack of functionality in the commercial EHR. In the EHR, orders, results, and progress notes related to the research study could *not* be separated and restricted from the patients' ongoing care as could occur in the paper-based health record. This research finding resulted in modifications of some of the healthcare organization's processes. For example, order entry for research-related care remained paper-based (Kahn et al. 2007, 665). Additionally, as a result of this finding, the EHR vendor created a clinical research advisory council to provide input into future product development (Kahn et al. 2007, 666). Finally, the researchers noted that the vignette assisted discussion by making generalized concepts concrete, tangible, and accessible to the responsible clinicians and executives (Kahn et al. 2007, 665).

The **case study** is another type of nonparticipant observation. Case studies are in-depth investigations of one person, one group, or one institution. Researchers conduct case studies to determine characteristics associated with a person, group, or institution. The characteristics then can shed light on similar persons, groups, or institutions. Often case studies suggest hypotheses that researchers subsequently investigate using other methods. Case studies are intensive, and researchers amass extensive details. Sources of data include administrative records, financial records, policy and procedure manuals, legal documents, government documents, surveys, and interviews. These many sources result in layer upon layer of detailed data, often called rich data.

Sigmund Freud conducted case studies at the individual person level (Flyvbjerg 2006, 229). This type of case study is called a clinical case study. Early research in medicine comprised clinical case studies. From a physician's presentation of detailed information about an individual patient, other physicians learned about similar patients.

Other case studies are at the group level and the institutional level. For example, at the group level researchers could investigate the influence that AIDS action groups have had on funding practices of the National Institutes of Health. At the institutional level, researchers studied the characteristics of ambulatory medical practices that were associated with the implementation and use of e-prescribing systems (Crosson et al. 2008, 365). Twelve medical practices representing a range of sizes and physician specialties were in the study. In the field, the researchers collected data through observation and interview before and after the implementation of an e-prescribing system. The data were entered into specialized software for the analysis of textual, graphical, audio, and visual data. The analyses revealed that successful implementations were associated with modest expectations, such as improved workflow, while unsuccessful implementations were associated with high expectations, such as flawless functioning and minimal disruption of routines. Finally, the researchers concluded that successful implementation of e-prescribing systems were associated with effective communication of the actual capabilities and limitations of the technology, with knowledge of the anticipated effects on the clinical workflow, and with timely access to high-quality technical support (Crosson et al. 2008, 368).

Participant Observation

In **participant observation**, researchers are also participants in the observed actions. They can participate overtly (openly) or covertly (secretly). For example, researchers in Australia wanted to determine the optimum time to repeat feedback on rates of hand washing to maximize the effects of the feedback and to most improve the rates (van de Mortel et al. 2000, 91). The researchers covertly observed the incidence of hand washing to establish a baseline. The researchers then posted feedback—bar charts displaying the rates of hand washing. Immediately after posting the feedback, the researchers overtly observed hand washing to assess the effect of their posting (intervention of providing feedback). Then, six months and 12 months later, the researchers again covertly observed the rates of hand washing. The baseline rate of hand washing was 61 percent; the rate was 83 percent immediately after intervention; and the six-month and twelve-month rates were 76 percent and 65 percent, respectively (van de Mortel et al. 2000, 93–94). Based on this pattern, the researchers concluded that feedback on the rates of hand washing should be provided every 12 months (van de Mortel et al. 2000, 95). Researchers using participant observation reflect the insiders' perspectives. This reflection can be both an advantage and a disadvantage. As insiders, the researchers have unique insights into the environment and context of the action. At the same time, however, as insiders, the researchers may share the biases and blind spots of insiders. Therefore, in participant observation, researchers attempt to maintain neutrality while in the "thick of the action."

Another aspect of participant observation is the ethical ambiguity of covert observation (Johnson 1992, 218). Covert observation is the deception of participants, and specifically in the previous research, deception of coworkers. It breaches the right to privacy and the principle of informed consent (Johnson 1992, 217–219; Herrera 1999, 332). Additionally, covert observation undermines human relationships by eroding trust and disregarding honesty. On the other hand, the ethical principal of utility—the greatest good for the greatest number—and the advancement of science may override the ethical breaches of covert observation (Johnson 1992, 220; Herrera 1999, 332). In general, researchers who are considering covert observation as their research method should assess whether the data could be collected using another method and should seek counsel from appropriate research oversight entities.

Ethnography

Ethnography is observational research that came to the life sciences from anthropology. It includes both qualitative and quantitative approaches and both participant and nonparticipant observation. Ethnographers typically investigate aspects of culture in naturalistic settings. For example, an HIM professional could choose ethnography to investigate how the culture of a nursing unit or clinic affects the timeliness and comprehensiveness of provider documentation. Are areas of the unit or clinic set aside for documentation, indicating that the culture of the unit or clinic values accurate and comprehensive documentation? Or, do providers attempt documenting in health records in corners or on ledges of the unit or clinic, indicating less attention to documentation?

Two key differences exist between ethnography and other types of research. First, in ethnography, the literature review results in initial research questions rather than clearly defined problems or focused research questions (Gay et al. 2006, 442–443). Second, ethnography is iterative, or cyclical (Byrne 2001, 82). As ethnographers collect data, they analyze them, revising their initial questions and creating new interpretations. They may seek other sources of data and participants and add alternate techniques for data collection. Therefore, ethnographers work in a cycle beginning with initial questions. They collect data about those questions. Based on their analysis of the initial data, they then revise their questions, interpretations, and techniques and collect more data about those revisions. This cyclical process contrasts with the linear processes of other research methods discussed in this chapter.

In order to understand cultures, ethnographers amass great volumes of detailed data while studying in the field. Therefore, another characteristic of ethnography is that the researchers live or work with the population they are studying. For example, researchers investigated the culture of clinical teaching conferences (Hill and Tyson 1997, 594). They attended 52 sessions of morning report with the faculty physicians, house officers, and medical students and timed the length of people's comments, the commentator's status, and the content of the comments (Hill and Tyson 1997, 594). In addition to the sessions of morning report, the researchers conducted 34 interviews lasting between 30 and 60 minutes with people from the three groups (Hill and Tyson 1997, 595). The quantitative aspect of this study is that the researchers tabulated the minutes and averaged the time that members of each group spoke. The qualitative aspect of this study is that the researchers analyzed the comments for themes.

Ethnography has other unique characteristics, such as the attention that ethnographers pay to the environment (furniture, instruments, space, lighting, schedules, brochures, and clothing). For example, the ethnographers in the previously described study recorded data on x-ray equipment and the placement of a table and a sign-in sheet (Hill and Tyson 1997, 596). In general, ethnographers also record details about members of the population, including jargon, feelings, points of view, beliefs, practices, and goals. In conclusion, the strength of ethnography is that researchers obtain insights not discoverable in other methods. Its weaknesses include volumes of data that are difficult to analyze, large investments of money and time, and the lack of generalizability and replicability.

Experimental Research

Experiments are another major category of research methods. These methods classify into two subcategories: experimental studies and quasi-experimental studies. Both subcategories involve treatments using the broad meaning of the term as some sort of intervention. The level of control that researchers establish differentiates experiments between experimental studies and quasi-experimental studies.

Campbell and Stanley (1963) wrote the classic text on experiments, defining and describing six major types of experiments, with three in the subcategory of experimental and three in the subcategory of quasi-experimental. Experimental studies include:

- Pretest–posttest control group method
- Solomon four-group method
- Posttest-only control group method

Quasi-experimental studies include:

- One-shot case study
- One-group pretest–posttest method
- Static group comparison

The key elements in the descriptions of these experiments are:

- Randomization
- Observation (pretest or posttest)
- Control group
- Treatment

Readers should be aware that, similar to the term *treatment,* researchers use the terms *pretest, posttest,* and *observation* broadly. They simply mean that they have measured the variable in some way.

To demonstrate the differences among these six subcategories, descriptions of research studies conducted in each of the six subcategories will be described. (See table 16.7.) The description will include how the studies representing the subcategories conform with or deviate from the four key elements. To highlight the differences, the research studies all involve the same research topic. This topic is the medical students' utilization of voice recognition software.

Table 16.7. Key elements of experimental and quasi-experimental studies*

Category/ Subcategory	Study Features	Elements			
		Randomization	Observation	Control Group	Treatment
Experimental					
Pretest–Posttest Control Group Method	Investigation of medical students' utilization of voice recognition software	X	X	X	X
	Random assignment to experimental and control groups				
	Observation to establish initial level of utilization (pretest)				
	Two-hour training session (treatment)				
	Observation to determine posttreatment utilization (posttest)				
	Potential that pretest exposure affected posttreatment performance				
Solomon Four-Group Method	Investigation of medical students' utilization of voice recognition software	X	X	X	X
	Random assignment to two experimental and two control groups				
	Observation to establish initial level of utilization (pretest)				
	Two-hour training session (treatment)				
	Observation to determine posttreatment utilization (posttest)				
	Controls for pretest exposure, but at the cost of double work because of double groups				
Posttest-Only Control Group Method	Investigation of medical students' utilization of voice recognition software	X	P	X	X
	Random assignment to experimental and control groups				
	Two-hour training session (treatment)				
	Observation to determine posttreatment utilization (posttest)				
	Controls for pretest exposure by eliminating pretest, but at cost of establishment of initial utilization level				
Quasi-Experimental					
One-Shot Case Study	Investigation of medical students' utilization of voice recognition software	0	P	0	X
	Two-hour training session (treatment)				
	Observation to determine posttreatment utilization (posttest)				
	Flaws of no pretest, no randomization, and no control group				
One-Group Pretest–Posttest Method	Investigation of medical students' utilization of voice recognition software	0	X	0	X
	Observation to establish initial level of utilization (pretest)				
	Two-hour training session (treatment)				
	Observation to determine posttreatment utilization (posttest)				
	Flaws of no control group and no randomization				
Static Group Comparison	Investigation of medical students' utilization of voice recognition software	0	P	X	X
	Assignment to experimental and control groups				
	Two-hour training session (treatment)				
	Observation to determine posttreatment utilization (posttest)				
	Flaws of no pretest and no randomization				

*X = Fully met; P = Partially met; 0 = Absent

Experimental Studies

Researchers conducted a pretest–posttest control group method to investigate medical students' utilization of voice recognition software. The researchers randomly assigned the first-year medical students to experimental and control groups. The researchers performed a pretest in which they established both groups' levels of utilization of voice recognition software. The researchers then conducted a two-hour training session (treatment). At the end of the academic year, the researchers measured both groups' utilization of voice recognition software. They could reasonably attribute differences in utilization to their treatment. However, the researchers should be cautious because the possibility exists that the students' higher level of utilization of the software is a function of their exposure during the pretest observation. Familiarity with the software from exposure could predispose the students to use it.

The key elements of this study include:

- Randomization (randomly assigned medical students to groups)
- Pretest and posttest observation (levels of utilization of voice recognition software before and after the training session)
- Control group
- Treatment (two-hour training session)

The Solomon four-group method is a complex variation of the pretest–posttest control group method. The purpose of the Solomon four-group method is to provide a way to control for the potential effect of exposure. For example, as noted in the previous study, taking a pretest may affect performance on a posttest. In the previous study of utilization of voice recognition software, how much of the utilization is due to mere familiarity with the software related to the original exposure? Using the Solomon four-group method, researchers create two experimental groups and two control groups rather than only one of each. They then administer the pretest to only one of the experimental groups and to only one of the control groups. However, they administer the posttest to *all* four groups. The difference in level of utilization between the two experimental groups would be the effect of the familiarity from pretesting. Therefore, the Solomon four-group method provides a valuable additional control. However, this additional control comes at a high price: everything is doubled.

The key elements of the Solomon four-group method are the same as those for the pretest–posttest control group method.

The posttest-only control group method is another method to offset the potential effect of familiarity related to exposure through pretesting. The posttest-only control group method is similar to the pretest–posttest control group method except that there is no pretest. In the research on utilization of voice recognition software, the researchers randomly assign half the first-year medical students to the experimental group and half to the control group. The researchers do not observe an initial level of utilization through a pretest. The experimental group receives the treatment of the training session, and the control group does not. Then, at the end of the academic year, the researchers measure the students' level of utilization of the software. This fairly simple method eliminates the potential bias introduced by pretesting.

The key elements of the posttest-only control group are randomization, posttest observation, control group, and treatment. For example, health educators used this method to observe the effects of endorsements by local opinion leaders and testimonials by teachers on schools' use of a Web-based smoking prevention program (Buller et al. 2007, 610–612). Randomization of the 394 public secondary schools occurred by region. There were three experimental groups that received the treatment: (1) received the endorsement and the testimonial, (2) received the endorsement only, and (3) received the testimonial only, as well as one control group that received neither the endorsement nor the testimonial. All four groups received the information on the Web-based smoking prevention program. The researchers found that the second experimental condition, the endorsements of opinion leaders such as directors of tobacco control coalitions, resulted in more teachers visiting the program's Web site and assigning their students to use it (Buller et al. 2007, 614).

Quasi-Experimental Studies

In the one-shot case study, researchers study one group only once following the treatment. For example, in the study of utilization of voice recognition software, researchers provide a two-hour training session on utilization of voice recognition software to all the first-year medical students at some point in the academic year. Then, at the end of the academic year, the researchers measure the students' level of utilization of the software. The researchers can make no credible statement about the effect of the training session on the utilization of voice recognition software because they (1) have not established with an observation (pretest) the level of utilization prior to the training (treatment) to use as a comparison and (2) have no other group of medical students (control group) to use as a comparison.

The key elements in this case are posttest observation and treatment.

The one-group pretest–posttest method corrects one flaw of the one-shot case study with the addition of the pretest. Therefore, the researchers investigating utilization of voice recognition software improve their experiment by adding some measurement, or pretest, that establishes the medical students' level of utilization prior to the training session. However, adding the pretest only minimally improves their investigation. Statements made by the researchers about the utilization of voice recognition software are still highly suspect because the researchers included no control group. Therefore, readers of this research could reasonably wonder whether other factors in the hospital or in society caused the level of utilization.

The key elements of this method are pretest and posttest observation and treatment.

The static group comparison corrects for the lack of a control group. Therefore, the static group comparison is similar to the one-shot case study except that researchers using the static group comparison add a second group, the control group. In the research on utilization of voice recognition software, the researchers allow half the students to choose to attend the training session. This group is the experimental group, and the half who choose not to receive the training are the control group. Then, at the end of the academic year, the researchers measure the students' level of utilization of the software. Unfortunately, a flaw of this study is that there is no random assignment to the groups. Perhaps all the technophiles joined the experimental group and all the technophobes joined the control group. In that case, the increased level of utilization of the experimental group could just be an effect of the group's inherent love of computers and not of the training session.

The key elements of the static group comparison are posttest observation, control group, and treatment.

Experimental research is important because this major category of research allows researchers to investigate cause and effect. It should be clear from these examples of research studies that true experimental studies are difficult to conduct. Nevertheless, experimental research studies are extremely powerful research methods because only they can establish cause and effect (causal relationship). The types classified as quasi-experimental studies begin to determine that a causal relationship could exist. Some experts state that very large quasi-experimental studies weakly determine a causal relationship. However, to truly establish causal relationships, researchers must use one of the types classified as an experimental study.

Secondary Analysis

Secondary analysis is the analysis of the original work of another person or organization. In secondary analysis, researchers reanalyze original data by combining data sets to answer new questions or by using more sophisticated statistical techniques (Cohen 1992, 172). Researchers make the distinction between **primary analysis** and **secondary analysis**. Primary analysis refers to analysis of original research data by the researchers who collected them. There are two types of secondary analysis: data mining and meta-analysis.

Reanalysis of secondary data is a powerful tool for health information managers because it allows them to compare their performance data with local, regional, state, and national benchmarks. For healthcare organizations in general, secondary analysis is an important tool because it allows organizations to compare their outcomes with the outcomes of industry leaders.

Data mining is the extraction and enumeration of patterns from data using algorithms (Fayyad 1997, 9). These patterns are nontrivial, previously undiscerned, and potentially useful (Fayyad 1997, 7). Data mining is considered secondary data analysis because data miners use databases created by others, often for purposes unrelated to research and data mining.

For example, researchers explored data from the clinical information system of the Ulster Community and Health Trust (Huang et al. 2007, 254). The clinical information system was used routinely for patient management (Huang et al. 2007, 254). The researchers' purpose was to improve the quality of diabetic treatment. They analyzed the clinical data of 2064 type 2 diabetic patients. Data mining allowed the researchers to determine the top 15 features (factors) that predicted patients' blood glucose control (Huang et al. 2007, 256). The researchers concluded that their model could become a part of routine medical practice, especially as the model provided support for evidence-based practice (Huang et al. 2007, 261).

Meta-analysis is the integrative analysis of findings from many studies that examined the same question. Studies that are included in a meta-analysis have common underlying characteristics (Cohen 1992, 172). Gene Glass coined the term meta-analysis (Cohen 1992, 172), and defined it as "the statistical analysis of a large collection of results from individual studies for the purpose of integrating findings" (Glass 1976, 3). Meta-analysis began as a sophisticated way to present a literature review but has become a research method in its own right.

The advantage of meta-analysis is that it weighs findings from many studies, some of which are contradictory. Researchers who use meta-analysis must specify their inclusion criteria; explain how they searched and found articles; code the studies' designs, methods, and outcomes; and analyze the coded data (Cohen 1992, 173–174).

For example, researchers conducted a meta-analysis that synthesized studies on the effects of decision aids on breast cancer patients' choices of surgical procedure and their knowledge of treatments for breast cancer (Waljee et al. 2007, 1068). Decision aids include brochures, pamphlets, audio and video tapes, and computer programs (Waljee et al. 2007, 1069). First, the researchers specified their inclusion criteria: to be included, the study must be an evaluation of a decision aid for stage I or II breast cancer treatment of breast-conserving surgery versus mastectomy. Second, the researchers explained their strategies to find all the studies. They listed their 16 search terms noting that their search terms were medical subject heading terms that the researchers "exploded" (librarians' term meaning expanding the search to the general topic). The researchers specified which reference databases they searched (MEDLINE, EMBASE, CINAHL, the Cochrane Network, and Health and Psychosocial Instructions [HAPI]). They also noted that they manually reviewed the reference lists of all the articles to identify additional studies. They also searched for unpublished works and abstracts from associations related to cancer and decision support. They included articles in all languages. Their search resulted in 116 articles and 7 unpublished abstracts, of which 11 articles (9 studies) met the search criteria: (a) three studies were **randomized clinical trials** (RCTs); (b) two studies were nonrandomized trials with control groups of which one study yielded three articles, and (c) four studies were nonrandomized trials without control groups. Third, all three researchers then extracted data independently. In cases of disagreement, consensus was obtained through discussion (Waljee et al. 2007, 1068). Finally, they conducted the meta-analysis statistical procedure called effect size analysis. *Effect size* is the strength of the impact of one factor on another (Shi 2008, 120). Integrating the results of these studies revealed that women who used a decision aid were 25 percent more likely to choose breast-conserving surgery over mastectomy than women who did not use a decision aid (Waljee et al. 2007, 1068). The analysis also indicated that average knowledge of treatment options was significantly increased by 24 percent for patients who received the decision aid as compared to the controls. Thus, using meta-analysis, the researchers synthesized the results from multiple studies in order to reach overall conclusions.

Several key points are important to remember about research design and methods. Research is the systematic, orderly set of procedures that individuals choose to expand their knowledge or to answer their question. They can investigate the same broad question or problem using several of the research designs. (See table 16.8.) Preliminary, exploratory investigations are often descriptive or correlational. As researchers refine these investigations, they conduct causal-comparative and experimental studies. The research design chosen depends on the purpose of the research. Certain methods, such as surveys and laboratory experiments, are associated with particular designs. However, methods can be associated with more than one design and overlap occurs. The key point is that how the problem or question is defined indicates the appropriate research design and method.

Table 16.8. Research designs in a progression of studies within one topic

Design	Example of Progression of Studies
Historical	The factors leading to the creation and expansion of The Medical Record (TMR) and the Regenstrief Medical Record System (RMRS) between 1970 and 1990
Descriptive	A survey of physicians to determine how and to what degree they use the computer-based patient record
Correlational	A study to determine the relationship among physicians' attributes, the setting, and use of the computer-based patient record
Evaluation	A study to evaluate the efficacy of the implementation of the computer-based patient record in an academic health center
Causal-Comparative (Quasi-Experimental)	A study to compare the use of the computer-based patient record of a group of physicians in a setting classified as low barrier and a group of physicians in a setting classified as high barrier
Experimental	A study to compare use of the computer-based patient record of two matched physician groups; one group trained in a low-barrier experimental computer laboratory and one group trained in a high-barrier experimental computer laboratory

Check Your Understanding 16.4

Instructions: Answer the following questions on a separate piece of paper.

1. Which research method uses self-report data?
2. What type of question is question 1?
3. Why would researchers choose to conduct a structured interview using an interview guide?
4. If researchers wanted to investigate the impact of changes in Medicare reimbursement on a region's healthcare, which method would they choose?
5. Why would researchers choose to conduct a questionnaire survey?
6. If researchers wanted to establish that a new drug caused a reduction in blood pressure, which research method would they choose?
7. When would researchers choose to conduct a meta-analysis?
8. In questions 3 through 7, what common characteristic determined the researchers' choice of method?

Statement of Hypothesis

Hypotheses differ between quantitative and qualitative research. In quantitative research, hypotheses are concrete and written in specific terms that are testable. In qualitative research, hypotheses are tentative suppositions. They are working possibilities that guide the initial data collection and are revised during the study based on the data obtained. This section discusses hypotheses in quantitative research.

Formulation of precise and accurate hypotheses is a difficult task. In the statement of hypothesis, the researcher states the research question in measurable terms. (See figure 16.6.) Therefore, the statement of the hypothesis is more specific than the research question. Some experts explain that the statement of the hypothesis operationalizes the research question. These experts mean that the hypothesis states the research question in a way that is quantifiable, computable, and uses defined variables. Moreover, the statement of the hypothesis becomes the basis of the statistical tests. Therefore, there are two errors to avoid in the statement of the hypothesis: writing an ambiguous hypothesis and writing an untestable hypoth-

Figure 16.6. Components of hypotheses

- Variables of the study as defined in the literature
- Predicted relationship(s) or difference(s) between and among variables
- Measurement (quantifiable, computable)
- Intent of research

esis. Finally, researchers should take care that the hypothesis actually reflects the intent of the research.

Researchers write null hypotheses and alternative hypotheses. The **null hypothesis** states that there is no association between the independent and dependent variables. (The word *null* means none.) The **alternative hypothesis** states that there is an association between the independent and dependent variables. Alternative hypotheses are one-tailed or two-tailed. If the researcher states that the association is more or less, the alternative hypothesis is a **one-tailed hypothesis**. If the researcher makes no prediction about the direction of the results (more or less), the alternative hypothesis is a **two-tailed hypothesis**. These hypotheses are matched pairs. For example:

- *Null hypothesis:* There is no difference in the levels of utilization of voice recognition software between the group of physicians receiving the training and the group not receiving it.
- *Alternative hypothesis (one-tailed):* The level of utilization of the group receiving the training is 10 percent higher than the level of the group not receiving it.
- *Alternative hypothesis (two-tailed):* There is a 10 percent difference in the levels of utilization of voice recognition software between the group of physicians receiving the training and the group not receiving it.

Researchers state what they believe in alternative hypotheses. Unfortunately, the properties of statistical techniques do not allow them to directly test the accuracy of the alternative hypotheses. Instead, statistical techniques test null hypotheses. Therefore, researchers also must write null hypotheses in order to conduct statistical analysis. If the null hypothesis is rejected, the alternative hypothesis is accepted.

Researchers establish an appropriate **level of significance** before performing statistical analyses. This level of significance is known as the alpha (α) level. The level of significance is the criterion used for rejecting the null hypothesis. Common alpha levels are 0.05 and 0.01. Researchers set the lower alpha level when they want to minimize the chance that they might erroneously reject the null hypothesis when it is actually true.

Power is the probability of identifying real relationships or differences between groups (Goodman and Berlin 1994, 200). Specifically, power is the likelihood of failing to reject a false null hypothesis. When researchers fail to reject a false null hypothesis, the researchers have wrongly determined that there is no relationship or difference when, in fact, there is. However, for researchers (and the public), the ramifications of failing to assert a difference (power) are less than falsely asserting a difference (level of significance). Therefore, typically, power is less stringent than the level of significance and is often set at 0.80.

Researchers can make two types of errors associated with rejecting or failing to reject null hypotheses (See table 16.9.).

Table 16.9. Type I and type II errors in significance testing

Error	Truth or Actuality
Fail to reject null hypothesis	Incorrect: Type II error (β) (false negative) Difference or association between groups' performance Correct: No difference or association between groups' performance
Reject null hypothesis	Incorrect: Type I error (α) (false positive) No difference or association between groups' performance Correct (power): Actual difference

A **type I error** occurs when the researcher erroneously rejects the null hypothesis when it is true; in actuality, there is no difference. A **type II error** occurs when the researcher erroneously fails to reject the null hypothesis when it is false; in actuality, there is a difference. For example:

- *Null hypothesis:* There is no difference in blood pressure levels between the group of patients receiving the new drug and the group receiving the placebo.
- *Alternative hypothesis (one-tailed):* The blood pressure of the group of patients receiving the new drug is 15 percent lower than the blood pressure of the group receiving the placebo.

A researcher committing a type I error would reject the null hypothesis. Continuing in the error, he or she would report the efficacy of the new drug. Unfortunately, the fact is that there is no difference between the blood pressures of the two groups of patients; the new drug does not work as predicted. Researchers who set the alpha level at 0.05 have a 5 percent chance of making this error whereas those who set the alpha level at 0.01 have a 1 percent chance of making the error. Thus, an alpha level of 0.01 is stricter than an alpha level of 0.05.

Beta (β) designates the probability of making a type II error. In the previous example, the researcher would make a type II error if he or she failed to reject the null hypothesis and it was indeed false. The researcher would erroneously state that there was no difference between the blood pressure of the group taking the new drug and the blood pressure of the group taking the placebo. In fact, there was a difference and the new drug was working as predicted. Beta is related to power because power is 1- β. Reflecting its relationship to power, β is often set at 0.20, meaning that the researcher has a 20 percent chance of failing to reject the null hypothesis when an association or difference actually exists.

Statistical tests for significance result in a p-value. A *p-value* indicates the probability of obtaining the result by chance if the null hypothesis is true. Therefore, if the *p*-value is 0.05, the probability that the difference occurred by pure chance is 5 percent. If the *p*-value obtained from the statistical test is less than or equal to the level of predetermined alpha value, the study's results are considered unlikely to be mere chance and the null hypothesis is rejected.

Researchers properly use the word *significance* in two ways (See table 16.10.). There is *statistical significance* that is related to significance testing. This meaning signifies that the association or difference is actual and not a random chance. This meaning is related to the reliability of the research findings. Statistical significance is based on calculations. The size of the sample is an element in the calculation. Because of its sheer size, a very large sample can create statistical significance. Researchers also use the term *significance* alone in the common, dictionary definition of the word. In this use, significance means importance or meaningfulness (or important or meaningful, in its adjective form). Significance alone relates to the importance of the finding and whether the association or difference can or should affect practice or policy. However, statistical significance does *not* guarantee clinical or practical significance. Statistically significant findings can be trivial. For example, researchers studying a managerial decision support system could find that an improved algorithm increased the speed of calculating staffing needs by a statistically significant 0.5 seconds. While statistically significant, managers are not likely to purchase a new decision support system for staffing based on half a second. However, in the previous study of collision avoidance systems where one second made the difference between a near-crash and a crash, 0.5 seconds would be both statistically significant and significant (McLaughlin et al. 2008, 14). Therefore, researchers should take care to write out the full phrase "statistical significance" when referring to the likelihood that their findings were not the result of random chance or a biased sample and use the word "significance" when they mean importance or meaningfulness.

The statement of the hypothesis is a crucial step in the development of the research plan. It leads to the establishment of the appropriate statistical techniques and the determination of the level of significance. These two actions, in turn, affect the interpretation of the consequences of the treatment.

Table 16.10. Meanings of significance in research

Use	Meaning
Statistical significance	Probability that a given finding actually exists and is not the result of a biased sample or random chance Reliable finding Not necessarily meaningful—because of the statistical formula for computation may be the result of a large sample size
Significance	Dictionary meaning of important, meaningful, or consequential Sometimes stated as clinical significance or practical significance Having implications for decision making, practice, or policy

Selection of a Research Method

In selecting a research method, researchers first and foremost should consider their purpose as reflected in their research question. If they want to establish a causal relationship, they should conduct one of the experimental studies. If they are breaking new ground in a poorly understood area of practice, they may want to consider an exploratory study in a qualitative design.

Other factors are associated with the researchers' expertise and resources. Researchers should establish a match between the method and the following factors:

- *Expertise:* Can the researcher conduct, interpret, and explain sophisticated statistical techniques, or are more basic statistical techniques within the researcher's comfort zone?
- *Skills:* Can the researcher conduct the laboratory experiments necessary for research? For example, to investigate physicians' utilization of clinical guidelines, is the researcher able to insert codes into an EHR? Is the researcher able to insert a time clock into the software and design a query mechanism?
- *Personal attributes:* If the researcher is considering interviewing people, is he or she able to easily establish rapport with people? Or do conversations with strangers make the researcher feel awkward?
- *Time:* Does the researcher have the time to devote to conducting the research plan well? For example, investigating the change in attitude of students in HIM programs from freshman year through graduation is a meritorious idea. However, graduate programs have time frames within which students must complete their studies. A four-year research study may not fit the time frame.
- *Money:* Can the researcher afford the postage for a census survey of 52,000 AHIMA members?
- *Potential subjects:* The Solomon four-group method is excellent and beautifully controlled; however, it requires double the number of subjects. If subjects are in short supply, would this method be feasible?

Finally, researchers should strive for **parsimony** or elegance. Parsimony means that explanations of phenomena should include the fewest assumptions and conditions. Researchers who have achieved parsimony have eliminated extraneous, unnecessary complications. Just as the best theory is the simplest, so too is the best method.

Validity and Reliability

There are three types of **validity**. Internal validity and external validity involve the integrity of the research plan. Validity without a modifier refers to an attribute of measurement instruments. Reliability involves the consistency of measurements.

Validity

Internal validity and external validity are key issues when implementing a research plan. **Internal validity** is an attribute of a study's design that contributes to the accuracy of its findings. Campbell and Stanley identified eight threats to internal validity (1963, 5). (See figure 16.7.) Threats to internal validity are potential sources of error that contaminate the study's results. These sources of error come from factors outside the study (confounding variables). Therefore, if internal validity is breached, researchers cannot state for certain that the independent variable caused the effect. **External validity** refers to the extent to which the findings can be generalized to other people or groups. *Generalizability* is the term that researchers use to mean the ability to apply the results to other groups, such as hospitals, patients, and states. Are the findings representative of many people or groups? Internal validity represents the bare minimum; internal validity combined with external validity is the ideal.

For example, researchers within the Department of Veterans Affairs (VA) evaluated the use of automated encoders in the VA system (Lloyd and Layman 1997, 73–74). Eight VA medical centers tested encoding software programs from three vendors. During the course of the study, an earthquake badly damaged one of the VA medical centers, which never reopened. Therefore, no final data on the software program were available from that center. This event represents the threat to internal validity of **mortality (attrition)**, meaning the loss of subjects. In addition, the VA centers were not covered by Medicare's inpatient prospective payment system (PPS) at the time. This uniqueness represents a threat to external validity because most hospitals are covered by the PPS. Thus, the findings lacked generalizability. Therefore, both internal validity and external validity are important considerations for researchers.

In terms of an instrument, validity means the extent to which the instrument measures what it is intended to measure. Multiple aspects of an instrument's validity are assessed. Two important aspects are content validity and construct validity. **Content validity** concerns whether the instrument's items relate to the topic (content). For example, an ICD-9-CM coding test with content validity would have items related to key aspects of coding, such as the definition of principle diagnosis, fifth digits, complications and comorbidities, V codes, E codes, and the neoplasm table. **Construct validity** is the instrument's ability to measure hypothetical, nonobservable traits called constructs. Classic examples of constructs are psychological concepts, such as intelligence, motivation, and anxiety. Although intelligence itself is not visible, its effects are. Therefore, if an instrument is intended to measure patient satisfaction, it should include issues associated with patient satisfaction. Researchers state in their journal articles the validity of the instruments they use. References about instruments also provide the validity of instruments.

Figure 16.7. Threats to internal validity

History:	Unplanned events occur during the research and affect the results
Maturation:	Subjects grow or mature during the period of the study
Testing:	Taking the first test affects subsequent tests; "practice effect"
Instrumentation:	Lack of consistency in data collection
Statistical Regression:	Subjects selected because of their extreme scores
Differential Selection:	Control group and experimental group differ and the difference could affect the study's findings
Experimental Mortality:	Loss of subjects during the study
Diffusion of Treatment:	Members of the control group learn about the treatment of the experimental group

Reliability

Reliability represents consistency. Instruments that have reliability are stable. Repeated administrations will result in reasonably similar findings. **Intrarater reliability** means that the same person repeating the test will have reasonably similar findings. **Interrater reliability** means that different persons taking the test will have reasonably similar findings. Thus, reliability means that, over time, a test or observation dependably measures whatever it was intended to measure.

Check Your Understanding 16.5

Instructions: Answer the following questions on a separate piece of paper.

1. In which hypothesis does the researcher state what he or she believes?
2. If the researcher believes that the treatment increases output, would he or she write a one-tailed or a two-tailed hypothesis?
3. What is the difference between a type I error and a type II error?
4. What does the p-value represent?
5. What issues are involved in internal validity?
6. Why is reliability important in tests?

Selecting an Instrument

An **instrument** is a standardized, uniform way to collect data. Common examples of instruments are interview guides and questionnaires, although many other types exist. (See figure 16.8.) Researchers can find standardized instruments in several reference books (figure 16.9) and in electronic databases. Of particular interest to HIM professionals are two electronic databases: Health and Psychosocial Instruments (HAPI) and Buros Institute of Mental Measurements. These databases provide descriptions and critiques of instruments.

Figure 16.8. Types of measurement instruments

Checklists	Projective techniques
Clinical screenings and assessments	Psychological tests
Coding schemes and manuals	Questionnaires
Educational tests	Rating scales
Index measures	Scenarios
Interview guides (schedules)	Vignettes
Personality tests	

Figure 16.9. Print sources of measurement instruments

Bowling, A. 2005. Measuring Health: A Review of Quality of Life Measurement Scales, 3rd ed. New York: Open University Press.

Chun, K-k, S. Cobb, and J.R.P. French, Jr. 1975. Measures for Psychological Assessment: A Guide to 3,000 Original Sources and Their Applications. Ann Arbor, MI: Survey Research Center, Institute for Social Research.

Herndon, R.M., ed. 1997. Handbook of Neurologic Rating Scales. New York: Demos Vermande.

Keyser, D.J., and R.C. Sweetland, eds. 1991. Test Critiques. Kansas City, MO: Test Corporation of America.

Maddox, T., ed. 2003. Tests: A Comprehensive Reference for Assessments in Psychology, Education, and Business, 5th ed. Austin, TX: Pro-Ed.

McDowell, I., and C. Newell. 1996. Measuring Health: A Guide to Rating Scales and Questionnaires, 2nd ed. New York: Oxford University Press.

Murphy, L.L., R.A. Spies, and B.S. Plake, eds. 2006. Tests in Print VII: An Index to Tests, Test Reviews, and the Literature on Specific Tests. Lincoln, NE: University of Nebraska Press.

Redman, B.K., ed. 2002. Measurement Tools in Clinical Ethics. New York: Springer.

Redman, B.K., ed. 2003. Measurement Tools in Patient Education, 2nd ed. New York: Springer.

Spies, R.A., and B.S. Plake, eds. 2005. The Sixteenth Mental Measurements Yearbook (Buros Mental Measurements Yearbooks). Lincoln, NE: University of Nebraska Press.

Spreen, O., and E. Strauss. 1998. A Compendium of Neuropsychological Tests: Administration, Norms, and Commentary, 2nd. ed. New York: Oxford University Press.

Factors in Selection

Factors that determine the selection of an instrument include:

- Purpose
- Satisfactory ratings for reliability and validity
- Clarity of language
- Brevity and attractiveness
- Match between the theories underpinning the instrument and the researcher's investigation
- Match between the level of measurement (nominal, ordinal, interval, or ratio scales of data) and the proposed statistical analyses
- Public domain or proprietary
- Cost

Of these factors, purpose is the most important. Researchers should match their purpose and the instrument's purpose. They should obtain the instrument and then read it in its entirety to be sure that it is collecting what they want to collect and that the terms in it match their meaning for the terms. For example, if the instrument is measuring social support, does it mean social support in the workplace or social support in the family and home? A researcher studying the effect of social support from colleagues and coworkers in the workplace should select an instrument about social support in the workplace. Selecting an instrument about social support in the family would be a grave error with negative consequences for the validity of the research. Thus, merely reading the description and critique in the reference database is insufficient.

Researchers should select instruments that other researchers have already developed and refined. The reliability and validity of these instruments are established. Development of a reliable and valid measure is a research project in and of itself. For example, construction of a questionnaire includes developing potential items (questions), conducting focus groups to explore the comprehensiveness of the instrument and its readability, analyzing the validity and reliability of the instrument, and pilot testing (Garvin 2005, 3-4). Researchers should undertake the difficult task of developing an instrument only after they have investigated and verified that one does not already exist.

Instruments may be in the public domain or proprietary. Instruments in the public domain can be copied and used freely. Instruments that are proprietary must be purchased and cannot be copied. However, researchers can often obtain samples of instruments for review at little or no cost. In addition, researchers must consider the quality of the research. Of what use is an instrument that collects inaccurate data only tangentially related to the researcher's topic? The instrument must match the purpose and contribute to the collection of accurate data that build knowledge.

Features of Instruments

Questions on instruments may be structured, semistructured, or unstructured. **Structured (closed-ended) questions** list all the possible responses. **Unstructured (open-ended) questions** allow free-form responses. In **semistructured questions**, researchers first ask structured questions and then follow with open-ended questions to clarify. The advantages of structured questions are that they are easier for the participant to complete and for the researcher to tabulate and analyze than unstructured questions. The disadvantages of structured questions are that they are restrictive and may not be the right questions (questionable validity). The advantages of unstructured questions are that they allow in-depth questions and may uncover aspects of a problem unknown to the researcher. The disadvantages of unstructured questions are that they are less reliable and are more difficult to quantify, tabulate, and analyze than structured questions.

Structured questions may be numeric items or categorical items. Numeric items request the respondent to enter a number. When feasible, numeric items are preferable to categorical items (Alreck and Settle 2004, 113). In writing a numeric item, researchers must be careful to be clear and to specify the unit of measure. For example, the question "How long ago was your last visit to the dentist?" does not give the respondent an explicit unit of measure. The respondent may write 365 days, 52 weeks, or 1 year.

Categorical items classify respondents into groupings. It is important to construct categories that:

- *Are all-inclusive:* All respondents must fit into a category, even if it is "other."
- *Are mutually exclusive:* Categories should not overlap and, thereby, confuse the respondents.
- *Form meaningful clusters:* Categories should make sense and be meaningfully distinct. The following set of categories does not form a reasonable, balanced progression: kindergarten to 12th grade, freshman, sophomore, junior, senior, and graduate school. A more meaningful set of categories is: high school education, associate degree, baccalaureate degree, and graduate degree.
- *Are sufficiently narrow or broad:* The number of categories for a question may range from two (yes or no, true or false) to six or eight. Respondents have difficulty seeing meaningful shades of meaning beyond eight categories. Alreck and Settle (2004, 112–113) recommend that, when in doubt, use the narrower (greater number) categories. Researchers can always combine categories, but cannot disaggregate broad categories into fine-grained categories if the detailed data were not collected. On the other hand, requesting participants to respond to too many, and unnecessarily narrow, categories may depress the response rate and introduce inaccuracy.

A type of categorical item is a scaled item. **Scales** are progressive categories such as size, amount, importance, rank, or agreement. (See table 16.11.) For example, an HIM researcher used a scale on her questionnaire that allowed respondents to categorize their feelings of capability regarding various skills related to coding (Garvin 2001, 30–31). (See figure 16.10.)

A commonly used scale is the **Likert scale**, named for its developer, Rensis Likert. A Likert scale records the respondents' level of agreement or disagreement. On a Likert scale, the categories are along a range: strongly agree, agree, neutral, disagree, and strongly disagree. Each category is also called a point. Therefore, a scale with five categories is a five-point scale.

Researchers, marketers, and others use a **semantic differential scale** to ascertain a group's perspective or image of a product, healthcare organization, or program. (See figure 16.11.) A semantic differential scale uses adjectives to rate the product, organization, or program. Adjectives that are polar opposites are placed on the ends of the continua. Up to 20 adjective pairs may be used. Half the items should begin with the positive adjective of the pair and the other half with the negative adjective. Identifying polar opposite adjectives and capturing the major attributes make this scale difficult to construct. However, a well-constructed semantic differential scale can provide a valuable profile of a product, organization, or program's image (Alreck and Settle 2004, 132–134).

Table 16.11. Common scales

Scale	Purpose	Example
Two-Point	Dichotomous question	Yes, no Favor, oppose True, false
Three-Point	Importance, interest, or satisfaction	Very, fairly, not at all
	Satisfaction with amounts	Too much (many), just (about) right, not enough (too few)
Four-Point	Generic	Excellent, good, fair, poor
	Measurement of amounts	Very much, quite a bit, some, very little
Likert (Five-Point)	Indication of agreement or disagreement	Strongly agree, agree, neutral, disagree, strongly disagree
Verbal Frequency (Five-Point)	Frequency	Always, often, sometimes, rarely (seldom), never
Expanded Likert (Seven-Point)	Extra discrimination desirable	Very strongly agree, strongly agree, agree, neutral, disagree, strongly disagree, very strongly disagree

Figure 16.10. Excerpt from survey questionnaire

Questionnaire on Coding Skills
Contained in AHIMA's Vision 2006

On a scale of 1 to 5, 5 being the most capable, please designate how capable you feel in the following areas:

1. Understanding the current clinical coding systems relevant to the organization:
   A. ICD-9-CM 5 4 3 2 1
   B. CPT 5 4 3 2 1
   C. DSM-IV 5 4 3 2 1
   D. SNOMED 5 4 3 2 1
   E. ICD-O 5 4 3 2 1
   F. ICD-10 5 4 3 2 1
2. Ability to gather clinical data from primary data sources 5 4 3 2 1
3. Understanding of the elements required for research and outcomes 5 4 3 2 1
4. Ability to participate in the design of studies 5 4 3 2 1

Source: Garvin 2001.

Figure 16.11. Semantic differential scale

Please mark with an "X" the space on each line below to show your opinion of the education received in your academic program.

Up-to-Date ____:____:____:____:____:____:____ Outdated
1 2 3 4 5 6 7

Low-Tech ____:____:____:____:____:____:____ High-Tech
1 2 3 4 5 6 7

Expensive ____:____:____:____:____:____:____ Economical
1 2 3 4 5 6 7

Easy ____:____:____:____:____:____:____ Hard
1 2 3 4 5 6 7

Availability of an Internet format is another important feature. Internet-based instruments have been developed for many paper-based instruments. Researchers are evaluating whether Internet-based instruments have similar reliability to their paper-based versions. Researchers found that for 16 existing self-report instruments, their Internet and paper-based versions had similar reliabilities (Ritter et al. 2004). Prior to using an instrument, researchers should validate that its reliability has been established for the format they intend to use. Moreover, as Internet-based surveys have become more common, their novelty has worn off and their response rates for some groups have declined. Thus, researchers should carefully review the literature for the response rates of their intended audience and factors affecting response rates. On the other hand, key advantages of Internet-based instruments include their ease of follow-up and direct data entry into analytical software. Thus, determining whether to use an Internet-based or paper-based instrument requires careful consideration.

In summary, obtaining or developing the proper instrument is a key step. Researchers should carefully consider the various factors as they review and select instruments. Carelessness or haste during this step can lead to unusable, unanalyzable data. Purpose should drive the decision.

Gathering the Data

All too often, researchers fail to plan how to gather data. Researchers who make mistakes during this phase of the research violate one of the factors of internal validity: instrumentation. They have contaminated data and may have compromised their ability to analyze their data. Researchers must write a step-by-step, day-by-day plan for gathering data prior to implementation.

Data Sampling Methods

A **sample** is a set of units selected for study. It is a subset of a target population, which is the large group that is the focus of the study. For example, researchers cannot poll all U.S. citizens for their opinions on storing their health data on the Internet, but they can identify a sample, meaning a group of citizens representative of the entire population. Individuals are one set of units. In other studies, the sets of units could be bacteria, mice, families, schools, television shows, historical documents, Web sites, and so on. There are two major types of samples: random and nonrandom.

Random Samples

Random sampling underpins many statistical techniques that HIM professionals encounter. To generate random samples, researchers can use either a feature of spreadsheet applications called the random number generator, an option of statistical packages called select cases, or a table of random numbers from a basic statistics textbook. The four types of random sampling are **simple random sampling**, **stratified random sampling**, **systematic sampling**, and **cluster sampling**. (See table 16.12.) Researchers using these methods attempt to make the sample as representative of the population as possible.

Table 16.12. Types of random sampling

Type of Sampling	Description
Simple	The selection of units from a population so that every unit has exactly the same chance of being included in the sample. When a unit has been selected, it is returned to the population so that the other units' chances remain identical.
Stratified	Some populations have characteristics that divide them. For example, the human population is male and female. The male and female subgroups are called strata (singular, stratum). The percentage of the stratum in the population should equal the percentage of the stratum in the sample. Therefore, the sample should be 50% male and 50% female. Other percentages would cast doubt on the results.
Systematic	Units of the sample are selected from a list by drawing every nth unit. For example, health information professionals could choose every fourth surgery on the surgical schedule for surgical case review.
Cluster	The sample is clusters of units. The population is first divided into clusters of units, such as family, school, or community.

Nonrandom Samples

Two common types of **nonrandom sampling** are convenience sampling and purposive sampling. **Convenience samples** cast doubt on the generalizability and usefulness of the research. **Purposive sampling**, on the other hand, serves a valuable function in qualitative research.

Researchers use convenience samples when they "conveniently" use any unit that is at hand. For example, HIM professionals investigating physician satisfaction with departmental services could interview physicians who came to the department. Unfortunately, this convenience sample ignores the opinions of all the physicians who did not come to the department, and these physicians may find services substandard. Therefore, use of a convenience sample diminishes the credibility of the research.

Purposive sampling is a strategy of qualitative research. In purposive sampling, researchers use their expertise to select both representative units and unrepresentative units. This strategy reflects the qualitative view that there are many truths. For example, Freud's work is purposive sampling because it focuses on unusual cases. Psychiatrists investigating the psychopathology of mass murderers would use purposive sampling because mass murder is not generalizable (Chadwick et al. 1984, 66). In an HIM example, the previously discussed study on the implementation and use of e-prescribing systems, the researchers used purposive sampling of the ambulatory medical practices (Crosson et al.

2008, 365). The researchers wanted to ensure that their study included practices in a range of sizes and physician specialties (Crosson et al. 2008, 365). Thus, purposive sampling has very specific applications.

Adequacy of the Sample Size

Sample size is the number of subjects the researcher determines should be included in the study in order to represent the population. The adequacy of the sample's size is a common concern. The size of the sample depends on the purpose of the study, the nature of the population, and the researchers' resources (Chadwick et al. 1984, 67). Some experts state that the general rule is to use the largest sample possible (Gall et al 2007, 176; Gay et al. 2006, 110). However, Kish (1995/1965) factored in utility to arrive at economic samples. An economic sample provides the level of detail needed to answer the question. Overall, although no absolute rule dictates the size of the sample, researchers should strive for a level of accuracy that makes the study worth conducting.

If a researcher's purpose is to explore areas of inconsistency between paper and electronic records, 90 randomly selected records at one academic health center may be sufficient (Mikkelsen and Aasly 2001, However, a study comparing the efficacy of various treatment **protocols** for breast cancer warrants a sample size in the thousands. If the researcher's purpose includes many variables, the sample size needs to be larger. Thus, purpose is a critical concern.

The nature of the population includes **heterogeneity** and typical response and attrition rates. Heterogeneity means variation or diversity. The more heterogeneous a population, the larger the sample. The sample needs to be larger to ensure that it includes all the diverse units in the population. Typical response rate is a factor for surveys. In the literature, other researchers report their response rates. The response rate is the number of people who returned the questionnaire or were reached for interview. If the typical response rate is 50 percent, the researcher will need to distribute twice as many surveys to achieve an adequate response. Attrition (mortality) rates are the numbers of subjects lost during the course of the study. Attrition is a threat to internal validity. High attrition rates also require a larger sample. Understanding the nature of the population contributes to the accuracy of the research.

Resources, namely time and money, also can affect sample size. Sometimes researchers must provide answers within a short time frame. For example, to respond in a timely fashion to a legislative initiative regarding photocopy charges, HIM professionals may conduct a quick survey of a small sample. Individual researchers often face financial constraints. These constraints sometimes result in smaller samples than purists would prefer.

Sample size calculation refers to the qualitative and quantitative procedures used to determine the appropriate sample size. Some experts have offered rules of thumb to calculate sample size. (See table 16.13.) These rules of thumb try to account for frequency of the behavior, numbers of variables, and statistical technique. Statistical formulae are also used to calculate adequate sample sizes (Osborn 2006, 145–149). Formulae depend on the sampling method used, such as simple random sampling or stratified random sample, and on the amount of information the researcher has about the population. For health information managers, Osborn's (2006) text offers excellent examples and step-by-step procedures. Finally, however, specific considerations should override reliance on these rules of thumb and formulae.

Table 16.13. Rules of thumb for sample size

Rule of Thumb	Source
General: minimum of 30 cases or responses	Bailey 1994, 97
Pilot study: 20–50 cases	Sudman 1976, 87
Descriptive study: minimum 10% of population	Gay et al. 2006, 110
Descriptive study: population 100 of fewer, survey entire population	Gay et al. 2006, 110
Descriptive study: minimum 20 percent of small population (~1,500)	Gay et al. 2006, 110
Correlational study: minimum of 30 cases or responses	Gall et al. 2007, 176
Causal-comparative and experimental research: 15–30 cases/comparison group	Gall et al. 2007, 176 Gay et al. 2006, 110
Major subgroup: minimum of 100 each Minor subgroups: minimum of 20–50 each/subgroup	Sudman 1976, 30
General: 200 cases or responses	Chadwick et al. 1984, 68

One commonly used formula for determining optimal sample size requires the researcher to know or to decide on the size of the population, the proportion of subjects needed, and an acceptable amount of error. The formula results in the number of responses needed from the sample. This number must be adjusted by the target audience's typical response rate to arrive at the number of instruments to be distributed. The following example walks through the formula for arriving at the sample size. (See figure 16.12.) Suppose the HIS director at a large academic health center wanted to determine the sample size for a study on the medical staff's opinion of electronic health records. In this instance, the director knows that the number of attending physicians on the medical staff is 800 but has little other information. Therefore, $p = 0.5$ and $(\beta) = 0.05$. Using the basic formula, the director calculates that, in this situation, a sample of 267 is needed if he or she is willing to accept 5 percent error due to variability in the sampling. Finally, the director determines the number of surveys to distribute by multiplying the sample size by the typical response rate. Thus, if half of the attending physicians typically respond to surveys, the director must double the sample and distribute 534 surveys for the opinion study.

Figure 16.12. Basic example of sample size calculation

Sample size = n Proportion of subjects needed = p
Size of the population = N Acceptable amount of error = B

Formula

$$n = \frac{Np\,(1 - p)}{(N - 1)\,\frac{(B^2)}{4} + (p)\,(1 - p)}$$

Data from the Case

$N = 800$
$p = .5$
$B = .05$

Calculations

$$n = \frac{(800)\,(.5)\,(1 - .5)}{(800 - 1)\,\frac{(.05^2)}{4} + (.5)\,(1 - .5)}$$

$$n = \frac{200}{(799)\,(.000625) + .25}$$

$$n = \frac{200}{.75}$$

$n = 267$

Data Collection Procedures

The research plan should consider every logistical detail of the collection of the data from start to finish. Lack of attention to detail at this point will breach factors of internal validity. Some issues related to data collection affect many of the methods; other issues are unique to the method. Data collection issues include:

- Obtaining approvals of oversight committees
- Listing each data element required to perform the appropriate statistical techniques
- Training for data collection procedures
- Performing a pilot study
- Considering the response rate
- Conducting the treatment
- Collecting the data
- Assembling the data for analysis

Federal regulations govern research on human subjects (Penslar and Porter 2001). The purpose of the regulations is to protect humans from researchers' abuses, such as those that occurred in the U.S. Public Health Services Syphilis Study (also known as the Tuskegee Syphilis Study; see chapter 18). To comply with federal regulations, organizations have **institutional review boards** (IRBs). IRBs (sometimes called human subjects committees) are administrative bodies established to protect the rights and welfare of human subjects recruited to participate in research activities associated with institutions. IRBs provide oversight for the research studies conducted within their institutions. As specified by both federal regulations and institutional policies, IRBs have the authority to review and to approve or reject research studies within their jurisdictions. They also may require modifications in research protocols. As human health and life are at stake, the federal government imposes severe penalties on institutions and individuals who fail to comply.

Prior to conducting studies, researchers must obtain written approvals from the IRB and other oversight entities of their organizations. To obtain approvals, researchers complete the organization's documentation, providing descriptions of their research plan and copies of their informed consent forms. (See chapter 18 for a complete discussion of IRBs.) Sufficient time must be allowed in their plan for the board to review the research, meet, and respond.

Researchers should compile a list of each data element required for each statistical analysis they plan to conduct. Prior to beginning data collection, researchers should ensure that their data collection strategies will obtain all the data. Therefore, it is advisable to conduct mock statistical analyses on fabricated data and to create tables and figures for the manuscript early in the planning of the research. For example, suppose researchers were investigating whether the time from heart transplant to the first rejection episode differed by ABO blood type and Rh factor. The blood types and Rh factors are not evenly distributed in the general population nor are they evenly distributed by national origin. Running mock statistical analyses would reveal that the researchers need a large sample size. Too often, graduate students have had to write in their theses or dissertations, "I did not have sufficient cases to run the statistical analysis." Planning can avoid this embarrassment.

Researchers and those they employ to assist them may require special training. For example, publishers of some psychological tests require verification of training to administer the tests. The researchers must obtain this verification (or select another instrument). To effectively conduct interviews or to observe vignettes, researchers and their assistants also need training.

Performing a **pilot study** (trial run) enhances the likelihood of its successful completion. When researchers conduct pilot studies, they work out the details of their research plan. The maxim, "The devil is in the details," is only too true. Pilot studies can reveal the following information:

- Biases in sample selection
- Volumes required
- Associated costs
- Performance features of equipment
- Defects, such as poorly worded cover letters, unclear questionnaire items, and leading questions in interviews
- Possible log jams (gridlock) in the mailing method
- Errors in the scoring key
- Discrepancies between the order of items on the data collection instrument and the order on the computer screen

Pilot studies demonstrate that the research study is logistically feasible. Even researchers conducting naturalistic studies perform simulations that test their instruments prior to the event. Pilot studies are as necessary as disaster drills.

Ensuring an adequate response rate is of particular concern for surveys. Low response rates jeopardize study accuracy and generalizability. Therefore, researchers strive to increase their response rates. To increase response rates, researchers can use the findings of Berdie and Anderson (1974). These researchers conducted the classic research study on the process of questionnaire surveys. Their research revealed many strategies to increase the response rate. (See figure 16.13.) Their primary recommendation was that researchers know their topic and their target population. This knowledge underpins decisions about the strategies and techniques to increase response rates.

Strategies to increase the response rate for questionnaire research include using a brief cover letter and multiple mailings. The cover letter should explain the purpose of the study and its benefits for the participants. Obtaining the sponsorship of a professional association or officials is desirable. Moreover, the letter should thank the responder, provide a deadline, and offer the study results. In the field of health information management, ensuring the confidentiality of the response also is particularly important. Key characteristics of effective cover letters are shown in figure 16.14. Multiple mailings in a timed sequence can significantly improve the response rate. For example, the tailored (total) design method on average achieves response rates of 74 percent (Dillman 2007, 27–28).

Internet surveys are becoming more prevalent because they are able to gather data from large samples directly and relatively inexpensively (Bethell et al. 2004). They are now being used to gather data on health status, access to care, and other health outcomes. Bethell and colleagues administered surveys both via the Internet and by telephone. The

Figure 16.13. Summary of Berdie and Anderson's strategies to increase the response rate in questionnaire surveys

General
1. Physical attractiveness of cover letter, postcard, and questionnaire
2. Quality of printing and paper
3. Pleasingly colored paper
4. Error-free documents
5. Incentives, such as an offer of the study's results or money ($0.25 maximum)

Cover Letter
1. Salutation's formality is tailored to the target population.
2. Prestigious sponsor
3. Time frame for response is exact (10 days) or "as soon as possible," depending on the population.
4. Tone of sincerity and honesty
5. Assurance of confidentiality

Questionnaire
1. Title
2. Easy to complete
3. Clear instructions included in the body of the questionnaire
4. Reasonable length
5. Contact information and return mailing address at the bottom

Mailing
1. Initial contact (postcard) that is an appeal for participation
2. Self-addressed, stamped return envelope
3. Properly timed follow-up

uncorrected response rate for the 13,400 e-mails surveys was 17.3 percent. Taking into account that, on average, 10 to 15 percent of e-mails are nonworking or dormant, the researchers concluded that the true response rate for the online survey was about 20 percent. The adjusted response rate for the telephone survey was 9.3 percent. In spite of six follow-up telephone calls, the one-time contact of the e-mail survey resulted in a higher response rate. Survey administration, statistical sampling, and weighted approaches to ensure representativeness were similar for the two survey strategies. The researchers concluded that, with the increasing resistance to telephone solicitations, Internet surveys represent an efficient, real-time strategy for data collection (Bethell et al. 2004).

Researchers also must be on guard for bias in response. For example, do persons who volunteer to participate in the research differ from those who do not volunteer? Do the persons who responded to the survey (responders) differ from those who did not (nonresponders)? Finally, how similar are the participants, nonparticipants, responders, and nonresponders to the population?

In conducting the study, researchers must be careful to follow the plan they have written. Deviations from the protocol result in potential bias and inaccurate data. For example, in questionnaire research, the Dillman (2007) method depends on a timed series of five contacts (151). Does the researcher have staff to track the responses and to make the multiple contacts?

Researchers must include a mechanism in the plan for compiling their data. If videotapes are involved, where will they be stored? Because sensitive data may be on personality tests, how will confidentiality be maintained? If the research includes measurement instruments, who will score them?

After researchers have collected the data, they must organize them in a way that allows analysis. In this step, the researchers must decide how they will enter the data into a software package. Who will enter the data? How will they ensure accuracy of data entry? Who will transcribe the contents of videotapes or audiotapes?

Data collection is a systematic, planned procedure that results in internal validity. Conducting a pilot study is a key step in ensuring a thorough and carefully conceived plan. The methods section of the study report documents the plan's execution. The methods section is also a recipe that other researchers can use to replicate the study. Therefore, careful attention to documentation and vigilant adherence to procedures are demanded.

Sources of Secondary Data

Researchers may choose to analyze or mine data that other researchers or agencies have gathered. As noted, analysis of secondary data is a powerful tool because it allows researchers to mine large databases at the regional, state, and national level. For example, researchers at an academic health center mined 667,000 de-identified EHRs, representing over 1 million

Figure 16.14. Sample cover letter

Letterhead	ZHIMA 1800 Carriage Oxford, ZB 31002 October 1, 2010 Dear Colleague:	
Purpose	The healthcare system and our field are rapidly changing. These changes place increasing demands on health information practitioners. Little research exists that explores stress and the buffers in directors of hospital health information management departments.	
Study's Importance Participant's Importance	Therefore, you have been randomly selected to participate in a national survey on stress in the workplace. Please take the time to complete and return the survey. The accuracy of the results and the possible benefits for the profession depend on your participation.	
Sponsor Time to Complete	This research is being sponsored by the AHIMA. The entire survey should take 15 to 20 minutes of your time. A detailed, personalized report on your coping resources is available. Should you wish to receive it, please write your name and address at the bottom of the pink Demographic Form.	Offer of Results
Time Frame	Please return the survey within 10 days in the postage-paid envelope.	SASE
	A vital concern of the health information management profession is confidentiality in research. The code number on your questionnaire is for mailing and follow-up purposes only. Only aggregate data will be reported, and at no time will the questionnaires be identified by respondent.	Confidentiality
Appreciation Contact Instruction	I truly appreciate your participation, and I think the findings of the survey will benefit many members of our profession in these stressful times. If you have any questions about the survey, please write or call me. Sincerely Jane Edwards, PhD 123 Anyplace Street Anytown, IL 12345 (123) 456-7890 Enclosures	

inpatient and outpatient visits (Mullins et al. 2006, 1353–1356). These data were compiled in clinical data repositories that received data from a variety of clinical and administrative sources (Mullins et al. 2006, 1352). The data mining software included three components: association analysis, predictive analysis, and pattern discovery. After discovering associations, the researchers verified them in the medical literature. Many of the associations were expected. However, the researchers listed novel (new) associations that they believed warranted further investigation (Mullins et al. 2006, 1362–1370). One such novel association was among psychoses, peptic ulcer disease, and paralysis (Mullins et al. 2006, 1370). The researchers concluded that non-hypothesis-driven (unsupervised) data mining of large clinical repositories is feasible (Mullins et al. 2006, 1370).

Health information researchers used data from the 1994 Health Care Cost Utilization Project-3 (HCUP-3) study (Rudman and Davey 2000, 3). The HCUP-3 data are health record data from inpatient hospital discharges. The researchers were investigating the type of injury or illness and medical cost of domestic violence. The researchers reported that for females, mental disorder, trauma, and pregnancy complications accounted for more than two-thirds of the admissions and that for all victims the average cost of the hospitalization was $8,159.81 (Rudman and Davey 2000, 7).

Another HIM researcher queried large databases of Medicare data to analyze reimbursement trends (Osborn 2001, 78). The researcher analyzed the data to identify problems in specific inpatient payment groups in order to reveal variations in charges and lengths of stay (Osborn 2001, 78). The analysis revealed that, for a specific hospital, its average length of stay was statistically significantly less than the national average, but its average charges were statistically significantly higher than the national average. The researcher concluded that analysis of data could identify potential areas in which a healthcare organization could improve its services (Osborn 2001, 84).

Several other sources of data are available to researchers. For example, several states post Medicaid data on the Internet. Specific examples of available data include:

- Labor force, earnings, and prices (Bureau of Labor Statistics)
- Crime, demographics, education, and health (Social Statistics Briefing Room)
- Statistics and information from 70 federal agencies (FedStats)
- Behavioral health (Behavioral Risk Factor Surveillance System [BRFSS] of the Centers for Disease Control and Prevention)
- Health statistics (National Center for Health Statistics, FASTATS A–Z)
- Health statistics, social indicators, and population health research (Area Resource File [ARF] of the Health Resources and Services Administration of the U.S. Department of Health and Human Services)
- Health information national trends survey (HINTS) (U.S. National Institutes of Health, National Cancer Institute)
- Medicare data (Medicare Provider Analysis and Review [MEDPAR] of Short-Stay Hospitals)
- Demographic data on U.S. population (Population Reference Bureau)
- Business, economic, and trade data from the federal government (STAT-USA)
- Hundreds of files from various state and federal governmental agencies (Statistical Resources on the Web)
- U.S. census data (U.S. Census Bureau)
- Medicaid data by state (see Medicaid programs of each state)

The problem is that in order to transform the data into information, researchers must understand the underlying structure of the data and how they were collected. Each data source has unique characteristics.

For example, one hospital database contained a field related to death, which is typically a discharge status. However, with its death field (Field 342), the hospital could track the number of intraoperative deaths, postoperative deaths, autopsied deaths, and medical examiner's cases. The death field was a multiple-entry field, with each category having a number (intraoperative death = 1; postoperative death = 2; autopsied death = 3; and medical examiner's case = 4). A surgeon requested a report on the number of intraoperative deaths. The worker who usually ran reports was on vacation and another worker attempted to run the query. This worker wrote the query as Field 342 = "1." As a multiple-entry field, the query should have been written as Field 342 contains "1." The erroneously written query excluded all intraoperative deaths that were also postoperative deaths (2), autopsied deaths (3), and medical examiner's cases (4). Some cases are all four. The case of a multiple stabbing victim illustrates the point. From the emergency room, the patient is initially brought to the operating room (OR). His wounds are explored and sutured. Postoperatively, the patient is sent to the intensive care unit. While in the ICU, he begins to bleed internally again and is brought back to the OR. While in the OR the second time, the patient dies. This patient is both a postoperative death and an intraoperative death (2 and 1). In addition, the body was sent for autopsy, and as a crime victim, the patient is a medical examiner's case (3 and 4). Therefore, researchers must either learn the underlying structure of the database and query it directly or download the data into a database or spreadsheet with which they are familiar.

Similar to the approach to literary databases, researchers must take a systematic and orderly approach. HIM professionals, such as Rudman and Davey (2000) and Osborn (2001), have queried large databases to analyze health data. Secondary analysis is a productive research method for HIM professionals.

Check Your Understanding 16.6

Instructions: Answer the following questions on a separate piece of paper.

1. Why would a researcher choose to use an instrument that someone else has created?
2. What is an adequate sample?
3. Would directors of departments of health information services be considered a heterogeneous population or a homogenous population?
4. Why are IRBs important?
5. What is a pilot study?
6. Why are survey researchers concerned about their response rates?
7. What common mistake do researchers make in data collection?

Preparing Data for Analysis

In the design of studies, researchers use procedures to maximize the integrity of their data. They attempt to prevent errors by constructing instruments that facilitate accurate and complete responses. They may insert field edits into their spreadsheet or database to support accurate data entry. However, despite researchers' best efforts, many different types of errors may occur. For example, researchers can transpose numbers in their data entry or participants can skip items. Thus, data must be prepared prior to analysis. In this preparation, researchers assess the quality of their data. They verify the accuracy and completeness of the data. This preparation minimizes the effects of these errors on their studies' results. All data require preparation; however, the data from data sources for secondary analysis and data mining require extensive preparation. Important aspects of data preparation are handling missing values and data cleansing.

Missing Values

Missing values are variables that do not contain values for some cases. For example, in the previously discussed study on breast cancer, occupation, menopausal status, and estrogen and progesterone receptor values were missing values

(Watzlaf et al 1996, 30–31). Missing values is a type of incomplete or coarse data (Heitjan and Rubin 1991, 2244).

Missing values must be resolved before statistical techniques can be applied. Methods to resolve missing values are case deletion, single imputation, and multiple imputation. Each of these methods has multiple techniques. A few representative and explanatory techniques are discussed.

In case deletion, a case with missing values is entirely deleted from the study. In a modified form of case deletion, a case is only excluded from calculations for which it has missing data. **Imputation** is the substitution of values for the missing values. A common single imputation is the substitution of the mean of the available values for the missing data. Both case deletion and single imputation have the advantage of simplicity. The disadvantages of both techniques are the loss of cases and the potential for bias because the missing data may not be random.

Techniques of multiple imputation involve several complex calculations, creation of subgroups, and multiple simulations. Statistical packages include multiple imputation. The advantages of multiple imputation are greater accuracy and less bias. One disadvantage is that large samples may be required.

Missing values are a common problem for researchers. However, this problem is important to address because, until shown otherwise, missing values are considered systematically biased. This systematic bias would corrupt the analysis of the data and undermine the integrity of the study. Finally, researchers should document the technique they use to resolve missing values.

Data Cleansing

Data cleansing (data cleaning, data scrubbing) is the "process of detecting, diagnosing, and editing faulty data" (Van den Broeck et al. 2005, 0966). Researchers note that data cleansing can consume 80 percent of the time of data mining (Sokol et al. 2001, 2). For other types of research, data cleansing may not be quite as arduous and time-consuming. However, the process still requires many hours of detailed work for which researchers should allow time.

Methods of data cleansing include finding duplications, checking internal consistency, and identifying outliers:

- Finding duplication often occurs during data entry when two completed questionnaires from the same subject are encountered (researchers need to have a method of determining which questionnaire to use—first received or most complete)
- Checking for internal consistency involves assessing gender and age against diagnosis or procedure, city against zip code, or other comparable attributes
- Detection of statistical outliers identifies values outside the expected range and may occur during the participants' completion of the instrument or the researchers' data entry (see box and whisker plot in the next section).

Once errors are detected they are corrected during data editing. According to Van den Broeck (2005), data editing is "changing the value of data shown to be incorrect" (0966). Only errors shown to be wrong should be corrected in data editing. Care should be taken not to manipulate the data.

As researchers clean their data, they should record their methods, the error types and rates, the error deletion and correction rates, and the outcomes with and without outliers (Van den Broeck et al. 2005, 0966). This information should then be documented in the scientific paper. This documentation thus avoids the appearance of data manipulation.

For example, in the previously described study on 667,000 individuals' health records, the researchers stated several procedures that they had performed to clean the data (Mullins et al. 2006, 1356–1357). To meet HIPAA requirements for de-identification, 18 identifiers were removed. The researchers omitted "time" as a variable because of formatting and extracted "first values" for several laboratory values. Narrative variables were converted to numeric (example: yes, don't know, no to −1, 0, +1).

Data preparation is integral to the quality of the study's results. It is important to allow sufficient time to resolve missing values and to conduct data cleansing.

Analyzing the Data

In this phase of the research process, researchers try to determine what they have found or what the data reveal. Many researchers fall into the common error of allowing too little time for analysis. Researchers should be sure to allocate sufficient time in their research plan to analyze and interpret the data.

Before conducting their study, researchers should determine which analytical techniques they will use. These techniques are specified in the methods section of the manuscript. The description of the analytical techniques should be clear so that other researchers can duplicate them.

Techniques for Quantitative Data Analysis

This section briefly describes a few common statistical techniques. For a detailed discussion, see a standard statistical text, such as *Statistical Applications for Health Information Management* (Osborn 2006). The purpose here is to suggest appropriate statistical techniques for general situations. The following three broad categories of statistical analysis are addressed:

- **Descriptive (summary) statistics** describe the data. Generally, researchers should begin with descriptive techniques to verify the accuracy of their data entry and to provide an overview of their respondents. Exploratory data analysis looks at the raw data. The raw data are presented in graphic displays. Two techniques of exploratory data analysis are box and whisker plots and stem and leaf diagrams. The stem and leaf diagram shows all the individual scores on a particular measure

(Gall et al. 2007, 152). Box and whisker plots are especially useful when the sets of data have hundreds or thousands of scores or the sets of data have unequal numbers of values. (See figure 16.15 and chapter 15) The shapes of these graphic displays allow researchers to see the range and distribution of scores. (See chapter 15.) Outliers become visible. Descriptive techniques include means, frequency distributions, and standard deviations. These statistical techniques are also called **univariate** because they involve one variable.

- **Inferential statistics** allow the researchers to make inferences about the population characteristics (parameters) from the sample's characteristics. Examples of inferential statistics include the paired *t*-test and the analysis of variance (ANOVA). Researchers investigating the differences between groups would use these statistical techniques.
- **Test statistics** examine the psychometric properties of measurement instruments. They describe and explore the validity and reliability of tests. Researchers conducting test statistics calculate the validity coefficient (correlation coefficient) and each item's validity. They also could perform factor analysis. Examples of approaches to verify reliability include test–retest and Kuder–Richardson formulae. Finally, test statistics include an index of difficulty, which is the percentage of persons correctly answering each item.

Most research data can be subjected to more than one statistical technique. Table 16.14 shows potential statistical tests for various combinations of data characteristics. The suggested statistical tests in the table are merely a starting point. Researchers should maximize the use of their data by using a variety of techniques to look at their data from multiple views. Multiple views of the data shed light on different aspects of the issue and expand the body of knowledge.

Figure 16.15. Box and whisker plot

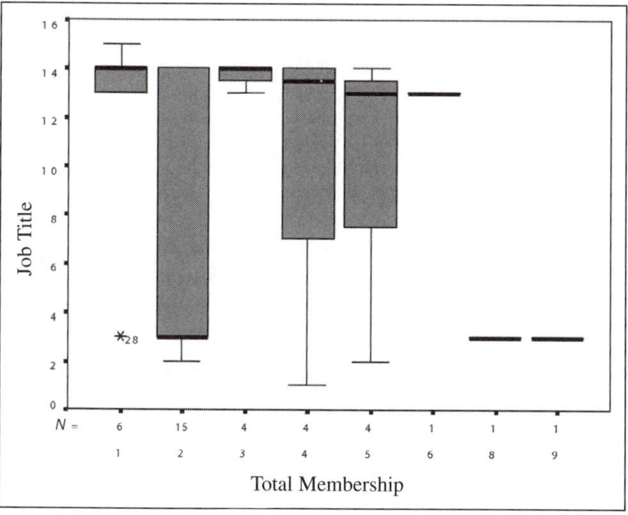

Table 16.14. Statistical test by characteristics of data

No. of Variables	Characteristics	Test
1	One group, normal*	Mean and standard deviation
	One group, nonnormal	Binomial test
	Two groups, normal	*t*-test
	Two groups, nonnormal	Chi-square
	Three+ groups, normal	ANOVA
	Three+ groups, nonnormal	Nonparametric
2	Both continuous	Correlation
	1 continuous, 1 discrete	ANOVA
	Both categorical	Chi-square
3+	One group	Multiple regression, factor analysis, repeated measures ANOVA, analysis of covariance
	Two+ groups	Multivariate ANOVA, discriminant function

*Normal distribution

Appropriate statistical techniques vary by:

- Purpose of the research (research design)
- Number of variables
- Type of data
- Nature of the target population
- Number, size, and independence of the groups

Purpose of the Research

Researchers should match their purpose and their statistical technique. Researchers whose purpose is to investigate the differences between groups would use statistical techniques of the paired *t*-test and the analysis of variance (ANOVA). On the other hand, researchers might be looking for relationships, such as in a correlational design. These researchers would want to know how the variables relate to one another. Therefore, these researchers would use correlational statistics. One correlational technique is the **bivariate** correlational coefficient. The bivariate correlational coefficient allows the researcher to describe the strength of the relationship between two variables in mathematical terms.

Number of Variables

The number of variables also affects the choice of statistical technique. **Multivariate** correlational methods involve many variables. For example, multiple linear regression examines the strength of relationship between several independent variables and one dependent variable. Other, more complex forms of regression exist.

Type of Data

Another factor in the choice of statistical technique is the type of data. There are five types of data:

- **Discrete data** are separate and distinct values or observations. Patients in the hospital represent discrete data because each patient can be counted.
- **Categorical data** are values or observations that can be sorted into a category (for example, gender).
- **Nominal data** are values or observations that can be labeled or named (nom = name). Therefore, the data can be coded (for example, Married = Y and Single = N or Male = 0 and Female = 1). Nominal data cannot be ranked or measured.
- **Ordinal data** represent values or observations that can be ranked (ordered). Ranking scales are common examples of ordinal data. For example, physicians often ask patients to evaluate the severity of their pain on a scale from 1 to 10. HIM professionals could use ordinal data when investigating customer satisfaction. For example, a health information manager could ask physicians how satisfied they are with the department's service on a scale from 1 to 5. However, because these rankings are subjective, the difference in satisfaction between 2 and 3 may be much less than the difference between 4 and 5.
- **Metric** data can be measured on some scale. Two subtypes are interval and ratio. The scale for **interval data** does not begin with a true zero. Time, as humans measure it, does not begin with a true zero. Interval data represent values or observations that occur on an evenly distributed scale. Time in years is an evenly distributed scale. The interval between 1985 and 1990 is the same as the interval between 1991 and 1996. On the other hand, the scale for **ratio data** does begin at a true zero. Height, weight, and temperature are examples of ratio data.

Metric data are **continuous data.** They represent values or observations that have an indefinite number of points along a continuum. For example, measurements made with a ruler can be a foot, an inch, a half-inch, a quarter, an eighth, to infinity. Continuous data also exhibit characteristics of the other types of data; they can be counted (discrete) and ordered (ordinal) and can be grouped.

The type of data depends on the way the variable is measured, not some inherent attribute of the variable. For example, height can be measured in inches or categorized as short or tall. Therefore, researchers should be careful to collect data in the form that matches their intended statistical technique.

Nature of the Target Population

The nature of the target population also affects the choice of statistical technique. For example, some statistical techniques are based on the assumption that the variable is normally distributed in the population. **Parametric techniques**, such as the *t*-test, ANOVA, and Pearson *r* correlation efficient, are used in these cases. However, this assumption is not always true. In some cases, researchers use **nonparametric (distribution-free) techniques** (for example, chi square and Spearman rho). Nonparametric techniques also are used for nominal and ordinal data. Osborn (2006) provides a powerful discussion on the use of parametric and nonparametric statistical tests by type of data (level of measurement, nominal to metric) (251–253).

Number, Size, and Independence of Groups

The selection of statistical test also depends on the number of samples or groups. In many instances, researchers want to compare two groups, the control group and the study group. However, in other types of studies, researchers may want to compare results from 10 different communities or all 50 states. The number of groups affects the choice of statistical test. Disparate sizes of groups also sometimes affect the choice of statistical test. Some statistical tests, however, are quite robust and can handle differences in sizes. For example, in many instances analysis of variance (ANOVA) can handle unequal group sizes. Researchers must take into account the inequality of sizes. For example, the smallest group size determines the precisions of estimates. The independence of the samples is also an issue. For instance, matched pairs of graduates and supervisors are used when an academic program wants to know the graduates' perspectives on the quality of the education and the supervisors' perspectives on the capabilities of graduates.

Techniques for Qualitative Data Analysis

Grounded Theory

Grounded theory is commonly used to analyze qualitative data. Researchers using grounded theory code, categorize, and compare their data. Grounded theory refers both to the theories generated using this technique and the technique itself. The term evolved because its early users spoke of their work being "grounded in data." Thus, the term emphasizes that the data generate the theories.

Grounded theory is an iterative or cyclical process. During data collection, researchers using grounded theory record and code their observations (called incidents). However, analysis begins during data collection. From the analysis, the researchers begin creating conceptual categories to fit their data. Both data collection and analysis may uncover gaps or discrepancies that require additional data collection or participants. The grounded theory technique has four stages:

1. Comparing incidents applicable to each category (includes comparing categories' relationships)
2. Integrating categories and their properties (cyclical process)
3. Delimiting theory (reducing and integrating core categories, tying theory to core categories, and achieving higher level conceptualizations)
4. Writing theory (validating theory by pinpointing data behind it) (Glaser 1965, 439–443)

Development of grounded theory consists of intertwined and concurrent data collection, data coding, categorization, and analysis. Because of the constant analysis and comparisons of categories, the theory and technique are sometimes called *constant comparative method.*

This process results in complex theories that fit the data closely. In grounded theory, researchers seek to develop theories that are unique to groups or settings, unlike quantitative researchers who seek to develop theories that are generalizable.

Content Analysis

Content analysis is the systematic and objective analysis of communication. Most often, researchers analyze written documentation. However, they may analyze other modes of communication, such as speech, body language, music, television shows, commercials, and movies. The purpose of content analysis is to describe and to make inferences and predictions about communication and its characteristics. Consumer groups who notify the public about the "most violent" or the "most sexually graphic" shows on television have used content analysis to compile their reports.

Researchers code the text or other means of communication. Coding is the labeling of words or word groups (segments) with annotations or scales. These labels are characteristics of the segments. To assess reliability, the agreement between and among coders may be checked. From the coding, researchers identify key terms, characteristics, or other attributes. The coded text (or communication) becomes the data. The data are then categorized into overarching themes. Some researchers also tabulate the frequency of coded data. Content analysis is "essentially a coding operation" (Babbie 2004, 318).

Healthcare personnel use content analysis. For example, researchers at a library of an academic health center conducted a study on the process of information retrieval (Crystal and Greenberg 2006, 1368). Specifically, the researchers explored how users judged the relevance of health information on the Web (Crystal and Greenberg 2006, 1368). The researchers explained that developers of search engines need to understand the criteria that users employ to judge the relevance of their "hits" (Crystal and Greenberg 2006, 1368). Given that searchers generate thousands to millions of "hits," developing search engines that make the process more efficient than the current process would serve users. The twelve participants in the study were students and various types of professionals. The participants searched the Web on twelve different health-related topics (Crystal and Greenberg 2006, 1372). The researchers helped the participants develop suitable queries, such as "health effects power lines," "cell phone cancer," "asthma car exhaust," "lead poisoning," and "pesticide risk developing countries" (Crystal and Greenberg 2006, 1372, 1382). The participants searched both surrogates (researcher developed mock document summaries) and the Web. The participants highlighted with their mouse any terms of interest. Additionally, the participants' interactions with the search engines were video captured (Crystal and Greenberg 2006, 1372). After the search, the researchers conducted and audiotaped "think-aloud" sessions with the participants. In these sessions, as the researchers and the participants jointly viewed the video record, the participants described their reactions to the document or summary. Finally, the researchers performed content analysis on the video logs and the audio tapes (Crystal and Greenberg 2006, 1373). The researchers found that the participants used many, diverse stratagems. The researchers classified the stratagems into categories. These categories were the participants' criteria for assessing the relevance of the Web document. The most common criteria was topic (Crystal and Greenberg 2006, 1378). Other criteria included affiliation (such as institution), authority (such as author or reference), and scope category (such as level or audience) (Crystal and Greenberg 2006, 1375). The researchers concluded that Web search engines could be improved by incorporating the criteria upon which users tend to rely (Crystal and Greenberg 2006, 1380–1381).

Statistical Software Packages

Many software packages are available to assist researchers in the analysis of quantitative and qualitative data. For basic descriptive statistics, researchers can use spreadsheet software, such as Excel. However, most researchers will choose to use dedicated analytical packages because these packages require less manipulation of the data than spreadsheet packages and because they perform many more analytical procedures. Other factors that influence the choice of software are type of data, planned analytical techniques, and cost.

Quantitative

Several software packages are commonly used to analyze data in quantitative studies. Freeware is also available on the Web, such as Amelia II. Amelia II includes the statistical technique of multiple imputation.

- Epi-Info is freeware from the Centers for Disease Control and Prevention. This integrated package, which includes word processing, database, and statistics, is designed for public health. The software allows the handling of epidemiological data in questionnaire format, calculating the required sample size, analyzing data, and presenting results.
- LISREL is a software package that conducts factor analysis. Factor analysis is used to evaluate the psychometric properties of measurement instruments. LISREL generates test statistics. For example, researchers used LISREL to evaluate the properties of a psychological test that predicts suicidal behavior (Aish and Wasserman 2001, 368).
- STATISTICA is a suite of analytical software. The suite provides a comprehensive array of software for data analysis, data management, data visualization,

and data mining procedures. The suite includes techniques for predictive modeling, clustering, classification, and exploration.

- Statistical Analysis System (SAS) is a powerful software package that integrates data access, data management, data analysis, and data presentation. Researchers use SAS to enter data, retrieve and manage data, analyze data with statistical and mathematical techniques, write reports, and generate graphics.
- Statistical Package for Social Sciences (SPSS) offers a broad array of analytical and graphic software. Its many components range from basic statistical techniques to advanced, specialized techniques. The basic statistics package performs counts and cross-tabs. Advanced techniques include factor analysis, regression, cluster analysis, binomial and multinomial logistic regression, and correspondence analysis.

Qualitative

Analytical software exists for qualitative studies. These software support the analysis of the multitudes of data in multiple media obtained during qualitative studies.

- ATLAS.ti is used to code and analyze text-based data from open-ended surveys, transcriptions of focus groups, or other sources. ATLAS.ti can be used to code other types of qualitative data, such as photographs. ATLAS.ti allows the retrieval of specific information based on search criteria. ATLAS.ti also has the ability to export data as an SPSS data set.
- CDC EZ-Text is a free software program from the U.S. Centers for Disease Control and Prevention (CDC). EZ-Text assists researchers to create, manage, and analyze semistructured qualitative databases. Investigators can use the software to enter data, create online code books, apply codes to specific response packages, develop case studies, conduct database searches to identify text passages, and export data in a wide array of formats for future analysis with other analytical software programs.
- Code-A-Text Integrated System for the Analysis of Interviews and Dialogues (C-I-SAID) is used to code, to label, and to analyze documents, transcripts, and sound files. This software allows researchers to specify codes and labels and to insert them into the document or sound file. Coded content of documents, transcripts, and sound files then can be analyzed. C-I-SAID produces descriptive statistics and tables and charts that support analysis. The software also assists researchers in categorizing the segments into themes, known as content analysis. C-I-SAID can be applied to field notes, open-ended questionnaires, and interviews. A multimedia version codes video and pictures.
- NVivo is a software that is used to analyze unstructured, qualitative data. It is used to code and analyze text-based data from open-ended surveys, transcriptions of focus groups, or other sources. NVivo allows researchers to retrieve specific quotes based on search criteria. The software can also create tabular data representing the counts of specific codes. The data can be exported to quantitative statistical packages.

In summary, analytical software packages exist for both quantitative and qualitative researchers. Researchers are encouraged to explore the capabilities of several packages. The choice of software depends on the type of data, the planned analytical techniques, and skills of the researcher.

Check Your Understanding 16.7

Instructions: Answer the following questions on a separate piece of paper.

1. How do descriptive and inferential statistics differ?
2. How many variables do bivariate statistical techniques involve?
3. What inferential statistical techniques emphasize differences in groups?
4. What are two types of continuous data?
5. Why must researchers know the type of data they are collecting?
6. Why might a researcher use Epi-Info as his or her statistical package?

Presenting Results

Researchers follow a two-step process when presenting their results. In the first step, they report their research findings with no commentary, explanation, or interpretation. This section of a manuscript is called research findings. In the second step, the researchers comment on, explain, and interpret their findings. This section of the manuscript is called discussion. Also included in the discussion are conclusions and recommendations for future research.

Researchers describe their results in the past tense; general truths are stated in the present tense. The style of writing for scientific manuscripts is objective, precise, and factual. Researchers avoid subjective interjections and emotional hyperbole. In the research findings, researchers must be careful to maintain a neutral tone. They are merely recording their findings in narrative form.

In research findings, researchers describe the results for each hypothesis. Restating the hypothesis aids the readers. Researchers state whether or not the results support the hypotheses. They also record characteristics about the sample and describe the results of the statistical analyses that investigate whether the sample is similar to or different from the population. Supplemental statistical analyses also are described. Researchers are careful to use the term *statistical significance*, as appropriate (Refer to table 16.10).

For research findings, researchers generate tables and graphs to support the readers' understanding of their findings. (See chapter 15 for more detailed descriptions of some common tables and graphs.) One rule of thumb is that data should be presented in only one way or mode (Day and Gastel 2006, 88). Researchers should present the particular data element in narrative text, in a table, or in a figure, but not in multiple modes. Graphics should clarify the data, not confuse the readers. Figure 16.16 lists 10 important points

Figure 16.16. Considerations for effective graphics

- Tables, graphs, and figures have titles.
- Tables have stubheads, spanner heads, and column heads for clarification.
- Sources are cited.
- Time frames and dates are noted.
- Multiple tables, charts, graphs, and figures are numbered.
- Both axes of graphs are labeled (bar titles, legends, scale captions).
- Keys show the meaning of shadings and colors.
- Scales start at zero.
- Wedges (slices) of a pie chart represent percentages, and the percentages convert to 360 degrees.
- Graphics are for emphasis; do not dilute the effect with clutter.

to remember when constructing graphics. Researchers must carefully consider which mode of communication is most effective for the particular data element. For example:

- *Tables* summarize data in a grid or matrix. The elements and numbers should be in the columns, not in the rows.
- *Pie charts* with their segments visually show the relationships among variables and the whole. They also can represent categorical data.
- *Bar charts* show comparisons between and among items. They often illustrate major characteristics in the distribution of data (male or female, age ranges). They can be used to represent categorical, nominal, or ordinal data.
- *Line charts* show comparisons over time.
- *Histograms* are similar to bar charts. They show major characteristics in the distribution of data and summarize data about variables whose values are numerical and measured on an interval scale. Histograms are used for large data sets.

Writing the discussion section requires energy and creativity. Too often, researchers shortchange this section. The discussion section is not a superficial repetition of the findings section. Rather, it is where researchers create new knowledge.

In the discussion section, researchers should compare their findings to the findings in the literature, explaining similarities and discrepancies. More important, they should provide some rationale to explain why their findings were the same or different. In writing this section, researchers should return to why they conducted the study in the first place. They should answer the following questions:

- What theoretical significance do their findings have?
- What practical significance do their findings have? (Refer to table 16.10.)
- How do their findings explicitly link to the larger body of knowledge?
- How have their findings improved the field's research model?
- How have their findings expanded the body of knowledge?
- What new definitions have they added to the field's area of practice?
- How do their findings support practitioners in the workplace?
- What problems do their findings solve?
- What valid conclusions can the researchers and the readers draw?

Researchers also state their assumptions and the limitations of their research. A researcher describing a questionnaire study might state that one assumption is that people are honest and that one limitation is that the study only reflects one point in time. Also, research always raises new questions. These new questions become the recommendations for further research.

The discussion section closes the presentation of the findings. To accurately represent the time and effort that went into the research study, the discussion section should be rich and insightful. Sufficient time for reflection and contemplation should be scheduled into the research plan. The researchers' goal should be to put usable information into the hands of practitioners in the workplace.

Disseminating Research

Knowledge is disseminated and examined through poster sessions, presentations at professional meetings, and journal articles. Researchers have an ethical obligation to disseminate their research because this new knowledge advances the health information profession and helps practitioners in the workplace. It is only common sense that in order for the researchers' information to be useful, it must be available and accessible to practitioners.

Poster sessions and presentations occur at professional meetings, conferences, and symposia. Often these events have been planned far in advance. Up to 12 months before a professional meeting, professional associations will issue a call for session proposals. (See figure 16.17.) In response to the call, researchers send brief descriptions of their proposed session. The meeting planners determine which proposals to accept based on the quality, number, and relevance of the topic to the theme of the conference.

Poster Sessions

Researchers must conform to poster guidelines when participating in a poster session. Prior to the event, meeting planners send out the requirements for the poster. These requirements state the size of the poster. Common size requirements are often three feet by five feet or four feet by six feet. Meeting planners will also state the session's time slot on the meeting agenda. Typically, poster sessions are three to five hours on one day. During that time, the researcher stands near the poster and answers questions about the research study.

Institutional printing departments offer services that enhance posters. Commercial printing companies with staffs of commercial artists and graphic designers also will print the posters. Researchers need to submit word documents or

Figure 16.17. Sample call for proposals

Call for Research Abstracts

Deadline for Abstracts: January 1, 20XX

Abstracts for the Summer Symposium are being solicited.

Topics:
- Workforce initiatives
- Innovations in service delivery
- Organizational or administrative issues in healthcare enterprises
- HIM best practices or performance improvement
- e-health implementations

Content of the research abstract should include:

- Title of presentation
- Name(s) of author(s) with title, credentials, and organization
- Method
- Brief results

Abstracts should be limited to 250 words. "To be considered, abstracts must be submitted by January 1, 20XX via the online submission form on the symposium Web site www.fictitious-URL.org/symposium 20XX." (Questions should be sent to Liz Qualef at the e-mail address listed at the bottom of this message.)

Selection of abstracts will be made through a peer-reviewed process.

Authors of accepted abstracts will then be asked to submit the complete scholarly paper by February 15, 20XX. Scholarly papers will be published in *Symposium Proceedings*. Content for the scholarly paper includes: (a) abstract; (b) title; (c) name(s) of author(s) with title; credentials, and organization; (d) literature review; (e) purpose or problem statement; (f) methods including analytical technique; (g) results; (h) discussion; and (i) conclusions and recommendations for future research.

Authors of accepted papers will also be asked to submit handouts for their presentation. The deadline for handouts is April 15. Presentations will be limited to 12 minutes, inclusive of questions. Due to the time constraints, authors are asked to focus their presentation and corresponding handouts on the sections of Results, Discussion, and Conclusions. For reference, interested parties will have the entire scholarly paper in the *Symposium Proceedings*.

For authors of accepted abstracts, half the registration will be waived.

Address to submit Research Abstracts:

Liz Qualef, PhD, RHIA
Professor and Chair
Blank University
Department of Health Information Management
School of Allied Health Sciences
City, ST 12345
School Fax: 252.428.XXXX
E-Mail: qualefl@xxxx.edu

PowerPoint slides. Web sites that offer printing of posters may be a cost-effective alternative. These Web sites may have templates that researchers can use. Posters typically include:

- Banner (header) with title of study, names of researchers, and institutional affiliation
- Abstract
- Purpose
- Method
- Results
- Discussion and conclusions

Posters should be colorful and readable at 10 feet. Charts and graphics are particularly striking. The posters can be laminated or mounted on poster board. Moreover, the researcher should take the time necessary to create a poster that looks professional.

Presentation

Professional presentations occur during sessions of regional, state, national, and international meetings. As described previously, researchers submit proposals in response to a call. Linking the response to the theme of the meeting increases the likelihood that the proposal will be accepted.

Presenters should remember their audience as they create and present their papers and PowerPoint slides. One researcher conducted research on the delivery of research papers (Edirisooriya 1996, 25). Over 7 years, she attended 126 sessions and viewed 748 presenters. Most presenters were allowed 12 minutes and found this limit inadequate. She found that 42 percent of presenters had not synthesized their data into information and, thus, wasted their time on unnecessary and trivial details (Edirisooriya 1996, 27). These presenters never reached the important points of their research. Edirisooriya recommended that presenters prepare for oral presentations by:

- Practicing their presentation
- Bringing all their materials
- Distilling their paper to four or five pages
- Showing eye-catching graphics (not tables with miniscule numbers)
- Focusing on results, discussion, and implications rather than background, theoretical framework, and rationales for analytical techniques

A more recent article reiterated these same ideas for effective presentations (Wineburg 2004, 13–14). Generally, presenters should be prepared to talk about their research. Merely reading the notes is inadequate. Rather, presenters should try to be animated and talk to the people in the room. Other details regarding the mechanics of creating an effective PowerPoint presentation are listed in figure 16.18.

Figure 16.18. Guidelines for effective PowerPoint presentations

- High contrast for visibility (black text on white background or dark blue background with white text and yellow highlights)
- Lots of white space
- Six by six rule (six words per line, six lines per slide)
- Upper- and lowercase (all caps hard to read)
- 18 minimum point size (24 recommended and 28 to 36 preferable)
- Two inches character height for every 20 ft between visual and audience
- Clear, simple fonts (Helvetica or Ariel)
- Colors limited to 2 or 3
- Colors' subliminal messages ("in the red")
- Red-green color blindness
- Color opposites on color wheel create "shimmer"
- Transitions limited to 1 or 2 and nondistracting
- Overuse of sounds annoying
- Bullets are points of the outline
- No paragraphs
- Consistent verb tenses
- Consistent tense of first words of parallel lines
- Simple graphs
- Proofread for spelling, math, grammar, numbering
- Handouts should have three slides and room for notes

Publication

Publication is important because it makes knowledge public. Practitioners, other researchers, and professionals in related fields can examine and critically analyze the research. Through publication, the HIM body of knowledge and the expertise of its professionals become available to the world.

Scientific manuscripts commonly are organized in a prescribed structure. An unpublished paper is known as a *manuscript*. A manuscript or paper that has been published in a journal is known as an *article*. The prescribed structure of scientific papers is called *IMRAD* (introduction, methods, results, and discussion) (Sollaci and Pereira 2004, 364).

This chapter has moved through the steps of research. In each step, the associated documentation is described. This documentation correlates with many sections of a research paper or journal article, including:

- Problem statement (introduction)
- Literature review
- Statement of hypothesis
- Method
- Results (including discussion)

At this time, the researcher must complete the documentation by writing the abstract and expanding and detailing the sections already written.

It seems strange that the abstract, the first section of a journal article, is written last. However, the abstract is written last because it encompasses the entire study, including the study's findings.

An **abstract** is a brief summary of the major parts of a research study. It only reports the contents of the research; no additional information is included. An abstract is important because it is used in bibliographic databases to index and retrieve an article. Readers use it to decide whether the article contains valuable information and whether they should read the entire article. In writing an abstract, an author should focus on the research's important information, objectives, results, and conclusions. Brevity and directness are keys to a good abstract.

Table 16.15 serves as a final checklist for the composition and revision of the manuscript. Authors submitting manuscripts to journals in the field of health information management should take note that the peer reviewers highly value the following characteristics of manuscripts: (1) accuracy, (2) potential for contribution, (3) reasonableness of conclusions, (4) readability and style, and (5) organization (Layman and Watzlaf 2003, 61). Common pitfalls are listed in figure 16.19. Careful attention to detail at this point has a high return on investment in terms of having journals accept the manuscripts. In preparing their manuscript for publication, researchers face two major remaining tasks: selecting the appropriate journal and following its submission guidelines.

Selecting the Appropriate Journal

Selecting the appropriate journal requires thought and investigation. Depending on the topic, researchers should consider journals in other disciplines, such as informatics, computer science, public health, epidemiology, healthcare management, allied health, nursing, bioethics, health services, health policy, and health education. As mentioned earlier, in health information management, research is published in two journals: the *Journal of the American Health Information Management Association* (*Journal of AHIMA*) and *Perspectives in Health Information Management* (*PHIM*).

Researchers can obtain lists of journals from a college or university library. They may also want to spend time at the library skimming through a number of journals. Reviewing the journals allows them to determine the journals' mission, foci, and audiences. This determination allows them to match their purpose, topic, research design, and style to the journal's scope, content, and audience.

First, researchers should determine their purpose. Is it altruism, service, or scholarship? Certain journals are better suited to one purpose than another. For example, some journals have a practice orientation and others have a research orientation.

For altruism and service, researchers may send their manuscripts to journals oriented to practice, such as the *Journal of AHIMA*. The researchers want to help their profession by putting effective techniques into the hands of practitioners. For example, if the researcher found that a particular graphical interface increased coder accuracy by 10 percent, he or she may decide to send that manuscript to the *Journal of AHIMA*.

In addition to altruism and service, some researchers want to advance scholarship in health information management. These researchers are building the field's body of knowledge. To build a body of knowledge, publication in high quality journals is essential. Quality, however, is not easily quantified and is more difficult to determine. For journals, direct measures of quality include:

- Being indexed in referenced in bibliographic databases, such as MEDLINE

Table 16.15. Organization of research publications

Section	Contents
Title Page	Concise and descriptive title, author, author's affiliation, grant information, disclaimer, corresponding author's address, telephone, fax, and e-mail
Abstract	Background, purpose, methods, results, conclusions or Context; objective; design, setting, and participants; interventions; main outcome measures; results, conclusions 45 to 250 words dependent upon call for papers or journal instructions 3 to 10 key words using medical subject headings (MeSH)
Introduction	Background; pertinent literature review that provides rationale for research; brief statement of research plan; purpose, objectives, or research question
Methods	Protocol with detail for replication Design, setting, and participants Definition of variables Reference established methods Sampling strategy Collection of data Statement about approval of IRB or other oversight entity Analytical strategy
Results	Core Important results followed by less important results Neutral reporting
Discussion	Relationship between results and purpose, objectives, or research question Evidence of relationship Similarities to and differences from previous research New knowledge in terms of theoretical framework Limitations Conclusions as related to purpose, objectives, or research question Implications for future research Recommendations as warranted Summary
Acknowledgment	Contributors whose level of involvement does not justify authorship
References	Citations per format in instructions
Tables	Consistent with narrative Expand abbreviations Format per instructions
Figures	Consistent with narrative Expand abbreviations Legend Format per instructions

- Having high rejection rates
- Scoring high impact factors (rate of citation of the journal's articles in a year)
- Being refereed

An indirect measure is the prestige of the journal. Prestige is the field's members' general opinion of the journal in comparison to other journals in the discipline. Thus, researchers publishing for scholarship should consider indexed and refereed journals with high rejection rates and high impact factors.

Second, researchers should match the content of their manuscript with the focus of the journal. For example, they should send manuscripts about research on the management of health information services to journals in the field of health information management. If their results have an impact on reimbursement or health policy, the researchers should consider journals with a broader base.

Third, researchers must match the design and method of their research to the types of designs and methods in the journal. Some journals include mostly experimental and quasi-experimental research; others include ethnographies, case studies, and personal histories. Researchers who match the design and method of their study with the types of typical designs and methods in the journal increase the likelihood of their manuscripts being accepted.

Fourth, researchers should strive for a match between their writing style and the preferences of the journal's audience. Journals that are oriented toward practice prefer brief articles written in simple, direct sentences. On the other hand, journals oriented toward scholarly work prefer a more formal and pedantic tone.

Finally, understanding the journal's audience combines the issues of topic and design. Researchers should submit their manuscripts to journals with audiences that would be interested in the topic. If the intended audience includes a broad range of fields, researchers should write manuscripts that are of interest to all potential readers. Moreover, researchers should clearly state how their manuscript affects and benefits the journal's intended audience.

Following the Journal's Submission Guidelines

Journals have rules for the format of manuscripts. The rules are both explicit and implicit. Explicit rules are openly stated; implicit rules are unwritten, but important. Editors and peer reviewers assume that researchers will naturally know and follow them. Different fields tend to have their own unique sets of implicit rules.

Journal editors state their explicit requirements for manuscripts in their style manual and submission guidelines. There are four major style manuals. (See figure 16.20.) Selection of style manual relates to the field. For example, journals in education generally require APA style whereas biomedical journals require AMA style. Journals in health information management use an adapted University of Chicago style. The variance in style manuals is illustrated in table 16.16.

The journal's submission guidelines include details such as the word-processing package, width of margins, length, and organizational structure. (See figure 16.21.) For instance,

Figure 16.19. Pitfalls in presenting research

- Allowing insufficient time to write the results or to develop the presentation
- Interjecting subjective commentary and emotional hyperbole
- Duplicating information in narrative and graphic forms
- Creating confusing or inconsistent graphics
- Believing that verbosity and inflated statements substitute for clarity and accuracy

Figure 16.20. Common style manuals

American Psychological Association. 2001. *Publication Manual of the American Psychological Association*, 5th ed. Washington, DC: APA. [Referred to as **APA Style**.]

Gibaldi, J. 2003. *MLA Handbook for Writers of Research Papers*, 6th ed. New York: Modern Language Association of America. [Referred to as **MLA Style**.]

Iverson, C. ed., 2007. *American Medical Association Manual of Style: A Guide for Authors and Editors*, 10th ed. New York: Oxford University Press.

University of Chicago Press. 2003. *Chicago Manual of Style*, 15th ed. Chicago: University of Chicago Press. [Referred to as **Chicago Style**.]

Table 16.16. Variation in style manuals

Organization	Book	Journal
AMA	Jencks C, Riesman D. *The Academic Revolution.* Chicago: University of Chicago Press; 1977.	Lloyd SC, Layman E. The effects of automated encoders on coding accuracy and coding speed. *Top Health Inf Manage* February 1997; 17(3):72–79.
APA	Jencks, C., & Riesman, D. (1977). *The academic revolution.* Chicago: University of Chicago Press.	Lloyd, S. C., & Layman, E. (1997, February). The effects of automated encoders on coding accuracy and coding speed. Topics in *Health Information Management,* 17(3), 72–79.
Chicago	Jencks, Christopher, and David Riesman. 1977. *The Academic Revolution.* Chicago: University of Chicago Press.	Lloyd, Susan C., and Elizabeth Layman. 1997 (February). The effects of automated encoders on coding accuracy and coding speed. *Topics in Health Information Management* 17(3):72–79.
MLA	Jencks, Christopher, and David Riesman. *The Academic Revolution.* Chicago: University of Chicago Press, 1977.	Lloyd, Susan C., and Elizabeth Layman. "The Effects of Automated Encoders on Coding Accuracy and Coding Speed." *Topics in Health Information Management* 17.3 (1997): 72–79.

Figure 16.21. Content of submission guidelines

- Information needed about the author and contact
- Style manual
- Length and representativeness of title
- Length of abstract in words
- Length of manuscript in maximum number of pages or number of words
- Font and font size
- Line spacing
- Justification
- Margins
- Pagination
- Inclusive (nonsexist) language
- Blinding (names of authors on separate page)
- Format of charts and tables
- Format of citations in text
- Format of references (sometimes vary slightly from style manual)
- General organizational structure of manuscript
- Word-processing software
- Number of paper copies
- Diskette or electronic submission

the editors of *PHIM* prefer an organizational structure that generally includes the following elements:

- Abstract (150 words or less and up to 10 key words)
- Introduction
- Background (literature review)
- Research question or hypothesis
- Methods
- Results
- Discussion
- Conclusion
- References

However, most editors state that the organizational structure is flexible and that researchers should adapt the structure to suit their research. Researchers can find guidelines in journals or on the publishers' Web sites.

A journal's implicit rules reflect the culture of its audience. Culture is reflected in the use of the first person, anthropomorphism, passive voice, and tone. For example, an audience of qualitative researchers would accept use of the first person whereas its use probably would cause an audience of experimental researchers to doubt the article's credibility. Purists reject anthropomorphism as giving human traits to inanimate objects. Audiences that reject first person and anthropomorphism also tend to prefer passive voice and a detached, neutral tone. Time spent skimming journals would provide insight into their implicit rules.

Some editors and peer reviewers assume that sloppy writing indicates sloppy research. Moreover, some editors and peer reviewers believe that the inability to follow submission guidelines indicates the inability to follow research protocols. Therefore, attention to detail is important. Researchers seeking more information about writing and publishing manuscripts should read the style manuals and review samples of submission guidelines. For grammar and clarity, Strunk and White's (2000) book on writing is a classic. First published in 1959 and periodically revised, its succinct discussions and precise examples provide clear guidance. Finally, researchers should carefully read *How to Write and Publish a Scientific Paper* by Day and Gastel (2006), which is dedicated to research writing and publishing.

Check Your Understanding 16.8

Instructions: Answer the following questions on a separate piece of paper.

1. How do the research findings and discussion sections differ?
2. What two factors should researchers consider when determining how to present a particular data element?
3. What three questions should a researcher answer when writing the discussion section?
4. What three factors should researchers consider when selecting a journal for manuscript submission?

Data Access and Confidentiality

When they access data, researchers pledge that they will keep them confidential. In their code of ethics, HIM professionals affirm that they will "uphold and defend the individual's right to privacy and the doctrine of confidentiality in the use and disclosure of information." This section describes the intersection of data access and protection of confidentiality.

Practical Considerations

Access to data depends on the type of data and their location. Data can range from totally uncontrolled to highly protected. For example, data on the Internet are easily accessed whereas data in health records require approvals from IRBs.

Data can be public or proprietary. Public data are often accessible under the Freedom of Information Act; some have been posted on the Internet. State registry data also are often accessible. Proprietary data require permission of the owner of the database.

Data can be individual or aggregate. Data that identify one individual are less accessible than aggregate data. Protections exist for identifiable data. To use identifiable data, researchers must obtain approvals from all involved IRBs. For example, researchers may need to obtain the approval of the IRB of the university where they work and from the IRB of the healthcare organization from which they received the identifiable data. Some organizations may require informed consents to review data. In addition, access to personally identifiable data has become more complex with the implementation of the regulations of the Health Insurance Portability and Accountability Act (HIPAA) of 1996. (See chapter 18 for additional information.)

After approvals or permissions are obtained, the location of data also affects ease of access. For data in databases, researchers can transfer the files over the Internet. For paper records, researchers must physically go to the site of storage where they must abide by the hours of operation and rules for security. In addition, they must arrange in some way to collect their data, for example, by entering them into a laptop.

Access to data becomes critical for researchers who conduct secondary analyses or combine their primary research with public databases. The key points for researchers who want to mine these rich resources are obtaining the approvals and allowing sufficient time.

Confidentiality

Confidentiality and anonymity are closely related concepts. *Confidentiality* pertains to the handling and maintenance of data so that the data are not divulged to others without the research participant's permission or divulged in ways contrary to the participant's understanding of the original disclosure. *Anonymity* pertains to data that have no identifiers linked to them and that cannot be traced back to the research participant.

Thus, confidentiality and anonymity are not synonymous and cannot be used interchangeably. Researchers must be careful in their use of the terms and not promise the more stringent concept of anonymity when they mean confidentiality.

The HIPAA regulations and its clauses related to de-identified data revolve around the concepts of confidentiality and anonymity.

Medical research, and by extension many other types of research in the United States, is covered under the Federal Policy for the Protection of Human Subjects (45 CFR Part 46 Subpart A) (HHS 2005). This federal policy is a set of regulations regarding research that 18 federal agencies share (NSF 2006). Because this federal policy is shared among many agencies, it is also known as the **Common Rule** (or, less commonly, *Subpart A*). These agencies fund research at institutions that provide written assurance to the funding agency that the institutions will comply with the requirements of the Common Rule.

At a minimum, the Common Rule requires the following:

- Institutional statement of principles regarding the institution's responsibilities in the protection of human subjects involved in its research studies
- IRB with sufficient staff
- List of IRB members that demonstrates representative capacity to contribute to IRB deliberations
- Written procedures that the IRB follows for reviewing proposed research and ongoing oversight
- Written procedures that ensure prompt reporting of unanticipated problems, serious or continuing noncompliance, and suspension or termination of IRB approval (Burrington-Brown and Wagg 2003, 56A)

Institutions that are covered entities under HIPAA and that conduct federally funded research must comply with the regulations of both HIPAA and the Common Rule. The regulations of HIPAA articulate with the Common Rule. For example, under the Common Rule, researchers must obtain informed consent. HIPAA adds that the researcher also must obtain a signed authorization before protected health information may be used or disclosed for research. Further, HIPAA expands the role of the IRB by giving it authority, under specific stipulations, to approve waivers or alterations to the requirement to obtain authorization.

Health data that have been de-identified may be used without restriction for research purposes. However, the IRB must ensure that the data have been de-identified in the correct manner, that is, de-identified using statistical verification or all of the following identifiers removed: names, addresses (except state), date (except year), telephone and fax numbers, e-mail addresses, Social Security numbers, health record numbers, health plan numbers, account numbers, certificate and license numbers, vehicle identifiers and serial numbers, device identifiers and serial numbers, URLs, IP addresses, biometric identifiers, full-face photographic images, and any other unique identifying number, characteristic, or code unless permitted by the privacy rule for re-identification (Gilles 2004, 52).

A disadvantage to using de-identified data is that contacting the patient or client to improve the response rate or to notify the patient about some malfunction of a device or side effect of a drug is impossible.

Researchers who are preparing to conduct research with health information are encouraged to read the in-depth discussions provided by Burrington-Brown and Wagg (2003), Gilles (2004), and Roth (2004a, 2004b, 2004c). Finally, researchers should familiarize themselves with state laws protecting privacy. Some state laws are more restrictive than HIPAA. Researchers must comply with the more restrictive regulations.

Research and the Practitioner

Research is a potential career for HIM professionals, according to Biedermann and Burrington-Brown (2004) who state that "HIM professionals are naturals for careers in research" (44). Moreover, an HIM researcher describes how HIM professionals can incorporate research into their roles as leaders of HIM Services Departments (Watzlaf 1995, 47–48). In practice, the roles of HIM professionals in research sort into four types:

- Researcher
- Support staff to researchers in healthcare organizations or health-related settings
- Employee of a research company or agency
- User of research in implementations of best practices in the workplace or in continuing education

First, many HIM professionals are researchers. They conduct research for several reasons, including service to the profession, personal interest, and condition of employment. HIM researchers have been involved in a wide array of research projects, such as:

- Developing Web-based reporting system for medication errors
- Coordinating a statewide patient safety education program
- Developing an information infrastructure to link rural hospitals to a tertiary care center (Bailey and Rudman 2004, 2)

Additionally, many of the citations in this chapter represent HIM professionals in the role of researcher.

Second, HIM professionals in the health information services departments of healthcare enterprises assist researchers in many ways, including:

- Assisting members of IRBs in the review of proposed studies that relate to data in health databases or paper records
- Evaluating and summarizing for administration the content of proposed studies that relate to data in health databases or paper records
- Identifying the location of the desired health data in databases, records, logs, reports, registers, or indexes
- Directing researchers and other authorized users to the location of health data
- Discussing with researchers the format of the data, such as paper records, microfilm, microfiche, and database
- Noting caveats, such as time frames and residual codes, related to the data
- Running computer queries to find cases
- Arranging access to computer databases and paper records
- Managing the work area reserved for researchers
- Obtaining signed confidentiality statements

Third, HIM professionals are employees of research companies or agencies. Research companies conduct various research-related activities, such as clinical trials or development of new pharmaceuticals. Research agencies often provide outcomes research that supports policymaking in healthcare. In these settings, HIM professionals may be responsible for collecting and coding data, managing clinical databases and protocols, providing decision support, and writing reports. HIM researchers note that these positions "blend [HIM] professional, clinical, and research skills with knowledge of business operations and insight into management of information systems" (Bailey and Rudman 2004, 2).

All HIM professionals can use the steps of research. Research provides a thorough, systematic approach. The problem-solving models of management and the decision-making models of decision sciences are based on the steps of research. Therefore, the logic of the approach allows HIM professionals to use research in their day-to-day activities. To find answers to common questions or solutions to everyday problems, research is a practical and effective tool. In the long term, the orderliness of the step-by-step approach saves time and results in the best decision.

Research results are made public in professional presentations, proceedings of meetings, and journals. The availability and accessibility of these results allow all HIM professionals to benefit. HIM professionals can put the results of the research into practice. For example, as a consequence of the medical sociologist's research on the chatter about patients in hospital elevators, orientation sessions specifically address the need to maintain confidentiality in all conversations and in all settings.

Relationship with the Professional Body of Knowledge

One of the defining characteristics of a profession is that it has a body of knowledge. By definition, a field of work without a body of knowledge becomes an occupation or a job. Therefore, as a means to build and expand knowledge, research is the foundation of a profession.

As an emerging profession, health information management is developing and articulating its body of knowledge. Leaders of AHIMA recognize the importance of knowledge in advancing practice and professional learning (Kloss 2000, 27). HIM professionals are conducting research in issues and topics related to health information. These topics and issues involve health information technology and systems, health data security and quality, management, benchmarks in practice and education, and informatics. (See figure 16.22.) This research is defining, expanding, and refining the body of knowledge for the HIM profession.

Use in HIM Practice: Data Quality

HIM practitioners can use research to improve their department's efficiency and effectiveness. They also can use research to improve their own performance as managers and administers. But which results should they rely on? Recent contradictory reports about widely used drugs raise skepticism about the research enterprise. The following section

Figure 16.22. Research topics in HIM

Compliance	Best practices in health information services
Use of computer applications in HIM education	Unique HIM instructional techniques
Information security	Information technology
Distance learning	Adoption and implementation of electronic health record
Vocabularies and terminologies	Role of technology in healthcare
Clinical education	Quality and use of coded data
Management issues	Impact of data quality in health outcomes
Graduate education	Data mining
Workforce retention and satisfaction	
Impact of HIPAA	
Managed care	
HIM curricular changes and their effectiveness	

gives HIM practitioners pointers and information on how to identify high-quality data in research.

Evaluating research begins with carefully, critically, and analytically reading the journal article. Cohen (1991) provides questions that analytical readers of research should ask themselves. As a demonstration, these questions will be applied to a journal article in *Perspectives in Health Information Management* (Watzlaf et al. 2004).

HIM researchers conducted a study to measure the awareness, use, and validity of the minimum content for electronic health records (EHRs) as recommended by the American Society for Testing and Materials (ASTM) (Watzlaf et al. 2004, 3). (See figure 16.23.)

1. Is the problem clearly stated? Are terms defined as needed? Has the problem been appropriately delimited?
   - Statements: "Therefore, it is important to assess if those who purchase and use these systems are aware that these standards exist, and to measure the extent of usage of these standards. It will also be helpful to see if the content of the standards are meeting users' needs, so future revisions can address any deficiencies or problem areas." "To our knowledge, no other survey-based study has been performed that examines the awareness, use, and fulfillment of user's needs of the most recent ASTM E1384 standards and E1633 coded values for the EHR."
   - Based on these statements, it appears the conditions of the first set of questions are met.

Figure 16.23. Key questions to evaluate research

1. Is the problem clearly stated? Are terms defined as needed? Has the problem been appropriately delimited?
2. Is the hypothesis stated? Does the hypothesis relate to the problem? Is the way the researcher intends to test the hypothesis clear?
3. To the best of the student's knowledge, is the literature review thorough, complete, and pertinent? Is the literature review clear and organized? Is the student convinced this problem is important? Does the literature review synthesize rather than merely summarize?
4. Does the study's design relate to the problem? Is the population clearly defined? Is the method of creating the sample clearly explained? Is bias reduced in sampling? Is the sample representative of the population?
5. Is the instrument specified? Is the instrument related to the problem? Does the researcher state the instrument's reliability and validity?
6. Does the researcher explain the method clearly enough and with sufficient detail that another person could replicate the study? Are confidential data protected?
7. Does the researcher use the best mode to present the results? Do tables, figures, and graphs have clear titles? Do the numbers "add up"?
8. Do the conclusions relate to the findings? Does the researcher provide alternative explanations? Does the researcher relate the findings back to the larger body of knowledge or theory?
9. Are all citations in the body of the article in the reference list? Is jargon kept to a minimum?

Source: Cohen 1991.

2. Is the hypothesis stated? Does the hypothesis relate to the problem? Is the way the researcher intends to test the hypothesis clear?
   - "The study is descriptive. Because there is no intent to make inferences, no hypothesis is needed."
   - The conditions of the second set of questions are not applicable.
3. To the best of the student's knowledge, is the literature review thorough, complete, and pertinent? Is the literature review clear and organized? Is the student convinced this problem is important? Does the literature review synthesize rather than merely summarize?
   - The authors explain the advantages of the EHR based on the Standard Guide. They cite Mary Brandt and Gretchen Murphy, AHIMA leaders. The authors also state, "To our knowledge, no other survey-based study has been performed that examines the awareness, use, and fulfillment of user's needs of the most recent ASTM E1384 standards and E1633 coded values for the EHR." "It is therefore important and timely to determine the awareness, use, and validity of the ASTM standards for the content and structure of EHRs and their corresponding coded values."
   - The final statement is most convincing. Based on these statements and the citation of professional leaders, it appears the conditions of the third set of questions are met.
4. Does the study's design relate to the problem? Is the population clearly defined? Is the method of creating the sample clearly explained? Is bias reduced in sampling? Is the sample representative of the population?
   - Yes, the design relates to the problem because there is little known on the topic. When little is known, the descriptive, cross-sectional design is appropriate. The population is stated in the article: U.S. healthcare facilities identified by the American Hospital Association; vendors of EHR/CPR systems as identified in Healthcare Informatics; vendors reviewed by the American Academy of Family Physicians; volunteers, organizations recognized by CPRI-HOST. Yes, sample creation is clearly explained.
   - Stratified random sample (stratification by state and type) reduces bias.
5. Is the instrument specified? Is the instrument related to the problem? Does the researcher state the instrument's reliability and validity?
   - The authors explain that they designed their own survey. The survey was piloted on a random sample of 5 to 10 facilities and organizations. To detect potential problems, two individuals were shadowed when completing the online survey. A draft of the survey was presented to the ASTM E1384 committee. Changes were made based on the comments. From the piloting it appears that the instrument relates to the problem. The instrument's reliability

and validity were not stated. As a new instrument, reliability and validity would need to be established, particularly if the researchers wanted to use this instrument again. Based on this information, it appears the conditions of the fifth set of questions are partially met.

6. Does the researcher explain the method clearly enough and with sufficient detail that another person could replicate the study?
   - Are confidential data protected?
   - Yes, because the method is very detailed, another researcher could replicate this study. It does not appear that confidential data were obtained; however, the researchers did go through their IRB.
   - Based on the clarity, I believe that the article met the conditions of the sixth set of questions.
7. Does the researcher use the best mode to present the results? Do tables, figures, and graphs have clear titles? Do the numbers "add up"?
   - Tables appear to be the best mode to present the results. Tables have clear titles. Authors explain when the numbers do not "add up."
   - Tables contain lots of data and seem long. Perhaps selected findings relevant to the audience could have been extracted. Overall, the article appears to meet conditions of the seventh set of conditions.
8. Do the conclusions relate to the findings? Does the researcher provide alternative explanations? Does the researcher relate the findings back to the larger body of knowledge or theory?
   - The authors concluded, "This study was able to provide some beginning information on the type of EHR system healthcare facilities have in place, as well as their awareness of ASTM standards and the specific minimum data elements they believe should be included in an EHR."
   - Comparing these conclusions, the problem statement, and the findings, it appears that they all relate.
   - The authors did not provide alternative explanations as they were conducting a descriptive study. They linked to the larger body of knowledge by extrapolating how their study supported the development of the longitudinal record. Overall, the article appears to have met the conditions of the eighth set of questions.
9. Are all citations in the body of the article in the reference list? Is jargon kept to a minimum?
   - All citations in the body of the article are in the reference list. ASTM and healthcare jargon is employed; however, it may have been difficult to communicate with the study participants without employing jargon. Also, the fields of healthcare and informatics seem particularly prone to jargon.
   - Overall, the article appears to have partially met the conditions of the eighth set of questions.

Reviewing a journal article requires that readers synthesize all they know about research with much of what they know about a topic. Practicing these skills keeps readers sharp and attuned to results that do not meet the characteristics of data quality.

Another skill to evaluate research is to sort out the meaning of statistics on the tables that report them. A sample statistical table from a research article is dissected below.

The researchers investigated the relationships between independent variables and dependent variables (Layman and Guyden 1999, 34). The independent variables were the coping mechanisms of self-disclosure, self-directed[ness], confidence, acceptance, structuring, problem solving, and coping resources. The dependent variable was burnout with its three subscales of emotional exhaustion (EE), depersonalization (DP), and personal accomplishment (PA).

The word *relationship* clues the reader that correlational statistical techniques are likely. The table's title lists the statistical technique as Pearson product–moment correlation. This title confirms the initial impression that correlational statistical techniques would be used. (See table 16.17.)

In the footnote, the researchers provide a key to the symbols (*, **, and ***). The asterisks meant the p-values were less than would be encountered through chance. The $p<0.05$ means that the probability of obtaining this extreme of a test statistic is 5 percent. The $p<0.01$ means that the probability of obtaining this extreme of a test statistic is 1 percent. The $p<0.001$ means that the probability of obtaining this extreme of a test statistic is 0.1 percent. Therefore, the researchers' findings were unlikely to be due to chance. A relationship existed between the emotional exhaustion and the coping resources (–0.4536).

Some of the findings have minus (–) signs in front of them. The minus signs show that an inverse relationship exists between the emotional exhaustion and coping resources (–0.4536). An inverse relationship means that the *more* emotionally exhausted the respondent was, the *fewer* coping resources the respondent had. Inverse relationships move in opposite directions. An alternative explanation of the relationship between emotional exhaustion and coping resources could be that the more coping resources the respondent had, the less emotionally exhausted the respondent was. Correlations cannot indicate which came first, the emotional exhaustion or the coping resources. We only know that the two variables are related.

The researchers state that the study was a cross-sectional, correlational design. As a quasi-experimental design, the study cannot show causation. Thus, the researchers cannot state what caused the lower levels of emotional exhaustion for some respondents. The researchers do not know whether the high levels of coping resources caused the lower levels of emotional exhaustion. The most the researchers can say is that the more coping resources the respondent recorded, the less emotionally exhausted the respondent was.

Table 16.17. Pearson product–moment correlation of burnout subscales and selected coping mechanisms

	Self-Disclosure	Self-Directed	Confidence	Acceptance	Solving Structuring	Problem Resources	Coping
EE	2.2489 (287) p = .000***	2.3245 (287) p = .000***	2.3993 (287) p = .000***	2.2821 (287) p = .000***	2.2948 (287) p = .000***	2.3048 (287) p = .000***	2.4536 (287) p = .000***
DP	2.2952 (287) p = .000***	2.2172 (287) p = .000***	2.3004 (287) p = .000***	2.2895 (287) p = .000***	2.1808 (287) p = .002**	2.2712 (287) p = .000***	2.3653 (287) p = .000***
PA	.2984 (287) p = .000***	.3731 (287) p = .000***	.5332 (287) p = .000***	.3398 (287) p = .000***	.3904 (287) p = .000***	.4970 (287) p = .000***	.5576 (287) p = .000***

Note. (coefficient / (cases) / two-tailed test).
*p < .05. **p < .01. ***p < .001.

Source: Layman and Guyden 1999.

Astute readers may note that the row of data labeled PA (personal accomplishment) does not have minus signs. The absence of the minus signs indicates that a positive relationship exists between the two variables. In positive relationships, the variables both move in the same direction. The *more* coping resources a respondent has, the *more* personally accomplished the respondent feels. To reiterate, the correlational design of the study precludes statements about causation.

Being able to determine the meaning of tables with statistical data is a powerful tool. Articles report data in tables and other graphics because these formats efficiently deliver information. However, if one cannot decode the table, the benefit is lost. Acquiring skills in statistical reporting is valuable for HIM professionals because they are data driven.

Researchers provide much information in journal articles. As the field of HIM increasingly moves to data mining and evidence-based practice, skills in evaluating the quality of data reported in journal articles become ever more important. Honing skills in research and data quality is a key task for HIM professionals who are preparing to lead the practice in the future.

Check Your Understanding 16.9

Instructions: Answer the following questions on a separate piece of paper.

1. What should researchers who use large databases for secondary analysis know about them?
2. How do public databases and proprietary databases differ?
3. The researcher's informed consent form stated that the patients' information would be anonymous. Later, in the application form for IRB approval, the researcher described a coding system to track respondents and nonrespondents. The IRB returned the application to the researcher with the stipulation that the informed consent must be changed. What raised the red flag?
4. What is the Common Rule?
5. A researcher is at an institution that is a covered entity and received federal funding for research. Which set of regulations applies to the researcher?
6. Why is research particularly important to an emerging profession, such as health information management?

Real-World Case

Electronic health records are being implemented throughout the healthcare system. Managing health records is a primary task of health information professionals. Over the years, the Council on Certification of AHIMA has conducted roles and functions studies. Periodically, the results of the roles and functions studies are reported (Rudman et al. 1996; Watzlaf et al. 1997). Beyond these studies, few studies on the roles of health information professionals in managing health records in paper and electronic environments have been conducted. In one study, dating back to 1984, researchers examined the effect of credentials on data quality (Green and Benjamin 1986). In studies from the mid-1990s, researchers investigated demographic characteristics related to job profiles, the effect of career moves on advancement, and factors associated with salaries (Mon et al. 1997a; Mon et al. 1997b; Rudman 1995). Thus, it is important to study the effects of the transition to electronic health records on the roles of health information professionals. This information can guide curriculum development, continuing education, and professional development.

An HIM researcher has begun the investigation of the effects of the transition to electronic health records on the roles of health information professionals (Rinehart-Thompson 2008a). The researcher conducted a descriptive, exploratory study. The researcher determined the population of "most-wired" hospitals from lists of acute care general hospitals that the American Hospital Association identified as "most-wired hospitals and health systems," "most wired small and rural organizations," and "most wireless" organizations. The resulting population was approximately 700 hospitals (multihospital systems affected the count). To investigate record retention practices, the researcher surveyed a representative, random sample of 250 of these "most-wired" hospitals. The survey was sent to the HIM professionals at the selected hospitals. The response rate was 33.6 percent.

The statistical analyses included frequencies, percentages, means, and standard deviations.

The study's results record the current status of practice in the transition to an electronic environment. In future studies, these current results can be used as a baseline for comparison. In terms of the respondents' responsibilities:

- 79 percent of the respondents stated that the HIM professional administered or oversaw the hospital's retention policy
- 8.8 percent of the respondents indicated that the HIM professional had sole responsibility for determining the retention period
- 81 percent stated that HIM professionals had varying degrees of involvement in determining retention periods
- 10 percent of the respondents indicated that HIM professionals had no involvement in determining retention periods
- 90 percent of the respondents cited state record retention laws as the most influential option for determining record retention periods
- 63 percent of the respondents reported permanent retention of paper records
- 58 percent of the respondents reported permanent retention of electronic records

Several of the study's results have implications for practice, professional development, and future research. In terms of practice, many of the respondents cited state retention laws as the determining factor for retention periods and more than half the respondents retained records permanently. Additional information is needed on these practices. Of the 31 states and the District of Columbia represented by the respondents, only one state's statutes implied permanent retention. The other respondent 30 states and the District of Columbia did not require permanent retention; instead, they required retention for a number of years after some event (entry, discharge, treatment, and such). In terms of professional development, the study delineates the role of HIM in record retention practices in the most wired hospitals. The study shows that HIM professionals have considerable influence in the establishment of retention policies and their administration. Thus, continuing education and curricula need to provide support for these responsibilities. Finally, in terms of future research, clarification of the HIM role in less-wired hospitals is needed. Moreover, to maintain knowledge on the status of the discipline, periodic updates on this study are needed as more and more hospitals complete the transition to an electronic environment. Research is also needed on the effect of the transition to EHRs on other core HIM functions.

This exploratory study described the current landscape of HIM practice in the most-wired hospitals. It demonstrates how research can guide leaders as they develop materials to support practice, refine HIM education, and provide opportunities in continuing education

Summary

High-quality research depends on a carefully conceived plan and impeccable execution. Researchers' plans are similar to the blueprints that architects use to construct buildings. Researchers use their plans to conduct their studies and to build new knowledge. Research is systematic, and health information professionals can adapt its step-by-step approach to practical problems in the workplace.

Knowing the purpose of the research is a consistent theme in this chapter. Purpose drives decisions in each of the steps of research. These steps are defining the problem, reviewing the literature, determining the design and method, selecting the instrument, collecting and analyzing the data, presenting the results, and interpreting the findings.

The purpose of research determines the approach, whether qualitative or quantitative. Qualitative research is often exploratory and preliminary; quantitative research investigates numerically measurable observations or tests hypotheses.

Purpose also assists researchers in clarifying their research question. Considering their purposes helps researchers to concentrate or narrow the focus of the question to a researchable issue. Purpose also can ensure that researchers investigate meaningful problems that need solutions or significant questions that need answers.

The literature review is guided by purpose. In research, preference is given to articles in refereed journals. Purpose aids researchers in discriminating between relevant and irrelevant articles and between related and tangential articles. Finally, one purpose of the literature review is to identify gaps in the body of knowledge that researchers can fill with their studies.

There are six common designs of research: historical, descriptive, correlational, evaluation, experimental, and causal–comparative. The design a researcher chooses depends on the purpose of the research. Associated with each design are many methods of research, including survey, observation, case study, ethnography, experiments, secondary analysis, and meta-analysis. As with the choice of design, purpose is crucial in the choice of method.

Purpose is also crucial in selecting the research instrument. Instruments are standardized means to collect data. Although many factors should be considered in the selection of an instrument, the most important is the researchers' purpose.

The importance of purpose may be less obvious in the collection and analysis of data. However, the higher the stakes, the larger the sample. Moreover, research that involves many variables also needs larger sample sizes. Therefore, purpose is a critical concern in the collection of data. Purpose also is involved in the analysis of data because statistical approaches vary by research design.

Moreover, purpose underlies the presentation of results and interpretation of findings. Researchers provide other HIM professionals with knowledge and techniques to answer questions and to solve problems in the workplace. Without presentation and interpretation, the knowledge and techniques would be unavailable to practitioners. Thereby, research in the field of health information management improves health information practices in the continuum of care.

HIM professionals are well suited to the role of researcher. Typically, persons in the field recognize their abilities to plan and organize. Their abilities with analytical expertise create a powerful toolbox of skills that HIM professionals can use to increase the field's body of knowledge.

References

AHIMA. 2008. e-HIM Practice Guidelines. http://www.ahima.org/e-him.

AHIMA Data Quality Management Task Force. 1998. Practice brief: Data quality management model. *Journal of AHIMA* 69(6).

Aish, A.M. and D. Wasserman. 2001. Does Beck's Hopelessness Scale really measure several components? *Psychological Medicine* 31(2):367–372.

Alreck, P.L. and R.B. Settle. 2004. *The Survey Research Handbook*. 3rd ed. New York: McGraw-Hill/Irwin.

Amatayakul, M.K. and M.A. Shah. 1992. *Research Manual for the Health Information Profession*. Chicago: AHIMA.

Ammenwerth, E. and N. de Keizer. 2005. An inventory of evaluation studies of information technology in health care: Trends in evaluation research 1982–2002. *Methods of Information in Medicine* 44(1):44–56.

Annual Reviews. 2008. Welcome to Annual Reviews. http://www.annualreviews.org.

Babbie, E. 2004. *The Practice of Social Research*. 10th ed. Belmont, CA: Wadsworth/Thomson Learning.

Bailey, J., and W. Rudman. 2004 (Sept. 20). The expanding role of the HIM professional: Where research and HIM roles intersect. *Perspectives in Health Information Management* 1(7):1–6.

Bailey, K.D. 1994. *Methods of Social Research*. 4th ed. New York: Free Press.

Becker, H.S., B. Geer, E.C. Hughes, and A.S. Strauss. 1961. *Boys in White: Student Culture in Medical School*. Chicago: University of Chicago Press.

Bednarz, D. 1985. Quantity and quality in evaluation research: A divergent view. *Evaluation and Program Planning* 8(4):289–306.

Bell, P.D. 2006 (Summer). Can factors related to self-regulated learning and epistemological beliefs predict learning achievement in undergraduate asynchronous web-based courses? *Perspectives in Health Information Management* 3(7):1–17.

Berdie, D.R. and J.F. Anderson. 1974. *Questionnaires: Design and Use*. Metuchen, NJ: Scarecrow Press.

Berner, E.S., R.K. Kasiraman, F. Yu, M.N. Ray, and T.K. Houston. 2005. Data quality in the outpatient setting: Impact of clinical decision support systems. *AMIA Annual Symposium Proceedings*,41–45. http://www.pubmedcentral.nih.org.

Bethell, C., J. Fiorillo, D. Lansky, M. Hendryx, and J. Knickman. 2004. Online consumer surveys as a methodology for assessing the quality of the United States health care system. *Journal of Medical Internet Research* 6(1):e2. http://www.jmir.org/2004/1/e2.

Biedermann, S.E. and J. Burrington-Brown. 2004. The research track: Career progressions in research for HIM professionals. *Journal of AHIMA* 75(10):44–46.

Bolin, D. and M. Goforth. 2005 (Nov.). Sideline documentation and its role in return to sport. *Clinical Journal of Sport Medicine* 15(6):405–409.

Bowling, A. 2005. *Measuring Health: A Review of Quality of Life Measurement Scales*. 3rd ed. New York: Open University Press.

Buller, D.B., W.F. Young, K.H. Fisher, and J.A. Maloy. 2007. The effect of endorsement by local opinion leaders and testimonials from teachers on the dissemination of a web-based smoking prevention program. *Health Education Research* 22(5):609–618.

Buros Institute. 1938–1995. The Mental Measurements Yearbook: *The Yearbook 1938–1995*. Highland Park, NJ: Buros Institute.

Buros Institute of Mental Measurements. 2003. *The Fifteenth Mental Measurements Yearbook*. http://www.unl.edu/buros.

Burrington-Brown, J. and D.G. Wagg. 2003. Practice brief: Regulations governing research. *Journal of AHIMA* 74(3):56A–56D.

Byrne, M. 2001. Ethnography as a qualitative research method. *Association of Operating Room Nurses Journal* 74(1):82–84.

Campbell, D.T. and J.C. Stanley. 1963. *Experimental and Quasi-Experimental Designs for Research*. Chicago: Rand McNally.

Chadwick, B.A., H.M. Bahr, and S.L. Albrecht. 1984. *Social Science Research Methods*. Englewood Cliffs, NJ: Prentice-Hall.

Chun, K.T., S. Cobb, and J.R.P. French Jr., eds. 1975. *Measures for Psychological Assessment: A Guide to 3,000 Original Sources and Their Applications*. Ann Arbor, MI: Survey Research Center, Institute for Social Research.

Cohen, P.A. 1992. Meta-analysis: Application to clinical dentistry and dental education. *Journal of Dental Education* 56(3):172–175.

Cohen, P.A. 1991. Criteria for evaluating research reports. Handout, educational research course. Augusta, GA: Medical College of Georgia.

Colaianni, L.A. 1994. Peer review in journals indexed in Index Medicus. *Journal of the American Medical Association* 272(2):156–158.

Crosson, J.C., N. Isaacson, D. Lancaster, E.A. McDonald, A.J. Schueth, B. DiCicco-Bloom, J.L. Newman, C.J. Wang, and D.S.Bell. 2008 (April). Variation in electronic prescribing implementation among twelve ambulatory practices. *Journal of General Internal Medicine* 23(4):364–371.

Crystal, A. and J. Greenberg. 2006. Relevance criteria identified by health information users during Web searches. *Journal of the American Society for Information Science and Technology* 57(10):1368–1382.

Day, R.A. and B. Gastel. 2006. *How to Write and Publish a Scientific Paper*. 6th ed. Westport, CT: Greenwood Press.

Department of Health and Human Services. 2005 (June 23). Protection of human subjects. *Code of Federal Regulations* 45 CFR 46. http://www.hhs.gov/ohrp/humansubjects/guidance/45cfr46.htm.

Deurenberg, R., J. Vlayen, S. Guillo, T.K. Oliver, B. Fervers, and J. Burgers. 2008 (March). Standardization of search methods for guideline development: An international survey of evidence-based guideline development groups. *Health Information and Libraries Journal* 25(1):23–30.

Dillman, D.A. 2007. *Mail and Internet Surveys: The Tailored Design Method*. 2nd ed.. Hoboken, NJ: John Wiley & Sons.

Dorr, D., L.M. Bonner, A.N. Cohen, R.S. Shoai, R. Perrin, E. Chaney, and A.S. Young. 2007 (March–April). Informatics systems to promote improved care for chronic illness: A literature review. *Journal of the American Medical Informatics Association* 14(2):156–163.

Edirisooriya, G. 1996. Research presentations in a democratic society: A voice from the audience. *Educational Researcher* 25(6):25–30.

Edmonson, S.R., K.A. Smith-Akin, and E.V. Bernstam. 2007 (Jan.). Context, automated decision support, and clinical practice guidelines: Does the literature apply to the United States practice environment? *International Journal of Medical Informatics* 76(1):34–41.

Englebardt, S.P. and R. Nelson. 2002. *Health Care Informatics: An Interdisciplinary Approach.* St. Louis, MO: Mosby, Inc.

Fayyad, U. 1997. Knowledge discovery in databases: An overview. *Inductive Logic Programming: Proceedings of the 7th International Workshop.* Book series: Lecture notes in computer science, Vol 1297. New York: Springer. http://www.springerlink.com/content/a07u771435m35318/fulltext.pdf.

Feldman, R.P. and J.T. Goodrich. 1999. The Edwin Smith surgical papyrus. *Child's Nervous System* 15(6–7):281–284.

Fenton, S. and M. Williams. 2005. Getting to know PubMed: An overview. *Journal of AHIMA* 76(3):60A–60D.

Field, A.E., W.C. Willett, L. Lissner, and G.A. Colditz. 2007. Dietary fat and weight gain among women in the Nurses' Health Study. *Obesity* 15(4):967–976.

Flexner, A. 1910. *Medical Education in the United States and Canada: A Report to the Carnegie Foundation for the Advancement of Teaching.* 1960 Reissue. Washington, DC: Health and Science Publications.

Flyvbjerg, B. 2006. Five misunderstandings about case-study research. *Qualitative Inquiry* 12(2):219–245.

Gall, M.D., J..P. Gall, and W.R. Borg. 2007. *Educational Research: An Introduction.* 8th ed. Boston: Allyn & Bacon.

Garrard, J. 2007. *Health Sciences Literature Review Made Easy: The Matrix Method.* 2nd ed. Sudbury, MA: Jones and Bartlett.

Garvin, J.H. 2001. Building on the vision: Exploratory research in future skill areas of the clinical data specialist as described in evolving HIM careers. *Educational Perspectives in Health Information Management* 4(1):19–32.

Garvin, J.H. 2005 (Fall). Development of a public health assessment tool to prevent Lyme Disease: Tool construction and validation. *Perspectives in Health Information Management* 2(10):1–25.

Gay, L.R., G.E. Mills, and P. Airasian. 2006. *Educational Research: Competencies for Analysis and Application.* 8th ed. Upper Saddle River, NJ: Pearson Education.

Giannangelo, K. and S.H. Fenton. 2008 (Spring). SNOMED CT survey: An assessment of implementation in EMR/EHR applications. *Perspectives in Health Information Management* 5(7):1–13.

Gibaldi, J. 2003. *MLA Handbook for Writers of Research Papers.* 6th ed. New York: Modern Language Association of America.

Gilles, K. 2004. Uncovering the relationship between IRBs and the HIPAA privacy rule. *Journal of AHIMA* 75(10): 48–49, 52.

Glaser, B.G. 1965 (Spring). The constant comparative method of qualitative analysis. *Social Problems* 12(4):436–445.

Glass, G.V. 1976. Primary, secondary, and meta-analysis of research. *Educational Researcher* 5(10):3–8.

Goodman, S.N. and J.A. Berlin. 1994 (Aug. 1). The use of predicted confidence intervals when planning experiments and the misuse of power when interpreting results. *Annals of Internal Medicine* 121(3):200–206.

Green, E. and C. Benjamin. 1986. Impact of medical record credential on data quality. *Journal of the American Medical Record Association* 57(11):29–38.

Haas, L.F. 1999. Papyrus of Ebers and Smith. *Journal of Neurology, Neurosurgery & Psychiatry* 67(5):578.

Heitjan, D.F. and D.B. Rubin. 1991 (Dec.). Ignorability and coarse data. *Annals of Statistics* 19(4):2244–2253.

Herndon, R.M., ed. 1997. *Handbook of Neurologic Rating Scales.* New York: Demos Vermande.

Herrera, C.D. 1999 (June). Two arguments for 'covert methods' in social research. *British Journal of Sociology* 50(2):331–343.

Hill, R.F. and E.P. Tyson. 1997. The culture of morning report: Ethnography of a clinical teaching conference. *Southern Medical Journal* 90(6):594–600.

Hopkins, R.B., K. Campbell, D. O'Reilly, J-E. Tarride, J. Bowen, G. Blackhouse, and R. Goeree. 2007 (Spring). Managing multiple projects: A literature review of setting priorities and a pilot survey of healthcare researchers in an academic setting. *Perspectives in Health Information Management* 4(4):1–16.

Huang, Y., P. McCullagh, N. Black, and R. Harper. 2007 (Nov.). Feature selection and classification model construction on type 2 diabetic patients' data. *Artificial Intelligence in Medicine* 41(3):251–262.

Iverson, C., ed. 2007. *American Medical Association Manual of Style: A Guide for Authors and Editors.* 10th ed. New York: Oxford University Press.

Jencks, C. and D. Riesman. 1977. *The Academic Revolution.* Chicago: University of Chicago Press.

Johnson, M. 1992. A silent conspiracy? Some ethical issues of participant observation in nursing research. *International Journal of Nursing Studies* 29(2):213–223.

Johnson, R.B. and A.J. Onwuegbuzie. 2004. Mixed methods research: A research paradigm whose time has come. *Educational Researcher* 33(7):14–26.

Kahn, M.G., D. Kaplan, R.J. Sokol, and R.P. DiLaura. 2007. Configuration challenges: Implementing translational research policies in electronic medical records. *Academic Medicine* 82(7):661–669.

Kesh, S. and W. Raghupathi. 2004. Critical issues in bioinformatics and computing. *Perspectives in Health Information Management* 1(9):1–8.

Keyser, D.J. and R.C. Sweetland, eds. 1991. *Test Critiques.* Kansas City, MO: Test Corporation of America.

Kish, L. 1995/1965. *Survey Sampling.* New York: John Wiley & Sons.

Kloss, L. 2000. Growing the HIM body of knowledge. *Journal of AHIMA* 71(10):27.

Koppel, R., J.P. Metlay, A. Cohen, B. Abaluck, A.R. Localio, S.E. Kimmel, and B.L. Strom. 2005. Role of computerized physician order entry systems in facilitating medication errors. *Journal of the American Medical Association* 293(10):1197–1203.

Layman, E.J. and J.A. Guyden. 1999 (Spring). The relationships among psychological type, coping mechanisms, and burnout in directors of hospital health information management departments. *Educational Perspectives in Health Information Management* 1(2):29–41.

Layman, E. and V. Watzlaf. 2003. Manuscript characteristics affecting reviewers' decisions for journals in health information management. *Educational Perspectives in Health Information Management* 5(1):48–85.

Leu, M.G., M. Cheung, T.R. Webster, L. Curry, E.H. Bradley, J. Fifield, and H. Burstin. 2008. Centers speak up: The clinical context for health information technology in the ambulatory care setting. *Journal of General Internal Medicine* 23(4):372–378.

Lloyd, S.C. and E. Layman. 1997. The effects of automated encoders on coding accuracy and coding speed. *Topics in Health Information Management* 17(3):72–79.

Maddox, T., ed. 2003. Tests: *A Comprehensive Reference for Assessments in Psychology, Education, and Business.* 5th ed. Austin, TX: Pro-Ed.

McDowell, I. and C. Newell. 1996. *Measuring Health: A Guide to Rating Scales and Questionnaires.* 2nd ed. New York: Oxford University Press.

McKibbon, K.A. and C.S. Gadd. 2004 (July 22). A quantitative analysis of qualitative studies in clinical journals for 2000 publishing year. *BMC Medical Informatics and Decision Making* 4:11. http://www.biomedcentral.com/content/pdj/1472-6947-4-11.pdf.

McLaughlin, S.B., J.M. Hankey, and T.A. Dingus. 2008. A method for evaluating collision avoidance systems using naturalistic driving data. *Accident Analysis and Prevention* 40(1):8–16.

Menachemi, N., A. Chukmaitov, C. Saunders, and R.G. Brooks. 2008. Hospital quality of care: Does information technology matter? The relationship between information technology adoption and quality of care. *Health Care Management Review* 33(1):51–59.

Metz, M.H. 2001. Intellectual border crossing in graduate education: A report from the field. *Educational Researcher* 30(5):12–18.

Mikkelsen, G. and J. Aasly. 2001(Oct.). Concordance of information in parallel electronic and paper-based patient records. *International Journal of Medical Informatics* 63(3):123–131.

Mon, D.T., K.R. Patena, and S. Khan. 1997a. Career trends in health information management: A look toward 2006, part I. *Journal of AHIMA* 68(9):92–98, 100–102, 104–105.

Mon, D.T., K.R. Patena, and S. Khan. 1997b. Career trends in health information management: A look toward 2006, part II. *Journal of AHIMA* 68(10):73–79.

Mullins, I.M., M.S. Siadaty, J. Lyman, K. Scully, C.T. Garrett, W.G. Miller, R. Muller, B. Robson, C. Apte, S. Weiss, I. Rigoutsos, D. Platt, S. Cohen, and W.A. Knaus. 2006. Data mining and clinical data repositories: Insights from a 667,000 patient data set. *Computers in Biology and Medicine* 36(12):1351–1377.

Mulrow, C.D. 1994. Systematic reviews: rationale for systematic reviews. *British Medical Journal* 309(6954):597–599.

Murphy, L.L., R.A. Spies, and B.S. Plake, eds. 2006. *Tests in Print VII: An Index to Tests, Test Reviews, and the Literature on Specific Tests.* Lincoln, NE: University of Nebraska Press.

National Institutes of Health. 2007 (June 19). The Nation's Medical Research Agency. http://www.nih.gov/about/NIHoverview.html.

National Science Foundation. 2006 (Sept. 21). Interpreting the Common Rule for the Protection of Human Subjects for Behavioral and Social Science Research. http://www.nsf.gov/bfa/dias/policy/hsfaqs.jsp.

Nickel, J.C. 2005. Management of urinary tract infections: Historical perspective and current strategies, Part 1: Before antibiotics. *Journal of Urology* 173(1):21–26.

Oniki, T.A., T.P. Clemmer, and T.A. Pryor. 2003 (March-April). The effect of computer-generated reminders on charting deficiencies in the ICU. *Journal of the American Medical Informatics Association* 10(2):177–187.

Osborn, C.E. 2001. DRG analysis reveals potential problems, trends. *Journal of AHIMA* 72(7):78–84.

Osborn, C.E. 2006. *Statistical Applications for Health Information Management.* 2nd ed. Sudbury, MA: Jones and Bartlett.

Penslar, R.L. and J.P. Porter. 2001. *IRB Guidebook.* Office for Human Research Protections. http://www.hhs.gov/ohrp/irb/irb_guidebook.htm.

Pluye, P., R.M. Grad, L.G. Dunikowski, and R. Stephenson. 2005. Impact of clinical information-retrieval technology on physicians: A literature review of quantitative, qualitative and mixed methods studies. *International Journal of Medical Informatics* 74(9):745–768.

Poissant, L., J. Pereira, R. Tamblyn, and Y. Kawasumi. 2005 (Sept.–Oct.). The impact of electronic health records on time efficiency of physicians and nurses: A systematic review. *Journal of the American Medical Informatics Association* 12(5):505–516.

Redman, B.K., ed. 2002. *Measurement Tools in Clinical Ethics*. New York: Springer.

Redman, B.K., ed. 2003. *Measurement Tools in Patient Education.* 2nd ed. New York: Springer.

Rinehart-Thompson, L.A. 2008a. Record retention practice among the nation's 'most wired' hospitals. *Perspectives in Health Information Management* 5(8):1–15.

Rinehart-Thompson, L.A. 2008b. Storage media profiles and health record retention practice patterns in acute care hospitals. *Perspectives in Health Information Management* 5(9):1–13.

Ritter, P., K. Lorig, D. Laurent, and K. Matthews. 2004. Internet versus mailed questionnaires: A randomized comparison. *Journal of Medical Internet Research* 6(3):e29. http://www.jmir.org/2004/3/e29/html.

Rosenthal, D.A. and E.J. Layman. 2008 Utilization of information technology in eastern North Carolina physician practices: Determining the existence of a digital divide. *Perspectives in Health Information Management* 5(3):1–20.

Roth, J.A. 2004a. Getting "hip" to other privacy laws, Part 1. *Journal of AHIMA* 75(2):50–52.

Roth, J.A. 2004b. Getting "hip" to other privacy laws, Part 2. *Journal of AHIMA* 75(3):48–50.

Roth, J.A. 2004c. Overdose of privacy law creates headaches for student health clinics. *Journal of AHIMA* 75(8):64–65, 67.

Roukema, J., R.K. Los, S.E. Bleeker, A.M. Van Ginneken, J. Van der Lei, and H.A. Moll. 2006. Paper versus computer: Feasibility of an electronic medical record in general pediatrics. *Pediatrics* 117(1):15–21.

Rudman, W.J. 1995. The effect of education on career advancement patterns of health information professionals. *Journal of* AHIMA 66(1):45–48.

Rudman, W.J., and D. Davey. 2000. Identifying domestic violence within inpatient hospital admissions using medical records. *Women & Health* 30(4):1–13.

Rudman, W.J., V.J.M. Watzlaf, M. Abdelhak, E. Borges, and P. Anania-Firouzan. 1996. Career paths, mobility, and advancement for health information managers. *Journal of AHIMA* 67(7):67–71.

Rudolph, F. 1990. *The American College and University: A History.* Athens: University of Georgia Press.

Sanders, D.L. and D. Aronsky. 2006. Biomedical informatics applications for asthma care: A systematic review. *Journal of the American Medical Informatics Association* 13(4):418–427.

Sasnett, B., and T. Ross. 2007 (Fall). Leadership frames and perceptions of effectiveness among health information management program directors. *Perspectives in Health Information Management* 4(8):1–15.

Shi, L. 2008. *Health Services Research Methods.* 2nd ed. Albany, NY: Delmar.

Silfen, E. 2006. Documentation and coding of ED patient encounters: An evaluation of the accuracy of an electronic medical record. *American Journal of Emergency Medicine* 24(6):664–678.

Singleton, R.A., Jr. and B.C. Straits. 2005. *Approaches to Social Research.* 4th ed. New York: Oxford University Press.

Sligar, S.R. and X. Zeng. 2008. Evaluation of Website accessibility of state vocational rehabilitation agencies. *Journal of Rehabilitation* 74(1):12–18.

Sokol, L., B. Garcia, J. Rodriguez, M. West, and K. Johnson. 2001 (August). Using data mining to find fraud in HCFA health care claims. *Topics in Health Information Management* 22(1):1–13.

Sollaci, L.B. and M.G. Pereira. 2004. The introduction, methods, results, and discussion (IMRAD) structure: A fifty-year survey. *Journal of the Medical Library Association* 92(3):364–371.

Sørby, I.D., and Ø. Nytrø. 2005. Does the electronic patient record support the discharge process? A study on physicians' use of clinical information systems during discharge of patients with coronary heart disease. *Health Information Management Journal* 34(4):112–119.

Spies, R.A. and B.S. Plake, eds. 2005. *The Sixteenth Mental Measurements Yearbook* (Buros Mental Measurements Yearbooks). Lincoln, NE: University of Nebraska Press.

Spreen, O. and E. Strauss. 1998. *A Compendium of Neuropsychological Tests: Administration, Norms, and Commentary*. 2nd ed. New York: Oxford University Press.

Strecher, V. 2007. Internet methods for delivering behavioral and health-related interventions (eHealth). *Annual Review of Clinical Psychology* 3:53–76.

Strunk, W., Jr. and E.B. White. 2000. *The Elements of Style*. 4th ed. New York: Longman.

Sudman, S. 1976. *Applied Sampling*. New York: Academic Press.

Sweetland, R.C. and D.J. Keyser, eds. 1991. *Tests: A Comprehensive Reference for Assessments in Psychology, Education, and Business*. 3rd ed. Austin, TX: Pro-Ed.

University of Chicago Press. 2003. *The Chicago Manual of Style*. 15th ed. Chicago: University of Chicago Press.

University of South Carolina Beaufort Library. 2007. Bare Bones 101: A Basic Tutorial on Searching the Web. http://sc.edu/beaufort/library/pages/bones/bones.shtml.

Van de Mortel, T., R. Bourke, L. Fillipi, J. McLoughlin, C. Molihan, M. Nonu, and M. Reis. 2000 (Aug.). Maximizing handwashing rates in the critical care unit through yearly performance feedback. *Australian Critical Care* 13(3):91–95.

Van den Broeck, J., S.A. Cunningham, R. Eeckels, and K. Herbst. 2005 (October). Data cleaning: Detecting, diagnosing, and editing data abnormalities. *PLoS [Public Library of Science] Medicine* 2(10)(e267):0966–0970.

Waljee, J.F., M.A.M. Rogers, and A.K. Alderman. 2007 (March 20). Decision aids and breast cancer: Do they influence choice of surgery and knowledge of treatment options? *Journal of Clinical Oncology* 25(9):1067–1073.

Watzlaf, V.J.M. 1995. The leadership role of the health information management professional in research. *Topics in Health Information Management* 15(3):47–58.

Watzlaf, V.J.M., J.H. Garvin, S. Moeini, and P. Firouzan. 2007. The effectiveness of ICD-10-CM in capturing public health diseases. *Perspectives in Health Information Management* 4(6):1–31.

Watzlaf, V., A. Katoh, and F. D'Amico. 1996. Obstacles encountered in the use of medical record and cancer registry abstract in breast cancer research. *Topics in Health Information Management* 17(1):25–33.

Watzlaf, V.J.M., W. Rudman, M. Abdelhak, P. Anania-Firouzan, and E. Rubinstein. 1997. Regional analyses of functions and demographics of health information managers. *Journal of AHIMA* 68(1):51–56.

Watzlaf, V., X. Zeng, C. Jarymowycz, and P.A. Firouzan. 2004. Standards for the content of the electronic health record. *Perspectives in Health Information Management* 1(1):1–21.

Wineberg, S. 2004. Must it be this way? Ten rules for keeping your audience awake during conferences. *Educational Researcher* 23(4):13–14.

Young, A.S., E. Chaney, R. Shoai, L. Bonner, A.N. Cohen, B. Doebbeling, D. Dorr, M.K. Goldstein, E. Kerr, P. Nichol, and R. Perrin. 2007 (Dec.). Information technology to support improved care for chronic illness. *Journal of General Internal Medicine* 22(Supplement 3):425–430.

Zhou, L. and G. Hripcsak. 2007. Temporal reasoning with medical data—A review with emphasis on medical natural language processing. *Journal of Biomedical Informatics* 40(2):183–202.

Chapter 17
Clinical Quality Management

Vicki L. Zeman, MA, RHIA

Learning Objectives

- Define quality within the context of clinical healthcare services
- State who has ultimate responsibility for the quality of services provided by a healthcare organization
- Differentiate among the three types of performance measures used in clinical quality improvement (QI): structure, process, and outcome
- Identify the benefits of having a QI program and how each clinical department selects areas for review
- Describe the reason for an annual appraisal of a QI plan/program
- Differentiate performance improvement initiatives of accrediting agencies, regulatory bodies, and payers
- Describe the significance of core performance measures in regard to data comparison, performance improvement, and data-driven accreditation
- Define the rationale behind the patient safety initiatives and the role played by the private sector and the government
- State the similarities and differences of the various quality measurement systems used in the healthcare environment
- Explain the significance of outcomes management, case management, clinical practice guidelines, and benchmarking in quality management
- Define the concept of sentinel event
- Recognize when root-cause analysis is required
- State the impact of the concepts of medical staff appointment/reappointment, credentialing, and clinical privileges on quality of care
- Recognize the functions of the executive committee and discuss the relevance of medical staff bylaws/rules and regulations in quality improvement
- Describe the medical staff quality applications required by the Joint Commission standards and summarize the medical staff's patient care review functions
- Define the utilization review process and its impact on quality of care
- Describe the importance of integrating risk management into any QI program
- Recognize the role of severity indexing in a QI program
- Describe the impact of the Agency for Healthcare Research and Quality on performance improvement
- Appreciate the significance of the Medicare Prescription Drug, Improvement, and Modernization Act of 2003 incentive payment initiative
- Define the importance of keeping QI data confidential and secure

Key Terms

Agency for Healthcare Research and Quality (AHRQ)
Agenda for Change
Benchmarking
Blood and blood component usage review
Bylaws/rules and regulations
Case management
Clinical privileges
Clinical Value Compass
Commission on Accreditation of Rehabilitation Facilities (CARF)
Core performance measures
Credentialing process
Disease management
Emergency preparedness
Evidence-based medicine
Health Plan Employer Data and Information Set (HEDIS)
Health record review
Incident report review
Independent practitioners
Infection review
Institute for Clinical Systems Improvement (ICSI)
Leapfrog group
Loss prevention
Loss reduction
Measure hierarchy
Medical care evaluation studies (audits)
Medication usage review
Mortality review
National Association of Healthcare Quality (NAHQ)
National Quality Forum
Occurrence/generic screening
ORYX initiative
Outcome measures
Peer review organization (PRO)
Performance improvement (PI)
Performance measure
Performance measurement system
Potentially compensable event (PCE)
Practice guidelines
Priority focus process (PFP)
Process measures
Quality
Quality assurance (QA)
Quality gap
Quality improvement (QI)
Quality improvement organization (QIO)
Quality management
Risk prevention
Root-cause analysis
Safe practices
Scope of work
Sentinel event
Severity indexing
Structure measures
Surgical review
Tax Equity and Fiscal Responsibility Act (TEFRA)
Temporary privileges
Ten-step monitoring and evaluation process
Universal Protocol
Utilization management
Utilization review (UR)
Verification service

In healthcare, **quality** means one thing to the patient and another to the healthcare provider. But to both, the objective of quality is to arrive at a desired outcome. Providing the best care in the most effective manner and for the least cost is something every healthcare organization strives to do. Improving healthcare quality is a fundamental consideration of the U.S. healthcare system today.

The world is constantly evolving, and change is a sure thing. Whether making a change is chaotic or measured and controlled often speaks to the success of those involved in the change process. The more measured and controlled the change process, the greater the chance of success. People in healthcare are survivors of phenomenal change, both measured and chaotic, over the past two decades. Health information management (HIM) professionals have been a distinct part of the change process.

The gurus of managing the change process—Deming, Juran, and Crosby, for example—have developed methods to measure and monitor systems and processes in organizations. Their theories give managers methods to use in bringing about measured, focused change before crisis occurs. With encouragement from accrediting bodies and government agencies, healthcare organizations are trying to achieve continued, measured, and focused change with the purpose of improving healthcare (McLaughlin and Kaluzny, 2006 18–27).

Healthcare professionals are struggling to use the **quality improvement** (QI) methods offered in the business sector. Healthcare is a highly complex environment involving many specially trained individuals with a strong commitment to their way of providing care. Finding ways to help such individuals work together effectively is a challenge.

This chapter discusses the history of quality management as well as how quality management is organized and evaluated in modern-day healthcare organizations. It then describes the clinical applications of QI efforts, focusing on the medical staff, nursing, and ancillary services. Finally, the chapter looks at using comparative data in the process of managing clinical quality.

Overview of Clinical Quality Management

Clinical **quality management** involves the evaluation of direct patient care. Clinical performance is often measured around diagnosis, medical condition, or care processes along with outcomes. The relationship between the way care is provided and the outcomes or results of the medical intervention is the focus of clinical quality management. Clinical quality management includes the process of quality improvement as it is applied in healthcare organizations. Although both the administrative and clinical aspects of healthcare systems may be the subjects of QI processes, the focus is on the clinical applications of QI in healthcare systems today.

Quality Improvement and the Use of Aggregate Data

Quality is assumed to give an enhanced worth or value to a product or service. Each person brings his or her unique perspective to the quality of a product or service he or she receives. If a person sees a service as having quality, it follows that the service was perceived as being good. Further, cost affects the perceived quality of a product or service. Consumers believe that the greater the quality of a product or service and the lower the cost, the greater the value of that product or service. Americans demand high-quality products or services for the lowest possible cost. W. Edwards Deming stated that "Quality has meaning only in terms of the customer, his needs, what he is going to use it for" (Walton 1986, 28). The **Agency for Healthcare Research and Quality** (AHRQ) defines quality of healthcare as "The degree to which health services for individuals and populations increase the likelihood of desired health outcomes and are consistent with current professional knowledge" (Wachter and Owens 2004, 2).

Individuals involved in QI processes in healthcare organizations must determine who the customers are, what they want, and what must be done to meet their expectations. Expectations must translate into performance requirements so that healthcare professionals can evaluate whether customers' needs are being met. This leads to developing statements of expectation or performance called performance measures. Aggregate data are analyzed to determine whether expectations are being met. The data are frequently analyzed and compared against other internal and external data in a process called **benchmarking**. This allows the organization an opportunity to determine whether it is providing the highest-quality care possible.

History of Quality Management in Healthcare

The evaluation of healthcare quality has been evolving for many years. Hippocrates said, "Do no harm," thereby making the physician responsible for a patient's care. In 1854, Florence Nightingale introduced new protocols for her nurses during the Crimean War. Changes were made in the ventilation and sanitation systems and in how the nurses related to their patients. These changes dramatically reduced mortality rates. In 1917, the American College of Surgeons (ACS) established minimum standards of care. In following years, the ACS began an accreditation program (Joint Commission 2008k).

These first steps led to the creation of the Joint Commission on Accreditation of Healthcare Organizations (JCAHO), now known as the Joint Commission, and standards for hospitals in 1952. The Joint Commission published its first set of standards for hospitals in 1953. In 1965, Congress passed the Social Security Amendments, which created Medicare and Medicaid, and initiated **utilization review** (UR) and **medical care evaluation studies** (audits) as a part of these programs. Evaluating clinical care was legislated in 1965 as part of Medicare and Medicaid. Medical care evaluation audits were mandated, and similar efforts were recommended by Joint Commission by the late 1960s. The Joint Commission used the term **quality assurance** (QA) to identify its patient care improvement efforts with the introduction of accreditation standards in 1980. QA focused on hospital-wide problem solving concentrating on the administrative or business operations of the organization. The QA standards allowed flexibility in the approach used by the organization. Problem lists were created and many problems were solved. Mainly administrative in nature, the problems focused on the environment and personnel working in the organization. In the mid-1980s, as problem lists became more legally challenging and the numbers of problems were reduced, the Joint Commission revised its standards.

In 1986, the Joint Commission launched a research and development project called the **Agenda for Change**. The Agenda for Change sought to develop better methods of evaluating healthcare effectiveness with regard to how the organization was governed and managed and how it provided clinical services. It included three initiatives that looked at the survey and accreditation process, education, and communication.

Developing valid and reliable quality performance measures that could be used as screens to identify potential problems became a major part of the survey and accreditation initiative. Another goal of this initiative was to have accreditation decisions more accurately reflect the quality of care rendered by the organization.

By 1990, the monitoring and evaluation process had been expanded to include medical staff review activities. In 1992, the monitoring and evaluation process was expanded to include a commitment to continuous improvement. In the mid-1990s, the Joint Commission introduced the concept of organizational performance improvement and began developing performance indicators.

The Joint Commission regional representatives worked with healthcare organizations; introduced measure-driven performance improvement systems; and attempted to coordinate the Joint Commission accreditation with other external review bodies, such as the **Health Care Financing Administration** (renamed in 2001 as the Centers for Medicare and Medicaid Services [CMS]). An organization could then use approved performance measures to screen their clinical performance to improve the quality of care.

In 1997, the **ORYX initiative** began. Also referred to as the Next Evolution in Accreditation, its purpose was to establish a continuous, data-driven accreditation process by using outcomes and performance measurement data focused on core performance measures. ORYX implementation applied to a variety of settings, including hospitals, long-term care organizations and healthcare networks.

Healthcare as an industry must strive to continually improve. It was slow to discover the link between improved processes and outcomes and increased effectiveness, efficiency, and cost savings. Some healthcare professionals still have a hard time recognizing the need to devote dollars to something that does not give an immediate payback.

The number of errors at any one hospital is likely to look insignificant, but the issue is compounded when data regarding errors are aggregated. In 2000, the Institute of Medicine (IOM) published information that brought attention to the issue of patient safety. *To Err is Human: Building a Safer Health System* asserted that 44,000 to 98,000 Americans die each year as a result of preventable errors. Shine (2002) states that, in actuality, these figures may be low because they do not include nursing home deaths or ambulatory care deaths. Moreover, many errors were never recorded in patient records. Shine further indicates that all the evidence gathered needs to do more than point to individual doctors. Information must be used to develop safer systems and processes less likely to fail. The numbers of adverse events and costs to society go far beyond anyone's expectation. Error reports show a gap between average care and best care. The IOM identified six dimensions around which to frame the measurement of quality (IOM 2001, 39–54):

- Safety
- Effectiveness
- Patient-centeredness
- Timeliness
- Efficiency
- Equity

Additionally, Wachter and Owens (2004) report in *The Genesis of Closing the Quality Gap* the need for continued analysis of reasons for the **quality gap**. Finding ways to increase the rate effective practice as applied to actual patient care is being analyzed. Many reasons for the gaps between best, evidence-based practice and current treatment choices include:

- A gap in the dissemination of knowledge from research to practitioners
- Failure to implement best practice due to skepticism surrounding the cost effectiveness, environment, or organizational culture of practice setting
- Research setting effectiveness not equating to an individual's practice setting

There is much interest and ongoing research in developing ways to close the quality gap that involves research and a variety of organizations.

Check Your Understanding 17.1

Instructions: Answer the following questions on a separate piece of paper.

1. What is quality? Why is it important to meet customers' expectations?
2. What role have the Joint Commission initiatives played in the evolution of measuring healthcare quality?
3. What agencies have been important in the development of modern quality improvement processes?
4. What impact has the Institute of Medicine had on the measurement of healthcare quality? What has the development of performance measures contributed to the improvement of quality healthcare?
5. Explain how the core performance measure sets enhance the accreditation process.

Organization of Quality Management in Healthcare Facilities

Quality management in healthcare facilities is organized to meet the needs of the organization. Today, most organizations have a program of continuous improvement in all functional areas. Data collection and analysis and resulting improvements have become an accepted way of doing business. An organization must address how it is going to achieve a successful QI program.

Organization, Accountability, and Ownership

The success of any QI program begins with a strong commitment from the executive level of the organization. This means that the governing body and the administration show, by example, their commitment to improving the quality of patient care. As an organization develops or revises a QI program, it must consider certain key elements. The elements of a QI program include:

- Clear statement of mission
- Supportive environment
- Available resources
- Leaders with adequate qualifications
- Adequate personnel
- Attitude of improvement
- Coordinated and integrated efforts
- Comprehensive and continuous care processes

Responsibility for QI activities must be clearly designated so that the program functions effectively. In addition, the methods of reporting should be made clear to all people involved in the QI program. (See figure 17.1.)

The governing body is ultimately responsible for the quality of care provided in any organization. Today, governing bodies are more involved in QI efforts than ever before. Board members are seeking training, asking questions, and insisting on seeing data confirming that care is improving within their organization. When a board expresses interest and concern about the quality of care being provided, it sets the bar for medical staff, administrative, and staff involvement.

Figure 17.1. Organizational communication and reporting

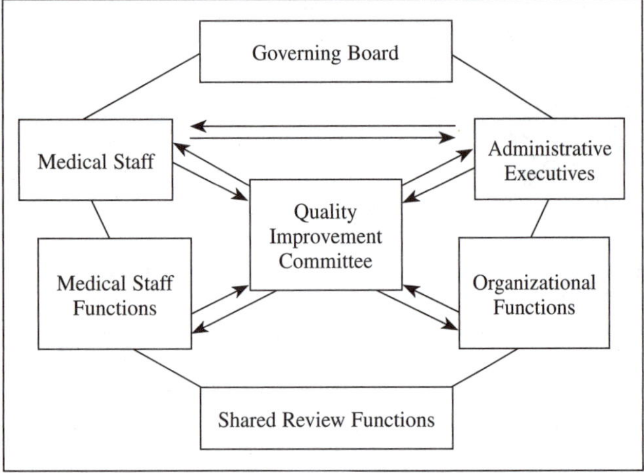

The Role of HIM Professionals

Many different types of professionals work in quality improvement. From a historical perspective, HIM professionals have been involved in QI from the time of medical evaluation audits in the mid-1960s. HIM professionals are a natural fit for performance improvement activities because they know the health record (still the primary data source) and understand the documentation process. The HIM professional can be involved in a variety of ways, including:

- Collecting data and information
- Organizing, interpreting, and reporting data in a meaningful way
- Knowing data sources
- Understanding clinical processes

In addition to the above ways of providing direct quality management involvement, the HIM professional role includes bringing basic guiding principles of solid information management to the attention of their organization. The HIM professional knows medical record documentation requirements and as a professional has a duty to uphold sound documentation principles (accuracy, integrity, reliability, and adequacy) and ask relevant questions for the organization. The HIM professional understands the need for data quality and with that has the responsibility and the need to develop and advocate the use of standards in a computerized environment. Additionally, influencing policy and procedure development is critical for organizations moving forward with an electronic health record (EHR). The HIM professional is in an excellent spot to help lead change management strategies in organizations undergoing considerable redesign. Technology is changing in a variety settings with each HIM professional self-educating in the areas that require their support and knowledge. One example is by taking opportunities to help with screen display design, checklist development and must entering policy setting as well as end-user training. All of which can be applied in the quality and safety management settings as well as generally in the healthcare environment (Hjort 2005, 56a–56g).

Other professionals, such as registered nurses, are currently involved in QI in many facilities because of their understanding of clinical processes and clinical decision making.

Quality Improvement and Management Program

Every healthcare organization needs to find QI methods that work for it. Organization-wide QI may be completed as part of health information service responsibilities, part of risk management, or a separate department in its own right. However they are designated, QI efforts must meet the needs of the facility.

The Joint Commission requires that organizational leadership set expectations, plan, and manage how to measure, assess, and improve in all aspects of providing care. (See figure 17.2.) A QI plan can be a separate document or incorporated into another planning document. CMS requires a plan in writing. Items commonly found in a plan include, but are not limited to:

- Statement of mission and vision
- Objectives
- Values
- Leadership
- Organizational structure
- Methodologies
- Performance measures
- Communication
- Annual plan appraisal

The QI plan needs to be evaluated on a regular basis to determine its effectiveness. An annual appraisal should include a review of measurement and assessment activities and of documented improvements. The annual appraisal also should include a plan for the future direction of the program.

Legislation affecting quality improvement at the federal level is the Medicare Prescription Drug, Improvement, and Modernization Act of 2003 (MMA) (PL 108-173). President George W. Bush signed this legislation into law in December, 2003. Section 646 is the portion of the legislation that directly affects healthcare quality. This section addresses the Medicare Health Care Quality Demonstration project. The goals are to:

- Improve patient safety
- Enhance quality of care
- Reduce scientific uncertainty and the unwarranted variation in medical practice that results in both lower quality and higher costs

This Medicare Health Care Quality Demonstration project is intended to identify, develop, test, and disseminate improvements to the U.S. healthcare system. It is hoped that through this project CMS can encourage providers by giving them incentives to redesign systems that lead to safer, higher-quality, and lower-cost healthcare for everyone. E-prescribing is being targeted because of the great potential to improve quality of care and lower healthcare costs. With the passage of the Medicare Improvements for Patients and Providers Act of 2008 (MIPPA), CMS announced that physicians who adopt and use qualified e-prescribing systems to transmit prescriptions to pharmacies will earn incentive payments for 2009. It is felt that e-prescribing can decrease adverse medication errors significantly. The projected numbers of adverse drug events is staggering (see figure 17.3). In its report on Preventing Medical Errors (July 2006), the IOM estimates that more than 1.5 million Americans are injured each year by drug errors. The true number may actually be considerably higher.

Figure 17.2. Organizational options for quality management programs

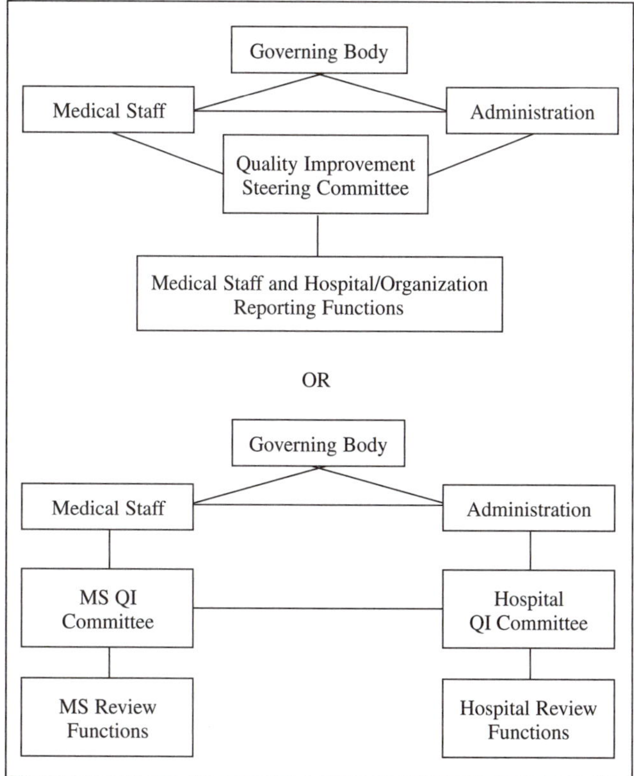

Figure 17.3. Adverse drug event reduction

Patient-Provider Relationship	Encourage a more active role by patients requiring better drug education, patient record keeping, patient communication with all providers (pharmacists, physicians, and nurses), and improved quality and accessibility of information.
Use Information Technologies to Reduce Drug Errors	Use point of care reference information, use electronic prescriptions, use electronic support systems for drug allergies and interactions, and high dosing, and internal monitoring systems to measure ADEs
Improved labeling and packaging of Medications	Improve drug nomenclature—drug names, abbreviations, and acronyms, improve drug industry and government collaboration, redesign the information about medications provided to patients using best methods research
Policy Recommendations–Research Support	Adverse drug event research efforts supported and funded by the federal government, regulatory agencies encourage adoption of technologies that reduce medication errors, accreditation agencies require more training in medication-management practices.

Source: IOM Report Brief 2006.

In addition, the Department of Health and Human Services (HHS) is piloting projects for e-prescribing at five sites. Each selected pilot offers unique perspectives to test various methodologies, user context, and the standards. The healthcare providers participating must use e-prescribing standards when prescriptions are ordered electronically for Medicare Part D coverage. The number of projects focused on quality of care continues to grow. The Agency for Healthcare Research and Quality (AHRQ) and CMS has information on many of the government-sponsored projects.

Definition of Quality Parameters

External regulators also are important factors in the quality puzzle. It is vital to understand who they are and what influence they have. The most influential external regulators in healthcare are voluntary accrediting agencies and the federal and state governments. A number of key judicial decisions also have had a profound impact on QI processes.

Judicial Decisions

Three landmark court decisions help explain the direction of quality improvement: *Darling v. Charleston Community Memorial Hospital* (1965), *Gonzales v. Nork and Mercy Hospital* (1973), and *Johnson v. Misericordia Community Hospital* (1981). All three cases established that healthcare facilities are responsible for selecting well-qualified professionals who provide acceptable standards of care.

Darling (1965) is a landmark case that established a hospital's responsibility for patient care. Touching directly on quality are the issues of the facility's responsibility to have effective methods of credentialing in place and effective mechanisms for continuing medical evaluation. The facility is responsible for knowing whether the care it provides meets acceptable standards of care. The evaluation of medical care involves all professionals and must be done regularly so that both hospital and medical staff understand the results of patient care. The hospital must provide more than a place to practice and tools for physicians and other healthcare providers.

The *Gonzales* (1973) case supports a facility's responsibility for patient care. The hospital must establish a system to monitor the work and abilities of its physicians and other healthcare providers. In essence, the hospital owes its patients a duty to care.

The *Johnson* (1981) case further supports the duty of the healthcare facility to select its medical staff and grant privileges using carefully defined criteria. In addition, the **bylaws/rules and regulations** adopted by the medical staff must be followed. Further, the hospital has a legal duty to ensure that the guidelines are followed. It must appoint and supervise qualified medical staff and give the medical staff direct responsibility for the quality of care.

Federal Legislation

The federal government has had a profound impact on the development of quality improvement over the past 35 years. (See table 17.1.) The Social Security Amendments of 1965 and the Medicare Conditions of Participation that followed in 1967 laid the groundwork for medical evaluation audits and UR if a facility was going to accept Medicare and Medicaid patients. In 1972, professional standard review organizations (PSROs) were legislated. The PSROs began to monitor the quality and appropriateness of Medicare and Medicaid patient care.

The **Tax Equity and Fiscal Responsibility Act of 1982** (TEFRA) not only introduced diagnosis-related groups (DRGs) but also **peer review organizations** (PROs) to replace PSROs. In 1985, legislation was passed to deny Medicare payment for substandard care. In addition, the Conditions of Participation were revised to require a written QA plan in any facility accepting federal funds for Medicare and Medicaid patients. Also in the mid-1980s the term *quality assurance* evolved into today's terminology, *quality improvement*.

In 1986, the Omnibus Budget Reconciliation Act (OBRA) required PROs to report adverse findings about healthcare providers to licensing and certifying agencies. That same year, the Health Care Quality Improvement Act (HCQIA) was passed to help protect peer review activities from liability and laid the foundation for the National Practitioner Data Bank.

Table 17.1. Major legislation relevant to clinical quality management

Date	Act	Description
1965	PL 89-97	Health coverage for citizens 65 years of age and older (effective July 1, 1966)
1972	PL 92-603	Professional standards review organizations created
1982	Tax Equity and Fiscal Responsibility Act	Peer review organizations and the prospective payment system (PPS) created
1983	PL 98-21	PPS for Medicare established
1985	Consolidated Omnibus Reconciliation Act	Denial of Medicare payments for substandard care authorized
1986	PL- 99-509	PROs required to report substandard care to licensing and certifying boards
1986	PL 99-660	Health Care Quality Improvement Act
1989	PL 101-239	Agency for Health Care Policy and Research created Outcome measures research
1990	PL 101-508	PROs required to inform licensing boards of physician sanctions
1996	PL 104-191	Health Insurance Portability and Accountability Act
2003	PL 108-173 Section 646	Medicare Modernization Act
2005	PL 109-41	Patient Safety and Quality Improvement Act

The Agency for Health Care Policy and Research (AHCPR) was legislated in 1989. This agency began to develop outcome measures and was a resource in outcomes assessment. In the mid-1990s, the agency name was changed to the Agency for Healthcare Research and Quality (AHRQ). This agency has worked diligently to provide clinical evidence for best practice. In 2003, the AHRQ, together with Stanford-UCSF (University of California, San Francisco) Evidence-based Practice Center, developed a plan to analyze literature on QI strategies. These analyses focused on translating research into practice, concentrating on what would increase the rate of effective practices as applied to patient care in actual practice settings. The aim of this program is to close the quality gap (Wachter and Owens 2004, 5–9).

In the 1990s, further federal efforts were undertaken to support QI in healthcare. In 1990, legislation was passed requiring PROs to report physician sanctions to licensing and medical boards. In addition, the National Practitioner Data Bank legislated in 1986 was activated.

In 2002, PROs were officially renamed **quality improvement organizations** (QIOs) to reflect changes in healthcare practice in recent years. The QIOs develop a response to the request for proposal (RFP) from CMS. The current **scope of work** is the ninth and runs August 1, 2008 through July 31, 2011. The work for this time period involves beneficiary protection, patient safety, and prevention (focus on clinics). The focus of work changes with each new scope of work. In addition, the QIO can submit RFPs on two projects focused on improving care coordination across care settings and preventing and improving care management for chronic kidney disease. QIOs work with healthcare organizations to improve the quality of healthcare as well as to monitor the care provided to Medicare patients. The current focus of QIOs is found in the section covering Quality Initiatives–CMS.

In January 2003, CMS published the final rule in the *Federal Register* requiring hospitals to develop and maintain a quality assessment and performance improvement program (QAPI). Hospitals are required to show measurable improvement on designated performance measures that have been linked to improved health outcomes and patient safety (CMS 2003). Beginning in 2005, the MMA's incentive payment initiative is available to organizations that are willing to report quality data using 10 performance measures and to have their data publicly displayed. These data are available through the HHS Web page titled Hospital Compare.

Legislative initiatives with the goal of improving the quality of care in the United States will most certainly continue. The federal government finances healthcare for a number of designated populations and has an interest in ensuring that the services provided are effective and appropriate within an increasingly integrated delivery system.

Accrediting Standards

As mentioned earlier, the idea of using standards to bring healthcare practice to a minimum level was initiated by the American College of Surgeons (ACS). Standards were used and refined over the years until the Joint Commission on Accreditation of Hospitals assumed responsibility for them. Today, the commission is known as the Joint Commission.

The Joint Commission's mission is to improve the quality of healthcare. Since 1953, it has worked to develop standards that help healthcare organizations measure and evaluate the care they provide. The use of clinical performance measures and continuous data-driven accreditation processes is currently being phased in.

However, the Joint Commission is not the only accrediting organization developing and using standards to encourage high-quality care. The **Commission on Accreditation of Rehabilitation Facilities** (CARF) has promoted high-quality healthcare in organizations serving patients who need rehabilitative treatment. The Accreditation Association for Ambulatory Health Care (AAAHC) is another private, nonprofit organization helping ambulatory healthcare organizations to improve the quality of their services. The Healthcare Facilities Accreditation Program (HFAP) of the American Osteopathic Association, one of two bodies authorized by CMS to accredit hospitals (the other being the Joint Commission), also has requirements for ongoing QI programs included in its accreditation standards.

In addition, QI efforts are being supported by organizations such as NCQA that accredits health plans mentioned earlier. The **Health Plan Employer Data and Information Set** (HEDIS) is used to collect data on managed care plans (see section on Quality in Ambulatory Care). Other health plans have developed or are working to develop quality measures. For example, Blue Cross/Blue Shield is using healthcare performance measures from the **Institute for Clinical Systems Improvement** (ICSI). These efforts support the growing interest in the public reporting of healthcare performance data.

The **National Association of Healthcare Quality** (NAHQ) promotes continuous QI efforts in healthcare organizations by certifying qualified professionals. This organization offers QI professionals educational opportunities regardless of the healthcare setting they work in.

Private Sector Initiatives

Frustration in the private sector over the disparate efforts of government and accrediting agencies to improve quality and safety of patients spawned initiatives in the private sector. Leapfrog group, a consortium of Fortune 500 companies and large private and public healthcare purchasers founded by The Business Roundtable, began a national initiative to reward hospitals for work that advanced patient safety and quality. The initial IOM report that found 98,000 Americans die every year from preventable medical errors made in hospitals recommended that large healthcare purchasers provide strong market reinforcement for quality and safety (IOM 2000). Initial foci or Leaps were on computerized physician order entry (CPOE), intensive care physician staffing (IPS), and evidence-based hospital referral (EBHR). The Leapfrog Group has collaborated with the National Quality Forum (NQF) on Safe Practices for Better Healthcare and Never Events (explained in more detail later in this chapter). Leapfrog rewards hospitals based on self-reporting. Results are shared with the goal of educating and informing those enrolled about patient safety and the need to compare provider performance on Leapfrog's quality and safety leaps and recognize and reward providers who make leaps to improve quality and safety. The 2008 focus is on (Thomson Healthcare 2007b):

- Acute Myocardial Infarction (AMI) and Pneumonia
- Resource use measures: AMI, Pneumonia, and EBHR (selected procedures)
- Other safety measures: rates of two hospital-acquired conditions

Another private sector quality and safety effort is being lead by the not-for-profit Bridges to Excellence (BTE). Again responding to the Institute of Medicine's recommendations, employers, physicians, health plans, and patients work together to encourage healthcare providers to redesign care processes. The Bridges to Excellence organization is guided by three principles (BTE 2008):

- Dedication to transforming care processes to reduce mistakes will require incentives, for which purchasers should create incentives
- Significant reduction in defects (misuse, underuse, overuse) will reduce waste and inefficiencies in the healthcare system
- Increased accountability and quality improvements will be encouraged by the release of comparative provider performance data, delivered to consumers in a compelling way

BTE has fostered continued support of providing quality care in a safe environment by partnering with organizations with similar missions such as the Leapfrog Group. A visit to either Web site will verify the strength of these private sector efforts.

Check Your Understanding 17.2

Instructions: Answer the following questions on a separate piece of paper.

1. What basic elements should be included in a quality improvement program?
2. Who is responsible for the overall quality of care in a healthcare organization?
3. Why are HIM professionals an appropriate choice to work in a quality improvement program?
4. How can HIM professionals fulfill their role in the QI environment?
5. What are the quality improvement goals of the MMA?
6. How have judicial decisions influenced quality improvement?
7. What role have the federal government and Joint Commission played in the development of QI processes?

Quality Management Process

Each stage of the evolution of quality management has involved some aspect of data collection, data analysis, and a resulting change to improve areas that are problematic. The focus of data collection efforts has been driven by diagnosis and procedure, problem, and, currently, clinical performance measures.

Creating a Culture of Service Excellence

Providing healthcare services is an incredibly personal experience for all parties. Safe, accurate, and caring behaviors and attitudes are required to provide healthcare that meets the expectations of patients, clients, or customers. Healthcare organizations strive to emphasize serviced-based patient-focused care. The mission of many healthcare facilities is to provide superior healthcare in a compassionate manner mindful of the dignity of each individual person. In order to foster an environment of customer service all levels of the organization must be involved and committed.

Generating pride in work performed by all employees and healthcare providers is key to providing excellent service. A culture that pays attention to details and treats all individuals with respect sounds simple, but in reality can take years to achieve. In addition, continual affirmation of a service of excellence culture is required of the organization. This is achieved by managing in a way that give employees a chance to succeed and recognizing and rewarding employees.

Managers can use clues to help determine whether or not service excellence is present. The red flags indicating low service standards include such things as high employee turnover, training that is "one time" in nature, and training to regulations rather than to the needs of the patient population. Ideas that help create an organization or department that strives for service excellence includes: hiring the right person for the right role, orienting all employees thoroughly, developing leaders within the organization, sharing information so staff understand the impact of their behaviors on the business of healthcare, managing people with success strategies in mind, recognizing employees for work well done, providing rapid feedback and responses to employees "on the line," and supporting improvement teams. Services and products are enhanced and a culture of service excellence established when managers understand what to look for.

The goal of creating a culture of service excellence is to provide an environment that recognizes and accepts the limitations of human performance. Technology and systems are developed with the spirit of service excellence and used to support and enhance care providers. The end result is that healthcare delivery is of high quality and consistently predictable with efficient use of all quality improvement methods.

Outcomes Management

Outcomes management is the systematic collection of healthcare end results using outcomes measurement. A physician, Dr. Paul Ellwood, introduced the concept of outcomes management as a method to improve the quality of care (Ellwood 1988, 1549–1556). Quality improvement during the late 1980s was strongly focused on outcomes as the best way to judge the quality of patient care. Many national organizations have worked to develop databases that allowed the comparison of outcomes. The Joint Commission's Core Measures (ORYX initiative), CMS's Clinical Performance Measures, the Cleveland Health Quality Choice Program (CHQC), the Institute for Clinical Systems Improvement (ICSI), and others have been involved in developing performance measures, collecting data, and analyzing outcomes.

The AHRQ, a part of the HHS, further seeks to determine how people are affected as result of their experience with healthcare services. Outcomes research is providing the clinician with potentially effective strategies to improve the quality of patient care. This is also referred to as *best practice* or *evidence-based practice*.

As a method of improving the quality of care, outcomes management looks for the best treatment process. A treatment process is determined and used, then data are collected and entered into a database. The data are analyzed and the treatment process altered as necessary. The goal is to find the best treatment possible to benefit patient care. These identified best practices then can be considered guidelines to help clinicians make the best decisions possible for their patients. Outcomes research has changed clinical practice. Being able to collect meaningful data, then analyze the types of treatments and the resulting outcomes, clinicians are able to provide better patient care more uniformly. See table 17.2.

Severity Indexing

Severity indexing is the process of identifying the level of resource consumption based on factors of clinical evidence. The more complications and co-morbid conditions present, the sicker the patient and the higher the resource consumption. This method of trying to judge the level of illness is useful for reimbursement, utilization, and quality of care programs. Reimbursement should be higher when more resources are consumed, length of stay (LOS) should be longer or shorter based on resources needed and degree of illness, and quality could be compromised when a patient requires more care because of complications or co-morbid conditions but does not receive it.

Table 17.2. Examples of health outcomes

Measure	Example
Mortality	Infant death rate
Physiologic measures	Blood pressure
Clinical events	Stroke
Symptoms	Difficulty breathing
Functional measures	SF-36, a 36-item health survey
Patients' experiences with care	Patient satisfaction survey

Source: Adopted from Clancy, C.M., and J.M. Eisenberg. 1998. Outcomes research: Measure the end results of health care. *Science* 282:245–246.

In 2007, the federal government revamped their Inpatient Prospective Payment System (IPPS) to include severity adjustment, in effect forcing healthcare organizations to improve their documentation practices and the data capture for reimbursement purposes. The available information for evaluating the quality of care was likewise improved. With healthcare organizations working hard to improve documentation in order to help substantiate their billing practices the quality of care can be more thoroughly and accurately evaluated. The overall impact results in establishing a clearer picture on care processes and outcomes. The improvement in the quality of data becomes a flashpoint for improving procedures and care processes in the healthcare organization.

With improved documentation available the information in databases used to analyze care becomes a more accurate picture of the care being provided. Determining how severely ill a patient is can provide valuable information about treatment process, why resources are used or length of stay is outside the norm. Severity indexing can be especially effective when an organization wants to determine reasons for longer or shorter LOS or to provide information supporting or refuting statistics regarding the quality of care rendered. Adopting and using severity indexing can also affect reimbursement by providing a more complete picture of the patient care. There are a number of databases from a variety of sources available that allow the healthcare organization to make accurate determinations about severity level of the care rendered, the appropriateness of care, and the level of reimbursement. The Medicare Severity-DRGs (MS-DRGs) and other severity of illness databases are designed to help improve hospital payment systems, risk-adjusted medical outcome studies, and measurement of hospital case mix. Examples of severity adjustment measures used today include:

- MS-DRGs—A product of HSS, Inc.
- 3M APR DRG Software—A product of 3M Health Information Systems
- APACHE IV—Benchmarks for mortality and resource use, Cerner Corporation

Evidence-based Practice

According to Centre for Evidence-Based Medicine, **evidence-based medicine** is "the conscientious and judicious use of current best evidence in making decisions about the care of individual patients (CEBM,2008)." The practice of evidence-based medicine means integrating individual clinical expertise with the best available external clinical evidence from systematic research (Sackett, 1996, 71–72). Research is at the root of this clinical approach. It complements the philosophical approach to continually measure performance on a clinical level. (See table 17.3.)

In order to support evidence-based practice in the U.S. the Agency for Healthcare Quality and Research (AHRQ) has established Evidence-based Practice Centers. EPCs develop evidence reports and technology assessments on relevant topics that are common or significant in the Medicare and Medicaid populations. The Centers review all scientific literature on clinical, behavioral, and organizational and financing topics, then produce evidence reports, as well as technical review and technology assessments. AHRQ's goal is to improve the quality, effectiveness and appropriateness of healthcare by translating evidence-based research findings. Five-year contracts are awarded to Centers all over the U.S. and Canada (AHRQ 2008).

Improving quality of care, advancing safety practices and evidence-based practice complement each other. Introducing a "most beneficial" approach to care for patients allows an opportunity to standardize treatment. Standardized expectations allow more accountability and measurement of outcomes. Evidence-based medicine utilizes methodologies that are based on research and the evaluation of the best external evidence to answer clinical questions. Important recommendations can be made to practitioners to help them determine optimal treatment courses. Is this the best diagnostic tool to use? Is the surgical or medical approach most optimal? Is this the best therapy for this diagnosis? A full discussion of outcomes and effectiveness research is presented in chapter 18.

Government Quality Initiatives

The Centers for Medicare and Medicaid Services has administered Medicare for many years. Efforts to contain costs and improve quality care for Medicare consumers have continued. The IOM reports *To Err is Human* (1999) and *Crossing the Quality Chasm* (2001) broadened the focus to include safety as well. CMS works to collaborate and demonstrate potential ways to improve care. Quality Improvement Organizations, the Hospital Quality Alliance and the Agency for Healthcare Research are several partners that work with Centers of Medicare and Medicaid Services. CMS continues to be diligent about trying to find ways to contain costs, improve quality, and keep patients safe.

Table 17.3. Evidence-based practice centers

Site	EPCs with a Specialized Focus
Blue Cross and Blue Shield Association	Technology Assessments
Duke University	Technology Assessments
ECRI Institute	Technology Assessments
Johns Hopkins University	
McMaster University	
Minnesota Evidence-based Practice Center	
Oregon Evidence-based Practice Center	Evidence Reports for the U.S. Preventive Services Task Force
RTI International—University of CA, San Francisco	
Southern California	
Stanford University—University of CA, San Francisco	
Tufts-New England Medical Center	Technology Assessments
University of Alberta	Technology Assessments
University of Connecticut	
University of Ottawa	
Vanderbilt University	

Source: http://www.ahrq.gov/clinic/ep.

Quality Improvement Organizations

The most current scope of work was granted as of August 2008. Each scope of work, a three period, adjusts to meet current perceived needs of the healthcare delivery system. The general focus is to improve quality and efficiency of the healthcare system. The new ninth scope of work (SOW) has six sections. Each Quality Improvement Organization must bid for a contract. All 53 QIOs will work on Beneficiary Protection, Patient Safety, and Core Prevention. Some QIOs will work on projects. The projects identified for this scope of work are: Chronic Kidney Disease, Care Transition, and Prevention: Efforts to Reduce Health Disparities among Diabetes Patients. Each QIO will submit their plan for addressing these initiatives.

Hospital Consumer Assessment of Healthcare Providers and Systems (HCAHPS)

The background for Hospital Consumer Assessment of Healthcare Providers and Systems (HCAHPS) is covered in the section on Quality Measurement in Ambulatory Care. Inpatient satisfaction surveys using the HCAHPS began in 2006. HCAHPS focuses on three goals. The first goal is to collect data on the patient perspective of care for comparison purposes. The second is to make the information available as a public reporting tool. Hospitals are incentivized to improve care from the patient's perspective. And the third goal is that public reporting will enhance accountability of healthcare organizations by increasing transparency of the quality of care provided in hospitals. CMS has been working with AHRQ to develop a survey instrument that is credible, useful, and practical. The survey has 27 questions about hospital experience. HCAHPS is administered 48 hours to 6 weeks after discharge to a random sample of adult patients. Survey administration can be done by hospital or by a survey vendor. The survey can be done using a variety of approaches—mail, telephone, mail with telephone follow-up or active interactive voice recognition. Hospitals can use this survey on its own or can combine it with their own survey questions. Results are published quarterly and are available on the Hospital Compare Web site.

Hospital Compare

Hospital Compare is a collaborative effort of CMS, and the Hospital Quality Alliance (HQA). The Hospital Quality Alliance is a public-private collaboration promoting the reporting of quality care in hospitals. HQA consists of organizations that represent consumers, hospitals, physicians, nurses, employers, accrediting organizations, and Federal agencies. Hospital Compare provides information on rates for heart attack, heart failure, pneumonia, asthma (children), or patients having surgery. Medicare and non-Medicare patient data are voluntarily submitted by hospitals. In addition, this site also reports the CMS Hospital Outcome of Care Measures. This data is compiled from claims and enrollment (Medicare) data. Patients admitted to the hospital for heart attack, heart failure, and pneumonia are included in this population. A 30-day Risk Adjusted Death Rate is used because this is the time period when deaths are most likely to be related to the care patients received while in the hospital. This information is intended to help the healthcare provider, patient, family, and friends compare quality of care provided in hospitals that submit data. Information on this site is also intended to encourage facilities to improve the care they provide.

Hospital Quality Incentive Demonstration

In 2003, CMS and the Premier Inc. Healthcare Alliance began a pay for performance project that has had a positive impact on the quality of care provided to patients receiving services at 250 hospitals in 36 states. There is a growing awareness that Medicare needs to change the way it pays for healthcare services. This demonstration project is designed to test new payment systems focused on improving the safety, quality, and efficiency of care delivered in hospitals. Payment for each discharge is contingent on the hospital's actual performance on a specific set of measures. The project is designed to determine if economic incentives can provide impetus to improve the quality of inpatient care.

The hospitals involved in these projects come in all shapes and sizes—large and small, urban, rural, teaching and non-teaching. The hospitals volunteer to submit their quality data on five high-volume inpatient conditions. The process and outcome measures used are acute myocardial infarction, coronary artery bypass graft, heart failure, pneumonia, and hip and knee replacement. The measures were developed by government and private organizations, including the National Quality Forum, the American Hospital Association, and the Leapfrog Group. The organizations testing the measures are the Joint Commission, CMS, and the AHRQ. The measures are monitored to determine whether care provided meets accepted evidence-based practice standards.

The process of collecting the data begins with hospitals submitting data to Premier, Inc. Premier than submits the data to CMS for validation and analysis. Improvements since the start of the projects have been remarkable as demonstrated in figure 17.4. The official close of the project is September 2009. CMS has submitted a proposal to Congress requesting that a percentage of a hospital's payment for each discharge be contingent on the hospital's actual performance.

Figure 17.4. Hospital Quality Incentive Demonstration (HQID)

The average Composite Quality Score (CQS)—from first to third year

- From 87.5 percent to 96.1 percent for patients with AMI (heart attack)
- From 84.8 percent to 97.4 percent for patients with coronary artery bypass graft (CABG)
- From 64.5 percent to 88.7 percent for patients with heart failure (HF)
- From 69.3 percent to 90.5 percent for patients with pneumonia (PN)
- From 84.6 percent to 96.9 percent for patients with hip and knee (HK) replacement

An aggregate of all quality measures within each clinical area improved by 4.4 percent between the project's second and third year for total gains of 15.8 percent over the project's first three years:

Premier Inc. 2006. Centers for Medicare and Medicaid Services (CMS). Premier Hospital Quality Incentive Demonstration Project: Project Findings from Year Two. Charolotte, NC.

Quality Improvement Strategies and Error Reductions

There are three main aspects to consider when developing strategies for quality improvement. The first is accountability regarding the clinical and administrative aspects of providing healthcare. Second is the focus of continuously reviewing and evaluating and improving the services provided by those working with patients. And third is developing ways to use information to evaluate clinical outcomes as defined by the patient and the healthcare system. Current climates in healthcare require that all three aspects be a part of any quality improvement effort (American College of Medical Quality 2005, 5).

There are many interested parties when it comes to determining the value of healthcare services. The patient, the direct care provider, the healthcare facility, the payer, the government through legislation and agencies, the accrediting organizations, and the list goes on. Measuring how well healthcare services are being delivered is being mandated by all groups previously named. Lack of a coordinated, systematic approach to measuring performance improvement leaves accountability for quality of care unsubstantiated.

Current performance measurement initiatives are focused on clinical effectiveness, patient safety, and patient satisfaction. The IOM has endorsed performance measures that are well researched, accepted by many stakeholders, and are evidence-based. Using standardized performance measures and benchmarking using databases to compare outcomes is one approach. The Joint Commission, federal agencies (especially IOM and AHRQ), CMS, professional associations, and others are building databases that allow comparisons of outcomes and they are making the results available to the public.

Patient satisfaction provides a different perspective to the healthcare delivery experience. The CAHPS patient satisfaction survey developed by AHRQ (figure 17.5) is being mandated by a variety of organizations including CMS,

Figure 17.5. CAHPS Hospital Survey

CAHPS® Hospital Survey

SURVEY INSTRUCTIONS

- You should only fill out this survey if you were the patient during the hospital stay named in the cover letter. Do not fill out this survey if you were not the patient.
- Answer all the questions by checking the box to the left of your answer.
- You are sometimes told to skip over some questions in this survey. When this happens you will see an arrow with a note that tells you what question to answer next, like this:
  ☐ Yes
  ☐ No → ***If No, Go to Question 1 on Page 1***

You may notice a number on the cover of this survey. This number is ONLY used to let us know if you returned your survey so we don't have to send you reminders.

Please note: Questions 1–22 in this survey are part of a national initiative to measure the quality of care in hospitals.

Please answer the questions in this survey about your stay at the hospital named on the cover. Do not include any other hospital stay in your answers.

YOUR CARE FROM NURSES

1. During this hospital stay, how often did nurses treat you with courtesy and respect?

[1]☐ Never
[2]☐ Sometimes
[3]☐ Usually
[4]☐ Always

2. During this hospital stay, how often did nurses listen carefully to you?

[1]☐ Never
[2]☐ Sometimes
[3]☐ Usually
[4]☐ Always

3. During this hospital stay, how often did nurses explain things in a way you could understand?

[1]☐ Never
[2]☐ Sometimes
[3]☐ Usually
[4]☐ Always

4. During this hospital stay, after you pressed the call button, how often did you get help as soon as you wanted it?

[1]☐ Never
[2]☐ Sometimes
[1]☐ Usually
[4]☐ Always
[9]☐ I never pressed the call button

YOUR CARE FROM DOCTORS

5. During this hospital stay, how often did doctors treat you with courtesy and respect?

[1]☐ Never
[2]☐ Sometimes
[3]☐ Usually
[4]☐ Always

6. During this hospital stay, how often did doctors listen carefully to you?

[1]☐ Never
[2]☐ Sometimes
[3]☐ Usually
[4]☐ Always

7. During this hospital stay, how often did doctors explain things in a way you could understand?

[1]☐ Never
[2]☐ Sometimes
[3]☐ Usually
[4]☐ Always

Source: Portion of CAHPS Hospital Survey 2008. https://www.cahps.ahrq.gov/content/products/Prod_Intro.asp?p=102&s=2.

health plans, NCQA, and a variety of payers. This information will provide facilities and direct care providers to improve services based on information from the patient.

Evidence-based practice uses well-researched and scientifically rigorous guidelines. Guidelines are being developed by a variety of entities. The guidelines offer a way to help standardize the healthcare delivered. The acceptance of these guidelines is growing, but there are many that reject the idea as "cookbook" medicine. Information technology in the form of a computerized medical record is a tool to help make the use of guidelines a meaningful part of healthcare delivery.

Reduction of errors and patient safety has exploded on the healthcare scene since the 1999 report by the IOM. As more data becomes available the black hole of adverse events deepens. Strategies for keeping patients safe, publicly acknowledging "never" events, and recognizing the complexity of an error-prone healthcare system has everyone's attention. Again, many organizations, agencies, facilities, and individual providers are trying help correct the systems. Patients are being strongly encouraged by some organizations and agencies to take more active roles in their healthcare delivery. The IOM recommends that a partnership be established between patient and provider. The report further recommends patients must understand more about their medications and providers must educate, consult, and listen to patients. Use of information technologies can reduce the number of medication errors with the use of e-prescriptions and point of care reference information, as well as linking patient history to e-prescriptions to identify interactions, allergies, and dosing. Improved labeling and packaging of medications is necessary and is linked to pharmaceutical nomenclature improvement. Medication safety is a crusade (IOM 2006).

The IOM identified certain aspects of care to be targeted for improvement. They are: efficiency, equity and patient-centeredness, transitions between providers, mortality (hospital-wide and physician-specific), and complex care situations with multiple providers delivering care. Approaches to measuring healthcare that are coordinated between providers, regulators, payers, and patients do not exist. There is much work to be done.

Patient Safety

Medical errors continue to make headlines in all parts of the United States. We were shocked in 1999 when the Institute of Medicine reported that between 48,000 and 98,000 patients are killed by medical errors each year. In 2001, the IOM's report, *Crossing the Quality Chasm: A New Health System for the 21st Century,* laid the groundwork for the January 2004 IOM Crossing the Quality Chasm Summit. The purpose of the summit was to offer guidance at the community and national levels about how best to provide patient-centered, high-quality care. The IOM released their most recent report in 2006. *Preventing Medication Errors* contains specific recommendations about how to reduce medical adverse drug events. The 2006 report raises grave concerns about the number and cost of errors in every step of the medication process. In addition, the report states that the projected 1.5 million adverse drug events (ADEs) are preventable and reports made by reputable agencies, government and private, about safety concerns continue to express urgency about the need to address performance measures addressed in the "chasm in quality" (IOM 2006).

The Joint Commission and state and federal governments have been working to improve the safety of patients by developing safety goals. Healthcare organizations are expected to comply with the safety goals in order to be accredited. The safety goals focus on known problematic areas. The Joint Commission recognizes that reliable systems design, high-quality care, and evidence-based expert solutions all complement each other as organizations work to improve patient safety.

Universal Protocol

Universal Protocol for ambulatory care, critical access hospitals, hospitals, and office-based surgery is accepted and promoted by the Joint Commission, relevant clinical specialties, and professional medical associations and organizations (figure 17.6). Universal Protocol incorporates the principles of eliminating wrong-site, wrong-procedure, and wrong-person surgery. The steps involved in this protocol include

- Preoperative verification process
- Marking of the operative site
- "Time out" before starting any procedure

The private sector is actively involved in the patient safety initiative as well. For example, the **Leapfrog Group**, a Washington-based coalition, is an example of a group that has effectively involved many healthcare organizations throughout the United States in its quality initiatives to make patients safe. Leapfrog has more than 2,000 hospitals participating in the Leapfrog Hospital Survey. In a June 2008 press release, Leapfrog reported that hospitals using their Leapfrog Hospital Survey have lower mortality and better quality than those who did not perform well on the survey or who did not participate. The public is free to check out ratings before making decisions on where to receive treatment. Public reporting allows healthcare organizations to be transparent about the safety and quality of care they provide.

The **National Quality Forum** (NQF), a not-for-profit organization in the private sector, focused on the development and implementation of strategies of patient safety and quality care. The NQF developed a set of 30 **safe practices** (figure 17.7) that are (1) likely to reduce harm to patients, (2) applied in a variety of healthcare settings, (3) enhance patient safety if implemented, and (4) have knowledge that can be useful to consumers, purchasers, providers, and researchers (NQF 2009). The NQF has also developed a list of serious events that should be publicly reported. The list is

Figure 17.6. Universal Protocol—Joint Commission

Implementation Expectations for the Universal Protocol for Preventing Wrong Site, Wrong Procedure, and Wrong Person Surgery™

These guidelines provide detailed implementation requirements, exemptions and adaptations for special situations.

- Pre-operative verification process

Verification of the correct person, procedure, and site should occur (as applicable):

- At the time the surgery/procedure is scheduled.
- At the time of admission or entry into the facility.
- Anytime the responsibility for care of the patient is transferred to another caregiver.
- With the patient involved, awake and aware, if possible.
- Before the patient leaves the preoperative area or enters the procedure/surgical room.

A preoperative verification checklist may be helpful to ensure availability and review of the following, prior to the start of the procedure:

- Relevant documentation (for example, H&P, consent).
- Relevant images, properly labeled and displayed.
- Any required implants and special equipment.
- Marking the operative site
- Make the mark at or near the incision site. Do NOT mark any non-operative site(s) unless necessary for some other aspect of care.
- The mark must be unambiguous (for example, use initials or "YES" or a line representing the proposed incision; consider that "X" may be ambiguous).
- The mark must be positioned to be visible after the patient is prepped and draped.
- The mark must be made using a marker that is sufficiently permanent to remain visible after completion of the skin prep. Adhesive site markers should not be used as the sole means of marking the site.
- The method of marking and type of mark should be consistent throughout the organization.
- At a minimum, mark all cases involving laterality, multiple structures (fingers, toes, lesions), or multiple levels (spine). Note: In addition to pre-operative skin marking of the general spinal region, special intraoperative radiographic techniques are used for marking the exact vertebral level).
- The person performing the procedure should do the site marking.
- Marking must take place with the patient involved, awake and aware, if possible.
- Final verification of the site mark must take place during the "time out."
- A defined procedure must be in place for patients who refuse site marking.
- Exemptions:
  - Single organ cases (for example, Cesarean section, cardiac surgery).
  - Interventional cases for which the catheter or instrument insertion site is not predetermined (for example, cardiac catheterization).
  - Teeth—BUT, indicate operative tooth name(s) on documentation *OR* mark the operative tooth (teeth) on the dental radiographs or dental diagram.
  - Premature infants, for whom the mark may cause a permanent tattoo.
- "Time out" immediately before starting the procedure must be conducted in the location where the procedure will be done, just before starting the procedure. It must involve the entire operative team, use active communication, be briefly documented, such as in a checklist (the organization should determine the type and amount of documentation) and must, at the least, include:
- Correct patient identity.
- Correct side and site.
- Agreement on the procedure to be done.
- Correct patient position.
- Availability of correct implants and any special equipment or special requirements.

The organization should have processes and systems in place for reconciling differences in staff responses during the "time out."

- Procedures for non-OR settings including bedside procedures.
- Site marking must be done for any procedure that involves laterality, multiple structures or levels (even if the procedure takes place outside of an OR).
- Verification, site marking, and "time out" procedures should be as consistent as possible throughout the organization, including the OR and other locations where invasive procedures are done.
- Exception: Cases in which the individual doing the procedure is in continuous attendance with the patient from the time of decision to do the procedure and consent from the patient through to the conduct of the procedure may be exempted from the site marking requirement. The requirement for a "time out" final verification still applies.

For more guidance, see the Frequently Asked Questions (FAQs) on the Joint Commission Web site.

Source: Joint Commission, http://www.jointcommission.org/NR/rdonlyres/E3C600EB-043B-4E86-B04E-CA4A89AD5433/0/universal_protocol.pdf, 2003.

titled "Never Events" and can be found at the NFQ's Web site. This list was ground breaking in 2002, and continues to evolve. Events are currently grouped into categories. The NQF has been at the forefront of developing a national reporting system that targets improved patient safety. The National Quality Forum is working with CMS, Leapfrog, the Joint Commission, and the AHRQ to establish its initiatives. There are many other private groups involved in safety and quality improvement.

Government agencies also have been involved in the patient safety movement. The IOM led the way with its 1999 report on medical errors. CMS, AHRQ, and the Food and Drug Administration (FDA) have been involved in developing safe practice protocols. The HHS has awarded grants to help study safer healthcare delivery practices. The Patient Safety Act of 2005 (PL 109-41) established a framework for healthcare organizations, physicians, and other healthcare providers to report patient safety events and perform aggregate data analysis of those events through Patient Safety Organizations. The legislation provides legal protection to organizations that share sensitive patient safety data. The legislation provides federal protection for privileged and confidential information. The intent is to increase the willingness of the clinicians to share information in this voluntary, provider-driven initiative. The intent of this legislation is to improve the quality, safety, and outcomes of patient care by learning about the underlying causes of risks in the healthcare delivery system.

Figure 17.7. National Quality Forum—Safe Practices

1. Create a healthcare culture of safety.
2. For designated high-risk, elective surgical procedures or other specified care, patients should be clearly informed of the likely reduced risk of an adverse outcome at treatment facilities that have demonstrated superior outcomes and should be referred to such facilities in accordance with the patient's stated preference.
3. Specify an explicit protocol to be used to ensure an adequate level of nursing based on the institution's usual patient mix and the experience and training of the nursing staff.
4. All patients in general intensive care units (both adult and pediatric) should be managed by physicians having specific training and certification in critical care medicine ("critical care certified").
5. Pharmacists should actively participate in the medication-use process, including, at a minimum, being available for consultation with prescribers on medication ordering, interpretation and review of medication orders, preparation of medication, dispensing of medication, and administration and monitoring of medications.
6. Verbal orders should be recorded whenever possible and immediately read back to the prescriber—for example, a healthcare provider receiving a verbal order should read or repeat back the information that the prescriber conveys in order to verity the accuracy of what was heard.
7. Use only standardized abbreviations and dose designations.
8. Patient care summaries or other similar records should not be prepared from memory.
9. Ensure that care information, especially changes in orders and new diagnostic information, is transmitted in a timely and clearly understandable form to all of the patient's current healthcare providers who need that information to provide care.
10. Ask each patient or legal surrogate to recount what he or she has been told during the informed consent discussion.
11. Ensure that written documentation of the patient's preference for life-sustaining treatments is prominently displayed in his or her chart.
12. Implement a computerized prescriber order entry system.
13. Implement a standardized protocol to prevent the mislabeling of radiographs.
14. Implement standardized protocols to prevent the occurrence of wrong-site procedures or wrong-patient procedures.
15. Evaluate each patient undergoing elective surgery for risk of an acute ischemic cardiac event during surgery and provide prophylactic treatment to high-risk patients with beta blockers.
16. Evaluate each patient upon admission, and regularly thereafter, for the risk of developing pressure ulcers. This evaluation should be repeated at regular intervals during care. Clinically appropriate preventive methods should be implemented consequent to the evaluation.
17. Evaluate each patient upon admission, and regularly thereafter, for the risk of developing deep vein thrombosis (DVT)/venous thromboembolism (VTE). Utilize clinically appropriate methods to prevent DVT/VTE.
18. Utilize dedicated antithrombotic (anticoagulation) services that facilitate coordinated care management.
19. Upon admission, and regularly thereafter, evaluate each patient for the risk of aspiration.
20. Adhere to effective methods of preventing central venous catheter-associated bloodstream infections.
21. Evaluate each pre-operative patient in light of his or her planned surgical procedure for the risk of surgical site infection and implement appropriate antibiotic prophylaxis and other preventive measures based on that evaluation.
22. Utilize validated protocols to evaluate patients who are at risk for contrast media-induced renal failure and utilize a clinically appropriate method for reducing risk of renal injury based on the patient's kidney function evaluation.
23. Evaluate each patient upon admission, and regularly thereafter, for risk of malnutrition. Employ clinically appropriate strategies to prevent malnutrition.
24. Whenever a pneumatic tourniquet is used, evaluate the patient for the risk of an ischemic and/or thrombotic complication and utilize appropriate prophylactic measures.
25. Decontaminate hands with either a hygienic hand rub or by washing with a disinfectant soap prior to and after direct contact with the patient or objects immediately around the patient.
26. Vaccinate healthcare workers against influenza to protect both them and patients from influenza.
27. Keep workspaces where medications are prepared clean, orderly, well lit, and free of clutter, distraction and noise.
28. Standardize the methods for labeling, packaging, and storing medications.
29. Identify all "high alert" drugs (for example, intravenous adrenergic agonists and antagonists, chemotherapy agents, anticoagulants and antithrombotics, concentrated parenteral electrolytes, general anesthetics, neuromuscular blockers, insulin and oral hypoglycemics, narcotics and opiates).
30. Dispense medications in unit-dose or, when appropriate, unit-of-use form, whenever possible.

Source: NQF 2003.

Minnesota was the first state to pass a law that requires the public reporting of 27 serious adverse events. Included on the list are medication errors and surgery on the wrong patient or body part. Reports submitted by hospitals are analyzed by the Minnesota Department of Health, and feedback is provided to the hospitals. Annual public reports describe adverse events, provide an aggregate analysis, and develop corrective action plans. Anyone can access information about safety in hospitals located in Minnesota. The numbers and variety of agencies and organizations looking at patient safety continues to grow (Minnesota Department of Health 2004). A number of states have followed suit. See figure 17.8 for a list of states that have adverse event reporting requirements with patient safety as the focus.

National Patient Safety Goals

Patient safety has evolved into a national passion. The government, accrediting organizations, and private organizations in a variety of sectors are targeting safety as a fertile area for improvement. The government under a variety of agencies has led the way. A few government agencies that have also been pioneers leading the way include the IOM, NIH, and the AHRQ, to name a few. As an accrediting body, the Joint Commission has developed the National Patient Safety Goals, Speak Up Program, Universal Protocol, and Do Not Use Abbreviations, Acronyms, and Symbols. (More detail can be found in the section on the Joint Commission's Patient Safety Initiatives.) Private organizations leading the way include the Leapfrog Group with their Hospital Rewards Program for hospitals that excel at patient safety. In addition, Patient Safety Organizations (PSOs) created through the Patient Safety Act of 2005 are intended to create a secure environment where healthcare providers—clinicians and healthcare organization—can analyze sensitive patient safety data. Ten PSOs have just been identified by AHRQ. See table 17.4.

Performance Indicator Development

Performance measures are quantifiable indicators used over time to determine whether structure, process, or outcome supports quality performance. They usually represent important aspects of care provided by the organization, department, or unit of service. Performance measure development has been a linchpin for clinical quality improvement. After important aspects of care are identified, it is then possible to establish criteria or data elements that will determine care patterns.

Figure 17.8. States requiring Adverse Events Reporting

California	Maine	Pennsylvania
Colorado	Maryland	Rhode Island
Connecticut	Massachusetts	South Carolina
District of	Minnesota	South Dakota
Columbia	Nevada	Tennessee
Florida	New Jersey	Utah
Georgia	New York	Vermont
Illinois	Ohio	Washington
Indiana	Oregon	Wyoming
Kansas		

Source: http://www.nashp.org/Files/shpsurveyreport_adverse2007.pdf.

Table 17.4. Patient safety organizations

Patient Safety Organizations	Location
California Hospital Patient Safety Organization	Sacramento, CA
ECRI Institute POS	Plymount Meeting, PA
Florida Patient Safety Corporation	Tallahassee, FL
Health Watch, Inc.	Easton, MD
Human Performance Technology Group	Collierville, TN
Institute for Safe Medication Practices (ISMP)	Horsham, PA
Missouri Center for Patient Safety	Jefferson City, MO
Peminic, Inc.	Fort Washington, PA
Sprixx	Santa Barbara, CA
University Healthsystem Consortium	Oak Brook, IL

Source: http://www.pso.ahrq.gov/listing/psolist.htm 2008.

The most common source of data is the health record. Data are collected and the professionals involved in the QI process analyze them. A determination is made as to whether the data provide the information that is needed. A decision then is made about how best to improve the care provided. Key performance measures addressing best practice have been developed and addressed in various ways during the evolution of quality improvement.

National Quality Forum

Besides patient safety standards development as described earlier, the NQF is known for its development of performance measures focused on clinical care. In 2007, the NQF began working with the CMS to develop quality measures for the CMS Physician Quality Reporting Initiative (PQRI). The areas of clinical focus include: cancer care, infectious diseases, non-medical doctor/doctor of osteopathy, surgery, and anesthesia at the individual clinician level. Healthcare stakeholders from every spectrum are included in the NQF's process of consensus development.

Overall the National Quality Forum has developed about 140 clinical measurement standards using their consensus development process. Organizations such as the Joint Commission and CMS look to the NQF for endorsement of their performance measures. Measures have been developed for a wide variety of conditions, including asthma and respiratory disease, bone and joint conditions, diabetes, heart disease, hypertension, mental health and substance abuse, and stroke; cross-cutting areas such as medication management, geriatrics, emergency care, obesity and prevention, immunization and screening; specialty areas including cardiac surgery, eye disease, and prenatal care; and patient experience with care instruments. With the support of member organizations, work on clinical measures continues to evolve.

National Quality Measures Clearinghouse

The National Quality Measures Clearinghouse (NQMC) is sponsored by AHRQ. The NQMC is a resource for organizations looking for clinical measures to evaluate the quality of clinical care. Measures are developed by a variety of organizations and individuals. The **measure hierarchy** is used to organize the measure set information. The levels of hierarchy are displayed in table 17.5. Interested reviewers can drill down to the desired level. A complete list of measure summaries and an index are available through the NQMC Web site. The information is organized alphabetically, by measure developer and submitter name. The site is updated weekly as measures and updates become available. More than 1,400 individual measure summaries are available.

There are a variety of performance measure resources available to organizations and healthcare providers. The AHRQ has a wealth of researched clinical performance measures to draw on. They also provide quality tools to help in evaluating the quality of care provided. Measures, data collection and analysis tools, as well as additional resources. Many professional organizations such as the American Academy of Family Physicians and American College of Surgeons are valuable resources for performance measures that are evidence-based. The development and acceptance of these measures has been a slow, but steadily accepted method of evaluating care processes and outcomes.

Quality Measurement in Ambulatory Care

The 1990s brought renewed interest in managed care and dramatic increases in the number of people who received healthcare services under its auspices. Health maintenance organizations, point-of-service plans, and preferred provider organizations have continued to evolve in the twenty-first century. Health plans that offer comprehensive ambulatory care services are aware of the need to measure the impact of the care provided in this sector. Consumer pressure to be responsive to patient demands has changed the ambulatory scene in the early 2000s. Health plans continue to develop methodologies that assess and compare care provided on an outpatient basis. A number of organizations have jumped to the forefront in the development of methodologies that look at quality of access, service, and care provided in the ambulatory setting. It is also worth noting that accreditation is becoming a more accepted norm among managed care organizations and health plans.

Table 17.5. Clinical Measurement Set organizational hierarchy

Hierarchy Name	Level	Description
Collection	Level 5 (highest)	Contains one or more sets, subsets, composites, or individual measures.
Set	Level 4	May contain one or more subsets, composites, or individual measures.
Subset	Level 3	May include one or more composites or individual measures.
Composite	Level 2	Is a measure that is an aggregate of scores from other measures. May stand alone or be combined with other measures or composites.
Measure	Level 1 (lowest)	May belong to a composite, subset, set, or collection.

Source: http://www.pso.ahrq.gov/listing/psolist.htm.

National Committee for Quality Assurance

The NCQA, a Washington-based nonprofit, private organization, is a leading source for information on quality of care provided by health plans. This organization accredits health plans and develops performance standards. Further, it sponsors, supports, and maintains HEDIS (Health Plan Employer Data and Information Set). It was founded in 1990 as an independent organization with the support of the Robert Wood Johnson Foundation, the large employer community and the managed care industry's main trade association. The NCQA began accrediting managed care organizations in 1991. Its mission is to improve the quality of healthcare by generating useful, understandable information about healthcare quality to help inform consumer and employer choice, and working to generate information and feedback to help physicians, health plans, and others to identify opportunities for improvement and make changes that enhance the quality of patient care.

HEDIS was developed through a combined effort of representatives from a variety of health plans and employers. This data set allows health plans to evaluate the quality of care provided by measuring their clinical practice using HEDIS performance standards (Millenson 1999, 340–348). More than 90 percent of health plans use HEDIS to measure the quality of care.

More than 60 different measures were designed to provide both purchasers and consumers of healthcare with information to compare the performance of managed care plans. Three methods are used in collecting HEDIS data: examining claims data, reviewing health records, or a combination of both. The health record can provide the most complete information, but it is the more time-consuming, costly, and difficult method. Health record review is time-consuming because a statistically valid sample of records must be reviewed. The stated minimum is 411 charts. It is costly because the reviewers must have technical skills that require higher salaries. Moreover, health records must be reviewed from the offices of many physicians because there is usually more than one primary care provider in any health plan.

HEDIS performance measures cover a number of areas: effectiveness of care, access and availability of care, satisfaction with care, health plan stability, utilization of services, cost of care, healthcare choices, and health plan descriptive information. HEDIS measures focus on the following:

- Controlling high blood pressure
- Beta-blocker treatment after a heart attack
- Breast cancer screening
- Cervical cancer screening
- Childhood immunizations
- Cholesterol screening (after heart attack)
- Diabetic care (HbA1c testing)
- Timeliness of prenatal care

More than 60 different standards fall into the following five major categories:

- Access and service
- Qualified providers
- Staying healthy (wellness and preventative services)
- Getting better
- Living with illness

These data can help employers and consumers make decisions that are best for their organizations. The decisions can include the cost and quality aspects of the health plan and can allow intelligent dialogue when making decisions about what health plan is best for an organization.

The NCQA continues to refine and evolve its commitment to quality. New initiatives begun by the NCQA include the Quality Plus program, which is intended to provide consumers and employers with new information about how well plans communicate with members, leverage technology, reward quality, as well as to promote wellness and disease management. Its purpose is to highlight health plans that are innovative with regard to member communications, care management, physician compensation, and other activities in the healthcare industry. The desired result of Quality Plus is to acknowledge innovation and allow early acceptance.

In addition, the NCQA has introduced Quality Compass. This is a database with a wealth of information from the nation's health plans. Plus, the NCQA is presenting its interactive survey system (ISS), a Web-based survey that collects information more quickly than the paper-based system currently used. It is intended to promote a quicker improvement process for health plans. The NCQA Web site has a wealth of information about HEDIS and all NCQA initiatives.

Institute for Clinical Systems Improvement

The Institute for Clinical Systems Improvement (ICSI) is an independent, nonprofit collaborative organization dedicated to providing evidence-based healthcare services to medical organizations in Minnesota. The medical organizations, located in North and South Dakota and Minnesota, range in size from 4 to 1,000 practitioners with a combined 9,000 physicians represented. Six Minnesota health plans sponsor ICSI. The primary sponsors are Blue Cross and Blue Shield of Minnesota, HealthPartners, Medica, Metropolitan Health Plan, PreferredOne, and UCare Minnesota.

ICSI describes itself as an objective voice championing healthcare quality and helping to define and implement best practices for patients. It promotes the move to increased public reporting of healthcare performance, thereby enhancing the value of healthcare. The ICSI program includes the following four components:

- Core commitment cycle
- Scientific groundwork for healthcare
- Support for improvement
- Minnesota health quality agenda

Carefully constructed clinical guidelines are made available to ICSI members. Each ICSI organization chooses at least four guidelines for intensive improvement and shares the results among all its members. An example of an ICSI guideline is shown in figure 17.9. ICSI tries to serve the healthcare community as an advocate for healthcare quality discussions. One unique approach ICSI has developed is that of providing best **practice guidelines** to patients and families in language they can understand. The most current strategy for ICSI is their R4R (Redesign for Results) program. ICSI is poised and committed to supporting Minnesota stakeholders in redesigning healthcare services with the outcome being better patient care.

Physician Quality Reporting Initiative (PQRI)

The Tax Relief and Health Care Act of 2006 (TRHCA) authorized the physician quality reporting system as a demonstration project through CMS. The Medicare, Medicaid, and SCHIP Extension Act of 2007 gave CMS the authority to make incentive payments in 2008. The Physician Quality Reporting Initiative (PQRI) is a voluntary reporting program targeting qualified professionals. It is a financial incentive (pay for performance) program that requires providers to

Figure 17.9. Sample: ICSI Guideline

Otitis Media in Children, Diagnosis and Treatment of (Guideline)

Scope and Target Population: Children greater than 3 months to age 18.

Clinical Highlights and Recommendations

- A clinical examination is necessary to diagnose acute otitis media. Diagnosis should be made with pneumatic otoscopy.
- Educate parents on measures to prevent the occurrence of otitis media.
- Children with low risk should use a wait-and-see approach to treatment.
- Refer the patient to an ear, nose, and throat specialist when the criteria are met.

Priority Aims and Suggested Measures

1. Increase the percentage of patients with a diagnosis of acute otitis media that were advised to "wait and see."
2. Improve appropriate antibiotic usage for otitis media infections.
3. Improve caregivers' knowledge of symptoms suggestive of otitis media, appropriate indicators for a provider visit, risk factors, and outcomes of otitis media.
4. Improve the percentage of patients with otitis media who receive an appropriate referral to an ear, nose, and throat specialist.

Source: http://www.icsi.org/guidelines_and_more/gl_os_prot/respiratory/otitis_media/otitis_media_in_children__diagnosis_and_treatment_of_633.html, 2008.

submit data on designated quality measures. The incentive payment is up to 1.5 percent of total allowed charges for covered Medicare Physician Fee Schedule services.

More than 100 quality measures have been designated as part of the PQRI initiative. The conditions included on the measure reporting list are common clinical conditions found on the Medicare Fee-For-Service claims. Diagnostic and procedures codes will be used to submit reports. ICD-9-CM is the diagnostic coding system, and the procedure codes are the Healthcare Common Procedure Coding System (HCPCS). Various aspects of care will be included as part of the reporting. Those aspects include:

- Prevention
- Management of chronic conditions
- Acute episode of care management
- Procedure-related care
- Resource utilization
- Care coordination

Reporting frequency and performance time frames are considered in the data collection plan. Professionals eligible for participation can select the measures that most closely reflect the services they provide. In 2008, the participants can select the desired reporting method. The methods are either claims-based or registry-based. Figure 17.10 demonstrates the decision tree and options available.

The Medicare PQRI is another pay for performance project being demonstrated through CMS. Potentially the patient and provider are winners in an arrangement that allows the provider to receive a financial bonus and the patient to receive better care that is evidenced-based on clinical guidelines. Physicians have been slow to participate in this program. Many physician practices may find this financial incentive insufficient to offset the costs of recording and submitting data as required. This demonstration continues to evolve and develop.

Consumer Assessment of Healthcare Providers and Systems

The Consumer Assessment of Healthcare Providers and Systems (CAHPS) is a program sponsored and administered by AHRQ. CAHPS has evolved into a source of coordinated

Figure 17.10. PQRI Participation Decision Tree

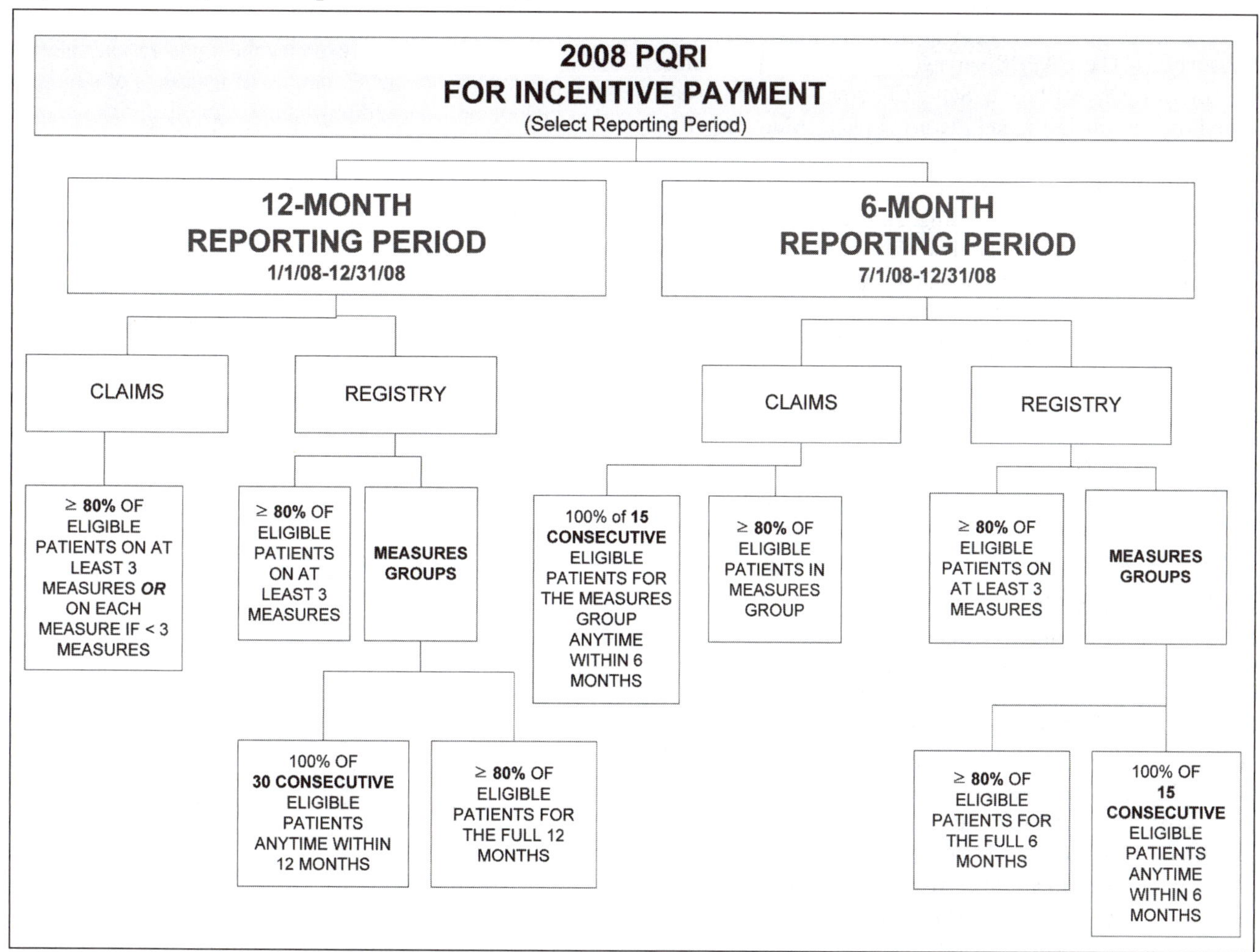

Source: http://www.cms.hhs.gov/PQRI/Downloads/PQRI2008ParticipationDecisionTree.pdf 2008.

survey instruments and reports intended to measure and communicate information on healthcare quality from the consumers' perspective. The original program (AHPS I, mid-1990s–2001) succeeded in developing questionnaires and reports for consumers enrolled in health plans. In 2002, the focus expanded and CAHPS II conducted research and developed survey products targeting ambulatory, hospital, nursing home, and dialysis center patients. During this second phase, surveys to assess consumer reaction were developed in various settings including physician offices, managed behavioral healthcare organization, dental plans, and tribal clinics. In 2007, CAHPS III shifted focus to the development of tools and resources supporting the use of CAHPS surveys. These tools are used by public and private purchasers (employers, state and federal agencies), quality measurement organizations (accrediting organizations, state healthcare organizations), provider organizations and health plans, as well as consumers and patients.

The National CAHPS Benchmarking Database (NCBD) contains ten years' worth of data from the Health Plan Survey as well as two years of data from the new Hospital Survey. CAHPS is best known for its Health Plan Survey which is well respected in the healthcare industry for obtaining consumers' perspective of their health plans. (Refer to figure 17.5.) The CAPHS survey is currently administered to Commercial, Medicaid, State Children's Health Insurance Program (SCHIP), and Medicare plans. More than 120 million enrollees have taken the CAHPS survey. The intent is to promote the comparison of results among users as a quality improvement tool—using the standardized data to identify relative strengths and weaknesses in performance, to determine where to improve and track progress over time. The data can also be used to make comparisons between Medicaid agencies using the benchmarks from the database. The NCBD is the source of CAHPS information for all types of care. Another role of the NCBD is as a supplier of primary data for conducting research on survey design and health plan and enrollee characteristics. CAHPS is another tool that can be used to improve the quality of healthcare in the United States. AHRQ's Report Card Compendium provides profiles of projects, organizations, and initiatives.

Patient Satisfaction

Patients bring a unique perspective to the evaluation of healthcare services. Patients have an opinion. Consumers are increasingly aware and informed about their healthcare services and providers. The move to obtain opinions from consumers is growing. CMS is requiring that facilities that are part of the inpatient prospective payment system must submit the CAHPS. The data from the CAHPS survey will be posted for public review on the Hospital Compare Web site. This survey has been endorsed by the National Quality Forum. The CAHPS survey is a tool used by many hospitals before the CMS requirement. (Refer to figure 17.5.) Hospitals are taking this patient evaluation tool seriously. Some hospitals have used the survey then added additional questions to personalize the survey. This tool can be useful as a quality measure of patient experience. Patients will have "patient-centered" information to review and help them decide where to get their care. The CAHPS and HCAHPS tools have become the standard for patient satisfaction surveying.

The Joint Commission's Quality Monitoring and Evaluation Process

The evolution of quality management included the development of a ten-step **monitoring and evaluation process** by the Joint Commission. The idea behind monitoring and evaluation is to continuously collect and analyze data and to address findings. The Joint Commission's ten-step process was developed to help healthcare organizations have a more prescribed methodology for assessing quality. The basic premise is still applicable today. (See figure 17.11.)

Donabedian's Quality Assessment Model

Avidas Donabedian's QA model has been used and accepted for many years. The model's approach to the assessment of healthcare is based on the following three measures (Donabedian 1980):

- **Structure measures** examine the organization's ability to provide services. Examples of measures of structure include policies and procedures, qualifications of staff, numbers of staff, physical space, and equipment.
- **Process measures** look at how care or service is provided to patients. The activities or protocols of care have some impact on the patient's outcome. Examples of process measures include protocols or methods of how treatment is delivered. For example, the patient's blood pressure is monitored hourly, patient education is completed before discharge, or the patient's discharge is determined to be appropriate. A healthcare provider (physician, nurse, or other allied health professional) usually carries out these functions.

Figure 17.11. Joint Commission's ten-step monitoring and evaluation process

Step 1.	Assign Responsibility
Step 2.	Delineate Scope of Care
Step 3.	Identify Important Aspects of Care
Step 4.	Identify Quality Indicators
Step 5.	Establish Thresholds for Evaluation
Step 6.	Collect and Organize Data
Step 7.	Evaluate Data—Trends and Patterns
Step 8.	Take Actions to Solve Problems
Step 9.	Assess the Actions and Document Improvement
Step 10.	Communicate Relevant Information to the Organizationwide Quality Improvement Program

Source: JCAHO 1988.

- **Outcome measures** assess the end results of the care or services provided. Examples of outcome measures include mortality reviews, complications, or any adverse events. Any of these could indicate an undesirable outcome and indicate the need for further investigation.

The Joint Commission's Performance Measurement System

The Joint Commission's evolution to core performance measures is a story unto itself. In the late 1980s and early 1990s, the Joint Commission began to develop a performance measurement system they called an Indicator Monitoring System (IMS) that would focus on clinical applications.

During this time, the Joint Commission determined that a program of continuous improvement was needed if a genuine impact on the quality of care was to be achieved. Additionally, the Joint Commission wanted to move from a process and structure orientation to one more focused on outcomes. The objective was to affect both administrative process and clinical patient care. One goal of the Agenda for Change initiative (discussed earlier) was to research and identify quality clinical performance measures. Identified performance measures represent sound clinical practice and reflect whether a healthcare organization is providing high-quality care to patients. The intention is to improve the quality of healthcare by improving performance in a given area of practice (for example, myocardial infarctions).

The complexity of the initial IMS project led first to the Orion project and then to the current ORYX initiative. The ORYX initiative integrates outcomes with performance measures and makes them both a part of a data-driven accreditation process. The use of nationally standardized performance measures has been considered a part of this initiative from the beginning. With the help of advisory panels, the Joint Commission identified measures that give an overall picture of an organization's healthcare services. Data collection began in 2002. The data collected provides valuable objective information about the patient care services. This evaluative information gives a basis for determining the level of standards compliance, and more importantly the outcomes achieved by an organization. Performance measurement data guides and supplements the survey process giving a targeted basis for the accreditation survey and for guiding the organization in improving the quality of healthcare provided within its walls (Joint Commission 2008i).

In an effort to coordinate accreditation with other external review bodies, data collected on several of the core measures are also required by the Centers for Medicare and Medicaid Services (CMS). At the heart of the ORYX project is the development of continuous improvement processes that focus on clinical areas. The next section in this chapter details the use of these standardized performance measures. This is a work in progress; currently hospitals have eight core measure sets to select from. Effective January 2008, the Joint Commission asks all hospitals with a daily census of ten or more to select four core measure sets. (See figure 17.12.) If the hospital does not have complementary services and must select fewer than the required number of core measures, the hospital can supplement the core measures with non-core measure sets. Each facility selects its own core measures based on the services it provides. For example, a hospital that does not provide obstetrical services would not be required to select measures from the pregnancy and related conditions category. Hospitals that serve patient populations having conditions that match two or more of the core measure sets are required to choose two measure sets. Hospitals should select measures that correlate to the greatest degree of high-risk, high-volume, and problem-prone areas within the organization. Data are submitted quarterly to Joint Commission (Joint Commission 2008i).

The ORYX requirements have been simplified for small hospitals. A hospital is designated as small when it has an average daily census of less than 10 and outpatient visits of fewer than 150 per month. Small hospitals are required to collect data internally on all selected measures or measure sets; generate either run charts or control charts on each measure, at least quarterly, for use in internal quality improvement activities; make data reports available for review by surveyors during on-site surveys; and produce reports upon request of Joint Commission for the purpose of data-monitoring activities (Joint Commission 2008i).

How an organization uses its selected core measures is evaluated during a Joint Commission accreditation on-site survey. The organization must demonstrate the reliability of the data, conduct credible analysis of the data, and initiate system and process improvements.

Core Performance Measures

Core performance measures are used to assess how well healthcare organizations provide care. They are currently being used by the Joint Commission and CMS, as well as healthcare plans such as Blue Cross. These organizations use data to understand what care is currently being provided and to determine where to focus QI activities and accreditation surveys. The use of statistically valid information becomes the basis for continuous **performance improvement** (PI). An organization can use the results of PI activities to determine its effectiveness in patient care over time. The organization

Figure 17.12. Performance Measurement Initiatives—Core Measure Sets

- Acute Myocardial Infarction (AMI)
- Heart Failure (HF)
- Pneumonia (PN)
- Surgical Care Improvement Project (SCIP)
- Pregnancy and Related Conditions (PR)
- Hospital Outpatient Department (HOP)
- Children's Asthma Care (CAC)
- National Hospital Inpatient Quality Measures-Hospital-based Inpatient Psychiatric Services (HBIPS)

Source: Joint Commission, http://www.jointcommission.org/PerformanceMeasurement, 2008.

can use the results to claim they provide high-quality care and can literally "prove" its excellence. Measures are recommended by accrediting organizations (Joint Commission) and the federal government (CMS and QIO) to allow comparability of like institutions.

Core performance measures are considered tools—standardized metrics—that provide an indication of an organization's performance. Core measures are defined as standardized sets of valid, reliable, and evidenced-based measures implemented by the Joint Commission for use within the ORYX initiative. Core measures are applied across accredited healthcare programs (Joint Commission 2008f). The use of core measures allows for benchmarking based on processes and outcomes of patient care. Core measures are designed to provide a comprehensive picture of the care provided in a given area. A core measure must:

- Demonstrate that it will have a significant impact on the health of specified populations
- Be precisely defined and specify requirements for data collection and for calculation of the core measure value or score
- Consistently identify the events it was designed to identify across healthcare organizations (reliability)
- Measure or capture what it is intended to measure (validity)
- Be interpretable (that is, its results must be easily understood by the users of the data, including accrediting organizations, providers, and consumers)
- Have the ability to be risk-adjusted or stratified (that is, the extent to which differences among population groups can be controlled or taken into account)
- Be assessed for availability and accessibility of the required data elements and the effort and cost of abstracting and collecting data
- Be useful in the accreditation process and support the organization's quality improvement efforts
- Be under the provider's control to influence the processes and outcomes being measured
- Be publicly available

In 1999, the Joint Commission gathered clinical professionals, healthcare provider organizations, state hospital associations, healthcare consumers, and performance measurement experts to determine where to focus attention. The core measures were introduced in July 2002, and the core measures methodology has been evolving to the current number. There are currently eight core measures that hospitals can select from to measure quality of care (refer to figure 17.12). If hospitals are unable to select four core measures, they will then use a combination of core and non-core measure data to submit to the Joint Commission.

With the introduction of these core performance measures, healthcare facilities will be expected to select a performance measurement system that meets Joint Commission's requirements and to send data to the Joint Commission on a routine basis. A **performance measurement system** must meet all parameters for data submission as determined by the Joint Commission. (See table 17.6.) Data from similar organizations will be compared and areas for improvement will be identified. If any undesirable patterns or trends are found, further monitoring and evaluation will follow. The performance measurement process can be used internally by hospitals for quality improvement activities and externally to help the Joint Commission focus survey activities. Also, public reporting is possible using the information in the core measure database.

The hospital quality measure sets currently utilized by Joint Commission and CMS are:

- Acute myocardial infarction
- Heart failure
- Pneumonia
- Asthma care for children
- Surgical infection prevention or the Surgical Care Improvement Project

The intent of this joint effort is to reduce data collection requirements put on healthcare organizations. The Joint Commission and CMS have worked together to ensure that these measures are comparable. Data will be calculated in an identical fashion.

Hospitals are not the only healthcare organizations involved in the Joint Commission's ORYX initiative. Long-term care, ambulatory care, home care, and behavioral health also are part of the initiative. In addition, data resulting from the

Table 17.6. Performance Measurement Systems—ORYX Core Measure Requirements

Attribute 1	Performance Measure Characteristics	Refers to characteristics of the performance measures for use in the ORYX initiative
Attribute 2	Data Collection and Receipt	Refers to the operational characteristics of measurement system
Attribute 3	Data Quality	Refers to the extent to which performance measures correctly identify events they were designed to identify
Attribute 4	Risk Adjustment Stratification	Refers to a process for reducing, removing, or clarifying the information and confounding patient factors that differ among comparison groups
Attribute 5	Technical Reporting Requirements	Refers to requirements related to the transmission of accredited healthcare organization data to the Joint Commission by performance measurement systems

Source: Joint Commission. http://www.jointcommission.org/NR/rdonlyres/64C5EDF0-253A-42CE-9DE5-C8AFE6755267/0/oryx_hap_cm_req.pdf, 2008.

performance measures is publicly reported. The Joint Commission Web site (also QualityCheck and the CMS Web site) make data available for the comparison of hospital performance (Joint Commission 2008i).

Data-Driven Accreditation

The Joint Commission is striving to make the accreditation process continuous and data driven. In January 2000, the Joint Commission surveyors used ORYX-specific presurvey reports to provide surveyors with information about performance measurement data. This data supplements the standards-based survey process. In the fall of 2002, the Joint Commission announced further changes to its accreditation process. The intent is to focus accreditation on operational systems critical to quality of care and safety issues. Period Performance Review (PPR) provides healthcare organizations the ability to evaluate themselves on an ongoing basis. PPR is a compliance assessment tool that provides opportunity for monitoring of performance measures to assure continuous compliance. The Joint Commission continues to develop ways for a more complete method to assure patient safety and quality care.

The core performance measure data will be instrumental in determining the focus of the clinical aspects of the survey. This approach to surveying uses the core performance measurement data, which is aggregated in an organization-specific manner. This is referred to as the **priority focus process** (PFP), which is an automated, rules-based tool. The intention is to make the accreditation process more relevant and valuable to healthcare organizations.

Joint Commission Patient Safety Initiative

The Joint Commission's National Patient Safety Goals (NPSGs) (see table 17.7) are central to their mission of

Table 17.7. Joint Commission's 2009 Hospital National Patient Safety Goals

Goal	Goal Name	Suggested Solution
1	Improve the accuracy of patient identification	Use at least 2 identifiers when providing care, treatment, and services Eliminate transfusion errors related to patient misidentification
2	Improve the effectiveness of communication among caregivers	Verify by reading back verbal orders, telephone orders, telephone or verbal reports of test results Standardize a list of abbreviations, acronyms, symbols, and dose designations *not* to be used Improve the timeliness of reporting and receipt of critical test and critical results and values by caregiver Implement a standardized way to communicate the hand-off of a patient Allow time to ask and respond to questions
3	Improve the safety of using medications	The organization has a list of medications that look and sound alike and updates the list yearly Label all medications not already labeled Take special precautions with patients who are using anticoagulant therapy
7	Reduce the risk of healthcare associated infections	Comply with WHO or CDC hand hygiene guidelines Manage as a sentinel event unanticipated death or major permanent loss of function related to a healthcare associated infection Use evidence-based practices to prevent healthcare associated infections due to multidrug resistant organisms (for example, MRSA) Use best or evidence based guidelines to prevent blood stream infections Use best practice for preventing surgical site infections
8	Accurately and completely reconcile medications across the continuum of care	Maintain a reconciled list of all medications taken by the patient and provide this list to all pertinent people including the patient Short duration medications are evaluated to make certain they don't react with any other medications
9	Reduce the risk of patient harm resulting from falls	Implement a fall reduction program that identifies all patients at risk for falling and evaluate the program regularly
13	Encourage patients' active involvement in their own care as a patient safety strategy	Identify ways for patient and family to report concerns about safety and encourage them to do so
15	The organization identifies safety risks inherent in its patient population	Patients at risk for suicide are identified
16	Improve recognition and response to changes in a patient's condition	Develop a way for staff to request additional assistance if a patient's condition worsens

Source: Adapted from Joint Commission's 2009 Hospital National Patient Safety Goals, http://www.jointcommission.org/NR/rdonlyres/40A7233C-C4F7-4680-9861-80CDFD5F62C6/0/09_NPSG_HAP_gp.pdf, 2008.

providing safe, high quality care. The Joint Commission acknowledges that more than 90 percent of U.S. hospitals use their standards to help guide and improve healthcare. *Improving America's Hospitals: A Report on Quality and Safety* (2008) has been received with enthusiasm. Many different organizations, providers, and payers have accessed the report validating the need for increased understanding of how to achieve safer, higher quality healthcare services. Healthcare organizations are expected to comply with the Joint Commission's national patient safety goals in order to be accredited. The Joint Commission's approach to all aspects of improving performance, whether safety or quality, is based on a theme of continual improvement. This approach uses systems redesign and a change in the culture of healthcare organizations as the focus of keeping errors from affecting patient care.

The Joint Commission uses an advisory group to help determine what safety goals are selected. The goals are selected based on the potential impact on patient care. Other factors taken into consideration include cost and practicality of implementation. The Joint Commission's Board of Governors makes the final approval for either deleting or adding goals to the NPSGs. It is strongly recommended that information about safety and quality be readily available for interested parties. This includes the public, providers, and payers. Private, not-for-profit organizations are also pushing for increased transparency regarding data on the quality and safety of healthcare providers—both organizations and direct care providers. The Joint Commission has made information on quality and safety issues at its Web site.

The Joint Commission's patient safety initiative is an integral part of the accreditation process. Commitment to a culture of safety is demonstrated by the number and variety of programs supported by the Joint Commission. The initiatives listed in table 17.8 involve patient safety in one way or another:

The extensive involvement of the Joint Commission in patient safety efforts speaks to a continued focus of providing higher quality, safer healthcare services.

Other Measurement Systems

A healthcare organization can measure the quality of the care provided in a variety of ways. Healthcare's complex nature has proved to be challenging, even difficult to evaluate. Evaluating the care provided to patients continues to evolve and change. Knowledge of current measurement systems being used in today's healthcare environment is necessary if one truly wants to provide the highest-quality healthcare. Six Sigma and Lean Six Sigma are two measurement systems being used extensively in healthcare organization. Refer to chapter 7 for detailed information on both of these measurement systems.

Clinical Value Compass

The **Clinical Value Compass** is a performance improvement approach developed to advance the association of quality and value. The "best care at the lowest cost" sums up this approach. A value equation may be represented as follows:

$$\text{Value} = \frac{f\,(\text{Quality} \times \text{Volume})}{\text{Costs}}$$

The name of this approach reflects its similarity to a directional compass. At the heart of the approach are four cardinal points:

- Functional status, risk status, and well-being (north)
- Costs (south)

Table 17.8. Safety Initiatives—Descriptions

Initiative	Description
Patient-related Standards	Approximately 50 percent of the Joint Commission's standards are related to safety. For example, medication's use, infection control, transfusions, and the like.
Sentinel Event Policy	Identifies events and requires action to prevent recurrence.
Sentinel Event Alert	Newsletter that describes underlying causes of SEs and recommends steps to prevent events.
Sentinel Event Advisory Group	Appointed group of professionals who are experts in safety that advise in the development of the National Patient Safety Goals.
National Patient Safety Goals	Specific goals targeted for improving the safety of patient when receiving healthcare services.
Universal Protocol	Protocol established to prevent wrong site, wrong procedure, and wrong person events.
Office of Quality Monitoring	Receives, evaluates, and tracks complaints and reports of concerns about healthcare organizations.
Patient Safety Research	Works to advance the field of patient safety and adverse event reporting systems.
Patient Safety Resources	A subsidiary that is focused on educating, training, consulting, and publishing information on keeping patients safe.
Speak Up Initiatives	Program that encourages patients to take an active, involved, and informed role in their healthcare.
Quality Check and Quality Reports	Methods for the public and accredited organizations to view performance measure results used in performance improvement initiatives.
Joint Commission International Client Safety	A virtual entity that will utilize a wide variety of experts to help provide safety solutions to healthcare organizations globally.
Legislative Efforts	Lobby for a non-punitive environment for the reporting of healthcare errors and patient safety.
Patient Safety Coalitions	Involved with a variety of groups with a common interest in patient safety.

Source: Joint Commission. http://www.jointcommission.org, 2008.

- Satisfaction with healthcare and perceived benefit (east)
- Clinical outcomes (west)

The clinical value compass (figure 17.13) gives providers a methodology to manage and improve healthcare services.

Providers will measure the value of care for similar patient populations, analyze the delivery processes, change delivery processes, test the changes, and determine whether the changes lead to better clinical outcomes at lower cost (value). The process is straightforward and begins with a selection of a population set. Then value measures are selected and defined. There will be at least one value measure for each quadrant of the value compass. Performance measures can be structure-, process-, or outcome-based. All key stakeholders can learn and see improvements that result in a healthcare experience that provides better value.

Check Your Understanding 17.3

Instructions: Answer the following questions on a separate piece of paper.

1. What can a manager do to ensure a high degree of customer service? Define and describe how performance measures are used in performance improvement processes.
2. How are the assessment approaches of structure, process, and outcome and performance measure development tied together?
3. Explain how outcomes management contributes to the clinical performance improvement and name two resources.
4. What core measures have the Joint Commission and CMS worked on together?
5. How do core measures contribute to making a data-driven accreditation process a reality?
6. What are five patient safety practices used by the Joint Commission, NFQ, Leapfrog, and CMS?
7. What federal agencies have been involved in developing safe practice protocols?
8. What contributions did managed care make to quality improvement?
9. Describe the role of the National Committee for Quality Assurance.
10. Explain why evidence-based medicine is an important component of improving clinical quality.
11. How can severity indexing contribute to improved patient care?

Quality Management in Clinical Applications

The first QA efforts using the Joint Commission model from 1980 focused on problems. The problems were most often administrative in nature. For example, the mechanics of moving patients through admitting to their rooms and placing safety devices in patient rooms and hallways were addressed in the first wave of QA efforts. Making changes in the clinical practice of physicians was approached more slowly. Clinical applications are the current focus of QI efforts.

Medical Staff Applications

The medical staff is a key player in the evaluation of clinical services and any clinical process improvement efforts. The medical staff organization (MSO) works closely with the healthcare organization's administration but is directly responsible and accountable to its governing body. The bylaws/rules and regulations guide the medical staff regarding the organization's structure, functions, and responsibilities. In addition, the MSO must be responsive to internal requests from the administration or the governing body as well as

Figure 17.13. Clinical Value Compass example

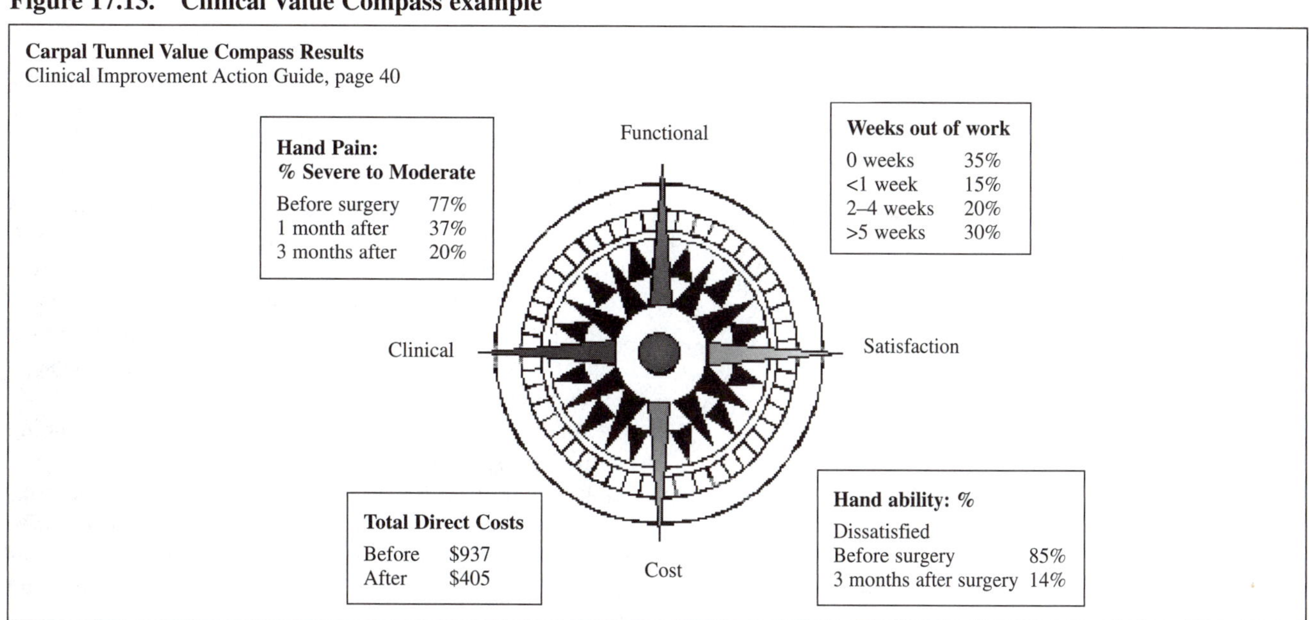

Source: Nelson et al. 1996.

external entities such as accrediting bodies and state and federal regulators. The MSO is expected to lead initiatives regarding patient safety and clinical quality improvement.

Organization of the Medical Staff

Like any organization, the medical staff, as a self-governing entity, needs to have structure. The Joint Commission's *Accreditation Manual for Hospitals* states "the medical staff and the governing body must work collaboratively" to provide the "quality and safety of care, treatment and services provided to patients" (2009a, 5). The medical staff bylaws provide an organizational structure to ensure communication with the governing body and high-quality patient care.

Committees are used to help most medical staffs function. The executive committee is the only medical staff committee required by the Joint Commission. It usually comprises either elected or appointed medical staff officers, department directors, and an administrative representative. Actual membership (size, composition, functions) is defined in the medical staff's own bylaws/rules and regulations (discussed later in this chapter). The majority of those serving on the executive committee must be fully licensed physicians. The members of the executive committee make decisions, determine policy, and act on behalf of the medical staff as a whole. In addition, this group provides leadership to the medical staff.

The executive committee makes recommendations directly to the governing board on matters such as:

- Structure of the medical staff
- Mechanisms used to review credentials
- Medical staff membership
- Delineation of clinical privileges
- Review of and actions on reports from medical staff committees, departments, and other groups

Many medical staffs today are organized into departments or divided into functioning units; only very small, uncomplicated medical staffs are not. The Joint Commission does not specify how a medical staff will organize. It is the responsibility of the medical staff to determine its method of self-governance with approval of the governing body. The bylaws/rules and regulations contain descriptions and definitions necessary to the operation of the medical staff.

A departmentalized medical staff must decide on the mechanism for acting and reporting. The Joint Commission recommends defining the leadership of each medical staff department. It further states that the department director must be qualified with appropriate education and training. The medical staff bylaws/rules and regulations specify the responsibilities of the department director:

- Determine clinical activities of the department
- Determine administrative responsibilities of the department
- Establish mechanisms for the surveillance of the clinical activities performed by all individuals in the department
- Establish criteria for clinical privileges for care provided within the department
- Recommend clinical privileges for each department member
- Determine the competence and qualifications of department personnel
- Integrate department functions into the organization
- Assess and improve the quality of services, treatment, and care provided within the department

The bylaws/rules and regulations of the medical staff provide the guidelines and framework or structure needed for the medical staff to function. In addition, the bylaws/rules and regulations define or describe:

- Medical staff structure
- Process for appointment to the medical staff
- Criteria and qualifications for appointment to the medical staff
- Executive committee organization and structure and authority
- Definition and qualifications plus roles and responsibilities of department chair
- Indicators for and implementation of suspension of medical staff membership or clinical privileges
- Methods of recommending membership or termination, suspension, or reduction in privileges
- Fair hearing and appeal process
- Medical staff membership
- Credentialing procedures

The bylaws/rules and regulations must be approved by the medical staff and by the governing body of the organization. When approved, they are intended to provide an agreement between the medical staff and the organization's administration.

Credentialing of the Medical Staff

Since its inception, the Joint Commission has supported healthcare organizations by developing processes to ensure that only the most qualified professionals practice in healthcare organizations. The Joint Commission's standards guide healthcare organizations in the **credentialing process**. Each healthcare organization must have its own credentialing process; thus, each healthcare organization will have a different process. Using the Joint Commission standards results in a credentialing process with a certain commonality among healthcare organizations. A sound credentialing process is the foundation of high-quality care.

Credentialing is the process of reviewing and validating qualifications, granting professional or medical staff membership, and awarding delineated privileges. Specific policies and procedures are used by healthcare organizations to accomplish this process. The credentialing process verifies the education, training, experience, current competence, and ability to perform the privileges requested or any other background information pertinent to an individual requesting membership on the medical staff. The medical staff bylaws/rules and regulations delineate what needs to be collected and reviewed and the process of approval or denial of medical staff membership and clinical privileges.

The credentialing process begins with a potential medical staff member submitting an application to the medical staff for membership and a request for clinical privileges. After the information on the application has been verified, the department chair reviews the request for clinical privileges and makes a recommendation. The application, the results of the verification process, and the department chair's recommendations are reviewed by a selected group of medical staff members. The credentials committee commonly performs this function. The recommendation goes from the credentials committee to the executive committee. The executive committee then reviews the recommendations and makes its recommendation to the governing board. The governing board reviews the information and makes the final decision to accept or reject the application. (See figure 17.14.)

The application to the medical staff contains categories of information as specified by the NCQA. Some of the suggested categories include:

- Licensure
- Hospital privileges
- Drug Enforcement Administration registration
- Medical education, including specialty board certification
- Malpractice insurance
- Liability claims history
- National Practice Data Bank (NPDB) queries (as required by law)
- Medical board sanctions
- Previous applications for medical staff membership and privileges

Items such as the above and additional items designated by the medical staff are included with the application. The Joint Commission references their requirements in MS.06.01.03 and MS.06.03.05.

During the credentialing process, each applicant to the medical staff requests specific clinical privileges. According to the Joint Commission, granting **clinical privileges** refers to the authorizing of a practitioner to provide specific patient care services within well-defined limits. The criteria for awarding clinical privileges must be detailed in the medical staff bylaws/rules and regulations. Criteria include, but are not limited to, preestablished definitions of minimum levels of current license status, training, experience, and competence and ability to perform the requested privilege (Joint Commission 2009a). The granting, renewal or denial of privileges must be objective and evidence-based.

Most healthcare organizations maintain lists of the procedures, services, and treatments that are most likely to be requested based on the services they offer. After the request for clinical privileges is made, the verification process begins. If the medical staff is departmentalized, the department director uses the criteria to make recommendations regarding the appropriateness of the requested privileges. If the medical staff is not departmentalized, the chief (president) of the medical staff or designee performs this function.

The delineation of privileges includes any limitations imposed on the individual provider, including the ability to admit, treat, or direct the course of treatment of patients admitted to the facility.

In today's healthcare environment, credentials are verified by either the healthcare organization (usually by a medical staff services professional) or a **verification service**. In

Figure 17.14. Flowchart of the credentialing process

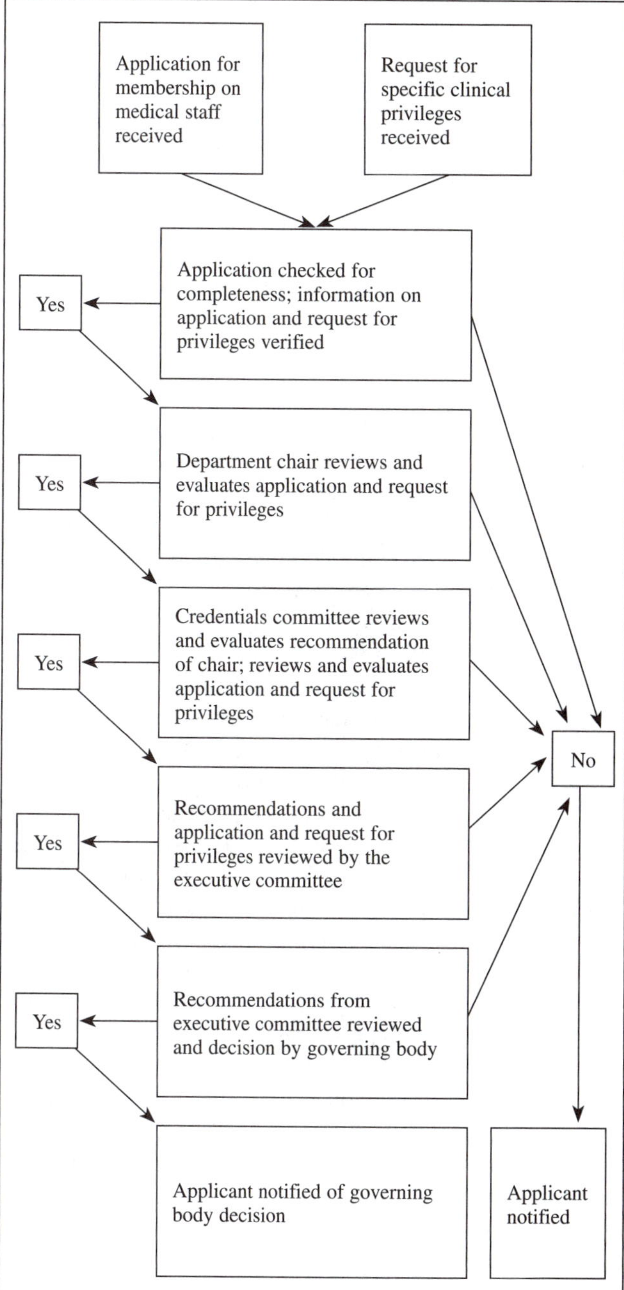

either case, primary sources should be checked when possible. According to the Health Care Quality Improvement Act and the Joint Commission, the NPDB must be queried when verifying applicants to the medical staff. All queries must be completed before any appointments are made or privileges awarded. In all cases, the verification process needs to be done in a timely manner specified in the bylaws.

Initial appointment and awarding of privileges is done for no more than a two-year period. Typically, appointment and designation of clinical privileges are done together. The credentialing process is ongoing. The reappointment and renewal or revision of clinical privileges is completed at least every two years. The reappointment and reappraisal process is continuous within the time line delineated in the medical staff bylaws.

The reappraisal process includes reviewing objective information collected on each individual who provides patient care services. Data are gathered and maintained on the practice patterns of all healthcare providers. The following may be included in the data:

- Procedures performed and the outcomes
- Pattern of blood and pharmaceutical usage
- Requests for tests and procedures
- Length of stay patterns
- Morbidity and mortality data
- Use of consultants

A credentials file is maintained on each member of the medical staff. This information is considered confidential and must be handled in accordance with established policies and procedures contained in the medical staff bylaws/rules and regulations. State and federal peer review and confidentiality legislation should be reviewed.

The initial granting of medical staff membership and privileges, along with any revisions or revocations of clinical privileges, must follow the medical staff bylaws/rules and regulations. All applicants have the right to appeal decisions and to have a fair hearing before a panel of their peers.

Temporary privileges may be awarded when special circumstances arise. There are two situations when the temporary granting of privileges applies. One is to fulfill an important care, treatment, or service need. The second is when a new applicant is awaiting review and approval of the Executive Committee and the Governing Body. The medical staff bylaws/rules and regulations specify how temporary privileges are applied. The Medical Staff Standard MS.06.13 states that the "privileges are granted for no more 120 days" and there are specific items requiring verification before this can be done (Joint Commission 2009a, MS 20). The Joint Commission requires that the chief executive officer or designee base the granting of temporary privileges on the recommendation of the president of the medical staff or designee. Temporary privileges must fall under state and federal regulations.

Medical staff bylaws/rules and regulations must specify the criteria used to appoint and reappoint or award clinical privileges. The medical staff and governing board approve the criteria. The bylaws must be applied to all applicants equitably. All individuals providing patient care services in the healthcare organization must be included in the credentialing process. It is imperative that the information be provided as part of the application and that the request for privileges is reviewed and verified. Failure to verify information jeopardizes the healthcare organization from a liability standpoint. Courts consistently hold healthcare organizations liable for failure to verify application/request for privileges information. Cases where healthcare organizations were found liable include *Candler General Hospital, Inc. v. Persaud* (1994), *Purcell and Tucson General Hospital v. Zimbelman* (1972), and *Insinga v. LaBella* (1989). Case law in this area continues to evolve.

Independent Practitioners and Credentialing

Individuals who provide healthcare services without supervision or direction are considered to be **independent practitioners**. Independent practitioners may work as employees of the organization or may work privately or through a group of physicians. Physicians, dentists, podiatrists, and clinical psychologists most commonly practice as independent practitioners.

Licensed independent practitioners other than physicians also must go through a credentialing process as described in the section on medical staff credentialing. Medical staff bylaws will delineate the process for credentialing independent practitioners. Independent practitioners go through an appointment and reappointment process and have specific privileges delineated within the scope of their license and the rules and regulations of the organization and medical staff. Independent practitioners must seek appointment and request specific clinical privileges and practice within that framework. The objective of this process is to guarantee patient safety by ensuring that only trained, competent, and qualified individuals provide healthcare services within the organization.

Other Medical Staff Quality Applications

Because the medical staff is responsible for ensuring the quality of care provided to patients treated in the healthcare facility, it is involved in collecting and analyzing data and improving both clinical and nonclinical functions in the organization. For the QI process to be successful, the medical staff must demonstrate leadership in QI activities. Data collection and analysis and recommendations are done on an ongoing basis, and changes are made to improve the patient care, treatment, and services offered in the organization. The medical staff and healthcare organization can then judge whether the services provided are meeting standards of care.

Patient Care Review

Physician leadership is critical to the success of the continuous PI program of any organization. Medical practice has changed remarkably over the past century. The practice of medicine has moved into the twenty-first century with the medical paradigm shifting from individuality to one of teamwork and collaboration. Physicians still work in an atmosphere of infallibility and have great difficulty acknowledging mistakes or lack of knowledge (Shine 2002). Yet they persist in looking for ways to provide the best possible medical care for their patients. Physicians, the government, and accrediting agencies continue efforts to determine the best way to collect information about patient care that allows a consistent and objective patient care review process.

Currently, PI incorporates the evaluation of outcomes and processes. The medical staff must lead the way in improving clinical and nonclinical processes used in organizations. Involvement of the medical staff in patient care review is critical. This means the medical staff is involved in measuring, assessing, and improving processes that depend on licensed physicians or other practitioners credentialed and privileged through the medical staff process. The Joint Commission (2009a) provides guidelines for the medical staff:

- Medical assessment and treatment of patients
- Information use about adverse privileging decision for any practitioner using the privileging process
- Use of medications
- Use of blood and blood components
- Operative and other procedures
- Appropriateness of clinical practice patterns
- Significant departures from established patterns of clinical practice
- Use of developed criteria for autopsies
- Sentinel event data
- Patient safety data

Health Record Review

Health record review is necessary to ensure that the documentation captured is complete and accurate and reflects the care provided to the patient. At a minimum, the team involved in this improvement process consists of medical staff, nursing, HIM, and administrative services. The review includes health record documentation on both open and closed cases, with the total number of records being reviewed at approximately 5 percent of the overall discharges. Elements being evaluated are identified in the Joint Commission standards. Findings must be shared with the healthcare organization's healthcare providers. Problems identified should be corrected, and the healthcare organization must be able to demonstrate how this is done.

Surgical Review

Data collection systems must be developed and used by healthcare organizations to evaluate all operative procedures. Both invasive and noninvasive procedures should be included in this improvement process. All procedures are a potential risk to the patient, and so the appropriateness of the procedure must be determined. The procedures established that have the greatest risk are reviewed closely as part of a **surgical review**. Procedural processes and outcomes need to be addressed. Again, the Joint Commission helps guide the medical staff and healthcare organization in developing a system to measure the use of operative and other procedures. The procedural processes to be measured include:

- Selection of the appropriate procedure
- Patient preparation for the procedure
- Performance of the procedure and patient monitoring
- Postprocedure care
- Postprocedure patient education

Medication Usage Review

Medication use is an important method of treatment in healthcare. Because of the growing number of available medications and the potential for adverse effects, such as short-term side effects, interactions of medications, and toxicity, it is essential that the healthcare organization measure the administration and use of medications as part of a **medication usage review**. Moreover, the healthcare facility should evaluate medication use. Priority is based on:

- Number of patients receiving a medication
- Risk versus therapeutic value
- Known or suspected problem-prone drugs
- Therapeutic effectiveness

In addition, attention should be given to medication processes. Again, the Joint Commission provides guidelines for data collection regarding:

- Ordering or prescribing medications
- Preparing and dispensing medications
- Administrating medications
- Monitoring the effects on patients of medications

Blood and Blood Component Usage Review

Blood and blood components are used to treat patients. Treatment has the potential of offering patients risks as well as benefits. The Joint Commission provides standards to guide the healthcare organization and the medical staff in performing a **blood and blood component usage review**. PI processes should examine the ordering, distribution, handling and dispensing, administration, and monitoring of the effects of blood and blood components. Other considerations include when blood and blood components are ordered but not indicated, when they are indicated but not given, or when they are administered incorrectly.

Mortality Review

A **mortality review** is an important outcome performance measure. Establishing a meaningful evaluation of mortality (death) is essential in the analysis of ongoing outcome and process improvement.

Infection Review

The medical staff and the healthcare organization should work together to provide an environment that reduces the risk of infections in both patients and healthcare providers. The healthcare organization should support activities that look for, prevent, and control infections. An **infection review** is done with the involvement of the medical staff. Information is collected regularly on endemic and epidemic nosocomial infections. As appropriate, the healthcare organization must report significant information to both internal groups and public health agencies.

The organization also must take the necessary steps to prevent and reduce the risk of infection in visitors to the facility. Monitoring should be ongoing, and the healthcare organization should support a process focused on reducing risks and lowering infection trends. Moreover, in today's healthcare environment, processes must be in place to prevent the transmission of disease resulting from bioterrorism activities.

Check Your Understanding 17.4

Instructions: Answer the following questions on a separate piece of paper.

1. Why is it essential to include the licensed, independent medical staff in the healthcare organization's quality improvement program?
2. How do the bylaws/rules and regulations support medical staff involvement in the organization's QI program?
3. How does the credentialing process help ensure the quality of care provided by the healthcare organization?
4. Why is it necessary to do regular reappointment and reappraisals of all members of the medical staff? Who is responsible for making sure this is done?

Nursing Staff Applications

Nursing leadership and nurses providing patient care services are part of the organization's overall quality improvement program. Nursing works with the governing body, medical staff, administration, and other healthcare providers to collect and analyze data, implement changes where necessary, and improve services. Focus is placed on areas where the largest numbers of patients are provided services, where there is the highest risk, or where there are known problems.

Nurses provide the majority of hands-on care. They not only provide direct nursing care but also work closely with other professionals in carrying out treatment plans. Their impact on the patient is all-embracing. Nursing professionals must provide care that is consistent with current literature and meets nationally recognized standards.

Nursing executives and staff must provide the appropriate guidance for all nursing care. Policies and procedures, standards of nursing practice, nursing standards of patient care, and standards to measure, assess, and improve patient outcomes must be defined, documented, available, and used to improve patient care processes. Nurses must work in conjunction with management, the medical staff, and other healthcare providers as part of an organization-wide PI program.

Ancillary Services Applications

All patients should receive information about the care they are provided. Information about how data are collected, used, and evaluated can be incorporated into this message. A number of individuals are involved in the data collection and analysis and system and process redesign. Data may be collected from patients about their experiences by using patient satisfaction surveys. In addition, patients need to be informed of the healthcare organization's process improvement activities.

Case Management

According the Case Management Society of America, **case management** (CM) is a collaborative process of assessment, planning, facilitation and advocacy for options and services to meet an individual's health needs through communication and available resources to promote quality cost-effective outcomes (URAC 2008). As the practice of healthcare delivery becomes more and more complex, finding methods and using tools to promote the efficient and appropriate delivery of healthcare services becomes the core of the treatment process. Additionally, chronic illness is gaining greater attention. In 2005, almost one half of all Americans—133 million people—lived with at least one chronic disease (CDC 2008). The realization is that the managing of chronic illness can improve the quality of life, increase productivity, and increase the activity of a great number of people. Many tools and strategies are used to help manage and coordinate the care of ambulatory or hospitalized patients.

The purpose of CM is to facilitate, coordinate, and follow the care of patients with complex care needs over a period of time. URAC defines case management as a collaborative process of assessment, planning, facilitation, and advocacy for options and services to meet a consumer's health needs through communication and available resources to promote high quality, cost effective outcomes. CM is used by healthcare facilities, hospitals, home care agencies, rehabilitation centers, insurance companies, and health plans. Case managers work to assure that the care and services needed are available at times and places that are most advantageous to the patient, client, or consumer. This role is often looked at from an advocacy perspective and may be especially useful in populations that are considered vulnerable.

Disease Management

The Disease Management Association of America defines **disease management** as "a system of coordinated healthcare interventions and communications for populations with conditions in which patient self-care efforts are significant" (DMAA 2008). Disease management emphasizes the provider-patient relationship in the development and execution of the plan of care, prevention strategies using evidence-based guidelines to limit complications and exacerbations, and evaluation based on outcomes that support improved overall health. Populations that benefit from disease management have chronic conditions with well-established evidence-based protocols. Patients involved are willing to be active participants in their healthcare. Patient education and communication with the healthcare provider are pivotal in the success of this effort. The specific components of disease management are listed in table 17.9.

Utilization Management

Ensuring the appropriate and efficient use of a facility's or health plan's resources is the focus of **utilization management** (UM). Utilization Review Accreditation Commission (URAC) defines utilization management as the evaluation of the medical necessity, appropriateness, and efficiency of the use of healthcare services, procedures, and facilities under the provisions of the applicable health benefits plan (URAC 2008). Utilization management is used in hospital and ambulatory settings. A UM program helps ensure that patients receive appropriate care in an efficient and cost-effective manner. UM programs are required by CMS, the Medicare and Medicaid Conditions of Participation, many state regulations, and managed care plans. Data collected as part of this program offer insight into the quality of care provided.

Utilization Review is a formal review of patient resource use. Data collected during this formal review help determine the appropriateness of the services provided. UR ensures the medical necessity of treatment provided and the cost-effective use of resources and identifies overuse or underuse of available services. Both the federal government and many state regulations require healthcare organizations to have a written UR plan. Although the Joint Commission does not require a written UR plan, it does require that UR incorporate a review of all patients, not just those who are federally funded.

History of Utilization Management

UR was legislated as part of the 1965 amendments to the Social Security Act. The focus of this legislation was on LOS review using physician reviewers. It also initiated medical care evaluation studies or audits. UR affected only federally funded patients until the Joint Commission published standards in the early 1970s. It then was expanded to include at least a sampling of patients with private payment sources.

Utilization Management Staffing

In hospitals, UR coordinators have a variety of backgrounds. RNs have moved into the field successfully because of their clinical backgrounds and rapport with physicians. Health information managers also can be successful in the field because of their knowledge of documentation practices, their clinical backgrounds, and their understanding of reimbursement requirements. UR coordinators must be able to work with physicians and employees of insurance companies and managed care organizations. In addition, they must be able to work with various committee structures and must be active participants on the UM committee.

The UM committee consists of individuals who provide clinical services to patients and those involved in reimbursement. It should include representatives from administration, nursing, HIM, UM, physicians, and others who are thought to play a role in the care and treatment of patients. The composition of the committee should be detailed in the UR plan. The purpose of the committee is to review and evaluate the medical necessity of care provided to patients and the appropriateness of treatment. In addition, the committee may be involved with the QI studies initiated by the QIO.

Table 17.9. Components of disease management

- Population identification process
- Evidence-based practice guidelines
- Collaborative practice models to include physician and support-service providers
- Patient self-management education (primary prevention, behavior modification programs, and compliance and surveillance)
- Process and outcomes measurement, evaluation, and management
- Routine reporting and feedback loop (may include communication with patient, physician, health plan and ancillary providers, and practice profiling)

Source: Disease Management Association of America. http://www.dmaa.org/dm_definition.asp, 2008.

Utilization Management Processes

In actuality, the UR process was implemented slowly. An organization must use screening criteria as a tool to make its determinations. Milliman Care Guidelines, a healthcare consulting organization, publishes the evidence-based guidelines used by many facilities today (Milliman Care Guidelines 2003–2008). These screening guidelines are a collection of best practices in a software package. The guidelines are drawn from a variety of sources providing pathway tables, flagged quality measures, and integrated medical evidence. Rationale for review is determined by the facility and is a part of the UR plan. Several types of review are common in healthcare organizations today (Milliman and Robertson 2008).

Preadmission Review

The preadmission review is done prior to the patient's admission. It is required by most managed care plans. Its purpose is to determine if the admission and procedure are medically necessary and appropriate in an acute care setting. The preadmission review identifies patients who are unsuitable for admission or for a particular procedure and then directs them to the appropriate care setting to obtain healthcare services.

Admission Review

The admission review is done at the time the patient is admitted to the facility. This review is done to determine or verify the medical necessity and appropriateness of admission.

Continued-Stay or Concurrent Review

Continued-stay or concurrent review ensures that the patient is remaining in the facility because of medical necessity and is being treated appropriately. The review ensures that the patient is evaluated at preset intervals to determine the appropriateness of care rendered and that beds are utilized efficiently. The specific interval is commonly tied to the diagnosis and procedure.

Discharge Planning

Discharge planning ensures that a patient is ready for placement in a nonacute setting when he or she leaves the facility. This process often begins either at preadmission or upon admission to ensure that the patient is placed or receives services needed at the time of discharge. Client education is an important part of the discharge planning process. Readiness for discharge is determined by preestablished criteria.

Retrospective Review

Retrospective review is completed after patient discharge. Its purpose is to determine medical necessity and appropriateness of services rendered. When care is determined to have been inappropriate or medically unnecessary, reimbursement is denied. The QIO is responsible for performing retrospective review on federally funded patients. Insurance companies and managed care organizations also do retrospective reviews. Reimbursement can be withdrawn when documentation does not support the medical necessity or appropriateness of care rendered. In addition, retrospective review can help determine problems with overutilization, underutilization, inefficient scheduling of services, and patterns of nonacute days.

Observation care is appropriate for patients with a condition that requires some time to determine whether admission is medically necessary. Various managed care plans have different criteria to determine the appropriate use of observation beds. In any case, care must be taken because the time spent in an observation bed is billed as an outpatient service and may not be covered under the patient's insurance.

Ancillary Services Review

Ancillary services review is tied to ordering, scheduling, and preparation for and performance of various tests and services. Data should be collected to determine whether ancillary services are being used in an efficient and effective manner. QI programs frequently address the appropriate use of ancillary services.

Medicare Review

Medicare review began with introduction of professional standard review organizations (PSROs). PSROs were nonprofit agencies made up of physicians who examined the medical necessity of care. In addition, energy was put into ensuring that the most economical care was rendered to meet the needs of the patient. PSROs introduced the concept of denying payment for care determined to be unnecessary. In addition, quality objectives were introduced to healthcare through the PSROs. Their effectiveness was questioned until their demise in the early 1980s.

TEFRA replaced the PSROs with peer review organizations (PROs). The PRO program was established to ensure that Medicare beneficiaries were provided services that are medically necessary, appropriate, and recognized as meeting professional standards of care. The name PRO was changed to quality improvement organization (QIO) in 2002.

QIOs monitor the appropriateness, effectiveness, and quality of care provided to Medicare beneficiaries. The QIO contracts with CMS to provide specific initiatives during a designated period of time (currently three years). Their current scope of work is focused on quality and safety-related issues, payment error prevention, and other areas. The ninth scope of work involves a shift to three core themes (StratisHealth 2008):

- Beneficiary protection (focus on case review of complaints, denials, certain notices)
- Patient safety (focus on hospitals and nursing homes)
- Prevention (focus on clinics), and two potential projects (improving care coordination across settings of care and preventing and improving care management for chronic kidney disease)

Notices of noncoverage were required by both the PSROs and the PROs and are still a part of the UR process. A notice of noncoverage is required for various situations, including:

- *Preadmission notice of noncoverage:* In this situation, the client is made aware prior to admission that care or services may not be covered or may be obtained at a lesser level of care. The client then is informed that if admission takes place, he or she will be responsible for all charges that result from the stay.
- *Admission notice of noncoverage:* In this situation, the patient is informed that acute care is not required and that he or she will be responsible for charges resulting after a specific grace period (48 hours).
- *Continued-stay notice of noncoverage:* In this situation, the patient is notified that acute care services are no longer required and that he or she will be responsible for charges after a specific grace period (48 hours).

The content and wording of the notices is prescribed by CMS through the QIOs. A policy and procedure regarding these notices must follow the prescribed methodology. The QIO monitors each notice of non-coverage and closely reviews these cases.

External Agency Review

Third- and fourth-party reviewers complete external agency reviews. Reviewers include commercial health insurance companies, managed care plans, and auditors. The focus of the reviews includes resource utilization, quality of care, reimbursement issues, and cases meeting specific criteria, such as readmission within seven days after discharge.

Medicaid Review

The Medicaid program was established by Title XIX of the Social Security Amendments of 1965. Federal money is distributed to each state under a block grant methodology and each state administers disbursement based on federal guidelines. Medicaid reviews differ from state to state. Range of services, qualifying factors, methods of payment, and LOS limitations are handled differently. UR plans also differ from state to state. However, most states do require a prior-approval process for inpatient care and selected outpatient procedures. Retrospective and prospective reviews may be a part of the process. Understanding each state's UR requirements is essential.

Managed Care Review

Managed care plans use UM to keep costs down and quality up. Each managed care plan will have a unique approach to doing UM. Managed care organizations frequently use preadmission certification. Continued-stay review is handled by the managed care organizations collecting information on the acuity and the timeliness of services. The managed care organization will request information both concurrently and retrospectively to determine medical necessity and appropriateness of care. UR coordinators work closely with a variety of managed care organizations to ensure that payment is made for services rendered.

Risk Management

Risk management is a program designed to reduce or prevent injuries and accidents and to minimize or prevent financial loss to the organization. The concept of reducing injuries and accidents has been around for thousands of years. The Code of Hammarabi (400 B.C.) actually addressed the issue of physician liability. When a physician inflicted certain injuries on a patient, punishment for the injuries was prescribed in the code. During the 1970s, the dramatic increase in malpractice claims supported the need for more aggressive management of risk in healthcare organizations. Risk management systems today are sophisticated programs that function to identify, reduce, or eliminate **potentially compensable events** (PCEs), thereby decreasing the financial liability of injuries or accidents to patients, staff, or visitors.

The Joint Commission and other accrediting bodies recommend risk management programs, state and federal laws and regulations give guidance with regard to risk management, and a variety of professional organizations offer professional guidelines that address the importance of risk management. Even third-party payers expect organizations to have systems in place to keep patients, staff, and visitors as safe as possible. Liability insurance carriers require and support an organization's efforts to develop and sustain risk management programs. Policies and procedures addressing risk must be developed and used to control injuries and accidents and to reduce the organization's financial liability.

Risk management policies and procedures are the foundation of managing the risk and quality in any organization. Figure 17.15 demonstrates the variety of information that is collected and used to monitor risk in a healthcare organization. The model provides a glimpse at how complex the risk management can be. Patient safety, the medical record and incident reporting (discussed later) are foundational pieces of this process. Complexity is further heightened by the fact

Figure 17.15 Risk management model

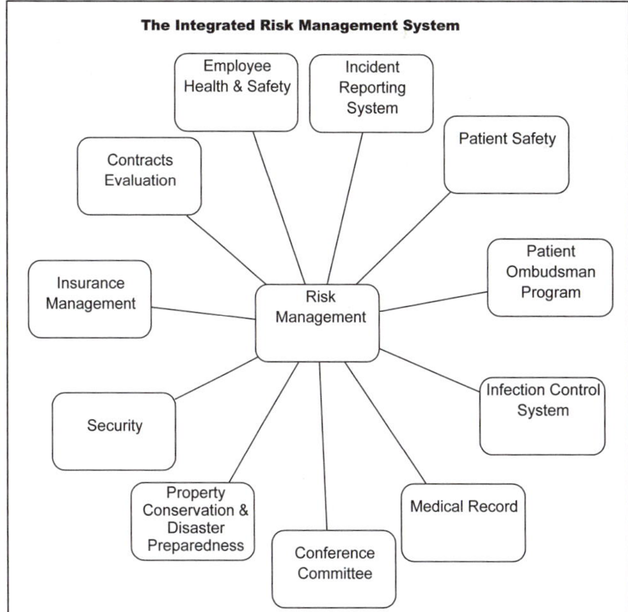

Source: ASHRM 2000, 78.

that collected information needs to be shared with the quality improvement efforts. Clinical and administrative data can be useful in preventing, improving, or identifying areas requiring quality improvement strategies. Collaborative efforts involving risk and quality management personnel will ensure both the safety and quality of patients, staff, and visitors.

Internally, an organization must collect information on injuries and accidents. Incident and event reporting is frequently organized with the help of the insurance carrier. Along with these data, occurrence/generic screening tools can be used to collect data on the risk management of patients. In addition, patient satisfaction surveys, mortality and morbidity reviews, infection control data, patient complaints, hazard reports, and claims management, as well as the development of appropriate policies and procedures to collect and analyze the data, all contribute to the well-being of the organization

The healthcare organization must provide personnel to support the efforts of risk management. This can be accomplished by hiring a risk manager who has adequate authority to make changes as necessary, or these duties can be part of the quality and safety areas of the organization. In either case, it is essential that the organization recognize the need to collect and analyze data, make changes, and improve current facility systems and to do so in conjunction with current efforts to improve the quality of care.

Risk Management Processes

For a risk management program to be successful, it must include certain processes. **Loss prevention** is a risk control strategy that includes developing and revising policies and procedures that are both facility-wide and department specific. It also involves educating staff, including medical personnel, healthcare executives, volunteers, and employees. Credentialing activities must be thorough. Compliance must be assured with federal, state, and accrediting bodies' standards, laws, and regulations. Complete and thorough patient education must be provided.

Another component of a successful risk management program is **loss reduction**. Loss reduction encompasses techniques used to manage events or claims that have already taken place. Ways to reduce losses incurred include:

- Investigating reported incidents or addressing occurrence reports promptly
- Reviewing claims made against the facility
- Managing workers' compensation programs
- Being knowledgeable about alternate dispute resolution processes
- Treating employee injuries on-site
- Implementing back-to-work programs
- Assisting with depositions or other pretrial activities
- Working closely with defense counsel

Another component of a successful risk management program is **risk prevention**. Some of the ways that risk prevention can be attained include:

- Educating all employees and medical staff to recognize and properly report all potentially adverse occurrences
- Ensuring that all employees and medical staff are doing their jobs to the best of their ability
- Developing early warning and reporting systems that identify areas of potential adverse effect
- Creating databases to track events and help point out areas where systems can be improved
- Making changes to systems requiring improvement and monitoring these areas to determine success
- Providing employees with appropriate safety training

In the name of patient safety, open disclosure policies are being adopted in many healthcare organizations. There is a strong call for greater transparency. Public disclosure of information is no longer kept behind locked doors as readily. With open disclosure policies healthcare organization and providers are admitting their mistakes, demonstrating the need to improve and apologizing to their customers. The result is a culture of greater credibility for the population served by the healthcare organization.

Risk Management Reporting Tools

Several areas require special mention because they are basic tools in an effective risk management program.

Incident Report Review

Incident report review is a process in which incident reports are analyzed or descriptions of adverse events are evaluated. Common examples include needle sticks; patient, employee, or visitor falls; and medication errors. Reviewing incident reports and developing a database of incidents with report capability can help identify patterns or trends that signal potential adverse events. (Refer to figure 17.15.)

Occurrence/Generic Screening

Occurrence/generic screening is a methodology where predefined criteria are used to review medical records to find cases that may indicate adverse patient outcomes. These criteria are not disease or procedure specific. Rather, they are generic in focus and include items such as whether an informed consent was signed, whether the patient was returned to the operating room, whether hospital-acquired infections were noted, and whether there was a failure to respond to significant x-ray or laboratory results.

Safety Programs

Every organization must have a safety program in place to focus on the environmental concerns of patient care. Fire, radioactive materials, and air quality are examples of areas addressed in a safety program. Federal and state laws require safety programs and accrediting bodies to have standards that address safety. Safety and risk are closely linked and data should be shared. (Refer to figure 17.15.)

Internal and External Disaster Preparedness Programs

An **emergency preparedness** program addresses disasters and emergency situations both inside and outside the healthcare organization. The September 11, 2001, tragedy involving the World Trade Center and the Pentagon created new challenges for this program. Management plans the response to crisis situations. The organization must have protocols on how patients will be treated, admitted, and discharged. The plan must be developed in cooperation with agencies and organizations within the community. All entities responding to emergency situations must be ready to work together to handle any type of disaster—fire, flood, hurricane have all occurred in the recent past. Natural disasters, such as Katrina, have had a devastating impact on patient care for thousands. Health information was lost, destroyed or otherwise made unavailable for hospitalized and ambulatory patients alike. Additionally, everyone working within organizations—hospitals and provider office practices—must be trained to respond to emergency and disaster situations.

The emergency preparedness plan must address certain areas, for example, how the organization will address the need for backup utilities, communication systems, and radioactive and chemical decontamination and isolation. Personnel must know their roles and responsibilities in a crisis situation. Practice sessions, also called disaster drills, should be held to help personnel react appropriately. Whether the emergency is internal or external to the organization, the appropriate policies and procedures need to be in place and well understood by the organization's personnel to ensure that the response is timely and meaningful.

Informed Consent Review

Healthcare organizations deal with many liability issues, including ensuring that clients understand and agree to treatment through the informed consent processes. Consent can be given either orally or in writing (expressed consent). It also may be implied through the actions or circumstances of the client's behavior.

Appropriate informed consent is one in which the client or patient acknowledges his or her understanding of the nature of the treatment or procedure to be performed. In addition, he or she must understand the risks, benefits, and alternatives to the treatment or procedure. The informed consent process involves an exchange of information between the healthcare provider and the patient or client, along with permission or assent. Failure to obtain informed consent can result in liability issues for both the healthcare organization and the healthcare provider. See chapter 8 for additional discussion of informed consent.

Sentinel Event Review

The Joint Commission's Sentinel Event Policy went into effect in 1998. Its purpose was to improve the quality of care. A **sentinel event** is an unexpected occurrence involving death or serious physical or psychological injury, or the risk thereof. Serious injury is defined as the loss of a limb or function. Events are deemed sentinel because they signal the need for immediate investigation and response. Examples of clinical events needing this kind of response are significant medication errors, significant adverse drug reactions, and confirmed transfusion reactions.

The organization may need to perform an intense analysis when the following occur:

- Patterns, trends, or variations of performance are significant or unexpected
- Performance differs significantly from performance in other, similar facilities
- Performance varies significantly from accepted standards
- A sentinel event occurs

Policies and procedures must be in place to respond to a sentinel event (Joint Commission 2009a).

When a sentinel event occurs, organizational leadership must support the process of investigation, analysis, and improvement. The expectation is that the organization will respond to all sentinel events. **Root-cause analysis** is the process used to identify the cause of the event. The organization looks for ways to decrease the likelihood of such an event happening again. The focus should be on organizational and clinical systems and processes, not on the person or people involved in the sentinel event.

Root-cause analysis examines both the clinical and administrative reasons for the event. After data collection and analysis, the organization should develop an action plan and move to make improvements in order to make such future events as unlikely as possible. The focus of the Joint Commission's survey process will be on how the organization has handled the sentinel event.

An organization is encouraged (but not required) to report sentinel events to the Joint Commission. A root-cause analysis and an action plan must be completed regardless. Healthcare organizations reporting a sentinel event can benefit by having an outside, objective third party review their action plan and by obtaining consultation as needed. In addition, the organization should show the public a sincere effort to remedy problems and for improvement.

Check Your Understanding 17.5

Instructions: Answer the following questions on a separate piece of paper.

1. What do utilization review and utilization management contribute to quality of care?
2. How do the different types of review (for example, preadmission, admission, continued stay, and discharge planning) support medical necessity, appropriateness of services, and length of stay review?
3. How does the notice of noncoverage affect the denial of reimbursement?
4. How does risk management contribute to the overall quality improvement program?
5. How do sentinel event policy and root-cause analysis contribute to the quality of care provided to patients?

Integration of Comparative Data into Clinical Quality Management

The Joint Commission and the nation's QIOs have developed performance measures requiring regular data collection. In addition, the healthcare organization needs to develop its own performance measures. Performance measures frequently are built around the categories of efficiency, effectiveness, safety, timeliness, and quality. Determining what data collection techniques will meet the needs of the QI process, which data displays and reporting methods are most effective, what to consider when analyzing and interpreting data, and how to affect systems and processes with meaningful changes all need to be considered. (Chapter 22 addresses the tools and techniques of PI. Those tools can be applied to clinical quality improvement.)

Data Collection and Reporting Techniques

To collect the required data, performance measures must be developed or identified that focus on the correct data elements. Clinical measures need to be detailed, diagnosis and procedure specific (usually), focused on process or outcome (most commonly), and selected by high-volume, high-risk, or known problems. It is necessary to determine what you want to know and how you can report it in numbers. The data can be reported as either meeting the element (for example, 98 percent of patients were free of infection) or not meeting the element (for example, 2 percent of the patients experienced infection). Each data element collected must be clearly defined, clearly understood, and agreed on by everyone involved in the data collection process. This helps ensure that the data collected support what the organization wants to know.

The scope of performance measurement activities requires clarity. The important areas of service are usually based on volume, risk, or known problem. The population targeted must be clearly identified and defined, and the sample size must be representative and allow for valid and reliable statistical measurement. (See chapters 16 and 18.) Descriptions of the raw data and data sources must be identified precisely so that everyone understands what the data elements will tell them. The medical record remains as the main data source.

It also is important to identify who will be involved in collecting and assessing the data, determining improvements, and performing ongoing evaluation. Data gathering is frequently done using forms, check sheets, surveys, questionnaires, or computer screens using database or spreadsheet applications as the tool to maintain consistency and accuracy. Further, it is necessary to determine how often data will be collected (daily, weekly, or monthly) and whether they will be collected concurrently or retrospectively and for how long.

Data displays need to be functional and credible and must meet the needs of reviewers. It is important to remember that effective data displays are visual supports that allow reviewers to understand data at a glance. Likewise, it is important to keep the data display simple by emphasizing no more than one or two points. Avoid spreadsheets or data summaries that are complex and overwhelming. Data display tools include, but are not limited to, pie charts, histograms, scatter charts, line charts, and bar graphs. (Refer to chapter 15.)

Narrative data also can be used effectively. Narrative information can address performance goals, data sources, and data collection procedures.

Data Analysis and Interpretation

The analysis and interpretation of data demonstrates whether a performance measure is being met. Changes plotted over time can answer questions about whether systems are doing what they are intended to do or whether they require change. Analysis and interpretation can help point out what change will have the most impact. The HIM professional and others involved in the QI activity can work together to use the displayed information to improve patient care. The HIM professional can be instrumental in ensuring that the data collected and displayed are accurate and truthfully represent actual performance (Spath and Hale 2003, 3–5).

The QI activities follow a problem-solving process of access, measure, analyze, and improve. Determining the best way to effect change can be challenging. Langley et al. (1996) recommend a combination of a thorough understanding of the current system or process, creative thinking, and use of improved technology, when possible. Some ideas for developing creative thinking include:

- Know current boundaries before making changes
- Rearrange the steps of the process
- Look for ways to level the current flow of tasks or activities
- Challenge why you are doing the QI activity
- Describe what would be ideal
- Do not allow the current process to continue

Different techniques can be used to improve the patient care process. Traditional approaches include training or education of personnel and administrative changes such as decreasing wait times, more thorough credentialing, and working closely with risk management to decrease liability.

Results Reporting and Follow-up

Because QI is an organization-wide effort, reporting lines must be clear and direct. Reporting begins with a hospital and medical staff committee or some other organizational unit such as infection control, safety, or utilization management and follows a clear and defined route. It is essential that communication be thorough and complete. The QI plan must delineate how reporting will flow through the organization. All levels of the organization must know that results will be shared throughout the organization.

After changes are made to improve systems or processes, there must be a way to determine whether the change was meaningful. This involves determining what needs to be known and selecting a few data elements that will give that information. If the changes have been successful, it may be necessary to either reduce the frequency of review for this performance measure or make an alternative change if no significant improvement can be identified.

For a quality management program to be effective, the risk management, safety, and disaster programs must work in conjunction with the QI program. Data collected to meet the needs of the different programs designed to keep patients, staff, and visitors safe and to allow response to community needs must be shared to benefit the overall organization. Developing methods for reporting and evaluating the results of the different programs and systems is a complex, continuous challenge. Results from any of the above areas can give an indication of high-quality care or point out areas requiring improvement or change.

Data Security and Confidentiality

The confidentiality and security of QI data must be addressed through effective policies and procedures. QI information must move through the organization's communication systems and yet be protected. State statutes may be used to help develop policies that are supported by legislation. Peer review activities are addressed by legislation in every state. Data must be kept in a secure environment, and access to the data must be carefully delineated and supported by statute whenever possible. Release of QI information must be handled in accordance with statutes, policies and procedures, and medical staff bylaws/rules and regulations.

Use of Computer-based Comparative Data

The computerization of healthcare data can offer healthcare providers, regulators, and payers a wealth of administrative and clinical information. Going back to Codman's pioneering work, it was recognized that good data can lead to the discovery of improved treatment practices (Neuhauser 2002; Millenson 1999). Then, beginning with the IOM's *To Err Is Human* (2000) and continuing through its 2003 report, *Priority Areas for National Action: Transforming Health Care Quality,* it was recognized that the need to collect, analyze, and distribute large quantities of data will help transform healthcare to a standard of best practice/best evidence. Computerization of data will enhance the ability to bridge the gap between best-evidence-based practice and actual practice.

The use of computerized data allows comparison of actual practice to best practice (benchmarking) and is critical to both regulatory and accreditation processes. The enormous volume of data has not prevented continued efforts to try and use the data effectively. The Joint Commission's ORYX initiative relies on the review of data trends and patterns to determine where to focus survey efforts. The Joint Commission-accredited organizations are encouraged to review their own data against data from similar organizations to determine their own PI opportunities. CMS is working with the Joint Commission to evaluate quality of care on designated diagnoses. Both the Joint Commission and CMS will utilize data submitted by organizations to analyze professional practice. This will give them information on whether an organization is exemplary, average, or substandard, which then gives focus for improvement opportunities and expectations. CMS is currently providing financial incentives to healthcare providers for submitting and publicly reporting their quality performance data to comply with the MMA.

Other computerized information systems are either available or under development. The true benefits of computers are their tireless ability to cross-check information and provide user feedback. Computerized physician order entry (CPOE) has received much attention in helping to reduce medication errors. More research is being done in this area to advance the safety of patients receiving healthcare services. Pharmacies also have gone to a variety of systems such as robotic medication distribution and bar-coding systems that help keep patients safe from receiving the wrong medication or wrong dosage. Alerts for drug interactions, smart systems that give clues to evidence-based practice, also will give necessary information to practitioners on the front lines. It is increasingly clear that insufficient access to, or management of, information plays a substantial role in the causes of medical errors. Further, physicians rarely recall *all* standards of care that can apply to a patient, especially in the time-limited, encounter-focused format based on patient complaint (Roland and Kannan 2003, 37).

The federal government is playing an instrumental role in accelerating the development and use of an electronic health record (EHR), and President Bush has stated on several occasions the need to develop one. The first annual National Healthcare Quality Report (NHQR) stated that as a nation we are making progress. Key findings included (AHQR 2003):

- High-quality healthcare is not yet a universal reality.
- Opportunities for preventive care are frequently missed.
- There is more to learn.
- Greater improvement is possible.

Former President Bush named David Brailer, MD, PhD, as the national coordinator for health information technology. Dr. Brailer is working to develop EHR systems that will enable physicians and other health professionals to electronically tap into a wealth of treatment information to better care for patients. Four major goals have been identified by federal leadership. They are (Rose 2004, 15–17):

Goal 1: Inform Clinical Practice—Information tools at point of care

Goal 2: Interconnect Clinicians—Interoperable health information infrastructure providing access to critical information

Goal 3: Personalize Care—Give consumers more access to and involvement in making health decisions

Goal 4: Improve Population Health—Expand public health monitoring, quality of care measurement and bring research advances into medical practice

The federal legislative process continues to spawn bills related to technology and healthcare quality. In 2005, the following legislative efforts were introduced: the Information Technology for Health Care Quality Act, the Patient Safety and Quality Improvement Act, the National Health Information Incentive Act, the 21st Century Health Information Act, and the Health Technology to Enhance Quality Act. Many of these legislative efforts are directed at promoting the adoption of standards, interoperability, and government funding to help support the move to electronic health information. Watching developments in this direction should be of great interest to healthcare organizations.

It is unequivocally believed that health information technology can improve care quality, reduce medical errors, and lower administrative costs.

Healthcare is an information-intense process. It is unfortunate that patient records and methods used to move information along the continuum of care have remained virtually stagnant. Electronic health information has unknown potential, yet little of it has been realized in today's healthcare environment (Kizer 2004b, 1). As we plan for the future by developing standards at the national, regional, and local levels, we must remember that computerized data must be kept in a secure environment. Passwords, fingerprints, retinal scans, and limited access are basic security features used to protect QI data. (The handling of computerized information is addressed thoroughly in chapters 2 and 5.) Adapting security and confidentiality practices for general computerized information is essential.

Public Reporting of Performance Data

Many feel that as healthcare becomes more transparent the ability to improve systems will be more completely accepted. AHRQ promotes public reporting as one more strategy to advance the quality improvement agenda in healthcare. Other organizations that support public reporting include the National Quality Forum, Ambulatory Care Quality Alliance, and the Hospital Quality Alliance.

Using measures to compare healthcare results are being developed or remodeled to fill this need. Again, AHRQ has Quality Indicators available to healthcare organizations. The measures were not developed for comparison purposes, but AHRQ is continually reviewing and improving the measures as well as providing information about how to best use their Quality Indicators for comparability. In addition, AHRQ has a Web site devoted to Talking Quality to consumers. The site has a compendium of more than 200 health plans, hospitals, medical groups, individual physicians, nursing homes, and other providers of care.

Data is being reported publicly in several venues. The government through the Medicare and Medicaid programs is making data on organizations available on their Hospital Compare Web site. (The Joint Commission has information available to the public on their Quality Check Web site. In addition, many state health departments have Web sites devoted to reporting hospital adverse events and hospital comparisons.)

Little research has been completed on the impact of public reporting, but C. Fung, et al. reports in the Annuals of Internal Medicine that evidence suggests that public reporting of performance data stimulates quality improvement activity at the hospital level. There is virtually nothing indicating the effect on direct patient care providers and practices. There is also no definite effect of public reporting on effectiveness, safety, and patient-centeredness (IOM 2001).

Influence of Information Technology on Quality and Data

The use of technology is indisputably at a high point within the U.S. healthcare system. In reality that technological advancement is in respect to diagnostic and treatment options, not necessarily in the use of information technology (IT). It has been only in the last several years that information technology has begun to flourish. In the March 2008 NQF Issue Brief, Paul Tang, MD asks "Wouldn't it be wonderful if the same data collected during the care process could be used automatically to trigger clinical decision support reminders and later aggregated and de-identified to appear in quality-measurement reports?" (NQF 2008). Performance measurement and information technology are made for each other in many respects.

The IOM, NQF, Joint Commission, NCQA and others support the use of IT and performance measurement especially in regard to patient safety issues. Applications such as computerized physician order entry, e-prescribing, computer generated alert systems, and clinical decision support systems reduce the number of errors, improve adherence to evidence-based practice guidelines, and thus improve healthcare delivery to patients. Further research is necessary to determine the true impact on patient outcomes. But most researchers believe it is not much of a leap from making patients safer to improved outcomes. Nearly every hospital in the United States reports on performance measurement data. Once IT and quality truly merge comparisons between organizations and providers will take on new meaning.

One of the beauties of marrying quality and IT is that IT requires use of standardization. It is through standardization of terms and technical specifications plus cooperation of the multiple parties involved in the care and safety of patients that better quality data will emerge. Most of the quality dataset needed for measuring performance consists of the same data necessary for clinical decision support systems. These datasets need to be developed and nurtured together so standardization can link the information for use at the level of direct patient care and performance measures. With better data made readily available through IT, HIM professionals can more accurately evaluate the quality of care provided in the United States.

Check Your Understanding 17.6

Instructions: Answer the following questions on a separate piece of paper.

1. Why is it necessary to clearly define performance measures, criteria, and data elements used in data collection?
2. What is the main source of data?
3. Explain how quality management, utilization management, risk management, and patient safety are interrelated.
4. Why must quality improvement data be kept confidential?
5. What are three ways in which an electronic health record will improve the quality of patient care?
6. What impact could poor communication practices have on a quality improvement program?

Summary

In the twentieth century, the American College of Surgeons paved the quality improvement (QI) road by establishing standards of care. In the last half of the twentieth century, the Joint Commission and other accrediting bodies have clearly led the way in developing modern QI initiatives. The federal government, through the Medicare Conditions of Participation and quality improvement organizations (QIOs), also has contributed to the development of high-quality patient care. In addition, judicial decisions have made, and will continue to make, significant progress toward improving healthcare.

Every healthcare organization has its own version of quality. In general, however, the attributes of quality must be both administrative and clinical in nature and involve both the medical and facility staff. The organization's focus should be on customer satisfaction, professional standards of care, and process and system performance. The organization must collect and analyze data and use the results to make improvements in its processes and systems and in the healthcare it provides. Instituting a methodology of performance improvement will bring ordered change and improve the quality of healthcare.

Numerous QI methodologies have been used over the years, beginning with the medical care evaluation audit. The Joint Commission has introduced several methodologies and is currently moving toward a data-driven, continuous accreditation process. Other accrediting organizations have developed methodologies that require assessing, measuring, and improving the quality of healthcare. Outcomes management practice guidelines are examples of techniques frequently used in healthcare to help ensure that patients receive high-quality care.

The medical staff must be a part of the organization's QI efforts. The QI process begins with a well-functioning credentialing process to ensure that the medical staff is qualified to perform requested clinical privileges. The medical staff's bylaws/rules and regulations must support the QI processes. Medical staff leadership is critical when evaluating clinical processes as part of the PI program. Moreover, the QI processes in any organization include a variety of programs.

The utilization management function contributes to high-quality healthcare by providing information on how effectively and efficiently the organization's resources are being used. Risk management contributes to patient safety by directly linking known risks to improving patient care. Use of generic criteria to monitor patient care helps to identify areas of risk, which enables the organization to be proactive in preventing or reducing injuries and accidents. The emergency preparedness program and safety programs also contribute to the quality of care.

Today, accrediting agencies, government agencies, and healthcare organizations use performance measures. Collecting information to evaluate an organization's processes is critical to improving the care the organization provides patients. Using effective data analysis and interpretation techniques helps determine whether the processes are effective.

Making meaningful changes is a constant challenge. Communicating performance measurement information to all parties who may benefit is difficult. Healthcare in the United States today is a highly technical, complex environment. All who practice in this environment must be aware of the need to continuously improve the processes and systems with which they work to achieve the quality and cost-effectiveness challenges facing the U.S. healthcare system.

References

Abdelhak, M., S. Grostick, M.A. Hanken, and E. Jacobs. 2001. *Health Information: Management of a Strategic Resource*. 2nd ed. Philadelphia: W.B. Saunders.

Agency for Healthcare Research and Quality. 2000. Fact Sheet: Outcomes Research. http://www.ahrq.gov/clinic/outfact.htm.

Agency for Healthcare Research and Quality. 2000 (July). *Quality of Care.* http://www.ahrq.gov.

Agency for Healthcare Research and Quality. 2001 (March). Reducing and preventing adverse drug events to decrease hospital costs. In *Research in Action 1.* AHRQ Publication No. 010020. Rockville, MD: AHRQ.

Agency for Healthcare Research and Quality. 2003 (March). Fact sheet: CAHPS and the National CAHPS benchmarking database. http://www.ahrq.gov.

Agency for Healthcare Research and Quality. 2003. *National Healthcare Quality Report* http://www.ahrq.gov/qual/nhqr03/nhqr03.htm

Agency for Healthcare Research and Quality. 2004 (July). HCUP Quality Indicators Archive. AHRQ Quality Indicators. Rockville, MD:AHRQ. http://222.qualityindicators.ahrq.gov/hcup_archive.htm.

Agency for Healthcare Research and Quality. 2004 (Aug.). *Closing the Quality Gap: A Critical Analysis of Quality Improvement Strategies.* Vol. 1 in *Series Overview and Methodology,* Technical Review. AHRQ Publication No. 04-0051-1. Rockville, MD: AHRQ.

Agency for Healthcare Research and Quality. 2005 (March). Fact sheet: Tools for hospitals and health care systems. AHRQ Publication No. 05-P016. Rockville, MD: AHRQ.

Agency for Healthcare Research and Quality. 2005. Health Care Report Compendium. http://www.talkingqulaity.gov/compendium.

Agency for Healthcare Research and Quality. 2005 (Jan.). Hypertension Care, Quality Improvement. http://www.ahrq.gov.

Agency for Healthcare Research and Quality. 2006a. Fact Sheet: Databases and Related Tools from the Healthcare Cost and Utilization Project (HCUP)–Update. AHRQ Pub No. 06-PO22. http://www.ahrq.gov.

Agency for Healthcare Research and Quality. 2006b. Fact Sheet: Inpatient Quality Indicators.http://www.qualityindicators.ahrq.gov/documentation.htm.

Agency for Healthcare Research and Quality. 2006c. *The Patient Safety and Quality Improvement Act of 2005.* http://www.ahrq.gov/qual/psoact.htm.

Agency for Healthcare Research and Quality. 2007. Evidence-based Practice Centers. http://www.ahrq.gov/clinic/epc.

Agency for Healthcare Research and Quality. 2008a. Surgical errors cost nearly $1.5 billion annually. *Research Activities.* No.337.1

Agency for Healthcare Research and Quality. 2008b. Patient Safety Organizations. http:www.pso.ahrq.gov.psos/overview.htm.

Agency for Healthcare Research and Quality. 2008c. CAHPS Hospital Survey. http://cahps.ahrq.gov.

Agency for Healthcare Research and Quality. 2008d. Evidence-based Practice Centers. http://www.ahrq.gov/clinic/epc/

American College of Medical Quality. 2005. *Core Curriculum for Medical Quality Management.* Sudbury, MA: Jones and Bartlett.

American Society for Healthcare Risk Management of the American Hospital Association. 2000. Risk Management Program Development Tool Kit, sample excerpt. http://www.ashrm.org/ashrm/samples/RMProgdev ToolKitSample.pdf, 12.

APR DRG Software–3M. 2008. http://solutions.3m.com.

Arrichiello, L. 2000. *HEDIS 101.* St. Paul, MN: Blue Cross/Blue Shield of Minnesota.

Berwick, D., A. Godfrey, and J. Roessner. 1991. *Curing Health Care: New Strategies for Quality Improvement.* San Francisco, CA: Josey-Bass Publishers.

Brandt, M. 1994. Clinical practice guidelines and critical paths: Roles of HIM professionals. *Journal of AHIMA* 65(2):54–59.

Bridges to Excellence. 2007. Overview, Mission, Rewarding quality across the healthcare system. http://www.bridgestoexcellence.org.

CAHPS. 2007: Program Brief: Assessing Health Care Quality from the Patients Perspective. http://www.cahps.ahrq.gove/content/cahpsOverview/0CAHPS-ProgramBrief.htm.

Candler General Hospital, Inc. v. Persaud, 212 GA App. 762, 442 S.E.2d 775 (1994).

Centers for Disease Control and Prevention. 2008 (March). Chronic Disease Overview. http://www.cdc.gov/NCCdphp/overview.htm.

Centers for Medicare and Medicaid Services. 2003. Quality Assessment Final Rule (42 CRF 482.21). http://www.cms.hhs.gov/CFCsAndCoPs/downloads/finalpatientrightsrule.pdf.

Centers for Medicare and Medicaid Services. 2005a (Jan.). Medicare begins performance-based payments for physician groups. http://www.cms.hhs.gov/researchers/demos/pgp.asp.

Centers for Medicare and Medicaid Services. 2005b. Medicare Program: Solicitation for Proposals for the Medicare Health Care Quality Demonstration Programs. Medicare Health Care Quality Demonstration System Redesign Incentives Leading to Improved Quality of Care. http://www.cms.hhs.gov/researchers/demos/mma646/SOLICITATION_09_07_2005.pdf.

Centers for Medicare and Medicaid Services. 2008a. Changes to the Hospital Inpatient Prospective Payment Systems and Fiscal year 2008 Rates. *Federal Register* 72 (162).

Centers for Medicare and Medicaid Services. 2008b. CMS/Premier Hospital Quality Incentive Demonstration Project: Project Overview and Finding from Year One. http://www.cms.hhs.gov/medicare.

Centers for Medicare and Medicaid Services. 2008c. CMS/Premier Hospital Quality Incentive Demonstration Project: Project Overview and Finding from Year Two. http://www.cms.hhs.gov/medicare.

Centers for Medicare and Medicaid Services. 2008d. Electronic Prescribing Incentive Fact Sheet: Introduction to e-Prescribing Incentive. http://www.cms.hhs.gov/EPrescribing.

Centers for Medicare and Medicaid Services. 2008e. HCAHPS Facts. http://www.cms.hhs.gov.

Centers for Medicare and Medicaid Services. 2008f. Quality Improvement Organizations: Statement of Work. http://www.cms.hhs.gov/Quality Improvement.

Centre for Evidence-Based Medicine. 2008. http://www.cebm.net/?o=1014 Orgs/04_9thsow.asp.

Cerner Corporation. 2005. White Paper: The APACHE IV Equations: Benchmarks for Mortality and Resource Use. http://www.cerner.org.

Crosby, P.B. 1979. *Quality Is Free: The Art of Making Quality Certain.* New York: Penguin Books.

Darling v. Charleston Community Memorial Hospital, 33 IL 2d 326 (1965).

Department of Health and Human Services. 2005. Hospital Compare: Hospital Care Quality Measures. http://www.hospitalcompare.hhs.gov/Hospital/Static/About-HospQuality.asp?dest=NAV|Home|About|Quality Measures#TabTop.

Department of Health and Human Services. *Federal Register* 42 CFR Part 3: Patient Safety and Quality Improvement; Proposed Rule. http://www.hhs.gov.

Disease Management Association of America. 2008. http://dmaa.org.

Donabedian, A. 1980. *Exploration in Quality Assessment and Monitoring.* Vol. 1: *The Definition of Quality and Approaches to Its Assessment.* Ann Arbor, MI: Health Administration Press.

Eckes, G. 2003. *Six Sigma for Everyone.* Hoboken, NJ: John Wiley and Sons.

Edgman-Levitan S., D. Shaller, K. McInnes, R. Joyce, K.L. Coltin, and P.D. Cleary. 2003. The CAHPS Improvement Guide: Practical Strategies for Improving the Patient Care Experience. CMS contract No. 500-95-0057. http://www.caphs.ahrq.gov.

Elliott, C., P. Shaw, P. Isaacson, and E. Murphy. 2000. *Performance Improvement in Healthcare: A Tool for Programmed Learning.* Chicago: AHIMA.

Ellwood, P.M. 1988. Shattuck Lecture: Outcomes management: A technology of patient experience. *New England Journal of Medicine* 23(9):1549–1556.

Frankel, A., E. Graydon-Baker, C. Neppi, T. Simmonds, M..Gustafson, and T.K. Gandhi. 2003. Patient safety leadership walkrounds. *Joint Commission Journal on quality and Safety* 29(1):16–26.

Gassiot, C., V. Searcy, and C. Giles. 2007. *The Medical Staff Services Handbook: Fundamentals and Beyond.* Sudbury, MA: Jones and Bartlett Publishers.

Goedert, J. 2004 (April). Crunching data: The key to Six Sigma success. *Health Data Management* 12(4):44–48.

Gonzales v. Nork and Mercy Hospital, 20 CA 3d 500 (1978).

Governance Institute. 2000. *The Board's Role in Monitoring Quality.* Washington, D.C.: Governance Institute.

Graham, O.N., ed. 1995. *Quality in Health Care: Theory, Application, and Evaluation.* Gaithersburg, MD: Aspen.

Guidelines for reporting hospital quality data. 2004. *Clinician Review* 14(3):46.

Healthcare Cost and Utilization Project, Nationwide Inpatient Sample. 2004 (June 9). Overview of disease severity measures. http://www.hcup-us.ahrq.gov/db/nation/nis/OverviewofSeveritySystems.pdf.

Health Grades. 2008a. About Us. http://www.healthgrades.com/about-us.

Health Grades. 2008b. Frequently Asked Questions. http://www.healthgrades.com.

Hjort, B. 2005. Practice Brief: The HIM Role in patient safety and quality of care. *Journal of AHIMA.* 76(1):56a–56g.

Hospital Compare. 2005. United States Department of Health and Human Services. http://www.hospitalcompare.hhs.gov/Hospital/Static/Data-Professionals.asp?dest=NAV.

Hospital Compare. 2008a. Hospital Quality Overview. http://www.hospitalcompare.hhs.gov/Hospital/Static/ConsumerInformation_tabset.asp.

Hospital Compare. 2008b. Hospital Process of Care Measures. http://www.hospital compare.hhs.gov/Hospital/Static/ConsumerInformation_tabset.asp.

Hospital Compare. 2008c. Hospital Outcome of Care Measures. http://www.hospital compare.hhs.gov/Hospital/Static/ConsumerInformation_tabset.asp.

Hospital Quality Alliance. 2007. Measure Build Out Table. http://www.hospitalqualityalliance.org.

Hospital Quality Alliance. 2008. Improving Care through Information. http://www.hospitalqualityalliance.org.

Hughes, Gwen. 2003. Practice brief: Using benchmarking for performance improvement. *Journal of AHIMA* 74(2):64A–D.

Institute for Clinical Systems Improvement. 2008a. Creating Patient-Centered and Value Driven Care: 2007 Annual Report. http://www.icsi.org.

Institute for Clinical Systems Improvement. 2008b. Health Care Guidelines: Otitis Media in Children, Diagnosis and Treatment of (Guideline). http://www.icsi.org/guidelines.

Institute of Medicine. 2000. *To Err Is Human: Building a Safer Health System.* Washington, D.C.: National Academy Press.

Institute of Medicine. 2003. *Priority Areas for National Action: Transforming Health Care Quality.* http://www.nap.edu/topics.php?topic=392&offset=30.

Institute of Medicine. 2005 (Dec.). Report Brief: Performance Measurement: Accelerating Improvement. http://www.nap.edu.

Institute of Medicine. 2006 (July). Report Brief: Preventing Medication Errors. http://www.nap.edu.

Institute of Medicine, Committee on Quality of Health Care in America. 2001. *Crossing the Quality Chasm: A New Health System for the 21st Century.* Washington, D.C.: National Academy Press.

Insinga v. LaBella FL, 543 So.2d 209 (1989).

Johnson v. Misericordia Community Hospital, 99 WI 2d 708 (1981).

Joint Commission. 1988. *The Joint Commission Guide to Quality Assurance.* Oakbrook Terrace, IL: Joint Commission.

Joint Commission. 1996. *When Bad Things Happen to Good Health Care Organizations: Meeting the Joint Commission Sentinel Event Policy Requirements Leaders Guide, Part 1.* Oakbrook Terrace, IL: Joint Commission.

Joint Commission. 2002 (March 18). A Comprehensive Review of Development and Testing for National Implementation of Hospital Core Measures.

Joint Commission. 2004. The Joint Commission announces the 2005 National Patient Safety goals and requirements. *Joint Commission Perspectives* 24(8): 1–3.

Joint Commission. 2008a. Facts about Quality Check and Quality Reports. http://www.jointcommission.org/QualityCheck.

Joint Commission. 2008b. Facts about the 2008 National Patient Safety Goals. http://www.jointcommission.org/Patient Safety.

Joint Commission. 2008c. Patient Safety: Our Commitment to Patient Safety. http://www.jointcommision.org/General Public/Patient Safety.

Joint Commission. 2008d. Facts about Speak Up Initiatives. http://www.jointcommission.org/GeneralPublic/Speak+Up/about_speakup.htm.

Joint Commission. 2008e. ORYX Risk Adjustment Guide. http://www.jointcommission.org.

Joint Commission. 2008f. Performance Measurement Initiatives. http://www.jointcommission.org.

Joint Commission. 2008g. Joint Commission Fact Sheets. Facts about the Periodic Performance Review. http://www.jointcommission.org.

Joint Commission. 2008h. Performance Measurement System Requirements for ORYX Listing Core, Core Test, and Non-Core Measure Implementation. http://www.jointcommission.org/PerformanceMeasurement/PerformanceMeasurementSystems/comm_guidelines_08.htm

Joint Commission. 2008i. Facts about ORYX for Hospitals. http://www.jointcommission.org.

Joint Commission. 2008j. Improving America's Hospitals: The Joint Commission's Annual Report on quality and Safety. http://www.jointcommissionreport.org.

Joint Commission. 2008k. A Journey Through the History of the Joint Commission. http://www.jointcommission.org/AboutUs/joint_commission_history.htm#1917.

Joint Commission. 2009a. *Comprehensive Accreditation Manual for Hospitals: The Official Handbook.* Oakbrook Terrace. IL: Joint Commission.

Joint Commission. 2009b. Hospital Nation Patient Safety Goals–2009. http://www.jointcommission.org.

Kizer, K.W. 2001. Establishing health care performance standards in an era of consumerism. *Journal of the American Medical Association* 286(10): 1212.

Kizer, K. 2004a (April 12). Conducting a dissonant symphony: NQF is working to bring more healthcare players into harmony on quality. *Modern Healthcare* 34(14):20.

Kizer, K. 2004b (June 17). Submission for the record to U.S. House of Representatives, subcommittee on health, hearing on healthcare information technology. http://www.waysandmeans.house.gov/hearings.asp?formmode=view&id=2244.

Langley, G.J., K.M. Nolan, T.W. Nolan, C.L. Norman, and L.P. Provost. 1996. *The Improvement Guide: A Practical Approach to Enhancing Organizational Performance.* San Francisco: Jossey-Bass.

Lazarus, I. 2003 (Jan. 1). Six Sigma raising the bar. *Managed Healthcare Executive.* http://www.managedhealthcareexecutive.com/mhe/article/articleDetail.jsp?id=43331.

Leape, L. 1990. Practice guidelines and standards: An overview. *Quality Review Bulletin* 16:42–43.

Leapfrog Group. 2008a. Fact Sheet: Never Events. http://www.leapfroggroup.org.

Leapfrog Group. 2008b. Leapfrog Group Position Statement on Never Events. http://www.leapfroggroup.org.

Leapfrog Group. 2008c. The Leapfrong Hospital Survey: What's New in the 2008 Survey (Version 5.0). http://www.leapfronggroup.org.

Lee, K. and C. McGreevey. 2002. Using comparison charts to assess performance measurement data. *Journal on Quality Improvement* 28(3):129–138.

Lumsdum, K. and M. Haglund. 1993 (Oct. 20). Mapping care. *Hospitals and Health Networks* 67(20):34–40.

Martin, G. 2008. How one hospital joined together to successfully implement MS-DRGs. *Journal of AHIMA–Coding Notes* 79(4):70–2.

McLaughlin C. and Kaluzney A. 2006. *Continuous Quality Improvement in Health Care.* 3rd ed. Jones & Bartlett, Inc. Sudbury, MA.

Medicare Prescription Drug, Improvement, and Modernization Act. 2003 (Dec. 8). Public Law 108-173. http://www.cms.hhs.gov/medicarereform/MMAactFullText.pdf.

Mellott, Susan, ed. 1996. *NAHQ Guide to Quality Management.* 6th ed. Glenview, IL: NAHQ.

Millenson, M. 1999. *Demanding Medical Excellence.* Chicago: University of Chicago Press.

Milliman and Robertson. 2002. *Milliman Care Guidelines.* Seattle: Milliman.

Milliman Care Guidelines. 2008. Delivering evidence-based knowledge at the point of care. http://www.careguidelines.com.

Minnesota Department of Health. 2004. Adverse Health Events Reporting Law: Implementation Update. http://www.health.state.mn.us/patientsafety/aeupdatefs04.pdf.

Minnesota Department of Health. 2007 (Oct.). Adverse Health Events Report Law: Minnesota's 28 Reportable Events. http://www.health.state.mn.us.

Minnesota Hospital Quality Report. 2008. http://www.mnhospitalquality.org.

Minnesota Statutes. 2007. Facility Requirements to report, analyze, and correct #144.7065. http://www.revisor.leg.state.mn.us.

Morrissey, J. 2003. Leapfrog works on weighted evaluation system. *Modern Healthcare* 33(42):8.

Mosser, G. and S. Scheitel. 2004. *Public Reporting of Health Performance in Minnesota: A Position Paper of the Board of the Institute for Clinical Systems Improvement.* Bloomington, MN: ICSI.

National Quality Forum. 2003. *Safe Practices for Better Healthcare: A Consensus Report.* Washington, D.C.: NQF.

National Quality Forum. 2007. Safe Practices for Better Healthcare, 2006 Update: A consensus report. http://www.qualityforum.org.

National Quality Forum. 2008. Wired for quality: The intersection of health IT and healthcare quality. *Issue Brief NQF* 8:1–7.

National Quality Forum. 2009. Safe Practices for Better Health. http://www.qualityforum.org/projects/ongoing/safe-practices.

National Committee for Quality Health Care. 2008a. Q&A for Pay for Performance. http://www.ncqhc.org.

National Committee for Quality Health Care. 2008b. Disease Management Measures. http://www.ncqa.org.

National Committee on Vital and Health Statistics, Subcommittee on Quality. 2008. 23 Building blocks for quality: The view from 2008. http://www.ncvhs.hhs.gov/080717rpt.pdf.

National Quality Measures Clearinghouse. 2008a. Measure Index. http://www.qualitymeasures.ahrq.gov.

National Quality Measures Clearinghouse. 2008b. Measure Hierarchy. http://www.qualitymeasures.ahrq.gov.

Nelson, E., J. Mohr, P. Batalden, and S. Plume. 1996. Improving health care, Part 1: The clinical value compass. *Journal on Quality Improvement* 22(4):243–255.

Neuhauser, D. 2002. Heroes and martyrs of quality and safety. *Quality and Safety in Health Care* 11:104–105.

Powell, J. and R. Stanley. 2008 (Sept.). Part of the Equation. A sober assessment of the CMS PQRI initiative reveals a promising future for the program. *Health Management Technology* 29(9):30–31.

Pozgar, G. 2004. *Legal Aspects of Health Care Administration*. 9th ed. Boston: Jones and Bartlett.

Prophet, S. 1997. Fraud and abuse implications for the HIM professional. *Journal of AHIMA* 68(4):52–56.

Purcell and Tucson General Hospital v. Zimbelman, 18 AZ App. 75, 500 P.2d 335 (1972).

Roland, T. and P. Kannan. 2003. E-service: A new paradigm for business in the electronic environment. *Communications of the ACM* 46(6):37–42.

Rose, E. 2004. Life after go-live, Part 4: Preventing error with an EMR. *Journal of Healthcare Information Management* 17(4):15–17.

Rust, R. 2003. E-service: A new paradigm for business in the electronic environment. *Communications of the ACM* 46(6):37–42.

Sackett, D.L., W.M. Rosenberg, C. Muir, J.A. Gray, R.B. Haynes, and W.S. Richardson. 1996. Evidence-based Medicine: What it is and what it isn't. *British Medical Journal*. International Edition. 312(7012):71 http://www.cebm.net.

Sautter, K.M., B.G. Bokhour, B. White, D. Min, G.J. Young, J.F. Burgess, M.D. Berlowitz, and R.C. Wheeler. 2007. The early experience of a hospital-based pay-for performance program.. *Journal of Healthcare Management* 52(2): 95–107.

Schaffer, W.A. 1991. Introducing data to medical staffs. In *Quantitative Methods in Quality Management: A Guide for Practitioners*. Edited by Longo, D.R. and D. Bohr. Chicago: American Hospital Publishing.

Schanz, S.J. 1999. *Developing and Implementing Clinical Practice Guidelines*. Chicago: AMA.

Schueler, J. 2000. Customer service through leadership: The Sidney way. *Training and Development* 54(10): 26.

Shine, K.I. 2002. Health care quality and how to achieve it. *Academic Medicine* 77(1):92.

Shojania, K.G. and Grimshaw, J.M. 2005. Evidence-based quality improvement: The state of the science. *Health Affairs* 24(1): 138–149.

Slee, V.N. and D.A. Slee. 1991. *Health Care Terms*. St. Paul, MN: Tringa Press.

Slovensky, D.J. 2001. Quality management and clinical outcomes. In *Health Information: Management of a Strategic Resource*. Rev. ed. Edited by Abdelhak, M. et al. Philadelphia: W.B. Saunders.

Spath, P.L. 2000. *Fundamentals of Health Care Quality Management*. Forest Grove, OR: Brown-Spath & Associates.

Spath, P.L. 2004. *Partnering with Patients to Reduce Medical Errors*. Chicago, IL: Health Forum, Inc.

Spath, P.L. 2005. *Leading Your Healthcare Organization to Excellence*. Chicago, IL: Health Administration Press.

Spath, P. and D. Hale. 2003. Comparative performance data can be change agent. *Hospital Case Management* 11(1):3–5.

StratisHealth. 2000. *The Sixth Scope of Work: National Priorities and Performance Measures*. Bloomington, MN: StratisHealth.

StratisHealth. 2008. StratisHealth Quality Report Update. http://www.stratishealth.org/index.php?submenu=Publications&src=gendocs&link=Pubs_quality_report_update&category=Publications.

Thielst, C.B. 2007. The Future of Healthcare Technology. *Journal of Healthcare Management* 52(1): 7–9.

Thomson Healthcare. 2006 (Sept.). Patient Safety. http://www.healthleadersmedia.com.

Thomson Healthcare. 2006 (Mar.). Outcomes Measures. http://www.healthleadersmedia.com.

Thomson Healthcare. 2007a. Disease Management. http://www.health leadersmedia.com.

Thomson Healthcare. 2007b. Quality Measures. http://www.healthleaders media.com.

Thomson Healthcare. 2007c. The Quality-Driven Consumer. http://www.healthleadersmedia.com.

Timmermans, S. and A. Mauck. (2005). The promises and pitfalls of evidence-based medicine. *Health Affairs* 14(1):18–27.

URAC. 2008. What is Care Management? http://www.urac.org/resources/careManagement.aspx.

Wachter, R. and D. Owens. 2004 (Aug.). *The Genesis of Closing the Quality Gap*. AHRQ Publication No. 04-0051-1. Rockville, MD: AHRQ.

Walton, M. 1986. *The Deming Management Method*. New York: Putnam Publishing Group.

Whitehouse. 2006. Fact Sheet: Health Care Transparency: Empowering Consumers to Save on Quality Care. http://www.whitehouse.gov/news/releases/2006/08/20060822.html.

Youngberg, B. J. 1990. *Essentials of Hospital Risk Management*. Rockville, MD: Aspen.

Part V

Knowledge-based Healthcare Data and Information

Chapter 18
Biomedical and Research Support

Valerie Watzlaf, PhD, RHIA, FAHIMA

Learning Objectives

- Explain the role of biomedical research in evaluating the safety and efficacy of diagnostic and therapeutic procedures in order to solve human problems
- Relate the measures outlined by the Nuremberg Code, the Declaration of Helsinki, and the Belmont Report for the protection of human subjects
- Describe the purpose and responsibilities as well as the overall management of the Institutional Review Board (IRB) for biomedical research
- Illustrate the different types of IRB submissions and the procedures that must be followed when conducting biomedical research
- Outline the contents of informed consent for the protection of human subjects as required by federal regulation
- Explain the procedures that should be followed when handling problems that include risks to human subjects engaged in biomedical research
- Outline the record keeping and retention requirements that are required by the IRB
- Discuss the role of the HIM professional both as researcher and as a supportive role to research conducted in healthcare facilities
- Discuss the Health Insurance Portability and Accountability Act (HIPAA) and its privacy provisions for the protection of human subjects
- Outline the various research designs for conducting biomedical research
- Describe the purpose of outcomes and effectiveness research
- Describe the various types of outcomes and effectiveness measures

Key Terms

Agency for Healthcare Research and Quality (AHRQ)
Attributable risk (AR)
Beneficence
Case-control study
Clinical trial
Cohort study
Controls
Cross-sectional study
Double-blinded study
Epidemiological studies
Experimental study
Food and Drug Administration (FDA)
Health Research Extension Act (1985)
Health services research (HSR)
Healthcare Cost and Utilization Project (HCUP)
Human subjects
Informed consent
Institutional Review Board (IRB)
Justice
Morality
National Committee for Quality Assurance (NCQA)
Observational study
Odds ratio
Office for Human Research Protections (OHRP)
Office of Research Integrity (ORI)
Outcomes and effectiveness research (OER)
Principal investigator
Privacy Rule
Prospective studies
Protected health information (PHI)
Protocol
Quality indicators (QIs)
Randomized clinical trials (RCTs)
Relative risk (RR)
Research
Respect for persons
Retrospective study
Single-blinded study
Sponsor
Vulnerable subjects

Biomedical research is a search for knowledge that often leads to advances in medicine. It uncovers what new drugs and other types of treatments, as well as new technology, are safe and effective for patients. When new treatments and technologies ultimately reach the consumers of healthcare, long-term studies of outcomes and effectiveness begin.

This chapter explores the various methods by which biomedical research is conducted. It also examines methods of assessing outcomes and effectiveness, including programs initiated by the **Agency for Healthcare Research and Quality** (AHRQ), the Joint Commission, and the **National Committee for Quality Assurance** (NCQA).

Clinical and Biomedical Research

Clinical and biomedical research studies are conducted to evaluate disease processes and interventions and the safety, effectiveness, and usefulness of drugs, diagnostic procedures, and preventive measures such as vaccines, mammography, and diets. The broad objective of these studies is to establish reproducible facts and theory that help solve human problems. The most common examples of these research studies are called **clinical trials** in which a specific type of clinical or biomedical intervention is tested to determine its effectiveness. **Health services research** examines the quality, access, cost, staffing, utilization, and safety of healthcare services in order to improve the overall quality of care provided to patients. For example, health services research studies may focus on examining the number and type of infections in an elderly cohort in order to determine the effect the infection has on extended length of stay, cost, coding, and reimbursement. Further research in this area may include siphoning out which infections are hospital-acquired and which are community-acquired and then determining which lead to additional cost, treatment, staffing, length of stay, while not providing additional reimbursement for the hospital and certainly not providing additional safety and quality for the patient (Watzlaf et al, 1998).

Ethical Treatment of Human Subjects

Human subjects are used in biomedical research studies. Because human subjects are involved, researchers are required to follow certain ethical principles that guide their behavior, **morality**, and character traits. Research ethics:

- Provide a structure for analysis and decision making
- Support and remind researchers to protect human subjects
- Provide workable definitions of benefits and risks

Risk versus benefit is critical in weighing the advantages of biomedical research. A benefit is a positive value of being part of the clinical research study. A benefit may be specific to the individual subject in that it provides a good therapeutic outcome, or it may be a direct advantage to society as a whole rather than to the individual subject.

Risks are concerned with the probability or magnitude of harm to the research subject. Stating that 1 in 100 patients may experience a certain risk suggests probability of harm. A rash as a minor effect of the treatment or liver failure as a major effect of the treatment suggests magnitude of harm.

The challenge for the researcher is to weigh risks to the subject against potential benefits. This is difficult because not all potential benefits and risks are known in advance and, as stated earlier, the benefit may be for society at large rather than for the individual subjects who assumed the risks. However, there are many clinical and biomedical research studies in which the benefits far outweigh the risks to the individual. For example, an individual with Stage IV pancreatic cancer may only see how the benefits outweigh the risks to enroll in a clinical trial that examines the effectiveness of a medication to stop the advancement of this devastating illness.

The Nuremberg Code and the Declaration of Helsinki

International guidelines also govern the ethical conduct of human research. The Nuremberg Code outlines research ethics that were developed during the trials of Nazi war criminals following World War II. The code was widely adopted as a standard for protecting human subjects in the 1950s and 1960s. The basic tenet of the Nuremberg Code is that "voluntary consent of the human subject is absolutely essential" (Nuremburg Code 1949, 181). It is the duty and responsibility of the individual initiating, directing, or conducting the experiment to ensure the quality of the informed consent. Additionally, the Nuremburg code requires that research be based on animal work, the risks be justified by the anticipated benefits, only qualified scientists conduct the research, and that physical and mental suffering be avoided. Research in which death is expected should not be conducted.

The Declaration of Helsinki is a code of ethics for clinical research approved by the World Medical Association in 1964. It was a reinterpretation of the Nuremberg Code directed toward medical research with a therapeutic intent. It is a statement of ethical principles that provides guidance to physicians and other participants in medical research involving human subjects, including research on identifiable human material or identifiable data. The document has been revised a number of times, most recently in October 2000 at the 52nd World Medical Association Assembly held in Edinburgh, Scotland.

Despite the Nuremberg Code and the Declaration of Helsinki, controversial ethical practices in biomedical research continued to be a problem. In 1966, Dr. Henry K. Beecher, an anesthesiologist, described 22 examples of research studies with controversial ethics that had been published by prominent researchers in major journals. Beecher's article increased public awareness of the ethical problems related to biomedical research, including:

- Lack of informed consent
- Coercion of, or undue pressure on, volunteers

- Use of a vulnerable population
- Information being withheld
- Available treatment being withheld
- Information about risks being withheld
- Subjects put at risk
- Risks to subjects that outweigh the benefits
- Deception
- Violation of rights

The U.S. Public Health Services Syphilis Study

A study conducted in the United States that brought ethical issues in research to the forefront was the U.S. Public Health Services Syphilis Study. This study was designed to study the natural history of syphilis in African-American men (see figure 18.1). At the time the study began, there was no treatment for syphilis. However, by the 1940s penicillin had proved to be safe and effective. The men enrolled in the study were denied treatment. They continued to be followed until 1972, when the first public accounts began to appear in the national press. The study resulted in 28 deaths, 100 cases of disability, and 19 cases of congenital syphilis.

After the press blew the whistle, Congress formed an ad hoc panel that determined the study should be stopped immediately and that oversight of human research was inadequate. It was recommended that federal regulations be implemented to protect human research in the future. In 1974, Congress authorized formation of the National Commission for the Protection of Human Subjects in Biomedical and Behavioral Research. The commission was charged with identifying the basic ethical principles that underlie the conduct of human research.

In 1979, the commission published the *Belmont Report: Ethical Principles and Guidelines for the Protection of Human Subjects of Research.* This report identifies the following three basic ethical principles that underlie all human subject research:

> ***Respect for persons*** requires that individuals be treated as autonomous human beings and not used as a means to an end. Elements of autonomy include the ability to understand and process information and the freedom to volunteer for research without coercion or undue influence from others. Respect for persons requires informed consent and respecting the privacy of research subjects.

Figure 18.1. Tuskegee syphilis study

> The Tuskegee Syphilis Study is a notorious chapter in medical research in the United States. From 1932 to 1972, the U.S. Public Health Service conducted research that had the stated purpose of obtaining more information about the clinical course of syphilis. The medical researchers from the U.S. Public Health Service experimented on 399 African American males in Macon County, Alabama. The medical researchers told the men that they were being treated for "bad blood." In fact, the researchers were deceiving the men and were denying them treatment for syphilis. Many of the men's wives were infected, and their children were subsequently born with congenital syphilis. The U.S. Public Health Service continued the study despite the advent of penicillin in 1947. The Tuskegee Syphilis Study is a symbol of unethical research.

> ***Beneficence*** is minimizing harms and maximizing benefits. Beneficence requires the best possible research design to achieve its goals. It also requires that researchers be able to perform the research and handle the risks.

> ***Justice*** requires that people be treated fairly and that benefits and risks be shared equitably among the population. Justice requires that subjects be selected equitably and that vulnerable populations or populations of convenience not be exploited.

The **Office for Human Research Protections** (OHRP) of the Department of Health and Human Services (HHS) monitors compliance with the federal regulations that govern the conduct of biomedical research (HHS 2005a). The federal regulations for the protection of human subjects include Title 45 CFR 46. The **Food and Drug Administration** (FDA) has a separate set of regulations governing human subjects research (21 CFR Part 56—IRBs and 21 CFR Part 50 Informed Consent). The basic requirements for IRBs and informed consent are similar between the HHS and FDA regulations.

Check Your Understanding 18.1

Instructions: Answer the following questions on a separate piece of paper.

1. What is the origin of the Nuremberg Code? What are its basic tenets?
2. List the three principles outlined in the *Belmont Report.*
3. A researcher fails to inform a study participant of the reasonable risks in a study on the effectiveness of a new chemotherapy agent. What ethical principle was violated?
4. List five ethical issues in the conduct of biomedical research in the United States cited by Beecher.
5. What study led to establishment of the *Belmont Report* and ultimate federal regulations for human subject protection?

Protection of Human Subjects

The HHS regulations contain three basic provisions for the protection of human subjects:

- Institutional Assurances of Compliance
- Institutional Review Board Review and Approval
- Informed Consent

Institutional Assurances of Compliance

An institutional assurance of compliance is a commitment of an institution to comply with HHS regulations for the protection of human subjects by documenting this commitment. The HHS will support non-exempt research covered by the regulations only if the organization has an Office of Human Research Protections (OHRP) approved assurance on file; the research has been reviewed and approved by the organization's IRB; and the IRB will continue to review the research, as necessary (HHS 2008a).

The Office for Human Research Protections

Protection of human subjects is required under the HHS Code of Federal Regulations (45 CFR 46). The Office for Human Research Protections (OHRP) is a federal agency that provides leadership and oversight on all matters related to the protection of human subjects participating in research conducted or supported by the HHS, as outlined in the regulations. It has formal agreements with more than 10,000 federally funded universities, hospitals, and other medical and behavioral research institutions in the United States and abroad. These organizations must agree to abide by the human subject protection regulations found in the Code of Federal Regulations. The OHRP's duties include:

- Establishing criteria for, and approving assurance of, compliance for the protection of human subjects with institutions engaged in HHS-conducted or HHS-supported human subject research
- Providing clarification and guidance on involving humans in research
- Developing and implementing educational programs and resource materials
- Promoting the development of approaches to enhance human subject protections

The OHRP also evaluates substantive allegations or indications of noncompliance with HHS regulations regarding the conduct of research involving human subjects (HHS 2005). It also provides education and development on the complex ethical and regulatory issues relating to human subjects protection in medical and behavioral research. The OHRP helps institutions assess and improve their own procedures for protecting human subjects through a quality improvement program.

Institutional Review Board (IRB)

The **Institutional Review Board** (IRB) is a committee established to protect the rights and welfare of human research subjects involved in research activities. The IRB members are appointed by the specific organization (HHS 2008).

The IRB determines whether research that is conducted is appropriate and that it protects human subjects as they participate in this research. The primary focus of the IRB is not on whether the type of research is appropriate for the organization to conduct but upon whether or not human subjects are adequately protected.

The purpose and responsibilities of the IRB is to protect the rights and welfare of human subjects as they engage in research activities. The IRB must abide by the regulations as listed in 45 CFR 46.111 and 21 CFR 56.111. The IRB must first determine if research is being conducted and then determine if human subjects are being protected. **Research** is defined by the regulations as "a systematic investigation, including research development, testing and evaluation, designed to develop or contribute to generalizable knowledge" [Federal Policy §___.102(d)]. **Human subjects** are defined by the regulations as "living individual(s) about whom an investigator (whether professional or student) conducting research obtains (1) data through intervention or interaction with the individual, or (2) identifiable private information" [Federal Policy §___.102(f)] (HHS 2008b). Research as defined here is different than quality improvement studies because quality improvement studies are not designed to contribute to "generalizable knowledge" but to add to the internal evaluation of healthcare organizations.

An IRB must review all research activities covered by the HHS regulations and approve, require changes to obtain approval, or disapprove any research activity. An IRB must perform continuing reviews of ongoing research as often as necessary per degree of risk, but not less than one year. The IRB has the authority to suspend or terminate approved research that is not being conducted in accordance with IRB requirements or that has caused unexpected or serious harm to the subject. If a suspension or termination occurs, the IRB must include a documented statement for the reason and must report this immediately to the investigator, appropriate institutional officials, and HHS.

The protection of human subjects is a shared responsibility between the institutional officials, the IRB, and the investigator. It should not rest solely with the IRB. The institutional official is responsible for choosing one or more IRB's to review research, providing enough space, staff, and other resources to support the IRB's review and record keeping responsibilities, provide education and training for the IRB staff and investigators, provide effective communication and guidance on human subject research, ensure that investigators carry out their research responsibilities with the utmost respect for human subjects, and serve as the point of contact for OHRP or designate another individual to undertake this responsibility.

The IRB is made up of at least five members with diversified backgrounds per federal regulation, such as including at least one member with a scientific background and at least one member in a non-scientific area. However, most organizations have more than that number. For example, many large universities are comprised of ten IRB committees, each functioning as a separate IRB under a central administration and support from the main IRB office. An IRB vice chairperson and several members with expertise in many diversified areas comprise the IRB committee. Also, the IRB office includes additional staff that reviews exempt or expedited research proposals.

A typical IRB in a large university may consist of the following individuals:

- *Chairperson:* Has ultimate responsibility for the review and approval of the research study protocol as it relates to human subject research.
- *Director, IRB office:* Manages the entire IRB office. Develops policies and procedures as they pertain to appropriate federal and state regulations pertaining to human subject research and protection. Provides continuing education to the organization at large.
- *Legal Counsel:* Advises the entire IRB office staff on legal issues pertaining to human subject research and protection.

- *Committee Vice-Chairpersons:* Conducts the IRB committee to review and approve research study protocol as it pertains to human subject protections.
- *Exempt/Expedited Vice-Chairpersons:* Conducts the organization and management of the review and approval of exempt or expedited research study protocols.
- *Education Coordinator:* Provides orientation and continuing education to IRB committee members, researchers, IRB staff and the research community.
- *Research Review Coordinators:* Reviews all IRB applications, attends all IRB committee meetings, ensures compliance with IRB policies and procedures, and records all minutes.
- *Adverse Event Coordinators:* Reviews and develops the response to all adverse related events that may occur as part of the research study protocol. Provides continuing education (University of Pittsburgh 2008a).

Conflict of Interest

No IRB member may participate in the review of a research project in which they have a conflict of interest. A conflict of interest may include serving as an IRB committee member to review a research study protocol in which one has a definite interest in the outcome of the specific medical device or medication. If this situation arises, the IRB committee member should remove himself or herself from the composition of the committee.

Before IRB submissions are reviewed, investigators may be required or recommended to complete different educational modules. These modules may include: Research integrity, conflict of interest, use of lab animals in research and education, human embryonic and stem cell research, HIPAA researchers privacy requirements, blood borne pathogens, chemical hygiene, responsible literature searching, IRB member education, research with children, and Good Clinical Practices module (recommended for those investigators involved in FDA regulated research) (University of Pittsburgh 2008b).

Procedures for IRB submission

Exempt, expedited and full board approval are the three major categories of IRB review for research study proposals. OHRP recommends that clear procedures be developed by organizations so that IRBs can determine whether research is exempt.

Exempt research activities include the involvement of human subjects in one or more of the categories listed below according to the HHS Federal Policy regulations (45 CFR 46.1.1(b)(1–6)). Research that is exempt does not mean that the researchers have no ethical obligations to the participants but that the regulatory requirements such as informed consent and yearly renewal from IRB do not apply to this type of research. The IRB still reviews research protocols to determine their exempt status.

Exempt research activities may include the involvement of human subjects in one or more of the following categories:

- Educational settings (45 CFR 46.101(b)(1)): Research conducted in educational settings involving normal educational practices such as testing different instructional methods (for example, differences in learning outcomes between distance education and traditional classroom)
- Use of educational tests, surveys, interviews, or observation (45 CFR 46.101 (b)(2)): Research conducted in any setting in which educational tests such as aptitude or achievement tests are conducted unless participants are identified in any way when data is collected
- Use of educational tests, surveys, interviews or observation (45 CFR 46.101 (b)(3)): Research conducted that is not exempt under paragraph (b)(2) if: (i) the human subjects are elected or appointed public officials or candidates for public office; or (ii) federal statute(s) require(s) without exception that the confidentiality of the personally identifiable information will be maintained throughout the research and thereafter
- Research involving the collection or study of existing data, documents, records, pathological specimens, or diagnostic specimens (45 CFR 46.101 (b)(4)): if these sources are publicly available or if the information is recorded by the investigator in such a manner that subjects cannot be identified, directly or through identifiers linked to the subjects
- Research and demonstration projects which are conducted by or subject to the approval of department or agency heads, and are designed to study, evaluate, or otherwise examine (45 CFR 46.101 (b)(5)): (i) Public benefit or service programs; (ii) procedures for obtaining benefits or services under those programs; (iii) possible changes in or alternatives to those programs or procedures; or (iv) possible changes in methods or levels of payment for benefits or services under those programs
- Taste and food quality evaluation and consumer acceptance studies (45 CFR 46.101 (b)(6)): (i) if wholesome foods without additives are consumed; or (ii) if a food is consumed that contains a food ingredient at or below the level and for a use found to be safe, or agricultural chemical or environmental contaminant at or below the level found to be safe, by the Food and Drug Administration or approved by the Environmental Protection Agency or the Food Safety and Inspection Service of the U.S. Department of Agriculture

Expedited research include those activities that (1) present no more than minimal risk to human subjects, and (2) involve only procedures listed in one or more of the following categories as authorized by 45 CFR 46.110 and 21 CFR 56.110. The categories for expedited IRB review include:

- Clinical studies of drugs and medical devices only when an investigational new drug application or medical device application is not required or when the medical device is cleared or approved for marketing and the medical device is being used in accordance with its cleared or approved labeling.
- Collection of blood samples by finger stick, heel stick, ear stick, or venipuncture
- Prospective collection of biological specimens for research purposes by noninvasive means. Examples include hair and nail clipping or placenta removed at delivery.
- Collection of data through noninvasive procedures (not involving general anesthesia or sedation) routinely employed in clinical practice, excluding procedures involving x-rays or microwaves. Examples include magnetic resonance imaging, electrocardiography, exercise testing, muscle strength testing, and so forth.
- Research involving materials (data, documents, records, or specimens) that have been collected, or will be collected solely for nonresearch purposes (such as medical treatment or diagnosis). (*Note*: Some research in this category may be exempt from the HHS regulations for the protection of human subjects (45 CFR 46.101(b)(4)). This listing refers only to research that is not exempt.)
- Collection of data from voice, video, digital, or image recordings made for research purposes.
- Research on individual or group characteristics or behavior (including, but not limited to, research on perception, cognition, motivation, identity, language, communication, cultural beliefs or practices, and social behavior) or research employing survey, interview, oral history, focus group, program evaluation, human factors evaluation, or quality assurance methodologies. (*Note*: Some research in this category may be exempt from the HHS regulations for the protection of human subjects (45 CFR 46.101(b)(2) and (b)(3)). This listing refers only to research that is not exempt.)
- Continuing review of research previously approved by the convened IRB as follows:
  - where (i) the research is permanently closed to the enrollment of new subjects; (ii) all subjects have completed all research-related interventions; and (iii) the research remains active only for long-term follow-up of subjects; or
  - where no subjects have been enrolled and no additional risks have been identified; or
  - where the remaining research activities are limited to data analysis.
- Continuing review of research, not conducted under an investigational new drug application or investigational device exemption where categories two (2) through eight (8) do not apply but the IRB has determined and documented at a convened meeting that the research involves no greater than minimal risk and no additional risks have been identified.
- An *expedited review procedure* consists of a review of research involving human subjects by the IRB chairperson or by one or more experienced reviewers designated by the chairperson from among members of the IRB in accordance with the requirements set forth in 45 CFR 46.110.

All other research projects that do not qualify under exempt or expedited review must be reviewed and approved at the full board level.

Once the category of submission is determined, the investigator must complete the proper forms for submission to the IRB. The types of forms that must be completed depend upon the level of review. Most IRB's are requiring research protocols be submitted electronically. An IRB protocol checklist is usually provided so that the investigator can determine what types of documents need to be completed and submitted. Please see Figure 18.2 for a copy of the IRB checklist used at the University of Pittsburgh IRB office.

Once the appropriate forms are submitted to the IRB, the investigator awaits a decision from the IRB committee. The decisions from the IRB can include one of the following four categories:

- Full approval
- Approval subject to modifications—protocol is recommended for approval pending inclusion of changes.
- Reconsideration—when there are a number of questions and concerns regarding the protocol and full board review and approval may be necessary once all questions and concerns are addressed.
- Disapproval—when major scientific or ethical problems cannot be resolved (University of Pittsburgh 2008c).

Management of Handling Problems Related to Risk of Human Subjects

Sometimes during the course of the research study protocol adverse events occur. When this happens the investigator must notify the IRB and complete an adverse event report. The adverse event report should include the following (University of Pittsburgh 2008d):

- Principal Investigator's (PI) name
- Title of the study
- IRB study number
- Date of the adverse event
- Date the adverse event was reported to the PI
- Subject ID
- Probability of the adverse event occurring
- Severity of the event
- Causality of the event (was it due to the study protocol or procedure)
- Seriousness or outcome of the event, such as death, life threatening, hospitalization, and so forth
- Whether the adverse event was seen before
- Number of subjects exposed to the intervention related to this adverse event
- Whether protocol modification is necessary and if so, a revised protocol and informed consent must be submitted
- Signature and date of the PI

Figure 18.2. IRB Scientific Reviewer Checklist

University of Pittsburgh
IRB Checklist for Scientific Reviewers
Revised May 2008

OSIRIS Section				
	TRIAGE	**Yes**	**No**	**NA**
T 3.0	Is risk level noted by investigators consistent with risks the study poses to subjects?	☐	☐	
	COVER SHEET	**Yes**	**No**	**NA**
CS 9.0	If not already listed, does this study require an IND or IDE?	☐	☐	☐
	OBJECTIVE, AIMS, BACKGROUND AND SIGNIFICANCE	**Yes**	**No**	**NA**
1.4	Is the research design adequate to yield scientifically sound data?	☐	☐	
	RESEARCH DESIGN AND METHODS	**Yes**	**No**	**NA**
2.1	Is the duration of the study drug intervention limited appropriately to that which is minimally necessary to evaluate efficacy?	☐	☐	☐
2.18	Is there a statistical justification for the sample size?	☐	☐	☐
2.18	Is the proposed statistical treatment of the data appropriate for the design of the study?	☐	☐	☐
2.3.1	Is a placebo being used where an effective treatment exists?	☐	☐	☐
2.6	Are the study procedures and study visits clearly outlined and described?	☐	☐	☐
2.6	Are all procedures described clearly defined as either research related or completed as part of the subject's clinical care? (regardless of study participation)	☐	☐	☐
	HUMAN SUBJECTS	**Yes**	**No**	**NA**
3.0	Is the study population appropriate for the goals of the study? (consider both the nature and size of the sample)	☐	☐	☐
3.5–3.11	Are adequate safeguards in place to protect any subject that would be categorized as vulnerable as defined by Subparts B, C and D? 46.111 (b)	☐	☐	☐
3.13	Are the criteria for inclusion of subjects appropriate?	☐	☐	
3.14	Are the criteria for exclusion of subjects appropriate?	☐	☐	
	RECRUITMENT	**Yes**	**No**	**NA**
4.4	Are methods of subject recruitment equitable, taking into consideration the nature and setting in which the research is being conducted? (46.111 (a) (3))	☐	☐	
4.4	Are the methods of recruitment legal, ethical and free from coercion or undue influence?	☐	☐	☐
	INFORMED CONSENT DOCUMENT—REQUIRED ELEMENTS	**YES**	**NO**	**NA**
4.9	Is there a clear statement that the study involves research?	☐	☐	
4.9	Is there a clear statement of the purpose of the study?	☐	☐	
4.9	Is the expected duration of the subject's participation included?	☐	☐	
4.9	Is there a description of procedures to be following during subject's participation?	☐	☐	
4.9	Are procedures which are experimental identified?	☐	☐	
4.9	Is there a complete and clear description of the potential risks (i.e., is quantitative information on the expected frequency of the listed side effects provided)?	☐	☐	
4.9	Are the potential benefits to the subjects (if any) clearly described? If there are no benefits is this clearly stated?	☐	☐	
4.9	If applicable, have all alternative treatments or courses of treatment that might be advantageous to the subject been satisfactorily described?	☐	☐	
4.9	Is there a statement describing the extent to which the confidentiality of subjects records will be maintained?	☐	☐	
4.9	For research that is more than minimal risk, is there an explanation of whether compensation for injury will be provided?	☐	☐	
4.9	Is there an explanation of whom to contact for questions about the research, research subject's rights, and in the event of a research-related injury?	☐	☐	

(Continued on next page)

Figure 18.2. (Continued)

4.9	For research that is more than minimal risk, is there a statement regarding treatment that is available if an injury were to occur as a result of the research?	☐	☐	
4.9	Is there a statement that participation in the research study is voluntary?	☐	☐	
4.9	Is there a statement that refusal to participate will involve no penalty or loss of benefits to which the subject is otherwise entitled?	☐	☐	
4.9	Is there a statement that the subject may discontinue participation at any time without penalty of loss of benefits to which the subject is otherwise entitled?	☐	☐	
4.9	Does the consent form contain exculpatory language?	☐	☐	
	INFORMED CONSENT DOCUMENT—ADDITIONAL ELEMENTS	**YES**	**NO**	**NA**
4.9	Is there a statement that the treatment or procedure may involve risks to the subject (or embryo or fetus, if the subject is or may become pregnant) which is currently unforeseeable?	☐	☐	☐
4.9	Is there a statement that indicates the anticipated circumstances under which the subject's participation may be terminated by the investigator without regard to the subject's consent?	☐	☐	☐
4.9	If subjects are expected to bear any additional costs for participation, are the costs identified?	☐	☐	☐
4.9	Are the consequences of a subject's decision to withdraw from the research and procedures for orderly termination of participation included?	☐	☐	☐
4.9	Is there a statement that significant new findings developed during the course of the research which may relate to the subject's willingness to continue participation will be provided to subjects?	☐	☐	☐
4.9	Is the approximate number of subjects involved in the study included?	☐	☐	☐
	INFORMED CONSENT PROCESS	**YES**	**NO**	**NA**
4.12	Is sufficient information provided about the informed consent process that will take place (including who will conduct the consent interview, whether there will be waiting period between informing the prospective participant and obtaining consent and steps that will be taken to minimize the possibility of coercion or undue influence)?	☐	☐	☐
4.12	Will informed consent be sought from each prospective subject or the subject's legally authorized representative to the extent required by §46.116? (46.111 (a) (4))	☐	☐	☐
4.12	Will informed consent be appropriately documented in accordance with and to the extent required by §46.117? (46.111 (a) (5))	☐	☐	☐
	POTENTIAL RISKS AND BENEFITS	**YES**	**NO**	**NA**
5.1-5.5	Are the risks to subjects reasonable in relation to the anticipated benefits, if any? (46.111 (a) (2))	☐	☐	
5.1–5.5	Are risks and benefits in the protocol consistent with risks/benefits in the consent?	☐	☐	☐
5.12	Are the potential benefits to the subject and/or society clearly described and outweigh the risks being incurred? (46.111 (a) (2))	☐	☐	
5.13	Does the research plan have adequate provision for monitoring the data collected to ensure the safety of the subjects? (46.111 (a) (6))	☐	☐	
5.2.2	Are the risks to the subject minimized by using procedures that are consistent with sound research design and, whenever appropriate, by using procedures already being performed on the subjects for diagnostic or treatment purposes? (46.111 (a) (1))	☐	☐	
5.4	Have appropriate statements regarding reproductive risks and birth control been included?	☐	☐	☐
5.8	Are there adequate provisions to protect the privacy of subjects and to maintain the confidentiality of data? (46.111 (a) (7))	☐	☐	
	COSTS AND PAYMENTS	**YES**	**NO**	**NA**
6.0	Are the financial obligations of the subject, the sponsor and the institution clearly described?	☐	☐	☐
6.1	Are costs/availability of the experimental drug/device following study completion addressed?	☐	☐	☐
6.1	Is there a clear description distinguishing between the costs related to research procedures versus clinical care procedures (done regardless of study participation)?	☐	☐	☐
6.2	Do all payments seem sufficient yet not large enough to be coercive?	☐	☐	☐
	QUALIFICATIONS AND SOURCE(S) OF SUPPORT/REFERENCES	**YES**	**NO**	**NA**
7.1	Do the principal investigator and co-investigators have the appropriate academic/clinical credentials and experience for this study?	☐	☐	
	Were appropriate references cited in the research protocol to support the research design and the risks and benefits of the study?	☐	☐	☐

Record Keeping and Retention

The IRB should prepare and maintain adequate documentation of all IRB activities. These activities may include (HHS 2008a):

- Copies of all research study protocols reviewed, sample consent forms, progress reports, and reports of injuries to subjects or adverse event reports
- Minutes of IRB committee meetings
- Records of continuing review activities
- Listing of IRB members and their responsibilities
- All written procedures for the IRB
- Statements of significant new findings provided to subjects

Informed Consent

Informed consent is more than just completing a form. It is a thoughtful and respectful explanation of information so that a person can decide whether to participate in a research study. The process that encompasses informed consent should not just regurgitate research study information but educate possible participants in terms they can understand. Informed consent should contain three fundamentals: information, comprehension, and voluntariness. The written presentation of information should document the basis for consent and for the participant's future reference. The consent document should also be revised when necessary to include changes to improve the consent procedure (HHS 2008c).

In most cases, biomedical research requires that subjects be given informed consent. Informed consent is a person's voluntary agreement to participate in research or to undergo a diagnostic, therapeutic, or preventive procedure. It is based on adequate knowledge and an understanding of relevant information provided by the investigators. In giving informed consent, subjects do not waive any of their legal rights nor do they release the investigator, sponsor, or institution from liability for negligence. Federal regulations require that certain information be provided each human subject. This information includes the following:

- A statement that the study involves research, the purpose of the research, the expected duration of subject participation, a description of the procedures to be followed, and the identification of procedures that are experimental.
- A description of reasonably foreseeable risks or discomforts. The description must be accurate and reasonable, and subjects must be informed of previously reported adverse events.
- A description of the benefits to the subject or others who may reasonably benefit from the research.
- A disclosure of the appropriate alternative procedures or courses of treatment, if any, that might be advantageous to the subject. When appropriate, a statement that supportive care with no additional disease-specific treatment is an alternative.
- A statement describing the extent to which confidentiality of records identifying the subject will be maintained. The statement should include full disclosure and description of approved agencies such as the Food and Drug Administration (FDA) that may have access to the records.
- For research involving more than minimal risk, an explanation as to whether any compensation or medical treatments are available if injury occurs, and, if so, what they consist of or where further information may be obtained. Injury is not limited to physical injury. Research-related injury may include physical, psychological, social, financial, or otherwise.
- An explanation of whom to contact for answers to pertinent questions about the research and research subjects' rights and who to contact in the event of a research-related injury to the subject.
- A statement that participation is voluntary and that the subject may discontinue participation at any time without penalty or loss of benefits to which he or she is otherwise entitled.

The regulations further require that additional consent information be provided when appropriate (Federal Policy 45 CFR 46.116), including:

- A statement that the treatment or procedure may involve risks to the subject (or embryo or fetus if the subject is pregnant) that are unforeseeable
- Anticipated circumstances under which the subject's participation may be terminated by the investigator without regard to the subject's consent
- Any additional costs that a subject may incur as a result of participating in the research
- The consequences of a subject's decision to withdraw from the research and procedures for orderly termination of participation by the subject
- A statement that significant new findings developed during the course of the research that may relate to the subject's willingness to continue participation will be provided to the subject
- The approximate number of subjects involved in the study

Federal regulations also require that informed consent be in a language that is understandable to the subject. If it is not, the consent form must be translated into the appropriate language. Subjects who are illiterate must have an interpreter present to explain the study and translate questions and answers between subject and investigator. A model consent form appears in Appendix 18A, at the end of this chapter. (In institutions where biomedical research is conducted, consent forms are usually maintained in storage facilities monitored by the **principal investigator**. Copies of the consent may or may not be kept in the medical record depending upon organizational policy. Consent forms often contain sensitive information such as that related to genetic testing. Results of tests related to genetic testing are not to be provided to insurers or other parties, and sometimes not to the subject. To help ensure that this information is not released inadvertently in the regular course of business related to the release of information process, some organizations choose to maintain these important documents separately. Examples of documents that are kept in the study center files are listed in figure 18.3.

The Joint Commission also has specific requirements regarding the protection of human research subjects. These are identified in the patients' rights chapter of The Joint Commission accreditation manual (Joint Commission 2008). The specific requirements related to human subject research appear in figure 18.4.

Vulnerable Subjects

HHS regulations include additional protections for vulnerable or special subject populations as subparts of 45 CFR Part 46. Federal regulations (HHS regulation 45 CFR 46.111(b) and FDA regulation 21 CFR 56.111(b)) require that "when some or all of the subjects are likely to be vulnerable to coercion or undue influence, additional safeguards have been included in the study to protect the rights and welfare of these subjects." When a subject has limited mental capacity or is unable to freely volunteer, the subject is considered vulnerable. Examples of **vulnerable subjects** include:

- *Children* may be vulnerable depending on age, maturity, and psychological state. There is potential for control, coercion, undue influence, or manipulation by parents, guardians, or investigators. The risk is greater for particularly young children.
- *Pregnant women, human fetuses, and neonates* may be vulnerable because of the increased potential risk to them. There is potential for interventions or procedures to cause greater risk for both the pregnant women and the fetus or neonate.
- *Mentally disabled individuals* have problems with capacity. They may not have freedom to volunteer because they may be institutionalized or hospitalized, are economically and educationally disadvantaged, and suffer from chronic diseases.
- *Educationally disadvantaged subjects* may have limitations on understanding the study they will be participating in; some may be illiterate. There is potential for undue influence and manipulation.
- *Economically disadvantaged subjects* may volunteer only because they will benefit economically. That is, because they will receive payment for participating in

Figure 18.3. Study center file contents

- Investigator's brochure
- Signed protocol
- Revised protocols (if applicable)
- Protocol amendments (if applicable)
- Continuing review documents
- Informed consent form (blank)
- HIPAA consent form (blank)
- Copies of signed consent forms
- Curriculum vitae (resumes) of principal investigator and coinvestigators
- Documentation of Institutional Review Board (IRB) or Ethical Review Board (ERB) compliance
- All correspondence between the investigator, IRB, or ERB, and study sponsor or contract research organization, relating to study conduct
- Copies of safety reports sent to FDA
- Lab certifications
- Normal laboratory value ranges for tests required by the protocol
- FDA's Clinical Investigator Information Sheet
- Clinical Research Associate monitoring log
- Drug invoices
- Study site signature log
- Financial disclosure statement

Figure 18.4. The Joint Commission standards for human subjects' research

Standard RI.01.03.05: The organization protects the patient and respects his or her rights during research, investigation, and clinical trials.

Elements of Performance:

1. The hospital reviews all research protocols and weighs the risks and benefits to the patient participating in the research.
2. To help the patient determine whether or not to participate in research, investigation, or clinical trials, the hospital provides the patient with all of the following information:
   - An explanation of the purpose of the research
   - The expected duration of the patient's participation
   - A clear description of the procedures to be followed
   - A statement of the potential benefits, risks, discomforts, and side effects
   - Alternative care, treatment, and services available to the patient that might prove advantageous to the patient
3. The hospital informs the patient that refusing to participate in research, investigation, or clinical trials, or discontinuing participation at any time, will not jeopardize his or her access to care, treatment, and services unrelated to the research.
4. The hospital documents the following in the research consent form: That the patient received information to help determine whether or not to participate in the research, investigation, or clinical trial.
5. The hospital documents the following in the research consent form: That the patient was informed that refusing to participate in research, investigation, or clinical trials, or discontinuing participation at any time will not jeopardize his or her access to care, treatment, and services unrelated to research.
6. The hospital documents the following in the research consent form: The name of the person who provided the information and the date the form was signed.
7. The research consent form describes the patient's right to privacy, confidentiality, and safety.
8. The hospital keeps all information given to subjects in the medical record or research file along with the consent forms.

Source: The Joint Commission. 2008. Rights and Responsibilities of Individuals: Pre-publication version. In *The Joint Commission Hospital Accreditation Program 2009* http://www.jointcommission.org.

the research, they may "volunteer." They may enroll in research only to receive monetary compensation or medical care they cannot otherwise afford.

- *Individuals with incurable or fatal diseases* may volunteer to participate out of desperation. In many cases, these individuals have failed many treatments and view volunteering in biomedical research as their last chance at surviving their illness. Also, because of disease progression or effects of medications, they may not have the mental capacity necessary to make an informed decision. These individuals may accept high risk because they are desperate for a cure, even when there is little or no prospect of direct benefit.
- *Prisoners* have limited autonomy and may not be able to exercise free choice. They may believe that they will receive adverse treatment or be denied certain privileges if they refuse to participate in the research study. In addition, cash payments may be an inducement to participate in research, thus it could be said that they are not truly volunteering but only participating for the cash benefit. Prisoners represent a population of convenience; that is, they are readily accessible and available. Studies on a contained population can be done more quickly and more cheaply. Lastly, prisoners may not realize benefits from their participation in research because of their incarceration and social and economic status.

Role of HIM Professional

Research

The role of the HIM professional and the IRB can take on two different functions. First, the HIM professional may serve as the PI for a particular research project. In this capacity, it is the HIM professional's responsibility to submit their research study to the appropriate level of IRB review and approval. The HIM professional should follow the IRB checklist (refer to figure 18.2). They should also complete any appropriate consent forms (Appendix 18A) so that they meet all of the essential rules and regulations that govern the IRB. As the PI of a research project, the HIM professional must follow all of the procedures just as they are written in their research study protocol. Since this is the original protocol that was approved by the IRB, any changes to this protocol should be submitted to the IRB again for review and approval. Second, the HIM professional can serve in a supportive role to investigators conducting research in healthcare facilities. In this capacity, they can provide education and information regarding the necessary policies and procedures that an investigator must follow when conducting research. They can also inform the PI about the proper procedures to follow when undergoing IRB review and approval and provide consultation on the development of the research study protocol and consent forms. They can also serve as a patient advocate by educating patients about their rights when involved in research. Finally, the HIM professional may be asked to serve as a member or consultant to the IRB as a subject matter expert in data and information handling, as well as the protection of patient privacy and confidentiality.

Privacy Considerations in Clinical and Biomedical Research

In response to a congressional mandate in the Health Insurance Portability and Accountability Act (HIPAA) of 1996, HHS issued regulations entitled Standards for Privacy of Individually Identifiable Health Information. Known as the **Privacy Rule**, the regulations protect medical records and other individually identifiable health information from being used or disclosed in any form. The rule became effective in April 2001, and organizations covered (covered entities) by the rule were expected to be in compliance by April 2003.

The Privacy Rule establishes a category of **protected health information** (PHI), which may be used or disclosed only in certain circumstances or under certain conditions. PHI is a subset of what is called individually identifiable health information. It includes what healthcare professionals typically regard as a patient's PHI, such as information in the patient's medical records as well as billing information for services rendered. PHI also includes identifiable health information about subjects of clinical research. Patient information considered "protected" is listed in figure 18.5.

The Privacy Rule defines the means by which human research subjects are informed of how their protected medical information will be used or disclosed. It also outlines their rights to access the information. The Privacy Rule protects the privacy of individually identifiable information while ensuring that researchers continue to have access to the medical information they need to conduct their research. Investigators are permitted to use and disclose PHI for research with individual authorization or without individual authorization under limited circumstances.

A valid Privacy Rule Authorization is an individual's signed permission that allows a covered entity to use or disclose the patient's PHI for the purpose(s) and to the recipient(s) stated in the authorization (HHS 2004b). When an authorization is obtained for biomedical research purposes, the Privacy Rule requires that it pertain only to a specific research study, not to future unspecified projects. Following are the core elements of the Privacy Rule Authorization:

- A description of the PHI to be used or disclosed, identifying the information in a specific and meaningful manner
- The names or other specific identification of the person or persons authorized to make the requested use or disclosure
- The names or other specific identification of the person or persons to whom the covered entity may make the requested use or disclosure

Figure 18.5. Deidentifying protected health information

The Privacy Rule allows covered entities to deidentify data by removing the following 18 elements that may be used to identify the individual or the individual's relatives, employers, or household members.

1. Names
2. All geographic subdivisions smaller than a state, including street address, city, county, precinct, ZIP code, except for the initial three digits of a ZIP code if, according to the current publicly available data from the Bureau of the Census:
   a. The geographic unit formed by combining all ZIP codes with the same three initial digits contains more than 20,000 people.
   b. The initial three digits of a ZIP code for all such geographic units containing 20,000 or fewer people are changed to 000.
3. All elements of dates (except year) for dates directly related to an individual, including birth date, admission date, discharge date, date of death; and all ages over 89 and all elements of dates (including year) indicative of such age, except that such ages and elements may be aggregated into a single category of age 90 or older.
4. Telephone numbers
5. Facsimile numbers
6. Electronic mail addresses
7. Social Security numbers
8. Medical record numbers
9. Health plan beneficiary numbers
10. Account numbers
11. Certificate/license numbers
12. Vehicle identifiers and serial numbers, including license plate numbers
13. Device identifiers and serial numbers
14. Web universal resource locators (URLs)
15. Internet protocol (IP) address numbers
16. Biometric identifiers, including fingerprints and voiceprints
17. Full face photographic images and any comparable images
18. Any other unique identifying number, characteristic, or code, unless permitted by the Privacy Rule for reidentification

Source: HHS 2004a.

- A description of each purpose of the requested use or disclosure
- Authorization expiration date or expiration event that relates to the individual or to the purpose of the use or disclosure
- Signature of the individual and date (If the individual's legally authorized representative signs the authorization, a description of his or her authority to act for the individual also must be provided.)

In addition, the authorization must include statements indicating:

- The individual has the right to revoke the authorization at any time and must be provided with the procedure for doing so
- Whether treatment, payment, enrollment, or eligibility of benefits can be contingent upon authorization, including research-related treatment and consequences of refusing to sign the authorization, if applicable
- Any potential risk that PHI will be redisclosed by the recipient and no longer protected by the Privacy Rule

In addition, the authorization must be written in plain language and a copy provided to the individual. Elements that are required in the HIPAA consent are shown in figure 18.6 optional elements are listed in figure 18.7.

For some types of research, it is impracticable for researchers to obtain written authorization from research participants. Therefore, the Privacy Rule contains criteria for waiver or alteration of the authorization requirement by an IRB or a Privacy Board. Under the Privacy Rule, either board may waive or alter, in whole or in part, the Privacy Rule's Authorization requirements for the use and disclosure of PHI in connection with a particular research project. For example, an IRB may partially waive the authorization requirement so that the covered entity can provide contact information to investigators so that they can contact and recruit subjects into their research study (HHS 2003).

It is believed that the Privacy Rule will promote participation in clinical trials. Reasons cited most often is concern about health insurance discrimination and loss of privacy should the information be released.

Oversight of Biomedical Research

Because of past abuses of human subjects in the conduct of biomedical research in the United States, Congress began hearings in 1981 to investigate scientific misconduct. Twelve cases of scientific misconduct were reported in the country between 1974 and 1981. Representative Albert Gore Jr., chairman of the Investigations and Oversight Subcommittee of the House Science and Technology Committee, held the first hearing. Continued abuses were reported throughout the 1980s, which resulted in the creation of several agencies that provide oversight of biomedical research.

Office of Research Integrity

In response to the public outcry over scientific misconduct in biomedical research, Congress passed the **Health Research Extension Act** in 1985 (PHS regulation 42 CFR 493). The act requires the secretary of HHS to issue a regulation requiring applicant or awardee institutions to establish "an administrative process to review reports of scientific fraud" and "report to the Secretary any investigation of scientific fraud which appears substantial."

Before 1986, reports of scientific misconduct were received by funding institutes within the Public Health Service (PHS). In 1986, the National Institutes of Health (NIH) assigned responsibility for receiving and responding to complaints of scientific misconduct to its Institutional Liaison Office. This was the first step in creating a central locus of responsibility for scientific misconduct within the HHS. In March 1989, the PHS created the Office of Scientific Integrity (OSI) and the Office of Scientific Review (OSIR) in the Office of the Assistant Secretary for Health (OASH).

Figure 18.6. Model HIPAA consent—required elements

Authorization to Use or Disclose (Release) Health Information that Identifies You for a Research Study

If you sign this document, you give permission to (name of health care providers) at (name of covered entity) to use or disclose (release) your health information that identifies you for the research study described here:

(provide a description of the research study, such as title and purpose)

The health information that we may use or disclose (release) for this research includes:

The health information listed above may be used by and/or disclosed (released) to:

(Name of covered entity) is required by law to protect your health information. By signing this document, you authorize (name of covered entity) to use and/or disclose (release) your information for this research. Those persons who receive your health information may not be required by Federal privacy laws (such as the Privacy Rule) to protect it and may share your information with others without your permission, if permitted by laws governing them.

Please note that (include the appropriate statement):

- You do not have to sign this Authorization, but if you do not, you may not receive research-related treatment (When the research involves treatment and is conducted by the covered entity or when the covered entity provides healthcare solely for the purpose of creating protected health information to disclose to a researcher).
- (Name of covered entity) may not condition (withhold or refuse) treating you on whether you sign this Authorization. (When the research does not involve research-related treatment by the covered entity or when the covered entity is not providing healthcare solely for the purpose of creating protected health information to disclose to a researcher)

Please note that (include the appropriate statement):

- You may change your mind and revoke (take back) this Authorization at any time, except to the extent that (name of covered entity) has already acted based on this Authorization. To revoke this Authorization, you mist write to: (name of covered entity and contact information) (Where the research study is conducted by an entity other than the covered entity)
- You may change your mind and revoke (take back) this Authorization at any time. Even if you revoke this Authorization, (name of persons at the covered entity involved in the research) may still use or disclose health information they already have obtained about you as necessary to maintain the integrity or reliability of the current research. To revoke this Authorization, you mist write to: (name of covered entity and contact information)

This Authorization does not have an expiration date.

Figure 18.7. Model HIPAA consent—optional elements

Authorization to Use or Disclose (Release) Health Information that Identifies You for a Research Study

Your health information will be used or disclosed when required by law.

- Your health information may be shared with a public health authority that is authorized by law to collect or receive such information for the purpose of preventing or controlling disease, injury, or disability, and conducting public health surveillance, investigations, or interventions.
- No publication or public presentation about the research described above will reveal your identity without another authorization from you.
- All information that does or can identify you is removed from your health information, the remaining information will no longer be subject to this authorization and may be used or disclosed for other purposes.
- **When the research for which the use or disclosure is made involves treatment and is conducted by a covered entity:** To maintain the integrity of this research study, you generally will not have access to your personal health information related to this research until the study is complete. At the conclusion of the research and at your request, you generally will have access to your health information that (name of covered entity) maintains in a designated record set that includes medical information or billing records used in whole or in part by your doctors or other healthcare providers at (name of covered entity) to make decisions about individuals. Access to your health information in a designated record set is described in the Notice of Privacy Practices provided to you by (name of covered entity). If it is necessary for your care, your health information will be provided to you or your physician.

In 1992, the OSI and the OSIR were consolidated to form the **Office of Research Integrity** (ORI) in the OASH (HHS 2005b). The creation of these groups removed responsibility for reviewing complaints of scientific misconduct from the funding agencies.

In 1993, the NIH Revitalization Act established the ORI as an independent agency within HHS. The role, mission, and structure of the ORI is focused on preventing misconduct and promoting research integrity principally through oversight, education, and review of institutional findings and recommendations. Responsibilities of the ORI include:

- Developing policies, procedures, and regulations related to the detection, investigation, and prevention or research misconduct and the responsible conduct of research
- Reviewing and monitoring research misconduct investigations conducted by applicant and awardee institutions
- Implementing activities and programs to teach the responsible conduct of research, promote research integrity, prevent research misconduct, and improve the handling of allegations of research misconduct
- Providing technical assistance to institutions that respond to allegations of research misconduct
- Conducting policy analyses, evaluations, and research to build the knowledge base in research misconduct and research integrity

The ORI within the HHS conducted a study which examined scientists' reports on suspected research misconduct. From this study, they found that investigators believe that the best way to detect and prevent research misconduct is to have the PI supervise research work closely by reviewing data and applying quality control procedures or audits on the data. They also found that more open communication is necessary to detect research misconduct and that anonymity is necessary for the person reporting the possible misconduct.

Polices and an effective training guide with a system for reporting were also found to be important (HHS 2008d).

Check Your Understanding 18.2

Instructions: Answer the following questions on a separate piece of paper.

1. In signing an informed consent, a subject releases the research sponsor from any liability or negligence. True or false?
2. A patient agrees to be a subject in a clinical trial assessing the effectiveness of the combination of two cancer agents. Because the patient is part of this research, all medical expenses are covered by the sponsoring organization. True or false?
3. Medical records of subjects in a research study may be released without patient authorization. True or false?
4. A subject may withdraw from a research study at any time. True or false?
5. Individuals who may be subject to undue influence to enroll in biomedical research are considered vulnerable. True or false?
6. Individuals who participate in clinical trials and biomedical research must sign the HIPAA consent form. True or false?
7. A patient's medical record number is considered protected health information (PHI). True or false?
8. What basic elements should be contained in an informed consent for human subjects?
9. Describe the relationship of the HIPAA Privacy Rule to clinical research.
10. What federal agencies provide oversight to biomedical research?

Types of Biomedical Research Designs

The more common types of designs for research involving human subjects include:

- Epidemiological studies
- Cross-sectional study
- Case-control studies
- Cohort studies
- Clinical trials

Epidemiological Studies

Epidemiology is the study of health and disease in populations rather than individuals. It examines epidemics as well as chronic diseases. The purpose of an **epidemiological study** is to compare two groups or populations of individuals, one group with the risk factor of interest and one without it. In such studies, the investigator attempts to identify risk factors for diseases, conditions, behaviors, or risks that result from particular causes, such as environmental factors and industrial agents.

The goal is to quantify the association between exposures and outcomes and to test hypotheses about causal relationships. Epidemiological research has several objectives:

- Identify the cause of disease and its associated risk factors
- Determine the extent of disease in a given community
- Study the natural history and prognosis of disease
- Evaluate new preventive and therapeutic measures and new modes of healthcare delivery
- Provide the foundation for public policy and regulatory decisions relating to environmental problems

Epidemiological studies may be observational or experimental. In an **observational study**, the exposure and outcome for each individual in the study is studied (observed). In an **experimental study**, the exposure status for each individual in the study is determined and the individuals are then followed to determine the effects of the exposure.

Observational studies are used to generate hypotheses for later experimental studies. They may consist of clinical observations at a patient's bedside. For example, Alton Ochsner observed that every patient he operated on for lung cancer had a history of cigarette smoking (Gordis 1996). If he had wanted to explore the relationship further, he would have compared the smoking histories of a group of his lung cancer patients with a group of his patients without lung cancer. This would be a case-control study. Research designs that are considered observational are cross-sectional studies, prospective cohort studies, retrospective cohort studies, and case-control studies

In biomedical research, experimental studies consist primarily of randomized clinical trials. In randomized clinical trials, individuals are randomly assigned to experimental and control groups in order to study the effect of an intervention, such as an experimental drug.

A major purpose of epidemiological studies is to determine risk. In prospective studies, a 2 × 2 table is a tool that is used to evaluate the association between exposure and disease. (See table 18.1.) The table is a cross-classification of exposure status and disease status. The total number of individuals with the disease is a + c, and the total number without disease is b + d. The total number exposed is a + b, and the total number not exposed is c + d.

The number of individuals who had both exposure and the disease is recorded in cell *a*; the number who had exposure, but no disease, is recorded in cell *b*; the number who had the disease, but no exposure, is recorded in cell *c*; and the number who had neither the disease nor exposure is recorded in cell *d*.

Cross-Sectional Study

In a **cross-sectional study**, both the exposure and the disease outcome are determined at the same time in each subject. A cross-sectional study may also be referred to as a prevalence study because it describes characteristics and health outcomes

Table 18.1. 2 × 2 table for classifying disease status and exposure status

		Disease Status		
		Yes	**No**	**Total**
Exposure Status	Yes	a	b	$a + b$
	No	c	d	$c + d$
		$a + c$	$b + d$	$a + b + c + d$

at a particular point in time. It provides quantitative estimates of the magnitude of a problem. After the population has been defined, the presence or absence of exposure and of disease can be established for each individual in the study. Each subject is then categorized into one of four subgroups that correspond to the 2 × 2 table that appears in table 18.2. An example of a cross-sectional study is determining the prevalence rate of individuals that receive yearly eye exams with type 2 diabetes mellitus.

The prevalence of disease in persons with exposure (a/a + b) is compared with persons without exposure (c/c + d). Alternatively, the prevalence of exposure in persons with the disease (a/a + c) is compared to the prevalence of exposure to persons without the disease (b/b + d).

A major advantage of the cross-sectional study is that it is relatively easy to conduct and may produce results in a short period of time. The disadvantage is that because exposure and disease are determined at the same time in each subject, the time relationship between exposure and onset of the disease cannot be established. It describes only what exists at the time of the study.

Case-Control Study

Case-control studies are a major component of epidemiological research. In them, persons with a certain condition (cases) and persons without the condition (**controls**) are studied by looking back in time. The objective is to determine the frequency of the risk factor among the cases and the frequency of the risk factor among the controls in order to determine possible causes of the disease. In a case-control study, if there is an association between exposure and disease, the prevalence of history of exposure will be higher in persons with the disease (cases) than in those without it (controls). For a case-control study, the 2 × 2 table in table 18.1 is modified in table 18.3. The proportion of cases exposed is a/a + c, and the proportion of controls exposed is b/b + d. For example, a researcher may be interested in examining the relationship between cell phone use and brain cancer. The researcher selects the cases as those individuals with brain cancer and the controls as those individuals without brain cancer but very much like the cases in all other characteristics. So, when selecting the controls, the researcher may choose a sibling or friend of the cases, as long as they do not have brain cancer. Then, the researcher may review cell phone records or conduct a person-to-person interview asking them questions about their past cell phone use. Odds ratios will be determined. If the odds ratio is 5, the researcher can conclude that those individuals who use cell phones are five times more likely to develop brain cancer than those individuals who do not use cell phones (see "Risk Assessment").

The advantages of case-control studies are that they are easy to conduct and cost-effective, with minimal risk to the subjects. Also, existing records may be used to conduct the studies. Case-control studies also allow the researcher to study multiple causes of disease. Although the use of existing medical records is advantageous, there are problems associated with using them for retrospective research. One major problem is that the cases are based on hospital admissions. Admissions are based on patient characteristics, severity of illness and associated conditions, and admission policies. All of these vary from hospital to hospital, making standardization of the study difficult. In addition, there are problems related to poor documentation, illegibility, and missing records. Lack of consistency in diagnostic and clinical services between hospitals also makes comparability difficult. Further, validation of the information can be difficult. An important aspect of epidemiological studies is the identification of risk. In studies using medical records, the population at risk is generally not defined.

Cohort Study

A **cohort study** is a prospective study in which the investigator selects a group of exposed individuals and unexposed individuals who are followed for a period of time to compare the incidence of disease in the two groups. The length of time for follow-up varies from a few days for acute diseases to several decades for cancer and cardiac diseases. If there is an association between exposure and disease, the incidence of disease is greater in the exposed group (a/a + b) than in the unexposed group (c/c + d). New cases of the disease are identified as they occur so that it can be determined whether a time relationship exists between exposure to disease and development of disease. The time relationship must be established if the exposure is to be considered the cause of the disease. For a cohort study, the 2 × 2 table in table 18.1 is modified in table 18.4.

Table 18.2. 2 × 2 table for cross-sectional studies

	Disease	No Disease	Totals	Prevalence of Disease for Exposed/Not Exposed
Exposed	a	b	$a + b$	$a/a + b$
Not Exposed	c	d	$c + d$	$c/c + d$
Totals	$a + c$	$b + d$	$a + b + c + d$	$a + b + c + d$
Prevalence of Exposure for Disease/No Disease	$a/a + c$	$b/b + d$		

Group a: Persons exposed with the disease
Group b: Persons exposed without the disease
Group c: Persons with the disease, but not exposed
Group d: Persons without disease and without exposure

Table 18.3. 2 × 2 table for case-control studies

	Cases (with disease)	Controls (without disease)
Exposed	*a*	*b*
Not exposed	*c*	*d*
Total	*a* + *c*	*b* + *d*
Proportions exposed	*a*/*a* + *c*	*b*/*b* + *d*

Table 18.4. 2 × 2 table for cohort studies

	Disease Develops	Disease Does Not Develop	Totals	Incidence Rates of Disease
Exposed	*a*	*b*	*a* + *b*	*a*/*a* + *b*
Not Exposed	*c*	*d*	*c* + *d*	*c*/*c* + *d*

One of the most famous cohort studies is the Framingham Study, which began in the 1950s. The research project was designed to monitor the incidence of coronary artery disease in more than 5,000 residents who were examined every two years for a period of 20 years. This study has provided important data demonstrating the relationship between the development of heart disease and risk factors such as smoking, obesity, diet, and high blood pressure.

Cohort studies offer several advantages. First, the researcher can control the data collection process throughout the study. Also, outcome events can be checked as they occur; many outcomes can be studied, including those that were not anticipated at the start of the study. The disadvantages of cohort studies are that they are costly and there is a long wait for the study results. Also, subjects may be lost to death, withdrawal, or follow-up.

One difference between case-control and cohort studies is that the former is a retrospective study and the latter is a prospective study. A **retrospective study** is conducted by reviewing records from the past; a **prospective study** is designed to observe events that occur after the subjects have been identified. The advantages and disadvantages of retrospective and prospective studies are outlined in tables 18.5 and 18.6.

Another difference is that in a cohort study the subjects are individuals with or without the disease and the focus is disease status; in the case-control study, the subjects are individuals who have been exposed or not exposed to the disease and the focus is exposure status.

Table 18.5. Advantages and disadvantages of retrospective studies

Advantages	Disadvantages
Short study time	Control group subject to bias in selection
Relatively inexpensive	Biased recall possible
Suitable for rare diseases	Cannot determine incidence rate
Ethical problems minimal	Relative risk is approximate
Hospital medical record may be used	
Small number of subjects	
No attrition problems	

Table 18.6. Advantages and disadvantages of prospective studies

Advantages	Disadvantages
Control group less susceptible to bias	Requires more time
No recall necessary	Costly
Incidence rate can be determined	Relatively common diseases only
Relative risk is accurate	Ethical problems may be considerable and influence study design
	Volunteers needed
	Results may not be generalizable to a larger population
	Requires a large number of subjects
	Problems with attrition

Clinical Trials

Clinical (medical) research is a specialized area of research that primarily investigates the efficacy of preventive, diagnostic, and therapeutic procedures. Efficacy involves both safety and effectiveness.

Clinical trials are the specific, individual studies within the field of clinical research. They offer a systematic way to introduce, evaluate, and monitor new drugs, treatments, and devices prior to their dissemination throughout the healthcare system. As a result, they have proved to be effective means of advancing knowledge about medicine and health and, thus, improving the quality of healthcare in the United States. Because clinical trials involve patients, they can begin only after the researcher has shown promising results in the laboratory or the results have been well documented in the literature.

The NIH supports thousands of clinical trials (NIH 2008). Private organizations such as drug companies and health maintenance organizations (HMOs) also support them. Trial sites are teaching and community hospitals, physician group practices, or health departments. Many clinical trials are multicentered; that is, a number of research institutions cooperate in conducting the study. In **randomized clinical trials** (RCTs), participants are assigned to a treatment or a control group. They may be **single-** or **double-blinded studies**, in which case the investigator, the participants, or both do not know who is in the treatment or control group until the end of the study.

Researchers conduct clinical trials using **protocols**. Protocols are sets of strict procedures that specify the language of informed consent, the types of subjects, the timing of treatments, the period of participation, and the evaluation of efficacy. For example, in RCTs, researchers must follow strict rules in assigning patients to groups. The rules ensure that both known and unknown risk factors will occur in approximately equal numbers between the group of patients receiving the treatment and the group of patients not receiving it.

Most clinical trials consist of three phases. In a phase 1 drug trial, studies are performed on 20 to 80 healthy volunteers who are closely monitored. The objective of phase 1 drug trials is to determine the metabolic and pharmacological actions of the drug in humans, to determine the side effects associated with increasing dosages, and to gain early evidence of effectiveness. Historically, phase 1 trials are considered the safest and usually involve administering a single dose to healthy volunteers. But they also can pose a high level of unknown risk because this is the first administration of a drug to a human. When the drug is highly toxic, such as cancer chemotherapies, cancer patients are usually the subjects for phase 1 trials.

In the phase 2 drug trial, the number of participants is usually increased to between 100 and 200. The purpose of this trial is to evaluate the drug's effectiveness for a certain indication in patients with the condition under study and to determine the short-term side effects and risks associated with the drug. Subjects included in phase 2 studies are usually those with the condition the drug is intended to treat. Phase 2 studies are randomized, well controlled, and closely monitored. They may include randomization to treatment and control groups and be double-blinded. Treatment and control groups allow for comparison between subjects who received the drug and those who did not.

Phase 3 drug trials involve the administration of a new drug to a larger number of patients in different clinical settings to determine its safety, effectiveness, and appropriate dosage. The number of subjects involved may range from several hundred to several thousand. Phase 3 trials are conducted only after evidence of effectiveness has been obtained. Phase 3 studies are designed to collect more information on drug effectiveness and safety for evaluating the drug's overall risk benefit.

The FDA, in collaboration with the **sponsor**, may decide to conduct a phase 4 postmarketing study to obtain more information about the drug's risks, benefits, and optimal use. Phase 4 studies may include studying different doses or schedules of administration than what was used in phase 2 studies, the use of the drug in other patient populations or other stages of the disease, or the use of the drug over a longer period of time. See table 18.7.

Risk Assessment

As stated earlier, one objective of epidemiological studies is to assess risk. Risk is the probability that an individual will develop a disease over a specified period of time, provided that he or she did not die as a result of some other disease process during the same time period. It is usually expressed as **relative risk** (RR). Before risk can be assessed properly, prevalence and incidence should be defined. Prevalence refers to the number of existing cases of a particular disease. Incidence refers to the number of new cases of a disease. The *prevalence rate* is therefore the number of existing cases of disease in a particular region during a specific time period divided by the number of individuals in the specific region for a specific time period. The *incidence rate* is the number of new cases of disease in a particular region during a specific time period divided by the number of individuals in the specific region for a specific time period. RR is calculated from cohort studies and compares the risk of some disease in two groups differentiated by some demographic variable such as sex or race. The group of interest is referred to as the exposed group and the comparison group is the unexposed group. The risk ratio is calculated as:

$$\frac{\text{Risk for exposed group or the incidence rate of the exposed group}}{\text{Risk for unexposed group or the incidence rate of the unexposed group}}$$

A relative risk of 1.0 indicates that there is identical risk in both groups. A RR that is greater than 1.0 indicates an increased risk for the exposed group; a RR of less than 1.0 indicates a decreased risk for the exposed group.

Odds Ratio

In a case-control study, the objective is to identify differences in exposure frequency associated with one group having the disease under study and the other group not having it. The incidence of disease in the exposed and unexposed populations is not known because persons with the disease (cases) and without the disease (controls) are identified at the onset of the study. Thus, RR cannot be calculated directly. So the question becomes: what are the odds that an exposed person will develop the disease? Or, put another way, what are the odds that a nonexposed person will develop the disease?

In a case-control study, the **odds ratio** compares the odds that the cases were exposed to the disease with the odds that

Table 18.7. Phases of clinical trials

Phase	I	II	III	IV
Number of Subjects	20–80	100–300	1000–3000	Multitudes postmarketing
Purpose	Evaluate safety Determine dosage Identify side effects	Evaluate safety Determine effectiveness	Collect more information about safe usage Confirm effectiveness Monitor side effects Compare to alternatives	Collect data on effect on specific groups (populations) Monitor long-term side effects

the controls were exposed. Using the 2 × 2 table in table 18.1 as a reference, the odds ratio is calculated as:

$$\frac{a/b}{c/d} = \frac{a \times c}{b \times c}$$

The odds ratio measures the odds of exposure of a given disease. For example, an odds ratio of 1.0 indicates that the incidence of disease is equal in each group; thus, the exposure may not be a risk factor for the disease of interest. An odds ratio of 2.0 indicates that the cases were twice as likely to be exposed as the controls. This implies that the exposure is associated with twice the risk of disease.

Attributable Risk

The **attributable risk** (AR) is a measure of the public health impact of a causative factor on a population. In this measure, the assumption is that the occurrence of a disease in an unexposed group is the baseline or expected risk for that disease. Any risk above that level in the exposed group is attributed to exposure to the risk factor. It is assumed that some individuals will acquire a disease, such as lung cancer, whether or not they were exposed to a risk factor such as smoking. The AR measures the additional risk of illness as a result of an individual's exposure to a risk factor. The AR is calculated as:

$$AR = \frac{\text{(Risk for exposed group)} - \text{(Risk for unexposed group)}}{\text{Risk for exposed group}} \times 100$$

Check Your Understanding 18.3

Instructions: Answer the following questions on a separate piece of paper.

1. Describe the relationship of the Privacy Rule to clinical research.
2. What are some of the common types of research designs used in studies of human subjects?
3. What are the objectives of epidemiological studies?
4. In what type(s) of studies are medical records used?
5. What are the characteristics of a case-control study?
6. What are the characteristics of randomized clinical trials?
7. What is relative risk?
8. What is attributable risk?

Outcomes and Effectiveness Research in Healthcare

The major objective of **outcomes and effectiveness research** (OER) is to understand the end results (outcomes) of particular healthcare practices and interventions. Examples of patient outcomes include ability to function, quality of life, satisfaction, and mortality. By linking the care that patients receive to the outcomes they experience, OER has become the key to developing better ways to monitor and improve the quality of care.

The history of outcomes research can be traced back to the 1860s when Florence Nightingale laid the foundation for collecting and evaluating hospital statistics (Burns 2005). Hospital mortality rates were the basic measures used for evaluating patient outcomes. The major finding was that mortality rates varied significantly from hospital to hospital.

The Flexner Report (1910), the Codman studies (1914), the establishment of hospital standards by the American College of Surgeons (1913), and the founding of the Joint Commission (1952) are landmarks in the development of outcomes research. More recently, the passage of Medicare (1965) and subsequent legislation has accelerated interest in outcomes research.

Outcomes and Effectiveness Research Strategies

OER may be conducted at the community, system, institutional, or patient level. At the community level, outcomes research focuses on the population as a whole or on specific communities. For example, the Dartmouth Atlas of Musculoskeletal Health Care (Center for the Evaluative Clinical Sciences 2000) has found that the rate for leg amputations in the southern tip of Texas is more than two times higher than the national average. The amputation rate in the Corpus Christi region is 3.7 leg amputations per 1,000 Medicare patients, three times higher than in Amarillo.

OER at the system level refers to the healthcare system as a whole. It may include the entire country or a specific region. Examples of geographic variations in medical care at the national level cited by the Dartmouth Atlas of Health Care include:

- In Bend, Oregon, the rate for back surgeries is 7.3 for every 1,000 Medicare recipients, more than four times higher than in Syracuse, New York, where there are 1.5 surgeries for every 1,000 Medicare recipients.
- Heart patients in Elyria, Ohio receive angioplasties at a rate more than seven times higher than in York, Pennsylvania, 360 miles away.
- Men in Baton Rouge, Louisiana undergo prostate removal surgery at a rate more than eight times higher than do men in Tuscaloosa, Alabama.

OER at the institutional level refers to the sites in which healthcare is delivered: hospitals, clinics, or HMOs. At the patient level, interest is on the interaction between one provider and one patient. An example outcome study performed at the institutional level is a review of medical records and clinical data of patients with a principal diagnosis of acute myocardial infarction that expire during hospitalization. A second example is the ongoing assessment of patient satisfaction.

There is no standard method for conducting outcomes research at the institutional level or any level. Donabedian (1966) proposed the first model for evaluating patient outcomes. His model focused on measuring the structure, process, and outcomes of medical care. Structure is the setting in which the healthcare is provided and the resources available to provide it. Process is the extent to which professionals perform according to accepted standards. Process is a set of activities that take place between providers. Outcomes include changes in the patient's condition, quality of life, and level of satisfaction. Characteristics of structure, process, and outcome appear in table 18.8. Other models used for the study of outcomes include the disease model and the health and wellness model. Epidemiological approaches are often used to study outcomes. In the hospital setting, the medical record often serves as the data source for outcomes studies.

Outcomes and Effectiveness Measures

Several types of measures are used in OER:

- *Clinical performance* measures are designed to evaluate the processes or outcomes of care associated with the delivery of clinical services. They allow for intra-organizational and inter-organizational comparisons to be used to improve patient health outcomes. Clinical measures should be condition specific or procedure specific or should address important functions of patient care, such as medication use and infection control.
- *Patient perceptions of care* and services focus on the delivery of clinical services from a patient's perspective. Aspects of care that may be addressed are patient education, wait times, medication use, pain management, practitioner bedside manner, communication regarding current care and future plans for care, and improvement in health status.
- *Health status* measures address the functional well-being of specific populations, both in general and in relation to specific conditions. They indicate changes that have occurred in physical functioning, bodily pain, social functioning, and mental health over time.
- *Administrative and financial performance* measures address the organizational structure for coordinating and integrating service, functions, or activities across organizational components. Examples of administrative and financial measures are those related to financial stability, utilization, length of stay (LOS), and credentialing.

Defining expected clinical outcomes is a major section of the protocols for clinical trials. The principal investigator or organization sponsoring the study must specifically state the expected outcomes of the clinical trial before the investigation can begin. Investigators also must state at what point the research study will stop if adverse events occur. Examples of study objectives and outcome variables are listed in figure 18.8.

Current Outcomes Movement

The current outcomes movement gained momentum in the 1980s when the prospective payment system (PPS) for

Table 18.8. Characteristics of structure, process, and outcome

Structure	Process	Outcome
System characteristics: Organization Specialty mix Workload Access/convenience	Technical: Visits Medications Referrals Test ordering Hospitalizations	Clinical endpoints: Symptoms and signs Laboratory values Death
Provider characteristics: Specialty training Preferences Job satisfaction	Interpersonal: Interpersonal manner Counseling Communication level	Health-related quality of life: Physical Mental Social Role
Patient characteristics: Diagnosis/condition Severity Comorbidity Health habits		Satisfaction with care: Access Convenience Quality General

Figure 18.8. Sample objectives and outcome variables for clinical research

Objective: to determine whether the treatment drug is safe and effective in patients with advanced chronic heart failure and is effective in reducing the incidence of cardiovascular hospitalization and/or mortality due to all causes.

Primary Outcome Variable: The primary outcome variable is the time from entry into the study to mortality from all causes of cardiovascular hospitalization. A hospitalization is a nonelective admission for medical therapy that results in at least one overnight stay. A cardiovascular hospitalization is one that is due to heart failure, myocardial infarction, coronary insufficiency, stroke, atrial or ventricular dysrhythmias, or symptomatic heart block.

Secondary Outcome Variable:

Time from study entry to all-cause mortality or all-cause hospitalization

Time from study entry to all-cause mortality or worsening heart failure hospitalization

Patient global assessment at the six-month visit

Six-minute walk test at the six-month visit

Other Outcomes of Interest:

All hospitalizations, classified by cause (heart failure, cardiovascular, vascular, nonvascular) in regard to frequency, length of stay, and cost

Number of emergency department visits classified by cause (heart failure or nonheart failure)

Mortality classified by cause (heart failure, cardiovascular, vascular, nonvascular)

All-cause mortality, all-cause hospitalization, cardiac transplant, and left ventricular assist device insertion

Myocardial infarction and cardiac revascularization

The safety and tolerability of the drug as determined by the occurrence of adverse events, permanent treatment withdrawals, changes in laboratory tests, physical exam, and ECG

Medicare inpatient care was implemented. The public and policy makers were concerned that Medicare patients were being forced out of hospitals because "their DRG had run out." The fear was that patients were being discharged based on their LOS rather than when they were clinically ready for discharge. William Roper, who became HCFA (Health Care Financing Administration, now the Centers for Medicare and Medicaid Services [CMS]) administrator in 1986, promoted the use of Medicare databases to monitor the quality of care through measurement of mortality rates, readmission rates, and other adverse outcomes.

Simultaneously, others were advancing the outcomes movement, which contained elements of research, measurement, and management. John Wennberg, director of the Center for the Evaluative Clinical Sciences at the Dartmouth Medical School, and others developed methods for exploring the impact of healthcare services on patient outcomes. Other research efforts on geographic variations in medical practice, appropriateness of care, and the poor quality of medical evidence to support various interventions and treatments resulted in establishment of the Agency for Health Care Policy and Research (AHCPR) in 1989. The Healthcare Research and Quality Act of 1999 changed the agency's name to the Agency for Healthcare Research and Quality (AHRQ). The mission of the AHRQ is to support health services research designed to improve the outcomes and quality of healthcare, reduce its costs, address patient safety and medical errors, and broaden access to effective services. The research sponsored by the AHRQ provides information that helps people make better decisions about healthcare. The goals and research priorities of the AHRQ include:

- Supporting improvement in health outcomes
- Strengthening quality measurement and improvement
- Identifying strategies to improve access, foster appropriate use, and reduce unnecessary expenditures

A component of the AHRQ is the AHRQ **quality indicators** (QIs). QIs are measures that address various aspects of quality. The various types of QIs include the following (AHRQ 2006):

- *Prevention QIs* identify hospital admissions that could have been avoided, at least in part, through high-quality outpatient care.
- *Inpatient QIs* reflect quality of care inside hospitals, including inpatient mortality for medical conditions and surgical procedures. Four dimensions are used to assess inpatient quality: volume, mortality for inpatient procedures, mortality for inpatient conditions, and utilization indicators.
- *Patient safety indicators* also reflect quality of care inside hospitals but focus on potentially avoidable complications and iatrogenic events. Patient safety indicators screen for problems that patients experience as a result of exposure to the healthcare system and that can be prevented by changes at the provider level or the area level. Provider-level indicators include only those cases where a secondary ICD-9-CM diagnosis code flags a potentially preventable complication. Area-level indicators capture all cases of potentially preventable complications in a given area either during a hospitalization or resulting in subsequent hospitalization. Area-level indicators are identified by both principal and secondary ICD-9-CM diagnoses codes.

Examples of AHRQ quality indicators appear in tables 18.9 through 18.11.

One must use caution when evaluating the results of assessments using the inpatient quality indicators. The data collected for these indicators were collected using the ICD-9-CM codes that appear on the UB-04. This represents administrative data and not research data. Limitations associated with using administrative data include:

- *Coding differences across hospitals:* Some hospitals code more thoroughly than others, making "fair" comparisons across hospitals difficult.
- *Ambiguity about when a condition occurs:* Most administrative data cannot distinguish whether a specific condition was present at admission or whether it occurred during the inpatient stay.
- *Limitations in ICD-9-CM coding:* The codes are often not specific enough to adequately describe a patient's condition, which makes it impossible to perfectly risk-adjust any administrative data set. This makes fair comparisons across hospitals difficult.

However, despite these limitations, QIs can assist individual hospitals in comparing their organizations with averages at the national, regional, or state level. The information can be used to investigate potential quality problems. Investigation may reveal quality problems for which quality improvement programs may be initiated, uncover problems in data collection that can be remedied through coding education, or determine what additional clinical information is required to understand the quality issues, beyond that obtained through administrative data alone.

An analytical tool that the AHRQ supports is the **Healthcare Cost and Utilization Project** (HCUP). The HCUP database, called HCUPnet, is an online query system that gives instant access to the largest set of all payer healthcare databases that are publicly available (AHRQ 2008). It contains Web-based tools that can be used to identify, track, analyze, and compare trends in hospital care at the national, regional, and state levels. HCUP data are used for research on hospital utilization, access, charges, quality, and outcomes. This database can be queried for information when doing internal assessments related to the AHRQ QIs. Figure 18.9 provides a snapshot of the interactive databases available at HCUPnet.

Table 18.9. AHRQ inpatient quality indicators

Type of Indicator	Definition	Indicators
Volume	Indirect measure of quality based on evidence suggesting that hospitals performing more of certain intensive, high-technology, or highly complex procedures may have better outcomes for these procedures.	Esophageal resection volume Pancreatic resection volume Pediatric heart surgery volume Abdominal aortic aneurysm (AAA) repair volume Coronary artery bypass graft (CABG) volume Percutaneous transluminal coronary angioplasty (PTCA) volume Carotid endarterectomy (CEA) volume
Mortality Indicators for Inpatient Conditions	Conditions where mortality has been shown to vary substantially across institutions and where evidence suggests that high mortality may be associated with deficiencies in the quality of care.	Acute myocardial infarction (AMI) mortality rate Congestive heart failure mortality rate Acute stroke mortality rate Gastrointestinal hemorrhage mortality rate Hip fracture mortality rate Pneumonia mortality rate
Mortality Indicators for Inpatient Procedures	Procedures where mortality has been shown to vary substantially across institutions and where evidence suggests that high mortality may be associated with deficiencies in the quality of care.	Esophageal resection mortality rate Pancreatic resection mortality rate Pediatric heart surgery mortality rate AAA repair mortality rate CABG mortality rate PTCA mortality rate CEA mortality rate Craniotomy mortality rate Hip replacement mortality rate
Utilization	Procedures whose use varies significantly across hospitals and for which questions have been raised about overuse, underuse, or misuse. High or low rates are likely to represent inappropriate or inefficient delivery of care.	Cesarean delivery rate Primary Cesarean delivery rate Vaginal birth after Cesarean (VBAC) rate VBAC rate, uncomplicated Laparoscopic cholecystectomy rate Incidental appendectomy in the elderly rate Bilateral cardiac catheterization rate

Source: AHRQ 2006.

Table 18.10. AHRQ patient safety indicators

Complications of anesthesia
Death in low-mortality DRGs
Decubitus ulcer
Failure to rescue
Foreign body left during procedure
Iatrogenic pneumothorax
Selected infections due to medical care
Postoperative hip fracture
Postoperative infection or hematoma
Postoperative physiologic and metabolic derangements
Postoperative respiratory failure
Postoperative pulmonary embolism or deep vein thrombosis
Postoperative sepsis
Postoperative wound dehiscence
Accidental puncture of laceration
Transfusion reaction
Birth trauma—injury to neonate
Obstetric trauma—vaginal with instrument
Obstetric trauma—vaginal without instrument
Obstetric trauma—Cesarean delivery
Obstetric trauma with 3rd degree lacerations—vaginal with instrument
Obstetric trauma with 3rd degree lacerations—vaginal without instrument
Obstetric trauma with 3rd degree lacerations—Cesarean delivery

Source: AHRQ 2006.

Table 18.11. AHRQ prevention quality indicators

Indicator Name
Diabetes short-term complication admission rate
Perforated appendix admission rate
Diabetes long-term complications admission rate
Pediatric asthma admission rate
Chronic obstructive pulmonary disease (COPD) admission rate
Pediatric gastroenteritis admission rate
Hypertension admission rate
Congestive heart failure (CHF) admission rate
Low birth weight rate
Dehydration admission rate
Bacterial pneumonia admission rate
Urinary tract infection admission rate
Angina without procedure admission rate
Uncontrolled diabetes admission rate
Adult asthma admission rate
Rate of lower-extremity amputation among patients with diabetes

Source: AHRQ 2006.

Figure 18.9. Text from HCUPnet Web page (partial)

National Statistics	Create your own statistics for national and regional estimates on hospital use for all patients from the HCUPNationwide Inpatient Sample (NIS).
For Children Only	Create your own statistics for national estimates on use of hospitals by children (age 0–17 years) from the HCUPKids' Inpatient Database (KID).
State Statistics	Create your own statistics on stays in hospitals for participating States from the HCUPState Inpatient Databases (SID).
Quick Statistics	Ready-to-use tables on commonly requested information from the HCUPNationwide Inpatient Sample (NIS), the HCUPKids' Inpatient Database (KID), or the HCUPState Inpatient Databases (SID).
AHRQ Quality Indicators	Ready-to-use national information on measures of healthcare quality based on the NIS, using theAHRQ Quality Indicators (QIs).

AHRQ 2006.

As an example, an organization wants to evaluate its congestive heart failure (CHF) mortality rate. CHF is a progressive, chronic disease with substantial short-term mortality, which varies across organizations. To begin the process, the researcher must review the definition of CHF mortality rate, which appears in table 18.12, and the ICD-9-CM codes used to retrieve the CHF information (table 18.13). The organization's data then can be compared with AHRQ QIs available at the HCUPnet Web site. (National data for the CHF mortality rate is displayed in figure 18.10.)

Use of Comparative Data in Outcomes Research

Healthcare organizations such as the National Commission for Quality Assurance (NCQA) and the Joint Commission have developed measures for evaluating the effectiveness of healthcare providers. The purpose of the measures developed by the NCQA is to provide purchasers of healthcare, primarily employers, with information about the cost and effectiveness of organizations with which they contract for services. The Joint Commission measures also are designed primarily to encourage organizations to improve their own performance and to provide a comprehensive picture of the care provided within the organization. A full discussion of NCQA's HEDIS measures and the Joint Commission's ORYX measures, as well as other performance measures used in healthcare and by healthcare providers, is presented in chapter 17.

Table 18.12. Congestive heart failure mortality rate

Relationship to quality	Better processes of care may reduce short-term mortality, which represents better quality.
Benchmark	State, regional, or peer group average
Definition	Number of deaths per 100 discharges with principal diagnosis code of CHF
Numerator	Number of deaths with a principal diagnosis code of CHF
Denominator	All discharges with a principal diagnosis of CHF. Age 18 years and older. Exclude patients with missing discharge disposition, transferring to another short-term hospital, MDC 14 and MDC 15.
Type of indicator	Mortality indicator for inpatient conditions
Empirical performance	Population rate (2002): 4.61 per 100 discharges at risk

Check Your Understanding 18.4

Instructions: Answer the following questions on a separate piece of paper.

1. What is the purpose of outcomes and effectiveness research?
2. What types of outcomes are studied?
3. What is the mission of the Agency for Healthcare Research and Quality (AHRQ)?
4. Who sponsors the Health Care Utilization Project (HCUP)? What is the purpose of its database?
5. What is the focus of the AHRQ quality indicators? What are their limitations?
6. What types of performance measures are used in outcomes and effectiveness research?

Real-World Case

The director of research at a large university hospital is searching for funding sources for two HIM professionals that are interested in collaborating with two administrative nurses to examine the best methods to properly train nurses when using an electronic health record (EHR). This experimental study will engage nurses in the use of the EHR by using interactive technology to train them on this system. In order to effectively perform the research, other methods of training will be developed and assessed. For example, a randomization technique will be used so that some nurses will receive hands-on classroom training while others will

Table 18.13. ICD-9-CM codes for congestive heart failure

398.31	Rheumatic heart failure	428.21	Acute systolic heart failure
402.01	Malignant hypertensive heart disease with CHF	428.22	Chronic systolic heart failure
402.11	Benign hypertensive heart disease w/ CHF	428.23	Acute or chronic systolic heart failure
402.91	Hypertensive heart disease w/ CHF	428.9	Heart failure NOS
404.01	Malignant hypertensive heart/renal disease w/ CHF	428.30	Diastolic heart failure NOS
404.03	Malignant hypertensive heart/real disease w/ CHF and renal failure	428.31	Acute diastolic heart failure
404.11	Benign hypertensive heart/renal disease w/ CHF	428.32	Chronic diastolic heart failure
404.13	Benign hypertensive heart/renal disease w/ CHF and renal failure	428.33	Acute or chronic diastolic heart failure
404.91	Hypertensive heart/renal disease NOS w/ CHF	428.40	Systolic/diastolic heart failure NOS
404.93	Hypertensive heart/renal disase w CHF and renal failure	428.41	Acute systolic/diastolic heart failure
428.0	Congestive heart failure	428.42	Chronic systolic/diastolic heart failure
428.1	Left heart failure	428.43	Acute/chronic systolic/diastolic heart failure
428.20	Systolic heart failure NOS		

receive Web-based hands-on training. Then the nurses' attitudes towards the training will be assessed as well as direct observations of how well they are able to navigate the EHR system. Funding sources of support for this type of research may be found through the hospital's internal foundation or through the Foundation of Research and Education (FORE) at AHIMA or through the American Nurses Association. IRB review and approval as well as informed consent will need to be obtained for each of the nurses participating in the research study. Since the study will take place over a two-year period, ongoing progress reports must be submitted to the IRB as well as yearly renewals. The investigators hope to publish the results in the peer-reviewed, online journal, *Perspectives in Health Information Management* or in the *Online Journal of Nursing Informatics*.

Summary

Biomedical and health services research conducted on human subjects should follow guidelines set forth in the *Belmont Report*, the Nuremberg Code, and the Declaration of Helsinki. Furthermore, biomedical research on human subjects requires a thorough evaluation and approval from the IRB. The IRB is a review board that examines research studies to determine if the rights of human subjects involved in the research are protected. The different levels of IRB approval depend upon the type of research conducted. Exempt, expedited, and full study protocols are the different levels of review. Informed consent is necessary when individuals are involved in research. Consent forms are necessary for research that is invasive or includes some type of intervention. The Office of Research Integrity and the Office for Human Research Protections are federal agencies that provide oversight of biomedical research.

Many study designs are used to conduct biomedical research, including cross-sectional studies, case-control studies, cohort studies, and clinical trials. In a cross-sectional study, the frequency of a risk factor and an outcome of interest in a geographically defined population are studied at one point in time. In a case-control study, the frequency of the exposure in the diseased cases is compared with the frequency of exposure in the controls. In a cohort study, individuals with the risk factor and individuals without the risk factor are followed over time for specific outcomes. Clinical trials are controlled studies that involve human subjects. They are designed to evaluate prospectively the safety and effectiveness of new drugs, devices, or behavioral interventions.

A major objective of biomedical and health services research is to quantify the risk of obtaining a particular disease resulting from exposure to a risk factor. Relative risk, odds ratio, and attributable risk are measures used to quantify or assess risk. Relative risk compares the incidence of disease in the exposed group to the incidence of disease in the control group. The odds ratio, the odds of exposure in a diseased group, is divided by the odds of exposure in the nondiseased group. Odds ratios are assessed in case-control studies while relative risk is assessed in cohort studies. Attributable risk is the proportion of total risk for a disease or outcome attributable to a particular exposure.

Various models for outcomes and effectiveness research are available and are commonly used in performance

Figure 18.10. National quality indicators—2001 national statistics
Deaths per 1,000 adult admissions with congestive heart failure (CHF) (excluding obstetric and neonatal admissions and transfers to another hospital) (IQI 16), by patient and hospital characteristics

	Adjusted Rate a/		
Patient/Hospital Characteristic	**Estimate**	**Standard Error**	***P*-Value: Relative to Marked Group b/**
Total U.S.	44.698	0.428	
Patient characteristic:			
Age Groups for Conditions Affecting Any Age			
18–44 b/	22.076	2.258	
45–64	25.679	0.967	0.142
65 and over	50.750	0.488	0.000
Age Groups for Conditions Affecting Primarily Elderly			
65–69 b/	35.905	1.379	
70–74	32.705	1.182	0.078
75–79	42.576	1.058	0.000
80–84	53.968	1.055	0.000
85 and over	72.328	0.927	0.000
Gender:			
Male b/	48.272	0.640	
Female	41.833	0.575	0.000
Median income of patient ZIP:			
Less than $25,000	42.678	1.475	0.232
$25,000–$34,999	45.843	0.818	0.258
$35,000–$44,999	44.267	0.827	0.739
$45,000 or more b/	44.627	0.699	
Location of patient residence:			
Metropolitan b/	43.573	0.479	
Micropolitan	47.994	1.251	0.001
Non-CBSA	50.439	1.470	0.000
Location of inpatient treatment:			
Northeast b/	49.514	0.939	
Midwest	43.447	0.920	0.000
South	44.069	0.649	0.000
West	41.512	1.129	0.000
Expected payment source:			
Private insurance b/	47.832	1.173	
Medicare	43.619	0.489	0.001
Medicaid	46.731	1.692	0.593
Other insurance	57.347	3.659	0.013
Uninsured/self pay/no charge	48.916	2.723	0.715
Hospital characteristic:			
Ownership/control:			
Private, not-for-profit b/	44.330	0.504	
Private, for-profit	43.841	1.101	0.686
Public	47.763	1.194	0.008

(Continued on next page)

Figure 18.10. (Continued)

Patient/Hospital Characteristic	Adjusted Rate a/		
	Estimate	Standard Error	*P*-Value: Relative to Marked Group b/
Teaching status:			
Teaching	44.817	0.823	0.863
Nonteaching b/	44.652	0.501	
Location of hospital:			
Metropolitan b/	43.344	0.470	
Micropolitan	49.545	1.312	0.000
Noncore	53.607	1.685	0.000
Bedsize:			
Less than 100	51.067	1.119	0.000
100–299 b/	44.933	0.658	
300–499	41.770	0.825	0.003
500+	43.189	1.061	0.163

Source: Agency for Healthcare Research and Quality's Healthcare Cost and Utilization Project, Nationwide Inpatient Sample. For relevant denominator sources, see Methods section.

a/ Rates are adjusted by age, gender, age-gender interactions, and APR-DRG risk of mortality score. When reporting is by age, the adjustment is by gender and APR-DRG risk of mortality score; when reporting is by gender, the adjustment is by age and APR-DRG risk of mortality score.

b/ Reference for *p*-value test statistics.

Weighted national estimate from HCUP Nationwide Inpatient Sample (NIS), 2001, Agency for Healthcare Research and Quality (AHRQ), based on data collected by individual statewide data organizations and provided to AHRQ through the HCUP partnership.

Total number of weighted discharges in the U.S. based on HCUP NIS = 37,187,641.

Source: AHRQ 2005b.

improvement (quality improvement) programs within healthcare organizations. The AHRQ sets a national agenda for the types of outcomes research that should be conducted and serves as a resource for individuals engaged in outcomes and health services research.

References

Agency for Healthcare Research and Quality. 2002. *AHRQ Quality Indicators—Guide to Inpatient Quality Indicators: Quality of Care in Hospitals—Volume, Mortality, and Utilization.* Revision 4. AHRQ pub. no. 02-R0204 (December 22, 2004). Rockville, MD: AHRQ.

Agency for Healthcare Research and Quality. 2004. *AHRQ Quality Indicators—Guide to Prevention Quality Indicators: Hospital Admission for Ambulatory Care Sensitive Conditions.* Revision 4. AHRQ pub. no.-2-R0203. Rockville, MD: AHRQ.

Agency for Healthcare Research and Quality. 2006. *AHRQ Quality Indicators—Guide to Patient Safety Indicators.* Version 2.1, Revision 3. AHRQ pub. no. 03-R203. Rockville, MD: AHRQ.

Agency for Healthcare Research and Quality. 2008. *HCUPnet, Healthcare Cost and Utilization Project.* Rockville, MD: AHRQ.

Burns, N and S. Grove. 2005. *The Practice of Nursing Research: Conduct, Critique, and Utilization.* Elsevier Saunders, 17

Center for the Evaluative Clinical Sciences at Dartmouth Medical School. 2000. Dartmouth Atlas of Healthcare. Hanover, NH: CECS. http://www.dartmouthatlas.org.

Department of Health and Human Services 2003. Institutional Review Boards and the HIPAA Privacy Rule. NIH pub.no. 03-5428. http://www.privacyruleandresearch.nih.gov/irbandprivacyrule.asp.

Department of Health and Human Services. 2004a. Clinical Research and the HIPAA Privacy Rule. NIH pub. no. 04-5495. http://www.privacyrule andresearch.nih.gov/clin_research.asp.

Department of Health and Human Services. 2004b. HIPAA Authorization for Research. NIH Pub. no. 04-5529. http://www.privacyruleandresearch.nih.gov/authorization.asp.

Department of Health and Human Services, 2005a. Office of Human Research Protections OHRP Fact Sheet. http://www.hhs.gov/ohrp/about/ohrpfactsheet.htm and fda.gov/oc/gcp/preambles/56fr28025.html.

Department of Health and Human Services, 2008a. Office of Human Research Protections Human Subject Assurance Training. http://www.ohrp-ed.od.nih.gov/CBTs/Assurance/login.asp.

Department of Health and Human Services. 2008b. Office of Human Research Protections IRB Guidebook. http://www.hhs.gov/ohrp/irb/irb_chapter1.htm.

Department of Health and Human Services, 2008c. Office of Human Research Protections IRB Guidebook. http://www.hhs.gov/ohrp/irb/irb_introduction.htm--under applying ethical principles).

Department of Health and Human Services. 2008d. The Office of Research Integrity Observing and Reporting Suspected Misconduct in Biomedical Research. The Gallup Organization, James A. Wells, Project Director.

Donabedian, A. 1966. Evaluating the quality of medical care. *Milbank Memorial Fund Quarterly: Health and Society* 44(3):166–203.

Gordis, L. 1996. *Epidemiology.* Philadelphia: W.B. Saunders.

Joint Commission. 2008. Rights and Responsibilities of Individuals: Pre-publication version. In *The Joint Commission Hospital Accreditation Program 2009* http://www.jointcommission.org.

Joint Commission on Accreditation of Healthcare Organizations. 2005. *Comprehensive Accreditation Manual for Hospitals.* Oakbrook Terrace, IL: Joint Commission.

National Institute of Health. 2008. Clinicaltrials.gov. http://clinicaltrials.gov.

The Nuremberg Code. 1949. Washington, D.C.: U.S. Government Printing Office. Reprinted in *Trials of War Criminals before the Nuremberg Military Tribunals under Control Council Law* 2(10):188–182. http://www.nihtraining.com/ohsrsite/guidelines/nuremberg.

University of Pittsburgh. 2008a. Institutional Review Board Reference Manual. Jurisdiction, Structure, and Responsibilities. http://www.irb.pitt.edu/manual/preface.pdf.

University of Pittsburgh. 2008b. Internet Based Studies in Education and Research. http://www.cme.hs.pitt.edu/servlet/IteachControllerServlet?actiontotake=faq&source=non-hipaa.

University of Pittsburgh. 2008c. Institutional Review Board Reference Manual. IRB Investigator Communications. http://www.irb.pitt.edu/manual/chapter4.pdf.

University of Pittsburgh. 2008d. Institutional Review Board IRB forms Adverse Event Reporting Form. http://www.irb.pitt.edu/irbforms/irbforms.htm.

Watzlaf, V., L. Kuller, and F. Ruben. 1998 (July). The Use of Medical Record and Financial Data to Examine the Cost of Infections in the Elderly. *Pharmacy Practice Management Quarterly.* 18(2).

Appendix 18A
Sample Informed Consent Document

Revised 6/2/08

SAMPLE INFORMED CONSENT DOCUMENT

Please note that some of the language contained in this sample consent document may not be appropriate for the type of study that you are conducting. If you would like assistance on how to modify the document for your study, please contact the IRB Office.

ONLY INCLUDE THIS HEADER ON ALL CONSENT PAGES IF YOU ARE SUBMITTING A PAPER APPLICATION. IF YOU ARE SUBMITTING AN ELECTRONIC SUBMISSION THROUGH OSIRIS (CURRENTLY REQUIRED FOR ALL NEW PROTOCOLS), PLEASE USE THE WATERMARK THAT IS AVAILABLE THROUGH THE SYSTEM.

(Division, Department, School, or Center Letterhead)

University of Pittsburgh
Institutional Review Board
Approval Date:
Renewal Date:
IRB Number:

CONSENT TO ACT AS A PARTICIPANT IN A RESEARCH STUDY

TITLE: Phase III Evaluation of Iometinol-300 as a Contrast Medium for CT Scans

PRINCIPAL INVESTIGATOR: Cynthia Curie, M.D.
Professor of Radiology
University of Pittsburgh
Room B-319, UPMC Presbyterian
Telephone: 412-647-xxxx

CO-INVESTIGATORS: Ray Rembrant, M.D.
Associate Professor of Radiology
University of Pittsburgh
Room B-325, UPMC Presbyterian
Telephone: 412-647-xxxx

SOURCE OF SUPPORT: January Laboratories, Inc.
Department of Radiology, UPMC

Why is this research being done?

You are being asked to participate in a research study in which we will test whether an "investigational" drug, called Iometinol-300, can further improve the pictures taken during CT scans, compared to drugs used currently. We will also test the safety of this "investigational drug". Computerized tomography (CT scan) is a method to take pictures of internal organs using X-rays. To increase the quality of these pictures, a drug ("X-ray dye") is often given by injection into a vein prior to the CT scan. Iometinol-300 is an "investigational" X-ray dye. This drug is considered "investigational" because it has not received approval from the Food and Drug Administration for general use.

Page 1 of 10 Participant's Initials______

Revised 6/2/08

In this research study, we will compare the CT scan pictures taken with the study drug, Iometinol-300, to those taken with the standard drug currently used in the radiology department. We will also evaluate if the study drug causes any changes to your body or blood.

Who is being asked to take part in this research study?

You are being invited to take part in this research study because you have already been scheduled for a CT scan of your head using the standard drug. The results of the CT scan using the standard drug will be compared to the results of an extra, research CT scan using the study drug to show us which of the two drugs was better for your particular case.

People invited to participate in this study must be between 18-60 years of age and, if female, cannot be pregnant. The study is being performed on a total of 60 individuals in three different medical centers in the United States. At this medical center, 20 individuals will participate.

What procedures will be performed for research purposes?

If you decide to take part in this research study, you will undergo the following procedures that are not part of your standard medical care:

Screening Procedures:

Procedures to determine if you are eligible to take part in a research study are called "screening procedures". For this research study, the screening procedures include:

1. For women who could possibly be pregnant, a small sample (about 1 teaspoonful) of blood will be taken from a vein in your arm for a pregnancy test. Pregnant women, or women who are currently breast-feeding an infant, will not be allowed to take part in this study.

Experimental Procedures:

If you qualify to take part in this research study, you will undergo the experimental procedures listed below. These procedures will take place in the radiology department.

1. Prior to the injection of the study drug and the extra, research CT scan, we will measure your blood pressure, temperature, and heart rate. In addition, we will obtain a blood sample (about 1 teaspoonful) from a vein in your arm for safety tests. This will require about 30 minutes of your time.
2. The study drug will be injected by vein followed by the extra, research CT scan.

Page 2 of 10 Participant's Initials______

Revised 6/2/08

Monitoring/Follow-up Procedures:

Procedures performed to evaluate the effectiveness and safety of the experimental procedures are called "monitoring " or "follow-up" procedures. For this research study, the monitoring/ follow-up procedures include:

1. One hour after the injection of the study drug, we will again measure your blood pressure, temperature, and heart rate. Thus, the study drug injection, research CT scan, and repeat safety measures will require about 1 hour of your time.

   You are free to leave the radiology department after these measures, but you will need to return 3 hours later for additional safety tests.

2. Four hours after the injection of the study drug, we will once again measure your blood pressure, temperature, and heart rate. These repeat safety measures will require about 15 minutes of your time.

   You are free to go home after these measures, but you will need to return the next day for final safety tests.

3. At about 24 hours (1 day) following injection of the study drug, we will measure your blood pressure, temperature, and heart rate. We will also obtain another sample (about 1 teaspoonful) of blood from your vein for follow-up safety tests. These procedures will require about 30 minutes of your time and will be performed in the radiology department.

4. The investigators will compare your scheduled CT scan using the standard drug to the research CT scan using the study drug.

What are the possible risks, side effects, and discomforts of this research study?

The possible risks of this research study may be due to the study drug, the blood tests, and/or the radiation exposure from the extra CT scan.

Risks of the Study Drug:

Previous human research studies using the study drug have shown that the nature and number of adverse events associated with its use are similar to those which occur with the standard drugs used for CT scans.

Infrequent adverse events (occur in 1–10%, or 1–10 out of 100 people): Itching, hives, nausea, and vomiting may be expected in 1-2% of the individuals who receive the study drug. These adverse events are usually mild in severity.

 Participant's Initials______

Revised 6/2/08

Rare adverse events (occur in less than 1% , or less than 1 out of 100 people): In about 1 out of every 10,000 injections (0.01%), more severe reactions (e.g., shortness of breath, chest pain, seizure) may occur. In some cases these reactions can be life-threatening.

As with any experimental procedure, there may be adverse events or side effects that are currently unknown and certain of these unknown risks could be permanent, severe, or life threatening.

A physician and emergency drugs and equipment will be readily available should you experience any adverse reactions from administration of the study drug.

Because participation in this study may harm a pregnancy, you and any person with whom you have sex must use an approved form of birth control. If you become pregnant or father a child while you are in this study, you must tell your doctor at once. Also, women must not breast feed while in this study. If you are a woman and you are able to become pregnant, you will have a *(insert the appropriate measurement: blood or urine)* test to make sure that you are not pregnant before you are permitted to undergo the experimental procedures. If you have questions, you are encouraged to speak with either the study doctor or your personal physician. **(Note: Additional examples of acceptable reproductive risk language appear on the IRB web site in a document entitled "Guidance for Reproductive Risk Language for Consents Revised February 22, 2008."**

Risks of the Blood Tests:

Bruising, soreness, or rarely, infection may occur as a result of the needle sticks to obtain blood from your vein.

Risks of Radiation Exposure:

Participation in this research study will involve exposure to radiation from the extra, research CT scan. The amount of radiation exposure that you will receive from this extra CT scan is about 1 rem (a unit of radiation exposure) to your head, with minimum exposure of other areas of your body. For comparison, radiation workers are permitted, by federal regulation, a maximum radiation exposure of 50 rems per year to any single body organ. There is no minimum amount of radiation exposure that is recognized as being totally free of the risk of causing genetic mutations (abnormal cells) or cancer. However, the risk associated with the amount of radiation exposure that you will receive from taking part in this study is felt to be low and comparable to everyday risks.

What are possible benefits from taking part in this study?

You will likely receive no direct benefit from taking part in this research study. Should the study drug be better than the standard drug, it is possible that you may receive some benefit from the higher quality CT scan. However, such a benefit cannot be guaranteed.

Page 4 of 10 Participant's Initials______

Revised 6/2/08

What treatments or procedures are available if I decide not to take part in this research study?

If you decide not to take part in this research study, you will have only the routine CT scan for which you were scheduled, using the standard drug.

If I agree to take part in this research study, will I be told of any new risks that may be found during the course of the study?

You will be promptly notified if, during the conduct of this research study, any new information develops which may cause you to change your mind about continuing to participate.

Will my insurance provider or I be charged for the costs of any procedures performed as part of this research study?

Neither you, nor your insurance provider, will be charged for the costs of any of the procedures performed for the purpose of this research study (i.e., the Screening Procedures, Experimental Procedures, or Monitoring/Follow-up Procedures described above). You will be charged, in the standard manner, for any procedures performed for your routine medical care (e.g., the CT scan for which you were already scheduled).

(NOTE—IF THE RESEARCH SUBJECTS OR THEIR HEALTH INSURANCE PROVIDER WILL BE RESPONSIBLE FOR ANY COSTS ASSOCIATED WITH THE RESEARCH, PLEASE INCLUDE THE FOLLOWING STATEMENTS):

If you participate in this research study, the cost of the experimental (device or drug, as applicable) and/or the costs of certain procedures performed for the purpose of the research study may be billed to your health insurance provider. You will be notified, in advance of undergoing the research procedures should your health insurance provider refuse to cover certain or all of these research costs and if any of these uncovered research costs will be billed directly to you. In this situation, you will be provided with a price estimate for the uncovered research costs that will be billed to you. If you decide to continue your participation in this research study, you will be required to meet with a hospital financial counselor to arrange for your advance payment of these uncovered research costs. If you do not have health care insurance, you will be provided with a price estimate for the research costs that will be billed to you. If, you decide to continue your participation in this research study, you will be required to meet with a hospital financial counselor to arrange for your advance payment of these research costs.

Will I be paid if I take part in this research study?

You will be paid a total of $150 if you complete all parts of this study. If, for whatever reason, you complete part but not all of the study, the terms of this payment will be as follows: 1) $20 for completing the initial temperature, blood pressure, and heart rate measurements and blood sample (if applicable); 2) an additional $50 for completing the extra, research CT scan using the new drug; 3) an additional $20 for completing the repeat measurements at 1 hour after injection of the study drug; 4) an additional $20 for completing the repeat measurements at 4 hours after injection of the study drug; and 5) an additional $40 for completing the repeat measurements and blood sample at 24 hours after injection of the study drug.

Page 5 of 10 Participant's Initials______

Revised 6/2/08

In addition, any parking fees related to your participation in this study will be paid for by the study.

Who will pay if I am injured as a result of taking part in this study?

For research that is NOT commercially sponsored but is conducted at Pitt or UPMC facilities utilize the following language:

If you believe that the research procedures have resulted in an injury to you, immediately contact the Principal Investigator who is listed on the first page of this form. Emergency medical treatment for injuries solely and directly related to your participation in this research study will be provided to you by the hospitals of UPMC. Your insurance provider may be billed for the costs of this emergency treatment, but none of those costs will be charged directly to you. If your research-related injury requires medical care beyond this emergency treatment, you will be responsible for the costs of this follow-up care. At this time, there is no plan for any additional financial compensation.

For research that IS commercially sponsored and the protocol is provided by the sponsor, please see Chapter 8 of the IRB Reference Manual for instructions.

Who will know about my participation in this research study?

Any information about you obtained from this research will be kept as confidential (private) as possible. All records related to your involvement in this research study will be stored in a locked file cabinet. Your identity on these records will be indicated by a case number rather than by your name, and the information linking these case numbers with your identity will be kept separate from the research records. You will not be identified by name in any publication of the research results unless you sign a separate consent form giving your permission (release).

Will this research study involve the use or disclosure of my identifiable medical information?

This research study will involve the recording of current and/or future identifiable medical information from your hospital and/or other (e.g., physician office) records. The information that will be recorded will be limited to information concerning the purpose of the CT scan that you were scheduled to undergo for your medical care, the results of this CT scan, and any adverse events that may have been associated with the approved X-ray dye used in this CT scan. This information will be compared to the research CT scan performed using the study drug for the purpose of evaluating the safety and effectiveness of the study drug.

This research study will result in identifiable information that will be placed into your medical records held at UPMC Presbyterian. The nature of the identifiable information resulting from your participation in this research study that will be recorded in your medical record includes the results of the additional CT scan performed for research purposes and information related to any adverse events you may suffer following the injection of the study drug.

Page 6 of 10 Participant's Initials______

Revised 6/2/08

Who will have access to identifiable information related to my participation in this research study?

In addition to the investigators listed on the first page of this authorization (consent) form and their research staff, the following individuals will or may have access to identifiable information (which may include your identifiable medical information) related to your participation in this research study:

Authorized representatives of the University of Pittsburgh Research Conduct and Compliance Office may review your identifiable research information (which may include your identifiable medical information) for the purpose of monitoring the appropriate conduct of this research study.

In unusual cases, the investigators may be required to release identifiable information (which may include your identifiable medical information) related to your participation in this research study in response to an order from a court of law. If the investigators learn that you or someone with whom you are involved is in serious danger or potential harm, they will need to inform, as required by Pennsylvania law, the appropriate agencies.

Authorized representatives of the sponsor of this research study, January Laboratories, Inc., will review and/or obtain identifiable information (which may include your identifiable medical information) related to your participation in this research study for the purpose of monitoring the accuracy and completeness of the research data and for performing required scientific analyses of the research data. Authorized representatives of the study sponsor may also be present during your participation in CT procedures performed as part of this research study. While the study sponsor understands the importance of maintaining the confidentiality of your identifiable research and medical information, the UPMC and University of Pittsburgh cannot guarantee the confidentiality of this information after it has been obtained by the study sponsor. The investigators involved in the conduct of this research study may receive funding from the sponsor to perform the research procedures and to provide the sponsor with identifiable research and medical information related to your participation in the study.

Authorized representatives of the U.S. Food and Drug Administration may review and/or obtain identifiable information (which may include your identifiable medical information) related to your participation in this research study for the purpose of monitoring the accuracy of the research data. While the U.S. Food and Drug Administration understands the importance of maintaining the confidentiality of your identifiable research and medical information, the University of Pittsburgh and UPMC cannot guarantee the confidentiality of this information after it has been obtained by the U.S. Food and Drug Administration.

Authorized representatives of the UPMC hospitals or other affiliated health care providers may have access to identifiable information (which may include your identifiable medical information) related to your participation in this research study for the purpose of (1) fulfilling orders, made by the investigators, for hospital and health care services (e.g., laboratory tests, diagnostic procedures) associated with research study participation; (2) addressing correct payment for tests and procedures ordered by the investigators; and/or (3) for internal hospital operations (i.e. quality assurance).

Page 7 of 10 Participant's Initials______

Revised 6/2/08

For how long will the investigators be permitted to use and disclose identifiable information related to my participation in this research study?

The investigators may continue to use and disclose, for the purposes described above, identifiable information (which may include your identifiable medical information) related to your participation in this research study for a minimum of seven years after final reporting or publication of a project.

May I have access to my medical information that results from my participation in this research study?

In accordance with the UPMC Notices of Privacy Practices document that you have been provided, you are permitted access to information (including information resulting from your participation in this research study) contained within your medical records filed with your health care provider.

Is my participation in this research study voluntary?

Your participation in this research study, to include the use and disclosure of your identifiable information for the purposes described above, is completely voluntary. (Note, however, that if you do not provide your consent for the use and disclosure of your identifiable information for the purposes described above, you will not be allowed to participate in the research study.) Whether or not you provide your consent for participation in this research study will have no effect on your current or future relationship with the University of Pittsburgh. Whether or not you provide your consent for participation in this research study will have no effect on your current or future medical care at a UPMC hospital or affiliated health care provider or your current or future relationship with a health care insurance provider.

Your doctor is involved as an investigator in this research study. As both your doctor and a research investigator, s/he is interested both in your medical care and the conduct of this research study. Before agreeing to participate in this research study, or at any time during your study participation, you may discuss your care with another doctor who is not associated with this research study. You are not under any obligation to participate in any research study offered by your doctor.

May I withdraw, at a future date, my consent for participation in this research study?

You may withdraw, at any time, your consent for participation in this research study, to include the use and disclosure of your identifiable information for the purposes described above. (Note, however, that if you withdraw your consent for the use and disclosure of your identifiable medical record information for the purposes described above, you will also be withdrawn, in general, from further participation in this research study.) Any identifiable research or medical information recorded for, or resulting from, your participation in this research study prior to the date that you formally withdrew your consent may continue to be used and disclosed by the investigators for the purposes described above.

To formally withdraw your consent for participation in this research study you should provide a written and dated notice of this decision to the principal investigator of this research study at the address listed on the first page of this form.

Page 8 of 10 Participant's Initials______

Revised 6/2/08

Your decision to withdraw your consent for participation in this research study will have no effect on your current or future relationship with the University of Pittsburgh. Your decision to withdraw your consent for participation in this research study will have no effect on your current or future medical care at a UPMC hospital or affiliated health care provider or your current or future relationship with a health care insurance provider.

If you decide to withdraw from study participation after you have received the study drug, you should participate in described monitoring follow-up procedures directed at evaluating the safety of the study drug.

If I agree to take part in this research study, can I be removed from the study without my consent?

It is possible that you may be removed from the research study by the researchers if, for example, your pregnancy test proves to be positive. If you are withdrawn from participation in this research study, you will continue to undergo the CT scan for which you were scheduled using the currently approved X-ray dye.

****

VOLUNTARY CONSENT

The above information has been explained to me and all of my current questions have been answered. I understand that I am encouraged to ask questions about any aspect of this research study during the course of this study, and that such future questions will be answered by a qualified individual or by the investigator(s) listed on the first page of this consent document at the telephone number(s) given. I understand that I may always request that my questions, concerns or complaints be addressed by a listed investigator.

I understand that I may contact the Human Subjects Protection Advocate of the IRB Office, University of Pittsburgh (1-866-212-xxxx) to discuss problems, concerns, and questions; obtain information; offer input; or discuss situations that have occurred during my participation.

By signing this form, I agree to participate in this research study. A copy of this consent form will be given to me.

______________________	______________________	__________
Participant's Signature	Printed Name of Participant	Date

Page 9 of 10 Participant's Initials______

Revised 6/2/08

CERTIFICATION of INFORMED CONSENT

I certify that I have explained the nature and purpose of this research study to the above-named individual(s), and I have discussed the potential benefits and possible risks of study participation. Any questions the individual(s) have about this study have been answered, and we will always be available to address future questions as they arise."

______________________________	______________________________
Printed Name of Person Obtaining Consent	Role in Research Study
______________________________	______________________________
Signature of Person Obtaining Consent	Date

IF THE RESEARCH STUDY INVOLVES CHILDREN OR DECISIONALLY IMPAIRED SUBJECTS, PLEASE SEE CHAPTER 6.0 FOR THE APPROPRIATE LANGUAGE/SIGNATURE SPACES.

Page 10 of 10 Participant's Initials______

Chapter 19
Expert Systems and Decision Support

J. Michael Hardin, PhD and Uzma Raja, PhD

Learning Objectives

- Understand the concept of decision support and the process of decision making
- Recognize the valuable assets contained within the organization's current data systems and how to better use the data
- Understand the background and history of decision support systems in general
- Identify the different structures used to develop decision support systems
- Differentiate among decision support systems and other information systems
- Identify the general types of decision support systems and recognize the key architectural differences
- Explain the concept of data warehousing and how it is applicable to decision support
- Understand the concept of data mining and types of data mining tools used in decision support systems
- Recognize the different classes of decision support systems found in healthcare
- Identify some of the basic models of artificial intelligence used in developing decision support systems
- Be familiar with some of the career opportunities related to decision support activities that are available to HIM professionals

Key Terms

Applied artificial intelligence
Artificial neural network (ANN)
Association rule analysis (rule induction)
Clinical decision support system (CDSS)
Clinical repository
Data miners
Data mining
Data warehouse
Data-based DSS
Decision support system (DSS)
Decision tree
Executive information system (EIS)
Expert system (ES)
Geographical information system (GIS)
Graphical user interface (GUI)
Graphics-based DSS
Health management information system (HMIS)
Hospital information system (HIS)
Hybrid online analytical processing (HOLAP)
Inference engine
Intellectual capital
Knowledge-based DSS
Linkage analysis
Machine learning
Model-based DSS
Multidimensional data structure
Multidimensional database management system (MDDBMS)
Multidimensional online analytical processing (MOLAP)
Natural language processing (NLP)
Normalization
Online analytical processing (OLAP)
Operations research (OR)
Relational database management system (RDMS)
Relational online analytical processing (ROLAP)
Return on investment (ROI)
Rule induction
Satisficing
Simon's decision-making model
Snowflake schema
Star schema
Structural decision
Structured query language (SQL)
Supervised learning
Text mining
Transactional systems
Unstructured decision
Unsupervised learning
Virtual reality (VR)

In *Future Health: Computers and Medicine in the Twenty-First Century,* Kaufman and Paterson (1995) identified seven goals that must be addressed in order to meet the future computing needs of physicians. Of critical importance, they observed, was the continued development and research of **decision support systems** (DSS) (Pickover 1995).

But what are expert and decision support systems? For many people in healthcare, the mention of these systems evokes notions of a computer application that assists the clinician in caring for patients. Based on symptoms and other data from the patient, the computer system formulates possible diagnoses for the patient's condition and presents these suggestions to the clinician. In difficult cases, possibly involving rare conditions, these suggestions may greatly assist the clinician in formulating a decision regarding the best course of treatment for the patient.

Computer systems that provide such aid and recommendations to clinicians in making clinical decisions for individual patients are an important group of expert and decision support systems used in healthcare. This group of systems typically is called **clinical decision support systems** (CDSS).

This chapter examines the many types of expert and decision support systems that are found in today's healthcare environment. It also describes the infrastructure requirements for decision support systems. Finally, this chapter looks at how artificial intelligence is applied in healthcare and discusses the roles of health information management (HIM) professionals in decision support.

Decision Support Systems

As business in general and healthcare in particular have entered into the twenty-first century, a new economic reality has emerged. Known by many different names, this new reality often is called "a knowledge economy" (Hardin et al. 1999). Businesses in a knowledge economy are more reliant on information, and this information resides in their employees and in their corporate data systems. The sum of all this knowledge represents a new form of business asset: **intellectual capital** (Stewart 1997). To be competitive and provide high-quality products and services in a knowledge economy, a business must learn to make right decisions quicker than their competitors do (Senge 1990).

The key point here is decision making. Decision making is a critical task for managers and clinicians. There is no shortage of computers and information technologies. What is important is not simply having information technology to collect data (although in healthcare this is very important as has been seen in the earlier chapters), but how a healthcare organization uses its information to make decisions. Stewart notes that "a corporation becomes a true knowledge company when it becomes aware of and involved in the 'deeper level,' where information is pursued for its own intrinsic value and not simply to automate or report on other activities" (1997, 6).

Expert and decision support systems enable business (healthcare) to move beyond automation of activities and begin to use computers to gain knowledge about its customers and its operations. DSSs include the establishment of repositories and data warehouses to efficiently store the organization's data in such a way as to make them accessible to managers as they make decisions. It also includes activities associated with **data mining**, which is the process of sorting through the organization's data to identify unusual patterns or to apply analytical models that will assist in predicting future events. Current applications of data-mining activities in healthcare include models to support fraud detection, utilization review, and clinical pathways.

DSSs also assist hospital chief financial officers (CFOs) in allocating financial resources (Friend 1992) and assist health plan administrators in managing the medical care market and formulating appropriate payment plans (Forgionne 1991). Additionally, DSSs assist hospital administrators in evaluating resource utilization (Cunningham and McKenna 1993) and improving the distribution of pharmaceuticals for inpatient patients (Zaki 1989). DSSs are being used and evaluated as tools to prevent medical errors and adverse events (Berner et al. 1999) in response to the serious issues noted in *To Err Is Human: Building a Safer Health System* (Kohn et al. 2000). The study described in this book shocked many people when it reported that as many as 98,000 people die annually in the United States as a result of medical errors such as:

- *Adverse events*, which are injuries to patients caused by medical mismanagement instead of the patient's underlying disease or medical condition
- *Medication-related errors*, such as accidental drug poisoning
- *Medication adverse events*, which are injuries resulting when, for example, an antibiotic drug is prescribed for a patient with a history of allergic reactions to the antibiotic

The 2001 Institute of Medicine (IOM) report entitled *Crossing the Quality Chasm: A New Health System for the 21st Century* recommends that greater use of DSSs by healthcare providers and organizations will improve the quality of care for patients and help minimize the likelihood of the occurrence of these serious problems.

Definition and Types

Although computers are integral to the implementation of decision support and expert systems, these systems are really about people—how they solve problems, how they think, how they use information and decide which information to use. In essence, these systems indicate how people make decisions. Hence, a study of decision support and expert systems also must incorporate some discussion of people issues.

A DSS is a computer-based system that gathers data from a variety of sources and assists in providing structure to the data using various analytical models and visual tools in order to facilitate and improve the ultimate outcome in decision-making tasks associated with nonroutine and nonrepetitive problems. However, this is but one of many definitions of a DSS. Because the goals involved in these systems have such breadth, no universally agreed-upon definition exists (Turban 1995). Nevertheless, this is a good working definition and captures the important characteristics commonly identified for DSSs. Table 19.1 provides a list of some of these characteristics.

Notice that the words *expert system* do not appear in the preceding definition. Was this an oversight? Well, yes and no. Most commonly, an **expert system** (ES) is a computer-based system that can perform problem-solving tasks equal to the performance of human experts and, in some cases, can actually exceed the abilities of human experts. ESs were developed as part of a branch of computer science known as **applied artificial intelligence**, and the vision of some of these efforts has been to replace human experts with computers.

Some people argue that although they have some unique features in their architecture, ESs also satisfy the concepts contained in the definition of DSS. Hence, an ES is simply one type of DSS. However, if the notion in the definition relating to the facilitation role of the DSS is seen as one in which the system suggests possible actions, but the final decision rests with the human decision maker, ESs may go beyond DSSs. Artificial intelligence and this view of ESs is discussed later in this chapter, but for now it suffices to include the ES as a type of DSS.

History and Background

The roots of DSS emanate from two articles that appeared in the early 1970s: "Models and Managers: The Concept of a Decision Calculus," by J.D. Little (1970), and "A Framework for Management Information Systems," by G.A. Gorry and M.S. Scott-Morton (1971). Using ideas from the research of Herbert Simon (1960, 1957) on how people—particularly managers—make decisions, these two works proposed computer-based systems to assist in unstructured decision making.

Simon argued that decisions were arrayed on a spectrum from highly structured to unstructured. **Structured decisions** arise from very established, repetitive kinds of problems, ones for which standard solutions are available. Examples of areas that provide such decisions are accounts receivable, patient entry, and so on. **Unstructured decisions** depend on the context that produced the need for the decision to provide a framework for the solution.

During World War II, a new branch of applied mathematics, **operations research** (OR), was developed to analyze situations arising out of the war and to propose mathematical models for their solutions. OR proved effective in providing solutions to structured problems arising in this context. After the war, this new discipline was applied to business problems, and a new business discipline, management science, was launched. During the 1950s and 1960s, these new disciplines assumed that decision makers could follow logical and systematic processes for arriving at business decisions by applying the scientific method to business problems. Thus, business problems were analyzed and classified into various general groups (for example, inventory control and scheduling). The key features of each of these general problems were analyzed, and elegant mathematical models and solutions were developed for them. Computer programs then were developed to perform the computations in a quick and efficient manner. Thus, by the late 1960s, the use of computers to provide assistance and support in the solution of structured decisions had become an important tool for business decision makers.

However, more research was still needed for unstructured decisions. According to Simon, unstructured decisions arose from those contexts in which there were no clear-cut solutions and for which the particular problem or decision at hand may never have been encountered previously and may never be encountered again. The set of possible alternatives as well as the relevant data may not be available to the decision maker in these complex decisions.

Table 19.1. Common characteristics of a decision support system

- Is used in semistructured or unstructured decision contexts
- Is intended to support decision makers rather than replace them
- Supports all phases of the decision-making process
- Focuses on the effectiveness of the decision-making process rather than its efficiency
- Is under the control of the DSS user
- Uses underlying data and models
- Facilitates learning on the part of the decision maker
- Is interactive and user-friendly
- Is generally developed using an evolutionary, iterative process
- Provides support for all levels of management from top executives to line managers
- Can provide support for multiple independent or interdependent decisions
- Provides support for individual, group-based, and team-based decision-making contexts

Source: Marakas 1999, 3.

Decision-Making Process

When faced with decisions, Simon (1960) observed that people use a three-phase approach. A schematic of **Simon's decision-making model** is shown in figure 19.1.

The Intelligence Phase

The first phase of Simon's decision-making model is the intelligence phase. In this phase, the decision maker is attentive to the organization's goals and is on alert for issues that run counter to those goals. The key activities of this phase are problem identification and organizational objective formulation, such as defining the objectives of the problem and what needs to be accomplished. Other activities during this phase may include breaking the problem down into smaller subproblems, problem classification, and data collection. However, the final outcome of this phase should be a careful statement of the problem to be solved or decision to be made.

Figure 19.1. Simon's decision-making model

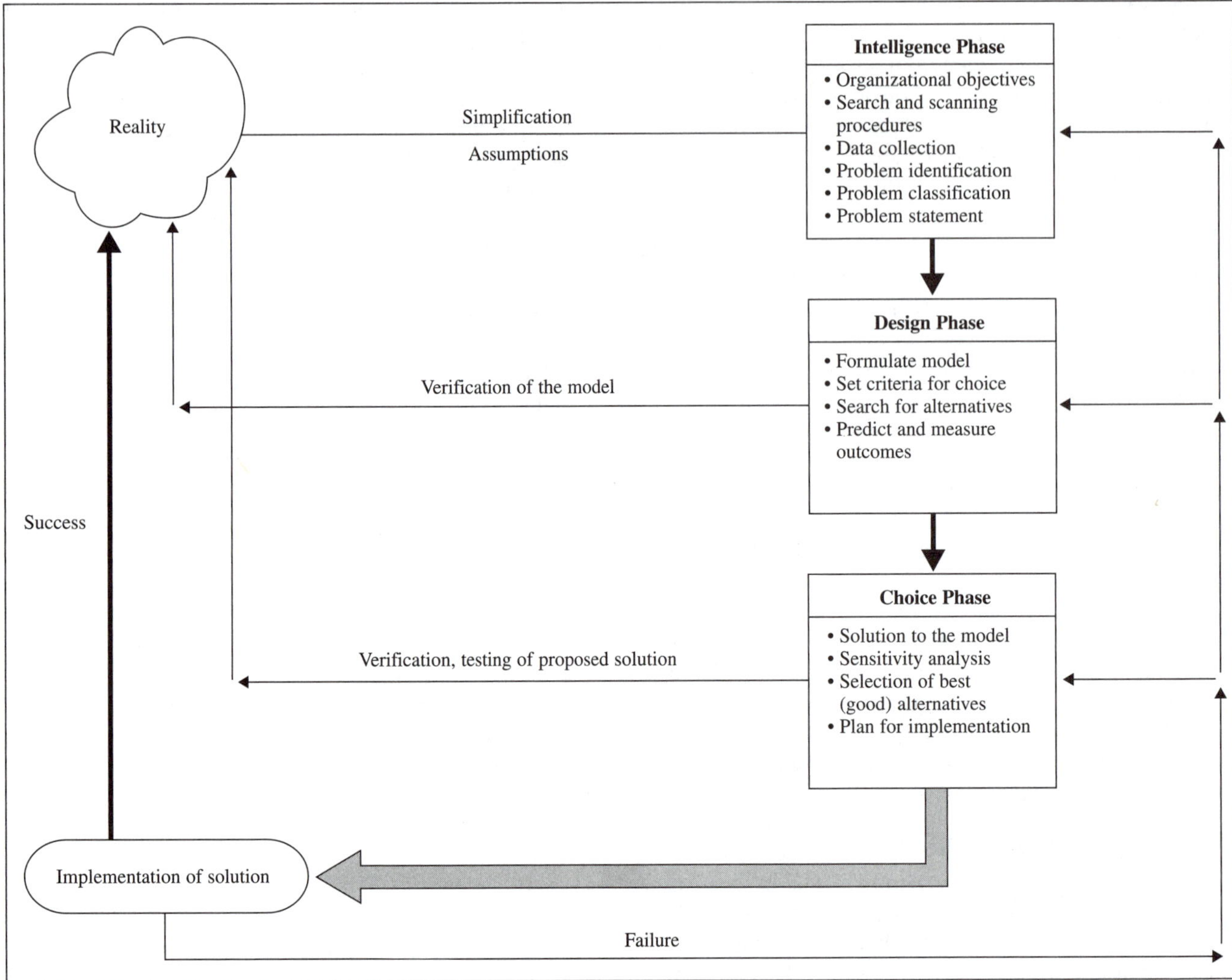

The Design Phase

In the design phase of the decision-making process, the decision maker identifies possible courses of action and the varieties of decision alternatives, locates the various knowledge sources of relevance to the problem, formulates a basic model for the problem, and determines the criteria to be used to evaluate possible alternatives. Also in this phase, the decision maker may seek to gather various data pertinent to the problem. In developing a model, the decision maker identifies various sets of variables to be included.

The sets of variables used in the modeling aspect of this phase include:

- Outcome, or dependent or target variable(s)
- Variables that can be manipulated or controlled
- Variables that cannot be controlled but are simply part of the context of the problem

The relationships among these variables also must be specified.

Often the decision maker has available standard decision-making models. For example, models developed in management science (such as linear and nonlinear programming, goal programming, integer programming) are helpful in this process; the decision maker simply identifies and gathers the appropriate data and information from within the organization to apply these models accurately to a given situation. Illustrative of this phase, one main aim of a data warehouse is to provide a convenient location from which to obtain any data needed in formulating and then solving such models.

The Choice Phase

In the choice phase, the decision maker applies the criteria decided on in the second phase and searches for the appropriate decision alternative. When the decision has been chosen, it must be evaluated and then a recommendation made as to the final solution to the given problem. Certainly, there is overlap between phases two and three with respect to enumerating the possible alternatives and in evaluating and selecting a decision alternative. This concept of postulating various decision alternatives and then selecting from among them is the classic view of decision making and is illustrated in figure 19.2.

A number of interesting questions can be posed about this process, including:

- How are the alternative decisions postulated?
- How many alternatives should be identified?
- What if there are too many alternatives (as is possible in complex problems)?
- What are possible strategies for selecting among the alternative decisions?

The answer to how the alternatives are postulated lies to a large degree in the creativity of the decision maker; however, having many sources of data and information available will enhance this activity. In choosing a possible criterion for selecting among alternatives, various options are available depending on the situation. For example, a problem involving the expenditure of capital may involve a large number of alternatives. Hence, the decision maker might select the criterion of maximizing the **return on investment** (ROI) and seek the alternative that gives the greatest ROI.

Because it can be difficult to determine exactly what the ROI will be for various investments, one might elect to use the criterion that the solution should make a "good" ROI possible. Because the definition of *good* in this case is fuzzy, some minimum ROI might be set and the first alternative accepted that exceeds this minimum. The general idea here is that the decision maker will accept any solution that meets the minimum requirements for a solution; it does not have to be the very best solution or even the optimal solution. Simply providing a solution to the problem that meets the requirements renders it a "good" solution. Such an approach is sometimes called a "good enough" solution or a **satisficing** solution (Simon 1977, 1976).

Figure 19.2. Classic view of decision making

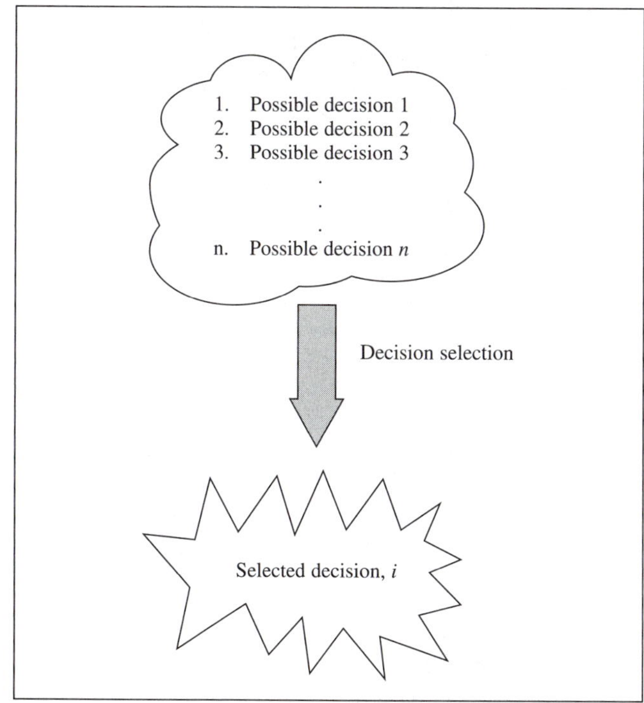

The preceding examples go through phase two of the decision-making process. The next question concerns how to go about searching through all the alternatives to identify one that fulfills the criterion. This search is part of phase three activities and has various options. One option is to use a "try-one-and-see" approach. The idea is simply to begin evaluating the criterion on a given alternative and see if it works. If it does, we are done; if not, we move on. Selection of alternatives is by chance, and so this option may be called a blind search.

Another option would be to use the mathematical optimization tools developed in operations research and management science and to attempt to select the analytically optimal alternative, one that either maximizes some objective such as ROI or minimizes something like loss. Both blind search and optimal searches, however, may take an exceedingly long time, even on a computer, so other options may need to be considered.

In some situations, other information might be incorporated into the search process. This additional information can be in the form of rules of thumb, hunches, or experience but is nevertheless felt to be accurate. When this type of information is used to help in the search, it is called a "heuristic" search. In cases where the criterion of satisficing is employed, search techniques such as genetic algorithms (a new area in artificial intelligence and machine learning) can be used.

Structure of Decision Support Systems versus Information Systems

Based on the account above of how people make decisions, it is easy to see various types of support that would be helpful to a decision maker. For example, having a data warehouse would facilitate the generation of solutions to ad hoc problems concerning patient case mix, patient payer mix, typical patient flow, length of stay, and so on. Another type of support is assistance in performing any of the searches mentioned. For any realistic problem, such searches would exceed the cognitive limits of most people. Computer-based DSSs were developed to meet these needs.

The functionality of a DSS will be much different from that of an information system (IS). ISs developed as managers began to recognize the need for periodic reports from the transactional or operational systems within the organization. **Transactional systems** perform electronic data processing and storage. They were among the first implementations of computer technology to business during the 1950s and 1960s and are still a primary application today. Such systems include payroll systems, patient billing systems, patient registration systems, accounting systems, and so on.

Tan (2001, 1998) applies the term **hospital information system** (HIS) to the transactional systems found in healthcare and uses the term **health management information system** (HMIS) for those systems whose purpose is to provide reports on routine operations and processing. Examples of HMISs are pharmacy inventory systems, radiological systems, and patient tracking systems. Many of these systems have been discussed in earlier chapters of this book. Neither the HIS nor the HMIS has decision support as its explicit purpose.

As stated earlier, DSS is about people and making decisions, not about data processing. Thus, the structure or architecture of the DSS will reflect this emphasis. Figures 19.3, 19.4, and 19.5 may be used to compare the differences among an HIS, an HMIS, and a DSS. Figure 19.3 presents a conceptual model of a typical HIS (or data-processing system). The key elements of the system relate to data acquisition and entry, storage, retrieval, record keeping, and so on. Typical outputs would include a patient bill, a listing of patient charges, and a list of patients admitted on a given day.

The HMIS presented in figure 19.4 includes some of the same elements as the HIS, in particular, data entry and storage. The key difference is that a standard reports element is added to the system. Thus, the outputs from the system will assist managers in monitoring the operations of the organization. For example, the system may generate a standard report on the number of admissions per week for the past six months. In addition, it could generate a report on the average cost per patient over a given period of time.

Figure 19.5 focuses on the role of the system as a decision tool. First, there is the user interface element. This element provides a friendly and interactive environment for user interaction with system. Ideally, this will be through a **graphical user interface** (GUI), allowing the user to point, click, drag, and drop icon objects on the computer screen to accomplish desired tasks. Input devices include the standard keyboard and the computer mouse.

The second element of the model identifies the sources of data that populate the DSS. These sources are those that a decision maker would turn to in order to obtain more information and knowledge about the problem's background and setting. Such sources would include data from the organization's operational and transactional systems (HIS, HMIS)

Figure 19.3. Conceptual model of a health information system

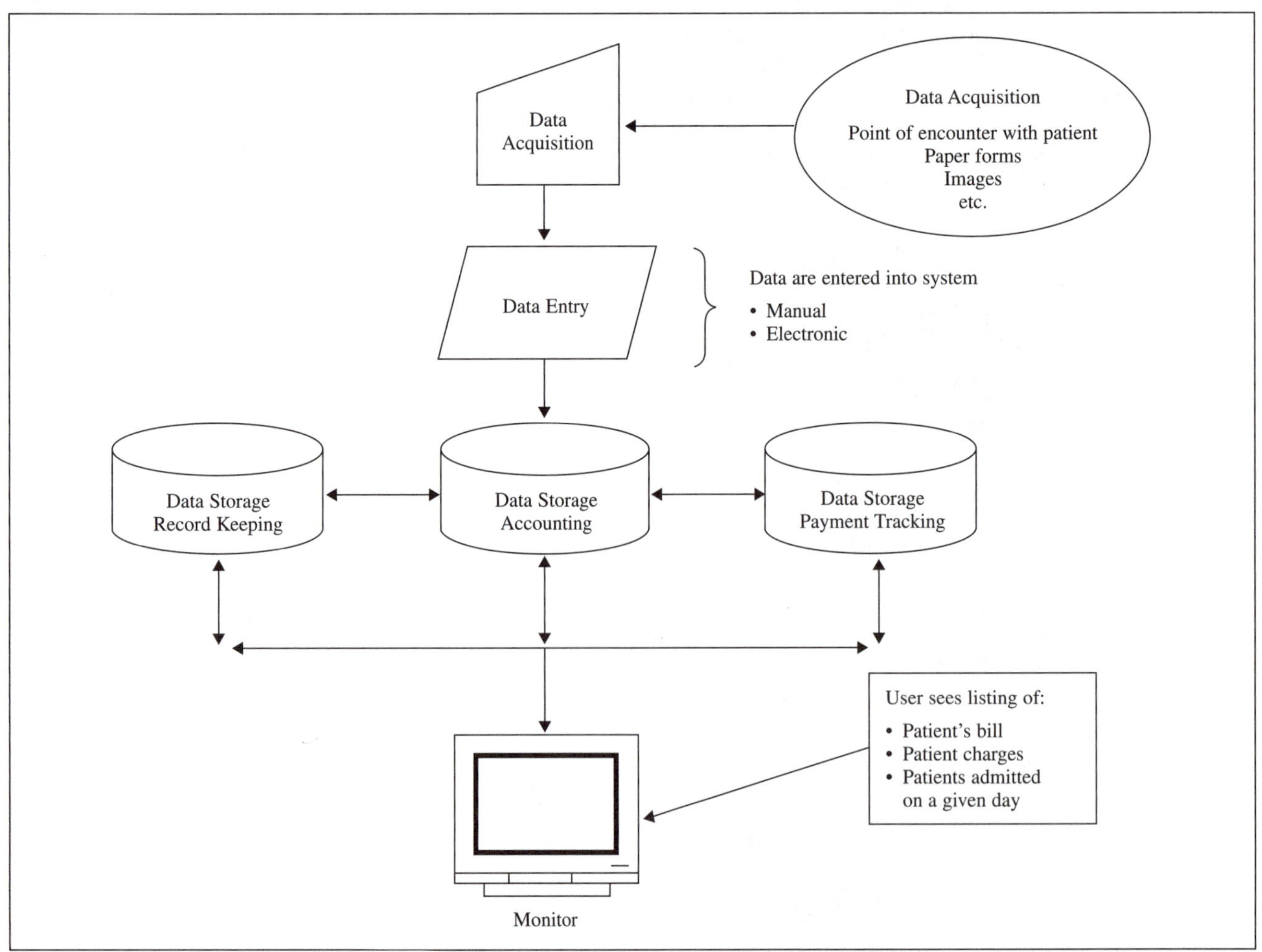

and could include other sources of external data such as state, regional, or national comparative data.

The DSS must contain some element or subsystem to manage all this information. This element may be divided into a database management subsystem and a model or knowledge-based management subsystem, depending on the sophistication of the DSS.

Perhaps the key element in the DSS is the one that assists in reasoning from the data and knowledge. This element enables the DSS to recognize and solve the problem. In expert systems, this element is often called the **inference engine**. Overall, it is where the DSS integrates the data and knowledge provided from the various sources, uses the structure of the problem as presented to it by the user, and applies its models and reasoning to suggest a feasible decision.

Finally, the DSS must communicate proposed decision options to the user or decision maker. Most often, this communication is accomplished through the same user interface that was used to specify the problem to the system, although it could use a separate system. DSSs can be classified according to the exact nature of the various elements represented in its model. These elements are discussed in the following subsections.

Figure 19.4. Conceptual model of a health information management system

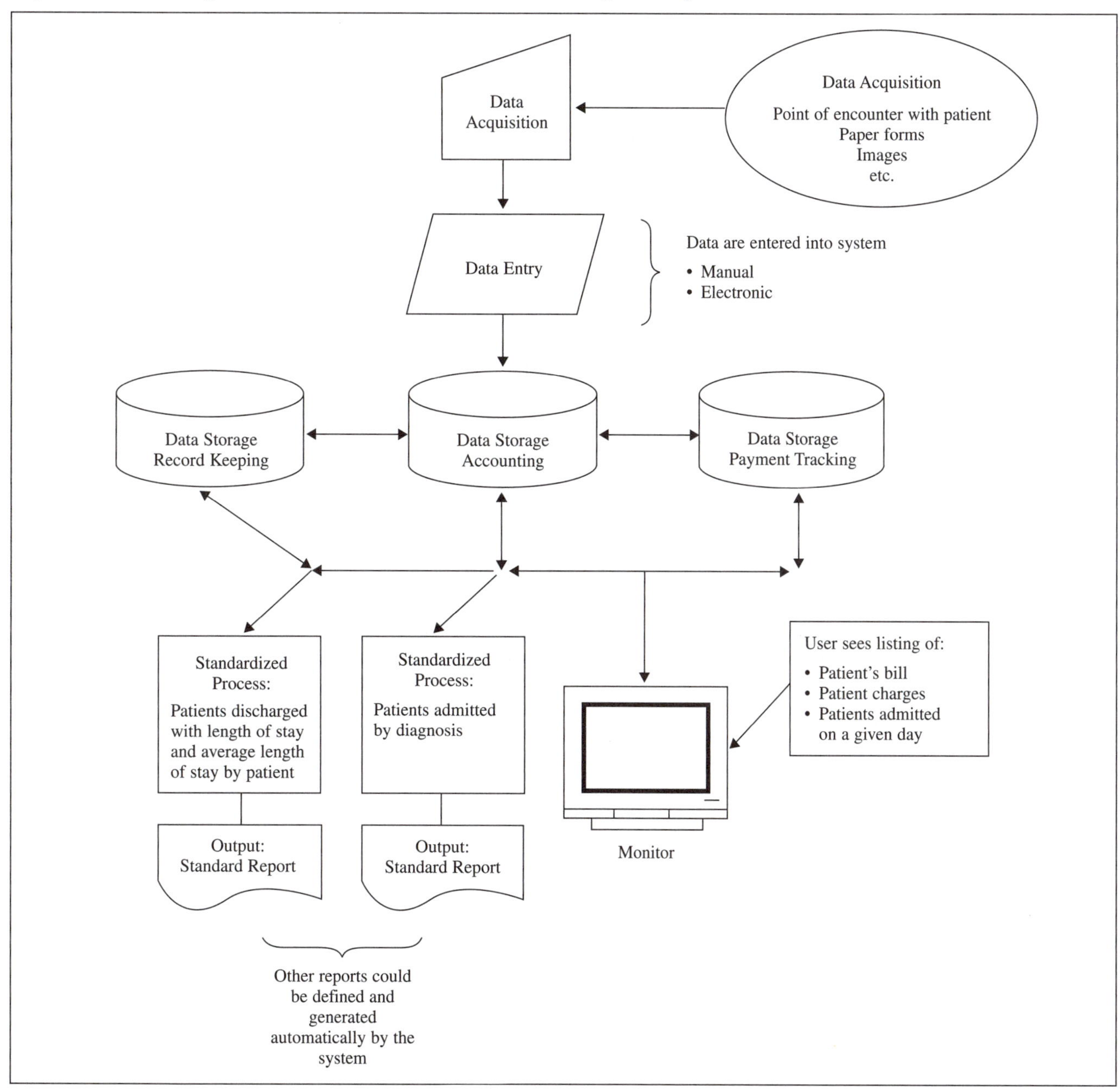

Data-based Decision Support Systems

A **data-based DSS** uses a database management approach for its overall organization. Its central focus is on providing access to the various data sources within the organization through one system. In essence, all the data and knowledge management is performed through the database subsystem. The input user interface generally allows the user to specify many forms of ad hoc queries through a graphical interface. The system uses its knowledge system to translate the user's requests into a query format acceptable to the database component. A typical implementation of this system allows the user to specify queries in a pick-and-click or drop-down manner via the GUI. The system then translates those requests into the database language **structured query language** (SQL). The SQL is submitted to the database system containing the various data sources, and a report is sent back to the user. In healthcare, the STARS system from ViPS, Inc. is an example of a data-based DSS. Most data warehouse systems also fall into this category of DSS.

Model-based Decision Support Systems

The famous statistician George Box once quipped, "All models are wrong, but some are useful" (1979, 202). A model is a generalized, abstract representation of the world in which

Figure 19.5. Conceptual model of a decision support system

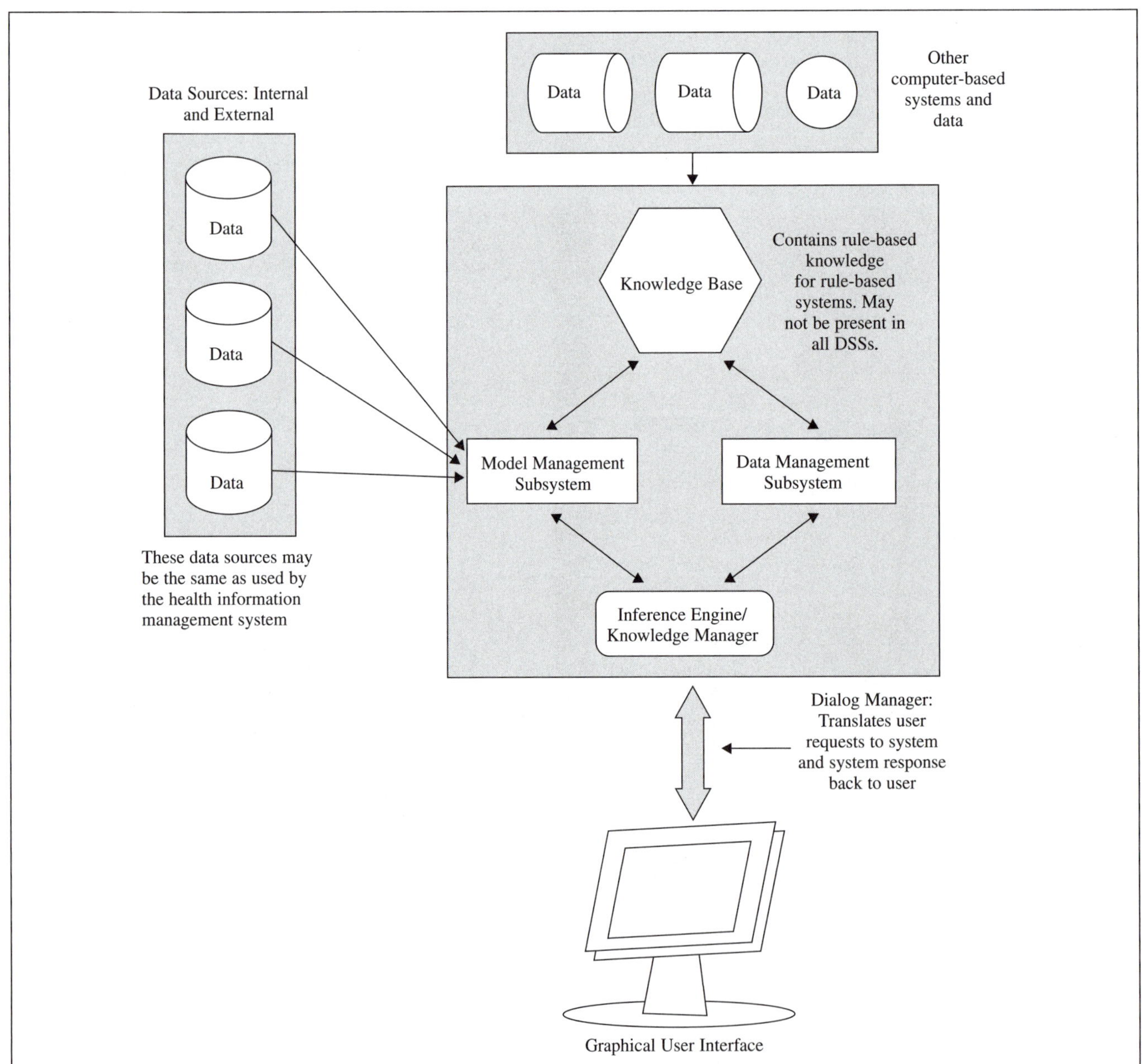

Adapted from Turban 1995, 88.

the decision or problem is located. In fact, all individuals depend on models to help interpret and organize everyday experiences. Experiences and decisions are interpreted and formed in terms of these mental models. These models are constructed from our experiences and education and those of the society in which we live.

A good **model-based DSS** attempts to include as many different models as can be accommodated to provide the user the greatest flexibility in framing the decision situation. For example, the SAS Enterprise Miner tool for data mining provides a large collection of models that the user can select and combine into an overall description of the problem. Other systems may provide specific models such as financial risk analysis or forecasting, depending on the area for which the DSS was developed.

In the model-based DSS, the key element is the subsystem that manages the system's models. The models make up the system's knowledge. The user describes the decision situation to the system in terms of the models available in the system or by using a modeling language. Internal and external data relevant to the needs of the model are accessed and supplied to it. The reasoning element in this system consists primarily of the modules needed to perform the computations or searches as required by the model. Results are provided via the user interface or output system.

Many examples of model-based DSS exist in healthcare. For example, the Episode Treatment Groups system from Symmetry Health Data Systems, Inc. can assist both buyers and providers of healthcare services with case-mix analysis of patients, provider profiling, and severity-of-illness adjustments when making quality of care and financial decisions.

Knowledge-based Decision Support Systems

A **knowledge-based DSS** is one in which the key element is the knowledge base. Knowledge-based DSSs are often referred to as rule-based systems because the knowledge is stored in the form of rules. For example, a simple rule system is the familiar IF, THEN, ELSE format—if a certain condition is true, then this is an indication of a certain other condition, else the condition is not indicated. By applying general rules of this form to a given situation, a decision is suggested to the user. The form of the rules can be generalized to allow them to have a probabilistic nature. For example, a rule might state that if a given condition is present, there is some probability that another condition is present.

In a knowledge-based DSS, the reasoning element is usually referred to as the inference engine mentioned earlier. The inference engine is a module that can apply and link the appropriate rules together based on the inputs provided by the user. Often the user in a dialog format supplies the input in these systems. The user interface asks the user a question and the user responds. Through the inference engine, the DSS applies the appropriate rule or rules and determines whether more input is needed. This iterative process between user and DSS continues until the DSS either is able to make a suggestion or determines that its knowledge base is not sufficient to make a determination.

Because many of the ideas of the knowledge-based DSS arose from the early work in artificial intelligence in computer science, it is often considered under the framework of expert systems. Examples of knowledge-based systems in healthcare include the early work of Shortliffe (1976) on his MYCIN system. The MYCIN system provided assistance in diagnosis and therapy selection for patients with blood-borne bacterial infections. Other systems that developed later along these lines are Quick Medical Reference (QMR) by Miller, Masarie, and Myers (1986) and DXplain (Barnett et al. 1987). Artificial intelligence and these types of systems are discussed in later sections of this chapter.

Graphics-based Decision Support Systems

Graphical tools are becoming more and more important in helping people make decisions. Perhaps the old adage that a picture is worth a thousand words really is true. **Graphics-based DSSs** exploit the human ability to glean patterns and insight from visual presentations of data. Thus, the key element in the architecture of a graphics-based DSS is the user interface. This interface must be carefully constructed and include both hardware and software. The hardware must be able to present detailed visualizations in a timely manner. Further, the type of graphic itself is of fundamental importance.

In a graphics-based DSS, the knowledge base is the collection of graphics that the system is capable of displaying. Common graphics include maps, histograms, and bar charts. However, many systems today involve a complex combination of various graphical displays for both output and input. Depending on the purpose of the DSS, various types of data also must be available to the system.

Many types of graphics-based DSSs have been developed for healthcare. In 1995, the Health Care Financing Administration (HFCA), now renamed the Centers for Medicare and Medicaid Services (CMS), contracted with Los Alamos National Laboratory to develop new techniques for reviewing Medicare claims to detect potentially fraudulent claims or providers. Los Alamos used a variety of new mathematical models and algorithms from the emerging area of **machine learning** and data mining to accomplish their tasks. One result of this work was development of a visualization system that gave the user the ability to spot potential patterns of fraud and abuse. In this case, the data/knowledge element of the system is the claims data, the reasoning element consists of the models and algorithms, and the user interface is the graphical display.

Similar graphical techniques have been developed by other people to detect fraud. These methods use a data-mining technique called **linkage analysis**. Linkage analysis portrays relationships discovered within data sets by a linked network graph. The graph shows interactions among items in the data set and has been applied to fraud investigations in money laundering (for example, Davis 1981; Davidson 1993). Netmap from Alta Europe, Daisy, and SAS's Enterprise Miner are examples of general software programs that implement this approach. Today, many healthcare organizations as well as government agencies are investigating linkage analysis as a DSS tool for containing the increasing cost of healthcare due to fraud and abuse.

Another important graphics-based DSS is the **geographical information system** (GIS). Begur, Miller, and Weaver (1997) reported their use of the package MAPINFO for the development of a graphics-based GIS system to assist in the routing of home healthcare nurses during their daily visits to ensure the shortest commuting distances and thereby minimizing travel expenses.

Check Your Understanding 19.1

Instructions: Answer the following questions on a separate piece of paper.

1. Why is decision support important for modern healthcare?
2. What are some of the challenges facing healthcare that decision support can assist in addressing?
3. What is a decision support system?
4. What is the key difference between a decision support system and an expert system?
5. Out of what discipline from World War II did the study and development of decision support systems come?
6. What are the three phases in Simon's model of the decision-making process?
7. Describe the classical view of decision making.
8. What is the key element in the architecture of a decision support system, and what does it do?
9. Name the four classes of decision support systems.
10. Name at least one important medical decision support system that can be classified as a knowledge-based DSS. Explain why it falls into this classification.

Infrastructure Requirements for Decision Support Systems

What types of organizational and technical infrastructures are required to enable the effective use of decision support systems? To implement effective DSSs, an organization first must have developed at least four key components: (1) a data warehouse or operational data store, (2) a set of data-mining or data-querying tools, (3) a trained group of data analysts or data miners, and (4) a trained group of data users. A definition and brief overview of these elements follows.

Data Warehouses

Data warehouse is a popular concept in information technology (IT) circles today. Almost any conference on IT contains a presentation on some aspect of the corporate data warehouse. The term was coined primarily by William Inmon (1992). Basically, a data warehouse is a database that has the following functions:

- Serves as a neutral storage area for data extracted from an organization's transactional systems
- Serves as a storage area organized around specific business functions or requirements
- Provides easy access to business data for analysis or data mining (that is, decision support)

Although various people have proposed different definitions of the data warehouse, all agree that one of its critical aspects is that it is a database. Its content is organized in a subject-specific, integrated, time-invariant, nonvolatile manner using one of several possible data models.

Because its architecture is so important, some people simply define data warehouse as architecture and not as an application or thing. Its architecture refers to how the system is put together or constructed; it is the system's blueprint. Thus, a data warehouse could be thought of as a collection of software systems that includes:

- A database engine allowing access, manipulation, and storage of transactional data
- An application software that allows business analysts to conduct complex business tasks, such as decision support
- A connectivity system that allows the system to communicate with the data sources as well as the end users (that is, client and server[s])

A simplified model of a data warehouse is shown in figure 19.6.

A comparison of the database components of a data warehouse and a transactional system shows that their underlying goals are very different. In a transactional system, the database has been constructed according to well-established principles of relational database design, in particular, **normalization**. Normalization seeks to eliminate redundancy in data storage. The design goal of a transactional system is to eliminate potential errors arising from updating, deleting, or inserting new records into the system, as well as minimizing data redundancy. Thus, a data model for these systems includes many tables, each containing non-redundant data. A data warehouse, on the other hand, is designed to assist the user in querying corporate data. Thus, the underlying design sacrifices data redundancy for query speed and ease of access and use. The data warehouse is not highly normalized.

Two well-known data models are used in designing data warehouses:

- The **star schema** seeks to represent the data within the business context by key business dimensions (time, location, and so on) and by the quantities of interest that are characterized by these dimensions (units sold, dollars spent, length of stay, and so on). For example, suppose the data of interest pertain to patient costs and lengths of stay over time. The star schema organizes the data around a central fact table containing these key business data items and relates the other dimensions of these data items (for example, physician, patient information, procedures, hospital service, time, and so on) through tables linked to

Figure 19.6. Simplified model of a data warehouse

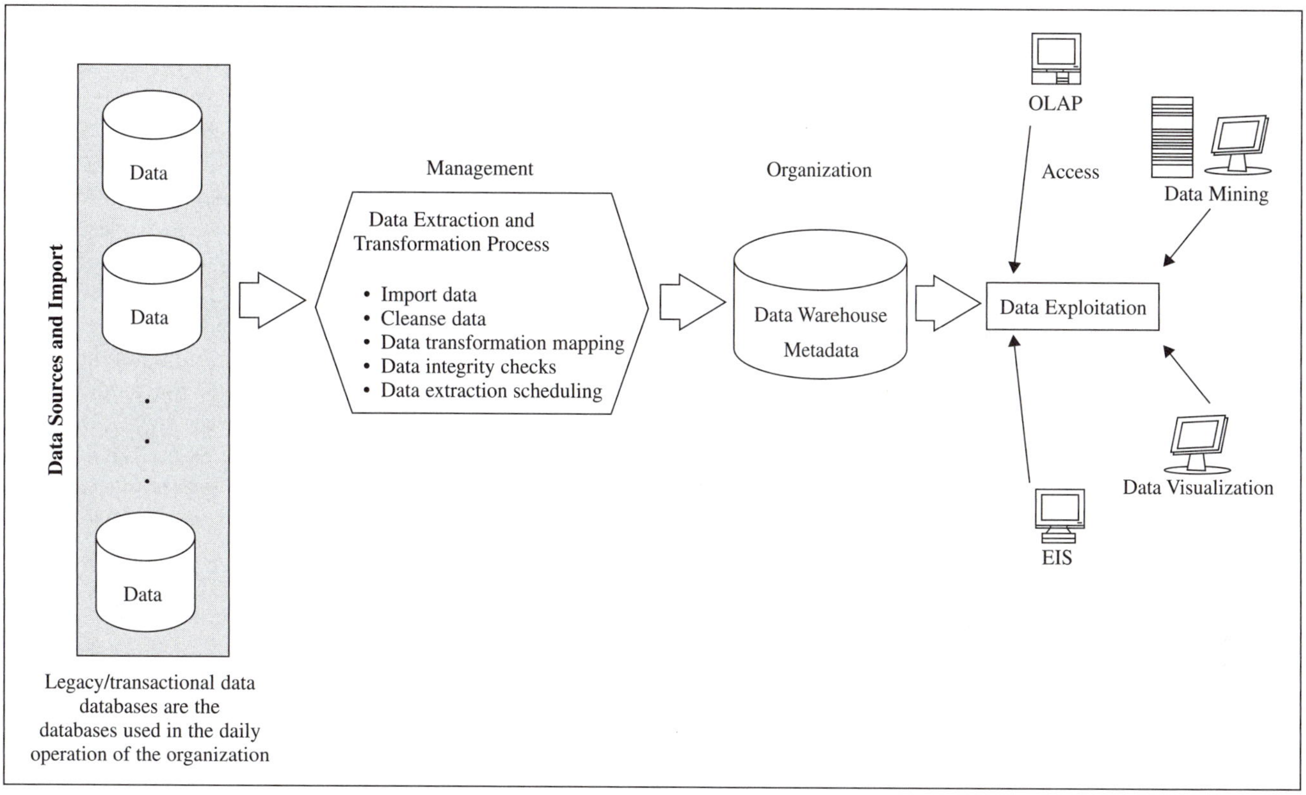

Data Sources and Import
Data
Data
Data
Legacy/transactional data databases are the databases used in the daily operation of the organization
Management
Data Extraction and Transformation Process
- Import data
- Cleanse data
- Data transformation mapping
- Data integrity checks
- Data extraction scheduling

Organization
Data Warehouse
Metadata
OLAP
Access
Data Mining
Data Exploitation
Data Visualization
EIS

the central fact table. The links are accomplished through variables called keys (for example, patient_ID). Figure 19.7 illustrates the star schema.

- The **snowflake schema** allows the dimensions in the star schema to be normalized. Figure 19.8 illustrates the general notion of the snowflake schema.

In healthcare, a closely associated idea is the **clinical repository**. The clinical repository likewise is a database that has been developed using a consistent clinical data model and clinical vocabulary and provides accurate clinical data from the various patient care systems. The clinical repository requires that the other health information and patient care systems be integrated with it to allow data to flow between it and the other systems. Thus, the clinical repository is like the data warehouse in that it serves as a database for storing data from transactional systems.

However, the data warehouse and the clinical repository differ in architecture. Because the clinical repository is integrated into the overall information system, its architecture is best described by the systems with which it interacts. The star and snowflake schemas are typically not utilized in its design. Further, although nonclinical data warehouses are static in nature (their data do not change except as specified on a periodic basis), the clinical repository is constantly changing as new clinical data are available for patient care. And finally, the nonclinical data warehouse is focused on retrospective analyses of business data; the business analyst wishes to tap the corporate data to assist with future decisions. However, the clinical repository is focused on assisting with patient care in a near real-time environment.

Introduction and Overview of Data-Mining Tools

Data-mining tools exploit the resources of the data warehouse. They enable the end user to query the warehouse, to drill down into the details of the information, to develop models for prediction, and to allow discovery algorithms to highlight new patterns of potential interest.

Online Analytical Processing

One set of tools is **online analytical processing** (OLAP). In discussing the data warehouse, it was mentioned that a key design feature is to recognize that complex business problems are multidimensional in nature. Thus, the data warehouse attempts to identify the key business dimensions of the data and organize the data around those dimensions.

OLAP is an application architecture that was developed to explore the multidimensional aspects of such business data. OLAP stores the data in a **multidimensional data structure** (multidimensional database, or MDDB) and enables the user to examine and view the data along dimensions that may be specific to the context and will be defined by the business rules of the organization. For example, total cost of stay in a hospital has dimensions of time, type of charges involved, and so on. Often this data structure is conceptualized as a data cube, where its dimensions represent the dimensions of the data and the data item of focus, such as cost or length of stay, is viewed as being located in one of the cells of the cube. This process is often referred to as slicing and dicing or drilling down into the data.

The MDDB is often stored in memory, which results in a very fast response to the user. The data in the MDDB are usually aggregated and many statistics are calculated prior to loading them into the system.

The OLAP database does not have to be part of the data warehouse, but it does extract data from it. The data warehouse database model, though, is often designed with OLAP in mind.

Although OLAP is based on the concepts of multidimensional databases, its implementation by different vendors has resulted in specialized data structures. Thus, OLAP tools have been categorized into several different groups, including:

- **Multidimensional online analytical processing** (MOLAP) vendors developed specialized multidimensional data structures, that is, **multidimensional database management systems** (MDDBMSs). A typical business context in which this has worked well is decision support for business problems involving applications of trend or time series analyses.
- **Relational online analytical processing** (ROLAP) vendors have sought to develop systems that can access the two-dimensional tables found in a typical **relational database management system** (RDBMS). Using these tables, the user can create a multidimensional view of the data without having to create the multidimensional data structure. ROLAP has been evolving rapidly among vendors, and various implementations are available.
- **Hybrid online analytical processing** (HOLAP) is actually a catchall group. With the rapidly changing landscape of technologies, vendors are adopting system

Figure 19.7. Example star schema for a data warehouse

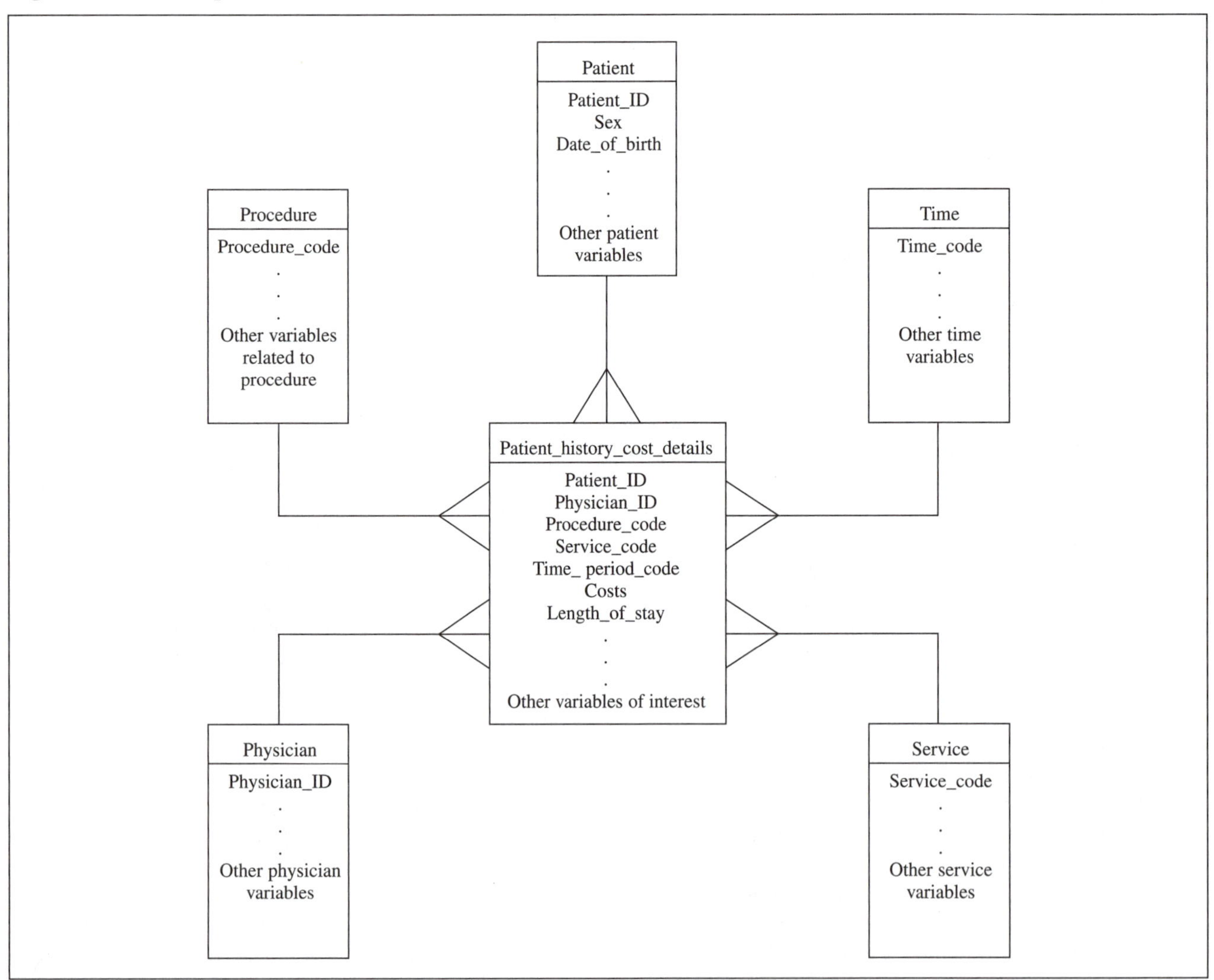

The symbol ——< indicates a one-to-many relationship.

architectures that blur the lines of distinction among these various groups.

As mentioned, the data structure on which OLAP is based can provide a convenient platform from which to perform other data mining. However, one important distinction must be noted: data mining and OLAP are different. As noted earlier, OLAP gives the user the ability to view and query the data in a multidimensional manner, but it is up to the user to determine which query to submit or what view is required to support a given decision problem. Data mining, on the other hand, seeks to learn from the data or to discover patterns not previously recognized by the user. Additionally, data mining seeks to search for new solutions to problems whereas OLAP must remain passive. Not all people agree with this distinction. Many vendors currently market systems as data-mining systems when, in essence, their true nature is OLAP. They simply provide the user an environment from which to provide drill downs into corporate data.

Machine Learning Techniques

Artificial neural networks (ANNs) and **decision trees** are examples of data-mining tools that use machine learning techniques called **supervised learning**. In supervised learning, the algorithm learns the inherent patterns hidden in the data that predict a specified outcome or target variable. This outcome or target variable must be present in the supplied data set in order for the supervised learning algorithm to proceed.

Another class of machine learning techniques is **unsupervised learning**. Unsupervised learning techniques seek to group cases or data records together that are similar or alike in certain respects. The goal of the analysis is to discover previously unknown groupings that exist in the data. A common unsupervised learning algorithm is k-nearest

Figure 19.8. General snowflake schema

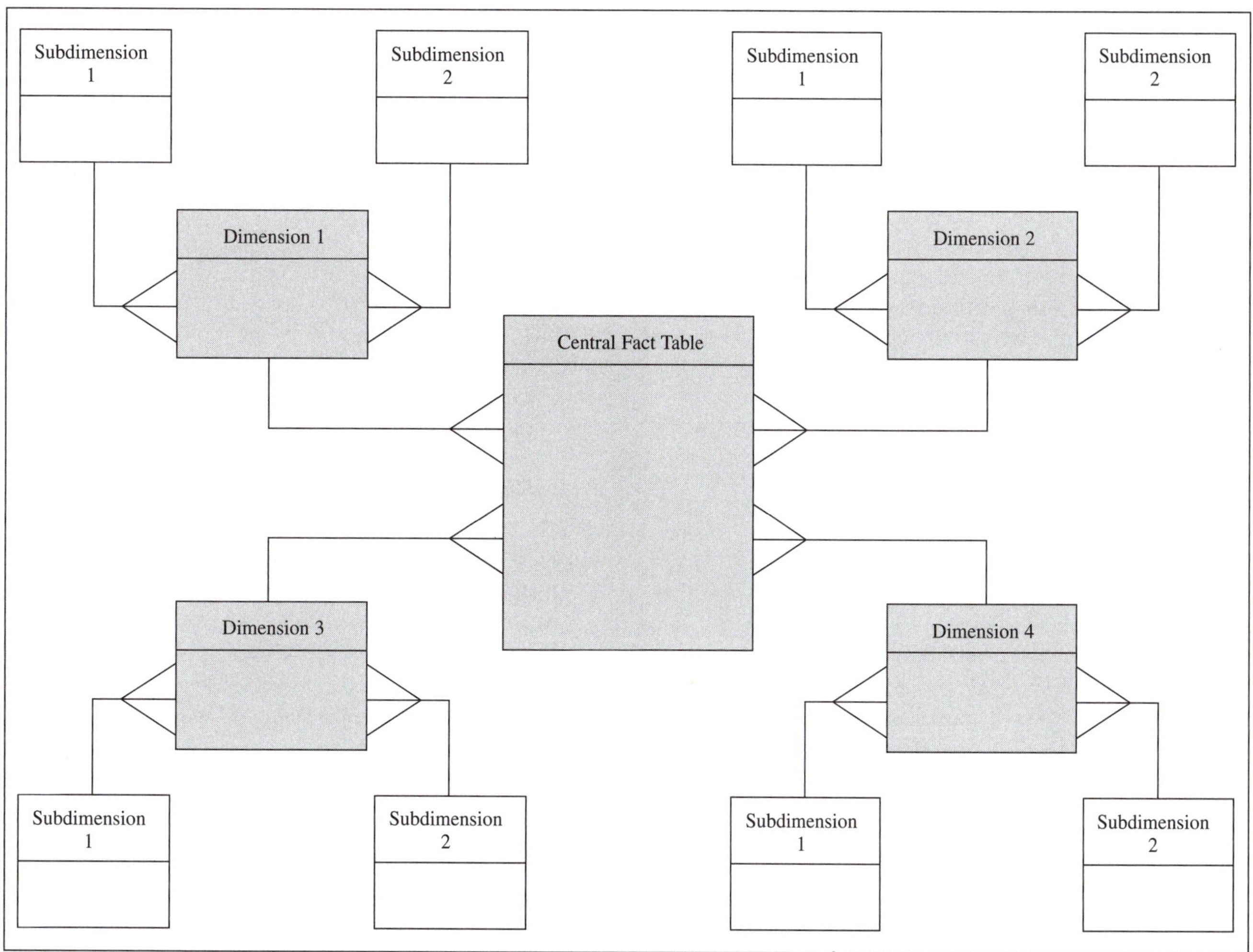

Notes:

1. All dimensions have been shown with exactly two subdimensions for illustrative purposes only. A dimension can have as many subdimensions as necessary.
2. Only generic table names are shown, for example, Dimension 1. In practice, the corresponding variables would appear in the table.

neighbor clustering, a technique applied when data attributes are numeric.

One last machine learning technique that has received a great deal of attention for data mining is **rule induction**, or **association rule analysis.** Association rule analysis does not fit neatly into either of the previous categories of learning techniques. Rule induction seeks to uncover the co-occurrences of items within the database. For example, the classic illustration of association rule analysis is the "market basket" analysis. In this case, the analyst wishes to determine customer-purchasing behaviors by examining associations among the various items customers place in their shopping baskets.

For instance, if the customer has placed milk in the basket, how likely is he or she to also place bread in the basket? If the customer has placed bread and cheese in the basket, how likely is he or she to also purchase soup? Thus, association rule analysis examines the co-occurrence of items in customers' baskets and produces sets of rules or associations that describe customer-buying behavior. A typical rule produced by an association rule analysis is as follows:

Milk & bread → cheese [support = 2%, confidence = 80%]

Support is the percentage of times that all three items occurred together in all the baskets examined; confidence is the percentage of time that cheese occurred given that both milk and bread were in the basket.

Although this type of analysis may seem of great use to retailers, how can it be used in healthcare? Suppose the "basket" was a person's tenure with a particular company. The various activities, projects, buildings, and jobs that the individual had or was involved in while with the company might be the items in the basket. Interesting questions that an association rule analysis could reveal include:

- Did people who worked in a specific building develop lung cancer?
- Did individuals in certain management positions also experience certain stress-related diseases?

Another example in healthcare is fraud detection. In this case, a basket would be a suspected provider or group of providers and the items in the basket would be the codes they billed. An association rule analysis then would suggest interesting co-occurrences of codes billed together. For example,

{short office visit and patient age >65} → {CBC ordered}
[support = 20%, confidence = 98%]

A payer integrity officer may find this association unusual and investigate whether the provider has some financial interest in the lab to which the patients are being referred.

Data Miners

Data miners are those individuals who use the data warehouse and the various analytical tools and software applications to support the decision-making activities of the organization. In this sense, they are decision support analysts. Moreover, data miners understand and can effectively use various data-mining algorithms such as those mentioned earlier.

In healthcare organizations, data miners may hold degrees in either a clinical or business area. Such an educational background is, in fact, helpful because it enables the data miner to better understand the context of the decision support problem. However, data miners will need to have other skills as well, including the ability to use relational databases, advanced statistics, and computer programming.

Data Users

Data users include a range of individuals within the organization. At one end of the spectrum is senior management. A senior manager uses reports prepared from the data, often extracting data from the data warehouse, in managing and making decisions for the business. In some cases, a senior manager might use a DSS called an **executive information system** (EIS). An EIS can provide easy access to a variety of corporate data without the need for programming or making requests to other information technologists. Such systems provide predefined queries and reports specifically tailored to address issues of continuing concern to management. For example, the CEO of a health system would be interested in always knowing the past week's number of patients admitted, average length of stay, and total dollars billed and collected. Using available data, an EIS would allow the CEO to generate such reports in her or his office.

Other data users include clinical staff and business staff. Clinical staff use patient data in the routine care of their patients; business staff use data in determining bills, sending out invoices, and crediting accounts.

Thus, many individuals in an enterprise use data. Data miners use data to develop answers for specific issues currently facing the organization, and others use data in their day-to-day jobs.

Check Your Understanding 19.2

Instructions: Answer the following questions on a separate piece of paper.

1. What are the three functions of a data warehouse?
2. What does normalization seek to do in a database?
3. What two well-known data models are used in constructing a data warehouse?
4. How is a data warehouse different from a clinical repository?
5. What do the acronyms OLAP, MOLAP, ROLAP, and HOLAP stand for?
6. What is supervised learning? What is unsupervised learning?
7. Name two important data-mining tools.

Uses of Decision Support Systems in Healthcare

Decision support systems are used in a variety of contexts in contemporary healthcare organizations.

Healthcare Decision Support

The term *healthcare decision support* is used here to cover a variety of DSSs used in healthcare, other than clinical decision support, executive decision support, or nursing decision support. In general, these systems all seek to provide the same assistance as a DSS in general, namely, to assist the user in the decision-making process within the domain of the system.

Examples of these systems include medication management and pharmacy order-entry DSSs. These systems assist in warning of possible drug interactions and prescribing errors (Poikonen and Leventhal 1999). Other examples of a healthcare DSS are alert and monitoring tools built into patient information systems.

During the last several years, healthcare has given a lot of attention to quality of care and has used the tools of total quality management (TQM) to measure progress in this arena. Various systems have been proposed and developed that assist in combining data from financial units within a hospital as well as from the clinical areas to allow both administrators and clinicians to examine quality improvement and cost efficiency of services provided to patients. Several recent articles discussing these systems can be found in Howe et al. (1999), Hohmann et al. (1998), and Dexter et al. (2001). These systems all fall within the definition of healthcare decision support.

Clinical and Medical Decision Support

CDSSs were mentioned at the beginning of this chapter. As noted earlier, for many people, the whole notion of the use of computers in medicine conjures up an image of the physician interacting with a computer system to reach a decision regarding a diagnosis for a patient. However, in the broadest sense, a CDSS is any computer system that assists a health professional in making clinical decisions. Some CDSSs include reminder and other alert systems as part of the integration with a general clinical information system.

The CDSS was one of the earliest applications of computers in healthcare. The research on CDSSs dates back to the late 1950s with papers by Ledley and Lusted (1959) and Warner et al. (1964). Particularly illustrative of the early work in CDSSs is Shortliffe's (1976) seminal work on the MYCIN system. MYCIN was developed to assist physicians in the selection of appropriate antibiotic therapy and was evaluated for patients with blood-borne bacterial infections (Yu et al. 1979). The system was designed using ideas that emerged out of the computer science field of artificial intelligence. Research in artificial intelligence provided new models for developing computer systems that could process and reason from "rules" provided to the system. Most software systems process numbers as input. "Knowledge" of the context of the numbers resides within the program and is "hard-coded" into the system.

Work in artificial intelligence and the resulting area of expert systems provides a means for a computer system to be supplied with a collection of rules that the system can then reason with or chain together to draw new inferences or make new decisions. A typical rule from the MYCIN is given in figure 19.9. Basically, a rule is a conditional statement expressed in an if-then format. Given a condition such that the "if" part of the statement is true, the "then" part of the rule indicates what conclusions are indicated. These rules may be referred to as production rules, condition-action rules, situation-action rules, or if-then rules.

MYCIN used a collection of about 450 rules that were elicited from in-depth interviews with medical experts in the area of antibiotics. The rules then were stored in the system's knowledge base. A knowledge base is the collection of all rules from which an ES can draw in reaching a decision. The component of the system that chains the rules together or reasons from the rules is the inference engine. Two common methodologies for performing this chaining process are forward chaining and backward chaining (Russell and Norvig 1995).

During these early years of research in CDSSs, several other systems also were developed. Gorry and Barnett (1968) developed a model for diagnosis using a sequential Bayesian reasoning system. Using this work, F. T. de Dombal and his colleagues developed a CDSS for diagnosing abdominal pain (de Dombal et al. 1969). In 1975, R.A. Miller and his associates presented the INTERNIST-I system (Pople et al. 1975; Miller et al. 1982). This system, initially called DIALOG, has undergone much development and research over the years and is now best known as QMR (Miller et al. 1986). In the late 1980s, Otto Barnett and his colleagues proposed the DXplain system (Barnett et al. 1987).

Today, there are many CDSSs, each attempting to address various areas in clinical care. Currently, many researchers are examining how best to integrate these systems into overall medical work flow, in particular, linking these systems to a patient's computer-based health record (Berner et al. 1999). Durieux et al. (2000) implemented clinical guidelines through a CDSS in an orthopedic surgery department. They found that the use of CDSS changed physician behavior and improved compliance guidelines. Gerbert et al. (2000) found that the use of CDSS could improve the decision making in primary care triage and potentially reduce healthcare costs.

Figure 19.9. A typical rule from the MYCIN system

Rule 507

IF:	(1) The infection which requires therapy is meningitis
	(2) Organisms were not seen on the stain of the culture
	(3) The type of infection is bacterial
	(4) The patient does not have a head injury defect, and
	(5) The age of the patient is between 15 years and 55 years
THEN:	The organisms that might be causing the infection are *Diplococcus pneumoniae* and *Neisseria meningitidis*

Source: Musen, Shahar, and Shortliffe 2001, chapter 16.

Dayton et al. (2000) found that CDSS could be useful in delivering online guidelines for TB treatment and become an effective resource for clinicians.

Executive Decision Support

Executive decision support systems, often called executive information systems (EISs), are special types of DSSs specifically designed to facilitate and support the decision-making needs of the organization's top executives. They provide easy access to both internal and external data sources relevant to monitoring critical success factors and making strategic decisions. EISs provide overall views of the organization's operations and offer a wide range of views of the data, including drill-down tools and various summarization tools. Table 19.2 lists some common characteristics of a typical EIS.

The term *EIS* was coined at the Massachusetts Institute of Technology (MIT) in the late 1970s and early 1980s (Marakas 1999). Originally, the EIS consisted of a mainframe computer program that pulled together various corporate data and packaged them in an easily readable and accessible format for decision makers. The intent was to assist corporate officers who were either unfamiliar or uncomfortable with working with computers.

Since the early days of EISs, however, the demand for such data and decision support has grown. Today, EISs support not only top-level executives, but also mid- and lower-level managers who require such support. With the advent of the PC and local area networks, such support can easily be offered to an organization's various levels of management.

Although EISs are types of decision support systems, it is important to note a few key differences. First, the EIS generally will not provide the sophisticated modeling and database capabilities that a DSS does. The EIS targets the top-level view and is not intended for the more in-depth analyses provided by a DSS. Second, the EIS is intended to allow executives to gain a quick view or "snapshot" of the organization as a whole, whereas a DSS often provides more detailed support in a particular area of the organization's operation. Third, generally speaking, EISs incorporate external data into the information given to the user, whereas DSSs typically use internal data.

Table 19.2. Characteristics of typical executive information systems

Characteristic	Description
Degree of use	High, consistent, without need of technical assistance
Computer skills required	Very low, must be easy to learn and use
Flexibility	High, must fit executive decision-making style
Principal use	Tracking, control
Decisions supported	Upper-level management, unstructured
Data supported	Company internal and external
Output capabilities	Text, tabular, graphical, trend toward audio/video in future
Graphic concentration	High, presentation style
Data access speed	Must be high, fast response

Source: Dobrzeniecki 1994.

The use of EISs in healthcare has grown over the years. Dobrzeniecki (1994) listed four examples of EIS use in healthcare settings:

- Baylor University Medical Center uses an EIS system called Performance Advisor to assist in creating flexible budgets that allow for different levels of customer activity. The program is a mainframe, general-ledger system.
- Meriter Hospital, in Madison, Wisconsin, adopted a product called Alternative View from Gerber Alley. This product provides an EIS for the hospital's clinical applications and has been part of its TQM effort.
- Samaritan Health Services, in Phoenix, Arizona, adopted the IBM product, Destiny, as its EIS system. The system provides a "briefing book" feature, which organizes information into several folders on key areas of interest. Users can monitor the various areas by selecting the appropriate folder. The system provides summary and trend information in graphical formats.
- The Florida Acute-Care and Teaching Hospitals Healthcare Cost Containment Board adopted MAXPAR, which allows executives to monitor financial, productivity, and physician-related data in all 220 acute care and teaching hospitals in the state of Florida. MAXPAR is an EIS product specifically designed for healthcare. A variety of summary information is available (for example, comparisons of practice patterns and average length of hospital stays for particular procedures).

Nursing Decision Support

The role of nursing in the care and treatment of patients is best thought of as complementary to the role of the physician. Physicians diagnose diseases, obtain medical histories, identify disease risks, and prescribe treatments. Nurses, on the other hand, contribute to the cure of patients through their special role of patient care. Nurses assess how patients respond to treatment and therapy and how they are coping with their conditions and treatments. Nurses develop patient care plans and seek ways to assess patients and alleviate suffering.

Nursing DSSs assist nursing staff in their delivery of patient care. Clearly, the decisions faced by nurses are broad and complex, making the development of such systems difficult. For this reason, to date, there are few nursing DSSs, although some systems have been developed that are similar to the clinical diagnostic DSSs mentioned earlier. For example, Lagina (1971) developed a computer diagnostic system to distinguish mild, moderate, and severe levels of anxiety among hospitalized patients. Ruland (1999) examined the use of decision support to elicit patient preferences and include them in the nursing care plan. He found that information about patient preferences changed the priorities if nurses care and become more aligned to the patient preferences. If there was a consistency in patient and nurses priorities, it resulted in higher preference achievement and greater patient satisfaction.

In a broad sense, however, decision support is built into current nursing information systems, especially those that are a part of emerging comprehensive patient information systems. These systems provide nurses with important, timely data on the patient and include alerting and monitoring mechanisms.

Artificial Intelligence Applications in Healthcare

Throughout this chapter, applications in healthcare and decision support have been mentioned from a branch of computer science called *artificial intelligence* (AI). AI is actually a fairly new branch that originated formally in 1956 when the term was coined (Russell and Norvig 1995). Although AI is generally thought of as being the development of programs for playing games such as chess, making robots, or creating computer systems that talk and interact with people, it is concerned primarily with understanding and building intelligent entities or agents in addition to studying intelligence. Thus, all the things mentioned are part of AI, plus more.

Four areas of AI are discussed in the following subsections.

Natural Language Processing

In 1950, Turning proposed his now-famous test for defining computer or machine intelligence. He proposed a test in which a human interrogator would ask questions and interact via teletype with a computer presumably in another location out of the interrogator's sight. A computer passed the test when the interrogator could tell whether he or she was interacting with a human or a computer at the other end.

For a computer system to pass this test, it must possess at least the capability of **natural language processing** (NLP). NLP is the ability of a computer to understand the full range of meaning contained in languages such as English. The system must be able to process the commands, instructions, or other input when provided by sentences as spoken in normal human discourse. Computer systems have excellent capabilities to process structured or constrained input where the user is limited to certain phrases or when a very specific manner in which to provide input to the system is prescribed. However, natural language has proved to be a very difficult capability for a computer system to acquire.

Recently, some systems have come to market with the ability to learn spoken language. Dictation programs that type as the user speaks have become widely available, and Microsoft Windows XP comes with speech recognition as a standard module. Nevertheless, the user must train these programs by providing as much as 30 minutes of spoken language to the system. Typically, these programs ask the user to read a predefined passage into the system. After the selection is read, training algorithms in the system process the recorded speech and train the system to recognize the user's unique speech patterns. Often such systems require additional training and adjustments. Once trained, however, the user can give verbal commands to the system and have them be performed.

In healthcare, NLP would be a tremendous tool for computer-assisted coding (AHIMA e-HIM Work Group on Computer-Assisted Coding 2004). Such information could be entered directly into the patient's computer-based health record, thus enhancing other decision support tools. Research and development of such systems is ongoing, however further testing and evaluation is needed before widespread adoption. Although NLP is an active area of research within both the computer science and informatics communities, many challenges still must be overcome. Issues such as a consistent or standard medical vocabulary must be addressed in addition to other technical issues in the speech recognition process.

Expert Systems

Earlier in this chapter, a distinction was made between decision support systems (DSSs) and expert systems (ESs). Discussion of both the knowledge-based DSS and the CDSS, particularly the MYCIN system, has introduced many of the features that characterize an expert system.

An ES attempts to replicate a human expert's ability to solve complex problems in a particular domain. In solving a particular problem, the system employs a set of rules obtained through a knowledge-gathering or engineering process by the developers of the ES. Reasoning is accomplished via an inference algorithm from AI. As mentioned previously, the reasoning component is the inference engine.

ES users are not experts in the particular problem domain. Rather, the ES is developed (ideally) as a surrogate for the expert. Thus, the user is typically inexperienced in the problem domain. In a sense, the goal of an ES is to capture an expert in the computer system.

One of the most difficult tasks in developing an ES is the capture of expert knowledge. This task is exceedingly difficult for several reasons. First, experts do not always know exactly how they arrive at their decisions. Often they have many years of experience and have developed an intuition about the problems and their solutions within the domain. Asking experts to state their knowledge in if-then rules becomes impossible. Second, even when if-then rules can be elicited from an expert(s), ensuring that the rules are consistent is a major challenge. Consistency of the rules means that when the rules are applied, the consequence will not contradict other rules in the collection or simply be circular.

Over the years, ESs have received mixed reactions from researchers and practitioners alike. The early work on MYCIN and other similar systems was groundbreaking. Many ES researchers and developers took as their goals the replacement of the expert with the computer. However, this goal was never fully accomplished. By the mid- to late 1980s, many clinicians questioned the idea of a system that treated the physician as a passive user, unable to solve a given diagnostic problem. Miller (1994) termed this early model of diagnostic support the "Greek oracle" model and noted its weaknesses. He observed that more recent systems have attempted to allow the user more control. The goal is no longer to allow the computer system to be the expert but, rather, to enhance the performance of the user.

In general, people are wary of giving a computer "expert status," especially in healthcare. In a few cases, ESs have been able to meet the goal of practically replacing the expert. An example is the XCON system developed in the 1980s by Digital Equipment Corporation (DEC) for use by sales and service people to configure DEC computer systems for customers. XCON was able to mimic the performance of computer engineers in configuring systems and was used by DEC for several years.

In healthcare, a variety of CDSSs have been developed using ES methodologies. Some of these systems have undergone rigorous evaluation (Berner et al. 1994). Yet, the reactions to these systems remain mixed. Carter observed the activity in this area as being one of "impressive creativity coupled with limited successes, small gains, [and] cynical resignation" (1999, 194). He concluded: "Do physicians really want help with the diagnostic process? This is a question of social and cognitive processes for which the answer to-date appears to be a very cool 'perhaps'" (1999, 194).

Artificial Neural Networks

ANNs are another important area in AI. They seek to provide mathematical models and computer algorithms that operate in a similar manner to the nervous system, in particular, the brain. The basis for ANNs consists of simple units called perceptrons (similar to the biological unit, neuron). These perceptrons are connected together and work in parallel. As data are presented to the ANNs, learning takes place through the adjustment and modification of weights embedded in the construction of the perceptron.

Research in ANNs began in the late 1940s and 1950s as an attempt to create programs that could reason similarly to human reasoning ability. Although the initial goal of the early researchers was never realized, over the years various ANN models have been developed that are very useful in pattern recognition, clustering, and predictive modeling. Many examples of ANN applications can be found in recent medical literature. Examples include applications involving the use of ANNs to assist radiologists in reading (classifying images), predicting patient outcomes, and developing clinical pathways.

Virtual Reality

Virtual reality (VR) is a recent area of AI. Jaron Lanier, founder of VPL research, coined the term in 1989 (Beier 2001). Since then, the term has been associated with a variety of closely related topics such as artificial reality, artificial life, virtual worlds, virtual environments, and cyberspace. VR is not purely an area of AI but, rather, it combines elements from computer simulation and computer graphics and visualization to provide an interactive, computer-mediated experience for the user. In the typical application, the user actually perceives himself or herself as an active participant in the "virtual" world constructed by the computer. To achieve this highly interactive, "virtual" experience, VR applications often require the user to wear some type of sensory device to achieve the immersive experience. Such devices range from a sensory glove or a head-mounted vision display, or both, to recent devices in which the user wears a complete sensory suit. These devices register the user's reactions to various actions occurring in the virtual environment and provide visual feedback and, in some cases, even physical sensations.

The application of VR to medical and healthcare issues has been rapidly occurring. However, most of the studies are in their infancy (Riva 2002). Some promising directions are in the application of VR to assist in simulating emergencies and training and in monitoring different healthcare workers' reactions. VR therapy in cases of mental health has been researched, yet good quality controlled experiments are yet to be seen in this area (Gregg and Nicholas 2007). More business-oriented VR applications include examining the location of new facilities, studying traffic flow patterns, and modeling local residents' reactions to real estate development.

Text Mining

Text mining (TM) refers to the discovery of knowledge from textual data. Physicians often express opinions in form of unstructured text that contain useful information not captured elsewhere. This information can be further utilized to develop intelligent models to improve healthcare process. However, statistical model building requires quantifiable, tangible information. TM can be used to convert text into numeric form that allows it to be used for analysis. There are several TM algorithms available that are suitable for a variety of problem domains (Raja et al. 2008).

TM has potential applications in the area of healthcare. Electronic clinical records contain information on all aspects of healthcare. Healthcare information systems collect large amounts of textual and numeric information about patients, visits, prescriptions, physician notes, and the like. The electronic documents encapsulate information that could lead to improvement in healthcare quality, promotion of clinical and research initiatives, reduction in medical errors, and reduction in healthcare costs. However, the documents that comprise the health record are wide ranging in complexity, length, and use of technical vocabulary, making knowledge discovery complex. Recent availability of commercial text mining tools provides a unique opportunity to extract critical information from textual data archives.

TM tools have been utilized in healthcare to analyze electronic medical records and identify patterns of emergency visits and physician on call (Cerrito 2005). TM can also lead to development of protocols to alleviate disparity in treatment. TM can be combined with other DM techniques to develop alerting systems for early detection of medical anomalies.

Check Your Understanding 19.3

Instructions: Answer the following questions on a separate piece of paper.

1. Name four types of decision support systems found in healthcare.
2. What are the main characteristics of a clinical decision support system?
3. What was the name of one of the earliest CDSSs?
4. What type of inference engine did the system given above use?
5. What are some of the difficulties in maintaining a CDSS?
6. What is a key characteristic of an EIS?
7. What makes the task of decision support for nursing so complex?
8. How can text mining benefit healthcare?

Healthcare in Web 2.0 Environment

Technology is changing the patterns of healthcare practice. Web 2.0 refers to new trends of World Wide Web technologies that support collaboration and information sharing. The proponents of Web 2.0 refer to it as a "web platform" where people can connect and share information (O'Reilly 2007). Use of blogs (for example, WordPress), video sharing sites (for example, YouTube) and social networking sites (for example, Facebook) are some examples of how Web 2.0 has changed the patterns of online information handling. As these technologies become widely accepted, the healthcare industry is trying to incorporate new technology to improve its performance. For example, Liverpool Women's clinic allows its midwives to access, review, and update medical records from the homes of patients at the clinic's servers. The solution—called "office on a stick"—provides a secure network access to healthcare workers (Merrill 2008). There are several examples of technology use in healthcare that is supported by the new generation of Internet applications. However, there is little evidence to indicate that the healthcare industry is ready to embrace Web 2.0.

We are far from a system where patient information is available in a format that can be accessed by doctors, pharmacies, insurance companies and, of course, patients. According to estimates, 75 percent of medical practices in the U.S. still do not use any form of electronic records (Burt et al. 2006). Where electronic records are available, there is a lack of standardization of formats to share the information with other stakeholders. The healthcare industry needs to get patient information into electronic databases that can be shared across multiple stakeholders and make the information interoperable. But more than that, with the increase in the use of social networking and customized content management solutions, patients will soon demand a networked decision-making framework to consult with doctors and not the prevailing centralized data management system. However, the sharing of information and availability of online contents carries new challenges of privacy and accuracy. Consumer and healthcare information needs to be protected and secure channels for information sharing have to be provided. Potential threats (for example, hacking) can jeopardize privacy and security of sensitive personal information.

Future Roles for HIM Professionals

In 2003, a task force was convened by the American Health Information Management Association (AHIMA). The group met to discuss the strategic directions of AHIMA and the evolution of the e-HIM initiative. Through a number of dialogues among the participants, including industry and academic leaders, this group charted new roles for HIM professionals in response to identified needs within healthcare organizations today. A variety of new roles related to the area of decision support were identified. Overall, the group found that HIM professionals will be increasingly required to provide, interpret, and use data as well as provide decision support over the continuum of healthcare. Several of the new roles identified by the group that are directly related to decision support are:

- Content expert (data sets, nomenclature, and classification standards)
- Data analyst
- Data facilitator/data information broker/data information presenter
- Data miner
- Data navigator
- Data quality and integrity monitor
- Data translator

Data analysts, navigators, and facilitators will perform many of the tasks often associated with a research specialist (RS). As outlined by Johns and Hardin (2006), the RS works to create and support decision- and knowledge-based activities within an organization by gathering and analyzing data. Typical job descriptions for RSs will include skills such as proficiency in Microsoft Access or SQL server, Visual Basic or Cold Fusion, and a statistical package such as SPSS or SAS.

The skills for a data miner and some data analysts are best described as a combination of the skills required above. In most cases, a data miner also should have at least a master's degree in an area such as health informatics, biostatistics (or applied statistics), epidemiology, or some quantitative health science field.

One difference between the data manager/navigator and some of the other roles listed is that the data miner will not necessarily be involved directly in the collection and management of data from the clinical or other setting. Instead, he or she will use the tools of data mining to better utilize the organization's data resources in making strategic and other business decisions.

In 2007, AHIMA produced "Vision 2016" and identified its key priorities as transformation of health information management to graduate level profession; realignment of the associates degree with work force needs and preparation of a quality pool of faculty by year 2016. Opportunities of higher degrees in HIM will enable the next generation of professionals in HIM to be equipped with more formal training. These trends will also attract HIM professional to academic careers in addition to become practitioners.

Future Development of Decision Support Systems

Many directions are possible for future development of DSSs. The incorporation of NLP into patient information systems may enable quick capture (extraction of discrete data from free text) of physicians' clinical observations. Another avenue of development is to help consumers of healthcare services make more informed decisions. Examples of this direction of development include the APACHE system and systems such as one that assists low-literacy women in making decisions about options of care and treatment for breast cancer. Jimison and Sher (1999) have written a helpful review that summarizes much of the activity in this area. Future directions also may include the development of systems that can guide nonexpert individuals in providing care for critically injured individuals during catastrophic events such as natural disasters when trained medical personnel are taxed to their limits and unable to meet the needs of all the people who need care.

Summary

Decision support systems will play an important role in the future of healthcare. Clinical decision support systems, which have received much attention in the past, will continue to play a key role—and perhaps an even more important role than before. As computer-based patient record and patient information systems emerge and develop, the incorporation of clinical decision support in the form of clinical reminders, clinical alerts, medication alerts, and drug interaction monitoring offers great potential for improving the quality of patient care and for eliminating many of the medical errors cited in recent reports. With strong mandates from both consumers and the government, the opportunities for advances in clinical decision support are numerous.

Other areas of decision support also offer great promise for the future. The development of data warehouses and the use of data-mining tools to exploit this vast mountain of data, will be an important competitive advantage for healthcare organizations. Many already are employing and studying the use of data-mining tools to identify medical errors and adverse events. In other examples, applications of this technology are proving beneficial in developing predictive models to assist in patient care and diagnosis, new facility location, clinical pathway development, identification of inappropriate utilization of healthcare resources, emergency vehicle scheduling in times of crisis, and improved quality of care for patients. The age of Web 2.0 technologies offers a new set of challenges and opportunities. While easy access to online records and information has potential cost and service benefits, the widespread use of such systems needs careful validation of patient record security.

References

AHIMA e-HIM Work Group on Computer-Assisted Coding. 2004. Practice brief: Delving into computer-assisted coding. *Journal of AHIMA* 75(10):48A–H (with Web extras).

Barnett, G.O., J.J. Cimino, J.A. Hupp, and E.P. Hoffer. 1987. DXplain—An evolving diagnostic decision-support system. *Journal of the American Medical Association* 258(1):67–74.

Begur, S.V., D.M. Miller, and J. Weaver. 1997. An integrated spatial DSS for scheduling and routing home-health-care nurses. *Interfaces* 27(4):35–48.

Beier, K.P. 2001. Virtual reality: A short introduction. University of Michigan Virtual Reality Laboratory (VRL). http://www-vrl.umich.edu/intro.

Berner, E.S., et al. 1994. Performance of four computer-based diagnostic decision support systems. *New England Journal of Medicine* 330(25):1792–1796.

Berner, E.S., R.S. Maisiak, C.G. Cobbs, and O.D. Taunton. 1999. A computer alert system to prevent injury from adverse drug events development and evaluation in a community teaching hospital. *Journal of the American Medical Informatics Association* 6(5):420–427.

Box, G.E.P. 1979. Robustness in the strategy of scientific model building. In *Robustness in Statistics*. Edited by Launer, R.L. and G.N. Wilkinson. New York: Academic Press.

Burt, C., E. Hing, and D. Woodwell. 2006. Electronic Medical Record Use of Office-Based Physicians: United States 2005. National Center for Health Statistics–NCHS Health E-Stats.

Carter, J.H. 1999. Design and implementation issues. In *Clinical Decision Support Systems: Theory and Practice*. Edited by Berner, E.S. New York: Springer.

Cerrito, P. and J.C. Cerrito. 2005. Data and text mining the electronic medical record to improve care and to lower costs. In *SUGI 31*. San Francisco, CA.

Cunningham, M. and O. McKenna. 1993. Market model addresses hospitals' need for decision support. *Journal of Medical Systems* 10:65–71.

Davidson, C. 1993. What your database hides away. *New Scientist* 137(1855):28–31.

Davis, R.H. 1981. Social network analysis: An aid in conspiracy investigations. *FBI Law Enforcement Bulletin* 50(12):11–19.

Dayton, C.S., J.S. Ferguson, D.B. Hornick, and M.W. Peterson. 2000. Evaluation of an Internet-based decision-support system for applying the ATS/CDC guidelines for tuberculosis preventive therapy. *Medical Decision Making* 20(1):1–6.

de Dombal, F.T., J.R. Hartley, and D.H. Sleeman. 1969. A computer-assisted system for learning clinical diagnosis. *Lancet* 1:145–148.

Dexter, P., S. Perkins, J.M. Overhage, K. Maharry, R. Kohler, and C.J. McDonald. 2001. A computerized reminder system to increase the use of preventive care for hospitalized patients. *New England Journal of Medicine* 345(13):965–970.

Dobrzeniecki, A. 1994. *Executive Information Systems.* Chicago: ITT Research Institute.

Durieux, P., R. Nizard, P. Ravaud, N. Mounier, and E. Lepage. 2000. A clinical decision support system for the prevention of venous thromboembolism effect on physician behavior. *Journal of the American Medical Association* 283(21):2816–2821.

Forgionne, G. 1991. Effectively marketing prepaid medical care with decision support systems. *Health Marketing Quarterly* 8(3/4):107–118.

Friend, D. 1992. Building an EIS your CFO will really use. *Chief Information Officer Journal* 5(1):32–36.

Gerbert, B., A. Bronstone, T. Maurer, R. Hofmann, and T. Berger. 2000. Decision support software to help primary care physicians triage skin cancer: A pilot study. *Archives of Dermatology* 136(2):187–192.

Gorry, G.A. and G.O. Barnett. 1968. Experience with a model of sequential diagnosis. *Computers and Biomedical Research* 1:490–507.

Gorry, G.A. and M.S. Scott-Morton. 1971. A framework for management information systems. *Sloan Management Review* 13:55–70.

Gregg, L. and N. Tarrier. 2007. Virtual reality and mental health: A review of literature. *Social Psychiatry and Psychiatric Epidemiology* 42(5):343–354.

Hardin, J.M., P. Miller, A. Whelton, and S. Bellile. 1999. A new role for HIM in the knowledge economy. *Journal of AHIMA* 70(7):56–59.

Hohmann, S., E.L. Buff, and G. Wietecha. 1998. Monitoring performance improvement using decision support systems. *Journal of AHIMA* 69(10):36–39.

Howe, R.S., M.B. Terpening, and S. Wadhwa. 1999. Disease management and clinical decision support. *Journal of Healthcare Information Management* 13(2):53–66.

Inmon, W.H. 1992. *Building the Data Warehouse.* New York: John Wiley & Sons.

Institute of Medicine, Committee on Quality of Health Care in America. 2001. *Crossing the Quality Chasm: A New Health System for the 21st Century.* Washington, D.C.: National Academy Press.

Jimison, H.B. and P.R. Sher. 1999. Decision support for patients. In *Clinical Decision Support Systems*. Edited by Berner, E. New York: Springer.

Johns, M.L. and J.M. Hardin. 2006. Research and decision support. Ch. 7 in *Ethical Challenges in the Management of Health Information: Process and Strategies for Decision-Making*. Edited by Harman, L.B. Sudbury, MA: Jones and Bartlett.

Kaufman, D.M. and G.I. Paterson. 1995. Preparing future physicians: How will medical schools meet the challenge? In *Future Health: Computers and Medicine in the Twenty-first Century*. Edited by Pickover, C.A. New York: St. Martin's Press.

Kohn, L.T., J.M. Corrigan, and M.S. Donaldson, eds. 2000. *To Err Is Human: Building a Safer Health System.* Washington, D.C.: National Academy Press.

Lagina, S. 1971. A computer program to diagnose anxiety levels. *Nursing Research* 20(6):484–492.

Ledley, R. and L. Lusted. 1959. Reasoning foundations of medical diagnosis. *Science* 130:9–21.

Little, J.D. 1970. Models and managers: The concept of a decision calculus. *Management Science* 16(8):B466–485.

Marakas, G.M. 1999. *Decision Support Systems in the 21st Century.* Upper Saddle River, NJ: Prentice-Hall.

Merrill, M. 2008 (Aug.). Midwives use new technology to remotely access patient info. Healthcare IT NewsDay Europe.

Miller, R.A. 1994. Medical diagnostic decision support systems—past, present, and future: A threaded bibliography and commentary. *Journal of the American Medical Informatics Association* 1(1):8–27.

Miller, R.A., F.E. Masarie, and J. Myers. 1986. Quick medical reference (QMR) for diagnostic assistance. *MD Computing* 3(5):34–48.

Miller, R.A., H.E. Pople, Jr., and J. Myers. 1982. Internist-I, an experimental computer-based diagnostic consultant for general internal medicine. *New England Journal of Medicine* 307(8):468–476.

O'Reilly, T. 2007. What is Web 2.0: Design patterns and business models for the next generation of software? *Communications and Strategies* 1(1):17.

Pickover, C.A., ed. 1995. *Future Health.* New York: St Martin's Press.

Poikonen, J. and J.M. Leventhal. 1999. Medication-management issues at the point of care. *Journal of Healthcare Information Management* 13(2):43–52.

Pople, H.E., J.D. Myers, and R.A. Miller. 1975. DIALOG: A model of diagnostic logic for internal medicine. In *Proceedings of the Fourth International Joint Conference on Artificial Intelligence.* Cambridge, MA: MIT Artificial Intelligence Laboratory Publications.

Raja, U., T. Mitchell, T. Day and J. M. Hardin. 2008 (Summer). Text mining in healthcare: Applications and opportunities. *Journal of Health Information Management Systems.*

Riva, Giuseppe. 2002. Virtual reality for health care: The status of research. *CyberPsychology & Behavior* 5(3): 219–225.

Ruland, C.M. 1999. Decision support for patient preference-based care planning: Effects on nursing care and patient outcomes. *Journal of American Medical Informatics Association* 6(4):304–312.

Russell, S. and P. Norvig. 1995. *Artificial Intelligence: A Modern Approach.* Upper Saddle River, NJ: Prentice-Hall.

Senge, P. 1990. *The Fifth Discipline: The Art and Practice of the Learning Organization..* New York: Doubleday.

Shams, K. and M. Farishta. 2001. Data warehousing: Toward knowledge management. *Topics in Health Information Management* 21(3):24–32.

Shortliffe, E.H. 1976. *Computer-based Medical Consultations: MYCIN.* New York: Elsevier.

Simon, H.A. 1957. *Models of Man*. New York: John Wiley & Sons.

Simon, H.A. 1960. *The New Science of Management Decision.* New York: Harper & Row.

Simon, H.A. 1976. *Administrative Behavior*. 3rd ed. New York: The Free Press.

Simon, H.A. 1977. *The New Science of Management Decision*. Rev. ed. Englewood Cliffs, NJ: Prentice-Hall.

Stewart, T.A. 1997. *Intellectual Capital.* New York: Doubleday/Currency.

Tan, J.K. 2001. *Health Management Information Systems: Methods and Practical Applications.* 2nd ed. Gaithersburg, MD: Aspen Publishers.

Tan, J.K. and S. Sheps, eds. 1998. *Health Decision Support Systems.* Gaithersburg, MD: Aspen Publishers.

Turban, E. 1995. *Decision Support and Expert Systems: Management Support Systems.* 4th ed. Englewood Cliffs, NJ: Prentice-Hall.

Turning, A. 1950. Computing machinery and intelligence. *Mind* 59:433–460.

Warner, H.R., R.M. Garner, and A.F. Toronto. 1964. Experience with Bayes' theorem for computer diagnosis of congenital heart disease. *Annals of the New York Academy of Science* 115:2–16.

Yu, V.L., et al. 1979. Antimicrobial selection by a computer: A blinded evaluation by infectious disease experts. *Journal of the American Medical Association* 242(12):1279–1282.

Zaki, A. 1989. Developing a DSS for a distribution facility: An application in the healthcare industry. *Journal of Medical Systems* 13:331–346.

Part VI

Management of Health Information Services

Chapter 20
Principles of Management

David X. Swenson, PhD

Learning Objectives

- Introduce the management discipline, the evolution of management thought, and the key functions and skills of management
- Identify significant trends in managerial models
- Understand that management approaches emerge in response to change drivers of a particular period
- Identify key theorists in the development of management practices
- Describe the four functions of management
- Describe the 10 roles of a manager
- Describe the relationship between management functions and skills and levels of management
- Identify different approaches to problem solving and decision making
- Describe the emergence and principles of corporate social responsibility
- Describe key practices for effective communication

Key Terms

85/15 rule
Acceptance theory of authority
Active listening
Administrative management
Balanced scorecard (BSC)
Baldridge Award
Bounded rationality
Break-even analysis
Bureaucracy
Business process reengineering (BPR)
Chain of command
Change drivers
Clinical communication space
Conceptual skills
Controlling
Corporate social responsibility
Critical path method
Decentralization
Discipline
Effectiveness
Efficiency
Emotional intelligence (EI)
Esprit de corps
Evidence-based management
Executive dashboard
Forecasting
Fourteen principles of management
Gantt chart
Goals
Groupthink
Hawthorne effect
Hierarchy of needs
Human relations movement
International Organization for Standardization (ISO)
Interpersonal skills
Intuition
Leading
Line authority
Linear programming
Management by objectives (MBO)
Management functions
Maslow's Hierarchy of Needs
Nonprogrammed decision
Operational plan
Operations management
Organizing
Paradigm
Piece-rate incentive
Planning
Program evaluation and review technique (PERT)
Programmed decisions
Queuing theory
Revenge effects
Role theory
Satisficing
Scalar chain
Scientific management
Self-monitoring
Simulation and inventory modeling
Span of control
Staff authority
Strategic plan
Sustainability
Tactical plan
Technical skills
Theory X and Y
Time and motion studies
Total quality management (TQM)
Triple bottom line
Vertical structure

Models for management originally were based on traditional ways of organizing people to accomplish tasks. For thousands of years, these typically involved small family cottage industries, military organizations, or church-directed structures. With the advent of the industrial revolution, migration to cities, and specialization of labor, the former methods of management no longer worked effectively. Workers did not necessarily carry on family traditions, could not be commanded to comply with orders, or did not serve out of dedication to some larger corporate value. New ways of thinking about management were needed.

Management theories are not just academic exercises; they are ways of describing how managers think about the way organizations work, which in turn influences their decisions and directs their efforts and behavior. The theories described in this chapter reflect the development of management theories over the decades, as well as newer approaches being developed. Many elements of even the early theories are still practiced widely. By being able to identify our working theories, we are better able to evaluate how appropriate they are for our settings and how we can revise them to work better.

In 1962, Thomas Kuhn published *The Structure of Scientific Revolutions.* Translated into 20 languages and cited by scholars in numerous fields, it has been a reference point for new management thinkers. Kuhn introduced the concept of a **paradigm**, a mental model or structure for perceiving, understanding, and responding to the world. Paradigms make thinking more efficient by drawing attention to certain things, but they also filter out exceptions to the rules where innovations may lie. He argued that scientific progress, rather than growing slowly and incrementally, more often occurs when complexity increases to a high degree and cannot be adequately dealt with by the current paradigm. A paradigm shift then occurs, and the old one is replaced with a new one.

A key idea in management is the recognition that management theories and practices grow out of the unique constellation of forces or **change drivers** that operate at the time. These large-scale forces consist of demographic, social, political, economic, technical, and, more recently, global and informational factors. In a competitive environment, each organization seeks to position itself to succeed against other organizations and does so by the effective and efficient allocation of its resources to respond to these demands.

In this chapter we will describe many of the historical and theoretical developments in management, most of which are still used today in organizations. The functions, skills, and roles of managers will be identified, along with trends in management theory related to problem solving. Finally, the importance of communication in organizations will be emphasized related to the increasing role of information in the healthcare workplace.

Landmarks in Management as a Discipline

A **discipline** is a field of study characterized by a knowledge base and perspective that is distinctive from other fields of study. The knowledge base and perspective form a foundation for the discipline's practices, guide research for continuing refinement, and create its literature base. As the study of management found its way into academic settings, theories and practices of management began to emerge. Changing social conditions and growing technological innovations often contributed to the way that management theories were framed.

Scientific Management

The late nineteenth and early twentieth centuries marked the emergence of many elements of modern management theory. The individuals profiled in the following subsections were key players in that development.

Max Weber

German sociologist, lawyer, and political economist Max Weber (1864–1920) was formulating his ideas of the ideal or prototypic organization. Recognizing the inefficiency that was occurring with high variability in standards, he proposed that organizations become bureaucracies. He believed that variability could be reduced by having a formally structured hierarchy of relationships, by formulating rules and regulations to standardize behavior, and by using trained specialists for jobs.

As a result, efficiency could be promoted, subjective judgment and favoritism could be eliminated, and planning could be based on the position rather than the person. At a time when organizational procedures were highly variable, bureaucratic theory offered the structure necessary to improve performance. In the modern marketplace where competitive advantage is maintained through innovation, **bureaucracy** has come more often to refer to slow decision making, unresponsiveness, ignoring the uniqueness of individuals, and rules without reasons.

Frederick Taylor

About the same time that Weber was forming his ideas about bureaucracy, Frederick W. Taylor (1856–1915) was a young engineer working at the Midvale Steel Company. He discovered that his company and most others had tremendous unused potential. Pay and working conditions were poor, waste and inefficiency were prevalent, and management decision making was unsystematic and not based on research of any sort. Taylor introduced new practices whose success led to his being recognized as the Father of Scientific Management. Although many of his ideas are commonly accepted today, they were revolutionary at the time.

Taylor defined the main objective of managers to be that of securing maximum prosperity for employer and employee. He viewed management and the workforce as interdependent and promoted the idea that people were inherently capable of hard work. The problem, he argued, was that the old management stifled workers and could be remedied by his four principles:

- Management should develop a scientific approach to work, involving precise, measurable guidelines for output; pay could be linked to performance.
- Management should select, train, and develop workers scientifically to be first class so that the right person has the right job.
- Management and workers should collaborate to ensure that the job matches plans.
- Management should provide equal division of work and responsibility between workers and management.

To implement his ideas, Taylor and his followers developed new techniques. **Time and motion studies**, for example, were conducted in which tasks were subdivided into their most basic movements. Detailed motions were timed to determine the most efficient way of carrying them out. After the one best way was found, the best worker match for the job was hired, tools and procedures were standardized, instruction cards were written to guide workers, and breaks were instituted to reduce fatigue. From implementing new practices, one mining company increased production from 12.5 to 47 tons of loaded pig iron per day and reduced the number of yard laborers from 600 to 140 with no reduction in output. A **piece-rate incentive** system also was developed in which workers received additional pay when they exceeded the standard output level for their task.

Taylor's principles were quickly embraced and later refined by Frank and Lillian Gilbreth, Henry Gantt, and others. The Gilbreths were a husband and wife team who developed many of the early ideas of ergonomics and work efficiency. Their original studies focused on bricklaying, part of Frank's background, in which they noticed that workers developed their own ways of working and that no two workers used the same method. The Gilbreths divided the process into detailed individual motions they called "therbligs" (Gilbreth nearly spelled backwards) to identify unnecessary or inefficient motions. Seeking the single best way to perform the tasks, they reduced the number of motions for bricklaying from 18 to 4.5, which resulted in much higher productivity, less fatigue, and better planning. Lillian (1878–1972) was known for her studies on finding innovative ways to design efficient kitchen and home living areas for patients with cardiac-limited conditions.

Frank Gilbreth

Frank Gilbreth (1868–1924) embraced time saving with a passion and gained notoriety with his experiments. For example, he would experiment to see whether it would be faster to button his vest from top to bottom or the reverse. He tried to shave with two razors, but the time saving was reduced by having to patch his several cuts. Two of his children wrote the popular book *Cheaper by the Dozen* in which they detailed the family's preoccupation with innovations.

Henry Gantt

Henry Gantt (1861–1919) worked for Taylor and was known for his promotion of favorable psychological work conditions. He may be best remembered for his development of the **Gantt chart**, which is still used for project management to show how the components of a task are scheduled over time. His chart contributed to development, in the late 1950s, of the program evaluation and review technique (PERT) developed by the U.S. Navy and the **critical path method** developed by Dupont. He also contributed his Task and Bonus Plan to management, which provided bonus payment for workers who exceeded their production standards for the day.

Many of these developments were rapidly applied to the growing market demand for popular products in the United States. Sears and Roebuck probably designed the first manufacturing assembly line for meeting mail-order delivery. In the automobile industry, Henry Ford (who employed Taylor) became intrigued by the moving conveyer belt of carcasses in a Chicago slaughterhouse. He quickly developed this idea into his assembly line for automobile manufacturing, streamlining production from a one-person assembly time of 12.5 hours to about 93 minutes per car. The idea was taken to its extreme in healthcare in the early 1970s when Russian ophthalmologists attempted to introduce assembly-line radial keratotomy, a surgery for correcting eye lens problems. The idea did not catch on widely, although there have been attempts in other countries to promote this idea to cut medical costs.

The legacy of **scientific management** is pervasive and persists in many areas of modern management. At a time when most businesses were growing in size and complexity, but lacked sound organization, Taylorism provided principles for increasing standardization and consistency. It emphasized the role of research in understanding how tasks were done, in selecting and training people, and in providing consistency in rules and procedures to promote efficiency. However, Taylorism was not without critics. Although scientific management helped managers routinize the internal workings of the business, it essentially ignored the external environment. In addition, critics complained that it was based on simplistic economic motivation, that workers were viewed as mechanistic parts of an organizational machine, and that senior management tasks were excluded from analysis.

Administrative Management

Attempting to compensate for scientific management's exclusion of senior management, **administrative management** argued that management was a profession and could be learned. The following subsections profile three individuals who played key roles in describing management functions.

Henry Fayol

Henry Fayol (1841–1925), a French engineer and director of mining, published a book summarizing his executive experiences in 1916. Fayol's major contribution includes a description of five functions of management and fourteen principles for organizational design and administration.

Fayol's five **management functions** have persisted with some variation into modern organizations and identify key functions that define the manager's role. These managerial functions were:

- **Planning** consists of examining the future and preparing plans of action to attain goals.
- **Organizing** includes the ways in which the managed system is designed and operated to attain the desired goals. It involves the way that tasks are grouped into departments and resources are distributed to them.
- **Leading** (sometimes also called directing) is the process of influencing the behavior of others. It involves motivating, creating shared culture and values, and communicating with all levels of the organization.
- **Controlling** refers to the monitoring of performance and use of feedback to ensure that efforts are on target toward prescribed goals, making course corrections as necessary.

Fayol's fifth function, coordination or unifying and harmonizing activity and effort has been absorbed by the other functions (primarily controlling) in modern versions.

Fayol formulated **fourteen principles of management** to guide managerial activities within the total organization. (See figure 20.1) Like his managerial functions, most have been incorporated into modern organizations and are widely accepted today. For example, authority was proposed as the right of an executive to give orders and expect obedience. Unity of command meant that each employee reports to only one boss. The **scalar chain**, or line of authority, ensured that everyone in the organization appears in the **chain of command** and reports to someone. **Esprit de corps** emphasized the work climate in which harmony and cohesion promoted good work.

Chester Barnard

Chester Barnard (1886–1961), a former president of the New Jersey Telephone Company and the Rockefeller Foundation, published *The Functions of the Executive* in 1938. In this book, he elaborated the role of top executives. He proposed that the leader needed information from those below, that the communication system is designed and implemented by the executive, and that the role of middle management is to implement plans and solve problems.

Barnard developed the **acceptance theory of authority**, which proposes that people have free will to choose whether they follow work orders. In addition, he emphasized that the measure of organizational cooperation is effectiveness and efficiency. **Effectiveness** refers to the degree to which the organization achieves its intended outcomes; **efficiency** refers to how well a minimum of resources is allocated to achieve the outcomes.

Figure 20.1. Fayol's fourteen principles

1. *Specialization of labor:* Work allocation and specialization allow concentrated activities, deeper understanding, and better efficiency.
2. *Authority:* The person to whom responsibilities are given has the right to give direction and expect obedience.
3. *Discipline:* The smooth operation of a business requires standards, rules, and values for consistency of action.
4. *Unity of command:* Every employee receives direction and instructions from only one boss
5. *Unity of direction:* All workers are aligned in their efforts toward a single outcome.
6. *Subordination of individual interests:* Accomplishing shared values and organizational goals take priority over individual agendas.
7. *Remuneration:* Employees should receive fair pay for work.
8. *Centralization:* Decisions are made at the top.
9. *Scalar chain:* Everyone is clearly included in the chain of command and line of authority from top to bottom of the organization.
10. *Order:* People should clearly understand where they fit in the organization, and all people and material have a place.
11. *Equity:* People are treated fairly and a sense of justice should pervade the organization.
12. *Tenure:* Turnover is undesirable and loyalty to the organization is sought.
13. *Initiative:* Personal initiative should be encouraged.
14. *Esprit de corps:* Harmony, cohesion, teamwork, and good interpersonal relationships should be encouraged.

Mary Parker Follett

Another major contributor to the administrative approach was Mary Parker Follett (1868–1933). In contrast to what was often considered a mechanistic view by Taylor, she was interested in broader social ideas and championed the role of relationships in organizations. Although she drew mixed attention in the late 1920s, she foresaw the development of a systems view of business, the role of empowered employees in organizational development, and the use of workgroups to implement solutions. Her ideas have enjoyed a revival in recent years, acknowledged by such management gurus as Peter Drucker and Henry Mintzberg. Follett promoted using teamwork and creative group effort, involving people in organizational development, and integrating the organization, which contained many elements of systems theory.

Humanistic Management

Although the United States has always touted itself as the home of democracy, the equity of power in the workplace has not always existed between workers and management. By the early 1900s, there were growing social pressures to treat workers in a more enlightened manner. Building on Barnard's and Follett's ideas that people should be treated fairly and that effective controls come from individual workers, the stage was set for a shift in management thought stimulated by an experiment at an electric power plant.

Hawthorne Studies

At the turn of the century, gas and electricity companies were intensely competitive about their respective products, and it appeared that electricity had edged out gas. To firm up its advantage, Thomas Edison and the Committee on Industrial Lighting proposed a study that would confirm the advantage of electric lighting. The Hawthorne plant of the Western Electric Company was elected to serve as the laboratory for examining the effects of illumination. From 1924 to 1932, Harvard professors Elton Mayo and Fritz Roethlisberger conducted the series of experiments. In some cases, the lighting in the plant was changed to see how it affected productivity. Although performance initially increased when illumination was improved, it paradoxically also improved when lighting was lowered to about the level of moonlight. The study concluded that although light was not the motivator they intended, positive attention and human relations improved performance—the so-called **Hawthorne effect**.

The Human Relations Movement

The **human relations movement** revolutionized thinking about how to treat workers to improve productivity. Sometimes referred to as the contented cow approach (contented cows give more milk), the belief was that satisfied workers are more productive. Interestingly, reexamination of the original research design and data suggests that financial incentives had a good deal to do with motivating people, and yet the impact of the human relations emphasis continues (Parson 1974). This movement reached its peak during the 1960s and 1970s.

Human Resources Management

In the 1950s, the field of psychology in the United States was just coming into its own prominence, as were theories of motivation. Observing that many problems derived from an inability to meet needs, Abraham Maslow (1908–1970) suggested that a **hierarchy of needs** might help to explain behavior and provide guidance for managers on how to better motivate workers.

His now-famous hierarchy, **Maslow's Hierarchy of Needs**, began with physiological existence needs and progressed through safety, social belongingness, self-esteem, and finally self-actualization or creativity needs. This developmental view of needs meant that to motivate people, lower-order needs should be satisfied before higher-order needs could serve as motivators. Although these were useful generalizations, in the emerging global economy with diverse populations, motivators can vary considerably by culture. What works as a management approach in American organizations may not work as well in other countries or cultures. (See chapter 23 for a full discussion of current human resources management principles, issues, and practices.)

Douglas McGregor

Douglas McGregor (1906–1964) recognized the shift in conceptual models from assumptions that workers were incapable of independent action to beliefs in their potential and high performance. He formulated the contrasting views as **theory X and Y** (1960). Theory X presumed that workers inherently disliked work and would avoid it, had little ambition, and mostly wanted security; therefore, managerial direction and control was necessary. Theory Y took a more enlightened view and assumed that work was as natural as play, that motivation could be both internally and externally driven, and that under the right conditions people would seek responsibility and be creative. Although theory Y is most favored at present, theory X may still be appropriate in some military, corrections, and immature workforce settings. In contrast, the innovative Saturn Corporation has based nearly all its auto manufacturing practices on theory Y.

Despite its simplicity, the human relations view brought management to focus on the human side of enterprise (to use McGregor's term). Managers and researchers began to consider the possible role of social and psychological factors on performance. This gave balance to a view of workers that was too heavily laden with mechanistic and economic explanations.

Operations Management

The innovations resulting from wars, the space race, and other international crises have often been the impetus for innovation. With World War II came the problems of planning, organizing, distributing, and monitoring huge collections of troops and materiel on a global basis. Advances in the fields of statistics, mathematics, and quantitative methods were brought to bear on decision making and strategy in an approach called operations research. **Operations management** later emerged as an application of these techniques in the business setting to better understand how products and services could be manufactured and delivered.

Techniques

A variety of techniques is now commonly found in many organizations, including:

- **Forecasting** is regularly used for planning in which previous conditions (such as sales and inventory) are projected into the future. Increasingly sophisticated software can provide projections of changes in technology, demographics, and human resources needs. However, in a rapidly changing environment, predictions based on past performance can be uncertain.
- **Linear programming** is used to identify an optimal decision given a set of planned constraints or limited resources.
- **Break-even analysis** helps planners determine when a project "breaks even," that is, the level of sales at which total revenues equal total costs. Revenues beyond that are profits.

- **Queuing theory** is a mathematical technique for determining the flow of customers or for designing optimal wait times for services.
- **Simulation and inventory modeling** is a recent development in management science based on computerization and systems concepts. The key components and processes of a system are represented in a computer model so that planners can experiment with different operating strategies and designs to get the best results before committing to their actual implementation.
- **Program evaluation and review technique** (PERT) was originally developed by the Navy in 1958 to coordinate the building of submarines. Now facilitated by powerful computer packages, PERT allows large, long-term, and complex projects to be shown graphically in order to clarify critical task sequences, potential bottlenecks, and the time required for them. For complex situations such as healthcare systems, computer decision support can help explore and optimize decisions.

Although many of these programs and techniques are challenging to learn, their ability to deal with vast amounts of data provides considerable advantage to the managers who can fully use them.

Contemporary Management

Although many aspects of older theories of management are still widely practiced in most organizations, research and practical experience have led to many new developments in the field. More contemporary approaches to management include management by objectives (MBO), total quality management (TQM), and an emphasis on excellence. Each of these has made a contribution to better understanding how effective management works, but none of them alone has yet succeeded in producing a comprehensive solution for managing organizations.

Peter Drucker and Management by Objectives

Often referred to as the guru of management gurus and Father of Modern Management, Peter Drucker (1909–2005) more clearly formulated the practice of strategy by integrating formulation, tactical planning, and budgeting into a single system of management (Kerker 2001). He revolutionized the role of strategy by wresting it from the hands of top management and making it everyone's job, helping workers understand how mission, strategy, goals, and performance were related. Because strategy was action oriented, starting in the 1950s, Drucker elaborated on the technique of **management by objectives** (MBO), in which clear target objectives could be stated and measured and could direct behavior. The four elements of an MBO system include (Drucker 1986):

- Top management's planning and setting of goals
- Managers with subordinates setting individual objectives related to organizational goals
- Autonomy in the means of achieving objectives
- Regular review of performance in obtaining objectives

Drucker's MBO approach was further developed by his promotion of the ideas that workers should be considered assets rather than liabilities, the corporation is an interpersonal community, and business is customer-centered (Byrne 2005). His style as a business consultant was also innovative, and he was described by one reviewer as an "iconoclast—the smasher of idols, seeker of proof, demander of evidence, gadfly, thorn in the side, and hard-nosed commentator on problems faced by our society (Bonaparte 1970, 23). As a consultant he would repeatedly ask his clients, "What is your business?" forcing them to consider the core of their work—still a valuable question for defining objectives and formulating strategy.

W. Edwards Deming and Quality

From the late 1970s to the mid-1980s, the United States was beset with a series of economic setbacks. Serious recessions, a growing trade deficit, government deregulation, and huge operating losses led to the downsizing of hundreds of thousands of workers. Quality became the focus as a means of increasing competitive position, and much of the idea was derived from W. Edwards Deming (1900–1993), an American statistician. Deming had initially developed his ideas in the 1940s (Walton 1986), but the American economy was booming at the time and seemed to believe it had found the "one best way" to do things. Consequently, American industry was inattentive to Deming's ideas about improvement and his statistical control procedures for monitoring quality. However, the Japanese were suffering from an all-but-destroyed economy and were eager to hear new ideas about production. They quickly adopted the concept of total quality management.

Total Quality Management

Total quality management (TQM) purported to overcome the limitations of MBO, criticizing the use of quotas because workers too often spent too much time trying to look good or protect themselves by seeking short-term objectives and ignoring long-term and critical outcomes. TQM offered a way to build in high performance by maximizing employee potential and continuous improvement of process. The **85/15 rule** of TQM proposes that 85 percent of problems encountered are the result of faulty systems rather than unproductive employees. The manager's job, then, becomes one of anticipating and removing barriers to high employee performance. Deming proposed his fourteen principles for TQM implementation. (See figure 20.2.)

Variations of TQM also were promoted by Juran and Crosby, and many of the ideas now find expression in a variation called **business process reengineering** (BPR). In the 1990s, when recognition of the high level of business competition was reaching a peak, Hammer and Champy (1993) published *Reengineering the Corporation.* They proposed that a radical redesign of the organization might be necessary to reduce costs, streamline operations, and improve quality of service. By the mid-1990s, the idea was often used to

Figure 20.2. Deming's 14 principles

1. Create a constancy of purpose toward continual improvement of products and services, with the objectives to stay in business, be competitive, and provide jobs.
2. Adopt the new philosophy for a new economic age by correcting superstitious learning, calling for a major change, and looking at the customer rather than competition.
3. Cease dependence on inspection to achieve quality by eliminating emphasis on mass inspection and building quality in from the beginning.
4. Don't award business based on price tag alone, and minimize total costs by developing trusting and loyal long-term relationships with single suppliers.
5. Constantly and continually improve production and service systems and thereby improve quality and decrease costs.
6. Institute training on the job, where barriers to good work are removed and managers provide a setting that promotes worker success.
7. Institute leadership with the aim of revising supervision to better help people, machines, and processes do a better job.
8. Drive out fear so everyone can work effectively toward company goals.
9. Break down barriers between departments so that various departments can work as a team and anticipate problems of production or use of a product or service.
10. Avoid asking for new levels of productivity and zero defects through slogans and targets because most problems of low productivity lie with the system rather than the worker.
11. Replace work standards such as quotas, numerical goals, and MBO with good leadership.
12. Remove barriers that rob people at all levels of their pride of workmanship; shift from numbers to quality.
13. Institute a program of education and self-improvement by emphasizing lifelong learning and employment.
14. Transformation of the workplace occurs through everyone's action.

justify downsizing, or the reduction of labor costs by laying off portions of the workforce, often without achieving the improvements desired.

The popularity of these approaches has demonstrated the growing importance of customer satisfaction, benchmarking, employee involvement, and teamwork. Quality has become a national goal. In 1987, Congress established a national award to recognize excellence in the manufacturing and service industries, small business, and, in 1999, healthcare and education. The **Baldridge Award,** named after the Secretary of Commerce, is based on meeting several criteria across industries: leadership, strategic planning, customer focus, information and analysis, human resources and process focus, and business results. The current criteria for the healthcare industry were more customized and include leadership, strategic planning, focus on patients, measurement/analysis/knowledge management, workforce focus, process management, and results (Baldridge National Quality Program 2008).

The **International Organization for Standardization** (ISO) is another example of the drive toward quality improvement. This non-governmental global organization established in 1987 provides over 17,000 quality standards for nearly every business, technology, and industry sector. Adopted by more than 157 countries, the generic standards can be applied to organizations of any size. It involves defining, executing, and auditing best practices in production or service delivery. Over 50,000 experts in a variety of fields annually review and update the standards to help organizations benchmark their processes (ISO.org 2008).

Peter and Waterman's *Search for Excellence*

Although elements of most major theories can be found within the practices of successful managers, developments and refinements in thinking have thrived to become part of management history. In 1982, Peters and Waterman published *In Search of Excellence.* Based on a sample of highly successful business firms, they described the management practices that led to their success. Eight characteristics were described that became the rage in management circles for a time, with managers hoping to reproduce in their own organizations what top firms had done. (See figure 20.3.) Although the eight practices are very important, a follow-up of the same organizations four years later showed disappointing results. In that short time, 66 percent had fallen from a top position and 19 percent were in a troubled position (Pascale 1990). The fall from excellence appears to be due to those organizations refocusing on their temporary success and not attending sufficiently to the dynamic and strategic processes that were required to keep them there.

Although researchers continue to search for the essential ingredients that will make firms most successful, the lesson from the excellence studies highlights some important principles, including:

- Whether you succeed or fail, try to understand what brought that about.
- When you succeed, recognize that the success factors are not static but, rather, are continually changing.
- Do not let past success strategies keep you from discovering new ones for the future.

Figure 20.3. Characteristics of highly successful firms

1. *A bias for action:* They establish a value for action and implementation rather than overanalyzing and delaying with endless committees.
2. *Close to the customer:* They listen and respond to customers to satisfy their needs.
3. *Autonomy and entrepreneurship:* They empower people and encourage innovation and risk taking.
4. *Productivity through people:* They increase employees' awareness that everyone's contributions lead to shared success.
5. *Hands on, value driven:* Their managers should be visible, involved, and know what is going on.
6. *Stick to the knitting:* They stay with the core business, what they do well, and avoid wide diversification.
7. *Simple form, lean staff:* They have fewer administrative layers and keep the structure simple.
8. *Simultaneous loose–tight properties:* They maintain dedication to core principles but encourage flexibility and experimentation in reaching goals.

- What may contribute to the success of one type of organization or competitive setting may not be as useful to other types and settings or at other stages of organizational development.

Check Your Understanding 20.1

Instructions: Answer the following questions on a separate piece of paper.

1. What are some of the important management concepts that have persisted over the decades? Why have they persisted?
2. Why have some management ideas been rapidly accepted while others have required years to become popular?
3. Using the example of the Gilbreth time-motion study, identify some complex activity you engage in (such as packing for a trip, dressing in the morning, and so on) and see how you can streamline the sequence to become more efficient.
4. Explore reasons why the top companies identified in Peters and Waterman's *In Search of Excellence* dropped from their top position within a few short years. How might that have been prevented?

Functions and Principles of Management

As mentioned earlier, Fayol identified four functions of management. Related to these functions are certain categories of skills that are needed to carry them out.

Managerial Functions

As theories of management began to be refined, so too did the formal nature of the manager's role. As organizations increased in diversity, complexity, and size, managers often shifted their expertise from expert knowledge in doing a task to expert knowledge in managing other people. As Mary Parker Follett is reputed to have said, "Management is the art of getting things done through people" (Stoner and Freeman 1989). Specific functions of management came to be defined, as did a range of skills and subroles that contribute to successful problem solving.

Fayol's management functions of planning, organizing, leading, and controlling continue to be useful categories for examining the work of the manager. After the enterprise is begun, these four stages become a cycle for continuous improvement in which the last function of control is fed back into planning for plan revision.

Planning

Planning is the first step in management and involves determining what should be accomplished and how. Although planning occurs at all levels, top-level or strategic planning is most critical in formulating the mission and providing direction for change. When these strategies are defined, they can be implemented at the lower levels of the organization. Planning provides competitive advantage over those who minimize the importance of planning, as reflected in higher levels of performance such as profits (Shrader et al.1984).

Plans are usually organized hierarchically, with a mission statement driving the enterprise by defining exactly what business the organization is in and what is valued. The **strategic plan** follows from the mission. It is formulated by top management, sets the priorities and positioning of the organization for a time period, and is based on the constellation of internal strengths and weaknesses and external opportunities and threats. These are translated through the lower levels of the organization by middle management, which formulates **tactical plans** for the organization's major divisions. At the lower departmental levels, these finally become **operational plans** that are implemented as daily activities.

Plans are usually expressed in terms of **goals**. Goals are statements of intended outcomes that provide a source of direction and motivation as well as a guideline for performance, decision making, and evaluation. Good goals cover key result areas of the strategy; have the characteristics of being specific, measurable, and challenging, but achievable; and are set for a given period of time.

Organizing

After the goals have been specified, the task changes to deciding how resources can be allocated to achieve them. Traditionally, division of labor has been used to divide work into separate jobs. This specialization allows for development of greater expertise and standardization of tasks and for clear selection and training criteria. However, too narrow or specialized a task, as in assembly-line work, may produce more boredom than productivity. As Bridges predicted in 1994, the emerging economy with downsized and flatter organizations often requires workers to take on multiple roles and, consequently, to have portfolios of skills rather than highly defined job descriptions. Such skill and role portfolios are often found in healthcare, where downsizing and staff shortages occur resulting in remaining staff assuming a broader range of duties (Apker 2001; Helseth 2007)

Jobs are most often organized by positions, and the positions are arranged hierarchically in the business by an organizational chart. (An example of a typical hospital organizational chart is shown in figure 20.4.) The organizational chart often includes departmental subdivisions and follows the scalar principle and unity of command discussed earlier. The **vertical structure** of the organization refers to the formal design of positions within departments and divisions, the lines of authority and responsibility, and the allocation of resources to them. Two kinds of authority are found in organizations. **Line authority** is the right of managers to direct the activities of subordinates under their immediate control; **staff authority** is related to the expert knowledge of specialists and involves their advising and recommending courses of action.

Each supervisor has a certain number of people who report to him or her, which is referred to as the span of management or the **span of control**. Although the span of control is determined more often by tradition or accident, there are several factors to consider in optimally balancing it. In general, the span is larger when work is routine and homogeneous, workers have similar tasks, rules and guidelines are available, people are well trained and motivated, workers are located together, and task times are short (Jacques 1996). Deciding how a combination of factors leads to a particular span has been facilitated by technology. For example, the Healthcare Management Council (HMC) provides a comprehensive measurement of organizational factors leading to a span of management recommendation. The HMC Span of Control Analysis considers organizational flatness, departmental fragmentation, and layers of management using organizational charts. The HMC report can be used by managers to optimize organizational structure, set staffing and financial targets, and determine needs (HMC 2007).

Related to span is delegation, in which managers transfer authority to subordinates to carry out a responsibility. With an increasing focus on customers and rapid response, frontline workers are now trained to make decisions that once were made levels above them. When authority and responsibility move from the organization's top levels to its lower levels where they can be competently exercised, centralized decision making becomes decentralized. Although **decentralization** enables top managers to take on new responsibilities or spend time with other priorities, it places an additional burden on workers. (See chapter 22 for further discussion of organizational structures and charts.)

Leading

The third managerial function accomplishes goals by influencing behavior and by motivating and inspiring people to high performance. At the turn of the century, an autocratic view of leadership was considered to be appropriate, but as humanistic views have prevailed over the decades, leadership has become decentralized and distributed throughout the organization.

Leading is most often accomplished by communicating, directing, and motivating, all intended to influence behavior to perform well. Power, the ability to influence, is central to leadership and derives from several sources, including:

- *Authority* or legitimate power comes from the right of the position in the organization to direct the activities of subordinates.
- *Reward power* is based on the leader's ability to withhold or provide rewards for performance.
- *Coercive power* maintains control over punishments.
- *Referent power* exists when the leader possesses personal characteristics that are appealing to the constituency, and the constituency follows out of admiration, charismatic impact, or the desire to be like the leader.

Figure 20.4. Sample hospital organizational chart

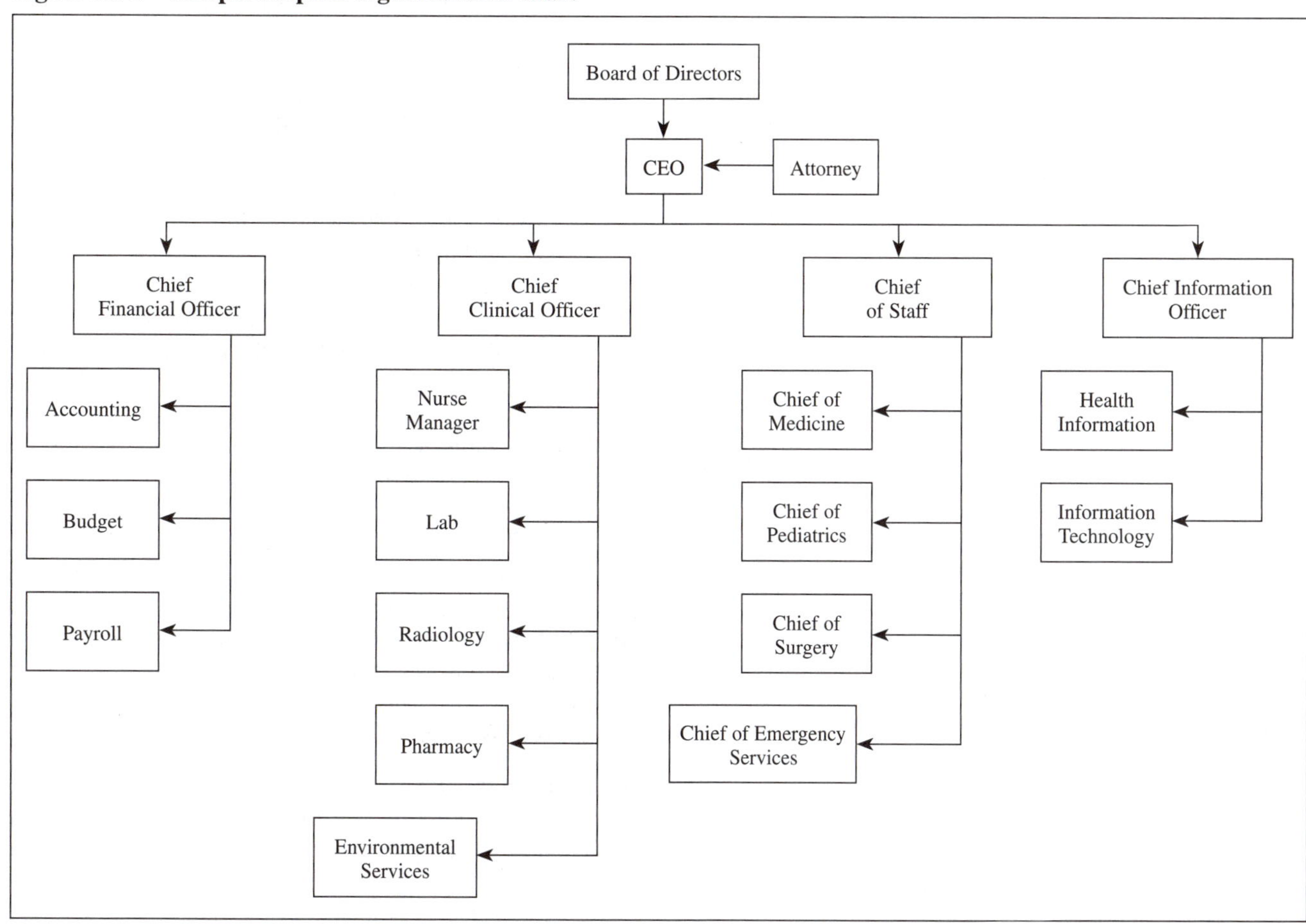

- *Expert power* occurs when the leader has knowledge or expertise that is of value (French and Raven 1959).
- *Information power* is based on the persuasive content of the person's message, apart from personal characteristics (Raven 1983).

Leadership behaviors and most models of leadership fall into two categories: task-oriented behaviors, and social or group-oriented behaviors. Task-oriented behaviors are directed toward defining tasks, creating structure and rules, ensuring production, and placing emphasis on quality and speed of output. Social orientation focuses on interpersonal behaviors that develop and maintain harmonious work relationships, encourage morale, reduce stress and conflict, and build worker satisfaction. Several models of leadership, such as the Blake-Mouton Managerial Grid, use these two dimensions and are discussed later in this chapter.

Controlling

The final managerial function refers to the monitoring of performance, determining whether it is on or off course in achieving the goals and making course corrections as needed. Managers are obligated to ensure that progress is made toward achieving goals, although recent trends indicate that employees are empowered to monitor themselves and each other, rather than being monitored from the top. This obviously requires selecting employees who have the maturity and integrity to accept this responsibility, but it corrects for the distortion and delay that can occur in a very hierarchical organization.

Significant breakthroughs have occurred in control with the development of the executive dashboard and balanced scorecard , introduced in 1992 (Kaplan and Norton 1996). The **executive dashboard** is often characterized as a manager's version of a pilot's cockpit dashboard; it contains all the critical information for leading the organization. The dashboard typically contains regularly updated information on key strategic measures such as forecasts, customer satisfaction, billings, profit, and so on.

The **balanced scorecard** (BSC) is an extension of strategic planning in which key performance indicators are measured at all levels of the organization and progress with workers and management receiving ongoing feedback. Categories of feedback usually include financial, customer satisfaction, internal processes (for example, quality, response time), and learning and growth. For example, using the BSC helped University and Hospital Clinics in Holmes County, Mississippi move much closer to break-even in its revenues, while Harrisburg Medical Center in Illinois reported achieving a consistent four percent margin over a four year period (Rural Health Resource Center 2008). The four functions of management vary in emphasis according to the level of management involved. (See figure 20.5.) In general, as one moves from first-line to middle management to top managers, planning increases, organizing increases, leading decreases, and controlling stays about the same (Jones and George 2006; Mahoney et al. 1965).

Figure 20.5. Management functions by level in the organization

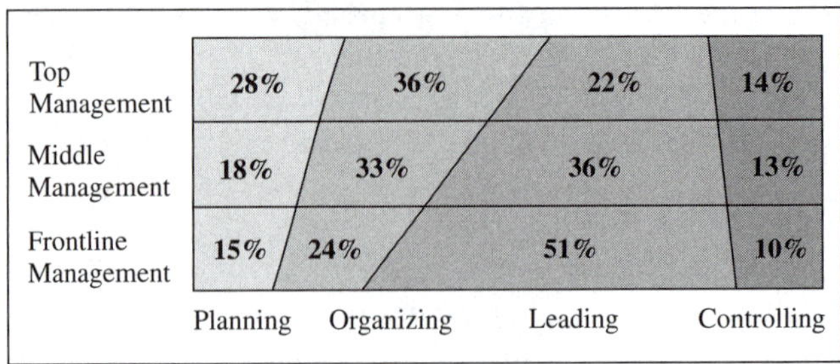

Managerial Skills

The categories of skills required to perform the four management functions are conceptual, interpersonal, and technical skills (Buhler, 2007; Katz 1974). As management has become increasingly complex, the requisite skills for carrying out the four managerial functions also vary by level in the organization. (See figure 20.6.)

Conceptual Skills

The need for **conceptual skills** has increased significantly over the decades. Where it once was important only to have good technical skills, now a successful manager must be able to understand diverse fields and deal with complex situations. According to Tenner (1996), the lack of sufficient conceptual and planning skills has led to revenge effects. **Revenge effects** are unexpected and usually undesired outcomes that emerge from good intentions but failure to understand the long-term or ripple effects of an action in an interconnected organization or system (Swenson 2008).

For example, the HIPPA privacy rule was intended to provide greater patient privacy protection and quality of care, while also enabling better information access to providers. The strong emphasis on privacy and apprehension about the consequences of inappropriate information release has led some facilities to be overly cautious in releasing information. The *Seattle Times* reported an incident in which a man was unable to obtain information on his injured mother when she was transferred from an assisted living facility to an emergency department with a broken ankle. In another instance, Leo Greenawalt, 20-year president of the Washington State Hospital Association, could only obtain information that his elderly father was in intensive care, despite the fact that Greenawalt thoroughly explained to the facility that HIPPA allowed him access to such information. As a result of overzealous restriction, patients, relatives, and other care providers have experienced frustrating delays in obtaining information (Burrington-Brown 2004).

Interpersonal Skills

Interpersonal skills involve the ability to work with and through others to accomplish goals. Depending on the nature of the work and the level of interaction needed among individuals, interpersonal skills may or may not be a critical skill

Figure 20.6. Functional skills by level in the organization

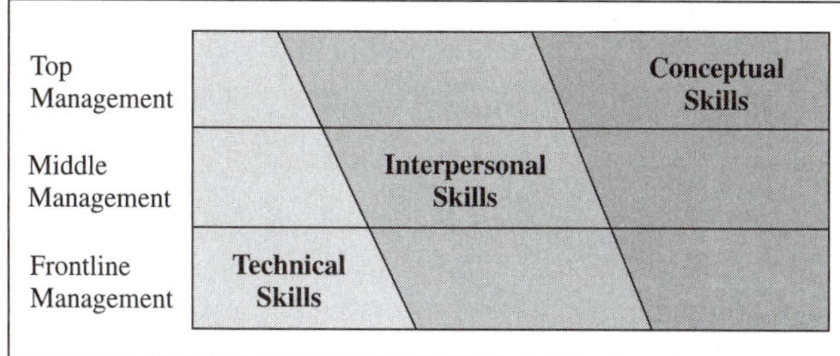

for employee success. However, managers, in their interactions with employees and with each other, need to cultivate impeccable interpersonal skills.

That the interpersonal domain is important is shown in a review of top management texts in which this was the only category that they all shared in common (Bigelow 1993). However, although managers spend up to 80 percent of their time in managing operations, an international survey of more than 700 communication and HR staff showed that the communication skills of operations managers was generally perceived as "poor," and only 14 percent were rated as "good" (Melcrum Research 2007).

Interpersonal competency is based on self-awareness and understanding, and the best managers are those who can articulate both their strengths and weaknesses (Goleman 1998). Yet, self-awareness is not enough and consistently high performers also demonstrate **self-monitoring** (Church 1997; Riggio and Reichard 2008). Self-monitoring refers to the ability to observe the reactions that one's behavior elicits in others and then adjusting one's behavior to improve the relationship. Other important interpersonal skills include communicating, motivating and influencing, managing conflict, credibility, and learning how to complement different ways of interacting (Page et al. 1999).

Emotional Intelligence

Effective managers can be considered different from successful managers (Luthans et al. 1988). Effective managers are identified as those who have satisfied and committed subordinates and produce results; in contrast, successful managers are those who have been promoted rapidly. Such promotions are often related to their interpersonal effectiveness. Although it has been around for a long time, Daniel Goleman popularized the idea in his 1995 book, *Emotional Intelligence,* and it is currently one of the most widely discussed topics in psychology. Advocates of **emotional intelligence** (EI) believe that awareness and use of feelings complements rational intelligence and experience, and it is the combination of these that is the key to success. (See figure 20.7.) Some people believe that emotions do not have a role in the workplace, but others, such as Angela Coke, Assistant Deputy Minister of the Ontario government's Ministry of Government Services, assert that "You can have different leadership styles but EI is the critical 'must have' for effective leadership . . ." (Reid 2008).

EI has caught the interest of many prominent organizations: Nearly 10 percent of Fortune 500 firms have used EI concepts in employee development efforts, and Johnson & Johnson initiated EI aptitude measuring for employees being considered for managerial potential in its consumer products division (Carey 2004). There is some supportive evidence for such use. Critics of the EI concept argue that it is not a distinct ability but, rather, a conglomerate of personality traits such as emotional stability, conscientiousness, and agreeableness. They believe that EI does not meet conventional standards of psychological measurement and that the criteria for measurement change over time. Additionally, they are concerned that claims of its predicting success are exaggerated and that self-reports used are subject to bias (Matthews et al. 2002).

Regardless of the criticism, organizations are eager to find something that will give their employees, managers, and leaders a competitive edge. Training programs, self-help books, and self-assessment instruments proliferate on EI. Executive coaching on interpersonal skills in the federal government, for example, has provided strong cost savings due to interpersonal issues (Salmon 2008). However, professionals should be cautious in expecting that a brief workshop will produce significant increases in these skills or personality features.

That managerial skills affect organizational performance is not a new idea, but studies examining an array of management skills challenged a common belief. They conclude that people management skills are more important to performance than are intellectual abilities (Carmeli and Tishler 2006; Strickland 2000). Other studies support the contention that interpersonal skills are strongly related to overall performance (Sy et al. 2005), successful conflict management (Jordan and Troth 2002), team performance (Druskat et al. 2005) and that such skills can be enhanced (Meyer et al. 2004).

Figure 20.7. Attributes of emotional intelligence (EI)

- Self-awareness: The ability to monitor, notice, and label one's feelings as they occur. This allows one to be more certain about feelings and to identify early vague feelings.
- Self-regulation: The ability to manage one's emotions and impulses. A person with this skill is often viewed as being reflective, comfortable with change and ambiguity, and able to control impulsiveness.
- Motivation: Being highly motivated is essential for focusing attention, mastering situations, showing creativity, and being productive and successful.
- Empathy: The ability to recognize emotions in others. This is important for teamwork as well as for helping adjust one's behavior to the emerging reactions of others.
- Social skills: The ability to handle relationships with others is central to being perceived as popular, effective with others, and having the qualities of a leader.

Source: Adapted from Goleman 1995.

Once-effective managers who are later derailed in their role have been distinguished from their more successful counterparts. The derailed managers tend to need less affiliation with others, are more impatient and do not listen well, and focus on task accomplishment to the dearth of relationships (Denton and van Lill 2006).

Technical Skills

Finally, understanding and mastering the technical information, methods, and equipment involved in a discipline constitute the **technical skills**. Although most important at the employee level of the organization, technical skills are still required for upper management so that there is a comprehensive understanding of the workings of the organization. However, conceptual and interpersonal skills are probably more useful in obtaining promotion in most organizations. This is true because, at higher levels in organizations, these types of skills are used more often and are more important than technical skills. For example, conceptual skills are more useful in the leading and planning function because they involve understanding the systems view of the total organization.

Managerial Roles

The activities of managers and leaders are typically organized around several roles. A role refers to a set of expectations about how a person is to behave from the perspective of oneself, peers, superiors, subordinates, consumers (patients), and others (such as legislators). **Role theory** has been a prominent framework for examining behavior in the field of sociology for decades, and it has been applied in management to clarify the wide range of responsibilities held.

Mintzberg's Role Studies

Henry Mintzberg (1939–), Cleghorn Professor of Management at McGill University, completed his dissertation at MIT on the roles of managers. Suspecting that what managers did might be difficult to classify in the categories covered in this chapter, he shadowed managers and recorded their actual activities. His findings defied many common assumptions about the work that managers do. It is widely believed that managers are systematic, reflective thinkers who carefully analyze situations before making decisions and acting. In practice, Mintzberg (1992) found that most chief executives spent less than 10 minutes on any activity and that supervising foremen in industry averaged one activity every 48 seconds. Managers opened 36 pieces of mail, attended eight meetings, and toured a building. Whatever was planned, something unexpected usually emerged. Another study of British middle and top-level managers showed that they were able to secure a half hour for concentrated work without interruption only once every two days. Mintzberg summarized his findings by saying that managers completed a great deal of work at an unrelenting pace, but the activities were characterized by variety, fragmentation, and brevity.

Mintzberg's subsequent research with managers showed that their activities could usually be described by 10 roles organized into three categories (table 20.1):

- *Interpersonal activity* arises from the manager's formal authority in the organization and is supportive of the informational and decisional activities. It includes the roles of figurehead for ceremonial and formal occasions, leadership for motivating and using power, and liaison to link and network for information and support.
- *Informational activity* includes the roles of monitor of performance information, disseminator of values and information, and spokesperson for the organization with outside groups.
- *Decisional activity* includes the roles of entrepreneur to promote improvement and change, disturbance handler to deal with disruptions, resource allocator for overseeing resources and setting priorities, and negotiator for arrangements with other organizations.

These roles are intricately intertwined and not easily separated by a particular problem when it comes to team management, where responsibilities are often distributed among team members. However, they provide a realistic portrayal of the wide range of skilled behaviors required of effective managers.

Comparing the workings of organizations during the twentieth century with those emerging in the twenty-first century, there is a clear need for a new way of thinking on the part of managers. Although the managerial skills used in conceptualization, relationships, and technology will persist, they will have to be applied in a different manner. The change drivers of globalization, demographic and marketplace diversity, information and technological changes, and other factors will mean

Table 20.1. Mintzberg's managerial roles

Managerial Activities	Related Roles
Interpersonal	• *Figurehead:* The manager represents the organization and is a symbol for ceremonial, social, legal, and inspirational duties. • *Liaison:* The manager maintains networks of relationships outside his or her organizational unit to gather information and favors. • *Leader:* The manager directs, guides, motivates, and develops subordinates.
Informational	• *Monitor:* The manager oversees internal and external information sources. • *Disseminator:* The manager communicates facts and values to others in the organization. • *Spokesperson:* The manager communicates with others outside the organization.
Decisional	• *Entrepreneur:* The manager promotes development and planned change in the organization. • *Disturbance handler:* The manager resolves crises and unexpected problems. • *Resource allocator:* The manager uses authority to allocate budget, personnel, equipment, services, and facilities. • *Negotiator:* The manager resolves dilemmas and disputes and determines the use of resources.

that managers will seldom be able to focus on the status quo as they have in the past. The new status quo is one of change and how people can be helped through transitions.

Again coming full circle, Taylor and other proponents of scientific management emphasized an important criterion for managerial success: It should be based on research whenever possible. As Pascale (1990) demonstrated in his diagram of the managerial fads from the 1960s to 1990s, many ideas were without empirical foundation, were short-lived, had limited application, and in some cases caused more problems than they solved.

In healthcare, as well as other fields of management, decisions are based more on political and value considerations than on empirical sources. With the increased interest in alternative approaches to healthcare (for example, acupuncture, nutrition), determining which methods are legitimate and produce the best outcomes can reduce liability and enhance sound program promotion. An emphasis on **evidence-based management**, or information-based management, is emerging in which more informed decisions are made based on the best clinical and research evidence that proposed practices will work. For example, Australia-based CSIRO works with healthcare organizations to determine factors that influence the use of health information by at-risk segments of a population and also develops performance measures for staff. Their procedures have increased the use of data and information by senior managers in strategic and daily planning. Increasingly, all levels of managers are having information available on performance evaluation and the outcomes of the decisions they make.

Check Your Understanding 20.2

Instructions: Answer the following questions on a separate piece of paper.

1. Discuss reasons for the four management functions changing in emphasis over the three levels of management. For example, why would there be less emphasis on the leadership function for top-level managers compared with the strong emphasis for first-line managers?
2. Examine a job description for a position in your field. What is the distribution of conceptual, interpersonal, and technical skills required?
3. Make a list of daily activities engaged in by observing or asking a manager what he or she does. Then, categorize the activities into Mintzberg's 10 managerial roles.
4. Draw an organizational chart of your college, a hospital, or some other organization with which you are familiar. Be sure to designate both line and staff positions.
5. What does quality mean in your work? Identify several tasks you perform, define quality for each task, and consider how you would measure it.

Trends in Management Theory

What we have seen in the several management theories presented in this chapter is that as change drivers have an impact on the marketplace and organizations, organizations must adapt in order to survive and thrive. Management theories become a template for thinking about the structure and processes by which business is conducted. As the marketplace changes, old theories may lose their explanatory power and be replaced with more accurate theories and principles for managing the organization. (See table 20.2.) At the same time, as managers become accustomed to, and develop expertise with, a certain viewpoint, they may become biased in its use and fail to see exceptions to it. A requisite skill for managers is to know when to use a particular framework and when to change it.

Although Taylor and others at the turn of the twentieth century faced a host of changes, the unrelenting pace of change is an even more constant companion to managers today. The successful manager must be able to see patterns of change and prepare others to respond to them.

Problem Solving and Decision Making

Problems are defined as impediments to the attainment of goals. While some managers view problems as negative and something to be avoided, problem solving can also be viewed as an opportunity for managers and organizations to build experience and resilience. Solving problems requires that they be framed or defined in useful and understandable ways, that creative approaches are applied to them, and that efficient methods are applied to recurrent problems. Problem solving involves understanding and resolving the barriers to goal attainment, while decision making refers to making the best choices from among available alternatives.

Steps in Problem Solving

Two primary responsibilities of managers are solving problems and making decisions. In the early years of management

Table 20.2. Paradigm shift in management

Traditional Management Paradigm	New Management Paradigm
Multilevel hierarchical organization	Flatter, distributed organization
Centralized decision making	Decentralized decision making
Status measured by amount of turf controlled	Status measured by success in achieving outcomes
Funding inputs and intentions	Funding outcomes
Face-to-face interaction	Telecommunication and virtual interaction
Homogenous staffing	Workforce diversity
Job description	Skill portfolio
Annual strategic plan	Learning organization
Financial bottom line	Triple bottom line
Efficiency and stability	Ongoing innovation
Mass services	Market segmentation
Work at central office	Satellite and home offices

practice, these activities were often based on personal preferences and limited experience, with little regard for long-term consequences. Since then, however, formal models of dealing with issues have been developed and managers are encouraged to proceed systematically through several stages, including:

1. Defining the problem and the desired outcome
2. Analyzing and understanding the nature of the problem
3. Generating alternatives
4. Selecting desired alternatives (decision making)
5. Planning and implementing the alternative
6. Evaluating and gathering feedback about the attained outcome

At each step in the problem-solving model, decisions need to be made that lead to the final choice of how to implement a means for solving the problem. Given the changing circumstances of the modern healthcare marketplace, it is unlikely that all the desires of information managers will be available. They will need to make decisions using less than perfect or less than complete information, and under ambiguous or risky circumstances.

Rational versus Administrative Decision Making

In recent years, the importance of rational decision making has become essential in management, and a variety of models have been developed. The Vroom-Yetton (1971) normative decision tree, which is discussed in detail later in this chapter, is an example of a system for responding to key questions, branching to alternatives, and arriving at a conclusion. For more complex decision making where there are several choices and criteria for selection, but the criteria cannot be ordered sequentially as in the Vroom-Yetton model, a decision matrix can be constructed for evaluating and comparing alternatives. (See figure 20.8.)

Using this method, the decision maker lists the criteria for a good outcome and then rates each possible alternative for the solution to the problem. Each alternative is identified, and each is rated on the extent to which it fulfills the desired outcome criteria. Finally, the criteria weightings are multiplied by the choice ratings and totaled. The alternative with the highest total is considered to provide the best combination of characteristics that meet the most important criteria. This can be a tedious process with very complex problems, and various computer programs and expert systems have been developed to systematically walk the user through the decision process and perform the calculations. An example is a simple expert system software program that prompts the user to answer questions about research data, and then recommends which statistical procedure to use to analyze it (Van Eck 2004).

Although this classical model of problem solving illustrates what managers should do, the most accurate assessment of a manager's effectiveness is determined by what he or she actually does.

Bounded Rationality

Most, if not all, problem solvers and decision makers operate within the limits of **bounded rationality**. Bounded rationality recognizes that problem situations can be overwhelmingly complex and in states of constant change, that not every fact about a situation can be known, and that people are not always rational. As a result, bounded rationality accounts for the limits of time and information, and encourages action despite uncertainty.

Intuition and Satisficing

Because of bounded rationality, managers often tend to rely on intuition and satisficing. **Intuition**, unconscious decision making based on similar conditions, can be useful as a quick way for highly experienced persons to make decisions when

Figure 20.8. Decision matrix

Example—Choosing the Job Offer That Best Meets Your Career Criteria

		Rating of extent to which this job meets each criterion (1 = high, 5 = low)		
Key decision criteria for a good job	**Rating of the Importance** (1 = high)	**Job Choice 1** Rating : Product	**Job Choice 2** Rating : Product	**Job Choice 3** Rating : Product
Criterion 1: Good pay	5	3 : 15	4 : 20	2 : 10
Criterion 2: Preferred region of country	2	2 : 4	3 : 6	4 : 8
Criterion 3: Interesting work	4	3 : 12	5 : 20	4 : 16
Additional criteria		↓	↓	↓
Total ratings for each choice		31	46	34

Step 1: Identify and rate (1–5, 5 high) the importance of the criteria for your desired job.

Step 2: Rate the extent to which each of the job choices meet your criteria (1–5, 5 high).

Step 3: Multiply each rating by the criteria rating.

Step 4: Total the products for all ratings and compare across the choices.

Decision: The higher product total of job choice 2 (for example, 46) offers greater fit with the applicants preferred criteria than do choices 1 and 3.

the current problem is similar to prior experiences. This kind of decision making is neither impulsive nor arbitrary but, rather, is based on decision pathways that have become so automatic as to become unconscious.

Satisficing is a less precise method than intuition and refers to a manager adopting the first alternative that is sufficient to meet the minimum requirement for a solution to the problem. Although this method is efficient and saves time and effort, it may have unexpected long-term effects. For example, the first apparent solution is not necessarily the most efficient in terms of time and money or the most appropriate. Without further analysis, the first solution is simply the first idea that appeared.

Programmed and Nonprogrammed Decisions

Decisions can be programmed or nonprogrammed. **Programmed decisions** are those in which a problem is so predictable, uniform, and recurring that rules have been developed to standardize or automate the procedure. Such rules enable managers to delegate authority to others to make decisions using predetermined criteria or to develop expert systems in which computers can make decisions. An example of such automation is an inventory system that automatically requests an order for restocking by a supplier when stock reaches a certain level.

Nonprogrammed decisions involve situations that are unpredictable, extremely complex, or ill defined. These situations defy simple decision criteria and usually require careful deliberation, often in consultation with others. Examples of nonprogrammed decisions include those found in market development, strategic management, and new product or service development.

Groupthink: The Hazards of Team Decision Making

There are many examples of disasters that share the common failure of groupthink. Since its conception there have been many crises identified which support the initial research on **groupthink**. These have included the historical Bay of Pigs invasion of Cuba (1961), Nixon's Watergate break-in debacle (1972), the *Exxon Valdez* oil spill (1989), the Union Carbide gas leak tragedy in Bhopal, India (1984), *Challenger* space shuttle accident (1986) as well as the more recent Bush administration's initiative in the Iraq war. Coined in 1952 by sociologist William H. Whyte and later extensively researched and popularized by psychologist Irving Janis (1972), the term refers to the tendency of a highly cohesive team to seek consensus. Subsequent research has shown this tendency to be relatively widespread and occurs when a team is very cohesive, there is high external pressure to perform, and few mechanisms are in place to correct for poor decision making.

The role of cohesion is an interesting one because most work teams desire to have high cohesion: close familiarity and homogeneity of styles, strong pride in and commitment to the team, and a shared mission and vision (Michalisin et al. 2004). The problem arises when cohesion is so high and pressure to succeed so great that pressure is exerted on members to conform to team processes that can result in poor decisions. Subsequent research (Baron 2005) suggests that some of the antecedents that contribute to groupthink are not as strong as Janis believed, nonetheless the effects of group conformity on decision making is ubiquitous.

Conditions for the Emergence of Groupthink

Janis originally proposed eight symptoms of groupthink grouped around three risky tendencies (figure 20.9).

- *Overconfidence* in the team's prowess can manifest as an illusion of invulnerability that leads team members to be overconfident and take excessive risks. They develop a collective rationalization that is used to discount warnings that would lead them to reconsider their underlying assumptions.
- *Tunnel vision* restricts the range of factors considered and can lead to a belief in the inherent morality of their cause, thereby ignoring the ethical consequences of their decisions. Outsiders are often viewed in stereotypical ways in which their threats are minimized.
- *Team pressures* further contribute to groupthink. Loyal members will disapprove of a member who questions the team and bring sanctions until he or she again conforms. Members also may self-censor when it appears that there is silent consensus, tunnel vision for viewing the problem, and group pressure to conform.

Figure 20.9. Symptoms of groupthink

Team's overestimation of its own power and morality

- *Illusion of invulnerability.* The illusion that they cannot go wrong leads to excessive optimism and risk taking.
- *Unquestioned belief in team's inherent morality.* Members believe their actions are correct leading them to ignore moral and ethnical implications.

Close-mindedness

- *Team rationalization to discount warnings.* They collectively minimize indications that would lead them to reconsider their assumptions and commitments.
- *Stereotypes of the opposition.* Outsiders are viewed as negative, evil, stupid to justify negotiations or to consider they could counter the team's efforts.

Pressure toward uniformity

- *Self-censorship.* Members tend to minimize and withhold expression of their dissenting views and counterarguments.
- *Illusion of shared unanimity.* Self-censorship and the false belief that silence means consent leads to the shared illusion that everyone agrees with the decision.
- *Pressure to conform.* Members who deviate from team norms by expressing doubts or arguing against its position are implicitly and explicitly pressured to conform.
- *Self-appointed "mind-guards."* Some members appoint themselves to protect the team from adverse information that might challenge their illusions.

Source: Janis 1982.

Consequences of Groupthink

The pressures to conform in groupthink often result in the restriction of information and the risk of poor decision making. Such restrictions can limit considerations of objectives, information search, alternative courses of action, examination of the risks of the preferred choice, and reassessment of the preferred choice. Moreover, they can bias the discussion and processing of the problem-solving process, and lead to a level of confidence that results in contingency plans being ignored or minimized.

In spite of, and in contrast to, these limitations, groupthink can have a beneficial effect on a group by contributing to morale following a devastating defeat and can provide encouragement when an otherwise positive outcome appears doubtful (Janis 1982). Although groupthink is more likely to occur in strong cultures, such cultures also have the benefit of being more resilient to outside pressures and can show higher performance when they can control groupthink (Sorenson 2002).

Countermeasures for Groupthink

The conditions that contribute to groupthink are ubiquitous, and it requires deliberate action by the team to minimize their adverse affects. By being aware of the risk of groupthink, alert to the symptoms, and intentionally implementing countermeasures, the team can maintain adequate cohesion without sacrificing decision quality. Instruments such as The Groupthink Profile (Swenson 2003) enable the team to better assess and discuss the implications of team cohesion, organizational self-correcting processes, pressure on the team, symptoms of groupthink, and countermeasures.

The use of countermeasures is especially important, and they can be internal or external. *Internal procedures* to reduce risk include using brainstorming, revisiting important decisions, monitoring the degree of consensus and disagreement, rotating the devil advocate's role among members, actively seeking contradictory information, and developing norms to challenge and question each other. In addition, the leader can refrain from stating an opinion that might affect opinions too early, and the team might be divided into subgroups to encourage different conclusions. *External procedures* include discussing decisions with outside experts and nonteam members and inviting external observers to provide feedback on meetings, decisions, and team processes. Such procedures increase awareness of group processes and enhance skills at arriving at better decisions.

Check Your Understanding 20.3

Instructions: Answer the following questions on a separate sheet of paper.

1. In what ways could you increase the feelings of cohesion for a team? What would be some indications of that cohesion?
2. What are some indications that cohesion has become excessive (for example, signs of groupthink)?
3. What actions might be taken to reduce the risks of groupthink?

Corporate Social Responsibility: Emergence and Principles

Numerous pressures are driving and shaping the growing emphasis on **corporate social responsibility** (CSR). Organizational ethical crises such as the World Com and Enron scandals, as well as political debates over healthcare issues have brought ethical and value considerations to strategic management. In addition, changing demographics and better educated groups are demanding higher standards of corporate performance. Regulatory pressures are requiring companies to include their social and environmental activities along with their financial disclosures. Furthermore, investors can now choose from among socially responsible portfolios. International nongovernmental organizations are growing in influence and bringing pressure on companies to become more ethically conscious.

Although philanthropy and CSR are often equated, there are important differences. Philanthropy involves discretionary allocation of resources to particular causes or specific stakeholders. It is often subject to whim, tends to be used to present a positive public image and reputation, and is often short term and discontinued as financial resources diminish (for example, unsustainable). In contrast, CSR is part of the strategic plan for the organization, and part of its bottom line, and while it may contribute to public image, the core intention is value-based rather than for publicity. Since CSR is the expression of a core value of the organization, it is sustainable over time.

Although economist Milton Friedman (1970) critically argued at one time that it is the primary (and only) responsibility of a corporation to maximize profits for its core stakeholders, and eschewed the idea of social responsibility, CSR is not at odds with financial stability. Several meta-analytic studies have shown organizations that promote CSR can also have a healthy bottom line (Mahoney and Roberts 2007; Margolis et al. 2007; Simpson and Kohers 2002).

While most organizations focus on the financial bottom line, those that embrace CSR emphasize the **triple bottom line** (Elkington 1994). This expanded criteria includes the sustainability of environmental and social performance of the organization as well, or people, planet, and profit. Viewing the world and business community as an ecosystem, **sustainability** refers generally to the ability to maintain certain resources or processes indefinitely, and more specifically to meet present needs without compromising ability to meet the needs of future generations (Our Common Future 1987).

From this view, the welfare of people (employees, patients, suppliers, other distant stakeholders) is placed before profits. Social issues are valued, such as services to disadvantaged and underserved populations, diversity, fair labor practices, insurance coverage, respectful treatment of employees, and the like. This also means organizations should focus on environmentally sound practices, such as promoting recycling, nonuse or safe disposing of hazardous materials, fair trade practices, and such.

CSR has been found to create many benefits for organizations (Hopkins 2005; Ling et al. 2007; O'Rourke 2004):

- Reputation is established around the intangibles of trust, consistency, quality, credibility, transparency, and investment in people, environment, and diversity
- Financing may be improved as evidenced by new financial indices, such as the FTSE4Good Index and Dow Jones Sustainability Index show
- CSR enhances employee morale, trust, satisfaction and motivation, and reduces turnover
- As much as 80 percent of the value of companies is investment in intellectual capital, which is preserved by positive relationships with internal stakeholders
- More accurate risk management can be achieved by clearer communication with and understanding of external stakeholders
- Technology makes services more available to underserved populations and non-industrialized countries
- Overall performance can be enhanced as indicated by competitive stock performance
- Understanding the wider implications of the organization in the community can help identify new services and products and develop strategic partnerships

The rapid growth of CSR, while exciting in its ethical implications, is still in early stages, and there are strong critics. The marketing function in organizations unfortunately too often considers it just another method of branding and public relations, but benefits are slowly changing such thinking. It is unclear how much emphasis it will continue to exert on leadership and strategic planning, but it is likely to continue for the near future.

Check Your Understanding 20.4

Instructions: Answer the following questions on a separate sheet of paper

1. Identify some of the national issues and crises that have contributed to interest in CSR. See if you can also identify some issues specific to healthcare.
2. Using the idea of the Triple Bottom Line, what are some measures you would add for environmental and social performance bottom lines in healthcare?
3. How would you construct an argument that CSR should be part of an organizations core strategy?

Managerial Communication

The exchange of information is central to health information management and one of the most frequently used definitions of *communication.* Although we often take communication for granted, miscommunication poses problems and risks in the healthcare field. It is important for professionals to understand important aspects of communication, including channels and barriers, the challenge of diversity, and ways communication can be improved.

Importance of Communication

As noted earlier in this chapter, Follett observed that managers get things done through people, and this in turn is accomplished by communicating with them. Communication is the interpersonal process by which information is transferred from one person to another. Nearly everything we do can potentially communicate something to someone, or more economically stated, "You cannot not communicate" (Watzlawick et al. 1968). Communication among providers in clinical settings constitutes about 80 percent of transactions, while about 30 percent of communication is considered interruptions (Coiera et al. 2002; Coiera et al. 2000). Still, ineffective communication remains a significant problem in most organizations. This is especially critical in healthcare where it has been found that lawsuits are less related to negligence and more to poor communication between provider and patient (Liebman and Hyman 2004), and errors in communication were the second most common errors in the recovery room (Kluger and Bullock 2002). For example, a survey of workers who voluntarily quit their organizations found that about 25 percent of their reasons were because they perceived their managers to be poor communicators (Supplee Group 2002). It has also been estimated that as much as 60 percent of time in operational tasks is wasted time, that involves searching for information or working with wrong information (Ameri and Dutta 2005). Similarly, a survey of 839 managers showed that while there was a glut of information available, there was a difference between quality and quantity of communication, and only half of managers believed that leaders spent sufficient time communicating effectively (Holton et al. 2008).

Formal and Informal Channels

Communication can take place through formal or informal channels. *Formal communication* consists of those intentional messages that are directed to people through their role relationships in the organization and usually through established channels such as e-mail, phone, face-to-face interaction, memo, letter, or other forms of announcement. This kind of communication usually focuses on task accomplishment and related matters. In contrast, *informal communication* may occur across role or department boundaries or organizational levels. It tends to employ face-to-face interactions and focuses on the interpersonal aspects of work, such as rumors and topics outside the immediate scope of the workplace. It is through informal communication that most relationships develop between employees and that influence is exercised.

Barriers to Communication

Complex organizations also have a variety of barriers to the richness or completeness of communication, both structural and interpersonal. *Structural barriers* include the distortion that can occur when a message is passed through several people, each adding or deleting information based on their own perceptions and needs. The increasing use of e-mail in organizations also eliminates the nonverbal cues of voice tone, volume, and inflection, as well as facial cues and gestures that add so much to face-to-face communication. *Interpersonal barriers* include distraction and partial listening, tendency to judge, assumption that we know what others mean, and fear of asking questions. In general, low-richness channels are one-way communication tools such as reports, bulletins, memos, and e-mail and high-richness channels include telephone and face-to-face interactions.

Diversity

As the workforce continues to become more diverse, there will be greater challenges to managerial communication. A Los Angeles multinational firm, for example, provides new employee orientation in 17 different languages. In many Asian countries where courtesy and "saving face" is very important, a person might say maybe when he really means no in order to avoid hurting feelings. Whereas most task-oriented Americans prefer to get right down to business, many South Americans prefer to spend time getting to know with whom they are doing business, and Arabs may have conversations where they shift from business to personal and other interests and then loop back several times.

Nonverbal communication also differs culturally: What may be a benign gesture in one place may be very offensive in another (Griffin 2008). For example, many Americans feel quite comfortable crossing their legs and leaning back in a chair, but showing the sole of the foot in such a manner is very offensive to most Arabs, and most Japanese would consider a slouched posture a sign of poor character. Beckoning by curling the index finger back is a common way for Americans to say "come here," but in Indonesia and Australia, such a gesture is used only for calling animals. Appreciating communication differences and customs is an important part of being an effective communicator, cosmopolitan traveler, and respected manager.

Suggestions for Increasing the Accuracy of Communications

To communicate effectively, managers must pay just as much attention to how their message is received and interpreted as they do to its content. The following practices can enhance the accuracy and acceptance of communication (Kirvin 2005; Spath 2007):

- Minimize "noise" that can distort the message. Make sure all parties are minimally distracted, can give their undivided attention, and have sufficient time to get their message across.
- Know what outcome you want to communicate through your message and then check to see if you get it.
- Monitor others' nonverbal behaviors for cues that they are following or are confused.
- Vary inflection for attention, but use the lower end of the voice range to communicate confidence, calmness, and confidence in the subject.
- Explain your reasoning to show and lead others to how you have formed your conclusions.
- Consider the effect that different interpersonal styles, cultural backgrounds, and experiences may have on interpretation of the message or how it is delivered.
- Use **active listening** in which you (or the other person) restate in your own words what you have heard the other person say.
- Respond to the feelings, attitudes, and values in the message as well as the content. Show empathy, concern, and compassion, as appropriate.
- Use examples or visual aids to make the message clearer.
- Ask for feedback and listen to it without being judgmental.
- Write clearly and concisely.

Remember that how well you model communication skills sets the norm for others.

Clinical Communication Space

As discussed throughout this chapter, communication is central to understanding error rates, providing performance feedback, and facilitating transition during change. **Clinical communication space** is the context and range of electronic and interpersonal information exchanged among staff and patients in the healthcare facility. Although electronic information is readily available, electronic medical records account for only about 10 percent of information exchange, with voice and e-mail accounting for another 25 percent. Even with improvements in electronic communications, most healthcare staff prefer real-time face-to-face communication (Martin et al. 2003) However, the pace of work sometimes leaves staff passing comments in the hall, calling on cell phones, and leaving Post-it notes where they hope they will be seen. To reduce errors in such impromptu communication, innovations such as SBAR have been introduced. This is a standard approach to staff communication that involves Situation, Background, Assessment, and Recommendations. The technique is implemented with a "tool kit" of notepads, record sheets, training booklets, posters, and pocket guides (SBAR 2008).

The work environment is characterized by many interactions and multiple interruptions, both electronic (pagers, telephones, e-mail) and interpersonal. These distractions, as well as information overload and memory limitations, create the risk of information errors and deficits (Patel et al. 2001). Most communication errors are usually between healthcare professionals in different disciplines (Gardner 2003). In addition, the hierarchical nature of most healthcare organizations is a source of miscommunication. As messages travel through several layers and channels, information is added or dropped out or modified.

Miscommunication rather than incompetence is at the root of most errors that plague healthcare facilities (Woolf et al. 2004). One error often begets another error, thereby producing a cascade of miscommunication. In a study of 75 error reports involving 15 physicians across five states, it was discovered that such a cascade was involved in 77 percent of the errors. Eighty percent of the cascades involved some form of miscommunication between physicians and medical records, including mishandling of patient requests and messages, inaccessible records, and inadequate reminder systems (Robeznieks 2004). In another study of 30 medical malpractice case files and 30 medical incident investigations, communication problems accounted for 76 percent of the cases (Stone 2002).

Medical errors have been estimated to cost the U.S. economy $37 billion annually (Grady, 2007). In 2007, the incidence of errors led Medicare to cease payment in 2008 for some complications that occur related to errors such as hospital acquired infections (Fabre 2007).

Although medical errors and injury to patients has been heavily documented and the analyses continue to grow, other outcomes from staff miscommunication have been less examined. A Microsoft survey of more than 38,000 people across 200 countries showed that about 17 hours (38 percent) of their 45 hour work week was spent on unproductive activities, largely due to poor communication, unclear objectives, and unproductive meetings (Microsoft Corporation 2005). Moreover, it has been estimated that improved telecommunications could save the healthcare industry as much as $80 billion annually (Girosi et al. 2005), and that electronic medical records along with automated warning systems can substantially reduce such errors (Gupta 2005). However, others argue that these error reductions and cost savings cannot be realized unless there are larger scale revisions in structure and policies regarding the healthcare system (Congressional Budget Office 2008).

Guidelines for Giving Feedback

Feedback enables people to monitor their own behavior and the reactions of others and to adjust their behavior and communication to be more effective. Feedback enables correction before (or soon after) errors occur and prevents their accumulation. Yet, effective feedback is not just "speaking your mind" to express yourself. If the purpose is to influence behavior, feedback must be used respectfully and strategically. The following characteristics of useful feedback should be kept in mind:

- *Relationship:* Become acquainted and develop a positive working relationship with people before giving feedback.
- *Requested:* People are most receptive when feedback is solicited rather than imposed on them.
- *Confidentiality:* Give feedback in private, especially when it is sensitive.
- *Needs of the recipient:* Effective feedback takes into consideration what the person needs rather than just serving your needs; it should be given to help, not hurt.
- *Practical:* Feedback focuses on what is said or done rather than why; the latter takes us away from a solution focus and toward speculation about motives.
- *Descriptive:* Feedback describes specific behavior and the recipient's reaction rather than judgments. Basing it on direct observation and providing examples can help reduce defensiveness and focus efforts.
- *Manageable amount:* Feedback should be given in a manageable amount; don't give too much feedback or too fast.
- *Balanced:* Provide both positive and negative constructive feedback; start with the positive, then present areas needing improvement, and end with positive.
- *Timing:* Give the feedback soon after the behavior has occurred.
- *Realistic:* The behavior to be changed should be something the receiver can do something about.
- *Listen and check:* The recipient may be asked to paraphrase what he or she has heard in the feedback to ensure accuracy of perception. Be attentive to the recipient's response to the feedback, and clarify and explain where needed.
- *Climate:* Create an environment in the organization in which the seeking and sharing of feedback is an expectation and a common occurrence.

Real-World Case

William Beaumont Hospital in Royal Oak, Michigan is a 1,061 bed facility with Level 1 trauma status and is a Magnet-designated hospital for nursing excellence. However, its 2004–2005 self-study revealed a troubling number of variance reports that led them to initiate a reengineering process to deal with patient handoffs between caregivers. They established goals for the performance standards governing handoffs, data needs to monitor high quality as patients were transferred from unit to unit, and setting team expectations for transfer of information and care. The project involved about 60 staff in four teams and subgroups. The teams focused on continuity of care, data elements to be included in the handoffs, performance standards, and training requirements. As a result, a Transport Procedure Checklist document was developed to ensure smooth transfer, fewer incident reports were reported, and patient safety was improved (H&HN Interviews 2006).

Summary

As the marketplace has expanded to a global perspective and workplace settings have become more diverse and complex, the discipline of management has likewise evolved. Classical management theories focused on formal authority, hierarchical avenues of communication and accountability, and operational efficiency. Weber's concept of bureaucracy, Taylor's scientific management, and Gilbreth's and Gantt's operational innovations provided such structure.

As management became professionalized, effective practices and responsibilities became more formal and were incorporated into the administrative model of management. In addition to describing the functions of planning, organizing, leading, and controlling, Fayol formulated 14 principles for management. Prior to emergence of the humanistic approach to management, Bernard proposed the acceptance view of authority and emphasized the balance of effectiveness and efficiency. The Hawthorne effect marked the shift from operations and authority to the human relations movement and attention to worker motivation. Maslow described a hierarchy of needs that provided managers with a model for targeting efforts to motivate workers, and McGregor recognized the shift from authoritarian to humanistic orientation in his Theory X and Y.

As technology and strategy were emphasized in response to international conflicts and competition, management science developed a variety of new tools. Operations management, statistical forecasting, break-even analysis, queuing, modeling, and PERT were used to reemphasize production to balance the renewed emphasis on people.

More contemporary approaches to management have emphasized improved quality of products and services through greater efficiency and increased focus on people. TQM, the Baldridge Award, and the search for best practices have fine-tuned many management and business processes.

Effective management involves not only understanding Fayol's four functions, but also understanding and developing conceptual skills for strategy, emotional intelligence or interpersonal skills for working effectively with people, and technical skills for dealing with the specific business field. Moreover, managers must learn to perform multiple roles while working at an unrelenting pace.

More recent theories have emphasized the complexity of modern organizations. Senge's (1990) emphasis on systems theory, for example, helps managers understand how the organization's components are connected much as a living system, and that change in one component can affect other components.

Change management requires strong leadership. Managers traditionally maintain a highly efficient workplace and establish procedures; leaders look to the future and promote change. Both solve problems and make decisions. Recurrent problems lend themselves to clear rules for programmed decisions that can be used routinely; unique, complex, or changing situations require careful thought when nonprogrammed decisions are made. Formal decision making progresses through several stages, including problem definition, problem analysis, generation of alternatives, selection of alternatives, plan implementation, and evaluation and feedback. In practice, managers more often use intuition or satisficing. Groupthink can produce riskier decisions and requires review of team norms periodically as well as implementation of countermeasures.

Corporate social responsibility has emerged as a strategic focus in recent years, partly due to concerns about inattention to environment and social issues that have been overshadowed by excessive attention solely to finances. It has also helped organizations consider their values and develop guidelines for congruence with those values. Communication errors can be costly in patient safety, liability risk, and staff relationships. Attention to clear communication, such as quality criteria, standards, and staff training can reduce distortion and error.

References

Ameri, F and D. Dutta. 2005. Product lifestyle management: Closing the knowledge loops. *Computer Aided Design and Application,* 2(5): 577–590.

Apker, J. 2001. Role development in the managed care era. *Journal of Applied Communication Research,* 29(2): 117–136.

Baldridge National Quality Program. 2008. *Healthcare criteria for performance excellence.* http://www.quality.nist.gov/PDF_files/2008_HealthCare_Criteria.pdf.

Baron, R.S. 2005. So right it's wrong: Groupthink and ubiquitous nature of polarized group decision making. *Advances in Experimental Social Psychology* 37: 219–252.

Bernard, Chester. 1938. *The Functions of the Executive.* Cambridge, MA: Harvard University Press.

Bigelow, J. 1993. Managerial skills texts: How do they stack up? *Journal of Management Education* 17(3): 399–415.

Bonaparte, T.H. 1970. *Peter Drucker: Contributions to business enterprise.* New York: NYU Press.

Bridges, W. 1994. *Jobshift: How to Prosper in a Workplace without Jobs.* Reading, MA: Addison-Wesley.

Buhler, P. M. 2007. Managing in the new millenium: Interpersonal skills. *Supervision* 68(7): 20–22.

Burrington-Brown, J. 2004. Does the Privacy Rule hinder patient care? *Journal of AHIMA* 75(9):72–73, 76.

Byrne, J.A. 2005 (Nov. 28). The man who invented management. *Business Week.* 97–106.

Carey, B. 2004 (July 14). A different kind of smart. *Los Angeles Times.*

Carmeli, A. and A. Tishler. 2006. The relative importance of the top management team's managerial skills. *International Journal of Manpower* 27(1):9–36.

Church, A.H. 1997. Managerial self-awareness in high performing individuals in organizations. *Journal of Applied Psychology* 82(2):281–292.

Coiera, E. 2000. When conversation is better than computation. *Journal of the American Medical Information Association* 7:277–286.

Coiera, E., R. Jayasuriya, M. Thorpe, and J. Hardy. 2000. Communication behaviors and information exchange patterns in a clinical setting. Report to NSW Health Department.

Coiera, E., R. Jayasuriya, J. Hardy, A. Bannon, and M. Thorpe. 2002. Communication loads on clinical staff in the emergency department. *Medical Journal of Australia* 176(9): 415–418.

Congressional Budget Office. 2008. Evidence on the costs and benefits of health information technology. Pub No. 2976. http://www.cbo.gov/ftpdocs/91xx/doc9168/05-20-HealthIT.pdf.

Denton, J. M. and J.B. van Lill.. 2006. Managerial derailment. *XIMB Journal of Management* 3(2):231–250.

Drucker, P. 1986. The appraisal of managerial performance. *Management Decision* 24(4):67–78.

Druskat, V.U., F. Sala, and G. Mount. 2005. *Linking Emotional Intelligence and Performance at Work.* Maywah, NJ: Lawrence Erlbaum.

Elkington, J. 1994. Towards the sustainable corporation: Win-win-win business strategies for sustainable development. *California Management Review* 36(2):90–100.

Fabre, J. 2007 (Sept. 26). The cost of medical errors just went up. http://www.nursingmasterminds.com/2007/09/cost-of-medical-errors-just-went-up.html.

French, J.R.P. and B. Raven. 1959. The bases of social power. In *Studies in Social Power.* Edited by Cartwright, D. Ann Arbor, MI: Institute for Social Research.

Friedman, M. 1970 (Sept. 13). The social responsibility of business is to increase its profits. *New York Times Magazine* 122(13):32–33.

Gardner, A. 2003 (Nov. 18). Tracking of medication errors rising: Report finds elderly most at risk in hospitals. Originally published by healthday.com. http://www. hon.ch/News/HSN/516102.html.

Gilbreth, F.B., Jr., and E.G. Carey. 1945. *Cheaper by the Dozen.* New York: Thomas Y. Crowell Company.

Girosi, F., R. Meili, and R. Scoville. 2005. *Extrapolating evidence of health information technology savings and costs.* Santa Monica, CA: RAND Corporation.

Goleman, D. 1995. *Emotional Intelligence.* New York: Bantam.

Goleman, D. 1998 (Nov.–Dec.). What makes a leader? *Harvard Business Review* 74(6):92–102.

Grady, P.A. 2007 (May 21). Testimony on FY 2008 Budget requests for NIH, Part II before HHS Appropriations Senate Subcommittee on Labor, US Senate. http://www.hhs.gov/asl/testify/2007/05/t20070521d.html.

Griffin, T.M. 2008. Effective intercultural communication. In *Effective multicultural teams: Theory and practice.* Edited by Halverson, C.B. and S.A. Tirmizi. Netherlands: Springer, 713–210.

Gupta, A. 2005. Medical errors: A leading cause of death in the United States. Medonomics: Insights into health care economics and policy. http://medonomics.blogspot.com/2007/06/medical-errors-leading-cause-of-death.html.

H&HN Interviews and research. 2006. Healthcare Benchmarks and Quality Improvement. http://www.hhnmag.com/hhnmag_app/jsp/printer_friendly.jsp?dcrPath=HHNMAG/PubsNewsArticle/data/2006August/0608HHN_gatefold&domain=HHNMAG.

Hammer, M. and J. Champy. 1993. *Reengineering the Corporation.* New York: Harper.

Healthcare Management Council. 2007. http://hmc-benchmarks.com.

Helseth, C. 2007 (Summer). Recruiting local people to fill health care needs. The Rural Monitor. http://www.raconline.org/newsletter/web/summer07.php.

Holton, V., F. Dents, and J. Rabbetts. 2008. Ashridge Management Index 2008: Meeting the challenges of the 21st century. http://www.ashridge.org.uk/website/IC.nsf/wFARATT/Ashridge%20Management%20Index%202008:%20Meeting%20the%20Challenges%20of%20the%2021st%20Century/$file/MeetingTheChallengesOfThe21stCentury.pdf.

Hopkins, M. 2005 (June 22). Can CSR pave the way for development?: From CSR to corporate social development. Paper presented to Second International Conference on CSR, London. http://mubs.mdx.ac.uk/Conferences/BPCSR05/07_csr_devcountries/Hopkins%20Paper%20Can%20CSR%20pave%20the%20way%20for%20development.pdf.

ISO.Org. 2008. http://www.iso.org/iso/isoinbrief_2008.pdf.

Jacques, E. 1996. *Requisite Organization.* Arlington, VA: Cason Hall.

Janis, I.L. 1972. *Groupthink: Psychological Studies of Policy Decisions and Fiascos.* Boston: Houghton Mifflin.

Jones, G.R. and J.M. George. 2006. Contemporary management. 4th edition. New York: McGraw-Hill Irwin.

Jordan, P. J., and A. Troth. 2005. Emotional conflict and conflict resolution. *Advances in Developing Human Resources* 4(1):62–79.

Kaplan, R.S. and D.P. Norton. 1996. *The Balanced Scorecard.* Boston: Harvard Business School Press.

Katz, R.L. 1974. Skills of an effective administrator. *Harvard Business Review* 52:90–102.

Kerker, S. 2001. Kerker reflects: Drucker's development of the strategy-focused organization. *New Corporate University Review* 9(1).

Kirvin, D. 2005 (March 28). Communication skills of the phlebotomist. Advance: For Medical Laboratory Professionals. http://laboratorian.advanceweb.com/Article/Communications-Skills-of-the-Phlebotomist-32805.aspx.

Kluger, M. and M. Bullock. 2002. Recovery room incidents: A review of 419 reports from the Anaesthetic Incident Monitoring Study (AIMS). *Anaesthesia* 57:1060–1066.

Kuhn, T.S. 1962. *The Structure of Scientific Revolutions.* Chicago: University of Chicago Press.

Liebman, C.B. and C.S. Hyman. 2004. A mediation skills model to manage disclosure of errors and adverse events to patients. *Health Affairs* 23:22–32.

Ling, A., S. Forrest, M. Fox, and S. Feilhauer. 2007 (June 22). Introducing GS SUSTAIN, Goldman Sachs Global Investment Research. http://www.unglobalcompact.org/docs/summit2007/gs_esg_embargoed_until030707pdf.pdf.

Luthans, F., R. Hodgetts, and S. Rosenkrantz. 1988. *Real Managers.* Cambridge, MA: Ballinger.

Mahoney, T.A., T.H. Jerdee, and S.J. Carroll. 1965. The job(s) of management. *Industrial Relations* 4(2):97–110.

Mahoney, L. and R.W. Roberts. 2007. Corporate performance, financial performance and ownership in Canadian firms. *Accounting Forum* 31(3):233–253.

Margolis, J.D., H.A. Elfenbein, and J.P. Walsh. 2007. Does it pay to be good? A meta-analysis and redirection of research on the relationship between corporate social and financial performance. Harvard University working paper. http://stakeholder.bu.edu/Docs/Walsh,%20Jim%20Does%20It%20Pay%20to%20Be%20Good.pdf.

Martin, K.L., L. Carter, D. Balciunas, F. Sotoudeh, D. Moore, and J. Westerfield. 2003. The impact of verbal communication on physician prescribing patterns in hospitalized patients with diabetes. *Diabetes Educator* 29(5):827–836.

Matthews, G., M. Zeidner, and R.D. Roberts. 2002. *Emotional Intelligence: Science and Myth.* Cambridge, MA: The MIT Press.

McGregor, D. 1960. *The Human Side of Enterprise.* New York: McGraw-Hill.

Melcrum Research. 2007. Making managers better communicators. An independent Melcrum Research Report. http://www.melcrum.com/offer/mmbc/07d/mmbc_xsum2007.pdf.

Meyer, B.B., T.B. Fletcher, and J. Parker. 2004. Enhancing emotional intelligence in the health care environment: An exploratory study. *Healthcare Manager* 23(3):225–234.

Michalisin, M.D., S.J. Karau, and C. Tangpong. 2004. Top management team cohesion and superior industry returns: An empirical study of the resource-based view. *Group and Organization Management* 29(1):125–140.

Microsoft Corporation. 2005 (March 15). Viewpoints from workers worldwide show technology and productivity increasingly intertwined. http://www.microsoft.com/presspass/features/2005/mar05/03-15PersonalProductivity.mspx.

Mintzberg, H. 1992. The manager's job: Folklore and fact. In *Managing People and Organizations*. Edited by Gabarro, J.J. Boston: Harvard Business School Publications.

Morgan, P. and K. Baker. 1985 (Nov.). Building a professional image: Improving listening behavior. *Supervisory Management.* 34–38.

O'Rourke, M. 2004 (April 1). Protecting your reputation. *Risk Management.* http://www.allbusiness.com/marketing-advertising/branding-brand-development/1004103-1.html.

Our common future. 1987. Chapter 2: Towards sustainable development. From A/42/427 Our common future: Report of the World Commission on Environment and Development. http://www.un-documents.net/ocf-02.htm.

Page, C., M. Wilson, and D. Meyer. 1999. A three domain, two dimensional model of managerial effectiveness. Paper presented at the Academy of Business and Administrative Sciences Conference, Barcelona, Spain.

Parson, H.M. 1974. What happened at Hawthorne? *Science* 183:922–932.

Pascale, R.T. 1990. *Managing on the Edge*. New York: Simon & Schuster.

Patel, V.L., J.F. Arocha, and D.R. Kaufman. 2001 (July/August). A primer on aspects of cognition for medical informatics. *Journal of the American Medical Information Association* 8(4):324–343.

Peters, T.J., and R.H. Waterman. 1982. *In Search of Excellence: Lessons from America's Best-Run Companies.* New York: Harper & Row.

Raven, B.H. 1983. Interpersonal influence and social power. In *Social Psychology*. Edited by Raven, B.H. and J.Z. Rubin. New York: John Wiley & Sons, 399–444.

Reid, S. 2008 (May/June). The resilient leader: Why EQ matters. *Ivey Business Journal*. http://www.iveybusinessjournal.com/article.asp?intArticle_ID=762.

Riggio, R.E. and R.J, Reichard. 2008. The emotional and social intelligences of effective leadership: An emotional and social skill approach. *Journal of Managerial Psychology* 23(2):169–185.

Robeznieks, A. 2004 (Aug.). Communication problems often initiate "cascades" of errors. *American Medical News*. Chicago: American Medical Association.

Rural Health Resource Center. 2008. Balanced Scorecard experiences. http://www.ruralcenter.org/?id=res_bscxp.

Salmon, G. L. 2008. The evolution of coaching in the U. S. Federal Government. *International Journal of Coaching in Organizations* 6(1):7–17.

SBAR: A communication technique for today's health care professional. 2008. http://www.saferhealthcare.com/index.php?Itemid=84&id=33&option=com_content&task=view

Senge, P. 1990. *The Fifth Discipline: The Art and Practice of the Learning Organization.* New York: Currency/Doubleday.

Shrader, C.B., L. Taylor, and D.R. Dalton. 1984. Strategic planning and organizational performance: A critical appraisal. *Journal of Management* 10(2):149–171.

Simpson, W.G., and T. Kohers. 2002. The link between corporate social and financial performance: Evidence from the banking industry. *Journal of Business Ethics* 35(2), 97–109.

Sorenson, J. B. 2002. The strength of corporate culture and reliability of firm performance. *Administrative Science Quarterly* 47(1):70–91.

Spath, P. 2007. Spread the word: Communication is the key to effective care. *For the Record* 19(8):36.

Stone, F. 2002 (April). An examination of the role of communication problems in preventable medical adverse events. Report no. AU/ACSC/110/2002-04 submitted in partial fulfillment of graduation requirements. Maxwell Air Force Base, AL. http://www.research.airuniv.edu/papers/ay2002/acsc/02-110.pdf.

Stoner, J.A.F. and R.E. Freeman. 1989. *Management.* Englewood Cliffs, NJ: Prentice-Hall.

Strickland, D. 2000. Emotional intelligence: The most potent factor in the success equation. *Journal of Nursing Administration* 30(3), 112–117.

Supplee Group. 2002 (Jan. 28). Press release: Employees cite poor managers as primary reason for quitting.

Swenson, D.X. 2003. The Groupthink Profile. http://www.behaviortrends.com.

Swenson, D.X. 2008. The Ouroboros Effect: The revenge effects of unintended consequences. http://www.faculty.css.edu/dswenson/web/Revenge.htm.

Sy, T., T. Tram, and L.A. O'Hara. 2005. Relation of employee and manager emotional intelligence to job satisfaction and performance. *Journal of Vocational Behavior* 68(3):461–473.

Tenner, E. 1996. *Why Things Bite Back: Technology and the Revenge of Unintended Consequences.* New York: Alfred A. Knopf.

Van Eck Computer Consulting. 2004. The decision tree for statistics. http://www.microsiris.com/Statistical%20Decision%20Tree.

Vogl, A.J. 2003 (Jan./Feb.). Does it pay to be good? *Across the Board.* http://www.management-issues.com/2006/8/24/research/does-it-pay-to-be-good.asp.

Vroom, V. and P. Yetton. 1971. *Leadership and Decision Making.* Pittsburgh: University of Pittsburgh Press.

Walton, M. 1986. *The Deming Management Method.* New York: Perigee Books.

Watzlawick, P., J.H. Beavin, and D.D. Jackson. 1968. *The Pragmatics of Human Communication.* New York: Norton.

Woolf, S.H., A.J. Kuzel, S.M. Dovey, and R.L. Phillips. 2004. A string of mistakes: The importance of cascade analysis in describing, counting and preventing medical errors. *Annals of Family Medicine* 2:317–326.

Chapter 21
Leadership Theory and Change Management

David X. Swenson, PhD

Learning Objectives

- Describe the functions of leadership
- Explain the differences between managers and leaders
- Discuss the key ideas of prominent leadership theories
- Recognize that a leadership approach needs to adjust to various situations
- Explain how leaders can fail in performance
- Identify ways of managing impaired leadership
- Identify the traits related to leadership effectiveness
- Appreciate how leadership theories have evolved from simple and two-dimensional models to complex, multidimensional, and situational models
- Recognize the stages and impact of organizational change
- Understand how to facilitate a transition in order to minimize stress to people and production

Key Terms

360-degree inventory
Adopter groups
Androgynous leadership
Appreciative inquiry
Autocratic leadership
Champion
Change agent
Change drivers
Charisma
Consideration
Contingency model of leadership
Critic
Delegation
Democratic leadership
Diffusion S curve
Early adopters
Early majority
Ending
Enhancers
Exchange relationship
Expectancy theory of motivation
Great person theory
Icarus Paradox
In-group
Initiating structure
Innovators
Inventor
Laggards
Late majority
Leader–member exchange
Leader–member relations
Leadership grid
Learning history
Least Preferred Coworker (LPC) scale
Lewin's stages of change
Neutral zone
Neutralizers
New beginnings
Normative Decision Model
Organization development (OD)
Organizational lifeline
Out-group
Path–goal theory
Peter Principle
Position power
Reductionism
Reflective learning cycle
Refreezing
Self-efficacy
Servant Leadership Model
Situational model of leadership
Sponsor
Stages of grief
Substitutes
Survey feedback
Synergy
System
Systems theory
Task structure
Team building
Trait approach
Transactional leadership
Transformational leadership
Unfreezing
Values-based leadership
Vertical dyad linkage
Worker immaturity–maturity

Permanent whitewater is the phrase often used to describe the turbulent nature of the emerging business environment that managers must understand and operate in daily (Vaill 1996). It is difficult enough to bring knowledgeable people together to plan for specific problems within a given time period, but change is now continuous and ubiquitous. Compounding the complexity of such planning is the growing uncertainty about the future and the need for an ongoing revision of plans to match the turbulent environment. Such a situation requires excellent leadership and an understanding of, and participation in, innovation throughout the organization.

This chapter examines the importance and role of leadership, several theories of leadership, and how organizations need to be prepared to manage continuous transitions.

Theory into Practice

Northwestern Clinic was a small healthcare facility. For several years it had operated in a cost-effective manner under the leadership of a physician executive. Following his retirement, the board of directors proposed that a change in leadership style was needed to remain competitive and responsive to the community. The directors recognized that such a shift, while desirable, would not be easy for the groups of stakeholders who were accustomed to their traditional way of operating.

The board invited an organization development consultant to assist in their restructuring efforts. They expected the consultant to spend some time diagnosing their facility and prescribing management solutions, much as the staff would deal with a patient. No such luck! The consultant explained that even a patient's response to treatment was more effective when they were fully engaged in their own health—so, too, was organization change. The consultant encouraged them to survey all staff (providing them confidentiality) regarding what did and did not work, what their image of a more effective organization might look like, and ideas to make their own departments work better.

The information was presented to the board and administrative team, and rather than telling the collected group what it meant, instead the consultant asked them to consider what it reflected about the organization. Overcoming initial reluctance to tell the "expert" what they expected him to tell them, they began a lively exploration of perceptions, problems, and hopes.

In the weeks and months that followed, the consultant encouraged the board, administrative team, and all levels of management to continue to involve staff in the shaping of the new organization. He suggested that it was the people who made the organization, and they should be involved in decisions that affected them. He also emphasized that they now had the skills to continue the change process without relying on him. Although the transition from recipient of advice to creator of their own organizational future was not an easy one, subsequent years were marked by high morale, lower turnover, improved communication, and better patient service.

Functions and Principles of Leadership

Leadership is the art of setting a direction and influencing people to move in that direction. Given the changing nature of the workplace and marketplace, leaders are in a unique position to influence the shaping of vision and mission in order to inspire people to put forth their best effort. Leaders also are the ones on which others rely to help make organizational change meaningful and to facilitate the transition to a new direction. Yet, clarifying exactly who leaders are and what they do is not an easy task. Several specialists in the field have lamented that despite so much research on the subject of leadership, there is little to show for it in the way of real insight and practical results (Bennis 1959; Burns 1978; Khurama 2007; Yukl 2006). There is a similar lack of consensus regarding what managers share in common (Hogan 2007; Kramer 2008).

Functions of Leadership

Leadership is a central strategic concern for most organizations because it makes a difference. Each year, the Hay Group and Chief Executive Magazine conduct a survey of the world's most-admired companies (Donlon 2007). Hay interviewed the top companies in 790 public companies and found that they were differentiated from the other companies by their exceptionally strong focus on several leadership areas. The leading companies provide "action learning" in which they develop leadership skills in response to real work mission-critical problems. In addition, they more often make leadership development activities available to a broad range of managers, managers are accountable for creating a motivating work climate, training is supported for interteam collaboration; and, in addition, people are assuming new leadership roles, working abroad to develop global awareness, and hiring from outside but orienting to the new culture. Nonetheless, fewer than half of organizations surveyed (46 percent) reported that they developed the talent of potential leaders by an in-depth consideration of the roles that will need to be filled in the future.

Leadership also affects financial performance, although the relationship between such performance and corporate governance has been difficult to clarify in the past. New financial indices have been developed to help determine this connection; for example, the FTSE Group and Institutional Shareholder Services launched a Corporate Governance Index. Based on best practices, this index provides a benchmark on 61 criteria (Baue 2004). The charisma of top leaders (including interpersonal skills) appears to have more impact on finances than task orientation in some cases (Koene et al. 2002). In a study of 353 Fortune 500 companies, diversity in leadership, specifically more women in executive leadership positions, also shows higher financial performance for such organizations (Guida 2004).

Part of the driving force for leadership training and development of leadership at all levels of the organization is the recognition that many Baby-Boomer executives and experienced managers will retire in the near future. It has been estimated that there may be an overall labor shortage by 2010, and if only 10 percent of these are leadership roles, this would still mean that there would be a shortage of one million leaders (Dychtwald et al. 2006; Fulmer and Bleak 2008). Nonprofit organizations are likewise challenged: a study by the Bridgespan Group, a Washington-based consultancy, reported that organizations would need to employ 640,000 senior managers between 2006–2016, and by 2016 will need to hire about 80,000 annually (Tierney 2006). Healthcare in particular is projected to experience a shortage of 62 percent (Aon Consulting 2008).

In modern organizations, leadership does not just reside at the top but, instead, permeates the organization. In a study by the Center for Creative Leadership, 70 percent of respondents believed that developing leadership at all levels of the organization was critical; 60 percent asserted the importance of developing staff with high potential and those who were emerging leaders. HR and training professionals have maintained a steady focus on providing leadership training, although a survey conducted by a coalition of HR and training groups found that 41 percent of people who participate in such training are neutral or dissatisfied with the training (Wellins and Pesci-Kelly 2003). Clearly, leadership development is a strong emphasis, but the more effective methods, focus, or utility has not yet been established. Among top-line executives, there is general agreement on the most important personality qualities required: leadership is essential, followed by ethics and strategy, with creativity and industry expertise less agreed upon (Schiller 2005).

The trend in modern organizations is to develop each employee's leadership potential to its full capacity. This allows the employees to exercise the empowerment they are given, demonstrate their value to the organization, and perhaps participate in leadership succession in the organization. Increasingly, succession planning emphasizes the character of the potential leaders. In a Chief Executive study (Dierick and McGill 2007), CEOs and their Boards highly valued the following: ability to build relationships, openness to change and growth, courage to make the right decisions, decisiveness, and ability to identify and develop talent. Yet, in spite of these desirable goals, only 35 percent of the sample said that a transition to new leadership would be successful if initiated today. This appears partly related to at least a quarter of executives not taking time to get acquainted with potential leaders more than two levels below them. As a result, about half of new leaders are not fully integrated into their companies, and the process takes longer than expected—from nine to 18 months. Even then, as many as 40 percent of executives fail at a cost of 10 to 20 times their salary.

Leadership versus Management

As seen in several chapters of this text, the workplace and the marketplace are beset with continuous adaptations to large-scale **change drivers** over which there is little control. Management must provide stability and consistency for workers and at the same time prepare them for the transition to new structures and processes. Managers and leaders must collaborate closely to ensure clear understanding and smooth transitions in ways that minimize disruption to people and production. Although the activities of leaders and managers can be distinguished, there is considerable overlap between the roles, and effective leaders and managers usually carry out both functions to some degree.

The terms *leader* and *manager* are often used interchangeably. Although they overlap, the two terms are technically—and in some aspects, practically—different. In general, the responsibility of managers is to ensure that current operations run smoothly whereas leaders strive to help the organization adapt to changing conditions. Managers tend to focus more on structured and analytical modes of thinking whereas leaders tend to use more flexible and creative modes. Managers are often more attentive to danger and uncertainty whereas leaders seek opportunities in undefined and unknown risk areas. Managers are said to determine the scope of problems whereas leaders search for alternative solutions. Managers seek methods and ask how something can be done whereas leaders seek motives and wonder why things are as they are and how they can be different. In general, then, managers work to create efficiency with the status quo whereas leaders move the organization into its unfolding future (Borkowski 2005). (See table 21.1.)

Table 21.1. Differences between managers and leaders

Managers	Leaders
Administer, replicate, and maintain	Innovate, originate, and develop
Emphasis on structure	Emphasis on people
Short-range view	Long-range view
Focus on bottom line	Focus on the horizon
Rely on control and rules	Rely on trust and inspiration
Avoid risks as problems	Take risks as opportunities
Do things right	Do the right thing
Uneventful early childhood	Developmental conflicts requiring reflection and mastery
Life seen as steady progression of positive events and security	Life punctuated with series of disruptions and challenges
Feel strong sense of belonging	Feel separateness; create rather than inherit identity
Transactional	Transformational

These differences have been attributed to the influence of different developmental experiences in these individuals' lives. When asked about their early family and personal experiences, managers often describe uneventful early childhoods and see life as a steady normative progression of positive events and security. Being involved in social and organized activities from an early age, they tend to gain a strong sense of belonging, identity, and self-esteem from others. In contrast, leaders more often describe disruptive experiences in early family and childhood in which they were confronted by conflicts and stresses. These crises required reflection and mastery through which self-efficacy was developed. Because confidence grows out of problem solving rather than relationships, leaders may be more attached to a vision that drives their achievement and inspires others than to an immediate situation (Hickman 1990; Kempster 2006; Kotter 1990; Zaleznik 1977).

Attesting to the relevance of developmental experiences, biographical data have been found to be predictive of good leadership over many years of research (Mumford et al. 1993; Tay et al. 2006; Taylor and Ellison 1967). At a time when human resources directors use caution about the types of questions they can ask in employment interviews, inquiring about the kinds of experiences that have led managers and leaders to be the kind of people they are can be insightful. It is important to remember that both roles are required in organizations, and it is in collaboration that leaders and managers provide balance for organizations in transition.

Flawed and Failed Leadership

A browse through most bookstores will show a series of unusual titles in the business section: *Crazy Bosses, When Smart People Work for Dumb Bosses, How to Work for an Idiot, Dinosaur Brains,* and so on. Such books reflect a serious problem in many organizations. The base rate for failed leadership has been estimated between 65 and 75 percent—based on employees reporting that the worst aspect of their job is their immediate supervisor (Hogan and Kaiser, 2004). In other studies, the failure rate of corporate executives in the United States from the 1980s to1990s was about 50 percent (DeVries 1992) and estimated between 55 to 60 percent by 2006 (Daley Group 2006).

Leaders are under greater scrutiny than before. The American Society for Training and Development asked 1,500 global managers and as many associates regarding current challenges for leadership. Three-quarters of leaders reported that they felt more pressure to perform and two-thirds believed that their performance was judged more stringently. This belief appeared justified in that about 60 percent of employees were more alert to the ethics of the leader and only 38 percent indicated that they had high confidence in the leader. This 38 percent corresponds to a study in which the same percent of employees would be willing to work for their same boss again (Curphy 2008). Leaders themselves were cautious in assessing their skills and felt that they were skilled in only a third of the required competencies. Creating further pressure and risk, 40 percent of the companies represented indicated that they did not have mechanisms in place to hold mediocre or poor leaders accountable for their performance (Kaplan-Leiserson 2004).

The consequences of these failures also are tragic. For example, it was found that near half of working Americans have experienced or observed workplace bullying, 37 percent have been directly bullied during their worklife, and such exposure adversely affects the psychological or physical health of nearly half of the target persons. Worst of all, an estimated 72 percent of the bullies are the bosses, leading to 40 percent of targets leaving their jobs (Zogby 2007). Reviews of research have established the connection between employee stress and bad bosses (Kelloway et al. 2005; Skogstad et al. 2007). Such malfeasance costs industries and the economy up to $5 billion annually, and it is estimated that half of the company's reputation is tied to the CEO's reputation. The risk and consequences also extend to the executives, and upwards of 75 percent have even considered quitting at some time (CEOGO 2003). The cost of a failed senior executive has been estimated between $750,000 and $1.5 million (DeVries and Kaiser 2003).

How is it that prominent organizational leaders such as U.S. Attorney General Alberto Gonzales, CEO Lloyd Blankfein of Goldman Sachs, CFO John Michael Kelly of Time Warner, Ed Zander of Motorola, and CEO Richard Fuld of Lehman Brothers and others in nearly daily news can fail their organizations? How is it that such talented people fall from success? It appears that there are three reasons: abuse of power, limited capacity, and personal impairments (Hale 2002).

Leaders throughout the organization and executives in particular have the right to exercise power to influence others and produce change. Power can become abused when a crisis requires a directive decision, but leadership continues the directive approach long after the crisis has passed. When there are insufficient checks and balances in the organization, such power can become excessive and often self-serving. This can even produce blind spots or compartmentalized thinking in which the person can entertain completely inconsistent values. For example, in the year before the accounting scandal brought down Enron, CEO Kenneth Lay toured the country presenting a training series on leadership ethics.

The question of what works and what does not work for leaders was examined in a five-year study of 200 management practices (Joyce et al. 2003). Their work concluded with a "4+2" formula for improved performance and organizational success. Four key areas were identified as essential: strategy, execution, culture, and structure. Sound strategy is based on a clear value proposition to the customer, valid stakeholder information, continual refinement, clear communication, and sticking to what you know best (similar to Peters' and Waterman's "excellence" criteria, which is discussed later in this chapter). Effective execution was based on meeting customer expectations, empowering decision making at lower levels, and reducing waste. Developing a healthy culture involved inspiring and empowering others to do their best, rewarding based on performance, encouraging an increase in quality performance, and promoting clear values. The structure finding indicated that leaders were more effective when they simplified processes, promoted open cooperation and communication, and used the best people on projects. Secondary areas were also discovered in which any combination of two improved success: promoting organizational talent, encouraging and rewarding innovation, inspiring board leadership in the organization, and strategically using mergers and partnerships. In contrast, they found that a failed leader more often had a lack of clear vision, difficulty in building teams, poor communication, mismatch in leadership style and situation, failure to execute plans, and poor interpersonal skills. These deficiencies generally affected the organization negatively.

In other cases, the successes and skills that led a person to promotion may be based on performance in a previous position unrelated to the new position. A successful manager who arose in a large or small company may not fare as well in the opposite-sized organization (Jahna 2002). Once referred to as the **Peter Principle** in which some people were promoted to their level of incompetency (Brown 2005; Peter and Hull 1969), leaders also may find themselves in a changing organization where their previous skills are outdated. For example, some managers may have an excellent understanding of such components as the financial process, but be unable to see the broader systemic view necessary for sound strategic planning.

Finally, leaders may have personal flaws or problems that interfere with a once successful style. Stress, alcohol abuse, anxiety, depression, and personality disorders can adversely affect a leader's judgment. Even unbridled success can exaggerate personality qualities and impair judgment as reflected in the *Icarus Paradox* (Miller 1990). In Greek mythology, Icarus was the son of Daedalus, who used wax to cover their arms with feathers so that they could fly like birds. Overcome with the thrill of flying, Icarus flew too near the sun. The heat from the sun melted the wax, causing Icarus to fall.

The **Icarus Paradox** proposes that successful styles and methods, unrestrained, can become their extreme, or, that our strengths can become our weaknesses: Builders become imperialists, pioneers become escapists, salespersons become drifters, and craftspersons become tinkerers. Systems can likewise fail for similar reasons. Two examples: an insurance company implemented an information system that initially increased the productivity of claims processing in the short run, but over time actually resulted in lower customer satisfaction and higher costs (Drummond 2008). Secondly, in its competition with Microsoft, Apple Computer criticized the software giant for its burdensome security system while Apple was essentially virus free. As Apple's popularity rose, it began acquiring the interest of hackers who put it through the same vulnerabilities as Windows had experienced (Kay 2008).

Although there are no completely successful prevention strategies, there are several practices that can reduce flawed leadership. When leaders are chosen or succession plans are in place, the "fit" between the leader's experience, style, and ability and the organization's culture and needs should be considered. Control mechanisms should be in place in the organization, usually a well-trained board of directors that monitors executive performance and development. Although charismatic leaders are inspiring and needed, especially during downturns and crises, they should be cautious in taking the organization in their personal direction rather than a strategic direction. Other warning signs include believing that they "own" the organization, having a short-term strategic focus, not wanting to hear adverse feedback, not modeling valued behavior, and contributing to intra-organizational competition.

Managing Flawed Leadership: Enhancers, Substitutes, and Neutralizers

The consequences of flawed leadership can be expensive in failed projects, financial costs, and employee turnover in the long term. Some ineffective leaders may remain in their positions for years when there is diffused responsibility, no accountability, replacements are scarce, or they have important political or family connections. Nonetheless, there are ways to respond to such leadership.

Kerr and Jermier (1978) proposed a situational model that helps distinguish when a leader can be improved, or when measures must be taken to dampen their adverse effects. Recognizing the effectiveness of self-directed teams, they questioned the degree to which a leader is actually needed, and whether other activities can provide substitutes for negligent leadership or neutralize the effects of abusive leadership. The flaw may not always reside in the leader, and they point out that a rigid organizational culture can also constrain the most creative of leaders and restrict their positive impact. Studies have been generally supportive of the model's application (Dionne et al. 2005; Howell et al. 1990), but some of the substitutes have not has as strong a moderating effect as predicted (Podsakoff et al. 1996; Yukl 2006).

To assess which strategy is most appropriate, Kerr and Jermier proposed a decision tree that helps plan whether **enhancer**, **substitute**, or **neutralizer** is most appropriate (see figure 21.1). The personal traits and personality are first considered and, if adequate, skills and knowledge are considered. If both of these are sufficient, then the leader's position should be enhanced and barriers or neutralizers to leadership removed. If the skills and knowledge are not adequate, then training or substitutes can be considered. In contrast, when the leader's personal traits or personality are not adequate, the feasibility of replacing the leader should be considered.

Figure 21.1. Kerr and Jermier decision tree

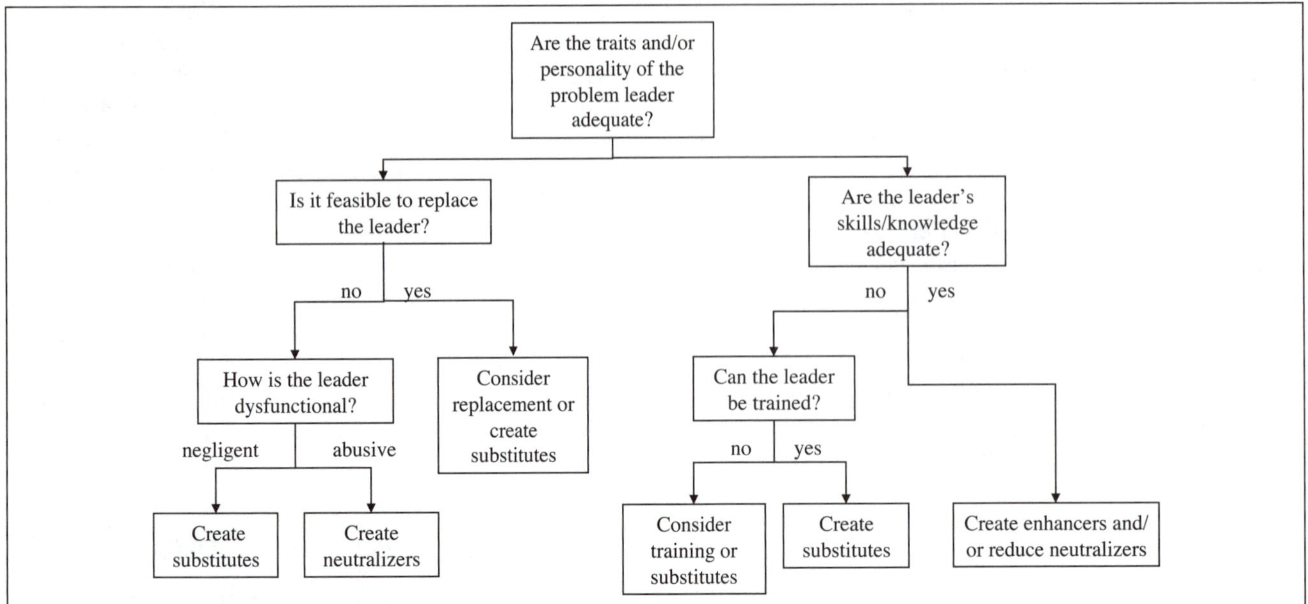

Source: Kerr and Jermier 1978.

When this is not possible, substitutes or neutralizers are considered.

Enhancement

Some leaders are less effective because they have not established their authority in the organization. Weakened positions may be due to subordinates not perceiving the leader's expertise, team spirit is not related to leadership efforts, subordinates are not dependent on the leader, the leader has low power, or workgroups are not cohesive related to leadership. The leader's influence can be enhanced by modifying these factors. Leader image can be improved by being a visible champion with important organizational responsibilities. Organizational climate can be modified by rewarding subordinates to increase confidence, emphasizing ceremony, and supporting subordinates; in other words, cohesion. Dependence on the leader can be enhanced by responding to crises that require immediate action and increasing leader centrality in providing information. Position power can be improved by changing title and status, increasing power to reward subordinates, and providing more resources for the leader to distribute.

Substitutes

If, however, the leader does not possess the leadership qualities required for the position or training is ineffective or unavailable, substitutes and neutralizers can be considered. The characteristics of subordinates to the leader can provide substitutes to the leader's lack of skill. Subordinates can have high ability, good experience, expert knowledge and training—all of which tend to replace the expertise of the absent leader. Subordinates who have a strong professional orientation, strong need for independence, or indifference to organizational rewards promote their focus on professional standards and internal locus of control rather than reliance on the leader. Characteristics of the task can also substitute for insufficient leadership and include feedback on the task, developing a routine, having tasks that do not vary in methods used, and having tasks that are intrinsically satisfying to the subordinate.

Finally, there are several organizational characteristics that can be substitutes. Formalizing the organization and organizational inflexibility minimizes leader's personal discretion and prescribed subordinate performance; group cohesion, degree of advisory and staff support, reward structures outside the leader's control, and physical separation between leader and subordinates.

Neutralizers

When a leader's behavior becomes abusive or produces adverse effects, but it is not feasible to replace the leader, efforts can be made to neutralize the negative effects. Subordinates whose performance is influenced by insightful self-monitoring (Anderson and Tolson 1989), professional standards, group cohesion and peer feedback, and objective performance feedback systems are less adversely affected. Other research shows that lack of leader expertise and an ineffective supportive leadership style has had little influence on highly authoritarian subordinates (Podsakoff et al. 1983). However, the use of neutralizers, while dampening an ineffective leader, may also create an influence vacuum from which a variety of dysfunctions can emerge (Kerr and Jermier 1978, 395).

In summary, some well-entrenched leaders may become dysfunctional under stress, have insufficient skill, or have a personality or management style mismatched with the situation. The Kerr-Jermier theory provides a description and alternatives to dealing with their behavior by enhancing their power in weakened positions, creating substitutes for their leadership when they are negligent, and finding ways to neutralize some of the effects of an abusive style.

Trends in Leadership Theory

The purpose of a theory is to serve as a template for examining some phenomenon, such as leadership. The theory labels important features, then uses them to describe, explain, and help predict what might happen if certain actions were pursued. Yet, unlike other areas of management, leadership theories have not coalesced into a clear picture; indeed, there are as many views on leadership currently as there were before the millennium. For example, Ralph Stogdill, one of the foremost researchers on the topic opined, "four decades of research on leadership have produced a bewildering mass of findings. . . . The endless accumulations of empirical data have not produced an integrated understanding of leadership" (1974, vii). Although there have been more recent efforts to construct a more general model (Goethals and Sorenson 2007), leadership continues to defy a comprehensive and integrated definition.

That leadership makes a difference is undisputed, but exactly how and why it makes a difference is still not well understood, and research reflects an inconsistent picture. For example, leadership has been found to be related to formation of subordinates' values, commitment (Lee 2005), empowerment and team effectiveness (Ozaralli, 2003), cohesion, commitment, trust, and motivation (Zhu et al. 2004). Supportive studies have shown that leadership accounts for 15–20 percent of the variance in organizational performance (Leadership Trust Foundation 2007), and 98 percent of corporate trainers believe that leadership can have a positive influence on financial stability (Chartered Institute 2005). In contrast, other studies suggest that although leaders shape organizational members' beliefs and behaviors, many external factors that affect the performance of organizations are beyond the influence of leaders (Bass and Avolio 1993). It also may be the case that when organizations are successful, such performance is attributed to leaders whereas the opposite attribution is made following failure. It is likely that such inconsistencies are due to methodological and measurement differences, as well as different styles of leadership being more or less effective in different situations (Smith et al. 1984). Nonetheless, some generalizations can be made.

Early theories were more basic views of leadership, consisting primarily of traits that leaders were expected to possess. As the limitations of these simple conceptualizations became evident, and the workplace and the marketplace became increasingly complex, the definitions and characteristics of effective leadership necessarily broadened to account for different circumstances. These situational or contingency views emphasize a leader's skills in assessing a situation and adjusting behavior accordingly. Although leadership theories have attempted to account for more complex behavior over time, nearly all of them continue to include task-oriented and people-oriented aspects (Judge et al. 2004).

Classical Approaches to Leadership Theory

The classical approaches to leadership refer to those early theories that formed the foundation for thinking about leadership and provided a basis for advancing research and new practices. Based on hierarchically structured organizations of the time, classical leadership theories tended to focus on the principled and effective use of authority. This emphasis began to change with the many social changes emerging in the early to mid-1900s. Inventions and innovations in manufacturing increased competition, which made managers more open to new ideas. Workers became increasingly better educated and skilled, thereby requiring managers with authoritative styles to adopt more democratic approaches. The workforce also became increasingly diverse, much like today, and this required a broader understanding of different cultures and motivational approaches.

Great Person Theory

The course of human history is marked with the contributions of great people. Such outstanding individuals originally led to the conception of leadership as an inborn ability, sometimes passed down through family, position, or social tradition, as in the cases of royal families in many parts of the world. The problem with the **great person theory** is that some of those who took positions of such greatness were terribly lacking, as in the case of such historical notables as Caligula in Rome, Idi Amin in Uganda, and Pol Pot in Cambodia. In the United States, there have been people who were leaders in one sphere, but who failed in others. General Ulysses S. Grant excelled as a general, which largely got him elected president, a role in which he performed miserably. Jeffrey Skilling, CEO of Enron, while a brilliant consultant and business strategist, was also considered to be unscrupulous, and his illegal manipulation of stocks led to the downfall of Enron, as well as Skilling's 24-year prison sentence.

Trait Approach

The **trait approach** gradually replaced the great person model and proposed that leaders possessed a collection of traits or personal qualities that distinguished them from nonleaders; in other words, they had "the right stuff." During the 1930s and 1940s, hundreds of studies on the trait approach to leadership were conducted, and as many as 18,000 traits were identified (Allport and Odbert 1936). Traits were often grouped into categories related to physical needs, values, intellect, personality, and skill characteristics. Some researchers have organized traits on the three leadership requirements of conceptual, interpersonal, and technical skills. Others add a fourth category—administrative skills—which includes the four managerial functions of planning, organizing, directing, and controlling (Yukl 2006).

Unfortunately, in much of the early research, only a weak relationship was discovered between traits and individuals who would emerge as leaders, and many leaders did not share all the traits in common. During later studies in which traits and skills were correlated with leader effectiveness rather than leader emergence, stronger connections appeared. Some of the more important traits included adaptability, social alertness, ambition, assertiveness, cooperativeness, decisiveness, dominance, energy, stress tolerance, and confidence. Skills included intelligence and conceptual abilities, creativity, tact, verbal fluency, work knowledge, organization, and persuasion (Stogdill 1974). Despite this extensive work, it appears that no single traits are absolutely required for leadership. Having certain traits and skills leads to a greater likelihood that such attributes may be more helpful in a situation and to leader effectiveness. However, meta-analysis, new statistical factor analysis techniques, and longitudinal research on the advancement of managers have led to a renewed interest in trait theory (Zaccaro et al. 2004).

Autocratic versus Democratic Leadership

As Douglas McGregor noted in his formulation of Theory X and Y, two types of environments and leaders corresponded to autocratic and democratic behaviors. In the late 1950s, stimulated by the Cold War between political democracies and communism, researchers at Iowa State University conducted studies on democratic and autocratic leaders (White and Lippitt 1960). They found that groups under **autocratic leadership** performed well as long as they were closely supervised, although levels of member satisfaction were low. In contrast, **democratic leadership** led members to perform well whether the leader was present or absent, and members were more satisfied. This kind of research led to the emphasis on participative management in many organizations, although the studies have been strongly criticized for studying groups of young boys at a summer camp and then generalizing the findings to corporate behavior (Lee 1982).

However, the autocratic–democratic dimension was useful for understanding a range of managerial behavior. Tannenbaum and Schmidt (1973) designed a continuum that described seven degrees of managerial involvement in a decision. (See figure 21.2). At one end of the continuum, the manager makes a decision alone and announces it; at the other, the manager encourages his or her subordinates to make their own decisions within prescribed limits. This model reflected a shift away from looking at the leader in isolation or in terms of a rigid or permanent style and suggested that a person had available a range of behaviors depending on the situation. But what behaviors made leaders successful?

Check Your Understanding 21.1

Instructions: Complete the following activities on a separate piece of paper.

1. Make two lists of effective and ineffective leaders. What makes them different from each other? Consider their personalities, limitations in skills or adaptability, and changes in the situation, as well as what is required of them.
2. Make a list of your traits and skills. Rank them in order of how effective they would make you as a leader in a given situation. Change the leadership situation and see which traits and skills might also change to give you an advantage or which ones might unexpectedly become a disadvantage. How could you develop these skills further?
3. Imagine you have been asked to be a consultant to an aspiring political or managerial figure. You are asked to recommend how this person should appear in order to increase his or her chances for election or promotion. What behaviors would you advise for and against? What ethical issues are involved in this type of image building?
4. What can an organization do to reduce the risk of having a flawed leader? Consider hiring practices and the impact of organizational change and crises.

Figure 21.2. Tannenbaum and Schmidt's leadership continuum

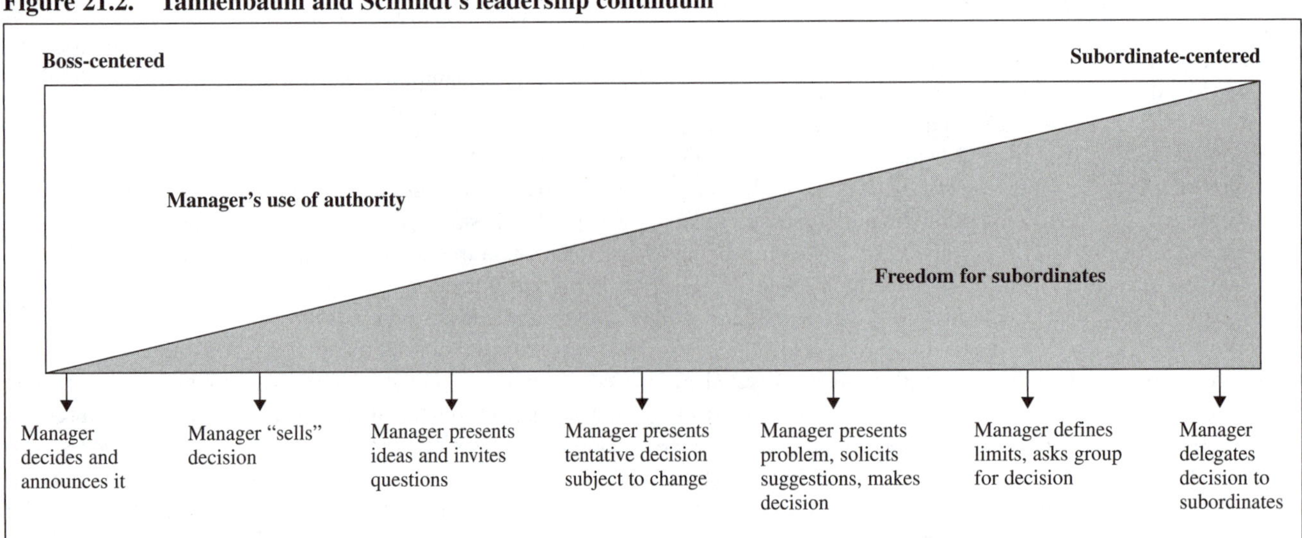

Behavioral Theories of Leadership

Earlier theories focused on what leaders should do and what was expected of them. In contrast, the emerging behavioral theories described what managers actually do. The emerging theories clearly emphasized a leader's orientation toward both tasks and people and enabled leaders to describe a variety of styles rather than just the "right" style.

Normative Decision Tree

Victor Vroom and Philip Yetton (1971) developed the **Normative Decision Model** in the early 1970s. Using a continuum similar to Tannenbaum and Schmidt's, they identified a series of intermediate questions and decisions that could be answered yes or no, and that would lead to each outcome. (See figure 21.3.) Crucial aspects of the situation related to the quality of the decision required, the degree of subordinate support for the decision, the amount of information available to leaders and followers, and how well structured or defined the problem was. A decision made exclusively by the leader without member input could create problems in acceptance, just as delegating a decision to a group could be costly in time and effort, if unnecessary. The Vroom-Yetton model enables a manager to decide on the level of decision-making involvement: autonomous, consultative, or delegative. A more recent revision of the model by Vroom and Jago (1988) replaced the limiting features of the yes or no response options with five choices. It also incorporated consideration for subordinate development, decision time, and the manager's rating of the criteria as new decision rules. The resulting formula is complex and most easily applied with a software program.

Another way to view both autocratic and democratic leadership continuum models is by describing them along a task-social dimension. For example, both the linear models of Tannenbaum and Schmidt and of Vroom and Jago allowed behavior to be described from a task to a social orientation. However, these linear models only allowed leaders to be placed along a single point on the continuum and did not allow them to favor both aspects at the same time. By "bending" the linear continuum into orthogonal axes (figure 21.4), it is possible to create a grid or a two-by-two table that has a greater area for describing more varieties of leadership behavior. Using this matrix format, a person could be described as having both task and social orientations, not just one or the other.

Ohio and Michigan Studies

During the 1950s and 1960s, researchers at Ohio State University examined the behavior of leaders in several hundred studies and reduced them to two categories: **consideration** and **initiating structure** (Shartle 1979). Consideration referred to attention to the interpersonal aspects of work, including respect for subordinates' ideas and feelings, maintaining harmonious work relationships, collaborating in teamwork, and showing concern for the subordinates' welfare. Initiating structure was more task-focused and centered on giving direction, setting goals and limits, and planning and scheduling activities. During the same period, researchers at the University of Michigan developed a similar model. Comparing effective and ineffective managers, they found that a key difference was that the former employee-centered managers focused more on the human needs of their subordinates whereas their less effective job-centered managers emphasized only goal attainment (Likert 1979). These two dimensions continue to be the foundation of organization and subordinate transformation in organizations (Vaishali and Kumar 2001; Vecchio et al. 2008).

Leadership Grid

Building on the Ohio State and Michigan studies, Blake and Mouton (1976) at the University of Texas identified the same two dimensions: concern for people and concern for production. Their **leadership grid** marked off degrees of emphasis toward orientation using a nine-point scale and finally separated the grid into five styles of management based on the combined people and production emphasis. For example, a score of 9,9 (emphasizing both people and production) was called "Team Management." Blake and Mouton considered it the best orientation because it emphasized harmonious cooperation in production to achieve goals. A score of 9,1, an "Authority-Compliance" orientation with an emphasis on production and operational efficiency, afforded little attention to human needs. The 1,9 "Country Club" orientation emphasized group harmony, esprit de corps, and cooperation over production. The 1,1 "Impoverished" orientation reflected inattention toward both relationships and work production. A mix of both dimensions, but less than a team orientation, is the 5,5 "Middle-of-the-Road" approach, which tries to balance the two. (See figure 21.5.) Although this model has been considered a key theory and it clearly presents a collaborative or team management approach as the ideal, subsequent contingency theories show that there are situations in which another emphases may be as effective.

Later Models of Leadership

To this point, most theories have emphasized identifying a cluster of traits or a single style or orientation for leadership. As research in leadership has continued, it has become apparent that successful leadership does not depend on style or skills alone but, rather, on matching a leader's style with the demands of a specific situation.

Fiedler's Contingency Model

Fred Fiedler at the University of Illinois designed his **contingency model of leadership** to compensate for the limitations of the classical and behavioral theories of leadership (1967). Fiedler kept the social-task orientation as the cornerstone of his theory and designed an innovative test to determine the leader's preferred style. The **Least Preferred Coworker (LPC) scale** presented a series of 16 to 22 bipolar adjectives along an eight-point rating scale. Sample items included unfriendly to friendly, uncooperative to cooperative, and hostile to supportive. When the leader described a least-preferred coworker with positive terms, he or she was considered to have

Figure 21.3. Normative decision tree

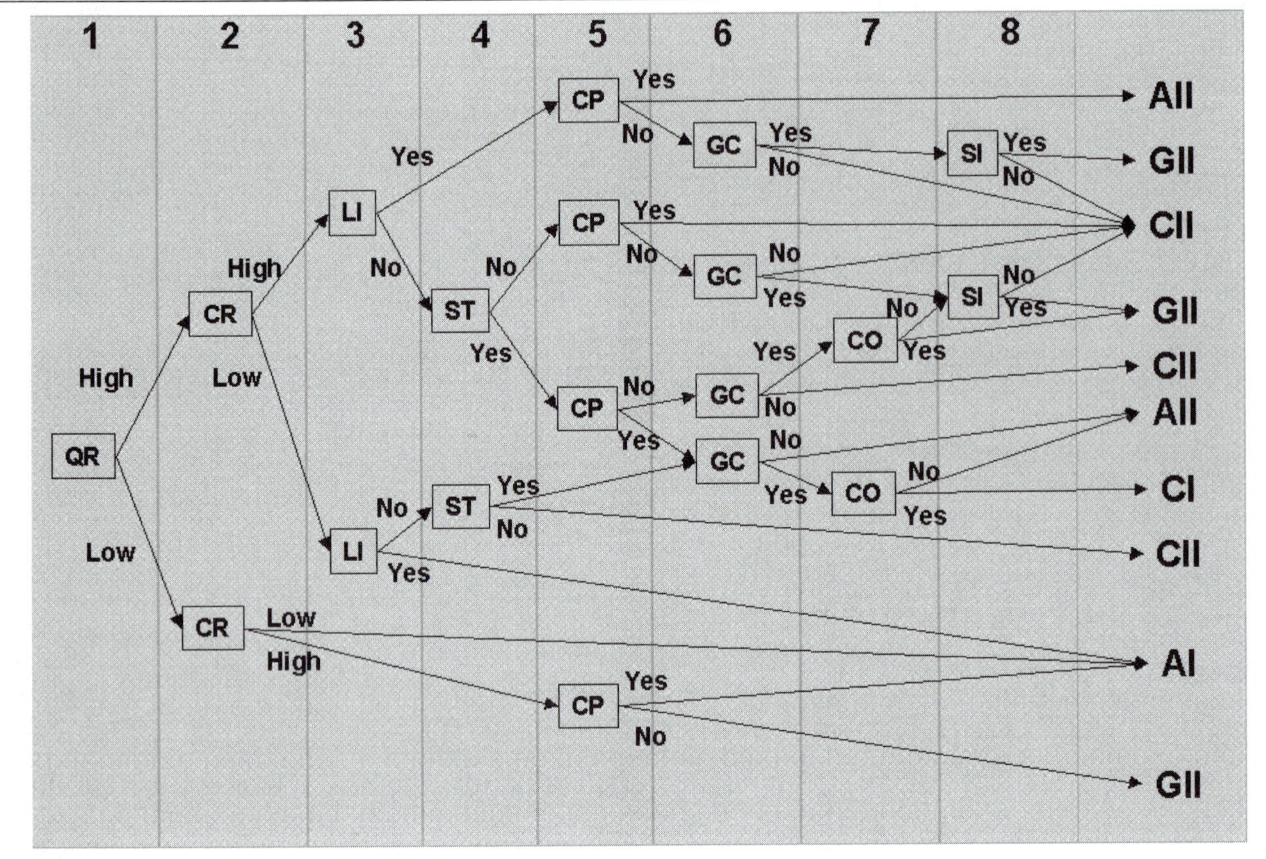

At each step in the process, a question is asked and the response determines the next branch and question. Each node of the tree has a critical criterion for determining the outcome, including:

- *Quality requirement (QR):* How important is the technical quality of the decision?
- *Commitment requirement (CR):* How important is subordinate commitment to the decision?
- *Leader's information (LI):* Do you (the leader) have sufficient information to make a high-quality decision on your own?
- *Problem structure (ST):* Is the problem well structured (e.g., defined, clear, organized, lends itself to solution, time limited, etc.)?
- *Commitment probability (CP):* If you were to make the decision by yourself, is it reasonably certain that your subordinates would be committed to it?
- *Goal congruence (GC):* Do subordinates share the organizational goals to be attained in solving the problem?
- *Subordinate conflict (CO):* Is conflict among subordinates over preferred solutions likely?
- *Subordinate information (SI):* Do subordinates have sufficient information to make a high-quality decision?

Decision Outcome	Description
Autocratic I (AI)	Leader solves the problem alone using information that is readily available.
Autocratic II (AII)	Leader obtains additional information from group members, then makes decision alone. Group members may or may not be informed.
Consultative I (CI)	Leader shares problem with group members individually and asks for information and evaluation. Group members do not meet collectively, and leader makes decision alone.
Consultative II (CII)	Leader shares problem with group members collectively but makes decision alone.
Group II (GII)	Leader meets with group to discuss situation. Leader focuses and directs discussion but does not impose will. Group makes final decision.

Figure 21.4 The shift from leadership continuum to matrix leadership model

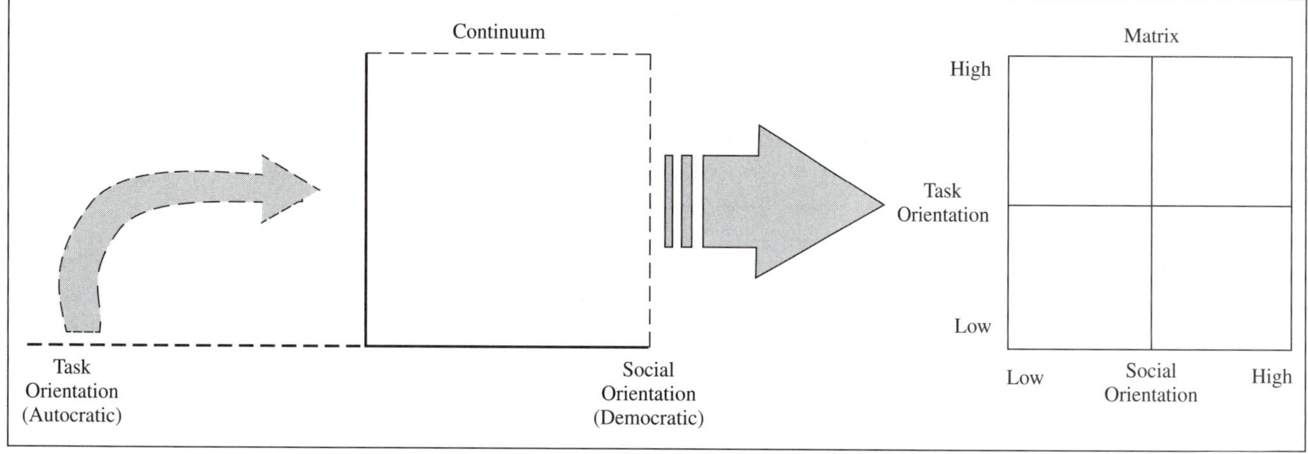

Figure 21.5. Leadership matrix models

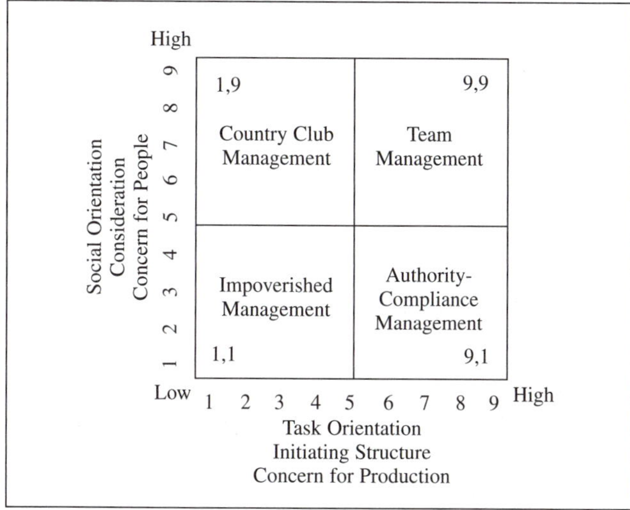

a relationship orientation. That is, although the leader might not want to work with the coworker, the leader's interpersonal orientation allows him or her to still perceive the coworker in a positive light. In contrast, a task-oriented leader would be one who described the LPC in negative terms; if he or she cannot work with the coworker, this biases the leader's view of the person on other behaviors.

The second aspect of Fiedler's model was the favorability of the situation in which the leader would operate. Because contingency means "depends on," the favorability or fit of a leader depends on the following three situational factors:

- **Leader–member relations**, or "group atmosphere," is much like social orientation and includes the subordinates' acceptance of, and confidence in, the leader as well as the loyalty and commitment they show toward the leader.
- **Task structure** is obviously related to task dimension described by other theories and refers to how clearly and how well defined the task goal, procedures, and possible solutions are.
- **Position power** refers to the authority the leader has to direct others and to use reward and coercive power.

In general, the greater the favorability to the leader, the more the subordinates can be relied on to carry out the task and the fewer challenges to leadership. Situations more favorable to leadership are those in which leader–member relations are positive, task structure is high, and position power is high. Situations in which these factors are reversed are considered unfavorable to leaders because they have less leverage to influence their followers. Task-oriented leaders tend to perform better in situations that are either high or low in favorability; relationship-oriented leaders do better under moderately favorable conditions.

Although the idea of a contingency or leadership style varying in effectiveness depending on circumstances has gained in popularity, research has not shown extensive support for certain aspects of Fiedler's model and its utility remains in dispute. The LPC, for example, does not appear to be exclusively related to task and relationship styles and may measure other, unrelated features. Fiedler originally believed that personality was "fixed" and that one should engineer or change a situation to be more compatible with a leader's style. Although Fiedler introduced a variety of useful strategies for changing the three contingencies, it is now clear that leaders have much more flexibility in applying their style than was once thought. Finally, several studies have shown that leaders in high- or low-favorability situations are about equally effective in goal attainment. Nonetheless, Fiedler's important contribution was his promotion of the idea of contingency.

Hersey and Blanchard's Situational Model

One of the more popular leadership models used for training, and one that has attempted to integrate other ideas from management, is Hersey and Blanchard's **situational model of leadership** (Hersey et al. 1996). As Dubrin (2004) points out, this is more a model than a theory because it does not explain why things happen but, rather, offers recommendations for behaving differently under various conditions.

To the already widely used task and social dimensions, Hersey and Blanchard added a third: the maturity of the followers. **Worker immaturity–maturity** is a concept borrowed from Chris Argyris, who suggested that job and psychological maturity also influences leadership style. Job maturity refers to how much work-related ability, knowledge, experience, and skill a person has; psychological maturity refers to willingness, confidence, commitment, and motivation related to work. Behaviors associated with maturity include initiative, dependability, perseverance, receptiveness to feedback, goal orientation, and minimal need for supervision. Argyris (1957) suggested that to apply a directive approach with mature workers can result in stifling their maturity and even in forcing them back to lower levels of maturity. Hence, adjusting leadership style to worker maturity is an important consideration. (See figure 21.6.)

Hersey and Blanchard also adapted the grid format of their predecessors and structured it in a developmental sequence. Borrowing the idea that teams and organizations progress through developmental stages of a life cycle (Edison 2008; Hwang and Park 2007), they suggested that leadership style should be adjusted to the stage of team development. For example, their Situation-1 (S1) involves high-task, but low-social, emphasis, thereby indicating that the leader should focus on task duties such as setting goals, identifying resources and constraints, and so on. As the team moves to Situation-2 (S2), task and social functions of the leader are both involved as members attempt to influence each other and to explore how their styles may conflict with or complement each other. In Situation-3 (S3), members clearly know the task and need little direction, but social interaction around team norms may require intervention and guidance. Finally, Situation-4 (S4) is the stage of high team performance in which both task and relationships require little intervention by the leader. Worker maturity is high, and the leader may be active only in encouraging higher performance and removing barriers to performance. Hersey and Blanchard also incorporated Tannenbaum and Schmidt's autocratic–democratic continuum, which they distributed across the developed stages and labeled telling, selling, participating, and delegating. (See figure 21.7.)

Figure 21.6. Argyris's worker immaturity–maturity continuum

Assertiveness & initiative	Passivity
Independence	Dependence
Wide behavioral choices	Limited behavioral range
Deep and strong interests	Shallow & casual interests
Past–future perspective	Present-centered perspective
Self-awareness & control	Low self-awareness

Figure 21.7. Situational leadership model

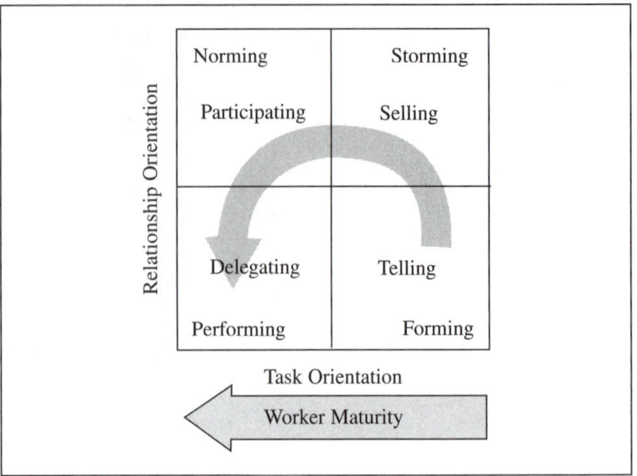

Path–Goal Theory

A more recent model of leadership, initially introduced by House (1971), is **path–goal theory**. While other theories have focused on the motivation of the leader, this one examines the motives and needs of the subordinates and how the leader can respond to them. This theory was based on the **expectancy theory of motivation** that proposes that one's effort will result in the attainment of desired performance goals. Path-goal theory states that a person's ability to perform certain tasks is related to the direction and clarity available that lead to organizational goals. For example, if a worker is unclear about what a task involves and what should be done, performance will be improved when clear instructions are given. The role of leaders, then, is to facilitate the path toward the goal by removing barriers to performance.

Path-goal theory identifies four different situations, each requiring a different facilitative response from leadership. (See figure 21.8.) When workers lack self-confidence, leaders provide support by being friendly, approachable, concerned about needs, and equitable. This increases the worker's confidence to achieve the work outcome. When the worker has an ambiguous job, the leader is more directive in providing the worker with direction, schedules, rules, and regulations that clarify the path. When workers do not have sufficient job challenge, the leader uses an achievement approach by setting challenging goals, continually seeking improvement, and expecting high performance. Finally, when the reward is mismatched with worker needs, the leader takes a more consultative or participative role in which workers share work problems, make suggestions, and are included in decision making to ensure more appropriate rewards. All four strategies result in improved task performance and satisfaction—again, the task and social dimensions.

Dyadic Relationship Theory

Some leadership theories are macro theories and attempt to explain leadership across large domains; but there also are

Figure 21.8. Path–goal theory

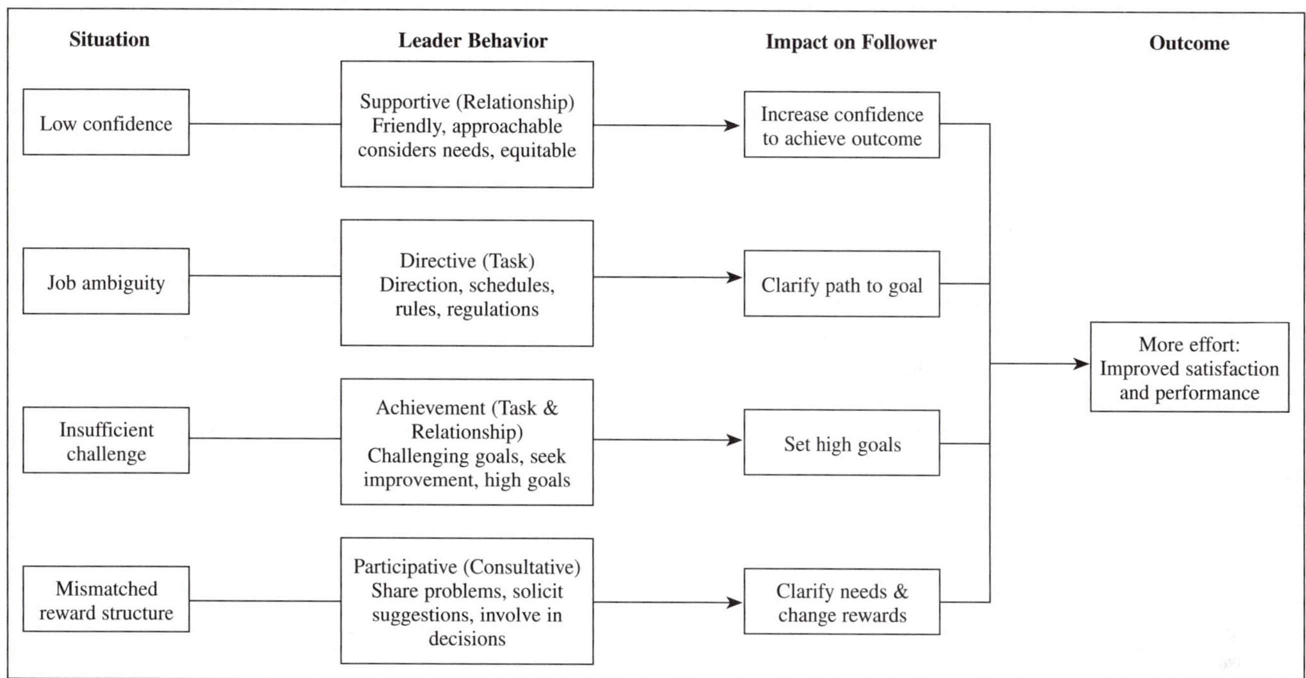

micro theories that focus on a specific context for leadership. **Leader–member exchange** (LMX) (Graen and Skandura 1987) and closely related **vertical dyad linkage** (VDL) represent micro theories that focus on dyadic relationships, or those between two people or between a leader and a small group. More specifically, they explain how **in-group** and **out-group** relationships form with a leader or mentor, and how **delegation** may occur.

VDL was first formulated in 1975 (Dansereau et al. 1975) to describe the single-person mentoring relationships that occur in organizations and was later supplemented by leader–member relations theory that applied the same idea to the leader's relations with groups. In these situations, leaders look for subordinates with high-performance and leadership potential that distinguishes them from subordinates with less potential. The best predictors of being selected for in-group, in addition to competence, include compatibility of the subordinate with the leader, interpersonal liking for each other, and being extraverted. Once identified, the leader and subordinates form an **exchange relationship**, in which a leader offers greater opportunities and privileges to a subordinate in exchange for loyalty, commitment, and assistance. The leader may delegate special responsibilities, offer interesting and desirable tasks, give opportunities for highly visible or skill-building projects, and provide mentoring.

Those subordinates who form a group around the leader are referred to as the in-group; those subordinates not included form the out-group. Being in the in-group may sound attractive, but it involves performance "beyond the call of duty." In-group members may spend longer hours, take work home or work during off-hours, and take on more difficult tasks compared to members in the out-group. The out-group expects to be treated fairly by the leader and as long as the exchanges are viewed as fair, there is little or no conflict between the in- and out-groups; they can remain fairly stable over time. However, when the out-group perceives that the in-group is receiving greater privileges for doing the same work as the out-group, the latter can feel resentment, alienation, and hostility, and show lower performance. There is evidence that once in the in-group, the halo effect can take over and ratings of the subordinate may be inflated (Duarte et al. 1993). The leader must ensure fair treatment and clear expectations for both groups. In addition, leaders can promote high-quality relationships with all employees by speaking with people personally, using active listening, not imposing the leader's view on issues discussed, and sharing expectations about the job and working relationship. A recent study of the theory supported its key hypothesis that when there was variance in employees' perceptions of equity and fairness, this negatively affected job satisfaction and feelings of wellbeing (Hooper and Martin 2008).

A review of leadership theories by Hogan and Kaiser (2004) shows the relationship among key factors in leader performance. Aspects of the personality of the leader are projected into one's leadership style, the latter of which may have some variance from situation to situation. This style is perceived by and interacts with employee attitudes and team functioning to facilitate the performance of others. This performance is finally expressed in organizational performance and its success or failure.

The Evolution of Leadership Theories

Although there are scores of leadership theories and unfortunately none yet that are comprehensive, we can speculate about the development of these theories over time and how they are changing (see figure 21.9). The Evolution of Leadership Theories figure shows the great person theory at the center, which emphasized a collection of various traits, often inconsistent and poorly defined. Its limitations led to a conceptualization of bipolar traits as shown in the Leadership Continuum of Tannenbaum and Schmidt (refer to figure 21.1). Although this was more descriptive than the simple trait approach, it was not possible to show that a leader could have *both* aspects of bipolar behaviors rather than their being mutually exclusive.

The Michigan (Likert 1961) and Ohio State (Halpin and Winer 1957) studies essentially took the bipolar dimension and bent it at right angles into coordinates so that behavior could be described as high or low on both dimensions. Hersey and Blanchard (1996) applied Bruce Tuckman's (1965) idea of stages of team development, thereby suggesting that leadership behaviors may need to change as team and organizational maturity progressed. The Modified Managerial Grid added a third dimension (one of the few theories to do so) to include effectiveness of leadership performance as well as whether it was social or task oriented.

Each of these theories were increasing in complexity and added contingencies to the model. Although the Vroom Yetton (1971) decision tree is a micro theory (focusing on decision making), it is representative of the use of multiple contingencies to show how a condition could direct the leader into a different style to match the situation. Contingency theory was clearly the focus of Fiedler's model that proposed that effective leadership style was a function of the combination of task structure, leader-member relations, and position power. Although systems theory is not explicitly about leadership, it is one of the more complex but thorough theories and techniques for describing the interconnections

Figure 21.9. Evolution of management theories

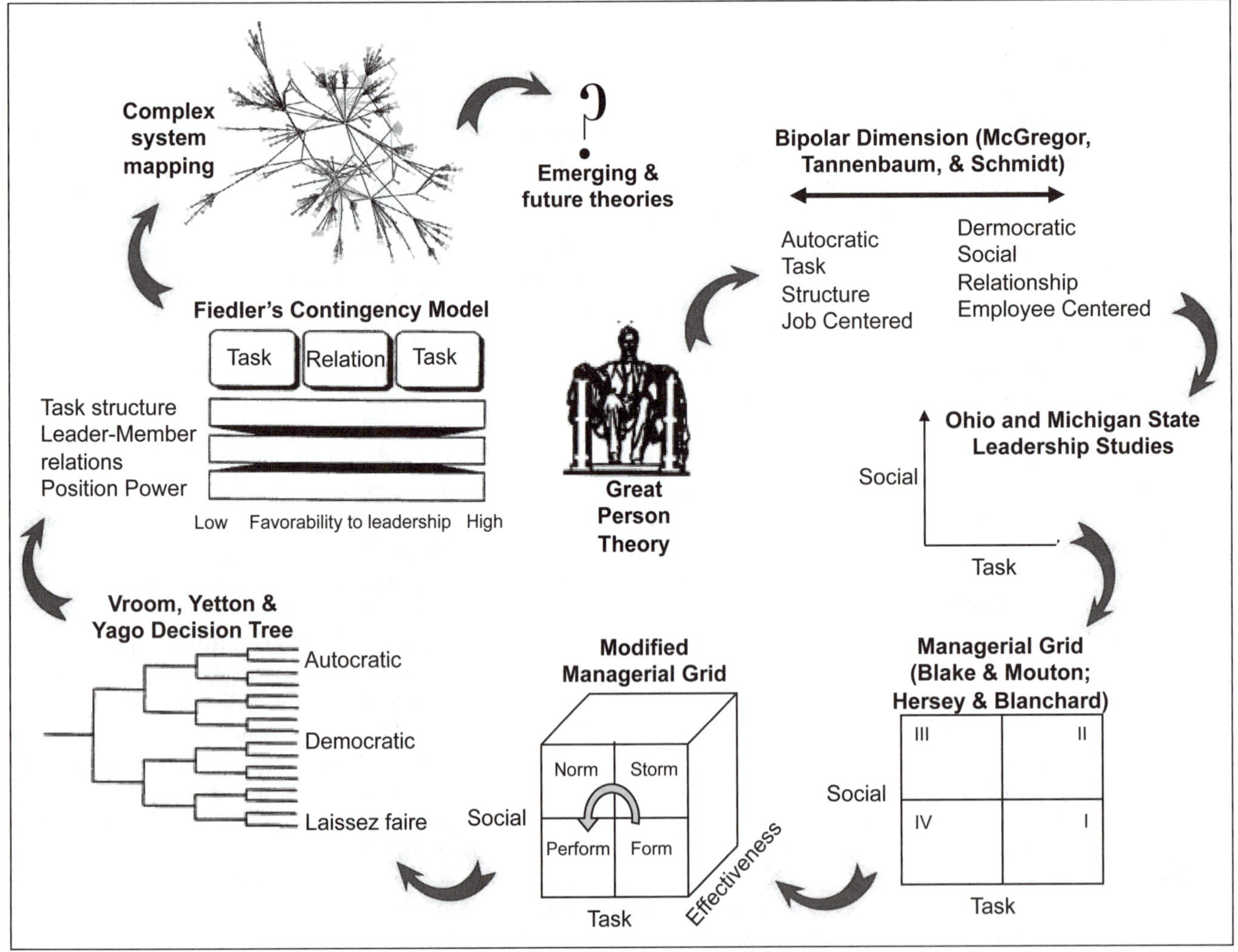

among factors in the leadership situation. While the very problem of high complexity may make it impractical for some people to use, computer technology and modeling software are making it more feasible.

In general, leadership theories have moved from simple and composite listing of traits to more detailed descriptions along task and social dimensions; to contingency theories that recommend flexible styles based on stage of development or combination of situational factors; to complex relationships among all of these in systems models. As much as there is no integrative theory at this time, it is also unclear what new leadership theories may emerge in the future.

Theories of Transactional and Transformational Leadership

This discussion goes back to the difference between managers and leaders discussed earlier. In 1978, when James MacGregor Burns published his Pulitzer prize-winning *Leadership,* he emphasized this distinction among political leaders, calling them transactional and transformational styles. **Transactional leadership** refers to the role of the manager who strives to create an efficient workplace by balancing task accomplishment with interpersonal satisfaction. In contrast, **transformational leadership** is considered more complex and powerful. In this leadership style, leaders promote innovation and organizational change. In the mid-1980s, Bernard Bass extended the model into the business world (1985). As you can see from the earlier presentation of differences between managers and leaders, managers tend to use transactional skills to improve organizational functioning, while leaders tend to use transformational skills for organizational change.

An important aspect of transformational leadership is **charisma**, or the ability to inspire and motivate people beyond what is expected with exceptionally high levels of commitment (Boerner and Dutschke 2008; Choi 2006). Charisma refers to influence by force of personality in which the leader inspires commitment, loyalty, and faith in a vision. Examples of people who have wielded such power include Winston Churchill, Martin Luther King, Jr., Michael Dell, and Barack Obama. Although the rhetoric and imagery can be stimulating to followers, there is a risk that with the leader's passing, leadership succession may fail and progress may falter.

In a five-year study, Bennis and Nanus (1985) conducted extensive interviews with 90 top leaders. Their study reinforced differences between transformational (leaders) and transactional (managers) roles, finding that transformational leaders were distinguished by their "four I's": idealized influence (leader as role model), inspirational motivation (team spirit and meaningfulness), intellectual stimulation (innovation and creativity), and individual consideration (mentoring).

Attempting to define the leadership practices of transformational leaders, Kouzes and Posner (1989) surveyed 550 middle and senior managers in private and public sectors. They used a series of questions that identified how leaders performed during their personal best leadership achievements. They reduced the results into five leadership practices and 10 behavioral commitments:

- Challenging the process included the search for opportunities and taking risks.
- Inspiring a shared vision involved envisioning the future and enlisting others.
- Enabling others to act was based on fostering collaboration and strengthening others.
- Modeling the way included setting an example and planning small wins.
- Encouraging the heart referred to recognizing and celebrating accomplishments.

Kouzes and Posner stressed that the relationship between leaders and followers has a **synergy**, in which the combination of their efforts produces more than either acting alone. This enthusiasm for change is essential in dealing more effectively with the innovations and changes that face modern organizations. Their work has led to the development of a Leadership Practices Inventory (Kouzes and Posner 2003) that has wide assessment use in leadership development in nursing (Tourangeau and McGilton 2004), hospital leadership (Capuano et al. 2005), dietetics (Arendt and Gregoire 2005), and information management (Lima 2006).

Values-based Leadership

The demoralizing impact of corporate scandals, layoffs due to downsizing, and stress, especially in the healthcare industry, has led to the resurgence of a focus on values and ethics in the workplace. Values are core beliefs that guide and motivate attitudes and actions and both form and express an organization's culture. Values make a difference to most people, and ethical leaders tend to promote more trust and loyalty among their employees (Sanford 2006; Verbos et al. 2007).

Role of Values

One of the significant consequences of the organization and its leaders not being perceived as highly ethical is that employees feel less loyalty and commitment and tend to leave the organization. In 2002, the national healthcare annual turnover rate averaged 19 percent (Gering and Connor 2002), and the cost of staff turnover ranged from 25 to 200 percent of annual compensation and benefits (Berk 2003; Burkholder 2003). By 2004, the turnover of allied health staff had become as high as 49 percent (Waldman et al. 2004).

Many organizations find that there are widespread conditions that mitigate employee retention. In our global marketplace, an international study of 10,000 employees in 32 nations reflected that only 34 percent are really loyal to their organizations, two-thirds do not believe their organization operates ethically, and 40 percent question their leader's personal integrity (Kidder 2000). Within the United States, "true loyalty," or the combination of high loyalty and commitment, is only 24 percent. Although two-thirds to three-quarters of employees are often proud of their work, would work above and beyond their requirements, and are highly motivated, they still consider leaving current positions. This discontent is related to questioning the fairness of pay and policy execution, as well as low recognition of achievement and insufficient job performance measures. Less than half of employees feel a sense of caring and concern for them in the organization, perceive that their judgment is trusted, or feel encouraged to be innovative (WalkerInformation 2001). Clearly, to retain talented people as well as to maintain a competitive position, organizational leadership must reestablish and promote ethical behavior and a culture of strong, consistent, and compatible values.

Many organizations believe that merely sending managers off to training will provide sufficient skill in ethical management. However, for the 75 percent of organizations that provide such training and consulting to their leadership teams at a cost of $15 billion, only about 10 percent actually translate it into behavior change (Hunter 2004). To fully effect change, managers and leaders must implement the values to be developed in an organization into their own behavior.

That ethics is increasingly a high priority and visible issue is shown by the Ethisphere 2008 report on and promotion of "The World's Most Ethical Companies." For this recognition they defined "ethical" performance as proactive engagement in the communities they serve, investment in quality and innovative sustainable business practices, and efforts made to influence and change the industry and profit fairly. In healthcare, they identified Fresenius Medical Care in Germany and Premier Healthcare in the United States. Becton Dickenson medical devices, Genzyme pharmaceuticals, and AFLAC insurance were other U.S. companies identified with notable ethical practices. Yet such awards are bittersweet, as the 2007 National Business Ethics Survey shows. The good news is that well-implemented ethics programs dramatically increase reports of misconduct, and organizations that combine strong ethical cultures with compliance reporting have the most reduction of ethics risk. The bad news is that only 25 percent of organizations have well-formed ethics and compliance programs, more than half of employees observed ethical violations during the past year, and 40 percent did not report for fear of retribution. To remedy the problem, the report encourages ethical leadership, supervisor reinforcement of practices, peer commitments to ethical practices, and such practices embedded into the culture of the organization.

Servant Leadership

The **values-based leadership** theories are similar to Burns's transformational leadership (1978), as well as other contingency theories such as path-goal leadership in which the leader's role is to empower and facilitate employee satisfaction and productivity. Prominent among values-based approaches is Robert Greenleaf's concept of servant leadership (Greenleaf 1991). Greenleaf was director of management research at AT&T for 38 years, as well as a Quaker with a strong contemplative orientation. To Greenleaf, servant leaders are those who put the needs, interests, and aspirations of others above their own. Larry Spears, CEO of the Greenleaf Center for Servant Leadership, describes it as seeking to "involve others in decision making, is strongly based in ethical and caring behavior, and it enhances the personal growth of workers while improving the caring and quality of organizational life" (Spears 1995, 142).

The values-based organization, represented by the **Servant Leadership Model**, promotes 10 essential values (Greenleaf 1991):

- *Listening* intently to clarify the will of the group as well as to hear one's own "inner voice" and seeking to discover what one's body, mind, and spirit are communicating
- *Empathize* with and understand others, assuming their good intentions, even when behaviors must be rejected
- *Healing* as a force for transformation and integration using the subtle communication of valuing the whole
- *Awareness* with courage to persist in recognizing and discussing what may be sensitive issues
- *Persuasion* rather than positional authority to build consensus and make decisions
- *Conceptualization* or vision must be balanced with daily realities
- *Foresight* requires learning lessons from the past, realities of the present, and consequences in the future using intuition
- *Stewardship* in which all stakeholders hold as their goal the greatest good for the larger society
- *Commitment* to the personal, professional, and spiritual growth of people
- *Community building* within the organization to replace what has been lost socially

Although servant leadership does not have strong evidence to support its effectiveness, its popularity has spread worldwide as well as to many of the best companies in the United States. Among the top companies are Southwest Airlines, TDIndustries, Men's Warehouse, Servicemaster, and Toro Company.

The strengths of the servant leadership concept include the following:

- It is compatible with the current surge of values and faith-based orientation in the lives of many people.
- There is anecdotal evidence of its success in prominent organizations.
- It has an intuitively desirable focus on values given a scandalous and postmodern environment.
- It contrasts serving others with the more traditional directive and hierarchical approach.

The weaknesses of the theory include the following:

- Some secular and non-faith-based settings may not be receptive to its religious overtones.
- The concepts are vaguely defined and difficult to measure.
- Its popularity exceeds its evidence.
- It may not account for all the facets of leadership.
- It is unclear how the concept works in a highly competitive or crisis environment.

Gender and Leadership

The idea of the "glass barrier" or "glass ceiling" was originally coined by Carol Hymowitz and Timothy Schellhardt in a 1986 *Wall Street Journal* article. The term refers to an unofficial barrier imposed to prevent certain groups, especially women, from progressing to higher levels of management in organizations. Since its introduction, the concept has raised awareness of the role and contribution of women and the importance of diversifying the workforce. There have been substantial increases in women's ascension into management and leadership in all fields and questions whether there are really differences between women and men's styles of management.

Women in Organizations

The role of women in organizations has changed dramatically over the decades. In 1972, women occupied only 17 percent of the supervisory and management positions in U.S. firms. In 2003, this had increased to about 40 percent. Research by the Catalyst organization showed that by 2008 women comprised about 46 percent of the total labor force, nearly 51 percent of the managerial, professional, and related occupations, and had gained nearly 15 percent of Fortune 500 Board seats (Catalyst 2008). A gender-centered perspective on leadership would propose that, through socialization, women develop a feminine leadership style that can be characterized by an emphasis on relationships through caring and nurturing, such as in collaborative projects and participatory decision making. In contrast, men develop a masculine style characterized by a focus on competition, domination, and task orientation. Early research on gender tended to support this dichotomy and that males were more often viewed as having desired leadership qualities (Megargee 1969). More recently, with the women's movement, challenges to the glass ceiling, and the increase in numbers of women entering managerial and leadership positions, there is a societal shift in gender perceptions.

It is sometimes difficult to tell how much of gender differences are due to true differences and how much are due to perceptual stereotypes. In a Pew survey of gender perceptions of political leadership during the 2008 Presidential election, there were notable differences reported. For example, on eight measures of leadership, women were perceived as surpassing males on compassion, creativity, honesty, sharing, and intelligence; being equal with them on hard work and ambition; and less endowed only on decisiveness (Pew Research 2008). More specifically, women were rated higher on working out compromises, keeping government honest, representing a broader range of constituency interests, standing up for what they believe, and dealing with social issues. Men, in contrast, were rated very high only on dealing with crime and public safety, and national security and defense. In spite of the advantage, most people (nearly 70 percent) assert that men and women are equally good leaders further attesting to the paradox in gender-related leadership.

In a perhaps less adversarial context, gender differences still exist in healthcare leadership. The American College of Healthcare Executives has conducted a survey of career attainment about every five years since 1990. Their 2006 survey showed that women executives were more likely to hold department head and other staff positions, while men continue to hold more top level executive positions (Lantz 2008). Given that woman comprise nearly 80 percent of the workforce for healthcare and are primary users of it, they are underrepresented in administration (Kirchheimer 2007). In a rating of top hospitals by Solucient in 2005, only 24 percent of the 474 top administrators were women (Dunham and Yhouse 2007).

Conflict appears to have somewhat of a mediating effect on whether male or female leaders are preferred in groups. Male leaders tend to be preferred when conflict occurs between groups, while a female leader is preferred when the conflict is within groups. It is possible that males are seen as more desirable for win-lose conflict issues between the groups, while a more relationship-centered female is viewed as useful in restoring harmony within the group that is essential to performance (Van Vugt and Spisak 2008). Their influence tactics also differ.

As gender awareness and efforts toward equity continue in business, distinctions are becoming increasingly blurred. In a study using a **360-degree inventory** assessing emotional intelligence of male and female executives, there were no significant differences in their competencies (Hopkins and Bilimoria 2008).

Gender Differences

In general, there is more evidence that there are actually few differences between men and women leaders in behavior, but that there are differences in perceptions of those behaviors (Bass and Avolio 1994; Kolb 1999). Leadership does not exist in a person but, rather, is a perceived relationship between people. The same behavior exhibited by men and women may be interpreted and labeled differently by the perceiver. This is due to gender-based stereotypes that include expectations about how gender roles should be performed.

In what has become a classic, the 1987 *Price-Waterhouse v. Hopkins* case reflected the prominent role of gender stereotype. Ann Hopkins was a high-performing and rapidly rising employee who during five years had brought in more clients than other candidates for company partnership. When she was denied partnership status, she sued. Allegedly, partners at what was then Price-Waterhouse (currently PricewaterhouseCooper) perceived her direct and assertive behavior as inappropriate for what they believed should be a feminine role. They told her she was "too macho, abrasive, and overbearing" and would be more promotable if she wore jewelry and makeup and walked and talked more femininely (Price-Waterhouse 1987). Price-Waterhouse was cited for sex discrimination, and the impact of gender stereotypes on people and organizations was brought to prominence. Although there may be advantages to women's leadership styles in some organizations, in organizations with a masculine culture women may experience prejudicial evaluations (Eagly and Carly 2003).

Androgynous Leadership

When the combination of leader effectiveness and gender is questioned, the answer becomes clearer, and middle managers who were described as successful more often possessed a combination of stereotypical masculine and feminine qualities or were **androgynous leaders** (Korabik 1990). As organizations continue to be diverse in the workforce and markets and complex in applying organizational strategy, androgynous managers and leaders may have greater flexibility in style to deal with such situations. They also may be perceived by others as more balanced.

Studies of gender leadership, particularly those examining the glass ceiling, have focused on external barriers to women's emergence as leaders. Although there is evidence for this, recent studies on self-efficacy show that the expectations by the women themselves may have a functional influence on their role seeking. **Self-efficacy**, or confidence in one's personal capabilities to do a job, affects the level of aspiration of potential leaders; those with low self-efficacy do not see themselves as capable and are less likely to seek a leadership role (McCormick, Tanguma, and Lopez-Forment 2003). In contrast to this view, women who are in leadership positions and have high efficacy tend to react to and reject the gender stereotype (Hoyt 2005). Self-efficacy also is related to how long a person will persist at a difficult task, use self-encouraging thoughts, and be resilient against setbacks. High-efficacy women faced with a high-stress situation tend to perceive it as a challenge whereas low-efficacy women tend to view it as threatening (Hoyt 2002).

Check Your Understanding 21.2

Instructions: Complete the following activities on a separate piece of paper.

1. Think of a decision you might be confronted with as a supervisor at work. Use the Vroom-Yetton decision tree to trace how you might choose whether to make the decision yourself, consult with others, or delegate the decision making to someone else.
2. Describe how your approach to leading people should change as they move through the stages of worker maturity. Explain what might happen if your style mismatches what they need at these stages.
3. Make two columns of leadership behaviors related to stereotypes of male and female roles. Make a third column in which you blend the two into an androgynous role. What are the advantages of this intermediate role over the other two?

The Learning Organization: Understanding and Participating in Change

When Peter Senge published *The Fifth Discipline: The Art and Practice of the Learning Organization* (1990), it was likely that not many people expected his ideas to influence management thinking as much as they have. As with Taylor's theory, the marketplace was ready for, and receptive to, new ways of thinking about increasingly complex organizations and how they could adapt to equally complex competitive environments.

Systems Theory

When introduced in the 1940s by von Bertalanffy and others, **systems theory** was a reaction against **reductionism** in which complex processes were reduced to their constituent elements and analyzed by their parts. Proponents of systems theory believe that important information is lost by too specific a focus and thus emphasize the interconnections, organization, and wholeness of these constituents rather than their inspection in isolation. In management, systems decisions implemented in good faith and with planning may have an adverse ripple effect in other parts of the organization or in relationship to the external environment.

The learning organization was an idea with a good fit for the questions that managers were asking: How do we adjust to all the changes in the marketplace (Argyris and Schon 1996; Senge 1990)? Systems theory's answer was learning. All **systems** (individual, team, organizational) adapt to a changing environment by learning. The more rapidly they learn, the faster they can take a stronger competitive position. This has led Robert Weiler, CEO of GIGA Information Group, to paraphrase the Darwinian principle: "It's not the strongest that survive, it's those most responsive and adaptive to change" (Pratt 2000). Arie de Geus (1997), a retired Royal Dutch/Shell Group executive who wrote *The Living Company,* takes an even stronger stance comparing organizations to living organisms that must adapt and evolve in competitive environments.

Proponents of systems theory suggest that organizational learning best takes place when a culture is formed that supports it. Such a culture is often described as emphasizing openness and communication, inquiry and feedback, adequate time for tasks, and mutual respect and support. This kind of organization also employs reflective learning in which people are alert to their experiences, consider what they reflect about the organization, and explore ways of improving performance. The Japanese push for quality has derived an interesting term, *Kaizen,* or "continuous improvement," to describe the importance of people in the learning organization. Like a *tsunami,* if each person learns from experience and applies something new each day of work, by the end of a year the organization has a "tidal wave" of small innovations that make a great difference.

Systems Thinking Skills

Contributing to the development of the learning organization are the disciplines or systems thinking skills identified by Senge (1990):

- *Personal mastery* refers to the lifelong discipline of continually clarifying personal values and vision, creativity, commitment, and intuition.
- *Mental models* are the conceptual maps we make of how things operate. They are representations based on our assumptions and beliefs that can limit our understanding of possibilities.
- *Building shared vision* emphasizes the consensual formulation of a compelling image of what the future or other goal might be.
- *Team learning* refers to the process of the team learning from its own experience that contributes to improving its performance.
- *Systems thinking* involves a way of thinking that considers the relationships among events, cycles and patterns of behavior, and awareness that everything is connected to everything else to some degree.

Consequences of Decisions

When managers do not consider the ripple effect of decisions throughout the organization, they can eventually face unexpected consequences that have adverse effects. For example, a mental health center had been losing staff due to stress, low morale, and overwork as well as having fewer billable contact hours. The center decided to involve staff in more administrative planning to increase their sense of involvement and buy-in. As a result of the mandatory involvement, staff members had even less time for clients, more conflict with administration, and fewer billable hours. As a result, even more staff left because of the unexpected pressures of seeing the larger administrative problem. In another example, lawmakers recognized the growing problem of an aging population and eagerly approved the concept of home healthcare. The intention was to make visits to ill persons in their homes and thereby save large costs to insurance companies, Medicare, and the patients themselves. Instead of saving money, however, many healthcare facilities came to rely on the services as a strong source of revenue and therefore encouraged more service. In 1998, the average home healthcare patient received about 80 visits a year, nearly four times as many as 10 years earlier (Daft 2000). However, by 1997, the Balanced Budget Act had begun mandating changes in reimbursement for home healthcare. This restriction of payment was found to have a direct effect on the number of visits (Long 2006). Many states now have limitations on the number of visits, with many limiting to 40 visits.

As organizations grow, expand their involvement with other organizations, and develop more complicated information systems in a continually changing and competitive environment, they will need to find better ways to respond. Efforts have been made to model some of these complex environments using systems theory. Simulation software such as PowerSim and Vensim can help managers create representations of various processes such as patient flows in order to identify bottlenecks, critical points, and intervention points. Figure 21.10 is a stock-and-flow diagram showing the management of psychiatric patients. Although these programs require much training, they exemplify the direction in which systems thinking is going with regard to management. Such modeling will eventually enable managers to explore how various innovations may affect their organizations.

Diffusion of Innovations

Innovations have occurred throughout history, but little attention was given to exactly how they were adopted until Rogers and Shoemaker (1971) clarified the process in their book, *Communication of Innovations.* Although Rogers and Shoemaker were not the first to develop ideas about diffusion, their presentation of the adopter categories or stakeholders and the **diffusion S-curve** came at a time when businesses were eager to understand consumers.

Categories of Adopter Groups

Viewing the organization in much the same way that marketers view market segments, Rogers and Shoemaker identified five **adopter groups** of an innovation that generally fits the normal curve (figure 21.11):

- **Innovators:** This venturesome group comprises about 2.5 percent of the organization and individuals who are eager to try new ideas. These individuals tend to be more cosmopolitan, to seek out new information in broad networks, and to be willing to take risks.
- **Early adopters:** This respectable group accounts for about 13.5 percent of the organization. The individuals in this group have a high degree of opinion leadership. They are more localized than cosmopolitan and often look to the innovators for advice and information. These are the leaders and respected role models in the organization, and their adoption of an idea or practice does much to initiate change.
- **Early majority:** This group comprises about 34 percent of the organization. Although usually not leaders, the individuals in this group represent the backbone of the organization, are deliberate in thinking and acceptance of an idea, and serve as a natural bridge between early and late adopters.
- **Late majority:** This skeptical group comprises another 34 percent of the organization. The individuals in this group usually adopt innovations only after social or financial pressure to do so.
- **Laggards:** The traditional members of this group are usually the last ones to respond to innovation and make

up as much as 16 percent of the organization. The laggards are often characterized as isolated, uninformed, and mistrustful of change and change agents, but they may serve a function by keeping the organization from changing too quickly.

When planning a change, each of these groups should be considered as a market segment whose needs must be responded to by leaders. In general, people who are more receptive to innovation are better educated and more literate and have stronger aspirations. In addition, they have higher socioeconomic status, occupational prestige, more income, and social mobility. Moreover, they are better socially networked, cosmopolitan, diverse in interests, and well integrated into the organization and the community (Rogers 1995).

Figure 21.10. A stock-and-flow diagram showing the management of psychiatric patients

Waiting Time
Admission Rate
Waiting List
Capacity Utilization
New Cases
Hospitalized Patients
Hospital Capacity
Recycling Patients
Discharge Rate
Treatment Duration
Medical Opinion
Fraction Recycling

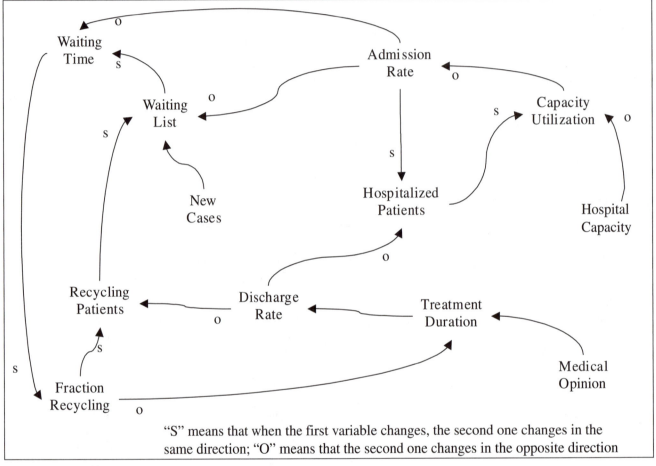

"S" means that when the first variable changes, the second one changes in the same direction; "O" means that the second one changes in the opposite direction

Source: Dangerfield 1999.

Figure 21.11. Characteristics of innovation stakeholders

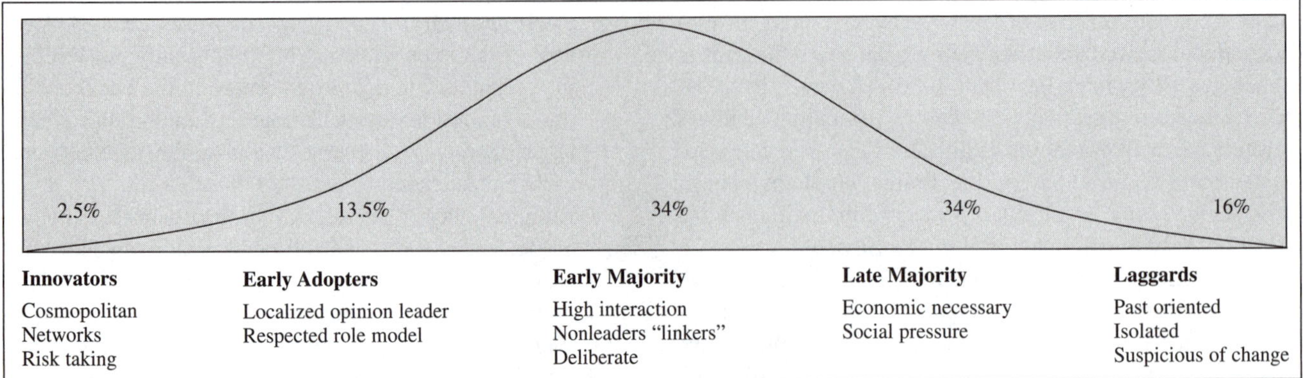

Diffusion Curve

Each of the adopter categories engages innovation at a different time and a different acceptance rate, as shown by the diffusion S curve. (See figure 21.12.) Note that during the early stages of diffusion, there is a shorter period between becoming aware of an innovation and adopting it. Over time, each adopter category becomes aware of the innovation but increasingly takes longer periods to adopt it, which can affect how well an innovation is introduced into the marketplace or how fully it is practiced in the organization. In addition, how quickly an innovation is accepted is based on a number of factors, including whether it offers an advantage relative to its alternative, its compatibility with the potential adopters' values and lifestyles, how easy it is to understand and use, the degree to with which it can be experimented, and the degree to which the results are visible to others (Rogers 1995). These diffusion patterns are relatively consistent for a variety of healthcare innovations, including healthcare technology (Cohen and Hanft 2004), coding technology (Fenton and Gamm 2008), and health students' intention to use online courses (Tung and Chang 2008).

Innovator Roles

In the late 1960s and early 1970s, the literature reflected a new interest in the roles of innovators within organizations who become gatekeepers or nodes for the flow of information (Allen and Cohen 1969). Four roles have been identified for the successful implementation of an innovation (Daft and Marcic 1998; Roberts 2007):

- **Inventor** (innovator): The individual who develops a new idea or practice in the organization. However, it is not sufficient to merely originate and understand the new idea. Rather, the idea must be facilitated by several other roles in the organization before it is adopted or brought to market (Daft 2000).
- **Champion:** Someone in the organization who believes in the idea, acknowledges the practical problems of financing and political support, and assists in overcoming barriers.
- **Sponsor:** Usually a high-level manager who approves and protects the idea, expedites testing and approval, and removes barriers within the organization.
- **Critic:** A crucial but sometimes overlooked role. This role is essential in challenging the innovation for shortcomings, presenting strong criteria, and, in essence, providing a reality test for the new idea.

In an innovative environment, all of these roles are important and good examples of how role responsibilities are distributed in an organization.

Management Fads, Fashions, and Trends

Innovations are not limited to products and services; they also extend to management theories and practices themselves. The competitive nature of most industries, including healthcare, as well as the need to use resources wisely, has led to a rich development of management techniques and practices. Although many of these are based on successful limited applications, they are too often quickly promoted beyond their evidentiary base and followed enthusiastically by a group. They become fads when they rise and fall quickly, fashionable when they rise quickly and fall slowly, and trends when they persist over a longer time (Aldag 1997). (See figure 21.13.)

Fads tend to proliferate during periods of uncertainty, when organizations search for innovative ways to fill what is perceived as a performance gap and to gain competitive advantage. Additional influence to adopt fads is often from popular management consultants and the popular media (who in turn are competing to sell their ideas) who speak to people's naive fascination with novelty. Many common practices have been considered as fads at some time in their emergence,

Figure 21.12. Diffusion S-curve

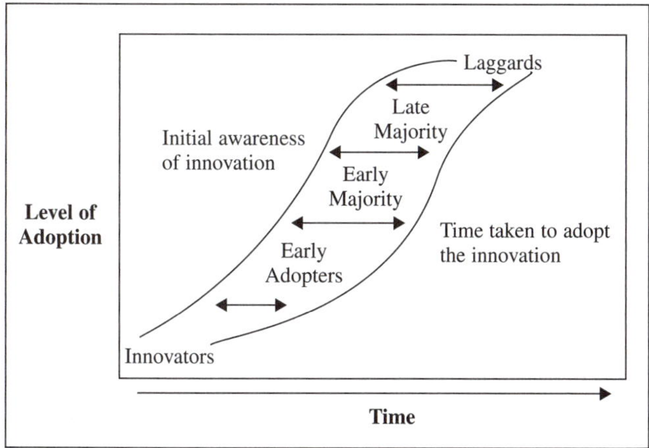

Figure 21.13. Fad, fashion, and trend curves

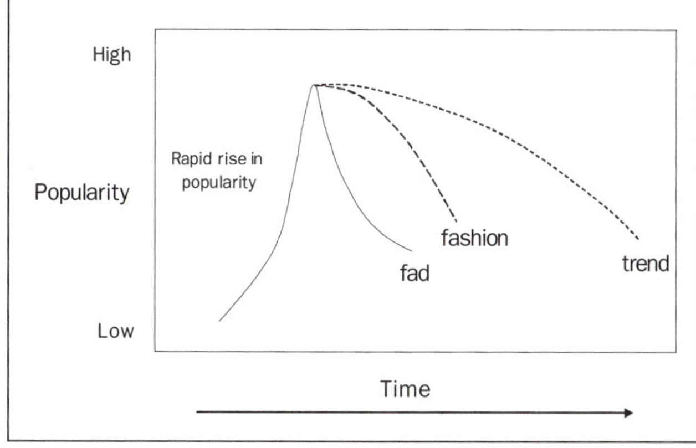

Source: Wasson 1978.

such as total quality management, managing by objectives, zero-based budgeting, managing by walking around, decentralizing, downsizing, and so on. Figure 21.14 shows the rise and fall of management practices based on their frequency of citation in Business Source Premier (a database of 4,600 journals) from 1950 to 2004.

Since 1993, Bain and Company has been frequently surveying senior executives from organizations around the world. The 11th of their surveys continues to show that the typical company uses 10 of the top 25 popular management "tools." Some of these tools persist and have found consistent value for organizations such as strategic planning, customer relationship management, and customer market segmentation. However, average satisfaction with tools in general has dropped slightly, as well as with some tools, such as corporate blogs, loyalty management tools, and shared service centers. Nearly three-quarters of the executives surveyed believed that they should be on the cutting edge of innovative techniques, but 81 percent also believed that the tools promised more than they actually delivered (Rigby and Bilodeau 2007). Despite the mixed evidence to support them, it appears that fads will continue to be a part of organizational strategies for improvement efforts.

The Problem with Fads

The major problem with fads is that they present the illusion of easy implementation, singular changes, and a quick fix to organizational problems. In practice, most significant changes require years. For example, shifting from traditional structures to team-based organizations has been estimated to take three to five years (Armstrong n.d.), and implementation of the balanced scorecard typically requires the same duration (Kaplan 2002). It took Motorola, the originator of the Six Sigma approach, 10 years to fully implement the concept. Such changes are clearly not a quick fix.

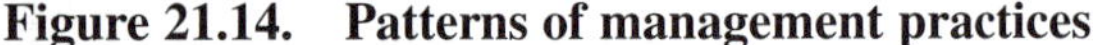

Figure 21.14. Patterns of management practices

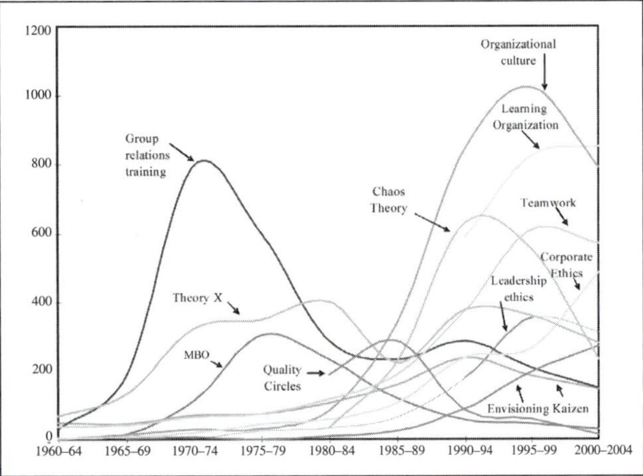

Source: Adapted from Business Source Premier 2004.

The fad management tool is often viewed as a singular fix to be implemented that has direct action on a problem. Such simplistic thinking ignores the complex systems that are modern healthcare facilities and communities. As system thinking suggests, an intervention often produces unexpected outcomes or "revenge effects" in which the intended solution becomes more of a problem than the problem it was designed to solve (Berringer 2004).

The overuse of fads can adversely affect employees who tend to become discouraged by unrealistic expectations, revised work procedures, and wasted resources (Birnbaum 2000; Byrne 1997). The initial enthusiasm fails to produce the expected results; in other cases, management support is lacking. As a result, even when good practices are initiated, many employees consider them just the next fad and fail to commit to them.

The enthusiasm with which fads are received appears to wax and wane over time, comprising what is typified as a fad life cycle. The steps of the fad life cycle are:

1. Some deficiency is perceived that requires a solution.
2. A management technique or theory is discovered that appears to solve the problem.
3. The euphoria of the fad's supporters leads to promotion within the organization.
4. Extension of the fad beyond its sound application ensures its eventual failure.
5. Derision and lowering of regard for the innovation begins to pervade the organization.
6. The fad is abandoned and may be replaced by a search for another solution (Chaulk and Sexty 2002).

The Failure of "Excellence"

Despite the wide popularity of Peters and Waterman's *In Search of Excellence,* the fad nature of the promotion became obvious after only a few years. Of the 43 companies they profiled, only a third remained in the top position. (See figure 21.15.) In a 2001 interview with *Fast Company* magazine, Peters admitted that he had no idea what he was doing when he wrote the book, he identified the eight principles only under pressure of a pending presentation (not after thoughtful consideration and data analysis), and he selected many companies on a much less-than-rigorous basis (Peters 2001). Nonetheless, the book was a useful turning point for many managers who started paying more attention to the human element in their organizations.

Fad management probably fails for four reasons. First, executive leadership for, and commitment to, the initiative lags and mid-level managers carry the burden for implementation. Second, there is a failure to deploy the innovation. There are no mechanisms to maintain the innovation, spread it beyond the pilot group trying it, or training beyond the introduction. Third, management seeks shortcuts and easy, superficial applications rather than try to understand in-depth

Figure 21.15. 43 "excellent" companies five years later

Excellent	Still Performing but Weakened Leadership	Weakened Position	Troubled Position
Rockwell	Bristol-Myers	Amdahl	Atari
Disney	Delta	Bechtel	Chesebrough-Ponds
Boeing	Dow	Caterpillar	Avon
DEC	Dupont	Dana	DataGeneral
Emerson	Hughes (GM)	Hewlett-Packard	Fluor
Frito-Lay	LeviStraus	Kodak	Kmart
IBM	Marriott	Raychem	National Semiconductor
Intel	Proctor & Gamble	Schlumburger	Revlon
Johnson & Johnson	Standard Oil	Texas Instruments	
Mars	Amoco	Tupperware (Dart)	
Maytag	3M	Wang	
McDonalds			
Merck			
Wal-Mart			

Source: Adapted from Peters 2001.

how the organization must customize the process. Fourth, proper metrics or measurements are not used as feedback to gauge progress and success, and thereby help revisions (Marash et al. 2003).

Not everyone agrees that management fads are a bad thing. Robert Cole of the University of California Haas School of Business has argued that adaptable companies learn how to use fads to improve quality and productivity (Cole 1999). Fads can motivate employees and bring attention to important organizational processes for revision. Exemplifying this is the American response to the Japanese Aquality challenge of the early 1980s. America was unprepared for the high market demand for high-quality goods, and the competition spurred U.S. businesses to focus more on quality.

From the end of World War II to the mid-1980s, management often held the belief that bigger is better and growth is good. By the end of the 1980s, productivity was declining, managerial overhead was increasing, and organizations were more seriously considering smaller size and efficiency (Tomasco 1987). Downsizing was popularly embraced as a way of reducing labor costs and improving performance, and nearly all the Fortune 1000 firms have utilized it. Reaching such faddish proportions, unfortunately downsizing has rarely delivered on its promise. In healthcare, downsizing has also been used to contain costs, but sometimes with unexpected consequences. For example, it has been proposed that the economic benefits of downsizing have been off set by the risks of being understaffed. In particular, the increase in methicillin resistant staphylococcus aureus infection has been related to overworked staff taking less time for hand washing (Napoli 2008).

Thinking Critically about New Approaches

New approaches should not be dismissed out of hand but, rather, should be thoughtfully examined for their utility in an organization or incorporation into a manager or leader's style. Several questions should be considered:

- What is the source of the new idea or practice? Does it come from a source that can be generalized to other settings?
- What is the evidence that it works?
- Can clear linkages between the practice and specific outcomes be measured?
- What does the level of enthusiasm or desperation about the fad suggest about the organization and what it really needs?
- What is needed to really implement the practice? It is rarely as simple or singular as the fad implies.

Change Management

A more global role for practitioners of organizational change is often referred to as the change agent. The **change agent** is a specialist in organizational development and facilitates the change brought about by the innovation. He or she may be internal or external to the organization, as in the case of a consultant specifically hired to assist with the change. **Organization development** (OD) is the process in which an organization reflects on its own processes and consequently revises them for improved performance. Beckhard has provided a widely accepted definition of OD: "Organization Development is an effort planned, organization-wide, and managed from the top, to increase organization effectiveness and health through planned interventions in the organization's processes, using behavioral-science knowledge" (1969, 9).

OD Consultant Functions

Blake and Mouton (1976) suggested that OD consultants might perform a range of five functions with management:

- *Acceptant function* uses counseling skills to help the manager sort out emotions to gain a more objective perspective of the organization
- *Catalytic function* helps collect and interpret data about the organization
- *Confrontation function* challenges the manager's thinking processes and assumptions
- *Prescriptive function* tells the manager what to do to correct a given situation
- *Theory and principle function* involves helping the client system internalize alternate explanations of what is occurring in the organization

Internal and External Change Agents

Change happens on its own but is usually most desirable when intentionally directed toward the benefit of the organization and its members. The role of the change agent is to facilitate this change process by utilizing reflective learning: drawing attention to important processes, helping people understand what the processes mean, and considering and implementing plans of action. Exactly who performs this role can be critical (Westcott 2005; Weick and Quinn 1995). There are advantages and disadvantages to using change agents from within the organization as well as from outside the organization. (See table 21.2.)

Advantages and Disadvantages of Using Internal Change Agents

Internal change agents have the clear advantage of being familiar with the organization, its history, subtle dynamics, secrets, and resources. Such people are often well respected, securely positioned, and have the strong interpersonal relationships to foster change. Moreover, there is an advantage to recognizing the internal expertise of employees, maintaining confidentiality of the process, and using people who are invested in the success of the outcome.

Yet, the strengths of internal change agents can be weaknesses. Coming from the inside, however reputable they are, their previous relationships with others in the organization could lead to accusations of bias. As a product of the organizational culture, internal change agents may be as blind to certain problems as those they seek to facilitate. Another disadvantage is that they are taken away from their regular duties to conduct the facilitation or perhaps become overextended in trying to handle both responsibilities. Finally, internal change agents may be subject to pressures and sanctions regarding the outcome whereas an external change agent would have no such obligations.

Advantages and Disadvantages of Using External Change Agents

The external change agent has the advantage of providing a fresh, outside view as well as having the knowledge base to compare performance across organizations. Not having direct connections to the organization, he or she usually feels more comfortable challenging norms and culture, questioning unusual or unfair practices, and generally noting events that others may be reluctant to comment on. Being from the outside, he or she may be seen as having new skills and being more objective, or at least less biased than an internal agent.

Table 21.2. Advantages and disadvantages of internal and external change agents

	Internal Change Agent	External Change Agent
Advantages	1. Knows the environment, culture, people, issues and hidden agendas 2. Develops and keeps expertise and resources internal 3. Creates and maintains norms of organization renewal from within 4. Provides higher security and confidentiality 5. May have trust and respect of others 6. Has strong personal investment in success	1. Provides fresh, outside, objective perspective 2. Willing to assert, challenge, and question norms 3. May have more legitimacy to insiders by not taking sides 4. Brings skills and techniques not available from within organization 5. Brings diverse organizational experiences to bear; benchmark comparisons
Disadvantages	1. May be biased; has already taken sides, or may be disliked or mistrusted by some stakeholders 2. Previous relationships may contribute to subgrouping or fragmentation 3. Takes CA away from other duties 4. May be enculturated and is "part of the problem" or does not see it 5. Is subject to organizational sanctions and pressures as an employee	1. May or may not be available when needed by the organization; may split time and commitments with other clients. 2. High expense 3. Takes time to become familiar with the system 4. May create codependency or may abandon the system.

Source: Weick and Quinn 1995.

The weaknesses of the external agents include not having a history with their client organization that could enhance their awareness of important dynamics. Becoming familiar with the organization takes time, and during a crisis they may move too quickly to conclusions based on limited information. Additionally, external change agents may be strongly influenced by the viewpoint of the administrators who contracted with them. External change agents must thoroughly evaluate the relevant people and processes of the organization. Moreover, external agents can be expensive, charging tens to hundreds of thousands of dollars for their consultation. For example, in one hospital system, a consulting group contracted over four years to implement a balanced scorecard system for the fee of about $2.3 million. Finally, a highly charismatic, directive, and successful agent could foster dependency with a client organization, leaving the organization reluctant to learn to manage its own change processes.

Internal versus External Change Agents

When an organization plans to use internal or external change agents, it should consider several questions, including:

- How confidential and proprietary is the information involved? Would either type of agent present a disclosure risk?
- Are there conflicts of interest? Is the external agent working with any competitor or internal agent loyal to conflicting parties?
- What level of commitment and availability is required? What is the potential effect of an external agent with many other clients or an internal agent with other work obligations?
- What skills are required for a successful change effort? What constellation of experience and skills do the external and internal agents offer?
- How important is it that stakeholders view the agent as being objective, fair, and neutral? Which type of agent would best be viewed this way? Explain your answer.
- To what extent does the culture of the organization require changing? Which type of agent is better positioned to influence the change?

Stages of OD

The work of change agents is captured in the seven stages of OD (Kolb and Frohman 1970):

1. *Scouting stage:* The change agent inquires and observes to determine how receptive the organization is, where the leverage points for change are located, and what the fit is between his or her skills and the system's requirements.
2. *Entry and contracting stage:* The working relationship between the change agent and key organizational members is built, expectations are set, roles are clarified, credibility is established, and resources and constraints are identified.
3. *Diagnosis, or data-gathering and feedback, stage:* This stage is one of the central features of OD. Rather than using the so-called medical model in which an expert makes the diagnosis and delivers it to the patient, the OD practitioner obtains data from the organization and involves the organization in interpreting the data and considering their implications.
4. *Planning stage:* The system moves toward a conclusion about the information. Responsibility is shifted from the change agent to the organization, which commits to the change and often formulates policy regarding it.
5. *Implementation stage:* The plan is carried out as designed and agreed to, with the change agent available for further consultation as needed.
6. *Evaluation stage:* This stage involves selecting appropriate measurements, monitoring the change process and its outcomes, and keeping people informed.
7. *Termination stage:* The change agent meets with key organizational members to review the change process, to determine what and how they have learned from the experience, and to end the consulting relationship.

Methods of OD

OD methods are quite varied and have grown out of extensive research and innovation in the behavioral sciences. Cummings and Huse (1989) identified more than 20 different techniques that practitioners use to promote change, and new ones are emerging regularly. Popular examples are discussed in the subsections that follow.

Survey Feedback

Survey feedback is widely used, especially during the diagnostic stage when questionnaires are used to identify attitudes and values about aspects of the change process. The results of the survey are presented to decision makers as feedback, with the intention that any discrepancies between what they believe and what is actually occurring in the organization will prompt corrective action. As with most OD techniques, the discussion is usually more important than the actual data, since it enables participants to engage each other, learn more about each others working styles, and build cohesion as a team.

Team Building

Team building involves identifying performance goals and then building cohesion by involving members in activities that enhance acquaintance, resolve conflicts, build healthy group norms, and build skills in reflecting on team processes to continue performance improvement. Team building activities can be as diverse as group "games" such as the "desert survival game," or highly sophisticated business simulations of real-world problems. What they have in common is an activity that enables participants to reflect on team dynamics.

Appreciative Inquiry

Appreciative inquiry is based on the belief that whatever is needed in organizational renewal already exists somewhere in the organization. It is a solution-oriented approach that seeks to identify where the change already works and how it can be amplified and transferred elsewhere in the organization.

Learning History

Learning history is the extensive and relatively long-term process of eliciting stories, experiences, and critical events in the life of the organization and its employees. These are collated into themes that reflect the values and processes of the organization that can be discussed by organization members. (See figure 21.16.). While powerful, this technique is time-consuming, involves many (if not all) members of the organization at some time, and can take them away from other tasks or require overtime or retreat scheduling.

Organizational Lifeline

Organizational lifeline is a graphic time line with annual demarcations that show important events in the life of the organization over the years. It can be used to assist new employees in understanding how the organization has arrived at where it is and to identify issues and change themes that are recurrent. This is one of the briefest of the preceding techniques and can be conducted in a single meeting as members identify significant events and reflect on how these have shaped organizational culture.

Stages of Change

People and organizations move through stages of change, and as they do, they have different needs and require different skills from the leader.

Lewin's Stages of Change

One of the first models of change was proposed by Kurt Lewin (1951), one of the early behavioral scientists who contributed to the knowledge base of information on group work, leadership, and organization development.

Lewin's model, or **Lewin's stages of change**, identified the initial stage of change as **unfreezing** the status quo, often by presenting the discrepancies between the status quo and the desired goals. Unfreezing often creates a state of cognitive dissonance, which is an uncomfortable awareness of two incompatible perceptions or beliefs, in this case, the discrepancy.

This motivates the person to resolve the dissonance, usually by changing the situation to make the perceptions congruent. This step marks the second stage of change or moving to the new desired state for the organization.

In the final stage of **refreezing**, the new behaviors are reinforced to become as stable and institutionalized as the previous status quo was. Lewin originally conceptualized this three-stage process as one in which the organization would plateau and stabilize for a time before the next change was required. More recent beliefs about organizational change characterize the change process as continuous with little respite for workers, managers, or leaders. The status quo has become one of dealing with continual change, which can be stressful as people learn to let go of past practices and make efforts to learning new ones.

Stages of Grieving

Elizabeth Kubler-Ross (1969) examined the stress of change in her classic study of the **stages of grief** experienced by terminally ill patients and their families. Change in the healthcare

Figure 21.16. Learning history

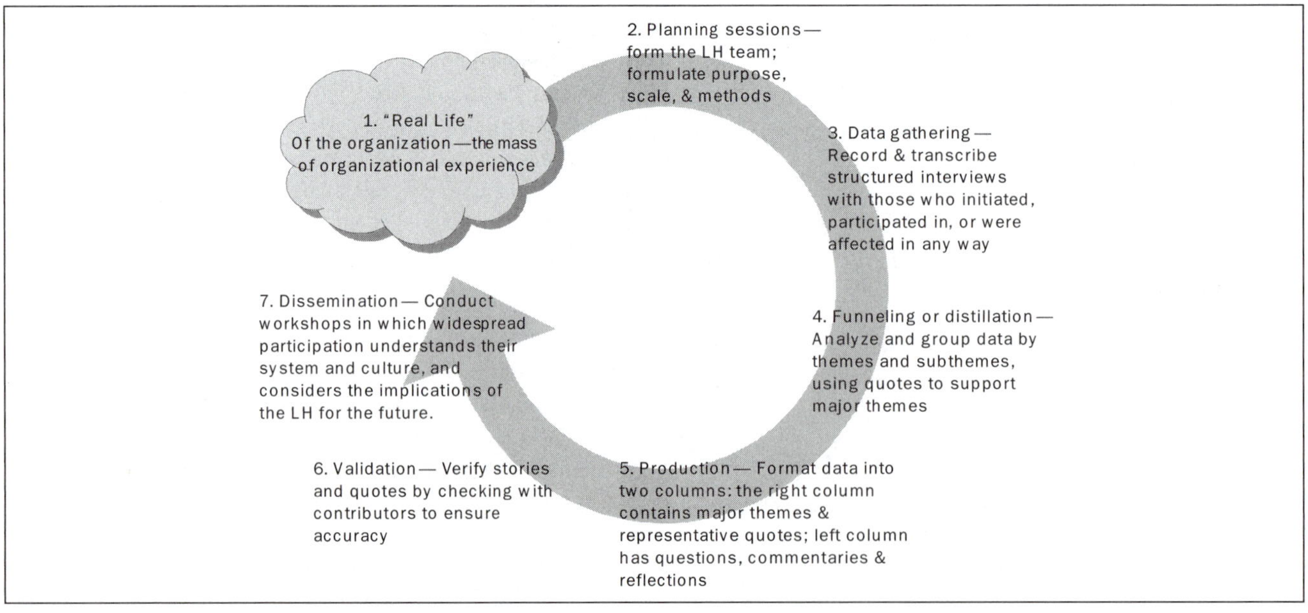

Source: Adapted from Cummings and Huse 1989.

system often involves mergers, acquisitions, downsizing, and other transitions that usually involve losses and grief. Her five-stage model has become useful in anticipating and working with people in a dramatic transition (Rogers 2000). The five stages of her model are (figure 21.17):

1. *Shock and denial:* Workers have difficulty believing the proposed transition. They may deny that change is imminent and go about business as usual rather than prepare for the adjustment. News of the change also may stun workers to the extent that they cannot concentrate or work efficiently, and they may isolate themselves.
2. *Anger:* Workers begin to understand the inevitability of the change. They may direct their resentment at the organization or the managers for allowing it to happen. In addition, they may engage in unproductive complaining, organize resistance, or even sabotage operations in attempts to reduce the threat.
3. *Bargaining:* Workers make a final attempt to avoid the change. They may actually try to bargain with managers to delay the change or work intensively to prove their value and reduce the risk of loss.
4. *Depression:* Workers may lose their self-esteem and be unresponsive to encouragement.
5. *Acceptance:* Workers begin to redirect their energy toward the new organization.

Resistance to Change

Kurt Lewin is credited with saying, "If you wish to understand something, try changing it." What he was referring to was the observation that when one attempts to change a system, the mechanisms that maintain it spring to its defense. Change does not come easily to most people, and in organizations, "resistance to change is experienced at almost every step" (DeWine 1994, 281). The first step for leaders who are trying to reduce resistance to change is to understand its source.

Resistance to change occurs for a number of reasons, including self-interest and anxiety about the unknown, different perceptions, suspiciousness, and conservatism. When confronted with change, the first thing most workers want to know is how it will affect them and their jobs. Because the turbulence of the marketplace makes many changes uncertain, workers may not receive satisfactory answers to their questions. Those who have attained expertise and status from their positions now may face new job descriptions or expanded or new duties. For example, many managers in downsized organizations have been reassigned as coaches to newly formed teams. This new role raises questions about their authority, status, and responsibility.

Other workers may resist change simply because they perceive the situation differently and believe the proposed change is unjustified. The result of ongoing change is to make many people uneasy about, and even mistrustful of, any innovation. Some people view all change as just another fad based on the whim of management rather than a survival strategy for the organization. And finally, some people are very conservative in their beliefs, are isolated in their social networks and information, and dislike the inconvenience of change.

Resistance can distract workers from their tasks, preoccupy them with gossiping, and contribute to stress and workplace violence. To confident change leaders, indications of resistance can be viewed as useful information about what stakeholders need before the transition can continue.

Figure 21.17. Kubler-Ross's stages of grief

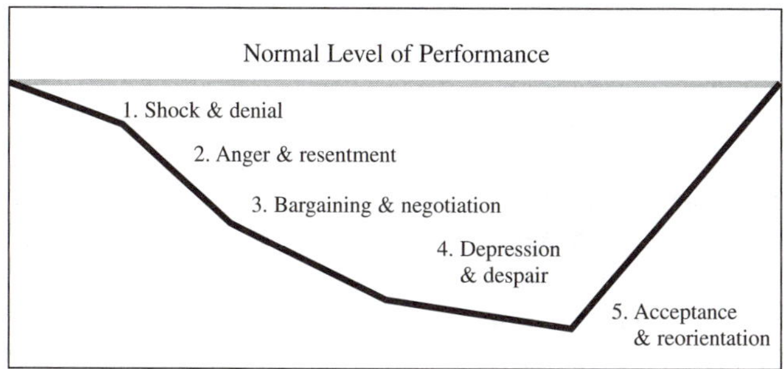

Source: Adapted fromKubler-Ross 1969.

Facilitation of Change

The purpose of transition management is to make the potential upheaval and chaos posed by planned changes less disruptive to the people and processes of healthcare. It might be helpful to think of a transition as a series of stages through which people move as they adjust to changes. Each stage has its own set of challenges and tasks to master, the successful completion of which forms the foundation for moving on to the next stage. The role of managers and leaders is to facilitate the movement from stage to stage.

Bridges's Stages of Facilitation

In recognition of the stresses that change imposes on the organization's employees, Bridges (2004) extended Lewin's three-stage model with recommendations for transition management to ease the struggle. The stages of his model are as follows:

1. The transition process begins with the recognition that the old way of doing things is **ending**. Workers begin to anticipate and experience losses with resulting grief, blame, shock, and fear. They need help in letting go of the way things were. The organization can facilitate the transition by providing reasons for the ending and by indicating what will not change. It is usually best to overcommunicate to ensure that everyone has

sufficient information about ongoing developments. Acknowledging losses and accepting grieving also can assist people in the ending stage.

2. The second stage, the **neutral zone**, begins when the old system has been left behind, but the new one has not yet been fully accepted. This stage fosters anxiety, uncertainty, and confusion. The organization can facilitate the transition by providing support, encouragement, reassurance, and protection. The employees need to know where they are and where they are going. One creative approach to gaining acceptance of the transition is to have employees generate innovative ideas about how they can move toward the new organization.
3. In the third stage, **new beginnings**, people accept, orient themselves, and engage in the new organization. New goals are created to provide direction, and the workers' relationships with the organization and their jobs are reinvented and integrated. Attitudes and behaviors that support the new beginning are supported by workers and role-modeled by leaders. Retraining, performance feedback, and recognition of new behavior serve to reinforce the transition.

Importance of Reflection

Reflection is the process of examining one's experience. It is an essential skill for developing leadership skills and an important component of team and organization development. However, reflection alone is not sufficient for changing behavior. Reflection involves awareness. Reflective learning, on the other hand, uses awareness to formulate an interpretation of what has been observed, considers what difference can be made by applying what has been learned, and executes the efforts toward change through deliberate action.

Several remarkably similar models of the **reflective learning cycle** have been developed over the years, including those by John Dewey (1938), David Kolb (1970), W. Edwards Deming (1986), and Donald Schon (1983). These models share the following four stages in common (figure 21.18):

Figure 21.18. Reflective learning process

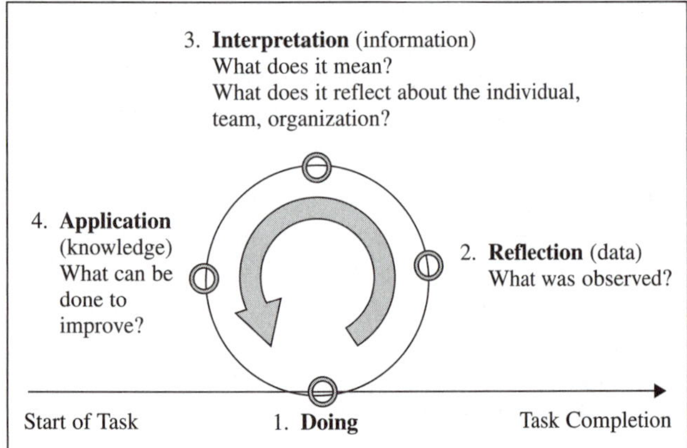

1. *Doing:* At this stage, people are concentrating and working directly on a task. Although most people reflect on a task after it is accomplished, this is often too late to make midcourse or more frequent changes. The reflective process should be used often, although too much reflection sometimes is used to avoid task completion.
2. *Reflection:* At this stage, the task is paused and the individual or team members reflect on how they have been working. What do they notice? The raw data become information as reflection progresses to the interpretation stage.
3. *Interpretation:* At this stage, one considers what the information means, what it reflects about the work process, and how various observations might be related.
4. *Application:* The application stage follows as information becomes knowledge and is applied to the work by doing something differently. Finally, the new knowledge is used to return to the action stage.

As the marketplace continues to change, organizations will have to adapt in order to maintain their competitive advantage. Organizational leaders play a key role in helping employees to reduce their resistance to change and to inspire and motivate them to accept it. By understanding leadership theories and the stages and techniques of planned change, and by using the reflective learning cycle, managers will be better prepared to meet the challenge.

Check Your Understanding 21.3

Instructions: Answer the following questions on a separate piece of paper.

1. If you were an OD consultant, what would you tell an executive team about a pending reorganization? What should the executive team expect?
2. If you were informed that your job was being eliminated due to reorganization, but that you could reapply for a new position, how would you react? What would you need to cope with the stress?
3. Make a list of reasons that people resist change. For each reason, suggest a way to reduce resistance.
4. Use the reflective learning process to examine a group meeting. What did you notice? What do you think your observations reflected about the group processes? What might you do differently to improve the next meeting?

Real-World Case

Several reports in recent years from the Institute of Medicine (IOM) have highlighted the need for new initiatives to improve patient safety, quality of care, and enhanced efficiency of the process of caring for patients. Specifically, the IOM recommended that new strategies be developed for educating health professionals. Supporting this, a survey of healthcare organizations in Minnesota revealed that three-quarters of respondents believed that having competence in using health information technologies would be "very to extremely important" for healthcare professionals by 2007–2012, and 70 percent had plans to implement computer-based documentation by 2007. Driven by these needs, the College of St. Scholastica in Duluth, Minnesota, proposed the Advancing Technology and Healthcare Education Now at St. Scholastica (ATHENS) initiative. The challenge is to provide students in health information management, nursing, physical therapy, occupational therapy, exercise physiology, and social work with the education necessary to competently use computer-based health information software applications and apply these tools to enhance their respective professions.

There is growing evidence that poor communication among professionals in different disciplines is a common source of medical errors. The new health professions' curriculum evolving from the ATHENS initiative will enable students to collaborate across disciplines using the electronic health record as a real-time, shared communication medium. Students will use software applications that are embedded with decision rules and alerts and evidence-based practice references, enabling more efficient and accurate clinical documentation, care planning, and results reporting, and creating a clinical data repository that integrates patient/client data from all sources for shared problem solving and decision making. This kind of professional development effort will reduce the communication barriers and challenges to transition management currently faced by most healthcare facilities (Athens Project 2005).

Summary

More recent theories have emphasized the complexity of modern organizations. Senge's emphasis on systems theory, for example, helps managers understand how the organization's components are connected much as a living system and that change in one component can affect other components. Such complexity also makes anticipating and planning for outcomes more challenging since long-term unexpected results can occur along with intended results. Theories of leadership have likewise become more complex over the decades, moving from the simple trait listings of the great person theory to more contingency and complex systems frameworks.

Change management requires strong leadership. Managers traditionally maintain a highly efficient workplace and establish procedures; leaders look to the future and promote change. Both solve problems and make decisions. Recurrent problems lend themselves to clear rules for programmed decisions that can be used routinely; unique, complex, or changing situations require careful thought when nonprogrammed decisions are made. Formal decision making progresses through several stages, including problem definition, problem analysis, generation of alternatives, selection of alternatives, plan implementation, and evaluation and feedback. In practice, managers more often use intuition or satisficing. Although high cohesion and strong organizational culture can be desirable, groupthink can produce riskier decisions and requires review of team norms periodically as well as implementation of countermeasures. Clear communication with consideration of all stakeholders can further reduce distortion and error.

Leadership theories provide a way to examine what is required in a situation to facilitate change through people. Classical approaches to leadership emphasized collections of traits that became unwieldy in practice. However, as society embraced democratic ideals, management began to reflect greater worker participation and involvement in decision making. Vroom and Yetton's normative model of decision making enables managers to decide when to make a decision alone and when to delegate. Studies from Ohio State University, the University of Michigan, and Blake and Mouton have enabled leadership styles to be described along a continuum of task and social dimensions. Building on the need for leaders to adjust their styles to meet the unique characteristics of each situation, more recent models have emerged, including Fiedler's leadership contingency model, work done by Hersey and Blanchard, path–goal theory, leader–member exchange, and servant leadership. Some theories appear first as fads, although even fads can increase organizational awareness of important processes. Gender continues to be an issue in many organizations, and while there are few differences in actual performance of most men and women leaders, stereotypes persist and executive positions are held more often by men than women.

Change goes through different stages in an organization, and each stage has its own group of stakeholders. Plotting actual change results in an S-shaped curve with a slow start, rapid development, and a plateau of saturation and adoption. Within the organization, innovations require the key roles of inventor, champion, sponsor, and critic. The change agent spearheads the organization's change efforts, though there are advantages and disadvantages to internal and external change agent roles.

A variety of tools and techniques for helping organizations change has been developed. Surveys, team-building activities, appreciative inquiry, and learning history are examples of structured approaches to helping organizations examine how they deal with change. Understanding the stages of change also can relieve resistance to change. The stages of change often parallel the stages of grief identified by Kubler-Ross in her classic study. Similarly, the stages of organizational change can be thought of as an end to the old ways, a neutral time of transition, and new beginnings.

References

Aldag, R. 1997 (March). Moving sofas and exhuming woodchuck. On relevance, impact and the following of fads. *Journal of Management Inquiry* 6(1):8–16.

Allen, T.J. and S.I. Cohen. 1969. Information flow in two R&D laboratories. *Administrative Science Quarterly* 14(1):12–19.

Allport, G.W. and H.S. Odbert. 1936. Trait-names: A psycho-lexical study. *Psychological Monographs* (47):171–220.

Anderson, L.R. and J. Tolson. 1989. Group members: self-monitoring as a possible neutralizer of leadership. *Small Group Research* 20(1):24–36.

Andersson, D. 1999. Avoiding the new executive failure trap. *Channel* 12(4). http://www.dom.semi.org/web/wchannel.nsf/0/6c527687b377f64b.88256792007dd5ca?OpenDocument.

Aon Consulting. 2008. 2008 Benefits and talent survey. http://insight.aon.com/?elqPURLPage=2942.

Arendt, S.W. and M.B. Gregoire. 2005. Dietetics students perceive themselves as leaders and report they demonstrate leadership in a variety of contexts. *Journal of the American Dietetic Association* 105(8):1289–1294.

Argyris, C. 1957. *Personality and Organization.* New York: Harper & Row.

Argyris, C. and D. Schon, 1996. *Organizational Learning II: Theory, Method & Practice.* Reading, MA: Addison Wesley.

Armstrong, R.V. (n.d.). FAQs about team-based organizations. http://www.rvarmstrong.com/TBOFAQs.htm.

Athens Project. 2005. Advancing Technology and Healthcare Education Now at St. Scholastica. http://www.css.edu/programs/athens.

Bass, B.M. 1985. *Leadership and Performance beyond Expectations.* New York: Free Press.

Bass, B. and B.J. Avolio. 1994. Shatter the glass ceiling: Women may make better managers. *Human Resource Management* 33:549–560.

Bass, B.M. and B.J. Avolio. 1993. Transformational leadership: A response to critics. In *Leadership Theory and Research: Perspectives and Directions.* Edited by Chemers, M.M. and R. Ayman. San Diego: Academic Press.

Baue, W. 2004 (Dec. 15). New indexes seek to link corporate governance and diversity to financial performance. *Sustainability Investment News.* http://www.socialfunds.com/news/article.cgi/1590.html.

Beckhard, R. 1969. *Organization Development: Strategies and Models.* Reading, MA: Addison Wesley.

Bennett. 1991 (June 6). Management: Downsizing does not necessarily bring an upswing in corporate profitability. *Wall Street Journal.*

Bennis, W. 1959. Leadership theory and administrative behavior: The problem of authority. *Administrative Science Quarterly* 4:259–301.

Bennis, W. and B. Nanus. 1985. *Leaders:The Strategy for Taking Charge.* New York: Harper & Row.

Berk, B. 2003 (Sept.). Bringing up the middle. *Healthleaders Magazine.* http://www.healthleaders.com/magazine/feature1.php?contentid'4212.

Berringer, G. 2004. Victim of the system or systems of the victim? http://www.systems-thinking.org/vossov/vos.htm.

Birnbaum, R. 2000. The life cycle of academic management fads. *Journal of Higher Education* 71(1):1–16.

Blake, R.R. and J.S. Mouton. 1976. *Consultation.* Reading, MA: Addison Wesley.

Boerner, S. and E. Dutschke. 2008. The impact of charismatic leadership on followers' initiative-oriented behavior: A study in German hospitals. *Health Care Management Review* 33(4):332–340.

Borkowski, N. 2005. *Organizational Behavior in Health Care.* Sudbury, MA: Jones and Bartlett.

Bridges, W. 2004. *Transitions: Making the Most of Change.* New York: Basic Books.

Brown, R. 2005. Why do so many executives fail after being appointed? Dunlop & Brown. http://www.dunlopbrown.com/talk.htm.

Burkholder, N. 2003 (Nov.). The real cost of turnover. http://www.staffing.org/updates/archive11062003.asp.

Burns, J.M. 1978. *Leadership.* New York: Free Press.

Business Source Premier. 1950–2004. Proprietary database available to scholarly libraries containing articles from scholarly and trade business journals on companies, industries, products, management, marketing, accounting, real estate, finance, insurance, business law, and technology.

Byrne, J. 1997 (June 23). Management theory: Of fashion of the month? *BusinessWeek* 47.

Capuano, T., J. Bokovoy, K. Hitchings, and J. Houser. 2005. Use of a validated model to evaluate the impact of the work environment on outcomes at a magnet hospital. *Health Care Management Review* 30(3):229–236.

Catalyst 2008. Women in business. http://www.catalyst.org/publication/132/us-women-in-business.

CEOGO. 2003. CEO reputation study 2003. Burson-Marsteller. http://www.ceogo.com.

Chartered Institute of Personnel and Development. 2005. Annual survey report, 2005. http://www.cipd.co.uk/NR/rdonlyres/271CD424-507C-4E4A-99B6-1FAD80573E4A/0/traindevtsurvrept05.pdf.

Chaulk, D. and R.W. Sexty. 2002. The management fad lifecycle phenomenon. Canadian evidence. Administrative Sciences Association of Canada/IFSAM Conference. Winnipeg, Manitoba.

Choi, J. 2006. A motivational theory of charismatic leadership: Envisioning, empathy and empowerment. *Journal of Leadership and Organizational Studies* 13(1):24–43.

Cohen, A.B. and R.S. Hanft. 2004. *Technology in American Health Care.* Ann Arbor, MI: University of Michigan Press.

Cole, R.E. 1999. *Managing Quality Fads: How American Business Learned to Play the Quality Game.* New York: Oxford Press.

Cummings, T.G. and E.F. Huse. 1989. *Organization Development and Change.* New York: West.

Curphy, G.J. 2008. http://www.leadershipkeynote.net.

Daft, R.L. 2000. *Management.* Fort Worth, TX: Dryden.

Daft, R.L. and D. Marcic. 1998. *Understanding Management.* Fort Worth, TX: Dryden.

Daley Group. 2006. Executive talent resource. http://stlbac.com/ExecutiveTalentResource.html.

Dansereau, F., G. Graen, and W. Haga. 1975. A vertical dyad linkage approach to leadership within formal organizations: A longitudinal investigation of the role-making process. *Organizational Behavior and Human Performance* 13:46–78.

de Geus, A. 1997. *The Living Company.* London: Nicholas Brealey Publishing.

Deming, W.E. 1986. *Out of the Crisis.* Cambridge: Massachusetts Institute of Technology, Center for Advanced Engineering Study.

DeVries, D.L. 1992. Executive selection: Advances but no progress. *Issues and Observations* 12:1–5.

DeVries, D.L. and R.B. Kaiser. 2003. Going sour in the suite: What you can do about executive derailment. In *Maximizing Executive Effectiveness.* Steckler, S., D. Sethi, and R.K. Prescot (coordinators). Workshop presented by the Human Resources Planning Society, Miami, FL.

Dewey, J. 1938. *Experience and Education.* New York: Collier.

DeWine, S. 1994. *The Consultant's Craft: Improving Organizational Communication.* New York: St. Martin's Press.

Dierick, C. and J. McGill. 2007 (April/May). The dark side of CEO succession. Chief Executive. http://www.chiefexecutive.net/ME2/dirmod.asp?sid=&nm=&type=Publishing&mod=Publications%3A%3AArticle&mid=8F3A7027421841978F18BE895F87F791&tier=4&id=5937728765724E6FA829D2DE7259A863.

Dionne, S.D., F.J. Yammarino, J.P. Howell, and J. Vila. 2005. Substitutes for leadership, or not? *The Leadership Quarterly* 16(1):161–193.

Donlon, J.P. 2007 (Dec.). Best companies for leaders. Chief Executive, http://www.chiefexecutive.net/ME2/dirmod.asp?sid=&nm=&type=Publishing&mod=Publications%3A%3AArticle&mid=8F3A7027421841978F18BE895F87F791&tier=4&id=2DAD55DBD2FE4497BA3649C78B3E24E6.

Drummond, H.D. 2008. The Icarus Paradox: An analysis of a totally destructive system. *Journal of Information Technology* 23(3):176–184.

Duarte, N.T., J.R. Goodson, and N.R. Klitch. 1993. How do I like thee? Let me appraise the ways. *Journal of Organizational Behavior* 14:239–249.

Dubrin, A.J. 2004. *Leadership: Research Findings, Practice and Skills*. New York: Houghton Mifflin.

Dunham, N. and J. Yhouse. 2007. Census of women chief administrators of the Solucient 100 Top Hospitals. Unpublished paper. University of Michigan, Ann Arbor.

Dychtwald, K., T. J. Erickson and R. Morison. 2006. *Workforce Crisis*. Boston, MA: Harvard Business School Press.

Eagly, A.H. and L.L. Carly. 2003. The female leadership advantage: An evaluation of the evidence. *Leadership Quarterly* 14(6):807–835.

Edison, T. 2008 (May-June). The team development lifecycle. Team dynamics. Defense AT&L. http://www.dau.mil/pubs/dam/2008_05_06/edis_mj08.pdf.

Ethisphere. 2008. http://ethisphere.com/wme2008.

Fenton, S.H. and L.D. Gamm. 2008 (Fall). Evaluation and Management documentation and coding technology adoption. Perspectives in Health Information Management, Computer Assisted Coding Conference Proceedings. http://library.ahima.org/xpedio/groups/public/documents/ahima/bok1_040477.html.

Fiedler, F.E. 1967. *A Theory of Leadership Effectiveness*. New York: McGraw-Hill.

Fulmer, R.M. and J.L. Bleak. 2008. The leadership advantage: How the best companies are developing their talent to pave the way for future success. New York: AMACOM.

Gering, J. and J. Connor. 2002 (Nov.). A strategic approach to employee retention. *Healthcare Financial Management*, 40–44.

Goethals, G.R. and G.J. Sorenson. 2007. *The Quest for a General Theory of Leadership*. Cheltenham, UK: Edward Elgar Publishing.

Graen, G. and T.A. Skandura. 1987. Toward a psychology of dyadic organizing. *Research in Organizational Behavior* 9:175–209.

Greenleaf, R.J. 1991. *Servant Leadership*. Mahwah, NJ: Paulist Press.

Guida, N. 2004. Catalyst study reveals financial performance is higher for companies with more women at the top. *Catalyst*. http://www.catalyst.org/press-release/2/catalyst-study-reveals-financial-performance-is-higher-for-companies-with-more-women-at-the-top.

Hale, B. 2002. Kenneth Lay: A fallen hero. BBC News. http://www.news.bbc.co.uk.

Halpin, A.W. and B.J. Winer. 1957. A factorial study of the leader behavioral descriptions. In *Leader Behavior: Its Description and Measurement*. Edited by Stogdill, R.M. and A.E. Coons. Columbus, OH: Bureau of Business Research, Ohio State University.

Hay Group. 1999. Press release: New Fortune/Hay Group ranking of the world's most admired companies.

Hersey, P., K.H. Blanchard, and D.E. Johnson. 1996. *Management of Organizational Behavior: Utilizing Human Resources*. 7th ed. Upper Saddle River, NJ: Prentice-Hall.

Hickman, C.R. 1990. *Mind of a Manager, Soul of a Leader*. New York: John Wiley & Sons.

Hogan, R. 2007. *Personality and the Fate of Organizations*. Hillsdale, NJ: Erlbaum.

Hogan, R. and R.B. Kaiser. 2004. What we know about leadership. *Review of General Psychology* 9(2):169–180.

Hooper, D.T. and R. Martin. 2008. Beyond personal leader-member exchange (LMX) quality: The effects of perceive LMX variability on employee reactions. *Leadership Quarterly* 19(1):20–30.

Hopkins M.M. and D. Bilimoria. 2008. Social and emotional competencies predicting success for male and female executives. *Journal of Management Development* 27(1):13–35.

House, R.J. 1971. A path-goal theory of leader effectiveness. *Administrative Science Leadership Review Quarterly* 16:321–339.

Howell, J.P., D.E. Bowen, P.W. Dorfman, S. Kerr, and P.M. Podsakoff. 1990. Substitutes for leadership: Effective alternatives to ineffective leadership. *Organizational Dynamics*, 20–38.

Howell, J.P., P.W. Dorfman, and S. Kerr. 1986. Moderator variables in leadership research. *Academy of Management Review* 11(1):88–102.

Hoyt, C. 2002 (Fall). Women leaders: The role of stereotype activation and leadership self-efficacy. Kravis Institute. *Leadership Review*. http://www.leadershipreview.org/2002fall/article2_fall_2002.asp.

Hoyt, C.L. 2005. The role of leadership efficacy and stereotype activation in women's identification with leadership. *Journal of Leadership and Organizational Studies* 11(4):2–14.

Hunter, J.C. 2004. *The World's Most Powerful Leadership Principle: How to Become a Servant Leader*. New York: Random House.

Hwang, Y-S., and S.H. Park. 2007. Organizational life cycle as a determinant of strategic alliance tactics: Research propositions. *International Journal of Management* 24(3):427–435.

Hymowitz, C. and T. Schellhardt. 1986 (March 24). The glass ceiling: Why women can't seem to break the invisible barrier that blocks them from the top jobs. Special report: The corporate woman, cover article. *Wall Street Journal*.

Jahna, S.R. 2002. Failure: The dreaded word in the CEOs' lexicon. *The CEO Refresher*. http://www.refresher.com/!jahnasr.html.

Joyce, W., N. Nohria, and B. Roberson. 2003. What really works. *Harvard Business Review* 81(7):43–52.

Judge, T.A., R.F. Piccolo, and R. Ilies. 2004. The forgotten ones? The validity of consideration and initiating structure in leadership research. *Journal of Applied Psychology* 89(1):36–51.

Kaplan, R.S. 2002. Building strategy focused organizations with the balanced scorecard. http://www.ddc.moph.go.th/module/webadmin/download_module/pdf/Kaplan_BSC.pdf.

Kaplan-Leiserson, E. 2004. Survey says: Leadership. *T+D* 58(3): 14.

Kay, R.L. 2008 (March 19). Apple's Icarus Effect. *BusinessWeek*. http://www.businessweek.com/technology/content/mar2008/tc20080317_287032.htm?chan=technology_technology+index+page_top+stories.

Kelloway, E.K., N. Sivanathan, L. Francis, and J. Barling. 2005. Poor leadership. In *Handbook of Work Stress*. Edited by Barling, J., E.K. Kelloway, and M.R. Frone. Thousand Oaks, CA: Sage, 89–112.

Kempster, S. 2006. Leadership learning through lived experience: A process of apprenticeship? *Journal of Management and Organization* 12(1):4–22.

Kerr, S. and J.M. Jermier. 1978. Substitutes for leadership: their meaning and measurement. *Organizational Behavior and Human Performance* 22:395–403.

Khurama, R. 2007. *From Higher Aims to Hired Hands: The Social Transformation of Business Schools and the Unfulfilled Promise for Management as a Profession.* Princeton, NJ: Princeton University Press.

Kidder, R.M. 2000 (Oct.). Want a loyal workforce? Build an ethical corporation. *Ethics Newsline.* http://www.globalethics.org/ewsline/members/issue.tmpl?articleid=10090003003140.

Kirchheimer, B. 2007. "A woman's place is in. . . ." *Modern Healthcare* 37(16):6–7.

Koene, B.A.S., A.L.W. Vogelaar, and J.L. Soeters. 2002. Leadership effects on organizational climate and financial performance: Local leadership effects in chain organizations. *The Leadership Quarterly* 13(2) 193–215.

Kolb, D.A., and A.L. Frohman. 1970. An organization development approach to consulting. *Sloan Management Review* 12(1):51–65.

Kolb, J.A. 1999. The effect of gender role, attitude toward leadership, and self-confidence on leader emergence: Implications for leadership development. *Human Resource Development Quarterly* 10(4):305–311.

Korabik, K. 1990. Androgyny and leadership style. *Journal of Business Ethics* 9:283–292.

Kotter, J.P. 1990. *A Force for Change: How Leadership Differs from Management.* New York: Free Press.

Kouzes, J. and B. Posner. 1989. *The Leadership Challenge: How to Get Extraordinary Things Done in Organizations.* San Francisco: Jossey-Bass.

Kouzes, J. and B. Posner. 2003. *The Leadership Practices Inventory.* Hoboken, NJ: Wiley.

Kramer, R.J. 2008. Have we learned anything about leadership development*? Conference Board Review* 45:26–30.

Kubler-Ross, E. 1969. *On Death and Dying.* New York: Simon & Schuster/Touchstone.

Lantz, P.M. 2008. Gender and leaderhsip in healthcare administration: 21st century progress and challenges. *Journal of Healthcare Management* 53(5):291–303.

Leadership Trust Foundation. 2007. Why leadership? http://www.leadership.org.uk/mainpages.asp?PageID=3.

Lee, J. 2005. The effects of leadership and leader-member exchange on commitment. *Leadership and Organization Development Journal* 26(8):655–672.

Lee, James. 1982. *The Gold and Garbage in Management Theories and Prescriptions.* Athens: Ohio University Press.

Lewin, K. 1951. *Field Theory in Social Science.* New York: Harper and Brothers.

Likert, R. 1961. *New Patterns of Management.* New York: McGraw Hill.

Likert, R. 1979. From production- and employee-centeredness to systems 1–4. *Journal of Management* (5):628–641.

Lima, L.A. Leadership in the information age: How chief information officers lead information technology workers [PhD thesis]. Bowling Green, OH: Bowling Green State University; 2006. http://rave.ohiolink.edu/etdc/view?acc%5Fnum=bgsu1151093030.

Long, L.C. Impact of Medicare payment policies for home healthcare on nursing services and patient outcomes [Doctoral dissertation]. Boston: University of Massachusetts; 2006. UMI Order AAI3221376.

Marash, S.A., P. Berman, and M. Flynn. 2003. *Fusion Management: Harnessing the Power of Six Sigma, Lean, ISO9001: 2000, Malcolm Baldrige, TQM and Other Quality Breakthroughs of the Past Century.* Fairfax, VA: QSU Publishing.

McCormick, M.J., J. Tanguma, and A.S. Lopez-Forment. 2003 (Spring). Gender differences in beliefs about leadership capabilities: Exploring the glass ceiling phenomenon with self-efficacy theory. Kravis Institute. *Leadership Review.* http://www.leadershipreview.org/2003spring/article2_spring_2003.asp.

Megargee, E.I. 1969. Influence of sex roles on the manifestation of leadership. *Journal of Applied Psychology* 53:377–382.

Miller, D. 1990. *The Icarus Paradox: How Exceptional Companies Bring about Their Own Downfall: New Lessons in the Dynamics of Corporate Success, Decline, and Renewal.* New York: Harper Business.

Mumford, M.D., J. O'Connor, T.C. Clifton, M.S. Connelly, and S.J. Zacarro. 1993. Background data constructs as predictors of leadership behavior. *Human Performance* 6(2):151–195.

Napoli, D. 2008. MRSA spread in part due to stressed health care systems. *Pediatric News* 42(8):13

Ozaralli, N. 2003. Effects of transformational leadership on empowerment and team effectiveness. *Leadership and Organization Development Journal* 24(6):16–47.

Peter, L.J. and R. Hull. 1969. *The Peter Principle: Why Things Always Go Wrong.* New York: William Morrow & Company.

Peters, T. 2001 (Dec.). Tom Peters's true confessions. *Fast Company* 53:78.

Peters, T.J. and R.H. Waterman. 1982. *In Search of Excellence: Lessons from America's Best-Run Companies.* New York: Harper & Row.

Pew Research. 2008. Men or women: Who's the better leader: Paradox in public attitudes. Pew Research Center. http://pewsocialtrends.org/pubs/708/gender-leadership

Podsakoff, P.M., S.B. MacKenzie, and W.H. Bommer. 1996. (Summer). Transformational leader behaviors and substitutes for leadership as determinants of employee satisfaction, commitment, trust, and organizational citizenship behaviors. *Journal of Management* 22(2):259–298.

Podsakoff, P.M., W.D. Toder, and R.S. Schuler. 1983. Leader expertise as a moderator of the effects of instrumental and supportive leader behavior. *Journal of Management* 9:176–185.

Pratt, D. 2000 (Sept. 14). Adaptation is key in the digital economy. *Barnstable Patriot.* http://www.barnstable-patriot.com/news_september_adaptation_is_key_in_the_digital_economy_archives_48_514.html.

Price-Waterhouse v. Ann B. Hopkins. 1987. Supreme Court of the United States. No. 87-1167. http://www.usdoj.gov/osg/briefs/1987/sg870104.txt.

Rigby, D. and B. Bilodeau. 2007. Management tools and trends 2007. Bain and Company. http://www.bain.com/bainweb/PDFs/cms/Public/Management%20Tools%202007%20BB.pdf.

Roberts, E.B. 2007 (Jan–Feb). Managing invention and innovation. *Research Technology Management.* http://www.iriinc.org/Content/ContentGroups/Research_Technology_Management/Volume_50_2007/Issue_Number_1_January_February_20071/Articles21/MANAGING_INVENTION_AND_INNOVATION.htm.

Rogers, E. 1995. *Diffusion of Innovations.* 4th ed. New York: Free Press.

Rogers, E. and F.F. Shoemaker. 1971. *Communication of Innovations: A Cross-Cultural Approach.* New York: Free Press.

Rogers, K.A. 2000. Transition management as an intervention for survivor syndrome. *Canadian Journal of Leadership Nursing* 13(4).

Sanford, K. 2006. The ethical leader. *Nursing Administration Quarterly* 30(1):5–10.

Schiller, M. 2005. Executive survey: What makes a great CEO? TheLadders.com. http://www.theladders.com/press-releases/abouttheladderspressdetail_051605.

Schon, D.A. 1983. *The Reflective Practitioner.* New York: Basic Books.

Senge, P. 1990. *The Fifth Discipline: The Art and Practice of the Learning Organization.* New York: Currency/Doubleday.

Shartle, C.L. 1979. Early years of the Ohio State University leadership studies. *Journal of Management* 5:126–134.

Skogstad, A., S. Einarsen, T. Torsheim, M.S. Aasland, and H. Hetland. 2007. The destructiveness of laissez-faire leadership behavior. *Journal of Occupational Health Psychology* 12:80–92.

Smith, J.L., K.P. Carson, and R.A. Alexander. 1984. Leadership: It can make a difference. *Academy of Management Journal* 27:765–776.

Spears, L. 1995. *Reflections on Leadership: How Robert K. Greenleaf's Theory of Servant Leadership Influenced Today's Top Management Thinkers.* New York: John Wiley & Sons.

Stogdill, R.M. 1974. *Handbook of Leadership: A Guide to Understanding Managerial Work.* Englewood Cliffs, NJ: Prentice-Hall.

Tannenbaum, T. and W. Schmidt. 1973 (May–June). How to choose a leadership pattern. *Harvard Business Review.* No. 73311. First published in 1958 (March–April) *Harvard Business Review* 36:95–101.

Tay, C., S. Ang, and L. Van Dyne. 2006. Personality, biographical characteristics, and job interview success: A longitudinal study of the mediating effects of interviewing self-efficacy and the moderating effects of internal locus of causality. *Journal of Applied Psychology* 91(2):446–454.

Taylor, C.W. and R.L. Ellison. 1967. Biographical predictors of scientific performance. *Science* 155(3766):1075–1080.

Tierney, T.J. 2006. The nonprofit sector's leadership deficit. The Bridgespan Group. http://www.bridgespangroup.org/PDF/LeadershipDeficitWhitePaper.pdf.

Tomasco, R. 1987. *Downsizing: Reshaping the Corporation for the Future.* New York: AMACOM.

Tourangeau, A.E. and K. McGilton. 2004. Measuring leadership practices of nurses using the leadership practices inventory. *Nursing Research* 53(3):182–189.

Tuckman, B.W. 1965. Developmental sequence in small groups. *Psychological Bulletin* 63:384–399.

Tung, F.C. and S.C. Chang. 2008. Nursing students' behavior intention to use online courses: A questionnaire survey. *International Journal of Nursing Studies* 45(9):1299–1309.

Vaill, P.B. 1996. *Learning as a Way of Being.* San Francisco. Jossey-Bass.

Vaishali, D.K.K. and M.P. Kumar. 2001. Transformational vs. transactional leadership and its effect on subordinates behavioral competencies: An empirical investigation. Presented at Second ARDC Conference on Human Resource Development in Asia, Bangkok, Thailand. November 29–December 4.

Van Vugt, M. and B. Spisak. 2008. Sex differences in leadership emergence during conflicts within and between groups. *Psychological Science* 19(9): (in press)

Vecchio, R.P., J.E. Justin, and C.L. Pearce. 2008. The utility of transactional and transformational leadership for predicting performance and satisfaction within a path-goal theory framework. *Journal of Occupational and Organizational Psychology* 81(1):71–81.

Verbos, A.K., J.A. Gerard, P.R. Forshey, C.S. Harding, and J.S. Miller. 2007. The positive ethical organization: Enacting a living code of ethics and ethical organization identity. *Journal of Business Ethics* 76(1):17–33.

Vroom, V. and P. Jago. 1988. *The New Leadership? Managing Participation in Organizations.* Englewood Cliffs, NJ: Prentice-Hall.

Vroom, V. and P. Yetton. 1971. *Leadership and Decision Making.* Pittsburgh: University of Pittsburgh Press.

Waldman, J.D., F. Kelly, S. Arora, and H.L. Smith. 2004 (Jan–March). The shocking cost of turnover in healthcare. *Health Care Management Review* 29:2–7.

WalkerInformation. 2001. Commitment in the workplace: The 2000 global employee relationship benchmark report. Walker Information Global Network and Hudson Institute. http://www.askemployees.com/why/docs/global.pdf.

Weick, K.E. and R.E. Quinn. 1995. Organizational change and development. *Annual Review of Psychology* 50:361–386.

Wellins, R., and J. Pesci-Kelly. 2003, (Jan. 29). Front-line leadership is a priority despite the recession. *Business Wire.*

Westcott, R.T. 2005. *The Certified Manager of Quality/Organizational Excellence Handbook.* Milwaukee, WI: American Society for Quality.

White, R.K. and R. Lippitt. 1960. *Autocracy and Democracy: An Experimental Inquiry.* New York: Harper.

Yukl, G. 2006. *Leadership in Organizations.* 6th ed. Upper Saddle River, NJ: Prentice-Hall.

Zaccaro, Kemp, and Bader. 2004. *The Nature of Leadership.* Thousand Oaks, CA: Sage.

Zaleznik, A. 1977 (May–June). Managers and leaders: Are they different? *Harvard Business Review* 55:68–78.

Zhu, W., I.K.H. Chew, and W.D. Spangler. 2004. CEO transformational leadership and organizational outcomes: The mediating role of human-capital-enhancing human resource management. *Leadership Quarterly* 16(1):39–52.

Zogby International, 2007. Zogby poll: As Labor Day nears, Workplace Bullying Institute Survey finds half of working Americans affected by workplace bullying. http://www.zogby.com/search/ReadNews.dbm?ID=1353.

Chapter 22
Work Design and Performance Improvement

Shirley Eichenwald Maki, MBA, RHIA, FAHIMA, and Pamela K. Oachs, MA, RHIA

Learning Objectives

- Describe how workflow, space and equipment, aesthetics, and ergonomics factor into the functionality of a work environment
- Identify alternate methods for distributing work assignments and for scheduling staff to assure adequate staffing to meet the department's or work unit's service requirements
- Explain the role job procedures play to support employees in delivering effective and efficient services
- Identify the criteria for developing effective performance standards and provide examples of both qualitative and quantitative standards
- Differentiate the process of standard setting when done through a benchmarking effort versus a work sampling effort
- Identify the steps involved in a work-sampling effort and the tools that can be used with certain steps
- Explain the difference between preventive and feedback controls
- Identify potential areas for improvement in departmental or work unit functions through observations and through variance analysis and establish a relevant action plan to address the problem(s) identified
- Differentiate effectiveness, efficiency, and adaptability as goals of process improvement efforts
- Describe the components of a system, how they relate to each other, and how they relate to process improvement
- Explain the purposes of the various CQI tools and techniques
- Select the appropriate tool(s) for use in different types of performance or process improvement efforts
- Discuss the similarities and differences between Lean and Six Sigma as process redesign methodologies

Key Terms

Affinity grouping
Benchmarking
Brainstorming
Business process reengineering
Check sheet
Common cause variation
Certainty factor
Closed systems
Compressed workweek
Continuous data
Continuous quality improvement (CQI)
Cybernetic systems
Cyclical staffing
DMAIC
Ergonomics
External customers
Feedback controls
Fishbone diagram
Flextime
Float employee
Flow process chart
Flowchart
Force-field analysis
Goal
Hard space
Histogram
Internal customers
Job procedure
Job sharing
Key indicator
Lean
Movement diagram
Multivoting technique
Narratives
Nominal group technique (NGT)
Objective
Off shoring
Open systems
Outsourcing
Parallel work division
Pareto chart
PDSA Cycle
Performance
Performance measurement
Playscript
Precision factor
Preventive controls
Procedure manual
Process redesign
Productivity
Qualitative standards
Quantitative standards
Run chart
Scatter diagram
Serial work division
Service quality
Shift rotations
Shift differentials
Six Sigma
Soft space
Special cause variation
Standard
Statistical process control (SPC) chart
System
Swimlane diagram
Telecommuting
Time ladder
Unit work division
Volume logs
Work
Work distribution analysis
Work distribution chart
Work division
Workflow
Work measurement
Work sampling

Management is commonly defined as getting work done through and with people. It may be thought of as both a science and an art. Management is a science because it is based on theory and principles that have been—and continue to be—tested and explored. It is an art because effective management depends on the use of sound judgment, intuition, communication, and interpersonal skills. Managers engage in specific functions, including planning, organizing, directing, and controlling, to create and facilitate effective work processes so that the desired outcome can be achieved in a cost-efficient manner.

Management of human resources is one of the most challenging and critical functions in a healthcare organization. Whether as a lead staff person, a supervisor, an assistant director, or a health information management (HIM) department director, to a great extent the practitioner's people and performance management skills are key factors impacting that practitioner's ability to successfully achieve organizational goals. Performance management does not occur by accident. Careful consideration of available staff resources and how the staff resources are organized is fundamental to delivering effective and efficient HIM departmental services.

This chapter introduces key concepts, tools, and techniques associated with designing, redesigning, and implementing effective and efficient work processes within an organization. It includes discussion of various methods of work division and work scheduling, management of work procedures, components of the work environment, elements of a performance management program, including methods for establishing performance standards; and various process improvement methodologies to continuously improve or to re-engineer workflow, work processes, and staff performance to accommodate changes in service requirements and fiscal limitations.

Functional Work Environment

Considering the fact that the average full time employee spends more waking hours in the work environment than in the home, it would be prudent for management to create a workplace infrastructure and ambiance that evokes comfort and productivity. Whether creating new space or evaluating current space, developing the work environment involves consideration of these fundamental elements: workflow, space and equipment, aesthetics, and ergonomics.

Departmental Workflow

The **workflow** in a departmental setting is the established path along which tasks are sequentially completed by any number of staff to accomplish a function. Well designed workflow is critical to achieving optimal efficiency when a function requires the coordinated activity of a group of employees. In a manual process environment, spatial relationships among people who perform tasks and the equipment required to perform them are critical factors in planning efficient workflow. In such situations, creating a layout diagram, sometimes called a **movement diagram** or layout flowchart, helps the manager to visualize the functions and related tasks performed in a defined work area and how they are related. (See figure 22.1.)

Space and Equipment

Workspace design can influence morale, productivity, and job satisfaction. The design of efficient office space involves a number of considerations. For example, in a paper-based health record environment, location of the file room is a primary consideration. If the file room is located on any floor other than ground level, it is important to determine how much weight the suspended floor can support. This is especially critical when planning for additional shelving to store paper medical records. The combined weight of the records and shelving can be extreme, and the floor must be designed to support weights of potential proportion.

The amount of space designated for the department is the major determining factor in considering office design and equipment specifications. Space is considered a precious and costly commodity in healthcare facilities and must be used efficiently. Designing efficient office space is a highly specialized and intricate process.

Department managers should understand basic facility planning techniques. They also must consider the facility's master plan in developing a plan for the department. This ensures maximum efficiency, consistency, and flexibility. The department plan also should address:

- Department's physical environment
- Office space utilization
- Space planning techniques, guidelines, and standards
- Office furniture and equipment

In an ideal situation, a move into a new space is the reason for engaging in space planning. Reorganization of a department because of changes in workforce numbers resulting from downsizing or from taking on new functions constitutes a space planning process. Departmental reorganization in response to changes in methods or functions, such as a move to home-based transcription or implementation of an electronic health record (EHR), can trigger a call for revised space planning. Sometimes the basic need to improve workflow and the appearance of a department can be a pivotal reason for space planning.

Remodeling existing space, as opposed to designing new space, presents special challenges. There may be space problems that cannot be changed, such as walls and pillars that cannot be moved and inadequate wiring. In addition, employees may resist changes and find it difficult to think creatively. In such instances, managers need to be inventive and creative in their space utilization.

Hard space and soft space are other considerations in designing efficient and effective space utilization. **Hard space** is space that cannot be converted easily to service

Figure 22.1. Movement diagram: Inefficient (top) and efficient (bottom)

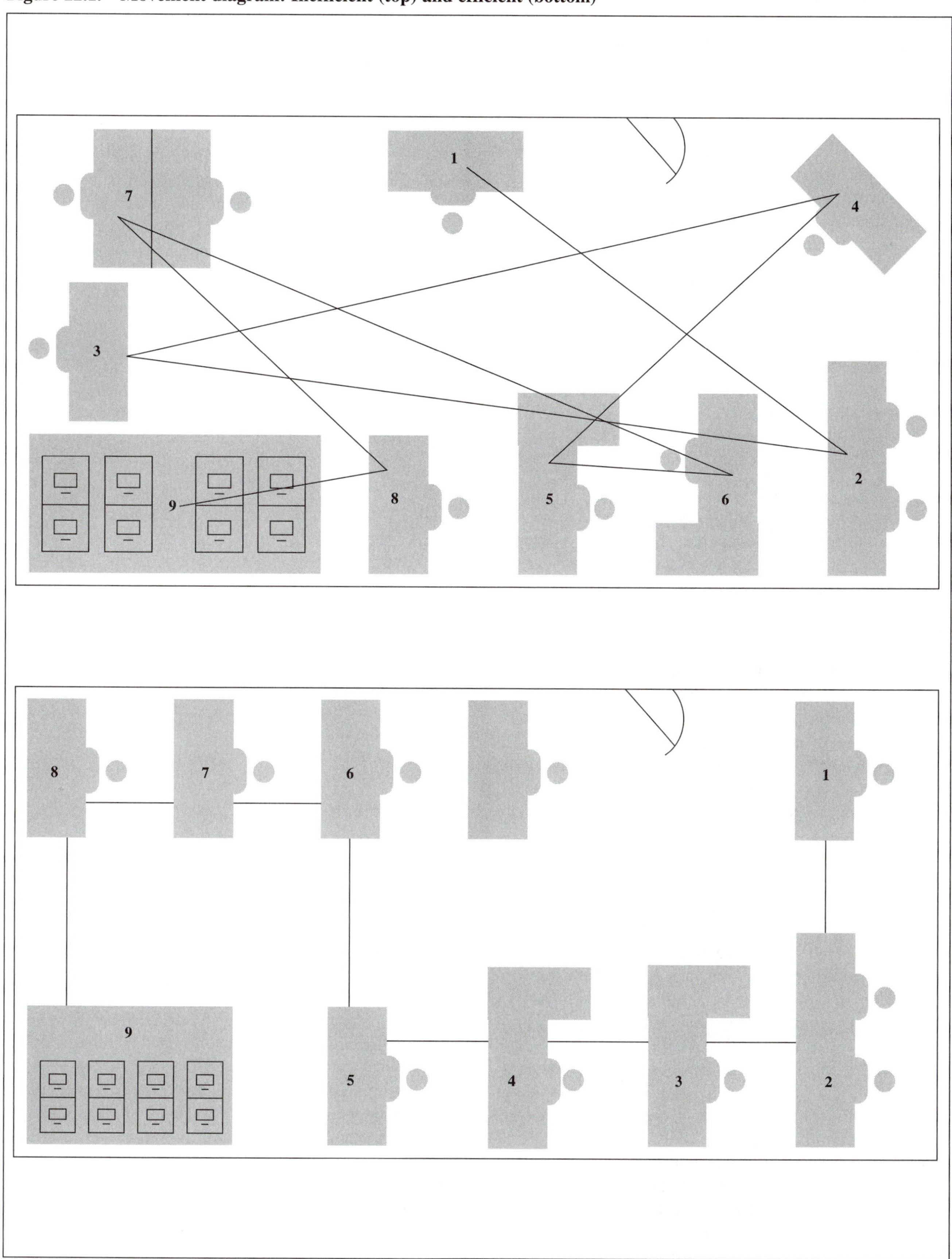

another function. For example, a file area could have certain structural needs or radiology may require lead walls. **Soft space** is space that is readily expandable or contractible to adjust to changing needs.

Determining how soft and hard space will be utilized is a major component of office space planning. Effective space planning has the following characteristics:

- Keeping costs to a minimum
- Contributing to the quality of the work
- Contributing to employee satisfaction
- Contributing to services provided by the department

Space needs change in the course of time and should be reevaluated periodically to determine whether principles of good space planning are being followed.

Four separate, self-explanatory types of office space are needed:

- Private office space
- General office space
- Service area
- Storage area

Another space consideration is personal space or the area of privacy surrounding an employee. Territoriality is a natural development because employees instinctively control the physical areas where they work.

Aesthetics

Aesthetics of the workplace have the most physiological as well as psychological effects on employees. Aesthetic elements include the lighting of both the office and the workspace, the colors of the walls and furniture, auditory impacts, and atmospheric condition and temperature.

Light should be of sufficient brightness and diffusion for the work situation. Exposures (north, south, east, and west in order of preference) to natural light must be considered when creating new space because natural light is best and easiest on the eyes. Luminance is the quality of light, and lux is a unit of measure. (Candlelight equals 10 lux. A well-lit office equals 500 to 700 lux, whereas the noonday sun produces 160,000 lux.) Desk or task lighting is more physically supportive than overhead florescent lighting alone. Many HIS functions include PC monitors, and the contrast between the print and the background can influence the employee's comfort level. Typically, a light background with dark print is least taxing on the eyes. Glare from light sources or PC screens can cause discomfort. Display screen fixtures can be used to help reduce glare. In addition, it is important to factor in the age of the staff; people over 40 have an increased level of discomfort from glare.

Color influences how people feel. For example, dark areas feel brighter or lighter when painted with light colors. Moreover, certain colors evoke a variety of sensations and feelings. Blues are cool, reds are warm, greens evoke luxury, and so on. When choosing color schemes, it is important to consider the area and who will occupy it. Neutral colors can have a calming effect and help avoid the subliminal friction that some primary colors trigger. Also, the finish of the paint should be considered. Matte surfaces absorb more light and reduce glare but are typically not cleanable. On the other hand, gloss surfaces are cleanable, but reflective, and can exacerbate glare.

Music and sound can be incorporated to improve working conditions and relieve both mental and visual fatigue. Certain kinds of music can reduce tension and make employees generally feel better. Sound conditioning and soundproofing are important considerations because a noisy office is seldom efficient. A certain level of routine office background noise is expected and usually is not irritating. However, loud or abrupt sounds can be alarming, distracting, and disruptive. Planning separate space for noisy work processes, such as copying and printing, is effective because it addresses the source of the noise. Carpeting, drapes, and partitioning can offer noise control because they absorb significant amounts of sound.

Air-conditioning regulates temperature, circulation, and moisture content and determines cleanliness. When considering normal ventilation for the space, at least 2,000 cubic feet per person per hour should be configured to maintain a healthy respiratory atmosphere. Air that is too warm or too cold is equally distracting, and a balance can be difficult to maintain. A range of 68 to 72 degrees Fahrenheit is generally acceptable to most people.

Ergonomics

The word **ergonomics** is derived from the Greek word *ergon,* which means "work," and *nomos,* which means "natural laws of." Developed in the 1950s by a group of scientists and engineers, the discipline of ergonomics has helped redefine the employee workspace with consideration for comfort and safety.

Questions to consider in office layout and design include:

- Do staff members assume fixed working postures that remain static for the majority of the workday? For example, do they sit at a keyboard all day?
- Do staff members perform repetitive motions such as filing, stamping, hole punching, and so on?
- Has the psychological stress caused by uncomfortable workstations been taken into consideration?

In effective ergonomic planning, the designer must know the work requirements of the job and the tasks involved. The physical traits of the worker assigned to each workstation also influence ergonomic considerations. For example, height or leg length or back waist length will determine specific needs. Another consideration is whether an individual or multiple persons share one workstation throughout the workweek. Finally, one must consider what equipment is currently available at the workstation and what equipment must be purchased to create an ergonomically correct work environment?

When the work environment is not ergonomically sound, common cumulative trauma disorders and repetitive strain injuries associated with office personnel can occur, including:

- Carpal tunnel syndrome is considered an occupational illness rather than an injury because it takes a long time to develop to the point of debilitation. The syndrome causes flexion, with ulnar deviation. Symptoms include tingling, numbness, and pain in the wrist and lower arm.
- Upper back and neck strain is caused by poor posture. Symptoms include tension headaches and muscle pain.
- Eyestrain is caused by incorrect viewing distances and poor illumination. Symptoms include burning, watery eyes, and headaches.

Good preventative, proactive ergonomic management includes educating staff on how to care for themselves to reduce potential ergonomic injuries or discomfort. A few simple principles help raise employees' awareness of their physical relationship with the work environment. Managers should encourage, if not insist, that staff working at a PC for the majority (more than two-thirds) of a shift take hourly neck, shoulder, and wrist roll breaks, along with stretch routines. In addition, employees should be aware of, and assessed on their use of, the ten basic principles of good sitting posture. (See figure 22.2.). These basic activities can help employees stop the tension cycle and reduce potential long-term problems.

Careful consideration and professional assessment of individual employee's work environment needs will help reduce or eliminate physical barriers to employee comfort and productivity. Preemptive, ergonomically correct practices markedly reduce employee absence and worker's compensation usage due to workplace injury.

Figure 22.2. Ten basic principles of good sitting posture

- Feet should rest flat on the floor or footrest.
- A fist-width space should be measurable between the back of the knees and the edge of the seat pan of the chair.
- The hips should be at a 90-degree angle (or slightly greater) in relation to the body. To help ensure this angle, the knees should be at or below hip height.
- The lower back (lumbar region) should be supported.
- Shoulders should be relaxed, not shrugged, slouched, or rolled forward.
- Elbows should rest comfortably at the side or on armrests. When typing, elbows should be at 90-degree angles and preferably supported by an adjustable armrest at an appropriate height.
- Wrists should be maintained in a neutral (straight) position while typing or using any variety of keyboard.
- Head and neck should be in an upright position. To confirm this, the ears should be directly over the shoulders, which are directly over the hips.
- Computer monitors should be positioned directly in front of the worker. The top line of print should be horizontal with the eyes when looking directly forward.
- Ergonomic aids should be used to help maintain comfortable posture. Examples include footrests, wrist rests for keyboard and mouse, antiglare screens for computer monitors, copy stands, and adjustable chair height for those working at a multitask station.

Check Your Understanding 22.1

Instructions: Answer the following questions on a separate piece of paper.

1. Name the fundamental elements addressed in good work environment planning.
2. Explain how a movement diagram (or layout flowchart) assists a manager during an office design or redesign effort.
3. Describe what types of impact aesthetic elements, such as lighting, the colors of the walls and furniture, noise and temperature have on employees.
4. Identify two simple actions employees can take to help stop the tension cycle and reduce potential long-term physical problems from ergonomic issues at their workstations.

Methods of Organizing Work

Staffing involves the determination of which types of employees are needed, how many of each type are needed, and what kind of work schedule is needed. The types of employees needed depend on the skills, experience, and education required by the specific work that must be done. The number of employees needed depends on the volume of work and the pattern of work division that has been selected for the work setting. Work scheduling is based on when employees are needed to provide the services they are responsible to deliver within the organization.

Work Division Patterns

The type of **work division** pattern used in a process-oriented department depends in large part on the nature of the work to be performed and the number of employees available to perform it. Three basic types of work division patterns are:

- **Serial work division:** The consecutive handling of tasks or products by individuals who perform a specific function in sequence. Often referred to as a production line work division, serial work division tends to create task specialists. This scenario is an example of a serial work division pattern: a receptionist receives a request for release of information, the request is passed to the release of information specialist who validates that the release is authorized and enters a request to the file room for the paper-based medical record to be pulled, the medical record is pulled by the file clerk and delivered to the release of information specialist who tags the pages in the medical record to be copied for release, an evening clerk photocopies the tagged pages and returns the medical record and copies to the release of information specialist who completes the entire process by preparing the requested information to be mailed to the requesting party. In this staffing model, each type of employee sequentially handles a step in the total release of information work process.

- **Parallel work division:** The concurrent handling of tasks. Multiple employees do identical types of tasks and basically see the process through from beginning to end. This scenario is an example of a parallel work division pattern: there are 3 release of information specialists in the department and each is responsible for receiving requests for release, for locating the medical record, identifying the content to be released, and preparing the content for distribution to the requestor. Thus, all three release of information specialists are expected to perform all of the tasks that comprise the release of information work process independent from the others.
- **Unit work division:** Simultaneous assembly in which everyone performs a different specialized task at the same time. The tasks are all related to the same end product but are not dependent on each other. The work is specialized, but the sequence of tasks is not fixed. Unit assembly is rarely used in HIS departments but is a typical work division pattern used in manufacturing. This scenario is an example of a unit work division pattern: one machinist makes the metal chair legs, another molds metal chair seats, and another molds metal chair backs. One employee takes four metal chair legs, one metal chair seat, and one metal chair back and assembles them into a complete chair.

Work Distribution Analysis

Work distribution analysis is a process for evaluating the types of work functions being performed in a department, the amount of time given to those functions, who is performing each function, and the way work is distributed among the employees. It is used to determine whether a department's current work assignments and job content are appropriate. Making time to perform this analysis can lead to one or more of the following observations:

- Large amounts of time are being dedicated to functions of minor importance
- Small amounts of time are being dedicated to functions of key importance
- There is too much or too little job function specialization
- There is duplication of efforts or functions
- Some employees are overloaded with work assignments
- Some employees do not have enough work to keep busy
- Staff are performing tasks inappropriate to their positions

Basic work distribution data can be collected in a **work distribution chart**, which is initially filled out by each employee and includes all responsible task content. (See table 22.1.) Task content should come directly from the employee's current job description. In addition to task content, each employee tracks each task's start time, end time, and volume or productivity within a typical a workweek. The results of a work distribution analysis can lead a department to redefine the job descriptions of some employees, redesign the office layout, or establish new or revised procedures for some department functions in order to gain improvements in staff productivity or service quality.

Work Scheduling

After management has determined the appropriate work distribution within a department and made adjustments accordingly, a work-scheduling system can be developed. Determining the work schedule for departmental staff involves more than simply assigning the correct number of work hours to each employee. Effective scheduling results in the following:

- A core of employees on duty at all times when services must be provided
- A pattern of hours (shifts) to be worked and days off that employees can be reasonably sure will not change except in extreme emergencies

Table 22.1. Work distribution chart

Position/ Employee	Supervisor/J. Johnson		Admissions Clerk/A. Jones		Discharge Clerk/B. Olson		File Clerk/R. Smith	
Activity	*Task*	*# of Hours*	*Task*	*# of Hours*	*Task*	*# of Hours*	*Task*	*# of Hours*
Release of information	Post requests; give depositions	2 10	Photocopy	8	Certify content	15	Retrieve records	10
Analysis	Chart IRS	2	File in MD box	3	Tag for incomplete	15	Collect charts	9
Filing	Audit file room	2	—	—	Pull for MDs	4	File and pull records	20
Administrative overhead	Attend meetings; supervise employees	12 10	Receive visitors; typing	14 14	Generate MD letters	5	—	—
Training	Read literature, etc.	2	Attend software training	1	Attend computer training	1	Attend computer training	1
Totals	40 hours/40 hours		40 hours/40 hours		40 hours/40 hours		40 hours/40 hours	

- Fair and just treatment of all employees with regard to hours assigned

Several staffing issues should be considered when devising an effective staff schedule. Answers to the following questions will help determine the department's course of action:

- How is the workweek defined by policy? The workweek is generally established to begin on Sunday, but organizational policy may dictate otherwise.
- What days of the week is the department open? How many and what hours and days are covered?
- What functions must be performed each day and within what time frame?
- How many full-time equivalents (FTEs) are needed to handle the work volume?

HIS departments often are on a standard Monday through Friday, eight-hour-day pattern but also may need evening or weekend coverage to handle specific functions that must be provided 24 hours per day, seven days a week. Uninterrupted work stretches should be no less than two days and no more than seven days. In other words, avoid scheduling staff either every other day or for more than seven days in a row.

Shift Rotation and Shift Differential

Employee schedules may involve **shift rotations** and **shift differentials** when the department has more than the standard Monday through Friday, eight-to-five staffing needs. Rotation among morning, afternoon, and evening shifts is not the ideal scheduling situation but is often necessary when coverage is needed and personnel have not been specifically hired to work afternoons or evenings on a regular basis. Specific start and end times should be determined for every shift, and at least 12 hours should elapse between the time an individual ends one shift and begins another. Time spent on the more undesirable shifts should not exceed time spent on the preferred shift. For example, a schedule of two weeks of days, one week of afternoons, and one week of evenings is acceptable, but a schedule of one week of days, one week of afternoons, and two weeks of evenings can create problems. In this case, it would be prudent to adopt **cyclical staffing**, which is the rotation of work schedule for a group of employees to allow for a fair distribution of evening and weekend shifts for each person within the group. **Float employees**, staff that are cross-trained in a number of departmental functions, can often be utilized to enable this particular type of scheduling.

In situations where weekend coverage is an issue, employees should have at least alternate weekends off. Many employers pay a slightly higher hourly wage to employees who work less desirable shifts (evening, night, weekend). This is referred to as a *shift differential.*

Mandatory activities and the minimal staff needed to cover them should be defined when determining weekend or holiday coverage. All employees should participate in holiday and weekend rotation. Holiday rotations should be posted one year in advance and weekend rotations at least three months in advance. Employees should be required to provide their own holiday or weekend replacements but should not be responsible for providing replacements when their absence is due to illness.

Vacation and Absentee Coverage

To keep productivity optimal, the HIS department manager must plan appropriately for vacation staffing and absentee coverage. Temporary FTEs hired to cover for vacationing employees are most desirable, but not always financially feasible. Moreover, some positions are too complex to be filled with float FTEs. For example, it is unlikely that a temporary assistant director could be hired to fill in for an assistant director on a two-week vacation. In such a case, key tasks that must be attended to must be identified and distributed appropriately among staff who will handle them while the employee is on vacation. Generally staff who are absent for more than a week can add undue stress on the remaining employees and adversely affect department service levels; thus, it would be advisable to hire temporary help when more than one week of absence is expected. See table 22.2.

Table 22.2. Sample vacation schedule

Employee	Title	Hire Date	Week #	7/1	7/8	7/15	7/22	7/29	8/5	8/12	8/19
Brown	Transcriptionist	2001	1					x			
Dorsey	Transcriptionist	2000	2	x							x
Grunch	Transcriptionist	1999	3		x				x	x	
Glass	Clerk	2000	2			x	x				

Diewell Community Hospital Vacation Policy

General Employees	Department Managers/Administrators
3 years or less = 1 week	3 years or less = 2 weeks
4 to 7 years = 2 weeks	4 to 7 years = 3 weeks
8 to 10 years = 3 weeks	8 years and over = 4 weeks
11 years and over = 4 weeks	

Alternate Work Schedules

Today's work environment has accepted some work scheduling alternatives to the regular 40-hour work week; for example:

- **Compressed workweek:** A week in which more hours are combined within fewer days (for example, four 10-hour days, three 12-hour days, seven 10-hour days with seven days off [seven on/seven off], and so on). This type of scheduling has advantages but may present child care issues and psychological or physical fatigue that could reduce efficiency and productivity.
- **Flextime** (also called *gliding time* or *bandwidth flextime*): Employees choose their arrival and departure times around a fixed core work time. For example, if management feels full coverage is essential between 10 a.m. and 2 p.m., employees could start as early as 5:30 a.m. or end as late as 6:30 p.m. and still provide the department with core coverage.
- **Job sharing:** Divides one job between two part-time employees, each with partial benefits (as they apply). In some organizations, the two employees split full-time benefits (for example, one takes insurance coverage and one takes vacation time). Job sharing may work well in some cases, but it also can be problematic depending on the compatibility of the two individuals involved. And should one person terminate employment, finding a compatible new job-sharing partner could present a challenge.
- **Telecommuting:** Employees work full- or part-time in their own homes. The first employees in HIS departments to take advantage of telecommuting were transcriptionists; they were soon followed by at-home coders. These telecommuters use computers (often provided by the facility) at home to transcribe or code information and then transmit it electronically back to the HIS department. The advantages to this type of work scheduling are that it saves space in the department, reduces long commutes to the workplace, retains parents who prefer to be home, and offers work opportunities to the physically challenged. On the other hand, employers may feel a loss of control when employees telecommute. And some employees in alternative work situations, such as telecommuters, need contact hours with other employees to avoid feeling disconnected from the department. (See chapter 24 for further discussion on managing telecommuters.)

In general, the benefits to employers of alternative work schedules include easier staff recruitment and better retention, increased morale, decreased absence and tardiness, and some productivity improvements. For employees, the benefits can include less home stress, reduced commuting time, and a perception of greater autonomy in the workplace.

Outsourcing

In some cases, flexible job arrangements may not be an option for employees. Another solution to the problem of a shortage of qualified staff is **outsourcing**. In this arrangement, the organization contracts with an independent company with expertise in a specific job function. The outside company then assumes full responsibility for performing the function rather than just supplying staff. Outsourcing functions (domestic and off-shore) provides access to staff as needed, even in a tight labor market; frees up internal resources for other things, eliminates some process or service "headaches," provides access to newest technologies quickly, and accelerates change. The disadvantages for the health information manager include less immediate control over the quantity and quality of the work, the need to know negotiation techniques, and the reliance on the vendor. HIPAA also requires special arrangements regarding security and confidentiality for outsourcing contractors. In an outsourced environment, the health information manager's responsibility shifts from supervising employees to managing a vendor relationship.

Common functions that are candidates for outsourcing in the HIM department include transcription, release of information, and most recently, coding. The outsourcing company may perform the functions either at the institution or partially or completely off-site. Advances in communication and security technology have resulted in many home-based workers being employed by such independent companies.

When healthcare organizations decide to use outsourcing, a manager is challenged to select the most appropriate vendor to provide the services desired. Specific key factors to consider when selecting a vendor or partner include:

- Commitment to quality
- Price
- References and reputation
- Cultural match
- Flexible contract terms
- Value-added capability
- Existing relationship

What leads to success when adopting an outsourcing vendor or contracted service? Senior executive support is a requisite for achieving success in outsourcing. The administration's confidence in the process is essential to creating the seamlessness necessary for continued, smooth functional operation. Administrative support can best be engaged when the manager understands the organization's goals for each outsourcing or contracted service effort being planned. Selecting the right vendor is a definite variable for a successful outsourcing. Good management of the relationship between the healthcare organization and the outsourcing partner includes properly constructed contracts, open communication among partners, and careful attention to personnel issues.

Suggestions for successful outsourcing arrangements include:

- Seeking assistance from someone skilled in negotiation when developing the contract with the vendor
- Engaging legal counsel to review the language of the contract to ensure that it complies with the HIPAA requirements

- Requiring competitive bidding for each outsourced service at regular intervals
- Establishing expectations and performance standards for contractors
- Monitoring compliance with performance standards
- Performing periodic customer surveys to assess satisfaction with the service

Off Shoring

Off shoring is a special case of outsourcing, where employees of the company are based overseas, most frequently in India, China, and the United Kingdom. The major benefits are cost savings and availability of a labor pool. Employees in foreign countries are generally paid much less than those in the United States and are extremely productive. There is also less turnover. HIM jobs such as transcription, coding, and insurance claims processing are very suited to these types of workers. Jobs most suitable for off shoring have the following characteristics:

- No face-to-face customer service requirements
- High information content
- High wage differential with workers in the destination country
- Low social networking requirement
- Little management or interaction with others in the organization

Those countries with young populations that speak English are preferred. The country also should have reliable utilities and suitable digital and voice networks.

As in any outsourcing arrangement, quality control and compliance with privacy and security standards are important issues to be addressed in contracts and performance monitoring.

Contracting for Services

When a manager is planning to contract for staffing in a transitional situation in order to meet organizational goals, various types of arrangements can be considered, including:

- *Full-service:* Contracting for staffing to handle a complete function within the department; for example, Cancer Registry function.
- *Project based:* Contracting for staffing to focus on completion of a specific project.
- *Temporary:* Contracting for staffing to cover for a transient event in order to keep productivity in line.

Clear definitions of the work or services needed as well as the performance expectations are crucial to a successful contract for services. Service-level agreements (SLAs) provide this detail in writing, plus price and payment terms, the reporting chain of command, terms for termination of the relationship, and confidentiality expectations of the vendor and vendor staff.

Work Procedures

Management has the responsibility to develop procedures for employees that fully aid them in effectively and efficiently carrying out their job functions. A **job procedure** is a structured, action-oriented list of sequential steps involved in carrying out a specific job or solving a problem.

Rules of Procedure Writing

To be effective, procedure writing requires considerable attention to detail. The following criteria facilitate the development of well-written procedures:

- Display the title of the procedure accurately and clearly.
- Number each step of the procedure for ready reference.
- Begin each activity with an action verb.
- Keep sentences short and concise.
- Include only procedures, not policies. Policy manuals should be maintained as separate documents; though it is appropriate to include references to related policies within the procedure so the employee can easily locate the policy within the Policy Manual as may be necessary or desired.
- Identify logical beginning and end points to simplify directions.
- Consider the audience and construct the procedure to be of most help to that audience. For example, new staff, temporary staff, or cross-trained staff who perform these procedures only occasionally need a basic, simplified version to ensure completion of a new or seldom-performed task.

In addition, the written procedure should provide completed ("filled in") samples of forms used during the procedure.

It is considered best practice to have an experienced employee who does the job write (or at least draft) the procedure because he or she knows it best. Supervisory personnel should collect all the written procedures and determine whether they are complete and follow a consistent format. Supervisory personnel are also responsible for ensuring that procedures are reviewed at least annually and updated in a timely way when the procedure is modified.

Procedure Formats

When determining the appropriate format for a procedure, the HIS manager needs to consider the audience as well as the complexity of the task. Several formats can be followed for procedural documentation, including:

- **Narratives:** Narrative formats are the most common for procedure writing. The author details the processes of the procedure in a step-by-step description method.
- **Playscript:** This format describes each player in the procedure, the action of the player, and the player's responsibility regarding the process from start to completion of a specific task within the procedure.
- **Flowcharts:** Flowcharts use standard flowcharting symbols provided in software programs such as PowerPoint and VISIO to depict the steps associated with a procedure. Figure 22.3 shows an example of procedure flowcharting applied in the HIS setting.

Figure 22.3. Loose chart filing flowchart

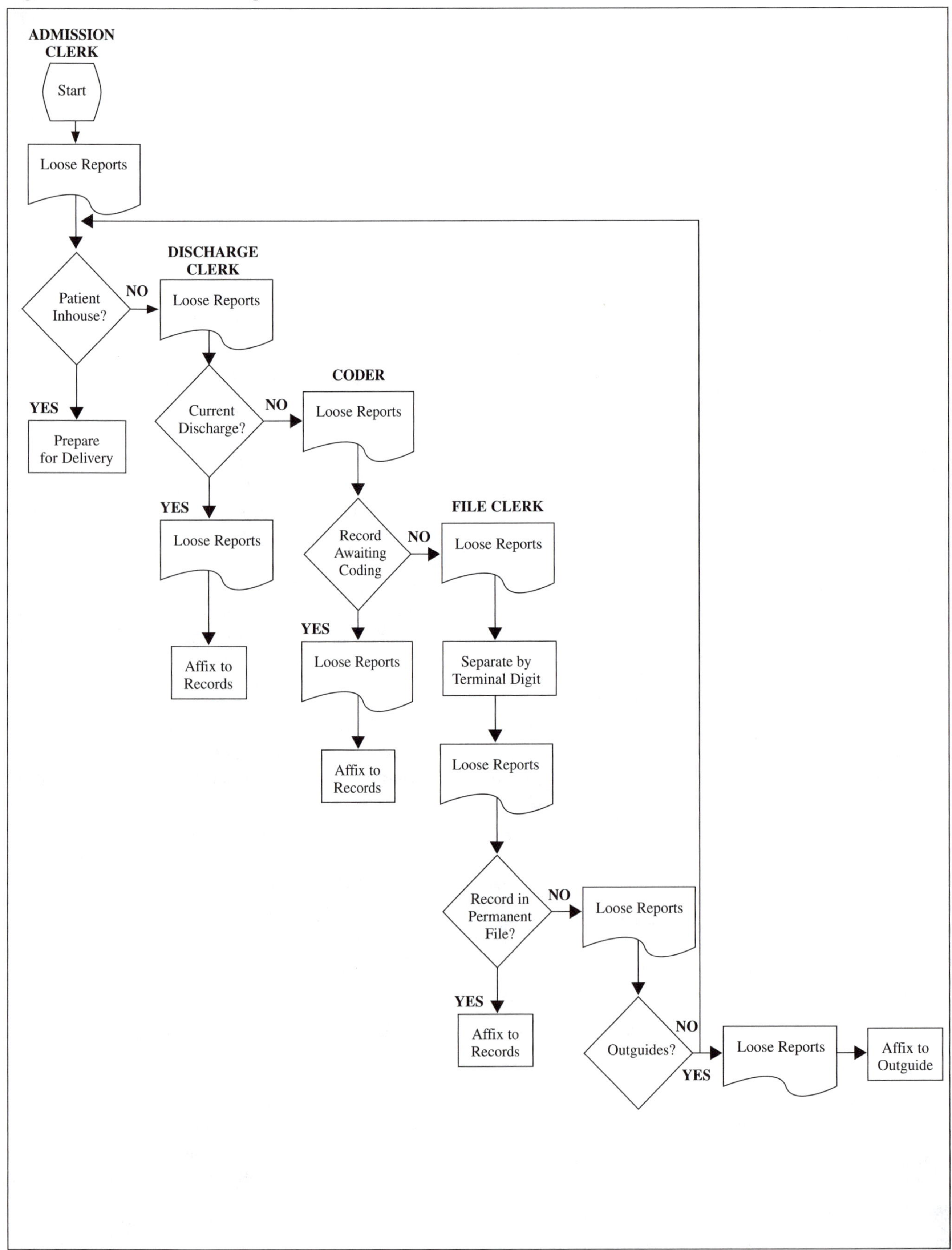

Sometimes a combination of narrative and flowchart formats is used. However, whatever format is chosen, all procedures should be available to employees at any time.

Procedure Manuals

A **procedure manual** is a compilation of all of the procedures used in a specific unit, department, or organization. Procedure manuals may be kept as hard copies that have been printed and bound together in a book or binder, or they may be maintained on an organization's secure Web site or intranet. The value associated with procedure manuals include:

- Promoting teamwork
- Promoting consistency in the work of employees
- Reducing training time
- Establishing guidance on the standards of the work unit
- Explaining what is expected of employees
- Answering employee questions

The manual's content and format are relatively straightforward. Procedure manuals should include the following elements:

- *Title page:* Name of the facility, name of the manual, name of the department, and date
- *Foreword:* Paragraph form, purpose of manual, suggestion for use by employees
- *Table of contents:* List of all procedures in the manual referenced to page number
- *Job procedures:* Step-by-step job procedures, including forms used in each procedure, and including completed forms together with explanations to ensure accurate completion of forms
- *General rules and regulations:* Information that includes department- or unit-specific details often influenced by state or federal law and regulatory agencies
- *Index*: Alphabetical list of topics covered in the manual (optional)

Check Your Understanding 22.2

Instructions: Answer the following questions on a separate piece of paper.

1. Looking at the sample vacation schedule in table 22.2, identify which weeks would the department be well advised to secure temporary help
2. List the potential problem areas a work distribution analysis can reveal.
3. Differentiate flextime, job sharing, and the compressed workweek as three unique alternatives to the regular 40-hour staffing schedule.
4. Explain what information is included in a service level agreement (SLA) and why it is needed.
5. Explain who should be involved with writing a job description and why.

Performance and Work Measurement Standards

Work is the task to be performed; **performance** is the execution of the task. Effective management involves discerning what work is to be done, what performance standards are achievable and appropriate, how performance can be measured in terms of efficiency and effectiveness, and how performance can be monitored for variances from the standards set. Most employees simply want to know for which tasks they are responsible, what is expected of them, and how they are performing relative to that expectation. Through performance standard-setting and measurement processes, managers can confirm the level of success of a work unit or identify opportunities for improvement.

A **standard** may be defined as a performance criterion established by custom or authority for the purpose of assessing factors such as quality, productivity, and performance. Managers are responsible for controlling all of the resources available to them, including men (staff), materials (supplies), machines (equipment), methods (procedures), and money (budget). Thus, managers are expected to set standards for each of these resources and then use them as ways to judge (assess, evaluate) the quality, productivity, and performance of those resources.

Criteria for Setting Effective Standards

To create viable, significant standards, it is important to be aware of the criteria commonly considered as the foundation for developing effective standard setting. Effective standards are:

- *Understandable:* The person(s) affected by the standard know what it means and it makes sense to them.
- *Attainable:* It is reasonable to expect that the person(s) affected by the standard can actually achieve it.
- *Equitable:* If more than one person is affected by the standard, all are held accountable for it.
- *Significant:* Meeting the standard is important to the goals of the work unit or organization; the effort it takes to meet the standard is worth it.
- *Legitimate:* The standard has been formally accepted within the organization and is documented in appropriate places and ways.
- *Economical:* The standard can be met and monitored without incurring costs that are beyond the value of that which is gained by having it. In other words, achieving the standard must be worth the expense associated with achieving it.

Types of Standards

Standards commonly are worded differently at various levels within the organization depending on whether they reflect a goal or an objective. A **goal** is a generalized statement of a unit, departmental, or organizational standard, typically without measurable content. An **objective** is a statement of end result in measurable terms with time and cost limits, as applicable. For example, the HIS department might have a general standard (most commonly called a goal) for its transcription function, such as "to support patient care through accurate and timely transcription of medical reports." The transcription function then might state a standard in objective form to make it more specific and measurable, for example, "to complete routine history and physical, operative, and consultation dictation within eight hours of dictation." Note that this objective is related directly to the timeliness aspect of the preceding goal statement.

Qualitative and Quantitative Standards

Objective level standards are also commonly characterized in two other ways: as quantitative standards and as qualitative standards.

Qualitative standards specify the level of **service quality** expected from a function, such as:

- *Accuracy rate:* For example, assignment of diagnostic and procedure codes for inpatient records is at least 98 percent accurate.
- *Error rate:* For example, mistakes in the assignment of diagnostic and procedure codes occur in no more than two percent of inpatient records coded.

Quantitative standards specify the level of measurable work, or **productivity**, expected for a specific function, such as:

- Number of units of work per specified period of time or amount of time allotted per unit of work (for example, 70 records per FTE per day or no more than 15 minutes are allotted to coding an inpatient record.)
- Turnaround time (for example, dictation must be transcribed within 24 hours.)
- Response time (for example, requests for information are responded to within seven working days of receipt.)

Quantity standards (also called productivity standards) and quality standards (also known as service standards) are generally used by managers to monitor individual employee performance and the performance of a functional unit or the department as a whole. To properly communicate performance standards, managers need to make the distinction between quantitative and qualitative standards and identify examples of each for the HIS functions.

Keeping the criteria for effective standards in mind and the difference between qualitative and quantitative standards, it is possible to set about developing standards for any of the resources under the control of management. Several examples of resource management standards are provided here:

- Standards related to "men" (staff resources)
  - *Qualitative (Quality):* Chart deficiency analyst accurately identifies chart completion status in 98 percent of charts analyzed.
  - *Quantitative (Productivity):* Coders code 25 to 30 inpatient discharges per eight-hour workday.
- Standards related to "materials" (supply resources)
  - *Qualitative (Quality):* Paper-based health record forms must be printed on 20-pound paper stock
  - *Quantitative (Productivity):* Each functional work unit in the department maintains no more than 1 weeks' volume of consumable supplies on hand
- Standards related to "money" (budget resources)
  - *Qualitative (Quality):* Major expense categories (salaries, supplies, postage, telephone, travel, and maintenance) must remain within plus or minus 3 percent of the budgeted amount monthly.
  - *Quantitative (Productivity):* Paid dollars per key statistic (P$PKS) must be less than $2 plus or minus the target P$PKS indicator established for the department.
- Standards related to "methods" (procedures)
  - *Qualitative (Quality):* An employee can effectively complete the entry of a release of information request into the ROI tracking system by following the steps outlined in the documented procedure.
  - *Quantitative (Productivity):* The steps outlined for completing the entry of a release of information request into the ROI tracking system can be completed in less than 1 minute per request.
- Standards related to "machines" (equipment)
  - *Qualitative (Quality):* The copier must be functioning properly 99 percent of the time; that is, less than 2 hours of downtime per month.
  - *Quantitative (Productivity):* The document imaging equipment must be able to process 30 to 40 images per minute.

Key Indicators

Key indicators are "live" (versus retrospective) measurement thresholds that alert a department or work unit to its current level of service. Key indicators allow managers to monitor critical service standards on a current basis so he or she can make timely staffing or process adjustments to ensure that department service performance remains on course. Common key indicators in HIS departments include:

- Transcription turnaround time
- Days outstanding in Accounts Receivable (A/R)
- Release of Information turnaround time
- Percentage of incomplete charts

These red flag indicators would certainly move a department manager to take corrective actions:

- The number and severity of complaints increase. When the number or severity of complaints increases, the circumstances surrounding the complaints need to be assessed immediately so that corrections to the process or personnel involved can be made.
- Compliance surveys to assess performance on accreditation, legal, or regulatory standards indicate that the organization has failed to comply in one or more areas. When

the organization fails to comply with one or more external standards during a survey, the organization needs to correct the variance(s) and return to compliance.

Methods of Communicating Standards

After standards have been created, they must be communicated to staff. All the above types of standards can be provided to staff in a number of ways, including through:

- *Written specifications:* For example, in job descriptions, performance evaluation forms, equipment specification sheets, and forms design guidelines
- *Documented rules, regulations, or policies:* For example, in policy manuals, regulations or accreditation manuals, and employee handbooks
- *Demonstration models:* For example, samples, videos, computer-based learning modules
- *Verbal confirmations:* For example, in departmental or work unit meetings, individual employee counseling sessions

Methods of Developing Standards

There are several methods that can be employed to develop performance standards in a work unit. Two approaches are commonly used: benchmarking comparable performance and measuring actual performance.

Benchmarking Comparable Performance

Benchmarking is based on researching the performance of similar organizations and programs or gathering data on standards established by national or local sources, such as professional associations and standard-setting organizations. Benchmarking has become a more prevalent approach to standard setting in HIS management in the past few years because this type of information is now being published regularly.

To engage in a benchmarking effort, the manager should first select key functions of the department that will be benchmarked (coding service, transcription service, release of information [ROI] service, and so on). Relating benchmarks to the specific process is critical. Thought must be given to the types of performance measure(s) desired as indicators (for coding, for example, payments remaining in accounts receivable due to uncoded records and payments remaining in accounts receivable due to coding disputes; for transcription, for example, turnaround time [dictation to charting] for consultations, operative reports, history and physicals).

When the key functional areas have been selected and the types of indicators identified, the research for benchmarks available through published sources (preferably) can begin. Investigation of benchmark standards gathered through this research must also involve a critical assessment of their relevance to the department's specific situation; then the standard can be successfully sold to the rest of the organization. Benchmarking involves the following steps:

1. Identifying peer organizations and departments that have achieved outstanding performance based on some key indicator (for example, 98 percent of health records coded within two days post-discharge)
2. Studying the best practices within the organization that make it possible to achieve that performance level
3. Acting to implement those best practices in one's own organization to achieve a similar performance

Before officially adopting a benchmark standard, a manager should routinely gather performance data in the department to match actual performance against the benchmark and then evaluate factors in department processes that must be changed to eventually move actual performance into the benchmark range.

Measurement of Actual Performance

Work measurement is the process of studying the amount of work accomplished and the amount of time it takes to accomplish it. It involves the collection of data relevant to the work, such as the amount of work accomplished per unit of time. Its purpose is to define and monitor productivity.

Work measurement can support a manager in many activities, including:

- Setting production standards
- Determining staffing requirements
- Establishing incentive pay systems
- Determining direct costs by function
- Comparing performance to standards
- Identifying activities for process and methods improvement

Gathering the information available through work measurement efforts will be invaluable to the manager in making administrative decisions. But how do managers know which method of work measurement will serve them best?

When selecting the work measurement technique that best suits his or her department, the manager should consider the following factors:

- Amount of financial resources available
- Availability of qualified personnel to take part in the study
- Amount of time available to devote to study
- Attitudes of employees toward participation in a study

Work measurement can be accomplished through a variety of techniques, including:

- *Analysis of historical (past performance) data:* The analysis of historical data generally uses work volume (direct or estimated) and hours paid from past records to establish the standard. When using historical data, managers are cautioned to keep in mind that volume figures are not adjusted for the level of quality and the number of hours paid is different from the number of hours actually worked.

- *Employee self-logging:* Employee self-logging is a form of self-reporting in which the employees simply track their tasks, volume of work units, and hours worked. Employee logging incorporates a **time ladder**, which is a form used by the employee to document the amount of time spent (worked) on various tasks. It can be modified to include the number of units produced per task throughout the day. **Volume logs** are sometimes used in conjunction with a time ladder to obtain information about the volume of work units received and processed in a day by simply keeping track of the number of products produced or activities done. (See table 22.3.)
- *Scientific methods:* The scientific methods of work measurement include time studies and the use of pre-established time/unit standards. For example, time studies use a stopwatch to record and document the time required to accomplish a specified task.
- *Work sampling:* **Work sampling** is a technique of work measurement that involves using statistical probability (determined through random sample observations) to characterize the performance of the department and its work (functional) units.

Each one of the varieties of work measurement techniques offers calculations of employee productivity in either unit/time or time/unit. For example, with the completion of a daily time ladder summary (see table 22.4), a manager can determine simple unit/time productivity statistics by dividing the number of units produced by the number of hours worked. Table 22.4 also contains the type of data needed to calculate the weekly activities of coders and a clerk's weekly activities.

Gathering the information available through any of these work measurement efforts will be invaluable to the manager in making administrative decisions. But how does a manager know which method of work measurement will serve them best? The manager should consider the following factors when attempting to select the work measurement method that best suits his or her department:

- Amount of financial resources available
- Availability of qualified personnel to take part in the study
- Amount of time available to devote to study
- Attitudes of employees toward participation in a study

A Focus on Work Sampling

Work sampling is an especially valuable method for developing performance standards. Work-sampling data can help the manager to:

- Catalog the activities being performed
- Determine the time devoted to each activity
- Identify inefficiencies
- Set employee performance standards

Work-sampling projects follow an established sequence of steps and use specific tools:

1. Decide which work activities to monitor during the study.
2. Design the form that will be used to record the observations collected during the study. The sample observation record form shown in table 22.5 captures activities by individuals and by units of function (supervisory, transcription, clerical, and coder).
3. Determine the best size of the study sample by using the precision interval method, a standard formula used

Table 22.3. Sample volume log

Task	Number of Worked Hours	Number of Units
Coding	40 worked hours	120 records
Loose filing	36 worked hours	48 inches

The coding standard calculates at three records per worked hour for this employee (120 records/40 hours) and a filing standard of 1.3 inches per worked hour (48 inches/36 hours). It does not capture any interruptions or unworked time in the eight-hour day but is a simple way to arrive at a ballpark figure.

Table 22.4. Sample daily time ladder summary

Unit: Reception Date: 07-04-02
Note: 7.5 worked hours (two 15-minute breaks)

Employee	Code/Task	Total Time (%)	Work Units
Jane	A. Answer phones	3hr/40%	64
	B. Write requisitions	1.75 hr/23%	92
	C. Personal/set up, etc.	.5 hr/7%	NA
	D. Mail handling	2.25 hr/30%	Incoming 80 Outgoing 100
Betty	A. Answer phones	5 hr/66%	100
	B. Write requisitions	.5 hr/7%	15
	C. Personal/set up, etc.	.5/7%	NA
	D. Mail handling	0	NA
	E. Stat chart delivery	1.5/20%	10

Table 22.5. Sample observation record form

	Mason	Davis	Perry	Kent	Martin	Carter	Roth	Evans	Larson	Owens .5 FTE	
Activity	**Supervisor**	**Transcriptionists**			**Clerical**				**Coders**		**Total**
Supervision											
Coding											
Transcription											
Record A & A											
Record retrieval/filing/transport											
Release of Information											
Assisting physicians											
Other clerical											
Idle: Gone, rest											
Total observations											

Observation Times:

1. 6.
2. 7.
3. 8. Recorded by: ____________
4. 9.
5. 10. Date: ____________

to determine sample size. The formula allows for various scenarios of desired **certainty factor** (confidence factor) and **precision factor** (acceptable error) in the study results. The certainty factor is a numerical representation of the confidence the manager has that the results will show the level of acceptable error. The precision factor is the level of tolerable error in the sampling process.

$$\text{Sample size} = 0.25 \times \left[\frac{\text{certainty factor }\%^2}{\text{precision factor }\%}\right]$$

Note that the 0.25 is a fixed (not variable) part of the formula.

If the precision factor is 5 percent, the confidence factor needed is 95 percent. (Note that the precision factor plus the confidence factor equal 100 percent.) For example:

$$25 \times (0.95 \div 0.025)^2 = 0.25 \times (38 \times 38) = 361$$

4. Determine the length of the study and establish appropriate observation times. When the sample size (total number of observations required) has been determined, the number of observations per day can be determined on the basis of the number of days, weeks, or months available to complete the study. The actual time of each observation each day must be determined by using a random observation generator (see figure 22.4) and a random numbers table (see figure 22.5). To create the observation generator, list the period of time the study will take place in a workday. (See figure 22.4, from 8 a.m. until 4 p.m., with 10-minute increments) and number each predetermined time increment. Then using a random numbers table

Figure 22.4. Observation generator

Time Block Number	Clock Time	Time Block Number	Clock Time
0	8:00 a.m.	25	12:10 p.m.
1	10	26	20
2	20	27	30
3	30	28	40
4	40	29	50
5	50	30	1:00 p.m.
6	9:00 a.m.	31	10
7	10	32	20
8	20	33	30
9	30	34	40
10	40	35	50
11	50	36	2:00 p.m.
12	10.00 a.m.	37	10
13	10	38	20
14	20	39	30
15	30	40	40
16	40	41	50
17	50	42	3:00 p.m.
18	11:00 a.m.	43	10
19	10	44	20
20	20	45	30
21	30	46	40
22	40	47	50
23	50	48	4:00 p.m.
24	12:00 p.m.	etc.	

Figure 22.5. Random numbers table (partial)

69	18	82	00	97	32	82	53	05	27
90	04	58	54	97	51	98	15	06	54
73	18	95	02	07	47	67	72	62	59
54	01	64	90	04	66	28	13	10	03
75	75	87	64	90	20	97	18	17	49
08	35	86	99	10	78	53	24	27	85
28	30	30	32	64	81	33	31	05	91
53	84	08	62	33	31	59	41	36	28
etc.									

Note: Entry may be made at any point, proceeding horizontally or vertically.

(figure 22.5 is a partial table of tables found in any statistics book), randomly select the first number and then a direction to read the numbers (horizontally, vertically, or diagonally). Looking at the first number, refer to the observation generator to find the time of day assigned that corresponding number. If it does not exist, proceed to the next number until the optimal number to complete the study has been selected. For example, if 500 observations were needed and 50 workdays were allotted to complete the study, 10 observations would need to be made each day of the 50-day study. (See figure 22.6.)

5. Explain the purpose of the study and how it is conducted to observers and staff. Orientation of observers and personnel is very important because it encourages consistency in data collection among observers and ensures that unbiased and reliable observations are collected on the basis of the observation schedule. At this point in the study, those who will be observed also must be informed of its purpose. It is important that workers perform normally throughout the process. They also should understand that the outcome of the study will be shared with them at the conclusion of the study period.
6. Collect and record observation data at random points. (See table 22.6.)
7. Report the results of the study. (See table 22.7, table 22.8, and table 22.9.)

Figure 22.6. Example of a first day's observation times

Observation Times		
1. 8:50 a.m.	6. 1:00 p.m.	
2. 9:40 a.m.	7. 1:10 p.m.	
3. 10:20 a.m.	8. 1:20 p.m.	Recorded by: ______
4. 12:00 noon	9. 2:20 p.m.	Department: ______
5. 12:40 p.m.	10. 2:30 p.m.	Date: ______

Check Your Understanding 22.3

Instructions: On a separate piece of paper, indicate whether the following statements are true or false. Then correct any false statement to make it true or explain why it is false.

1. A standard is a criterion established by custom or authority for the purpose of assessing quality, productivity, or performance.
2. Turnaround times are examples of qualitative standards and error rates are examples of quantitative standards
3. Work sampling is a work measurement methodology that relies on statistical probability to characterize the performance of the functional work units in a department.
4. Men (staff), money (budget), materials (supplies), machines (equipment), and methods (procedures) are the basic resources under the control of a manager.

Table 22.6. First day's observations, Cure-All Hospital's HIM department

	Mason	Davis	Perry	Kent	Martin	Carter	Roth	Evans	Larson	Owens .5 FTE	
Activity	**Supervisor**	**Transcriptionists**			**Clerical**				**Coders**		**Total**
Supervision											2
Coding											0
Transcription											24
Record A & A											10
Record retrieval/filing/transport											16
Release of information											8
Assisting physicians											8
Other clerical											15
Idle: Gone, rest											10
Total observations	10	10	10	10	10	10	10	10	10	3	93

Table 22.7. Observation summary, Cure-All Hospital's HIM department

Activity	Previous Observation Days	3/10/00	Study Total	% Total
Supervision	—	2	90	2.2
Coding	—	0	18	0.4
Transcription	—	24	1,053	25.9
Record A & A	—	10	540	13.3
Filing/retrieval/transport	—	16	618	15.2
Release of information	—	8	381	9.4
Assisting physicians	—	8	273	6.7
Other clerical	—	15	711	17.5
Idle: Gone, rest	—	10	378	9.4
Total observations	—	93	4,062	100.0

Note: This particular work sampling effort involved a total work sampling of 500 planned observations (10 observations per workday for 50 days). This number of observations gives a ±2.75% precision interval for = >10% activities, a 5.5% accuracy rate, and 94.5% confidence level.

Table 22.8. Work sampling results, Cure-All Hospital's HIM department: Actual activity vs. expectations

Activity	Normal Range of Expectations	Department Expectations	Department Actual	Estimated Variation
Supervision	NA	15%	2.2%	−13%
Coding	2–4.5%	3%	0.4%	−2%
Transcription	30–40%	30%	25.9%	−4%
Record A & A	10–13%	12%	13.3%	+1%
Record retrieval/filing	2–5%	3%	15.2%	+12%
Release of information	6–9%	7%	9.4%	+2%
Assisting physicians	6–10%	8%	6.7%	−1%
Other clerical	8–13%	10%	17.5%	+7%
Idle: Gone, rest	7–14%	12%	9.4%	−3%
Total	NA	100%	100%	NA

Table 22.9. Work sampling results, Cure-All Hospital's HIM department

Activity Area/Expected %	% of Time	Minutes*	Hours*	Work Volume for Period	Work Units
Supervision/15%	2%	4,560	76	NA	NA
Coding/3%	1%	0.01 × 228,000 or 2,280	0.01 × 3,800 or 38 hours	775	Dx coded
Transcription/30%	26%	0.26 × 228,000 or 59,280	0.26 × 3,800 or 988	150,000	Lines transcribed
Record assembly and analysis/12%	13%	29,640	494	2,964	Records analyzed
Record filing, retrieval, etc./3%	15%	34,200	570	11,400	Records pulled/filed
Release of information/7%	9%	20,520	342	1,050	Requests handled
Assisting physician/8%	7%	15,960	266	NA	NA
Other clerical/10%	18%	41,040	684	NA	NA
Idle: Gone, rest/12%	9%	20,520	342	NA	NA
Total	100%	—	—	—	—

Notes: Working days in the period: 50 days
Current workforce: 9.5 FTE, including the supervisor
Work minutes/day per FTE: 480 minutes (8 hr × 60)
Total study work hours: 3,800 hours (9.5 FTE × 8 × 50)
Total study work minutes: 228,000 minutes (9.5 FTE × 480 × 50) or (3,800 × 60)

*Minutes and hours are calculated based on the percentage of total time represented by each activity area. For example, 2% of 228,000 minutes = 4,560 minutes; 2% of 3,800 hours = 76 hours.

Performance Measurement

Performance measurement is the process of comparing the outcomes of an organization, work unit, or employee to pre-established performance standards. The results of the performance measurement process generally are expressed as percentages, rates, ratios, averages, and other quantitative assessments. Performance measurement is used to assess quality and productivity in clinical services and in administrative services. Examples of performance measures maintained by acute care hospitals in clinical services include the rate of nosocomial infection, the percentage of surgical complications, the average length of stay, and the ratio of live births to stillbirths. Examples of performance measures maintained by an administrative service such as the HIS department include transcription lines transcribed and turnaround times per report type, turnaround times for ROI requests, and days in A/R due to uncoded patient discharges.

Performance measurement is a fundamental management activity that supports two of the basic functions of management: controlling and planning. The control function is concerned with ensuring that the work unit or organization is doing what it should be doing in the right way. The planning function is concerned with defining the expectations of performance (standards or objectives), the processes required for achieving those expectations (procedures), and the desired outcomes of performance (or goals). The goals, objectives, standards, and processes established during the planning process become the criteria used in the control process to evaluate actual performance.

Performance Controls

In the control process, specific monitors (controls) are established for the purpose of identifying undesirable circumstances occurring in a work process that could lead to an undesirable outcome so appropriate intervention can be introduced into the process.

The characteristics of effective performance controls include:

- *Flexibility* refers to the fact that controls must be adaptable to real changes in the requirements of a process. For example, a budget is a control on the use of money. Money budgeted in one category (equipment) may need to be spent in another category (travel) because of a change in a program, a new law or regulation, and so on.
- *Simplicity* refers to the fact that those involved in the process must find the controls understandable and reasonable.
- *Economy* implies that controls should not cost more than they are worth. The time and money spent to implement a control should be in line with the level of risk (loss) involved if the process fails to meet performance expectations. For example, potential loss of a life calls for a significant investment in controls; potential criminal liability calls for significant investment in controls; while the potential for having to pay for a day of overtime to correct clerical errors calls for a minimal investment in controls.
- *Timeliness* suggests that controls should be implemented so as to detect potential variances within a time frame that allows for corrective action before any adverse effect has occurred. For example, the accuracy of a record number assignment should be confirmed at the time of registration or the coding checked before a bill is mailed or transmitted in order to avoid the adverse effects associated with errors that are then transmitted to other areas of the organization or outside the organization (for example, the insurance carrier).
- *Focus on exceptions* demands that controls are targeted at those aspects of a process that are most likely to vary significantly from expectation. For example, a new transcriptionist who is likely to make more errors that could do damage to customer service ratings is generally monitored (controlled) more closely and more frequently than one who is experienced and has performed well for the past year.

There are two general types of controls: preventive (self-correcting) and feedback (non-self-correcting). **Preventive controls** are front-end processes that guide work in such a way that input and process variations are minimized. Simple things such as standard operating procedures, edits on data entered into computer-based systems, and training processes are ways to reduce the potential for error by using preventive controls.

Feedback controls are back-end processes that monitor and measure output, and then compare it to expectations and identify variations that then must be analyzed so corrective action plans can be developed and implemented. Processes with feedback controls in place are also called cybernetic processes or systems. Some may be self-regulating (such as thermostatic systems), but most are non-self-regulating, meaning that they require intervention by an oversight agent (a supervisor, manager, or auditor) to identify the variance and take action to correct it. A customer survey or routine performance reviews are examples of this type of control.

Variance Analysis

In the context of performance measurement, when variations are identified (that is, actual performance does not meet or significantly exceeds expectations), further analysis is needed. Analysis of the resources involved in the work (people, procedures, supplies, equipment, and money) is conducted to help determine what, if any, changes should be made. Changes may involve activities such as additional staff training; modifications in procedures, adjustments in workflow, revision of policies; purchases of updated equipment. As a result, the analysis and the changes to address findings may also lead to revisions in performance criteria and expectations.

Assessment of Departmental Performance

When establishing an employee performance assessment program, the steps in the control (evaluation) process include:

1. Monitoring and measuring outcomes performance
2. Comparing performance to established goals and standards
3. Evaluating variance and developing action plans
4. Taking appropriate action

Monitoring and Measuring Performance

Monitoring and measuring performance involves taking an aggregate look at performance over a period of time. Options include operating with an employee self-reporting method such as self-logging, using computerized monitoring to audit productivity, manually auditing work samples, or relying on customer feedback to measure performance.

Effective outcomes performance monitoring depends on both employee performance measurement and management execution. The focus of the effort is on service indicators such as turnaround time, cost and revenue reports, and customer feedback. Consider this practical application of department outcomes performance monitoring. Assume that one established expectation of the department is that routine response to an authorized release of information (ROI) request occurs within five working days of receipt of the request in the department.

The first step in controlling this function would be to set up a data collection and reporting activity to obtain information that can be used to monitor the time it takes the department to respond to a routine ROI. (See table 22.10.)

Next, the department should determine the kinds of controls it wants to establish. The department wants to monitor routine requests, but how are "routine requests" defined? A routine request may be any request that is not stat or emergency (that is, it does not have to be handled within minutes, hours, or some stipulated amount of time under five working days). For example, a subpoena for a record that must be handled within three days or a request for a record needed for an appointment in a clinic the next morning would not be considered routine requests.

Table 22.10. ROI requests

On June 6, 2000, Total Routine ROI Requests in Processing: 130					
Days Since Receipt	**6–10 Days**	**11–15 Days**	**16–20 Days**	**>20 Days**	**Summary**
Number of total	12 9%	15 12%	2 2%	1 1%	30 24%
Unable to locate record	0	2	0	1	3 10%
Incomplete record	12	12	2	0	26 87%
Issue with authorization	0	0	0	0	0
Unavailable record	0	1	0	0	1 3%
Other	0	0	0	0	0

The line related to ROI requests in the middle of the performance report shown in table 22.11 indicates the average number of days it took the HIS department to respond to routine ROI requests in January (3), February (3), March (6), and April (5). However, it is important to note that these numbers tell nothing about the routine ROI requests the department received in each of those months which have not yet been responded to.

Table 22.11. Sample health information services performance report

Indicator	January 2006	February 2006	March 2006	April 2006
DCEs	5,000	5,400	5,360	5,500
Labor cost per DCE: <$10.00	$10.00	9.25	9.33	9.90
FTE budgeted at 50	50	50	50	48
Days in assembly/analysis at end of month <2days	1	2	2	3
Delinquency rate <50%	35%	40%	43%	45%
Coding: Days in AR due to uncoded records <5 days	3	5	4	5
Lines transcribed	120,000	130,000	128,000	132,000
Transcription: TAT for H&Ps <24 hours	12	16	18	26
ROI requests received	200	245	300	260
Release of Info: TAT <5 days	3	3	6	5
File pull requests	2,000	2,200	2,300	2,500
Retrieval rate: >95%	%94	%96	%93	%91%
Loose filing inches received	100 average 25/week	120 average 30/week	80 average 20/week	130 average 32/week
Loose filing inches at end of month: <16	15	20	12	15
Filing: Misfiles <1%	.05%	.08%	.06%	.08%
Resignations: <1%	0	0	0	2/50 = 4%
Education hours	4	16	2	8
Unproductive hours (sick, vacation): <15%	10%	12%	20%	10%

The average turnaround time number was calculated by dividing the total response days attributed to the volume of routine requests that were responded to within the reporting period by the volume of routine requests responded to. For example, if the department responded to 300 routine requests in the month of May and 100 were responded to in six days, 100 in two days, and 100 in four days, the average turnaround time in May would be four days:

$$\frac{(600 \text{ days} + 200 \text{ days} + 400 \text{ days})}{300 \text{ requests}} = 4 \text{ days (average)}$$

Having the information on a monthly basis to include as part of the regular performance reporting within the department allows the manager to review monthly trends and identify potential focus areas for future process improvement activities.

The underlying data indicate that a considerable number of requests are not responded to within the five-working-days expectation (for example, 100 [or 33 percent] were responded to in six working days). In this case, the direct supervisor of the ROI function would likely want access to data of this nature more often than once a month. For example, a weekly report showing the number of routine requests in the system for five days or more that have not yet been answered would allow the supervisor or ROI clerk to identify problem requests and take corrective actions over the course of the following week.

Comparing Performance to Established Goals and Standards

The next step in monitoring and measuring outcome performance is to compare current performance against established goals (standards). Continuing with the example in the preceding section, when comparing performance against the standard performance indicator of responding to routine ROIs within five days, the data in table 22.11 show an upward trend in March and April.

Evaluating Variance and Developing Action Plans

When comparisons are done, the manager should evaluate any variances and develop an action plan specific to each. For example, in an evaluation of the performance variance in responding to routine ROI requests, the direct supervisor would likely begin to collect data that will provide the following types of information in order to uncover the factors that have triggered the variances:

- How many open ROI requests exist with a date of receipt of more than five working days?
- What is the aging profile of those open ROI requests; that is, how many are 6 to 10 working days, 10 to 15 working days, 16 to 20 working days, or more than 20 days?
- What are the reasons the requests are still open?
- In what time increments since receipts of the request has the requesting party been notified of the delay and the reason for the delay?

After the variances have been evaluated, an action plan can be formulated to address areas for performance improvement; for example:

- Establish a procedure to ensure weekly contact with the requestor to determine continuing need for the information and update on the status of the request
- Flag the incomplete record with a ROI REQUEST PENDING to ensure that it is routed to ROI immediately when required documentation is complete
- Track the missing record
- Check the status of the unavailable record and contact the current user to obtain the record so that ROI can occur and then (if necessary) the record can be returned to the user.

Taking Appropriate Action

The supervisor, working with the ROI staff, will take the actions put forth in the plan and then continue to monitor the ROI function to determine if the actions taken are effective in resolving the identified performance variance.

Check Your Understanding 22.4

Instructions: Answer the following questions on a separate piece of paper.

1. Define performance measurement and explain why it is a major responsibility of management.
2. Explain the purpose of monitors (or controls) placed on the functions performed in a work unit.
3. Provide examples of the types of changes or actions a manager might take to address performance issues revealed when he or she completes an analysis of performance variances in the department.

Performance Improvement (PI)

Clearly, the reason managers set performance standards and routinely measure departmental performance against those standards is to ensure the department is serving its internal and external customers in ways that meet their needs and expectations. A natural outcome of any performance measurement system is the identification of variances from performance expectations and thus the opportunity to engage in performance improvement activities to bring performance back into line.

The Joint Commission (2009) has standards that specifically require accredited organizations to have PI efforts as an integral aspect of their day-to-day operations, as follows

- LD.04.04.01 The leaders establish priorities for performance improvement.
- LD.04.04.03 New or modified services or processes are well designed.
- PI.01.01.01 The hospital collects data to monitor its performance.
- PI.02.01.02 The hospital compiles and analyzes data.
- PI.03.01.01 The hospital improves performance.

The Role of Customer Service

All process improvement environments today focus on the customer and work to create a true customer orientation within the work environment by listening and responding to customers, thinking about their needs, and using that information to modify and improve the way our systems work for them.

In the process of customer orientation, management and staff must:

- Identify the customers
- Define quality from a customer perspective
- Determine how to judge service
- Obtain regular feedback

Customers are the people, external and internal, who receive and are affected by the work of the organization or department. They have names and needs, and are the reason(s) for the collective work of the organization.

Internal customers are located within the organization. They may be anyone within the work unit who is affected by the HIS function. Physicians and clinical staff need high-quality, expedient patient health information in order to deliver high-quality patient care. Administrative staff members are customers of the information harvested from collective databases for use in planning facilities and services. And not least among the department's internal customers are the HIS department staff who work in each of the functional areas and rely on each other in various ways to get their work done.

External customers reside outside the organization. Physicians seen by patients who originated at the facility for care are considered external customers, as are payers who need information so they can reimburse their enrollees in a timely manner. Regulatory agencies look to HIS for data on conditions of accreditation or participation. Vendors assist HIS, with the department's direct input, in making optimal selections of products. Public health agencies look to HIS for information and data on the health status of the community population in order to earmark services the population needs to maintain a healthy existence.

Identification of Performance Improvement Opportunities

In a department that employs performance standards and engages in routine performance measurement, opportunities for performance improvement present themselves as a natural outcome of that effort. Even when a department is lacking a formal performance measurement program, these common symptoms of performance problems are easily observable by department managers and staff; when observed they present obvious opportunities for performance improvement effort, as well:

- Inaccuracies and errors in work
- Complaints from customers
- Delays in getting things done or lots of interruptions
- Low employee morale or high rates of absenteeism or turnover
- Poor safety records and on-the-job injuries

When inaccuracies and errors are evident in the work products of a group of employees, an investigation of the underlying cause(s) is required and appropriate actions taken to address them so the inaccuracies and errors are eliminated.

Customer complaints indicate that performance is not meeting expectations. Managers need to consider each complaint and determine whether it is circumstantial or a signal of something bigger that needs to be investigated and resolved through an improvement effort.

Delays in getting things done or continuous interruptions to a process can warn of roadblocks to success. Delays give time to revisit the current workflow and analyze what might be improved. If transcribed operative reports are not on the patients' charts within the prescribed time, the reason for the delay should be identified and the improvement activity be planned to eliminate the delay.

Low employee morale and a high rate of absenteeism or turnover are serious indicators that something needs to be improved. While not always the case, commonly these indicators are a sign that there are training, procedural, or task-related problems that underlie the employees' behavior. High turnover and absenteeism are budget draining and call for an investigation followed by a defined plan of action to avert a continued pattern.

Poor safety records or injuries are indicative of urgent process improvement opportunities. Work-related injuries and accidents are management markers regarding a poorly designed or configured work environment, poor equipment, or poor training. Again, work injuries are a costly burden for both the individual employee and the organization.

Collecting meaningful performance data, being alert, and observing and listening to customers and key staff are all ways to identify improvement opportunities. It is a continuous process that has no tolerance for complacency. Excellence is not an accident; it is an intended outcome that requires a manager's commitment and continuous attention.

Principles of Performance Improvement

The concepts of performance improvement, work improvement, process improvement, and methods improvement are essentially synonymous. They all relate to a management philosophy that is, at its core, systems oriented; that is, a management philosophy that views the work processes in an organization as being systematic in nature and seeks to constantly improve them by adjusting various components of the system.

A **system** is set of related elements (components) that are linked together according to a plan in order to meet a specific objective to achieve desired outcomes. Systems come in manual, automated, and hybrid forms. The basic systems model demonstrates that a system is made up of the following components (figure 22.7):

- *Input:* Resources available to system, namely men (staff), money, methods (procedures), machines (equipment), and materials (supplies).
- *Process:* The transformation of the inputs. What is done to or with the inputs that result in something being accomplished?

- *Output:* The finished product or the result of the process, such as an educated student, a transcribed report, a coded record, and so on.
- *Controls* and *standards:* The expectations of what the output should be and the mechanisms in place to monitor, track, and observe how well actual performance measures up to expectations.
- *Feedback:* Information that is reported when output is compared to the standards to identify how well actual output and standards (desired output) mesh. Feedback sometimes comes in the form of customer complaints and certainly feedback can and should come in the form of compliments to staff, as well, when performance expectations are met.
- *External environment:* Anything outside the system that affects how the system functions (for example, laws or regulations set by the local, state, or federal government). In HIS departments, external factors that commonly affect its systems include:
  - The HIPAA regulations related to patient information confidentiality and security
  - Medicare's Conditions of Participation requirements for patient's medical record content
  - MS-DRGs and Present on Admission (POA) regulations which impact coding and reimbursement systems in hospitals
  - A tight labor market, which makes it difficult to hire well qualified employees for specialized jobs

Systems such as those described here also are called **open systems** because they are affected by what is going on around them and must adjust as the environment changes and **cybernetic systems** because they have standards, controls, and feedback mechanisms built into them. On the other hand, a **closed system** operates in a self-contained environment; that is, it is not affected by outside factors. A mechanical system (engines, motors, and so on) is the best example of a closed system.

Figure 22.7. Basic systems model

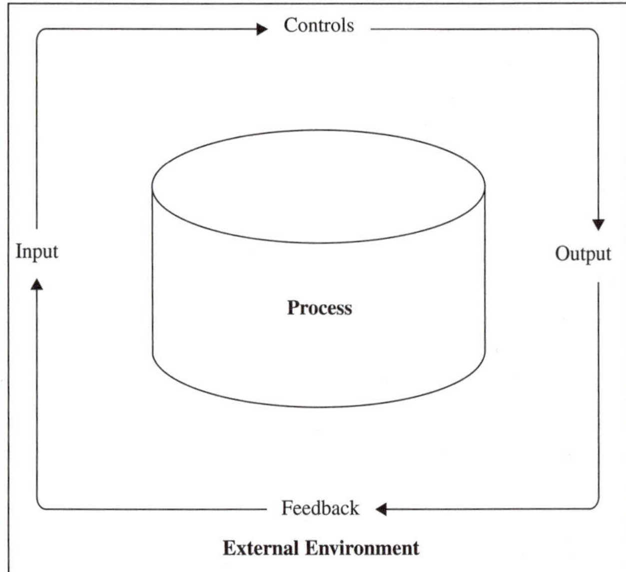

The aim of all performance, work, method or process, or improvement efforts is to increase the effectiveness, efficiency, or the adaptability of the systems that are operating within an organization.

- *Effectiveness:* How closely the output of a system matches what is expected of it. If a department is effective, it is getting done what it is supposed to get done.
- *Efficiency:* How well the department is using its resources; that is, is the department getting the most bang for its buck, or is it wasting staff time, money, or any other of its resources?
- *Adaptability:* The ease with which the system can adjust when circumstances require it to change to meet new demands or expectations. Adaptable systems respond appropriately to changing needs.

Check Your Understanding 22.5

Instructions: On a separate sheet of paper, indicate whether the following sentences are true or false and correct any false statement to make it true or to explain why it is false.

1. The components of an open, cybernetic system are input, process, and output.
2. An efficient process or system is one that uses its resources wisely; that is, it does not waste staff, supplies, money, and so on.
3. The Joint Commission requires accredited hospitals to collect data, aggregate it, and analyze it for the purpose of identifying opportunities for change and making improvements in processes.
4. Customers are the government agencies and public health organizations who have established regulations and policies that affect the way the department does its work.

Process Improvement Methodologies

The principle methodologies available to healthcare facilities interested in PI are continuous quality improvement and business process reengineering. These approaches have the same goal and use many of the same tools. However, they differ in focus and breadth of improvement effort.

Continuous Quality Improvement

Continuous quality improvement (CQI), frequently referred to as total quality management (TQM) or service excellence, is a management philosophy that seeks to "involve healthcare personnel in planning and executing a continuous flow of improvements to provide quality healthcare that meets or exceeds expectations" (McLaughlin and Kaluzny 199, 3). Its focus is on improving the quality of services provided to customers, whether internal (employees) or external (patients, physicians, payers). The approach is to make efforts to meet or exceed customer expectations by conducting small tests of change aimed at improving the quality of services. Of course, not all customer expectations can be met at the same time. In fact, some customers have expectations that conflict with the expectations of other customers. However, the goal is worth pursuing, even when only partly achievable.

CQI casts off the notion of ignoring problems until they become too big to ignore. Rather, it subscribes to the theory of seeking ways to improve the system through the testing of small, incremental changes with the expectation that, over time, the changes will continually improve the quality of care that health facilities provide to their patients (Berwick 1989). To achieve this, CQI relies on the gathering and analysis of data that can be used to make informed decisions.

More than a buzzword in healthcare, CQI is a way of thinking, a way of being, a way of managing, and a way of conducting business. It can be applied to individuals as well as organizations. The expression "If it ain't broke, don't fix it" is alien to the CQI philosophy. Moreover, CQI does not seek to blame problems on individuals but, instead, suggests that systems or processes may have inherent flaws that contribute to problems.

CQI attempts to involve people in the examination and improvement of existing systems. Several principles are incorporated into the CQI philosophy, including:

- *Constancy of variation:* Systems will always produce some normal variation in their output; the manager's job is to reduce the amount of variation as much as possible so that the process can become more stable and produce a more reliable output. Managers should not assume that any variation is a defect but, rather, should monitor and measure data over time to ensure that any variation is, in fact, caused inherently by the system. This type of variation is **common cause variation**. A greater-than-expected variation is a **special cause variation**. Sometimes a change is initiated with the express purpose of producing an improvement effort, in which case it should be encouraged. Other times, changes result in negative outputs and these must be eliminated. An example of variation in HIS departments might be found in the coding and processing of records. A coder may complete 20 records one day, but only 18 the next. The variation is not due to the clerk's lack of productivity, but perhaps to the size of the records that day. In other words, the change is attributed to common cause variation. A significant drop in coding might indicate that a special cause is in effect. Perhaps the coder was assigned duties that day in addition to coding.
- *Importance of data:* Far too often, decisions for improvement are based on faulty assumptions. CQI recognizes the importance of collecting sufficient data so that informed decisions can be made. Omachonu states "that the ability to collect, analyze, and use data is a vital component of a successful performance improvement process. Healthcare organizations that do not devote sufficient attention to data collection may be able to speak of only marginal success in their process improvement journey" (1999, 71). Individuals planning a CQI effort must take time to develop appropriate data collection methods and instruments (written surveys, direct observation, focus group interviews, reviews of medical records with criteria forms). Appropriate analysis must follow data collection to provide the knowledge on which improvement efforts can be built (White 2002).
- *Vision and support of executive leadership*: CQI gurus such as W. Edwards Deming and Brian Joiner stress that acceptance of the CQI philosophy must funnel down from the top to truly permeate the organization's culture. Executive leadership must communicate a clear vision and mission statement that every employee can understand and share.
- *Focus on customers*: To be successful, the organization must know and understand what its customers need and want. One way to obtain customer feedback is to administer satisfaction surveys on a regular basis. Any needs that are identified should be addressed.
- *Investment in people*: The CQI philosophy assumes that people want to do their jobs well. However, because this philosophy is relatively new, some employees may need training on how they can more adequately serve their customers. Management can empower employees by giving them opportunities to learn and grow and feel more competent in performing their jobs.
- *Importance of teams*: Because CQI seeks to improve processes that may extend beyond the boundaries of individual departments, the people directly involved with the processes must work together. Teams should include individuals with different expertise and from different levels of the organization. Team members should be knowledgeable about portions of the process and able to contribute to the improvement effort. Having members from different areas on the team brings fresh perspectives and opens communication. A good team also is able to communicate its purpose and activities to other parts of the organization.

Improvement Models

Several models exist for structuring PI. One that is frequently used in hospitals is Hospital Corporation of America's FOCUS-PDCA model. This model includes five steps before initiating its PDCA (Plan, Do, Check, Act) cycle. The five initial steps of the FOCUS-PDCA include:

1. Find a process to improve.
2. Organize a team that knows the process.
3. Clarify the current knowledge of the process.
4. Understand causes of special variation.
5. Select the process improvement.

A different, but highly effective, model that can be used for any process targeted for improvement is the Langley, Nolan, and Nolan Foundation for Improvement Model (1994). It is presented here because of its simplicity. The model has two parts. The first part requires an individual or team to answer three fundamental questions; the second part requires initiation of the PDSA (Plan, Do, Study, and Act) cycle.

The three fundamental questions that must be answered for any improvement project are:

- *What is my aim?* This question forces the responder to determine his or her overall goal.
- *How will I know a change is an improvement?* This question requires the responder to define measures (preferably quantitative, but also some qualitative) that will indicate progress made toward his or her goal. These measures will enable the individual or team to collect data.
- *What changes have the potential to result in improvement?* This question requires the responder to brainstorm a number of changes that might lead to improvement. He or she must recognize that not all changes do result in improvement.

After changes have been brainstormed, one change deemed to have significant potential for affecting improvement should be tried. This is a small test of change made with one change strategy. If it is successful, other changes may be added. The change strategy is tested using the **PDSA cycle**.

PDSA is a trial and learning cycle. (See figure 22.8.) It is essentially the same as PDCA, both of which are at times referred to as the Deming Cycle or the Deming Wheel. The phases of the cycle break down as follows:

1. During the plan phase, preparations are made for implementing the selected change. This is the time to consider who, what, where, when, and how. In addition, this is the time to plan how to collect data that will be used in determining the progress of the implementation. It may be necessary to develop a data collection instrument. Having already determined what the measurements will be, it also may be necessary to collect baseline data before implementing the change. Finally, this phase is the time to decide how often and how long to collect data before the results are analyzed.
2. During the do phase, the change strategy is implemented and data are collected. Perhaps the change strategy and the data collection will go on for two weeks before the analysis. The length of time depends on how frequently data were collected and how long the PDSA cycle is intended to last.
3. During the study phase, the data are analyzed. Is progress being made toward the defined aim? Are there any unanticipated problems? This phase indicates whether a change is an improvement. If it appears to be, the decision will likely be to continue the change strategy. If it is not showing as much improvement as expected, it may be necessary to adjust the change strategy. If it shows no improvement, it may be time to abandon the change strategy and test another one.
4. During the act phase, the knowledge obtained from the PDSA trial and learning cycle is applied, which leads to three possible actions: continue with the current change strategy, adjust it, or try a new one. At this point, a second PDSA cycle is implemented to continue the quest for knowledge about what affects the process and what permits progress. The more knowledge, the greater the likelihood of a successful improvement effort.

Figure 22.8. PDSA cycles expedite improvement

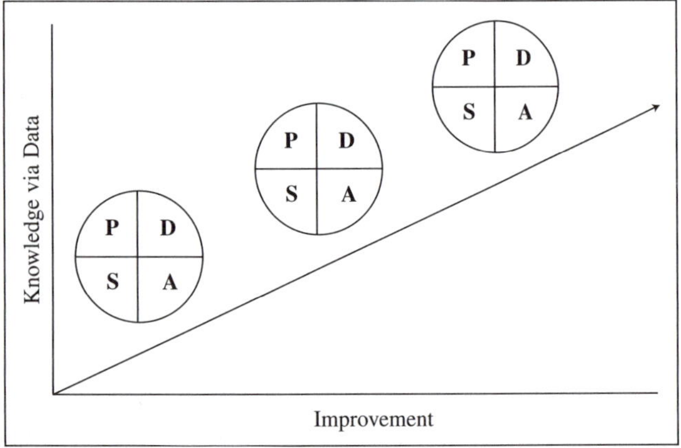

Basic PI Tools

A number of tools and techniques are frequently used with PI initiatives (Brassard and Ritter 1993; Johnson and McLaughlin 1999; Cofer and Greeley 1993). Some of them are used to facilitate communication among employees; others are used to assist people in determining the root causes of problems. Some tools show areas of agreement or consensus among team members; others permit the display of data for easier analysis. The following section presents a brief description and discussion of the purpose of tools and techniques commonly used by improvement teams (White 2002).

Work Distribution Chart

A **work distribution** chart can be helpful in determining the nature of the work being performed in the unit, which employees are performing the activities, and the amount of time spent on each activity. As mentioned earlier, a work distribution chart shows job activities, time spent on them, and the names or titles of the employees who perform them. It can be helpful in determining whether adequate time is available and appropriate for each task and whether employees are overburdened or have time for additional responsibilities. In addition, it can help the manager assess whether the work is organized and distributed appropriately.

Work distribution charts can be formulated in a variety of ways but frequently are tables with work tasks forming the row headings and a double column of employee names and hours spent on tasks forming the column headings. (Refer to table 22.1.) Data for the work distribution chart come from self-reported activities and hours or parts of hours spent on tasks gathered by employees over a designated period of time. Actual data collection time varies depending on what is needed to get a representative sample of activities and times. When adequate data have been collected, the manager compiles them, clusters similar job tasks together, and completes the chart.

Movement Diagram

A **movement diagram** is a visual depiction of the layout of the workspace with all the furniture, equipment, doorways, and so on sketched in. Superimposed on the layout are the movements of either individuals or things (for example, documents, files, and the like). (Refer to figure 22.1.) The movement diagram can be used to evaluate the workflow and to redesign one that is more efficient. An inefficient workflow is depicted in figure 22.1 (top), that is, long distances between connected points in the workflow, crisscrossing paths, and paths that backtrack in the work space. A redesigned movement diagram in figure 22.1 (bottom) depicts a smoother workflow resulting in improved efficiency.

Flow Process Chart

A **flow process chart** is useful in operations analysis. (See figure 22.9.) It charts the flow of work of a material or a task but is limited to the flow of only one unit at a time. Each step of a particular process is shown in chronological order and in great detail (for example, the distance a material moves in each step, the time needed, the quantity moved, and specific notes about the process). Standard symbols are used on the chart to indicate specific processes. An operation is symbolized with a circle, transportation with an arrow, storage with a triangle, inspection with a rectangle, and a delay with a figure resembling an uppercase D. When the symbols are connected with a line, the manager can see the actual flow of work.

The flow process chart is an excellent method for indicating time problems with workflow. It can show duplication and inefficiency and also can be useful in verifying procedures or planning a workstation redesign (Liebler et al. 1992). Some flow process charts include two charts in one: a chart showing the current flow of work and a second chart proposing a redesigned workflow.

Brainstorming

Brainstorming is a technique used to generate a large number of creative ideas. It encourages team members to think "outside the box" and offer ideas. There are some variations in using the technique—one can use an unstructured method for brainstorming or a structured method. The unstructured method involves having a free flow of ideas about a situation. The team leader writes down each idea as it is offered so all can see. There should be no evaluative discussion about the worthiness of the idea because we want to do nothing that will inhibit the flow of ideas. Each idea is captured and written for the team to consider at a later point.

Structured brainstorming uses a more formal approach. The team leader asks each person to generate a list of ideas

Figure 22.9. Flow process chart

	PRESENT		PROPOSED		DIFFERENCE		
	NO.	TIME	NO.	TIME	NO.	TIME	
○ OPERATIONS							Job__________
⇨ TRANSPORTATIONS							Date__________
□ INSPECTIONS							Man Material
D DELAYS							
▽ STORAGES							Chartered by __________
DISTANCE TRAVELED		FT.		FT.		FT.	

DETAILS OF (PRESENT/PROPOSED) METHOD	OPERATION	TRANSPORT	INSPECTION	DELAY	STORAGE	DISTANCE IN FEET	QUANTITY	TIME	ANALYSIS WHY	NOTES	ACTION CHANGE
1	○	⇨	□	D	▽						
2	○	⇨	□	D	▽						
3	○	⇨	□	D	▽						
4	○	⇨	□	D	▽						
5	○	⇨	□	D	▽						
6	○	⇨	□	D	▽						

for themselves and then, one by one, the team leader proceeds around the room eliciting a new idea from each member. The process may take several rounds. As team members run out of new ideas, they pass and the next person offers an idea until no one can produce any fresh ideas.

Brainstorming is highly effective for identifying a number of potential processes that may benefit from improvement efforts and for generating solutions to particular problems. It helps people to begin thinking in new ways and gets them involved in the process. It is an excellent method for facilitating open communication.

Affinity Grouping

Affinity grouping allows the team to organize and group similar ideas together. Ideas that are generated in a brainstorming session may be written on Post-it notes and arranged on a table or posted on a board. Without talking to each other, each team member is asked to walk around the table or board, look at the ideas, and place them in groupings that seem related or connected to each other. Each member is empowered to move the ideas in a way that makes the most sense. As a team member moves the ideas back or places them in other groupings, the other team members consider the merits of the placement and decide if further action is needed. The goal is to have the team eventually feel comfortable with the arrangement. The natural groupings that emerge are then labeled with a category. This tool brings focus to the many ideas generated. (See figure 22.10.)

Nominal Group Technique

Nominal group technique (NGT) is a process designed to bring agreement about an issue or an idea that the team considers most important. It produces and permits visualization of team consensus. In NGT, each team member ranks each idea according to its importance. For example, if there were six ideas, the idea that is most important would be given the number 6. The second most important idea would be given the number 5. The least important idea would have the number 1. After each team member has individually ranked the list of ideas, the numbers are totaled. The ideas that are deemed most important are clearly visible to all. Those ideas that people did not think were as important are also made known by their low scores. NGT demonstrates where the team's priorities lie.

Figure 22.10. Affinity grouping

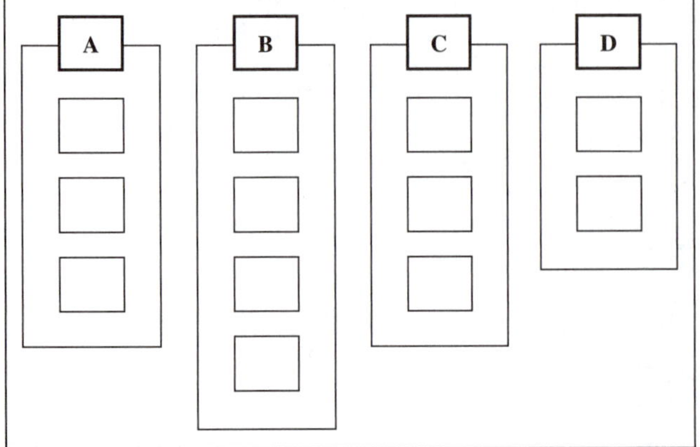

Multivoting Technique

The **multivoting technique** is a variation of NGT and has the same purpose. Rather than ranking each issue or idea, team members are asked to rate the issue using a distribution of points or colorful dots. Weighted multivoting is a variation of this process. For example, a team member may be asked to distribute 25 points among ten total issues. Thus, one issue of particular importance to him or her may receive 12 points, four others may receive some variation of the remaining 12 points, and five others may receive no points. After the voting, the numbers are added and the team is able to see which issue has emerged as particularly important to its members.

This process also can be done with colored dots. For example, if there are eight items on a chart, each team member may be given four dots to distribute on the four items that are most important to him or her. This method particularly enables team members to see where consensus lies and what issue has been deemed most important by the team as a whole.

Flowchart

Whenever a team examines a process with the intention of making improvements, it must first thoroughly understand the process. Each team member comes to the team with a unique perspective and significant insight about how a portion of the process works. To help all members understand the process, a team will undertake development of a flowchart. (Refer to figure 22.3) This work allows the team to thoroughly understand every step in the process and the sequence of steps. It provides a picture of each decision point and each event that must be completed. It readily points out places where there is redundancy and complex and problematic areas.

Root-Cause Analysis (Fishbone Diagram)

When a team first identifies a problem, it may use a **fishbone diagram**, also known as a cause-and-effect diagram, to help it determine the root causes of the problem. (See figure 22.11.) The problem is placed in a box on the right side of the paper. A horizontal line is drawn, somewhat like a backbone, with diagonal bones, like ribs, pointing to the boxes above and below the backbone. Each box contains a category. The categories may be names that represent broad classifications of problem areas (for example, people, methods, equipment, materials, policies and procedures, environment, measurement, and so on). The team determines how many categories it needs to classify all the sources of problems. Usually, there are about four. After constructing the diagram, the team brainstorms possible sources of the problem. These are then placed on horizontal lines extending from the diagonal category line. The brainstorming of

Figure 22.11. Fishbone diagram

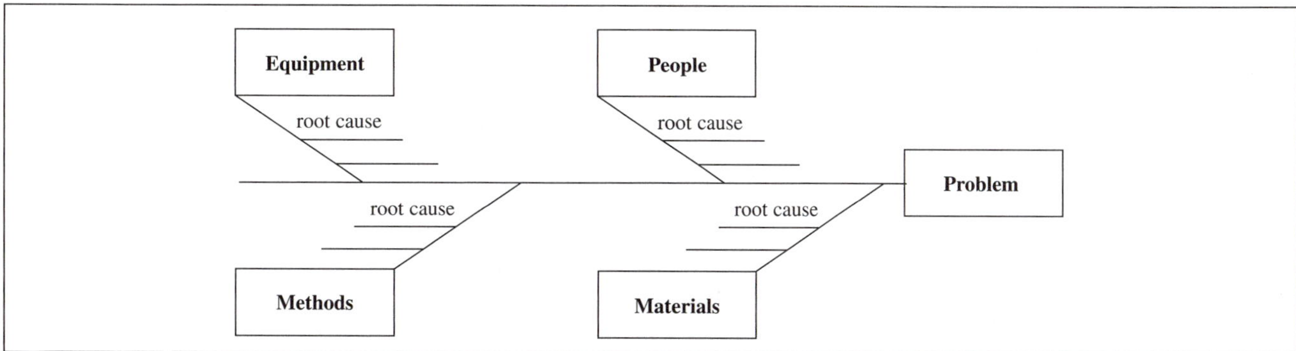

root causes continues among team members until all ideas are exhausted. The purpose of this tool is to permit a team to explore, identify, and graphically display all the root causes of a problem.

After identifying a number of causes of a problem, a team may decide to begin working to remove one of them. CQI involves continually making efforts to improve processes; certainly removing one cause and then working to remove another cause will eventually improve the process. The question may arise, however, about which cause to remove first. Techniques such as multivoting or NGT, previously discussed, can help bring consensus among the team about what to work on first.

Pareto Chart

When a team decides to use multivoting or NGT to determine consensus among the members about the most important problem to tackle first, each team member places a number or mark next to an item indicating his or her opinion about the item's importance. When the numbers are tallied, the items can be ranked according to importance. This ranking can then be visually displayed in a **Pareto chart**. (See figure 22.12.) A Pareto chart looks like a bar chart except that the highest-ranking item is listed first, followed by the second highest, down to the lowest-ranked item. Thus, the Pareto chart is a descending bar chart. This visualization of how the problems were ranked allows team members to focus on those few that have the greatest potential for improving the process. The Pareto chart is based on the Pareto principle, which states that 20 percent of the sources of the problem are responsible for 80 percent of the actual problems. By concentrating on the vital few sources, a large number of actual problems can be eliminated.

Figure 22.12. Pareto chart

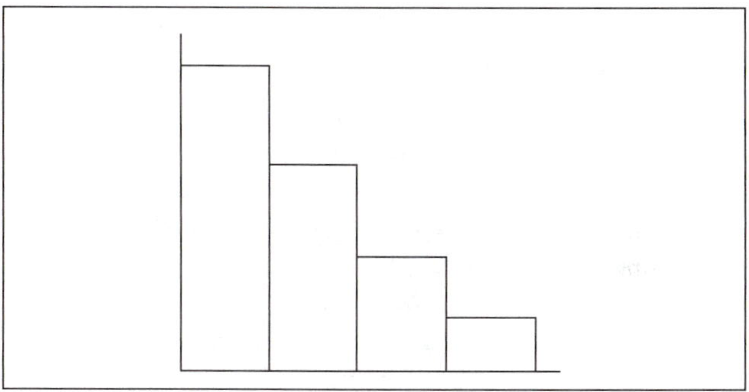

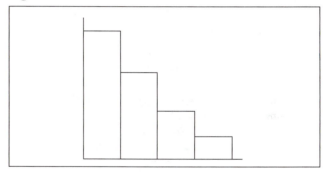

Figure 22.13. Force-field analysis

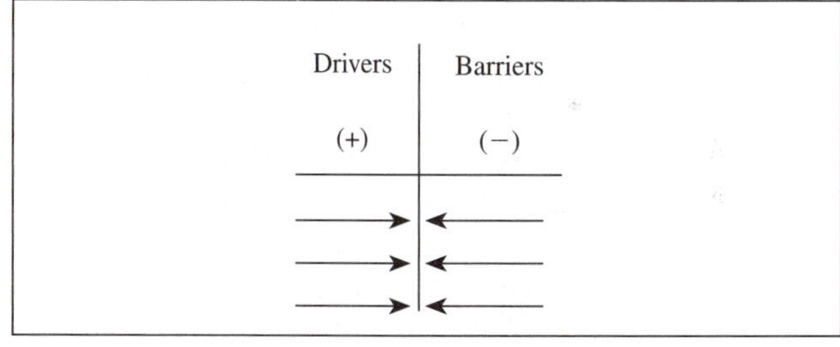

Force-Field Analysis

A **force-field analysis** also visually displays data generated through brainstorming. The team leader draws a large *T* formation on a board. (See figure 22.13.) Above the crossbar and on the left side of the T is written the word *drivers*, and above the bar and written on the right side of the T is written the word *barriers*. Team members are then asked to brainstorm and list on the chart under the crossbar the reasons or factors that would contribute to a change for improvement and those reasons or factors that can create barriers. Thus, the force field enables team members to identify factors that support or work against a proposed solution. Often the next step in this activity is to work on ways that either eliminate barriers or reinforce drivers.

Check Sheet

A **check sheet** is a data collection tool permitting the recording and compiling of observations or occurrences. It consists of a simple listing of categories, issues, or observations on the left side of the chart and a place on the right for individuals to record checkmarks next to the item when it is observed or counted. (See figure 22.14.) After a period of time, the checkmarks are counted and the patterns or trends can be revealed.

A check sheet is a simple tool that allows a clear picture of the facts to emerge. It enables data to be collected. After

Figure 22.14. Check sheet

	1	2	Total
A	~~////~~	///	8
B	////	////	8
C	//	/	3

data are collected, several tools can be used to display the data and help the team more easily analyze them.

Scatter Diagram

A **scatter diagram** is a data analysis tool used to plot points of two variables suspected of being related to each other in some way. For example, to see whether age and blood pressure are related, one variable (age) would be plotted on one line of the graph, and the other variable (blood pressure) would be plotted on the other line. After several people's blood pressures are plotted along with their ages, a pattern might emerge. If the diagram indicates that blood pressure increases with age, the data could be interpreted as revealing a positive relationship between age and blood pressure. (See figure 22.15.)

In some cases, a negative relationship might exist, such as with the variables "age" and "flexibility" or with the number of hours of training and number of mistakes made. Whenever a scatter diagram indicates that the points are moving together in one direction or another, conclusions can be drawn about the variables' relationship, either positive or negative. In other cases, however, the scatter diagram may indicate no linear relationship between the variables because the points are scattered haphazardly and no pattern emerges. In this case, the conclusion would have to be that the two variables have no apparent relationship.

Histogram

A **histogram** (figure 22.16) is a data analysis tool used to display frequencies of response. (See also chapter 15.) It offers a much easier way to summarize and analyze data than having them displayed in a table of numbers. A histogram displays **continuous data** values that have been grouped into categories. The bars on the histogram reveal how the data are distributed. For example, an HIM administrator may want to show the number of minutes it takes to respond to patient requests for information. Minutes may be categorized into four groupings, for example, 1–30 minutes, 31–60 minutes, 61–90 minutes, and more than 90 minutes. Checkmarks may be recorded indicating the category of minutes taken to respond to the request. After a period of time, the checkmarks are added and the histogram is plotted with the frequencies shown on the vertical, or *y* axis, and the minute intervals shown on the horizontal, or *x* axis.

Figure 22.15. Scatter diagram

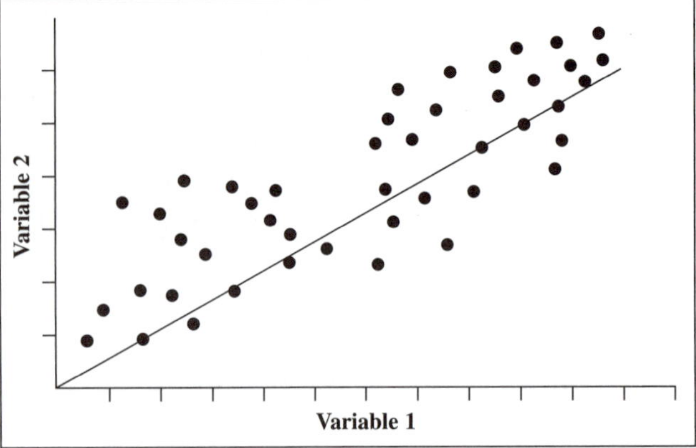

Figure 22.16. Histogram

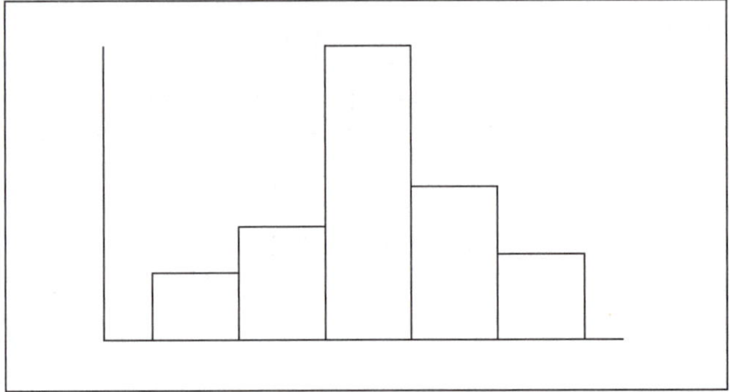

This graph indicates the different intervals patients had to wait for their requests to be filled. A histogram can give an excellent idea of how well a process is performing. Thus, it can show how frequently data values occur among the various intervals, how centered or skewed the distribution of data is, and what the likelihood of future occurrences is.

Run Chart

A **run chart** displays data points over a period of time to provide information about performance. (See figure 22.17.) Measured points of a process are plotted on a graph at regular time intervals to help team members see whether there are substantial changes in the numbers over time. For example, suppose an HIS manager wanted to reduce the number of incomplete records in the HIS department. The manager might first plot on a graph the number of incomplete records each month for the past six months and then enact a change in the processing of records designed to improve the process. Following the improvement effort, data would continue to be collected on the number of incomplete records and would continue to be plotted on the graph. If the run chart shows that the number of incomplete charts has actually decreased, the HIS manager could attribute the decrease to the improvement effort.

A run chart is an excellent tool for providing visual verification of how a process is performing and whether an improvement effort appears to have worked.

Statistical Process Control Chart

A **statistical process control (SPC) chart** looks like a run chart except that it has a line displayed at the top, called an upper control limit (UCL), and a line displayed at the bottom, called a lower control limit (LCL). (See figure 22.18.) These lines have been statistically calculated from the data generated in the process and represent three units of dispersion above and below the midline (three standard deviations) (Omachonu 1999).

Like the run chart, the SPC chart plots points over time to demonstrate how a process is performing. However, the two control limit lines enable the interpreter to determine whether the process is stable, or predictable, or whether it is out of control. Remembering the constancy of variation principle, it is easy to see the purpose of the SPC chart. The SPC chart indicates whether the variation occurring within the process is a common cause variation or a special cause variation. It indicates whether it is necessary to try and reduce the ordinary variation occurring through common cause or to seek out a special cause of the variation and try to eliminate it.

Business Process Redesign

Used extensively in the mid-1980s and early 1990s, **business process reengineering** has met with significant criticism in the healthcare sector because of the fear it has invoked among healthcare workers. As would be expected, reengineering frequently results in the loss of jobs. Because salaries and benefits comprise 50 to 60 percent of a healthcare facility's total expenses, a drop in personnel can have a significant impact on reducing expenditures and is often used as an effective strategy in reengineering. Due to negative connotations related to downsizing, restructuring, and outsourcing, the perception of reengineering went from a strategy an organization does to something that is done to the organization. Although the term *reengineering* itself is not always favorable in organizations today, business process redesign is still a focus strategy for rethinking and drastically improving overall performance.

Figure 22.17. Run chart

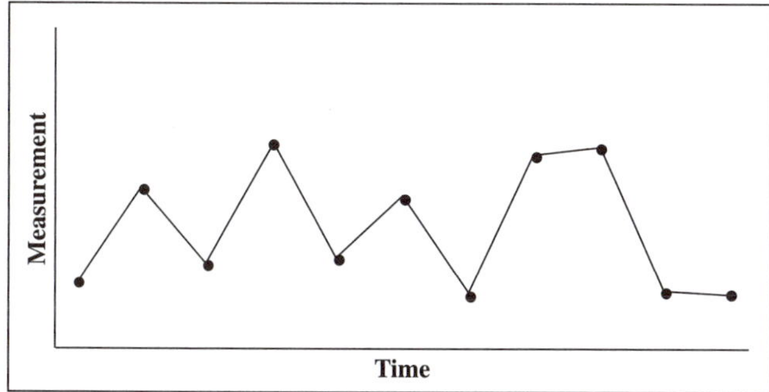

Figure 22.18. Statistical process control chart

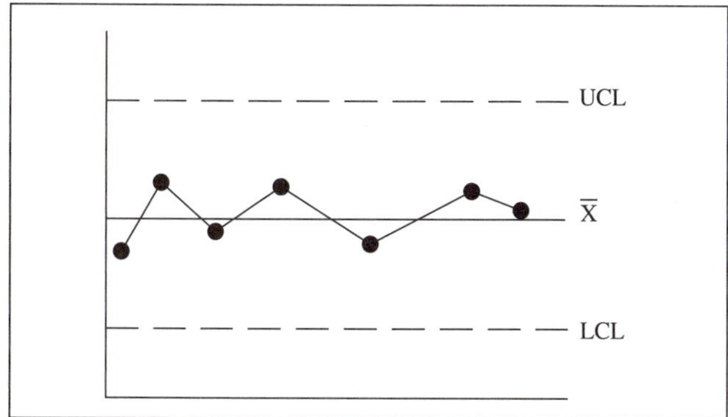

Models and Methodologies

Business Process Reengineering

Unlike CQI which focuses on conducting small tests of change to achieve continuous but incremental improvement over time, business process reengineering (BPR) focuses on the potential redesign of the entire process to achieve improvement. (See table 22.12 for a comparison of reengineering and quality management.) Reengineering implies making massive changes to the way a facility delivers healthcare services. In *Reengineering the Corporation: A Manifesto for Business Revolution,* Hammer and Champy (1993, 32) defined reengineering as "the fundamental rethinking and radical redesign of business processes to achieve dramatic improvements in critical contemporary measures of performance such as cost, quality, service, and speed".

Philosophy of Reengineering

Business process reengineering has entered the healthcare sector after first being successfully applied in the wider business community. In reengineering, the entire manner and purpose of a work process is questioned. The goal is to achieve the desired process outcome in the most effective and efficient manner possible. Thus, the results expected from reengineering efforts include:

- Increased productivity
- Decreased costs
- Improved quality
- Maximized revenue
- More satisfied customers

However, it should be clearly understood that the main focus is on reducing costs (Palmer 1995).

Table 22.12. Reengineering compared to quality management

Reengineering		Quality Management	
Rethinking and Radical Redesign	Focus	Incremental Improvements	Focus
Rethink	Think outside of the box	Quality planning	Focus on the customer
Redesign	Think both process and outcome	Quality control	Measure and monitor performance
Retool	Use technology to control and define work processes	Quality improvement	Use data, eliminate boundaries, and empower work

Process of Reengineering

When an organization decides to use reengineering as an improvement strategy, it commits itself to looking at selected processes within the organization in fine detail. Processes are selected for reengineering based on a number of criteria, including:

- Frequency and severity of problems created by the process, such as slow turnaround time or excessive waiting time
- Impact on customer satisfaction
- Complex processes involving multiple departments, procedures, and employees
- The feasibility of actually creating improvement (Umiker 1998)

Selecting a process for reengineering raises several questions, including:

- What is the intended purpose of the process? Is that purpose being accomplished efficiently?
- Is the process absolutely necessary? Could any redundancies or non-value-added activities be eliminated?
- Which employees are involved in the process, and which ones are actually needed? In other words, what are the minimum qualifications and minimum number of employees needed to do the job?
- Is the process as efficient as it could be, or are there more efficient means for accomplishing the goal?
- Is the process contributing to the efficiency of other processes that may be affected by its results?
- Is there an opportunity to combine processes and to train or use employees to perform more functions than they currently perform?
- Can any steps of the process be eliminated?
- Is outsourcing a feasible and more cost-effective alternative?
- Would new equipment or new technologies improve the process?

Many of the tools and techniques used in systems analysis and CQI also are used in reengineering. In reengineering, it is essential to thoroughly understand how the process contributes to how the organization functions and to determine whether a better method exists. Therefore, observation of processes, customer input, interviews with employees, and the use of cross-functional teams to discuss the current steps of the process are frequently used methods for obtaining data. Data must be collected for a sufficient period of time to actually reflect the effectiveness of the process.

In addition, the data must be analyzed appropriately and the analysis should include the input of individuals qualified to interpret the findings. Thus, a team composed of individuals involved in various aspects of the process should be permitted access to the data and should give input about alternative strategies. Moreover, the team can investigate the acceptability of new technologies that might allow for greater efficiency. Before new technologies are adopted, however, the team should thoroughly analyze the potential benefits, costs, and feasibility of using them in the organization.

After a reengineered process has emerged, new policies and procedures must be written and distributed to the people involved in the process. In addition, employees should be thoroughly trained in the redesigned process. However, it is important that they be given adequate time to master the process. Managers play an important role in reengineering through their support, encouragement, and commitment to the process.

Factors for Success in Reengineering Efforts

One critical factor for the success of the reengineering effort is the visible and persistent commitment of senior administration. A second critical factor is management's commitment to excellence. Managers must demonstrate a can-do attitude in working through the change. In addition, the fact that change is needed to address an unacceptable problem must be effectively communicated throughout the organization. Having everyone, or almost everyone, acknowledge that a problem exists creates a great deal of buy-in. Employees, including physicians, should be encouraged to overcome any reluctance to participate in the change process due to fears about restructuring. Many healthcare organizations make the mistake of not including their physicians in critical decision making. The likelihood of a successful reengineering effort increases when every stakeholder is involved in the process.

Reengineering takes anywhere from one to three years to achieve. The organization should realize that change cannot be achieved overnight and should avoid trying to change too many processes at one time. Instead, it should focus its efforts on a few processes at a time. A great deal of planning, information gathering, and analysis must occur before an actual redesign can be implemented. When the planning phase has been completed, the organization should revise or develop policies and procedures accordingly and distribute them throughout the organization.

Finally, implementation of the redesigned processes requires patience. Glitches may occur with any new system, but with careful monitoring and persistent adjusting, reengineering can produce significant PI.

Lean

Lean is a management strategy described as a philosophy based on "the continuous pursuit of improving the processes, eliminating all non-value-added activities, and reducing waste within an organization" (Rizzardo and Brooks 2003). Lean is known for its focus on the reduction of waste and is based on the Japanese success story of Toyota. Toyota's steady growth from a small company to one of the largest automobile companies in the world through the use of Lean principles has made Lean a hot topic in management science in the 21st century.

Lean implementation focuses on eliminating waste and creating a smooth workflow. Through analysis of the process versus a prime focus on the end goal, quality problems are exposed and waste reduction occurs naturally as a consequence. The goals of the organization remain the same; the approach toward achieving the goals differs in the Lean methodology. Lean works to eliminate non-value-added work, or waste, brought about by a lack of error detection, confused responsibilities, unnecessary work, disconnects, and workarounds. Waste can be defined as anything that does not add value to a product or service from the standpoint of the customer. Lean is about creating a continually improving system that is capable of achieving more while using less.

Lean has been applied in many industries, not just manufacturing. It has been used in healthcare with significant improvements in quality and efficiency. The principles of removing activities that do not add value can be applied anywhere. Value in a hospital setting maybe described as patient comfort, competent caregivers, or patient discharge after achieving the desired outcomes. Anything that helps treat the patient is value-added; everything else is waste. Toyota identified seven areas of waste: delay, over processing, inventory, transportation, motion, overproducing, and defects. Zidel (2006) gives examples of how these areas of waste may relate to healthcare. (See table 22.13.) There are a number of Lean tools and techniques used in manufacturing; several have a strong application to the healthcare industry. The following tools are described in Zidel (2006). They seem simple, but when intentionally used can uncover large amounts of waste:

Table 22.13. Seven areas of waste related to healthcare

Delay	Waiting for bed assignments, waiting to be discharged, waiting for treatment, waiting for supplies, waiting for approval, waiting for the physician
Over processing	Excessive paperwork, redundant processes, unnecessary tests, multiple bed transfers
Inventory	Lab specimens awaiting analysis, ER patients awaiting a room assignment, patients awaiting diagnostic tests, excess supplies kept on hand, dictation awaiting transcription
Transportation	Transporting lab specimens, transporting patients, transporting medication, transporting supplies or equipment
Motion	Searching for charts, searching for supplies, delivering medications, nurses caring for patients in different areas
Overproducing	Mixing drugs in anticipation of patient needs, creating paperwork packets for an anticipated patient arrival
Defects	Medication errors, wrong-site surgery, improper labeling of specimens, assignment of duplicate medical record numbers

Source: Zidel 2006.

- The 5 Whys—In this technique, simply ask "why" in every situation until you discover the root cause of the problem. Usually this process takes approximately five times before the root cause is identified.
- 5 S—The 5 S's are Sort, Straighten, Scrub, Standardize, and Sustain. This method, simply stated, is housekeeping.
  - Sort—Get rid of everything that is not used or expected to be used
  - Straighten—Organize what is kept, have a place for everything, and keep everything in its place
  - Scrub—Clean the area
  - Standardize—Establish procedures to keep the area organized
  - Sustain—Maintain the gains and avoid backsliding
- Visual Controls—The visual controls tool is used to create a workplace where all that is needed is displayed and immediately available. There are four levels of visual controls:
  - Visual Indicator—Something that just informs, that is, a sign on a patient's door with special instructions
  - Visual Signal—An alert or alarm, that is, as a nurse call light
  - Visual Control—A mechanism to control behavior, such as a needle box that automatically closes when full to eliminate the risk of overfilling.
  - Visual Guarantee—A mechanism that allows only a correct response, that is, a medication dispensing machine that will not dispense a medication without proper identifiers. A visual guarantee is foolproof.

In addition, the following two tools as described by Jones and Mitchell (2006) have applicability in the healthcare setting:

- *Value Stream Mapping:* This is a visual method of documenting both material and information flows of a process. It is a flow diagram that identifies all the value-added and non-value-added activities in the process. This is first developed to analyze the current process and eliminate non-value-added steps; then it is developed again to illustrate the improved, streamlined process. The value stream shows all the actions (both value-added and non-value-added) and related information required to bring a patient through the process from the start to the end of his visit.
- *Pull System:* This is a method of controlling the flow of resources by replacing only what the customer has consumed. Pull systems consist of production based on actual consumption, small volumes, low inventories, management by sight, and better communication. To create value, services must be in line with demand; no

less, no more. Delivering services in line with demand means that work, material, and information should be "pulled" toward the task when needed.

Identifying the value streams, mapping and understanding each action in the value stream, and identifying and implementing immediate and future improvements using Lean tools and techniques are all a part of building a culture of continuous improvement in the organization.

Six Sigma

Historically, healthcare has been a follower with regard to quality improvement methods. In the mid-1980s, William Smith, an engineer, developed the concept of **Six Sigma**. Motorola was the first company to adopt the concept and turn itself from a company on the edge of bankruptcy to a highly profitable firm. When Motorola won the coveted Malcolm Baldridge National Quality Award in 1988, the "best-kept secret" was suddenly on the lips of all the nations' CEOs (Misra 2008). That best-kept secret, in actuality, is not innovative in the sense that it is new knowledge; actually, it embraces tenets similar to Deming's PDCA. More emphatically, it is a culmination of "old notions" with a technology twist: data informatics. The evidence that gave the old innovation a new visibility is the evidence that the success of the Six Sigma initiative is modeled and measured by data that are collected, cleaned, and considered strategically both in the lines of service and as an outcome. They are data that are, in most cases, already being captured but not leveraged. It was not until 2001–2002, however, that healthcare organizations looked seriously at the Six Sigma concept (Lazarus 2003). Healthcare has been slow to adopt this concept because the extensive training involved is expensive, and physician and administrative buy-in is hard to come by. In recent years, however, a number of healthcare organizations have implemented Six Sigma successfully.

Some doubted that Six Sigma could be applied to the healthcare industry because of the human variability of patients. However, the 2000 Institute of Medicine report highlighting the alarming statistic of 98,000 deaths linked to medical errors soon resulted in a movement to review statistical data in the healthcare industry with industry eyes. Industry is customer driven and so is healthcare. Industry relies on feedback regarding success and failure in relevant data and so does healthcare. Healthcare leaders became invested in enlisting this philosophy of excellence, reducing costs, lowering lengths of stay, and raising the bar for high-quality healthcare. The healthcare industry leaders that have embraced Six Sigma are quick to share their successes as the industry continues to come to understand the richness of the data that are captured and how to understand their inherent value.

Six Sigma uses a methodology not completely unique. It is reputed to use a scientific methodology that involves the following steps: define, measure, analyze, improve, and control (**DMAIC**). (See figure 22.19.) Each step has substeps that are referred to as "tollgates." The tollgates provide detailed directions on what must be done to complete each step before moving on to the next step (Eckes 2003, 29–65).

Figure 22.19. DMAIC improvement methodology

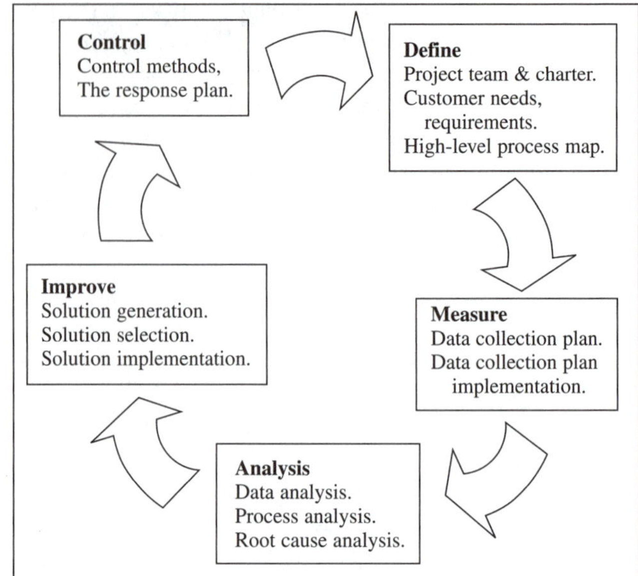

Source: Eckes 2003, p. 29.

Six Sigma uses many of the same tools used by other quality management systems. However, two tools unique to Six Sigma are (1) the critical quality tree (CQT) used in the define stage and (2) the process map used to identify the steps of a current process under review. In addition, Six Sigma uses "soft" tools that do not have a math basis; however, soft tools can be tricky to use because they have a subjective quality to them. Examples of some basic soft tools are a set of ground rules, a team agenda, a parking lot to track ideas not immediately pertinent, and activity or progress reports.

Six Sigma focuses on improving management and clinical processes. Statistical analysis is used to find the most defective part of a process, and rigorous control procedures are used to ensure sustained improvement. The goal of Six Sigma is to control for defects so that a 0.00034 percent defect rate is achieved (Lazarus 2003, 1).

Six Sigma can be used successfully in healthcare. It provides a systematic approach to validate data and focuses on the most meaningful improvements. As in other quality management concepts, the customer defines acceptable performance with the focus on delivery, quality, and cost. This definitely parallels the healthcare mainstay of cost, quality, and access (Lazarus 2003, 1). Successful implementation of Six Sigma in healthcare organizations has produced benefits such as the following:

- Higher productivity
- Fewer errors and adverse effects
- Improved organizational communication
- Improved patient satisfaction

- Better physician satisfaction
- Better nursing satisfaction
- Increased patient flow
- Short patient wait times
- Better use of advanced technologies

Lean Six Sigma

The uses of Lean methods along with Six Sigma techniques have been successful. Despite numerous debates over which process improvement methodology is best, it may be that the two methods work quite well together. Lean provides tools to identify and implement value-added activities designed to streamline processes and improve efficiency as a result of waste reduction. Six Sigma focuses on reducing variation through statistical analysis, validation of data, and measuring improvements. Lean and Six Sigma complement each other with goals aimed toward overall improvement, organizational buy-in, and a culture change that promotes continuous improvement via a structured methodology and identified tools and techniques.

Workflow Analysis and Process Redesign

Whatever the methodology or strategy used, workflow analysis and **process redesign** are necessary components of overall organizational improvement. The study of workflow as "who does what when" has become a critical part of process analysis and design methodologies.

Process and Workflow Theory

The delivery of healthcare is increasingly complex, therefore the related workflows are also increasingly complex. As the use of technology becomes critical in all aspects of patient care, understanding how the work flows within and between processes is critical. The success of information technology projects is not solely dependent on the technology, but rather on the people and the process. A business process is defined as "a collection of interrelated work tasks initiated in response to an event that achieves a specific result for a customer of the process" (Sharp and McDermott 2001, 58). A process must remain customer focused; redundancy, delay, and error must be avoided. The goal of workflow analysis is business process re-design.

Workflow analysis should be done any time work involves multiple departments or functions and prior to identifying an IT solution. It is important to ensure all the stakeholders are a part of the analysis, the entire process is considered when making improvements, the business process is accurately identified, and the team does not get stalled in over-analysis of the current process. HIM professionals are well suited for workflow analysis because they can see the big picture of the overall healthcare process, they understand how healthcare professionals work together toward quality patient care, and they understand information flow and the users of the information.

Sharp and McDermott (2001) describe the steps in workflow analysis as follows:

1. Frame the process.
2. Understand the current (as-is) process.
3. Design the new (to-be) process.
4. Develop use case scenarios.

Outside of the actual methodology of workflow analysis, related key concepts include understanding the organizational structure and managing change.

An essential, necessary distinction in workflow analysis is the difference between a process versus a function. A process, as stated earlier, is a collection of interrelated work tasks done in response to an event that achieves a specific result for a customer. A function is an occupation or a department that focuses on related activities and similar skills. See Table 22.14 for an example distinguishing a process from a function. If a function is identified erroneously as a process for analysis, work methods will be defined for the benefit of the individual function, not to optimize the manner in which work flows through the function and through other areas of the organization as a whole. Focusing on functions and not business process perpetuates the development of functional silos or stovepipes. This should be avoided in process redesign.

Once a process is identified, framing that process is crucial in establishing and documenting the process boundaries. This will clarify the scope of the process, both what is within as well as outside of the scope. Documenting all the pertinent information about the process is called developing the process frame. In the process frame, one must:

- Describe the process triggers, steps, results and stakeholders
- Understand the environment including the mission, vision, goals, and culture
- State the case for analysis

Table 22.14. Process vs. Function

Coding Process (Interdepartmental, Multiple Skill Set)	Coding Function (Intradepartmental, One Skill Set)
Register patient	Go to worklist and select case
Generate clinical documentation about patient assessment and services provided in the course of patient care	Obtain clinical documentation and charges
Enter charges	Review and determine adequacy of information
Process medical record for completeness and accuracy	Apply coding rules and select codes
Generate codes for billing and clinical databases	Enter codes into databases for billing and clinical systems
Analyze remittance advice and denials	

Source: AHIMA. 2006. Resource Book: Optimizing Investment in the EHR.

The purpose of analysis is to understand processes to identify bottlenecks, sources of delay, rework due to errors, role ambiguity, duplication, unnecessary steps, and handoffs. This understanding of the current (as-is) process will lead to a redesigned future (to-be) process that can then be tested through a use case analysis.

Tools and Techniques

As with continuous quality improvement, there are several process mapping tools that can assist with workflow analysis and process redesign. Process mapping shows the activities of the process including the sequence and flow of the work. Tool selection will depend on the level of precision needed and the nature of the process being mapped. Tools may be simple or complex, paper-based, automated, or Web-based. Some of these tools are the same or similar to the CQI tools.

Workflow Diagram

The workflow diagram is a physical illustration of where there is movement of information. This may also be known as a movement diagram (refer to figure 22.1).

Process Flowchart

The flowchart is a common analysis tool that visually illustrates each step in a process and the sequence of the steps. Flowcharts can be at a high level defining major steps in the process or it can be detailed, defining each step including decision points in the process (refer to figure 22.3).

Top Down Process Map

The top down process map identifies the least number of steps necessary in a process. The main steps are worded broadly and simply with each step showing only 3–4 sub tasks in more detail (see figure 22.20).

Swimlane Diagram

A **swimlane diagram** shows an entire business process from beginning to end and is especially popular because it highlights relevant variables (who, what, and when) while requiring little or no training to use and understand. The swimlane diagram is often used to identify the current (as-is) process as well as design the new (to-be) process (see figure 22.21).

Process Simulation Software

Process simulation software can show the flow of work, individuals, or movement of information in varying existing or hypothetical situations. This software can show movement in existing situations and can show various alternative designs to help identify the most appropriate workflow.

These tools and techniques assist in analyzing current workflows to focus on facts rather than opinions, to truly understand the existing process, and to document all aspects of the process. Additionally, process maps can bring stakeholders to a common understanding to move forward with process redesign.

Figure 22.20. Top-down process maps

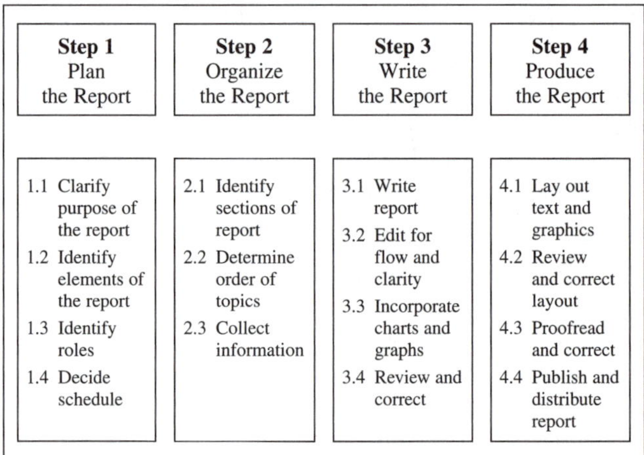

Step 1
Plan
the Report
Step 2
Organize
the Report
Step 3
Write
the Report
Step 4
Produce
the Report
1.1 Clarify purpose of the report
1.2 Identify elements of the report
1.3 Identify roles
1.4 Decide schedule
2.1 Identify sections of report
2.2 Determine order of topics
2.3 Collect information
3.1 Write report
3.2 Edit for flow and clarity
3.3 Incorporate charts and graphs
3.4 Review and correct
4.1 Lay out text and graphics
4.2 Review and correct layout
4.3 Proofread and correct
4.4 Publish and distribute report

Source: AHIMA 2006. Resource Book: Optimizing Investment in the EHR.

Figure 22.21. Sample swimlane diagram

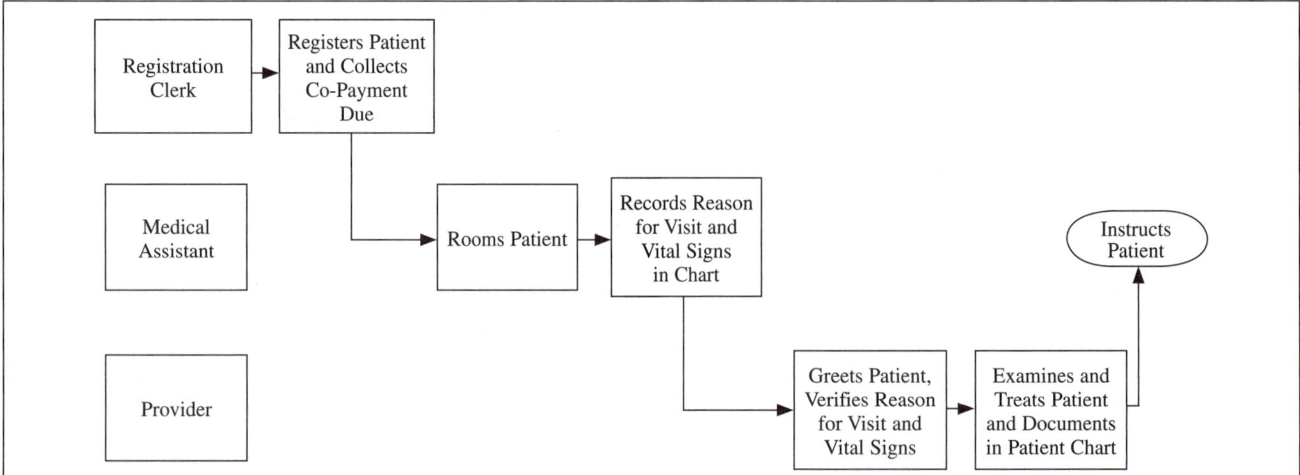

Source: AHIMA 2006. Resource Book: Optimizing Investment in the EHR.

Use Case Analysis

A use case analysis is a technique to determine how users will interact with a system. It uses the designed future (to-be) process and describes how a user will interact with the system to complete process steps and how the system will behave from the user perspective. The purpose of use case analysis is to bridge the gap between user needs and system functionality. A use case analysis helps identify system requirements, design the user interface, facilitate documentation, create test plans, and develop training and support plans. It is critical to list all use case scenarios that impact each and every user so that no case is overlooked. Priority should go to developing use case scenarios that focus on those areas that have the most impact on the success of the project such as those that affect workflows of multiple users.

Identifying all potential use cases is valuable to ensure that nothing is overlooked and all users are involved. More value emerges when each use case is not only identified but also described. Basic elements of a use case description are the use case name, a description of the use case, the users of the system for that use case, pre-conditions that must be in place before the use case can be tested, the normal sequence of steps, the post conditions or results expected, any alternate steps as needed, and any variations or issues known to that particular use case that are important to know. See example in figure 22.22.

Check Your Understanding 22.6

Instructions: On a separate piece of paper, indicate whether the following statements are true or false. Then correct any false statement to make it true or explain why it is false.

1. The goal of CQI—to meet or exceed the expectations of all the organization's customers—is generally attainable and achievable.
2. A manager's job with regard to performance improvement is to seek ways to reduce the amount of normal variation that occurs within systems and processes.
3. Obtaining and using actual data to inform managers who need to make decisions is a critically important element of the CQI philosophy.
4. Six Sigma came to the attention of healthcare CEOs in the late 1990s as a completely new and innovative approach to managing quality and cost in healthcare.
5. Lean is particularly focused on the elimination of waste.

Real-World Case

A lengthy, inefficient process for discharging inpatients is a common concern of hospitals. It not only causes frustration for patients and family members, but also leads to delays for incoming patients from Admitting, the Post Anesthesia Care Unit, or the Emergency Department.

When Valley Baptist Medical Center in Harlingen, Texas, faced this issue, it decided to apply Lean, Six Sigma, and change management techniques within one pilot unit. A multidisciplinary project team led by a Black Belt included

Figure 22.22. Use case description

Use Case Name
Physician orders medication(s) for a patient.
Description
When a physician determines that the patient needs a medication, he or she will complete the ordering process for medication administration.
Actor(s)
Physician; a nurse may also place the medication order (with a separate use case).
Preconditions
• The patient must currently be admitted in the hospital or receiving treatment in the ER. • The physician has active privileges at the facility. • The electronic medication ordering system is functioning properly.
Normal Sequence of Steps
• Physician signs on to the system using a password. • System validates the password and displays the patient search screen. • Physician enters the patient's medical record number. • System verifies the medical record number and displays the patient's electronic medical record. • Physician selects the medication module. • System verifies the user is allowed access to the module and displays the medication module. • Physician selects the medication from drop-down list. • System verifies the medication name. • Physician enters the dosage amount, frequency, method of administration. • System verifies the dosage amount, frequency, method of administration. • Physician submits the medication order by selecting the Submit button.
Postconditions
• The order is submitted to the pharmacy information system. • The pharmacy receives electronic notification of pending order. • A pending order is recorded in the patient's electronic medical record.
Alternative Sequence of Steps
• If the physician does not have the medical record number, he or she may enter the patient's last name and the first name. The system will then provide a list of patient names that the physician may choose from. • An additional free text field may be provided to the physician to record any additional notes or messages in relation to the medication being ordered.
Comments, Issues, and Design Notes
• When searching for a patient's electronic medical record, it may be necessary to also be able to search by patient date of birth. • For the fields of amount, frequency, and method of administration, it may be necessary to create drop-down lists that can be selected from instead of allowing free text. This will allow more control of the data entry and reduce data entry errors.

Used with permission from College of St. Scholastica HIM graduate student, D. Parisian, 2008.

nursing staff, case managers, an information technology Green Belt, and the chief medical officer, also a Green Belt.

The project was to reduce the time between when a discharge order for a patient was entered into the computer and when the room was ready for the next patient. During the initial scoping of this project, the team divided the process into four components:

1. From discharge order entry to discharge instructions signed
2. From discharge instructions signed to patient leaving
3. From patient leaving to room cleaned
4. From room cleaned to discharge entered in the computer (thus indicating the bed was ready for another patient)

Because of the hospital's commitment to customer service, the team was asked to concentrate on the first two components. The goal was for this first sub-process to be completed in less than 45 minutes.

To minimize the time a bed was empty, the team realized it also would need to address the time between when a patient's room was cleaned and the time a discharge was entered into the computer, or the second sub-process. This would address the problem that arises when Admitting does not have the necessary information to assign a new patient to a clean and empty bed.

Mapping the Process

The team began with a process map to visually understand how the process was currently working. When several nurses were asked to help develop a detailed process map on the discharge process, they initially could not reach consensus, since they each followed their own methods for discharging the patient. This lack of standard operating procedures had led to widespread process variation.

The team developed a representative process map, printed a large copy and placed it in the nurses' lounge. Each staff member was encouraged to review the map and add comments on the flow. After a week, the team retrieved the inputs and revised the "as-is" process map accordingly.

Elements of Lean thinking were combined with this map to help identify "muda" (a Lean term, Japanese for waste). To understand which steps were not contributing to timely discharge, aspects of the existing process were categorized as value-added, non-value-added, and value-enablers.

Using the Lean concepts, the team completed the revised map—identifying rework loops, non-value-added steps, communication flows and staff movement, and adding key metrics. It was apparent from the map that many of the current steps were needed for discharge; however, it also showed significant non-value-added time components and rework.

Baseline data revealed the "from-discharge-order-entry-to-patient-leaving" sub-process required 184 minutes with a standard deviation of 128 minutes. The second sub-process of "patient leaving-to-discharge-in-computer" had an average of 36 minutes with a standard deviation of 36 minutes. When compared against an upper specification limit of 45 minutes, the first sub-process had a yield of 7 percent while the second sub-process did better, with a yield of 25 percent compared to its upper specification of 5 minutes.

Behind the Waste and Variation

The most important tool for determining the critical drivers of waste and variation was the Lean process map. The staff segmented the process into key steps and used the value-added and non-valued-added times to understand the delays and rework involved.

The segments of the process were:

- Secretary processes discharge order entry
- Discharge order processed to nurse begins (delay)
- Nurse begins computer entry (to create discharge instructions)
- Computer entry to patient signature

Using Mood's Median to test various hypotheses, the team found that three factors were critical drivers of waste and variation.

1. Clarification: In 21 percent of the cases, clarification from the physician was needed before the nurse could enter the information in the computer. The team confirmed that clarification processes added a significant amount of time. The median of the process increased from 12 minutes to 45 minutes when clarification was required, indicating both a statistical significance and a practical significance ($p = 0.01$).
2. Handoff: The current process required a handoff as the charge nurse placed vital signs and other relevant information in the computer system, printed out the discharge instructions and then placed them in a bin for the primary nurse to pick up. In many cases, the primary nurse would then review the information with the patient and obtain the patient's signature.
3. In a small number of cases, however, the primary nurse completed all tasks without any handoff. The use of Mood's Median revealed a statistically significant difference between no handoff versus the more common handoff approach. The median increased from 9 minutes when one nurse completed all tasks, to 73 minutes when a handoff between nurses was required ($p = 0$). Without a signal for the handoff, the patient's paperwork often waited up to an hour before it was acted on.
4. Aftercare: Finally, the team tested the hypothesis that when aftercare was required (for example, the social services department ordering equipment), there was an increase in median cycle time from 121 minutes in the current process to 160 minutes when aftercare was required ($p = 0.035$).

The process generally suffered from rework and a lack of visual signals which caused additional delays. In addition, little thought had been given to correct sequencing or designating some activities which could be done ahead as set-up items for the discharge process.

Improving the Process

Since variations in the "as is" process were contributing greatly to long cycle times and delays, a new standard operating procedure (SOP) was developed containing six steps:

- Unit secretary enters discharge order
- Unit secretary tells primary nurse via spectra link phone that he or she is next in the process
- Primary nurse verifies order and provides the assessment
- Primary nurse enters information into computer system
- Primary nurse prints instructions and information
- Primary nurse reviews instructions and obtains patient signature

Only value-added steps were targeted, but steps causing bottlenecks and rework also were moved from workflow on the day of discharge to set-up activities. A daily meeting would coordinate these activities and patients would be assessed the day before discharge. The charge nurse, case manager, primary nurse, and other professionals participated in the daily meeting and a new tool was developed to help document and assign tasks to be completed prior to discharge. Areas reviewed were: lines, elimination (Foley's), activity level, diets and tube feeding, consults, aftercare orders and medical records. The daily meetings reduced the need for physician clarifications and aftercare on the day of discharge—two significant causes for delays.

Having the primary nurse complete all discharge tasks eliminated the bottlenecks created by time-consuming handoffs, the need for signaling those handoffs, and the fact that the charge nurse, who has many responsibilities, was not always readily available.

With the first sub-process of their deliverable improved—from discharge order entry to patient leaving—the team focused on getting information into the computer so the bed could be filled. A session was conducted with transporters and unit secretaries to determine the best way to improve the computer entry process. It was immediately clear that the current process was not working. Unit secretaries were not always aware when a patient was transferred from the unit. No signal was provided when a transporter moved a patient. Since the secretaries performed numerous activities (not always at the nurses station), they could easily forget a patient had been discharged.

A small discharge slip was developed containing the patient name, room number, and time of call. The transporter would pick up the patient and then go to the nurses' station and ask the secretary to provide the time on the computer. The transporter would write the time and hand the slip to the secretary. This served as a trigger and transferred the process from the transporter to the secretary.

Maintaining Improvement

Two tactics employed simultaneously helped to sustain the improvements. The first was the use of change acceleration process (CAP) and the second was an ongoing tracking system. Four CAP sessions were guided by the Black Belt and process owner, increasing understanding as to why the initiative was undertaken, providing baseline data, and establishing the rationale for improvements.

Each session also included exercises to help participants better appreciate Lean and Six Sigma, with a catapult exercise as a learning tool. Participants split into groups and worked to meet customer needs. They then reviewed the process, made adjustments, and developed standard operating procedures. Upon execution, the new plan showed improved performance.

A tracking system included three components:

- A daily report of the prior day's discharges, including discharge times, primary nurse, and unit secretary responsible for discharging the patient from the computer
- A performance tracker to ensure individual accountability for primary nurses and unit secretaries in terms of mean, standard deviation, and yield
- A control chart that tracked the means and standard deviations

Summary: Process in Control

With the process now in control, the components were remeasured. The from-discharge-order-entry-to-patient-leaving sub-process showed a mean improvement of 74 percent with a 70 percent decrease in the standard deviation. The second sub-process, from patient-leaving-to-discharge-in-computer, showed an improvement of 90 percent in the mean and 58 percent in the standard deviation. (See the following table.) With success in this unit, a translation effort would be undertaken for the entire hospital. This will be an ongoing effort requiring change management for the entire hospital and training sessions on the new standard operating procedures.

	From Discharge Order Entry to Patient Leaving Upper Specification Limit: 45 Minutes		**From Patient Leaving to Discharge in Computer** Upper Specification Limit: 5 Minutes	
	Baseline	**Current**	**Baseline**	**Current**
Mean	184.8	47.8	36.6	3.47
Standard Deviation	128.7	37.2	36.1	16.9
Yield	6.9%	61.7%	24.6%	95.4%

Source: Debusk and Rangel, Jr. 2001–2008.

Summary

Excellence in management requires the manager to be knowledgeable about the components of systems and work processes, to be aware of the quality and productivity expectations of the customers served by them, and have the ability to define, execute, monitor and analyze performance based on standards that have been developed through benchmarking and specific types of work measurement methodologies. When variations in performance are identified, they are addressed in a timely way through actions plans which may well include efforts focused on process improvement to achieve greater effectiveness, efficiency, and adaptability of the systems involved.

Continuous quality improvement and business process redesign are two fundamental approaches to improving processes and performance in healthcare organizations. These approaches share many similarities: all are focused on bettering the system to provide high-quality service in a cost-effective manner. They also use similar data-gathering and analysis tools. The differences in the approaches reflect the breadth of change, the duration of the change effort, and the specific focus area for the change. CQI is a test of small changes with the intention of improving services to customers over time. Business process reengineering involves a massive reexamination of processes with the main purpose of reducing costs. Lean and Six Sigma are commonly being used in healthcare organizations to improve healthcare service delivery.

References

AHIMA. 2006. *Optimizing investment in the EHR: Workflow analysis as the foundation for success* [Workshop resource book]. Chicago: AHIMA.

Berwick, D.M.. 1989. Continuous improvement as an ideal in health care. *New England Journal of Medicine* 320(1):53–56.

Brassard, M. and D. Ritter. 1993. *The Memory Jogger II.* Methuen, MA: GOAL/QPC.

Cofer, J.I. and H.P. Greele. 1993. *Quality Improvement Techniques for Medical Records.* Marblehead, MA: Opus Communications.

DeBusk, C. and A. Rangel, Jr. 2000. Creating a Lean Six Sigma hospital discharge process: An iSixSigma Case Study. *iSixSigma.* http://healthcare.isixsigma.com/library/content/c040915a.asp.

Eckes, G. 2003. *Six Sigma for Everyone.* Hoboken, NJ: John Wiley & Sons.

Hammer, M. and J. Champy. 1993. *Reengineering the Corporation: A Manifesto for Business Revolution.* New York: HarperBusiness.

Hughes, G. 2003. Practice brief: Using benchmarking for performance improvement. *Journal of AHIMA* 74(2):64A–D.

Institute of Medicine. 2000. *To Err is Human.* Washington, D.C.: National Academies Press.

Joint Commission. 2009. Comprehensive Accreditation Manual. Oakbrook Terrace, IL. Joint Commission.

Jones, D. and A. Mitchell. 2006. *Lean thinking for the NHS.* A report commissioned by the NHS.

Johns, M.L. 1997. *Information Management for Health Professionals.* Albany, NY: Delmar.

Johnson, S.P. and C.P. McLaughlin. 1999. Measurement and statistical approaches in CQI. In *Continuous Quality Improvement in Health Care.* Edited by McLaughlin, C.P. and A.D. Kaluzny. Gaithersburg, MD: Aspen Publishers.

Keister, J. 2001. Workflow automation: Streamlining the way things get done. *For the Record* 13(16):16–20.

Lazarus, I. 2003 (Jan. 1). Six Sigma raising the bar. *Managed Healthcare Executive.* http://www.managedhealthcareexecutive.com.mhe/article/articleDetail.jsp?id=43331.

Langley, G.J., K.M. Nolan, and T.W. Nolan. 1994 (June). The foundation of improvement. *Quality Progress.* 81–86.

Liebler, J.G., R.E. Levine, and J. Rothman. 1992. *Management Principles for Health Professionals.* 2nd ed. Gaithersburg, MD: Aspen Publishers.

McLaughlin, C.P. and A.D. Kaluzny. 1999. *Continuous Quality Improvement in Health Care: Theory, Implementation and Applications.* 2nd ed. Gaithersburg, MD: Aspen Publishers.

Misra, K.B. 2008. *Handbook of Performability Engineering.* London: Springer.

Omachonu, V.K. 1999. *Healthcare Performance Improvement.* Norcross, GA: Engineering and Management Press.

Palmer, L. 1995. Reengineering healthcare: The future awaits us all. *Journal of AHIMA* 66(2):32–35.

Rizzardo, D. and R. Brooks. 2003. Understanding Lean Manufacturing. http://www.mtech.umd.edu/MTES/understand_lean.html.

Senge, P.M. 1990. *The Fifth Discipline: The Art and Practice of the Learning Organization.* New York: Currency/Doubleday.

Sharp, A. and P. McDermott. 2001. *Workflow Modeling: Tools for Process Improvement and Application Development.* Norwood, MA: Arctech House.

Six Sigma. 2004. Deming Cycle, PDCA. http://www.isixsigma.com/dictionary/Deming_Cycle,_PDCA-650.htm.

Umiker, W. 1998. *Management Skills for the New Health Care Supervisor.* 3rd ed. Gaithersburg, MD: Aspen Publishers.

White, A. 2002. Performance improvement. In *Health Information Management Technology: An Applied Approach.* Edited by M.L. Johns. Chicago: AHIMA.

Zidel, T.G. 2006 (January/February). Quality toolbox: A Lean toolbox – using Lean principles and techniques in healthcare. *Journal for Healthcare Quality*—Web Exclusive. http://www.mainenetwork.org/upload_files/Tom%20Zidel%20-%20Lean%20Toolbox%20-%20JHQ%20JanFeb06.pdf.

Chapter 23
Human Resources Management

Madonna M. LeBlanc, MA, RHIA

Learning Objectives

- Differentiate among the concepts of chain of command, scope of command, and unity of command
- Differentiate among the hierarchical, bureaucratic, and team-based approaches to organization and management
- Develop organizational charts that accurately represent an organization's formal structure
- Construct mission, vision, and values statements
- Distinguish the unique responsibilities associated with each level of management in the organization: supervisor, middle manager, executive manager, and board director
- Identify the activities associated with the human resources (HR) management function in an organization
- Associate key federal legislation with each of the human resources management activities
- Develop position descriptions, performance standards, staffing structures, and work schedules for use as tools in human resources management
- Explain how job descriptions are used in employee recruitment and selection
- Identify effective steps for conducting an interview
- Discuss the roles that employee orientation and communication plans play in the development and retention of staff
- Articulate the benefits of teamwork in an organization and identify the steps in creating an effective team (team building)
- Identify and differentiate among the four methods of job evaluation
- Describe the relationship among performance standards, performance review, and performance counseling
- Identify the key steps a manager should take in performance counseling and disciplinary action
- Select the appropriate conflict management technique to use in each specific conflict situation
- Explain the process for handling employee complaints and grievances
- Identify the obligations an organization has to maintain the security of employee information and records
- Anticipate the impact of current workforce trends on the organization's human resources management activities

Key Terms

360-degree evaluation
Ability (achievement) tests
Age Discrimination in Employment Act (1967)
Americans with Disabilities Act (ADA) (1990)
Aptitude tests
Authority
Behavioral description interview
Benefits
Board of governors (board of trustees, board of directors)
Bureaucracy
Chain of command
Civil Rights Act, Title VII (1964)
Civil Rights Act (1991)
Communication plan
Compensable factors
Compensation and benefits
Compromise
Conflict management
Constructive confrontation
Control
Delegation of authority
Disciplinary action
Discrimination
Effort
Employee record
Employment-at-will
Equal Employment Opportunity Act (1972)
Equal Pay Act (EPA) (1963)
Executive managers
Exempt employees
Exit interview
Factor comparison method
Fair Labor Standards Act (FLSA) (1938)
Family and Medical Leave Act (FMLA) (1993)
Flexible work schedules
Grievance
Grievance procedures
Harassment
Hay method of job evaluation
Hierarchy
Hiring
Honesty (integrity) tests
Interviews
Job classification method
Job evaluation

Job ranking
Job specification
Labor-Management Relations Act (Taft-Hartley Act)
Labor-Management Reporting and Disclosure Act (Landrum-Griffin Act)
Labor relations
Layoffs
Mental ability (cognitive) tests
Middle managers
Mission statement
National Labor Relations Act (Wagner Act)
Nonexempt employees
Occupational Safety and Health Act (OSHA) (1970)
Organization
Organizational chart
Orientation
Panel interview
Performance counseling
Performance review
Performance standards
Point method
Policy
Position (job) description
Pregnancy Discrimination Act (1978)
Procedure
Progressive discipline
Recruitment
Reference check
Reliability
Responsibility
Resume
Retention
Selection
Skill
Span of control (scope of command)
Staffing structure
Structured interview
Supervisory managers
Team building
Termination
Testing
Uniformed Services Employment and Reemployment Rights Act (1994)
Union
Unity of command
Validity
Values statement
Vision statement
Workers' Adjustment Retraining and Notification (WARN) Act
Working conditions

The process of management cannot be practiced or examined meaningfully outside the social, cultural, and ethical contexts in which human organizations of all kinds operate. In modern industrial societies, human resources represent every organization's most valuable asset.

Healthcare organizations are extremely complex. They must operate as effective and efficient businesses in a very tight financial environment. They also must employ a variety of well-educated technical specialists and professional employees to provide or support increasingly sophisticated healthcare services. Contemporary healthcare managers work in a unique environment that is characterized by the need to control costs and, at the same time, meet the needs of healthcare consumers and healthcare workers.

Managers work at many levels within healthcare organizations: as supervisors of functional units, as middle managers of departmental units or service lines, and as executive managers of multiple departmental units or service lines. At each level of management, the practice of managing the human resources within the prescribed scope of **authority** and **responsibility** is critical to the manager's success and the success of the entire organization.

Managing human resources (HR) is both an art and a science. Managers can learn much in this arena by partnering with HR management specialists, observing experienced colleagues, reflecting regularly on their own experiences, and continuing to develop their competencies throughout their careers.

This chapter is not meant to provide a comprehensive background in human resources management. The purpose of this chapter is to present a general introduction to the subject of managing human resources within the context of health information management (HIM) operations. The chapter begins with a brief overview of the principles and nature of organizations and a discussion of the roles of the various levels of management. Its primary focus is the interrelationship of HIM managers and HR professionals and the roles of the supervisor and middle manager as frontline implementers of the HR policies and practices of healthcare organizations.

Principles of Organization

Organization is the planned coordination of the activities of more than one person for the achievement of a common purpose or goal. It is accomplished through the division of labor, and it is based on a hierarchy of authority and responsibility (Schein 1980). Jobs and the people who perform them are arranged in a way that accomplishes the goals of the organization. Various organizational tools are used to communicate the structure, the purpose, and the methods for accomplishing the shared work of the organization's members.

Organizations are somewhat like sports teams in that they have specific positions, a predefined set of rules, and a shared goal (in the case of sports teams, the goal is winning).

Organizations also use communications tools that are similar to a players roster (position descriptions), a rule or playbook (policies and procedures), and a record of wins and losses (a budget and financial records).

Like other types of businesses, healthcare institutions are a type of formal organization. That is, they have established goals and a specific purpose for existing. Although purpose, structure, and methods vary widely, all healthcare organizations use common systems and tools to achieve their goals.

Nature of Organizations

By nature, humans are social creatures. They are biologically designed to live within groups of their own kind. Moreover, they continuously form and reform informal and formal groups of various sizes (two members to billions of members) and longevity (a few seconds to a few centuries). No two groups have identical purposes, membership, or rules. Therefore, every human group is unique.

There is an endless variety of groups. Groups range from relatively informal friendships, families, and social clubs to extremely formal businesses, educational institutions, and national governments. They can be loose, unstructured, and temporary. An example of an extremely loose, short-term group might be that of a dozen people who ride on a bus together on a given morning. But even the most informal groups have a purpose and a set of more or less well-communicated rules. In this example, the group's purpose is to get from point A to point B. The rules require that the bus driver follow a pre-established route and the riders pay a pre-established fare.

Although every group of humans is unique, interactions among humans follow predictable patterns. Human behavior has been studied for centuries. Theories on organizational behavior have been offered ever since humans learned how to communicate with each other. Although few principles of organizational behavior go unchallenged, centuries of observation have produced some basic rules. For example, one unchanging principle of organizational behavior seems to be that the group's structure affects the way its members interact with each other. And these structural effects can have both positive and negative consequences for the group as a whole as well as for its individual members.

Organizational Structures

At least until recent decades, formal organizations such as healthcare and manufacturing institutions have tended to be structured as relatively inflexible hierarchies. In a **hierarchy**, every member of the organization is assigned a specific rank. Each rank, in turn, carries a specific level of decision-making authority as well as specific responsibilities within the institution. Hierarchies are authoritarian in nature. In other words, they are strictly controlled by a powerful elite group working "at the top" of the organization. These few individuals make almost every significant decision on behalf of the entire organization.

Historically, large governmental institutions have tended to be organized as rigid bureaucratic structures. In a **bureaucracy**, as in a hierarchy, positions within the formal organization are assigned specific ranks. Hierarchical ranks are based on levels of decision-making **authority**. In contrast, bureaucratic ranks are based on levels of technical expertise.

The purpose of bureaucratic organizations is to conduct highly complex and regulated processes. The structure of the bureaucratic organization reflects the processes it was designed to carry out. Therefore, bureaucracies operate according to well-established and often inflexible rules. Each individual within the bureaucracy is responsible for carrying out only a small, well-defined element of the larger process. The Social Security Administration is a good example of a government bureaucracy. It was created in 1935, with the sole purpose of implementing the Social Security Act.

Both hierarchies and bureaucracies depend on authoritarian **chains of command**. Two principles that are inherent in a traditional chain-of-command structure are span of control (scope of command) and unity of command. **Unity of command**, one of Henri Fayol's 14 Principles of Management, is expressed as each employee being accountable to only one boss. **Span of control**, Luther Gulick's adaptation of European military strategy, defines one manager overseeing the work of many employees. The structures of military organizations, for example, are organized around extremely rigid chains of command. Gulick determined there are organizational variables that impact the number of subordinates a manager can effectively command. It became apparent that a narrow versus a broad span of control is somewhat dependent on the complexity of the functions for which each employee was responsible (Gulick and Urwick 1937). The higher the complexity of employee functions, the narrower the span of control required to manage those employees effectively and vice versa. (See figures 23.1 and 23.2).

Figure 23.1. Narrow span of control

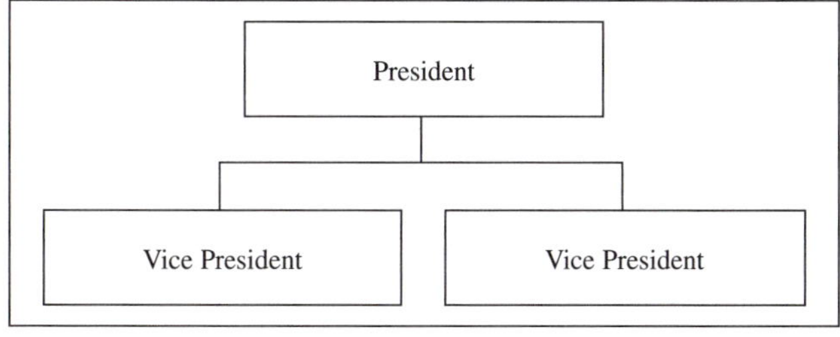

Figure 23. 2. Broad span of control

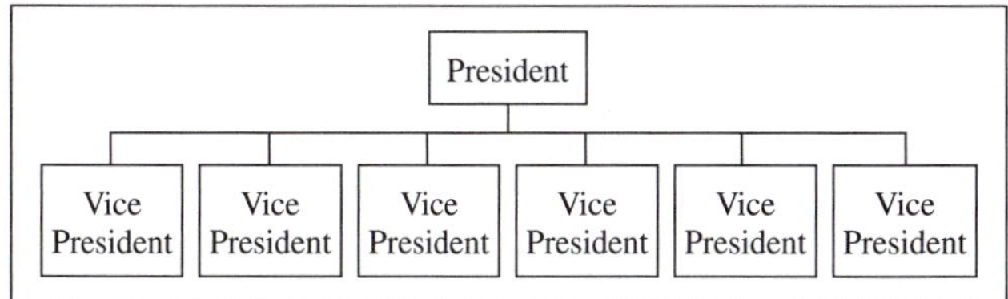

In modern times, organizational structure has been studied systematically since the early 20th century. In the subsequent decades, a number of new management theories were suggested, and each theory seems to have required innovations in organizational structure. The period of economic rebuilding after World War II ushered in the current era of business thinking. Business and management theorists W. Edwards Deming and Joseph M. Juran began developing modern management systems during the early 1950s.

Today's management systems are modern in that they are moving away from the traditional authoritarian models that have prevailed since the Industrial Revolution. Most of all, they are modern in that they recognize the potential value of change and treat change as an opportunity rather than as a threat.

Modern management systems are based on the objective statistical analysis of data and information. They emphasize the **benefits** of sharing authority among employees and managers. They also favor interdisciplinary and cross-functional cooperation and teamwork over bureaucratic regulation and authoritarian control. Modern management systems value continual learning and demand systems thinking (Senge 1990, 6–8). Systems thinking is simply an objective way of looking at work-related ideas and processes with the goal of allowing people to uncover ineffective patterns of behavior and thinking and then finding ways to make lasting improvements.

In large part, modern management systems represent a rejection of the traditional authoritarian, hierarchical, and bureaucratic approaches to organization and management. However, because traditional management systems have been the accepted norm since the Industrial Revolution began in the early 18th century, they have proved difficult to displace. They continue to be the core organizational structures in place in most businesses today. Management theorists continue to lead the movement to establish information-based management systems and team-based organizational structures in all types of business endeavors, including the business of healthcare delivery. (See chapter 20 for a fuller discussion of the evolution of management theory.)

Organizational Charts

An **organizational chart** is a graphic representation of an organization's formal structure. It shows the organization's various activities and the specific members or categories of members assigned to carry out its activities. The chart for a very small organization might list the actual names of employees or individual position titles. The chart for a very large organization might list the various functional groups or departments responsible for each area of operations. By looking at an organizational chart you can see not only the major functions, but the chain of command, the relationships between functions or departments, the lines of authority, the lines of communication, the span of control and the unity of command. Therefore, at a glance, you can see if there are any problems; for example, is one subordinate reporting to two supervisors or one supervisor with too many subordinates? Traditionally, the reporting relationships among individuals and groups also are indicated according to accepted labeling conventions. For example, a solid line between two elements on a chart indicates a direct reporting relationship and a broken line indicates an indirect reporting relationship. (See figures 23.3, 23.4, and 23.5 for examples of organizational charts developed for different types of healthcare organizations.)

Three key elements need to be addressed when initially organizing personnel or reviewing a current organizational structure:

- What activities need to be accomplished—transcription, filing, coding, data abstracting?
- What duties are related to those activities—supervision, transcription, proofreading, delivery of reports?
- How many and what types of personnel are required for these activities? What kinds?

Once the personnel structure and types have been determined, the specific department work units and number of personnel in each can be determined, authority relationships can be determined, and the organizational chart can be drawn to reflect those decisions. Organizational charts are excellent tools to use in employee orientation to aid new employees in understanding the entire organizational structure.

There are four basic types of organization charts:

- *Vertical:* Most commonly used, the vertical chart shows levels of the organization in a step arrangement, with the chief executive officer (CEO) at the top. This format is easy to read and understand.
- *Horizontal:* Reads from left to right and is advantageous in that it emphasizes functional leadership and minimizes hierarchal levels.
- *Circular*: Shows various levels in a concert of circles around the CEO; hierarchy is not emphasized.
- *Inverted pyramid:* Becoming more common in work settings that embrace the Total Quality Management (TQM) philosophy; positioning the CEO at the bottom of the chart—at the tip of the inverted pyramid.

Several computer software programs can be utilized to facilitate illustration of the organizational chart, such as Visio, Microsoft Word, and PowerPoint. Each program provides the shapes commonly used to create these charts. Whatever computer-assisted design program used, following rules for organizational chart construction assures a universal method for both creating and understanding these charts. (See figure 23.6.)

Today's healthcare organizations are somewhat less concerned with official lines of authority. Instead, they are concerned with the interrelationships of work groups and functions. Individual departments and interdepartmental work groups sometimes develop detailed organizational charts as a first step in redesigning work processes. The charts then can be used as the basis for creating workflow diagrams and flowcharts. The purpose of these graphic tools is to help work teams visualize current and proposed processes and then suggest and implement improvements.

Some organizations also include organizational charts in their official position (job) descriptions. In this context, the charts put the work of a specific position or employee into the larger context of how the whole organization works as a system of interdependent processes.

Mission, Vision, and Values Statements

Modern organizations use a variety of communication devices to convey their purpose and goals to their members and the communities they serve. A **mission statement** is a short description of the general purpose of an organization or group. For healthcare organizations, the mission statement usually includes a broad definition of the services the organization provides and the communities and patrons it serves. Similarly, a **vision statement** is a short description of the organization's ideal future state. One way to distinguish between an organization's mission and its vision is to think of the concepts in the following way:

- The mission is a *realistic* expression of what the organization actually does at the current time.
- The vision is an *idealistic* portrayal of what the organization would like to become sometime in the future.

Most healthcare organizations update their mission and vision statements regularly as part of the strategic planning

Figure 23.3. Sample organizational chart for an acute care hospital

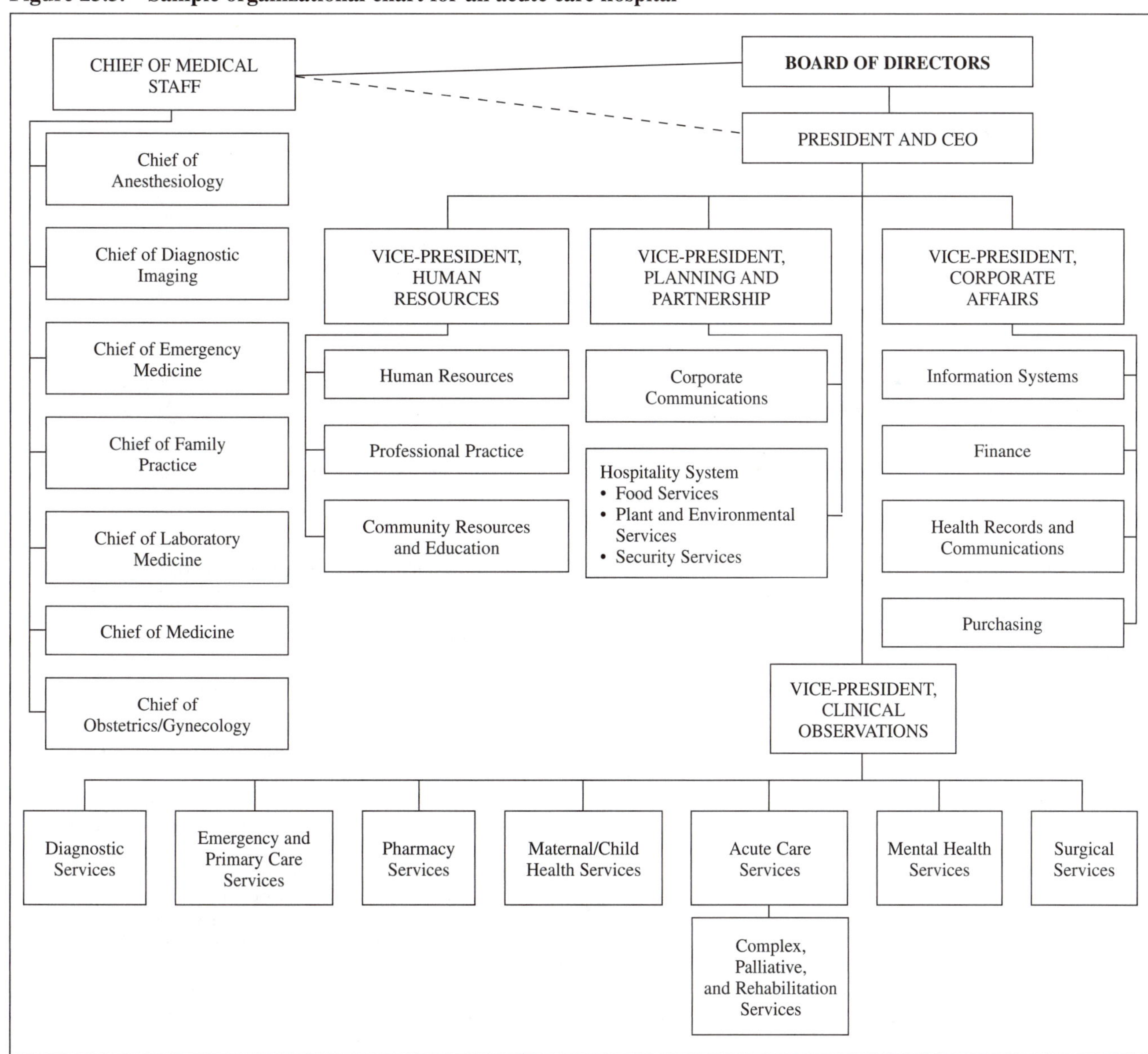

process. The organization shares its mission and vision statements internally with its employees and medical staff and externally with its patrons and the community it serves. The statements are meant to inform, guide, and inspire.

Healthcare organizations use mission and vision statements at many different levels. An individual organization usually develops statements for the enterprise as a whole. A multifacility healthcare system usually develops statements for the system as a whole, as well as for each individual facility within it. Departments, work teams, and even temporary task forces often develop vision and mission statements. These groups use the statements to express and communicate their specific purpose and goals. Figure 23.7 provides examples of vision and mission statements from healthcare organizations. (See chapter 28 for a broader discussion of strategic planning.)

Many healthcare organizations also develop **values statements** that communicate their social and cultural belief system. The organization's values statement provides a way to support the type of behavior the organization wishes to

Figure 23.4. Sample organizational chart for an ambulatory care clinic

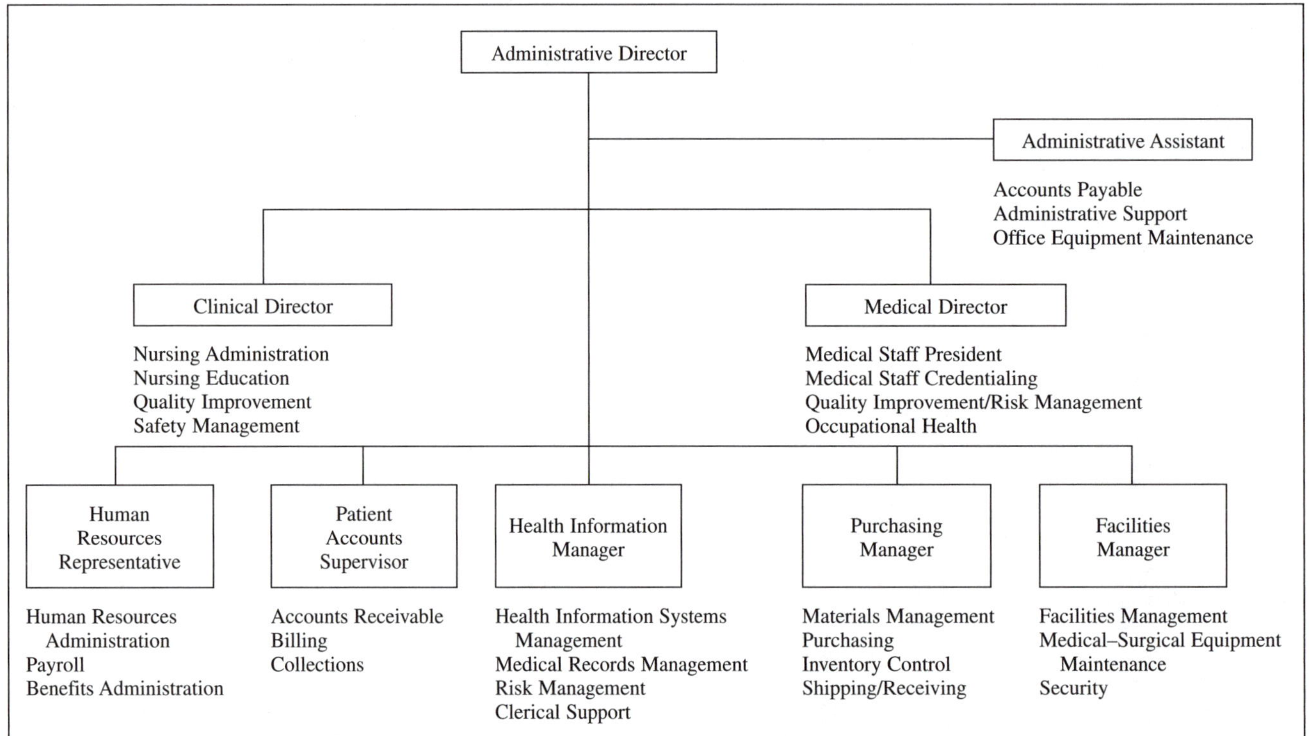

Figure 23.5. Sample organizational chart for a managed care organization

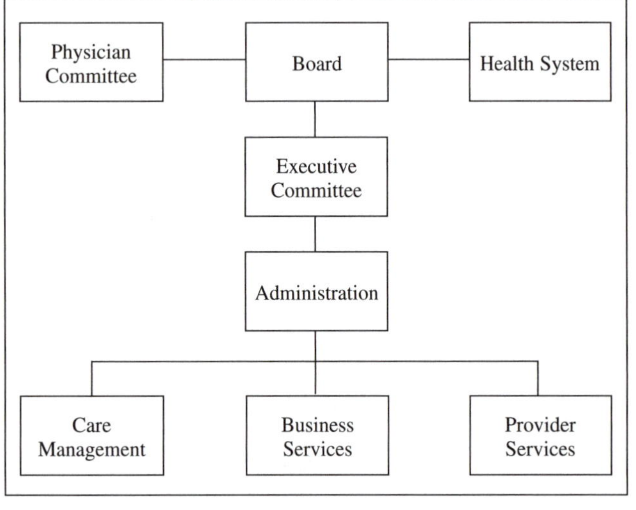

Figure 23.6. Rules for organization chart construction

- Fully identify the chart (for example, Hospital XYZ Health Information Services).
- Start at the top.
- Use rectangular boxes to show each work unit (for example, coding, transcription, etc.) or individual.
- Vertical placement denotes relative position within a hierarchy.
- Horizontal row denotes same or similar organizational rank.
- Solid lines show flow of line authority.
- Dotted lines show flow of functional/staff authority.
- Lines of authority enter at the top center of a box and exit at the bottom center of the box.
- Side entry is acceptable when showing staff relationships.
- Titles of each position should be placed in the box.
  - Include # FTE occupying a single job title when several employees hold an identical position, if not providing a box per employee.
  - Name of individuals is optional.
  - If done, must be updated in a timely manner.
- Include the supervisor to whom the work unit reports.
- Include the date chart was approved.

Figure 23.7. Sample mission and vision statements

General Hospital Affiliated with a Larger Healthcare System

Lutheran Hospital's **mission** is to improve the health of the communities we serve by providing high-quality services in a responsible and caring way.

Our **vision** is to become the leader in promoting healthy life-styles in an atmosphere of spiritual support, dignity, compassion, and mutual respect for all.

Community General Hospital

Anytown General Hospital's **mission** is to provide quality health services and technology to meet the changing healthcare needs of the people of southwestern Minnesota.

Anytown General Hospital's **vision** is to become the hospital of choice for residents of Polk, Sunny Isle, and Spring counties, a position we strive to strengthen by our long-term commitment to:

- Teamwork
- Service excellence
- Compassionate care
- Cost consciousness
- Continuous improvement

Academic Medical Center

Prairie University Hospital's **mission** is to provide the most up-to-date medical and surgical services available in the three-state area and to train medical students and graduate physicians to meet current and future challenges in healthcare.

Our **vision** is the achievement of healthy communities and progress toward the future of healthcare for Montana, western North Dakota, and northwestern South Dakota.

Specialty Hospital

The **mission** of Women's Hospital of Somewhereville is to meet the healthcare needs of our patients and to exceed their service expectations.

Our **vision** is of a hospital:

- Providing services with compassion and kindness
- Striving for performance improvement
- Fostering pride and integrity
- Aiming for increased cost-effectiveness and productivity

Specialty Clinic within an Academic Medical Center

The **mission** of the Midwest Asthma Center is to:

- Provide optimal medical care for persons with asthma and related illnesses
- Develop new knowledge about asthma and its management through medical research
- Promote improved understanding about asthma and related illnesses through providing educational programs and materials for our patients, for other healthcare providers, and for the community

The **vision** of the Midwest Asthma Center is to provide the highest quality of integrated comprehensive care for persons with asthma and related illnesses and to be one of the centers of excellence in the world for asthma treatment, research, and education.

Primary Care Physicians' Practice

The **mission** of Coastal Shores Primary Care Associates is to serve the unique needs of individuals and families by providing high-quality, coordinated, primary care medical services through an efficient, accessible, and responsive network of caring providers.

Our **vision** is to be the primary care medical group of choice in the Atlantic County area by delivering high-quality, individualized, and efficient patient care.

encourage among its members. For example, the Benedictine Health System based in Duluth, Minnesota, clearly identifies "hospitality, stewardship, respect and justice" as its organizational core values (Benedictine Health System 2002, 1).

Check Your Understanding 23.1

Instructions: On a separate piece of paper, indicate whether the following statements are true or false (T or F) If the statement is false, explain why it is false.

1. Systems thinking is a subjective way to look at work-related ideas and processes.
2. Bureaucratic ranks are based on levels of technical expertise.
3. Today's healthcare organizations are increasingly concerned with official lines of authority.
4. Healthcare organizations develop mission statements to communicate their social and cultural belief systems.

Levels of Management

As noted earlier in this chapter, the various levels of management in organizations have different levels of responsibility and decision-making authority.

Supervisory Management

Supervisory managers (supervisors) oversee the organization's efforts at the staff level and monitor the effectiveness of everyday operations and individual performance against pre-established standards. Further, supervisory managers are responsible for ensuring that the organization's human assets are used effectively and that its policies and procedures are carried out consistently.

Supervisory managers work in small (2- to 10-person) functional work groups or teams. They often perform hands-on functions in addition to supervisory functions. They play an important role in staff training and recruitment and retention efforts. Supervisory managers direct daily work, create work schedules, and monitor the quality of the work and the productivity of the staff. They are important resources in revising procedures and conducting performance reviews because they are familiar with the work of the unit and the performance of individual staff members.

Supervisory managers usually have advanced technical **skills** that allow them to perform the most complex functions of the work team. However, most supervisors have limited financial authority and must seek the approval of higher-level managers before spending money or **hiring** staff. Depending on the size and structure of the organization, HIM supervisors report to another supervisory-level manager or to a department-level manager or assistant manager.

Effective supervisory managers are extremely important in healthcare organizations because the greatest part of the healthcare organization's resources is expended at the operational level. Labor costs represent the greatest investment that the organization makes. Staff and supervisory healthcare workers include nurses, clinical therapists, diagnostic technicians, dietary workers, laboratory workers, environmental support staff, and administrative support staff.

In healthcare organizations, registered health information technicians (RHITs) or health information administrators (RHIAs) often fill roles as supervisory managers. They provide vital administrative services and support patient care by protecting the accuracy and confidentiality of clinical databases and health records. They also ensure the financial health and future of their organizations by providing high-quality clinical coding services.

Middle Management

Middle management is concerned primarily with facilitating the work performed by supervisory- and staff-level personnel as well as by executive leaders. The responsibilities of middle managers include the following:

- Developing, implementing, and revising the organization's policies and procedures under the direction of executive managers
- Executing the organizational plans developed at the board and executive levels
- Providing the operational information that executives need to develop meaningful plans for the organization's future

Middle managers oversee operations of a broader scope in their work as managers or assistant managers of departments or disciplinary functions. For example, they may be responsible for overseeing all the functions in a health information services (HIS) department or for directing the functions in two or more related departments, such as HIS, admission or registration services, and quality improvement services.

Middle managers can change department-level policies and procedures when necessary. For example, when a department manager finds that an employee is not following a specific procedure, he or she investigates and analyzes the department's systems and processes to determine whether the problem is with the employee's performance or with shortcomings in the processes themselves. In contrast, supervisory managers enforce the policies and procedures that relate directly to the activities of their own work group or team. For example, when a supervisor finds that an employee is not following a specific procedure, he or she takes action to correct that individual's performance.

Typically, middle managers are responsible for performing a limited number of hands-on analytical and decision-making functions related directly to the departments they manage. In an HIS department, for example, an HIM professional in an assistant director position might be responsible for tracking the quality of clinical databases and overseeing coding compliance programs. HIS department managers participate on a number of permanent and temporary interdisciplinary committees within the organization and serve as resources to the committees on subjects that relate to the organization's information resources. They also initiate interdepartmental efforts to address issues that go beyond department-level operations. In small healthcare organizations, the HIM director may play additional managerial roles in risk management, quality management, or utilization management.

Depending on the size and structure of the organization, HIS middle managers report to a department-level director or an executive-level manager (vice-president) on the organization's senior management team. In a multifacility healthcare delivery network, the HIS director might report to the vice-president of operations (sometimes referred to as the chief operating officer, or COO) or the vice-president of information services (sometimes called the chief information officer, or CIO). In a small community hospital, the HIS director might report to the CEO, the CFO (chief financial officer), or the COO.

Executive Management and Governance

The third managerial level in healthcare organizations can be divided into executive management and governance. The governance body is often called the **board of governors (board of directors, board of trustees)**.

Role of Executive Management

Executive managers are directly employed by the organization. They are hired by either the board or the organization's CEO with the board's approval. In publicly owned organizations, the stockholders elect board members. In privately owned organizations, the board members are appointed.

Executive managers are primarily responsible for working with the board to set the organization's future direction and establish its strategic plan. To that end, executive managers work to ensure that the organization uses its assets wisely, fulfills its current mission, and works toward achieving a meaningful vision for the future. Executive managers oversee broad functions, departments, or groups of departments. Executive managers are also responsible for establishing the policies of healthcare organizations and leading their quality improvement and compliance initiatives. In addition, executive managers work with community leaders to make sure that the healthcare organization contributes to the well-being of the community it serves.

Depending on the complexity of the organization, the titles of executive managers vary. The different titles include chief executive officer, president, executive vice-president, senior vice-president, vice-president, and director. Executive managers may report to other executive managers, to higher-level vice-presidents, or to the CEO.

In most organizations, the CEO is the highest-ranking executive manager. CEOs sometimes hold more than one title. For example, the head of an organization might have the title president and CEO. The CEO or president reports directly to the organization's board of directors.

Role of the Governing Board

Healthcare organizations such as hospitals, healthcare businesses, and multifacility healthcare delivery networks are organized as legal entities, or corporations. Every state has laws that dictate how corporations are to be structured and run within its jurisdiction. However, all state incorporation laws are consistent in one area: responsibility for the operation of each healthcare organization ultimately lies with its board of governors. Thus, the board is the final authority in setting the organization's strategic direction, mission and vision, and general philosophy and ethical base. The name and structure of the board depend on the profit-making status of the organization, among other factors.

Typically, the board consists of a chairperson and 10 to 20 board members. It represents the interests of the organization's owners. Any number of different entities may own large healthcare organizations, including federal, state, and local governments; investment groups; educational institutions; and religious organizations. Moreover, healthcare organizations may be owned privately or publicly. In publicly owned for-profit entities, investors purchase stock on national and international stock exchanges and receive a share of the profits in the form of dividends. Many private healthcare organizations operate as not-for-profit charitable organizations. In not-for-profit organizations, any excess income is reinvested in the organization rather than being paid out in profits or dividends.

Check Your Understanding 23.2

Instructions: On a separate piece of paper, indicate whether the following statements are true or false (T or F). If the statement is false, explain why it is false.

1. Supervisory managers set the organization's future direction and establish its goals.
2. In general, middle managers perform the daily work of the organization.
3. Vice-presidents are representatives of the executive level of management.
4. The ultimate responsibility for the organization's operation lies with its chief executive officer.
5. In publicly owned healthcare entities, investors buy stock and receive dividends.

Role of the Human Resources Department

Payroll and benefits consume the majority of most healthcare organizations' financial resources. Therefore, adequate time and attention must be paid to the management of HR. Effective HR management is also important for reasons beyond financial impact. HR management factors affect the attitudes and morale of healthcare workers and other employees and, therefore, affect their ability to perform their work effectively, as well. Obviously, employee morale becomes extremely important when the work involves caring for patients directly or indirectly supporting those who provide hands-on care.

Entities such as hospitals, large physician groups, and managed care organizations commonly have a dedicated HR department that acts as a reference and support for managers at all levels. However, every manager must have an understanding of the principles of HR management in order to implement them effectively within the scope of the manager's authority and responsibility. Every manager must also know how to appropriately and effectively work with the organization's HR department.

The HR department is responsible for several types of interrelated activities. Mathis and Jackson (2002) describe HR management as a set of closely related activities focused on contributing to an organization's success by enhancing its productivity, quality, and service. Each of these interrelated activities is shown in figure 23.8 Mathis and Jackson also emphasize the importance of performing HR activities with the organization's unique mission, culture, size, and structure in mind as well as the greater social, political, legal, economic, technological, and cultural environment in which it operates.

Human Resources Planning and Analysis

HR planning and analysis ensure the long-term health of the organization's human assets. Internal trends such as the aging of the workforce or the changing nature of the skill mix required to handle the organization's evolving product lines must be addressed. The impact of external trends such as workforce shortages and evolving workforce expectations also must be assessed.

Figure 23.8. HR management activities

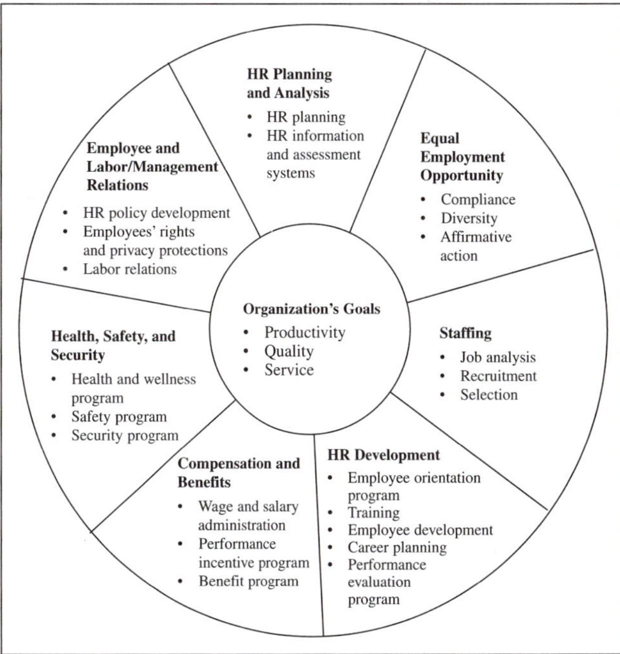

Adapted from Mathis and Jackson 2002, 4.

Equal Employment Opportunity Practices

The HR department takes the lead in ensuring that the various laws and regulations associated with equal employment opportunity (EEO) laws are scrupulously applied in the organization's hiring and promotion practices. Federally enacted EEO legislation includes the **Age Discrimination in Employment Act** (ADEA) of 1967, the **Americans with Disabilities Act** (ADA) of 1990, the **Civil Rights Act, Title VII** (1964) and **the Civil Rights Act** (1991), the **Equal Employment Opportunity Act** of 1972, the **Pregnancy Discrimination Act,** and the **Uniformed Services Employment and Reemployment Rights Act** of 1994 (Anthony et al. 1996; Buhler 2002). The Equal Employment Opportunity Commission (EEOC) was created by Title VII of the Civil Rights Act of 1964 as the agency responsible for investigating discrimination claims emanating from the Civil Rights Act of 1991.

Discrimination and harassment are two important concepts related to fair employment practices. **Discrimination** refers to practices that result in people being treated differently based solely on their differences. **Harassment** refers to practices that create a hostile work environment. Both are clearly illegal under the EEO laws.

Rights of Employees and Employers

Although many of the basic rights of employees are defined in law, others are expectations that may be debated within organizations. For example, **employment-at-will** is a well-established concept: either an employer or an employee can terminate an employment relationship without providing either notice or reason. On the other hand, what are the privacy rights of employees? Can an employer monitor employees' e-mail and voicemail? Organizations are well advised to address the rights of employees and the rights of the employer in an employee handbook to clarify expectations for employees and supervisors. A well-developed employee handbook also improves the organization's legal position should the organization be called on to defend its actions in a court proceeding.

Staffing

The HR department also helps managers to define staffing needs; develop job descriptions; and recruit, screen, and select staff. After an employee is brought into the organization, the HR department plays a significant role, in partnership with the employee's direct supervisor, by spearheading the employee's immediate **orientation** to the organization's policies, practices, and procedures. The HR department is also active in addressing the employee's ongoing training and development requirements.

Compensation and Benefits Program

The organization's **compensation and benefits** program is probably the most prominent activity associated with HR management because it is so directly connected to the employee's pocketbook. This activity involves the establishment of basic definitions of employment and compensation status for the organization (for example, full-time versus part-time, temporary versus permanent, independent contractor versus employee, wage versus salary). The **Fair Labor Standards Act** (FLSA) of 1938 and the **Equal Pay Act** (EPA) of 1963 serve as fundamental legislative mandates in this area.

The HR department also leads the development and administration of the organization's benefits program, job evaluation and classification systems, wage and salary systems, and incentive pay systems.

Social Security, unemployment compensation, and workers' compensation are three benefits organizations are required to offer. Other common benefits offered to employees voluntarily by the organization are health insurance, retirement plans, wellness programs, holidays (time off with pay), vacation time, and employee assistance programs.

The **Family and Medical Leave Act** (FMLA) of 1993 is an example of one legislative initiative that has had a major impact on the benefit programs, as well as on staffing activities (Anthony et al. 1996). Leaves of absence can be granted for a variety of reasons, including personal or family illness, pregnancy, or military service.

Health and Safety Program

The HR department is also involved in activities designed to protect the health, safety, and security of the workforce. Healthcare organizations have given substantial attention to safety management since the enactment of the **Occupational Safety and Health Act** (OSHA) of 1970. Its intended purpose is "to assure, so far as possible, every working man or woman in the nation safe and healthful **working conditions** and to preserve our human resources." This act established a national reporting system for accidents and injuries on the job and led to the development of specific safety management programs in most businesses. More recently, health-related hazards associated with the use of technology or chemical substances in the workplace, injuries due to workplace violence, and employee security concerns have begun to receive special attention by HR professionals (Anthony et al. 1996).

Labor Relations

Employee and labor and management relations are established through the day-to-day interactions between employees and their managers. However, the organization's managers and employees often seek leadership and support from the HR department. The HR department sets the stage for developing and sustaining the quality of these critical relationships by establishing and communicating to both managers and employees the contracts, policies, practices, and rules that constitute the organization's expectations of its employees.

HR management activities associated with **unions** and collective bargaining are referred to as **labor relations**. Labor organizations (unions) enter into negotiations with employers on behalf of groups of employees who have elected to join a union. The negotiations relate to compensation and safety and health concerns. In a unionized environment, three laws that came into existence over a period of 25 years (1935–1960) constitute a code of practice for unions and management. HR departments pay strict attention to these three acts (Mathis and Jackson 2002; Anthony et al. 1996):

- National Labor Relations Act (Wagner Act)
- Labor-Management Relations Act (Taft-Hartley Act)
- Labor-Management Reporting and Disclosure Act (Landrum-Griffin Act)

For the manager who oversees a group of employees covered by a union contract, these laws represent the basic rules for their interactions with employees in the areas of pay, benefits, safety, health, and performance evaluation.

Check Your Understanding 23.3

Instructions: On a separate piece of paper, indicate whether the following statements are true or false (T or F). If the statement is false, explain why it is false.

1. Internal and external environmental trends are significant factors in HR planning and analysis.
2. The Fair Labor Standards Act is one piece of the EEO legislation package passed in the early 1960s.
3. A national system for reporting workplace accidents and injuries was mandated by the Americans with Disabilities Act.
4. Orientation for new employees and the ongoing training of employees are solely the responsibility of the HR department.
5. The Fair Labor Standards Act, the Wagner Act, and the Equal Pay Act provide key guidelines for managing union relationships.

Role of the HIM Manager in Human Resources

Because the day-to-day management of the organization's human resources is the responsibility of supervisory, middle, and executive managers, every manager is responsible for the same HR activities as the HR professionals. In an HIS department, for example, the supervisor of coding services would be responsible for the day-to-day management of clinical coding specialists. Managers at all levels can use any of a variety of HR tools and processes to handle these responsibilities efficiently and effectively.

Tools for Human Resources Planning

Several tools may be used to plan and manage staff resources. Position descriptions, for example, outline the work and qualifications needed to perform a job. Performance standards establish the organization's expectations of how well a job must be done and how much work must be accomplished. Routine staff meetings and regular written communications (via departmental Web sites, bulletin boards, and newsletters, for example) establish a routine process for up-to-date information flow for employees.

Staffing Structures and Work Scheduling

In addition to these basic tools, managers establish **staffing structures** and use work schedules to ensure that there is adequate coverage and staff to complete the required work. Schedules are developed first to provide adequate coverage during the hours the organization or department is open for business.

In hospitals, it is not uncommon to find some part of the HIM department open 24 hours a day, seven days a week. This schedule ensures that HIM staff will be available to provide information for admissions to the hospital and emergency department, support patient discharges and transfers, and handle other HIM functions. In some healthcare organizations, the demand for HIM services outside regular business hours is limited. In such cases, HIM functions can be provided by business office staff, nursing staff, or emergency department staff who have been cross-trained to perform basic HIM tasks.

Another scheduling consideration is space. Space limitations on the number of workstations in the department or the number of employees who can work in the file room may require that employees work in shifts or on weekends.

In addition, staff preferences need to be considered in creating the work schedule. Balancing the demands of the organization with individual requests for flexible start times makes scheduling an important part of the manager's responsibility. Organizations are commonly establishing **flexible work schedules** to accommodate employee needs to adjust work schedules to lifestyles. (These flexible scheduling options—compressed workweek, flextime, job sharing, and telecommuting—are discussed in detail in chapter 24.)

Written policies and procedures that explain the department's staffing requirements and scheduling procedures help the manager to remain fair and objective and help the staff to understand the rules. The amount of personal time off, such as sick leave or vacation, also factors into the development of a staff schedule and the overall assessment of the number of staff positions required.

In addition, most healthcare organizations establish some type of job classification system that combines jobs with similar levels of responsibility and qualifications into job grades that determine salary ranges and benefit packages. For instance, all supervisory-level managers might be classified into one salary and benefit category, but each would have a unique job description. Job classifications also may determine whether an employee belongs to a union or is a candidate for unionization at the time a union attempts to organize the workforce.

Position Descriptions

A **position (job) description** outlines the work to be performed by a specific employee or group of employees with the same responsibilities. Position descriptions generally consist of three parts: a summary of the position's requirements and purpose, its functions, and the qualifications needed to perform the job. Position descriptions also include the official title of the job.

A **job specification** is a document (or a section of the position description document) that is focused on the knowledge, skills, abilities, and characteristics required of an individual in order to perform the job. These specifications may include the following (Buhler 2002):

- Educational level and professional certifications
- Experience
- General characteristics (team player, good writing skills)
- Specific knowledge (foreign language proficiency, software program proficiency)

Position descriptions, including the job specification, are used during the recruitment process to explain the work to prospective candidates. They also enable managers and HR staff to set appropriate salaries and wages for various positions. Moreover, they may be used to resolve performance problems. For that reason it is essential that position descriptions are written in a criteria-based language directly correlated to the established job functions. The manager can use the position description to clarify the tasks the employee is expected to perform.

Generally, job descriptions are needed in the following circumstances:

- When an entirely new kind of work is required
- When a job changes and the old description no longer reflects the work
- When a change in technology or processes dramatically affects the work to be accomplished
- When employee job performances are evaluated, either during probationary periods or annually

Sometimes top performers outgrow their job descriptions. They may find more efficient ways of doing part of their assigned tasks and want more interesting or meaningful work. Some employees request updated job descriptions to support an increase in salary and benefits or a change in title.

When writing new position descriptions, managers may use existing descriptions of other, related jobs or interview staff who are currently performing some of the tasks intended for the new job. They also might ask staff members to keep a record of how they spend their time for a period that reflects a comprehensive cycle of their work. Staff with more repetitive daily activities may only need to record their activities for a week. In contrast, staff with more diverse tasks may need a month to document the scope of their duties.

Performance Standards

In addition to a position description, **performance standards** are often developed for the key functions of the job. These standards indicate the level of acceptable execution for each function. Performance standards are usually set for both quantity and quality and should be as objective and measurable as possible.

Some organizations establish measures that reflect various levels of performance. For example, one measure of a coder's performance might be coding a specified number of charts per day, perhaps no fewer than 20 charts per day. Other organizations might establish several levels of expected performance, for example:

30–35 charts per day	Outstanding
25–29 charts per day	Exceeds expectations
20–24 charts per day	Meets expectations
15–19 charts per day	Needs improvement
Fewer than 14 charts per day	Unsatisfactory

The following example shows how a quality standard might be used as a performance indicator of coding accuracy. For example:

96%–100% accuracy	Outstanding
92%–95% accuracy	Exceeds expectations
89%–94% accuracy	Meets expectations
84%–88% accuracy	Needs improvement
Less than 84%	Unsatisfactory

In the preceding example, a definition for coding accuracy might be helpful. For example, accurate coding includes capturing accurate codes and sequencing them appropriately for all diagnoses and procedures that affect reimbursement.

Standards that are measurable and relevant to an employee's overall performance are helpful in setting clear expectations. They also are useful in providing constructive feedback. (See chapter 22 for a full discussion of performance standards and measurement.)

Policies and Procedures

Policies and procedures are critical tools that may be used to ensure consistent quality performance. A **policy** is a statement about what an organization or department does. For example, a policy might state that patients are allowed to review their health records under certain conditions such as when a clinical professional is present or in the HIM department. Policies should be clearly stated and comprehensive. They must be developed in accordance with applicable laws, and they must reflect actual practice. And because they may be used as documentation of intended practice in a lawsuit, policies should be developed very carefully.

A **procedure** describes how work is to be done and how policies are to be carried out. Procedures are instructions that ensure high-quality, consistent outcomes for tasks done, especially when more than one person is involved.

One of the benefits of developing a procedure is that time is taken to analyze the best possible method for completing a process. This analysis may begin by developing a flowchart to document workflow, decision points, and the flow required to complete a procedure. (Flowcharting is discussed in detail in chapter 22.)

After a flowchart is completed, the steps in the process are written down in the order in which they are to be performed. When more than one person is involved in completing a procedure, each person who performs a task is documented. Anyone generally competent to perform a task should be able to complete it after reading a well-written procedure. This usually takes several drafts that have been reviewed by people who actually perform the work. Moreover, it might be useful to ask someone unfamiliar with the job to try to complete the task according to the written procedure.

Writing a procedure also offers a great opportunity to identify ways to streamline the process. Are supplies available and organized in a way that makes work efficient? Would it be faster to complete one type of task for all of the work, or should each job be completed before the next task is begun? The following rules of writing procedures help in creating procedures that are specific and directive:

- Title accurately and state procedure objective clearly: What exactly is the procedure intended to accomplish?
- Number each step
- Begin each step with an action verb (that is, Open; Confirm; Count)
- Keep sentences short and concise
- Include only procedures *not* policy
- Identify logical beginning and end points (that is, *Begin* and *Finally*)
- Consider the audience to determine the level of detail needed to accurately complete each procedure.

For example, a receptionists' initial procedure for the process of logging in information requests might include the following steps:

1. Begin by opening all incoming mail daily before 10 a.m.
2. Confirm that the date on the date stamp is accurate and stamps all mail in the upper right-hand corner.
3. Sort requests for medical information into three categories: legal, medical, or insurance.
4. Count the requests in each category, clip or bind the requests for each category together, write the count on a sticky note, and place the note on the top request of each bundle.
5. Finally, forward processed external medical requests for information to the ROI coordinator by 10 a.m. for entering the request details into the ROI module of the department's computerized information system.

This example, although only the first five steps in a full procedure, shows how a detailed procedure would be useful in training a new receptionist or ROI coordinator or in providing instructions to anyone needed to perform this task in the regular employee's absence. It also highlights the fact that the receptionist would need to be trained to identify different types of information requests and the ROI coordinator trained on the ROI module of the department's computerized information system.

Several tools may be used to effectively communicate the purpose, scope, and details of the work done by employees in the organization. The procedure as written should also have any sample forms utilized in the task attached, completed or filled out to indicate the proper processing. (See figure 23.9.) The manager is responsible for developing and maintaining these tools. However, the manager's role does not end here. Given the tools described so far, he or she is ready to hire, train, and interact with employees.

Tools for Recruitment and Retention

Recruitment is the process of finding, soliciting, and attracting new employees. **Retention** is the ability to keep valuable employees from seeking employment elsewhere.

Staff Recruitment, Selection, and Hiring

Armed with a position description, the manager is ready to begin recruiting candidates for a new or open position. However, the manager should be sure to understand the organization's recruitment and hiring policies and to seek the assistance of the HR department before the vacancy is publicized. This preparation ensures that the organization's legal obligations and policies and procedures are followed throughout the recruitment, selection, and hiring process.

Recruitment

The first thing to consider in recruiting candidates to fill a staff opening is whether to promote someone from inside the organization or to look for candidates outside the organization. The advantage of promoting from within is that the practice often motivates employees to perform well, learn new skills, and work toward advancement. To advertise a vacancy internally, the organization might post it on facility bulletin boards or list it in the organization's newsletter or Web site. The department manager may announce an opening at a routine staff meeting or use any other communication channels available. Management must communicate an opportunity for promotion to all staff rather than to just the employee who is the most likely candidate. Because employees see widespread posting as a fair practice, it communicates the underlying message that internal candidates are considered first whenever possible.

When the position cannot be filled from within, however, there are several ways to advertise it externally. For example, the organization might run an ad in a newspaper, post the job on Internet recruitment sites, announce the opportunity at professional meetings, contact people who have previously applied or expressed interest in working at the organization, or work through a professional recruiter.

In most cases, the approach used depends on the nature of the open position. For example, the facility might run an ad for a file room position in a local newspaper, but not in a professional journal. On the other hand, the facility might turn to a professional recruiter when trying to fill a department director or experienced coding position.

As in every industry, job seekers looking for professional-level healthcare positions submit detailed resumes. A **resume** describes the candidate's educational background and work experience and usually includes information on personal and professional achievements. Candidates often submit a

Figure 23.9. Sample flowchart procedure

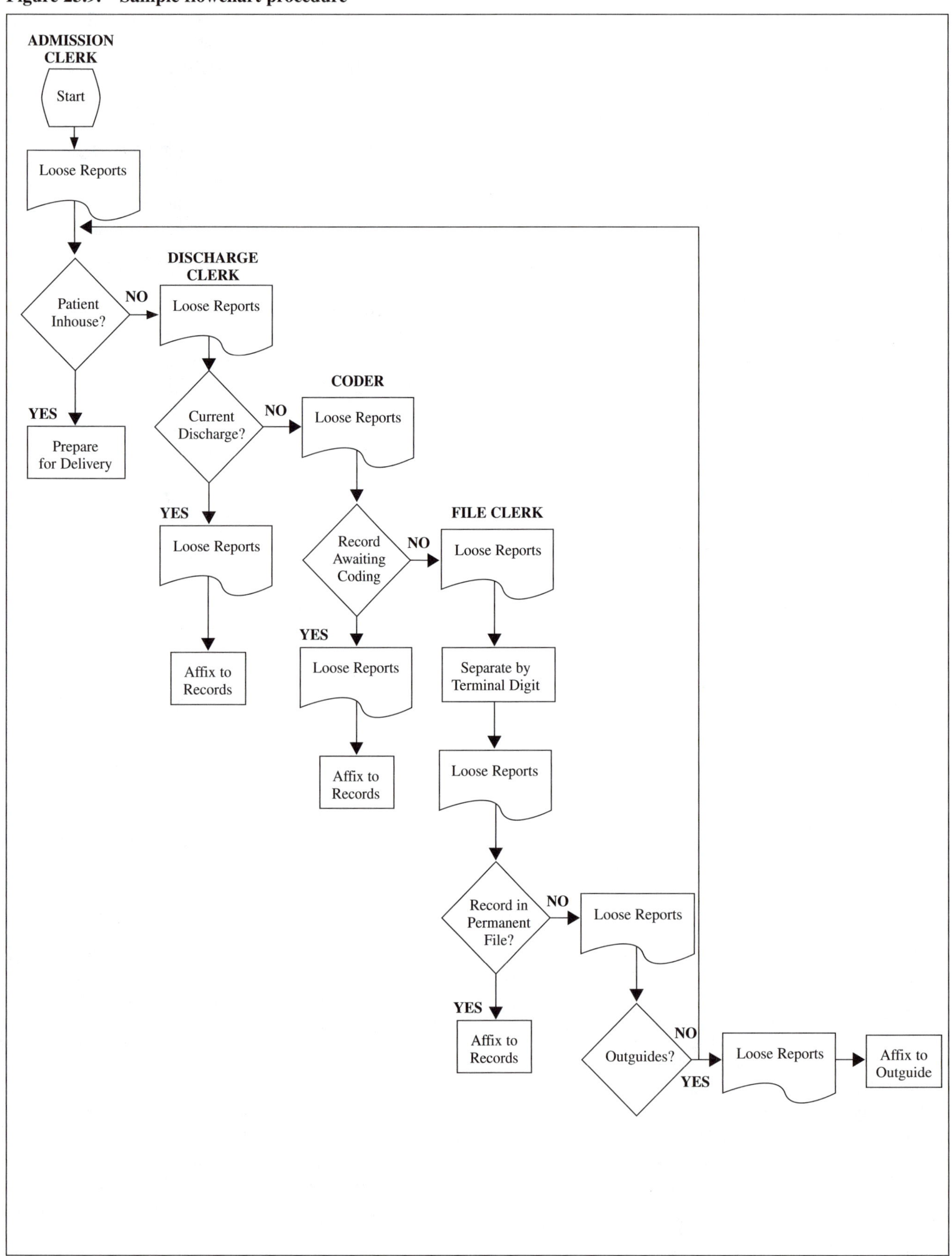

cover letter describing the type of position in which they are interested along with the resume. Today, it is common for candidates to submit, and organizations to accept, application letters and resumes through electronic systems.

Most organizations ask every candidate to complete a formal job application. People seeking entry-level positions may be asked to complete an application rather than to submit a resume. In many cases today, completion of applications can be done online.

Selection

When a sufficient pool of applicants has been recruited, the **selection** process can begin. The goal of the selection process is to identify the candidate most qualified to fill the position.

Testing applicants with reliable and valid instruments designed to objectively assess the applicants' fit for the position and **interviews** are the two basic tools employed in the selection process. **Testing** is commonly conducted during the applicant's first visit to the facility. **Reliability** of a test refers to the consistency with which a test measures an attribute. **Validity** refers to a test's ability to accurately and consistently measure what it purports to measure. Testing practices are under increasing legal scrutiny, which places a special burden on organizations to ensure that tests used are clearly job related. HR professionals are generally familiar with a variety of **ability (achievement) tests**, **aptitude tests**, **mental ability (cognitive) tests**, personality tests, and **honesty (integrity) tests** that are suitable for use in the organization (Anthony et al. 1996; Buhler 2002). Many healthcare organizations also perform routine drug testing on candidates for employment in order to create a drug-free work environment.

Mathis and Jackson (2002) agree that the selection interview is generally considered the most important phase of the selection process. They also describe three effective interview formats:

- **Structured interview** uses a set of standardized questions that are asked of all applicants.
- **Behavioral description interview** requires applicants to give specific examples of how they have performed a specific procedure or handled a specific problem in the past.
- **Panel interview** includes a team of people who interview applicants at one time.

Interviewing is one of the most important skills that managers need for selecting new staff. Unfortunately, many managers receive little formal training in interviewing techniques or have little practical experience. Even supervisors and managers with many years of experience sometimes dread the interviewing process. This shortcoming can be overcome through self-education, mentoring by more experienced managers, or instructional sessions with HR professionals in the organization.

Failure to adequately prepare for conducting the interview has consequences that are very serious for the organization and the applicant. Reviewing the position description, reading the applicant's resume and application form, and preparing appropriate and relevant questions are important steps to take before beginning an interview.

The interview itself has four basic purposes:

- Obtain information from the applicant about his or her past work history and future goals
- Give information to the applicant about the organization's mission and goals and the nature of the employment opportunity
- Evaluate the applicant's work experience, attitude, and personality as a potential fit for the organization
- Give the applicant an opportunity to evaluate the organization as a potential fit for his or her current and future employment goals

EEO regulations dictate the types of questions that may be asked during interviews and on job applications. For example, questions pertaining to age, religious affiliation, and marital status should be avoided in most cases. These regulations apply during all activities associated with the interview, including during formal interview sessions and during less formal lunches or dinners or hallway and elevator small talk, when it is very easy to inadvertently lapse into discussions on these topics. Managers should always seek the advice of HR professionals when they are uncertain about which questions to ask.

Healthcare organizations, like other employers, must be certain to conduct careful background checks of potential employees. Managers or HR professionals also check the references of candidates and communicate with the past employers of candidates via telephone or correspondence. Checking references involves confirming the information provided by applicants on resumes and applications. **Reference checks** or a background investigation should also be conducted specifically to assess the applicants' fit with the position and to validate the accuracy of information the applicants provide on their applications and during their interviews. According to Mathis and Jackson (2002, 73), a recent survey of employers revealed that the false information furnished most commonly by candidates for employment dealt with past lengths of employment, salary history, criminal record, and job titles.

Hiring

After all the internal and external interviews, tests, and reference and background checks are complete, the hiring manager usually has enough information to make a hiring decision. In some organizations, the manager shares the hiring decision with key department staff, HR staff, and executive staff, depending on the level of the position.

When the details of the job offer have been approved by the HR department, a formal job offer should be made. The

HR department should prepare a letter that describes the duties and responsibilities of the position, states the employment start date, and explains the salary and benefits package. In addition, the hiring manager may choose to communicate the offer to the candidate through a personal telephone contact, which is subsequently confirmed by an official letter (Anthony et al. 1996).

Staff Retention

It is normal to have a certain level of staff turnover. Employees move, retire, or seek other careers. A manager can do little to prevent turnover resulting from changes in the personal lives of employees. However, the actions of managers and the policies of the organization can have an impact, either positive or negative, on staff retention. The following questions should be considered:

- Does the organization support continued education either financially or through flexible work schedules?
- Do employees have opportunities to advance their careers within the organization?
- Are salaries and benefits competitive with similar organizations?
- Do working conditions provide a comfortable and safe environment?

Although individual managers may have limited influence on some of these factors, they must always be aware of the impact that broader organizational HR policies and practices have on employees. Gone unnoticed or left unaddressed, concerns in these areas are often what make employees look for other jobs. For example, employees can become dissatisfied when they feel that they are being treated unfairly or that HR practices are needlessly rigid. In some cases, employees become dissatisfied simply because they do not know the rationale for a particular HR policy or because a concern they have voiced about an unsafe condition in their work area is not acted on by the manager. The challenge to the manager is to anticipate or, at the very least, to find ways to be informed as soon as possible when employees express an HR-related concern.

Staff turnover is expensive in terms of both lost productivity and recruitment and training costs. To ensure effective management, turnover should be monitored across time and benchmarked with the rest of the organization and other organizations in the community or geographic area. Routine employee satisfaction surveys can help provide information about how employees feel about their jobs and insights into how the facility might improve working conditions. Conducting routine **exit interviews** with employees who leave the organization is another way to obtain information on how employees feel about their jobs and what issues cause them to leave.

New Employee Orientation and Training

One of the key ingredients in employee satisfaction is the feeling of being knowledgeable and competent. This feeling begins with an effective orientation and training program for new employees. Just as the manager prepared for the interview and selection of the new employee, he or she must plan how the new employee will learn about the organization, the department, and the job.

Most large organizations have a formal new employee orientation process. This process may involve a one-on-one session with HR, group training with new employees from all over the organization, or some form of computer-based training.

In general, orientation programs in healthcare organizations address the organization's mission and vision, goals, and structure; general employment policies; employee conduct standards; communication processes; and confidentiality policies. Orientation also may include a tour of the facility and cover computer access and responsibilities. When the organization provides this type of orientation, the manager must understand the material covered and feel comfortable answering any questions or directing the new employee to the appropriate resource for follow-up.

The manager must be very patient during the employee's first days and schedule adequate time to spend with the new hire. Everyone learns in different ways and at a different pace. The first days not only establish how the employee will do the job but also contribute to the employee's ongoing relationships with the manager and other staff. (A full discussion of the development of new employee orientation programs is presented in chapter 24.)

Tools for Effective Communication

Maintaining regular and effective communication with staff is one of the ongoing challenges in managing human resources. Communication is important because it contributes significantly to the morale of the staff and their ability to contribute to the department's operations as a whole. To address this challenge, a manager should establish a **communication plan** that includes routine and timely opportunities for both verbal and written information sharing within the department or work group. The plan should include, at minimum, the following types of communication:

- Daily personal contact with every employee to maintain a sense of connectedness and, as necessary, to create opportunities for casual discussions of emerging work-related changes or issues
- Web-based or traditional bulletin boards located in an area convenient to staff to publicize official announcements, permissible personal news, written status updates, and written highlights from departmental meetings
- Weekly status meetings with the staff for each functional unit in the department in larger organizations or the entire department in smaller organizations
- Monthly departmental meetings with highlights recorded for posting
- Quarterly performance discussions with individual employees
- Ad hoc verbal or electronic (e-mail) status updates, as appropriate, to alert staff to information of interest from organizational meetings

On a day-to-day basis, when problems emerge that require resolution within the department or when decisions are made that affect the employees in the department, the management team is responsible for establishing a unique communication plan that conforms to the situation. Such a plan identifies the full range of employees affected by the problem or the decision and defines the specific approach that managers will take to engage or inform each person appropriately.

In general, keeping staff well informed is a key factor in developing and sustaining a healthy level of trust in the relationship between employees and managers. Communication plans are simple tools that managers can use to ensure that this critical aspect of their responsibilities is handled with the level of routine and regular attentiveness it requires.

Tools for the Empowerment of Staff

Creating an environment that encourages and allows employees to use and develop their problem-solving and decision-making competencies is an established HR management practice that has many benefits. For example, it increases the manager's capacity and productivity, improves the quality and timeliness of decision making, enhances employee morale, and contributes to improved employee retention.

Team Building

Most people today want to work collaboratively with others; thus, the need for **team building**. The team may consist of people who perform the same function within the same department, for example, a coding team. The team may bring together people who perform different functions within the same department to solve a shared problem or people from across the organization with different expertise to implement a new computer system or to study an issue that would affect the overall organization (for example, improvements in the employee evaluation system).

At their best, teams increase the creativity and improve the quality of problem solving. Often team-based decisions are more widely accepted than managerial decisions because team members enlist support for the decisions from their peers and coworkers. In addition, teams can use their collective energy to produce more work than individuals can. Moreover, teamwork establishes strong relationships among employees. Teamwork also can enrich jobs and provide variety in work assignments. Finally, teams can develop new leaders and expose employees to issues that would not be within the usual scope of their jobs.

One thing that binds team members together is having a common purpose. The purpose for an ongoing work team, for example, might be to ensure cross-training, improve procedures, and monitor quality and productivity. In other cases, teams are created for a specific purpose. Some teams exist for long periods of time because they have an ongoing reason to exist. Other teams function for limited periods of time and disband after their purpose has been fulfilled.

However, having a common purpose is only one element of an effective team. The team also must have an effective leader. This individual must be able to create agendas and organize meetings, lead discussions, and ensure that the work moves forward. The team may either appoint or elect its leader, depending on its purpose and the experience and expertise of its members.

In addition, effective teams set ground rules. For instance, team members might decide that all meetings will start on time, minutes will be recorded, decisions will be reached by consensus, and everyone will participate in discussions. The early establishment of rules can reduce conflict as the team moves forward. Teams work through the same type of decision-making process described earlier in this chapter. However, their strength lies in engaging the collective brainpower of all of their members, and so the team leader should use techniques that effectively engage every member of the team.

Not all teams are effective, and the causes for problems vary. For example, a team without a clear purpose could create a product that does not accomplish the work it was designed to accomplish. A leader who dominates the team could reduce its effectiveness and frustrate its members. Members who do not participate, have insufficient expertise, or are unconcerned with the team's success could cause the team to fail. And members who work outside the team or do not support its decisions can create dissension and reduce support for the outcome.

Managing staff teams is an important aspect of every manager's responsibilities. Careful consideration should be given to developing the team's purpose and composition. Team members need to feel that their work is important and that their contributions make a difference. A well-run team can be an effective and productive force. A poorly run team can waste time and frustrate and demoralize its members.

Delegation of Authority

Managers have specific responsibilities and the authority to act within the scope of those responsibilities. A manager's responsibilities can never be delegated to another person; that is, the manager always remains the one accountable for outcomes in areas within his or her designated scope. However, with appropriate preparation and decision-making guidelines in place, managers can and should delegate the authority to make and act on decisions to employees as individuals or teams. **Delegation of authority** expands the manager's capacity, improves the timeliness of decisions, and develops the competencies of other staff members.

When delegating authority, managers make it possible for staff to succeed by preparing them in advance as follows:

- Explaining exactly what needs to be done
- Describing clear expectations
- Setting clear deadlines
- Granting authority to make relevant decisions
- Ensuring appropriate communication and outcomes reporting
- Providing the resources needed to complete the assigned task

See chapter 24 for an expanded discussion of empowerment and delegation as workforce retention strategies.

Check Your Understanding 23.4

Instructions: On a separate piece of paper, indicate whether the following statements are true or false (T or F). If the statement is false, explain why it is false.

1. To lead effectively, every manager should have an understanding of HR management principles.
2. To be effective, communications with employees should be expressed in written form.
3. Position descriptions outline the work that employees are expected to perform.
4. Performance standards are developed to indicate the time frame in which each function of a job must be executed.
5. Procedures are written explanations of how to perform tasks.
6. In healthcare organizations, individuals applying for entry-level positions must submit a resume and a cover letter.
7. The interview process is intended to give the applicant an opportunity to evaluate the organization as a potential fit for his or her current and future employment goals.
8. Staff turnover is expensive in terms of lost productivity and recruitment and training costs.
9. A manager's responsibilities include new employee orientation and training.
10. Trust between managers and employees is enhanced by keeping employees well informed.
11. One thing that teams have in common is that their members are usually from the same department.
12. Managers can delegate responsibilities, but not authority.

Compensation Systems

Employee compensation systems basically serve to reward employees equitably for their service to the organization. Organizations also use compensation systems to enhance employee loyalty and encourage greater productivity.

The FLSA, the EPA, and several of the EEO laws (for example, Title VII of the Civil Rights Act, Age Discrimination in Employment Act, and the ADA) all have provisions that affect compensation systems. Provisions of the FLSA, for example, cover minimum wage, overtime pay, child labor restrictions, and equal pay for equal work regardless of sex. Federal regulations specify exemptions from some or all of the FLSA provisions for a number of groups of employees (Myers 1998). These groups are referred to as **exempt employees.** Covered groups are referred to as **nonexempt employees.**

Managers who control employee work schedules and process employee timecards at the close of each pay period become quite familiar with the provisions of the FLSA that relate to overtime pay. In general, the FLSA requires that employers pay time and a half for all hours that covered (nonexempt) employees work in excess of forty per week. Some organizations institute overtime pay for all worked hours in excess of eight hours per day. In calculations of worked hours, the FLSA specifies that rest periods of up to 20 minutes each be counted as worked time, but meal periods of thirty minutes or more are not counted as worked time. Time spent in mandated job-related training is considered worked time, and significant travel time (beyond the usual time required to commute to and from work) associated with a work-related event is counted as worked time. Compensatory time, taken in lieu of overtime pay, may be used when it is part of the organization's compensation plan (Myers 1998).

Because of the complexities and sensitivities associated with compensation issues, HR professionals are a manager's best advisor when questions related to compensation regulations and practices arise.

Compensation Surveys

The HR department routinely consults compensation surveys published by government agencies and professional and trade associations. In some cases, an HR department may choose to conduct an independent survey to obtain data more specific to the organization's needs. Often consultants experienced with survey design and data analysis are employed by the organization to either assist in or do the survey project to ensure a successful outcome from this costly activity. Compensation surveys provide benchmark data that the organization can use to evaluate or establish its compensation system for unique jobs within the organization or for jobs throughout the organization (Myers 1998).

Job Evaluations

Job evaluation projects are undertaken by an organization to determine the relative worth of jobs as a first step toward establishing an equitable internal compensation system. Job evaluation is the process of applying predefined **compensable factors** to jobs to determine their relative worth (Myers 1998, 630). Myers defines a compensable factor as "a characteristic used to compare the worth of jobs" and adds that "the EPA requires employers to consider [several] compensable factors in setting pay for similar work performed by both females and males." These factors include skill, **effort**, responsibility, and working conditions.

Four job evaluation methods are commonly used:

- **Job ranking** is the simplest and the most subjective method of job evaluation. It involves placing jobs in order from highest to lowest in value to the organization.
- **Job classification method** involves matching a job's written position description with a description of a classification grade. Jobs in the federal government are graded on the basis of this method of job evaluation.
- **Point method** is a commonly used system that places weight (points) on each of the compensable factors in a job. The total points associated with a job establish its relative worth. Jobs that fall within a specific range of points fall into a grade associated with a specific wage or salary.
- **Factor comparison method** is a complex quantitative method that combines elements of both the ranking and point methods. Factor comparison results indicate the degree to which different compensable factors vary by

job, making it possible to translate each factor value more easily into a monetary wage (Mathis and Jackson 2002).

In recent years, the **Hay method of job evaluation,** officially known as the Hay Guide Chart-Profile Method of Job Evaluation, has been used extensively. It is adaptable to many types of jobs and organizations and easy for individuals within organizations to learn to use. The method is essentially a modification of the point method that numerically measures the levels of three major compensable factors: the know-how, problem-solving, and accountability requirements of each job (Myers 1998; Mathis and Jackson 2002).

Performance Management

Most organizations use some form of **performance review** system to evaluate the performance of individual employees. Although performance reviews should be a part of regular communications between managers and employees, formal performance review discussions are routinely held on an annual or biannual basis. The functions of performance reviews include the following:

- Assessment of the employee's performance compared to performance standards or previously set performance goals
- Development of performance goals for the future year
- Development of a plan for professional development

Reviews also may include employee self-assessments. In some organizations, other employees may contribute information to the reviews of colleagues and coworkers. In the case of a supervisory manager, his or her staff may participate in the evaluation. This form of evaluation to which managers, peers, and staff contribute is called a **360-degree evaluation.**

Many organizations' base pay increases on the results of annual performance reviews. Whether or not the evaluation affects salary, the annual review is an opportunity to formally discuss past accomplishments, career development, and expectations for future performance.

Periodic Performance Reviews

Performance management is an ongoing challenge. Information about performance should be collected regularly and shared with employees, whether their jobs involve coding clinical records or directing a department. Good performance results should be shared to encourage and reward ongoing success.

Performance issues are rarely resolved by ignoring them. Understanding the causes of problems and working with employees to resolve them are important management tasks. Actions that can be taken to improve performance include retraining, streamlining responsibilities, reestablishing expectations, and monitoring progress.

Performance Counseling and Disciplinary Action

When actions taken to improve performance are unsuccessful, more formal counseling and even **disciplinary action** may be required. Most organizations have formal processes in place to ensure that all staff is treated fairly and that employment laws are followed. Managers should consult with the HR department to ensure that any disciplinary actions comply with approved procedures.

The steps described in establishing performance standards, hiring and training employees, and conducting routine performance reviews are all necessary before doing **performance counseling** or taking disciplinary action. Moreover, steps to improve performance should be taken in all cases.

Performance counseling usually begins with informal counseling or a verbal warning. No record of these actions is maintained in the employee's file.

The **progressive discipline** process begins with a verbal warning. When a second offense occurs, the process progresses to a written reprimand with formal documentation of the problem and delineation of the steps needed to correct it. Employees may be required to submit a step-by-step action plan to resolve issues and improve their performance. A third offense results in suspension, and a fourth offense generally results in dismissal.

In some environments, disciplinary actions include suspension from employment without pay or demotion to a job with lower expectations and less pay. In some cases, more than one of these actions may be taken. Generally, however, suspension and demotion are less popular than the use of binding performance improvement plans because suspension and demotion create a punitive atmosphere. Such punitive actions also affect the morale of other employees and staff. Empowering employees to create a plan of action places the responsibility for performance improvement in their own hands.

Regardless of the counseling and disciplinary actions mandated by the organization, managers should take some key steps of their own, including:

- Discussing performance problems and consequences for poor performance with the employee in a clear and direct manner
- Supporting the employee's efforts to improve performance or resolve performance issues
- Documenting the steps taken to improve performance
- Carefully following the organization's HR policies
- Consulting HR professionals before taking action
- Keeping performance issues confidential
- Following the same process for all employees

Termination and Layoff

One of the most difficult duties of a line manager is delivering the actual notification of **termination** to an employee. The HR department is a vital resource for advising and supporting the manager through this process to ensure that accepted HR practices as established by the organization are adhered to. Buhler (2002) presents these simple, general guidelines:

- State your position and end the discussion
- Be sensitive to appropriate timing for the discussion
- Be prepared with all of the appropriate severance information
- Treat the employee with dignity and respect

Layoffs are essentially unpaid leaves of absence initiated by the employer as a strategy for downsizing staff in response to a change in the organization's status (for example, an unexpected or a seasonal downturn in business volume). In many cases, employees may be called back to work at some future date.

The **Workers' Adjustment Retraining and Notification (WARN) Act** requires that organizations employing more than 100 people give the employees and the community a 60-day notice of its intent to close the business or to lay off 50 or more members of its workforce.

Conflict Management

Sometimes problems arise because of conflicts among employees. It is not unusual for people to disagree. Indeed, sometimes a difference of opinion can increase creativity. However, conflict can also waste time, reduce productivity, and decrease morale. When taken to the extreme, it can threaten the safety of employees and cause damage to property.

Conflict management focuses on working with the individuals involved to find a mutually acceptable solution. There are three ways to address conflict:

- **Compromise:** In this method, both parties must be willing to lose or give up a piece of their position.
- **Control:** In this method, interaction may be prohibited until the employees' emotions are under control. The manager also may structure their interactions. For example, the manager can set ground rules for communicating or dealing with specific issues. Another form of control is personal counseling. Personal counseling focuses on how people deal with conflict rather than on the cause of specific disagreements.
- **Constructive confrontation:** In this method, both parties meet with an objective third party to explore their perceptions and feelings. The desired outcome is to produce a mutual understanding of the issues and to create a win-win situation.

Grievance Management

Employees have the right to disagree with management and can express their opinions or complaints in a variety of ways. They should be encouraged to bring problems and concerns directly to their manager. When they do not achieve satisfaction at that level, the manager should explain other options to the employee. For example, dissatisfied employees should understand that they can either take their issues to the next management level or discuss them with HR staff.

Organizations establish **grievance procedures** that define the steps an employee can follow to seek resolution of a disagreement they have with management on a job-related issue. A complaint becomes a **grievance** when it has been documented in writing. At that point, the formal grievance procedure is set in motion.

Employees who belong to a union should follow the grievance procedures set by their union. Union contracts usually specify the types of actions employees can take and the time frames for filing grievances. The contracts usually specify time frames for responses and define the formal process for elevating the consideration or resolution of a grievance. Grievances taken to the highest levels will likely have to be resolved through mediation or arbitration.

Each of these steps takes time and can cost money. Therefore, managers should try to avoid grievances by maintaining open and effective communication with their staff.

Maintenance of Employee Records

Official **employee records** must be maintained under the control of the HR department. Any personnel records maintained under the control of the manager must be kept secure at all times.

Federal legislation such as Title VII of the Civil Rights Act of 1964, the Age Discrimination in Employment Act, the Immigration Reform and Control Act, and the FLSA place numerous record-keeping and reporting requirements on the HR department. The Environmental Protection Agency (EPA) and the Occupational Safety and Health Administration (OSHA) also have record-keeping requirements. Myers (1998, 125–126) outlines several additional record-keeping obligations, as follows:

- Employers must protect the confidentiality of personnel records and files.
- Employers must protect the health records of employees.
- Employers must avoid intruding into the personal lives of employees, such as their other associations, alcohol use, spending habits, and financial obligations unless there are valid job-related reasons for making such intrusions.
- Employers must prevent the public disclosure of personal information that may be embarrassing to an employee.
- Employers must protect the results of employment-related tests, including written tests used in making selection decisions, and the results of both pre-employment and random drug testing.

Current Human Resources Trends

According to the U.S. Department of Labor (2007), the following workforce trends in employment are likely to affect the labor market in the United States during the first decade of the 21st century:

- Women will constitute a greater proportion of the labor force than in the past, with 59.4 percent of all U.S. women in the workforce in 2006. In the healthcare industry, women are more than 50 percent of the workforce. Slightly over 73 percent of the women in the workforce have children under the age of 18, and one-third of women in the workforce hold college degrees.
- Minority racial and ethnic groups will account for a growing percentage of the overall labor force. Immigrants will expand this growth.
- The average age of the U.S. population will increase, and more workers who retire from full-time jobs will work part-time.
- As a result of these and other shifts, employers in a variety of industries will face shortages of qualified workers.

From this information, it is obvious that employers must be prepared to function with an increasingly diverse workforce in terms of gender, age, health status, race, and ethnicity. In general, the management of an increasingly diverse workforce is receiving considerable attention in the HR literature, and some organizations are initiating diversity-training programs. Mathis and Jackson (2002) identify three content areas that are often included in diversity training programs:

- *Legal awareness:* Federal and state laws and regulations on equal employment opportunity and the consequences of violating these laws and regulations
- *Cultural awareness:* Attempts to deal with stereotypes, typically through discussions and exercises
- *Sensitivity training:* Attempts to sensitize people to the differences among them and how their words and behaviors are perceived by others

According to Gillian Flynn (1998), mixed reviews regarding the effectiveness of the diversity training received from both public- and private-sector organizations suggest that either the programs or their implementation is ineffective. There seems to be considerable work still to be done within healthcare organizations and HIM departments to prepare for the anticipated growth in the multicultural profile of HR assets over the coming decade.

The Department of Labor data also indicate that employees will increasingly seek ways to gain more control over their time. The time pressure associated with trying to balance work and personal lives (especially when both parents are working outside the family home) coupled with the time pressure associated with increasingly long commutes appear to be driving this concern to the surface in HR management. Flextime, job sharing, and home-based (telecommuting) staffing options are emerging as viable solutions to the workforce retention issue. Within transcription and coding work units in HIM services, flextime and home-based staffing options are being implemented to address the labor shortages already affecting departmental operations. (See chapter 25 for a full discussion of these staffing alternatives.)

Check Your Understanding 23.5

Instructions: On a separate piece of paper, indicate whether the following statements are true or false (T or F). If the statement is false, explain why.

1. Employee compensation systems are used to enhance employee loyalty.
2. Minimum wage and overtime policies are impacted by the Taft-Hartley Act.
3. All employees are subject to the provisions of the Fair Labor Standards Act.
4. Trade associations and government agencies are routine sources for compensation benchmark data.
5. The Equal Pay Act requires employers to consider compensable factors when setting pay for similar work performed by both females and males.
6. Job ranking is the most commonly used method for conducting job evaluations.
7. The Hays method is a popular, specialized point method for conducting job evaluations.
8. Formal performance review sessions are routinely done on an annual basis.
9. A 180-degree evaluation involves evaluation feedback from supervisors, peers, and self-assessment.
10. The first step in a progressive disciplinary process is a verbal, undocumented warning.
11. Compromise is a method of conflict resolution with the goal of arriving at a win-win outcome.
12. Grievances taken to the highest levels for resolution will likely be resolved through mediation or arbitration.
13. Organizations are obliged to avoid intrusions into an employee's personal life unless there is a valid job-related reason for doing so.
14. U.S. Department of Labor statistics (2000–2006) indicate that a surplus of qualified labor will be available in most industries over the next decade.
15. Flextime and home-based staffing alternatives are being employed in health information services to address labor shortage issues.

Real-World Case

A coding specialist position is being added to the HIS department of a large metropolitan medical center. The purpose of the new position is to help the current staff to handle its increased workload since the implementation of the outpatient prospective payment system for Medicare patients earlier in the year. Figure 23.10 shows the resume of one of the numerous candidates applying for the coding specialist

Figure 23.10. Sample resume

Sample Traditional Resume

EXPERIENCE

HIM Services February 2003 to present	Consultant, Interim Manager. Project-based work that has included departmental assessments, policy and procedure development, origination of job descriptions, Joint Commission preparation, cost benefit analyses, and interim management. Interim management responsibilities ranged from small single-facility departments to departments consisting of approximately 100 FTEs at 19 sites.
Apple Hill Clinic (Ambulatory Care) October 1998 to February 2003	Medical Record Manager. Managed 20 medical record and 25 transcription FTEs at main clinic with oversight responsibilities for HIM function at seven additional satellite locations.
Northern and Centerville April 1997 to October 1998	Medical Record Manager. In addition to responsibilities at Centerville Hospital, took on management responsibilities for 15 medical record and transcription FTEs at Northern Hospital and Medical Center.
Centerville Hospital April 1992 to October 1998	Utilization Management/Quality Assurance Director. Directed 26 FTEs constituting the medical record, transcription, pre-admission, admitting, utilization management, quality assurance, social service departments, and guest relations function.

SPECIAL SKILLS

Computers and Systems Implementation	Implemented digital dictation system at Northern Hospital and Medical Center and Centerville Hospital. Directed upgrade of digital system at St. Joseph's Hospital. Implemented word processing systems at Lakeview School, Centerville Hospital, Northern Hospital and Medical Center, and Apple Hill Clinic. Implemented bar coding at City Clinic. Implemented electronic messaging to facilitate communication between medical records and unit staff at Apple Hill Clinic. Implemented HIS system at Centerville Hospital and Northern Hospital and Medical Center.

HONORS, AWARDS RECEIVED

Unsung Hero Award	2005, City Clinic
Outstanding Leadership Award	1997, Centerville Hospital

PROFESSIONAL ACTIVITIES

Chairman	Health Information Technology Professional Practice Committee, AHIMA, 2006–2007
President	Washington State Health Information Management Association, 2005–2006

Source: Hughes, G. 2000. "How to Write an Effective Resume." *Journal of AHIMA* 71(6): 64–65.

position. The director of the department has already developed a detailed job description for the new position. A registered health information administrator (RHIA) was hired six months ago to supervise the department's five-person outpatient services team, and this new supervisor is a bit nervous about taking on this part of her new job. The director of the department has delegated responsibility for leading the process of selecting the person to fill the new coding specialist position to the new supervisor.

Summary

Management is key in setting the healthcare organization's direction, establishing its policies, and maximizing its assets. Included among its assets are the people who carry out the organization's mission: the human resources staff. Managers are diffused throughout the organization with different responsibilities assigned at different levels and yet all have important roles to play in creating and maintaining an environment that is prudent in handling its financial resources, focused on providing high-quality services to its customers, and attentive to the basic human needs of its workforce.

Effective management of human resources begins with attention given to the adoption of appropriate policies, procedures, and practices in each of the seven HR activity areas: HR planning and analysis; equal employment opportunity; staffing; HR development; compensation and benefits; health, safety, and security; and employee and labor and management relations. HR professionals working in close partnership with the organization's managers hire and retain qualified employees by following these guidelines and fostering good working relationships between employees and management.

Effective recruitment, selection, and hiring practices involve the consistent use of the tools designed to identify the best-qualified candidates for each position. Once hired, ensuring that employees are well oriented and trained is the critical first step toward a successful long-term outcome. Subsequently, maintaining open and meaningful communications with employees, setting realistic performance expectations for employees, engaging employees in ways that give them appropriate control of their work schedule and environment, delegating appropriate levels of decision-making authority, and providing them with opportunities for ongoing staff development all serve to enhance employee morale and increase job satisfaction.

Managing human resources is both a science and an art. As such, it is learned through a combination of study and observation. Published HR management resources are readily available to provide the knowledge foundation associated with this field. In the workplace, HR professionals are available to serve as advisors to managers who want to handle this complex aspect of their management responsibilities knowledgably and artfully.

References

Anthony, W.P., P.L. Perrewe, and K.M. Kacmar. 1996. *Strategic Human Resource Management.* Orlando, FL: Harcourt Brace & Company.

Benedictine Health System. 2002. Advancing the BHS ministry through a renewed commitment to mission, values. *BHS System Spirit & Life* 6(3):1.

Buhler, P. 2002. *Human Resources Management.* Avon, MA: F+W Publications.

Department of Labor, Bureau of Labor Statistics. 2007. Women in the labor force: A databook. http://www.bls.gov/cps/wlf-intro-2007.pdf.

Flynn, G. 1998. The harsh reality of diversity programs. *Workforce* 12:26–35.

Gulick, L. and L. Urwick, eds. 1937. *Papers on the science of administration.* New York: Institute of Public Administration.

Hughes, Gwen. 2000. How to write an effective resume. *Journal of AHIMA* 71(6):64–65.

Mathis, R.L. and J.H. Jackson. 2002. *Human Resource Management: Essential Perspectives.* 2nd ed. Cincinnati: South-Western Publishers.

Myers, D.W. 1998. *1999 U.S. Master Human Resources Guide.* Chicago: CCH.

Schein, E.H. 1980. *Organizational Psychology.* 3rd ed. Englewood Cliffs, NJ: Prentice-Hall.

Senge, P.M. 1990. *The Fifth Discipline.* New York: Doubleday/Currency.

Chapter 24
Training and Development

Karen R. Patena, MBA, RHIA

Learning Objectives

- Understand the continuum of employee training and development
- Appreciate the role of staff development in retaining a competent workforce
- Know how to respond to various learning styles and to the needs of adult learners
- Learn how to respond to the needs of a culturally diverse workforce or the needs of employees with disabilities
- Know how to apply appropriate delivery methods to various training needs
- Learn how to develop an orientation program for new employees
- Learn how to prepare and conduct appropriate in-service education programs for various healthcare employees
- Prepare employees for e-HIM roles
- Identify alternative staffing trends and discuss their role in workforce retention
- Know how to apply appropriate methods for developing employee potential
- Learn how to assess the needs of current employees for continuing education
- Prepare a training and development plan for a health information management department
- Comply with the requirements of laws and regulations affecting workforce training

Key Terms

Accountability
Adult learning
Asynchronous
Audioconferencing
Authority
Blended learning
Career development
Coaching
Competency
Compressed workweek
Computer-based training
Continuing education
Cross-training
Cultural competence
Customer service training
Delegation
Development
Distance learning
Diversity training
e-HIM
e-learning
Electronic performance support system
Employment contract
Empowerment
Ethics training
Flex years
Flextime
Habit
Human Resources Department (HR)
Incentive
In-service education
Intranet
Job description
Job rotation
Job sharing
Job specification
Just-in-time training
Learning content management system
Learning curve
Learning management system
Lecture
M-learning
Massed training
Mentor
Motivation
Multiuser virtual environments (MUVEs)
Needs assessment
Offshoring
On-the-job training
Orientation
Outsourcing
Pay for performance
Productivity
Promotion
Reinforcement
Reverse mentoring
Role playing
Self-directed learning
Simulations
Spaced training
Strategic management
Synchronous
Task analysis
Team building
Telecommuting
Trainee
Train the trainer
Trainer
Training
Training and development model
Virtual reality
Web-based training
Wikis

As a service industry, healthcare relies on the availability of competent workers. The growth of new technologies, the application of new vocabulary and processes, and the decreasing numbers of employees with adequate skills to respond to the new environment mean that healthcare organizations must frequently assume responsibility for preparing and developing their own labor pool, unless they choose to outsource or use employees overseas. Providing the necessary training to workers is costly in terms of both money and time. Using overseas workers creates its own training needs in areas such as ethics or the English language. Moreover, after the organization has made the investment, it must do what it can to protect its investment by retaining its workforce.

Human resources are the healthcare institution's most valuable asset. Managing employees requires recognizing and meeting the needs of the employees as well as those of the organization. Healthcare organizations must provide employees with the tools for career success and personal achievement if they are to win their long-term commitment.

This chapter focuses on training and retaining employees in the healthcare organization. It describes the orientation process and different methods for training new employees as well as current employees taking on new job responsibilities. It discusses **adult learning** strategies, techniques for delivering employee training, including the increasing use of e-learning methods, and ways to enhance job satisfaction. Special training issues, such as diversity, training overseas workers, and preparing for e-HIM roles are addressed. Finally, the chapter describes how to implement a departmental employee training and development plan.

Training Program Development

Traditional management theory differentiated between training for lower-level, technical employees and development for management staff who needed to improve skills such as decision making and interpersonal communication. However, this distinction has become outdated in the twenty-first century as organizations take a more comprehensive approach to improving employee performance. Today, the terms **training** and **development** are often used interchangeably, with the primary goal being to improve knowledge, skills, abilities, attitudes, and social behavior of workers at all levels. As employees who make up the organization grow, so does the organization.

Training programs should accommodate employees with special needs, such as providing equipment and locations that are accessible to those with disabilities or instructions in another language for employees for whom English is a second language. In addition, the organization should develop diversity-training programs. **Diversity training** facilitates an environment that fosters tolerance and appreciation of individual differences within the organization's workforce.

Training and development programs should be viewed as a vital part of the **strategic management** of healthcare institutions. The standards of accreditation organizations as well as healthcare plans require the demonstration of high-quality, efficient healthcare delivery. To remain financially viable, healthcare organizations must emphasize **productivity**, performance, and profitability. Managers should identify goals and objectives, first for their departments and then for individual employees, and then define the skills and knowledge necessary to achieve the objectives. This goal-oriented approach should challenge and encourage the workforce to achieve organizational goals while helping individual employees reach their highest potential.

Investment in training programs helps the organization to accomplish goals on an individual, group, and organizational level. Other important reasons for providing employee training and development include:

- To introduce new employees to the organization
- To provide a path for employee promotion and retention
- To improve employee performance and productivity
- To update skills for employees in new or restructured positions resulting from organizational or technological change
- To reduce organizational problems caused by absenteeism, turnover, poor morale, or substandard quality
- To deliver high-quality healthcare within budgetary constraints

As presented in table 24.1, one way to view training and development needs is as a continuum of five conceptual areas: orientation, on-the-job training, staff development through internal in-service education programs, staff development through external and professional continuing education programs, and career development beyond the current job (Fottler et al. 1998, 201). Each concept differs in objectives, diversity of skills, degree of emphasis on career development, training location, and frequency of delivery. Healthcare organizations are unique, so their development programs should be unique as well. A 50-bed long-term care facility has very different staffing and training needs than that of a large acute care academic medical center. There is no best way to deliver training; it must fit the context of the institution.

However, investment in employee development does not end with training. Organizations need to find ways to gain the commitment of employees so that they will remain productive. Retaining good employees and developing their potential is an area of great importance, particularly in an industry that has a shortage of qualified workers.

Elements of Workforce Training

The goal of any institution's training program is to provide employees the skills they need to perform their jobs. Because employees are at different stages in their **career development**, the training program must be flexible and able to adapt to meet many needs. At any given time, some new employees

Table 24.1. Employee development continuum

Concept	Objectives	Scope of Skill Diversity	Emphasis on Personal/Career Growth	Training Site	Frequency
Orientation training	To introduce staff to the mores, behaviors, and expectations of the organization	Narrow ↑	Narrow ↑	Internal	Single instance
Training	To teach staff specific skills, concepts, or attitudes			Internal	Sporadic
In-service education	To teach staff about skills, facts, attitudes, and behaviors largely through internal programs			Internal	Continuous
Continuing education	To facilitate the efforts of staff members to remain current in the knowledge base of their trade or profession through external programs designed to achieve external standards			External	Continuous
Career development	To expand the capabilities of staff beyond a narrow range of skills toward a more holistically prepared person	↓ Broad	↓ Broad	Internal and external	Continuous

Source: Fottler et al. 1998, 201.

will need to know basic information about the organization and long-term employees will want to improve their ability to contribute at higher levels within the organizational structure. Today's workforce needs both technical skills and so-called soft skills, such as **team building** and critical thinking. For example, electronic health records (EHRs) are increasingly becoming an integral part of the healthcare work setting. Thus, whatever the primary task, most employees need to develop skills in using personal computers and related devices.

New Employee Orientation

After employees have been recruited and selected, the first step is to introduce them to the organization and their immediate work setting and functions. New employee **orientation** includes a group of activities that introduce the employee to the organization's mission, policies, rules, and culture; the department or workgroup; and the specific job he or she will be performing. In addition to the basic skills needed to do the job, the employee needs to experience a period of **socialization** in which he or she learns the values, behavior patterns, and expectations of the organization.

Needs Assessment

As with all training programs, the orientation must be customized to the particular employee. New employees will require a more in-depth orientation than current employees who are starting a different position within the same institution. In a large facility, new employee orientation is usually coordinated by the **human resources department** (HR); in a small facility, it may be performed entirely by the employee's supervisor. The orientation may consist of a brief and informal presentation, or it may be a formal program that takes place over several days on a regularly scheduled basis. Formal programs typically begin with presentations by HR and other department heads before the new employee is introduced to his or her immediate supervisor. The supervisor then continues the orientation process within the employee's assigned department.

To develop an orientation program, it is helpful to begin with a **task analysis** to determine the specific skills required for the job. The **job description** and the **job specification** are excellent sources for this part of the process. Beyond specific tasks, all new employees need to understand matters common to the institution, such as personnel policies, benefits, and safety regulations. Federal and state governments and accreditation organizations also may require certain subjects to be included in the orientation program.

Requirements

Although the orientation program is typically done at a single point in time, a new employee may not feel completely competent for as long as a year from the date he or she was hired. The program should attempt to make employees feel that they made the right choice in accepting the position. For this to happen, they should feel welcome, comfortable in their new environment, positive about their supervisor, and confident that they are learning the skills they need to do the job. An orientation program should not just be for completing paperwork.

An effective tool used in orienting new workers is the orientation checklist (figure 24.1), which helps the employer know that the employee is receiving the information he or she needs to begin the job and serves as an agenda for presenting the information in a logical manner. Rather than presenting everything the new employee needs to know all at once, it is helpful to spread the orientation over several days.

In addition, it is helpful to present policies and requirements that all employees must know, such as insurance programs, payroll requirements, and personnel policies, in an employee handbook given to new employees during the orientation. The handbook provides a handy reference after the immediate orientation period has ended. However, the facility must be careful not to include content that expresses or could imply conditions of an **employment contract**. If the employee views the handbook as a contract, it becomes a legally binding agreement. Employer or employee could be held liable if any conditions set out in the handbook are not strictly followed. Thus, the employee handbook must be viewed as advisory in nature and not as a legal document.

The requirements of an orientation program may be expressed on three levels: organizational, departmental, and individual.

At the *organizational level,* the orientation program provides the information that every employee who works for the company needs to know. This information typically includes:

- Background and mission of the organization
- Policies and procedures that apply to all employees, such as confidentiality agreements or infection control procedures
- **Ethics training**, including how to recognize ethical dilemmas and draw upon codes of conduct to resolve problems (See chapter 11 for discussion of ethical issues concerning HIM in detail)
- Cultural diversity sensitivity and antiharassment training
- Employee benefits (paid time off, insurance coverage)
- Safety regulations
- Employee orientation handbook
- Tour of the facility

At the *departmental level,* orientation information typically includes:

- Departmental policies and procedures
- Introduction to other employees
- Tour of department
- Work hours
- Time sheet requirements
- Training in operation of equipment (for example, photocopying machines or computers)
- Safety regulations specific to the department

Figure 24.1. Sample orientation checklist

Orientation Checklist

Supervisor ______________________ Date ______________________

Employee ______________________ Department ______________________

Before Worker Arrives

(Check off tasks when completed.)

___ 1. Prepare other employees.
___ 2. Have desk and supplies ready.
___ 3. Arrange for luncheon escort.

First Day

___ 1. Attend hospital orientation program.
___ 2. Receive employee handbook and (if applicable) union contract information.
___ 3. Receive benefit information.
___ 4. Review safety and security regulations, including infection control procedures.
___ 5. Introduce to immediate associates.
___ 6. Introduce to the workplace.
___ 7. Give overview of the job.
___ 8. Ask whether new employee has any questions.

Second Day

___ 1. Discuss confidentiality policy.
___ 2. Give job instructions.
___ 3. Review compensation.
___ 4. Explain hours of work.
___ 5. Discuss attendance requirements.
___ 6. Explain performance review.
___ 7. Explain quality and quantity standards.
___ 8. Encourage employee to ask questions.
___ 9. Explain where to store work overnight.

Third Day

___ 1. Explain telephone system, computer system, and fax and copier machines.
___ 2. Explain reasons for rules and policies.
___ 3. Explain insurance plans.
___ 4. Ask whether the new employee has any questions.

Fourth Day

___ 1. Give employee opportunity to describe how he or she is getting along.
___ 2. Discuss departmental policies in addition to hospital policies.
___ 3. Explain hospital continuing education program.

Fifth Day

___ 1. Describe vacation system.
___ 2. Explain bulletin board policy.

Sixth Day

___ 1. Encourage employee to talk to supervisor when necessary.
___ 2. Administer postorientation assessment.
___ 3. Give orientation evaluation form to employee to complete.

Orientation Completed ______________________ (Date)

Signature of Employee ______________________ Signature of Supervisor ______________________

Source: Adapted from Keeling and Kallaus 1996, 148.

At the *individual level,* the new employee learns specific job tasks that, at a minimum, should include:

- Specific, measurable objectives for productivity and performance
- An explanation of each job task by the supervisor, followed by a demonstration and an opportunity for the employee to demonstrate the task

The new employee's individual orientation is usually the longest portion of the orientation program.

Components of an Orientation Program

An orientation program should be developed with input from HR, other department heads, and the employee's supervisor. For a typical new employee in the HIM department of an acute care hospital, the orientation program might follow the schedule shown in figure 24.1. The first portion of the program introduces the employee to the institution and is typically led by the director of education or the director of HR. The employee is given a handbook and any required forms to complete for payroll and insurance. The director of safety and security then introduces safety regulations.

To introduce the employee to the individual job setting as quickly as possible, the general portion of the orientation could be completed within the first half-day. The employee then could meet the immediate supervisor and be matched with a "buddy" to escort him or her to lunch and back to the department. Ideally, the buddy should have the same job as the new employee. On the afternoon of day one, the new worker should be introduced to coworkers, given a tour of the department, and shown his or her workstation. The first day could end with a basic overview explanation of the job's duties, including an opportunity for questions.

The individual portion of the orientation should continue as described in the suggested schedule, with some portion of each day devoted to job training and work rules so that the new employee can gradually understand the requirements of the job and become socialized to the work environment. As the new employee is trained and tested in each important aspect of the job, the supervisor should document his or her demonstrated competency. This documentation will help the organization to comply with the standards of the Joint Commission.

Orientation of Overseas Workers

The demand for health information technicians to fill positions such as transcription, coding, and insurance claims processing exceeds the current U.S. supply. Also, pressure to reduce cost continues to mount on healthcare providers. As with many other industry sectors, U.S. healthcare providers have discovered there are many benefits to be gained as a result of moving some of their work to employees who live overseas (often referred to as **offshoring**). Most frequently these employees are located in India, China, Pakistan, the Philippines, and the United Kingdom, where English is frequently spoken. This has resulted in some unique requirements for training. In addition to the requirements for orientation of all new employees, orientation training for overseas workers may include English proficiency, American etiquette, and cultural differences. Specific training requirements should be included in a service agreement. For those in the United States supervising the workers, issues of **cultural competence** are essential. For example, many Asian countries are much more respectful of the impact of personal lives of employees, which requires breaks for religious practice and other personal obligations.

Quality control is an important issue. Tasks to be performed, acceptable turnaround times, quantity and quality standards, and how the performance measures will be tracked and reported should be spelled out. It is especially important to specify accountability for confidentiality because data are at risk when they are transmitted overseas. HIPAA requirements, including those pertaining to business associate contracts, may be applicable to overseas workers and should be included.

Assessment

After the orientation process, all the participants should be asked for feedback. A form should be developed and completed by the new employee. Figure 24.2 presents an example of a form for evaluating the general portion of the orientation program. Typical questions include:

- Was the program relevant to your job and needs?
- What part of the program was most useful to you?
- What part of the program was least useful to you?

In addition, supervisors should be asked to evaluate the effectiveness of the orientation process. For example, they should be asked for feedback on the employee's ability to apply his or her newly acquired job skills and for an assessment of the employee's comfort level with the department.

On-the-Job Training

Preparing staff to carry out the tasks and functions of their particular jobs should be an ongoing effort for both new and experienced employees. A variety of methods are available to employers. Effective training programs begin with a **needs assessment** and blend an appropriate combination of methods, media, content, and activities into a curriculum that is matched to the specific education, experience, and skill level of the audience.

On-the-job training is a method of teaching an employee to perform a task by actually performing it. Along with teaching basic skills, on-the-job training gives employees and supervisors opportunities to discuss specific problem areas and initiates socialization among the new employees and their coworkers. On-the-job training offers a number of advantages, including its relatively low cost compared to outside training programs and the fact that work is still in progress while the employee is being trained. However, employees may feel burdened if they are held responsible for work they do not accomplish during the training period and the learning process may be less than optimal if the work setting is disrupted by ongoing distractions and pressures.

Training may be performed by either a supervisor or a coworker with particular expertise. The selection of an appropriate trainer is critical to the success of this method. Even though they are very capable at performing the job being taught, some employees may not be effective teachers and may omit vital steps if not motivated to do the teaching.

Requirements of the Job

The training program should begin by reviewing the job description and the job specification. Job descriptions and job specifications should include a list of tasks performed for a job; the skills, ability, and knowledge required; and the expected quality and quantity standards of performance. Next, a performance analysis should be completed to assess the gap between expected performance and the employee's current performance level. In the case of a new employee, this may be verified through a written **competency** assess-

Figure 24.2. Sample orientation evaluation form

Employee Orientation Program Evaluation Form

Date:____________________

Job Title: ____________________

1. Please rate each of the following items to indicate your reaction to the session. If ranking is less than average, please comment on the back of this form.

Item	Poor	Adequate	Average	Good	Excellent
Objective 1: Applicability to your job, responsibilities, and needs					
Objective 2: Enough examples and chances to practice so you can apply your new skills at work					
Objective 3: Opportunity for discussion with other participants					
Objective 4: Length of the program relative to its objectives					

2. Which part of the program was of most value to you? Why?

3. Which part of the program was of least value to you? Why?

4a. Please use the following scale to comment on each instructor's ability to lead the program where:

1 = Needs improvement 2 = Adequate 3 = Good 4 = Excellent

Item	Instructor 1	Instructor 2
Organization/preparation of subject matter	1 2 3 4	1 2 3 4
Presentation of subject matter	1 2 3 4	1 2 3 4
Clarity of instructions	1 2 3 4	1 2 3 4
Ability to control time	1 2 3 4	1 2 3 4
Ability to link content to your job functions	1 2 3 4	1 2 3 4
Ability to stimulate productive discussions	1 2 3 4	1 2 3 4
Ability to create a productive learning environment	1 2 3 4	1 2 3 4

4b. Please comment on the instructors' abilities to lead the program:

5. How would you rate your overall reaction to the program? 1 2 3 4

6. How would you rate your level of skill/knowledge:

   a. Before the program? 1 2 3 4

   b. After the program? 1 2 3 4

7. Other comments:

Source: O'Connor et al. 2002.

ment. What the employee does not know or cannot do becomes the basis for on-the-job training. The requirements may include any of the following:

- Physical skills (for example, operation of equipment)
- Academic knowledge (for example, medical terminology or English spelling and grammar)
- Knowledge of institutional policies (for example, safety regulations)
- Technical skills, which may include both physical and mental skills (for example, use of computer programs)

Components of on-the-Job Training

On-the-job training offers a variety of delivery options, including:

- One-on-one training by a supervisor or an experienced peer
- Job rotation
- Computer-based training
- Coaching or mentoring
- Informal learning during meetings or discussions with supervisors and peers

One-on-one training is the technique used most often. In this type of training, the employee learns by first observing a demonstration and then performing the task. For this type of training to be effective, organizations may offer **train-the-trainer** workshops in which the **trainer** learns skills in communication and instruction. It is important to select a person to serve as a trainer who is not only competent in the job content, but also able to teach and interact effectively with the **trainee.** One-on-one training by the supervisor gives the supervisor an opportunity to observe how the trainee is doing and to make adjustments to meet the employee's skill level. A trainee who learns quickly can move through the steps at a faster pace; a trainee who learns slowly may need an opportunity for additional practice or a second demonstration.

In **job rotation**, the employee moves from job to job at planned intervals. This method is most useful for supervisory jobs, where the employee needs to learn a variety of tasks performed by several different employees, as well as their interrelationships. In **cross-training**, the employee learns to perform the jobs of many team members. This method is most useful when work teams are involved.

Computer-based training, including **Web-based training**, provides an opportunity to supplement job task performance with additional knowledge and simulation. It is effective in situations where repetition aids learning, for example, with medical terminology and tasks that cannot be duplicated entirely in the practice session, such as role-playing with different release of information (ROI) scenarios.

After the trainee has demonstrated the ability to do the job, **coaching** should continue by the supervisor or an expert peer on an ongoing basis. The experienced worker observes or reviews the work of the employee in a nonthreatening manner, offering advice and suggestions for revising techniques to improve productivity and efficient work performance. In a formalized arrangement in which a specific person is assigned to follow up on a regular basis, the coach is referred to as a **mentor**. In this scenario, the mentor meets with the trainee on a regular basis and often gives advice on career growth and development within the organization.

It is estimated that approximately two-thirds of training actually results from informal interactions between the employee and his or her coworkers. Learning occurs even though it is not formally designed or monitored by the organization, for example, during hallway conversations or on lunch breaks when a work topic is discussed and other employees or supervisors offer suggestions or corrections.

On-the-job training methods can be used individually or in combination and should be adapted to each learner. Whatever technique is used, on-the-job training should follow the steps presented in figure 24.3.

Figure 24.3. Steps in on-the-job training

Step 1: Preparation of the learner

a. Put the learner at ease; relieve the tension.
b. Explain why he or she is being taught.
c. Create interest, encourage questions, find out what the learner already knows about his or her job or other jobs.
d. Explain the whole job and relate it to some job the worker already knows.
e. Place the learner as close to the normal working position as possible.
f. Familiarize the worker with the equipment, materials, tools, and trade terms.

Step 2: Presentation of the operation

a. Explain quantity and quality requirements.
b. Go through the job at the normal work pace.
c. Go through the job at a slow pace several times, explaining each step. Between operations, explain the difficult parts or those in which errors are likely to be made.
d. Again, go through the job at a slow pace several times; explain the key points.
e. Have the learner explain the steps as you go though the job at a slow pace.

Step 3: Do a tryout

a. Have the learner go through the job several times, slowly, explaining each step to you. Correct mistakes and, if necessary, do some of the complicated steps the first few times.
b. Run the job at the normal pace.
c. Have the learner do the job, gradually building up skill and speed.
d. As soon as the learner demonstrates ability to do the job, let the work begin, but don't abandon him or her.

Step 4: Follow-up

a. Designate to whom the learner should go for help if he or she needs it.
b. Gradually decrease supervision, checking work from time to time against quality and quantity standards.
c. Correct faulty work patterns that begin to creep into the work, and do it before they become a habit. Show why the learned method is superior.
d. Compliment good work; encourage the worker until he or she is able to meet the quality/quantity standards.

Source: Dessler 2007.

Training Overseas Workers

Training overseas workers on the job may be performed by a combination of remote Web-based training provided from the United States and on-site group or one-on-one training. The trainer may be based in the country or brought overseas from the United States. Areas of training for overseas workers may include workshops to improve proficiency in English writing and verbal communication, medical terminology, and data quality control. Instruction in the technology and equipment related to the job, such as voice recognition technology for transcriptionists or computer-assisted coding may be provided. For those desiring career advancement, topics such as leadership development and supervision should be added. Cross training provides opportunity for competent employees to experience greater task variety in their jobs and also affords flexibility in shifting resources for workload or attendance fluctuation.

Assessment

By its nature, on-the-job training provides an opportunity for immediate assessment of its effectiveness. The trainer can observe the employee's skills as part of the performance tryout and can question the employee on his or her knowledge of policies, procedures, and other academic knowledge that may be required. If the assessment reveals areas of weakness, the training can be adjusted to reinforce knowledge or repeat steps performed incorrectly.

When the employee is working on his or her own, the supervisor should check the quantity and quality of the employee's work against performance standards from time to time. If the employee's performance is below standard, the training can be repeated before bad performance becomes a **habit**.

Finally, the employee should be encouraged to ask questions both during and after the training and should receive positive and negative feedback as appropriate.

Staff Development through In-Service Education

The healthcare industry grows and changes constantly. Whether it is a new law passed by the state or the federal government, new reimbursement regulations, updates to ICD-9-CM or CPT codes, new or revised accreditation standards, or new e-HIM roles, change is a permanent factor. Preparing workers for such changes requires continuous training and retraining.

The third step in the employee development continuum is **in-service education** (refer to table 24.1), a continuous process that builds on the basic skills learned through new employee orientation and on-the-job training. In-service education is concerned with teaching employees specific skills and behaviors required to maintain job performance or to retrain workers whose jobs have changed. Although in-service education may include external programs, it is primarily developed and delivered at the work site or through computer-based training.

Needs Assessment

The need for in-service education may be triggered by many events, including:

- A restructuring of the department or organization
- Annual updates to coding or reimbursement requirements
- Implementation of electronic health records
- A decline in productivity or morale or an increase in absenteeism
- A new organizational policy or procedure
- An external requirement imposed by accreditation or licensing organizations, such as an annual renewal of CPR certification or retraining in infectious disease precautions or safety procedures

The amount of in-service education needed varies with the event and the education and experience of the employee. Downsizing or reorganizing organizational structure often causes changes in an individual employee's job responsibilities. Employees may need to learn other job functions within the workgroup or may even be placed in a new department. This can require a series of formal training sessions, including on-the-job training.

Renewal of training, required by external organizations, may be subject to defined content and duration, often including a test or demonstration of the employee's competence. On the other hand, implementation of a new policy or procedure may simply include distributing the information accompanied by a short meeting.

Decisions need to be made regarding the appropriate format of the in-service education. The following types of questions should be asked:

- Should the instruction be given as **massed training** in a highly concentrated session or as **spaced training** in several shorter sessions?
- Should the task be broken down into parts or be taught as a single unit?
- How will competence be assessed? Is the topic a skill that needs to be demonstrated by the learner, or is it a level of knowledge that should be tested with a written assessment?

As with other training categories, periodic analysis of actual-versus-desired job performance will create a list of topics that should be addressed with in-service education.

Requirements

Unlike orientation programs, which are delivered primarily at one point in time, in-service education programs need to be available on a continuing basis. Depending on the size of the organization, some programs, such as a refresher on the response to the institution's disaster plan, may be offered on a monthly basis. The HR department may coordinate programs on topics that affect the organization as a whole. Programs specific to health information management, such as a coding update, are more likely to be developed by a supervisor or manager in the HIM department.

Finally, some topics serve the needs of more than one department. For example, a program on coding updates may be given by the coding supervisor to employees from the HIM, patient accounting, and physician billing departments. This type of program probably would take place in a more formal setting and require coordination with other department managers.

Examples of in-service education topics and the individuals within the organization who are likely to have responsibility for them are shown in figure 24.4.

Steps in Conducting In-Service Education

Presenting an effective in-service program requires planning. The time frame depends on the complexity of the material and the number of participants but should include enough time to prepare materials and publicize the event. Generally, a formal in-service program should follow these steps:

1. *Set objectives.* Is the purpose of the program to teach a new job task to an individual or to improve morale within the department?
2. *Determine the audience.* Is the training intended for one employee or 50 employees? Are the participants from the same department or from several departments?
3. *Determine whether the content should be delivered as a unit or in parts (massed or spaced).* This may be determined by the availability of the employee as well as the topic.
4. *Determine the best method of instruction.* The education and experience of the audience, the time available, and the cost of preparing and delivering the instruction should all be taken into consideration. Is there a qualified expert in-house? Are videos or computer-based materials available for rent or purchase? Is space available to train a large group at one time? (See the discussions of adult learning strategies and delivery methods later in this chapter.)
5. *Prepare a budget.* If a specific amount has been allocated, the plan should be compared to the predetermined budget and revised, if necessary. Approval should be obtained if the proposal is a new one. In addition, the proposal should include the costs of photocopying materials, speaker fees, and training resources.
6. *Publicize the program.* Flyers and electronic notices should be posted to announce the program and should include the date, time, location, topic, and a summary of the content. When it is important to know the number of attendees in advance, the notice should include a method for RSVP.
7. *If appropriate, prepare handout materials.* Handouts would include materials to be used for instruction as well as documents to reference following the program. At a minimum, an agenda of the topics and a schedule should be developed.
8. *Practice, practice, practice*! The person presenting the program should be adequately prepared and comfortable with the content. Also, a training room should be scheduled ahead of time, and any needed equipment should be checked to ensure that it is available and in good working order. Anyone planning to use a computer or a projector should know how to operate it.
9. *Use a variety of methods and be alert to your audience.* In addition to the lecture, the presenter should engage the audience through interactive questioning and activities. People learn by doing. Opportunities should be provided from time to time for questions and periodic breaks when the program lasts more than two hours.
10. *Obtain feedback from the audience.* It is important to give the participants an opportunity to document their reactions to the training. To that end, an evaluation form should be created and distributed. A sample in-service education evaluation form is shown in figure 24.5.

Figure 24.4. Examples of responsibility for in-service education

Organizationwide: The human resources department typically assumes responsibility for the following topics and may include staff from other departments in the planning and presentation:
- Fire and safety awareness
- Disaster plan implementation
- Infectious disease/universal precautions
- Diversity training
- Team building
- HIPAA training

Multiple Departments: The health information manager may work with managers of several departments to coordinate presentation of the following topics:
- ICD-9-CM or CPT annual updates
- Medical terminology training
- Use of office productivity software for employee productivity measurement
- Health record documentation

Health Information Management Department: The health information manager may develop in-service training within the department for the following topics:
- Release of information
- Fire, safety, and disaster preparedness
- Electronic health record (EHR) implementation
- Use of new photocopier

Assessment

Because some amount of cost, in terms of both time and resources, is usually involved with in-service training, it is important to determine whether its objectives have been met. Three methods for assessing the impact of in-service education are:

- *Completion of an evaluation form at the conclusion of the program:* Immediate feedback provides an assessment of the effectiveness of the delivery methods. Is

Figure 24.5. Sample in-service education evaluation form

In-Service Education Evaluation Form

To help us improve the quality of future programs, please complete the following evaluation of today's session.

Please use the following scale to answer questions 1–5:

1 = Needs Improvement 2 = Satisfactory 3 = Excellent

1. How satisfied were you with the content of the presentation?	1	2	3
2. How would you rate the organization of the presentation?	1	2	3
3. How would you rate the effectiveness of visual media used in the presentation?	1	2	3
4. How would you rate the delivery of the presentation?	1	2	3

5. How satisfied were you with the following aspects of the program?

a. Meeting location	1	2	3
b. Parking	1	2	3
c. Accessibility	1	2	3
d. Registration process	1	2	3
e. Meeting room setup/seating	1	2	3
f. Handout materials	1	2	3

6. What is one thing you learned that you did not know prior to attending?
7. What would you like to have learned more about?
8. Please provide any additional comments that could improve future programs.

the employee energized and ready to put the material to use, or was the material overwhelming?

- *Formal or informal feedback from the employee's supervisor:* Within a few days of the program, the supervisor should be contacted to determine whether the learner has applied the new skills and knowledge on the job.
- *Follow-up with the employee at a later time:* Thirty days after the in-service program, the attendees should be asked to validate the value of the program. Are they able to perform their job better? Is there something they feel they did not learn that should have been included? This may be accomplished easily via an e-mail message.

Special Issues for Staff Development

Several issues must be considered in training programs that apply to all levels, from orientation programs to staff development.

Diversity, Sensitivity, and Antiharassment Training

The September 11, 2001 terrorist attacks had a profound effect on training in the United States. Awareness of the impact of culture on the workforce became an important issue, yet people were afraid to discuss differences for fear of offending others. Organizations found it was important to learn about issues such as the effect of culture on communication and learning styles.

Diversity training attempts to develop sensitivity among employees about the unique challenges facing diverse religious, ethnic, and sexual orientation groups, as well as those with disabilities, and strives to create a more harmonious working environment. It is important to help all employees from diverse backgrounds feel part of the team, respected, committed, and productive; and to understand how to respond appropriately to other employees, customers, or patients. The emphasis should be on learning from each other's viewpoints. Training should be provided for the entire organization, with additional specific training for management staff. Figure 24.6 emphasizes the suggested focus of a diversity sensitivity training program.

A training course about ethnic minorities might begin with a review of various cultures from a social studies perspective (that is, location of the country, climate, customs, or food preferences). Other topics that might be included later would be cultural norms, such as communication styles (strong eye contact or standing close when conversing), use of first versus formal names, or tolerance of jokes. Of particular importance to the HIM employee is the perspective of some cultures on the issue of privacy, which may require that permissions be obtained to comply with the Health Insurance Portability and Accountability Act (HIPAA) of 1996.

Figure 24.6. The four Cs of working with diversity

- Check and test assumptions
- Communicate empathy and respect
- Create a climate of inclusion
- Challenge inappropriate behavior

Source: Bagshaw, M. 2004. Is diversity divisive? A positive training approach. In *Training for Diversity, Industrial and Commercial Training* 36(4): 156, Emerald Group Publishing Limited.

A booklet might be prepared about each group that provides knowledge of the culture, communication helps, and tips for nonjudgmental respect. Employees might be advised to read the material and then follow up with a discussion. When the training course has been completed, an employee advisory group might be formed to advise management staff regarding barriers and issues of concern to diverse employees. A calendar with various cultural and religious celebrations might be posted on the company intranet.

For those employees needing training in the English language and American culture, topics might include English reading and writing skills, focusing on general as well as medical terms. Interpersonal skills, **customer service training,** and the U.S. corporate culture also might be helpful.

Employee harassment is prohibited under Title VII of the Civil Rights Act. Antiharrassment training must cover all types of unlawful harassment based on sex, race, religion, national origin, disability, or sexual orientation. It should be included in new employee orientation and repeated periodically with other training required by accreditation or law. The trainer should be carefully chosen and should be an expert in discrimination laws. The training must be substantial to be effective (that is, the requirement may not be met by simply requiring employees to view a video). Suggested stages for diversity training include:

- Antiharassment and sensitivity training
- Cultural awareness and competence
- Development of multicultural teams
- Full inclusion of minority groups into every level of the organization

Many companies produce materials to help with diversity training, including videos, facilitator materials, printed materials, and cases for **role playing**.

Preparing the HIM Staff for e-HIM

The AHIMA **e-HIM** initiative seeks to promote the migration from paper to an electronic health information infrastructure, reinvent how institutional and personal health information and records are managed, and deliver measurable cost and quality results from improved information management. A task force was convened to articulate a vision for the future state of HIM, including roles for HIM professionals and an action plan to achieve the vision.

Future roles for HIM professionals include:

- Business process engineer
- Clinical research protocol designer and manager
- Clinical trials manager
- Clinical vocabulary manager
- Consumer advocate
- Data analyst
- Data facilitator
- Data/information broker
- Data/information presenter
- Data sets, nomenclature, and classification standards developer
- Data miner
- Data navigator
- Data quality and integrity monitor
- Data resource manager
- Data security, privacy, and confidentiality manager
- Data translator
- Information system designer
- Work and data flow analyst

The task force recommended that HIM professionals continuously transform their knowledge, skills, and abilities to keep pace with the competencies needed for the new roles. Competencies are needed in areas such as data analysis, data integration, privacy and security, methods of encryption and deidentification, clinical vocabulary development and maintenance, and public health surveillance. Providing training for these topics should become a focus of the HIM department's training and development plan for all employees. Other examples of career roles in information technology include:

- Applications analyst
- Project manager
- Team leader
- Marketing or sales associate

Working in Teams

Team-building training helps employees learn to work in groups that have the authority to make decisions. Emphasis is on the group rather than individual achievement. Skills are taught that help members diagnose and devise solutions to problems. Exercises such as constructing items within a group encourage creativity. Conflict-resolution training focuses on communication skills needed to resolve gridlock. Facilitators may work with a group, asking group members and leaders to identify problem issues at the beginning of the session. The group then ranks the themes identified, and that becomes the agenda for problem solving. A byproduct of team training is improved employee attitudes and satisfaction.

Check Your Understanding 24.1

Instructions: Answer the following questions on a separate piece of paper.

1. What are the purposes of an employee orientation program?
2. What are the three levels of an orientation program? List two items typically included at each level.
3. Who is responsible for conducting employee orientation programs?
4. What are some suggestions for making a new employee feel welcome in the new department?
5. What are two additional topics to be included in orientation training for overseas workers?
6. What are the advantages and disadvantages of on-the-job training?
7. What are two examples of skills that are often included in on-the-job training programs?
8. Which is the most common technique used for on-the-job training? What key factor is essential to the success of this method?

9. When is job rotation a useful training technique?
10. What features characterize the major steps in on-the-job training?
11. What is the purpose of in-service education?
12. List two events that suggest a need for in-service education.
13. What HIM in-service topics might be of interest to other departments? Describe at least one.
14. What printed items should always be distributed at a formal in-service program?
15. What three methods are used to assess the effectiveness of an in-service education program?
16. What is the purpose of AHIMA's e-HIM initiative and what topics should be included in training programs to develop employees for new roles?
17. What topics should be included in diversity-training programs?
18. Describe two skills that are desired as a result of customer service training.

Adult Learning Strategies

Training has been defined as the process of providing individuals with the materials and activities they need to develop the knowledge, skills, abilities, attitudes, and behaviors desired in the workplace. Learning is what occurs in the individual, the changes in behavior, knowledge, attitudes, abilities, and skills that are desired. In the healthcare work environment, learning translates into achieving the goals of the institution, including improved job performance. The objective is for employees to develop effective work habits. To accomplish this objective, it is important to understand how employees learn and the factors that affect the learning environment.

Characteristics of Adult Learners

One of the most difficult tasks faced by employees is achieving balance. Ideally, people shift their time between the demands of work, the demands of home, and their own needs. Everyone wants to accomplish more with fewer and fewer hours. Although a low level of stress is positive, too much can lead to burnout. Therefore, training must be viewed as an integral part of the work environment and not as an add-on requirement. The individuals responsible for training need to understand that time is a very valuable resource.

Because time is scarce, employees need to see relevance in the activities that consume their time. They will be more willing to accept tasks that can be accomplished quickly, provide satisfaction or tangible benefits, and can be completed within short time frames.

Three fundamental concepts in helping adults learn are motivation, reinforcement, and knowledge of results.

Motivation

Motivation is the inner drive to accomplish a task. At different stages in life, adults are motivated by specific needs. Understanding that employees differ in the relative importance of these needs at any given time is important in designing a training program. For example, a newly credentialed health information technician in his early 20s with no dependents may be interested in working long hours. He may demonstrate an eagerness to devote extra hours to training that will advance his career. On the other hand, a young parent may value time to attend his or her children's school activities and want to limit time spent away from home.

Employees will be more motivated when they perceive a need for the training. The trainer should call attention to the important aspects of the job and help employees understand how to perform these tasks efficiently and effectively.

Moreover, employees should see a direct connection between the knowledge gained and the work goal. It is helpful when the trainer explains the reason for performing a task in a certain order and relates policies to objectives. For example, coders may be instructed to review a record in a specific order, beginning with a discharge summary and then lab reports. It is helpful when the trainer explains that the purpose of this process is to ensure appropriate evidence of diagnoses to comply with reimbursement requirements. Work that is interesting and challenging, and provides an opportunity for growth, provides the strongest motivation.

Reinforcement

Reinforcement is a condition following a response that results in an increase in the strength of that response. It is associated with motivation in that the strength of the response is a factor of the perceived value of the reinforcer. For example, the young parent who values time with his or her children may be negatively reinforced by a pay increase given after a training course when the increase requires additional work hours. However, money would serve as a reinforcer for the new health information technician discussed earlier. Reinforcement is most effective when it occurs immediately after a correct response.

Incentive pay systems are a form of positive reinforcement. For example, transcriptionists might be compensated based on the number of lines correctly transcribed rather than on an hourly rate.

Knowledge of Results

Adults like feedback on their performance. It is important to understand the concept of the **learning curve**. When a new task is learned, productivity may decrease while a great deal of material is actually being learned. Later, there is little new learning, but productivity may increase greatly. Either situation can be frustrating, so guidance and feedback are important to help employees understand what they have accomplished. In addition, it is important to explain that the employee may reach a plateau where improvement slows or levels off and that this is normal.

Education of Adult Learners

When an organization wants its workers to improve their work habits, it must demonstrate that it values the effort behind the improvements. The organizational climate must support the continued learning and growth of its employees. Some actions the administration might take to indicate this commitment include:

- Providing training during work hours rather than outside the employees' regular work schedules
- Conducting the training off-site to avoid interruptions from day-to-day activities
- Compensating voluntary education with incentives such as bonuses or promotions

Adults will remember and understand material that is relevant and has value to them. Therefore, it is important to present an overall picture along with the objectives they are expected to accomplish. Performance standards should be realistic and attainable. Setting artificially high standards reduces motivation and results in feelings of frustration, anxiety, and stress. Thus, employees should feel challenged, but not overwhelmed.

Consideration should be given to the importance of motivation, reinforcement, and knowledge of results. Setting individual goals that challenge employees and satisfy their particular motivators is the ideal. Training methods that allow for the design of individualized programs, such as computer-based training or print-based programmed learning modules, should be considered. Programmed learning modules lead learners through subject material that is presented in short sections, followed immediately by a series of questions that require a written response based on the section just presented. Answers are provided in the module for immediate feedback.

Learning is accomplished best by doing; therefore, it is important to provide as many hands-on activities as possible. In general, people recall 10 percent of what they hear, 20 percent of what they both see and hear, and almost all of what they simultaneously see, hear, and do (Fallon and McConnell 2007, 194). Therefore, the most effective training includes a combination of verbal instruction, demonstration, and hands-on experience. Correct responses should be reinforced immediately. Recognition by the trainer or feedback about achievement may be just as effective as monetary rewards in providing reinforcement.

Adults learn better in small units because their attention span is usually not long. In addition, they want to be in control of the situation and learn at their own pace. Where possible, training should be delivered in a modular fashion over a longer period of time. The employee who learns quickly can move forward whereas the slower learner can devote more time to a specific activity.

Learning Styles

Just as there are many personalities, there are many ways people learn. It would seem appropriate, then, that the greatest amount of learning will take place if the teaching method matches the learning style of the learner. If relevancy, meaning, and emotion are attached to the material taught, the learner will learn. Learners tend to progress only as far as they need to in order to achieve their goal. Therefore, the best time to learn is when it is seen as useful, which has made **just-in-time training** popular.

Although an individual may have a preferred learning style, other approaches may be sometimes be used. Learning styles are influenced by factors such as age, maturity, and experience, and they may change over time. In general, active learning is more effective than passive learning. Younger workers prefer concrete, sequential learning, whereas older adults prefer more ambiguity, which permits them to draw on their own experience. Following are various models for categorizing learning styles:

- *Sensory:* The learner may prefer *auditory* (prefers to listen), *visual* (prefers to read), or *kinesthetic* (prefers to practice) learning.
- *Personality:* Various personality traits shape our orientation to the world.
- *Information processing:* People differ in how they receive and process information.
- *Social interaction:* Gender and social context determine learning style.
- *Instructional and environmental preference:* Sound, light, structure, and learning relationships affect perceptions.

Various teaching techniques may be used to address different learning styles. These include:

- Individual tasks (reading, answering questions)
- Working with a partner (exchanging ideas, problem solving)
- Lecture to a group
- Working in groups (role playing, simulations)

When addressing a group with various ages and learning styles, the trainer might offer a project with broad guidelines for group completion. For example, some students might contribute text, some might create graphics, and some might build a database, for example.

Computer technology and the advent of **e-learning** have offered the ability to deliver content to match a variety of learning styles. Some students may prefer to read text; others may prefer to interact with graphics or solve problems. The material can be delivered in a variety of modes in a cost-efficient manner and at a pace consistent with an individual's learning style.

Additional resources for information about adult learning are the American Society for Training and Development, the Association for Workplace Learning and Performance Professionals, and Workforce, an organization that provides a variety of HR tools, including a magazine and an e-newsletter.

Training Learners with Special Needs

Trainers should be aware of the necessity of addressing issues of diversity and disability when preparing training programs.

Diversity

Content of training programs should be developed in a culturally sensitive manner. For example, speaking in an informal, or offhanded manner may be offensive to some. It also is inappropriate in some cultures to question or challenge an instructor, or communal learning may be more valued than success of the individual. Males may be more used to dominating a discussion; females may need to be encouraged to contribute.

English as Second Language

In addition to considering cultural diversity issues when creating training programs, many healthcare institutions include employees where a language other than English may be primary, either in the United States or overseas. If the number of such employees is significant, thought should be given to obtaining materials written in the primary language. Developing English proficiency in writing or oral communication should be provided if this is needed.

Disabilities

In general, employers are required to make reasonable accommodation for workers with disabilities. This may include altering training materials, modifying equipment, and making existing facilities accessible and usable. However, companies are *not* required to train employees on equipment they are not capable of running, or for jobs where using such equipment would cause a drop in productivity.

The U.S. Department of Education has established minimum requirements for developers of electronic and information technology to ensure accessibility for those with or without disabilities. When designing training programs for use on computer, keep in mind that adjustments may need to be made so that users with disabilities are able to use the program if it requires use of a keyboard and monitor. Some programs may be developed using voice recognition software or screen readers. Web design should be compliant with requirements of the Americans with Disabilities Act (ADA). If graphics, audio, or video are to be used, a text alternative should accompany them to be accessible with a screen reader. Options for the user to control animation, flashing or blinking objects, or color contrast should be provided, as well as an option to extend time available on timed responses.

Check Your Understanding 24.2

Instructions: Answer the following questions on a separate piece of paper.

1. What role does motivation play in developing a training program?
2. Give an example of a reinforcer other than a monetary reward.
3. Performance standards should be set higher than may reasonably be accomplished. Explain why you agree or disagree with this statement.
4. What two characteristics of adult learners should be considered when developing training programs?
5. Describe the five models for categorizing learning styles.
6. What adaptations should be made to accommodate diversity and disability issues in training?

Delivery Methods

There are many techniques for delivering training, just as there are many purposes of training. Factors that influence selection of a training method include:

- Purpose of the training
- Level of education and experience of the trainees
- Amount of space, equipment, and media available for training
- Number of trainees and their location
- Cost of the method in comparison to desired results
- Need for special accommodation due to disability or cultural differences among the trainees

When the purpose of training is to increase the level of knowledge or to introduce new policies, a different method is appropriate than when the goal is to teach a hands-on skill. Training that requires a lot of room and equipment located near the employees' work area will require a different method than training that needs to be delivered across a distance. Instruction in essential skills or license requirements may justify a higher expenditure than instruction that is helpful, but not mandatory.

Table 24.2 presents the time and location requirements for various training delivery methods. Some subjects, such as demonstration of a new fire safety procedure, are best taught to a group of learners at the same time and place, for example, in a traditional classroom setting. Other subjects, such as use of computers, may be taught at a time and place convenient for employees to learn. **Audioconferencing** is a method used to train people located in different offices, but

Table 24.2. Location and time factors of various training methods

	Same Time	Different Time
Same Space	Traditional: Face-to-face meetings Classes	Work station: VCR Computer Interactive video disk
Different Space	Real-time distance learning: Audioconferencing Interactive television (two-way video and two-way audio) Satellite courses (one-way video and two-way audio) Synchronous computer communications	Asynchronous distance learning: Correspondence courses Video-based telecourses Online computer courses (computers and modems) Multimedia on demand (just-in-time)

Source: Levenburg, N., and H. Major. 1998. Distance learning: implications for higher education in the 21st century. Originally published in *The Technology Source.*

at one time. Each office can be equipped with a speaker and a transmitter, which enables learners to listen and respond to the same material presented by an instructor located at another site.

A recent trend is toward **blended learning**, using several delivery methods, therefore gaining the advantages and reducing the disadvantages of each method alone.

Self-Directed Learning

Self-directed learning allows students to progress at their own pace. It presents material, questions the learner, and provides immediate responses with either positive or negative reinforcement. Providing an employee with the opportunity to control the learning situation is a clear advantage. It is suitable for delivery to one or many employees and is a solution for employees who cannot attend sessions outside work hours because of home or family responsibilities.

Self-directed learning (sometimes called directed reading) was originally delivered via textbooks. Although computers have replaced them in some cases, textbooks still work very well at a relatively low cost. Learners are presented with text and diagrams and then respond to questions. Answers to the questions are provided on another page in the same book for easy checking and feedback. Other advantages to using texts are that they are easily portable and may be supported by other media, such as audiotapes. One disadvantage is that learners may not learn much more than the information in the traditional textbook and the cost of development may not be paid back unless the book is used several times.

An example of a subject using directed reading is medical terminology. Text and diagrams of a body system are presented, for example, and the learner is asked to label anatomical structures and to answer multiple-choice or fill-in-the-blank questions. An audiotape may be provided to give the pronunciation of the terms introduced in the text.

The same idea can be presented using computer-based training, with the learner interacting with diagrams, text questions, or pronunciation requested via a computer program.

Computer-based Training

Computer-based training (CBT) is a method designed to provide individual learners with flexible training at their own pace. The students must have access to a computer on which the program is installed. Similar to text-based programmed learning, the explanatory material is presented and followed by a series of questions. The text is accompanied by sounds or drawings to maintain interest and to present the material in a creative way. After each question is answered, there is an immediate response or reinforcement by the computer. In most systems, students can repeat sections of the material until they have mastered it. Students can work on different topics, at varying speeds, and in several languages. The cost of developing CBT courses is higher than classroom instruction or texts, but once developed, the cost of delivery is less because the course can be used multiple times. It is especially useful for content that does not change frequently, such as basic medical terminology or general ROI policies.

CBT is usually delivered via CD-ROM or DVD-ROM. Both provide an excellent way to deliver text, audio, video clips, and animation, and both are particularly useful for providing simulations of work situations. The advantage of DVD-ROM is a large storage capacity and high quality, with up to two hours of full-screen digital video.

The advantages of CBT include lower training costs, reduction in travel or time away from work for workshops, and better learning retention than with traditional classroom teaching. In addition, interactive technology has been demonstrated to reduce learning time by an average of 50 percent.

Electronic Performance Support Systems

Electronic Performance Support Systems (EPSSs) are sets of computerized tools and displays that automate training and documentation, and integrate this automation with the computer application. It is true just-in-time training, providing information at the time it is needed. These systems are especially useful for complex jobs with multiple steps. An EPSS prompts the user through a series of questions, similar to a checklist. Training time can be reduced significantly through the use of an EPSS, and quality of work is enhanced. An EPSS is relatively easy to update as policies or requirements change, ensuring that the user has the most up-to-date information available.

Classroom Learning

Classroom learning is still the most popular method of instruction. It enables immediate feedback and can improve communication skills. When the goal is to train a large number of employees on largely factual knowledge within a short period of time, classroom learning may be the best choice. When the intention is to convey information, this method is effective and economical. However, it is not as appropriate for developing problem-solving skills or improving interpersonal competence.

Teaching a class used to mean using the **lecture** method in which the instructor delivers content and the student listens and observes, primarily one-way communication. This technique usually involves little active participation by the learner. However, because students learn more by doing, today's classroom instruction usually combines lecture with small group discussion, role playing, student presentations, videos, or other means where dialogue is facilitated. Using a combination of methods has proved to be highly effective. Videotape is useful for presenting events or demonstrations not easily accomplished in lectures, such as scenarios on interpersonal communication or conflict resolution or viewing surgical procedures. The class itself may be videotaped and the video used to deliver the same material to other shifts or workers unable to attend the class.

Role playing is an activity where learners are presented with a hypothetical situation they may encounter on the job, and they act out the response. It is useful for tasks such as interviewing, grievance handling, team problem solving, or communication difficulties.

Seminars and Workshops

Seminars or workshops offer training over the course of one or more days and usually consist of several sessions on specific topics related to an overall theme. Some sessions are large, general classes and others are small, "break-out" classes on topics of limited interest. The cost of workshops and seminars, especially when they are held outside the workplace, is usually high because of the costs of materials, room rental, refreshments, and speaker fees. This training is typically conducted by experts on a subject and may be held in-house or offered by professional organizations, public or private colleges, or vocational schools. It is often used to develop new skills or to retrain employees whose jobs have been affected by changes in the organization, external requirements, or new policies or procedures.

Simulations

Simulations are training approaches that utilize devices or programs replicating tasks away from the job site; when computer based they are known as **virtual reality** simulations. A typical simulation provides the learner with a fictional scenario of a problem, and the learner interacts through an interface device and decides what action to take next, as if it were a real experience. These simulations are similar to playing a video game. Learning occurs in two parts. First, the learner is immersed in a true representation of an actual situation, and second, the learner is required to manage several rules and relationships involved in the process. Learning is acquired through understanding the relationships among the complex processes, learning through exploration. Simulation is helpful for training managers or supervisors.

Distance Learning

Distance learning offers a delivery mode in which the physical classroom, the instructor, and the students are not all present at the same time and in the same location. Distance-learning systems remove barriers associated with location and timing, both individually and simultaneously. This is a particularly important issue for adult learners. In addition, distance learning supports self-directed and individual learning styles.

Methods that support different locations, but same-time delivery, include live audio- or videoconferencing or **synchronous** computer conferencing, where instructors "meet" students at the same time via Internet or intranet delivery. Delivery of courses at both different locations and times is accomplished via **asynchronous** Internet or intranet Web-based courses or independent study courses offered through a combination of print-based, video, and computer-based training materials. With asynchronous delivery, instructors and students send messages one way and receive a response later, which is useful when they are in different time zones or have difficulty arranging schedules to meet at the same time.

E-learning

E-learning refers to training courses delivered electronically. Although most often used to designate Web-based training, the term also may be used to refer to self-directed computer-based training, video or audioconferencing, or electronic performance support systems (EPSS). There is increased demand for online training because traditional methods lack the flexibility and broad-based delivery necessary to meet the rising demand for updated skills in many areas of healthcare.

Electronic training is most successful when:

- There is a large audience to train.
- Employees are geographically dispersed at several sites or work varied schedules.
- Just-in-time training is required.
- The purpose is to gain knowledge or learn applications.
- There is a blend of solid instructional design, instructor creativity, and proven technology.

Advantages of e-learning include flexibility of class time and place, consistency of delivery, reduced time and cost of training, and the ability to reuse and easily maintain content. Drawbacks include technical problems, such as connectivity or availability for large blocks of time, and student issues with motivation or distraction. Trainers may not be available for some time, and therefore a lag may occur between the time a problem arises and the time it can be solved. Figure 24.7 shows a breakdown of frequency of common e-learning delivery methods. Table 24.3 shows classroom versus e-learning advantages and disadvantages.

Figure 24.7. e-learning delivery methods

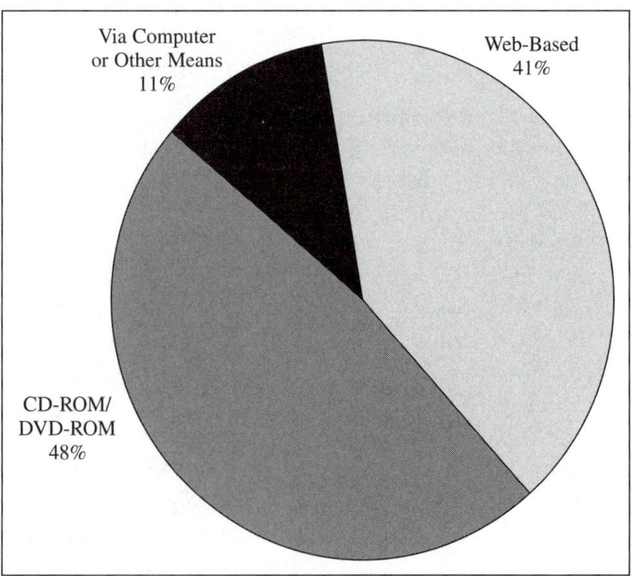

Source: Adapted from Mondy and Noe 2005, 214.

Table 24.3. Classroom versus e-learning advantages and disadvantages

	Classroom	Asynchronous Web-based	Synchronous Web-based
Advantages	• High-quality delivery • Immediate Q and A	• Just-in-time training • Self-paced learning • Consistency • Training materials easy to update • Flexible time and place • Cost-effective	• High-quality delivery • Immediate Q & A • Rapid, low-cost content
Disadvantages	• Expensive • Training too soon or too late	• Motivation can be difficult • Lack of classroom collaboration • Delay in trainer response	• Higher cost per student than asynchronous • Instructor and students need to be available at same time
Best for:	• Multiple students with similar skills • Training in single location • Interpersonal skills	• Basic training • Students in multiple locations	• Basic training • Students in multiple locations • Highly interactive knowledge sharing
Worst for:	• Students of varying skill levels • Consistency across learner groups	• Observing interpersonal skills/feedback • Real-time knowledge sharing	• Students of varying skill levels • Observing interpersonal skills/feedback

Source: Adapted from *Workforce Management Magazine* 2001.

Live Audio or Video-based Courses

With audio- or videoconferencing, employees in several locations can learn together via telephone lines or satellite transmission. Audioconferencing enables students to listen to material delivered by a presenter while looking at handout material or books. At selected points in the presentation, the instructor pauses and students interact and share comments or ask questions about the material. The advantage of audioconferencing is its relatively low cost compared to video or computer delivery. Moreover, it eliminates the time and expense of travel to the instruction site. It is useful for the same kind of purpose as the lecture method, which is to deliver specific content to a large group of people.

Interactive videoconferencing is delivered via satellite, television, or, most recently, computer and offers one- or two-way video together with two-way audio. With one-way video, students receive the image of the instructor and demonstrations and can both see and hear the presenter, but the instructor cannot see the students. Two-way video permits both parties to see each other and to interact. Improved technology is enhancing the quality as well as reducing the cost of this delivery method.

A *teleconferencing network* usually consists of video and audio recording equipment and a satellite service to broadcast the signal to televisions in a remote location. Videoconferencing permits additional flexibility in delivering courses that may be enhanced through visual as well as audio presentation, such as those that include demonstrations or simulation exercises. It is useful for training employees in organizations with multiple sites, such as integrated delivery networks with inpatient and outpatient facilities. The expense is justified for large organizations that do extensive training.

Web-based Courses

The most frequent mode of distance learning is the Web-based course. Driving this phenomenon are two main factors: universal availability, and cost savings. The Internet has become a familiar entity in the lives of most people. Internet-based training permits on-demand training, removing both time and space barriers. The medium is familiar to most individuals and requires a minimum of instruction in the specific courseware used to deliver the course. This method provides instruction when, where, and at a pace suited to each learner. The instruction can be delivered in several forms.

Web-based courses can be delivered synchronously, with employees and trainers interacting via chat rooms, whiteboards, or application sharing at a predetermined time with review of materials. This closely mimics a traditional classroom setting. Another option is asynchronous delivery, where students and instructors interact through e-mail or discussion forums. It is not necessary to be online at the same time and is therefore more convenient than synchronous delivery. The discussion board format is the most frequently used, where students post comments and then review and respond at different times. Materials also can be posted for review at the student's convenience.

Software can be distributed simultaneously to students via e-mail. Students can interact with other students and the instructor through a variety of communication tools. The most common form of delivery today is to access courses developed by training organizations or universities via a Web site. Course authoring tools are now readily available that permit trainers to develop e-learning courses easily and quickly without professional course developers. Most rapid e-learning tools also incorporate search tools, bookmarking, and data tracking. Employees are issued a log-on name and password to access the course. Material can be presented using a variety of methods, including text, audio, or video. Relevant material can be accessed through hypertext links embedded in the Web site, which students can access with the click of a mouse.

Software for delivering Web-based courses is developed as **learning management systems** (LMSs) and **learning content management systems** (LCMSs). LMSs manage the learning process, tracking grades and access, presenting the content, and collating statistics on use. LCMSs provide a technical framework to develop the content and permit sharing and reusing content. Most courseware used by colleges and universities has both components. Rapid e-learning tools can be linked to learning management systems to facilitate course development.

Intranets are private computer networks that use Internet technologies but are protected with security features and can only be accessed by employees of the organization. Many hospitals use intranets to distribute policies, procedures, and education courses on a variety of topics. Material on CD-ROM can be installed and delivered via intranets for employee self-study, as well as other customized courses for specific employee needs.

The advantages of Web-based courses include the availability of the delivery medium (the Internet or intranet), which brings the course to the employee's computer at home or work, and the ability to easily update materials. Multimedia materials, including audio, video, graphics, and animation, provide an interesting way to deliver material and have been shown to result in faster learning and greater retention. They also are well suited to adult learners, meeting their needs for education on their terms of time and location. Although sometimes expensive to develop, the cost of using multimedia materials is usually less compared to the cost of classroom or seminar courses for large numbers of employees.

It is important to remember to start with an understanding of the specific performance goals to be attained with training. Using an authoring tool without good instructional design that is focused on outcomes will likely not achieve success.

Social Networks

The increasing popularity of social networking Web sites provides another opportunity for e-learning. These sites provide an online community where participants can share information, including file attachments, Web site bookmarks, or multimedia files. Web logs (*blogs*) provide a Web page where users can post text, images, and links to other Web sites. While blogs originally started as a type of online personal diary; they are now used for a variety of purposes, including communication within organizations, and can be helpful for distributing training materials. **Wikis** are a collection of Web pages that together form a collaborative Web site. A wiki can be modified by its users. Healthcare organizations may use wikis as a tool where trainers or supervisors can post material and employees can respond and discuss questions.

MUVEs refer to online, multiuser virtual environments, and are also known as *virtual worlds*. They can be used to simulate a work environment that can be accessed over the Internet. Users create representations of themselves (avatars) and interact with other users. Healthcare organizations can use a MUVE in a variety of "soft skills" training exercises such as interpersonal communication, decision making, and leadership. Individuals can role-play to practice skills, try real world experiences, and learn from their mistakes. Team building scenarios can be also be developed. MUVEs can also be used for technical training. Group or individual orientation for new hires in a simulation of the actual hospital or HIM department can be provided. Other benefits of using a MUVE include:

- Participants can be in multiple locations
- Hands-on, interactive learning
- Capable of being stored on an organization's intranet and used repeatedly
- Integration into learning management systems

M-Learning

M-learning, or mobile learning, is an electronic learning mode in which content typically delivered via the Internet to computers can be received via personal digital assistant devices (PDAs), therefore expanding the accessibility to a true anytime, anyplace level. Issues to consider are the type of device (small handheld versus tablet PC) and type of connectivity. Screens on a tablet PC are larger, permitting more information to be transmitted. Information can be downloaded from a PC to a mobile device and then accessed later away from the organization, or the device can be directly connected to the Internet via wireless connection. As with any form of e-learning, good instructional design is important. M-learning is not appropriate for very long courses with a great deal of material but is appropriate for delivering key points and short updates. It is an effective way to deliver multimedia information to a large number of people quickly. Following review of the material, participants might respond to questions or use social networking tools such as blogs or wikis, providing an interactive learning environment.

Intensive Study Courses

Intensive study courses allow a great deal of material to be compressed into a small time frame. A common example is the weekend college, where students attend 10 to 12 hours per day on Saturday and Sunday. These courses are usually delivered on a college campus or at a hotel setting and require an overnight stay. This training method is suited for teaching special skills that can best be learned in a setting away from day-to-day operations. Examples of courses include cultural awareness, training in teamwork and empowerment, and management development.

A popular exercise is to take the organization's leadership team to an outdoor setting where they learn spirit and cooperation and the need to rely on others in order to overcome physical obstacles. The process builds trust to be transferred back to the work setting.

Check Your Understanding 24.3

Instructions: Answer the following questions on a separate piece of paper.

1. What factors should be considered in selecting a training method?
2. How is computer-based training as a learning method different from self-directed learning with textbooks?
3. When is it appropriate to deliver training in a classroom setting?
4. What training obstacles are reduced with e-learning?
5. How would a healthcare organization use its intranet to deliver training?
6. Describe how social networks and MUVE's can be used for training.
7. What topics are appropriate for intensive study training?

Workforce Retention

A 1998 study by Aon Consulting identified five factors that influence employee commitment to an organization (Odgers and Keeling 2000, 214). They include:

- A fearless corporate culture
- Job satisfaction
- Opportunities for personal growth
- Organizational direction
- The company's recognition of employees' need for work–life balance

Many employees leave organizations because of their need for flexibility. As personal lives become more complex, managers must learn to permit their employees more control over their own time if they are to gain their loyalty.

Turnover and Its Impact

Today's employees have different work expectations than their parents had. They want control of their careers and an employer that rewards them based on their performance. The "traditional" worker felt the employer was responsible for providing a career path and, in return, deserved the employee's long-term commitment to the job. Concerned with job security and stability, yesterday's worker preferred a predictable job, with some opportunity for growth, but desired direction with a small amount of creativity.

The "emerging" worker of the twenty-first century values growth over predictability, is concerned with opportunities for creativity, and understands that job security must be earned. Personal opportunity for growth, although it requires a job change, is preferred over remaining in a position that is stable but lacks opportunity for advancement.

The costs of hiring and training employees are quite significant. Therefore, organizations should try to minimize turnover by understanding what will retain employees.

Reasons that employees stay in organizations include:

- *Culture and work environment:* Employees prefer good communication and friendly workplace relationships.
- *Compensation:* Pay should be fair, based on performance and effort required for the job.
- *Training and development:* There should be opportunities for mentoring and career growth.
- *Role of the supervisor:* A supervisor should demonstrate high performance and good relationships with staff.
- *Growth and earnings potential:* There should be opportunities for new skill development and consequent financial rewards.

Organizations need to develop retention skills in managers. Pay should be fair, and job flexibility should be provided. Peer coaches may help employees work through difficulties that may cause them to leave. In addition, screening questions during the hiring process may help identify employees who have a high level of integrity and are less likely to suddenly resign.

Alternative Staffing Structures

One important benefit that can enhance job satisfaction is the ability to balance demands of work and personal life. Alternative staffing structures offer flexibility in hours, location, and job responsibilities as a method to attract and retain employees. Electronic-based health information can be managed in places and at times and by people other than those physically located in the institution. As security and technology advance, new staffing arrangements will present both opportunities and challenges for the health information manager. Alternative staffing structures are discussed in Chapter 22 as methods of work design. The use of alternative staffing structures also present challenges and opportunities for orientation, training and development of employees who do their work in remote locations, in off-peak hours, or as outsourced employees under contract. This will require knowledge of how to manage new legal, technical, and personal issues.

Flextime

Flextime generally refers to the employee's ability to work by varying his or her starting and stopping hours around a core of midshift hours, such as 10 a.m. to 1 p.m. Depending on their position and the institution, employees may have a certain degree of freedom in determining their hours. For example, an employee may be given flexibility to start any time between 6 a.m. and 8 a.m. and leave after having worked seven hours.

Compressed workweeks permit employees to work longer days and three or four days per week rather than the usual five eight-hour days. The advantages of this arrangement include increased productivity due to fewer start-and-stop periods, a reduction in commuting time, and additional days off for personal time. The disadvantages may include fatigue and a greater impact of absenteeism and tardiness.

Another option is **flex years**. With this option, employees may choose (at six-month intervals) the number of hours they work each month for the next year. Flex years are particularly attractive to parents of young children, who can work more hours during the school year and fewer hours during vacation periods, for example. In the HIM department, this may be a good option if an event such as an accreditation survey or the installation of a new computer system necessitates a heavier workload requiring more hours for a short period of time, but fewer hours later.

The advantages of flextime programs include a decrease in tardiness and absenteeism caused by taking time to handle personal matters, more productivity during the hours worked, the ability to adjust hours to the workload, and the opportunity to share limited resources across more employees and hours. Flextime programs also lessen the distinction between employees and supervisors and encourage the delegation of duties. However, such programs can be complex to administer and do not work well in situations where workers depend on the physical presence of others for interactive job responsibilities.

However, it is important to ensure that the flextime arrangement does not violate provisions of the Fair Labor Standards Act, the Occupational Safety and Health Act (OSHA), or antidiscrimination laws. To avoid problems, the facility's policy should be clear regarding the positions that are eligible for flextime; the work schedule should not be viewed as a reward for only certain employees. In addition, it is important to understand the impact of flextime on benefit plans, which may require employees to work a certain number of hours in a given time period. For example, nonexempt employees may have different regulations than exempt employees regarding overtime pay.

Even with its minor drawbacks, flextime appears to be a viable arrangement and, in most institutions, improves morale, encourages employee responsibility, and results in an overall increase in productivity.

Successful flextime programs have the following conditions in common:

- A person appointed to oversee the program, develop policies and procedures, and resolve differences between supervisors and employees
- A written policy that clearly states the positions that are open to flextime and those that are not
- An orientation program for supervisors when the program is first introduced or as part of a new supervisor's introduction to the organization
- A job function that will benefit from flexibility, for example, one that has high and low workloads at different time periods and one that permits the employee to work independently

Job Sharing

Job sharing is a work arrangement in which two or more people share one full-time job. For example, one employee may work mornings and another works afternoons, but it also can mean working different days or weeks. A distinction must be made between job sharing and part-time work. In job sharing, one full-time job is split and all employees sharing the job may perform parts of the same project. Part-time jobs involve employees who work fewer than full-time hours and perform their jobs independently of others.

The main advantage of job sharing is that it enables organizations to attract employees who otherwise may not work because of personal responsibilities. This is an attractive option for parents and employees who want to attend school. The success of job sharing depends on the individuals in the job. They must be mature and cooperative and must want to work toward achieving the objectives of the job. Frequent communication is important regarding the status of projects or unplanned events that may alter the work requirements for a given day.

The disadvantages of job sharing include lack of continuity, particularly when one employee starts a task in the morning and another is responsible for completing it later in the day, as well as decreased productivity when the employees are not cooperative or fail to communicate well. Job sharing also may cause confusion for other employees or the public, who have to interact with several individuals rather than one.

Home-based Work

Computer technology has created a new option for employees who work at home **telecommuting**. HIM departments have seen an increase in the number of coders and medical transcriptionists who choose this option. Telecommuting provides an opportunity for employees to become employed who cannot travel from home for reasons such as physical or personal limitations and helps resolve the problem of shortages of qualified employees in critical job functions. It is an excellent alternative for physically challenged individuals. Individuals who choose this option are employees of the institution and are covered by the same policies and benefits as those who work on-site. The employer usually provides a computer and any networking hardware and software, and the employee is required to submit a detailed time sheet of hours worked.

The advantages of telecommuting include freedom from the time, expense, and physical requirements of commuting; the ability to work flexible hours; increased productivity; lack of distractions from other employees; and an increase in personal time. Telecommuting may be offered as an incentive to retain competent employees when wage increases may not be an option. Moreover, the institution benefits from a reduced need for physical space and improved recruitment.

The disadvantages of telecommuting include employee difficulty in separating work and personal life and feelings of isolation. The "invisible" employee also creates unique challenges for the supervisor. One way to resolve this issue is to have the employee and the manager enter into a telecommuting agreement that defines the expectations of both parties regarding location, hours, equipment, and confidentiality. (See figure 24.8 for a sample agreement.)

Figure 24.8. Sample telecommuting agreement

Telecommuting Agreement

I have read and understand the attached Telecommuting Policy, and agree to the duties, obligations, responsibilities, and conditions for telecommuters described in that document.

I agree that, among other things, I am responsible for establishing specific telecommuting work hours, furnishing and maintaining my remote work space in a safe manner, employing appropriate telecommuting security measures, and protecting company assets, information, trade secrets, and systems.

I understand that telecommuting is voluntary and I may stop telecommuting at any time. I also understand that the company may at any time change any or all of the conditions under which I am permitted to telecommute, or withdraw permission to telecommute.

Note: The following elements are recommended specific to the situation.

1. Remote work location:

____
Address of employee residence or work premises

____
Work phone number, fax number, etc.

____
Description of work space at remote location

2. Telecommuting schedule:

____
On a weekly basis as follows

____
On a monthly basis as follows

____
No regular schedule (separate permission for each telecommuting day)

3. Regular telecommuting work hours:

   From ______ to ______

____
Meal break/other breaks

4. General description of the activities and functions to be completed by the telecommuter:
5. Frequency of communication with company (that is, check voice mail, e-mail, etc.):
6. Productivity requirements or expectations (if applicable):
7. Company assets to be used at remote work location (description, ID numbers, and value):
8. Company information systems to be accessed from remote work location (list):
9. Noncompany services, equipment, software, and data to be used at remote work location (list):
10. Equipment and services to be provided by the telecommuter (list):
11. Security measures to be used by telecommuter and expectations (virus protection and frequency of program updates, use of personal firewalls for computer, shredding company documents, etc.):
12. Expectations for childcare for infants or young children during work hours:
13. Obligation to comply with company rules, policies, and procedures while telecommuting:
14. Other

This sample form was developed by AHIMA for discussion purposes only. It should not be used without review by your organization's legal counsel to ensure compliance with local and state laws.

Source: Dougherty and Scichilone 2002.

Suggested items to include in the agreement include work schedule, communication frequency and methods, goals, performance measures, confidentiality requirements, equipment maintenance responsibilities, and environmental safety requirements.

A particular issue for the HIM department is the confidentiality and security of personal health information transmitted over networks as records are sent for coding and dictation is sent for transcription. In addition, the information needs to be secured while in the employee's home, where it can be subject to physical damage or be viewed by the employee's family members or friends. The HIPAA security standards, in particular, provide specific requirements for remote access, including secure transmission, assurance of data integrity, and authentication methods.

As with flextime, clearly stated policies should be in place regarding who is eligible for telecommuting arrangements and their impact on benefit plans. Workers' compensation issues have not been fully resolved. If an employee trips in the home, for example, is this a workers' compensation injury? The answer appears to center on whether the individual was doing work at the time of the injury.

Although many issues still need answers, it appears that telecommuting will increasingly become an important option for HIM departments as a way to recruit and retain satisfied employees.

Outsourcing

In some cases, flexible job arrangements may not be an option for employees. Another solution to the problem of a shortage of qualified staff is **outsourcing**. In this arrangement, the institution contracts with an independent company with expertise in a specific job function. The outside company then assumes full responsibility for performing the function rather than just supplying staff. Thus, the health information manager's responsibility shifts from supervising employees to managing a vendor relationship.

Common functions that are candidates for outsourcing in the HIM department include transcription, release of information, and coding. The outsourcing company may perform the functions either at the institution or partially or completely off-site. Advances in communication and security technology have resulted in many home-based workers being employed by such independent companies.

The advantages of outsourcing to the health information manager include the ability to complete work efficiently and with high quality while avoiding the problem of staff recruitment and supervision. With the increase in companies providing these services, outsourcing also can mean a reduction in cost because of competitive bidding. The advantages to the employees of outside companies include flextime and telecommuting—the ability to work varying hours, an increase in personal time, and increased morale. The disadvantages for the health information manager include less immediate control over the quantity and quality of the work, the need to know negotiation techniques, and the reliance on the vendor. HIPAA also requires special arrangements regarding security and confidentiality for outsourcing contractors.

Suggestions for successful outsourcing arrangements include:

- Seeking assistance from someone skilled in negotiation when developing the contract with the vendor
- Engaging legal counsel to review the language of the contract to ensure that it complies with the HIPAA requirements
- Requiring competitive bidding for each outsourced service at regular intervals
- Establishing expectations and performance standards for contractors
- Monitoring compliance with performance standards
- Performing periodic customer surveys to assess satisfaction with the service

Employee Development

In addition to the need to balance work and personal life, employees often look for opportunities for personal growth. By nature, they want to learn new skills and further their careers. A significant amount of training should be devoted to developing the ability of employees to help themselves and to realize that they are the ones responsible for their advancement.

Empowerment

Empowerment is the concept of providing employees with the tools and resources to solve problems themselves. In other words, employees obtain power over their work situation by assuming responsibility. Empowered employees have the freedom to contribute ideas and perform their jobs in the best possible way. The idea of empowerment actually began as part of total quality management programs, which many organizations initiated in order to improve the quality of service provided to customers and to increase their competitiveness in the marketplace. A high-quality organization strives to understand and improve work processes in order to prevent problems.

Healthcare organizations that empower their employees believe that all employees can perform—and truly want to perform—to their highest potential when given the proper resources and environment. Because they perform jobs on a regular basis, they are intimately familiar with the steps in the process. What the employees may lack are skills in analysis and problem solving. Training sessions in skills such as data analysis, use of control charts, or flowcharting will help employees to identify problems, develop alternatives, and recommend solutions.

To perform effectively, employees also need to be given responsibility, authority, and the trust to make decisions and act independently within their area of expertise. Figure 24.9 offers suggestions on how managers can empower their employees.

Figure 24.9. How to empower employees

- Get others involved in selecting their work assignments and the methods for accomplishing tasks.
- Create an environment of cooperation, information sharing, discussion, and shared ownership of goals.
- Encourage others to take initiative, make decisions, and use their knowledge.
- When problems arise, find out what others think and let them help design the solutions.
- Stay out of the way; give others the freedom to put their ideas and solutions into practice.
- Maintain high morale and confidence by recognizing successes and encouraging high performance.

Source: Schermerhorn 2005, 328.

Empowered employees are less likely to complain or feel helpless or frustrated when they cannot resolve a problem on their own. Moreover, they are more likely to feel a sense of accomplishment and to be more receptive to solutions that they develop themselves. In addition, they tend to demonstrate commitment and self-confidence and to produce high-quality work.

One disadvantage that is frequently mentioned by managers is that empowerment involves too much time for meetings and discussion and takes employees away from the "real work." Actually, it is much more efficient to take the time necessary to prevent problems than to solve them after they occur. In the long run, empowered employees work more efficiently and productively.

Indeed, some managers are afraid to share power. They feel that they have worked hard to gain the power they have and are reluctant to give it up. But the manager who empowers others usually increases his or her own power because a high-performing unit reflects the manager's expertise.

An example of empowerment in the HIM department would be to train employees in the ROI function to solve a slow turnaround issue. The employees are probably more aware than the supervisor of problems that prevent them from filling requests for information (missing charts, insufficient fees, incomplete records). With proper training in brainstorming and flowcharting, as well as a supportive environment, the employees may be able to develop a procedure that can be performed differently to prevent delays.

Delegation

Delegation is the process of distributing work duties and decision making to others. To be effective, delegation should be commensurate with **authority** and responsibility. A manager must assign responsibility, which is an expectation that another person will perform tasks. At the same time, authority, or the right to act in ways necessary to carry out assigned tasks, must be granted. An employee cannot be expected to perform a job for which he or she is not given authority to obtain resources. Authority should equal responsibility when work is delegated. Finally, **accountability** must be created, which is the requirement to answer to a supervisor for results. An employee must be empowered to act, given the necessary tools and skills, and held accountable for the quality of his or her work.

Successful delegation includes:

- Assigning responsibility
- Granting authority
- Creating accountability

Guidelines for delegating are presented in figure 24.10. As an employee development tool, delegation can provide employees the opportunity to try new tasks previously performed by someone in a higher position and leads to empowerment because employees are given the opportunity to contribute ideas and fully utilize their skills. At the same time, the manager should remain available to provide assistance and support.

Sometimes managers have difficulty delegating because they feel that only they can do the job correctly. In other cases, they feel threatened by the idea that another employee can do their tasks and perhaps do them better. This thinking can lead to poor morale and result in talented employees leaving the organization. In addition, it can lead to managers being overburdened with work that could be done by others and to employees being denied opportunities to learn new skills.

In some situations, employees may be unwilling to accept delegated responsibilities when they feel that they are unqualified to do the tasks or that they are being dumped on. Dumping can involve assigning an employee unpleasant or unpopular work that seems to have little value or asking an employee to take on work in addition to an already demanding workload. This results in resentment or anger. Employees may feel this way when they have a poor working relationship with their supervisor, know that others have refused the same task, or have been taken advantage of in the past.

To avoid these problems, employees should be selected who are either competent to perform the tasks or willing to undergo the necessary training. People are more willing to accept tasks that they understand, have a choice in doing, and recognize value added to the organization and their personal growth. Managers should set checkpoints, monitor how the

Figure 24.10. Ground rules for effective delegation

- Carefully choose the person to whom you delegate.
- Define the responsibility; make the assignment clear.
- Agree on performance objectives and standards.
- Agree on a performance timetable.
- Give authority; allow the other person to act independently.
- Show trust in the other person.
- Provide performance support.
- Give performance feedback.
- Recognize and reinforce progress.
- Help when things go wrong.
- Don't forget *your* accountability for performance results.

Source: Schermerhorn 2005, 264.

delegate is doing, and allow the opportunity for questions and feedback.

Delegation is a skill that matches the right employee with the right task. It requires communication, support, and an environment that fosters risk taking. It is essential in order to identify and develop successors and is important if a manager wishes to provide a path to advance in the organization. Effective delegation actually leads to a more efficient and productive department overall and mutually benefits the manager, the employee, and the institution.

Coaching and Mentoring

Both new employees and experienced employees who may be ready for a change can benefit from coaching or mentoring. As discussed earlier in this chapter, coaching is an ongoing process in which an experienced person offers performance advice to a less experienced person. However, coaching goes beyond teaching. A good coach is also a counselor, a resource person, a troubleshooter, and a cheerleader. Coaches deal with improving attitudes, morale, and career development in addition to giving instruction in specific tasks.

Effective coaches are dedicated leaders who display a high level of competence and are able to push or pull employees to their highest level of performance. They are role models who set a good example; show workers what is expected and how to get the job done well; provide praise or constructive feedback, where appropriate; and are ready to help with routine work alongside the employee, if necessary. Department managers are well-positioned to share their knowledge and expertise of the job they manage.

Coaching starts with orientation of the new employee and continues throughout his or her time with the organization. The more time the coach spends walking around observing and listening to employees, the more opportunities there will be to support, praise, and offer advice.

Helping employees should be done in a manner that encourages self-sufficiency. For example, when an employee comes forward with a problem, a good coach does not simply give the answer but, rather, asks the employee for suggestions. In other words, the coach's response should be "What do you think?" rather than "Here's what you should do."

Coaches defend and support their employees. They are facilitators who remove obstacles and obtain resources to enable and empower their staffs. It is important to praise performance above and beyond the expected, for example, when the employee completes a task ahead of schedule or offers to help a colleague. It is equally important to praise the worker who consistently meets objectives or improves in an area that was below standard, in other words, for doing what is expected. To be effective, both positive and negative feedback must be timely, specific, and in the right setting (privately or publicly depending on the circumstance). Good coaches direct negative feedback at the behavior they wish to correct, not at the person.

However, coaching can be done poorly. This happens when criticism is overused or praise is undeserved. In addition, the approach needs to be adjusted to the employee. Good coaching takes time to allow flexibility and encourage the employee to perform correctly without jumping in too quickly with advice.

Mentoring is a form of coaching. A mentor is a senior employee who works with employees early in their careers, giving them advice on developing skills and career options. Several employees may be assigned as protégés to the mentor, but contact is usually one-on-one. Through the mentoring relationship, employees have an advisor with whom they can solve problems, analyze and learn from mistakes, and celebrate successes. Many organizations have formal mentoring programs where protégés are matched with potential mentors. Other managers voluntarily offer to work with up-and-coming employees.

Mentors share their knowledge of management styles and teach prospective supervisors specific job or interpersonal skills. They may assign challenging projects that allow employees to explore real-life learning experiences while still under the guidance of an experienced teacher.

A recent use of mentoring is helpful in teaching diversity tolerance. In **reverse mentoring**, an employee from a minority group will provide mentoring to management staff, sharing their day-to-day perspectives and providing cultural awareness to the manager.

Successful mentoring depends on effective interaction between mentor and protégé. Mentors must be chosen who enjoy passing on their experience and knowledge to others.

Promotion

Promotion may be another tool to encourage employee development and commitment. When tied to training programs, it can become a powerful incentive. Promotion usually refers to the upward progression of an employee in both job and salary. However, it also can mean a lateral move to a different position with similar job skills or to a change within the same job as a result of completing higher education or credentialing requirements. To attract, retain, and motivate employees, organizations should provide a career development system that promotes from within.

When tied to promotion, career development programs offer an incentive to ambitious employees. Goals can be incorporated into the performance review process. In the HIM department, clerical employees can be encouraged to take classes that would lead to an associate's degree in health information technology or a bachelor's degree in health information administration, making them eligible for certification exams. In addition, employees may be encouraged to enter coding certificate programs and achieve coding certification.

The higher the status of the person in the organization, the more likely it is that promotion will work as a motivator. To improve employee performance, promotion should be awarded based on competence, not on seniority. In some organizations, union contracts emphasize seniority and thus restrict the organizations' ability to use competence as a sole criterion.

Promotion based on performance is usually measured by appraising past performance against standards. However, past performance does not always predict future potential. Some organizations use testing instruments to assess this capability.

Succession planning is a specific type of promotional plan in which senior-level position openings are anticipated and candidates are identified from within the organization. The candidates are given training through formal education, job rotation, and mentoring so that they can eventually assume these positions.

To be effective, promotion criteria should be published in a formal policy and procedure, which usually includes job postings of open positions, so that all employees have the opportunity to apply for consideration. When promotions appear to be given to favored employees, or when the procedure is shrouded in secrecy, promotion ceases to be attractive.

Incentive Programs

Voluntary employee turnover can be disruptive to an organization. Both high and low performers are more likely to leave than are average performers. It is important to try to retain high performers. The usual way to do this is through a **pay for performance** system. In order for these systems to be successful, it is important for the employee to make a connection between pay and performance. Incentive plan effectiveness is affected by differences in employee personalities and values. Each person is motivated by different needs, and they will not pursue rewards they do not find valuable. Therefore, an effective incentive program links effort directly to a reward, and the reward must be valued.

Rewards may be in the form of pay or other items, such as vacations, flexible work hours, prizes, or recognition on a plaque or bulletin board, or in a personal note. One reward system allows employees to select a reward from a catalog or Web site, allowing the employee to select something they value.

Incentives may be given based on the following structures:

- Pay for item completed (lines transcribed, charts coded)
- Pay based on success of a team achieving goals (this encourages collaboration, but high-performing individuals are not recognized)
- Pay based part on the individual and part on team performance
- Pay based on a standard rate plus premium if productivity exceeds the standard
- Merit pay given annually as a salary increase

An incentive plan may fail if it appears there is an emphasis on quantity without an associated focus on quality, or if the reward is not valued (such as increased pay given to an employee who would rather have time off). Finally, incentive programs must be accompanied with effective management.

The best incentive programs demonstrate that effort must be instrumental in obtaining the reward. Under the control of the employee, employees should support and value the plan, and employee goals should be SMART—Specific, Measurable, Attainable, Relevant, and Timely.

Continuing Education

Continuing education (CE) is a requirement of most professionals, including those in HIM. It usually requires a person to complete a certain number of hours of education within a given time period to maintain a credential or license status. Accrediting organizations, such as the Joint Commission also include CE in their standards. The HIM field is changing rapidly, primarily in the areas of technology, e-HIM, and legal and regulatory requirements. It is important that credentialed professionals remain current in their knowledge of the profession so that they can provide high-quality skills to the organizations for which they work.

CE refers to keeping up with changes in the profession or to improving skills required to perform the same job. It is different from career development, which is geared toward preparing an individual for a new job. Sometimes this line is blurred. In HIM, management development programs may be essential for the current position when one is already a supervisor, for example. On the other hand, preparing a technical employee to assume a new management role would be considered career development. Some organizations have tuition reimbursement policies to encourage career development.

CE programs are most often provided by external organizations, such as the American Health Information Management Association (AHIMA) or its local chapters. Career development, by contrast, usually includes a combination of job rotation through progressively increasing job responsibilities in-house and externally taught formal classes and workshops.

As part of the formal performance appraisal process, CE goals should be set for all employees. A record should be kept in the employee's personnel file that indicates the number of CE hours earned as well as the topic, place, and person who provided the education. Management should support the individual's achievement by providing time off to attend workshops, flexible scheduling for formal classes offered at educational institutions, and financial reimbursement.

CE programs are delivered via many different formats to suit the individual learner. These include classroom as well as computer-based modules or Web-based courses that all employees can access, regardless of where they live or their personal or physical limitations. Continued skill development should be an important requirement for all HIM employees.

Check Your Understanding 24.4

Instructions: Answer the following questions on a separate piece of paper.

1. Describe two techniques organizations can implement to reduce employee turnover.
2. In what work situations would an HIM department benefit from a flextime work arrangement?
3. What is one advantage to the employee of working compressed workweeks? To the department?
4. What potential problems with flextime should a manager be wary of? Give the possible solution to each problem.
5. What is the difference between job sharing and traditional part-time employment?
6. What items should be included in a telecommuting agreement?
7. What two functions does the HIM department commonly outsource?
8. What factors help ensure the success of an outsourcing arrangement?
9. In what three ways can managers empower employees?
10. What two reasons might managers have for not empowering employees?
11. How are the concepts of delegation and empowerment related?
12. What three actions must be done for effective delegation?
13. When might an employee resist accepting delegated responsibilities?
14. What are the basic characteristics of effective coaches?
15. How does mentoring differ from coaching? How is it similar?
16. On what should promotion be based if it is to motivate?
17. Why do incentive programs fail?
18. Why do HIM professionals need continuing education?

Departmental Employee Training and Development Plan

Every healthcare organization and every HIM department have unique training needs. The level of education and experience of the employees, the tasks they perform, and the resources available will change the focus of training efforts. As table 24.1 shows, employee development is a continuum of concepts. The content, objectives, and frequency of a training program are all dependent on the specific situation that exists in an organization.

Training and Development Model

The following **training and development model** can be applied on various levels and will help an organization's HR department or a health information manager identify and fulfill the training needs of their employee group:

1. Perform a needs analysis.
2. Set training objectives.
3. Design the curriculum.
4. Determine the location and method of delivery.
5. Pilot the program.
6. Implement the program.
7. Evaluate the effectiveness of the program.
8. Make changes as needed.
9. Provide feedback to interested groups.

The plan should be approved and supported by upper management. Implementing a training program requires a substantial investment of time, money, and personnel. Developing a curriculum based on a systematic evaluation of needs is a much wiser investment than creating a program around the latest hot topic.

Perform a Needs Analysis

The needs analysis is critical to the design of the plan. This approach typically focuses on three levels: the organization, the specific job tasks, and the individual employee. The outcome of the needs analysis is an understanding of where training is needed in the organization (entry-level, remedial, or management development), based on the firm's strategic mission and goals. In addition, a list of the tasks to be learned at each level (based on the job description and the job specification, the specific skills, and knowledge required) and an analysis of the deficiencies in knowledge and skills between the desired level and the current level of employees are completed.

This information can be obtained through observation, employee and manager interviews, surveys, tests, and task analysis of the job descriptions and job specifications.

Set Training Objectives

After the needs have been established, specific, measurable training objectives should be set. Objectives specify what the employee should be able to accomplish upon completion of the training program. These are based on the deficiencies that have been identified between the desired and current performance levels. It is important to set objectives before starting the program so that the results can be evaluated following completion of training.

Design the Curriculum

The curriculum is the subject content of the program that will be taught, including the sequence, activities, and materials. A budget needs to be prepared that identifies costs and available resources. Are there individuals within the organization who can develop and teach the program, or is it necessary to purchase an externally prepared program? Do materials such as videos or computer-based modules need to be produced? Do printed materials need to be developed and reproduced? Will the program be available over the Internet?

After these decisions are made, the curriculum must be organized into a program that supports adult learning and the stated objectives. All program elements need to be carefully prepared to ensure quality and effectiveness.

Determine the Location and Method of Delivery

Where and when the program should be delivered is an important part of the training plan. When space is available and the instructor and materials are available internally, a classroom setting might be suitable. On the other hand, when employees work over several shifts and days or in remote locations, computer-based CD-ROMs and Web-based delivery might permit the employee to more readily achieve the training objectives.

Pilot the Program

It is important to validate the program by introducing it to a test audience. When computer technology is part of the program delivery, all computer programs should be tested to make sure they work with a variety of hardware and Web browsers. Following completion of the program by a few employees, feedback should be obtained and the program revised, if necessary.

Implement the Program

The tested program now can be given to the entire audience for which it has been developed. When necessary, train-the-trainer workshops should be conducted for instructors who may not have formal training experience.

Evaluate the Effectiveness of the Program

Two issues should be addressed in evaluating training programs. The first is selecting the method of evaluation; the second is identifying the outcomes that will be measured.

Evaluation is most frequently assessed using a survey (refer to figures 24.2 and 24.5). Opinions obtained immediately after the training and again after a period of time are valuable in assessing the effectiveness of the program for both trainees and managers. In addition, pretests and posttests help identify the level of knowledge or skill that has actually been learned.

When possible, an excellent method for evaluating the training program is to conduct a controlled experiment. A control group that receives no training is compared to a group that received training. Data are obtained from both groups both before and after training. It is then possible to determine the extent to which the training program caused a change in performance in the training group.

Four outcomes can be measured in evaluating effective training programs:

- *Reaction:* What is the reaction of the trainees immediately after the program? Are they excited about what they learned?
- *Learning:* What have the trainees actually learned? Can they now use a new software program?
- *Behavior:* Have supervisors noticed a change in employee behavior? Has morale improved?
- *Results:* How does the actual level of performance compare with the established objectives? Can the employees assign codes more accurately?

Make Changes as Needed

When the results of the evaluation show less-than-expected results, it is important to determine where changes may be helpful. This may include a change in the materials, the location or time of program delivery, or the subject content. In any case, it is important to adjust. A program that is not meeting the desired objectives is costly.

Provide Feedback to Interested Groups

After tallying the results of the evaluations and making any adjustments that are needed, it is important to provide feedback to the course developers, managers and supervisors of the involved departments, and the trainees. Communication is vital to maintaining interest and support for the training program. Feedback demonstrates a desire to respond to the needs of everyone involved in this important activity.

Laws and Regulations Impacting Training

In developing training programs, healthcare organizations must recognize that special accommodations may be required to address the needs of both a culturally diverse workforce and employees with disabilities. Employers need to understand the requirements affecting training that are included under Title VII of the 1964 Civil Rights Act, the 1991 Civil Rights Act, and the ADA. If completion of a training program is part of the selection process for a particular job, the organization must be able to demonstrate that the requirements are valid and do not discriminate against, or have a negative impact on, women, minorities, or disabled individuals. For example, the vocabulary in written documents used for training should match the level required for the job, and training equipment and locations should be accessible to individuals with mobility disabilities.

In order for employers to avoid liability for harassment and discrimination acts of their employees, they must not only implement antidiscrimination policies, but also provide training to ensure that employees understand their rights and responsibilities. The courts interpret this as exercising reasonable care to prevent harassment. The training should cover all types of harassment, be provided for all employees shortly after they are hired and again periodically, be of substantial length, and permit the employee to repeat as necessary until competence is demonstrated.

Inadequate training exposes employers to potential liability for negligent training if they fail to train adequately and an employee harms a third party.

OSHA was established by the federal government to ensure safe working conditions. Among its many requirements is training to reduce unsafe acts. Hospitals are required to train employees in fire safety and other job-related safety measures. The training must be provided in the worker's native language (other than English, if necessary) and the worker must be able to demonstrate proficiency following the training.

The Allied Health Reinvestment Act of 2005 encourages individuals to seek and complete high-quality allied health education and training by providing funding for their studies. Grants are provided to healthcare organizations for advertising campaigns and for partnerships between healthcare facilities and allied health educational programs. Scholarships may be given to applicants who agree to serve two years in a rural or other medically underserved area with allied health personnel shortages.

The ADA requires employers to provide reasonable accommodations for physical or mental limitations with regard to many employment-related functions, including training. For example, this would require that accommodations be made to computer-based training to provide accessibility through voice recognition or screen readers, if necessary. The World Wide Web Consortium's Web Accessibility Initiative publishes information about ADA Compliance for Web sites. Section 508 of the Rehabilitation Act of 1973 provides accessibility standards for electronic and information technology.

Finally, the Joint Commission requires staff orientation and continuing education to meet requirements of a particular position, and defines several topics for training, including cultural diversity sensitivity.

Check Your Understanding 24.5

Instructions: Answer the following questions on a separate piece of paper.

1. What are the steps in a typical training and development plan?
2. What are three outcomes of a needs analysis?
3. What is the relationship between setting objectives and evaluating a training program?
4. What are three items to consider in designing a training program?
5. What are four outcomes that should be measured in program evaluation?
6. Discuss two laws that affect training programs and describe their impact.

Real-World Case

The employees of the HIM department in Midwest Community Hospital, a 100-bed facility located in the Chicago suburbs, have just returned from a meeting. Their director, Gary Smith, announced that the hospital was recently acquired by a large integrated delivery system, Hometown Health Systems. Hometown Health Systems has just implemented an electronic health record system and intends to ensure that the HIM department employees receive the necessary training to be prepared to assume their new e-HIM roles. Gary has been with the organization for 30 years and has indicated his intention to retire when the facilities merge, which is scheduled to occur in about six months. Hometown's corporate director of health information systems, Jane Winters, will assume responsibility for managing the department, with an assistant director to be appointed at Midwest who will assume day-to-day supervisory responsibilities.

Jane knows that three employees at Midwest might be qualified to assume the position and would like to fill it through promotion. All three candidates have positive and negative factors, some of which could be remedied with training. Gary and Jane plan to discuss the best approach to selecting the new supervisor and Gary has been asked to assist in the process by preparing the selected employee for the transition. After returning from the meeting, Gary begins to review the three employees in his mind.

Bob has worked in the ROI area of the department for three years and recently obtained his RHIT credential after attending a local community college program. He is enthusiastic about working in the department and has frequently suggested new procedures, which has led to some friction with Gary, whose motto is "If it ain't broke, don't fix it!" Bob has been frustrated by the lack of available technology in the HIM department. Now that he has the credential, he has mentioned that he may want to begin looking elsewhere if his ideas are not appreciated at Midwest.

Sherry is a coder who has worked at Midwest for about one year. She began her employment at the hospital in the outpatient registration area. Six months after completing AHIMA's online coding program, she assumed the coding position in the HIM department. She is a single parent who is a self-proclaimed workaholic. In her spare time, she works at home as a coder for a physician's office to increase her income.

Linda currently works as the lead file clerk in the department. Of the three employees, she is the only one with supervisory experience, although she has had no formal management training. Gary had promoted her to the lead position because of her excellent attendance record and seniority. However, her employees have complained frequently to Gary that she "takes over" and corrects their work without explaining what they did wrong. Gary also knows that she does not feel comfortable disciplining employees and that she finds doing the job herself easier than working with the employee responsible for the job.

Gary will meet next Monday with Jane and is still unsure how to solve this dilemma.

Summary

Employees are the healthcare institution's most valuable asset. The decreasing availability of qualified employees means that responsibility for developing staff increasingly rests with the employer. Workforce development and retention must become part of the institution's strategic plan.

Training and development needs can be viewed on a continuum of five conceptual areas: orientation, training, in-service education, continuing education, and career development. Each healthcare organization's training program must be able to adapt to the different needs of its employees.

New employees need to be introduced to the rules and culture of the organization, the department, and the specific job duties they will be performing. This function is typically performed through a formal orientation program that provides employees with information regarding organizational policies and procedures, benefits, safety regulations, and an introduction to the work area. Finally, employees begin learning the duties and responsibilities of the specific jobs they will be performing. Preparing staff to carry out their specific job tasks should be an ongoing effort. Methods used to accomplish this include on-the-job-training, job rotation, and cross-training.

In-service education builds on basic skills provided during orientation and on-the-job training. It also is used when departments are restructured or when external requirements require employees to update their competency. This training needs to be available on a continuous basis and may be conducted by department managers in formal training sessions or through self-directed learning methods. AHIMA's e-HIM initiative, to promote the migration from paper to an electronic health information infrastructure, will require the training of HIM professionals in new competencies needed to fulfill future roles.

Future HIM professionals also will need training in diversity sensitivity and team building skills as they prepare to carry out the e-HIM vision.

The techniques used to deliver training should be matched with the purpose of the training, the trainee's level of education and experience, location, and budget. Self-directed learning permits students to determine the pace of the learning. A number of DVDs or CD-ROMs provide computer-based training for this purpose. Classroom lectures are useful for training large numbers of employees on factual knowledge in a short time period. E-learning methods overcome a number of obstacles of traditional training methods and provide anytime, anywhere instruction in a cost-effective mode. Some of these methods include electronic performance support systems, live teleconferencing, and synchronous or asynchronous Web-based courses including social networks and virtual worlds.

Because training programs require a considerable investment of both time and money, the organization should encourage commitment to long-term employment. An important factor in maintaining job satisfaction is recognition by the company of employee needs for work–life balance. Alternative staffing arrangements permit employees to vary work hours and locations while still satisfying the organization's need for productivity. Options include flextime programs, job sharing, and telecommuting. For those who wish to work on a limited basis or for employers who cannot find qualified staff, outsourcing may be an option. Using employees based overseas is a viable, cost-effective option for jobs with little face-to-face contact and high information content, including transcription, coding, and insurance claims processing. Internet technologies have created solutions to issues related to training these employees, as well as ensuring the security of information transfer.

Another factor that enhances employee job satisfaction is the opportunity for personal growth. Employees should be empowered with the tools and resources to solve problems themselves. Successful managers delegate effectively. Effective delegation leads to a more efficient and productive department and mutually benefits the manager, the employee, and the institution.

Employees just beginning their careers may benefit from mentoring. Mentors advise and teach specific job and interpersonal skills. Coaching is a process that begins in orientation and continues throughout the employee's time with the organization. Coaches act as role models, provide praise and constructive feedback, and help with routine work when needed.

Promotion can be a powerful incentive for employees when tied to career development programs. It should be awarded on competence, not seniority, and the criteria should be based on objective standards. Incentive programs that reward effort with something the employee values, such as pay, vacations, or other recognition, also may help reduce turnover and improve productivity.

Employees who hold professional credentials must complete CE requirements to remain current in their knowledge of the profession as it moves forward with its e-HIM vision. Continued skill development should be an important requirement for all HIM employees.

Because the training needs of every department are unique, it is important to develop a formal training and development plan. The plan begins with a needs analysis and the establishment of measurable objectives. A curriculum is then designed to meet those needs.

A successful and effective plan for employee training and development requires a substantial investment of time, money, and personnel. It should be approved and supported by upper management and based on a systematic evaluation of needs.

References

AHIMA, CHIA, AAMT, MTIA. 2006 (May 4). Joint Position Statement issued. Regulation of Health Information Processing in an Outsourcing Environment.

AHIMA e-HIM Task Force. 2003 (Aug. 15). Vision of the e-HIM future: A report from the AHIMA e-HIM Task Force. Supplement to *Journal of AHIMA.*

American Society for Training and Development.2008. http://www.astd.org.

Bagshaw.M. 2004. Is diversity divisive? A positive training approach. 2004. In *Training for Diversity, Industrial and Commercial Training* 36(4), 153–157. Emerald Group Publishing Ltd. http://site.ebrary.com/lib/uic. Document ID: 10058614.

Dessler, G. 2007. *Human Resources Management.* 11th ed. Upper Saddle River, NJ: Pearson Prentice-Hall.

Dougherty, M. and R. Scichilone. 2002. Practice brief: Establishing a telecommuting or home-based employee program. *Journal of AHIMA* 73(7):72A–L.

Fallon, L. and C. McConnell. 2007. *Human Resource Management in Healthcare.* Sudbury, MA: Jones and Bartlett.

Fottler, H., S. Hernandez, and C. Joiner, eds. 1998. *Essentials of Human Resource Management in Health Service Organizations.* Albany, NY: Delmar.

Gale, S. 2008. Dial M for mobile learning .*Workforce Management Magazine*. http://www.workforce.com/archive/feature/25/56/00/index_printer.php.

Gale, S. 2008. Do-it-yourself e-learning .*Workforce Management Magazine*. http://www.workforce.com/section/11/feature/25/53/42/index_printer.html.

Heiphetz, A. and S. Liverman. 2008. Using robotic avatars in Second Life simulations and training. http://www.ahg.com.

Johnson, M. 2004 (Summer). Harassment and Discrimination Prevention Training: What the Law Requires. *Labor Law Journal* 55(2), 119–129. ABI/INFORM Global database. Document ID: 695028321.

Keeling, B. and N. Kallaus. 1996. *Administrative Office Management.* 11th ed. Cincinnati, OH: South-Western.

Levenburg, N. and H. Major. 1998. Distance learning: Implications for higher education in the 21st century. Originally published in *The Technology Source.* http://www.technologysource.org/article/distance_learning__implications_for_higher_education_in_the_21st_century.

Mondy, R. and R. Noe. 2005. *Human Resource Management.* 9th ed. Upper Saddle River, NJ: Pearson Prentice Hall.

O'Connor, B.N., M. Bronner, and C. Delaney. 2002. *Training for Organizations.* 2nd ed. Cincinnati, OH: South-Western.

Odgers, P. and B. Keeling. 2000. *Administrative Office Management.* 12th ed. Cincinnati, OH: South-Western.

O'Neal.H. and R. Perez. 2006. *Web-based Learning Theory, Research and Practice.* Mahwah, N.J.: Lawrence Erlbaum Associates, Inc.

Schermerhorn, J. 2005. *Management.* 8th ed. New York: John Wiley & Sons.

U.S. Department of Education. 2001 (modified 8/31/2007). Requirements for accessible electronic and information technology (E&IT) design. http://www.ed.gov/print/fund/contract/apply/clibrary/software.html.

Workforce Management Magazine. 2001. Pros and cons of training modes. http://www.workforce.com/archive/article/22/13/14.php.

World Wide Web Consortium's Web Accessibility Initiative. http://www.w3c.org/WAI.

Zachary, M. 2004. Labor law for supervisors: training for the disabled. *Supervision* 65(5), 23–26. http://www.ABI/INFORM Global database. Document ID: 628502271.

Chapter 25
Financial Management

Nadinia Davis, MBA, CIA, CPA, RHIA, FAHIMA

Learning Objectives

- Read, understand, and use balance sheets and income statements
- Explain the difference between financial accounting and managerial accounting
- Recognize the importance of accounting to nonfinancial managers
- Calculate and identify the components of basic financial ratios
- Explain the importance of internal controls and their role in financial management
- Describe the components of operational and capital budgets
- Discuss the impact of claims processing and reimbursement on financial statements
- Describe the financial management functions of HIM professionals

Key Terms

Accounting
Accounting rate of return
Accounts payable
Accounts receivable
Accrue
Acid-test ratio
Activity-based budget
Asset
Balance sheet
Bill hold
Budget cycle
Buildings
Capital budget
Cash
Charge description master (CDM)
Claims processing
Conceptual framework of accounting
Conservatism
Consistency
Contra-account
Corporation
Corrective controls
Cost accounting
Cost justification
Cost report
Credits
Current ratio
Debits
Debt ratio
Debt service
Depreciation
Detective controls
Direct costs
Direct method of cost allocation
Discharged, no final bill (DNFB)
Disclosure
Double distribution
Entity
Equipment
Equity
Expenses
Favorable variance
Financial Accounting Standards Board (FASB)
Financial data
Financial transaction
Fiscal year
Fixed budget
Fixed costs
Flexible budget
Forecasting
For-profit organizations
Fund balance
General ledger
Generally accepted accounting principles (GAAP)
Generally accepted auditing standards (GAAS)
Going concern
Government Accounting Standards Board (GASB)
Historical cost
Income statement
Indirect costs
Interim period
Internal controls
Internal rate of return (IRR)
Inventory
Journal entry
Liabilities
Liquidity
Long-term assets
Managerial accounting
Matching
Materiality
Mortgage
Net assets
Net income
Net loss
Net present value
Not-for-profit organizations
Operational budget
Overhead costs
Owner's equity
Partnership
Payback period
Permanent budget variance
Preventive controls
Profitability index
Public Company Accounting Oversight Board (PCAOB)
Purchase order
Ratio analysis
Reliability
Request for proposal (RFP)
Retained earnings
Return on equity (ROE)
Return on investment (ROI)
Revenue
Revenue Principle
Securities and Exchange Commission (SEC)
Simultaneous equations method
Sole proprietorship
Stable monetary unit
Statement
Statement of cash flow
Statement of retained earnings
Statement of stockholder's equity
Step-down allocation
Temporary budget variance
Time period
Unallocated reserves
Unfavorable variance
Variable costs
Variance
Variance analysis
Zero-based budget

A physician treats a patient. A hospital admits a woman in labor. A professional association offers continuing education for its members. All these are examples of organizations providing services for which they receive compensation. How organizations arrange to provide those services, determine compensation, and handle the flow of funds that these activities both require and generate is guided by financial management.

This chapter focuses on the concepts and tools associated with planning and controlling the financial resources required to operate a department or a work unit. It presents operations, labor, and capital budgeting processes and techniques; reviews organizational and departmental financial performance measures; and explores techniques for improving financial performance at the departmental level. Finally, the chapter acquaints readers with the language of financial and managerial accounting so as to enhance their understanding of the role of the HIM professional as a manager.

Healthcare Financial Management

The process of financial management involves various players within the organization's financial arena. Table 25.1 lists and describes the roles of the financial personnel who work in hospitals. However, healthcare financial management also involves a number of players outside the financial arena. For example, health information management (HIM) professionals are involved with reimbursement through the coding function. Record retention and release of information activities help support claims auditing and claims denial appeals. HIM professionals play an important role in documentation improvement activities, including clinical training to support medical necessity. Figure 25.1 illustrates the potential relationship between HIM and the financial personnel in a hospital.

HIM professionals are familiar with **financial data** as one of the components of a health record: the data related to payers and billing. To financial managers, financial data are the individual elements of organizational financial transactions. (The term *financial* refers to money and, as is discussed later, money is the measurement of financial transactions.) A **financial transaction** is the exchange of goods or services for payment or the promise of payment. Financial data are compiled into informational reports for users. The degree of detail that users require depends on their needs and is largely influenced by the relationship of the user to the originator of the transaction.

Financial transactions that originate at the department level require review by that department. For example, the pharmacy department will review its drug transactions; and the HIM department will review its purchases of supplies and services. On the administrative level, however, such detail is not usually required. Instead, informative summaries are often more useful. For example, an organization administrator does not usually need to know the number of cases of copier paper purchased in each department. Instead, he or she would look at the total office supply purchases and evaluate whether they were at appropriate and expected levels. Additional detail or explanation would not be required unless the purchases were unusual. The accumulation and reporting of financial data within an organization is an accounting function.

Accounting

Accounting is an activity as well as a profession. Just as there are many HIM roles and functions, so are there diverse accounting roles and functions. The accounting activity involves the collection, recording, and reporting of financial data. Accountants are both the individuals who perform these activities and many of those who use the reported data. Accounting is important because it is the language that organizations use to communicate with each other to effect transactions, determine investment strategies, and evaluate performance.

The **conceptual framework of accounting** underlies all accounting activity and is based on the following ideas:

- The benefits of the financial data should exceed the costs of obtaining them.
- The data must be understandable.
- The data must be useful for decision making. In other words, the data must be relevant, reliable, and comparable.

Although some of these requirements are similar to general data quality concerns, they are discussed specifically with financial data in mind.

Accounting Concepts and Principles

Concepts and principles that define the parameters of accounting activity are briefly discussed here and summarized in figure 25.2.

Concepts

An **entity** is a person or organization, such as a corporation or professional association. A business owner, for example, must not commingle business and personal data. This concept can be very difficult for small business owners, who may not understand why business receipts are not the same as personal income. It can be equally difficult for large corporations that own many different companies.

When analysis of an entity's financial data shows that the organization can continue to operate for the foreseeable future, the organization is considered a **going concern**. Assuming that a business is going to continue, projections of future activities can be made based on historical trends and assumptions about future conditions. The concept of going concern also places constraints on the organization to maintain sufficient financial and other resources to ensure future stability and growth.

Table 25.1. Financial personnel and their roles in a hospital

Position	Typical or Minimum Background	Financial Roles
Board of directors or trustees	Depends on the needs of the facility	Ultimate responsibility for the fiscal integrity of the organization
Chief executive officer (CEO)	Generally, master's-prepared in public administration, hospital administration, or business administration; occasionally, clinical background	Overall responsibility for administration of the organization
Chief financial officer (CFO)	Certified public accountant (CPA) or certified management accountant (CMA)	Overall responsibility for related departments, including patient accounts, internal auditing, and often HIM
Controller or accounting manager	CPA	Oversees accounting and cash disbursement, including payroll
Patient accounts manager	Bachelor's degree	Oversees claims processing

Figure 25.1. Organization of the non-physician side of the hospital

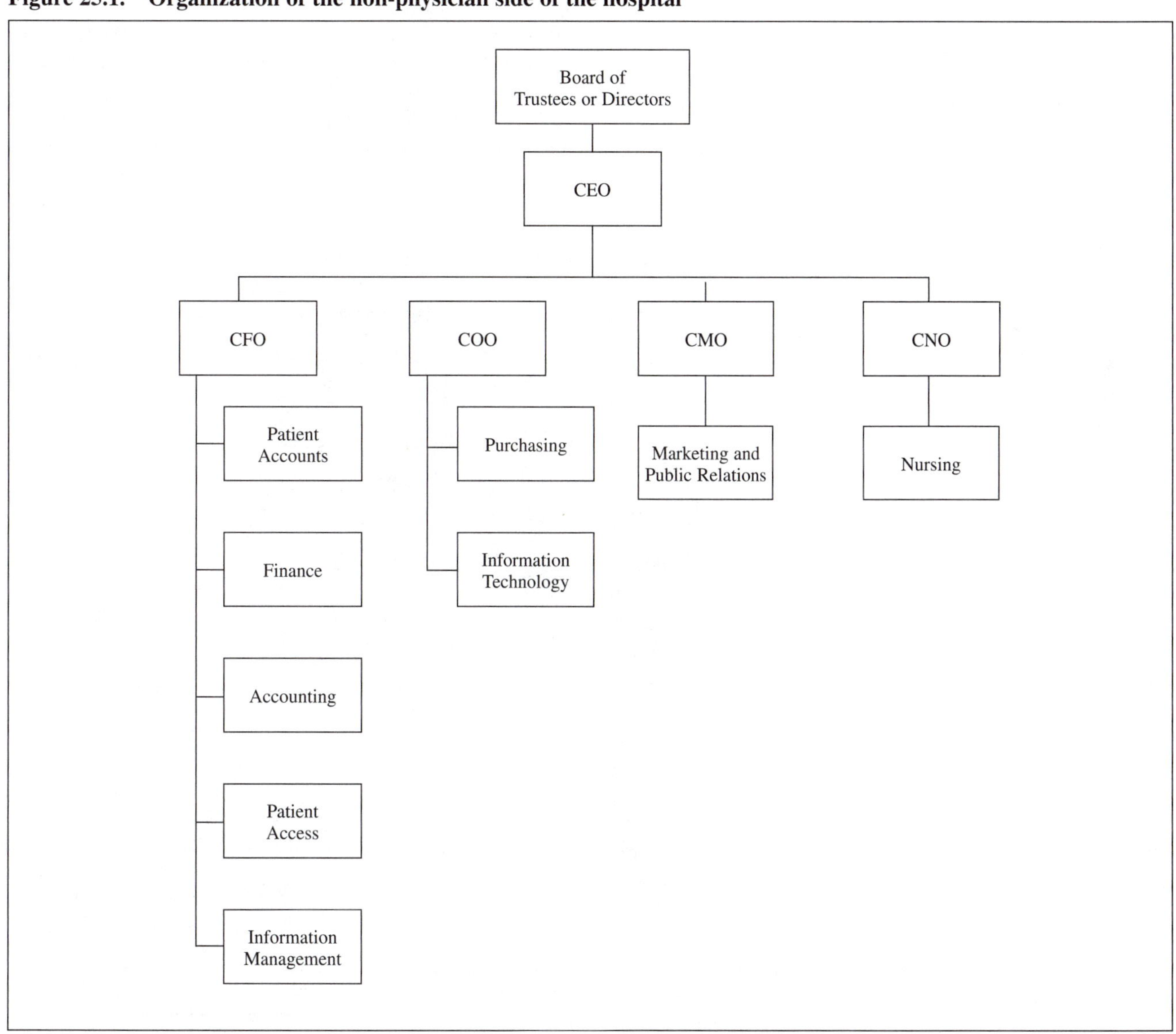

Figure 25.2. Basic accounting concepts and principles

Basic Accounting Concepts

- *Entity:* The financial data of different entities are kept separate.
- *Going concern:* Organizations are assumed to continue indefinitely, unless otherwise stated.
- *Stable monetary unit:* Money is the measurement of financial transactions.
- *Time period:* Financial data represent a specified time period.
- *Conservatism:* Resources must not be overstated, and liabilities must not be understated.
- *Materiality:* The financial data collected by an organization are relevant to its goals and objectives.

Basic Accounting Principles

- *Reliability:* Amounts represent the transactions that occurred.
- *Cost:* Transactions are recorded at historical cost.
- *Revenue:* In order to record revenue, it must be earned and measurable.
- *Matching:* Expenses are recorded in the same period as the related revenue.
- *Consistency:* When an accounting rule is followed, all subsequent periods must reflect the same rule.
- *Disclosure:* Financial reports must be accompanied by helpful explanations, when necessary.

All of an entity's transactions must be quantified using a standard measurement or **stable monetary unit**. In the United States, financial transactions are recorded in U.S. dollars and cents.

Financial data represent transactions during a specified period of time: hour, day, week, month, quarter, year, and so on. The specific **time period** depends on the use of the data. The **fiscal year** (also called the financial year) is defined by the tax year. Individuals generally have a tax year that coincides with the calendar year. Organizations, on the other hand, use fiscal years that correspond to their business needs, usually their business cycle, which represents the total activities of the organization. For example, the U.S. government's fiscal year ends September 30.

For financial reporting purposes, a fiscal year is divided into quarters (three-month periods) and months. Because the months generally end on the last calendar day, the quarters can be of slightly different duration. For example, the first quarter of a fiscal year that begins April 1 includes April, May, and June: 91 days. The second quarter of that same fiscal year includes July, August, and September: 92 days. Figure 25.3 illustrates the extent of the difference in a nonleap year. Over time, it is common to compare similar quarters from year to year, particularly when the business cycle has predictable peaks and valleys.

Not all financial data represent completed transactions within the period represented. Sometimes estimates are involved, or transactions are completed between periods. When amounts are estimated, efforts must be made to ensure that their use does not misrepresent the actual financial transaction. Therefore, financial data must comply with **conservatism** in that they fairly represent the financial results of the period and do not overstate or understate information in a significant (material) way.

Materiality refers to the thresholds below which items are not considered significant for reporting purposes. These thresholds may be a dollar value or a percentage of a dollar value. To a $100,000 professional association with $100,000 in income, $10,000 is a significant (material) amount. To a $100 billion oil company, $10,000 is not material. This issue arises when determining the significance of errors, potential liabilities, and the necessity for disclosures. Items that are considered immaterial individually may, when added to other immaterial items, be of concern on this basis.

Principles

Accounting principles support the quality of financial data. Because they are data, financial data must possess the same data quality characteristics, such as timeliness and validity, as any other type of data. In financial data, **reliability** refers to whether the data actually represent what occurred and are free of material error both in the current period and over time. Transactions are recorded at their **historical cost** measured at the time of the transaction. For some transactions, such as the purchase of equipment or investment in marketable securities, there may be a change in the actual or perceived value of the underlying asset or liability. In those cases, adjustments or **disclosures** are made when reporting the financial data. The **Revenue Principle** states that earnings as a result of activities and investments may only be recognized when they have been earned, can be measured,

Figure 25.3. Impact of days in the month on fiscal quarter and semi-annual reporting (nonleap year)

Month	# of Days	Quarter	# of Days	Half	# of Days
January	31				
February	28				
March	31	Quarter I	90		
April	30				
May	31				
June	30	Quarter II	91	First Half	181
July	31				
August	31				
September	30	Quarter III	92		
October	31				
November	30				
December	31	Quarter IV	92	Second Half	184

and have a reasonable expectation of being collected. For an organization to generate **revenue**, it must incur expenses, for example, payroll, rent, travel, and raw materials. Whenever possible, expenses are recorded in the same period as the associated revenue, thereby **matching** the expenses and revenues. Some accounting rules include variations. The principle of **consistency** requires that the method not change over the life of the asset. Thus, the financial data are prepared in the same way from one period to the next. In fact, organizations sometimes change their choices. Consistency then requires that financial data be restated to show the effect of the change applied to previous periods. Interestingly, some allowed financial accounting rules differ from tax accounting rules, producing different results. Sometimes the financial data alone do not provide enough information for users of the data to make informed decisions. The impact of a building fire, a potential or ongoing lawsuit, or an expiring collective bargaining agreement cannot be reflected in the financial data when no financial transaction has occurred. Therefore, notes or disclosures that help the user to make informed decisions must accompany all financial reports.

Authorities

Just as clinical data are organized and reported in predetermined formats for ease of communication, financial data also are organized and reported in specific ways. Theoretically, organizations can design their own accounting systems and reporting mechanisms. Internally, this is often the case, as will be seen with budgeting. However, organizations that want to borrow funds or attract investors must follow generally accepted rules that apply to their industry and accounting in general. Four major sources of accounting and reporting rules apply to healthcare organizations: the Financial Accounting Standards Board (FASB), the Securities and Exchange Commission (SEC), the Centers for Medicare and Medicaid Services (CMS), and the Internal Revenue Service (IRS).

Financial Accounting Standards Board

The **Financial Accounting Standards Board** (FASB) is an independent organization that sets accounting standards for businesses in the private sector. Its counterpart, the **Government Accounting Standards Board** (GASB), sets standards for accounting for government entities. The FASB promulgates the rules by which financial data are compiled, reported, reviewed, and audited. These rules, which include the conceptual framework, are referred to as **generally accepted accounting principles** (GAAP) and **generally accepted auditing standards** (GAAS).

Securities and Exchange Commission

The **Securities and Exchange Commission** (SEC) is a federal agency that regulates public and some private transactions involving the ownership and debt of organizations. The SEC sets standards regarding reporting financial data, disclosures, timing, marketing, and execution of these transactions. Public transactions take place through an exchange, such as the New York Stock Exchange (NYSE) or the National Association of Securities Dealers Automated Quotation System (NASDAQ). Organizations whose ownership interests (stocks) are traded on these exchanges are called public companies.

Internal Revenue Service

The tax status of an organization influences its administration. The IRS regulates and collects federal taxes. Healthcare organizations fall into one of two major tax categories: for-profit and not-for-profit. The primary differences between for-profit and not-for-profit organizations are related to the level of accountability and the distribution of profits. Within these categories are several legal structures, such as sole proprietorship, partnership, and corporation. A summary of legal structures is provided in table 25.2. The primary differences between for-profit and not-for-profit organizations are related to the level of accountability and the distribution of profits.

Public Company Accounting Oversight Board

Historically, the accounting profession has been largely self-regulated. The FASB and GASB, although technically independent, have strong ties to the profession. Although IRS and SEC standards and regulations constrained the specific representation of financial activities, the accounting profession was free to accomplish its reporting and other activities without government intervention. However, that changed in 2002. The federal government responded to the collapse of ENRON, WorldCom, and others with the Sarbanes-Oxley Act, which restricted the professional services of independent auditors of public companies and, among other things, created the **Public Company Accounting Oversight Board** (PCAOB). As of this writing, the PCAOB has issued five standards and 10 rules pertaining to auditing, independence, ethics, and technical issues (Standards and Related Rules 2008). The impact of Sarbanes-Oxley has been significant with respect to the way that public accountants do business; however, the overall impact of the PCAOB remains to be seen.

Centers for Medicare and Medicaid Services

CMS (formerly called the Health Care Financing Administration [HCFA]) is the federal agency that administers the

Table 25.2. Common legal structures of non-governmental organizations

Structure	Description	Healthcare Examples
Sole proprietorship	One owner; all profits are owner's personal income	Solo practitioners
Partnership	Two or more owners; all profits are owners' personal income	Physician group practices
Corporation	One or many owners; profits may be either retained or distributed as dividends. Dividends are income to the owners. May be public or private. "Owners" may be individuals, other organizations, or an interest group.	Hospitals, insurance companies

Medicare program and the federal portion of the Medicaid program. The federal government is the largest single payer of healthcare expenses in the United States. Although CMS does not set accounting rules, it enforces the federal regulations regarding the reimbursement for Medicare and the federal portion of the Medicaid program and sets standards for the documentation and reporting of transactions related to such reimbursement. Since CMS requires significant reporting from participant organizations, its influence on the financial activities and data collection should not be underestimated.

Financial Organization

The way an entity organizes itself depends on its financing, its leadership, and its tax status. The three basic forms of business organization are the sole proprietorship, the partnership, and the corporation. Other organizational entities, such as trusts, and variations such as Limited Liability Corporations (LLCs) are beyond the scope of this discussion.

- **Sole proprietor:** An independent coding consultant who operates from home and has no employees may choose to operate as a sole proprietor. The owner, or proprietor, is the leader of the organization and is responsible for all aspects of the business. Income from the business flows through the owner's individual tax return. If the consultant's business expands, employees or subcontractors can be added without changing the organizational structure. Many physicians are solo practitioners and therefore sole proprietors.
- **Partnership:** Two or more consultants who want to be in business together may choose a partnership structure. Partners share in the responsibility for the business, and income still flows through the individuals' tax returns. Partners do not need to share equally in the financial or other business responsibilities. A partnership agreement details the contractual arrangement. Because a partnership is a separate legal and accounting entity from the individuals, a tax identification number is required for the partnership, and the partnership may be required to file its own tax returns detailing the income allocated to each partner. Partnerships survive as entities only so long as the partners remain together. A change in ownership dissolves the original partnership and a new one must be created.
- **Corporation:** A corporation is a legal entity that exists separately from its owner(s). Corporations pay their own taxes and have their own legal rights and responsibilities. In fact, the owner(s) of the corporation may have nothing to do with its leadership or day-to-day operations. A corporation is typically governed by a board of directors or trustees, and the day-to-day operations are led by one or more administrators who report to the board. The corporation's income after taxes may or may not be distributed in whole or in part to the owner(s). This after-tax distribution is a dividend and is taxable income to the owner(s). This two-tiered taxation, on the corporation and then again on the distributed dividend, is referred to as "double taxation" and may make this structure less attractive to individuals.

The underlying purpose of the organization drives another consideration in the financial organization of the business. Is the purpose of the business to generate income for the owners, or is there a more altruistic foundation? The answer to this question helps to define the tax status the organization will be able to obtain.

For-Profit Organizations

For-profit organizations may be sole proprietorships, partnerships, or corporations. In this context, "profits" are the funds remaining after all current obligations have been met, including taxes. Inherently, the underlying goal of for-profit organizations is to increase the wealth of the owners. Increase in wealth can be accomplished through the generation of profits to be distributed to the owners, or by increasing the value of the organization so that the owners' investment is more valuable. The leadership of the organization may distribute the profits to the owners or otherwise invest them as they see fit. For-profit organizations may be privately or publicly owned.

Private ownership may be by an individual, a group of individuals, or an organization. Physician practices, urgent care centers, and freestanding ancillary care organizations are often privately owned. The distribution of profits from a privately owned organization is at the discretion of the owners or as defined by contract among owners.

Public ownership means that the ownership interest in the organization may be bought and sold in the financial marketplace. For example, Tenet Healthcase Corporation (THC) is a publicly held organization with hospitals in numerous states. Its stock is traded on the NYSE under the symbol *THC*. A publicly held organization's board of directors determines the distribution of profits. Boards are constrained in these determinations by contractual obligations, such as mortgage contracts and preferred stock obligations, stockholder expectations, and strategic organizational goals.

Not-for-Profit Organizations

Not-for-profit organizations are not owned but, instead, are held in trust for the benefit of the communities they serve. Many hospitals fall into this tax category. Other not-for-profit organizations include professional associations such as the American Health Information Management Association (AHIMA), charitable organizations such as the American Red Cross, and educational foundations, such as the Foundation on Research and Education (FORE). The IRS defines numerous types of not-for-profit organizations, some of which are summarized in table 25.3. The two categories of not-for-profit organizations discussed here are: 501(c)(6) and 501(c)(3).

501(c)(6)

Most professional associations are organized under 501(c)(6), which gives them some federal tax benefits and the

Table 25.3. Common not-for-profit tax status

Not-for-Profit	Description	Healthcare Examples
501(c)(3)	Largely exempt from taxes, donations to these organizations can be tax-deductible. Underlying purpose of the organization must be charitable or educational.	Charities, AHIMA's Foundation on Research and Education (FORE)
501(c)(6)	Partially exempt from taxes. May lobby and sell goods and services. Underlying purpose must benefit the interest group or public.	Professional associations, some hospitals
501(c)(4)	Business leagues	N/A
501(c)(14)	Credit unions	N/A
501(c)(19)	Veterans' organizations	N/A

freedom to engage in some activities unrelated to their organizational purpose. For example, organizations under 501(c)(6) may lobby and sell goods and services but are largely involved in activities that benefit their major interest group, which may be defined as paid membership. 501(c)(6) organizations may be subject to state sales tax, both as purchaser and seller. AHIMA and most of its component state associations are 501(c)(6) organizations.

501(c)(3)

On the other hand, 501(c)(3) organizations are largely exempt from federal taxes but must confine their activities to the public benefit. Donations to 501(c)(3) organizations are generally tax deductible (for the donor) to the extent that no goods or services have been received in return. For that reason, charities are generally 501(c)(3) organizations and many 501(c)(6) organizations have charitable components that are separately incorporated. For example, AHIMA is a 501(c)(6) organization that has a 501(c)(3) component, FORE. 501(c)(3) organizations may also be exempt from state sales tax under certain circumstances.

Tax Status Issues

It is important to understand the underlying tax status of an organization because tax status affects the organization's business decision making and long-term strategies. Undistributed profits from a for-profit organization may stay in the business and be available for investment or future distribution. There is no necessity to identify the future use for these funds, although stockholders may ultimately press for distribution when undistributed profits appear excessive. Occasionally, portions of undistributed profits are held in reserve for specific uses.

On the other hand, profits from a not-for-profit organization stay in the business. Because all such profits must be used for the benefit of the community the organization serves, the future use of these profits should be clearly defined. Excessive unrelated business income or high unrestricted reserves (effectively, too much savings) may result in the loss of not-for-profit status. For further information about tax exemptions of organizations, see IRS Publication 557 (IRS 2008).

Sources of Financial Data

Just as a health record is constructed from the data collected, financial records are also composed of data. Health records are built from medical decision making; financial records originate with financial decision making, the smallest component of which is the transaction.

Transactions

Virtually every financial transaction consists of three fundamental steps:

1. Goods or services are provided.
2. A transaction is recorded.
3. Compensation is exchanged.

Each step may require a number of additional steps, depending on the service and the industry. In addition, the steps are not always performed in the same order. Independent contractors that perform hospital coding represent a simple example. The contractor codes the charts, submits an invoice, and receives a check from the hospital. In this case, four specific steps may be needed to support the transaction: keeping a log to track the charts that have been coded, preparing an invoice to bill the hospital, keeping a list of the invoices sent, and checking the invoices off when they are received.

In a hospital, multiple individuals and departments perform services and provide administrative support for financial transactions. Four areas are of particular concern in the context of this discussion: clinical services, patient accounts, health information management, and administration.

Clinical Services

Just as contract coders keep track of the records they have coded, so do clinical, or patient care, services providers keep track of the services they perform. The documents of original entry or source documents enable the healthcare facility to verify that the services were provided and to communicate to supporting departments that a transaction has been initiated. The source document includes two elements: the clinical documentation and the billing documentation.

Clinical documentation is a record of who has seen the patient and why and what tests or treatments were performed, in other words, everything clinically relevant that happened to the patient during his or her interaction with the organization.

Along with the recording of clinical documentation is the capture of the associated billing information. Regardless of the reimbursement system (discussed in chapter 14), the organization must capture the billable event in such a way that the financial transaction can be completed. Therefore, when a medication is administered to a patient, the clinical record reflects the medication, dosage, time, date and route of administration, and the clinical personnel who administered it. At the same time, the charge for the drug must be communicated to patient accounts. This detailed tracking of billable events also supports the cost accounting function, which is discussed later in this chapter.

Patient Accounts

The patient accounts department is responsible for collecting recorded transactions, billing the payer (claim), and ensuring the correct receipt of reimbursement. This department depends on the reliable recording of services. This means that the capture of billing information must be timely and accurate in order to complete the financial transaction efficiently. In addition to the clinical support staff and departments, the patient accounts department relies on the HIM department for coded data.

Health Information Management

The HIM department is responsible for, among other things, identifying and recording the appropriate clinical codes to describe the patient's interaction with the organization. (Refer to chapters 4 and 5.) In some cases, this coding drives the reimbursement to the facility; in other cases, it is used to support the billing.

Increasingly, the reimbursement requirements mandated by CMS and other plans and payers are commingling clinical data with the coding data that describe them. For example, the Minimum Data Set (MDS) used in long-term care combines the clinical data with the codes. The HIM department should be responsible for assigning or ensuring the accuracy of the codes.

In addition to the coding activity, the HIM department is responsible for aggregating and maintaining the documentation that supports the reimbursement.

Administration

Financial transactions occur throughout the facility. Employees are paid, equipment and supplies are purchased, and departments perform services for each other. The finance department accumulates and analyzes all of the financial data. Ultimately, the entire management team participates in the review and analysis of financial data.

Uses of Financial Data

Financial data are generated virtually everywhere in a healthcare facility. Managerial and supervisory personnel use these data for four key purposes: to track reimbursement, to control costs, to plan future activities, and to forecast results.

Reimbursement

Healthcare facilities are service organizations that derive almost all their income from clinical activities. Therefore, a key use of financial data is to track reimbursement and ensure that the desired amount of profit is generated. In the current industry environment, where payers often dictate the amount of reimbursement, the provider is increasingly unable to control pricing as a method of managing desired profit. Therefore, the cost of providing services has become the controllable factor.

Control

Controlling costs is best done at the departmental level. For example, the CEO of a hospital does not shop around for the best price on copier paper, and the CFO does not monitor employee productivity in the food services department. Each department is charged with responsibility for ensuring prudent management of financial and other resources. Departments are given this charge through the budget process, which is one of the outcomes of administrative planning.

Planning

Administrative planning reflects the organization's mission. From that mission, goals and objectives are derived that help move the organization toward achieving its mission. Financial data are used to analyze trends, develop budgets, and plan for the future. Planning cannot be accomplished by using historical data alone because the industry changes, sometimes rapidly. Therefore, the administration must forecast future scenarios.

Forecasting

Forecasting is the prediction of future behavior based on historical data as well as environmental scans. It can be as simple as predicting the profits of an organization on the basis of anticipated changes in reimbursement. It also can involve complicated predictions of consumer behavior based on market research and news reports.

Check Your Understanding 25.1

Instructions: Answer the following questions on a separate piece of paper.

1. If an insurance company representative were to contact the HIM department about a claims audit, to which financial personnel should he or she be directed and why?
2. Given that DRG payments are predetermined, why would a hospital not record revenue on the basis of the working DRG?
3. Big Medical Center earned a lot more revenue than expected this year but does not expect to earn as much next year. To make the financial reports more consistent, a junior accountant suggests that the hospital record some of next year's expenses this year. Would you agree or disagree that this is a good strategy? Why?
4. What influence does CMS have on in a hospital's financial management?
5. If a hospital's HIM department has excess coding or transcription staff, can the hospital sell coding or transcription services to other hospitals (based on what has been covered so far in this chapter)? Why or why not?

Basic Financial Accounting

A basic understanding of the mechanics of financial accounting helps department managers to understand the impact of their financial transactions on the overall organization. The system of recording financial transactions is based on balancing the *purpose* of the transactions with their impact on the organization. For example, a facility purchases drugs with the purpose of ensuring that sufficient and appropriate drugs are on hand to treat patients. The purchase of the drugs increases the facility's pharmaceutical **inventory**. The impact of that purchase is the outlay of cash. After the cash is spent on drugs, it cannot be spent on something else. Recording both the increase in inventory and the outlay of cash enables the organization to understand and communicate information about its activities. Fundamental to this communication is an understanding of the components of financial data and their relationship to each other.

Assets

An **asset** is something that is owned or due to be received. In a transaction, the compensation that has been earned by providing goods or services becomes an asset as soon as it has been earned. Examples of assets include cash, inventory, accounts receivable, buildings, and equipment.

Cash

Cash consists of monetary instruments and those instruments that can be converted into cash quickly. The latter are often referred to as cash equivalents. Included in cash are funds that are maintained in bank accounts. It is important to remember that, for accounting purposes, currency and bank accounts are both considered cash. At the point of sale, such as purchasing lunch in the cafeteria, currency may be tendered. CMS, on the other hand, does not deliver reimbursement to a hospital in truckloads of currency; instead, it wires funds between financial institutions. Nevertheless, both are considered cash to the hospital. Cash is only recorded, and becomes an asset, when it has been received.

Inventory

An organization has inventory if it maintains goods on hand that it intends to sell to a client. Drugs are part of a hospital's pharmaceutical inventory because they are effectively on hand to be sold to patients. It is important to distinguish between goods that are available for sale and goods that are used by the organization in other ways. Photocopy paper is inventory to the office supply store. To the hospital HIM department, it is used for general business purposes and is considered a supply. In this case, the hospital is the client (the consumer of the goods). Because hospitals are primarily service organizations, and the provision of goods is incidental to the services provided, hospitals tend not to have a great deal of inventory other than supplies.

Accounts Receivable

When an organization has delivered goods and/or services, payment for same is expected. Remember that the second step in a transaction is to record the transaction. Because the revenue has been earned upon delivery or provision of the goods and services, the organization must have some way to keep track of what is owed as a result. **Accounts receivable** then is merely a list of the amounts due from various customers (in this case, patients). Payment on the individual amounts is expected within a specified period. A schedule of those expected amounts is prepared in order to track and follow up on payments that are overdue (late). Figure 25.4 shows one way to prepare a simple aged accounts receivables report. This list also could be sorted by discharge date or payer and the amounts subtotaled.

Building

Many organizations own the **buildings** in which they reside. These buildings are assets to the organization because they are part of its physical plant, its infrastructure. If an organization leases space for its operations, that space is not considered an asset because the organization does not own it. Buildings are considered **long-term assets** because they are typically owned for many years.

Equipment

Equipment is another long-term asset. Hospitals include CT scanners, computer systems, and vehicles in this category. Each organization decides what items are relevant to this category, depending on industry conventions and materiality. For example, a large hospital would rarely consider a $500 personal computer to be equipment whereas an independent coding consultant might view it as a significant, long-term investment.

Purchase Price

In acquiring a piece of equipment (and certain other assets), the transaction is recorded at the purchase price. For example, the hospital purchases digital mammography equipment for $200,000. The hospital then would have a $200,000 asset in equipment. However, the equipment gradually wears out from use over time. That $200,000 asset is not worth $200,000 four years after it was purchased. To provide better information about the financial value of its equipment, the organization provides an estimate of this decrease in value every year. This estimate is called **depreciation.**

Depreciation

Depreciation is an example of a **contra-account**. This estimate of the cumulative decrease in value of an asset actually reduces the cost of the underlying asset. Thus, the mammography equipment purchased for $200,000 may have accumulated depreciation of $75,000 after two years. At that point, its value to the organization is $125,000. The cumulative or accumulated depreciation is associated with its underlying assets when the value of those assets is being reported.

Mammograph	$200,000
Accumulated Depreciation	$75,000
Asset Value	$125,000

Liabilities

Liabilities are essentially debts. They are amounts that are owed, often due to the acquisition of an asset.

Accounts Payable

Accounts payable is a liability that is created when the organization has received goods or services but has not yet remitted the compensation. Referring to the accounts receivable discussion, the provider of the goods and services records a receivable when payment is not received at the point of the sale. On the other side of that transaction is the organization for which the goods and services were provided. When the recipient of the goods and services does not intend to pay immediately, the amount is recorded by the recipient as an account payable. The recipient also records either the acquisition of an asset or the recognition of an expense (discussed later in this chapter).

Notes Payable

A note is a financial obligation that has specific terms of payment in the form of a contract. Effectively, a note is a type of loan. The creation of the note may be associated with the purchase of goods or services, and the material goods may be guaranteed by the value of specific assets (collateral). For example, the organization may need $50,000 more than it has on hand in order to purchase a CT scanner. It might take a two-year loan from the bank (or the vendor), using the scanner as collateral. If the organization does not pay the loan back on a timely basis, the lender is entitled by contract to take possession of the scanner.

Mortgage

A **mortgage** is a liability that is created when the organization borrows money and uses a physical asset, such as a building, as collateral.

Figure 25.4. Aged accounts receivable

A/C #	D/C	SER	0–30 days	31–60 days	61–90 days	91–120 days	> 120 days	Total A/R
46153153	04/15/09	ED					149	
46160492	07/06/09	ED				25		
46162518	07/31/09	REC			10			
46162874	08/31/09	REC			30			
46163484	08/07/09	ED					165	
46162580	07/30/09	ED				114		
46125122	06/19/08	OP					16	
46160520	07/06/09	ED				50		
46169245	10/09/09	OP	175					
46165628	09/30/09	REC		266				
46163713	08/12/09	OP			52			
46166048	09/04/09	ED		280				
46161964	07/23/09	OP				94		
46162506	07/30/09	OP				94		
46164953	08/25/09	OP			52			
46169231	10/09/09	ED	25					
46157104	05/30/09	ED					50	
46124652	06/15/08	OBN					84	
46126673	07/09/08	OP					148	
46122161	05/20/08	OP					207	
Total Amounts			**$200**	**$546**	**$144**	**$377**	**$819**	**$2,086**
Total Number of Accounts			**2**	**2**	**4**	**5**	**7**	**20**

Source: Adapted from Schraffenberger 2007, 357.

Equity/Fund Balance/Net Assets

All financial accounting is based on an equation that pictures the organization holistically, balancing what is owned against what is owed: assets versus liabilities. **Equity** (or **owner's equity**) is the arithmetic difference between assets and liabilities. In a not-for-profit environment, the difference between assets and liabilities is referred to as the **fund balance** or just **net assets**. These relationships can be expressed in the following equation:

Assets − liabilities = net assets (equity)

The purchase of a building illustrates this equation. The purchase of a house typically involves a deposit of cash and an assumption of a mortgage. The building is an asset whose value is, historically, the price that was paid at the time of the purchase. The mortgage is a liability. As mortgage payments are made, the amount of the mortgage owed declines. The deposit of cash is the owner's equity in the building. As mortgage payments are made, the amount of owner's equity in the building increases. For example, Dr. James purchases an office building for $200,000. She makes a down payment (or deposit) of $50,000 and assumes a mortgage of $150,000. As the mortgage is paid over 30 years, the historical value of the house remains the same, the amount of the mortgage decreases, and the owner's equity in the property increases. When the mortgage is completely paid, the owner's equity in the house equals the historical value of the house, as shown here:

	Assets		Liabilities		Equity
At purchase	$200,000	−	$150,000	=	$ 50,000
After 10 years	$200,000	−	$100,000	=	$100,000
After 20 years	$200,000	−	$ 50,000	=	$150,000
After 30 years	$200,000	−	- 0 -	=	$200,000

Earlier, it was stated that an equation balances what is owned and what is owed. Therefore, another way to look at the accounting equation is:

Assets = liabilities + net assets (equity)

Using the previous mortgage example, the second version of the equation proves useful. At every step in the following calculation, the equations balance. An increase in assets increases equity. A decrease in assets decreases equity. An increase in assets with an equal increase in liabilities has no impact on equity. Notice that increasing a liability reduces equity in the same manner that decreasing an asset does.

	Assets		Liabilities		Equity
At purchase	$200,000	=	$150,000	+	$ 50,000
After 10 years	$200,000	=	$100,000	+	$100,000
After 20 years	$200,000	=	$ 50,000	+	$150,000
After 30 years	$200,000	=	- 0 -	+	$200,000

Assets, liabilities, and equity/fund balance are the components of the **balance sheet** (discussed later in this chapter). Before that, however, it is important to understand the revenue and expense components of financial information.

Revenue

Revenue consists of earned, known amounts. It is the compensation that has been earned by providing goods and services to the client or patient as well as amounts received or earned from other sources.

Sources of Revenue

Patient services is the main source of revenue for a healthcare facility. Indeed, depending on the nature of the facility, patient services may be its only source of revenue. Examples of nonclinical services include employee food services, donated services, monetary donations, and copy fees.

Categories of Revenue

How an organization describes its revenue depends on industry convention, materiality, and whether the revenue is recurring or unusual. Revenue from any source increases equity. A coding consultant works for a week at a client hospital and earns $1,500. He receives a check from the hospital and deposits it in his bank account. This increases his cash asset by the amount of the deposit: $1,500. The increase in the asset, absent an associated liability, increases equity by the same amount. Most organizations can group their revenue sources into at least two categories: operating and nonoperating.

Operating Revenue

A hospital considers patient services revenue to be operating revenue. Because the hospital is in the business of serving patients, patient services is its main source of revenue and thus falls under the heading of operating revenue. Consider food services. Inpatients must be fed, so food services is a patient service and thus an operating expense. The employee cafeteria also generates revenue, but the revenue it generates is unrelated to patient services. In the HIM department, small revenue streams may be generated through release of information activities or through contracting services out to other facilities. Since the pricing of these activities is generally cost-based, it is more appropriately thought of as an offset or quasi-reimbursement of the underlying cost.

Nonoperating Revenue

Another dilemma is investment income. A hospital with a large endowment that generates significant income may want to highlight this investment revenue in a separate category. Investment income is one example of nonoperating income. Other examples include gift shop sales and unrestricted monetary donations.

Expenses

It is unlikely that revenue is generated without any reduction of cash or liability being incurred. The consultant coder in the previous example must purchase codebooks and coding software, travel from home to client and back, and engage in continuing education (CE). **Expenses**, then, represent the utilization of resources by the organization in order to generate revenue. The consultant coder uses cash to purchase a codebook. The codebook helps to generate revenue for one year, at which time it expires. Therefore, the price of the codebook is an expense to the coder.

This simple example illustrates the impact on the accounting equation of the financial transactions discussed thus far.

October Activity					
	Assets	–	Liabilities	=	Equity
Beginning balance	$1,500	–	- 0 -	=	$1,500
Purchase codebook	<100>	–		=	<100>
Pay health insurance	<100>	–		=	<100>
Receive payment from client	$1,200	–		=	$1,200
Purchase computer (on credit)	<200>	–	800	=	<1,000>
Receive payment from client	$1,300	–		=	$1,300
Attend CE session	<80>	–		=	<80>
Ending balance	$3,520	–	800	=	$2,720

Purchasing

As previously stated, healthcare organizations typically cannot affect revenue by raising prices. Therefore, they must attempt to control expenses as much as possible. One way to do this is through the purchasing function. Individuals responsible for purchasing activities must adhere to their facility's policies and procedures, which may vary somewhat from the basic descriptions in the following section.

Organization

Organizations handle the purchasing function differently, depending on their size and needs. Large organizations tend to maintain a central purchasing and distribution department that is responsible for the acquisition of supplies and equipment.

Significant savings can be obtained by purchasing supplies in bulk and distributing them as needed to departments. Central purchasing also has the benefit of minimizing the space required for storage of items on hand. Central purchasing systems should be designed to minimize the risk of loss due to misappropriation of stored items. The periodic comparison, by counting, of items on hand with the items recorded and the itemized distribution of stored items can assist in this process.

In order to obtain the benefits of purchasing in large quantities, some facilities combine their purchasing efforts. Hospital associations, for example, may offer coordinated purchasing on behalf of multiple facilities. Nevertheless, the control over the use of the items remains with the department.

Maintaining a central purchasing and distribution department results in direct administrative costs to the organization (for example, salary, facility maintenance, and administrative processing). Therefore, the control benefits of centralized purchasing must be weighed against the cost of such operations. Savings also can be obtained by limiting the source of supplies to one or two key vendors who offer discounts to the organization. In this scenario, department managers would order items as needed, but only from approved vendors.

Finally, an organization may choose to allow individual departments to make purchases independently. Although this can result in additional supply and equipment costs, there may be overall savings in not maintaining a central purchasing department. The major disadvantages of independent, or decentralized, purchasing are the need for supply storage space in the ordering department and the allocation of managerial resources to purchasing.

Regardless of the purchasing system used, controls must be in place to ensure the efficient execution of approved transactions. Purchase orders, shipping/receiving documents, and invoices are the key controls over the purchase process.

Purchase Orders

The **purchase order** system ensures that purchases have been properly authorized prior to ordering. Authorization is often tied to dollar limits or the budget process. Purchase orders are numbered sequentially so that all orders can be verified. In a paper environment, a purchase order is a paper form on which all details of the intended purchase are reported. Purchase orders for routine, budgeted items often require only the authorization of a supervisor or manager. For large-dollar items, as specified in the organization's policy and procedure manual, additional authorization may be required. In a computer-based system, there may be no physical form; however, authorization levels are still required.

The purchase order shows that the appropriate individual with the appropriate authorization ordered the specific items. The order is then forwarded to the vendor. The originator of the order keeps a copy, and another copy is sent to the accounts payable department. When there is a central receiving department, that department also should receive a copy of the order. In a computer-based system, access to the orders may suffice.

Shipping/Receiving Documents

Items received from a vendor contain a packing slip, also known as a *shipping/receiving document.* This document lists the quantities and descriptions of the items sent from the vendor, but not usually the price. The recipient of the items must verify that the items received match the ones that were ordered. The verified shipping/receiving document is forwarded to accounts payable.

Invoices

The vendor sends an invoice (bill or request for payment) directly to accounts payable. The accounts payable department matches the invoice to the shipping/receiving document and the purchase order on file. When all the documents match, the invoice can be processed and payment scheduled. Invoices generally have terms: for example, payable upon receipt or within 30 days. Some vendors offer discounts for early payment, such as "2/10, net 30", which means that the seller will grant a 2 percent discount for payment within 10 days; otherwise, the full amount is due within 30 days. Other terms may include interest charges for late payment. The facility's accounting department has to balance expected payments (receivables) with obligations (payables). Departments such as HIM often receive invoices directly and it is important to forward all invoices to the accounting department immediately upon receipt and verification so that accounting has the information it needs to make appropriate and timely decisions about payment.

Statements

A **statement** is merely a list of outstanding invoices the vendor has sent, but for which no payment has been received. Some companies send statements that include all activity for the period, including payment. The statement is one way the vendor lets the customer know that payments are late. Statements are not payable without supporting documentation. When there is no purchase order, receiving document, and invoice, accounts payable will not remit payment.

Statements received for which there is no underlying documentation should be treated as suspicious. Purchases may have been made without proper authorization. Additionally, there are unscrupulous organizations that send only statements when no transaction has taken place in the hope that the receiving organization's controls are lax and payment will be made. This is particularly true of certain fraudulent subscriptions and advertising schemes.

Inventory Slips

The purchase of large quantities is supplies inventory and may be recorded as an asset at the time of purchase. Items are then removed from assets and recorded as expenses as they are used. This same system may be used to track pharmacy inventory (by patient rather than department). In a centralized purchasing system, some mechanism must be in place to track the distribution of items to other departments. Frequently paper based, a form is completed requesting items and verifying their receipt. These systems are purely internal because items are on hand. The financial transaction consists of moving the responsibility for the expense of the items from the purchasing department to the requesting department. Table 25.4 shows some common accounts and what they represent.

Recording Transactions

As previously discussed, financial transactions begin with the documents of original entry or source documents. Whether the organization's transactions are recorded on paper or via computer, there must be a way to determine the origination of the transaction. The originating document details the parties involved in the transaction, the amount of the transaction, the type of financial impact involved (revenue or expense, asset or liability), and the individual responsible for the transaction.

Double-Entry Bookkeeping

All financial transactions are recorded with the accounting equation in mind. To simplify the recording of transactions, accountants use special terminology to reflect the maintenance of a balanced equation.

Debits and Credits

Visually, transactions have two sides: left and right. **Debits** are shown on the left; **credits** are shown on the right. Each account has two sides: increase and decrease. In asset accounts, the left-hand debit side represents the natural balance of the account and debits increase the account. Conversely, credits decrease an asset account. Obviously, for the accounting equation to balance, the opposite is true of liability and equity accounts. The right-hand credit side of liability and equity accounts represents the natural balance, and credits increase the accounts. Instead of using minus signs or brackets to represent the increases and decreases, debits and credits provide an additional safeguard against clerical error because every transaction must balance.

Look at the coding consultant example again, using debits and credits.

October Activity								
	Assets		–	**Liabilities**		=	**Equity**	
	Debit	**Credit**		**Debit**	**Credit**		**Debit**	**Credit**
Beginning balance	$1,500		–	- 0 -		=		$1,500
Purchase codebook		100	–			=	100	
Pay health insurance		100	–			=	100	
Receive payment from client	$1,200		–			=		$1,200
Purchase computer (on credit)		200	–		800	=	1,000	
Receive payment from client	$1,300		–			=		$1,300
Attend CE session		80	–			=	80	
Ending balance	$3,520		–		800	=		$2,720

Table 25.4. Common accounts

<table>
<tr><th>Account</th><th>Description</th><th>Example</th></tr>
<tr><td colspan="3">Assets</td></tr>
<tr><td>Cash</td><td>Money. Typically, money is represented by several accounts, depending on how the money is stored (for example, in different banks).</td><td>Bank account</td></tr>
<tr><td>Inventory</td><td>Goods that are available for sale.</td><td>Pharmaceuticals</td></tr>
<tr><td>Accounts receivable</td><td>Amounts owed the organization for goods and services.</td><td>Claims to payers that have not yet been paid</td></tr>
<tr><td>Building</td><td>Permanent structures. The land on which they are built is often listed separately.</td><td>Office building</td></tr>
<tr><td>Equipment</td><td>Represents items that are used to generate revenue or to support the organization during more than one business cycle.</td><td>Photocopier
CT scanner</td></tr>
<tr><td colspan="3">Liabilities</td></tr>
<tr><td>Accounts payable</td><td>Amounts the organization owes but has not yet paid.</td><td>Supplies purchased on credit</td></tr>
<tr><td>Loans payable</td><td>Amounts the organization has borrowed that will be paid over more than one business cycle.</td><td>Bank loan</td></tr>
<tr><td>Mortgage payable</td><td>Amounts the organization has borrowed to finance the purchase of buildings and equipment.</td><td>Building mortgage</td></tr>
<tr><td colspan="3">Equity</td></tr>
<tr><td>Capital/stock/fund balance</td><td>In a sole proprietorship or partnership, capital is the owner's equity in the organization.
In a corporation, stock is the amount invested by owners in the corporation.
In a not-for-profit organization, the fund balance is the amount represented by the difference between assets and liabilities.</td><td></td></tr>
<tr><td>Retained earnings/ reserves</td><td>In a corporation, retained earnings are profits that have not been distributed.
Reserves are amounts that have been designated for a specific purpose.</td><td></td></tr>
<tr><td>Revenue</td><td>Temporary account that captures amounts earned by the organization in the current fiscal year.</td><td rowspan="2">The difference between revenue and expenses is net income (profits or losses). These accounts are closed at the end of every fiscal year and the net income is moved to Retained Earnings/Reserves.</td></tr>
<tr><td>Expenses</td><td>Temporary account that captures amounts disbursed by the organization in the current fiscal year to support the generation of revenue.</td></tr>
</table>

Impact on Individual Accounts

Assets involve multiple accounts as described previously: cash, accounts receivable, and building. Similarly, liabilities have their own accounts. Revenues and expenses fall into the equity section. This system of debits and credits enables us to understand immediately whether a transaction increases or decreases a particular account. Individual accounts increase and decrease in value; however, the overall equation always remains in balance.

Keeping Track of Transactions

Financial transactions are recorded, or posted, to the accounts described earlier according to a system of journal entries.

Journal Entry

Each **journal entry** contains at least one debit and one credit. For every transaction, the sum of the debits must equal the sum of the credits. Ensuring that the debits and credits equal is one aspect of ensuring the accuracy of financial data. Other aspects include posting to the correct accounts and in the correct time period. The following tabulation illustrates the purchase of supplies on credit. The supplies are delivered on February 24, and the supplier's invoice is paid on March 15. Note that no financial transaction is recorded until the supplies are received.

Date	Description	Debit	Credit
2/24	Supplies expense	$300	
	Accounts payable		$300
	Purchase office supplies		
3/15	Accounts payable	$300	
	Cash		$300
	Pay 2/24 office supply invoice		

The accounts payable amount is eliminated when the invoice is paid. It is common business practice to record, or **accrue**, liabilities as they are incurred. This accrual basis of accounting enables organizations to understand their total liabilities continuously and to match expenses with the associated revenue. Some organizations, such as small professional associations and sole proprietorships, only record transactions when the cash is paid or received. This cash basis of accounting is analogous to the way individuals handle their private transactions.

In the preceding tabulation, the supplies expense entry is a debit to increase that account. Expenses are temporary equity accounts that close annually. Revenue increases net income; expenses reduce net income. Therefore, revenue accounts have a natural credit balance and expenses have a natural debit balance.

It should be noted that all the financial accounting examples in this chapter relate to corporate and not-for-profit accounting. Government accounting activity, although a system of debits and credits, is significantly different in some respects. For example, a supply purchase would be recorded (encumbered) at the time the supplies were budgeted and then reduced at the time they were ordered. Government accounting is outside the scope of this discussion.

General Ledger

In a paper-based accounting system, journal entries are recorded chronologically in a general journal and their component debits and credits are posted to the individual accounts. The list of all the individual accounts is referred to as the **general ledger**. In a computer-based environment, only the original journal entry is posted. The computer stores the entries and generates summaries of the individual accounts on request.

The example in figure 25.5 is based on this chapter's original description of a financial transaction. The result of this completed transaction is an increase in cash and an increase in equity (revenue). Note that the amount in accounts receivable is eliminated when the reimbursement is received.

Nonfinancial managers are rarely required to make actual journal entries to record financial transactions. However, they do initiate the transactions and receive reports that detail them. Often the reports only show the department's side of the transaction. For example, a purchase of supplies would appear to the manager on a list of expenses and be added to a summary of all supply expenses on another report. The cash and accounts payable portions of the transaction would not show because they are controlled by the accounting department. Another example is the discharged, no final bill (DNFB), which is discussed later in this chapter. The DNFB lists individual patient accounts, which are accounts receivable to the organization. Managerial reporting activity is also discussed later is this chapter.

Figure 25.5. Example of a financial transaction

Service provided:
Physician sees in the office a new patient, whose chief complaint is an itchy rash.

Transaction recorded:

Clinical record: History and physical/progress note reflect examination of rash and notation that the patient encountered poison ivy while weeding his garden. OTC topical ointment prescribed, and free sample distributed with instructions.

Billing record: Encounter form—office visit code 99201 and ICD-9-CM code 692.6 circled.

Journal entry:

	Debit	Credit
Accounts Receivable—Patient X	60	
Patient Service Revenue		60

Reimbursement received:

Journal entry:

	Debit	Credit
Cash	60	
Accounts Receivable—Patient X		60

Financial Statements

At the departmental level, individual financial transactions are reviewed for data quality and compliance with policies and procedures. On an administrative level, the overall impact of transactions is generally of more interest than the individual transactions; therefore, summary reports are prepared. These summaries also are used to communicate with lending institutions, potential investors, and regulatory agencies. A variety of summaries are useful for analyzing an organization's financial activities. The three key reports are the income statement, the statement of changes in retained earnings, and the balance sheet.

Income Statement

The **income statement** summarizes the organization's revenue and expense transactions during the fiscal year. The income statement can be prepared at any point in time and reflects results up to that point. The income statement contains only income and expense accounts and reflects only the activity for the current fiscal year.

The arithmetic difference between total revenue and total expenses is **net income**. When total expenses exceed total revenue, net income is a negative number, or a **net loss**. Net income increases equity; net loss decreases equity.

At the end of the fiscal year, all income statement accounts are closed and the net results are added to, or subtracted from, the appropriate equity account (fund balance). For the purposes of periodic reporting, fund balances are adjusted in this manner every time this report is prepared. However, at the end of the fiscal year, the income and expense accounts are actually closed so that the new fiscal year begins at zero.

Retained Earnings

The **statement of retained earnings** expresses the change in retained earnings from the beginning of the balance sheet period to the end. Retained earnings are affected, for example, by net income/loss, distribution of stock dividends, and payment of long-term debt. Net income/loss is carried forward from the income statement. When the income statement accounts are closed, the net income/loss is transferred to equity. The "mechanics" of this transaction are to take the balance in each revenue and expense account and record the opposite amount so that all of the income statement accounts have a zero balance. The net dollar amount of the debits and credits is recorded to equity. The statement of changes in retained earnings (fund balance) highlights this transaction. The ending balance in Retained Earnings is then reported on the balance sheet.

Balance Sheet

The **balance sheet** is a snapshot of the accounting equation at a point in time. Because every financial transaction affects the equation, theoretically, the balance sheet will look different after every transaction. To ensure a meaningful evaluation, the balance sheet is typically reviewed on a periodic basis (monthly, quarterly, semiannually, and annually). It is often compared to balance sheets from previous fiscal years in order to analyze changes in the organization.

The balance sheet lists the major account categories grouped under their equation headings: assets, liabilities, and equity/fund balance. Figure 25.6 shows a set of simple statements, as described earlier. The dollar amount shown next to each account category is the total in each category on the ending date listed at the top of the report. Figure 25.7 shows the relationship between the income statement, the statement of retained earnings, and the balance sheet.

Analysis Statements

A number of other types of summary statements are required by users to analyze an organization's financial activity and position. Depending on the organization and their use, the additional financial statements may be required by GAAP as part of a complete financial summary report. Figure 25.8 shows a two-year comparative balance sheet and three simple examples of statements that help to explain the changes

Figure 25.6. Financial statements with the associated Income Statement and Statement of Changes in Fund Balance

Sample Hospital
Statement of Revenues and Expenses

	12/31/08 (000)
Revenue	
Net patient service revenue	$650
Unrestricted gifts	40
Other	95
Total Revenue	$785
Expenses	
Salaries and wages	$430
Fringe benefits	95
Supplies	175
Total expenses	$700
Income from operations	$ 85
Nonoperating gains	
Unrestricted gifts	$ 15
Excess of revenues over expenses	$100

Sample Hospital
Statement of Changes in
Unrestricted Fund Balance

	2008 (000)
Beginning Balance January 1	$ 900
Excess of Revenues over Expenses	100
Ending Balance December 31	$1,000

Sample Hospital
Balance Sheet

	12/31/08 (000)
Assets	
Cash	$ 500
Accounts receivable	600
Inventory	400
Building	2,500
Total assets	$4,000
Liabilities	
Accounts payable	600
Mortgage	2,000
Total Liabilities	$2,600
Fund Balance	
Restricted funds	400
Unrestricted funds	1,000
Total Fund Balance	$1,400
Total Liabilities and Fund Balance	$4,000

from one year to the next. These statements are included for completeness of discussion and are not statements that HIM professionals generally need to analyze.

Cash Flow

The **statement of cash flow** (also called the *statement of changes in financial position*) details the reasons that cash changed from one balance sheet period to another. It shows the analyst whether cash was used to purchase equipment or to pay down debt and whether any unusually large transactions took place.

Stockholder's Equity

The **statement of stockholder's equity** (also called the *statement of fund balance*) details the reasons for changes in each of the stockholder's equity accounts, including retained earnings.

Ratio Analysis

After the financial statements have been prepared, they are ready for **ratio analysis**. Financial analysts can use financial statements, particularly the balance sheet, to determine whether an organization is using its resources similarly or

Figure 25.7. Relationship between the income statement, fund balance, and the balance sheet

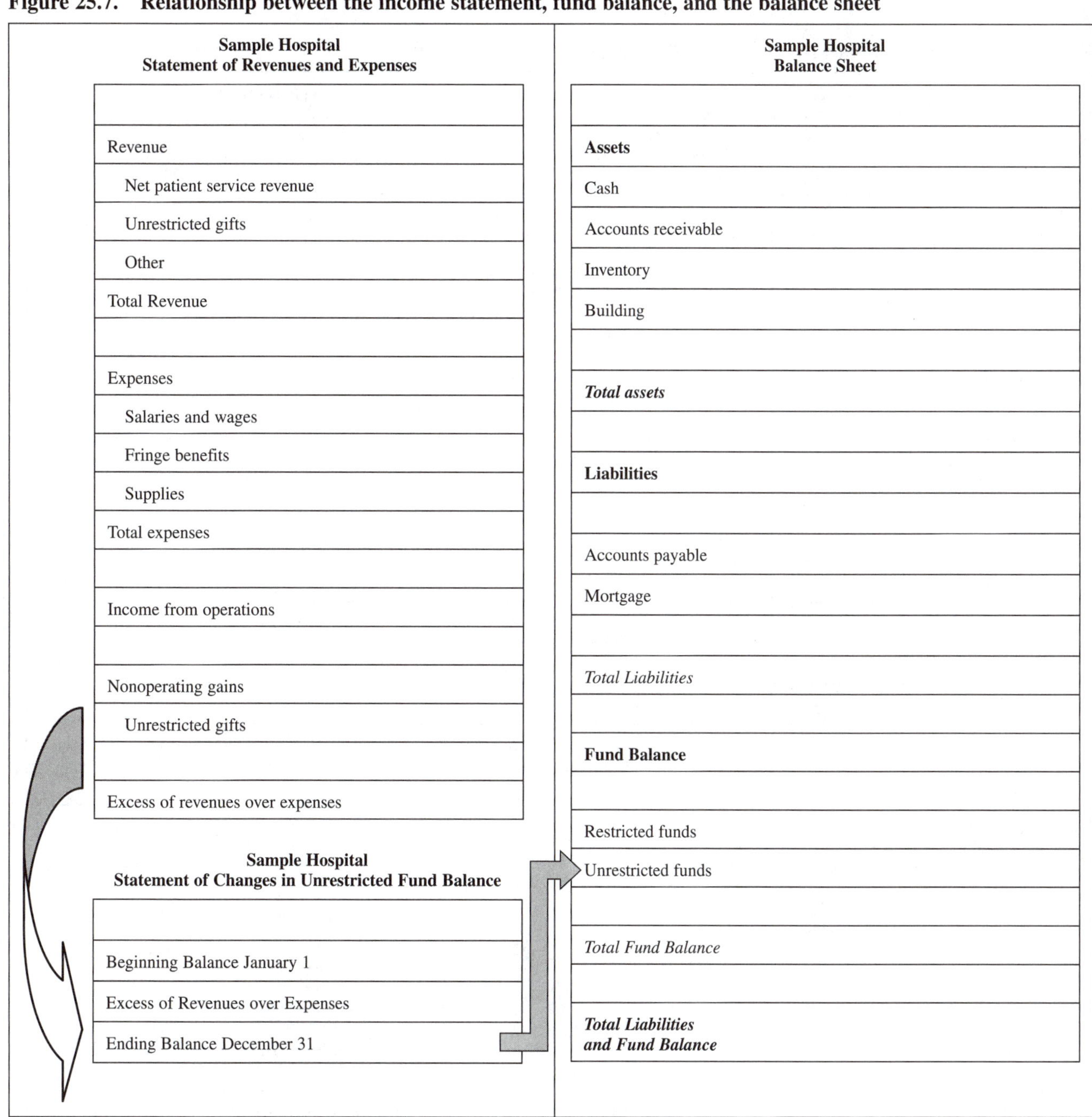

differently from other organizations in the same industry. In retail sales, analysts compare inventory turnover; that is, how quickly inventory is sold. In any industry, one of the most common reasons to analyze financial statements is to lend money to the organization or to invest in it. Thus, the organization's use of assets compared to its liabilities is extremely important. Changes in an organization's ratios are of particular interest.

Ratios, as a comparative tool, are only meaningful within the context of the organization's industry. It is not useful to compare a ratio for a hospital against a ratio for an automobile manufacturer, except to state that one would expect the ratios to be different. Whether an organization's particular ratio is inherently good or bad depends on expected ratios for similar organizations in that industry.

The Healthcare Financial Management Association publishes industry ratio medians annually as a member service. Some state hospital associations also publish ratio information.

Liquidity and Debt Service

A key issue to lenders and investors is the organization's ability to discharge its financial obligations. **Liquidity** refers to the ease with which assets can be turned into cash. This is important because payroll, loan payments, and other financial obligations are typically paid in cash. **Debt service** is the extent to which those financial obligations are loans.

Figure 25.8. 2-year comparative balance sheet with analytical statements

Sample Hospital
Statement of Revenues and Expenses

	12/31/08 (000)	12/31/07 (000)
Revenue		
Net patient service revenue	$650	$500
Unrestricted gifts	40	30
Other	95	70
Total Revenue	$785	$600
Expenses		
Salaries and wages	$430	$290
Fringe benefits	95	90
Supplies	175	180
Total expenses	$700	$560
Income from operations	$ 85	$ 40
Nonoperating gains		
Unrestricted gifts	$ 15	$ 10
Excess of revenues over expenses	$100	$ 50

Sample Hospital
Statement of Revenues and Expenses

	2008 (000)	2007 (000)
Beginning Balance January 1	$ 900	$850
Excess of Revenues over Expenses	100	50
Ending Balance December 31	$1,000	$900

Sample Hospital
Balance Sheet

	12/31/08 (000)	12/31/07 (000)
Assets		
Cash	$ 500	$ 650
Accounts receivable	600	750
Inventory	400	350
Building	2,500	2,150
Total assets	$4,000	$3,900
Liabilities		
Accounts payable	600	500
Mortgage	2,000	2,100
Total Liabilities	$2,600	$2,600
Fund Balance		
Restricted funds	400	400
Unrestricted funds	1,000	900
Total Fund Balance	$1,400	$1,300
Total Liabilities and Fund Balance	$4,000	$3,900

Current Ratio

An organization's ability to pay current liabilities with current assets is very important to lenders. Current assets include cash, short-term investments, accounts receivable, and inventory. Current assets implicitly will be (or could be) converted to cash at some point within a year, through collections, sales, or other business activity. Current liabilities include accounts payable and the current portion of loan obligations. Again, the term *current* implies that the liability will be discharged within a year. The **current ratio** compares total current assets with total current liabilities:

$$\frac{\text{Total current assets}}{\text{Total current liabilities}}$$

From the balance sheet in figure 25.6, one can take the current assets (cash plus accounts receivable plus inventory) and divide them by the current liabilities (accounts payable) to determine the current ratio:

$$\frac{1{,}500{,}000}{600{,}000} = \frac{15}{6} = \frac{2.5}{10}$$

The current ratio indicates that for every dollar of current liability, \$2.50 of current assets could be used to discharge the liability, which even common sense tells us is good.

Acid-Test Ratio

Inventory is a current asset because it is presumed that inventory will be sold, or turned over, within one fiscal year. However, inventory can become obsolete very quickly (for example, in the fashion and computer industries). Pharmaceuticals can expire before they are used. For expensive items such as motor vehicles, saleable merchandise may be retained in inventory longer than expected or desirable. Therefore, a stricter measure of an organization's ability to pay current liabilities is needed. The **acid-test ratio** compares current liabilities to the current assets that are truly liquid, that is, able to be turned into cash quickly:

$$\frac{(\text{Cash} + \text{short-term investments} + \text{net current receivables})}{\text{Total current liabilities}}$$

Short-term investments include money market funds, certificates of deposit, and treasury bills, for example. Using the balance sheet in figure 25.6, the acid-test ratio is:

$$\frac{1{,}100{,}000}{600{,}000} = \frac{1.1}{6.0} = \frac{1.83}{1.00}$$

In this example, the acid-test ratio reveals that for every dollar of current liabilities, \$1.83 of current assets could be used immediately or sold quickly to discharge the liabilities.

Debt Ratio

Looking back to the mortgage example, the organization's building asset was purchased using 10 percent cash and 90 percent mortgage. Ninety percent of that asset was financed with debt. Looking at all the liabilities and all the assets together gives the analyst an overall picture of how the assets were acquired. The **debt ratio**, therefore, is total liabilities divided by total assets.

It is important to remember that all ratio analysis is industry specific and varies somewhat depending on the economic environment. Therefore, ratio analysis can be used to compare similar organizations at a specific point in time or the same organization at different points in time. However, a hospital ratio would never be compared with a professional association ratio.

Profitability

The preceding examples illustrate how organizations can evaluate their ability to pay their bills. Another measure of an organization's health is its profitability. Profitability refers to an organization's increase in value: how well does it invest its assets? As with other ratios, profitability measures are only meaningful as benchmarks against like organizations or in trending a single organization over time.

Return on Investment

Return on investment (ROI) measures the increase in the value of an asset. In a savings account, this increase is measured as the amount of interest received in a period. The beginning balance in the account is the measurement of the asset. Interest received in the period is the return. Thus:

$$\text{ROI} = \frac{\text{Interest earned in the period}}{\text{Asset value at the beginning of the period}}$$

Return on individual investments can be calculated in this manner. For an entire organization, interest earned is replaced by earnings, usually after taxes. Asset value is replaced by total assets

$$\text{ROI} = \frac{\text{Earnings (after taxes)}}{\text{Total assets}}$$

Return on Equity

ROI does not tell the whole story because it only indirectly measures the liabilities incurred in order to acquire or generate the asset. Generating sufficient overall profits to ensure ongoing operations, as well as maintaining and upgrading assets, is especially of interest to users of financial information. An organization may use several profitability ratios to gauge overall performance. **Return on equity** (ROE) is an important indicator for determining an organization's efficiency or profitability level. It measures the excess of revenue over expenses (net income) for an accounting period compared to the total fund balance (equity)

To illustrate, examine the acquisition of technology to generate income.

Purchase: \$100,000 (invest in transcription system)
Liability: \$90,000 (long-term loan from bank)
Net income: \$30,000 (after taxes)

$$\text{ROI} = \frac{\$30{,}000}{\$100{,}000} = 30\%$$

$$\text{ROE} = \frac{\$30{,}000}{\$10{,}000} = 300\%$$

Additional measures of return are discussed later in the section on capital projects.

Check Your Understanding 25.2

Instructions: Answer the following questions on a separate piece of paper.

1. List three assets and three liabilities.
2. Why are revenue and expense accounts part of owner's equity?
3. What inventory does a hospital have?
4. What is the difference between a debit and a credit?
5. Why is knowledge of accounting important to nonfinancial managers?
6. A lender wants to know how quickly a borrower would be able to repay a debt. What is the best ratio to use for this analysis? Why?

Basic Management Accounting

To obtain appropriate compensation for goods and services provided, the organization must understand and measure the resources used to manufacture, acquire, or otherwise produce those goods and services. The measurement of those resources is monetary and is referred to as their cost. In manufacturing and other goods-oriented businesses, sales are compared to the cost of goods sold, which are composed of raw materials and other manufacturing costs. Calculation of manufacturing cost of goods sold, by products, salvage, and waste is outside the scope of this discussion. In a service industry, the underlying costs consist largely of human resources, supplies, and the tools of the trade.

Management accounting focuses on the internal communication of accounting and financial data for the purpose of facility-based decision making. Management accountants use the same transaction data that is summarized in a financial statement. They also use a variety of additional data, such as prevailing interest rates and staffing levels, to provide meaningful information required by management.

Describing Costs

Cost accounting is the discipline of identifying and measuring costs and is a unique subset of the accounting profession. However, a general understanding of the terminology helps nonfinancial managers participate in and support the process. There are numerous ways to describe costs, but the most important for purposes of this discussion are discussed here.

Direct Costs

Direct costs are traceable to a specific good or service provided. To a hospital, the cost of a specific medication can be matched to the specific patient to whom it was administered. Room charges are another example. Similarly, to a consulting firm, the hours that a consultant coder spends coding are directly linked to the services provided to a specific facility.

Indirect Costs

Indirect costs are incurred by the organization in the process of providing goods or services; however, they are not specifically attributable to an individual product or service. The cost of providing security services at a hospital or clerical support at the switchboard are indirect costs with respect to patient care. To the consulting firm, the cost of CE for its coding staff is an indirect cost of providing services to a particular client.

The classification of costs as direct or indirect depends on the relationship of the cost to the client, department, product, service, or activity in question. Payroll in the security department is an indirect cost to patient care, but it is a direct cost to the security department. Therefore, the distinction between direct and indirect costs is important in understanding the broader financial impact of activities within the facility. In developing capital projects (discussed later in this chapter) such as the development and implementation of an electronic health record, an understanding of the associated costs (and, conversely, the cost savings) is crucial in making realistic financial estimates and projections.

Fixed Costs

For planning and analysis, it is useful to classify costs as fixed or variable. **Fixed costs** remain the same, despite changes in volume. For example, a manager's base salary does not change, regardless of patient volume or other changes in activity. Mortgage payments also are not dependent on activity. In figure 25.9, the copy machine depreciation expense does not vary, regardless of the number of requests.

Variable Costs

Variable costs are sensitive to volume. Medication is a good example. The more patients are treated, the more medication is used. Paper medical record documentation is another example. The larger the volume of patients, the more paper is used. In figure 25.10, the cost of paper used to print release of information requests rises proportionately with the number of requests.

Semi-Fixed Costs

Costs may behave in a combination of fixed and variable ways and volume is not the only change agent. For example, consider the coding function. Base coding salaries are fixed. Increases in discharges may require a temporary coding consultant. If the consultant charges on a per-chart basis, the cost of coding services rises variably with that volume. Similarly, the combination of personnel and paper costs for release of information have a combined mixed variability, as illustrated in figure 25.11.

On the other hand, nursing base salaries are also a fixed cost. However, hospitals do not staff nursing for full capacity. Therefore, increases in census require the use of part-time or per diem nurses, who are added based on established patient-to-nurse ratios. The full cost of nursing services, then, goes up in steps. Figure 25.12 illustrates this type of personnel cost variability, as applied to the copy cost example. (For a detailed discussion of cost classifications, see Chapter 11 in Cleverley and Cameron's *Essentials of Health Care Finance* [2003]).

Figure 25.9. Fixed cost

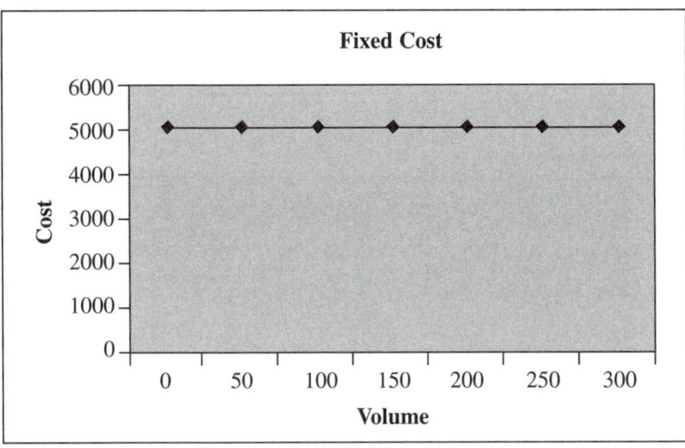

Figure 25.10. Variable cost

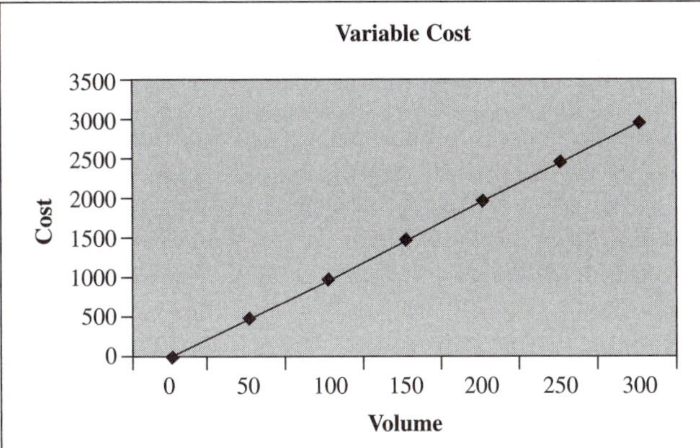

Figure 25.11. Mixed cost

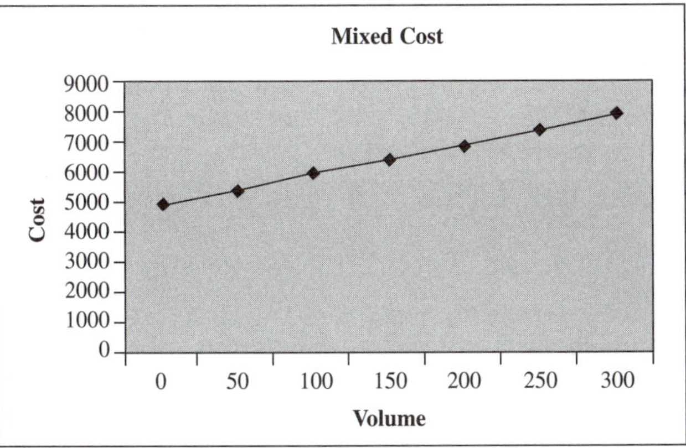

Figure 25.12. Step mixed cost

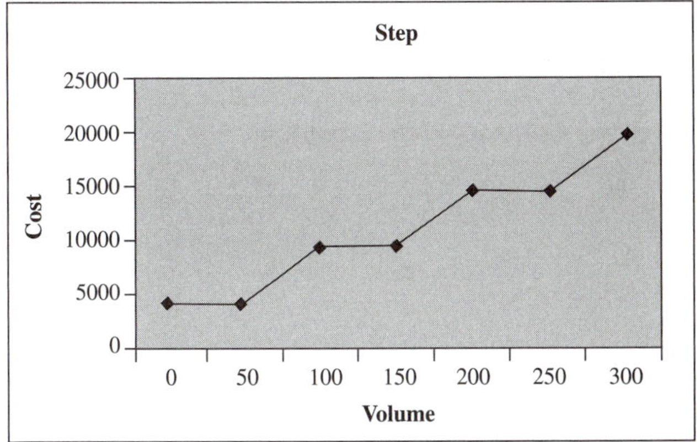

Cost Reports

Prior to implementation of prospective payment systems (PPSs), Medicare reimbursement to hospitals was related directly to the costs incurred by the facilities. Individual facility **cost reports** were submitted to Medicare, identifying the direct and indirect costs of providing care to Medicare patients. Direct costs include nursing and radiology; indirect costs include medical records and information systems. Preparation of cost reports requires the definition of products or services, establishment of cost centers, and identification of service units (Dunn 1999, 64–65). The expense of nonrevenue-producing cost centers is allocated to revenue-producing cost centers in order to fully understand the cost of providing services. Although cost reporting is no longer used to directly determine Medicare reimbursement, some payers still use cost reports to make reimbursement decisions. In addition, CMS uses cost reports to help determine facility-specific and regional cost adjustment factors for healthcare PPSs.

Allocation of Overhead

The attribution of indirect or **overhead costs** to revenue-producing service units illustrates the budget concept that all activities must support the mission of the organization. There are four methods of allocation of overhead:

- **Direct method of cost allocation** distributes the cost of overhead departments solely to the revenue-producing areas. Allocation is based on each revenue-producing area's relative square footage, number of employees, or actual usage of supplies and services. (See figure 25.13.)
- **Step-down allocation** distributes overhead costs once, beginning with the area that provides the least amount of nonrevenue-producing services.
- **Double distribution** allocates overhead costs twice, which takes into consideration the fact that some overhead departments provide services to each other.
- **Simultaneous equations method** distributes overhead costs through multiple iterations, allowing maximum distribution of interdepartmental costs among overhead departments.

The last three methods of cost allocation above assume that overhead cost centers (such as housekeeping) perform services for each other as well as for revenue-producing areas. Therefore, overhead costs are distributed among overhead cost centers as well as revenue-producing areas.

Although each of these methods may produce slightly different results, the ultimate goal is to allocate overhead costs appropriately. Appropriate allocation enables the facility to express the full cost of providing services.

Figure 25.13. Direct allocation vs. step allocation

	NonRevenue-Producing Department		Revenue-Producing Department	
	HIM Department	Business Office	Medicine	Laboratory
Direct method:				
Overhead costs before allocation	$360,000	$240,000	$400,000	$250,000
Allocation				
HIM (# discharges processed)	($360,000)		$340,000	$20,000
Business office (# labor hours used)		($240,000)	$80,000	$160,000
Total overhead after allocation	$0	$0	$820,000	$430,000
Step method:				
Overhead costs before allocation	$360,000	$240,000	$400,000	$250,000
Allocation				
HIM (# discharges processed)	($360,000)	$50,000	$300,000	$10,000
Business office (# labor hours used)		($290,000)	$90,000	$200,000
Total overhead after allocation	$0	$0	$790,000	$460,000

Charge Description Master

Chapter 14 discusses the various types of reimbursement to healthcare providers. Regardless of the reimbursement method, however, the facility must be able to evaluate the underlying cost of providing services and to compare its actual reimbursements to the potential reimbursements based on charges. To do this, all individual patient charges are captured in the patients' accounts. The charges themselves and the underlying costs of the services provided are maintained in a database called the **charge description master** (CDM). (Several alternative terms are used for the database, such as charge data master and chargemaster.) Using the individual patient charges and the associated clinical codes, the patient accounts department is able to prepare reimbursement claims.

The CDM collects information on all the goods and services the facility provides to its clients. Responsibility for maintaining the database varies among facilities, and multiple departments contribute to the data. Because many of the charges are associated with CPT/HCPCS codes, the HIM department should be involved in the routine maintenance of this database.

The purpose of the CDM is to facilitate charge capture by centralizing and standardizing charge data within the facility. Grocery stores do this by linking UPC symbols to the price and description of grocery items. The customer sees the evidence of this activity on the grocery bill but does not see that the database also contains the cost of the item, the vendor, and the underlying general ledger information. Similarly, the CDM enables the facility to capture and record patient charges as they are incurred. For the charges to be captured accurately, the CDM must be updated routinely as new services emerge, costs change, and CPT code descriptions change. Use of a properly updated CDM also helps the facility administratively by enabling the statistical reporting of charge-related activities.

The components of the CDM vary, depending on the needs of the healthcare organization. At a minimum, the fields for each record include (Schraffenberger 2007, 135):

- *Charge code:* The facility's internal tracking number
- *Item description:* The facility's description of the item
- *General ledger (GL) key:* The reference to the facility's accounting system
- *Revenue code:* The three-digit Medicare billing reference
- *Insurance code mapping:* Multiple fields to reference alternative billing codes for the item for different payers
- *Charge:* The charge for the item
- *Activity date/status:* Whether the item is currently being used

Figure 25.14 provides an example of a CDM and its components.

Maintenance of the CDM is a multidisciplinary activity. For example, the HIM department knows the clinical codes, the patient accounts department knows the general ledger codes, the pharmacy department knows the drugs and their costs, and the finance department knows the associated charge formulas. Pharmacy cannot realistically update radiology's data nor can finance update charges without knowledge of underlying costs.

To coordinate the update effort, a single department, usually finance, should be assigned responsibility for ensuring timely updates. The finance department then should enlist the assistance of other disciplines, including HIM. Update frequency depends on the data element to be updated, but certainly whenever underlying costs change. For example, pharmacy charges may be updated every time inventory is replenished. The entire CDM must be reviewed at least annually. Identification and substantiation of actual costs provide the foundation for the development of what an organization

Figure 25.14. Sample charge description master

Charge Code	Item Description	CPT/HCPCS Code				G/L Key	Activity Date
		INS Code A	Rev Code A	INS Code B	Rev Code B		
54100128	CONTINUOUS SPAG	94640	410	94640	410	3	6/15/2008
54100060	IPPB TX SUBSEQUENT	94640	410	94640	410	3	5/16/2008
54100037	IPPB THERAPY, INITIAL	94640	410	94640	410	3	8/1/2008
54100011	PENTAMADINE AEROSOL TX	94640	410	94640	410	3	7/26/2008
54100540	PR STRNGT/ENDURANCE PER 15 MIN	97535	410	G0237	410	3	6/25/2008
54100243	PULM REHAB 1 ON 1 PER 15 MIN	97110	410	G0238	410	3	5/24/2008
54100250	PULM REHAB THERAP PROC GRP	97150	410	G0239	410	3	4/25/2008
54100458	PR BREATHING RETRAINING	97535	419	G0237	419	3	7/3/2008
55400139	ALS AMBULANCE; GROUND PER MILE	A0425	540	A0425	540	3	8/14/2008
55400014	BLS AMBULANCE; GROUND PER MILE	A0425	540	A0425	540	3	7/21/2008
57400186	SIMP/COMP PL GEN W/O REPROGRAM	95970	740	95970	740	3	7/13/2008
57400194	SIMP PL GEN W/REPROGRAM	95971	740	95971	740	3	8/8/2008
57400202	CX BRAIN PL GEN W/RPG 1ST HR	95978	740	95978	740	3	7/15/2008
58000068	HEMOPERFUSION	90997	801	90997	801	3	3/12/2008
58200015	INCENTER DIALYSIS-PED OP <12KG	90999	821	90999	821	3	7/8/2008
58200023	INCENTER DIALYSIS-PED OP >24KG	90999	821	90999	821	3	6/15/2008
58200031	INCENTER DIALYSIS-PED OP 12–24	90999	821	90999	821	3	5/16/2008
58500000	HOME CCPD DAILY CHARGE-PED	90947	851	90947	851	3	8/1/2008
59201780	ELECTRONIC ANALY OF CI 1ST HR	95974	920	95974	920	3	7/26/2008
59201772	ELECTRONIC ANALY CI ADDL 30 MIN	95975	920	95975	920	3	6/25/2008

charges for its services. The subsections below follow those charges through the revenue cycle from here (even though they are not technically cost accounting topics).

Claims Processing

Claims processing involves accumulating charges for services, submitting claims for reimbursement, and ensuring that claims are satisfied. As this chapter has already discussed, this is the responsibility of the patient accounts department. However, the patient accounts department can only process what the service providers have accumulated and what HIM has coded.

Claims processing is often outsourced in nonhospital ambulatory care because physician offices and other small facilities often do not have the resources to perform this complex activity effectively. The activity of submitting a claim is often called dropping a bill. Because reimbursement for clinical services provided is the healthcare facility's largest source of revenue, timely, accurate claims processing is necessary.

Sometimes facilities adopt a **bill hold** policy. This policy dictates a waiting period between the patient's discharge date and claim submission (dropping the bill). Bill hold assumes that there will be a delay in accumulating the charges incurred by a patient. By incorporating this predicted delay into normal operations, the facility creates a preventive control to avoid underbilling or having to submit late charges to the payer. In acute care, the typical bill hold ranges from three to five days; in ambulatory care, it is 7 to 10 days (Schraffenberger 2007, 161). The determination of the duration of the bill hold is based on the needs of the facility.

Third-party payers generally will not reimburse a claim that does not include the clinical diagnostic and procedural codes. This is true whether the reimbursement is based on a PPS, actual charges, or some other method. For this reason, the patient accounts department cannot drop a bill until the patient record has been coded. Therefore, timely, accurate coding is critical to the reimbursement process and directly affects the facility's cash flow.

Accounts Receivable

During a patient's encounter with a healthcare provider, individual services are performed and associated charges are incurred. Each charge is recorded in a subledger for the specific patient account. Because each charge represents a completed transaction, the amount of the charge becomes revenue (earned and measurable) and receivable. However, from a practical standpoint, the claim to the payer is not rendered until after patient discharge, at which time the charges incurred by the patient during his or her stay are finalized. For example:

4/15	Accounts Receivable—Patient	$5,500	
	Patient Services Revenue		$5,500
	Total charges for account #0146589		

Cumulating charges and postdischarge billing work well for ambulatory care and most acute care encounters. For long-term care, however, interim billing is necessary. When an interim bill is dropped, the reimbursement received reduces the accounts receivable for that patient.

Posting the receivable and dropping the bill are two different activities. To monitor timely claims processing, a summary report of patient receivables is frequently generated. This summary report has no standard title. It is sometimes called DNFB (**discharged, no final bill**) or merely accounts receivable (AR).

Components of Accounts Receivable

The individual charges for a patient's account are collected in a database. The actual components of the database vary, depending on the needs of the facility. Patient identifying data and financial data collected at registration are components of the database. Individual charges incurred also are collected. Maintenance of patients' accounts in a database enables the facility to analyze these financial data in a number of ways.

Review and Analysis of Accounts Receivable

Department managers review the patient account database for different reasons. The pharmacy department may request a listing of all pharmaceutical charges in order to compare the posted charges with its records. This detective control enables the pharmacy department to ensure that all dispensed medications are charged. The chief financial officer (CFO), on the other hand, may target one number: total charges for patients who have been discharged, but for whom no final bill has been dropped. When the total charges exceed a predetermined threshold, the CFO will require an explanation from the patient accounts department.

A predetermined threshold may be a dollar amount or a time period, such as days in accounts receivable. For example, an acceptable level of unbilled charges may be $1,000,000 in one hospital and $200,000 in another. A dollar threshold would be determined taking into consideration the cash flow needs of the facility as well as the facility's historical experience in accurate billing, including average discharges during the bill hold period.

An alternative or concomitant threshold would be days in accounts receivable, which refers to the number of days an invoice has been outstanding after it has been billed. Of course, the first step is to send out the final bill. Because one common reason for no final bill is the lack of clinical codes, the HIM department may be involved in delivering the explanation.

The HIM department participates in ensuring timely claims processing by timely coding of the clinical records. Therefore, effective coding management includes the routine analysis of the DNFB. Figure 25.15 illustrates a portion of a DNFB. Notice that the report lists the outstanding charges by the patient's last name. The patient's account number and discharge date enable the HIM department to locate the patient's clinical record. The sample report indicates that

Fig 25.15. Example DNFB attributable to HIM

Sample Hospital
Failed Bills 12/10/08
Responsibility: Health Information Management
Inpatients
Service: INP

A/C Number	Pt Name	Admission	Discharge	Days in AR	Estimated Charges	Error
473829382	Grost, Nancy	11/21/08	11/24/08	18	25,970	Final Abstract
473829825	Black, Paul	11/27/08	11/29/08	13	14,728	Final Abstract
473830256	Sands, Marie	11/05/08	12/05/08	5	267,548	Principal Diagnosis Final Abstract
473830537	Abbott, Michael	12/03/08	12/07/08	3	45,928	Principal Diagnosis Final Abstract
473830539	Chang, Lin	12/01/08	12/07/08	3	67,283	Principal Diagnosis Final Abstract
473830614	Reese, Dewayne	12/05/08	12/07/08	3	22,510	Principal Diagnosis Final Abstract

Total Unbilled Accounts 6 Total Estimated Charges 443,967

Errors
6 Final Abstract
4 Principle Diagnosis

patient number 473830256 was discharged five days before the report was prepared and that the estimated accumulated charges are $267,548. The reason listed for failure to drop the bill is "final abstract" and "principle diagnosis." Seeing this, the HIM department manager would have located the record, determined why it had not been coded, and taken action to solve whatever problem had prevented its coding. Typical problems include lack of a pathology report, uncertainty as to principal diagnosis (outstanding physician query), and backlog in the coding function. Table 25.5 lists some common coding delays and actions that can be taken to solve the underlying problem. When the DNFB is actively worked, the manager would ideally have identified this high-dollar account and worked with coding staff to identify any issues and resolve them promptly.

Because the patients' account data are maintained in a database, theoretically, they can be retrieved in whatever format is useful to the manager. Many facilities' computer systems include sophisticated report-writing functions that enable managers to query the database for the desired data and retrieve a report in the desired format, as needed. Of course, this situation is ideal; other systems do not provide this capability. The facility's information systems (IS) department should be able to provide the manager with a customized report routinely.

The frequency with which managers review the accounts receivable data depends on the facility's policies and procedures as well as on the impact on claims processing. To proactively manage the outstanding receivables, some HIM managers review the data daily and take action on large-dollar accounts. Because the entire AR report may contain hundreds of accounts, the manager may request a report of all accounts with an amount over $40,000 that were discharged over two days ago. Even with a bill-hold policy of three or four days, a targeted report enables the HIM department to prioritize the processing of high-dollar accounts quickly. Another useful way to handle this data is to obtain an electronic download daily of the AR listing. This enables the manager to review the list in a number of different ways as circumstances dictate.

The priority of coding high-dollar accounts quickly must be balanced against the need to maintain the even distribution of workload and orderly processing of all records in the HIM department. Ten $5,000 accounts are financially equivalent to one $50,000 account. Failure to process those 10 accounts because the routine was disrupted in order to process the one higher dollar account is not good financial management. Therefore, routine, timely processing of all records can obviate prioritization by dollars.

In addition to proactively monitoring receivables, HIM personnel also support claims management by providing clinical documentation for a variety of purposes. For example, a payer may deny payment for a technical or clinical reason. Failure to provide supporting documentation on a timely basis results in loss of reimbursement. HIM managers who outsource their ROI function must work closely with the vendor to ensure that documentation needed by patient accounts for claims management is processed timely. Further, when the claims processing and denials management functions are also outsourced, the HIM manager may find himself or herself working not only with patient accounts, but also with the vendors, who may or may not have a smooth, ongoing relationship. On a practical level, detailed contract management and continuous, thorough communication among the parties are essential in these situations.

Impact of Accounts Receivable on Financial Statements

Accounts receivable represents a current asset. Delays in processing claims cause receivables to age. Aged receivables can negatively affect a facility's ability to borrow money. Failure to claim and collect receivables affects cash, which in turn negatively affects the facility's ability to discharge its current liabilities, the largest of which is payroll. Therefore,

Table 25.5. Remedies for common coding delays

Reason for Failure to Code	Underlying Issue(s)	Possible Actions
Lack of pathology report	Pathology department may not have completed the analysis.	Ask the pathology department for an estimated completion date and a STAT dictation.
	Pathologist may not have dictated the report.	Ask the pathology department for a STAT dictation or a verbal confirmation of the pathology diagnosis.
	Pathology reports may not have been in the charts.	Search the reports for the missing one. In a computer-based environment, coders should have the ability to search for the reports online.
Uncertain principal or additional diagnosis	Waiting for a response to a physician query	Elevate the query to the managerial level. Meet the physician on the nursing unit during morning rounds, if necessary.
Coding backlog	Coder(s) out sick	Prioritize coding by receivable size instead of discharge date.
	Coder(s) on vacation	Consider overtime pay for staff to fill in.
	Coding function understaffed	Assign qualified supervisory personnel to assist and/or support coders.
		Plan vacation coverage in advance to avoid affecting the facility's cash flow.
		Long-term understaffing can impair coding quality. Outsourcing should be considered. Coding quality and DNFB impact are typical justifications for approving additional coding staff.

in a facility for which reimbursement is the largest revenue item and payroll is the largest expense, there is a direct relationship between getting paid and paying employees. Thus, the role of HIM becomes a critical component of maintaining the facility's fiscal integrity.

Internal Controls

In any industry, **internal controls** must be in place to safeguard assets and to ensure compliance with policies and procedures. Internal controls may be designed to prevent the theft of cash or to ensure that a patient receives the correct medication. The three major categories of internal controls are preventive, detective, and corrective controls.

Preventive

Preventive controls are implemented prior to the activity's taking place because they are designed to stop an error from happening. In financial management, pretransaction supervisory review and authorization is a preventive control. Computer data-entry validation is another preventive control. Data-entry validation prevents the user from entering "64," for example, as a day of the month. Preventive controls are sometimes more costly than their effect warrants. In those cases, controls must be put in place to find and correct errors.

Detective

Detective controls are designed to find errors that have already been made. Detective controls tend to be less expensive than preventive controls and can be implemented at many levels. Quantitative record reviews and computer exception reports are examples of detective controls. In accounting, the summing of debits and credits is a detective control because the two sums must always be equal. Footing and cross-footing financial reports is another detective control. (See figure 25.16.)

Corrective

When an error or other problem has been detected, action must be taken to correct the error, solve the problem, or design controls to prevent future errors or problems. The error or problem must be analyzed to determine the cause. When a correction can be made, it is documented and implemented. However, some errors, such as amputation of an incorrect limb, cannot be corrected. In these cases, analysis of the root cause is important so that the error can be prevented in the future. In financial management, very few errors cannot be corrected. Typical errors include posting transactions to an incorrect account, posting transactions that have not been completed, and posting incorrect amounts. Even financial statement errors can be corrected and the reports redistributed. Problems that cannot always be corrected include theft of assets and failure to invest funds on a timely basis. These problems require analysis and development and implementation of controls for the future.

Corrective controls are designed to fix problems that have been discovered, frequently as a result of detective controls. Many errors and problems occur routinely, such as failing to complete forms, making computation errors, and wrongly posting transactions. Therefore, procedures must be in place to ensure the timely and accurate correction of the error or solution to the problem. In the HIM department, the

Figure 25.16. Footing and cross-footing financial reports

SUMMING OF DEBITS AND CREDITS

	Debit	Credit
Cash	$1,345	
Photocopy paper		$974
Toner		$362

In this journal entry, the debit ($1,345) does not match the credits ($1,336). This means that an error has been made. Reference back to the original documentation will reveal that the sales tax on the items was not accounted for.

FOOTING AND CROSS-FOOTING

	January	February	March	Year-to-date (Cross-foot)
Payroll	20,000	20,000	20,000	60,000
Benefits	6,000	6,000	6,000	24,000
Office supplies	1,000	1,000	1,000	3,000
Equipment service	400	500	600	500
				87,500?
Monthly Totals	27,400 (Foot)	27,400	27,400	82,200?

The foot is the sum of the columns; the cross-foot is the sum of the rows. Notice that in this example the sums do not match. Footing and cross-footing reports that are supposed to represent arithmetic totals is a very useful detective control, particularly with manually prepared or PC-prepared reports. A simple error in creating a formula in a spreadsheet program can cause an entire report to be wrong.

incomplete chart system is a corrective control. Incomplete charts have been detected, the source of the error identified, and the responsible individual contacted for completion of the chart. In financial management, supervisory review of transactions is typically used to detect errors and problems. The ability to correct errors in journal entries is essential.

Internal controls may be present at every level of the organization. In a service organization, such as a hospital, controls over expenditures are some of the most important responsibilities of individual managers. Two key methods of exerting such controls are through purchasing and analysis of budget variances.

Budgets

Managers must have some understanding of **managerial accounting** in order to control the financial aspects of their departments' operations. As stated earlier, managers must work within budgets that have been developed based on their organization's goals and objectives. Therefore, it is not sufficient for a manager merely to review for accuracy the financial transactions generated by the department during the period. Rather, the transactions must be compared to the expected or budgeted transactions to ensure that the goals and objectives of both the department and the organization are being met. Managerial accounting is the development, implementation, and analysis of systems that track financial transactions for managerial control purposes; it includes both budget and cost analysis systems.

Types of Budgets

In addition to the most familiar budgets, operating and capital budgets (discussed next), organizations develop and monitor other budgets, including financial budgets, cash flow budgets, and incremental budgets. These budgets are the responsibility of the finance department.

The development and monitoring of budgets is guided by the facility's policy and procedures manual and the management styles of the administrative and departmental management team. Therefore, it is extremely important for department managers to understand the facility's budgeting methods, including how administration uses budgets.

At best, a budget is a manager's best guess at the outcomes of future financial transactions. Unexpected events that influence those transactions, such as declining census, increase in interest rates, and staffing changes, create budget variances. Some budgets are specifically designed to take these fluctuations into consideration. A budget can represent virtually any projected set of circumstances. Therefore, there are many different types of budget methodologies. Common methodologies include fixed, flexible, activity-based, and zero-based budgets.

The most common type of budget is a **fixed budget**. Budget amounts are based on expected capacity. Fixed budgets do not change when expected capacity changes. For example, the HIM department would budget file folder expense on the basis of the estimated number of discharges and the historical need to replace worn folders. When the number of discharges materially increases or declines, the file folder expense will increase or decrease, thus creating a budget variance.

Flexible budgets are based on projected productivity. In this case, the HIM department would budget file folder expense at several levels of discharges. As the actual discharges become known, the budget reflects the estimate at that level of activity. Used primarily in manufacturing, this method of budgeting also is useful for projecting personnel budgets in service areas, such as nursing units, where increased activity has a direct impact on staffing and supplies.

Activity-based budgets are based on activities or projects rather than on departments. Typically used for construction projects, an activity-based budget can be useful for any project that spans multiple budget lines or departments and for projects that span more than one fiscal year. Computer system installation and implementation should be controlled using an activity-based budget.

Different budget methodologies are developed to meet the needs of the organization. Fixed and flexible budgets are characteristic of operating budgets. Activity-based budgets are more often used for capital projects. All three types of budgets can be used by virtually any organization. **Zero-based budgets**, on the other hand, apply to organizations for which each budget cycle poses the opportunity to continue or discontinue services based on the availability of resources. Every department or activity must be justified and prioritized annually in order to effectively allocate the organization's resources. Professional associations and charitable foundations, for example, routinely use zero-based budgeting.

Operational Budgets

The purpose of an **operational budget** is to allocate and control resources in a manner consistent with the organization's goals and objectives. These goals and objectives are tied to the organization's mission. Each department also should have its own mission, goals, and objectives that identify how it contributes to the organization's overall mission. Every item in the operational budget should have a direct relationship to a departmental goal that supports an organizational goal.

The budget process begins with the board of directors or trustees, who approve the fiscal assumptions for the upcoming year. Those assumptions are quantified and communicated to the department managers, who develop budgets based on those assumptions. Typical assumptions include the desired growth in revenue and target cost reductions.

Budget Cycle

The operational **budget cycle** generally coincides with one fiscal year. The purpose of the operational budget is the quantification of the projected results of operations for the coming fiscal year. This process begins three to four months before the end of the current fiscal year. Projected budgets should be collected, compiled, reviewed, and approved prior to the start of the new fiscal year.

Fiscal Period

An organization's budget year coincides with its fiscal year on file with the IRS. Although the actual operational budget generally only applies to one fiscal year, financial managers often project multiple years of budgets with a variety of scenarios in order to test the financial impact of current decision making.

Interim Periods

In a computerized environment, it is relatively easy to generate financial reports as frequently as needed by management. However, monthly budget reporting is most common. Any period that represents less than an entire fiscal year is an **interim period**. Figure 25.17 provides a sample budget report for an HIM department for May. The budgeted amounts for each item are listed next to the actual amounts for the month. As is common, the year-to-date (in this case, January through May) budget and actual amounts also are included. It is useful for budget reports to show the differences between budgeted and actual amounts. Such differences are called variances. Many budget reports also show the percentage variance for each item, based on the budget. Managers may be required to explain variances that exceed a particular dollar value or a specified percentage.

In the budget report shown in figure 25.17, there is a large variance in May's budgeted expense for printer paper. By following that line item across to the year-to-date amount, it is evident that there is no year-to-date variance in the budget. This illustrates a timing difference between the expected expense and the actual expense. The budget may have placed that expense in April, even though the actual expense occurred in May. These types of temporary variances are the result of normal business activities, and although they may require explanation, they are usually not of concern.

Budget Components

The components of an operational budget generally follow the format of the income statement and list revenue items and expense items. Every department is different, depending on its unique activities. However, budget reports tend to be uniform throughout the organization. Therefore, line items that do not apply to a particular department are likely to be listed with zero values rather than be omitted.

Revenues

In the HIM department, there is little, if any, revenue. Occasionally, a facility with excess capacity will contract out transcription services. Copy fees are another potential source of revenue; however, because such fees should be cost based, they are probably more appropriately considered a reimbursement (reduction of expenses).

Expenses

The HIM department budget consists primarily of expenses. Expenses may be incurred as a result of financial transactions outside or within the organization. Some departments, such as housekeeping and facilities maintenance, perform services for other facility departments. Therefore, charges from these departments may appear on the budget. Such charges are generally carried forward through the cost allocation process and usually are not estimated by individual managers.

Ordinarily, the single largest expense in a healthcare facility is payroll. This is typical for service organizations. Payroll can be a difficult expense to project because employees have different anniversary dates and different salary increases.

The cost of employee benefits is part of payroll but is often listed separately. Facilities rarely expect department managers to calculate benefits budgets because this is a human resources–controlled line item. The cost of benefits tracks with payroll.

The next largest expense account is often supplies. Clinical supplies are a substantial item on the cardiology or radiology department budget, whereas office supplies might be a large item for health information management.

Cost of goods sold is a manufacturing concept that refers to the underlying cost of making the finished goods. This concept applies to healthcare providers in the sense that there is a cost basis for providing services. For every inpatient treated, there are payroll, utility, office supplies, pharmaceutical, and

Figure 25.17. HIM department budget report for May

Description	May Budget	May Actual	May Variance	YTD Budget	YTD Actual	YTD Variance
Payroll	$25,000	$22,345	$2,655	$125,000	$110,321	$14,679
Fringe benefits	$8,000	$7,360	$640	$40,000	$37,870	$2,130
Contract services	$5,000	$8,000	($3,000)	$25,000	$40,000	($15,000)
Office supplies	$150	$145	$5	$750	$975	($225)
Printer paper	$100	$250	($150)	$500	$500	—
Postage	$95	$97	($2)	$475	$456	$19
Travel	$0	$0	—	$0	$0	—
Continuing education	$0	$0	—	$0	$45	($45)

equipment costs that the facility incurred. Unlike manufacturing, in which the cost of producing items is tracked very closely, healthcare facilities historically have not been good at tracking the underlying costs of providing services to individual patients. The costs of providing care are often analyzed in the aggregate.

Management of the Operating Budget

When the operating budget has been developed and approved, it is the responsibility of the department management to ensure that the budget goals are met. As a general rule, in meeting goals, revenue should meet or exceed budget and expenses should meet or be less than budget. However, because expenses support revenues, an increase in revenues (perhaps due to unexpected volume) may signal an expected increase in expenses, such as variable expenses. This is particularly true when the patient census exceeds expectations. Despite the logical and expected nature of these results, managers are required to investigate and explain differences between budgeted and actual amounts on a regular basis.

Identification of Variances

A **variance** is the arithmetic difference between the budgeted amount and the actual amount of a line item. **Variance analysis** places accountability for financial transactions on the manager of the department that initiated the transaction.

Variances are often calculated on the monthly budget report. The organization's policies and procedures manual defines unacceptable variances or variances that must be explained. In identifying variances, it is important to recognize whether the variance is favorable or unfavorable and whether it is temporary or permanent.

Timing

The problems identified by variance analysis and the action that must be taken depend largely on whether the variance is temporary or permanent. Temporary variances are generally self-limiting.

Temporary budget variances are not expected to continue in subsequent months. For example, a department may budget for a large purchase of file folders in May. When that purchase does not actually take place until July, there will be a temporary variance in the May and July monthly report and a temporary variance in the May and June year-to-date numbers. Figure 25.18 illustrates this point. In this example, the HIM department budgeted $260 per month for department supplies, plus an additional $9,750 in May for file folders. Because of an unexpectedly low census, the file folders were not needed until July. This created a temporary, favorable variance in expenditures in May and June.

In contrast, **permanent budget variances** do not resolve during the current fiscal year. In the preceding example, a variance still would have existed at the end of December (the close of the fiscal year) if the file folders had been budgeted in November. The department supplies variance then would be a permanent variance during the current and subsequent fiscal year, unless the subsequent year's budget can include the purchase.

Impact

In addition to identifying whether timing is an issue, the variance analysis is expected to identify whether the variance is favorable of unfavorable. This is often obvious from the budget report but should be stated clearly when discussing the variance.

Favorable variances occur when the actual results are better than budget projections. Actual revenue in excess of budget is a favorable variance. **Unfavorable variances** occur when the actual results are worse than what was budgeted. Actual expenditure in excess of budget is an unfavorable variance. Note that the terms *favorable* and *unfavorable* refer to the impact on the organization rather than to the magnitude or direction of the variance. Sometimes the terms *negative* and *positive* are used instead. This can be confusing because a negative expense variance is favorable. Therefore, it is extremely important to ensure that the manager understands and correctly uses the language of the organization.

Explanation of Variances

The analysis of budget variances is a financial management control. Administration may review the monthly budget report first and then ask questions of the appropriate manager. In other instances, the department managers are automatically required to respond to certain variances.

Figure 25.18. Examples of budget variances

May Budget Report						
	May Budget	**May Actual**	**May Variance**	**YTD Budget**	**YTD Actual**	**YTD Variance**
Department supplies	10,000	250	9,750	11,000	1,250	9,750
June Budget Report						
	June Budget	**June Actual**	**June Variance**	**YTD Budget**	**YTD Actual**	**YTD Variance**
Department supplies	250	250	0	11,250	1,500	9,750
July Budget Report						
	July Budget	**July Actual**	**July Variance**	**YTD Budget**	**YTD Actual**	**YTD Variance**
Department supplies	250	10,000	−9,750	11,500	11,500	0

In general, the reason for a temporary budget variance is the timing of the transaction. Looking back to the department supplies and file folder example in figure 25.18, there is a very simple explanation for the temporary variance. In wording the explanation to administration, the department manager should state:

- Nature of the variance (favorable or unfavorable, temporary or permanent)
- Exact amount of the variance
- Cause of the variance
- Any ameliorating circumstances or offsetting amounts

Amount

In the analysis of variance, materiality is an issue. Rarely will a manager be required to explain a $5 variance. Clearly, the cost of a manager's time to explain such an insignificant amount far exceeds the benefit of knowing why the variance has occurred. In fact, because budgets are largely estimates, it would be quite odd if the actual amounts always matched the budgeted amounts. Therefore, dollar and percentage limits are set in the organization's policies and procedures manual. Variances that exceed these limits must be explained in detail.

Cause

For the preceding file folder variance example, the explanation might be something like the following: "In department supplies, the favorable, temporary variance of $9,750 will resolve in July when the budgeted expenditure for file folders is processed." For such a temporary variance, no additional explanation is usually necessary; however, the administration may prefer more detail. In that case, the relationship between low census and the need for file folders could be added to the explanation.

Temporary variances are not typically of serious concern to administrations. However, permanent variances can be a problem because management of departmental budgets is an important indicator of the competence of department managers.

Whether a variance is temporary or permanent depends on the answers to two questions:

- Are the subsequent transactions that will compensate for the variance likely to occur within the same fiscal year?
- Is it reasonably certain the transactions will occur as predicted?

If the compensating transactions are unlikely to take place during the current fiscal year, the result is a permanent variance in the current budget report. Sometimes the manager may not know when—or if—the transactions will actually take place. For example, the manager may have budgeted $2,000 for attendance at an unspecified CE conference in June. A conflict with the Joint Commission survey prevented the manager from attending the conference, creating a favorable expense variance. As long as the manager believes the amount will be spent appropriately at some time during the fiscal year, the variance is temporary. For example, the manager may be able to attend a conference later in the year. However, if the manager knows that there is no chance of attending a conference and appropriately spending the budgeted amount, the variance should be explained as permanent.

Additional explanation is probably necessary for a permanent variance. An expenditure that must be deferred until the next fiscal year is particularly important. In that case, the explanation might be as follows: "In department supplies, there is a favorable, permanent variance of $9,750. Because of an unexpectedly low census, the purchase of additional file folders for discharged patient records was not necessary this year. This amount is included in next year's budget."

Circumstances

Managers may have the opportunity to utilize favorable variances in one line item to offset unfavorable variances in another line item. For example, unused travel budget may be used for CE. The explanation of these circumstances will generally be carried forward through all remaining variance analyses for the remainder of the fiscal year.

The ability to work with the departmental budget as a whole as opposed to justifying line items is entirely dependent on the administration of the budget process. One typical example of offsetting variances occurs when an employee leaves and cannot be replaced immediately. Several things may happen. The vacancy may cause a favorable variance in payroll expense until the position is filled or an unfavorable variance in payroll expense if other employees are paid overtime to help fill the vacancy. Both of these variances are permanent. Alternatively, the vacancy may cause a permanent, favorable variance in payroll expense and a permanent, unfavorable variance in consulting expenses when the vacant position is outsourced. In the latter case, the two variances at least partially offset each other, which must be explained in the monthly variance report.

Capital Budget

Unlike the operational budget, which looks primarily at projected income statement activity for the next fiscal year, the **capital budget** looks at long-term investments. Such investments are usually related to improvements in the facility infrastructure, expansion of services, or replacement of existing assets. Capital investments focus on either the appropriateness of an investment (given the facility's investment guidelines) or choosing among different opportunities to invest. The capital budget is the facility's plan for allocating resources over and above the operating budget.

Funding for the capital budget may come from diverse sources. For example, donations or grants may fund a building project or **retained earnings** or **unallocated reserves** may fund equipment purchases. Federal and state government funds may be available to offset the cost of capital investments. Regardless of the source of the funds, capital investments are defined by facility policy and selected using financial analysis techniques.

Large-Dollar Purchases

From a departmental perspective, capital budget items are large-dollar purchases, as defined by facility budget policies and procedures. Capital budget items usually have a useful life in excess of one fiscal year, making them long-term assets, and a dollar value in excess of a predetermined amount, often $500 or $1,000. The most common HIM department capital budget items include shelving, office furniture, photocopying equipment, and computer equipment. Computer software, and even some computer hardware, has a limited useful life and is often included in the operating budget. Some organizations maintain a separate capital budget and process for computer-related equipment and software. In addition, in such cases, control over the acquisition of the related long-term assets may rest with the information technology or information systems department.

Acquisitions

The acquisition of long-term assets may be controlled by the purchasing department. The purchasing department may already have a contract with a specific vendor to provide certain types of equipment or furniture. In the absence of an existing contract, it may still be the purchasing department's responsibility to ensure the appropriate acquisition of assets through the **request for proposal** (RFP) process. The RFP process is a preventive control designed to eliminate bias and to ensure competitive pricing in the acquisition of goods and services.

Cost-Benefit Analysis

An old photocopying machine breaks down at least once a week. Repair of the machine takes up to two days and is increasingly expensive. During the downtime, ROI clerks must use a machine located two floors below the HIM department and shared by three other departments. It seems obvious to HIM department personnel that a new machine is needed. Including a new machine in the HIM department's capital budget request is certainly warranted. However, funding for a new machine is based on specific, detailed cost justifications and is weighed in comparison to all departments' requests. Facility administration may be forced to choose between a new copier for the HIM department and several new computers for the patient accounts department. All other factors being equal, increased efficiency and productivity in claims processing is likely to be chosen over increased efficiency in release of information. For this reason, HIM managers should include cost savings calculations in such requests.

Depreciation

As discussed earlier, certain long-term assets, such as equipment and furniture, wear out over time and must be replaced. Such assets contribute to revenue over multiple fiscal periods. Therefore, the cost of these assets is not recorded as an expense at the time of purchase. Rather, the current asset, cash, is exchanged for a long-term asset, equipment. A portion of the historical cost of equipment then is moved from asset into expense each fiscal year and cumulated into the contra-account: accumulated depreciation. Eventually, the cost of equipment has been expensed and equipment account value is zero. The purpose of depreciation is to spread the cost of an asset over its useful life. (See tables 25.6 and 25.7.)

Note that the depreciation of long-term assets does not necessarily have a direct relationship to the activity of actually using the asset. It is not unusual to depreciate an asset over five years and then continue to use it for another five. For example, a facility whose equipment is fully depreciated and whose current assets are heavily financed with debt obligations may be unable to reinvest in new equipment. This is another example of how ratio analysis affects lending decisions.

Capital Projects

A facility's ability to invest in capital projects is very important to the continued success of its operations. Because buildings deteriorate, equipment wears out, and new technology is important to healthcare delivery, capital improvements must be implemented. Individual departments request equipment purchases and facility improvements as the needs arise. Facility administration must choose among the suggested projects to optimize use of its resources.

In addition to capital improvements, facilities may make capital investments that improve operational efficiency. Some of these capital investments require broader analysis than the cost of the equipment. Replacing a manual incomplete record tracking system, for example, with a computer-based system involves an analysis of employee time and departmental space allocations as well as the associated equipment and software costs. Medical staff relationship improvement is another factor that is difficult to quantify but should be considered.

Facility administration looks at capital projects differently than it reviews operational activities. Theoretically, operational activities contribute to the generation of revenue for the facility. For example, all hospital activities either provide healthcare services or in some way support departments that provide healthcare services. A hospital may elect to perform its own printing rather than outsource the printing function; however, it is unlikely to provide printing services to the general public. Printing forms supports clinical and administrative services internally; running a printing business does not. Therefore, the justification for operational budget amounts generally rests on the extent to which the underlying activities support the mission of the facility at the projected productivity levels. Capital projects, on the other hand, although still mission-supportive, often leverage the facility to higher levels of productivity, increased efficiency, or expansion of services and capacity.

Finally, budgeted capital funds generally must be expended in the time period for which they were approved. Even when allocated, capital budget items may be prioritized and timed so that purchases are made only with administrative approval. Actual funding may not meet anticipated levels or unforeseen circumstances may change administrative priorities.

For capital budgets, supporting the mission of the facility is not sufficient justification. Capital projects also must satisfy predetermined levels of return on the projected investment.

Cost Justification

All departments in a facility compete for finite facility resources. Therefore, department managers must be familiar with cost justification techniques and with their facility's method of analyzing capital projects. Typical **cost justifications** are based on increased revenue, increased efficiency, improved customer service, and reduced costs. The analysis of a capital project is based on the estimated ROI, including the weight of costs versus the benefits to be derived from the project. The specific cost-benefit analysis method used by facility administration depends on the characteristics of the project as well as the preferences of the analyst. When no specific cash inflows are expected, return may be based on depreciation or other cost savings. Sometimes the capital budget includes the allocation of resources for assets whose acquisition will attract or retain valuable personnel or physician relationships. Even in such cases, the acquisition should be analyzed financially, not just politically.

Payback Period

The **payback period** is the time required to recoup the cost of an investment. Mortgage refinancing analysis frequently uses the concept of payback period. Mortgage refinancing is considered when interest rates have dropped. Refinancing may require up-front interest payments, called points, as well as a variety of administrative costs. In this example, the payback period is the time it takes for the savings in interest to equal the cost of the refinancing.

Payback Period

Investment:	$100,000
Cash In:	$50,000 per year
Payback Period:	2 years (100,000 / 50,000)

The advantage of using a payback period to analyze investments is that it is relatively easy to calculate and understand. For example, a payback period can be used to describe the time it takes for the savings in payroll costs to equal the cost of productivity-enhancing equipment. In the previous

Table 25.6. Sample depreciation methods

Method	Description	Formula
Straight Line	The cost of the asset is expensed equally over the expected life of the asset. The estimated sale value of the asset at the end of its useful life is called the residual value and is subtracted from the cost prior to depreciation.	$\frac{\text{Cost} - \text{residual value}}{\text{\# of years (useful life)}}$
	Example: Copy machine purchased at a cost of $5,000 Useful life = 4 years Residual value = $200 Annual depreciation = $\frac{\$5{,}000 - \$200}{4} = \$1{,}200$ per year	
Units of Production	The cost of the asset is expensed over the expected life of the asset, measured in usage. In this case, usage would a number of copies.	$\frac{\text{Cost} - \text{residual value}}{\text{\# of copies (useful life)}}$
	Example: Copy machine purchased at a cost of $5,000 Useful life = 100,000 copies Residual value = $200 Depreciation rate = $\frac{\$5{,}000 - \$200}{100{,}000} = \$0.048$ (4.8 cents) per copy Annual depreciation = $0.048 times the number of copies actually made	
Accelerated	There are several accelerated depreciation methods, all of which are designed to expense more of the asset's value early in its useful life. One such method is called double declining balance (DDB). DDB expenses the asset at double the straight-line method, based on the book value rather than on the historical cost.	Book value times twice the straight line rate Straight line rate = $\frac{\text{annual depreciation}}{\text{cost} - \text{residual value}}$
	Example: Copy machine purchased at a cost of $5,000 Useful life = 100,000 copies Residual value = $200 Straight line rate = $1,200/$4,800 = 25% Annual depreciation = Book value times 50%	

Note: These examples of depreciation methods are just a few of the acceptable methods in use today for various purposes. The reader should be aware that there are other methods and that not all methods are acceptable for income tax purposes or for GAAP. Accounting for income taxes is beyond the scope of this discussion.

photocopy machine example, the payroll costs would be calculated based on downtime incurred when using a copier in another area of the building.

The disadvantage of a payback period is that it ignores the time value of money. Because the funds used for one capital investment could have been invested elsewhere, there is always an inherent opportunity cost of choosing one investment over another. Hence, there is an assumed rate of return against which investments are compared and a benchmark rate of return under which a facility will not consider an investment.

Accounting Rate of Return

Another simple method of capital project analysis is the **accounting rate of return**. This method compares the projected annual cash inflows, minus any applicable annual depreciation, divided by the initial investment. Co[illegible] purchase of a CT scanner. Reimbursement from use [illegible] machine is the cash inflow. Depreciation is easily calculat[illegible] based on the initial investment.

Accounting Rate of Return

Investment:	$100,000
Straight Line Depreciation over 5 years:	$20,000 per year
Cash In:	$50,000 per year
ARR:	30% [(50,000 – 20,000) / 100,000]

Accounting rate of return is another example of a simple method of capital project analysis. However, it also ignores the time value of money. In addition, accounting rate of return is based on an estimate. If the analyst incorrectly projects annual cash inflows, the projected rate of return will be incorrect.

Table 25.7. Sample depreciation schedule

Copy machine purchased at a cost of $5,000
Useful life = 100,000 copies
Residual value = $200

Straight Line-Depreciation (25% of Cost minus Residual Value annually)

	Book Value at Beginning of Year	Depreciation	Accumulated Depreciation	Book Value at End of Year
Year 1	$5,000	$1,200	$1,200	$3,800
Year 2	3,800	1,200	2,400	2,600
Year 3	2,600	1,200	3,600	1,400
Year 4	1,400	1,200	4,800	200
Year 5	200			

Units of Production (4.8 cents per copy annually)

	Book Value at Beginning of Year	Number of Copies Used	Depreciation	Accumulated Depreciation	Book Value at End of Year
Year 1	$5,000	20,000	$960	$960	$4,040
Year 2	4,040	20,000	960	1,920	3,080
Year 3	3,080	22,000	1,056	2,976	2,024
Year 4	2,024	25,000	1,200	4,176	824
Year 5	824	25,000	624	4,800	200

Notice that in units of production the useful life is based on the number of copies used—not on the time in service. In this example, the copier does not become fully depreciated until year 5. Also, the depreciation cannot exceed the cost less the residual value; therefore, the depreciation in year 5 is only $624.

Double Declining Balance (50% of book value annually)

	Book Value at Beginning of Year	Depreciation	Accumulated Depreciation	Book Value at End of Year
Year 1	$5,000	$2,500	$2,500	$2,500
Year 2	2,500	1,250	3,750	1,250
Year 3	1,250	625	4,375	625
Year 4	625	425	4,800	200
Year 5	200			

Notice that in DDB, the final depreciation entry in year 4 reduces the book value to the residual value (50% of $625 is really $375.50, but we added $49.50 to make the depreciation 425 so that book value drops to $200 at the end of year 4).

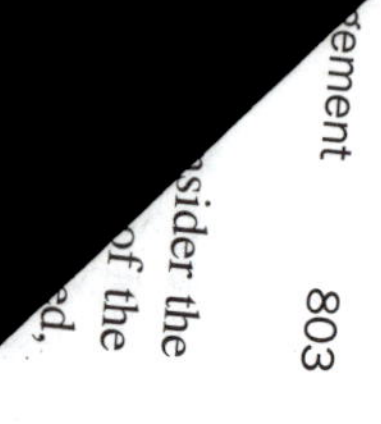

ed to analyze marketable securities ase in market value of the securi- l investment is the ROI. When an ed with the investment, the income rket value of the securities in calculating return. In ... g the ROI among different securities, the tax implications must be considered. Long-term gains are taxed differently than short-term gains. Tax-exempt investments result in different returns than taxable investments.

With respect to capital investments, the equation is similar. Divide the controllable operating profits by the controllable net investment. Operating profits are the cash inflow minus the direct costs of operation.

Return on Investment

Investment:	$100,000
Straight Line Depreciation over 5 years:	$20,000 per year
Operating Costs:	$5,000 per year
Cash In:	$50,000 per year
ROI:	25% [(50,000 – 25,000) / 100,000]

As with accounting rate of return and payback period, ROI is easy to calculate and understand. Similarly, it does not consider the time value of money.

Net Present Value

To take into consideration the time value of money, the analyst must establish an interest rate at which money could have otherwise been invested. From that implied interest rate and the projected future cash inflows of the investment, the present value of the cash inflows is calculated. Present value is the current dollar amount that must be invested today in order to yield the projected future cash inflows at the implied interest rate. **Net present value** is the calculated present value of the future cash inflows compared to the initial investment.

The advantage of using net present value to analyze investments is that it considers the time value of money. When choosing among like investments, net present values can be reliably compared to determine the financial advantages of the investment.

Net Present Value

Investment:	$100,000
Cash In:	$25,000 per year (revenue minus depreciation and operating costs)
Interest Rate:	7%
NPV:	$2,341 (based on 5 years of service)

As with other analysis tools, analysts may have to estimate the projected cash flows. However, the main disadvantage of net present value is that the interest rate is subjective. Therefore, it is best used to compare multiple investment opportunities rather than to analyze one investment alone. Another disadvantage of using net present value is that it requires some knowledge of mathematics to calculate as well as to accept its validity and understand its relevance. Fortunately, financial calculators and computer spreadsheet programs have made the calculation of net present value relatively simple.

Internal Rate of Return

Internal rate of return (IRR) is the interest rate that makes the net present value calculation equal zero. In other words, it is the interest rate at which the present value of the projected cash inflows equals the initial investment. IRR considers the time value of money. Both individual and multiple investments can be evaluated. As with net present value, knowledge of mathematics is helpful. The main disadvantage is that a project may have multiple IRRs.

Internal Rate of Return

Investment:	$100,000
Cash In:	$25,000 per year (revenue minus depreciation and operating costs)
NPV:	$0 (based on 5 years of service)
Interest Rate:	8%

Profitability Index

Facilities cannot automatically invest in seemingly profitable projects. For example, a $500,000 radiology equipment investment may have a present value of cash inflows of $1,500,000, for a net present value of $1,000,000. At the same time, a $10,000 pharmacy computer system yields a net present value of $30,000. This seems to be a great investment; however, the facility's capital budget may be limited to $100,000. In this case, a **profitability index** helps the organization prioritize investment opportunities. For each investment, divide the present value of the cash inflows by the present value of the cash outflows. In this example, the pharmacy system has a higher profitability index, as illustrated below:

Radiology		Pharmacy
$1,500,000	Present value of cash inflows	$40,000
$500,000	Present value of cash outflows	$10,000
3	Profitability index	4

Check Your Understanding 25.3

Instructions: Answer the following questions on a separate piece of paper.

1. Compare and contrast financial accounting and managerial accounting.
2. Compare and contrast operational budgets and capital budgets.
3. A not-for-profit organization offers a variety of programs and services. Each functional department in the organization plays some role in delivering all these programs and services. What type of operational budget would be most effective in this environment? Why?
4. Why would an organization choose a fiscal year that does not coincide with the calendar year?
5. The HIM department has a YTD budget for a payroll of $100,000. The actual YTD amount is $98,000. Is this a favorable or an unfavorable variance?

Real-World Case

Bright Hospital is a 270-bed, not-for-profit community hospital. Its largest percentage of patients consists of mothers and newborns, followed by a mix of cardiovascular-related admissions. It has an emergency department staffed by hospital employees. Bright's fiscal year follows the calendar year, ending December 31. In August, Bright began its year-end budget process by establishing its financial assumptions for the following two years. Bright assumed that revenue would remain constant, that it would continue its existing contracts with payers, that its Medicare population percentage would not change, and that no major infrastructure maintenance would be required in the upcoming fiscal year. No major capital projects were anticipated. In its operational budget, administration plans to include resources for a Joint Commission steering committee and related activities to prepare for the anticipated accreditation visit in the subsequent year. Administration distributed operational and capital budget compilation packages to department managers for completion and return by September 30.

Bright Hospital does not have a large marketing department. It has one marketing professional on staff whose responsibilities include the development and publishing of brochures and coordination of patient satisfaction surveys, which are compiled and analyzed by an outside vendor. In the past two years, there has been a slight, but continuing, decline in patient satisfaction among maternity patients. Suggestions for improvement have varied, but common complaints center on the lack of soothing ambiance in labor and delivery and the hospital policy prohibiting overnight visitors.

The maternity and newborn departments have been very concerned about declining patient satisfaction. They are worried that the current year's slight decline in maternity admissions is the result of that dissatisfaction and that patients are traveling a little further to give birth at a neighboring medical center, at which some of their physicians also have privileges. The departments would like to renovate the maternity and newborn wing, forming a women's center with increased emphasis on wellness and ancillary services. This would be a two-year capital project that would require marketing support and some minor disruption of services during construction.

The cardiology department is very excited. It has just learned that a well-respected cardiologist has retired to the area and is exploring the idea of opening a small consulting practice. The cardiologist has not yet applied for privileges at any area hospitals, but it is known that she is used to working in a facility with its own cardiac catheterization lab. Because the current chief of the medical staff at Bright is a personal friend of the cardiologist, the cardiology department believes that she could be lured on staff if the hospital had its own lab. Based on the volume of patients that Bright currently sends out to another facility for cardiac catheterization, the cardiology department believes that patient care would be facilitated by the expansion and that the increased revenue would help justify the cost.

The HIM department has recently lost several employees to retirement and promotions within the facility. It is currently down two coders and a file clerk, and has reduced its weekend coverage to one person, day shift only. Transcription is handled largely by the department, with an outside service processing any overflow. The HIM department would like to outsource all of its transcription and move to a Web-based coding system that would allow the coders to telecommute. This plan would improve productivity, decrease transcription and coding delays, and shorten billing time. In addition, the computer-based storage of documents involved in these changes would facilitate release of information. All three departments submitted capital budget requests for the projects described.

Summary

Management roles in any healthcare facility require some knowledge of accounting and financial management. The ability to read, understand, and interpret pertinent financial reports is a desirable business skill. Because of the close ties between reimbursement and HIM, this basic skill is even more important. Although the financial accounting methodologies of compiling and analyzing financial statements may not be needed routinely, the managerial accounting skills involving budget preparation and analysis are critical. Also important is an awareness of the preventive, detective, and corrective controls that managers must implement to ensure the accuracy of financial data.

Operational budgets are developed annually to allocate resources for the normal functioning of the facility, according to its mission. Operational budgets focus on revenues and expenses. Capital budgets separately identify and analyze long-term asset acquisitions that are designed to maintain and improve the facility's infrastructure, improve operational efficiency, or expand business, for example. Capital budget requests are analyzed for their cost versus benefit as well as return on investment.

Efficient claims processing has a direct impact on the ability of a facility to fund its operations, including paying its bills and meeting payroll obligations. HIM plays a direct role in ensuring efficient claims processing by participating in charge description master review, participating in the analysis and minimization of the AR totals, and ensuring efficient and accurate coding of records.

References

Cleverley, W. and A. Cameron. 2003. *Essentials of Health Care Finance*. 5th ed. Sudbury, MA: Jones and Bartlett.

Dunn, R. 1999. *Finance Principles for the Health Information Manager.* Chicago: AHIMA.

Schraffenberger, L.A., ed. 2007. *Effective Management of Coding Services*. 3rd ed. Chicago: AHIMA.

Tax Exempt Status for Your Organization. 2008. Pub. 557. Internal Revenue Service. http://www.irs.gov/pub/irs-pdf/p557.pdf.

Standards and Related Rules. 2008. Public Company Accounting Oversight Board (PCAOB). http://www.pcaobus.org/Standards/Standards_and_Related_Rules/index.aspx.

Chapter 26
Project Management

Patricia B. Seidl, RHIA, CCDM

Learning Objectives

- Identify how a project differs from an organization's daily operations
- Describe the components of a project
- Discuss reasons for project success versus project failure
- Describe different project team structures
- Understand the responsibilities of the project manager
- Know the project management process and recognize the technical and people skills involved
- Identify the components of a project proposal document
- Understand the steps in planning and organizing a project
- Estimate work, duration, and resource requirements
- Understand how to anticipate and manage project risk
- Know how to track a project's progress and analyze variances
- Describe the types of plan revision
- Understand the concept of scope management
- Recognize the components of a communication plan

Key Terms

Assumptions
Baseline
Change control
Contingency
Critical path
Dependency
Duration
Issue log
Predecessor
Project charter
Project components
Project definition
Project deliverables
Project management life cycle
Project management software
Project network
Project office
Project plan
Project schedule
Project scope
Project team
Resources
Risk
Roles and responsibilities
Scheduling engine
Scope creep
Sponsor
Stakeholders
Statement of work
Subprojects
Successor
Task
Variances
Work
Work breakdown structure
Work products

Although health information management (HIM) professionals practice in many diverse healthcare delivery systems and domains, there is a common responsibility across all lines of business: leading or participating in projects. It is important to understand the concepts and best practices of project management in order to engage fully and effectively as a project team member. Although there are many different types, all projects have similar attributes: their objectives benefit the organization, they all follow the project management process, similar characteristics of the project manager are needed, they all involve a project team, and they all result in some type of outcome.

Projects consist of organizational and behavioral components. Organizational or structural components guide the team toward its end goals. Behavioral components include the concepts of leading, motivating, politics, and interpersonal communication.

This chapter describes the different elements of a project and the different types of projects that healthcare organizations might undertake. It also focuses on how projects are managed and tracked to ensure their success.

The Project

An organization undertakes a project because it has determined the need for some type of change. This need may be the result of a company's strategic agenda, such as implementation of a new computer system, or it may be in response to passage of a new government regulation. After the need for the project has been acknowledged, the project enters the project management life cycle or process.

Every project has an identified sponsor. The **sponsor** is the facility employee with the most vested interest in the project's success. It is a good practice to select someone who has responsibility for the organization's departments, divisions, and personnel that will be affected by the project. The project will open up many issues that, in some situations, must be resolved by an authority figure. It is much easier to obtain a decision or consensus when the sponsor already has established control over the areas involved in the project. The sponsor often approves the budget for the project and is ultimately responsible for the project expenditures.

The project also has **stakeholders**. A stakeholder is anyone in the organization who is affected by the project product. Stakeholders include personnel who are on the project team, personnel whose daily work will be changed because of the project's product, and the managers and executives for those departments involved in the project. Each stakeholder has different concerns relative to the project's objectives and goals. The **project team** wants to produce a high-quality product. Departmental personnel worry about their ability to adapt to the procedures and skills required by the new or changed product. Department managers and executives must support the functional changes that may be needed as a result of the project. Each stakeholder will evaluate the project's success based on these concerns and the expectations they hold for how the project will benefit them.

Definition of a Project

A Guide to the Project Management Body of Knowledge (*PMBOK Guide*) describes a project as "a temporary endeavor undertaken to create a unique product, service, or result" (PMI 2008, 5). A project has the following characteristics:

- Specific objectives or goals to be achieved
- Defined start and end date
- Defined set of resources assigned to perform the required work
- Specific deliverables or work products
- Defined budget or cost

A project differs from the day-to-day operations of an organization. Operations are concerned with the everyday jobs needed to run the business. The personnel involved in the operational aspects of the business perform the same functions on a routine basis. This work does not end. In contrast, a project has a precise, expected result produced by defined **resources** within a specific time frame.

Project Parameters

A well-defined project has specific objectives. After the project's objectives have been defined, all project activities should be focused on meeting them. The project activities result in project deliverables or **work products**. When the project activities have concluded and the project deliverables have been completed, the project ends.

The process of documenting project parameters is discussed later in this chapter.

Project Components

Lewis (2008) writes that a project's objectives include cost, performance, time, and scope. Cost is the project budget, performance relates to the quality of the project work, time is the schedule, and **project scope** is the magnitude of the work to be done. He illustrates the relationship with the expression "Cost is a function of Performance, Time, and Scope." Should the cost, performance, or schedule variable change, the relationship dictates that the scope will change (Lewis 2008, 127–128). The project manager and the sponsor must acknowledge this relationship and be willing to make the trade-offs that will be needed when the variables change.

When developing the **project plan**, the project manager translates the objectives into three **project components**: scope, resources, and schedule. These components have a strong dependency. If one of the three components changes then one of the other two parameters must change as well. This is often illustrated as a triangle. (See figure 26.1.)

Project resources are not just people. A resource is any physical asset needed to complete a **task**. This includes facilities, equipment, materials, and supplies. Resources also

Figure 26.1. Illustration of project components

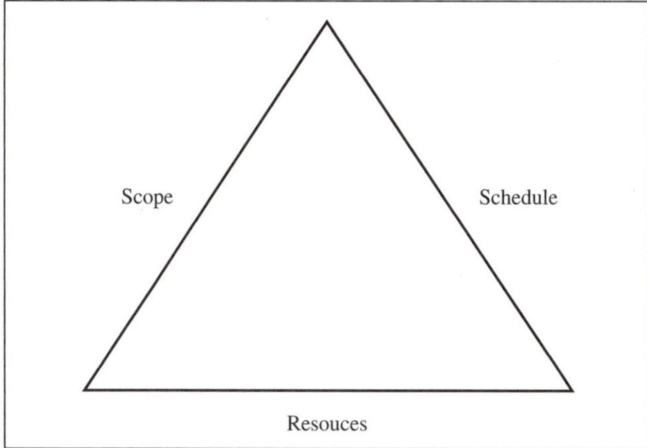

can include individuals from outside organizations, such as suppliers or vendors.

One reason why many projects fail to meet their objectives within the expected time frame and budget is that their scope begins to grow as they progress. For example, new functions or features are added to a software implementation. This is commonly known as **scope creep**. The requestor presents each change as a small revision with low impact on time line or cost. However, several minor changes soon add up to a more significant modification to the original work or cost estimate. The project manager must be diligent to prevent scope creep, which is discussed in detail later in this chapter.

Project Assumptions

Assumptions are scope-limiting parameters. They provide constraints on what is and is not included in the project. For example, if the project is to design a training program, the number of personnel to be trained will need to be defined. This assumption affects the number of copies for any training materials (impacting the cost) and the amount of time it will take to train everyone (impacting the schedule.)

Assumptions define answers to unknown questions. For instance, at the beginning of the project, the project manager may not know what personnel will be assigned to the project and thus will not know the skill set that will be available. One assumption might be that a project team member from a particular department on a cross-departmental project is a decision maker. In other words, when the project team meets to design the user interface for a software implementation, the decisions can be made in that meeting and will not be deferred to a person outside the team. If this assumption does not prove to be true, the project manager is faced with a potential delay because the process required for decision making was not accounted for in the **project schedule**.

Assumptions directly affect the project estimates for the resource and time line requirements. Therefore, it is critical that the project manager obtain agreement from the sponsor and the stakeholders on all assumptions. A lack of buy-in by all the project participants puts the objectives at **risk**. Many projects immediately start down the path of failure because the assumptions were not addressed adequately at the project start.

Types of Projects

There are many different types of projects. Although they share some attributes, projects can be vastly different in several aspects. Some projects are short term and completed in the span of weeks; other projects take years to complete. One project may involve only a single department; another may require participation across the facilities in an integrated delivery system (IDS).

Following are types of projects in which HIM professionals may be involved:

- Instituting new or revised procedures to address new regulations
- Improving the management of the revenue cycle
- Evaluating the effectiveness of a compliance program
- Instituting a productivity benchmarking program
- Merging two HIM departments
- Creating a new employee orientation program
- Implementing a new business procedure or process
- Implementing new technology such as EHRs

A complex project may comprise several **subprojects**. The subprojects share common milestones and objectives but may be managed by different project managers. Subproject information may be compiled into one report to show information across all associated projects.

Project Risk versus Project Value

Projects are undertaken to specifically incorporate some requirement or business need. Although the organization certainly expects a positive outcome, there are always some risks to the organization as well. One of the project manager's responsibilities is to mitigate risk. However, the organization will need to weigh the cost of potential risks against the perceived value to be gained.

Project risk can take many forms and be of either a technical or psychological nature. For example, implementing a state-of-the-art computer system may provide leading-edge technology that sets the organization apart from its competitors. However, the availability of personnel who can provide support for new technology may be limited.

Another example would be a project that introduces a significant change to a department employee's responsibilities. However, the change positions the employee out of his or her comfort zone. Before the project begins, an employee may be considered an expert in his or her job responsibilities. At the conclusion of the project, the same employee may have new duties and will not have the same proficiency in them. This could cause self-esteem problems. It is not uncommon for employee turnover to occur during a project because of this threat to job security.

Check Your Understanding 26.1

Instructions: Answer the following questions on a separate piece of paper.

1. Why does an organization start a project?
2. What are the similar responsibilities of the project's sponsor and stakeholders? What are examples of different responsibilities?
3. How do projects and organizational processes differ?
4. What is scope creep?

Project Management

The *PMBOK Guide* defines project management as "the application of knowledge, skills, tools, and techniques to project activities to meet the project requirements" (PMI 2008, 6). Project management is concerned with completing a project within the expected cost and time line with high-quality results. This is not easy to accomplish and, as a consequence, interest in project management best practices is very high. Many organizations are starting to stress the importance of solid project management methodologies and are establishing project offices to support the organization's project managers. A **project office** is responsible for defining project management procedures, conducting risk analyses on projects, and mentoring project managers.

Overview of Project Management

The discipline of project management has emerged as organizations have come to realize that projects cannot succeed without it. Projects have customarily been deemed successful when they meet their objectives and do not exceed their approved cost and estimated schedule. Lewis (2008) proposes a different definition of project success. He challenges the commonly held belief that a project has failed when it does not meet its cost, performance, time, or scope targets by questioning how these targets were established. The targets may have been unrealistic and therefore impossible to meet. By citing several studies, Lewis concludes that it is how closely the project outcomes align with the perceptions held by the key project personnel that determines project success (105–110). As an example, if a project comes in under budget but ends up solving the wrong problem, is it successful? A project may meet the schedule but have unexpected and undesirable consequences. As Thomas K. Connellan, a speaker, trainer, consultant, and senior principal of a customer relationship management consulting firm, once said, "There is no point in doing well that which you should not be doing at all."

Kliem (2004) proposes a paradigm shift, noting that project performance has not improved dramatically over the years despite a proliferation of tools, techniques, and expertise. His proposal is to change from a prevailing paradigm that relies too much on the mechanics of project management (for example, creating a project plan) to subjective factors that play a major role in effective leadership. Under this new paradigm a project is defined as a focused, integrated human endeavor to achieve a specific common purpose. The implications of this new paradigm are illustrated in table 26.1 (Kliem 2004, 29, 47–52).

Project success relies on a balance between project management as a scientific discipline and people-oriented project leadership.

Table 26.1. Implications of the new paradigm

Implication	Prevailing Paradigm	New Paradigm
Results	Best tool or most efficient process becomes an end in itself	Excellence comes from delivering a product or service that achieves a desired result
Interdependence	Places value on defining all the elements of a project in precise detail	Places more value on how to define and improve the relationship of those elements to achieve desired results
Why	Emphasis on determining what must be done which leads to implementing counterproductive tools, techniques and methodology	Ask why to determine if a tool, technique or methodology advances the goal of the project
Responsiveness	When a project deviates from the plan, force feeding tools, techniques and concepts that don't contribute to the goals of the project	Determine why certain actions must happen. Actions should be one that provide the most leverage to achieve desired results
Qualitative	Relying on quantitative aspects at the expense of people. Uses measures that reflect great efficiencies at the expense of effectiveness.	Recognizes that quantification is not the only driver of a project and that quantification is reflective of qualitative factors such as beliefs and values.
Dynamic	Unrealistic emphasis on maintaining control thereby imposing project management principles and practice instead of adapting them.	Projects are seen as dynamic entities. A project and its environment constantly changes and this reality should be accepted.
People	People are another resource along with time, money and equipment	Puts people at the center of the project. It is people who must participate not only in the formulation of plans, but also in the implementation of all the tools, techniques, and practices of project management.

The Project Management Life Cycle

Every project follows a **project management life cycle** regardless of its size or duration. Each process in the life cycle has its own importance. Any one of the processes cannot be eliminated or minimized without endangering the success of the project. As listed in table 26.2, the project management life cycle consists of a number of processes, which are later discussed in detail.

The Project Team

By definition, a project results in an end product through the completion of task activities. The execution of these task activities is the responsibility of the project team. A project team is composed of individuals who possess the knowledge and skill set to produce the project deliverables and work products.

The type of project determines the size of the project team and the originating location of the resources. A project that affects only one department will typically have project team members from only that department. A project with organization-wide objectives will have a cross-departmental team, whereas a project for an IDS will include representatives from all the system's facilities.

There are three types of project team structure: functional, projectized, and matrixed (PMI 2008, 28–32).

Functional Team Structure

In a strictly functional organization, the project is thought to affect only one department. The functional manager may assume responsibility for managing the project. The team members are primarily from the functional department, and the functional manager confers with other functional managers on any issues affecting those departments.

Table 26.2. Project management life cycle

Project definition	This process will determine the project objectives, activities, assumptions, high-level cost estimate, and anticipated schedule.
Planning and organization	A detailed project plan is developed that delineates the tasks to be performed, the resources necessary for each task, and the estimated task duration, start, and finish. The project team is assembled.
Tracking and analysis	By tracking project progress and analyzing it against the original plan, the project manager is able to determine when the project is not moving forward as planned.
Project revisions	When the analysis reveals project deviations, the plan may need to be modified in order to still meet the project objectives.
Change control	This is the process of managing change requests to the original project definition.
Communication	This process occurs throughout the project life cycle. Project information is collected from, and disseminated to, all stakeholders.

Projectized Team Structure

The projectized organization has dedicated resources that are involved only in project work. Team members report to the project manager not only on project assignments, but also as their direct manager.

Matrixed Team Structure

The matrixed organization maintains the functional organization. Team members report to a functional manager and remain employees of that department. The team members receive their project assignments from the project manager.

In a matrixed organization, assigning the members of the project team can pose a dilemma for the stakeholders and the project manager. Typically, the best people to have on a project team are the ones who most intimately understand the processes and procedures affected by the project. However, these people have operational responsibilities in their respective departments that do not disappear while the project is in progress. Depending on the scope of the project, the time commitment required of the project team can be quite significant.

It is important to define the **roles and responsibilities** of the project team. In a matrixed organization, the project team members do not report to the project manager in an organizational structure. However, the project manager holds team members accountable for their tasks.

Check Your Understanding 26.2

Instructions: On a separate piece of paper, prepare a grid that lists examples of the types of projects an HIM professional may be involved in. For each project list the following:

- The project objectives
- The factors that will be used to measure project success
- The factors that may contribute to project failure
- The members of the project team

The Project Manager

The project manager is the individual with responsibility for directing the project activities from initiation through closure. Depending on the size of the project, the project manager may be a dedicated resource or may be performing these duties along with other operational assignments. For example, for a project confined to a single department, an assistant director may be asked to manage the project while the department director takes on the sponsor role. In other situations, one of the team members may be asked to be the project leader while still performing specific task assignments for the project.

In circumstances where the project manager is not fully devoted to the project, it is easy for the project management duties to fall by the wayside, especially because many of these may produce intangible results. (The functions of the project manager are discussed in a subsequent section of this chapter.) The project sponsor must ensure that an adequate percentage of the project manager's time is allocated to these responsibilities.

Competencies and Skills

A project manager must possess both functional and behavioral skills. Some of his or her responsibilities are purely operational, for example, preparing a project plan. However, several skills are required that touch on the human side of projects. All projects result in a change in the organization. Facilitating an organization through the impact of these changes requires attributes that are described as "soft skills."

Project managers are very often in the position of having great responsibility, but little authority, because the project team members do not report to them from an organizational perspective. Thus, project managers must get results from the team members through leadership and influence.

Project managers should possess the following skills:

- General management skills of planning, directing, organizing, and prioritizing
- Leadership skills of influencing, motivating, providing vision, and resolving conflict
- Communication skills of being able to interact with all levels of an organization and of being able to understand different communication styles and mediums
- Facilitation skills, including negotiation, consensus building, and meeting management
- Analytical skills, including innovative thinking, problem solving, and decision making

Functions

The project manager performs several functions over the course of the project management life cycle. These functions are described in table 26.3.

The Project Management Process

A project follows a defined process regardless of size, type, or industry. The process is scalable, meaning that the depth to which a particular process is performed may vary according to project length, scope, or other parameters. However, to ensure the success of the project, all these processes must be performed to some degree.

Project Definition

Project definition sets the expectation for the what, when, and how of the project. As noted under the project parameters section of this chapter, every project comprises three components: What is to be done (scope), the resources needed to accomplish the objectives, and the amount of time required to complete the project. The project definition process formally documents these variables for the project. This process is important for several reasons. First, it provides all project stakeholders, team members, and other personnel with the same information about the project—what it will accomplish, when it will be done, and what resources it will require. Second, it is then used as the basis for understanding when requested changes are out of the project's scope.

Table 26.3. Functions of the project manager

Set the project expectations.	As noted earlier, project success is tied to the perception that the project met the objectives. The project manager has responsibility for properly setting the project expectations and continually resetting them as the project progresses.
Create the project plan and recruit the project team.	The project manager generates a project schedule with the estimated work effort. The project team is organized, with each team member understanding his or her roles and responsibilities. The project manager leads team development efforts to form an effective, motivated team. He or she uses interpersonal skills to establish a rapport with team members.
Manage project control.	When the project is under way, the project manager must have a clear understanding of its status. Informal and formal communication methods are used to determine project progress. The project manager maintains the project plan to perform variance analysis. The project manager works with the project team to bring tasks to closure by facilitating decision-making and issue resolution. The project manager facilitates the removal of any obstacles that prevent the team from producing the project deliverables.
Recommend plan revisions.	If a plan is not progressing as scheduled, the project manager must determine what actions need to be taken to put the project back on track. He or she gains consensus on the changes from the sponsor and the stakeholders, and monitors any new risks to the plan.
Execute change control.	The project manager institutes a policy and procedure for managing change requests. He or she keeps everyone focused on the end goal.
Prepare, document, and communicate project information.	Project documentation is a key facet of project communication. The project manager creates the communication plan that will be used to determine when, how, and what information is to be gathered and distributed. He or she facilitates the dissemination of information throughout the organization. Although the project team members create much of the documentation through the project deliverables, the project manager is responsible for ensuring that documentation exists and is available.

Determine Project Scope and Define Project Deliverables

The definition of the project starts with determining its goals. The project's goals or objectives should be measurable. If they are not, it will be impossible for the project manager and the stakeholders to determine whether the project is successful. (Examples of objectives are shown in table 26.4.)

The next step in defining the project is to determine the tangible end results of the project. These are typically called **project deliverables**. The project deliverables indicate when the project activities have been completed. Typical deliverables for a software implementation include:

- System requirements
- User interface design document
- Test plans
- Training and procedure manuals
- Production software

Estimate the Project Schedule and Cost

The next step in project definition is to estimate how long the project will take and how much it will cost. At this point in the process, the project may not have been approved, so this information is needed in order for the stakeholders to make an informed decision. This also poses a dilemma for the project manager. He or she may not have enough detailed information about the project to make an estimate. (A detailed analysis occurs in the project planning phase.)

In this case, the project manager has a few options. One is to evaluate a past project that is similar in scope and to extract pertinent information from it that can be used in estimating the new project. A second option is to confer with professional colleagues who have experience in the proposed project. If a similar project is unavailable for analysis, a third alternative is for the project manager to use his or her expert judgment and intuition based on other professional experiences. Another opportunity would be available if the project manager were working with a vendor. The vendor would likely have experience in these types of projects and could assist the project manager in formulating estimates.

Table 26.4. Examples of project objectives

Type of Project	Non-Measurable Objective	Measurable Objective
As part of EHR implementation, conduct process improvement project for the Release of Information function	Decrease time spent on ROI activities	Improve average release of information turnaround time from 5 days to 3 days
Implementation of EHR system	Decrease required FTEs for file room activities	Decrease file room FTEs from 3 to 1
Institute a home coding program	Improve coder satisfaction	Decrease staff turnover by 20%

Prepare the Project Proposal

As stated above, one of the purposes of the project definition phase is to set project expectations. The project manager now should be ready to record the project objectives, scope, deliverables, expected time line, and anticipated cost in a written document. This document is known by various names. Typical names include **project charter**, **statement of work**, and project definition document or business plan.

The project proposal contains several topics. The following information should be included:

- *Summary:* The summary provides an overview of the project and can provide any relevant background history and reasons why the project is being proposed.
- *Objectives:* The objectives state the project's goals.
- *Project activities:* This section is a high-level description of the major project tasks and maps out how the project will produce the project deliverables. These activities will be detailed during the project planning phase.
- *Assumptions:* Assumptions provide input on the estimates for the resource and time line requirements. Inclusion of the assumptions in the project definition document sets the stage for their acknowledgment and agreement. Assumptions may or may not prove to be true as the project progresses. The importance of identifying assumptions is that when one does not prove to be true, one of the project components will likely need to be altered.
- *Roles and responsibilities:* This section defines the types of resources needed on the project and delineates who does what. Its concept is not dissimilar to defining a department's organizational structure. The purpose is to ensure that everyone is aware of everyone's duties and the lines of authority. It is a good idea to include a project organizational chart. The project manager usually does not have management authority over the team, so documenting the roles is crucial in understanding how the team will function.
- *Schedule and cost:* Schedule and cost information is provided at a very high level because it will be further refined during the project planning phase. Cost estimates will include those for personnel, equipment, and supplies. If an external company will be providing some project services, this section should indicate whether the engagement is based on time and materials or fixed-fee pricing.
- *Deliverables:* The discussion of deliverables is another component of setting expectations. By documenting the tangible output from the project, everyone will understand when the project tasks are complete. This section can be specific by including the following types of information for each deliverable:
  - Type (for example, Microsoft Word)
  - Expected length or size
  - Number of copies provided
  - Mode of delivery (for example, via e-mail)

Check Your Understanding 26.3

Instructions: On a separate piece of paper, prepare a project proposal document for one of the projects you listed in Check Your Understanding 26.2. Include the project objectives, deliverables, high-level project activities, assumptions, and roles and responsibilities. What needs to be considered when estimating the project cost?

Project Planning

After a project has been approved, it moves into the planning phase. The purpose of this phase is to further refine the project work effort, time line, and cost. During the project planning phase, the project manager creates a project plan that details the tasks to be performed, the resources needed to perform each task, the estimated work effort, and the estimated start and finish dates.

The project manager may use **project management software** to aid this process. Also known as a **scheduling engine**, project management software can provide the tools to automate some of the functions the project manager must perform. However, a software tool cannot perform the behavioral roles required of the project manager. Beware of software product literature promising a successful project simply by using it!

Identify Project Activities

When a project is initiated, the project manager is faced with the following question: how do we complete the project objectives and produce the project deliverables? Creating a project plan that lists each activity provides the road map to answer this question. For example, when a person decides to go on a vacation, he or she does not simply go to the airport. First, he or she has to decide where to go and how to get there and then make the appropriate reservations and so on.

A project plan starts with a **work breakdown structure** (WBS), or task list. The WBS is a hierarchical list of steps needed to complete the project. This structure provides levels that are similar to the concept of a book outline. Each level drills down to more detail. The lowest level is the task level, which is the level to which resources are assigned and work effort estimates are made.

A good place to begin in building the WBS is with the deliverables. Every deliverable should have a set of corresponding tasks to produce it. After every deliverable has been covered, the next area to address is the tasks that do not produce deliverables as such. What kind of tasks are they? One such task would be project management. Although project management tasks certainly produce plenty of documentation, the output is not a deliverable for the project itself, meaning that it does not contribute to the project objectives.

When creating the WBS, the project manager is faced with determining the level of task detail to be included. When the task level is not itemized enough, it will be difficult to assess the progress on the task. Having too much detail presents its own problems if the project manager is using project management software because he or she will spend too much time managing the project plan instead of doing the actual project. The level of detail directly correlates to the project manager's ability to control the project. He or she must determine the level of detail that provides this control.

Table 26.5 is an illustration of too much detail in a project plan. The list on the left represents steps, not tasks. The project plan should not be thought of as a to-do list. The list on the right represents a more manageable level of detail.

Construct the Project Network

When all the tasks have been defined, the next step is to determine the **dependency** among tasks. The tasks in the project plan cannot all start at the same time. For example, training on a new computer system cannot begin until the training materials have been completed and the system has been thoroughly tested.

The definition of dependencies among the project tasks is the first step in scheduling the project. The purpose of the project schedule is to provide information on when the particular tasks can begin and when they are scheduled to end. The overall **project network** is defined through these dependencies.

Figure 26.2 shows an example of a project schedule for a training program project.

There are a few types of dependencies:

- *Finish-to-start:* This means that the first, or **predecessor**, task must finish before the dependent, or **successor**, task can start. Finish-to-start is the most common type of dependency.
- *Start-to-start:* This states that the successor task cannot start until the predecessor task begins. An example of this relationship would be in a computer system implementation where outdated hardware must be replaced. The hardware for the users from the old system cannot be swapped out with the hardware for the new system until the old system is taken offline when the conversion process begins.
- *Finish-to-finish:* In this definition, the successor task cannot finish until the predecessor task finishes. An example of this dependency would be completing training materials when the system testing for a computer system is complete. The materials cannot be finished until the project manager is assured, via testing, that all modifications to the software have been completed.

Table 26.5. Illustration of steps vs. tasks

Steps	Tasks
Invitations	**Invitations**
Shop for invitations Choose invitation Purchase invitations Address invitations Purchase stamps Mail invitations	Select and purchase invitations Mail invitations

Estimate Activity Duration and Work Effort

After the tasks have been defined, the project manager determines who will perform each task (resources), the amount of effort it will take to complete the task (work), and how long it will take to finish the task (duration). **Work** and **duration** are two different values. For example, if Emily is assigned to a task for 24 hours of work effort, how long will it take her to complete the task? It depends on how much of Emily's overall workday she devotes to this particular task. If she spends 100 percent of her day on this task and the assumption is that she is scheduled to work eight hours a day, she can complete the task in three days. If she can only dedicate 50 percent of her time to the task, she will complete the task in six days.

This calculation is shown in table 26.6. If multiple resources can be assigned to the task, the task duration can be reduced.

Estimating the work effort for tasks is difficult and can be time-consuming, especially if the organization does not have much experience in the type of project being performed.

It is best to get estimates from the people who will be performing the work. If the team has not been assigned, the functional manager of the area may be called on to provide this information. Either way, the project manager may still encounter unrealistic values because people tend to underestimate the effort in those instances where historical information is unavailable. Some people overcompensate in their estimate if they do have experience in projects, knowing that unforeseen circumstances may arise.

And, unfortunately, Parkinson's Law, which says that "Work expands to fill the time," complicates the estimating situation. Typically, if a resource is told that 16 hours of work effort are allocated for a task, he or she will expend all 16 hours.

The assumptions for the project also play a role in defining the estimates. For example, if an assumption is that a software engineer knowledgeable in the applicable software language will be assigned to the project, the work estimates will be lower than if the assumption is that an inexperienced resource will be assigned.

After the work effort values have been determined and the task durations calculated, the project network reflects a more realistic time frame. The project finish date is calculated

Figure 26.2. Example of a project schedule for a training program

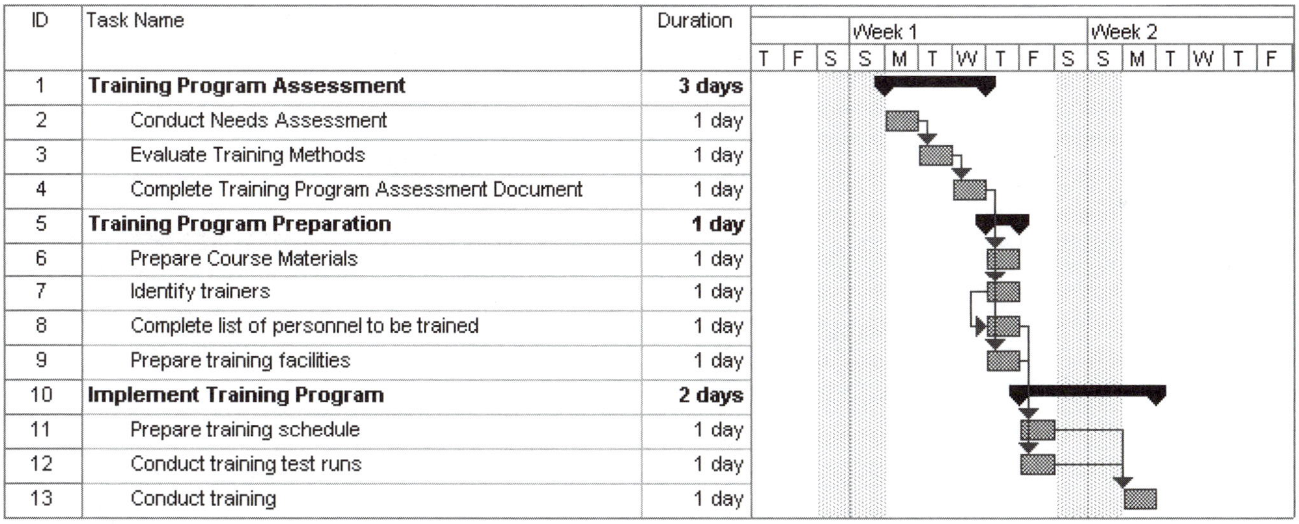

ID	Task Name	Duration
1	**Training Program Assessment**	**3 days**
2	Conduct Needs Assessment	1 day
3	Evaluate Training Methods	1 day
4	Complete Training Program Assessment Document	1 day
5	**Training Program Preparation**	**1 day**
6	Prepare Course Materials	1 day
7	Identify trainers	1 day
8	Complete list of personnel to be trained	1 day
9	Prepare training facilities	1 day
10	**Implement Training Program**	**2 days**
11	Prepare training schedule	1 day
12	Conduct training test runs	1 day
13	Conduct training	1 day

Week 1 / Week 2: T F S S M T W T F S S M T W T F

Table 26.6. Calculation of duration based on work and percentage of day

Situation	Resources	Work	Percentage of Day	Duration
Emily is the only resource assigned to a task and will focus on that task until it is complete.	Emily	40 hours	100%	5 days
Emily is the only resource assigned to a task and can only dedicate half of her time to the task.	Emily	40 hours	50%	10 days
Emily and John are assigned to a task and can share the responsibilities. They will focus on this task until it is complete.	Emily John	20 hours 20 hours	100%	2.5 days
Emily and John are assigned to a task and can share the responsibilities. They can dedicate half of their time to this task.	Emily John	20 hours 20 hours	50% 50%	5 days

based on the task dependencies and task durations. Figure 26.3 shows how the project tasks from figure 26.2 are now scheduled.

If a project manager is using project management software, the **critical path** for the project can be determined. The critical path is the series of specific tasks that determine the overall project duration.

The critical path is important for the project manager to understand because any change in the start or finish of one of the tasks on the critical path means the expected project finish date will change. Changes to the critical path can happen in a variety of ways, including:

- The duration of a task may change because the work effort or resource availability changes.
- The expected start date for the task changes because the finish date for a predecessor task changes.
- The finish date for a task changes because a resource's availability is changed. Perhaps a person schedules vacation or training for a week or his or her availability for the project changes because he or she is assigned additional duties outside the project.

The project manager also can use the critical path to determine how to shorten the overall project schedule. It is typical for the stakeholders of a project to already have a predetermined expected finish date for the project when it is proposed. It is not uncommon for this date to be earlier than the project finish date calculated by the scheduling engine software. The project manager is faced with the situation of fitting the tasks into this predetermined schedule. The way to do this is to look at the critical path tasks to determine how they could be accomplished sooner.

A project plan for an office move is displayed in figure 26.4. Each task is flagged as to whether or not it is on the critical path. It is easy to see in this illustration that if the start or finish of task 10 (Order office furniture) changes, it will not affect the project end date. However if the dates for task 6 changes (Finalize lease on office space), there will be an impact on the overall finish date.

Figure 26.3. Example of a project task schedule

ID	Task Name	Duration
1	**Training Program Assessment**	**19 days**
2	Conduct Needs Assessment	8 days
3	Evaluate Training Methods	8 days
4	Complete Training Program Assessment Document	3 days
5	**Training Program Preparation**	**15 days**
6	Prepare Course Materials	15 days
7	Identify trainers	10 days
8	Complete list of personnel to be trained	10 days
9	Prepare training facilities	10 days
10	**Implement Training Program**	**33 days**
11	Prepare training schedule	3 days
12	Conduct training test runs	3 days
13	Conduct training	30 days

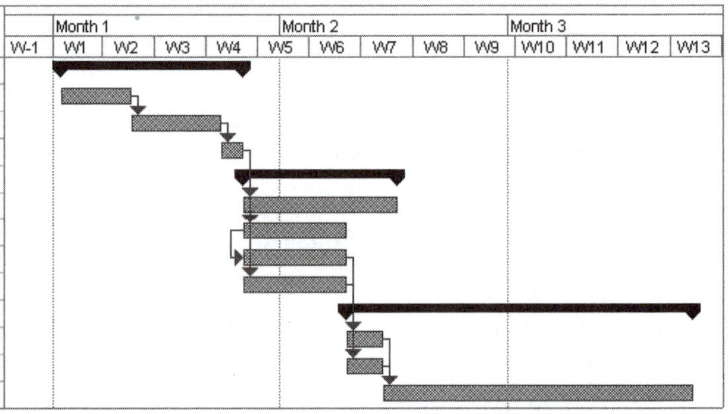

Month 1 Month 2 Month 3
W-1 W1 W2 W3 W4 W5 W6 W7 W8 W9 W10 W11 W12 W13

Figure 26.4. Example of a project path with a critical path shown

ID	Task Name	Start	Finish	Critical
1	**Office Move**	**Jan 3**	**Mar 8**	**Yes**
2	**Office Space**	**Jan 3**	**Mar 8**	**Yes**
3	**Identify requirements for new office space**	**Jan 3**	**Jan 5**	**Yes**
4	**Identify potential office sites**	**Jan 6**	**Jan 12**	**Yes**
5	**Make final decision on office space**	**Jan 13**	**Jan 21**	**Yes**
6	**Finalize lease on office space**	**Jan 24**	**Jan 27**	**Yes**
7	**Design office space**	**Jan 28**	**Mar 1**	**Yes**
8	**Assign office space**	**Mar 2**	**Mar 8**	**Yes**
9	**Office Equipment**	**Jan 24**	**Mar 4**	**No**
10	Order office furniture	Jan 24	Jan 26	No
11	Order new office equipment	Mar 2	Mar 4	No
12	Order phone system	Mar 2	Mar 2	No
13	**Moving Companies**	**Jan 28**	**Feb 16**	**No**
14	Select the move day	Jan 28	Jan 28	No
15	Obtain estimates from moving companies	Jan 31	Feb 15	No
16	Hire movers	Feb 16	Feb 16	No

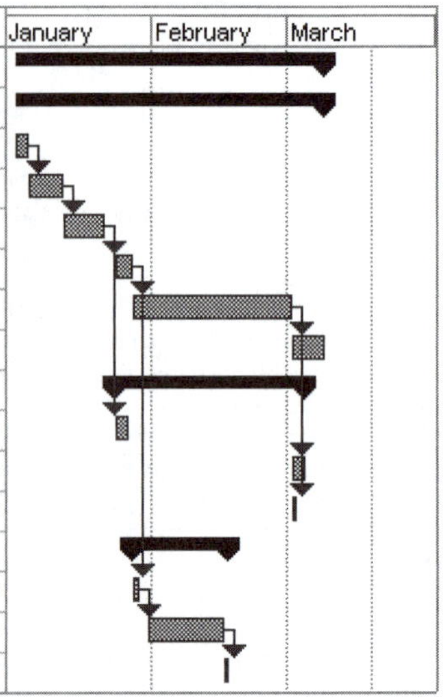

January February March

Conduct Risk Analysis

With the project network calculated, the project manager has a plan for the project schedule, work effort, and cost. However, it is a very ideal project; it assumes that all the tasks will occur as scheduled and estimated. For example, as soon as a predecessor task finishes, the successor task begins. It also assumes that the resources will be available on the exact day the task is scheduled to begin. At this point, the project is not accommodating delays such as illness, a delay in hardware acquisition, or the learning curve encountered when using a new technology.

If one thing can be accurately predicted about a project, it is that it will not progress as scheduled. To account for the inevitable changes, the project manager should perform a risk analysis and adjust the project schedule, work effort, or cost projections to incorporate any anticipated risk.

To conduct a risk analysis, the project manager first documents the types of risks that may occur. He or she then assigns a probability factor and an impact factor. The probability factor indicates the odds of the particular risk occurring. The impact factor designates the effect the risk will have on the project if it does occur. These two factors are then multiplied together to calculate the risk factor.

A **contingency** should be put in place for any risk with a high-risk factor. The contingency describes what the project team will do if the risk is realized. For example, to mitigate the risk of losing a key project team member, the project manager would ensure that the project documentation is kept up-to-date. The impact of the contingency should be reflected in the project plan. For the example cited, the project manager would make sure that a task is in the project plan for updating project documentation.

An example of a risk analysis can be illustrated by using a situation you may be familiar with—planning a vacation. (See table 26.7.) For this example, the vacation will be to a Caribbean island in October, which happens to be during hurricane season.

As with assumptions, the project manager should obtain consensus from the project team, project sponsor, and stakeholders for the contingency plans. After the initial risk assessment is documented, a synopsis can be included in the project manager's status report. This synopsis could include any changes to the risk factors, realized and unrealized risks, and changes to contingency plans. After the threat of the risk is over, it can be removed from the report.

Check Your Understanding 26.4

Instructions: Prepare a work breakdown structure for the project you initiated in Check Your Understanding 26.3. Include the following for the tasks: task name, predecessor task(s), associated deliverable(s), and a list of the team members who will work on the task. Then answer the following questions on a separate piece of paper.

1. What methods can be used to estimate the work effort for a task?
2. What are some potential risks to the project you selected in Check Your Understanding 26.3? What contingencies can be put in place to mitigate this risk?

Project Implementation

When the project planning is complete, the organization is ready to begin the project. The project manager has prepared the project schedule, identified the work effort requirements, and anticipated potential delays. Before the project begins, he or she will capture a **baseline** of the project schedule and work effort. The baseline is a copy of the original estimates for the project. It is captured so that the progress of the project can be compared to the original plan. This comparison is discussed in further detail later in this chapter.

Hold a Project Kickoff Meeting

It is customary to hold a project kickoff meeting when the project gets under way. This meeting sets the tone for the project and helps everyone understand its importance. A typical agenda for the meeting includes the following items:

- Executive presentation, during which the sponsor or key stakeholder presents the background on the project with a particular emphasis on why the organization is embarking on this endeavor
- Project objectives
- Project organization chart
- Team roles and responsibilities

Table 26.7. Example of risk analysis

Risk Description	Probability Factor Low = 1 Medium = 3 High = 5	Impact Factor Range is 1–10 Low = 1 High = 10	Risk Factor (Probability × Impact)	Contingency
Forget to pack an item	5	3	15	Prepare a packing list
Traffic congestion on the way to the airport	1	10	10	Check road construction hotline and radio traffic reports; allow extra travel time
Rain during the vacation	3	8	24	Plan some indoor activities
Luggage doesn't make it to the destination	1	10	10	Purchase additional baggage insurance
Hurricane strikes the resort	5	10	50	Purchase trip cancellation insurance

- High-level WBS (approach)
- Project schedule
- Key assumptions and constraints
- Project control and communication, including project tracking, meeting schedule, project documentation, change control procedure, and issue tracking

Perform Project Tasks and Produce Deliverables

The project team now has responsibility for performing the scheduled tasks and producing the project deliverables. The project manager has responsibility for ensuring that all participants understand what is to be done and when.

At this point in the project, the team may become bogged down in indecisiveness, resistance to change, and bureaucracy. The project manager works with the team, the stakeholders, and the project sponsor to keep the project moving by getting issues resolved and decisions made. The project manager may use various problem-solving and decision-making techniques to facilitate this process. (See chapter 20 for more information on this subject.)

Track Progress and Analyze Variance

When the project is under way, the project manager needs to follow how it is progressing. He or she must be able to provide the following information to the stakeholders and the project team:

- Will the project be completed on time?
- Will the project cost more than planned?
- Will the project objectives be met?

The project manager can answer these questions only by actively tracking the project's progress and analyzing its progress against the original plan.

Project Tracking

The project is tracked through the process of collecting actual progress and remaining effort from the project team members. Each team member should provide information on a periodic basis. The frequency of progress information depends on the duration of the project. For a short project of less than two months in duration, updates may be needed more than once a week. Longer projects may require a weekly progress report. In determining tracking frequency, the project manager should consider the effort of obtaining the information and updating the project plan against the level of information needed to perform the variance analysis and, more importantly, should be able to adequately respond to required plan revisions when a project is in trouble.

Each project team member should report the following information for each task:

- Actual start date or new scheduled start date (when the task was not started on time)
- Percentage of complete or actual work
- Remaining work or expected finish date
- Actual and remaining cost
- Actual finish date (for completed tasks)
- Issues

It is usually difficult to obtain actual progress from the project team members. There are both procedural and psychological reasons for this. With regard to procedural reasons, the project manager has to set up a mechanism for getting the information. This may be a hard-copy report, or it may be automated through project management software. Unfortunately, the process of getting the information can be tedious and project managers often neglect it to pursue other project management processes that they deem to be more important.

With regard to psychological reasons, people are inclined to overestimate their progress. They tend to tell someone what they believe that person wants to hear rather than report true progress. People also may become defensive about their progress, especially in situations where they are behind schedule or over budget. Although some personal accountability may be involved, often the reason for the delay or overrun is not directly within the team member's control. The project manager can set the right tone for the data collection process by letting the team know how the information will be used. Honesty from team members should not result in punitive measures, unless an individual has been consistently negligent in his or her project responsibilities. When a project team member is not performing as needed, the project manager needs to address this issue. (Refer to chapter 20 for management strategies that can be used to resolve this situation.)

Variance Analysis and Project Revision

After updating the project schedule with the task progress, the project manager compares the task start date, expected finish date, estimated work effort, estimated cost, and estimated duration to what was originally planned. As stated above, all projects do not progress as originally planned. The project manager must concentrate on those **variances** that are substantially affecting the project's time line, budget, and objectives. For example, a task may start later than planned, but if it is not on the project's critical path, the delay will not affect the project finish date. However, if the task is on the critical path, the project manager must determine how to make up the delay and still complete the project on schedule. A task may have started on time but consume a higher work effort than originally estimated. Unless other tasks in the plan consume less than the original estimate, the overall project will exceed the work estimates and thus the cost estimate.

Figure 26.5 shows a report for the office move project plan that can be used to assess the variances. The work and cost variances are shown directly to the right of the task name. The right side of the report is known as a Gantt chart. The Gantt chart was developed by Henry L. Gantt as a method to illustrate the time needed for each task. On the figure 26.5 report, there are two bars for each task. The top bar shows the start and finish dates as they have been rescheduled based on tracking information. The bottom bar shows the baseline dates. The report shows that due to the fact that task 5 will not finish according to the original schedule, tasks 6 and 7

Figure 26.5. Example of a project plan with information to assess variances

ID	Task Name	Work Variance	Cost Variance
1	**Office Move**	**45 hrs**	**$14,500.00**
2	**Office Space**	**10 hrs**	**$1,000.00**
3	Identify requirements for new office space	0 hrs	$0.00
4	Identify potential office sites	10 hrs	$1,000.00
5	Make final decision on office space	0 hrs	$0.00
6	Finalize lease on office space	0 hrs	$0.00
7	Design office space	0 hrs	$0.00
8	Assign office space	0 hrs	$0.00
9	**Office Equipment**	**0 hrs**	**$10,000.00**
10	Order office furniture	0 hrs	$10,000.00
11	Order new office equipment	0 hrs	$0.00
12	Order phone system	0 hrs	$0.00
13	**Moving Companies**	**35 hrs**	**$3,500.00**
14	Select the move day	0 hrs	$0.00
15	Obtain estimates from moving companies	35 hrs	$3,500.00
16	Hire movers	0 hrs	$0.00

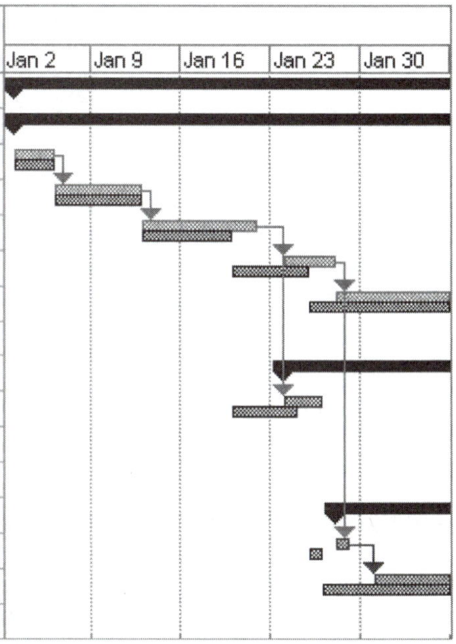

Jan 2 Jan 9 Jan 16 Jan 23 Jan 30

also will be delayed. These tasks are on the critical path; therefore, the delay must be addressed if the project is to remain on schedule. (Refer to figure 26.4.)

To get the project back on track, the project manager must evaluate the available options. All these options are a variant of the variables that make up the project parameters: scope, performance, cost, and time line. The project manager needs to clearly document the options and ramifications of each and present the documentation to the project's stakeholders. The sponsor and the stakeholders will make the decision based on what is most important to the success of the project. For example, in a software implementation, it may be more important for the new system to contain all the desired functionality than it is for the implementation to meet the budget. The sponsor may be willing to do this to obtain department satisfaction and compliance with the new system.

Table 26.8 shows the types of plan revisions the project manager may propose and the risks involved in using each option.

Establish Change Control

In addition to proposing project revisions to keep the project on track, the project manager is usually faced with requests for changes to the original project scope. These requests can be the result of any of the following:

- Change in a departmental procedure
- New or revised organizational initiative
- New or revised regulatory requirement
- Desired change in the design of a system function

Changes to project scope are inevitable and should not be automatically considered a form of project failure. It is the way project changes are handled that can have a negative impact on the success of the project. The most important factor in scope change is for the stakeholders to understand the impact of the requested change and, if approved, be willing to accept the ramifications the change will have on the project's schedule and cost. In other words, the project manager must be in control of the changes. Just as in plan revision, all changes to the plan will affect the final project outcome in terms of scope, work, time line, or cost. When the project manager, sponsor, and other stakeholders do not acknowledge the impact of the change by approving a corresponding modification to one of the other variables, the quality of the project suffers.

Table 26.8. Potential risks in revising a project plan

Options for Plan Revision	Potential Risks
Decrease the scope of work by removing some of the project requirements. Requirements may be eliminated or deferred to a subsequent project.	Project objectives may be compromised.
Eliminate the nice-to-have features of the project to decrease the scope of work.	Project objectives may be compromised.
Add more resources to get the work done faster.	Project cost may be compromised.
Ask team members to get the work done by putting in extra time.	Project cost may be compromised.
Evaluate the project plan to determine whether some tasks can start sooner. Look for finish-to-start dependencies to determine whether the tasks can overlap.	Quality may suffer when shortcuts are taken to shorten the schedule.

The procedure for **change control** should be established at the beginning of the project in order to set the proper expectations for how scope modifications will be handled. The process should be as follows:

1. The requestor completes a change request form.
2. An impact analysis is performed. Its purpose is to determine the effect the change will have on the project. For example, there may be a positive impact on the relationship to the system's objectives, but the request may increase the work effort.
3. The request is presented to the stakeholders for approval. If the change is approved, the stakeholders have indicated they are willing to accept the ramification on the project time line or cost. In other words, the benefits of the change outweigh the goal to stay within the original project budget.

Communicate Project Information

One of the success factors for a project is good project communication. All involved parties need to be kept apprised of the project's progress, understand any outstanding issues, understand the change control requests, and understand the project politics. Several forms of project communication are used during the project: project status meetings, project status reports, issue logs, and project plans.

Project Status Meetings

A project status meeting is a formal meeting attended by the project team members. Its purpose is to report accomplishments, to review the status of in-progress project tasks, and to discuss issues that are impeding the completion of any tasks.

There are a few cautions for the project manager when conducting the meeting. The first is that project team members may feel pressure to report a rosy picture of the task progress because they are among their peers. A task may be behind schedule to the point that it will most likely delay the overall project schedule, but a team member may be reluctant to report this to avoid being held accountable for the entire project missing its target finish date. Although formal status meetings are important for a project, the informal status reporting from the team members is just as important. The project manager should spend time with team members outside the meeting where the team member may feel that the environment is more conducive to an honest appraisal of the task progress.

The second problem with some status meetings is that participants become bogged down in discussions that cannot be resolved in the meeting. For example, team members may be discussing an issue in terms of what it is instead of actually resolving it. Although everyone must understand all project issues, it is not good use of the status meeting time to discuss the issue unless all the decision makers are in the room. Generally, issues should be handled in separate meetings outside the project status meeting.

Project Status Reports

A project status report is the formal documentation of the project progress. Again, although formal documentation is a required component of the project, the project manager should supplement this reporting with ad hoc conversations with the team members and stakeholders. This informal reporting, sometimes referred to as "walk around" status reporting, can elicit information on the politics, conflicts, personality disputes, and bureaucracy that tend to impede task progress.

The frequency of status reports varies depending on the overall project duration. A short project may require weekly reporting whereas a long project may require monthly reporting. Whatever frequency is selected, it should support the project manager's ability to react to changes, delays, and issues.

Topics to be included in a status report include:

- Objectives for the period
- Accomplishments during the period
- Explanation of any differences
- Objectives for next period
- Issues

When the task-tracking procedure and the formal status report follow the same frequency schedule (for example, both are completed on a weekly basis), the project manager may choose to collect this information on the same form. The feasibility of this also depends on the method selected for tracking. When task tracking is automated via project management software, the ability to also collect task status information may or may not be supported.

Issue Log

Issues are items that prevent the completion of a project task. Because all projects introduce some type of change, it is inevitable that issues will arise. The purpose of the **issue log** is to document the issues so that the project manager can ensure that they are resolved in a timely manner. The issue log should include:

- A description of each issue
- Name of the team member assigned to resolve the issue
- Priority (for example, high, medium, low)
- Date the issue was opened
- Status (open, deferred, or closed)
- The required resolution date
- A descriptive status of the issue
- Resolution date and description of the resolution

After the issue log is established, the team needs to actively work toward resolving the issues. This is where the skills of negotiation, conflict management, and innovative thinking are critical. Consensus among the affected parties is always the best solution in any issue, but in some situations the project sponsor must be called on to end a deadlock.

The issue log also can be used to capture ideas and topics that are not either specifically pertinent to the project or within its scope. These topics are often referred to as "parking lot" items. Placing them on the issue log (with a separate priority or status) is a good time management technique that ensures that the ideas will not be forgotten.

Project Plans

Reports generated from the project plan can provide information on the status of the project tasks. These reports are usually produced for the stakeholders to provide a snapshot of the project. When the project manager is using project management software, it is able to produce a variety of reports, including:

- Gantt chart that visually displays the task start and finish dates along with the percent of progress completed
- Tasks that are behind schedule
- Task list displaying the critical path tasks
- Tasks exceeding the original work estimate
- Resource reports showing the estimated work for each resource broken down by week or month

An example of a resource report is shown in figure 26.6.

Prepare the Final Report

When the project has been concluded, it is good practice to produce a final project report. The purpose of the report is to bring closure to the endeavor by documenting the project's final outcome. The topics to be included in the report include:

- List of the project objectives with a description of how each objective was accomplished
- List of the project deliverables
- Final project budget, detailing the comparison of the original estimate to the actual cost
- Final project schedule, detailing the comparison of the original dates to the actual dates

Celebrate Success

Projects can be very stressful to an organization. Therefore, it is important for the stakeholders and the project manager to provide the leadership to motivate team members and departments throughout the project duration. One of the ways this can be accomplished is by emphasizing the project's importance by celebrating accomplishments. For example, several social events might be held during the project to honor key project milestones. The project stakeholder could thank project participants for the effort expended thus far and encourage the same level of commitment for the remaining project activities.

After the project is completed, a more formal celebration may take place. All project contributors should be invited and recognized for their efforts.

Check Your Understanding 26.5

Instructions: Answer the following questions on a separate piece of paper.

1. What project progress information should project team members provide to the project manager?
2. What are some of the barriers to obtaining accurate progress information from team members?
3. What is change control?
4. What are some of the problems with formal project communications methods?

Figure 26.6. Example of a resource report

ID	Resource Name	Work	Details	January	February	March	April
1	Chief Relocation Officer	30 hrs	Work	30h			
	Identify requirements for new office space	*20 hrs*	Work	20h			
	Make final decision on office space	*5 hrs*	Work	5h			
	Finalize lease on office space	*5 hrs*	Work	5h			
2	Office Manager	257 hrs	Work	64.87h	137.78h	54.35h	
	Identify potential office sites	*20 hrs*	Work	20h			
	Design office space	*100 hrs*	Work	8.7h	86.95h	4.35h	
	Assign office space	*10 hrs*	Work			10h	
	Order office furniture	*30 hrs*	Work	30h			
	Order new office equipment	*30 hrs*	Work			30h	
	Order phone system	*10 hrs*	Work			10h	
	Select the move day	*2 hrs*	Work	2h			
	Obtain estimates from moving companies	*50 hrs*	Work	4.17h	45.83h		
	Hire movers	*5 hrs*	Work		5h		

Real-World Case

Reimbursement rules require that the chargemaster drive a facility's charges. To receive the optimal reimbursement for services rendered, the chargemaster must be up-to-date and all-inclusive and must meet any payer rules and regulations.

The facility has decided to undergo a review of its chargemaster to ensure that it meets the above criteria. In addition to the comprehensive evaluation, one of the other objectives of the project will be to institute the procedures to ensure that all additions, revisions, and deletions meet the chargemaster standards.

Summary

The art of project management encompasses a wide variety of responsibilities and skills. Project management does not just involve the creation and maintenance of a project plan. Organizations need to realize that good project management does not just happen. The concepts of project management must be understood and embraced at all levels of the organization. When the organization's executives do not support good project management methodology, the risk of project failure will outweigh any perceived benefits.

When a project begins, all parties must understand its objectives. The lack of a common vision for what the project will achieve is the first opportunity for the project to fail. All stakeholders must be willing to commit the required resources to the project and to support the procedural changes that will inevitably occur as a result of the project. All project personnel also can contribute to the success of the project by keeping proposed project changes to a minimum.

A project adheres to the project management life cycle. Depending on the size and type of project, each process is scalable. In other words, the extent to which each process is performed may vary, but all processes should be included in every project.

The project manager is in a unique position in situations where a project crosses departmental boundaries. He or she has responsibility for the project success, but generally little authority over the members of the project team. The project manager must possess technical, functional, and analytical skills as well as leadership, influential, and motivational abilities.

References

Kliem, R.L. 2004. *Leading High-Performance Projects.* Boca Raton, FL: J. Ross Publishing.

Lewis, J.P. 2008. *Mastering Project Management.* New York: McGraw-Hill.

Project Management Institute. 2008. *A Guide to the Project Management Body of Knowledge.* Newtown Square, PA: PMI.

Chapter 27
Strategic Thinking: Strategic Management and Leading Change

Susan E. McClernon, MHA, CHE

Learning Objectives

- Define and describe strategic management as an essential set of skills for strategic thinking and leading change in health information management (HIM) services
- Explore the skills that strategic health information managers and thinkers possess
- Distinguish strategic management from strategic planning and strategic thinking
- Know the steps of the strategic management and strategic thinking process
- Understand tools and approaches that complement the strategic management and thinking process
- Describe the benefits of strategic management and relate these to leadership and management principles and to the change management process
- Appreciate the importance of managing risk in a highly turbulent environment
- Apply theoretical knowledge in the area of a comprehensive environmental assessment
- Identify the concepts of *driving force* and *areas of excellence*
- Plan for the future through scenario building, strategic leverage, and innovation
- Describe techniques for considering future HIM and healthcare challenges and identifying strategic options
- Identify examples of innovative strategic management and strategic thinking as applied to HIM practice
- Understand how HIM strategies fit into broader information strategies and the overall strategy of the organization
- Describe the qualities and attributes of a strategic leader in HIM

Key Terms

Area of excellence
Balanced Scorecard methodology
Coalition building
Critical issues
Driving force
Environmental assessment
Kolb's "Learning Loop"
Innovation
Mission
Operations improvement planning
Paradigm
Process innovations
Scenarios
Service innovations
Storytelling
Strategic goal
Strategic management
Strategic objectives
Strategic planning
Strategic profile
Strategic thinking
Strategy
Strategy map
Strength, Weaknesses, Opportunities, and Threats (SWOT analysis)
Vision

Setting strategy is often viewed as the work of senior managers and boards of trustees. Strategy is thought of as being handed down from on high, embodied in slogans and generally not very relevant to the day-to-day work of most employees in the organization. Sometimes strategy is detailed in a three- to five-year strategic plan that lays out goals and key actions to meet the organization's goals. But strategy is no longer the sole purview of senior managers, planning departments, or consultants. The ability to develop effective strategies is a key attribute of successful managers and leaders at all levels in today's organizations. Employers cite strategic thinking, which includes strategic management and change leadership as competencies they look for in health information management (HIM) professionals (AHIMA 2004). Managers and directors should be able to lead the development of strategic plans at their department or division level as well as contribute significantly in strategic thinking and planning at an organizational level.

Simply stated, a **strategy** is the art and science of planning and marshalling resources for their most efficient and effective use. A strategy "provides the blueprint by which the end can be attained under conditions of direct combat. This is true whether the 'war' is actual military conflict or market competition" (Luke et al. 2004, 4). Strategy means consciously choosing to be clear about your company's direction in relation to what's happening in the dynamic environment (Olsen 2007, 10). **Strategic management** is a process a leader uses for assessing a changing environment to create a vision of the future, determining how the organization fits into the anticipated environment based on its mission, vision, and knowledge of its strengths, weaknesses, opportunities, and threats, and then setting in motion a plan of action to position the organization accordingly.

Strategic planning is not the same as operations improvement planning. **Strategic planning** "is the formalized roadmap that describes how your company executes the chosen strategy. A plan spells out where an organization is going over the next year or more and how it's going to get there. A strategic plan is a management tool that serves the purpose of helping an organization do a better job, because a plan focuses the energy, resources, and time of everyone in the organization in the same direction" (Olsen 2007, 12). **Operations improvement planning** focuses on improving how existing programs and services are carried out. By definition, it is internally focused and is one part of how to implement strategic thinking.

Management theories about the importance of strategy and how to set strategy are changing. This reconsideration is a reflection of the speed of change in every facet of contemporary life including healthcare. **Strategic thinking** is "the process of thinking that goes on in the head of the CEO and the key people around him or her that helps them determine the look for the organization at some point in to the future. Strategic thinking is different from strategic planning and operational planning. In fact, strategic thinking is the framework for the strategic and operational improvement plans. It combines an understanding of a strategic plan and an operational plan which support strategic thinking within an organization" (Robert 1998, 24–25).

This chapter explores the importance of strategic thinking and planning to effective management and describes approaches to making and communicating strategic choices. It discusses the importance of strategic management and strategic thinking for organizational learning and illustrates how HIM professionals can use strategy to shape and effect change in their department and organization.

Skills of Strategic Managers and Strategic Thinkers

The definition of strategy is straightforward, but the skills for setting and executing strategy are far from simple. HIM professionals must take advantage of opportunities to learn and develop skills for strategic management and thinking, including

- Monitoring industry trends in healthcare and information management
- Reflecting on how trends can affect existing and new products and services
- Considering how changes in one area can affect others in the organization
- Considering how a strategic course for change is set for their departments and organizations
- Helping others visualize the need for change and recruiting them as partners in moving a change agenda
- Implementing and measuring strategic plans effectively
- Questioning the status quo on a continuing basis and leading innovative change
- Being self-reflective and lifelong learners

Strategy is no longer a management domain reserved for senior managers. Today, all managers must develop skills and competencies that enable them to think and act strategically. These skills include sharpening their ability to observe the world around them. Strategic managers watch for changes in the larger environment beyond the healthcare industry, including political, economic, social, and technological changes. Such changes may involve staff attitudes, public policy, ethics, or inventions and innovations within the healthcare industry or externally. Managers must consider how these changes are affecting—or might affect—healthcare and the organizations in which they work. For example, shifts in public attitudes regarding the value placed on personal privacy have implications for health information policies and practices regarding patients who request access to their personal medical records.

Strategic managers develop skills reflecting the implications and opportunities afforded by trends. Whether reading a journal or discussing new ideas with others, strategic managers are always testing new ideas, identifying those that have merit and discarding those that do not. They are creating links between the trends and the value-adding actions they can take. For example, federal programs to adjust physician reimbursement on the basis of certain quality parameters suggest a need to elevate organizational standards for data integrity so that pay-for-performance determinations are accurate and fair.

Effective strategic managers and thinkers are creative in how they make associations among trends, ideas, and new opportunities. These associations are not always direct as in the examples about privacy and public policy or data quality and pay for performance. Making strategy choices may be the result of drawing lessons from analogous situations. When faced with an unfamiliar problem or opportunity, experienced managers often learn from similar situations they have seen or heard about and apply what they have learned to current situations (Gavetti and Rivkin 2005, 54–63). For example, faced with a shortage of trained coders, the HIM director institutes a coder-training program sponsored by her healthcare organization in partnership with a local community college and modeled on a similar program used to address the shortage of nurses in the community.

Strategic managers also continually look for opportunities to improve on the status quo. They do not accept the old adage, "If it's not broken, don't fix it." They always look for ways to make things better and are willing to take some risks and evaluate new approaches through trial and error. They know that standing still is really moving backward. They understand that no action may be less tolerable than trying something even if does not fully succeed. For example, the quality of coded data for inpatient services is at 94 percent and the data quality manager thinks that adjusting staff assignments may make better use of staff skills and improve performance.

New managers may lack the confidence to initiate change and may have few analogous experiences to draw on. Still, they should guard against accepting or perpetuating artificial barriers to creativity characterized by common squelchers, such as "We've never done that before," "We have always done it that way," or "That's not my job." Confidence comes from experience, and experience requires action and thoughtful reflection on what did and did not work.

Finally, strategic managers learn to help their organization contribute to new thinking and new ideas. They know that the best solutions represent the best thinking of all the stakeholders. Thus, strategic managers learn techniques to bring out the best thinking of all staff, superiors, colleagues, and other constituents for their change agenda. As Drucker (1996, xii) says, "The only definition of a leader is someone who has followers." For example, in pursuit of a goal to decrease the amount of printing of electronic records by physicians, the health information manager knew that support from nursing and other staff in the patient care units was essential for success. He oversaw implementation of a multifaceted plan to reduce the rate of printing on the units and shared credit with nursing when the print rate began to decline.

The skills of the strategic manager are learned. Learning begins by recognizing the importance of strategy to today's successful managers. For HIM professionals, the learning begins with their professional course work and directed learning experiences. Skills are learned and subsequently sharpened through work experience; particularly opportunities to be part of—and to lead—change management projects.

From Strategic Planning to Strategic Management and Thinking

Strategic planning was described in the management literature in the 1960s and the decades that followed. It was a prominent and highly touted organizational function. Strategic planning was developed to prevent organizations from "crisis planning" when they realized that their competitors outpaced them in innovation and they quickly had to develop reactive strategies to keep this from happening again. Early applications were characterized by rigorous and formal analysis of data to deduce a desired future and the steps to achieve it. In large corporations, departments of planners prepared forecasts with the aid of computer analysis. The complex reports were delivered to senior managers who were largely uninvolved in the process.

These approaches have fallen out of favor for several key reasons. First, forecasting the future, particularly in such rapidly changing times, is difficult. Also, by the time a complex three- to five-year plan is finalized and delivered to senior managers, it is undoubtedly out-of-date. In order to stay strong and viable as an organization, the HIM professional must engage the best thinking of everyone, look at where the organization is today, where it needs to be in the future, and then find the path to the new vision as a team. When departmental and organizational strategies are updated at least annually, the effort will result in plans that make real organizational change. If customers, employees, and all levels of managers are involved in strategy development, the plan is likely to be seen as relevant and likely to be implemented. In addition, for strategic planning and thinking to really be more than an improved operational plan, it needs to include innovative strategies that not only help redefine the organization's existing products and services but creates new products and services that strategically move the organization forward toward its vision.

No one phrase is the accepted successor for this type of comprehensive strategic planning. In fact, today managers and directors in many organizations are likely to still hear the activity referred to as strategic planning. However, it is important to get beneath the words to understand the process being followed. It may be called strategic planning, but it may embody many of the newer concepts that often are called strategic management and thinking. For example:

- It is framed by organizational values, vision, and mission.
- It takes into account possible futures scenarios, rather than trying to forecast only one future.

- It is truly the work of management, even when guided by consultants, and has broad input and participation.
- It is action oriented and measured, with a commitment to bringing about change.
- It results in organizational innovation, change, and learning.

Strategic thinking is a way of introducing innovation into decision making and engaging others in the change process. With the rapid changes in HIM practice, this discussion of strategic thinking is not academic. The skills that distinguish a strategic thinker include the following:

- Ability to plan (consensus building) and strategy formation (leadership)
- Flexibility and creativity
- Comfort with uncertainty and risk
- A sense of urgency and vision of how to move change forward positively
- How to gain a powerful core of organizational supporters
- An ability to communicate the vision and plans

Strategic management and thinking should be viewed as a component of each of the five functions of management discussed in chapter 20. Every aspect of management involves a strategic management component, as described here.

With organizational learning as a centerpiece, this approach unifies change management, strategy development, and leadership. In all three, managers learn by observing and reflecting on the results of their experiences. This concept is best depicted in **Kolb's "Learning Loop,"** shown in figure 27.1 (Kolb 1988, 68–88). To undertake deliberate change, individuals reflect on their experiences and become aware of new patterns and trends that they did not previously perceive. They form new ways of looking at the opportunities and the implications of their experiences. They evaluate new theories about what can and should be, and then apply these theories and test their implications. They observe and reflect on the results of their experiences, thus beginning the loop again.

Figure 27.1. Kolb's "Learning Loop"

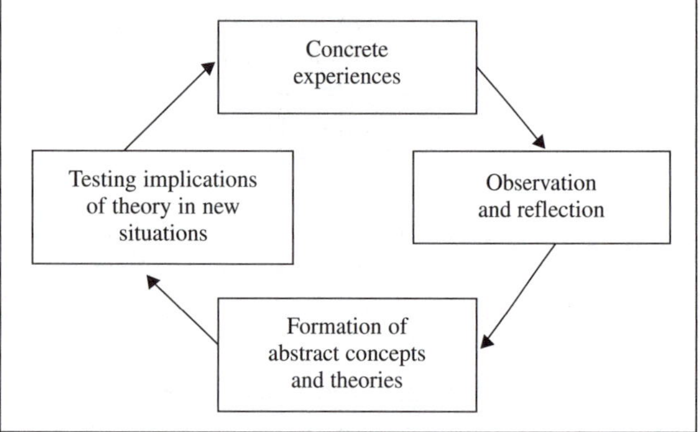

Source: Kolb 1988.

Elements of Strategic Thinking and Strategic Management

As shown in figure 27.2, strategic thinking and strategic management is a logical process that comprises a number of steps that may be explicit or implicit. It begins with a current description and internal assessment of the organization and an assessment of the external environment.

Based on the findings and conclusions from the assessment, a new or updated strategic profile and a vision statement of how the organization would like things to be in the future are developed. For example, the vision for a managed care health plan might be to have fully engaged patients who are full partners with the health plan in maintaining their health. Obviously, a few key strategies are needed for this vision to be realized and these must be identified and understood. Strategies are the most important directional goals to pursue to achieve the vision. Once the core strategies are identified, a set of strategic goals for each strategy need to be developed that define a series of longer-term action steps of how to achieve each strategy. For example, a strategy for the health plan may be to develop a campaign to include patients in focusing on the aspects of self health. Some of the strategic goals might involve a way to develop incentives for patients to engage in wellness activities, to use their personal health records (PHRs), and to provide easy access to computer and health literacy education. The next step would be to take each strategic goal and identify the strategic objectives or short-term action plans that are needed to accomplish each strategic goal.

Major strategic goals and objectives that are needed to move toward the vision are described. These become more precise than the overall vision and strategy. For example, providing all citizens with access to lifetime electronic PHRs might be a strategy to achieve the vision of empowered consumers. The vision and strategy describe where the organization wants to go, and the strategic goals and objectives describe what must be accomplished and how to get there. The strategies are how the organization intends to pursue its vision. The strategic goals and objectives are the specific action plans needed to implement these strategies.

Although depicted as a circular process, overall strategic management is never so neat and organized, and the best strategies may emerge from trial and error. But effective strategy will not emerge without a clear idea of where the leader wants to move the organization and a realistic assessment of the issues to overcome. Moreover, strategic management will not happen in isolation. Stakeholders, whether staff, customers, patients, or senior managers, must be engaged in each phase of the process.

Each step involves learning, which in turn enables plans to be improved upon, therefore making subsequent efforts more effective. Thus, experience sharpens and clarifies understanding of the issues, allowing managers to be more precise in setting goals. Strategies and tactics are continually modified with experience. Strategic management, like Kolb's "Learning Loop", is a process that leads to organizational learning and improvement over time. (Refer to figure 27.2.)

In contrast to traditional strategic planning, where all steps are neatly outlined before implementation is begun, strategic management requires a willingness to learn and change as the leader guides an organization through the process. In a fast-paced, changing environment, constant review of strategy, goals and objectives is required.

Check Your Understanding 27.1

Instructions: On a separate piece of paper, answer the following questions.

1. In two sentences, describe how strategic thinking relates to strategic planning and operational planning.
2. List three skills of a strategic thinker.

Create a Commitment to Change with Vision

The organization's vision sets the broad directional strategy leaving the details to be worked out. A **vision** is a picture of the desired future (Kemp et al. 1993). Kotter (2002, 72) explains that an effective vision statement has the following characteristics:

- Conveys a picture of what the future will look like
- Appeals to the long-term interests of the stakeholders
- Sets forth realistic and achievable goals
- Is clear enough to provide guidance in decision making
- Is flexible so that alternative strategies are possible as conditions change
- Is easy to describe and communicate

An organization may never realize a vision in its entirety. Today's technology may not yet support lifetime PHRs or autocoding of 100 percent of cases, but that does not mean these bold visions should not be sketched. All health information may never be in digital form, but that does not mean this should not be a vision. Visions must be worth pursuing; otherwise, why would others become engaged?

Visions should evoke a sense of excitement and urgency from those closest to the process. If the designers are not getting excited about the possibilities the vision presents, others are not likely to generate excitement. A sense of urgency is essential to overcome the forces that protect the status quo.

Figure 27.2. Elements of strategic planning

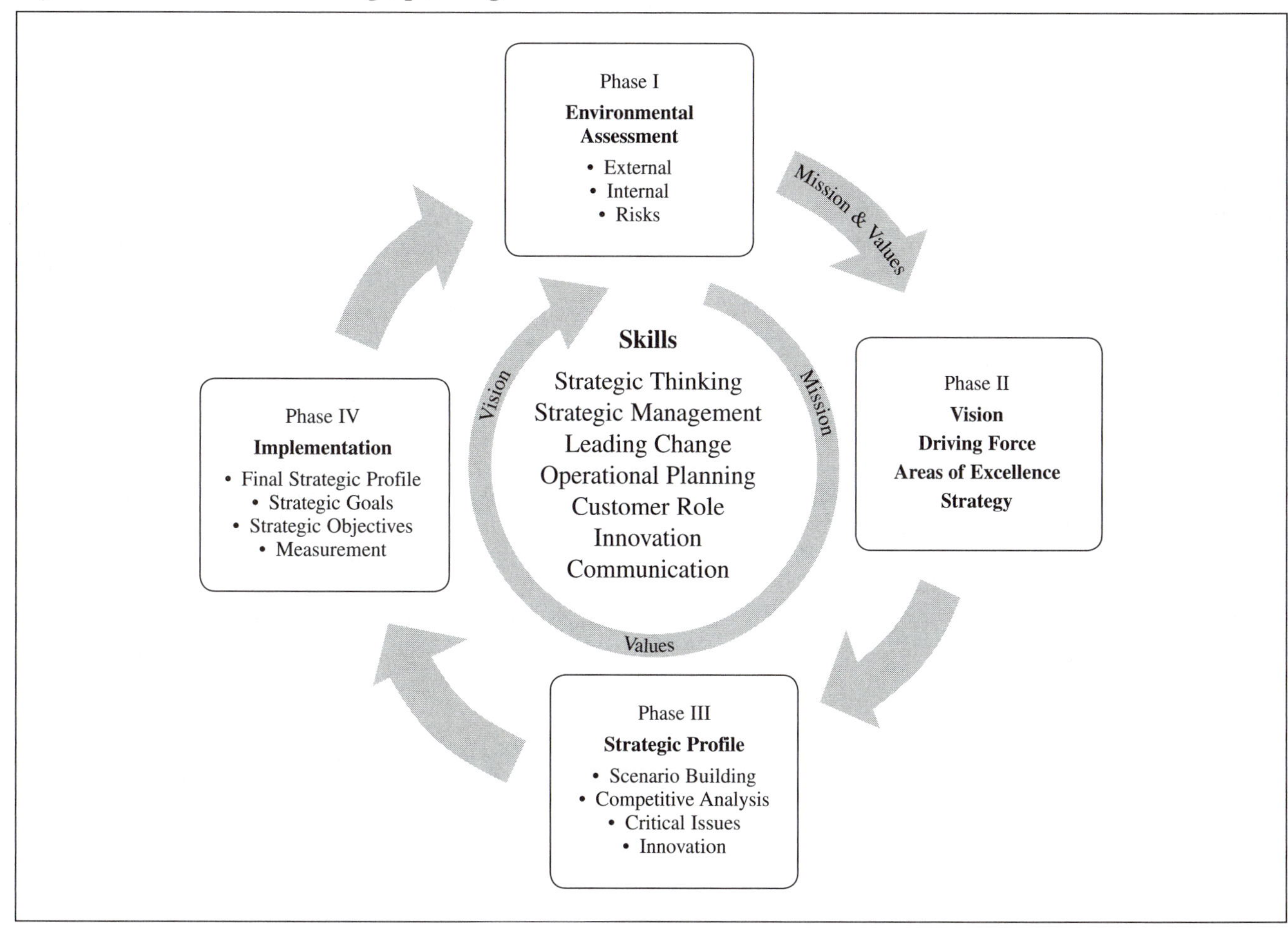

According to Kouzes and Posner (1995, 94), "A vision describes a bold and ideal image of the future." It is the catalyst for change. They also state, "if leaders are going to take us to places we've never been before, constituents of all types demand that they have a sense of direction" (Kouzes and Posner 1995, 95).

A vision states the direction for organizational change and helps motivate people to take action. In 2003, the American Health Information Management Association (AHIMA) convened an interdisciplinary panel of experts to craft a vision for electronic health information management (e-HIM):

> Electronic health information management is the body of knowledge and practice that assures the availability of health information to facilitate real-time healthcare delivery and critical health-related decision making for multiple purposes across diverse organizations, settings, and disciplines.

This vision statement describes features of e-HIM that work in real time to support critical decision making across healthcare. The vision reflects a more diverse field with a critical charge. It has been used to help catalyze the field to embrace e-HIM as a change strategy.

In 2005, AHIMA's Board of Directors again looked to the future to consider how the field of HIM is changing and the impact of the changes on the profession and on the professional association. It reaffirmed the vision crafted in 2003 and articulated new insights about strategies that would secure a strong future for the profession.

Designing a compelling vision requires a solid understanding of the internal and external environment. It also requires the ability to break free of the current paradigm and to think creatively about a new reality for the future. **Paradigm** is broadly defined as a philosophical or theoretical framework of any kind based on theory and experimentation (*Merriam-Webster* online).

The following are examples of vision statements for HIM. A director of HIM services for a health system envisions services that make the fullest use of technology to provide high-quality, cost-effective information to authorized users. He expressed this idealized vision as follows:

> It is our goal to utilize state-of-the-art information technology and best practices grounded in applied research in every phase of our operation so that we are able to deliver accurate information in digital form to support patient care and healthcare operations. This ambitious goal will require us to become more externally focused, to gain a deeper understanding of user needs, and to work closely with others within and outside our organization. It will also require health information services staff to work together to question all current practices and be willing to try new approaches even if they are not all successful.

This vision lays out a substantial challenge, yet it provides focus. First, the overarching vision is to be able to deliver all information in digital form to all users of HIM services. It acknowledges that technology is only as good as the enabling processes; therefore, it promises use of best practices. These practices are not to be just what we might think are best but, rather, are practices substantiated by applied research that demonstrates their validity. The vision statement acknowledges that achieving this vision will require new ways of working. First, success will require gaining a deeper understanding of the needs of those who rely on the information and of those whose collaboration is needed to achieve the vision. Second, it will require effective teamwork among HIM staff that must become more comfortable with both change and risk taking.

In another example, an HIM consultant for a long-term care system was having difficulty gaining support for her vision of what an EHR could contribute to the residents, staff, and the overall organization. She developed the following description of her vision:

> All members of the care team have immediate access to complete and accurate information for each resident. This information recaps care delivered and presents the status of all health, social, ADL, and other resident-specific issues being managed. Information needs to be entered just once and is available for a variety of patient care, quality improvement, and administrative uses. Summary reports are used as the basis for shift change briefings and for periodic care conferences. The information system prompts caregivers to actions that need to be taken and alerts them to changes in status that require special vigilance. Data entered into the system summarizing observations, care given, orders, and activities produce a record of care that meets licensing and other external requirements. The system also automatically accumulates the information needed for care and operations management and for external reporting.

This vision highlights the benefits of implementing an EHR from the perspective of improving management of the care process every day. It underscores the fact that information for management and internal and external reporting should be a byproduct of the system, thereby reducing the redundant paperwork that currently requires so much staff time. A careful parsing of the vision reveals the major features and functions required of a system. For example, the system must be capable of producing a change-of-shift summary report recapping care processes and the status of all resident problems being managed. It also must accumulate the data needed for minimum data set (MDS) and other reporting. The vision serves as a starting point for creating a more detailed set of specifications and evaluating potential system vendors.

Visions also can be more narrowly focused on a particular project. For example, a data quality manager for a multispecialty group practice clinic prepared the following vision statement to help the physicians and coding staff rally around a proposed project to improve the timeliness and accuracy of billing processes through the use of computer-assisted coding tools:

> During each patient visit, the physician enters problems, treatments, orders, and follow-up plans into his or her handheld personal assistant device (PDA). PDA data are periodically uploaded to the clinical data repository throughout the day and data are combined there with other patient-specific reports and information. Codes are auto-assigned by the systems and missing data are flagged. Clinical data analysts review each visit record to check the accuracy of the auto-

generated codes and determine whether the information substantiates the codes assigned. A visit record is either marked for billing or flagged as incomplete with supplementary information requested from the physician or referred service. Ninety percent of visits are billed within one business day, 95 percent within three business days, and the balance within five business days.

This vision statement has three major elements. First, it sets an aggressive goal of billing 90 percent of visits on the day of service. To do so, physicians must initiate the process using electronic tools to eliminate time-consuming handling of handwritten information. The new role of clinical data analyst is introduced, reflecting the role of coding specialists with advanced data quality and compliance management skills.

These vision statements relate to HIM challenges. However, it is important that the HIM vision complement the organization's overall vision and mission. For example, the organization's vision is to be known for its advanced clinical services in cardiac and oncology care. To achieve this vision, the organization is pursuing a strategy of attracting clinical talent with national reputations and expanding clinical research programs. This overall vision and these strategies should be accounted for when crafting the HIM vision and strategies.

Strategic managers must understand the overall organizational goals and take them into account when crafting their own plans. First, they seek ways to support and further the overall goals of the organization through the priorities they set for their areas of responsibility. For example, will the cancer registry program need to be upgraded to support the more sophisticated information needs of a world-class oncology service? As a practical matter, it is hard to sell a plan that is out of step with priorities. Advancing the organization's goals through synergistic efforts is the mark of a successful manager.

Check Your Understanding 27.2

Instructions: Based on an expanded understanding of the elements of a vision statement, write a concise, two-sentence vision statement that describes your department or organization's Electronic Health Record future state in the next three years. On a separate piece of paper, explain how the statement meets the elements of an effective vision statement as outlined by Kotter.

Begin with a Current Profile

The beginning stage in developing a strategic plan is to develop a good understanding of the organization's current profile. This approach assesses the current mission, values, and vision of the organization or department, completes an internal analysis of the trends within the organization or department, and conducts an external assessment of trends. The final step in completing the current profile is to assess the potential impact of the uncertainties and risks in the internal and external environment on the organization's strategic thinking and plan. Based on all the information and intelligence gathered throughout this profiling process, the strategic thinking tools and techniques described here are then utilized to develop a strategic future profile.

Assess the Current Mission, Values, and Vision

It is important to review the current mission, values, and vision of the organization and department. A **mission** statement is defined as an enduring statement of purpose for an organization that identifies the scope of its operations in services and products, its market terms, and reflects its values and priorities (Abrahams 1999, 14). As described earlier, the mission differs from the vision. It is also important to understand the organizational values that are used to describe the basic philosophy, principles, or ideals of the organizational culture and behavioral expectations. Any strategic plan needs to be developed in accordance with the mission, vision, and values of the organization in order to drive change that will be supported by staff and senior leaders.

Understanding Environmental Assessment Trends

Knowledge of the internal and external environment is essential to vision and strategy formulation. An **environmental assessment** is conducted, which is defined as a thorough review of the internal and external conditions in which an organization operates (Jennings 2000, 39). This data-intensive process is the continuous process of gathering and analyzing intelligence about trends that are—or may be—affecting HIM and the healthcare organization and industry. It is both internally focused on the healthcare organization and HIM and externally focused on industry, market, and environmental trends.

Internal Assessment

It is important to fully evaluate and understand the current internal environment of both the department and the organization. This is a critical step to understand the organization's current strategic direction. It is also an opportunity to begin to gain multiple perspectives from key stakeholders on the current state. During this step in the process, differing perspectives that are held by various key stakeholders will emerge. Key themes of consensus will also begin to show.

The current description needs to include a recent **strategic profile** that identifies the existing key services or products of the department or organization, the nature of its customers and users, the nature of its market segments, and the nature of its geographic markets (Robert 1998, 60–61). Another critical step in the assessment process is to conduct a SWOT (strengths, weaknesses, opportunities, and threats) analysis of the department and organization. **SWOT analysis** "evaluates the internal organization based on its strengths compared to competitors and regional and societal demands, weaknesses compared to competitors or related to just the internal functions, opportunities for the advancing ahead of competitors or serving a patient population not served well currently, and threats from external or internal agents that could stymie the organization's success" (Dunn 2007, 123). This process should involve all key stakeholders and will be an opportunity to begin consensus building. At this point in the process, key planning assumptions, data analysis and, identification of potential risks and uncertainties should be identified.

Internal environmental assessment as adapted from the work of Bryson (1995, 90–92) includes analysis of

- *Performance indicators:* Budget targets and results, financials, performance and productivity measures, staff and customer feedback
- *Resources:* Budgeted staff, information technology, and educational resources, programs, competencies, organizational culture
- *Present strategy:* Organization-wide strategy and priorities, information management strategy, information systems plans and priorities, compliance programs, products and services, business processes

External Assessment

External environmental assessment as adapted from Bryson (1995, 87–89) includes analysis of:

- *Forces and trends:* Political, economic, demographic, social, technological, and educational
- *Resource constraints:* Healthcare reimbursement systems, patient and customer trends, regulators, competitors
- *Collaborators:* Current and potential collaborators
- *Trends* in industry and other related organizations

Other key areas to review and collect information for the external assessment phase of the strategic plan include the following:

- Demographics
- Innovative trends in the industry
- Technology
- Market structure
- Market share
- Market dynamics
- Customers
- Competitors
- Centers of excellence

An HIM manager, who focuses exclusively on his or her own area of responsibility, whether managing a department, a service, or a project, will have a difficult time succeeding as a strategic manager. Understanding the environment provides the context for the tough decisions involved in setting direction, designing strategy, and leading change. Some ways to develop access to be better able to gather external assessment information in your environment include:

- Taking inventory of sources of internal and external information to identify and fill information gaps
- Building performance measures to gain perspective on trends over time
- Becoming involved in projects and task forces within the organization to interact with a wide range of coworkers
- Developing a personal reading list to follow the thinking of experts in the field
- Reading what futurists are saying about how things will change
- Becoming active in professional associations, AHIMA, and other groups
- Building a network of professional colleagues
- Making full use of the information resources that AHIMA and other organizations make available
- Contributing to the professional body of knowledge when developing new HIM practice solutions

How to Manage Uncertainty

Analyzing the changing environment and envisioning the future is at the same time an analytic and a highly creative activity. Understanding internal and external trends and forces of risks and uncertainties requires analysis of:

- Relationships between trends
- Sequence of events
- Causes and effects
- Priority among items

As a strategic thinker, this is a critical skill that will require the leader to understand that there is risk and uncertainty as an organization begins to predict possible future trends and design strategies that might work based on those different scenarios. It also gives the leader an opportunity to find ways for identifying strategies to avoid some of the possible pitfalls or counteract external or internal forces. The key uncertainties or risks (see figure 27.3) to review as adapted from Jennings (2000, 7–14) include:

- Demand structure—for example, market and industry trends
- Supply structure—for example, employees, physicians
- Competitors—for example, Information Technology, outsourcing
- External forces—for example, payers, employers, customer trends
- Regulation—for example, federal or state government
- Time—for example, when are the forces of uncertainty predicted to potentially change or not change

Another aspect that is helpful in reviewing the key forces that may bring risk and uncertainty is to understand there are three levels of uncertainty to consider about each of the preceding forces. Based on Jennings (2000, 10–13), part of the strategic process must evaluate the levels of uncertainty and degrees of risk by whether they are:

- Clear trends—for example, moving from a paper medical record to the PHR

Figure 27.3. Sources of uncertainty

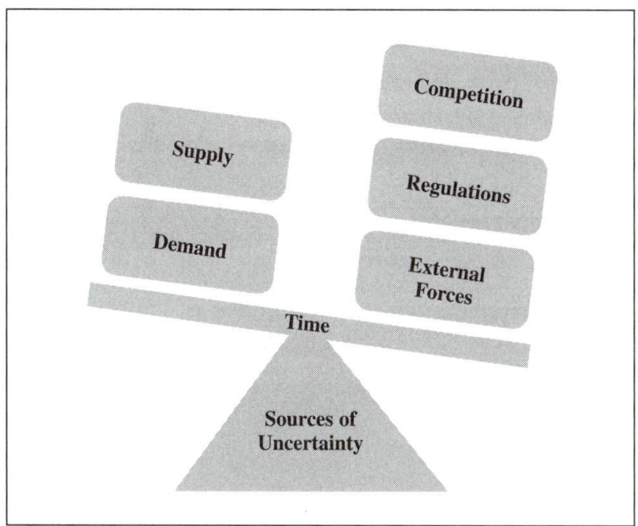

- Unknowns that are knowable—for example, consumer preferences of the PHR
- Residual uncertainty—for example, fate of IT companies that make PHRs

When assessing the levels of uncertainty, it is important to understand that elements may be things the leaders won't really be able to totally understand or they may become clearer over time. It is important to decide whether it is important to continue tracking each of the risks or uncertainties or if they pass the "so what?" test. These levels of uncertainty will be helpful to include in the next phase that focuses on tools for strategic thinking, especially the scenario building exercise.

Tools for Strategic Thinking—Scenario Building

To bring out the best strategic thinking of a team or work group, it is often helpful to use techniques that help participants consider factors from different perspectives. A number of group process techniques such as brainstorming, nominal group technique, and others help unleash each individual's creative talent.

Storytelling is another powerful group process technique. Stories are defined as one way we transmit an organization's truths, insights, and commitments. Using compelling stories is a powerful way to persuade people by uniting an idea with an emotion. In a story, you not only weave a lot of information into the telling but you also arouse your listener's emotions and energy. Essentially, a story expresses how and why life changes (McKee 2003). Telling stories about the future suggested by the trends has a number of advantages, including:

- Most people are comfortable with this approach.
- Findings are presented in an understandable and real-world context.
- Stories are memorable, making it easier for others to remember essential points.
- Stories generate excitement and are fun to develop.

One storytelling technique that is used in more sophisticated strategy planning is that of scenarios. The word *scenario* literally means a script of a play or story, or a projected sequence of events. **Scenarios** are "focused descriptions of fundamentally different futures presented in coherent script-like or narrative fashion" (Schoemaker 1993, 193–213). They are plausible stories about how the future might unfold. They are not meant to predict but, rather, simply to interpret and clarify how environmental trends may play out.

Scenarios are based on analysis and interaction of environmental variables. Environmental assessment is an important preparatory step in scenario development. Based on study of the environment, two to four scenario themes reflecting alternate possible futures using differing potentials around the key forces or risks of uncertainties described earlier are developed. Stories or scenarios are constructed that describe how each of these themes might be played out. These scenarios or stories are refined through input and further study until they reflect the group's best thinking about what futures might be in store for the organization under various circumstances.

To understand how the clinical coding function might change in the future, an AHIMA task force studied environmental trends and developed four scenarios, each highlighting a slightly different, but plausible, future (Johns 2000, 26–33):

- The first scenario described the impact on coding if a breakthrough technology became available that would automate a great deal of the coding that is now being done manually or with the help of encoders.
- The second scenario described the impact on coding functions if healthcare organizations were strategically committed to using information to improve the quality of care information and hence the organization's strategic positioning.
- The third scenario involves the role of coding in an increasingly regulatory environment in which healthcare spending is ratcheted down and investments in technology are constrained.
- The fourth scenario involves greater consumer involvement in making healthcare decisions and maintaining personal health information.

One can quickly see that all are plausible scenarios. The future of coding will be affected by all these factors, but one or more may have a greater impact than others. Strategic managers would develop contingency plans to account for the variables that may shape the future.

AHIMA also used scenarios to consider how medical transcription would be affected by technology. The steering group for this future project also prepared four likely future scenarios concerning medical transcription practice and a set of strategic actions to ensure that the field is well prepared to adapt regardless of which of the scenarios actually proves true (Fuller and Dennis 2005, 48–51).

The HIM professional should build a portfolio of techniques that a leader can use to bring out the best thinking of others; peruse the business shelves of major bookstores for guidebooks containing exercises and techniques to improve group process; observe techniques used by facilitators to improve how groups work and think together; keep a notebook or computer file of such techniques and practice them whenever the opportunity arises. Effective strategic managers know how to facilitate groups to help them think and work well together.

Check Your Understanding 27.3

Instructions: Answer the following questions on a separate sheet of paper.

1. List four ways that you, as a leader, do external "environmental scanning" in your everyday life (for example, read the Sunday newspaper, belong to listservs, and so on).
2. Explain how—and how well—you, as a leader, stay in touch with new developments and trends in each of the following sectors:
   - Your community
   - The healthcare industry and related industries
   - The nation
   - The world
3. Identify two additional "external environmental assessment" activities that you can incorporate into your professional life that would help you improve your rating in the exercise above by improving your grasp of the external environment.
4. In groups of four to six, reach consensus on the three most important ways that a new HIM professional can stay current with practice trends in HIM. You will need a flip chart and markers for this exercise.

   In your small group:
   - First, work quietly for five minutes to construct a group list. Write the best ideas on a piece of paper.
   - Allow each member of the group to contribute one idea. Write each idea on the flip chart. Go around the group until all ideas have been contributed. Do not repeat identical ideas.
   - When all ideas have been contributed, ask the group to rate the importance of each idea using the following scale: 5 points for very important, 3 points for somewhat important, 1 point for minimally important, and 0 points for those suggestions you do not think are at all important.
   - Tally the scores of each rater to produce a total score per idea. Rewrite the ideas in order of the most to least important based on the group's ratings.

Note: The group process technique used in this exercise is called the *nominal group technique*. Begin your facilitator's notebook with this technique.

Create a Platform for Strategic Innovation

Techniques such as scenario development and environmental assessment are useful in formulating strategy because they include a focus on both the internal and external environments. However, one should not expect to identify exciting new strategies by only looking at the past, looking inward, or looking within the healthcare industry. Take time to look outside the organization and industry; look to the future in formulating innovative strategy. New or innovative services or products come from identifying potential new needs based on determining the possible future scenarios that might occur and actually differentiate the organization's services or products from others. "Product or **service innovations** create new market opportunities, and in many industries are the driving force behind growth and profitability. **Process** or service **innovations** enable firms to produce existing products or services more efficiently. As such, process and service innovations are one of the main determinants of productivity growth" (Robert 1998, 45–46). It takes understanding the department and organization's strategic capabilities and anticipating what future needs will come from predicting future trends. It takes a willingness to be able to take risks and think strategically. For example, having access to personal health information on the Internet 24 hours a day is an innovation in healthcare. Many of the innovations in healthcare have come from unexpected stress (computerized dictation systems), research and development, and a willingness to test new services or products with the ultimate goal of improving the health of a population. The strategic plan needs to include time for thoughtful development of service and product innovations.

From Vision to Strategy

As defined earlier, a strategy is an action or set of actions that moves the organization toward its vision. Strategic management is about pursuing a new set of activities or new ways of carrying out current activities that move the organization toward its vision. It may take the form of new or redesigned programs or services. It may involve implementing new systems, outsourcing certain operations, or merging functions with another organizational entity. It also may entail phasing out an outdated program or adopting new technologies. Finally, it may be aimed at bringing an organization into compliance with new regulations or finding new ways to reduce operating costs.

It is important to remember that strategic management is not the same as operations improvement. Operations improvement is internally focused whereas strategic management seeks to improve the position of the organization in the broader world in which it operates.

To illustrate the thought process involved in moving from vision to strategy, consider the sample shown earlier in figure 27.2 based on the vision statement presented earlier in this chapter to move from a predominantly paper record to a digital record.

Understanding the Driving Force

The most important strategic thinking skill to understand prior to determining strategy is to understand the driving force of the department or organization. **Driving force** is the concept of what a department or organization uses to determine which products or services to offer, which markets to seek, and which customers to attract (Robert 2000, 63–65). With intentional analysis, it is critical to understand the driving force or strategic drive that propels a department or organization forward toward its vision. After the internal and external assessments, decide if that same driving force should continue or if there is a strategic need to change to a different driving force to achieve the organization's vision. According to Robert, every organization is composed of 10 important strategic areas, or driving forces, but only one of these is strategically most important to the company and is the engine that propels, or drives, the company forward to success (1998, 64–65). For example, AHIMA's driving force is defined as a user or customer class organization that is strategically focusing its business around a describable and specific category of customers—HIM professionals. AHIMA responds by providing a wide variety of services and products that are aimed at this user class. Therefore, it is helpful to keep the key driving force in mind when it determines its future strategies. It becomes the major filter of determining what new strategies or initiatives will continue moving the organization toward its vision.

Defining Areas of Excellence

Understanding and developing an **area of excellence** is another key concept of strategic thinking. This concept is a describable skill, competence, or capability that a department or company cultivates to a level of proficiency greater than anything else it does (Robert 1998, 109). To determine a strategic direction, the leader must develop a clear understanding of current key areas of excellence in the organization and what areas of excellence will be needed to achieve the new vision. Over time, the strategy of an organization, like a person, can become stronger and healthier or it can get weaker and sicker. What determines the future of the strategy are the areas of excellence that a department or organization deliberately cultivates to keep the strategy strong and healthy (Robert 1998, 109). For an HIM director, understanding special capabilities, such as managing the collection of patient and clinical quality data to improve quality of patient care, can be an important area of excellence. It becomes much easier to make difficult choices involving resources and time allocation if it is clear which strategies and areas of excellence are being pursued.

Strategic Goals and Strategic Objectives

The next step in strategic planning is to develop strategic goals to carry out each strategy. For example, implementing the strategy "Acquire and implement electronic signature software" requires research about technology vendors that offer software compatible with the clinical data repository. It requires budgeting for this technology, securing support for the action plan, issuing an RFP, checking references, and so on.

Building a strategy grounded in a vision provides a context in which one can continually assess whether the organization is on track and if it is making progress. The AHIMA Board of Directors identified six key strategies in its 2005 future visioning session that were supported by the e-HIM vision and a deep understanding of the external environment. They were cast as transformative "from-to" statements, reflecting the key changes that AHIMA must lead over the next decade:

- From variable health record content and formats to standardization
- From passive responsiveness to vendors to system-building certification of offerings
- From exclusivity to inclusive membership driven by role, aspirations, and interests
- From academic only to academic and performance-based certification
- From autonomy and self-sufficiency to working alliance with like-minded bodies
- From traditional leadership to governance adept at advancing change

For each key area for strategic action, a strategy map was designed that began with a brief description of the current state in 2005 and a desired state in 2015. A **strategy map** is a tool described as providing a visual representation of an organization's critical objectives and the relationships among them that drive organizational performance (Norton et al. 2000, 2). A set of short-term strategic goals and objectives undertaken in 2005–2006 were determined along with future milestones that should be met along the way to 2015. Two sample strategy maps are shown in figures 27.4 and 27.5. Depicting change as a road map is a useful way to help others understand the goals and the course of change.

Check Your Understanding 27.4

Instructions: Complete the following steps on a separate piece of paper.

1. Prepare a template for the strategy worksheet shown in figure 27.3 using your PC word-processing or presentation software (Microsoft Word or PowerPoint). Complete the figure using real sources of uncertainty that will impact the vision you outlined in Check Your Understanding 27.2.
2. Select AHIMA's vision statement to identify the driving force and one area of excellence. Then describe the strategy to achieve that area of excellence in one or two sentences on the form.
3. In the space provided on the form, write at least two strategic goals that would need to be pursued to address the preceding identified strategy.
4. Identify one or more strategic objectives that would need to be implemented to move toward each goal.
5. Finally, describe the logic you followed in determining the strategy, setting strategic goals, and developing strategic objectives.

Customer Role in Strategic Thinking

An important part of strategic planning that is often overlooked, yet vital to developing effective strategy, is the role of the customer. Traditional ways of collecting customer information include methods such as consumer focus groups, patient advisory boards, and patient surveys. If set up correctly, these tools can be effective in gathering information within the proper context of strategic planning. Unfortunately, the strategic planning process often ignores customers or users or involves them too late to provide effective feedback. In the case of the PHR, it would mean involving patients and their families in the design of the strategies, strategic goals and objectives, and implementation plan for the PHR. During this process, the organization would begin to understand their needs and expectations and develop ways

Figure 27.4. Strategy map: From variable health record content and formats to standardization

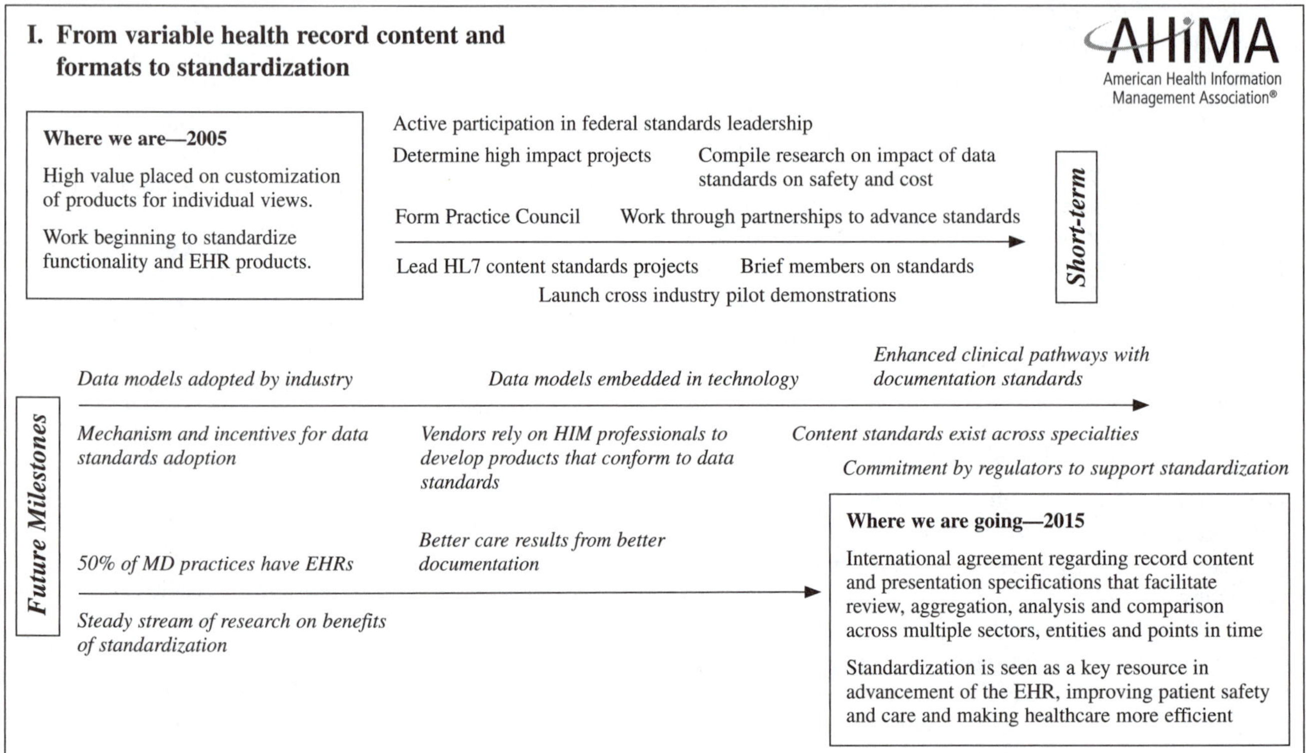

Figure 27.5. Balanced scorecard with strategy map

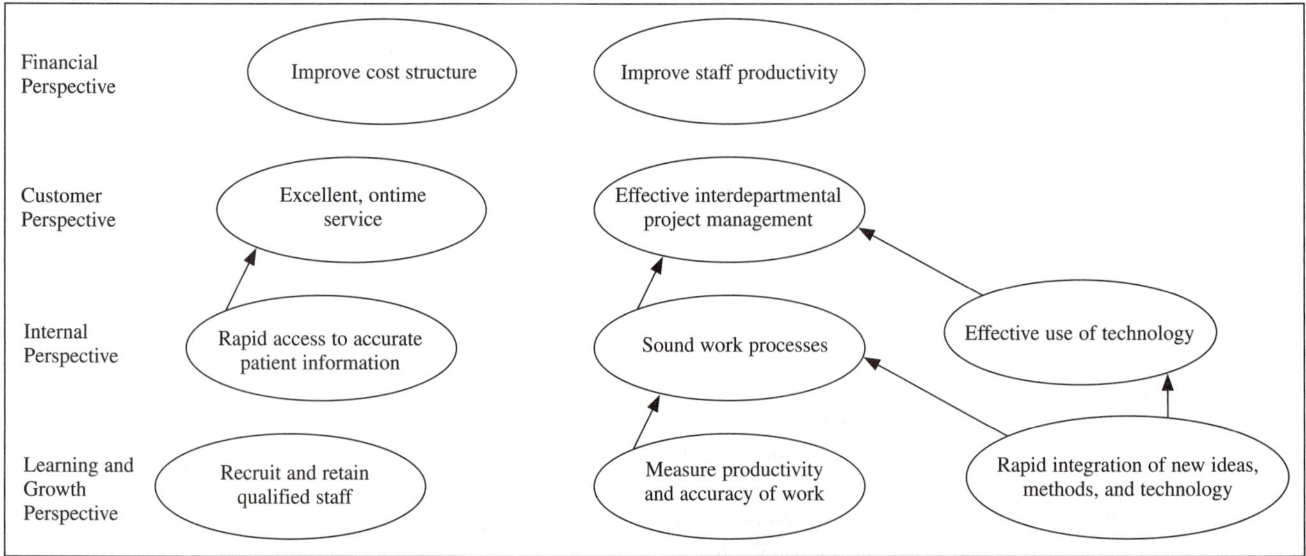

to provide a truly innovative product and service from the customers' perspective. These customers are often readily available, whether it involves using volunteers, staff members, or their family members who are customers of the PHR. Also, physicians and office staff who get calls from patients on a regular basis are well-versed in understanding what their customers want and need.

Determine Impact of Competition

Developing ways to understand the department or organization's competitors is also valuable during the strategic planning process. Innovations or changes are also being planned by the competition. Take time to understand what the organization's key competitor's current and potential strengths and weaknesses are. The organization's strategies should be developed in order to have the most influence on increasing its market share. Once the manager has selected a strategic direction, he or she should take time to evaluate and anticipate any impact that competitors, current or future, might have on the strategy.

Strategic Management Implementation

Porter advises that the "essence of strategy is deciding what not to do" (1996, 61–78). He urges managers to view strategy as a series of trade-offs. Major change will impact current activities and may well require their modification or even elimination. No organization has the resources to take on major new programs without considering their impact on current programs. Making trade-offs is difficult for most managers. Letting go of even a marginal program may produce a backlash. However, resources must be reallocated to those programs that will enable the organization to operate at a new level of strategy.

Develop Strategic Findings and Conclusions

After reviewing all of the information from both internal and external assessments, a shared list of findings is developed with the strategic planning team. Based on these findings, the leader should determine if there are further informational needs or data points that will be important for developing a set of strategic conclusions. Strategic findings and conclusions help solidify the new vision, strategic driving force, and areas of excellence, which leads to identifying key strategies for achieving the vision. After completing all the above aspects of strategic planning, the leaders will now need to put a strategic "stake in the ground" to move forward.

The Role of Strategic Goals

Strategic goals and objectives should not be confused with operational tactics or tactical planning. Often strategic plans are written as operational goals or objectives rather than at a strategic level. A **strategic goal** is defined as a long-term, continuous strategic area that identifies key activities, strategic objectives, that need to be performed to achieve the new organizational vision (Olsen 2004, 37). Strategic goals are needed to describe how to carry out each of the selected key strategies. For example, if the strategy is to have 95 percentile performance on timely billing to payers, the strateigic goal might be to reduce the accounts receivable days attributable to coding backlogs, and strategic objectives may include authorizing overtime, hiring contract coders, and redesigning the record completion processes. It is important to look at the range of strategies being pursued to be clear about priorities, identify opportunities for synergy and integration, and identify strategies that no longer add value. When formulating strategies, question whether the leaders are getting too deeply into how something will be done. Remember that strategy is *what* the organization is going to do; goals and objectives are *how* the organization plans to do it.

The Role of Strategic Objectives

Strategic objectives are more detailed ways to meet a strategic goal and include timelines, resource allocation needs, and assigning responsibility of who will be accountable for implementation. From the above example, the strategic objectives would state, in more detail, the person responsible and the action steps of how to authorize more overtime, who and how to hire the contract coders, and who and how the record completion process will be redesigned. For example, for the strategic objective of hiring contract coders, the objective would state who the organization will be contracting with, how many contract coders are needed, the timelines for implementation, and who is responsible for making it happen.

Importance of Implementation and Action Plans

In order for any strategic plan to become effective and to ensure a successful implementation plan, detailed strategic goals and objectives must be written and supported by those responsible for the implementation. (See figure 27.6.) This requires having involvement in design and understanding of the rationale for and the outline of detailed responsibilities and expectations required of all leaders and staff in the department or organization. The strategic goals and objectives need to be clearly outlined, with assignments for who will be accountable, timelines, allocation of resources, and measurements that will be used to track success of implementation.

Identify Critical Issues

Critical issues are the bridge between the current strategic profile and the future strategic vision and profile of a

Figure 27.6. Detailed implementation plan

Strategy #1: Transcribed reports currently become part of the EHR through scanning only; content is not in digital form.			
Strategic Goal	**Strategic Objectives**	**Implementation Plan**	**Measurements**
A. Physicians are able to review and modify dictated reports online within 3rd quarter of fiscal year.	1. Implement electronic signature software. 2. Design and pilot test a process whereby physicians can authenticate, make changes to, and reassign a transcribed report online. 3. Design a phased plan for implementation of online physician review that is coordinated with the availability of online access to electronic reports.	TIMELINE: RFP -First Quarter Purchased by 2nd Quarter Installed by 3rd Quarter WHO'S RESPONSIBLE: HIM Supervisor and IT Supervisor RESOURCE NEEDS: Capital and Operating budget support, 0.5 FTE Medical Staff HIM Committee	Physicians' dictation achieved: By Q3 = 100% By Q4 = 75% Physician Quality Survey of Dictation System: Score 4.0–5 = 100% Score 3.5–3.99 = 80% Score 3.0–3.49 = 60%
B. Voice recognition converts dictated reports to digital information for storage in the EHR	1. Implement voice recognition in the emergency, cardiac cath, and imaging departments. 2. Upgrade the EHR to accept input from voice recognition in structured reports. 3. Design and pilot test a plan for storing output in the EHR.	TIMELINE: 1st quarter WHO'S RESPONSIBLE: HIM Transcription Manager, Departmental reps from ER, CC, and Imaging RESOURCE NEEDS: Capital and Operating budget	Voice recognition conversion in place: Q1 = 100% Q2 = 75%

department or organization that leadership has deliberately decided to pursue (Robert 2000, 165–168). The strategic direction of the organization has been decided and this identification of critical issues is the beginning of managing in the new direction, usually focused on four areas including structure, systems and processes, skills and competencies, and compensation (Robert 2000, 165).

Support for the Change Program

Sound change strategies and tactics alone do not ensure success. Success depends on great execution, including securing support for the needed organizational change efforts. Healthcare organizations are highly complex with many competing priorities. Gaining approval, even for the best-designed efforts, may be difficult.

An experienced HIM director with support from the IT director tried for three consecutive budget cycles to get funding for a document-imaging program. The request was accompanied by a solid return on investment (ROI) picture in terms of reductions in full-time equivalents, cost of storage, and increased productivity. In year four, the director tied the request not merely to how change would affect the HIM service, but also how it would support improved access to health information, reduce errors caused by illegibility, and improve communication among caregivers. In light of the Joint Commission's patient safety goals, the HIM director enlisted the help of nursing leadership to make the budget case. Nursing spoke to how this solution would improve access to information at the patient care bedside and would help link various electronic documentation systems already in place. The caregivers stressed the need to link the systems to help them do their jobs better. By taking this approach, the document-imaging system was presented to the board of directors by the organization's Patient Safety Council chairperson and was approved by the board without hesitation.

Take a Systems Approach

According to Tichy (1983), "the development of change strategy involves simultaneous attention to three [organizational] systems—technical, political, and cultural." The technical systems are concerned with the business we are in and how we conduct that business (for example, the process we use to manage patient information). Political systems involve the distribution of power and influence in the organization (for example, the authority of the medical staff, the approval and decision-making processes). Cultural systems are the style and values that define how the organization typically operates.

Major change throws the organization into chaos as existing systems are deliberately unglued. This is a time of great vulnerability, and managers must be vigilant, watching for and thoughtfully addressing unintended effects that could make it difficult to achieve realignment. Managers must be sensitive to the very real emotional relationships among individuals in a group and how change will affect relationships between individuals and between the manager and others. Times of change are times of high stress and anxiety. This may play out in a number of ways. For example, in times of great change, employees may be more inclined to look for other employment opportunities as it is threatening and unsettling to go through change. Some turnover in staff may be an acceptable and unavoidable result, but the manager should be attentive and sensitive so that turnover does not derail the ability to carry out the project.

The technical, political, and cultural systems are highly interdependent, and any change will have intended and unintended impact on all three systems. For example, when implementing new technology such as EHRs or other major systems, the focus is often on features and functions of the system. Securing the right champions for the system and understanding how it affects the work and formal and informal interactions of staff is more challenging and important to successful implementation than the features and functions. The successful strategic manager leading wide-scale technology change will be the one who excels at helping people get behind and involved in the change. The manager who focuses only or primarily on installing the hardware and software will not succeed. Managers should not let these challenges keep them from pursuing the strategies their organization needs. However, success will depend on how well change is managed from a systems perspective. The manager must attend to all three system aspects throughout the implementation process. He or she also should be aware that implementation is not complete until all three systems are back in a new alignment after the changes are in place.

Create the Structure for Change

Organizational structure is an important element to ensure success of the change process. Once a new vision and strategies are determined, the current structure is reviewed and focus placed on how to best restructure to achieve the new vision. As strategic goals and objectives are identified, the goals and objectives are assigned to a leader. If it is difficult to assign the goals and objectives to a current position or if too much is being assigned to one position, reconsider the structure. Structure is an organizational function often overlooked and yet important to successful implementation. Another important aspect of consideration regarding structure is where the department is positioned within the structure of the organization. This placement in the structure is important to understanding how allocation of resources and capital will be made. The importance of structure for accomplishing an organization's strategic goals and objectives should not be underestimated.

Manage the Politics of Change

Organizational change is a political process. Change leadership requires the courage to persevere even in the face of criticism; however, plowing ahead without considering the political implications may be folly. According to Bryson, managing the politics of change requires "finding ideas (visions, goals, strategies) that people can support and that further their interests . . . and making deals in which something is traded in exchange for that support" (1995, 225).

Political savvy entails skill in mediating and shaping conflicts that are inevitable when people are offered real choices with real consequences. Deliberately enlist the support of thought and opinion leaders. Reach out to those who may be most threatened by the proposed change; do not wait for them to come to you. Early engagement may turn potential resisters into supporters. At the very least, it will help change leaders build their arguments and communication plan to address the concerns of those who oppose the change.

Coalition building is one technique for managing the political dimensions of change. Change may threaten to shift the balance of power, and employees or coworkers who feel threatened may react by joining together to increase their own power so as to influence the course of events. Coalitions can be a force for thwarting change, or leaders can use coalition building as a way to build support for change. The example of the manager who gained the support of nursing to move ahead on the document management system project illustrates the power of coalition building.

The first step in building a coalition is to honestly assess subgroups in terms of how they will view the proposed change. Before embarking on a major change, the following questions should be considered carefully:

- Who will be most affected by the change?
- What benefits (for example, power) might these individuals perceive they will lose?
- Are their fears real? If so, what options are available to help overcome their fears?
- Does the change have the potential to create new benefits for these individuals?
- Can a negative reaction be avoided by engaging individuals or groups in the process?
- If the leader is not successful in getting them on board, is their influence likely to be strong enough to derail the change plan?

Even when a leader is not successful in getting resisters on board, he or she will have better information about the strength of their feelings and their resolve to oppose change. At the same time, leaders are always working to diffuse potential resistance and to focus on building support for the change.

Create a Sense of Urgency

Kotter asserts that "by far the biggest mistake people make when trying to change organizations is to plunge ahead without establishing a high enough sense of urgency" (1995, 59–67). Leaders may overestimate the extent to which they can force change on the organization.

To increase the sense of urgency, leaders must remove or minimize the sources of complacency. Some examples of how this might be done include:

- Engaging employees, customers, and coworkers in a dialogue about change through a series of meetings

- Convening a project steering committee with representatives from all stakeholder groups
- Identifying opinion leaders and securing their support early
- Presenting believable stories or scenarios that illustrate the potential futures that may occur if action is not taken
- Creating new vehicles for communication, such as a project newsletter

Communicate, Communicate, Communicate

Communication is key to engaging others in the vision and change process. DePree sums it up by saying that "if you're a leader and you are not sick and tired of communicating you probably aren't doing a good enough job" (1992, 100).

A benchmarking study of how companies have successfully communicated change showed that communication is critical at three stages of the change process: as it is being planned, throughout implementation, and after it is complete (Powers 1997, 30–33). Effective communication was shown to be critical at each stage, even to the point of releasing partial information when details are incomplete.

At the planning stage, leaders should communicate the need for change and the vision. Remember, if followers do not accept the vision, the rest of the change process is likely to be very rocky. Communicating results, even when they are incomplete, is an important reinforcement. It makes the change real and maintains the necessary momentum.

Communication is most effective if the message is tailored to the recipient. The leader identifies needs and opportunities to customize the organization's message to subgroups that have a particular set of issues. For example, the message to the medical staff will be different from the message to staff in health information services. Before implementing the use of report templates to expedite dictation, the manager may design a tactical plan that details all the elements of the communication plan for each of the constituent groups affected by, or with an interest in, the project.

The communication plan must offer groups the opportunity to "talk back." Kotter reminds us that the "downside of two-way communication is that feedback may suggest that you are on the wrong course and that the vision and plans need to be reformulated. But in the long run, swallowing your pride and reworking the vision and plan is far more productive than heading off in the wrong direction—or in a direction that others won't follow" (2002, 100).

Kotter (2002, 90) also reminds us that communication comes in two forms—words and actions—and that the most effective communication is characterized by deeds. "Behavior from important people that is inconsistent with the vision overwhelms other forms of communication." Leaders become the symbols for the change. Their motivations may be questioned and their actions scrutinized. Others will watch the leaders' actions for signals of commitment to the course of action and rightly insist on their integrity.

Ethics and integrity must be front and center all the time, but particularly during times of important change. At these times, the political, cultural, and technical systems are out of alignment. There is opportunity for events to take unexpected turns. Leaders' actions are closely scrutinized and their motives may be suspect.

Implementing Strategic Change

Once a vision and strategies are designed, the change management team is in place, and the guiding coalitions are organized, the hard work of implementation begins. Implementation requires all the managerial skills described in chapter 20, including planning, budgeting, monitoring, and producing results.

Create and Communicate Short-term Wins

Major change takes time. The organization's vision may be compelling and its strategies right on target, but if short-term results cannot be demonstrated, the leaders may lose support and the momentum for change may begin to erode. The best way to sustain change efforts is to sequence the implementation plan in such a way that short-term successes are clearly demonstrated and celebrated. For example, in implementing a new compliance plan, the data quality manager for a group practice reported statistics to the chiefs of service showing the monthly claims rejection rate. As this rate began to decline, the manager organized special events such as a dessert party and recognition event for office managers and staff at each improvement milestone. These touches garnered attention and maintained momentum for the project.

The implementation plan can be deliberately seeded with a number of short-term projects that have a high likelihood of success. This tactic enables the implementation team to work together to assess how much effort and how many resources will be required for later phases. It demonstrates that the program of planned change is real and not just talk. Moreover, it strengthens the courage and commitment of the leaders and the guiding coalitions.

New programs can be launched quickly by using techniques such as rapid prototyping, demonstration projects, or pilot tests. The details do not always need to be fully worked out to create visible demonstrations. The leader may not need to secure approval for full implementation as testing an approach to see its value is often accepted as a pilot. In test mode, all operational details do not need to be worked out before "going live." The leader need not anticipate all the intricacies up front but should just begin the journey and adjust as he or she is implementing the pilot stage. Prototyping and pilot tests also offer a way to show others how redesigned processes or new technology might work when fully implemented.

Check Your Understanding 27.5

Instructions: Complete the following exercises on a separate sheet of paper.

1. Describe two ways to utilize structure and coalition building to achieve more successful strategy implementation.
2. Describe three ways to communicate to others how the selected strategy could maintain the momentum for change.
3. Think back to an experience when you were involved in an organizational or personal change (for example, new computer program implemented at the company where you worked last summer; a committee you were on that was planning an event or new program). Describe two events or actions that advanced the change agenda and two events that impeded it (for example, all employees were given a half-day of training and a gift for completing the training course).

Pace and Refine Change Plans

Implementation requires managing interdependent projects at various stages of design, development, and deployment. One of the most difficult implementation challenges is deciding what phases should be advanced first and how fast or slow to move through them. Sequencing and pacing change requires thorough knowledge of the organization and its capacity for change, again considering all organizational components—cultural, political, and technical—and the available financial and managerial resources.

The higher the stakes, the more likely it is that a proposed change will be controversial. If the only viable approach is likely to meet with resistance, more time and effort are needed up front to gain acceptance before the approach is implemented. The importance of two-way communication throughout the process cannot be overemphasized.

The timing of change is critical. Change leaders can cite examples of projects that moved too quickly and projects that moved too slowly. Lawrence sums up this challenge: "I have become convinced that the real art of leadership lies in careful pacing. Pacing means moving simultaneously in a variety of areas and keeping each area progressing so that the combined cadence does not tear the organization apart. I'm positive that nobody gets timing 100 percent right. But the winners do it less wrong" (Walton, 1998, 291–308).

Implementation is a process of guiding, adjusting, and improving as the plan moves forward. "Invariably, the organizational, strategic and leadership choices made during the earlier phases are only partially informed. As experience and events provide feedback to the organization, adjustments are almost always called for" (Walton, 1998, 347–366).

Implementing change is a highly iterative process. Leaders should expect that their plans and tactics will need to be modified as they gain experience. They should create budgets and timetables that permit frequent course corrections.

Maintain Momentum and Stay the Course

Because leading change is a process of learning and adjusting, change leaders must learn to tolerate—and even enjoy—uncertainty. Change sponsors are eager to see their well-crafted strategies take hold and inevitably feel discouraged by a lengthy process. In addition to celebrating short-term wins, other ways to maintain momentum and keep moving include:

- Working quickly to resolve the thorny issues.
- Reiterating what will happen if change either does not occur or is watered down by compromise. If possible, focus on the consequences due to external trends.
- Keeping focused on the prize. Put every action in context. Regularly revisit the vision, goals, and strategies to regenerate a sense of purpose. Help others by making the goals as tangible as possible.
- Remembering that resistance to change is natural. Do not take it personally.
- Rethinking the tactics, sequence, and pace regularly to keep from getting bogged down. If momentum slows, institute actions that will produce short-term gains. Keep moving forward.
- Maintaining the sense of urgency. Although it is important to celebrate short-term wins, do not let these celebrations mitigate the sense of urgency the organization has created. Also, do not let intermediate gains be mistaken for the bigger goals.

For maximum and sustained impact, the change being introduced must become part of the fabric of the organization. It must become the way the organization operates, thinks, and behaves. At some point, it must become part of the culture. Even after change is implemented, there often continues to be a tug backward toward the old reality. So strong is the effect of culture, leaders should be on the lookout for signs of slippage and for opportunities to reinforce the value of the new reality. To ensure that change is lasting and to prepare the organization for more change, leaders should:

- Quantify the impact, benefits, and value of the changes and use data to identify the direction for future change
- Continue intensive communication on issues facing HIM and the organization
- Integrate change competencies and behaviors into performance appraisal and management development programs
- Approach strategy, change, and organizational development as a continuous process

Measure Your Results

Environmental assessment was shown to be an important prerequisite to launching major change. It is also the way to measure the impact of change and to determine what further change is needed. Any time strategic change is undertaken, the measures by which its success will be judged should be made part of the performance measures data set. Environmental assessment, both internal and external, must become a core competency of the organization and part of its routine work. It need not be an elaborate system, but it should be systematic and ongoing and it must include information on performance, trends, attitudes, and satisfaction.

The **strategy map** provides a visual framework for integrating the four perspectives of a balanced scorecard (Kaplan and Norton 2004, 55). The **balanced scorecard methodology** is a technique for measuring organizational performance across the following four perspectives (Kaplan and Norton 2004, 31):

- *Financial perspective:* How must the organization be financially responsible as a whole?
- *Customer perspective:* To achieve the vision, how should the organization appear to internal and external customers?
- *Internal process perspective:* To satisfy customers, which operational processes must the organization excel at?
- *Learning and growth perspective:* How will the organization enhance its ability to change and improve?

A strategy map enables examination of the cause-and-effect relationships among the preceding perspectives. Figure 27.5 shows a sample balanced scorecard using the above four perspectives based on a strategy map for improving the real and perceived value of HIM services. Figure 27.6 shows a sample detailed implementation plan using the balanced scorecard methodology to demonstrate how a strategy is more clearly defined using a strategic goal, strategic objective, implementation plan, and measurements

Real-World Case

According to coverage in the *Journal of the American Health Information Management Association,* consumer-maintained or accessible personal health records (PHRs) is a trend that is gaining momentum and is an important component of the national health information strategy. Some healthcare systems already offer PHR views into their EHRs. As consumers become more knowledgeable about healthcare matters, they seek access to more information about their own and their family members' health and healthcare. The employer- and insurance-sponsored consumer-directed health plans also are encouraging patients to become more knowledgeable about health and healthcare.

This trend affects HIM, as practitioners become not only patient advocates in the emerging e-world, but also knowledge and content experts. The *Journal of AHIMA* describes the impact of this consumer trend on HIM as a "sea change." This is a way of describing a profound change from which there is no turning back. AHIMA also sponsors a consumer Web site, MyPHR.com, and a consumer education campaign.

Although great change is forecasted, just what form it will take is not at all clear. This lack of clear direction presents a real-life strategic challenge for HIM professionals who must consider plausible alternate futures when constructing visions and formulating strategies.

Summary

HIM is a dynamic profession that offers great opportunities to advance and contribute in a variety of important roles. Professional course work has required that HIM leaders consider the attributes of a professional and the responsibilities of professionalism. In this book, readers have learned about managing systems, resources, and people. This chapter introduces them to the HIM professional as a strategic leader and thinker, a role that probably does not feel comfortable to all managers.

In truth, it will require experience to perfect the skills of strategic management and it will require a commitment to lifelong learning. One of the first ways to apply the lessons of this chapter is to evaluate options for entry-level positions as an HIM professional.

In the course of interviewing for positions, look closely at the organizational environment to identify evidence that constructive change is valued. What is the organization's strategic focus? Does its culture value idea sharing and innovation? What is the vision for HIM services? How is the political environment and how are decisions made? Are there any examples of change projects that have been very successful? Have any change projects failed? What lessons were learned from successful or failed projects?

Even seasoned managers are learning and improving their abilities every day. There is no such thing as a master manager who knows it all. What is important is to keep the lessons in mind as one gains experience and grows in confidence as a strategic manager. This chapter has explored the following five lessons (Bryson 1995, 225):

Lesson 1: Leading change is more than a process to be managed, it is a way of thinking and acting.

Managing change is a central strategic challenge for all organizations. The challenge may be even greater in healthcare organizations because their cultures tend to be averse to change and their governance structures and decision-making processes are more complicated than those of the typical business organization. Leading change requires a vision, and it often requires building new organizational capabilities, such as environmental scanning, creative group process, and a more external focus.

Lesson 2: Leading change must be approached as a central and fundamental role of all managers.

The best way to learn how to become more strategic is just to begin. Leading change requires creativity and imagination grounded in good information, managerial competence, and effective decision making. Do not expect to get it exactly right the first time, the second time, or any time. It is better to make mistakes than to take no risks. As lessons are learned, they should be chronicled so that the "learning loop" helps improve future decisions.

Lesson 3: Effective change happens only after others are engaged in a meaningful and personal way and their acceptance is earned.

All change is ultimately about increasing effectiveness. To be successful, a leader must first understand what the "customers" want and need and how to deliver real value. This requires information and continuous two-way communication about issues, ideas, and trends. Acceptance for change strategies must be earned. Leaders must be politically savvy, learning to communicate the rationale for change, the expected results, and the consequences of no action. They must be sensitive to the fact that it takes time to disseminate a change message and for the message to be assimilated at a personal level. Change projects should move at a deliberate pace, but a pace that takes the needs of others into account.

Lesson 4: Successful organizations will have a bias for action because learning to lead change is a byproduct of leading change while knowing how to be successful.

A bias for preserving the status quo is strong in most organizations. This must be replaced with a bias for action. Leading change is a learning process, and success increases the sense of possibility and the excitement to tackle the next challenge. Organizations that are on the move are energized, and this energy will be felt by their employees, coworkers, superiors, and customers. Learning to lead change is an essential skill in today's fast-paced world of work.

Lesson 5: There is great opportunity for HIM professionals who understand that leadership, change, and learning are intertwined.

Our society talks a great deal about leadership, change, and learning. What is only now becoming clear is that these concepts are really intertwined. As Beer, Eisenstat, and others state, "One cannot contemplate dramatic change occurring within an organization without the exercise of some leadership. And the organization does not change fundamentally without significant reorientation and learning by its leaders and members. Without learning, the attitudes, skills, and behavior needed to formulate and implement a new strategic task will not develop" (1993, 217). The goal is to reorient organizations to value strategic thinking that includes innovation and change. This takes time, perseverance, and courage. Nonetheless, this is the goal strategic managers should have for the organizations they are privileged to lead.

References

Abrahams, J. 1999. *The Mission Statement Book*. Berkeley: Ten Speed Press.

American Health Information Management Association. 2004 (June). Study: Employment of HIM professionals in the U.S.: Current patterns and future prospects. Chicago: AHIMA.

Beer, M., R.A. Eisenstat, et al. 1993. Why change programs don't produce change. In *The Learning Imperative: Managing People for Continuous Innovation*. Edited by R. Howard. Boston: Harvard Business School Press.

Bryson, J.M. 1995. *Strategic Planning for Public and Nonprofit Organizations*. Rev. ed. San Francisco: Jossey-Bass.

DePree, M. 1992. *Leadership Jazz*. New York: Dell Publishing.

Drucker, P. 1996. Not enough generals were killed. In *The Leader of the Future*. Edited by F. Hesselbein and M. Goldsmith. San Francisco: Jossey-Bass.

Dunn, R.T. 2007. *Haimann's Healthcare Management*, Eighth Edition. Chicago. Health Administration Press.

Fuller, S.R. and J. Callahan Dennis. 2005. Transcription's future(s): AAMT and AHIMA outline scenarios for the years ahead. *Journal of AHIMA* 76(7):48–51.

Gavetti, G. and J.W. Rivkin. 2005. How strategists really think: Tapping the power of analogy. *Harvard Business Review* 83(4):54–63.

Jennings, M.C. 2000. *Health Care Strategy for Uncertain Times*. San Francisco: Josey-Bass.

Johns, M. 2000. A crystal ball for coding. *Journal of AHIMA* 71(1):26–33.

Kaplan, R.S. and D.P. Norton. 2004. *Strategy Maps: Converting Intangible Assets into Tangible Outcomes*. Boston: Harvard Business School Press.

Kemp, E.,R. Funk, and D and Eadie. 1993. Change in chewable bites: Applying strategic management at EEOC. *Public Administration Review*, 130.

Kolb, D.A. 1988. Integrity, advanced professional development, and learning. In *Executive Integrity*. Edited by S. Srivastra. San Francisco: Jossey-Bass.

Kotter, J.P. 1995. Leading change: why transformation efforts fail. *Harvard Business Review* 73(2):59–67.

Kotter, J.P. 2002. *Heart of Change: Real-Life Stories of How People Change Their Organizations*. Boston: Harvard Business School Press.

Kouzes, J.M. and B.Z. Posner. 1995. *The Leadership Challenge: How to Keep Getting Extraordinary Things Done in Organizations*. San Francisco: Jossey-Bass.

Lawrence, D.M. 1998. Leading discontinuous change: Ten lessons from the battlefront. In *Navigating Change*. Edited by D.C. Hambrick, D.A. Nadler, and M.L. Tushman. Boston: Harvard Business School Press.

Luke, R.D., Walstrom, S.L., Plummey, P.M. 2003. *Healthcare Strategy: In Pursuit of Competitive Advantage*. Chicago: Health Administration Press.

McKee, Robert. 2003 (June). Storytelling that moves people: A conversation with screenwriting coach Robert McKee. *Harvard Business Review*, 81(6).

Merriam-Webster online. 2008. http://www.merriam-webster.com/dictionary.

Norton, R., S. Kaplan and P. David. 2000 (Oct.). Having trouble with your strategy? Then map it. *Harvard Business Review.*

Olsen, E., 2004. *Strategic Planning for Dummies*, Indianapolis, IN, John Wiley & Sons.

Porter, M.E. 1996. What is strategy? *Harvard Business Review* 74(6):61–78.

Powers, V.J. 1997. Benchmarking study illustrates how best-in-class achieve alignment, communicate change. *Communication World* 14(2):30–33.

Robert, M. 1998. *Strategy Pure and Simple II.* New York: McGraw-Hill.

Schoemaker, P.J.H. 1993. Multiple scenario development: Its conceptual and behavioral foundation. *Strategic Management Journal* 14:193–213.

Society for Healthcare Strategy and Market Development. *Futurescan 2008: Healthcare Trends and Implications 2008–2013.* Chicago: Health Administration Press.

Tichy, N.M. 1983. *Managing Strategic Change: Technical, Political and Cultural Dynamics.* New York: John Wiley & Sons.

Walton, E. 1998. Senior leadership and discontinuous change. In *Navigating Change.* Edited by D.C. Hambrick, D.A. Nadler, and M.L. Tushman. Boston: Harvard Business School Press.

Xuckerman, A.M., Sollenberger, .K., 2006. *Advancing Strategic Planning in Healthcare,* Frontiers, National Science Foundation, Arlington, VA, 56.

Appendices, Glossary, and Index

Appendix A
Sample Documentation Forms

Figure A.1a. Admission record (Face Sheet) in paper format

University of Anystate Hospitals

ADMISSION RECORD

PATIENT LABEL

Health Record #	Admission Date/Time	Discharge Date/Time	Service	Station	Room #	Patient Type	Financial Class.	BL/Account #

Location(s)	Language	Sex	Race	Marital Status	Date of Birth	Age

Patient

Patient Name and Address	SSN Primary Telephone #	Patient Employer	Telephone #

Guarantor / **Employers**

Guarantor Name and Address	SSN Relationship	Guarantor Employer	Telephone #

Insurance

Insurance 1	Insurance 2

Miscellaneous

Emergency Contact Home: Work:	Spouse Home: Work:

Admission Dx/Presenting Complaint	Arrival Mode	Admission Type/Source

Admitting Physician	Attending Physician	Referring Physician	Primary Care Physician

Alerts	Previous Admission Date

For Emergency Department Use Only
Allergies LMP T R P BP Time Signature

Diagnoses/Procedures	**DRG/Code(s)**
Principal Diagnosis:	
Other Diagnoses:	
Principal Operation/Procedure:	
Other Operation(s)/Procedure(s):	

Physician Signature: ________________ Date: ________

ADMISSION RECORD
000001 (11/2002)

Figure A.1b. Electronic admission records

Last Name	First Name	Middle Name	Sex	Race	Ethnic Group
Johnson	Kelly	Ann	Female	White	
Birth Date	**Age**	**Medical Record Number**	**Financial Number**	**Marital Status**	**Religion**
10/20/1930	78Y	9041	13060	Married	Roman Catholic
Organ Donor	**Living Will**	**Confidentiality Level**	**Facility**	**Building**	**Nurse\Ambulatory**
YES	Yes, on file		ATHENS MC	HSC Bldg	HIM 999
Registration Date	**Registration Time**	**Attending Physician**	**Encounter Type**	**Admit Type**	**Admitting Diagnosis**
01/21/2009	11:06		Inpatient		

Residence Address | Billing Address | Employer Information | Primary Guarantor Information | Next of Kin | Emergency Contact

Street Address	Street Address2	City	State	Zipcode	Phone Number
1258 Jack Avenue		San Francisco	CA	94101	415.555.1212
Pager Number					

Last Name	First Name	Middle Name	Sex	Race	Ethnic Group
Johnson	Kelly	Ann	Female	White	
Birth Date	**Age**	**Medical Record Number**	**Financial Number**	**Marital Status**	**Religion**
10/20/1930	78Y	9041	13060	Married	Roman Catholic
Organ Donor	**Living Will**	**Confidentiality Level**	**Facility**	**Building**	**Nurse\Ambulatory**
YES	Yes, on file		ATHENS MC	HSC Bldg	HIM 999
Registration Date	**Registration Time**	**Attending Physician**	**Encounter Type**	**Admit Type**	**Admitting Diagnosis**
01/21/2009	11:06		Inpatient		

Residence Address | Billing Address | Employer Information | Primary Guarantor Information | Next of Kin | Emergency Contact

Search for Employer...

Employer Name	Occupation	Street Address	City	State	State (C)
Thebes Corporation	Telemarketer	5400 Union Street	San Francisco		CA
Zipcode					
94101					

Last Name	First Name	Middle Name	Sex	Race	Ethnic Group
Johnson	Kelly	Ann	Female	White	
Birth Date	**Age**	**Medical Record Number**	**Financial Number**	**Marital Status**	**Religion**
10/20/1930	78Y	9041	13060	Married	Roman Catholic
Organ Donor	**Living Will**	**Confidentiality Level**	**Facility**	**Building**	**Nurse\Ambulatory**
YES	Yes, on file		ATHENS MC	HSC Bldg	HIM 999
Registration Date	**Registration Time**	**Attending Physician**	**Encounter Type**	**Admit Type**	**Admitting Diagnosis**
01/21/2009	11:06		Inpatient		

Residence Address | Billing Address | Employer Information | Primary Guarantor Information | Next of Kin | Emergency Contact

Search for Next of Kin...

NOK's Relationship to Person	Last Name	First Name	Street Address	Street Address2	City
Friend	Smith	Jackie	3625 Blush Road		San Francisco
State	**Zipcode**	**Phone Number**			
CA	94101	415.525.1212			

Figure A.2. Combined consent to treatment and consent to the use and disclosure of protected health information

University of Anystate Hospitals

PATIENT LABEL

CONSENT FOR TREATMENT AND DISCLOSURE OF PROTECTED HEALTH INFORMATION
PAGE 1 OF 2

To the Patient (or his/her parent, guardian, or legal representative):

Before University of Anystate Hospitals and Clinics or any of its departments can provide inpatient or outpatient services to you, you will need to understand the services you are to receive, give the hospital your consent to perform those services, and agree to pay for them. You will also need to understand the ways the hospital uses the information in your health record and agree to allow the hospital to use that information.

Part I of this form covers your consent to treatment and explains other important matters related to your healthcare. Part II explains the use of your personal health information. You may ask a member of the admissions staff to read this form to you, and we encourage you to ask any questions you may have about it. When you fully understand the form's content, please sign it in the place indicated on the back of the form. Thank you very much for helping us to fulfill the hospital's responsibility to you and the rest of the community we serve.

Part I: Treatment-Related Information

Consent to the Treatment

You authorize your physician and/or other qualified medical providers to perform medical treatments and services on your behalf. You also consent to all of the hospital medical and/or diagnostic services ordered for you during your outpatient visit or inpatient stay in the hospital. This consent includes testing for infections such as hepatitis B and HIV and providing blood or body fluids for such tests in order to protect you and/or those who care for you.

Payment for Services and Insurance

You are directly responsible for paying for the services provided during your hospital visit or stay. The hospital will work directly with the third parties who provide coverage of your medical expenses, including health insurance companies, Medicare, Medicaid, Workers' Compensation, and various types of liability, accident, and disability insurance providers. By signing this form, you attest that your insurance coverage is current, valid, and effective and that you will promptly pay any required copayment amounts and unpaid deductibles. If your stay qualifies for Medicare coverage, the benefits you will receive include coverage for the physician services that were performed as part of your hospital care.

You guarantee payment to the hospital for all noncovered services and any unpaid, billed amounts not covered by insurance benefits when your insurance plan allows the hospital to bill you for any unpaid balances. You understand and accept that your physician's orders may include services not paid by insurance plans but will be provided to you by the hospital. Also, you accept that insurance plans may deny payment for what you believed were covered services, resulting in your responsibility for paying for these services. You may be billed for the professional component of any hospital services, such as the professional component for clinical laboratory tests.

Valuables

You accept full responsibility for your valuables, especially money or jewelry. The hospital does not accept any liability for your valuables. The hospital expects you will entrust any valuables to family or friends for safekeeping. Alternatively, you may deposit them in the safe that the hospital provides for that purpose. This is especially important when you are an inpatient, but this responsibility also extends to when you are an outpatient and must change into a hospital gown, remove jewelry, or undergo sedation during a medical procedure.

Special Note for Medicare or CHAMPUS Beneficiaries

You acknowledge and certify by your signature that all of the information you have provided to the hospital for Medicare or CHAMPUS benefits is correct. You also agree to allow the hospital or others who have information on your Medicare or CHAMPUS benefits claim to provide this information to Medicare or CHAMPUS or their agents in order for them to determine your eligibility for benefits. To carry out this activity, the hospital may use a copy rather than the original of this consent form. You also acknowledge that you have received a copy of the *Important Message from Medicare* or the *Important Message from CHAMPUS* form. This acknowledgement does not waive your rights for a review or make you liable for payment.

Figure A.2. (Continued)

University of Anystate Hospitals

PATIENT LABEL

CONSENT FOR TREATMENT AND DISCLOSURE OF PROTECTED HEALTH INFORMATION
PAGE 2 OF 2

Part II: Health Record-Related Information

Consent to the Use and Disclosure of Protected Health Information

You agree to honestly, completely, and correctly provide all requested information. You also agree to permit the hospital to share your health record as applicable under the law with your physician, your insurers, Medicare, Medicaid, or their designated agents. They may review your record and copy it in full or in part in order to obtain billing and payment information. Insurers (private or government) may also use your health record to determine whether they cover your services. You agree to allow the hospital to use the record created during this visit to meet any reporting requirements related to your care and to collect payment for the services you received. You agree to allow your physicians to send copies of your health records to other physicians, hospitals, and healthcare facilities as they deem necessary for continuity of care. You also agree to have your name posted on scheduling boards and outside your hospital room.

Specific Uses of Your Protected Information

The hospital originates and maintains health records describing your health history, symptoms, examination and test results, diagnoses, treatment, and any plans for future care or treatment. This information serves as:

- The basis of care planning and treatment
- A means of communication among the many healthcare professionals who contribute to your care
- A source of information for applying diagnosis and surgical information to your bill
- A means by which a third-party payer (usually your insurance company or a government healthcare program) can verify that the services billed were actually provided
- A tool for routine healthcare operations, such as assessing quality and reviewing the competence of healthcare professionals

Your signature acknowledges that you received the *Notice of Information Practices,* which provides a description of information uses and disclosure practices. You accept and understand that:

- You have the right to review the notice prior to signing this consent.
- The hospital reserves the right to change the notice and its information practices, for past, current, or future information. The new notice will contain the effective date on its first page and be made available on our Web site.
- You have the right to object to the use of your health information for the hospital's patient directory.
- You have the right to request restrictions on the use or disclosure of your health information to carry out treatment, payment, or healthcare operations and to correct error(s) in your record. The hospital, however, is not required to agree to the restrictions requested.
- You may revoke in writing the consent that you provide to the hospital. The revocation does not apply to any uses of your information made by the hospital in reliance upon this consent form and on the belief that your consent was still effective.

I certify that I have read (or had read to me) both parts of this form and fully understand and agree to the content.

Patient/Agent: ______________________________ Date: ______________

If you are signing as the patient's agent, please state your relationship to the patient (parent, guardian, or legal representative): ______________________________

Witness (when form is accepted verbally,
by telephone, or by electronic means): ______________________ Date: ______________

CONSENT FOR TREATMENT AND DISCLOSURE
000002 (11/2002)

Figure A.3. Acknowledgment of notice of privacy practices

Anytown Community Hospital

ACKNOWLEDGMENT OF NOTICE OF PRIVACY PRACTICES

PATIENT LABEL

I understand that as part of my healthcare, this organization originates and maintains health records describing my health history, symptoms, examination and test results, diagnoses, treatment, and any plans for future care or treatment. I understand that this information serves as:

- A basis for planning my care and treatment
- A means of communication among the many health professionals who contribute to my care
- A source of information for applying my diagnosis and surgical information to my bill
- A means by which a third-party payer can verify that services billed were actually provided
- And a tool for routine healthcare operations such as assessing quality and reviewing the competence of healthcare professionals

I understand and have been provided with a *Notice of Information Practices* that provides a more complete description of information uses and disclosures. I understand that I have the right to review the notice prior to signing this consent. I understand that the organization reserves the right to change their notice and practices and prior to implementation will mail a copy of any revised notice to the address I've provided. I understand that I have the right to object to the use of my health information for directory purposes. I understand that I have the right to request restrictions as to how my health information may be used or disclosed to carry out treatment, payment, or healthcare operations and that the organization is not required to agree to the restrictions requested. I understand that I may revoke this consent in writing, except to the extent that the organization has already take action in reliance thereon.

☐ I request the following restrictions to the use or disclosure of my health information:

____

____

Signature of Patient or Legal Representative Date

Witness Date

Notice Effective Date or Version

☐ Accepted ☐ Denied

Signature Title Date

ACKNOWLEDGMENT OF PRIVACY NOTICE
100093 (1/2002)

Figure A.4. Discharge order in paper format

University of Anystate Hospitals

PATIENT, PETUNIA P.
000000001
DOB: 08/14/1949

PHYSICIAN ORDERS

Drug Allergies: Codeine

Date/Time	RN Signature	Physician Order/Physician Signature
10/11/04	Claire Barton, RN	(1) Admit via surgery (2) NPO (3) CBC, urinalysis (4) BCP 8
6:00 a.m.		(5) Prothrombin time, PTT (6) Type and screen (7) PA chest X-ray
		(8) EKG (9) Prep abdomen
		(10) Start IV fluids: 1000 cc D5LR at 125 cc/h via 18g Jelco (11) Mefoxin 2 g IV at 7:45 a.m.
		Myron P Gynesurg MD 10/11/04
10/11/04	Claire Barton, RN	(12) Morphine sulfate 2 mg PCA IV RR q.1.0-1.5.h.
10:00 a.m.		(13) Mefoxin 2 g IV in 8 h then discontinue
		(14) D5LR 1000 cc at 125 cc/h (15) Liquid diet (16) Bed rest
		(17) Vital signs every 4 h Myron P Gynesurg MD 10/11/04
10/11/04	Nancy Nurse, RN	Telephone order from Dr. Gynesurg:
2:00 p.m.		(18) Morphine sulfate 2 mg IV push Myron P Gynesurg MD 10/12/04
10/11/04	Nancy Nurse, RN	Telephone order from Dr. Gynesurg:
3:00 p.m.		(19) Temporarily discontinue PCA pump until vital signs return to normal
		(20) Vital signs every hour Myron P Gynesurg MD 10/12/04
10/12/04	Nancy Nurse, RN	(21) Remove Foley
12:05 p.m.		(22) Begin to ambulate (23) Soft diet
		(24) Vital signs every 4 h Myron P Gynesurg MD 10/12/04
10/13/04	Nancy Nurse, RN	(25) Discontinue morphine
12:15 p.m.		(26) Darvacet-N 100 mg, one or two tablets q.4h. as needed for pain (27) Solid diet Myron P Gynesurg MD 10/13/04
10/14/04	Nancy Nurse, RN	(28) Discontinue IVs
8:00 a.m.		(29) Discharge to home—see discharge instruction sheet Myron P Gynesurg MD 10/14/04

PHYSICIAN ORDERS
000010 (11/2002)

Figure A.5. Obstetric admission record in paper format

Anytown Community Hospital

OBSTETRIC ADMITTING RECORD
PAGE 1 OF 2

PATIENT LABEL

Admission Date ____ / ____ / ____ Time____________
☐ Ambulatory ☐ Stretcher ☐ Oriented to Unit
☐ Wheelchair ☐ Transfer from ________ ☐ Safety/Security

G	T	Pt	A	L	LMP / /	EDD / /	Weeks
						EDD by Fetal Assessment / /	

Race/Ethnicity ____________________ Age ________
Advance Directives ☐ None ☐ Living Will ☐ Medical Power of Attorney
Organ Donor ☐ Yes ☐ No
Pain ☐ No ☐ Yes (site: _____)
Intensity 0 ______________________ 10
None Highest
Last Oral Intake
Fluids ____ / ____ / ____ Time ________
Solids ____ / ____ / ____ Time ________

Allergy/Sensitivity ☐ None ☐ Latex
☐ Other: ____________________

Reasons for Admission
☐ Onset of Labor
☐ Induction of Labor
☐ Spontaneous Abortion
☐ Cesarean Section
☐ Primary ☐ Repeat
(Reason for primary: ____________)
☐ Tubal Ligation
☐ Vaginal Bleeding
☐ ROM ☐ Premature ☐ Prolonged
☐ Preterm Labor
Reasons for Admission: ____________________

Observation Evaluation
☐ Fetal Status
☐ Ultrasound
☐ Amniocentesis
☐ NST ☐ CST
☐ Medical Complications
____
____
☐ Obstetric Complications
____
____

Medications ☐ None

Type/Dose	Last Taken	With Patient No	With Patient Yes	Disposition
		☐	☐	
		☐	☐	
		☐	☐	

MD/CDM Phone # | Support Person/Relationship Phone #:

Personal Effects	Disposition		
Item	With Patient	With Support Person	Other (Describe)

Patient Triage Data
Contractions ☐ None ☐ Palpation ☐ Tocotransducer
Frequency __________ Duration __________ Intensity __________
Began on ____ / ____ / ____ Time____________
Pain intensity 0 ____________________ 10
None Highest
Membranes ☐ Intact ☐ Bulging
☐ Ruptured (date ____ / ____ / ____ Time ____________)
☐ Nitrazine test ☐ pos ☐ neg ☐ Sterile speculum exam
☐ Fern test ☐ pos ☐ neg (findings: ____________)

Fluid ☐ Clear ☐ Bloody ☐ Meconium stained
☐ Foul odor ☐ No foul odor ☐ None observed
Vaginal Bleeding ☐ None ☐ Normal show
☐ Bleeding (describe: ____________)
Cervical Exam By: ____________
Station ______ Effacement ________ Dilatation ______cm
Presentation ☐ Vertex ☐ Transverse lie
☐ Face/brow ☐ Compound
☐ Breech ☐ Unknown
(type: ____________)

Physical Assessment

Height	Weight Pregrav/Grav	T	P	R	BP

Detail Abnormal Findings

System	Normal	Abnormal	System	Normal	Abnormal
HEENT	☐	☐	Respiratory	☐	☐
Neurologic	☐	☐	Abdomen	☐	☐
Skin	☐	☐	Gastrointestinal	☐	☐
Breasts	☐	☐	Urinary	☐	☐
Extremities	☐	☐	Genitalia	☐	☐
Cardiovascular	☐	☐			

Initial Problems Identified ☐ None	Plan
1.	
2.	
3.	

Fetal Evaluation Data
Multiple Gestation ☐ No ☐ Yes
Fundal Height _____ cm
Fetal Weight (est.) _____
FHR __________
☐ Fetoscope ☐ Fetal Monitor
☐ Doppler ☐ Other: ____________

	Presentation	Position
1.		
2.		
3.		

Specimens Obtained (Check all that apply)

Urine Test	Time	Results	Blood Test	Time	Results
☐ Urinalysis			☐ Hgb		
☐ C+S			☐ Hct		
☐ Glucose			☐ VDRL/RPR		
☐ Albumin			☐ Type/Screen		
☐ Ketones			☐		
☐ pH			Cervical Culture		
☐ Blood			☐ GBS		
☐ Toxicology			☐		
Admitting Signature		Date/Time	Examiner Signature		Date/Time

Figure A.5. (Continued)

Anytown Community Hospital

OBSTETRIC ADMITTING RECORD
PAGE 2 OF 2

PATIENT LABEL

Significant Prenatal Data
Prenatal Records Available on Admission
☐ No ☐ Yes Source ______
First Visit by 13 Weeks ☐ Yes ☐ No
Regular Care ☐ Yes ☐ No
Prenatal Classes ☐ Yes ☐ No

Pediatric Provider

Lab Findings
☐ None
Blood Type & Rh ____
Rubella Titer ____
Serology ____
HBsAg ____
HIV ____
GBS ____
____ ____
____ ____

General Health ☐ Healthy
☐ Functional Deficit (Type ______)
☐ Recent Exposure to Communicable Disease
Type/Date ______ ___/___/___
☐ Illness (≤14 days prior to admission)
Type/Treatment ______
☐ Chronic Condition ______

Nutritional Status ☐ Well-nourished ☐ Malnourished ☐ Obese
☐ Special Diet ______
Eating Disorder ☐ None ☐ Identify ______
Nutritional Problems ☐ None ☐ Identify ______

Fetal Assessment Tests
☐ None

Date	Test	Result
/		
/		
/		
/		

Problems Identified ☐ None

	Active	Resolved
1. ______	☐	☐
2. ______	☐	☐
3. ______	☐	☐
4. ______	☐	☐

Hospitalizations ☐ None
1. ___/___/___ Reason ______
2. ___/___/___ Reason ______

Plans for Birth and Hospital Stay ☐ Birth Plan Attached
Support Person Present in L&D ☐ No ☐ Yes ______
Other Family Members in L&D ☐ No ☐ Yes ______
Anesthesia ☐ None ☐ Local ☐ Epidural ☐ Spinal ☐ General
Delivery Site/Position ______
Personal Requests ______

Adoption ☐ No ☐ Yes Contact with Infant ☐ No ☐ Yes
Adoption Contact ______
Feeding Preference ☐ Breast ☐ Bottle
☐ Tubal Ligation Authorization Signed ☐ Yes ☐ No
☐ Circumcision Authorization Signed ☐ Yes ☐ No

Psychosocial Data ☐ See Prenatal Records
Emotional Status ☐ Happy ☐ Ambivalent ☐ Concerned
☐ Depressed ☐ Angry ☐ Other ______
Communication Barriers ☐ **None**
☐ Language ☐ Interpreter ______
☐ Vision ☐ Reading ☐ Writing ☐ Hearing
☐ Speech ☐ Other ______
Support System
Marital Status S M Sep D W Father involved ☐ Yes ☐ No
Other Support ☐ None ☐ ______
Occupation ______
Religion ☐ N/A ☐ ______
Personal/Cultural/Religious Customs Affecting Care and/or Learning
☐ None ☐ Identify ______

Basic Needs Met	Yes	No	If No, Explain
Food	☐	☐	
Clothing	☐	☐	
Housing	☐	☐	
Transportation	☐	☐	
Finances	☐	☐	

Life Stress	No	Yes	If Yes, Explain
Physical Abuse	☐	☐	
Emotional Abuse	☐	☐	
Major Change	☐	☐	
Self-Care Needs	☐	☐	
Serious Illness	☐	☐	
Other ______	☐	☐	

Substance Abuse	No	Yes	If Yes, Amount/Day, Last Use
Tobacco	☐	☐	______
Alcohol	☐	☐	______
Prescribed Drugs	☐	☐	______
Illicit Drugs	☐	☐	______

Educational Needs	Mother	Support Person	Comments
Stages/Phases of Labor	☐	☐	
Coping Techniques	☐	☐	
Infant Feeding	☐	☐	
Infant Care	☐	☐	
Other ______	☐		

Preferred Learning Methods	Yes	No
One-on-One Instruction	☐	☐
Group Instruction	☐	☐
Written Information	☐	☐
Audio/Visual Information	☐	☐
Demonstration/Practice	☐	☐

Discharge Planning Data Planned Length of Stay _____ Days

Home Setting	Yes	No
Heat, running water, refrigeration	☐	☐
Infant Care Supplies/Car Seat	☐	☐
Phone in home	☐	☐
Transportation available	☐	☐
Adult assistance available	☐	☐

Referrals
☐ RN Case Manager ☐ Utilization Review ☐ Other ______
☐ Home Care RN ☐ Social Service
☐ Nutritionist/Dietitian ☐ Pediatric Provider

MD/CNM
Notified by ______ Date/Time ______

Admitting
Signature ______ Date/Time ______

OBSTETRIC ADMITTING RECORD
200305 (06/2003)

Figure A.6. Consultation report

Anytown Community Hospital

CONSULTATION REPORT
PAGE 1 OF 2

PATIENT, BLUTO P.
070095111
DOB: 04/01/1930

I was asked by Dr. Doctor to evaluate Mr. Patient for consideration of left VATS talc pleurodesis.

CHIEF COMPLAINT: Shortness of breath

HISTORY OF PRESENT ILLNESS: Mr. Patient is a 73-year-old male who has a history of metastatic pancreatic cancer. He was found to have left pleural effusion and underwent thoracentesis. He returned with a recurrent effusion. He was admitted on 05/12/2003 and underwent left chest tube thoracostomy and an attempt at talc pleurodesis through the chest tube. He has had residual pneumothorax and continues to drain from the left chest tube. He was referred for the purpose of left VATS talc pleurodesis.

PAST SURGICAL HISTORY: His past surgical history is remarkable for Whipple procedure.

PAST MEDICAL HISTORY: His past medical history is remarkable for prostate cancer and pancreatic cancer.

MEDICATIONS: Avalide and pancrease

ALLERGIES: He has no known drug allergies.

FAMILY/SOCIAL HISTORY: Remarkable for being married. He drinks socially.

REVIEW OF SYSTEMS: Remarkable for no history of seizure or stroke, no history of previous pneumonia, no history of previous myocardial infarction, no history of previous liver failure, renal failure. He has had no swelling in his legs.

PHYSICAL EXAMINATION: He is 5 feet 6 inches tall. He weighs 158 pounds. His blood pressure is 126/70. His pulse is 62. His respiratory rate is 20. His temperature is 97.1. His neurological exam is remarkable for a normal affect. He is oriented × 3. His gross motor examination is 5/5 in all four extremities. His head and neck exam is remarkable for no icteric sclerae. He has no oral lesions. His neck demonstrates no cervical or supraclavicular adenopathy. He has no carotid bruits. His chest exam is remarkable for no use of accessory muscles, no dullness to percussion. He has a left chest tube in place with no air leak. He has serous-appearing drainage from his left chest tube. His breath sounds are remarkable for a slight decrease in breath sounds in the left lateral lung. His cardiovascular exam is remarkable for no lift, heave, or thrill. He has a normal S1, S2 without murmurs. Abdomen is remarkable for well-healed Whipple incision. His abdomen is nontender, nondistended without evidence of masses or organomegaly. His extremities are without clubbing, cyanosis, or edema.

His chest CT shows a loculated left pneumothorax with small residual effusion. He has chest tube in place. This is a small caliber tube. His chest X ray shows loculated left pneumothorax.

Figure A.6. (Continued)

Anytown Community Hospital

PATIENT, BLUTO P.
070095111
DOB: 04/01/1930

CONSULTATION REPORT
PAGE 2 OF 2

His laboratory studies are further remarkable for urinalysis that is normal, an EKG that is normal sinus rhythm, sodium of 133, potassium 3.8, chloride 95, BUN 19, creatinine 1.1, PPTT of 11.8, INR of 0.9, PTT of 29.

My impression is that Mr. Patient is a 73-year-old male with metastatic pancreatic cancer status post Whipple. He has a recurrent left pleural effusion. He has undergone previous tube thoracostomy and pleurodesis and now has a residual left pneumothorax and residual chest tube drainage from his malignant effusion.

I have recommended to Mr. Patient that we proceed with left VATS talc pleurodesis today. He understands that his risks include, but are not limited to, death (1–2%), bleeding requiring blood transfusion, infection, prolonged air leak from the cut surface of his lung, and a 30% chance of recurrent effusion. Understanding these risks as well as the alternative of continued drainage, he wishes to proceed today with left VATS talc pleurodesis.

Thank you very much for allowing me to participate in his care.

Signature:

5/17/03

James W. Medman, MD — Date

d: 05/17/2003
t: 05/20/2003
JWM, MD/mc

Figure A.7. Initial nursing assessment

Midwest Medical Center

INITIAL NURSING ASSESSMENT

PATIENT LABEL

Baseline Information

Date:	Time:	Age:	Arrived: AMB WC Stretcher EMS Carried Other:	Primary MD:

Initial/Chief Complaint/History of Present Illness:

T: PO R TM	P:	R:	BP: R L	⊕ O_2 Sats %	Sex: M F	Height:	Weight: Actual: Stated:

⊕ Tetanus/Immunizations:	Pneumococcal Vaccine ☐ No ☐ Yes Most Recent Date:
⊕ Pregnant ☐ No ☐ Yes LNMP:	Influenza Vaccine ☐ No ☐ Yes Most Recent Date:

Allergies: ☐ None ☐ Medications ☐ Latex ☐ Food ☐ Anesthesia ☐ Other

List Names and Reactions:

TB Assessment (Initiate airborne isolation if 4 or more criteria are checked yes)

Persistent Cough > 2 weeks ☐ No ☐ Yes	Abnormal Chest X-Ray	☐ No ☐ Yes	Respiratory Isolation Ordered ☐ No ☐ Yes
Fever > 100.4 (night sweats) ☐ No ☐ Yes	Physician Order for AFB (smear/culture)	☐ No ☐ Yes	
Unexplained Weight Loss ☐ No ☐ Yes	Recent Exposure to Person with Suspected TB or +PPD	☐ No ☐ Yes	

RN/LPN Signature: ______________________________

☐ See Home Medication Orders Medication/Over the Counter/Herbal History ☐ Investigation Drugs/Devices

Medication	Dose	Freq	Last Dose	Medication	Dose	Freq	Last Dose

Hospitalizations/Surgeries:

Medical History

Neurological	☐ No	☐ Yes		Sensory Impairment	☐ No	☐ Yes	
Cardiovascular	☐ No	☐ Yes		Endocrine	☐ No	☐ Yes	
Hypertension	☐ No	☐ Yes		Blood Disorder	☐ No	☐ Yes	
Respiratory	☐ No	☐ Yes		Cancer	☐ No	☐ Yes	
Gastrointestinal	☐ No	☐ Yes		Psychological	☐ No	☐ Yes	
Renal/Urological	☐ No	☐ Yes		Tobacco Use	☐ No	☐ Yes	
Gynecological	☐ No	☐ Yes		Alcohol/Drug Use	☐ No	☐ Yes	
Musculoskeletal	☐ No	☐ Yes		Infectious Disease	☐ No	☐ Yes	
Integumentary	☐ No	☐ Yes		Cough/Cold Past 2 Weeks	☐ No	☐ Yes	
EENT	☐ No	☐ Yes		Anesthesia	☐ No	☐ Yes	

Source of Information ☐ Patient ☐ Family ☐ Unable to Obtain ☐ Other | ☐ Medications Sent Home with Patient: ____________

Arrival Date:	Arrival Time:	T: PO R TM	P:	R:	BP: R L	O_2 Sats %: (If applicable)

RN Initial: ____________ **RN Signature:** ______________________ **Date:** ________ **Time:** ____________ **Unit:** __________

RN Initial: ____________ **RN Signature:** ______________________ **Date:** ________ **Time:** ____________ **Unit:** __________

INITIAL NURSING ASSESSMENT
000039 (10/2002)

Figure A.8. Patient care plan

University of Anystate Hospital

PATIENT CARE PLAN
PAGE 1 OF 2

PATIENT LABEL

Admitting Physician:

Admission Date: | Diagnosis: | Isolation:

Operative/Special Procedures: Date: | Allergies:

Vital Signs

- ☐ TPR
- ☐ BP
- ☐ Neuro checks
- ☐ Circ. checks
- ☐ Weight
- ☐ Telemetry
- ☐ Transport S Tele

Diet and Fluids

Diet:
- ☐ NPO
- ☐ Regular
- ☐ Other
- ☐ Snack
- ☐ Tube Feedings
- ☐ Supplemental
- ☐ Restrict
- ☐ Force
- ☐ Ice Chips

Fluids:
- ☐ Intake
- ☐ Output
- ☐ Others

Activity

- ☐ Bedrest
- ☐ BRP
- ☐ Up in Chair
- ☐ Ambulate
- ☐ Up Ad Lib
- ☐ Head of Bed
- ☐ Foot of Bed
- ☐ TCDB
- ☐ Leg Exercises
- ☐ Others

Hygiene

- ☐ Self
- ☐ Assist
- ☐ Complete
- ☐ Tub/Shower
- ☐ Mouth/Denture Care
- ☐ Shampoo
- ☐ Skin Care
- ☐ Others

Bladder/Bowel

Bladder:
- ☐ Strain Urine
- ☐ Check Voiding
- ☐ Cath PRN
- ☐ Foley Cath
  - ☐ Date Inserted
- ☐ S.P. Cath
- ☐ Condom Cath
- ☐ Irrigate Cath q. ____ h. with:
- ☐ Bladder Irrigation
- ☐ IDEO Conduit
- ☐ Incontinent

Bowel:
- ☐ Check BMs
- ☐ Suppository
- ☐ Enema
- ☐ Ostomy
- ☐ Incontinent
- ☐ Others

Treatments

- ☐ S&A
  - ☐ Self
- ☐ NG
- ☐ Gomco
  - ☐ Clamp
  - ☐ Irrigate
- ☐ Chest Tube
- ☐ Wound
- ☐ Others:

Respiratory

- ☐ Ventilator
- ☐ O_2
  - ☐ Mask
  - ☐ Nasal Cannula
  - ☐ AMT
- ☐ Suction
- ☐ Triflow
- ☐ IPPB/HHN
- ☐ Others

Tube Feeding

Type of Tube	Type and Strength of Feeding	Rate	Count	Irrigation	Bag ▲

Safety Measures

- ☐ Siderails
  - ☐ Upper
  - ☐ Lower
- ☐ Restraints
- ☐ Seizure Precautions
- ☐ High Risk for Falls
- ☐ Self-Injury Precautions

IV Therapies

#	Solution	Additives	Rate	Count

Site Care/Tubing Change

Start/Date					
Type/Size					

Blood Transfusions

Figure A.8. (Continued)

University of Anystate Hospital

PATIENT CARE PLAN
PAGE 2 OF 2

PATIENT LABEL

Date	Daily Lab Work	Date	Lab Work	Date	X-Ray/Special Procedures

Date	Preps for Procedures

Special Equipment	Miscellaneous
☐ Traction ____ ☐ Trapeze ____ ☐ ______Bed ☐ ______Mattress ☐ Sheepskin ☐ Crutches ☐ Walker ☐ Teds ☐ Others ____	
Therapies	
☐ Physical ____ ☐ Speech ____ ☐ OT ____	
Transportation	
☐ Wheelchair ☐ Stretcher ☐ Ambulatory ☐ Bed	
Consultations	

PATIENT CARE PLAN
000072 (10/2002)

Figure A.9. Clinical pathway

University of Anystate Hospitals

CLINICAL PATHWAY:
CESAREAN SECTION DELIVERY
PAGE 1 OF 3

PATIENT LABEL

This document should be considered a *guideline.* Outcomes will vary depending on the patient's severity of illness and other factors/conditions that affect or alter expected outcomes.

Key: Fill in appropriate location for nursing unit. Initial completed intermediate and discharge outcomes. Circle any variances and document on variance log. Once variance is resolved, date and inital clinical pathway.

Expected Discharge Outcomes	Preop Date ________ Time ________	Operative/Recovery Date ________ Time ________
	Nursing Unit ________	Nursing Unit ________
Cardiovascular • Hemodynamically stable • Chest clear to auscultation bilaterally	Stable BP (< 140/90 or no increases > 30 mm systolic or > 15 mm diastolic) ________ Chest clear ________	Stable BP (< 140/90 or no increases > 30 mm systolic or > 15 mm diastolic) ________
Gastrointestinal • Bowel sounds present • Tolerates regular diet • Passing flatus	NPO	
Genitourinary • Normal bladder function		Foley patent, draining clear yellow urine ________ UOP ≥ 30 cc/h ________
Reproductive • Delivery of well newborn • Involution progressing • Minimal physical discomfort • Breast: Skin and nipples intact	Adequate prenatal care ________ Reassuring father ________ No signs/symptoms of uterine/vaginal bleeding ________	Fundus firm, lochia small to moderate ________ Pain control initiated ________ EBL ≤ 1000 cc ________ Delivery of well newborn ________
Integumentary • Incision intact with evidence of healing • No signs/symptoms of infection		Abdominal dressing dry and intact ________
Psychosocial • Patient/family demonstrates adjustment to parental role		
Education • Patient/family able to identify problems that require immediate medical attention • Patient/family able to verbalize understanding of care needs (wound, etc.)	States/understands plan of care ________	
Discharge Planning • Patient/family able to verbalize support system(s) and/or support system for home care established • Patient/family able to manage continuing care needs • Patient discharged	Patient/family identifies support system for home care ________	

Date	Initials	Signature	Date	Initials	Signature	Date	Initials	Signature

Figure A.9. (Continued)

University of Anystate Hospitals

CLINICAL PATHWAY:
CESAREAN SECTION DELIVERY
PAGE 2 OF 3

PATIENT LABEL

This document should be considered a *guideline.* Outcomes will vary depending on the patient's severity of illness and other factors/conditions that affect or alter expected outcomes.

Key: Fill in appropriate location for nursing unit. Initial completed intermediate and discharge outcomes. Circle any variances and document on variance log. Once variance is resolved, date and inital clinical pathway.

Expected Discharge Outcomes	Postoperative Day Date ________ Time ________	Postop Day #1 Date ________ Time ________
	Nursing Unit ________	Nursing Unit ________
Cardiovascular • Hemodynamically stable	Able to turn, cough, and deep-breathe every 2 h ________ Chest clear ________	Ambulates with assistance ________ Chest clear ________
Gastrointestinal • Bowel sounds present • Tolerates regular diet • Passing flatus	Tolerates clear liquids, no nausea or vomiting ________	Bowel sounds present ________ Tolerates regular diet ________
Genitourinary • Normal bladder function	Foley patent, draining clear yellow urine ________ UOP > 240 cc/8 h ________	Normal bladder function ________ UOP < 240 cc/8 h ________
Reproductive • Delivery of well newborn • Involution progressing • Minimal physical discomfort • Breast: Skin and nipples intact	Fundus firm, lochia small to moderate ________ Pain controlled ________	Fundus firm, lochia small to moderate ________ Pain controlled ________
Integumentary • Incision intact with evidence of healing • No signs/symptoms of infection	Abdominal dressing dry and intact ________ Afebrile (<100.4°F) ________	Wound edges approximated, no signs/symptoms of infection ________ Afebrile (<100.4°F)
Psychosocial • Patient/family demonstrate adjustment to parental role	Demonstrates appropriate parent/infant interaction ________	Demonstrates appropriate parental/infant interaction________
Education • Patient/family able to identify problems that require immediate medical attention • Patient/family able to verbalize understanding of care needs (wound, etc.)	States/understands postop plan of care ________ Initiates breast-feeding ________	Establishes infant feeding ________
Discharge Planning • Patient/family able to verbalize support system(s) and/or support system for home care established • Patient/family able to manage continuing care needs • Patient discharged		Discusses plan for discharge________

Date	Initials	Signature	Date	Initials	Signature	Date	Initials	Signature

Figure A.9. (Continued)

University of Anystate Hospitals

CLINICAL PATHWAY:
CESAREAN SECTION DELIVERY
PAGE 3 OF 3

PATIENT LABEL

This document should be considered a *guideline.* Outcomes will vary depending on the patient's severity of illness and other factors/conditions that affect or alter expected outcomes.

Key: Fill in appropriate location for nursing unit. Initial completed intermediate and discharge outcomes. Circle any variances and document on variance log. Once variance is resolved, date and inital clinical pathway.

Expected Discharge Outcomes	**Postop Day #2** Date ________ Time ________	**Postop Day # 3/Discharge Outcomes** Date ________ Time ________
	Nursing Unit ________	Nursing Unit ________
Cardiovascular • Hemodynamically stable	Participates in self-care ________ Ambulates in hall ________ Chest clear ________ Stable BP (<140/90 or no increases > 30 mm systolic or > 15 mm diastolic ________	Responsible for self-care ________ Vital signs within normal ________ Chest clear ________
Gastrointestinal • Bowel sounds present • Tolerates regular diet • Passing flatus	Active bowel sounds ________ Passing flatus ________ Tolerates regular diet ________	Active bowel sounds ________ Passing flatus ________ Tolerates regular diet ________
Genitourinary • Normal bladder function	Bladder function normal ________ UOP >240 cc/8 h ________	Normal bladder function ________
Reproductive • Delivery of well newborn • Involution progressing • Minimal physical discomfort • Breast: Skin and nipples intact	Fundus firm, lochia small to moderate ________ Pain controlled ________	Delivery of well newborn ________ Involution progressing ________ Minimal physical discomfort ________ Breasts and nipples intact ________
Integumentary • Incision intact with evidence of healing • No signs/symptoms of infection	Wound edges approximated, no signs/symptoms of infection ________ Remains afebrile (<100.4°F) ________	Incision intact with evidence of healing ________ No signs/symptoms of infection ________
Psychosocial • Patient/family demonstrates adjustment to parental role	Parental adjustment progressing ________ Demonstrates appropriate parental–infant interaction ________ Patient/family verbalizes thoughts/ feelings about childbirth ________	Patient/family demonstrates adjustment to parental role ________
Education • Patient/family able to identify problems that require immediate medical attention • Patient/family able to verbalize understanding of care needs (wound, etc.)	Verbalizes/demonstrates self-care knowledge and skills ________ Demonstrates infant feeding ________	Patient/family able to identify problems that require immediate medical attention ________ Patient/family able to verbalize understanding of care needs (wound, infant feeding) ________
Discharge Planning • Patient/family able to verbalize support system(s) and/or support system for home care established • Patient/family able to manage continuing care needs • Patient discharged	Support system for home care established ________	Patient/family able to verbalize support system(s) and/or support system for home care established ________ Verbalizes understanding of follow-up care ________ Discharged home ________

Date	Initials	Signature	Date	Initials	Signature	Date	Initials	Signature

CLINICAL PATHWAY: C-SECTION
300111 (5/2004)

Figure A.10a. Graphic vital signs

University of Anystate Hospitals

GRAPHIC VITAL SIGNS

PATIENT LABEL

Date																																
Hospital Day/Postop																																
Hour			a.m.			p.m.			a.m.			p.m.			a.m.			p.m.			a.m.			p.m.			a.m.			p.m.		
	°C	°F	12 (2400)	4 (0400)	8 (0800)	12 (1200)	4 (1600)	8 (2000)	12 (2400)	4 (0400)	8 (0800)	12 (1200)	4 (1600)	8 (2000)	12 (2400)	4 (0400)	8 (0800)	12 (1200)	4 (1600)	8 (2000)	12 (2400)	4 (0400)	8 (0800)	12 (1200)	4 (1600)	8 (2000)	12 (2400)	4 (0400)	8 (0800)	12 (1200)	4 (1600)	8 (2000)
Temperature	40.0	104																														
	39.5	103																														
	38.9	102																														
	38.4	101																														
	37.8	100																														
	37.2	99																														
	36.7	98																														
	36.1	97																														
	35.6	96																														
P																																
R																																
BP																																
S&As (time/results)	a.m.																															
	p.m.																															
Height: _____ Weight: _____			_____ Bed/Chair/Stand						_____ Bed/Chair/Stand						_____ Bed/Chair/Stand						_____ Bed/Chair/Stand						_____ Bed/Chair/Stand					

	Stool				24-H				24-H				24-H				24-H				24-H
	Shift	7-3	3-11	11-7	Total	7-3	3-11	11-7	Total	7-3	3-11	11-7	Total	7-3	3-11	11-7	Total	7-3	3-11	11-7	Total
Intake	Tube Feedings																				
	Oral																				
	Intravenous																				
	Piggyback																				
	Blood																				
	Shift Total																				
Output	Voided																				
	Catheter																				
	Gastric																				
	Emesis																				
	Shift Total																				

GRAPHIC VITAL SIGNS
000029 (11/2002)

Figure A.10b. Electronic plotted vital signs

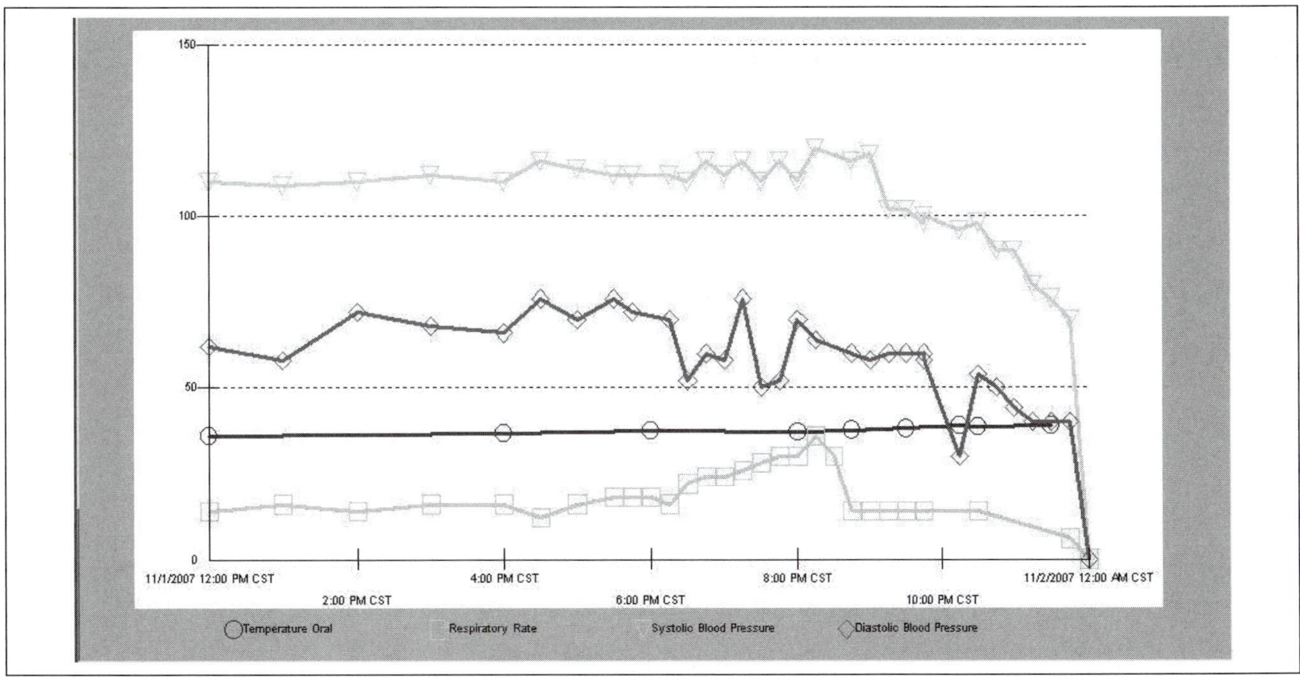

Figure A.11a. Medication administration record

University of Anystate Hospitals and Clinics

PATIENT LABEL

MEDICATION ADMINISTRATION RECORD

Site Codes: A = L upper arm
B = R upper arm
C = L hip
D = R hip
E = L thigh
F = R thigh
G = Abdomen
H = Chest

IV Site Codes: 1 = L extremity
2 = R extremity
3 = Central line
4 = Other

Reasons Doses Not Given: Ⓝ = NPO Ⓡ = Refused Ⓢ = Sleeping
Ⓟ = On pass Ⓞ = Other
Ⓣ = Testing (DC) = Discontinued

Drug/Dose/Route	Order #	Scheduled	Start	Stop	7–3	3–11	11–7

Stat/One-Time Medications	Date	Time	Site	Initials

Initials	Signature	Initials	Signature	Initials	Signature

MEDICATION ADMINISTRATION RECORD
000028 (11/2002)

Figure A.11b. Electronic medication administration

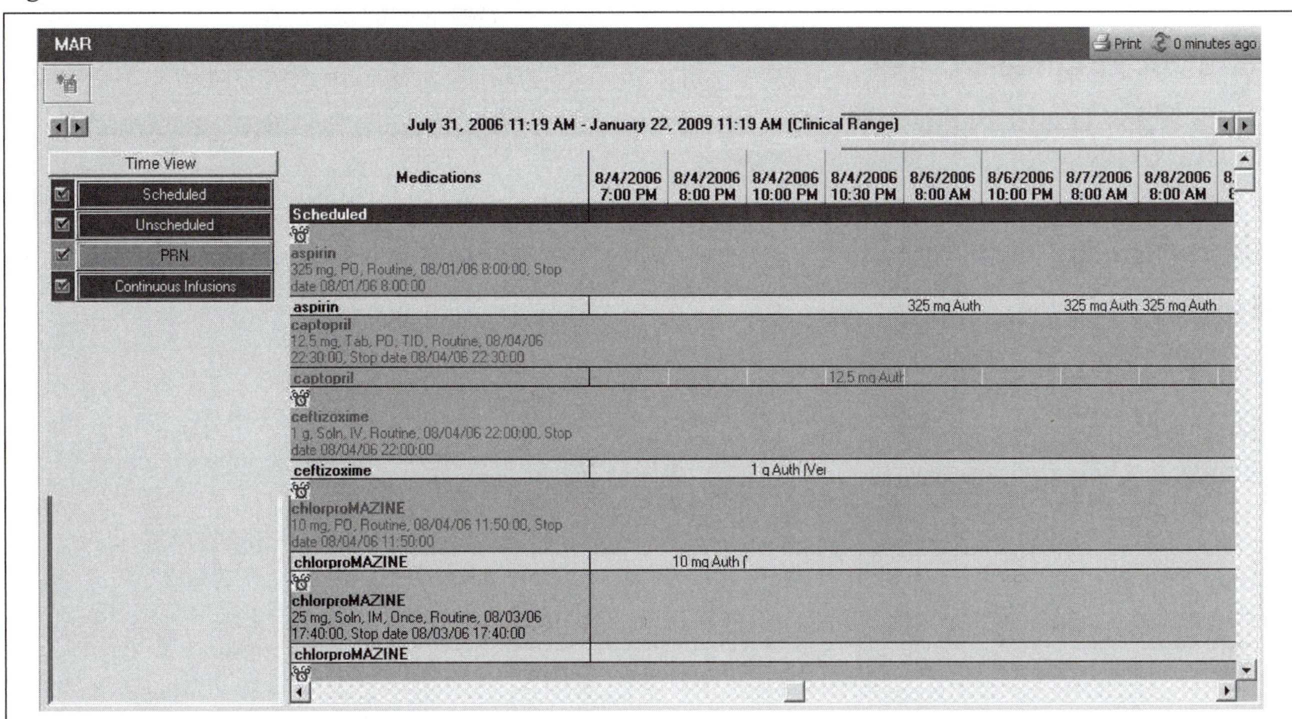

Figure A.12a. Laboratory report

Midwest Medical Center

LABORATORY SERVICES REPORT: COAGULATION

PATIENT, WYLIE C.
090241237
DOB: 10/10/1918

ADMISSION DATE: 05/14/03

ADMITTING PHYSICIAN: M. D. Doctor

SPECIMEN DATE: 05/20/03

COLLECTED TIME: 4:55 p.m.

WEEKDAY: Tuesday

——ROUTINE COAGULATION——		UNITS	REFERENCE	
PT	**17.6 H**	SEC	11.2–13.8	
INR	1.9			(1)
PTT	32.0	SEC	22.1–32.5	(2)

H = High

Footnotes

(1) The INR therapeutic range (1.5–4.0) for patients on warfarin therapy will depend on the clinical disorder being treated.

(2) Effective August 19, 2002, the suggested therapeutic range may vary from 40.9–68.3 sec for inpatients on heparin therapy.

Figure A.12b. Electronic lab report

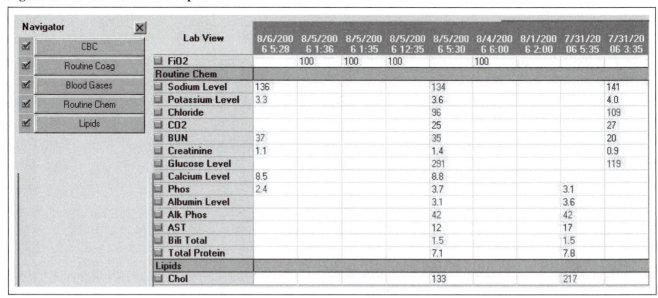

Navigator

- CBC
- Routine Coag
- Blood Gases
- Routine Chem
- Lipids

Lab View	8/6/200 6 5:28	8/5/200 6 1:36	8/5/200 6 1:35	8/5/200 6 12:35	8/5/200 6 5:30	8/4/200 6 6:00	8/1/200 6 2:00	7/31/20 06 5:35	7/31/20 06 3:35
FiO2		100	100	100		100			
Routine Chem									
Sodium Level	136				134				141
Potassium Level	3.3				3.6				4.0
Chloride					96				109
CO2					25				27
BUN	37				35				20
Creatinine	1.1				1.4				0.9
Glucose Level					291				119
Calcium Level	8.5				8.8				
Phos	2.4				3.7			3.1	
Albumin Level					3.1			3.6	
Alk Phos					42			42	
AST					12			17	
Bili Total					1.5			1.5	
Total Protein					7.1			7.8	
Lipids									
Chol					133			217	

Figure A.13. Echocardiographic report

Anytown Community Hospital

ECHOCARDIOGRAPHIC REPORT

TEST, PATIENT
009999999
DOB: 04/01/1930

DATE: 06/02/2003

REFERRING PHYSICIAN: Dr. Doctor

INDICATION FOR STUDY: Murmur

TAPE: House 528

Outpatient Study

Two-dimensional and M-mode echocardiograms were performed

The left atrium is at the upper limits of normal size at 3.7 cm compared to an aortic root diameter of 2.9 cm. The left ventricle is at the upper limits of normal size with a normal internal dimension of 5.6 cm in diastole and 3.3 cm in systole. There is normal wall thickness. There is hyperdynamic left ventricular systolic performance. The ejection fraction is estimated at greater than 70%. No specific regional wall motion abnormalities were identified. The cardiac valves appear structurally normal. No intracardiac masses were identified and a pericardial effusion was not visualized.

Conventional as well as color-flow Doppler imaging was performed. There are findings of mitral regurgitation which is estimated to be at least moderate to severe, if not severe. There is tricuspid regurgitation with peak right ventricular systolic pressure of 31 mmHg. No other significant valvular stenoses or regurgitation were identified.

IMPRESSION:

1. The left atrium and left ventricle at the upper limits of normal size with a hyperdynamic left ventricular systolic performance.
2. There is evidence of mitral regurgitation which is at least moderate to severe. Would consider transesophageal echocardiography to further assess the severity of the mitral regurgitation as well as potentially its etiology.

Signature: Philip Default

Philip Default, MD

6/2/03

Date

d: 06/02/2003
t: 06/02/2003

Figure A.14. Electrocardiograph report

University of Anystate Hospitals

GRAPHIC EKG REPORT

PATIENT, PETUNIA P.
000000001
DOB: 08/14/1949

NAME: Patient, Petunia

TECHNICIAN: SKH

PROCEDURE DATE/TIME: 10/11/04 9:59:02

CARDIOLOGIST: Julius W. Cardiolini, MD

SEX/RACE: Female, White

REPORT DATE: 10/08/04

REQUESTED BY: M. Gynesurg, MD

RESULTS: Normal EKG

PR	200	Normal sinus rhythm rate: 59
QRST	73	
QT	407	
QTc	403	
Axes		
P	28	
QRS	36	
T	35	

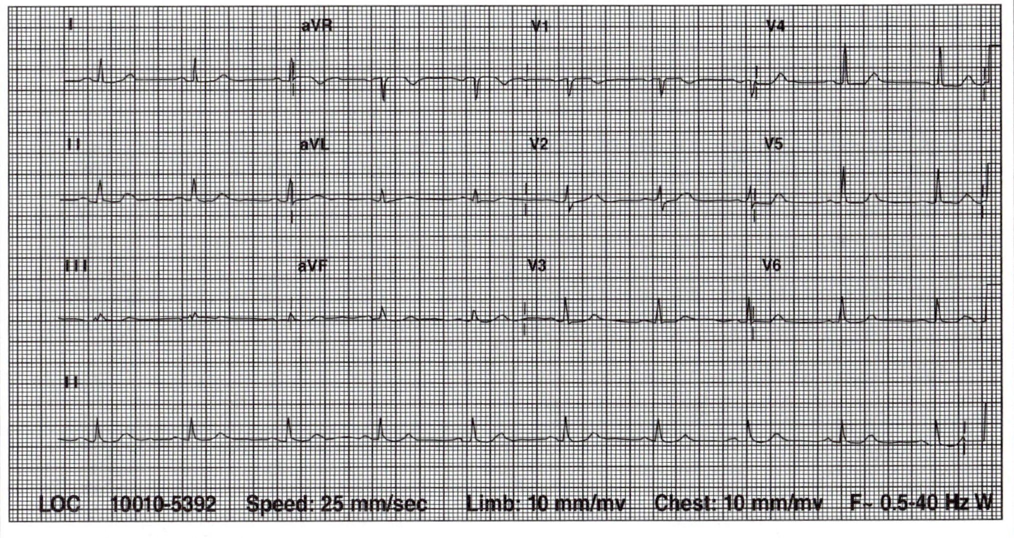

Julius W. Cardiolini, MD
Cardiologist

10/8/04
Date

Figure A.15. Informed consent for operation with blood products

University of Anystate Hospitals

PATIENT LABEL

INFORMED CONSENT FOR OPERATION/ PROCEDURE/ANESTHESIA INCLUDING BLOOD AND BLOOD PRODUCTS

1. I give permission to Dr.(s) ______________________________ to perform the following procedure(s): ______________________________

   ____

   ______________________ on ______________________ (patient's name).
2. I understand that during the procedure(s), new findings or conditions may appear and require an additional procedure(s) for proper care.
3. My physician has explained the following items:
   - the nature of my condition
   - the nature and purpose of the procedure(s) that I am now authorizing
   - the possible complications and side effects that may result, problems that may be experienced during recuperation, and the likelihood of success
   - the benefits to be reasonably expected from the procedure(s)
   - the likely result of no treatment
   - the available alternatives, including the risks and benefits
   - the other possible risks that accompany any surgical and diagnostic procedure (in addition to those already discussed). I acknowledge that neither my physician nor anyone else involved in my care has made any guarantees or assurances to me as to the result of the procedure(s) that I am now authorizing.
4. I know that other clinical staff may help my physician during the procedure(s).
5. I understand that the procedure(s) may require that I undergo some form of anesthesia, which may have its own risks.
6. Any tissue or specimens taken from my body as a result of the procedure(s) may be examined and disposed of, retained, preserved, or used for medical, scientific, or teaching purposes by the hospital.
7. I understand that my procedure(s) may be photographed or videotaped and that observers may be present in the room for the purpose of advancing medical care and education.
8. I understand that during or after the procedure(s) my physician may find it necessary to give me a transfusion of blood or blood products. My physician has explained the alternatives to, and possible risks of, transfusion.
9. I understand what my physician has explained to me and have had all my questions fully answered.
10. Additional comments: ______________________________

    ____

After talking with my physician and reading this form, I give my consent to the procedure(s) described above.

Signature of Patient or
Legal Representative: ______________________ Date: ______ Time: ________

If Legal Representative, Relationship to Patient: ______________________

Witness: ______________________________

Verbal or Telephone Consent

Name of Legal Representative: ______________________ Date: ______ Time: ________

Relationship to Patient: ______________________________

Witness: ______________________ Witness: ______________________

I have explained the risks, benefits, potential complications, and alternatives of the treatment to the patient and have answered all questions to the patient's satisfaction, and he/she has granted consent to proceed.

Physician Signature: ______________________ Date: ______ Time: ________

INFORMED CONSENT FOR OPERATION
000015 (11/2002)

Figure A.16. Anesthesia record

University of Anystate Hospitals

ANESTHESIA RECORD
PAGE 1 OF 2

PATIENT LABEL

Date: ____________________ Time: __________
Age: ____ Sex: ____ Height: ____ Weight: ____ BP: ____ P: ____ R: ____ T: ________
Lab: ____ Status: ____________________
Allergies: ____________________________________ Last Intake: ________________
Premediation: ____

☐ **Patient reassessed immediately prior to induction. Condition satisfactory for planned anesthesia.**

Vital Signs

Time

Systolic ⋁
Diastolic ⋀
Pulse
Respiration ○
Spon ●
Assist ⊙
Controlled
Surgery Start/End ⊗
Anesthesia Start/End x
Anesthesia Start ________
Anesthesia End ________

240
220
200
180
160
140
120
100
80
60
40
20
15
10
5

Machine Check
Initials
Patient Position

☐ General
☐ Regional
☐ Local
☐ Monitored
☐ IVs (spinal/EPI needle)

Position
Prep
Site
Agent
Paresthesia
Catheter
Sensory Block TO

☐ Heat/Moisture Exchanger
☐ Warming Blanket
☐ Fluid Warmer
☐ Bair Hugger

Endotracheal Tube
Cuff Inflated
Laryngoscope Blade
Stylet
Direct Vision
Blind

Figure A.16. (Continued)

University of Anystate Hospitals

ANESTHESIA RECORD
PAGE 2 OF 2

PATIENT LABEL

Monitors
- ☐ NIBP ☐ R ☐ L
- ☐ APB ☐ R ☐ L
- ☐ T (site): _______
- ☐ Pulse oximeter (site): _______
- ☐ ECG (lead): _______
- ☐ Airway gas monitor
- ☐ FiO_2 analyzer
- ☐ Pulmonary artery
- ☐ CVP
- ☐ EEG
- ☐ Stethoscope (site): _______
- ☐ SSEP
- ☐ Peripheral nerve stimulator
- ☐ Capnography

Remarks

Fluid		Fluid		Fluid		Fluid		Fluid		Fluid	
Start	Finish	Start	Finish	Start	Finish	Start	Finish	Start	Finish	Start	Finish

Operation			Recovery Room Time: _________ BP P T °F Endotracheal In ☐ Out ☐ Condition SpO_2 %
Surgeon	Anesthesiologist	Date	

Preanesthesia Evaluation

Review of Clinical Data

- ☐ Yes ☐ No Patient Medical History Reviewed
- ☐ Yes ☐ No Current Medications Reviewed
- ☐ Yes ☐ No Allergies Reviewed
- ☐ Yes ☐ No ☐ N/A Lab Results Reviewed
- ☐ Yes ☐ No ☐ N/A CXR Results Reviewed
- ☐ Yes ☐ No ☐ N/A EKG Results Reviewed

Pertinent Physical Exam

	Normal	Abnormal	Comments
EENT			
Respiratory			
Cardiac			
Mental Status			

Anesthesia History

- ☐ Yes ☐ No Past Hx of Anesthesia Complications
- ☐ Yes ☐ No Family Hx of Anesthesia Complications
- ☐ Yes ☐ No History of Malignant Hyperthermia

ASA Classification

1 2 3 4 5 E

Airway Evaluation

- Dentures: ☐ None ☐ Upper ☐ Lower
- Capped Teeth: ☐ None ☐ Yes
- Condition of Teeth: ☐ Good ☐ Fair ☐ Poor
- Estimated Intubation Difficulty:
  ☐ Normal ☐ Moderately Difficult ☐ Difficult

Anesthesia Plan

- ☐ General
- ☐ Spinal
- ☐ Epidural
- ☐ Regional Block
- ☐ Rapid Sequence Intubation
- ☐ MAC
- ☐ Epidural for POPM

☐ Alternatives, risks of anesthesia, and potential complications were discussed. Patient and/or guardian state understanding and acceptance of anesthesia plan.

Comments:

Anesthesiologist Date

ANESTHESIA RECORD
000017 (11/2002)

Figure A.17a. Operative report

Midwest Medical Center

OPERATIVE REPORT
PAGE 1 OF 2

PATIENT, TWEETY PYE
00555066
DOB: 02/18/1948

DATE: 06/02/2003

SURGEON: Douglas Default

ASSISTANT: Stanley Cutter

ANESTHETIC: Spinal

PREOPERATIVE DIAGNOSES:

1. Intrauterine pregnancy, term, previous cesarean section, voluntary repeat cesarean section
2. Multiparity, voluntary sterilization

POSTOPERATIVE DIAGNOSES:

1. Intrauterine pregnancy, term, previous cesarean section, voluntary repeat cesarean section
2. Multiparity, voluntary sterilization
3. Delivery of viable unengaged 6 pound 2 ounce female, APGAR 8–9

OPERATION:

1. Low-segment transverse cesarean section
2. Bilateral partial salpingectomy

COMPLICATIONS: None

DRAINS: One Foley catheter in urinary bladder

ESTIMATED BLOOD LOSS: Approximately 500 to 600 cc

PACKS: None

DESCRIPTION OF OPERATION: After satisfactory level of spinal anesthesia was obtained, the patient was placed in the dorsal supine position with mild left lateral uterine displacement. The lower abdominal skin tissues were prepped with a Hibiclens solution. She was then draped with sterile drapes in a sterile manner.

There was a previous transverse skin scar on the lower abdominal skin. A repeat transverse skin incision was made very carefully with sharp dissection. The fascia of the anterior abdominal wall was incised in a lateral crescentic manner exposing the rectus muscles, which were then bluntly divided in the midline exposing the peritoneum, which was then carefully incised in a vertical manner. There was a wetting amount of peritoneal fluid. The peritoneum reflection over the lower anterior uterine segment was then incised in a superficial transverse manner, and the "bladder flap" was gently pushed off the lower segment without difficulty.

Figure A.17a. (Continued)

Midwest Medical Center

PATIENT, TWEETY PYE
00555066
DOB: 02/18/1948

OPERATIVE REPORT
PAGE 2 OF 2

A transverse uterine incision was made very carefully with both sharp and blunt dissection. The myometrium was noted to be only 2 to 3 mm in thickness. The amniotic fluid was clear. The unengaged vertex was delivered through the uterine and abdominal incision without difficulty. The nasal and oropharynx were suctioned with bulb suction prior to the newborn's initial inspiration. The remainder of the delivery was accomplished without difficulty. The cord was clamped and severed, and the newborn was handed crying and in good condition to the awaiting nursery personnel.

The placenta was then manually removed from a fundal location showing a central insertion of a three-vessel cord. There were no visible extensions of the uterine incision. Both tubes and ovaries appeared normal for pregnant state. The uterine incision was then closed with a running interlocking #1 chromic suture.

With the patient's strong desire for permanent sterilization, approximately 1 to 1.5 cm segment of the isthmic portion of each fallopian tube was isolated with Babcock clamps, doubly ligated and excised, and sent to the laboratory labeled as portion of left and right fallopian tube, respectively. Hemostasis was deemed adequate. Both tubes appeared occluded.

The abdominal cavity was irrigated with copious amounts of warm normal saline. The first sponge, needle, and instrument counts were correct. The parietal peritoneum was then closed with a running 0 chromic suture. Hemostasis was deemed adequate in the subfascial space. The fascia was then approximated with running 0 PDS suture. Hemostasis was deemed adequate in the subcutaneous tissue. The skin was then approximated with running 3-0 Vicryl subcuticular suture. Sterile dressing was placed upon the incision.

The patient tolerated the procedure quite well and was sent to the recovery room in good condition. The newborn was taken to the nursery by the nursery personnel in good condition. The second and third sponge, needle, and instrument counts were corrected.

Signature:

Douglas D Default | 6/2/03

Douglas D. Default, MD | Date

d: 06/02/2003
t: 06/04/2003
DDD, MD/sf

Figure A.17b. Electronic operative report

SURGEON: CHANDLER BLOCK, DO

PRE-OPERATIVE DIAGNOSIS:
Painful Swallowing

POST-OPERATIVE DIAGNOSIS:
Significant Barrett's esophagus, acute GE junction inflammation secondary to reflux. Moderate gastritis.

OPERATION: Gastroscopy, biopsy, and Clo test.

According to his wife, this male is being seen at the request of Dr. Swenson, after developing painful swallowing. The patient and his wife were told the reasons for the procedure and the possible esophageal dilation including other risks.

PROCEDURE: Following local anesthesia with Cetacaine, 25 mg of Demerol and 1 mg of Versed IV, the GIF-100 was with some difficulty passed into the esophagus where starting at about 28 cm to the GE junction, scattered area of what looked like typical Barrett's esophagus. It was a little more prominent distally at the GE junction where there was no stricturing process. The scope was easily passed into the small hiatus hernia into the stomach where the gastric mucosa and the body and the antrum were significantly inflamed and, therefore, Clo test was taken of pyloric ring and duodenum which was negative. The scope was then withdrawn back up into the esophagus where random biopsy from the inflamed area was taken.

IMPRESSION: I wonder if the patient has had a greater degree of reflux during hospitalization when he has had more bed rest.

PLAN: Anti-reflux program, Prevacid.

Figure A.18a. Surgical pathology report

Midwest Medical Center

SURGICAL PATHOLOGY CONSULTATION

PATIENT, SWEETPEA C.
007770021
DOB: 12/18/1931

ADMITTING PHYSICIAN: M. D. Doctor

CONSULT PHYSICIAN 1:

CONSULT PHYSICIAN 2:

ACCESSIONED IN LAB: 05/20/2003

ACCESSION #: S-03-010101

DATE OF SURGERY: 5/20/2003

SPECIMEN: A-Vag Mucosa

CLINICAL DATA: Cystocele/rectocele, stress incontinence

GROSS: Received are four wrinkled, variegated, pink/tan portions of vaginal mucosa, which are $7 \times 6 \times 1$ cm in aggregate dimension. Representative portions of each are submitted for microscopic evaluation. M/1/pg.

MICROSCOPIC COMMENT: Sections are of squamous mucosa. There are no atypia.

DIAGNOSIS: Squamous mucosa, multiple portions exhibiting no atypia (vaginal)

Signature: Walter Q. Pathman — 5/20/03

Walter Q. Pathman, MD — Date

d: 05/20/2003
t: 05/23/2003
WQP, MD/jt

Figure A.18b. Electronic surgical pathology report

SURGICAL PATHOLOGY REPORT

SPECIMEN STATED TO BE:
Distal esophageal bx's

CLINICAL DIAGNOSIS:
Dysphagia

MACROSCOPIC:
The specimen consists of tan soft tissue fragments aggregating 0.3 cm - all embedded.

MICROSCOPIC:
Sections show benign ulcerated/inflammatory squamous mucosa, nonspecific features.

DIAGNOSIS:
Benign ulcerated/inflammatory squamous mucosa.

Figure A.19a. Discharge summary

Midwest Medical Center

DISCHARGE SUMMARY

SAYLORMEN, POPEYE T.
333333333
DOB: 02/09/1961

PHYSICIAN/SURGEON: Philip P. Heartstopper, MD

DATE OF DISCHARGE: 05/18/2003

PRINCIPAL OPERATION AND PROCEDURE: OPCAB × 3, left internal mammary artery of the LAD, saphenous vein graft to D-1, and saphenous vein graft to OM-1

HISTORY OF PRESENT ILLNESS: Mr. Saylormen was seen at the request of Dr. Doctor regarding surgical treatment of ischemic heart disease. He is a 42-year-old male with a family history of coronary artery disease. He smokes a pipe and had a previous myocardial infarction approximately three years ago. His current status is postangioplasty. While working on a construction project, he developed anginal-type symptoms and was seen in the emergency room and then admitted to the hospital for further evaluation.

ADMITTING DIAGNOSIS: Coronary artery disease

HOSPITAL COURSE: The patient underwent cardiac catheterization and was found to have significant three-vessel coronary artery disease. It was felt that he would benefit from undergoing an OPCAB procedure. On 05/14/03, the patient underwent OPCAB × 3 as described above. The patient tolerated the procedure well and returned to the Cardiothoracic Intensive Care Unit hemodynamically stable. On postoperative day one, he was weaned from mechanical ventilation, extubated, and transferred to the Cardiothoracic Step-Down Unit, where he continued on a progressive course of recovery. On postoperative day four, he was up and about in his room and the halls without difficulty. Upon discharge, he was tolerating his diet well. His lungs were clear. His abdomen was soft, and his incisions were unremarkable. His vital signs were stable. He was in normal sinus rhythm. His heart rate was in the 70s and 80s. Blood pressure had been running consistently in the low 110s/60s. He was afebrile. Oxygen saturations on room air were reported at 97%.

LABORATORY DATA AT DISCHARGE: BUN 14, Creatinine 0.9, H&H 8.8 and 25.4

MEDICATIONS AT DISCHARGE: Lisinopril 5 mg q.d.; Lipitor 80 mg q.d.; metoprolol 50 mg q.d.; aspirin 81 mg q.d.; Darvocet-N 100—one to two tablets every 4–6 hours as needed for pain; iron sulfate 325 mg q.d. × 30 days; and Colace 100 mg b.i.d. × 30 days

DIET: He may follow a regular diet.

FINAL DIAGNOSIS: Coronary artery disease

DISPOSITION: No lifting greater than 10 pounds. No driving for 4–6 weeks. He may shower but he should not take a tub bath. Follow up with Dr. Doctor in 1–2 weeks.

Philip P. Heartstopper, MD — Date: 5/18/03

d: 05/18/2003
t: 05/19/2003
PPH, MD/mb

Figure A.19b. Electronic discharge summary

PRINCIPAL DIAGNOSIS: Severe osteoarthritis post-traumatic right knee treated by below operation.

SUMMARY: Patient is a 47-year-old gentleman with severe post-traumatic osteoarthritis of his right knee for planned right total knee arthroplasty. He was evaluated medically by Dr. Dell Dobson and felt to be in satisfactory condition for this surgery.

HOSPITAL COURSE: On 12-10, the patient did have right LCS cemented total knee arthroplasty with percutaneous placement of a Stryker pain pump under general endotracheal anesthesia.

In the postoperative period he was started on a rehab program and using CPM first postop day. He did well with this; initially had some bleeding from his incision but this was handled with just a compressive dressing. By 12-13, he had 0-85 degrees of flexion and he was able to a good quad set and arrangements were made for transfer home using a CPM at home and then return in about another week for staple removal.

DISCHARGE MEDICATIONS: Lortab 5 for pain.

____
MICK THOMPSON, MD

Figure A.20. Physician's order sheet in paper format

University of Anystate Hospital

PHYSICIAN ORDERS

PATIENT LABEL

Drug Allergies

Date and Time	RN Signature	

PHYSICIAN ORDERS
000122 (02/2003)

Figure A.21. Example of a HIPAA-compliant authorization form

Midwest Medical Center

CONSENT FOR DISCLOSURE OF HEALTH INFORMATION

PATIENT LABEL

(1) I hereby authorize (name of provider) to disclose the following information from the health records of:

Patient Name: ______________________ Date of Birth: ______________________

Address: ____

Telephone: ______________________ Patient Number: ______________________

Covering the period(s) of healthcare:

From (date) ______________________ to (date) ______________________

From (date) ______________________ to (date) ______________________

(2) Information to be disclosed:

- ☐ Complete health record(s)
  - ☐ Discharge summary
  - ☐ Progress notes
  - ☐ History and physical examination
  - ☐ Laboratory test results
  - ☐ Consultation reports
  - ☐ X-ray reports
- ☐ Photographs, videotapes, digital or other images
- ☐ Other (please specify) ______________________

I understand that this will include information relating to (check if applicable):

- ☐ AIDS (acquired immunodeficiency syndrome) or HIV (human immunodeficiency virus) infection
- ☐ Psychiatric care
- ☐ Treatment for alcohol and/or drug abuse

(3) This information is to be disclosed to ______________________ for the purpose of ______________________.

(4) I understand this authorization may be revoked in writing at any time, except to the extent that action has been taken in reliance on this authorization. Unless otherwise revoked, this authorization will expire on the following date, event, or condition: ______________________

____

(5) The facility, its employees, officers, and physicians are hereby released from any legal responsibility or liability for disclosure of the above information to the extent indicated and authorized herein.

Signature of Patient or Legal Representative	Date	Signature of Witness	Date

CONSENT FOR DISCLOSURE OF HEALTH INFORMATION
000089 (9/2001)

Figure A.22. Example of a request for accounting of disclosures

Anytown Community Hospital

REQUEST FOR ACCOUNTING OF DISCLOSURES

PATIENT LABEL

Date of Request: ______________________________

Patient Name: ______________________________

Date of Birth: ____________________ Health Record Number: ____________________

Patient Address: ______________________________

Address to Send Disclosure Accounting (if different from above):

____

Dates Requested

I would like an accounting of all disclosures for the following time frame.

From: ____________________ To: ____________________

(Please note: The maximum time frame that can be requested is six years prior to the date of request.)

Fees

First request in a 12-month period: Free

Subsequent requests: (Insert cost-based fee per entity)

The fee for this request will be: ____________

I understand that there is a fee for this accounting and wish to proceed. I also understand that the accounting will be provided to me within 60 days unless I am notified in writing that an extension of up to 30 days is needed.

______________________________ ____________________

Signature of Patient or Legal Representative Date

For Healthcare Organization Use Only:

Date Received: ____________________ Date Sent: ____________________

Extension Requested: ☐ No ☐ Yes, Reason ____________________

Patient Notified in Writing on This Date: ____________________

Staff Member Processing Request: ____________________

REQUEST FOR ACCOUNTING OF DISCLOSURES
300252 (10/2002)

Appendix B
AHIMA Code of Ethics and Standards of Ethical Coding

The Standards of Ethical Coding are based on the American Health Information Management Association's (AHIMA's) Code of Ethics. Both sets of principles reflect expectations of professional conduct for coding professionals involved in diagnostic and/or procedural coding or other health record data abstraction.

A Code of Ethics sets forth professional values and ethical principles and offers ethical guidelines to which professionals aspire and by which their actions can be judged. Health information management (HIM) professionals are expected to demonstrate professional values by their actions to patients, employers, members of the healthcare team, the public, and the many stakeholders they serve. A Code of Ethics is important in helping to guide the decision-making process and can be referenced by individuals, agencies, organizations, and bodies (such as licensing and regulatory boards, insurance providers, courts of law, government agencies, and other professional groups).

The AHIMA Code of Ethics (which appears later in this appendix) is relevant to all AHIMA members and credentialed HIM professionals and students, regardless of their professional functions, the settings in which they work, or the populations they serve. Coding is one of the core HIM functions, and due to the complex regulatory requirements affecting the health information coding process, coding professionals are frequently faced with ethical challenges. The AHIMA Standards of Ethical Coding are intended to assist coding professionals and managers in decision-making processes and actions, outline expectations for making ethical decisions in the workplace, and demonstrate coding professionals' commitment to integrity during the coding process, regardless of the purpose for which the codes are being reported. They are relevant to all coding professionals and those who manage the coding function, regardless of the healthcare setting in which they work or whether they are AHIMA members or nonmembers.

These Standards of Ethical Coding have been revised in order to reflect the current healthcare environment and modern coding practices. The previous revision was published in 1999.

2004 American Health Information Management Association Code of Ethics

Preamble

The ethical obligations of the health information management (HIM) professional include the protection of patient privacy and confidential information; disclosure of information; development, use, and maintenance of health information systems and health records; and the quality of information. Both handwritten and computerized medical records contain many sacred stories—stories that must be protected on behalf of the individual and the aggregate community of persons served in the healthcare system. Healthcare consumers are increasingly concerned about the loss of privacy and the inability to control the dissemination of their protected information. Core health information issues include what information should be collected, how the information should be handled, who should have access to the information, and under what conditions the information should be disclosed.

Ethical obligations are central to the professional's responsibility, regardless of the employment site or the method of collection, storage, and security of health information. Sensitive information (genetic, adoption, drug, alcohol, sexual, and behavioral information) requires special attention to prevent misuse. Entrepreneurial roles require expertise in the protection of the information in the world of business and interactions with consumers.

Professional Values

The mission of the HIM profession is based on core professional values developed since the inception of the Association in 1928. These values and the inherent ethical responsibilities for AHIMA members and credentialed HIM professionals include providing service; protecting medical, social, and financial information; promoting confidentiality; and preserving and securing health information. Values to the healthcare team include promoting the quality and advancement of healthcare, demonstrating HIM expertise and skills, and promoting interdisciplinary cooperation and collaboration. Professional values in relationship to the employer include protecting committee deliberations and complying with laws, regulations, and policies. Professional values related to the public include advocating change, refusing to participate or conceal unethical practices, and reporting violations of practice standards to the proper authorities. Professional values to individual and professional associations include obligations to be honest, bringing honor to self, peers and profession, committing to continuing education and lifelong learning, performing association duties honorably, strengthening professional membership, representing the profession to the public, and promoting and participating in research.

These professional values will require a complex process of balancing the many conflicts that can result from competing interests and obligations of those who seek access to health information and require an understanding of ethical decision-making.

Purpose of the American Health Information Management Association Code of Ethics

The HIM professional has an obligation to demonstrate actions that reflect values, ethical principles, and ethical guidelines. The American Health Information Management Association (AHIMA) Code of Ethics sets forth these values and principles to guide conduct. The code is relevant to all AHIMA members and credentialed HIM professionals and students, regardless of their professional functions, the settings in which they work, or the populations they serve.

The AHIMA Code of Ethics serves six purposes:

- Identifies core values on which the HIM mission is based.
- Summarizes broad ethical principles that reflect the profession's core values and establishes a set of ethical principles to be used to guide decision-making and actions.
- Helps HIM professionals identify relevant considerations when professional obligations conflict or ethical uncertainties arise.
- Provides ethical principles by which the general public can hold the HIM professional accountable.

- Socializes practitioners new to the field to HIM's mission, values, and ethical principles.
- Articulates a set of guidelines that the HIM professional can use to assess whether they have engaged in unethical conduct.

The code includes principles and guidelines that are both enforceable and aspirational. The extent to which each principle is enforceable is a matter of professional judgment to be exercised by those responsible for reviewing alleged violations of ethical principles.

The Use of the Code

Violation of principles in this code does not automatically imply legal liability or violation of the law. Such determination can only be made in the context of legal and judicial proceedings. Alleged violations of the code would be subject to a peer review process. Such processes are generally separate from legal or administrative procedures and insulated from legal review or proceedings to allow the profession to counsel and discipline its own members although in some situations, violations of the code would constitute unlawful conduct subject to legal process.

Guidelines for ethical and unethical behavior are provided in this code. The terms "shall and shall not" are used as a basis for setting high standards for behavior. This does not imply that everyone "shall or shall not" do everything that is listed. For example, not everyone participates in the recruitment or mentoring of students. A HIM professional is not being unethical if this is not part of his or her professional activities; however, if students are part of one's professional responsibilities, there is an ethical obligation to follow the guidelines stated in the code. This concept is true for the entire code. If someone does the stated activities, ethical behavior is the standard. The guidelines are not a comprehensive list. For example, the statement "protect all confidential information to include personal, health, financial, genetic and outcome information" can also be interpreted as "shall not fail to protect all confidential information to include personal, health, financial, genetic, and outcome information."

A code of ethics cannot guarantee ethical behavior. Moreover, a code of ethics cannot resolve all ethical issues or disputes or capture the richness and complexity involved in striving to make responsible choices within a moral community. Rather, a code of ethics sets forth values and ethical principles, and offers ethical guidelines to which professionals aspire and by which their actions can be judged. Ethical behaviors result from a personal commitment to engage in ethical practice.

Professional responsibilities often require an individual to move beyond personal values. For example, an individual might demonstrate behaviors that are based on the values of honesty, providing service to others, or demonstrating loyalty. In addition to these, professional values might require promoting confidentiality, facilitating interdisciplinary collaboration, and refusing to participate or conceal unethical practices. Professional values could require a more comprehensive set of values than what an individual needs to be an ethical agent in their personal lives.

The AHIMA Code of Ethics is to be used by AHIMA and individuals, agencies, organizations, and bodies (such as licensing and regulatory boards, insurance providers, courts of law, agency boards of directors, government agencies, and other professional groups) that choose to adopt it or use it as a frame of reference. The AHIMA Code of Ethics reflects the commitment of all to uphold the profession's values and to act ethically. Individuals of good character who discern moral questions and, in good faith, seek to make reliable ethical judgments, must apply ethical principles.

The code does not provide a set of rules that prescribe how to act in all situations. Specific applications of the code must take into account the context in which it is being considered and the possibility of conflicts among the code's values, principles, and guidelines. Ethical responsibilities flow from all human relationships, from the personal and familial to the social and professional. Further, the AHIMA Code of Ethics does not specify which values, principles, and guidelines are the most important and ought to outweigh others in instances when they conflict.

Code of Ethics 2004

Ethical Principles: The following ethical principles are based on the core values of the American Health Information Management Association and apply to all health information management professionals.

Health information management professionals:

I. Advocate, uphold and defend the individual's right to privacy and the doctrine of confidentiality in the use and disclosure of information.

II. Put service and the health and welfare of persons before self-interest and conduct themselves in the practice of the profession so as to bring honor to themselves, their peers, and to the health information management profession.

III. Preserve, protect, and secure personal health information in any form or medium and hold in the highest regard the contents of the records and other information of a confidential nature, taking into account the applicable statutes and regulations.

IV. Refuse to participate in or conceal unethical practices or procedures.

V. Advance health information management knowledge and practice through continuing education, research, publications, and presentations.

VI. Recruit and mentor students, peers and colleagues to develop and strengthen the professional workforce.

VII. Represent the profession accurately to the public.

VIII. Perform honorably health information management association responsibilities, either appointed or elected, and preserve the confidentiality of any privileged information made known in any official capacity.

IX. State truthfully and accurately their credentials, professional education, and experiences.

X. Facilitate interdisciplinary collaboration in situations supporting health information practice.

XI. Respect the inherent dignity and worth of every person.

How to Interpret the Code of Ethics

The following ethical principles are based on the core values of the American Health Information Management Association and apply to all health information management professionals. Guidelines included for each ethical principle are a noninclusive list of behaviors and situations that can help to clarify the principle. They are not to be meant as a comprehensive list of all situations that can occur.

I. Advocate, uphold, and defend the individual's right to privacy and the doctrine of confidentiality in the use and disclosure of information.

Health information management professionals **shall:**

1.1. Protect all confidential information to include personal, health, financial, genetic, and outcome information.

1.2. Engage in social and political action that supports the protection of privacy and confidentiality, and be aware of the impact of the political arena on the health information system. Advocate for changes in policy and legislation to ensure protection of privacy and confidentiality, coding compliance, and other issues that surface as advocacy issues as well as facilitating informed participation by the public on these issues.

1.3. Protect the confidentiality of all information obtained in the course of professional service. Disclose only information that is directly relevant or necessary to achieve the purpose of disclosure. Release information only with valid consent from a patient or a person legally authorized to consent on behalf of a patient or as authorized by federal or state regulations. The need-to-know criterion is essential when releasing health information for initial disclosure and all redisclosure activities.

1.4. Promote the obligation to respect privacy by respecting confidential information shared among colleagues, while responding to requests from the legal profession, the media, or other nonhealthcare-related individuals, during presentations or teaching and in situations that could cause harm to persons.

II. Put service and the health and welfare of persons before self-interest and conduct themselves in the practice of the profession so as to bring honor to themselves, their peers, and to the health information management profession.

Health information management professionals **shall:**

2.1. Act with integrity, behave in a trustworthy manner, elevate service to others above self-interest, and promote high standards of practice in every setting.

2.2. Be aware of the profession's mission, values, and ethical principles, and practice in a manner consistent with them by acting honestly and responsibly.

2.3. Anticipate, clarify, and avoid any conflict of interest, to all parties concerned, when dealing with consumers, consulting with competitors, or in providing services requiring potentially conflicting roles (for example, finding out information about one facility that would help a competitor). The conflicting roles or responsibilities must be clarified, and appropriate action must be taken to minimize any conflict of interest.

2.4. Ensure that the working environment is consistent and encourages compliance with the AHIMA Code of Ethics, taking reasonable steps to eliminate any conditions in their organizations that violate, interfere with, or discourage compliance with the code.

2.5. Take responsibility and credit, including authorship credit, only for work they actually perform or to which they contribute. Honestly acknowledge the work of and the contributions made by others verbally or written, such as in publication.

Health information management professionals **shall not:**

2.6. Permit their private conduct to interfere with their ability to fulfill their professional responsibilities.

2.7. Take unfair advantage of any professional relationship or exploit others to further their personal, religious, political, or business interests.

III. Preserve, protect, and secure personal health information in any form or medium and hold in the highest regards the contents of the records and other information of a confidential nature obtained in the official capacity, taking into account the applicable statutes and regulations.

Health information management professionals **shall:**

3.1. Protect the confidentiality of patients' written and electronic records and other sensitive information. Take reasonable steps to ensure that patients' records are stored in a secure location and that patients' records are not available to others who are not authorized to have access.

3.2. Take precautions to ensure and maintain the confidentiality of information transmitted, transferred, or disposed of in the event of a termination, incapacitation, or death of a healthcare provider to other parties through the use of any media. Disclosure of identifying information should be avoided whenever possible.

3.3. Inform recipients of the limitations and risks associated with providing services via electronic media (such as computer, telephone, fax, radio, and television).

IV. Refuse to participate in or conceal unethical practices or procedures.

Health information management professionals **shall:**

4.1. Act in a professional and ethical manner at all times.

4.2. Take adequate measures to discourage, prevent, expose, and correct the unethical conduct of colleagues.

4.3. Be knowledgeable about established policies and procedures for handling concerns about colleagues' unethical behavior. These include policies and procedures created by AHIMA, licensing and regulatory bodies, employers, supervisors, agencies, and other professional organizations.

4.4. Seek resolution if there is a belief that a colleague has acted unethically or if there is a belief of incompetence or impairment by discussing their concerns with the colleague when feasible and when such discussion is likely to be productive. Take action through appropriate formal channels, such as contacting an accreditation or regulatory body and/or the AHIMA Professional Ethics Committee.

4.5. Consult with a colleague when feasible and assist the colleague in taking remedial action when there is direct knowledge of a health information management colleague's incompetence or impairment.

Health information management professionals **shall not:**

4.6. Participate in, condone, or be associated with dishonesty, fraud and abuse, or deception. A noninclusive list of examples includes:

- Allowing patterns of retrospective documentation to avoid suspension or increase reimbursement
- Assigning codes without physician documentation
- Coding when documentation does not justify the procedures that have been billed
- Coding an inappropriate level of service
- Miscoding to avoid conflict with others
- Engaging in negligent coding practices
- Hiding or ignoring review outcomes, such as performance data
- Failing to report licensure status for a physician through the appropriate channels
- Recording inaccurate data for accreditation purposes
- Hiding incomplete medical records
- Allowing inappropriate access to genetic, adoption, or behavioral health information
- Misusing sensitive information about a competitor
- Violating the privacy of individuals

V. Advance health information management knowledge and practice through continuing education, research, publications, and presentations.

Health information management professionals **shall:**

5.1. Develop and enhance continually their professional expertise, knowledge, and skills (including appropriate education, research, training, consultation, and supervision). Contribute to the knowledge base of health information management and share with colleagues their knowledge related to practice, research, and ethics.

5.2. Base practice decisions on recognized knowledge, including empirically based knowledge relevant to health information management and health information management ethics.

5.3. Contribute time and professional expertise to activities that promote respect for the value, integrity, and competence of the health information management profession. These activities may include teaching, research, consultation, service, legislative testimony, presentations in the community, and participation in their professional organizations.

5.4. Engage in evaluation or research that ensures the anonymity or confidentiality of participants and of the data obtained from them by following guidelines developed for the participants in consultation with appropriate institutional review boards. Report evaluation and research findings accurately and take steps to correct any errors later found in published data using standard publication methods.

5.5. Take reasonable steps to provide or arrange for continuing education and staff development, addressing current knowledge and emerging developments related to health information management practice and ethics.

Health information management professionals **shall not:**

5.6. Design or conduct evaluation or research that is in conflict with applicable federal or state laws.

5.7. Participate in, condone, or be associated with fraud or abuse.

VI. Recruit and mentor students, peers and colleagues to develop and strengthen professional workforce.

Health information management professionals **shall:**

6.1. Evaluate students' performance in a manner that is fair and respectful when functioning as educators or clinical internship supervisors.

6.2. Be responsible for setting clear, appropriate, and culturally sensitive boundaries for students.

6.3. Be a mentor for students, peers and new health information management professionals to develop and strengthen skills.

6.4. Provide directed practice opportunities for students.

Health information management professionals **shall not:**

6.5. Engage in any relationship with students in which there is a risk of exploitation or potential harm to the student.

VII. Accurately represent the profession to the public.

Health information management professionals **shall:**

7.1 Be an advocate for the profession in all settings and participate in activities that promote and explain the mission, values, and principles of the profession to the public.

VIII. Perform honorably health information management association responsibilities, either appointed or elected, and preserve the confidentiality of any privileged information made known in any official capacity.

Health information management professionals **shall:**

8.1. Perform responsibly all duties as assigned by the professional association.

8.2. Resign from an association position if unable to perform the assigned responsibilities with competence.

8.3. Speak on behalf of professional health information management organizations, accurately representing the official and authorized positions of the organizations.

IX. State truthfully and accurately their credentials, professional education, and experiences.

Health information management professionals **shall:**

9.1. Make clear distinctions between statements made and actions engaged in as a private individual and as a representative of the health information management profession, a professional health information organization, or the health information management professional's employer.

9.2. Claim and ensure that their representations to patients, agencies, and the public of professional qualifications, credentials, education, competence, affiliations, services provided, training, certification, consultation received, supervised experience, and other relevant professional experience are accurate.

9.3. Claim only those relevant professional credentials actually possessed and correct any inaccuracies occurring regarding credentials.

X. Facilitate interdisciplinary collaboration in situations supporting health information practice.

Health information management professionals **shall:**

10.1. Participate in and contribute to decisions that affect the well-being of patients by drawing on the perspectives, values, and experiences of those involved in decisions related to patients. Professional and ethical obligations of the interdisciplinary team as a whole and of its individual members should be clearly established.

XI. Respect the inherent dignity and worth of every person.

Health information management professionals **shall:**

11.1. Treat each person in a respectful fashion, being mindful of individual differences and cultural and ethnic diversity.

11.2. Promote the value of self-determination for each individual.

Acknowledgement

Adapted with permission from the Code of Ethics of the National Association of Social Workers.

Resources

National Association of Social Workers. "Code of Ethics." 1999. Available online from www.socialworkers.org/pubs/code/code.asp.

Harman, L.B., ed.. 2001. *Ethical Challenges in the Management of Health Information.* Gaithersburg, MD: Aspen.

AHIMA Code of Ethics, 1957, 1977, 1988, and 1998.

Revised and adopted by AHIMA House of Delegates—July 1, 2004

Standards of Ethical Coding

Coding professionals should:

1. Apply accurate, complete, and consistent coding practices for the production of high-quality healthcare data.
2. Report all healthcare data elements (e.g. diagnosis and procedure codes, present on admission indicator, discharge status) required for external reporting purposes (e.g. reimbursement and other administrative uses, population health, quality and patient safety measurement, and research) completely and accurately, in accordance with regulatory and documentation standards and requirements and applicable official coding conventions, rules, and guidelines.
3. Assign and report only the codes and data that are clearly and consistently supported by health record documentation in accordance with applicable code set and abstraction conventions, rules, and guidelines.
4. Query provider (physician or other qualified healthcare practitioner) for clarification and additional documentation prior to code assignment when there is conflicting, incomplete, or ambiguous information in the health record regarding a significant reportable condition or procedure or other reportable data element dependent on health record documentation (e.g., present on admission indicator).
5. Refuse to change reported codes or the narratives of codes so that meanings are misrepresented.
6. Refuse to participate in or support coding or documentation practices intended to inappropriately increase payment, qualify for insurance policy coverage, or skew data by means that do not comply with federal and state statutes, regulations, and official rules and guidelines.
7. Facilitate interdisciplinary collaboration in situations supporting proper coding practices.
8. Advance coding knowledge and practice through continuing education.
9. Refuse to participate in or conceal unethical coding or abstraction practices or procedures.
10. Protect the confidentiality of the health record at all times and refuse to access protected health information not required for coding-related activities (examples of coding-related activities include completion of code assignment, other health record data abstraction, coding audits, and educational purposes).
11. Demonstrate behavior that reflects integrity, shows a commitment to ethical and legal coding practices, and fosters trust in professional activities.

Revised and approved by the House of Delegates, September, 2008.

Resources

AHIMA Code of Ethics: http://www.ahima.org/about/ethics.asp

ICD-9-CM Official Guidelines for Coding and Reporting: http://www.cdc.gov/nchs/datawh/ftpserv/ftpicd9/icdguide07.pdf .

AHIMA's position statement on Quality Health Data and Information: Available at http://www.ahima.org/dc/positions.

AHIMA's position statement on Uniformity and Consistency of Healthcare Data (DRAFT).

AHIMA Practice Brief titled "Managing an Effective Query Process:" Available at http://www.ahima.org/infocenter/briefs.asp.

How to Interpret the Standards of Ethical Coding

The following ethical principles are based on the core values of the American Health Information Management Association and the AHIMA Code of Ethics and apply to all coding professionals. Guidelines for each ethical principle include examples of behaviors and situations that can help to clarify the principle. They are not meant as a comprehensive list of all situations that can occur.

1. ***Apply accurate, complete, and consistent coding practices for the production of high-quality healthcare data.***

   Coding professionals and those who manage coded data shall:

   1.1. Support selection of appropriate diagnostic, procedure and other types of health service related codes (e.g. present on admission indicator, discharge status).

   Example:
   Policies and procedures are developed and used as a framework for the work process, and education and training is provided on their use.

   1.2. Develop and comply with comprehensive internal coding policies and procedures that are consistent with official coding rules and guidelines, reimbursement regulations and policies, and prohibit coding practices that misrepresent the patient's medical conditions and treatment provided or are not supported by the health record documentation.

   Example:
   Code assignment resulting in misrepresentation of facts carries significant consequences.

   1.3. Participate in the development of institutional coding policies and ensure that coding policies complement, and do not conflict with, official coding rules and guidelines.

   1.4. Foster an environment that supports honest and ethical coding practices resulting in accurate and reliable data.

   Coding professionals **shall not**:

   1.5. Participate in improper preparation, alteration, or suppression of coded information.

2. ***Report all healthcare data elements (e.g. diagnosis and procedure codes, present on admission indicator, discharge status) required for external reporting purposes (e.g. reimbursement and other administrative uses, population health, public data reporting, quality and patient safety measurement, research) completely and accurately, in accordance with regulatory and documentation standards and requirements and applicable official coding conventions, rules, and guidelines.***

   Coding professionals **shall**:

   2.1. Adhere to the ICD coding conventions, official coding guidelines approved by the Cooperating Parties,[1] the CPT rules established by the American Medical Association, and any other official coding rules and guidelines established for use with mandated standard code sets.

   Example:
   Appropriate resource tools that assist coding professionals with proper sequencing and reporting to stay in compliance with existing reporting requirements are available and used.

   2.2. Select and sequence diagnosis and procedure codes in accordance with the definitions of required data sets for applicable healthcare settings.

   2.3. Comply with AHIMA's standards governing data reporting practices, including health record documentation and clinician query standards.

3. ***Assign and report only the codes that are clearly and consistently supported by health record documentation in accordance with applicable code set conventions, rules, and guidelines.***

   Coding professionals **shall**:

   3.1. Apply skills, knowledge of currently mandated coding and classification systems, and official resources to select the appropriate diagnostic and procedural codes (including applicable modifiers), and other codes representing healthcare services (including substances, equipment, supplies, or other items used in the provision of healthcare services).

   Example:
   Failure to research or confirm the appropriate code for a clinical condition not indexed in the classification, or reporting a code for the sake of convenience or to affect reporting for a desired effect on the results, is considered unethical.

4. ***Query provider (physician or other qualified healthcare practitioner) for clarification and additional documentation prior to code assignment when there is conflicting, incomplete, or ambiguous information in the health record regarding a significant reportable condition or procedure or other reportable data element dependent on health record documentation (e.g. present on admission indicator).***

   Coding professionals **shall**:

   4.1. Participate in the development of query policies that support documentation improvement and meet regulatory, legal, and ethical standards for coding and reporting.

   4.2. Query the provider for clarification when documentation in the health record that impacts an externally reportable data element is illegible, incomplete, unclear, inconsistent, or imprecise.

4.3. Use queries as a communication tool to improve the accuracy of code assignment and the quality of health record documentation, not to inappropriately increase reimbursement or misrepresent quality of care.

Example:
Policies regarding the circumstances when clinicians should be queried are designed to promote complete and accurate coding and complete documentation, regardless of whether reimbursement will be affected.

Coding professionals **shall not**:

4.4. Query the provider when there is no clinical information in the health record prompting the need for a query.

Example:
Query the provider regarding the presence of gram-negative pneumonia on every pneumonia case, regardless of whether there are any clinical indications of gram-negative pneumonia documented in the record.

5. ***Refuse to change reported codes or the narratives of codes so that meanings are misrepresented.***

Coding professionals **shall not**:

5.1. Change the description for a diagnosis or procedure code or other reported data element so that it does not accurately reflect the official definition of that code.

Example:
The description of a code is altered in the encoding software, resulting in incorrect reporting of this code.

6. ***Refuse to participate in or support coding or documentation practices intended to inappropriately increase payment, qualify for insurance policy coverage, or skew data by means that do not comply with federal and state statutes, regulations, and official rules and guidelines.***

Coding professionals **shall**:

6.1. Select and sequence the codes such that the organization receives the optimal payment to which the facility is legally entitled, remembering that it is unethical and illegal to increase payment by means that contradict regulatory guidelines.

Coding professionals **shall not**:

6.2. Misrepresent the patient's clinical picture through intentional incorrect coding or omission of diagnosis or procedure codes, or the addition of diagnosis or procedure codes unsupported by health record documentation, to inappropriately increase reimbursement, justify medical necessity, improve publicly reported data, or qualify for insurance policy coverage benefits.

Examples:
A patient has a health plan that excludes reimbursement for reproductive management or contraception; so rather than report the correct code for admission for tubal ligation, it is reported as a medically necessary condition with performance of a salpingectomy. The narrative descriptions of both the diagnosis and procedures reflect an admission for tubal ligation and the procedure (tubal ligation) is displayed on the record.

A code is changed at the patient's request so that the service will be covered by the patient's insurance.

Coding professionals **shall not**:

6.3. Inappropriately exclude diagnosis or procedure codes in order to misrepresent the quality of care provided.

Examples:
Following a surgical procedure, a patient acquired an infection due to a break in sterile procedure; the appropriate code for the surgical complication is omitted from the claims submission to avoid any adverse outcome to the institution.

Quality outcomes are reported inaccurately in order to improve a healthcare organization's quality profile or pay-for-performance results.

7. ***Facilitate interdisciplinary collaboration in situations supporting proper coding practices.***

Coding professionals **shall**:

7.1. Assist and educate physicians and other clinicians by advocating proper documentation practices, further specificity, and re-sequence or include diagnoses or procedures when needed to more accurately reflect the acuity, severity, and the occurrence of events.

Example:
Failure to advocate for ethical practices that seek to represent the truth in events as expressed by the associated code sets when needed is considered an intentional disregard of these standards.

8. ***Advance coding knowledge and practice through continuing education.***

Coding professionals **shall**:

8.1. Maintain and continually enhance coding competency (e.g., through participation in educational programs, reading official coding publications such as the Coding Clinic for ICD-9-CM, and maintaining professional certifications) in order to stay abreast of changes in codes, coding guidelines, and regulatory and other requirements.

9. ***Refuse to participate in or conceal unethical coding practices or procedures.***

   Coding professionals **shall**:

   9.1. Act in a professional and ethical manner at all times.

   9.2. Take adequate measures to discourage, prevent, expose, and correct the unethical conduct of colleagues.

   9.3. Be knowledgeable about established policies and procedures for handling concerns about colleagues' unethical behavior. These include policies and procedures created by AHIMA, licensing and regulatory bodies, employers, supervisors, agencies, and other professional organizations.

   9.4. Seek resolution if there is a belief that a colleague has acted unethically or if there is a belief of incompetence or impairment by discussing their concerns with the colleague when feasible and when such discussion is likely to be productive. Take action through appropriate formal channels, such as contacting an accreditation or regulatory body and/or the AHIMA Professional Ethics Committee.

   9.5. Consult with a colleague when feasible and assist the colleague in taking remedial action when there is direct knowledge of a health information management colleague's incompetence or impairment.

   Coding professionals **shall not**:

   9.6. Participate in, condone, or be associated with dishonesty, fraud and abuse, or deception. A non-exhaustive list of examples includes:

   - Allowing inappropriate patterns of retrospective documentation to avoid suspension or increase reimbursement
   - Assigning codes without supporting provider (physician or other qualified healthcare practitioner) documentation
   - Coding when documentation does not justify the diagnoses and/or procedures that have been billed
   - Coding an inappropriate level of service
   - Miscoding to avoid conflict with others
   - Adding, deleting, and altering health record documentation
   - Copying and pasting another clinician's documentation without identification of the original author and date
   - Knowingly reporting incorrect present on admission indicator
   - Knowingly reporting incorrect patient discharge status code
   - Engaging in negligent coding practices

10. ***Protect the confidentiality of the health record at all times and refuse to access protected health information not required for coding-related activities (examples of coding-related activities include completion of code assignment, other health record data abstraction, coding audits, and educational purposes).***

    Coding professionals **shall**:

    10.1. Protect all confidential information obtained in the course of professional service, including personal, health, financial, genetic, and outcome information.

    10.2. Access only that information necessary to perform their duties.

11. ***Demonstrate behavior that reflects integrity, shows a commitment to ethical and legal coding practices, and fosters trust in professional activities.***

    Coding professionals **shall**:

    11.1. Act in an honest manner and bring honor to self, peers, and the profession.

    11.2. Truthfully and accurately represent their credentials, professional education, and experience.

    11.3. Demonstrate ethical principles and professional values in their actions to patients, employers, other members of the healthcare team, consumers, and other stakeholders served by the healthcare data they collect and report.

[1]The Cooperating Parties are the American Health Information Management Association, American Hospital Association, Centers for Medicare and Medicaid Services, and National Center for Health Statistics.

Source: AHIMA House of Delegates. 2008 (Sept.) "AHIMA Standards on Ethical Coding."

Appendix C
Answers to Check Your Understanding Exercises

Chapter 2

Check Your Understanding 2.1

1. b
2. d
3. d
4. a
5. c.
6. c
7. a
8. d

Check Your Understanding 2.2

1. b
2. g
3. a
4. d
5. h
6. c
7. e
8. f

Check Your Understanding 2.3

1. a
2. b
3. f
4. e
5. d
6. c

Check Your Understanding 2.4

1. c
2. e
3. a
4. h
5. j
6. f
7. d
8. g
9. i
10. b

Check Your Understanding 2.5

1. T
2. T
3. T
4. T
5. T
6. T
7. T
8. F
9. T
10. T

Check Your Understanding 2.6

1. c
2. d
3. d
4. c
5. a
6. b
7. c

Check Your Understanding 2.7

1. T
2. T
3. T
4. F
5. T
6. T
7. T
8. T

Chapter 3

Check Your Understanding 3.1

1. Informatics applies information management in the context of computer-based systems that are designed to support specific types of users in performing their work (for example, decision-making support). Information management, however, is a more generalized discipline with similar aims that are applied in both paper-based and computer-based environments.
2. Healthcare professionals use data and information constantly throughout their day to perform work for patients. They need to review previous and current clinical, financial, and demographic patient data and information as well as document new findings. Patient information is crucial for sharing and planning patient care with the healthcare team of professionals, for proper consultation and appropriate referrals, and for appropriate patient interaction from patient visits to patient billing.
3. Due to the ease and availability of Web-based commerce, online banking, ATMs, and other technologies, healthcare appears to lag behind. The healthcare industry is just beginning to adopt Web-based services for patients such as appointment scheduling, demographic and insurance updates, and e-mail contact with physicians or clinicians. This perception may be changed by informing healthcare consumers of the advances in healthcare technology, the importance of privacy and standards when sharing patient information, and the subjectivity of clinical practice, which makes healthcare different from other industries.

Check Your Understanding 3.2

1. The goal of healthcare informatics is to understand the structure, dynamics, and design of information systems, which are composed of people, technology, and organizational factors. This understanding allows optimum flow and use of information for every task in every context for every user. The healthcare informatics discipline focuses on the development of computer-based applications that are specifically designed to support different types of users in performing their work or meeting their needs. Healthcare informatics makes it possible for organizations to improve communications, achieve better outcomes, improve processes, and make administration more efficient.
2. Two IOM reports, one released in 1999 and the second in 2001, were based on the work of the IOM's Committee on the Quality of Healthcare in America, which identified major issues associated with deaths attributable to preventable medical errors and called for a transformation of healthcare delivery in the United States. The IOM's third and fourth reports were also from the IOM's Committee on the Quality of Health Care in America. The 2002 report argued that the federal government should lead the development of clinical standards for measuring care, and called for financial incentives for organizations that improve quality. The 2003 report proposed the Consolidated Health Informatics (CHI) initiative in which the DHHS, DoD, and VA work with the NCVHA to identify appropriate clinical data standards. This report mandated that EHRs operate as a part of a national network of health information accessible by all healthcare organizations. In all these landmark reports, information technology (IT) needs and benefits were included in the call to action.
3. The National Health Information Network (NHIN) is a government-sponsored initiative also referred to as the "Medical Internet." The purpose of this initiative is to provide a comprehensive view of a patient's health information at the point of care through the development of a interconnected, knowledge-based network of interoperable information systems. Providers of care will be able to electronically exchange information among all electronic health records so that a complete EHR can be assembled whenever and wherever a patient presents for care.
4. Barriers include a current lack of standards, which are necessary for interoperability and data sharing; insufficient funding; a lack of ongoing economic incentives, which are needed to sustain infrastructure operations; and public concern over privacy.
5. An HIM professional can get involved in RHIO and HIE initiatives by creating policies, establishing processes, developing communication plans, and ensuring that solid HIM principles are considered.
6. The federated approach is not fully integrated; rather, it consists of distinct, distributed, disparate, and decentralized databases. Centralization only occurs with an EMPI for demographic data. This approach is favored because it does not require a unique national patient identifier, it allows contributing organizations to retain ownership and control of their data, and new computer systems are not required, which allows for an easier transition to the regional EHR. Drawbacks include the lack of a centralized database, standardization, and a unified data model. The lack of these things makes decision support and reporting difficult.

Check Your Understanding 3.3

1. Structured data include laboratory test results; demographic data such as name, address, and birth date; financial data such as dollar amounts charged for services; and codes that represent case-mix types. Unstructured data include transcribed radiology reports and histories and physicals.

Discrete data is another term for structured data and includes, for example, ICD-9-CM codes, patient weight and height measurements, and dollar amounts. Examples of free text data include handwritten progress notes and transcribed pathology reports

2. When a healthcare professional searches for discrete data or structured data, the database search engine can easily find, retrieve, and manipulate the data element. Free-text data, or unstructured data, cannot be easily retrieved or manipulated.
3. Both diagnostic images and document images are bit-mapped data. All document images and some diagnostic images are based on analog documents (paper or photographic film) that must be scanned to digitize the data for electronic storage. However, some diagnostic images are based on digital modalities, such as images resulting from computed radiography (CR), magnetic resonance (MR), and computed tomography (CT).
4. Examples of real audio include digital heart sounds, voice annotation, and voice recognition. Cardiac catheterizations, ultrasounds, and echocardiograms are examples of motion or streaming data. Examples of signal or vector data include fetal heart monitor, ECGs (electrocardiograms), and EEGs (electroencephalograms).
5. Possible answers:
   a. Speech recognition technology employs basic natural language processing capabilities as it translates spoken words (natural language voice bytes) into text. However, speech recognition technology does not yet employ the advanced capabilities of natural language processing; for instance, speech recognition technology is not yet capable of taking two sound-alike terms (such as ileum and ilium) with different meanings and then selecting the correct term based on an analysis of the context.
   b. Natural language processing technology and Boolean searching differ from each other in that the former considers sentence structure (syntax), meaning (semantics), and context to accurately extract data from free text. For example, "no shortness of breath, chest pain aggravated by exercise" and "no chest pain, shortness of breath aggravated by exercise" look the same to a Boolean word search engine when it identifies occurrences of "chest" and "pain" in the same sentence. Natural language processing technology, however, would discern the syntactical and semantic differences between these two phrases.

Check Your Understanding 3.4

1. Bar coding is commonly used in healthcare; examples include labels, patient wristbands, specimen containers, and medication packets. Optical character recognition (OCR) technology is used on a limited basis; examples include the indexing of scanned documents and the digitizing of text documents. Intelligent character recognition (ICR) technology is being adopted slowly; examples include pen-based and handheld input devices. Radio frequency identification (RFID) is rapidly evolving; examples include the tracking of moveable patients, clinicians, medications, and equipment. Intelligent document recognition (IDR) has recently been developed; examples include document and form-type identification.
2. Electronic data interchange (EDI) was the healthcare industry's first venture into direct electronic transmission of data between the computer system of one organization and the computer system of another organization (often called a business partner). By 2000, EDI as a term (not as a concept) had become dated and was replaced by e-commerce and e-health. E-health now refers to the practice of e-commerce within the healthcare industry.
3. As healthcare organizations collaborate to exchange patient information, multiple databases in multiple formats poses problems. As a result, healthcare providers are developing strategic enterprise master patient index (EMPI) initiatives because this technology, through an indexing scheme, ties a patient's information together across separate systems and databases, providing access to multiple repositories of information about overlapping patient populations.
4. An object-oriented database associated with a clinical data repository can contain several types of unstructured data (for example, streaming video, free text, real audio, or vector graphic data).
5. An ED/CM system is any electronic system that manages an organization's analog and digital documents or content to significantly improve business work processes.
   - Document imaging technology electronically captures, stores, identifies, retrieves, and distributes documents that are not generated digitally or are generated digitally but are stored on paper.
   - Workflow/business process management (BPM) technology allows computers to add and extract value from document content as the documents move throughout an organization. The documents can be automatically assigned, routed, activated, and managed through system-controlled rules that mirror business operations.

- Computer output laser disk (COLD)/enterprise report management (ERM) technology electronically stores, manages, and distributes documents that are generated in a digital format and whose output data are report-formatted. These documents can be distributed through fax, e-mail, Web, and hard copy.
- Automated forms processing technology allows users to electronically enter data into online forms and electronically extract the data from the online forms for data manipulation. The form document is stored in a form format, as the user sees it on the screen, for ease of interpretation.
- Digital signature management technology offers both signer and document authentication for analog or digital documents. Signer authentication is the ability to identify the person who digitally signed the document. Document authentication ensures that the document and the signature cannot be altered.

6. Secure clinical messaging is not dependent upon time zones, it can be done in each clinical user's own timeframe, it gives clinical recipients time to think over and respond to issues appropriately, and it does not require all participants to be available at the same time.
7. Web browser-based systems are more complex than Web-enabled systems. Web browser-based systems use Web-based programming languages (such as HML, SGML, XML, or Java) as the system's code so that the Web browser acts as the primary desktop interface for accessing information directly from the organization's data repositories. Web-enabled systems do not use Web-based programming language. Instead, authorized users must access data in Web-enabled systems through a Web page from which the organization's applications (which may be written, for example, in Visual Basic) are then launched.
8. The clinical workstation (clinician/physician portal) provides the clinician with a single point of access with a common user interface (and a single log-on password) to launch and view information from disparate applications.
9. Web portals provided by providers/payers allow patients to schedule appointments, ask questions of their providers via secure messaging, request prescription renewals, securely view all or portions of their provider-based EHR, and pay bills online.
10. Web-based intranets are designed to enhance communication among an organization's internal employees and facilities. An employee handbook may be found on an organization's intranet. Web-based extranets are designed to enhance communication among an organization's business partners. A medical supply company might use an extranet to check an organization's inventory level to determine when to reorder.
11. Benefits of open source technology are its availability, extensibility to be customized, and the collaborative nature of this technology allowing users and developers to interact and improve upon the product. Drawbacks include the need for skilled developers within the organization and the lack of technical support.
12. Under an application service provider (ASP) or software as a service (SaaS) model, a healthcare organization can gain quick access to functioning application software with the cost distributed over time and based on a set monthly or transaction-based fee structure. The organization is spared the burden of maintaining the system using internal technical staff because maintenance is the responsibility of the ASP/SaaS. The drawbacks for the organization are that it must accept an off-the-shelf software application, it will lose control over the timing of upgrades, it remains responsible for firewalls and HIPAA compliance, and it must be prepared to transition its data from the ASP/SaaS's control should the contract be dissolved.

Check Your Understanding 3.5

1. Data repositories are structured on relational and object-oriented database models that are well suited for online transaction processing (OLTP), and the data are updated in real time by current transactions. Data warehouses are structured on multidimensional database models that are well suited for online analytical processing (OLAP), and the data are historical in nature, subject-oriented, and nonvolatile.
2. Clinical decision support systems provide information that assists clinicians in making decisions related to patient care. Examples include reminders and alerts, clinical guideline advice, and benchmarking data. Expert decision support systems also provide information that assists clinicians. Expert decision support systems, however, first apply a set of rules or protocols to patient information, then provide a problem analysis, and finally offer advice similar to that which might be expected to be given by an expert serving as a consultant.
3. Artificial intelligence technology performs functions normally associated with humans, such as language, reasoning, learning, and problem solving.

Check Your Understanding 3.6

1. Distinct examples of diagnostic tests that involve physiological signal processing include electrocardiograms (EKGs), electroencephalograms (EEGs), electromyograms (EMGs), fetal tracings, digital blood pressure (BP) monitors, and digital thermometers.
2. Patient data that are typically collected and viewed (accessed) by care providers using point-of-care systems include order entry data, medication administration data, vital signs, input/output data, and lab test results.
3. Providers are recognizing the enormous variation in how they diagnose, treat, and care for patients. Therefore, they are looking to standardize care for both quality assurance and cost-containment purposes. Automation (computerization) of care plans, guidelines, pathways, and protocols promotes easier access to information by clinicians and easier ongoing maintenance.
4. Second- and third-generation telehealth applications rely on patient interaction and consultation, whereas first-generation applications relied on the transfer of patient information only. (The use of guided robotics is evident in third-generation telehealth applications. Telesurgeons in New York City, for example, can perform a gallbladder surgery on a patient in France via robots fed by high-speed signals sent across the Atlantic Ocean through fiber-optic cables.)
5. These IOM reports defined a computer-based patient record (CPR) as "an electronic patient record that resides in a system specifically designed to support users by providing accessibility to complete and accurate data, alerts, reminders, clinical decision support systems, links to medical knowledge and other aids." An electronic medical record (EMR) composed of digitized, bit-mapped images cannot provide the full functionality of the CPR as defined here. Alerts, reminders, links to medical knowledge, and so on are not functional components of a patient record that is primarily composed of digitized images of documents.
6. The EHR-S Functional Model and Standard laid the foundation for the first generation standards-based EHR and defined the EHR's components.
7. Examples of services using e-health technology that healthcare organizations offer include PHRs, patient appointment scheduling, patient registration, pre-visit health screening, post-visit patient education, and information on health conditions.
8. The e-health culture in a healthcare organization is characterized by quick response to communications from patients and customers and a high comfort level with working in partnership with a variety of other organizations.
9. The shared data record is a PHR supported by the provider and maintained by both the provider and the patient. In the EHR extension model, the provider allows access for an authorized patient to the record for review and extraction purposes only. PHRs built on the provider-sponsored information management model use communication vehicles between provider and patient so that reminders, appointment scheduling, prescription refills, and monitoring tools for disease management can be handled by the PHR system.
10. Consumers use Web 2.0/Health 2.0 tools such as blogs, social networks, content communities, wikis, and podcasts to collaborate with others in discussions and communities, obtain and share information, and to create their own content. The lack of control and restrictions over Web 2.0/Health 2.0 tools presents legal and ethical concerns that must be addressed by healthcare providers such as privacy, confidentiality and liability issues.

Check Your Understanding 3.7

1. Public key infrastructure (PKI) is a type of encryption technology. It involves a private key (known to one computer) and a public key that is given to a second computer. The second computer receives an incoming message from the first computer and decodes it with the public key and its own private key. PKI is becoming the standard encryption technology for securing data transfers and online authentication. Public key infrastructure is receiving much attention within the healthcare industry because secure data transfers and online authentication are vital in meeting the HIPAA security regulations.
2. In general, the major benefits of using biometrics to verify identity are that biometrics ensure unique positive identification without the fear of replication or duplication, and biometrics are reliable personal identifiers. The major drawback of using biometrics is that, because biometric methods are so reliable, individuals might feel that their privacy is threatened or compromised when they are tracked by such devices. Fingerprints are the oldest and most popular type of biometric because they are accurate and easy to obtain. Fingerprint scanning requires the subject to pause and place a finger on a device while the imprint match is made. This is problematic for individuals with no or deformed fingers. Retinal and iris scanning are very accurate types of biometrics. However, they are not as popular as fingerprint scanning because of the close eye contact users must make with the scanning device. These scans are problematic for subjects who wear eyeglasses or contact lenses. Facial image recognition is the least obtrusive type of biometric. However, it requires the matching of dynamic

images, which is more technologically difficult than the matching of static images such as fingerprints or retinal/iris scans.
3. Proxy services are special-purpose programs allowing network administrators to permit or deny user access to specific applications or features of applications. Filtering services allow routers to make permit/deny decisions for each piece of information that attempts to enter or leave a private network.
4. Delegating responsibility to users for examining their audit histories is one way to establish user trust. Another way to instill user trust is to frequently sample system usage by organizational managers and publish results of audit trails.

Check Your Understanding 3.8

1. As the patient record evolves into an EHR, the domains of HIM professional practice (clinical data quality, the legal and regulatory integrity of the record, and the privacy and security of the patient record) are transitioning from the paper-based environment into the electronic environment. Informatics is defined as information management applied in a computer-based environment, so HIM professionals functioning in an EHR environment are key players (along with IT professionals) within the informatics discipline.

Chapter 4

Check Your Understanding 4.1

1. The HIM profession has been changed by government sponsorship and regulation of healthcare, the advent of computers, advances in medical practice, socioeconomic changes, and progress in higher education.
2. The information technology field is not specific to healthcare. It requires more in-depth knowledge of computer science, but less or no training in clinical processes, the healthcare industry, and other specifics of the HIM curriculum.
3. One of the HIM professional's principal roles is to develop systems that collect accurate and timely clinical information and make it available to decision makers. Collection may be from many sources with a wide variety of uses.
4. Other healthcare professionals collect and use these data in the direct provision of patient care. HIM professionals perform a variety of tasks associated with the data, including information management as well as data manipulation for use by others.
5. Unlike the other forms of data for which health information managers are responsible, reference data are not derived from individual patient data.

Check Your Understanding 4.2

1. The benefits gained from HIM planning include making information available; ensuring appropriate access, security, and confidentiality; and making the process of accessing and retrieving information in clinical and administrative processes more efficient.
2. Data modeling defines the data that are required, whereas process or workflow modeling identifies how and when the data will be captured.
3. A data dictionary defines all of the unique data elements in the data set and contains the definition, data attributes, edits, and authentication requirements.
4. In data modeling, understanding how data are used and their sources can help to identify what data are needed. For process and workflow modeling, an understanding of the care process can assist in identifying what data can be collected and used by whom. Knowledge of the data meanings can help suggest data edits.

Check Your Understanding 4.3

1. A student would expect to learn about HIPAA regulations when studying Healthcare privacy, confidentiality, security, and ethical issues. However the content is often interrelated and may be cross-referenced in multiple knowledge clusters.
2. Health services organization and delivery includes e-health delivery systems, accreditation standards including the Joint Commission, and regulatory and licensure requirements.
3. The elements of healthcare data, content, and structure are:
    - structure and use of health information
    - health information media
    - type and content of health records
    - data quality assessment and integrity
    - secondary data sources
    - healthcare data sets
    - health information archival systems
    - National Healthcare Information Infrastructure
    - data collection tools
4. For performing research using health information, the following curriculum topics are useful:
    - biomedical sciences
    - healthcare statistics
    - biomedical research
    - quality management of healthcare statistics and research
    - quality management and performance improvement

Check Your Understanding 4.4

1. AHIMA is addressing a global future by continually reviewing and revising the core professional characteristics.
2. Membership in more than one professional association may be helpful if one's career involves more than one domain of practice.
3. Key services provided by professional associations include:
   - networking opportunities
   - continuing education
   - certification
   - advocacy
4. The International Medical Informatics Association (IMIA) and the International Federation of Health Record Organizations (IFHRO) are both examples of international associations dealing with health information.
5. CSA stands for Component State Association. Under the Federation Model, membership in AHIMA automatically allows core services at the component state level. Among other benefits, CSAs provide local access to professional education, networking and representation, keeping members informed of regionally significant HIM issues.
6. The code of ethics instructs all HIM professionals to advance health information management knowledge and practice through continuing education, research, publications, and presentations and to conduct themselves in the practice of the profession so as to bring honor to themselves, their peers, and the HIM profession.
7. Both are important to continuing documentation accuracy. AHDI members focus on transcription with a mission directed at clinical documentation accuracy, privacy, and security at the data capture level. AHDI certifies medical transcriptionists. ACDIS' mission is to bring clinical documentation improvement specialists together for the purpose of improving documentation, sharing strategies and resources.
8. The benefits of certification include the following.
   - Certification demonstrates to colleagues and superiors a dedication to high-quality healthcare and to the highest standards of health information management.
   - Certification presents solid evidence to employers that an employee has been trained and tested to implement best practices and apply current technological solutions, abilities that, in turn, advance the organization.
   - Certification sets a person apart from uncredentialed job candidates. In recent AHIMA-sponsored research groups, healthcare executives and recruiters cited these reasons for preferring credentialed personnel: assurance of current knowledge through continued education, possession of field-tested experience, and verification of base-level competency.
   - Certification has value for employers because it supports a worker's commitment to upholding industry standards and regulations, thereby potentially saving organizations from fines and penalties due to errors or noncompliance.
   - Certification is a beneficial addition to a resume because it provides recognition of a candidate's capabilities. Because credentials appear after a person's name, they announce expertise with every signature.
   - Certification is maintained by abiding by the AHIMA Code of Ethics and completing the required continuing education activities.
9. Of the organizations listed in this chapter, professional certification is offered by the following: AHIMA, AHDI, HIMSS, and NCRA
10. RHIA applicants must pass AHIMA's RHIA examination and must hold one of the following educational requirements:
    - a baccalaureate degree from a CAHIIM-accredited health information administration (HIA) program
    - a baccalaureate degree from an accredited college or university and a certificate in HIA from a CAHIIM-accredited program
    - a degree from a foreign HIA baccalaureate program with which AHIMA has a reciprocal agreement (AHIMA currently has an agreement with the Health Information Management Association of Australia at the baccalaureate level)
11. Certification records are audited annually on a random sample of 2 percent of the reporting population.
12. Continuing education activities are reported to AHIMA through completion of a continuing education (CE) report form either on paper or via their Web site.

Chapter 5

Check Your Understanding 5.1

1. There are many possible answers to this question. An ICD-9-CM code is an example of data that would become information when aggregated into a report showing the top discharge diagnoses for the month.
2. Individuals within an organization need different levels of information. For example, a chief executive officer (CEO) might need a more advanced analysis of discharge statistics than a unit manager might need. A monthly report might already be information for the unit manager but might need to be inserted into a database for comparison with other facilities to become information for the CEO.
3. Data and information in an organization spans every area and is not limited to the patient record. This data and information comes in many forms and can be contained in many information systems. Enterprise Content and Records Management (ECRM) allows the organization to manage all the information in all of the systems.
4. Examples of explicit knowledge include procedure manuals, research results, clinical guidelines, policies, computer programs, and training manuals.
   Examples of tacit knowledge include employee skills, judgment, experience, and guiding principles.
   With the predicted large number of healthcare worker retirements and a shortage of healthcare workers, it is important to have a successful transfer of knowledge when an employee leaves an organization.
   With the importance of evidence-based medicine it is important to have the most accurate, up-to-date, evidence to base decisions. This evidence can be both explicit and tacit knowledge.

Check Your Understanding 5.2

1. The Joint Commission IM plan begins with a needs assessment because each organization has unique information needs. No one information management plan would work for all.
2. Patient-specific, aggregate, comparative, and knowledge-based information go into the model. The Joint Commission identifies five categories of information uses: clinical decision making, organizational decision making, research, performance improvement, and education (of patients, families, and healthcare providers).
3. The basic principles of information management are treating information as an essential organizational resource, obtaining top executive support for information systems (IS) planning and management, and developing an IS strategic plan and vision.
4. Healthcare organizations are information intensive. So much patient and ancillary information is created that it is imperative that it be managed effectively.
5. User-centered design makes sure that the user is involved throughout the entire design and development process. This ensures that the new IS system meets the users' needs.

Check Your Understanding 5.3

1. These models have some characteristics in common, but their structures are different. The AHIMA model includes the dimensions of data quality and the MRI lists principles of documentation. The MRI model divides documentation into both information capture and report generation.
   a. Timeliness and accuracy
   b. AHIMA strives to include all healthcare data, but the MRI model limits the characteristics to clinical documentation. They are compatible.
2. The 10 dimensions of data quality are accuracy, accessibility, comprehensiveness, consistency, currency, definition, granularity, precision, relevancy, and timeliness.
3. There are many possible answers to this question. Please refer to the examples provided in the chapter.

Check Your Understanding 5.4

1. Database design and management knowledge is important to HIM professionals because they are essential participants in the design, development, and maintenance of organizational databases. Communication between IS and HIM professionals is important for successful IS systems. If HIM professionals have database knowledge it assists in the communication.
2. Today, the most common type of database is the relational database.
3. Database design helps eliminate unnecessary redundancy and promotes data accuracy. Update, addition, and deletion errors are essentially eliminated in a well-designed relational database.
4. A data model is a "picture" or abstraction of real conditions. It shows how data are related within a database.
5. The conceptual data model has the highest level of abstraction; the physical model the lowest. The conceptual model is both software and hardware independent, the logical model is hardware independent, and the physical model is software specific. The physical model is essentially obsolete because most databases today are relational and do not require a physical-level model.

6. Entity relationship diagrams (ERDs) are used as communication tools among database developers and users at the conceptual level for any type of database and at the logical level for a relational database. Unified modeling language (UML) is a modeling language used to show a "picture" of an object-oriented database.
7. The components of an ERD are entity (relation), relationship, and attribute.
8. In an ERD, an entity is represented as a rectangle; a relationship is represented as a triangle.
9. 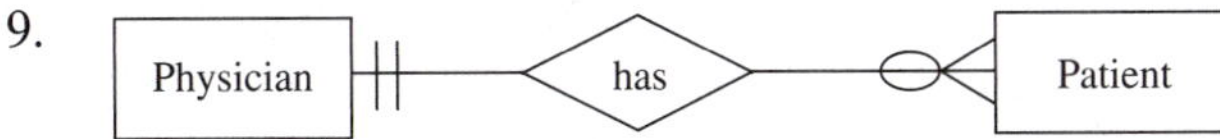

Check Your Understanding 5.5

1. A data dictionary contains detailed, agreed-upon database or enterprise-wide data element definitions. A data dictionary is important for data consistency and in facilitating comparisons or aggregations of data across systems.
2. A list of terms and data elements would be housed in an enterprise-wide data dictionary. A system catalog would also include information about data tables, relationships, and other information pertinent to the development and maintenance of the database.
3. Data maps or crosswalks are connections or paths between classifications and vocabularies.
4. AHIMA's recommended guidelines for development of data dictionaries include: design a plan, develop an enterprise data dictionary, ensure collaborative involvement, develop an approvals process, identify and retain details of data versions, design for flexibility and growth, design room for expansion of field values, follow established guidelines, adopt nationally recognized standards, beware of differing standards for the same concepts, use geographic codes, test the information system, provide ongoing education, assess the consistency.

Check Your Understanding 5.6

1. The data administrator is responsible for managing the data that may be stored within a database. Database administrators manage the technical aspects of a database and focus on managing the data within the database. According to the AHIMA definition of data resource manager, the data resource manager also retrieves data and information from the database. The data analyst investigates and compiles data for research, auditing, quality assessment and other purposes.
2. For multiple reasons discussed in the chapter, health information managers would be excellent candidates for data administrators, data resource managers, and data analyst.

Check Your Understanding 5.7

1. *Data integrity* is the assurance that data have been accessed or modified only by those authorized to do so and in a manner appropriate to the database. Data integrity is controlled by the database design. Numerous data integrity constraints or rules are built into databases.
2. Data security focuses on access authorization; that is, preventing unauthorized users from obtaining entry into the database. Data integrity includes access issues, but is also concerned with what happens to the data after they are accessed.
3. The authorization management features of the DBMS define users, assign passwords, define user groups, and assign access privileges.

Check Your Understanding 5.8

1. Graphs should:
   - show the data
   - induce the viewer to think about the substance rather than the methodology, graphic design, the technology or other things
   - avoid distorting what the data have to say
   - present many numbers in a small space
   - make large data sets coherent
   - encourage the eye to compare different pieces of data
   - reveal the data at several levels of detail
   - serve a reasonably clear purpose
   - be closely integrated with the statistical and verbal descriptions of the data set
2. The following are some basic guidelines for graphical excellence:
   - A well-designed presentation of interesting data is a matter of substance, statistics, and design.
   - Complex ideas should be communicated with clarity, precision, and efficiency.
   - Excellent graphics give the viewer the greatest number of ideas in the shortest time with least ink in the smallest space.
3. The steps for designing and giving presentations are:
   1. Define your purpose.
   2. Profile your audience.
   3. Map your structure.
   4. Add drama and impact.
   5. Rehearse until perfect.
   6. Deliver with style.
   7. Review and revise.

   There are many possible examples for each of the steps.
4. Examples of strategies to optimize the impact of PowerPoint presentations include: use both visual and verbal methods in your presentation, segment your story into bites, have a clear direction for your viewer, use visuals to persuade, less is more, and present one point per slide.

Chapter 6

Check Your Understanding 6.1

1. Strategic information systems (IS) planning is important because it ensures that the IS plans are well aligned and integrated with the organization's overall strategic plans. Information systems generally require an enormous financial investment and require considerable resources (hardware, software, network, and personnel) to implement and maintain. Too often, they fail because of poor planning and inadequate involvement from key stakeholders, including clinicians and senior leadership. Most healthcare institutions have competing IS needs, and the strategic IS planning process enables leaders to set priorities and make informed decisions based on current and future needs.

   If the IS plan is not aligned with the organization's overall strategic plan, the organization may end up not having in place the information infrastructure or systems needed to support its strategic directions or initiatives. This can lead to cost overruns, the acquisition of ineffective or inadequate systems, low staff morale, and dissatisfied patients.
2. Senior-level managers and clinicians from key areas within the healthcare enterprise, including, but not limited to, information systems, medical staff, nursing, ancillary departments, and finance, should be involved in strategic IS planning. Senior-level input is critical. Different organizations might choose different individuals to lead the effort. In some cases, the chief information officer (CIO) is the best person. In other situations, a well-respected physician or senior administrator should be the leader. Whoever is selected should be well-respected within the organization, have strong communication and project management skills, and have the power or clout to make things happen.
3. If an organization's overall strategic plan and the IS plan are not integrated or aligned, the healthcare organization runs the risk of not having in place the information infrastructure or systems needed to support its strategic directions or initiatives. This misalignment or lack of integration can lead to cost overruns, the acquisition of ineffective or inadequate systems, low staff morale, high staff turnover, and dissatisfied patients.
4. A healthcare organization should examine its current information systems before embarking on a new IS initiative. It should have a good handle on what systems are currently used, to what extent they meet the needs of end users, which ones will likely need to be replaced or upgraded, and which ones are likely to be obsolete. An organization also should examine how well existing systems support its strategic plans. If it moves forward without conducting this internal assessment of existing systems, it runs the risk of failing to identify needs or of acquiring new systems that are not needed.
5. A healthcare organization can prioritize its IS projects or needs in a number of ways. One way is to identify all proposed IS projects and hold an intensive retreat where key stakeholders rank and score each project in terms of its priority to the organization's mission and strategic goals. Another approach is to have senior leadership establish IS priorities as part of the strategic planning process.

Check Your Understanding 6.2

1. The systems development life cycle (SDLC) typically begins after the board of directors or senior administration has given the "go ahead" and approved funding for an IS project. Many institutions use the SDLC to select, implement, and evaluate healthcare information systems. IS priorities are generally established as part of the strategic IS planning process, after which the SDLC begins.
2. The four main phases of the SDLC are analysis, design, implementation, and maintenance and evaluation.
   - In the analysis phase, the organization further explores the need for a new IS, pinpoints problems with the existing system, identifies user needs, and establishes specifications. The primary focus is on the business problem, independent of any technology that might be used to implement a solution to the problem.
   - In the design phase, the organization considers how the new system will be designed or selected. Will it be built in-house, by an outside developer, or purchased from a vendor? Most organizations begin by exploring what products are currently available from vendors through submission of a request for information (RFI). Responses to the RFI are used to narrow down the list to vendors who will be invited to respond to the subsequent request for proposal (RFP). Organizations may use a variety of other methods to assess vendors and their products, including contacting current users, attending user conferences, and hosting vendor demonstrations. Informal and formal mechanisms are used to obtain key stakeholder input on the various products. This phase ends with final contract negotiations for procurement of the system.

- In the implementation phase, plans are made and executed to implement the new information system. This can be a lengthy process. Strong project management and leadership are required to coordinate the various activities. Key activities may include, but are not limited to, preparing the site, installing necessary hardware and software, preparing data tables, building interfaces, establishing a stable infrastructure, training staff, testing the new system, identifying and correcting errors, preparing documentation to support system use, implementing conversion plans, and testing backup and disaster recovery procedures.
- In the maintenance and evaluation phase, problems in the new system are addressed. IT staff must be available to correct any problems and to identify new problems before they occur. For critical patient care systems, adequate technical staff and procedures must be in place for responding to system problems at all hours of the day, including weekends. Ongoing training must take place, and methods for monitoring data quality, integrity, and security should be established. It also is important to evaluate the new system on an ongoing basis to assess the degree to which it is contributing to the institution's goals and meeting user needs.

3. The RFI is generally sent to an extensive list of vendors and is used to assess the products available and to identify those vendors who offer products likely to meet the facility's needs. It typically outlines the facility's needs in general and broad terms. Responses from the RFI are used to narrow down the list of vendors to those who will be invited to respond to the RFP. In contrast to the RFI, the RFP includes detailed specifications and guidelines that the vendor should follow in submitting a bid.
4. The HIM professional can be an active participant throughout the SDLC. In the analysis phase, he or she may be able to assist in identifying problems with the current system, assessing user needs, and determining user specifications. In the design phase, he or she may be able to assist in evaluating vendors and their products and also could provide valuable input when security and confidentiality issues are raised. Because the HIM professional has an understanding of both clinical and financial data, he or she could provide a broad perspective on how systems are integrated or how they interact with each other. In the implementation phase, the HIM professional could assume an active role in rolling out the new system through testing, training staff, and identifying problems.

Chapter 7

Check Your Understanding 7.1

1. Patient-specific data consist of data elements that describe characteristics about an individual patient, such as height, sex, principal diagnosis, and blood pressure. These data are contained in the health record of the specific patient and are identifiable as belonging to that patient.

   Aggregate data are data that have been extracted (or abstracted) from individual patient health records and collected into a database to describe characteristics about groups of patients. An example of aggregate data might be the number of men over age 50 who have had a myocardial infarction in the past year. Although identifying data may be kept in a database, aggregate data are generally presented and used without identifying individual patients.
2. The adage about comparing apples to oranges is applicable in healthcare data. To accurately collect, comb, compare, analyze, and interpret data, it is critical that data elements be defined in a common manner. For example, in studying the link between maternal risk factors and fetal death, it is important that everyone use the same definition of fetal death and the same definitions of the risk factors. If data elements are not defined in a uniform way, conclusions drawn from the data may be erroneous.
3. Healthcare data sets and core data elements provide standardized lists of data that should be collected and definitions (that have been determined by experts, usually through a process of negotiation and collaboration) of data elements. The data sets are then either mandated by a controlling agency, such as the federal government, or adopted by common consent in the healthcare industry. One example of a standardized definition is the one for principal diagnosis. The definition, as a result of a collaborative project in the 1960s, was adopted as part of the Uniform Hospital Discharge Data Set (UHDDS). It was subsequently adopted as part of a federal requirement under the prospective payment system (PPS) and is used across the United States to identify the principal diagnosis for all discharged hospital inpatients.
4. The National Center for Health Statistics (NCHS) sponsored the original conference on discharge data abstract systems that resulted in adoption of the UHDDS. It continues, along with the National Committee on Vital and Health Statistics (NCVHS) to be an active organization in developing standardized data, most notably in the area of standardized code sets such as ICD-9-CM and CPT.

5. Before the widespread use of technology, data were collected and analyzed manually within hospitals and other healthcare facilities. The data were used internally but rarely reported or compared with the data of external organizations. As long as data definitions were applied consistently within an organization, there was no need to be concerned with external data definitions. The advent of computer systems allowed healthcare facilities to use data for clinical and administrative decision making and to develop comparative databases. Regulatory agencies such as federal and state agencies and The Joint Commission began to demand sophisticated comparative data. Third-party payers and other external data organizations also developed reporting systems that required use of consistent and uniform data submission.
6. The MDS provides a structured way to organize resident information and to document problems identified in the assessment process. Documentation of a problem triggers a resident assessment protocol (RAP), which requires that the LTC facility evaluate the nature of the problem, the complications and risk factors associated with it, factors to consider in developing the care plan, and the need for referrals or further evaluation. LTC personnel use these data to outline a specific and personalized plan of care for the resident and to assess the resident's progress related to the indicated problems.
7. Data Elements for Emergency Department Systems (DEEDS) is a data set that supports the uniform collection of data in hospital-based emergency departments. The Essential Medical Data Set (EMDS) complements DEEDS and was designed to build a medical history of each individual emergency patient.
8. The common purpose for the use of data generated through the Health Plan Employer Data and Information Set (HEDIS) and ORYX is to evaluate outcomes of care by providing information about the effectiveness of interventions and treatments for specific diseases. Healthcare facilities can compare their success rates with those of other facilities to determine areas for performance improvement.
9. Clinical data provide the basis for evaluating patient progress and response to treatment. They also can provide information on the patient's long-term functional status following various treatment modalities. Because all these outcomes measurement systems focus on improving the quality of care for patients with specific disease conditions, it is critical to collect clinical data about the patient's disease, condition, treatment, functional status, survival, and so on in order to determine the efficacy and effectiveness of interventions.
10. The purpose of the National Health Information Network is to develop the technology, standards, and work processes that support electronic exchange of health information across organizational lines. The goal of NHIN is to increase patient safety, reduce medical errors, increase efficiency and effectiveness of healthcare, and contain costs through the use of information technology by exchanging critical information electronically in a secure and standard manner. A national health information network (NHIN) defines three dimensions of the infrastructure that provide a means for conceptualizing the capture, storage, communication, processing, and presentation of information for each group of information users:
    - Personal health dimension
    - Healthcare provider dimension
    - Population health dimension

Check Your Understanding 7.2

1. The transition from data sets to healthcare informatics standards has been evolutionary. The original data sets, such as the UHDDS and the UACDS, contained a list of data elements recommended or required for inclusion in a patient's record. They also contained definitions of the data elements, such as the UHDDS definition of principal diagnosis. In some cases, the data set also defined the manner in which data should be collected, such as using the postal zip code as a standard element in describing a patient's address.

    Healthcare information standards describe accepted methods for collecting, maintaining, and/or transferring healthcare data between computer systems. They are more inclusive than data sets in that they also specify hardware and/or software configurations, the mechanics of collecting and storing data, and the methods of transferring data. In addition, they are intended for computer-to-computer communication.
2. The computer revolution and the widespread use of technology have propelled the healthcare industry to develop standards that facilitate communication among providers, payers, regulators, researchers, and other users of healthcare data. Without healthcare informatics standards that set uniform definitions and link individualized platforms, data stored in specific computer systems could not be transmitted to other entities. The wealth of data stored in healthcare organization (HCO) systems would not be available for the variety of reimbursement, research, evaluation, and assessment purposes for which it is commonly used today.

3. The American Society for Testing and Materials (ASTM) Standard E1384 establishes structure and content standards for electronic health record systems. It describes data elements to be included in computerized records and gives clear definitions of these data elements. The Electronic Health Record System (EHR-S) Functional Model and Standards addresses the content and structure of an EHR. For HIM professionals charged with leading the selection or implementation of systems, knowledge of these standards is critical in supporting professional credibility.
4. The ASTM, Health Level Seven (HL7), the Accredited Standards Committee X12 (referred to as AST X12), and the creators of electronic data interchange (EDI) have been actively involved in developing healthcare informatics standards that are applicable to electronic systems for health data management.
5. The report is found at http://www.nahit.org/images/pdfs/HITTermsFinalReport_051508.pdf with the following definitions.

   Electronic medical record: An electronic record of health-related information on an individual that can be created, gathered, managed, and consulted by authorized clinicians and staff within one healthcare organization.

   Electronic health record (EHR): An electronic record of health-related information on an individual that conforms to nationally recognized interoperability standards and can be created, managed, and consulted by authorized clinicians and staff across more than one healthcare organization.

   Personal health record (PHR): An electronic record of health-related information on an individual that conforms to nationally recognized interoperability standards and that can be drawn from multiple sources while being managed, shared, and controlled by the individual.

Check Your Understanding 7.3

1. The coding of healthcare data spans a variety of software systems where value sets may include entire classifications, nomenclatures, or reference terminologies. SNOMED CT, LOINC ICD and CPT/HCPCS codes represent clinical information and are used to communicate information about individual patients as well as to perform studies related to aggregate groups of patients. To generate high-quality data, coding systems must rely on data standards that set clear and concise definitions, conventions, and processes for coding. For coded data to be comparable across institutions, both data producers and data users must adhere to standard code sets and data standards. Increasingly coded data is generated by software applications with oversight from humans rather than resulting from a manual process of coders reviewing individual records and selecting the appropriate codes.
2. Historically, healthcare consumers have received an identifier number called a medical record number at the time of admission or encounter with each healthcare provider. The result is that many consumers have health records at a variety of clinics, hospitals, emergency centers, nursing homes, and so on. These records are maintained in the facility and are not easily linked. Thus, healthcare can easily become fragmented because information about an individual is not coordinated. A unique healthcare identification number that would be used in every site of care would provide an effective means of linking the records of an individual consumer across disparate systems and would improve the quality of care.
3. Use of the Social Security number (SSN) as a unique identification number is considered inappropriate due to privacy, confidentiality, and security issues.
4. The extensible markup language (XML) was developed as a universal language to facilitate the storage and transmission of data published on the Internet. It allows each healthcare data item to be tagged with a descriptor that clearly defines and differentiates it from all other data items. Moreover, it allows data to be organized in a meaningful and searchable form and serves as an exchange standard for information transmitted over the Internet.

Chapter 8

Check Your Understanding 8.1

1. The primary purpose of patient health information is patient care and treatment.
2. Six other purposes or uses of patient health information are
   - support for clinical decision making and communication
   - documentation of services
   - evaluation of quality and efficacy of care
   - research
   - education
   - information for management as required by law and regulations

3. The Joint Commission promotes voluntary accreditation and develops and publishes standards to help improve the safety and quality of healthcare in the United States. A large portion of the Joint Commission's standards focus on information and documentation.

   The Centers for Medicare and Medicaid Services (CMS) includes requirements for records in its Conditions of Participation. The Conditions of Participation spell out requirements that facilities must meet to be part of CMS programs.

   State licensure has regulations for content of records and information that must be reported.

   The bylaws of individual facilities contain requirements and procedures that must be followed by the medical staff.
4. A longitudinal health record is a birth-to-death record that acts as an ongoing reference for and about the patient. The problem with achieving a longitudinal health record with a hybrid system is that the patient has paper records in multiple settings which cannot be linked.
5. The provider is responsible for ensuring the quality of health record documentation. Health information managers ensure that providers understand the regulations and standards for proper documentation.

Check Your Understanding 8.2

1. d Orders
2. c Physical examination
3. j Ancillary notes
4. a Care path
5. b History
6. g Advance directives
7. i Discharge summary
8. f Nursing notes
9. h Emergency record
10. e Consultations

Check Your Understanding 8.3

1. Source oriented
2. Universal chart order
3. Integrated
4. Problem oriented
5. Hospice
6. Ancillary
7. Long-term care
8. Shadow record

Check Your Understanding 8.4

1. The contract system, or outsourcing, of transcription saves money, provides for handling of overload, and can do all the work for the facility or partial work, as needed. Internal or in-house transcription provides internal control and protects confidentiality.
2. The formal education of medical transcriptionists at business schools or community colleges includes terminology, medical science, anatomy and physiology, English grammar, and other course work. Candidates for certification must also pass a certification examination.
3. Voice recognition technology will turn medical transcriptionists into editors and proofreaders.
4. The four benefits of an incentive pay plan would include the ability to reward productivity, motivate employees, reduce turnover, and provide a system for fair and equitable pay.
5. Factors to consider when determining the number of transcriptionists a facility needs include the kind and amount of information to be typed, specialties, whether the organization is a teaching facility, the presence of clinics, and additional nontranscription duties involved.

Check Your Understanding 8.5

1. Quantitative analysis is a review of the record for completeness and accuracy. For example, a quantitative analysis checks that the proper reports for the proper patient exist, that signatures are in place, and that the organization of the record is correct. Qualitative analysis is a more thorough review of the quality and accuracy of the documentation, ensuring that it meets standards and regulations.
2. Concurrent review, which may be qualitative or quantitative, is accomplished while patients are in the facility or under active treatment. Because the analysis is done in the location where the providers are, providers can easily be reminded of items that need to be accomplished to complete the chart, missing signatures that need to be obtained, and reports that need to be filed with the chart.
3. Universal chart order means leaving a paper record in the same order for permanent filing that was used in the nurse's area during the patient's hospitalization. This method saves personnel time, and allows providers quick retrieval of needed materials because the order for the record is always the same.
4. Open-record review is done concurrently with the patient's stay in the facility; closed-record review is done retrospectively, after the patient is discharged.
5. Incomplete records can hold up a facility's billing process and affect the timely reimbursement for patient care.

6. Incomplete records can be stored in an incomplete file area by either patient number or physician name. Some facilities do not have a separate incomplete file area but, instead, store incomplete records with all other records by patient number. If incomplete charts are filed by number in either a separate or permanent filing area, personnel must pull the records for the providers who wish to work on them.
7. Incomplete records are not finished; they become delinquent when they are not completed within a specified time frame, such as within 14 days after discharge. The definition of when a record becomes delinquent is set by the facility.
8. The HIM professional educates providers in proper documentation and sets up procedures within the HIM department to provide lists of what is needed to complete the record, to conduct concurrent analysis, , to flag or mark what needs to be signed, and to complete other tasks to make it easier for providers to complete records quickly.
9. Authentication proves authorship. Authentication in paper records is accomplished with a signature or initials handwritten in ink. An electronic signature is a computer password used to authenticate an electronic report or document. Autoauthentication is a process by which providers can state, in advance, that dictated reports can be considered signed automatically if not corrected within a certain period of time.
10. Concurrent review processes often include notification of outstanding signatures. Facilities have discontinued retrospective notification because signing orders and notes after the patient has been discharged has no effect on the patient care process.
11. There must be control of the design and content of forms to ensure that the forms are compatible with the paper record and with imaging and microfilming systems.
12. The four parts of the forms control process are developing forms according to guidelines, controlling printing and the use of forms, educating providers about guidelines, and preventing duplication of unneeded forms.
13. Providers wanting a new form should go through the approval process to ensure control of forms, especially as the transition to imaging or computerized systems continues. The person developing the form may be unaware of the impact the form may have on the patient care process.
14. Bar codes and bar code labels are used to allow for indexing in imaging or computer systems.

Check Your Understanding 8.6

1. In a serial numbering system, each patient receives a new number at each visit or hospitalization. In a unit numbering system, the patient is assigned a number during the first encounter and keeps it permanently.
2. Terminal-digit filing allows for a more even distribution of files within the filing area and thus a more even distribution of work. In straight numerical filing, newer records are at the end of the file and most of the file work will be concentrated in the area with the new files.
3. The main factors in determining how long to maintain a health records are patient care needs, state laws, federal regulations, accreditation standards, and facility policies.
4. The major advantage of microfilming health records is that it saves space.
5. By using optical imaging in the chart completion process, images of the chart can be accessed remotely and reviewed by simultaneous users.
6. The four primary steps in a good record retention program are conducting inventory, determining storage format and location, assigning retention periods, and destroying unnecessary records.

Check Your Understanding 8.7

1. The master patient index (MPI) is the key locator for records in a numerical filing system because it contains the patient numbers by which the records are filed.
2. Accurate information in an MPI ensures the correct identification of both the patient and the record.
3. Some of the reasons why incorrect patient information is obtained are that someone other than the patient provides the information, incorrect spelling, different names and/or initials are used for the same patient, clerical mistakes, and language differences.
4. The consequence of a patient having duplicate health record numbers is that providers will not have the proper information for patient care, resulting in duplicate testing and poor-quality healthcare.

Chapter 9

Check Your Understanding 9.1

1. F
   NAHIT distinguishes an EHR as interoperable and EMR as not. EHR is described by HL7, EHR-S FM, and CCHIT certification criteria, whereas EMR has many local meanings.
2. T
3. T
4. T
5. T
6. T
7. F
   The federal government only uses the term *EHR* as described by the CCHIT, which is a federally recognized certifying body.
8. T
9. F
   E-prescribing is a special type of medication ordering process that generates a prescription and is used only in an ambulatory/out-patient environment.
10. T

Check Your Understanding 9.2

1. A, B, C, F, G, H
2. A, B, C, E
3. A, B, F, H
4. A, B
5. A, C, D, E, H
6. D
7. A, F
8. C, E

Check Your Understanding 9.3

1. CDR—clinical data repository
2. CDS—clinical decision support
3. CDW—clinical data warehouse
4. COW—computers on wheels
5. ECRM—electronic content and records management
6. RAID—redundant array of independent [or inexpensive] disks
7. SAN—storage area network
8. **Client/server architecture:** Computer architecture where powerful computers house the applications and process data (servers), supporting local data capture and retrieval by other computers (clients)
9. **Full server redundancy:** Contingency plan where duplicate servers process EHR transactions simultaneously so that if one crashes, processing fails over to the other server
10. **Integration:** The ability to exchange data between systems without requiring an interface
11. **Interface:** A protocol that helps data to be passed from one disparate system to another
12. **Semantic interoperability:** Information exchange where not only the format of the message is the same, but the meaning of the content is the same because of using a standard vocabulary
13. **Source systems:** Systems that supply data to the EHR, such as a laboratory information system
14. **Storage management:** The people, and now software, that keep track of where data are stored, making it accessible, and managing archival and retention processes.

Check Your Understanding 9.4

1. *Minimum necessary use requirement*—documentation of treatment relationships can support more granular access controls
2. *Individual right to request restriction*—discrete data can support specific restrictions if agreed upon by the covered entity
3. *Confidentiality of PHI when transmitted over the Internet*—data encryption can protect data transmitted in an open network
4. *Emergency operation procedures*—"break the glass" technology can support more granular access controls
5. *Authentication*—stronger forms of authentication can be applied and monitored
6. E
7. D
8. Z, E, and D
9. D
10. E

Check Your Understanding 9.5

1. Change, value, leadership, workflow, ownership, different systems between hospital and practice, security and privacy, patient acceptance, learning how to use system
2. Payback period calculates the number of years it will take to begin gaining positive financial results (sometimes described as how long it takes to pay for the system). IRR is a measure that considers the time value of money, or helps compare the percent of earnings a given investment will yield.
3. *ASP* is a model where the data and applications are housed (hosted) at a vendor site. The financial agreement is similar to a lease, where monthly payments are made for the duration of the time the application is being used by the organization. *An EHR acquisition model* is one in which the organization acquires a license to use the application and implements it internally and retains its own data. Usually there is a large upfront cost and then periodic maintenance fees.

4. Executives should provide the leadership necessary to achieve EHR benefits, by demonstrating their commitment and support, establishing appropriate expectations, and fostering a culture of quality and productivity improvement.
5. Most states require the accuracy and integrity of records in electronic form to be demonstrated.

Check Your Understanding 9.6

a. 6
b. 4
c. 5
d. 2
e. 3
f. 1
g. 12
h. 8
i. 11
j. 10
k. 7
l. 9

Chapter 10

Check Your Understanding 10.1

1. The four sources of law governing Americans are common law, statutory law, constitutional law, and administrative law.
2. Cases typically heard in federal courts include federal crimes such as racketeering and bank robbery, constitutional issues, and civil actions in which the parties do not live in the same state.
3. The court of last resort is the U.S. Supreme Court.
4. The two most common types of civil cases in healthcare are torts and contracts.
5. In a court, the *trier of fact* is the judge or the jury.
6. The result of a trial is called a *verdict* or *judgment.*
7. Crimes that are wrongful acts against public health, safety, and welfare are covered by *criminal laws.*
8. The *prosecutor* in a criminal case is the attorney who, on behalf of the government, prosecutes an accused for a crime; the defendant is the person or group accused in a criminal or civil court action. The prosecutor has the burden of proving the charges against the defendant.
9. The *defendant* may plead guilty and be sentenced to probation or imprisonment and/or pay a fine or may plead not guilty, which results in a trial. The trial can result in a verdict of either guilty or not guilty. If found not guilty, the charges are dismissed. If found guilty, the defendant will be sentenced to probation or imprisonment and/or be required to pay a fine. The defendant has the right to appeal.
10. The three categories of torts are *negligent torts*, *intentional torts*, and *product liability*. Most healthcare cases arise from negligent torts.
11. *Negligence* results when a person does not act as a reasonably prudent person would act under the same circumstances. A negligent tort may result from a person committing an act or failing to act as a reasonably prudent person would or would not in the given circumstances. Typically, negligence is careless conduct that is outside the generally accepted standard of care.
12. The four elements of negligence are the duty to use due care, the breach of the duty to use due care, the injury (harm) that occurred, and the conduct that caused the injury/harm.
13. *False imprisonment* might occur in a hospital through the inappropriate use of restraints or the refusal to allow a patient to leave.
14. *Truth and privilege* are the available defenses to a defendant accused of defamation of character.
15. Healthcare providers may be held liable for a negligent disregard for patients' rights to privacy.
16. A *contract* is an agreement, whether written or oral, that, in most cases, is legally enforceable through the U.S. legal system.
17. A *contract case* arises when there is a breach of an agreement. This means that one party charges the other with failing to meet one or more of the obligations in the contract.

Check Your Understanding 10.2

1. The two sections of a health record are demographic and clinical. The *demographic section* includes, among other items, the patient's name, sex, age, insurance information, and the person to contact in case of emergency. The *clinical section* contains the patient's complaint, history of present illness, medical history, family history, social history, continuing documentation of ongoing medical care, report of diagnostic tests, x-ray reports, surgery and other procedure reports, consultant reports, nursing documentation, various graphs, and the final diagnoses.
2. Licensure is mandatory and government sponsored; accreditation is voluntary and not government sponsored.
3. National patient information confidentiality standards in the Health Insurance Portability and Accountability Act of 1996 (HIPAA) were promulgated in December 2000.

4. A plaintiff may make a claim of unauthorized disclosure of health information against a hospital (because of the breach of its duty to maintain confidentiality of information) on the basis of any job-related acts of the hospital's employees or agents and the consequences of any unauthorized disclosure, whether by employees, agents, or medical staff members.
5. The holding regarding privacy issued by the court in *Griswold v. Connecticut* was that the right to privacy limits governmental authority to regulate contraception, abortion, and other decisions affecting reproduction.
6. Federal/state laws; administrative policy; medical practice; varied purposes
7. Privacy, transactions and code sets, and security
8. Privacy Act of 1974, Freedom of Information Act, Controlled Substance Act, Medicare Conditions of Participation for Hospitals, Conditions of Participation for Clinics, Rehabilitation Agencies, and Public Health Agencies as Providers of Outpatient Physical Therapy and Speech-Language Pathology, Conditions of Participation for Home Health Agencies, Confidentiality of Alcohol and Drug Abuse Patient Records.

Check Your Understanding 10.3

1. Because they are the provider's business records, the healthcare provider (physician or hospital) that maintains the health records owns them.
2. The patient
3. The primary focus is how and for what purpose patient health information can be used.
4. Health plans, clearinghouses, and healthcare providers
5. No. The standard HIPAA rule is that it preempts state law if it is contrary to that state law except if one or more of the following conditions are met:
   - The Secretary of HHS determines that the provision of state law is necessary
   - To prevent fraud and abuse related to providing or paying for healthcare
   - To ensure appropriate state regulation of insurance and health plans
   - For state reporting on healthcare delivery or costs
   - For public health, safety, or welfare if the Secretary determines that the intrusion into privacy is warranted when balanced against this need
   - For the purpose of regulating the manufacture, registration, distribution, dispensing, or other control of controlled substances
   - The provision of state law relates to the privacy of individually-identifiable health information and is more stringent that a provision in the HIPAA privacy rule
   - The provision of state law provides for reporting disease or injury, child abuse, birth, or death, or for the conduct of public health surveillance, investigation, or intervention
   - The provision of state law requires a health plan to report, or to provide access to, information for management audits, financial audits, program monitoring and evaluation, or licensure or certification of facilities or individuals
6. How covered entities may use and disclose PHI; the patient's rights regarding the covered entities' uses and disclosures; and the covered entities' obligations for protecting the patient's PHI
7. At the time of the first service delivery, including service delivered electronically. In emergency situations, covered entities providing care must provide the notice as soon as practicable after the emergency treatment situation is resolved. The covered entity is to make a good faith effort to obtain the patient's written acknowledgement of receipt of the notice. This requirement also is delayed until practicable in emergency treatment situations. If receipt is not obtained for any reason, including the patient refusing to provide the acknowledgement, the covered entity is required to document its good faith efforts and the reason why the acknowledgement was not obtained.
8. Oral, paper, and electronic
9. Oral information; psychotherapy notes; information compiled in anticipation of, or for use in, a civil, criminal, or administrative action or proceeding; PHI the covered entity maintains that is subject to or exempted from the Clinical Laboratory Improvements Amends (CLIA) of 1988
10. The most striking feature of the privacy rule is the individual's right to obtain an accounting of disclosures of his or her health information.
11. The types of disclosures that do not need to be included in an accounting are:
    - To carry out treatment, payment, and healthcare operations
    - To the patient who is the subject of the PHI
    - Those that are incidental
    - Those pursuant to patient authorization
    - For facility directory or to family or caregivers
    - For national security or intelligence purposes
    - To correctional institutions or law enforcement under specific circumstances
    - PHI included in a limited data set
    - Those made prior to the compliance date for the covered entity
12. The patient's request can be denied without giving the patient an opportunity to request review of the denial. In addition to the PHI types noted earlier to which the patient is not given access, access can be denied:

    If the covered entity is a correctional institution or a covered entity acting under the direction of the correctional institution and such access would jeopardize the health, safety, security, custody, or rehabilitation of the individual or others

When PHI was created or obtained during research that includes treatment—the access is suspended while the research is in progress as long as the patient agreed to the access denial when consenting to participate in the research and the patient had to have been advised that the right would be reinstated upon completion of the research

If the PHI is contained in records subject to the Privacy Act of 1974 and is also not available for access under the privacy act

13. According to HIPAA the patient or his or her legal representative may authorize the release of information.
14. The circumstances listed in the Privacy Rule under which a facility may deny a patient's request for access to his or her own health information without providing the patient the opportunity to have the denial reviewed are when the confidential medical information is excluded from the right of access and was obtained from someone other than a healthcare provider under a promise of confidentiality.
15. Unless otherwise authorized by the patient, the organization may only release information to the news media that states the patient's general condition in terms of good, fair, or poor. No information may be released that reveals the patient's diagnosis. Furthermore, information may only be released on those patients that the news media identify by name.
16. The provider may release information to an employer when:
    - The care provider is a member of the employer's workforce or provides healthcare to the patient at the employer's request.
    - The care relates to a medical surveillance of the workplace or to a work-related illness or injury.
    - The information that is disclosed consists of findings concerning a work-related illness or injury or a workplace-related medical surveillance.
    - The employer needs the findings to comply with its obligations under federal and state laws.
17. Although the release of certain medical information is statutorily mandated under certain circumstances, a court may view the release to the wrong agency as a breach of confidentiality.

Check Your Understanding 10.4

1. No, the patient only must be given an opportunity to object (opt out) of the hospital's directory.
2. Only members of the clergy may receive this information. They may receive the information even if they do not ask for the patient by name.
3. When a patient is incapacitated or in an emergency situation and cannot object to being included in the facility's directory, the covered provider may disclose the information as noted if the disclosure is:

   In the patient's best interest as determined by the provider using professional judgment
4. Disclosure to family, friends, or other caregivers identified by the patient relevant to their involvement with the patient's care. The requirement for patient authorization typically extends to a request by a patient's family members, including the spouse. However, healthcare providers may discuss general information about the patient's condition with family members without authorization unless the patient has instructed otherwise. If the patient is incapacitated, the physician and other caregivers may discuss health information and treatment plans with the next of kin or the patient's representative; however, that is defined by a given state, to the extent necessary to make medical decisions on the incapacitated patient's behalf. The privacy rule permits the hospital to disclose to a family member, other relative, close personal friend, or any person identified by the patient health information directly relevant to that person's involvement in the patient's care or payment for healthcare [Section 164.510(b)(1)(i)].

Check Your Understanding 10.5

1. Yes. Except as permitted or required under the HIPAA Privacy Rule, a valid patient authorization is required for the use or disclosure of PHI [45 CFR §164.508(a)(1)].
2. The authorization must include a specific description of the information to be used or disclosed. In addition, the name or other specific identification of the person(s) authorized to request and receive the requested information must be included. Further, the authorization must include the expiration date or event that relates to the individual or the purpose of the use or disclosure. The patient must be given the right to revoke the authorization in writing, the exceptions to this right, and a description of how he or she may revoke it. The authorization also must advise the patient that information released pursuant to the authorization may be subject to redisclosure by the recipient and may no longer be protected. Finally, the patient must sign and date the authorization.

   If a personal representative signs the authorization, a description of his or her authority to act for the patient must be included in the authorization form. Further, the form must be written in plain language. The patient must be advised that the hospital will not condition treatment, payment, enrollment in a health plan, or eligibility for benefits on his or her providing authorization for the requested information. The authorization must include a description of each purpose for the requested information. Further, the authorization must contain a statement to the effect that the patient may inspect or copy the information and may refuse to sign it. The hospital must disclose to the patient whether the release of the information will result in direct or indirect remuneration to the facility from a third party. If there is remuneration, the authorization must state that such remuneration will result. Also, the patient is entitled to a copy of the signed authorization.

3. Authorizations for uses and disclosures of health information created for research that includes treatment of the patient must contain additional elements. For example, there must be a description of the extent to which the information will be used or disclosed to carry out treatment, payment, or healthcare operations. The authorization must further include a description of any health information that could be disclosed but will not be disclosed for facility directories or public health purposes. However, the facility may not include a limitation affecting its right to release information required by law.
4. For an unemancipated minor, the legal representative is the parent, guardian, or other person acting in loco parentis.
5. The two categories of uses and disclosures that the HIPAA Privacy Rule specifically refers to as requiring patient authorization are psychotherapy notes and marketing.

Check Your Understanding 10.6

1. Treatment, payment and healthcare operations
2. No, patients and patient representatives have access to PHI without signing an authorization form (45 CFR §164.524).
3. Yes, because this is for continuation of care. The privacy rule, in sections 164.501 and 164.506(c)(1) and (2), permits the facility and healthcare providers to use or disclose confidential information for:
   - Providing, coordinating or managing healthcare and related services by one or more healthcare providers, including with a third party
   - Consulting between healthcare providers relating to a patient
   - Referring a patient for healthcare from one healthcare provider to another
4. Treatment, payment and healthcare operations; patient or patient representative; as required by law; public health activities; abuse, neglect, or domestic violence reporting; health oversight; judicial and administrative proceedings; Law enforcement; coroners, medical examiners, funeral directors; organ procurement organization; research; to avert a serious threat to health and safety; specialized governmental functions; fundraising; marketing exception
5. Common types of information reported for public health purposes include vital statistics (births and deaths); communicable diseases; child, adult, and elder abuse; wounds, such as from stabs and gunshots; and conditions affecting the ability to drive.
6. If the violation is committed with the intent to sell, transfer, or use PHI for commercial advantage, personal gain or malicious harm, the fine is not more than $250,000, imprisonment for not more than 10 years, or both.

Check Your Understanding 10.7

1. The physician–patient privilege may be created when a physician contracts to care for a particular group of people and a person from that group seeks care, when a physician enters into an express contract with a patient or his or her representative for care, and when a physician engages in conduct from which a patient can imply that a contract exists.
2. The care provider can be released from the privilege through words or actions. For example, a patient who places his or her treatment at issue in a trial cannot continue to claim a privilege to protect the information.
3. Both the HHS (for Medicare) and the state Medicaid agency may request information from the health record to support the healthcare provider's bill submitted for payment and for investigative purposes such as pursuant to the federal fraud and abuse statutes.
   Other examples could include:
   - food and drug administration/public health or legal authorities charged with preventing or controlling disease, injury or disability
   - correctional institutions
   - workers compensation agents
   - organ and tissue donation organizations
   - military command authorities
   - health oversight agencies
   - funeral directors, coroners and medical directors
   - national security and intelligence agencies
   - protective services for the President and others
   - to advert a serious threat to health or safety
   - lawsuits and disputes (response to a court or administrative order)
4. *Metadata* is data about the data. It includes data about the content, context, location and other characteristics of data stored in a system. A subpoena may specifically include a request for information such as time stamps for accesses to information, creating records, and changing records. Further, a subpoena for "any and all information" goes beyond what would be disclosed in the paper record environment.

5. E-discovery will have a significant impact on disclosure processes, retention and destruction, spoliation, and business continuity planning. During pretrial conferences, attorneys for the parties meet to reach agreement on matters related to discovery, such as document discovery. The HIM professional will need to work with the organization's attorney prior to a pretrial conference to identify relevant information and its availability. Typically the HIM professional knows which departments feed clinical information into the legal health record. Therefore, they must also become familiar with what systems are used by these different departments to assist legal counsel in determining what information is relevant to the subpoena and whether it is available.
6. The custodian of records, typically the health information manager, may be called as a witness to identify the record as the one subpoenaed. He or she also may be called to testify as to policies and procedures relevant to the following:
    - Creation of the record
    - Maintenance of the record to prevent it from being altered
    - Maintenance of the record to prevent it from being accessed without proper authorization

Check Your Understanding 10.8

1. For QI purposes to ensure following policies and procedures; to measure employee performance; as a basis to request additional staff; as part of the annual evaluation process.
2.
    - turnaround time for requests
    - number of requests processed per employee per month
    - number of subpoenas processed per employee per month
3. Education that reinforces the organization's policies and the importance of following those policies. Staff also must be provided with and express an understanding of the expectations for them to follow ROI policies and procedures.
4. Yes, as the investigation relates to an alleged violation of HIPAA regulation by ROI staff. The ROI manager works with the Privacy Officer in such investigations pursuant to the organization's investigation policy. The investigation process may include the HR department to impose disciplinary action.

Check Your Understanding 10.9

1. The process of granting a physician membership in the hospital medical staff is called *credentialing*.
2. Typically, the documentation reviewed for the initial medical staff membership appointment includes medical education, including medical school, residencies, postdoctoral studies, and fellowships; license to practice; medical practice experience; and a search of the National Practitioner Data Bank (NPDB) regarding judgments and settlements above a specific amount in medical malpractice cases.
3. To grant specific privileges, the medical staff may require the physician to obtain a consultation before performing specific procedures; to have operative procedures proctored by an observing or assisting physician; or to have certification beyond a license, such as board certification in a particular medical specialty.
4. At reappointment, the medical staff may review, among other factors, the physician's blood usage patterns, lengths of stay, infection rates, complications and complication rates, health record documentation, closed malpractice claims, and the outcomes of focused studies. Physicians who have gained additional training since the last appointment may seek privileges not previously held. For any new privileges requested, the physician may be required to submit to consultation or proctoring.
5. Third parties such as the Joint Commission and state and federal regulatory organizations may review credentialing files as part of their accrediting and licensing functions. Some states statutorily protect credentialing files from discovery in legal proceedings. However, when a plaintiff alleges negligent credentialing against a hospital, there is a question as to whether the protection will hold up.
6. Concurrent review consists of evaluating medical care as it is being given; retrospective review occurs after patient discharge.
7. Quality improvement and concurrent review files should be kept confidential because these review activities involve collecting outcomes and performance data on physician performance and may have an impact on continued medical staff membership.

Check Your Understanding 10.10

1. An *incident* is an occurrence that is inconsistent with the standard of care.
2. The attorney–client privilege doctrine and the attorney work product doctrine.
3. It is created and kept in the normal course of business; made at or near the time of the matter recorded; and made by a person within the business with knowledge of the events recorded.
4. *Authenticity* of the record means "it is what it purports to be". Authenticity relates both to the information being created and the system being used to create and store that information. As to the system, reliability includes such features as user access controls, system security, access tracking and auditing capabilities, and operational stability (dependability and availability). These features are particularly important because the general concern is that electronically stored information can be easily changed. Methods to verify the author of entries made in the health record is referred to as *authentication*. In paper records authentication is most often accomplished by a handwritten signature and initials, both in ink. Authentication in an EHR can include electronic or digital signatures and computer keys. The auto-authentication process can be used. This process states that an entry is considered authenticated if the author fails to review and affirmatively approve or disapprove the entry within a specified time period.
5. The purpose of the health record; state and federal laws, regulations, and standards defining health record content; internal documents; risks the organization faces if its health record does not meet business record or legal health record requirements or the rules of evidence especially if it is an EHR.
6. Incident reports should be protected because they contain facts about occurrences; therefore, hospitals strive to protect their confidentiality. Incident reports may be protected under statutes protecting quality improvement (QI) studies and activities or attorney–client privilege. Protection under the latter doctrine may be based on whether the primary purpose of the incident report is to provide information to the hospital's attorney or liability insurer.
7. The health information manager and the risk manager work as a team. The risk manager depends on the health information manager to alert him or her to potentially compensable events. These are events that could result in a settlement or judgment against the facility, further resulting in a payout of funds whether through insurance or from facility internal funds. The health information manager also can advise the risk manager when an attorney requests a copy of a health record. The risk manager then can review records identified by any of these methods to determine whether further action is necessary from a risk management standpoint.

Chapter 11

Check Your Understanding 11.1

1. b Employer
2. c Public interest
3. a Patients and the healthcare team
4. d Oneself and one's peers and professional associations
5. d Oneself and one's peers and professional associations
6. a Patients and the healthcare team
7. d Oneself and one's peers and professional associations
8. b Employer
9. d Oneself and one's peers and professional associations
10. b Employer
11. a Patients and the healthcare team
12. d Oneself and one's peers and professional associations
13. a Patients and the healthcare team
14. a Patients and the healthcare team
15. d Oneself and one's peers and professional associations
16. b Employer
17. c Public interest
18. c Public interest
19. a Patients and the healthcare team
20. d Oneself and one's peers and professional associations
21. b Employer
22. a Patients and the healthcare team

Check Your Understanding 11.2

1. e
2. b
3. d
4. a
5. f
6. g
7. c

Check Your Understanding 11.3

1. e Self-determination
2. d Promote good
3. g Do no harm
4. h Fairness in applying rules
5. a Right or wrong
6. b Reasoned discourse
7. c Right to be let alone
8. f Healthcare communication
9. j Electronic protection of information
10. i Establishes privacy and security standards

Chapter 12

Check Your Understanding 12.1

1. A *primary data source* is created by the healthcare professionals providing the care. The medical record is considered a primary data source. A *secondary data source* is made up of data taken from a primary data source and put in a different format, such as a registry.
2. *Patient-identifiable data* are facts that can be connected with a particular patient, such as a single laboratory value. *Aggregate data* are data that have been grouped together, such as the number of discharges for a month. There is no way to determine information about a particular patient from these groups of data.
3. Secondary sources are created to put the information from the primary record into a format that is easier to query and manipulate. For example, it is difficult and time consuming for a cancer registrar to determine the number of patients with each type of cancer by looking at individual records. A database, which is a secondary record, can be queried to provide this information in a report from the secondary data that has been entered, thus speeding up the process.
4. An *internal user* is someone within the facility or enterprise, such as a cancer committee. An external user is someone or some agency outside of the facility or enterprise, such as the state vital records office.

Check Your Understanding 12.2

1. HIM departments use facility-specific indexes to locate data as requested by internal and external users. The operation index, for example, could be used to locate medical records for patients with a specific operation for a quality assessment study. It could also be used to provide information to external users. For example, residents often must provide data on the types of operations they have performed during their residency to the appropriate board for certification in their specialty.
2. The master population index allows users to locate patients by name and to find out their medical record number. It contains demographic information about the patient such as medical record number, name, address, dates of previous hospital admissions, name of attending physician, and date of birth.
3. Disease and operations indexes allow users to find medical records of patients with a particular diagnosis or operation. At minimum, they include the patient's health record number and disease/operation codes. They may also include other data such as physician or surgeon and date of discharge or operation as determined by the facility.
4. The purpose of the physician index is to locate medical records of patients that have been treated by a particular physician. It must, at a minimum, include the physician's name or a code number assigned and the patient's name and/or health record number.

Check Your Understanding 12.3

1. Registries are collections of secondary data related to a patient's specific diagnosis, condition, or procedure. They are created and maintained to provide specific information from the medical record in an easily retrievable form.
2. Case definition refers to the process used by each registry to define the cases to be included in it. Case finding is a method used to identify patients who have been seen and/or treated in the facility for the particular disease or condition of interest to the registry.
3. A facility-based registry contains data used to provide information for the improved understanding of a specific disease or condition within a particular facility such as a hospital. A population-based registry contains data showing trends and changes in the incidence of the disease or condition within a geographic area covered by the registry, such as a city or state.
4.
   - Cancer registry
     - *Case definition:* the types of cancer to be included in the registry
     - *Case finding:* HIM discharge processing, disease index, review of cancer-related reports such as pathology, and lists of patients receiving cancer-related services such as radiation therapy
   - Trauma Registry
     - *Case definition:* trauma registries usually include cases with diagnosis codes for traumas such as fractures, burns, and open wounds.
     - *Case finding:* disease index or deaths in services with frequent trauma diagnoses
   - Birth Defects Registry
     - *Case definition:* varies; may include cases found within the first year of life or cases within the first five years of life; may include stillborn

- *Case finding:* disease index; labor and delivery logs; pathology and autopsy reports; ultrasound reports; cytogenetic reports; information from rehabilitation centers and children's hospitals; and birth, death, and fetal death certificates
- Diabetes registry
  - *Case definition:* may limit by type of diabetes or age of patient
  - *Case finding:* review of medical records, ICD-9-CM diagnosis codes, medication lists, identification by physician, and information from health plans
- Implant registry
  - *Case definition:* may include all implants or only certain types such as cochlear implants
  - *Case finding:* identifies patients who have the implant of interest to the registry
- Transplant registry
  - *Case definition/case finding:* physicians identify patients needing transplants
- Immunization registry
  - *Case definition:* all children in a population area or only those seen in public clinics are included; may include adults for immunization such as pneumonia and influenza vaccines
  - *Case finding:* electronic entry at birth from electronic vital records system or manual entry at birth from birth and death certificates

5.
- Cancer registry: For a facility-based registry, patient records are reviewed to collect demographic information, type and site of the cancer, diagnostic methodologies, and treatment methodologies. For a population-based registry, information is submitted by facilities within the population covered
- Trauma registry: Abstracting data from the medical record including demographic information, hospital care provided, status of patient at the time of admission, diagnosis and procedure codes, abbreviated injury scale, and injury severity score.
- Birth defects registry: Abstracting information from the sources used in case finding. Abstracted information includes demographic information, diagnosis codes, birth weight, status at birth, autopsy, cytogenetic reports, mother's and father's use of alcohol and drugs, and family history of birth defects.
- Diabetes registry: Abstracting information from physician office or clinic record including demographic information and laboratory values.
- Implant registry: Abstracting information from the health record including demographic data and data required by the FDA.
- Transplant registry
  - *Recipient information:* demographic data, patient diagnosis, medical urgency, functional status, life support status, and previous transplants
  - *Donor information/living donor:* relationship to recipient, clinical information, organ recovery information, and histocompatibility
  - *Donor information/deceased donor:* cause and circumstances of death, organ procurement and consent process, medications taken, and other donor history
- Immunization registry: Data is abstracted from vital records. The abstracted data includes core immunization data elements from the Centers for Disease Control and the National Vaccine Advisory Committee

6.
- Cancer registry: Annual report including aggregate data on the cancer cases for the year
- Trauma registry: Sometimes an annual report or performance improvement reports such as delays in abdominal surgery
- Birth defects registry: No standard reports
- Diabetes registry: Laboratory monitoring, patient follow up, incidence of diabetes
- Implant registry: Reporting to the FDA and the manufacturer
- Transplant registry: Information on donors and recipients as well as survival rates, length of time on the waiting list for an organ, and death rates
- Immunization registry: Immunization rates are automatically reported to schools

7.
- Cancer registry: Review of medical records for treatment in the last year, contacting the patient's physician, contacting the patient, newspaper obituaries, and/or Internet sites
- Trauma registry: Follow up is done by some, but not all, registries; emphasis is on patient's quality of life
- Birth defects registry: Not routinely done
- Diabetes registry: Done to ensure appropriate continued care
- Implant registry: Follow up is done to assess performance of the implant over time
- Transplant registry: At intervals throughout the first year and then annually
  - *Living donor:* complications of the procedure, length of hospital stay
  - *Recipient:* status at time of follow up, functional status, graft status, treatment
- Immunization registry: Follow up reminders that immunizations are due, by postcard, telephone call, or autodialed call

8. • Cancer registry: American College of Surgeons, North American Association of Central Cancer Registries, and Centers for Disease Control
   • Trauma registry: American College of Surgeons
   • Birth defects registry: None
   • Diabetes registry: None
   • Implant registry: None
   • Transplant registry: None
   • Immunization registry: Centers for Disease Control (CDC)
9. • Cancer registry: On-the-job training, seminars, and/or cancer registry program in a college; AHIMA's online Cancer Registry program
   • Trauma registry: Varies; may use RHITs, RHIAs, RNs, LPNs, EMTs or other health professionals or workshops and on-the-job training
   • Birth defects registry: None specified
   • Diabetes registry: None specified
   • Implant registry: None specified
   • Transplant registry: None specified
   • Immunization registry: None specified
10. • Cancer registry: Certified Cancer Registrar (CTR) is provided by the National Cancer Registrar's Association and requires passing an examination provided by the National Board for Certification of Registrars
   • Trauma registry: Certified Specialist Trauma Registry (CSTR) is provided through the American Trauma Society Registrar Certification Board. Certification requires passing an examination.
   • Birth defects registry: None
   • Diabetes registry: None
   • Implant registry: None
   • Transplant registry: None
   • Immunization registry: Proposed for Centers for Disease Control

Check Your Understanding 12.4

1. The MEDPAR file provides data on Medicare patients including demographic patient data, provider data, Medicare coverage, total charges, charges by service, diagnosis and procedure codes, and DRGs.
2. The limitation of MEDPAR data is that it only includes data on Medicare cases.
3. The National Practitioner Data Bank was developed to make information on malpractice claims, sanctions by Boards of Medical Examiners, and professional review actions available among all states. Before, a physician who had incurred such actions could move to another state and practice without anyone in the new state knowing his or her background. The Health Care Quality Improvement Act of 1986 mandated the creation of the NPDB.

   The Healthcare Integrity and Protection Data Bank was developed because there was no central repository for information on healthcare fraud and abuse. The Data Bank was mandated by the Health Insurance Portability and Accountability Act of 1996.
4. Information that must be reported to the National Practitioner Data Bank includes practitioner information, the reporting entity, and the judgment or settlement against the practitioner. Information that must be reported to the Healthcare Integrity and Protection Data Bank includes final adverse actions resulting in unnecessary costs to the program, improper payment, services that fail to meet professionally-recognized standards of care or that are medically unnecessary, adverse patient outcomes, failure to provided covered or needed care in violation or contraction arrangements, and delays in diagnosis or treatment.
   There may be an overlap between the two data banks, so one report is made to both, and the information is then sorted to the appropriate data bank.
5. Healthcare organizations use the National Practitioner Data Bank in the credentialing process. They must query the data bank when the physician initially applies for medical staff privileges and every two years thereafter.

   Federal and state government agencies and health plans may access the Healthcare Integrity and Protection Data Bank. Practitioners, providers, and suppliers may only query about themselves.
6. Health information managers contribute to public health databases by providing accurate information from the medical records of patients in their facilities.
7. The databases using data from health records include the National Hospital Discharge Survey, the National Ambulatory Medical Care Survey, the National Survey of Ambulatory Surgery, the National Nursing Home Survey, and the National Hospital Ambulatory Medical Care Survey.
8. A clinical trial is a research project in which new treatments and tests are investigated to see whether they are safe and effective.

   Clinical trial databases are developed to help physicians and patients find clinical trials.

   The Food and Drug Administration Modernization Act of 1997 mandated the development of a national clinical trials database.
9. The source of data for the Healthcare Cost and Utilization Project is data collected at the state level on claims data from the UB-04 or discharge abstracted data including the UHDDS reported by individual hospitals and, in some cases, ambulatory care centers.
10. The UMLS is of interest to health information managers because it includes data from the ICD, CPT and HCPCS coding systems.
11. HIEs have been developed to provide longitudinal health information at the point of care.
12. HIEs include patient-specific data for patient care.

Check Your Understanding 12.5

1. The factors to be considered in determining the quality of data are its validity, reliability, completeness, and timeliness.
2. Errors in data that are used to make decisions concerning new treatment methods, healthcare policy, and physician credentialing and privileging may cause serious problems.
3. One method used to check validity in secondary data is the computer edit. Reliability may be checked through the interrater reliability method of having more than one person abstract data for the same case. Uniform terminology also improves reliability by ensuring that the same definitions are used for all concepts.
4. Security refers to controlling access to all health information. Confidentiality refers to efforts to guarantee the privacy of personal health information.
5. Methods used to control access to a health information system include the establishment of passwords, role-based access, control of physical access to hardware and printouts, and encryption.
6. Factors to consider in developing a physical security program include placing computers in areas that are not available to unauthorized people, ensuring that reports and printouts are not left where they can be seen, and encrypting sensitive data. Sensitive data, such as HIV status, should be encrypted.
7. Methods include employee training in confidentiality and the development of policies and procedures concerning who may access data.
8. Increased use of automated data entry is a current trend in the collection of secondary data. The development of the electronic patient record will ensure that less data will have to be abstracted from the medical record into secondary records. Emphasis by stakeholders on issues such as ownership of secondary data has increased. The HIM stewardship role is becoming increasingly important in the area of secondary data.
9. Registries and secondary data sources maintained by covered entities are covered by HIPAA.
10. The Notice of Privacy Practices given to each patient on the initial encounter notifies the patient about data that may be included in secondary data sources and released to outside entities.
11. *Deidentification* is the process of removing patient-identifiable data from a data source. Under HIPAA, this may be accomplished by stripping off certain elements to ensure that the patient's information has been deidentified or using statistical and scientific principles and methods to minimize the risk that the information might be used to identify an individual.

Chapter 13

Check Your Understanding 13.1

1. A classification is a system that arranges similar diseases and procedures and organizes related entities for easy retrieval. An example of a classification system is ICD-10-CM. A nomenclature is a system of names or terms used for a particular discipline created to facilitate communication by eliminating ambiguity. An example of a nomenclature is the Diagnostic Statistical Manual (DSM).
2. A terminology differs from classifications and nomenclatures in that classifications and nomenclatures categorize and aggregate content and a terminology represents the entire content for a particular subject area or discipline.

Check Your Understanding 13.2

1. The original purpose of ICD-9-CM was to report morbidity data.
2. The four essential characteristics of ICD-10-PCS are:
   - **Completeness:** Content coverage is adequate for all known procedures
   - **Expandability:** The structure allows incorporation of new procedures as unique codes
   - **Standardized terminology:** Definitions for all the terms used in ICD-10-PCS are specific and consistent
   - **Multiaxial structure:** Each code character has the same meaning within the specific procedure section and across procedure sections to the extent possible
3. The primary function of CPT is to report physician services.
4. The topography code in ICD-O describes the site of origin of the neoplasm.

Check Your Understanding 13.3

1. Semantic interoperability is the ability to exchange data across electronic systems in which the meaning of the information being shared is understood.
2. a) A clinical terminology that would be a good candidate to represent laboratory data is LOINC.
   b) A clinical terminology that would be a good candidate to represent nursing documentation is the CCC.
   c) A clinical terminology that would be a good candidate to represent problem list information is SNOMED-CT.
3. In SNOMED-CT, a concept is the most granular unit of representation. A concept is a single clinical meaning indentified by a unique numeric identifier. Relationships identify how concepts within SNOMED-CT are linked to one another.

Check Your Understanding 13.4

1. Permanence is important in clinical terminologies to preserve the longitudinal uniformity of a clinical terminology or classification.
2. Another name for context representation is grammar, which means that the meaning of a term is more than just the term because some terms have multiple meanings. To fully understand a term, all of the modifying words and terms related to the original term must be considered.
3. Mapping is the process where content in one code set (classification/terminology) is linked to content in another code set that has the same or substantially similar meaning. Mapping allows data captured with one code set to be used for other purposes.

Chapter 14

Check Your Understanding 14.1

1. Until the late 1800s, Americans paid their own healthcare expenses or, if they did not have means to pay for care, they received charity care or no care at all. During the early part of the 20th century, both legislative and private efforts were initiated to cover the cost of healthcare. These efforts resulted in the development of private insurance systems for those who could afford it and public welfare for those who could not. Medicare and Medicaid, the first federal program developed specifically to provide funding for healthcare costs for specific populations, were instituted in 1965.
2. As a result of spiraling demand for healthcare services throughout the 1970s and early 1980s, the cost of funding Medicare and Medicaid services skyrocketed. The federal government developed the first prospective payment system for hospital inpatients in 1983 in order to control and manage the costs of the Medicare and Medicaid programs. Since that time prospective payment methodologies have been developed for other segments of healthcare such as long-term care, home healthcare, and ambulatory services.
3. According to table 14.1, percentage change in health insurance coverage status from 2005 to 2006 is –0.5%.
4. The Centers for Medicare and Medicaid Services (CMS) administers the Medicare and Medicaid programs. This agency was known as the Health Care Financing Administration (HCFA) until 2001.
5. To counteract labor shortages during World War II, employers added health insurance coverage for hospital, surgical, and medical expenses to their accident and life insurance plans as a way of attracting workers.

Check Your Understanding 14.2

1. Fee-for-service reimbursement occurs when a patient pays cash for services on a retrospective basis (after the service has been rendered). Until the advent of managed care, capitation, and other prospective payment systems in the 1980s, most private insurance plans and government-sponsored programs also reimbursed providers on a retrospective fee-for-service basis. Fee-for-service is rarely used today because the government and most private insurers now compensate providers according to predetermined discounted rates rather than on a fee-for-service basis.
2. Private commercial insurance plans are financed through the payment of a pre-established monthly premium by each individual or family covered under the plan. The insurance company sets aside the premiums from all the people covered under the plan into a special fund, which is then used to pay claims for medical care.
3. When a claim for medical care is submitted to an insurance company, the company reviews the claim to determine whether the services described in the claim are covered by the patient's policy. The company also reviews the documentation provided with the claim to ensure that the services provided were medically necessary. If the claim is approved, payment is then made to either the provider or the policyholder.
4. Many employers have developed self-insurance programs to cover healthcare services for their workforce. Employer-based self-insurance programs often enter into administrative services only (ASO) contracts with private insurers. The employer funds the plan and the private insurer administers the self-insurance plan on behalf of the employer.
5. Medicaid pays for healthcare services for financially needy individuals.
6. TRICARE is a healthcare program for active-duty members of the military and other qualified family members, TRICARE-eligible retirees and their family members, and eligible survivors of members of the uniformed services. CHAMPVA is an acronym for the Civilian Health and Medical Program–Veterans Administration. It is a healthcare program for dependents and survivors of permanently and totally disabled veterans, survivors of veterans who died from service-related conditions, and survivors of military personnel who died in the line of duty.
7. Medicare Part B is a voluntary healthcare program in which a Medicare beneficiary pays a monthly premium in order to extend or supplement Medicare coverage for services not covered by Medicare Part A such as physician services, emergency and outpatient services, laboratory and x-ray services, physical and occupational therapy services, and durable medical equipment.

8. Medicare Advantage, often referred to as Medigap insurance, was established by the Balanced Budget Act of 1997 to expand the options for participation in private healthcare plans.
9. Medigap is private health insurance that pays, within limits, most of the healthcare service charges not covered by Medicare Part A. These policies, which must meet federal standards, are offered by Blue Cross and Blue Shield and various commercial health insurance companies.
10. Title XVIII of the Social Security Act, or Health Insurance for the Aged and Disabled, established the Medicare program, which became effective in July 1966. Title XIX of the Social Security Act established the Medicaid program, effective as of the same date. Medicare is a federally-funded health insurance program that covers most Americans over the age of 65. In 1973, several additional groups became eligible for Medicare benefits, including those entitled to Social Security or Railroad Retirement disability cash benefits, most persons with end-stage renal disease, and certain individuals over 65 who were not eligible for paid coverage but elected to pay for Medicare benefits. Medicaid was designed as a cost-sharing program between the federal and state governments. It pays for healthcare services provided to many low-income Americans and is administered by state governments.
11. Medicaid allows states to add health coverage to public assistance programs for low-income groups, families with dependent children, the aged, and the disabled. Eligibility criteria are determined within each state and the criteria vary from state to state. However, to be eligible for federal funds, states are required to provide Medicaid coverage to certain individuals defined by the federal government. Low income is only one test for Medicaid eligibility. Other financial resources are also compared against eligibility standards.
12. Preferred provider organizations (PPOs) represent contractual agreements between healthcare providers and a self-insured provider or a health insurance carrier. Beneficiaries of PPOs select providers from a list of participating providers who have agreed to furnish healthcare services to the covered population. Point-of-service (POS) plans are similar to HMOs in that subscribers select a primary care physician from a network of participating physicians. However, POSs are different in that subscribers are allowed to seek care from providers outside the network as long as they pay a greater share of the charges for out-of-network services.
13. The State Children's Health Insurance Program (SCHIP) is a program initiated by the Balanced Budget Act of 1997. It allows states to expand existing insurance programs by providing additional federal funds to states so that Medicaid eligibility can be expanded to include a greater number of uninsured children.
14.
    - Inpatient hospitalization: Medicare Part A
    - Prescription eyeglasses: No Medicare coverage
    - Emergency department visits: Medicare Part B
    - Dental care: No Medicare coverage
    - Ambulatory surgery center services: Medicare Part B
    - Hospice care: Medicare Part A
15. TRICARE offers three options to its beneficiaries: TRICARE Prime, TRICARE Extra, and TRICARE standard. TRICARE Prime provides the most comprehensive healthcare coverage at the lowest cost. TRICARE Extra is a cost-effective preferred provider network (PPO) option.
16. Federal workers are covered by the Federal Workers' Compensation program, while other nonfederal workers are generally covered by individual State Workers' Compensation coverage. In general, these programs cover healthcare costs and lost income associated with work-related injuries and illnesses.
17. A staff model health maintenance organization (HMO) directly employs physicians and other healthcare professionals to provide healthcare services to members.
18. In an independent practice association (IPA), the HMO enters into a contract with an organized group of physicians who join together for purposes of fulfilling the HMO contract but retain their individual practices. The IPA serves as an intermediary during contract negotiations. In a staff model HMO, physicians are directly employed by the HMO, are salaried, and are considered employees of the HMO. In general, the physician practice in a staff model HMO is limited to HMO clients.
19. Managed care is the generic term used to describe prepaid health plans that integrate the financial and delivery aspects of healthcare services. Managed care organizations work to control the cost of, and access to, healthcare services at the same time that they strive to meet high-quality standards. Types of managed care plans available in the United States are:
    - Health maintenance organizations (HMOs)
    - Preferred provider organizations (PPOs)
    - Point-of-service (POS)
    - Exclusive provider organizations (EPOs)
    - Integrated delivery systems (IDSs)
20. Management services organizations (MSOs) provide practice management services, including administration and support, to individual physician practices. MSOs are usually owned by a group of physicians or a hospital.

Check Your Understanding 14.3

1. A prospective payment system is in place when the amount of payment is determined in advance.
2. Usual, customary, and reasonable (UCR) charges represent the amount a third-party payer will reimburse a provider for a particular service or procedure based on the amount considered to represent reasonable compensation for those services in a specific geographic area.
3. The most typical cost share ratio is 80:20. This means that 80 percent of the costs are paid by the third-party payer and 20 percent of the costs are paid by the patient.
4. The most common utilization control associated with managed fee-for-service reimbursement is utilization review of the health services planned for, or provided to, patients. The review may be done on either a prospective (before admission) or retrospective (after discharge) basis. Prospective review is often referred to as *precertification*.
5. If a group of patients used more services than a managed care plan originally calculated in its contract, the plan would show a loss for the period. Conversely, if the group used fewer services than estimated, the plan would show a profit for the period.
6. *Bundled payments* are lump-sum payments to providers to compensate them for all of the healthcare services delivered to a patient for a specific illness or over a specified period of time. Bundled payments are also called *episode-of-care* (EOC) payments and include capitated payments, global payments, global surgery payments, Medicare ambulatory surgery center rates, and Medicare prospective payment systems.
7. *Capitation* is a payment methodology based on per-person premiums or membership fees rather than on itemized per-procedure or per-service charges. The capitated managed care organization (MCO) negotiates a contract with an employer or government agency representing a specific group of individuals. The MCO agrees to provide all of the contracted healthcare services that the covered individuals need over a specified period of time. Capitated premiums are calculated on the projected cost of providing covered services per patient or member per month.

Check Your Understanding 14.4

1. Congress set the stage for prospective payment when it passed the Tax Equity and Fiscal Responsibility Act of 1982 (TEFRA) requiring implementation of the MS-DRG-based prospective payment system in 1983. In 1983, Congress enacted legislation mandating the first Medicare PPS for Medicare Part A coverage.
2. Prior to the implementation of the MS-DRG-based inpatient PPS, Medicare Part A payments to hospitals were based on traditional fee-for-service reimbursement. Reasonable cost and/or per-diem costs were used to determine payment.
3. The MS-DRG prospective payment rate is based on the patient's principal diagnosis as well as complications, comorbidities, principal procedure, and other procedures.
4. The computer software program that assigns the appropriate DRG according to information provided for each episode of care is called a *MS-DRG grouper*.
5. The Medicare acute care prospective payment system excludes the following types of hospitals:
   - Psychiatric and rehabilitation hospitals and psychiatric and rehabilitation units within larger medical facilities
   - Long-term care hospitals, defined as hospitals with an average length of stay of 25 days or more
   - Children's hospitals
   - Cancer hospitals
   - Critical access hospitals
6. DRGs are organized within 25 major diagnostic categories (MDCs). Most MDCs are based on a particular organ system of the body, although others are constructed to include multiple organ systems.
7. Case mix refers to the types or categories of patients treated by a hospital. The DRG system allows a hospital to relate its case mix to the costs incurred for inpatient care. This information supports administrative decisions about services to be offered to its patient population.
8. The Balanced Budget Act of 1997 mandated implementation of a skilled nursing facility prospective payment system (SNF PPS). The system was implemented on July 1, 1998.
9. Resident assessment data are standardized data collected about all residents of skilled nursing facilities (SNFs). They are collected from the Minimum Data Set, Version 2.0 (MDS 2.0). This is a data collection tool that includes the minimum core of defined and categorized patient assessment questions and serves as the basis for documentation and reimbursement in a SNF.
10. The resource-based relative value scale (RBRVS) was implemented by HCFA (now CMS) in 1992 as a reimbursement system for physician services covered under Medicare Part B. The system reimburses physicians according to a fee schedule based on predetermined values assigned to specific services.
11. The outpatient prospective payment system (OPPS) does not apply to critical access hospitals (CAHs) or hospitals in Maryland that are excluded because they qualify under the Social Security Act for payment under the state's payment plan. In addition, Indian Health Service hospitals and hospitals located outside the 50 states, the District of Columbia and Puerto Rico are excluded.

12. Discounting applies to the practice of multiple surgical procedures furnished during the same operative session. The full APC rate is paid for the surgical procedure with the highest weight, and other surgical procedures performed at the same time are reimbursed at 50 percent of the APC rate.
13. Home health agencies use the Outcome and Assessment Information Set (OASIS) to collect data elements that represent core items for the comprehensive assessment of adult home care patients.
14. The home health resource group (HHRG) is a classification system established for the prospective reimbursement of covered home care services to Medicare beneficiaries during a 60-day episode of care. Covered services include skilled nursing visits, home health aide visits, therapy services, medical social services, and nonroutine medical supplies.
15. An inpatient rehabilitation facility is required to complete a patient assessment instrument (PAI) on all patients upon both admission to and discharge from the facility.
16. CMS provides IRFs with IRVEN to collect the IRF-PAI in a database that can be transmitted electronically to a nationwide IRF database. This data is used in assessing clinical characteristics of patients in rehabilitation settings. Eventually it can be used to provide survey agencies with a means to objectively measure and compare facility performance and quality and to allow researchers to develop improved standards of care.
17. LTC hospitals are defined as having an average inpatient length of stay of more than 25 days.
18. A short-stay outlier is an adjustment to the payment rate for stays that are considerably shorter than the average length of stay for a particular LTC-DRG. A case would qualify for short-stay outlier status when the length of stay is between one day and up to and including 5/6 of the average length of stay for the LTC-DRG. Both the average length of stay and the 5/6 of the average length of stay periods are published in the *Federal Register*. Payment under the short-stay outlier is made using different payment methodologies.
19. The prospective systems for long-term care hospitals and inpatient psychiatric facilities both use the current MS-DRGs for inpatient hospitals.
20. Patient-level or case-level adjustments are provided for age, specified DRGs, and certain comorbidity categories. Payment adjustments are made for eight age categories beginning with age 45 at which point costs are statistically increased as the patient ages.

    The IPF receives a MS-DRG payment adjustment for a principal diagnosis that groups to 1 of 15 psychiatric DRGs. There is also a variable per diem adjustment to recognize higher costs in the early days of a psychiatric stay.

    The IPF prospective payment system also includes an outlier policy for those patients who require more expensive care than expected in an effort to minimize the financial risk to the IPF.

    The prospective payment system also includes regulations on payments when there is an interrupted stay, meaning the patient is discharged from an IPF and returns to the same or another facility before midnight on the third consecutive day.

Check Your Understanding 14.5

1. The coder's primary responsibility is to data accuracy.
2. The main factor in ensuring the quality of clinical coding is the quality of the clinical documentation.
3. The quality assessment process for coding consists of:
    - Documenting the current coding process
    - Taking baseline measurements
    - Setting up benchmarks using comparative data
    - Continuing to evaluate coding in an ongoing manner

Check Your Understanding 14.6

1. Encoders use extensive user interaction. Automated coders use natural language processing.
2. Speech recognition is one emerging technology that will affect classification and clinical terminologies because it can improve the accuracy of documenting the clinician's intent and it can make documentation easier. Other emerging technologies include handheld computers and personal digital assistants (PDAs), which will facilitate point-of-care data entry.

Check Your Understanding 14.7

1. A coordination of benefits (COB) transaction is an electronic transmission from a healthcare provider to a healthcare plan. The purpose of a COB is to determine relative payment responsibilities for healthcare claims and payment information.
2. A remittance advice is sent by the third-party payer to the provider to explain payments made by the payer.
3. The CMS-1500 form is a standardized billing form used to bill third-party payers for reimbursement for provider services such as physician office visits. Though its precursor was the Attending Physician Statement (APS) (or COMB-1), the CMS-1500 currently has no alternate name.
4. Medicare carriers process Part B claims for services by physicians and medical suppliers and might include such agencies as a Blue Shield plan, a commercial insurance company, or another organization that contracts with Medicare. Carriers are responsible for performing the following functions:
    - Determining the charges allowed by Medicare
    - Maintaining the quality of performance records
    - Assisting in fraud and abuse investigations

- Assisting both suppliers and beneficiaries as needed
- Making payments to physicians and suppliers for Part B-covered services

Medicare fiscal intermediaries (FIs) process Part A claims and hospital-based Part B claims for institutional services, including inpatient hospital claims, and claims from SNFs, home health agencies, and hospice services. They also process outpatient claims for supplemental medical insurance (Medicare Part B). The same types of organizations that serve as Medicare carriers might also contract as fiscal intermediaries. FIs are responsible for the following functions:

- Determining costs and reimbursement amounts
- Maintaining records
- Establishing controls
- Safeguarding against fraud and abuse or excess use
- Conducting reviews and audits
- Making payments to providers for covered services
- Assisting both providers and beneficiaries, as needed

5. A Medicare Administrative Contractor is a newly established contracting entity that will administer both Medicare Part A and Part B as of 2011. MACs will replace the carriers and fiscal intermediaries.
6. The CMS implemented the Correct Coding Initiative (CCI) in 1996 to develop correct coding methodologies to improve the appropriate payment of Medicare Part B claims. The CCI edits explain what procedures and services cannot be billed together on the same day of service for a patient.
7. The Correct Coding Initiative (CCI) policies are based on national and local policies and coding edits, coding guidelines developed by CMS, analysis of standard medical and surgical practices, and review of current coding practices.

Check Your Understanding 14.8

1. Generally, third-party payers update fee schedules on an annual basis.
2. A physician or other healthcare provider who participates in the Medicare program must agree to accept assignment for all covered services provided to Medicare patients. To accept assignment means that the provider or supplier accepts, as payment in full, the allowed charge from the Medicare fee schedule. The provider or supplier is prohibited from balance billing, which means the patient cannot be held responsible for charges in excess of the Medicare fee schedule.
3. Physicians, practitioners, and suppliers must notify Medicare by December 31 of each year whether they intend to participate in the Medicare program during the coming year. Medicare participation means that the provider or supplier agrees to accept assignment for all covered services provided to Medicare patients.

   Nonparticipating providers (nonPAR) do not sign a participation agreement with Medicare but may or may not accept assignment. If the nonPAR physician elects to accept assignment, he or she is paid 95 percent (5 percent less than participating physicians) of the Medicare Physician Fee Schedule or MFS. NonPAR providers who choose not to accept assignment are subject to Medicare's limiting charge policy.
4. The limiting charge policy states that a physician may not charge a patient more than 115 percent of the nonparticipating fee schedule. Under the limiting charge policy, the provider collects the full amount from the patient and Medicare reimburses the patient.
5. A chargemaster lists the individual charges for every element of every service provided and serves as a provider's standard fee schedule. Chargemasters provide a reference so that fees billed to various payers are standardized. Chargemasters simplify the work of the billing department.
6. An inaccurate chargemaster can adversely affect facility reimbursement as well as compliance and data quality. Negative results that may occur because of an inaccurate chargemaster include overpayment, underpayment, undercharging for delivery of healthcare services, claims rejections, and fines or penalties.
7.
   - *Description of service:* Examples might be the evaluation and management visit, observation, or emergency room visit.
   - *CPT/HCPCS code:* Must correspond to the description of the service
   - *Revenue code:* A three-digit code that describes a classification of a product or service provided to the patient. These revenue codes are required by CMS for reporting services.
   - *Charge amount:* The amount that the facility charges for the procedure or service. This does not necessarily equal what the facility will be reimbursed by the third-party payer.
   - *Charge or service code:* An internally assigned number that is unique to the facility. It identifies each procedure listed on the chargemaster and identifies the department or revenue center that initiated the charge. The charge code can be useful for revenue tracking and budget analysis.
   - *General ledger key:* A two or three digit number that assigns a line item to a section of the general ledger in the hospital's accounting system.
   - *Activity/Status Date:* Indicates the most recent activity of an item
8. The chargemaster is generally maintained by representatives from health information management, clinical services, the business office, and compliance and information systems.

9. Revenue cycle management involves many different processes, and people all working to make sure that the healthcare facility is properly reimbursed for the services that are provided. Effective management of the revenue cycle is essential to improving the facility's revenues. Delays in payment, denied claims, and other lost revenues have a tremendous impact on the financial health of the facility. The major functions of revenue cycle management typically include admitting and access management, case management, charge capture, health information management, patient financial services and business office, finance, compliance, and information technology.
10. A good physician query form should:
    - Be clearly and concisely written
    - Contain precise language
    - Present the facts from the medical record and identify why clarification is needed
    - Present the scenario and ask the physician to make a clinical interpretation of a given diagnosis or condition based on treatment, evaluation, monitoring, and services provided. "Open-ended" questions that allow the physician to document the specific diagnosis are preferable to multiple-choice questions or questions requiring only a "yes" or "no" response. Queries that appear to lead the physician to provide a particular response could lead to allegations of inappropriate upcoding and should be avoided.
    - Be phrased such that the physician is allowed to specify the correct diagnosis. The form should not indicate the financial impact of the response to the query. The form should not be designed so that only the physician signature is provided.
    - Include patient name, admission date, medical record number, name and contact information (phone number and e-mail address) of the coding professional, specific question and rationale, place for the physician to document his or her response, and a place for the physician to sign and date his or her response
11. Coding compliance programs focus on preventing accusations of fraud and abuse. The Office of the Inspector General (OIG) of the Department of Health and Human Services (HHS) provides guidance for healthcare organizations in developing compliance programs.
12. *Upcoding* is the practice of assigning a reimbursement code specifically for the purpose of obtaining a higher level of payment. It is most often found when reimbursement-grouping systems are used. *Unbundling* is the practice of using multiple codes that describe individual components of a procedure rather than an appropriate single code that describes all steps of the procedure performed.
13. From Bowman 2004:
    - Inconsistent documentation
    - Incomplete progress notes
    - Undocumented care
    - Test results not addressed in the physician documentation
    - Historical diagnoses being documented as current diagnoses
    - Long-standing, chronic conditions that are not documented
    - Lack of documentation of postoperative complications
    - Illegibility
    - Documentation not completed on time
14.
    - DRG Coding Accuracy
    - Variations in case mix
    - Discharge status (transfers versus discharges)
    - Services provided under arrangement
    - 72-hour window
    - Medical necessity
    - Evaluation and management (E/M) services
    - Chargemaster Description
15. Benefits of effective corporate compliance include a commitment to responsible conduct toward employees and the community, an accurate view of behavior related to fraud and abuse, identification and prevention of criminal and unethical conduct, and high-quality patient care improvements

Chapter 15

Check Your Understanding 15.1

1. Zip code—Nominal
2. Blood pressure—Ratio
3. Heart failure classification I, II, III, IV—Nominal/ordinal
4. Age—Ratio
5. Ethnicity—Nominal
6. Martial status—Nominal
7. Length of stay—Ratio
8. Discharge disposition (home, SNF, and so on)—Nominal
9. Weight—Ratio
10. Level of education—Nominal/ordinal
11. The number of procedures currently being performed is 1,500 per year:
    250 days × 6 procedures = 1,500 per year

    The number of procedures that must be done to accommodate the current patients plus the transfers equals 1986: 1500 + 486 = 1986

    If 486 additional exams are needed then the Cardiac Cath Lab would need to perform an additional 2 procedures each day"

486/250 = 1.94 or 2 additional exams per day

If the lab is currently performing 6 procedures per day in an 8 hour work day then each exam takes 1.33 hours. They would need to add 2.66 hours to their work day:

8 hours/6 exams = 1.33 hours for each exam.

1.33 × 2 = 2.66 additional hours per exam day.

12.

	Family Practice	Internal Medicine	Cardiology
January	11.4%	38.6%	50.0%
February	15.8%	39.5%	44.7%
March	18.2%	31.8%	50.0%
April	20.9%	32.6%	46.5%
May	18.4%	39.5%	42.1%
June	12.5%	35.0%	52.5%
July	16.2%	27.0%	56.8%
August	18.6%	23.3%	58.1%
September	25.6%	15.4%	59.0%
October	20.0%	20.0%	60.0%
November	10.5%	21.1%	68.4%
December	8.1%	40.5%	51.4%
Total	16.70%	30.60%	52.70%

Check Your Understanding 15.2

1. Medicare admissions outnumber Commercial insurance admissions 3 to 2. —Ratio
2. At the annual state HIM meeting, 85 of the registrants were female and 35 were male. Therefore 0.71 of the registrants were female. —Proportion
3. Of the 250 patients admitted in the last six months, 36 percent had Type II diabetes mellitus. —Rate

Check Your Understanding 15.3

1. a. Inpatient census: (120 + 22) – 18 = 124
   b. Daily inpatient census: [(120 + 22) – 18] +1 = 125
   c. Inpatient service days: [(120 + 22) – 18] +1 = 125
2. a. Inpatient census: (12 + 6) – 2 = 16
   b. Daily inpatient census: [(12 + 6) – 2 +1] = 17
3. a. Inpatient census:
   10 (remaining patients) +
   2 (admissions from ESD) +
   1 (transfer from Surgery unit) = 13
   b. Daily inpatient census:
   10 (remaining patients) +
   2 (admissions from ESD) +
   1 (transfer from Surgery unit) + 1 (A & D) = 14

Check Your Understanding 15.4

1.

Inpatient Unit	Service Days	Bed Count	Occupancy Rate
Medicine	580	36	(580 × 100)/(36 × 30) = 58000/1080 = 53.7%
Surgery	689	42	(689 × 100)/(42 × 30) = 68900/1260 = 54.7%
Pediatric	232	18	(232 × 100)/((18 × 30) = 23200/540 = 43.0%
Psychiatry	889	35	(889 × 100)/(35 × 30) = 88900/1050 = 84.7%
Obstetrics	222	10	(222 × 100)/(10 × 30) = 22200/300 = 74.0%
Newborn	222	15	(222 × 100)/(15 × 30) = 22200/450 = 49.3%

2. [(580 + 689 + 232 + 889 + 222) × 100] / [(36 + 42 + 18 + 35 + 10) × 30] = 261200/4230 61.7%
3. January–June (15672 × 100) / (156 × 181) = 1567200/28236 = 55.5%

   July–December (25876 × 100) / (200 × 184) = 2587600/36800 = 70.3%

   January–December [(15672 + 25876) × 100] / (156 × 181) + (200 × 184) = 4154800 / (28236 + 36800) = 4154800/65036 = 63.9%

   181 is the number of days in January through June

   184 is the number of days in July through December

Check Your Understanding 15.5

1. a. Total length of stay = 72 + 70 + 72 + 136 + 32 + 81 + 68 + 80 + 63 + 84 = 758
   b. Number of patients discharged = 12 + 10 + 12 + 17 + 8 + 9 + 11 + 10 + 14 + 12 = 115
   c. Average length of stay = 758/115 = 6.6 days

Check Your Understanding 15.6

1. Gross death rate for adults and children: (22 × 100) / 1250 = 1.76%
2. Net death rate for adults and children: [(22 – 5) × 100]/ (1250 – 5) = 1700/1245 = 1.37%
3. Fetal death rate: (4 × 100) / 150 + 4) = 400/154 = 2.60%
4. Newborn death rate: (2 × 100) / 152 = 1.32%
5. Gross death rate – all patients: [(22 + 2) × 100] / (1250 + 152) = 2400/1402 = 1.71%
6. Maternal death rate: 1 × 100)/155 =100/155 = 0.65%

Check Your Understanding 15.7

1. Gross autopsy rate: (12 × 100) / 25 = 1200/25 = 48.0%
2. Net autopsy rate: (12 × 100) / (25 – 2) = 1200/23 = 52.2%
3. Hospital autopsy rate: [(12 + 1) × 100] / (25 + 1) = 1300/26 = 50.0%

Check Your Understanding 15.8

1. Nosocomial infection rate: (4 × 100) / 57 = 400/57 = 7.0%
2. Consultation rate (June): (47 × 100) / 149 = 4700/149 = 31.5%
3. Total weights in table.

MS-DRG	MS-DRG Title	Rel. Wt.	No. of Pts.	Total Wt.
179	Respiratory infections and inflammations w/o CC/MCC	1.2754	5	6.3770
187	Pleural effusion w CC	1.1947	2	2.3894
189	Pulmonary edema and respiratory failure	1.3660	3	4.0980
194	Simple pneumonia and pleurisy w CC	1.0235	1	1.0235
208	Respiratory system diagnosis w ventilator support <96 hours	2.2463	1	2.2463
280	Acute myocardial infarction, discharged alive w MCC	1.7391	3	5.2173
299	Peripheral vascular disorders w MCC	1.2220	2	2.4440
313	Chest pain	0.5489	4	2.1956
377	G.I. hemorrhage w MCC	1.3367	1	1.3367
391	Esophagitis, gastroent and misc digest disorders w MCC	0.9565	1	0.9565
547	Connective tissue disorders w/o CC/MCC	0.9565	1	0.9565
552	Medical back problems w/o MCC	0.7839	1	0.7839
684	Renal failure w/o CC/ MCC	0.9835	1	0.9835
812	Red blood cell disorders w/o MCC	0.7780	2	1.5560
872	Septicemia w/o MV 96+ hours w/o MCC	1.3783	1	1.3783
918	Poisoning and toxic effects of drugs w/o MCC	0.6886	1	0.6886
Total			30	34.6311

Case mix = 34.6311/30 = 1.1544

Check Your Understanding 15.9

1. Crude death rate for men: (1,207,476/145,999,746) × 10,000 = 82.7%
2. Crude death rate for women: (1,240,286/150,410,658) × 10,000 = 82.5%
3. Crude death rate for group: (1,240,286 + 1,207,476)/ (150,410,658 + 145,999,746) × 10,000 = 2,447,762/296,410,404 = 82.5%
4. Crude death rate for men ages 35 – 44: (53,309/21,940,039) × 10,000 = 24.3%
5. Crude death rate for women ages 35 – 44: (31,476/21,922,425) × 10,000 = 14.4%

Check Your Understanding 15.10

1. The *incidence rate* is the probability or risk of illness in a population over a period of time.
   The *prevalence rate* is the proportion of persons in a population who have a particular disease at a specific point in time or over a specified period of time.
2. *Notifiable disease* is one for which regular, frequent, and timely information on individual cases is considered necessary to prevent and control disease.
3. Incidence rate of HIV: (65,000/296,410,404) × 100,000 = 21.9%

Check Your Understanding 15.11

1. table
2. pie chart
3. line graph
4. bar chart
5. histogram
6. box plot

Check Your Understanding 15.12

1. 2,418 = Mean
2. 2,540 = Median
3. 2,540 = Mode
4. 1,095 = Range
5. 139,617.1 = Variance
6. 373.7 = Standard deviation

Check Your Understanding 15.13

1. The *normal distribution* is a family of distributions that are symmetrical and bell-shaped. Since it is symmetrical, 50 percent of the observations fall above the mean and 50 percent fall below the mean. In a normal distribution, the mean, median, and mode are equal.
2. When a distribution is asymmetrical it is said to be skewed. *Skewness* is the horizontal stretching of the distribution to one side so that one tail of the distribution is longer than the other.

Chapter 16

Check Your Understanding 16.1

1. Research is thoughtful, planned activity that expands or refines knowledge.
2. Health records are important to clinical research because clinical research, as opposed to epidemiology, focuses on the individual patient. Many protocols of clinical trials state that specific data will be obtained from health records.
3. Theories are made up of concepts that are abstract ideas generalized from particular instances, interrelationships that are assumed to exist among these concepts, and consequences that are assumed to follow logically from the relationships proposed in the theory.
4. The "best" theories are often the simplest theories.
5. An advantage of models is that they aid comprehension. Models include all known properties of theories and describe theories graphically or on a smaller scale.
6. The research of health information professionals is considered applied research because it involves the use of research to improve practice.
7. Knowing their purpose is important to researchers because purpose determines research approach.
8. *Inductive reasoning* involves creating conclusions based on a limited number of observations; *deductive reasoning* involves creating conclusions based on generalizations. Therefore, induction begins with the specific and deduction begins with the general.

Check Your Understanding 16.2

1. The seven basic steps of research are defining the problem, reviewing the literature, determining the design and method, selecting the instrument, gathering the data, analyzing the data, and presenting the results.
2. A well-developed research question should be stated clearly and exactly; have theoretical significance, practical worth, or both; have obvious and explicit links to a larger body of knowledge; advance knowledge in a definable way; and be worthwhile.
3. The three rich sources of meaningful research questions are:
    - Research models
    - Recommendations of previous researchers
    - Gaps in the field's body of knowledge detected during the review of the literature
4. Conducting a literature review is important because it results in the researcher "owning" the body of knowledge. In other words, he or she knows the theories; the names of key researchers, theorists, and collaborators; the sources of data; the common research designs; and the gaps in the body of knowledge.
5. Five data sources, other than journal articles, that researchers should consider when doing a comprehensive search are videos, audiotapes, Web sites, government reports, and statistical data (such as census data, economic data, crime data, and Medicare data).
6. Journal articles from refereed journals should constitute the bulk of the literature review because articles in refereed journals have been evaluated for quality prior to publication.
7. A director of health information services might select the productivity standard recommended in a peer-reviewed journal rather than one recommended in a popular magazine because health information experts have evaluated the quality of the recommendations in the peer-reviewed journal.
8. Researchers use key terms (MeSH headings) to identify journal articles related to their topic.
9. A researcher might use bibliographic software because it saves time for the researcher by automatically converting the bibliographic information to the particular style required by a professor or journal.
10. Studies with contradictory results should be included in the review of the literature because readers could perceive the absence of contradictory studies as evidence of bias. Evidence of bias detracts from the credibility of the literature review.
11. In the review of the literature, readers should expect information about the study's design, time frame, method, sample, response rate, statistical techniques, and findings.

Check Your Understanding 16.3

1. The purpose of the study determines a researcher's choice of a research design.
2. A researcher would use correlational research to investigate the relationship between a supervisor's level of stress and the number of his or her subordinates.
3. An example of a direct relationship would be the higher the number of subordinates managed by the supervisor, the higher the level of the supervisor's stress.
4. The key characteristic of experimental research is control.
5. Quasi-experimental (for example, causal-comparative research) lacks random assignment to a group and manipulation of treatment.
6. The independent variable causes an effect in the dependent variable.
7. In a double-blind study, administrative assistants or researchers removed from the study know which subjects are in the study group. Neither the participants nor the researchers directly conducting the study knows which subjects are in the study control.

8. A longitudinal design is more credible than a cross-sectional study because it eliminates the possibility that the study occurred at some unrepresentative point in time. For an important topic, such as cancer, the investment of time is justifiable.

Check Your Understanding 16.4

1. A survey uses self-report data.
2. Question 1 is a written question on an interview guide or a query on a questionnaire.
3. A researcher may choose a structured interview because it is easier to quantify, tabulate, and analyze than an unstructured interview. An interview guide provides the list of questions so all the researchers ask the same questions.
4. If researchers wanted to investigate the impact of the Hill-Burton Act on a region's healthcare, they would most likely choose to use the case study method.
5. Researchers would choose to conduct a questionnaire survey because it is efficient, it takes less time than other methods, and it generates great numbers of responses at a relatively low cost.
6. If researchers wanted to establish that a new drug causes a reduction in blood pressure, they would choose an experiment (randomized clinical trial or double-blind study), such as the pretest-posttest control group method, the Solomon four-group Method, or the posttest-only control group method.
7. Researchers might conduct a meta-analysis when many studies examined the same question, when the studies have common underlying characteristics, or when some of the studies' findings are contradictory.
8. The common characteristic that determined the researchers' choice of method in questions 3 through 7 was purpose (or definition of the question or problem).

Check Your Understanding 16.5

1. The alternative hypothesis states what the researcher believes.
2. If the researcher believes that the treatment increases output, the researcher would write a one-tailed hypothesis.
3. A type I error occurs when the researcher erroneously rejects the null hypothesis when it is true. A null hypothesis states that there is no difference between the groups. Rejecting the null implies that there is a difference in the groups. In the type I error, the researcher has said a difference exists when none does (that is, the drug really does not help the patient). A type II error occurs when the researcher erroneously fails to reject the null hypothesis when it is false. Failing to reject the null hypothesis implies that there is no difference in the groups. In a type II error, the researcher says no difference exists when a difference does exist (that is, the drug helps the patient but the researcher says it does not).
4. The *p*- value represents the probability that the difference occurred by pure chance.
5. Internal validity ensures that the effect seen was caused by the independent variable. If internal validity is breached, the researcher cannot state that the independent variable caused a particular effect on the dependent variable. The issues involved in internal validity are history, maturation, testing, instrumentation, statistical regression, differential selection, experimental mortality, and diffusion of treatment.
6. Reliability is important because it represents the tests' dependability. Reliable tests result in the same or similar outcomes for multiple subjects in multiple situations. For example, scholastic aptitude tests or AHIMA's registration examination have the characteristic of reliability.

Check Your Understanding 16.6

1. A researcher would choose to use an instrument that someone else has created because the reliability and validity of the instrument are established. Construction of a reliable and valid measure is difficult. An established instrument can be matched to the purpose and theory of the researcher. In addition, it has the following characteristics: clarity of language, brevity and attractiveness, and a match between the levels of measurement.
2. An adequate sample depends on the purpose of the study, the nature of the population, and the resources available to the researcher(s).
3. Directors of HIS departments would be considered a homogenous population (mostly female and white with similar educational backgrounds).
4. Institutional review boards (IRBs) are important because they help organizations comply with federal regulations and protect human subjects from abuses.
5. A pilot study is a "trial run." It shows that it is logistically feasible for the research study to be conducted on a larger scale.
6. Researchers are concerned about their response rates because low response rates could breach both internal and external validity of a study. A low response rate could represent bias, introduce inaccuracy, and/or make generalization to the population impossible.
7. Two common mistakes that researchers make in data collection are lack of planning and deviation from the original plan.

Check Your Understanding 16.7

1. Descriptive (summary) statistics describe the data through techniques such as means, frequency distributions, and variations. Inferential statistics allow the researchers to make inferences about the population characteristics (parameters) based on the characteristics of the sample.
2. Bivariate statistical techniques involve two variables.
3. Paired *t* test and analysis of variance (ANOVA) are inferential statistical techniques that emphasize differences in groups.
4. The two types of continuous data are interval data and ratio data.
5. Researchers must know the type of data that they are collecting because certain statistical techniques require data of a particular kind.
6. Researchers might use Epi-Info because it is especially designed for their type of study, epidemiological. It makes conducting the research easier by calculating the proper sample size and setting up the entry of data from questionnaires. In addition, Epi-Info is a dedicated statistical package. This means that Epi-Info requires less manipulation of the data and performs many statistical procedures. Finally, the software is free from the Centers for Disease Control and Prevention.

Check Your Understanding 16.8

1. The research findings and discussion sections differ in content and tone. The research findings section contains only the findings of the analysis of the data. No commentary about the findings is included. In the discussion section, researchers interpret and explain their findings and compare them to other researchers' findings. The researchers also comment on the significance of their study in terms of expanding the field's body of knowledge or of adding to a theory. The discussion section is more creative than the research findings section.
2. First, they should consider that they should present the element in only one mode (narrative, table, or figure). Second, they should consider which mode would be most meaningful and understandable to the reader.
3. A researcher should answer any three of the following questions when writing the discussion section:
   - What theoretical significance or practical worth do the findings have?
   - How do the findings link explicitly to the larger body of knowledge?
   - How have the findings improved the field's research model?
   - How have the findings expanded the body of knowledge?
   - What new definitions have the findings added to the field's area of practice?
   - How do the findings support practitioners in the workplace?
   - What problems do the findings solve?
   - What valid conclusions can the researchers and the readers draw from the findings?
   - How can other researchers expand or improve this research study?
4. When selecting a journal for manuscript submission, researchers should consider the journal's scope, content, and audience. Researchers should try to find a journal that matches their purpose, topic, and research design. They should apply the style to their manuscript and make revisions before submission.

Check Your Understanding 16.9

1. When using large databases for secondary analysis, researchers should know whether the database is public or proprietary, individual or aggregate, and the means of access. In all cases, they will need to obtain approvals or permissions from relevant oversight entities and, in the case of individually identifiable data, additional approvals or permissions may be required.
2. Public databases are in the public domain (freely available), while proprietary databases are the property of an entity (access requires permission).
3. The discrepancy between the researcher's use of the term "anonymous" in the informed consent and the researcher's intent to track respondents. Anonymity demands that the researcher cannot link the response and the responder. The code would link the respondents to their data, so their data would no longer be anonymous.
4. The Common Rule is the set of regulations that stipulate the protection of human subjects in federally funded research under seventeen agencies.
5. Both HIPAA and the Common Rule apply to this researcher. Any state regulations that may be more stringent may also apply.
6. Research is important to an emerging profession, such as health information management, because the key characteristic of a profession is a body of knowledge. Research builds the body of knowledge.

Chapter 17

Check Your Understanding 17.1

1. The definition of quality will change based on the perspective of the individual. Products or services must meet the expectations of the individual(s) for whom they are provided. Failure to meet expectations means the product or service does not meet the basic standard of quality.
2. The Joint Commission has promoted quality of care since its inception. The organization's role has been to provide support and leadership for healthcare organizations in a variety of capacities and with the goal of improving quality. The focus of using data—collecting and analyzing data—is to improve performance at the core of their initiatives.
3. The agencies involved in today's quality of care issues are the Joint Commission, state and federal agencies including the Food and Drug Administration (FDA), the Centers for Disease Control (CDC), and the Centers for Medicare and Medicaid Services (CMS).
4. The Institute of Medicine (IOM) has identified six dimensions around which to frame the measurement of quality: safety, effectiveness, patient-centeredness, timeliness, efficiency, equity. The IOM has also continued to explore in more detail areas of concern regarding safety such as the area of adverse events and medication errors. These measures are helping HIM professionals devise ways and focus attention on pertinent areas to help close the quality gap.
5. The core performance measures enhance the accreditation process by providing a way to look at and measure the quality of clinical practice in a healthcare organization.

Check Your Understanding 17.2

1. The basic elements of a quality improvement (QI) program are:
   - Statement of mission
   - Supportive environment
   - Sufficient resources
   - Leaders with qualifications to provide direction
   - Sufficient staff
   - An organizational attitude that focuses on the importance of improvement
   - Coordinated and integrated effort
   - Continuous monitoring
2. The governing board/body is responsible for the overall care provided by a healthcare organization.
3. The HIM profession has a history of being involved in the evaluation of high-quality care and of having an understanding of QI. The backgrounds of HIM professionals in documentation, clinical data management, disease processes, and data analysis, as well as an understanding of the interdisciplinary responsibility for patient care quality add to the richness of the HIM vantage point.
4. HIM professionals can provide support to QI programs in the areas of research, data collection, use and development of spreadsheets and databases, data analysis (interpreting data in a meaningful way), data source evaluation, clinical process improvement, and documentation evaluation and improvement. HIM professionals in managerial roles can advocate for using data and the analysis of information to make decisions and suggest improvements in how care is provided.
5. The goals of the Medicare Modernization Act (MMA) are to:
   - Improve patient safety
   - Enhance quality of care
   - Reduce scientific uncertainty and the unwarranted variation in medical practice that results in both lower quality and higher costs
6. Judicial decisions have influenced QI because they have provided the foundation for the hospital industry's responsibility for patient care. They have provided direction about what kinds of information to monitor regarding patient care, the work/services of physicians, and the processes necessary for selecting medical staff and granting of privileges.
7. The federal government and Joint Commission have both set parameters regarding the quality of patient care. Both agencies have continued to find ways to examine clinical practice and use evidence-based medicine to improve care provided to patients. The federal government uses legislation to provide direction, and the Joint Commission develops and publishes accreditation standards to support quality of care initiatives.

Check Your Understanding 17.3

1. Managers must aware of the expectations of patients, be aware of red flags indicating a problem with services provided, provide orientation and training that gives staff the tools to provide excellent service and create an environment that solicits staff input for providing superior care. Performance measures are statements of expectation or performance. In QI processes, these indicators are tools that help measure the quality of care.
2. Structure, process, and outcome are part of an assessment model that provides a perspective of or orientation to the indicator statements used to measure the quality of care. For example, a statement may measure the qualifications of staff, which would be a statement developed around structure because it addresses the people who provide care.

3. Core measures, statements of outcomes, and clinical practice guidelines are all names of tools that can be used to measure the performance of an organization. They are all different in approach, definition, and process.
4. The core measurement areas identified for hospitals by the Joint Commission and CMS are:
   - Acute myocardial infarction (AMI)
   - Heart failure (HF)
   - Pneumonia (PN)
   - Pregnancy and pregnancy-related conditions
   - Surgical care improvement project
   - Asthma care for children
5. Core performance measures require that healthcare facilities send data to the Joint Commission on a routine basis. Data from similar organizations will be compared, and areas for improvement will be identified that will be evaluated upon Joint Commission accreditation review.
6. Students can visit the Web sites of these organizations to find specific items.
   - The Joint Commission
     - improve accuracy of patient identification
     - improve effectiveness of communication
     - improve safety of using high-alert medication
     - eliminate wrong-site, wrong-patient, wrong-procedure surgery
     - improve the safety of using infusion pumps
     - improve the effectiveness of clinical alarm systems
     - reduce the risk of healthcare-acquired infections
   - NQF
     - promote a culture of safety by reducing errors
     - match healthcare needs with service delivery capabilities to reduce healthcare errors
     - facilitate information transfer and clear communication to reduce healthcare errors
     - specific setting or processes of care targeted to reduce healthcare errors
     - increase the safe use of medications to reduce healthcare errors
   - Leapfrog (4 quality and safety practices)
     - use computer physician order entry (CPOE)
     - use evidence-based hospital referral
     - use ICU physician staffing
     - use the Leapfrog practices score (the NQF's 27 safe practices)
   - CMS
     - use of best practice guidelines
     - encourage use of shared decision making between providers and patients
     - appropriate use of culturally and ethnically sensitive care
     - provide incentives to improve safety, quality, and efficiency
     - reduce scientific uncertainty through examination of service variation and outcomes measurement
7. CMS, AHRQ, and the Food and Drug Administration (FDA) have been involved in developing safe practice protocols.
8. Managed care uses a system of checks and balances to ensure that patients receive the necessary care. The National Committee for Quality Assurance (NCQA) supports managed care organizations in evaluating their quality of care. The Health Plan Employer Data and Information Set (HEDIS) was developed to evaluate the quality of care provided by managed care plans.
9. The National Committee for Quality Assurance (NCQA) accredits health plans and develops performance standards.
10. Evidence-based medicine is an important component to improving clinical quality because the medicine practiced is based on best scientific evidence available. When using evidence-based medicine a balance is struck between externally researched evidence and provider expertise. In addition, current practice is applied thus providing patients the most up to date practice available. A more consistent practice results with everyone having access to the same evidence-based information.
11. Severity indexing improves patient care because it provides information about the level of resource consumption. It allows those evaluating quality to determine whether a patient received sufficient resources and, therefore, adequate or high-quality care.

Check Your Understanding 17.4

1. It is important to include the licensed, independent medical staff in the healthcare organization's QI plan because the medical staff is a key player in providing healthcare in an organization, giving specific direction for virtually all patient care services.
2. The bylaws and rules and regulations of an organization provide the medical staff with structure, functions, and responsibilities. The bylaws set the parameters for how the medical staff functions in all capacities, including process improvement.
3. The credentialing process, when completed thoroughly and correctly, ensures that medical staff members are qualified and competent to provide the patient care services requested. Thus, it should eliminate unqualified or incompetent practitioners.
4. Reappointment/reappraisal ensures that the practice patterns of the medical staff are reviewed on a regular basis. The governing body is responsible for timely and appropriate reappointment and reappraisal.

Check Your Understanding 17.5

1. Utilization review (UR) and utilization management (UM) provide information about the appropriateness and necessity of patient care. UR helps ensure, in an efficient manner, that patients receive all needed services.
2. The different types of healthcare reviews (preadmission, admission, continued stay, and discharge planning) provide information about appropriateness and medical necessity at different times during the patient's encounter. This time line begins before admission and continues to discharge and ensures effective and efficient use of resources and patient care.
3. A notice of noncoverage informs the patient, physician, family, and the organization that services are no longer covered and that the patient or family will have to assume responsibility for all remaining costs.
4. Risk management programs contribute to an organization's overall QI plan because they identify, reduce, or eliminate events that potentially jeopardize patients, staff, and visitors. Identifying and preventing these events contributes to the overall safety and quality of patient care.
5. Sentinel events are catastrophic events that require a system of intensive inquiry (called root-cause analysis) that leads to improvements in patient care systems.

Check Your Understanding 17.6

1. Clearly defined indicators, criteria, and/or data elements in data collection programs provide better information to use to address the system or process in question. Better, clearer information leads to more meaningful improvements.
2. The main data source of performance improvement data is the medical record.
3. Quality management is the foundation of providing high quality patient care. Risk management is a program designed to reduce injury or accidents to everyone who works in a healthcare organization. Reducing the likelihood of injuries to patients being treated in the organization or identifying likely PCEs is one aspect of providing a safer, higher quality environment. Utilization management assures the effective and efficient use of a healthcare organization resources so the patient gets the right services and treatment in a timely way. This assures that the patient is provided the necessary care in the most reasonable amount of time. Patient safety programs provide the patient with an environment that is as secure as possible. Keeping the patient from hazardous materials or unnecessary treatments and assuring appropriate medication use and administration equates to a higher quality of care for the patient.
4. QI data are sensitive information. They offer insight into an organization's inner workings and highlight what is most right and most wrong. Information is collected on the people who provide patient care and those who receive it. All information collected must be kept private and confidential. Laws, statutes, and professional organizations all encourage such safeguarding of this information.
5. Provide decision support to the direct care providers such as allergic or interaction alerts (cross-check information).
    - Provide improved communication of test results by having all information available for better diagnosis.
    - Provide more accurate and complete information (large volumes of data) about all aspects of patient care.
    - Improve the quality of care by allowing quicker more complete analysis of data (benchmarking) involving practice patterns leading to a quicker understanding of what is best for patient care.
6. Communication is how an organization shares information. To be effective, information must flow freely from top to bottom and vice versa. Good communication increases clarity of understanding. Information is collected in many different areas for many different reasons. The results of QI efforts must be shared with all pertinent parties. There must be an openness to ensure that when areas for improvement are found, all appropriate staff and individuals work toward improvement. The challenge of collecting, analyzing, and improving does not just happen because of the efforts of one or two people. Effective communication can create an environment of sharing and caring, which then can lead to effective improvement of patient care services.

Chapter 18

Check Your Understanding 18.1

1. The Nuremberg Code outlines research ethics to guide the conduct of research involving human subjects. It was developed during the trials of Nazi war criminals following World War II. Its basic tenets are:
    - Informed consent is essential
    - Research should be based on prior animal work
    - The risks should be justified by the anticipated benefits
2. (1) Respect for persons, (2) beneficence, (3) justice
3. Respect for persons

4. Answer should include five of the following:
   - Lack of informed consent
   - Coercion or undue pressure on volunteers
   - Use of a vulnerable population
   - Withholding of information
   - Withholding available treatment
   - Withholding information about risks
   - Putting subjects at risk
   - Risks to subjects that outweigh the benefits
   - Deception
   - Violation of rights
5. The Public Health Service syphilis study

Check Your Understanding 18.2

1. False The researcher, the research sponsor and/or organization in which the research is conducted are not exculpable for any harm caused to the human subject.
2. False Only medical expenses related to the experimental portion of the research study are covered. Diagnostics such as x-ray, MRIs, etc., drugs and other treatments provided that are considered standard of care are the responsibility of the patient and/or the patient's insurance company unless otherwise noted.
3. False Release of patient information is restricted to those identified in the informed consent. The subject must authorize the release of information to any other party.
4. True A subject may withdraw from a research study at any time without penalty.
5. True Individuals who have diminished autonomy are considered vulnerable. Autonomy means the ability to understand and process information (mental capacity) and the freedom from control or influence of other (voluntariness).
6. True
7. True
8. A statement that the study involves research, the purpose of the research, the expected duration of subject participation, a description of the procedures to be followed, and the identification of procedures that are experimental.

   A description of reasonably foreseeable risks or discomforts. The description must be accurate and reasonable, and subjects must be informed of previously reported adverse events.

   A description of the benefits to the subject or others who may reasonably benefit from the research.

   A disclosure of the appropriate alternative procedures or courses of treatment, if any, that might be advantageous to the subject. When appropriate, a statement that supportive care with no additional disease-specific treatment is an alternative.

   A statement describing the extent to which confidentiality of records identifying the subject will be maintained. The statement should include full disclosure and description of approved agencies, such as the Food and Drug Administration (FDA) that may have access to the records.

   For research involving more than minimal risk, an explanation as to whether any compensation or medical treatments are available if injury occurs, and, if so, what they consist of or where further information may be obtained. Injury is not limited to physical injury. Research-related injury may include physical, psychological, social, financial, or otherwise.

   An explanation of whom to contact for answers to pertinent questions about the research and research subjects' rights and who to contact in the event of a research-related injury to the subject.

   A statement that participation is voluntary and that the subject may discontinue participation at any time without penalty or loss of benefits to which he or she is otherwise entitled.

   The regulations further require that additional consent information be provided when appropriate (Federal Policy 45 CFR 46.116), including:

   A statement that the treatment or procedure may involve risks to the subject (or embryo or fetus if the subject is pregnant) that are unforeseeable.

   Anticipated circumstances under which the subject's participation may be terminated by the investigator without regard to the subject's consent.

   Any additional costs that a subject may incur as a result of participating in the research.

   The consequences of a subject's decision to withdraw from the research and procedures for orderly termination of participation by the subject.

   A statement that significant new findings developed during the course of the research that may relate to the subject's willingness to continue participation will be provided to the subject.

   The approximate number of subjects involved in the study.
9. The HIPAA Privacy Rule protects medical records and other individually identifiable information from disclosure. It informs human subjects about how information about them will be used or disclosed. It also outlines their rights to access the information.
10. Office of Research Integrity (ORI) and Office of Human Research Protections

Check Your Understanding 18.3

1. The Privacy Rule provides individuals with certain rights about how their health information will be used and disclosed as well as how they can gain access to health records and information about when the PHI was released without their permission.
2. Epidemiological studies
   Case-control studies
   Cohort studies
   Cross-sectional study
   Clinical trials
3. Identify the cause of disease and associated risk factors
   - Determine the extent of disease in a given community
   - Study the natural history and prognosis of disease
   - Evaluate the preventive and therapeutic measures and new modes of healthcare delivery
   - Provide the foundation for public policy and regulatory decisions relating to environmental problems
4. Medical records may be used in cross-sectional, case-control, or prospective studies. However, use of medical records may be problematic in that generalizability to a larger population is limited when only hospitalized patients are studied. In addition, medical records may be illegible, have poor documentation, or be unavailable. However, if the specific data items are known to be present in the medical record, then it may be a good tool for epidemiological studies. Also, use of other types of data collection methods may be necessary to validate what is found in the medical record.
5. In case-control studies, groups are defined on the basis of an outcome and then assessed on the basis of past exposure to possible risk factors. Case-control studies are quick and easy to conduct and inexpensive. However, because a case-control study is a retrospective study, recall bias may be a limitation or disadvantage of this type of study design.
6. Randomized controlled clinical trials (RCCTs) are considered the gold standard for studying interventions. If properly designed, they can eliminate bias. In an RCCT, subjects are randomly assigned to either an experimental or control group. The experimental group receives the experimental treatment, and the control group receives a placebo or the standard method of treatment. If neither the subject nor the investigator is made aware of the treatment assignment until the conclusion of the study, it is called a double-blind study.
7. Relative risk is a ratio that compares the risk of disease or the incidence rate between two groups; it is also referred to as *risk ratio.*
8. Attributable risk is a measure of the public health impact of a causative factor on a population. It is assumed that the occurrence of a disease in an unexposed group is the baseline or expected risk for that disease. Any risk above that in the exposed group is the result of exposure to the risk factor. It is assumed that some individuals will acquire a disease whether or not they are exposed to the risk factor.

Check Your Understanding 18.4

1. The major objective of outcomes and effectiveness research is to understand the benefits, outcomes and end results of healthcare practices and interventions.
2. - Patient function
   - Quality of life
   - Patient satisfaction
3. The mission of the AHRQ is to support research designed to improve the outcomes and quality of healthcare, reduce its costs, address patient safety and medical errors, and broaden access to effective services. This information helps consumers make better decisions about healthcare.
4. The AHRQ is the sponsor of the HCUP. HCUP is a robust online query system that provides instant access to the largest set of all payer healthcare databases that are publicly available. It can be used to identify, track, analyze, and compare trends in hospital care at the national, regional, and state levels.
5. - Prevention quality indicators—used to identify hospital admissions that could have been avoided
   - Inpatient quality indicators—used to assess quality of care including inpatient mortality and utilization
   - Patient safety quality indicators—indicators to evaluate potentially avoidable complications and iatrogenic events
   - Inpatient quality indicators—used to assess quality of care including inpatient mortality and utilization
   - Patient safety quality indicators—indicators to evaluate potentially avoidable complications and iatrogenic events
6. - Structure—the setting in which healthcare is provided and the resources available to provide it
   - Process—the extent to which professionals perform to acceptable levels
   - Outcomes—changes in patient's condition, quality of life, and level of satisfaction

Chapter 19

Check Your Understanding 19.1

1. Because healthcare is a very information- and decision-intensive environment, with human lives as well as the financial soundness of organizations at stake, decision support systems are indispensable.
2. Some of the challenges facing healthcare that decision support can assist in addressing include locating and allocating financial resources, assisting health plan administrators in managing the medical care market and formulating appropriate payment plans, assisting hospital administrators in evaluating resource utilization, and preventing medical errors and adverse events.
3. A decision support system (DSS) is a computer-based system that gathers data from a variety of sources and assists in providing structure to this data by using various analytical models and visual tools. A decision support system facilitates and improves the outcomes of decision-making tasks associated with nonroutine and nonrepetitive problems.
4. Expert systems are designed to replace the expert. Decision support systems are designed to provide decision support for the decision maker, not to replace the decision maker.
5. The study and development of decision support systems evolved from the World War II discipline of operations research (also called *management science*).
6. The three phases in Simon's model of the decision making process are the intelligence phase, the design phase, and the choice phase.
7. The classical view of decision making involved postulating various decision alternatives and then selecting one from among them.
8. The key element in the DSS is the one that assists in "reasoning." The reasoning process considers the data and knowledge that has been provided and attempts to recognize and solve the problem. In expert systems, this key element is often called the inference engine.
9. The four classes of decision support systems are data-based, knowledge-based, model-based, and graphics-based.
10. An early medical DSS developed by Shortliffe and called MYCIN is an important medical decision support system that can be classified as a knowledge-based DSS. It used a knowledge base composed of rules (such as the one illustrated in figure 19.9 in the chapter), and an inference engine to "reason" from the rule base.

Check Your Understanding 19.2

1. A data warehouse serves as a neutral storage area for data extracted from an organization's transactional systems, is organized around specific business functions or requirements, and provides easy access to business data for analysis or data mining (decision support).
2. Normalization in a database seeks to eliminate redundancy in data storage.
3. Two well-known data models used for constructing a data warehouse are the star schema and the snowflake schema.
4. The architecture of a data warehouse and a clinical repository differ significantly. Because the clinical repository is integrated into the overall information system, its architecture is best described by the systems with which it interacts. Though used in the design of a data warehouse, the star and snowflake schemas are typically not used in the design of the clinical repository. While nonclinical data warehouses will be static in nature (their data does not change except as specified on a periodic basis), the clinical repository will constantly be changing as new clinical data are available for patient care. The nonclinical data warehouse is focused on retrospective analyses of business data. The business analyst uses the nonclinical data warehouse to tap into corporate data to assist with future decisions. The clinical repository, however, is focused on assisting with patient care in a near real-time environment.
5.
   - OLAP—online analytical processing
   - ROLAP—relational online analytical processing
   - MOLAP— multidimensional online analytical processing
   - HOLAP—hybrid online analytical processing
6. In supervised learning, the algorithm learns the inherent patterns hidden in the data that predict a specified outcome or target variable. In supervised learning algorithms, this outcome or target variable must be present in the supplied data set in order for the algorithm to proceed. Unsupervised learning techniques seek to group together cases or data records that are similar or alike in certain respects. The goal of the analysis is to discover previously unknown groupings that exist in the data.
7. Important data-mining tools include artificial neural networks, decision trees, k-nearest neighbor clustering, and rule induction.

Check Your Understanding 19.3

1. The four types of decision support systems found in healthcare are clinical decision support systems (CDSSs), executive decision support systems, healthcare decision support systems, and nursing decision support systems.
2. A clinical decision support system (CDSS) is software that integrates information on the characteristics of individual patients with a computerized knowledge base for the purpose of generating patient-specific assessments or recommendations designed to aid clinicians and patients in making clinical decisions.
3. The name of one of the earliest CDSSs was MYCIN.
4. MYCIN used a knowledge base containing the production rules for the system, and an inference engine that "reasoned" based on the rules in the knowledge base.
5. Some of the difficulties in maintaining a CDSS include maintaining the rule base or the knowledge base to keep it current, eliciting the rules from medical experts (not all experts will agree on what is the most appropriate rule for a given situation), and ensuring that the knowledge base does not contain contradictory rules or rules that would lead to circular reasoning. All of these issues are part of what is often referred to as knowledge engineering in expert systems. Some have called it the Achilles' heel of expert systems.
6. The following are key characteristics of an EIS:
   - Generally, modeling and database capabilities are not as sophisticated as a DSS
   - Targets the top-level view and is not intended for the more in-depth analyses provided in a DSS
   - Is intended to allow executives to gain a "view" or "snapshot" of the organization as a whole, whereas a DSS often provides more detailed support in a particular area of the organization's operation
   - EISs typically incorporate external data into the information given to the user, while DSSs typically use internal data
7. The task of decision support for nursing is complex because the decisions faced by nurses are themselves broad and complex, making the development of nursing decision support systems difficult.
8. Electronic clinical records contain information on all aspects of healthcare. Healthcare information systems collect large amounts of textual and numeric information about patients, visits, prescriptions, physician notes etc. Text mining can help extract critical information from electronic clinical records to improve healthcare quality, promote clinical and research initiatives, reduce medical errors, and reduce healthcare costs.

Chapter 20

Check Your Understanding 20.1

1. The following are important management concepts that have persisted over the decades:
   - *Efficiency:* The early time and motion studies of Taylor, the Gilbreths, and others are still relevant to most organizations. The early studies are carried on in today's just-in-time inventory process, project management efforts, and emphasis on quality management.
   - *Management functions:* The four management functions of planning, organizing, leading, and controlling (plus Fayol's fifth function, coordination) have persisted in nearly all organizations and will likely continue to do so in the future.
   - *Fayol's 14 principles,* though modified in some cases, are still sound management concepts that are regularly practiced.

   These concepts have persisted because they enable managers to structure and monitor the functions of a business, regardless of size. They also create a common culture across organizations so that relocated or transferred staff encounter a shorter learning curve and require less time to adjust.
2. New management concepts, theories, and ideas have often been readily and quickly accepted because those who are in a position to adopt them have been ready to do so. These individuals see the need, understand the mechanism for implementing the idea, and understand that adoption of the idea presents obvious benefits. Because of limited or specialized applications at the time they were proposed, resistance to replacing established practices, and apprehension over uncertainty about new ideas, other ideas have required years to be accepted and adopted.
3. For example, the learner could time how long it typically takes to pack for a short trip and compare this time to packing time if a section of the closet is sectioned off with travel clothes already lightly folded, ready for placement in a suitcase. A travel kit of toiletries could be assembled and held ready for any trip. Socks, underwear, handkerchiefs, and so on, could be folded in stacks and placed in a special travel drawer for rapid packing. Another example might be to coordinate the several activities in making a dinner so that all of the dishes are done at the same time.
4. It appears that many of the executives in *In Search of Excellence* believed in Taylor's "one best way" of doing something and that the discovery of "that one way" in their own business led to their initial success. Some of the executives were so proud that

they spent the next few years writing and giving workshops on how others could use the methods that made them successful. They ultimately failed because they stopped paying as much attention to their own businesses and how they made them successful in the first place. If they had recognized that success is a dynamic and ongoing process and continued reinventing new and successful ways to do business in a changing environment, they might have enjoyed longer success.

Check Your Understanding 20.2

1. Staff at different levels of the organization have different challenges and different responsibilities, and the required mix of the four management functions in any one employee often change to account for these differences. For example, while top executives certainly do provide a certain amount of leadership at the top levels of an organization, front-line supervisors and managers need to provide even more daily one-on-one and face-to-face leadership to their subordinates to accomplish goals.
2. An instructor in management, for example, must understand the purpose, principles, and concepts of management as described in this text. Interpersonal skills are used to encourage, challenge, coach, and motivate learners to do their best on assignments. Technically, the instructor must be able to design instructional materials, lecture, facilitate teamwork, and otherwise communicate instructional information.
3. For example, a manager of a museum store meets with staff to recognize best monthly sales performance (figurehead role), sends a memo on group tours planned for the next month (disseminator), coaches an employee who seems frequently late to work (disturbance handler), and so on.
4. See figure 20.4 (Sample Hospital organizational chart). The learner should create a chart similar to this.
5. For example, a student working part-time at a pizza store might define quality in terms of quickly attending to new customers, accurately getting the order from the customer, preparing the pizza quickly and in an attractive manner, serving the correct pizza slice to the correct person at each table, attending to other customer needs (for example, refills), and presenting the bill in a timely manner so the customers do not have to wait unnecessarily when they have finished. To get feedback on each key area of quality, a customer satisfaction card could be placed at each table.

Check Your Understanding 20.3

1. Cohesion refers to the interpersonal forces that influence a group to remain together and act with unity. There are several ways in which cohesion can be promoted, including: having a team name and identity, acquaintance and familiarity among members, shared goals, similarity of styles, team successes, smaller team size, and responding to a common "enemy" or competitor.
2. As much as cohesion is generally desirable, when it is excessive it can interfere with effective group functioning. Indicators of excessive cohesion include a lack of conflict, agreement in meetings but disagreeing privately, under-estimating the capability of competitors, believing that only the group holds the high ethical ground, making rapid decisions without considering alternatives or consequences, avoiding external opinions or evaluation, and not making contingency plans.
3. Groupthink can be reduced by encouraging members to voice disagreements and concerns, not having leadership exert too much influence early in discussions, splitting the group into subgroups, having a devil's advocate argue for opposing points of view, inviting external observers to meetings, seeking external evaluation of group processes, and revisiting previous decisions to ensure soundness of arguments and decisions.

Check Your Understanding 20.4

1. There have been numerous national issues and crises that have brought the role of ethics in organizations to the fore: the financial mismanagement of Enron and WorldCom are recent examples of devastating lapses of ethical judgment, deliberate malfeasance, and disregard for the effects on stakeholders. The financial services "bailout" and failure of bank and mortgage companies to properly manage their holdings is another example of negligence for the ethical responsibilities of these institutions. In the healthcare industry, reports of medical errors, inequity in benefits and salaries for employees in contrast to executive salaries, and providing services for indigent patients have driven wider consciousness of the need for ethics.
2. Environmental measures of CSR for the Triple Bottom Line might include: monitoring purchasing only from vendors who hold values and practices consistent with sustainability, local purchasing whenever possible to reduce carbon footprint of excessive transportation, reviewing products that have excessive or non-recyclable packaging, energy loss through insufficient temperature and lighting controls, etc. Social performance bottom lines could be examined by identifying employee training over periods of time, staff turnover, morale and organizational commitment

surveys, number of employees who volunteer in the community, etc.

3. Incorporating CSR into organizations requires a sound argument. Constructing such an argument might include how CSR is consistent with the vision and mission of the organization, finding benchmarking or competitive organizations who are already taking such a position, finding examples of enhanced public image and support for CSR-oriented hospitals, or number of staff who attend programs on ethical issues and training.

Chapter 21

Check Your Understanding 21.1

1. This list can be organized in several ways. For example, it could be interpreted as "good" and "bad" leaders as well as along effectiveness dimensions. Effectiveness refers to the extent to which their leadership served others and contributed to goal attainment. Effective leaders might include heads of state, business leaders, social leaders, and others (for example, Franklin Roosevelt, Lee Iacoca of Chrysler, Congressional Representative Shirley Chisholm, etc.). Ineffective leaders—those whose performance did not serve their people or resulted in poor outcome—might include: Saddam Hussein, Kenneth Lay of Enron, Imelda Marcos of the Philippines, etc. Discuss how some leaders may attain temporary prominence (such as Hitler), but it does not serve others in the long run.
2. For example, assume you are very skilled and comfortable with providing structure and direction. This would be advantageous during the early stages of supervision or team formation, but as the supervisee or team gained experience and responsibility, such control would likely be perceived as restraining and inappropriate. As the supervisor, you might develop more flexibility in style, assess people's means of demonstrating responsibility, and empower them to perform more independently.
3. You might identify the range of behaviors that are associated with perceptions of effective or ineffective leadership, but emphasize that the person should not try to misrepresent or portray who he or she is not. Positive behaviors might include being a good listener, gate-keeping conversations, showing intelligence (but not too much), and taking a conventional ethical position. You might advise against speaking out too strongly, joking too much, or criticizing other leaders. The primary ethical issue is whether such behavioral practice can be viewed as manipulation.
4. The organization should examine what it most needs at the time and the direction it is developing, and select a leader who can best help them transition in that direction. The leader's ability to understand complex situations (for example, systems thinking), communication skills, experience in the field, stress management, and absence of dysfunctional behaviors (for example, alcohol abuse, anger problems, etc.) should be examined. Employees throughout the organization can be involved in reviewing applicants and background materials.

Check Your Understanding 21.2

1. For a specific decision you made, answer yes or no to each of the eight questions for the decision tree. When the questions have been answered, you will have identified the type of decision format recommended by the Normative Decision Tree (for example, autocratic, consultative, or group delegation). Compare the recommended decision with the procedure you used.
2. In general, leadership tends to be more directive, structured, and autocratic in the beginning and then more participative and delegative as people learn their roles, tasks become routine, skills become more developed, and they require less direct supervision. If knowledgeable and mature workers are overly supervised and controlled, they can become demoralized, resentful, and less productive.
3. Table may include the following:
   - Male stereotypes: Competitive, aggressive, directive, logical
   - Female stereotypes: Collaborative, passive, permissive, emotional
   - Androgynous characteristics: Achieving, visionary, transformational, effective

   Emphasize that any time stereotypes are used, the group stereotyped has important qualities overlooked. Also note that the gender dimension roughly corresponds to the task and social dimensions found in leadership and organizational studies, and that both are important to utilize.

Check Your Understanding 21.3

1. You might inform them of the disruptive nature of organizational change, and that the timing of it should be considered, given fluctuations in production or cash flows. You should also indicate that when new skills and perspectives are being learned, performance usually temporarily drops off—things get worse before they get better. Finally, during change people need a lot of reassurance and information, and clear communication is essential from top management.

2. You might start by reexamining what you want from your job and for your career, and whether job elimination might be an opportunity for change. Should you decide to stay, you would need to assess your skills related to the revised job, and decide how to present them as strengths. The stress of prospective unemployment can be high, and one should rely on a strong support group, be well rested, develop a plan and schedule for pursuing another job, talk with others to express your feelings, and identify your resources and resiliencies that will help you get through the transition.
3. People resist change for many reasons, among them: fear of losing what they value, they don't understand the reason for change, fear of failure, and lack of trust. Examples of measures to reduce these resistances include (respectively): showing people what they will continue doing that is important to them, providing clear rationale for the change, providing skills to help them succeed in the new organization, and building trust and respect before the change is introduced.
4. For example, you might notice that a few members of the group tend dominate the discussion, while others are very quiet. You might speculate and share with the group that you wonder if this reflects a split in the group, different levels of commitment, or lack of information by the low participators. A discussion of these possible meanings can help to decide what the group might want to do differently next meeting. For example, lack of information might be prevented by circulating the agenda and background information so all members can attend prepared to discuss the issue.

Chapter 22

Check Your Understanding 22.1

1. The fundamental elements that must be addressed in good work environment planning are workflow, space, equipment, aesthetics, and ergonomics.
2. A movement diagram helps the manager to visualize the functions and related tasks performed in a defined work area.
3. Lighting should be sufficiently bright; exposure to natural light is easiest on the eyes, desk or task lighting is more physically supportive than overhead fluorescent lighting, PCs with a light background with dark print is least taxing on the eyes, and glare from light or PC screens should be avoided. Color influences how people feel; neutral colors have a calming effect. The finish of the paint should also be considered; matte surfaces absorb more light and reduce glare but generally are not easily cleaned. Certain kinds of music can reduce tension; sound proofing can keep an office less noisy; carpeting, drapes and partitioning all affect the noise level because they absorb sound. Air that is too warm or cold can be distracting so temperature is also important for an effective work space.
4. Two simple actions employees can take to reduce tension and long-term physical problems are hourly neck, shoulder and wrist roll breaks along with stretching; and using good sitting posture.

Check Your Understanding 22.2

1. Temporary help should be secured for the weeks of 7/15 and 7/22 because the sole clerk is on a two-week vacation.
2. Work distribution analysis can reveal the following potential problem areas:
   - There is too much or too little job function specialization
   - There is duplication of efforts of functions
   - Some employees are overloaded while others do not have enough work to keep them busy
   - Large amounts of time are spent on functions of minor importance
   - Small amounts of time are spent on functions of key importance
3. Flextime allows employees to choose their arrival and departure times around a fixed core work time; job sharing divides one job between two part-time employees, each with partial benefits as applicable; and the compressed workweek is a week in which more hours are combined within fewer days.
4. A service level agreement (SLA) includes the detail of what services are needed and the performance expectations, price and payment terms, the reporting chain of command, terms for termination of the agreement, and confidentiality expectations of the vendor and vendor staff.
5. Using the documentation that has been gathered by the employee in the position, that individual's supervisor or manager should write the job description.

Check Your Understanding 22.3

1. True
2. False Turnaround times are examples of quantitative standards and error rates are examples of qualitative standards.
3. True
4. True

Check Your Understanding 22.4

1. Performance measurement is the process of comparing the outcomes of an organization, work unit, or employee to pre-established performance standards. Performance measurement is a fundamental management activity that supports two basic functions of management: controlling and planning. The manager must ensure the work unit or organization is doing what it should be doing in the right way; and the manager must define the expectations of performance, the processes required to achieve those expectations, and the desired outcomes of performance.
2. The purpose of monitors (or controls) is to identify undesirable circumstances occurring in a work process that could lead to an undesirable outcome; this is so appropriate intervention can be introduced to improve the process.
3. Examples of changes to address performance issues could be additional staff training, modifications in procedures, adjustments in workflow, revision of policies, or purchase of updated equipment.

Check Your Understanding 22.5

1. False The components of an open, cybernetic system are input, process, output, controls/standards, feedback, and external environment.
2. True
3. True
4. False One example of external customers are the government agencies and public health organizations who have established regulations and policies that affect the way a department does its work.

Check Your Understanding 22.6

1. False An organization has many customers and sometimes the expectations of one group of customers conflict with those of another group. Nevertheless, the goal of CQI is an admirable one and should be pursued because it can only serve to improve an organization's performance.
2. True
3. True
4. True
5. True

Chapter 23

Check Your Understanding 23.1

1. False
2. True
3. False
4. False

Check Your Understanding 23.2

1. False
2. False
3. True
4. False
5. True

Check Your Understanding 23.3

1. True
2. False
3. True
4. False
5. False

Check Your Understanding 23.4

1. True
2. True
3. False
4. True
5. False
6. True
7. True
8. False
9. False
10. True
11. False
12. True

Check Your Understanding 23.5

1. True
2. False
3. False
4. True
5. True
6. False
7. True
8. True
9. False
10. True
11. False
12. True
13. True
14. False
15. True

Chapter 24

Check Your Understanding 24.1

1. The purposes of the employee orientation program are to introduce the employee to the:
   - Organization's mission, policies, rules, and culture
   - Department or workgroup
   - Specific job he or she will be performing

The orientation program also provides a period of socialization in which the employee learns the values, behavior patterns, and expectations of the organization.

2. The three levels of an orientation program and items reviewed, discussed, or accomplished at each level include the following:
   - Organizational level: Background and mission, policies and procedures, employee benefits, safety regulations, employee handbook, facility tour
   - Departmental level: Policies and procedures, introduction to other employees, tour of the department, work hours, time sheet, equipment operation, safety regulations
   - Individual level: Specific objectives for productivity and performance, instruction, and demonstration of specific job tasks
3. The orientation in large institutions may be conducted by the director of human resources or the director of education. In smaller organizations, the orientation is often conducted by the employee's supervisor. The departmental and individual portions of the orientation at both large and small organizations are typically performed by the employee's supervisor.
4. There are many things that can be done to make a new employee feel welcome in a new department. For example, the employee can be matched with a "buddy" on the first day who can escort him or her to lunch. On the first day, the new employee should also be introduced to coworkers, given a tour of the department, and shown his or her workstation.
5. Orientation of overseas workers should include English proficiency, American etiquette, and cultural understanding, as well as quality standards such as turnaround time and performance expectations. In addition, training on HIPAA requirements and confidentiality are important.
6. Advantages of on-the-job training include its relatively low cost and the fact that work is still in progress while the employee is being trained. It also gives employee and supervisor opportunities to discuss specific problem areas and initiates socialization among employees and their coworkers. Disadvantages include distractions in the workplace and a feeling of pressure if employees do not accomplish work during the training period.
7. Skills that are often developed in on-the-job training include physical skills, academic knowledge, knowledge of institutional policies, and technical skills.
8. The most common technique used for on-the-job training is one-on-one training. For this to be successful, a trainer must be selected who is competent in the job content and capable of teaching and interacting effectively with the trainee. Train-the-trainer workshops may be offered to develop skills in communication and instruction.
9. Job rotation is a useful training technique for employees who are supervisors and need to learn a variety of tasks performed by several subordinate employees.
10. The major steps in on-the-job training include:
    - Preparing the learner by putting him or her at ease and providing an overview of the job
    - Presenting the operation step by step
    - Having the learner demonstrate the steps
    - Following up with encouragement and correction, if necessary
11. In-service education is a continuous training process used to build on basic skills and to teach skills required to maintain job performance or retrain workers whose jobs have changed.
12. Events that suggest a need for in-service education include a restructuring of the department and/or organization, annual updates to coding or reimbursement requirements, implementation of new software or hardware, a decline in productivity or morale or an increase in absenteeism, a new organizational policy or procedure, or an external requirement imposed by accreditation or licensing organizations.
13. HIM in-service topics that might be of interest to other departments include ICD-9-CM or CPT annual updates, medical terminology, use of office productivity software for employee productivity measurement, and health record documentation.
14. Printed items that should be distributed at formal in-service programs include an agenda, a program schedule, materials or handouts to be used for instruction, and reference documents for post-training reinforcement.
15. The effectiveness of an in-service program can be assessed by:
    - Completion of an evaluation form at the conclusion of the program
    - Formal or informal feedback from the employee's supervisor
    - Follow-up with the employee at a later time
16. The purpose of AHIMA's e-HIM initiative is to:
    - Promote the migration from paper to the electronic health record (EHR)
    - Reinvent how institutional and personal health information and records are managed
    - Deliver measurable cost and quality results from improved information management.
17. Topics for training programs might include data analysis, data integration, privacy and security, encryption and deidentification methods, clinical vocabulary development and maintenance, and public health surveillance.
18. Diversity training programs might include topics such as review of other cultures from a social studies perspective, cultural norms such as communication styles, and perspectives of other cultures on privacy

issues. Some employees may need training in English reading and writing skills, interpersonal communication skills, and customer service. Describe two skills that are desired as a result of customer service training.

Skills to be developed in customer service training include communication and listening skills, as well as sensitivity training.

Check Your Understanding 24.2

1. Motivation plays a role in developing a training program because individual employee needs vary and even a single employee may have needs that differ at different points in his or her life or career. By calling attention to the relevance of training to specific needs and connecting the knowledge learned with a work goal, training can be facilitated for each employee.
2. Reinforcers other than monetary awards include a job schedule that allows more time with family or an opportunity for career advancement.
3. Performance standards should usually not be set higher than may reasonably be accomplished because they may reduce motivation and result in feelings of frustration, anxiety, and stress. Standards should be high enough to challenge employees, but not overwhelm them.
4. Adult learners typically like to control the speed of instruction and learn better when training is broken into manageable chunks. Training for adult learners should therefore be delivered in a modular fashion and over a longer period of time because adults learn better in smaller units and want to control the pace of their learning.
5. The five models are:
   - *Sensory:* Does the learner prefer to listen, read, or practice in order to learn best?
   - *Personality:* One's personality traits affect how a person views the world
   - *Information processing:* People differ in how they receive and process information
   - *Social interaction:* Learning style differs by gender and social context
   - *Instructional and environmental preference:* The environment and its structure determine learning style.
6. Trainers should accommodate diversity through acting in a culturally sensitive manner, such as encouraging females of non-Western cultures to participate more, and should adapt computer use to accommodate disabilities, such as using ADA-compliant Web design or voice recognition.

Check Your Understanding 24.3

1. Factors that influence selection of a training method include:
   - Purpose of the training
   - Level of education and experience of the trainees
   - Amount of space, equipment, and media available for training
   - Number of trainees and their location
   - Cost of the method
   - Need for special accommodation due to disability or cultural differences
2. Computer-based training differs significantly from textbook learning. In computer-based training, the computer immediately responds to questions or reinforces answers. Textbooks, in this respect, are much less interactive than computer-based training programs. In addition, in computer-based learning, learners can repeat the interactive segments until they have fully mastered the material. The cost of developing computer-based training is higher than for a textbook, but the cost of delivery is less because the course can be used without an instructor and may be repeated as many times as necessary for learners to gain mastery of the material.
3. Classroom training is appropriate when the goal is to train a large number of employees on largely factual knowledge within a short period of time, but it is not appropriate for developing problem-solving skills or improving interpersonal communication skills.
4. Distance learning removes training barriers associated with location and timing, both for individuals and groups. Learners can attend at a time and place of their choosing.
5. There are many ways that a healthcare organization can use an intranet to deliver training. Intranets are useful for distributing policies and procedures as well as for uploading educational courses for employee self-study. Material on CD-ROM can be installed and delivered to the employee's desktop, or customized for specific needs.
6. Social networking sites can be used to share files or web site bookmarks. Blogs can be used to distribute training materials. Wikis can be used to build a collaborative web site. MUVE's can simulate work environments and scenarios and can be used to practice role-play of leadership or anti-harassment situations. Teams can work together to solve problems.
7. Topics appropriate for intensive study include cultural awareness, training on teamwork and empowerment, or management development.

Check Your Understanding 24.4

1. Organizations can reduce employee turnover by providing fair compensation, job flexibility, good communication, opportunities for mentoring and career growth, and good screening during the hiring process to seek employees with a high level of integrity.
2. An HIM department would benefit from a flextime arrangement when a workload has peaks and valleys, when equipment must be shared across employees and hours, and when employees need time to handle personal matters away from work.
3. An advantage for the employee of a compressed workweek is a reduction in commuting time and additional days off for personal time. An advantage to the department is increased productivity because of fewer start-and-stop periods.
4. One potential problem with flextime is that employees who work in positions that require interaction with others may be ineligible, which can produce feelings of favoritism or discrimination. This can be avoided with written policies that clearly state the positions that are open to flextime and those that are not. Another problem may be the increased fatigue of employees working long days in compressed workweeks. This can be avoided with an appropriate employee and supervisor orientation to explain appropriate work techniques and with extra break time.
5. In job sharing, two or more people share one full-time job and everyone sharing the job may perform parts of the same project. In traditional part-time employment, employees work less than full-time hours and perform their jobs independently of others.
6. A telecommuting agreement should include work schedule, communication frequency and methods, performance measures, confidentiality requirements, equipment maintenance responsibilities, and environmental safety requirements.
7. Functions that are commonly outsourced in an HIM department include transcription, release of information, and coding.
8. Factors that ensure the success of an outsourcing arrangement include:
   - Having assistance from someone skilled in negotiation when developing the contract
   - Engaging legal counsel to review the language of the contract
   - Requiring competitive bidding
   - Establishing expectations and performance standards for contractors
   - Monitoring compliance with performance standards
   - Performing periodic customer surveys to assess satisfaction with the service
9. Managers can empower employees by:
   - Getting others involved in selecting their work assignments and methods for accomplishing tasks
   - Creating an environment of cooperation, information sharing, discussion, and shared ownership of goals
   - Encouraging others to take initiative and make decisions
   - When problems arise, finding out what others think and letting them help design solutions
   - Giving others the freedom to put their ideas and solutions into practice
   - Recognizing successes and encouraging high performance
10. Managers may not empower employees because:
    - They feel that meetings take up too much time and take employees away from their "real work"
    - They may be afraid to share power with others
11. Delegation can provide employees the opportunity to try new tasks. Trying new tasks leads, in turn, to empowerment because employees can contribute ideas and fully use their skills.
12. Successful delegation includes assigning responsibility, granting authority, and creating accountability.
13. Employees may resist accepting delegated responsibilities if they feel unqualified to do the tasks or are being assigned too much work or unpopular work that has little value.
14. Effective coaches are dedicated leaders who display a high level of competence and can push or pull employees to their highest level of performance. They are role models, they provide praise or constructive feedback, and they are ready to help with routine work alongside the employee, if necessary. They defend and support their employees.
15. Mentors are senior employees who work with employees early in their careers. Mentoring is a form of coaching in that it helps employees become self-sufficient but is usually done on a one-on-one basis. Mentors share their knowledge of management styles and teach interpersonal skills, primarily for future job advancement. A coach, on the other hand, may work with several employees at the same time and is concerned more with helping them do the best job they can in their current job by removing obstacles and offering suggestions.
16. Promotion should be awarded on performance and competence, not on seniority, if it is to serve as a motivator. Promotion criteria should be published so that all employees have the opportunity to apply for consideration.
17. Incentive programs fail when there is an emphasis on quantity without a focus on quality, if the reward is not valued and not linked to the amount of effort displayed, or there is ineffective management of the reward program.

18. HIM professionals need continuing education to remain current in their knowledge of the field, which is changing rapidly, and so that they can provide high-quality skills to their organizations.

Check Your Understanding 24.5

1. The steps in a typical training and development plan include:
   - Performing a needs analysis
   - Setting training objectives
   - Designing the curriculum
   - Determining the location and method of delivery
   - Piloting the program
   - Implementing the program
   - Evaluating the effectiveness of the program
   - Making changes as needed
   - Providing feedback to interested groups
2. Outcomes of the needs analysis include:
   - An understanding of where training is needed in the organization
   - A list of the tasks to be learned at each level (entry, remedial, and management development)
   - An analysis of the deficiencies in employee knowledge and skills (accomplished by a comparison of desired and current levels of competence)
3. Objectives specify what employees should be able to accomplish upon completion of the training program. These should be set before starting the program so that results can be evaluated after completion.
4. Among the items to consider when designing a training program are the curriculum, the budget, who will teach the program, materials to be developed, location, and method of delivery.
5. Four outcomes to be measured in program evaluation include reaction of the trainees, what the trainees have learned, behavioral change, and results.
6. The Occupational Safety and Health Act of 1970 was passed to assure safe working conditions. Hospitals must train employees in safety measures, in the worker's native language.

   The Allied Health Reinvestment Act of 2005 encourages individuals to complete allied health education. It provides grants to healthcare organizations and scholarships to applicants.

   The Americans with Disabilities Act of 1990 requires employers to provide reasonable accommodations for physical or mental limitations regarding training, such as providing accessibility to computer-based training.

   Section 508 of the Rehabilitation Act of 1973 provides accessibility standards for electronic and information technology.

Chapter 25

Check Your Understanding 25.1

1. The HIM department is responsible for the coding of the records. While this is important in the billing process, the actual claims are filed by the patient accounts department. Therefore, the insurance company should be referred to the patient accounts department for resolution. If there is an individual who is specifically responsible for handling billing audits, that individual is an appropriate referral. Part of the claims audit may involve a review of the medical records. In that case, the HIM department will provide access to the records in the department, if necessary.
2. Revenue is recorded when known and earned. While the working DRG gives the "known" amount in an acute care situation, the revenue is technically not earned until discharge. Therefore, revenue is not recorded until after discharge. In longer term care situations, this is not the case. Interim payments are requested periodically and the associated revenue booked.
3. This is not a good strategy as it violates the Matching Principle. While the hospital should certainly make every effort to capture all of the associated expenses for THIS fiscal year, NEXT year's expenses must be booked next year. If some of next year's expenses are actually paid this year, they would not be booked as expenses but rather as assets under the heading "prepaid expenses."
4. The federal government is the largest single payer of healthcare expenses in the United States. Although the CMS does not set accounting rules, it enforces the federal regulations regarding the reimbursement for Medicare and the federal portion of the Medicaid program and sets standards for the documentation and reporting of transactions related to such reimbursement.
5. Purely on the basis of the information in this chapter, yes the hospital can sell these services. The hospital would book nonoperating revenue. However, a not-for-profit hospital may potentially incur income tax liability—a problem if the revenue is substantial, since the income is unrelated to its main business.

Check Your Understanding 25.2

1. *Examples of assets:* Cash, marketable securities, accounts receivable, inventory, building, equipment, land.
   Examples of liabilities: Accounts payable, notes payable, mortgage.
2. The excess of revenue over expenses increases the value of the organization. Conversely, the excess of expenses over revenue decreases the value of the organization. The net value of the organization (assets minus liabilities) is expressed in owner's equity (aka fund balance)
3. Anything that it sells as part of the services it provides. Typically, medications are inventory. Durable medical equipment may be considered inventory. In general, medical supplies may be considered inventory; however, for practical purposes they are more likely to be considered expenses in the provision of patient services.
4. Debits are on the left and credits are on the right. In a double-entry bookkeeping system, all transactions have two sides, represented by an equal dollar amount of debits and credits. Assets and expenses are increased by debits. Liabilities, revenue, and owners equity are increased by credits. In this manner, all transactions preserve the balance of the accounting equation: assets minus liabilities equals owners equity.
5. Nonfinancial managers are routinely asked to justify their activities in terms of their contribution to the financial well-being of the organization. Therefore, an understanding of accounting helps managers communicate with financial decision makers.
6. *Current Ratio:* An organization's ability to pay current liabilities with current assets is important to lenders. Current assets implicitly will be (or could be) converted to cash at some point within a year, either through collections, sales, or other business activity. The current ratio compares total current assets with total current liabilities.

Check Your Understanding 25.3

1. *Comparison:* Both branches of accounting deal with the recording, reporting, and analysis of transactions.
   Contrast: Financial accounting focuses on the financial statements and the needs of the users of those statements. Managerial accounting focuses on internal measurements of financial performance, such as budgets.
2. *Comparison:* Both types of budgets allocate the resources of the organization; both can originate at the department or administrative level; both can be analyzed and controlled at the departmental or administrative level.
   Contrast: Operational budgets are prepared annually. Capital budgets are prepared on an as-needed basis. Operational budgets last for one fiscal year. Capital budgets last for the life of the project. Operational budgets are measured and controlled by analyzing monthly and YTD variables from budget to actual amounts. Capital budgets are also measured in terms of return on investment.
3. In this particular situation, an activity-based budget may be more effective than a budget developed along organizational lines. With an activity-based budget, the financial effectiveness of the programs and services can be evaluated more easily. A zero-based budget may also be effective in ensuring that only effective programs and services are carried forward from one year to the next. Either a fixed or variable budget could be developed; however, it would be most effective on an activity basis rather than by department.
4. An organization whose activities do not follow a typical calendar year might find a noncalendar fiscal year more effective. For example, a not-for-profit organization that holds elections and an annual meeting in early summer might have trouble implementing a calendar year budget, since the fiscal accountability would be split between two administrations. Therefore, a fiscal year that ends as one administration leaves office would be more practical.
5. This is a favorable variance, since the payroll amount is actually less than budgeted. However, for a complete analysis, other line items, such as temporary employees and consulting expenses, must be analyzed. For example, a $2,000 favorable payroll variance due to the resignation of a coder may be offset by a $3,000 consulting fee for temporary coding services.

Chapter 26

Check Your Understanding 26.1

1. A project is undertaken because the organization has determined the need for some type of change. This need may be the result of a company's strategic agenda, such as the implementation of a new computer system, or may be due to the passage of a new government regulation.

   Some departments in an organization are primarily project oriented. For example, the information technology department is constantly in the process of implementing new or upgraded systems. Other departments, such as the registration department, can be thought of as primarily operations departments. These types of departments may undertake a project to improve a process.
2. Each project has an identified sponsor. The sponsor is the company employee with the most vested interest in the successful completion of the project. The project also has stakeholders. A stakeholder is anyone in the organization who is affected by the project product.

   Both the sponsor and the stakeholders need to support the project to its successful conclusion. They need to ensure that issues are responded to, change factors are addressed, and that the appropriate resources are dedicated to the project. The main difference between the sponsor and the stakeholders is that the sponsor is the ultimate authority figure and has final say in any issue disputes. A stakeholder may be able to make budget decisions related to his or her area, but the sponsor usually approves the overall budget and any budget overruns that occur. The project manager generally has responsibility for the successful completion of the project objectives but usually does not have authority over the project team. The project manager must work with the sponsor and the stakeholders since they are typically the functional managers for the project team.

   The stakeholders and sponsor often make up the oversight committee, sometimes named the steering committee.
3. A project differs from the day-to-day operations of an organization. Operations are concerned with the everyday jobs needed to run the business. The personnel involved in the operational aspects of the business perform the same functions on a routine basis. This work does not end. By contrast, a project has a precise, expected result produced by defined resources within a specific time frame.
4. One of the reasons that many projects fail to meet the project objectives within the expected time frame and budget is that the scope begins to grow as the project progresses. For example, new functions or features are added to a software implementation. This change is commonly known as *scope creep*. The requester presents each change as a small revision with a low impact to the timeline or cost. Soon there are several minor changes that add up to a more significant modification to the original work or cost estimates. The project manager must be diligent to prevent scope creep. Examples:
   - Class assignment: What happens if your instructor asks for a 10-page document that is due in two weeks, but then two days prior to the due date, changes it to 25 pages? You'd want a new due date right? The scope changed, the resources stayed the same, so the timeline needs to be modified.
   - Building a house: If the foundation has been poured and you decide to have a den and additional bedroom added, this changes the scope. On the other hand, if you decide instead to upgrade to marble counters, you haven't created an impact on the schedule, but you have created an impact on the cost.

Check Your Understanding 26.2

Requires instructor guidance.

Check Your Understanding 26.3

Requires instructor guidance for the preparation of the project proposal document.

The cost estimates will include personnel, equipment, and supplies. If an external company will be providing some project services, the answer should indicate if the engagement is based on time and materials or fixed fee pricing.

The skill set of the project team members will have an impact on the cost. It is a good idea to document the assumptions on which the cost estimates were based. If the project team members will receive raises during the project timeline, this should be reflected as well. Any costs associated with contingency plans should also be detailed.

Check Your Understanding 26.4

Requires instructor guidance for preparation of the work breakdown structure.

1. Methods that can be used for estimating work effort include evaluating a previous project that was similar in scope, conferring with professional colleagues who have experience in this particular type of project, and working with the vendor in those cases where a vendor is involved in the project.
2. Requires instructor guidance.

Check Your Understanding 26.5

1. Each project team member should report the following information for each task:
   - Actual start date or new scheduled start date (when the task was not started on time)
   - Percentage of complete or actual work
   - Remaining work or expected finish date
   - Actual and remaining cost
   - Actual finish date (for completed tasks)
   - Issues
2. People are inclined to overestimate their progress. They tend to tell someone what they believe that person wants to hear rather than report true progress. People also may become defensive about their progress, especially in situations where they are behind schedule or over budget.
3. The process of determining the effect a requested scope change will have on the project in terms of work, schedule and cost and the acceptance of that change by the project stakeholders.
4. Project team members may feel pressure to report a rosy picture of the task progress especially in the case where a task is behind schedule to the point it may delay the overall project schedule. Another problem with status meetings is that participants become bogged down in discussions that cannot be resolved in the meeting. Team members may be reluctant to discuss issues related to politics, conflicts, personality disputes, and bureaucracy when that information will be documented in minutes or a formal status report.

Chapter 27

Other than answer listed here, the Check Your Understanding exercises in this chapter require instructor guidance.

Check Your Understanding 27.1

2. Strategic thinker skills:
   - Ability to plan (consensus building) and strategy formation (leadership)
   - Flexibility and creativity
   - Comfort with uncertainty and risk
   - A sense of urgency and vision on how to move change forward positively
   - How to gain a powerful core of organizational supporters
   - An ability to communicate the vision and plans

Glossary

Abbreviated Injury Scale (AIS): A set of numbers used in a trauma registry to indicate the nature and severity of injuries by body system

Ability (achievement) tests: Tests used to assess the skills an individual already possesses

Abstract: Brief summary of the major parts of a research study

Abstracting: 1. The process of extracting information from a document to create a brief summary of a patient's illness, treatment, and outcome 2. The process of extracting elements of data from a source document or database and entering them into an automated system

Accept assignment: A term used to refer to a provider's or a supplier's acceptance of the allowed charges (from a fee schedule) as payment in full for services or materials provided

Acceptance theory of authority: A management theory based on the principle that employees have the freedom to choose whether they will follow managerial directions

Access control: 1. A computer software program designed to prevent unauthorized use of an information resource 2. The process of designing, implementing, and monitoring a system for guaranteeing that only individuals who have a legitimate need are allowed to view or amend specific data sets

Accession number: A number assigned to each case as it is entered in a cancer registry

Accession registry: A list of cases in a cancer registry in the order in which they were entered

Accountability: Responsibility for a specific activity

Accounting: 1. The process of collecting, recording, and reporting an organization's financial data 2. A list of all disclosures made of a patient's health information

Accounting rate of return: The projected annual cash inflows, minus any applicable depreciation, divided by the initial investment

Accounts payable (A/P): Records of the payments owed by an organization to other entities

Accounts receivable (A/R): Records of the payments owed to the organization by outside entities such as third-party payers and patients

Accreditation: 1. A voluntary process of institutional or organizational review in which a quasi-independent body created for this purpose periodically evaluates the quality of the entity's work against preestablished written criteria 2. A determination by an accrediting body that an eligible organization, network, program, group, or individual complies with applicable standards

Accreditation Association for Ambulatory Health Care (AAAHC): Association that requires that the history and physical examination, laboratory reports, radiology reports, operative reports, and consultations be signed in a timely manner

Accredited Standards Committee (ASC) X12N: A committee of the National Standards Institute that develops and maintains standards for the electronic exchange of business transactions, such as 837—Health Care Claim, 835—Health Care Claim Payment/Advice, and others

Accrue: The process of recording known transactions in the appropriate time period before cash payments or receipts are expected or due

Acid-test ratio: A ratio in which the sum of cash plus short-term investments plus net current receivables is divided by total current liabilities

Active listening: The application of effective verbal communications skills as evidenced by the listener's restatement of what the speaker said

Activities of daily living (ADL): The basic activities of self-care, including grooming, bathing, ambulating, toileting, and eating

Activity-based budget: A budget based on activities or projects rather than on functions or departments

Acute care: Medical care of a limited duration that is provided in an inpatient hospital setting to diagnose and treat an injury or a short-term illness

Acute care prospective payment system (PPS): The reimbursement system for inpatient hospital services provided to Medicare and Medicaid beneficiaries that is based on the use of diagnosis-related groups as a classification tool

Administrative information: Information used for administrative and healthcare operations purposes such as billing and quality oversight

Administrative information systems: A category of healthcare information systems that supports human resources management, financial management, executive decision support, and other business-related functions

Administrative law: A body of rules and regulations developed by various administrative entities empowered by Congress; falls under the umbrella of public law

Administrative management: A subdivision of classical management theory that emphasizes the total organization rather than the individual worker and delineates the major management functions

Administrative services only (ASO) contract: An agreement between an employer and an insurance organization to administer the employer's self-insured health plan

Adopter groups: Groups of adopters (such as innovators, early adopters, early majority, late majority, and laggards) of an innovation that generally fits the normal curve

Adult learning: Self-directed inquiry aided by the resources of an instructor, colleagues and fellow students, and educational materials

Advance Beneficiary Notice (ABN): A statement signed by the patient when he or she is notified by the provider, prior to a service or procedure being done, that Medicare may not reimburse the provider for the service, wherein the patient indicates that he will be responsible for any charges

Advance directive: A legal, written document that describes the patient's preferences regarding future healthcare or stipulates the person authorized to make medical decisions in the event the patient is incapable of communicating his or her preferences

Affinity grouping: A technique for organizing similar ideas together in natural groupings

Age Discrimination in Employment Act (1967): Federal legislation that prohibits employment discrimination against persons between the ages of forty and seventy and restricts mandatory retirement requirements except where age is a bona fide occupational qualification

Agency for Healthcare Research and Quality (AHRQ): The branch of the U.S. Public Health Service that supports general health research and distributes research findings and treatment guidelines with the goal of improving the quality, appropriateness, and effectiveness of healthcare services

Aggregate data: Data extracted from individual health records and combined to form de-identified information about groups of patients that can be compared and analyzed

All-patient diagnosis-related groups (AP-DRGs): A case-mix system developed by 3M and used in a number of state reimbursement systems to classify non-Medicare discharges for reimbursement purposes

All-patient refined diagnosis-related groups (APR-DRGs): An expansion of the inpatient classification system that includes four distinct subclasses (minor, moderate, major, and extreme) based on the severity of the patient's illness

Alternative hypothesis: A hypothesis that states that there is an association between independent and dependent variables

Ambulatory care: Preventative or corrective healthcare services provided on a nonresident basis in a provider's office, clinic setting, or hospital outpatient setting

Ambulatory payment classification (APC) system: The prospective payment system used since 2000 for reimbursement of hospitals for outpatient services provided to Medicare and Medicaid beneficiaries

Ambulatory surgery center or ambulatory surgical center (ASC): Under Medicare, an outpatient surgical facility that has its own national identifier; is a separate entity with respect to its licensure, accreditation, governance, professional supervision, administrative functions, clinical services, record keeping, and financial and accounting systems; has as its sole purpose the provision of services in connection with surgical procedures that do not require inpatient hospitalization; and meets the conditions and requirements set forth in the Medicare Conditions of Participation

Ambulatory Surgery Center Prospective Payment System (ASC PPS): The system that resulted from the Medicare Modernization Act (MMA) of 2003 extensively revising the ASC payment system with changes going into effect on January 1, 2008

American Association of Medical Colleges (AAMC): The organization established in 1876 to standardize the curriculum for medical schools in the United States and to promote the licensure of physicians

American College of Healthcare Executives (ACHE): The national professional organization of healthcare administrators that provides certification services for its members and promotes excellence in the field

American College of Radiology and the National Electrical Manufacturers Association (ACR-NEMA): Digital Imaging and Communications in Medicine (DICOM) was originally created to permit the interchange of biomedical image waveforms and related information through a cooperative effort between ACR and NEMA

American College of Surgeons (ACS): The scientific and educational association of surgeons formed to improve the quality of surgical care by setting high standards for surgical education and practice

American Health Information Community: Group formed in 2005 for leadership toward a connected system and standards development

American Health Information Management Association (AHIMA): The professional membership organization for managers of health record services and healthcare information systems as well as coding services; provides accreditation, certification, and educational services

American Hospital Association (AHA): The national trade organization that provides education, conducts research, and represents the hospital industry's interests in national legislative matters; membership includes individual healthcare organizations as well as individual healthcare professionals working in specialized areas of hospitals, such as risk management

American Medical Association (AMA): The national professional membership organization for physicians that distributes scientific information to its members and the public, informs members of legislation related to health and medicine, and represents the medical profession's interests in national legislative matters

American Medical Informatics Association (AMIA): The membership organization composed of individuals, institutions, and corporations that develop and use information technologies in healthcare

American National Standards Institute (ANSI): The organization that accredits all U.S. standards development organizations to ensure that they are following due process in promulgating standards

American Nurses Association (ANA): The national professional membership association of nurses that works for the improvement of health standards and the availability of healthcare services, fosters high professional standards for the nursing profession, and advances the economic and general welfare of nurses

American Society for Testing and Materials (ASTM): A national organization whose purpose is to establish standards on materials, products, systems, and services

American Society for Testing and Materials Standard E1384 (ASTM E1384)—Standard Guide for Description of Content and Structure of an Automated Primary Record of Care: A standard that identifies the basic information to be included in electronic health records and requires the information to be organized into categories

Americans with Disabilities Act (ADA) (1990): Federal legislation that makes it illegal to discriminate against individuals with disabilities in employment, public accommodations, public services, transportation, and telecommunications

Analog: Data or information that is not represented in an encoded, computer-readable format

Analysis phase: The first phase of the systems development life cycle during which the scope of the project is defined, project goals are identified, current systems are evaluated, and user needs are identified

Ancillary systems: Electronic systems that generate clinical information (such as laboratory information systems, radiology information systems, pharmacy information systems, and so on)

Ancillary systems applications: *See* **ancillary systems**

Androgynous leadership: Managers who are described as successful more often possessed a combination of stereotypical masculine and feminine qualities

Application programming interface (API): A set of definitions of the ways in which one piece of computer software communicates with another or a programmer makes requests of the operating system or another application; operates outside the realm of the direct user interface

Application service provider (ASP): A third-party service company that delivers, manages, and remotely hosts standardized applications software via a network through an outsourcing contract based on fixed, monthly usage or transaction-based pricing

Application systems analyst: Systems analysts with a clinical background in nursing, medicine, or other health professions, including HIM

Applied artificial intelligence: An area of computer science that deals with algorithms and computer systems that exhibit the characteristics commonly associated with human intelligence

Applied healthcare informatics: Automated information systems applied to healthcare delivery business and workflow processes, including the diagnosis, therapy, and systems of managing health data and information within the healthcare setting

Applied research: A type of research that focuses on the use of scientific theories to improve actual practice, as in medical research applied to the treatment of patients

Appreciative inquiry: Is based on the belief that whatever is needed in organizational renewal already exists somewhere in the organization

Aptitude tests: Tests that assess an individual's general ability to learn a new skill

Architecture: The configuration, structure, and relationships of hardware (the machinery of the computer including input/output devices, storage devices, and so on) in an information system

Area of excellence: A describable skill, competence, or capability that a department or company cultivates to a level of proficiency

Artificial intelligence (AI): High-level information technologies used in developing machines that imitate human qualities such as learning and reasoning

Artificial neural network (ANN): A computational technique based on artificial intelligence and machine learning in which the structure and operation are inspired by the properties and operation of the human brain

Assets: The human, financial, and physical resources of an organization

Association for Healthcare Documentation Integrity (AHDI): Formerly the American Association for Medical Transcription (AAMT), the AHDI has a model curriculum for formal educational programs that includes the study of medical terminology, anatomy and physiology, medical science, operative procedures, instruments, supplies, laboratory values, reference use and research techniques, and English grammar

Association of Clinical Documentation Improvement Specialists (ACDIS): Formed in 2007 as a community in which clinical documentation improvement professionals could communicate resources and strategies to implement successful programs and achieve professional growth

Association rule analysis (rule induction): The process of extracting useful if/then rules from data based on statistical significance; *See* **rule induction**

Assumptions: Undetermined aspects of a project that are considered to be true (for example, assuming that project team members have the right skill set to perform their duties)

ASTM Continuity of Care Record (CCR): Document containing standard content for referrals

Asynchronous: Occurring at different times

Attending Physician Statement (APS) (or COMB-1): The standardized insurance claim form created in 1958 by the Health Insurance Association of America and the American Medical Association

Attributable risk (AR): A measure of the impact of a disease on a population (for example, measuring additional risk of illness as a result of exposure to a risk factor)

Attributes: 1. Data elements within an entity that become the column or field names when the entity relationship diagram is implemented as a relational database 2. Properties or characteristics of concepts

Audioconferencing: A learning technique in which students in different locations can learn together via telephone lines while listening to a presenter and looking at handouts or books

Audit: A review process conducted by healthcare facilities (internally and/or externally) to identify variations from established baselines; *See* **external review**

Audit controls: The mechanisms that record and examine activity in information systems

Audit trail: A chronological set of computerized records that provides evidence of information system activity (log-ins and log-outs, file accesses) used to determine security violations

Authentication: 1. The process of identifying the source of health record entries by attaching a handwritten signature, the author's initials, or an electronic signature 2. Proof of authorship that ensures, as much as possible, that log-ins and messages from a user originate from an authorized source

Authority: The right to make decisions and take actions necessary to carry out assigned tasks

Authorization: The granting of permission to disclose confidential information; as defined in terms of the HIPAA privacy rule, an individual's formal, written permission to use or disclose his or her personally identifiable health information for purposes other than treatment, payment, or healthcare operations

Authorization management: The process of protecting the security and privacy of the confidential data in a database

Autoauthentication: A procedure that allows dictated reports to be considered automatically signed unless the health information management department is notified of needed revisions within a certain time limit

Autocoding: The process of extracting and translating dictated and then transcribed free-text data (or dictated and then computer-generated discrete data) into ICD-9-CM and CPT evaluation and management codes for billing and coding purposes

Autocratic leadership: Iowa State University researchers showed that groups under this leadership performed well as long as they were closely supervised, although levels of member satisfaction were low

Autodialing system: A method used to automatically call and remind patients of upcoming appointments

Automated code assignment: Uses data that have been entered into a computer to automatically assign codes; uses natural language processing (NLP) technology—algorithmic (rules based) or statistical—to read the data contained in a CPR

Automated forms-processing (e-forms) technology: Technology that allows users to electronically enter data into online, digital forms and electronically extract data from online, digital forms for data collection or manipulation

Autonomy: A core ethical principle centered on the individual's right to self-determination that includes respect for the individual; in clinical applications, the patient's right to determine what does or does not happen to him or her in terms of healthcare

Availability: The accessibility for continuous use of data

Average daily census: The mean number of hospital inpatients present in the hospital each day for a given period of time

Average length of stay (ALOS): The mean length of stay for hospital inpatients discharged during a given period of time

Balance billing: A reimbursement method that allows providers to bill patients for charges in excess of the amount paid by the patients' health plan or other third-party payer (not allowed under Medicare or Medicaid)

Balance sheet: A report that shows the total dollar amounts in accounts, expressed in accounting equation format, at a specific point in time

Balanced Budget Refinement Act (BBRA) of 1999: The amended version of the Balanced Budget Act of 1997 that authorizes implementation of a per-discharge prospective payment system for care provided to Medicare beneficiaries by inpatient rehabilitation facilities

Balanced scorecard (BSC) methodology: A strategic planning tool that identifies performance measures related to strategic goals

Baldridge Award: A congressional award that recognizes excellence in several areas of business

Bar chart: A graphic technique used to display frequency distributions of nominal or ordinal data that fall into categories

Bar-code medication administration record (BC-MAR) system: System that uses bar-coding technology for positive patient identification and drug information

Bar-coding technology: A method of encoding data that consists of parallel arrangements of dark elements, referred to as bars, and light elements, referred to as spaces, and interpreting the data for automatic identification and data collection purposes

Baseline: The original estimates for a project's schedule, work, and cost

Basic research: A type of research that focuses on the development and refinement of theories

Bed count (complement): The number of inpatient beds set up and staffed for use on a given day

Bed count day: A unit of measure that denotes the presence of one inpatient bed (either occupied or vacant) set up and staffed for use in one twenty-four-hour period

Bed turnover rate: The average number of times a bed changes occupants during a given period of time

Behavioral description interview: An interview format that requires applicants to give specific examples of how they have performed a specific procedure or handled a specific problem in the past

Behavioral healthcare: A broad array of psychiatric services provided in acute, long-term, and ambulatory care settings; includes treatment of mental disorders, chemical dependency, mental retardation, and developmental disabilities, as well as cognitive rehabilitation services

Benchmarking: An analysis process based on comparison

Beneficence: A legal term that means promoting good for others or providing services that benefit others, such as releasing health information that will help a patient receive care or will ensure payment for services received

Benefit: Healthcare service for which the healthcare insurance company will pay

Bill hold period: The span of time during which a bill is suspended in the billing system awaiting late charges, diagnosis and procedure codes, insurance verification, or other required information

Bills of Mortality: Documents used in London during the seventeenth century to identify the most common causes of death

Bioethics: A field of study that applies ethical principles to decisions that affect the lives of humans, such as whether to approve or deny access to health information

Biotechnology: The field devoted to applying the techniques of biochemistry, cellular biology, biophysics, and molecular biology to addressing practical issues related to human beings, agriculture, and the environment

Bit-mapped data: Data made up of pixels displayed on a horizontal and vertical grid or matrix

Bivariate: An adjective meaning the involvement of two variables

Blanket authorization: An authorization for the release of confidential information from a certain point in time and any time thereafter

Blended learning: A training strategy that uses a combination of techniques—such as lecture, Web-based training, or programmed text—to appeal to a variety of learning styles and maximize the advantages of each training method

Blogs: Web logs provide a Web page where users can post text, images, and links to other Web sites

Blood and blood component usage review: Evaluation of how blood and blood components are used using Joint Commission guidelines

Blue Cross and Blue Shield (BC/BS): The first prepaid healthcare plans in the United States; Blue Shield plans traditionally cover hospital care and Blue Cross plans cover physicians' services

Blue Cross and Blue Shield Association: The national association of state and local Blue Cross and Blue Shield plans

Blue Cross and Blue Shield Federal Employee Program (FEP): A federal program that offers a fee-for-service plan with preferred provider organizations and a point-of-service product

Board of governors (board of trustees, board of directors): The elected or appointed group of officials who bear ultimate responsibility for the successful operation of a healthcare organization

Body of Knowledge (BoK): The collected resources, knowledge, and expertise within and related to a profession

Bounded rationality: The recognition that decision making is often based on limited time and information about a problem and that many situations are complex and rapidly changing

Boxplot: Tool in the form of a graph that displays five-number data summary

Brainstorming: A group problem-solving technique that involves the spontaneous contribution of ideas from all members of the group

Break-even analysis: A financial analysis technique for determining the level of sales at which total revenues equal total costs beyond which revenues become profits

Breast Imaging Reporting and Data System Atlas (BI-RADS): A comprehensive guide providing standardized breast imaging terminology and a report organization, assessment structure, and classification system for mammography, ultrasound, and MRI of the breast

Bridge technology: Technology such as document imaging and/or clinical messaging that provides some, but not all, the benefits of an EHR

Bubble chart: A type of scatter plot with circular symbols used to compare three variables; the area of the circle indicates the value of a third variable

Budget cycle: The complete process of financial planning, operations, and control for a fiscal year; overlaps multiple fiscal years

Buildings: A long-term (fixed) asset account that represents the physical structures owned by the organization

Bundled payments: A period of relatively continuous medical care performed by healthcare professionals in relation to a particular clinical problem or situation

Bureaucracy: A formal organizational structure based on a rigid hierarchy of decision making and inflexible rules and procedures

Business intelligence (BI): The end product or goal of knowledge management

Business process reengineering (BPR): The analysis and design of the workflow within and between organizations

Bylaws/rules and regulations: Operating documents that describe the rules and regulations under which a healthcare organization operates

Capital budget: The allocation of resources for long-term investments and projects

Capitation: A method of healthcare reimbursement in which an insurance carrier prepays a physician, hospital, or other healthcare provider a fixed amount for a given population without regard to the actual number or nature of healthcare services provided to the population

Care Map: A proprietary care-planning tool similar to a clinical protocol that outlines the major aspects of treatment on the basis of diagnosis or other characteristics of the patient

Care path: A care-planning tool similar to a clinical practice guideline that has a multidisciplinary focus emphasizing the coordination of clinical services

Career development: The process of growing or progressing within one's profession or occupation

Case definition: A method of determining criteria for cases that should be included in a registry

Case fatality rate: The total number of deaths due to a specific illness during a given time period divided by the total number of cases during the same period

Case finding: A method of identifying patients who have been seen or treated in a healthcare facility for the particular disease or condition of interest to the registry

Case law: *See* **common law**

Case management: 1. The ongoing, concurrent review performed by clinical professionals to ensure the necessity and effectiveness of the clinical services being provided to a patient 2. A process that integrates and coordinates patient care over time and across multiple sites and providers, especially in complex and high-cost cases 3. The process of developing a specific care plan for a patient that serves as a communication tool to improve quality of care and reduce cost

Case manager: 1. A professional nurse who coordinates the daily progress of a patient population by assessing needs, developing goals, individualizing plans of care on an ongoing basis, and evaluating overall progress 2. A medical professional (usually a nurse or a social worker) who reviews cases to determine the necessity of care and to advise providers on payer's utilization restrictions

Case mix: A description of a patient population based on any number of specific characteristics, including age, gender, type of insurance, diagnosis, risk factors, treatment received, and resources used

Case study: A type of nonparticipant observation in which researchers investigate one person, one group, or one institution in depth

Case-control (retrospective) study: A study that investigates the development of disease by amassing volumes of data about factors in the lives of persons with the disease (cases) and persons without the disease

Case-mix group (CMG) relative weights: Factors that account for the variance in cost per discharge and resource utilization among case-mix groups

Case-mix index (CMI): The average relative weight of all cases treated at a given facility or by a given physician, which reflects the resource intensity or clinical severity of a specific group in relation to the other groups in the classification system; calculated by dividing the sum of the weights of diagnosis-related groups for patients discharged during a given period divided by the total number of patients discharged

Cash: The actual money that has been received and is readily available to pay debts; a short-term (current) asset account that represents currency and bank account balances

Categorical data: *See* **scales of measurement**

Categorically needy eligibility: Categories of individuals to whom states must provide coverage under the federal Medicaid program

Causal relationship: A type of relationship in which one factor results in a change in another factor (cause and effect)

Causal-comparative research: A research design that resembles experimental research but lacks random assignment to a group and manipulation of treatment

Cause-specific death rate: The total number of deaths due to a specific illness during a given time period divided by the estimated population for the same time period

Census: The number of inpatients present in a healthcare facility at any given time

Census survey: A survey that collects data from all the members of a population

Center for Drug Evaluation and Research (CDER) Data Standards Manual: A compilation of standardized nomenclature monographs for sharing information regarding manufactured drug dosage forms

Centers for Medicare and Medicaid Services (CMS): The division of the Department of Health and Human Services that is responsible for developing healthcare policy in the United States and for administering the Medicare program and the federal portion of the Medicaid program; called the Health Care Financing Administration (HCFA) prior to 2001

Certainty factor: The defined certainty percentage rate with which an occurrence must present itself to satisfy quality standards

Certification: 1. The process by which a duly authorized body evaluates and recognizes an individual, institution, or educational program as meeting predetermined requirements 2. An evaluation performed to establish the extent to which a particular computer system, network design, or application implementation meets a prespecified set of requirements

Certification Commission for Healthcare Information Technology (CCHIT): A recognized certification body for electronic health records and their networks; a private, nonprofit initiative

Certified coding associate (CCA): An AHIMA credential awarded to entry-level coders who have demonstrated skill in classifying medical data by passing a certification exam

Certified coding specialist (CCS): An AHIMA credential awarded to individuals who have demonstrated skill in classifying medical data from patient records, generally in the hospital setting, by passing a certification examination

Certified coding specialist–physician-based (CCS–P): An AHIMA credential awarded to individuals who have demonstrated coding expertise in physician-based settings, such as group practices, by passing a certification examination

Certified in healthcare privacy and security (CHPS): Credential that recognizes advanced competency in designing, implementing, and administering comprehensive privacy and security protection programs in all types of healthcare

organizations; requires successful completion of both the CHP and the CHS exams (jointly sponsored by AHIMA and HIMSS)
Certified medical transcriptionist (CMT): A certification that is granted upon successful completion of an examination
Certified professional in health information management systems (CPHIMS): Credential (managed jointly by HIMSS, AHA Certification Center, and applied measurement professionals) that certifies knowledge of healthcare information and management systems and understanding of psychometrics (the science of measurement; requires baccalaureate or graduate degree plus associated experience)
Chain of command: A hierarchical reporting structure within an organization
Champion: Someone in the organization who believes in the idea, acknowledges the practical problems of financing and political support, and assists in overcoming barriers
Change agent: A specialist in organizational development and facilitates the change brought about by the innovation
Change control: The process of performing an impact analysis and obtaining approval before modifications to the project scope are made
Change drivers: Forces in the external environment of organizations or industries that force organizations or industries to change the way they operate in order to survive
Change management: Way in which an organization fosters and directs change in conjunction with process improvement
Charge description master (CDM): *See* **chargemaster**
Chargemaster: A financial management form that contains information about the organization's charges for the healthcare services it provides to patients; *See* **charge description master (CDM)**
Charisma: The ability to inspire and motivate people beyond what is expected with exceptionally high levels of commitment
Chart tracking: A system that identifies the current location of a record or information
Charting by exception: A method of charting only abnormal or unusual findings or deviations from the prescribed plan of care; also known as focus charting
Check sheet: A tool that permits the systematic recording of observations of a particular phenomenon so that trends or patterns can be identified
Chief executive officer (CEO): The senior manager appointed by a governing board to direct an organization's overall long-term strategic management
Chief financial officer (CFO): The senior manager responsible for the fiscal management of an organization
Chief information officer (CIO): The senior manager responsible for the overall management of information resources in an organization
Chief information security officer (CISO): IT leadership role responsible for ensuring that a healthcare organization's information systems are secure and safe from tampering or misuse; role has grown as a direct result of HIPAA security regulations
Chief information technology officer (CITO): IT leadership role that guides an organization's decisions related to technical architecture and evaluates latest technology developments and their applicability or potential use in the organization
Chief medical informatics officer (CMIO): An emerging position, typically a physician with medical informatics training, that provides physician leadership and direction in the deployment of clinical applications in healthcare organizations
Chief nursing officer (CNO): The senior manager (usually a registered nurse with advanced education and extensive experience) responsible for administering patient care services
Chief operating officer (COO): The role responsible for managing day-to-day activities of an organization
Circuit: The geographic area covered by a U.S. Court of Appeals
Civil law: The branch of law involving court actions among private parties, corporations, government bodies, or other organizations, typically for the recovery of private rights with compensation usually being monetary
Civil Rights Act (1991): The federal legislation that focuses on establishing an employer's responsibility for justifying hiring practices that seem to adversely affect people because of race, color, religion, sex, or national origin
Civil Rights Act, Title VII (1964): The federal legislation that prohibits discrimination in employment on the basis of race, religion, color, sex, or national origin
Civilian Health and Medical Program of the Uniformed Services (CHAMPUS): A federal program providing supplementary civilian-sector hospital and medical services beyond that which is available in military treatment facilities to military dependents, retirees and their dependents, and certain others
Civilian Health and Medical Program-Veterans Administration (CHAMPVA): The federal healthcare benefits program for dependents of veterans rated by the VA as having a total and permanent disability, for survivors of veterans who died from VA-rated service-connected conditions or who were rated permanently and totally disabled at the time of death from a VA-rated service-connected condition, and for survivors of persons who died in the line of duty
Claim: An itemized statement of healthcare services and their costs provided by a hospital, physician office, or other healthcare provider; submitted for reimbursement to the healthcare insurance plan by either the insured party or the provider
Claims processing: The process of accumulating claims for services, submitting claims for reimbursement, and ensuring that claims are satisfied
Client/server architecture: A computer architecture in which multiple computers (clients) are connected to other computers (servers) that store and distribute large amounts of shared data

Clinic outpatient: A patient who is admitted to a clinical service of a clinic or hospital for diagnosis or treatment on an ambulatory basis

Clinical (or critical) pathway: A tool designed to coordinate multidisciplinary care planning for specific diagnoses and treatments; *See* **critical path and Care Map**

Clinical Care Classification (CCC): Two interrelated taxonomies, the CCC of Nursing Diagnoses and Outcomes and the CCC of Nursing Interventions and Actions, that provide a standardized framework for documenting patient care in hospitals, home health agencies, ambulatory care clinics, and other healthcare settings

Clinical care plans: Care guidelines created by healthcare providers for individual patients for a specified period of time

Clinical communication space: The context and range of electronic and interpersonal information exchanged among staff and patients

Clinical data: Data captured during the process of diagnosis and treatment

Clinical data repository (CDR): A central database that focuses on clinical information

Clinical data specialist: Specialist who concentrates on assuring accurate and complete coding, validating the information contained in databases for internal and external uses, and providing information for clinical research across the entire integrated health care delivery system

Clinical data warehouse (CDW): *See* **data warehouse**

Clinical decision support (CDS): *See* **clinical decision support system**

Clinical decision support system (CDSS): A special subcategory of clinical information systems that is designed to help healthcare providers make knowledge-based clinical decisions

Clinical document architecture (CDA): HL7 electronic exchange model for clinical documents (such as discharge summaries and progress notes)

Clinical informatics: A field of information science concerned with the management of data and information used to support the practice and delivery of patient care through the application of computers and computer technologies

Clinical information system (CIS): A category of a healthcare information system that includes systems that directly support patient care

Clinical messaging: The function of electronically delivering data and automating the workflow around the management of clinical data

Clinical messaging system: Secure messaging systems that are important, pervasive tools included in a broad set of contextual collaboration tools for clinicians

Clinical pathways: *See* **clinical practice guidelines**

Clinical practice guidelines: A detailed, step-by-step guide used by healthcare practitioners to make knowledge-based decisions related to patient care and issued by an authoritative organization such as a medical society or government agency

Clinical privileges: The authorization granted by a healthcare organization's governing board to a member of the medical staff that enables the physician to provide patient services in the organization within specific practice limits

Clinical project manager: One who is responsible for managing and frequently participating in defining the scope of work, developing project plans, and maintaining schedules; he or she will finalize the budget, develop plans for minimizing risks, and will be responsible for implementing improvement processes

Clinical repository: A frequently updated database that provides users with direct access to detailed patient-level data as well as the ability to drill down into historical views of administrative, clinical, and financial data; *See* **data warehouse**

Clinical systems analyst: *See* **systems analyst**

Clinical terminology: A set of standardized terms and their synonyms that record patient findings, circumstances, events, and interventions with sufficient detail to support clinical care, decision support, outcomes research, and quality improvement

Clinical transformation: A comprehensive, ongoing approach to care delivery excellence that offers value while measurably improving quality, enhancing service, and reducing costs through the effective alignment of people, process, and technology

Clinical trial: A controlled research study involving human subjects that is designed to evaluate prospectively the safety and effectiveness of new drugs, tests, devices, or interventions

Clinical value compass: Performance improvement approach that measures the association of quality and value

Clinical workstation: A single point of access that includes a common user interface to view information from disparate applications and to launch applications

Clinical/medical decision support system: A special subcategory of clinical information systems that is designed to help healthcare providers make knowledge-based clinical decisions

Clinician/physician Web portals: The media for providing clinician/physician access to the provider organization's multiple sources of data from any network-connected device

Closed records: The records of patients who have been discharged from the hospital or whose treatment has been terminated

Closed systems: Systems that operate in a self-contained environment

Closed-record review: A review of records after a patient has been discharged from the organization or treatment has been terminated

Cluster sampling: The process of selecting subjects for a sample from each cluster within a population (for example, a family, school, or community)

CMS-1500: A Medicare claim form used to bill third-party payers for provider services (for example, physician office visits)

Coaching: 1. A training method in which an experienced person gives advice to a less-experienced worker on a formal or informal basis 2. A disciplinary method used as the first step for employees who are not meeting performance expectations

Coalition building: A technique used to manage the political dimensions of change within an organization by building the support of groups for change

Coded data: Data that are translated into a standard nomenclature of classification so that they may be aggregated, analyzed, and compared

Coding: The process of assigning numeric representations to clinical documentation

Cohort study: A study, followed over time, in which a group of subjects is identified as having one or more characteristics in common

Coinsurance: Cost sharing in which the policy or certificate holder pays a preestablished percentage of eligible expenses after the deductible has been met

Collaborative Stage Data Set: A new standardized neoplasm-staging system developed by the American Joint Commission on Cancer

College of American Pathologists (CAP): Organization of board-certified pathologists that serves patients, pathologists, and the public by fostering and advocating excellence in the practice of pathology and laboratory medicine

College of Healthcare Information Management Executives (CHIME): A membership association serving chief information officers through professional development and advocacy

Commission on Accreditation of Health Informatics and Information Management Education (CAHIIM): The accrediting organization for educational programs in health informatics and information management

Commission on Accreditation of Rehabilitation Facilities (CARF): A private, not-for-profit organization that develops customer-focused standards for behavioral healthcare and medical rehabilitation programs and accredits such programs on the basis of its standards

Common cause variation: The source of variation in a process that is inherent within the process

Common Framework: A set of tools critical to achieving an interoperable environment that supports modern healthcare practice, including precisely defined and uniform technical standards as well as common policies and methods

Common law: Unwritten law originating from court decisions where no applicable statute exists; *See* **case law**

Common Rule: Federal Policy for the Protection of Human Subjects (45 CFR Part 46 Subpart A) that is a set of regulations regarding research that 18 federal agencies share; these agencies fund research at institutions that provide written assurance to the funding agency that the institutions will comply with the requirements of this policy

Communication plan: A documented approach to identifying the media and schedule for sharing information with affected parties

Community of Practice (CoP): The community for those interested in clinical terminologies and vocabularies

Comorbidity: A medical condition that coexists with the primary cause for hospitalization and affects the patient's treatment and length of stay

Comparative data: Data that are used for benchmarking or other comparisons within or across healthcare organizations

Compensable factor: Characteristic used to compare the worth of jobs (for example, skill, effort, responsibility, and working conditions)

Compensation and benefits: The payment package offered to employees in return for work

Competencies: Demonstrated skills that a worker should perform at a high level

Compliance: 1. The process of establishing an organizational culture that promotes the prevention, detection, and resolution of instances of conduct that do not conform to federal, state, or private payer healthcare program requirements or the healthcare organization's ethical and business policies 2. The act of adhering to official requirements

Compliance program guidance: The information provided by the Office of the Inspector General of the Department of Health and Human Services to help healthcare organizations develop internal controls that promote adherence to applicable federal and state guidelines

Complication: A medical condition that arises during an inpatient hospitalization (for example, a postoperative wound infection)

Compressed workweek: A work schedule that permits a full-time job to be completed in less than the standard five days of eight-hour shifts

Compromise: A mutual agreement

Computer output to laser disk (COLD): *See* **Computer Output Laser Disk/Enterprise Report Management (COLD/ERM) technology**

Computer Output Laser Disk/Enterprise Report Management (COLD/ERM) technology: Technology that electronically stores the documents and distributes them with fax, email, Web, and traditional hard-copy print processes

Computer virus: A software program that attacks computer systems and sometimes damages or destroys files

Computer-assisted coding: The process of extracting and translating dictated and then transcribed free-text data (or dictated and then computer-generated discrete data) into ICD-9-CM and CPT evaluation and management codes for billing and coding purposes

Computer-based training: A type of training that is delivered partially or completely using a computer

Computerized provider order entry (CPOE): Systems that allow physicians to enter medication or other orders and receive clinical advice about drug dosages, contraindications, or other clinical decision support

Concept: A unit of knowledge or thought created by a unique combination of characteristics

Conceptual data model: The highest level of data model, representing the highest level of abstraction, independent of hardware and software

Conceptual framework of accounting: The concept that the benefits of financial data should exceed the cost of obtaining them and that the data must be understandable, relevant, reliable, and comparable

Conceptual skills: One of the three managerial skill categories that includes intellectual tasks and abilities such as planning, deciding, and problem solving

Concurrent analysis: A review of the health record while the patient is still hospitalized or under treatment

Conditions of Participation: The administrative and operational guidelines and regulations under which facilities are allowed to take part in the Medicare and Medicaid programs; published by the Centers for Medicare and Medicaid Services, a federal agency under the Department of Health and Human Services

Confidentiality: A legal and ethical concept that establishes the healthcare provider's responsibility for protecting health records and other personal and private information from unauthorized use or disclosure

Conflict management: The process of working with individuals to find a mutually acceptable solution to a problem that has arisen between them

Confounding (extraneous, secondary) variable: An event or a factor that is outside a study but occurs concurrently with the study

Consent: A means for residents to convey to healthcare providers their implied or expressed permission to administer care or treatment or to perform surgery or other medical procedures

Conservatism: The concept that resources must not be overstated and liabilities not understated

Consideration: In an Ohio State University examination of the behavior of leaders in the 1950s and 1960s, referred to attention to the interpersonal aspects of work, including respect for subordinates' ideas and feelings, maintaining harmonious work relationships, collaborating in teamwork, and showing concern with the subordinates' welfare

Consistency: The idea that all time periods must reflect the same accounting

Consolidated Health Informatics (CHI): The notion of adopting existing health information interoperability standards throughout all federal agencies

Consolidated Health Informatics (CHI) initiative: The effort to achieve CHI through federal agencies spearheaded by the Office of National Coordinator for Health Information Technology

Construct validity: The ability of an instrument to measure hypothetical, nonobservable traits

Constructive confrontation: A method of approaching conflict in which both parties meet with an objective third party to explore perceptions and feelings

Consultant: Employed outside of the healthcare provider arena, he or she works for an external firm or independently; may be responsible for operational assistance with e-HIM conversions, revenue cycle and coding auditing, compliance, privacy and security, or any of the HIM-related functions

Consultation: The response by one healthcare professional to another healthcare professional's request to provide recommendations and opinions regarding the care of a particular patient/resident

Consultation rate: The total number of hospital inpatients receiving consultations for a given period divided by the total number of discharges and deaths for the same period

Consumer health: Providing services that accommodate more knowledgeable patients while helping them to become more informed and to participate as partners in their own healthcare

Consumer informatics: The field of information science concerned with the management of data and information used to support consumers by consumers (the general public) through the application of computers and computer technologies

Content: The substantive or meaningful components of a document or collection of documents

Content analysis: A method of research that provides a systematic and objective analysis of communication effectiveness, such as the analysis performed on tests

Content validity: The extent to which an instrument's items represent the content that the instrument is intended to measure

Context: The text that illustrates a concept or the use of a designation

Context-sensitive: Templates that react to the nature of the data being entered and to tailor that tailor the template to the specific data entry needs

Contingency: A plan of action to be taken when circumstances affect project performance

Contingency model of leadership: Designed by Fred Fiedler at the University of Illinois to compensate for the limitations of the classical and behavioral theories of leadership; Fiedler kept the social-task orientation as the cornerstone of his theory and designed an innovative test to determine the leader's preferred style

Contingency planning: An administrative security requirement in which applications should be categorized by criticality and backup plans, disaster recovery plans, and emergency mode operations plans developed in accordance with the criticality of the application and its information

Continuing education: A type of training that enables employees to remain current in the knowledge base of their profession

Continuity of care document: Document that is the result of harmonizing the ASTM International Continuity of Care Record (CCR) standard content for referrals with the HL7 CDA standard for document construction; now widely used in creating PHRs

Continuity of care record (CCR): Documentation of care delivery from one healthcare experience to another

Continuous data: Data that represent measurable quantities but are not restricted to certain specified values

Continuous quality improvement (CQI): 1. A management philosophy that emphasizes the importance of knowing and meeting customer expectations, reducing variation within processes, and relying on data to build knowledge for process improvement 2. A continuous cycle of planning, measuring, and monitoring performance and making knowledge-based improvements

Continuous record review: *See* **open-record review**

Continuous speech input: The quality of speech/voice recognition technology that does not require users to pause between words to allow the computer to distinguish between the beginnings and endings of words

Continuous variables: Discrete variables measured with sufficient precision

Continuum of care: The range of healthcare services provided to patients, from routine ambulatory care to intensive acute care

Contra-account: Any account set up to adjust the historical value of a balance sheet account (for example, cumulative depreciation is a contra-account to an equipment [fixed-asset] account)

Contract law: A branch of law based on common law that deals with written or oral agreements that are enforceable through the legal system

Contract service: An entity that provides certain agreed-upon services for the facility, such as transcription, coding, or copying

Control: One of the four management functions in which performance is monitored in accordance with organizational policies and procedures

Control group: A comparison study group whose members do not undergo the treatment under study

Controlled Substances Act: The legislation that controls the use of narcotics, depressants, stimulants, and hallucinogens

Controlling: The monitoring and maintenance of a project's structure

Convenience sampling: A type of nonrandom sampling in which researchers use any unit at hand

Coordination of benefits (COB) transaction: The electronic transmission of claims and/or payment information from a healthcare provider to a health plan for the purpose of determining relative payment responsibilities

Core data elements/core content: A small set of data elements with standardized definitions often considered to be the core of data collection efforts

Core measure/core measure set: Standardized performance measures developed to improve the safety and quality of healthcare (for example, core measures are used in the Joint Commission on Accreditation's ORYX initiative)

Core performance measures: Measures that are considered tools—standardized metrics—that provide an indication of an organization's performance

Corporate social responsibility: A responsibility of an organization that is part of its strategic plan, part of its bottom line, and the core intention is value-based

Corporation: An organization that may have one or many owners in which profits may be held or distributed as dividends (income paid to the owners)

Corrective controls: Internal controls designed to fix problems that have been discovered, frequently as a result of detective controls

Correlational research: A design of research that determines the existence and degree of relationships among factors

Cost accounting: The specialty branch of accounting that deals with quantifying the resources expended to provide the goods and services offered by the organization to its customers/clients/patients

Cost justification: A rationale developed to support competing requests for limited resources

Cost outlier: Exceptionally high costs associated with inpatient care when compared with other cases in the same diagnosis-related group

Cost outlier adjustment: Additional reimbursement for certain high-cost home care cases based on the loss-sharing ratio of costs in excess of a threshold amount for each home health resource group

Cost report: A report that analyzes the direct and indirect costs of providing care to Medicare patients

Court of Appeals: A branch of the federal court system that has the power to hear appeals on the final judgments of district courts

Covered entity (CE): To make a good faith effort to obtain the patient's written acknowledgment of receipt of the HIPAA Privacy Notice

CPT® (Current Procedural Terminology): A comprehensive, descriptive list of terms and numeric codes used for reporting diagnostic and therapeutic procedures and other medical services performed by physicians; published and updated annually by the American Medical Association

Credentialing or credentialing process: The process of reviewing and validating the qualifications (degrees, licenses, and other credentials), of physicians and other licensed independent practitioners, for granting medical staff membership to provide patient care services

Credits: The amounts on the right side of a journal entry

Criminal law: A branch of law that addresses crimes that are wrongful acts against public health, safety, and welfare, usually punishable by imprisonment and/or fine

Critic: This role is essential in challenging the innovation for shortcomings, presenting strong criteria, and, in essence, providing a reality test for the new idea

Critical issues: The bridge between the current strategic profile and the future strategic vision and profile of a department or organization that leadership has deliberately decided to pursue

Critical path/critical path method: In project management, the sequence of tasks that determine the project finish date

Cross-sectional study: A biomedical research study in which both the exposure and the disease outcome are determined at the same time in each subject

Cross-training: The training to learn a job other than the employee's primary responsibility

Crosswalk: *See* **data map**

Crude birth rate: The number of live births divided by the population at risk

Crude death rate: The total number of deaths in a given population for a given period of time divided by the estimated population for the same period of time

Cultural competence: Skilled in awareness, understanding, and acceptance of beliefs and values of the people of groups other than one's own

Current Dental Terminology (CDT): A medical code set of dental procedures, maintained and copyrighted by the American Dental Association (ADA), referred to as the Uniform Code on Dental Procedures and Nomenclatures until 1990

Current Procedural Terminology (CPT): Published by the AMA, this codebook has become widely used as a standard for outpatient and ambulatory care procedural coding in contexts related to reimbursement; it is updated every year on January 1

Current ratio: The total current assets divided by total current liabilities

Customer relationship management (CRM): A management system whereby organizational structure and culture and customer information and technology are aligned with business strategy so that all customer interactions can be conducted to the long-term satisfaction of the customer and to the benefit and profit of the organization

Customer service training: Training that focuses on creating a true customer orientation within the work environment

Cybernetic systems: Systems that have standards, controls, and feedback mechanisms built in to them

Cyclical staffing: A transitional staffing solution where workers are brought in for specific projects or to cover in busy times

Daily inpatient census: The number of inpatients present at census-taking time each day, plus any inpatients who were both admitted and discharged after the census-taking time the previous day

Dashboard: A launching pad from which one is able to drill down to further detail about a given aspect of the patient's care

Data: The dates, numbers, images, symbols, letters, and words that represent basic facts and observations about people, processes, measurements, and conditions

Data administrator: An emerging role responsible for managing the less technical aspects of data, including data quality and security

Data capture: The process of recording healthcare-related data in a health record system or clinical database

Data cleansing: The process of detecting, diagnosing, and editing faulty data

Data confidentiality: The extent to which personal health information is kept private

Data content standards: Standards that make it possible to exchange health information using electronic networks that reach across the country and around the world

Data definition language (DDL): A special type of software used to create the tables within a relational database, the most common of which is structured query language

Data dictionary: A descriptive list of the data elements to be collected in an information system or database whose purpose is to ensure consistency of terminology

Data display: A method for presenting or viewing data

Data element: An individual fact or measurement that is the smallest unique subset of a database

Data Elements for Emergency Department Systems (DEEDS): A data set designed to support the uniform collection of information in hospital-based emergency departments

Data exchange standards: Protocols that help ensure that data transmitted from one system to another remain comparable

Data integrity: 1. The extent to which healthcare data are complete, accurate, consistent, and timely 2. A security principle that keeps information from being modified or otherwise corrupted either maliciously or accidentally

Data integrity specialist: One who is responsible for assuring quality and accuracy of medical information in any form, electronic or hybrid

Data manipulation language (DML): A special type of software used to retrieve, update, and edit data in a relational database, of which the most common is structured query language

Data map: Term that describes the connections, or paths, between classifications and vocabularies; *see* **crosswalk**

Data mart: A well-organized, user-centered, searchable database system that usually draws information from a data warehouse to meet the specific needs of users

Data miners: Those individuals who extract data from a database with the intention of quantifying and filtering them

Data mining: The process of extracting information from a database and then quantifying and filtering discrete, structured data

Data model: A picture or abstraction of real conditions used to design the definitions of fields and records and their relationships in a database

Data modeling: The process of determining the users' information needs and identifying relationships among the data

Data quality management: A managerial process that ensures the integrity (accuracy and completeness) of an organization's data during data collection, application, warehousing, and analysis

Data quality manager/data quality analyst: One who is responsible for data management functions that involve formalized continuous quality improvement activities for data integrity throughout the organization, beginning with the data dictionary and policy development, as well as data quality monitoring and audits

Data quality model: A managerial process that ensures the integrity (accuracy and completeness) of an organization's data during data collection, application, warehousing, and analysis; also called data management model

Data repository: An open-structure database that is not dedicated to the software of any particular vendor or data supplier, in which data from diverse sources are stored so that an integrated, multidisciplinary view of the data can be achieved; also called a central data repository or, when related specifically to healthcare data, a clinical data repository

Data resource manager: A role that ensures that the organization's information systems meet the needs of people who provide and manage patient services

Data security: The process of keeping data safe from unauthorized alteration or destruction

Data set: A list of recommended data elements with uniform definitions that are relevant for a particular use

Data types: A technical category of data (text, numbers, currency, date, memo, and link data) that a field in a database can contain

Data warehouse: A database that makes it possible to access data from multiple databases and combine the results into a single query and reporting interface; *See* **clinical repository**

Data warehousing: The acquisition of all the business data and information from potentially multiple, cross-platform sources, such as legacy databases, departmental databases, and online transaction-based databases, and then the warehouse storage of all the data in one consistent format

Database: An organized collection of data, text, references, or pictures in a standardized format, typically stored in a computer system for multiple applications

Database administrator: The individual responsible for the technical aspects of designing and managing databases

Database life cycle (DBLC): A system consisting of several phases that represent the useful life of a database, including initial study, design, implementation, testing and evaluation, operation, and maintenance and evaluation

Database management system (DBMS): Computer software that enables the user to create, modify, delete, and view the data in a database

Data-based DSS: Decision support system that focuses on providing access to the various data sources within the organization through one system

Debit: The amount on the left side of an account entry that represents an increase in an expense or liability account or a decrease in a revenue or asset account

Debt ratio: The total liabilities divided by the total assets

Debt service: The current obligations of an organization to repay loans

Decentralization: The shift of decision-making authority and responsibility to lower levels of the organization

Decision support system (DSS): A computer-based system that gathers data from a variety of sources and assists in providing structure to the data by using various analytical models and visual tools in order to facilitate and improve the ultimate outcome in decision-making tasks associated with nonroutine and nonrepetitive problems

Decision tree: A structured data-mining technique based on a set of rules useful for predicting and classifying information and making decisions

Deductive reasoning: The process of developing conclusions based on generalizations

Deemed status: An official designation indicating that a healthcare facility is in compliance with the Medicare Conditions of Participation; to qualify for deemed status, facilities must be accredited by the Joint Commission on Accreditation of Healthcare Organizations or the American Osteopathic Association

Default judgment: A court ruling against a defendant in a lawsuit who fails to answer a summons for a court appearance

Defendant: In civil cases, an individual or entity against whom a civil complaint has been filed; in criminal cases, an individual who has been accused of a crime

Deidentification: The process in which users of secondary data will need to remove identifying data so that data can be used without violating the patient's privacy

Delegation: The process by which managers distribute work to others along with the authority to make decisions and take action

Delegation of authority: The act of assigning responsibility

Delinquent health record: An incomplete record not finished or made complete within the time frame determined by the medical staff of the facility

Democratic leadership: Iowa State University researchers showed that members under this leadership performed well whether the leader was present or absent and members were more satisfied

Demographic data: *See* **demographic information**

Demographic information: Information used to identify an individual, such as name, address, gender, age, and other information linked to a specific person

Dental informatics: A field of information science concerned with the management of data and information used to support the practice and delivery of dental healthcare through the application of computers and computer technologies

Department of Health and Human Services (HHS): The cabinet-level federal agency that oversees all the health- and human-services–related activities of the federal government and administers federal regulations

Dependency: The relationship between two tasks in a project plan

Dependent variable: A measurable variable in a research study that depends on an independent variable

Depreciation: The allocation of the dollar cost of a capital asset over its expected life

Derived attribute: An attribute whose value is based on the value of other attributes (for example, current date minus date of birth yields the derived attribute age)

Descriptive research: A type of research that determines and reports the current status of topics and subjects

Descriptive statistics: A set of statistical techniques used to describe data such as means, frequency distributions, and standard deviations; statistical information that describes the characteristics of a specific group or a population

Design phase: The second phase of the systems development life cycle during which all options in selecting a new information system are considered

Designated record set: A group of records maintained by or for a covered entity that may include patient medical and billing records; the enrollment, payment, claims adjudication, and cases or medical management record systems maintained by or for a health plan; or information used, in whole or in part, to make patient care-related decisions

Detective control: An internal control designed to find errors that have already been made

Development: The process of growing or progressing in one's level of skill, knowledge, or ability

Diagnosis-related group (DRG): A unit of case-mix classification adopted by the federal government and some other payers as a prospective payment mechanism for hospital inpatients in which diseases are placed into groups because related diseases and treatments tend to consume similar amounts of healthcare resources and incur similar amounts of cost; in the Medicare and Medicaid programs, one of more than 500 diagnostic classifications in which cases demonstrate similar resource consumption and length-of-stay patterns

Diagnostic image data: Bit-mapped images used for medical or diagnostic purposes (for example, chest x-rays or computed tomography scans)

Diffusion S curve: Curve that shows that each of the adopter categories engages innovation at a different time and a different acceptance rate

Digital: 1. A data transmission type based on data that have been binary encoded 2. A term that refers to the data or information represented in an encoded, computer-readable format

Digital dictation: A process in which vocal sounds are converted to bits and stored on computer for random access

Digital Imaging and Communication in Medicine (DICOM): A standard that promotes a digital image communications format and picture archive and communications systems for use with digital images

Digital signature management technology: The practice of validating the identity of an individual sending data through the use of an electronic signature

Direct costs: Resources expended that can be identified as pertaining to specific goods and services (for example, medications pertain to specific patients)

Direct method of cost allocation: A budgeting concept in which the cost of overhead departments is distributed solely to the revenue-producing areas

Discharge analysis: An analysis of the health record at or following discharge

Discharge planning: The process of coordinating the activities related to the release of a patient when inpatient hospital care is no longer needed

Discharge summary: A summary of the resident's stay at the long-term care facility that is used along with the post-discharge plan of care to provide continuity of care for the resident upon discharge from the facility

Discharged, no final bill (DNFB) report: A report that includes all patients who have been discharged from the facility but for whom, for one reason or another, the billing process is not complete

Disciplinary action: Steps taken, such as suspension from employment without pay or demotion to a job with lower expectations and less pay, when actions taken to improve performance are unsuccessful

Discipline: A field of study characterized by a knowledge base and perspective that is different from other fields of study

Disclosure: The act of making information known; in the health information management context, the release of confidential health information about an identifiable person to another person or entity

Discounting: The application of lower rates of payment to multiple surgical procedures performed during the same operative session under the outpatient prospective payment system; the application of adjusted rates of payment by preferred provider organizations

Discrete data: Data that represent separate and distinct values or observations; that is, data that contain only finite numbers and have only specified values

Discrete variables: A dichotomous or nominal variable whose values are placed into categories

Discrimination: The act of treating one entity differently from another

Disease index: A list of diseases and conditions of patients sequenced according to the code numbers of the classification system in use

Disease management: Emphasizes the provider-patient relationship in the development and execution of the plan of care, prevention strategies using evidence-based guidelines to limit complications and exacerbations, and evaluation based on outcomes that support improved overall health

Disease registry: A centralized collection of data used to improve the quality of care and measure the effectiveness of a particular aspect of healthcare delivery

Disposition: For outpatients, the healthcare practitioner's description of the patient's status at discharge (no follow-up planned; follow-up planned or scheduled; referred elsewhere; expired); for inpatients, a core health data element that identifies the circumstances under which the patient left the hospital (discharged alive; discharged to home or self-care; discharged and transferred to another short-term general hospital for inpatient care; discharged and transferred to a skilled nursing facility; discharged and transferred to an intermediate care facility; discharged and transferred to another type of institution for inpatient care or referred for outpatient services to another institution; discharged and transferred to home under care of organized home health services organization; discharged and transferred to home under care of a home intravenous therapy provider; left against medical advice or discontinued care; expired; status not stated)

Distance learning: A learning delivery mode in which the instructor, the classroom, and the students are not all present in the same location and at the same time

Diversity training: A type of training that facilitates an environment that fosters tolerance and appreciation of individual differences within the organization's workforce and strives to create a more harmonious working environment

DMAIC: Methodology used by Six Sigma that involves the following steps: define, measure, analyze, improve, and control

Do not resuscitate (DNR) order: An order written by the treating physician stating that in the event the patient suffers cardiac or pulmonary arrest, cardiopulmonary resuscitation should not be attempted

Document: Any analog or digital, formatted, and preserved "container" of data or information

Document image data: Bit-mapped images based on data created and stored on analog paper or photographic film

Document imaging technology: The practice of electronically scanning written or printed paper documents into an optical or electronic system for later retrieval of the document or parts of the document if parts have been indexed

Document management technology: Technology that organizes and assembles, secures, and shares documents, and includes such functions as document version control, check in-check out control, document access control, and text and word searches

Documentation: The methods and activities of collecting, coding, ordering, storing, and retrieving information to fulfill future tasks

Double distribution: A budgeting concept in which overhead costs are allocated twice, taking into consideration that some overhead departments provide services to each other

Double-blind study: A type of clinical trial conducted with strict procedures for randomization in which neither researcher nor subject knows whether the subject is in the control group or the experimental group

DRG grouper: A computer program that assigns inpatient cases to diagnosis-related groups and determines the Medicare reimbursement rate

Driving force: The concept of what a department or organization uses to determine which products or services to offer, which markets to seek, and which customers to attract

Duration: The amount of time, usually measured in days, for a task to be completed

Early adopters: Accounts for about 13.5 percent of the organization; the individuals in this group have a high degree of opinion leadership; they are more localized than cosmopolitan and often look to the innovators for advice and information; these are the leaders and respected role models in the organization, and their adoption of an idea or practice does much to initiate change

Early majority: comprises about 34 percent of the organization; although usually not leaders, the individuals in this group represent the backbone of the organization, are deliberate in thinking and acceptance of an idea, and serve as a natural bridge between early and late adopters

e-commerce: The use of the Internet and its derived technologies to integrate all aspects of business-to-business and business-to-consumer activities, processes, and communications

e-Discovery: Refers to Amendments to Federal Rules of Civil Procedure and Uniform Rules Relating to Discovery of Electronically Stored Information; wherein audit trails, the source code of the program, metadata, and any other electronic information that is not typically considered the legal health record is subject to a motion for compulsory discovery

e-forms: Electronic forms used to collect specific data for a registry

Edit: A condition that must be satisfied before a computer system can accept data

Effectiveness: The degree to which stated outcomes are attained

Efficiency: The degree to which a minimum of resources is used to obtain outcomes

Effort: The mental and physical exertion required to perform job-related tasks

e-health: The application of e-commerce to the healthcare industry, including electronic data interchange and links among healthcare entities

e-HIM: The application of technology to managing health information

EHR collaborative: A group of healthcare professional and trade associations formed to support Health Level Seven, a healthcare standards development organization, in the development of a functional model for electronic health record systems

Eighty-five/fifteen (85/15) rule: The total quality management assumption that 85 percent of the problems that occur are related to faults in the system rather than to worker performance

e-learning: The use of the Internet and its derived technologies to deliver training and education

Electronic data interchange (EDI): A standard transmission format using strings of data for business information communicated among the computer systems of independent organizations

Electronic document/content management system (EDM): A storage solution based on digital scanning technology in which source documents are scanned to create digital images of the documents that can be stored electronically on optical disks

Electronic health information management: *See* **e-HIM**

Electronic health record (EHR): An electronic record of health-related information on an individual that conforms to nationally recognized standards and that can be created, managed, and consulted by authorized clinicians and staff across more than one healthcare organization

Electronic medical record (EMR): An electronic record of health-related information on an individual that can be created, gathered, managed, and consulted by authorized clinicians and staff within a single healthcare organization

Electronic medication administration record (EMAR): System designed to prevent medication errors by checking a patient's medication information against his or her bar-coded wristband

Electronic performance support system (EPSS): Sets of computerized tools and displays that automate training, documentation, and phone support; that integrate this automation into applications; and that provide support that is faster, cheaper, and more effective than traditional methods

Electronic records management technology: Systems that create and preserve electronic records

Electronic signature: 1. Any representation of a signature in digital form, including an image of a handwritten signature 2. The authentication of a computer entry in a health record made by the individual making the entry

Emergency Care Research Institute (ECRI): Group that is currently working with the FDA to produce a map of the Universal Medical Device Nomenclature System to Global Medical Device Nomenclature to coordinate their practices that may lead to a merger in the near future

Emergency Maternal and Infant Care Program (EMIC): The federal medical program that provides obstetrical and infant care to dependents of active-duty military personnel in the four lowest pay grades

Emergency Medical Treatment and Active Labor Act (EMTALA): To ensure that emergency patients are made aware of their rights, transfer and acceptance policies and procedures must be delineated to ensure that facilities comply with this act

Emergency outpatient: A patient who is admitted to the emergency department or equivalent service of a hospital for diagnosis and treatment of a condition that requires immediate medical services, dental services, or related healthcare services

Emergency preparedness: A state of readiness to react to an emergency situation

Emotional intelligence (EI): The sensitivity and ability to monitor and revise one's behavior based on the needs of and responses by others

Empiricism: The quality of being based on observed and validated evidence

Employee record: The document in which an employee's information relating to job performance and so on is kept

Employer-based self-insurance: An umbrella term used to describe health plans that are funded directly by employers to provide coverage for their employees exclusively in which employers establish accounts to cover their employees' medical expenses and retain control over the funds but bear the risk of paying claims greater than their estimates

Employment contract: A legal and binding agreement of terms related to an individual's work, such as hours, pay, or benefits

Employment-at-will: Concept that employees can be fired at any time and for almost any reason based on the idea that employees can quit at any time and for any reason

Empowerment: The condition of having the environment and resources to perform a job independently

Encoder: Specialty software used to facilitate the assignment of diagnostic and procedural codes according to the rules of the coding system

Encounter: The direct personal contact between a patient and a physician or other person who is authorized by state licensure law and, if applicable, by medical staff bylaws to order or furnish healthcare services for the diagnosis or treatment of the patient

Encryption: The process of transforming text into an unintelligible string of characters that can be transmitted via communications media with a high degree of security and then decrypted when it reaches a secure destination

Ending: The transition process begins with the recognition that the old way of doing things is being terminated

Enhancers: Enhancement of a leader's influence can be done by modifying factors such as subordinates not perceiving the leader's expertise, team spirit not related to leadership efforts, subordinates not dependent on the leader, the leader has low power, or workgroups are not cohesive related to leadership

Enterprise master patient index (EMPI): An index that provides access to multiple repositories of information from overlapping patient populations that are maintained in separate systems and databases

Enterprise (or electronic) content and records management (ECRM): Systems that enable scanning and indexing of paper documents and other content in digital form

Entity: An individual person, group, or organization

Entity relationship diagram (ERD): A specific type of data modeling used in conceptual data modeling and the logical-level modeling of relational databases

Environmental assessment: A thorough review of the internal and external conditions in which an organization operates

Environmental Protection Agency (EPA) Substance Registry System (SRS): Interoperability standard for chemicals that provides a common basis for identification of chemicals, biological organisms, and other substances listed in EPA regulations and data systems

Epidemiological data: Data used to reveal disease trends within a specific population

Epidemiological studies: Studies that are concerned with finding the causes and effects of diseases and conditions

Episode-of-care (EOC) reimbursement: A category of payments made as lump sums to providers for all healthcare services delivered to a patient for a specific illness and/or over a specified time period; also called bundled payments because they include multiple services and may include multiple providers of care

e-prescribing (e-Rx): A type of ordering application that generates a prescription to be filled by a retail pharmacy that is not exactly equivalent to a medication order that is directed to the clinical pharmacy in a hospital

Equal Employment Opportunity Act (1972): Federal legislation prohibiting discrimination in the workplace based on gender, race, religion, or national origin

Equal Pay Act of 1963 (EPA): The federal legislation that requires equal pay for men and women who perform substantially the same work

Equipment: A long-term (fixed) asset account representing depreciable items owned by the organization that have value over multiple fiscal years (for example, the historical cost of a CT scanner is recorded in an equipment account)

Ergonomics: A discipline of functional design associated with the employee in relationship to his or her work environment, including equipment, workstation, and office furniture adaptation to accommodate the employee's unique physical requirements so as to facilitate efficacy of work functions

Esprit de corps: Enthusiasm among the members of a group supporting the group's existence

Essential Medical Data Set (EMDS): A recommended data set designed to create a health history for an individual patient treated in an emergency service

Established Name for Active Ingredients and FDA Unique Ingredient Identifier (UNII) Codes: Interoperability standard for active ingredients in medications

Ethical agent: An individual who promotes and supports ethical behavior

Ethical decision making: The process of requiring everyone to consider the perspectives of others, even when they do not agree with them

Ethicist: An individual trained in the application of ethical theories and principles to problems that cannot be easily solved because of conflicting values, perspectives, and options for action

Ethics: A field of study that deals with moral principles, theories, and values; in healthcare, a formal decision-making process for dealing with the competing perspectives and obligations of the people who have an interest in a common problem

Ethics training: The act of teaching others about moral principles, theories, and values

Ethnography: A method of observational research that investigates culture in naturalistic settings using both qualitative and quantitative approaches

European Committee for Standardization: A business facilitator in Europe, removing trade barriers for European industry and consumers; through its services it provides a platform for the development of European Standards and other technical specifications

Evaluation research: A design of research that examines the effectiveness of policies, programs, or organizations

Evidence: Something that provides proof

Evidence-based management: A management system in which practices based on research evidence will be effective and produce the outcomes they claim

Evidence-based medicine: Healthcare services based on clinical methods that have been thoroughly tested through controlled, peer-reviewed biomedical studies

Exchange relationship: Relationship in which a leader offers greater opportunities and privileges to a subordinate in exchange for loyalty, commitment, and assistance

Exclusive provider organization (EPO): Hybrid managed care organization that provides benefits to subscribers only when healthcare services are performed by network providers; sponsored by self-insured (self-funded) employers or associations and exhibits characteristics of both health maintenance organizations and preferred provider organizations

Executive dashboard: An information management system providing decision makers with regularly updated information on an organization's key strategic measures

Executive information system (EIS): An information system designed to combine financial and clinical information for use in the management of business affairs of a healthcare organization

Executive manager: A senior manager who oversees a broad functional area or group of departments or services, sets the organization's future direction, and monitors the organization's operations

Exempt employees: Specific groups of employees who are identified as not being covered by some or all of the provisions of the Fair Labor Standards Act

Exit interview: The final meeting an employee has with his or her employer before leaving the organization

Expectancy theory of motivation: Proposes that one's effort will result in the attainment of desired performance goals

Expenses: Amounts that are charged as costs by an organization to the current year's activities of operation

Experimental (study) group: A group of participants in which the exposure status of each participant is determined and the individuals followed forward to determine the effects of the exposure

Experimental research: 1. A research design used to establish cause and effect 2. A controlled investigation in which subjects are assigned randomly to groups that experience carefully controlled interventions that are manipulated by the experimenter according to a strict protocol; *See* **experimental study**

Experimental study: *See* **experimental research**

Expert decision support system: A decision support system that uses a set of rules or encoded concepts to construct a reasoning process

Expert system (ES): A type of information system that supports the work of professionals engaged in the development or evaluation of complex activities that require high-level knowledge in a well-defined and usually limited area

Explanation of Benefits (EOB): A statement issued to the insured and the healthcare provider by an insurer to explain the services provided, amounts billed, and payments made by a health plan

Explicit knowledge: Documents, databases, and other types of recorded and documented information

Extended care facility: A healthcare facility licensed by applicable state or local law to offer room and board, skilled nursing by a full-time registered nurse, intermediate care, or a combination of levels on a twenty-four-hour basis over a long period of time

Extensibility: Intention that the vocabulary be extended by users or applications developers

Extensible markup language (XML): A standardized computer language that allows the interchange of data as structured text

External customers: Customers that reside outside the organization

External review (audit): A performance or quality review conducted by a third-party payer or consultant hired for the purpose

External validity: An attribute of a study's design that allows its findings to be applied to other groups

Extranet: A system of connections of private Internet networks outside an organization's firewall that uses Internet technology to enable collaborative applications among enterprises

Facility-based registry: A registry that includes only cases from a particular type of healthcare facility, such as a hospital or clinic

Factor comparison method: A complex quantitative method of job evaluation that combines elements of both the ranking and point methods

Fair Labor Standards Act of 1938 (FLSA): The federal legislation that sets the minimum wage and overtime payment regulations

Family and Medical Leave Act of 1993 (FMLA): The federal legislation that allows employees time off from work (up to twelve weeks) to care for themselves or their family members with the assurance of an equivalent position upon return to work

Family numbering: A filing system, sometimes used in clinic settings, in which an entire family is assigned one number

Favorable variance: The positive difference between the budgeted amount and the actual amount of a line item, that is, when actual revenue exceeds budget or actual expenses are less than budget

Federal Employees' Compensation Act (FECA): The legislation enacted in 1916 to mandate workers' compensation for civilian federal employees, whose coverage includes lost wages, medical expenses, and survivors' benefits

Federal Register: The daily publication of the U.S. Government Printing Office that reports all changes in regulations and federally mandated standards, including HCPCS and ICD-9-CM codes

Fee schedule: A list of healthcare services and procedures (usually CPT/HCPCS codes) and the charges associated with them developed by a third-party payer to represent the approved payment levels for a given insurance plan; also called table of allowances

Feedback controls: Back-end processes that monitor and measure output, and then compare it to expectations and identify variations that then must be analyzed so corrective action plans can be developed and implemented

Fee-for-service basis: *See* **Traditional fee-for-service (FFS) reimbursement**

Felony: A serious crime such as murder, larceny, rape, or assault for which punishment is usually severe

Fetal autopsy rate: The number of autopsies performed on intermediate and late fetal deaths for a given time period divided by the total number of intermediate and late fetal deaths for the same time period

Fetal death (stillborn): The death of a product of human conception before its complete expulsion or extraction from the mother regardless of the duration of the pregnancy

Fetal death rate: A proportion that compares the number of intermediate or late fetal deaths to the total number of live births and intermediate or late fetal deaths during the same period of time

Financial Accounting Standards Board (FASB): An independent organization that sets accounting standards for businesses in the private sector

Financial and administrative applications: Type of source system (such as Registration-Admission Discharge Transfer [R-ADT], patient accounting, MPI, order communication, and the like) used by hospitals and physicians' offices

Financial data: The data collected for the purpose of managing the assets of a business (for example, a healthcare organization, a product line); in healthcare, data derived from the charge generation documentation associated with the activities of care and then aggregated by specific customer grouping for financial analysis

Financial transaction: The exchange of goods or services for payment or the promise of payment

Fiscal intermediary (FI): An organization that contracts with the Centers for Medicare and Medicaid Services to serve as the financial agent between providers and the federal government in the local administration of Medicare Part B claims

Fiscal year: One business cycle or tax year, which may or may not coincide with the calendar year

Fishbone diagram: A performance improvement tool used to identify or classify the root causes of a problem or condition and to display the root causes graphically

Fixed budget: A type of budget based on expected capacity

Fixed costs: Resources expended that do not vary with the activity of the organization (for example, mortgage expenses do not vary with patient volume)

Flex years: A work arrangement in which employees can choose, at specific intervals, the number of hours they want to work each month over the next year

Flexible budget: A type of budget that is based on multiple levels of projected productivity (actual productivity triggers the levels to be used as the year progresses)

Flexible work schedule: *See* **flextime**

Flextime: A work schedule that gives employees some choice in the pattern of their work hours, usually around a core of midday hours

Float employee: An employee who is not assigned to a particular shift or function and who may fill in as needed in cases of standard employee absence or vacation

Flow process chart: *See* **flowchart**

Flowchart: A graphic tool that uses standard symbols to visually display detailed information, including time and distance, of the sequential flow of work of an individual or a product as it progresses through a process

Focus group: Group of members of the population that are questioned for research purposes

Focused studies: Studies in which a researcher orally questions and conducts discussions with members of a group

Food and Drug Administration (FDA): The federal agency responsible for controlling the sale and use of pharmaceuticals, biological products, medical devices, food, cosmetics, and products that emit radiation, including the licensing of medications for human use

Force-field analysis: A performance improvement tool used to identify specific drivers of, and barriers to, an organizational change so that positive factors can be reinforced and negative factors reduced

Forecasting: To calculate or predict some future event or condition through study and analysis of available pertinent data

Foreign key: A key attribute used to link one entity or table to another

For-profit organizations: The tax status assigned to business entities that are owned by one or more individuals or organizations and that earn revenues in excess of expenditures that are subsequently paid out to the owners or stockholders

Foundational applications (for EHR): Applications including those that capture patient and provider demographic and administrative information, maintain and create custom patient lists, maintain problem lists, retain allergy information, manage medication lists, access and view test results during the ordering process, and perform medication reconciliation

Fourteen principles of management: Henri Fayol's key points in the formulation of the administrative approach to management

Fraud and abuse: The intentional and mistaken misrepresentation of reimbursement claims submitted to government-sponsored health programs

Freedom of Information Act (FOIA): The federal law, applicable only to federal agencies, through which individuals can seek access to information without the authorization of the person to whom the information applies

Free-text data: Data that are narrative in nature

Frequency distribution: A table or graph that displays the number of times (frequency) a particular observation occurs

Frequency polygon: A type of line graph that represents a frequency distribution

Fund balance: In a not-for-profit setting, the entity's net assets or resources remaining after subtracting liabilities that are owed; in a for-profit organization, the owner's equity

Gantt chart: A graphic tool used to plot tasks in project management that shows the duration of project tasks and overlapping tasks

General ledger: A master list of individual revenue and expense accounts maintained by an organization

Generalizability: The ability to apply research results, data, or observations to groups not originally under study

Generally accepted accounting principles (GAAP): An accepted set of accounting principles and recognized procedures central to financial accounting and reporting

Generally accepted auditing standards (GAAS): The way in which organizations record and report financial transactions so that financial information is consistent between organizations

Geographic information system (GIS): A decision support system that is capable of assembling, storing, manipulating, and displaying geographically referenced data and information

Geographic practice cost index (GPCI): An index developed by the Centers for Medicare and Medicaid Services to measure the differences in resource costs among fee schedule areas compared to the national average in the three components of the relative value unit: physician work, practice expenses, and malpractice coverage

Geographical information system (GIS): A decision support system that is capable of assembling, storing, manipulating, and displaying geographically referenced data and information

Gesture recognition technology: A method of encoding handwritten, print, or cursive characters and of interpreting the characters as words or the intent of the writer

Global Medical Device Nomenclature (GMDN): A collection of internationally recognized terms used to accurately describe and catalog medical devices, in particular, the products used in the diagnosis, prevention, monitoring, treatment or alleviation of disease or injury in humans

Global payment: A form of reimbursement used for radiological and other procedures that combines the professional and technical components of the procedures and disperses payments as lump sums to be distributed between the physician and the healthcare facility

Goal: A specific description of the services or deliverable goods to be provided as the result of a business process

Going concern: An organization that can be assumed to continue indefinitely unless otherwise stated

Government Accounting Standards Board (GASB): The federal agency that sets the accounting standards to be followed by government entities

Graphical user interface (GUI): A style of computer interface in which typed commands are replaced by images that represent tasks (for example, small pictures [icons] that represent the tasks, functions, and programs performed by a software program)

Graphics-based decision support system: A decision support system in which the knowledge base consists primarily of graphical data and the user interface exploits the use of graphical display

Great person theory: Outstanding individuals originally led to the conception of leadership as an inborn ability, sometimes passed down through family, position, or social tradition, as in the cases of royal families in many parts of the world

Grievance: A formal, written description of a complaint or disagreement

Grievance procedures: The steps employees may follow to seek resolution of disagreements with management on job-related issues

Gross autopsy rate: The number of inpatient autopsies conducted during a given time period divided by the total number of inpatient deaths for the same time period

Gross death rate: The number of inpatient deaths that occurred during a given time period divided by the total number of inpatient discharges, including deaths, for the same time period

Grounded theory: Researchers using this theory code, categorize, and compare their data; term refers both to the theories generated using this technique and the technique itself

Group health insurance: A prepaid medical plan that covers the healthcare expenses of an organization's full-time employees

Group model health maintenance organization: Type of health plan in which an HMO contracts with an independent multispecialty physician group to provide medical services to members of the plan

Group practice without walls (GPWW): A type of managed care contract that allows physicians to maintain their own offices and share administrative services

Grouper: A computer software program that automatically assigns prospective payment groups on the basis of clinical codes

Groupthink: An implicit form of group consensus in which openness and effective decision making are sacrificed to conformity

Habit: An activity repeated so often that it becomes automatic

Harassment: The act of bothering or annoying someone repeatedly

Hard space: Space that cannot be converted easily to service another function

Hard-coding: The process of attaching a CPT/HCPCS code to a procedure located on the facility's chargemaster so that the code will automatically be included on the patient's bill

Hawthorne effect: A research study that found that novelty, attention, and interpersonal relations have a motivating effect on performance

Hay method of job evaluation: A modification of the point method of job evaluation that numerically measures the levels of three major compensable factors: know-how, problem-solving ability, and accountability

Health care provider dimension (HCPD): One of three dimensions of the National Health Information Infrastructure privacy concept that addresses the needs of providers for complete and accurate patient data

Health information exchange (HIE): The exchange of health information electronically between providers and others with the same level of interoperability, such as labs and pharmacies

Health information management (HIM): An allied health profession that is responsible for ensuring the availability, accuracy, and protection of the clinical information that is needed to deliver healthcare services and to make appropriate healthcare-related decisions

Health Information Management and Systems Society (HIMSS): A national membership association that provides leadership in healthcare for the management of technology, information, and change

Health information manager (or director): One who is responsible for the enterprise-wide direction of HIM functions

Health Information Security and Privacy Collaboration (HISPC): This project originally included 3 phases and 34 states and territories in the United States. In the first phase, the 34 teams followed a defined process to assess variances in organization-level business policies and state laws that affect HIE. The second phase focused on identification and proposal of practical solutions while preserving privacy and security requirements in the applicable federal and state laws. In 2008, the third phase, developing detailed plans and implementing solutions, was underway.

Health information technology (HIT): A term that encompasses the technical roles that process health data and records, such as classification, abstracting, retrieval, and so on

Health Information Technology Standards Panel (HITSP): This organization serves as a cooperative partnership between the public and private sectors for achieving a wide acceptance and usable standards; its specific mission is to enable and support widespread interoperability among healthcare software applications as they interact in a local, regional, and NHIN for the United States

Health Insurance Portability and Accountability Act (HIPAA) of 1996: The federal legislation enacted to provide continuity of health coverage, control fraud and abuse in healthcare, reduce healthcare costs, and guarantee the security and privacy of health information

Health Level Seven (HL7): A standards development organization accredited by the American National Standards Institute that addresses issues at the seventh, or application, level of healthcare systems interconnections

Health maintenance organization (HMO): Entity that combines the provision of healthcare insurance and the delivery of healthcare services, characterized by: (1) organized healthcare delivery system to a geographic area, (2) set of basic and supplemental health maintenance and treatment services, (3) voluntarily enrolled members, and (4) predetermined fixed, periodic prepayments for members' coverage

Health management information system (HMIS): An information system whose purpose is to provide reports on routine operations and processing (for example, a pharmacy inventory system, radiological system, or patient-tracking system)

Health Plan Employer Data and Information Set (HEDIS): A set of performance measures developed by the National Commission for Quality Assurance that are designed to provide purchasers and consumers of healthcare with the information they need to compare the performance of managed care plans

Health record review: A concurrent or ongoing review of health record content performed by caregivers or HIM professionals while the patient is still receiving inpatient services to ensure the quality of the services being provided and the completeness of the documentation being maintained; also called health record analysis

Health Research Extension Act (1985): Federal legislation that established guidelines for the proper care of animals used in biomedical and behavioral research

Health savings accounts: Savings accounts designed to help people save for future medical and retiree health costs on a tax-free basis, part of the 2003 Medicare bill

Health science librarian: A professional librarian who manages a medical library

Health services research: Research conducted on the subject of healthcare delivery that examines organizational structures and systems as well as the effectiveness and efficiency of healthcare services

Health systems agency: An agency that promotes and provides community-based health planning services

Health 2.0: Web 2.0 technologies and tools used in the healthcare industry

Healthcare Common Procedure Coding System (HCPCS): A classification system that identifies healthcare procedures, equipment, and supplies for claim submission purposes; the three levels are as follows: I, Current Procedural Terminology codes, developed by the AMA; II, codes for equipment, supplies, and services not covered by Current Procedural Terminology codes as well as modifiers that can be used with all levels of codes, developed by CMS; and III (eliminated December 31, 2003 to comply with HIPAA), local codes developed by regional Medicare Part B carriers and used to report physicians' services and supplies to Medicare for reimbursement

Healthcare Cost and Utilization Project (HCUP): A group of healthcare databases and related software tools developed through collaboration by the federal government, state governments, and industry to create a national information resource for patient-level healthcare data

Healthcare informatics: The field of information science concerned with the management of all aspects of health data and information through the application of computers and computer technologies

Healthcare Information Security and Privacy Collaboration (HISPC): Partnership consisting of a multidisciplinary team of experts and the National Governor's Association (NGA) working with approximately 40 states to assess and develop plans to address variations in organization-level business policies and state laws that affect privacy and security practices which may pose challenges to interoperable HIE

Healthcare information standards: Guidelines developed to standardize data throughout the healthcare industry (for example, developing uniform terminologies and vocabularies)

Healthcare Information Technology Standards Panel (HITSP): Private organization formed in 2005; funded by the federal government to address standards harmonization and gaps, especially in light of using a nationwide health information network

Healthcare Integrity and Protection Data Bank (HIPDB): A national database that collects information on cases of healthcare fraud and abuse

Healthcare provider: A provider of diagnostic, medical, and surgical care as well as the services or supplies related to the health of an individual and any other person or organization that issues reimbursement claims or is paid for healthcare in the normal course of business

Heterogeneity: The state or fact of containing various components

Heuristic thought: Exploratory thinking that helps in solving certain types of problems but offers no guarantees

Hierarchy: An authoritarian organizational structure in which each member is assigned a specific rank that reflects his or her level of decision-making authority within the organization

Hierarchy of needs: Maslow's theory that suggested that human needs are organized hierarchically from basic physiological requirements to creative motivations; *See* **Maslow's hierarchy of needs**

Hill-Burton Act: The federal legislation enacted in 1946 as the Hospital Survey and Construction Act to authorize grants for states to construct new hospitals and, later, to modernize old ones; *See* **Hospital Survey and Construction Act**

Hiring: Engaging the services of an individual in return for compensation

Histocompatibility: The immunologic similarity between an organ donor and a transplant recipient

Histogram: A graphic technique used to display the frequency distribution of continuous data (interval or ratio data) as either numbers or percentages in a series of bars

Historical cost: The resources expended by an organization to acquire an asset

Historical research: A research design used to investigate past events

History: The pertinent information about a patient, including chief complaint, past and present illnesses, family history, social history, and review of body systems

Home Assessment Validation and Entry (HAVEN): A type of data-entry software used to collect Outcome and Assessment Information Set (OASIS) data and then transmit them to state databases; imports and exports data in standard OASIS record format, maintains agency/patient/employee information, enforces data integrity through rigorous edit checks, and provides comprehensive online help

Home health agency (HHA): A program or organization that provides a blend of home-based medical and social services to homebound patients and their families for the purpose of promoting, maintaining, or restoring health or of minimizing the effects of illness, injury, or disability

Home health prospective payment system (HHPPS): The reimbursement system developed by the Centers for Medicare and Medicaid Services to cover home health services provided to Medicare beneficiaries

Home health resource group (HHRG): A classification system with 80 home health episode rates established to support the prospective reimbursement of covered home care and rehabilitation services provided to Medicare beneficiaries during 60-day episodes of care

Home healthcare (HH): The medical and/or personal care provided to individuals and families in their place of residence with the goal of promoting, maintaining, or restoring health or minimizing the effects of disabilities and illnesses, including terminal illnesses

Honesty (integrity) tests: Tests designed to evaluate an individual's honesty using a series of hypothetical questions

Hospice: An interdisciplinary program of palliative care and supportive services that addresses the physical, spiritual, social, and economic needs of terminally ill patients and their families

Hospice care: The medical care provided to persons with life expectancies of six months or less who elect to forgo standard treatment of their illness and to receive only palliative care

Hospital ambulatory care: Hospital-directed preventive, therapeutic, and rehabilitative services provided by physicians and their surrogates to patients who are not hospital inpatients or home care patients

Hospital autopsy: A postmortem (after death) examination performed on the body of a person who has at some time been a hospital patient by a hospital pathologist or a physician of the medical staff who has been delegated the responsibility

Hospital autopsy rate: The total number of autopsies performed by a hospital pathologist for a given time period divided by the number of deaths of hospital patients (inpatients and outpatients) whose bodies were available for autopsy for the same time period

Hospital death rate: The number of inpatient deaths for a given period of time divided by the total number of live discharges and deaths for the same time period

Hospital discharge abstract system: A group of databases compiled from aggregate data on all patients discharged from a hospital

Hospital information system (HIS): The comprehensive database containing all the clinical, administrative, financial, and demographic information about each patient served by a hospital

Hospital inpatient autopsy: A postmortem (after death) examination performed on the body of a patient who died during an inpatient hospitalization by a hospital pathologist or a physician of the medical staff who has been delegated the responsibility

Hospital newborn inpatient: A patient born in the hospital at the beginning of the current inpatient hospitalization

Hospital outpatient: A patient who receives services in one or more of the facilities owned and operated by a hospital

Hospital Survey and Construction Act: *See* **Hill-Burton Act**

Hospital-acquired conditions (HAC): Eight conditions (not present on admission) identified by CMS as "reasonably preventable"

Hospital-acquired infection rate: The number of hospital-acquired infections for a given time period divided by the total number of inpatient discharges for the same time period

Hospitalization insurance (HI) (Medicare Part A): A federal program that covers the costs associated with inpatient hospitalization as well as other healthcare services provided to Medicare beneficiaries

Human Genome Nomenclature (HUGN): Interoperability standard for exchanging information regarding the role of genes in biomedical research and healthcare

Human Genome Organisation (HUGO): Manages the Human Genome Nomenclature as a confidential database containing more than 16,000 records

Human relations movement: A management philosophy emphasizing the shift from a mechanistic view of workers to concern for their satisfaction at work

Human subjects: Individuals whose physiologic or behavioral characteristics and responses are the object of study in a research program

Human–computer interface: The device used by humans to access and enter data into a computer system, such as a keyboard on a PC, personal digital assistant, voice recognition system, and so on

Hybrid online analytical processing (HOLAP): A data access methodology that is coupled tightly with the architecture of the database management system to allow the user to perform business analyses

Hybrid record: A health record that includes both paper and electronic elements

HyperText Markup Language (HTML): A standardized computer language that allows the electronic transfer of information and communications among many different information systems

Hypothesis: A statement that describes a research question in measurable terms

Icarus Paradox: Proposes that successful styles and methods, unrestrained, can become their extreme, or, that our strengths can become our weaknesses: Builders become imperialists, pioneers become escapists, salespersons become drifters, and craftspersons become tinkerers

ICD-9-CM (International Classification of Diseases, Ninth Revision, Clinical Modification): A classification system used in the United States to report morbidity and mortality information

Identifier standards: Recommended methods for assigning unique identifiers to individuals (patients and clinical providers), corporate providers, and healthcare vendors and suppliers

Identity management: In the master patient index, policies and procedures that manage patient identity, such as prohibiting the same record number for duplicate patients or duplicate records for one patient

Implementation phase: The third phase of the systems development life cycle during which a comprehensive plan is developed and instituted to ensure that the new information system is effectively implemented within the organization

Imputation: The substitution of values for the missing values

Incentive: Something that stimulates or encourages an individual to work harder

Incentive pay: A system of bonuses and rewards based on employee productivity; often used in transcription areas of healthcare facilities

Incidence: The number of new cases of a specific disease

Incidence rate: A computation that compares the number of new cases of a specific disease for a given time period to the population at risk for the disease during the same time period

Incident: An occurrence in a medical facility that is inconsistent with accepted standards of care

Incident report review: An analysis of incident reports or an evaluation of descriptions of adverse events

Income statement: A statement that summarizes an organization's revenue and expense accounts using totals accumulated during the fiscal year

Indemnity plans: Health insurance coverage provided in the form of cash payments to patients or providers

Independent practice organization (IPO) or association (IPA): An open-panel health maintenance organization that provides contract healthcare services to subscribers through independent physicians who treat patients in their own offices; the HMO reimburses the IPA on a capitated basis; the IPA may reimburse the physicians on a fee-for-service or a capitated basis

Independent practitioners: Individuals working as employees of an organization, in private practice, or through a physician group who provide healthcare services without supervision or direction

Independent variable: An antecedent factor that researchers manipulate directly

Index: An organized (usually alphabetical) list of specific data that serves to guide, indicate, or otherwise facilitate reference to the data

Indian Health Service (IHS): The federal agency within the Department of Health and Human Services that is responsible for providing federal healthcare services to American Indians and Alaska natives

Indirect costs: Resources expended that cannot be identified as pertaining to specific goods and services (for example, electricity is not allocable to a specific patient)

Individually-identifiable health information: Personal information that can be linked to a specific patient, such as age, gender, date of birth, and address

Inductive reasoning: A process of creating conclusions based on a limited number of observations

Infant mortality rate: The number of deaths of individuals under one year of age during a given time period divided by the number of live births reported for the same time period

Infection review: Evaluation of the risk of infection among patients and healthcare providers, looking for, preventing, and controlling the risk

Inference engine: Specialized computer software that tries to match conditions in rules to data elements in a repository (when a match is found, the engine executes the rule, which results in the occurrence of a specified action)

Inferencing: Determining the intended degree of automation in classification; the intention that validation on input be possible

Inferential statistics: A set of statistical techniques that allows researchers to make generalizations about a population's characteristics (parameters) on the basis of a sample's characteristics

Informatics: A field of study that focuses on the use of technology to improve access to, and utilization of, information

Information: Factual data that have been collected, combined, analyzed, interpreted, and converted into a form that can be used for a specific purpose

Information assets: Information that has value for an organization

Information capture: The process of recording representations of human thought, perceptions, or actions in documenting patient care, as well as device-generated information that is gathered and computed about a patient as part of health care

Information management: The acquisition, organization, analysis, storage, retrieval, and dissemination of information to support decision-making activities

Information privacy coordinator/privacy officer: Works in collaboration with managers to assess risks to health information security and privacy, monitor organizational privacy compliance issues, and establish policy and procedures to address security risks

Information science: The study of the nature and principles of information

Information system (IS): An automated system that uses computer hardware and software to record, manipulate, store, recover, and disseminate data (that is, a system that receives and processes input and provides output); often used interchangeably with information technology (IT)

Information technology (IT): Computer technology (hardware and software) combined with telecommunications technology (data, image, and voice networks); often used interchangeably with information system (IS)

Information technology (IT) acquisition strategy: Strategy where, as much as possible, all older applications are replaced with new applications from a single vendor, with newer architecture and more clinically oriented approaches

Information technology professional: An individual who works with computer technology in the process of managing health information

Informed consent: 1. A legal term referring to a patient's right to make his or her own treatment decisions based on the knowledge of the treatment to be administered or the procedure to be performed 2. An individual's voluntary agreement to participate in research or to undergo a diagnostic, therapeutic, or preventive medical procedure

In-group: Refers to those subordinates who form a group around the leader

Initiating structure: Leaders in this group were more task-focused and centered on giving direction, setting goals and limits, and planning and scheduling activities

Injury Severity Score (ISS): An overall severity measurement maintained in the trauma registry and calculated from the abbreviated injury scores for the three most severe injuries of each patient

Innovators: Comprises about 2.5 percent of the organization and individuals who are eager to try new ideas; these individuals tend to be more cosmopolitan, to seek out new information in broad networks, and to be willing to take risks

Inpatient: A patient who is provided with room, board, and continuous general nursing services in an area of an acute care facility where patients generally stay at least overnight

Inpatient bed occupancy rate (percentage of occupancy): The total number of inpatient service days for a given time period divided by the total number of inpatient bed count days for the same time period

Inpatient psychiatric facility (IPF): A healthcare facility that offers psychiatric medical care on an inpatient basis; CMS established a prospective payment system for reimbursing these types of facilities using the current DRGs for inpatient hospitals

Inpatient rehabilitation facility (IRF): A healthcare facility that specializes in providing services to patients who have suffered a disabling illness or injury in an effort to help them achieve or maintain their optimal level of functioning, self-care, and independence

Inpatient Rehabilitation Validation and Entry (IRVEN): A computerized data-entry system used by inpatient rehabilitation facilities

Inpatient service day (IPSD): A unit of measure equivalent to the services received by one inpatient during one twenty-four-hour period

In-service education: Training that teaches employees specific skills required to maintain or improve performance, usually internal to an organization

Institute for Clinical Systems Improvement (ICSI): A collaboration of healthcare organizations that provides an objective voice dedicated to supporting healthcare quality and helping its members identify and achieve implementation of best practices for their patients

Institute of Electrical and Electronics Engineers (IEEE): A national organization that develops standards for hospital system interface transactions, including links between critical care bedside instruments and clinical information systems

Institute of Electrical and Electronics Engineers (IEEE) 1073: Interoperability standard for electronic data exchange

Institute of Medicine (IOM): A branch of the National Academy of Sciences whose goal is to advance and distribute scientific knowledge with the mission of improving human health

Institutional review board (IRB): An administrative body that provides oversight for the research studies conducted within a healthcare institution

Instrument: A standardized and uniform way to collect data

Insured: A holder of a health insurance policy

Insurer: An organization that pays healthcare expenses on behalf of its enrollees

Integrated delivery network (IDN): *See* **integrated delivery system**

Integrated delivery system (IDS): A system that combines the financial and clinical aspects of healthcare and uses a group of healthcare providers, selected on the basis of quality and cost management criteria, to furnish comprehensive health services across the continuum of care

Integrated health record: A system of health record organization in which all of the paper forms are arranged in strict chronological order and mixed with forms created by different departments

Integrated provider organization (IPO): An organization that manages the delivery of healthcare services provided by hospitals, physicians (employees of the IPO), and other healthcare organizations (for example, nursing facilities)

Integration: The complex task of ensuring that all elements and platforms in an information system communicate and act as a uniform entity; or the combination of two or more benefit plans to prevent duplication of benefit payment

Integrity: The state of being whole or unimpaired

Integrity constraints: Limits placed on the data that may be entered into a database

Intellectual capital: The combined knowledge of an organization's employees with respect to operations, processes, history, and culture

Intelligent character recognition (ICR) technology: A method of encoding handwritten, print, or cursive characters and of interpreting the characters as words or the intent of the writer

Intelligent document recognition (IDR) technology: Technology that automatically recognizes analog items, such as tangible materials or documents, or recognizes characters or symbols from analog items, enabling the identified data to be quickly, accurately, and automatically entered into digital systems

Interface: The zone between different computer systems across which users want to pass information (for example, a computer program written to exchange information between systems or the graphic display of an application program designed to make the program easier to use)

Interface terminology: Concerned with facilitating clinician documentation within the standardized structure (for example, menus, drop-down boxes) needed for an EHR; provides a limited set of words and phrases in a manner that is consistent with a clinician's thought process used while documenting

Interim period: Any period that represents less than an entire fiscal year

Internal controls: Policies and procedures designed to protect an organization's assets and to reduce the exposure to the risk of loss due to error or malfeasance

Internal customers: Customers located within the organization

Internal rate of return (IRR): An interest rate that makes the net present value calculation equal zero

Internal validity: An attribute of a study's design that contributes to the accuracy of its findings

International Classification for Nursing Practice (ICNP): Unified nursing language system into which existing terminologies can be cross-mapped

International Classification of Diseases (ICD): Used by more than 100 countries worldwide to classify diseases and other health issues; the classification system facilitates the storage and retrieval of diagnostic information and serves as the basis for compiling mortality and morbidity statistics reported by World Health Organization members

International Classification of Diseases, 11th Revision (ICD-11): Edition of ICD that is underway; a significant difference is that it will be designed to include linkages to standardized healthcare terminologies to facilitate processing and use of the data for a variety of purposes such as research

International Classification of Diseases for Oncology (ICD-O-3), 3rd Revision: A classification system used for reporting incidences of malignant disease

International Classification of Diseases, 9th Revision, Clinical Modification (ICD-9-CM): A derivative work of the International Classification of Diseases, 9th Revision, as developed by the World Health Organization; ICD-9-CM is used in the United States only to code and classify diagnoses from inpatient and outpatient records, as well as inpatient procedures

International Classification of Diseases, 10th Revision, Clinical Modification (ICD-10-CM): Modified for the reporting of morbidity data, ICD-10-CM contains a substantial increase in content over ICD-9-CM

International Classification of Diseases, 10th Revision, Procedure Coding System (ICD-10_PCS): A new procedural coding system to replace the Tabular List of Procedures, Volume 3 of ICD-9-CM

International Classification of Primary Care (ICPC-2): Classification used for coding the reasons of encounter, diagnoses, and interventions in an episode-of-care structure

International Classification on Functioning, Disability and Health (ICF): Classification of health and health-related domains that describe body functions and structures, activities, and participation

International Federation of Health Record Organizations (IFHRO): Organization that supports national associations and health record professionals to implement and improve health records and the systems that support them

International Health Terminology Standards Development Organisation (IHTSDO): An international non-profit organization based in Denmark that distributes SNOMED CT (Systematized Nomenclature of Medicine-Clinical Terminology Terms)

International Medical Informatics Association (IMIA): Worldwide not-for-profit organization that promotes medical informatics in healthcare and biomedical research

International Organization for Standardization (ISO): A non-governmental global organization established in 1987 that provides more than 17,000 quality standards for nearly every business, technology, and industry sector

Interoperability: The ability, generally by adoption of standards, of systems to work together

Interoperable: Adjective form of interoperability

Interoperate: Verb form of interoperability

Interpersonal skills: One of the three managerial skill categories that includes skills in communicating and relating effectively to others

Interrater reliability: A measure of a research instrument's consistency in data collection when used by different abstractors

Interrogatories: Discovery devices consisting of a set of written questions given to a party, witness, or other person who has information needed in a legal case

Interval data: A type of data that represents observations that can be measured on an evenly distributed scale beginning at a point other than true zero

Interval-level data: The intervals between successive values are equal

Interval scale: Situation where the intervals between adjacent scale values are equal with respect to the attributes being measured

Intervention: 1. A clinical manipulation, treatment, or therapy 2. A generic term used by researchers to mean an act of some kind

Interview: A formal meeting, often between a job applicant and a potential employer

Interview guide: A list of written questions to be asked during an interview

Interview survey: A type of research instrument with which the members of the population being studied are asked questions and respond orally

Intranet: A private information network that is similar to the Internet and whose servers are located inside a firewall or security barrier so that the general public cannot gain access to information housed within the network

Intrarater reliability: A measure of a research instrument's reliability in which the same person repeating the test will get reasonably similar findings

Intuition: Unconscious decision making based on extensive experience in similar situations

Inventor: Individual who develops a new idea or practice in the organization

Inventory: Goods on hand and available to sell, presumably within a year (a business cycle)

Investor-owned hospital chain: Group of for-profit healthcare facilities owned by stockholders

Issue log: A form of documentation that describes the questions, concerns, and problems that must be solved in order for a task to be completed

Job classification method: 1. A method of job evaluation that compares a written position description with the written descriptions of various classification grades 2. A method used by the federal government to grade jobs

Job description: A list of a job's duties, reporting relationships, working conditions, and responsibilities

Job evaluation: The process of applying predefined compensable factors to jobs to determine their relative worth

Job procedure: A structured, action-oriented list of sequential steps involved in carrying out a specific job or solving a problem

Job ranking: A method of job evaluation that arranges jobs in a hierarchy on the basis of each job's importance to the organization, with the most important jobs listed at the top of the hierarchy and the least important jobs listed at the bottom

Job rotation: A work design in which workers are shifted periodically among different tasks

Job sharing: A work schedule in which two or more individuals share the tasks of one full-time or one full-time-equivalent position

Job specifications: A list of a job's required education, skills, knowledge, abilities, personal qualifications, and physical requirements

Joint Commission: A private, not-for-profit organization that evaluates and accredits hospitals and other healthcare organizations on the basis of predefined performance standards; formerly the Joint Commission on Accreditation of Healthcare Organizations (JCAHO)

Journal entry: An accounting representation of a financial transaction or transfer of amounts between accounts that contains at least one debit and one credit and in which the dollar value of the debits and the credits is the same

Judge-made law: Unwritten law originating from court decisions where no applicable statute exists; *See* **common law or case law**

Jurisdiction: The power and authority of a court to hear and decide specific types of cases

Justice: The impartial administration of policies or laws that takes into consideration the competing interests and limited resources of the individuals or groups involved

Just-in-time training: Training provided anytime, anyplace, and just when it is needed

Key attributes: Common fields (attributes) within a relational database that are used to link tables to one another

Key indicator: A quantifiable measure used over time to determine whether some structure, process, or outcome in the provision of care to a patient supports high-quality performance measured against best practice criteria

Knowledge: The information, understanding, and experience that give individuals the power to make informed decisions

Knowledge assets: Assets that are the sources of knowledge for an organization (for example, printed documents, unwritten rules, workflows, customer knowledge, data in databases and spreadsheets, and the human expertise, know-how, and tacit knowledge within the minds of the organization's workforce)

Knowledge base: A database that not only manages raw data but also integrates them with information from various reference works

Knowledge management: 1. The process by which data are acquired and transformed into information through the application of context, which in turn provides understanding 2. A management philosophy that promotes an integrated and collaborative approach to the process of information asset creation, capture, organization, access, and use

Knowledge-based data: The sources of knowledge for an organization (for example, printed documents; unwritten rules; workflows; customer knowledge; data in databases and spreadsheets; and the human expertise, know-how, and tacit knowledge within the minds of the organization's workforce); also called knowledge-based assets

Knowledge-based DSS: Decision support system in which the key element is the knowledge base; often referred to as a rule-based system because the knowledge is stored in the form of rules (for example, the IF, THEN, ELSE format)

Kolb's "Learning Loop": A theory of experiential learning involving four interrelated steps: concrete experiences, observation and reflection, formation of abstract concepts and theories, and testing new implications of theory in new situations

Laboratory information system (LIS): System that, in addition to producing lab results, manages workload balancing, supplies inventories, Medicare medical necessity checking, billing, public health reporting, and generates custom reports for clinical or quality management

Labor relations: Human resources management activities associated with unions and collective bargaining

Labor-Management Relations Act (Taft-Hartley Act): Federal legislation passed in 1947 that imposed certain restrictions on unions while upholding their right to organize and bargain collectively

Labor-Management Reporting and Disclosure Act (Landrum-Griffin Act): Federal legislation passed in 1959 to ensure that union members' interests were properly represented by union leadership; created, among other things, a bill of rights for union members

Laggards: Members of this group are usually the last ones to respond to innovation and make up as much as 16 percent of the organization; they are often characterized as isolated, uninformed, and mistrustful of change and change agents, but they may serve a function by keeping the organization from changing too quickly

Late majority: Skeptical group that comprises another 34 percent of the organization; individuals in this group usually adopt innovations only after social or financial pressure to do so

Layoff: A suspension of work, usually temporary

Leader–member exchange: Micro theory that focuses on dyadic relationships, or those between two people or between a leader and a small group; explains how in-group and out-group relationships form with a leader or mentor, and how delegation may occur

Leader–member relations: Group atmosphere much like social orientation, includes the subordinates' acceptance of, and confidence in, the leader as well as the loyalty and commitment they show toward the leader

Leadership grid: Blake and Mouton's grid that marked off degrees of emphasis toward orientation using a nine-point scale; and finally separated the grid into five styles of management based on the combined people and production emphasis.

Leading: One of the four management functions in which people are directed and motivated to achieve goals

Lean: Management strategy known for its focus on the reduction of waste and is based on the Japanese success story of Toyota

Leapfrog Group: Organization that promotes healthcare safety by giving consumers the information they need to make better-informed choices about the hospitals they choose

Learning content management system: Training software development tools that assist with management, sharing, and reuse of course content

Learning curve: The time required to acquire and apply certain skills so that new levels of productivity and performance exceed prelearning levels (productivity often is inversely related to the learning curve)

Learning history: The extensive and relatively long-term process of eliciting stories, experiences, and critical events in the life of the organization and its employees

Learning management system: A software application that assists with managing and tracking learners and learning events and collating data on learner progress

Least preferred coworker (LPC) scale: Presents a series of 16 to 22 bipolar adjectives along an eight-point rating scale; sample items included unfriendly to friendly, uncooperative to cooperative, and hostile to supportive

Lecture: A one-way method of delivering education through speaking in which the teacher delivers the speech and the student listens

Legacy system: A type of computer system that uses older technology but may still perform optimally

Legal health record: The subset of all patient-specific data created or accumulated by a healthcare provider that may be released to third parties in response to legally permissible requests

Length of stay (LOS): The total number of patient days for an inpatient episode, calculated by subtracting the date of admission from the date of discharge

Level of significance: 1. The relative intensity of services given when a physician provides one-on-one services for a patient (such as minimal, brief, limited, or intermediate) 2. The relative intensity of services provided by a healthcare facility (for example, tertiary care); also called level of service

Lewin's stages of change: One of the first models of change proposed by Kurt Lewin (1951), one of the early behavioral scientists who contributed to the knowledge base of information on group work, leadership, and organization development; *see* **refreezing** and **unfreezing**

Lexicon: 1. the vocabulary used in a language or a subject area or by a particular speaker or group of speakers 2. A collection of words or terms and their meanings for a particular domain, used in healthcare for drug terms

Lexicon Logical Observation Identifier Names and Codes (LOINC): Generally accepted as the exchange standard for laboratory results; the goal is not to replace the laboratory fields in facility databases but, rather, to provide a mapping mechanism

Liability: 1. A legal obligation or responsibility that may have financial repercussions if not fulfilled 2. An amount owed by an individual or organization to another individual or organization

Licensure: The legal authority or formal permission from authorities to carry on certain activities that by law or regulation require such permission (applicable to institutions as well as individuals)

Likert scale: An ordinal scaling and summated rating technique for measuring the attitudes of respondents; a measure that records level of agreement or disagreement along a progression of categories, usually five (five-point scale), often administered in the form of a questionnaire

Line authority: The authority to manage subordinates and to have them report back, based on relationships illustrated in an organizational chart

Line graph: A graphic technique used to illustrate the relationship between continuous measurements; consists of a line drawn to connect a series of points on an arithmetic scale; often used to display time trends

Linear programming: An operational management technique that uses mathematical formulas to determine the optimal way to allocate resources for a project

Linkage analysis: A technique used to explore and examine relationships among a large number of variables of different types

Liquidity: The degree to which assets can be quickly and efficiently turned into cash, for example, marketable securities are generally very liquid, the assumption being that they can be sold for their full value in a matter of days, whereas buildings are not very liquid, because they cannot usually be sold quickly

Literature review: A systematic and critical investigation of the important information about a topic; may include books, journal articles, theses, dissertations, periodicals, technical and research reports, proceedings of conferences, audiovisual media, and electronic media

Litigation: A civil lawsuit or contest in court

Logical (or conceptual) repository: The compilation of multiple physical repositories

Logical data model: The second level of data model that is drawn according to the type of database to be developed

Logical Observation Identifier Names and Codes (LOINC): A database protocol developed by the Regenstrief Institute for Health Care aimed at standardizing laboratory and clinical codes for use in clinical care, outcomes management, and research

Longitudinal: A type of time frame for research studies during which data are collected from the same participants at multiple points in time

Longitudinal health record: A permanent, coordinated patient record of significant information listed in chronological order and maintained across time, ideally from birth to death

Long-term assets: Assets whose value to the organization extends beyond one fiscal year; for example, buildings, land, and equipment are long-term assets

Long-term care: Healthcare services provided in a nonacute care setting to chronically ill, aged, disabled, or mentally handicapped individuals

Long-term care hospital (LTCH): A healthcare organization that provides medical, nursing, rehabilitation, and subacute care services to residents who need continual care

Loss prevention: A risk management strategy that includes developing and revising policies and procedures that are both facility-wide and department specific

Loss reduction: A component of a risk management program that encompasses techniques used to manage events or claims that already have taken place

Low-utilization payment adjustment (LUPA): An alternative (reduced) payment made to home health agencies instead of the home health resource group reimbursement rate when a patient receives fewer than four home care visits during a 60-day episode

Machine learning: An area of computer science that studies algorithms and computer programs that improve employee performance on some task by exposure to a training or learning experience

Maintenance and evaluation phase: The fourth and final phase of the systems development life cycle that helps to ensure that adequate technical support staff and resources are available to maintain or support the new system

Major diagnostic category (MDC): Under diagnosis-related groups (DRGs), one of 25 categories based on single or multiple organ systems into which all diseases and disorders relating to that system are classified

Major medical insurance (catastrophic coverage): Prepaid healthcare benefits that include a high limit for most types of medical expenses and usually require a large deductible and sometimes place limits on coverage and charges (for example, room and board)

Malpractice: The improper or negligent treatment of a patient, as by a physician, resulting in injury, damage, or loss

Managed care: 1. Payment method in which the third-party payer has implemented some provisions to control the costs of healthcare while maintaining quality care 2. Systematic merger of clinical, financial, and administrative processes to manage access, cost, and quality of healthcare

Managed care organization (MCO): A type of healthcare organization that delivers medical care and manages all aspects of the care or the payment for care by limiting providers of care, discounting payment to providers of care, and limiting access to care

Management by objectives (MBO): A management approach that defines target objectives for organizing work and comparing performance against those objectives

Management functions: Traditionally, the tasks of planning, organizing, directing, coordinating, and controlling

Management information system (MIS): A computer-based system that provides information to a healthcare organization's managers for use in making decisions that affect a variety of day-to-day activities

Management service organization (MSO): An organization, usually owned by a group of physicians or a hospital, that provides administrative and support services to one or more physician group practices or small hospitals

Managerial accounting: The development, implementation, and analysis of systems that track financial transactions for management control purposes, including both budget systems and cost analysis systems

Many-to-many relationship: The concept (occurring only in a conceptual model) that multiple instances of an entity may be associated with multiple instances of another entity

Mark sense technology: Technology that detects the presence or absence of hand-marked characters on analog documents; used for processing questionnaires, surveys, and tests, such as filled-in circles by Number 2 pencils on exam forms

Maslow's Hierarchy of Needs: A theory developed by Abraham Maslow suggesting that a hierarchy of needs might help explain behavior and guide managers on how to motivate employees; *See* **hierarchy of needs**

Massed training: An educational technique that requires learning a large amount of material at one time

Master patient index (MPI): A list or database created and maintained by a healthcare facility to record the name and identification number of every patient who has ever been admitted or treated in the facility

Master planning committee: *See* **steering committee**

Matching: A concept that enables decision makers to look at expenses and revenues in the same period to measure the organization's income performance

Materiality: The significance of a dollar amount based on predetermined criteria

Maternal death rate (hospital based): For a hospital, the total number of maternal deaths directly related to pregnancy for a given time period divided by the total number of obstetrical discharges for the same time period; for a community, the total number of deaths attributed to maternal conditions during a given time period in a specific geographic area divided by the total number of live births for the same time period in the same area

Maternal mortality rate (community based): A rate that measures the deaths associated with pregnancy for a specific community for a specific period of time

Mean: A measure of central tendency that is determined by calculating the arithmetic average of the observations in a frequency distribution

Measure hierarchy: Used to organize the measure set information

Measures of central tendency: The typical or average numbers that are descriptive of the entire collection of data for a specific population

Median: A measure of central tendency that shows the midpoint of a frequency distribution when the observations have been arranged in order from lowest to highest

Medicaid: An entitlement program that oversees medical assistance for individuals and families with low incomes and limited resources; jointly funded between state and federal governments

Medical care evaluation studies (medical audits): Audits required by the Medicare Conditions of Participation that dictate the use of screening criteria with evaluation by diagnosis and procedure

Medical device: Device used by a physician for a patient that has a condition where a body part does not achieve any of its primary intended purposes such as a heart valve; can be used for life support, such as anesthesia ventilators, as well as for monitoring of patients, such as fetal monitors and other uses such as incubators

Medical foundation: Multipurpose, nonprofit service organization for physicians and other healthcare providers at the local and county level; as managed care organizations, medical foundations have established preferred provider organization, exclusive provider organizations, and management service organizations, with emphases on freedom of choice and preservation of the physician-patient relationship

Medical identity theft: Committed by family, friends and acquaintances, and strangers who steal someone's identity in order obtain medical care, services or equipment either because they do not have medical care or their insurance does not cover the needed services

Medical informatics: A field of information science concerned with the management of data and information used to diagnose, treat, cure, and prevent disease through the application of computers and computer technologies

Medical informatics professionals: Individuals who work in the field of medical informatics

Medical Literature, Analysis, and Retrieval System Online (MEDLINE): A computerized, online database in the bibliographic Medical Literature Analysis and Retrieval System (MEDLARS) of the National Library of Medicine

Medical staff bylaws: A collection of guidelines adopted by a hospital's medical staff to govern its business conduct and the rights and responsibilities of its members

Medical staff classifications: Categories of clinical practice privileges assigned to individual practitioners on the basis of their qualifications

Medical Subject Headings database (MeSH): The National Library of Medicine's (NLM's) controlled vocabulary for indexing journal articles

Medical transcription: *See* **transcription**

Medical transcriptionist: A medical language specialist who types or word-processes information dictated by providers

Medically needy option (Medicaid): An option in the Medicaid program that allows states to extend eligibility to persons who would be eligible for Medicaid under one of the mandatory or optional groups but whose income and resources fall above the eligibility level set by their state

Medicare: A federally funded health program established in 1965 to assist with the medical care costs of Americans sixty-five years of age and older as well as other individuals entitled to Social Security benefits owing to their disabilities

Medicare Administrative Contractor (MAC): Newly established contracting entities that will administer Medicare Part A and Part B as of 2011; MACs will replace the carriers and fiscal intermediaries

Medicare Advantage (Medicare Part C): Optional managed care plan for Medicare beneficiaries who are entitled to Part A, enrolled in Part B, and live in an area with a plan;

types include health maintenance organization, point-of-service plan, preferred provider organization, and provider-sponsored organization

Medicare carrier: A health plan that processes Part B claims for services by physicians and medical suppliers (for example, the Blue Shield plan in a state)

Medicare fee schedule (MFS): A feature of the resource-based relative value system that includes a complete list of the payments Medicare makes to physicians and other providers

Medicare prospective payment system: The reimbursement system for inpatient hospital services provided to Medicare and Medicaid beneficiaries that is based on the use of diagnosis-related groups as a classification tool

Medicare Provider Analysis and Review (MEDPAR) database system: A database containing information submitted by fiscal intermediaries that is used by the Office of the Inspector General to identify suspicious billing and charge practices

Medicare Summary Notice (MSN): A summary sent to the patient from Medicare that summarizes all services provided over a period of time with an explanation of benefits provided

Medication reconciliation: Checking medications each time a patient transfers to another level of care

Medication usage review: An evaluation of medication use and medication processes

Medigap: A private insurance policy that supplements Medicare coverage

Mental ability (cognitive) tests: Tests that assess the reasoning capabilities of individuals

Mentor: An advisor; an experienced individual who coaches another individual who is at the beginning stages of his or her career

Message format standards: Protocols that help ensure that data transmitted from one system to another remain comparable

Meta-analysis: A specialized form of systematic literature review that involves the statistical analysis of a large collection of results from individual studies for the purpose of integrating the studies' findings

Metadata: Descriptive data that characterize other data to create a clearer understanding of their meaning and to achieve greater reliability and quality of information

Metadata registry: Used to store characteristics of data that are necessary to clearly describe, inventory, analyze, and classify data

Metric: Data that can be measured on some scale; two subtypes are interval and ratio

Microfilming: A photographic process that reduces an original paper document into a small image on film to save storage space

Middle managers: The individuals in an organization who oversee the operation of a broad scope of functions at the departmental level or who oversee defined product or service lines

Migration path: A series of steps required to move from one situation to another

Minimum Data Set 2.0 (MDS): The instrument specified by the Centers for Medicare and Medicaid Services that requires nursing facilities (both Medicare certified or Medicaid certified) to conduct a comprehensive, accurate, standardized, reproducible assessment of each resident's functional capacity

Minimum Data Set for Long-Term Care-Version 2.0 (MDS 2.0): A federally mandated standard assessment form that Medicare- and Medicaid-certified nursing facilities must use to collect demographic and clinical data on nursing home residents

Misdemeanor: A crime that is less serious than a felony

Missing values: Variables that do not contain values for some cases

Mission statement: A short description of an organization or group's general purpose for existing

Mixed methods research: Research that combines quantitative and qualitative techniques within a single study and across related studies

m-learning: Mobile learning; the application of e-learning to mobile computing devices and wireless networks

Mode: A measure of central tendency that consists of the most frequent observation in a frequency distribution

Model: The representation of a theory in a visual format, on a smaller scale, or with objects

Model-based DDS: Decision support system that attempts to include as many different models as can be accommodated to provide the user the greatest flexibility in framing the decision situation

Moral values: A system of principles by which one guides one's life, usually with regard to right or wrong

Morality: A composite of the personal values concerning what is considered right or wrong in a specific cultural group

Morbidity: A diseased state

Morphological: Refers to the study and description of word formation in a language, including inflection, derivation, and compounding

Morphology: In ICD-O-3, this code describes the characteristics of the tumor itself, including cell type and biologic activity

Mortality (attrition): 1. A term referring to the incidence of death in a specific population 2. The loss of subjects during the course of a clinical research study

Mortality review: A review of deaths as part of an analysis of ongoing outcome and performance improvement

Mortgage: A loan that is secured by a long-term asset, usually a building

Motion for summary judgment: A request made by the defendant in a civil case to have the case ruled in his or he favor based on the assertion that the plaintiff has no genuine issue to be tried

Motion (or streaming) video/frame data: A medium for storing, manipulating, and displaying moving images in a format, such as frames, that can be presented on a computer monitor

Motivation: The drive to accomplish a task

Movement diagram: A chart depicting the location of furniture and equipment in a work area and showing the usual flow of individuals or materials as they progress through the work area

Multiaxial: Coding system with more than one axis, such as in the Diagnostic and Statistical Manual of Mental Diseases (DSM)

Multidimensional analysis: Simultaneous analysis of data from multiple dimensions using different data elements

Multidimensional data structure: A structure whereby data are organized according to the dimensions associated with them

Multidimensional database management system (MDDBMS): A database management system specifically designed to handle data organized into a data structure with numerous dimensions

Multidimensional online analytical processing (MOLAP): A data access methodology that is coupled tightly with a multidimensional database management system to allow the user to perform business analyses

Multimedia: The combination of free-text, raster or vector graphics, sound, and motion video/frame data

Multivariate: A term used in reference to research studies indicating that many variables were involved

Multivoting technique: A decision-making method for determining group consensus on the prioritization of issues or solutions

Narratives: The author details the processes of the procedure in a step-by-step description method

National Alliance for Health Information Technology (NAHIT): A partnership of government and private-sector leaders from various healthcare organizations working to use technology to achieve improvements in patient safety, quality of care and operating performance; founded in 2002

National Association for Home Care (NAHC): The nation's largest trade association representing the interests and concerns of home care agencies, hospices, and home care aide organizations

National Association of Healthcare Quality (NAHQ): An organization devoted to advancing the profession of healthcare quality improvement through its accreditation program

National Cancer Institute (NCI) Thesaurus: Interoperability standard that describes anatomical locations for clinical, surgical, pathological, and research purposes

National Cancer Registrars Association (NCRA): An organization of cancer registry professionals that promotes research and education in cancer registry administration and practice

National Center for Health Statistics (NCHS): The federal agency responsible for collecting and disseminating information on health services utilization and the health status of the population in the United States

National Committee for Quality Assurance (NCQA): A private not-for-profit accreditation organization whose mission is to evaluate and report on the quality of managed care organizations in the United States

National Committee on Vital and Health Statistics (NCVHS): A public policy advisory board that recommends policy to the National Center for Health Statistics and other health-related federal programs

National conversion factor (CF): A mathematical factor used to convert relative value units into monetary payments for services provided to Medicare beneficiaries

National Correct Coding Initiative (NCCI): A series of code edits on Medicare Part B claims

National Council for Prescription Drug Programs (NCPDP): An organization that develops standards for exchanging prescription and payment information

National Drug Code (NDC) Directory: A list of all drugs manufactured, prepared, propagated, compounded, or processed by a drug establishment registered under the Federal Food, Drug, and Cosmetic Act

National Drug Codes (NDC): Codes that serve as product identifiers for human drugs, currently limited to prescription drugs and a few selected over-the-counter products

National Health Care Survey: A national public health survey that contains data abstracted manually from a sample of acute care hospitals or from discharged inpatient records or that are obtained from state or other discharge databases

National health information network (NHIN): System that links various healthcare information systems together, allowing patients, physicians, healthcare institutions, and other entities nationwide to share clinical information privately and securely

National Hospital and Palliative Care Organization (NHPCO): Organization whose mission is to lead and mobilize social change for improved care at the end of life

National Information Infrastructure-Health Information Network Program (NII-HIN): A national quasi-governmental organization that provides oversight of all healthcare information standards in the United States

National Institutes of Health (NIH): Federal agency of the Department of Health and Human Services comprising a number of institutes that carry out research and programs related to certain types of diseases, such as cancer

National Labor Relations Act (Wagner Act): Federal pro-union legislation passed in 1935, later amended by the Taft-Hartley Act

National Library of Medicine (NLM): The world's largest medical library and a branch of the National Institutes of Health

National Practitioner Data Bank (NPBD): A data bank established by the federal government through the 1986 Health Care Quality Improvement Act that contains information on professional review actions taken against physicians and other licensed healthcare practitioners, which healthcare organizations are required to check as part of the credentialing process

National provider identifier (NPI): An eight-character alphanumeric identifier used to identify individual healthcare providers for Medicare billing purposes

National Quality Forum: A private, not-for-profit membership organization created to develop and implement a strategy nationwide to improve the measurement and reporting of healthcare quality

National Vaccine Advisory Committee (NVAC): A national advisory group that supports the director of the National Vaccine Program

National Vital Statistics System (NVSS): A federal agency responsible for the collection of official vital statistics for the United States

Nationwide health information network (NHIN): Network envisioned by the government whereby health information may be exchanged securely and seamlessly to authorized parties across the country

Natural language processing (NLP): *See* **natural language processing technology**

Natural language processing technology: The extraction of unstructured or structured medical word data, which are then translated into diagnostic or procedural codes for clinical and administrative applications

Naturalism: A philosophy of research that assumes that multiple contextual truths exist and bias is always present

Naturalistic observation: A type of nonparticipant observation in which researchers observe certain behaviors and events as they occur naturally

Needs assessment: A procedure performed to determine what is required, lacking, or desired by an employee, a group, or an organization

Need-to-know principle: The release-of-information principle based on the minimum necessary standard that means that only the information needed by a specific individual to perform a specific task should be released

Negative (inverse) relationship: A relationship in which the effects move in opposite directions

Negligence: A legal term that refers to the result of an action by an individual who does not act the way a reasonably prudent person would act under the same circumstances

Neonatal mortality rate: The number of deaths of infants under twenty-eight days of age during a given time period divided by the total number of births for the same time period

Net autopsy rate: The ratio of inpatient autopsies compared to inpatient deaths calculated by dividing the total number of inpatient autopsies performed by the hospital pathologist for a given time period by the total number of inpatient deaths minus unautopsied coroners' or medical examiners' cases for the same time period

Net death rate: The total number of inpatient deaths minus the number of deaths that occurred less than 48 hours after admission for a given time period divided by the total number of inpatient discharges minus the number of deaths that occurred less than 48 hours after admission for the same time period

Net income: The difference between total revenues and total expenses

Net loss: The condition when total expenses exceed total revenue

Net present value: A formula used to assess the current value of a project when the monies used were invested in the organization's investment vehicles rather than expended for the project; this value is then compared to the allocation of the monies and the cash inflows of the project, both of which are adjusted to current time

Network administrators: The individuals involved in installing, configuring, managing, monitoring, and maintaining network computer applications and responsible for supporting the network infrastructure and controlling user access

Network model health maintenance program: Program in which participating HMOs contract for services with one or more multispecialty group practices

Network provider: A physician or another healthcare professional who is a member of a managed care network

Neural networks: Nonlinear predictive models that, using a set of data that describe what a person wants to find, detect a pattern to match a particular profile through a training process that involves interactive learning

Neutral zone: Begins when the old system has been left behind, but the new one has not yet been fully accepted

Neutralizers: When a leader's behavior becomes abusive or produces adverse effects, but it is not feasible to replace the leader, efforts can be made to neutralize the negative effects; subordinates whose performance is influenced by insightful self-monitoring professional standards, group cohesion and peer feedback, and objective performance feedback system are less adversely affected

New beginnings: Stage in which people accept, orient themselves, and engage in the new organization

Newborn (NB): An inpatient who was born in a hospital at the beginning of the current inpatient hospitalization

Newborn autopsy rate: The number of autopsies performed on newborns who died during a given time period divided by the total number of newborns who died during the same time period

Newborn death rate: The number of newborns who died divided by the total number of newborns, both alive and dead

Nomenclature: A recognized system of terms used in a science or art that follows preestablished naming conventions; a disease nomenclature is a listing of the proper name for each disease entity with its specific code number

Nominal data: *See* **nominal-level data**

Nominal group technique: A group process technique that involves the steps of silent listing, recording each participant's list, discussing, and rank ordering the priority or importance of items

Nominal-level data: Data that fall into groups or categories that are mutually exclusive and with no specific order (for example patient demographics such as third-party payer, race, and sex)

Nonexempt employees: All groups of employees covered by the provisions of the Fair Labor Standards Act

Nonmaleficence: A legal principle that means "do no harm"

Nonparametric (distribution-free) technique: A type of statistical procedure used for variables that are not normally distributed in a population

Nonparticipant observation: A method of research in which researchers act as neutral observers who do not intentionally interact or affect the actions of the population being observed

Nonparticipating provider: A healthcare provider who did not sign a participation agreement with Medicare and so is not obligated to accept assignment on Medicare claims

Nonprogrammed decision: A decision that involves careful and deliberate thought and discussion because of a unique, complex, or changing situation

Nonrandom sampling: A type of convenience or purposive sampling in which all members of the target population do not have an equal or independent chance of being selected for a research study

Normal distribution: A theoretical family of continuous frequency distributions characterized by a symmetric bell-shaped curve, with an equal mean, median, and mode, any standard deviation, and with half of the observations above the mean and half below it

Normalization: 1. A formal process applied to relational database design to determine which variables should be grouped together in a table in order to reduce data redundancy across and within the table 2. Conversion of various representational forms to standard expressions so that those that have the same meaning will be recognized by computer software as synonymous in a data search

Normative decision model: Model developed by Victor Vroom and Philip Yetton in the early 1970s; using a continuum similar to Tannenbaum and Schmidt's, they identified a series of intermediate questions and decisions that could be answered yes or no, and that would lead to each outcome

Nosocomial (hospital-acquired) infection: An infection acquired by a patient while receiving care or services in a healthcare organization

Nosology: The branch of medical science that deals with classification systems

Not Elsewhere Classified (NEC): Indicates that you have more information but no place to put it; also means that any additional information will be lost forever if it is assigned the NEC label

Not Otherwise Specified (NOS): Indicates that there is no additional information

Not-for-profit organizations: An organization that is not owned by individuals, where profits may be held for a specific purpose or reinvested in the organization for the benefit of the community it serves

Notice of Privacy Practices: A statement (mandated by the HIPAA Privacy Rule) issued by a healthcare organization that informs individuals of the uses and disclosures of patient-identifiable health information that may be made by the organization, as well as the individual's rights and the organization's legal duties with respect to that information

Notifiable disease: A disease that must be reported to a government agency so that regular, frequent, and timely information on individual cases can be used to prevent and control future cases of the disease

Null hypothesis: A hypothesis that states there is no association between the independent and dependent variables in a research study

Nursing informatics: The field of information science concerned with the management of data and information used to support the practice and delivery of nursing care through the application of computers and computer technologies

Object: The basic component in an object-oriented database that includes both data and their relationships within a single structure

Objective: A statement of the end result expected, stated in measurable terms, usually with a time limitation (deadline date) and often with a cost estimate or limitation

Object-oriented database (OODB): A type of database that uses commands that act as small, self-contained instructional units (objects) that may be combined in various ways

Object-oriented database management system (OODBMS): A specific set of software programs used to implement an object-oriented database

Observational research: A method of research in which researchers obtain data by watching research participants rather than by asking questions

Observational study: An epidemiological study in which the exposure and outcome for each individual in the study is observed

Occasion of service: A specified identifiable service involved in the care of a patient that is not an encounter (for example, a lab test ordered during an encounter)

Occupational Safety and Health Act of 1970 (OSHA): The federal legislation that established comprehensive safety and health guidelines for employers

Occurrence/generic screening: A risk management technique in which the risk manager reviews the health records of current and discharged hospital inpatients with the goal of identifying potentially compensable events

Odds ratio: A relative measure of occurrence of an illness; the odds of exposure in a diseased group divided by the odds of exposure in a nondiseased group

Office for Human Research Protections (OHRP): The department within the Department of Health and Human Services that monitors compliance with federal regulations governing the conduct of biomedical research

Office of Research Integrity (ORI): Organization that provides integrity in biomedical and behavioral research, monitoring incidents of research misconduct and facilitating responsible research conduct through educational, preventive, and regulatory activities

Office of the National Coordinator of Health Information Technology (ONC): Office that provides leadership for the development and implementation of an interoperable health information technology infrastructure nationwide to improve healthcare quality and delivery

Offshoring: Outsourcing jobs to countries overseas, wherein local employees abroad perform jobs that domestic employees previously performed

Omnibus Budget Reconciliation Act (OBRA) of 1989: Federal legislation that mandated important changes in the payment rules for Medicare physicians; specifically, the legislation that requires nursing facilities to conduct regular patient assessments for Medicare and Medicaid beneficiaries

One-tailed hypothesis: An alternative hypothesis in which the researcher makes a prediction in one direction

One-to-many relationship: A relationship that exists when one instance of an entity is associated with multiple instances of another entity

One-to-one relationship: A relationship that exists when an instance of an entity is associated with only one instance of another entity, and vice versa

Ongoing records review: *See* **open-record review**

Online analytical processing (OLAP): A data access architecture that allows the user to retrieve specific information from a large volume of data

Online analytical processing (OLAP) engine: An optimized query generator that can retrieve the correct information from the warehouse to accommodate what-if queries

Online/real-time analytical processing (OLAP): *See* **online analytical processing**

Online/real-time transaction processing (OLTP): The real-time processing of day-to-day business transactions from a database

On-the-job training: A method of training in which an employee learns necessary skills and processes by performing the functions of his or her position

Open-record review: A review of the health records of patients currently in the hospital or under active treatment; part of the Joint Commission survey process

Open-source technology: Applications whose source (human-readable) code is freely available to anyone who is interested in downloading the code

Open systems: Processes that are affected by what is going on around them and must adjust as the environment changes

Operation index: A list of the operations and surgical procedures performed in a healthcare facility that is sequenced according to the code numbers of the classification system in use

Operational budget: A type of budget that allocates and controls resources to meet an organization's goals and objectives for the fiscal year

Operational plan: The short-term objectives set by an organization to improve its methods of doing business and achieve its planned outcomes

Operationalize: Formulating the question in terms that are capable of generating data and that satisfactorily capture the issues of the question or problem

Operations improvement planning: Focuses on improving how existing programs and services are carried out; is internally focused and is one part of how to implement strategic thinking

Operations management: The application of mathematical and statistical techniques to production and distribution efficiency

Operations research (OR): A scientific discipline primarily begun during World War II that seeks to apply the scientific method and mathematical models to the solution of a variety of management decision problems

Optical character recognition (OCR) technology: A method of encoding text from analog paper into bit-mapped images and translating the images into a form that is computer readable

Optical imaging technology: The process by which information is scanned onto optical disks

Order communications: In hospitals, type of data that may be directed to many of the applications that support CPOE and EMAR and other applications that have been relatively stand-alone applications

Ordinal data: Data with inherent order and with higher numbers usually associated with higher values; also referred to as ordinal-level data

Ordinal-level data: Data in which the order of the numbers is meaningful, not the number itself

Organization: The planned coordination of the activities of more than one person for the achievement of a common purpose or goal

Organization development (OD): The process in which an organization reflects on its own processes and consequently revises them for improved performance

Organizational chart: A graphic representation of an organization's formal structure

Organizational lifeline: A graphic time line with annual demarcations that show important events in the life of the organization over the years

Organizing: The process of coordinating something, such as activities

Orientation: A set of activities designed to familiarize new employees with their jobs, the organization, and its work culture

Orthographic: Refers to the correctness of spelling or the representation of the sounds of a language by written or printed symbols

ORYX: *See* **ORYX initiative**

ORYX initiative: A Joint Commission initiative that supports the integration of outcomes data and other performance measurement data into the accreditation process; often referred to as ORYX

Outcome and Assessment Information Set (OASIS): A standard core assessment data tool developed to measure the outcomes of adult patients receiving home health services under the Medicare and Medicaid programs

Outcome measures: The process of systematically tracking a patient's clinical treatment and responses to that treatment, including measures of morbidity and functional status, for the purpose of improving care

Outcomes and effectiveness research (OER): A type of research performed to explain the end results of specific healthcare practices and interventions

Outcomes management: The process of systematically tracking a patient's clinical treatment and responses to that treatment, including measures of morbidity and functional status, for the purpose of improving care

Out-group: Those subordinates not included in the group formed around the leader

Out-of-pocket expenses: Healthcare costs paid by the insured (for example, deductibles, copayments, and coinsurance) after which the insurer pays a percentage (often 80 or 100 percent) of covered expenses

Outpatient: A patient who receives ambulatory care services in a hospital-based clinic or department

Outpatient code editor (OCE): A software program linked to the Correct Coding Initiative that applies a set of logical rules to determine whether various combinations of codes are correct and appropriately represent the services provided

Outpatient prospective payment system (OPPS): The Medicare prospective payment system used for hospital-based outpatient services and procedures that is predicated on the assignment of ambulatory payment classifications

Outpatient visit: A patient's visit to one or more units located in the ambulatory services area (clinic or physician's office) of an acute care hospital

Outsourcing: The hiring of an individual or a company external to an organization to perform a function either on site or off site

Overhead costs: The expenses associated with supporting but not providing patient care services

Overlap: Occurs when a patient has more than one medical record number assigned across more than one database

Overlay: Occurs when one patient record is overwritten with data from another patient's record

Owner's equity: The value of the investment in an organization by its owners

Packaging: A payment under the Medicare outpatient prospective payment system that includes items such as anesthesia, supplies, certain drugs, and the use of recovery and observation rooms

Panel interview: An interview format in which the applicant is interviewed by several interviewers at the same time

Par level: The accepted, standard inventory level for all supplies and equipment in an organization

Paradigm: A philosophical or theoretical framework within which a discipline formulates its theories and makes generalizations

Parallel work division: A type of concurrent work design in which one employee does several tasks and takes the job from beginning to end

Parametric technique: A type of statistical procedure that is based on the assumption that a variable is normally distributed in a population

Pareto chart: A bar graph that includes bars arranged in order of descending size to show decisions on the prioritization of issues, problems, or solutions

Parsimony: Explanations of phenomena should include the fewest assumptions and conditions

Partial hospitalization: A term that refers to limited patient stays in the hospital setting, typically as part of a transitional program to a less intense level of service; for example, psychiatric and drug and alcohol treatment facilities that offer services to help patients reenter the community, return to work, and assume family responsibilities

Participant observation: A research method in which researchers also participate in the observed actions

Partnership: The business venture of two or more owners for whom the profits represent the owners' personal income

Path–goal theory: States that a person's ability to perform certain tasks is related to the direction and clarity available that lead to organizational goals

Patient information coordinator: Helps consumers manage their personal health information, including personal health histories and release of information; also helps customers understand managed care services and access to health information resources

Patient Medical Record Information (PMRI): Information in which SNOMED CT is part of a core set of terminology

Patient/member Web portals: The media for providing patient/member access to the provider organization's multiple sources of data from any network-connected device

Patient-identifiable data: Data in the health record that relates to a particular patient identified by name

Patient-specific data: *See* **patent-identifiable data**

Pay for performance: The Integrated Healthcare Association initiative in California based on the concept that physician groups would be paid for documented performance

Payback period: A financial method used to evaluate the value of a capital expenditure by calculating the time frame that must pass before inflow of cash from a project equals or exceeds outflow of cash

Payer of last resort (Medicaid): A Medicaid term that means that Medicare pays for the services provided to individuals enrolled in both Medicare and Medicaid until Medicare benefits are exhausted and Medicaid benefits begin

Payment status indicator (PSI): An alphabetic code assigned to CPT/HCPCS codes to indicate whether a service or procedure is to be reimbursed under the Medicare outpatient prospective payment system

PDSA cycle (Plan-do-study-act): A performance improvement model designed specifically for healthcare organizations

Peer review: A service that provides diagnostic and therapeutic services for patients under the age of fourteen years

Peer review organization (PRO): Until 2002, a medical organization that performs a professional review of medical necessity, quality, and appropriateness of healthcare services provided to Medicare beneficiaries; now called quality improvement organization (QIO)

Peer-reviewed journal: A type of professional or scientific journal for which content experts evaluate articles prior to publication

Per member per month (PMPM): *See* **per patient per month**

Per patient per month (PPPM): A type of managed care arrangement by which providers are paid a fixed fee in exchange for supplying all of the healthcare services an enrollee needs for a specified period of time (usually one month but sometimes one year)

Performance: Execution of a task

Performance counseling: Guidance provided to an individual in an attempt to improve his or her work performance

Performance improvement (PI): The continuous study and adaptation of a healthcare organization's functions and processes to increase the likelihood of achieving desired outcomes

Performance measure: A quantitative tool used to assess the clinical, financial, and utilization aspects of a healthcare provider's outcomes or processes

Performance measure/measurement system: System designed to improve performance by providing feedback on whether goals have been met

Performance measurement: The process of comparing the outcomes of an organization, work unit, or employee against preestablished performance plans and standards

Performance review: An evaluation of an employee's job performance

Performance standards: The stated expectations for acceptable quality and productivity associated with a job function

Permanence: The notion that terminologies and classifications must be permanent if they are to be useful for longitudinal reporting; concepts may be inactivated but must never be deleted

Permanent budget variance: A financial term the refers to the difference between the budgeted amount and the actual amount of a line item that is not expected to reverse itself during a subsequent period

Persistence: The notion that some vocabularies are intended, at least initially, primarily for a specific study or a specific site; if a vocabulary is intended to be persistent, there should be a means of updating or some kind of change management

Personal digital assistant (PDA): A hand-held microcomputer, without a hard drive, that is capable of running applications such as e-mail and providing access to data and information, such as notes, phone lists, schedules, and laboratory results, primarily through a pen device

Personal health dimension (PHD): One of three dimensions of the National Health Information Infrastructure privacy concept that supports individuals in managing their own wellness and healthcare decision making

Personal health record (PHR): An electronic or paper health record maintained and updated by an individual for himself or herself

Peter Principle: Principle in which some people were promoted to their level of incompetency

Pharmacy Information System (PIS): Ancillary system application in a hospital or physician's office that generates clinical (pharmacological) information

Physical data model: The lowest level of data model with the lowest level of abstraction

Physical data repository: A repository organized into data fields, data records, and data files, storing structured, discrete, clinical, administrative, and financial data as well as unstructured, patient free-text, bit-mapped, real audio, streaming video, or vector graphic data

Physician assistant (PA): A healthcare professional licensed to practice medicine with physician supervision

Physician index: A list of patients and their physicians that is usually arranged according to the physician code numbers assigned by the healthcare facility

Physician-hospital organization (PHO): An integrated delivery system formed by hospitals and physicians (usually through managed care contracts) that allows for cooperative activity but permits participants to retain some level of independence

Physiological signal processing systems: Systems that store vector graphic data based on the human body's signals and create output based on the lines plotted between the signals' points

Picture archiving and communication system (PACS): System that digitizes medical images

Pie chart: A graphic technique in which the proportions of a category are displayed as portions of a circle (like pieces of a pie)

Piece-rate incentive: An adjustment of the compensation paid to a worker based on exceeding a certain level of output

Pilot study: A trial run on a smaller scale

Pixel: An abbreviation for the term *picture element,* which is defined by many tiny bits of data or points

Placebo: A medication with no active ingredients

Plaintiff: The group or person who initiates a civil lawsuit

Planning: An examination of the future and preparation of action plans to attain goals; one of the four traditional management functions

Playscript: This format describes each player in the procedure, the action of the player, and the player's responsibility regarding the process from start to completion of a specific task within the procedure

Point method: A method of job evaluation that places weight (points) on each of the compensable factors in a job whereby the total points associated with a job establish its relative worth and jobs that fall within a specific range of points fall into a pay grade with an associated wage

Point-of-care information system: A computer system that captures data at the location (for example, bedside, exam room, or home) where the healthcare service is performed

Point-of-care (POC) patient charting system: Guides the user in the necessary data to collect in the context of the specific patient at the location where the healthcare service is performed

Point-of-care review: *See* **open-record review**

Point-of-service (POS) plan: A type of managed care plan in which enrollees are encouraged to select healthcare providers from a network of providers under contract with the plan but are also allowed to select providers outside the network and pay a larger share of the cost

Policy: 1. A governing principle that describes how a department or an organization is supposed to handle a specific situation 2. Binding contract issued by a healthcare insurance company to an individual or group in which the company promises to pay for healthcare to treat illness or injury

Policy development: Includes establishing data security, confidentiality, retention, integrity, and access standards; developing training programs that empower others to carry out the information policies; advocating for data privacy, confidentiality, and appropriate access

Policyholder: An individual or entity that purchases healthcare insurance coverage

Polyhierarchy: Multiple relationships should exist for every concept

Population health dimension (PHD): One of three dimensions of the National Health Information Infrastructure privacy concept that addresses protecting and promoting the health of the community

Population-based registry: A type of registry that includes information from more than one facility in a specific geopolitical area, such as a state or region

Population-based statistics: Statistics based on a defined population rather than on a sample drawn from the same population

Position (job) description: A document that outlines the work responsibilities associated with a job

Position power: Refers to the authority the leader has to direct others and to use reward and coercive power

Positive (direct) relationship: A relationship in which the effect moves in the same direction

Positivism: A philosophy of research that assumes that there is a single truth across time and place and that researchers are able to adopt a neutral, unbiased stance and establish causation; *See* **quantitative approach**

Post–acute care: Care provided to patients who have been released from an acute care facility to recuperate at home

Postneonatal mortality rate: The number of deaths of persons aged 28 days up to, but not including, one year during a given time period divided by the number of live births for the same time period

Postoperative infection rate: The number of infections that occur in clean surgical cases for a given time period divided by the total number of operations within the same time period

Potentially compensable event (PCE): An event (for example, an injury, accident, or medical error) that may result in financial liability for a healthcare organization

Power: The probability of identifying real relationships or differences between groups

Practice guidelines: Protocols of care that guide the clinical care process

Practice management system (PMS): Software designed to help medical practices run more smoothly and efficiently

Precision factor: The definitive tolerable error rate to be considered in calculations of productivity standards

Predecessor: A task that affects the scheduling of a successor task in a dependency relationship

Preemption: In law, the principle that a statute at one level supercedes or is applied over the same or similar statute at a lower level (for example, the federal HIPAA privacy provisions trump the same or similar state law with certain exceptions)

Preferred provider organization (PPO): A managed care arrangement based on a contractual agreement between healthcare providers (professional and/or institutional) and employers, insurance carriers, or third-party administrators to provide healthcare services to a defined population of enrollees at established fees that may or may not be a discount from usual and customary or reasonable charges

Pregnancy Discrimination Act (1978): The federal legislation that prohibits discrimination against women affected by pregnancy, childbirth, or related medical conditions by requiring that affected women be treated the same as all other employees for employment-related purposes, including benefits

Premium: Amount of money that a policyholder or certificate holder must periodically pay an insurer in return for healthcare coverage

Present on admission (POA): A condition present at the time the order for inpatient admission occurs; conditions that develop during an outpatient encounter, including the emergency department, observation, or outpatient surgery

Prevalence rate: The proportion of people in a population who have a particular disease at a specific point in time or over a specified period of time

Preventive controls: Internal controls implemented prior to an activity and designed to stop an error from happening

Primary analysis: The analysis of original research data by the researchers who collected them

Primary care manager (PCM): The healthcare provider assigned to a TRICARE enrollee

Primary care physician (PCP): 1. Physician who provides, supervises, and coordinates the healthcare of a member and who manages referrals to other healthcare providers and utilization of healthcare services both inside and outside a managed care plan 2. The physician who makes the initial diagnosis of a patient's medical condition

Primary data source: A record developed by healthcare professionals in the process of providing patient care

Primary key: An explanatory notation that uniquely identifies each row in a database table

Primary source: An original work of a researcher who conducted an investigation

Principal diagnosis: The disease or condition that was present on admission, was the principal reason for admission, and received treatment or evaluation during the hospital stay or visit

Principal investigator: The individual with primary responsibility for the design and conduct of a research project

Principal procedure: The procedure performed for the definitive treatment of a condition (as opposed to a procedure performed for diagnostic or exploratory purposes) or for care of a complication

Priority focus process (PFP): A process used by the Joint Commision to collect, analyze, and create information about a specific organization being accredited in order to customize the accreditation process

Privacy: The quality or state of being hidden from, or undisturbed by, the observation or activities of other persons or freedom from unauthorized intrusion; in healthcare-related contexts, the right of a patient to control disclosure of personal information

Privacy Act of 1974: The legislation that gave individuals some control over information collected about them by the federal government

Privacy Rule: The federal regulations created to implement the privacy requirements of the simplification subtitle of the Health Insurance Portability and Accountability Act of 1996

Privacy standards: Rules, conditions, or requirements developed to ensure the privacy of patient information

Privilege: The professional relationship between patients and specific groups of caregivers that affects the patient's health record and its contents as evidence; the services or procedures, based on training and experience, that an individual physician is qualified to perform; a right granted to a user, program, or process that allows access to certain files or data in a system

Privileging process: The process of evaluating a physician's or other licensed independent practitioner's quality of medical practice and determining the services or procedures he or she is qualified to perform

Problem-oriented medical record (POMR): A way of organizing information in a health record in which clinical problems are defined and documented individually; also called problem-oriented health record

Procedure: A document that describes the steps involved in performing a specific function

Procedure manual: A compilation of all of the procedures used in a specific unit, department, or organization

Process and workflow modeling: The process of creating a representation of the actions and information required to perform a function, including decomposition diagrams, dependency diagrams, and data flow diagrams

Process innovations: Enable firms to produce existing products or services more efficiently

Process measures: Specific measures that enable the assessment of the steps taken in rendering a service; also called process indicators

Process redesign: Change and improvements made that increase efficiency

Productivity: A unit of performance defined by management in quantitative standards

Profession: In HIM, characteristics include: professional associations; code of ethics; unique body of knowledge that must be learned through formal education; system of training with entry by examination or other formal prerequisites (certification); professional cohesion; professional literature

Professional component (PC): 1. The portion of a healthcare procedure performed by a physician 2. A term generally used in reference to the elements of radiological procedures performed by a physician

Profitability index: An index used to prioritize investment opportunities, where the present value of the cash inflows is divided by the present value of the cash outflows for each investment and the results are compared

Program evaluation and review technique (PERT) chart: A project management tool that diagrams a project's time lines and tasks as well as their interdependencies

Programmed decisions: An automated decision made by people or computers based on a situation being so stable and recurrent that decision rules can be applied to it

Programmers: Individuals primarily responsible for writing program codes and developing applications, typically performing the function of systems development and working closely with system analysts

Programs of All-Inclusive Care for the Elderly (PACE): A state option legislated by the Balanced Budget Act of 1997 that provides an alternative to institutional care for individuals fifty-five years old or older who require the level of care provided by nursing facilities

Progress notes: The documentation of a patient's care, treatment, and therapeutic response that is entered into the health record by each of the clinical professionals involved in a patient's care, including nurses, physicians, therapists, and social workers

Progressive discipline: A four-step process for shaping employee behavior to conform to the requirements of the employee's job position that begins with a verbal caution and progresses to written reprimand, suspension, and dismissal upon subsequent offenses

Project charter: A document that defines the scope and goals of a specific project

Project components: Related parameters of scope, resources, and scheduling with regard to a project

Project definition: First step in the project management life cycle that sets expectations for the what, when, and how of a project the organization wants to undertake
Project deliverables: The tangible end results of a project
Project management life cycle: The period in which the processes involved in carrying out a project are completed, including project definition, project planning and organization, project tracking and analysis, project revisions, change control, and communication
Project management software: A type of application software that provides the tools to track a project
Project network: The relationship between tasks in a project that determines the overall finish date
Project office: A support function for project management best practices
Project plan: A plan consisting of a list of the tasks to be performed in a project, a defined order in which they will occur, task start and finish dates, and the resource effort needed to complete each task
Project schedule: The portion of the project plan that deals specifically with task start and finish dates
Project scope: 1. The intention of a project 2. The range of a project's activities or influence
Project team: A collection of individuals assigned to work on a project
Promotion: The act of being raised in position or rank
Proportion: A type of ratio in which the elements included in the numerator also must be included in the denominator
Proportionate mortality ratio (PMR): The total number of deaths due to a specific cause during a given time period divided by the total number of deaths due to all causes
Prosecutor: An attorney who prosecutes a defendant accused for a crime on behalf of a local, state, or federal government
Prospective: In research studies, subjects are followed into the future to examine relationships between variables and later occurrences
Prospective payment system (PPS): A type of reimbursement system that is based on preset payment levels rather than actual charges billed after the service has been provided; specifically, one of several Medicare reimbursement systems based on predetermined payment rates or periods and linked to the anticipated intensity of services delivered as well as the beneficiary's condition
Prospective studies: Studies designed to observe outcomes or events that occur after the identification of a group of subjects to be studied
Protected health information (PHI): Under HIPAA, all individually identifiable information, whether oral or recorded in any form or medium, that is created or received by a healthcare provider or any other entity subject to HIPAA requirements
Protocol: In healthcare, a detailed plan of care for a specific medical condition based on investigative studies; in medical research, a rule or procedure to be followed in a clinical trial; in a computer network, a protocol is used to address and ensure delivery of data
Public assistance: A monetary subsidy provided to financially needy individuals
Public Company Accounting Oversight Board (PCAOB): A not-for-profit organization that oversees the work of auditors of public companies
Public health: An area of healthcare that deals with the health of populations in geopolitical areas, such as states and counties
Public Health Service (PHS): Services concerned primarily with the health of entire communities and population groups
Public key infrastructure (PKI): A system of digital certificates and other registration authorities that verify and authenticate the validity of each party involved in a secure transaction
Purchase order: A paper document or electronic screen on which all details of an intended purchase are reported, including authorizations
Purposive sampling: A strategy of qualitative research in which researchers use their expertise to select representative units and unrepresentative units to capture a wide array of perspectives
Qualitative analysis: A review of the health record to ensure that standards are met and to determine the adequacy of entries documenting the quality of care
Qualitative approach: *See* **naturalism**
Qualitative standards: Service standards in the context of setting expectations for how well or how soon work or a service will be performed
Quality: The degree or grade of excellence of goods or services, including, in healthcare, meeting expectations for outcomes of care
Quality assurance (QA): A set of activities designed to measure the quality of a service, product, or process with remedial action, as needed, to maintain a desired standard
Quality gap: The difference between approved standards, criteria, or expectations in any type of process and actual results
Quality improvement (QI): A set of activities that measures the quality of a service or product through systems or process evaluation and then implements revised processes that result in better healthcare outcomes for patients, based on standards of care
Quality improvement organization (QIO): An organization that performs medical peer review of Medicare and Medicaid claims, including review of validity of hospital diagnosis and procedure coding information; completeness, adequacy, and quality of care; and appropriateness of prospective payments for outlier cases and nonemergent use of the emergency room; until 2002, called peer review organization
Quality indicator (QI): A standard against which actual care may be measured to identify a level of performance for that standard
Quality management: Evaluation of the quality of healthcare services and delivery using standards and guidelines

developed by various entities, including the government and independent accreditation organizations

Quantitative analysis: A review of the health record to determine its completeness and accuracy

Quantitative approach: *See* **positivism**

Quantitative standards: Measures of productivity in the context of setting expectations for how efficiently or effectively work will be performed

Questionnaire survey: A type of survey in which the members of the population are questioned through the use of electronic or paper forms

Queuing: Involves a process of making the record available to a particular user

Queuing theory: An operations management technique for examining customer flow and designing ideal wait or scheduling times

Radio frequency identification (RFID): An automatic recognition technology that uses a device attached to an object to transmit data to a receiver and does not require direct contact

Radiology Information System (RIS): Ancillary system application in a hospital or physician's office that generates clinical (radiological) information

Random sampling: An unbiased selection of subjects that includes methods such as simple random sampling, stratified random sampling, systematic sampling, and cluster sampling

Randomization: The assignment of subjects to experimental or control groups based on chance

Randomized clinical trial (RCT): A special type of clinical trial in which the researchers follow strict rules to randomly assign patients to groups

Range: A measure of variability between the smallest and largest observations in a frequency distribution

Raster image: A digital image or digital data made up of pixels in a horizontal and vertical grid or a matrix instead of lines plotted between a series of points

Rate: A measure used to compare an event over time; a comparison of the number of times an event did happen (numerator) with the number of times an event could have happened (denominator)

Ratio: 1. A calculation found by dividing one quantity by another 2. A general term that can include a number of specific measures such as proportion, percentage, and rate

Ratio analysis: Mathematical computations that compare elements of an organization's financial statements

Ratio data: Data with a defined unit of measure, a real zero point, and with equal intervals between successive values; also called ratio-level data

Ratio-level data: *See* **ratio data**

Real audio (or sound) data: The storing, manipulating, and displaying of sound in a computer-readable format

Record locator service (RLS): A key infrastructure component of the Common Framework to support connectivity and interoperability

Recruitment: The process of finding, soliciting, and attracting employees

Reductionism: Complex processes are reduced to their constituent elements and analyzed by their parts

Redundancy: As data are entered and processed by one server, they are simultaneously being entered and processed by a second server

Redundant array of independent (or inexpensive) disks (RAID): A method of ensuring data security

Reengineering: Fundamental rethinking and radical redesign of business processes to achieve significant performance improvements

Reference check: Contact made with an individual that a prospective employee has listed to provide a favorable account of his or her work performance or personal attributes

Reference data: Information that interacts with the care of the individual or with the healthcare delivery system, such as a formulary, protocol, care plan, clinical alert, or reminder

Reference terminology: A set of concepts and relationships that provide a common consultation point for the comparison and aggregation of data about the entire healthcare process, recorded by multiple individuals, systems, or institutions

Referential integrity: Concept that involves constraints placed on the primary and foreign keys within the database

Referred outpatient: An outpatient who is provided special diagnostic or therapeutic services by a hospital on an ambulatory basis but whose medical care remains the responsibility of the referring physician

Reflective learning cycle: Uses awareness to formulate an interpretation of what has been observed, considers what difference can be made by applying what has been learned, and executes the efforts toward change through deliberate action

Refreezing: Lewin's final stage of change in which the new behaviors are reinforced to become as stable and institutionalized as the previous status quo was

Regional health information network (RHIN): System that links various healthcare information systems in a region together so that patients, healthcare institutions, and other entities can share clinical information

Regional health information organization (RHIO): An organization that manages the local deployment of systems promoting and facilitating the exchange of healthcare data within a national health information network

Registered health information administrator (RHIA): A type of certification granted after completion of an AHIMA-accredited four-year program in health information management and a credentialing examination

Registered health information technician (RHIT): A type of certification granted after completion of an AHIMA-accredited two-year program in health information management and a credentialing examination

Registry: A collection of a limited set of information about a patient and often disease specific

Rehabilitation services: Health services provided to assist patients in achieving and maintaining their optimal level of function, self-care, and independence after some type of disability

Reinforcement: The process of increasing the probability of a desired response through reward

Relational database: A type of database that stores data in predefined tables made up of rows and columns

Relational database management system (RDBMS): A database management system in which data are organized and managed as a collection of tables

Relational online analytical processing (ROLAP): A data access methodology that provides users with various drill-down and business analysis capabilities similar to online analytical processing

Relationship: A type of connection between two terms

Relative risk (RR): A ratio that compares the risk of disease between two groups

Relative value unit (RVU): A measurement that represents the value of the work involved in providing a specific professional medical service in relation to the value of the work involved in providing other medical services

Reliability: A measure of consistency of data items based on their reproducibility and an estimation of their error of measurement

Religious Non-Medical Health Care Institutions (RNHCI): Type of hospital excluded from Medicare's acute care PPS but still paid on the basis of reasonable cost, subject to payment limits per discharge or under a separate PPS

Remittance advice (RA): An explanation of payments (for example, claim denials) made by third-party payers

Remote connectivity: Ability to access a system from a location other than where the system is based (for example, a hospital or physician's office

Report generation: The process of analyzing, organizing, and presenting recorded patient information for authentication and inclusion in the patient's healthcare record; the formatting and structuring of captured information

Request for information (RFI): A written communication often sent to a comprehensive list of vendors during the design phase of the systems development life cycle to ask for general product information

Request for production: A discovery device used to compel another party to produce documents and other items or evidence important to a lawsuit

Request for proposal (RFP): A type of business correspondence asking for very specific product and contract information that is often sent to a narrow list of vendors that have been preselected after a review of requests for information during the design phase of the systems development life cycle

Research: An inquiry process aimed at discovering new information about a subject or revising old information

Research and decision support analyst: Ensures the quality of data and information generated through clinical investigations and other research projects

Research data: Data used for the purpose of answering a proposed question or testing a hypothesis

Research frame: The overarching structure of the research project

Research method: The particular strategy used by a researcher to collect, analyze, and present data

Research methodology: A set of procedures or strategies used by researchers to collect, analyze, and present data

Resident Assessment Instrument (RAI): A uniform assessment instrument developed by the Centers for Medicare and Medicaid Services to standardize the collection of skilled nursing facility patient data; includes the Minimum Data Set 2.0, triggers, and resident assessment protocols

Resident assessment protocols (RAPs): A summary of a long-term care resident's medical condition and care requirements

Resident Assessment Validation and Entry (RAVEN): A type of data-entry software developed by the Centers for Medicare and Medicaid Services for long-term care facilities and used to collect Minimum Data Set assessments and to transmit data to state databases

Resource Utilization Groups, Version III (RUG-III): A case-mix–adjusted classification system based on Minimum Data Set assessments and used by skilled nursing facilities

Resource-based relative value scale (RBRVS): A Medicare reimbursement system implemented in 1992 to compensate physicians according to a fee schedule predicated on weights assigned on the basis of the resources required to provide the services

Resources: The labor, equipment, or materials needed to complete a project

Respect for Persons: The principle that all people are presumed to be free and responsible and should be treated accordingly

Respite care: A type of short-term care provided during the day or overnight to individuals in the home or institution to temporarily relieve the family home caregiver

Responsibility: The accountability required as part of a job, such as supervising work performed by others or managing assets or funds

Restitution: The act of returning something to its rightful owner, of making good or giving something equivalent for any loss, damage, or injury

Resume: A document that describes a job candidate's educational background, work experience, and professional achievements

Retained earnings: Undistributed profits from a for-profit organization that stay in the business

Retention: 1. The process whereby inactive health records are stored and made available for future use in compliance with state and federal requirements 2. The ability to keep valuable employees from seeking employment elsewhere

Retention schedules: Timetables specifying how long various records are to be maintained according to rules, regulations, standards, and laws

Retrospective: A type of time frame that looks back in time

Retrospective payment system: Type of fee-for-service reimbursement in which providers receive recompense after health services have been rendered; also called retrospective payment method

Retrospective study: A type of research conducted by reviewing records from the past (for example, birth and death certificates and health records) or by obtaining information about past events through surveys or interviews

Return on equity (ROE): A more comprehensive measurement of profitability that takes into consideration the organization's net value

Return on investment (ROI): The financial analysis of the extent of value a major purchase will provide

Revenge effects: Unintended and typically negative consequences of a change in technology

Revenue: The charges generated from providing healthcare services; earned and measurable income

Revenue codes: A three- or four-digit number in the chargemaster that totals all items and their charges for printing on the form used for Medicare billing

Revenue Principle: States that earnings as a result of activities and investments may only be recognized when it has been earned, can be measured, and has a reasonable expectation of being collected

Reverse mentoring: The opposite of the usual coaching process where the younger goes to the older instructor

Risk: 1. The possibility of injury or loss 2. The probable amount of loss foreseen by an insurer in issuing a contract

Risk analysis: An assessment of possible security threats to the organization's data

Risk prevention: One component of a successful risk management program

Role playing: A training method in which participants are required to respond to specific problems they may actually encounter in their jobs

Role theory: Thinking that attempts to explain how people adopt specific roles, including leadership roles

Roles and responsibilities: The definition of who does what on a project and the hierarchy for decision making

Root-cause analysis: A technique used in performance improvement initiatives to discover the underlying causes of a problem

Rule induction: *See* **association rule analysis**

Run chart: A type of graph that shows data points collected over time and identifies emerging trends or patterns

RxNorm: A clinical drug nomenclature developed by the Food and Drug Administration, the Department of Veterans Affairs, and HL7 to provide standard names for clinical drugs and administered dose forms

Safe practices: Behaviors undertaken to reduce or prevent adverse effects and medical errors

Sample: A set of units selected for study that represents a population

Sample size: The number of subjects needed in a study to represent a population

Sample size calculation: The qualitative and quantitative procedures to determine an appropriate sample size

Sample survey: A type of survey that collects data from representative members of a population

Satisficing: A decision-making process in which the decision maker accepts a solution to a problem that is satisfactory rather than optimal

Scalar chain: A theory in the chain of command in which everyone is included and authority and responsibility flow downward from the top of the organization

Scale: Measure with progressive categories, such as size, amount, importance, rank, or agreement

Scales of measurement: A reference standard for data collection and classification; *See* **categorical data**

Scanning: The process by which a document is read into an optical imaging system

Scatter chart: *See* **scatter diagram**

Scatter diagram: A graph that visually displays the linear relationships among factors

Scenarios: Stories describing the current and feasible future states of the business environment

Scheduling engine: A specific functionality in project management software that automates the assignment of task start-and-finish dates and, as a result, the expected project finish date

Scientific inquiry: A process that comprises making predictions, collecting and analyzing evidence, testing alternative theories, and choosing the best theory

Scientific management: A principle that states that the best management is a science based on laws and rules and that secures maximum prosperity for both employer and employee

Scope creep: A process in which the scope of a project grows while the project is in process, virtually guaranteeing that it will be over budget and behind schedule

Scope of command: The number and type of employees who report to a specific management position in a defined organizational structure

Scope of work: The time period an organization is under contract to perform as a quality improvement organization

Secondary analysis: A method of research involving analysis of the original work of another person or organization

Secondary data source: Data derived from the primary patient record, such as an index or a database

Secondary release of information: A type of information release in which the initial requester forwards confidential information to others without obtaining required patient authorization

Secondary source: A summary of an original work, such as an encyclopedia

Secure messaging systems: A system that eliminates the security concerns that surround e-mail, but retains the benefits of proactive, traceable, and personalized messaging

Securities and Exchange Commission (SEC): The federal agency that regulates all public and some private transactions involving the ownership and debt of organizations

Security: 1. The means to control access and protect information from accidental or intentional disclosure to unauthorized persons and from unauthorized alteration, destruction, or loss 2. The physical protection of facilities and equipment from theft, damage, or unauthorized access; collectively, the policies, procedures, and safeguards designed to protect the confidentiality of information, maintain the integrity and availability of information systems, and control access to the content of these systems

Security standards: Statements that describe the processes and procedures meant to ensure that patient-identifiable health information remains confidential and protected from unauthorized disclosure, alteration, and destruction

Selection: The act or process of choosing

Self-directed learning: An instructional method that allows students to control their learning and progress at their own pace

Self-efficacy: Confidence in one's personal capabilities to do a job

Self-monitoring: The act of observing the reactions of others to one's behavior and making the necessary behavioral adjustments to improve the reactions of others in the future

Semantic clinical drug (SCD): Standardized names created in RxNorm for every clinical drug; consists of components and a dose form

Semantic Clinical Drug (SCD) of RxNorm: *See* **semantic clinical drug**

Semantic differential scale: A measure that records a group's perception of a product, organization, or program through bipolar adjectives on a seven-point continuum, resulting in a profile

Semantics: The meaning of a word or term; sometimes refers to comparable meaning, usually achieved through a standard vocabulary

Semistructured question: A type of question that begins with a structured question and follows with an unstructured question to clarify

Sentinel event: According to the Joint Commission, an unexpected occurrence involving death or serious physical or psychological injury, or the risk thereof

Serial numbering system: A type of health record identification and filing system in which patients are assigned a different but unique numerical identifier for every admission

Serial work division: A system of work organization where each task is performed by one person in sequence

Serial-unit numbering system: A health record identification system in which patient numbers are assigned in a serial manner but records are brought forward and filed under the last number assigned

Servant Leadership Model: Model for a values-based organization that promotes 10 essential values: Listening, Empathy, Healing, Awareness, Persuasion, Conceptualization, Foresight, Stewardship, Commitment, and Community building

Service innovations: Changes that create new market opportunities and in many industries are the driving force behind growth and profitability

Service quality: Level specified by qualitative standards that is expected from a function

Severity indexing: 1. The process of using clinical evidence to identify the level of resource consumption 2. A method for determining degrees of illness

Shift differential: An increased wage paid to employees who work less desirable shifts, such as evenings, nights, or weekends

Shift rotation: The assignment of employees to different periods of service to provide coverage, as needed

Simon's decision-making model: A model proposing that the decision-making process moves through three phases: intelligence, design, and choice

Simple random sampling: The process of selecting units from a population so that each one has exactly the same chance of being included in the sample

Simulation: A training technique for experimenting with a real-world situation by means of a computerized model that represents the actual situation

Simulation and inventory modeling: The key components of a plan that are computer simulated for testing and experimentation so that optimal operational procedures can be found

Simulation observation: A type of nonparticipant observation in which researchers stage events rather than allowing them to happen naturally

Simultaneous equations method: A budgeting concept that distributes overhead costs through multiple iterations, allowing maximum distribution of interdepartmental costs among overhead departments

Single-blinded study: A study design in which (typically) the investigator but not the subject, knows the identity of the treatment and control groups

Situational model of leadership: Hersey and Blanchard's model that is more a model than a theory because it does not explain why things happen but, rather, offers recommendations for behaving differently under various conditions

Six Sigma: Disciplined and data-driven methodology for getting rid of defects in any process

Skill: The ability, education, experience, and training required to perform a job task

Skilled nursing facility (SNF): A long-term care facility with an organized professional staff and permanent facilities (including inpatient beds) that provides continuous nursing and other health-related, psychosocial, and personal services to patients who are not in an acute phase of illness but who primarily require continued care on an inpatient basis

Skilled nursing facility prospective payment system (SNF PPS): A per-diem reimbursement system implemented in July 1998 for costs (routine, ancillary, and capital) associated with covered skilled nursing facility services furnished to Medicare Part A beneficiaries

SMART goals: Stands for goals that are specific, measurable, attainable, realistic, and timely

Smart peripherals: Medical instruments that have information processing components including medication dispensing devices, robotics, smart infusion pumps, and vital signs monitoring equipment

Snowflake schema: A modification of the star schema in a relational database in which the dimension tables are further divided to reduce data redundancy

Social Security Act 1935: The federal legislation that originally established the Social Security program as well as unemployment compensation, and support for mothers and children; amended in 1965 to create the Medicare and Medicaid programs

Social Security number (SSN): A unique numerical identifier assigned to every U.S. citizen

Socialization: The process of influencing the behavior and attitudes of a new employee to adapt positively to the work environment

Soft space: Space that is readily expandable or contractible to adjust to changing needs

Software as a Service (SaaS): Software that is provided through an outsourcing contract

Sole proprietorship: A venture with one owner in which all profits are considered the owner's personal income

Source systems: An information system that operates independently of a CPR system but provides data to it

Source-oriented health record: A system of health record organization in which information is arranged according to the patient care department that provided the care

Spaced training: The process of learning a task in sections separated by time

Span of control: The number of subordinates reporting to a supervisor

Special cause variation: An unusual source of variation that occurs outside a process but affects it

Specialty clinical applications: Systems for intensive care, perioperative or surgical services, cardiology, oncology, emergency medicine, labor and delivery, infection control, and others; many of these specialty clinical applications have been less mainstream, in that they are less widely used and frequently not able to be integrated as well with financial and administrative data or other ancillary systems

Speech recognition technology: Technology that translates speech to text

Spoliation: The intentional destruction, mutilation, alteration, or concealment of evidence

Sponsor: A person or an entity that initiates a clinical investigation of a drug (usually the drug manufacturer or research institution that developed the drug) by distributing it to investigators for clinical trials; a person in an organization that supports, protects, and promotes an idea within the organization; the company position with the ultimate responsibility for a project's success

Stable monetary unit: The currency used as the measurement of financial transactions

Staff authority: The lines of reporting in the organizational chart in which the position advises or makes recommendations

Staff model health maintenance organization: A type of health maintenance that employs physicians to provide healthcare services to subscribers

Staffing structure: The arrangement of staff positions within an organization

Stages of grief: Elizabeth Kubler-Ross' examination of the stress of change experienced by terminally ill patients; the five stages of grief are: shock and denial, anger, bargaining, depression, and acceptance

Staging system: A method used in cancer registers to identify specific and separate different stages or aspects of the disease

Stakeholder: An individual within the company who has an interest in, or is affected by, the results of a project

Standard: 1. A scientifically based statement of expected behavior against which structures, processes, and outcomes can be measured 2. A model or example established by authority, custom, or general consent or a rule established by an authority as a measure of quantity, weight, extent, value, or quality

Standard deviation: A measure of variability that describes the deviation from the mean of a frequency distribution in the original units of measurement; the square root of the variance

Standard of care: An established set of clinical decisions and actions taken by clinicians and other representatives of healthcare organizations in accordance with state and federal laws, regulations, and guidelines; codes of ethics published by professional associations or societies; regulations for accreditation published by accreditation agencies; usual and common practice of equivalent clinicians or organizations in a geographical regions

Standards development organization (SDO): A private or government agency involved in the development of healthcare informatics standards at a national or international level

Star schema: A visual method of expressing a multidimensional data structure in a relational database

State Children's Health Insurance Program (SCHIP): The children's healthcare program implemented as part of the Balanced Budget Act of 1997; sometimes referred to as the Children's Health Insurance Program, or CHIP

State workers' compensation insurance funds: Funds that provide a stable source of insurance coverage for work-related illnesses and injuries and serve to protect employers from underwriting uncertainties by making it possible to have continuing availability of workers' compensation coverage

Statement: A list of unpaid invoices; sometimes a cumulative list of all transactions between purchaser and vendor during a specific time period

Statement of cash flow: A statement detailing the reasons why cash amounts changed from one balance sheet period to another

Statement of retained earnings: A statement expressing the change in retained earnings from the beginning of the balance sheet period to the end

Statement of stockholder's equity: A statement detailing the reasons for changes in each stockholder's equity accounts

Statement of work: A document that defines the scope and goals of a specific project

Statistical process control chart: A type of run chart that includes both upper and lower control limits and indicates whether a process is stable or unstable

Statute of limitations: A specific time frame allowed by a statute or law for bringing litigation

Statutory law: Written law established by federal and state legislatures

Steering committee: An interdisciplinary oversight committee set up to guide and manage the strategic planning process

Stem and leaf plots: A visual display that organizes data to show its shape and distribution, using two columns with the stem in the left-hand column and all leaves associated with that stem in the right-hand column; the "leaf" is the ones digit of the number, and the other digits form the "stem"

Step-down allocation: A budgeting concept in which overhead costs are distributed once, beginning with the area that provides the least amount of non-revenue-producing services

Storytelling: A group process technique in which group members create stories describing the plausible future state of the business environment

Straight numeric filing system: Records are filed in numerical order according to the number assigned

Strategic goal: An observable and measurable end result having one or more objectives to be achieved within a more or less fixed timeframe

Strategic IS planning: A process for setting IS priorities within an organization; the process of identifying and prioritizing IS needs based on the organization's strategic goals with the intent of ensuring that all IS technology initiatives are integrated and aligned with the organization's overall strategic plan

Strategic management: The art and science of formulating, implementing, and evaluating cross-functional decisions that enable an organization to achieve its objectives

Strategic objectives: More detailed ways to meet a strategic goal that include timelines, resource allocation needs, and assigning responsibility of who will be accountable for implementation

Strategic plan: A broad organization-wide plan by which the facility accomplishes its strategic goals

Strategic planning: A disciplined effort to produce fundamental decisions that shape and guide what an organization is, what it does, and why it does it

Strategic profile: Identifies the current existing key services or products, the nature of its customers and users, the nature of its market segments, and the nature of its geographic markets

Strategic thinking: The framework for the strategic and operational improvement plans; it combines an understanding of a strategic plan and an operational plan which support strategic thinking within an organization

Strategy: A course of action designed to produce a desired (business) outcome

Strategy map: A visual representation of the cause-and-effect relationships among the components of an organization's strategy

Stratified random sampling: The process of selecting the same percentages of subjects for a study sample as they exist in the subgroups (strata) of the population

Strength, Weaknesses, Opportunities, and Threats (SWOT analysis): A strategic planning method used to evaluate the strengths, weaknesses, opportunities, and threats involved in a project or in a business venture

Structure: A term from Donabedian's model of quality assessment that assesses an organization's ability to provide services in terms of both the physical building and equipment and the people providing the healthcare services

Structure and content standards: Common data elements and definitions of the data elements to be included in an electronic patient record

Structure measures: Indicators that measure the attributes of the healthcare setting (for example, adequacy of equipment and supplies)

Structured analysis: A pattern identification analysis performed for a specific task

Structured (close-ended) question: A type of question that limits possible responses

Structured data: Binary, computer-readable data

Structured decision: A decision made by following a formula or a step-by-step process

Structured interview: An interview format that uses a set of standardized questions that are asked of all applicants

Structured Product Labeling (SPL): Used by LOINC, which was adopted as a federal health information interoperability standard for the electronic exchange of laboratory test orders and drug label section headers

Structured query language (SQL): A fourth-generation computer language that includes both DDL and DML components and is used to create and manipulate relational databases

Subacute care: A type of step-down care provided after a patient is released from an acute care hospital (including nursing homes and other facilities that provide medical care, but not surgical or emergency care)

Subprojects: Smaller components of a larger project

Substitutes: The characteristics of subordinates to the leader can provide substitutes to the leader's lack of skill; subordinates can have high ability, good experience, expert knowledge and training—all of which tend to replace the expertise of the absent leader

Successor: A task in a dependency relationship between two tasks that is dependent on the predecessor task

Supervised learning: Any learning technique that has as its purpose to classify or predict attributes of objects or individuals

Supervisory managers: Managers who oversee small (two- to ten-person) functional workgroups or teams and often perform hands-on functions in addition to supervisory functions

Supplemental medical insurance (SMI) (Medicare Part B): A voluntary medical insurance program that helps pay for physicians' services, medical services, and supplies not covered by Medicare Part A

Surgical review: Evaluation of operative and other procedures, invasive and noninvasive, using Joint Commission guidelines

Survey: A method of self-report research in which the individuals themselves are the source of the data

Survey feedback: The results of the survey are presented to decision makers as feedback, with the intention that any discrepancies between what they believe and what is actually occurring in the organization will prompt corrective action

Sustainability: Refers generally to the ability to maintain certain resources or processes indefinitely, and more specifically to meet present needs without compromising ability to meet the needs of future generations

Swimlane diagram: Diagram that shows an entire business process from beginning to end and is especially popular because it highlights relevant variables (who, what, and when) simply while requiring little or no training to use and understand

Synchronous: Occurring at the same time

Synergy: The combination of efforts produces more than acting alone

Syntactic: Refers to the formal properties of language

Syntax: A term that refers to the comparable structure or format of data, usually as they are being transmitted from one system to another

System: A set of related and highly interdependent components that are operating for a particular purpose

System catalog: An integrated data dictionary (which is a component of a database management system) that generally contains information on data tables and relationships in addition to data definitions

Systematic literature review: Methodical approach to literature review that reduces the possibility of bias; characterized by explicit search criteria to identify literature, inclusion, and exclusion criteria to select articles and information sources, and evaluation against consistent methodological standards

Systematic sampling: The process of selecting a sample of subjects for a study by drawing every *n*th unit on a list

Systematized Nomenclature of Dentistry (SNODENT): A clinical vocabulary developed by the American Dental Association (ADA) for data representation of clinical dentistry content

Systematized Nomenclature of Medicine (SNOMED): A comprehensive clinical vocabulary developed by the College of American Pathologists that is the most promising set of clinical terms available for a controlled vocabulary for healthcare

Systematized Nomenclature of Medicine Clinical Terminology (SNOMED CT): A comprehensive, controlled clinical vocabulary developed by the College of American Pathologists

Systematized Nomenclature of Medicine Reference Terminology (SNOMED RT): A concept-based terminology consisting of more than 110,000 concepts with linkages to more than 180,000 terms with unique computer-readable codes

Systems analyst: An individual who investigates, analyzes, designs, develops, installs, evaluates, and maintains an organization's healthcare information systems; is typically involved in all aspects of the systems development life cycle; and serves as a liaison among end users and programmers, database administrators, and other technical personnel

Systems development life cycle (SDLC): A model used to represent the ongoing process of developing (or purchasing) information systems

Systems theory: A reaction against reductionism; proponents of this theory believe that important information is lost by too specific a focus and thus emphasize the interconnections, organization, and wholeness of these constituents rather than their inspection in isolation

Tacit knowledge: The actions, experiences, ideals, values, and emotions of an individual that tend to be highly personal and difficult to communicate (for example, corporate culture, organizational politics, and professional experience)

Tactical plan: A strategic plan at the level of divisions and departments

Target population: A large group of individuals who are the focus of a study

Task: The steps to be performed in order to complete a project or part of a project

Task analysis: A procedure for determining the specific duties and skills required of a job

Task structure: Refers to how clearly and how well defined the task goal, procedures, and possible solutions are

Tax Equity and Fiscal Responsibility Act of 1982 (TEFRA): The federal legislation that modified Medicare's retrospective reimbursement system for inpatient hospital stays by requiring implementation of diagnosis-related groups and the acute care prospective payment system

Taxonomy: The principles of a classification system, such as data classification, and the study of the general principles of scientific classification

Team building: The process of organizing and acquainting a team, and building skills for dealing with later team processes

Technical component (TC): The portion of radiological and other procedures that is facility based or nonphysician based (for example, radiology films, equipment, overhead, endoscopic suites, and so on)

Technical skills: One of the three managerial skill categories, related to knowledge of the technical aspects of the business

Telecommuting: A work arrangement (often used by coding and transcription personnel) in which at least a portion of the employee's work hours is spent outside the office (usually in the home) and the work is transmitted back to the employer via electronic means; *See* **telestaffing**

Telehealth: A telecommunications system that links healthcare organizations and patients from diverse geographic locations and transmits text and images for (medical) consultation and treatment; also called telemedicine
Telestaffing: *See* **telecommuting**
Temporary Assistance for Needy Families (TANF): A federal program that provides states with grants to be spent on time-limited cash assistance for low-income families, generally limiting a family's lifetime cash welfare benefits to a maximum of five years and permitting states to impose other requirements
Temporary budget variance: The difference between the budgeted and actual amounts of a line item that is expected to reverse itself in a subsequent period; the timing difference between the budget and the actual event
Temporary privileges: Privileges granted for a limited time period to a licensed, independent practitioner on the basis of recommendations made by the appropriate clinical department or the president of the medical staff
Ten characteristics of data quality: Characteristics of a data quality model by AHIMA: accuracy, accessibility, comprehensiveness, consistency, currency, definition, granularity, precision, relevancy, and timeliness
Ten-step monitoring and evaluation process: The systematic and ongoing collection, organization, and evaluation of data related to indicator development promoted by the Joint Commission in the mid-1980s
Terminal-digit filing system: A system of health record identification and filing in which the last digit or group of digits (terminal digits) in the health record number determines file placement
Termination: The act of ending something (for example, a job)
Terminology: A set of terms representing the system of concepts of a particular subject field; a clinical terminology provides the proper use of clinical words as names or symbols
Test statistics: A set of statistical techniques that examines the psychometric properties of measurement instruments
Testing: The act of performing an examination or evaluation
Text mining: The process of extracting and then quantifying and filtering free-text data
Theory: A systematic organization of knowledge that predicts or explains the behavior or events
Theory X and Y: A management theory developed by McGregor that describes pessimistic and optimistic assumptions about people and their work potential
360-degree evaluation: A method of performance evaluation in which the supervisors, peers, and other staff who interact with the employee contribute information
Time and motion studies: Studies in which complex tasks are broken down into their component motions to determine inefficiencies and to develop improvements
Time ladder: A form used by employees to document time spent on various tasks
Time period: A specific span of dates to which data apply
Topography: Code that describes the site of origin of the neoplasm and uses the same three- and four-character categories as in the neoplasm section of the second chapter of ICD-10
Tort: An action brought when one party believes that another party caused harm through wrongful conduct and seeks compensation for that harm
Total length of stay (discharge days): The sum of the days of stay of any group of inpatients discharged during a specific period of time
Total quality management (TQM): A management philosophy that includes all activities in which the needs of the customer and the organization are satisfied in the most efficient manner by using employee potentials and continuous improvement
Traditional fee-for-service (FFS) reimbursement: A reimbursement method involving third-party payers who compensate providers after the healthcare services have been delivered; payment is based on specific services provided to subscribers
Train the trainer: A method of training certain individuals who, in turn, will be responsible for training others on a task or skill
Trainee: A person who is learning a task or skill
Trainer: A person who gives instruction on a task or skill
Training: A set of activities and materials that provide the opportunity to acquire job-related skills, knowledge, and abilities
Training and development model: A nine-step plan designed to help the health information manager or human resources department identify the training needs of an employee group
Trait approach: Proposes that leaders possess a collection of traits or personal qualities that distinguishes them from nonleaders
Transaction standards: Standards that support the uniform format and sequence of data during transmission from one healthcare entity to another
Transactional leadership: Refers to the role of the manager who strives to create an efficient workplace by balancing task accomplishment with interpersonal satisfaction
Transactional system: A computer-based information system that keeps track of an organization's business transactions through inputs (for example, transaction data such as admissions, discharges, and transfers in a hospital) and outputs (for example, census reports and bills); also called transaction-processing system
Transcription: The process of deciphering and typing medical dictation
Transformation: Mappings to other vocabularies; identifying what mappings are supported for the intended purpose
Transformational leadership: Leaders promote innovation and organizational change
Transparency: Refers to the degree to which patients included in secondary data sets are aware of their inclusion
Traumatic injury: A wound or injury included in a trauma registry

Treatment: The manipulation, intervention, or therapy; a broad term used by researchers to generically mean some act, such as a physical conditioning program, a computer training program, a particular laboratory medium, or the timing of prophylactic medications

Triangulation: The use of multiple sources or perspectives to investigate the same phenomenon

TRICARE: The federal healthcare program that provides coverage for the dependents of armed forces personnel and for retirees receiving care outside military treatment facilities in which the federal government pays a percentage of the cost; formerly known as Civilian Health and Medical Program of the Uniformed Services

TRICARE Extra: A cost-effective preferred provider network TRICARE option in which costs for healthcare are lower than for the standard TRICARE program because a physician or medical specialist is selected from a network of civilian healthcare professionals who participate in TRICARE Extra

TRICARE Prime: A TRICARE program that provides the most comprehensive healthcare benefits at the lowest cost of the three TRICARE options, in which military treatment facilities serve as the principal source of healthcare and a primary care manager is assigned to each enrollee

TRICARE Prime Remote: A program that provides active-duty service members in the United States with a specialized version of TRICARE Prime while they are assigned to duty stations in areas not served by the traditional military healthcare system

TRICARE Senior Prime: A managed care demonstration TRICARE program designed to better serve the medical needs of military retirees, dependents, and survivors who are 65years old and older

TRICARE Standard: A TRICARE program that allows eligible beneficiaries to choose any physician or healthcare provider, which permits the most flexibility but may be the most expensive

Trier of fact: The judge or jury hearing a civil or criminal trial

Triple bottom line: This expanded criteria (beyond the financial bottom line) includes the sustainability of environmental and social performance of the organization as well, or people, planet, and profit

Two-tailed hypothesis: A type of alternative hypothesis in which the researcher makes no prediction about the direction of the results

Type I error: A type of error in which the researcher erroneously rejects the null hypothesis when it is true

Type II error: A type of error in which the researcher erroneously fails to reject the null hypothesis when it is false

UB-04 (Uniform Bill-04): The single standardized Medicare form for standardized uniform billing, implemented in 2007 for hospital inpatients and outpatients; this form will also be used by the major third-party payers and most hospitals

Unallocated reserves: Monies that have not been assigned a specific use

Unbundling: The practice of using multiple codes to bill for the various individual steps in a single procedure rather than using a single code that includes all of the steps of the comprehensive procedure

Unfavorable variance: The negative difference between the budgeted amount and the actual amount of a line item, where actual revenue is less than budget or where actual expenses exceed budget

Unfreezing: In Lewin's stages of change, the initial stage of change is unfreezing the status quo, often by presenting the discrepancies between the status quo and the desired goals; often creates a state of cognitive dissonance, which is an uncomfortable awareness of two incompatible perceptions or beliefs, in this case, the discrepancy; *see* **Lewin's stages of change** and **refreezing**

Unified Medical Language System (UMLS): A program initiated by the National Library of Medicine to build an intelligent, automated system that can understand biomedical concepts, words, and expressions and their interrelationships

Unified Medical Language System (UMLS) Metathesaurus: A list containing information on biomedical concepts and terms from more than 100 healthcare vocabularies and classifications, administrative health data, bibliographic and full-text databases, and expert systems

Unified Medical Language System (UMLS) Semantic Network: A categorization of all UMDNS concepts in the UMLS Metathesaurus

Unified Medical Language System (UMLS) SPECIALIST Lexicon: An English-language lexicon containing biomedical terms

Unified modeling language (UML): A common data-modeling notation used in conjunction with object-oriented database design

Uniform Ambulatory Care Data Set (UACDS): A data set developed by the National Committee on Vital and Health Statistics consisting of a minimum set of patient/client-specific data elements to be collected in ambulatory care settings

Uniform Hospital Discharge Data Set (UHDDS): A core set of data elements adopted by the U.S. Department of Health, Education, and Welfare in 1974 that are collected by hospitals on all discharges and all discharge abstract systems

Uniformed Services Employment and Reemployment Rights Act (1994): Federal legislation that prohibits discrimination against individuals because of their service in the Armed Forces Reserves, National Guard, or other uniformed services

Union: A collective bargaining unit that represents groups of employees and is authorized to negotiate with employers on the employees' behalf in matters related to compensation, health, and safety

Unique identification number: A combination of numbers or alphanumeric characters assigned to a particular patient

Unique identifier: A type of information that refers to only one individual or organization

Unique physician identification number (UPIN): A unique numerical identifier created by the Health Care Financing

Administration (now called the Centers for Medicare and Medicaid Services) for use by physicians who bill for services provided to Medicare patients

Unit numbering system: A health record identification system in which the patient receives a unique medical record number at the time of the first encounter that is used for all subsequent encounters

Unit work division: A method of work organization where each task is performed by one person at the same time that another person is doing a task, but one does not have to wait for the other

Unity of command: A human resources principle that assumes that each employee reports to only one specific management position

Univariate: A term referring to the involvement of one variable

Universal chart order: A system in which the health record is maintained in the same format while the patient is in the facility and after discharge

Universal Medical Device Nomenclature System (UMDNS): A standard international nomenclature and computer coding system for medical devices, developed by ECRI

Universal protocol: A written checklist developed by the Joint Commission to prevent errors that can occur when physicians perform the wrong procedure, for example

Unstructured data: Nonbinary, human-readable data

Unstructured decision: A decision that is made without following a prescribed method, formula, or pattern

Unstructured (open-ended) question: A type of question that allows free-form responses

Unsupervised learning: Any learning technique that has as its purpose to group or cluster items, objects, or individuals

Upcoding: The practice of assigning diagnostic or procedural codes that represent higher payment rates than the codes that actually reflect the services provided to patients

User-centered design: A concept that involves the user throughout the entire design and development process; involving the user throughout the entire process enables the developers to make sure the users' needs are met; in healthcare, it translates to patient-centered, caregiver-centered, support staff-centered, employee-centered, and the like

Usual, customary, and reasonable (UCR) charges: Method of evaluating providers' fees in which the third-party payer pays for fees that are "usual" in that provider's practice, "customary" in the community, and "reasonable" for the situation

Utilization management: 1. The planned, systematic review of the patients in a healthcare facility against care criteria for admission, continued stay, and discharge 2. A collection of systems and processes to ensure that facilities and resources, both human and nonhuman, are used maximally and are consistent with patient care needs

Utilization review (UR): The process of determining whether the medical care provided to a specific patient is necessary according to preestablished objective screening criteria at time frames specified in the organization's utilization management plan

Utilization Review Act: The federal legislation that requires hospitals to conduct continued-stay reviews for Medicare and Medicaid patients

Validity: 1. The extent to which data correspond to the actual state of affairs or that an instrument measures what it purports to measure 2. A term referring to a test's ability to accurately and consistently measure what it purports to measure

Values-based leadership: Theory similar to other contingency theories such as path-goal leadership; *see* **path-goal theory**

Values statement: A short description that communicates an organization's social and cultural belief system

Variability: The dispersion of a set of measures around the population mean

Variable: A factor

Variable costs: Resources expended that vary with the activity of the organization, for example, medication expenses vary with patient volume

Variance: A measure of variability that gives the average of the squared deviations from the mean; in financial management, the difference between the budgeted amount and the actual amount of a line item; in project management, the difference between the original project plan and current estimates

Variance analysis: An assessment of a department's financial transactions to identify differences between the budget amount and the actual amount of a line item

Vector graphic (or signal tracing) data: Digital data that have been captured as points and are connected by lines (a series of point coordinates) or areas (shapes bounded by lines)

Vendor neutral: Classifications and terminologies must be neutral so that they can be readily used as national standards by all vendors without conferring a competitive advantage to any one of them

Vendor system: A computer system developed by a commercial company not affiliated with the healthcare organization

Verification service: An outside service that provides a primary source check on information that a physician makes available on an application to the medical staff

Vertical dyad linkage: Formulated in 1975 to describe the single-person mentoring relationships that occur in organizations and was later supplemented by leader–member relations theory that applied the same idea to the leader's relations with groups

Vertical structure: The levels and relationships among positions in an organizational hierarchy

Virtual reality (VR): An artificial form of reality experienced through sensory stimuli and in which the participant's actions partly affect what happens

Vision: A picture of the desired future that sets a direction and rationale for change

Vision statement: A short description of an organization's ideal future state

Vital statistics: Data related to births, deaths, marriages, and fetal deaths

Vocabulary: A list or collection of clinical words or phrases and their meanings

Vocabulary standard: A common definition for medical terms to encourage consistent descriptions of an individual's condition in the health record

Voice recognition technology: A method of encoding speech signals that do not require speaker pauses (but uses pauses when they are present) and of interpreting at least some of the signals' content as words or the intent of the speaker

Volume logs: Forms used (sometimes in conjunction with time ladders) to obtain information about the volume of work units received and processed in a day

Voluntary Disclosure Program: A program unveiled in 1998 by the OIG that encourages healthcare providers to voluntarily report fraudulent conduct affecting Medicare, Medicaid, and other federal healthcare programs

Vulnerable subjects: A subject that has limited mental capacity or is unable to freely volunteer

Web browser–based (or Web native) architectures: Systems and applications written in one or more Web programming languages; also called Web browser-based systems

Web content management systems: Systems in which information placed in a Web site can be labeled and tracked so that it can be easily located, modified, and reused

Web portal: A Web site entryway through which to access, find, and deliver information

Web services: an open, standardized way of integrating disparate, Web browser-based and other applications

Web services architecture: A way of integrating Web-based applications using open standards over an Internet protocol backbone; it allows organizations to share data across different system platforms behind a firewall without being tied to one operating system or programming language

Web 2.0: The second generation of Internet-based services that emphasizes online collaboration and sharing among users; some of these applications and technologies include blogs, social networks, content communities, wikis, and podcasts

Web-based systems and applications: Systems and applications that use Internet technology

Web-based training: Instruction via the Internet that enables learners to work when, where, and at a pace suited to them and offers interaction with other students and the instructor via the listserv

Webmasters: Individuals who support Web applications and the healthcare organization's intranet and Internet operations

Wireless technology: A type of technology that uses wireless networks and wireless devices to access and transmit data in real time

Work: The effort, usually described in hours, needed to complete a task

Work breakdown structure: A hierarchical structure that decomposes project activities into levels of detail

Work distribution analysis: An analysis used to determine whether a department's current work assignments and job content are appropriate

Work distribution chart: A matrix that depicts the work being done in a particular workgroup in terms of specific tasks and activities, time spent on tasks, and the employees performing the tasks

Work division: The way in which tasks are handled within an organization

Worker immaturity–maturity: Concept borrowed from Chris Argyris, who suggested that job and psychological maturity also influences leadership style; job maturity refers to how much work-related ability, knowledge, experience, and skill a person has; psychological maturity refers to willingness, confidence, commitment, and motivation related to work

Work measurement: The process of studying the amount of work accomplished and how long it takes to accomplish work in order to define and monitor productivity

Work products: Documents produced during the completion of a task that may be a component of, or contribute to, a project deliverable

Work sampling: A work measurement technique that uses random sample measurements to characterize the performance of the whole

Workers' Adjustment and Retraining Notification (WARN) Act: Federal legislation that requires employers to give employees a 60-day notice in advance of covered plant closings and covered mass layoffs

Workers' compensation: The medical and income insurance coverage for certain employees in unusually hazardous jobs

Workflow: Any work process that must be handled by more than one person

Workflow technology: Technology that automatically routes electronic documents into electronic in-baskets of its department clerks or supervisors for disposition decisions

Working conditions: The environment in which work is performed (surroundings) and the physical dangers or risks involved in performing the job (hazards)

World Health Organization (WHO): Responsible for maintaining the International Classification of Diseases (ICD)

World Organization of National Colleges, Academies, and Academic Associations of General Practitioners/Family Physicians (WONCA): Developed the International Classification of Primary Care (ICPC-2), a coding terminology for the classification of primary care

XML: *See* **Extensible markup language**

X12N: Referring to standards adopted for electronic data interchange

Zero-based budget: Types of budgets in which each budget cycle poses the opportunity to continue or discontinue services based on available resources so that every department or activity must be justified and prioritized annually to effectively allocate resources

Index

(continued)